THE OFFICIAL GUIDE TO
AMERICAN HISTORIC INNS

Rated "Outstanding" by Morgan Rand

Winner of Benjamin Franklin Award
Best Travel Guide

Winner of Travel Publishing News
Best Travel Reference

Winner of Benjamin Franklin Award
Best Directory

Comments from print media:

"... helps you find the very best hideaways (many of the book's listings appear in the National Register of Historic Places)." — **Country Living**

"I love your book!" — **Lydia Moss, Travel Editor, McCall's**

"Delightful, succinct, detailed and well-organized. Easy to follow style . . ." — **Don Wudtke, Los Angeles Times**

"This is one of the best guidebooks of its kind. It's easy to use, accurate and the thumbnail sketches give the readers enough description to choose among the more than 1,000 properties detailed . . ." — **Dallas Morning News**

". . . thoughtfully organized and look-ups are hassle-free . . . well-researched and accurate . . . put together by people who know the field. There is no other publication available that covers this particular segment of the bed & breakfast industry - a segment that has been gaining popularity among travelers by leaps and bounds. The information included is valuable and well thought out." — **Morgan Directory Reviews**

"The Official Guide to American Historic Inns (published by American Historic Inns) shares their picks with USA Today." — **USA Today** (10 great places for a Valentines's Day getaway, Feb. 7, 2003)

"This is the best bed & breakfast book out. It outshines them all!" — **Maggie Balitas, Rodale Book Clubs**

Comments from innkeepers:

"Your book is wonderful. I have been reading it as one does a novel." — Olallieberry Inn, Cambria, Calif.

"We want to tell you how much we love your book. We have it out for guests to use. They love it, each featured inn stands out so well. Thank you for the privilege of being in your book." — Fairhaven Inn, Bath, Maine

"What a wonderful book! We love it and have been very pleased with the guests who have made reservations using your book." — Vermont innkeeper

"We have had fantastic response. Thanks!" — Liberty Rose Colonial B&B, Williamsburg, Va.

"We've been with you for years and we are doing wonderfully through your books. We get a lot of business from it." — Homestead Inn, New Milford, Conn.

"We get many good leads from you throughout the year. Anything that we can do to support, we'll be glad to. Thanks for a great publication." — A Grand Inn-Sunset Hill House, Sugar Hill, N.H.

"Your guide has high praises from guests who use it." — The Inn on South Street, Kennebunkport, Maine

"Thank you for all the time and work you put into this guidebook. We have had many guests find our inn because of you." — The Kaleidoscope Inn & Gardens, Nipomo, Calif.

＊＊＊＊＊＊＊＊＊＊＊＊＊

Dedicated to our favorite guests —
you who love and visit America's historic bed &
breakfasts and country inns. Your support and
patronage has kept innkeepers passionate and
excited about sharing the memories and spirit of
their historic inn. We hope you will be greatly
refreshed by your journeys.

＊＊＊＊＊＊＊＊＊＊＊＊＊

THE OFFICIAL GUIDE
— TO —
AMERICAN HISTORIC INNS

BED & BREAKFASTS AND COUNTRY INNS

N I N T H   E D I T I O N

BY DEBORAH EDWARDS SAKACH

Published By

AMERICAN HISTORIC INNS INCORPORATED

PO Box 669
Dana Point
California
92629-0669
www.iLoveInns.com
E-mail:comments@iLoveInns.com

The Official Guide to American Historic Inns — Bed & Breakfasts and Country Inns

FRONT COVER (CLOCKWISE FROM TOP LEFT):

La Residence Country Inn, Napa, Calif.
Photo by David Livingston

Litchfield Plantation, Island, S.C.
Photo by Louise Parsons

The Captain Lord Mansion, Kennebunkport, Maine
Photo by Warren Jagger Photography, Inc.

Two Meeting Street Inn, Charleston, S.C.
Photo by American Historic Inns, Inc.

BACK COVER (FROM TOP):

Castle Inn Riverside, Wichita, Kan.

Victoria-On-Main B&B, Whitewater, Wis.
Photo by Peter Hlavacek

Great Oak Manor, Chestertown, Md.

Grand Victorian Inn, Bellaire, Mich.
Photo by Don Rutt

Castle Hill Inn & Resort, Newport, R.I.

COVER DESIGN:
David Sakach

PRODUCTION MANAGER:
Andy Prizer

SENIOR EDITOR:
Shirley Swagerty

ASSISTANT EDITORS:
Tiffany Crosswy, Patricia Purvis, Stephen Sakach

DATABASE ASSISTANTS:
Valerie Christy, Jamee Danihels, Chaya Prizer

PROGRAMMING AND CARTOGRAPHY:
Chris Morton

DIGITAL SCANNING:
Jamee Danihels

Publisher's Cataloging in Publication Data
Sakach, Deborah Edwards
American Historic Inns, Inc.
The Official Guide to American Historic Inns

1. Bed & Breakfast Accommodations - United States, Directories, Guide Books.
2. Travel - Bed & Breakfast Inns, Directories, Guide Books.
3. Bed & Breakfast Accommodations - Historic Inns, Directories, Guide Books.
4. Hotel Accommodations - Bed & Breakfast Inns, Directories, Guide Books.
5. Hotel Accommodations - United States, Directories, Guide Books.
I. Title. II Author. III Bed & Breakfast, The Official Guide to American Historic Inns

ISBN: 1-888050-20-9
Softcover
Printed in the United States of America.
10 9 8 7 6 5 4 3 2 1

Contents

How To Use This Book

Welcome! You hold in your hands the most comprehensive collection of our nation's best historic bed & breakfast and country inns. Most were built in the 17th, 18th or 19th centuries, but a few inns from the early 20th century have been included. The National Register of Historic Places requires that buildings be constructed prior to 1950 in order to gain historic standing, and we follow this guideline as well.

When you stay at a historic inn, not only do you enjoy a unique getaway, you also promote and support the preservation of our nation's architectural and cultural heritage. Most of these homes are owned privately and have been restored with the private funds of individual families. They are maintained and improved by revenues collected from bed & breakfast guests.

With a few exceptions, we have omitted homestays. These are B&Bs with only one or two rooms, often operated casually or as a hobby.

Accommodations

Among the listings, you'll find B&Bs and country inns in converted schoolhouses, lighthouses, 18th-century farmhouses, Queen Anne Victorians, adobe lodges and a variety of other unique places, both new and old.

The majority of inns included in this book were built in the 17th, 18th, 19th or early 20th centuries. We have stated the date each building was constructed at the beginning of each description. Many of the inns are steeped in the traditions of Colonial America, the Victorian Era, The Civil War, Spanish colonization or the Old West. Many are listed in the National Register of Historic Places.

A Variety of Inns

A **Country Inn** generally serves both breakfast and dinner and may have a restaurant associated with it. Many have been in operation for years, some since the 18th century as you will note in our "Inns of Interest" section. Although primarily found on the East Coast, a few country inns are in other regions of the nation.

A **Bed & Breakfast** facility's primary focus is lodging. It can have from three to 20 rooms or more. The innkeepers often live on the premises. Breakfast usually is the only meal served and can be a full-course, gourmet breakfast or a simple buffet. B&B owners often pride themselves on their culinary skills.

As with country inns, many B&Bs specialize in providing historic, romantic or gracious atmospheres with amenities such as canopied beds, fireplaces, spa tubs, afternoon tea in the library and scenic views.

Some give great attention to recapturing a specific historic period, such as the Victorian or Colonial eras. Many display antiques and other furnishings from family collections.

A **Homestay** is a room available in a private home. It may be an elegant stone mansion in the best part of town or a charming country farm. Homestays have one to three guest rooms. Because homestays are often operated as a hobby-type business and open and close frequently, only a very few such properties are included in this publication.

A Note About Innkeepers

Your innkeepers are a tremendous resource. Most knowledgeable innkeepers enjoy sharing regional attractions, local folklore, area history, and pointing out favorite restaurants and other special features of their areas. Unlike hotel and motel operators, innkeepers often bring much of themselves into creating an experience for you to long remember. Many have personally renovated historic buildings, saving them from deterioration and often, the bulldozer. Others have infused their inns with a unique style and personality to enliven your experience with a warm and inviting environment.

Area Codes

Although we have made every effort to update area codes throughout the book, new ones appear from time to time. Please be sure to dial 411 and ask the operator to help you should your call not go through.

How to Use This Book

Note: We try to keep the use of codes to a minimum, but they help create a more comprehensive listing for each of the inns and B&Bs. We encourage you to read this entire section, as it will help plan a getaway that is just right for you.

Baths

Most bed & breakfasts and country inns provide a private bath for each guest room, however, some do not. We have included the number of rooms and the number of private baths in each facility. The code "*PB*," indicates how many guest rooms include a private bath.

Beds

K, Q, D, T indicates King, Queen, Double or Twin beds available at the inn.

Children

Many innkeepers go out of their way to provide a wonderful atmosphere for families. In fact, more and more inns are catering to families.

However, this is always a sensitive subject. We do not list whether children are allowed at inns or B&Bs in this guide because it is illegal in several states to discriminate against persons of any age. Occasionally innkeepers do "discourage" children as guests. Some innkeepers consider their inn a place for romance or solitude, and often do not think younger guests fit into this scheme. Also, many inns are filled with fine antiques and collectibles, so it may be an inappropriate place for very small children. If you plan to bring your children, always ask your innkeeper if children are welcome, and if so, at what age.

Meals

Continental breakfast: Coffee, juice and toast or pastry.

Continental-plus breakfast: A continental breakfast plus a variety of breads, cheeses and fruit.

Full breakfast: Coffee, juice, breads, fruit and an entree.

Full gourmet breakfast: May be a four-course candlelight offering or especially creative cuisine.

Vegetarian breakfast: Entrees can cater to special vegetarian diets and are created without meat.

Country breakfast: Hearty country fare may include fresh farm eggs gathered on the premises or sausages and cheeses made in the area.

Gourmet lunch: Specially creative sandwiches, soups or other items not normally found in a lunch box.

Gourmet dinner: May include several courses and finer cuisine, usually featuring local produce, fish, fowl, etc. prepared with creative flair.

Teas: Usually served in the late afternoon with cookies, crackers or other in-between-meal offerings.

Always find out what meals, if any, are included in the rates. Not every establishment in this guidebook provides breakfast, although most do. Please do not assume meals are included in the rates featured in the book.

Rates

Rates are usually listed in ranges, i.e., $65-175. The LOWEST rate is almost always available during off-peak periods and may only apply to the least expensive room. Rates are always subject to change and are not guaranteed. You should always confirm the rates when making the reservations. Rates for Canadian listings usually are listed in Canadian dollars. Rates are quoted for double occupancy.

Breakfast and other meals MAY or MAY NOT be included in the rates.

Minimum stays

Many inns require a two-night minimum stay on weekends. A three-night stay often is required during holiday periods or special events.

Cancellations

Cancellation policies are individual for each bed & breakfast. It is not unusual to see 7- to 14-day cancellation periods or more. Please verify the inn's policy when making your reservation.

Rooms

Under some listings, you will note that suites are available. We typically assume that suites include a private bath.

Additionally, under some listings, you will note a reference to cottages. A cottage may be a rustic cabin tucked in the woods, a seaside cottage or a private apartment-style accommodation.

Fireplaces

When fireplaces are mentioned in the listing they may be in guest rooms or in common areas and are abbreviated as "FP." A few have fireplaces that are non-working because of city lodging requirements. Please verify this if you are looking forward to an evening in front of a crackling fire.

Historic Interest

Many of the inns included have listed items of historic interest nearby that guests can visit. To help you plan your trip, most of the inns also have included the distance to the sites of significant historic interest.

Smoking

The majority of country inns and B&Bs, especially those located in historic buildings, prohibit smoking; therefore, if you are a smoker, we advise you to call and specifically check with each inn to see if and how they accommodate smokers.

State maps

The state maps have been designed to help travelers find an inn's location quickly and easily. Each city shown on the maps contains one or more inns. As you browse through the guide, you will notice coordinates next to each city name, i.e. "C3." The coordinates designate the location of inns on the state map.

Media coverage

Some inns have provided us with copies of magazine or newspaper articles written by travel writers about their establishments and we have indicated that in the listing. Articles written about the inns may be available either from the source as a reprint, through libraries or from the inn itself. Also, TV coverage, catalogue and movie appearances are included.

Comments from guests

Over the years, we have collected reams of guest comments about thousands of inns. Our files are filled with these documented comments. At the end of some descriptions, we have included a guest comment received about that inn.

Descriptions

This book contains descriptions of more than 2,600 inns, and each establishment was reviewed carefully prior to being approved for this guide. Many inns and B&Bs were turned away from this guide because they did not meet our standards. We also do not allow innkeepers to write their own descriptions. Our descriptions are created from visits to the inns, interviews with innkeepers and from a bulk of other information, including ratings, guest comments and articles from top magazines and newspapers.

Inspections

Since 1981, we have had a happy, informal team of inn travelers and prospective innkeepers who report to us about new bed & breakfast discoveries and repeat visits to favorite inns.

Although our staff usually sees many inns each year, inspecting inns is not the major focus of our travels. We visit as many as possible and meet the innkeepers. Some inns are grand mansions filled with classic, museum-quality antiques. Others are rustic, such as reassembled log cabins, renovated barns or historic lighthouses. We have enjoyed them all and cherish our memories of each establishment, pristine or rustic.

Only rarely have we come across a truly disappointing inn, poorly kept or poorly managed. This type of lodging usually does not survive because an inn's success depends upon repeat guests and enthusiastic word-of-mouth referrals from satisfied guests. We do not promote these types of establishments.

Traveler or tourist

Travel is an adventure into the unknown, full of surprises and rewards. A seasoned "traveler" learns that even after elaborate preparations and careful planning, travel provides the new and unexpected. The traveler learns to live with uncertainty and considers it part of the adventure.

To the "tourist," whether "accidental" or otherwise, new experiences are disconcerting. Tourists want no surprises. They expect things to be exactly as they had envisioned them. To tourists we recommend staying in a hotel or motel chain where the same formula is followed from one locale to another.

We have found that inngoers are travelers at heart. They relish the differences found at these unique bed & breakfasts and country inns. This is the magic that makes traveling from inn to inn the delightful experience it is.

What if the inn is full?

Ask the innkeeper for recommendations. They may know of an inn that has recently opened or one nearby but off the beaten path. Call the local Chamber of Commerce in the town you hope to visit. They may also know of inns that have recently opened. Please let us know of any new discoveries you make.

We want to hear from you!

We've always enjoyed hearing from our readers and have carefully cataloged all letters and recommendations. If you wish to participate in evaluating your inn experiences, use the Inn Evaluation Form in the back of this book. You might want to make copies of this form prior to departing on your journey.

We hope you will enjoy this book so much that you will want to keep an extra copy or two on hand to offer to friends and family. Many readers have called to purchase our books for hostess gifts, birthday presents, or for seasonal celebrations. It's a great way to introduce your friends to America's enchanting country inns and bed & breakfasts.

Visit us online at iLoveInns.com!

Would you like more information about the inns listed in this book? For color photos, links to the inns' web sites and more, search our web site at **www.iLoveInns.com**. You'll find thousands of inns from the United States and Canada. As winner of Yahoo! Internet Magazine's "Best B&B Site," we think you'll agree it's *the only online bed & breakfast guide you will ever need.*™ "

How to Read an Inn Listing

Anytown ❶ G6

An American Historic Inn
❷ 123 S Main St
Anytown, VT 12345-6789
(123)555-1212 (800)555-1212 Fax:(123)555-1234
❸ E-mail: americaninn@mail.com
Web: www.americaninn.com

❹ **Circa 1897.** Every inch of this breathtaking inn offers something special. The interior is decorated to the hilt with lovely furnishings, plants, beautiful rugs and warm, inviting tones. Rooms include four-poster and canopy beds combined with the modern amenities such as fireplaces, wet bars and stocked refrigerators. Enjoy a complimentary full breakfast at the inn's gourmet restaurant. The chef offers everything from a light breakfast of fresh fruit, cereal and a bagel to heartier treats such as pecan peach pancakes and Belgium waffles served with fresh fruit and crisp bacon.

❺

❻ **Historic Interest:** Indian Burial Grounds (15 miles), Fort Morgan (30 miles).

❼ Innkeeper(s): David & Rebecca Prizer. ❽ $125-195. ❾ 13 rooms with PB, 10 with FP, 1 suite and 1 conference room. ❿ Breakfast and afternoon tea included in rates. ⓫ Types of meals: full breakfast, gourmet breakfast and early coffee/tea. Dinner, picnic lunch, gourmet lunch, banquet service, catering service and room service available. Restaurant on premises. ⓬ Beds: KQTC.

⓭ Phone, turndown service, ceiling fan, TV and VCR in room. Air conditioning. Fax, copier and bicycles on premises. Handicap access. Antiques, fishing, parks, shopping, theater and watersports nearby.

⓮ Publicity: *Beaufort, Southern Living, Country Inns, Carolina Style, US Air, Town & Country.*

⓯ *"A dream come true!"*

---

① **Map coordinates**
Easily locate an inn on the state map using these coordinates.

② **Inn address**
Mailing or street address and all phone numbers for the inn.

③ **E-mail and web address**
Many inns have included their e-mail and web addresses. Use the e-mail address to contact innkeepers regarding reservations or other questions. Often, additional information, including color photographs, can be found on the inn's web site.

④ **Description of inn**
Descriptions of inns are written by experienced travel writers based on visits to inns, interviews and information collected from inns.

⑤ **Drawing of inn**
Many listings include artistic renderings.

⑥ **Historic interest**
Indicates items of special historic significance near the inn's location.

⑦ **Innkeepers**
The name of the innkeeper(s).

⑧ **Rates**
Rates are quoted for double occupancy. The rate range includes off-season rates and is subject to change.

⑨ **Rooms**
Number and types of rooms available.
PB-Private Bath FP-Fireplace HT-Hot Tub

⑩ **Included meals**
Types of meals included in the rates.

⑪ **Available meals**
This section lists the types of meals that the inn offers. These meals may or may not be included in the rates.

⑫ **Beds**
King, Queen, Double, Twin

⑬ **Amenities and activities**
Information included here describes other amenities or services available at the inn. Nearby activities also are included.

⑭ **Publicity**
Newspapers, magazines and other publications which have featured articles about the inn.

⑮ **Guest comments**
Comments about the inn from guests.

Alabama

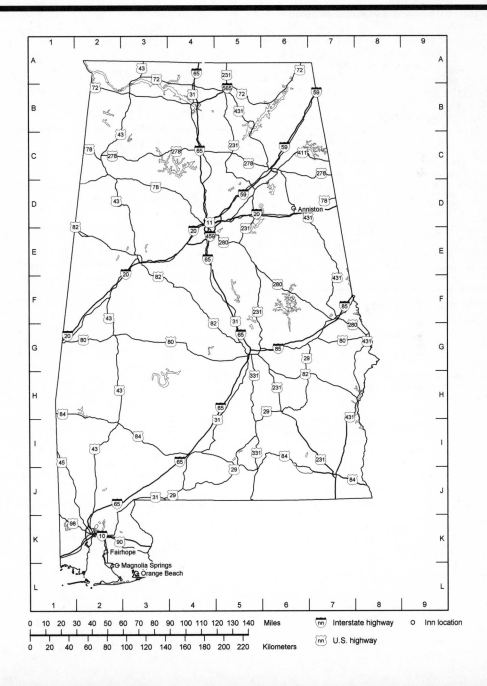

0 10 20 30 40 50 60 70 80 90 100 110 120 130 140   Miles

0   20   40   60   80   100 120 140 160 180 200 220   Kilometers

nn Interstate highway   ○ Inn location

nn U.S. highway

Anniston
D6

The Victoria, A Country Inn & Restaurant

1604 Quintard Ave, PO Box 2213
Anniston, AL 36202-2213
(256)236-0503 (800)260-8781 Fax:(256)236-1138
Web: www.thevictoria.com

Circa 1887. This Victorian estate, an Alabama landmark, occupies almost an entire square block on Quintard Avenue, Anniston's major thoroughfare. The first floor of the main house has four dining rooms, a lounge and a glass-enclosed veranda. The guest rooms in the house are furnished with antiques, while those in the hotel feature reproduction pieces. Covered walkways, verandas and gazebos flow among the massive hardwoods, gardens, courtyard and pool.

Historic Interest: Saint Michaels and All Angels Episcopal Church (1 mile), Tyler Hill Square (2 miles), Grace Episcopal Church (1/2 mile).

Innkeeper(s): Jean Ann Oglesby. $89-319. 60 rooms with PB, 4 with FP, 1 cottage and 4 conference rooms. Breakfast included in rates. Types of meals: Full bkfst and room service. Restaurant on premises. Beds: KQD. Data port, cable TV, clock radio and telephone in room. Air conditioning. TV, VCR, fax, copier, swimming, fireplace and fine dining on premises. Limited handicap access. Weddings, small meetings, family reunions and seminars hosted. Amusement parks, antiquing, live theater, parks and shopping nearby.

Publicity: *Southern Living, New York Times, Anniston Star, Birmingham Post Herald, Decatur Daily, Birmingham News and Good Housekeeping.*

Fairhope
K2

Bay Breeze Guest House

742 S Mobile St
Fairhope, AL 36533
(866)928-8976 Fax:(251)929-2389

Circa 1938. A white shell driveway leads to this gracious home, located on three acres of landscaped gardens of camellias and azaleas on Mobile Bay. A wide sandy beach and 462-foot private pier gives guests an unparalleled experience. The pier is popular for waterside picnics, naps, fishing, sunbathing and an occasional barbecue. Furnished with family heirlooms and period antiques,

the rooms also offer stained glass, Oriental rugs and quilts. Guests are treated to bountiful breakfasts in view of pelicans in flight or diving into the bay. Southern hospitality is extended in a variety of ways throughout your stay.

Innkeeper(s): Bill & Becky Jones. $130-160. 5 rooms, 1 with PB and 4 suites. Breakfast included in rates. Types of meals: Full bkfst. Beds: Q. Cable TV, reading lamp, ceiling fan, clock radio and desk in room. Air conditioning. VCR, fax, copier, swimming, bicycles, parlor games, telephone and fireplace on premises. Antiquing, fishing, golf, parks, shopping and water sports nearby.

Church Street Inn B&B

51 S Church St
Fairhope, AL 36532-2343
(866)928-8976 Fax:(251)929-2389

Circa 1921. Guests at Church Street choose from three bedchambers, each decorated with family antiques and heirlooms. The home, listed in the National Register, contains many original features, including a clawfoot tub in the Ashley Anne room. Breakfasts offer a warm sumptuous continental-plus breakfast in the dining room. Fairhope, a small town on Mobile Bay, offers a quaint downtown area with galleries, boutiques, antique shops and restaurants.

Innkeeper(s): Marisha Chavers. $120. 3 rooms with PB. Breakfast included in rates. Types of meals: Cont plus. Beds: KQ. Cable TV, reading lamp, ceiling fan, clock radio and desk in room. Air conditioning. Telephone and fireplace on premises. Antiquing, fishing, golf, parks, shopping and water sports nearby.

Magnolia Springs
L2

Magnolia Springs

14469 Oak St
Magnolia Springs, AL 36555
(251)965-7321 (800)965-7321
E-mail: info@magnoliasprings.com
Web: www.magnoliasprings.com

Circa 1897. A canopy of ancient oak trees line the streets leading to the Magnolia Springs bed & breakfast. Softly framed by more oaks, and in springtime, pink azaleas, the National Register inn with its dormers and spacious wraparound porch offers an inviting welcome. Warm hospitality enfolds guests in the Great Room with its pine walls and ceilings and heart pine floors, as well as the greeting from the innkeeper. Curly pine woodwork is found throughout the home, which was originally an area hotel. Guest rooms are appointed with a variety of carefully chosen antiques. Breakfast favorites often include pecan-topped French toast, bacon, grits, fresh fruit with cream dressing and blueberry muffins. Guests may also request a special breakfast to accommodate dietary needs. The innkeepers will recommend some memorable adventures, or simply stroll to Magnolia River and enjoy the area.

Innkeeper(s): David Worthington. $97-164. 5 rooms, 4 with PB and 1 suite. Breakfast, afternoon tea and snacks/refreshments included in rates. Types of meals: Full bkfst and early coffee/tea. Beds: KQDT. Data port, cable TV, reading lamp, ceiling fan, telephone, turn-down service and desk in room. Central air. Fax and copier on premises. Weddings, small meetings and family reunions hosted. Amusement parks, antiquing, art galleries, beach, canoeing/kayaking, fishing, golf, hiking, museums, parks, shopping and water sports nearby.

Publicity: *Southern Living, Fox 10 Mobile and HGTV-Bob Vila's Restore America.*

Orange Beach   *L3*

The Original Romar House

23500 Perdido Beach Blvd
Orange Beach, AL 36561-3007
(251)974-1625 (800)487-6627 Fax:(251)974-1163
E-mail: original@gulftel.com
Web: www.bbonline.com/al/romarhouse/

Circa 1924. From the deck of the Purple Parrot Bar, guests at this seaside inn can enjoy a cocktail and a view of the Gulf of Mexico. Each of the guest rooms is named and themed after a local festival and decorated with authentic Art Deco furnishings. Stained and beveled glass windows add to the romantic atmosphere. A full Southern breakfast is served each morning, and in the evening, wine and cheese is served in the Purple Parrot Bar.

Innkeeper(s): Darrell Finley. $79-139. 6 rooms with PB, 1 suite, 1 cottage and 1 conference room. Breakfast included in rates. Types of meals: Full bkfst. Beds: Q. Reading lamp, ceiling fan, clock radio and turn-down service in room. Air conditioning. VCR, spa, bicycles, library, parlor games, telephone, fireplace and heated swimming pool on premises. Weddings, small meetings and family reunions hosted. Amusement parks, antiquing, fishing, golf, parks, shopping, water sports, night clubs and seafood restaurants nearby.

Alaska

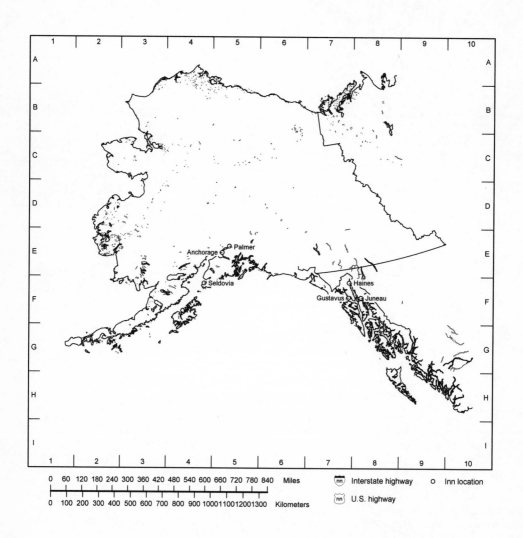

1 2 3 4 5 6 7 8 9 10

A B C D E F G H I

Anchorage ○ ○ Palmer

○ Seldovia

○ Haines

Gustavus ○ ○ Juneau

0 60 120 180 240 300 360 420 480 540 600 660 720 780 840   Miles

0 100 200 300 400 500 600 700 800 900 1000 1100 1200 1300   Kilometers

🛡 Interstate highway   ○ Inn location

🛡 U.S. highway

Anchorage   E5

Anchorage Mahogany Manor Historic Downtown Inn

204 East 15th Ave.
Anchorage, AK 99501
(907)278-1111 (888)777-0346 Fax:(907)258-7877
E-mail: mahoganymanor@compuserve.com
Web: www.mahoganymanor.com

Circa 1947. This elegant inn in the heart of Anchorage stands on a half-acre on the crest of a hill with views of the countryside and mountains. From the rare woods used in construction, to the Alaskan artwork, to the unique floor-to-ceiling indoor waterfall, the beauty of this inn competes with the natural beauty surrounding it. The library is full of books on Alaska for explorers planning their next journey or for guests relaxing at the end of the day. The four guest bedrooms, including a three-room family suite, come with robes and slippers. A hearty continental breakfast is available to guests whenever they want it in the full-service guest kitchen that is stocked with delights like juice, fruit, rolls, breads, pastries, yogurt and hot and cold cereals. Hot drinks are always available, and hors d'oeuvres or dessert are offered each evening, as well. The inn is a perfect place for releasing creative energies at corporate meetings, and it's excellent for creating lifetime memories at family events. It has a swimming pool and outdoor whirlpool.

Innkeeper(s): Mary Ernst, CTC & Russ Campbell. $129-309. 4 rooms, 2 with PB, 1 with FP, 2 suites and 1 conference room. Breakfast, afternoon tea and snacks/refreshments included in rates. Types of meals: Cont plus, veg bkfst, early coffee/tea and room service. Beds: KQDT. Modem hook-up, data port, cable TV, VCR, reading lamp, stereo, clock radio, telephone, coffeemaker, turn-down service, desk, voice mail, fireplace, hair dryers, iron, ironing board, robes and slippers in room. Fax, copier, spa, library, parlor games, fireplace, laundry facility and gift shop on premises. Weddings, small meetings, family reunions and seminars hosted. Antiquing, art galleries, bicycling, canoeing/kayaking, cross-country skiing, downhill skiing, fishing, golf, hiking, horseback riding, museums, parks, shopping, sporting events, tennis, water sports, Performing Arts Center, Egan Convention Center and federal buildings and hospitals nearby.

Publicity: *Anchorage Daily News, Alaska Business Monthly and MSNBC documentary.*

Gustavus   F7

Gustavus Inn at Glacier Bay

PO Box 60
Gustavus, AK 99826-0060
(907)697-2254 (800)649-5220 Fax:(907)697-2255
E-mail: dave@gustavusinn.com
Web: www.gustavusinn.com

Circa 1928. Established by the Lesh family in 1965, today the third generation continues to offer expert guidance to experience the best of Glacier Bay National Park. This New England-style country inn sits in the Salmon River meadow overlooking Icy Strait. Two of the guest bedrooms boast oceanviews. Enjoy family-style meals in the original homestead dining room. Homemade sourdough pancakes and rhubarb sauce are house specialties. The American plan rate includes transportation to the inn and to Bartlett Cove in the park, fishing poles, bikes and an afternoon guided nature walk. Direct flights are available from Seattle.

Historic Interest: Historic homestead built in 1928, restored in 1993.

Innkeeper(s): David & JoAnn Lesh. $300. 13 rooms, 11 with PB and 2 suites. Breakfast, afternoon tea, snacks/refreshments and dinner included in rates. Types of meals: Full gourmet bkfst, veg bkfst, early coffee/tea and gourmet lunch. Restaurant on premises. Beds: QDT. Reading lamp, clock radio and desk in room. TV, VCR, fax, copier, bicycles, library, child care, parlor games, telephone, fireplace, laundry facility, gift shop and transportation to guided nature walk at the National Park on premises. Limited handicap access. Weddings, family reunions and seminars hosted. Art galleries, beach, bicycling, canoeing/kayaking, fishing, golf, hiking, parks, shopping, Glacier Bay National Park, scenic boat cruises, whale watching, flightseeing and Spirit of Adventure nearby.

Publicity: *New York Times, LA Times, Conde Nast, Savieur, Forbes, Alaska Magazine, Alaska Southeaster, Charles Kurault ON THE ROAD and Keith Famie's Cooking Adventures.*

Haines   F7

The Summer Inn B&B

PO Box 1198
Haines, AK 99827-1198
(907)766-2970 Fax:(906)766-2970
E-mail: summerinnb&b@wytbear.com
Web: www.summerinn.wytbear.com

Circa 1912. This historic farmhouse has an infamous beginning, it was built by a member of a gang of claimjumpers who operated during the Gold Rush. The home affords stunning mountain and water views. The home is comfortably furnished, and one guest bathroom includes a clawfoot tub original to the home. Breakfasts include fresh fruit and entrees such as sourdough pancakes with ham. The area offers many activities, including museums and a historic walking tour, skiing, snowshoeing, ice fishing, hiking, fishing and much more.

Historic Interest: Built in 1912 by member of Soapy Smith's Gang.

$80-110. 5 rooms. Breakfast included in rates. Types of meals: Full bkfst, early coffee/tea, afternoon tea and snacks/refreshments. Beds: DT. Reading lamp and alarm clocks in room. Fax, library, telephone and BBQ on premises. Cross-country skiing, fishing, golf, live theater, parks, shopping, tennis, water sports and birding nearby.

Publicity: *American History April 2000 and Historic Sears Mail Order Houses Roebucks.*

Juneau   F8

Alaska's Capital Inn

113 W Fifth St
Juneau, AK 99801
(907)586-6507 (888)588-6507 Fax:(907)586-6508
E-mail: innkeeper@alaskacapitalinn.com
Web: www.alaskacapitalinn.com

Circa 1906. This American Four Square-style home was built of old growth Douglas Fir by gold rush pioneer John Olds. Olds was one of the first miners in the Juneau area after word got out about the discovery of gold, and he became the mayor. The inn is furnished in period antique pieces and newer Stickley pieces. A gourmet breakfast is served on china and with silver and it incorporates local seafood specialties. A lucky guest might awake to a treat like a smoked salmon omelet or a crab quiche. The inn has seven guest bedrooms. It is within the downtown historic district, next door to a park with a 100-year-old lilac tree, and it has mountain views. The inn has a yard with room for croquet and secluded areas to swing in the hammock. Its rear porch is a perfect place to eat breakfast or just relax.

Innkeeper(s): Linda Wendeborn & Mark Thorson. $99-275. 5 rooms with PB, 2 with FP and 2 suites. Breakfast included in rates. Types of meals: Country bkfst, early coffee/tea and afternoon tea. Beds: KQT. Modem hook-up, cable TV, VCR, reading lamp, clock radio, telephone, turn-down service, fireplace, hair dryers, irons and robes in room. Fax, spa, bicycles and parlor games on premises. Small meetings hosted. Art galleries, beach, bicycling, canoeing/kayaking, cross-country skiing, downhill skiing, fishing, hiking, live theater, museums, parks, shopping, tram ride and wildlife viewing nearby.

Publicity: HGTV "If walls could talk."

Alaskan Hotel

167 S Franklin St
Juneau, AK 99801-1321
(907)586-1000 (800)327-9347 Fax:(907)463-3775
E-mail: akhotel@ptialaska.net
Web: www.ptialaska.net/~akhotel

Circa 1913. Restored to its original Victorian design and decor, this is the city's oldest operating hotel and is listed in the National Register of Historic Places. Opened in 1913, it is an example of the architectural transition from the 19th to 20th century. Choose a guest bedroom with a private or shared bath, or stay in a more spacious studio. Baggage storage and a coin op laundry are available. Visit the hotel's historic bar and enjoy live entertainment.

Innkeeper(s): Bettye Adams. $60-90. 43 rooms, 21 with PB. Beds: DT. Telephone in room. Fax and copier on premises. Small meetings hosted. Cross-country skiing, downhill skiing, fishing, golf and shopping nearby.

Silverbow Inn & Bakery

120 2nd St
Juneau, AK 99801-1215
(907)586-4146 (800)586-4146 Fax:(907)586-4242
E-mail: info@silverbowinn.com
Web: www.silverbowinn.com

Circa 1914. For more than 100 years, Alaska's oldest operating bakery has been located here. The innkeepers, an architect and urban planner, have brought the building to life with a luxurious lobby and romantic restaurant. The inn offers B&B and European-style pension rooms. Freshly made bagels, breads and pastries are served at breakfast. Within two blocks are the state capitol, convention center, waterfront and shopping district.

Innkeeper(s): Jill Ramiel/Ken Alper. $68-148. 6 rooms with PB and 2 conference rooms. Breakfast, afternoon tea and snacks/refreshments included in rates. Types of meals: Cont and early coffee/tea. Restaurant on premises. Beds: QT. Cable TV, VCR, reading lamp, refrigerator, snack bar, clock radio, telephone, desk and voice mail in room. Fax, copier, library, parlor games, social hour with wine and cheese and bakery on premises. Weddings, small meetings, family reunions and seminars hosted. Antiquing, cross-country skiing, downhill skiing, fishing, live theater, parks and shopping nearby.

Publicity: Travel & Leisure, Destinos and Frommers Choice 2000.

Palmer   E5

Colony Inn

325 E Elmwood
Palmer, AK 99645-6622
(907)745-3330 Fax:(907)746-3330

Circa 1935. Historic buildings are few and far between in Alaska, and this inn is one of them. The structure was built to house teachers and nurses in the days when President Roosevelt was sending settlers to Alaska to establish farms. When innkeeper Janet Kincaid purchased it, the inn had been empty for some time. She restored the place, including the wood walls, which now create a cozy ambiance in the common areas. The 12 guest rooms are nicely appointed, and 10 include a whirlpool tub. Meals are not included, but the inn's restaurant offers breakfast and lunch. The inn is listed in the National Register.

Innkeeper(s): Janet Kincaid. $90. 12 rooms with PB. Types of meals: Full bkfst and lunch. Restaurant on premises. Beds: QDT. Cable TV, reading lamp, clock radio and telephone in room. Parlor games and fireplace on premises. Weddings, small meetings and family reunions hosted. Antiquing, cross-country skiing, downhill skiing, fishing, golf, parks, shopping and tennis nearby.

"Love the antiques and history."

Seldovia   F4

Seldovia Rowing Club Inn

343 Bay St
Seldovia, AK 99663
(907)234-7614 Fax:(907)234-7514
E-mail: rowing@ptialaska.net
Web: www.ptialaska.net/~rowing/

Circa 1930. Majestic mountain peaks and crystal clear waters serve as the scenery at this bed & breakfast, the first in south central Alaska. The home is located on the historic Seldovia  boardwalk, just steps from the water. There are two guest suites; each affords a water view. A full breakfast is delivered to your room. Innkeeper Susan Mumma has been welcoming guests for nearly 20 years. Seldovia offers many attractions, including fishing, mountain biking, hiking, kayaking or just enjoy the amazing scenery.

Innkeeper(s): Susan Mumma. $110. 2 suites. Breakfast included in rates. Types of meals: Full gourmet bkfst. Beds: Q. Cable TV, VCR, CD player, refrigerator, telephone and desk in room. Library, parlor games and fireplace on premises. Limited handicap access. Weddings and family reunions hosted. Cross-country skiing, fishing and water sports nearby.

Publicity: Alaska Magazine and Alaska's Best Places Milepost.

Arizona

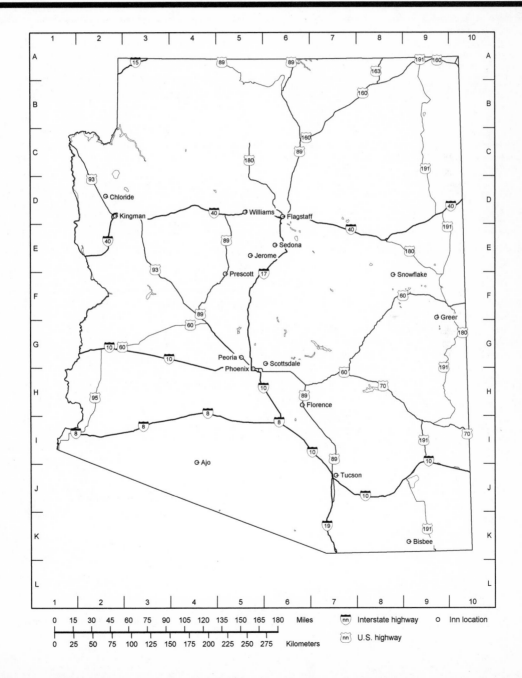

0 15 30 45 60 75 90 105 120 135 150 165 180   Miles

0 25 50 75 100 125 150 175 200 225 250 275   Kilometers

nn Interstate highway   ○ Inn location

nn U.S. highway

Ajo I4

Guest House Inn

700 W Guest House Rd
Ajo, AZ 85321-2754
(520)387-6133

Circa 1927. Originally built for copper mining executives and their visitors, the stately guest quarters were lavishly furnished and maintained until the mine closed. Now privately owned and renovated, this ranch-style bed & breakfast reflects the relaxing ambiance of southwest living as well as the rich traditions. Unpretentious guest bedrooms feature spacious and comfortable furnishings with individual heating and cooling controls. A sumptuous breakfast is served daily in the stately dining room accented by a large, locally-crafted banquet table. The lush Sonoran Desert boasts spectacular vistas and a mild climate. Visit the nearby Mexican border, the Gulf of California and Kitt Peak National Observatory. Phoenix and Tuscon are a two-hour drive.

Historic Interest: Provided lodging for mining company executives and guests.

Innkeeper(s): Mike Walker. $79-89. 4 rooms with PB. Breakfast included in rates. Types of meals: Full bkfst. Beds: QT. Reading lamp, refrigerator, ceiling fan, clock radio, hair dryer, ironing board and iron in room. Air conditioning. TV, VCR, telephone and fireplace on premises. Bicycling, golf, hiking, museums, shopping, National Monument and wildlife refuge nearby.

Bisbee K9

Bisbee Grand Hotel, A B&B Inn

61 Main Street, Box 825
Bisbee, AZ 85603
(520)432-5900 (800)421-1909
E-mail: bisbegrandhotel@msn.com
Web: www.bisbeegrandhotel.com

Circa 1906. This National Register treasure is a stunning example of an elegant turn-of-the-century hotel. The hotel originally served as a stop for mining executives, and it was restored back to its Old West glory in the 1980s. Each of the rooms is decorated with Victorian furnishings and wall coverings. The suites offer special items such as clawfoot tubs, an antique Chinese wedding bed, a fountain or four-poster bed. Try the Old Western Suite with an authentic covered wagon modified to fit a queen-size bed. The Grand Western Salon boasts the back bar fixture from the Pony Saloon in Tombstone. After a full breakfast, enjoy a day touring the Bisbee area, which includes mine tours, museums, shops, antiquing and a host of outdoor activities.

Historic Interest: Located in downtown historic Bisbee, features 110-year-old back bar fixture.

Innkeeper(s): Bill Thomas. $50-150. 8 rooms and 7 suites. Breakfast included in rates. Types of meals: Full bkfst.

Chloride D2

Shep's Miners Inn

9827 2nd St
Chloride, AZ 86431
(928)565-4251 (877)565-4251 Fax:(928)565-3643
E-mail: miners4251@frontiernet.net
Web: www.shepsminersinn.com

Circa 1890. Originally a Butterfield stagecoach stop and general store, this renovated 1890 adobe inn is perfect for experiencing the history of the Old West. The inn sits on five acres at the foot of the Cerbat Mountains in an old silver mining town in the high desert. Some of the guest bedrooms feature wall paintings by Tony Mafia, who is now a famous Brussels artist. Dine in Yesterday's Restaurant, the inn's full-service establishment. Visit nearby Indian petroglyphs and mountainside murals by Roy Purcell. A variety of tours are available. Centrally located, take easy day trips to the Grand Canyon, Kingman and Laughlin, Nevada. Ask about special packages offered.

Historic Interest: All adobe construction, originally stage coach stop for Butterfield Stage Line.

Innkeeper(s): John & Bonnie McNeely. $35-65. 15 rooms with PB and 1 suite. Restaurant on premises. Beds: QDT. Reading lamp, ceiling fan and clock radio in room. TV, VCR, fax, copier, library, pet boarding, parlor games, telephone and gift shop on premises. Limited handicap access. Weddings, small meetings, family reunions and seminars hosted. Amusement parks, antiquing, art galleries, beach, bicycling, canoeing/kayaking, fishing, golf, hiking, horseback riding, live theater, museums, parks, shopping, sporting events, tennis, water sports and wineries nearby.

Publicity: *Mohave Co. Standard, AZ Republic, KAAA, KZZZ Radio, CH 77 TV, Universal Soldier and Wild Rider.*

Flagstaff D6

Birch Tree Inn

824 W Birch Ave
Flagstaff, AZ 86001-4420
(928)774-1042 (888)774-1042 Fax:(928)774-8462
E-mail: info@birchtreeinn.com
Web: www.birchtreeinn.com

Circa 1917. Situated in a cool Ponderosa Pine forest, this pristine white bungalow with blue shutters and trim is surrounded by an inviting wraparound veranda supported with Corinthian columns. The inn's guest rooms represent a variety of styles. A full breakfast and afternoon refreshments are served. Nearby are hiking trails and ski runs. Historic downtown Flagstaff is within walking distance for shops, restaurants and entertainment. The Grand Canyon and Sedona are each an hour's drive away.

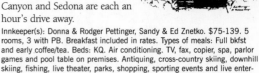

Innkeeper(s): Donna & Rodger Pettinger, Sandy & Ed Znetko. $75-139. 5 rooms, 3 with PB. Breakfast included in rates. Types of meals: Full bkfst and early coffee/tea. Beds: KQ. Air conditioning. TV, fax, copier, spa, parlor games and pool table on premises. Antiquing, cross-country skiing, downhill skiing, fishing, live theater, parks, shopping, sporting events and live entertainment nearby.

Publicity: *Arizona Daily Sun, Arizona Republic, San Francisco Chronicle, New York Times, Phoenix Gazette and Orange County Register.*

"Charming hosts and wonderful food- like visiting old friends."

Comfi Cottages

1612 N Aztec St
Flagstaff, AZ 86001-1106
(928)774-0731 (888)774-0731 Fax:(928)773-7286
E-mail: pat@comficottages.com
Web: www.comficottages.com

Circa 1920. Each of the seven cottages has been thoughtfully decorated and features a variety of styles. One cottage is decorated in a Southwestern motif, while the others feature antiques and English-Country decor. Five cottages include fireplaces, and all include kitchens stocked with full equipment and all staples. They also have the added luxury of a washer and dryer. Sleds and bicycles are available for guest use, as well as picnic tables, a barbecue grill and picnic baskets. The Grand Canyon and national parks are close by, and the cottages are in the perfect location to enjoy all Flagstaff has to offer.

Historic Interest: The cottages are located near the many activities available in historic downtown Flagstaff. Several Indian ruins are within 50 miles of the cottages.

Innkeeper(s): Ed & Pat Wiebe. $120-260. 7 cottages. Breakfast and snacks/refreshments included in rates. Types of meals: Full bkfst. Beds: KQDT. Cable TV, VCR, ceiling fan and telephone in room. Bicycles, laundry facility, sleds, BBQ and picnic tables on premises. Limited handicap access. Small meetings, family reunions and seminars hosted. Antiquing, cross-country skiing, downhill skiing, fishing, golf, hiking, live theater, parks, shopping, sporting events, tennis, water sports and Indian ruins nearby.

Publicity: *Arizona Republic, Arizona Daily Sun, Washington Post, Phoenix Magazine and Fodor's and Frommer's Guide.*

"A delightful stay; the view of the San Francisco Peaks was gorgeous."

Florence   H6

Inn at Rancho Sonora

9198 N Hwy 79
Florence, AZ 85232
(520)868-8000 (800)205-6817 Fax:(520)868-8000
E-mail: rancho@c2i2.com
Web: www.ranchosonora.com

Circa 1930. A natural desert setting of huge saguaro cacti and vegetation, fresh air, blue sky, abundant birds and wildlife is the backdrop for this adobe inn. The original integrity has been preserved while providing comfort with modern conveniences. Guest bedrooms open onto a secluded courtyard. For longer stays or spacious privacy, a kitchen suite or cottages offering complete living quarters are available. A plentiful continental breakfast buffet in the dining room is enhanced by expansive views. An outdoor fireplace, heated pool and waterfall spa add bliss to the stress-free environment.

Innkeeper(s): Linda Freeman. $59-150. 6 rooms with PB, 1 with FP, 1 suite, 3 cottages and 1 conference room. Breakfast included in rates. Types of meals: Cont plus. Beds: KQDT. Modem hook-up, data port, TV, VCR, reading lamp, refrigerator, ceiling fan, clock radio, telephone, coffeemaker, desk, hot tub/spa, satellite TV and fireplace in room. Central air. Fax, copier, spa, fireplace and laundry facility on premises. Antiquing, golf, hiking, outlet mall and Indian ruins nearby.

Publicity: *Los Angeles Times.*

Greer   F9

White Mountain Lodge

PO Box 143
Greer, AZ 85927-0143
(928)735-7568 (888)493-7568 Fax:(928)735-7498

Circa 1892. This 19th-century lodge affords views of Greer meadow and the Little Colorado River. The guest rooms are individually decorated in a Southwestern or country style. The common rooms are decorated with period antiques, Southwestern art and Mission-style furnishings. The Lodge's living room is an ideal place to relax with its stone fireplace. While dining on the hearty breakfasts, guests not only are treated to entrees that range from traditional country fare to the more gourmet, they also enjoy a view from the picture window. The cookie jar is always filled with homemade goodies and hot drinks are available throughout the day. The inn is near excellent hiking trails.

Innkeeper(s): Charles & Mary Bast. $95-155. 6 cabins with PB, 4 with FP and 1 conference room. Breakfast and snacks/refreshments included in rates. Types of meals: Full gourmet bkfst, veg bkfst and early coffee/tea. Beds: KQT. TV, VCR, reading lamp, refrigerator, ceiling fan, clock radio, coffeemaker, desk, hot tub/spa and two rooms with whirlpool tubs in room. Fax, copier, spa, telephone and fireplace on premises. Small meetings and family reunions hosted. Antiquing, art galleries, cross-country skiing, downhill skiing, fishing, golf, hiking, museums and shopping nearby.

Publicity: *Independent & Arizona Republic, Arizona Foothills, Vista Magazine, KOY Radio, Channel 3 and Phoenix Magazine.*

Jerome   E5

Ghost City Inn

541 Main St. (Hwy. 89A)
Jerome, AZ 86331
(928)634-4678 (888)634-4678
E-mail: innkeeper@ghostcityinn.com
Web: www.ghostcityinn.com

Circa 1890. Porches and verandas stretch across the front of this inn, overlooking the town, Verde Valley and the red rocks of Sedona. Originally built as a boarding house for mining company employees, the old hotel has been refurbished by the innkeepers. (Dave is an architect.) Many guest rooms are furnished with Victorian antiques. In the morning, an abundant selection of breakfast items are offered, in addition to a main course such as strawberry cream cheese stuffed, caramelized French toast topped with whipped cream and more strawberries or a green chili tortilla strata with sour cream and salsa. There is an outdoor Jacuzzi for soaking and enjoying starlit nights, or you can enjoy the shops, restaurants and galleries of the historic landmark town of Jerome.

Innkeeper(s): Allen & Jackie Muma. $85-125. 6 rooms, 2 with PB, 2 with FP and 1 suite. Breakfast included in rates. Types of meals: Full gourmet bkfst. Beds: QD. TV, VCR, reading lamp, ceiling fan, clock radio and fireplace in room. Air conditioning. Spa on premises. Weddings and family reunions hosted. Antiquing, art galleries, canoeing/kayaking, fishing, golf, hiking, museums, parks and shopping nearby.

Publicity: *Boston Globe, Sunset, AZ Highways, Biz AZ and Fox 10 Truly Arizona.*

Jerome Grand Hotel

PO Box H, 200 Hill St
Jerome, AZ 86331
(928)634-8200 (888)817-6788 Fax:(928)639-0299
E-mail: hotel@wildapache.net
Web: www.jeromegrandhotel.net

Circa 1926. Originally the United Verde Hospital, this five-story Spanish Mission building made of poured-in-place, reinforced concrete is one of the highest structures in Verde Valley, promising spectacular scenic views. The inn is a A National Historic Landmark Hotel. Restoration has preserved all of the exterior, while most of the interior remains original. Phones in the guest bedrooms and suites are serviced by an antique switchboard. The lobby offers round-the-clock hospitality, and the gift shop also is open 24 hours. A restaurant and lounge provide indoor and outside seating.

Innkeeper(s): Larry & LaWanda Altherr. $85-195. 22 rooms, 19 with PB and 3 suites. Types of meals: Early coffee/tea. Restaurant on premises. Beds: QT. Cable TV, ceiling fan and telephone in room. Central air. Weddings, small meetings and family reunions hosted. Antiquing, art galleries, golf, hiking, museums, parks and shopping nearby.

Kingman   D2

Hotel Brunswick

315 E Andy Devine Ave
Kingman, AZ 86401
(928)718-1800 Fax:(928)718-1801
E-mail: rsvp@hotel-brunswick.com
Web: www.hotel-brunswick.com

Circa 1909. Built at the turn of the 20th century, the Hotel Brunswick was, for awhile, the tallest building in three counties. The hotel was built to accommodate the many railroad passengers who traveled through Kingman. Later in the century, the hotel fell into disrepair until the current owners purchased the property, restoring the historic charm. Each of the guest rooms has been appointed individually. Rooms range from the spacious honeymoon suite to the cozy, economical Cowboy and Cowgirl rooms. In addition to the accommodations, the hotel includes a European-style café, Mulligan's Bar, and a full-service business center. Your hosts can arrange a massage service or create a honeymoon package with flowers and champagne. Kingman, a stop along the famed Route 66, maintains many historic buildings and sites.

Innkeeper(s): Mr. Gerard Guedon. $25-110. 24 rooms, 7 with PB and 8 suites. Breakfast included in rates. Types of meals: Cont plus, early coffee/tea and gourmet dinner. Restaurant on premises. Beds: QDT. Modem hook-up, cable TV, VCR, reading lamp, refrigerator and telephone in room. Air conditioning. Fax, copier and laundry facility on premises. Limited handicap access. Weddings, small meetings, family reunions and seminars hosted. Antiquing, canoeing/kayaking, fishing, golf, hiking, horseback riding, museums, parks, shopping, water sports and ghost towns nearby.

Publicity: *Kingman Daily Miner, Standard News, Arizona Holidays and TV 77.*

Peoria   G5

Old Town B&B

8276 W Monroe St
Peoria, AZ 85345
(623)412-7797 Fax:(623)412-7797
E-mail: oldtowninnkeeper@cox.net
Web: www.oldtownbb.com

Circa 1947. Half an acre of gardens with a gazebo, arch and fountains surrounds this red brick home. Socialize in the Victorian parlor, watch a video, or relax on one of the outdoor patios. Stay in one of the cozy guest bedrooms in the main house. The Country Cottage Room boasts a clawfoot tub and the Americana Room is adorned with quilts and antiques. The nearby bungalow offers a four-room Caribbean-style getaway. Enjoy breakfast delicacies in the dining room. The B&B is close to the Glendale historic district, antique shops, as well as the Peoria and Surprise Sports Complexes for baseball spring training. Popular activities include fishing and boating at Lake Pleasant Regional Park and hiking and picnicking at White Tank Mountain Park.

Innkeeper(s): Vicki & Tom Hunt. $75-125. 3 rooms. Breakfast included in rates. Types of meals: Full bkfst and early coffee/tea. Beds: Q. Reading lamp, ceiling fan, clock radio, turn-down service and desk in room. Central air. TV, VCR, fax, copier, parlor games, telephone and laundry facility on premises. Weddings and small meetings hosted. Antiquing, fishing, golf, shopping, sporting events and water sports nearby.

Phoenix   H5

Maricopa Manor

15 W Pasadena Ave
Phoenix, AZ 85013
(602)274-6302 (800)292-6403 Fax:(602)266-3904

Circa 1928. Secluded amid palm trees on an acre of land, this Spanish-style house features four graceful columns in the entry hall, an elegant living room with a marble mantel and a music room. Completely refurbished suites are very spacious and distinctively furnished with style and good taste. Relax on the private patio or around the pool while enjoying the soothing sound of falling water from the many fountains.

Historic Interest: Arizona Biltmore Resort (2 miles), Heard Museum (3 miles), Pueblo Grand Indian Ruins and Museum.

Innkeeper(s): Jeff Vadheim. $99-249. 7 suites, 4 with FP. Breakfast included in rates. Types of meals: Cont plus. Beds: KQ. Cable TV, VCR, reading lamp, stereo, refrigerator, ceiling fan, clock radio, telephone and desk in room. Air conditioning. TV, fax, copier, spa, swimming, library, parlor games and off-street parking on premises. Limited handicap access. Amusement parks, antiquing, golf, live theater, parks, shopping, sporting events, tennis, water sports and restaurants nearby.

Publicity: *Arizona Business Journal, Country Inns, AAA Westways, San Francisco Chronicle, Focus and Sombrero.*

"I've stayed 200+ nights at B&Bs around the world, yet have never before experienced the warmth and sincere friendliness of Maricopa Manor."

Prescott — F5

Dolls & Roses Victorian Bed & Breakfast

109 N Pleasant St
Prescott, AZ 86301
(928)776-9291 (800)924-0883 Fax:(928)778-2642
E-mail: dollsandroses@yahoo.com
Web: www.dollsandroses-bb.com

Circa 1883. Each of the guest rooms at this historic 19th-century Victorian is decorated with a rose theme. The English Rose is a spacious room with a sitting area decorated with a love seat and antique rocker. The Rose Garden has an antique clawfoot tub. The historic home is decorated in Victorian style with antiques and a collection of porcelain dolls. A full breakfast is served each morning featuring specialty egg dishes. Historic downtown is within walking distance.

Historic Interest: Built in 1883.

Innkeeper(s): Donna Perkins. $99-149. 4 rooms with PB. Breakfast included in rates. Types of meals: Full bkfst and snacks/refreshments. Beds: KQ. Reading lamp and ceiling fan in room. Air conditioning. TV, VCR, fax, copier, parlor games, telephone and fireplace on premises. Weddings, small meetings and family reunions hosted. Antiquing, art galleries, bicycling, fishing, golf, hiking, horseback riding, live theater, museums, parks, shopping, tennis, water sports and seasonal town square events nearby.

Pleasant Street Inn

142 S Pleasant St
Prescott, AZ 86303-3811
(928)445-4774 (877)226-7128 Fax:(928)445-4774
E-mail: jeannew@cableone.net
Web: www.pleasantstreetinn-bb.com

Circa 1906. Pleasant Street Inn was moved to its present site, in the heart of historic Prescott, in 1991. Rooms at this quaint, Victorian inn are stylishly decorated with comfort in mind. The PineView Suite boasts a sitting room and fireplace. Another suite includes a sitting room and private, covered deck. Prescott, which served twice as the state territorial capital, offers a variety of museums and art galleries to explore, as well as the historic Court House Square. Nearby Prescott National Forest is a perfect place to enjoy hiking, climbing and other outdoor activities.

Innkeeper(s): Jeanne Watkins. $95-135. 4 rooms with PB and 2 suites. Breakfast included in rates. Types of meals: Full bkfst. Beds: KQD. Modem hook-up, data port, reading lamp, refrigerator, ceiling fan, fireplace and private deck in room. Central air. TV, VCR, fax, parlor games and telephone on premises. Small meetings, family reunions and seminars hosted.

Prescott Pines Inn

901 White Spar Rd
Prescott, AZ 86303-7231
(928)445-7270 (800)541-5374 Fax:(928)778-3665
E-mail: info@prescottpinesinn.com
Web: www.prescottpinesinn.com

Circa 1934. A white picket fence beckons guests to the veranda of this comfortably elegant country Victorian inn, originally the Haymore Dairy. There are masses of fragrant pink roses, lavenders and delphiniums, and stately ponderosa pines that tower above the inn's three renovated guesthouses, which were once shelter for farm hands. A three-bedroom, two-bath on-site chalet that sleeps up to ten guests is perfect for a family or group. Seven of the eleven rooms are equipped with kitch-enettes and three have fireplaces. The acre of grounds includes a garden fountain and romantic tree swing. A full breakfast is offered at an additional charge.

Innkeeper(s): Harry & Debbie Allen. $65-269. 11 rooms with PB, 3 with FP. Types of meals: Full bkfst and early coffee/tea. Beds: KQ. Cable TV, reading lamp, refrigerator, ceiling fan, clock radio and telephone in room. Air conditioning. TV, fax, copier, parlor games and fireplace on premises. Small meetings and family reunions hosted. Antiquing, hiking, live theater, parks and shopping nearby.

Publicity: *Sunset, Arizona Republic News and Arizona Highways.*

"The ONLY place to stay in Prescott! Tremendous attention to detail."

Scottsdale — G6

Arizona Trails

PO Box 18998
Scottsdale, AZ 85269
(480)837-4284 (888)799-4284 Fax:(480)816-4224
E-mail: aztrails@arizonatrails.com
Web: www.arizonatrails.com

Circa 1940. Many of Arizona's B&Bs, inns and hotels that this reservation service represents are historic or depict Southwestern style. Some are situated on or near historic sites including the Cochise stronghold, Tombstone, the OK Corral, Grand Canyon, Indian cliff dwellings and archaeological sites. Listings include a restored adobe Victorian inn, an authentic stagecoach stop where a mercantile store was converted to a bed & breakfast and the renowned Fred Harvey Historic Hotel, frequented by celebrities from the early days of Hollywood. Exclusive getaway locations feature desert or mountain settings with panoramic views. Accommodations range from one guest bedroom to 80, with seasonal rates. Breakfasts vary from continental fare to regional recipes. A travel consultant will assist in planning custom itineraries and packages.

Innkeeper(s): Roxanne Boryczki. $85-495. Breakfast, afternoon tea and snacks/refreshments included in rates. Types of meals: Full gourmet bkfst, veg bkfst and early coffee/tea. Beds: KQDT. Modem hook-up, data port, cable TV, VCR, reading lamp, stereo, refrigerator, ceiling fan, snack bar, clock radio, telephone, coffeemaker, turn-down service, desk, hot tub/spa and voice mail in room. Central air. Fax, spa, swimming, sauna, stable, bicycles, tennis, library, pet boarding, parlor games, fireplace and laundry facility on premises. Limited handicap access. Weddings, small meetings, family reunions and seminars hosted. Antiquing, art galleries, bicycling, cross-country skiing, downhill skiing, fishing, golf, hiking, horseback riding, museums, parks, shopping, sporting events, tennis and wineries nearby.

Sedona — E6

Briar Patch Inn

3190 N Hwy 89A
Sedona, AZ 86336-9602
(928)282-2342 (888)809-3030 Fax:(928)282-2399
E-mail: briarpatch@sedona.net
Web: www.briarpatchinn.com

Circa 1943. Getting in touch with nature should come easy at this cluster of cottages on 9 acres found along the lush banks of Oak Creek and located three miles north of the town of Sedona. Fireplaces, shaded patios and privacy help guests relax along with massages offered in your own cottage. Each cottage is different in size, layout and unique decor, which includes

Arizona Indian and Mexican art. Healthy breakfasts can be enjoyed by the fireplace in the lounge, on a tray in the cottages or creekside. Throughout the year, small workshops in painting, Navajo weaving, Indian arts and other self-enrichment classes are given.

Innkeeper(s): Rob Olson. $169-325. 17 cabins. Breakfast, afternoon tea and snacks/refreshments included in rates. Types of meals: Full bkfst. Beds: KQT. Reading lamp, refrigerator and ceiling fan in room. Air conditioning. Fax, copier, swimming, library, telephone, fireplace and BBQ area on premises. Weddings, small meetings, family reunions and seminars hosted. Antiquing, cross-country skiing, downhill skiing, fishing, golf, hiking, shopping and tennis nearby.

Publicity: *Sedona Magazine.*

Snowflake   F8

Osmer D. Heritage Inn

161 North Main
Snowflake, AZ 85937
(928)536-3322 (866)486-5937 Fax:(928)536-4834
E-mail: mulcherjdp@netscape.net
Web: www.heritage-inn.net

Circa 1890. A loving heritage surrounds this restored inn boasting two-story brick buildings. The decor is Victorian, and the antique furnishings can be purchased. Visit the adjacent antique shop to find more treasures. For solitude or socializing, ample common rooms include the parlor with DVD, library and reception room. Gas-log stoves highlight guest bedrooms and a honeymoon suite. Several rooms feature romantic spa tubs for two. Linger over a hearty gourmet breakfast in the dining room. French or cowboy steak-dinner parties can be arranged. After a day of touring historic pioneer homes, relax in the large hot tub.

Innkeeper(s): J. Dean & Sandra Porter. $65-120. 11 rooms with PB, 11 with FP, 2 suites and 1 conference room. Breakfast and snacks/refreshments included in rates. Types of meals: Full gourmet bkfst, early coffee/tea, lunch, picnic lunch and gourmet dinner. Restaurant on premises. Beds: Q. Data port, cable TV, VCR, reading lamp, clock radio, telephone, fireplace, Jacuzzi spa for eight people and exercise equipment in room. Air conditioning. Fax, copier, spa, library, parlor games, fireplace, laundry facility, antique shop next door and gift shop on premises. Limited handicap access. Weddings, small meetings and seminars hosted. Antiquing, art galleries, bicycling, downhill skiing, fishing, golf, hiking, horseback riding, museums, parks, shopping, tennis, tours of historic pioneer homes and cabins, national parks, three Indian Reservation day trips and casinos on Indian land nearby.

Publicity: *Country Register and Antique Register.*

Tucson   J7

Adobe Rose Inn

940 N Olsen Ave
Tucson, AZ 85719-4951
(520)318-4644 (800)328-4122 Fax:(520)318-4644
E-mail: hookjim@aol.com
Web: www.aroseinn.com

Circa 1933. This three-diamond-rated inn is located in the historic Sam Hughes neighborhood just a few blocks from the University of Arizona campus. The inn boasts an exquisite stained-glass window, beamed ceilings and a kiva fireplace. Airy guest rooms are decorated with a romantic, Southwestern flavor. The Arizona Room includes a fireplace and a huge hand-painted tile tub. The Rainbow's End, which overlooks the pool, offers a beehive fireplace. The innkeeper also offer

two cottages, one with a refrigerator and microwave oven and another with a galley kitchen.

Historic Interest: Located in Sam Hughes neighborhood which is placed in National Historic Register.

Innkeeper(s): Jim and Marion Hook. $65-165. 6 rooms, 3 with PB, 2 with FP and 2 suites. Breakfast and snacks/refreshments included in rates. Types of meals: Full gourmet bkfst, veg bkfst and early coffee/tea. Beds: KQT. Cable TV, VCR, reading lamp, refrigerator, ceiling fan, clock radio, telephone, coffeemaker and desk in room. Air conditioning. Spa, swimming, parlor games and fireplace on premises. Small meetings and family reunions hosted. Antiquing, art galleries, bicycling, golf, hiking, live theater, museums, parks, shopping, sporting events, tennis and water sports nearby.

Casa Alegre B&B

316 E Speedway Blvd
Tucson, AZ 85705-7429
(520)628-1800 (800)628-5654 Fax:(520)792-1880
E-mail: alegre123@aol.com
Web: www.casaalegreinn.com

Circa 1915. Innkeeper Phyllis Florek decorated the interior of this Craftsman-style home with artifacts reflecting the history of Tucson, including Native American pieces and antique mining

tools. Wake to the aroma of fresh coffee and join other guests as you enjoy fresh muffins, fruit and other breakfast treats,  such as succulent cottage cheese pancakes with raspberry preserves. The Arizona sitting room opens onto serene gardens, a pool and a Jacuzzi. An abundance of shopping and sightseeing is found nearby.

Historic Interest: The innkeeper serves on the board of directors of the West University Historic District and is full of information about historic sites and the history of the area.

Innkeeper(s): Phyllis Florek. $90-135. 4 rooms with PB, 1 with FP. Breakfast included in rates. Types of meals: Full gourmet bkfst. Beds: Q. Cable TV, reading lamp, ceiling fan and clock radio in room. VCR, fax, spa, swimming, parlor games, telephone and fireplace on premises. Weddings, small meetings and family reunions hosted. Antiquing, live theater, parks, shopping, sporting events and restaurants nearby.

Publicity: *Arizona Daily Star, Travel Holiday and Arizona Times.*

"An oasis of comfort in Central Tucson."

The El Presidio B&B Inn

297 N Main Ave
Tucson, AZ 85701-8219
(520)623-6151 (800)349-6151
Web: www.bbonline.com/az/elpresidio

Circa 1886. The cobblestone courtyards, fountains, and lush gardens surrounding El Presidio are filled with an old-world Southwestern ambiance. The inn is comprised of a Victorian-Territorial adobe built around a traditional zaguan, or large central hall, plus separate suites  in the former carriage house and gate house. Innkeeper Patti Toci conducted a 10-year, award-winning restoration of this inn. Rooms are immaculate, romantic and richly appointed. Gourmet breakfasts are served in a dining room that overlooks the courtyard. Beverages are served throughout the day. This inn was voted the "Best B&B in

Tucson" for 1995-96 and the "Best B&B in Southern Arizona" for 1998. Restaurants and museums are nearby.

Innkeeper(s): Patti Toci. $95-125. 3 suites. Breakfast included in rates. Beds: Q. TV and telephone in room. Live theater, shopping, restaurants and museums nearby.

Publicity: *Gourmet, Travel & Leisure, Glamour, Tucson Home & Garden, Arizona Highways, Innsider and Zagat Survey.*

"Thank you again for providing such a completely perfect, pampering, relaxing, delicious, gorgeous vacation 'home' for us."

Elysian Grove Market Bed & Breakfast Inn

400 W Simpson St
Tucson, AZ 85701-2283
(520)628-1522
E-mail: info@elysiangrove.com
Web: www.elysiangrove.com

Circa 1920. Originally built as a corner market, this adobe home has been transformed with charm. It is located next to the downtown arts district, in an Historic Barrio. Wood floors, 14-foot ceilings, skylights and wood-burning fireplaces are accented by folk art and antique furnishings from the Southwest and Mexico. Guest bedrooms boast tribal rugs and comfortable vintage beds. Two rooms have French doors that open onto the garden of cactus, flowers and fountains, and two others have been converted from what were the wine cellars. Mexican tile and pull chain toilets add to the ambiance in the bathrooms. The fully equipped kitchen was once the meat locker. Music is played during a tasty breakfast that includes pan dulce (a pastry), cheese, fresh fruit and beverages.

Innkeeper(s): Deborah Lachapelle. $85. 5 rooms, 1 with PB. Breakfast included in rates. Types of meals: Cont plus. Beds: QDT. Fully equipped kitchen and fireplaces on premises. Weddings hosted. Bicycling, golf, hiking and shopping nearby.

Publicity: *Tucson LifeStyles Magazine, New York Times, Spacio Casa Magazine, Better Homes & Gardens and Wallpaper Magazine.*

La Posada Del Valle

1640 N Campbell Ave
Tucson, AZ 85719-4313
(520)795-3840 (888)404-7113 Fax:(520)795-3840

Circa 1929. This Southwestern adobe has 18-inch-thick walls, which wraparound to form a courtyard. Ornamental orange trees and lush gardens surround the secluded property. All the rooms have private entrances and open to the patio or overlook the courtyard and fountain. Furnishings include antiques and period pieces from the '20s and '30s. Breakfasts are served in a dining room that offers a view of the Catalina Mountains. The University of Arizona, University Medical Center, shops, dining and more all are within walking distance.

Innkeeper(s): Karin Dennen. $75-149. 5 rooms with PB and 1 cottage. Breakfast included in rates. Types of meals: Full gourmet bkfst. Beds: KQT. Cable TV, reading lamp and clock radio in room. Air conditioning. VCR, fax, library, telephone, fireplace, off-street parking and fireplace in living room on premises. Weddings, small meetings and family reunions hosted. Antiquing, downhill skiing, live theater, parks, shopping and sporting events nearby.

Publicity: *Gourmet, Los Angeles Times, USA Today, Travel & Leisure, Channel 4 Television and Sunset.*

The Peppertrees B&B Inn

724 E University Blvd
Tucson, AZ 85719-5045
(520)622-7167 (800)348-5763
E-mail: pepperinn@gci-net.com
Web: www.peppertreesinn.com

Circa 1905. Inside this historic home, you will find English antiques inherited from the innkeeper's family. There is a patio filled with flowers and a fountain. Each of two newly built Southwestern-style guest houses features two bedrooms, two bathrooms, a kitchen, laundry and a private patio. Blue-corn pecan pancakes and Scottish shortbread are house specialties. Peppertrees is within walking distance to the University of Arizona, shops, theaters, museums and restaurants.

Innkeeper(s): Marjorie G. Martin. $88-185. 4 rooms, 3 with PB and 1 cottage. Breakfast included in rates. Types of meals: Full gourmet bkfst. Beds: KQT. TV, ceiling fan, telephone and microwaves in room. Air conditioning. Weddings, small meetings and family reunions hosted. Hiking, live theater, museums, shopping and sporting events nearby.

Publicity: *Tucson Guide, Travel Age West, Country, Tucson Homes & Gardens, Sunset, Tucson Lifestyle, Arizona Highways and Arizona Business Magazine.*

"We have not yet stopped telling our friends what a wonderful experience we shared at your lovely home."

The Royal Elizabeth Bed & Breakfast Inn

204 S Scott Ave
Tucson, AZ 85701
(520)670-9022 (877)670-9022 Fax:(520)629-9710
E-mail: inn@royalelizabeth.com
Web: www.royalelizabeth.com

Circa 1878. Listed in the National Register, this adobe mansion was built with a Victorian design. Imparting a casual elegance, the inn's original trim and millwork are enhanced by modern renovations. Refreshments in the parlor are enjoyed throughout the day. Some of the spacious guest bedrooms can be made into adjoining suites. They feature fine linens, period antiques, Jacuzzi tubs, dish network TV, VCR and a refrigerator concealing armoire. Gourmet breakfast is served in the grand dining hall. A pool and spa offer refreshment. Historic downtown has much to offer only a few blocks away.

Innkeeper(s): Jack Nance & Robert Ogburn. $90-180. 6 rooms with PB and 4 suites. Breakfast, afternoon tea and snacks/refreshments included in rates. Types of meals: Full gourmet bkfst, veg bkfst and early coffee/tea. Beds: QD. Modem hook-up, cable TV, VCR, reading lamp, refrigerator, ceiling fan, clock radio, telephone and desk in room. Central air. Fax, copier, spa, swimming, library and parlor games on premises. Small meetings, family reunions and seminars hosted. Antiquing, art galleries, bicycling, golf, hiking, horseback riding, live theater, museums, parks, shopping, sporting events, tennis and wineries nearby.

Publicity: *HGTV.*

Williams D5

The Red Garter Bed & Bakery

137 W Railroad Ave
Williams, AZ 86046
(928)635-1484 (800)328-1484
E-mail: historicinn@redgarter.com
Web: www.redgarter.com

Circa 1897. An 1897 saloon and bordello, this two-story Richardsonian Romanesque brick building listed in the National Register now offers lodging and a bakery in a small-town setting. Twelve-foot ceilings and antique furnishings reflect the old western ambiance while modern amenities ensure comfort and convenience. Overlook the ponderosa pine forest and the Grand Canyon Railway Depot in Best Gal's Room with an adjoining sitting room. Big Bertha's Room boasts a vintage footed bathtub, and a stay in The Madam's Room includes original skylights and a smaller parlor with second Queen-size bed. Enjoy a fresh-baked continental-plus breakfast before riding on the steam train or touring historic Route 66.

Historic Interest: Built by a German tailor in 1897 as the Grand Canyon's whorehouse and saloon, the Red Garter sits on historic Route 66 across from the Grand Canyon Railway. Richardsonian Romanesque in design, it boasted a two-story outhouse and housed an opium den at the rear of the building. While clients seldom left their names, Governor George W.P. Hunt was an occasional poker player in the saloon downstairs.

Innkeeper(s): John Holst. $70-120. 4 rooms with PB and 1 conference room. Breakfast and afternoon tea included in rates. Types of meals: Cont plus. Beds: Q. Cable TV, reading lamp, ceiling fan and clock radio in room. Telephone and gift shop on premises. Weddings, small meetings and family reunions hosted. Antiquing, art galleries, bicycling, cross-country skiing, downhill skiing, fishing, golf, hiking, horseback riding, museums, shopping, Grand Canyon National Park, Walnut Canyon, Sunset Crater, Waputki National Monuments, Native American ruins and Sedon/Oak Creek Canyon nearby.

Publicity: *AZ Republic "Brothel Reborn as B&B" - April 2000, Atlanta Constitution Journal "Honeymooners Find Quiet in Arizona Bordello" - Nov. 97, Abenteuer & Reisen USA: "Freudenhaus als Nachtquartier" - Nov. 95, "Creame De La Chrom" - July 98, Der Tages Spiegel, Reise (Berlin) - Sept. 98, BBC Route 66 Special, NPR Historic Route 66 interview, GEO - Feb. 98, Trailer Life - Sept. 98, Arizona Highways - Oct. 01 and Oct. 02; Route 66 Magazine - Fall 96; Romantic Traveling - Summer 98; Passport Newsletter - June 97.*

Arkansas

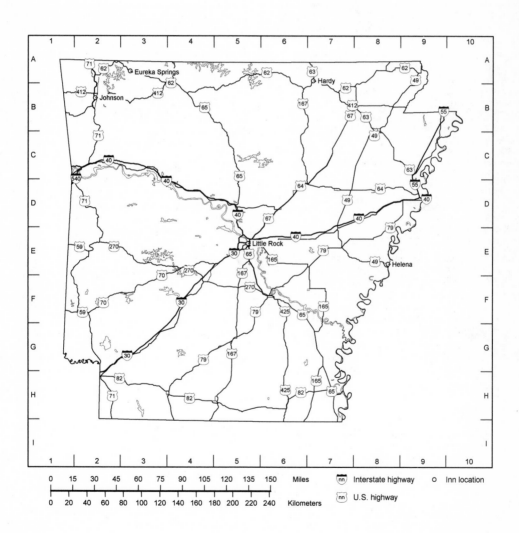

		Miles
0 15 30 45 60 75 90 105 120 135 150		

		Kilometers
0 20 40 60 80 100 120 140 160 180 200 220 240		

⬡ Interstate highway   ○ Inn location

⬡ U.S. highway

Eureka Springs   A3

11 Singleton House B&B

11 Singleton St
Eureka Springs, AR 72632-3026
(479)253-9111 (800)833-3394

Circa 1895. This pink Queen Anne Victorian is highlighted with bird-shaped exterior brackets. Guest rooms are whimsically decorated with an eclectic collection of folk art and antique family treasures. Some rooms offer two beds.

Breakfast is served on the balcony overlooking colorful wildflower gardens, lily-filled goldfish pond and scenic wooded view. Created by a local artist, the garden features a unique birdhouse collection and winding stone paths. Guests may stroll one block down a wooded footpath to shops and restaurants, ride the trolley through town or enjoy a horse and carriage ride through the historic district.

Innkeeper(s): Barbara Gavron. $65-125. 5 rooms with PB, 1 suite and 1 cottage. Breakfast and afternoon tea included in rates. Types of meals: Full bkfst, veg bkfst and early coffee/tea. Beds: QDT. Cable TV, reading lamp, refrigerator, hot tub/spa and most with ceiling fans in room. Air conditioning. Fax, copier, library and parlor games on premises. Family reunions hosted. Antiquing, Passion Play, dinner train and music shows nearby.
Publicity: *Arkansas Gazette, The Houston Post* and *The Wichita Eagle-Beacon.*

"All the many little surprises were so much fun. We enjoyed the quietness of sitting on the porch and walking through your garden."

1881 Crescent Cottage Inn

211 Spring St
Eureka Springs, AR 72632-3153
(479)253-6022 (800)223-3246 Fax:(501)253-6234

Circa 1881. This Victorian inn was home to the first governor of Arkansas after the Civil War. Two long verandas overlook a breathtaking valley and two mountain ranges. The home is graced by a beautiful tower, spindlework and coffered ceilings.

A huge arch joins the dining and living rooms, which, like the rest of the inn, are filled with antiques. All of the guest rooms feature Jacuzzi tubs, and two have a fireplace. The inn is situated on the quiet, residential street at the beginning of the historic loop. A five-minute walk into town takes guests past limestone cliffs, tall maple trees, gardens and refreshing springs. Try a ride on a horse carriage or on the steam engine train that departs nearby.

Historic Interest: Excluding a few new areas, the entire town of Eureka Springs is a National Historic District and filled with beautiful homes, buildings and shops to explore. The Crescent Cottage is listed in the National Register and designated as a state and city landmark.

Innkeeper(s): Ray & Elise Dilfield. $99-145. 4 rooms with PB, 2 with FP and 1 suite. Breakfast included in rates. Types of meals: Full bkfst and early coffee/tea. Beds: Q. Cable TV, VCR, refrigerator, ceiling fan, hot tub/spa and private Jacuzzi in room. Air conditioning. Fax, copier and parlor games on premises. Weddings and family reunions hosted. Amusement parks, antiquing, fishing, golf, hiking, live theater, parks, shopping, sporting events, tennis, water sports and boating nearby.
Publicity: *Country Home, Country Inn, Ft.Lauderdale News, Minneapolis Tribune, "Victorian Express"* and *"America's Painted Ladies."*

1884 Bridgeford House B&B

263 Spring St
Eureka Springs, AR 72632-3154
(479)253-7853 (888)567-2422 Fax:(479)253-5497
E-mail: innkeeper@bridgefordhouse.com
Web: www.bridgefordhouse.com

Circa 1884. Victorian charm abounds at this Queen Anne-Eastlake home, located in the heart of the historic district. Experience generous Southern hospitality upon arrival, when offered homemade treats. Several guest bedrooms feature a double Jacuzzi, fireplace and deck. Savor a gourmet breakfast served on fine china and flatware. The bed & breakfast is just a few blocks from gift boutiques, antique shops, spas, restaurants and much more.

Historic Interest: Pea Ridge National Park (30 min.), War Eagle Mill & Cavern (30 min.), North Arkansas Railway (1 block).
Innkeeper(s): Jeff & Nadara (Sam) Feldman. $99-165. 5 rooms with PB. Breakfast included in rates. Types of meals: Full bkfst, early coffee/tea, snacks/refreshments and room service. Beds: KQ. Cable TV, VCR, reading lamp, refrigerator, clock radio and fans in room. Air conditioning. Telephone on premises. Weddings, small meetings and family reunions hosted. Antiquing, fishing, golf, live theater, shopping and water sports nearby.
Publicity: *Times Echo Flashlight, Arkansas National Tour Guide and Country Almanac.*

"You have created an enchanting respite for weary people."

1908 Ridgeway House B&B

28 Ridgeway Ave
Eureka Springs, AR 72632-3025
(479)253-6618 (877)501-2501
E-mail: rheureka@ipa.net
Web: www.ridgewayhouse.com

Circa 1908. Declared a stress-free environment, this renovated two-story, white Colonial Revival in the historic district has four columns, original woodwork and a spiral staircase going between the first- and second-floor verandas. Tastefully decorated guest bedrooms and suites are furnished with antiques and offer access to a veranda or deck overlooking the Ozark Mountains. Some boast a Jacuzzi, parlor, kitchen, cable TV and VCR. Keith's breakfasts are so satisfying, lunch won't be needed. An afternoon dessert is also prepared, and hot and cold beverages always are available.

Innkeeper(s): Keith & Gayla Hubbard. $99-149. 5 rooms with PB, 1 with FP and 2 suites. Breakfast and snacks/refreshments included in rates. Types of meals: Full gourmet bkfst and early coffee/tea. Beds: KQ. Cable TV, VCR, reading lamp, stereo, refrigerator, ceiling fan, clock radio, coffeemaker and hot tub/spa in room. Central air. TV, fax, library, parlor games, telephone and fireplace on premises. Small meetings hosted. Antiquing, art galleries, beach, bicycling, canoeing/kayaking, fishing, golf, hiking, horseback riding, live theater, museums and shopping nearby.

"True southern hospitality at its best."

5 Ojo Inn B&B

5 Ojo St
Eureka Springs, AR 72632-3220
(479)253-6734 (800)656-6734 Fax:(479)363-9492
E-mail: bnbinns@5ojo.com
Web: www.5ojo.com

Circa 1900. Guests at 5 Ojo choose between four restored buildings ranging in vintage from an 1891 Victorian to a 1940s cottage. Rooms are decorated with antiques but include modern amenities such as refrigerators and coffeemakers. Most rooms include whirlpool tubs and fireplaces. The Carriage House Cottage and the Anniversary Suite are ideal places for honeymooners or those celebrating a

special occasion. Among its romantic amenities, the Anniversary Suite includes a private porch with a swing. Gourmet breakfasts are served in the Sweet House's dining room, but private dining can be arranged. Eureka Springs with its 63-65 springs, has been a sought after spa town for more than a century.

Innkeeper(s): Richard & Jan Grinnell. $79-149. 10 rooms with PB, 7 with FP, 2 suites and 1 cottage. Breakfast included in rates. Types of meals: Full gourmet bkfst. Beds: QT. Cable TV, reading lamp, refrigerator, ceiling fan, clock radio, coffeemaker, desk and nine with Jacuzzi tubs for two in room. Air conditioning. TV, VCR, fax, spa, library, parlor games and telephone on premises. Weddings, small meetings and family reunions hosted. Antiquing, art galleries, fishing, golf, live theater, parks, shopping, sporting events, water sports, massage therapy and Victorian village nearby.

Publicity: *Arkansas Democrat Gazette, Southern Living and Country Inns.*

Candlestick Cottage Inn

6 Douglas St
Eureka Springs, AR 72632-3416
(479)253-6813 (800)835-5184
E-mail: candleci@mynewroads.com
Web: www.candlestickcottageinn.com

Circa 1888. Woods and foliage surround this scenic country home, nestled just a few blocks from Eureka Springs historic district. Guests are sure to discover a variety of wildlife strolling by the home, including an occasional deer. Breakfasts are served on the tree-top porch, which overlooks a waterfall and fish pond. The morning meal begins with freshly baked muffins and fresh fruit, followed by an entree. Innkeepers Bill and Patsy Brooks will prepare a basket of sparkling grape juice and wine glasses for those celebrating a special occasion. Guest rooms are decorated in Victorian style, and some include two-person Jacuzzis.

Innkeeper(s): Bill & Patsy Brooks. $65-129. 6 rooms with PB. Breakfast included in rates. Types of meals: Full bkfst. Beds: Q. Cable TV, reading lamp, refrigerator, clock radio and Jacuzzi in room. Air conditioning. Telephone on premises. Weddings and small meetings hosted. Antiquing, fishing, parks and shopping nearby.

Cliff Cottage Inn - Luxury B&B Suites & Historic Cottages

Heart of Historic Downtown
Eureka Springs, AR 72632
(479)253-7409 (800)799-7409
E-mail: cliffctg@aol.com
Web: www.cliffcottage.com

Circa 1880. The only bed & breakfast in the heart of historic downtown, it is comprised of three splendid houses in a row, just 17 steps down to the shops and restaurants of Main Street. Cliff Cottage, an 1880 Eastlake Victorian, is Sears' first kit home and is a State and National Historic Landmark. It features suites with private front porches overlooking downtown and decks tucked into the three-story high rock bluff behind. The Place Next Door is a Victorian replica boasting two upstairs suites with balconies. The Artist's Cottage is a renovated 1910 Craftsman. Two elegant suites include pure-air whirlpool tubs, 20 shower settings, wetbars, a porch and a deck. A compli-

mentary bottle of champagne or white wine is chilled in the refrigerator; a coffeemaker with imported tea, coffee, hot chocolate and chai are provided. A full gourmet breakfast is delivered each morning. The innkeeper will gladly arrange massages, horseback rid-

ing, carriage rides, canoe trips and discounted golf.

Innkeeper(s): Sandra CH Smith. $181-227. 7 rooms, 6 suites and 1 cottage. Types of meals: Full gourmet bkfst and early coffee/tea. Beds: KQ. Cable TV, VCR, reading lamp, refrigerator, ceiling fan, snack bar, clock radio, hot tub/spa, fireplaces and Jacuzzis in room. Air conditioning. Library, parlor games, telephone, fireplace and art gallery on premises. Weddings, small meetings, family reunions and seminars hosted. Amusement parks, antiquing, canoeing/kayaking, fishing, golf, horseback riding, live theater, parks, shopping, tennis and water sports nearby.

Publicity: *Arkansas Democrat Gazette, Country Inns, Modern Bride, Southern Living,* One of the Top Four Most Romantic Inns of the South by *Romantic Destinations Magazine,* Winter 2003 published by *Southern Bride,* 3 Star AAA and received the American Bed & Breakfast Association highest rating as well as an Award for Excellence.

Gaslight Inn

19 Judah St
Eureka Springs, AR 72632
(479)253-8887 (888)253-8887 Fax:(479)253-2278
E-mail: info@gaslightsquare.com
Web: www.gaslightsquare.com

Circa 1895. Exquisitely furnished with museum-quality antiques and vintage treasures from the 1890s, this upscale Victorian inn sits on a secluded hill in the historic district of the village. Elegant surroundings and a comfortable ambiance are the hallmarks of this award-winning inn. Chat over champagne, fruit and cheese in the splendid parlor. Romantic suites feature Jacuzzis with separate showers, fireplaces, cable TV and private entrances. Indulge in the pampered delight of a gourmet breakfast. Relax on the veranda or stroll the impressive gardens with a fountain, covered pavilion and fish pond. Walk into town to explore the galleries, museums and shops. Wedding, honeymoon and deluxe packages are available.

Innkeeper(s): Cynthia & Thomas Morin. $110-150. 5 rooms with PB, 4 with FP and 2 suites. Beds: QD. Cable TV, refrigerator, ceiling fan, clock radio and hot tub/spa in room. Central air. Fax, copier, spa, telephone, fireplace and wedding gazebo on premises. Limited handicap access. Weddings, small meetings and family reunions hosted.

Heart of The Hills Inn

5 Summit St
Eureka Springs, AR 72632
(479)253-7468 (800)253-7468
E-mail: hearthills@earthlink.net
Web: www.heartofthehillsinn.com

Circa 1883. Two suites and a Victorian cottage comprise this antique-furnished homestead located just four blocks from downtown. Suites have been restored and decorating in an 1880s style. The cottage is located beside the inn and is decorated in Victorian-country style. The cottage also offers a private deck that overlooks the garden. The village trolley stops at the inn, but the inn is within walking distance of town. Trolley tickets available for purchase at the Inn.

Innkeeper(s): Lee Crawford. $80-139. 3 rooms with PB, 2 suites and 1 cottage. Breakfast and snacks/refreshments included in rates. Types of meals: Full bkfst and early coffee/tea. Beds: KD. Cable TV, VCR, refrigerator and coffeemaker in room. Air conditioning. TV, parlor games, telephone, private decks, double Jacuzzi and quiet garden area on premises. Small meetings and family reunions hosted. Antiquing, art galleries, fishing, golf, live theater, shopping and water sports nearby.

Publicity: *Carroll County Tribune's Peddler and KHOG (ABC) Fayetteville/Fort Smith.*

"The decor and atmosphere of your inn was breathtaking; we were able to relax and not want for a thing."

The Heartstone Inn & Cottages

35 King's Hwy
Eureka Springs, AR 72632-3534
(479)253-8916 (800)494-4921 Fax:(479)253-5361
E-mail: info@heartstoneinn.com
Web: www.heartstoneinn.com

Circa 1903. A white picket fence leads to this spacious Victorian inn and its pink and cobalt blue wraparound porch filled with potted geraniums and Boston ferns. Located on the Eureka Springs historic loop the inn offers English country antiques, private entrances and pretty linens.

Private Jacuzzis, refrigerators and VCRs are available. Pamper yourself in the inn's massage therapy studio. Walk to shops, restaurants and galleries or hop on the trolley to enjoy all the pleasures of the town. Golf privileges at a private club are extended to guests. The New York Times praised the inn's cuisine as the "Best Breakfast in the Ozarks."

Historic Interest: Pea Ridge Civil War Battle Ground (20 miles), War Eagle Mill (20 miles).

Innkeeper(s): Rick & Cheri Rojek. $92-145. 12 rooms, 11 with PB, 4 with FP, 6 suites and 2 cottages. Breakfast and snacks/refreshments included in rates. Types of meals: Full gourmet bkfst. Beds: KQ. Cable TV, VCR, refrigerator, ceiling fan, clock radio, coffeemaker, fireplace and Jacuzzi in room. Air conditioning. Fax, copier, spa, parlor games, telephone, massage therapy and gift shop on premises. Weddings and family reunions hosted. Amusement parks, antiquing, art galleries, bicycling, canoeing/kayaking, fishing, golf, hiking, horseback riding, live theater, parks, shopping and restaurants nearby.

Publicity: *Innsider, Arkansas Times, New York Times, Arkansas Gazette, Southern Living, Country Home, Country Inns and USA Today.*

"Extraordinary! Best breakfasts anywhere!"

Palace Hotel & Bath House

135 Spring St
Eureka Springs, AR 72632-3106
(479)253-7474
E-mail: phbh@ipa.net
Web: www.palacehotelbathhouse.com

Circa 1901. The Palace Hotel and Bath House has been extensively renovated. The lobby and guest rooms are furnished in Victorian antiques, recalling opulent turn-of-the-century beginnings. Each guest room has a double-sized water-jet tub and a wet bar. Built on the edge of a cliff, the hotel features a lower mineral-bath level. The bath house is equipped with original six-foot-long clawfoot tubs, and the Victorian-era Eucalyptus steam barrels are still in service. Each tub is situated in a private alcove.

Historic Interest: Built in 1901, we are the only operating historic bath house in Eureka Springs, a town founded because of its healing waters.

Innkeeper(s): Steve & Francie Miller. $149-169. 8 suites. Breakfast included

in rates. Types of meals: Cont plus. Beds: K. Cable TV, refrigerator, ceiling fan, telephone, coffeemaker, turn-down service and hot tub/spa in room. Air conditioning. Spa, full-service spa with mineral baths, eucalyptus steam treatment, clay mask and massage therapy on premises. Antiquing, art galleries, canoeing/kayaking, fishing, golf, hiking, horseback riding, parks, shopping and water sports nearby.

Publicity: *Country Home, Southern Living, Ladies Home Journal, The New York Times, USA Weekend, Washington Post, National Geographic Traveler and Bon Appetit.*

Sleepy Hollow Inn

92 South Main
Eureka Springs, AR 72632
(479)253-5561 (800)805-6261
E-mail: sleepyhollowbnb@aol.com
Web: www.estc.net/sleepyhollow

Circa 1881. Ideal for honeymooners or those in search of privacy, this three-story Victorian cottage with gingerbread trim provides a romantic retreat. Fine attention to detail has been given to the inn's elegant decor. Guest bedrooms and a luxurious main suite encompass all of the second floor, and a third-story guest bedroom boasts a view of impressive limestone cliffs. For the ultimate in intimacy and seclusion, the entire cottage is available to one or two couples at a time, offering the freedom to relax and make  this a vacation home away from home. Soak in the antique clawfoot tub or snuggle up on the porch swing. Fresh-baked pastries and other treats await in the spacious kitchen. Red bud trees give shade to the peaceful garden setting across the street from a historical museum. Chilled champagne and wedding packages are available.

Innkeeper(s): Janet Fyhrie. $129. 4 rooms, 2 with PB, 3 suites and 2 cottages. Breakfast and snacks/refreshments included in rates. Types of meals: Cont plus and early coffee/tea. Beds: QD. Cable TV, reading lamp, stereo, refrigerator, ceiling fan, snack bar, clock radio, telephone, coffeemaker, hot tub/spa and fireplace in room. Central air. Spa, fireplace and private parking on premises. Amusement parks, antiquing, art galleries, beach, canoeing/kayaking, fishing, golf, hiking, horseback riding, live theater, museums, parks, shopping, tennis, water sports and vintage train rides nearby.

Publicity: *Bestfares.com Magazine.*

"Truly a delightful experience. The love and care going into this journey back in time is impressive."

Hardy　　　　　　　　　　　　A7

The Olde Stonehouse B&B Inn

511 Main St
Hardy, AR 72542-9034
(870)856-2983 (800)514-2983 Fax:(870)856-2193
E-mail: info@oldestonehouse.com
Web: www.oldestonehouse.com

Circa 1928. The stone fireplace gracing the comfortable living room of this former banker's home is set with fossils and unusual stones, including an Arkansas diamond. Lace tablecloths, china and silver make breakfast a special occasion. Each room is decorated to keep the authentic feel of the Roaring '20s. The bedrooms have antiques and ceiling fans. Aunt Jenny's room boasts a clawfoot tub and a white iron bed, while Aunt Bette's room is filled with Victorian-era furniture. Spring River is only one block away and offers canoeing, boating and

fishing. Old Hardy Town caters to antique and craft lovers. The innkeepers offer "Secret Suites," located in a nearby historic home. These romantic suites offer plenty of amenities, including a Jacuzzi for two. Breakfasts in a basket are delivered to the door each morning. The home is listed in the National Register. Murder-mystery weekends, romance packages, golf, canoeing and fly-fishing are available.

Historic Interest: Olde Hardy Town 19th-century commercial buildings (2 blocks), Old Court House and Jail (2 blocks), Railroad Station/Museum at Mammoth Springs (18 miles), vintage car museum.

Innkeeper(s): Charles & JaNoel Bess. $79-149. 6 rooms with PB and 2 suites. Breakfast and snacks/refreshments included in rates. Types of meals: Full bkfst, early coffee/tea and picnic lunch. Beds: QD. Reading lamp, stereo, refrigerator, ceiling fan, clock radio and desk in room. Air conditioning. TV, VCR, fax, copier, library, parlor games, telephone, fireplace, guest refrigerator, coffee service and phones on premises. Small meetings hosted. Antiquing, fishing, live theater, parks, shopping, water sports, museums, fly fishing with guide available and murder mystery weekends nearby.

Publicity: *Memphis Commercial Appeal, Jonesboro Sun, Vacations, Southern Living, Arkansas at Home, Democrat Gazette and Midwest Living.*

"For many years we had heard about 'Southern Hospitality' but never thought it could be this good. It was the best!"

Helena E8

Edwardian Inn

317 S Biscoe
Helena, AR 72342
(870)338-9155 Fax:(870)338-4215

Circa 1904. In his book Life on the Mississippi, Mark Twain wrote, "Helena occupies one of the prettiest situations on the river." William Short, cotton broker and speculator, agreed and built his stately home here. The Edwardian Inn boasts a large rotunda and two verandas wrapping around both sides of the house. Inside are wood carpets and floor designs imported from Germany that are composed of 36 pieces of different woods arranged in octagon shapes. Polished-oak paneling and woodwork are set off with a Victorian-era decor.

Innkeeper(s): John Crow. $75-110. 12 rooms with PB, 3 suites and 1 conference room. Breakfast included in rates. Types of meals: Full bkfst, early coffee/tea and snacks/refreshments. Beds: KQD. Cable TV, reading lamp, ceiling fan, clock radio, telephone and desk in room. Air conditioning. VCR, fax, copier, library, parlor games and fireplace on premises. Limited handicap access. Weddings, small meetings, family reunions and seminars hosted. Antiquing, fishing, golf, live theater, parks and shopping nearby.

Publicity: *Arkansas Times, Dallas Morning News, Southern Living, Country Inns and USA.*

"The Edwardian Inn envelopes you with wonderful feelings, smells and thoughts of the Victorian era."

Johnson B2

Johnson House B&B

5371 S 48th St, PO Box 431
Johnson, AR 72741-0431
(501)756-1095

Circa 1882. This elegant country home on the rolling hillside was built with handmade bricks and offers authentic Ozark hospitality. Gracefully restored and filled with wonderful

antiques, the inn's peaceful ambiance enhances a pleasant stay. Relax fireside in the front parlor that boasts an intricately painted ceiling. Large guest bedrooms reflect an old-fashioned charm and comfort. The window-filled dining room is perfect for lingering over a mouth-watering breakfast. Stroll the gardens, browse the Smokehouse Antique Shop, play a game of horseshoes or croquet. Enjoy an Arkansas sunset from the upstairs veranda.

Innkeeper(s): Mary K. Carothers. $105. Types of meals: Full bkfst and picnic lunch. Reading lamp, ceiling fan, clock radio, turn-down service and desk in room. Air conditioning. VCR, telephone, fireplace, croquet, horseshoes and shuffle on premises. Weddings, small meetings, family reunions and seminars hosted. Antiquing, live theater, shopping and sporting events nearby.

Little Rock E5

The Empress of Little Rock Small Luxury Hotel and B&B

2120 Louisiana St
Little Rock, AR 72206-1522
(501)374-7966 (877)374-7966 Fax:(501)375-4537
E-mail: hostess@theEmpress.com
Web: www.theEmpress.com

Circa 1888. Day lilies, peonies and iris accent the old-fashioned gardens of this elaborate, three-story Queen Anne Victorian. A grand center hall opens to a double staircase, lit by a stained-glass skylight. The 7,500 square feet include a secret card room at the top of the tower. The Hornibrook Room features a magnificent Renaissance Revival bedroom set with a high canopy. The Tower Room mini-suite has a king-size Austrian bed. The two-course gourmet breakfast is served in the dining room "before the Queen" by candlelight.

Historic Interest: At one time it was the first women's college in the state. Arkansas territorial restoration, old state house, state capitol, Villa Marre, MacArthur's birthplace (1-2 miles), Toltec Indian Mounds (5 miles).

Innkeeper(s): Sharon Welch-Blair & Robert Blair. $125-195. 5 rooms with PB, 3 with FP, 3 suites and 1 conference room. Breakfast and snacks/refreshments included in rates. Types of meals: Full gourmet bkfst, veg bkfst, early coffee/tea and picnic lunch. Beds: KQT. Data port, cable TV, reading lamp, refrigerator, ceiling fan, snack bar, clock radio, telephone, coffeemaker, turn-down service, desk, luxury robes, complimentary liquors, antique fireplace with gas logs, feather beds and high-speed Internet access in room. Central air. VCR, fax, copier, library, parlor games, fireplace, secret garden with Gothic summer house, spa and award winning gardens on premises. Weddings, small meetings and family reunions hosted. Antiquing, art galleries, bicycling, fishing, golf, hiking, horseback riding, live theater, museums, parks, shopping, sporting events, tennis, water sports, tours, high tea, bridal brunches and portraits nearby.

Publicity: *National Geographic Traveler, Nation's Business, Victorian Home, Victorian Decorator & Life Styles, Southern Living and Home and Garden Television.*

"Staying at the Empress of Little Rock was a 'dream come true!' We've read about and admired it for years. It was definitely a trip to a more gracious time—one that we should all try to implement more in our daily lives."

California

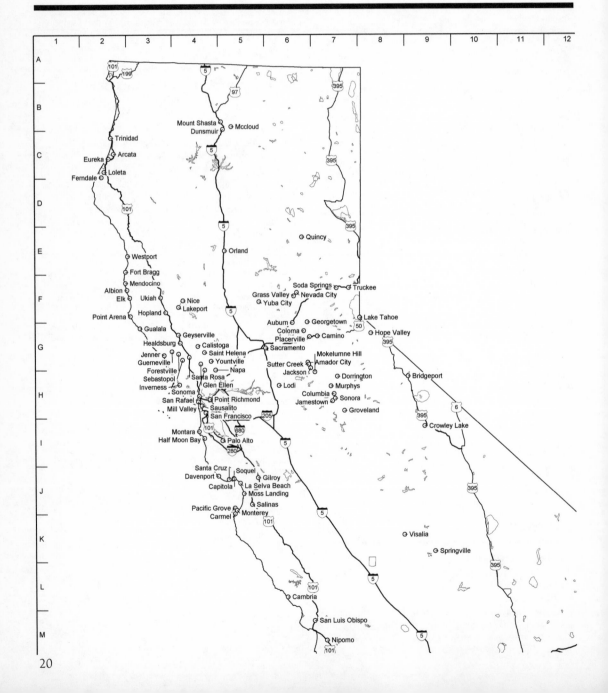

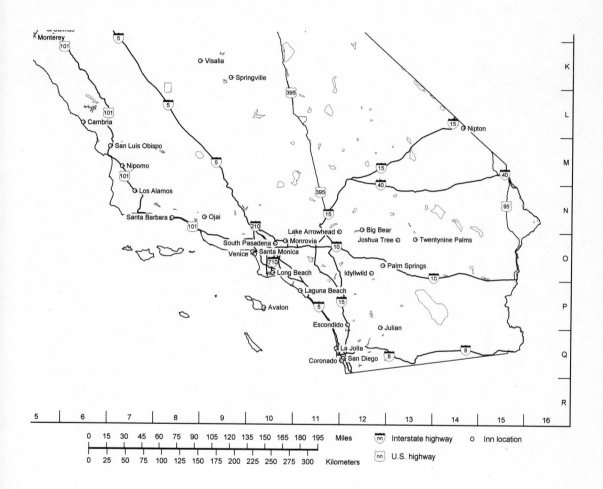

Monterey
101
Salinas
5
Visalia
Springville
395
5
Cambria
101
15
Nipton
San Luis Obispo
15
Nipomo
101
40
5
Los Alamos
40
95
Santa Barbara
Ojai
101
210
395
15
Lake Arrowhead
Big Bear
South Pasadena
Monrovia
Joshua Tree
Twentynine Palms
Venice
Santa Monica
10
710
Palm Springs
Long Beach
Idyllwild
10
Laguna Beach
5
15
Avalon
Escondido
Julian
La Jolla
Coronado
San Diego
8
8

5   6   7   8   9   10   11   12   13   14   15   16

0 15 30 45 60 75 90 105 120 135 150 165 180 195   Miles

0 25 50 75 100 125 150 175 200 225 250 275 300   Kilometers

K
L
M
N
O
P
Q
R

nn Interstate highway   o Inn location

nn U.S. highway

Albion   F3

Fensalden Inn

33810 Navarro Ridge Rd
Albion, CA 95410-0099
(707)937-4042 (800)959-3850
E-mail: inn@fensalden.com
Web: www.fensalden.com

Circa 1860. Originally a stagecoach station, Fensalden looks out over the Pacific Ocean as it has for more than 100 years. The Tavern Room has witnessed many a rowdy scene, and if

you look closely you can see bullet holes in the original redwood ceiling. The inn provides 20 acres for walks, whale-watching, viewing deer and bicycling. Relax with wine and hors d'oeuvres in the evening.

Innkeeper(s): Lyn Hamby. $125-225. 8 rooms with PB, 8 with FP, 3 suites, 1 cottage and 2 conference rooms. Breakfast included in rates. Types of meals: Full bkfst. Beds: Q. Refrigerator and Bungalow has Jacuzzi tub in room. Telephone and fireplace on premises. Limited handicap access. Weddings, small meetings, family reunions and seminars hosted. Antiquing, fishing, live theater, parks, shopping and water sports nearby.

Publicity: *Sunset, Focus, Peninsula and Country Inns.*

"Closest feeling to heaven on Earth."

Amador City   G6

Mine House Inn

PO Box 245
Amador City, CA 95601-0245
(209)267-5900 (800)646-3473
E-mail: minehse@cdepot.net
Web: www.minehouseinn.com

Circa 1870. Mine House Inn was headquarters for one of the most profitable gold mines in the mother lode of 1853, known as the Keystone Mine. Each room in this inn is named for its original function. All are furnished with authentic 19th-century antiques. Rooms include the Vault, Bookkeeping, Directors, Mill Grinding and Assay rooms. Over $24 million of gold was processed into gold bars in the Retort Room. The acre of land surrounding the inn is shaded by 200-year-old oaks and pines. Just steps away is the historic downtown of Amador City with shops and fine restaurants. Within easy driving distance are the towns of Volcano and Columbia.

Historic Interest: Abandoned gold mines, Keystone mine and ruins are across the highway. Knight Foundry in Sutter Creek is two miles away. It is the last operational water-powered foundry in U.S.

Innkeeper(s): Allen & Rose Mendy. $95-245. 13 rooms, 6 with PB and 5 suites. Breakfast included in rates. Types of meals: Full bkfst and gourmet dinner. Beds: KQ. Reading lamp, Some rooms have fireplaces and suites are in adjacent 1930s guest house and have Jacuzzi tubs for two in room. Air conditioning. Swimming, outdoor spa in enclosed gazebo and inn limousine for wine country tours on premises. Family reunions hosted. Antiquing, cross-country skiing, downhill skiing, fishing, live theater, shopping, water sports and wineries nearby.

Publicity: *Fun Times, LA Times and HGTV restore America.*

"We enjoyed the nostalgia and the decor and the challenge of trying to crack the safe."

Arcata   C2

Hotel Arcata

708 9th St
Arcata, CA 95521-6206
(707)826-0217 (800)344-1221 Fax:(707)826-1737

Circa 1915. This historic landmark hotel is a fine example of Beaux Arts-style architecture. Several rooms overlook Arcata's downtown plaza, which is just outside the front door. A variety of rooms are available, each decorated in turn-of-the-century style. All rooms include pedestal sinks and clawfoot tubs. The hotel offers a full-service, renown Japanese restaurant, offering excellent cuisine,

and there are many other fine restaurants within walking distance. Guests also enjoy free use of a nearby full-scale health club. The starting point of Arcata's architectural homes tour is within walking distance of the hotel.

Innkeeper(s): Virgil Moorehead. $120-200. 32 rooms with PB, 7 suites and 1 conference room. Breakfast included in rates. Types of meals: Cont, lunch, dinner and room service. Restaurant on premises. Beds: KQT. Cable TV, reading lamp, telephone and desk in room. Fax, copier and free health club privileges on premises. Limited handicap access. Weddings, small meetings, family reunions and seminars hosted. Parks, shopping, state parks, beaches, redwoods, rivers and theater nearby.

Auburn   G6

Powers Mansion Inn

164 Cleveland Ave
Auburn, CA 95603-4801
(530)885-1166 Fax:(530)885-1386

Circa 1898. This elegant Victorian mansion was built by Harold Power with the proceeds from his gold mine. Many prominent people, including engineer Herbert Hoover, visited here. The parlor and the second floor halls contain notes and memorabilia concerning its history. The luxury of the inn is typified by the honeymoon suite, which has a heart-shaped whirlpool tub and a fireplace at the foot of the brass bed.

Innkeeper(s): Trudy & Jamie Sessions. $119-229. 12 rooms with PB, 2 with FP and 1 conference room. Types of meals: Full bkfst. Beds: Q. TV in room. Telephone on premises.

Publicity: *Sierra Heritage Magazine.*

"The rooms are so relaxing and the breakfast is fantastic."

Avalon   P10

Hotel Metrople

205 Crescent Ave
Avalon, CA 90704
(310)541-8528 (800)541-8528 Fax:(310)510-2534
E-mail: metropol@catalinas.net
Web: www.hotel-metropole.com

Circa 1888. This luxurious beachfront hotel, which is just an easy walk from the ferry, exudes a casual elegance with a Mediterranean ambiance. Newly remodeled guest bedrooms with ocean, mountain or courtyard views feature data ports, Frette linens, robes and slippers. Many rooms also boast

Jacuzzis, fireplaces, DVD/CD players, fireplaces and balconies. The spacious and private Beach House is also available. Before exploring the island, enjoy a generous continental breakfast of granola, cereals, fruit, muffins, Danishes, croissants and bagels with cream cheese. Lounge on the rooftop sundeck with a relaxing Jacuzzi. Spa services are available. Stroll through the adjacent open-air Metropole Market Place with boutiques, art galleries and restaurants.

$125-795. 48 rooms, 39 with PB and 8 suites. Breakfast included in rates. Types of meals: Full gourmet bkfst, veg bkfst, early coffee/tea, lunch and room service. Restaurant on premises. Beds: KQD. Cable TV, reading lamp, CD player, snack bar, clock radio, telephone, turn-down service, desk, hot tub/spa, voice mail, most have fireplace, DVD, robes and slippers in room. Central air. Fax, copier and spa on premises. Limited handicap access. Weddings, small meetings, family reunions and seminars hosted. Art galleries, beach, bicycling, canoeing/kayaking, fishing, golf, hiking, horseback riding and water sports nearby.

Big Bear   N12

Gold Mountain Manor Historic B&B

1117 Anita, PO Box 2027
Big Bear, CA 92314
(909)585-6997 (800)509-2604 Fax:(909)585-0327
E-mail: info@goldmountainmanor.com
Web: www.goldmountainmanor.com

Circa 1928. This spectacular log mansion was once a hideaway for the rich and famous. Eight fireplaces provide a roaring fire in each room in fall and winter. The Lucky Baldwin Room offers a hearth made from stones gathered in the famous Lucky

Baldwin mine nearby. In the Clark Gable room is the fireplace Gable and Carole Lombard enjoyed on their honeymoon. Gourmet country breakfasts and afternoon hors d'oeuvres are served. In addition to the guest rooms, there are home rentals.

Historic Interest: Small Historic Museum in Big Bear City (1 mile) and gold mining.

Innkeeper(s): Trish & Jim Gordon. $125-225. 7 rooms with PB, 7 with FP, 2 suites and 1 conference room. Afternoon tea and snacks/refreshments included in rates. Types of meals: Full gourmet bkfst and early coffee/tea. Beds: Q. Reading lamp, ceiling fan, desk, hot tub/spa and suites have Jacuzzi in room. VCR, fax, spa, bicycles, library, parlor games, telephone, fireplace and pool table on premises. Weddings, small meetings, family reunions and seminars hosted. Cross-country skiing, downhill skiing, fishing, parks, sporting events, water sports and hiking/forest nearby.

Publicity: *Best Places to Kiss, Fifty Most Romantic Places and Kenny G holiday album cover.*

"A majestic experience! In this magnificent house, history comes alive!"

Bridgeport   H9

The Cain House

340 Main St
Bridgeport, CA 93517
(760)932-7040 (800)433-2246 Fax:(760)932-7419

Circa 1920. The grandeur of the Eastern Sierra Mountains is the perfect setting for evening refreshments as the sun sets, turning the sky into a fiery, purple canvas. The innkeeper's experiences while traveling around the world have influenced The Cain House's decor to give the inn a European elegance with a casual western atmosphere. Travelers can take a short

drive to the ghost town of Bodie where 10,000 people once lived in this gold-mining community. Outdoor enthusiasts can find an abundance of activity at Lake Tahoe, which is an hour-and-a-half away.

Innkeeper(s): Chris & Marachal Gohlich. $90-145. 7 rooms with PB. Breakfast and snacks/refreshments included in rates. Types of meals: Full bkfst and early coffee/tea. Beds: KQ. Cable TV, refrigerator, telephone and desk in room. Air conditioning. TV, fax, copier, parlor games and fireplace on premises. Family reunions hosted. Cross-country skiing, fishing, parks, tennis and water sports nearby.

Publicity: *Los Angeles Times, Mammoth Times and Sunset Magazine.*

Calistoga   G4

Fannys

1206 Spring St
Calistoga, CA 94515-1637
(707)942-9491 Fax:(707)942-4810
E-mail: info@fannysnapavalley.com
Web: www.fannysnapavalley.com

Circa 1915. In a shingled Craftsman-cottage style, painted forest green and red, this inn offers an inviting shaded porch with swing, rockers and spots for dining. Inside, comfortable interiors include over-stuffed chairs, a fireplace, library and upstairs guest rooms with plank floors and window seats. The innkeeper, a former restaurateur, provides a full breakfast and knowledgeable touring suggestions.

Innkeeper(s): Deanna Higgins. $120-180. 2 rooms with PB. Breakfast included in rates. Types of meals: Country bkfst. Beds: Q. Reading lamp, ceiling fan and clock in room. Air conditioning. Fax, library, parlor games, telephone and fireplace on premises. Weddings hosted. Antiquing, golf, parks, shopping and winery tours & tasting nearby.

Foothill House

3037 Foothill Blvd
Calistoga, CA 94515-1225
(707)942-6933 (800)942-6933 Fax:(707)942-5692
E-mail: gus@calicom.net
Web: www.foothillhouse.com

Circa 1892. This country farmhouse overlooks the western foothills of Mount St. Helena. Graceful old California oaks and pockets of flowers greet guests. Each room features country antiques, a four-poster bed, a fireplace and a small refrigerator. Breakfast is served in the sun room or is delivered personally to your room in a basket. Three rooms offer private Jacuzzi tubs.

Historic Interest: Old Faithful Geyser (1 mile), Petrified Forest (3 miles).

Innkeeper(s): Doris & Gus Beckert. $175-325. 4 suites, 4 with FP. Breakfast and snacks/refreshments included in rates. Types of meals: Full gourmet bkfst and early coffee/tea. Beds: KQT. Cable TV, VCR, reading lamp, stereo, refrigerator, ceiling fan, clock radio, telephone, turn-down service, robes, bottled water, coffee and tea in room. Air conditioning. Fax, copier, library, parlor games and fireplace on premises. Weddings, small meetings and family reunions hosted. Amusement parks, antiquing, fishing, parks, shopping, water sports, wineries, balloon rides, glider port and health spas nearby.

Publicity: *Sunset Magazine, San Francisco Examiner, Herald Examiner and Baltimore Sun.*

"Gourmet treats served in front of an open fire. Hospitality never for a moment flagged."

Hotel d'Amici

1436 Lincoln Avenue
Calistoga, CA 94515
(707)942-1007 Fax:(707)963-3150
E-mail: amici@rutherfordgrove.com
Web: www.rutherfordgrove.com

Circa 1920. Hotel d'Amici is a cross between a modern California-style lodging and an Italian villa, seemingly a perfect mix for an inn in California's famous Napa Valley. Each of the four suites is decorated impeccably, and two of the suites include a fireplace. The other two share a balcony that looks out to downtown Calistoga with views of Mt. St. Helena. Aside from the multitude of wineries in the area, other attractions include the Calistoga Old Faithful Geyser and the Petrified Forest. Both are within eight miles of the inn. Guests can walk to Calistoga's famous spas, as well as shops and restaurants.

Innkeeper(s): Roger Asbill. $150-225. 4 suites. Breakfast included in rates. Types of meals: Cont. Restaurant on premises. Beds: Q. Cable TV, reading lamp, refrigerator, ceiling fan, clock radio, telephone and coffeemaker in room. Central air. Fireplace on premises. Antiquing, art galleries, bicycling, golf, hiking, horseback riding, museums, parks, shopping, water sports and wineries nearby.

Publicity: *Los Angeles Times Travel Section.*

Scarlett's Country Inn

3918 Silverado Trl
Calistoga, CA 94515-9611
(707)942-6669 Fax:(707)942-6669
E-mail: scarletts@aol.com
Web: members.aol.com/scarletts

Circa 1900. Formerly a winter campground of the Wappo Indians, the property now includes a restored farmhouse. There are green lawns and country vistas of woodland and vineyards. Each room has a private entrance. Breakfast is often served beneath the apple trees or poolside.

Historic Interest: Old Bale Mill (2 miles), Beringer and Charles Krug Wineries (4 miles), Schramsberg Champagne Cellars (2 miles), Sharpsteen Museum (4 miles), graveyard in Boothe State Park (2 miles).

Innkeeper(s): Scarlett Dwyer. $135-205. 3 rooms with PB, 1 with FP, 2 suites and 1 cottage. Breakfast and afternoon tea included in rates. Types of meals: Full gourmet bkfst, early coffee/tea and room service. Beds: Q. TV, reading lamp, refrigerator, snack bar, clock radio, telephone, turn-down service and desk in room. Air conditioning. Fax, copier, swimming and parlor games on premises. Small meetings and family reunions hosted. Antiquing, fishing, parks, shopping, water sports, ballooning, gliders and winetasting nearby.

Publicity: *Daily News.*

"Wonderful, peaceful, serene."

Scott Courtyard

1443 2nd St
Calistoga, CA 94515-1419
(707)942-0948 (800)942-1515 Fax:(707)942-5102
E-mail: info@scottcourtyard.com
Web: www.scottcourtyard.com

Circa 1940. Located in the heart of Napa Valley, this delightfully different California-style inn features two-room suites with fireplaces and private entrances. The romantic ground-level Rose Suite has a large sitting room with fireplace, day bed and

library. The adjoining Burgandy Suite is perfect for couples traveling together. Named for its view of the mountains, the second-floor Palisades Suite boasts a four-poster bed and a small balcony overlooking the pool. A full gourmet breakfast is served in the dining room or garden with fresh-brewed coffee from a local roastery. Enjoy evening wine and cheese. Explore the extensive gardens with grapevines, flowers, fruit and nut trees. Swim in the pool or relax by the fire in the social room. Visit local shops, wineries, museums, spas, art galleries and restaurants just two blocks away.

Innkeeper(s): Diane Byrne, Dave and Susan DeVries. $160-225. 4 suites. Breakfast included in rates. Types of meals: Full bkfst. Beds: KQT. Cable TV, clock radio, coffeemaker, fireplace, central heating, refrigerator, iron, hair dryer and dressing gown in room. Central air. Fax, copier, swimming, library, telephone, Internet connection, social room with vaulted ceiling, gardens, complimentary wine and fruit and cheese each evening on premises. Antiquing, art galleries, bicycling, fishing, golf, hiking, horseback riding, museums, parks, shopping, tennis, wineries, mud baths, massage, ballooning, glider rides and natural wonders and historical sites nearby.

Publicity: *Sunset Magazine, Access Press and The Best Places to Kiss in Northern California.*

Trailside Inn

4201 Silverado Trl
Calistoga, CA 94515-9605
(707)942-4106 Fax:(707)942-4702
E-mail: h.gray@att.net
Web: www.trailsideinn.com

Circa 1932. This secluded valley farmhouse overlooks Three Palms Vineyard and the distant Sterling Winery. Each accommodation is a tastefully decorated suite with its own porch, private entrance, small kitchen, private bath and fireplace. Furnished with country antiques and old quilts, two suites have an extra bedroom to accommodate a family of four. House specialties are banana and blueberry breads, freshly baked and brought to your room. Complimentary wine and mineral water also are offered.

Historic Interest: Robert Louis Stevenson State Park (3 miles), Beringer Winery (4 miles), Calistoga (3 miles).

Innkeeper(s): Lani Gray. $165-185. 3 suites, 3 with FP. Breakfast included in rates. Types of meals: Cont plus. Beds: QDT. Complimentary wine in room. Swimming on premises.

Publicity: *San Francisco Examiner and Wine Country Review.*

"If Dorothy and Toto were to click their heals together they would end up at the Trailside Inn."

Cambria   L6

Olallieberry Inn

2476 Main St
Cambria, CA 93428-3406
(888)927-3222 Fax:(805)927-0202
E-mail: olallieinn@olallieberry.com
Web: www.olallieberry.com

Circa 1873. This restored Greek Revival home features rooms decorated with fabrics and wall coverings and furnished with period antiques. Eight of the guest rooms feature fireplaces. Butterfly and herb gardens and a 120-year-old redwood grace the front yard. The cheery gathering room boasts a view of the Santa Rosa Creek. Full breakfast with fresh breads, fruits and a special entree start off the day, and wine and hors d'oeuvres are served in the afternoon. The inn is within walking distance to restaurants and shops.

Historic Interest: Hearst Castle is six miles from the inn.
Innkeeper(s): Marilyn & Larry Draper. $115-207. 9 rooms with PB, 6 with FP and 1 suite. Breakfast and snacks/refreshments included in rates. Types of meals: Full gourmet bkfst and early coffee/tea. Beds: KQ. Reading lamp and eight with fireplace in room. Fax, parlor games, telephone and fireplace on premises. Limited handicap access. Weddings, small meetings, family reunions and seminars hosted. Antiquing, fishing, shopping, water sports, wineries and Hearst Castle nearby.

Publicity: *Los Angeles Times and Elmer Dills Radio Show.*

"Our retreat turned into relaxation, romance and pure Victorian delight."

The Squibb House

4063 Burton Dr
Cambria, CA 93428-3001
(805)927-9600 Fax:(805)927-9606
E-mail: innkeeper@squibbhouse.com
Web: www.squibbhouse.com

Circa 1877. A picket fence and large garden surround this Victorian inn with its Italianate and Gothic Revival architecture. Guests may relax in the main parlor, stroll the gardens or sit and rock on the porch. The home was built by a Civil War veteran and young school teacher. The downstairs once was used as a classroom while an addition was being made in the town's school. Each guest room has a fire stove.

Historic Interest: Heart Castle is six miles away, and further attractions include the San Luis Obispo Mission and San Miguel Mission, both about 35 miles from the home.
Innkeeper(s): Kory. $105-185. 5 rooms with PB, 5 with FP. Breakfast included in rates. Types of meals: Cont plus. Beds: Q. Reading lamp in room. Parlor games, telephone, fireplace and retail shop in historic 1885 carpentry shop on premises. Weddings and small meetings hosted. Antiquing, fishing, golf, parks, shopping, Hearst Castle, wine tasting and galleries nearby.

Publicity: *Cambrian.*

Camino   G7

The Camino Hotel-Seven Mile House

4103 Carson Rd, PO Box 1197
Camino, CA 95709-1197
(530)644-7740 Fax:(530)647-1416
E-mail: inquire@caminohotel.com
Web: www.caminohotel.com

Circa 1888. Once a barracks for the area's loggers, this inn now caters to visitors in the state's famed gold country. Just east of Placerville, historic Camino is on the Old Carson Wagon Trail in Apple Hill. Nine guest rooms are available, including the E.J. Barrett Room, a favorite with honeymooners. Other rooms feature names such as Pony Express, Stage Stop and Wagon Train. The family-oriented inn welcomes children, and a local park offers a handy site for their recreational needs.

Popular area activities include apple picking, antiquing, hot air ballooning, white-water rafting, hiking and wine tasting. The inn also offers a Self-Indulgence Package, on-site wine tasting and an in-house masseuse.

Innkeeper(s): Paula Nobert. $68-98. 9 rooms, 3 with PB and 1 conference room. Breakfast and snacks/refreshments included in rates. Types of meals: Full bkfst, early coffee/tea and picnic lunch. Beds: QDT. Reading lamp, clock radio, turn-down service and coolers in room. Parlor games, telephone, fireplace, homemade chocolate chip cookies, wine tasting room and two mas-

sage therapists on premises. Weddings, small meetings, family reunions and seminars hosted. Antiquing, cross-country skiing, downhill skiing, fishing, golf, live theater, parks, shopping, water sports, wine tasting, white-water rafting and hot air ballooning nearby.

Publicity: *Better Homes & Gardens, Sunset and Sierra Heritage.*

Capitola   J5

Inn at Depot Hill

250 Monterey Ave
Capitola, CA 95010-3358
(831)462-3376 (800)572-2632 Fax:(831)462-3697
E-mail: reserve@innsbythesea.com
Web: www.innatdepothill.com

Circa 1901. Once a railroad depot, this inn offers rooms with themes to represent different parts of the world: a chic auberge in St. Tropez, a romantic French hideaway in Paris, an Italian coastal villa, a summer home on the coast of Holland and a traditional English garden room, to name a few. Most rooms have garden patios with hot tubs. The rooms have many amenities, including a fireplace, white marble bathrooms and feather beds. Guests are greeted with fresh flowers in their room. Gourmet breakfast, tea, wine, hors d' oeuvres and dessert are offered daily.

Innkeeper(s): Tom Cole. $200-385. 12 rooms, 12 with FP, 4 suites and 1 conference room. Breakfast and snacks/refreshments included in rates. Beds: KQT. Cable TV, VCR, reading lamp, stereo, clock radio, telephone, turn-down service, desk and hot tub/spa in room. TV, fax, spa and fireplace on premises. Limited handicap access. Small meetings, family reunions and seminars hosted. Amusement parks, antiquing, fishing, golf, live theater, parks, shopping and water sports nearby.

Publicity: *Country Inn, Santa Cruz Sentinel, McCalls, Choices & Vacation, San Jose Mercury News, Fresno & Sacramento Bee, San Francisco Focus, American Airline Flight, SF Examiner and Sunset Magazine.*

"The highlight of our honeymoon. Five stars in our book!"

Carmel   J5

Happy Landing Inn

PO Box 2619
Carmel, CA 93921-2619
(831)624-7917 Fax:(831)624-4844

Circa 1926. Built as a family retreat, this early Comstock-design inn has evolved into one of Carmel's most romantic places to stay. The Hansel-and-Gretel look is accentuated with a central garden and gazebo, pond and flagstone paths. There are cathedral ceilings and the rooms are filled with antiques. Breakfast is brought to your room.

Innkeeper(s): Robert Ballard and Dick Stewart. $95-185. 7 rooms with PB, 3 with FP and 2 suites. Breakfast and afternoon tea included in rates. Types of meals: Cont plus. Beds: KQD. Cable TV, reading lamp and telephone in room. TV and fireplace on premises. Limited handicap access. Weddings and family reunions hosted. Antiquing, art galleries, beach, golf, hiking, horseback riding, live theater, parks, shopping, water sports, wineries and restaurants and beach nearby.

Publicity: *San Francisco Chronicle and Monterey Herald.*

"Just what the doctor ordered!"

Sandpiper Inn-by-the-Sea

2408 Bay View Ave
Carmel, CA 93923-9118
(831)624-6433 (800)633-6433 Fax:(831)624-5964
E-mail: sandpiper-inn@redshift.com
Web: www.sandpiper-inn.com/virtualtour

Circa 1929. Only a half block from miles of pristine coastline, this early California-style inn is set in a quiet residential neighborhood of million-dollar estates. There are 17 guest rooms, all individually decorated in English and French antiques. Several

offer fireplaces or ocean views. For a more intimate stay, guests can request one of the three cottage rooms. With its beautifully furnished interiors, the inn has been a favorite getaway spot for a host of famous people. An expanded continental buffet breakfast is served in the dining room. In the afternoon, guests are invited to enjoy tea or a glass of imported Amontillado sherry.

Innkeeper(s): Bill Lee. $115-250. 17 rooms with PB, 3 with FP. Breakfast and afternoon tea included in rates. Types of meals: Cont plus and early coffee/tea. Beds: KQ. Reading lamp, clock radio, desk and 6 with ocean view in room. Fax, parlor games, telephone, fireplace and 3 cottage rooms on premises. Antiquing, golf, live theater, parks, shopping, tennis and water sports nearby.

The Stonehouse Inn

PO Box 2939
Carmel, CA 93921
(831)624-4569 (800)748-6618

Circa 1906. This quaint Carmel country house boasts a stone exterior, made from beach rocks collected and hand shaped by local Indians at the turn of the century. The original owner, "Nana" Foster, was hostess to notable artists and writers from the San Francisco area, including Sinclair Lewis, Jack London and Lotta Crabtree. The romantic Jack London room features a dramatic gabled ceiling, a brass bed and a stunning view of the ocean. Conveniently located, the inn is a short walk from Carmel Beach and two blocks from the village.

Innkeeper(s): Terri Navailles. $139-199. 6 rooms. Breakfast included in rates. Types of meals: Full bkfst. Beds: KQDT. Reading lamp in room. Telephone on premises. Weddings and family reunions hosted. Fishing, live theater, parks, shopping and water sports nearby.
Publicity: *Travel & Leisure and Country Living.*
"First time stay at a B&B — GREAT!"

Vagabond's House Inn

PO Box 2747, Dolores & 4th
Carmel, CA 93921-2747
(831)624-7738 (800)262-1262 Fax:(831)626-1243
E-mail: innkeeper@vagabondshouseinn.com
Web: www.vagabondshouseinn.com

Circa 1940. Shaded by the intertwined branches of two California live oaks, the stone-paved courtyard of the Vagabond's House sets the tone of this romantic retreat. The inn is comprised of a cluster of white stucco cottages built into a slope. Some include kitchens, but all feature a fireplace and

an antique clock. In the morning, continental breakfast is delivered to you near the camellias or in the privacy of your room.
Historic Interest: Carmel Mission (2 miles), Robinson Jeffers' Tor House (1 mile).
Innkeeper(s): Dawn Dull. $125-205. 11 rooms with PB, 9 with FP. Types of meals: Cont plus. Beds: KQD. Cable TV, reading lamp, refrigerator, clock radio, telephone and desk in room. TV, fax and copier on premises. Weddings hosted. Antiquing, fishing, live theater, parks and shopping nearby.
Publicity: *Arrington's Bed & Breakfast Journal - "Best Inns on West Coast" & "Best Inn to visit again & again," Diversion and Cat Fancy.*
"Charming & excellent accommodations and service. Very much in keeping with the character and ambiance of Carmel's historic setting."

Coloma   G6

Coloma Country Inn

345 High Street
Coloma, CA 95613-0502
(530)622-6919 Fax:(530)626-4959
E-mail: info@colomacountryinn.com
Web: www.colomacountryinn.com

Circa 1852. Surrounded by the Sierra Nevada foothills, this country inn bed & breakfast sits on five private acres in the midst of the 300-acre Marshall Gold Discovery State Park. Guest bedrooms in the historic two-story clapboard main farmhouse are decorated and furnished with American and English antiques, handmade quilts and fresh flowers. Many of the baths include clawfoot tubs. The original 1898 carriage house features a Cottage Suite that offers a more secluded, spacious stay with kitchenette and private brick courtyard. After breakfast explore the quiet grounds with a pond, gazebo and gorgeous gardens. Swing in an old walnut tree or play horseshoes.
Historic Interest: Built in 1852, one of the oldest surviving original structures from the Gold Rush era.
Innkeeper(s): Kerry & Candie Bliss. $110-175. 5 rooms with PB, 2 suites, 1 cottage and 1 conference room. Breakfast and snacks/refreshments included in rates. Types of meals: Full gourmet bkfst, early coffee/tea, picnic lunch and afternoon tea. Beds: QDT. Reading lamp and ceiling fan in room. Air conditioning. Fax, parlor games, telephone, fireplace, pond, formal gardens, horseshoes and swing in old walnut tree on premises. Weddings, small meetings, family reunions and seminars hosted. Antiquing, art galleries, canoeing/kayaking, downhill skiing, fishing, golf, hiking, live theater, museums, parks, shopping, water sports, wineries, gold panning, white water rafting, olive oil tasting and local farmer's markets nearby.
Publicity: *Country Living, Los Angeles Times, Country Inns, Sunset, Motorland and New York Times.*

Columbia   H7

Columbia City Hotel & Restaurant

22768 Main St
Columbia, CA 95310
(209)532-1479 (800)532-1479 Fax:(209)532-7027

Circa 1856. Built in 1856 during the height of the Gold Rush Era, this two-story Victorian was known as the "What Cheer House." Now a state historical site, it has been authentically restored by the State of California, and the state owns the hotel's antique furniture and fixtures. The hotel was listed in Sunset Magazine's February 2000 issue as one of the 24 best bed & breakfasts. No televisions or telephones intrude on the historic ambiance of the hotel's 10 guest rooms. Indoor plumbing is the only historical compromise. Each room has a half-bath, and showers are down the hall. The beautifully restored restaurant offers fine selections of French cuisine, The hotel hosts family reunions, meetings, and weddings. Inquire about the Getaway Lodging, Dinner and Theatre Package for two.

Innkeeper(s): Tom Bender. $105-125. 10 rooms and 1 conference room. Breakfast included in rates. Types of meals: Cont plus, early coffee/tea and gourmet dinner. Restaurant on premises. Beds: QDT. Central air. Parlor games on premises. Weddings, small meetings, family reunions and seminars hosted. Antiquing, art galleries, cross-country skiing, downhill skiing, fishing, golf, hiking, horseback riding, live theater, museums, parks, shopping, tennis and wineries nearby.

Fallon Hotel

11175 Washington St
Columbia, CA 95310-1870
(209)532-1479 (800)532-1479 Fax:(208)532-7027

Circa 1857. The Fallon Hotel, restored and operated by the State of California Parks and Recreation Department, still boasts the main-floor theater where productions are featured year-round. Original furnishings from the hotel's Gold-Rush days have been repaired, polished and reupholstered, including a fine Turkish loveseat in the parlor. Bradbury & Bradbury redesigned the nine wallpaper patterns featured. The best rooms are upstairs with balconies overlooking the town's four blocks of saloons, cash stores, an ice cream parlor, blacksmith shop and the stage coach that periodically rambles through town.

Innkeeper(s): Tom Bender. $60-125. 14 rooms, 1 with PB and 1 suite. Breakfast included in rates. Types of meals: Cont plus. Beds: DT. Telephone on premises. Limited handicap access. Antiquing, downhill skiing, fishing, live theater, water sports and wine tasting nearby.

Publicity: *Home & Garden, Innsider, Motorland and Sunset.*

"Excellent service."

Coronado   Q12

Glorietta Bay Inn

1630 Glorietta Blvd
Coronado, CA 92118-2913
(619)435-3101 (800)283-9383 Fax:(619)435-6182
E-mail: rooms@gloriettabayinn.com
Web: www.gloriettabayinn.com

Circa 1908. Encounter resplendent grandeur at this Edwardian mansion, built for the renown John D. Spreckels and now a historic landmark. Major restoration has preserved many of the original light fixtures, sconces and chandeliers, brass banisters, marble stairs, copper-clad glass doors, hardwood floors and ornate woodwork. The Music Room boasts a baby grand player piano, guest library and board games. Thoughtful modernization of suites and guest bedrooms includes heat and air conditioning, data ports, voicemail, cable TV and whirlpool tubs. A generous continental breakfast buffet is served in the Verandah Room. The swimming pool is a popular gathering place, and afternoon refreshments are enjoyed on the patio. Enjoy a docent-led walking tour of the island on Tuesdays, Thursdays and Saturdays.

$150-585. 100 rooms with PB, 1 with FP and 19 suites. Breakfast and snacks/refreshments included in rates. Types of meals: Cont. Beds: KQD. Modem hook-up, data port, cable TV, VCR, reading lamp, CD player, refrigerator, ceiling fan, clock radio, telephone, coffeemaker, turn-down service, desk, hot tub/spa, voice mail and fireplace in room. Air conditioning. Fax, copier, spa, swimming, library, parlor games, fireplace and laundry facility on premises. Family reunions hosted. Antiquing, art galleries, beach, bicycling, fishing, golf, hiking, horseback riding, live theater, museums, parks, shopping, tennis and water sports nearby.

Publicity: *New York Times, Los Angeles Times, Home and Garden TV and Travel Channel.*

Crowley Lake   I9

Rainbow Tarns B&B at Crowley Lake

505 Rainbow Tarns Road
Crowley Lake, CA 93546
(760)935-4556 (888)588-6269
E-mail: info@rainbowtarns.com
Web: www.rainbowtarns.com

Circa 1920. Just south of Mammoth Lakes, at an altitude of 7,000 feet, you'll find this secluded retreat amid three acres of ponds, open meadows and the High Sierra Mountains. Country-style here includes luxury touches, such as a double Jacuzzi tub, queen-size bed, down pillows, comforters and a skylight for stargazing. In the '50s, ponds on the property served as a "U-Catch-Em." Folks rented fishing poles and paid 10 cents an inch for the fish  they caught. Nearby Crowley Lake is still one of the best trout-fishing areas in California. Romantic country weddings are popular here. Guests are free to simply relax in the peaceful setting, but hiking, horseback riding and skiing all are available in the area. In the afternoons, guests are treated to snacks and wine.

Innkeeper(s): Brock & Diane Thoman. $95-140. 3 rooms with PB. Breakfast included in rates. Types of meals: Full bkfst and early coffee/tea. Beds: QD. Limited handicap access.

Publicity: *Mammoth-Sierra, Bishop Vacation Planner, Eastern Sierra Fishing Guide, Sunset and Scenic 395.*

Davenport   J4

Davenport Oceanview B&B

31 Davenport Ave
Davenport, CA 95017
(831)425-1818 (800)870-1817 Fax:(831)423-1160

Circa 1906. Captain John Davenport came here to harvest the gray whales that pass close to shore during migration. The oldest building remaining originally was used as a public bath. It later became a bar, restaurant and dance hall before conversion into a private home. Completely renovated, it now houses four of the inn's rooms.

Historic Interest: The Wilder Ranch State Park is five miles away. Davenport Jail, Giovvini Cheesehouse, Old Davenport Pier and the St. Vincent DePaul Catholic Church, built in 1902, are nearby.

Innkeeper(s): Bruce & Marcia McDougal. $115-155. 12 rooms with PB. Types of meals: Full bkfst, lunch and dinner. Restaurant on premises. Beds: KQ. TV and telephone in room. Guests are given a breakfast voucher for restaurant breakfast menu on premises.

Publicity: *Monterey Life, Travel & Leisure, Sacramento Bee and Peninsula Time Tribune.*

"The warmth of the rooms, the people who work here and the ocean keeps us coming back year after year."

Dorrington H7

The Dorrington Hotel & Restaurant

3431 Hwy 4, PO Box 4307
Dorrington, CA 95223
(209)795-5800 Fax:(866)995-5800

Circa 1852. This historic hotel was built by Dorrington's town founders as a hotel and restaurant for those traveling through the area on stagecoach. More than a century later, guests still arrive for that purpose. Guest rooms are decorated in country style with antiques and brass beds topped with handmade quilts. A separate accommodation, "Cabin Sweet Cabin" offers a kitchenette, stone fireplace and whirlpool tub and may be rented apart from the bed and breakfast. The innkeepers want their guests to have a relaxing stay, free from the modern world, so there are no televisions or phones in guest rooms. Continental fare in the mornings, and Northern Italian cuisine nightly in the restaurant. According to legend, the ghost of the hotel's former mistress sometimes walks the hallways.

Innkeeper(s): Bonnie Saville. $85-125. 5 rooms. Breakfast included in rates. Types of meals: Cont and early coffee/tea. Restaurant on premises. Beds: Q. Weddings and small meetings hosted. Antiquing, cross-country skiing, downhill skiing, fishing, live theater, parks, shopping and water sports nearby.

Publicity: *Robert Conrad's Series "Search and Rescue."*

"The Dorrington has always existed in the dreams of all those out there that love romance."

Dunsmuir Q12

Dunsmuir Inn

5423 Dunsmuir Ave
Dunsmuir, CA 96025-2011
(530)235-4543 (888)386-7684 Fax:(530)235-4154
E-mail: jerryrig@joimail.net
Web: www.dunsmuirinn.net

Circa 1925. Comfortably situated in the Sacramento River canyon, this country inn is a perfect home base for the assortment of outdoor activities available. Old-fashioned flower gardens and the family orchard surround picnic tables and barbecue facilities. Stay in a guest bedroom or suite with a clawfoot tub. A hearty breakfast starts the day right. Sit on the front porch swing before taking a stroll along the Historic District. A short scenic walk to the river offers white water rafting, kayaking, world class trout fishing and popular swimming holes. Gold panning is still a favorite pastime to try. Go skiing and sledding nearby, or ice fish at Castle Lake. Visit breathtaking Mount Shasta and Mossbrae Falls. Ask the innkeepers about driving tours and sightseeing suggestions.

Innkeeper(s): Jerry & Julie Iskra. $75-85. 5 rooms with PB and 1 suite. Breakfast included in rates. Types of meals: Country bkfst, veg bkfst, early coffee/tea, picnic lunch and snacks/refreshments. Beds: KD. TV, VCR, reading lamp, ceiling fan and turn-down service in room. Air conditioning. Fax and telephone on premises. Family reunions hosted. Antiquing, bicycling, canoeing/kayaking, cross-country skiing, downhill skiing, fishing, golf, hiking, parks and world class trout fishing nearby.

Elk F3

The Harbor House Inn

5600 S Hwy 1
Elk, CA 95432
(707)877-3203 (800)720-7474 Fax:(707)877-3452
E-mail: innkeeper@theharborhouseinn.com
Web: www.theharborhouseinn.com

Circa 1916. The Harbor House Inn rests on a cliff overlooking Greenwood Cove and the Pacific Ocean. Built by a lumber company for executives visiting from the East, the inn is constructed entirely of redwood. All of the antique-filled guest rooms include a fireplace, and some have decks with spectacular ocean views. Guests are treated to both a full breakfast as well as an award winner four-course dinner. A path winds through the inn's gardens down to a private beach below.

Innkeeper(s): Elle Haynes. $295-450. 10 rooms with PB, 9 with FP, 4 cottages and 1 conference room. Breakfast and dinner included in rates. Types of meals: Full gourmet bkfst. Restaurant on premises. Beds: KQ. Reading lamp, CD player, clock radio, coffeemaker and desk in room. Fax, copier, telephone and fireplace on premises. Weddings and seminars hosted. Antiquing, art galleries, beach, bicycling, canoeing/kayaking, fishing, golf, hiking, horseback riding, live theater, museums, parks, shopping and wineries nearby.

Publicity: *Travel & Leisure, Sunset, Departures and Wine Spectator-Award of Excellence.*

"The Harbor House has become the most luxurious Inn along this seaside coast."

Sandpiper House Inn

5520 S Hwy 1
Elk, CA 95432
(707)877-3587 (800)894-9016 Fax:(707)877-1822
E-mail: aled@earthlink.net
Web: www.sandpiperhouse.inn

Circa 1916. A garden path leads Sandpiper guests to a garden sitting area overlooking the California coast. The path continues onward to a private beach. The historic home was built by a local lumber company. The living room and dining room have virgin redwood paneling. Guest quarters are appointed to look like rooms in an English country home. Canopied beds, Oriental rugs and polished wood floors create a romantic ambiance. Rooms offer either ocean or countryside views, and four have a fireplace. Gourmet breakfasts are served on tables set with lace and fresh flowers. In-house massages also are available.

Innkeeper(s): Ed & Althea Haworth. $155-260. 5 rooms with PB, 4 with FP and 2 suites. Breakfast and snacks/refreshments included in rates. Types of meals: Full gourmet bkfst and early coffee/tea. Beds: KQ. Reading lamp and refrigerator in room. Parlor games, telephone, fireplace and in-house massage therapy on premises. Fishing, live theater, parks, shopping, water sports and wineries nearby.

Escondido P12

Zosa Gardens B&B

9381 W Lilac Rd
Escondido, CA 92026-4508
(760)723-9093 (800)711-8361 Fax:(760)731-7616
E-mail: zosamd@aol.com
Web: www.zosagardens.com

Circa 1940. Escondido, located in northern San Diego County, is the setting for this Spanish Hacienda. The home rests on 22 well-landscaped acres atop a bluff in the Monserate Mountains.

Rooms bear flowery themes. Angel-lovers should try the Angel Room. The Master Suite includes a fireplace. In the evenings, gourmet tidbits are served with a selection of local wines. Billiards, hiking trails, a tennis court and massages are available. Golf courses, restaurants and other sites are just minutes away.

Innkeeper(s): Noli & Nena Zosa. $145-250. 15 rooms with PB, 3 with FP, 3 suites and 2 cabins. Breakfast and snacks/refreshments included in rates. Types of meals: Full gourmet bkfst. Beds: KQ. Desk, hot tub/spa and Jacuzzi in room. Air conditioning. VCR, fax, copier, spa, swimming, tennis, parlor games, telephone and fireplace on premises. Limited handicap access. Weddings, small meetings, family reunions and seminars hosted. Amusement parks, antiquing, fishing, golf, live theater, parks, shopping, sporting events, tennis, water sports, Buddhist Monastery, wineries and hot air balloons nearby.

Publicity: On The Town Getaways.

Eureka   C2

Abigail's 'Elegant Victorian Mansion' B&B Lodging

1406 C St
Eureka, CA 95501-1765
(707)444-3144
E-mail: info@eureka-california.com
Web: www.eureka-california.com

Circa 1888. One of Eureka's leading lumber barons built this picturesque home, a National Historic Landmark, from 1,000-year-old virgin redwood. Original wallpapers, wool carpets and antique light fixtures create a wonderfully authentic Victorian ambiance. A tuxedoed butler and your hosts, decked in period attire, greet guests upon arrival. Croquet fields and Victorian gardens surround the inn. The hosts provide complimentary "horseless" carriage rides. The beds in the well-appointed guest quarters are topped with custom-made mattresses. There is a video library of vintage silent films. The inn has been host to many historic personalities, including actresses Lillie Langtry and Sarah Bernhardt, and many senators and representatives. The Pacific Ocean, beaches and the Giant Redwoods are only a few minutes away.

Historic Interest: Historic Fort Humboldt State Park, Redwood parks, Clark Historic Museum, Maritime Museum, historic "Old Town" (all within walking distance).

Innkeeper(s): Doug & Lily Vieyra. $85-215. 4 rooms, 2 with PB, 1 suite and 1 conference room. Afternoon tea and snacks/refreshments included in rates. Beds: Q. Reading lamp, refrigerator, clock radio, telephone, turn-down service, desk, chocolate truffles and B&B guidebooks in room. Air conditioning. VCR, fax, copier, sauna, bicycles, library, parlor games, croquet field, antique automobiles and horseless carriages on premises. Small meetings and seminars hosted. Antiquing, beach, horseback riding, live theater, tennis, water sports, carriage rides, bay cruise, sailing and Giant Redwoods nearby.

Publicity: New York Times, San Francisco Chronicle, Boston Globe, LA Times, Wall Street Journal, Jay Leno, "H & G" TV and Outbreak.

The Carter House Victorians

301 L St
Eureka, CA 95501
(707)444-8062 (800)404-1390 Fax:(707)444-8067
E-mail: reserve@carterhouse.com
Web: www.carterhouse.com

Circa 1884. Superior hospitality is offered in these Victorian inns that grace the historic district. Perched alongside Humboldt Bay, the inn promises appealing views. Proud of their AAA four-diamond rating, luxurious guest bedrooms and suites feature fireplaces, antique furnishings and spas. Begin each morning with a highly acclaimed breakfast. Renowned for regional, seasonal cuisine, for many ingredients are grown in the garden or bought from local purveyors. Restaurant 301 boasts a coveted international Wine Spectator Grand Award, maintaining in its cellars an extensive collection of the world's finest vintages.

Historic Interest: Redwood forests, historic architecture, wildlife/bird sanctuary, Victorian Sawmill (all within 10 miles).

Innkeeper(s): Mark & Christi Carter. $99-497. 32 rooms with PB, 15 with FP, 15 suites, 2 cottages and 1 conference room. Breakfast and afternoon tea included in rates. Types of meals: Full gourmet bkfst, early coffee/tea, snacks/refreshments, hors d'oeurves, wine, gourmet dinner and room service. Restaurant on premises. Beds: KQDT. Cable TV, VCR, reading lamp, stereo, refrigerator, snack bar, clock radio, telephone, turn-down service, desk and hot tub/spa in room. Fax, copier, spa, fireplace, bedtime tea & cookies and wine & hors d'oeuvres before dinner available on premises. Limited handicap access. Small meetings, family reunions and seminars hosted. Antiquing, fishing, live theater, parks, shopping, sporting events, water sports and beaches nearby.

Publicity: Sunset, U.S. News & World Report, Country Home, Country Living, Bon Appetit, San Francisco Focus, Northwest Palate, Gourmet, Art Culinare, San Francisco Chronicle, Wine Spectator, New York Times Magazine and Organic Gardening.

Cornelius Daly Inn

1125 H St
Eureka, CA 95501-1844
(707)445-3638 (800)321-9656 Fax:(707)444-3636
E-mail: innkeeper@dalyinn.com
Web: www.dalyinn.com

Circa 1905. This 6,000-square-foot Colonial Revival mansion is located in the historic section of Eureka. The inn's gracious atmosphere includes four wood-burning fireplace and a third floor ballroom. Enjoy the romantic French bedroom suite with dressing table, armoire and bedstead in Annie Murphey's Room. It offers a fireplace and a view over the Victorian garden. Miss Martha's Room features antique twin beds with inlaid pearl. Breakfast is served fireside in the inn's formal dining room or garden patio. In the evenings, refreshments are served.

Historic Interest: The Carson Mansion, historic Old Town, Fort Humboldt and a Victorian sawmill are among the nearby historic attractions.

Innkeeper(s): Donna & Bob Gafford. $90-160. 5 rooms, 3 with PB, 1 with FP and 2 suites. Breakfast and snacks/refreshments included in rates. Types of meals: Full gourmet bkfst and early coffee/tea. Beds: QT. Reading lamp, clock radio, Antique furnishings, plush robes and beautiful carpets in room. VCR, fax, copier, library, parlor games, telephone, fireplace, game room and billiard table on premises. Weddings, small meetings, family reunions and seminars hosted. Antiquing, fishing, live theater, shopping, redwood park and ocean nearby.

"A genuine delight."

Old Town Bed & Breakfast Inn

1521 3rd St
Eureka, CA 95501-0710
(707)443-5235 (888)508-5235 Fax:(707)442-4390
E-mail: info@oldtownbnb.com
Web: www.oldtownbnb.com

Circa 1871. This early Victorian was built in the Greek Revival style as the original family home of lumber baron William Carson. It was constructed of virgin redwood and Douglas fir and moved three blocks to its current location in 1905. Called a "Humboldt County jewel" by the local visitors and convention bureau, the inn is the original bed & breakfast of the area and was opened in 1983. Spacious guest rooms offer heirloom quilts, antiques, and TV/VCRs. (There's a large movie collection to peruse.) In the morning, a variety of gourmet breakfasts are served under the light of oil lamps and beside a flickering fireplace.

Innkeeper(s): Steve & Karen Albright. $110-140. 4 rooms with PB, 1 with FP. Breakfast included in rates. Types of meals: Country bkfst, veg bkfst and early coffee/tea. Beds: KQ. Cable TV, VCR and clock radio in room. Fax, library, telephone, fireplace, large movie collection and library with computer/modem/fax on premises. Family reunions hosted. Antiquing, art galleries, beach, bicycling, canoeing/kayaking, fishing, golf, hiking, horseback riding, live theater, museums, parks, shopping, tennis, water sports, eco-tours, Redwood State National and zoo nearby.

Publicity: *Times-Standard, Country, San Francisco Chronicle, Sunset, San Francisco Examiner and L.A.Times.*

"From the moment we opened the door, we knew we had chosen a special place to stay."

Ferndale   C2

Gingerbread Mansion Inn
PO Box 40, 400 Berding St
Ferndale, CA 95536-1380
(707)786-4000 (800)952-4136 Fax:(707)786-4381
E-mail: innkeeper@gingerbread-mansion.com
Web: gingerbread-mansion.com

Circa 1899. Built for Dr. H.J. Ring, the Gingerbread Mansion is now the most photographed of Northern California's inns. Near Eureka, it is in the fairy-tale Victorian village of Ferndale (a National Historical Landmark). Gingerbread Mansion is a unique combination of Queen Anne and Eastlake styles with elaborate gingerbread trim. Inside are spacious and elegant rooms including two suites with "his" and "her" clawfoot bathtubs. The Empire Suite is said to be the most opulent accommodation in Northern California. Another memorable choice would be "The Veneto", an imaginative experience where guests stay within a piece of artwork. Extensive formal English gardens beautifully surround the mansion and it is a stroll away to Victorian shops, galleries and restaurants. A Wilderness park and bird sanctuary are a half mile away.

Historic Interest: Victorian shops and galleries along Main Street, The Ferndale Museum, wilderness park and bird sanctuary (one-half mile).

Innkeeper(s): Tom Amato & Maggie Dowd. $150-400. 11 rooms with PB, 5 with FP and 5 suites. Breakfast and afternoon tea included in rates. Types of meals: Full bkfst and early coffee/tea. Beds: KQT. Reading lamp, clock radio, turn-down service and desk in room. Library, parlor games, telephone, fireplace and gardens on premises. Small meetings and family reunions hosted. Antiquing, fishing, hiking, live theater, parks and shopping nearby.

Publicity: *San Francisco Focus, Sunset, Travel Holiday, Country Inns, Los Angeles Times, Sunset, PBS (Inn Country USA), HGTV-Restore America and Outbrook (Warner Bros.).*

"Absolutely the most charming, friendly and delightful place we have ever stayed."

Shaw House B&B Inn
PO Box 1369
Ferndale, CA 95536-1369
(707)786-9958 (800)557-7429 Fax:(707)786-9758

Circa 1854. The owners of Ferndale's most historic structure note that the Shaw House was opened to the public in 1860 (six years after its construction) "to serve man and beast". A carpenter Gothic house with gables, bays and balconies it is set back on an acre of garden. An old buckeye tree frames the front gate, and in the back, a secluded deck overlooks a creek. Nestled under the wallpapered gables are several guest rooms filled with antiques and fresh flowers.

Historic Interest: Listed in the National Register.

Innkeeper(s): Jan Culbert. $85-185. 8 rooms with PB. Breakfast and afternoon tea included in rates. Types of meals: Full bkfst. Beds: QD. Telephone on premises. Antiquing, fishing and live theater nearby.

Publicity: *Travel & Leisure and New York Times.*

"Lovely place and lovely people." — Willard Scott

The Victorian Inn
400 Ocean Ave
Ferndale, CA 95536
(707)786-4949 (888)589-1808 Fax:(707)786-4558
E-mail: innkeeper@a-victorian-inn.com
Web: www.a-victorian-inn.com

Circa 1890. Built with redwood from North Coast Humboldt County, this elegant inn truly reflects its name in decor and location. It is situated in an ideal Victorian village, close to the beach. The former front parlors now display a luxurious collection of rare gems and fine jewelry. Ceilings as tall as 14 and 16 feet accent the spacious guest bedrooms and suites. Vintage fixtures and furnishings are featured including clawfoot tubs, iron and brass beds. The Pacifica Room boasts a turreted sitting area and a fireplace. Breakfast is served in Curley's, the on-site restaurant and tavern offering fine dining daily.

Innkeeper(s): Lowell Daniels & Jenny Oaks. $85-175. 12 rooms with PB, 1 with FP, 4 suites and 4 conference rooms. Breakfast included in rates. Types of meals: Full gourmet bkfst, veg bkfst, early coffee/tea, gourmet lunch, picnic lunch, snacks/refreshments and gourmet dinner. Restaurant on premises. Beds: KQD. Cable TV, VCR, reading lamp, refrigerator, ceiling fan, clock radio, telephone, desk and fireplace in room. Fax, copier, library, parlor games, fireplace and gift shop on premises. Small meetings, family reunions and seminars hosted. Antiquing, art galleries, beach, bicycling, canoeing/kayaking, fishing, golf, hiking, live theater, museums, parks and shopping nearby.

Publicity: *"The Majestic," starring Jim Carrey, "Outbreak," starring Dustin Hoffman and was also filmed here.*

Forestville   G4

Case Ranch Inn B&B
7446 Poplar Dr.
Forestville, CA 95436
(707)887-8711 Fax:(707)887-8607
E-mail: info@caseranchinn.com
Web: www.caseranchinn.com

Circa 1894. Enjoy the Russian River Valley and surrounding wine country at this Victorian inn, a Sonoma County historical landmark. The quiet rural location covers two acres of lawn, gardens, fruit trees and a large deck with fountain. Gather on comfy wicker furniture by the fire in the large parlor. Offering the intimacy and personal service of a traditional B&B, idyllic guest suites feature soothing toiletries, plush robes, pillowtop mattresses and down comforters. Enjoy a satisfying breakfast in the dining room. Natural and organic ingredients are used, and special dietary needs are easily accommodated. The front wrap-around porch is great to watch visiting deer and quail.

Innkeeper(s): Diana Van Ry & Allen Tilton. $140-215. 3 rooms with PB. Breakfast and snacks/refreshments included in rates. Types of meals: Full gourmet bkfst, veg bkfst and early coffee/tea. Beds: Q. Modem hook-up, reading lamp, CD player, refrigerator and clock radio in room. Central air. Fax, telephone, luxury suite and vacation cottage on premises. Small meetings and seminars hosted. Antiquing, art galleries, beach, bicycling, canoeing/kayaking, fishing, golf, hiking, horseback riding, live theater, museums, parks, shopping, tennis and wineries nearby.

Publicity: *CABBI's annual directory.*

Fort Bragg   E2

Avalon House

561 Stewart St
Fort Bragg, CA 95437-3226
(707)964-5555 (800)964-5556 Fax:(707)964-5555
E-mail: anne@theavalonhouse.com
Web: www.theavalonhouse.com

Circa 1905. This redwood California Craftsman house was extensively remodeled in 1988 and furnished with a mixture of antiques and willow furniture. Some rooms feature fire-

places, whirlpool tubs and ocean views and decks. The inn is in a quiet residential area, three blocks from the Pacific Ocean, one block west of Hwy. 1, and two blocks from the Skunk Train depot.

Innkeeper(s): Anne Sorrells. $85-155. 6 rooms with PB, 4 with FP. Breakfast included in rates. Types of meals: Full bkfst and early coffee/tea. Beds: QD. Reading lamp, clock radio and spa in room. Telephone and fireplace on premises. Weddings, small meetings and family reunions hosted. Antiquing, fishing, live theater, parks, shopping, water sports, whale watching and Skunk Train nearby.

Publicity: *Advocate News.*

"Elegant, private and extremely comfortable. We will never stay in a motel again."

Grey Whale Inn

615 N Main St
Fort Bragg, CA 95437-3240
(707)964-0640 (800)382-7244 Fax:(707)964-4408

Circa 1915. As the name implies, whales can be seen from many of the inn's vantage points during the creatures' migration season along the West Coast. The stately four-story red-

wood inn features airy and spacious guest rooms with neighborhood ocean views. Some rooms include a fireplace, whirlpool tub for two or private deck. Near the heart of downtown Fort Bragg, it's an easy walk to the Skunk Train, shops, galleries, a microbrewery and restaurants. There is also a fireside lounge, TV/VCR room and a recreation area with pool table.

Historic Interest: The Georgia Pacific Logging Museum and the Guest House Museum are two blocks away, while the Kelley House Museum and Ford House are a 10-mile drive.

Innkeeper(s): Michael Dawson. $100-200. 14 rooms with PB, 4 with FP and 1 conference room. Breakfast included in rates. Types of meals: Full bkfst. Beds: KQDT. Cable TV, reading lamp, refrigerator, clock radio, telephone, desk and hot tub/spa in room. VCR, fax, copier, library, parlor games and fireplace on premises. Limited handicap access. Weddings, small meetings, family reunions and seminars hosted. Antiquing, fishing, live theater, parks, shopping, whale watching, golf, hiking, bicycling and microbrewery nearby.

Publicity: *Inn Times, San Francisco Examiner, Travel, Fort Bragg Advocate News, Mendocino Beacon, Los Angeles Times, Sunset and Contra Costa Times.*

"We are going to return each year until we have tried each room. Sunrise room is excellent in the morning or evening."

Old Stewart House Inn

511 Stewart St
Fort Bragg, CA 95437-3226
(707)961-0775 (800)287-8392
E-mail: pat@oldstewarthouseinn.com
Web: www.oldstewarthouseinn.com

Circa 1876. This is the oldest house in Fort Bragg and was built for the founding partner of the town mill. The Victorian theme is enhanced by rooms that may feature amenities such as a fireplace, as well as period furnishings. Within a three-block area of the inn are the Skunk Train Depot, restaurants, shops and beaches. Also nearby are ocean cliffs, stands of redwood, waterfalls and botanical gardens.

Innkeeper(s): Jim and Pat McKeever. $100-145. 5 rooms with PB, 2 with FP and 2 cabins. Breakfast and snacks/refreshments included in rates. Types of meals: Full bkfst. Beds: Q. TV, spa, library, parlor games, telephone and fireplace on premises. Limited handicap access. Antiquing, fishing, golf, live theater, parks, shopping, tennis and water sports nearby.

Georgetown   G6

American River Inn

PO Box 43, Gold Country
Georgetown, CA 95634-0043
(530)333-4499 (800)245-6566 Fax:(530)333-9253
E-mail: ariinnkeeper@aol.com
Web: www.americanriverinn.com

Circa 1853. Just a few miles from where gold was discovered in Coloma stands this completely restored miners' boarding house. Mining cars dating back to the original Woodside Mine Camp are on-site. The lode still runs under the inn. There is a Jacuzzi, croquet field, chipping

green and complimentary mountain bikes. In the evenings, guests are treated to complimentary wines and hors d'oeuvres. Georgetown was a designated site for the California gold discovery celebration.

Innkeeper(s): Maria, Will & Betty. $85-115. 12 rooms, 7 with PB, 1 with FP and 1 conference room. Types of meals: Full gourmet bkfst. Beds: KQ. Fax, copier and spa on premises. Limited handicap access. Fishing and hiking nearby.

Publicity: *Los Angeles Times, Sunset, Gourmet, Westways and 50 Romantic Getaways.*

"Our home away from home. We fell in love here in all its beauty and will be back for our fourth visit in April, another honeymoon for six days."

Geyserville G4

Hope-Merrill House & Hope Bosworth House

PO Box 42
Geyserville, CA 95441-9637
(707)857-3356 (800)825-4233 Fax:(707)857-4673
E-mail: moreinfo@hope-inns.com
Web: www.hope-inns.com

Circa 1870. The Hope-Merrill House is a classic example of the Eastlake Stick style that was so popular during Victorian times. Built entirely from redwood, the house features original wainscoting and silk-screened wallcoverings. A swimming pool, vineyard and gazebo are favorite spots for guests to relax. The Hope-Bosworth House, on the same street, was built in 1904 in the Queen Anne style by an early Geyserville pioneer who lived in the home until the 1960s. The front picket fence is covered with roses. Period details include oak woodwork, sliding doors, polished fir floors and antique light fixtures.

Innkeeper(s): Cosette & Ron Scheiber. $124-250. 12 rooms with PB, 5 with FP and 1 suite. Breakfast included in rates. Types of meals: Full gourmet bkfst, early coffee/tea and picnic lunch. Beds: Q. Reading lamp, ceiling fan and desk in room. Fax, copier, telephone, fireplace, coffee, tea and hot chocolate available 24 hours a day on premises. Weddings, small meetings and family reunions hosted. Antiquing, parks, shopping, water sports, wineries and redwoods nearby.

Publicity: *New York Times, San Francisco Chronicle, San Diego Union, Country Homes, Sunset, Sacramento Union, Los Angeles Times and Bay Area Back Roads.*

Gilroy J5

The 1890 Chesbro House

7541 Church St
Gilroy, CA 95020
(408)842-3750
E-mail: info@chesbrohouse.com
Web: www.chesbrohouse.com

Circa 1890. A visit to this Eastlake Victorian provides a taste of the gracious past. The home was built in the heart of the historic district for the current owner's great-grandfather, a pioneer physician whose descendants of four generations have since lived here. The all-redwood Painted Lady boasts rooftop iron cresting, ornate ceiling medallions, original woodwork and period fixtures. Have tea in the antique-filled front parlor, or relax in the Arts and Crafts-style sitting room. Guest bedrooms feature heirlooms and furnishings of wicker, brass, walnut and marble. A wholesome and hearty breakfast may include Big Sur omelette, turkey sausage and home-baked fig muffins. A century-old trumpet vine adorns the front porch, while a variety of old fruit trees shade the garden.

Innkeeper(s): Dick & Elizabeth Barratt. $125-145. 2 rooms, 1 with PB. Breakfast included in rates. Types of meals: Full gourmet bkfst, veg bkfst, early coffee/tea and afternoon tea. Beds: KQ. Cable TV, VCR, reading lamp, ceiling fan, clock radio, telephone and desk in room. Amusement parks, antiquing, beach, bicycling, fishing, golf, hiking, live theater, museums, parks, shopping and wineries nearby.

Publicity: *Gilroy Business Focus, Ripon College (WI) Magazine, Gilroy Dispatch, Out and About, Valley Adviser and Silicon Valley Handbook.*

Country Rose Inn - B&B

PO Box 2500
Gilroy, CA 95021
(408)842-0441 Fax:(408)842-6646
E-mail: countryrosebnb@earthlink.net
Web: www.countryrose-b-n-b.com

Circa 1920. Amid five acres, and set between Morgan Hill and Gilroy, a half-hour's drive south of San Jose, is the aptly named Country Rose Inn. A roomy Dutch Colonial manor, this inn was once a farmhouse on a chicken ranch. Every room features a rose theme, including wallpaper and quilted bedspreads. Each window offers a relaxing view of grazing horses, fertile fields, or the tranquil grounds, which boast magnificent 100-year-old oak trees. The inn is 20 minutes north of the San Juan Bautista Mission.

Historic Interest: San Juan Bautista Mission.

Innkeeper(s): Rose Hernandez. $149-239. 5 rooms with PB, 1 with FP, 1 suite and 2 conference rooms. Types of meals: Full bkfst and early coffee/tea. Beds: KQDT. Reading lamp, clock radio, turn-down service and desk in room. Air conditioning. Fax, library, telephone and fireplace on premises. Weddings, small meetings and seminars hosted. Antiquing, golf, live theater, parks, shopping, wineries, Bonfante Gardens Theme Park, Monterey Peninsula and Henry W. Coe State Park nearby.

"The quiet, serene country setting made our anniversary very special. Rose is a delightful, gracious hostess and cook."

Glen Ellen G4

Glenelly Inn & Cottages

5131 Warm Springs Rd
Glen Ellen, CA 95442-9739
(707)996-6720 Fax:(707)996-5227
E-mail: glenelly@glenelly.com
Web: www.glenelly.com

Circa 1916. Scenic beauty is enchanting year-round at this historic, traditional French Colonial bed & breakfast in the heart of the Valley of the Moon. Experience a graciousness and hospitality that instill a comfortable leisure. Guest bedrooms boast private entrances with verandas or decks, country antique furnishings, firm beds with Norwegian down comforters, fine linens and lots of pillows. Most of the private bathrooms include clawfoot tubs with showers. A gourmet breakfast buffet can be enjoyed by the cobblestone fireplace in the Common Room or al fresco on the flagstone patio. Massage and spa services are available. Swing in the hammock or soak in the in-ground Jacuzzi surrounded by garden scents and sky sights. Ask about family packages.

Historic Interest: Built in 1916 as a country resort.

Innkeeper(s): Kristi Jeppesen. $150-250. 10 rooms, 8 with PB, 4 with FP and 2 cottages. Breakfast and snacks/refreshments included in rates. Types of meals: Full gourmet bkfst, early coffee/tea and picnic lunch. Beds: QDT. Reading lamp, ceiling fan, clock radio and fireplace in room. TV, VCR, fax, copier, spa, library, parlor games, telephone and fireplace on premises. Antiquing, art galleries, bicycling, golf, hiking, horseback riding, live theater, museums, parks, shopping, tennis, water sports and wineries nearby.

Grass Valley   F6

Annie Horan's

415 W Main St
Grass Valley, CA 95945-6403
(530)272-1516 (800)771-4676
E-mail: mauryhorn@yahoo.com
Web: www.anniehoran.com

Circa 1873. Mine owner James Horan built this splendid
Victorian house for his wife Mary. Today the exterior, parlor and
guest quarters are as they were at the height of Gold Country
opulence. Follow in the footsteps of Mark Twain, Bret Harte and
Presidents Grant, Harrison and Cleveland, who visited the shops,
pubs, restaurants and other spots located just beyond the inn.
Historic Interest: James Horan built the first Catholic Church in Grass Valley
and built this home for his wife. Their daughter, Annie, ran it as a boarding
house from 1900-1954.
Innkeeper(s): Maury Horn. $69-109. 4 rooms with PB. Breakfast included in
rates. Types of meals: Country bkfst and early coffee/tea. Beds: Q. Ceiling fan
and clock radio in room. Central air. TV, parlor games, telephone, laundry
facility and massage on premises. Amusement parks, antiquing, bicycling,
canoeing/kayaking, cross-country skiing, downhill skiing, fishing, golf, hiking,
live theater, parks, shopping, water sports and wineries nearby.

Swan-Levine House

328 S Church St
Grass Valley, CA 95945-6709
(530)272-1873

Circa 1897. Originally built by a local mine owner, this Queen
Anne Victorian was converted into a hospital by Dr. John Jones,
and it served the area as a medical center until 1968.
Innkeepers/artists Howard and Margaret Levine renovated the
house including a printmaking studio and guesthouse. The old
surgery is now a guest room with rose-painted walls and octagonal white floor tiles and provides a grand view from the wicker-furnished turret.
Innkeeper(s): Howard & Peggy Levine. $85-110. 4 rooms with PB, 1
with FP and 1 suite. Types of meals: Full bkfst. Beds: KQT. Fireplace in
suite in room.
Publicity: *Country Living Magazine.*

*"You made us feel at home. An atmosphere of open-hearted friend-
ship is rather rare these days."*

Groveland   H7

All Seasons Groveland Inn

18656 Main Street
Groveland, CA 95321
(209)962-0232 (800)595-9993 Fax:(209)962-0250
E-mail: jjenkins@goldrush.com
Web: www.allseasonsgrovelandinn.com

Circa 1897. One of the first houses built in the area, this 1897
Victorian inn with classic details and wraparound porch sits
above the fog and below the snow. Enjoy Gold Country lodging with guaranteed year-round access to Yosemite National
Park. Handcrafted murals with exotic wall treatments such as a
waterfall, bird's nest and billowing clouds are featured in
themed guest bedrooms depicting Yosemite. Custom-made
bedding accents antique furnishings. Most rooms boast Jacuzzi
tubs, fireplaces, coffee stations and private decks. Generous

upscale amenities are sure to please. There are guest refrigerators in the kitchen. A wishing well adorns the lawn and garden
that includes an arch of roses inside the white picket fence.
Innkeeper(s): Judy Thompson & Josie Tamez. $81-200. 5 rooms with PB, 4
with FP. Beds: QT. Modem hook-up, clock radio, telephone, coffeemaker, desk
and fireplace in room. Air conditioning. Fax, sauna, parlor games, laundry
facility and refrigerators for each room on premises. Weddings and family
reunions hosted. Antiquing, art galleries, beach, bicycling, canoeing/kayaking,
cross-country skiing, downhill skiing, fishing, golf, hiking, horseback riding,
live theater, museums, parks, shopping, tennis, water sports, wineries and
panning for gold nearby.
Publicity: *San Jose Mercury Independent Journal.*

The Groveland Hotel at Yosemite National Park

18767 Main St, PO Box 481
Groveland, CA 95321-0481
(209)962-4000 (800)273-3314 Fax:(209)962-6674

Circa 1849. Located 23 miles from Yosemite National Park, the
1992 restoration features both an 1849 adobe building with
18-inch-thick walls constructed during the Gold Rush and a
1914 building erected to house workers for the Hetch Hetchy
Dam. Both feature two-story balconies. There is a Victorian
parlor, a gourmet restaurant and a Western saloon. Guest
rooms feature European antiques, down comforters, some
feather beds, in-room
coffee, phones with
data ports, and hair
dryers. The feeling is
one of casual elegance.
Innkeeper(s): Peggy A. & Grover C. Mosley. $135-210. 17 rooms with PB, 3
with FP, 3 suites and 1 conference room. Breakfast included in rates. Types
of meals: Cont plus, early coffee/tea, picnic lunch and room service.
Restaurant on premises. Beds: QT. Data port, reading lamp, ceiling fan, clock
radio, telephone, desk and hair dryers in room. Air conditioning. VCR, fax,
copier, library, parlor games and fireplace on premises. Limited handicap
access. Weddings, small meetings, family reunions and seminars hosted.
Antiquing, cross-country skiing, downhill skiing, fishing, golf, parks, shopping,
tennis and water sports nearby.
Publicity: *Sonora Union Democrat, Los Angeles Times, Peninsula, Sunset
(February 2001-Wests Best Inns), Stockton Record, Country Inns
Magazine (Top 10 inns in U.S.) and Wine Spectator Award of Excellence
for our wine list.*

Gualala   G3

North Coast Country Inn

34591 South Hwy One
Gualala, CA 95445
(707)884-4537 (800)959-4537 Fax:(707)884-1833
E-mail: innkeeper@northcoastcountryinn.com
Web: www.northcoastcountryinn.com

Circa 1944. Overlooking the Pacific Ocean, the six guest
rooms that comprise North Coast Country Inn are tucked
into a pine and redwood forested hillside. Each is furnished
with antiques, and include a fireplace, some wet-bar kitchenettes and private deck. There is a very private and secluded
hot tub on the hillside or
you may relax in the gaze-
bo. Breakfast is served in
the breakfast room. Barking
sea lions are often heard in
the distance.
Innkeeper(s): Maureen Topping &

Bill Shupe. $146-215. 6 rooms with PB, 6 with FP and 1 conference room. Breakfast and snacks/refreshments included in rates. Types of meals: Full gourmet bkfst, veg bkfst, early coffee/tea and picnic lunch. Beds: KQ. Reading lamp, refrigerator, ceiling fan, clock radio, coffeemaker, turn-down service, hot tub/spa and fireplace in room. TV, VCR, fax, spa, parlor games, telephone, fireplace and gift shop on premises. Weddings, small meetings, family reunions and seminars hosted. Antiquing, art galleries, beach, bicycling, canoeing/kayaking, fishing, golf, hiking, horseback riding, live theater, parks, shopping, tennis and wineries nearby.

Publicity: *San Francisco Examiner, Wine Spectators, Wine Trader, Motortrend, Los Angeles Times and San Francisco Chronicle.*

"Thank you so much for a very gracious stay in your cozy inn. We have appreciated all the special touches."

Guerneville   G3

Fern Grove Cottages
16650 Highway 116
Guerneville, CA 95446-9678
(707)869-8105 Fax:(707)869-1615

Circa 1926. Clustered in a village-like atmosphere and surrounded by redwoods, these craftsman cottages have romantic fireplaces, private entrances, and are individually decorated. The cottages were built in the 1920s and served as little vacation houses for San Francisco families visiting the Russian River. Some units have a kitchen or wet bar, some have double whirlpool tubs and other cottages are suitable for families. Guests enjoy use of the swimming pool. The cottages are just a few blocks from shops and restaurants, as well as a swimming beach on the river. Visit a nearby redwood state reserve or the Russian River Valley wineries for wine tasting and tours.

Innkeeper(s): Mike & Margaret Kennett. $79-219. 21 cottages with PB, 14 with FP and 1 conference room. Breakfast included in rates. Types of meals: Cont plus. Beds: KQ. Cable TV, reading lamp, refrigerator and clock radio in room. Swimming, fireplace and guest barbecue area on premises. Small meetings, family reunions and seminars hosted. Antiquing, beach, canoeing/kayaking, fishing, golf, parks, shopping, tennis, water sports, wineries, Armstrong Redwood State Park, wineries and ocean nearby.

Ridenhour Ranch
12850 River Rd
Guerneville, CA 95446-9276
(707)887-1033 (888)877-4466 Fax:(707)869-2967
E-mail: ridenhourinn@earthlink.net
Web: www.ridenhourranchhouseinn.com

Circa 1906. Located on a hill overlooking the Russian River, this ranch house is shaded by redwoods, oaks and laurels. There are eight guest rooms, including two cottages overlooking the informal gardens. Guests can relax in the hot tub below the majestic oak trees. The Korbel Champagne cellars are next door, and it's a five-minute walk to the river. The ranch offers easy access to wineries in Napa and Sonoma, old-growth redwoods, the Russian River and the dramatic Sonoma coast.

Innkeeper(s): Chris Bell & Meilani Naranjo. $105-185. 8 rooms with PB, 1 with FP and 1 suite. Breakfast and snacks/refreshments included in rates. Types of meals: Full gourmet bkfst and early coffee/tea. Beds: KQ. Cable TV and ceiling fan in room. Parlor games and fireplace on premises. Antiquing, bicycling, fishing, golf, hiking, live theater, parks, shopping and water sports nearby.

Publicity: *Los Angeles Times, Orange County Register and Los Altos Town Crier.*

"Your hospitality and food will ensure our return!"

Half Moon Bay   I4

Mill Rose Inn
615 Mill St
Half Moon Bay, CA 94019-1726
(650)726-8750 (800)900-7673
E-mail: info@millroseinn.com
Web: www.millroseinn.com

Circa 1903. This Victorian country inn is part of the original Miramontes land grant and played an important part in local coastal history. English country gardens bloom year-round under the magical hand of innkeeper and landscape designer Terry Baldwin. Canopy beds, clawfoot tubs, hand-painted fireplaces and an inside garden spa create an opulent setting in which to relax.

Innkeeper(s): Eve & Terry Baldwin. $190-360. 6 rooms with PB, 5 with FP and 1 conference room. Types of meals: Full bkfst. Beds: KQ. TV, spa and telephone on premises.

Publicity: *New York Times, LA Times, Dallas Morning News and Sunset Magazine.*

"One of the loveliest retreats this side of the Cotswolds." - San Diego Union

Old Thyme Inn
779 Main St
Half Moon Bay, CA 94019-1924
(650)726-1616 (800)720-4277 Fax:(650)726-6394
E-mail: innkeeper@oldthymeinn.com
Web: www.oldthymeinn.com

Circa 1898. Spend enchanted nights in this "Princess Anne" Victorian inn located on the historic Main Street of Old Town, Half Moon Bay. Its lush, aromatic English flower and herb garden with a bubbling fountain provides a perfect backdrop for casual conversations or romantic tete-a-tetes. Just 28 miles from San Francisco and less than one hour from San Jose and the Silicon Valley, the inn is within walking distance of a crescent-shaped beach, art galleries, shops and fine dining. Furnished in antiques and adorned with the innkeeper's art collection, it offers seven freshly decorated guest rooms, each with a queen bed and hypoallergenic featherbed and down comforter. Two rooms have both Jacuzzis and fireplaces. Savor the inn's tantalizing full breakfast before a day of relaxing or sightseeing.

Historic Interest: San Francisco is just 25 miles away, Filoli Gardens nearby.

Innkeeper(s): Rick & Kathy Ellis. $130-300. 7 rooms with PB, 3 with FP. Breakfast included in rates. Types of meals: Full bkfst. Beds: Q. TV, VCR, reading lamp, stereo, refrigerator, clock radio, desk, hot tub/spa, some with Jacuzzi tubs and fireplaces in room. Fax, telephone and fireplace on premises. Small meetings and family reunions hosted. Antiquing, fishing, golf, live theater, parks, shopping and water sports nearby.

Publicity: *California Weekends, Los Angeles, San Mateo Times, San Jose Mercury News, Herb Companion and San Francisco Examiner.*

Zaballa House

324 Main St
Half Moon Bay, CA 94019-1724
(650)726-9123 Fax:(650)726-3921
E-mail: zaballa@zaballahouse.com
Web: zaballahouse.com

Circa 1858. The Zaballa House is the oldest building still standing in Half Moon Bay. The inn features an elegant reception room, a breakfast nook and a parlor with comfortable Victorian-style chairs. Guest rooms have such amenities as 10-foot ceilings, vaulted ceilings, fireplaces, clawfoot tubs and garden views. Some rooms have double-size whirlpool tubs, kitchenettes, and private entrances.

Historic Interest: Historical walking tour of Half Moon Bay.

Innkeeper(s): Marian, Susanne & Janie . $109-275. 21 rooms, 17 with FP, 4 suites and 1 conference room. Breakfast and snacks/refreshments included in rates. Types of meals: Full bkfst. Beds: Q. Cable TV, reading lamp, refrigerator, ceiling fan, clock radio, telephone and desk in room. Fax, copier and fireplace on premises. Small meetings, family reunions and seminars hosted. Antiquing, fishing, live theater, parks, shopping, water sports and flower market nearby.

Publicity: *Half Moon Bay Review, San Francisco Examiner and Los Angeles Times.*

"The hospitality extended to us made us feel very welcome."

Healdsburg   G4

Calderwood Inn

25 West Grant St
Healdsburg, CA 95448-4804
(707)431-1110 (800)600-5444
E-mail: talktous@calderwoodinn.com
Web: www.calderwoodinn.com

Circa 1902. This romantic Queen Anne Victorian is surrounded by lush acres of redwoods, cedars and cypress trees. Each of the six rooms has been decorated with elegant, yet comfortable antiques. Two rooms offer claw-foot tubs, while others include amenities such as fireplaces and whirlpool tubs. Window seats, down comforters and four-poster beds are some of the romantic touches guests might find in their rooms. Fresh seasonal fruit and baked goods accompany the morning entree. Appetizers, wine and port are served in the evenings.

Historic Interest: Luther Burbank Home & Gardens, Sonoma County Museum are some of the area's historic sites.

Innkeeper(s): Jennifer & Paul Zawodny. $145-245. 6 rooms with PB and 1 conference room. Breakfast and snacks/refreshments included in rates. Types of meals: Full gourmet bkfst and early coffee/tea. Beds: KQ. TV, CD player, clock radio, fireplace, whirlpool, clawfoot tub, hair dryer, game chest and iron/ironing board in room. Library, parlor games, telephone, fireplace, appetizers, wine, port, cookies, Internet access, two large porches for relaxing, player piano, gardens, fountains and koi ponds on premises. Antiquing, fishing, hiking, live theater, water sports, gift shop, 100+ Sonoma County wineries and renowned Sonoma restaurants nearby.

Camellia Inn

211 North St
Healdsburg, CA 95448-4251
(707)433-8182 (800)727-8182 Fax:(707)433-8130
E-mail: info@camelliainn.com
Web: www.camelliainn.com

Circa 1869. Just two blocks from the tree-shaded town plaza, this Italianate Victorian townhouse elegantly graces a half-acre of award-winning grounds. Architectural details include ceiling medallions, ornate mahogany and Palladian windows. Gather in the double parlor with twin marble fireplaces and antiques. Spacious guest bedrooms feature inlaid hardwood floors with Oriental rugs and chandeliers. Many feature whirlpool tubs for two, gas-log fireplaces, canopy beds, sitting areas and private entrances. The Memento can be used as a family suite with an adjoining room. Savor a hearty breakfast buffet fireside in the main dining room. Relax in the swimming pool, and enjoy the more than 50 varieties of camellias.

Innkeeper(s): Ray, Del and Lucy Lewand. $99-209. 9 rooms with PB, 4 with FP and 1 suite. Breakfast included in rates. Types of meals: Full bkfst. Beds: QD. Fax on premises. Antiquing and fishing nearby.

Publicity: *Sunset, Travel & Leisure, New York Times, San Fernando Valley Daily News, San Diego Union, Sacramento Bee, Healdsburg Tribune, Washington Post, Cooking Light and Food & Travel.*

"A bit of paradise for city folks."

Grape Leaf Inn

539 Johnson St
Healdsburg, CA 95448-3907
(707)433-8140 (866)433-8140 Fax:(707)433-3140
E-mail: info@grapeleafinn.com
Web: www.grapeleafinn.com

Circa 1900. This magnificently restored Queen Anne home was built in what was considered the "Nob Hill" of Healdsburg. It was typical of a turn-of-the-century dream house. It is situated near the Russian River and the town center. Twenty-five skylights provide an abundance of sunlight, fresh air and stained glass. Twelve guest rooms offer whirlpool tubs and showers for two. The innkeepers make the most of their wine country location, hosting a wine tasting each evening

with a display of at least five Sonoma County wines. Each guest room is named for a wine variety, such as Zinfandel or Merlot. The inn is just a few blocks from many of Healdsburg's fine restaurants and shops.

Innkeeper(s): Richard & Kae Rosenberg. $165-325. 12 rooms with PB. Breakfast and snacks/refreshments included in rates. Types of meals: Full bkfst. Beds: KQ. Ten with whirlpool tub/showers for two and five with fireplace in room. Air conditioning. Full wine & cheese tastings on premises. Antiquing, fishing, shopping, water sports and over 100 wineries nearby.

Publicity: *Sonoma County Guide and Historic Homes of Healdsburg.*

"It was our first time at a real one and we were delighted with our lovely accommodations, delicious breakfasts and most of all you graciousness in trying to please your guests. Thank you for making our 38th anniversary a very special one that we will always remember."

Haydon Street Inn

321 Haydon St
Healdsburg, CA 95448-4411
(707)433-5228 (800)528-3703 Fax:(707)433-6637
E-mail: innkeeper@haydon.com
Web: www.haydon.com

Circa 1912. Architectural buffs will have fun naming the several architectural styles found in the Haydon House. It has the curving porch and general shape of a Queen Anne Victorian, the expansive areas of siding and unadorned columns of the Neo-Classic style and the exposed roof rafters of the Craftsman. The decor is elegant and romantic, with antiques. The Turret Room includes a clawfoot tub and a fireplace. Two rooms are located in the inn's Victorian Cottage, and both have whirlpool tubs. The Pine Room offers a pencil-post bed with a Battenburg lace canopy, while the Victorian Room includes fine antiques and a four-poster mahogany bed.

Innkeeper(s): Dick & Pat Bertapelle. $120-250. 8 rooms with PB, 1 with FP. Breakfast, afternoon tea and snacks/refreshments included in rates. Types of meals: Full gourmet bkfst and early coffee/tea. Beds: QD. TV, reading lamp, ceiling fan, clock radio, desk, hot tub/spa, double whirlpool tubs (two rooms) and also in the cottage is a large suite with hot tub on the private patio in room. Air conditioning. VCR, fax, parlor games, telephone and fireplace on premises. Family reunions and seminars hosted. Antiquing, fishing, parks, shopping, water sports, biking and wine tasting nearby.

Publicity: *Los Angeles and San Francisco.*

"Adjectives like class, warmth, beauty, thoughtfulness with the right amount of privacy, attention to details relating to comfort, all come to mind. Thank you for the care and elegance."

Healdsburg Inn on The Plaza

110 Matheson St, PO Box 1196
Healdsburg, CA 95448-4108
(707)433-6991 (800)431-8663 Fax:(707)433-9513
E-mail: reservations@healdsburginn.com
Web: www.healdsburginn.com

Circa 1900. A former Wells Fargo building, the inn is a renovated brick gingerbread overlooking the plaza in historic downtown Healdsburg. Ornate bay windows, embossed wood paneling and broad, paneled stairs present a welcome entrance. There are fireplaces and the halls are filled with sunlight from vaulted, glass skylights. A solarium is the setting for breakfast and evening wine and hors d'oeuvres. A large covered balcony extends along the entire rear of

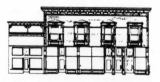

the building. Shops on the premises sell gifts, toys, quilts and fabric. An antique shop and art gallery can be found there, as well. The surrounding area is full of things to do, including wineries and wine-tasting rooms.

Innkeeper(s): Genny Jenkins & LeRoy Steck. $255-295. 10 rooms with PB, 9 with FP and 1 conference room. Breakfast and snacks/refreshments included in rates. Types of meals: Full gourmet bkfst and early coffee/tea. Beds: KQT. Cable TV, VCR, reading lamp, refrigerator, ceiling fan and telephone in room. Air conditioning. TV, fax, copier, parlor games, fireplace and wine tasting on premises. Small meetings, family reunions and seminars hosted. Antiquing, fishing, parks, shopping, water sports, wineries, balloon, canoe and historic walking tour nearby.

Publicity: *Healdsburg Tribune, Los Angeles Daily News, New York Times and San Francisco Chronical Travel Section.*

"The first-thing-in-the-morning juice and coffee was much appreciated."

Madrona Manor, Wine Country Inn & Restaurant

1001 Westside Road
Healdsburg, CA 95448-0818
(707)433-4231 (800)258-4003 Fax:(707)433-0703
E-mail: info@madronamanor.com
Web: www.madronamanor.com

Circa 1881. This handsome estate consists of five historic structures including the Mansion, Schoolhouse and a Gothic-style Carriage House. Embellished with turrets, bay windows, porches and a mansard roof, the stately inn is surrounded by eight acres of manicured lawns, terraced flower and vegetable gardens and wooded areas. Elegant antique furnishings abound. The inn's noteworthy five-star restaurant offers California cuisine featuring fresh local ingredients served in romantic dining rooms.

Historic Interest: Luther Burbank home (15 miles), Simi Winery (3 miles).

Innkeeper(s): Joe & Maria Hadley. $185-445. 17 rooms with PB, 5 suites and 2 conference rooms. Breakfast included in rates. Types of meals: Full gourmet bkfst and dinner. Restaurant on premises. Beds: KQ. Telephone in room. Air conditioning. Fax, fireplace and data port on premises. Limited handicap access. Weddings, small meetings, family reunions and seminars hosted. Antiquing, bicycling, fishing, parks, shopping, sporting events, water sports and wineries nearby.

Publicity: *Travel & Leisure, Conde Naste, Gourmet, Woman's Day Home Decorating Ideas, US News, Diversions, Money, Good Housekeeping, Wine Spectator, Wine and Spirits and Great Country Inns of America.*

"Our fourth visit and better every time."

Raford House

10630 Wohler Rd
Healdsburg, CA 95448-9418
(707)887-9573 (800)887-9503 Fax:(707)887-9597
Web: www.rafordhouse.com

Circa 1880. Situated on more than four acres of rose gardens and fruit trees, this classic Victorian country estate was originally built as a summer home and ranch house in the 1880s and is now owned by Rutz Cellars. Just 70 miles north of San Francisco, Raford House is nestled in the heart of Sonoma County wine country, minutes away from award-winning wineries and many fine restaurants. Located close to the Russian River, between Healdsburg and the beautiful California coast, the area has scenic country roads and rugged coastlines.

$135-195. 6 rooms with PB. Breakfast and snacks/refreshments included in rates. Types of meals: Full bkfst and early coffee/tea. Beds: Q. Reading lamp, BOSE wave CD player, Gilchrist & Soames bath products and in-room massage available upon request in room. Fax, parlor games, telephone and satellite TV on premises. Antiquing, fishing, live theater, parks, shopping and water sports nearby.

Publicity: *Los Angeles Times, Travel & Leisure and Country and Wine Spectator Magazine.*

"Truly a 'serendipity' experience! Wonderful, welcoming ambiance, great food, lovely hosts. I am 'renewed.'"

Hope Valley   G8

Sorensen's Resort

14255 Hwy 88
Hope Valley, CA 96120
(530)694-2203 (800)423-9949
E-mail: sorensensresort@yahoo.com
Web: www.sorensensresort.com

Circa 1876. Where Danish sheepherders settled in this 7,000-foot-high mountain valley, the Sorensen family built a cluster of fishing cabins. Thus began a century-old tradition of valley hospitality. The focal point of Sorensen's is a "stave" cabin — a
reproduction of a 13th-century Nordic house. Now developed as a Nordic ski resort, a portion of the Mormon-Emigrant Trail and Pony Express Route pass near the inn's 165 acres. In the summer, river rafting, fishing,

pony express re-rides and llama treks are popular Sierra pastimes. Lake Tahoe lies 20 miles to the north. Breakfast is included in the rates for bed & breakfast units only. All other cabins are equipped with kitchens.

Historic Interest: Alpine County Museum (12 miles), Old Indian Trade Ports, Emigrant Road.

Innkeeper(s): John & Patty Brissenden. $95-350. 33 rooms, 31 with PB, 23 with FP, 28 cottages and 2 conference rooms. Types of meals: Full bkfst, early coffee/tea, lunch, picnic lunch, snacks/refreshments and gourmet dinner. Restaurant on premises. Beds: QD. Reading lamp and refrigerator in room. Copier, sauna, library, parlor games, telephone, fireplace, e-mail hook-up, complimentary wine and tea and cocoa on premises. Limited handicap access. Weddings and family reunions hosted. Antiquing, cross-country skiing, downhill skiing, fishing, parks and water sports nearby.
Publicity: *Sunset, San Francisco Chronicle, Los Angeles Times, Motorland, Outside, New York Times* and *Travel & Leisure.*

"In one night's stay, I felt more comfortable, relaxed, and welcome than any vacation my 47 years have allowed. Thank you for the happiness you have given my children."

Hopland   F3

The Hopland Inn

13401 Highway 101
Hopland, CA 95449
(707)744-1890 (800)266-1891 Fax:(707)744-1219
E-mail: info@hoplandinn.com
Web: www.hoplandinn.com

Circa 1890. Enter the elegance and charm of this 1890 Victorian-era historic hotel. The Fireside Library with its rich wood bookshelves, marble fireplace and high back chairs is an inviting place to read a good book, and there are more than 4,000 volumes to choose from. Enjoy a full selection of Mendocino wines, fine liquors and ales at the mahogany bar with polished brass and marble accents. Guest bedrooms are appointed with floral period-style wallcoverings and antiques. The large and airy dining room with high ceilings opens onto a courtyard surrounded by lush flora. The more intimate Pomo Room is also available for special functions, holiday parties and rehearsal dinners diligently prepared by executive chef Sean Forsha. The innkeepers will help plan visits to local wineries as well as other interesting local attractions.

Historic Interest: Architecture.

Innkeeper(s): Sean and Sanchia Forsha. $100-175. 21 rooms with PB. Breakfast included in rates. Types of meals: Cont plus and dinner. Restaurant on premises. Beds: KQT. Reading lamp, ceiling fan, clock radio, telephone and voice mail in room. Air conditioning. Library, parlor games, fireplace, swimming pool and dinner served Thursday through Tuesday nights on premises. Small meetings, family reunions and seminars hosted. Antiquing, bicycling, hiking, water sports, wineries and casino nearby.
Publicity: *Johansen, Best Places of Northern California Guidebook* and inspected/rated by California Association of Beds & Breakfasts.

"We appreciate your attention to details and efforts which made our visit so pleasant."

Idyllwild   O12

Creekstone Inn

54950 Pine Crest Ave
Idyllwild, CA 92549
(909)659-3342 (800)409-2127
E-mail: creekstoneinn@pe.net

Circa 1942. Situated amid towering evergreens, Creekstone Inn provides a peaceful setting for those hoping to get away from it all. The historic chalet's past includes time spent as a soda fountain, a restaurant, general store, and even the setting for a movie. Its restoration included refurbishing the original wooden paneling and the local stones from which the inn was constructed. Most of the nine guest rooms include a fireplace, and three offer the added luxury of double Jacuzzi tubs. The décor is country in style, and furnishings include antiques. Guests are pampered with a gourmet breakfast featuring fresh fruit, perhaps strawberries with cream and homemade entrees such as quiche or French toast. After breakfast, explore the mountain village of Idyllwild, which offers shops, restaurants and miles of wondrous hiking trails.

Innkeeper(s): Judy Smith. $105-155. 9 rooms with PB, 7 with FP. Breakfast included in rates. Types of meals: Full gourmet bkfst and early coffee/tea. Beds: Q. Modem hook-up, cable TV, reading lamp, clock radio, seven with fireplace, three with spa and TV on request in room. Parlor games, telephone, fireplace and refrigerator on premises. Limited handicap access. Weddings, small meetings, family reunions and seminars hosted. Antiquing, art galleries, cross-country skiing, fishing, hiking, horseback riding, live theater, parks and shopping nearby.

Inverness   H4

Ten Inverness Way

10 Inverness Way, PO Box 63
Inverness, CA 94937-0063
(415)669-1648 Fax:(415)669-7403
E-mail: inn@teninvernessway.com
Web: www.teninvernessway.com

Circa 1904. Shingled in redwood, this handsome bed & breakfast features a stone fireplace, a sunny library with many good books, and close access to a wonderful hiking area. After an afternoon of hiking, guests can enjoy a soak in the garden hot tub. Inverness is located on Tomales Bay, offering close access to nearby beaches at Point Reyes National Seashore. The Golden Gate Bridge is 45 minutes from the inn.

Innkeeper(s): Teri Mowery. $125-200. 5 rooms, 4 with PB and 2 suites. Breakfast and afternoon tea included in rates. Types of meals: Full gourmet bkfst, veg bkfst, early coffee/tea, picnic lunch and snacks/refreshments. Beds: Q. Reading lamp, ceiling fan and clock radio in room. Fax, copier, spa, library, parlor games, telephone, fireplace and gift shop on premises. Weddings, small meetings, family reunions and seminars hosted. Antiquing, art galleries, beach, bicycling, canoeing/kayaking, fishing, golf, hiking, horseback riding, live theater, museums, parks, shopping, water sports and wineries nearby.

Publicity: *Los Angeles Times, New York Times, Travel & Leisure, Sunset, Gourmet and San Francisco Chronicle.*

"Everything we could have wanted for our comfort was anticipated by our hosts. Great hot tub. Lovely rooms and common areas."

Jackson   G6

Court Street Inn

215 Court St
Jackson, CA 95642-2309
(209)223-0416 (800)200-0416 Fax:(209)223-5429
E-mail: dave@courtstreetinn.com
Web: www.courtstreetinn.com

Circa 1875. This cheery yellow and white Victorian-era house is accentuated with a porch stretching across the entire front and decorated with white wicker furniture. Behind the house, a two-story brick structure that once served as a museum for Indian artifacts now houses guests. Afternoon refreshments are served in the dining room under an embossed, carved tin ceiling. Guests relax in front of a marble fireplace in the parlor topped by a gilded mirror. Guest rooms are decorated in antiques. Downtown is only two blocks away.

Historic Interest: Amador County Museum (one-half block), Kennedy Mine Tailing Wheels (one-half mile), Chaw Se' Indian Ground Rock State Park (15 miles).

Innkeeper(s): Dave & Nancy Butow. $115-240. 7 rooms, 3 with PB, 6 with FP, 2 suites, 1 cottage and 1 conference room. Breakfast, afternoon tea and snacks/refreshments included in rates. Types of meals: Full gourmet bkfst and early coffee/tea. Beds: KQ. Modem hook-up, cable TV, ceiling fan, clock radio, hot tub/spa, fireplace and in room. Central air. VCR, fax, copier, spa, telephone and gift shop on premises. Limited handicap access. Weddings, small meetings, family reunions and seminars hosted. Antiquing, art galleries, bicycling, canoeing/kayaking, cross-country skiing, downhill skiing, fishing, golf, hiking, horseback riding, live theater, museums, parks, shopping and wineries nearby.

Publicity: *Amador Dispatch, Sunset and Vacations.*

"Thank you for creating such a warm, relaxing atmosphere. We enjoyed our stay very much and we'll recommend your hospitality."

Gate House Inn

1330 Jackson Gate Rd
Jackson, CA 95642-9539
(209)223-3500 (800)841-1072 Fax:(209)223-1299
E-mail: info@gatehouseinn.com
Web: www.gatehouseinn.com

Circa 1902. This striking Victorian inn is listed in the National Register of Historic Places. Set on a hillside amid lovely gardens, the inn is within walking distance of a state historic park and several notable eateries. The inn's country setting, comfortable porches and swimming pool offer many opportunities for relaxation. Accommodations include three rooms, a suite and a romantic cottage with a gas log fireplace and whirlpool tub. All of the guest rooms feature queen beds and elegant furnishings. Nearby are several lakes, wineries and golf courses.

Historic Interest: Chaw Se' Indian State Park (8

miles), Kennedy Wheels State Park (one-half mile), Setters Fort/Mill (25 miles).

Innkeeper(s): Mark & Donna Macola. $130-205. 6 rooms with PB, 3 with FP, 1 suite and 2 cottages. Breakfast included in rates. Types of meals: Full bkfst, early coffee/tea and afternoon tea. Beds: Q. Reading lamp, ceiling fan, clock radio and desk in room. Air conditioning. Fax, copier, swimming, parlor games, telephone and fireplace on premises. Weddings, small meetings and family reunions hosted. Antiquing, cross-country skiing, downhill skiing, fishing, live theater, parks, shopping, water sports and casino nearby.

"Most gracious, warm hospitality."

Windrose Inn

1407 Jackson Gate Rd
Jackson, CA 95642-9575
(209)223-3650 (888)568-5250 Fax:(209)223-3793
E-mail: info@windroseinn.com
Web: www.windroseinn.com

Circa 1897. This Victorian farmhouse overlooking Jackson Creek was built in the Mother Lode Country just North of Jackson, a town that had two of the most productive gold mines a century ago. The inn has a large wraparound porch and gardens with sitting areas, a gazebo, a pond, a creek with a footbridge and a bench on the bank. There's a hammock for two slung between walnut trees. Guestrooms are elegantly appointed with items such as a mahogany sleigh bed, clawfoot bathtubs, fireplaces and a champagne bubble bath spa tub for two. The inn's gourmet breakfasts offer eggs, meats, scones or croissants, potatoes or pancakes. Activities include visiting gold rush sites like Columbia, a fully restored gold mining town an hour from the inn. You may also go hiking or biking, enjoy river and lake sports, take tours of the mines or visit museums, wineries or antique stores.

Innkeeper(s): Paula & Bruce Stanbridge. $109-199. 4 rooms, 2 with FP and 1 suite. Breakfast and snacks/refreshments included in rates. Types of meals: Full gourmet bkfst, veg bkfst, early coffee/tea and picnic lunch. Beds: Q. Reading lamp, ceiling fan, turn-down service, hot tub/spa and fireplace in room. Air conditioning. Fax, copier, parlor games, telephone, fireplace, pond, creek and gourmet picnic baskets available for $25 on premises. Weddings, small meetings, family reunions and seminars hosted. Antiquing, art galleries, bicycling, canoeing/kayaking, cross-country skiing, downhill skiing, fishing, golf, hiking, live theater, museums, parks, shopping and wineries nearby.

Publicity: *Amador Ledger Dispatch, SF Chronicle, LA Times, Davis Daily, Daily Republic, D'vine Magazine and Amador Magazine.*

Jamestown   H7

1859 Historic National Hotel, A Country Inn

18183 Main St, PO Box 502
Jamestown, CA 95327
(209)984-3446 (800)894-3446 Fax:(209)984-5620
E-mail: info@national-hotel.com
Web: www.national-hotel.com

Circa 1859. Located between Yosemite National Park and Lake Tahoe, in Gold Country, this is one of the 10 oldest continuously operating hotels in the state. The inn maintains its original redwood bar where thousands of dollars in gold dust were once spent. Original furnishings, Gold Rush period antiques, brass beds, lace curtains and regal comforters grace the guest bedrooms. A soaking room is an additional amenity, though all rooms include private baths. Enjoy a daily bountiful buffet breakfast. Arrange for romantic dining at the on-site gourmet restaurant, considered to be one of the finest in the Mother Lode. Order a favorite liquor or espresso from the saloon, or try the area's wine tasting. Favorite diversions include gold panning, live theatre and antiquing, golf and shopping.

Historic Interest: Railtown 1897 State Historic Park, located in Jamestown, is a few blocks from the hotel.

Innkeeper(s): Stephen Willey. $90-140. 9 rooms with PB and 1 conference room. Breakfast included in rates. Types of meals: Cont plus, early coffee/tea, gourmet lunch, picnic lunch, snacks/refreshments and gourmet dinner. Restaurant on premises. Beds: QT. Cable TV, reading lamp and desk in room. Air conditioning. TV, VCR, fax, parlor games and telephone on premises. Weddings, small meetings, family reunions and seminars hosted. Antiquing, cross-country skiing, downhill skiing, fishing, live theater, parks and water sports nearby.

Publicity: *Bon Appetit, California Magazine, Focus, San Francisco Magazine, Gourmet* and *Sunset.*

Jamestown Hotel

18153 Main Street
Jamestown, CA 95327-9748
(209)984-3902 (800)205-4901 Fax:(209)984-4149
E-mail: info@jamestownhotel.com
Web: www.jamestownhotel.com

Circa 1858. Restored to its original elegance, experience historic lodging and fine dining at this Gold Country hotel near Yosemite. Built in 1858, it has also been a bordello, hospital, bus depot and boarding house during the last 150 years. Antique furnishings accent the guest bedrooms, named after that era's famous women. Many include a sitting room. Choose accommodations with a whirlpool bath or a clawfoot tub and vintage pull-chain toilet. Lunch, dinner and Sunday brunch offer California and continental cuisine with a twist. The cocktail lounge boasts a fireplace and an old fashioned oak bar with a full drink selection. Relax on the open balcony overlooking the town.

Innkeeper(s): Annette & Norbert Mede. $80-175. 11 rooms with PB. Breakfast included in rates. Types of meals: Full bkfst, lunch, picnic lunch, snacks/refreshments and dinner. Beds: KQ. Ceiling fan, clock radio, hot tub/spa, some with whirlpool tubs, hair dryers and televisions in room. Central air. Restaurant, bar and business center on premises. Limited handicap access. Weddings, small meetings, family reunions and seminars hosted. Antiquing, art galleries, canoeing/kayaking, cross-country skiing, downhill skiing, fishing, golf, hiking, horseback riding, live theater, museums, parks, shopping, tennis, water sports and wineries nearby.

Publicity: *Country Inns* and *Gourmet.*

The Palm Hotel B&B

10382 Willow St
Jamestown, CA 95327-9761
(209)984-3429 (888)551-1852 Fax:(209)984-4929

Circa 1890. Enjoy Gold Country at this Victorian, which was home to Albert and Amelia Hoyt, publishers of the Mother Lode Magnet. In the 1890s, the home served as a boarding house. Today, it offers eight guest rooms with lacy curtains, fresh flowers, clawfoot tubs, marble showers and robes. A full breakfast is served each morning along with The Palm's special blend of coffee. The inn is located two-and-a-half hours from San Francisco and about an hour from Yosemite Valley, and it is within walking distance of Main Street, boutiques, galleries, restaurants and Railtown State Park.

Innkeeper(s): Rick & Sandy Allen. $95-165. 8 rooms with PB. Breakfast included in rates. Types of meals: Full bkfst. Beds: KQD. Cable TV, reading lamp, refrigerator, clock radio and desk in room. Central air. Fax, copier, parlor games and telephone on premises. Limited handicap access. Small meetings and family reunions hosted. Antiquing, fishing, golf, live theater, parks, shopping, water sports, Railtown State Park and Yosemite and Calaveras Big Trees nearby.

Publicity: *Avalon Bay News, San Jose Mercury News, Sacramento Bee,*
Modesto Bee, San Francisco Chronicle, Sonora Union Democrat, Central Valley Chronicles on KVIE TV and *Central Sierra Bank 1999 calendar.*

"The simple elegance of our room and ambiance of the Palm in general was a balm for our souls."

Royal Carriage Inn

18239 Main St
Jamestown, CA 95327-0219
(209)984-5271 Fax:(209)984-1675
E-mail: info@royalcarriageinn.com
Web: www.royalcarriageinn.com

Circa 1922. Guests can experience a bit of the Old West at the Royal Hotel, which was built in the early '20s to provide luxurious lodging for travelers. The hotel originally had a ballroom and restaurant, and for those who preferred to ignore Prohibition, there was a secret "back bar." Rooms are decorated in Victorian style with turn-of-the-century antiques. In addition to the hotel guest rooms, there are secluded cottages. Jamestown is California's second oldest gold mining town and has been the site of more than 150 movies and television shows. Jamestown offers shops, antique stores, restaurants and gold mining attractions. The innkeepers can arrange for theater and golf packages.

Innkeeper(s): George Costa. $55-110. 19 rooms, 17 with PB, 2 suites, 3 cottages and 1 conference room. Breakfast included in rates. Types of meals: Cont plus and early coffee/tea. Beds: QT. Reading lamp, ceiling fan and some with TV in room. Air conditioning. TV, library, parlor games, telephone and fireplace on premises. Small meetings and seminars hosted. Antiquing, downhill skiing, fishing, golf, live theater, parks, shopping, water sports and steam train rides nearby.

Publicity: *Local newspaper.*

Jenner   G3

Jenner Inn & Cottages

10400 Hwy 1, PO Box 69
Jenner, CA 95450
(707)865-2377 (800)732-2377 Fax:(707)865-0829
E-mail: innkeeper@jennerinn.com
Web: www.jennerinn.com

Circa 1904. Located on three acres, this New England cottage-style inn began as a hotel with general store and post office to accommodate needs of the local lumber industry. Destroyed by fire and rebuilt by ship builders, the parlor features a beamed ceiling and oak floors and is comfortably furnished. The inn consists of waterside cottages tucked into nooks and crannies of the village. There are suites with fireplaces and kitchenettes, or you may select an entire rental home with panoramic views of the ocean and river. The decor varies from contemporary to rustic or Victorian. All have sun decks. A favorite meal at the inn's restaurant includes Dungeness Crab Cakes, Sonoma Green Salad, Seared Salmon Filet and Swiss Chocolate Pie. Visit Bodega Bay, wineries, Point Reyes or simply enjoy driving along the scenic country roads. Located close to beautiful sandy beaches.

Historic Interest: The Sonoma Coast State Beaches are 15 miles of sandy beaches.

Innkeeper(s): Richard Murphy. $98-278. 20 rooms with PB, 10 with FP, 2 suites, 2 cottages, 2 cabins and 1 conference room. Breakfast and afternoon tea included in rates. Types of meals: Full bkfst, early coffee/tea and dinner. Restaurant on premises. Beds: KQD. Reading lamp, refrigerator, ceiling fan, clock radio, hot tub/spa and private decks in room. Fax, copier, spa, parlor games, telephone and fireplace on premises. Weddings, small meetings, family reunions and seminars hosted. Antiquing, fishing, golf, live theater, parks, shopping, water sports, hiking, bicycling, kayaking canoeing, bird watching, whale watching, farms and wineries nearby.

Joshua Tree   O13

Joshua Tree Inn

61259 29 Palms Hwy, PO Box 340
Joshua Tree, CA 92252-0340
(760)366-1188 Fax:(760)366-3805
E-mail: frontdesk@JTinn.com
Web: Joshuatreeinn.com

Circa 1940. Escape to the peaceful grandeur of the Mojave Desert at this secluded hacienda-style inn on four acres, only five miles from the national park. Feel enveloped by the awesome mountains while relaxing on the vine-covered veranda.

 The square horseshoe design allows for privacy with each ground-level guest bedroom and suite facing the large pool and courtyard. Stay in the legendary Gram Parsons Room, named after the songwriter/musician who was one of the many celebrity guests. Two- and three-bedroom cottages, some with fireplaces and outdoor spas, are also available nearby. Hike, climb or simply stargaze from a lounge chair.

Innkeeper(s): Yvo Kwee & Margo. $85-275. 10 rooms with PB, 2 suites and 1 conference room. Types of meals: Cont, early coffee/tea and afternoon tea. Beds: KQDT. Cable TV, reading lamp, ceiling fan, clock radio and telephone in room. VCR, fax, copier, swimming, parlor games and fireplace on premises. Weddings, small meetings, family reunions and seminars hosted. Antiquing, golf, live theater, parks, shopping, tennis and Joshua Tree National Park nearby.

Publicity: *Los Angeles Times and Press Enterprise.*

"Quiet, clean and charming."

Julian   P12

Butterfield B&B

2284 Sunset Dr
Julian, CA 92036
(760)765-2179 (800)379-4262 Fax:(760)765-1229
E-mail: butterfield@abac.com
Web: butterfieldbandb.com

Circa 1935. On an ivy-covered hillside surrounded by oaks and pines, the Butterfield is a peaceful haven of hospitality and country comfort. Overlooking the countryside, several of the charming guest bedrooms feature fireplaces and fluffy feather beds. A delicious gourmet breakfast is served in the gazebo during summer or by a warm fire in cooler months. The parlor is a delightful place to enjoy hot beverages and afternoon treats. Whether it is scheduling an in-room massage, or arranging a horse-drawn carriage, the innkeepers are always happy to oblige.

Innkeeper(s): Ed & Dawn Glass. $130-175. 5 rooms with PB, 2 with FP and 1 cottage. Breakfast and snacks/refreshments included in rates. Types of meals: Full gourmet bkfst and early coffee/tea. Beds: QD. Cable TV, VCR and ceiling fan in room. Air conditioning. Library on premises. Antiquing, fishing, golf, live theater, parks and shopping nearby.

Publicity: *South Coast and Travel Agent.*

Villa De Valor - Hildreth House, circa 1898

2020 Third Street
Julian, CA 92036
(760)765-3865 (877)968-4552 Fax:(760)765-3862
E-mail: villadevalor@aol.com
Web: www.villadevalor.com

Circa 1898. Gracing the heart of the historic district, this formal Victorian bed & breakfast offers a getaway full of elegance and charm. Innkeeper Valorie proudly displays her personal artwork throughout the inn for all to enjoy. A parlor invites conversation. Romantic suites feature private entrances, fireplaces, spacious sitting areas, period furnishings and nostalgic amenities. Intimate table settings accent gourmet candlelight breakfasts. Later, indulge in sweet treats by the fire. Breathe in the mountain air and enjoy the view from the front porch, unwind in an aromatherapy sauna or just relax in the backyard garden gazebo with the sounds of a soothing fountain.

Historic Interest: Built circa 1898, belonged to Julian's physician Dr. Hildreth, known in its day as the most elegant home in Julian, located in the historic district.

Innkeeper(s): Valorie Ashley. $165-185. 3 rooms with PB, 3 with FP, 2 suites and 1 cottage. Breakfast and snacks/refreshments included in rates. Types of meals: Full gourmet bkfst, veg bkfst and early coffee/tea. Beds: QD. Cable TV, VCR, reading lamp, refrigerator, ceiling fan, clock radio, coffeemaker, desk, fireplace, formal parlor sitting area and CD player in room. Library, parlor games, telephone, fireplace, gift shop and evergreen garden with gazebo and water fountain pond on premises. Weddings, small meetings, family reunions and seminars hosted. Antiquing, art galleries, bicycling, fishing, hiking, horseback riding, live theater, museums, parks, shopping, wineries, gold mine, star gazing and carriage rides nearby.

Publicity: *San Diego Union Tribune, Orange County Register, Winner of Arrington's 2003 "Best Art Collection" and 2004 "Best Antiques," feature story in fall issue 2003 Inn Traveler, Winner of Arrington's 2003 Book of Lists and Best Art Collection.*

Kenwood   G4

A Wine Country Teahouse

9556 Frederica Avenue
Kenwood, CA 95452
(707)833-6998
E-mail: info@winecountryteahouse.com
Web: www.winecountryteahouse.com

Circa 1906. Experience the peaceful serenity of the Far East while staying at this authentic Japanese teahouse built by two carpenters from Komatsu, Ishikawa Prefecture, who used traditional construction methods. Situated in Northern California's wine country, the inn is surrounded by two state parks as well as many regional and historic sites. Generous hospitality is enjoyed in receiving a welcome bottle of wine and a cheese platter, fruit basket, snacks, beverages and chocolates. The delightful atmosphere is accented with flowers, candles and incense. Feel pampered in the Central Tatami Room after bathing with the personal care products provided and sleep soundly on a luxurious futon. Wake up to a healthy breakfast. Relax on a private patio and gazebo. Ask about special spa packages.

Historic Interest: The original property and dwellings were built before 1906 - the great Earthquake. The Japanese teahouse was built in 1990 by two carpenters from Komatsu, Japan. They used traditional methods of construction that have been used in Japan for centuries. The teahouse is authentically built and retains rich cultural heritage of Japan's history and art.

Innkeeper(s): Ken Joachim. $175-250. Breakfast, afternoon tea and snacks/refreshments included in rates. Types of meals: Cont plus, picnic lunch

and dinner. Beds: Q. Cable TV, VCR, reading lamp, stereo, refrigerator, snack bar, clock radio, telephone, coffeemaker, hot tub/spa, welcome bottle of wine and cheese platter, fruit basket, hot and cold beverages, snacks, chocolates, flowers, candles, incense and basket of bathroom amenities in room. Air conditioning. Spa, swimming, bicycles, library, guest patio and gazebo, private off-street parking and 7-foot high fence to retain Japanese environment on premises. Weddings hosted. Antiquing, art galleries, beach, bicycling, canoeing/kayaking, fishing, golf, hiking, horseback riding, live theater, museums, parks, shopping, sporting events, tennis, water sports and wineries nearby.
Publicity: *April newsletter on Sonoma.com.*

Muir Manor B&B

8790 Sonoma Hwy
Kenwood, CA 95452
(707)833-6996 Fax:(707)833-6398
E-mail: info@muirmanor.com
Web: www.muirmanor.com

Circa 1913. Set amongst vineyards, this two-acre Prairie-style country estate with breathtaking views was given historic designation by Sonoma County. A fireplace, library and game table are located in the Victorian breakfast parlor. The sitting parlor offers a reading nook and small visitors center. Romantic guest bedrooms and suites feature four-poster and sleigh beds. The spacious Red Room boasts a soaking tub with shower and a private balcony overlooking the pond and hazelnut trees. Fresh produce from the orchard and garden provides ingredients for seasonal breakfast recipes like artichoke cheese frittata, scones and poached pears. Relax on the wraparound porch facing mountain vistas.

Innkeeper(s): Kathy & Ray Yahr. $130-190. 4 rooms with PB, 1 suite and 1 conference room. Breakfast and afternoon tea included in rates. Types of meals: Full gourmet bkfst, veg bkfst and early coffee/tea. Beds: KQ. Data port, reading lamp, desk and clock in room. Central air. Fax, copier, library, parlor games, telephone and fireplace on premises. Small meetings and family reunions hosted. Amusement parks, antiquing, art galleries, beach, bicycling, golf, hiking, horseback riding, parks, shopping and wineries nearby.
Publicity: *Travel Holiday.*

La Jolla   Q11

The Bed & Breakfast Inn at La Jolla

7753 Draper Ave
La Jolla, CA 92037
(858)456-2066 (800)582-2466 Fax:(858)456-1510
E-mail: bedbreakfast@innlajolla.com
Web: www.innlajolla.com

Circa 1913. This historic gem truly is a treasure, surrounded by the coastal beauty of La Jolla. The home was designed for George Kautz and was built by Irving Gill in his Cubist style. John Philip Sousa and his family lived in the house for several years during the 1920s. The guest rooms and suites offer beautiful furnishings and romantic décor. The Holiday room includes a massive four-poster, canopy bed, hardwood floors topped with antique Oriental rugs and a fireplace. Other rooms include amenities such as clawfoot tubs and fireplaces; some rooms offer ocean and sunset views. The gourmet breakfasts are a treat, rivaled only by the setting. Guests partake of their morning meal either in the dining room by candlelight or in the high garden. Californians have long enjoyed the splendor of La Jolla, a charming village with a spectacular coastline. Guests can walk to the many unique shops or take a stroll along the beach and enjoy an unforgettable sunset. A short drive out of La Jolla will take guests to the myriad of sites in San Diego.

After a day exploring the area, guests return to the inn and enjoy a sampling of wine and cheese.

Innkeeper(s): Judy Robertson. $179-399. 15 rooms with PB, 4 with FP, 2 suites and 1 conference room. Breakfast and snacks/refreshments included in rates. Types of meals: Early coffee/tea and picnic lunch. Beds: KQT. Data port, cable TV, reading lamp, CD player, refrigerator, snack bar, clock radio, telephone, turn-down service, desk, some with VCR, mini bar and ceiling fans and phone with data ports in room. Central air. VCR, fax, bicycles, library, parlor games, fireplace, picnic lunches, beach chairs, towels and tennis rackets on premises. Weddings, small meetings, family reunions and seminars hosted. Amusement parks, antiquing, art galleries, beach, bicycling, canoeing/kayaking, fishing, golf, hiking, live theater, museums, parks, shopping, sporting events, tennis and water sports nearby.
Publicity: *New York Times, Los Angeles Times, Glamour, Country Inns, Travel & Leisure and ABC.*

La Jolla Inn

1110 Prospect St
La Jolla, CA 92037-4533
(858)454-0133 (888)855-STAY Fax:(858)454-2056

Circa 1946. Relax at this delightful hotel in an upscale seaside village outside of San Diego. The pleasant European decor is highlighted by sublime vistas of the Pacific Ocean. Most of the guest bedrooms and suites boast flower-bedecked balconies with incredible views. Made-to-order continental breakfasts are served on the sun deck, facing La Jolla Cove. Stroll the many unique shops and enjoy the variety of nearby restaurants. Grab a bike to explore more of the scenic local area.

Innkeeper(s): Anthony Torbati. $150-400. 23 rooms with PB and 2 suites. Breakfast and afternoon tea included in rates. Types of meals: Cont. Beds: KQT. Cable TV, reading lamp, refrigerator, clock radio and telephone in room. Air conditioning. Fax, copier, bicycles, library and sun deck on premises. Weddings, small meetings, family reunions and seminars hosted. Amusement parks, fishing, golf, live theater, parks, shopping, sporting events, tennis and water sports nearby.
Publicity: *Diversions, Coastal Living, San Diego Edge Magazine and New York Times.*

La Selva Beach   J5

Aptos Beach Inn - Center for Soul

1258 San Andreas Road
La Selva Beach, CA 95076
(831)728-1000 (888)523-2244 Fax:(831)728-8294
E-mail: innkeeper@aptosbeachinn.com
Web: www.aptosbeachinn.com

Circa 1867. An historic replica of Abraham Lincoln's Springfield home, this Neo-Georgian farmhouse sits on three acres within an easy walk to a 22-mile sandy beach. The upscale amenities and variety of activities found at an oceanside resort are enjoyed at this coastal inn. Play tennis on grass or clay courts. Volleyball, badminton and croquet are also popular favorites. Choose a selection from the book and video library to enjoy by the fire in a spacious suite or guest bedroom that feature robes, adjustable massage beds, and two-person, eight-jet spa tubs with showers. Muffins, fruit salad, peach pancakes and scrambled eggs with cheese are some of the breakfast foods served. Swim or surf at nearby Manresa and Sand Dollar state beaches.

Historic Interest: First farm house of this stature built by German farmer who brought modern farming techniques to the Pajaro Valley. It is also a replica of Abraham Lincoln's Springfield home. Photographed and visited by Ansel Adams.

Innkeeper(s): Susan Van Horn. $185-225. 5 rooms with PB, 5 with FP, 1 suite and 3 conference rooms. Breakfast included in rates. Types of meals: Country bkfst, veg bkfst, picnic lunch and snacks/refreshments. Beds: KQT. Modem hook-up, data port, cable TV, VCR, reading lamp, ceiling fan, clock radio, hot tub/spa and fireplace in room. Fax, copier, library, fireplace and two clay tennis courts on premises. Limited handicap access. Weddings, small meetings, family reunions and seminars hosted. Antiquing, art galleries, beach, bicycling, canoeing/kayaking, fishing, golf, hiking, horseback riding, live theater, museums, parks, shopping, tennis, water sports and wineries nearby.

Laguna Beach   P11

Eiler's Inn

741 S Coast Hwy
Laguna Beach, CA 92651-2722
(949)494-3004 Fax:(949)497-2215
Web: www.eilersinn.com

Circa 1940. This New Orleans-style inn surrounds a lush courtyard and fountain. The rooms are decorated with antiques and wallpapers. Wine and cheese is served during the evening in front of the fireplace. Named after Eiler Larsen, famous town greeter of Laguna, the inn is just a stone's throw from the beach on the ocean side of Pacific Coast Highway.

Innkeeper(s): Maria Mestas. $110-275. 12 rooms with PB, 1 with FP and 1 suite. Breakfast included in rates. Types of meals: Cont plus and afternoon tea. Beds: KQD. TV and telephone in room. Fireplace on premises. Weddings, small meetings and seminars hosted. Amusement parks, antiquing, fishing, live theater and shopping nearby.

Publicity: *California Bride, Los Angeles Magazine, Westways, The Tribune and Daily News.*

"Who could find a paradise more relaxing than an old-fashioned bed and breakfast with Mozart and Vivaldi, a charming fountain, wonderful fresh-baked bread, ocean air."

Lake Arrowhead   N11

Bracken Fern Manor

815 Arrowhead Villas Rd, PO Box 1006
Lake Arrowhead, CA 92352-1006
(909)337-8557 Fax:(909)337-3323
E-mail: bfm@dreamsoft.com
Web: www.brackenfernmanor.com

Circa 1929. Opened during the height of the '20s as Lake Arrowhead's first membership resort, this country inn provided refuge to Silver Screen heroines, the wealthy and the prominent. Old letters from the Gibson Girls found in the attic bespoke of elegant parties, dapper gentlemen, the Depression, Prohibition and homesick hearts. Each room is furnished with antiques collected from a lifetime of international travel. There is also a game parlor, wine tasting cellar, library, art gallery and garden Jacuzzi and sauna. Wine is offered in the afternoon. The Crestline Historical Society has its own museum and curator and a map of historical sites you can visit.

Historic Interest: Lake Arrowhead's first private membership resort with electricity, opened in 1929 by Bugsy Segal.

Innkeeper(s): Cheryl Weaver. $80-225. 10 rooms, 9 with PB and 3 suites. Breakfast included in rates. Types of meals: Full bkfst and early coffee/tea. Beds: KQDT. Reading lamp, refrigerator and hot tub/spa in room. VCR, telephone, fireplace, Jacuzzi, art gallery and garden & wine cellar on premises. Weddings, small meetings, family reunions and seminars hosted. Antiquing, cross-country skiing, downhill skiing, fishing, live theater, shopping and water sports nearby.

Publicity: *Mountain Shopper & Historic B&B, The Press Enterprise, Sun and Lava.*

"My husband brought me here for my 25th birthday and it was everything I hoped it would be - peaceful, romantic and so relaxing .... Thank you for the wonderful memories I will hold close to my heart always."

Lake Tahoe   F8

Royal Gorge's Rainbow Lodge

9411 Hillside Dr PO Box 1100
Lake Tahoe, CA 95728
(530)426-3871 (800)500-3871 Fax:(530)426-9221

Circa 1928. Located in the Sierras by a bend of the Yuba River, this old mountain lodge is a nostalgic, picturesque getaway spot. The lodge was built using local granite and hand-hewn timber. A mountain decor permeates the 32 guest rooms. There are two dining rooms, featuring fine Californian and French cuisine. The Engadine Cafe offers breakfast, lunch, dinner and Sunday brunch. The cocktail lounge, which offers a bar menu throughout the day and into the evening, is decorated with a variety of photographs documenting the area's history. Chairs and tables have been set up for those who wish to relax and enjoy the river view. The lodge is adjacent to the Royal Gorge Ski Area, which is the largest cross-country ski area in North America. Summer activities include hiking, mountain biking and fishing.

Innkeeper(s): Alan Davis. $145-165. 32 rooms, 10 with PB, 2 suites and 1 conference room. Breakfast included in rates. Types of meals: Country bkfst, veg bkfst, early coffee/tea, gourmet lunch, picnic lunch, snacks/refreshments and gourmet dinner. Restaurant on premises. Beds: QDT. Reading lamp in room. TV, fax, library, parlor games, telephone and fireplace on premises. Small meetings hosted. Antiquing, beach, bicycling, canoeing/kayaking, cross-country skiing, downhill skiing, fishing, golf, hiking, museums, parks, water sports and wineries nearby.

Publicity: *Sunset and Sacramento News.*

Lakeport   F4

Forbestown B&B Inn

825 N Forbes St
Lakeport, CA 95453-4337
(707)263-7858 Fax:(707)263-7878
E-mail: forbestowninn@zapcom.net
Web: www.forbestowninn.com

Circa 1863. Beckoned by an inviting front porch, this early California farmhouse-style inn is located just a few blocks from downtown Lakeport and Clear Lake. Appealing guest bedrooms are tastefully decorated and furnished with oak antiques. A delicious breakfast is served by a vintage window wall in the dining room or in the secluded garden. Enjoy a refreshing swim in the pool as one of the day's pleasant activities.

Innkeeper(s): Wally & Pat Kelley. $84-125. 4 rooms with PB. Types of meals: Full bkfst, early coffee/tea and snacks/refreshments. Beds: KQ. Reading lamp, ceiling fan and clock radio in room. Air conditioning. TV, VCR, fax, swimming, library, parlor games, telephone, fireplace, wood stove and internet access on premises. Weddings, small meetings, family reunions and seminars hosted. Antiquing, bicycling, fishing, golf, hiking, parks, shopping, water sports, wineries, festivals, local events and birding nearby.

Publicity: *Sunset.*

Thompson House

3315 Lakeshore Blvd
Lakeport, CA 95453
(707)263-4905 Fax:(707)263-6276
E-mail: thompsonhouse@thompsonhouse.net
Web: www.thompsonhouse.net

Circa 1895. This Spanish stucco home's interior is decorated in an English Tudor style. Located on two acres, the home's grounds include lawns, a gazebo and space for 300-400 people for garden weddings and parties. Owners of Anthony's Restaurant nearby, the innkeepers offer kitchen dinners for 40 once a month at the inn and a 10% discount at Anthony's is also offered on Thursday. A 1,400-square-foot suite is the only accommodation offered. It's comprised of a bedroom with a romantically draped four-poster bed, a private bath and a living room with ceiling fan, fireplace and a wall of bookcases. Porcelain dolls, crafted by the innkeeper, are displayed. A popular breakfast item is puff pastry filled with home-canned fruits, home-baked muffins and fruit compote. The grounds feature a horseshoe pit. Berries are grown on the property and there's a grape arbor, roses, azaleas, rhododendrons and fruit and nut trees.

Innkeeper(s): Jan & Bill Thompson. $125. 1 suite, 1 with FP. Breakfast included in rates. Types of meals: Cont plus. Beds: Q. Cable TV, VCR, reading lamp, CD player, refrigerator, ceiling fan, clock radio, coffeemaker and coffee/tea available in room. Air conditioning. Fax, copier, library, parlor games, telephone, laundry facility and fireplace on premises. Weddings, small meetings, family reunions and seminars hosted. Antiquing, art galleries, beach, bicycling, canoeing/kayaking, fishing, golf, hiking, horseback riding, live theater, museums, parks, shopping, tennis, water sports, wineries and water slides nearby.

Publicity: *Lake County Record Bee.*

Lodi
H6

Wine & Roses

2505 W Turner Rd
Lodi, CA 95242-4643
(209)334-6988 Fax:(209)371-6116
Web: www.winerose.com

Circa 1902. Attracted by the excellent reputation for food, lodging and service, guests such as Margaret Thatcher and Martha Stewart have stayed at this historic inn. Luxury guest bedrooms, some with a fireplace, are tucked among the gardens and around the ancient canopy of trees. Old-fashioned features such as beamed ceilings, built-in bookshelves and bench seats mingle with  the modern-day technology of modem hook-ups, spa tubs, VCRs and refrigerators. Each room has a private trellised veranda or balcony for enjoying quiet moments. The restaurant offers excellent dining in its beautiful garden setting. A winery building on the property is host to the community's wine industry and includes a banquet facility. The inn is located off I-5, an ideal midway stop between Los Angeles and San Francisco for honeymooners, tourists and corporate travelers.

Innkeeper(s): Rachelle Navarec. $149-295. 10 rooms with PB, 4 suites and 1 conference room. Breakfast included in rates. Types of meals: Full gourmet bkfst, early coffee/tea, picnic lunch, snacks/refreshments, gourmet dinner and room service. Restaurant on premises. Beds: Q. Reading lamp, ceiling fan, clock radio and telephone in room. Air conditioning. TV, fax, copier and fire-

place on premises. Limited handicap access. Weddings, small meetings, family reunions and seminars hosted. Antiquing, fishing, live theater, shopping, sporting events and water sports nearby.

Publicity: *Los Angeles, Business Tribune and Country Inns.*

"Hospitality here exceeds Southern hospitality. I feel as if I am somewhere in time."

Loleta
C2

Southport Landing

444 Phelan Rd
Loleta, CA 95551
(707)733-5915

Circa 1898. Situated on more than two acres, this early Colonial Revival with its wraparound front porch offers spectacular views of the hills and Humboldt Bay National Wildlife Refuge. Besides the inn's traditional country manor atmosphere with its period antiques, guests will enjoy the uninterrupted silence and the bounty of wildlife. There are five individually decorated guest rooms all with dramatic views of the hillside or the bay. A third-floor game room features a pool table, ping-pong, darts and cards. The country breakfasts include items such as local sausage, homemade muffins and fresh pastry. Snacks are provided in the evening. Hiking, bird-watching, bicycling and kayaking available locally.

Historic Interest: Redwood forests, Arcata Marsh, Somoa Dunes, Lost Coast are located nearby.

Innkeeper(s): Denise Flynn. $110-150. 5 rooms, 4 with PB. Breakfast included in rates. Types of meals: Country bkfst, early coffee/tea and afternoon tea. Beds: Q. Reading lamp, clock radio and turn-down service in room. TV, VCR, fax, library, parlor games, telephone and fireplace on premises. Limited handicap access. Weddings, small meetings and family reunions hosted. Antiquing, art galleries, beach, bicycling, canoeing/kayaking, fishing, golf, hiking, live theater, museums, parks, shopping, wineries, bird watching and beachcombing nearby.

"Our greatest B&B experience!"

Long Beach
O10

Lord Mayor's B&B Inn

435 Cedar Ave
Long Beach, CA 90802-2245
(562)436-0324 (800)691-5166 Fax:(562)436-0324
E-mail: innkeepers@lordmayors.com
Web: www.lordmayors.com

Circa 1904. This collection of carefully restored homes includes the Main House where the city's first mayor lived. Granite pillars flank the veranda of this historical landmark with a golden oak wood interior. The Eastlake Room boasts a family heirloom fainting couch. Hand-carved Austrian twin beds accent Margarita's Room. The Hawaiian Room has a small clawfoot tub. A four-poster bed and Dutch wardrobe adorn Beppe's Room. The Apple and Cinnamon Houses are suitable for families or large groups. The  Garden House, a studio that was originally part of the horse barn, provides tranquil privacy. Breakfast is a tasty assortment of home-baked treats and a hot entree. Enjoy the city garden, or walk to the nearby convention center, restaurants and beach.

Innkeeper(s): Laura & Reuben Brasser. $85-140. 12 rooms, 10 with PB, 1 cottage and 1 conference room. Breakfast and snacks/refreshments included in rates. Types of meals: Full bkfst and early coffee/tea. Beds: QDT. Reading lamp and clock radio in room. TV, VCR, fax, library and telephone on premises. Weddings, small meetings, family reunions and seminars hosted. Antiquing, art galleries, beach, bicycling, golf, live theater, museums, parks, Aquarium of Pacific, Gateway to Catalina and Island and Carnival Cruise Line terminal nearby.

Publicity: *KCET Magazine, Daily News Los Angeles, Press Telegram and Yellow Brick Road.*

"Your hospitality and beautiful room were respites for the spirit and body after our long trip."

The Turret House Victorian B&B

556 Chestnut Ave
Long Beach, CA 90802-2213
(562)983-9812 (888)488-7738 Fax:(562)437-4082
E-mail: innkeepers@turrethouse.com
Web: www.turrethouse.com

Circa 1906. This Queen Anne Victorian does, of course, display a turret as one of its delightful architectural features. The home, located in a Long Beach historic district, remained in the same family until it was purchased by the current owners. The decor is elegant and romantic. Fine linens top the beds and the wallpapers and furnishings are all coordinated with similar prints and colors. Each room has a clawfoot tub, and bubble bath is provided for a relaxing soak. The breakfasts are an imaginative gourmet treat. Guests might partake of a menu with a granola parfait, followed by cranberry scones and spinach parasol pie. There are two Victorian parlors to enjoy, and a proper afternoon tea is served with succulent treats such as a mocha cheesecake or rich peanut butter pie. Long Beach offers plenty of shops and restaurants, and the city is well situated for those enjoying the many attractions in Southern California.

$110-150. 5 rooms with PB. Breakfast and afternoon tea included in rates. Types of meals: Full gourmet bkfst and early coffee/tea. Beds: KQT. Reading lamp, ceiling fan, clock radio, turn-down service, table and chairs and balcony in room. Air conditioning. TV, VCR, fax, parlor games, telephone, fireplace and piano on premises. Weddings, small meetings, family reunions and seminars hosted. Amusement parks, antiquing, art galleries, beach, bicycling, canoeing/kayaking, fishing, golf, hiking, horseback riding, live theater, museums, parks, shopping, sporting events, tennis, water sports, wineries, aquarium and Queen Mary nearby.

Publicity: *Press Telegram, L.A. Daily News, L.A. Times, Long Beach Press Telegram, Signal Hill News and Local cable station.*

Los Alamos   N7

1880 Union Hotel & Victorian Mansion

362 Bell Street (135)
Los Alamos, CA 93440
(805)344-2744 (800)230-2744 Fax:(805)344-3125
E-mail: unionhotel2003@yahoo.com
Web: www.unionhotelvictmansion.com

Circa 1880. The casual Western facade of the Union Hotel is in sharp contrast with its intensely decorated interiors. Richly upholstered and carved furnishings, Egyptian burial urns and an enormous Tiffany grandfather clock furnish the parlor. Fantasy guest rooms in the Victorian mansion include the Egyptian room, entered through a one-ton stone door. An enormous pillared bed is draped in white, and there is a private soaking tub, fireplace and King Tut statue.

Innkeeper(s): Christine Mary Williams. $150-250. 18 rooms, 10 with PB, 7

with FP, 7 suites and 2 conference rooms. Breakfast included in rates. Types of meals: Country bkfst, veg bkfst, early coffee/tea and afternoon tea. Restaurant on premises. Beds: KQD. VCR, reading lamp, refrigerator, hot tub/spa, fireplace, claw foot tubs and pull chain toilets in room. Central air. Fax, copier, spa, library, parlor games, telephone, fireplace, gift shop, great spot for retreats, historic stagecoach stop, "Stagecoach Murder Mystery," English hedge maze, frog pond, gardens and gazebo on premises. Weddings, small meetings, family reunions and seminars hosted. Antiquing, art galleries, beach, bicycling, canoeing/kayaking, fishing, golf, hiking, horseback riding, live theater, museums, parks, shopping, water sports, wineries and Thursday & Sunday Historic Hotel tours by appointment nearby.

Publicity: *Los Angeles Times, The Good Life, Pacific Coast, Huell Howser "California Gold," Jon Bon Jovi "Bang a Drum" and Say-Say-Say.*

"The entire weekend was a fairy tale turned into a reality by you and the rest of your staff."

McCloud   B5

McCloud River Inn

325 Lawndale Ct
McCloud, CA 96057-1560
(530)964-2130 (800)261-7831 Fax:(530)964-2730

Circa 1900. Nestled within the beauty of Shasta National Forest rests this country Victorian. Five serene acres of lawns and woodland create a peaceful setting at this home, on the National Register of Historic Places. The interior has been painstakingly restored, and each of the five guest rooms has its own individual charm. Breakfasts are a treat, and a typical menu might include a savory Greek quiche, homemade pastries and a selection of fresh fruits. Shops and historic sites are within walking distance, and it's a 15-minute drive to Mt. Shasta Ski Park.

Innkeeper(s): Ron & Marina Mort. $75-145. 5 rooms with PB and 2 suites. Breakfast included in rates. Types of meals: Full bkfst. Beds: QDT. Reading lamp, desk and some with Jacuzzi tub in room. Air conditioning. Fax, copier, parlor games, telephone and gift shop on premises. Small meetings hosted. Antiquing, bicycling, cross-country skiing, downhill skiing, fishing, golf, hiking, parks, shopping, water sports and train excursions nearby.

Publicity: *Sunset, Berkeley Guide, Siskiyou County Railroad Gazette, Siskiyou County Scene and Miami Herald.*

Mendocino   F2

Agate Cove Inn

11201 Lansing, PO Box 1150
Mendocino, CA 95460-1150
(707)937-0551 (800)527-3111
E-mail: info@agatecove.com
Web: www.agatecove.com

Circa 1860. Perched on a blufftop above the Pacific Ocean, Agate Cove Inn offers splendid ocean views in a two-acre setting of gardens and 100-year-old cypress trees. Most rooms boast stunning ocean views or garden vistas and have fireplaces and decks. Select from a spa tub, showers for two or deep-soaking tub. Down comforters and feather beds invite snuggling in the king or queen beds. TVs, VCRs and CD players as well as daily morning newspapers are additional amenities. Guests enjoy a full country breakfast with freshly baked muffins or the innkeeper's award-winning bread. Eggs Benedict, omelettes, French toast and other entrees are served along with baked apples, poached pears and homemade applesauce as accompaniments. The Farmhouse breakfast room offers a spectacular ocean view. Fine dining, hiking, art walks and other activities may be arranged with the help of the inn's knowledgeable staff.

Innkeeper(s): Dennis & Nancy Freeze. $129-299. 10 rooms with PB, 9 with FP. Types of meals: Full bkfst. Beds: KQ. Cable TV, VCR, CD player, fireplace, ocean view, feather bed, down comforter, hair dryer, sherry, newspaper delivery, HBO and spa or soaking tub in room. Fax, telephone, cottages, Internet connection, concierge service, refrigerator, CD library, video library and paperback book exchange on premises.

Publicity: *Karen Brown's California: Charming Inns & Itineraries, The Annual Directory of American and Canadian B&Bs, More Weekends for Two in Northern California, America's Wonderful Little Hotels & Inns, Richmond Times-Dispatch, Arrington's Publishing Book of Lists, PC World Magazine, LA Times, Sky West, Angeleno, The Northern California Best Places Cookbook, Wine Spectator, Sunset Magazine, Passport Newsletter, Country Inns Magazine, Avenues Auto Club Magazine, St. Louis Dispatch, Travel Holiday Magazine, Inns & Retreats Newsletter, The Province Newspaper, Glamour Magazine, Sacramento Magazine and Fine Living channel.*

"Warmest hospitality, charming rooms, best breakfast and view in Mendocino."

Brewery Gulch Inn

9401 Coast Hwy One N
Mendocino, CA 95460-9767
(707)937-4752 (800)578-4454 Fax:(707)937-1279
E-mail: info@brewerygulchinn.com
Web: www.brewerygulchinn.com

Circa 1864. Ten acres of bliss are found at this distinctive Craftsman-style inn, built with eco-salvaged, old virgin redwood timbers from Big River. Sitting next to the original historic farmhouse on a scenic hillside, Arts and Crafts furnishings and ocean views create an eye-pleasing decor. The romantic guest bedrooms boast fireplaces, private decks, and pampering touches including terry robes and CD players. Mouth-watering breakfast al fresco on the common deck or fireside is prepared with organic ingredients by a French-trained chef. Relax in the fireplaced Great Room with afternoon wine and hors d'oeuvres.

Innkeeper(s): Glenn Lutge. $150-295. 10 rooms with PB, 10 with FP. Breakfast and snacks/refreshments included in rates. Types of meals: Full gourmet bkfst, early coffee/tea and picnic lunch. Beds: KQT. Modem hook-up, data port, cable TV, VCR, reading lamp, stereo, clock radio, telephone, turndown service, desk and fireplace in room. Fax, copier, library, parlor games, fireplace and gift shop on premises. Limited handicap access. Weddings hosted. Antiquing, art galleries, beach, bicycling, canoeing/kayaking, fishing, golf, hiking, horseback riding, live theater, museums, parks, shopping, tennis, water sports, wineries and Skunk steam engine train nearby.

Publicity: *Coastal Living, Food & Wine, Sunset Magazine, San Francisco Chronicle, Appellation, Steppin' Out, KGO Radio, was Travel & Leisure Magazine's Inn of the Month in November of 2001 and was chosen as one of 12 Great Gateways by Diablo Magazine.*

Glendeven Inn

8205 N. Coast Hwy 1
Mendocino, CA 95456
(707)937-0083 (800)822-4536
E-mail: innkeeper@glendeven.com
Web: www.glendeven.com

Circa 1867. Offering a delightful taste of the coast, this wonderfully restored New England-Style farmhouse is set on two and a half acres of ever-flowering gardens with ocean vistas to the south. Before leaving for dinner, enjoy early-evening gatherings in the living room with wine and hors d'oeuvres. Experience first-class accommodations in the Main House, Stevenscroft Annex or Carriage House. All

well-lit guest bedrooms feature elegant luxury, tasteful antique furnishings and fine art. Most include fireplaces, private decks and views of the Pacific. A hot country breakfast is delivered to each room daily. Browse the contemporary gallery showcasing the work of local artists.

Innkeeper(s): Sharon & Higgins. $110-240. 10 rooms with PB. Breakfast included in rates. Types of meals: Full bkfst. Beds: KQ.

Publicity: *USA Today, San Francisco Examiner and Santa Rosa Press Democrat.*

"We just returned from our stay at your beautiful inn and had to let you know how wonderful and very special we felt for the two days we were there."

The Headlands Inn

Corner of Howard and Albion Streets
Mendocino, CA 95460
(707)937-4431 (800)354-4431 Fax:(707)937-0421
E-mail: innkeeper@headlandsinn.com
Web: www.headlandsinn.com

Circa 1868. A historic village setting by the sea complements this New England Victorian Salt Box. The quaintness of the past combines with amenities of the present. Meet new friends sharing afternoon tea and cookies in the parlor. Almost all of the romantic guest bedrooms feature fireplaces, comfortable feather beds with down comforters, fresh flowers and bedside chocolates. A cottage provides more spacious privacy. Indulge in a full breakfast delivered to the room with homemade treats and creative entrees. The front porch is an ideal spot for ocean views. Lawn seating gives ample opportunity to enjoy the year-round English garden.

Historic Interest: The Inn was built in 1868 as a small barbershop on Main St. in Mendocino, Calif. In 1884 the building became a "high class" restaurant, The Oyster and Coffee Saloon. The owner at that time was W.J. Wilson, and he used the upstairs as an annex to The Wilson Hotel. George Switzer purchased the house in 1893 and moved it to the present location. It was transported by horses pulling the house over logs. John & Bessie Strauss bought the house in 1924 and resided there until 1979.

Innkeeper(s): Denise & Mitch. $100-195. 7 rooms with PB, 6 with FP and 1 cottage. Breakfast and snacks/refreshments included in rates. Types of meals: Full gourmet bkfst and veg bkfst. Beds: KQ. Reading lamp, clock radio, desk, hair dryers, robes, fireplace and cottage has cable TV/VCR and refrigerator in room. Fax, copier, parlor games, telephone and fireplace on premises. Weddings and family reunions hosted. Antiquing, art galleries, beach, bicycling, canoeing/kayaking, fishing, golf, hiking, horseback riding, live theater, museums, parks, shopping, tennis and wineries nearby.

Publicity: *"Best Places to Kiss" Romantic Travel Guide and "Best Places to Stay" Travel Guide.*

"If a Nobel Prize were given for breakfasts, you would win hands down. A singularly joyous experience!!"

The Inn at Schoolhouse Creek

N Hwy 1, PO Box 1637
Mendocino, CA 95460
(707)937-5525 (800)731-5525 Fax:(707)937-2012
E-mail: innkeeper@schoolhousecreek.com
Web: www.schoolhousecreek.com

Circa 1860. The Inn at School House Creek offers private cottages and rooms on its eight acres of rose gardens, forests and meadows. (The inn's gardens have been featured in several magazines.) Many cottages include views of the ocean and all offer a fireplace. Located three miles from Mendocino, the inn was a motor court in the '30s. Private beach access to Buckhorn Cove allows guests to enjoy whale watching, sea lions and the crashing waves of the Pacific. Organize your day to include a picnic lunch (available by advance notice) to enjoy at a secluded waterfall in the redwoods. Then take a sunset soak in the inn's ocean view hot tub. The next morning's breakfast may include Fruit Basket Breakfast Pudding with whipped cream, eggs, fruit and a variety of freshly baked muffins and breads, jams and juices.

Innkeeper(s): Steven Musser & Maureen Gilbert. $115-255. 15 rooms with PB, 15 with FP, 2 suites and 9 cottages. Breakfast included in rates. Types of meals: Full bkfst, early coffee/tea and picnic lunch. Beds: KQD. Cable TV, VCR, telephone, hot tub/spa, some with whirlpools, kitchens, refrigerators and microwaves in room. Fax, spa, parlor games, fireplace and evening hors d'oeuvres on premises. Weddings, small meetings, family reunions and seminars hosted. Fishing, golf, hiking, live theater, parks, shopping, tennis and water sports nearby.

John Dougherty House

571 Ukiah St
Mendocino, CA 95460
(707)937-5266 (800)486-2104
E-mail: jdhb@wshift.com
Web: www.jdhouse.com

Circa 1867. Experience pleasant stays in private, upscale accommodations with generous amenities, English gardens and ocean vistas. Innkeepers Marion and David exchanged a corporate metropolitan life for a rural, picture-perfect bed & breakfast location in the historic district that

offers everything needed for a relaxing getaway. All of the guest bedrooms feature Early-American antiques, hand-stenciled walls, Currier and Ives prints, four-poster beds, woodburning fireplaces and jetted tubs. Many rooms boast bay, garden or village views. The Captain's Room includes an upstairs veranda. The historic water tower has an 18-foot beamed ceiling and a sitting area. Two-room suites or nearby cottages provide spacious seclusion. Walk to the cliffs of Mendocino Headlands State Park to watch the waves, sea lions and osprey.

Historic Interest: Located in Mendocino Historic Village.

Innkeeper(s): David & Marion Wells. $105-240. 8 rooms with PB, 7 with FP, 2 suites, 1 cottage and 2 cabins. Breakfast included in rates. Types of meals: Full gourmet bkfst and early coffee/tea. Beds: KQ. Cable TV, reading lamp, refrigerator, clock radio and several with jet tubs in room. TV, parlor games, telephone, fireplace and antiques on premises. Antiquing, fishing, golf, live theater, parks, shopping, tennis and water sports nearby.

Publicity: Mendocino Beacon, Country Home, Los Angeles Times (Travel Section August 2001) and San Francisco Times/Tribune.

"A treasure chest of charm, beauty and views."

Joshua Grindle Inn

PO Box 647
Mendocino, CA 95460-0647
(707)937-4143 (800)474-6353
E-mail: stay@joshgrin.com
Web: www.joshgrin.com

Circa 1879. Sitting atop a two-acre knoll, this welcoming home overlooks the village. It is easy to park and forget about the car with shops, restaurants, the beach and hiking trails just a short stroll away. Hospitality is generous, with the friendly staff attending to every need. Relax on the front veranda and

watch the whales in the distance. Chat with fellow guests over evening refreshments in the parlor. Tastefully decorated guest bedrooms are comfortable and exceptionally clean. Enjoy a full gourmet breakfast each morning, then escape to the private gardens for a quiet moment of reflection. The luxury Grindle Guest House, an ocean-view vacation rental is also available.

Innkeeper(s): Charles & Cindy Reinhart. $150-250. 10 rooms with PB, 6 with FP. Breakfast and snacks/refreshments included in rates. Types of meals: Full gourmet bkfst. Beds: KQT. Reading lamp, clock radio, desk, luxurious robes, coffee/tea, cookies, wine and hair dryer in room. Fireplace, parlor with wine, refreshments, gardens, picnic grounds and croquet on premises. Art galleries, bicycling, canoeing/kayaking, hiking, live theater, parks, shopping, fine dining, botanical gardens, scenic railroad and music/food festivals nearby.

Publicity: Peninsula, Copley News Service, Orange Coast Magazine, San Francisco Magazine, Sacramento Magazine, AT&T Commercial, San Francisco News and AAA 4 Diamond.

"We are basking in the memories of our stay. We loved every moment."

The Larkin Cottage

44950 Larkin Rd
Mendocino, CA 95460
(707)937-2567 Fax:(707)937-4714
E-mail: stay@larkincottage.com
Web: www.larkincottage.com

Circa 1940. If you're searching for a touch of romance, a stay at this cozy, one-bedroom cottage might be just the place. In addition to the bedroom, the cottage includes a living room, kitchen and a private deck. Antiques, lacy curtains, and a fireplace add to the romance of the cottage's interior, and the garden setting provides quiet and privacy. Although breakfast isn't provided, the owners stock the cottage with plenty of goodies, including coffee, tea, fruit juice, bagels, pastries, fresh fruit, cookies, cheese, crackers and even wine and sherry. The cottage is just one mile out of Mendocino, and close to the beach, as well.

Innkeeper(s): Bob & Diann Gerbo. $135-150. 1 cottage. Snacks/refreshments included in rates. Types of meals: Cont plus and early coffee/tea. Beds: Q. Cable TV, VCR, reading lamp, stereo, refrigerator, clock radio, telephone, coffeemaker, full kitchen and fireplace in room. Fax, copier and bicycles on premises. Antiquing, art galleries, beach, bicycling, canoeing/kayaking, fishing, golf, hiking, horseback riding, live theater, parks, shopping, tennis and wineries nearby.

MacCallum House Inn

45020 Albion St
Mendocino, CA 95460
(707)937-0289 (800)609-0492 Fax:(707)937-2243
E-mail: reservations@maccallumhouse.com
Web: www.maccallumhouse.com

Circa 1882. Built by William H. Kelley for his newly wed daughter, Daisy MacCallum, the MacCallum House Inn is a splendid example of New England architecture in the Victorian village of Mendocino. Besides the main house, accommodations include the barn, carriage house, greenhouse, gazebo and water tower rooms.

Innkeeper(s): Jed & Megan Ayers and Noah Sheppard. $120-325. 19 rooms with PB. Types of meals: Full gourmet bkfst. Beds: KQT. 24-hour Internet access in room. Complimentary wine hour on premises. Limited handicap access.

Publicity: California Visitors Review.

Mendocino Hotel

PO Box 587
Mendocino, CA 95460-0587
(707)937-0511 (800)548-0513 Fax:(707)937-0513

Circa 1878. In the heart of Mendocino on Main Street, the Mendocino Hotel originally was established as a temperance hotel for lumbermen. An Old West facade was added. The historic Heeser House, home of Mendocino's first settler, was annexed by the hotel along with its  acre of gardens. Many of the guest rooms and suites boast tall, four-poster and canopy beds or fireplaces and coastal views. The hotel has several dining rooms and is a member of the National Trust Historic Hotels of America.

Innkeeper(s): Dwight Goldstein, General Manager. $85-275. 51 rooms, 37 with PB, 20 with FP, 6 suites and 1 conference room. Types of meals: Cont, lunch, gourmet dinner and room service. Restaurant on premises. Beds: KQDT. TV, copier and telephone on premises. Antiquing, fishing, live theater and water sports nearby.

Publicity: *Los Angeles Times, Tribune, Wine Spectator, Gourmet, Bon Appetit, Press Democrat and Country Inns.*

"The hotel itself is magnificent, but more importantly, your staff is truly incredible."

Packard House

PO Box 1065
Mendocino, CA 95460
(707)937-2677 (888)456-3267 Fax:(707)937-1323

Circa 1878. One of four landmark homes on Executive Row, this Carpenter's Gothic Victorian was built for the town chemist. The original watertower is listed in the National Register. Elegantly furnished with an eclectic blend of old and new, antiques and custom-made pieces dwell easily with an extensive collection of fine art. Luxurious items like fine linens, soft robes, slippers and Spanish sherry add to the enchantment of the gorgeous guest bedrooms. Anticipate the pleasure of two-person jet tubs, fireplaces, VCRs and CD players, as well as colorful garden or ocean views. Mouth-watering breakfasts are served in the dining room, as are wine and appetizers in the afternoon.

Historic Interest: Village of Mendocino declared a National Landmark.
Innkeeper(s): Maria & Dan Levin. $125-255. 5 rooms with PB, 5 with FP and 1 suite. Breakfast and snacks/refreshments included in rates. Types of meals: Full gourmet bkfst and early coffee/tea. Beds: KQ. Cable TV, VCR, reading lamp, stereo, refrigerator, clock radio, telephone, desk, hot tub/spa and fireplace in room. Fax, spa, library, parlor games, fireplace, gift shop and video library on premises. Antiquing, art galleries, beach, bicycling, canoeing/kayaking, fishing, golf, hiking, horseback riding, live theater, museums, parks, shopping, tennis, water sports and wineries nearby.

Sea Gull Inn

44960 Albion St
Mendocino, CA 95460
(707)937-5204 (888)937-5204
E-mail: seagull1@mcn.org
Web: www.seagullbb.com

Circa 1878. Shaded by a giant holly tree, this house built in 1878 was one of the area's first bed & breakfast inns. Relax on the front porch or in the lush private garden. Stay in a spacious upstairs or first-floor guest bedroom or a private cot-

tage with antiques, fresh flowers and original artworks. A variety of amenities are offered from sitting areas to ocean views. A light breakfast is delivered to the room at a prearranged time and a morning newspaper is available upon request. Walk to the village shops and art galleries. Visit the Mendocino Art Center or the botanical coastal gardens. Tour Anderson Wine Valley and take the Skunk Train at Fort Bragg through the mountains and redwoods.

Historic Interest: Built in 1878, one of Mendocino's first bed and breakfast inns; some of the gardens are the original ones.
Innkeeper(s): Marlene McIntyre. $55-165. 9 rooms with PB and 1 cottage. Breakfast included in rates. Types of meals: Cont plus. Beds: QD. Cable TV and desk in room. Fax, parlor games, telephone and laundry facility on premises. Antiquing, art galleries, beach, bicycling, canoeing/kayaking, fishing, golf, hiking, horseback riding, live theater, museums, parks, shopping, water sports, wineries, scuba diving, whale watching and Mendocino Coast Botanical Gardens nearby.

Sea Rock B&B Inn

11101 Lansing St
Mendocino, CA 95460
(707)937-0926 (800)906-0926
E-mail: searock@mcn.org
Web: www.searock.com

Circa 1930. Enjoy sea breezes and ocean vistas at this inn, which rests on a bluff looking out to the Pacific. Most of the accommodations include a wood-burning Franklin fireplace and feather bed. Four guest rooms are available in the Stratton House, and each affords a spectacular ocean view. There are six cottages on the grounds, most offering a sea view. The innkeepers also offer deluxe accommodations in four special suites. Each has an ocean view, wood-burning fireplace, private entrance and a deck, whirlpool or ocean view tub. The grounds, which now feature gardens, were the site of an 1870s brewery. The inn is less than half a mile from Mendocino.

Innkeeper(s): Susie & Andy Plocher. $149-299. 14 rooms with PB, 14 with FP, 8 suites and 6 cottages. Breakfast included in rates. Types of meals: Cont plus. Beds: KQ. Cable TV, VCR, reading lamp, clock radio, telephone and desk in room. Fireplace on premises. Antiquing, fishing, golf, live theater, parks, shopping, tennis and water sports nearby.

Publicity: *California Visitors Review and Sunset Magazine.*

The Stanford Inn By The Sea

PO Box 487
Mendocino, CA 95460-0487
(707)937-5615 (800)331-8884 Fax:(707)937-0305

Circa 1856. Tucked against a forested hillside, this inn is comprised of a combination of buildings from an 1856 homestead to a 1930s cottage, and the more recent 1969 and 1996 inn that offers views of the ocean from each room.
The ten acres also include an expansive lawn studded with flower gardens that slope down to a duck pond and redwood barn where the inn's llamas and horses graze. Guest bedrooms 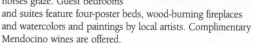 and suites feature four-poster beds, wood-burning fireplaces and watercolors and paintings by local artists. Complimentary Mendocino wines are offered.

Historic Interest: Mendocino Village (immediately adjacent).
Innkeeper(s): Joan & Jeff Stanford. $215-325. 41 rooms with PB, 31 with FP, 7 suites, 3 cottages and 4 conference rooms. Breakfast and afternoon tea included in rates. Types of meals: Full gourmet bkfst, veg bkfst, early coffee/tea, snacks/refreshments, gourmet dinner and room service. Restaurant on premis-

es. Beds: KQT. TV, spa, sauna, telephone, massage and yoga on premises. Limited handicap access. Art galleries, beach, bicycling, canoeing/kayaking, live theater, museums, parks, shopping and water sports nearby.

Publicity: *Oakland Tribune, Brides, Contra Costa Times, San Francisco Chronicle, Bayarea Backroads and Channel 4 KRON San Francisco.*

"As working parents with young children, our weekends away are so terribly few in number, that every one must be precious. Thanks to you, our weekend in Mendocino was the finest of all."

Whitegate Inn

499 Howard St
Mendocino, CA 95460
(707)937-4892 (800)531-7282 Fax:(707)937-1131
E-mail: staff@whitegateinn.com
Web: www.whitegateinn.com

Circa 1883. When it was first built, the local newspaper called Whitegate Inn "one of the most elegant and best appointed residences in town." Its bay windows, steep gabled roof, redwood siding and fish-scale shingles are stunning examples of Victorian architecture. The house's original wallpaper and candelabras adorn the double parlors. There, an antique 1827 piano, at one time part of Alexander Graham Bell's collection, and inlaid pocket doors take you back to a more gracious time. French and Victorian antique furnishings and fresh flowers add to the inn's elegant hospitality and old world charm. The gourmet breakfasts are artfully presented in the inn's sunlit dining room. The inn is just a block from the ocean, galleries, restaurants and the center of town.

Historic Interest: Mendocino Headlands State Park surrounds the village, which was once the property of the original lumber mill.

Innkeeper(s): Richard & Susan Strom. $159-289. 6 rooms with PB, 6 with FP and 2 cottages. Breakfast and snacks/refreshments included in rates. Types of meals: Full gourmet bkfst and early coffee/tea. Beds: KQT. Cable TV, VCR, reading lamp, refrigerator, snack bar, clock radio, telephone and desk in room. Fax, copier, fireplace, welcome basket, evening sherry, wine and cheese on premises. Weddings, small meetings, family reunions and seminars hosted. Antiquing, fishing, golf, horseback riding, live theater, parks, shopping, tennis, water sports and whale watching nearby.

Publicity: *Innsider, Country Inns, Country Home, Glamour, Santa Rosa Press Democrat, San Francisco Chronicle, Bon Appetit, Victoria Magazine, Sunset, San Francisco Examiner, Victorian Decorating and Country Gardener.*

Mill Valley   H4

Mountain Home Inn

810 Panoramic Hwy
Mill Valley, CA 94941-1765
(415)381-9000 Fax:(415)381-3615

Circa 1912. At one time the only way to get to Mountain Home was by taking the train up Mount Tamalpais. With 22 trestles and 281 curves, it was called "the crookedest railroad in the world." Now accessible by auto, the trip still provides a spectacular view of San Francisco Bay. Each guest room has a view of the mountain, valley or bay.

Innkeeper(s): Josh Sperry. $175-325. 10 rooms with PB, 5 with FP and 1 conference room. Breakfast included in rates. Types of meals: Full bkfst, lunch and gourmet dinner. Beds: KQ. Reading lamp, clock radio and telephone in room. Fax, copier and fireplace on premises. Weddings, small meetings and family reunions hosted. Parks and shopping nearby.

Publicity: *San Francisco Examiner and California.*

"A luxurious retreat. Echoes the grand style and rustic feeling of national park lodges." — *Ben Davidson, Travel & Leisure*

Mokelumne Hill   H7

Hotel Leger

8304 Main St
Mokelumne Hill, CA 95245
(209)286-1401
E-mail: acanty2298@aol.com
Web: www.hotelleger.com

Circa 1851. Three ghosts are said to reside at this 150-year-old inn that was built with French architecture. Scenically located in historic Gold Country, experience the nostalgia of the Mother Lode era with easy access to modern city life. Guest bedrooms and a suite feature antique furnishings and Victorian beds covered with down-filled duvets. Three rooms boast fireplaces. Breakfast and afternoon tea are welcome repasts. A restaurant and saloon offer menus for lunch and dinner. Relax in the spa after visiting nearby historical sites. The landscaped quarter-acre is a popular wedding spot complete with available horse-drawn carriage.

Innkeeper(s): Ron and Jane Pitner. $50-150. 13 rooms, 7 with PB, 3 with FP, 1 suite and 1 conference room. Breakfast and afternoon tea included in rates. Types of meals: Cont plus, veg bkfst, early coffee/tea, picnic lunch, snacks/refreshments, dinner and room service. Restaurant on premises. Beds: QDT. Turn-down service and fireplace in room. Swimming, parlor games and fireplace on premises. Weddings, small meetings, family reunions and seminars hosted. Antiquing, art galleries, bicycling, canoeing/kayaking, cross-country skiing, downhill skiing, fishing, golf, hiking, horseback riding, museums, parks, shopping, wineries, gold panning, caves and national forests nearby.

Monrovia   O10

Chez Noel

210 W Colorado Blvd
Monrovia, CA 91016
(626)256-6622 (877)256-6622

Circa 1886. It's rare to find 19th-century homes in the Los Angeles area, so Chez Noel is a rare find. The Eastlake Victorian was built by a Civil War captain. The home is decorated in an eclectic style and features artwork created by the innkeepers. Healthy, gourmet breakfasts include items such as whole-grain French toast, homemade muffins and fresh fruit. Chez Noel is located in Old Town Monrovia. Pasadena is five minutes away, and most popular local attractions are less than 40 minutes from the inn, including Disneyland and Knott's Berry Farm.

Innkeeper(s): Scott & Cammie Noel. $110-150. 3 rooms with PB. Breakfast included in rates. Types of meals: Full gourmet bkfst, early coffee/tea, picnic lunch and snacks/refreshments. Beds: KQT. Reading lamp in room. Air conditioning. VCR, fax, bicycles, library, parlor games, telephone and fireplace on premises. Amusement parks, antiquing, downhill skiing, golf, live theater, parks, shopping, sporting events, old town Monrovia, Pasadena nearby and Disneyland nearby.

Montara   I4

The Goose & Turrets B&B

835 George St, PO Box 937
Montara, CA 94037-0937
(650)728-5451 Fax:(650)728-0141
E-mail: rhmgt@montara.com
Web: goose.montara.com

Circa 1908. Now a haven focusing on comfort and hospitality, this classic bed & breakfast once served as Montara's first post office, the town hall, and a country club for Spanish-American War veterans. Large living and dining room
areas are filled with art
and collectibles. Sleep
soundly in one of the
tranquil guest bedrooms
then linger over a leisure-
ly four-course breakfast. Stimulating conversation comes easily during afternoon tea. There are plenty of quiet spots including a swing and a hammock, to enjoy the fountains, orchard, rose, herb and vegetable gardens.

Historic Interest: The historic district of Half Moon Bay is eight miles away. Pescadero and a historic mansion and gardens are about 15 miles away.

Innkeeper(s): Raymond & Emily Hoche-Mong. $145-190. 5 rooms with PB, 3 with FP. Breakfast and afternoon tea included in rates. Beds: KQDT. Reading lamp, clock radio and desk in room. Library, parlor games, tele-
phone, bocce ball court and piano on premises. Antiquing, bicycling, fishing, golf, hiking, horseback riding, parks, water sports, nature reserves, whale watching, aero sightseeing and birding nearby.

Publicity: San Diego Union, Tri-Valley, Los Angeles Times, Pilot Getaways, AOPA Magazine, San Jose Mercury News, Half Moon Bay Review, Peninsula Times Tribune, San Mateo Times, Contra Costa Times and The Wall Street Journal.

"You have truly made an art of breakfast and tea-time conversation. We will be back."

Monterey   J5

The Jabberwock

598 Laine St
Monterey, CA 93940-1312
(831)372-4777 (888)428-7253 Fax:(831)655-2946
E-mail: innkeeper@jabberwockinn.com
Web: www.jabberwockinn.com

Circa 1911. Set in a half-acre of gardens, this Craftsman-style inn provides a fabulous view of Monterey Bay with its famous barking seals. When you're ready to settle in for the evening, you'll find huge Victorian beds
complete with lace-edged sheets
and goose-down comforters.
Three rooms include Jacuzzi
tubs. In the late afternoon, hors
d'oeuvres and aperitifs are served
on an enclosed sun porch. After
dinner, guests are tucked into
bed with homemade chocolate chip cookies and milk. To help guests avoid long lines, the innkeepers have tickets available for the popular and nearby Monterey Bay Aquarium.

Historic Interest: Historic adobes and Cannery Row are within walking distance of The Jabberwock.

Innkeeper(s): Joan & John Kiliany. $145-265. 7 rooms with PB, 4 with FP. Types of meals: Full gourmet bkfst and early coffee/tea. Beds: KQ. Reading lamp, clock radio and three with Jacuzzi in room. Fax, copier, parlor games, telephone and fireplace on premises. Weddings, small meetings and family reunions hosted. Antiquing, fishing, live theater, parks, shopping, water sports and restaurants nearby.

Publicity: Sunset, Travel & Leisure, Sacramento Bee, San Francisco Examiner, Los Angeles Times, Country Inns, San Francisco Chronicle, Diablo and Elmer Dill's KABC-Los Angeles TV.

"Words are not enough to describe the ease and tranquility of the atmosphere of the home, rooms, owners and staff at the Jabberwock."

Moss Landing   J5

Captain's Inn

Moss Landing, CA
E-mail: capt@captainsinn.com
(831)633-5550
Web: www.captainsinn.com

Circa 1906. A meticulously restored historic Pacific Coast Steamship Company building and a newly built boathouse comprise this coastal getaway only an hour from San Jose. Relax in front of the parlor fireplace or peruse the reading library and browse through area guidebooks. The inn's nautical décor includes a touch of whimsy in the guest bedrooms that are furnished with antiques and thoughtful amenities like robes, plush-top mattresses and feather pillows. Stay in a room with a fireplace and soaking or clawfoot tub for two. Continental fare is available to early risers. Later in the dining room, a home-cooked breakfast full of traditional classics and recipes from German grandmothers are served. Walk to ocean beaches, shops and art studios.

Innkeeper(s): Captain Yohn & Melanie Gideon. Call for rates. 10 rooms with PB. Breakfast and snacks/refreshments included in rates. Types of meals: Full bkfst and early coffee/tea. Beds: KQ. Clock radio, telephone, voice mail, fireplace, fresh flowers, soaking tubs, comforters, quilts with feather pillows and cozy robes in room. TV on premises. Antiquing, art galleries, beach, bicy-
cling, fishing, hiking, shopping and wineries nearby.

Publicity: "Selected Best Sleep in North Monterey County" by locals, Monterey Magazine, 2003," Official Bed and Breakfast for Spector Dance's ballet performances: Summer fest 2003, Huell Howser's California's Golden Coast, PBS, KCET-LA, June on the Road with Bette, KVIE-PBS, Sacramento, Travels with Romney Dunbr and Cable TV.

Mount Shasta   B5

Mount Shasta Ranch B&B

1008 W.A. Barr Rd
Mount Shasta, CA 96067-9465
(530)926-3870 Fax:(530)926-6882
E-mail: mbenton1@snowcrest.net
Web: www.stayinshasta.com

Circa 1923. This large two-story ranch house offers a full view of Mt. Shasta from its 60-foot-long redwood porch. Spaciousness abounds from the 1,500-square-foot living room with a massive rock fireplace to the large suites with private bathrooms that include large tubs and roomy showers. A full country breakfast may offer cream cheese-stuffed French toast or fresh, wild blackberry crepes. Just minutes away, Lake Siskiyou boasts superb fishing, sailing, swimming, and 18 hole golf course with public tennis courts.

Historic Interest: Built in 1923 by HD "Curley" Brown as a thoroughbred horse ranch.

Innkeeper(s): Bill & Mary Larsen. $60-115. 9 rooms, 4 with PB, 1 cottage and 1 conference room. Breakfast included in rates. Types of meals: Full bkfst, early coffee/tea and afternoon tea. Beds: Q. Cable TV, reading lamp, ceiling fan and desk in room. Air conditioning. VCR, fax, copier, library, parlor games, telephone and fireplace on premises. Small meetings, family reunions and seminars hosted. Antiquing, cross-country skiing, downhill skiing, fishing, parks, shopping and water sports nearby.

Murphys H7

Dunbar House, 1880

271 Jones St
Murphys, CA 95247-1375
(209)728-2897 (800)692-6006 Fax:(209)728-1451
E-mail: innkeep@dunbarhouse.com
Web: www.dunbarhouse.com

Circa 1880. A picket fence frames this Italianate home, built by Willis Dunbar for his bride. The porch, lined with rocking chairs, is the perfect place to take in the scenery of century-old gardens decorated by fountains, birdhouses and swings. A collection of antiques, family heirlooms and comfortable furnishings fill the interior. The two-room garden suite includes a bed dressed with fine linens and a down comforter and a two-person Jacuzzi spa. Guests can enjoy the morning fare in the dining room, garden or opt for breakfast in their room.

Historic Interest: Columbia State Park (10 miles), Big Trees State Park (14 miles).

Innkeeper(s): Bob & Barbara Costa. $190-245. 5 rooms with PB, 5 with FP and 2 suites. Breakfast and afternoon tea included in rates. Types of meals: Full gourmet bkfst, early coffee/tea and room service. Beds: KQ. Cable TV, VCR, reading lamp, stereo, refrigerator, ceiling fan, snack bar, telephone, turn-down service and desk in room. Air conditioning. TV, fax, copier, library, parlor games and fireplace on premises. Antiquing, cross-country skiing, downhill skiing, fishing, live theater, parks, shopping and water sports nearby.

Publicity: *San Francisco Chronicle, Los Angeles Times, Gourmet, Victorian Homes, Country Inns, Travel & Leisure and Search & Rescue.*

"Your beautiful gardens and gracious hospitality combine for a super bed & breakfast."

Trade Carriage House

230 Big Trees Rd
Murphys, CA 95247
(209)728-3404 (800)800-3408 Fax:(209)728-2527
E-mail: sales@realtyworld-murphys.com
Web: www.realtyworld-murphys.com

Circa 1930. A white picket fence surrounds the Trade Carriage House, originally built in Stockton and later moved to Murphys. There are two bedrooms, both furnished with antiques and wicker pieces. A sunroom overlooks a private deck. Three doors down is a second vacation home, Tree Top House, that boasts a deck overlooking the treetops. This home has two bedrooms and two baths, a pine vaulted ceiling and, like the Trade Carriage House, is within two blocks of historical Main Street, with shops, restaurants and local wineries. Nearby are the gold rush towns of Columbia and Sonora. Main Street Lodge is a third vacation house situated across the street from Murphys' famous donkeys, Cass and Clarissa attached. Murphys is located between Lake Tahoe and Yosemite.

Innkeeper(s): Cynthia Trade. $130-150. 3 cottages. Beds: QD. Cable TV, reading lamp, refrigerator and telephone in room. Air conditioning. One apartment on premises. Antiquing, cross-country skiing, downhill skiing, fishing, golf, live theater, parks, shopping, tennis, water sports and major area for wineries nearby.

Napa H4

1801 Inn

1801 First Street
Napa, CA 94559
(707)224-3739 (800)518-0146 Fax:(707)224-3932
E-mail: Innkeeper@the1801inn.com
Web: www.the1801inn.com

Circa 1903. The innkeepers at this Queen Anne Victorian have created a setting perfect for romance. The guest rooms feature Victorian decor, Oriental rugs atop hardwood floors and beds dressed with fine linens and soft comforters. Each guest bathroom has a large soaking tub and each bedchamber has a fireplace. The turn-of-the-century inn is located in Old Town Napa and is close to the multitude of wineries in the valley, as well as antique shops and restaurants.

Historic Interest: The 1801 Inn is also known as the distinguished Hunter-Prouty House. Designed in 1903 by architect William Corlett, the house exhibits some of the most magnificent design elements in the city and remains a well known historical site in Napa. The house retains the original hardwood floors and crown mouldings in the entry way, living room, dining room and main floor suites. One of which is the original master bedroom of the home and its expansive bay window looks out onto Jefferson Street.

Innkeeper(s): Darcy, Ramona, Brenna. $165-325. 8 rooms with PB, 8 with FP, 5 suites and 3 cottages. Breakfast and snacks/refreshments included in rates. Types of meals: Full gourmet bkfst, veg bkfst, early coffee/tea and picnic lunch. Beds: KQ. Cable TV, VCR, reading lamp, stereo, ceiling fan, clock radio, telephone, coffeemaker, desk, hot tub/spa, fireplace and 5 suites have spacious two-person soaking tubs with separate showers and 3 cottages have Jacuzzi tubs. All rooms have sensual bath amenities and luxurious robes in room. Central air. Fax, copier, spa, fireplace, video and CD library, 24 hour complimentary minibar with homebaked cookies, fruit, soda, juices, port and sherry. Custom gourmet baskets, lunches, dinners, cakes, wine and champagne made to order on premises. Limited handicap access. Family reunions hosted. Amusement parks, antiquing, art galleries, bicycling, canoeing/kayaking, fishing, golf, hiking, horseback riding, live theater, museums, parks, shopping, wineries, The Wine Train, Copia, hot air balloon rides, The Culinary Institute of America, The Napa Opera House and gondola rides on the lazy Napa river nearby.

Beazley House

1910 1st St
Napa, CA 94559-2351
(707)257-1649 (800)559-1649 Fax:(707)257-1518
E-mail: innkeeper@beazleyhouse.com
Web: www.beazleyhouse.com

Circa 1902. Nestled in green lawns and gardens, this graceful shingled mansion is frosted with white trim on its bays and balustrades. Stained-glass windows and polished-wood floors set the atmosphere in the parlor. There are six rooms in the main house, and the carriage house features five more, many with fireplaces and whirlpool tubs. The venerable Beazley House was Napa's first bed & breakfast inn.

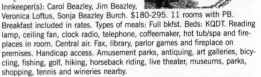

Innkeeper(s): Carol Beazley, Jim Beazley, Veronica Loftus, Sonja Beazley Burch. $180-295. 11 rooms with PB. Breakfast included in rates. Types of meals: Full bkfst. Beds: KQDT. Reading lamp, ceiling fan, clock radio, telephone, coffeemaker, hot tub/spa and fireplaces in room. Central air. Fax, library, parlor games and fireplace on premises. Handicap access. Amusement parks, antiquing, art galleries, bicycling, fishing, golf, hiking, horseback riding, live theater, museums, parks, shopping, tennis and wineries nearby.

Publicity: *Los Angeles Times, USA Today, Sacramento Bee, Yellow Brick Road, Emerge, Bay Area Backroads, Wine Spectator 25th Anniversary Edition, HGTV's Dream Drives, San Francisco Chronicle and North Bay Biz.*

"There's a sense of peace & tranquility that hovers over this house, sprinkling magical dream dust & kindness."

Belle Epoque

1386 Calistoga Ave
Napa, CA 94559-2552
(707)257-2161 (800)238-8070 Fax:(707)226-6314
E-mail: lynnette@napabelle.com
Web: www.napabelle.com

Circa 1893. This luxurious Victorian inn has won awards for "best in the wine country" and "best breakfast in the nation." Enjoy the experience in the wine cellar and tasting room where guests can casually sip Napa Valley wines. The inn, which is one of the most unique architectural structures found in the wine country, is located in the heart of Napa's Calistoga Historic District. Beautiful  original stained-glass windows include a window from an old church. Six guest rooms offer a whirlpool tub. A selection of fine restaurants and shops are within easy walking distance, as well as the riverfront, art museums and the Wine Train Depot.

Innkeeper(s): Lynnette & Steve Sands. $205-350. 9 rooms with PB, 6 with FP, 3 suites and 1 conference room. Breakfast and snacks/refreshments included in rates. Types of meals: Full gourmet bkfst and early coffee/tea. Beds: KQ. Cable TV, VCR, reading lamp, ceiling fan, clock radio, telephone, desk and whirlpools in room. Air conditioning. Fax, copier, parlor games and fireplaces on premises. Weddings hosted. Amusement parks, antiquing, golf, live theater, parks, shopping, sporting events and tennis nearby.

"At first I was a bit leery, how can a B&B get consistent rave reviews? After staying here two nights, I am now a believer!"

Blue Violet Mansion

443 Brown St
Napa, CA 94559-3349
(707)253-2583 (800)959-2583 Fax:(707)257-8205
E-mail: bviolet@napanet.net
Web: www.bluevioletmansion.com

Circa 1886. English lampposts, a Victorian gazebo, and a rose garden welcome guests to this blue and white Queen Anne Victorian. Listed in the National Register, the house originally was built for a tannery executive. There are three-story bays, and from the balconies guests often view hot air balloons in the early morning. Rooms are available with two-person spas and fireplaces. A full breakfast is served in the dining room. In the evenings, desserts are presented and elegant dinners are served in the grand salon. Nearby is the wine train and restaurants. The Official Hotel Guide gave the Blue Violet Mansion a gold award in 1996, voting it "Best Bed & Breakfast in North America."

Historic Interest: Napa County Landmarks prestigious Award of Merit for historical restoration 1993.

Innkeeper(s): Melanie Jones. $199-359. 17 rooms with PB, 15 with FP, 3 suites and 3 conference rooms. Breakfast and snacks/refreshments included in rates. Types of meals: Full bkfst, picnic lunch, gourmet dinner and room service. Restaurant on premises. Beds: KQ. Stereo, refrigerator, ceiling fan, snack bar, clock radio, telephone, turn-down service, most with one- and two-person spa, balcony and in room massage in room. Air conditioning. VCR, fax, copier, spa, swimming, parlor games, fireplace and massage on premises. Limited handicap access. Weddings, small meetings, family reunions and seminars hosted. Amusement parks, antiquing, fishing, live theater, parks, shopping and water sports nearby.

Candlelight Inn

1045 Easum Drive
Napa, CA 94558-5524
(707)257-3717 (800)624-0395 Fax:(707)257-3762
E-mail: mail@candlelightinn.com
Web: www.candlelightinn.com

Circa 1929. Located on a park-like acre with gardens, this elegant English Tudor-style house is situated beneath redwood groves and towering trees that shade the banks of Napa Creek. Seven rooms feature a marble fireplace and two-person marble Jacuzzi inside the room. The Candlelight Suite offers cathedral ceilings, stained-glass windows and a private sauna. The inn's breakfast room has French doors and windows overlooking the garden. Breakfast is served by candlelight.

Innkeeper(s): Mark & Wendy Tamiso. $125-350. 10 rooms with PB, 7 with FP, 2 suites and 1 cottage. Breakfast and snacks/refreshments included in rates. Types of meals: Full gourmet bkfst and early coffee/tea. Beds: KQT. Cable TV, reading lamp, clock radio, telephone, hot tub/spa, voice mail and fireplace in room. Air conditioning. Fax, swimming and parlor games on premises. Small meetings, family reunions and seminars hosted. Amusement parks, antiquing, art galleries, bicycling, canoeing/kayaking, golf, hiking, horseback riding, live theater, museums, parks, shopping, wineries, hot air ballooning and spas nearby.

"We still haven't stopped talking about the great food, wonderful accommodations and gracious hospitality."

Cedar Gables Inn

486 Coombs St
Napa, CA 94559-3343
(707)224-7969 (800)309-7969 Fax:(707)224-4838
E-mail: info@cedargablesinn.com
Web: www.cedargablesinn.com

Circa 1892. This gracious country manor was designed by English architect Ernest Coxhead, who patterned the home after designs prevalent during Shakespeare's time. The innkeepers received an award of merit for their restoration efforts and it's clearly deserved. Guests ascend winding staircases to reach their posh rooms decorated in rich colors and filled with antiques. Each room features its own color scheme and unique touches. The Churchill Chamber, the original master bedroom, is adorned in grays, tans and black and boasts ornate furnishings, a gas fireplace and a two-person whirlpool tub. Four guest rooms include gas fireplaces, and others feature clawfoot, whirlpool or Jacuzzi tubs. A complete breakfast is served either in the dining room or in the bright sun room, a perfect start to a full day exploring Napa Valley.

Historic Interest: Aside from the area's bounty of historic wineries, museums and Old Grist Mill are some of the historic sites.

Innkeeper(s): Bob & Tammy Korman. $179-329. 9 rooms with PB, 4 with FP and 1 suite. Breakfast included in rates. Types of meals: Full bkfst. Beds: Q.

Publicity: *California Visitor's Review.*

"Charming and elegant, yet strikingly cozy. This place tops the list in atmosphere and hospitality."

Churchill Manor

485 Brown St
Napa, CA 94559-3349
(707)253-7733 Fax:(707)253-8836
Web: www.churchillmanor.com

Circa 1889. Listed in the National Register of Historic Places, each room of this stately Napa Valley manor is individually decorated with fine European antiques. All rooms have fireplaces, five have two-person showers and eight have vintage soaking bathtubs. Priceless artifacts have been preserved, such as the

original bath and fireplace tiles in Edward's Room and Rose's Room trimmed with 24-karat gold. Guests are treated to delicious breakfasts and freshly baked cookies and refreshments in the afternoons. In the
evening, there is a complimentary two-hour wine and cheese reception. The breakfast buffet offers an abundant selection of fresh fruits, fresh-baked croissants and muffins, gourmet omelets and French toast made-to-order as each guest arrives. The innkeepers add Victorian flavor by keeping complimentary tandem bicycles and a croquet set on hand for their guests. The Napa Wine Train Topia and historic downtown Napa are within walking distance.

Historic Interest: Churchill Manor, which is listed in the National Register, is located in the National Register Historic District of Old Town Napa.

Innkeeper(s): Joanna Guidotti & Brian Jensen. $155-270. 10 rooms with PB, 6 with FP and 3 conference rooms. Breakfast included in rates. Beds: KQ. Reading lamp, clock radio, telephone and desk in room. Air conditioning. TV, VCR, fax, copier, bicycles, library, parlor games, fireplace, grand piano and croquet on premises. Limited handicap access. Weddings, small meetings, family reunions and seminars hosted. Amusement parks, antiquing, fishing, live theater, parks, shopping, water sports, wineries, mud baths and galleries nearby.

Publicity: *Napa County Record, Food & Beverage Journal, ABC-KGO TV and San Francisco Bay Guardian.*

"Retaining the ambiance of the 1890s yet providing comfort for the 1990s."

Hennessey House-Napa's 1889 Queen Anne Victorian B&B

1727 Main St
Napa, CA 94559-1844
(707)226-3774 Fax:(707)226-2975
E-mail: inn@hennesseyhouse.com
Web: www.hennesseyhouse.com

Circa 1889. Colorful gardens surround this gracious Victorian, once home to Dr. Edwin Hennessey, a Napa County physician and former mayor. Pristinely renovated, the inn features

stained-glass windows and a curving wraparound porch. A handsome hand-painted, stamped-tin ceiling graces the dining room. The inn's romantic rooms are furnished in antiques and some offer fireplaces, feather beds and spa tubs. The bathrooms all feature marble floors
and antique brass fixtures. There is a sauna and a garden fountain. The innkeepers serve gourmet breakfasts with specialties such as blueberry-stuffed French toast and Eggs Florentine. Tea and cookies are offered at 3 p.m., and later in the evening,

wine and cheese is served. Walk to inviting restaurants and shops. Nearby are the world-famous Napa Valley wineries. The innkeepers will be happy to make recommendations or reservations for wineries, the area's spas and mud baths, hot air balloons, the Wine Train, horseback riding, cycling and hiking.

Historic Interest: Historic Old Town Napa.

Innkeeper(s): Gilda and Alex Feit. $119-299. 10 rooms with PB, 6 with FP. Breakfast included in rates. Types of meals: Full bkfst. Beds: KQT. Reading lamp, ceiling fan, telephone, some with Jacuzzi and some with fireplace in room. Air conditioning. TV, fax, sauna and fireplace on premises. Weddings, small meetings, family reunions and seminars hosted. Antiquing, shopping, walk to inviting restaurants, shops and COPIA-The American Center for Wine, Food and the Arts and wine train packages nearby.

Publicity: *AM-PM Magazine.*

"A great place to relax in Napa!"

Inn of Imagination

470 Randolph Street
Napa, CA 94559
(707)224-7772 Fax:(707)202-0187
E-mail: info@innofimagination.com
Web: www.innofimagination.com

Circa 1920. A whimsical décor is encountered in this classic example of Spanish Revival architecture located in the historic Arroyo Grande section. The inn is listed in the National Register and features 12-foot ceilings, hardwood floors and a showcase fireplace. The solarium/library will whet any imaginative appetite with books and murals. Guest bedrooms celebrate the wit and creativity of Lewis Carroll, Dr. Seuss or Jimmy Buffett. Expansive gardens include arbors, a gazebo, sculpture, swings and so much more.

Innkeeper(s): Kim & Nancy Thomas. $180-280. 3 rooms with PB. Breakfast included in rates. Types of meals: Cont plus. Beds: Q. Refrigerator and coffeemaker in room. Air conditioning. Library, parlor games, telephone and fireplace on premises. Antiquing, art galleries, bicycling, golf, hiking, museums, parks, shopping, tennis and wineries nearby.

Publicity: *Bon Appetit December 2003.*

"The Inn of Imagination redefines wine country accommodations."
— Bon Appetit

Inn on Randolph

411 Randolph St
Napa, CA 94559-3374
(707)257-2886 (800)670-6886 Fax:(707)257-8756
E-mail: innonrandolph@aol.com
Web: www.innonrandolph.com

Circa 1860. Located in Napa's historic district, this shuttered Gothic Revival is a city landmark and one of the oldest homes in the valley. Common rooms feature antique Victorian furnishings, hardwood floors and a sweeping spindled staircase. A hand-painted flower mural, white wicker and sleigh bed are just a few of the romantic touches featured in the five guest rooms located in the original house. Besides privacy, the Randolph and Laurel cottages each offer two separate, but adjoining rooms decorated in antiques, fireplaces and whirlpool tubs for two. The Arbor Cottage overlooks a semi-private stone patio and is complete with a fireplace, kitchenette, two-person walk-in shower and whirlpool tub for two. Breakfast begins with freshly ground coffee, tea and juice, followed by a hot entree such as peach and strawberry French toast or Mexican quiche served with fresh salsa. Wine tasting, shopping, bicycling and golf are nearby.

Innkeeper(s): Deborah Coffee. $144-289. 10 rooms with PB, 7 with FP.

Breakfast and snacks/refreshments included in rates. Types of meals: Full bkfst and early coffee/tea. Beds: KQT. Ceiling fan, telephone, turn-down service, robes, cottages have TV, VCR and CD player and 8 with whirlpool tubs in room. Fax, library, parlor games and fireplace on premises. Antiquing, golf, live theater, parks and shopping nearby.

"You reinforced our reason for staying in lovely bed & breakfasts."

La Residence Country Inn

4066 Howard Lane
Napa, CA 94558-1635
(707)253-0337 Fax:(707)253-0382
Web: www.laresidence.com

Circa 1870. This inn offers luxurious accommodations for those exploring the enchanting Napa Valley wine country. The uniquely decorated rooms in the French-style farmhouse or Gothic Revival Mansion are spacious and well-appointed, with fine antiques and designer fabrics. Many rooms also feature fireplaces, patios or balconies. Guests will be impressed with the lovely gardens and pool area at the inn, not to mention the discreet but attentive service. Be sure to inquire about excursions into the winery-rich valley.

Innkeeper(s): David Jackson, Craig Claussen. $195-350. 23 rooms with PB, 19 with FP, 8 suites and 1 conference room. Breakfast and snacks/refreshments included in rates. Types of meals: Full bkfst, early coffee/tea and room service. Beds: KQ. Reading lamp, stereo, clock radio, telephone and hot tub/spa in room. Air conditioning. Fax, copier, spa, swimming, child care, parlor games and fireplace on premises. Limited handicap access. Weddings, small meetings, family reunions and seminars hosted. Antiquing, golf, live theater, parks, shopping, tennis, wineries, ballooning, biking and glider riding nearby.
Publicity: *Travel & Leisure.*

Napa Inn

1137 Warren St
Napa, CA 94559-2302
(707)257-1444 (800)435-1144 Fax:(707)257-0251
E-mail: info@napainn.com
Web: www.napainn.com

Circa 1877. The older of the two Victorian homes that comprise this inn was built in 1877 and is listed in the National Register. The other, a stately Queen Anne, was built in 1899. Located in historic downtown Napa on a tranquil tree-lined street, many world-class wineries are minutes away. Thoughtfully appointed guest bedrooms and suites feature antiques and artwork as well as an assortment of upscale amenities. Many include fireplaces, whirlpools or clawfoot tubs and balconies or patios. Each morning a menu of exquisite homemade cuisine is served for breakfast. Relax with refreshments in the gardens or by the fire in the parlor.

Historic Interest: The Buford House is in the National Historic Register.
Innkeeper(s): Brooke & Jim Boyer. $120-295. 14 rooms with PB, 14 with FP, 1 with HT, 4 suites, 1 cottage and 2 conference rooms. Breakfast and snacks/refreshments included in rates. Types of meals: Full bkfst. Beds: KQ. Modem hook-up, data port, cable TV, VCR, reading lamp, CD player, refrigerator, ceiling fan, snack bar, clock radio, telephone, coffeemaker, desk, hot tub/spa, fireplace and 6 with whirlpool tubs in room. Air conditioning. Fax, copier, library, parlor games, gift shop and wireless Internet access on premises. Limited handicap access. Weddings, small meetings and family reunions hosted. Antiquing, golf, horseback riding, parks, shopping, hot air balloon rides, limousine wine tours, Napa Valley Wine Train, Copia and Opera House nearby.
Publicity: *New York Times and San Francisco Examiner.*

"Best night's sleep this side of the Atlantic Ocean! Thank you for your warm welcome and delicious breakfast."

Old World Inn

1301 Jefferson St
Napa, CA 94559-2412
(707)257-0112 (800)966-6624 Fax:(707)257-0118
E-mail: theoldworldinn@aol.com
Web: www.oldworldinn.com

Circa 1906. The decor in this exquisite bed & breakfast is second to none. In 1981, Macy's sought out the inn to showcase a new line of fabrics inspired by Scandinavian artist Carl Larrson. Each romantic room is adorned in bright, welcoming

colors and includes special features such as canopy beds and clawfoot tubs. The Garden Room boasts three skylights, and the Anne Room is a must for honeymoons and romantic retreats. The walls and ceilings are painted in a warm peach and blue, bows are stenciled around the perimeter of the room. A decorated canopy starts at the ceiling in the center of the bed and falls downward producing a curtain-like effect. A buffet breakfast is served each morning and a delicious afternoon tea and wine and cheese social will curb your appetite until dinner. After sampling one of Napa's gourmet eateries, return to the inn where a selection of desserts await you.

Innkeeper(s): Sam Van Hoeve. $145-250. 10 rooms with PB, 6 with FP, 1 suite and 1 cottage. Breakfast, afternoon tea and snacks/refreshments included in rates. Types of meals: Full gourmet bkfst and early coffee/tea. Beds: KQT. Cable TV, VCR, reading lamp, refrigerator, ceiling fan, clock radio, telephone and hot tub/spa in room. Air conditioning. Fax, spa, parlor games and fireplace on premises. Antiquing, fishing, golf, live theater, parks, shopping, sporting events and tennis nearby.
Publicity: *Napa Valley Traveller.*

"Excellent is an understatement. We'll return."

Stahlecker House B&B Country Inn & Garden

1042 Easum Dr
Napa, CA 94558-5525
(707)257-1588 (800)799-1588 Fax:(707)224-7429
E-mail: stahlbnb@aol.com
Web: www.stahleckerhouse.com

Circa 1949. This country inn is situated on the banks of tree-lined Napa Creek. The acre and a half of grounds feature rose and orchard gardens, fountains and manicured lawns. Guests often relax on the sun deck. There is an antique refrigerator stocked with soft drinks and lemonade. Full, gourmet breakfasts are served by candlelight in the glass-wrapped dining room that overlooks the gardens. In the evenings, coffee, tea and freshly made chocolate chip cookies are served. The Napa Wine Train station is five minutes away. Wineries, restaurants, antique shops, bike paths and hiking all are nearby.

Innkeeper(s): Ron & Ethel Stahlecker. $148-268. 4 rooms with PB, 4 with FP and 1 suite. Breakfast and snacks/refreshments included in rates. Types of meals: Full gourmet bkfst and afternoon tea. Beds: QT. TV, reading lamp, clock radio, telephone, turn-down service, desk, hot tub/spa and Couple Spa/Couple Shower in room. Air conditioning. Library, parlor games, fireplace and croquet on premises. Antiquing, fishing, golf, hiking,

live theater, parks, shopping, tennis, wineries and hot air balloons nearby.
Publicity: *Brides Magazine and Napa Valley Traveler.*

"Friendly hosts and beautiful gardens."

Tall Timbers Chalets

1012 Darms Ln
Napa, CA 94558
(707)252-7810 Fax:(707)252-1055
Web: www.talltimberscottages.com

Circa 1930. Flowers decorate the exterior of these little cottages, painted white with dark and light green trim. The chalets were built between 1930 and 1940, and the grounds were the site of several movies during the 1930s. Each cottage includes a bedroom, bathroom, sitting room and kitchen. The sitting rooms include a sofa bed, so the cottages can accommodate four guests comfortably. Dozens of wineries, shops and restaurants are nearby.
Innkeeper(s): Mary Sandmann-Montes. $65-150. 8 cottages with PB. Breakfast included in rates. Types of meals: Cont plus. Beds: Q. Cable TV and refrigerator in room. Air conditioning. Fax and telephone on premises. Weddings, small meetings, family reunions and seminars hosted. Antiquing, golf, parks and vineyard and winery tours nearby.

Nevada City   F6

Deer Creek Inn

116 Nevada St
Nevada City, CA 95959
(530)265-0363 (800)655-0363 Fax:(530)265-0980

Circa 1860. A prominent local citizen who served as postmaster, as well as holding several other important city and county posts built this Queen Anne Victorian. The inn boasts many original features, including an abundance of stained glass, which frames many of the windows. Guest rooms and common areas are decorated with period antiques. Beds are topped with down comforters, and some rooms include a canopy bed or clawfoot tub. Each room is named for one of the women who have owned the house throughout the years. Breakfasts, served on a veranda overlooking Deer Creek, include several courses, beginning with a fruit dish such as poached pears in apricot nectar. This is followed by an egg dish, perhaps a mushroom and spinach strata accompanied by honey maple sausage and potatoes. Finally, guests are treated to a special entrée. One delectable example is orange pecan French toast topped with hot orange-maple syrup. During California's gold rush, hundreds of pounds of gold were discovered in Deer Creek, which runs behind the inn's one-acre property. This local gold rush was the catalyst that created Nevada City, a quaint historic town that offers shops, walking tours, carriage rides, art galleries and museums. Two state parks represent the area's mining history, and there are plenty of outdoor activities, as well.
Innkeeper(s): Chuck & Elaine Matroni. $135-179. 5 rooms with PB and 1 conference room. Breakfast and snacks/refreshments included in rates. Types of meals: Full bkfst and early coffee/tea. Beds: KQ. Data port, reading lamp, ceiling fan, clock radio, desk and Roman tub in room. Central air. TV, VCR, fax, parlor games and telephone on premises. Family reunions hosted. Antiquing, art galleries, beach, bicycling, canoeing/kayaking, cross-country skiing, fishing, golf, hiking, horseback riding, live theater, museums, parks, shopping, tennis, water sports and wineries nearby.

Emma Nevada House

528 E Broad St
Nevada City, CA 95959-2213
(530)265-4415 (800)916-3662 Fax:(530)265-4416
E-mail: mail@emmanevadahouse.com
Web: www.emmanevadahouse.com

Circa 1856. The childhood home of 19th-century opera star Emma Nevada now serves as an attractive Queen Anne Victorian inn. English roses line the white picket fence in front, and the forest-like back garden has a small stream with benches. The Empress' Chamber is the most romantic room with ivory Italian linens atop a French antique bed, a bay window and a massive French armoire. Some rooms have whirlpool baths and TV. Guests enjoy relaxing in the hexagonal sunroom and on the inn's wraparound porches. Empire Mine State Historic Park is nearby.
Historic Interest: Malakoff Diggins (20 miles), Nevada City Historical District (3 blocks).
Innkeeper(s): Laura DuPee. $130-200. 6 rooms with PB, 2 with FP. Breakfast and afternoon tea included in rates. Types of meals: Full bkfst and early coffee/tea. Beds: Q. Reading lamp, desk and clawfoot and Jacuzzi tubs in room. Air conditioning. Fax, library, parlor games, telephone and fireplace on premises. Weddings and small meetings hosted. Antiquing, downhill skiing, fishing, live theater, parks, shopping and water sports nearby.
Publicity: *Country Inns, Gold Rush Scene, Sacramento Focus, The Union, Los Angeles Times, San Jose Mercury News, Sacramento Bee and Karen Browns.*

"A delightful experience: such airiness and hospitality in the midst of so much history. We were fascinated by the detail and the faithfulness of the restoration. This house is a quiet solace for city-weary travelers. There's a grace here."

Grandmere's Inn

449 Broad St
Nevada City, CA 95959-2430
(530)265-4660
E-mail: grandmeresinn@oro.net
Web: grandmeresinn.com

Circa 1856. Aaron Sargent, U.S. Congressman, senator and author of the women's suffrage bill, was the first owner of this white Colonial Revival house. He and his wife often received Susan B. Anthony here. Shaker pine furnishings and white wooden shutters predominate the spacious interior design. Lavish creature comforts include six pillows on the four-poster beds. Huge country breakfasts may include onion-caraway quiche, cornbread and the inn's trademark, Grandmere's French Toast. A half acre of terraced gardens cascade behind the inn.
$145-220. 6 rooms with PB. Types of meals: Full bkfst. Beds: Q. Weddings hosted. Antiquing, fishing, live theater, shopping and restaurants nearby.
Publicity: *Country Living, Gourmet, Sierra Heritage and New York Times.*

The Parsonage B&B

427 Broad St
Nevada City, CA 95959-2407
(530)265-9478 Fax:(530)265-8147

Circa 1865. Guests in search of California history would do well to stop in Nevada City and at the Parsonage. The Gold Rush town is a registered National Monument, and the home is one of the older homes in the state, dating to the 1860s. Innkeeper Deborah Dane's family has been in California since Gold Rush days, and the home features many heirlooms. Although used to house Methodist ministers for 80 years, the home was in a quite ungodly state by the time Deborah found it. She painstakingly restored the gem and filled it with beautiful antiques and delightful, elegant decor. Special furnishings, knickknacks and artwork are located throughout, including an amazing carved mahogany bed the Dane family brought along the Oregon Trail. In addition to her flair for restoration and decorating, Deborah is a dietitian and Cordon Bleu graduate, so be prepared for a gourmet breakfast that's as healthy as it is delicious.

Innkeeper(s): Deborah Dane. $100-150. 6 rooms with PB, 1 with FP, 1 cottage and 1 conference room. Breakfast included in rates. Types of meals: Full bkfst and early coffee/tea. Beds: QT. Cable TV, reading lamp, refrigerator, ceiling fan, snack bar, clock radio and desk in room. Air conditioning. Fax, copier, library, telephone and fireplace on premises. Weddings, small meetings, family reunions and seminars hosted. Antiquing, cross-country skiing, downhill skiing, fishing, golf, live theater, shopping and water sports nearby.

Publicity: *Country Inns.*

US Hotel Bed & Breakfast Inn

233B Broad St
Nevada City, CA 95959-2501
(530)265-7999 (800)525-4525 Fax:(530)265-7998
E-mail: info@ushotelbb.com
Web: www.ushotelbb.com

Circa 1856. Spacious and luxurious, this historic brick building with 12-foot ceilings boasts scenic downtown views from any one of five balconies. Peruse the extensive collection of books about the local area's history and people as well as an interesting selection of vintage books. Recently renovated to provide modern amenities, the air-conditioned guest bedrooms feature high-speed DSL computer hookups. Down comforters and feather pillows top canopy beds. Antique clawfoot tubs grace the large bathrooms. A three-course breakfast is a satisfying repast with a fresh fruit dish, just-baked bread or sweet and gooey coffee cake and an egg entree served with meats. Beverages and light snacks are available during the day. Sitting in the foothills of the Sierra Nevada mountains, an assortment of activities and annual festivals are offered.

Historic Interest: During the Gold Rush days our inn served the community as a full service hotel for travelers and gold panners. Lota Crabtree was one of the original entertainers at this hotel.

Innkeeper(s): Catherine Bennett and Lesli Steiner. $119-199. 8 rooms with PB and 1 conference room. Breakfast and snacks/refreshments included in rates. Types of meals: Full gourmet bkfst, early coffee/tea, picnic lunch and room service. Beds: KQ. Modem hook-up, data port, cable TV, VCR, reading lamp, stereo, refrigerator, ceiling fan, snack bar, clock radio, telephone, desk and DSL in room. Central air. Fax, copier, parlor games and library has a collection of books published before 1930 and extensive history books of the area and its people on premises. Weddings, small meetings, family reunions and seminars hosted. Antiquing, art galleries, bicycling, canoeing/kayaking, cross-country skiing, downhill skiing, fishing, golf, hiking, horseback riding, live theater, museums, parks, shopping, wineries and river beaches nearby.

Publicity: *Union Newspaper and Nevada City Scene.*

Nice   F4

Featherbed Railroad Company B&B

2870 Lakeshore Blvd, PO Box 4016
Nice, CA 95464
(707)274-4434 (800)966-6322
E-mail: rooms@featherbedrailroad.com
Web: featherbedrailroad.com

Circa 1940. Located on five acres on Clear Lake, this unusual inn features guest rooms in nine luxuriously renovated, painted and papered cabooses. Each has its own featherbed and private bath, most have Jacuzzi tubs for two. The Southern Pacific cabooses have a bay window alcove, while those from the Santa Fe feature small cupolas.

Innkeeper(s): Lorraine Bassignani. $102-180. 9 rooms with PB. Breakfast included in rates. Types of meals: Full bkfst. Beds: QDT. Cable TV and VCR in room. TV and spa on premises.

Publicity: *Santa Rosa Press Democrat, Fairfield Daily Republic, London Times, Travel & Leisure and Bay Area Back Roads.*

Nipomo   M7

The Kaleidoscope Inn & Gardens

130 E Dana St
Nipomo, CA 93444
(805)929-5444 Fax:(805)929-5440
E-mail: info@kaleidoscopeinn.com
Web: www.kaleidoscopeinn.com

Circa 1887. Romantic and historic, this splendidly restored Victorian home is ocean close on the Central Coast. Built entirely from redwood in 1887, the original gingerbread, moon and sun detailing reflect its architectural heritage. Spacious guest bedrooms with stained-glass windows and 14-foot ceilings feature many luxuries. CD players, robes, hair dryers, down comforters, quilts, and private baths are delightful pleasures. Wake up to a fabulous gourmet breakfast. Roam the acre of lush gardens before touring nearby Hearst Castle. Special packages are available. Local golf courses offer reduced playing fees. Outdoor weddings, receptions and special events are popular around the Heart Gazebo under the lawn's shade trees. Dancing is enjoyed on the brick patio.

Historic Interest: Victorian home built entirely from redwood in 1887. Architectural details include stained glass windows in every room of the original structure, gingerbread, moon and sun detailing and 14-foot ceilings.

Innkeeper(s): Carolayne, Holley & Kevin Beauchamp. $125. 4 rooms with PB. Breakfast included in rates. Types of meals: Full bkfst. Beds: KQ. Reading lamp in room. TV, VCR, library, parlor games, telephone and fireplace on premises. Weddings, small meetings and family reunions hosted. Antiquing, fishing, golf, live theater, parks, shopping, water sports, Hearst Castle, wineries, missions, beaches, hiking, biking and spas nearby.

"Beautiful room, chocolates, fresh flowers, peaceful night's rest, great breakfast."

Nipton L14

Hotel Nipton

HC 1, BOX 357, 107355 Nipton Rd
Nipton, CA 92364-9735
(760)856-2335

Circa 1904. This Southwestern-style adobe hotel with its wide verandas once housed gold miners and Clara Bow, wife of movie star Rex Bell. It is decorated in period furnishings and historic photos of the area. A  1920s rock and cactus garden blooms, and an outdoor spa provides the perfect setting for watching a flaming sunset over Ivanpah Valley, the New York Mountains and Castle Peaks. Later, a magnificent star-studded sky appears undimmed by city lights.

Historic Interest: Gold mining town started in 1885.

Innkeeper(s): Gerald & Roxanne Freeman. $70. 5 rooms. Breakfast included in rates. Types of meals: Cont and early coffee/tea. Beds: DT. Reading lamp in room. Air conditioning. Fax, library, parlor games and Jacuzzi on premises. Weddings, small meetings, family reunions and seminars hosted. Amusement parks, fishing, golf, live theater, parks, shopping, sporting events, water sports and golf and stables nearby.

Publicity: *Los Angeles Times, New York Times, National Geographic Traveler, Town & Country, U.S. News & World Report.* and *Breakdown.*

"Warm, friendly, unpretentious, genuine. The hotel's historical significance is well-researched and verified."

Ojai N9

The Moon's Nest Inn

210 E Matilija St
Ojai, CA 93023-2722
(805)646-6635 Fax:(805)646-4995
Web: www.moonsnestinn.com

Circa 1874. Built in 1874, The Moon's Nest Inn is the oldest building in the small town of Ojai (OH hi). The city's first school house and community center, the structure was later used as a residence and then an inn. Three years ago the new owners renovated the inn, adding heating and air conditioning, private baths and balconies. They enclosed the gardens and pond with walls and vines to accent the property and the magnificent old oak trees, creating an oasis within the convenient small town location. The Ojai Valley is often referred to as Shangri-La. This may be because the area was used as the location for the original film by that name, or because the valley is surrounded by millions of acres of the Los Padres National Forest. The region offers seashores, lake shores, mountains, hiking trails and streams.

Historic Interest: The Ojai Valley Historical Museum is in the historic old St. Thomas Chapel. The Ojai Center for the Arts presents community theater productions and works of California artists. The city also boasts the oldest tennis tournament in America.

Innkeeper(s): Char Carper. $115-175. 7 rooms, 5 with PB and 1 conference room. Breakfast and snacks/refreshments included in rates. Types of meals: Full gourmet bkfst, veg bkfst and early coffee/tea. Beds: QDT. Central air. TV, VCR, fax, library, parlor games, telephone, modem hook-up and afternoon wine on premises. Weddings, small meetings, family reunions and seminars hosted. Antiquing, art galleries, bicycling, canoeing/kayaking, fishing, golf, hiking, live theater, museums, parks, shopping, tennis and wineries nearby.

Ojai Valley Inn & Spa

905 Country Club Rd
Ojai, CA 93023
(805)646-5511 (800)422-6524 Fax:(805)646-7969
E-mail: info@ojairesort.com
Web: www.ojairesort.com

Circa 1923. Rich in history, this Spanish Colonial landmark is a 220-acre luxury mountain resort surrounded by the Topa Topa Mountains with impressive views. Lavish guest bedrooms and suites, most with private terraces and some with fireplaces, are decorated in contemporary California Mission style. Numerous upscale and personal amenities are sure to pamper and please. Choose between casual or more formal dining, the cuisine and atmosphere is wonderful either way. An abundance of inn activities include a championship golf course, full-service spa, tennis center, art studio, bicycles, swimming pools, whirlpools, horseback riding, hiking and bird watching. A variety of off-site excursions are also offered.

$279-2500. 206 rooms, 184 with PB, 15 with FP and 26 suites. Types of meals: Full gourmet bkfst, early coffee/tea, gourmet lunch, snacks/refreshments, gourmet dinner and room service. Restaurant on premises. Beds: KQ. Data port, cable TV, reading lamp, snack bar, clock radio, telephone, coffeemaker and desk in room. Air conditioning. Fax, copier, spa, swimming, stable, bicycles, tennis, fireplace and gift shop on premises. Limited handicap access. Weddings, small meetings, family reunions and seminars hosted. Antiquing, art galleries, bicycling, fishing, golf, hiking, horseback riding, shopping and tennis nearby.

The Theodore Woolsey House

1484 E Ojai Ave
Ojai, CA 93023-9623
(805)646-9779 Fax:(805)646-4414
E-mail: twhouse@mindspring.com
Web: www.theodorewoolseyhouse.com

Circa 1887. This historical landmark appears as a Connecticut farmhouse in the middle of sunny California. The house is full of antiques and hand-woven rugs. The living room boasts a custom-made walnut piano. All the bedrooms are decorated with nostalgic period lace curtains and original furniture. To give your stay a romantic twist, add some extras such as flowers and champagne or breakfast in bed. All guests will enjoy an expanded continental breakfast of fresh fruits, coffee cakes, flavored yogurt, cereals and freshly-squeezed juices.

Innkeeper(s): Ana Cross. $85-150. 5 rooms, 6 with PB, 3 with FP and 1 cottage. Types of meals: Cont plus. Beds: QD.

Orland E5

Inn at Shallow Creek Farm

4712 County Rd DD
Orland, CA 95963
(530)865-4093 (800)865-4093

Circa 1900. This vine-covered farmhouse was once the center of a well-known orchard and sheep ranch. The old barn, adjacent to the farmhouse, was a livery stop. The citrus orchard, now restored, blooms with 165 trees. Apples, pears, peaches, apricots, persimmons, walnuts, figs, and pomegranates are also grown here. Guests can meander about and examine the Polish crested chickens, silver guinea fowl, Muscovy ducks, and African geese. The old caretaker's house is now a four-room guest cottage. Hundreds of narcissus grow along the creek that flows through the property.

Innkeeper(s): Mary & Kurt Glaeseman. $65-90. 4 rooms, 2 with PB and 1 suite. Breakfast included in rates. Types of meals: Full bkfst and early coffee/tea. Beds: QT. Reading lamp, ceiling fan, telephone and desk in room. Air conditioning. Library, parlor games and fireplace on premises. Antiquing, fishing, parks and birding nearby.

Publicity: *Adventure Road, Orland Press Register, San Francisco Focus, Chico Enterprise Record and Minneapolis Star.*

"Now that we've discovered your country oasis, we hope to return as soon as possible."

Pacific Grove   J5

Centrella B&B Inn

612 Central Ave
Pacific Grove, CA 93950-2611
(831)372-3372 (800)433-4732 Fax:(831)372-2036
E-mail: concierge@innsbythesea.com
Web: www.centrellainn.com

Circa 1889. Pacific Grove was founded as a Methodist resort in 1875, and this home, built just after the town's incorporation, was billed by a local newspaper as, "the largest, most commodious and pleasantly located boarding house in the Grove." Many a guest is still sure to agree. The rooms are well-appointed in a comfortable, Victorian style. Six guest rooms include fireplaces. The Garden Room has a private entrance, fireplace, wet bar, Jacuzzi tub and a canopy bed topped with designer linens. Freshly baked croissants or pastries and made-to-order waffles are common fare at the inn's continental buffet breakfast. The inn is within walking distance of the Monterey Bay Aquarium, the beach and many Pacific Grove shops.

Innkeeper(s): Marijo Harr. $119-279. 26 rooms with PB, 6 with FP, 2 suites and 5 cottages. Breakfast and snacks/refreshments included in rates. Types of meals: Cont plus. Beds: KQT. Reading lamp and telephone in room. VCR, fax, copier, fireplace and TVs upon request on premises. Antiquing, golf, parks and water sports nearby.

Publicity: *Country Inns, New York Times and San Francisco Examiner.*

"I was ecstatic at the charm that the Centrella has been offering travelers for years and hopefully hundreds of years to come. The bed— perfect! I am forever enthralled by the old beauty and will remember this forever!"

Gatehouse Inn

225 Central Ave
Pacific Grove, CA 93950-3017
(831)649-8436 (800)753-1881 Fax:(831)648-8044
E-mail: lew@redshift.com

Circa 1884. This Italianate Victorian seaside inn is just a block from the Monterey Bay. The inn is decorated with Victorian and 20th-century antiques and touches of Art Deco. Guest rooms feature fireplaces, clawfoot tubs and down comforters. Some rooms have ocean views. The dining room boasts opulent Bradbury & Bradbury Victorian wallpapers as do some of the guest rooms. Afternoon hors d'oeuvres, wine and tea are served. The refrigerator is stocked for snacking.

$125-195. 9 rooms with PB, 6 with FP. Breakfast, afternoon tea and snacks/refreshments included in rates. Beds: KQT. Reading lamp, clock radio, telephone and turn-down service in room. Fax, copier, parlor games and fireplace on premises. Weddings and family reunions hosted. Antiquing, fishing, live theater, parks, shopping and water sports nearby.

Publicity: *San Francisco Chronicle, Monterey Herald, Time, Newsweek, Inland Empire and Bon Appetit.*

"Thank you for spoiling us."

Gosby House Inn

643 Lighthouse Ave
Pacific Grove, CA 93950-2643
(831)375-1287 (800)527-8828 Fax:(831)655-9621
E-mail: info@foursisters.com
Web: www.foursisters.com/inns/gosbyhouseinn.html

Circa 1887. Built as an upscale Victorian inn for those visiting the old Methodist retreat, this sunny yellow mansion features an abundance of gables, turrets and bays. During renovation the innkeeper slept in all the rooms to determine just what antiques were needed and how the beds should be situated. Eleven of the romantic rooms include fireplaces and many offer canopy beds. The Carriage House rooms include fireplaces, decks and spa tubs. Gosby House, which has been open to guests for more than a century, is in the National Register. There is a $20 fee for an additional guest in room, except for children less than 5 years old. Gosby House is one of the Four Sisters Inns. The Monterey Bay Aquarium is nearby.

Innkeeper(s): Kalena Mittelman. $95-185. 22 rooms with PB, 11 with FP. Breakfast, afternoon tea, wine and hors d'oeuvres included in rates. Types of meals: Full bkfst and early coffee/tea. Beds: KQD. Telephone, turn-down service, hot tub/spa, bath robes, newspaper and 8 with TV in room. TV, fax, copier, bicycles, fireplace on premises. Limited handicap access. Antiquing, shopping and Monterey Bay Aquarium nearby.

Publicity: *San Francisco Chronicle, Oregonian, Los Angeles Times and Travel & Leisure.*

Grand View Inn

557 Ocean View Blvd
Pacific Grove, CA 93950-2653
(831)372-4341
Web: www.pginns.com

Circa 1910. Overlooking Lover's Point beach on the edge of Monterey Bay, this site was chosen by noted marine biologist Dr. Julia Platt to build this Edwardian-style home. As the first mayor of Pacific Grove, she was also one of those responsible for preserving the landmark beach and park for future generations. All of the guest rooms offer unsurpassed ocean views and are elegantly appointed with authentic and reproduction antiques. Guests will delight in strolling the gardens surrounding the inn or venturing outdoors to walk along the seashore. A full breakfast and afternoon tea are served in the ocean-view dining room.

Historic Interest: The world-famous 17-Mile Drive along the ocean to Pebble Beach and Carmel, Cannery Row and Monterey Bay made famous by John Steinbeck. Old Fisherman's Wharf is also located nearby.

Innkeeper(s): Susan & Ed Flatley. $175-375. 11 rooms with PB. Breakfast and afternoon tea included in rates. Types of meals: Full bkfst and early coffee/tea. Beds: KQ. Reading lamp, turn-down service and some with TV in room. Parlor games, telephone, fireplace, picnic lunches, gift baskets and flowers available on premises. Limited handicap access. Antiquing, fishing, golf, live theater, parks, shopping, tennis and water sports nearby.

Green Gables Inn

104 5th St
Pacific Grove, CA 93950-2903
(831)375-2095 (800)722-1774 Fax:(831)375-5437
E-mail: info@foursisters.com
Web: www.foursisters.com/inns/greengablesinn.html

Circa 1888. This half-timbered Queen Anne Victorian appears as a fantasy of gables overlooking spectacular Monterey Bay. The parlor has stained-glass panels framing the fireplace and bay windows looking out to the sea. A favorite focal point is an antique carousel horse. Most of the guest rooms have panoramic views of the ocean, fireplaces, gleaming woodwork, soft quilts and teddy bears, and four rooms have spa tubs. Across the street is the  Monterey Bay paved oceanfront cycling path. (Mountain bikes may be borrowed from the inn.) There is a $20 fee for an additional guest in room, except for children less than 5 years old. Green Gables is one of the Four Sisters Inns.

Innkeeper(s): Lucia Root. $155-260. 11 rooms, 7 with PB, 6 with FP and 5 suites. Breakfast, afternoon tea and snacks/refreshments included in rates. Types of meals: Full bkfst and early coffee/tea. Beds: KQD. Cable TV, VCR, reading lamp, stereo, ceiling fan, snack bar, clock radio, telephone, turn-down service, hot tub/spa, terry robes and newspaper in room. Fax, copier, bicycles, library, parlor games, fireplace and afternoon wine and hors d'oeuvres on premises. Limited handicap access. Antiquing, art galleries, beach, bicycling, canoeing/kayaking, fishing, golf, hiking, horseback riding, live theater, museums, parks, shopping, tennis, water sports, wineries and aquarium nearby.

Publicity: *Travel & Leisure and Country Living.*

Inn at 213 Seventeen Mile Dr

213 Seventeen Mile Dr
Pacific Grove, CA 93950-2400
(831)642-9514 (800)526-5666 Fax:(831)642-9546
E-mail: innkeeper@innat17.com
Web: www.innat17.com

Circa 1925. The only challenging part of a visit to this 1920s craftsman-style house is figuring out where the deep blue sea ends and clear skies begin. Located in the heart of the Monterey Peninsula, this two-story, three-building inn offers sea or garden views from the main house, while you will find rustic ambiance, surrounded by oak and redwood trees, in the cottage and redwood chalet rooms. Relax in the spa beneath the tall trees in the gardens, which are often visited by deer and monarch butterflies, or enjoy a glass of champagne while observing Koi in the fountain ponds. Or, spend time in the wood-paneled dining, sitting and reading rooms while enjoying complimentary hors d'oeuvres and planning a day full of activities.

Innkeeper(s): Tony, Glynis Greening, Sally Goss. $145-240. 14 rooms with PB and 1 cottage. Breakfast and snacks/refreshments included in rates. Types of meals: Full gourmet bkfst and veg bkfst. Beds: KQ. Data port, cable TV, refrigerator, clock radio and telephone in room. VCR, fax, copier, spa, library, parlor games and fireplace on premises. Limited handicap access. Weddings, small meetings, family reunions and seminars hosted. Antiquing, art galleries, beach, bicycling, canoeing/kayaking, fishing, golf, hiking, live theater, museums, parks, shopping, sporting events, tennis, water sports, wineries, Monterey Bay Aquarium and The Monarch Butterfly Sanctuary nearby.

Martine Inn

255 Ocean View Blvd
Pacific Grove, CA 93950
(831)373-3388 (800)852-5588 Fax:(831)373-3896
E-mail: don@martineinn.com
Web: www.martineinn.com

Circa 1890. This turn-of-the-century oceanfront manor sits atop a jagged cliff overlooking the coastline of Monterey Bay. Bedrooms are furnished with antiques, and each room contains a fresh rose and a silver Victorian bridal basket filled with fresh fruit. Thirteen rooms also boast fireplaces. Some of the museum-quality antiques were exhibited in the 1893 Chicago World's Fair. Other bedroom sets include furniture that belonged to Edith Head, and there is an 1860 Chippendale Revival four-poster bed with a  canopy and side curtains. Innkeeper Don Martine has a collection of old MGs, five on display for guests. Twilight wine and hors d'oeuvres are served, and chocolates accompany evening turndown service. The inn is a beautiful spot for romantic getaways and weddings.

Historic Interest: Pacific Grove Historic Walking Tour.

Innkeeper(s): Don Martine. $129-329. 24 rooms with PB, 13 with FP, 1 suite and 6 conference rooms. Breakfast and snacks/refreshments included in rates. Types of meals: Full gourmet bkfst, early coffee/tea, picnic lunch, afternoon tea and dinner. Beds: KQD. Reading lamp, refrigerator, telephone, turn-down service, desk and with 48 hour notice dinner is available in room. TV, fax, copier, spa, library, parlor games, fireplace, evening wine and DSL Internet on premises. Limited handicap access. Weddings, small meetings, family reunions and seminars hosted. Antiquing, art galleries, beach, bicycling, canoeing/kayaking, fishing, golf, hiking, horseback riding, live theater, museums, parks, shopping, sporting events, tennis, water sports, wineries, Monterey Bay Aquarium and Cannery Row nearby.

Publicity: *Sunday Oregonian, Bon Appetit, Vacations APAC and Fresno Bee.*

"Wonderful, can't wait to return."

Old St. Angela Inn

321 Central Ave
Pacific Grove, CA 93950-2934
(831)372-3246 (800)748-6306 Fax:(831)372-8560
Web: www.sueandlewinns.com

Circa 1910. This Cape-style inn once served as a rectory then a convent. Guest rooms are decorated with period antiques. Three rooms include a fireplace, and two offer a cast-iron stove. Six rooms have a whirlpool tub. Breakfasts are served in a glass solarium. The ocean is a block away and it's just a short walk to the aquarium or fisherman's wharf.

Innkeeper(s): Lewis Shaefer & Susan Kuslis. $110-225. 9 rooms with PB. Breakfast, afternoon tea and snacks/refreshments included in rates. Types of meals: Full gourmet bkfst and early coffee/tea. Beds: KQT. Reading lamp, refrigerator, telephone and hot tub/spa in room. Fax, spa, parlor games and fireplace on premises. Small meetings and family reunions hosted. Antiquing, fishing, live theater, parks, shopping and water sports nearby.

Publicity: *Best Places to Kiss.*

"Outstanding inn and outstanding hospitality."

Seven Gables Inn

555 Ocean View Blvd
Pacific Grove, CA 93950-2653
(831)372-4341
Web: www.pginns.com

Circa 1886. At the turn of the century, Lucie Chase, a wealthy widow and civic leader from the East Coast, embellished this Victorian with gables and verandas, taking full advantage of its spectacular setting on Monterey Bay. All guest rooms feature wonderful ocean views, and there are elegant antiques, intricate Persian carpets, chandeliers and beveled-glass armoires throughout. A full breakfast and afternoon tea are served in a dining room that features wraparound ocean views. Sea otters, harbor seals and whales often can be seen from the inn.

Historic Interest: The world-famous 17-Mile Drive along the ocean to Pebble Beach and Carmel, Cannery Row and Monterey Bay made famous by John Steinbeck. Old Fisherman's Wharf is also located nearby.

Innkeeper(s): The Flatley Family. $175-385. 14 rooms with PB. Breakfast and afternoon tea included in rates. Types of meals: Full bkfst, early coffee/tea and picnic lunch. Beds: KQ. Turn-down service and some with fireplace in room. Limited handicap access. Antiquing, fishing, golf, live theater, parks, shopping, tennis and water sports nearby.

Publicity: *Travel & Leisure and Country Inns.*

"Our stay was everything your brochure said it would be, and more."

Palm Springs 013

Casa Cody Country Inn

175 S Cahuilla Rd
Palm Springs, CA 92262-6331
(760)320-9346 (800)231-2639 Fax:(760)325-8610
E-mail: casacody@aol.com
Web: www.casacody.com

Circa 1910. Casa Cody, built by a relative of Wild Bill Cody and situated in the heart of Palm Springs, is the town's oldest continuously operating inn. The San Jacinto Mountains provide a scenic background for the tree-shaded spa, the pink and purple bougainvillea and the blue waters of the inn's two swimming pools. Each suite has a small kitchen and features terra cotta and turquoise  Southwestern decor. Several have wood-burning fireplaces. There are Mexican pavers, French doors and private patios. The area offers many activities, including museums, a heritage center, boutiques, a botanical garden, horseback riding and golf.

Historic Interest: Village Heritage Center, Village Theater and numerous historic estates within blocks; Mooten Botanic Gardens and Indian Canyons within minutes.

Innkeeper(s): Elissa Goforth. $59-229. 23 rooms, 24 with PB, 10 with FP, 8 suites and 2 cottages. Breakfast included in rates. Types of meals: Cont plus. Beds: KQT. Cable TV, reading lamp, refrigerator, ceiling fan, telephone, desk, hot tub/spa and kitchen in room. Air conditioning. TV, fax, copier, spa and swimming on premises. Weddings, small meetings, family reunions and seminars hosted. Antiquing, bicycling, live theater, hiking, horseback riding, tennis, golf, ballooning and polo nearby.

Publicity: *New York Times, Washington Post, Los Angeles Times, San Diego Union Tribune, Seattle Times, Portland Oregonian, Los Angeles, San Diego Magazine, Pacific Northwest Magazine, Sunset, Westways, Alaska Airlines Magazine and Huel Howser California Gold.*

"Outstanding ambiance, friendly relaxed atmosphere."

Ingleside Inn

200 W Ramon Rd
Palm Springs, CA 92264-7385
(760)325-0046 (800)772-6655 Fax:(760)325-0710

Circa 1925. This posh, intimate hotel has been hosting the rich and famous since the 1930s when it was converted from a private estate into a luxurious hostelry. Among its notable guests are Greta Garbo, Greer Garson, President Ford, Marlon Brando, Goldie Hawn, John Travolta and many more. Each of the inn's suites and rooms is individually decorated. The spacious accommodations include amenities such as whirlpool tubs, steam rooms, sitting rooms, private porches and refrigerators stocked with drinks and snacks. Guests can enjoy the mountainous scenery while relaxing by the Olympic-size pool or in the Jacuzzi. Ingleside guests also receive special tee times at several local golf courses. The inn's restaurant, Melvyn's, is a multiple award winner. The two dining rooms are romantic in decor and the menu selection is vast, featuring everything from chateaubriand to shrimp scampi. Lunch and a gourmet Sunday brunch also are served. The inn is a Palm Springs historic site.

Innkeeper(s): Armida Pedrin. $95-395. 30 rooms with PB, 13 with FP, 2 suites and 2 conference rooms. Snacks/refreshments included in rates. Types of meals: Full bkfst, early coffee/tea, lunch, dinner and room service. Restaurant on premises. Beds: KQT. Modem hook-up, data port, cable TV, VCR, reading lamp, refrigerator, clock radio, telephone, coffeemaker, turn-down service, desk, hot tub/spa and fireplace in room. Central air. Fax, copier, spa, swimming, fireplace and laundry facility on premises. Weddings, small meetings, family reunions and seminars hosted. Antiquing, art galleries, bicycling, golf, horseback riding, live theater, museums, parks, shopping, tennis, Joshua Tree National Park, Palm Springs Aerial Tramway and Indian Canyons nearby.

Publicity: *LA Times, NY Times, NY Post, Sunset Magazine, USA Today, Chicago Tribune, London Daily Mirror, 60 Minutes, Eye on LA, Wheel of Fortune, Phil Donahue Show, Jeopardy and KTLA News.*

Orchid Tree Inn

261 S Belardo Rd
Palm Springs, CA 92262-6329
(760)325-2791 (800)733-3435 Fax:(760)325-3855
E-mail: info@orchidtree.com
Web: www.orchidtree.com

Circa 1915. Nineteen buildings comprise this desert retreat offering a variety of Mediterranean, ranch, and modern designs representing more than 50 years of Palm Springs architecture. Said to be the oldest continuously operating lodging establishment in Palm Springs, the inn's mature, lush gardens meander throughout the three acres of property and offer excellent mountain views. Each accommodation has its own decorating style including Mission Oak, Prairie, ranch oak, lodge pole pine, Mexican folk and wicker. Restored in 1999, some units feature private whirlpools and fireplaces. A deluxe continental breakfast is offered November through May.

Historic Interest: Aqua Caliente Indian Canyon, buildings by Frank Lloyd Wright and other major architects are nearby.

Innkeeper(s): Robert Weithorn & Karen Prince-Weithorn. $70-395. 40 rooms with PB, 7 with FP, 8 suites, 1 cottage, 8 cabins and 1 conference room. Types of meals: Cont plus, early coffee/tea and room service. Beds: KQDT. Cable TV, reading lamp, clock radio, telephone, desk, one suite with private steam room, some rooms with hot tub/spa, refrigerators, microwave ovens and most with full kitchens in room. Central air. TV, VCR, fax, copier, spa, swimming, bicycles, tennis, library, parlor games, fireplace, laundry facility, data ports and shuffleboard on premises. Weddings, small meetings, family reunions and seminars hosted. Amusement parks, antiquing, art galleries, bicycling, cross-country skiing, fishing, golf, hiking, horseback riding, live theater, museums, shopping, tennis, aerial tramway, Joshua Tree National Park and more than 110 restaurants within five blocks nearby.

Sakura, Japanese B&B Inn

1677 N Via Miraleste at Vista Chino
Palm Springs, CA 92262
(760)327-0705 (800)200-0705 Fax:(760)327-6847

Circa 1945. An authentic Japanese experience awaits guests of this private home, distinctively decorated with Japanese artwork and antique kimonos. Guests are encouraged to leave their shoes at the door, grab kimonos and slippers and discover what real relaxation is all about. Futon beds, and in-room refrigerators and microwaves are provided. Guests may choose either American or Japanese breakfasts, and Japanese or vegetarian dinners also are available. The Palm Springs area is home to more than 100 golf courses and hosts annual world-class golf and tennis charity events. A favorite place for celebrity watching, the area also is the Western polo capital and offers the famous 9,000-foot aerial tram ride that climbs through several temperature zones. There are cycling trails, theater, horseback riding in the canyons and fine dining, skiing and antiquing. During the summer months, the innkeepers conduct tours in Japan.

Innkeeper(s): George & Fumiko Cebra. $45-90. 3 rooms, 2 with PB and 1 suite. Breakfast included in rates. Types of meals: Full bkfst, early coffee/tea, picnic lunch, afternoon tea and dinner. Beds: Q. Weddings, small meetings and family reunions hosted. Amusement parks, antiquing, cross-country skiing, fishing, live theater, parks and shopping nearby.

Villa Royale Inn

1620 South Indian Trail
Palm Springs, CA 92264
(760)327-2314 (800)245-2314 Fax:(760)322-3794
E-mail: info@villaroyale.com
Web: www.villaroyale.com

Circa 1940. Rich European decor and furnishings create the ambiance of a secluded Mediterranean inn at this romantic retreat that graces more than three well-landscaped acres. Meander on paths through lush garden courtyards. Distinctive guest bedrooms and villas feature thick robes, down duvets and herbal toiletries. Antiques, wooden beams, tile floors, French doors leading out to private patios, fireplaces and kitchens are among the lavish amenities. Early risers read the morning paper while drinking coffee or tea on the poolside patio. Linger over a made-to-order breakfast served al fresco. Two swimming pools and a spa highlight a stress-free stay. The inn's award-winning Europa Restaurant offers fine dining and warm service in an intimate setting.

Innkeeper(s): Amy Aquino. $99-329. 31 rooms with PB, 17 with FP and 11 suites. Breakfast included in rates. Types of meals: Full bkfst, gourmet dinner and room service. Restaurant on premises. Beds: KQT. Cable TV, reading lamp, clock radio, telephone, thick terry cloth robes and some with kitchens in room. Air conditioning. Fax, spa, swimming, fireplace, private patio and spa on premises. Weddings, small meetings and family reunions hosted. Antiquing, golf, hiking, horseback riding, live theater, parks, shopping, tennis and water parks nearby.

The Willows Historic Palm Springs Inn

412 W Tahquitz Canyon Way
Palm Springs, CA 92262
(760)320-0771 (800)966-9597 Fax:(760)320-0780
E-mail: innkeeper@thewillowspalmsprings.com
Web: www.thewillowspalmsprings.com

Circa 1924. This beautiful Italianate Mediterranean estate was once the abode of Marion Davies, mistress of William Randolf Hearst. Carole Lombard and Clark Gable stayed here as part of

"the world's longest honeymoon," and Albert Einstein was also a guest. The building's architecture includes the construction of a second shell inside the exterior to provide a natural cooling effect with the air pocket created. Mahogany beams, hardwood floors, a grand piano and a carved fireplace accentuate the Great Hall. It's difficult to choose a room, but for your first trip you might try the Rock Room with a shower flowing onto a protruding piece of San Jacinto Mountain and a double tub built into a rock. The Marion Davies Room offers fine antiques, a balcony with view, and a fireplace. Its bath has a stone floor, silver chandelier, chaise lounge and double tub as well as a shower with a private garden view. The arches of the inn's veranda are set off with long drapes and there are frescoed ceilings and views out over the pool. Guests enjoy wine and hors d'oeuvres in the evening, sometimes with live music, and in the morning, a full gourmet breakfast is served within view of a hillside waterfall. Cross the street to Le Vallauris, an excellent French restaurant, or walk to several historical sites.

$295-575. 8 rooms with PB, 4 with FP and 1 conference room. Breakfast and snacks/refreshments included in rates. Types of meals: Full gourmet bkfst, early coffee/tea and room service. Beds: KQ. Modem hook-up, data port, cable TV, VCR, reading lamp, refrigerator, clock radio, telephone, turndown service, desk and voice mail in room. Central air. Fax, copier, spa, swimming, parlor games and fireplace on premises. Weddings, small meetings and family reunions hosted. Antiquing, bicycling, golf, hiking, horseback riding, live theater, museums, parks, shopping and tennis nearby.

Publicity: *Travel & Leisure, Los Angeles, Avenues, Westways Departures, Chicago Tribune, Los Angeles Times, Country Inns, Gourmet, Instyle and New York Times.*

Palo Alto I5

Adella Villa B&B

122 Atherton Ave.
Palo Alto, CA 94027-4021
(650)321-5195 Fax:(650)325-5121
E-mail: tricia@best.com
Web: www.adellavilla.com

Circa 1923. This Italian villa is located in an area of one-acre estates five minutes from Stanford University. One guest room features a whirlpool tub; four guest rooms have showers. The music room boasts a 1920 mahogany Steinway grand piano. There is a seasonal swimming pool set amid manicured gardens.

Innkeeper(s): Tricia Young.
$115-165. 5 rooms with PB. Breakfast, afternoon tea and snacks/refreshments included in rates. Types of meals: Full gourmet bkfst and early coffee/tea. Beds: KQ. Modem hook-up, cable TV, VCR, reading lamp, stereo, clock radio, telephone, desk and DSL in room. Fax, copier, swimming, library, fireplace, laundry facility and DVD on premises. Amusement parks, antiquing, art galleries, beach, bicycling, golf, live theater, museums, parks, shopping, sporting events, tennis and wineries nearby.

Publicity: *L.A. Times- Reader's Choice.*

"This place is as wonderful, gracious and beautiful as the people who own it!"

Placerville   G6

Chichester-McKee House B&B

800 Spring St
Placerville, CA 95667-4424
(530)626-1882 (800)831-4008
E-mail: info@innlover.com
Web: www.innlover.com

Circa 1892. This fanciful Victorian home, with all its gables, gingerbread and fretwork draws the breath of many a passerby. The house is full of places to explore and admire, including the parlor, library and conservatory.
Guest rooms are filled with family treasures and antiques, and the home features fireplaces and stained glass. Breakfast at the inn includes freshly baked goods and delicious entrees. Evening refreshments are a treat, and the special blends of morning coffee will wake your spirit.
Ask the innkeepers about the discovery of a gold mine beneath the dining room floor and for advice on adventures in the Placerville and Sierra Foothills area.
Historic Interest: Marshall State Historic Gold Discovery Park, Gold Bug Park Mine, Apple Hill.

Innkeeper(s): Doreen & Bill Thornhill. $105-135. 4 rooms. Breakfast and snacks/refreshments included in rates. Types of meals: Full gourmet bkfst and early coffee/tea. Beds: QT. VCR, library, parlor games, telephone and fireplace on premises. Small meetings and family reunions hosted. Antiquing, cross-country skiing, fishing, live theater, parks, shopping, water sports and wineries nearby.
Publicity: *Hi Sierra, Mountain Democrat, Sierra Heritage, Crosscut and Thomas Kincade Victorian Christmas III painting.*

Shafsky House B&B Inn

2942 Coloma St
Placerville, CA 95667
(530)642-2776 Fax:(503)642-2109
E-mail: shafsky@directcon.net
Web: www.shafsky.com

Circa 1902. Gold Country hospitality is offered at this Queen Anne Victorian located just a stroll to the historic district and the shops of Old Hangtown. Enjoy a welcome snack and refreshments in the elegant parlor. Pleasantly decorated guest bedrooms are furnished with antiques and offer individually controlled heat and air conditioning as well as feather beds and goosedown comforters during winter. The two-room Lighthouse Suite also boasts a sitting room for a private breakfast, and a lace curtain-enclosed poster bed. Cozy slippers are provided for no-shoes comfort. Arrangements can be made for special occasions, or a personalized bouquet of flowers.
Historic Interest: Built in 1902 for Albert Shafsky who owned the first department store in Placerville and was also mayor of the town.

Innkeeper(s): Rita Timewell and Stephanie Carlson. $115-145. 3 rooms, 2 with PB and 1 suite. Breakfast and snacks/refreshments included in rates. Types of meals: Full gourmet bkfst. Beds: KQ. Reading lamp, coffeemaker and turn-down service in room. Air conditioning. TV, VCR, library, parlor games, telephone, fireplace and satellite TV on premises. Weddings, small meetings, family reunions and seminars hosted. Antiquing, art galleries, canoeing/kayaking, cross-country skiing, fishing, golf, hiking, horseback riding, live theater, museums, parks, shopping, tennis, water sports, wineries and Apple Hill nearby.
Publicity: *Mountain Democrat and KNCI Radio Station.*

Point Arena   F3

Coast Guard House Historic Inn

695 Arena Cove
Point Arena, CA 95468
(707)882-2442 Fax:(707)882-3233
E-mail: coast@mcn.org
Web: www.coastguardhouse.com

Circa 1901. This National Register, Cape Cod-style home was built by the Lifesaving Service and later was used by the U.S. Coast Guard. A collection of photographs and memorabilia also is displayed. Guest rooms are decorated in arts and crafts and all afford ocean or canyon views. The Boathouse, a replica of the ground's original boathouse, is a romantic cabin with a woodburning stove, private patio and spa with an ocean view. The Point Arena Lighthouse and Museum, as well as many shops and restaurants are just a few miles away.
Historic Interest: Built in 1901 by Life Saving Service.

Innkeeper(s): Mia & Kevin Gallagher. $125-245. 7 rooms. Breakfast included in rates. Types of meals: Full bkfst.

Point Richmond   H4

East Brother Light Station Inc

117 Park Pl
Point Richmond, CA 94801
(510)233-2385
E-mail: info@ebls.org
Web: www.ebls.org

Circa 1873. For guests in search of the unique and a fabulous ocean setting, the East Brother Light Station might be just the ticket. Guests must access this historic, working lighthouse by boat, as it is located on an island about 10 minutes from the shore. Upon reaching the lighthouse, guests climb a ladder to get to facilities and the accommodations. From there, guests can take a guided tour of the lighthouse or relax and enjoy the views. The guest rooms are decorated in period Victorian style, and all offer bay views. Two rooms include a private bath. Guests are greeted with hors d'oeuvres and pampered with a gourmet dinner and homemade breakfast.

Innkeeper(s): Curt and Carolyn Henry. $290-410. 5 rooms, 2 with PB, 1 with FP. Breakfast and dinner included in rates. Types of meals: Full gourmet bkfst and early coffee/tea. Beds: QD. Period and nautical furnishings in room. Library, parlor games, gift shop, lighthouse, fog horn and horseshoes on premises. Weddings, small meetings, family reunions and seminars hosted. Beach and fishing nearby.
Publicity: *Uncommon Lodgings, Sunset Magazine, Islands, Bay Area Backroads and PBS Legendary Lighthouses.*

Quincy   E6

The Feather Bed

542 Jackson St PO Box 3200
Quincy, CA 95971-9412
(530)283-0102 (800)696-8624
E-mail: info@featherbed-inn.com
Web: www.featherbed-inn.com

Circa 1893. Englishman Edward Huskinson built this Queen Anne house shortly after he began his mining and real estate ventures. Ask for the secluded cottage with its own deck and clawfoot tub. Other rooms in the main house overlook down-

town Quincy or the mountains. Check out a bicycle to explore the countryside.

Historic Interest: County Historic Designation.
Innkeeper(s): Bob Janowski. $90-150. 7 rooms with PB, 4 with FP, 1 suite and 2 cottages. Breakfast and snacks/refreshments included in rates. Types of meals: Full gourmet bkfst and early coffee/tea. Beds: QT. TV, reading lamp, ceiling fan, telephone, desk and radio in room. Air conditioning. VCR, fax, copier, bicycles, library, parlor games and fireplace on premises. Limited handicap access. Antiquing, cross-country skiing, fishing, parks, shopping, water sports and theater nearby.
Publicity: *Parade, Focus, Reno Gazette, Bay Area Back Roads, San Francisco Chronicle, Country Accents and Sunset.*

"After living and traveling in Europe where innkeepers are famous, we have found The Feather Bed to be one of the most charming in the U.S. and Europe!"

Sacramento G6

Amber House

1315 22nd St
Sacramento, CA 95816-5717
(916)444-8085 (800)755-6526 Fax:(916)552-6529
E-mail: info@amberhouse.com
Web: www.amberhouse.com

Circa 1905. These three historic homes on the city's Historic Preservation Register are in a neighborhood of fine historic homes eight blocks from the capitol. Each room is named for a famous poet, artist or composer and features stained glass, English antiques, and amenities such as bath robes and fresh flowers. Ask about the Van Gogh Room where you can soak in the heart-shaped Jacuzzi tub-for-two or enjoy one of the rooms with marble baths and Jacuzzi tubs in either the adjacent 1913 Mediterranean mansion or the 1895 Colonial Revival. A gourmet breakfast can be served in your room or in the dining room at a time you request.

Historic Interest: California State Capitol, State Railroad Museum, Crocker Art Museum, Governor's Mansion, Old Sacramento State Historic Park (all within 8 to 22 blocks).
$149-299. 14 rooms with PB, 3 with FP and 1 conference room. Breakfast included in rates. Types of meals: Full gourmet bkfst and early coffee/tea. Beds: KQ. Cable TV, VCR, reading lamp, CD player, refrigerator, clock radio, telephone, turn-down service, desk, hot tub/spa, voice mail, hair dryer, iron/ironing board and breakfast in room. Air conditioning. TV, fax, bicycles, library, parlor games and fireplace on premises. Weddings, small meetings and seminars hosted. Antiquing, cross-country skiing, downhill skiing, fishing, live theater, parks, shopping and water sports nearby.
Publicity: *Travel & Leisure and Village Crier.*

"Your cordial hospitality, the relaxing atmosphere and delicious breakfast made our brief business/pleasure trip so much more enjoyable."

Inn At Parkside

2116 Sixth Street
Sacramento, CA 95818
(916)658-1818 (800)995-7275 Fax:(916)658-1809
E-mail: info@innatparkside.com
Web: www.innatparkside.com

Circa 1936. A gracious welcome is extended while staying at this elegant inn, the Historic Fong Mansion, just two blocks from downtown sites and activities, the State Capitol and

Sutter's Fort. The ballroom invites dancing on its spring-loaded maple floor. A guest kitchenette is available at any time. Exquisite guest bedrooms are furnished with authentic museum pieces, and boast modern amenities to enjoy. Morning brings an award-winning breakfast to savor. The intimate yet elaborate spa room features a Jacuzzi tub for two, stained-glass ceiling, original artwork, and wall-to-wall mirror. Southside Park offers landscaped grounds, walking or jogging trails and tennis courts.

Innkeeper(s): Bill Swenson, Will Sawyer, Philip Hartshorn. $115-289. 7 rooms with PB and 2 conference rooms. Breakfast included in rates. Types of meals: Full gourmet bkfst and early coffee/tea. Beds: KQ. Modem hook-up, cable TV, VCR, reading lamp, stereo, refrigerator, ceiling fan, snack bar, clock radio, telephone, turn-down service, desk, hot tub/spa, fireplace and high-speed Internet access in room. Central air. Fax, copier, lap pool, small gym, fishing lake, playground and park on premises. Limited handicap access. Weddings, small meetings, family reunions and seminars hosted. Antiquing, art galleries, canoeing/kayaking, cross-country skiing, downhill skiing, fishing, golf, hiking, horseback riding, live theater, museums, parks, shopping, sporting events, tennis, water sports and wineries nearby.
Publicity: *Sacramento Bee.*

Saint Helena G4

Adagio Inn of St. Helena

1417 Kearney St.
Saint Helena, CA 94574
(707)963-2238 (800)823-2446 Fax:(707)963-5598
E-mail: innkeeper@adagioinn.com
Web: www.adagioinn.com

Circa 1890. Gracing a quiet neighborhood in the historic district of the Napa Valley wine country, this 1890 Edwardian home has been recently renovated to offer the comfort and amenities of a fine country inn. Chat over fireside afternoon refreshments in the parlor while the baby grand piano is played. Guest bedrooms and suites are splendidly decorated in a relaxed European elegance and feature plush robes, upscale bath products, hair dryer, refrigerator, cable TV, CD selection and player. Evening turndown service is also provided. The Concerto Suite boasts a clawfoot tub and shower. A jetted whirlpool tub for two is enjoyed in the Sonata Suite. The Prelude boasts a private deck with two-person spa. Savor a lavish breakfast in the dining room or on the veranda.

Historic Interest: 1890 Eduardian, fully restored. Edwardian furnishings.
Innkeeper(s): Polly Keegan. $200-275. 3 suites. Breakfast and afternoon tea included in rates. Types of meals: Full gourmet bkfst and early coffee/tea. Beds: K. Cable TV, VCR, reading lamp, CD player, refrigerator, clock radio, telephone, turn-down service and hot tub/spa in room. Central air. Fax, copier, spa, parlor games and fireplace on premises. Antiquing, art galleries, bicycling, canoeing/kayaking, golf, hiking, live theater, museums, parks, shopping, tennis, wineries, Napa Valley wine country, hot springs, spas and mudbaths nearby.

Ambrose Bierce House

1515 Main St
Saint Helena, CA 94574-1851
(707)963-3003 Fax:(707)993-9367
E-mail: ambrose@napanet.net
Web: www.ambrosebiercehouse.com

Circa 1872. A white iron archway welcomes guests to this three-story Victorian, once home to short story writer Ambrose Bierce. (Gregory Peck visited the house and starred as Bierce in the movie Old Gringo.) Guest rooms offer high ceilings, antiques, fine linens, fresh flowers and high beds. Rooms offer special features such as Jacuzzi tubs, a fireplace and canopy beds. Enjoy evening wine or early morning coffee from the balcony while admiring the massive redwood providing the shade, or listen to the classical music that plays softly in the parlor. At breakfast, expect entrees such as eggs Benedict or Belgian waffles as well as freshly baked croissants. Champagne is offered each morning. John is a hobby winemaker (200 cases a year) and Lisa is famous for her award-winning landscaping and flowerbeds. Galleries, shops and restaurants are a stroll away in historic downtown.

Innkeeper(s): John & Lisa Wild-Runnells. $169-269. 3 rooms with PB, 1 with FP and 1 suite. Breakfast included in rates. Types of meals: Full gourmet bkfst, early coffee/tea and snacks/refreshments. Beds: Q. Cable TV, VCR, reading lamp, stereo, clock radio and hot tub/spa in room. Central air. Fax, copier, parlor games, telephone, fireplace, coffeemaker, refrigerator and hot tub on premises. Antiquing, art galleries, bicycling, canoeing/kayaking, fishing, golf, hiking, horseback riding, museums, parks, shopping, tennis and wineries nearby.

Shady Oaks Country Inn

399 Zinfandel Ln
Saint Helena, CA 94574-1635
(707)963-1190 Fax:(707)963-9367
E-mail: shadyoaks@napanet.net
Web: www.shadyoaksinn.com

Circa 1880. This country inn is secluded on two acres among the finest wineries in the Napa Valley. There are two buildings, a 1920s home and a winery. The winery features original stone walls and is now a luxurious guest suite. Rooms boast fine linens, antiques, a private deck or a view of the gardens and vineyards. Wine and cheese are served fireside each evening in the parlor or on the Roman-pillared patio. A gourmet champagne breakfast is the subject of rave reviews by guests and may include eggs Benedict or Belgian waffles.

Innkeeper(s): Lisa Wild-Runnells & John Runnells. $139-249. 5 rooms with PB, 3 with FP and 1 suite. Breakfast included in rates. Types of meals: Full gourmet bkfst and early coffee/tea. Beds: KQ. Modem hook-up, reading lamp, ceiling fan, clock radio and telephone in room. Central air. Fax, copier, parlor games and fireplace on premises. Limited handicap access. Weddings, small meetings, family reunions and seminars hosted. Antiquing, art galleries, bicycling, fishing, golf, hiking, horseback riding, live theater, museums, parks, shopping, tennis and wineries nearby.

"Can't decide which is the most outstanding, the rooms, the breakfast or the sensational hospitality." — Rocky Mountain News

Salinas J5

Barlocker's Rustling Oak Ranch B&B

25252 Limekiln Rd
Salinas, CA 93908
(831)675-9121 Fax:(831)675-2060
E-mail: mbarlocker@yahoo.com
Web: www.rustlingoaksranch.com

Circa 1940. One-hundred-year old oaks shade the grounds of this 16-acre ranch. Guest rooms feature a variety of options, or choose the cottage. It offers knotty pine walls, a kitchen, pellet stove and two bedrooms. There are horseshoe pits, a trampoline and horseback riding opportunities. Nearby are several wineries, the Monterey Bay Aquarium and John Steinbeck's home.

Innkeeper(s): Margaret & Calum Barlocker. $90-150. 5 rooms, 4 with PB and 1 cottage. Breakfast included in rates. Types of meals: Full bkfst and early coffee/tea. Beds: KQT. Reading lamp, ceiling fan and clock radio in room. VCR, fax, copier, swimming, stable, bicycles, library, pet boarding, child care, parlor games, telephone and fireplace on premises. Limited handicap access. Weddings, small meetings and family reunions hosted. Antiquing, golf, parks and shopping nearby.

San Diego Q12

A Victorian Heritage Park Inn

2470 Heritage Park Row
San Diego, CA 92110-2803
(619)299-6832 (800)995-2470 Fax:(619)299-9465
E-mail: innkeeper@heritageparkinn.com
Web: www.heritageparkinn.com

Circa 1889. Situated on a seven-acre Victorian park in the heart of Old Town, this inn is two of seven preserved classic structures. The main house offers a variety of beautifully appointed guest rooms, decked in traditional Victorian furnishings and decor. The opulent Manor Suite includes two bedrooms, a Jacuzzi tub and sitting room. Several rooms offer ocean views, and guest also can see the nightly fireworks show at nearby Sea World. A collection of classic movies is available, and a different movie is shown each night in the inn's parlor. Guests are treated to a light afternoon tea, and breakfast is served on fine china on candlelit tables. The home is within walking distance to the many sites, shops and restaurants in the historic Old Town.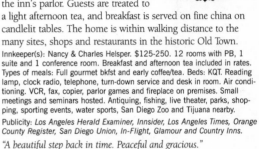

Innkeeper(s): Nancy & Charles Helsper. $125-250. 12 rooms with PB, 1 suite and 1 conference room. Breakfast and afternoon tea included in rates. Types of meals: Full gourmet bkfst and early coffee/tea. Beds: KQT. Reading lamp, clock radio, telephone, turn-down service and desk in room. Air conditioning. VCR, fax, copier, parlor games and fireplace on premises. Small meetings and seminars hosted. Antiquing, fishing, live theater, parks, shopping, sporting events, water sports, San Diego Zoo and Tijuana nearby.

Publicity: *Los Angeles Herald Examiner, Innsider, Los Angeles Times, Orange County Register, San Diego Union, In-Flight, Glamour and Country Inns.*

"A beautiful step back in time. Peaceful and gracious."

Carole's Bed & Breakfast Inn

3227 Grimm Ave
San Diego, CA 92104
(619)280-5258 (800)975-5521

Circa 1904. Relax on the large deck and patio area amidst the many gardens of this delightful Craftsman-style home. Located in North Park, it is just minutes from the city's historic area and tourist attractions. Paneled walls, beamed ceilings and hardwood floors with Oriental carpets create warmth, beauty and period ambiance. The inn offers eight guest bedrooms, two garden studios, a one-bedroom house and a two-bedroom apartment. Before starting on the day's adventures, enjoy a generous continental breakfast that includes items such as homemade muffins, freshly baked bread, fruit in season and hot beverages. The San Diego Zoo, Balboa Park, Scripps Aquamuseum, Mission Bay, Old Town San Diego and The Wild Animal Park are just some of the many nearby excursions.

Innkeeper(s): Carole Dugdale/Michael O'Brien. $89-189. 8 rooms, 3 with PB and 1 cottage. Breakfast included in rates. Types of meals: Cont plus, veg bkfst and early coffee/tea. Beds: KQ. Cable TV, reading lamp, refrigerator, ceiling fan, clock radio, telephone, coffeemaker and desk in room. Pool, A/C and there is a one-bedroom house and a two-bedroom apartment on premises. Family reunions hosted. Antiquing, art galleries, beach, bicycling, golf, hiking, museums, parks, shopping and tennis nearby.

San Francisco   H4

Andrews Hotel

624 Post St
San Francisco, CA 94109-8222
(415)563-6877 (800)926-3739 Fax:(415)928-6919

Circa 1906. This historic hotel originally was constructed in
1905 as a Turkish bath. After being damaged by earthquake,
the Andrews was rebuilt in 1906 and transformed into a hotel.
Today it offers 48 guest rooms; each decorated in a pleasant,
modern style. High ceilings and bay windows are a reminder of
the hotel's turn-of-the-century construction. In the mornings,
guests will find continental breakfast fare just outside their
door. In the afternoons, a complimentary glass of wine is available to guests at the hotel's restaurant and bar, Fino. The
Andrews Hotel is located two blocks west of Union Square.

Innkeeper(s): Barbara, Brando. $105-175. 48 rooms with PB and 5 suites.
Breakfast included in rates. Types of meals: Cont, early coffee/tea, afternoon
tea, gourmet dinner and room service. Restaurant on premises. Beds: KQDT.
Cable TV, VCR, reading lamp, clock radio, telephone, desk, all rooms with
ceiling fans, 10 rooms with refrigerators and wireless high-speed Internet
access for a special rate in room. TV, fax, copier, child care, restaurant and
bar and video library on premises. Weddings hosted. Antiquing, golf, live theater, parks, sporting events and tennis nearby.

Archbishop's Mansion

1000 Fulton St (at Steiner)
San Francisco, CA 94117-1608
(415)563-7872 (800)543-5820 Fax:(415)885-3193

Circa 1904. This French Empire-style manor was built for the
Archbishop of San Francisco. It is designated as a San Francisco
historic landmark. The grand stairway features redwood paneling, Corinthian columns and a stained-glass dome. The parlor
has a hand-painted ceiling. Each of the guest rooms is named
for an opera. Rooms have antiques, Victorian window treatments and embroidered linens. Continental breakfast is served
in the dining room, and guests also are treated to a complimentary wine and cheese reception each night.

Innkeeper(s): Greg Horner. $165-425. 15 rooms with PB, 11 with FP and 5
suites. Breakfast included in rates. Types of meals: Cont. Beds: KQ. Cable TV,
VCR, reading lamp, clock radio, telephone, turn-down service, desk and hot
tub/spa in room. Fax, copier and fireplace on premises. Weddings and small
meetings hosted. Parks nearby.

Publicity: *Travel-Holiday, Travel & Leisure and Country Inns.*

"The ultimate, romantic honeymoon spot."

The Chateau Tivoli

1057 Steiner St
San Francisco, CA 94115-4620
(415)776-5462 (800)228-1647 Fax:(415)776-0505
E-mail: mail@chateautivoli.com
Web: www.chateautivoli.com

Circa 1892. Built for lumber magnate Daniel Jackson, this
10,000-square-foot mansion is painted in 22 colors with highlights of glimmering gold leaf accentuating its turrets and towers. It has been named "The Greatest Painted Lady in the
World" by Elizabeth Pomada and Michael Larson, authors of
the Painted Ladies series. Antiques and art from the estates of
Cornelius Vanderbilt, Charles de Gaulle and J. Paul Getty are
featured throughout. Canopy beds, marble baths, fireplaces and
balconies recall San Francisco's Golden Age of Opulence.

Chateau Tivoli holds the California Heritage Council's 1989
award for best restoration of a Victorian house in California.
During the week, guests are served continental-plus fare. On
weekends, a champagne brunch is served. Complimentary
wine and cheese is offered in the evening. All rooms offer data
ports with computer-dedicated lines for guests.

Innkeeper(s): Geraldine & Stephen Shohet. $99-265. 9 rooms, 7 with PB, 2
with FP. Breakfast included in rates. Types of meals: Cont plus and
snacks/refreshments. Beds: KQD. Data port in room. TV, fax, copier, telephone and e-mail access on premises. Victoriana and jazz nearby.

Publicity: *Bay City Guide, Elle Decor, Northern California Jewish Bulletin
and Country Inns.*

*"The romance and charm has made Chateau Tivoli the place to stay
whenever we are in San Francisco."*

Edward II Inn & Suites

3155 Scott St
San Francisco, CA 94123-3311
(415)922-3000 (800)GRE-ATINN Fax:(415)931-5784
E-mail: innkeeper@edwardii.com
Web: www.edwardii.com

Circa 1914. Only blocks away from the yacht harbor, this
three-story European-style inn was originally built for the 1915
World's Fair. Film enthusiasts may recognize this hotel from
the movie "Beaches." Recently renovated and tastefully decorated, the inn offers a wonderful experience for the business traveler or vacationer. Spacious guest bedrooms and suites feature a
variety of amenities to choose from. Most of the romantic
suites boast fireplaces and Jacuzzi tubs. Some also include
refrigerators or kitchens. Start the day with fresh-baked goods,
juice and gourmet coffee before embarking to exciting city sites.

Innkeeper(s): Bob and Denise Holland. $82-235. 32 rooms, 14 with PB, 7
with FP, 7 suites, 1 cottage and 1 conference room. Breakfast included in
rates. Types of meals: Cont plus. Beds: QDT. Modem hook-up, cable TV, VCR,
reading lamp, refrigerator, ceiling fan, clock radio, telephone, coffeemaker,
desk, hot tub/spa and fireplace in room. Fax, copier, parlor games, fireplace
and gift shop on premises. Weddings and family reunions hosted. Antiquing,
art galleries, beach, bicycling, canoeing/kayaking, fishing, golf, live theater,
museums, parks, shopping, sporting events, water sports and wineries nearby.

Publicity: *Romantic Valentine pick for San Francisco's "Evening Magazine,"
Sunset Magazine, Beaches and Voted top 3 "Best Romantic Hotel" in best
of city search 2002 Bay Area.*

Golden Gate Hotel

775 Bush St
San Francisco, CA 94108-3402
(415)392-3702 (800)835-1118 Fax:(415)392-6202
E-mail: info@goldengatehotel.com
Web: www.goldengatehotel.com

Circa 1913. News travels far when there's a bargain. Half of
the guests visiting this four-story Edwardian hotel at the foot of
Nob Hill are from abroad. Great bay windows on each floor
provide many of the rooms with gracious
spaces at humble prices. An original bird
cage elevator kept in working order floats
between floors. Antiques, fresh flowers,
and afternoon tea further add to the
atmosphere. Union Square is two-and-a-
half blocks from the hotel.

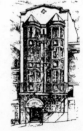

Innkeeper(s): John & Renate Kenaston. $85-130.
25 rooms, 14 with PB. Breakfast and afternoon tea
included in rates. Types of meals: Cont. Beds: QDT.
Cable TV, reading lamp, clock radio, telephone and
wireless DSL Internet access in room. TV, fax and

fireplace on premises. Antiquing, live theater and restaurants nearby.

Publicity: *Toronto Globe & Mail, Los Angeles Times, Melbourne Sun (Australia) and Sunday Oregonian.*

"Stayed here by chance, will return by choice!"

Grove Inn

890 Grove St
San Francisco, CA 94117-1712
(415)929-0780 (800)829-0780 Fax:(415)929-1037
E-mail: grovinn@jps.net
Web: www.grovinn.com

Circa 1885. Part of the historic Alamo Square area, a hilltop park with spectacular panoramic views, this restored Italianate-Victorian was built in the 1800s. Proprietors Rosetta and Klaus have been actively involved in historic preservation since 1970. The inn is conveniently located near the Civic Center, close to bus lines and taxis. Quiet and comfortable guest bedrooms boast fluffy feather beds, high ceilings, double-paned windows and modern amenities. Enjoy a continental breakfast before exploring the city's limitless sites and attractions. Walk to the top of Telegraph Hill to the 210-foot-tall Coit Tower for a stunning sight of the the bridge, bay and Alcatraz island.

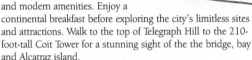

Historic Interest: Inn built in 1861 as a family home.

Innkeeper(s): Klaus & Rosetta Zimmermann. $75-110. 19 rooms, 14 with PB, 2 with FP, 1 suite and 1 conference room. Breakfast included in rates. Types of meals: Cont. Beds: QDT. Modem hook-up, TV, clock radio, telephone, desk and refrigerator in some rooms in room. Fax and copier on premises. Antiquing, art galleries, beach, bicycling, golf, live theater, museums, parks, shopping and tennis nearby.

Publicity: *NBC Los Angeles and Merian (German magazine).*

Hotel Drisco

2901 Pacific Avenue
San Francisco, CA 94115
(415)346-2880 (800)634-7277 Fax:(415)567-5537

Circa 1903. Built as a luxury hotel in the prestigious Pacific Heights residential district in 1903, many notables, from presidents to authors to musicians, have stayed here. The Edwardian building has been renovated and redesigned boasting a luxurious English-European decor. Elegant suites and guest bedrooms feature upscale amenities to enhance business or relaxation. Plush robes, city and bay views, two-line speakerphones with data port, CD players, personalized voicemail, VCRs, daily newspapers and turndown service offer comfort and convenience. A continental breakfast includes yogurt, cereals, bagels, muffins, pastries, and beverages. Morning towncar services are available during weekdays. Work out in the Fitness Room.

Historic Interest: Built in 1903 as a hotel by Frank Drisco.

Innkeeper(s): Gerard Lespinette. $245-425. 48 rooms with PB, 19 suites and 1 conference room. Breakfast and afternoon tea included in rates. Types of meals: Cont plus and early coffee/tea. Beds: KT. Data port, cable TV, VCR, CD player, refrigerator, snack bar, clock radio, telephone, coffeemaker, turndown service, desk and voice mail in room. Fax, copier and parlor games on premises. Limited handicap access. Weddings, small meetings, family reunions and seminars hosted. Amusement parks, antiquing, art galleries, beach, bicycling, golf, hiking, horseback riding, live theater, museums, parks, shopping, tennis and wineries nearby.

Publicity: *The Best Places to Kiss, American Way, Travel Holiday and Celebrated Living.*

The Inn San Francisco

943 South Van Ness Ave
San Francisco, CA 94110-2613
(415)641-0188 (800)359-0913 Fax:(415)641-1701
E-mail: innkeeper@innsf.com
Web: www.innsf.com

Circa 1872. Built on one of San Francisco's earliest "Mansion Rows," this 21-room Italianate Victorian is located near the civic and convention centers, close to Mission Dolores. Antiques, marble fireplaces and Oriental rugs decorate the opulent grand double parlors. Most rooms have feather beds, Victorian wallcoverings and desks, while deluxe rooms offer private spas, fireplaces or bay windows. There is a rooftop deck with a 360-degree view of San Francisco. Complimentary beverages are always available. The inn is close to the opera, symphony, theaters, Mission Dolores, gift and jewelry centers and antique shopping.

Innkeeper(s): Marty Neely & Connie Wu. $95-265. 21 rooms, 19 with PB, 3 with FP, 3 suites and 1 cottage. Breakfast included in rates. Types of meals: Full bkfst and afternoon tea. Beds: QD. TV, reading lamp, refrigerator, clock radio, telephone, desk, hot tub/spa, one suite with redwood hot tub, flowers and truffles in room. Fax, fireplace, garden, rooftop view sundeck and parlor on premises.

Publicity: *Innsider, Sunset Magazine, San Francisco Chronicle and American Airlines Magazine.*

"Breakfast; marvelous. The best B&B we've visited. We were made to feel like family."

The No Name Victorian B&B

847 Fillmore St
San Francisco, CA 94117-1703
(415)899-0060 Fax:(415)899-9923
E-mail: reservations@bbsf.com
Web: bbsf.com/InnDB/Content_n/showInn_n.asp?InnId=2&region=0

Circa 1890. Located in the historic district of Alamo Square, this Victorian sits close to the Civic Center, Opera House, Davies Symphony Hall and Union Square. An 1830s wedding bed from mainland China adorns the honeymoon room. The other rooms are tastefully decorated in antiques and antique reproductions. There's a family accommodation with a private entrance, full kitchen and a crib.

Innkeeper(s): Richard & Susan Kreibich. $79-145. 5 rooms, 3 with PB, 4 with FP and 1 suite. Breakfast included in rates. Types of meals: Full bkfst and early coffee/tea. Beds: QT. Reading lamp in room. Spa, parlor games, telephone and fireplace on premises. Weddings and family reunions hosted. Live theater, parks, shopping, sporting events, opera, symphony and ballet nearby.

Petite Auberge

863 Bush St
San Francisco, CA 94108-3312
(415)928-6000 (800)365-3004 Fax:(415)775-5717
E-mail: petiteauberge@jdvhospitality.com
Web: www.jdvhospitality.com

Circa 1917. An ornate baroque design with curved bay windows highlight this five-story hotel that has now been transformed into a French country inn. This Joie de Vivre property boasts antiques, fresh flowers and country accessories. Most guest bedrooms feature working fireplaces. Take a short walk to

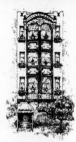

the Powell Street cable car. In the evenings, wine and cheese are served. There is an extra fee for an additional guest in room, except for children less than five years old.

Innkeeper(s): Lou Rosenberger. $139-239. 26 rooms with PB, 17 with FP and 1 suite. Breakfast and afternoon tea included in rates. Types of meals: Full gourmet bkfst and early coffee/tea. Beds: KQ. Refrigerator, telephone, turn-down service and terry robes in room. TV, fax, copier, fireplace and valet parking on premises. Limited handicap access. Antiquing, live theater, parks, shopping, sporting events, historic sites, museums and cable nearby.

Publicity: *Travel & Leisure, Oregonian, Los Angeles Times and Brides.*

"Breakfast was great, and even better in bed!"

Stanyan Park Hotel

750 Stanyan St
San Francisco, CA 94117-2725
(415)751-1000 Fax:(415)668-5454

Circa 1904. In the National Register of Historic Places, many of the guest rooms of this restored Victorian inn overlook Golden Gate Park. Rooms are decorated in period decor and the turret suites and bay suites are good choices for special occasions or for longer stays. All the suites include kitchens, dining rooms and parlors. Guests enjoy an expanded continental breakfast and evening tea service. Museums, horseback riding and biking are available in the park, as well as the Japanese Tea Garden.

Innkeeper(s): John Brocklehurst. $130-325. 36 rooms, 30 with PB and 6 suites. Types of meals: Cont plus. Beds: QT. Cable TV, reading lamp, clock radio, telephone, desk and suites have kitchens in room. TV, fax, copier and bicycles on premises. Limited handicap access. Live theater, parks, shopping and sporting events nearby.

Publicity: *Metropolitan Home, New York Times and Sunset Magazine.*

San Luis Obispo   M7

Garden Street Inn

1212 Garden St
San Luis Obispo, CA 93401-3962
(805)545-9802 (800)488-2045 Fax:(805)545-9403
E-mail: innkeeper@gardenstreetinn.com
Web: www.gardenstreetinn.com

Circa 1887. Enjoy scenic Edna Valley Wine Country while staying at this restored 1887 Italianate Queen Anne home that reflects a classic Victorian décor. Relax with a book in the Goldtree Library or sit outside on spacious decks. Gather for evening wine and cheese at the daily Innkeeper Reception. Well-appointed guest bedrooms and suites offer a variety of pleasing amenities that may include a fireplace, clawfoot tub, Jacuzzi, sitting room and private deck. Savor a complete breakfast in the McCaffrey Morning Room accented by original stained-glass windows. Downtown is just one block away; visit the historic 1772 Mission. Experience an excursion to the sand dunes of Pismo Beach or tour the opulent and remarkable Hearst Castle.

Innkeeper(s): Sharyn McCoy. $140-200. 13 rooms with PB, 5 with FP and 4 suites. Breakfast included in rates. Types of meals: Full gourmet bkfst, veg bkfst and early coffee/tea. Beds: KQ. Cable TV, reading lamp, CD player, clock radio, telephone, desk, hot tub/spa and televisions and hot tubs CD players in suites in room. Air conditioning. Fax, copier, spa, library, parlor games, fireplace, gourmet wines and hors d'oeuvres on premises. Limited handicap access. Weddings, small meetings and seminars hosted. Antiquing, art galleries, beach, bicycling, canoeing/kayaking, fishing, golf, hiking, horseback riding, live theater, museums, parks, shopping, sporting events, water sports and wineries nearby.

Publicity: *Times-Press-Recorder, Telegram-Tribune, San Francisco Chronicle, Los Angeles Times, Orange County Register and Los Angeles Daily News.*

"We appreciate your warmth and care."

San Rafael   H4

Casa Soldavini

531 C St
San Rafael, CA 94901-3809
(415)454-3140 Fax:(415)454-3140

Circa 1932. The first Italian settlers in San Rafael built this home. Their grandchildren now own it and proudly hang pictures of their family. Grandfather Joseph, a wine maker, planned and planted what are now the lush gardens surrounding the home. The many Italian antiques throughout the house complement the Italian-style decor. A homemade breakfast is included, and snacks and beverages are served throughout the day.

Innkeeper(s): Linda Soldavini Cassidy. $95-135. 3 rooms, 1 with PB. Breakfast included in rates. Types of meals: Cont plus, afternoon tea and snacks/refreshments. Beds: Q. Cable TV, VCR, CD player, ceiling fan, snack bar, clock radio, telephone, coffeemaker, turn-down service and voice mail in room. Fax, copier, bicycles, pet boarding, parlor games and fireplace on premises. Amusement parks, antiquing, art galleries, beach, bicycling, canoeing/kayaking, fishing, golf, hiking, horseback riding, live theater, museums, parks, shopping, sporting events, tennis, water sports and wineries nearby.

Santa Barbara   N8

Bath Street Inn

1720 Bath St
Santa Barbara, CA 93101-2910
(805)682-9680 (800)341-2284 Fax:(805)569-1281
E-mail: bathstin@silcom.com
Web: www.bathstreetinn.com

Circa 1890. Arriving at this three-story Queen Anne Victorian home, the front porch beckons and the warm hospitality that has become a tradition at this inn quickly begins. Inside, comfortable chairs and a roaring fire require closer inspection while partaking of evening wine and cheese. Spacious guest bedrooms in the renovated main house feature unique architectural details and pampering amenities including fresh flowers. The Balcony Room under the eaves boasts a view from the historic "eyelid" balcony. The Partridge Room features a clawfoot tub and hardwood floors and overlooks the Santa Ynez Mountains. Other rooms offer sitting areas, double Jacuzzis and fireplaces; some are located in the newer yet compatible Summer House. Linger over a gourmet breakfast in the formal dining room. Enjoy afternoon tea in the back garden, surrounded by wisteria and blossoming orange trees.

Innkeeper(s): Marie Christensen. $90-240. 12 rooms with PB, 4 with FP and 1 suite. Breakfast, afternoon tea and snacks/refreshments included in rates. Types of meals: Full bkfst and early coffee/tea. Beds: KQT. Cable TV, reading lamp, refrigerator, clock radio, telephone and hot tub/spa in room. Air conditioning. Fax, copier and fireplace on premises. Limited handicap access. Antiquing, fishing, live theater, parks, shopping, sporting events, water sports and wineries nearby.

Publicity: *Los Angeles Times, Sunset and Elmer Dills.*

"Like going to the home of a favorite aunt." — Country Inns

Bayberry Inn

111 West Valerio Street
Santa Barbara, CA 93101
(805)569-3398 Fax:(805)569-1120
E-mail: info@bayberry.sbcoxmail.com
Web: www.bayberryinnsantabarbara.com

Circa 1894. Designated an historic Structure of Merit by the city, this Federal-style home graces a quiet residential neighborhood within walking distance to downtown. Well-appointed guest bedrooms feature a Victorian decor accented by elegant queen-size canopy beds and fresh flowers. Some include an antique clawfoot tub, fireplace or private entrance. A leisurely gourmet breakfast is served on the garden deck. Play a game of English croquet before afternoon wine and cheese. Chairs and towels are provided for beach excursions. Every evening a homemade dessert is offered. An assortment of beverages are always available. Make a reservation for an in-room massage or local day spa services.

Innkeeper(s): Jill & Kenneth Freeland. $109-229. 9 rooms with PB, 4 with FP. Breakfast and afternoon tea included in rates. Types of meals: Full gourmet bkfst, early coffee/tea, snacks/refreshments and room service. Beds: KQ. Cable TV, reading lamp, CD player, ceiling fan, clock radio and some with private decks in room. Fax, copier, library, parlor games, telephone, fireplace and afternoon wine and cheese on premises. Weddings, small meetings, family reunions and seminars hosted. Antiquing, art galleries, beach, bicycling, canoeing/kayaking, fishing, golf, hiking, horseback riding, live theater, museums, parks, shopping, sporting events, tennis, water sports and wineries nearby.

Publicity: *Santa Barbara News-Press, Pacific Coast Business Times and Santa Barbara Independent.*

Cheshire Cat Inn & Spa

36 W Valerio St
Santa Barbara, CA 93101-2524
(805)569-1610 Fax:(805)682-1876
E-mail: cheshire@cheshirecat.com
Web: www.cheshirecat.com

Circa 1894. This elegant inn features three Queen Anne Victorians, a Coach House and three cottages surrounded by fountains, gazebos and lush flower gardens. The guest bedrooms and suites are furnished with English antiques, Laura Ashley fabrics and wallpapers or oak floors, pine furniture and down comforters. Some boast fireplaces, Jacuzzi tubs, private balconies, VCRs and refrigerators. Wedgewood china set in the formal dining room or brick patio enhances a delicious breakfast. Local wine and hors d'oeuvres are served in the evening. Spa facilities offer massage and body treatments.

Historic Interest: Santa Barbara Beautiful Award.
Innkeeper(s): Christine Dunstan. $160-400. 21 rooms with PB, 7 suites and 1 conference room. Breakfast included in rates. Types of meals: Full bkfst and room service. Beds: KQT. Cable TV, reading lamp, refrigerator, ceiling fan, telephone and hot tub/spa in room. Fireplace and spa facilities on premises. Small meetings, family reunions and seminars hosted. Amusement parks, antiquing, fishing, live theater, shopping, sporting events and water sports nearby.

Publicity: *Two on the Town, KABC, Los Angeles Times, Santa Barbara, American In Flight and Elmer Dills Recommends.*

"Romantic and quaint."

Glenborough Inn

1327 Bath St
Santa Barbara, CA 93101-3630
(805)966-0589 (800)962-0589 Fax:(805)564-8610
E-mail: info@glenborough.com
Web: www.glenboroughinn.com

Circa 1885. The Victorian and California Craftsman-style homes that comprise the Glenborough are located in the theatre and arts district. Antiques, rich wood trim and elegant fireplace suites with canopy beds are offered. Some rooms also have mini refrigerators or whirlpools tubs. There's always plenty of hospitality and an invitation to try the secluded garden hot tub. Homemade breakfasts, served in the privacy of your room, have been written up in Bon Appetit and Chocolatier. Bedtime cookies and beverages are served, as well. It's a three-block walk to restaurants, shops and the shuttle to the beach.

Historic Interest: Walking distance to historic downtown Santa Barbara, Mission Santa Barbara (1 1/4 mile).
Innkeeper(s): Marlies Marburg. $110-325. 18 rooms with PB, 12 with FP and 6 cottages. Breakfast included in rates. Types of meals: Full bkfst. Beds: KQD. TV, reading lamp, ceiling fan, clock radio, telephone, desk, hot tub/spa, coffeemaker, robes and some with A/C and mini-fridge in room. Fax, spa, parlor games and fireplace on premises. Antiquing, fishing, live theater, parks, shopping, sporting events and water sports nearby.

Publicity: *Houston Post, Los Angeles Times and Pasadena Choice.*

"Only gracious service is offered at the Glenborough Inn."

The Old Yacht Club Inn

431 Corona Del Mar
Santa Barbara, CA 93103-3601
(805)962-1277 (800)676-1676 Fax:(805)962-3989

Circa 1912. One block from famous East Beach, this California Craftsman house was the home of the Santa Barbara Yacht Club during the Roaring '20s. It was opened as Santa Barbara's first B&B and has become renowned for its gourmet food and superb hospitality.

Innkeeper(s): Eilene Bruce. $110-220. 12 rooms with PB and 1 conference room. Breakfast included in rates. Types of meals: Full gourmet bkfst, early coffee/tea and gourmet dinner. Beds: KQ. TV, reading lamp, telephone and hot tub/spa in room. Fax, copier, bicycles, fireplace, wine social, beach chairs and beach towels on premises. Small meetings and seminars hosted. Antiquing, fishing, live theater, shopping, sporting events and water sports nearby.

Publicity: *Los Angeles, Valley, Bon Appetit and Gourmet.*

"One of Santa Barbara's better-kept culinary secrets."

Prufrock's Garden Inn By The Beach

600 Linden Ave
Santa Barbara, CA 93101
(805)566-9696 (877)837-6257 Fax:(805)566-9404
E-mail: innkeepers@prufrocks.com
Web: www.prufrocks.com

Circa 1904. Tucked between a mountain wilderness, flower fields and an ocean, this inn is located one block from State Beach Park and 10 minutes from the City Center. Santa Barbara Independent named it a "Most Romantic Getaway," and the LA. Times voted it a "Readers' Favorite." Other recognitions include being pictured in Land's End catalog and a "Community Beautiful" award. Explore Salt Marsh Park and waterfront bluffs, or visit specialty shops and cafes. The inn is close to an Amtrak station. A quote from The Love Song of J. Alfred Prufrock, by TS Eliot is lived out at this inn: "Time for you and time for me, before the taking of a toast and tea."

Historic Interest: The Old Mission and historic county courthouse are about 12 minutes away in Santa Barbara. Other nearby historic attractions include adobes and a state historic park.

Innkeeper(s): Judy & Jim Halvorsen. $119-249. 7 rooms, 5 with PB. Breakfast, afternoon tea and snacks/refreshments included in rates. Types of meals: Full bkfst and early coffee/tea. Beds: Q. Reading lamp, turn-down service, sitting area and daybeds in room. VCR, bicycles and gardens on premises. Small meetings, family reunions and seminars hosted. Antiquing, beach, bicycling, fishing, hiking, live theater, parks, shopping, sporting events, wineries and tide pools nearby.

Publicity: *Santa Barbara Independent's "Most Romantic Getaway," Carpinteria's "Community Beautification" award, pictured in Land's End catalog and LA Times "Reader's favorite."*

Simpson House Inn

121 E Arrellaga
Santa Barbara, CA 93101
(805)963-7067 (800)676-1280 Fax:(805)564-4811
E-mail: reservations@simpsonhouseinn.com
Web: www.simpsonhouseinn.com

Circa 1874. The Simpson House is currently the only bed and breakfast in North America holding a Five Diamond award from AAA. If you were one of the Simpson family's first visitors, you would have arrived in Santa Barbara by stagecoach or by ship. The railroad was not completed for another 14 years. A stately Italianate Victorian house, the inn, a historic landmark, is situated on an acre of English gardens hidden behind a 20-foot-tall eugenia hedge. In the evenings, guests are treated to a sampling of local wines, as well as a lavish Mediterranean hors d'oeuvre buffet. The evening turndown service includes delectable chocolate truffles. The innkeepers can arrange for in-room European spa treatments, and guests can workout at a nearby private health club. Guests also receive complimentary passes for the Santa Barbara trolley.

Historic Interest: The Inn and gardens have been named one of California's best examples of Victorian Italianate style. The main house and old Barn have been authentically restored, decorated and preserved.

Innkeeper(s): Dixie Adair Budke Ph.D. $215-600. 15 rooms with PB, 11 with FP, 4 suites and 4 cottages. Breakfast, afternoon tea and snacks/refreshments included in rates. Types of meals: Full gourmet bkfst, veg bkfst, early coffee/tea and room service. Restaurant on premises. Beds: KQT. Data port, cable TV, VCR, reading lamp, stereo, refrigerator, snack bar, clock radio, telephone, coffeemaker, turn-down service, desk, hot tub/spa, voice mail and fireplace in room. Air conditioning. Fax, copier, bicycles, library, parlor games, fireplace, gift shop, croquet and spa services on premises. Limited handicap access. Weddings, small meetings, family reunions and seminars hosted. Antiquing, art galleries, beach, bicycling, canoeing/kayaking, fishing, golf, hiking, horseback riding, live theater, museums, parks, shopping, sporting events, tennis, water sports, wineries and Historic downtown Santa Barbara nearby.

Publicity: *Country Inns, Santa Barbara, LA Magazine, Avenues, Sunset, San Diego Magazine, USA Today, Los Angles Times, Travel & Leisure, Gourmet, Bon Appetit, Chicago Tribune, Philadelphia Inquirer and NY Times.*

"Perfectly restored and impeccably furnished. Your hospitality is warm and heartfelt and the food is delectable. Whoever said that 'the journey is better than the destination' couldn't have known about the Simpson House."

Tiffany Country House

1323 De La Vina St
Santa Barbara, CA 93101-3120
(805)963-2283 (800)999-5672
E-mail: upham.hotel@verizon.net
Web: www.tiffanycountryhouse.com

Circa 1898. This Victorian house features a steep front gable and balcony accentuating the entrance. Colonial diamond-paned bay windows and a front veranda welcome guests to an antique-filled inn. The Windsor room is a favorite with its secluded garden entrance, garden window seat, Jacuzzi tub and fireplace. The Penthouse occupies the entire third floor and includes a living room with a fireplace, a terrace offering mountain views and a Jacuzzi tub. Other rooms are just as interesting, with antique furniture, cozy atmosphere and comfortable beds. Fine restaurants and shops are within walking distance.

Innkeeper(s): Jan Martin Winn. $165-350. 7 rooms with PB, 5 with FP. Types of meals: Full bkfst. Beds: KQ. Telephone and Jacuzzi tub (five rooms) in room.

"We have stayed at a number of B&Bs, but this is the best. We especially liked the wonderful breakfasts on the porch overlooking the garden."

The Upham Hotel & Country House

1404 De La Vina St
Santa Barbara, CA 93101-3027
(805)962-0058 (800)727-0876 Fax:(805)963-2825
E-mail: upham.hotel@verizon.net
Web: www.uphamhotel.com

Circa 1871. Antiques and period furnishings decorate each of the inn's guest rooms and suites. The inn is the oldest continuously operating hostelry in Southern California. Situated on an  acre of gardens in the center of downtown, it's within easy walking distance of restaurants, shops, art galleries and museums. The staff is happy to assist guests in discovering Santa Barbara's varied attractions. Garden cottage units feature porches or secluded patios and several have gas fireplaces.

Innkeeper(s): Jan Martin Winn. $165-400. 50 rooms with PB, 8 with FP, 4 suites, 3 cottages and 3 conference rooms. Breakfast included in rates. Types of meals: Cont plus, early coffee/tea and snacks/refreshments. Beds: KQ. Cable TV, reading lamp, ceiling fan, clock radio, telephone, desk and master suite has hot tub/spa in room. Fax, copier and fireplace on premises. Small meetings, family reunions and seminars hosted. Antiquing, golf, live theater, parks, shopping and water sports nearby.

Publicity: *Los Angeles Times, Santa Barbara, Westways, Santa Barbara News-Press and Avenues.*

"Your hotel is truly a charm. Between the cozy gardens and the exquisitely comfortable appointments, The Upham is charm itself."

Santa Cruz J5

The Adobe on Green Street B&B

103 Green Street
Santa Cruz, CA 95060
(831)469-9866 (888)878-2789 Fax:(831)469-9493
E-mail: info@adobeongreen.com
Web: www.adobeongreen.com

Circa 1949. It is an easy walk to local attractions from this authentic adobe brick bed & breakfast situated in an impressive historic neighborhood. Awarded as an Environmentally Friendly Inn, this peaceful garden retreat is furnished in Mission style with antiques and international art. A gorgeous sitting room offers tea service and a video library for in-room viewing. Spacious guest bedrooms, some with private entrances and patios include cable TV and a VCR. Choose The Courtyard Room or The Ohlone which feature Whirlpool tubs and fireplaces. A generous gourmet breakfast is served daily and special dietary needs are considered. Relax in the steam room or arrange for an aromatherapy massage. Ask about special romantic packages offered.

Historic Interest: Adobe Revival.

Innkeeper(s): Judith Hutchinson & Arnold Leff. $105-225. 4 rooms with PB, 2 with FP. Breakfast included in rates. Types of meals: Full gourmet bkfst, veg bkfst, early coffee/tea, snacks/refreshments and room service. Beds: Q. Data port, cable TV, VCR, reading lamp, CD player, ceiling fan, clock radio, telephone and desk in room. Fax, copier, bicycles and parlor games on premises.

Babbling Brook B&B Inn

1025 Laurel St
Santa Cruz, CA 95060-4237
(831)427-2437 (800)866-1131 Fax:(831)427-2457
Web: www.babblingbrookinn.com

Circa 1909. This inn was built on the foundations of an 1870 tannery and a 1790 grist mill. Secluded, yet within the city, the inn features a cascading waterfall, historic waterwheel and meandering creek on one acre of gardens and redwoods.

Country French decor, cozy fireplaces, and deep-soaking whirlpool tubs are luxurious amenities of the Babbling Brook. In the evenings, complimentary wine and cheese are served.

$165-270. 13 rooms with PB, 13 with FP and 1 conference room. Breakfast and snacks/refreshments included in rates. Types of meals: Full bkfst and early coffee/tea. Beds: KQT. Cable TV, reading lamp, clock radio, telephone, desk and hot tub/spa in room. TV, fax, parlor games and fireplace on premises. Limited handicap access. Weddings hosted. Amusement parks, antiquing, fishing, golf, live theater, parks, shopping, sporting events, water sports and wineries nearby.

Publicity: *Country Inns, Yellow Brick Road, Times-Press-Recorder, Reno Air Magazine and Romantic Homes Magazine.*

"We were impressed with the genuine warmth of the inn. The best breakfast we've had outside our own home!"

Chateau Victorian

118 1st St
Santa Cruz, CA 95060-5402
(831)458-9458

Circa 1885. This Victorian is within a block of the waterfront and offers seven guest rooms. The romantic Bay Side Room is a favorite of guests, as it offers a marble fireplace and a clawfoot

tub with an overhead shower. Breakfasts, including a variety of tempting fruits and pastries, can be enjoyed on the patio, dining room or on the secluded side deck. After a day of exploring Santa Cruz and its surroundings, evening refreshments are a perfect touch. The inn

is within walking distance to downtown, the wharf, a variety of restaurants, the Boardwalk Amusement Park and the beach.

Innkeeper(s): Alice June. $125-155. 7 rooms with PB, 7 with FP. Breakfast included in rates. Types of meals: Cont plus. Beds: Q. Telephone and fireplace on premises. Small meetings hosted. Amusement parks, antiquing, fishing, live theater, shopping and water sports nearby.

Publicity: *Times Tribune, Santa Cruz Sentinel and Good Times.*

"Certainly enjoyed our most recent stay and have appreciated all of our visits."

Cliff Crest Bed & Breakfast Inn

407 Cliff St
Santa Cruz, CA 95060-5009
(831)427-2609 (831)252-1057 Fax:(831)427-2710

Circa 1887. Warmth, friendliness and comfort characterize this elegantly restored Queen Anne Victorian home. An octagonal solarium, tall stained-glass windows, and a belvedere overlook Monterey Bay and the Santa Cruz

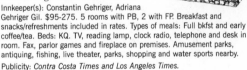

Mountains. The mood is airy and romantic. The spacious gardens were designed by John McLaren, landscape architect for Golden Gate Park. Antiques and fresh flowers fill the rooms, once home to William Jeter, lieutenant governor of California.

Innkeeper(s): Constantin Gehriger, Adriana Gehriger Gil. $95-275. 5 rooms with PB, 2 with FP. Breakfast and snacks/refreshments included in rates. Types of meals: Full bkfst and early coffee/tea. Beds: KQ. TV, reading lamp, clock radio, telephone and desk in room. Fax, parlor games and fireplace on premises. Amusement parks, antiquing, fishing, live theater, parks, shopping and water sports nearby.

Publicity: *Contra Costa Times and Los Angeles Times.*

"Delightful place, excellent food and comfortable bed."

Compassion Flower Inn

216 Laurel Street
Santa Cruz, CA 95060
(831)466-0420 Fax:(831)466-0431
E-mail: reservations@compassionflowerinn.com
Web: www.compassionflowerinn.com

Circa 1865. Shoes are left at the door of this lovingly restored Gothic Revival Victorian. Period furnishings of mahogany and oak reside well with artistic mosaics, stencils and faux and marbelized finishes. Several common rooms provide delightful opportunities to relax. Themed guest bedrooms include the romantic Lover's Suite boasting a sunken tub. Enjoy an organic breakfast that may feature fresh-baked muffins and an herb asparagus omelette. Gather on the garden patio and deck, or soak in the Jacuzzi. The convenient downtown location ensures a short walk to the beach and famous boardwalk.

Innkeeper(s): Andrea Tischler & Maria Mallek. $115-175. 4 rooms, 2 with PB, 2 with FP and 1 suite. Breakfast and veg bkfst included in rates. Types of meals: Full gourmet bkfst and veg bkfst. Beds: D. Reading lamp, telephone and fireplace in room. Fax, copier, spa, library, parlor games and fireplace on premises. Weddings, small meetings, family reunions and seminars hosted. Amusement parks, antiquing, art galleries, beach, bicycling, canoeing/kayaking, fishing, golf, hiking, museums, parks, shopping, tennis, water sports and wineries nearby.

Publicity: *Boston Globe, People Magazine, New York Times, CNN, San Francisco and San Jose TV stations, 60 Minutes and French TV.*

Santa Monica   O10

Channel Road Inn

219 W Channel Rd
Santa Monica, CA 90402-1105
(310)459-1920 Fax:(310)454-9920
E-mail: info@channelroadinn.com
Web: www.channelroadinn.com

Circa 1910. This shingle-clad building is a variation of the Colonial Revival Period, one of the few remaining in Los Angeles. The abandoned home was saved from the city's wrecking crew by owner Susan Zolla, with the encouragement of the local historical society. The rooms feature canopy beds, fine linens, custom mattresses and private porches. Chile Cheese Puffs served with salsa are a popular breakfast speciality. The Pacific Ocean is one block away, and guests often enjoy borrowing the inn's bicycles to pedal along the 30-mile coastal bike path. In the evening, the inn's spectacular cliffside spa is popular.

Innkeeper(s): Christine Marwell. $165-350. 14 rooms with PB, 2 with FP and 1 suite. Breakfast, afternoon tea and snacks/refreshments included in rates. Types of meals: Full bkfst and early coffee/tea. Beds: KQT. Cable TV, VCR, reading lamp, refrigerator, ceiling fan, clock radio, telephone, desk and hot tub/spa in room. Fax, copier, spa, bicycles and fireplace on premises. Limited handicap access. Antiquing, fishing, live theater, parks, shopping, sporting events, water sports, beach, bike path and Paul Getty Museum nearby.

Publicity: *New York Times, Los Angeles, Brides and Country Inns.*

"One of the most romantic hotels in Los Angeles."

Santa Rosa   G4

Pygmalion House B&B Inn, Hideaway

331 Orange St
Santa Rosa, CA 95401-6226
(707)526-3407 Fax:(707)526-3407

Circa 1880. This historic Victorian, which has been restored to its 19th-century grandeur, is just a few blocks from Santa Rosa's Old Town, "Railroad Square" and many antique shops, cafes, coffeehouses and restaurants. The home is filled with a unique mix of antiques, many of which belonged to famed Gypsy Rose Lee. Each of the Victorian guest rooms includes a bath with a clawfoot tub. Breakfast includes homemade entrees, freshly baked breads and fresh fruit.

Innkeeper(s): Caroline Berry. $89-129. 6 rooms with PB. Breakfast included in rates. Beds: KQ. Cable TV, reading lamp and turn-down service in room. Central air. Fax, copier, library, telephone and fireplace on premises. Antiquing, golf, live theater, parks, shopping, wineries and mall nearby.

Sausalito   H4

Gables Inn Sausalito

62 Princess St
Sausalito, CA 94965
(415)289-1100 (800)966-1554 Fax:(415)339-0536
E-mail: gablesinns@aol.com
Web: www.gablesinnsausalito.com

Circa 1869. Sitting 200 yards from the water with a view of the bay, this beautifully restored 1869 pioneer-style inn with Gothic Revival elements is just five minutes north of the Golden Gate Bridge. Ferry service to San Francisco is a three-minute walk. Stroll to more than 200 shops, art galleries and gourmet restaurants. Some of the nine guest bedrooms and the honeymoon suite boast amenities such as fireplaces, oversized spa tubs and balcony vistas. A continental-plus breakfast includes cereal, fresh juice, pastries and fruit. Wine, cheese and fruit are served in the afternoons and evenings. Muir Woods National Park is 30 minutes away and the Napa Valley wine country is an hour's drive.

Innkeeper(s): Abraham & Patricia Chador. $155-300. 9 rooms with PB, 7 with FP and 1 conference room. Breakfast and snacks/refreshments included in rates. Types of meals: Cont plus, veg bkfst and early coffee/tea. Beds: KQ. Cable TV, VCR, reading lamp, clock radio, telephone, desk, hot tub/spa and voice mail in room. Fax, copier, library, fireplace and evening wine and cheese on premises. Limited handicap access. Weddings and family reunions hosted. Antiquing, art galleries, beach, bicycling, canoeing/kayaking, fishing, golf, hiking, horseback riding, live theater, museums, parks, shopping, tennis, water sports and wineries nearby.

Sebastopol   G4

Vine Hill Inn

3949 Vine Hill Rd
Sebastopol, CA 95472
(707)823-8832 Fax:(707)824-1045
E-mail: innkeeper@vine-hill-inn.com
Web: www.vine-hill-inn.com

Circa 1897. Situated between picturesque apple orchards and vineyards, this Victorian farmhouse is an eclectic country-style bed & breakfast. An intimate ambiance is imparted, with gathering places to play games or converse. Spacious guest bedrooms boast antiques, Egyptian towels and bathrobes. Choose between a clawfoot tub or Jacuzzi. Relax on private decks or porches with gorgeous views. Savor a satisfying breakfast that may include fresh fruit, chicken sausage, frittata and beverages. A swimming pool provides added enjoyment.

Innkeeper(s): Kathy Deichmann. $135-175. 4 rooms with PB. Breakfast included in rates. Types of meals: Full gourmet bkfst. Beds: Q. Reading lamp in room. Central air. Fax, copier, swimming, library, parlor games, telephone and fireplace on premises. Weddings, small meetings, family reunions and seminars hosted. Antiquing, art galleries, beach, bicycling, canoeing/kayaking, fishing, golf, hiking, horseback riding, live theater, parks, shopping and wineries nearby.

Sequoia National Park   K9

Plantation B&B

33038 Sierra Hwy 198
Sequoia National Park, CA 93244-1700
(559)597-2555 (800)240-1466 Fax:(559)597-2551
E-mail: relax@plantationbnb.com
Web: www.plantationbnb.com

Circa 1908. The history of orange production is deeply
entwined in the roots of California, and this home is located on
what once was an orange plantation. The original 1908 house
burned in the 1960s, but the current home was built on its

foundation. In keeping with the home's
plantation past, the innkeepers decorated the bed and breakfast with a "Gone
With the Wind" theme. The comfortable, country guest rooms sport names
such as the Scarlett O'Hara, the Belle
Watling, and of course, the Rhett Butler.
A hot tub is located in the orchard, and
there also is a heated swimming pool.

Innkeeper(s): Scott & Marie Munger. $129-219. 7 rooms with PB, 2 with FP
and 2 suites. Breakfast and snacks/refreshments included in rates. Types of
meals: Full gourmet bkfst and early coffee/tea. Beds: KQDT. Cable TV, VCR,
reading lamp, ceiling fan and hot tub/spa in room. Air conditioning. Fax, spa,
swimming, parlor games, telephone and fireplace on premises. Small meetings and family reunions hosted. Antiquing, cross-country skiing, fishing, golf,
parks, shopping, sporting events and water sports nearby.

Publicity: *Exeter Sun, Kaweah Commonwealth, Los Angeles Times, Fresno
Bee, Visalia Delta Times, Westways Magazine and Sunset Magazine.*

"Scarlett O'Hara would be proud to live on this lovely plantation."

Soda Springs   F7

Rainbow Lodge

PO Box 1100
Soda Springs, CA 95728
(530)426-3871 (800)500-3871 Fax:(530)426-9221

Circa 1920. Built alongside a bend in the Yuba River, this
recently renovated mountain lodge features original stone from
local granite and woodwork of hand-hewn timber. Historical
photos are displayed in the Sierra Cocktail Lounge to reflect the
romantic past. Gather to play games by the large fireplace.
Linger over a delicious complimentary breakfast after a comfortable night's sleep. The on-site Engadine Cafe also offers
French and Californian cuisine for lunch and dinner. Enjoy
year-round activities using shuttle buses for skiing trails or bicycles for area rides.

Historic Interest: Donner Party Museum 10 miles.

Innkeeper(s): Alan Davis/Anelle Erasmus. $95-165. 30 rooms. Breakfast
included in rates. Types of meals: Full gourmet bkfst, veg bkfst, early
coffee/tea, gourmet lunch, picnic lunch, snacks/refreshments and gourmet
dinner. Restaurant on premises. Beds: QDT. Reading lamp and clock radio in
room. TV, bicycles, library, parlor games, telephone and fireplace on premises. Weddings, small meetings and seminars hosted. Beach, bicycling, canoe-
ing/kayaking, cross-country skiing, downhill skiing, fishing, golf, hiking, museums, water sports and wineries nearby.

Sonoma   H4

Brick House Bungalows

313 First St E
Sonoma, CA 95476
(707)996-8091 Fax:(707)996-7301
E-mail: info@brickhousebungalows.com
Web: www.brickhousebungalows.com

Circa 1907. Just one hour north of San Francisco, in the heart of
Sonoma Wine Country, this 1907 brick house was built to reflect
an Italian stone farmhouse. The four bungalows were gradually
added in later years. Kitchenettes, fireplaces, fine linens, vibrant
patterned fabrics, distressed leather couches, antique Kilim carpets and private patios enhance a luxurious stay. In-suite massage
and spa services are available. Lush gardens and a secluded central courtyard impart a tranquil atmosphere for a perfect getaway.
Relax on the hammock or sip complimentary wine by the fire.
Enjoy many cultural events, museums, restaurants and shopping
one-half block away in Historic Sonoma Plaza.

Innkeeper(s): BJ Clarke, Joe Gough. $125-275. 5 cottages, 4 with FP and 2
suites. Breakfast included in rates. Types of meals: Cont plus. Beds: KQ.
Cable TV, VCR, reading lamp, stereo, refrigerator, ceiling fan, clock radio, telephone, coffeemaker, desk and fireplace in room. Fax, child care, parlor
games, fireplace and laundry facility on premises. Family reunions hosted.
Amusement parks, antiquing, art galleries, bicycling, golf, hiking, horseback
riding, live theater, museums, parks, shopping, tennis, wineries, hot air balloons and historical wineries nearby.

Publicity: *Tuscan Magazine and voted among "The Top 10 B&Bs in America"
by Arrington's B&B Journal.*

Hidden Oak Inn

214 E Napa St
Sonoma, CA 95476-6721
(707)996-9863
E-mail: vep@sonic.net
Web: www.hiddenoakinn.com

Circa 1914. This shingled California craftsman bungalow, now
painstakingly restored features a vine-covered gabled roof and
front porch with stone pillars. Located a block from the historic
Sonoma Plaza, the inn offers spacious rooms furnished with
antiques and wicker. Tasty breakfasts are served, and there is a
therapeutic hot tub on the premises. The innkeepers maintain
a small fleet of complimentary bicycles for touring the area's
award-winning wineries, and they also provide local health club
passes for their guests.

Innkeeper(s): Valerie & Don Patterson. $145-225. 3 rooms with PB.
Breakfast and afternoon tea included in rates. Types of meals: Cont plus and
early coffee/tea. Beds: KQ. Bicycles on premises. Small meetings and family
reunions hosted. Antiquing, golf, horseback riding, parks, shopping, sporting
events and wineries nearby.

"The room was delightful and breakfast was excellent."

Sonoma Hotel

110 W Spain St
Sonoma, CA 95476-5696
(707)996-2996 (800)468-6016 Fax:(707)996-7014
E-mail: sonomahotel@aol.com
Web: www.sonomahotel.com

Circa 1879. Located on the renowned Sonoma Plaza, this historic inn was recently remodeled. French-country furnishings
and antiques fill the lobby. Guest rooms also are decorated

with French-country furnishings. Maya Angelou wrote "Gather Together in My Name" while staying here. Wine service is offered to guests between 5 p.m. and 6 p.m., and in the morning, a continental breakfast is served.

Restaurants, antique stores, spas, and museums are within steps of the inn and a short walk away from the tree-lined plaza are several wineries.

Historic Interest: Mission San Francisco Solano, Bear Flag Revolt, Casa Grande Indian Servants Quarters (all within walking distance).

Innkeeper(s): Timothy Farfan & Craig Miller. $110-245. 16 rooms with PB. Breakfast included in rates. Types of meals: Cont, early coffee/tea and dinner. Restaurant on premises. Beds: QDT. Fax, copier and telephone on premises. Antiquing, wineries, spas and shops nearby.

Publicity: *Press Democrat, California Getaway Guide, Americana and House Beautiful.*

"Great food and service! I was so pleased to see such a warm and lovable place."

Trojan Horse Inn

19455 Sonoma Hwy
Sonoma, CA 95476-6416
(707)996-2430 (800)899-1925 Fax:(707)996-9185

Circa 1887. This Victorian home rests on one acre on the banks of Sonoma Creek. Recently restored, the pristine interior offers antiques and a romantic country decor. The Bridal Veil Room has a four-poster bed, wood-burning stove and windows overlooking a magnolia tree, while a private Jacuzzi tub is a popular feature in the Grape Arbor Room. Bicycles, an additional outdoor Jacuzzi, flower gardens and grand old bay and spruce trees add to the experience.

Innkeeper(s): Joe & Sandy Miccio. $160-185. 6 rooms with PB, 1 with FP and 1 conference room. Types of meals: Full bkfst and early coffee/tea. Beds: Q. Reading lamp, ceiling fan and hot tub/spa in room. Air conditioning. Spa, bicycles, telephone and fireplace on premises. Limited handicap access. Small meetings and family reunions hosted. Antiquing, live theater and shopping nearby.

Publicity: *Contra Costa Times, Mobil Travel Guide and Sonoma Index Tribune.*

"We came for one night and stayed for four."

Victorian Garden Inn

316 E Napa St
Sonoma, CA 95476-6723
(707)996-5339 (800)543-5339 Fax:(707)996-1689
E-mail: Vgardeninn@aol.com
Web: www.victoriangardeninn.com

Circa 1870. Authentic Victorian gardens cover more than an acre of grounds surrounding this Greek Revival farmhouse. Pathways wind around to secret gardens, and guests can walk to world-famous wineries and historical sites. All rooms are

decorated with the romantic flair of the innkeeper, an interior designer. Ask to stay in the renovated water tower or in the Woodcutter's Cottage which offers a private deck. Enjoy a therapeutic spa in the gardens.

Historic Interest: Northernmost mission in California chain; home of General M.G. Vallejo; historic Sonoma Plaza, site of 1846 "Bear Flag Rebellion" (establishment of California Republic); Sonoma Barracks - all within 4 blocks.

Innkeeper(s): Donna Lewis. $129-259. 4 rooms, 3 with PB, 2 with FP and 1 suite. Breakfast included in rates. Types of meals: Cont plus, veg bkfst, early coffee/tea, snacks/refreshments and room service. Beds: QDT. Refrigerator, ceiling fan, clock radio, telephone, coffeemaker, hot tub/spa and some with fireplaces in room. Air conditioning. Spa, swimming, sauna, library, parlor games, fireplace, laundry facility and beautiful gardens on premises. Antiquing, live theater, wineries, therapeutic spa, beautiful gardens and restaurants nearby.

Publicity: *Denver Post and Los Angeles Times.*

"I'll be back! So romantic, this place is for lovers! What a perfect spot for a honeymoon! Great! Wonderful! Fabulous! We could not have asked for anything more."

Sonora   H7

Barretta Gardens Inn Bed & Breakfast

700 Barretta St
Sonora, CA 95370-5131
(209)532-6039 (800)206-3333 Fax:(209)532-8257
E-mail: barrettagardens@hotmail.com
Web: www.barrettagardens.com

Circa 1900. Three porches offer views over an acre of lawns and gardens and terraced hillside to Sonora. Living room with fireplace and two parlors are gathering places for guests. Request the Odette Suite and you'll enjoy an original chandelier, 10-foot ceiling, floor-to-ceiling mirror, a 10-foot-high armoire and a Victorian queen bed as well as a whirlpool tub and a solarium/sitting room. The Isabelle room has a whirlpool tub, stained glass and a wall of windows for sunset views. Breakfast is served under the chandelier in the dining room or on the breakfast porch. Pecan-apple puffed pancakes with sausage are a favorite entree, and there are gratins, crepes and fresh french pastries. Walk to shops and restaurants or drive to Jamestown to try the steam train or Columbia State Park. Yosemite National Park is an hour away.

Innkeeper(s): Bruno & Sally Trial. $100-250. 5 rooms with PB and 2 suites. Breakfast and snacks/refreshments included in rates. Types of meals: Full gourmet bkfst and veg bkfst. Beds: KQ. Cable TV, VCR, clock radio, desk, hot tub/spa, wireless Internet access and some with hot tub in room. Central air. Fax, parlor games, telephone and fireplace on premises. Weddings, small meetings and family reunions hosted. Antiquing, bicycling, cross-country skiing, downhill skiing, fishing, golf, hiking, horseback riding, live theater, parks, shopping, tennis, water sports and wineries nearby.

Publicity: *Los Angeles Times, Modesto Bee and Travel Channel.*

Bradford Place Inn & Gardens

56 Bradford Ave
Sonora, CA 95370
(209)536-6075 (800)209-2315 Fax:(209)532-0420
E-mail: innkeeper@bradfordplaceinn.com
Web: bradfordplaceinn.com

Circa 1889. Located in the foothills of the Sierra Nevada and in the center of town, this is a two-story Queen Anne-style house with white picket fence, gabled red roof and wraparound veranda. It was originally constructed for a Wells Fargo agent. A well on the property was one of the area's three original water sources for the gold rush camp that developed here in the 1850s. In addition to the usual amenities, Bradford Place also offers in-room expanded cable television, phones with data ports as well as cookies and a garden filled with flowers. Breakfasts feature a gourmet entree and the inn's specialty, "Mother Lode Skillet," a serving of eggs, potatoes and ham. Guests have the option of being served in the parlor before the fireplace, on the veranda, or in their room, until 11:00 a.m. The historic county courthouse is next door, and guests can walk to cafes, antique stores, bookstores and shops. Nearby is Columbia (three miles) Jamestown and Murphys, and there are giant sequoias and caverns to explore. Other activities include gold panning, river rafting, trout fishing, horseback riding and carriage rides.

Innkeeper(s): Dottie Musser, John Eiseman. $85-175. 4 rooms with PB, 1 with FP, 1 suite and 1 conference room. Breakfast, afternoon tea and snacks/refreshments included in rates. Types of meals: Country bkfst and veg bkfst. Beds: Q. Data port, TV, VCR, reading lamp, CD player, refrigerator, ceiling fan, clock radio, telephone, coffeemaker, desk, satellite TV, microwave and refrigerator in room. Central air. Fax, parlor games, fireplace, laundry facility, parking, microwave and refrigerator on premises. Small meetings and seminars hosted. Antiquing, art galleries, canoeing/kayaking, cross-country skiing, downhill skiing, fishing, golf, hiking, horseback riding, live theater, museums, parks, shopping, sporting events, tennis, water sports, wineries, horse drawn carriage rides, rafting, caverns, sequoias, steam train rides and county fairgrounds nearby.

Lavender Hill B&B

683 S Barretta St
Sonora, CA 95370-5132
(209)532-9024 (800)446-1333
E-mail: lavender@sonnet.com
Web: www.lavenderhill.com

Circa 1900. In the historic Gold Rush town of Sonora is this Queen Anne Victorian inn. Its four guest rooms include the Lavender Room, which has a mini-suite with vanity, desk, sitting area and clawfoot tub and shower. After a busy day fishing, biking, river rafting or exploring nearby Yosemite National Park, guests may relax in the antique-filled parlor, the sitting room or the library. Admiring the inn's gardens from the wraparound porch is also a favorite activity. Be sure to ask about dinner theater packages.

Innkeeper(s): Gail Golding. $95-150. 4 rooms with PB. Breakfast included in rates. Types of meals: Full bkfst, early coffee/tea and afternoon tea. Beds: KQ. Reading lamp, ceiling fan, clock radio and desk in room. Air conditioning. TV, library, parlor games, telephone, movies, afternoon refreshments and wood burning stove on premises. Antiquing, cross-country skiing, downhill skiing, fishing, golf, live theater, parks, shopping, water sports and wineries nearby.

Publicity: *Roseville Times and Union Democrat.*

Soquel   J5

Blue Spruce Inn

2815 S Main St
Soquel, CA 95073-2412
(831)464-1137 (800)559-1137 Fax:(831)475-0608

Circa 1875. The Blue Spruce is located four miles south of Santa Cruz and one mile from Capitola Beach and the Monterey Bay Marine Sanctuary. Spa tubs, fireplaces and colorful gardens add to the pleasure of this renovated farmhouse.

The Seascape is a favorite room with a private entrance and a bow-shaped Jacuzzi tub for two. The Carriage House offers skylights above the bed, a king-size featherbed and an in-room Jacuzzi. Plush robes and private baths are features and in the morning, hearty gourmet breakfasts, the inn's specialty, are served. Afterwards enjoy a ride along the beach or a hike through the redwoods.

Historic Interest: Redwood Forests (5 miles), Santa Cruz Mission (4 miles), Carmel-by-the-Sea (30 miles), Monterey (20 miles).

Innkeeper(s): Nancy, Wayne & Carissa Lussier. $110-240. 6 rooms with PB, 6 with FP. Breakfast included in rates. Types of meals: Full bkfst and early coffee/tea. Beds: KQ. Cable TV, reading lamp, clock radio, telephone, desk, four with Jacuzzi tubs, five with deck or patio and private entrance in room. TV, parlor games and fireplace on premises. Antiquing, beach, golf, parks, shopping and wineries nearby.

Publicity: *L.A. Weekly, Aptos Post, San Francisco Examiner and Village View.*

"You offer such graciousness to your guests and a true sense of welcome."

South Pasadena   O10

The Artists' Inn B&B

1038 Magnolia St
South Pasadena, CA 91030-2518
(626)799-5668 (888)799-5668 Fax:(626)799-3678
E-mail: artistsinn@artistsinns.com
Web: www.artistsinns.com

Circa 1895. A poultry farm once surrounded this turn-of-the-century home. Today, the streets are lined with trees and a variety of beautiful homes. Interior designer Janet Marangi restored the historic ambiance of the cheery, yellow home and cottage, filling them with antiques and original artwork. Each of the guest rooms captures a different artistic style. Soft, soothing colors enrich the Impressionist room, which includes a clawfoot tub and antique brass bed. The 18th Century English room is filled with pieces by Gainsborough, Reynolds and Constable and includes a romantic canopied bed. Fireplaces and Jacuzzis are offered in the inn's five newest cottage suites. There are plenty of helpful amenities, including hair dryers, toiletries and desks in each room. The innkeeper creates a breakfast menu with freshly made breads, homemade granola, fruit and a special entree. The home is just a few blocks from South Pasadena's many shops, boutiques, cafes and restaurants.

Historic Interest: The historic Mission West district is a short distance from the inn. The Norton Simon Museum of Art, Old Town Pasadena, Mission San Gabriel and the Huntington Library are other nearby historic attractions.

Innkeeper(s): Janet Marangi. $115-205. 10 rooms with PB and 4 suites. Breakfast and afternoon tea included in rates. Types of meals: Full gourmet bkfst, early coffee/tea and picnic lunch. Beds: KQDT. Reading lamp, stereo, ceiling fan, clock radio, desk, fresh flowers, TV, Jacuzzis and fireplace in room. Air conditioning. Fax, parlor games, telephone and fireplace on premises. Weddings, small meetings and family functions hosted. Amusement parks, antiquing, art galleries, live theater, parks, shopping, sporting events and Gold Line lightrail nearby.

Publicity: *Pasadena Star News, San Marino Tribune, Stanford, Pasadena Weekly, South Pasadena Review, Recommended by Elmer Dills, Travel & Leisure, New York Times and West Ways.*

Bissell House

201 Orange Grove Ave
South Pasadena, CA 91030-1613
(626)441-3535 (800)441-3530 Fax:(626)441-3671
E-mail: info@bissellhouse.com
Web: www.bissellhouse.com

Circa 1887. Adorning famous Orange Grove Avenue on historic Millionaire's Row, this restored three-story Victorian mansion is a cultural landmark that offers an elegant ambiance and inviting hospitality. Spacious guest bedrooms feature antique furnishings, tasteful décor and modern conveniences that include DSL. Linger over a scrumptious full breakfast in the formal dining room served with crystal glassware, vintage silver and fresh flowers. Apricot bread pudding, egg strata, ginger scones, crème brulee and lemon soufflé French toast are some of the popular specialties. Swim in the pool surrounded by lush foliage or relax in the gorgeous English garden. Visit nearby Old Town Pasadena with a small-town atmosphere and big-city entertainment, boutiques, and upscale restaurants.

Historic Interest: Architectural land once owned by Bissell Carpet Sweeper family, located on "Millionaire's Row."

Innkeeper(s): Russell & Leonore Butcher. $140-185. 6 rooms with PB. Breakfast, afternoon tea and snacks/refreshments included in rates. Types of meals: Full gourmet bkfst, veg bkfst and early coffee/tea. Beds: QD. Data port, reading lamp, clock radio, desk, hot tub/spa and DSL in room. Central air. TV, VCR, fax, copier, spa, swimming, library, parlor games, telephone, fireplace and gift shop on premises. Family reunions hosted. Antiquing, art galleries, golf, hiking, horseback riding, live theater, museums, parks, shopping, sporting events, tennis and wineries nearby.

Springville   K9

Springville Inn

35634 Highway 190
Springville, CA 93265-9747
(559)539-7501 (800)4TH-EINN Fax:(559)539-7502
E-mail: info@springvilleinn.com
Web: www.springvilleinn.com

Circa 1911. At the gateway to the Giant Sequoia National Monument this inviting inn with Old West-style architecture sits on three acres in the foothills of the Sierra Nevada Mountains. It is considered to be the town's first permanent building, originally offering food, drink and lodging to travelers. Boasting a California Country decor, the Kemmerling Family has painstakingly and lovingly restored the inn to once again provide warm hospitality. Relaxation is easy in the comfortable common areas and pleasant guest bedrooms. Award-winning American gourmet cuisine starts the day. Explore the beauty of this majestic region in Tule River County.

Innkeeper(s): Carleen & Kevin Kemmerling. $120-225. 8 rooms with PB, 2 suites and 1 conference room. Breakfast included in rates. Types of meals: Cont plus and gourmet dinner. Restaurant on premises. Beds: KQD. Modem hook-up, data port, cable TV, reading lamp, ceiling fan, clock radio, telephone, coffeemaker and voice mail in room. Air conditioning. Fax, copier, fireplace and laundry facility on premises. Limited handicap access. Weddings, small meetings, family reunions and seminars hosted. Antiquing, art galleries, bicycling, canoeing/kayaking, cross-country skiing, fishing, golf, hiking, horseback riding, live theater, parks, shopping, tennis, water sports and wineries nearby.

Sutter Creek   G6

Foxes In Sutter Creek

77 Main St, PO Box 159
Sutter Creek, CA 95685
(209)267-5882 (800)987-3344 Fax:(209)267-0712
E-mail: innkeeper@foxesinn.com
Web: www.foxesinn.com

Circa 1857. Known for its elegant furnishings, this English farmhouse home offers luxurious accommodations and amenities. Canopy beds and armoires are found in the guest bedrooms and suites. Most feature old-fashioned tubs with showers and fireplaces, some boast a built-in music system, library or sitting area. The Fox Den and the Hideaway also boast a private entry. Choose breakfast from a menu. Cooked to order

and presented on a silver service, it will be delivered to the room when desired. For a change of scenery, arrange to be served in the gazebo.

Innkeeper(s): Bob VanAlstine. $155-215. 7 rooms with PB, 5 with FP. Types of meals: Full bkfst. Beds: Q. Cable TV and VCR in room.

Publicity: *San Francisco Focus, Sunset, Bon Appetit and Travel & Leisure.*

"Foxes is without a doubt the most charming B&B anywhere."

Grey Gables B&B Inn

161 Hanford St
Sutter Creek, CA 95685-1687
(209)267-1039 (800)473-9422 Fax:(209)267-0998
E-mail: reservations@greygables.com
Web: www.greygables.com

Circa 1897. The innkeepers of this Victorian home offer poetic accommodations both in the delightful decor and by the names of their guest rooms. The Keats, Bronte and Tennyson rooms afford garden views, while the Byron and Browning rooms include clawfoot tubs. The Victorian Suite, which encompasses the top floor, affords views of the garden, as well as a historic churchyard. All of the guest rooms boast fireplaces. Stroll

down brick pathways through the terraced garden or relax in the parlor. A proper English tea is served with cakes and scones. Hors d'oeuvres and libations are served in the evenings.

Historic Interest: Property was once owned by Patrick Riordan, Archbishop of San Francisco.

Innkeeper(s): Roger & Susan Garlick. $130-224. 8 rooms with PB, 8 with FP. Breakfast and afternoon tea included in rates. Types of meals: Full gourmet bkfst and early coffee/tea. Beds: KQT. Reading lamp, ceiling fan and clock radio in room. Air conditioning. Fax, copier, parlor games, telephone and fireplace on premises. Limited handicap access. Antiquing, cross-country skiing, downhill skiing, fishing, live theater, parks, shopping, water sports and wineries nearby.

The Hanford House B&B Inn

61 Hanford St Hwy 49
Sutter Creek, CA 95685
(209)267-0747 (800)871-5839 Fax:(209)267-1825
E-mail: bobkat@hanfordhouse.com
Web: www.hanfordhouse.com

Circa 1929. Hanford House is located on the quiet main street of Sutter Creek, a Gold Rush town. The ivy-covered brick inn features spacious, romantic guest rooms; eight have a fireplace. The Gold Country Escape includes a Jacuzzi tub, canopy bed, sitting area and a private deck. Guests can enjoy breakfast in their room or in the inn's cheerful breakfast room. Guests can relax in the front of a fire in the Hanford Room, which doubles as facilities for conferences, retreats, weddings and social events. Wineries, antique shops and historic sites are nearby.

Innkeeper(s): Bob & Karen Tierno. $110-249. 9 rooms with PB, 8 with FP, 3 suites and 1 conference room. Breakfast, afternoon tea and snacks/refreshments included in rates. Types of meals: Full gourmet bkfst and early coffee/tea. Beds: KQ. Cable TV, reading lamp, ceiling fan and telephone in room. Air conditioning. VCR and fax on premises. Limited handicap access. Weddings, small meetings, family reunions and seminars hosted. Antiquing, fishing, golf, live theater, water sports, skiing, Gold Rush historic sites and 25 wineries nearby.

Publicity: *Best Places to Kiss and 50 Best Inns in Wine Country.*

Sutter Creek Inn

PO Box 385
Sutter Creek, CA 95685-0385
(209)267-5606 Fax:(209)267-9287
E-mail: info@suttercreekinn.com
Web: www.suttercreekinn.com

Circa 1859. Relax in hammocks or chaise lounges at this grandmother of western B&Bs. Nestled among trees and vines on huge grounds, many of the guest bedrooms open onto latticed enclaves, arbors or patios. Most rooms offer fireplaces, Jane Way's famous swinging beds and tubs for two. A full country breakfast is served family style in the dining room. The area offers a variety of activities, including golfing, panning for gold, touring wineries, and visiting historical sites. Massage is available by appointment.

Innkeeper(s): Jane Way. $85-185. 17 rooms with PB. Breakfast included in rates. Types of meals: Full bkfst. Beds: QDT. Antiquing, cross-country skiing, fishing, live theater, water sports and wineries nearby.

Publicity: *Fun Times, Motorland and Country Inns.*

Trinidad   C2

Trinidad Bay B&B

PO Box 849
Trinidad, CA 95570-0849
(707)677-0840

Circa 1949. Enjoy ocean and garden views from your room at this New England Cape Cod-style home, which is located on Northern California's beautiful coast. Guests in two of the inn's four rooms can enjoy breakfast delivered to their door. Redwood National Park is just 25 minutes from the inn, or you can hike Trinidad Head and the cliff trails or stroll from the inn to shops and the beach. In the evening, walk to the village restaurants.

Innkeeper(s): Corlene & Don Blue. $135-180. 4 rooms with PB, 1 with FP. Breakfast, afternoon tea and snacks/refreshments included in rates. Types of meals: Full bkfst and early coffee/tea. Beds: KQ. Reading lamp, refrigerator, snack bar and clock radio in room. Parlor games, telephone and fireplace on premises. Antiquing, bicycling, fishing, hiking, live theater, parks, shopping, Redwood National Park, whale watching and restaurants nearby.

"We went away with wonderful memories of the warmth you extended."

Truckee   F7

Hania's Bed & Breakfast

10098 High St
Truckee, CA 96161
(530)582-5775 (888)600-3735 Fax:(530)828-8884

Circa 1884. Situated above historic downtown Truckee, this white farmhouse Victorian framed by a white picket fence offers visitors a panoramic view of mountains and the town. A hot tub, especially inviting during sunsets and on starry nights, is popular with guests. Inside, the interiors are decorated in a Southwestern decor and offer a touch of European elegance. Guest rooms feature log furnishings. Breakfast specialties include eggs a la Hania, Polish-style potato pancakes and crepes with cinnamon apple served in the dining area. In the afternoon, complimentary wine is offered from a rustic bar in front of the wood stove. Restaurants are just downhill, and factory stores as well as the old jail are nearby.

Innkeeper(s): Hania Davidson. $135. 4 rooms with PB. Breakfast, afternoon tea and snacks/refreshments included in rates. Types of meals: Full gourmet bkfst, veg bkfst and early coffee/tea. Beds: Q. Modem hook-up, cable TV, VCR, reading lamp and telephone in room. Fax, spa, library, fireplace and refrigerator with refreshments on premises. Limited handicap access. Weddings, small meetings and family reunions hosted. Antiquing, art galleries, beach, bicycling, canoeing/kayaking, cross-country skiing, downhill skiing, fishing, golf, hiking, horseback riding, museums, parks, shopping, tennis and water sports nearby.

Publicity: *San Francisco Chronicle and Reno Gazette Journal.*

Richardson House

10154 High St
Truckee, CA 96161-0110
(530)587-5388 (888)229-0365 Fax:(530)587-0927
Web: www.richardsonhouse.com

Circa 1887. Guests enjoy views of the rugged Sierra Nevadas and the charm of a historic Old West town while at Richardson House. The historic Victorian bears the name of the prominent lumber baron who built it, Warren Richardson. Each guest room is individually appointed with timely antiques and accessories and the elegant touch of fresh flowers, fine linens, feather beds and down comforters. Some rooms offer views of the Sierra Mountains, while others have views of gardens. The gingerbread-adorned gazebo is the highlight of the Victorian gardens, a perfect setting for a memorable wedding. Inside, the parlor is set up for relaxation with a player piano, television, VCR and stereo. The innkeepers also provide a well-stocked, 24-hour refreshment center. Freshly baked cookies are another treat.

Innkeeper(s): Jim Beck. $100-175. 8 rooms, 6 with PB. Breakfast included in rates. Types of meals: Full gourmet bkfst and early coffee/tea. Beds: KQDT. Reading lamp, clock radio and desk in room. Air conditioning. VCR, fax, copier, parlor games, telephone, morning paper, books and videos on premises. Limited handicap access. Weddings, small meetings and family reunions hosted. Cross-country skiing, downhill skiing, fishing, golf, hiking, parks, shopping and water sports nearby.

The Truckee Hotel

10007 Bridge St
Truckee, CA 96161-0211
(530)587-4444 (800)659-6921 Fax:(530)587-1599
E-mail: thetruckeehotel@sierra.net
Web: www.truckeehotel.com

Circa 1873. As guests enter the historic Truckee Hotel they are suddenly transported back to the Victorian era, and one can almost imagine the days when the hotel served as a stagecoach stop. Eventually, the hotel became home to railroad workers who were building the Transcontinental Railroad. By the turn of the 20th century, the hotel once again served vacationers to the Truckee area. The interior boasts a rich, authentic Victorian decor. In guest rooms, antiques, canopy beds and clawfoot tubs add to the historic romance. Weekend guests enjoy afternoon tea service, and the hotel has a restaurant and bar that serve lunch and dinner daily, as well as Sunday brunch. There is also a gift boutique and cigar shop on the premises. The area offers many places to go, including Donner Lake and the historic Emigrant Trail. More than one dozen ski areas are 25 miles away.

Innkeeper(s): Jenelle Potvin. $50-135. 37 rooms, 8 with PB. Breakfast included in rates. Types of meals: Cont plus. Beds: KQDT. VCR, fax, parlor games, telephone and fireplace on premises. Weddings, small meetings, family reunions and seminars hosted. Antiquing, cross-country skiing, downhill skiing, fishing, golf, parks, shopping, tennis and water sports nearby.

Twentynine Palms   O13

Roughley Manor

74744 Joe Davis Dr
Twentynine Palms, CA 92277
(760)367-3238 Fax:(760)367-4483
E-mail: jan@roughleymanor.com
Web: www.roughleymanor.com

Circa 1924. In the spring, vistas of wildflowers may be seen from this 25-acre estate near Joshua Tree National Park. Palms and cypress trees shade the three-story historic stone house and the inn's Tamarisk tree is home to a family of great horned owls that nest here every year. The inn is appealingly decorated with polished maple floors providing the backdrop for comfortable furnishings and antiques. There are five fireplaces. The Great Room is partially covered by a 22-by-36-foot braided rug made by Fanny Bryce. In addition to the guest rooms in the main house and the museum, there are seven creatively decorated cottages, each with a kitchenette and some with a fireplace. In spring, the inn is famous for its free Serendipity Tea where more than 200 women join in the festivity and wear hats, long dresses and may come barefoot as long as they bring a fabulous dessert.

Innkeeper(s): Jan and Gary Peters. $125-150. 9 rooms with PB, 4 with FP and 7 cottages. Breakfast, afternoon tea and snacks/refreshments included in rates. Types of meals: Full gourmet bkfst and early coffee/tea. Beds: KQ. TV, reading lamp, stereo, refrigerator, snack bar, telephone, turn-down service and hot tub/spa in room. Central air. VCR, fax, library, parlor games, fireplace and laundry facility on premises. Small meetings hosted. Antiquing and hiking nearby.

Publicity: *Sunset Magazine, New York Post, LA Times, Wild Bird Magazine and San Bernardino Sun.*

Ukiah   F3

Vichy Hot Springs Resort & Inn

2605 Vichy Springs Rd
Ukiah, CA 95482-3507
(707)462-9515 Fax:(707)462-9516
E-mail: vichy@vichysprings.com
Web: www.vichysprings.com

Circa 1854. This famous spa, now a California State Historical Landmark (# 980), once attracted guests Jack London, Mark Twain, Robert Louis Stevenson, Ulysses Grant and Teddy Roosevelt. Nineteen rooms and eight cottages comprise the property. Some of the cottages are historic and some are new. The 1860s naturally warm and carbonated mineral baths remain unchanged. A hot soaking pool and historic, Olympic-size pool await your arrival. A magical waterfall is a 30-minute walk along a year-round stream.

Historic Interest: Sun House Museum California Historic Landmark (4 miles west), tallest trees in the world- Montgomery Woods (18 miles west, Redwoods).
Innkeeper(s): Gilbert & Marjorie Ashoff. $115-265. 26 rooms with PB, 8 with FP, 8 cottages and 1 conference room. Breakfast included in rates. Types of meals: Full bkfst. Beds: QT. Reading lamp, refrigerator, clock radio, telephone and desk in room. Air conditioning. Fax, copier, spa, swimming, fireplace, mineral baths, massages and facials on premises. Limited handicap access. Family reunions and seminars hosted. Antiquing, fishing, live theater, museums, parks, water sports, wineries and redwood parks nearby.
Publicity: *Sunset, Sacramento Bee, San Jose Mercury News, Gulliver (Japan), Oregonian, Contra Costa Times, New York Times, San Francisco Chronicle, San Francisco Examiner, Adventure West, Gulliver (Italy) and Bay Area Back Roads (TV).*

Venice   O10

Venice Beach House

15 Thirtieth Avenue
Venice, CA 90291
(310)823-1966 Fax:(310)823-1842
E-mail: info@venicebeachhouse.com
Web: www.venicebeachhouse.com

Circa 1911. Built by Warren and Carla Wilson in 1911 in the Craftsman style of architecture, this faithfully restored home is listed in the National Register. The Wilsons' friends and family included the founder of Venice, Abbot Kinney and a close-knit group of Hollywood stars and local personalities. An ever-growing circle of friends and family are invited to share its casual elegance. Romantic guest bedrooms and spacious suites are tastefully decorated and well-furnished. James Peasgood's Room boasts a double Jacuzzi, cathedral wood ceiling and private balcony. Enjoy the ocean vista in the Pier Suite with a fireplace and sitting room. Tramp's Quarters with a pine beam ceiling and the Olympia Suite with oversized dual shower offer delightful garden views. After breakfast explore the scenic area by bicycle or walk to the beach to rollerblade, surf and people-watch.

Innkeeper(s): Brian Gannon. $130-195. 9 rooms, 3 with PB, 1 with FP and 2 suites. Breakfast included in rates. Types of meals: Cont plus. Beds: KQDT. Modem hook-up, data port, cable TV, reading lamp, clock radio, telephone, desk and DSL high-speed Internet access in room. Fax, bicycles, library, fireplace and Venice Beach on premises. Amusement parks, beach, bicycling, canoeing/kayaking, hiking, shopping, water sports, roller blading and surfing nearby.
Publicity: *Washington Post and MTV.*

"In one of the most popular beach towns in the world, by far the most charming accommodation is the Venice Beach House." — *Washington Post*

Visalia   K8

Ben Maddox House B&B

601 N Encina St
Visalia, CA 93291-3603
(559)739-0721 (800)401-9800 Fax:(559)625-0420
E-mail: innkeeper@benmaddoxhouse.com
Web: www.benmaddoxhouse.com

Circa 1876. Sequoia National Park is just 40 minutes away from this late 19th-century home constructed completely of redwood. The parlor, dining room and front guest bedrooms remain in their original pristine state and are tastefully furnished in period antiques. Other guest bedrooms boast a Jacuzzi bathtub or separate sitting area. Enjoy a leisurely breakfast served at private tables in the historic dining room or on the deck. The grounds feature a swimming pool, finch aviary, gardens and 100-year-old trees. Ask about small group special events such as weddings, showers, rehearsal dinners, family reunions, corporate retreats and meetings.

Historic Interest: Sequoia/King's Canyon National Parks (40 minutes), Tulare Co. Museum (10 minutes).
Innkeeper(s): Brenda & Michael Handy. $85-135. 6 rooms with PB. Breakfast included in rates. Types of meals: Full bkfst. Beds: KQ. Cable TV, reading lamp, refrigerator, clock radio, telephone and data port in room. Air conditioning. Swimming, complimentary soft beverages and pool on premises. Antiquing, cross-country skiing, fishing, live theater, parks, shopping, sporting events, water sports, Sequoia National park, historic downtown area and restaurants nearby.
Publicity: *Southland, Fresno Bee and has 3-diamond rating for AAA and CABBI.*

Spalding House

631 N Encina St
Visalia, CA 93291-3603
(559)739-7877 Fax:(559)625-0902
E-mail: spaldinghouse@mediaone.net
Web: www.thespaldinghouse.com

Circa 1901. This Colonial Revival home, built by a wealthy
lumberman, has been restored and decorated with antiques
and reproductions. The elegant interior includes polished wood
floors topped with Oriental rugs and rich wallcoverings. The
music room features a 1923 Steinway player grand piano. The
library, which boasts some of the home's rich woodwork,
includes shelves filled with books. Breakfasts include fresh
fruit, yogurt, muffins and entrees such as a cheese blintz, apple
crepe or French toast. The home is near downtown Visalia, as
well as Sequoia National Park.

Innkeeper(s): Wayne & Peggy Davidson. $85. 3 suites. Breakfast included in
rates. Types of meals: Full gourmet bkfst. Beds: QD. Reading lamp, ceiling
fan and clock radio in room. Air conditioning. Fax, copier, library, parlor
games, telephone and fireplace on premises. Antiquing, cross-country skiing,
downhill skiing, fishing, golf, live theater, parks, shopping, tennis, water
sports and Sequoia National Park nearby.

Westport   E3

Howard Creek Ranch

40501 N Hwy One, PO Box 121
Westport, CA 95488
(707)964-6725 Fax:(707)964-1603
E-mail: howardcreekranch@mcn.org
Web: www.howardcreekranch.com

Circa 1871. First settled as a land grant of thousands of acres,
Howard Creek Ranch is now a 60-acre farm with sweeping
views of the Pacific Ocean, sandy beaches and rolling moun-

tains. A 75-foot bridge spans a
creek that flows past barns and
outbuildings to the beach 200
yards away. The farmhouse is
surrounded by green lawns, an
award-winning flower garden,
and grazing cows, horses and

llama. This rustic rural location offers antiques, a hot tub,
sauna and heated pool. A traditional ranch breakfast is served
each morning.

Innkeeper(s): Charles & Sally Grigg. $75-160. 15 rooms, 13 with PB, 5 with
FP, 3 suites and 3 cabins. Breakfast included in rates. Types of meals: Full
gourmet bkfst. Beds: KQD. Reading lamp, refrigerator, ceiling fan, desk and
hot tub/spa in room. Fax, spa, swimming, sauna, library, parlor games, telephone and fireplace on premises. Antiquing, art galleries, beach, bicycling,
canoeing/kayaking, fishing, hiking, horseback riding, live theater, museums,
shopping, wineries and farm animals nearby.

Publicity: *California, Country, Vacations, Forbes, Sunset and Diablo.*

"This is one of the most romantic places on the planet."

Yountville   G4

Maison Fleurie

6529 Yount St
Yountville, CA 94599-1278
(707)944-2056 (800)788-0369 Fax:(707)944-9342
E-mail: info@foursisters.com
Web: www.foursisters.com/inns/maisonfleurie.html

Circa 1894. Vines cover the two-foot thick brick walls of the
Bakery, the Carriage House and the Main House of this French
country inn. One of the Four Sisters Inns, it is reminiscent of a
bucolic setting in Provence.
Rooms are decorated in a
warm, romantic style, some
with vineyard and garden
views. Rooms in the Old
Bakery have fireplaces. A pool

and outdoor hot tub are avail-
able and you may borrow bicycles for wandering the countryside. In the evenings, wine and hors d'oeuvres are served.
Yountville, just north of Napa, offers close access to the multitude of wineries and vineyards in the valley. There is a $20 fee
for an additional guest in room, except for children less than 5
years old.

Innkeeper(s): Rachel Retterer. $130-225. 13 rooms with PB, 7 with FP.
Breakfast and afternoon tea included in rates. Types of meals: Full gourmet
bkfst. Beds: KQD. Telephone, turn-down service, hot tub/spa, terry robes
and newspaper in room. Fax, bicycles, fireplace, outdoor pool and hot tub
on premises. Limited handicap access. Weddings hosted. Antiquing and
wineries nearby.

"Peaceful surroundings, friendly staff."

Yuba City   F5

Harkey House B&B

212 C St
Yuba City, CA 95991-5014
(530)674-1942 Fax:(530)674-1840

Circa 1875. An essence of romance fills this Victorian Gothic
house set in a historic neighborhood. Every inch of the home
has been given a special touch, from the knickknacks and photos in the sitting room to the quilts and furnishings in the
guest quarters. The Harkey Suite features a poster bed with a
down comforter and extras such as an adjoining library room
and a gas stove. Full breakfasts of muffins, fresh fruit, juice and
freshly ground coffee are served in a glass-paned dining room
or on the patio.

Historic Interest: Located in the oldest part of Yuba City.

Innkeeper(s): Bob & Lee Jones. $90-195. 4 rooms, 3 with PB, 2 with FP,
1 cottage and 1 conference room. Breakfast included in rates. Types of
meals: Full bkfst and early coffee/tea. Beds: Q. Cable TV, reading lamp,
stereo, ceiling fan, clock radio, telephone, turn-down service, desk and hot
tub/spa in room. Air conditioning. TV, VCR, spa, library, parlor games, fireplace and CD on premises. Weddings, small meetings and family reunions
hosted. Antiquing, fishing, live theater, parks, shopping, water sports and
birding nearby.

Publicity: *Country Magazine.*

"This place is simply marvelous...the most comfortable bed in travel."

Colorado

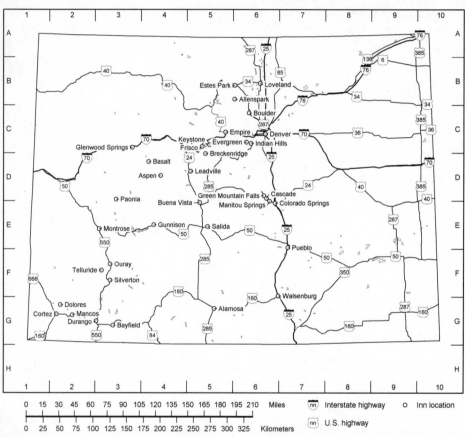

Map legend:
- nn Interstate highway
- nn U.S. highway
- o Inn location

Miles scale: 0 15 30 45 60 75 90 105 120 135 150 165 180 195 210
Kilometers scale: 0 25 50 75 100 125 150 175 200 225 250 275 300 325

Alamosa   G5

Cottonwood Inn & Gallery: A B&B Inn

123 San Juan Ave
Alamosa, CO 81101-2547
(719)589-3882 (800)955-2623 Fax:(719)589-6437
E-mail: relax@cottonwoodinn.com
Web: www.cottonwoodinn.com

Circa 1912. This refurbished Colorado Arts-and-Crafts inn is filled with antiques and paintings by local artists. Blueberry pancakes and banana crepes with Mexican chocolate are the inn's specialties. A favorite day trip is riding the Cumbres-Toltec Scenic Railroad over the La Manga Pass, site of an Indiana Jones movie. The inn offers five rooms, four suites and a carriage house.

Historic Interest: Cumbres-Toltec Scenic Railroad, highest and longest narrow gauge RR in North America (30 minutes), Fort Garland (20 minutes), San Luis, oldest town in Colorado (45 minutes), Great Sand Dunes National Monument (30 minutes).

Innkeeper(s): Deborah Donaldson. $56-125. 10 rooms, 6 with PB and 4 suites. Breakfast and afternoon tea included in rates. Types of meals: Full gourmet bkfst, veg bkfst and gourmet dinner. Beds: KQD. Cable TV, reading lamp, refrigerator, clock radio, telephone, coffeemaker and desk in room. Fax, library, child care, parlor games and courtyard hot tub on premises. Small meetings, family reunions and seminars hosted. Antiquing, art galleries, bicycling, cross-country skiing, fishing, golf, hiking, horseback riding, live theater, museums, parks, shopping, sporting events, tennis, historical train, sand dunes and hot springs nearby.

Publicity: *Colorado Expressions, Rocky Mountain News, Country Inns, Denver Post, Milwaukee Journal, Channel 4 Denver and Colorado Get Away.*

"Your place is so inviting, and with the front porch and birds singing, our visit was so peaceful and relaxing."

Allenspark   B6

Allenspark Lodge

PO Box 247, 184 Main St
Allenspark, CO 80510-0247
(303)747-2552 Fax:(303)747-2552
Web: www.allensparklodge.com

Circa 1933. Since its opening in the 1930s, this lodge has welcomed visitors with a combination of beautiful scenery and hospitality. The lodge was constructed out of Ponderosa pine, and its rustic interior still maintains exposed log walls and a fireplace of native stone. Rooms are comfortable and each has its own unique atmosphere. Three rooms include antique clawfoot tubs. There is plenty to do in the area, no matter the season. Skiing, snowshoeing, hiking, backpacking, horseback riding and birdwatching are among the options.

Innkeeper(s): Bill & Juanita Martin. $70-140. 14 rooms, 7 with PB, 1 with FP and 1 conference room. Breakfast included in rates. Types of meals: Full bkfst. Beds: QDT. Reading lamp, ceiling fan and desk in room. Fax, spa, library, espresso coffee bar and snack bar on premises. Weddings, small meetings, family reunions and seminars hosted. Antiquing, cross-country skiing, downhill skiing, fishing, golf, live theater, parks, shopping, tennis, water sports, horseback riding, extensive hiking and cross-country trails nearby.

Publicity: *New England Hiking Holidays, Travelers Magazine, Mobile Travel Guide, Sunset Magazine and Frommers Travelguide.*

Aspen   D4

Independence Square B&B

404 S Galena St
Aspen, CO 81611-1820
(970)920-2313 (800)633-0336 Fax:(970)920-2020
E-mail: reservations@indysquare.com
Web: www.indysquare.com

Circa 1889. Located one block away from Aspen Mountain in the downtown area, this completely restored red brick historic landmark offers guests the intimacy of an inn with all the amenities of a large hotel. All 28 guest rooms are decorated in French-country furnishings featuring queen beds, down comforters and wet bars. Guests are invited to enjoy the rooftop Jacuzzi and sun deck or partake in the complimentary apres-ski wine and cheese every afternoon during ski season. A continental breakfast buffet is offered every morning. Ski lockers, airport transportation and complimentary use of the Aspen Athletic Club are available.

Innkeeper(s): Jami Downs. $125-360. 28 rooms with PB. Breakfast included in rates. Types of meals: Cont. Beds: Q. Cable TV, reading lamp, refrigerator, clock radio and telephone in room. Air conditioning. Fax, copier and (in winter season) complimentary wine and cheese on premises. Weddings, small meetings and family reunions hosted. Cross-country skiing, downhill skiing, fishing, golf, live theater, parks, shopping and tennis nearby.

Little Red Ski Haus

118 East Cooper Ave.
Aspen, CO 81612
(970)925-3333 (866)630-6119 Fax:(970)925-7123
E-mail: info@littleredskihaus.net
Web: www.littleredskihaus.net

Circa 1888. People from all over the world stay at this historic Victorian bed & breakfast that is known to be the area's first. Little Red is in the historic registry and boasts a recent $1 million renovation. An elegant fireplace with an antique mantel graces the parlor and an upright piano is in the music room. Antiques furnish the elegant guest rooms. Enjoy a full gourmet breakfast in the Prospector's Cellar. In the afternoon and evening, guests gather in this charming room that boasts a fireplace and full service bar. Guests can also find time to meet friends and enjoy the hot tub deck. Located close to town, shuttle busses go to the nearby slopes. The gondola is walking distance away.

Innkeeper(s): Beverly Fiore. $137-389. 13 rooms with PB, 2 suites and 1 conference room. Breakfast included in rates. Types of meals: Full gourmet bkfst, picnic lunch and afternoon tea. Beds: KQT. Modem hook-up, data port, cable TV, VCR, reading lamp, ceiling fan, clock radio, telephone, turn-down service, desk, hot tub/spa, voice mail, some with whirlpool tubs and others have instant steam showers in room. Spa, library, parlor games, fireplace, laundry facility, ski lockers and boot room on premises. Limited handicap access. Weddings, small meetings, family reunions and seminars hosted. Antiquing, art galleries, bicycling, canoeing/kayaking, cross-country skiing, downhill skiing, fishing, golf, hiking, horseback riding, live theater, museums, parks, shopping, tennis, water sports, snowmobiling, hot air ballooning, rodeos, white-water rafting, snowshoeing, ice skating, rock climbing, paragliding, Jeep trips and motorcross trips nearby.

Publicity: *Aspen Magazine, Boulder Daily Camera, Aspen Times, Aspen Daily News, Du Page County Dairy Herald, Denver Post, Ski Magazine - voted November 2003 "Inn of the Month," ABC Chicago Affiliate, Janet Davies Show and In Gear Cable TV Show.*

Sardy House

128 E Main St
Aspen, CO 81611-1714
(970)920-2525

Circa 1892. This Queen Anne Victorian was built by J. William Atkinson, an owner of the Little Annie Mine and Aspen's first freight company. The mansion is built with thick brick walls, sandstone detailing, and wood ornamental trim. A Colorado blue spruce on the grounds is more than 90 feet tall, the tallest in Aspen. There are deluxe guest rooms and six suites. Dinner is available nightly.

Innkeeper(s): Bob Bayless. $125-800. 20 rooms with PB and 1 conference room. Types of meals: Full bkfst. Restaurant on premises. Beds: KQT. TV, spa, swimming, sauna and telephone on premises.

Publicity: *Country Inns.*

"I was overwhelmed by your attention to details. A job well done!"

Basalt   D4

Shenandoah Inn

600 Frying Pan Rd
Basalt, CO 81621
(970)927-4991 (800)804-5520 Fax:(970)927-4990

Circa 1897. On the banks of the Frying Pan River, the Shenandoah Inn has been restored into a peaceful country inn. The innkeepers completed an amazing restoration of the house, which was very dilapidated when they discovered the property.

In addition to restoring the 1960-era main house, they brought back to life a century-old log cabin. Innkeepers Bob and Terri Ziets can tell an array of fascinating stories about the former occupants, as well as their own exhaustive work. The idyllic setting includes decks for relaxing and a riverside hot tub. On a chilly day, enjoy a hot drink in front of the 16-foot rock fireplace in the living room. Rooms are decorated with antiques, and beds are topped with down quilts. The historic cabin is especially well suited to honeymooners in search of privacy, or families, as it sleeps up to five guests. Breakfasts are a treat. Peach-stuffed French toast is a possibility, accompanied by gourmet coffee and a fruit appetizer. Everything is homemade, from the freshly baked breads to the preserves and apple butter.

Innkeeper(s): Bob & Terri Ziets. $105-175. 4 rooms with PB and 1 cabin. Breakfast included in rates. Types of meals: Full bkfst and early coffee/tea. Beds: KQT. Turn-down service, robes, fresh flowers and candy in room. VCR, fax, spa, library, parlor games, telephone and fireplace on premises. Weddings, small meetings and family reunions hosted. Antiquing, cross-country skiing, downhill skiing, fishing, golf, live theater, parks, shopping, tennis, water sports, horseback, kayak and rafting nearby.

Publicity: *Denver Post, Aspen Times, Valley Journal, Health, Roaring Fork Sunday and Washington Observer.*

Bayfield   G3

Wit's End Guest Ranch

254 Country Rd 500
Bayfield, CO 81122
(970)884-4113 (800)236-9483 Fax:(970)884-3261
E-mail: witsend@bwn.net
Web: www.witsendranch.com

Circa 1870. When the owners of this guest ranch bill their place as "luxury at the edge of the wilderness," it isn't just a snappy slogan, it's true. If a half million acres of wilderness and stunning views of snow capped mountain peaks don't entice you, the historic lodge's interior should. Picture polished exposed beams and wood-paneled or log walls, a mix of Victorian and country French furnishings and just enough antlers to create that rustic, lodge atmosphere. Each guest room includes a stone fireplace. There is also an assortment of cabins to consider, some more than a century old. The cabins include a living room, stone fireplace, kitchen and a private porch or deck. There is a full-service, fine-dining restaurant and a tavern often hosting live musical groups from nearby Durango. Now an Orvis endorsed fly-fishing lodge, the inn offers fly fishing in ponds, rivers and lakes. The San Juan River is rated third in the nation for fine fly fishing. (Fly-tying clinics and instruction are offered and there's a fly-fishing lodge.) Other activities include hay rides, mountain biking, dog sled rides, snowshoeing, sleigh rides and watersports. Horseback and trail riding, of course, are a major part of the fun. The ranch offers a full children's program with many interesting activities. As is typical of dude ranches, rates are quoted for weekly visits.

$5417-5826. 4 rooms and 34 cabins. Breakfast, snacks/refreshments and dinner included in rates. Types of meals: Full gourmet bkfst and gourmet lunch. Restaurant on premises. Beds: Q. VCR, reading lamp, refrigerator, snack bar, clock radio, telephone, turn-down service, desk, hot tub/spa and luxury furniture and decor in room. Fax, copier, spa, swimming, stable, bicycles, tennis, library, parlor games, fireplace, full children's program, riding and tours on premises. Weddings, small meetings, family reunions and seminars hosted. Antiquing, cross-country skiing, downhill skiing, live theater, parks, shopping, sporting events, water sports, snowmobiling, Jeep tours, fly fishing program, retail shop and boutique nearby.

Publicity: *Jeopardy, Wheel of Fortune, Quicksilver, Family Feud, Country Inns, Country Living, Learning Channel, Homes & Garden, Great Country Inns & Network and Prize of Wheel of Fortune.*

Boulder   C6

The Alps Boulder Canyon Inn

38619 Boulder Canyon Dr # 18298
Boulder, CO 80302-9654
(303)444-5445 (800)414-2577 Fax:(303)444-5522
E-mail: info@alpsinn.com
Web: www.alpsinn.com

Circa 1870. The entrance to this Adirondack-style lodge is through the original log cabin, which dates to 1879 when it was a stagecoach stop. Located on 24 forested acres, the inn adjoins

the preserve with miles of scenic trails, picnic and camping areas. Rooms feature mountain views and most have double Jacuzzi tubs, fireplaces and sitting areas. The inviting dining room boasts polished wood floors and small tables with twig back chairs. The common areas feature lodge and simple English-country decor. Stuffed French toast with apple cider syrup is a popular entree for the inn's breakfast buffet.

Innkeeper(s): John & Jeannine Vanderhart. $118-250. 12 rooms with PB, 12 with FP. Breakfast and snacks/refreshments included in rates. Types of meals: Full bkfst, early coffee/tea and afternoon tea. Beds: KQ. Reading lamp, ceiling fan, clock radio and telephone in room. VCR, fax and fireplace on premises. Weddings and small meetings hosted. Antiquing, cross-country skiing, downhill skiing, fishing, golf, live theater, parks, shopping, sporting events, tennis and water sports nearby.

Publicity: *Country Inns and Geraldo Rivera Show.*

"We felt so personally welcome, at tea time, at every time."

Briar Rose B&B

2151 Arapahoe Ave
Boulder, CO 80302-6601
(303)442-3007 Fax:(303)786-8440

Circa 1896. Known locally as the McConnell House, this English-style brick house is situated in a neighborhood originally comprised of bankers, attorneys, miners and carpenters. The inn recently was selected as "Best Bed and Breakfast Inn" in Boulder County by the readers of the Boulder Weekly. Fresh flowers, handmade feather comforters and turndown service with chocolates are among the inn's offerings.

Historic Interest: Historic Boulder offers walking tours of the town, including tours of four historic districts and a cemetery.

Innkeeper(s): Bob & Margaret Weisenbach. $119-199. 9 rooms with PB, 2 with FP. Breakfast and afternoon tea included in rates. Types of meals: Cont plus and early coffee/tea. Beds: QDT. TV, reading lamp, ceiling fan, clock radio, telephone, turn-down service, desk and modem hook-up in room. Air conditioning. Fax, copier, parlor games and fireplace on premises. Weddings, small meetings and family reunions hosted. Antiquing, cross-country skiing, downhill skiing, fishing, live theater, parks, shopping, sporting events, many summer festivals, hiking and biking nearby.

Publicity: *Inn Country USA.*

The Inn on Mapleton Hill

1001 Spruce St
Boulder, CO 80302-4028
(303)449-6528 (800)276-6528 Fax:(303)415-0470
E-mail: maphillinn@aol.com
Web: www.innonmapletonhill.com

Circa 1899. Sitting in a quiet residential neighborhood in the historic district, this century-old, red brick Edwardian is two blocks from the downtown Pearl River Mall. Emma Clark, a widowed dressmaker who took in boarders, first occupied the home. Today the guest bedrooms are furnished with period antiques and reproductions that include four-poster beds, clawfoot tubs, rockers, wicker chairs, Victorian writing desks, lace curtains and vintage art. Breakfast is served in the Great Room with its marble and wood fireplace. Feast on a hot entrée such as orange-flavored French toast or an egg dish as well as homemade granola, freshly baked breads, seasonal fruit salad, cereals and yogurt. Refreshments are also available in the late afternoon. The inn is located on the edge of the Rockies where a national park, waterfalls, hiking and biking trails are nearby.

Innkeeper(s): Judi & Ray Schultze. $93-175. 7 rooms, 4 with PB, 2 with FP and 1 suite. Breakfast included in rates. Types of meals: Full bkfst, early coffee/tea, afternoon tea and snacks/refreshments. Beds: QD. Modem hook-up, reading lamp, clock radio, telephone and desk in room. Air conditioning. TV, fax, copier, library, parlor games and fireplace on premises. Small meetings hosted. Amusement parks, antiquing, art galleries, bicycling, canoeing/kayaking, cross-country skiing, downhill skiing, fishing, golf, hiking, horseback riding, live theater, museums, parks, shopping, sporting events, tennis and water sports nearby.

Pearl Street Inn

1820 Pearl St
Boulder, CO 80302-5519
(303)444-5584 (888)810-1302
E-mail: kate@pearlstreetinn.com
Web: www.pearlstreetinn.com

Circa 1895. Located in downtown Boulder, the Pearl Street Inn is composed of a restored Victorian brick house and a new contemporary-style addition. The guest rooms overlook a tree-shaded

courtyard garden where a full gourmet breakfast is served. Antiques, cathedral ceilings, bleached oak floors and fireplaces are featured in all rooms.

Innkeeper(s): Kate Beeman. $119-179. 8 rooms with PB, 8 with FP and 1 conference room. Types of meals: Full gourmet bkfst. Beds: KQDT. TV, fax, copier and telephone on premises.

"Enter the front door and find the sort of place where you catch your breath in awe."

Breckenridge D5

Bed & Breakfasts on North Main Street

303 N Main St
Breckenridge, CO 80424
(970)453-2975 (800)795-2975

Circa 1880. Located in the National Historic District, the 1885 Williams House and exceptionally private 1880 Willoughby Cottage have been meticulously restored to offer Victorian charm, romance and period antiques. Two parlors in the Williams House feature manteled fireplaces and comfortable seating. Relax over afternoon refreshments. Ask for the Deluxe Room and enjoy a mountain view, fireplace and whirlpool tub for two. The three-room Cottage boasts a parlor, fireplace, double whirlpool, shower, TV/VCR, stereo, kitchenette and front porch swing. Stay in the 1997 Barn Above the River on a willow-lined riverbank with private balconies/patios and a fireplace. Start the day with a scrumptious candlelit breakfast. Soak in the outdoor hot tub at day's end. The town trolley and skier shuttles are just around the corner.

Innkeeper(s): Fred Kinat & Diane Jaynes. $89-325. 11 rooms, 10 with PB, 6 with FP and 1 cottage. Breakfast included in rates. Types of meals: Full bkfst and early coffee/tea. Beds: KQT. Cable TV, reading lamp, some with ceiling fans, telephones and claw-footed tubs in room. VCR, spa, parlor games, telephone, fireplace, boot/glove dryers and ski and bike storage on premises. Bicycling, cross-country skiing, downhill skiing, fishing, golf, hiking, horseback riding, live theater, shopping, tennis, water sports, snowmobiling, ice skating, music festivals, bike/rollerblade path, historic tours and boating nearby.
Publicity: *Denver Post, Rocky Mountain News, Summit Daily News, Los Angeles Times* and *Sunset Magazine.*

Buena Vista E5

Trout City Berth & Breakfast

East Highway 24/285
Buena Vista, CO 80908
(719)495-0348

Circa 1880. Restored in 1987, this unique inn provides an opportunity to sleep in an elegantly decorated Victorian Pullman car or in the Drover's caboose. Located on 40 scenic acres in the San Isabel National Forest, the inn has the 1880 reconstructed depot on its historic narrow-gauge railway site. Depot rooms, dining room and game room/gift shop all are decorated in Victorian style. A wildlife area, mountain trails and trout stream pass through the property. The surrounding region boasts some of the world's best fishing, whitewater rafting, mountain climbing, rock hounding and trail riding, shopping and summer theater.

Innkeeper(s): Juel & Irene Kjeldsen. $50-70. 4 rooms with PB and 1 conference room. Breakfast included in rates. Types of meals: Full bkfst. Beds: DT. VCR, telephone, movies and hiking on premises. Weddings and family reunions hosted. Antiquing, bicycling, fishing, live theater, parks, shopping and water sports nearby.

Cascade D6

Eastholme In The Rockies

4445 Hagerman Ave
Cascade, CO 80809
(719)684-9901 (800)672-9901
E-mail: info@eastholme.com
Web: www.eastholme.com

Circa 1885. Although Cascade is only six miles from Colorado Springs, guests will feel as though they are staying in a secluded mountain getaway at this Victorian inn, in the National Register. An affluent New Yorker built the historic hotel, which accommodates the many guests traveling the Ute Pass. The previous innkeeper redecorated the inn, added double Jacuzzi tubs and fire-

places in the two cottages and a gazebo for small weddings. The decor is Victorian, but rooms are uncluttered and airy. Several rooms are furnished with antiques original to the hotel. Three different homemade breads and entrees such as frittatas with herbed potatoes are served during breakfast service.

Historic Interest: Listed on Colorado and National Registers of Historic Places, Ute Pass landmark.

Innkeeper(s): Deborah & Ken Rice. $75-150. 8 rooms, 6 with PB, 3 with FP, 2 suites, 2 cottages and 1 conference room. Breakfast and snacks/refreshments included in rates. Types of meals: Full gourmet bkfst, veg bkfst, early coffee/tea and room service. Beds: QDT. Cable TV, VCR, reading lamp, CD player, refrigerator, ceiling fan, hot tub/spa, guest kitchen on second floor and cottages with Jacuzzi tubs in room. Library, parlor games, telephone, fireplace, outdoor hot tub, wedding gazebo, stone patio, 40-foot front porch, balcony and great view on premises. Weddings, small meetings, family reunions and seminars hosted. Antiquing, art galleries, bicycling, canoeing/kayaking, cross-country skiing, fishing, golf, hiking, horseback riding, live theater, museums, parks, shopping, sporting events, tennis, wineries, climbing, rafting, Pikes Peak, Manitou Springs, Cripple Creek and Woodland Park nearby.

Publicity: *Country Magazine, Denver Post, Colorado Springs Gazette, Rocky Mountain News, AAA rating and BBIC rating.*

Rocky Mountain Lodge & Cabins

4680 Hagerman Ave
Cascade, CO 80809-1818
(719)684-2521 (888)298-0348 Fax:(719)684-8348
E-mail: info@rockymountainlodge.com
Web: www.rockymountainlodge.com

Circa 1936. Surrounded by mountains, this rustic log lodge is snuggled within the Ute Pass about five miles from Manitou Springs. There are five rooms in the lodge, as well as a cottage and cabin. Rooms are decorated in an upscale country style; poster and sleigh beds are topped with quilts and fluffy comforters. The great room includes a huge rock fireplace and plenty of places to relax. Three-course breakfasts are served to all guests staying in the lodge rooms. The cottage and cabin are within walking distance from the main lodge. The cabin dates to 1909 and includes two bedrooms, a living room with a fireplace and a kitchen. The two-story cottage, built during the 1930s, includes a bedroom and sitting area upstairs and a kitchenette and dining room downstairs.

Innkeeper(s): Brian and Debbie Reynolds. $90-150. 5 rooms with PB, 1 cottage and 1 cabin. Breakfast, afternoon tea and snacks/refreshments included in rates. Types of meals: Full gourmet bkfst, veg bkfst and early coffee/tea. Beds: QDT. Cable TV, VCR, reading lamp and clock radio in room. Fax, spa, library, telephone, fireplace, refrigerator, microwave and evening dessert on premises. Weddings, small meetings and family reunions hosted. Amusement parks, antiquing, art galleries, bicycling, fishing, golf, hiking, horseback riding, live theater, museums, parks, shopping, sporting events, tennis and white water rafting nearby.

Chipita Park   D6

Chipita Lodge B&B

9090 Chipita Park Rd
Chipita Park, CO 80809
(719)684-8454 (877)CHI-PITA Fax:(719)684-8234

Circa 1927. Overlooking Chipita Lake and at the base of Pikes Peak, this native stone and log lodge features a hot tub and gazebo with views of mountains on its two-acre knoll-top location. Formerly the local post office and general store, the lodge boasts rooms with fresh Western decor as well as rooms with Native American influences. A three-course breakfast is served with country-style entrees. Evening and afternoon refreshments are offered before the large stone fireplace in the handsome gathering room or on the deck overlooking the lake. The Garden of the Gods, Manitou Springs and Cripple Creek are nearby.

Innkeeper(s): Kevin & Martha Henry. $88-126. 3 rooms with PB and 1 conference room. Breakfast and snacks/refreshments included in rates. Types of meals: Full gourmet bkfst. Beds: Q. Modem hook-up, reading lamp, CD player, ceiling fan, clock radio and turn-down service in room. Fax, copier, spa, parlor games, telephone and fireplace on premises. Weddings and small meetings hosted. Amusement parks, antiquing, art galleries, cross-country skiing, fishing, golf, hiking, horseback riding, live theater, museums, parks, shopping, sporting events and wineries nearby.

Publicity: *Denver Post.*

Colorado Springs   E6

Cheyenne Canon Inn

2030 W Cheyenne Blvd
Colorado Springs, CO 80906
(719)633-0625 (800)633-0625 Fax:(800)633-8826
E-mail: info@cheyennecanoninn.com
Web: cheyennecanoninn.com

Circa 1921. This massive, 10,000-square foot mansion features Arts and Crafts-style architecture. The manor was built as an upscale casino and bordello. During its heyday, the famous guests included the Marx Brothers and Lon Chaney. The casino room now serves as the location for the inn's nightly wine and cheese hour. The room has more than 100 panes of glass affording views of Cheyenne Canon and Cheyenne Mountain. The guest rooms and adjacent honeymoon cottage are decorated with treasures and antiques from around the world. There is a greenhouse spa on the second floor and complimentary beverages and fruit always are available. Modem outlets, TVs and in-room phones are among the amenities for business travelers. Downtown Colorado Springs is minutes away, and hiking trails and waterfalls are across the street.

Historic Interest: Cripple Creek is an hour's drive from the inn, and closer attractions include cliff dwellings, Old Colorado City and the Broadmoor Hotel.

Innkeeper(s): Keith Hampton. $95-200. 10 rooms with PB, 4 with FP, 3 suites, 1 cottage and 2 conference rooms. Types of meals: Full bkfst, early coffee/tea, snacks/refreshments and gourmet dinner. Beds: KQ. Cable TV, ceiling fan, telephone, turn-down service and hair dryers in room. Air conditioning. Fax, library and day spa on premises. Weddings, small meetings and seminars hosted. Antiquing, fishing, golf, hiking, live theater, parks, shopping, sporting events and gambling nearby.

Publicity: *Denver Post, Colorado Source, Beacon, National Geographic Traveler and Country Inns.*

"It truly was 'home away from home.' You have made it so welcoming and warm. Needless to say our breakfasts at home will never come close to the Cheyenne Canon Inn!!"

Holden House-1902 Bed & Breakfast Inn

1102 W Pikes Peak Ave
Colorado Springs, CO 80904-4347
(719)471-3980 (888)565-3980 Fax:(719)471-4740
E-mail: mail@holdenhouse.com
Web: www.holdenhouse.com

Circa 1902. Built by the widow of a prosperous rancher and businessman, this Victorian inn has rooms named after the Colorado towns in which the Holden's owned mining interests. The main house, adjacent carriage house and Victorian house next door include the Cripple Creek, Aspen, Silverton, Goldfield and Independence suites. The inn's suites boast fireplaces and oversized tubs for two. Guests can relax in the living room with fireplace, front parlor, veranda with mountain views or garden with gazebo and fountains. There are friendly cats in residence.

Historic Interest: Miramont Castle, McAllister House, Glen Eyrie Castle, The Pioneer's Museum, the Broadmoor Hotel & Carriage House Museum, Cliff

Dwellings Museum, Pikes Peak, and Garden of the Gods Park are among the area's many historic attractions.

Innkeeper(s): Sallie & Welling Clark. $135-150. 5 suites, 5 with FP. Breakfast included in rates. Types of meals: Full bkfst, early coffee/tea and afternoon tea. Beds: Q. TV, reading lamp, refrigerator, ceiling fan, clock radio, telephone, turn-down service, desk, tubs for two, fireplaces, modem hookups and hair dryer in room. Air conditioning. VCR, fax, copier, parlor games and fireplace on premises. Antiquing, fishing, live theater, museums, parks, shopping, sporting events, historic sites, hiking, biking and horseback riding nearby.

Publicity: *Denver Post, Victorian Homes, Pikes Peak Journal, Glamour, Country Inns, Vacations, Rocky Mountain News, Cats and KKTV.*

"Your love of this house and nostalgia makes a very delightful experience."

Lennox House Bed & Breakfast

1339 N Nevada Ave
Colorado Springs, CO 80903-2431
(719)471-9265 (800)471-9282 Fax:(719)471-0971
E-mail: info@lennoxhouse.com
Web: www.lennoxhouse.com

Circa 1890. Whether traveling for pleasure or business, visitors to this recently renovated Queen Anne Victorian will find an abundance of comforts and generous amenities. Surrounded by historical homes on tree-lined streets, the inn is centrally located to enjoy all that downtown has to offer, as well as nearby Pikes Peak National Forest. Original woodwork highlights the custom-designed interior. Guest bedrooms feature fireplaces, tub-for-two, canopy beds and modern conveniences that enhance a delightful stay. A satisfying breakfast is served every morning at a flexible time. Snacks, beverages and use of a refrigerator and microwave are available around the clock. Enjoy an extensive video collection and small gift shop. Ask about special packages offered.

Innkeeper(s): Mark & Lisa Kolb. $99-129. 4 rooms with PB and 1 suite. Breakfast and snacks/refreshments included in rates. Beds: KQ. Cable TV, VCR, reading lamp, telephone and voice mail in room. Air conditioning. Fax, laundry facility and video collections on premises. Hiking and shopping nearby.

Room at the Inn A Victorian Bed & Breakfast

618 N Nevada Ave
Colorado Springs, CO 80903-1006
(719)442-1896 (888)442-1896 Fax:(719)442-6802
E-mail: roomatinn@pcisys.net
Web: www.roomattheinn.com

Circa 1896. A Colorado pioneer built this Queen Anne Victorian, a delightful mix of turret, gables and gingerbread trim. While restoring their century-old Victorian, the innkeepers discovered several hand-painted murals had once decorated the interior. Original fireplace mantels and a collection of antiques add to the nostalgic ambiance. Fresh flowers, turn-down service and a bountiful breakfast are just a few of the amenities. Several rooms include a fireplace or double whirlpool tub.

Innkeeper(s): Dorian & Linda Ciolek. $99-180. 8 rooms with PB, 4 with FP and 2 suites. Breakfast, afternoon tea and snacks/refreshments included in rates. Types of meals: Full bkfst and early coffee/tea. Beds: Q. Reading lamp, telephone, turn-down service, desk, clocks and whirlpool tubs in room. Air conditioning. VCR, fax, copier, parlor games, fireplace and spa on premises. Limited handicap access. Small meetings, family reunions and seminars hosted. Antiquing, fishing, live theater, parks, shopping, sporting events, museums and fine arts center nearby.

Publicity: *Denver Post and Colorado Springs Gazette-Telegraph.*

Cortez   G2

Grizzly Roadhouse B & B

3450 Highway 160 South
Cortez, CO 81321-9619
(970)565-7738 (800)330-7286 Fax:(970)565-7243
E-mail: grizbb@fone.net
Web: grizzlyroadhouse.com

Circa 1940. Experience true Pueblo history on 40 acres of evergreen hills and canyons a few miles away from Colorado's Mesa Verde Pueblo Ruins. Amidst the pristine setting of Southwest Colorado lies this country Roadhouse next door to a Victorian cottage. Here you can spend each morning and evening on a private deck gazing at the prism of colors in the sky from the sun as it meets the red mesas. Each day, host Michelle Eagle Boyer prepares authentic pueblo food from family recipes, such as blue corn pancakes, chili rellenos and corn quiche, along with American favorites such as homemade bread and muffins. In this surreal setting, spend nights soaking in the spa while observing clear, starry skies and days fishing at the McPhee Reservoir, hiking or rafting along the Dolores River or skiing during the winter.

Innkeeper(s): Jacob & Michelle Eagle Boyer. $69-89. 4 rooms with PB, 1 cottage and 1 conference room. Breakfast and snacks/refreshments included in rates. Types of meals: Full gourmet bkfst, veg bkfst, early coffee/tea, picnic lunch and afternoon tea. Beds: Q. TV, VCR, reading lamp, stereo, refrigerator, ceiling fan, snack bar, clock radio, telephone, coffeemaker, turn-down service, desk and hot tub/spa in room. Air conditioning. Copier, spa, library, parlor games and laundry facility on premises. Small meetings and family reunions hosted. Amusement parks, antiquing, art galleries, bicycling, canoeing/kayaking, cross-country skiing, downhill skiing, fishing, golf, hiking, horseback riding, museums, parks, shopping, sporting events, tennis and water sports nearby.

Denver   C6

The Adagio Bed & Breakfast

1430 Race Street
Denver, CO 80206
(303)370-6911 (800)533-3241 Fax:(303)377-5968
E-mail: Adagio@adagiobb.com
Web: www.adagiobb.com

Circa 1892. Experience affordable luxury at this recently renovated historic Victorian inn. Hardwood floors, wainscoting and a grand staircase resonate architectural details that befit the era. The richly appointed parlor includes one of the original fireplaces, traditional furnishings, a guitar and grand piano. The harmony of music and hospitality is also enjoyed in the romantic guest bedrooms that are named for famous composers. The Copland and Brahms Suites boasts two-person tubs. A ceiling mural with images of a nighttime sky and full moon graces the Holst Suite. DSL computer hookups are available. The restored dining room is perfect for hosting private parties, receptions or business meetings. Chef Armstrong's commercial kitchen is well-equipped to serve elegant evening meals upon request. Relax in the backyard, popular for garden weddings.

Innkeeper(s): Todd Armstrong & Helen Strader. $75-160. 6 rooms with PB, 2 with FP and 1 conference room. Breakfast and snacks/refreshments included in rates. Types of meals: Full bkfst and veg bkfst. Beds: KQT. Modem hook-up, cable TV, VCR, reading lamp, refrigerator, ceiling fan, clock radio, telephone, desk, hot tub/spa, robes and DSL computer hookups available in room. Air conditioning. Fax, copier, spa, library, parlor games and fireplace on premises. Weddings, small meetings, family reunions and seminars hosted. Amusement parks, antiquing, art galleries, bicycling, golf, hiking, horseback riding, live theater, museums, parks, shopping, sporting events and tennis nearby.

Publicity: *Don Kennedy's "Inn for the Night," Denver Post, McCalls Quilting, Colorado Jobs and News 4-Internet marketing feature.*

Capitol Hill Mansion Bed & Breakfast

1207 Pennsylvania St
Denver, CO 80203-2504
(303)839-5221 (800)839-9329 Fax:(303)839-9046
E-mail: info@capitolhillmansion.com
Web: www.capitolhillmansion.com

Circa 1891. Although only open since 1994, owners James R. Hadley and Carl S. Schmidt II have mastered the art of innkeeping at this beautiful 1891 ruby sandstone mansion. Choose from eight antique-appointed guest rooms, all with private baths, some with a whirlpool tub for two, a fireplace or balcony. Each of the guest rooms is uniquely decorated. The Gold Banner Suite features a brass bed, fireplace and cozy sitting area. The Pasqueflower Room on the third floor boasts a six-foot, round whirlpool tub located in the turret of the mansion. Enjoy a full breakfast each morning and Colorado wine in the evening. Experience the Victorian luxury of yesterday in present-day Denver.

Historic Interest: The Capitol Hill Mansion is one block from the Molly Brown Home and only four blocks from the Governor's Mansion. Guests can walk to several other historic homes, including the Grant-Humphreys Mansion.

Innkeeper(s): Jay Hadley & Carl Schmidt II. $85-175. 8 rooms with PB, 2 with FP and 3 suites. Breakfast included in rates. Types of meals: Full bkfst. Beds: KQT. Cable TV, reading lamp, stereo, refrigerator, clock radio, telephone, whirlpool tubs, fireplaces and parlor games in room. Air conditioning. Fax, copier, parlor games and CD player on premises. Limited handicap access. Weddings, small meetings and family reunions hosted. Amusement parks, antiquing, cross-country skiing, downhill skiing, fishing, golf, live theater, parks, shopping, sporting events, tennis and water sports nearby.

Publicity: *Yellow Brick Road, Life on Capitol Hill, Journal Constitution, Denver Post, Rocky Mountain News, Westword and Citysearch.com.*

Castle Marne - A Historic Urban Inn

1572 Race St
Denver, CO 80206-1308
(303)331-0621 (800)926-2763 Fax:(303)331-0623
E-mail: jim@castlemarne.com
Web: www.castlemarne.com

Circa 1889. This 6,000-square-foot fantasy was designed by William Lang and is on the National Register. It is constructed of hand-hewn rhyolite stone. Inside, polished oak, cherry and

black ash woodwork enhance the ornate fireplaces, period antiques and opulent Victorian decor. For special occasions ask for the Presidential Suite with its tower sitting room, king-size tester bed, whirlpool tub in the solarium and private balcony.

Historic Interest: Downtown Historic District (7 minutes), State Capitol (2 minutes), Byers-Evans Museum (5 minutes), Molly Brown House Museum (3 minutes), State Historical Society (4 minutes), Four Mile House (20 minutes).

Innkeeper(s): The Peiker Family. $100-250. 9 rooms with PB, 2 suites and 1 conference room. Breakfast and afternoon tea included in rates. Types of meals: Full bkfst and gourmet dinner. Beds: KQDT. Two rooms with 2-person hot tub and three with private balconies in room. Fax, copier, parlor games and telephone on premises. Antiquing, cross-country skiing, downhill skiing, fishing, live theater and water sports nearby.

Publicity: *Denver Post, Innsider, Rocky Mountain News, Los Angeles Times, New York Times, Denver Business Journal, Country Inns, Brides and U.S. Air.*

"The beauty, service, friendliness, delicious breakfasts - everything was so extraordinary! We'll be back many times."

Historic Queen Anne Bed & Breakfast Inn

2147-2151 Tremont Pl
Denver, CO 80205-3132
(303)296-6666 (800)432-4667 Fax:(303)296-2151
E-mail: travel@queenannebnb.com
Web: www.queenannebnb.com

Circa 1879. Recipient of the Outstanding Achievement Award by the Association of American Historic Inns, this Queen Anne Victorian was designed by Colorado's most famous architect, Frank Edbrooke. Furnishings, chamber music and art add to the Victorian experience. In an area of meticulously restored homes and flower gardens, the inn is two blocks from the center of the central business district.

Innkeeper(s): The King Family. $75-175. 14 rooms with PB, 2 with FP and 4 suites. Breakfast included in rates. Types of meals: Full bkfst and early coffee/tea. Beds: KQDT. Modem hook-up, cable TV, reading lamp, stereo, refrigerator, ceiling fan, clock radio, telephone, desk and hot tub/spa in room. Central air. VCR, fax, copier, bicycles, library, parlor games and afternoon Colorado Wine on premises. Weddings and seminars hosted. Amusement parks, antiquing, art galleries, bicycling, cross-country skiing, downhill skiing, golf, hiking, horseback riding, live theater, museums, parks, shopping, sporting events and tennis nearby.

Publicity: *New York Times, USA Today, Travel Holiday, New Woman, Bon Appetit and Conde Nast Traveler.*

"A real dream, a real home away from home."

The Oxford Hotel

1600 17th St
Denver, CO 80202-1204
(303)628-5400 (800)228-5838 Fax:(303)628-5408
E-mail: rmorrow@theoxfordhotel.com
Web: www.theoxfordhotel.com

Circa 1891. The Oxford Hotel, Denver's oldest operating hotel, was designed by Colorado's leading architect. The hotel is listed in the National Register. The morning paper is delivered to each individually decorated guest room, and complimentary coffee and shoe shine services are available. Guests also enjoy limousine service, round-the-clock room service, turndown service and privileges at the adjacent Oxford Club, a fitness center with a spa and salon.

Historic Interest: The Oxford Hotel is located in the downtown historic district and affords close access to an art museum and many other historic Denver sites.

Innkeeper(s): Mike Case. $139-359. 80 rooms and 1 suite. Types of meals: Full bkfst, lunch, dinner and room service. Restaurant on premises. Beds: QD. Antiques in room. Spa, salon and health club on premises. Antiquing nearby.

"Your staff, from the maids to the front desk, is wonderful. The Hotel has great character and you are doing things right."

Dolores   G2

Rio Grande Southern Hotel

101 S 5th St, PO Box 516
Dolores, CO 81323-0516
(970)882-7527 (800)258-0434
E-mail: riogrande@hubwest.com
Web: www.riograndesouthernhotel.com

Circa 1893. Once filled with mining and railroad millionaires, this historic Victorian hotel has been providing comfortable lodging for more than 100 years. Teddy Roosevelt is also said to have been a guest. Tastefully decorated guest bedrooms and suites offer pleasant amenities. Most rooms feature clawfoot tubs. Rumor has it that Zane Grey stayed in Room Four while writing parts of Riders of the Purple Sage. Enjoy fine dining Tuesday through Sunday in the relaxing ambiance of the on-site restaurant that specializes in Southwestern cuisine. Located on the picturesque town square at the base of the San Juan Mountains, the Dolores River Valley is a popular recreation area.

Innkeeper(s): Fred & Cathy Green. $55-140. 5 rooms with PB and 4 suites. Breakfast included in rates. Types of meals: Full bkfst, lunch and picnic lunch. Restaurant on premises. Beds: QD. Reading lamp in room. Library, parlor games and telephone on premises. Weddings, small meetings, family reunions and seminars hosted. Antiquing, art galleries, bicycling, canoeing/kayaking, cross-country skiing, downhill skiing, fishing, golf, hiking, horseback riding, live theater, museums, parks, shopping, sporting events, tennis, water sports and wineries nearby.

Durango   G3

Blue Lake Ranch

16919 Hwy 140
Durango, CO 81326
(970)385-4537 (888)258-3525 Fax:(970)385-4088
E-mail: bluelake@frontier.net
Web: www.bluelakeranch.com

Circa 1910. Built by Norwegian immigrants in 1910, this beautiful Victorian farmhouse has become a luxurious country inn and estate on 200 acres that include spectacular flower gardens, wildlife and splendid mountain views. The Ranch provides a magical experience in a magnificent private setting. It is filled with comforts such as down quilts, family antiques and vases of fresh flowers. The property is designated as a wildlife refuge. There is a cabin overlooking trout-filled Blue Lake and a cottage on the river. Enjoy a European/Southwest buffet breakfast. Named by American Historic Inns as one of the ten most romantic inns, 2001.

Innkeeper(s): Paula Alford, Shirley Isgar & Tracy West. $95-325. 16 rooms with PB, 13 with FP, 2 suites, 2 cottages, 1 cabin and 1 conference room. Breakfast included in rates. Types of meals: Full gourmet bkfst. Beds: K. VCR, telephone and some with kitchen in room. TV, fax, child care, gardens, lake, river and fishing on premises. Limited handicap access. Weddings, small meetings, family reunions and seminars hosted. Antiquing, bicycling, cross-country skiing, downhill skiing, fishing, golf, hiking, live theater, parks, shopping, sporting events, tennis, water sports, mountain climbing, river rafting, Mesa Verde National Park and Durango Silverton Train nearby.

Publicity: *Town & Country, Conde Nast Traveler, National Geographic Traveler, Sunset, Country Living, Metropolitan Home and USA Today.*

"We have been visiting the Ranch for the last 15 years and each stay gets better. The setting is ideal and the staff incredible — so beautiful and relaxing."

Gable House Bed & Breakfast

805 E 5th Ave
Durango, CO 81301-5358
(970)247-4982
E-mail: ghbb@frontier.net
Web: creativelinks.com/gablehouse

Circa 1892. In a picturesque, quiet neighborhood, within walking distance of the downtown historic district, nostalgia awaits at this elegant Queen Anne Victorian home listed in the national and state historic registers. Once inside the private hedge with iron gate, a relaxing journey unfolds. The parlor is perfect for learning about the area from hostess Heather. Antique-filled guest bedrooms and suite are spacious yet inti-

mate, boasting private entrances. A deliciously prepared breakfast is highlighted with elegant table settings of Blue Willow china and vintage silver. The balconies or lawn chairs offer a restful view of the manicured grounds and flower beds.

Historic Interest: Seven blocks away from Durango & Silverton Narrow Gauge Train Station.

Innkeeper(s): Heather Bryson. $95-150. 4 rooms, 1 with PB, 1 suite and 1 conference room. Breakfast included in rates. Types of meals: Full gourmet bkfst, veg bkfst, early coffee/tea and afternoon tea. Beds: QDT. Reading lamp, clock radio and turn-down service in room. TV, VCR, bicycles, library, parlor games, telephone, fireplace and laundry facility on premises. Weddings, small meetings, family reunions and seminars hosted. Antiquing, art galleries, bicycling, canoeing/kayaking, cross-country skiing, downhill skiing, fishing, golf, hiking, horseback riding, live theater, museums, parks, shopping, sporting events and water sports nearby.

Publicity: *Victorian Home, Durango Magazine and Dallas Morning News.*

Leland House B&B Suites

721 East Second Ave
Durango, CO 81301-5403
(970)385-1920 (800)664-1920 Fax:(970)385-1967

Circa 1927. The rooms in this Craftsman-style brick building are named after historic figures associated with this former apartment house and Durango's early industrial growth. The decor features unique cowboy and period antiques designed for

both comfort and fun. In addition to regular rooms with queen-size beds, the suites also include queen sofa beds or fold-outs for those traveling with a child, friends or family. Gourmet breakfasts include inn specialties of homemade granola, cranberry scones and a variety of entrees like Southwest burritos and multi-grain waffles. Located in the historic district downtown, guests can take walking tours or enjoy specialty shops, restaurants, galleries and museums nearby.

Innkeeper(s): Kirk & Diane Komick. $109-320. 10 rooms with PB, 6 with FP, 6 suites and 1 conference room. Breakfast and snacks/refreshments included in rates. Types of meals: Full gourmet bkfst, veg bkfst, early coffee/tea and afternoon tea. Beds: Q. Modem hook-up, cable TV, reading lamp, refrigerator, ceiling fan, clock radio, telephone and coffeemaker in room. Air conditioning. VCR, fax, copier and fireplace on premises. Weddings, small meetings and family reunions hosted. Antiquing, art galleries, bicycling, canoeing/kayaking, cross-country skiing, downhill skiing, fishing, golf, hiking, live theater, museums, parks, shopping, tennis and water sports nearby.

"It is great! Charming and warm, friendly staff and superb food. Marvelous historic photo collection."

The Rochester Hotel

721 East Second Ave
Durango, CO 81301-5403
(970)385-1920 (800)664-1920 Fax:(970)385-1967
E-mail: stay@rochesterhotel.com
Web: www.rochesterhotel.com

Circa 1892. This Federal-style inn's decor is inspired by many Western movies filmed in and around the town. The building is an authentically restored late-Victorian hotel with the charm and luxury of the Old West, completely furnished in antiques from the period. The inn is situated on a beautifully landscaped setting that features a flower-filled courtyard, and is

located just one block from historic Main Avenue downtown. The inn is close to all major attractions, museums, galleries, shops, restaurants, and outdoor activities.

Historic Interest: Listed in National Register of Historic Places.

Innkeeper(s): Kirk & Diane Komick. $139-209. 15 rooms with PB, 2 suites and 2 conference rooms. Breakfast included in rates. Types of meals: Full gourmet bkfst, picnic lunch and afternoon tea. Beds: KQ. Cable TV, reading lamp, ceiling fan, clock radio, telephone and desk in room. Air conditioning. VCR, fax and copier on premises. Limited handicap access. Weddings, small meetings, family reunions and seminars hosted. Antiquing, cross-country skiing, downhill skiing, fishing, live theater, parks, shopping, water sports and Mesa Verde National Park nearby.

Publicity: *Conde Naste Traveler, Denver Post and National Geo Adventure.*

"In a word — exceptional! Far exceeded expectations in every way."

Empire   C5

Mad Creek B&B

PO Box 404
Empire, CO 80438-0404
(303)569-2003 (888)266-1498

Circa 1881. There is just the right combination of Victorian décor with lace, flowers, antiques and gingerbread trim on the façade of this mountain town cottage. The home-away-from-home atmosphere is inviting and the Eastlake furnishings are comfortable. Relax in front of the rock fireplace while watching a movie, peruse the library filled with local lore or plan an adventure with local maps and guide books. Empire was once a mining town, conveniently located within 20 to 60 minutes of at least six major ski areas.

Innkeeper(s): Myrna & Tonya Payne. $75-105. 3 rooms with PB. Breakfast, afternoon tea and snacks/refreshments included in rates. Types of meals: Full bkfst and early coffee/tea. Beds: KQD. Reading lamp, ceiling fan, toiletries and down comforters in room. TV, VCR and outdoor hot tub and gazebo where breakfast is served when weather permits among the beautiful wildflower gardens on premises. Weddings and family reunions hosted. Antiquing, cross-country skiing, downhill skiing, fishing, horseback riding, parks, shopping, water sports and gambling nearby.

The Peck House

PO Box 428
Empire, CO 80438-0428
(303)569-9870 Fax:(303)569-2743
E-mail: info@thepeckhouse.com
Web: www.thepeckhouse.com

Circa 1862. Built as a residence for gold mine owner James Peck, this is the oldest hotel still in operation in Colorado. Many pieces of original furniture brought here by ox cart remain in the inn, including a red antique fainting couch and walnut headboards. Rooms such as the Conservatory provide magnificent views of the eastern slope of the Rockies, and a panoramic view of Empire Valley can be seen from the old front porch.

Innkeeper(s): Gary & Sally St. Clair. $60-100. 11 rooms, 9 with PB and 1 suite. Breakfast included in rates. Types of meals: Cont and gourmet dinner. Restaurant on premises. Beds: QDT. Reading lamp in room. Fax, spa, library, telephone and fireplace on premises. Small meetings and seminars hosted. Antiquing, art galleries, bicycling, cross-country skiing, downhill skiing, fishing, hiking, horseback riding, museums, parks, shopping and tennis nearby.

Publicity: *American West, Rocky Mountain News, Denver Post and Colorado Homes.*

Estes Park   B6

Anniversary Inn

1060 Mary's Lake Rd
Estes Park, CO 80517
(970)586-6200
E-mail: thebert@gte.net
Web: www.estesinn.com

Circa 1890. High in the Colorado Rockies, at 7,600 feet, this authentic log home is surrounded by spectacular views. There are two acres with a pond and river nearby. An exposed-log living room is dominated by a massive mossrock fireplace. The guest rooms boast stenciled walls and other country accents. The full breakfasts are served on a glass-enclosed wrap-around porch. The inn specializes in honeymoons and anniversaries and features a honeymoon cottage.

$100-175. 4 rooms with PB, 1 with FP and 1 cottage. Breakfast and snacks/refreshments included in rates. Types of meals: Full gourmet bkfst. Beds: Q. Reading lamp, stereo, refrigerator, hot tub/spa and refrigerator in room. TV, VCR, library, parlor games, telephone and fireplace on premises. Weddings and family reunions hosted. Antiquing, art galleries, cross-country skiing, fishing, golf, hiking, horseback riding, shopping, backpacking, snowshoeing and Rocky Mountain National Park nearby.

Publicity: *Denver Post, Columbus Dispatch and Rocky Mountain News.*

"The splendor and majesty of the Rockies is matched only by the warmth and hospitality you showed us during our stay."

The Baldpate Inn

PO Box 700, 4900 S. Hwy 7
Estes Park, CO 80517-4445
(970)586-6151 (866)577-5397
E-mail: baldpatein@aol.com
Web: www.baldpateinn.com

Circa 1917. Cradled in a grove of aspens on the side of Twin Sisters Mountain, this early 1900s inn is listed in the National Register of Historic Places. Adjacent to Rocky Mountain National Park, Baldpate is surrounded by 15 acres of private forest. Enjoy an unparalleled view of the valley below. Relax in the lobby and library with massive stone fireplaces and an inviting ambiance. Admire the collection of keys from around the world and photos of notables including Teddy Roosevelt and Henry Ford. Comfortable guest bedrooms and private cabins boast a country mountain decor with down comforters and handmade quilts. Savor a three-course gourmet breakfast. The dining room is open to the public for lunch and dinner, so reservations are encouraged. Weddings and other celebrations are popular here.

Innkeeper(s): Lois Smith, MacKenzie Smith, Jen & Pete Macakanja. $95-160. 12 rooms, 2 with PB, 4 cabins and 1 conference room. Breakfast and snacks/refreshments included in rates. Types of meals: Full gourmet bkfst, early coffee/tea and picnic lunch. Restaurant on premises. Beds: KQDT. Reading lamp in room. TV, VCR, library and parlor games on premises. Weddings, small meetings and seminars hosted. Hiking, horseback riding, shopping and Rocky Mountain National Park nearby.

Publicity: *Bon Appetit, Taste of Home, Rocky Mountain News, Country Living and Discovery Channel.*

"This place unlocked my heart!"

Black Dog Inn

650 S. Saint Vrain Ave.
Estes Park, CO 80517
(970)586-0374
E-mail: blkdoginn@aol.com
Web: www.blackdoginn.com

Circa 1910. Imagine relaxing in a private romantic whirlpool enjoying a warm fire while surrounded by views of the majestic Rocky Mountains. Travelers are sure to enjoy this romantic getaway and mountain retreat. All rooms have private baths with marble showers, and two rooms include Jacuzzi tubs and fireplaces. Tasteful family antiques decorate each room. The innkeepers invite guests to enjoy the many seasons of the Rockies.

Historic Interest: Stanley Hotel (one-half mile), Historical Museum (one-quarter mile), Enos Mills Cabin (8 miles), McGregor Ranch Museum (3 miles).

Innkeeper(s): Norm & Dee Pritchard. $85-165. 4 rooms with PB, 3 with FP and 3 suites. Breakfast and snacks/refreshments included in rates. Types of meals: Full gourmet bkfst and early coffee/tea. Beds: Q. Reading lamp, refrigerator, ceiling fan and tubs for two in room. VCR, library, parlor games, telephone, fireplace and 100+ movies on premises. Weddings, small meetings and seminars hosted. Antiquing, cross-country skiing, fishing, golf, hiking, horseback riding, shopping, boating, snowshoeing, river rafting, fly fishing, white water rafting, rock climbing, backpacking and Rocky Mt. National Park nearby.

Publicity: *Rocky Mountain News, Denver Post, Country Inns and Historic Inns.*

"The peace and tranquility are so refreshing."

Eagle Manor-A Bed and Breakfast Place

441 Chiquita Lane
Estes Park, CO 80517-1013
(970)586-8482 (888)603-3578 Fax:(970)586-1748
E-mail: mike@eaglemanor.com
Web: www.eaglemanor.com

Circa 1917. Elk and deer often roam across the grounds that surround Eagle Manor. The historic home boasts Rocky Mountain views. Frank Bond, a local pioneer built the home. There are four guest rooms, and all guests enjoy amenities such as an indoor swimming pool, sauna, and outdoor hot tub. Enjoy a game of billiards in the manor's great room, which is warmed by a fireplace. The stunning wilderness around Estes Park includes a host of activities, including rock climbing, hiking, whitewater rafting, horseback riding and a variety of festivals and seasonal events.

Innkeeper(s): Mike Smith. $125-145. 4 rooms, 3 with PB and 1 suite. Breakfast and snacks/refreshments included in rates. Types of meals: Full bkfst, veg bkfst and early coffee/tea. Beds: QT. Cable TV, VCR, reading lamp, clock radio and telephone in room. Fax, copier, spa, swimming, library, parlor games, fireplace, billiard table and basketball half court on premises. Weddings, small meetings, family reunions and seminars hosted. Antiquing, art galleries, bicycling, canoeing/kayaking, cross-country skiing, downhill skiing, fishing, golf, hiking, horseback riding, live theater, museums, parks, shopping, sporting events, tennis and wineries nearby.

Romantic RiverSong B&B

1765 Lower Broadview Rd
Estes Park, CO 80517
(970)586-4666 Fax:(970)577-0699
E-mail: romanticriversong@earthlink.net
Web: www.romanticriversong.com

Circa 1927. This Craftsman-style country inn sits on a private wildlife habitat of 27 acres adjacent to Rocky Mountain National Park. Each of the enchanting guest bedrooms, appropriately named after ten local wildflowers, exudes a romantic charm. They all feature fireplaces, large antique, jetted, sunken or whirlpool tubs and unique showers such as a rock wall waterfall and a rooftop shower for two. Stargaze through skylights, and enjoy spectacular views from private decks. Start the day with RiverSong coffee or Mexican hot chocolate. A generous breakfast includes a fruit starter, a savory, potato or sweet main entree, and perhaps John Wayne casserole with sour cream peach muffins. Outdoors, the breath-taking scenery is enhanced by extensive varieties of birds, trout streams and deer. Close by are some of the nation's best hiking and snowshoeing trails. RiverSong's forte is offering fantastic wedding packages.

Historic Interest: A very well-maintained classic mountain Craftsman inn that has been tastefully added on. The inn has a grand history of family fun and hospitality when it was a private lodge. The tradition is carried on today. The Motto is "Romantic RiverSong, your new mountain home."

Innkeeper(s): Gary & Sue Mansfield. $150-295. 10 rooms with PB, 9 with FP, 5 suites and 4 cottages. Breakfast, afternoon tea and snacks/refreshments included in rates. Types of meals: Full gourmet bkfst, veg bkfst, early coffee/tea and dinner. Beds: KQ. Reading lamp, CD player, ceiling fan, turn-down service, desk, hot tub/spa, fireplace, heat-radiating floors, skylights and libraries in room. Spa, library, telephone, fireplace, gift shop, ponds, mountain stream, hiking trails and tree swings on premises. Handicap access. Weddings and seminars hosted. Antiquing, art galleries, bicycling, canoeing/kayaking, cross-country skiing, fishing, golf, hiking, horseback riding, live theater, museums, parks, shopping, Rocky Mountain National Park and Forest, rock climbing, Nature seminars and animal and bird watching nearby.

Publicity: *Selected Colorado's most Romantic Bed and Breakfast, Romantic Inns of America, Rocky Mountain News, "10 Best Inns of Colorado", Channel 7 Valentine week most romantic, channel 7 on "Colorado Getaways" and Discovery Channel featured on "Great Country Inns" series.*

Evergreen   C6

Bears Inn B&B

27425 Spruce Lane
Evergreen, CO 80439
(303)670-1205 (800)863-1205 Fax:(303)670-8542
E-mail: innkeepers@bearsinn.com
Web: www.bearsinn.com

Circa 1924. Guests have been drawn to the stunning mountain views and tradition of hospitality at this historic lodge since the 1920s. Originally a summer resort, this bed and breakfast is now open for year-round enjoyment. The comfortable rustic interior boasts exposed logs and hardwood floors. Gather to read or relax by the inviting, large stone fireplace in the Great Room. Guest bedrooms are decorated and furnished to reflect a theme. Antiques and clawfoot tubs add a nostalgic elegance. Native American fabrics decorate the Dakota Room. Linger over a gourmet candlelight breakfast each morning. Soak up the scenery on the spacious deck with a gas log campfire, or in the outdoor hot tub. Ask about murder mystery events. Biking, hiking, fishing, ice skating, cross-country skiing- these are some of the myriad of local activities available. Take a gold mine tour or visit Denver just 35 miles away.

Innkeeper(s): Vicky Bock. $110-180. 11 rooms with PB, 1 suite and 1 conference room. Breakfast and snacks/refreshments included in rates. Types of meals: Country bkfst, veg bkfst and afternoon tea. Beds: KQ. Modem hookup, data port, cable TV, VCR, reading lamp, clock radio and telephone in room. Fax, copier, spa, library, parlor games and fireplace on premises. Small meetings, family reunions and seminars hosted. Amusement parks, antiquing, art galleries, bicycling, canoeing/kayaking, fishing, golf, hiking, horseback riding, museums, parks and shopping nearby.

Frisco   C5

Frisco Lodge

321 Main Street
Frisco, CO 80443
(970)668-0195 (800)279-6000 Fax:(970)668-0149
E-mail: info@friscolodge.com
Web: www.friscolodge.com

Circa 1885. Originally built as a stagecoach stop, this historic lodge in the Rocky Mountains has been renovated recently as a unique bed & breakfast. Use of an Internet workstation is welcomed in the living room where reading by the fire or watching TV also are enjoyed. Eight types of accommodations are offered. Victorian deluxe or classic are in the main lodge with one or two bedrooms, shared or private bath. The ensuite building includes standard, queen and king deluxe, or a two-room suite with Jacuzzi tub and mini kitchen. A one-bedroom cottage with a studio area, full kitchen, bath, dining and living room also is available. Savor a satisfying buffet breakfast full of delicious delights. Later, partake of afternoon snacks on one of the scenic decks. An outdoor hot tub overlooks the courtyard and native flower and water garden.

Historic Interest: Built in 1885, the lodge is steeped in local and Colorado history.

Innkeeper(s): Susan Wentworth. $55-260. 18 rooms, 12 with PB, 4 suites, 1 cottage and 1 conference room. Breakfast, afternoon tea and snacks/refreshments included in rates. Types of meals: Full gourmet bkfst. Beds: KQDT. Modem hook-up, data port, cable TV, VCR, reading lamp, refrigerator, ceiling fan, snack bar, clock radio, telephone, coffeemaker, desk, hot tub/spa, fireplace and high-speed Internet access in room. Fax, copier, spa, library, parlor games and fireplace on premises. Weddings, small meetings and family reunions hosted. Antiquing, art galleries, bicycling, canoeing/kayaking, cross-country skiing, downhill skiing, fishing, golf, hiking, horseback riding, live theater, museums, parks, shopping, sporting events, tennis, water sports, mountain biking, wilderness area and sailing nearby.

Glenwood Springs   C3

Glenwood Springs Victorian B & B

1020 Colorado Ave
Glenwood Springs, CO 81601-3320
(970)945-0517

Circa 1909. Decorative shingles in shades of purple and white with gingerbread trim accent the historic wood frame of this Victorian Stick house. Restored to reflect its original era, oak moldings and wainscoting mingle with wallpapers and lace as well as French, American and English antique furnishings. The parlor boasts an oak and marble fireplace mantle and chandelier. Lavish guest bedrooms include robes, comforters, quilts and fine linens. Ask about in-room mini spa treatments. An elegant and hearty breakfast is served in the dining room with crystal, silver and china. Enjoy afternoon tea with treats.

Innkeeper(s): Renee Pogrow. $100-135. 3 rooms, 1 with PB. Breakfast, afternoon tea and snacks/refreshments included in rates. Types of meals: Full gourmet bkfst, veg bkfst and early coffee/tea. Beds: Q. Reading lamp, clock radio, robes and fans in room. TV, VCR, library, parlor games, telephone, fire-

place, front porch, gifts and mini spa treatments on premises. Weddings and family reunions hosted. Amusement parks, antiquing, art galleries, bicycling, canoeing/kayaking, cross-country skiing, downhill skiing, fishing, golf, hiking, horseback riding, live theater, museums, parks, shopping, tennis, wineries, hot springs, vapor caves and caverns nearby.

Green Mountain Falls   D6

Outlook Lodge B&B

6975 Howard St, PO Box 586
Green Mountain Falls, CO 80819
(719)684-2303 (877)684-7800

Circa 1889. Outlook Lodge was originally the parsonage for the historic Church in the Wildwood. Located at the 7,800-foot altitude above the secluded mountain village of Green Lake at the foot of Pikes Peak, the inn is within 13 miles of Colorado Springs and Manitou Springs. Hand-carved balustrades surround a veranda that frames the alpine village view, and many original parsonage furnishings are inside. Antiques and quilts decorate the lodge rooms and two-bed suites. Hearty mountain breakfasts are offered, which include egg bakes, pancakes and freshly baked breads. Ride the cog railroad, fish the trout streams, hike or ice skate in winter on Green Mountain Falls Lake by the gazebo.

Innkeeper(s): Pat & Diane Drayton. $85-115. 5 rooms with PB. Breakfast included in rates. Types of meals: Full bkfst and early coffee/tea. Beds: Q. Reading lamp, clock radio and desk in room. TV, parlor games, telephone, fireplace and hot tub on premises. Small meetings, family reunions and seminars hosted. Hiking and Pikes Peak nearby.

Publicity: *Denver Post and Colorado Springs Gazette.*

"Found by chance, will return with purpose."

Gunnison   E4

Mary Lawrence Inn

601 N Taylor St
Gunnison, CO 81230-2241
(970)641-3343 Fax:(970)641-6719

Circa 1885. A local entrepreneur and saloon owner built this Italianate home in the late 19th century, but the innkeepers named their home in honor of Mary Lawrence, a later resident. Lawrence, a teacher and administrator for the local schools, used the building as a boarding house. The innkeepers have created an inviting interior with touches such as patchwork quilts, antique furnishings and stenciled walls. A variety of treats are served each morning for breakfast, and the cookie jar is kept full. The inn offers convenient access to the area's bounty of outdoor activities.

Historic Interest: In the hills near Gunnison are several mining ghost towns. A local museum is open during the summer months. Self-guided tours of the historic buildings are available. The Crested Butte historic district is 30 miles away.

Innkeeper(s): Janette McKinny. $69-135. 7 rooms with PB and 2 suites. Breakfast included in rates. Types of meals: Full gourmet bkfst and early coffee/tea. Beds: KQT. Reading lamp and clock radio in room. Fax, copier, library, parlor games, telephone and hot tub on premises. Family reunions hosted. Cross-country skiing, downhill skiing, fishing, live theater, parks, shopping and water sports nearby.

Publicity: *Rocky Mountain News, Denver Post and Gunnison Country.*

"You two are so gracious to make our stay a bit of 'heaven' in the snow."

The Ranch House B&B

233 County Road 48
Gunnison, CO 81230
(970)642-0210 (866)895-0986 Fax:(970)642-0211

Circa 1875. Originally a hand-hewn log cabin, this 1875 ranch/Victorian inn provides guests comfort in the midst of glorious views. At the entrance to beautiful Ohio Creek Valley and 25 miles from Crested Butte Historic District, the inn offers three guest bedrooms that accommodate children. Hearty and lite breakfasts are offered each morning. The hearty country breakfasts of egg dishes, bacon/sausage, hash browns, homemade baked goods and fresh fruit is perfect for the guest who intends to go hiking, biking, rafting, fishing, climbing, horseback riding, hunting, skiing, wrangling, snowmobiling or snowshoeing. An afternoon snack awaits hungry guests each afternoon in the ranch house dining room. End your evening by watching the stars as you soak in the hot tub or sit around the fire pit.
Innkeeper(s): Steve & Tammy Shelafo. $75-100. 3 rooms, 2 with PB. Breakfast and snacks/refreshments included in rates. Types of meals: Country bkfst and early coffee/tea. Beds: Q. TV, VCR, reading lamp and clock radio in room. Fax, copier, spa, bicycles, telephone, laundry facility, satellite TV and picnic area on premises. Antiquing, art galleries, bicycling, canoeing/kayaking, cross-country skiing, downhill skiing, fishing, golf, hiking, horseback riding, museums, parks, shopping and water sports nearby.

Indian Hills   C6

Mountain View B&B

4754 Picutis Rd
Indian Hills, CO 80454
(303)697-6896 (800)690-0434 Fax:(303)697-6896

Circa 1920. Two-and-a-half acres surround this mountain home, which was built as a writer's retreat. In the mid-1950s, the home served as a lodge. The innkeepers hail from Great Britain and Germany and have decorated the home in European style. In addition to rooms in the main house, there is a cottage decorated in Southwestern style. Breakfasts include items such as homemade coffeecake accompanied with a savory egg casserole entrée. The bed & breakfast is a half-hour from downtown Denver.
Innkeeper(s): Graham & Ortrud Richardson. $80-175. 5 rooms with PB, 2 suites and 1 cottage. Breakfast and snacks/refreshments included in rates. Types of meals: Full gourmet bkfst, veg bkfst, early coffee/tea and room service. Beds: Q. Modem hook-up, cable TV, VCR, reading lamp, stereo, refrigerator, ceiling fan, snack bar, clock radio, telephone, coffeemaker, turndown service, desk and hot tub/spa in room. Air conditioning. Fax, spa, fireplace and CD player in cabin on premises. Antiquing, art galleries, bicycling, cross-country skiing, fishing, golf, hiking, horseback riding, parks and shopping nearby.
Publicity: Denver Post.

Keystone   C5

Ski Tip Lodge

764 Montezuma Rd.
Keystone, CO 80435
(970)496-4950 (800)742-0905 Fax:(970)496-4940
E-mail: dwilcox@vailresorts.com
Web: www.skitiplodge.com

Circa 1880. Built as a stagecoach stop in the 1880s, it was refurbished into the state's first ski lodge in 1940. The unique atmosphere has been retained while adding a gourmet restaurant and offering Keystone Resort amenities. Wood-burning fireplaces and antique furniture enhance two inviting sitting rooms. Uncluttered guest bedrooms boast a quiet, comfortable decor with no phones or televisions. Indulge in a delicious breakfast. Relax on the patio overlooking the beaver ponds with spectacular mountain views. Enjoy the pool and hot tubs, restaurants and shopping. Kid's Night Out, summer festivals, winter fireworks, torchlight parades, stargazing workshops, wine tasting, skating, yoga, boat rentals and gondola rides are some of the many seasonal activities available. Shuttle service is provided.
Historic Interest: Built as a stagecoach stop in 1880s and was refurbished into the state's first ski lodge in 1940.
Innkeeper(s): David Wilcox. $70-210. 12 rooms, 9 with PB and 2 suites. Breakfast and afternoon tea included in rates. Types of meals: Full bkfst, early coffee/tea, snacks/refreshments and dinner. Restaurant on premises. Beds: Q. Reading lamp, clock radio and dresser in room. Fax, copier, library, telephone and fireplace on premises. Weddings, small meetings and family reunions hosted. Bicycling, canoeing/kayaking, cross-country skiing, downhill skiing, fishing, golf, hiking, horseback riding, parks, shopping, mountain biking, white-water rafting, festivals, free weekly events, scenic wagon rides, sailing, swimming, 4-wheel drive tours, historical tours, fitness center/spa, snowboarding, ice skating, snowshoeing, snowmobiling, horse-drawn sleigh rides, wine tasting, yoga, storytelling, marshmallow roasting, guest welcome receptions, gold panning and night skiing (with each reservation guests receive a Mountain Passport giving them many of these activities for free) nearby.
Publicity: Country Inns, Country Living, Innsider and 5280.

Leadville   D5

The Apple Blossom Inn Victorian B&B

120 W 4th St
Leadville, CO 80461-3630
(719)486-2141 (800)982-9279 Fax:(719)486-0994
E-mail: applebb@amigo.net
Web: www.theappleblossominn.com

Circa 1879. Featuring comfort and hospitality, this elegant Victorian home sits on downtown's historic Millionaire's Row. The living room features an antique fireplace, perfect for relaxing with friends. Spacious guest bedrooms are furnished with feather beds and terry cloth robes and boast stained glass windows and fireplaces. Escape from city life to this quiet location, perfect for enjoying the area's many outdoor activities.

Innkeeper(s): Elizabeth Lang. $79-149. 5 rooms with PB, 2 with FP and 2 suites. Breakfast and afternoon tea included in rates. Types of meals: Full gourmet bkfst and early coffee/tea. Beds: KQDT. Reading lamp, clock radio and desk in room. Parlor games, telephone and fireplace on premises. Weddings, small meetings and family reunions hosted. Antiquing, cross-country skiing, downhill skiing, fishing, golf, hiking, live theater, parks, shopping, tennis and water sports nearby.
Publicity: Rocky Mountain News and Denver Post.

"We have stayed at other bed & breakfasts, but the Apple Blossom Inn really felt like home."

The Ice Palace Inn Bed & Breakfast

813 Spruce St
Leadville, CO 80461-3555
(719)486-8272 (800)754-2840 Fax:(719)486-0345

Circa 1899. Innkeeper Kami Kolakowski was born in this historic Colorado town, and it was her dream to one day return and run a bed & breakfast. Now with husband Giles, she has created a restful retreat out of this turn-of-the-century home built with lumber from the famed Leadville Ice Palace. Giles and Kami have filled the home with antiques and pieces of history from the Ice Palace and the town. Guests are treated to a mouth-watering gourmet breakfast with treats such as stuffed French toast or German apple pancakes. After a day enjoying Leadville, come back and enjoy a soak in the hot tub.

Historic Interest: The Baby Doe Tabor Museum, National Mining Hall of Fame, Tabor Opera House and Healy House are among Leadville's historic attractions, and all are near the Ice Palace Inn.

Innkeeper(s): Giles & Kami Kolakowski. $89-149. 5 rooms with PB, 5 with FP. Breakfast, afternoon tea and snacks/refreshments included in rates. Types of meals: Full gourmet bkfst, early coffee/tea and room service. Beds: KQDT. TV, VCR, reading lamp, ceiling fan, clock radio, turn-down service and desk in room. Spa, library, parlor games, telephone, fireplace and hot tub on premises. Weddings, small meetings, family reunions and seminars hosted. Antiquing, cross-country skiing, downhill skiing, fishing, live theater, parks, shopping and water sports nearby.

Publicity: Herald Democrat, The Denver Post, The Great Divide, Good Morning America, CNN and The Fox Report.

The Leadville Country Inn

127 E 8th St
Leadville, CO 80461-3507
(719)486-2354 (800)748-2354 Fax:(719)486-0300
E-mail: info@leadvillebednbreakfast.com

Circa 1892. Colorado's spectacular scenery follows along the route of the Silver Kings into Leadville at a height of 10,200 feet. Staying in this restored Victorian adds more magic to your experience. Built by a mining executive, this Queen Anne offers a romantic turret and many original features. There is a hot tub in the garden. The inn is often selected for anniversaries and is a popular romantic getaway for couples.

Innkeeper(s): Maureen & Gretchen Scanlon. $70-160. 9 rooms with PB. Breakfast included in rates. Types of meals: Full gourmet bkfst, early coffee/tea and snacks/refreshments. Ceiling fan and some with TV in room. VCR and spa on premises. Weddings, small meetings, family reunions and seminars hosted. Antiquing, cross-country skiing, downhill skiing, fishing, hiking and shopping nearby.

Publicity: Rocky Mountain News, Herald Democrat, Country Travels, Sunset Magazine and Denver Post.

"This Inn has more charm than a love story written for entertainment."

Peri & Ed's Mountain Hide Away

201 W 8th St
Leadville, CO 80461-3529
(719)486-0716 (800)933-3715 Fax:(719)486-2181

Circa 1879. This former boarding house was built during the boom days of Leadville. Families can picnic on the large lawn sprinkled with wildflowers under soaring pines. Shoppers and history buffs can enjoy exploring historic Main Street, one block away. The surrounding mountains are a natural playground offering a wide variety of activities, and the innkeepers will be happy to let you know their favorite spots and help with directions. The sunny Augusta Tabor room features a sprawling king-size bed with a warm view of the rugged peaks.

Innkeeper(s): Eva Vigil. $49-129. 10 rooms with PB, 2 with FP and 2 cottages. Breakfast included in rates. Types of meals: Full bkfst. Beds: KQDT. Ceiling fan and clock radio in room. VCR, spa, library, parlor games and telephone on premises. Family reunions hosted. Antiquing, cross-country skiing, downhill skiing, fishing, live theater, parks and shopping nearby.

Loveland   B6

Sylvan Dale Guest Ranch

2939 North County Road 31D
Loveland, CO 80538-9763
(970)667-3915 (877)667-3999 Fax:(970)635-9336
E-mail: ranch@sylvandale.com
Web: www.sylvandale.com

Circa 1920. There is room to roam at this scenic, 3200-acre, family-owned dude ranch in the foothills. Accommodations are furnished in a traditional Western and warm country decor. Each comfortable, air-conditioned cabin is equipped with a refrigerator, coffeemaker, fireplace and outside deck. The two-story Wagon Wheel Bunkhouse includes a full kitchen and gathering room in the common area. Two-bedroom suites are offered in the original Jessup Lodge and the J-House that has a living room and covered porch overlooking the Big Thompson River. Gather for a hearty breakfast in the Antique Dining Room. Play volleyball, horseshoes or tennis. Outdoor enthusiasts may try fly fishing, horseback riding and cattle drives. Relax by the river or hike the extensive nature trails.

Historic Interest: Homesteaded in 1864, original building, inside kitchens, Dude Ranch since 1920s. Native American archeological sites.

Innkeeper(s): Susan Jessup, David Jessup. $75-235. 25 rooms, 10 with PB, 3 with FP, 2 suites, 12 cabins and 4 conference rooms. Breakfast included in rates. Types of meals: Country bkfst, veg bkfst, early coffee/tea and picnic lunch. Beds: KQDT. Reading lamp, refrigerator, clock radio, coffeemaker, desk, fireplace and guest houses have full kitchens in room. Air conditioning. TV, VCR, fax, copier, swimming, stable, tennis, library, parlor games, telephone, fireplace, gift shop, fly fishing, volleyball, horseshoes, tennis and picnic areas on premises. Limited handicap access. Weddings, small meetings, family reunions and seminars hosted. Antiquing, art galleries, bicycling, canoeing/kayaking, cross-country skiing, downhill skiing, fishing, golf, hiking, horseback riding, live theater, museums, parks, shopping, sporting events, tennis, water sports and wineries nearby.

Publicity: Reunions Magazine, AAA, Fly Fish America, Channel 9 News, numerous fishing videos, local news stories and Cattle Week.

Mancos   G2

Bauer House

100 Bauer Ave
Mancos, CO 81328
(970)533-9707 (800)733-9707
E-mail: bauerhse@fone.net
Web: www.bauer-house.com

Circa 1890. Built by town founder George Bauer, this three-story brick and stone Victorian home displays several of the prominent family's possessions as well as old newspapers, pictures and bank ledgers. Guest bedrooms and a suite feature a classic decor with antique furnishings and splendid mountain views. The third-floor Southwest-style penthouse includes a kitchen with a bar. Bobbi makes a changing creative menu for each day's breakfast. Enjoy popular favorites like her signature eggs Benedict, stuffed pancakes, homemade waffles or stratas accompanied by fresh fruit, muffins and breads. Relax on porches and patios, visit the inn's antique shop or take a ride to historic sites on the Bauer House Buggy (a horseless carriage). Practice on the putting green, play croquet or bocce ball. The entrance to Mesa Verde National Park is seven miles away.

Innkeeper(s): Bobbi Black. $75-125. 5 rooms with PB. Breakfast, afternoon tea and snacks/refreshments included in rates. Types of meals: Full gourmet bkfst, early coffee/tea and picnic lunch. Beds: QT. Reading lamp, ceiling fan, clock radio, turn-down service, desk and penthouse has kitchenette in room. VCR, fax, copier, parlor games, telephone, fireplace and computer e-mail on premises. Weddings, small meetings, family reunions and seminars hosted. Antiquing, fishing, golf, live theater, parks, shopping, sporting events, tennis and water sports nearby.

Publicity: *"Colorado Homes & Life Styles," "Four Corners Style," Denver Post, Durango Herald, Arrington's Book of Lists* - voted #5 two years in a row by inngoers for Best Customer Service in North America and CBS.

"Bobbi went out of her way to make our visit to Mancos more enjoyable. She is an excellent ambassador for the Mancos Valley and quite an interesting person to know. The Bauer House should be recommended as the place to stay, to anyone visiting the area!"

Manitou Springs   E6

Cliff House at Pikes Peak

306 Canon Ave
Manitou Springs, CO 80829-1712
(719)685-3000 (888)212-7000 Fax:(719)685-3913
E-mail: information@thecliffhouse.com
Web: www.thecliffhouse.com

Circa 1874. Built as a boarding house and stagecoach stop, this rambling Queen Anne Victorian later became a resort hotel catering to those who visited the local mineral springs. Distinguished guests include President Theodore Roosevelt, Thomas Edison, Clark Gable, Henry Ford, J. Paul Getty and Crown Prince Ferdinand. Listed in the National Register, the inn has been meticulously restored to retain its historical integrity while offering the most luxurious elegance and comfort. Share afternoon tea or a glass of wine in the intimate music room by the fire. Romantic guest bedrooms and suites boast two-person spa tubs, gas fireplaces, skylights, steam showers with body sprays, heated toilet seats, towel warmers, terry-lined silk robes and mountain views. Enjoy a breakfast buffet in the formal dining room. Sitting in a rocker on the veranda is perfect for gazing at Pikes Peak.

Innkeeper(s): Paul York. $145-475. 55 rooms with PB, 38 suites and 6 conference rooms. Types of meals: Cont, afternoon tea and room service. Restaurant on premises. Beds: KQT. Data port, cable TV, VCR, CD player, refrigerator, telephone, coffeemaker, voice mail, terry-lined silk robes, hair dryers, heated toilet seats, 500-thread-count Egyptian linens, closet safe, iron and ironing board in room. Bicycling, fishing, golf, horseback riding, Jeep tours, balloon rides, white water rafting, rock climbing and spa nearby.

Publicity: *Sunset, Wine Spectator, Mountain Living, Food Art Magazine, Conde Nast Traveler, Gourmet, The Los Angeles Times, The New York Times, The Denver Post and The Rocky Mountain News.*

Gray's Avenue Hotel

711 Manitou Ave
Manitou Springs, CO 80829-1809
(719)685-1277 (800)294-1277 Fax:(719)685-1847

Circa 1886. This 1886 Queen Anne shingled Victorian inn is in the Manitou Springs Historic Preservation District, which is listed in the National Register of Historic Places. It was one of Manitou Spring's original hotels. The four guest rooms and three suites are comfortably appointed — from the cozy Bird Room with its bay window to the Orange Suite, which has three rooms, each with a double bed. Start off your day with a hearty breakfast, including courses like waffles with fresh straw-

berries and whipped cream, bacon, fresh fruit, coffee and tea. Then relax on the large front porch, stroll through the town with its shops and restaurants or put on your hiking boots to explore the incredible natural wonderland. Within walking or driving distance is the Cog Railroad, Pikes Peak, the Cave of the Winds, Cliff Dwellings, the Air Force Academy, the Commonwheel Artist Co-op and a number of museums and art galleries. Hikers will enjoy Mueller State Park, Waldo Canyon, Intemann and Barr Trails, Garden of the Gods and more. Airport pickup and return can usually be arranged.

Innkeeper(s): Kevin Abney. $75. 7 rooms with PB, 3 with FP and 3 suites. Breakfast and snacks/refreshments included in rates. Types of meals: Full bkfst, veg bkfst and early coffee/tea. Beds: KQDT. Cable TV, reading lamp, clock radio and three with fireplace in room. VCR, fax, copier, spa, library, parlor games, telephone, fireplace and massages on premises. Small meetings and family reunions hosted. Antiquing, art galleries, bicycling, fishing, golf, hiking, horseback riding, live theater, museums, parks, shopping, sporting events and tennis nearby.

Peacock Bed & Breakfast

41 Lincoln Ave.
Manitou Springs, CO 80829
(719)685-0123 (866)685-0123
E-mail: info@peacockbedandbreakfast.com
Web: www.peacockbedandbreakfast.com

Circa 1895. Fully restored, this large, three-story Queen Anne Victorian with white balconies and a wraparound veranda has had an interesting history since being built in 1897. From a bordello to a missionary training center, now it is a perfect place for a romantic getaway, spiritual retreat or special treat in the foothills of the Rocky Mountains. Enjoy breathtaking views of the valley and majestic Pikes Peak. Stay in the Marrakech Suite, reminiscent of a colorful Moroccan tent. The living room boasts a VCR and CD player and French doors lead onto a private patio. A full-service kitchen is included. Other delightful guest bedrooms with wicker, mahogany, and antique furnishings feature an assortment of amenities such as Jacuzzis, a clawfoot tub, DVDs, skylights and a gas fireplace. A breakfast buffet offers a hot entrée and delicious accompaniments. Relax in the outdoor hot tub in the garden.

Historic Interest: The Peacock is a fully restored Queen-Anne Victorian with original woodwork, hardwood floors, stained glass and a Van Briggle fireplace.

Innkeeper(s): Devonna Faith. $90-155. 7 rooms with PB, 2 with FP and 1 suite. Breakfast and snacks/refreshments included in rates. Types of meals: Full gourmet bkfst, veg bkfst and early coffee/tea. Beds: QT. Cable TV, VCR, reading lamp, stereo, refrigerator, ceiling fan, snack bar, telephone, coffeemaker, hot tub/spa and fireplace in room. Central air. Spa, library, laundry facility and wraparound veranda with incredible views on premises. Antiquing, art galleries, bicycling, canoeing/kayaking, cross-country skiing, fishing, golf, hiking, horseback riding, live theater, museums, parks, shopping, sporting events, tennis, wineries, Pikes Peak, Garden of the Gods, Royal Gorge, Olympic Training Center and Air force Academy nearby.

Red Crags B&B Inn

302 El Paso Blvd
Manitou Springs, CO 80829-2308
(719)685-1920 (800)721-2248 Fax:(719)685-1073
E-mail: info@redcrags.com
Web: www.redcrags.com

Circa 1880. Well-known in this part of Colorado, this unique, four-story Victorian mansion sits on a bluff with a combination of views that includes Pikes Peak, Manitou Valley, Garden of the Gods and the city of Colorado Springs. There are antiques throughout the house. The formal dining room features a rare cherrywood Eastlake fireplace. Two of the suites include double whirlpool tubs. Outside, guests can walk through beautifully landscaped gardens or enjoy a private picnic area with a barbecue pit and a spectacular view. Wine is served in the evenings.

Innkeeper(s): Howard & Lynda Lerner.
$85-185. 8 rooms with PB, 8 with FP and 5 suites. Breakfast, afternoon tea and snacks/refreshments included in rates. Types of meals: Full bkfst and early coffee/tea. Beds: K. Reading lamp, clock radio, desk, two two-person jetted tubs, feather beds, phones and TV available upon request in room. Fax, copier, parlor games, telephone, fireplace and spa/hot tub on premises. Weddings, small meetings, family reunions and seminars hosted. Antiquing, cross-country skiing, fishing, golf, live theater, parks, shopping, sporting events, tennis, Pikes Peak and Olympic Training Center nearby.

Publicity: *Rocky Mountain News, Bridal Guide, Denver Post, Los Angeles Times, Springs Woman and Colorado Springs Gazette.*

"What a beautiful, historical and well-preserved home - exceptional hospitality and comfort. What wonderful people! Highly recommended!"

Rockledge Country Inn

328 El Paso Blvd
Manitou Springs, CO 80829-2319
(719)685-4515 (888)685-4515 Fax:(719)685-1031
E-mail: info@rockledgeinn.com
Web: www.rockledgeinn.com

Circa 1912. Honored by The Denver Post as Colorado's Most Romantic Bed and Breakfast, this five-acre estate with views of Pike's Peak, was originally built for a wealthy entrepreneur with stonework quarried locally. Each spacious suite is distinctively decorated and features gener-

ous upscale amenities. Feel pampered by luxury linens and feather mattresses with European down duvets and pillows. Many boast fireplaces and Jacuzzi tubs. Breakfast is always a culinary event. The inn is minutes from the historic district of Manitou Springs and downtown Colorado Springs. Visit nearby Garden of the Gods for breathtaking scenery, minutes from the downtown historic district.

Historic Interest: Built in 1912 by the oilman who had the first oil gusher in US, Spindeltop in Beaumont, TX.
Innkeeper(s): Deena & Bob Stuart. $175-295. 5 suites, 4 with FP and 1 cottage. Breakfast included in rates. Types of meals: Full gourmet bkfst, veg bkfst, early coffee/tea, afternoon tea, snacks/refreshments and gourmet dinner. Beds: KQ. Modem hook-up, cable TV, VCR, reading lamp, stereo, refrigerator, clock radio, telephone, coffeemaker, turn-down service, desk and hot tub/spa in room. Air conditioning. Fax, copier, spa, library, parlor games, fireplace and gift shop on premises. Limited handicap access. Weddings, small meetings, family reunions and seminars hosted. Antiquing, art galleries, bicycling, cross-country skiing, fishing, golf, hiking, horseback riding, live theater, museums, parks, shopping, sporting events, tennis, water sports and wineries nearby.

Publicity: *"Colorado's Most Romantic B&B" and The Denver Post.*

Two Sisters Inn-A Bed and Breakfast

10 Otoe Pl
Manitou Springs, CO 80829-2014
(719)685-9684 (800)274-7466
E-mail: info@twosisinn.com
Web: www.twosisinn.com

Circa 1919. Voted the most romantic place in Pikes Peak, this Victorian inn was originally built by two sisters as the Sunburst boarding house. Now celebrating its 14th anniversary, the inn

continues to be a favorite. A honeymoon cottage in the back garden, a beautiful stained-glass door, hardwood floors, a stone fireplace in the parlor and a library are among the special features. A three-course breakfast (a winner of a national innkeeper breakfast contest) features inspired mouth-watering dishes. Nestled at the base of Pikes Peak, it is one block from the center of the historic district and close to mineral springs, art galleries, shops, restaurants and the beginning of the historic Manitou Springs Walking Tour. The Garden of the Gods and the Cog Railway are one mile away while the Cave of the Winds and Cliff Dwellings are within a quarter of a mile. Guests come back to the inn for the fine cuisine and the camaraderie with the caring innkeepers.

Innkeeper(s): Wendy Goldstein & Sharon Smith. $69-125. 5 rooms, 4 with PB. Breakfast included in rates. Types of meals: Full gourmet bkfst. Beds: D. Reading lamp, refrigerator and clock radio in room. Telephone and fireplace on premises. Antiquing, bicycling, hiking and shopping nearby.

Publicity: *Rocky Mountain News, Gazette Telegraph, The Denver Post and Country Inns.*

"The welcome is so sincere you'll want to return again and again."

Victoria's Keep Bed & Breakfast Inn

202 Ruxton Ave
Manitou Springs, CO 80829
(719)685-5354 (800)905-5337 Fax:(719)685-5913
E-mail: info@victoriaskeep.com
Web: www.victoriaskeep.com

Circa 1892. A stream passes by the wraparound front porch of this Queen Anne Victorian. Stained glass windows and a turret complete the picture. The home is furnished in period antiques, and there are coordinated wallpapers. Every room has a fireplace of its own as well as Queen beds. Most have whirlpool tubs for two and feather beds. Afternoon dessert is offered, and in the morning a gourmet breakfast is served.

Historic Interest: Turret, antique lighting, William Morris wallpaper.
Innkeeper(s): Gerry & Donna Anderson. $80-185. 6 rooms, 2 with PB, 5 with FP and 4 suites. Breakfast, afternoon tea and snacks/refreshments included in rates. Types of meals: Full gourmet bkfst, veg bkfst and early coffee/tea. Beds: Q. Reading lamp, CD player, refrigerator, clock radio, hot tub/spa and fireplace in room. Air conditioning. TV, VCR, library, parlor games, telephone and fireplace on premises. Small meetings and family reunions hosted. Antiquing, art galleries, bicycling, canoeing/kayaking, fishing, golf, hiking, horseback riding, live theater, museums, parks, shopping, sporting events and United States Olympic Training Center nearby.

Montrose   E3

The Uncompahgre Lodge B&B

21049 Uncompahgre Rd
Montrose, CO 81401-8750
(970)240-4000 (800)318-8127 Fax:(970)249-5124

Circa 1914. Once the local schoolhouse, this modified prairie-style brick building boasts a penthouse and small bell tower. The inn's tall windows provide views of the surrounding mountains and country setting. Some of the guest rooms allow for as many as six people, with two queen beds and one king-size bed, making it comfortable for families with children. The French Country Room offers a two-person Jacuzzi with mirror, a king bed, CD music, candles and an electric log fireplace popular in both winter and summer because it crackles, flickers and smells like pine but does not generate heat. The great room, formerly the old auditorium and stage area, is the location for breakfast and catered affairs.

Innkeeper(s): Barbara & Richard Helm. $58-105. 9 rooms with PB and 1 conference room. Breakfast and afternoon tea included in rates. Types of meals: Full bkfst and early coffee/tea. Beds: KQ. Cable TV, VCR, reading lamp, ceiling fan, clock radio and desk in room. Fax, copier, spa, library, telephone, billiard room and piano on premises. Limited handicap access. Weddings, small meetings, family reunions and seminars hosted. Antiquing, cross-country skiing, downhill skiing, fishing, golf, live theater, parks, shopping, tennis, water sports and Black Canyon of Gunnison National Park nearby.

Publicity: *Montrose Daily Press and Denver Post.*

Ouray   F3

Christmas House B&B Inn

310 Main
Ouray, CO 81427
(970)325-4992 (888)325-9627 Fax:(970)325-4992

Circa 1889. Peace and goodwill abound at this delightful romantic Victorian lodge surrounded by the San Juan Range of the Rocky Mountains. The tiny town, population 700, is nine blocks long and six blocks wide. It sits at the northern end of the portion of Highway 550 known as "The Million Dollar Highway" because of its spectacular views. The inn has five deluxe suites, each with a double whirlpool tub and awesome views. Four have fireplaces and private entrances. Guests can enjoy the Dickensesque English Ivy suite with its antique Victorian bed and breathtaking mountain view. Or they may choose the Mistletoe (perfect for honeymooners and other lovers) with its fireplace and pink half canopy bed. Breakfast is a celebration of menus with names like "Joy To The World," "Up on the Housetop" and "Feliz Navidad." Happy, hungry guests will enjoy entrees like maple/rosemary grilled ham, crepes, waffles, omelets and juices.

Innkeeper(s): George Allyson Crosby. $95-170. 5 suites, 4 with FP. Breakfast and snacks/refreshments included in rates. Types of meals: Full gourmet bkfst, veg bkfst, early coffee/tea and gourmet dinner. Beds: QT. Modem hook-up, data port, cable TV, VCR, reading lamp, stereo, refrigerator, ceiling fan, clock radio, telephone, coffeemaker, turn-down service, desk, hot tub/spa, fireplace, private Jacuzzis for two, private entrances, private & shared saunas for two, robes and dryers in room. Air conditioning. TV, fax, copier, sauna, library, parlor games, fireplace, gift shop, video/CD library, telescope, local menus, ice and iron/board on premises. Antiquing, art galleries, bicycling, canoeing/kayaking, cross-country skiing, downhill skiing, fishing, golf, hiking, horseback riding, live theater, museums, parks, shopping, tennis, water sports, wineries, Jeep tours and rentals, mine tours, ballooning, mountain biking, ice climbing, sledding, snowmobiling, snowshoeing and ice skating nearby.

Publicity: *Westwind, West Life and KJYE.*

St. Elmo Hotel

426 Main St, PO Box 667
Ouray, CO 81427-0667
(970)325-4951 Fax:(970)325-0348
E-mail: steh@rmi.net
Web: www.stelmohotel.com

Circa 1898. The inn was built by Kitty Heit, with views of the amphitheater, Twin Peaks and Mt. Abrams, and it has operated as a hotel for most of its life. Rosewood sofas and chairs covered in red and green velvet, and a piano furnish the parlor. The Bon Ton Restaurant occupies the stone-walled basement, and it's only a short walk to the hot springs.

Historic Interest: The Town of Ouray is a National Historical District.

Innkeeper(s): Dan & Sandy Lingenfelter. $85-140. 9 rooms with PB and 2 suites.

Breakfast included in rates. Restaurant on premises. Beds: KQ. Spa and sauna on premises. Antiquing, cross-country skiing, downhill skiing, fishing and water sports nearby.

Publicity: *Colorado Homes & Lifestyles.*

"So full of character and so homely, it is truly delightful. The scenery in this area is breathtaking."

Wiesbaden Hot Springs Spa & Lodgings

625 5th St
Ouray, CO 81427
(970)325-4347 Fax:(970)325-4358
E-mail: lodge@wiesbadenhotsprings.com
Web: www.wiesbadenhotsprings.com

Circa 1879. Built directly above natural mineral hot springs, this historic lodging establishment has a European flair. Below the main lodge and into the mountain is the natural Vaporcave, where the hot springs flow from thousands of feet below the earth's surface into a 108 degree soaking pool. The remains of an adobe where Chief Ouray resided while using the sacred water for its medicinal and healing qualities can be seen on the property. The Vaporcave, outdoor swimming pool and Lorelei, a privately rented outdoor soaking spa are all continually flowing hot springs. Therapeutic massage, Raindrop, LaStone and Dry Brushings are also offered as well as Aveda Concept Spa facials, wraps and polishes. The Wiesbaden is considered a place of unequaled ambiance.

Innkeeper(s): Linda Wright-Minter. $120-335. 20 rooms with PB, 2 with FP, 2 suites and 2 cottages. Types of meals: Early coffee/tea. Beds: KQDT. Cable TV, reading lamp, refrigerator and telephone in room. Spa, swimming and fireplace on premises. Weddings, small meetings and family reunions hosted. Antiquing, cross-country skiing, downhill skiing, fishing, golf, parks, shopping, tennis and water sports nearby.

Publicity: *Travel & Leisure, National Geographics Traveler, Spa, Sunset, Money, Lifestyles, New York Times and many other publications.*

Paonia   D3

The Bross Hotel B&B

312 Onarga AVe.
Paonia, CO 81428
(970)527-6776 Fax:(970)527-7737
E-mail: brosshotel@paonia.com
Web: www.paonia-inn.com

Circa 1906. A group of artisans, carpenters and craftspeople restored this turn-of-the-century western hotel to its original splendor with front porch and balcony. Wood floors and trim, dormer windows and exposed brick walls all add to the Victorian decor. For pleasure, relax in the sitting area or library/TV/game room. A conference room and communications center is perfect for business. Guest bedrooms feature antiques and handmade quilts. Some can be adjoined into suites. Breakfast is an adventure in seasonal culinary delights that cover the antique back bar in the dining room. Visit Black Canyon, Gunnison National Park, Grand Mesa, West Elk and Ragged Wilderness areas.

Innkeeper(s): Linda Lentz . $100. 10 rooms with PB and 1 conference room. Breakfast and snacks/refreshments included in rates. Types of meals: Full gourmet bkfst, veg bkfst and early coffee/tea. Beds: KQDT. Modem hook-up, data port, ceiling fan and telephone in room. TV, VCR, fax, copier, spa, library and parlor games on premises. Weddings, small meetings, family reunions and seminars hosted. Antiquing, art galleries, bicycling, canoeing/kayaking, cross-country skiing, fishing, golf, hiking, horseback riding, museums, parks, shopping, wineries, dinosaur dig and explore the many activities of the Black Canyon of the Gunnison National Park nearby.

Publicity: *Denver Post and Grand Junction Sentinel.*

Pueblo E7

Abriendo Inn

300 W Abriendo Ave
Pueblo, CO 81004-1814
(719)544-2703 Fax:(719)542-6544
E-mail: info@abriendoinn.com
Web: www.abriendoinn.com

Circa 1906. Upon entering this inn, it becomes apparent why it was chosen "Pueblo's Best Weekend Getaway" and "Best Bed and Breakfast Inn for the Colorado Front Range." Special details include curved stained-glass windows, a spiral staircase and parquet floors. Comfortably elegant guest

bedrooms feature canopy or brass beds, heart-shaped double whirlpool tubs, cable TV, VCR, microwave and small refrigerator. A typical breakfast served at flexible

times, might include a fruit cup, tomato-basil frittata, nectarine kuchen, cheddar toast, Dutch crumb muffin and beverages. A 24-hour complimentary snack/refreshment center is an added convenience. Enjoy the one acre of park-like grounds and a wraparound porch lined with wicker rockers and chairs for a relaxing change of pace.

Historic Interest: Historic Union Avenue District (within 4 blocks), where Bat Masterson walked the streets & site of "Old Monarch," the Hanging Tree.

Innkeeper(s): Mark and Cassandra Chase . $74-130. 10 rooms, 9 with PB and 1 suite. Breakfast included in rates. Types of meals: Full gourmet bkfst, veg bkfst, early coffee/tea and snacks/refreshments. Beds: KQ. Modem hookup, data port, cable TV, VCR, reading lamp, refrigerator, ceiling fan, snack bar, clock radio, telephone, desk and whirlpool tub for two in room. Air conditioning. TV, fax, copier, parlor games, fireplace and gift shop on premises. Family reunions hosted. Antiquing, art galleries, beach, bicycling, canoeing/kayaking, cross-country skiing, fishing, golf, hiking, horseback riding, live theater, museums, parks, shopping, sporting events, tennis and water sports nearby.

Publicity: Pueblo Chieftain, Rocky Mountain News, Denver Post, Colorado Springs Gazette, Sunset Magazine and Boulder Daily Camera.

"This is a great place with the friendliest people. I've been to a lot of B&Bs; this one is top drawer."

Salida E5

River Run Inn

8495 Co Rd 160
Salida, CO 81201
(719)539-3818 (800)385-6925 Fax:(801)659-1878

Circa 1895. This gracious brick home, a National Register building, is located on the banks of the Arkansas River, three miles from town. It was once the poor farm, for folks down on their luck who were willing to work in exchange for food and lodging. The house has been renovated to reflect a country-eclectic style and has six guest rooms, most enhanced by mountain views. The location is ideal for anglers, rafters, hikers, bikers and skiers. A 13-bed, third floor is great for groups. A full country breakfast, afternoon cookies and refreshments, evening brandy and sherry are offered daily.

Innkeeper(s): Sally Griego & Brad Poulson. $98-110. 6 rooms with PB and 1 conference room. Breakfast and snacks/refreshments included in rates. Types of meals: Full gourmet bkfst, veg bkfst, early coffee/tea, picnic lunch and dinner. Beds: KQT. Reading lamp in room. TV, VCR, library, parlor games, tele-

phone, fishing and lawn games on premises. Weddings, small meetings, family reunions and seminars hosted. Antiquing, art galleries, bicycling, canoeing/kayaking, cross-country skiing, downhill skiing, fishing, golf, hiking, horseback riding, live theater, museums, parks, shopping, tennis, water sports, wineries and snowshoeing nearby.

Publicity: Men's Journal, Denver Post, Colorado Springs Gazette, CBS Denver, The Travel Channel and MSNBC.com.

"So glad we found a B&B with such character and a great owner as well."

Thomas House

307 E 1st St
Salida, CO 81201-2801
(719)539-7104 (888)228-1410
E-mail: office@thomashouse.com
Web: www.thomashouse.com

Circa 1888. This home was built as a boarding house to help accommodate the thousands of railroad workers and travelers who passed through Salida. Today, the home still serves as a restful place for weary travelers drawn to the Colorado wilderness. The inn is deco-

rated with antiques, collectibles and contemporary furnishings. Each guest room is named for a mountain. The Mt.

Princeton suite includes a bedroom, private bath with an antique clawfoot tub and a separate sitting area. The innkeepers keep reading materials on hand, and there is an outdoor hot tub as well. Breakfasts are continental, yet hearty, with a variety of freshly baked breads and muffins, yogurt, granola, cheese and fruit.

Innkeeper(s): Tammy & Steve Office. $66-120. 6 rooms with PB, 1 suite and 1 cottage. Breakfast included in rates. Types of meals: Full bkfst and early coffee/tea. Beds: KQT. Reading lamp, refrigerator, ceiling fan, clock radio and suite has kitchenette in room. Spa, library, telephone and shared kitchen on premises. Small meetings and family reunions hosted. Antiquing, cross-country skiing, downhill skiing, fishing, live theater, parks, shopping, water sports and art galleries nearby.

Silverton F3

The Wyman Hotel & Inn

1371 Greene St
Silverton, CO 81433
(970)387-5372 (800)609-7845 Fax:(970)387-5745
E-mail: thewyman@frontier.net
Web: www.thewyman.com

Circa 1902. A stately building renown for its ballroom in the early 1900s, this modern luxury inn is listed in the National Register of Historic Places. Enjoy the smoke-free environment with two common rooms that offer access to a large video library. Well-appointed guest bedrooms are comfortably furnished with antiques and boast spectacular views. Stay in a romantic suite with a whirlpool bath for two. Highly acclaimed gourmet breakfasts are served in the Dining Room accented by the music of Mozart. Sunnyside souffle with roasted potatoes is one of the mouth-watering entrees that may accompany homemade baked goods, fresh fruit and Costa Rican coffee. An elegant, four-course dinner by candlelight features signature dishes such as Veal Piccata and Thai Shrimp and Scallops in Coconut Curry. Rent mountain bikes for a closer look at the San Juan

Mountains. Visit Mesa Verde National Park and Anasazi ruins or the Durango and Silverton Narrow Gauge Railroad.

Innkeeper(s): Lorraine & Tom Lewis. $120-215. 17 rooms with PB and 5 suites. Breakfast and afternoon tea included in rates. Types of meals: Full gourmet bkfst, early coffee/tea and snacks/refreshments. Beds: KQ. Data port, TV, VCR, reading lamp, ceiling fan, clock radio, telephone, turn-down service, desk, two-person whirlpools (suites), whirlpool tubs (five rooms), feather beds and down duvets in room. Fax, copier, library, art gallery, videos, wine and cheese social hour and candlelight dinner available at additional charge on premises. Weddings, small meetings and family reunions hosted. Cross-country skiing, fishing, hiking, horseback riding, live theater, parks, shopping, folk and music festival, mountain biking, jeeping to ghost towns, snowshoeing, sledding and downhill skiing at the new Silverton Mountain nearby.

Publicity: *The Denver Post, The New York Times, Albuquerque Journal, The Gazette, Douglas County News-Press, The Salt Lake Tribune, Austin American Statesman, Outdoor Channel, The Travel Channel, Denver's KUSA News and winner of national award for Best Hospitality and Best Breakfast in U.S. B&Bs.*

"Everything and everyone great, hospitable and helpful. We had to change plans and leave at 6:15 a.m. and could not stay for breakfast so Tom was up at crack of dawn to fix us something. So very beyond the call and much appreciated!!!"

Telluride   F3

New Sheridan Hotel

231 W Colorado Ave, PO Box 980
Telluride, CO 81435-0980
(970)728-4351 (800)200-1891 Fax:(970)728-5024
E-mail: info@newsheridan.com
Web: www.newsheridan.com

Circa 1895. This charming hotel reflects the Victorian ambiance of a historic mining town. The building was redecorated recently to its former glory and is the only remaining original Victorian hotel and bar in Telluride. Much of the bar's interior is original, including a cherrywood back bar with carved lions imported from Austria. The adjoining Sheridan Opera House hosted such stars as Sarah Bernhardt, Lillian Gish and William Jennings Bryan. Guests can relax in their cozy guests rooms or in the library or parlor. Fluffy terry robes, in-room ceiling fans, a fitness room and rooftop hot tubs await to pamper you. The hotel is a two-block walk from ski lifts and gondola.

Historic Interest: All the sites of charming, historic Telluride are within 10 blocks of the hotel.

Innkeeper(s): Ray Farnsworth. $90-400. 32 rooms, 24 with PB and 6 suites. Breakfast included in rates. Types of meals: Full bkfst and gourmet dinner. Restaurant on premises. Beds: KQ. Clock radio, telephone and desk in room. Fax, copier, fireplace and computer on premises. Limited handicap access. Small meetings, family reunions and seminars hosted. Antiquing, cross-country skiing, downhill skiing, fishing, live theater, parks, shopping, water sports and concerts. Horseback riding nearby.

Publicity: *Rocky Mountain News, San Francisco Examiner, Inn Style, Ski, Bon Appetit, Sunset and Arizona Republic.*

Walsenburg   F6

La Plaza Inn

118 West Sixth
Walsenburg, CO 81089
(719)738-5700 (800)352-9237 Fax:(719)738-6220

Circa 1907. Stay in the relaxed comfort of this historic stucco inn painted in traditional Southwest colors. Relax in the large well-appointed lobby or second-floor sitting room. Each guest bedroom imparts its own ambiance and is nicely furnished

with a mixture of period pieces. Many of the suites feature fully equipped kitchens. Breakfast is individually served or a buffet is set up in the on-site cafe and bookstore that boasts original 15-foot tin ceilings. Sit in the refreshing shade of the back yard. Enjoy the scenic area by skiing local mountains, hiking nearby trails or engaging in water activities and other outdoor sports.

Innkeeper(s): Martie Henderson. $75-90. 11 rooms with PB, 6 suites and 1 conference room. Breakfast included in rates. Types of meals: Country bkfst, veg bkfst, early coffee/tea and lunch. Restaurant on premises. Beds: KQDT. Modem hook-up, data port, cable TV, VCR, reading lamp, refrigerator, ceiling fan, snack bar, telephone, coffeemaker and desk in room. Air conditioning. Fax, copier, library, parlor games, cafe and bookstore on premises. Weddings, small meetings, family reunions and seminars hosted. Antiquing, art galleries, bicycling, canoeing/kayaking, cross-country skiing, fishing, golf, hiking, live theater, museums, parks, shopping, tennis and water sports nearby.

Winter Park   C5

Bear Paw Inn

871 Bear Paw Dr, PO Box 334
Winter Park, CO 80482
(970)887-1351
E-Mail: bearpaw@rkymtnhi.com
Web: www.bearpaw-winterpark.com

Circa 1989. Secluded, quiet and romantic, this massive award-winning log lodge is exactly the type of welcoming retreat one might hope to enjoy on a vacation in the Colorado wilderness, and the panoramic views of the Continental Divide and Rocky Mountain National Park are just one reason. The cozy interior is highlighted by log beams, massive log walls and antiques. There are two guest rooms, both with a Jacuzzi tub. The master has a private deck with a swing. Guests can snuggle up in feather beds topped with down comforters. Winter Park is a Mecca for skiers, and ski areas are just a few miles from the Bear Paw, as is ice skating, snowmobiling, horse-drawn sleigh rides and other winter activities. For summer guests, there is whitewater rafting, golfing, horseback riding and bike trails. There are 600 miles of bike trials, music festivals and much more.

Innkeeper(s): Rick & Sue Callahan. $170-215. 2 rooms with PB. Breakfast and snacks/refreshments included in rates. Types of meals: Full gourmet bkfst and early coffee/tea. Beds: Q. TV, reading lamp, refrigerator, turn-down service, feather beds, finest linens, Jacuzzi tubs and chocolates in room. Fax, copier, telephone, fireplace, 3-course gourmet breakfast and homemade afternoon treats each day on premises. Weddings, small meetings, family reunions and seminars hosted. Antiquing, cross-country skiing, downhill skiing, fishing, live theater, shopping, water sports, hot air balloons, mountain bikes and summer rodeos nearby.

Publicity: *Cape Cod Life, Boston Globe, Los Angeles Times, Continental Airlines Quarterly, Denver Post, Rocky Mountain News, Log Homes Illustrated, Colorado Country Life, voted "Outstanding Hospitality" by the Colorado Travel Writers and given 10 stars and chosen "Best Date Getaway" by the editors of Denver City Search.*

"Outstanding hospitality."

Connecticut

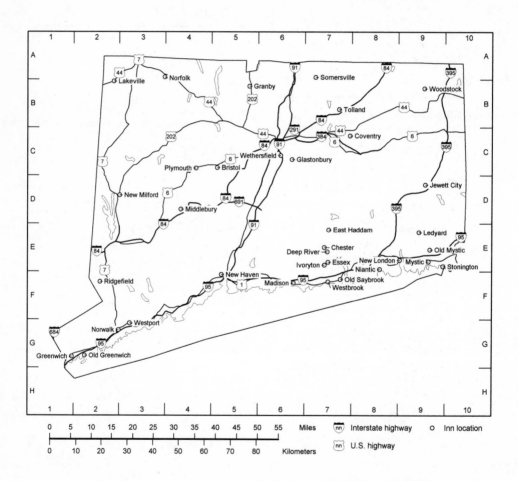

	1	2	3	4	5	6	7	8	9	10

A — 7 — 44 Lakeville — Norfolk — Granby — Somersville — 91 — 84 — 395 — Woodstock

B — 202 — 44 — Tolland — 84 — 44 — 291 — 384 — 44 — Coventry — 6 — 395

C — 7 — 202 — 44 — 91 — 6 — Wethersfield — 384 — 6 — Glastonbury — 395

Plymouth — Bristol

D — New Milford — 6 — Middlebury — 84 — 691 — 84 — 91 — 395 — Jewett City

E — 84 — 7 — Deep River — Chester — East Haddam — Ledyard — Old Mystic — 95

Ridgefield — Ivoryton — Essex — New London — Mystic — Stonington

Niantic

F — 95 — New Haven — 1 — Madison — 95 — Old Saybrook — Westbrook

G — 684 — Norwalk — Westport — 95

Greenwich — Old Greenwich

H

	1	2	3	4	5	6	7	8	9	10

0 5 10 15 20 25 30 35 40 45 50 55   Miles

0 10 20 30 40 50 60 70 80   Kilometers

nn Interstate highway   o Inn location

nn U.S. highway

Bozrah   C5

Bozrah House B&B

347 Salem Turnpike, Rt 82
Bozrah, CT 06334-1515
(860)823-1551 (888)488-7073 Fax:(860)823-1551
E-mail: bozrahhouse@aol.com
Web: www.bozrahouse.com

Circa 1892. Surrounded by an acre of grounds, this 1890s
Victorian bed & breakfast features gardens filled with annuals
and perennials. Distinctly furnished guest bedrooms are light
and airy, boasting comfort and cleanliness as highest priorities.
Share in the bounty of a full country candlelight breakfast. The
location is convenient for visits to Foxwoods and Mohegan Sun
Casinos and the famous village of Mystic.

Innkeeper(s): Ed & Maxine Hadley. $85-120. 3 rooms with PB. Breakfast
included in rates. Types of meals: Country bkfst. Beds: QD. Air conditioning.
TV, fax, copier and telephone on premises. Antiquing, art galleries, beach,
canoeing/kayaking, fishing, golf, hiking, live theater, museums, parks, shopping, sporting events and wineries nearby.

Bristol   C5

Chimney Crest Manor

5 Founders Dr
Bristol, CT 06010-5209
(860)582-4219 Fax:(860)589-8645

Circa 1930. This Tudor mansion possesses an unusual castle-
like arcade and a 45-foot living room with a stone fireplace at
each end. Many of the rooms are embellished with oak paneling and ornate plaster ceilings. One suite includes a thermo
spa. The inn is located in the historically registered Federal Hill
District, an area of large colonial homes.

Historic Interest: American Clock and Watch Museum (3 blocks), New
England Carousel Museum (one-half mile).

Innkeeper(s): Dante & Cynthia Cimadamore. $95-185. 5 rooms with PB, 1
with FP, 3 suites and 1 conference room. Breakfast included in rates. Types
of meals: Full bkfst and early coffee/tea. Beds: KQ. Cable TV, ceiling fan,
turn-down service, fireplace and spa or view in room. Air conditioning. TV,
VCR, fax, telephone and fireplace on premises. Weddings, small meetings,
family reunions and seminars hosted. Amusement parks, antiquing, cross-
country skiing, downhill skiing, golf, museums, parks and tennis nearby.

Publicity: PM Magazine and Record-Journal.

*"Great getaway — unbelievable structure. They are just not made
like this mansion anymore."*

Chester   E7

123 Main Bed & Breakfast

123 Main St.
Chester, CT 06412
(860)526-3456 Fax:(860)526-1003

Circa 1866. Originally built in the 1800s as the South District
schoolhouse, this inn has been recently restored and renovated
in keeping with the Victorian style, while adding a contemporary flair. The spacious dining room with high ceiling and 12-
over-12 windows doubles as a game or reading room. Shiny
pine floors, ceiling fans and hand-crocheted curtains enhance
the antique furnishings in the guest bedrooms and suite. A full
breakfast is prepared on weekends with lighter fare served on
the weekdays. Enjoy alfresco dining on the veranda during

warm weather. Landscaped grounds are filled with colorful and
creative flower beds, trees and fruit.

Innkeeper(s): Chris & Randy Allinson. $95-150. 5 rooms, 3 with PB, 1 suite
and 1 conference room. Breakfast and snacks/refreshments included in rates.
Types of meals: Full bkfst, veg bkfst, early coffee/tea and picnic lunch. Beds:
QT. Reading lamp, ceiling fan, clock radio and desk in room. Fax, parlor
games and telephone on premises. Weddings and small meetings hosted.
Antiquing, art galleries, beach, bicycling, canoeing/kayaking, cross-country
skiing, fishing, golf, hiking, horseback riding, live theater, museums, parks,
shopping, sporting events, tennis, water sports, wineries, Mystic Seaport,
Foxwoods & Mohegan Sun casinos, Wadsworth Atheneum, Camelot cruise
lines, Deep River Navigation system and Essex Steam Train nearby.

Publicity: Hartford Courant, New London Day, Main Street News and New
York Magazine.

The Inn at Chester

318 W Main St
Chester, CT 06412-1026
(860)526-9541 (800)949-7829 Fax:(860)526-4387
E-mail: innkeeper@innatchester.com
Web: www.innatchester.com

Circa 1778. More than 200 years ago, Jeremiah Parmelee built a
clapboard farmhouse along a winding road named the
Killingworth Turnpike. The Parmelee Homestead stands as a
reflection of the past and is an inspiration for the Inn at Chester.
Each of the rooms is individually appointed with Eldred Wheeler
Reproductions. The Lincoln Suite has a sitting room with a fireplace. Enjoy lively conversation or live music while imbibing
your favorite drink at the inn's tavern, Dunk's Landing. Outside
Dunk's Landing, a 30-foot fireplace soars into the rafters. Fine
dining is offered in the inn's post-and-beam restaurant.

Innkeeper(s): Leonard Lieberman. $105-215. 42 rooms with PB, 2 with FP,
1 suite and 3 conference rooms. Breakfast included in rates. Types of meals:
Cont plus, lunch and gourmet dinner. Restaurant on premises. Beds: KQDT.
Cable TV, reading lamp, telephone and desk in room. Air conditioning. VCR,
fax, copier, sauna, bicycles, tennis, library, parlor games and fireplace on
premises. Limited handicap access. Weddings, small meetings, family
reunions and seminars hosted. Antiquing, cross-country skiing, downhill skiing, fishing, golf, live theater, parks, shopping and water sports nearby.

Publicity: New Haven Register, Hartford Courant, Pictorial Gazette, Discover
Connecticut, New York Times, Connecticut Magazine and Food Network.

Coventry   C7

Bird-In-Hand

2011 Main St
Coventry, CT 06238-2034
(860)742-0032 (877)348-0032

Circa 1731. Prepare for a remarkable journey back in time at this
former 18th-century tavern. Original wide-board floors, fireplaces
and raised paneled walls reflect that era. Romantic canopy beds
and Jacuzzi tubs boast added comfort to the guest bedrooms. A
secret closet may have harbored runaway
slaves during the Underground
Railroad. Spacious privacy is
offered in the cottage.
Conferences and small weddings are accommodated easily.
Local universities, Caprilands
Herb Farm and Nathan Hale Homestead all are nearby.

Historic Interest: Enjoy the Victorian era with a tour of Roseland Cottage, a
nearby 19th-century, pink, Gothic Revival summer house in Woodstock. The
Windham Textile and History Museum is up the road in Willimantic, and the
Nathan Hale Homestead is nearby.

Innkeeper(s): Susan Crandall. $75-150. 4 rooms with PB, 3 with FP and 1 cottage. Breakfast included in rates. Types of meals: Country bkfst and early coffee/tea. Beds: QT. Cable TV, VCR, reading lamp, refrigerator, clock radio, telephone and fireplace in room. Air conditioning. Fax, copier, parlor games and fireplace on premises. Small meetings and seminars hosted. Antiquing, art galleries, canoeing/kayaking, fishing, hiking, live theater, museums, sporting events and wineries nearby.

Publicity: *Journal Inquirer and Willimantic Chronicle.*

"We were delighted then, to find such a jewel in the Bird-In-Hand."

Deep River E7

Riverwind

209 Main St
Deep River, CT 06417-2022
(860)526-2014 (866)526-2014
E-mail: innkeeper@riverwindinn.com
Web: www.riverwindinn.com

Circa 1790. Embrace the warmth of this wonderful bed & breakfast built in 1790 with post and beam construction, wood ceilings and a 12-foot stone fireplace. Mingle in one of a variety of common rooms or bask in privacy. Sip a glass of sherry in the keeping room, watch a movie, grab a book from the library, or play a game in one of the upstairs sitting rooms. Air-conditioned guest bedrooms boast a delightful décor accented by stenciling and tasteful furnishings. The new Moonlit Suite on the third floor is already very popular and offers total privacy. A sitting room with fireplace and a two-person Jacuzzi enhances its romantic ambiance. Sit outside on an Adirondack chair or relax in a rocker on the wraparound porch.

Innkeeper(s): Roger & Nicky Plante. $110-225. 8 rooms with PB. Breakfast included in rates. Types of meals: Full bkfst. Beds: QD. Weddings hosted. Antiquing, live theater, museums, hiking trails, great restaurants, casinos and Connecticut River nearby.

Publicity: *Hartford Courant, Country Living, Country Inns, Country Decorating, New York Travel & Leisure, New York Times, Boston Globe and Los Angeles Times.*

"Warm, hospitality, a quiet homey atmosphere, comfortable bed, well thought-out and delightful appointments, delicious light hot biscuits — a great find!"

East Haddam E7

Bishopsgate Inn

7 Norwich Rd
East Haddam, CT 06423-0290
(860)873-1677 Fax:(860)873-3898

Circa 1818. This Colonial house is furnished with period antiques, and each floor of the inn has a sitting area where guests often relax with a good book. Four of the guest rooms include a fireplace and the suite has a sauna. The innkeepers serve a hearty breakfast. Although secluded on two acres, the inn is a short walk to the Goodspeed Opera House and shopping.

Innkeeper(s): Kagel Family. $105-165. 6 rooms with PB, 4 with FP and 1 suite. Breakfast and afternoon tea included in rates. Types of meals: Full bkfst and early coffee/tea. Beds: KQD. Reading lamp, clock radio, desk and sauna in room. Air conditioning. Small meetings and family reunions hosted. Antiquing, cross-country skiing, downhill skiing, fishing, live theater, parks, shopping and water sports nearby.

Publicity: *Boston Globe, Discerning Traveler, Adventure Road and Manhattan Cooperator.*

". . . Attention to detail, ambiance and amenities . . . Bishopsgate is truly outstanding."

Essex E7

Griswold Inn

36 Main St
Essex, CT 06426-1132
(860)767-1776 Fax:(860)767-0481

Circa 1776. One of the country's oldest continuously operating inns, the Griswold is also known for its important maritime art collection. On Sundays, indulge in the popular Hunt Breakfast that was originally served at the request of the British after they invaded the harbor during the War of 1812. Enjoy lively music nightly in the handsome Tap Room. Dine on fine New England fare in one of the five dining rooms: The Covered Bridge, The Gun Room, The Library, The Essex Room and The Steamboat Room.

Historic Interest: Important historic houses line many of the lanes of Essex. Changing exhibits of early river valley life can be seen at the Connecticut River Museum. Mystic Seaport and Gillette's Castle are also on the "must see" list.

Innkeeper(s): Douglas & Joan Paul. $95-200. 31 rooms with PB, 8 with FP and 1 conference room. Breakfast included in rates. Types of meals: Cont, lunch and dinner. Beds: KQDT. Air conditioning. Fax, copier and telephone on premises. Weddings, small meetings and family reunions hosted. Antiquing, bicycling, hiking, live theater, shopping, art galleries, steam train and boating and historic homes nearby.

Publicity: *Yankee Magazine, House Beautiful, New York Times and New York Magazine.*

"A man in search of the best inn in New England has a candidate in the quiet, unchanged town of Essex, Connecticut." — Country Journal

Glastonbury C6

Butternut Farm

1654 Main St
Glastonbury, CT 06033-2962
(860)633-7197 Fax:(860)659-1758

Circa 1720. This Colonial house sits on two acres of landscaped grounds amid trees and herb gardens. Prize-winning goats, pigeons, chickens, ducks, geese and pheasants are housed in the old barn on the property. Eighteenth-century Connecticut antiques are placed throughout the inn, enhancing the natural beauty of the pumpkin-pine floors and eight brick fireplaces.

Innkeeper(s): Don Reid. $90-110. 4 rooms with PB, 2 with FP and 1 suite. Breakfast included in rates. Types of meals: Full bkfst. Beds: DT. VCR, reading lamp, stereo, clock radio and telephone in room. Air conditioning. TV, fax, fireplace and one apartment on premises. Antiquing, cross-country skiing, downhill skiing, fishing, live theater, parks, shopping and sporting events nearby.

Publicity: *New York Times, House Beautiful, Yankee and Antiques.*

Granby B5

The Dutch Iris Inn B&B

239 Salmon Brook Street
Granby, CT 06035
(860)844-0262 (877)280-0743 Fax:(860)844-0248
E-mail: info@dutchirisinn.com
Web: www.dutchirisinn.com

Circa 1812. For many years this historic Colonial was used as a summer home. Some of the inn's antiques were the original furnishings, including a Louis XIV couch, Chickering grand piano, fainting couch, four-poster bed and marble-top dresser. Relax in the keeping room by a roaring fire, where the previous owners did the cooking. Several guest bedrooms feature working fireplaces. A customized breakfast menu is savored by candlelight and classical music. Half of the six acres feature perennial and bulb gardens, as well as wild blackberries and blueberries. Sip a cold beverage in a rocking chair on the side porch.

Innkeeper(s): Kevin & Belma Marshall. $109-149. 6 rooms with PB, 3 with FP. Breakfast and snacks/refreshments included in rates. Types of meals: Full bkfst, early coffee/tea and picnic lunch. Beds: KQ. Modem hook-up, cable TV, VCR, reading lamp, clock radio, telephone, wireless Internet access, fireplace and two with whirlpool tubs in room. Air conditioning. Parlor games and fireplace on premises. Weddings and family reunions hosted. Amusement parks, antiquing, art galleries, beach, bicycling, canoeing/kayaking, cross-country skiing, downhill skiing, fishing, golf, hiking, horseback riding, live theater, museums, parks, shopping, tennis, wineries, private schools: Westminster, Ethel Walker, Avon Olf Farm, Suffield Academy, Loomis Chaffee and Miss Porter's nearby.

Greenwich G1

Stanton House Inn

76 Maple Ave
Greenwich, CT 06830-5698
(203)869-2110
E-mail: shinn@aol.com
Web: shinngreenwich.com

Circa 1900. It took 150 years for one of the Saketts to finally build on the land given them in 1717. The manor they built was remodeled on a grand scale at the turn-of-the-century under architect Sanford White. In the '40s, the house became a tourist home and received visitors for many years. Renovated recently, it now offers spacious rooms decorated in a traditional, country inn style.

Innkeeper(s): Tog & Doreen Pearson. $115-229. 24 rooms with PB, 6 with FP and 2 suites. Breakfast included in rates. Types of meals: Cont. Beds: KQDT. Cable TV, reading lamp, refrigerator, clock radio, telephone, desk, voice mail and suites with two-person whirlpool tub in room. Air conditioning. TV, fax, copier, swimming, fireplace and valet on premises. Weddings, small meetings and family reunions hosted. Antiquing, live theater, parks and shopping nearby.

Publicity: Foster's Business Review and NY Times Business Travel.

"For a day, or a month or more, this is a special place."

Ivoryton E7

The Copper Beech Inn

46 Main St
Ivoryton, CT 06442-1004
(860)767-0330 (888)809-2056
E-mail: info@copperbeechinn.com
Web: www.copperbeechinn.com

Circa 1887. An elegant setting, fine dining and splendid service are the hallmarks of this historic Victorian estate. Luxury suites in the restored Main House feature period antiques, oriental rugs and rich fabrics. Queen Anne and Chippendale reproductions grace the guest bedrooms with whirlpool baths in the renovated Carriage House. Some boast private decks overlooking the woodlands. After exploring the scenic countryside, enjoying the area's shoreline, visiting museums and shopping in quaint villages, indulge in an exquisite

meal from the inn's award-winning restaurant and wine cellar. Special events and weddings are easily accommodated.

Historic Interest: Connecticut River Museum (4 miles), Goodspeed Opera House (15 miles), Ivoryton Playhouse (1/2 mile), Mystic Seaport (25 miles).
Innkeeper(s): Barbara & Ian Phillips. $135-325. 13 rooms with PB. Breakfast included in rates. Types of meals: Cont plus and gourmet dinner. Restaurant on premises. Beds: KQT. Cable TV, reading lamp, CD player, clock radio, telephone, hot tub/spa, some with fireplaces, choice of down or non-allergenic comforter and pillows, comfy bath robes, extra firm mattresses, hair dryers and UltraBath Hydro massage whirlpool tub in room. Air conditioning. Limited handicap access. Weddings, small meetings and seminars hosted. Antiquing, art galleries, fishing, live theater, museums, parks, shopping, water sports and designer outlet shopping nearby.
Publicity: Los Angeles Times, Bon Appetit, Connecticut, Travel & Leisure, Discerning Traveler, Wine Spectator, The New York Times, Conde Nast Johansens and Select Registry.

"The grounds are beautiful ... just breathtaking ... accommodations are wonderful."

Jewett City D9

Homespun Farm Bed and Breakfast

306 Preston Rd, Route 164
Jewett City, CT 06351
(860)376-5178 (888)889-6673
E-mail: relax@homespunfarm.com
Web: www.homespunfarm.com

Circa 1740. The Brewster family, whose great-great grandfather arrived on the Mayflower, owned this Colonial farmhouse for 250 years. Now the Bauers have lovingly renovated the home, which is listed in the National Register. Furnished with antiques and period reproductions, the inn's tasteful decor is accented with an artistic hand-stenciled wood floor and wall border. A sitting room overlooks the golf course and offers gorgeous sunset views. Charming guest bedrooms are well suited for romance, families or business. Luxury abounds with plush robes, candles, aromatherapy personal products, fresh flowers and fine linens on the handmade white oak and pencil post beds. Farm-fresh eggs are part of a scrumptious candlelight breakfast served in the Keeping Room. The extensive grounds, a Certified National Wildlife Federation Backyard Habitat, feature a koi pond, kitchen garden, orchard, grape arbor and flower gardens that welcome birds and butterflies.

Innkeeper(s): Kate & Ron Bauer. $95-140. 2 rooms with PB, 2 with FP and 1 suite. Breakfast and snacks/refreshments included in rates. Types of meals: Country bkfst, veg bkfst and early coffee/tea. Beds: QT. Cable TV, VCR, reading lamp, clock radio and fireplace in room. Air conditioning. Fax, library, parlor games, telephone, fireplace and laundry facility on premises. Small meetings and family reunions hosted. Antiquing, art galleries, bicycling, canoeing/kayaking, fishing, golf, hiking, horseback riding, live theater, museums, parks, shopping, sporting events, wineries, Foxwood Casino and Mohegan Sun Casino nearby.
Publicity: The New London Day, Ghost Investigator Vol. 3 by Linda Zimmerman, Inn Traveler Magazine "Top 15 B&B in America having most charm" 2003 and 2004.

Lakeville B2

Wake Robin Inn

106 Sharon Road, Route 41
Lakeville, CT 06039
(860)435-2000 Fax:(860)435-6523
E-mail: info@wakerobininn.com
Web: www.wakerobininn.com

Circa 1899. Once the Taconic School for Girls, this inn is located on 11 acres of landscaped grounds in the Connecticut Berkshires. A library has been added as well as a year-round dining deck. The recently renovated property also includes private cabins. A popular restaurant is on premises.

Historic Interest: Wake Robin Inn opened in 1899 as The Taconic School for girls.
Innkeeper(s): Michael Bryan Loftus. $149-269. 38 rooms, 36 with PB. Breakfast included in rates. Types of meals: Full bkfst, early coffee/tea, picnic lunch, snacks/refreshments and dinner. Restaurant on premises. Beds: KQDT. Cable TV, reading lamp, refrigerator, ceiling fan, clock radio, telephone, turndown service and fireplace in room. Air conditioning. Fax, copier, fireplace and gift shop on premises. Weddings, small meetings, family reunions and seminars hosted. Antiquing, art galleries, bicycling, canoeing/kayaking, cross-country skiing, downhill skiing, fishing, golf, hiking, horseback riding, live theater, museums, parks, shopping, sporting events and wineries nearby.
Publicity: *Connecticut Magazine.*

"A new sophistication has arrived in Lakeville, Conn. with the restoration of the Wake Robin Inn."

Ledyard   E9

Applewood Farms Inn

528 Colonel Ledyard Hwy
Ledyard, CT 06339-1649
(860)536-2022 (800)717-4262 Fax:(860)536-6015

Circa 1826. Five generations of the Gallup family worked this farm near Mystic. The classic center-chimney Colonial, furnished with antiques and early-American pieces, is situated on 33 acres of fields and meadows. Stone fences meander through the property and many of the original outbuildings remain. It is in the National Register, cited as one of the best surviving examples of a 19th-century farm in Connecticut.

Innkeeper(s): Frankie & Tom Betz. $125-290. 4 rooms with PB, 4 with FP and 1 suite. Breakfast included in rates. Types of meals: Full bkfst and early coffee/tea. Beds: KDT. Air conditioning. VCR, fax, copier, spa, pitch & putt golf green and hot tub spa on premises. Weddings, small meetings and family reunions hosted. Amusement parks, antiquing, cross-country skiing, fishing, live theater, parks, shopping, sporting events, water sports and Indian casinos nearby.
Publicity: *Country, New Woman, Travel Host, New York Post and Getaways Magazine.*

"This bed & breakfast is a real discovery."

Stone Croft Inn

515 Pumpkin Hill Road
Ledyard, CT 06339
(860)572-0771
Web: www.stonecroft.com

Circa 1807. Perfect for a romantic getaway or a tranquil retreat, this 1807 sea captain's estate exudes a quiet country elegance and smoke-free environment. The Main House, a sunny Georgian Colonial, and the Grange, a recently converted post and beam barn with granite fieldstone foundation, are both listed in The National Register of Historic Places. Choose to stay in a guest bedroom or luxury suite with a fireplace, two-person whirlpool bath, towel warmer and separate shower. The Great Room, Red Room and Snuggery offer gathering and reading spots in the Main House. Breakfast and dinner are served in the Grange's ground floor dining room or through the French doors on the outdoor stone terrace overlooking the landscaped grounds with a water garden and grapevine-shaded pergola. Ask about special packages.
Innkeeper(s): Lyn & Joan Egy. $150-300. 10 rooms with PB, 10 with FP, 10 with HT. Breakfast included in rates. Types of meals: Full bkfst, veg bkfst and early coffee/tea. Restaurant on premises. Beds: KQ. Data port, cable TV, reading lamp, clock radio, desk, hot tub/spa and fireplace in room. Central air. Fax, copier, spa, library, parlor games and telephone on premises. Limited

handicap access. Weddings, small meetings, family reunions and seminars hosted. Amusement parks, antiquing, art galleries, beach, bicycling, canoeing/kayaking, fishing, golf, hiking, horseback riding, live theater, museums, parks, shopping, tennis, water sports, wineries and casino nearby.
Publicity: *30 Strategic Retreats New York Magazine, Getaways for Gourmets in the Northeast, Passport to New England, Select Registry Restaurant: 4 Stars, Hartford Courant Restaurant: 3 1/2 Stars (and rising), Connecticut Magazine and Best Restaurant Connecticut Magazine 2000.*

Madison   F6

Madison Beach Hotel

PO Box 546, 94 W Wharf Rd
Madison, CT 06443-0546
(203)245-1404 Fax:(203)245-0410

Circa 1800. Since most of Connecticut's shoreline is privately owned, the Madison Beach Hotel is one of the few waterfront lodgings available. It originally was constructed as a stagecoach stop and later became a popular vacation spot for those who stayed for a month at a time with maids and chauffeurs. Art Carney is said to have driven a Madison Beach Hotel bus here when his brother was the manager.  Rooms are furnished in a variety of antiques and wallpapers. Many rooms have splendid views of the lawn and the Long Island Sound from private porches.

Innkeeper(s): Roben & Kathleen Bagdasarian. $80-250. 35 rooms with PB, 6 suites and 1 conference room. Breakfast included in rates. Types of meals: Cont plus, early coffee/tea, lunch, picnic lunch, dinner and room service. Restaurant on premises. Beds: QT. Cable TV, clock radio, telephone and suites have refrigerator in room. Air conditioning. TV, fax and copier on premises. Limited handicap access. Weddings, small meetings, family reunions and seminars hosted. Antiquing, fishing, live theater, shopping, sporting events and water sports nearby.
Publicity: *New England Travel.*

"The accommodations were wonderful and the service was truly exceptional."

Tidewater Inn

949 Boston Post Road
Madison, CT 06443-3236
(203)245-8457 Fax:(203)318-0265
E-mail: info@thetidewater.com
Web: www.TheTidewater.com

Circa 1900. Experience the pleasures of coastal living at this recently renovated French farmhouse-style inn with comfortable yet elegant antiques and estate furnishings from the 1930s. A beamed sitting room features a large fireplace. Guest bedrooms boast floral wallpaper, four-poster or canopy beds. The Cottage suite also offers a sitting room, Jacuzzi for two, refrigerator, VCR and private patio. Favorite breakfast items include a melon boat, California egg puff, tomato salad, bacon, apple coffee cake and Top of the Mountain French toast with sausages and maple syrup. Appreciate the two nicely landscaped acres from backyard Adirondack chairs, front porch rockers or under an umbrella in the English garden.
Innkeeper(s): Jean Foy & Rich Evans. $110-185. 9 rooms with PB, 2 with FP and 1 suite. Breakfast, afternoon tea and snacks/refreshments included in rates. Types of meals: Full gourmet bkfst and early coffee/tea. Beds: KQDT. Modem hook-up, cable TV, VCR, reading lamp, refrigerator, telephone, desk, hot tub/spa, voice mail, fireplace and hair dryer in room. Air conditioning. Fax, copier, library, fireplace, guest refrigerator (stocked), butler's basket, daily newspapers, area maps and brochures and area restaurant menus on premises. Antiquing, art galleries, beach, bicycling, canoeing/kayaking, fishing, hiking, live theater, museums, parks, shopping, water

sports, wineries, outlet malls, steam train and Long Island Sound and Connecticut River cruises nearby.
Publicity: *New York Times, New Britain Herald, Shore Line Times* and *CT Channel 3* feature.

Middlebury   D4

Tucker Hill Inn

96 Tucker Hill Rd
Middlebury, CT 06762-2511
(203)758-8334 Fax:(203)598-0652

Circa 1923. There's a cut-out heart in the gate that opens to this handsome three-story estate framed by an old stone wall. The spacious Colonial-style house is shaded by tall trees. Guests enjoy a parlor with fireplace and an inviting formal dining room. Guest rooms are furnished with a flourish of English country or romantic Victorian decor.

Innkeeper(s): Susan & Richard Cebelenski. $95-145. 4 rooms, 2 with PB. Breakfast included in rates. Types of meals: Full bkfst, early coffee/tea and afternoon tea. Beds: QT. Cable TV, VCR, reading lamp, ceiling fan, clock radio and desk in room. Air conditioning. Fax, parlor games, telephone and fireplace on premises. Small meetings and family reunions hosted. Amusement parks, antiquing, cross-country skiing, golf, live theater, parks, shopping, tennis and lake nearby.
Publicity: *Star, Waterbury American Republican* and *Voices.*

"Thanks for a special visit. Your kindness never went unnoticed."

Mystic   E9

Harbour Inne & Cottage

15 Edgemont St
Mystic, CT 06355-2853
(860)572-9253
E-mail: harbourinne@earthlink.net
Web: www.harbourinne-cottage.com

Circa 1898. Known as Charley's Place after its innkeeper, this New England inn located on the Mystic River is comfortably decorated with cedar paneling and hardwood floors throughout. A large stone fireplace and piano are featured in the common room. There is a gazebo, six-person hot tub at the cottage, picnic area and boat dock on the grounds. The inn is minutes from the Olde Mystic Village, Factory Outlet Stores and casinos.

Innkeeper(s): Charles Lecouras, Jr. $55-250. 6 rooms with PB, 1 with FP and 1 cottage. Types of meals: Cont. Beds: D. Cable TV, refrigerator, desk and hot tub/spa in room. Air conditioning. Telephone, fireplace, picnic area, gazebo, boat dock and spas on premises. Weddings, small meetings and family reunions hosted. Antiquing, fishing, golf, live theater, museums, parks, shopping, tennis, water sports, nautilus submarine, aquarium and casino nearby.

Pequot Hotel Bed and Breakfast

711 Cow Hill Road
Mystic, CT 06355
(860)572-0390 Fax:(860)536-3380
E-mail: pequothtl@aol.com
Web: www.pequothotelbandb.com

Circa 1840. Year-round accommodations are available at this authentically restored bed & breakfast, originally built as a stagecoach stop in 1840. Relax and chat in one of the two large parlors. A spacious screened porch features comfortable wicker fur-

nishings. Gorgeous guest bedrooms, two with fireplaces and one boasting a whirlpool tub for two, are wonderful retreats to feel pampered in. A complete breakfast includes juices, fresh fruit, egg entree, french toast, blueberry pancakes, quiche, breads, cereal and hot beverages. The 23 acres include extensive perennial flower and herb gardens, a grape arbor and 3 acres of Christmas trees. Visit downtown and the seaport only two miles away.

Historic Interest: Built in 1840 as a stagecoach stop and as a secret meeting place for the Freemasons.
Innkeeper(s): Nancy & Jim Mitchell. $95-175. 3 rooms with PB, 2 with FP. Breakfast, afternoon tea and snacks/refreshments included in rates. Types of meals: Country bkfst, veg bkfst and early coffee/tea. Beds: QDT. Reading lamp, ceiling fan, desk, fireplace and one with large whirlpool tub in room. Air conditioning. TV, VCR, fax, copier, library, parlor games, telephone, fireplace and laundry facility on premises. Antiquing, art galleries, beach, bicycling, canoeing/kayaking, fishing, golf, hiking, horseback riding, live theater, museums, parks, shopping, sporting events, tennis, water sports and wineries nearby.

The Whaler's Inn

20 E Main St
Mystic, CT 06355-2646
(860)536-1506 (800)243-2588 Fax:(860)572-1250
E-mail: sales@whalersinnmystic.com
Web: www.whalersinnmystic.com

Circa 1901. This classical revival-style inn is built on the historical site of the Hoxie House, the Clinton House and the U.S. Hotel. Just as these famous 19th-century inns offered, the Whaler's Inn has the same charm and convenience for today's visitor to Mystic. Once a booming ship-building center, the town's connection to the sea is ongoing, and the sailing schooners still pass beneath the Bascule Drawbridge in the center of town. More than 75 shops and restaurants are within walking distance.

Innkeeper(s): Richard Prisby. $85-249. 49 rooms with PB and 1 conference room. Types of meals: Cont plus, gourmet lunch and gourmet dinner. Restaurant on premises. Beds: KQD. Reading lamp, desk, cable TV, telephone, voice mail, data port, alarm clock, air conditioning, eight luxury rooms with water views, Jacuzzi tubs and fireplaces in room. TV, telephone and business center on premises. Limited handicap access. Small meetings, family reunions and seminars hosted. Antiquing, fishing, parks, shopping, water sports, walk to Mystic Seaport and harbor & schooner cruises nearby.

New Haven   F5

Three Chimneys Inn at Yale University

1201 Chapel St
New Haven, CT 06511-4701
(203)789-1201 (800)443-1554 Fax:(203)776-7363
E-mail: chimneysnh@aol.com
Web: www.threechimneysinn.com

Circa 1870. Gracing the historic Chapel West District, this elegantly restored Painted Lady Victorian mansion is just a block from Yale University. Art museums, boutiques and an assortment of ethnic restaurants are within walking distance. Savor afternoon tea and treats in the library/parlor, and evening wine served fireside. A guest pantry and honor bar offers other snacks and beverages. Work out in the mini exercise facility. Deluxe guest bedrooms feature Georgian and Federal decor, Oriental rugs, antiques, collectibles and four-poster beds with Edwardian privacy drapes. Enjoy reading one of several newspapers delivered daily. Breakfasts are an award-winning affair, and special dietary needs are accommodated with advance notice.

$205-215. 11 rooms with PB and 2 conference rooms. Breakfast included in rates. Types of meals: Full bkfst. Beds: KQ. Modem hook-up, data port, cable TV, VCR, reading lamp, clock radio, desk, EuroShower wands, two-line phone with data port and individual HV/AC in room. Air conditioning. Fax, copier, telephone, fireplace, private on-site parking, space is available for business/social gatherings as well as catering and exercise room on premises. Small meetings and seminars hosted. Live theater, parks, shopping, sporting events, dining and museums nearby.

Publicity: *Yankee Magazine editors pick since 1999, The Advocate Business Times, Best of New Haven, Best University B&B National Trust, 4-Star Mobil and National Trust Inn.*

New London   E9

Queen Anne Inn Bed & Breakfast

265 Williams Street
New London, CT 06320
(860)447-2600 (800)347-8818 Fax:(860)443-0857
E-mail: info@queen-anne.com
Web: www.queen-anne.com

Circa 1903. Several photographers for historic house books have been attracted to the classic good looks of the Queen Anne Inn. The traditional tower, wraparound verandas and elaborate frieze invite the traveler to explore the interior with its richly polished oak walls and intricately carved alcove. Period furnishings include brass beds and some rooms have their own fireplace.

Historic Interest: The Mystic Seaport, Mystic Marine and an aquarium are a 15-minute drive. Other nearby historic attractions include the Eugene O'Neil Homestead, Goodspeed Opera House and the Nautilus submarine and museum.

Innkeeper(s): Kasey Goss, Sue Ortaldo & Scott Danforth. $95-175. 8 rooms with PB, 2 with FP and 1 suite. Breakfast included in rates. Types of meals: Full bkfst, veg bkfst, early coffee/tea, lunch, afternoon tea, snacks/refreshments and dinner. Beds: KQDT. Modem hook-up, data port, cable TV, reading lamp, refrigerator, clock radio, telephone, desk, one room with private balcony and fireplace in room. Air conditioning. Fax, copier and fireplace on premises. Weddings, small meetings, family reunions and seminars hosted. Amusement parks, antiquing, art galleries, beach, bicycling, canoeing/kayaking, fishing, golf, live theater, museums, parks, shopping, water sports, wineries and Foxwoods and Mohegan casinos nearby.

Publicity: *New York Newsday and New London Day Features.*

"Absolutely terrific — relaxing, warm, gracious — beautiful rooms and delectable food."

New Milford   D3

Heritage Inn

34 Bridge St
New Milford, CT 06776-3530
(860)354-8883 Fax:(860)350-5543
E-mail: bette@heritageinnct.com
Web: www.heritageinnct.com

Circa 1870. Once a warehouse for locally grown tobacco, the inn is located directly across from the restored train depot and adjacent to small community stores. The front porch is graced with wooden chairs. A turn-of-the-century decor features blue

and white floral carpeting, swag curtains and framed prints. Suites are available. In the morning, a full breakfast features French toast, pancakes and omelets.

Innkeeper(s): Bette Bottge. $110-125. 20 rooms with PB. Breakfast, afternoon tea and snacks/refreshments included in rates. Types of meals: Full bkfst and veg bkfst. Beds: QD. Data port, cable TV, reading lamp, ceiling fan, clock radio, telephone and desk in room. Air conditioning. Fax and copier on premises.

Publicity: *Litchfield County Times.*

Homestead Inn

5 Elm St
New Milford, CT 06776-2995
(860)354-4080
Web: www.homesteadct.com

Circa 1853. Built by the first of three generations of John Prime Treadwells, the inn was established 80 years later. Victorian architecture includes high ceilings, spacious rooms and large verandas. There is a small motel adjacent to the inn.

Innkeeper(s): Bill Greenman. $91-135. 14 rooms with PB. Types of meals: Cont plus. Beds: KQDT. Cable TV and telephone in room. Air conditioning. TV on premises.

Publicity: *Litchfield County Times, ABC Home Show and Food & Wine.*

"One of the homiest inns in the U.S.A. with most hospitable hosts. A rare bargain to boot."

Niantic   E8

Fourteen Lincoln Street, a Chef-Owned Bed & Breakfast

14 Lincoln Street
Niantic, CT 06357
(860)739-6327 Fax:(860)739-6327

Circa 1879. Once a 19th-century New England church, this fully restored bed & breakfast graces a seaside village. A relaxed, elegant decor features oil paintings and antique Oriental carpets that accent comfortable sitting areas. Serene guest chambers in subtle hues boast Jacuzzi tubs and modem hookups. Choose to sleep on the choir loft or sanctuary level in a carved four-poster, pewter knot, ornate Louis XVI or sleigh bed. At this chef-owned B&B, breakfast and afternoon tea are given great gastronomical attention. A bountiful herb-garden inspired breakfast is served with heirloom baked goods and edible flower jellies. Several times a year weekend cooking classes are offered.

Historic Interest: The inn is housed in a restored 19th-century village church.

Innkeeper(s): Cheryl Jean. $155-185. 4 rooms with PB. Breakfast and afternoon tea included in rates. Types of meals: Full gourmet bkfst and early coffee/tea. Beds: KQDT. Modem hook-up, cable TV, VCR and telephone in room. Central air. Fax, copier, library, fireplace, lovely outdoor terrace and flower gardens on premises. Weddings, small meetings, family reunions and seminars hosted. Antiquing, art galleries, beach, bicycling, fishing, golf, hiking, live theater, museums, parks, shopping, water sports, wineries, Coast Guard Academy and Mystic Aquarium nearby.

Inn at Harbor Hill Marina

60 Grand St
Niantic, CT 06357
(860)739-0331 Fax:(860)691-3078
E-mail: info@innharborhill.com
Web: www.innharborhill.com

Circa 1890. Arise each morning to panoramic views of the Niantic River harbor at this traditional, late-19th-century inn. Travel by boat or car to neighboring cities and enjoy the finest culture New England has to offer. This three-story, harbor-front inn offers rooms filled with antiques and seaside décor. Some have balconies and fireplaces. Experience true adventure at sea on a chartered fishing trip, or spend the day in town shopping or relaxing on the beach, all within walking distance. During the summer, guests can listen to outdoor concerts in the park while overlooking Long Island Sound. Whatever the day has in store, guests can start each morning the right way with a fresh, continental breakfast on the wraparound porch overlooking the marina and gardens.

Innkeeper(s): Sally Keefe. $90-195. 8 rooms with PB, 1 suite and 1 conference room. Breakfast and snacks/refreshments included in rates. Types of meals: Cont plus. Beds: QT. Cable TV, reading lamp, ceiling fan, clock radio, desk, balcony rooms and fireplaces in room. Air conditioning. Fax, copier, parlor games, telephone and fireplace on premises. Weddings, small meetings and family reunions hosted. Antiquing, art galleries, beach, canoeing/kayaking, fishing, golf, live theater, museums, parks, shopping, water sports, wineries and Mohegan Sun and Foxwoods Casinos nearby.

Norfolk   A3

Blackberry River Inn

538 Greenwoods Road W
Norfolk, CT 06058
(860)542-5100 Fax:(860)542-1763
E-mail: blackberry.river.inn@snet.net
Web: www.blackberryriverinn.com

Circa 1763. In the National Register, the Colonial buildings that comprise the inn are situated on 27 acres. A library with cherry paneling, three parlors and a breakfast room are offered for guests' relaxation. Guest rooms are elegantly furnished with antiques. Guests can choose from rooms in the main house with a fireplace or suites with a fireplace or Jacuzzi. The Cottage includes a fireplace and Jacuzzi. A full country breakfast is included.

$75-225. 18 rooms with PB and 1 cottage. Breakfast and afternoon tea included in rates. Types of meals: Full bkfst. Cable TV in room. Air conditioning. Swimming, library, fireplace, hiking and fishing on premises. Weddings hosted. Antiquing, canoeing/kayaking, cross-country skiing, downhill skiing, golf, horseback riding, shopping, tennis, sleigh rides, hay rides, auto racing and music festivals nearby.

Manor House

69 Maple Ave
Norfolk, CT 06058-0447
(860)542-5690 Fax:(860)542-5690
E-mail: innkeeper@manorhouse-norfolk.com
Web: www.manorhouse-norfolk.com

Circa 1898. Charles Spofford, designer of London's subway, built this home with many gables, exquisite cherry paneling and grand staircase. There are Moorish arches and Tiffany windows. Guests

can enjoy hot-mulled cider after a sleigh ride, hay ride, or horse and carriage drive along the country lanes nearby. The inn was named by "Discerning Traveler" as Connecticut's most romantic hideaway.

Historic Interest: Norfolk is a historic community with many historic homes; the Yale Chamber Music Festival is held at one such historic estate. Litchfield County has many museums and historic homes to tour.

Innkeeper(s): Hank & Diane Tremblay. $125-250. 9 rooms with PB, 4 with FP, 1 suite and 1 conference room. Breakfast and afternoon tea included in

rates. Types of meals: Full gourmet bkfst, early coffee/tea and room service. Beds: KQDT. Reading lamp, ceiling fan, clock radio, desk and three with double whirlpools in room. Fax, library, parlor games, telephone and fireplace on premises. Weddings, small meetings, family reunions and seminars hosted. Antiquing, cross-country skiing, downhill skiing, fishing, live theater, parks, shopping, sporting events and water sports nearby.

Publicity: *Good Housekeeper, Gourmet, Boston Globe, Philadelphia Inquirer, Innsider, Rhode Island Monthly, Gourmet, National Geographic Traveler and New York Times.*

"Queen Victoria, eat your heart out."

Norwalk   G2

Silvermine Tavern

194 Perry Ave
Norwalk, CT 06850-1123
(203)847-4558 (888)693-9967 Fax:(203)847-9171
E-mail: innkeeper@silverminetavern.com
Web: www.silverminetavern.com

Circa 1790. The Silvermine consists of the Old Mill, the Country Store, the Coach House and the Tavern itself. Primitive paintings and furnishings, as well as family heir-

looms, decorate the inn. Guest rooms and dining rooms overlook the Old Mill, the waterfall and swans gliding across the millpond. Some guest rooms offer items such as canopy bed or private decks. In the summer, guests can dine al fresco and gaze at the mill pond.

Historic Interest: Lockwood Matthews Mansion (10 miles).

Innkeeper(s): Frank Whitman, Jr. $115-150. 10 rooms with PB and 1 suite. Breakfast included in rates. Types of meals: Cont, lunch and dinner. Restaurant on premises. Beds: QDT. Reading lamp, clock radio, desk and some with canopied beds in room. Air conditioning. VCR, fax, copier, parlor games, telephone and fireplace on premises. Weddings, small meetings, family reunions and seminars hosted. Antiquing, fishing, parks and shopping nearby.

Old Greenwich   G2

Harbor House Inn

165 Shore Rd
Old Greenwich, CT 06870-2120
(203)637-0145 Fax:(203)698-0943

Circa 1890. This turn-of-the-century inn is decorated with unique, Old World flair. Guest rooms feature poster beds and sturdy, comfortable furnishings. Each room includes a mini refrigerator and a coffee maker, and there are laundry facilities on the premises. Business travelers will appreciate the availability of a fax machine and copier, and the inn offers a conference room. Restaurants and shops are nearby, and the inn is 45 minutes by train from New York City.

Innkeeper(s): Rosemarie Stuttig & Dawn Browne. $109-275. 23 rooms and 1 conference room. Breakfast included in rates. Types of meals: Cont. Beds: QDT. Cable TV, VCR, refrigerator, clock radio and telephone in room. Air conditioning. Fax, copier and bicycles on premises. Weddings, small meetings and family reunions hosted. Antiquing, beach, fishing, live theater, parks and shopping nearby.

Publicity: *Local newspapers.*

Old Mystic   E9

The Old Mystic Inn

52 Main St, Box 733
Old Mystic, CT 06372-0733
(860)572-9422
E-mail: omysticinn@aol.com
Web: www.oldmysticinn.com

Circa 1784. Charles Vincent ran the Old Mystic Bookstore from this house for 35 years. Although it once housed 20,000 old books and maps, it has been renovated to a bed & breakfast inn. The old maps and drawings hung around the stairwell have been preserved. There are wide board floors and stone fireplaces in all the rooms. Furnishings include replica Colonial period pieces.

Innkeeper(s): Michael Cardillo. $125-185. 8 rooms with PB, 6 with FP. Breakfast and snacks/refreshments included in rates. Types of meals: Country bkfst and early coffee/tea. Beds: Q. Reading lamp and two with whirlpool tubs in room. Air conditioning. Gazebo and Saturday evenings complimentary wine and cheese is served on premises. Weddings, small meetings, family reunions and seminars hosted. Antiquing, parks and water sports nearby.

Publicity: *New Jersey Monthly and New London Day.*

"A real delight and the breakfast was sumptuous!"

Red Brook Inn

PO Box 237
Old Mystic, CT 06372-0237
(860)572-0349
E-mail: redbrookin@aol.com
Web: www.redbrookinn.com

Circa 1740. If there was no other reason to visit Mystic, a charming town brimming with activities, the Red Brook Inn would be reason enough. The Crary Homestead features three unique rooms with working fireplaces, while the Haley Tavern offers seven guest rooms, some with canopy beds and fireplaces. Two have whirlpool tubs. Innkeeper Ruth Keyes has beautiful antiques decorating her inn. Guests are sure to enjoy her wonderful country breakfasts. A special winter dinner takes three days 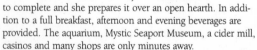 to complete and she prepares it over an open hearth. In addition to a full breakfast, afternoon and evening beverages are provided. The aquarium, Mystic Seaport Museum, a cider mill, casinos and many shops are only minutes away.

Historic Interest: Mystic Seaport Museum.

Innkeeper(s): Ruth Keyes. $129-189. 10 rooms with PB, 7 with FP and 3 conference rooms. Breakfast included in rates. Types of meals: Full bkfst. Beds: QDT. Reading lamp and desk in room. TV, VCR, tennis, library, parlor games, telephone, fireplace, terrace and parlors on premises. Small meetings, family reunions and seminars hosted. Amusement parks, antiquing, fishing, live theater, museums, parks, shopping, sporting events, water sports and casino nearby.

Publicity: *Westerly Sun, Travel & Leisure, Yankee, New York, Country Decorating, Philadelphia Inquirer, National Geographic Traveler and Discerning Traveler.*

"The staff is wonderful. You made us feel at home. Thank you for your hospitality."

Old Saybrook   F7

Deacon Timothy Pratt Bed & Breakfast Inn C.1746

325 Main Street
Old Saybrook, CT 06475
(860)395-1229 Fax:(860)395-4748
E-mail: bnbinns@pratthouse.net
Web: www.pratthouse.net

Circa 1746. Built prior to the Revolutionary War, this slate blue house is an outstanding example of center chimney Colonial-style architecture. Listed in the National Register, the inn's original features include six working fireplaces, hand-hewn beams, wide board floors, a beehive oven and built-in cupboard. Four-poster and canopy beds, Oriental rugs and period furnishings accentuate the New England atmosphere. Fireplaces and Jacuzzi tubs invite romance and relaxation. On weekends a multi-course, candlelight breakfast is served in the elegant dining room. Enjoy homemade muffins or scones, fresh fruit and entrees such as heart-shaped blueberry pancakes or eggs Benedict. Among the variety of local historic house museums to visit, the William Hart house is across the street. The area offers many shopping and dining opportunities as well as galleries to explore. Beaches, a state park and river cruises also are available.

Innkeeper(s): Shelley Nobile. $100-190. 7 rooms with PB, 7 with FP, 7 with HT, 2 suites and 1 conference room. Breakfast, afternoon tea and snacks/refreshments included in rates. Types of meals: Full bkfst and veg bkfst. Beds: QDT. Modem hook-up, data port, cable TV, reading lamp, stereo, clock radio, telephone, turn-down service, desk, fireplace, Jacuzzi, Queen canopy or four-poster bed, cot and twin rollaway available, comfortable sitting areas, hair dryer, iron and modem line in room. Air conditioning. TV, library, parlor games, guest refrigerator, complimentary soft drinks, tea, cookies, sherry and massage therapy on premises. Weddings, small meetings, family reunions and seminars hosted. Antiquing, art galleries, beach, bicycling, canoeing/kayaking, cross-country skiing, downhill skiing, fishing, golf, hiking, horseback riding, live theater, museums, parks, shopping, sporting events, tennis, wineries, casinos, spas, playhouses and factory outlet malls nearby.

Publicity: *Fodor's New England Travel Guide, America's Favorite Inns Book, Elle Magazine, Coastal Living Magazine, Inn Traveller, Entrepreneur's Business Start-Ups Magazine, Inn Spots & Special Places in New England, Waterside Escapes by Woodpond Press, Arrington Publishing Awards: Most Historical Charm, Best Interior Design & Decor and Best Location for walking to shops & restaurants.*

Plymouth   C4

Shelton House B&B

663 Main St (Rt 6)
Plymouth, CT 06782
(860)283-4616 Fax:(860)283-4616

Circa 1825. This home's most famous resident was a carriage maker whose wares were sold as far away as Chicago. The Greek Revival is listed in the National Register and was a stop on the town's bicentennial homes tour. Antiques and reproductions decorate the interior. Beds are topped with fine quality linens and soft, fluffy comforters. There are three tranquil acres of grounds, shaded by trees. After breakfast, guests can take a trip to historic Litchfield, which is just 12 miles down the road. Antique shops, restaurants, skiing and other activities are all nearby.

Innkeeper(s): Pat & Bill Doherty. $85-100. 4 rooms, 2 with PB. Breakfast and afternoon tea included in rates. Types of meals: Full bkfst. Beds: QDT. Reading lamp, desk, robes, window fans and alarm clocks in room. Air conditioning. Fax, parlor games, telephone, fireplace, pineapple fountain and perrenial gardens on premises. Amusement parks, antiquing, cross-country skiing, fishing, golf, live theater, museums, parks, shopping and soaring center nearby.

"Accommodations were excellent. Breakfast was great. I was pampered and I loved it."

Ridgefield   F2

West Lane Inn

22 West Ln
Ridgefield, CT 06877-4914
(203)438-7323 Fax:(203)438-7325
E-mail: westlanein@aol.com
Web: www.westlaneinn.com

Circa 1849. This National Register Victorian mansion on two acres features an enormous front veranda filled with black wrought iron chairs and tables overlooking a manicured lawn. A polished oak staircase rises to a third-floor landing and lounge. Chandeliers, wall sconces and floral wallpapers help to establish an intimate atmosphere. Although the rooms do not have antiques, they feature amenities such as heated towel racks, extra-thick towels, air conditioning, remote control cable TVs, VCRs and desks.

Innkeeper(s): Maureen Mayer & Deborah Prieger. $125-195. 16 rooms with PB, 2 with FP and 1 suite. Breakfast included in rates. Types of meals: Cont and room service. Beds: Q. Cable TV, VCR, reading lamp, refrigerator, telephone, desk and modem in room. Air conditioning. Fireplace on premises. Small meetings hosted. Antiquing, cross-country skiing, golf, live theater, shopping, award winning restaurants, boutiquing and movies nearby.
Publicity: *Stanford-Advocate, Greenwich Times and Home & Away Connecticut.*

"Thank you for the hospitality you showed us. The rooms are comfortable and quiet. I haven't slept this soundly in weeks."

Riverton   B4

Old Riverton Inn

436 E River Rd
Riverton, CT 06065
(860)379-8678 (800)378-1796 Fax:(860)379-1006
E-mail: innkeeper@rivertoninn.com
Web: rivertoninn.com

Circa 1796. Originally a stagecoach stop between Hartford and Albany and now listed in the National Register of Historic Places, this Colonial inn sits on an acre in a quaint village setting overlooking the wild and scenic designated west branch of the Farmington River. The enclosed Grindstone Terrace, named after the floor made of quarried grindstone from Nova Scotia, features a raised fireplace and white wrought iron furniture. Decorated in early-American style, one of the guest bedrooms boasts a fireplace. A country breakfast is served in the dining room, and the Hobby Horse Bar with Vermont flagstone floors has saddles on kegs for bar stools.

Innkeeper(s): Mark & Pauline Telford. $90-200. 12 rooms, 11 with PB, 1 with FP, 1 suite and 1 conference room. Breakfast included in rates. Types of meals: Country bkfst, lunch and dinner. Restaurant on premises. Beds: KQDT. Modem hook-up, cable TV, reading lamp, clock radio, telephone, desk and fireplace in room. Air conditioning. Fax, copier, library, parlor games and fireplace on premises. Weddings, small meetings, family reunions and seminars hosted. Antiquing, beach, bicycling, canoeing/kayaking, cross-country skiing, fishing, golf, hiking, horseback riding, museums, parks, shopping and wineries nearby.

Somersville   A7

The Old Mill Inn B&B

63 Maple St
Somersville, CT 06072
(860)763-1473
E-mail: omibnb@cox.net
Web: www.oldmillinnbnb.com

Circa 1860. Giant maples and landscaped grounds create a private, peaceful ambiance at this Greek Revival home, secluded along the banks of the Scantic River. There is a hammock set up for those hoping for a nap among the trees, or perhaps you'd prefer a trip up the river on the inn's canoe. The grounds also are decorated with a gazebo. Rooms feature romantic decor, with comforters, fine linens and furnishings such as a brass bed or a wicker loveseat. In the evenings, hors d'oeuvres and beverages are served in the fireplaced parlor. One of your innkeepers is an  accomplished chef and professional cake decorator, so guests should expect something wonderful during the gourmet breakfast service. The innkeepers provide bicycles for those who wish to tour the area, and there is a spa on premises. The inn is often the site of weddings, parties and family reunions.

Innkeeper(s): Jim & Stephanie D'Amour. $85-95. 6 rooms. Types of meals: Full gourmet bkfst and early coffee/tea. Beds: KD. Spa, bicycles, parlor games, fireplace and sun deck outside rooms on second level on premises. Weddings and family reunions hosted. Antiquing, fishing, shopping, museums, Basketball Hall of Fame, golfing, horseback riding and Six Flags New England nearby.

"We loved staying here! You are both delightful. P.S. We slept like a log."

Stonington   E9

Another Second Penny Inn

870 Pequot Trail
Stonington, CT 06378
(860)535-1710 Fax:(860)535-1709
E-mail: historic@secondpenny.com
Web: www.secondpenny.com

Circa 1710. Stay in a quiet country setting of gardens, fields, and forests at this five-acre bed & breakfast inn, the recently restored Edward Denison House, a 1710 Center Chimney Colonial. The traditional decor is inviting and warm with candles in the windows, elegant colors and comfortable furnishings. Secluded hideaways encourage conversation or reading. Delightful guest bedrooms and a suite feature jetted tubs, fireplaces, handmade quilts and comforters. An incredible breakfast served on antique china and in crystal goblets may include sauteed apple and yogurt parfait, homemade doughnut muffins, cereals, scrambled eggs with cream cheese and crab alongside baked tomatoes and stuffed mushrooms, and sorbet or light pudding. Play badminton or croquet, and visit nearby Mystic Seaport.

Historic Interest: The house was built in 1710. See our web site for a complete history.

Innkeeper(s): Jim and Sandra Wright. $80-185. 3 rooms with PB, 2 with FP, 1 suite and 1 conference room. Breakfast and snacks/refreshments included in rates. Types of meals: Full bkfst, veg bkfst, early coffee/tea and picnic lunch. Beds: KQT. Modem hook-up, cable TV, VCR, reading lamp, CD player, refrigerator, clock radio, telephone, desk, hot tub/spa, voice mail and fireplace in room. Air conditioning. Fax, library, parlor games, fireplace, coffee, tea, hot chocolate, cookies available 24 hours a day, gardens, fields and forests on premises. Weddings, small meetings, family reunions and seminars hosted. Amusement parks, antiquing, art galleries, beach, bicycling, canoeing/kayaking, fishing, golf, hiking, live theater, museums, parks, shopping, sporting events, tennis, water sports, wineries, Mystic Seaport, Mystic Aquarium and casinos nearby.

Tolland   B7

Tolland Inn

63 Tolland Green, PO Box 717
Tolland, CT 06084-0717
(860)872-0800 (877)465-0800 Fax:(860)870-7958

Circa 1790. This late 18th-century Colonial offers seven guest rooms, three with sitting rooms. A first-floor room and two second-floor suites offer both a hot tub and fireplace. All rooms have private baths, air conditioning and phones. The inn is decorated in antiques and hand-built furniture throughout. Susan was raised in Nantucket and is a third-generation innkeeper, while Stephen is a designer and builder of fine furniture. Guests are invited to enjoy breakfast and afternoon tea, fireside in cool weather. The inn is convenient to UCONN, Old Sturbridge Village, Brimfield Antique Shows, Caprilands.

Innkeeper(s): Susan & Stephen Beeching. $95-179. 7 rooms with PB, 4 with FP, 3 suites and 1 conference room. Breakfast and afternoon tea included in rates. Types of meals: Full gourmet bkfst and early coffee/tea. Beds: KQ. Cable TV, VCR, reading lamp, refrigerator, telephone, desk and hot tub/spa in room. Spa, library, parlor games and fireplace on premises. Small meetings, family reunions and seminars hosted. Antiquing, cross-country skiing, fishing, live theater, parks, shopping and sporting events nearby.

Publicity: *Journal Inquirer, Hartford Courant and Tolland County Times.*

Westbrook   F7

Angels Watch Inn

902 Boston Post Rd
Westbrook, CT 06498-1848
(860)399-8846 Fax:(860)399-2571
E-mail: info@angelswatchinn.com
Web: www.angelswatchinn.com

Circa 1830. Appreciate the comfortable elegance of this stately 1830 Federal home that sits on one acre of tranquil grounds. Maintaining a fine reputation of impeccable standards, the inn caters to body, mind and spirit. Savor chocolate-dipped strawberries upon arrival. Furnished with antiques, renovated guest bedrooms feature bathrobes, personal care amenities, fireplaces and refrigerators stocked with complimentary beverages. Choose a whirlpool bath or dual clawfoot soaking tubs. Start the day with fresh juice, warm muffins, cereal and yogurt; followed by Samuels' Clouds, a delectable fruit dish and an entree like Angel Puffs, scrambled eggs with seasoned garden vegetables served over flaky pastry puffs with a white cheese sauce and sauteed mushrooms. Sit on a bench in the front of the house or relax in the park-like backyard. Wellness professionals are available for services by appointment.

Historic Interest: The Inn was built in 1830. The property on which the Inn stands is rich with history. "Deeded to Samuel Bates in the Twenty-sixth reign of Queen Anne of England, Scotland, Wales and France." In 1737 Robert Bates deeded the property to Ephram Kelsey and it remained in the Kelsey Family for over 150 years. It was part of a 51-acre parcel which extended

from the Patchogue River to Long Island Sound. It was owned then by ship builders and sea captains.

$115-185. 5 rooms with PB, 5 with FP. Breakfast, afternoon tea and snacks/refreshments included in rates. Types of meals: Full gourmet bkfst, veg bkfst, early coffee/tea, picnic lunch and gourmet dinner. Beds: KQT. Cable TV, VCR, reading lamp, stereo, refrigerator, ceiling fan, snack bar, clock radio, turn-down service, desk, hot tub/spa and fireplace in room. Air conditioning. Fax, spa, bicycles, library, child care, parlor games, telephone, fireplace and laundry facility on premises. Antiquing, art galleries, beach, bicycling, canoeing/kayaking, cross-country skiing, downhill skiing, fishing, golf, hiking, horseback riding, live theater, museums, parks, shopping, sporting events, tennis, water sports and wineries nearby.

Publicity: *The Hartford Courant, New Haven Register, Main Street News, Pictorial and ABC affiliate Positively Connecticut.*

Captain Stannard House

138 S Main Street
Westbrook, CT 06498-1904
(860)399-4634
E-mail: vern@stannardhouse.com
Web: www.stannardhouse.com

Circa 1865. An inn for all seasons, this historic Georgian-style bed & breakfast exudes a casual country elegance that offers comfort and hospitality. Situated in a small shoreline village on Long Island Sound, Pilot's Point marina is within walking distance. Play chess, shoot pool, watch TV or chat by the fire in one of the common areas. Enjoy the peaceful gardens. A guest refrigerator is available for use as needed. Tastefully furnished with antiques, spacious guest bedrooms include in-room temperature control. Linger over a full breakfast in the dining room at a table for two. Just one block from the beach, passes and sand chairs enhance a fun day in the sun. Ask about special events and theme weekends.

Historic Interest: Original home of Captain Stannard.

Innkeeper(s): Lee & Vern Mettin. $95-185. 9 rooms with PB, 1 suite and 3 conference rooms. Breakfast and snacks/refreshments included in rates. Types of meals: Full bkfst, early coffee/tea and picnic lunch. Beds: QDT. Cable TV, reading lamp, clock radio and turn-down service in room. Air conditioning. TV, VCR, bicycles, library, parlor games, telephone, fireplace, laundry facility, billiard table and piano on premises. Weddings, small meetings, family reunions and seminars hosted. Antiquing, art galleries, beach, bicycling, canoeing/kayaking, fishing, golf, hiking, horseback riding, live theater, museums, parks, shopping, tennis, water sports and wineries nearby.

Publicity: *Best Places to Kiss, Connecticut Magazine and travel guides.*

"Excellent accommodations."

Talcott House

161 Seaside Ave
Westbrook, CT 06498
(860)399-5020

Circa 1890. This restored Newport-style Georgian manor offers an ideal location on Long Island Sound. From the expansive lawn guests can enjoy the view as the sun sets over the Sound. The home is less than a mile from Pilots Point Marina. The rooms all face the oceanfront; one boasts a private veranda. The inn is listed on the local historic register. The Mystic Seaport, Gillette Castle, Essex Village and the Essex Steam Train are among the area's attractions. A full breakfast is served on the weekends and a continental breakfast on the weekdays.

Innkeeper(s): Barbara Slusser. $140-185. 3 rooms with PB. Breakfast included in rates. Types of meals: Full gourmet bkfst and early coffee/tea. Beds: QD. Reading lamp, ceiling fan, clock radio and desk in room. Swimming, telephone, fireplace, piano and refrigerator on premises. Limited handicap access. Weddings, small meetings and family reunions hosted. Antiquing, art galleries, beach, bicycling, canoeing/kayaking, fishing, hiking, live theater, parks, shopping, tennis, water sports, wineries and two casinos nearby.

Welcome Inn

433 Essex Rd
Westbrook, CT 06498-1504
(860)399-2500 Fax:(860)399-1840

Circa 1895. This handsome Victorian farmhouse is located on a half acre of grounds with tall trees, mature plantings and flowerbeds. A descendant of one of the town's founding fathers built the home, which features antiques and family heirlooms. A full breakfast is prepared and often features fresh vegetables and regional fruits from neighboring orchards. Westbrook, on the Connecticut coastline, offers appealing historic homes and museums. Popular activities include outlet shopping, the Essex Steam Train, river cruises, local theatre and the Goodspeed Opera House. There are more than 400 antique dealers in the surrounding area. In winter, a popular activity is bundling up for a romantic carriage ride complete with sleigh bells and white horses.

Innkeeper(s): Helen P. Spence. $79-149. 4 rooms with PB. Breakfast and snacks/refreshments included in rates. Types of meals: Full gourmet bkfst, veg bkfst and early coffee/tea. Beds: QD. Modem hook-up, cable TV, reading lamp, ceiling fan, clock radio, split of wine & candies and masseuse upon request in room. Air conditioning. Fax, copier, library, parlor games, telephone and fireplace on premises. Weddings, small meetings, family reunions and seminars hosted. Antiquing, art galleries, beach, bicycling, canoeing/kayaking, fishing, golf, hiking, live theater, museums, parks, shopping, tennis, water sports and wineries nearby.

Westbrook Inn B&B

976 Boston Post Rd
Westbrook, CT 06498-1852
(800)342-3162 Fax:(860)399-8023
E-mail: info@westbrookinn.com
Web: www.westbrookinn.com

Circa 1876. A wraparound porch and flower gardens offer a gracious welcome to this elegant Victorian inn. The innkeeper, an expert in restoring old houses and antiques, has filled the B&B with French and American period furnishings, handsome paintings and wall coverings. Well-appointed guest bedrooms and a spacious two-bedroom cottage provide comfortable accommodations. A full breakfast features homemade baked goods that accompany a variety of delicious main entrees. Complimentary beverages are available throughout the day. Enjoy bike rides and walks to the beach. Nearby factory outlets and casinos are other popular activities.

Innkeeper(s): Glenn & Chris. $99-179. 9 rooms with PB, 1 cottage and 1 conference room. Breakfast and snacks/refreshments included in rates. Types of meals: Full bkfst, early coffee/tea, afternoon tea and room service. Beds: QT. Cable TV, reading lamp, refrigerator, clock radio, telephone, turn-down service, desk, 10 rooms furnished with antiques and period decor and one two-bedroom cottage with full kitchen in room. Air conditioning. VCR, fax, copier, bicycles, library, parlor games and picturesque gardens on premises. Weddings, small meetings and family reunions hosted. Antiquing, beach, fishing, golf, live theater, parks, shopping, sporting events, tennis, water sports, casinos, outlet mall and walk to beaches and downtown nearby.

Publicity: Arrington's Bed & Breakfast Journal ("Best Inn with Nearby Attractions" - 2003).

Westport G3

The Inn at National Hall

2 Post Rd W
Westport, CT 06880-4203
(203)221-1351 (800)628-4255 Fax:(203)221-0276
E-mail: info@innatnationalhall.com
Web: www.innatnationalhall.com

Circa 1873. This exquisite inn is consistently named as one of the nation's best, and it is quite deserving of its four-star and five-diamond rating. The inn is situated on the Saugatuck River and guests can meander by the water on the boardwalk. The renovation of this National Register gem cost upwards of $15 million, and the result is evident. Rooms are masterfully appointed with the finest fabrics and furnishings. The Acorn Room is a stunning example. Walls are painted a deep red hue, and guests slumber atop a massive canopy bed enveloped in luxurious yellow fabrics. The conference room is filled with regal touches. Guests can enjoy a European-style continental breakfast in the Drawing Room. There are ample amenities, valet and room service. Gourmet dinners can be enjoyed at the inn's restaurant. Westport's posh boutiques, art galleries and antique shops are a stone's throw away.

Innkeeper(s): Gary Bedell. $225-700. 16 rooms with PB, 1 with FP, 8 suites and 1 conference room. Breakfast included in rates. Types of meals: Cont plus, early coffee/tea and gourmet dinner. Restaurant on premises. Beds: KQT. Cable TV, VCR, reading lamp, stereo, refrigerator, clock radio, telephone, turn-down service and desk in room. Air conditioning. Fax, copier, parlor games and fireplace on premises. Weddings, small meetings, family reunions and seminars hosted. Antiquing, beach, live theater, parks, shopping and tennis nearby.

Publicity: Architectural Digest and Country Inns.

Wethersfield C6

Chester Bulkley House B&B

184 Main St
Wethersfield, CT 06109-2340
(860)563-4236 Fax:(860)257-8266

Circa 1830. Offering the best of both worlds, this renovated Greek Revival structure is ideally located in the historic village of Old Weathersfield with its quaint sites, museums and shops, yet the inn also boasts a 10-minute drive to downtown Hartford with ballet, Broadway shows, opera and the symphony. Hand-carved woodwork, wide pine floors, working fireplaces and period pieces enhance the comfortable ambiance. Cut flowers, pillow chocolates and other thoughtful treats ensure a pleasant and gracious stay for business or leisure.

Innkeeper(s): Tom Aufiero. $90-105. 5 rooms, 3 with PB and 1 suite. Breakfast included in rates. Types of meals: Full bkfst, early coffee/tea, afternoon tea and room service. Beds: KQDT. Ceiling fan and clock radio in room. Air conditioning. Fax, telephone and fireplace on premises. Weddings, small meetings, family reunions and seminars hosted. Antiquing, downhill skiing, fishing, live theater, parks, shopping and sporting events nearby.

Woodstock B9

Elias Child House B&B

50 Perrin Rd
Woodstock, CT 06281
(860)974-9836 (877)974-9836
E-mail: afelice@earthlink.net
Web: www.eliaschildhouse.com

Circa 1700. Nine fireplaces warm this heritage three-story colonial home, referred to as "the mansion house" by early settlers. There are two historic cooking hearths, including a beehive oven. Original floors, twelve-over-twelve windows and paneling remain. A bountiful breakfast is served fireside in the dining room and a screened porch and a patio provide nesting spots for reading and relaxing. The inn's grounds are spacious and offer a pool and hammocks. Woodland walks on the 47 acres and antiquing are popular activities.

Historic Interest: Roseland Cottage, Sturbridge Village and Brimfield (20 minutes), Pequot Indian Museum, Putnam antique center, Windham Textile Museum.

Innkeeper(s): Anthony Felice, Jr. & MaryBeth Gorke-Felice. $100-135. 3 rooms with PB, 4 with FP and 1 suite. Breakfast included in rates. Types of meals: Country bkfst and early coffee/tea. Beds: QDT. Reading lamp, clock radio, turn-down service, suite has two fireplaces, sitting room and two baths (one with a clawfoot tub) in room. Air conditioning. VCR, fax, copier, swimming, bicycles, parlor games, telephone, fireplace, hearth-cooking demonstrations and cross-country skiing on premises. Small meetings and family reunions hosted.

Publicity: *Time Out New York, Best Fares Magazine, Distinction, Wine Gazette, Car & Driver Magazine, Worcester Telegram and Gazette.*

"Comfortable rooms and delightful country ambiance."

The Inn at Woodstock Hill

94 Plaine Hill Rd
Woodstock, CT 06281-2912
(860)928-0528
E-mail: innwood@snet.net
Web: www.woodstockhill.com

Circa 1850. This classic Georgian house with its black shutters and white clapboard exterior reigns over 14 acres of rolling farmland. Inside are several parlors, pegged-wood floors, English country wallpapers and floral chintzes. Four-poster beds and wood-burning fireplaces enhance the special ambience.

Historic Interest: National Register.

Innkeeper(s): Richard Naumann. $100-200. 19 rooms with PB, 6 with FP and 1 conference room. Types of meals: Full gourmet bkfst. Restaurant on premises. Beds: KQT. TV, VCR, telephone, phone,TV and broadband Internet at no charge on premises. Limited handicap access. Fishing nearby.

Publicity: *Hartford Courant, Worcester Telegram, Connecticut Magazine and Country Inns.*

"You can go to heaven, I'll just stay here!"

Delaware

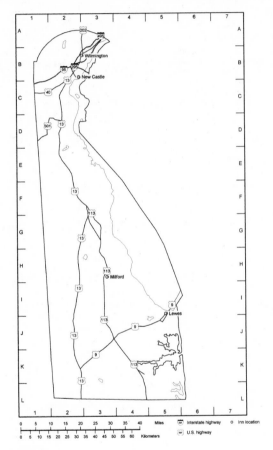

blueberry scones. Bicycles are available to explore the area. An interesting collection of historic houses and churches dating from 1631 are found in Lewes. The Cape May Ferry is here, as well as sea charters. One of the country's largest outlet malls is nearby.

Innkeeper(s): Patricia & Leon Rockett. $65-85. 5 rooms. Breakfast included in rates. Types of meals: Early coffee/tea. Beds: QDT. Reading lamp, refrigerator, ceiling fan, clock radio and desk in room. Air conditioning. VCR, bicycles, library, pet boarding, parlor games, telephone, fireplace and pool table on premises. Small meetings hosted. Amusement parks, antiquing, art galleries, fishing, golf, live theater, parks, shopping, sporting events, tennis, water sports, movies and gourmet restaurants nearby.

Zwaanendael Inn

142 2nd St
Lewes, DE 19958-1396
(302)645-6466 (800)824-8754 Fax:(302)645-7196
E-mail: innkeeper@zwaanendael.com
Web: www.zwaanendaelinn.com

Circa 1926. In the heart of the historic district, this inn has 23 individually decorated guest rooms. All rooms feature antique beds and turndown service. The inn also offers conference facilities, catering and convenient access to antiquing, beaches, dining and sightseeing. Five suites also are available. The shore is just one mile from the inn. Prime Hook National Wildlife Refuge and Cape Henlopen State Park are nearby.

Innkeeper(s): Mike Cryne. $45-275. 23 rooms, 18 with PB, 5 suites and 1 conference room. Breakfast included in rates. Types of meals: Early coffee/tea. Restaurant on premises. Beds: KQDT. Reading lamp, telephone, turn-down service and some with TV in room. Air conditioning. Fax, copier and Swan's Nest Cafe on premises. Limited handicap access. Weddings, small meetings, family reunions and seminars hosted. Antiquing, fishing, parks, shopping and water sports nearby.

Publicity: *New York Times, Mid-Atlantic Country* and *National Geographic.*

Lewes — I5

Kings Inn

151 Kings Hwy
Lewes, DE 19958-1459
(302)645-6438

Circa 1888. High ceilings, stained-glass windows and hardwood floors highlight this nine-bedroom Victorian. The décor is eclectic and full of art. Relax on the front or back porch overlooking the wisteria arbor. Choose a guest bedroom with a queen, double or twin bed and a Jacuzzi for two. Breakfast is served in the sunroom and usually includes freshly baked items such as banana, pumpkin and cranberry breads and cinnamon

Milford — H3

Causey Mansion Bed & Breakfast

2 Causey Ave
Milford, DE 19963-1936
(302)422-0979

Circa 1763. Originally a Georgian-style home, this stately inn was renovated in 1849 to a Greek Revival mansion. It is on the National Register of Historic Places, and was the home of two governors, one from the 18th century and one from the 19th century. Two of the original slave quarters are still on the three-acre property near the beaches of Delaware Bay and the Atlantic Ocean. The inn itself has a large porch and a solarium, and sits on a meticulously landscaped yard. It offers five guest bedrooms. A hearty breakfast is served each morning. Guests may then explore the beautiful natural and historic surroundings. Swimming, tennis and golf, fishing, boating and antiquing are available nearby. Or guests may prefer to relax with a book in the library or stroll through the formal boxwood gardens.

Innkeeper(s): Kenneth & Frances Novak. $85. 5 rooms, 4 with PB and 1 suite. Breakfast and snacks/refreshments included in rates. Types of meals: Full bkfst and early coffee/tea. Beds: QDT. Desk in room. Air conditioning. TV, VCR, library, parlor games and telephone on premises. Weddings and small meetings hosted. Antiquing, beach, canoeing/kayaking, fishing, golf, live theater, museums, shopping and tennis nearby.

The Towers B&B

101 NW Front St
Milford, DE 19963-1022
(302)422-3814 (800)366-3814
E-mail: mispillion@ezol.com
Web: www.mispillion.com

Circa 1783. Once a simple colonial house, this ornate Steamboat Gothic fantasy features every imaginable Victorian architectural detail, all added in 1891. There are 10 distinct styles of gingerbread as well as towers, turrets, gables, porches and bays. Inside, chestnut and cherry woodwork, window seats and stained-glass windows are complemented with  American and French antiques. The back garden boasts a gazebo porch and swimming pool. Ask for the splendid Tower Room or Rapunzel Suite.

Historic Interest: Historic districts in Milford, town of Lewes, Dickinson Plantation, historic city of Dover.
Innkeeper(s): Daniel & Rhonda Bond. $95-135. 4 rooms with PB and 2 suites. Breakfast included in rates. Beds: QD. Reading lamp, ceiling fan and clock radio in room. Air conditioning. Swimming, telephone and fireplace on premises. Antiquing, fishing, live theater, parks, shopping and water sports nearby.
Publicity: *Washington Post, Baltimore Sun, Washingtonian and Mid-Atlantic Country.*

"I felt as if I were inside a beautiful Victorian Christmas card, surrounded by all the things Christmas should be."

New Castle B2

William Penn Guest House

206 Delaware St
New Castle, DE 19720-4816
(302)328-7736 Fax:(302)328-0403

Circa 1682. William Penn slept here. In fact, his host Arnoldus de LaGrange witnessed the ceremony in which Penn gained possession of the Three Lower Colonies. Mrs. Burwell, who lived next door to the historic house, "gained possession" of the house one day about 44 years ago while her husband was away. After recovering from his wife's surprise purchase, Mr. Burwell rolled up his sleeves and began restoring the house. Guests may stay in the very room slept in by Penn.

Innkeeper(s): Irma & Richard Burwell. $75-95. 4 rooms, 1 with PB. Types of meals: Cont. Beds: KDT. Telephone in room. TV on premises. Museums nearby.
Publicity: *Asbury Press.*

"An enjoyable stay, as usual. We'll return in the spring."

Wilmington B3

Darley Manor Inn

3701 Philadelphia Pike
Wilmington, DE 19703-3413
(302)792-2127 (800)824-4703 Fax:(302)798-6143

Circa 1790. Charles Dickens once stayed in this 18th-century Colonial manor, and one of the guest rooms bears his name. Tasteful rooms are furnished with period antiques and reproductions. One of the suites includes porch railings from the "White House" in Richmond, Va., while two suites boast working fireplaces. A leisurely, full breakfast is served in the dining room with a selection of entrees. Darley Manor is close to many restaurants, shops and Brandywine Valley attractions.

Historic Interest: The Longwood Gardens, Old New Castle, Brandywine River Museum and historic Philadelphia are all within 30 minutes from the inn.
Innkeeper(s): Ray & Judith Hester. $85-109. 6 rooms with PB, 3 with FP and 4 suites. Breakfast, afternoon tea and snacks/refreshments included in rates. Types of meals: Country bkfst and early coffee/tea. Beds: Q. Data port, cable TV, VCR, reading lamp, CD player, refrigerator, ceiling fan, clock radio, telephone, turn-down service, desk and suites with refrigerator in room. Air conditioning. Fax, parlor games, fireplace, garden Jacuzzi in season and business center on premises. Antiquing, art galleries, canoeing/kayaking, fishing, golf, hiking, live theater, museums, parks, shopping, sporting events, tennis and wineries nearby.
Publicity: *Wilmington News Journal.*

"Comfort cannot be beat and hospitality is tops. It is truly a world apart."

White House Bed & Breakfast

2311 Newport Gap Pike (The Cedars)
Wilmington, DE 19808
(302)999-1495 Fax:(302)994-3914

Circa 1902. Previously called the Spring Hill Estate, this Colonial Revival home is embellished with elegant Victorian furnishings and accents. The innkeepers are proud of the personal attention given to make each stay a cherished one. A spacious living room boasts cozy sitting areas, movie entertainment and a fireplace. Large guest bedrooms feature antique brass or canopy beds with quilts or comforters and Oriental carpets on hardwood floors. Wicker, lace, crystal, soft music and a fresh rose create a setting on the terrace for an entree of banana pancakes, Belgian waffles or an omelette. Dinners can be arranged with advance notice. Three-and-a-half acres of appealing landscaping include trees, plants, a gazebo and lily pond with frogs and fish. The grounds are perfect for weddings or other special occasions.

Innkeeper(s): Eric & Sandra Semke. $98-125. 4 rooms. Breakfast and snacks/refreshments included in rates. Types of meals: Full gourmet bkfst, veg bkfst, early coffee/tea and afternoon tea. Beds: QD. Reading lamp, ceiling fan, clock radio and turn-down service in room. Air conditioning. TV, VCR, fax, spa, parlor games, telephone and fireplace on premises. Museums, parks, shopping, sporting events, tennis, wineries, Weddings, bridal and baby showers, anniversary parties and special occasion parties hosted. Antiquing, art galleries, beaches, canoeing/kayaking, fishing, golf, hiking and horseback riding nearby.
Publicity: *Wilmington News Journal (Reader's Choice Award), The Reading News Journal (Reader's Choice Award) and second best Bed & Breakfast in Delaware for 2002 and 2003.*

"My extended family and I wish to thank you for the excellent service and exquisite meal you provided to us."

Florida

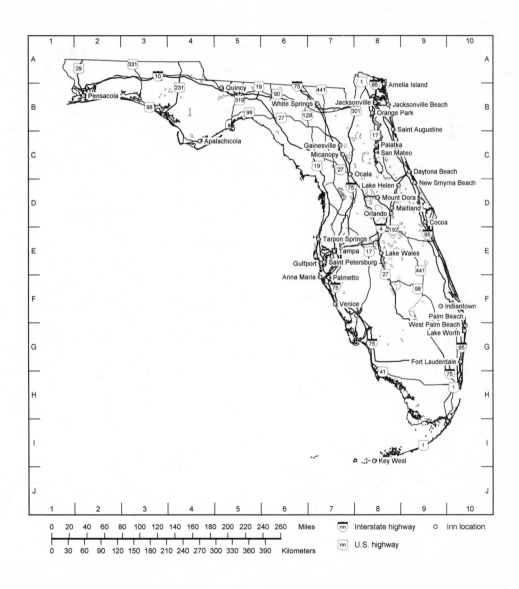

	Miles	
0 20 40 60 80 100 120 140 160 180 200 220 240 260	Miles	
0 30 60 90 120 150 180 210 240 270 300 330 360 390	Kilometers	

Interstate highway   ○ Inn location

U.S. highway

Amelia Island   B8

Amelia Island Williams House

103 S 9th St
Amelia Island, FL 32034-3616
(904)277-2328 (800)414-9258 Fax:(904)321-1325
E-mail: topinn@williamshouse.com
Web: www.williamshouse.com

Circa 1856. It's not this grand Antebellum mansion's first owner, but its second for whom the house is named. Marcellus Williams and his wife, a great-great-granddaughter of the King of Spain, are its most esteemed residents. Among their many influential guests, the two once hosted Jefferson Davis, and, ironically, the first owners used part of the home for the Underground Railroad. It will be hard for guests to believe that the home was anything but opulent. Antiques from nine different countries decorate the home. The guest rooms are romantic; the gourmet breakfast served on the finest china; and the lush, fragrant grounds are shaded by a 500-year-old oak tree. The innkeepers also have restored the historic home next door, which was used as an infirmary during the Civil War. Four of the guest rooms are housed here, complete with clawfoot or Jacuzzi tubs.

Innkeeper(s): Paul & Nancy Barnes. $170-245. 8 rooms with PB, 5 with FP and 2 suites. Breakfast and afternoon tea included in rates. Types of meals: Full gourmet bkfst. Beds: KQ. Cable TV, VCR, reading lamp, ceiling fan, clock radio, telephone, coffeemaker, turn-down service, desk, hot tub/spa, video library, robes, iron, flowers, chocolates, towels for beach and daily maid service in room. Air conditioning. Fax, copier, bicycles, parlor games, fireplace and video library on premises. Limited handicap access. Weddings and family reunions hosted. Antiquing, canoeing/kayaking, fishing, golf, live theater, parks, shopping, sporting events, tennis, water sports, sailing and zoo nearby.
Publicity: *Country Inns, Southern Living, Southern Accents, Victoria, Veranda, Palm Beach Life, National Geographic Traveler, Jacksonville Magazine, 2002 Award Best B&B on Amelia Island, Superior Small Lodging, Arrington's Journal - voted "Most Elegant Inn 2002 & 2003," Waters Edge Magazine, CNN International Travel and Inn Country USA.*

Bailey House

28 S 7th St
Amelia Island, FL 32034-3960
(904)261-5390 (800)251-5390 Fax:(904)321-0103
E-mail: bailey@bellsouth.net
Web: www.bailey-house.com

Circa 1895. This elegant Queen Anne Victorian was a wedding present that steamship agent Effingham W. Bailey gave to his bride. He shocked the locals by spending the enormous sum of $10,000 to build the house with all its towers, turrets, gables and verandas. The parlor and dining room open to a fireplace in a reception hall with the inscription "Hearth Hall - Welcome All." A spirit of hospitality has reigned in this home from its beginning.

Historic Interest: The historic seaport is within walking distance, Fort Clinch (2 miles).

Innkeeper(s): Tom & Jenny Bishop. $139-199. 10 rooms with PB, 7 with FP. Breakfast included in rates. Types of meals: Full bkfst and early coffee/tea. Beds: KQT. Cable TV, reading lamp, ceiling fan and telephone in room. Air conditioning. TV, fax, copier, bicycles and fireplace on premises. Small meetings hosted. Antiquing, fishing, golf, live theater, parks, shopping, sporting events, tennis, water sports and history museum nearby.
Publicity: *Victorian Homes, Innsider, Southern Living, Victorian Homes, Saint Petersburg Times, Jacksonville, Travel Network and Romantic Inns.*

The Fairbanks House

227 S 7th St
Amelia Island, FL 32034
(904)277-0500 (888)891-9939 Fax:(904)277-3103
E-mail: email@fairbankshouse.com
Web: www.fairbankshouse.com

Circa 1885. The living and dining room fireplace tiles of this Italianate-style mansion bring to life scenes from Shakespeare's works and "Aesop's Fables." Other features include polished hardwood floors, intricately carved moldings and eight other fireplaces that grace spacious rooms. Each of the guest rooms is furnished with a four-poster or canopied king, queen or twin bed, Jacuzzi and clawfoot tubs or showers. Guests can step outside to enjoy an inviting courtyard,  swimming pool and gardens bursting with roses, palms and magnolias. The Fairbanks House was named Florida's "Most Sophisticated and Romantic Bed & Breakfast" by The Best Romantic Escapes in Florida. The inn is a smoke-free property, which includes the grounds.

Innkeeper(s): Bill & Theresa Hamilton. $180-295. 12 rooms with PB, 9 with FP, 3 suites and 3 cottages. Breakfast included in rates. Types of meals: Full gourmet bkfst. Beds: KQT. Cable TV, reading lamp, ceiling fan, telephone, hair dryer and ironing board in room. Air conditioning. Bicycles, fireplace, beach towels, beach chairs, swimming pool and social hour on premises. Antiquing, beach, fishing, golf, live theater, parks, shopping, sporting events, tennis, water sports and restaurants nearby.
Publicity: *Country Inns, Veranda, Southern Living, Amelia Now, Islander, Florida Living, New York Times and Mother's Day.*

Hoyt House B&B

804 Atlantic Ave
Amelia Island, FL 32034-3629
(904)277-4300 (800)432-2085 Fax:(904)277-9626
E-mail: reservations1@hoythouse.com
Web: www.hoythouse.com

Circa 1905. A centerpiece of the historic district, this 1905 Queen Anne Victorian mansion blends warm hospitality and delightful comforts with the grace of a bygone era. Feel the ocean breeze from a swing or rockers on broad porches while sipping lemonade or iced tea. Relax by a fireplace in one of the gathering rooms. Elegant guest bedrooms feature a private bath, some include a whirlpool tub. Enjoy a chef's breakfast, afternoon tea and evening wine. Bike to the sea to take in the island sunshine, birds and dolphins. Beach gear is provided. Explore fascinating shops and dine in excellent restaurants all within an easy stroll.

Innkeeper(s): Gayl Blount. $129-189. 10 rooms with PB, 2 with FP and 1 conference room. Breakfast and snacks/refreshments included in rates. Types of meals: Full bkfst and picnic lunch. Beds: KQ. TV, reading lamp, telephone, hair dryers and first floor rooms with ceiling fans in room. Air conditioning. VCR, fax, copier, modem, bicycles, beach gear and complimentary evening wine and beer on premises. Limited handicap access. Weddings, small meetings, family reunions and seminars hosted. Antiquing, fishing, golf, live theater, parks, shopping, sporting events, tennis and water sports nearby.
Publicity: *The Washington Times, PBS, Southern Living, Intimate Destinations and Jacksonville Times-Union.*

Apalachicola   C4

Gibson Inn

57 Market Street
Apalachicola, FL 32320-1774
(850)653-8282 Fax:(850)653-3521

Circa 1907. Originally owned by the Gibson sisters, this impressive cypress and pine Victorian inn has been meticulously returned to its turn-of-the-century grandeur. Located in the heart of the historic district, the inn was picked as one of two buildings in the state for restoration and preservation. Relax with a drink in the nautical bar or view the Apalachicola Bay from a rocker on one of the wraparound verandas. Guest bedrooms are furnished with wrought iron or four-poster beds, armoires and other period antiques. Linger over breakfast in the dining room. Mystery weekends and weddings have increased the inn's popularity.
Historic Interest: National Register.
Innkeeper(s): Michael Koun & Charlene Carter. $90-140. 31 rooms with PB and 1 conference room. Breakfast included in rates. Types of meals: Cont, lunch and dinner. Beds: KQT. Cable TV, telephone and voice mail in room. Air conditioning. TV and copier on premises. Limited handicap access. Weddings and small meetings hosted. Antiquing, art galleries, beach, bicycling, fishing, golf, live theater and shopping nearby.
Publicity: *Travel & Leisure and Tallahassee Democrat.*

Cocoa   D9

Indian River House

3113 Indian River Dr
Cocoa, FL 32922-6501
(321)631-5660 Fax:(321)631-5268
E-mail: suzanne@indianriverhouse.com
Web: www.indianriverhouse.com

Circa 1900. Built at the turn of the 20th century, this historic home offers four comfortable guest rooms. The home is casually decorated, and a few antiques have been placed among the furnishings. The home is located along the Intracoastal Waterway, and guests only have to walk a few feet to reach the inn's dock where they can fish or just enjoy the scenery. Breakfasts include items such as freshly baked biscuits, fresh fruit, eggs Benedict or perhaps French toast. The home offers close access to many attractions, including the sites of Orlando, the Daytona Speedway, National Seashore and Wildlife Refuge, fishing, kayaking and biking. Space shuttle launches can be seen from the front porch.
Innkeeper(s): Suzanne LaMee Bender. $95. 4 rooms with PB, 2 with FP. Breakfast and snacks/refreshments included in rates. Types of meals: Full bkfst and veg bkfst. Beds: KQ. Reading lamp and clock radio in room. Central air. TV, VCR, fax, copier, bicycles, library, parlor games, telephone and fireplace on premises. Antiquing, art galleries, beach, bicycling, fishing, horseback riding, live theater, museums, parks, shopping, tennis, water sports and kayaking nearby.

Daytona Beach   C9

Coquina Inn B&B

544 S Palmetto Ave
Daytona Beach, FL 32114-4924
(386)254-4969 (800)805-7533
E-mail: coquinabnb@aol.com
Web: www.coquinainndaytonabeach.com

Circa 1912. Located in the Daytona Beach Historic District, this handsome house boasts an exterior of coquina rock blended from shells, arched windows and a wrought-iron balcony on

the second floor. The Jasmine Room is accentuated with a seven-foot canopy bed draped in a delicate netting. French leather chairs, a fireplace and a Victorian tub are featured. The Hibiscus Room is decorated

with an iron canopy bed, wicker settee chair and coffee table and includes a French door that leads to a private balcony.
Historic Interest: Sugar Mill Gardens (5 miles), Gamble House (8 miles), Tomoka State Park & Museum (14 miles).
Innkeeper(s): Ann Christoffersen & Dennis Haight. $80-110. 4 rooms with PB, 1 with FP. Breakfast included in rates. Types of meals: Full gourmet bkfst. Beds: QD. TV, ceiling fan, clock radio and fresh flowers in room. Air conditioning. Bicycles, telephone and fireplace on premises. Antiquing, fishing, live theater, shopping, sporting events and water sports nearby.
Publicity: *Country Inns, Florida Sports, Sun Sentinel, Southern Living and Miami Herald.*

"Better than chocolate. A little bit of heaven on earth."

Fort Lauderdale   G10

Caribbean Quarters Inn

3012 Granada St
Fort Lauderdale, FL 33304
(954)523-3226 (888)414-3226
E-mail: cqbandb@aol.com
Web: www.caribbeanquarters.com

Circa 1939. With its unique South Florida architecture, this three-story hotel features a courtyard with plantation-style wooden verandas and French doors that open onto the interior. Lush tropical plants and flowers are everywhere. The decor throughout is Caribbean with a hint of the 1930s. A variety of guest bedrooms and suites with white gauzy mosquito netting hangs over beds with floral spreads. Rattan or wicker furnishings grace sitting areas. Innkeeper Bernie is a professional cook who oversees the breakfast service of fresh fruit, cereals, baked goods and juices. Situated in the older part of the city, the inn is only half a block from the beach or the water taxi on the inland waterway.
Innkeeper(s): Bernd Metz. $95-250. 15 rooms with PB and 5 suites. Breakfast included in rates. Types of meals: Cont plus and room service. Beds: KQDT. Modem hook-up, data port, cable TV, VCR, reading lamp, refrigerator, ceiling fan, telephone and coffeemaker in room. Air conditioning. Spa, laundry facility and sun deck on premises. Weddings, small meetings and family reunions hosted. Antiquing, art galleries, beach, bicycling, fishing, golf, hiking, live theater, museums, parks, shopping, tennis and water sports nearby.

The Pillars at New River Sound

111 North Birch Rd
Fort Lauderdale, FL 33304
(954)467-9639 (800)800-7666 Fax:(954)763-2845
E-mail: guestservices@pillarshotel.com
Web: www.pillarshotel.com

Circa 1939. One of the original homes remaining on the central Fort Lauderdale beach, this completely restored main house boasts British Colonial architecture blended with island plantation decor. Custom furnishings, artwork, oak hardwood floors and painted paneled walls evoke a warm, inviting ambiance. The reception area features a library and baby grand piano. Luxurious guest bedrooms and suites with marble bathrooms offer comfort and style with extraordinary amenities to meet most any business or personal need. French doors open to a waterfront courtyard and swimming pool. Enjoy a daily newspaper and a generous continental-plus breakfast. The 100-

foot sun dock is directly on the Intracoastal Waterway near the palm-lined promenade. Complimentary iced tea is served poolside. Massage services are available.

Innkeeper(s): Philip Lu. $133-455. 23 rooms with PB, 5 suites and 1 conference room. Types of meals: Cont plus, early coffee/tea, lunch, gourmet dinner and room service. Beds: KQT. Modem hook-up, data port, cable TV, VCR, reading lamp, refrigerator, ceiling fan, clock radio, telephone, turn-down service, desk, voice mail and Ethernet connection in room. Air conditioning. Fax, copier, swimming, library, parlor games and high-speed wireless Internet on premises. Limited handicap access. Weddings, small meetings, family reunions and seminars hosted. Antiquing, art galleries, beach, bicycling, canoeing/kayaking, fishing, golf, live theater, museums, parks and water sports nearby.

Publicity: *Inn of the Month- Travel & Leisure Magazine December 2001 and Top Ten Romantic Inn American Historic Inns 2003.*

Gainesville   C7

Magnolia Plantation Cottages and Gardens

309 SE 7th Street
Gainesville, FL 32601-6831
(352)375-6653 Fax:(352)338-0303

Circa 1885. This restored French Second Empire Victorian is in the National Register. Magnolia trees surround the house. Five guest rooms are filled with family heirlooms. All bathrooms feature clawfoot tubs and candles. There are also private historic cottages available with Jacuzzis. Guests may enjoy the gardens, reflecting pond with waterfalls and gazebo. Bicycles are also available. Evening wine and snacks are included. The inn is two miles from the University of Florida.

Innkeeper(s): Joe & Cindy Montalto. $90-250. 5 rooms with PB, 5 with FP and 6 cottages. Breakfast and afternoon tea included in rates. Types of meals: Full bkfst. Beds: Q. TV, reading lamp, ceiling fan, clock radio, turn-down service, desk, cottages have Jacuzzi, fireplace, full kitchen and private garden in room. Air conditioning. VCR, fax, bicycles, library, telephone, fireplace and cocktail hour on premises. Antiquing, live theater, parks, shopping and sporting events nearby.

Publicity: *Florida Living Magazine and Inn Country USA.*

"This has been a charming, once-in-a-lifetime experience."

Sweetwater Branch Inn B&B

625 E University Ave
Gainesville, FL 32601-5449
(352)373-6760 (800)595-7760 Fax:(352)371-3771
E-mail: reservations@sweetwaterinn.com
Web: www.sweetwaterinn.com

Circa 1885. Seven fountains highlight the handsome gardens of this Queen Anne Victorian, listed in the National Register. Next to the University of Florida, the inn offers a spacious banquet hall, attractive parlor and dining room and finely appointed guest rooms. Poached pears with English custard and Sweetwater Crepes are specialties of the inn. The gazebo and the inn's grounds attract special events such as weddings. The nearby historic district offers dining, theater and music.

Innkeeper(s): Cornelia Holbrook. $75-150. 14 rooms with PB, 7 with FP, 4 suites, 2 cottages and 3 conference rooms. Breakfast included in rates. Types of meals: Full gourmet bkfst, early coffee/tea, gourmet lunch, afternoon tea, gourmet dinner and room service. Beds: QT. Data port, cable TV, reading lamp, refrigerator, ceiling fan, clock radio, telephone, desk and hot tub/spa in room. Air conditioning. Fax, bicycles, library, fireplace, irons/ironing boards and blow dryers on premises. Limited handicap access. Weddings and small meetings hosted. Antiquing, fishing, golf, live theater, parks and sporting events nearby.

Publicity: *Sun Sentinel, Tampa Tribune, Inn Country and USA Feature.*

"You have met every need we could possibly have. It has been a wonderful stay."

Gulfport   E7

The Peninsula Inn & Spa

2937 Beach Blvd
Gulfport, FL 33707
(727)346-9800 (888)9000-INN Fax:(727)343-6579
E-mail: inn_spa@yahoo.com
Web: www.innspa.net

Circa 1905. Combining the architectural styles of New England and Southern Vernacular, this boutique inn is a landmark in the waterfront historic district. Reminiscent of a Raj, the old-world atmosphere exudes British Colonial ambiance and decor and is embellished by hosting the foreign office of the Kingdom of Mandalay. Well-appointed suites and guest bedrooms are found on the second and third floors. On the first floor, savor gourmet dishes at the highly acclaimed Six Tables, or enjoy more casual fare in our Palm Lounge which offers a full service bar adjacent to a covered veranda and private, open-air alcove. Play croquet on the north side lawn. Relaxing and rejuvenating spa services offered here on the premises include massage, reflexology and skin care. Customized packages are popular at this premier location for special functions and intimate weddings.

Historic Interest: Built at the turn of the 19th century.

Innkeeper(s): Laurie Kozbelt & Amy Grabowski. $110-189. 11 rooms with PB. Breakfast included in rates. Types of meals: Cont plus, early coffee/tea, gourmet lunch, afternoon tea and gourmet dinner. Restaurant on premises. Beds: KQT. Modem hook-up, data port, cable TV, reading lamp, ceiling fan, clock radio, telephone and turn-down service in room. Central air. Fax, copier, tennis, library, parlor games, fireplace, gift shop and spa services on premises. Weddings, small meetings, family reunions and seminars hosted. Amusement parks, antiquing, art galleries, beach, bicycling, canoeing/kayaking, fishing, hiking, live theater, museums, parks, shopping, water sports, wineries, golf, tennis and swimming at country club nearby.

Publicity: *St. Petersburg Times, Edmonton Journal, Calgary Herald, Tampa Bay Illustrated, Gourmet Magazine, Tampa Bay Wedding & Party Planner Magazine, Spa Life Magazine, Fox News and Tampa Bay's Best.*

Holmes Beach   F7

Harrington House Beachfront B&B Inn

5626 Gulf Dr N
Holmes Beach, FL 34217-1666
(941)778-5444 (888)828-5566 Fax:(941)778-0527
E-mail: ahinns@harringtonhouse.com
Web: www.harringtonhouse.com

Circa 1925. A mere 40 feet from the water, this gracious home, set among pine trees and palms, is comprised of a main house and two beach houses. Constructed of thick coquina blocks, the house features a living room with a 20-foot-high beamed ceiling, fireplace, '20s wallpaper and French doors. Many of the guest rooms have four-poster beds, antique wicker furnishings and French doors opening onto a deck that overlooks the swimming pool and Gulf of Mexico. Some offer Jacuzzi-type tubs and fireplaces. Kayaks are available for dolphin watching, and bicycles are available for island sightseeing.

Innkeeper(s): Jo & Frank Davis. $129-249. 16 rooms with PB. Breakfast included in rates. Types of meals: Full gourmet bkfst. Beds: KQDT. TV, VCR, refrigerator, ceiling fan, telephone and desk in room. Air conditioning. Limited handicap access. Weddings, small meetings, family reunions and seminars hosted. Amusement parks, antiquing, fishing, live theater, shopping, sporting events and water sports nearby.

Publicity: *Southern Living, Sarasota Herald Tribune, Island Sun, Palm Beach Post, Tampa Tribune, Glamour, Atlantic Monthly and Travel Holiday.*

"Elegant house and hospitality."

Indiantown   F9

Seminole Country Inn

PO Box 1818-15885 SW Warfield Blvd
Indiantown, FL 34956
(772)597-3777 Fax:(561)597-2883

Circa 1926. Selected as one of the top 20 inns in Florida by the St. Petersburg Times, this historic inn is located halfway between Palm Beach and Lake Okeechobee in a citrus and cattle ranch area. Wallis Simpson was once a guest here because the Duchess was the niece of the inn's builder, a banker and railroad man. A wind-

ing staircase that leads to an upstairs sitting room highlights an inviting lobby. Guest rooms are filled with antiques and period decor. A restaurant is in the inn's dining room, an impressive site to behold with tall Palladium windows and 20-inch-thick walls. The menu features a wide variety of Southern favorites mingled with a bit of nouveau cuisine and is acclaimed for its fine offerings. An assortment of interesting events and tours are available such as traditional Thanksgiving and Christmas dinners, trail rides, barbecues and swamp tours. Innkeeper(s): Jonnie Flewelling. $65-125. 22 rooms with PB and 2 conference rooms. Types of meals: Cont, lunch, picnic lunch and gourmet dinner. Restaurant on premises. Beds: KQD. Cable TV, reading lamp, stereo, clock radio, telephone and desk in room. Air conditioning. VCR, fax, copier, swimming, bicycles, parlor games, fireplace and native border gardens on premises. Small meetings hosted. Antiquing, bicycling, fishing, golf, hiking, horseback riding, live theater, parks, shopping, tennis, water sports, eco tours and bird watching nearby.
Publicity: *St. Petersburg Times and The Sun Sentinel.*

Jacksonville   B8

Dickert House

1804 Copeland St
Jacksonville, FL 32204-4617
(904)387-4762 Fax:(904)387-4003
E-mail: info@dickert-house.com
Web: www.dickert-house.com

Circa 1915. Dickert House is located in a lush, quiet neighborhood just off the St. Johns River, and guests can take in the view from the home's patio. Each of the suites features its own special décor, and most include a bedroom, bathroom and spacious sitting room. The suite in the carriage house is a perfect place for honeymooners. A canopy trailed with ivy shades the bed, and the French doors in the sitting room are draped with lace and a bit more ivy. The Irish Suite is perfectly named with its bedroom done in a rich emerald hue. The massive Sunflower Suite is as bright and welcoming as a bouquet of flowers, and includes two bedrooms, a sitting room and bath with a whirlpool tub. The sitting room is painted in a warm shade of lemon, and the master bedroom walls are painted a rich cornflower with a king-size bed topped with an English country comforter. Be sure to take a tour of the incredible gardens, which include jasmine, camellias, impatiens, amaryllis and roses to name a few. Along the way, you'll discover fountains, one

with a family of koi. With all of this opulence, one would expect a gourmet breakfast, and guests are pampered not only with the morning meal, but also with a proper English afternoon tea. Innkeeper(s): Betty Dickert. $99-199. 10 rooms, 6 with PB, 1 with FP, 6 suites and 1 conference room. Types of meals: Full gourmet bkfst, veg bkfst, early coffee/tea and room service. Beds: KQDT. Modem hook-up, cable TV, VCR, reading lamp, ceiling fan, clock radio, telephone, turn-down service, desk, hot tub/spa, computer with high-speed Internet, use of fax, wine and hors d'oeuvres in room. Central air. Fax, copier, spa, bicycles, library, parlor games, fireplace and laundry facility on premises. Limited handicap access. Weddings, small meetings, family reunions and seminars hosted. Antiquing, art galleries, beach, bicycling, fishing, golf, live theater, museums, parks, shopping, sporting events and tennis nearby.

House on Cherry St

1844 Cherry St
Jacksonville, FL 32205-8702
(904)384-1999 Fax:(904)387-4007

Circa 1909. Seasonal blooms fill the pots that line the circular entry stairs to this Federal-style house on tree-lined Cherry Street. It was moved in two pieces to its present site on St. Johns River in the historic Riverside area. Traditionally decorated rooms include antiques, collections of hand-carved decoy ducks and old clocks that chime and tick. Most rooms overlook the river. Your host is a nationally published writer.
Innkeeper(s): Victoria Freeman. $85-115. 4 suites. Breakfast and snacks/refreshments included in rates. Types of meals: Cont. Beds: QT. TV, reading lamp, ceiling fan, clock radio, telephone, desk, some refrigerators and flowers in room. Air conditioning. VCR, fax, copier, parlor games and fishing on premises. Small meetings, family reunions and seminars hosted. Antiquing, live theater, parks, shopping, sporting events and water sports nearby.
Publicity: *Southern Living, Florida Wayfarer, Tampa Tribune, New York Times and Florida Secrets.*

St. John's House B&B

1718 Osceola St
Jacksonville, FL 32204
(904)384-3724

Circa 1914. In the national historic district of old Riverside, this Prairie-style residence sits just one block from the serene St. Johns River. Spacious guest bedrooms feature handmade quilts. The Carriage House offers a private entrance and boasts French doors into a bath with a clawfoot tub. A delicious, healthy breakfast is served in the formal dining room or on the sun porch. A variety of sports, entertainment, parks, water activities and numerous sites are close by. All of northeast Florida and southeast Georgia are easily accessible from this convenient location. Innkeeper(s): Joan Moore & Dan Schafer. $75-110. 3 rooms, 2 with PB. Breakfast included in rates. Types of meals: Full bkfst and veg bkfst. Beds: QD. Cable TV, reading lamp, ceiling fan, clock radio, telephone, coffeemaker, desk, iron, ironing boards, VCR and one with refrigerator in room. Central air. VCR, fax and fireplace on premises. Antiquing, art galleries, beach, fishing, golf, live theater, museums, parks, shopping, sporting events and tennis nearby.

Jacksonville Beach   B8

Fig Tree Inn

185 4th Ave S
Jacksonville Beach, FL 32250
(904)246-8855 (877)217-9830

Circa 1915. Whether staying here for a romantic getaway or to cheer for a favorite football team, this cedar shake bed & breakfast inn with Victorian accents offers an inviting and relaxing atmosphere. Sip a cool beverage in a rocker or swing on the acclaimed front porch. Games, books and magazines as well as an extensive video library are in the parlor. Wireless high-speed Internet service is available. Stay warm by the fire on cool nights. Themed guest bedrooms feature a handmade willow and canopy bed, Jacuzzi and clawfoot tub. The backyard's namesake produces enough fruit to make fig walnut pancakes, fig jelly and preserves served on scones. A light meal is served weekdays, a full breakfast is enjoyed on weekends. The kitchen can be used at any time. Walk to the beach, only half a block away.

Innkeeper(s): Dawn & Kevin Eggleston. $75-350. 6 rooms with PB. Breakfast, afternoon tea and snacks/refreshments included in rates. Types of meals: Full gourmet bkfst, veg bkfst, early coffee/tea, picnic lunch and room service. Beds: QT. Modem hook-up, cable TV, VCR, reading lamp, refrigerator, ceiling fan, clock radio, telephone, coffeemaker, desk, robes, hair dryer, iron, ironing board and wireless high-speed Internet in room. Fax, copier, bicycles, library, parlor games, fireplace, laundry facility and video library on premises. Weddings, small meetings, family reunions and seminars hosted. Amusement parks, antiquing, art galleries, beach, bicycling, canoeing/kayaking, fishing, golf, hiking, horseback riding, live theater, museums, parks, shopping, sporting events, tennis and water sports nearby.

Key West   18

Andrews Inn

0 Whalton Ln
Key West, FL 33040
(305)294-7730 (888)263-7393 Fax:(305)294-0021
E-mail: info@seascapetropicalinn.com
Web: www.andrewsinn.com

Circa 1920. You may never run with the bulls in Pamplona or hunt rhinoceros in the wilds of Africa, but at this Key West inn, you won't be far from the spirit of Hemingway. The famed author's estate adjoins the property of the historic Andrews Inn, separated only by a fence. Aside from this claim to fame, the inn is within easy walking distance of Duval Street, shops and restaurants. The grounds are lush with tropical plants and there's a swimming pool, as well. Continental-plus breakfasts include a variety of goodies, but champagne adds an extra touch of elegance to the morning meal.

Innkeeper(s): Sally Garratt. $119-205. 6 rooms with PB. Breakfast and snacks/refreshments included in rates. Types of meals: Cont plus. Beds: KQ. Cable TV, ceiling fan, clock radio and telephone in room. Air conditioning. Swimming on premises. Weddings, small meetings and family reunions hosted. Antiquing, art galleries, beach, bicycling, canoeing/kayaking, fishing, golf, live theater, museums, parks, shopping, tennis and water sports nearby.

Blue Parrot Inn

916 Elizabeth St
Key West, FL 33040-6406
(305)296-0033 (800)231-2473
E-mail: bluparotin@aol.com
Web: www.blueparrotinn.com

Circa 1884. This Bahamian-style inn is decorated in a pleasing, tropical style and all the rooms are air conditioned. The grounds are lush and peaceful. Continental-plus breakfasts of fresh fruit, bagels, muffins and quiche are served poolside. There is plenty of space around the pool to relax and tan. The inn is located in a historic neighborhood and is near shops and restaurants. The ocean is just a few blocks away. Kittens are in residence.

Innkeeper(s): Larry Rhinard & Frank Yaccino. $79-487. 9 rooms, 7 with PB and 2 suites. Breakfast included in rates. Types of meals: Cont. Beds: KQD. Cable TV, reading lamp, refrigerator, ceiling fan, clock radio, telephone, voice mail and air conditioning in room. Fax, copier, swimming, bicycles and parlor games on premises. Limited handicap access. Weddings, small meetings and family reunions hosted. Antiquing, fishing, live theater, parks, shopping and water sports nearby.

Center Court-Tropical Inn & Cottages

915 Center St
Key West, FL 33040
(305)296-9292 (800)797-8787 Fax:(305)294-4104
E-mail: info@centercourtkw.com
Web: www.centercourtkw.com

Circa 1873. Built by a ship's captain, this historic yet upscale inn with suites, cottages and villas is listed in the National Register of Historic Places. Located on a quiet lane near Duval Street, the contemporary decor is accented by a tropical flair. Honeymoon suites feature Jacuzzis, private decks, hammocks and gas barbecue grills.

Cottages can accommodate up to 10 people; some boast a private pool. Enjoy an expanded continental breakfast served every morning and a complimentary happy hour on weekends. Common areas include three pools and two Jacuzzis.

Innkeeper(s): Naomi R. Van Steelandt. $98-598. 26 rooms, 7 with PB and 18 cottages. Types of meals: Cont plus. Beds: KQD. Reading lamp, stereo, refrigerator, clock radio, desk, hot tub/spa, TV, phone, ceiling fan, A/C, beach towels, beach bags, in-room safe and hair dryer in room. Telephone, VCR, fax, copier, spa, computer access, exercise pavilion and swimming pools on premises. Weddings, small meetings and family reunions hosted. Antiquing, fishing, golf, live theater, parks, shopping, water sports and the famous Duval Street nearby. Publicity: *Town & Country, Florida Keys Magazine* and *Toronto Sun*.

Chelsea House

707 Truman Ave
Key West, FL 33040-6423
(305)296-2211 (800)845-8859 Fax:(305)296-4822
E-mail: info@chelseahousekw.com
Web: www.chelseahousekw.com

Circa 1890. In the heart of historic Old Town, this two-story Victorian mansion has been restored, showcasing hardwood floors, tongue-and-groove wood walls, 14-foot-high ceilings and antique furnishings. In addition to the main house, there are three other buildings. The Pool House offers rooms next to the pool and sun decks. The recently renovated Garden Rooms overlook the tropical gardens and pool. Rocking chairs sit on raised decks. The Suites Building features studio-style and two-room suites, with French doors opening to private porches. A continental breakfast is served daily.

Innkeeper(s): Jim & Gary. $69-245. 21 rooms with PB. Breakfast included in rates. Types of meals: Cont plus and snacks/refreshments. Beds: KQDT. Modem hook-up, cable TV, VCR, reading lamp, refrigerator, ceiling fan, clock radio and telephone in room. Central air. Fax, copier, swimming, library, parlor games and pet friendly rooms on premises. Weddings, small meetings and family reunions hosted. Antiquing, art galleries, beach, bicycling, canoeing/kayaking, fishing, golf, live theater, museums, parks, shopping, tennis and water sports nearby.

Conch House Heritage Inn

625 Truman Ave
Key West, FL 33040-3233
(305)293-0020 (800)207-5806 Fax:(305)293-8447
E-mail: conchinn@aol.com
Web: www.conchhouse.com

Circa 1889. This restored Victorian inn is located in a historic Key West neighborhood and is listed in the National Register. In 1895, the home was purchased by Lance and Herminia Lester, and it has remained in the family ever since. The inn is surrounded by a picturesque white picket fence. The interior is light, airy and elegant. Walls are painted in bright colors and the home has a spacious, uncluttered feel. Rooms are appointed with elegant antiques. The continental-plus breakfast includes locally made Cuban bread.

Innkeeper(s): W. Sam Holland Jr. $98-228. 6 rooms with PB, 1 with FP. Breakfast included in rates. Types of meals: Cont plus. Beds: KQD. Cable TV, reading lamp, ceiling fan, clock radio and telephone in room. Air conditioning. Fax, copier, swimming and bicycles on premises. Limited handicap access. Antiquing, fishing, golf, live theater, parks, shopping, tennis and water sports nearby.

Publicity: *National Newspaper.*

The Curry Mansion Inn & Museum

511 Caroline St
Key West, FL 33040-6604
(305)294-5349 (800)253-3466 Fax:(305)294-4093
E-mail: frontdesk@currymansion.com
Web: www.currymansion.com

Circa 1892. This three-story white Victorian was billed as the most elaborate home on Caroline Street when it was built in 1867 by Florida's first millionaire. The inn still contains original features such as bookcases, chandeliers and fireplaces, as well as an abundance of antiques. The innkeepers use the inn to display some of their beautiful collectibles, including a family Limoges service for 120. Guests enjoy Key West's mild weather while enjoying a full breakfast with made-to-order omelettes. Piano music serenades guests at a nightly "cocktail" party with hors d'oeuvres and a full open bar.

Historic Interest: The mansion is within blocks of a variety of historic sites, including the Little White House, Hemingway's Home and a Historical Society museum, near Mallory Square.

Innkeeper(s): Edith Amsterdam. $140-275. 28 rooms with PB and 10 suites. Breakfast and snacks/refreshments included in rates. Types of meals: Full gourmet bkfst. Beds: KQ. Cable TV, reading lamp, refrigerator, ceiling fan, clock radio, telephone, desk and hot tub/spa in room. Air conditioning. VCR, fax, copier, swimming and library on premises. Weddings, small meetings, family reunions and seminars hosted. Antiquing, fishing, live theater, shopping, water sports, swimming and boating nearby.

Publicity: *Mariner Outboards SLAM, New York Times, Southern Living and Colonial Homes.*

"Everything was so tastefully tended to. We truly felt like 'Royalty.' We certainly will not consider returning to Key West unless we are able to book accommodations at the Curry Mansion."

Cypress House

601 Caroline St
Key West, FL 33040-6674
(305)294-6969 (800)525-2488 Fax:(305)296-1174
E-mail: cypresskw@aol.com
Web: www.cypresshousekw.com

Circa 1888. There's much to see and do in popular Key West, and Cypress House is an ideal place for those visiting the area. The National Register inn was built by one of Key West's first settlers, and it still maintains many original features. Guest rooms are airy and spacious, decorated in a variety of styles. A continental breakfast with muffins, bagels, fresh fruit and more is served daily. A cocktail hour also is included in the rates. The inn is just a block from Duval Street, which offers shops, galleries, eateries and plenty of nightlife.

Innkeeper(s): Dave Taylor. $99-300. 22 rooms, 14 with PB and 2 suites.

Breakfast included in rates. Types of meals: Cont plus. Beds: KQD. Cable TV, ceiling fan, clock radio, telephone and refrigerator in room. Air conditioning. Swimming on premises. Weddings, small meetings, family reunions and seminars hosted. Antiquing, fishing, live theater, parks, shopping and water sports nearby.

Duval House

815 Duval St
Key West, FL 33040-7405
(305)294-1666 (800)223-8825 Fax:(305)292-1701
E-mail: duvalhs@attglobal.net
Web: www.duvalhousekeywest.com

Circa 1880. Seven historic houses, painted in island pastel shades, surround a lush tropical garden and a pool. Located on an estate in the heart of the historic Old Town, guests relish the cozy spaces to relax such as the hammock for two, gazebo, sun decks and private balconies. The inn's white picket fences and plentiful porches are bordered by tropical trees, flowers and vines. A continental-plus  breakfast is served from the pool house. Rooms have wicker and antique furniture, Victorian armoires and Bahamian fans.

Historic Interest: Hemingway House (1 block).

Innkeeper(s): Sarah Goldstein. $110-325. 25 rooms with PB and 4 suites. Breakfast included in rates. Beds: KQ. Cable TV and telephone in room. Air conditioning. Swimming and parlor games on premises. Antiquing, shopping, water sports, spa and historic touring nearby.

Publicity: *Palm Beach Post, Orlando Sentinel, Brides, Vacations, Honeymoon, St. Petersburg Times and Sun Sentinel.*

"You certainly will see us again."

Eaton Manor Guest House

1024 Eaton St
Key West, FL 33040-6925
(305)294-9870 (800)305-9870 Fax:(305)294-1544

Circa 1896. Nestled in a Key West historic district, Eaton Manor Guest House is just minutes from local attractions, as well as the Lands End Marina. The home features a tropical fish theme. Rooms are decorated with wicker furnishings and beds are topped with fish bedspreads, fish sheets and towels with fish motifs. Fish lamps also add to the whimsy. The front office boasts a massive saltwater aquarium and the exterior has a hand-painted mural of an underwater reef. Breakfasts include items such as homemade blueberry or chocolate chip muffins, Belgian waffles, fresh fruit and freshly brewed coffee.

Innkeeper(s): Delaine & Jim Lowry. $49-249. 27 rooms, 19 with PB. Breakfast included in rates. Types of meals: Cont. Beds: KQDT. Cable TV, refrigerator, ceiling fan, telephone and voice mail in room. Central air. Copier and spa on premises. Weddings, small meetings, family reunions and seminars hosted. Antiquing, beach, bicycling, canoeing/kayaking, fishing, golf, live theater, shopping, water sports, harbor walk and Duval Street nearby.

Eden House

1015 Fleming St
Key West, FL 33040-6962
(305)296-6868 (800)533-5397 Fax:(305)294-1221
E-mail: mike@edenhouse.com
Web: www.edenhouse.com

Circa 1924. Once a hot spot for writers, intellectuals and European travelers, this Art Deco hotel was improved by innkeeper Mike Eden. He added a 10-person Jacuzzi, patios, gazebos an elevated sun deck, waterfalls and hammocks. Ceiling fans and wicker furniture reflect the tropical atmosphere found in each guest bedroom. The Goldie Hawn movie, "Criss Cross" was filmed here. Enjoy cold refreshments upon arrival and a complimentary happy hour. Cafe Med, the inn's restaurant, offers island cuisine

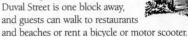

with a Mediterranean twist. Try the popular Linguine Fruit DiMare-linguine tossed with scallops, shrimp, mussels, clams, olive oil, garlic, fresh tomato, crushed red pepper and Italian parsley. Smoking is allowed outside only.

Historic Interest: Conch houses on property were built in 1889 and 1874. Innkeeper(s): Mike Eden. $80-350. 39 rooms, 34 with PB and 6 suites. Types of meals: Full bkfst, veg bkfst, early coffee/tea and gourmet lunch. Restaurant on premises. Beds: QDT. Cable TV and ceiling fan in room. Air conditioning. TV, VCR, fax, bicycles, telephone, heated pool and spa, elevated sun deck, hammock, porch swings, five waterfalls, lush gardens and happy hour daily on premises. Weddings, small meetings and family reunions hosted. Antiquing, art galleries, beach, bicycling, canoeing/kayaking, fishing, golf, live theater, museums, parks, shopping, tennis and water sports nearby. Publicity: *Chicago Tribune, Woman's Day, Southern Living, Miami Herald and New York Times.*

The Garden House

329 Elizabeth Street
Key West, FL 33040-6804
(305)296-5368 (800)695-6453 Fax:(305)292-1160
E-mail: info@the-garden-house.com
Web: www.the-garden-house.com

Circa 1938. "Most Fun Inn Key West" is the motto at this inn, which is centrally located in the historic district. This Caribbean Conch-style house is a secluded tropical paradise surrounded by lush foliage, including several rare hibiscus, and a miniature rose bed on the upper sun deck. Enjoy a nightly social hour. Quietly inviting guest bedrooms and a suite feature air conditioning, refrigerators and comfortable furnishings. Some rooms boasts intimate porches. A daily continental breakfast offers hot beverages and juice, assorted breads and muffins and fresh coffee cake. Relax in the heated pool and spa. Rent a bike to explore the island. Indulge in local activities like diving, fishing, snorkeling, sailing, kayaking, waterfront dining, parasailing and windsurfing.

Historic Interest: All within walking distance of Garden House: Audubon House, Mel Fisher's Museum, Hemingway House, Truman's Little White House, Wrecker's Museum, Historic Seaport, Mallory Square, Curry Mansion, Sloppy Joe's, Capt. Tony's.

Innkeeper(s): John & Connie Manasco. $120-179. 10 rooms with PB. Breakfast included in rates. Types of meals: Cont. Beds: KQD. Cable TV, reading lamp, ceiling fan, clock radio, telephone, desk, and mini refrigerator in room. Air conditioning. Fax, copier, swimming, bicycles, ice machine, soda machine, heated pool/spa, rental bikes and free beer and wine happy hour served poolside nightly on premises. Antiquing, art galleries, beach, bicycling, canoeing/kayaking, fishing, golf, hiking, live theater, museums, parks, shopping, water sports and wineries nearby.

Heron House

512 Simonton St
Key West, FL 33040-6832
(800)294-1644 Fax:(305)294-5692
E-mail: heronkyw@aol.com
Web: www.heronhouse.com

Circa 1856. Orchid gardens in a rain forest-style landscape is an inviting aspect of Heron House, one of the oldest homes remaining in Key West. With its Conch architecture, the inn showcases many beautiful features, including hand-crafted wood walls, marble baths, stained-glass transoms and Chicago brick patios. Rated

four diamonds by AAA, there are many other amenities such as private decks and balconies and French doors. Suites with wet bars and sitting areas also are available. Duval Street is one block away, and guests can walk to restaurants and beaches or rent a bicycle or motor scooter.

Innkeeper(s): Fred Geibelt. $119-369. 23 rooms. Breakfast included in rates. Types of meals: Cont plus. Beds: KQD. Telephone in room. TV on premises. Publicity: *Sun Sentinel.*

Island City House

411 William St
Key West, FL 33040-6857
(305)294-5702 (800)634-8230 Fax:(305)294-1289
E-mail: info@islandcityhouse.com
Web: www.islandcityhouse.com

Circa 1889. The oldest operating guest house in Key West, the Island City House was built for a wealthy Charleston merchant who later converted it to a small hotel, anticipating the arrival of the railroad in 1912. Restored by two active preservationists, Island City House and Arch House provide suites in beautifully restored environs with turn-of-the-century decor. Private porches and ceiling fans are historical amenities that remain. The Cigar House is a cypress wood building with spacious suites in an elegant island decor with rattan and wicker. Many of its accommodations offer porches with hammocks overlooking the pool.

Innkeeper(s): Amy & Sean Kelley. $120-325. 24 suites. Breakfast included in rates. Types of meals: Cont plus. Beds: KQD. Cable TV, reading lamp, refrigerator, ceiling fan, clock radio, telephone and desk in room. Air conditioning. VCR, fax, copier, swimming, bicycles and parlor games on premises. Antiquing, fishing, golf, live theater, parks, shopping, tennis and water sports nearby.

Publicity: *Palm Beach Daily News, London Times, Miami Herald, Palm Beach Post and Travel & Leisure Magazine.*

"We enjoyed relaxing on our hammock on the veranda of the Cigar House. We'll be back."

Key West B&B, The Popular House

415 William St
Key West, FL 33040-6853
(305)296-7274 (800)438-6155 Fax:(305)293-0306
E-mail: relax@keywestbandb.com
Web: www.keywestbandb.com

Circa 1890. This pink and white Victorian sits elegantly behind a white picket fence. It was constructed by shipbuilders with sturdy heart-pine walls and 13-foot ceilings. With two stories of porches, the inn is located in the center of the Historic District.

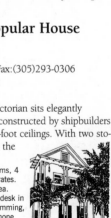

Innkeeper(s): Jody Carlson. $59-285. 8 rooms, 4 with PB and 1 suite. Breakfast included in rates. Types of meals: Cont plus and early coffee/tea. Beds: KQDT. Reading lamp, ceiling fan and desk in room. Air conditioning. Fax, copier, spa, swimming, sauna, bicycles, parlor games, telephone and specimen garden on premises. Weddings, small meetings, family reunions and seminars hosted. Antiquing, fishing, live theater, shopping, water sports, historic tours and museums nearby.

Publicity: *Palm Beach Life, South Florida, Food Arts, London House & Gardens, Conde Naste Traveler and New York Times.*

"The essence of charming."

Key West Harbor Inn

219 Elizabeth St
Key West, FL 33040
(305)296-2978 (800)608-6569 Fax:(305)294-5858
E-mail: kwharborinn@yahoo.com
Web: www.keywestharborinn.com

Circa 1850. This elegant three-story mansion is surrounded by ornate Victorian homes in Old Town Key West. It's steps away from Historic Key West Seaport's boardwalk and two blocks from Duval Street. Built in a different location in 1850 by a local physician, the mansion was bought by two women who moved the inn in 1950 to its current location so that the home would face the harbor with its beautiful sunsets. The inn's many guest bedrooms include touches like four poster beds, French doors leading to verandas and views of the tropical gardens or the harbor. The home, the Pool House and the Carriage House are surrounded by a walled tropical garden, which adds an air of wild seclusion. Guests enjoy the swimming pool and Jacuzzi and all kinds of local water sports, including snorkeling in the only living reef in North America, treasure hunting, deep sea fishing, sea kayaking, jet skiing, dolphin watching and touring the beautiful local sights.

Innkeeper(s): Steve & Alexis. $100-350. 11 rooms with PB. Breakfast and snacks/refreshments included in rates. Types of meals: Cont plus. Beds: KQ. Data port, cable TV, CD player, refrigerator, ceiling fan, clock radio, telephone, hair dryers and some with full wet bars with sink in room. Air conditioning. Spa and swimming on premises. Canoeing/kayaking, fishing, water sports, snorkeling, jet skis and dolphin eco-tours nearby.

The Mermaid & Alligator

729 Truman Ave
Key West, FL 33040-6423
(305)294-1894 (800)773-1894 Fax:(305)295-9925
E-mail: mermaid@joy.net
Web: www.kwmermaid.com

Circa 1904. Anticipate warm hospitality and a casual elegance at this Victorian home in the heart of Old Town. Enjoy the eclectic mix of local and Caribbean artwork and antiques. Private guest bedrooms offer distinctive personalities. The romantic Caribbean Queen Room features a four-poster bed, large Roman soaking tub and access to the wraparound veranda. After a full breakfast, relax in the garden or swim in the pool. Snorkel, scuba dive or search for shells at the nearby beach. Duval Street's many shops, restaurants and galleries are just three blocks away.

Innkeeper(s): Dean Carlson & Paul Hayes. $108-248. 9 rooms with PB and 1 cottage. Breakfast included in rates. Types of meals: Full bkfst. Beds: Q. Reading lamp, CD player, ceiling fan, clock radio, desk, hair dryer, iron and ironing board in room. Air conditioning. TV, VCR, fax, swimming, library, parlor games and telephone on premises. Antiquing, art galleries, beach, bicycling, canoeing/kayaking, fishing, golf, live theater, museums, parks, shopping, tennis and water sports nearby.

Seascape

420 Olivia St
Key West, FL 33040-7411
(305)296-7776 (800)765-6438 Fax:(305)296-6283
E-mail: info@seascapetropicalinn.com
Web: www.seascapetropicalinn.com

Circa 1889. This inviting restored two-story clapboard inn with blue shutters offers privacy among the hustle and bustle of Key West's Old Town. It features tropical gardens, a heated pool/spa and sundecks. Seascape is located a few blocks from

the Atlantic Ocean and the Gulf of Mexico and is walking distance to restaurants and shops. There are 10 accommodations including bed & breakfast rooms, studio apartments and a two-bedroom cottage. Guest rooms feature white wicker and tropical furnishings as well as a unique collection of local art. Breakfast is served under the shade of the sapodilla tree on a private courtyard. Guests may join the hosts for the complimentary wine hour in season. The inn was featured on the front page of the New York Times travel section and has received several excellent recommendations by travel writers.

Innkeeper(s): Tom & Nancy Coward. $89-269. 6 rooms with PB and 4 cottages. Breakfast included in rates. Types of meals: Cont. Beds: KQT. Fishing, live theater and water sports nearby.
Publicity: *New York Times, San Francisco Chronicle and Florida Keys Magazine.*

Simonton Court

320 Simonton St
Key West, FL 33040-6869
(305)294-6386 (800)944-2687 Fax:(305)293-8446
E-mail: simontoncourt@aol.com
Web: www.simontoncourt.com

Circa 1870. Just three blocks from the Gulf of Mexico and a stroll from famous Duval Street on Key West Island is Simonton Court. This secluded two-acre estate with rustling palm trees and fragrant tropical flowers is one of the most romantic properties on the island. There are secluded pools and hot tubs for guests to enjoy. The estate boasts 26 guest rooms ranging from individual cottages with kitchenettes to restored historic buildings. Enjoy a poolside breakfast, and then walk or bike through town. Or charter a boat and go fishing, diving or sailing.

Innkeeper(s): Terry Sullivan. $129-499. 26 rooms. Cable TV, VCR, refrigerator, ceiling fan and telephone in room. Air conditioning. Lushly landscaped gardens on premises. Weddings, small meetings and seminars hosted. Antiquing, live theater and shopping nearby.

Travelers Palm-Historic Inn & Cottages

915 Center Street
Key West, FL 33040
(305)294-9560 (800)294-9560 Fax:(305)294-4104
E-mail: info@travelerspalm.com
Web: www.travelerspalm.com

Circa 1880. Choose from delightful accommodations in Old Town Key West. Take a bike or walk to the beach and local sites. Bahamian Conch-style cottage apartments on Catherine Street offer a peaceful garden setting located only three blocks from popular Duval Street. For a romantic escape, Newton Street is an intimate hideaway in a neighborhood within an easy walk to town. The tropical casual décor reflects the lush surroundings of heliconias, orchids and other fragrant flowers.

Innkeeper(s): Naomi Van Steelandt. $58-308. 10 rooms with PB. Beds: KQDT. Modem hook-up, data port, cable TV, VCR, reading lamp, stereo, refrigerator, ceiling fan, clock radio, telephone, coffeemaker and voice mail in room. Central air. Fax, copier, swimming, bicycles, library, child care and laundry facility on premises. Weddings, family reunions and seminars hosted. Antiquing, art galleries, beach, bicycling, canoeing/kayaking, fishing, golf, live theater, museums, shopping, tennis, water sports, Ft. Jefferson National Park, Ft. Zachery Taylor State Park, Mel Fisher Museum, Historic Seaport and Mallory Square nearby.

Treetop Inn Historic B&B

806 Truman Ave
Key West, FL 33040-6426
(305)293-0712 (800)926-0712 Fax:(305)294-3668
E-mail: treetopinninfo2@aol.com
Web: www.treetopinn.com

Circa 1898. Treetop Inn, a Florida plantation-style home, was built at the beginning of the 20th century by a prominent cigar maker. The picturesque home is listed in the National Register. The exterior grounds are surrounded by a picket fence and the lush grounds include a small swimming pool. The three guest rooms are comfortable and decorated in a light, airy style. Wicker furnishings and some antique pieces add to the historic ambiance. Guests can walk to shops, beaches, restaurants and other Key West offerings.
Innkeeper(s): Richard Rettig. $125-225. 5 rooms with PB. Breakfast included in rates. Types of meals: Cont. Beds: K. Cable TV, reading lamp, refrigerator, ceiling fan, clock radio, coffeemaker and voice mail in room. Air conditioning. Swimming and telephone on premises. Antiquing, art galleries, beach, bicycling, canoeing/kayaking, fishing, golf, live theater, museums, parks, shopping, tennis and water sports nearby.
Publicity: *Travel Holiday Magazine.*

Westwinds

914 Eaton St
Key West, FL 33040-6923
(305)296-4440 (800)788-4150 Fax:(305)293-0931
E-mail: frontdesk@westwindskeywest.com
Web: www.westwindskeywest.com

Circa 1900. Hospitality, intimacy and relaxation are the hallmarks of every stay at Westwinds. The Victorian buildings feature tin roofs, clapboard and gingerbread trim. Though situated in the historic seaport district of Old Town, the gardens are lush with tropical trees, shrubs and a waterfall. The lounge has a library, television, refrigerator and Internet access. Choose a guest bedroom, suite or cottage. Enjoy conversation and meeting new friends over a continental breakfast with fresh fruits, juices, croissants and local honey. Swim in the heated, in-ground pool.
Historic Interest: Victorian architecture.
Innkeeper(s): Claire Tucker. $80-195. 19 rooms with PB, 5 suites, 1 cottage and 1 conference room. Breakfast included in rates. Types of meals: Cont. Beds: KQDT. Reading lamp, ceiling fan, clock radio and telephone in room. Air conditioning. TV, fax, copier, swimming, bicycles, library, parlor games, laundry facility and gift shop on premises. Limited handicap access. Weddings, small meetings, family reunions and seminars hosted. Art galleries, beach, bicycling, canoeing/kayaking, fishing, golf, hiking, live theater, museums, shopping, water sports, snorkeling, diving and writers workshops nearby.
Publicity: *NY Times and Conde Nast Traveler.*

Whispers-Gideon Lowe House

409 William St
Key West, FL 33040-6853
(305)294-5969 (800)856-7444 Fax:(305)294-5141
E-mail: info@whispersbb.com
Web: www.whispersbb.com

Circa 1845. Tropical elegance awaits each guest at this mid 19th-century, three-story Greek Revival home, listed in the National Register of Historic Places. Ample verandas and shuttered windows reveal the early Bahamian influence, while tall white walls and ceilings fans cool the antique Victorian-decorated rooms, which offer a romantic touch of canopies and lace. Lounge in the tropical garden, complete with a pond for fish and a pool and hot tub for guests. Welcome each bright and glorious day in Key West with croissants dipped in egg nog and spiced rum, fresh fruit and a special lemon dill omelet wrapped around honey maple ham, cheese and sautéed asparagus. Other amenities include use of a private beach and health club nearby.
Innkeeper(s): John & Bonita Marburg. $99-175. 7 rooms with PB. Breakfast included in rates. Types of meals: Full gourmet bkfst and veg bkfst. Beds: KQ. Cable TV, reading lamp, refrigerator, ceiling fan, clock radio, coffeemaker, private baths, color cable TV and refrigerator in room. Air conditioning. Fax, spa, bicycles, telephone, gourmet breakfast, pool, spa, sundeck and complimentary passes to health club and beach on premises. Antiquing, art galleries, beach, bicycling, canoeing/kayaking, fishing, golf, hiking, live theater, museums, parks, shopping, tennis and water sports nearby.
Publicity: *National Geographic Traveler.*

Lake Helen   D8

Clauser's B&B

201 E Kicklighter Rd
Lake Helen, FL 32744-3514
(386)228-0310 (800)220-0310 Fax:(386)228-0475
E-mail: clauserinn@totcon.com
Web: www.clauserinn.com

Circa 1890. This three-story, turn-of-the-century vernacular Victorian inn is surrounded by a variety of trees in a quiet, country setting. The inn is listed in the national, state and local historic registers, and offers eight guest rooms, all with private bath. Each room features a different type of country decor, such as Americana, English and country. Guests enjoy hot tubbing in the Victorian gazebo or relaxing on the inn's porches, which feature rockers, a swing and cozy wicker furniture. Borrow a bike to take a closer look at the historic district. Stetson University, fine dining and several state parks are nearby.
Innkeeper(s): Tom & Marge Clauser. $100-140. 8 rooms with PB, 1 with FP. Breakfast and snacks/refreshments included in rates. Types of meals: Full bkfst and early coffee/tea. Beds: KQ. Reading lamp, ceiling fan, telephone, desk, hot tub/spa and private screened porch in room. Air conditioning. VCR, fax, copier, spa, bicycles, library, parlor games, fireplace and nature trail through forest on premises. Limited handicap access. Small meetings, family reunions and seminars hosted. Amusement parks, antiquing, fishing, live theater, parks, sporting events, water sports and atlantic beaches nearby.

Lake Wales   E8

Chalet Suzanne Country Inn & Restaurant

3800 Chalet Suzanne Dr
Lake Wales, FL 33859-7763
(863)676-6011 (800)433-6011 Fax:(863)676-1814
E-mail: info@chaletsuzanne.com
Web: www.chaletsuzanne.com

Circa 1924. Situated on 70 acres adjacent to Lake Suzanne, this country inn's architecture includes gabled roofs, balconies, spires and steeples. The superb restaurant has a glowing reputation and offers a six-course candlelight dinner. Places of interest on the property include the Swiss Room, Wine Dungeon, Gift Boutique, Autograph Garden, Chapel Antiques, Ceramic Salon,

Airstrip and the Soup Cannery. The inn has been transformed into a village of cottages and miniature chateaux, one connected to the other seemingly with no particular order.

Historic Interest: This wonderful inn is located in a National Historic District.
Innkeeper(s): Vita Hinshaw & Family. $169-229. 30 rooms with PB. Breakfast included in rates. Types of meals: Full bkfst, lunch, gourmet dinner and room service. Beds: KDT. Cable TV, reading lamp, refrigerator, clock radio, telephone and desk in room. Air conditioning. TV, VCR, fax, copier, swimming, library and parlor games on premises. Limited handicap access. Weddings, small meetings, family reunions and seminars hosted. Amusement parks, antiquing, fishing, golf, live theater, parks, shopping, sporting events, tennis and water sports nearby.
Publicity: *National Geographic Traveler, Southern Living, Country Inns, Uncle Ben's 1992 award and Country Inn Cooking.*

"I now know why everyone always says, 'Wow!' when they come up from dinner. Please don't change a thing."

Lake Worth   G10

Mango Inn
128 N Lakeside Dr
Lake Worth, FL 33460
(561)533-6900 (888)626-4619 Fax:(561)533-6992
E-mail: info@mangoinn.com
Web: www.mangoinn.com

Circa 1915. After a stay at Mango Inn, you'll want to take the decorator back to your own home and redo everything inside and out. Inside the historic home are eight unique guest rooms, each with luxurious and imaginative décor. From the Seagrape Room with its verdant walls and a bed that includes a picket fence headboard trailed with ivy to the romantic Rose Room with a gingham comforter and rose-covered walls. The poolside cottage is a private retreat with a four-poster bed and French doors that lead out to a private patio. For a longer stay, try the picturesque Little House, a 1,200-square-foot cottage with two bedrooms, two bathrooms, a living room, dining room, full kitchen and laundry facilities. Breakfast treats might include the inn's signature mango-cashew muffins, and the meal is served either by the fireplace in the dining room or on a veranda that looks out to the pool. The innkeepers offer a variety of special packages to add an extra touch of elegance and romance to your stay. The shops of Palm Beach are just a few miles away, and Lake Worth offers plenty of antique shops.
Innkeeper(s): Erin & Bo Allen. $75-235. 8 rooms with PB and 1 cottage. Breakfast included in rates. Types of meals: Full gourmet bkfst, early coffee/tea and picnic lunch. Beds: Q. Cable TV, VCR, reading lamp, refrigerator, ceiling fan, clock radio and telephone in room. Central air. Fax, swimming, bicycles and fireplace on premises. Weddings and family reunions hosted. Antiquing, art galleries, beach, bicycling, canoeing/kayaking, fishing, golf, horseback riding, live theater, museums, parks, shopping, sporting events, tennis and water sports nearby.

Sabal Palm House B&B Inn
109 N Golfview Rd
Lake Worth, FL 33460
(561)582-1090 (888)722-2572 Fax:(561)582-0933
E-mail: mrbsph@aol.com
Web: www.sabalpalmhouse.com

Circa 1936. Located across from the Intracostal Waterway and just minutes from white, sandy Atlantic beaches, this two-story, 1936 Key West Colonial-style home welcomes each guest with its tall ceilings, covered balconies, antique furniture and fine art. Surrounded by palm trees, bushes and white picket fences, guests will feel embraced in the sunny climate and romantic, European-tropical courtyard. Each detail in the recently reno-

vated home was carefully preserved, from the oakwood floors to the tropical elegance of its original architecture and décor. With ample activities to fill both day and night in the surrounding area, the comfort of coming home to freshly cut flowers and a turned-down bed each night soothes the weariest of travelers and allows them to truly relax and enjoy their stay in one of Florida's most intriguing cities. Sabal Palm House is the only four-diamond inn located between Miami and Orlando.
Innkeeper(s): Colleen & John Rinaldi. $85-195. 7 rooms with PB and 1 suite. Breakfast and afternoon tea included in rates. Types of meals: Full gourmet bkfst, veg bkfst and early coffee/tea. Beds: KQT. Ceiling fan, clock radio, telephone, turn-down service, desk, two with Jacuzzi tubs, wine and appetizer in room. Central air. TV, fax, copier, bicycles, parlor games and evening appetizers with wine and beer on premises. Family reunions hosted. Amusement parks, antiquing, art galleries, beach, bicycling, canoeing/kayaking, fishing, golf and horseback riding nearby.
Publicity: *Palm Beach Post, Sun Sentinel, Miami Herald and New York Post.*

Maitland   D8

Thurston House
851 Lake Ave
Maitland, FL 32751-6306
(407)539-1911 (800)843-2721 Fax:(407)539-0365
E-mail: thurstonbb@aol.com
Web: www.thurstonhouse.com

Circa 1885. Just minutes from busy Orlando and the many attractions found nearby, this classic Queen Anne Victorian inn boasts a lakefront, countryside setting. Two of the inn's screened porches provide views of Lake Eulalia. Two parlors provide additional relaxing spots, and many guests like to stroll the grounds, which feature fruit trees and several bountiful gardens.
Innkeeper(s): Carole Ballard. $140-160. 4 rooms with PB. Breakfast and snacks/refreshments included in rates. Types of meals: Full bkfst and early coffee/tea. Beds: Q. Reading lamp, ceiling fan, clock radio, telephone and desk in room. Air conditioning. VCR, fax, copier, library, parlor games and fireplace on premises. Antiquing, fishing, live theater, parks, shopping and sporting events nearby.
Publicity: *New York Times, US Air, Fort Lauderdale Sun Sentinel, Orlando Sentinel, Florida Living, Country Almanac, Palm Beach Post and WESH-TV - Channel 2 News.*

"Gracious hosts. What a jewel of a place. We couldn't have enjoyed ourselves more!"

Micanopy   C7

Herlong Mansion
402 NE Cholokka Blvd
Micanopy, FL 32667
(352)466-3322
E-mail: info@herlong.com
Web: www.herlong.com

Circa 1845. This mid-Victorian mansion features four two-story, carved-wood Roman Corinthian columns on its veranda. The mansion is surrounded by a garden with statuesque old oak and pecan trees. Herlong Mansion features leaded-glass windows, mahogany inlaid oak floors, 12-foot ceilings and floor-to-ceiling windows in the dining room. Guest rooms with Jacuzzi tubs are available. All rooms are furnished with antiques.

Historic Interest: St. Augustine is about one and one-half hours from the mansion. The Marjorie Kinnan Rawlings Home is eight miles away. Micanopy is the oldest inland town in Florida, and has been the site for several movies. Innkeeper(s): Julia & Lon Boggs. $99-189. 11 rooms with PB, 3 suites, 2 cottages and 1 conference room. Breakfast and snacks/refreshments included in rates. Types of meals: Full bkfst. Beds: KQDT. Cable TV, reading lamp, ceiling fan, clock radio, turn-down service, desk, coffeemaker, robes, stereo, CD player and 2-person Jacuzzi tubs available in some rooms in room. Central air. TV, VCR, library, parlor games, telephone and fireplace on premises. Limited handicap access. Weddings, small meetings, family reunions and seminars hosted. Antiquing, art galleries, bicycling, canoeing/kayaking, fishing, golf, hiking, horseback riding, museums, parks, shopping, sporting events and Marjorie Kinnan Rawlings House nearby.
Publicity: *Country Inns, Travel & Leisure, National Geographic Traveler, Southern Living, Florida Living and Florida Trend.*

Mount Dora   D8

Magnolia Inn

347 E 3rd Ave
Mount Dora, FL 32757-5654
(352)735-3800 (800)776-2112 Fax:(352)735-0258
E-mail: info@magnoliainn.net
Web: magnoliainn.net

Circa 1926. This Mediterranean-style inn in Central Florida offers elegant accommodations to its guests. Guests will enjoy the convenience of early coffee or tea before sitting down to the inn's full breakfasts. Guests can take a soak in the inn's spa,

relax in the hammock by the garden wall or swing beneath the magnolias of this one-acre estate. Just an hour from Disney World and the other Orlando major attractions, Mount Dora is the antique capital of Central Florida. Known as the Festival City, it is also recommended by Money magazine as the best retirement location in Florida. It's also the site of Renninger's Antique Extravaganzas. Romantic carriage rides and historic trolley tours of the downtown, two blocks from the inn, are available.
Innkeeper(s): Dave & Betty Cook. $139-250. 5 rooms with PB. Breakfast included in rates. Types of meals: Full bkfst and early coffee/tea. Beds: KQ. TV, reading lamp, CD player, ceiling fan and clock radio in room. Air conditioning. Fax, copier, spa, parlor games, telephone and fireplace on premises. Antiquing, fishing, live theater, parks, shopping and water sports nearby.
Publicity: *Mount Dora Topic and Mediterranean Villa on one acre.*

Mount Dora Historic Inn

221 E 4th Ave
Mount Dora, FL 32757
(352)735-1212 (800)927-6344 Fax:(352)735-9743
E-mail: info@mountdorahistoricinn.com
Web: www.mountdorahistoricinn.com

Circa 1886. This century-old Victorian is on half an acre in quaint Mount Dora. Just a quarter of a mile from the water and 25 minutes from Orlando, the inn offers four guest bedrooms. Early risers may enjoy coffee and tea. The full six-course gourmet breakfast includes fruit, a breakfast casserole and homemade bread. Afternoon tea also is served. Guests are encouraged to enjoy all the local area has to offer: nature walks, antique and craft stores, gourmet restaurants and horse-drawn carriage rides.
Innkeeper(s): Lindsay & Nancy Richards. $85-125. 4 rooms with PB. Breakfast, afternoon tea and snacks/refreshments included in rates. Types of meals: Full gourmet bkfst, veg bkfst, early coffee/tea and room service. Beds: KQ. Modem hook-up, reading lamp, refrigerator, ceiling fan, telephone and turn-down service in room. Central air. Fax, copier, parlor games and laundry facility on premises. Amusement parks, antiquing, art galleries, bicycling, canoeing/kayaking, fishing, golf, hiking, horseback riding, live theater, museums, parks, shopping, tennis, water sports and wineries nearby.

New Smyrna Beach   D9

Little River Inn B&B

532 N Riverside Dr
New Smyrna Beach, FL 32168-6741
(386)424-0100 (888)424-0102 Fax:(386)424-5732
E-mail: little-river-inn@juno.com
Web: www.little-river-inn.com

Circa 1883. Located on two acres of brick pathways, gardens and oak trees, this historic Inn offers wide, wraparound verandas and a cozy second floor porch. Guests enjoy views of scenic Indian River Lagoon and a variety of

birds and wildlife that take refuge in the nature preserve. Spacious rooms are appointed pleasantly and each has a special theme. Gourmet breakfasts are served in the dining room with colorful views of the gardens and grounds, which include fountains, a tennis court and a hammock. Nearby, New Smyrna Beach offers antique shops, galleries, marinas and "the world's safest bathing beach."
Innkeeper(s): Doug & Joyce MacLean. $99-159. 7 rooms, 5 with PB and 1 conference room. Breakfast and snacks/refreshments included in rates. Types of meals: Full gourmet bkfst, veg bkfst, early coffee/tea, gourmet lunch, picnic lunch and gourmet dinner. Beds: KQ. Data port, cable TV, VCR, reading lamp, stereo, refrigerator, ceiling fan, snack bar, clock radio, telephone, coffeemaker, turn-down service and hot tub/spa in room. Central air. Fax, copier, spa, tennis, library, parlor games and fireplace in living room on premises. Limited handicap access. Weddings, small meetings, family reunions and seminars hosted. Amusement parks, antiquing, art galleries, beach, bicycling, canoeing/kayaking, fishing, golf, hiking, horseback riding, live theater, museums, parks, shopping, sporting events, water sports and wineries nearby.

"Our retreat turned into relaxation, romance and pure Victorian delight."

Night Swan Intracoastal B&B

512 S Riverside Dr
New Smyrna Beach, FL 32168-7345
(386)423-4940 (800)465-4261 Fax:(386)427-2814
E-mail: info@nightswan.com
Web: www.nightswan.com

Circa 1906. From the 140-foot dock at this waterside bed & breakfast, guests can gaze at stars, watch as ships pass or perhaps catch site of dolphins. The turn-of-the-century home is decorated with period furnishings, including an antique baby grand piano, which guests are invited to use. Several guest rooms afford views of the Indian River, which is part of the Atlantic Intracoastal Waterway. Seven rooms include a whirlpool tub. The innkeepers have created several special packages, featuring catered gourmet dinners, boat tours or romantic baskets with chocolate, wine and flowers.

Innkeeper(s): Martha & Chuck Nighswonger. $95-175. 15 rooms with PB, 4 suites and 1 conference room. Breakfast and snacks/refreshments included in rates. Types of meals: Full bkfst and early coffee/tea. Beds: KQ. Cable TV, reading lamp, refrigerator, ceiling fan, clock radio, telephone, desk and seven whirlpool tubs in room. Air conditioning. Fax, library and fireplace on premises. Weddings, small meetings, family reunions and seminars hosted. Antiquing, fishing, live theater, parks, shopping and water sports nearby.
Publicity: *Ft. Lauderdale Sun Sentinel and Florida Living.*

Ocala   C7

Ritz Historic Inn

1205 E Hwy 40
Ocala, FL 34471
(352)671-9300 (888)382-9390 Fax:(352)671-9302
E-mail: ritztowers@hotmail.com
Web: www.ritzhistoricinn.com

Circa 1925. A park-like setting surrounds this historic, award-winning inn that is listed in the National Register. The style and grace of yesterday mingles elegantly with today's modern conveniences. Choose to stay in a designer-decorated Executive or Standard Suite. Enjoy large sitting rooms, hardwood floors, balconies with picturesque views and generous amenities. Relax over a continental breakfast. Stroll the lush gardens and ornate courtyards. The mosaic-tiled pool with waterfall fountain is a luxurious place to swim and soak up the sun.

Innkeeper(s): Anthony & Diana Piccione. $79-249. 32 suites, 16 with FP and 3 conference rooms. Breakfast included in rates. Types of meals: Cont plus and early coffee/tea. Beds: KQDT. Data port, cable TV, VCR, reading lamp, refrigerator, ceiling fan, clock radio, telephone, coffeemaker, desk, hot tub/spa and fireplace in room. Central air. Fax, spa, swimming and "Magnolia Room" jazz club on premises. Limited handicap access. Weddings, small meetings, family reunions and seminars hosted. Amusement parks, antiquing, art galleries, bicycling, canoeing/kayaking, golf, hiking, horseback riding, live theater, museums, parks, shopping and water sports nearby.
Publicity: Ocala Star Banner, "Boys Night Out" WC Fields, guests including WC Fields, Gregory Peck, Elvis, Katharine Hepburn, Spencer Tracy, John Travolta, Johnny Wiesmuller and others.

Seven Sisters Inn

820 SE Fort King St
Ocala, FL 34471-2320
(352)867-1170 Fax:(352)867-5266
E-mail: sistersinn@aol.com
Web: www.sevensistersinn.com

Circa 1888. This highly acclaimed Queen Anne-style Victorian is located in the heart of the town's historic district. In 1986, the house was judged "Best Restoration Project" in the state by Florida Trust Historic Preservation Society. Guests may relax on the large covered porches or visit with other guests in the club room. A gourmet breakfast features different entrees daily, which include blueberry French bread, three-cheese stuffed French toast, egg pesto and raspberry-oatmeal pancakes. Inquire about candlelight and murder- mystery dinners.

Historic Interest: Marjorie Kinan Rawlings House, who authored "The Yearling," is 30 minutes away.
Innkeeper(s): Ken Oden & Bonnie Morehardt. $119-269. 14 rooms with PB, 3 with FP, 5 suites and 1 conference room. Breakfast and afternoon tea included in rates. Types of meals: Full gourmet bkfst, picnic lunch and gourmet dinner. Beds: KQT. TV, reading lamp, ceiling fan, clock radio, telephone, turn-down service and desk in room. Air conditioning. Fax, copier, parlor games, fireplace and off-grounds pet boarding available on premises. Weddings, small meetings, family reunions and seminars hosted. Antiquing, fishing, golf, live theater, shopping, water sports, national forest and Silver Springs attractions nearby.
Publicity: Southern Living, Glamour, Conde Nast Traveler and Country Inns (one of 12 best).

Orange Park   B8

The Club Continental Suites

2143 Astor St
Orange Park, FL 32073-5624
(904)264-6070 (800)877-6070 Fax:(904)215-9503

Circa 1923. This waterfront estate was constructed for the Palmolive family and overlooks the St. Johns River. The architecture is Italian Renaissance with stucco and clay tile roof. Formal grounds include gardens with fountains, giant oaks and an elegant courtyard. Riverfront views are enjoyed. There are seven tennis courts, a marina and the pre-Civil War River House Pub, as well as the Club Continental Restaurant, a dinner club. A complimentary breakfast is served daily. Lunch is served Tuesday through Friday; brunch is available on Sunday.

Innkeeper(s): Caleb & Karrie Massee. $80-165. 22 rooms with PB, 2 with FP, 4 suites and 2 conference rooms. Breakfast included in rates. Types of meals: Cont, gourmet lunch and dinner. Beds: KQ. Cable TV, reading lamp, refrigerator, clock radio, telephone, desk and hot tub/spa in room. Air conditioning. TV, fax, copier, swimming, tennis, fireplace, dinner, gourmet lunches Tuesday-Friday and Sunday brunch on premises. Weddings, small meetings, family reunions and seminars hosted. Antiquing, fishing, live theater, parks, shopping and sporting events nearby.
Publicity: Miami Herald, Sun Sentinel and Tampa Tribune.

"Superb dining with spectacular grounds."

Orlando   D8

The Courtyard at Lake Lucerne

211 N Lucerne Circle E
Orlando, FL 32801-3721
(407)648-5188 (800)444-5289 Fax:(407)246-1368
E-mail: info@orlandohistoricinn.com
Web: www.orlandohistoricinn.com

Circa 1885. This award-winning inn, precisely restored with attention to historical detail, consists of four different architectural styles. The Norment-Parry House is Orlando's oldest home. The Wellborn, an Art-Deco Modern Building, offers one-bedroom suites with kitchenettes. The I.W. Phillips is an antebellum-style manor where breakfast is served in a large reception room with a

wide veranda overlooking the courtyard fountains and lush gardens. The Grand Victorian Dr. Phillips House is listed in the National Register of Historic Places. For an enchanting treat, ask for the Turret Room.

Innkeeper(s): Charles Meiner. $89-225. 30 rooms with PB and 1 conference room. Breakfast included in rates. Types of meals: Cont plus. Beds: KQD. Cable TV, reading lamp, refrigerator, clock radio, telephone, desk and hot tub/spa in room. Air conditioning. TV, copier and fireplace on premises. Weddings, small meetings and family reunions hosted. Amusement parks, antiquing, fishing, live theater, shopping, sporting events and water sports nearby.
Publicity: Florida Historic Homes, Miami Herald, Southern Living and Country Victorian.

"Best-kept secret in Orlando."

Palatka   C8

Azalea House

220 Madison St
Palatka, FL 32177-3531
(386)325-4547
E-mail: azaleahouse@gbso.net
Web: www.theazaleahouse.com

Circa 1878. Located within the Palatka Historic District, this beautifully embellished Queen Anne Victorian is painted a cheerful yellow with complementing green shutters. Bay windows, gables and verandas have discrete touches of royal blue, gold, white and aqua on the gingerbread trim, a true "Painted Lady." There are oak, magnolia and palm trees and an 85-year-old, grafted camellia tree with both pink and white blossoms. Double parlors are furnished with period antiques including an arched, floor-to-ceiling mirror. A three-story heart and curly pine staircase leads to the guest rooms. Breakfast is served on fine china in the formal dining room. Two blocks away is the mile-wide north flowing St. John's River. An unaltered golf course designed by Donald Ross in 1925 is nearby, as well as the Ravine State Botanical Garden. It's 25 minutes to Crescent Beach.

Innkeeper(s): Doug & Jill de Leeuw. $75-135. 6 rooms, 4 with PB. Breakfast and snacks/refreshments included in rates. Types of meals: Full bkfst and early coffee/tea. Beds: Q. Reading lamp, ceiling fan, telephone, turn-down service and alarm clocks in room. Air conditioning. Swimming, fireplace and porch swings on premises. Weddings and small meetings hosted. Antiquing, fishing, golf, live theater, parks, shopping and water sports nearby.
Publicity: American Treasures and 2002 B&B Calendar.

Palm Beach   G10

Palm Beach Historic Inn

365 S County Rd
Palm Beach, FL 33480-4449
(561)832-4009 Fax:(561)832-6255
E-mail: innkeeper@palmbeachhistoricinn.com
Web: www.palmbeachhistoricinn.com

Circa 1923. Visitors are welcomed into a lobby with the look of an elegant European parlor. Intimate, comfortable, meticulously clean accommodations with every modern convenience await each guest. Besides choice lodging, travelers will enjoy being just one block from the beach. Also a few short steps away are a variety of entertainment options, gift and antique shopping, spectacular dining experiences, and tours of legendary mansions and art galleries. Recreational activities range from horseback riding, tennis and golf to snorkeling, scuba diving or fishing. Ask the concierge for advice in exploring this tropical paradise.

Historic Interest: Flagler Museum is more than a mile away. World-famous Worth Ave., known for its 1920s Mizner architecture, is within walking distance, two blocks from the inn. Even closer is the historic Town Hall, located right across the street.
Innkeeper(s): Sean & Jody Herbert. $85-325. 9 rooms with PB and 4 suites. Breakfast included in rates. Types of meals: Cont. Beds: KQD. Cable TV, reading lamp, stereo, refrigerator, clock radio, telephone, desk and built in hair dryers in room. Air conditioning. VCR, fax, copier, library and parlor games on premises. Family reunions hosted. Fishing, live theater, parks, shopping, sporting events and water sports nearby.
Publicity: PB Today and PB Society.

Palmetto   F7

The Palmetto House B&B

1102 Riverside Dr
Palmetto, FL 34221
(941)723-1236 (800)658-4167 Fax:(941)723-1507
E-mail: info@thepalmettohouse.com
Web: www.thepalmettohouse.com

Circa 1912. This gracious historic manor, along with its three cottages, is situated directly on the Manatee River with views of moss-draped oaks and waterfront sunsets. Overlooking the Regatta Pointe Marina, the inn's acre of gardens include hibiscus, sabal palms, plumbago and Royal Palms. In the National Register, the home has been newly renovated. Guest rooms offer Victorian or Arts and Crafts furnishings and decor and most rooms have Jacuzzi tubs, walk-in-showers as well as a plethora of amenities. Breakfast is served in the dining room or on the inviting sunroom, but beforehand be sure to enjoy early morning coffee along the river or on the courtyard. The Ringling Museum, Anna Maria Island, Marie Selby Botanical Gardens and the Mote Aquarium are area attractions.

Historic Interest: The inn is a Sears Roebuck catalog house on the site of an early settlers' cabin. The Cortez Historic Fishing Village, Gamble Plantation and Manatee Village Historical Park are within 15 miles.
Innkeeper(s): Bob & Linda Gehring. $100-160. 7 rooms with PB, 2 suites and 2 cottages. Breakfast and snacks/refreshments included in rates. Types of meals: Full bkfst and afternoon tea. Beds: KQ. Cable TV, VCR, reading lamp, ceiling fan, clock radio, telephone, turn-down service, desk, hot tub/spa and voice mail in room. Central air. Fax, copier, spa, swimming, library and parlor games on premises. Weddings, small meetings, family reunions and seminars hosted. Amusement parks, antiquing, art galleries, beach, bicycling, canoeing/kayaking, fishing, golf, live theater, museums, parks, shopping, sporting events, tennis, water sports, wineries, Anna Maria Island, DeSoto National Memorial, Ringling Museum, Mote Aquarium and Marie Selby Botanical Gardens nearby.
Publicity: Bradenton Herald and Sarasota Herald Tribune.

Pensacola   B2

Noble Manor

110 W Strong St
Pensacola, FL 32501-3140
(850)434-9544
E-mail: info2@noblemanor.com
Web: www.noblemanor.com

Circa 1905. This two-story home offers Tudor Revival-style architecture. It is set on lavish grounds planted with camellias, azaleas and roses. The inn is decorated with traditional furnishings, antiques and fine art prints, and guests will enjoy a dramatic central staircase and handsome fireplaces. Breakfast is served in the dining room. A front porch and a gazebo with a hot tub are among guests' favorite spots. Pensacola's North Hill Historic District is a historic preservation area. Nearby are Civil War forts and a restored 1800s area.

Innkeeper(s): John & Carol Briscoe. $79-125. 5 rooms with PB, 3 with FP and 1 conference room. Breakfast and snacks/refreshments included in rates. Types of meals: Cont plus and early coffee/tea. Beds: KQ. Cable TV, reading lamp, ceiling fan and clock radio in room. Central air. Spa, swimming, library, telephone and fireplace on premises. Weddings and small meetings hosted. Antiquing, art galleries, beach, live theater, museums, parks and sporting events nearby.

Springhill Guesthouse

903 N Spring St
Pensacola, FL 32501
(850)438-6887 (800)475-1956 Fax:(850)438-9075

Circa 1900. Traditional comfort and antiques augment this spacious yet intimate Queen Anne Victorian. Generous and creative hospitality is the home's hallmark. The Turret Suite boasts two hand-crafted fireplaces, a guest bedroom with sitting area, parlor, full kitchen and dining area. The Bay Suite features a parlor with a fireplace, a dining area and a butler's pantry kitchen. It can sleep up to four people. Both of the well-decorated suites offer privacy and a romantic ambiance. Books, games and videos are available. Breakfast is provided at Hopkins House, a local landmark and family restaurant, or with continental fare in your room. Relax on the front porch or enjoy the landscaped grounds with a New Orleans-style patio area.

Innkeeper(s): Michael & Rita Widler. $79-149. 2 suites, 2 with FP. Breakfast included in rates. Types of meals: Country bkfst and early coffee/tea. Beds: Q. Modem hook-up, data port, cable TV, VCR, reading lamp, refrigerator, clock radio, telephone, coffeemaker, desk, fireplace and full kitchens in room. Central air. Fax, copier, parlor games and laundry facility on premises. Weddings hosted. Amusement parks, antiquing, art galleries, beach, canoeing/kayaking, fishing, golf, hiking, live theater, museums, parks, tennis and water sports nearby.

Quincy B5

Allison House Inn

215 N Madison St
Quincy, FL 32351
(850)875-2511 (888)904-2511 Fax:(850)875-2511

Circa 1843. Crepe myrtle, azaleas, camellias and roses dot the acre of grounds that welcomes guests to the Allison House. A local historic landmark located in the 36-block historic district, the inn is in a Georgian, English-country style with shutters and an entrance portico. It was built for General Allison, who became Governor of Florida. There are two parlors, and all the rooms are appointed with English antiques. Homemade biscotti is always available for snacking and for breakfast, English muffins and freshly baked breads are offered. Walk around the district and spot the 51 historic homes and buildings. Nearby dining opportunities include the historic Nicholson Farmhouse Restaurant.

Innkeeper(s): Stuart & Eileen Johnson. $85-150. 6 rooms with PB. Breakfast and snacks/refreshments included in rates. Types of meals: Full bkfst. Beds: KQD. Modem hook-up, cable TV, reading lamp, ceiling fan, clock radio, telephone, individual air conditioning controls and hair dryers in room. TV, fax and bicycles on premises. Limited handicap access. Family reunions hosted. Antiquing, art galleries, bicycling, golf, horseback riding, live theater, sporting events and tennis nearby.

McFarlin House B&B Inn

305 E King St
Quincy, FL 32351
(850)875-2526 (877)370-4701 Fax:(850)627-4703
E-mail: inquiries@mcfarlinhouse.com
Web: mcfarlinhouse.com

Circa 1895. Tobacco farmer John McFarlin built this Queen Anne Victorian, notable for its left-handed turret and grand, wraparound porch. The home, which is listed in the National Register, boasts original woodwork, hand-carved mantels, Italian tile work and stained glass. Romantic guest rooms are decorated with Victorian furnishings, and each is unique. The Southern Grace includes a fireplace and whirlpool tub for two.

In the King's View, the double whirlpool tub is set in front of bay windows. The Pink Magnolia Room is located in the home's turret. The Ribbons and Roses Room includes a six-foot-long clawfoot tub, a fireplace and a canopy bed draped in netting. Breakfast begins with two different baked goods, followed by a main course, perhaps an omelet or quiche. McFarlin House is located in a Quincy historic district, just a short drive from Florida's capital city, Tallahassee.

Innkeeper(s): Richard & Tina Fauble. $85-175. 9 rooms with PB. Breakfast and snacks/refreshments included in rates. Types of meals: Full bkfst. Beds: KQD. Modem hook-up, cable TV, VCR, reading lamp, stereo, refrigerator, ceiling fan, clock radio, telephone and hot tub/spa in room. Central air. Fax, spa and fireplace on premises. Weddings, small meetings, family reunions and seminars hosted. Antiquing, art galleries, fishing, golf, museums and sporting events nearby.

Saint Augustine B8

Agustin Inn

29 Cuna St
Saint Augustine, FL 32084-3681
(904)823-9559 (800)248-7846 Fax:(904)824-8685
E-mail: www.agustin@aug.com
Web: www.agustininn.com

Circa 1903. Situated in the historic walking district of our nation's oldest city, this Victorian inn captures the ambiance of old downtown St. Augustine. Innkeepers Robert and Sherri Brackett, members of Historic Inns of St. Augustine and Superior Small Lodging, have furnished the home in comfortable elegance. The twelve guest bedrooms boast mahogany or canopy beds and oval Jacuzzi tubs. Some of the bedrooms have private entrances and terraces where early coffee or tea and evening wine and hors d'oeuvres can be enjoyed while overlooking the fragrant courtyards. Sherri's full homemade breakfasts are satisfying and may feature Belgian waffles with fried apples and bananas, delicious omelets, and home fries with buttermilk biscuits. Venturing out on the cobblestone streets offers a variety of activities and historical sites.

Innkeeper(s): Robert & Sherri Brackett. $89-185. 12 rooms with PB. Breakfast and snacks/refreshments included in rates. Types of meals: Full bkfst and early coffee/tea. Beds: Q. Reading lamp, ceiling fan and Jacuzzi tubs in room. Central air. TV, fax, copier and telephone on premises. Limited handicap access. Antiquing, art galleries, beach, fishing, golf, museums, parks and shopping nearby.

Alexander Homestead B&B

14 Sevilla St
Saint Augustine, FL 32084-3529
(904)826-4147 (888)292-4147 Fax:(904)823-9503
E-mail: bonnie@alexanderhomestead.com
Web: www.alexanderhomestead.com

Circa 1888. Green pastel hues dotted with white create a fanciful, tropical look at this Victorian bed & breakfast. Polished wood floors, colorful rugs and a mix of antiques and family pieces set the stage for a nostalgic getaway. Oversized tubs, lace, scented sachets and fresh flowers are just a few treats awaiting guests. The plentiful breakfasts are served in the elegant dining room. In the evening, guests also may enjoy a cordial in the Victorian parlor. The inn is located in St. Augustine's downtown historic area, so there is plenty of nearby activity.

Innkeeper(s): Bonnie Alexander. $115-195. 4 rooms with PB, 3 with FP. Breakfast and

afternoon tea included in rates. Types of meals: Country bkfst, early coffee/tea, picnic lunch, snacks/refreshments and room service. Beds: QT. Modem hook-up, cable TV, reading lamp, clock radio, desk, hot tub/spa and one with whirlpool Jacuzzi tub in room. Central air. Fax, bicycles, telephone and fireplace on premises. Weddings and family reunions hosted. Antiquing, art galleries, beach, bicycling, canoeing/kayaking, fishing, golf, live theater, museums, parks, shopping, tennis and water sports nearby.
Publicity: *US Air, Florida Living, Palm Beach Post, Orlando Sentinel and WPEC TV 12 West Palm Beach.*

"We want to thank you for the 'oasis' we found in your home. Everything was perfection. We feel the love that you extend to your guests."

Bayfront Westcott House

146 Avenida Menendez
Saint Augustine, FL 32084-5049
(904)824-4301 (800)513-9814 Fax:(904)824-1502
E-mail: westcott@aug.com
Web: www.westcotthouse.com

Circa 1890. Dr. John Westcott, a man notable for his part in building the St. John Railroad and linking the Intracoastal Waterway from St. John's River to Miami, built this stunning vernacular Victorian. The elegant inn overlooks Matanzas bay, affording guests an enchanting view both inside and out. The interior is filled with Victorian furnishings, from marble-topped tables to white iron beds. The inn is located in St. Augustine's historic district, and plenty of historic sites, restaurants and shops are within walking distance.
Innkeeper(s): Janice & Robert Graubard. $95-250. 9 rooms with PB, 3 with FP. Breakfast and snacks/refreshments included in rates. Types of meals: Full gourmet bkfst, veg bkfst, early coffee/tea, afternoon tea and room service. Beds: KQ. Modem hook-up, cable TV, reading lamp, ceiling fan, telephone, turn-down service, hot tub/spa and fireplace in room. Central air. Fax, copier, bicycles, parlor games and fireplace on premises. Weddings hosted. Amusement parks, antiquing, art galleries, beach, bicycling, canoeing/kayaking, fishing, golf, hiking, live theater, museums, parks, shopping, sporting events, tennis, water sports, wineries and marina nearby.
Publicity: *Country Homes and AAA Magazine.*

Carriage Way B&B

70 Cuna St
Saint Augustine, FL 32084-3684
(904)829-2467 (800)908-9832 Fax:(904)826-1461
E-mail: bjohnson@aug.com
Web: www.carriageway.com

Circa 1883. A two-story veranda dominates the facade of this Victorian. Painted creamy white with blue trim, the house is located in the heart of the historic district. It's within a three-block walk to restaurants and shops and the Intracoastal Waterway. Guest rooms reflect the charm of a light Victorian touch, with brass canopy and four-poster beds. Many furnishings have been in the house for 60 years. The "Cottage"offers two guest rooms, a comfortable living/dining room and a kitchenette. A full gourmet breakfast is provided in the morning.
Historic Interest: Castillo de San Marcos, museums, Fountain of Youth.
Innkeeper(s): Bill Johnson & son, Larry. $89-199. 11 rooms with PB, 1 with FP. Breakfast and snacks/refreshments included in rates. Types of meals: Full bkfst, early coffee/tea and picnic lunch. Beds: KQD. Ceiling fan and telephone in room. Air conditioning. TV, fax, copier and bicycles on premises. Weddings, small meetings and family reunions hosted. Amusement parks, antiquing, fishing, live theater, parks, shopping, sporting events and water sports nearby.
Publicity: *Miami Herald, Florida Times Union, Palm Beach Post and Sunday Oklahoman.*

Casa De La Paz Bayfront B&B

22 Avenida Menendez
Saint Augustine, FL 32084-3644
(904)829-2915 (800)929-2915
E-mail: innkeeper@casadelapaz.com
Web: www.casadelapaz.com

Circa 1915. Overlooking Matanzas Bay, Casa de la Paz was built after the devastating 1914 fire leveled much of the old city. An ornate stucco Mediterranean Revival house, it features clay barrel tile roofing, bracketed eaves, verandas and a lush walled courtyard. The home is listed in the National Register of Historic Places. Guest rooms offer ceiling fans, central air, hardwood floors, antiques, a decanter of sherry, chocolates and complimentary snacks.
Historic Interest: Fountain of Youth, Castillo de San Marcos, Lightner Museum, Flagler College (walking distance).
Innkeeper(s): Sherri & Marshall Crews. $130-275. 7 rooms with PB, 3 with FP. Breakfast included in rates. Types of meals: Full bkfst and early coffee/tea. Beds: KQ. Cable TV, reading lamp, ceiling fan and telephone in room. Air conditioning. TV, parlor games and fireplace on premises. Antiquing, fishing, live theater, parks, shopping, sporting events and water sports nearby.
Publicity: *Innsider, US Air Magazine, Southern Living and PBS.*

"We will always recommend your beautifully restored, elegant home."

Casa De Solana, B&B Inn

21 Aviles St
Saint Augustine, FL 32084-4441
(904)824-3555 (888)796-0980 Fax:(904)824-3316
E-mail: info@cascadesolana.com
Web: www.casadesolana.com

Circa 1763. Spanish military leader Don Manuel Solana built this home in the early European settlement, and Spanish records show that a Solana child was the first European child born in America. The thick coquina-shell walls (limestone formed of broken shells and corals cemented together), high ceilings with

dark, hand-hewn beams and polished hand-pegged floors are part of the distinctive flavor of this period. Five Minorican fireplaces are in the house. A Southern breakfast is served in an elegant dining room.
Innkeeper(s): Joe Finnegan. $109-229. 10 rooms with PB and 2 suites. Breakfast included in rates. Types of meals: Full bkfst. Beds: KQD. Cable TV, reading lamp, stereo, clock radio, telephone, desk, most with fireplace, whirlpool tubs and balconies in room. Air conditioning. TV and fireplace on premises. Amusement parks, antiquing, fishing, golf, live theater, parks, shopping, tennis and water sports nearby.
Publicity: *Times Union, House Beautiful, Palm Beach Post, Innsider, North Florida Living, Jacksonville Today and PM Magazine.*

Casablanca Inn on The Bay

24 Avenida Menedez
Saint Augustine, FL 32084
(904)829-0928 (800)826-2626
E-mail: innkeeper@casablancainn.com
Web: www.casablancainn.com

Circa 1914. One of Henry Flagler's engineers built this Mediterranean Revival home with its panoramic Matanzas Bay views. Situated in the historic district, Fort Castillo de San

Marcos is seen easily from the sprawling veranda. The inn is furnished and decorated with antiques and one-of-a-kind collectibles appropriately placed for comfort and style. Choose from guest bedrooms or suites offering private sun decks and entries, pillow-top mattresses, Jacuzzis and decorative fireplaces. Hospitality is generous with a sumptuous two-course breakfast. Complimentary beverages and fresh-baked cookies are extra enjoyable when gathered on a porch in a rocker overlooking the ocean. Designated off-street parking is provided, with many attractions, shops, museums and restaurants within an easy walk. Bikes are available for further fresh-air exploration. Voted "Best B&B" by the local residents.

Innkeeper(s): Brenda & Tony Bushell. $99-299. 20 rooms with PB and 10 suites. Breakfast, afternoon tea and snacks/refreshments included in rates. Types of meals: Full gourmet bkfst and early coffee/tea. Beds: QT. Modem hook-up, data port, TV, reading lamp, ceiling fan, clock radio, telephone, desk and hot tub/spa in room. Central air. Fax, bicycles, fireplace and complimentary refreshments available 24 hours on premises. Small meetings and seminars hosted. Antiquing, art galleries, beach, bicycling, canoeing/kayaking, fishing, golf, hiking, horseback riding, live theater, museums, parks, shopping, sporting events, tennis, water sports, wineries, boating, World Golf Village and Jacksonville Jaguars (NFL) nearby.
Publicity: *Atlanta Journal and featured on St. Augustine Ghost tour.*

Castle Garden B&B

15 Shenandoah St
Saint Augustine, FL 32084-2817
(904)829-3839
E-mail: castleg@aug.com
Web: www.castlegarden.com

Circa 1860. This newly-restored Moorish Revival-style inn was the carriage house to Warden Castle. Among the seven guest rooms are three bridal rooms with in-room Jacuzzi tubs and sunken bedrooms with cathedral ceilings. The innkeepers offer packages including carriage rides, picnic lunches, gift baskets and other enticing possibilities. Guests enjoy a homemade full, country breakfast each morning.

Historic Interest: Castle Warden next door, Fort Mantanza's (200 yards to south), Alligator Farm, Saint Augustine Lighthouse (nearby).

Innkeeper(s): Bruce & Brian Kloeckner. $69-199. 7 rooms with PB and 3 suites. Breakfast included in rates. Types of meals: Full bkfst, early coffee/tea and picnic lunch. Beds: KQT. TV and ceiling fan in room. Air conditioning. Telephone and common sitting room with cable on premises. Antiquing, fishing, golf, live theater, shopping, tennis, water sports and ballooning nearby.

Cedar House Inn Victorian B&B

79 Cedar St
Saint Augustine, FL 32084-4311
(904)829-0079 (800)233-2746 Fax:(904)825-0916
E-mail: info@cedarhouseinn.com
Web: www.cedarhouseinn.com

Circa 1893. A player piano entertains guests in the parlor of this restored Victorian, which offers plenty of relaxing possibilities. Enjoy refreshments on the veranda or simply curl up with a good book in the library. Innkeepers Russ and Nina Thomas

have preserved the home's luxurious heart-of-pine floors and 10-foot ceilings. They highlighted this architectural treasure with period furnishings and reproductions. Guests rooms

are decked in Victorian decor and boast either clawfoot or Jacuzzi tubs. The innkeepers also offer an outdoor Jacuzzi spa. Elegant breakfasts are served either in the dining room or on the veranda. Guests may borrow bicycles perfect for exploring historic Saint Augustine or nearby beaches.

Historic Interest: The inn is within walking distance of the Lightner Museum, downtown historical sites and the historic district.
Innkeeper(s): Russ & Nina Thomas. $119-215. 6 rooms with PB, 3 with FP, 1 suite and 1 conference room. Breakfast and snacks/refreshments included in rates. Types of meals: Full gourmet bkfst. Beds: Q. Reading lamp, ceiling fan, clock radio, desk and hot tub/spa in room. Air conditioning. Fax, spa, bicycles, parlor games, telephone and fireplace on premises. Weddings, small meetings, family reunions and seminars hosted. Antiquing, art galleries, beach, bicycling, canoeing/kayaking, fishing, golf, live theater, museums, parks, shopping, tennis, water sports, wineries and historic sites and museums nearby.
Publicity: *Palm Beach Times, Palm Beach Post, Southern Living and New York Times.*

"What a special 'home' to spend our honeymoon! Everything was terrific! We feel this is our place now and will be regular guests here! Thank you!"

Centennial House

26 Cordova St
Saint Augustine, FL 32084-3627
(904)810-2218 (800)611-2880 Fax:(904)810-1930
E-mail: innkeeper@centennialhouse.com
Web: www.centennialhouse.com

Circa 1899. In the heart of the historic district on the horse-drawn carriage route, this meticulously restored Victorian home maintains 19th century aesthetics with generous modern amenities. Relax in the garden courtyard and enjoy the landscaped grounds of this premier inn. Impressive suites and guest bedrooms are sound insulated and offer almost every luxury imaginable for leisure or business. The inn is handicap accessible. Savor a complete gourmet breakfast each morning. Special dietary requests are met with gracious hospitality. It is an easy stroll to a wide variety of local sites and attractions.

Historic Interest: Sketchy records make it difficult to pinpoint the bed and breakfast's construction date, but census reports show that it had to be built sometime from 1899 to 1904. Which actually makes the Centennial House relatively new in comparison to surrounding St. Augustine, a city that historians widely acknowledge as the nation's oldest. And, in actuality, the Centennial House, a home originally inhabited by turn-of-the-century St. Augustine councilman J.D. Oliveros, has received a few modern-day architectural upgrades that promise to keep it looking both old and new well into this century and the next.
Innkeeper(s): Geoff & Ellen Fugere. $110-235. 8 rooms with PB, 3 with FP and 1 conference room. Breakfast and snacks/refreshments included in rates. Types of meals: Full bkfst and early coffee/tea. Beds: KQ. Data port, cable TV, VCR, reading lamp, clock radio, telephone, turn-down service, desk, most with whirlpools, hair dryer, robes, down pillows, Egyptian cotton towels, video library, soft drinks, 19th-century aesthetics, soundproof insulation and wireless Internet connection in room. Air conditioning. Fax, copier, parlor games and video library on premises. Limited handicap access. Weddings, family reunions and seminars hosted. Amusement parks, antiquing, art galleries, beach, bicycling, canoeing/kayaking, fishing, golf, hiking, horseback riding, live theater, museums, parks, shopping, sporting events, tennis, water sports and wineries nearby.

Inn on Charlotte Street

52 Charlotte St
Saint Augustine, FL 32084-3647
(904)829-3819 Fax:(904)810-2134
E-mail: innoncharlotte@webtv.net
Web: www.innoncharlotte.com

Circa 1914. Majestic palms accentuate the exterior of this brick home, adorned by a sweeping second-story veranda. The inn is located among many historic gems within Saint

Augustine's historic district. Innkeeper Vanessa Noel has been an innkeeper for more than 30 years, hosting guests in Maine and New Hampshire. Now she has brought her considerable talents to Saint Augustine, a perfect vacation spot for history buffs. Noel has decorated the inn with antiques, over-stuffed sofas and wicker. Some rooms include a Jacuzzi tub, fireplace or private veranda. The inn is within walking distance to many shops and restaurants, as well as the Castillo de San Marcos. Golf, sailing and fishing are other popular local activities.

Innkeeper(s): Vanessa Wyatt Noel. $85-165. 6 rooms with PB, 2 with FP. Breakfast, afternoon tea and snacks/refreshments included in rates. Types of meals: Country bkfst, veg bkfst and early coffee/tea. Beds: KQ. Reading lamp, ceiling fan, hot tub/spa and fireplace in room. Central air. TV, VCR, fax, copier, library, parlor games, telephone and fireplace on premises. Small meetings and seminars hosted. Amusement parks, antiquing, art galleries, beach, bicycling, canoeing/kayaking, fishing, golf, live theater, museums, parks, shopping, sporting events, tennis, water sports, wineries and historical re-enactments nearby.
Publicity: *Southern Living.*

Kenwood Inn

38 Marine St
Saint Augustine, FL 32084-4439
(904)824-2116 (800)824-8151 Fax:(904)824-1689
E-mail: kenwood@aug.com
Web: www.thekenwoodinn.com

Circa 1865. Originally built as a summer home, the Kenwood Inn has taken in guests for more than 100 years. Early records show that it was advertised as a private boarding house as early as 1886. Rooms are decorated in periods ranging from the simple Shaker decor to more formal colonial and Victorian styles.

Historic Interest: Lightner Museum, Oldest House Museum, Bridge of Lions (walking distance).
Innkeeper(s): Mark & Kerrianne Constant. $115-225. 14 rooms with PB and 4 suites. Breakfast included in rates. Types of meals: Cont. Beds: KQD. TV, reading lamp and ceiling fan in room. Air conditioning. Fax, swimming, telephone and fireplace on premises. Antiquing, fishing, live theater, shopping and water sports nearby.
Publicity: *Palm Beach Post, Florida Living, Southern Living and Seabreeze.*

"It's one of my favorite spots for a few days of relaxation and recuperation."

Old City House Inn & Restaurant

115 Cordova St
Saint Augustine, FL 32084-4413
(904)826-0113
E-mail: relax@oldcityhouse.com
Web: www.oldcityhouse.com

Circa 1873. Strategically located in the center of a city immersed in history, this award-winning inn and restaurant was a former stable. Recently it was locally voted the "best of St. Augustine." A red-tiled roof, coquina walls, veranda and courtyard add to the Spanish atmosphere. Guest bedrooms boast hand-carved, four-poster beds and high-speed Internet. Some rooms feature Jacuzzi tubs. An expansive daily gourmet break-

fast is included. The on-site restaurant is open for lunch and dinner. Unique salads, fresh fish and chicken create the midday menu, while dinner selections boast

standards such as Filet Mignon or a more unusual Thai coconut milk beef curry with sesame rice. Choose an appetizer of baked brie, Asian crab cakes or escargot.

Historic Interest: Castillo de San Marcos (1/4 mile), Ripley's Believe It or Not Museum (1/2 mile), Lightner Museum (across street).
Innkeeper(s): James & Ilse Philcox. $85-205. 7 rooms with PB. Breakfast included in rates. Types of meals: Full bkfst, early coffee/tea, gourmet lunch and gourmet dinner. Restaurant on premises. Beds: Q. Cable TV, reading lamp, ceiling fan, clock radio, telephone, hot tub/spa, four-poster hand-carved beds, some with Jacuzzis and high-speed Internet available in room. Air conditioning. TV, VCR, fax, copier and bicycles on premises. Limited handicap access. Antiquing, fishing, live theater, shopping and water sports nearby.
Publicity: *Florida Times Union, Florida Trend and Ft. Lauderdale Sun Sentinal.*

Old Powder House Inn

38 Cordova St
Saint Augustine, FL 32084-3629
(904)824-4149 (800)447-4149 Fax:(904)825-0143
E-mail: kalieta@aug.com
Web: www.oldpowderhouse.com

Circa 1899. Be immersed in four centuries of history while visiting this enchanting Victorian bed & breakfast inn. Relax on a shaded veranda with iced tea or lemonade as horse-drawn carriages pass by towering oak and pecan shade trees. Perfect for a romantic getaway, lace curtains and hardwood floors grace antique-filled guest bedrooms. Gather in the formal dining room for a generous gourmet breakfast. Throughout the day enjoy hot or cold beverages and fresh-baked treats. Wine and cordials are offered in the evening. Each visit promises to be unforgettable with warm hospitality and elegant service. Located in the heart of the city's historic district, it is an easy stroll to museums, famous landmarks, quaint restaurants and shops.

Innkeeper(s): Katie & Kal Kalieta. $85-205. 11 rooms, 9 with PB and 2 suites. Breakfast and snacks/refreshments included in rates. Types of meals: Full gourmet bkfst, early coffee/tea and picnic lunch. Beds: KQDT. Reading lamp, refrigerator, ceiling fan, clock radio and hot tub/spa in room. Air conditioning. Fax, copier, parlor games, telephone, fireplace, outdoor Jacuzzi, daily social hour includes wine and tea/coffee with cordials and sweets on premises. Weddings, small meetings, family reunions and seminars hosted. Antiquing, fishing, golf, live theater, parks, shopping, tennis and water sports nearby.

"If you're looking for a retreat into a world of elegance and repose, try The Old Powder House Inn." - West Palm Beach Post

Penny Farthing Inn

83 Cedar St
Saint Augustine, FL 32084-4311
(904)824-2100 (800)395-1890
E-mail: penny@aug.com
Web: www.pennyfarthinginn.net

Circa 1890. Experience a simpler era at this Victorian bed and breakfast in historic downtown. Built in 1887, the main house was transformed into an elegant and inviting inn in 1990. Relax by the fire in the parlor, use the gaming table or read in the comfortable sitting area. Share conversation over afternoon refreshments that include snacks, wine, beer and other beverages. Suites and bedchambers are furnished with period antiques and boast covered porches. Several rooms feature clawfoot soaking

tubs, or choose Brittany's Secret, decorated in wicker and white lace with a two-person whirlpool bath. Ponce de Leon arrived in this city to find the Fountain of Youth, those who come now find rejuvenation.

Innkeeper(s): Paul Schwartz and Connie Goodwin. $89-199. 7 rooms with PB, 1 with FP and 3 suites. Breakfast included in rates. Types of meals: Full gourmet bkfst. Beds: QT. Cable TV, reading lamp, refrigerator and ceiling fan in room. Air conditioning. Bicycles, library, telephone, fireplace and parking on premises. Weddings, small meetings and seminars hosted. Antiquing, fishing, golf, live theater, parks, shopping, sporting events, tennis and water sports nearby.

Southern Wind B&B

18 Cordova St
Saint Augustine, FL 32084
(904)825-3623 (800)781-3338 Fax:(904)810-5212
E-mail: swind@aug.com
Web: www.southernwindinn.com

Circa 1915. Horse-drawn carriages pass by this Flagler-style inn, built of coquina masonry with columns and wraparound verandas. Located in the historic district, a gracious elegance and casual relaxation is found in abundance and reflected in the exquisite blend of antiques and period furnishings. Guest bedrooms offer pillow-top mattresses, down pillows, fluffy robes, two-person Jacuzzis, bottled spring water, and assorted amenities that pamper and soothe. Linger over a lavish breakfast presented on vintage china in the formal dining room. Savor popular stuffed French toast entrees such as banana pecan, apple cinnamon and cream cheese, or pineapple macadamia nut, or Savory Bacon Crepes with fresh basil cream sauce, and Southwest Frittatas. More delicious delights are served in the afternoon with wine and lemonade. Relax on porch rockers overlooking the front garden and fountain.
Innkeeper(s): Alana & Bob Indelicato. $99-229. 10 rooms with PB. Breakfast and afternoon tea included in rates. Types of meals: Full gourmet bkfst, veg bkfst, early coffee/tea, picnic lunch and snacks/refreshments. Beds: KQ. Cable TV, reading lamp, refrigerator, ceiling fan, clock radio, telephone, desk and hot tub/spa in room. Central air. Fax, copier, bicycles, parlor games, fireplace and fireplace in parlor on premises. Weddings, family reunions and seminars hosted. Antiquing, art galleries, beach, bicycling, canoeing/kayaking, fishing, golf, hiking, horseback riding, live theater, museums, shopping, tennis, water sports and wineries nearby.
Publicity: *Boston Globe, Palm Coast Recorder and Gainsville Sun and Ponte Vedre Lifestyle.*

St. Francis Inn

279 Saint George St
Saint Augustine, FL 32084-5031
(904)824-6068 (800)824-6062 Fax:(904)810-5525
E-mail: info@stfrancisinn.com
Web: www.stfrancisinn.com

Circa 1791. Long noted for its hospitality, the St. Francis Inn is nearly the oldest house in town. A classic example of Old World architecture, it was built by Gaspar Garcia, who received a Spanish grant to the plot of land. Coquina was the main building material. A buffet breakfast is served. Some rooms have whirlpool tubs and fireplaces. The city of Saint Augustine was founded in 1565.
Historic Interest: The nation's oldest house (free admission for guests at the St. Francis Inn), Saint Augustine Antigua.
Innkeeper(s): Joe Finnegan. $109-229.
14 rooms with PB, 8 with FP, 4 suites, 1 cottage and 2 conference rooms. Breakfast included in rates. Types of meals: Full bkfst. Beds: KQDT. Cable TV, reading lamp, refrigerator, ceiling fan, telephone, desk and whirlpool tubs in room. Air conditioning. TV, fax, copier, swimming, bicycles, parlor games, fireplace and whirlpool tubs on premises. Weddings, small meetings, family reunions and seminars hosted. Antiquing, fishing, parks, shopping, sporting events and water sports nearby.

Publicity: *Orlando Sentinel.*

"We have stayed at many nice hotels but nothing like this. We are really enjoying it."

Victorian House B&B

11 Cadiz St
Saint Augustine, FL 32084-4431
(904)824-5214 (800)709-5710

Circa 1897. Enjoy the historic ambiance of Saint Augustine at this turn-of-the-century Victorian, decorated to reflect the grandeur of that genteel era. Stenciling highlights the walls, and the innkeepers have filled the guest rooms with canopy beds and period furnishings complementing the heart of pine floors. A full breakfast includes homemade granola, fresh fruit, a hot entree and a variety of freshly made breads.
Innkeeper(s): Ken & Marcia Cerotzke. $99-185. 8 rooms with PB and 4 suites. Breakfast and snacks/refreshments included in rates. Types of meals: Full gourmet bkfst. Beds: KQDT. Reading lamp, ceiling fan and one with refrigerator in room. Air conditioning. Fax and bicycles on premises. Family reunions hosted. Antiquing, fishing, live theater, museums, parks, shopping, water sports, fine restaurants and historic sites nearby.

Whale's Tale

54 Charlotte St
Saint Augustine, FL 32084-3647
(904)829-5901 (888)989-4253
E-mail: whale@oldcity.com
Web: www.WhalesTaleBandB.com

Circa 1910. Whale's Tale is within one or two blocks from the Bay Front, Castillo de San Marcos, Plaza de Constitution, St. George Street and within a mile of dozens of historic sites, including the Fountain of Youth, Victorian Village, The Fort and Mission de Nombre de Dias. The Lightener Museum is three blocks away. The home itself is historic, built in the early 20th century. Gardens and two tall palm trees mark the front of the house, and there's a porch off all the rooms. The décor includes lacy curtains, turn-of-the-century antiques and patchwork quilts. A full breakfast is served each morning and the innkeepers have a repertoire of 14 different breakfasts, such as Whale's Tale quiche on a hash brown potato crust and apple-peach smoothies. The innkeepers are happy to help guests find a special restaurant or plan daily activities. Parking on the premises and a dozen restaurants are nearby.
Historic Interest: Built in 1565, oldest city in the United States, occupied by Spanish English, and during the Civil War it was occupied at different times by the Confederates and the Union, a refuge for slaves from Georgia and the Carolinas.
Innkeeper(s): Betty & Denis Cunningham. $89-149. 7 rooms with PB. Breakfast included in rates. Types of meals: Full bkfst and veg bkfst. Beds: Q. Reading lamp and ceiling fan in room. Central air. Telephone on premises. Weddings, small meetings, family reunions and seminars hosted. Antiquing, art galleries, beach, bicycling, canoeing/kayaking, fishing, golf, hiking, horseback riding, live theater, museums, parks, shopping, sporting events, tennis, water sports and wineries nearby.

"The perfect setting for celebrating our first wedding anniversary. We have told all our friends about your beautiful establishment. Thanks for such a wonderful place."

Saint Petersburg E7

Inn at the Bay Bed and Breakfast

126 4th Ave NE
Saint Petersburg, FL 33701
(727)822-1700 (888)873-2122 Fax:(727)896-7412
E-mail: info@innatthebay.com
Web: www.innatthebay.com

Circa 1910. Conveniently located on Tampa Bay, this newly renovated inn is near many of the state's popular attractions. The plush guest bedrooms and suites, themed in regional motifs, showcase Florida. Allergy-free feather beds and whirlpool tubs soothe and rejuvenate. Hospitality is abundant in the provision of thoughtful amenities like fluffy robes, lighted makeup mirrors, cable TV and Internet access. After a delicious breakfast, enjoy reading the daily newspaper in the garden gazebo.

Innkeeper(s): Dennis & Jewly Youschak. $119-250. 12 rooms with PB and 1 conference room. Breakfast included in rates. Types of meals: Full bkfst and early coffee/tea. Beds: KQ. Data port, cable TV, VCR, reading lamp, CD player, refrigerator, ceiling fan, clock radio, telephone, coffeemaker, turn-down service, desk, hot tub/spa, voice mail and one with fireplace in room. Central air. Fax, copier, parlor games and fireplace on premises. Limited handicap access. Weddings, small meetings, family reunions and seminars hosted. Amusement parks, antiquing, art galleries, beach, canoeing/kayaking, fishing, golf, hiking, horseback riding, live theater, museums, parks, shopping, sporting events and water sports nearby.

La Veranda Bed & Breakfast

111 5th Ave. N
Saint Petersburg, FL 33701
(727)824-9997 (800)484-8423 ext. 8417 Fax:(727)827-1431
E-mail: info@laverandabb.com
Web: www.laverandabb.com

Circa 1910. Featuring Old World charm in an urban setting, this classic Key West-style mansion is only two blocks from the waterfront. Antiques, Oriental rugs and artwork accent the gracious elegance. Lounge by the fire in the living room or on one of the large wicker-filled wraparound verandas overlooking lush tropical gardens. Romantic one- and two-bedroom suites boast private entrances, as well as indoor and outdoor sitting areas. A gourmet breakfast with Starbucks coffee is served on settings of china, silver and crystal. Corporate services are available with assorted business amenities. When dialing the inn's toll-free number, be sure to enter pin #8417.

Innkeeper(s): Nancy & Lou Meuse. $99-249. 5 rooms, 1 with PB and 4 suites. Breakfast and snacks/refreshments included in rates. Types of meals: Full gourmet bkfst, veg bkfst, early coffee/tea, afternoon tea and room service. Beds: KQT. Cable TV, VCR, reading lamp, CD player, refrigerator, ceiling fan, snack bar, clock radio, telephone, turn-down service, desk and fireplace in room. Air conditioning. Fax, copier, bicycles, library, fireplace and laundry facility on premises. Weddings, small meetings, family reunions and seminars hosted. Amusement parks, antiquing, art galleries, beach, bicycling, canoeing/kayaking, fishing, golf, hiking, live theater, museums, parks, shopping, sporting events, water sports and wineries nearby.

Publicity: *NY Daily Times and Interstate 75.*

Lee Manor Inn

342 3rd Ave N
Saint Petersburg, FL 33701-3821
(727)894-3248 (866)219-7260 Fax:(727)895-8759
E-mail: info@leemanorinn.com
Web: www.leemanorinn.com

Circa 1937. Comfortable and convenient, this historic 21-room inn is located downtown. This city oasis is relaxing for the leisure or business traveler. Furnished with antiques, the vintage hotel offers Old World charm and warm hospitality. Each guest bedroom features amenities that include a hair dryer, television, refrigerator and coffee maker with supplies. Danish, fruit, waffles, toast, juice and hot beverages are offered every morning for a complimentary continental breakfast. The Pier, Baywalk, County Courthouse, Tropicana Field, museums, theaters and shops all are nearby.

Innkeeper(s): Dave Anderson & Brenda Martin. $69-169. 21 rooms with PB and 2 suites. Breakfast included in rates. Types of meals: Cont. Beds: QDT. Modem hook-up, data port, cable TV, reading lamp, refrigerator, ceiling fan, clock radio, telephone and coffeemaker in room. Air conditioning. VCR, fax, copier and library on premises. Weddings and family reunions hosted. Antiquing, art galleries, beach, bicycling, canoeing/kayaking, fishing, golf, hiking, horseback riding, live theater, museums, parks, shopping, sporting events, tennis and water sports nearby.

Mansion House B&B

105 5th Ave NE
Saint Petersburg, FL 33701
(727)821-9391 (800)274-7520 Fax:(727)821-6906
E-mail: mansion1@ix.netcom.com
Web: www.mansionbandb.com

Circa 1901. The first mayor of St. Petersburg once lived here, and the inn is so named in the English tradition that states the home of a mayor shall be known as the mansion house. The home's architecture is Arts and Crafts in style, and has been completely restored, winning awards for beautification and enhancement. The Pembroke Room, in the inn's carriage house, is especially remarkable. Wicker pieces and hand-painted furnishings by Artist Marva Simpson, exposed beams painted a rich teal green, and trails of flowers and ivy decorating the lace-covered windows create the ambiance of an English seaside cottage. The Edinburgh Room is another beauty with its canopy bed topped with luxurious coverings. Guests can walk from the home to a natural harbor, restaurants, popular local parks and the beach. Busch Gardens, museums, an arboretum and a botanical garden are other nearby attractions.

Innkeeper(s): Rose Marie Ray. $119-220. 12 rooms with PB and 4 conference rooms. Breakfast and snacks/refreshments included in rates. Types of meals: Full gourmet bkfst, veg bkfst, early coffee/tea, picnic lunch and afternoon tea. Restaurant on premises. Beds: KQT. Modem hook-up, data port, cable TV, reading lamp, ceiling fan, clock radio, telephone and desk in room. Central air. VCR, fax, copier, library, parlor games, laundry facility, swimming pool and courtyard/garden on premises. Weddings, small meetings, family reunions and seminars hosted. Amusement parks, antiquing, art galleries, beach, bicycling, canoeing/kayaking, fishing, golf, hiking, horseback riding, live theater, museums, parks, shopping, sporting events, tennis, water sports and eco-nature tours nearby.

Publicity: *Michelin Green Guide, Frommer's Unofficial Guide to B&Bs of the South and American Bed & Breakfast Book.*

Sunset Bay Inn

635 Bay St, NE
Saint Petersburg, FL 33701
(727)896-6701 (800)794-5133 Fax:(727)898-5311
E-mail: wrbcom@aol.com
Web: www.sunsetbayinn.com

Circa 1911. After restoring this historically designated Georgian Colonial Revival, the inn is now a AAA four-diamond property with luxurious traditional decor. A sunroom with comfy furniture boasts the original Cuban red tile floor. Read by the fireplace in the salmon-painted living room. Beverages and baked goods always are available in the butler's pantry. Romantic guest bedrooms feature a variety of amenities to pamper and please including robes, wine, whirlpool tubs, VCRs

and CD players. Breakfast is enjoyed in the elegant green dining room or outside on the veranda. A lush courtyard separates the main house from the carriage house in an intimate setting.
Innkeeper(s): Bob & Martha Bruce. $130-270. 8 rooms, 3 suites and 1 conference room. Breakfast and snacks/refreshments included in rates. Types of meals: Full bkfst, early coffee/tea and picnic lunch. Beds: KQT. Modem hook-up, data port, cable TV, VCR, reading lamp, stereo, refrigerator, ceiling fan, clock radio, telephone, coffeemaker, turn-down service, desk, hot tub/spa, hair dryers, iron and ironing board and plush robes in room. Central air. Fax, copier, bicycles, library, parlor games, fireplace, laundry facility and gift shop on premises. Weddings, small meetings, family reunions and seminars hosted. Antiquing, art galleries, beach, bicycling, fishing, golf, hiking, live theater, museums, parks, shopping, sporting events, tennis, water sports and wineries nearby.
Publicity: *Southern Living, Florida Magazine, Tampa Tribune, Palm Beach Post, Fort Lauderdale-Sun Sentinel, St. Petersburg Times, CBS, 48 Hours, The Black Stallion and Budweiser beer commercial.*

San Mateo   C8

Ferncourt B&B

150 Central Ave
San Mateo, FL 32187-0758
(386)329-9755
E-mail: ferncourt@gbso.net

Circa 1889. This Victorian "painted lady," is one of the few remaining relics from San Mateo's heyday in the early 1900s. Teddy Roosevelt once visited the elegant home. The current owners have restored the Victorian
atmosphere with rooms decorated with bright, floral prints and gracious furnishings. Awake to the smells of brewing coffee and the sound of a rooster crowing before settling down to a full gourmet

breakfast. Historic Saint Augustine is a quick, 25-mile drive.
Innkeeper(s): Jack & Dee Morgan. $65-85. 6 rooms, 5 with PB. Breakfast included in rates. Types of meals: Full gourmet bkfst and early coffee/tea. Beds: KQD. Reading lamp and ceiling fan in room. Air conditioning. Parlor games, telephone and fireplace on premises. Small meetings and family reunions hosted. Antiquing, fishing, golf, live theater, parks and shopping nearby.

"First class operation! A beautiful house with an impressive history and restoration. Great company and fine food."

Tampa   E7

The Bayshore Ryan House

203 West Verne Street
Tampa, FL
(813)253-3142 Fax:(813)253-3104
E-mail: innkeeper@bayshoreryanhouse.com
Web: www.bayshoreryanhouse.com

Circa 1906. Centrally located in historic Hyde Park within walking distance to just about everything including the downtown area, this bed & breakfast is the perfect solution for a business trip, vacation or romantic getaway. Listed in the National and Local Registers, the home was built in 1902 and is furnished in period antiques. It has been renovated with modern conveniences for comfort and ease. Themed luxury suites boast high-speed Internet with computer-friendly data ports, double whirlpool baths, ceiling fans, cable TV and VCRs. Relax on a rocking chair on the large front porch. There is a 24-hour snack bar and a wine and cheese hour on the weekends. The gracious southern hospitality that is extended is easy to surrender to. Soak in the backyard hot tub.

Innkeeper(s): John and Cindy Ryan. $99-500. 4 rooms with PB, 4 with HT. Breakfast included in rates. Types of meals: Full bkfst and early coffee/tea. Beds: KQ. Data port, cable TV, VCR, ceiling fan, telephone, desk, hot tub/spa, double whirlpools, plush robes and high-speed Internet in room. Antiquing, art galleries, beach, bicycling, canoeing/kayaking, fishing, golf, hiking, live theater, museums, parks and water sports nearby.

Don Vicente de Ybor Historic Inn & Restaurant

1915 Republica de Cuba
Tampa, FL 33605
(813)241-4545 Fax:(813)367-2917
E-mail: donvicentehotel@hotmail.com
Web: www.donvicenteinn.com

Circa 1895. Sitting in the center of the entertainment district, this historic Mediterranean Revival inn was built by the founder of Ybor City. The Old World European decor, architecture and furnishings have transformed it into a premier boutique hotel. Opulent splendor is found in the quiet guest bedrooms and suites featuring Persian carpets and down comforters over pillowtop mattresses. After a pleasurable breakfast, sit on one of the patios adorned with tropical plants and plan the day's events. Many sites and activities are within an easy walk. The waterfront is five minutes away.
Innkeeper(s): Tessa Shiver. $99-199. 16 rooms with PB, 2 suites and 2 conference rooms. Breakfast included in rates. Types of meals: Cont plus, early coffee/tea and lunch. Restaurant on premises. Beds: KQ. Data port, cable TV, reading lamp, clock radio, telephone, pillow top mattresses, fluffy down comforters and persian carpets in room. Central air. Fax on premises. Limited handicap access. Weddings, small meetings, family reunions and seminars hosted. Amusement parks, antiquing, art galleries, beach, bicycling, live theater, museums, shopping, sporting events and entertainment district nearby.
Publicity: *Tampa Tribune and St. Petersburg Times.*

Tarpon Springs   E7

Spring Bayou Inn

32 W Tarpon Ave
Tarpon Springs, FL 34689-3432
(727)938-9333

Circa 1905. This large Victorian house is surrounded by a wraparound veranda and a balcony. Inside, glowing curly pine paneling adorns the staircase and fireplace. The parlor offers a baby grand piano. Stroll to the nearby bayou surrounded by high green banks and huge oak trees, a block from the inn. The sponge docks, made famous by Greek sponge divers, are within walking distance, as well, or you can browse the antique shops, choose from a variety of restaurants or take in a cultural event.
Innkeeper(s): Sharon Birk, Linda & John Hall. $80-125. 5 rooms with PB. Types of meals: Full gourmet bkfst. Beds: KQD. Fireplace, baby grand piano and wraparound porch on premises. Antiquing and shopping nearby.
Publicity: *Florida Home & Garden Magazine, Sunshine Magazine, Miami Today and Palm Beach Post.*

"Lots to do in the area, and the decor was very nice."

Venice   F7

Horse and Chaise Inn, LLC

317 Ponce de Leon
Venice, FL 34285
(941)488-2702
E-mail: innkeeper@horseandchaiseinn.com
Web: www.horseandchaiseinn.com

Circa 1926. The architectural style of this two-story Mediterranean Revival is historically significant, as it was adopted as the city's official theme. Ornate stucco trim frames the large front door. Relax in the living room accented by a massive fireplace. Vintage prints from the Venice Archives grace the walls of the guest bedrooms, which reflect the heritage of the area. Sitting on three acres, the fragrant garden and shaded deck are enjoyable places to rest. Bicycles are available for further adventure, or stroll to the beach. Ask about special packages that are offered including golf, wedding, picnic for two, romantic dinner or in-room massage.

Innkeeper(s): Jon & Lois Steketee. $95-150. 10 rooms with PB and 4 suites. Breakfast included in rates. Types of meals: Full bkfst. Beds: KQT. Cable TV, reading lamp, refrigerator, ceiling fan and clock radio in room. Air conditioning. Fax, bicycles, telephone, fireplace and laundry facility on premises. Limited handicap access. Weddings and family reunions hosted. Antiquing, art galleries, beach, bicycling, canoeing/kayaking, fishing, golf, hiking, live theater, museums, parks, shopping, sporting events, tennis and water sports nearby.

West Palm Beach   G10

Casa de Rosa

520 27th St
West Palm Beach, FL 33407
(561)833-1920 (888)665-8666 Fax:(561)835-3566
E-mail: elaine@casaderosa.com
Web: www.casaderosa.com

Circa 1924. This historic Florida house has recently been fully restored, including its extensive gardens, offering guests a private enclave while visiting West Palm Beach. Freshly decorated guest spaces include the inviting parlor, a brand new kitchen and the dining room. (If you can pull yourself away from the joys of the garden, pool and arched verandas.) Two gazebos, a cottage garden, rock garden and rose garden offer additional inspiration. Four guest rooms provide a selection of size and décor.

Innkeeper(s): Elaine & Frank Calendrillo. $110-195. 4 rooms with PB and 1 cottage. Breakfast included in rates. Types of meals: Full gourmet bkfst and snacks/refreshments. Beds: KQ. Cable TV, ceiling fan, telephone and hair dryer in room. Central air. Fax, copier, swimming, library, daily room service, wine, soft drinks, juices, ice tea, lemonade, fireplace in living room and spa service available on premises. Antiquing, art galleries, beach, bicycling, canoeing/kayaking, fishing, golf, horseback riding, live theater, museums, parks, shopping, tennis and water sports nearby.

Hibiscus House

501 30th St
West Palm Beach, FL 33407-5121
(561)863-5633 (800)203-4927 Fax:(561)863-5633
E-mail: info@hibiscushouse.com
Web: www.hibiscushouse.com

Circa 1922. Built for the mayor of West Palm Beach, the Hibiscus House offers guest rooms individually decorated with antiques. The poolside cottage accommodates up to six people and includes a kitchen and two bathrooms. Two-course breakfasts are served daily with fine china and crystal. Complimentary cocktails also are served.

Innkeeper(s): Raleigh Hill and Colin Rayner. $75-270. 8 rooms with PB, 1 with FP, 2 suites and 1 cottage. Breakfast included in rates. Types of meals: Full bkfst. Beds: Q. Cable TV, reading lamp, ceiling fan, clock radio, telephone and desk in room. Air conditioning. TV, VCR, fax, swimming, library, parlor games and fireplace on premises. Weddings, small meetings and family reunions hosted. Antiquing, fishing, golf, live theater, parks, shopping, sporting events, tennis and water sports nearby.

Publicity: *Palm Beach Life, Ocean Drive and Miami Herald.*

"You have such a warm and beautiful home. We have told everyone of our stay there."

Tropical Gardens Bed and Breakfast

419 32nd St
West Palm Beach, FL 33407
(561)848-4064 (800)736-4064 Fax:(561)848-2422
E-mail: tropgard@bellsouth.net
Web: www.tropicalgardensbandb.com

Circa 1937. A relaxed and colorful atmosphere is found at these historic Key West-style accommodations located in a secluded, tropical setting only minutes from beaches, city life and the airport. Guest bedrooms and cottages with cypress ceilings, crown molding, French doors and wicker furniture are comfortable retreats. An expanded continental buffet breakfast with fresh-squeezed Florida orange juice starts the day's adventures. Lounge by the pool, or enjoy the lush native foliage in the quiet courtyard. Bicycles are available.

Innkeeper(s): John and Cornelia Wilson. $80-150. 4 rooms, 2 with PB and 2 cottages. Breakfast included in rates. Types of meals: Cont plus. Beds: QT. Modem hook-up, data port, cable TV, VCR, reading lamp, stereo, refrigerator, ceiling fan, clock radio, telephone, coffeemaker, turn-down service, fireplace and pool in room. Central air. Fax, copier, swimming, tennis, library, parlor games and pool on premises. Small meetings, family reunions and seminars hosted. Antiquing, art galleries, beach, bicycling, canoeing/kayaking, fishing, golf, hiking, live theater, museums, parks, shopping, tennis and water sports nearby.

White Springs   B7

White Springs Bed and Breakfast Inn

PO Box 403
White Springs, FL 32096
(386)397-1665 (888)412-1665 Fax:(386)397-1665
E-mail: kgavronsky@aol.com
Web: www.whitesprings.org

Circa 1905. Formerly known as the Kendrick-Lindsey House in the historic district near the Suwannee River, this Vernacular inn is listed in the National Register. Recently restored with modern conveniences, a Victorian ambiance remains with original woodwork and staircase, heart of pine floors, stained-glass window, tin roof, four fireplace mantels and two clawfoot tubs. The parlor is perfect for watching movies, listening to a CD or playing the piano. The suites and guest bedrooms are furnished in an assortment of English Country Cottage, French Country and Victorian decor. A delicious full breakfast is served on fine china in the formal dining room. Enjoy the landscaped grounds with a rose garden and shade trees.

Innkeeper(s): Kerry & Jake Gavronsky. $75-85. 4 rooms with PB, 2 with FP. Breakfast and snacks/refreshments included in rates. Types of meals: Full gourmet bkfst, early coffee/tea, afternoon tea and room service. Beds: KQDT. Data port, cable TV, reading lamp, ceiling fan, clock radio, coffeemaker, turn-down service and fireplace in room. Air conditioning. VCR, fax, copier, bicycles, library, parlor games, telephone, fireplace, gift shop, refrigerator upstairs for guest convenience, flexible breakfast time and check-in times and VCR and movie tapes available on premises. Amusement parks, antiquing, art galleries, bicycling, canoeing/kayaking, fishing, golf, hiking, horseback riding, museums, parks, shopping, water sports, white water rafting and walking tour of homes nearby.

Georgia

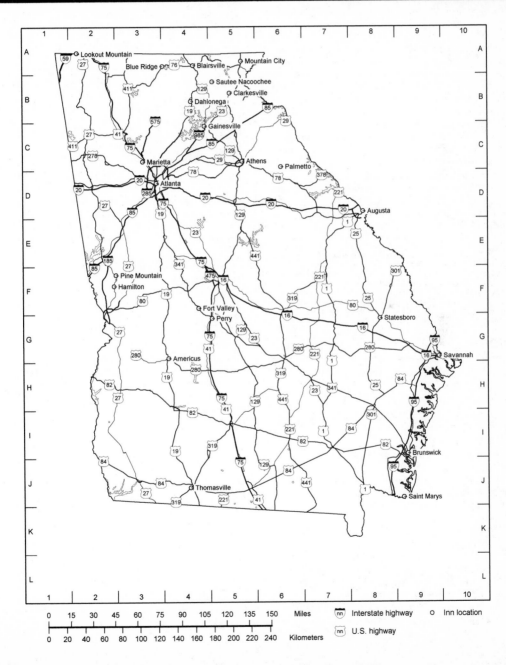

0 15 30 45 60 75 90 105 120 135 150 Miles

0 20 40 60 80 100 120 140 160 180 200 220 240 Kilometers

[nn] Interstate highway   o Inn location

[nn] U.S. highway

Americus
G4

Americus Garden Inn Bed & Breakfast

504 Rees Park
Americus, GA 31709
(229)931-0122 (888)758-4749
E-mail: info@americusgardeninn.com
Web: www.americusgardeninn.com

Circa 1847. Original wood floors, stained glass, high ceilings and a grand hall stairway showcase this 1847 pre-Civil War Antebellum mansion that adorns more than an acre in a historic residential district. Complimentary refreshments are available all the time. A library offers use of movies, books and games. Each of the casually elegant guest bedrooms combines antiques with modern comfort and upscale amenities, including personal care products, hair dryers and irons. Some rooms feature Jacuzzi or garden tubs, private balconies, kitchenettes and wheelchair access. An incredible "skip a lunch" breakfast begins with six choices of juice, then breads or muffins before a specialty fruit dish. A hot egg and cheese entrée is accompanied by the pancake of the day, one of the more than 20 varieties prepared. Meander through the flower-lined pathways to the koi pond or swing in the gazebo.

Historic Interest: Built in 1847, the building was restored to its original glory between 1994-1998. Throughout the inn, you can see elements from the 1840s, 1890s and 1920s. Original wood floors, stained glass, unique hall stairway, 12-foot ceilings even the koi pond is from the 1920s.

Innkeeper(s): Mr. & Mrs. Kim and Susan Egelseer. $100-150. 8 rooms with PB and 1 conference room. Breakfast and snacks/refreshments included in rates. Types of meals: Full bkfst and early coffee/tea. Beds: KQD. Data port, cable TV, VCR, reading lamp, ceiling fan, clock radio, telephone, turn-down service, desk, hot tub/spa, voice mail, bath gel, shampoo, conditioner, moisturizer, hair dryer, iron/board, some with Jacuzzi, garden tub, private balcony, kitchenette and wheelchair accessibility in room. Central air. Fax, library, parlor games, free movie library, books, games and 24 hour complimentary refreshments on premises. Limited handicap access. Small meetings and seminars hosted. Antiquing, fishing, golf, hiking, live theater, museums, parks, shopping and sporting events nearby.

Athens
C5

The Nicholson House Inn

6295 Jefferson Rd
Athens, GA 30607-1714
(706)353-2200
E-mail: 1820@nicholsonhouseinn.com
Web: www.nicholsonhouseinn.com

Circa 1820. For a distinctive stay in this classic city, this Antebellum inn depicts the splendor of the Old South. Built in Colonial Revival style, the meticulously renovated home boasts a historic elegance that is accented with Civil War artifacts, antiques from the early 19th century and limited-edition prints. Two parlors and an extensive library are delightful common areas to enjoy. Evening sherry is offered. Spacious guest bedrooms all with private bath provide personal luxury. Morning brings a healthy and hearty breakfast of fresh fruit, a hot entree, warm breads, cereal, gourmet coffee and juice served in the formal dining room. Relax in a rocking chair on the veranda or stroll among the 34 wooded acres with natural springs, towering trees, colorful flowers and plants. Downtown is just five miles away where the state's Antebellum Trail begins, and there are many museums.

Historic Interest: Inn was a stagecoach stop on "Old Federal Road" for most of the 1800s.

Innkeeper(s): Celeste & Harry Neely. $99-139. 8 rooms with PB. Breakfast included in rates. Types of meals: Full bkfst. Beds: KQ. Cable TV and telephone in room. Air conditioning.

Atlanta
D3

Beverly Hills Inn

65 Sheridan Dr NE
Atlanta, GA 30305-3121
(404)233-8520 (800)331-8520 Fax:(404)233-8659
E-mail: mit@bhi.com
Web: www.beverlyhillsinn.com

Circa 1929. Period furniture and polished-wood floors decorate this inn located in the Buckhead neighborhood. There are private balconies, kitchens and a library with a collection of  newspapers and books. The governor's mansion, Neiman-Marcus, Saks and Lord & Taylor are five minutes away.

Innkeeper(s): Mit Amin. $99-160. 18 suites. Breakfast included in rates. Types of meals: Cont plus. Beds: QD. Cable TV, reading lamp, refrigerator, clock radio and telephone in room. Air conditioning. TV and health club privileges on premises. Small meetings and family reunions hosted. Antiquing, parks and shopping nearby.

Publicity: *Travel & Leisure, Country Inns, Southern Living, Time and CNN.*

"Our only regret is that we had so little time. Next stay we will plan to be here longer."

Gaslight Inn B&B

1001 St Charles Ave NE
Atlanta, GA 30306-4221
(404)875-1001 Fax:(404)876-1001
E-mail: innkeeper@gaslightinn.com
Web: www.gaslightinn.com

Circa 1913. Flickering gas lanterns outside, original gas lighting inside and seven working fireplaces add to the unique quality of this inn. Beautifully appointed guest rooms offer individual decor. The Ivy Cottage is a romantic Cape Cod style bungalow with a living room and kitchen. The regal English Suite boasts a four-poster bed covered in rich blue hues and a private deck. The Rose Room features a fireplace and four-poster bed covered with lace. Located in the Virginia Highlands neighborhood, the inn is approximately ten minutes from downtown and is served by Atlanta's public transportation system.

Innkeeper(s): Mark Hall. $95-195. 8 rooms with PB, 3 with FP, 5 suites and 2 cottages. Breakfast included in rates. Types of meals: Cont plus and early coffee/tea. Beds: KQ. Cable TV, VCR, reading lamp, stereo, refrigerator, ceiling fan, snack bar, clock radio, telephone, desk and hot tub/spa in room. Air conditioning. Fax, copier, spa, sauna, library and fireplace on premises. Limited handicap access. Weddings, small meetings, family reunions and seminars hosted. Amusement parks, antiquing, live theater, parks, shopping and sporting events nearby.

Publicity: *Vacations Magazine, CNN Travel Guide Show, Discover Channel, CBS's 48 hours and Travel Channel.*

"Best B&B I've ever stayed in."

King-Keith House B&B

889 Edgewood Ave NE
Atlanta, GA 30307
(404)688-7330 (800)728-3879 Fax:(404)584-8408
E-mail: kingkeith@mindspring.com
Web: www.kingkeith.com

Circa 1890. One of Atlanta's most photographed houses, this 1980 Queen Anne Victorian sits among live oaks and prominent homes in the restored neighborhood of Inman Park. Listed in the National Register, it boasts twelve-foot ceilings and carved fireplaces. Play the baby grand piano in one of the elegant public rooms and 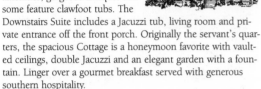 stroll through the private gardens. Enjoy complimentary snacks and beverages. Romantic guest bedrooms offer a variety of pleasing amenities, gorgeous antiques and some feature clawfoot tubs. The Downstairs Suite includes a Jacuzzi tub, living room and private entrance off the front porch. Originally the servant's quarters, the spacious Cottage is a honeymoon favorite with vaulted ceilings, double Jacuzzi and an elegant garden with a fountain. Linger over a gourmet breakfast served with generous southern hospitality.

Innkeeper(s): Jan & Windell Keith. $90-175. 6 rooms with PB, 1 suite and 1 cottage. Breakfast included in rates. Types of meals: Full gourmet bkfst and early coffee/tea. Beds: KQDT. Cable TV, reading lamp, refrigerator, ceiling fan, snack bar, clock radio, telephone, desk, hair dryer and cottage with Jacuzzi and fireplace in room. Air conditioning. Parlor games on premises. Weddings, small meetings, family reunions and seminars hosted. Antiquing, golf, live theater, parks, shopping, sporting events, tennis and restaurants nearby.

Publicity: *Southern Living and Cover Victorian Homes.*

Laurel Hill Bed and Breakfast

1992 McLendon Ave.
Atlanta, GA 30307
(404)377-3217 Fax:(404)377-0756
E-mail: dhinman@bellsouth.neet
Web: www.laurelhillbandb.com

Circa 1920. Two English Tudor-style cottages from the 1920s have been combined and meticulously restored in this historic Lake Claire neighborhood, just four miles from downtown. Classic period furnishings are accented by bold contemporary wall colors to create an ambiance that blends the best of yesterday and today. Luxurious guest suites enhance relaxation and romance. Dave is a fully trained chef and makes breakfast a scrumptious delight. Savor afternoon tea on Saturdays and Sundays. Meander along walking paths on the tranquil grounds with landscaped sitting areas. The scenic hilltop setting overlooks native Georgia oaks, pines and laurels. Bikes are available to explore this picturesque area. Decatur town square is just two miles away.

Historic Interest: Located in historic Lake Claire.

Innkeeper(s): Dave Hinman. $80-150. 5 suites. Breakfast and snacks/refreshments included in rates. Types of meals: Full bkfst and veg bkfst. Beds: KQ. Data port, cable TV, VCR, reading lamp, stereo, ceiling fan, clock radio, telephone, turn-down service, voice mail and two with hot tub/spa in room. Central air. Fax, copier, spa, bicycles, parlor games, fireplace and laundry facility on premises. Weddings, small meetings, family reunions and seminars hosted. Antiquing, art galleries, bicycling, golf, hiking, live theater, museums, parks, shopping, sporting events and tennis nearby.

Augusta   D8

The Azalea Inn

312-334 Greene St
Augusta, GA 30901
(706)724-3454 (877)292-5324 Fax:(706)724-1033
E-mail: azaleabnb@aol.com
Web: www.theazaleainn.com

Circa 1895. Three tastefully restored Victorian homes comprise the Azalea Inn, located in the Olde Town Historic District. Elegantly furnished suites with 11-foot ceilings also offer fireplaces and large whirlpool tubs. Breakfast is delivered to your room in a basket. The inn is within walking distance to the Riverwalk on the Savannah River, fine restaurants, museums, antique shops and unique boutiques.

Innkeeper(s): David Tremaine, Andrew Harney. $99-179. 21 rooms with PB, 13 with FP and 4 suites. Types of meals: Cont plus. Beds: KQ. Cable TV, reading lamp, refrigerator, ceiling fan, clock radio, telephone, desk, whirlpool tubs and suites with glassed in sunporches in room. Air conditioning. Fax and fireplace on premises. Limited handicap access. Small meetings and family reunions hosted. Antiquing, fishing, golf, live theater, parks, shopping, sporting events, tennis, water sports and historic sites nearby.

Publicity: *Georgia Journal, Augusta Magazine and S.C. State Newspaper.*

"Third time and loved it!"

The Partridge Inn

2110 Walton Way
Augusta, GA 30904-6905
(706)737-8888 (800)476-6888 Fax:(706)731-0826
E-mail: info@partridgeinn.com
Web: www.partridgeinn.com

Circa 1879. The original structure of this inn was built prior to the Civil War, and it was Morris Partridge who purchased the house in the 1890s and transformed it into an inn. By 1929, the inn had blossomed into a 129-room hostelry with a quarter-mile of porches and balconies. Throughout its history, the inn has hosted prominent personalities, such as senators, actors and even a president. For those on an extended stay, some rooms offer small  kitchens. Guests enjoy use of an on-site swimming pool as well as a nearby health spa. There are plenty of dining options here. The Bar & Grill is a popular spot for lunch or an informal dinner, and often is host to jazz ensembles. Bambu on Hickman is Augusta's sushi serving fusion cafe that has received excellent reviews. Visit the inn's web site for golf and vacation packages.

Innkeeper(s): David Jones. $89-150. 155 rooms with PB, 43 suites and 7 conference rooms. Types of meals: Lunch and room service. Restaurant on premises. Beds: KQD. Cable TV, reading lamp, refrigerator, clock radio, desk, coffeemakers, iron/board, high-speed Internet and roll-in handicap shower in room. Air conditioning. Fax, copier, telephone, swimming pool, two-line phone and airport shuttle on premises. Limited handicap access. Weddings, small meetings, family reunions and seminars hosted. Amusement parks, antiquing, parks, shopping, sporting events, Paine College, Augusta Tech, State University and Medical College of Georgia nearby.

Queen Anne Inn

406 Greene St
Augusta, GA 30901
(706)723-0045 (877)460-0045 Fax:(706)826-7920

Circa 1890. This inviting three-story inn, filled with marble-topped antiques, stained glass windows and working fireplaces offers a special family suite in its handsome turret. Shaded by tall trees, the inn's veranda is a favorite spot for relaxing after returning from the Savannah River Walk, which starts three blocks away. Rooms are furnished with antique beds such as a Second Empire, an ornate Eastlake and a high-backed sleigh bed. The parlors offer fringed Victorian pieces, Oriental carpets and original paintings. Breakfast is continental, or you can walk down the tree-shaded street to a local cafe, which provides Queen Anne guests a full hot breakfast. Evening in-suite dining is available by selecting room service dinners from quality restaurants working with the inn. The family tower suite offers parents with children a chance to enjoy an elegant inn, yet have quiet quarters for themselves and their young children in a special section of the inn. Best of all, your well-traveled schoolteacher/innkeepers can arrange baby-sitting services for families. A shuttle service is offered as well.

Innkeeper(s): Val & Bill Mundell. $69-99. 7 rooms with PB. TV, VCR, fax, bicycles, library, parking and Jacuzzi on premises. Antiquing, bicycling, canoeing/kayaking, golf, hiking, shopping and museums nearby.

Publicity: *Applause.*

"Thank you so much for taking such good care of my husband on his first trip to Augusta."

Blairsville   A4

Misty Mountain Inn & Cottages

4376 Misty Mountain Ln
Blairsville, GA 30512-5604
(706)745-4786 (888)647-8966 Fax:(706)781-1002
E-mail: mistyinn@alltel.net
Web: www.jwww.com/misty

Circa 1890. This Victorian farmhouse is situated on a four-acre compound and also features six mountain-side cottages located in the woods surrounding the inn. There are four spacious guest rooms in the main house with private baths and fireplaces. All

are decorated in country antiques with hand-crafted accessories, quilts and green plants. Two cottages boast antique beds and Jacuzzi tubs. The lofted bedroom cottages can comfortably sleep more than two people, while offering lofted bedrooms, living rooms and eat-in kitchens. Flea markets, festivals, antique craft shops, lakes, waterfalls and hiking trails are located nearby.

Historic Interest: Close to Union County Historic Courthouse, Misty Mountain Train Museum, Blue Ridge Scenic Railway, Young Harris College, Georgia Mountain Fair, Vogel State Park and the Appalachian Trail.

$65-90. 4 rooms with PB, 10 with FP and 6 cottages. Types of meals: Full bkfst and early coffee/tea. Beds: QT. Reading lamp, ceiling fan, clock radio, desk and fireplace & private balcony in room. Air conditioning. Fax, copier and telephone on premises. Limited handicap access. Weddings, small meetings and family reunions hosted. Antiquing, fishing, golf, parks, shopping, water sports and riding nearby.

Blue Ridge   A4

Blue Ridge Inn

477 W First St
Blue Ridge, GA 30513-4582
(706)632-0222 Fax:(706)258-4525
E-mail: blueridgeinn@tds.net
Web: www.blue-ridge-inn.com

Circa 1890. In a scenic mountain setting, this three-story Victorian home known as the Kincaid House, is one of the area's oldest, built in 1890. Recently renovated, the original hand carved woodwork and heartpine floors are beautifully restored. Chat with new friends in the elegant parlor or relax on a porch rocking chair. Stay in one of the guest suites or bed-rooms with a fireplace and antique clawfoot tub. A hearty country breakfast is accompanied by homemade bread and biscuits served in the formal dining room with lace and vintage furnishings. Dogwood and apple trees add shade to the country garden with crape myrtle, flowers and herbs. Visit the Victorian Tea Room and antique shop or the Excursion train depot just one block away in the downtown area. Boat on Lake Blue Ridge or go whitewater rafting on Ocoee River.

Historic Interest: Our home is one of the oldest in Blue Ridge. It was built in 1890, the Kinkaid House.

Innkeeper(s): Rick and Caroline Hanken. $79-99. 7 rooms, 5 with PB, 4 with FP and 2 suites. Breakfast, afternoon tea and snacks/refreshments included in rates. Types of meals: Country bkfst, veg bkfst and early coffee/tea. Beds: KQD. Cable TV, VCR, reading lamp, refrigerator, ceiling fan, snack bar and fireplace in room. Central air. Fax, parlor games and fireplace on premises. Weddings and family reunions hosted. Antiquing, art galleries, bicycling, canoeing/kayaking, fishing, golf, hiking, horseback riding, parks, shopping and The Victorian Tea Room nearby.

Publicity: *Blue Ridge Chamber of Commerce.*

Brunswick   I9

Brunswick Manor

825 Egmont St
Brunswick, GA 31520-7825
(912)265-6889 Fax:(912)265-7879

Circa 1886. Nestled in the heart of historic Old Town Brunswick, this Victorian inn features the original carved-oak staircase, high ceilings and Victorian mantels with beveled mirrors, plus many antique bric-a-brac and period reproductions. Guests may relax on the rockers or antique wicker swing on the columned veranda and enjoy the moss-draped oaks and tall palm trees. A stroll through the gardens leads to the greenhouse, fish pond, fountain, patio and arbor-covered hot tub. The inn boasts a Country Inns/Waverly Fabrics award-winning nautical room. A full, complimentary breakfast is offered each morning and afternoon tea is always a treat.

Historic Interest: Fort Frederica, Coastal Historic Museum, Jekyll Island Historic District.

Innkeeper(s): Claudia & Harry Tzucanow. $80-90. 7 rooms with PB and 3 suites. Breakfast, afternoon tea and snacks/refreshments included in rates. Types of meals: Full gourmet bkfst, early coffee/tea, picnic lunch and gourmet dinner. Beds: QT. Modem hook-up, cable TV, VCR, reading lamp, refrigerator, ceiling fan, snack bar, coffeemaker, desk, robes, sherry, fruit and cheese, mints, antiques and designer linens in room. Central air. Fax, copier, spa, library, parlor games, laundry and laundry facility on premises. Weddings, small meetings, family reunions and seminars hosted. Antiquing, art galleries, beach, bicycling, canoeing/kayaking, fishing, golf, live theater, museums, parks, shopping, tennis, water sports and historic tours nearby.

Publicity: *Southern Homes, Bon Appetit, Country Inns, Brunswick News and PBS.*

"Your great charm and warm hospitality is your legacy. We've never stayed in such a room and house full of such treasures before. We'd say one of the best B&Bs in the country!"

McKinnon House B&B

1001 Egmont St
Brunswick, GA 31520-7554
(912)261-9100 (866)261-9100

Circa 1902. This 1902 Victorian built by lumber magnate L.T. McKinnon, a local naval stores/lumber baron, was once featured in the movie Conrack. Just 10 miles from Fort Frederica, 12 miles from Fort King George, and 10 miles from Christ Church and St. Simon's Light House, the inn is formally landscaped with a Victorian garden on the side. It has 17 Corinthian columns made of Georgia cypress on the exterior and Georgia marble front steps that lead to double front doors with stained glass. Its nine working fireplaces have intricately carved mantelpieces. The home is filled with family heirlooms and antiques from Charleston and New Orleans. Fresh flowers and candles add to the ambiance. Sleep in one of three guest rooms and arise to a breakfast including treats like fresh fruit, gourmet coffee, a hot entrée, side meats and homemade rolls, muffins or biscuits.

Innkeeper(s): Jo Miller. $90-200. 3 rooms with PB, 3 with FP. Breakfast and snacks/refreshments included in rates. Types of meals: Full bkfst. Beds: KDT. Reading lamp and fireplace in room. Central air. TV, VCR, telephone and fireplace on premises. Weddings and family reunions hosted. Antiquing, art galleries, beach, bicycling, canoeing/kayaking, fishing, golf, hiking, live theater, museums, parks, shopping, tennis and water sports nearby.

Publicity: *Conrack.*

Clarkesville   B5

Glen-Ella Springs Hotel

1789 Bear Gap Rd
Clarkesville, GA 30523
(706)754-7295

Circa 1875. Situated just south of the Tallulah Gorge State Park, this renovated hotel listed in the National Register of Historic Places is an outstanding example of early 19th- and 20th-century inns that dotted the state's countryside. Now a premier country inn, relax on a plethora of porches. A great stone fireplace is the focal point of the parlor that is decorated in bright chintzes. Local handcrafted pieces and antiques furnish the guest rooms that feature luxurious private baths. Two suites feature stone fireplaces. Enjoy breakfast and dinner by reservation in the dining room. Bordered by Panther Creek, the grounds include a swimming pool, 17 acres of meadows, flower and herb gardens and original mineral springs.

Historic Interest: Listed in the National Register of Historic Places.

Innkeeper(s): Barrie & Bobby Aycock. $125-200. 16 rooms with PB, 2 with FP and 1 conference room. Types of meals: Full gourmet bkfst and dinner. Restaurant on premises. Beds: KQT. Fax, copier, swimming and telephone on premises. Limited handicap access.

Publicity: *Atlanta, Georgia Journal, Country Inns* and chosen as *"Georgia's Favorite Bed & Breakfast"* by *Georgia Magazine.*

"Quality is much talked about and too seldom found. With you folks it's a given."

Cumberland Island   J9

Greyfield Inn

Grand Avenue
Cumberland Island, GA 32035
(904)261-6408 (888)241-6408 Fax:(904)321-0666

Circa 1900. The Thomas Carnegies built this four-story home on the barrier island of Cumberland Island. Guests seeking seclusion have the advantage of 1,300 private acres on an island most of which has been designated as a National Seashore. Only 300 persons a day are allowed to visit, a stipulation of the National Park Service. The mansion affords elegant dining opportunities and picnics are available. There's an honor bar in the old gun room, and guests enjoy mingling fireside in the living and dining room or out on the swing on the tree shaded porch. Expansive views of the Intracoastal Waterway may be seen from the inn's balcony. All guest rooms are furnished in family antiques and traditional pieces including four-poster beds, high boys and lounge chairs. Enjoy one of the inn's bicycles and tour the island to view wild horses, deer, an occasional bobcat, armadillos and a variety of birds. Hiking in the marshes, beach combing and clam digging are favored activities. Plan on making phone calls before arriving on the island since only a radio phone is available.

Innkeeper(s): Zachary Zoul and Beth Fisher. $395-575. 17 rooms, 10 with PB, 7 with FP, 3 suites and 2 cottages. Breakfast, afternoon tea, snacks/refreshments and dinner included in rates. Types of meals: Full gourmet bkfst and early coffee/tea. Restaurant on premises. Beds: KQDT. Reading lamp, ceiling fan, turn-down service, fireplace, robes and iron/ironing board in room. Central air. Fax, swimming, bicycles, library, parlor games, fireplace, gift shop and fishing equipment on premises. Handicap access. Weddings, small meetings, family reunions and seminars hosted. Beach, bicycling, canoeing/kayaking, fishing, hiking and Jeep tour with naturalist nearby.

Publicity: *Southern Living and Atlanta Journal.*

Dahlonega   B4

The Royal Guard Inn

65 S. Park St
Dahlonega, GA 30533-1232
(706)864-1713 (877)659-0739

Circa 1938. Shaded by tall magnolias, a large wraparound veranda accents this Cape Cod-style house, located one block from the town square. Afternoon tea or wine and cheese is offered. A delicious full breakfast is served and includes a variety of dishes including egg casseroles, French toast, waffles, pancakes, fresh fruit and a number of side dishes.

Innkeeper(s): Suzanne & Steve. $95-110. 4 rooms with PB. Breakfast included in rates. Types of meals: Full gourmet bkfst. Beds: Q. Air conditioning. Library, parlor games, fireplace and books on premises. Antiquing, canoeing/kayaking, fishing, golf, hiking, horseback riding, live theater, parks, shopping, tennis, water sports, gold mining/panning and tubing nearby.

Fort Valley   F4

The Evans-Cantrell House

300 College St
Fort Valley, GA 31030-3742
(478)825-0611 (888)923-0611 Fax:(478)822-9925
E-mail: evanscantrell@yahoo.com
Web: www.bbonline.com/ga/evanscantrell/

Circa 1916. Innkeepers Norman and Cyriline Cantrell are only the second residents of this majestic home, which was constructed by A.J. Evans, who built an empire reaching into agriculture, commerce and finance. The Italian Renaissance Revival-style architecture with two covered porches is the perfect package for what guests discover inside. Brightly painted walls, traditional furnishings and glorious woodwork create an atmosphere reminiscent of early America. The dining room boasts the table and chairs that were built originally for the home. A beautiful mahogany-stained staircase leads up to the guest rooms, each of which is named for one of A.J. Evans' children. The innkeepers are happy to accommodate special culinary needs during the breakfast service. The inn is a 1995 recipient of the Georgia Historic Preservation Award.

Historic Interest: The Evans-Cantrell House is located in Fort Valley's Everett Square Historic District, and innkeepers will provide guests with a walking tour map. Historic Macon, Indian mounds, P.O.W. memorial to all wars and Andersonville's National Memorial is about 35 minutes away.

Innkeeper(s): Norman & Cyriline Cantrell. $85-105. 4 rooms with PB and 1 suite. Breakfast, afternoon tea and snacks/refreshments included in rates. Types of meals: Full bkfst, veg bkfst and early coffee/tea. Beds: QD. Cable TV, reading lamp, ceiling fan, clock radio, telephone, turn-down service, desk and non-working fireplace in room. Central air. TV, VCR, fax, library and parlor games on premises. Amusement parks, antiquing and shopping nearby.

Publicity: *Georgia Journal and Macon.*

"Award Winning! We must get your efforts a Georgia Trust Award!! Keep up the good work!!!"

Gainesville   C4

Dunlap House

635 Green St N W
Gainesville, GA 30501-3319
(770)536-0200 (800)276-2935 Fax:(770)503-7857

Circa 1910. Located on Gainesville's historic Green Street, this inn offers 9 uniquely decorated guest rooms, all featuring period furnishings. Custom-built king or queen beds and remote-controlled cable TV are found in all of the rooms, several of which have romantic fireplaces. Guests may help themselves to coffee, tea and light refreshments in the inn's common area. Breakfast may be enjoyed in guests' rooms or on the picturesque veranda, with its comfortable wicker furniture. Road Atlanta, Mall of Georgia, Lake Lanier, Brenau University, Riverside Academy and the Quinlan Art Center are nearby.

Innkeeper(s): David & Karen Peters. $85-155. 9 rooms with PB, 2 with FP. Breakfast and snacks/refreshments included in rates. Types of meals: Full bkfst and early coffee/tea. Beds: KQ. Cable TV, reading lamp, clock radio, telephone, desk, laptop computer and phone hook-up in room. Air conditioning. TV and copier on premises. Limited handicap access. Weddings, small meetings and family reunions hosted. Antiquing, fishing, golf, live theater, parks, shopping, water sports, Road Atlanta Racing and Lake Lanier nearby.

Publicity: *Southern Living, Atlanta Journal Constitution, Country Inns and North Georgia Journal.*

Hamilton   F2

Magnolia Hall B&B

127 Barnes Mill Rd
Hamilton, GA 31811
(706)628-4566
E-mail: kgsmag@juno.com
Web: www.magnoliahallbb.com

Circa 1890. Fancy gingerbread trim decorates the wide veranda of this two-story Victorian settled in an acre of magnolias and century-old hollies, near the courthouse. Heart-pine floors, tall ceilings, antiques, a grand piano and china, crystal and silver service for breakfast, set the mood for a gracious inn stay. One of the house specialties is Baked Georgia Croissant with fresh peaches and toasted almonds. It's ten miles to Callaway Gardens and 20 miles to Warm Springs.

Innkeeper(s): Dale & Kendrick Smith. $105-125. 5 rooms with PB and 2 suites. Breakfast and snacks/refreshments included in rates. Types of meals: Full gourmet bkfst and early coffee/tea. Beds: QT. Cable TV, VCR, reading lamp, clock radio, turn-down service, desk and refreshments in room. Air conditioning. Parlor games, telephone, fireplace, rockers and porch swing on premises. Limited handicap access. Amusement parks, antiquing, fishing, golf, parks, shopping, sporting events, tennis, water sports, Wild Animal Park and FDR Home nearby.

Publicity: *Victorian Homes, Georgia Journal, Georgia Magazine and National Geographic Traveler.*

Little St. Simons Island   I9

The Lodge on Little St. Simons Island

PO Box 21078
Little St. Simons Island, GA 31522-0578
(912)638-7472 (888)733-5774 Fax:(912)634-1811
E-mail: LSSI@mindspring.com
Web: www.LittleStSimonsIsland.com

Circa 1917. Deer roam freely and birds soar over 10,000 acres of pristine forests, fresh water ponds, isolated beaches and marshland. There are more than 280 species of birds, and guests can enjoy horseback riding on miles of private trails. There are seven miles of isolated beach to enjoy, as well as boating, canoeing, fishing, birdwatching, swimming and naturalist programs. All activities are included in the rates. To ensure solitude and privacy, the innkeepers allow only 30 overnight guests at a time. Full-Island rates, ranging from $7,700 to $8,000 are available. The inn is accessible only by boat. Breakfast, lunch and dinner, served family style, are included in the rates. The Lodge also offers extras such as marsh cruises, oyster roasts, beach picnics and crab boils.

Historic Interest: Fort Frederica National Monument (neighboring island), Fort George (13 miles), Jekyll Island Club and historic district homes of turn-of-the-century millionaires (Jekyll Island).

Innkeeper(s): Bo Taylor. $600-675. 13 rooms with PB, 2 suites and 3 conference rooms. Breakfast, lunch and dinner included in rates. Types of meals: Full bkfst. Beds: KQT. Reading lamp, ceiling fan, suites with fireplace and coffee maker in room. Air conditioning. Fax, copier, swimming, stable, bicycles, telephone, fireplace, boats, interpretive guides, fishing and fishing gear, kayaks and horseback riding on premises. Weddings, small meetings, family reunions and seminars hosted.

Publicity: *Forbes, Conde Nast, Meeting Destinations, Gourmet, Today Show, Great Country Inns, Southern Living, Coastal Living, Andrew Harper's Hideaway Report, Atlanta Good Morning and CNN Travel.*

"The staff is unequaled anywhere."

Lookout Mountain A2

The Chanticleer Inn

1300 Mockingbird Lane
Lookout Mountain, GA 30750
(706)820-2002 (800)4CH-ANTI Fax:(706)820-7976
E-mail: info@stayatchanticleer.com
Web: www.stayatchanticleer.com

Circa 1934. The local mountain stone exteriors of this inn and the surrounding Country French cottages appear much as they did when first built atop this scenic location. Extensive interior renovations provide modern comfort and technology. Relax by the fire in the large living room and watch a video. An outdoor pool beckons the more active-minded. Hardwood floors, English antiques and a country theme create a pleasant ambiance. Gracious guest bedrooms and suites, some that can be adjoining and several with fireplaces, whirlpool tubs, air and heat controls. Savor a hot Southern-style buffet breakfast. Enjoy five acres of landscaped grounds, patios with benches and a swimming pool.

Innkeeper(s): Kirby & Judy Wahl. $99-279. 17 rooms with PB, 1 with FP, 4 suites, 5 cottages and 1 conference room. Breakfast and afternoon tea included in rates. Types of meals: Full bkfst and early coffee/tea. Beds: KQD. Cable TV, VCR, reading lamp, refrigerator, ceiling fan, clock radio, telephone, desk, hot tub/spa, voice mail, fireplace and down mattresses in room. Air conditioning. Fax, copier, swimming, parlor games, fireplace and historic house that is now a wedding and banquet facility with full catering that is located across the street on premises. Weddings, small meetings, family reunions and seminars hosted. Antiquing, art galleries, bicycling, canoeing/kayaking, fishing, golf, hiking, museums, parks, shopping, sporting events, tennis and spa nearby.

Publicity: *Lookout Mountain Mirror, Chattanooga Times Free Press, Blue Ridge Country Magazine, Southern Living Magazine, Memphis Sentinel, Chattanooga Convention and Visitors Bureau Publication.*

Marietta C3

Sixty Polk Street, A B&B

60 Polk St
Marietta, GA 30064-2349
(770)419-1688 (800)845-7266 Fax:(770)590-7959

Circa 1872. This French Regency Victorian has been completely restored. Period antiques decorate the rooms. Guests are encouraged to enjoy the library or relax in the parlor. Afternoon treats are served in the dining room, and guests are treated to a hearty Southern breakfast. Marietta offers an abundance of antique stores, restaurants and museums, as well as a delightful town square. The inn is just 30 minutes from Atlanta.

Historic Interest: Sixty Polk Street is within walking distance of the Marietta Square and Northwest Marietta Historic District. Kennesaw Mountain National Battlefield and Confederate and national cemeteries also are found in the area.
Innkeeper(s): Joe & Glenda Mertes. $95-175. 4 rooms with PB, 1 with FP and 1 suite. Breakfast included in rates. Types of meals: Full bkfst. Beds: KQ. Telephone on premises. Antiquing, golf and live theater nearby.

Publicity: *North Georgian Journal and Victorian Homes Magazine.*

"Better than dreamed of."

Whitlock Inn

57 Whitlock Ave
Marietta, GA 30064-2343
(770)428-1495 Fax:(770)919-9620

Circa 1900. This cherished Victorian has been restored and is located in a National Register Historic District, one block from the Marietta Square. Amenities even the Ritz doesn't provide

are in every room, and you can rock on the front verandas. An afternoon snack also is served. There is a ballroom grandly suitable for weddings and business meetings.

Historic Interest: Kennesaw Mountain Battlefield & Civil War National Park (3 miles), numerous historic homes, several from Civil War era (within 6 blocks).
Innkeeper(s): Alexis Edwards. $100-125. 5 rooms with PB and 3 conference rooms. Breakfast included in rates. Types of meals: Cont plus. Beds: KQT. Cable TV, reading lamp, ceiling fan, clock radio, telephone and desk in room. Air conditioning. Fax and copier on premises. Weddings, small meetings, family reunions and seminars hosted. Amusement parks, antiquing, live theater, parks, shopping and sporting events nearby.

Publicity: *Marietta Daily Journal.*

"This is the most beautiful inn in Georgia and I've seen nearly all of them."

Mountain City A5

The York House

PO Box 126
Mountain City, GA 30562-0126
(706)746-2068 (800)231-9675 Fax:(706)746-0210
E-mail: yorkhouse@alltel.net

Circa 1851. Bill and Mollie York opened The York House as an inn in 1896, and it has operated continuously ever since. Two stories of shaded verandas overlook tall hemlocks, Norwegian spruce, lawns and mountains. Adjacent to the Old Spring House is a stand of pines that provides a romantic setting for weddings.

Breakfast is carried to the room each morning on a silver tray, and each room is plumbed with natural spring water.

Historic Interest: National Register.
Innkeeper(s): Al & Edie Wiggirs. $69-129. 13 rooms with PB, 1 with FP and 1 conference room. Breakfast included in rates. Types of meals: Full gourmet bkfst, veg bkfst and early coffee/tea. Beds: KQD. Cable TV, VCR, reading lamp, stereo, refrigerator, ceiling fan, clock radio, telephone and coffeemaker in room. Central air. Fax, stable, parlor games, fireplace, shuffleboard, badminton and croquet on premises. Limited handicap access. Weddings, small meetings and family reunions hosted. Antiquing, art galleries, canoeing/kayaking, downhill skiing, fishing, golf, hiking, horseback riding, live theater, museums, parks, shopping, tennis, water sports and wineries nearby.

Publicity: *Blue Ridge Country and Mountain Review.*

Palmetto C6

Serenbe Bed & Breakfast

10950 Hutcheson Ferry Rd
Palmetto, GA 30268-2233
(770)463-2610 Fax:(770)463-4472
E-mail: steve@serenbe.com
Web: www.serenbe.com

Circa 1905. Enjoy a truly unique experience at this 800-acre farm in rural Georgia. Choose from a variety of accommodations, such as a lake house with large, screened porch or a converted 1930s horse barn. Over 100 farm animals provide an interactive experience for children, from feeding goats and holding rabbits, to gathering eggs and visiting with cows, pigs and horses. Families can enjoy a hayride or roast marshmallows over a campfire. Activities for all ages include canoeing, fishing, a hot tub under the stars or a picnic on a granite rock near a waterfall. Rates include a full country breakfast, afternoon southern tea and sweets at bedtime. Just south of Atlanta, many city attractions also are conveniently available.

Innkeeper(s): Steve & Marie Nygren. $140-225. 15 rooms, 12 with PB, 3 cottages and 1 conference room. Breakfast and afternoon tea included in rates. Types of meals: Country bkfst. Beds: KQDT. Reading lamp, ceiling fan and hot tub/spa in room. Central air. TV, VCR, fax, copier, spa, swimming, bicycles, library, child care, parlor games, telephone and fireplace on premises. Handicap access. Weddings, small meetings, family reunions and seminars hosted. Amusement parks, antiquing, art galleries, bicycling, canoeing/kayaking, fishing, golf, hiking, horseback riding and parks nearby.

Publicity: *Country Inns Magazine, I Do Magazine and HGTV.*

Perry   G5

Henderson Village

125 South Langston Circle
Perry, GA 31069-9684
(478)988-8696 (888)615-9722 Fax:(912)988-9009
E-mail: info@hendersonvillage.com
Web: www.hendersonvillage.com

Circa 1838. Experience the southern charm of this country resort that spans 18 bucolic acres just two hours south of Atlanta. Play darts or ping pong in the Game Room and visit the tropical bird aviary. A library offers CDs, books and videos for in-room use. Elegant guest accommodations boast antiques and reproductions, feather beds, terry cloth robes, stereo systems, and turndown service. Many feature gas fireplaces. The Wynne House rooms access a wraparound veranda with a porch swing, wicker chairs and rockers. Most of the suites in the Holland House include Jacuzzi tubs and separate sitting rooms. A central hall parlor and a private porch is appealing in Hodge House. Tenant Cottages provide added privacy and assorted amenities. Breakfast can be delivered to the room or enjoyed in one of the dining rooms of Langston House Restaurant. The swimming pool is open year-round. Fly fishing, biking, walking trails, horseback riding, sporting clays and horse-drawn carriage rides are among the many activities available. The Wimberly Conference Center is perfect for special events.

Innkeeper(s): Heather Bradham. $125-325. 24 rooms, 19 with PB, 18 with FP, 5 suites and 2 conference rooms. Breakfast included in rates. Types of meals: Country bkfst, gourmet lunch, gourmet dinner and room service. Restaurant on premises. Beds: KQT. Cable TV, VCR, reading lamp, stereo, ceiling fan, clock radio, telephone, coffeemaker, turn-down service and fireplace in room. Central air. Fax, copier, bicycles, library, pet boarding, parlor games and fireplace on premises. Weddings, small meetings, family reunions and seminars hosted. Antiquing, art galleries, bicycling, fishing, golf, hiking, horseback riding, live theater, museums, parks, shopping and tennis nearby.

Publicity: *Southern Living, House Beautiful and GPTV.*

Pine Mountain   F3

Chipley Murrah House B&B

207 Harris St
Pine Mountain, GA 31822-1011
(706)663-9801 (888)782-0797

Circa 1895. Completely renovated, this Queen Anne Victorian home features extensive moldings and 12-foot ceilings. The comfortable furnishings tastefully blend distinctive antiques with updated pieces. Relax on swings, rockers and wicker on

the large wraparound porch. Enjoy pure Southern hospitality served with a full breakfast. Accommodations also include a three family cottages with complete kitchen. Visit the Callaway Gardens, only one mile away; walk one block to downtown.

Innkeeper(s): Paul & Donna Haynes. $85-200. 4 rooms with PB and 3 cottages. Breakfast included in rates. Reading lamp, refrigerator, clock radio, desk and claw foot tubs with showers in room. Air conditioning. VCR, fax, parlor games, telephone, fireplace, swimming pool and putting green on premises. Weddings, small meetings and family reunions hosted. Antiquing, fishing, golf, parks, shopping, sporting events, tennis and water sports nearby.

Saint Marys   J9

Spencer House Inn B&B

200 Osborne Street
Saint Marys, GA 31558-8361
(912)882-1872 (888)800-1872 Fax:(912)882-9427
E-mail: info@spencerhouseinn.com
Web: www.spencerhouseinn.com

Circa 1872. A white picket fence surrounds this Victorian era house, painted a pleasant pink with white trim on the wide two-level veranda. The Inn is in the St. Marys' Historic District

and is on the National Register. Heart-pine floors, original moldings and high ceilings are features of the rooms. Carefully selected reproductions, fine antiques, coordinated fabrics and rugs have been combined to create a sunny, fresh decor. There are four-poster beds and clawfoot soaking tubs. Breakfast is buffet style with peaches and cream, bread pudding or frittatas as specialties. The Inn is one block to the ferry to Georgia's largest barrier island, Cumberland Island, with 17 miles of white sand beaches, live oak forests, salt marshes and wild horses. Okefenokee National Wildlife Refuge is 45 minutes away.

Innkeeper(s): Mary & Mike Neff. $100-175. 14 rooms with PB and 1 suite. Breakfast included in rates. Types of meals: Full bkfst, early coffee/tea and picnic lunch. Beds: KQDT. Cable TV, reading lamp, ceiling fan, clock radio, telephone and HBO in room. Air conditioning. Fax, library, parlor games, elevator and limited handicap access on premises. Weddings, small meetings, family reunions and seminars hosted. Antiquing, fishing, golf, shopping, sporting events, Cumberland Island National Seashore, Okefenokee Swamp, Kings Bay Submarine Base and new waterfront park nearby.

Publicity: *Seabreeze and Water's Edge Magazine.*

"I don't see how it could be improved!"

Sautee Nacoochee   B5

The Stovall House

1526 Hwy 255 N
Sautee Nacoochee, GA 30571
(706)878-3355
E-mail: info@stovallhouse.com
Web: www.stovallhouse.com

Circa 1837. This house, built by Moses Harshaw and restored in 1983 by Ham Schwartz, has received two state awards for its restoration. The handsome farmhouse has an extensive wraparound porch providing vistas of 26 acres of cow pastures and mountains. High ceilings, polished walnut woodwork and decorative stenciling provide a pleasant backdrop for the inn's collec-

tion of antiques. Victorian bathroom fixtures include pull-chain toilets and pedestal sinks. The inn has its own restaurant.

Historic Interest: Sautee Nacoochee Arts and Community Center (1 mile), Museum of Indian and local history, Stovall Covered Bridge (1 mile).

Innkeeper(s): Ham Schwartz. $84-92. 5 rooms with PB. Breakfast included in rates. Types of meals: Cont and dinner. Restaurant on premises. Beds: KQDT. Ceiling fan and clock radio in room. Air conditioning. Library, parlor games, telephone and fireplace on premises. Weddings, small meetings and family reunions hosted. Amusement parks, antiquing, fishing, live theater, parks, shopping and water sports nearby.

Publicity: *Atlanta Journal and GPTV - Historic Inns of Georgia.*

"Great to be home again. Very nostalgic and hospitable."

Savannah   G9

17 Hundred 90 Inn

307 e President St
Savannah, GA 31419
(912)236-7122 (800)487-1790 Fax:(912)236-7143
E-mail: innkeeper@17hundred90.com
Web: www.17hundred90.com

Circa 1790. Secluded by Spanish moss-draped oaks in the historic district, Savannah's oldest inn offers a richly wonderful experience. Perfectly restored and decorated in old southern tradition, the original furnishings and Scalamandre fabric will delight antique lovers. All but two of the guest bedrooms feature fireplaces. Amenities include nightly turndown service, a CD player, coffeemaker, mini bar, data ports and TV. A complimentary bottle of wine and a superb breakfast can be delivered to the room or enjoyed downstairs. Listen to Jack Rogers play the piano at the award-winning restaurant that serves lunch and dinner. Hors d'oeuvres are available in the low-key lounge, a favorite place to gather. The sites and attractions of River Street are only four blocks away.

Innkeeper(s): Tena Norrid. $129-169. 14 rooms with PB, 6 with FP and 1 conference room. Breakfast, afternoon tea, hors d'oeuvres and wine included in rates. Beds: KQ. Modem hook-up, cable TV, VCR, reading lamp, refrigerator, clock radio, telephone, turn-down service, desk, hot tub/spa, voice mail and fireplace in room. Air conditioning. Fax, copier, spa, library and V Library on premises. Handicap access. Antiquing, art galleries, beach, bicycling, canoeing/kayaking, fishing, golf, hiking, horseback riding, live theater, museums, parks, shopping, water sports and wineries nearby.

The Azalea Inn

217 E Hungtingdon St
Savannah, GA 31401
(912)236-6080 (800)582-3823 Fax:(912)236-0127
E-mail: info@azaleainn.com
Web: www.azaleainn.com

Circa 1889. A prominent Savannah resident who served as a captain in the state militia and was a member of the Cotton Exchange built Azalea Inn. All of the guest rooms are furnished with a four-poster bed, and two include a whirlpool tub. The spacious Captain's Suite, named to honor the original owner, includes a four-poster canopy bed, sitting area and a private deck. The inn is located in a beautiful residential neighborhood within the historic district and a block and a half east of Forsyth Park.

Innkeeper(s): John McAvoy & Jessie Balentine. $140-260. 9 rooms, 7 with PB. Breakfast included in rates. Types of meals: Full gourmet bkfst. Beds:

KQ. Cable TV, ceiling fan, clock radio, coffeemaker, fireplace, bathrobes, iron and ironing board in room. Central air. Fax, copier, swimming, telephone and fireplace on premises. Weddings, family reunions and seminars hosted. Antiquing, art galleries, beach, bicycling, canoeing/kayaking, fishing, golf, horseback riding, live theater, museums, parks and shopping nearby.

Foley House Inn

14 W Hull St
Savannah, GA 31401-3903
(912)232-6622 (800)647-3708 Fax:(912)231-1218
E-mail: foleyinn@aol.com
Web: www.foleyinn.com

Circa 1896. Moss-draped Chippewa Square, where Forrest Gump waited for the bus with his box of chocolates, is the backdrop for this elegant townhouse mansion. Tastefully furnished with English, French and American antiques, this Victorian inn offers Southern hospitality and European charm. The magnificent double parlor boasts a graceful comfort amidst treasured pieces. A video library provides a variety of movies. Guest bedrooms feature canopied and four-poster beds. Most include gas fireplaces, and some have oversize whirlpool baths and private balconies. Enjoy a delicious hot and cold breakfast as well as sweet and savory treats with afternoon tea. Relax in one of the two delightful courtyards. The inn is located in the heart of the historic district, making it an easy stroll to theaters, symphony, art galleries, antique stores and restaurants. The staff will gladly make tour and dinner reservations.

Innkeeper(s): Beryl and Don Zerwer. $215-345. 18 rooms with PB, 14 with FP, 3 suites and 1 conference room. Breakfast, afternoon tea and snacks/refreshments included in rates. Types of meals: Full gourmet bkfst, early coffee/tea and room service. Beds: KQD. TV, VCR, telephone, turn-down service, Jacuzzi, private balcony and fireplace in room. Air conditioning. Fax, copier, library, fireplace, laundry facility, gift shop, evening hot and cold hors d'oeuvres, afternoon tea and sweets, data ports, film library, concierge service, health club access and day spa services on premises. Small meetings and family reunions hosted. Antiquing, art galleries, beach, bicycling, fishing, golf, live theater, museums, parks, shopping, sporting events, tennis, deep-sea fishing and Atlantic Ocean beaches nearby.

Publicity: *The Discerning Traveler and Travel Holiday Magazine (2001).*

"Our stay was wonderful due to the warmth and friendliness of the staff and no request was too much trouble."

The Granite Steps

126 E Gaston St
Savannah, GA 31401
(912)233-5380 Fax:(912)236-3116
E-mail: info@granitesteps.com
Web: www.granitesteps.com

Circa 1881. Aptly named for its majestic granite double curved entry steps, this magnificent Italianate mansion graces the National Historic Landmark District. Meticulously restored, renovated and redecorated, the original hardwood and marble floors are enhanced by fourteen-foot ceilings. Gather for afternoon wine and hors d'oeuvres in the double parlor highlighting twin mirrors above two marble fireplaces and play an antique rosewood Chickering piano. Relax on wicker furnishings in the bright and airy sunroom. Borrow a book or watch TV in the library. Luxurious guest bedrooms and suites boast an assortment of amenities that may include a Jacuzzi, fireplace, balcony, canopy, six-poster or sleigh bed and a private entrance. A gourmet breakfast is served daily in the opulent dining room. Elegant surroundings, Southern hospitality and distinguished service make this inn a perfect place for special events.

Innkeeper(s): Donna Sparks/Mary Strickler. $275-500. 7 rooms with PB, 7 with FP, 5 suites and 1 conference room. Breakfast, afternoon tea and snacks/refreshments included in rates. Types of meals: Full gourmet bkfst, early coffee/tea and room service. Beds: KQ. Modem hook-up, data port, cable TV, VCR, reading lamp, CD player, refrigerator, snack bar, clock radio, telephone, turn-down service, desk, hot tub/spa and voice mail in room. Central air. Fax, copier, spa, library and fireplace on premises. Limited handicap access. Weddings, small meetings, family reunions and seminars hosted. Antiquing, art galleries, beach, bicycling, canoeing/kayaking, fishing, golf, hiking, horseback riding, live theater, museums, parks, shopping, tennis and water sports nearby.

Publicity: *Savannah Magazine, Atlanta Journal, USA Today and Midnight in the Garden of Good and Evil.*

Planters Inn

29 Abercorn Street
Savannah, GA 31401
(912)232-5678 (800)554-1187 Fax:(800)232-8893
E-mail: planinn@aol.com
Web: www.plantersinnsavannah.com

Circa 1913. Opening onto historic Reynolds Square, this elegant award-winning inn is a boutique-style property with a rich background. Offering intimacy with deluxe service, lavish attention is paid to details. Using the finest fabrics and Baker furnishings, some guest bedrooms boast fireplaces, refrigerators and balconies as well as four-poster rice beds. Overlook the park and bustling Riverfront from the penthouse hospitality suite where continental breakfast is served. An evening wine hour is enjoyed in the impressive lobby. Dinner room service is available from the Olde Pink House next door. Nightly chocolates and turndown service are added delights.

Innkeeper(s): Natalie A. Miller. $115-185. 60 rooms with PB and 1 conference room. Breakfast included in rates. Types of meals: Cont plus and room service. Beds: QT. Modem hook-up, data port, TV, clock radio, telephone, coffeemaker, turn-down service, some with fireplace, refrigerator and balconies in room. Central air. Fax, copier, child care, fireplace and laundry facility on premises. Limited handicap access. Weddings, small meetings and family reunions hosted. Antiquing, art galleries, beach, bicycling, canoeing/kayaking, fishing, golf, live theater, museums, parks, shopping, water sports, fitness center and spa nearby.

The President's Quarters Inn and Guesthouse

225 E President St
Savannah, GA 31401-3806
(912)233-1600 (888)592-1812 Fax:(912)238-0849
E-mail: PQSav@aol.com
Web: www.presidentsquarters.com

Circa 1855. In the heart of Savannah's Historic District, The President's Quarters is comprised of Federal-style townhouses constructed by the W.W. Gordon estate. In 1870 Robert E. Lee paid a call here. Nineteen presidents are thought to have visited Savannah and the rooms at the inn today offer suitable accommodations for such dignitaries. Antique period furnishings, working fireplaces, four-poster rice beds, canopy or carved beds are featured, and the suites boast additional amenities such as balconies, hand-painted ceilings and loft bedrooms. Special services include fruit, afternoon hors d'oeuvres, nightly turndown service with cordials and local sweets and 24-hour

concierge service. Breakfast is served in your room or in the courtyard. River Street is three blocks away.

Historic Interest: Four diamond award winner.

Innkeeper(s): Tina Norrid. $137-250. 19 rooms with PB, 19 with FP and 8 suites. Types of meals: Full bkfst and snacks/refreshments. Beds: KQD. Turn-down service in room. TV, VCR, fax, copier, telephone, data ports and elevator on premises. Limited handicap access.

Publicity: *Country Inns, Southern Homes, London Herald, Working Women and Travel Holiday.*

"President's Quarters was truly a home away from home." - Karl Malden

Savannah's Bed & Breakfast Inn

117 W Gordon St at Chatham Sq
Savannah, GA 31401
(912)238-0518
E-mail: bnbinn@sysconn.com
Web: www.savannahbnb.com

Circa 1853. Across from Chatham Square in the historic district, this bed & breakfast offers an economic choice. Two rowhouses are joined with a back balcony. The air-conditioned garden suites and guest bedrooms are most pleasantly decorated with original artwork and four-poster beds. Enjoy sipping morning coffee in the garden. A delicious breakfast is served in the sunny dining room.

Innkeeper(s): Robert McAlister. $79-140. 13 rooms with PB and 2 suites. Breakfast included in rates. Types of meals: Full bkfst. Beds: QT. Cable TV, reading lamp, ceiling fan, clock radio and telephone in room. Air conditioning. TV on premises. Weddings, small meetings, family reunions and seminars hosted. Antiquing, fishing, golf, live theater, parks and shopping nearby.

Publicity: *New York Times, Chicago Tribune and Atlanta Constitution.*

"Enjoyed it tremendously. Food was good and service gracious."

Sonja's RSVP B&B Reservation Service of Savannah

611 E 56th St
Savannah, GA 31405
(912)232-7787 (800)729-7787 Fax:(912)353-8060

Circa 1848. Stay at one of 15 small inns with under ten rooms, a two-bedroom townhouse, carriage house or garden suite that are all available through this free reservation service. The inns are owner-operated and selected for their location in the historic district, southern charm and hospitality. Amenities include off-street parking, whirlpool baths, antique furnishings, breakfast, afternoon wine and refreshments. Several offer handicapped access and accept children and small pets. Call Sonja's Monday through Friday from 9:30 to 5:00 for help in selecting the perfect inn.

Innkeeper(s): Sonja Lazzaro. Call for rates. 250 rooms with PB. Breakfast and afternoon tea included in rates. Types of meals: Full bkfst, early coffee/tea and snacks/refreshments. Beds: KQDT. Cable TV, VCR, reading lamp, CD player, refrigerator, snack bar, telephone, coffeemaker, many with fireplace and some will accept small pets in room. Central air. Fax, pet boarding, fireplace and laundry facility on premises. Limited handicap access. Art galleries, museums and shopping nearby.

William Kehoe House

123 Habersham St
Savannah, GA 31401-3820
(912)232-1020 (800)820-1020 Fax:(912)231-0208
E-mail: classmanagement@aol.com
Web: www.williamkehoehouse.com

Circa 1892. A wealthy Irish businessman built this Renaissance Revival manor. The interior has been impeccably restored and decorated in Victorian style with antiques, reproductions and original artwork. In
honor of the original owner, the individually decorated guest rooms are named for a county in Ireland. Each day begins with a gourmet, Southern-style breakfast. Fresh fruit, and home-baked breads accompany such entrees  as eggs Savannah, bacon, grits and potatoes. The staff is always happy to assist guests and can direct you to fine restaurants, shops and attractions in the Savannah area.

$205-345. 14 rooms with PB, 2 suites and 2 conference rooms. Breakfast and snacks/refreshments included in rates. Types of meals: Full gourmet bkfst, early coffee/tea and afternoon tea. Beds: KQT. Cable TV, reading lamp, ceiling fan, clock radio, telephone, turn-down service and desk in room. Air conditioning. Fax, copier and hors d'oeuvres on premises. Limited handicap access. Small meetings hosted. Antiquing, fishing, live theater, parks, shopping and water sports nearby.

Publicity: *Hideaway, Atlanta Homes & Lifestyles, Discerning Traveler and Romantic Inns of America.*

Statesboro   G8

Historic Statesboro Inn

106 S Main St
Statesboro, GA 30458-5246
(912)489-8628 (800)846-9466 Fax:(912)489-4785
E-mail: frontdesk@statesboro.com
Web: www.statesboroinn.com

Circa 1904. Visitors to the Georgia Southern University area often seek out this inn, a turn-of-the-century Neoclassical/Victorian home with 15 guest rooms, all beautifully furnished and featuring special amenities such as fireplaces, whirlpool baths or screened porches. The unique architecture includes bay windows, multiple gables and Tuscan columns, beautifully detailed woodwork and ceilings. It is believed Blind Willie wrote the song "Statesboro Blues" in the Hattie Holloway Cabin on the grounds. Special dinner parties, receptions and conferences may be accommodated.

Historic Interest: First house in Statesboro wired for electricity. The Brannen house on the property is the oldest house in Statesboro built in 1881. The Hatty-Holloway cabin used to house owners staff was the house of the famous blues guitarist Blind Willie McTell who wrote Statesboro Blues made famous by the Allman Brothers Band.
Innkeeper(s): Tony and Michele Garges, John and Melissa Armstrong. $85-130. 16 rooms with PB, 2 with FP, 1 suite and 2 conference rooms. Breakfast included in rates. Types of meals: Country bkfst, veg bkfst, picnic lunch, snacks/refreshments, gourmet dinner and room service. Restaurant on premises. Beds: KQD. Modem hook-up, data port, cable TV, VCR, reading lamp, refrigerator, ceiling fan, clock radio, telephone, coffeemaker, desk, voice mail and fireplace in room. Central air. Fax, copier, library, pet boarding, par-

lor games, fireplace, laundry facility and gift shop on premises. Limited handicap access. Weddings, small meetings, family reunions and seminars hosted. Antiquing, fishing, golf, hiking, live theater, museums, parks, shopping, sporting events and two state parks nearby.

Thomasville   J4

1884 Paxton House Inn

445 Remington Ave
Thomasville, GA 31792-5563
(229)226-5197 Fax:(229)226-9903
E-mail: 1884@rose.net
Web: www.1884paxtonhouseinn.com

Circa 1884. The picturesque residential neighborhood in the renowned Plantation Region is the perfect setting for this award-winning, historic Gothic Victorian Landmark Home, listed in the National Register. Unique architecture, a grand circular staircase, 12 ornamental fireplaces, 13-foot ceilings, heart-pine floors, a courting window and nine-foot doors reflect remarkable craftsmanship. Museum-quality reproductions, classic antiques, designer fabrics and international collections impart an 18th-century style. Luxurious suites and garden cottages offer upscale amenities that include Egyptian bath towels, terry robes, data ports and sound spas. Breakfast is served with settings of fine china and silver. Indulge in family recipes passed down by generations of Southern chefs. Rock on the wraparound veranda, swim in the indoor lap pool or take a moonlit stroll through the gardens.

Innkeeper(s): Susie M. Sherrod. $155-350. 9 rooms with PB, 3 suites and 2 cottages. Breakfast, afternoon tea and snacks/refreshments included in rates. Types of meals: Full gourmet bkfst, veg bkfst and early coffee/tea. Beds: KQ. Data port, cable TV, VCR, reading lamp, refrigerator, ceiling fan, clock radio, telephone, coffeemaker, turn-down service, desk, hot tub/spa, wet bar (some rooms), private baths with tub/shower (all suites and rooms), iron and ironing board, sound spa, hair dryer, terry robes, goose-down pillows and full-length mirror in room. Central air. Fax, copier, spa, swimming, library, parlor games, fireplace, computer center, lap pool, gift shop, VCR, phone, 2 computer centers for guests with fiber optic connection, lemonade social and teas available by reservation only and $15 per person 12 and older on premises. Small meetings hosted. Amusement parks, antiquing, art galleries, bicycling, fishing, golf, horseback riding, live theater, museums, parks, shopping, sporting events and tennis nearby.

Publicity: *Fodor's* (named the South's and America's "Best" B&B Inn), *Frommer's* (Four Flags), *Southern Living, Travel and Leisure, Georgia Journal* ("Best B&B Inn" in the Plantation region of Georgia), *American Automobile Association, Times Picayune* ("Special Inns of the Southeast"), *The Sun* ("provides us with a true glimpse of Southern living"), *St. Louis Times* ("the charm of the 1800s still attracts visitors to Thomasville...[Susie Sherrod's] efforts result in a spectacular variety of blossoms") and on *WALB* television.

Dawson Street Inn

324 N. Dawson Street
Thomasville, GA 31792
(229)226-7515 Fax:(229)226-7570

Circa 1856. Steeped in history, this antebellum home, known as the Ephraim G. Ponder House, is listed in the National Register. Meticulous renovations showcase original details including two grand staircases, 12-foot ceilings, plaster medallions, woodwork, crown moldings and 10 fireplaces. Period furniture highlights the parlor and formal living room. Elegant suite-size guest bedrooms feature antique sleigh, four-poster brass and rice beds. Wicker furnishings accent sitting areas. Tropical fruit bowls, hot baked goods, eggs Benedict, French toast strata, clafouti or Southwest quiche are some of the delights served for breakfast in the dining room. Take a refreshing swim in the pool. The Charleston-style grounds instill a relaxed feeling with old brick, stone walls, iron gates, lush lawn, magnolias, boxwoods, azaleas and dogwoods.

Innkeeper(s): Daniel & Alice (Randy) Mitchell. $125-135. 6 rooms with PB, 6 with FP. Breakfast included in rates. Types of meals: Full gourmet bkfst, veg bkfst and early coffee/tea. Beds: KQD. Cable TV and ceiling fan in room. Air conditioning. Fax, copier, swimming, parlor games, telephone and fireplace on premises. Amusement parks, antiquing, art galleries, beach, canoeing/kayaking, fishing, golf, hiking, horseback riding, live theater, museums, parks, shopping and tennis nearby.

Melhana The Grand Plantation

301 Showboat Lane
Thomasville, GA 31792
(229)226-2290 (888)920-3030 Fax:(229)226-4585
E-mail: info@melhana.com
Web: www.melhana.com

Circa 1825. More than 50 acres surround the historic Melhana Plantation comprised of 30 buildings including the manor, The Hibernia Cottage and a village. There are 30 buildings, all in the National Register. Traditional décor includes furnishings and amenities such as king- and queen-size four-poster beds, desks, paintings, puffy down comforters and handmade duvets. Some accommodations offer marble Jacuzzis and veranda entrances. Most include views of expansive green lawns, the Avenue of Magnolias, camellia gardens, the sunken garden or the plantation's pasture land. The inn's elegantly appointed restaurant has received acclaims from prestigious critics for its Southern cuisine, enhanced by herbs garnered from private kitchen gardens. To fully enjoy the plantation, consider arranging for horseback riding, quail hunting or a carriage ride, but be sure to allow time to linger on the veranda or to enjoy the indoor swimming pool, theater and fitness center.

Historic Interest: During his visit in 1895, Presidential Candidate McKinley was quoted by the reporters of the Thomasville Times Enterprise to say that the skies of Thomasville, Georgia were as blue and as clear as those of Italy. Indeed President McKinley made much of Thomasville's genteel hospitality, piney woods and beautiful spring season, characteristics which may have been forgotten by socialites and travelers over the course of the century, but certainly have not faded. Melhana Plantation Resort elegantly recreates the luxurious lifestyle enjoyed by those who came to Thomasville at the turn of the century in search of days filled with recreation, hunting, sport and leisure. The beautifully restored plantation offers its guests a taste of an era of luxury long past. Visitors to Melhana will be overwhelmed by the peaceful elegance of this historic 1825 plantation, now reborn as a unique plantation.

Innkeeper(s): Charlie & Fran Lewis. $285-450. 38 rooms, 37 with PB, 14 suites, 2 cottages and 3 conference rooms. Breakfast, afternoon tea and snacks/refreshments included in rates. Types of meals: Full gourmet bkfst, gourmet lunch, picnic lunch, gourmet dinner and room service. Restaurant on premises. Beds: KQ. Data port, cable TV, clock radio, telephone, turn-down service, desk, hot tub/spa and voice mail in room. Central air. Fax, copier, swimming, tennis, library, parlor games, fireplace and laundry facility on premises. Weddings, small meetings, family reunions and seminars hosted. Antiquing, art galleries, beach, canoeing/kayaking, fishing, golf, horseback riding, live theater, parks, tennis, hunting and sporting adventures nearby.

Serendipity Cottage

339 E Jefferson St
Thomasville, GA 31792-5108
(229)226-8111 (800)383-7377 Fax:(229)226-2656
E-mail: goodnite@rose.net
Web: www.serendipitycottage.com

Circa 1906. Gracing a serene, residential historic district, this bed & breakfast inn is only three blocks from award-winning downtown. The house has been restored for utmost comfort and relaxation and is furnished with antiques and collectibles. Each pampering guest bedroom offers generous amenities that include an iron, VCR, hair dryer, phone, cable TV, data port, robes, sound spa and turndown service with chocolates. Sip an early-morning hot beverage before savoring a multi-course breakfast served on the sun porch that overlooks the garden. Ask for a wake-up call, if needed. Homemade cookies, cream sherry and soft drinks provide pleasurable treats.

Innkeeper(s): Kathy & Ed Middleton. $100-135. 4 rooms with PB, 2 with FP. Breakfast included in rates. Types of meals: Full bkfst and early coffee/tea. Beds: QD. Cable TV, VCR, reading lamp, refrigerator, ceiling fan, clock radio, telephone, turn-down service and complimentary sherry in room. Air conditioning. Bicycles, parlor games and fireplace on premises. Antiquing, fishing, live theater, parks, shopping, sporting events and plantation tours nearby.

"Thank you for the wonderful weekend at Serendipity Cottage. The house is absolutely stunning and the food delicious."

Hawaii

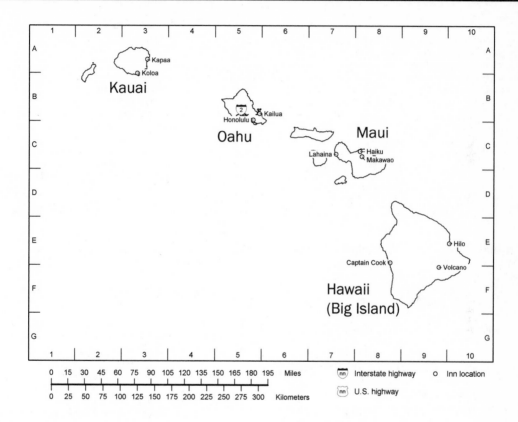

Miles: 0 15 30 45 60 75 90 105 120 135 150 165 180 195

Kilometers: 0 25 50 75 100 125 150 175 200 225 250 275 300

[nn] Interstate highway   o Inn location

[nn] U.S. highway

Hawaii (Big Island)

Captain Cook   E8

Affordable Hawaii At Pomaika'I

83-5465 Mamalahoa Hwy
Captain Cook, HI 96704-8303
(808)328-2112 (800)325-6427 Fax:(808)328-2255

Circa 1932. Experience ecotourism at this Japanese Hawaiian bed & breakfast on four acres. A century-old working Kona coffee/macadamia nut farm, the lush surroundings include tropical fruit, exotic flowers and birds. Stay in the guest bedroom of the restored farmhouse with private bath. Enjoy use of videos, games and a library. The light and airy Greenhouse Rooms are in the large addition with a private entrance behind the house. Ideal for families or honeymooners, secluded island living is found in the Coffee Barn, with an outdoor hot water shower. Breakfast is a delicious meal with a daily special and homemade jam, jellies and breads. Overlook Keei Bay and the Pacific Ocean from the large lanai.

Historic Interest: Century old Japanese Hawaiian coffee/macadamia nut farm. Farmhouse is one of the oldest in area (1932).

Innkeeper(s): Nita Isherwood & Pomaika'i Coulon. $60-75. 4 rooms with PB. Breakfast included in rates. Types of meals: Country bkfst. Beds: QD. Reading lamp, ceiling fan and clock radio in room. TV, VCR, fax, copier and laundry facility on premises. Weddings, small meetings, family reunions and seminars hosted. Art galleries, beach, bicycling, canoeing/kayaking, fishing, golf, hiking, horseback riding, museums, parks, shopping, tennis and water sports nearby.

Publicity: *Best of Both Worlds, Hawaii and A & E.*

Hilo   E10

Maureen's Bed & Breakfast

1896 Kalanianaole Ave
Hilo, HI 96720-4918
(808)935-9018 (800)935-9018 Fax:(808)961-5596
E-mail: info@maureenbnb.com
Web: www.maureenbnb.com

Circa 1932. Known to locals as the Saiki Mansion, named after its original owner, this fully restored home has a baronial ambiance that befits an Aloha experience. The rich blend of redwood and cedar line the 30-foot vaulted living room ceiling, walls, double staircases and wraparound balcony. The Japanese Tea Room is elegant in cherry wood. Antique furnishings made of koa (a precious wood native to Hawaii) as well as mahogany and oak add to the luxury of silk paintings and tapestries. The guest bedrooms boast mountain views of Mauna Kea or the relaxing sounds of ocean surf. A satisfying breakfast includes island specialties with macadamia nuts, tropical fruits and Kona coffee. The koi ponds or botanical gardens with fragrant flowers and colorful plants can be enjoyed from the front and rear lanais. Across the street, a beach park offers swimming.

Innkeeper(s): Maureen Goto. $50-100. 5 rooms with PB. Breakfast included in rates. Types of meals: Full gourmet bkfst and veg bkfst. Beds: KQDT. Ceiling fan and clock radio in room. TV, VCR, fax, library, parlor games, telephone and fireplace on premises. Antiquing, art galleries, beach, bicycling, canoeing/kayaking, fishing, golf, hiking, horseback riding, museums, parks, shopping, tennis, water sports and wineries nearby.

Shipman House Bed & Breakfast Inn

131 Kaiulani St
Hilo, HI 96720-2529
(808)934-8002 (800)627-8447 Fax:(808)934-8002
E-mail: bighouse@bigisland.com
Web: www.hilo-hawaii.com

Circa 1899. Locals know Shipman House as "The Castle," no doubt because of both its size and grandeur. The manor, a mix of Italianate and Queen Anne styles, is listed on both the state and national historic registers. The home's former mistress, Mary Shipman, not only was the granddaughter of a Hawaiian chiefess, but a friend of Queen Lili'uokalani. Jack London and his wife once stayed here for a month as guests of the Shipmans. The grounds still feature many of the plants, palms and flowers nurtured by the Shipmans. Inside, the innkeeper has decorated the home with a mix of antiques and traditional furnishings, many pieces are original to the house. There is a cottage available as well, secluded by trees and foliage. A lavish, continental-plus breakfast buffet is served on the home's lanai, offering such items as homemade granola, local fruit (and there are 20 different varieties of fruit trees on the property), freshly baked breads, homemade passionfruit butter, and pancakes, waffles or French toast. With advance notice.

Innkeeper(s): Barbara & Gary Andersen. $154-209. 5 rooms with PB and 1 cottage. Breakfast and snacks/refreshments included in rates. Types of meals: Cont plus, veg bkfst and early coffee/tea. Beds: QT. Reading lamp, refrigerator, ceiling fan, clock radio, desk, fresh flowers, maps and robes in room. Fax, copier, library, parlor games, telephone, fireplace, botanical garden and views

on premises. Antiquing, beach, bicycling, canoeing/kayaking, downhill skiing, fishing, golf, hiking, live theater, museums, parks, shopping, sporting events, wineries and volcano observatories nearby.

Publicity: *New York Times, Los Angeles Times, Boston Globe, Honolulu Advertiser, Sunset Magazine, Victorian Homes, Wings Magazine, Travel & Leisure, Island Magazine, Hawaii Magazine, PBC documentary on non-resort vacations on Hawaii Island and HGTV.*

Volcano   F9

Aloha Junction Bed & Breakfast

19-4037 Post Office Ln, PO Box 91
Volcano, HI 96785
(808)967-7289 (888)967-7286 Fax:(808)967-7289
E-mail: junction@aloha.net
Web: www.bbvolcano.com

Circa 1927. Sugar mill managers from the Hamakua Coast originally stayed at this plantation retreat home for their vacations. Situated on a little more than an acre of mountain rain forest, the lush surroundings melt away any stress. The rooms are comfortable and large, boasting 10-foot ceilings. A typical tropical breakfast may include a fresh papaya boat filled with bananas and coconut, made-to-order free-range eggs and signature macadamia nut pancakes. Hawaii Volcanoes National Park is less than a mile away. Be sure to visit Green Sand and Black Sand Beaches.

Historic Interest: Built in 1927, this old house was built for the sugar plantation CEOs during their summer holidays. Located just outside the Hawaii Volcanoes National Park.

Innkeeper(s): Robert & Susan Hughes. $75-99. 4 rooms, 1 with PB and 1 suite. Breakfast included in rates. Types of meals: Full bkfst and early coffee/tea. Beds: KQT. Modem hook-up, cable TV and desk in room. VCR, fax, copier, spa, library, parlor games, telephone, fireplace and gift shop on premises. Parks, thermal hot ponds, green sand beach and black sand beach nearby.

Kilauea Lodge

PO Box 116
Volcano, HI 96785-0116
(808)967-7366 Fax:(808)967-7367
E-mail: stay@kilauealodge.com
Web: www.kilauealodge.com

Circa 1938. Guests are pampered at this gorgeous tropical paradise, only a mile from the entrance to Volcanoes National Park. Fluffy towels, towel warmers, robes, cozy, comfortable beds and rich decor create a feeling of warmth and romance in each of the guest rooms. Fresh flowers and original art add to the majesty of the lodge. The wonderful, gourmet meals are served in front of the lodge's historic  Fireplace of Friendship, which is decked with all sorts of artifacts. The innkeepers offer truly memorable meals, praised by such publications as Bon Appetit and Gourmet Magazine. The inn has an interesting history. Built as a YMCA, it later was used during World War II as offices and a military bivouac.

Historic Interest: Historical Hilo Town is 26 miles away and the Volcano Art Center and the original Volcano House, built in the 1890s, are only two miles away.

Innkeeper(s): Lorna & Albert Jeyte. $125-175. 14 rooms with PB, 8 with FP, 3 cottages and 1 conference room. Breakfast included in rates. Types of meals: Full bkfst, dinner and room service. Restaurant on premises. Beds: KQT. Reading lamp, coffeemaker, desk, heaters and heated towel warmers in room. TV, VCR, fax, copier, library, parlor games, telephone, fireplace, gazebo and hot tub on premises. Limited handicap access. Weddings, small meetings, family reunions and seminars hosted. Antiquing, art galleries, beach, bicycling, golf, hiking, live theater, museums, parks, shopping, wineries and volcano viewing nearby.

Publicity: *National Geographic Traveler, Bon Appetit, Pacific Business News and Conde Nast.*

"Your rooms were outstanding both for cleanliness and decor. As to the dinner we had, it was superb, and as far as I'm concerned the best four-course dinner I have ever eaten."

Volcano Inn

19-3820 Old Volcano Highway
Volcano, HI 96785
(808)967-7293 (800)997-2292 Fax:(808)985-7349
E-mail: volcano@volcanoinn.com
Web: www.volcanoinn.com

Circa 1928. If sleeping next to a volcano is on your adventure list, Volcano Inn and its cedar cottages are located on a lush, three-acre spread adjacent to Volcanoes National Park in a rain forest setting. Some of the cottages can sleep five to seven guests, so families and groups are welcome. Among the features are private entrances, fresh flower bouquets, in-room refrigerators, chocolates at check-in and in the afternoon, tea service. Breakfast is served in a light-filled dining room and includes egg dishes, freshly baked breads, poha and ohelo berry jams and cereals. Your hosts will assist you in organizing excursions to Waipio Valley and the Mauna Kea Observatory, or you may wish to go horseback riding or take a helicopter tour.

Historic Interest: The Inn was built in 1928 by the Mist family and was used primarily as a summer house to escape the heat and crowds of city life. We are still researching the finer aspects of construction such as our beautiful wood floors and the lava rock fireplace. However, this is probably one of the first properties to have been established in Volcano.

Innkeeper(s): Joan Prescott-Lighter. $90-130. 8 rooms with PB, 1 suite and 1 cottage. Breakfast and afternoon tea included in rates. Types of meals: Full gourmet bkfst, veg bkfst, early coffee/tea and picnic lunch. Beds: KQDT. Cable TV, VCR, reading lamp, refrigerator, clock radio, coffeemaker, desk, hair dryers and robes in room. Fax, copier, stable, bicycles, library, parlor games, telephone, fireplace, laundry facility, gardens, exercise room, running/walking paths and gift shop on premises. Antiquing, art galleries, beach, bicycling, golf, hiking, horseback riding, live theater, museums, parks, shopping, tennis, wineries and Hawaii Volcanoes National Park nearby.

Kauai

Kapaa A3

Lani-Keha Bed & Breakfast

848 Kamalu Rd
Kapaa, HI 96746
(808)822-1605 (800)821-4898 Fax:(808)822-2429
E-mail: lanikeha@hawaiian.net
Web: www.lanikeha.com

Circa 1948. Against the backdrop of mountains and island beauty, solitude surrounds this plantation home built in the the sugar cane heyday. Sprawling on a three-acre estate of lawns and fruit trees, the tropical decor features rattan furnishings. Pleasant guest bedrooms offer leisurely comfort, with thoughtful fruit baskets. The casual atmosphere extends to the kitchen where breakfast fixings are provided for self-preparation and is open to use for other meals, too. Grove Farm Homestead and Kauai Museum are must-see places to visit.

Innkeeper(s): Karena Biber & Criss Kidder. $65. 3 rooms with PB. Breakfast included in rates. Beds: KT. Cable TV, VCR, reading lamp, ceiling fan, clock radio and desk in room. Fax, library, telephone, fireplace, laundry facility, BBQ and full kitchen use on premises. Art galleries, beach, bicycling, canoeing/kayaking, fishing, golf, hiking, horseback riding, live theater, museums, parks, shopping, sporting events, tennis and water sports nearby.

Koloa B3

Poipu Plantation Resort

1792 Pee Rd
Koloa, HI 96756-9535
(808)742-6757 (800)634-0263 Fax:(808)742-8681
E-mail: plantation@poipubeach.com
Web: www.poipubeach.com

Circa 1938. Just steps away from the ocean in sunny Poipu Beach, this peaceful resort offers accommodations with ocean and garden views. Spacious suites and guest bedrooms in the 1938 Plantation House include a delicious breakfast served in the Lanai Room. Also on this acre of fragrant Hawaiian gardens, vacation rental cottages feature one or two bedrooms, full-size kitchens, air conditioning and private decks. The owner and staff share the spirit of "aloha" and gladly arrange helicopter tours, horseback riding, boating or snorkeling excursions, personalized suggestions for hikes, directions to favorite beaches and other island delights.

Innkeeper(s): Chris Moore. $95-250. 14 rooms, 5 with PB and 9 cottages. Breakfast included in rates. Beds: KQT. TV, VCR, reading lamp, ceiling fan, telephone, some with whirlpool tubs and wet bars in room. Air conditioning. Fax, copier, spa, child care, laundry facility, BBQ and beach supplies on premises. Weddings, small meetings, family reunions and seminars hosted. Golf, hiking, horseback riding, shopping, tennis, snorkeling, surfing, swimming, scuba and gourmet dining nearby.

Maui

Haiku C8

Haikuleana Plantation Inn

555 Haiku Rd
Haiku, HI 96708-5884
(808)575-2890 Fax:(808)575-9177

Circa 1860. A true plantation house, the Haikuleana sits in the midst of pineapple fields and Norfolk pine trees. With high ceilings and a tropical decor, the inn has been licensed  since 1989 and boasts all of the flavor of Hawaiian country life. The porch looks out over exotic gardens. Beaches and waterfalls are nearby.

Innkeeper(s): Ralph H. & Jeanne Elizabeth Blum. $100-150. 3 rooms with PB. Breakfast and snacks/refreshments included in rates. Types of meals: Full gourmet bkfst, veg bkfst and early coffee/tea. Beds: KQT. TV, reading lamp, ceiling fan, clock radio, telephone and hot tub/spa in room. VCR, fax, copier, spa, library and parlor games on premises. Weddings, small meetings, family reunions and seminars hosted. Antiquing, art galleries, beach, bicycling, fishing, golf, hiking, horseback riding, live theater, parks, shopping and water sports nearby.

Publicity: *Honolulu Advertiser, Maui News, Los Angeles Times and Portland Oregonian.*

"Great, great, extra great! Maui is paradise thanks to your daily guidance, directions and helpful hints."

Lahaina   C7

Lahaina Inn

127 Lahainaluna Rd
Lahaina, HI 96761-1502
(808)661-0577 (800)669-3444 Fax:(808)667-9480
E-mail: inntown@lahainainn.com
Web: www.lahainainn.com

Circa 1938. In the center of Old Lahaina Town, this elegant inn is filled with Victorian antiques and inviting decor. Each guest room or spacious parlor suite boasts balconies with exciting views of the harbor or mountains. Romantic antique beds, lamps and Oriental rugs add warmth and luxury to the rooms. There are both ceiling fans and air conditioning. An antique sideboard outside the guest rooms is stocked each morning with steaming Kona coffee, tea, juice, croissants and muffins. The inn has been featured in many articles and newspapers and was named to the list of "Top Ten Romantic Inns" by American Historic Inns.

Historic Interest: A walking tour of this charming Hawaiian town includes such sites as the Baldwin House, Government Market, a courthouse, fort and canal. The Hauola Stone, a stop of the tour, was believed to have been used by Hawaiians as a healing place.

Innkeeper(s): Melinda A Mower. $99-169. 9 rooms and 3 suites. Breakfast included in rates. Types of meals: Cont and early coffee/tea. Restaurant on premises. Beds: KQDT. Stereo, ceiling fan and telephone in room. Air conditioning. Fax, copier and Internet access on premises. Antiquing, beach, golf, shopping, tennis and harbor activities nearby.

Publicity: *Tour & Travel News, Hawaii Magazine, Honolulu, Pacific Business News, Glamour, Travel & Leisure and Conde Nast Traveler.*

"Outstanding lodging and service. Ahhh! Paradise. Fantastic. Excellent. Exquisite."

Makawao   C8

Banyan Tree House

3265 Baldwin Ave
Makawao, HI 96768-9629
(808)572-9021 Fax:(808)573-5072
E-mail: banyan@hawaii-mauirentals.com
Web: www.hawaii-mauirentals.com

Circa 1926. Banyan Tree is composed of three bedrooms in a Hawaiian plantation-style house and four cottages. Ethel Smith Baldwin, a prominent local citizen who served as secretary of the Red Cross and founded a flourishing artist organization, was the most well-known inhabitant of this house. The home was built by the Maui Agricultural Company, of which Baldwin's husband was president. The lush setting includes two acres of gardens, with tree swings and hammocks. Guests in the main house enjoy a full restaurant kitchen. Three of the cottages include kitchenettes, and one has a full kitchen. The house has a full kitchen, spacious living room, fireplace, formal dining room and a lanai with a view of the ocean. It is popular for groups, families and workshops. Tropical Hawaii is the decorating theme throughout the rooms and cottages. Beach activities, galleries, shops and restaurants all are nearby.

Innkeeper(s): Suzy Papanikolas. $85-325. 7 rooms with PB, 1 with FP, 4 cottages and 1 conference room. Beds: QDT. Reading lamp, refrigerator, clock radio, telephone, coffeemaker and desk in room. Fax, copier, spa, swimming, child care, laundry facility, cable TV, VCR, CD player, library, parlor games and fireplace in Plantation House on premises. Small meetings, family reunions and seminars hosted. Antiquing, art galleries, beach, bicycling, canoeing/kayaking, fishing, golf, hiking, horseback riding, live theater, museums, parks, shopping, water sports and wineries nearby.

Oahu

Honolulu   B5

The Manoa Valley Inn

2001 Vancouver Dr
Honolulu, HI 96822-2451
(808)947-6019 Fax:(808)946-6168
E-mail: manoavalleyinn@aloha.net
Web: www.aloha.net/~wery/

Circa 1915. This exquisite home offers the best of two worlds, a beautiful, country home that is also surrounded by a tropical paradise. Each restored room features lavish decor with ornate beds, ceiling fans and period furniture. Little amenities, such as the his and her robes, create a romantic touch. Breakfasts with kona coffee, juices, fresh fruits and baked goods are served. The inn's common rooms offer unique touches. The Manoa Valley is a perfect location to enjoy Hawaii and is only blocks away from the University of Hawaii.

Historic Interest: The Honolulu Art Academy, founded by an early missionary, features a unique architectural mix of Polynesian design and missionary style. The Iolani Place was built by King David Kalakaua and was the home of Hawaiian royalty until the demise of the monarchy in 1893.

Innkeeper(s): Theresa Wery. $99-150. 8 rooms, 5 with PB and 1 cottage. Breakfast included in rates. Types of meals: Cont. Beds: KQD. TV, ceiling fan, telephone and daily maid service in room. Fax, copier, billiard room and iron on premises. Weddings and small meetings hosted. Museums and art museums nearby.

Publicity: *Travel Age, Travel Holiday, Travel & Leisure and LA Style.*

"A wonderful place!! Stepping back to a time of luxury!"

Kailua   B5

Be Back Hawaii All Islands Reservation Service

3429 Kanaina Ave
Kailua, HI 96815
(808)732-6618 (877)4BE-BACK Fax:(808)732-6618
E-mail: beback@lava.net
Web: www.bebackhawaii.com

Circa 1900. Explore the Hawaiian Islands with the help of a personal vacation planner and stay at some of the finest bed & breakfasts each island has to offer, with accommodations ranging from a comfortable guest house to the native adventure of a tree house. Perhaps listening to the waves crash along the warm shore from a beach cottage, or enjoying the privacy of a secluded vacation home depicts the ideal relaxing location. Whatever the taste, guests can experience one or all of the islands with the expertise of Hawaii's knowledgeable Brigitte Baccus, personal travel consultant and Hawaii specialist, who will set up "Island Exploring" stays or offer assistance in choosing the perfect Inn or bed & breakfast to spend an entire vacation. With more than 20 years of experience, Be Back Hawaii offers the magnificence of the islands that everyday tourists so often miss and helps guests discover a new view of the Hawaiian Islands.

Innkeeper(s): Brigitte Baccus. $50-250. Types of meals: Cont plus.

Idaho

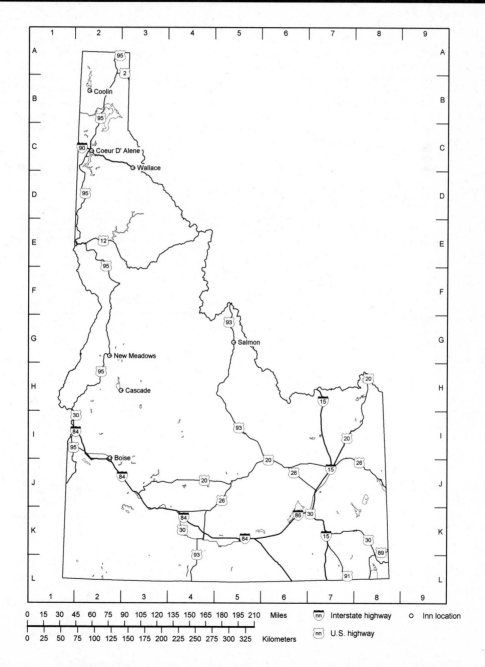

	1	2	3	4	5	6	7	8	9

A

B Coolin

C Coeur D' Alene

Wallace

D

E 12

F

G Salmon

New Meadows

H Cascade

I Boise

J

K

L

| Miles | 0 | 15 | 30 | 45 | 60 | 75 | 90 | 105 | 120 | 135 | 150 | 165 | 180 | 195 | 210 |

0 25 50 75 100 125 150 175 200 225 250 275 300 325   Kilometers

Interstate highway   ○ Inn location

U.S. highway

Boise   I2

A J.J. Shaw House Bed & Breakfast Inn

1411 W Franklin Street
Boise, ID 83702
(208)344-8899 (877)344-8899 Fax:(208)344-6677
E-mail: jjshaw@earthlink.net
Web: www.jjshaw.com

Circa 1907. J.J. Shaw House, a graciously restored Queen
Anne Victorian, was named for its builder, a lumber baron and
one of the founding fathers of Boise. Tastefully decorated rooms
include antiques and special touches, such as the trail of ivy
that adorns the ceiling of Shaw's Retreat. Gertrude's Chamber
includes a four-poster bed and a rose-colored, antique clawfoot
tub encircled by a curtain of lace. In other rooms, guests might
enjoy a jetted tub or a view of the local mountains. Breakfasts
with fresh fruit cups with French creme, stuffed French toast
with blueberry syrup and Canadian bacon provide an excellent
start to your days in Boise. Hyde Park and the Capitol building
are within walking distance. Bogus Basin Ski Resort is just 16
miles from the home.
Historic Interest: Built in 1907 by lumber baron John James Shaw, a Boise
founding father.

Innkeeper(s): Junia Stephens. $79-119. 5 rooms with PB, 1 suite and 1
conference room. Breakfast and snacks/refreshments included in rates. Types
of meals: Full gourmet bkfst. Beds: KQT. Modem hook-up, data port, reading
lamp, refrigerator, ceiling fan, clock radio, telephone, coffeemaker, desk and
jetted tub in room. Air conditioning. Fax, library, parlor games, fireplace and
handmade afternoon treats on premises. Weddings, small meetings, family
reunions and seminars hosted. Antiquing, art galleries, bicycling,
canoeing/kayaking, cross-country skiing, downhill skiing, fishing, golf, hiking,
horseback riding, live theater, museums, parks, shopping, sporting events,
tennis, water sports and wineries nearby.

Publicity: *Idaho Statesman, Idaho State Journal, Touched by an Angel, Idaho
Statesman News, Channel 7 "Eye on Idaho" and Sunset Magazine.*

Idaho Heritage Inn

109 W Idaho St
Boise, ID 83702-6122
(208)342-8066 Fax:(208)343-2325
Web: www.idheritageinn.com

Circa 1904. This Colonial Revival home, set back on a tree-
lined street near downtown, was once the home of Senator
Frank Church and is in the National Register. Because of its
location in the historic Warm Springs district, geothermal water
is used for heating and bathing. Period furnishings and wall

coverings are found
throughout. Bicycles are
available for enjoying the
nearby greenbelt, which
winds along the Boise
River.

Innkeeper(s): Betti & Craig Newburn. $75-115. 6 rooms with PB, 3 suites
and 1 cottage. Breakfast included in rates. Types of meals: Full gourmet bkfst
and early coffee/tea. Beds: Q. TV, reading lamp, refrigerator, telephone and
desk in room. Air conditioning. VCR, fax, bicycles, parlor games and fireplace
on premises. Small meetings and seminars hosted. Antiquing, cross-country
skiing, downhill skiing, fishing, golf, parks, shopping, sporting events, tennis
and water sports nearby.

Publicity: *Idaho Statesman, Denver Post, San Antonio Sun and NY Times.*

"Thanks so much for the hospitality and warmth."

Cascade   H3

Wapiti Meadow Ranch

Johnson Creek Rd, HC 72
Cascade, ID 83611
(208)633-3217 Fax:(208)633-3219
E-mail: wapitimr@aol.com
Web: www.wapitimeadowranch.com

Circa 1926. Experience a wilderness adventure with backcountry luxury at this ranch that features cabins and a log and
stone lodge. Sitting in a lush mountain valley surrounded by
national forest and rivers, this tranquil retreat offers an abundance of amenities and activities. A great room features a massive stone fireplace, player piano, games and books. The well-
appointed, cabins include bedrooms, kitchenettes stocked
with snacks and refreshments, living rooms, full baths, fresh
flowers and daily maid service. Hearty breakfasts, lunches that
can be packed for day trips, enjoyed on the porch or on garden picnic tables and dinners that are a culinary event are all
included. After a day of fly fishing, horseback riding, swimming, tubing, basketball, volleyball, badminton, horseshoes,
croquet, hiking, biking, snowmobiling or cross-country skiing,
the hot tub beckons and soothes.

Innkeeper(s): Diana & Barry Bryant. $100-200. 9 rooms, 6 with FP, 2
suites, 4 cabins and 2 conference rooms. Breakfast, afternoon tea,
snacks/refreshments and dinner included in rates. Types of meals: Full
gourmet bkfst, early coffee/tea and gourmet lunch. Beds: KQT. Reading lamp,
refrigerator, snack bar, coffeemaker, desk, fireplace, quiet, solitude and clear
mountain air in room. Fax, copier, spa, stable, bicycles, library, parlor games,
telephone, fireplace, laundry facility, gift shop, fishing, hiking, wildlife viewing
and horseback riding on premises. Weddings, small meetings, family reunions
and seminars hosted. Bicycling, canoeing/kayaking, cross-country skiing,
downhill skiing, fishing, hiking and horseback riding nearby.

Coeur d' Alene   C2

Baragar House B&B

316 Military Dr
Coeur d' Alene, ID 83814-2137
(208)664-9125 (800)615-8422
E-mail: stay@baragarhouse.com
Web: www.baragarhouse.com

Circa 1926. Built by a lumber baron, this expansive
Craftsman-style bungalow is a pleasurable retreat. Guest bedrooms include the Country Cabin accented with murals of a
mountain stream and clouds. The
floral-themed Garden Room has a
canopied window seat and
antique vanity. The
Honeymoon Suite is especially
appealing with an oversized
bathroom boasting a clawfoot
tub under a bay window. Ask about how to sleep under the
stars. "Wreck your diet" breakfasts are served daily, though
special dietary needs are graciously accommodated. Enjoy the
indoor spa and sauna.

Innkeeper(s): Bernie & Carolyn Baragar. $99-139. 3 rooms, 1 with PB.
Breakfast and snacks/refreshments included in rates. Types of meals: Full
gourmet bkfst, veg bkfst and early coffee/tea. Beds: QD. Cable TV, VCR, reading lamp, refrigerator, ceiling fan, snack bar, clock radio, coffeemaker and
desk in room. Air conditioning. Fax, spa, swimming, sauna, tennis, library,
parlor games, telephone and laundry facility on premises. Amusement parks,

antiquing, art galleries, beach, bicycling, canoeing/kayaking, cross-country skiing, downhill skiing, fishing, golf, hiking, horseback riding, live theater, museums, parks, shopping, tennis, water sports and wineries nearby.

Publicity: *Coeur d'Alene Press and Spokesman Review.*

"Thank you for the hospitality and most exquisite honeymoon setting."

Gregory's McFarland House

601 E Foster Ave
Coeur d' Alene, ID 83814
(208)667-1232 (800)335-1232

Circa 1905. This yellow and white three-story historic home, shaded by tall trees, offers a wraparound porch with swaying swing, a deck and summerhouse, overlooking green lawns and gardens. English chintz, Oriental rugs and antiques are found throughout. A three-course gourmet breakfast is offered in the glass conservatory, next to the scenic deck. The inn has a resident minister and professional photographer, so it is popular for weddings and for renewing marriage vows. Water skiing, fishing, bird watching, skiing and digging for garnets are favorite activities. Coeur d'Alene Lake, within walking distance, is considered one of the most beautiful lakes in the world. Spokane is 30 minutes away and the international airport 45 minutes.

Innkeeper(s): Winifred, Carol & Stephen Gregory. $90-195. 5 rooms with PB, 4 suites and 1 conference room. Breakfast included in rates. Types of meals: Full gourmet bkfst. Beds: KQ. Reading lamp, ceiling fan, clock radio, turn-down service, desk and bath robes in room. VCR, parlor games, telephone, fireplace and central air conditioning on premises. Weddings, small meetings, family reunions and seminars hosted. Amusement parks, antiquing, cross-country skiing, downhill skiing, fishing, golf, live theater, parks, shopping, sporting events, tennis and water sports nearby.

The Roosevelt Inn

105 E Wallace Ave
Coeur d' Alene, ID 83814-2947
(208)765-5200 (800)290-3358 Fax:(208)664-4142
E-mail: info@therooseveltinn.com
Web: www.therooseveltinn.com

Circa 1905. This turn-of-the-century, red brick home was named for President Roosevelt and is the oldest schoolhouse in town. Roosevelt translates to Rosefield in Dutch, and the innkeepers have created a rosy theme for the inn. The Bell Tower Suite and the Honeymoon Suite are the favorite room requests, but all rooms offer Victorian antiques and some have lake views. Coeur d' Alene has been recognized by National Geographic Magazine as one of the five most beautiful lakes in the world. The area offers the world's longest floating boardwalk and Tubb's Hill Nature Park. A variety of shops and restaurants are within a five minute stroll from the inn. The natural surroundings offer mountain biking, boating, skiing and hiking.

Innkeeper(s): John & Tina Hough. $79-289. 15 rooms, 12 with PB, 3 with FP, 6 suites and 2 conference rooms. Breakfast and snacks/refreshments included in rates. Types of meals: Full gourmet bkfst, veg bkfst, early coffee/tea and afternoon tea. Beds: Q. Data port, cable TV, reading lamp, CD player, clock radio, coffeemaker and turn-down service in room. Central air. TV, VCR, fax, copier, spa, sauna, library, parlor games, telephone, fireplace, rose greeting in room and exercise room on premises. Limited handicap access. Weddings, small meetings, family reunions and seminars hosted. Amusement parks, antiquing, art galleries, beach, bicycling, canoeing/kayaking, cross-country skiing, downhill skiing, fishing, golf, hiking, horseback riding, live theater, museums, parks, shopping, sporting events, tennis, water sports and wineries nearby.

Coolin   B2

Old Northern Inn

PO Box 177, 220 Bayview
Coolin, ID 83821-0177
(208)443-2426 Fax:(208)443-3856

Circa 1890. This historic inn was built to serve guests riding the Great Northern rail line. Today, travelers come to enjoy trout-filled Priest Lake and all its offerings. The inn is located on the lake shore, and guests enjoy use of a small marina and private beach. There is also a volleyball court, but guests are welcome to simply sit and relax on the spacious deck. The natural surroundings are full of wildlife, and it's not unusual to see deer, caribou and even a moose. The hotel itself is a two-story log and shingle structure, quite at home among the tall cedars. The interior is warm and inviting. There is a common area with a stone fireplace and country furnishings, as well as a view of mountains and the lake. Rooms are decorated with turn-of-the-century antiques, and the suites include a small sitting room. Huckleberry pancakes have been a staple at the inn's breakfast table since the 19th century. In the afternoons, wine, cheese and fruit are served.

Innkeeper(s): Terri Wright. $90-140. 6 rooms with PB and 2 suites. Breakfast included in rates. Types of meals: Full bkfst and early coffee/tea. Beds: Q. Reading lamp and desk in room. Fax, copier, swimming, parlor games, telephone and fireplace on premises. Limited handicap access. Small meetings and family reunions hosted. Antiquing, fishing, golf, shopping, tennis and water sports nearby.

Publicity: *Seattle Times.*

New Meadows   G2

Hartland Inn

211 Norris Hwy 95
New Meadows, ID 83654-0215
(208)347-2114 (888)509-7400 Fax:(208)347-2535

Circa 1911. This handsome, three-story house was built by the president of the PIN Railroad. The mansion's pleasant interiors include a sunny sitting room and a formal dining room. Guest rooms offer polished wood floors and ceiling fans, and some include period antiques. Breakfast includes strata, muffins and fruit smoothies. Enjoy the area's mountains, forests, rivers, lakes and scenic drives. The Little Salmon River is three blocks away.

Innkeeper(s): Stephen & JoBeth Mehen. $130. 5 rooms, 3 with PB, 4 with FP and 4 suites. Breakfast included in rates. Types of meals: Full bkfst and early coffee/tea. Beds: QD. Cable TV, reading lamp, ceiling fan and telephone in room. VCR, fax, spa, library and fireplace on premises. Weddings, small meetings and family reunions hosted. Antiquing, art galleries, bicycling, canoeing/kayaking, cross-country skiing, downhill skiing, fishing, golf, hiking, horseback riding, parks and water sports nearby.

Salmon   G5

Greyhouse Inn B&B

1115 Hwy 93 South
Salmon, ID 83467
(208)756-3968 (800)348-8097
E-mail: osgoodd@salmoninternet.com
Web: www.greyhouseinn.com

Circa 1894. The scenery at Greyhouse is nothing short of wondrous. In the winter, when mountains are capped in white and the evergreens are shrouded in snow, this Victorian appears as a safe haven from the chilly weather. In the summer, the rocky peaks are a contrast to the whimsical house, which looks like something out of an Old West town. The historic home is known around town as the old maternity hospital, but there is nothing medicinal about it now. The rooms are Victorian in style with antique furnishings. The parlor features deep red walls and floral overstuffed sofas and a dressmaker's model garbed in a brown Victorian gown. Outdoor enthusiasts will find no shortage of activities, from facing the rapids in nearby Salmon River to fishing to horseback riding. The town of Salmon is just 12 miles away.

Innkeeper(s): David & Sharon Osgood. $70-90. 7 rooms, 5 with PB, 1 cottage and 2 cabins. Breakfast included in rates. Types of meals: Country bkfst, veg bkfst, picnic lunch and dinner. Beds: KQDT. VCR, reading lamp, ceiling fan, clock radio and desk in room. TV, bicycles, library, parlor games, telephone, laundry facility, carriage house and two log cabin rooms on premises. Weddings, small meetings and family reunions hosted. Antiquing, bicycling, canoeing/kayaking, cross-country skiing, downhill skiing, fishing, golf, hiking, horseback riding, live theater, museums, parks, shopping, float trips, hot springs and mountain biking nearby.

"To come around the corner and find the Greyhouse, as we did, restores my faith! Such a miracle. We had a magical evening here, and we plan to return to stay for a few days. Thanks so much for your kindness and hospitality. We love Idaho!"

Wallace   C3

The Beale House

107 Cedar St
Wallace, ID 83873-2115
(208)752-7151 (888)752-7151

Circa 1904. This attractive, three-story Colonial Revival home is listed in the National Register of Historic Places, as is the entire town of Wallace. Original parquet wood floor, antiques and memorabilia combine to lend an authentic aura of the past. Each of the five guest rooms offers a unique feature, such

as a fireplace, balcony or wall of windows. The innkeepers are well versed in their home's history, and guests are welcome to look over a photographic record of the house and its former owners. A backyard hot tub provides views of the mountains and creek, while the large front porch invites slowing down with its swing and rocking chairs. Guests can enjoy birdwatching on the property. Recreational activities abound in the vicinity, famous for its silver mines. There are also museums nearby.

Historic Interest: Town of Wallace, Cataldo Mission, Route of the Hiawatha biking trail.

Innkeeper(s): Jim & Linda See. $115-180. 5 rooms, 1 with FP and 1 suite. Breakfast included in rates. Types of meals: Full bkfst. Beds: QDT. Turn-down service in room. VCR, spa, library, telephone and fireplace on premises. Weddings hosted. Antiquing, bicycling, cross-country skiing, downhill skiing, fishing, golf, hiking, live theater, museums, parks, shopping, water sports, bird watching, popular biking trails include the Route of the Hiawatha and the Trail of the Coeur d' Alenes and tours of silver and gold mines nearby.

Publicity: *Shoshone News Press, Spokesman Review, Silver Valley Voice, Off the Beaten Path/Guide to Unique Places, Northern Rockies: Best Places Guide to the Outdoors, Travel Holiday and Americas Most Charming Towns and Villages.*

Illinois

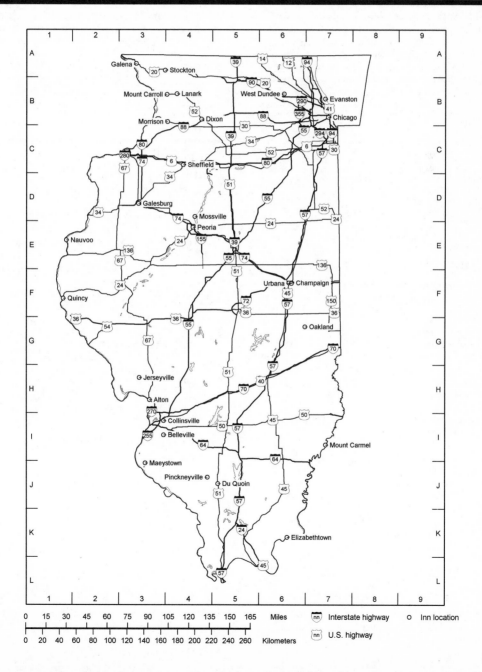

	Miles
0 15 30 45 60 75 90 105 120 135 150 165	
0 20 40 60 80 100 120 140 160 180 200 220 240 260	Kilometers

Interstate highway ○ Inn location

U.S. highway

153

Alton H3

Beall Mansion, An Elegant B&B

407 East 12th St
Alton, IL 62002-7230
(618)474-9100 (866)843-2325 Fax:(618)474-9090

Circa 1903. An eclectic blend of Neoclassic, Georgian and Greek Revival styles, the mansion was designed as a wedding gift by world renown architect, Lucas Pfeiffenberger. Original woodwork, eleven and a half-foot ceilings, leaded-glass windows, pocket doors, crystal chandeliers and imported marble and bronze statuary reflect the era's opulence. Elegantly appointed guest bedrooms are unique in size and decor. Each includes a private bath with shower and clawfoot tub or whirlpool for two, imported marble floor and chandelier. Voted "Illinois Best Bed & Breakfast" by Illinois Magazine's first Annual Readers Poll.

Innkeeper(s): Jim & Sandy Belote. $97-462. 5 rooms with PB, 2 with FP, 1 suite and 2 conference rooms. Types of meals: Full gourmet bkfst and early coffee/tea. Beds: KQD. Modem hook-up, cable TV, reading lamp, ceiling fan, clock radio, telephone, turn-down service, fireplace, whirlpool for two, iron and ironing board, toiletries including our own homemade lavender bath salts, radiator heat and high-speed wireless Internet in room. Central air. Fax, copier, parlor games, fireplace, veranda, hammock, badminton, horseshoes and croquet on premises. Weddings, small meetings, family reunions and seminars hosted. Amusement parks, antiquing, art galleries, bicycling, canoeing/kayaking, fishing, golf, hiking, horseback riding, live theater, museums, parks, shopping, sporting events, tennis, water sports and wineries nearby.

Publicity: *Illinois Magazine, Illinois Now, AAA Midwest Motorist, St. Louis Post Dispatch, Pequot Press, NorthShore Magazine, Show Me St. Louis, News 4 St. Louis, The Telegraph, Edwardsville Intelligencer, DeForest Times, Big Beautiful Woman Magazine, The Daily Journal* and inspected and approved by the Illinois Bed and Breakfast Association.

Belleville I3

Swans Court B&B

421 Court St
Belleville, IL 62220-1201
(618)233-0779 (800)840-1058 Fax:(618)277-3150

Circa 1883. This home, designated by the Department of the Interior as a certified historic structure, was once home to David Baer, known as the "mule king of the world." Baer sold more than 10,000 mules each year to British troops in World War I and to American troops in World War II. The home is furnished almost entirely in antiques. Innkeeper Monty Dixon searched high and low to fill her B&B with authentic pieces, creating a nostalgic ambiance. The library offers a selection of books, games and puzzles for guests to enjoy. The home is located in a historic neighborhood, within walking distance to shops and restaurants. Belleville is convenient to St. Louis, and there are historic sites, Lewis & Clark sites and a state park nearby.

Innkeeper(s): Ms. Monty Dixon. $65-90. 4 rooms, 2 with PB, 2 with FP. Breakfast and snacks/refreshments included in rates. Types of meals: Full bkfst. Beds: QD. Reading lamp, ceiling fan, clock radio, telephone and folding tables upon request in room. Air conditioning. VCR, library, parlor games and fireplace on premises. Limited handicap access. Weddings, small meetings, family reunions and seminars hosted. Antiquing, golf, live theater, shopping, sporting events and tennis nearby.

"We feel like we have made a new friend. We appreciated all of the nice little touches, such as the fresh flowers."

Champaign F6

Golds B&B

2065 County Road 525 E
Champaign, IL 61822-9521
(217)586-4345

Circa 1874. Visitors to the University of Illinois area may enjoy a restful experience at this inn, west of town in a peaceful farmhouse setting. Antique country furniture collected by the innkeepers over the past 25 years is showcased in the inn and is beautifully offset by early American stenciling on its walls. Seasonal items from the garden are sometimes used as breakfast fare.

Innkeeper(s): Rita & Bob Gold. $45-50. 3 rooms, 1 with PB. Breakfast included in rates. Types of meals: Cont plus and early coffee/tea. Beds: QT. Reading lamp and clock radio in room. Air conditioning. VCR, telephone and fireplace on premises. Antiquing, fishing, live theater, parks and shopping nearby.

Chicago B7

China Doll Short-Term Rental Apartments

738 West Schubert Avenue
Chicago, IL 60614
(773)525-4967 (866)361-1819 Fax:(773)525-3929

Circa 1895. Everything needed is included for a wonderful visit to the Windy City. Stay in a self-contained, one-bedroom garden apartment with exposed brick walls. It is complete with an entertainment system, fireplace, private Jacuzzi, sauna and a fully stocked island kitchen with customized breakfast foods per advance request. A larger accommodation of one to two bedrooms with up to six rooms is available on the second-floor, and features a private deck. A laundry room facility is the only shared amenity. Chinese-Mandarin and English are spoken.

Innkeeper(s): Jim & Yanan Haring. $135-175. 1 room with PB, 1 with FP. Breakfast, afternoon tea and snacks/refreshments included in rates. Types of meals: Cont plus. Beds: QDT. Modem hook-up, data port, cable TV, VCR, reading lamp, stereo, refrigerator, snack bar, clock radio, telephone, coffeemaker, desk, voice mail and fireplace in room. Air conditioning. Fax, copier, spa, library, fireplace, laundry facility, sauna and conference room with projector on premises. Art galleries, beach, bicycling, cross-country skiing, fishing, golf, hiking, live theater, museums, parks, shopping, sporting events and tennis nearby.

Gold Coast Guest House B&B

113 West Elm Street
Chicago, IL 60610-2805
(312)337-0361 Fax:(312)337-0362
E-mail: Sally@bbchicago.com
Web: www.bbchicago.com

Circa 1873. Built just after the Great Chicago Fire, this 19th-century brick row house is situated in the heart of the Gold Coast in one the city's most exclusive neighborhoods. The bed & breakfast is only one of three historic buildings still standing on Elm Street. Recently restored, the B&B is decorated in a combination of antiques and contemporary furnishings. Four tastefully appointed guest rooms offer private baths, TV, ceiling fans and air conditioning. One upstairs guest room features a bay window and the original brick fireplace. Fresh multi-grain bread, fruit, apple-cinnamon tea bread, English muffins and assorted cereals are served in the second-floor dining room. The B&B is a five-minute walk to the shops on the "Magnificent Mile" and to the lakeshore, public transportation, restaurants, museums and theaters.

Innkeeper(s): Sally Baker. $99-199. 4 rooms with PB and 1 conference room. Breakfast, afternoon tea and snacks/refreshments included in rates. Types of meals: Cont plus, veg bkfst and early coffee/tea. Beds: QT. Data port, cable TV, VCR, reading lamp, CD player, ceiling fan, clock radio, telephone, coffeemaker, desk, hair dryers and ironing board in room. Air conditioning. Fax, laundry facility, evening wine & Brie available, 8,000-square-foot health club one block away and modest daily fee for guests on premises. Small meetings and family reunions hosted. Amusement parks, antiquing, art galleries, beach, bicycling, golf, hiking, live theater, museums, parks, shopping, sporting events, tennis, water sports, The Magnificent Mile/Michigan Ave., Rush Street nightlife, River North Galleries and three museums nearby.

Publicity: *Washington Post, Inns & Retreats, "Hus" of Sweden, Mexico City Times, Kansas City Magazine, Michigan Living and ABC's 190 North.*

House Of Two Urns

1239 N Greenview Ave
Chicago, IL 60622-3318
(773)235-1408 (800)835-9303 Fax:(773)235-1410

Circa 1912. This historic townhouse offers guests a unique experience in the Windy City. The house is built in late Victorian style, and innkeeper Kapra Fleming has decorated the B&B in an eclectic style with antiques and family heirlooms. Kapra has included many thoughtful amenities, such as robes, hair dryers, slippers and an alarm clock. Rooms are inviting and tastefully furnished. The spacious loft suite includes a queen and full bed, as well as a private bath. The continental-plus breakfasts include items such as French toast with almonds and bananas or chocolate chip scones. The home is located in the Wicker Park section of Chicago, less than three miles from downtown and six miles from McCormick Center.

Innkeeper(s): Kapra Fleming. $82-150. 4 rooms and 1 suite. Breakfast included in rates. Types of meals: Cont plus and early coffee/tea. Beds: KQD. Cable TV, VCR, reading lamp, refrigerator, ceiling fan, clock radio, telephone, desk and hair dryer in room. Fax and limited Internet access on premises. Family reunions hosted. Antiquing, live theater, parks, shopping, sporting events and water sports nearby.

Windy City Urban Inn

607 W Deming Pl
Chicago, IL 60614
(773)248-7091 (877)897-7091 Fax:(773)529-4183
E-mail: stay@windycityinn.com
Web: www.windycityinn.com

Circa 1886. Built as a Victorian mansion, it is now an eclectic urban inn proudly reflecting its namesake city. Chicago memorabilia and art are featured in the decor. The guest bedrooms and coach house apartments continue the regional theme, each named after a well-known local author. Relish the luxury of whirlpool tubs, fireplaces, and plush robes. The common rooms offer wonderful places to relax, read, or play the piano. Enjoy refreshments in the colorful courtyard garden with ivy-covered brick walls.

Innkeeper(s): Mary & Andy Shaw. $115-325. 7 rooms, 4 with PB, 3 with FP, 3 suites and 1 conference room. Breakfast and snacks/refreshments included in rates. Types of meals: Cont plus and early coffee/tea. Beds: KQ. Modem hook-up, data port, cable TV, VCR, reading lamp, stereo, refrigerator, ceiling fan, snack bar, clock radio, telephone, coffeemaker, desk, hot tub/spa and fireplace in room. Central air. Fax, copier, spa, library, parlor games and fire-

place on premises. Weddings, small meetings, family reunions and seminars hosted. Antiquing, art galleries, beach, bicycling, fishing, golf, hiking, live theater, museums, parks, shopping and sporting events nearby.

Publicity: *Time Magazine.*

Wooded Isle Suites

5750 S Stony Island Ave
Chicago, IL 60637-2049
(773)288-6305 (800)290-6844 Fax:(773)288-8972
E-mail: reserve@woodedisle.com
Web: www.woodedisle.com

Circa 1914. Although neither bed & breakfast nor country inn, this collection of two- and three-room apartment suites serves as a convenient, relaxing alternative to hotel travel. The suites are located in Chicago's Hyde Park area and are convenient to the many museums, shops, restaurants and attractions in the downtown area and Lake Michigan. The early 20th-century complex originally served as housing for employees of the Illinois Central Railroad Hospital. Each suite includes a long list of practical amenities, such as a kitchen stocked with pots, pans, dishes, coffee makers, coffee, tea bags and more. The decor is a pleasant, contemporary style.

Innkeeper(s): Charlie Havens & Sara Pitcher. $147-189. 13 suites. Beds: Q. Cable TV, refrigerator, ceiling fan, clock radio, telephone, desk, microwave, stove and answering machine in room. Air conditioning. Laundry facility on premises. Fishing, live theater, parks, sporting events, water sports, museums and antique bookstores nearby.

"We have all had very positive experiences at Wooded Isle. Everyone has been pleasant and tuned in to our joy."

Collinsville   13

Maggie's B&B

2102 N Keebler Ave
Collinsville, IL 62234-4713
(618)344-8283

Circa 1900. A rustic two-acre wooded area surrounds this friendly Victorian inn, once a boarding house. Rooms with 11-foot ceilings are furnished with exquisite antiques and art objects collected on worldwide travels. Downtown St. Louis, the Gateway Arch and the Mississippi riverfront are just 10 minutes away.

Historic Interest: Cahokia Indian Mounds (3 miles), Gateway Arch (15 miles), Gateway International Racetrack (3 miles), Fairmont Racetrack (1 mile), Our Lady of the Snows (10 miles).

Innkeeper(s): Maggie Leyda. $45-100. 5 rooms, 3 with PB, 2 with FP and 1 conference room. Breakfast included in rates. Types of meals: Full bkfst and early coffee/tea. Beds: KQDT. Cable TV, VCR, reading lamp, ceiling fan, clock radio and turn-down service in room. Air conditioning. TV, spa, library, telephone and fireplace on premises. Limited handicap access. Weddings, small meetings and family reunions hosted. Amusement parks, antiquing, fishing, live theater, parks, shopping and sporting events nearby.

Publicity: *USA Today, Cooking Light, Collinsville Herald Journal, Innsider, Belleville News, Democrat, Saint Louis Homes & Gardens, Edwardsville Intelligences, St. Louis Business Journal and St. Louis Post Dispatch.*

"We enjoyed a delightful stay. You've thought of everything. What fun!"

Dixon B4

Crawford House Inn

204 E Third St
Dixon, IL 61021
(815)288-3351

Circa 1869. In 1869, Joseph Crawford, who counted Abraham Lincoln among his friends, built the Italianate Victorian style house that now bears his name. His descendants maintained the family home until the 1950s when it was converted into a nursing facility and then lawyer offices. Enjoying life today as a B&B, Crawford House offers its guests a glimpse into small-town America. Three guest rooms have either king- or queen-size feather beds; bathrooms are shared. Breakfasts are served in the dining room and are presented with white linens, china and stemware. Gourmet breakfasts include juice, coffee, an egg entree, fresh baked goods and seasonal fruits. Dixon has just been named "Petunia Capital of the United States," and its streets are lined with colorful beds of the blooms all summer long. At the center of five state parks, the area is popular for cycling. Scenic country roads and paths offer opportunities for walking and horseback riding, as well. Visits can be made to the Ronald Reagan boyhood home, the John Deere Historical Site or local antique stores. Rock River is two blocks away for boating, fishing and canoeing, and across the street is the historical courthouse square where summertime concerts are popular in the evenings. Cross-country skiing and snowmobiling are available during the winter months.

Innkeeper(s): Lyn Miliano. $65-85. 3 rooms, 1 with FP. Breakfast included in rates. Types of meals: Full gourmet bkfst. Beds: KQ. Cable TV, VCR, reading lamp, ceiling fan and clock radio in room. Air conditioning. Library, parlor games and fireplace on premises. Small meetings hosted. Antiquing, bicycling, canoeing/kayaking, fishing, golf, hiking, horseback riding, live theater, museums, parks, shopping, tennis and water sports nearby.

Du Quoin J5

Francie's Inn

104 S Line St
Du Quoin, IL 62832-2344
(618)542-6686 (877)877-2657
E-mail: martha@franciesinnonline.com
Web: www.franciesinnonline.com

Circa 1908. This solid three-story home on three acres served as an orphanage for 39 years. The inside is decorated with a Victorian flair, and the rooms feature extravagant touches such as puffy comforters, as well as writing desks and lounge chairs. The Ciara room has a brass and iron bed, while the Desiree room boasts a view of the front and side grounds. The Van Arsdale Suite has a four-poster bed, antique wardrobe and clawfoot tub, and a first-floor room, The Willow, offers a king bed and sofa sleeper. Breakfasts are served on the balcony, back deck or in the Tea Room, which seats 30 and is an ideal location for a wedding reception or business function. There's a wide veranda that stretches across the front and rear of the inn. Southern Illinois University and Shawnee National Forest is nearby.

Innkeeper(s): Bruce & Martha Crawford. $69-115. 6 rooms with PB. Types of meals: Full bkfst. Beds: KQT. TV and telephone in room. Wireless Internet access on premises. Shopping nearby.

Elizabethtown K6

River Rose Inn B&B

1 Main St PO Box 78
Elizabethtown, IL 62931-0078
(618)287-8811 Fax:(208)330-8715

Circa 1914. Large, shade trees veil the front of this Greek Gothic home, nestled along the banks of the Ohio River. From the grand front entrance, guests look out to polished woodwork and a staircase leading to shelves of books. Rooms are cheerful and nostalgic, decorated with antiques. Each guest room offers something special. One has a four-poster bed, another offers a fireplace. The Scarlet Room has its own balcony and whirlpool tub, and the Rose Room has a private patio with a swing. The Magnolia Cottage is ideal for honeymooners and includes a whirlpool tub for two, fireplace and a deck that overlooks the river. Breakfasts are served in the dining room where guests can enjoy the water views.

Innkeeper(s): Don & Elisabeth Phillips. $69-109. 5 rooms with PB, 2 with FP and 1 cottage. Breakfast included in rates. Types of meals: Full gourmet bkfst and early coffee/tea. Beds: QT. Cable TV, VCR, reading lamp, ceiling fan, clock radio and four rooms with whirlpool tubs in room. Air conditioning. Fax, copier, spa, swimming, library, parlor games, telephone and fireplace on premises. Amusement parks, antiquing, fishing, golf, parks, shopping, water sports, hiking and biking nearby.

Publicity: *Chicago Tribune and Midwest Living.*

Evanston B7

The Homestead

1625 Hinman Ave
Evanston, IL 60201-6021
(847)475-3300 Fax:(847)570-8100
E-mail: office@thehomestead.net
Web: www.thehomestead.net

Circa 1927. This hotel, the only lodging in Evanston's Lakeshore Historic District, was built by a local architect. The Colonial structure is very much unchanged from its beginnings in the 1920s. Several rooms offer views of Lake Michigan, which is just two blocks away. Northwestern University also is just a two-block walk from the hotel. The inn harbors the nationally renowned restaurant, Trio, acclaimed for its contemporary cuisine.

Innkeeper(s): David Reynolds. $120-140. 35 rooms, 15 suites and 1 conference room. Breakfast included in rates. Types of meals: Cont and gourmet dinner. Restaurant on premises. Beds: QDT. Cable TV, reading lamp, refrigerator, telephone and desk in room. Air conditioning. Fax, copier, library and fireplace on premises. Small meetings and seminars hosted. Live theater, parks, sporting events, tennis and water sports nearby.

Margarita European Inn

1566 Oak Ave
Evanston, IL 60201-4298
(847)869-2273 Fax:(847)869-2353

Circa 1927. This stately inn, once the proper home to young area working women, has a proud tradition in the city's history. The Georgian architecture is complemented by an impressive interior, featuring arched French doors, vintage period molding and a large parlor with floor-to-ceiling windows. Near the lakefront and Northwestern University, it also boasts a library, rooftop garden and VaPenisero, a restaurant serving regional Italian specialties. Guests often enjoy renting a bike and exploring the area's many attractions, including 24 nearby art galleries.

Innkeeper(s): Barbara & Tim Gorham. $79-150. 42 rooms, 22 with PB and 1 conference room. Breakfast included in rates. Types of meals: Cont and early coffee/tea. Restaurant on premises. Beds: KQDT. Reading lamp, ceiling fan, clock radio, telephone and desk in room. Air conditioning. Fireplace on premises. Weddings, small meetings, family reunions and seminars hosted. Antiquing, live theater, shopping, sporting events and Northwestern University nearby.

Galena   A3

Belle Aire Mansion Guest House

11410 Route 20 West
Galena, IL 61036
(815)777-0893
E-mail: belleair@galenalink.com
Web: www.belleairemansion.com

Circa 1836. At the end of a tree-lined lane this pre-Civil War, Federal-style home sits on 11 landscaped acres with a barn and a windmill. A comfortable decor includes antiques and reproductions. The kitchen is a popular gathering place for snacks and conversation. Videos, books, toys and games are found in the living room. Guest bedrooms and suites feature double whirlpool tubs and fireplaces or parlor stoves. The Canopy Suite boasts a separate sitting room, and Ruthie's includes a clawfoot tub. Pecan French toast, locally made breakfast sausage, melon and banana bread are a favorite morning meal. Relax on one of the porches overlooking flowers and greenery. The surrounding region contains a treasure trove of historic sites to visit.

Historic Interest: Eighty-five percent of Galena on Historic Register (2 1/2 miles).
Innkeeper(s): Lorraine & Jan Svec. $95-185. 5 rooms with PB, 3 with FP and 2 suites. Breakfast and snacks/refreshments included in rates. Types of meals: Country bkfst, veg bkfst and early coffee/tea. Beds: KQT. TV, VCR, reading lamp, CD player, refrigerator, clock radio, coffeemaker, hot tub/spa and fireplace in room. Air conditioning. Parlor games and telephone on premises. Weddings and family reunions hosted. Antiquing, art galleries, bicycling, cross-country skiing, downhill skiing, fishing, golf, hiking, horseback riding, live theater, museums, parks, shopping and wineries nearby.
Publicity: *Chicago Sun-Times and Dubuque Telegraph Herald.*

"Loved the house and the hospitality!"

Bernadine's Stillman Inn & Tea Room

513 Bouthillier St
Galena, IL 61036-2703
(815)777-0557 (866)777-0557 Fax:(815)777-8097
E-mail: Stillman@galenalink.com
Web: www.stillmaninn.com

Circa 1858. Two gorgeous acres of gardens with a courtyard and waterfall surround this luxury inn that was originally known as part of the Nelson Stillman Estate, belonging to one of the wealthiest men in this lead-mining, riverboat town of the 1800s. Relax on wicker furniture on one of the two covered porches. Play the piano in the parlor. Stay in a romantic Victorian guest bedroom or suite with a double whirlpool, fireplace, beverage-filled mini-refrigerator, VCR, CD player and matching robes. Plan the day's activities with advice shared over a satisfying breakfast. The Tea Room offers breakfast and

lunch menus as well as afternoon and cream teas. Visit the gift shop and artist gallery.

Historic Interest: Built in 1858. We still have the original 1858 Carriage House.
Innkeeper(s): Bernadine and Dave Anderson. $80-265. 7 rooms with PB, 5 with FP and 3 suites. Breakfast included in rates. Types of meals: Full gourmet bkfst, veg bkfst, lunch, picnic lunch, afternoon tea, snacks/refreshments and gourmet dinner. Restaurant on premises. Beds: Q. Cable TV, VCR, reading lamp, CD player, refrigerator, ceiling fan, clock radio, coffeemaker, fireplace, matching robes, complimentary beverages and coffeemaker in room. Air conditioning. Fax, copier, parlor games, telephone, fireplace, laundry facility, tea room and lounge on premises. Weddings, small meetings, family reunions and seminars hosted. Antiquing, art galleries, bicycling, canoeing/kayaking, cross-country skiing, downhill skiing, fishing, golf, hiking, horseback riding, live theater, museums, parks, shopping and wineries nearby.
Publicity: *Chicago Tribune 2002 - Best Winter Package, New York Times 2003 - The Place to Stay and Chicago Magazine 2003 - Places to Stay.*

Farmers' Guest House

334 Spring St
Galena, IL 61036-2128
(815)777-3456 (888)459-1847 Fax:(815)777-3514
E-mail: farmersgh@galenalink.net
Web: www.farmersguesthouse.com

Circa 1867. This two-story brick Italianate building was built as a bakery and served as a store and hotel, as well. Rows of arched, multi-paned windows add charm to the exterior. The rooms are decorated with antiques, lace curtains and floral wallpapers. The accommodations include seven rooms with queen-size beds, one room with a double bed, and two, two-room king Master Suites. There's a bar, featured in the movie "Field of Dreams." A hot tub is offered in the backyard. The inn also has a cabin in the woods available for rent.

Innkeeper(s): Kathie, Jess Farlow. $125-195. 10 rooms with PB, 2 with FP, 2 suites and 1 cabin. Breakfast included in rates. Types of meals: Full bkfst. Beds: KQD. Cable TV, reading lamp, CD player, coffeemaker and hot tub/spa in room. Central air. VCR, fax, library, parlor games, telephone, fireplace, hot tub and evening wine and cheese hour on premises. Small meetings, family reunions and seminars hosted. Antiquing, art galleries, bicycling, cross-country skiing, downhill skiing, golf, hiking, horseback riding, live theater, museums, parks, shopping, wineries and hot air ballooning nearby.
Publicity: *Better Homes & Gardens, Country Discoveries, Comforts at Home, Country Extra and Field of Dreams.*

"Neat old place, fantastic breakfasts."

Park Avenue Guest House

208 Park Ave
Galena, IL 61036-2306
(815)777-1075

Circa 1893. A short walk from Grant Park sits this attractive Queen Anne Victorian with turret and wraparound porch. Gardens and a gazebo add to this peaceful neighborhood charm, as does the original woodwork throughout. The Helen Room features a gas fireplace, TV, tub and shower, while Miriam Room's brass bed highlights a cheerful floral decor and a fireplace. The Anna Suite also has a fireplace and boasts a comfortable sitting room in the inn's turret area and the Lucille Room is tastefully furnished in mauve, gray and white tones. The Inn has a permanent display of 165 house Dickens Village. The holiday decorations, including twelve Christmas trees, are not to be missed.

Innkeeper(s): Sharon Fallbacher. $95-135. 4 rooms with PB, 3 with FP and

1 suite. Snacks/refreshments included in rates. Types of meals: Full bkfst and early coffee/tea. Beds: QT. Cable TV, reading lamp, ceiling fan and desk in room. Air conditioning. VCR, telephone and fireplace on premises. Weddings, small meetings and family reunions hosted. Antiquing, cross-country skiing, downhill skiing, fishing, live theater, shopping, casino and riverboat nearby.

Publicity: *Gail Greco Romance of Country Inns, Daily Herald, Country Inns, Chicago Tribune, Better Homes & Gardens, Gourmet and Midwest Living.*

The Steamboat House Bed and Breakfast

605 S. Prospect
Galena, IL 61036
(815)777-2317 Fax:(815)776-0712

Circa 1855. Truly elegant as well as historic, this brick Gothic Revival, pre-Civil War mansion was built for a renowned Mississippi River steamboat captain. The inn exudes luxury while imparting a welcome, friendly ambiance. Main-floor parlors include a library and billiards room. A central parlor on the second floor offers early-morning Gevalia coffee and tea. Enjoy midweek afternoon treats or wine and cheese on the weekends. Each guest bedroom features a fireplace, heirloom furniture, vintage photographs and original artwork. The formal dining room is set with antique china, crystal and silver for a breakfast that is sure to please. Relax on the front porch overlooking roses.

Historic Interest: One of the finest examples of Gothis Revival architecture in the Midwest. The mansion was built from an Andrew Jackson Downing plan for Daniel Harris, one of the best known steamboat captains on the Mississippi River.

Innkeeper(s): Glen and Char Carlson. $95-135. 5 rooms with PB, 5 with FP. Breakfast and snacks/refreshments included in rates. Types of meals: Full gourmet bkfst, veg bkfst and early coffee/tea. Beds: QT. Cable TV, VCR, reading lamp, clock radio, fireplace and heirloom antique furnishings in room. Central air. Library, parlor games, telephone, fireplace, billiard room, original parlors and large covered front porch on premises. Weddings, small meetings, family reunions and seminars hosted. Antiquing, art galleries, bicycling, canoeing/kayaking, cross-country skiing, downhill skiing, fishing, golf, hiking, horseback riding, live theater, museums, parks, shopping, sporting events, tennis, water sports, wineries, historic district and trolley tours nearby.

Galesburg   D3

Seacord House

624 N Cherry St
Galesburg, IL 61401-2731
(309)342-4107

Circa 1891. A former county sheriff and businessman built this Eastlake-style Victorian, which is located in the town's historic district. The home was named for its builder, Wilkens Seacord, a prominent local man whose family is mentioned in Carl Sandburg's autobiography. In keeping with the house's historical prominence, the innkeepers have tried to maintain its turn-of-the-century charm. Victorian wallpapers, lacy curtains and a collection of family antiques grace the guest rooms and living areas. The bedrooms, however, feature the modern amenity of waterbeds. For those celebrating romantic occasions, the innkeepers provide heart-shaped muffins along with regular morning fare.

Historic Interest: Built in 1894, house has natural woodwork on first floor and working pocket doors.

Innkeeper(s): Gwen and Lyle. $50. 3 rooms. Breakfast included in rates. Types of meals: Cont plus. Fax on premises.

Jerseyville   H3

The Homeridge B&B

24818 Homeridge Drive
Jerseyville, IL 62052-1127
(618)498-3442

Circa 1867. This red brick Italianate Victorian features ornate white trim, a stately front veranda and a cupola where guests often take in views of sunsets and the surrounding 18 acres. The home was constructed by Cornelius Fisher, just after the Civil War. In 1891, it was purchased by Senator Theodore

Chapman and remained in his family until the 1960s. The innkeepers have filled the 14-room manor with traditional and Victorian furnishings, enhancing the high ceilings and ornate woodwork typical of the era. Guests are invited to take a relaxing dip in the inn's swimming pool or enjoy a refreshment on the veranda.

Innkeeper(s): Sue & Howard Landon. $95. 4 rooms with PB. Breakfast included in rates. Types of meals: Full bkfst, early coffee/tea and afternoon tea. Beds: KQDT. Reading lamp, ceiling fan, clock radio and desk in room. Air conditioning. VCR, fax, copier, swimming, bicycles, library, parlor games, telephone and fireplace on premises. Weddings, small meetings, family reunions and seminars hosted. Amusement parks, antiquing, cross-country skiing, fishing, live theater, parks, shopping, sporting events and water sports nearby.

Publicity: *Chicago Sun Times, Midwest Living Magazine, Midwest Living Magazine and St. Louis Post Dispatch.*

"A most beautiful, entertaining, snow-filled few days."

Lanark   B4

Standish House

540 W Carroll St
Lanark, IL 61046-1017
(815)493-2307 (800)468-2307

Circa 1882. Four generations of Standishes are associated with this Queen Anne Victorian house. The current owner is Norman Standish, descendant of Captain Myles Standish. Furnishings include English antiques from the 17th and 18th centuries and canopy beds. The second Saturday of November each year the

innkeepers recreate the First Thanksgiving and they sponsor a series of lectures on early American history and Myles Standish for school groups. A full breakfast is served by candlelight in the formal dining room.

Historic Interest: First two Blackhawk Indiana War Battlefields (nearby), historic Galena and lead mines (nearby), restored river boat gambling (near Mississippi River).

Innkeeper(s): Ingrid Standish. $60-70. 5 rooms, 1 with PB. Breakfast included in rates. Types of meals: Full bkfst. Beds: Q. A living museum of Early American history and the pilgrims on premises. Antiquing, cross-country skiing, downhill skiing, fishing, live theater and water sports nearby.

Publicity: *Northwestern Illinois Dispatch, Country, Midwest Living, Daily Telegraph, Daily Leader, Taste of Homes and Chicago Tribune.*

"Absolutely beautiful! Immaculate, enjoyable, comfortable, very refreshing."

Maeystown   J3

Corner George Inn

Corner of Main & Mill
Maeystown, IL 62256
(618)458-6660 (800)458-6020
E-mail: cornrgeo@htc.net
Web: www.cornergeorgeinn.com

Circa 1884. This inn is located in a restored hotel listed in the National Register of Historic Places. The inn originally served as both a hotel and saloon, but eventually served as a general store. Rooms in the inn are named after prominent local citizens and include Victorian appointments and antiques. The Summer Kitchen, a rustic cottage, once served as a smoke house, bakery and kitchen for the hotel's earliest owners. The cottage features original limestone walls and exposed beams. Another suite is also available in an 1859 rock house, and it includes two bedrooms. Breakfasts include entrees such as baked Victorian French toast, fresh fruit and homemade muffins or coffeecake.

Historic Interest: The inn consists of four completely restored structures, an 1884 hotel and saloon (main building), an 1890s summer Kitchen guest cottage and two 1860s Civil War rock houses.

Innkeeper(s): David & Marcia Braswell. $79-159. 7 rooms with PB, 3 suites, 1 cottage and 1 conference room. Breakfast included in rates. Types of meals: Full bkfst. Beds: QD. Reading lamp and fresh flowers in room. Central air. Library, parlor games, telephone and gift shop on premises. Weddings, small meetings, family reunions and seminars hosted. Antiquing, fishing, golf, hiking, live theater and wineries nearby.

Publicity: *Midwest Living, Midwest Motorist, St. Louis Magazine, Belleville News Democrat and Show Me St. Louis.*

Morrison   B4

Hillendale B&B

600 W Lincolnway
Morrison, IL 61270-2058
(815)772-3454 Fax:(815)772-7023
E-mail: hillend@clinton.net
Web: www.hillend.com

Circa 1891. Guests at Hillendale don't simply spend the night in the quaint town of Morrison, Ill., they spend the night in France, Italy, Hawaii or Africa. Each of the guests rooms in this Tudor manor reflects a different theme from around the world. Travelers and innkeepers Barb and Mike Winandy cleverly decorated each of the guest quarters. The Kimarrin room reflects Mayan culture with photographs of antiquities. The Outback, a private cottage, boasts a fireplace and whirlpool spa for two along with Australian decor. The Failte room includes a rococo Victorian antique highback bed, fireplace and Irish-themed decor. And these are just a few of the possibilities. Barb creates wonderful breakfasts full of muffins, breads and special entrees. Stroll the two-acre grounds and you will encounter a three-tier water pond, which sits in front of a teahouse, built by the original owner after a trip to Japan. One of the tiers houses Japanese Koi and another a water garden. The area has riverboat gambling and plenty of outdoor activities.

Historic Interest: The home is near several historic sites, including Albany Indian Burial Mounds, Dillion Home Museum and Carlton House, Morrison Historic Society. Hillendale is part of the Blackhawk Chocolate Trail.

Innkeeper(s): Barb & Mike Winandy. $70-180. 10 rooms with PB. Breakfast included in rates. Types of meals: Full bkfst. Beds: KQT. Cable TV, VCR, read-

ing lamp, refrigerator, ceiling fan, clock radio, telephone, desk and selected amenities in select rooms only in room. Air conditioning. Fax, copier, fireplace, pool table and fitness room on premises. Small meetings hosted. Antiquing, cross-country skiing, fishing, live theater, parks and gambling nearby.

Publicity: *New York Times, Sterling Gazette, Whiteside News Sentinel, Midwest Living, Home & Away and Moline Dispatch.*

"We've never been any place else that made us feel so catered to and comfortable. Thank you for allowing us to stay in your beautiful home. We feel very privileged."

Mossville   D4

Old Church House Inn

1416 E Mossville Rd, PO Box 295
Mossville, IL 61552
(309)579-2300

Circa 1869. Discover this restored Colonial to be a true sanctuary. The inn once served as a country church but now promises hospitality and relaxation. Each guest bedroom offers a unique feature, such as an antique carved bedstead, feather beds, handmade quilts and lacy curtains. A cup of tea and fresh-baked cookies can be enjoyed by a warm fire or among the garden's colorful flowers. Chocolates are a pleasant treat at turndown in the evening.

Innkeeper(s): Dean & Holly Ramseyer. $115. 2 rooms, 1 with PB. Breakfast included in rates. Types of meals: Cont plus, early coffee/tea, picnic lunch and room service. Beds: Q. Reading lamp, clock radio and turn-down service in room. Air conditioning. Telephone and fireplace on premises. Weddings and small meetings hosted. Antiquing, cross-country skiing, fishing, live theater, shopping, sporting events, water sports and bike trail nearby.

Publicity: *Chillicothe Bulletin, Journal Star, Country Inns and The Chicago Tribune.*

"Your hospitality, thoughtfulness, the cleanliness, beauty, I should just say everything was the best."

Mount Carmel   I7

Living Legacy Homestead

3759 N 900 Blvd
Mount Carmel, IL 62863
(618)298-2476 (877)548-3276 Fax:(618)298-2476

Circa 1870. This turn-of-the-century German homestead stands on 10 hilltop acres with a panoramic view of the local area. The eight farm buildings are full of artifacts and equipment that reflect their original functions. These include the shop and garage, smokehouse, scale shed, machine shed, hen house, corncrib and feed house and, of course, the outhouse. The barn hayloft, constructed using wooden pegs, is available for large group functions. The property was bought in 1902 by second-generation German immigrants. Their grand-daughter, innkeeper Edna Schmidt Anderson, was born at the Farmstead and returned home following her parents' deaths. Accommodations include the Heritage Room in the farmhouse, the detached Summer Cottage and some rustic bunk house rooms with tractor themes: Ford, Oliver, John Deere and Case. Guests enjoy a full country breakfast in the 1860 Log Room, a part of the original log cabin, which has exposed interior log walls. Lunch, dinner, picnics, snacks and refreshments are available upon request. Guests may choose to study nature, reflect quietly or go on hikes, picnics and other outdoor activities. An amphitheater made of barn beams offers an exquisite view of the sunset. The inn is located near the Beall Woods State Park and Historic New Harmony, Ind. Guests may tour the grounds by themselves or with a guide.

Innkeeper(s): Edna Schmidt Anderson. $30-75. 4 rooms, 2 with PB, 1 cottage and 1 conference room. Breakfast included in rates. Types of meals: Full bkfst, early coffee/tea, lunch, picnic lunch, snacks/refreshments and dinner. Beds: DT. Reading lamp, ceiling fan and clock radio in room. Air conditioning. Library, parlor games, telephone, Treasures Gift Shop in attic loft and nature walks on premises. Limited handicap access. Small meetings, family reunions and seminars hosted. Antiquing, fishing, parks and historic village nearby.

Mount Carroll B4

Prairie Path Guest House

1002 N Lowden Rd
Mount Carroll, IL 61053-9476
(815)244-3462
E-mail: fernatppath@grics.net
Web: www.bbonline.com/il/prairiepath/

Circa 1876. Thirty-five acres of woods and fields surround this historic Victorian country home. If warm hospitality and natural beauty seem appealing, then this is the right place. Comfortable guest bedrooms feature hand stenciling, patchwork quilts, marble-top dressers, antiques and even Grandma's feather bed. Homemade jellies and jams accompany a hearty breakfast. Gaze at the deer, wild birds and other wildlife from the upstairs veranda's porch swing.

Innkeeper(s): Delos (Buster) & Fern Stadel. $60-89. 3 rooms, 1 with PB. Breakfast and snacks/refreshments included in rates. Types of meals: Country bkfst, veg bkfst, early coffee/tea and afternoon tea. Beds: Q. Cable TV, VCR, reading lamp, ceiling fan and clock radio in room. Central air. Library, parlor games, telephone and gift shop on premises. Antiquing, art galleries, beach, bicycling, canoeing/kayaking, cross-country skiing, downhill skiing, fishing, golf, hiking, horseback riding, live theater, museums, parks, shopping and wineries nearby.

Publicity: *Chicago Tribune, Dallas Morning News, Quad City Times and Wisconsin State Journal.*

Nauvoo E1

Nauvoo Grand-A Bed & Breakfast Inn

2015 Parley Street
Nauvoo, IL 62354
(217)453-2767
Web: www.bbonline.com/il/nauvoogrand

Circa 1904. Across from the state's oldest winery, this historic treasure boasts intricately detailed brick, Victorian trim, etched and stained glass, carved woodwork, copper hardware and pressed metal ceilings. Experience the tranquil ambiance of the past in the elegant parlor with ebonized oak furniture. In the evening, dessert is enjoyed in the exquisite library. Spacious guest bedrooms on three floors feature antique furnishings and modern amenities like DVD players. Some boast jetted tubs and scenic views overlooking the one-acre grounds and surrounding orchards and vineyards. In the formal dining room savor a complete gourmet breakfast served on Spode china.

Historic Interest: Original moldings, ceilings, hardware, stained glass, etc. dating back to the turn of the century.

Innkeeper(s): Gloria Laswell. $115. 5 rooms with PB. Breakfast and snacks/refreshments included in rates. Types of meals: Full gourmet bkfst. Beds: Q. Cable TV, reading lamp, CD player, clock radio, telephone and DVD

player in room. Central air. Library on premises. Antiquing, fishing, golf, hiking, horseback riding, live theater, museums, shopping, wineries, midwest's largest historic preservation site with more than 2 dozen restored homes and business from the 1840s, all furnished and with tours offered by guides in period costume free to the public nearby.

Oakland G6

Inn on The Square

3 Montgomery
Oakland, IL 61943
(217)346-2289 Fax:(217)346-2005

Circa 1878. This inn features hand-carved beams and braided rugs on wide pine flooring. The Tea Room has oak tables, fresh flowers and a hand-laid brick fireplace. Guests may wander in the forest behind the inn or relax in the library with a book or

jigsaw puzzle. Guest rooms have oak poster beds and handmade quilts. The Pine Room boasts an heirloom bed with a carved headboard. In addition to guest rooms, the inn houses

shops selling ladies apparel, gifts and antiques. The Amish communities of Arthur and Arcola are 14 miles away.

Innkeeper(s): Linda & Gary Miller. $65. 3 rooms with PB, 1 with FP and 1 conference room. Breakfast included in rates. Types of meals: Full bkfst, early coffee/tea, lunch and picnic lunch. Restaurant on premises. Beds: D. TV, reading lamp, ceiling fan, clock radio, desk and homemade cookies in room. Air conditioning. VCR, library, parlor games, telephone and fireplace on premises. Weddings, small meetings, family reunions and seminars hosted. Antiquing, golf, live theater, parks, shopping, sporting events, tennis, water sports, Amish Community, forest preserve, Lincoln sites and boating nearby.

Publicity: *Amish Country News, PM, Midwest Living and Country Living.*

Peoria E4

Randolph Terrace Historic Bed & Breakfast

201 W Columbia Ter
Peoria, IL 61606
(309)688-7858 (877)264-8266 Fax:(309)688-7858
E-mail: rthbb@horizon222.net
Web: www.rthbb.com

Circa 1914. Built for a prominent local civic leader, this beautiful Georgian Revival home has been restored to its original elegance. The common areas include a living room, east room, sun room and library. Appointed with European antiques, the luxurious guest bedrooms and suites offer spacious comfort. Robes and hair dryers are thoughtful amenities. A candlelight breakfast is served on china and crystal with a romantic flair. Flower gardens and greenery surround a brick patio.

Innkeeper(s): Kia Vega, Mercedes Vega. $95-145. 4 rooms with PB, 1 suite and 1 conference room. Breakfast, afternoon tea and snacks/refreshments included in rates. Types of meals: Full bkfst and veg bkfst. Beds: Q. Reading lamp, clock radio, turn-down service and suite has desk in room. Central air. TV, VCR, fax, copier, library, parlor games and telephone on premises. Small meetings, family reunions and seminars hosted. Antiquing, art galleries, bicycling, fishing, golf, hiking, live theater, museums, parks, shopping, sporting events, tennis and water sports nearby.

Pinckneyville J4

Oxbow B&B

3967 State Rt 13/127
Pinckneyville, IL 62274
(618)357-9839 (800)929-6888

Circa 1929. Most of the renovations and reconstruction to this country inn have been done by innkeeper Al. Sitting on ten acres, the bed & breakfast includes the Oxbow house with antique-filled guest bedrooms named after people and places of the Civil War. The Shiloh Room boasts a seven-foot headboard, marble-top dresser and mirrored washstand. A four-poster canopy bed made from aged barn timbers is the highlight of the Pilot Knob Room. A luxurious honeymoon suite is featured in the converted Oxbow Barn. A loft meeting room and in-ground swimming pool are enjoyed in the Shannon Barn. Two windmills and a woodworking shop also grace the grounds that provide ample parking.

Historic Interest: Oxbow B&B is near several historic sites, including Fort Kaskaskia, St. Mary River Covered Bridge, Charter Oak Schoolhouse, Pierre Menard Home, The Old Slave House and Fort De Chartres. The Perry County Historical Jail is only one mile from the home.

Innkeeper(s): Al & Peggy Doughty. $50-70. 5 rooms with PB and 1 suite. Breakfast included in rates. Types of meals: Full bkfst. Beds: Q. Spa, swimming, library, exercise equipment and pool table on premises. Antiquing, fishing and water sports nearby.

Quincy F1

The Kaufmann House B&B

1641 Hampshire St
Quincy, IL 62301-3143
(217)223-2502

Circa 1885. Gardens, tall trees and a fountain set the scene for this restored Queen Anne-style house. Ask for the Gray Antique Room with walnut antiques, sleigh couch, clawfoot tub and bay window views of the terraced gardens. The Patriot Room features Lincoln memorabilia, a sitting area, white iron bed and private balcony. Honeymooners are delighted by the gracious Robin Green Room. Enjoy a candlelight continental breakfast that may include hot scones and croissants, Swiss fingers and fresh fruit. Explore the surrounding scenic area on the bicycle built for two.

Innkeeper(s): Emery & Bettie Kaufmann. $75. 3 rooms with PB, 2 suites and 1 conference room. Breakfast included in rates. Types of meals: Full gourmet bkfst and early coffee/tea. Beds: QDT. Reading lamp, clock radio and desk in room. Air conditioning. VCR, bicycles, library, telephone and fireplace on premises. Weddings, small meetings, family reunions and seminars hosted. Antiquing, fishing, golf, live theater, parks, shopping, tennis and water sports nearby.

Sheffield C4

Chestnut Street Inn

301 E Chestnut St
Sheffield, IL 61361
(815)454-2419 (800)537-1304
E-mail: gail@chestnut-inn.com
Web: www.chestnut-inn.com

Circa 1854. Originally built in Italianate style, this mid-19th-century reborn Colonial Revival is the dream-come-true for innkeeper Gail Bruntjen. She spent more than 15 years searching for just the right country home to open a bed & breakfast. With its gracious architectural character and well-organized interior spaces, the Chestnut Street Inn fit the bill. Classic French doors open to a wide foyer with gleaming chandeliers and a floating spindle staircase. Sophisticated chintz fabrics and authentic antiques highlight each room. The four guest rooms offer down comforters, four-poster beds and private baths. Guests will be delighted by the gourmet selections offered every morning such as broccoli mushroom quiche, homemade breads and fresh fruit, all exquisitely presented by candlelight on fine China and crystal. Afternoon tea and evening snacks are served in the public rooms. Antiquing, shops, bicycling, hiking, golf and fishing are located nearby.

Innkeeper(s): Gail Bruntjen. $75-175. 4 rooms with PB, 1 with FP, 1 suite and 1 conference room. Breakfast, afternoon tea and snacks/refreshments included in rates. Types of meals: Full bkfst and early coffee/tea. Beds: KQT. Cable TV, VCR, reading lamp, turn-down service and desk in room. Air conditioning. Library, parlor games, telephone and fireplace on premises. Weddings and small meetings hosted. Antiquing, bicycling, fishing, golf, parks and shopping nearby.

Publicity: *The Illinois Review and Illinois Country Living.*

"Without a doubt, the best B&B I've ever been to."

Stockton A3

Hammond House B&B

323 N Main St
Stockton, IL 61085-1115
(815)947-2032
E-mail: haas@blkhawk.net
Web: www.hammondhouse.com

Circa 1900. Experience the rich heritage, tranquility and generous amenities offered at this serenely located restored Colonial Revival bed & breakfast inn. The mansion was built by widower Merwin Hammond for his new bride who requested the finest and largest home in the area. Relax on the double deck off the main floor or in the wicker furniture on the pillared front porch. Watch a video on the large-screen TV in the great room. Romantic, themed guest suites feature welcome baskets, chocolate and a bottle of wine. A continental breakfast is enjoyed in the dining room accented by the original second-floor skylight. Browse through the gift shop's extensive assortment of treasures for every season and occasion.

Innkeeper(s): LaVonneda & Spencer Haas. $65-175. 5 rooms with PB, 3 suites and 1 conference room. Breakfast and snacks/refreshments included in rates. Types of meals: Cont plus and early coffee/tea. Beds: QT. Cable TV, VCR, reading lamp, stereo, refrigerator, ceiling fan, snack bar, clock radio, coffeemaker, desk, hot tub/spa, complimentary welcome baskets, bottle of wine or sparkling cider, snacks and treats in room. Central air. Fax, copier, spa, library, telephone and gift shop on premises. Small meetings and family reunions hosted. Antiquing, art galleries, bicycling, canoeing/kayaking, cross-country skiing, downhill skiing, fishing, golf, hiking, horseback riding, live theater, museums, parks, shopping, tennis, water sports and wineries nearby.

Urbana   F6

Lindley House

312 W Green St
Urbana, IL 61801-3222
(217)384-4800
E-mail: lindley@shout.net
Web: www.lindley.cc

Circa 1895. Designed by architect Rudolph Gill from the University of Illinois for Dr. Austin Lindley, a prominent physician, this classic Queen Anne Victorian displays many of the whimsical architectural details popular during this era. The facade features imposing gables, an octagonal turret and a curved porch. Gleaming parquet floors in the four public rooms, a magnificent oak gingerbread staircase, beveled- and stained-glass windows are all part of the interior Victorian detailing. All second-floor queen guest rooms are decorated in antiques. The spacious third-floor king suite offers a sitting area, wet bar and private bath. There is also a two bedroom carriage house. Fresh fruit, homemade breads, a by-request hot dish and Columbian coffee are offered in the morning. Lindley House is located close to restaurants, parks, sports activities and the University of Illinois.

Innkeeper(s): Carolyn Baxley. $85-150. 5 rooms, 2 with PB, 1 suite and 1 cottage. Breakfast included in rates. Types of meals: Cont plus. Beds: KQDT. Cable TV, VCR, reading lamp, CD player, refrigerator, ceiling fan, clock radio and telephone in room. Air conditioning. Parlor games, fireplace and Internet access on premises. Weddings, small meetings and family reunions hosted.

West Dundee   B6

The Mansion Bed & Breakfast

305 Oregon Avenue
West Dundee, IL 60118
(847)426-7777 Fax:(847)426-5777
Web: www.themansionbedandbreakfast.com

Circa 1907. Exquisite woodwork, leaded stained-glass windows and lighting fixtures are some of the magnificent details of this impressive 1907 Tudor mansion that was once an iron-ore baron's private estate. Gather for conversation, board games or to read a book in the library. Romantic guest bedrooms and suites offer deluxe accommodations with an assortment of delightful amenities including some rooms with whirlpool tubs or Jacuzzis, four-poster or canopy beds, antique furnishings and a private terrace. An exceptional variety of nearby dining opportunities include a microbrewery and restaurant, Italian cuisine, elegant American and authentic Mexican food. The one-acre grounds feature a gazebo for hosting special events. Banquets can also be arranged.

Innkeeper(s): Steve Fang & Eda Tomasone. $89-179. 4 rooms with PB and 2 suites. Beds: KQ. Cable TV, VCR, reading lamp, clock radio, telephone and hot tub/spa in room. Air conditioning. Library, parlor games and fireplace on premises. Weddings, small meetings, family reunions and seminars hosted.

Indiana

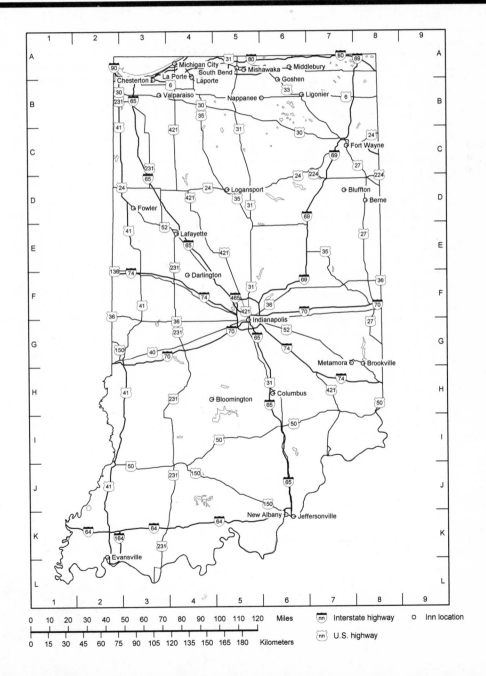

0 10 20 30 40 50 60 70 80 90 100 110 120   Miles

0 15 30 45 60 75 90 105 120 135 150 165 180   Kilometers

| nn | Interstate highway | o | Inn location |

| nn | U.S. highway |

163

Berne   D8

Historic Schug House Inn

706 W Main St
Berne, IN 46711-1328
(260)589-2303

Circa 1907. This Queen Anne home was built in 1907 by Emanuel Wanner. It was constructed for the Schug family, who occupied the home for 25 years, and whom the innkeepers chose the name of their inn. Victorian features decorate the home, including inlaid floors, pocket doors and a wrap-around porch. Guest rooms boast walnut, cherry and oak furnishings. Fruit, cheeses and pastries are served on antique china each morning in the dining room. Horse-drawn carriages from the nearby Old Order Amish community often pass on the street outside.

Innkeeper(s): John Minch. $40-45. 9 rooms with PB and 1 conference room. Breakfast included in rates. Types of meals: Cont. Beds: KQDT. TV and telephone on premises.

Bloomington   H4

Grant Street Inn

310 N Grant St
Bloomington, IN 47408-3736
(812)334-2353 (800)328-4350 Fax:(812)331-8673
E-mail: gsi@grantstinn.com
Web: www.grantstinn.com

Circa 1883. Built originally before the turn of the century by William P. Rogers, dean of the Indiana University Law School, for his bride Belle, the home served as both a private home and student residence until 1990. It was moved to its present location at 7th and Grant Street in the historic district and restored to its original elegance of hardwood flooring, crown moldings and raised porches. There are 24 individually decorated rooms, all featuring antique-style furnishings. All of the rooms offer private baths, TV and phones. Some of the rooms feature fireplaces and separate entrances. Suites offer the romance of Jacuzzi tubs and fireplaces. Guests can enjoy a leisurely full breakfast in the breakfast room. The inn is located within walking distance of Indiana's largest antique mall and cultural events at Indiana University.

Historic Interest: The inn is a short drive to Lake Monroe, Brown County and McCormick's Creek State Park.

Innkeeper(s): Bob Bohler. $109-179. 24 rooms with PB, 14 with FP and 2 suites. Breakfast included in rates. Types of meals: Full bkfst. Beds: KQT. Cable TV, clock radio, telephone and desk in room. Air conditioning. Fax, copier and fireplace on premises. Limited handicap access. Antiquing, fishing, golf, live theater, parks, shopping, sporting events, tennis and water sports nearby.

Bluffton   D7

The Washington Street Inn

220 E Washington St
Bluffton, IN 46714
(260)824-9070

Circa 1896. Many original features are found in this restored 1896 Queen Anne Victorian home. The staircase and two fireplace mantels are finished in rich cherry wood. Several rooms still feature hardwood floors. Guest bedrooms and baths are furnished in Victorian decor. A guest kitchen boasts a refrigerator, microwave, table and chairs. A game room/library also is available. The main living area, two porches and large fenced-in backyard provide ample space to roam and relax. The inn is close to restaurants, an antique mall and a state park. Downtown is only two blocks away. A Wabash River walkway also is nearby.

Innkeeper(s): Gene & Ruthann Kyle. $75. 4 rooms. Breakfast included in rates. Types of meals: Full bkfst. Beds: QD. Cable TV, reading lamp, clock radio, telephone and some with VCR in room. Air conditioning. VCR, parlor games and fireplace on premises. Weddings and small meetings hosted. Antiquing, cross-country skiing, fishing, golf, parks and tennis nearby.

Brookville   G8

The Hermitage Bed and Breakfast

650 East 8th St
Brookville, IN 47012
(765)647-5182 (877)407-9198

Circa 1835. J. Ottis Adams and T.C. Steele, two renown Indiana artists, set up their home and art studios on this large estate that spans 6.5 acres. The Hoosier Group painted here in the heart of the scenic Whitewater River Valley for several years. Join Martha for a tour of this 19-room house, and then converse over refreshments in the living room or studios. A library features a wood-burning fireplace, antique books and magazines. A 112-foot-long veranda with vintage furniture and a hammock overlooks the picturesque grounds. The adjacent Town Park and nearby lake offer many outdoor activities. Visit the historic region of Metamora, a Canal town and South Central area's covered bridge communities.

Innkeeper(s): Martha Shea. $75. 6 rooms with PB and 1 conference room. Breakfast and snacks/refreshments included in rates. Types of meals: Full gourmet bkfst, early coffee/tea and dinner. Beds: KDT. Reading lamp, ceiling fan, clock radio, turn-down service and desk in room. Air conditioning. TV, VCR, bicycles, library, parlor games and fireplace on premises. Weddings, small meetings, family reunions and seminars hosted. Antiquing, beach, bicycling, canoeing/kayaking, downhill skiing, fishing, golf, hiking, horseback riding, parks, shopping, sporting events, tennis, water sports, wineries, Historic Canal Town and Metamora nearby.

Publicity: *Outdoor Indiana.*

Chesterton   B3

The Gray Goose

350 Indian Boundary Rd
Chesterton, IN 46304-1511
(219)926-5781 (800)521-5127 Fax:(219)926-4845
E-mail: graygoose@niia.net
Web: www.graygooseinn.com

Circa 1939. Situated on 100 wooded acres, just under one hour from Chicago, this English country inn overlooks a private lake. Guests can see Canadian geese and ducks on the lake and surrounding area. Rooms are decorated in 18th-century English, Shaker and French-country styles. Some of the rooms feature fireplaces, Jacuzzi and poster beds. Complimentary snacks, soft drinks, coffee and tea are available throughout the day. Strains of Mozart or Handel add to the ambiance.

Historic Interest: The Dunes State and National Lakeshore is less than three miles from the inn.

Innkeeper(s): Tim Wilk & Chuck Ramsey. $90-185. 8 rooms with PB, 3 with FP, 3 suites and 1 conference room. Breakfast, afternoon tea and snacks/refreshments included in rates. Types of meals: Full gourmet bkfst and early coffee/tea. Beds: KQ. TV, VCR, reading lamp, ceiling fan, clock radio, telephone, desk, hot tub/spa and one room with fireplace and Jacuzzi in room. Air conditioning. Fax, copier, library, fireplace, snack/service bar, large screened gazebo and gift shop on premises. Weddings, small meetings, family reunions and seminars hosted. Antiquing, cross-country skiing, downhill skiing, fishing, golf, live theater, parks, shopping, sporting events, tennis and water sports nearby.

Publicity: *Insider, Post-Tribune, Glamour, Country Inns, Midwest Living, Indianapolis Star and Indianapolis Woman.*

"Extremely gracious! A repeat stay for us because it is such a wonderful place to stay."

Columbus   H6

The Columbus Inn
445 5th St
Columbus, IN 47201-6206
(812)378-4289 Fax:(812)378-4289
E-mail: columbusinn@voyager.net
Web: www.thecolumbusinn.com

Circa 1895. Dances, basketball games and poultry shows once convened in the auditorium of the old Columbus City Hall during its years as the focal point of town. The original terra-cotta floors, enormous brass chandeliers and hand-carved oak woodwork now welcome overnight guests. Lavishly decorated rooms feature reproduction antiques such as cherry sleigh beds. Twelve-foot-high windows and 21-foot ceilings grace the Charles Sparrell Suite with its separate sleeping level.

Historic Interest: In the National Register.

Innkeeper(s): Chester Dingus. $119-279. 34 rooms with PB, 5 suites and 3 conference rooms. Breakfast included in rates. Types of meals: Full gourmet bkfst, early coffee/tea, afternoon tea and gourmet dinner. Beds: QD. Cable TV, reading lamp, refrigerator, clock radio, telephone and desk in room. Air conditioning. TV, VCR, fax, copier and parlor games on premises. Limited handicap access. Weddings, small meetings, family reunions and seminars hosted. Amusement parks, antiquing, downhill skiing, fishing, live theater, parks, shopping, sporting events and water sports nearby.

Publicity: *Chicago Sun-Times, Country Inns, Home & Away, Cincinnati Enquirer, Glamour, Innsider and InnReview.*

"A delicious and beautifully served breakfast was the crowning glory of our stay."

Darlington   F4

Our Country Home
RR 1 Box 103
Darlington, IN 47940
(765)794-3139

Circa 1850. A favorite activity at this country home is a moonlight carriage ride along country roads. (You can opt for carriage driving classes!) Abundant fields of corn and beans surround the 12-acre property, and there are horses and a barn. The innkeepers provide full country breakfasts of muffins, potatoes, eggs, bacon and pancakes. Private candlelight dinners can be reserved as well. Guest rooms are decorated in a country style. There's a bicycle built for two, and guests often cycle the back roads for hours and then come home to soak in the hot tub later that evening under the stars.

Innkeeper(s): Jim & Debbie Smith. $95-205. 4 rooms. Breakfast included in rates. Types of meals: Full bkfst, lunch, picnic lunch and dinner. Restaurant

on premises. Beds: Q. TV, VCR, ceiling fan and turn-down service in room. Air conditioning. Spa, swimming, stable, bicycles, library, carriage rides and horse camps for kids in the summer on premises. Weddings, small meetings and family reunions hosted. Bicycling, golf, horseback riding, live theater, museums, shopping and sporting events nearby.

Publicity: *Journal Review, The Park County Guild and Indianapolis TV Channel 59.*

"Just what the doctor ordered, a very relaxing, rejuvenating and back to nature weekend."

Evansville   K2

Starkey Inn
214 SE First St
Evansville, IN 47713
(812)425-7264 (800)580-0305 Fax:(812)425-7333
E-mail: webmaster@starkeyinn.com
Web: www.starkeyinn.com

Circa 1850. A prominent attorney built this Greek Revival mansion for his bride who longed for a fashionable city home typical to those in the South. The current owner Marti T. Starkey, also an attorney, has made extensive renovations to ensure modern comfort while retaining its original integrity. Two of the children's names are still found etched on an upstairs window. Tastefully decorated guest bedrooms boast antique furnishings including four-poster and sleigh beds. Using recipes from a well-worn cookbook, host Veda serves favorites like cheese strata, French toast with peaches, lemon yogurt muffins and quick quiche. Choose to eat in the dining room, kitchen, or even breakfast in bed. Only a block from the Ohio River, it is a short walk to the historic city's main street shops and restaurants.

Innkeeper(s): Veda & Walt Taylor & Marti T. Starkey. $85-185. 5 rooms, 3 with PB, 3 with FP and 1 suite. Breakfast included in rates. Types of meals: Full bkfst, early coffee/tea and room service. Beds: KQD. Reading lamp, clock radio, telephone, desk and hot tub/spa in room. Central air. TV, VCR, fax, copier, library, parlor games, fireplace and laundry facility on premises. Weddings, small meetings, family reunions and seminars hosted. Antiquing, art galleries, bicycling, downhill skiing, fishing, golf, live theater, museums, parks, shopping, sporting events, tennis and water sports nearby.

Fort Wayne   C7

The Carole Lombard House B&B
704 Rockhill St
Fort Wayne, IN 46802-5918
(219)426-9896 (888)426-9896

Circa 1895. Jane Alice Peters, a.k.a. Carole Lombard, spent her first six years in this turn-of-the-century home located in Ft. Wayne's historic West-Central neighborhood. The innkeepers named two guest rooms in honor of Lombard and her second husband, Clark Gable. Each of these rooms features memorabilia from the Gable-Lombard romance. A video library with a collection of classic movies is available, including many of Lombard's films. The innkeepers provide information for a self-guided architectural tour of the historic area.

Historic Interest: On Oct. 6, 1908, Jane Alice Peters was born in the handsome house at the foot of Rockhill Street. The world knew her as Carole Lombard.

Innkeeper(s): Bev Fiandt. $75-85. 4 rooms with PB. Breakfast included in rates. Types of meals: Full bkfst and early coffee/tea. Beds: KQDT. Cable TV, reading lamp, clock radio and telephone in room. Air conditioning. VCR, bicycles and fireplace on premises. Small meetings hosted. Antiquing, live theater, parks and sporting events nearby.

Publicity: *Playboy and Michigan Living.*

"The elegance and ambience are most appreciated."

Fowler D3

Pheasant Country B&B

900 E 5th St
Fowler, IN 47944-1518
(765)884-1252 (765)714-2896
E-mail: pheasantcountryinn@yahoo.com
Web: www.pheasantcountryinn.com

Circa 1940. Situated on a tree-lined brick street in the heart of the small town's historic area east of the Benton County Court House, this English Colonial inn is just 25 minutes northwest of Purdue University. Feel welcomed by the friendly hospitality. Relax amid European antiques in the smoke-free environment that is pleasantly scented with flower and mint aromas. Guest bedrooms feature generous amenities. Wake up to a bountiful breakfast of scones, waffles, egg dishes and beverages while classic music plays in the background. Bicycles are available for leisurely exploring the surrounding scenery.

Historic Interest: Historic house located in historic area on a brick street.

Innkeeper(s): June Gaylord. $49-89. 4 rooms, 1 with PB. Breakfast, afternoon tea and snacks/refreshments included in rates. Types of meals: Full gourmet bkfst, veg bkfst, early coffee/tea, gourmet lunch, gourmet dinner and room service. Beds: Q. Cable TV/VCR, videos, phone, clock, hair dryer, ironing board, iron, basket of toiletries, fruit basket, fresh flowers, coffeemaker, newspaper, magazines, chocolates, bottled water, central air and ceiling fan in room. Costa Rican coffee, herbal teas, computer, copier, library, gift & antique shop, massage/yoga instructor and bicycles on premises. Small meetings hosted. Art galleries, bicycling, canoeing/kayaking, golf, hiking, horseback riding, live theater, museums, parks, tennis, Purdue sporting events and convocations, antique auctions every weekend, Wabash River, hunting (pheasant, rabbit, turkey and deer) nearby.

Publicity: Benton Review, Lafayette Journal & Courier and Lafayette - WLFI-TV.

Goshen B6

Prairie Manor B&B

66398 US Hwy 33
Goshen, IN 46526-9482
(574)642-4761

Circa 1925. Local craftsman created this elegant English-style country manor home. The home's original features have remained unchanged, including the original window seats, arched doorways and a winding staircase. The inn's 12 acres include a swimming pool and play area for children. Breakfasts include items such as crepes filled with fresh strawberries and bananas topped with a yogurt-whipped cream sauce or baked eggs with fresh herbs and three cheeses. Homemade breads, such as raspberry cream cheese coffeecake, also are served.

Innkeeper(s): Jean & Hesston Lauver. $65-95. 3 rooms with PB, 1 suite and 2 conference rooms. Breakfast and snacks/refreshments included in rates. Types of meals: Full bkfst, veg bkfst and early coffee/tea. Beds: QT. Modem hook-up, cable TV, reading lamp, ceiling fan, clock radio and desk in room. Air conditioning. Fax, swimming, stable, library, parlor games, telephone, fireplace and laundry facility on premises. Weddings, small meetings, family reunions and seminars hosted. Antiquing, art galleries, bicycling, canoeing/kayaking, cross-country skiing, fishing, golf, hiking, live theater, museums, parks, shopping, sporting events and tennis nearby.

Indianapolis G5

The Old Northside Bed & Breakfast

1340 North Alabama St.
Indianapolis, IN 46202
(317)635-9123 (800)635-9127 Fax:(317)635-9243
E-mail: garyh@hofmeister.com
Web: www.oldnorthsideinn.com

Circa 1885. This Romanesque Revival mansion is fashioned out of bricks, and the grounds are enclosed by a wrought-iron fence. Border gardens and an English side garden complete the look. Rooms are decorated with a theme in mind. The Literary Room, which includes a fireplace and Jacuzzi tub, is decorated to honor Indiana authors. Another room honors the Hollywood's golden years. The home has many modern conveniences, yet still retains original maple floors and hand-carved, mahogany woodwork. Full breakfasts are served in the formal dining room or on the patio. Guests can walk to many city attractions.

Innkeeper(s): Gary Hofmeister. $85-185. 7 rooms. Breakfast and snacks/refreshments included in rates. Types of meals: Full bkfst. Beds: K. Cable TV, VCR, clock radio, telephone, desk and hot tub/spa in room. Central air. Fireplace on premises. Small meetings hosted. Antiquing, art galleries, bicycling, live theater, museums, parks, shopping and sporting events nearby.

Speedway B&B

1829 Cunningham Dr
Indianapolis, IN 46224-5338
(317)487-6531 (800)975-3412 Fax:(317)481-1825

Circa 1906. This two-story white columned inn reflects a plantation-style architecture. The inn is situated on an acre of lawn and trees. The bed & breakfast has a homey decor that includes a wood-paneled common room and elegantly furnished guest rooms. Breakfast includes items such as homemade coffee cake and Danish or sausage and egg casserole. Nearby attractions include President Harrison's home, the Hall of Fame Museum and the largest city park in the nation, Eagle Creek Park.

Innkeeper(s): Pauline Grothe. $65-135. 5 rooms with PB. Breakfast included in rates. Types of meals: Full bkfst. Beds: KQD. Cable TV, reading lamp, clock radio and telephone in room. Air conditioning. VCR, fax, bicycles, parlor games and fireplace on premises. Weddings, small meetings, family reunions and seminars hosted. Antiquing, cross-country skiing, fishing, golf, live theater, parks, shopping, sporting events, tennis and water sports nearby.

"It is people like you who have given B&Bs such a good reputation."

Stone Soup Inn

1304 N Central Ave.
Indianapolis, IN 46202-2616
(317)639-9550 (800)639-9550 Fax:(317)917-9086
E-mail: stonesoupinn@iquest.net
Web: www.stonesoupinn.com

Circa 1901. Situated in a historic neighborhood near downtown, this neo-Colonial features a Mission-style décor with a touch of Victorian. Complimentary beverages and snacks are provided in the Butler's Pantry. Guest bedrooms include phones with voice mail and VCRs with a large video selection to choose from. The popular Lily Room features a sleigh bed and a bay window overlooking the pond. The exquisite Blue Room boasts a working fireplace. Some rooms also have small kitchenettes. A favorite breakfast specialty is the inn's Cheese-egg Bake. Ask about the Historic Theater District Getaway package, or the Old Northside Historic Walking Tour. Massages and spa services can be arranged. Wine gift baskets and flower arrangements are available upon request.

Innkeeper(s): Jordan Rifkin & Jeneane Life. $85-135. 8 rooms, 6 with PB, 1 with FP. Types of meals: Full bkfst. Beds: QDT. Cable TV, VCR, reading lamp, CD player, refrigerator, ceiling fan, clock radio, telephone, coffeemaker and desk in room. Central air. Fax and parlor games on premises. Small meetings and family reunions hosted. Antiquing, art galleries, live theater, museums, parks and wineries nearby.

The Tranquil Cherub

2164 N Capitol Ave
Indianapolis, IN 46202-1251
(317)923-9036 Fax:(317)923-8676
E-mail: reservations@tranquilcherub.com
Web: www.tranquilcherub.com

Circa 1890. Visitors to the bustling Indianapolis area will appreciate the quiet elegance of the Tranquil Cherub, a Classical Revival home, five minutes from downtown. Guests may choose from the blue and taupe Wedgwood Room, which offers a mural headboard, or the Gatsby Room highlighted by an Art Deco-era four-poster cannonball bed. The jade-green and navy Rogers Room features stained glass and an oak bedroom set that originated in an old Chicago hotel. Grannies Suite comprises the third floor and is a spacious accommodation with an eclectic selection of antiques. Breakfast is served in the oak-paneled dining room or on a back deck overlooking the lily ponds.

Historic Interest: President Benjamin Harrison home (1 mile), James Whitcomb Riley museum home (2 miles), Morris-Bulter house (1 mile).

Innkeeper(s): Thom & Barbara Feit. $85-125. 4 rooms, 3 with PB, 2 with FP and 1 suite. Breakfast and snacks/refreshments included in rates. Types of meals: Full gourmet bkfst, veg bkfst and early coffee/tea. Beds: KQT. Data port, cable TV, reading lamp, ceiling fan, snack bar, clock radio, telephone, desk and fireplace in room. Central air. VCR, fax, copier, library, fireplace and gift shop on premises. Small meetings, family reunions and seminars hosted. Antiquing, art galleries, bicycling, golf, hiking, live theater, museums, shopping, sporting events, tennis, wineries and hospital nearby.

Publicity: *Indianapolis Star and Indianapolis Monthly.*

Jeffersonville   K6

1877 House Country Inn

2408 Utica-Sellersburg Rd
Jeffersonville, IN 47130
(812)285-1877 (888)284-1877

Circa 1877. Sugar maples shade the lawn of this inn, located on more than two acres. There are two guest rooms and a cottage available on the property. The renovated farmhouse is decorated with country pieces and memorabilia collected for several years by the innkeepers. Strawberry soufflé, savory bread pudding and poppyseed bread are favorites served at the inn that also have been included in the food section of the local paper.

Innkeeper(s): Steve & Carol Stenbro. $89-149. 3 rooms with PB, 3 with FP. Breakfast and snacks/refreshments included in rates. Types of meals: Full gourmet bkfst. Beds: QDT. Cable TV, VCR, ceiling fan, cottage with Jacuzzi tub and fireplace in room. Air conditioning. Fax, copier, Internet and gazebo with 8-person hot tub on premises. Small meetings hosted. Amusement parks, antiquing, downhill skiing, fishing, golf, live theater, parks, shopping, sporting events, tennis, wineries, boating, gambling and swimming nearby.

Publicity: *Courier Journal, New Albany Tribune and Midwest Living.*

The Old Bridge Inn

131 W Chestnut St
Jeffersonville, IN 47130
(812)284-3580 Fax:(812)284-3561

Circa 1840. A neoclassical property in Jeffersonville's historic districts, the Old Bridge Inn is within walking distance of the Ohio River and has a delightful garden that is a mix of perennials and herbs. It offers four guest bedrooms, and a daily multi-course breakfast that includes tasty items such as fruit, muffins, granola or muesli, a breakfast casserole or Belgian waffles. Complimentary beverages are available throughout the day. Guests may venture out to nearby attractions like the falls of the Ohio State Park, the Howard Steamboat Museum and Churchill Downs.

Innkeeper(s): Linda Williams. $60-115. 4 rooms with PB, 1 with FP, 1 suite and 1 conference room. Breakfast included in rates. Types of meals: Full bkfst, early coffee/tea, gourmet lunch, picnic lunch, afternoon tea and gourmet dinner. Beds: QD. TV, reading lamp, clock radio and fireplace in room. Central air. TV, fax, copier, library, pet boarding, telephone, fireplace and gift shop on premises. Weddings, small meetings, family reunions and seminars hosted. Amusement parks, antiquing, art galleries, downhill skiing, fishing, golf, hiking, live theater, museums, parks, shopping, sporting events, tennis, water sports and wineries nearby.

La Porte   A4

Hidden Pond B&B

5342 N US Hwy 35
La Porte, IN 46350-8279
(219)879-8200 Fax:(219)879-1770
E-mail: edberent@adsnet.com
Web: www.bbonline.com/in/hiddenpond/

Circa 1918. Ten wooded acres with wetlands, pond and meadows surround this country house and its hot tub, heated pool and gazebo. Each guest room offers picturesque views and country decor. An egg entree, breakfast meat and pastries are provided at breakfast. Your hosts will advise you on nearby excursions and activities such as the Blue Chip Casino, La Porte antique shops and the Indiana Dunes along the shores of Lake Michigan. Or you can try your hand at angling for one of the pond's inhabitants and simply enjoying nature. Chicago is 60 miles away.

Innkeeper(s): Sue & Ed Berent. $89-159. 4 rooms, 3 with PB and 1 conference room. Breakfast and snacks/refreshments included in rates. Types of meals: Full gourmet bkfst, veg bkfst, early coffee/tea, gourmet lunch and gourmet dinner. Beds: KT. Modem hook-up, reading lamp, ceiling fan, clock radio, desk and hot tub/spa in room. Air conditioning. TV, fax, copier, spa, library, parlor games, telephone and fireplace on premises. Small meetings, family reunions and seminars hosted. Amusement parks, antiquing, art galleries, beach, bicycling, fishing, golf, hiking, horseback riding, live theater, museums, parks, shopping, sporting events, tennis, water sports and wineries nearby.

Publicity: *South Bend Trib, La Porte Herald Argus, Michigan City Dispatch and Gary Post Tribune.*

Lafayette   E4

Historic Loeb House Inn

708 Cincinnati St
Lafayette, IN 47901
(765)420-7737 Fax:(765)420-7805
Web: www.loebhouseinn.com

Circa 1882. This pristine brick Italianate manor was once the home of a prominent Lafayette family, but was later turned into apartments. In 1996, it was painstakingly restored to its former glory. The home boasts crown molding and ceiling medallions, gleaming woodwork and intricate wood floors. Fine Victorian antiques and appointments decorate the inn. Three guest rooms include a fireplace, and the private baths include either a whirlpool or clawfoot tub. Guests are pampered in Victorian style with a full breakfast, afternoon tea and turndown service. The home is located in Lafayette's Centennial historic district and is close to many local sites, including Purdue University.

Innkeeper(s): Jan Alford & Dick Nagel. $85-175. 5 rooms with PB, 3 with FP, 1 suite and 1 conference room. Breakfast, afternoon tea and snacks/refreshments included in rates. Types of meals: Full bkfst and early coffee/tea. Beds: D. Cable TV, reading lamp, ceiling fan, telephone, turn-down service and desk in room. Air conditioning. Fax, copier, parlor games, fireplace, pantry stocked with snacks and beverages and ice machine on premises. Weddings, small meetings and seminars hosted. Amusement parks, antiquing, golf, live theater, parks, shopping, sporting events, tennis, water sports and festivals nearby.

Publicity: *Purdue Magazine and Lafayette Journal & Courier.*

The Perrin House Historic Bed and Breakfast

1219 Main Street
Lafayette, IN 47901
(765)420-7628
E-mail: lodgings@perrinhouse.net
Web: www.PerrinHouse.net

Circa 1863. A place of warmth and solace, this 1863 Queen Anne Victorian mansion with its graceful architecture adorns the premier Perrin Historic District, Lafayette's first planned residential area that conformed to geographic contours. Relax with snacks and refreshments on the large front porch. Stroll through the sunny flower garden or enjoy the shaded landscape of the secluded brick patio. Spacious and elegantly decorated guest bedrooms offer pampering retreats for leisure and practical comfort for business. Beds with pillow top mattresses and down comforters, central air conditioning, antique furnishings, data ports and fresh flowers are some of the pleasurable features to expect. One grand room boasts a fireplace and canopy bed. After a country fresh breakfast, explore the scenic area on available bikes. Walk downtown to the nearby Riehle Plaza on the Wabash Riverfront.

Historic Interest: From the moment you walk into the foyer and throughout every room, you will feel the air of history because of the grand and elegant architecture.
Innkeeper(s): Melinda and Burt Etchison. $85-135. 4 rooms with PB, 2 with FP. Breakfast and snacks/refreshments included in rates. Types of meals: Full gourmet bkfst, veg bkfst, early coffee/tea, gourmet lunch, picnic lunch, afternoon tea and gourmet dinner. Beds: KQT. Data port, reading lamp, ceiling fan, clock radio, turn-down service, fireplace, antiques and original artwork from local artists in room. Central air. Library, parlor games, telephone and laundry facility on premises. Weddings, small meetings, family reunions and seminars hosted. Amusement parks, antiquing, art galleries, bicycling, canoeing/kayaking, cross-country skiing, fishing, golf, hiking, horseback riding, live theater, museums, parks, shopping, sporting events and water sports nearby.

Ligonier   B6

Solomon Mier Manor Bed Breakfast and Antiques

508 South Cavin Street
Ligonier, IN 46767-1802
(260)894-3668

Circa 1899. This turn-of-the-century Queen Anne-Italianate manor boasts hand-painted ceilings, intricate woodwork and stained-glass windows. The ornate carved staircase is especially

appealing with its staircase library. Antiques fill the guest rooms and common areas. The home is eligible to be on the National Register and originally was home to Solomon Mier, one of the area's first Jewish residents who came to the Ligonier area in search of religious tolerance and word of the railroad to come. Guests will find many areas of interest, such as the Shipshewana Flea Market & Auction and the on-site antique shop.

Historic Interest: The home was built in 1899 and has 100-year-old stained-glass windows, hand-carved woodwork, and hand-painted ceilings. The Manor is furnished throughout with period antiques and objects d'art.
Innkeeper(s): Ron & Doris Blue. $60-70. 4 rooms with PB. Breakfast, afternoon tea and snacks/refreshments included in rates. Types of meals: Full bkfst and early coffee/tea. Beds: KQDT. Reading lamp, ceiling fan and telephone in room. Air conditioning. TV, VCR, bicycles, library, parlor games, fireplace and gift shop on premises. Family reunions and seminars hosted. Fishing, golf, museums, parks, shopping and tennis nearby.

Publicity: *Goshen News.*

"Complete and beautiful experience."

Logansport   D5

Inntiquity, A Country Inn

1075 State Rd 25 N
Logansport, IN 46947
(574)722-2398 (877)230-7870 Fax:(574)739-2217
E-mail: inntiqui@ffni.com
Web: www.intiquity.com

Circa 1849. Sitting on 23 acres with flower and herb gardens, two ponds, a manicured croquet lawn and undeveloped land, this elegantly converted dairy barn has been family-owned since 1849. Well-appointed suites and guest bedrooms, two with fireplaces, feature plush robes, canopy beds with fine linens, turndown service, sitting rooms, Jacuzzi tubs and candles. Indulge in quiet moments relaxing on a private deck. A satisfying breakfast and snacks are provided. The on-site restaurant offers lunch and dinner menu selections. Ride one of the available bicycles to view the local sites.

Historic Interest: Family owned since 1849 land grant. Converted dairy barn with countless surviving conveniences that did not require electricity, original architectural pieces, many saved from local families.
Innkeeper(s): Lee & George Naftzger. $80-125. 11 rooms with PB, 2 with FP and 10 suites. Breakfast and snacks/refreshments included in rates. Types of meals: Full gourmet bkfst, veg bkfst, early coffee/tea, gourmet lunch, gourmet lunch, afternoon tea and gourmet dinner. Restaurant on premises. Beds: KQ. Data port, cable TV, VCR, reading lamp, stereo, clock radio, telephone, coffeemaker, turn-down service, desk, hot tub/spa and fireplace in room. Central air. Fax, copier, spa, bicycles, library, parlor games, fireplace, laundry facility, gift shop, deck access to every room and two ponds on premises. Limited handicap access. Weddings, small meetings, family reunions and seminars hosted. Amusement parks, antiquing, art galleries, beach, canoeing/kayaking, cross-country skiing, fishing, golf, hiking, horseback riding, live theater, museums, parks, shopping, tennis, water sports, Ivt-Tech and IUPUI Kokomo nearby.
Publicity: *Inn Travel Book Logansport Pharos Tribune Kokomo Newspaper.*

Metamora   G7

The Thorpe House Country Inn

19049 Clayborne St, PO Box 36
Metamora, IN 47030
(765)647-5425 (888)427-7932
E-mail: thorpe_house@hotmail.com
Web: www.metamora.com/thorpehouse

Circa 1840. The steam engine still brings passenger cars and the gristmill still grinds cornmeal in historic Metamora. The Thorpe House is located one block from the canal. Rooms feature original pine and poplar floors, antiques, stenciling and country accessories. Enjoy a hearty breakfast selected from the inn's restaurant menu. (Popular items include homemade biscuits, egg dishes and sourdough pecan rolls.) Walk through the village to explore more than 100 shops.

Historic Interest: Indian mounds, historic Brookville, Laurel, and "village of spires" Oldenburg are within 10 minutes. Historic Connersville and Batesville are within one-half hour.

Innkeeper(s): Mike & Jean Owens. $70-125. 5 rooms with PB and 1 suite. Breakfast and snacks/refreshments included in rates. Types of meals: Country bkfst, veg bkfst, early coffee/tea, lunch and picnic lunch. Restaurant on premises. Beds: KDT. Reading lamp, refrigerator, snack bar, clock radio, telephone and coffeemaker in room. Central air. TV, VCR, fax, parlor games and gift shops, pottery studio on premises. Family reunions hosted. Amusement parks, antiquing, art galleries, beach, bicycling, canoeing/kayaking, fishing, golf, hiking, horseback riding, museums, parks, shopping, water sports, flea markets and bird sanctuary nearby.

Publicity: *Cincinnati Enquirer, Chicago Sun-Times and Midwest Living.*

"Thanks to all of you for your kindness and hospitality during our stay."

Michigan City   A4

Brickstone B&B

215 W 6th St
Michigan City, IN 46360
(219)878-1819
E-mail: brickstone@comcast.net
Web: http:mywebpages.comcast.net/brickstone/

Circa 1880. Originally the parsonage of the First Congregational Church, the Brickstone offers a Great Room with fireplace and a wicker-filled screened porch. There are four guest rooms, each decorated in a style reflecting one of the four seasons. All feature fresh flowers and double or single Jacuzzi tubs. A breakfast buffet is provided in the morning and afterward you can walk or take a bicycle to the marina, beach or zoo. Guests often enjoy walking across to the Light House Mall Outlet Center.

Innkeeper(s): Jim & Sidney Hoover. $80-140. 4 rooms with PB. Breakfast included in rates. Types of meals: Full gourmet bkfst and early coffee/tea. Beds: QT. Reading lamp, clock radio, desk and fan in room. VCR, fax, library and telephone on premises. Weddings hosted. Antiquing, fishing, golf, live theater, parks, shopping and water sports nearby.

The Hutchinson Mansion Inn

220 W 10th St
Michigan City, IN 46360-3516
(219)879-1700
Web: www.hutchinsonmansioninn.com

Circa 1875. Built by a lumber baron in 1875, this grand, red-brick mansion features examples of Queen Anne, Classic Revival and Italianate design. The mansion boasts 11 stained-glass panels and the front parlor still has its original plaster friezes, ceiling medallion and a marble fireplace. The dining room's oak-paneled walls include a secret panel. The library is stocked with interesting books and games, and classical compositions and Victorian parlor music are piped in. The second floor offers a host of places perfect for relaxation, including a small game room, mini library and a sun porch. Rooms are filled with antiques and

unusual pieces such as the Tower Suite's octagonal/post Gothic-style bed. The carriage house suites include a sitting room, refrigerator and either a whirlpool or large, soaking tub.

Historic Interest: The mansion is nestled in Michigan City's historic district and a short distance from other gracious homes. The Barker Mansion, a house museum, is only three blocks away. A lighthouse museum is less than a mile from the inn. Bailly Homestead and Chellberg Farm, a turn-of-the-century Swedish farm, are 15 minutes away.

Innkeeper(s): Mary DuVal. $95-150. 10 rooms with PB and 4 suites. Breakfast included in rates. Types of meals: Full bkfst. Beds: QD. Telephone and fresh flowers in room. Central air. Fax, library, game room furnished with antiques and off-street parking on premises. Small meetings and family reunions hosted. Antiquing, beach, cross-country skiing, fishing, golf, horseback riding, live theater, museums, shopping, tennis, wineries, National Lakeshore, stables, shopping and hiking nearby.

Publicity: *Midwest Living, Midwest Motorist, Heritage Country, Indianapolis Star, Michigan Living, South Bend Tribune and Chicago Tribune.*

"Beautiful, romantic inn, exceptional hospitality, your breakfasts were fabulous."

Middlebury   A6

Patchwork Quilt Country Inn

11748 CR 2
Middlebury, IN 46540
(574)825-2417 Fax:(574)825-5172
E-mail: patchworkinn@aol.com
Web: www.patchworkquiltinn.com

Circa 1875. Located in the heart of Indiana's Amish country, this inn offers comfortable lodging and fine food. Some of the recipes are regionally famous, such as the award-winning Buttermilk Pecan Chicken. All guest rooms feature handsome quilts and country decor, and The Loft treats visitors to a whirlpool tub and kitchenette. Ask about the three-hour guided tour of the surrounding Amish area. The smoke-free inn also is host to a quilt and gift shop.

Historic Interest: 1875 farmhouse, original recipes in the restaurant.

Innkeeper(s): John & Adrienne Cohoat. $79-129. 14 rooms with PB, 1 suite and 6 conference rooms. Breakfast included in rates. Types of meals: Country bkfst, lunch, picnic lunch, snacks/refreshments and gourmet dinner. Beds: QD. Modem hook-up, TV, reading lamp, refrigerator, clock radio, coffeemaker, three with whirlpool tubs and some with VCR in room. Central air. VCR, fax, copier, library, parlor games, telephone, fireplace, laundry facility, gift shop, game and fitness center, nature trail, meditation cabin, campfire area and movies on premises. Weddings, small meetings, family reunions and seminars hosted. Amusement parks, antiquing, art galleries, bicycling, canoeing/kayaking, cross-country skiing, downhill skiing, fishing, golf, hiking, horseback riding, live theater, museums, parks, shopping, sporting events, tennis, water sports, wineries and Amish buggy rides and tours nearby.

Publicity: *Elkhart Truth, Goshen News, Fox 28 TV and WCRT radio.*

Mishawaka   A5

The Beiger Mansion Inn

317 Lincoln Way E
Mishawaka, IN 46544-2012
(574)256-0365 (800)437-0131 Fax:(574)259-2622
E-mail: Ron@BeigerMansion.com
Web: www.beigermansion.com

Circa 1903. This Neoclassical limestone mansion was built to satisfy Susie Beiger's wish to copy a friend's Newport, R.I., estate. Palatial rooms that were once a gathering place for local society now welcome guests who seek gracious accommodations. On the premises is a restaurant with a full bar and a pub. Notre Dame, St. Mary's and Indiana University in South Bend are nearby.

Innkeeper(s): Ron Montandon & Dennis Slade. $115-125. 6 rooms with PB and 1 suite. Breakfast included in rates. Types of meals: Full bkfst and gourmet dinner. Restaurant on premises. Beds: Q. Cable TV, reading lamp, clock radio, telephone and desk in room. Air conditioning. TV, VCR, fax, copier and fireplace on premises. Weddings, small meetings, family reunions and seminars hosted. Antiquing, fishing, golf, live theater, parks, sporting events and tennis nearby.

Publicity: *Tribune*.

"Can't wait until we return to Mishawaka to stay with you again!"

Nappanee — B6

Homespun Country Inn

302 N Main St
Nappanee, IN 46550
(574)773-2034 (800)311-2996 Fax:(574)773-3456
E-mail: home@hoosierlink.net
Web: www.homespuninn.com

Circa 1902. Windows of stained and leaded glass create colorful prisms at this Queen Anne Victorian inn built in 1902. Quarter-sawn oak highlights the entry and first-floor common rooms. Comfortable antiques and family heirlooms accent the inn. Two parlors offer areas to read, do a jigsaw puzzle or watch satellite TV or a movie. Each guest bedroom displays photos of the home's original occupants. Early risers enjoying a cup of coffee or tea might see a passing horse and buggy while sitting on the porch swing. Breakfast is served in the dining room. Ask about the assortment of special packages and how to add a Homespun Memory Gift Bag to a reservation.

Innkeeper(s): Dianne & Dennis Debelak. $65-79. 5 rooms with PB. Breakfast and snacks/refreshments included in rates. Types of meals: Full bkfst and early coffee/tea. Beds: QDT. Cable TV, VCR, reading lamp, ceiling fan, clock radio and night lights in room. Air conditioning. Fax, copier, parlor games, telephone and fireplace on premises. Small meetings, family reunions and seminars hosted. Antiquing, golf, live theater, parks, shopping, sporting events and tennis nearby.

Publicity: *The Elkhart Truth*.

"We have been telling all our friends about how wonderful your establishment is."

The Victorian Guest House

302 E Market St
Nappanee, IN 46550-2102
(574)773-4383
E-mail: vghouse@bnin.net
Web: www.victorianb-b.com

Circa 1887. Listed in the National Register, this three-story Queen Anne Victorian inn was built by Frank Coppes, one of America's first noted kitchen cabinet makers. Nappanee's location makes it an ideal stopping point for those exploring the heart of Amish country, or visiting the South Bend or chain of lakes areas. Visitors may choose from six guest rooms, including the Coppes Suite, with its origi-

nal golden oak woodwork, antique tub and stained glass. Full breakfast is served at the antique 11-foot dining room table. Amish Acres is just one mile from the inn.

Innkeeper(s): Vickie Hunsberger. $119. 6 rooms with PB. Breakfast and afternoon tea included in rates. Types of meals: Full bkfst, early coffee/tea and snacks/refreshments. Beds: QT. Cable TV, reading lamp, ceiling fan, clock radio, telephone and turn-down service in room. Air conditioning. Weddings, small meetings, family reunions and seminars hosted. Antiquing, live theater, shopping, sporting events and water sports nearby.

Publicity: *Goshen News*.

New Albany — K6

Honeymoon Mansion B&B & Wedding Chapel

1014 E Main St
New Albany, IN 47150-5843
(812)945-0312 (800)759-7270 Fax:(812)945-6615
E-mail: landon@honeymoonmansion.com
Web: www.honeymoonmansion.com

Circa 1850. The innkeepers at Honeymoon Mansion can provide guests with the flowers, wedding chapel and honeymoon suite. All you need to bring is a bride or groom. An ordained minister is on the premises and guests can marry or renew their vows in the inn's Victorian wedding chapel. However, one need not be a newlywed to enjoy this bed & breakfast. Canopy beds, stained-glass windows and heart-shaped rugs are a few of the romantic touches. Several suites include marble Jacuzzis flanked on four sides with eight-foot-high marble columns, creating a dramatic and elegant effect. The home itself, a pre-Civil War Italianate-style home listed in the state and national historic registers, boasts many fine period features. Gingerbread trim, intricate molding and a grand staircase add to the Victorian ambiance. Guests are treated to an all-you-can-eat country breakfast with items such as homemade breads, biscuits and gravy, eggs, sausage and potatoes.

Innkeeper(s): Landon Caldwell. $49-179. 12 rooms, 6 with PB, 1 with FP, 6 suites and 2 conference rooms. Breakfast included in rates. Types of meals: Full bkfst. Beds: QD. Cable TV, VCR, reading lamp, stereo, ceiling fan, clock radio and hot tub/spa in room. Air conditioning. Parlor games and fireplace on premises. Limited handicap access. Weddings, small meetings, family reunions and seminars hosted. Amusement parks, antiquing, cross-country skiing, downhill skiing, fishing, live theater, parks, shopping, sporting events, water sports, three state parks, three caves, Culbertson Mansion and riverboat casino nearby.

Publicity: *Courier-Journal, Evening News, Tribune.* and *WHAS TV*.

South Bend — A5

English Rose Inn

116 S Taylor St
South Bend, IN 46601
(574)289-2114 Fax:(574)287-1311
E-mail: info@englishroseinn.com
Web: www.englishroseinn.com

Circa 1892. A stunning Queen Anne Victorian, the English Rose is indeed adorned in a fanciful light pink hue. A prominent local doctor built the turn-of-the-20th-century home. The innkeeper has filled the inn with antiques and period-style decorations. The inviting guest rooms include quilt-topped beds with coordinating linens and special touches, such as a delicate tea set. Guests can enjoy the multi-course, private breakfast in the privacy of their room. The inn is close to Notre Dame, as well as historic sites such as Tippecanoe Place and the Copshalom Home.

Innkeeper(s): Barry & Susan Kessler. $75-165. 5 rooms with PB. Breakfast and snacks/refreshments included in rates. Types of meals: Full bkfst. Beds: QDT. Cable TV, reading lamp, clock radio, coffeemaker and desk in room. Central air. VCR, fax, parlor games, telephone, fireplace and laundry facility on premises. Small meetings, family reunions and seminars hosted. Antiquing, art galleries, canoeing/kayaking, fishing, golf, hiking, live theater, museums, parks, shopping, sporting events, tennis and wineries nearby.

Oliver Inn

630 W Washington St
South Bend, IN 46601-1444
(574)232-4545 (888)697-4466 Fax:(574)288-9788
E-mail: oliver@michiana.org
Web: www.oliverinn.com

Circa 1886. This stately Queen Anne Victorian sits amid 30 towering maples and was once home to Josephine Oliver Ford, daughter of James Oliver, of chilled plow fame. Located in South Bend's historic district, this inn offers a comfortable library and nine inviting guest rooms, some with built-in fireplaces or double Jacuzzis. The inn is within walking distance of downtown and is next door to the Tippecanoe Restaurant in the Studebaker Mansion.

Innkeeper(s): Richard & Venera Monahan. $95-165. 9 rooms, 7 with PB, 2 with FP, 3 suites and 1 conference room. Breakfast and snacks/refreshments included in rates. Types of meals: Full bkfst and early coffee/tea. Beds: KQ. Cable TV, reading lamp, ceiling fan, telephone, desk, hot tub/spa and several with double whirlpool tubs in room. Air conditioning. Fax, parlor games, fireplace and baby grand with computer disk system on premises. Weddings, small meetings, family reunions and seminars hosted. Antiquing, canoeing/kayaking, cross-country skiing, fishing, live theater, museums, parks, shopping, sporting events, water sports, fine dining, Amish country and Notre Dame nearby.

Queen Anne Inn

420 W Washington St
South Bend, IN 46601-1526
(574)234-5959 (800)582-2379 Fax:(574)234-4324
E-mail: Pauline@queenanne.net
Web: www.queenanneinn.net

Circa 1893. Samuel Good, a local who made his fortune from the Gold Rush, built this Queen Anne, Neo-Classical home which was later moved to its present neighborhood. Frank Lloyd Wright-designed bookcases, oak floors and panelling, crystal chandeliers, hand-painted silk wallpaper, and a mirrored, mahogany buffet enhance the warm, rich interior. Special teas are served on Thursdays and Saturdays. Amenities are

available for business travelers.

Innkeeper(s): Pauline & Bob Medhurst. $70-109. 6 rooms, 5 with PB, 1 with FP, 1 suite and 1 conference room. Breakfast included in rates. Types of meals: Full bkfst, early coffee/tea, picnic lunch and afternoon tea. Beds: KQDT. TV, reading lamp, snack bar, clock radio, telephone, desk and television in room. Air conditioning. VCR, fax, copier, bicycles, library, parlor games and laundry facility on premises. Weddings, small meetings, family reunions and seminars hosted. Antiquing, art galleries, beach, canoeing/kayaking, fishing, golf, hiking, museums, parks, shopping, sporting events and water sports nearby.

Publicity: *South Bend Tribune, Indiana Business and Romantic Getaways.*

Valparaiso B3

The Inn at Aberdeen

3158 South SR 2
Valparaiso, IN 46385
(219)465-3753 Fax:(219)465-9227

Circa 1890. An old stone wall borders this inn, once a dairy farm, horse farm and then hunting lodge. Recently renovated and expanded, this Victorian farmhouse is on more than an acre. An elegant getaway, there's a solarium, library, dining room and parlor for relaxing. The inn offers traditional Queen Anne furnishings in the guest rooms. The Timberlake Suites include fireplaces, two-person Jacuzzi tubs and balconies. The Aberdeen Suite includes a living room and fireplace, while the Alloway Suite offers a living room, kitchenette and a balcony. A conference center on the property is popular for executive meetings and special events, and  there is a picturesque gazebo overlooking the inn's beautifully landscaped lawns and English gardens. Golf packages and mystery weekends have received enthusiastic response from guests. There is a golf course, spa and microbrewery adjacent to the inn.

Innkeeper(s): Bill Simon. $99-185. 11 suites, 10 with FP and 1 conference room. Breakfast and snacks/refreshments included in rates. Types of meals: Full gourmet bkfst and early coffee/tea. Beds: KQ. Cable TV, VCR, reading lamp, ceiling fan, clock radio, telephone, desk and hot tub/spa in room. Air conditioning. Fax, copier, swimming, bicycles, tennis, library, parlor games, fireplace, snack bar and gazebo on premises. Limited handicap access. Weddings, small meetings, family reunions and seminars hosted. Antiquing, cross-country skiing, downhill skiing, fishing, golf, live theater, parks, shopping, sporting events, tennis and water sports nearby.

Publicity: *Midwest Living, Chicago Magazine, Chicago Tribune, Country Inns and Indiana Business Magazine ("Best Retreat Site").*

"Every time we have the good fortune to spend an evening here, it is like a perfect fairy tale, transforming us into King and Queen."

Iowa

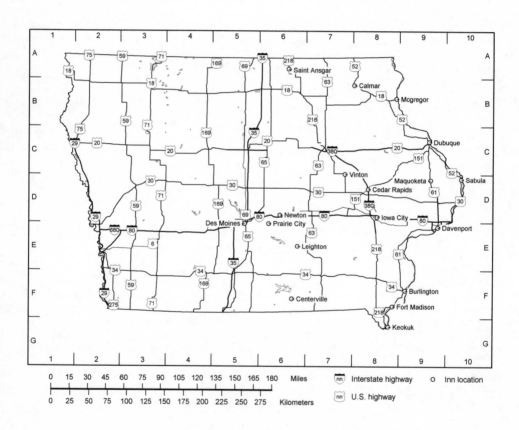

0 15 30 45 60 75 90 105 120 135 150 165 180   Miles

0 25 50 75 100 125 150 175 200 225 250 275   Kilometers

[nn] Interstate highway   ○ Inn location

[nn] U.S. highway

Bentonsport F8

Mason House Inn of Bentonsport

21982 Hawk Dr
Bentonsport, IA 52565
(319)592-3133 (800)592-3133

Circa 1846. A Murphy-style copper bathtub folds down out of the wall at this unusual inn built by Mormon craftsmen, who stayed in Bentonsport for three years on their trek to Utah. More than half of the furniture
is original to the home, including a nine-foot walnut headboard and a nine-foot mirror. This is the oldest operating pre-Civil War steamboat inn in Iowa.

Guests can imagine the days when steamboats made their way up and down the Des Moines River, while taking in the scenery. A full breakfast is served, but if guests crave a mid-day snack, each room is equipped with its own stocked cookie jar.

Innkeeper(s): Chuck & Joy Hanson. $64-95. 8 rooms with PB, 1 cottage and 1 conference room. Breakfast included in rates. Types of meals: Full bkfst and early coffee/tea. Beds: KQD. Reading lamp and filled cookie jar in room. Air conditioning. Telephone and fireplace on premises. Limited handicap access. Weddings, small meetings, family reunions and seminars hosted. Antiquing, cross-country skiing and shopping nearby.

Publicity: *Des Moines Register, Decatur Herald & Review, AAA Home & Away and Country Magazine.*

"The attention to detail was fantastic, food was wonderful and the setting was fascinating."

Burlington F9

Mississippi Manor

809 N 4th St
Burlington, IA 52601-5008
(319)753-2218
E-mail: pczajkowski@mchsi.com
Web: www.mississippimanor.com

Circa 1877. Located just four blocks from the Mississippi River in the National Landmark District, this Victorian Italianate manor house was built by a lumber baron who incorporated European craftsmanship into the fine architectural detailing.

Inside, the inn is elegantly decorated and includes four guest rooms with private baths. Two spacious suites offer wood burning fireplaces. A continental breakfast is included in the rates. The inn is close to downtown and the Mississippi River.

Innkeeper(s): Florence Paterno. $75-95. 4 rooms with PB, 2 with FP. Breakfast included in rates. Types of meals: Cont plus. Beds: QT. Cable TV, reading lamp, ceiling fan, clock radio and telephone in room. Air conditioning. VCR, parlor games and fireplace on premises. Weddings, small meetings, family reunions and seminars hosted. Antiquing, fishing, golf, parks, shopping, tennis, water sports, magnificent park system and arboretum nearby.

Publicity: *Hawkeye.*

Schramm House B&B

616 Columbia St
Burlington, IA 52601
(800)683-7117 Fax:(319)754-0373

Circa 1866. "Colossal" would be an excellent word to describe this Queen Anne Victorian. The home is an impressive site in this Burlington historic district. The exterior is brick on the first story with clapboard on the second, and a third-story tower is one of the architectural highlights. Inside, the parquet floors and woodwork have been restored to their 19th-century grandeur. The home was built just after the Civil War by a local department store owner. Additions were made in the 1880s. Eventually, the home was converted into apartments, so the innkeepers took on quite a task refurbishing the place back to its original state. The Victorian is decorated with the innkeepers collection of antiques. One particularly appealing guest room includes an exposed brick wall and tin ceiling. Breakfast might begin with a baked pear topped with toasted almonds and a raspberry sauce. From there, freshly baked muffins arrive, followed by an entree, perhaps a frittata or French toast. All courses are served with fine china and crystal. The home is just six blocks from the Mississippi, and don't pass up a walk down the historic Snake Alley.

Innkeeper(s): Sandy & Bruce Morrison. $95-150. 5 rooms with PB. Breakfast included in rates. Types of meals: Full bkfst and early coffee/tea. Beds: Q. Reading lamp, ceiling fan, clock radio, turn-down service, desk, robes and hair dryers in room. VCR, fax, library, parlor games, telephone and fireplace on premises. Weddings and small meetings hosted. Antiquing, fishing, golf, parks, shopping and tennis nearby.

Publicity: *Hawk Eye.*

Calmar B8

Calmar Guesthouse

103 W North St
Calmar, IA 52132-7605
(563)562-3851

Circa 1890. This beautifully restored Victorian home was built by John B. Kay, a lawyer and poet. Stained-glass windows, carved moldings, an oak-and-walnut staircase and gleaming woodwork highlight the gracious interior. A grandfather clock ticks in the living room. In the foyer, a friendship yellow rose is incorporated into the stained-glass window pane. Breakfast is served in the formal dining room. The Laura Ingalls Wilder Museum is nearby in Burr Oak. The Bily Brothers Clock Museum, Smallest Church, Luther College and Norwegian Museum are located nearby.

Historic Interest: The Norwegian Museum is 10 minutes away. The Smallest Church, Bily Brothers Clocks Museum and Luther College are nearby.

Innkeeper(s): Lucille Kruse. $59-65. Breakfast included in rates. Types of meals: Cont and early coffee/tea. Beds: Q. Cable TV, reading lamp and clock radio in room. Air conditioning. VCR, bicycles, library, parlor games and telephone on premises. Small meetings hosted. Antiquing, cross-country skiing, downhill skiing, fishing, live theater, parks, shopping, sporting events and water sports nearby.

Publicity: *Iowa Farmer Today, Calmar Courier, Minneapolis Star-Tribune, Home and Away and Iowan.*

"What a delight it was to stay here. No one could have made our stay more welcome or enjoyable."

Cedar Rapids   D8

Belmont Hill Victorian B&B

1525 Cherokee Dr NW
Cedar Rapids, IA 52405
(319)366-1343 Fax:(319)366-1351
E-mail: belmonthil@aol.com
Web: www.belmonthill.com

Circa 1882. Built by Cedar Rapids brickyard owner, Philip
Wolff, both buildings here were constructed with three courses
of brick, resulting in 14-inch-thick walls. The gracious Italianate
architecture along with a secluded location at the edge of a
woodland, creates a magical setting. English gardens surround
the old criss-cross wooden doors to the pristinely renovated
Carriage House. The Belmont Suite, located in the upper floor,
offers a walnut bed handcrafted in the Amanas along with
antiques and luxurious linens. Breakfast is provided in the dining room of the Main House.

Innkeeper(s): Ken and Shelley Sullens. $99-152. 3 rooms with PB and 1
suite. Breakfast included in rates. Types of meals: Full gourmet bkfst, early
coffee/tea, afternoon tea and snacks/refreshments. Beds: KQ. TV, VCR, reading lamp, clock radio, turn-down service and desk in room. Air conditioning.
Telephone, fireplace and perennial gardens on premises. Limited handicap
access. Small meetings hosted. Antiquing, fishing, golf, live theater, parks,
shopping, sporting events, tennis and water sports nearby.
Publicity: *Cedar Rapids Gazette and KGAN News.*

"What a place and what a setting."

Centerville   F6

One of A Kind

314 W State St
Centerville, IA 52544
(641)437-4540 Fax:(641)437-4540

Circa 1867. This large, three-story brick home with mansard
roof and tall bays is the second oldest house in town. The
innkeeper has filled the inn with "One of a Kind" craft and decorative items for sale, created on the premises or by local artisans.
There is also a tea room, popular for its chicken soup and homemade croissant sandwiches, so of course you can expect a
yummy breakfast, as well. Guest quarters are decorated with
antiques and reproductions spiced with a variety of collectibles.
The largest fish hatchery in the world is a short drive away at
Lake Rathbun, but there is plenty to do within walking distance.

Innkeeper(s): Jack & Joyce Stufflebeem. $40-70. 5 rooms, 3 with PB.
Breakfast and snacks/refreshments included in rates. Types of meals: Full
bkfst, early coffee/tea, lunch, picnic lunch, afternoon tea and gourmet dinner.
Beds: QDT. Cable TV, reading lamp, ceiling fan and turn-down service in
room. Air conditioning. VCR, fax, copier, parlor games, telephone and tea
room on premises. Weddings, small meetings and family reunions hosted.
Antiquing, fishing, golf, live theater, parks, shopping, sporting events, tennis
and water sports nearby.

Davenport   E9

Fulton's Landing Guest House

1206 E River Dr
Davenport, IA 52803-5742
(563)322-4069 Fax:(563)322-8186

Circa 1871. Enjoy views of the Mississippi River from the
porches of this stone, Italianate home, which is listed in the
National Register. The guest rooms are decorated with antiques,

including ceiling fans. After enjoying the
morning meal, guests have a variety of
activities to choose. Riverboat gambling,
shopping and downtown Davenport
all are nearby.

Innkeeper(s): Pat & Bill Schmidt. $85-125. 4
rooms with PB. Breakfast included in rates.
Types of meals: Full gourmet bkfst. Beds: Q.
Cable TV, reading lamp, ceiling fan, clock
radio, telephone and desk in room. Air condi-
tioning. Fax, copier, bicycles and fireplace on premises. Antiquing, cross-
country skiing, fishing, live theater, parks, shopping, sporting events and
water sports nearby.

*"I have never felt more pampered and cared for staying away from
home."*

Des Moines   E5

Butler House on Grand

4507 Grand Ave
Des Moines, IA 50312
(515)255-4096 (866)455-4096
E-mail: info@butlerhouseongrand.com
Web: www.butlerhouseongrand.com

Circa 1923. Constructed entirely from steel and concrete with
an all-brick veneer, this American Tudor home has withstood
change of ownership and renovations. This bed & breakfast
proudly showcases the work of area designers and artists
throughout its tasteful decor. Both floors offer a common area
with refrigerator and snack bar. Some of the suites and guest
bedrooms feature spa tubs, fireplaces and VCRs. A fruit starter
is served first, then breads, an egg dish and bacon or sausages
for a full breakfast. Prairie flowers and other indigenous plants
grace the landscaped grounds.

Innkeeper(s): Clark Smith & Lauren Kernan Smith. $90-160. 7 rooms.
Breakfast and snacks/refreshments included in rates. Types of meals: Full
gourmet bkfst, veg bkfst and early coffee/tea. Beds: QD. Modem hook-up,
cable TV, VCR, reading lamp, clock radio, telephone, turn-down service,
desk, two suites with spa tubs, four with ceiling fans, two with fireplaces and
four with VCR in room. Air conditioning. Fax, copier, library, parlor games,
fireplace, refrigerator, snack bar and hot tub on premises. Small meetings and
family reunions hosted. Amusement parks, antiquing, art galleries, bicycling,
fishing, golf, hiking, horseback riding, live theater, museums, parks, shopping, tennis and wineries nearby.
Publicity: *Des Moines Register, Better Homes & Gardens, Intro Magazine
and BH&G TV.*

Dubuque   C9

The Hancock House

1105 Grove Ter
Dubuque, IA 52001-4644
(563)557-8989 Fax:(563)583-0813
E-mail: chuckdbq@aol.com
Web: www.thehancockhouse.com

Circa 1891. Victorian splendor can be found at The Hancock
House, one of Dubuque's most striking examples of Queen
Anne architecture. Rooms feature period furnishings and offer
views of the Mississippi River states of
Iowa, Illinois and Wisconsin. The
Hancock House, listed in the
National Register, boasts several
unique features, including a fire-
place judged blue-ribbon best at
the 1893 World's Fair in Chicago.

Guests can enjoy the porch swings, wicker furniture and spectacular views from the wraparound front porch.

Innkeeper(s): Chuck & Susan Huntley. $80-175. 9 rooms with PB, 3 with FP and 4 suites. Breakfast included in rates. Types of meals: Full bkfst and early coffee/tea. Beds: Q. Cable TV, reading lamp, clock radio, desk and feather mattress in room. Air conditioning. Fax, copier, parlor games, telephone, fireplace and gift shop on premises. Small meetings, family reunions and seminars hosted. Antiquing, cross-country skiing, downhill skiing, fishing, golf, live theater, parks, shopping, sporting events, tennis, water sports and riverboat casino nearby.

Publicity: *Victorian Sampler (Cover).*

The Mandolin Inn

199 Loras Blvd
Dubuque, IA 52001-4857
(563)556-0069 (800)524-7996 Fax:(563)556-0587
E-mail: innkeeper@mandolininn.com
Web: www.mandolininn.com

Circa 1908. This handicapped-accessible three-story brick Edwardian with Queen Anne wraparound veranda boasts a mosaic-tiled porch floor. Inside are inlaid mahogany and rosewood floors, bay windows and a turret that starts in the parlor and ascends to the second-floor Holly Marie Room, decorated in a wedding motif. This room features a seven-piece Rosewood bedroom suite and a crystal chandelier. A gourmet breakfast is served in the dining room with a fantasy forest mural from the turn of the century. There is an herb garden outside the kitchen. Located just 12 blocks away, is the fabulous National Mississippi River Museum and Aquarium. The inn can equally accommodate both business and pleasure travel.

Innkeeper(s): Amy Boynton. $85-150. 8 rooms, 6 with PB and 2 conference rooms. Breakfast included in rates. Types of meals: Full gourmet bkfst and early coffee/tea. Beds: KQ. Cable TV, reading lamp, clock radio and desk in room. Central air. Fax and telephone on premises. Weddings, small meetings, family reunions and seminars hosted. Antiquing, cross-country skiing, downhill skiing, live theater, parks, shopping, sporting events and water sports nearby.

"From the moment we entered the Mandolin, we felt at home. I know we'll be back."

The Richards House

1492 Locust St
Dubuque, IA 52001-4714
(563)557-1492

Circa 1883. Owner David Stuart estimates that it will take several years to remove the concrete-based brown paint applied by a bridge painter in the '60s to cover the 7,000-square-foot, Stick-style Victorian house. The interior, however, only needed a tad of polish. The varnished cherry and bird's-eye maple woodwork is set aglow under electrified gaslights. Ninety stained-glass windows, eight pocket doors with stained glass and a magnificent entryway reward those who pass through.

Historic Interest: Five historic districts are in Dubuque.

Innkeeper(s): Michelle A. Stuart. $45-105. 7 rooms, 4 with PB, 4 with FP, 1 suite and 1 conference room. Breakfast included in rates. Types of meals: Full bkfst, early coffee/tea, afternoon tea and snacks/refreshments. Beds: Q.

Cable TV, VCR, reading lamp, telephone and desk in room. TV, fax, parlor games and fireplace on premises. Weddings, small meetings and family reunions hosted. Antiquing, cross-country skiing, downhill skiing, fishing, live theater, parks, shopping and water sports nearby.

Publicity: *Collectors Journal and Telegraph Herald.*

"Although the guide at the door had warned us that the interior was incredible, we were still flabbergasted when we stepped into the foyer of this house."

Fort Madison   F8

Kingsley Inn

707 Avenue H (Hwy 61)
Fort Madison, IA 52627
(319)372-7074 (800)441-2327 Fax:(319)372-7096
E-mail: kingsley@interl.net
Web: www.kingsleyinn.com

Circa 1858. Overlooking the Mississippi River, this century-old inn is located in downtown Fort Madison. Though furnished with antiques, all 17 rooms offer modern amenities and private baths (some with whirlpools and fireplaces) as well as river views. A two-bedroom, two-bath suite also is available. There is a restaurant, Alphas on the Riverfront, on the premises.

Historic Interest: A museum and historic fort are nearby. Historic Nauvoo, Ill., known as the "Williamsburg of the Midwest," is only 11 miles from the inn.

Innkeeper(s): Alida Willis. $85-185. 17 rooms with PB, 1 suite and 1 conference room. Breakfast included in rates. Types of meals: Full bkfst. Restaurant on premises. Beds: KQD. Data port, cable TV, reading lamp and telephone in room. Air conditioning. TV, VCR, fax, elevator and off-street parking on premises. Weddings, small meetings, family reunions and seminars hosted. Antiquing, fishing, shopping, casino and historic sites including Nauvoo, IL nearby.

Publicity: *Midwest Living.*

Iowa City   D8

Golden Haug Bed & Breakfast

517 E Washington St
Iowa City, IA 52240-1832
(319)338-6452
E-mail: imahaug@avalon.net
Web: www.goldenhaug.com

Circa 1919. Located in a historic downtown neighborhood, this Foursquare Arts and Crafts two-story home is within steps of the original town park and is a short walk to the University of Iowa. DSL high-speed Internet access is available as well as other modern amenities that complement the whimsical décor and antique furnishings. Relax outdoors on the porch or deck. Comfortable guest bedrooms and suites offer a two-person whirlpool or clawfoot soaking tub, fireplace, TV and VCR. A satisfying gourmet breakfast is served daily with popular favorites that may include glazed ham balls, sticky buns and the inn's special French toast. Enjoy a stroll through the landscaped levels and pocket gardens. Lake McBride and Coralville Reservoir are ten miles away.

Historic Interest: Built in 1919, our B&B has the antique woodwork and lighting of the era.

Innkeeper(s): Nila Haug. $100-150. 5 rooms with PB, 1 with FP and 4 suites. Breakfast included in rates. Types of meals: Full gourmet bkfst, veg bkfst and early coffee/tea. Beds: KQT. Modem hook-up, data port, cable TV, VCR, reading lamp, ceiling fan, clock radio, telephone, desk, fireplace and DSL high-speed Internet access in room. Central air. Off-street parking and porch on premises. Antiquing, art galleries, beach, bicycling, canoeing/kayaking, cross-country skiing, fishing, golf, hiking, horseback riding, live theater, museums, parks, shopping, sporting events, tennis and water sports nearby.

Keokuk   G8

The Grand Anne

816 Grand Ave
Keokuk, IA 52632-5030
(319)524-6310 (800)524-6310 Fax:(319)524-6310
Web: www.bbonline.com/ia/grandanne

Circa 1897. Situated high on a hill overlooking the Mississippi River, this exquisitely restored Queen Anne Victorian, listed in the National Register, is a dramatic testimony to the craftsmanship of the renowned architect, George F. Barber. Signature details include the candle-snuffer porch and tower rooms with bent-glass windows, an oak-paneled reception hall with coffered ceiling and staircase with hand-turned spindles. A conservatory and two spacious parlors feature wainscoting and intricate moldings. A refrigerator is stocked with soda. Enjoy a full breakfast in the formal dining room. One of the parlors opens to a screened porch viewing formal gardens and expansive lawns.

Historic Interest: Historic Nauvoo, Ill., is a 20-minute drive via the scenic river route. The inn is listed in the National Register of Historic Places.

Innkeeper(s): Sandra Kleopfer. $95-140. 5 rooms with PB. Breakfast included in rates. Types of meals: Full bkfst. Beds: Q. Cable TV, VCR and CD player in room. Air conditioning. Parlor games and telephone on premises. Antiquing, bicycling, cross-country skiing, fishing, golf, live theater, parks, shopping, tennis, water sports and boating nearby.

Publicity: *Country Inns, The Iowan and Des Moines Register.*

Leighton   E6

Dutchman's Bed & Breakfast

1345 Highway 163-49 MM
Leighton, IA 50143-8055
(641)626-3092

Circa 1918. Located in the rural countryside, this historic home has been in the family for more than 100 years and is now listed in the National Register. Beautiful arbors and flowers fill the back yard and the screened-in porch provides a place to read and relax or smoke. Tastefully furnished guest bedrooms feature antiques. Hearty breakfasts include specialties such as homemade cinnamon rolls and caramel French toast. The town of Pella, known as "A Touch of Holland," just five miles away, hosts the famous Tulip Festival and is filled with shops and treasures including imported Dutch lace and authentic Delft.

Innkeeper(s): Mr. and Mrs. Vernon Van Gorp. $58. 3 rooms, 2 with PB. Breakfast and snacks/refreshments included in rates. Types of meals: Full gourmet bkfst, early coffee/tea and afternoon tea. Beds: D. TV, VCR, reading lamp, CD player, ceiling fan, clock radio and desk in room. Central air. Parlor games, telephone and laundry facility on premises. Weddings, family reunions and seminars hosted. Antiquing, art galleries, beach, bicycling, fishing, golf, hiking, live theater, museums, parks, shopping, sporting events, tennis, water sports and canoeing nearby.

Maquoketa   D9

Squiers Manor B&B

418 W Pleasant St
Maquoketa, IA 52060-2847
(319)652-6961
E-mail: innkeeper@squiersmanor.com
Web: www.squiersmanor.com

Circa 1882. Innkeepers Virl and Kathy Banowetz are ace antique dealers, who along with owning one of the Midwest's largest antique shops, have refurbished this elegant, Queen Anne Victorian. The inn is furnished with period antiques that are beyond compare. Guest rooms boast museum-quality pieces such as a Victorian brass bed with lace curtain wings and inlaid mother-of-pearl or an antique mahogany bed with carved birds and flowers. Six guest rooms include whirlpool tubs, and one includes a unique Swiss shower. The innkeepers restored the home's original woodwork, shuttered-windows, fireplaces, gas and electric chandeliers and stained- and engraved-glass windows back to their former glory. They also recently renovated the mansion's attic ballroom into two luxurious suites. The Loft, which is made up of three levels, features pine and wicker furnishings, a sitting room and gas-burning wood stove. On the second level, there is a large Jacuzzi, on the third, an antique queen-size bed. The huge Ballroom Suite boasts 24-foot ceilings, oak and pine antiques, gas-burning wood stove and a Jacuzzi snuggled beside a dormer window. Suite guests enjoy breakfast delivered to their rooms. Other guests feast on an array of mouth-watering treats, such as home-baked breads, seafood quiche and fresh fruits. Evening desserts are served by candlelight.

Historic Interest: The area has 70 sites listed in the National Register.

Innkeeper(s): Virl & Kathy Banowetz. $80-195. 8 rooms with PB and 3 suites. Breakfast included in rates. Types of meals: Full gourmet bkfst. Beds: KQT. Small meetings hosted. Antiquing, cross-country skiing, downhill skiing, fishing, parks, shopping and water sports nearby.

Publicity: *Des Moines Register Datebook and Daily Herald.*

"We couldn't have asked for a more perfect place to spend our honeymoon. The service was excellent and so was the food! It was an exciting experience that we will never forget!"

McGregor   B8

McGregor Manor

320 4th St
McGregor, IA 52157
(563)873-2600
E-mail: mmanor@mhtc.net
Web: www.mcgregorinn.com

Circa 1897. Restored to its 1897 elegance, this classic Victorian bed & breakfast is a delightful retreat with panoramic views of the surrounding hills. Relax on the large wraparound porch. Each guest bedroom reflects the inn's warmth and hospitality. The Marge Goergen Room, named after a local photographer, boasts a curved turret window and is accented with her original prints. Enjoy scenes of the mighty Mississippi in the Captain Jack Room with huge bay windows. Stay in a quilted room overlooking the wildflower garden, or one that features the river city of New Orleans. Food is plentiful from a generous breakfast to afternoon tea and evening dessert. Explore the scenic area and ask about Mystery To Go for adventure and intrigue.

Innkeeper(s): David & Carolyn Scott. $70-80. 4 rooms with PB. Breakfast and snacks/refreshments included in rates. Types of meals: Full bkfst. Beds: Q. Reading lamp and clock radio in room. Air conditioning. TV, VCR, fax, library, parlor games, telephone, fireplace, gift shop and mystery dinners on premises. Weddings, small meetings, family reunions and seminars hosted. Antiquing, canoeing/kayaking, fishing, hiking, horseback riding, museums, parks and shopping nearby.

Publicity: *Country Magazine, St. Paul Pioneer Press and KCRG.*

Newton   D6

La Corsette Maison Inn

629 1st Ave E
Newton, IA 50208-3305
(641)792-6833 Fax:(641)792-6597
Web: www.lacorsette.com

Circa 1909. This unusual Mission-style building has an arts-and-crafts interior. All the woodwork is of quarter-sawn oak, and the dining room furniture was designed by Limbert.

Stained and beveled glass is found throughout. French bedchambers feature reproduction and antique furnishings. One of the suites includes a fireplace and double whirlpool tub. The inn's restaurant has received four-and-one-half stars from the Des Moines Register's Grumpy Gourmet. The mansion also has three working wood-burning fireplaces.

Historic Interest: Jasper County Courthouse (7 blocks), Saint Stevens Episcopal Church (3 blocks).

Innkeeper(s): Kay Owen. $85-225. 7 rooms with PB, 3 with FP and 2 suites. Breakfast included in rates. Types of meals: Full bkfst, picnic lunch and gourmet dinner. Restaurant on premises. Beds: KQD. TV, fax and telephone on premises. Antiquing, cross-country skiing, downhill skiing and fishing nearby.

Publicity: *Cedar Rapids Gazette, American Airlines, Innsider, Midwest Living, AAA Home and Away, Des Moines Register, Bon Appetit, Conde Nast Traveler and Chicago Sun Times.*

"We shall return. You and your house are an inspiration."

Prairie City   E6

The Country Connection B&B

9737 West 93rd St S
Prairie City, IA 50579
(515)994-2023
E-mail: ctryctnbnb@aol.com
Web: www.iowa-country-bed-breakfast.com

Circa 1910. In a friendly, working farm community, this sixth generation Four Square home sits on three scenic acres. Original walnut woodwork reflects a rich heritage enhanced by family heirlooms, antiques and keepsakes. Grandma's spinning wheel, homemade dolls, wedding quilts and the family Bible brought from Ireland and wonderful are just some of the lovingly displayed treasures of the past. Play a game by the fire or read a book from the library at the top of the stairs or. In the evening, old-fashioned homemade ice cream is served as a bedtime treat. Each guest bedroom features delightful amenities. Grandpa's Getaway on the first floor is a favorite of honey-

mooners. Romantic extras can be arranged in advance. A hearty country breakfast is served in an elegant candlelit setting with vintage china, crystal and lace. Open year-round, there are many nearby attractions to visit.

Innkeeper(s): Jim & Alice Foreman. $50-75. 3 rooms, 1 with PB. Breakfast and snacks/refreshments included in rates. Types of meals: Country bkfst. Beds: Q. TV, reading lamp, ceiling fan and desk in room. Central air. VCR, library, parlor games and telephone on premises. Amusement parks, antiquing, art galleries, bicycling, hiking, live theater, museums, parks, shopping, sporting events, tennis, water sports and Neal Smith National Wildlife Refuge nearby.

Sabula   D10

Castle B&B

616 River St
Sabula, IA 52070
(319)687-2714

Circa 1898. This home's location offers views of the Mississippi River from its location along the riverbank. Built more than a century ago, the home has a cream, brick exterior. Guests enjoy the carved staircase and views of the river from their rooms. Take your early morning coffee out to the screened-in wraparound porch. A full breakfast is served. Children and pets are welcome.

Innkeeper(s): Joan W. Thompson. $50-80. 3 rooms. Breakfast included in rates. Types of meals: Country bkfst, early coffee/tea and snacks/refreshments. Beds: KQ. Cable TV, VCR, reading lamp, clock radio and telephone in room. Air conditioning. TV and laundry facility on premises. Weddings, small meetings, family reunions and seminars hosted. Antiquing, bicycling, cross-country skiing, downhill skiing, fishing, hiking, horseback riding, parks, shopping and river boat gambling nearby.

Publicity: *The Iowan Magazine.*

Saint Ansgar   A6

Blue Belle Inn B&B

PO Box 205, 513 W 4th St
Saint Ansgar, IA 50472-0205
(641)713-3113 (877)713-3113
E-mail: innkeeper@bluebelleinn.com
Web: www.bluebelleinn.com

Circa 1896. This home was purchased from a Knoxville, Tenn., mail-order house. It's difficult to believe that stunning features, such as a tin ceiling, stained-glass windows, intricate woodwork and pocket doors could have come via the mail, but these original items are still here for guests to admire. Rooms are named after books special to the innkeeper. Four of the rooms include a whirlpool tub for two, and the Never Neverland room has a clawfoot tub. Other rooms  offer a skylight, fireplace or perhaps a white iron bed. During the Christmas season, every room has its own decorated tree. The innkeeper hosts a variety of themed luncheons, dinners and events, such as the April in Paris cooking workshop, Mother's Day brunches, the "Some Enchanted Evening" dinner, Murder Mysteries, Ladies nights, Writer's Retreats, quilting seminars and horse-drawn sleigh rides.

Innkeeper(s): Sherrie Hansen. $70-160. 6 rooms, 5 with PB, 2 with FP, 2 suites and 2 conference rooms. Breakfast included in rates. Types of meals: Full gourmet bkfst, early coffee/tea, gourmet lunch, afternoon tea, snacks/refreshments, gourmet dinner and room service. Restaurant on premises. Beds: KQT. TV, VCR, reading lamp, stereo, clock radio, desk and Jacuzzi for two in room. Air conditioning. Fax, library, parlor games, telephone, fireplace, kitchenette, Internet access, piano, treadmill and movies on premises. Weddings, small meetings, family reunions and seminars hosted. Antiquing, canoeing/kayaking, fishing, golf, parks, shopping, water sports and hunting nearby.

Publicity: *Minneapolis Star Tribune, Post-Bulletin, Midwest Living, Country, AAA Home & Away, Des Moines Register, Country Home, Iowan Magazine, American Patchwork and Quilting and HGTV Restore America.*

Vinton   C7

Lion & The Lamb B&B

913 2nd Ave
Vinton, IA 52349-1729
(319)472-5086 (888)390-5262 Fax:(319)472-5086
E-mail: lionlamb@lionlamb.com
Web: www.lionlamb.com

Circa 1892. This Queen Anne Victorian, a true "Painted Lady," boasts a stunning exterior with intricate chimneys, gingerbread trim, gables and turrets. The home still maintains its original pocket doors and parquet flooring, and antiques add to the nostalgic flavor. One room boasts a 150-year-old bedroom set. Breakfasts, as any meal in such fine a house should, are served on china. Succulent French toast topped with powdered sugar and a rich strawberry sauce is a specialty.

Innkeeper(s): Richard & Rachel Waterbury. $75-109. 6 rooms with PB, 2 with FP. Breakfast included in rates. Types of meals: Full bkfst and early coffee/tea. Beds: KQ. TV, reading lamp, ceiling fan and coffeemaker in room. Air conditioning. Parlor games and telephone on premises. Weddings, small meetings, family reunions and seminars hosted. Antiquing, cross-country skiing, fishing, golf, live theater, parks, shopping, tennis and water sports nearby.

Publicity: *Cedar Valley Times, Waterloo Courier, Cedar Rapids Gazette, Country Discoveries Magazine and KWWL-Channel 7 Neighborhood News.*

"It is a magical place!"

Kansas

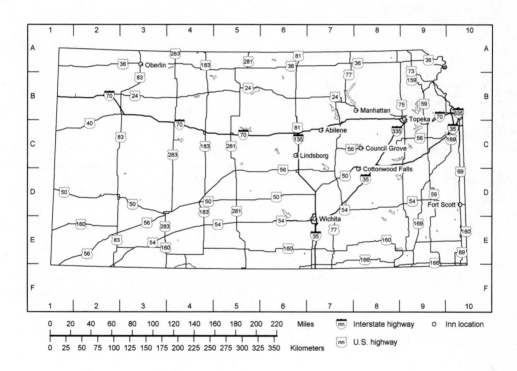

0 20 40 60 80 100 120 140 160 180 200 220   Miles

0 25 50 75 100 125 150 175 200 225 250 275 300 325 350   Kilometers

Interstate highway   Inn location

U.S. highway

Abilene   C7

Victorian Reflections B&B Inn

820 NW 3rd St
Abilene, KS 67410-3316
(785)263-7774

Circa 1900. Beautifully preserved and reflecting a relaxed, bygone age, this Queen Anne showpiece offers a restful setting. Marvel at the hand-carved staircase and luxurious formal living room. The mansion features spacious guest bedrooms and suites. After breakfast relax on the balcony or large porch. A tandem bike is available for exploring the area. Walk to historic downtown to enjoy live professional theater and historic restaurants. Visit local tours mansions and attractions, as well as the Eisenhower library, home and museum. The son of the inn's original owner was the childhood best friend of the former President Eisenhower.

Innkeeper(s): Cary & Alicia Mock. $65-95. 7 rooms, 5 with PB and 2 suites. Breakfast and snacks/refreshments included in rates. Types of meals: Full bkfst and early coffee/tea. Beds: KQDT. TV, VCR and reading lamp in room. Central air. Parlor games, telephone, fireplace, movie library, tandem bike, large porch, balcony and reading on premises. Weddings, small meetings, family reunions and seminars hosted. Antiquing, bicycling, live theater, museums, parks, shopping and tennis nearby.

Cottonwood Falls   D8

1874 Stonehouse B&B on Mulberry Hill

Rt 1, Box 67A
Cottonwood Falls, KS 66845
(620)273-8481
E-mail: tranquility@stonehousebandb.com
Web: www.stonehousebandb.com

Circa 1874. More than 100 acres surround this historic home, which is one of the state's oldest native stone homes that are still in use. Each guest bedroom offers something special. The Rose Room includes a sleigh bed, while the Blue Room and Yellow Room boast views of either the quarry pond or the Flint Hills. The new Prairie Flower Suite has a Jacuzzi for two, double shower, fireplace and four-poster feather bed. After breakfast explore the property and see wildlife, an old stone barn and corral ruins. The Cottonwood River runs through the land at one point and provides fishing opportunities. Tallgrass Prairie National Preserve is only five miles away.

Innkeeper(s): Joe & Billie Altenhofen. $95-150. 3 rooms with PB. Breakfast included in rates. Types of meals: Full gourmet bkfst. Beds: KQT. Reading lamp, ceiling fan and clock radio in room. Air conditioning. VCR, fax, library, parlor games, telephone, fireplace, nature trail, turkey, deer, quail, kennel facilities, stocked pond, old stone barn and coral ruins on premises. Antiquing, art galleries, bicycling, fishing, golf, hiking, horseback riding, parks, shopping, hunting and weaving nearby.

Publicity: Arrington's Bed & Breakfast Journal as one of the top 15 Bed and Breakfast Country Inns in the "Best Literary Selections" category for 2003.

"I have never felt so pampered. Our walk around the countryside was so peaceful and beautiful."

Council Grove   C8

The Cottage House Hotel

25 N Neosho St
Council Grove, KS 66846-1633
(620)767-6828 (800)727-7903 Fax:(620)767-6414
E-mail: cottagehouse@cgtelco.net
Web: www.cottagehousehotel.com

Circa 1898. The inn is located in Council Grove, the rendezvous point on the Santa Fe Trail. The building grew from a boarding house to an elegant home before it became the hotel of a local banker. The home's original section dates to 1872, and the home was built in stages until 1898. Listed in the National Register of Historic Places, the inn has been completely renovated and is a beautiful example of Victorian architecture in a prairie town. There is a honeymoon cottage on the premises, as well.

Historic Interest: National Register.

Innkeeper(s): Connie Essington. $72-155. 26 rooms with PB, 2 cottages and 2 conference rooms. Breakfast included in rates. Types of meals: Cont plus. Beds: KQD. Modem hook-up, data port, cable TV, VCR, reading lamp, refrigerator, ceiling fan, clock radio, telephone, coffeemaker, desk, hot tub/spa and whirlpool tubs in room. Air conditioning. Fax, copier, spa, sauna, library and parlor games on premises. Limited handicap access. Weddings, small meetings, family reunions and seminars hosted. Antiquing, fishing, golf, hiking, horseback riding, museums, parks, shopping, sporting events, tennis, water sports and riverwalk nearby.

Publicity: Manhattan Mercury, Gazette, Globe & Mail, Kansas City Star, Wichita Eagle, Midwest Living and Kansas Magazine.

"A walk back into Kansas history; preserved charm and friendliness."

Fort Scott   D10

Lyons' Victorian Mansion Bed & Breakfast and Spa

742 S National Ave
Fort Scott, KS 66701-1319
(620)223-3644 (800)784-8378
E-mail: relax@lyonsmansion.com
Web: www.lyonsmansion.com

Circa 1876. For a business trip, vacation or romantic getaway, this landmark Victorian mansion is a luxurious choice. This gracious home has parlors to gather and Paradise, a full service spa. Spacious guest bedrooms offer King-size beds, refined comfort and modern technology with refreshment centers and dedicated computer lines. The suites feature oversized jetted whirlpools that are made to look like antique clawfoot tubs. Enjoy a hearty breakfast in the grand dining room, unless a breakfast basket delivered to the door is preferred. The grounds are showcased by a gazebo, fish ponds, picnic areas and an enclosed star-lit hot tub. Ask about the creative specialty packages offered.

Innkeeper(s): Pat & Larry Lyons. $79-150. 7 rooms, 6 with PB and 1 suite. Breakfast included in rates. Types of meals: Full bkfst. Three suites with whirlpool in room.

Lindsborg C6

Swedish Country Inn

112 W Lincoln St
Lindsborg, KS 67456-2319
(785)227-2985 (800)231-0266 Fax:(785)227-2795
E-mail: info@swedishcountryinn.com
Web: www.swedishcountryinn.com

Circa 1904. Founded in the 1860s by Swedish immigrants, the town of Lindsborg is still known as "Little Sweden," maintaining its heritage through a variety of cultural events, festivals, galleries, shops and restaurants. The Swedish Country Inn adds to the town's ethnic flavor. All the furnishings have been imported from Sweden. Bright, airy rooms feature pine furnishings, handmade quilts and hand-painted cupboards. A Swedish-style buffet breakfast is served each morning, with items such as meatballs, lingonberries, herring, knackebread, fruit, cheese, cold meats and fresh baked goods. The Christmas season is an especially festive time to visit this inn and picturesque small town.

Innkeeper(s): Becky Anderson. $55-101. 19 rooms with PB, 2 suites and 1 conference room. Breakfast, afternoon tea and snacks/refreshments included in rates. Types of meals: Full gourmet bkfst and early coffee/tea. Beds: QD. Data port, cable TV, VCR, reading lamp, clock radio, telephone, desk and sauna in room. Central air. Fax, copier, sauna, bicycles, parlor games, fireplace and massage by appointment on premises. Weddings, small meetings, family reunions and seminars hosted. Antiquing, art galleries, bicycling, fishing, golf, hiking, horseback riding, live theater, museums, parks, shopping, tennis and wineries nearby.

Publicity: *Midwest Living.*

Manhattan B8

Shortridge House Bed & Breakfast

529 Pierre
Manhattan, KS 66502
(785)565-0086

Circa 1871. In the heart of downtown, this completely restored Greek Revival Italianate home is close to the university as well as shops and businesses. Furnished with Victorian antiques, the warm hospitality is friendly and inviting. Enjoy complimentary drinks and snacks. Select from the book and video library. Guest bedrooms include Internet access and feature a Jacuzzi tub in a large bathroom. A bountiful breakfast is served in the formal dining room or on the balcony when weather allows. Seasonal fruit, fresh baked goods, Belgium waffles, blueberry and walnut pancakes, ham and egg casserole or fresh herb frittata with thick-cut bacon or sausage is some of the mouth-watering foods that are made with organic ingredients when possible. Relax on the enclosed brick patio garden with a fountain. Konza Prairie is only ten minutes away for a hike in the flint hills.

Historic Interest: One of the grandest homes built in the city by the original founders, represents an era of grand hospitality and gentility.

Innkeeper(s): James Sherow and Bonnie Lynn-Sherow. $85-95. 2 rooms. Breakfast and snacks/refreshments included in rates. Types of meals: Full gourmet bkfst, veg bkfst and early coffee/tea. Beds: QDT. Modem hook-up, cable TV, VCR, reading lamp, ceiling fan, clock radio, telephone, turn-down service and desk in room. Air conditioning. Fax, copier, spa, bicycles, library, parlor games, balcony and enclosed patio with fountain on premises. Antiquing, art galleries, canoeing/kayaking, fishing, golf, hiking, horseback riding, live theater, museums, parks, shopping, sporting events and tennis nearby.

Oberlin A3

The Landmark Inn at The Historic Bank of Oberlin

189 S Penn
Oberlin, KS 67749
(785)475-2340 (888)639-0003

Circa 1886. In 1886, this inn served as the Bank of Oberlin, one of the town's most impressive architectural sites. The bank lasted only a few years, though, and went through a number of uses, from county courthouse to the telephone company. Today, it serves as both inn and a historic landmark, a reminder of the past with rooms decorated Victorian style with antiques. One room includes a fireplace; another has a whirlpool tub. In addition to the inviting rooms, there is a restaurant serving dinner specialties such as buttermilk pecan chicken and roasted beef with simmered mushrooms. The inn is listed in the National Register.

Innkeeper(s): Gary Anderson. $69-109. 7 rooms with PB, 1 with FP, 1 suite and 2 conference rooms. Breakfast included in rates. Types of meals: Full gourmet bkfst, early coffee/tea, gourmet lunch, afternoon tea, snacks/refreshments, gourmet dinner and room service. Restaurant on premises. Beds: QD. Cable TV, VCR, reading lamp, ceiling fan, clock radio, telephone and desk in room. Air conditioning. Fax, sauna, bicycles, library, parlor games and fireplace on premises. Limited handicap access. Weddings, small meetings, family reunions and seminars hosted. Antiquing, golf, parks, shopping and tennis nearby.

Publicity: *Kansas Magazine, Dining out in Kansas, Wichita Eagle-Beacon, Salina Journal, Hays Daily News, 2001 Bed & Breakfast Calendar, KSN TV-Wichita, KS, High Plains Public TV and Kansas Public TV Taste of Kansas.*

Topeka B9

1878 Sage Inn & Stagecoach Station, LLC

13553 SW K-4 Hwy (Dover)
Topeka, KS 66420-0003
(785)256-6050 (866)466-6736 Fax:(785)256-6291
E-mail: sageinn@inlandnet.net
Web: www.historicsageinn.com

Circa 1865. Constructed from limestone, this rustic country inn opened in 1865 as a hotel, expanding to a stagecoach station in 1878. It has retained its original limestone walls and pine floors and is now listed in the National Register. The Colonial guest bedroom boasts a clawfoot tub and four-poster bed, the Victorian features a slipper tub and shower. Expect a European flair in the Cosmopolitan, with a walk-in shower and the exotic Explorer offers a tub/shower combo. Browse the on-site antique/gift shop. Located on the historic Southwest Trail, the link which connected the Oregon Trail to the Santa Fe Trail, it is within 15 minutes of Topeka, an hour from Kansas City and Wichita.

Innkeeper(s): Mike & Debra Stufflebean. $75-85. 4 rooms with PB. Breakfast included in rates. Types of meals: Country bkfst. Beds: KQD. TV, reading lamp, stereo, clock radio, extra pillows, blankets and portable heaters in room. Air conditioning. VCR, parlor games, telephone, gift shop, full body massage, antiques, lounge with snack bar and candlelight dinner by reservation on premises. Antiquing, fishing, golf, horseback riding, live theater, parks, shopping, Echo Cliff Park, duck pond and driving and hiking in the Flinthills nearby.

Wichita E7

Castle Inn Riverside

1155 N River Blvd
Wichita, KS 67203
(316)263-9300
E-mail: info@castleinnriverside.com
Web: www.castleinnriverside.com

Circa 1886. A stunning example of Richardsonian Romanesque architecture, the historic Campbell Castle is now a luxurious inn. High ceilings, a showpiece staircase, hand-crafted inlaid wood floors, stained-glass windows, delicately carved fretwork and original hardware grace the Castle. Relax in the Parlour, Library or Billiards Room. Enjoy a sampling of wine, cheese, gourmet coffee and tea, after-dinner liqueurs and dessert. Each well-appointed guest bedroom and suite offers elegance and privacy. Most feature antique fireplaces and many boast two-person Jacuzzi tubs. Generous in-room amenities include TV, VCR, phone and data port. This estate resort is just a few minutes from downtown and nearby attractions like Exploration Place, Old Town and the Wichita Art Museum.

Historic Interest: The area offers several historic attractions, including nearby Old Town, a Native American center and several museums.

Innkeeper(s): Terry & Paula Lowry. $125-275. 14 rooms with PB, 12 with FP, 1 suite and 1 conference room. Breakfast included in rates. Types of meals: Full gourmet bkfst and snacks/refreshments. Beds: KQ. Data port, TV, VCR, reading lamp, clock radio, telephone and desk in room. Air conditioning. Fax, copier, parlor games and fireplace on premises. Limited handicap access. Weddings, small meetings, family reunions and seminars hosted. Antiquing, fishing, live theater, parks, shopping, sporting events and water sports nearby.

Publicity: *Country Inns, Midwest Living, Travel Holiday, Runners World, The Wichita Business Journal, PBS and HGTV.*

Inn at the Park

3751 E Douglas Ave
Wichita, KS 67218-1002
(316)652-0500 (800)258-1951 Fax:(316)652-0525
E-mail: iap@innatthepark.com
Web: www.innatthepark.com

Circa 1910. This popular three-story brick mansion offers many special touches, including unique furnishings in each of its 12 guest rooms, three of which are suites. Most of the rooms feature fireplaces. The inn's convenient location makes it ideal for business travelers or those interested in exploring Wichita. The inn's parkside setting provides additional opportunities for relaxation or recreation. Close to shops, restaurants, Old Town, Exploration Place and museums.

Innkeeper(s): Judy Hess and/or Jan Lightner. $89-164. 12 rooms with PB, 8 with FP, 3 suites and 1 conference room. Breakfast included in rates. Types of meals: Cont plus and early coffee/tea. Beds: KQ. Cable TV, VCR, reading lamp, refrigerator, clock radio, telephone, turn-down service, desk and hot tub/spa in room. Air conditioning. TV, fax, copier, spa and fireplace on premises. Antiquing, live theater, shopping and conference facility nearby.

Publicity: *Wichita Business Journal.*

"This is truly a distinctive hotel. Your attention to detail is surpassed only by your devotion to excellent service."

Little River House B&B

6137 Fairfield Rd
Wichita, KS 67204
(316)838-3127

Circa 1920. In a quiet neighborhood on the Little Arkansas River, this restored cottage is surrounded by flower beds. A living room with a Queen sofa bed and two dining areas offer plenty of places to relax. Furnished in a classic style with antiques and Oriental rugs, the guest bedroom features a four-poster bed. The fully equipped kitchen is stocked with fresh breakfast foods and ingredients. Enjoy snacks and beverages as well as stuffed cookie and candy jars. Relax on the intimate front porch, or view the scenic woods from the back patio. Birding, walking and jogging are popular activities, or explore the local area on one of the bikes available. Popular music concerts with a pipe organ/piano are available next door.

Innkeeper(s): Michael & Karen Coup. $99-129. Breakfast and snacks/refreshments included in rates. Types of meals: Country bkfst, veg bkfst, early coffee/tea and dinner. Beds: KQ. Modem hook-up, cable TV, VCR, reading lamp, stereo, refrigerator, snack bar, clock radio, telephone, coffeemaker, desk and voice mail in room. Central air. Fax, copier, bicycles, library, parlor games, laundry facility, fully furnished kitchen, dishwasher and fans on premises. Weddings hosted. Amusement parks, antiquing, art galleries, bicycling, golf, hiking, live theater, museums, parks, shopping, sporting events, tennis and virgin prairies nearby.

Kentucky

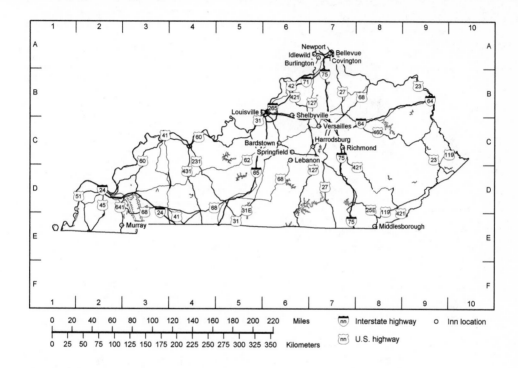

	1	2	3	4	5	6	7	8	9	10

Newport
Idlewild
Burlington
Bellevue
Covington
75
42 71
421
127
265
Louisville
31
Shelbyville
Versailles
Harrodsburg
Bardstown
Springfield
Lebanon
Richmond
41
60
60
231
431
82
65
68
127
27
51
24
45
641
68
24
41
68
31E
31
Murray
27
75
421
25E 119 421
75
Middlesborough
41
119
23
64
84
460
23
119

```
0   20  40  60  80  100 120 140 160 180 200 220   Miles
0  25  50  75 100 125 150 175 200 225 250 275 300 325 350  Kilometers
```

(nn) Interstate highway   o Inn location
(nn) U.S. highway

Bardstown   C6

A Rosemark Haven
714 N Third St
Bardstown, KY 40004
(502)348-8218
E-mail: arosemarkhaven@aol.com
Web: www.arosemarkhaven.com

Circa 1830. This antebellum mansion is listed in the National
Register of Historic Places. The inn features elegantly carved
woodwork, stained glass, yellow poplar and ash floors, a grand
entrance foyer and spiral staircase. There is a lookout on top of
the house. The inn is furnished with antiques.
Innkeeper(s): Rosemary Sweeney. $115-160. 7 rooms with PB, 5 with FP.
Types of meals: Full gourmet bkfst. Beds: K.
Publicity: *Kentucky Travel Guide.*

The Homestead B&B
3944 Bloomfield Road
Bardstown, KY 40004
(502)349-1777

Circa 1785. Slow down and relax while staying at this 1785
log home built from huge hand-hewn native Tulip (yellow)
poplar. Later additions include a Victorian wing and a slave
wing. Restoration has preserved its rich heritage and The
Homestead is now an Historic Kentucky Landmark. The quaint
and peaceful setting is best appreciated from one of the porches or a swing overlooking the bridge and water. Antique furnishings accent the primitive interior and a grand buffalo head
adorns the fireplace mantle in the living room. Guest bedrooms
boast a rustic to Victorian décor. Farm-fresh eggs are gathered
for a hearty country breakfast that includes homemade jams,
jellies and preserves. Shop for treasures in the gift shop.
Historic Interest: Three story log home built in 1785 with the slave wing
added in 1830. Logs are native Tulip (yellow) Poplar.
Innkeeper(s): Joanne Hobbs. $95-125. 3 rooms, 1 with PB. Breakfast includ-
ed in rates. Types of meals: Country bkfst, early coffee/tea, picnic lunch and

183

dinner. Beds: QDT. Cable TV, CD player, ceiling fan, telephone and turn-down service in room. Central air. VCR, fireplace and gift shop on premises. Small meetings hosted. Amusement parks, antiquing, art galleries, fishing, golf, hiking, horseback riding, live theater, museums, parks and shopping nearby.

Jailer's Inn

111 W Stephen Foster Ave
Bardstown, KY 40004-1415
(502)348-5551 (800)948-5551 Fax:(502)349-1837
E-mail: cpaul@jailersinn.com
Web: www.jailersinn.com

Circa 1819. As the innkeepers say, guests can come and "do time" at this inn, which was used as a jail as late as 1987. However, today, accommodations are bit less restrictive. Each of the elegant guest rooms is individually appointed. From the Victorian Room to the Garden Room, each captures a different theme. Two guest rooms include a double Jacuzzi tub. Only one guest room resembles a jail cell, it contains two bunks, as well as the more luxurious addition of a waterbed. In the summer, the full breakfasts are served in a courtyard. The inn is located in the heart of historic Bardstown.

Historic Interest: Tours of "My Old Kentucky Home," conducted by guides in antebellum costumes, are a popular attraction. Lincoln's birthplace and boyhood home and the oldest cathedral west of Alleghany are nearby, as is the Getz Museum of Whiskey History.
Innkeeper(s): Paul McCoy. $70-125. 6 rooms with PB. Breakfast included in rates. Types of meals: Full bkfst and early coffee/tea. Beds: KQD. Cable TV, reading lamp, ceiling fan, clock radio, turn-down service and desk in room. Air conditioning. VCR, parlor games, telephone and fireplace on premises. Weddings, small meetings and family reunions hosted. Antiquing, live theater, parks and shopping nearby.
Publicity: *Vacations, New Choices, Kentucky Standard, USA Weekend, New York Times, Cincinnati Enquire, Honeymoon Magazine, Country Inns, Southern Living, Courier Journal Newspaper, Travel Channel, Food Channel, Nashville's Crossroads and Jeopardy.*

"Wonderful experience! A very special B&B."

Old Talbott Tavern

107 W Stephen Foster Ave, PO Box 365
Bardstown, KY 40004-0036
(502)348-3494 (800)482-8376 Fax:(502)348-3404
E-mail: talbotts@bardstown.com
Web: www.talbotts.com

Circa 1779. Old Talbott Tavern is the oldest continuously operating "western" stagecoach inn in America. The stone building is filled with antiques, and there are murals painted by King Philippe of France and his entourage. If you look closely, you'll find bullet holes left by Jesse James. There are five guest rooms, including two suites. In addition to the unusual Kentucky Bourbon Bar and gift shop, the inn's full service restaurant offers five dining/meeting rooms, popular for group bookings as well as business and special occasion dining.
Innkeeper(s): The Kelley Family. $70-125. 5 rooms with PB.

Bellevue   A7

Christopher's B&B

604 Poplar St
Bellevue, KY 41073
(859)491-9354 (888)585-7085

Circa 1889. The former home of Bellevue Christian Church, this unique inn sits in one of the area's three historic districts. The spacious building was transformed into a delightful residence and B&B featuring the original hardwood floors and stained-glass windows. Tastefully decorated and furnished in a Victorian style, the gracious guest bedrooms and suite feature Jacuzzi tubs and VCRs.
Innkeeper(s): Brenda Guidugli. $89-169. 3 rooms with PB and 1 suite. Breakfast and snacks/refreshments included in rates. Types of meals: Full bkfst and early coffee/tea. Beds: KQ. Modem hook-up, data port, cable TV, VCR, reading lamp, CD player, refrigerator, ceiling fan, snack bar, clock radio, telephone, coffeemaker, desk and Jacuzzi in room. Central air. Fireplace, Continental plus breakfast is available and included in rates on weekdays and single and double Jacuzzi tubs on premises. Amusement parks, antiquing, art galleries, golf, live theater, museums, parks, shopping, sporting events, Newport Aquarium, Newport on the Levee, Millennium Peace Bell and various restaurants along Ohio River to choose from nearby.
Publicity: *Midwest Living, The Cincinnati Enquirer, The Kentucky Post, Kentucky Monthly, Arts Across Kentucky, AAA Home Away, City Beat, Places To Go and voted by inngoers in Arrington's Bed and Breakfast Journal 2003 & 2004 Book of Lists as "one of the Top 15 B&Bs/Inns for best design and decor."*

Burlington   A7

Burlington's Willis Graves B&B

5825 Jefferson St
Burlington, KY 41005
(859)689-5096 (888)226-5096
E-mail: inn@burligrave.com
Web: www.burligrave.com

Circa 1830. Situated on an acre and a half of lawn and garden, this brick Federal house is located next to the county fairgrounds. Once hidden behind aluminum siding, the home is now filled with antiques and is listed in the National Register. Handsome mantels, vintage artwork and original floorboards add to the inn's historic integrity. Guest bedrooms feature high-speed Internet access, and the suite boasts a spa bathroom with a whirlpool and steam shower. Explore the nearby shops and restaurants, or drive to the Covington riverfront area.
Innkeeper(s): Nancy & Bob Swartzel. $95-175. 3 rooms with PB and 1 suite. Breakfast included in rates. Types of meals: Full bkfst and early coffee/tea. Beds: QD. Modem hook-up, cable TV, VCR, reading lamp, stereo, refrigerator, clock radio, telephone, turn-down service, desk and suite with spa bathroom featuring whirlpool steam shower in room. Air conditioning. Parlor games on premises. Antiquing, downhill skiing, fishing, golf, horseback riding, parks, shopping and restaurants nearby.
Publicity: *The Courier-Journal, Kentucky Monthly Magazine and Cincinnati Magazine.*

"If a historic setting and elegant surroundings is your definition of the perfect getaway, consider northern Kentucky's historic Burlington's Willis Graves (BWG) Bed and Breakfast. The proprietors have perfected every detail of the ambience of the 19th century. I say this from experience, having been a recent guest at this sophisticated retreat."

Covington
A7

Amos Shinkle Townhouse

215 Garrard St
Covington, KY 41011-1715
(859)431-2118 (800)972-7012 Fax:(859)491-4551

Circa 1854. This restored mansion has won several preservation awards. It features a Greco-Italianate facade with a cast-iron filigree porch. Inside there are lavish crown moldings and Italianate mantels on the fire-places. Sixteen-foot ceilings and Rococo Revival chandeliers add to the formal elegance. Guest rooms boast four-poster or massive Victorian-style beds and period furnishings. Here, Southern hospitality is at its finest.

Historic Interest: National Register.
Innkeeper(s): Don Nash & Bernie Moorman. $95-165. 7 rooms with PB and 1 conference room. Breakfast included in rates. Types of meals: Full bkfst. Beds: KQD. TV and telephone in room. Air conditioning. Fax and copier on premises.
Publicity: *Everybody's News, Cleveland Plain Dealer, New York Times, Country Inn, Washington Post, Southern Living, ComAir Wing Tips, National Geographic Traveler, "Best BnB in Cincinnati" Cincinnati Magazine (10/02), "Best BnB in Kentucky" (6/03) Kentucky Monthly, Arts across Kentucky, Ohio Magazine and Louisville Magazine.*

"It's like coming home to family and friends."

Harrodsburg
C7

Bauer Haus

362 N College
Harrodsburg, KY 40330-1116
(859)734-6289 (877)734-6289

Circa 1880. This Queen Anne Victorian, sans gingerbread, features a wicker-filled front porch, complete with swing. In the National Register, it was built on one of the first outlots in Harrodsburg. The town is the state's oldest settlement, established in 1774. Inside the parlor, archways adorn the mantel and date back to the early 19th century. The spacious guest bedrooms are furnished with antiques in a traditional decor.

Coffee or tea is served to each room before the breakfast seating. Lower-fat dishes and fresh fruit accompany low-fat, made-from-scratch breakfast cakes or muffins. Adjacent to the main house is the new carriage house, with deluxe accommodations featuring a fireplace, whirlpool tub, TV/VCR and small kitchen.
Innkeeper(s): Dick & Marian Bauer. $79-135. 4 rooms with PB. Breakfast and snacks/refreshments included in rates. Types of meals: Full bkfst and early coffee/tea. Beds: QDT. Reading lamp and clock radio in room. Air conditioning. VCR, parlor games, telephone and fireplace on premises. Small meetings, family reunions and seminars hosted. Antiquing, fishing, golf, live theater, water sports and historic sites nearby.

Canaan Land Farm B&B

700 Canaan Land Rd
Harrodsburg, KY 40330-9220
(859)734-3984 (888)734-3984

Circa 1795. This National Register farmhouse, one of the oldest brick houses in Kentucky, is appointed with antiques, quilts and feather beds. A flock of sheep, goats and other

assorted barnyard animals graze the pastures at this working farm. In 1995, the innkeepers reconstructed an 1815 historic log house on the grounds. The log house includes three guest rooms and two working fireplaces.
Historic Interest: In 1992, Canaan Land Farm was named a Kentucky historic farm. Nearby Shakertown, a restored Shaker village, features daily craft demonstrations, riverboat rides and tours.
Innkeeper(s): Mark & Ann Fryer. $75-125. 7 rooms with PB, 2 with FP. Breakfast included in rates. Types of meals: Full bkfst. Beds: QDT. Reading lamp and desk in room. VCR, spa, swimming, parlor games, telephone and fireplace on premises. Weddings, family reunions and seminars hosted. Antiquing, fishing, golf, horseback riding, parks, shopping and water sports nearby.
Publicity: *Danville Advocate and Lexington Herald Leader.*

"You truly have a gift for genuine hospitality."

Shaker Village of Pleasant Hill

3501 Lexington Rd
Harrodsburg, KY 40330-9218
(859)734-5411 (800)734-5611 Fax:(859)734-7278
E-mail: diana@shakervillageky.org
Web: www.shakervillageky.org

Circa 1809. A living history museum, this 19th-century Shaker village is set atop a pleasant meadow and includes 2,800 acres of farmland. Guest rooms are in 15 of the 33 restored buildings where Shakers once lived. Guest rooms are furnished with Shaker reproductions and hand-woven rugs. The entire village is a National Historic Landmark. Costumed interpreters work at 19th-century crafts and describe Shaker culture and craft. A dining room in the village serves bountiful Kentucky fare and Shaker recipes and the Summer Kitchen is available for lunch from May through October.

Innkeeper(s): James Thomas. $78-225. 81 rooms with PB, 8 suites, 2 cottages and 4 conference rooms. Types of meals: Full bkfst, lunch and dinner. Beds: DT. Cable TV and telephone in room. Air conditioning. TV, VCR, fax, copier and fireplace on premises. Small meetings, family reunions and seminars hosted. Antiquing, fishing, golf, hiking, live theater, shopping, historic sites and state park nearby.
Publicity: *Southern Living, Traveler, New York Times, Architectural Digest, HGTV and Good Morning America.*

Idlewild
A7

First Farm Inn

2510 Stevens Rd
Idlewild, KY 41080
(859)586-0199 (800)277-9527
E-mail: firstfarm@goodnews.net
Web: www.firstfarminn.com

Circa 1870. Elegantly updated, this 1870s farm house and historic wooden barn with tobacco rails are surrounded by 21 acres of rolling hills, ponds stocked with bass, centuries-old maple trees, gardens and horses. Situated above the Ohio River, where Kentucky joins Ohio and Indiana, city sites and country pleasures are equally accessible. Spend a few hours learning about horses and riding one of the quiet and friendly equines. Lessons begin with grooming, moving into the arena, then graduating to trail rides around the farm, along the creek and through the woods. Schedule a massage with a licensed therapist in a spacious guest bedroom furnished with antique oak heirlooms from five generations. Indulge in a bountiful home-made breakfast of fresh fruit, assorted breads and an entree served family style around the big dining room table. Sit by the fire or play the grand piano. Relax in the outdoor hot tub; swing or rock on the veranda.

Historic Interest: Built in 1870s, surrounded by 200+ year-old trees. Historic wooden barn with tobacco rails.

Innkeeper(s): Jen Warner & Dana Kisor. $90-135. 2 rooms with PB. Breakfast included in rates. Types of meals: Full gourmet bkfst, veg bkfst and early coffee/tea. Beds: Q. Data port, TV, VCR, reading lamp, ceiling fan, clock radio and telephone in room. Central air. Fax, copier, spa, stable, library, parlor games, fireplace, horseback riding lessons, porch swing, porch rockers, tire swing, hammock, cats, dogs, horses, grand piano, fishing pond and hiking on premises. Small meetings hosted. Amusement parks, antiquing, art galleries, downhill skiing, fishing, golf, hiking, horseback riding, live theater, museums, parks, shopping, sporting events, tennis and Perfect North ski slopes nearby.

Publicity: *Kentucky Monthly, Cincinnati Monthly, Chicago Herald, Columbus Parent, Kentucky Post, Cincinnati Enquirer, Louisville Courier-Journal, Indianapolis Monthly, City Beat, The Downtowner and Channel 12 One Tank Trip.*

Lebanon   C6

Myrtledene B&B

370 N Spalding Ave
Lebanon, KY 40033-1557
(502)692-2223 (800)391-1721

Circa 1833. Once a Confederate general's headquarters at one point during the Civil War, this pink brick inn, located at a bend in the road, has greeted visitors entering Lebanon for more than 150 years. When General John Hunt Morgan returned in 1863

to destroy the town, the white flag hoisted to signal a truce was flown at Myrtledene. A country breakfast usually features ham and biscuits as well as the innkeepers' specialty, peaches and cream French toast.

Historic Interest: Headquarters of confederate General John Hunt Morgan. Morgan rode his mare up to front hall stairs.

Innkeeper(s): James F. Spragens. $85. 4 rooms, 2 with PB, 1 with FP and 1 conference room. Breakfast included in rates. Types of meals: Full gourmet bkfst, early coffee/tea and afternoon tea. Beds: DT. Reading lamp, clock radio, turn-down service, Makers Mark bourbon and bourbon chocolates in room. Air conditioning. VCR, library, parlor games, telephone and fireplace on premises. Weddings, small meetings, family reunions and seminars hosted. Antiquing, fishing, live theater, parks, shopping and water sports nearby.

Publicity: *Lebanon Enterprise, Louisville Courier-Journal, Lebanon/Marion County Kentucky and Sunnyside.*

"Our night in the Cabbage Rose Room was an experience of another time, another culture. Your skill in preparing and presenting breakfast was equally elegant! We'll be back!"

Louisville   B6

1853 Inn at Woodhaven

401 S Hubbard Ln
Louisville, KY 40207-4074
(502)895-1011 (888)895-1011
E-mail: info@innatwoodhaven.com
Web: www.innatwoodhaven.com

Circa 1853. This Gothic Revival, painted in a cheerful shade of yellow, is still much the same as it was in the 1850s, when it served as the home on a prominent local farm. The rooms still feature the outstanding carved woodwork, crisscross window designs, winding staircases, decorative mantels and hardwood

floors. Guest quarters are tastefully appointed with antiques, suitable for their 12-foot, nine-inch tall ceilings. Complimentary coffee and tea stations are provided in each room. There are several common areas in the Main House and Carriage House, and guests also take advantage of the inn's porches. Rose Cottage is octagon shaped and features a 25-foot vaulted ceiling, a king bed, fireplace, sitting area, double whirlpool, steam shower and wraparound porch. The National Register home is close to all of Louisville's attractions.

Innkeeper(s): Marsha Burton. $85-225. 8 rooms with PB, 3 with FP, 6 suites and 1 cottage. Breakfast included in rates. Types of meals: Full gourmet bkfst, picnic lunch and gourmet dinner. Beds: KQ. Cable TV, reading lamp, stereo, ceiling fan, clock radio, telephone, desk, coffee, tea and hot chocolate facility in room. Air conditioning. Fax, copier, library, parlor games, fireplace, five rooms with double whirlpools and four rooms with steam showers on premises. Limited handicap access. Weddings, small meetings, family reunions and seminars hosted. Amusement parks, antiquing, golf, live theater, parks, shopping, sporting events, tennis and water sports nearby.

Publicity: *Courier Journal, New York Times, WAVE and WHAS.*

1888 Historic Rocking Horse Manor B&B

1022 S 3rd St
Louisville, KY 40203-2952
(502)583-0408 (888)467-7322 Fax:(502)558-36077
E-mail: rockinghorse1888@cs.com
Web: www.rockinghorse-bb.com

Circa 1888. Gleaming woodwork, elegant rugs and period light fixtures create a restful elegant ambiance in this 1888 Richardsonian Romanesque mansion located in historic Old Louisville near Churchill Downs. The inn has a Victorian parlor, a library, an exercise facility and a third-floor sitting area with a mini-office for those who need to momentarily re-enter the 21st century. It has five guest rooms with whimsical names like Chelsea's Garden and The Irish Rose Room. The two-room suite is perfect for families or romantic getaways. Breakfast is an event each morning with such delights as strawberry yogurt parfait, apple brunch biscuit, New Orleans French Toast and homemade hash browns. Complimentary evening snacks and beverages are also available.

Innkeeper(s): Richard Lowrimore. $79-169. 5 rooms with PB, 1 suite and 1 conference room. Breakfast and snacks/refreshments included in rates. Types of meals: Full gourmet bkfst, veg bkfst and early coffee/tea. Beds: KQDT. Modem hook-up, cable TV, reading lamp, ceiling fan, clock radio, telephone, turn-down service, desk and hot tub/spa in room. Central air. VCR, fax, sauna, bicycles, library, parlor games, fireplace and exercise facility on premises. Small meetings and family reunions hosted. Amusement parks, antiquing, art galleries, bicycling, golf, live theater, museums, parks, shopping, tennis, wineries and Caesar's Casino nearby.

Publicity: *The Courier Journal, Kentucky Monthly and WHAS.*

Aleksander House

1213 S First St
Louisville, KY 40203
(502)637-4985 (866)637-4985 Fax:(502)635-1398

Circa 1882. French impressionist paintings, French Toile wall coverings in the dining room, gas light fixtures, 12-foot ceilings, fireplaces and walnut woodwork create the pleasant decor of this three-story Italianate Victorian. Ask for Katharine's Room on the third floor and enjoy a four-poster bed, writing desk and settee. Pecan waffles served with glazed peaches and cream or eggs Benedict are popular breakfast entrees. Mystery weekend packages are offered on occasion. The inn is listed in the National Register.

Innkeeper(s): Nancy R Hinchliff. $95-169. 5 rooms, 3 with PB, 2 with FP

and 1 suite. Breakfast and snacks/refreshments included in rates. Types of meals: Full gourmet bkfst, veg bkfst and early coffee/tea. Beds: KQDT. Modem hook-up, data port, TV, VCR, reading lamp, refrigerator, ceiling fan, snack bar, clock radio, telephone, coffeemaker, desk, terry cloth robes, irons, ironing boards and hair dryers in room. Central air. Fax, copier, library, pet boarding, parlor games, fireplace and video library on premises. Small meetings, family reunions and seminars hosted. Amusement parks, antiquing, art galleries, bicycling, golf, hiking, horseback riding, live theater, museums, parks, shopping, tennis, wineries and river boating nearby.
Publicity: *Country Inns, Louisville Magazine, Today's Woman Magazine, The Courier-Journal, Country Register and Channel 11-WGN.*

Central Park B&B

1353 S Fourth St
Louisville, KY 40208-2349
(502)638-1505 (877)922-1505 Fax:(502)638-1525
E-mail: centralpar@win.net
Web: www.centralparkbandb.com

Circa 1884. This three-story Second Empire Victorian is listed in the National Register, and it is located in the heart of "Old Louisville," amid America's largest collection of Victorian homes. Enjoy the fine craftsmanship of the home's many amenities, including the reverse-painted glass ceiling of the front porch and the polished woodwork and stained glass. Among its 18 rooms are seven guest rooms, all with private baths and two with whirlpool tubs. There are 11 fireplaces, some with carved mantels and decorative tile. The Carriage House suite has a full kitchen. Antiques are found throughout. The University of Louisville and Spalding University is within easy walking distance. Across the street is Central Park.
Innkeeper(s): Mary & Joseph White. $89-169. 7 rooms with PB and 3 suites. Breakfast and snacks/refreshments included in rates. Types of meals: Full bkfst and early coffee/tea. Beds: KQ. Cable TV, reading lamp, telephone, turn-down service, desk, hair dryers and computer port in room. Air conditioning. Fireplace on premises. Weddings, small meetings, family reunions and seminars hosted. Antiquing, live theater, shopping, sporting events and fine dining nearby.

DuPont Mansion B&B

1317 South Fourth Street
Louisville, KY 40208
(502)638-0045
E-mail: hwarren9@bellsouth.net
Web: www.dupontmansion.com

Circa 1879. Meticulously restored, this historically significant Italianate mansion features original, ornate marble fireplaces, inlaid flooring, 15-foot ceilings and crystal chandeliers. The grand Victorian decor is accented by period antique furnishings. Spacious common areas and a courtesy kitchen offer added comfort and convenience. Each of the romantic guest bedrooms and suite boast a whirlpool tub, and most include fireplaces. Linger over breakfast in the banquet-style dining room with a typical feast of fruit, broccoli-cheese quiche, bacon, cranberry-orange scones, fresh-squeezed orange juice and gourmet coffee. Popular local sites like Churchill Downs and the Kentucky Derby, Louisville Slugger Museum and many others are all within a 10-minute range.
Historic Interest: House was built in 1879, original hardwood floors, ornate woodwork, beautiful windows, 15 ft. ceilings, gorgeous Italian marble fireplace.
Innkeeper(s): Sarah Leber. $119-199. 8 rooms, 6 with PB, 7 with FP and 2 suites. Breakfast and snacks/refreshments included in rates. Types of meals: Full gourmet bkfst and early coffee/tea. Beds: KQ. Modem hook-up, cable TV, VCR, reading lamp, ceiling fan, clock radio, telephone, Jacuzzi and fireplace in room. Central air. Library, fireplace and laundry facility on premises. Weddings, small meetings, family reunions and seminars hosted. Amusement parks, antiquing, art galleries, fishing, golf, hiking, horseback riding, live theater, museums, parks, shopping, sporting events, tennis, water sports and wineries nearby.
Publicity: *Courier Journal.*

Fleur de Lis Bed & Breakfast

1452 S. Fourth St
Louisville, KY 40208
(502)635-5764 Fax:(502)485-0451
E-mail: fleurdelis@kentucky-lodging.com
Web: www.kentucky-lodging.com

Circa 1896. Named for the city's symbol, this Victorian house sits in historic Old Louisville. It was built, as were many of the area's fine mansions, by money earned from the railroad. Encompassing 6,000 square feet, the inn's adventure begins in a grand foyer and staircase with a rare leaded-glass front door. Stained-glass windows accent the living room, library and formal dining room. The inn recently has been restored to retain its original character while enhancing comfort with today's technology. Spacious guest bedrooms feature luxurious furnishings, rich hardwood floors and woodwork, 13-foot ceilings, fireplaces and some whirlpool tubs. A hearty breakfast and afternoon refreshments are pleasurable highlights.
Innkeeper(s): Sharon Portman. $129-159. 5 rooms with PB, 5 with FP, 1 suite and 1 conference room. Breakfast, afternoon tea and snacks/refreshments included in rates. Types of meals: Full gourmet bkfst, veg bkfst and early coffee/tea. Beds: KQT. Data port, cable TV, VCR, reading lamp, ceiling fan, clock radio, telephone, turn-down service, hot tub/spa and fireplace in room. Central air. Fax, library, fireplace and gift shop on premises. Weddings, small meetings, family reunions and seminars hosted. Amusement parks, antiquing, art galleries, bicycling, fishing, golf, hiking, horseback riding, live theater, museums, parks, shopping, sporting events and tennis nearby.

Pinecrest Cottage and Gardens - A Bed and Breakfast

2806 Newburg Rd
Louisville, KY 40205
(502)454-3800 Fax:(502)452-9791
E-mail: pinecrest@insightbb.com
Web: www.pinecrestcottageandgardens.com

Circa 1775. On more than six landscaped acres including century-old trees, three ponds and a dozen perennial flower beds stands the Pinecrest Cottage, a 1,400-square-foot, five-room guesthouse with one bedroom. Guests are afforded full privacy, and may even cook their own breakfast with food provided in the fully stocked kitchen. Summer visitors enjoy tennis and swimming on the grounds. Fall visitors enjoy the colors of autumn, and winter visitors see the landscape blanketed with snow. Nearby attractions include Churchill Downs and Derby museum, Louisville Slugger Museum, the Louisville Zoo, and various restaurants and antique shops.
Innkeeper(s): Nancy Morris. $110-165. 1 room with PB, 1 with FP. Breakfast and snacks/refreshments included in rates. Types of meals: Cont plus. Beds: K. Modem hook-up, data port, cable TV, VCR, reading lamp, stereo, refrigerator, clock radio, telephone, coffeemaker, desk and fireplace in room. Central air. Fax, copier, swimming, tennis and fireplace on premises. Amusement parks nearby.
Publicity: *Courier Journal.*

Tucker House Bed & Breakfast

2406 Tucker Station Rd
Louisville, KY 40299
(502)297-8007 Fax:(502)266-7561
E-mail: tuckerhouse1840@aol.com
Web: www.tuckerhouse1840.com

Circa 1840. A state landmark, this meticulously restored brick, Federal-style farmhouse is listed in the National Register. The ambiance of early country living is enhanced by original poplar

floors and trim, seeded-glass windows, solid brick walls and seven fireplaces. The parlor holds two historical book collections. Distinctive guest chambers feature thick robes, big towels and soft linens. Freshly brewed coffee and other refreshments are available in the common room that leads to a relaxing deck. A hearty breakfast is served on antique china in the formal dining room or on Kentucky Bybee pottery in the cheery gathering room. Five acres of spectacular surroundings include formal gardens, woods, a spring-fed lake and a swimming pool.
Innkeeper(s): Devona & Steve Porter. $105-125. 4 rooms with PB and 2 conference rooms. Breakfast and snacks/refreshments included in rates. Types of meals: Country bkfst, veg bkfst and early coffee/tea. Beds: QD. TV, VCR, reading lamp, clock radio, telephone, turn-down service, desk and hot tub/spa in room. Central air. Fax, copier, swimming, stable, library, parlor games, fireplace, lake and woods on premises. Weddings, small meetings, family reunions and seminars hosted. Amusement parks, antiquing, art galleries, bicycling, fishing, golf, hiking, horseback riding, live theater, museums, parks, shopping and sporting events nearby.
Publicity: Louisville Courier-Journal, Today's Woman and New York Times.

Middlesborough E8

The Ridge Runner B&B

208 Arthur Hts
Middlesborough, KY 40965-1728
(606)248-4299

Circa 1890. Bachelor buttons, lilacs and wildflowers line the white picket fence framing this 20-room brick Victorian mansion. Guests enjoy relaxing in its turn-of-the-century parlor filled with Victorian antiques. Ask for the President's Room and you'll enjoy the best view of the Cumberland Mountains. (The  innkeeper's great, great-grandfather hosted President Lincoln the night before his Gettysburg address, and the inn boasts some heirlooms from that home.) A family-style breakfast is provided and special diets can be accommodated if notified in advance. Cumberland Gap National Park is five miles away, and the inn is two miles from the twin tunnels that pass through the Cumberland Gap. Pine Mountain State Park is 12 miles away. Guests also enjoy a visit to the P. 38 restoration project housed at the local airport.
Historic Interest: Restoration of a P-38 fighter plane, Abraham Lincoln artifacts and museum.
Innkeeper(s): Alan & Susan Meadows and Irma Gall. $70-80. 4 rooms, 2 with PB. Breakfast and snacks/refreshments included in rates. Types of meals: Early coffee/tea. Beds: DT. Reading lamp, ceiling fan, turn-down service and desk in room. Telephone on premises. Small meetings and family reunions hosted. Antiquing, parks and shopping nearby.
Publicity: Lexington Herald Leader, Blue Ridge Country, Indianapolis Star, Daily News, Courier Journal and Country Inn.

Murray E2

The Diuguid House B&B

603 Main St
Murray, KY 42071-2034
(270)753-5470 (888)261-3028

Circa 1895. This Victorian house features eight-foot-wide hallways and a golden oak staircase with stained-glass window. There is a sitting area adjoining the portico. Guest rooms are generous in size.
Historic Interest: Listed in the National Register.

Innkeeper(s): Karen & George Chapman. $45. 3 rooms. Breakfast included in rates. Types of meals: Full bkfst and early coffee/tea. Beds: QT. Reading lamp, clock radio, turn-down service and desk in room. Air conditioning. TV, parlor games and telephone on premises. Weddings, small meetings and family reunions hosted. Antiquing, fishing, live theater, parks and water sports nearby.
Publicity: Murray Ledger & Times.

"We enjoyed our visit in your beautiful home, and your hospitality was outstanding."

Newport A7

Cincinnati's Weller Haus B&B

319 Poplar St
Newport, KY 41073-1108
(859)431-6829 (800)431-4287 Fax:(859)431-4332
E-mail: innkeepers@wellerhaus.com
Web: www.wellerhaus.com

Circa 1880. Set in Taylor Daughter's Historic District and five minutes from downtown Cincinnati, this inn consists of two historic homes. The inn has received awards for preservation, and special features include original woodwork and doors. Secluded gardens are inviting, and there is a wrought iron fence setting off the property. A full breakfast is served by candlelight. Rooms offer antiques and suites feature double Jacuzzi tubs. A sky-lit great room has cathedral ceilings, and an ivy-covered gathering kitchen is open for snacks and drinks. Guests enjoy walking to the Newport Aquarium, Newport on the Levee and the Riverboat Row Restaurants as well as downtown Cincinnati stadiums. Other attractions include live theater and water sports. Business travelers are provided telephones, in room desks, high-speed Internet and a copy machine and fax are on the premises. Private space is available for small meetings. Breakfast can accommodate business schedules.
Innkeeper(s): Valerie & David Brown. $89-180. 5 rooms with PB. Breakfast included in rates. Types of meals: Full bkfst and early coffee/tea. Beds: QDT. Modem hook-up, cable TV, VCR, ceiling fan, telephone, suites have Jacuzzi for two and high-speed Internet access in room. Air conditioning. Small meetings and seminars hosted. Amusement parks, antiquing, fishing, live theater, museums, shopping, sporting events and water sports nearby.
Publicity: Downtowner, Bellevue Community News, Cincinnati Enquirer, Country Inns, Kentucky Monthly and Arrington's Bed & Breakfast Journal & the Book of Lists.

"You made B&B believers out of us."

Richmond C7

The Bennett House B&B and Events

419 W Main St
Richmond, KY 40475-1458
(859)623-7876
E-mail: smart@bennetthousebb.com
Web: www.bennetthousebb.com

Circa 1889. Rich in history this renovated, three-story Queen Anne with Romanesque detailing was well built with a stone foundation and two-foot-thick brick wall running through the center of the house. Retaining its integrity, many original features include stained glass, solid cherry and walnut woodwork, hand-carved mantles, fireplaces, tiles and floors. Relax in spacious guest bedrooms offering Southern hospitality. A savory breakfast is presented on fine china and may include the inn's signature Bennett House Hot Cinnamon Roll. The grounds are a delightful assortment of gardens, patios, creek rock walkways and a goldfish pond.

Innkeeper(s): Richard Smart. $75. 4 rooms, 3 with PB. Breakfast and snacks/refreshments included in rates. Types of meals: Full bkfst. Beds: KQ. Modem hook-up, cable TV, reading lamp, telephone, desk and fireplace in room. Central air. Fireplace on premises. Weddings, small meetings, family reunions and seminars hosted. Antiquing, art galleries, fishing, golf, hiking, horseback riding, parks, shopping and sporting events nearby.

Shelbyville   B6

The Wallace House

613 Washington St
Shelbyville, KY 40065-1131
(502)633-2006

Circa 1805. Relax in the peace and quiet of this Federal-style house that is listed in the National Register of Historic Places. It is conveniently situated midway between Louisville and Frankfort. Enjoy the slow pace on the front porch swings. Spacious guest bedrooms feature antique furnishings. Three suites include a private breakfast room to linger leisurely over a generous continental-plus morning meal. Located in the downtown historic district, it is an easy walk to the park, shops, restaurants and theater. Play golf or go swimming nearby.

Historic Interest: Kentucky Horse Park (50 miles), Shakertown (50 miles), Churchill Downs Derby Museum (30 miles).

Innkeeper(s): Evelyn Laurent. $75-85. 4 rooms with PB and 3 suites. Types of meals: Cont plus. Beds: Q. Cable TV, reading lamp, refrigerator and clock radio in room. Air conditioning. Telephone on premises. Antiquing, fishing, live theater and shopping nearby.

Springfield   C6

1851 Historic Maple Hill Manor Bed & Breakfast

2941 Perryville Rd (Hwy 150)
Springfield, KY 40069-9611
(859)336-3075 (800)886-7546 Fax:(859)336-3076
E-mail: stay@maplehillmanor.com
Web: www.maplehillmanor.com

Circa 1851. In a tranquil country setting on 14 acres, this Greek Revival mansion with Italianate detail is considered a Kentucky Landmark home and is listed in the National Register of Historic Places. Numerous architectural features include 14-foot ceilings, nine-foot windows, 10-foot doorways and a grand cherry spiral staircase. Guest bedrooms provide spacious serenity, and some boast fireplaces or Jacuzzis. Enjoy a full country breakfast, and then take a peaceful stroll through flower gardens and the fruit orchard, or relax on a patio swing or porch rocker. The local area has a rich abundance of attractions including Bardstown, Shaker Village, Bourbon, historic Civil War areas and Lincoln Trails. Lexington and Louisville are within an hour's drive.

Historic Interest: Bardstown's My Old Kentucky Home and Stephen Foster Musical (15 miles), Danville's Constitution Square (20 miles), Perryville's Civil War Battlefield (10 miles), Harrodsburg's Old Fort Harrod (18 miles), Shaker Village at Pleasant Hill (25 miles), Hodgenville's Lincoln Birthplace and Museum (25 miles).

Innkeeper(s): Todd Allen & Tyler Horton. $95-150. 7 rooms with PB, 2 with FP, 4 suites and 1 conference room. Breakfast and afternoon tea included in rates. Types of meals: Full gourmet bkfst, veg bkfst, early coffee/tea, picnic lunch, snacks/refreshments, gourmet dinner and room service. Beds: QDT. Reading lamp, CD player, ceiling fan, snack bar, clock radio, turn-down service, two with Jacuzzi, fireplace, radio alarm clock, designer linens, antique furnishings, rollaway beds available and some with TV and VCR in room. Air conditioning. TV, VCR, fax, copier, library, parlor games, telephone, fireplace, laundry facility, orchard, nature walking paths, flower gardens, snack bar, complimentary homemade evening desserts, alpaca and llama farm, Kentucky hand-crafted gift gallery and Murder Mystery Events on premises. Weddings, small meetings, family reunions and seminars hosted. Antiquing, art galleries, bicycling, fishing, golf, hiking, horseback riding, live theater, museums, parks, shopping, tennis, water sports, wineries, My Old Kentucky Home, Bernheim Forest, Kentucky Railway Museum and Kentucky bourbon distilleries nearby.

Publicity: *Southern Living, Danville's Advocate-Messenger, Springfield Sun, Cincinnati's Eastside Weekend, Louisville Courier Journal, Lexington Herald-Leader, Arts Across Kentucky and Kentucky Monthly.*

"Thank you again for your friendly and comfortable hospitality."

Versailles   C7

1823 Historic Rose Hill Inn

233 Rose Hill
Versailles, KY 40383-1223
(859)873-5957 (800)307-0460

Circa 1823. This Victorian mansion, in the National Register, was occupied at different times by both Confederate and Union troops during the Civil War. Near Lexington, the home maintains many elegant features, including original stained-glass windows, 14-foot ceilings and hardwood floors fashioned from timber on the property. The decor is comfortable, yet elegant. Four guest baths include double Jacuzzis. Guests enjoy relaxing in the library, the parlor, or on the porch swing on the veranda. The home's summer kitchen is now a private cottage with a kitchen, two bedrooms and  a Jacuzzi. The Cottage and Auntie's Attic are perfect for those traveling with children or for guests with well-behaved dogs. The innkeepers offer a hearty, full breakfast with specialties such as Mexican eggs, or Banana-filled French toast in the dining room. In summer it's often served on the veranda overlooking the water gardens, lawns and trees where cardinals fly about. Walk to the historic districts, antique shops restaurants and a museum. Additional attractions include Shaker Village, scenic drives past bucolic horse farms, Keeneland Race Track, Kentucky Horse Park and a wildlife sanctuary.

Innkeeper(s): Sharon Amberg . $99-169. 5 rooms with PB, 1 suite and 1 cottage. Breakfast included in rates. Types of meals: Full bkfst and early coffee/tea. Beds: KQDT. TV, VCR, reading lamp, ceiling fan and telephone in room. Library and A/C on premises. Small meetings and family reunions hosted. Antiquing, fishing, golf, parks, shopping, sporting events, horse farm tours, Kentucky Horse Park, Shaker Village and Keeneland nearby.

Louisiana

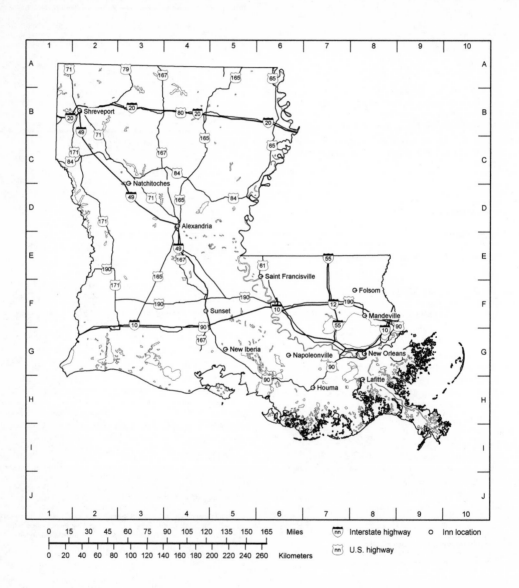

Alexandria   *D4*

Inglewood Plantation

6287 Old Baton Rouge Hwy.
Alexandria, LA 71302
(318)487-8340 (888)575-6288 Fax:(318)443-1808

Circa 1836. Family-owned for generations, this 3,500-acre working farm is one of the few in the area to survive the Civil War. Secluded in a grove of majestic oaks and pecan trees, accommodations include two cottages: Matt's Cabin (originally a sharecropper's home) and the 1850s Schoolhouse. The entire plantation house, in a National Register Historic District, can be leased for a two-night minimum. Enjoy homemade banana or wheat bread topped with hand-harvested mayhaw jelly, cereals, fresh fruit and beverages. Lawn games, tennis courts, swimming pool, ping pong, jungle gym, swings and porches with rocking chairs offer pleasurable activities for all ages.

Innkeeper(s): Georgia. $125-160. 2 cottages. Breakfast included in rates. Types of meals: Cont. Beds: QT. TV, VCR, reading lamp, refrigerator, ceiling fan, clock radio, telephone, coffeemaker, fireplace, fresh garden bouquets and bathrobes in room. Central air. Fax, swimming, stable, tennis, library, fireplace, front porch rocking chairs, RV parking, croquet, tree swings, jungle gym and 1,500 acre nature preserve on premises. Family reunions hosted. Amusement parks, antiquing, art galleries, fishing, golf, live theater, museums, parks, shopping, water sports, spa and cajun dancing nearby.

Publicity: *Southern Living Magazine, Chef John Folse B&B Cookbook, Elle and PBS Chef John Folse's Cooking series.*

Folsom   *F8*

Woods Hole Inn Bed & Breakfast

78253 Woods Hole Lane
Folsom, LA 70437
(985)796-9077 Fax:(985)796-9077
E-mail: ssmalley@woodsholeinn.com
Web: www.woodsholeinn.com

Circa 1850. Perfect for a romantic getaway or secluded relaxation, the wooded country setting infuses this inn with a tranquil ambiance. Three private suites feature separate drives and entrances, antique furnishings, river stone fireplaces and equipped kitchenettes. The Cabin, built in the mid 1800s, boasts a rustic décor with tin roof, screened porch and clawfoot tub. The Cypress Suite, named after the trees that surround it, includes a deep soaking tub and walk-in shower with a stained-glass window. A vaulted ceiling, four-poster bed and French doors that lead to an enclosed patio accent the Courtyard Suite. A light breakfast is set up each evening to enjoy as desired the next morning. Special requests are accommodated. Explore the scenic area on an available bicycle.

Historic Interest: Our cabin was built in the 1850s and refurbished to modern standards but maintaining the country cabin feel.

Innkeeper(s): Sam & Marsha Smalley. $115-138. 3 rooms with PB, 3 with FP, 2 suites, 1 cabin and 1 conference room. Breakfast, afternoon tea and snacks/refreshments included in rates. Types of meals: Cont plus. Beds: Q. Cable TV, VCR, reading lamp, refrigerator, ceiling fan, clock radio, coffeemaker and fireplace in room. Central air. Fax, copier, bicycles, gift shop, horseback riding, tubing and canoeing on premises. Weddings, small meetings, family reunions and seminars hosted. Amusement parks, antiquing, art galleries, beach, bicycling, canoeing/kayaking, fishing, hiking, horseback riding, live theater, museums, parks, shopping, tennis, water sports and wineries nearby.

Houma   *H7*

Grand Bayou Noir

1143 Bayou Black
Houma, LA 70361
(985)872-6207 Fax:(985)873-6562

Circa 1936. Experience relaxation and tranquility at this historic Georgian home on the bank of Big Bayou Black, surrounded by four acres of gardens and old oak trees in the heart of Cajun Country. Formal living and dining rooms boast a fireplace and piano. Original wood floors highlight the home. Well-appointed guest bedrooms feature baths with bidets. A private balcony, separate entrance and a sitting room accompany the suite. After breakfast, take a bike ride or watch the world go by from rockers on the large screened porch. If a nap beckons, hammocks are an easy remedy or bask in one of the two hot tubs.

Innkeeper(s): Tim & Debbie Ellender. $90-130. 3 rooms with PB and 1 suite. Breakfast included in rates. Types of meals: Country bkfst, early coffee/tea, snacks/refreshments and gourmet dinner. Beds: Q. Cable TV, reading lamp, ceiling fan, clock radio and desk in room. Central air. Spa, bicycles, telephone and laundry facility on premises. Limited handicap access. Weddings, small meetings and family reunions hosted. Beach, bicycling, canoeing/kayaking, fishing, golf, museums, parks, shopping and water sports nearby.

Lafitte   *H8*

Victoria Inn & Gardens

4707 Jean Lafitte Blvd
Lafitte, LA 70067
(504)689-4757 (800)689-4797 Fax:(504)689-3399
E-mail: info@victoriainn.com
Web: www.victoriainn.com

Circa 1874. Located on the site of the Mulligan Plantation, this inn consists of three West Indies-style homes on more than six acres of landscaped gardens. The grounds include an  antique rose garden, a parterre herb garden and an iris pond. A private pier and swimming pool extend out into the lake, which was once the field of this Louisiana sugar plantation. All of the rooms are uniquely furnished and the galleries offer a place to relax and enjoy the tropical breezes. Swamp tours, fishing charters, hiking or canoeing in the National Park are available.

Innkeeper(s): Roy & Dale Ross. $85-175. 14 rooms with PB, 7 suites and 1 conference room. Breakfast included in rates. Types of meals: Full gourmet bkfst, veg bkfst, early coffee/tea, afternoon tea and snacks/refreshments. Beds: QDT. Data port, cable TV, VCR, reading lamp, ceiling fan, clock radio, coffeemaker, desk, hot tub/spa and voice mail in room. Central air. Fax, copier, swimming, library, parlor games, telephone, fireplace, laundry facility and gift shop on premises. Limited handicap access. Weddings, small meetings, family reunions and seminars hosted. Amusement parks, antiquing, art galleries, beach, bicycling, canoeing/kayaking, fishing, golf, hiking, live theater, museums, parks, shopping, sporting events, tennis and water sports nearby.

Publicity: *Times Picayune, Shreveport Times, San Francisco Examiner, Lonely Planet and Discovery.*

"You contributed greatly to the fine memories of our 35th wedding anniversary."

Mandeville   F8

Cozy Corner Guest House

736 Lafayette St
Mandeville, LA 70448
(504)626-9189

Circa 1889. Sections of this historic house date back more than a century. The guesthouse includes two comfortable bedrooms, each with a private bath and eclectic furnishings. Upon arrival, guests are treated to refreshments, and in the mornings, an English-style breakfast is served. The home is five blocks from Mandeville Lake, and 30 minutes from downtown New Orleans. Borrow a bicycle from the innkeepers and enjoy the 31-mile bike path that runs through the area.

Innkeeper(s): Barbara & Chris Clark. $85-95. 2 rooms with PB. Breakfast included in rates. Types of meals: Country bkfst, veg bkfst, afternoon tea and snacks/refreshments. Beds: KQ. Cable TV, refrigerator, ceiling fan, clock radio, telephone and coffeemaker in room. Central air. VCR, swimming, bicycles and laundry facility on premises. Antiquing, beach, bicycling, canoeing/kayaking, fishing, golf, hiking, live theater, shopping and wineries nearby.

"Your warm home and generous hospitality makes us eager to return."

Myrtle Grove   G8

Woodland Plantation

21997 Hwy 23
Myrtle Grove, LA 70083
(504)656-9990 (800)231-1514 Fax:(504)656-9995
E-mail: Spiritsofwood@cs.com
Web: www.woodlandplantation.com

Circa 1834. The only remaining plantation home on the west bank of the Mississippi River in the Delta, this classic Raised Creole cottage with Greek Revival details is featured on the label of Southern Comfort. The Big House, Overseers House, brick slave cabin, sugar mill and pumping station sit on a broad meadow covering 54 acres. Relax on large front and back porches. Suites are furnished with well-placed fine antiques. Enjoy scenic views. Breakfast is a satisfying start to the day. Explore four distinct natural habitats. Watch videos that impart a cultural background. Take a marsh or swamp tour, or fish in this premier sportsman's destination. Visit New Orleans' French Quarter only 35 miles away.

Historic Interest: Featured on the label of Southern Comfort Liquor. Occupied by Union Troops during the Civil War. Only plantation with brick slave quarters, only remaining plantation in the Deep Delta south of New Orleans on the West Bank.

Innkeeper(s): Foster Creppel. $100-150. 9 rooms with PB, 1 suite and 2 conference rooms. Breakfast included in rates. Types of meals: Country bkfst, veg bkfst, gourmet lunch, picnic lunch, afternoon tea, snacks/refreshments and gourmet dinner. Restaurant on premises. Beds: KQDT. Reading lamp, ceiling fan, clock radio, telephone and desk in room. Central air. TV, VCR, fax, copier, pet boarding, child care, parlor games, fireplace, laundry facility, restaurant and bar on premises. Limited handicap access. Weddings, small meetings, family reunions and seminars hosted. Amusement parks, antiquing, art galleries, beach, bicycling, canoeing/kayaking, fishing, golf, hiking, live theater, museums, parks, shopping, sporting events, water sports, marsh and swamp tours and video of natural and cultural history nearby.

Publicity: *Southern Living, Times Picayune, Jaguar Magazine, Whereyat, Louisiana Cooking, Public Television, Food Network and WWOZ local New Orleans radio station.*

Napoleonville   G6

Madewood Plantation House

4250 Highway 308
Napoleonville, LA 70390-8737
(985)369-7151 (800)375-7151 Fax:(985)369-9848
E-mail: madewoodpl@aol.com
Web: www.madewood.com

Circa 1846. Six massive ionic columns support the central portico of this striking Greek Revival mansion, a National Historic Landmark. Framed by live oaks and ancient magnolias, Madewood, on 20 acres, across from Bayou Lafourche. It was designed by Henry Howard, a noted architect from Cork, Ireland. There are elegant double parlors, a ballroom, library, music room and din-ing room where regional specialties are served by candlelight.

Historic Interest: Swamp tours, other plantations (one-half hour).

Innkeeper(s): Keith Marshall. $229-259. 8 rooms with PB, 1 with FP, 2 suites and 1 conference room. Breakfast and dinner included in rates. Types of meals: Full bkfst. Beds: KQDT. Copier on premises.

Publicity: *Travel & Leisure, Travel Holiday, Los Angeles Times, Country Home, Country Inns (1 of 12 best inns in 1993) and Top 54 inns in US National Geographic Traveler 1999.*

"We have stayed in many hotels, other plantations and English manor houses, and Madewood has surpassed them all in charm, hospitality and food."

Natchitoches   C3

Breazeale House B&B

926 Washington St
Natchitoches, LA 71457-4730
(318)352-5630 (800)352-5631

Circa 1899. This three-story Victorian home boasts a porch accentuated with white columns on the first level and an expansive balcony with balustrades on the second floor. Stained-and leaded-glass windows with white shutters and trim offer an inviting exterior. Eleven fireplaces afford a warm backdrop to the inn's antique Victorian furnishings. A popular breakfast menu includes crescent rolls with ham and cheese, eggs, muffins and fruit.

Innkeeper(s): Jack & Willa Freeman. $70-100. 5 rooms, 4 with PB. Breakfast included in rates. Types of meals: Full bkfst, early coffee/tea, afternoon tea and room service. Beds: Q. Reading lamp and ceiling fan in room. Air conditioning. Fax, swimming, telephone and fireplace on premises. Weddings, small meetings, family reunions and seminars hosted. Antiquing, fishing, golf, shopping, sporting events, tennis and water sports nearby.

Judge Porter House B & B

321 2nd St
Natchitoches, LA 71457-4373
(318)352-9206 (800)441-8343 Fax:(318)238-2573
E-mail: judgeporter@judgeporterhouse.com
Web: www.judgeporterhouse.com

Circa 1912. Delightful treats and elegant treasures ensure a pleasant stay at this impressive home in the National Historic Landmark District. A Queen Anne influence in the wraparound two-story gallery blends with Colonial Revival architecture reflected in the huge columns on brick pillars. Almost half of the 33 windows are more than eight feet tall. High ceilings, heart pine floors and five fireplaces showcase exquisite mid

19th-century antiques and European cut crystal chandeliers. Two comfortable parlors provide books, newspapers, magazines, videos and refreshments. The quiet guest bedrooms and private guest house offer mahogany and rosewood tester and four-poster beds, silk brocade drapes, tapestry chairs and most every luxurious amenity desired. The multi-course candlelight breakfast in the formal dining room is truly a feast for the senses.

Innkeeper(s): John Puchet. $105-135. 5 rooms, 4 with PB. Breakfast and snacks/refreshments included in rates. Types of meals: Full gourmet bkfst, veg bkfst and early coffee/tea. Beds: Q. Data port, cable TV, VCR, reading lamp, ceiling fan, snack bar, clock radio, telephone, coffeemaker, fireplace, robes, complimentary wine, soft drinks, coffee/tea, chocolates and snacks in room. Central air. Library, parlor games, fireplace, laundry facility and two parlors on premises. Small meetings and family reunions hosted. Antiquing, art galleries, bicycling, canoeing/kayaking, fishing, golf, hiking, horseback riding, live theater, museums, parks, tennis, Fish Hatchery Aquarium and Bayou Pierre Gator Park and Show nearby.

Publicity: *Southern Living, Southern Lady and Gourmet.*

Levy-East House B&B

358 Jefferson St
Natchitoches, LA 71457-4382
(318)352-0662 (800)840-0662
E-mail: judy@levyeasthouse.com
Web: www.levyeasthouse.com

Circa 1838. In a quaint town, this luxurious 1838 Greek Revival house is located in the heart of the Historic Landmark District. Recently restored and tastefully renovated, this B&B captures the spirit of an earlier time. Many of the fine antiques are lovingly refinished heirlooms that have been in the home for more than a century. Romantic guest bedrooms with elegant window dressings boast whirlpool baths, plush terry robes, piped-in music and carafes of cream sherry, to name a few of the lavish amenities. After indulging in early morning coffee, enter the formal dining room with a Victorian table set with fine china, silver and crystal accented by candelabras. Breakfast may include Creole baked eggs with cheese grits and strawberry bread or French toast sundaes.

Innkeeper(s): Judy and Avery East. $125-200. 4 rooms with PB. Breakfast included in rates. Types of meals: Full gourmet bkfst and early coffee/tea. Beds: Q. Cable TV, VCR, reading lamp, CD player, refrigerator, ceiling fan, telephone, turn-down service and whirlpool baths in room. Central air. Fax and copier on premises. Antiquing, art galleries, fishing, golf, hiking, museums, shopping, tennis, Cane River plantations, historic homes, Kisatchie National Forest, trolley rides, paddle boats, Bayou Pierre Gator Park and Show, Fish Hatchery Aquarium and Briarwood - the Caroline Dorman Nature Preserve nearby.

Publicity: *Southern Living, Southern Lady Magazine, Gourmet Magazine, D Magazine, PBS series - "A Taste of Louisiana" and Chef John Folse's "Hot Beignets & Warm Boudoirs" cookbook.*

Maison Louisiane Historic Bed & Breakfast

332 Jefferson St.
Natchitoches, LA 71457
(318)352-1900 (800)264-8991 Fax:(318)354-1566
E-mail: kfidelak@aol.com
Web: www.maisonlouisiane.com

Circa 1898. Incredible detail was given to preserve the architectural integrity of this recently restored Queen Anne Victorian. Listed in the National Register, it sits on two acres in the historic district within an easy walk to downtown. An elegant style reflects a French decor. Play the piano or a game of chess in the salon or parlor room. Refreshments are found at the honor bar in the breezeway overlooking the rear garden. Well-appointed guest bedrooms and a private cottage called the

Garden Suite offer exquisite furnishings and lavish amenities. Melt-in-your-mouth crepes stuffed with fresh strawberries, chocolate mousse with warm maple syrup, smothered Southern cottage fries and apple-smoked bacon may be part of a scrumptious meal served in the formal dining room or as breakfast in bed. Relax on the front porch, upstairs gallery or rear balcony.

Innkeeper(s): Keri & Ben Fidelak. $75-150. 5 rooms with PB and 1 conference room. Breakfast included in rates. Types of meals: Full gourmet bkfst, early coffee/tea, gourmet lunch and gourmet dinner. Beds: KQDT. Modem hook-up, cable TV, VCR, reading lamp, stereo, refrigerator, ceiling fan, snack bar, clock radio, telephone, coffeemaker, desk, fireplace, range and microwave in guest house in room. Central air. Fax, copier, spa, library, parlor games and fireplace on premises. Weddings, small meetings, family reunions and seminars hosted. Antiquing, art galleries, bicycling, canoeing/kayaking, fishing, golf, hiking, horseback riding, museums, parks, sporting events, tennis, water sports, site of the filming of "Steel Magnolias" and Bayou Pierre Alligator Park nearby.

Publicity: *Steel Magnolias.*

Tante Huppe Inn

424 Jefferson St
Natchitoches, LA 71457
(318)352-5342 (800)482-4276
Web: www.tantehuppe.com

Circa 1830. A prominent French family built this Greek Revival home, which contains furnishings original to the house. There are three suites; each can accommodate up to four guests. Each suite has a kitchen and patio, as well as a private entrance. Natchitoches was founded in 1714, and the inn is located in town historic district.

Innkeeper(s): Robert "Bobby" DeBlieux. $95. 3 suites. Types of meals: Cont. Beds: QD. Cable TV, VCR, reading lamp, refrigerator, ceiling fan, clock radio and telephone in room. Air conditioning. Library and beautiful swimming pool on premises. Antiquing, fishing, golf, live theater, parks, shopping, sporting events, tennis and water sports nearby.

New Iberia G5

A New Iberian B&B

416 Iberia St.
New Iberia, LA 70560
(337)367-5888
E-mail: anewiberian@aol.com
Web: www.anewiberian.com

Circa 1898. The main house, called "The Enchanted Cajun Victorian," and the carriage house were built with locally grown and milled cypress by Dutch settlers in the 1800s and have been recently restored. Enjoy a quiet conversation or a cool drink in the sitting parlor with bay windows. The guest suites in the main house offer one and two bedrooms with a private porch and entrance. The Jeff Bradley Carriage House is a two-bedroom cottage adjacent to the garden area where fish, birds and butterflies reside amidst colorful flowers. Breakfast is brought to the cottage. For the suites, it is served in the main dining room. Cajun sausage, fresh breads, sliced and whole fruits, jams, jellies, yogurt and beverages are some of the usual delights. Ask about taking a swamp tour to fully explore the region.

Innkeeper(s): Michel & Elaine LaBoeuf. $55-150. 5 rooms, 3 with PB, 1 with FP and 1 cottage. Breakfast and snacks/refreshments included in rates. Types of meals: Cont plus, veg bkfst, picnic lunch and afternoon tea. Beds: QD. Modem hook-up, data port, TV, reading lamp, stereo, ceiling fan, telephone, coffeemaker, turn-down service, desk, fireplace and pond and gardens in room. Central air. VCR, fax, parlor games and fireplace on premises. Limited handicap access. Weddings, small meetings and family reunions hosted. Antiquing, art galleries, bicycling, canoeing/kayaking, fishing, golf, hiking, horseback riding, parks, shopping, water sports and Swamp Tours nearby.

New Orleans   G8

1822 Bougainvillea House

924 Gov. Nicholls St.
New Orleans, LA 70116-3106
(504)525-3983 Fax:(504)522-5000
E-mail: patkahn@aol.com
Web: www.1822bougainvillea.com

Circa 1822. Built by a plantation owner in 1822, this French Quarter guesthouse boasts the romantic mystique of its historical background. Each luxurious suite includes a bedroom, living/dining room, bath, private entrance and either a patio or balcony. Some feature antique furnishings. Dine on culinary delights at famous restaurants nearby, walk along the levee by the river, shop at the Royal Street boutiques, and plan a visit during Mardi Gras, Creole Christmas or one of the many popular local festivals. Arrange an excursion to the world-class Audubon Zoo, the swamps or take a walking tour of haunted mansions.

Innkeeper(s): Pat Kahn. $90-250. 5 suites. Types of meals: Early coffee/tea. Beds: KQD. Cable TV, reading lamp, refrigerator, ceiling fan, clock radio, telephone, coffeemaker and desk in room. Central air. Fax, copier, bicycles and laundry facility on premises. Amusement parks, antiquing, art galleries, beach, bicycling, fishing, golf, horseback riding, live theater, museums, parks, shopping, sporting events and tennis nearby.

"We love your home and always enjoy our visits here so much!"

A Creole House Hotel

1013 Saint Ann St
New Orleans, LA 70116-3012
(504)524-8076 (800)535-7858 Fax:(504)581-3277
E-mail: ach5555@aol.com
Web: big-easy.org

Circa 1830. Experience classic Southern hospitality at this 1830s townhouse built by a French Creole family, and now listed in the National Register. Enjoy the quiet refuge, authentic ambiance and friendly local flavor located just two blocks from Bourbon Street in the famous French Quarter. Each air-conditioned guest bedroom and suite boasts a different décor from period furnishings to contemporary. Some face one of the delightful courtyards, and others are in the main townhouse. Stay in a two-bedroom suite that features a Jacuzzi. Wake up any time to hot coffee and freshly baked pastries. A very helpful staff will assist your tour planning.

Innkeeper(s): Brent Kovach. $49-189. 29 rooms. Breakfast included in rates. Types of meals: Cont. Beds: KQDT. Reading lamp, clock radio, telephone and desk in room. Air conditioning. Fax, copier and fireplace on premises. Antiquing, fishing, golf, live theater, parks and sporting events nearby.

Avenue Inn Bed & Breakfast

4125 St. Charles Avenue
New Orleans, LA 70115
(504)269-2640 (800)490-8542 Fax:(504)269-2641
E-mail: info@avenueinnbb.com
Web: www.avenueinnbb.com

Circa 1891. Set among timeless oaks on famous St. Charles Street is this 1891 Thomas Sully mansion. The inn has high ceilings and hardwood floors, and its nine guest rooms are furnished with period pieces. Come during Mardi Gras and you can sit on the big front porch and watch the 18 Mardi Gras parades that come down St. Charles Avenue. The French Quarter, Central Business District, Convention Center as well as Tulane and Loyola Universities are all within 1 3/4 miles. Antique shops, restaurants and night spots are within walking distance.

Historic Interest: 1891 Thomas Sully designed Queen Anne Mansion.
Innkeeper(s): Joe & Bebe Rabhan. $69-299. 17 rooms with PB, 5 with FP. Breakfast included in rates. Types of meals: Cont. Beds: KQD. Modem hook-up, data port, cable TV, reading lamp, ceiling fan, clock radio, telephone, desk and voice mail in room. Central air. VCR, fax, copier and fireplace on premises. Weddings, small meetings, family reunions and seminars hosted. Amusement parks, antiquing, art galleries, bicycling, canoeing/kayaking, fishing, golf, live theater, museums, parks, shopping, restaurants, cultural events and sightseeing nearby.

Bonne Chance B&B

621 Opelousas Ave
New Orleans, LA 70114
(504)367-0798 Fax:(504)368-4643
E-mail: watsondolores@aol.com
Web: www.bonne-chance.com

Circa 1890. This recently renovated two-story Eastlake pale pink Victorian with gentle lavender and green trim boasts four balconies and a porch with fretwork and columns. Antique furnishings and Oriental rugs are found throughout, and fully furnished apartments with kitchens are available. A secluded courtyard with fountain and gardens are in the rear of the inn. A free five-minute ferry boat ride takes you to the French Quarter.

Innkeeper(s): Dolores Watson. $85-175. 3 suites. Breakfast included in rates. Types of meals: Cont plus. Beds: Q. Cable TV, reading lamp, refrigerator, ceiling fan, clock radio, telephone, desk and three apartments with fully equipped kitchens in room. Air conditioning. VCR, fax, copier and library on premises. Amusement parks, antiquing, fishing, golf, live theater, parks, shopping, sporting events, tennis and French Quarter nearby.
Publicity: *New Orleans.*

Chateau du Louisiane

1216 Louisiana Ave
New Orleans, LA 70115
(504)723-6192 (800)734-0137 Fax:(504)269-2603
E-mail: chateau@accesscom.net
Web: www.chateaulouisiane.com

Circa 1885. Built in Greek Revival style, Chateau du Louisiane is located on the edge of New Orleans' famous Garden District. The home, along with the myriad of other historic homes and buildings, is listed in the National Register of Historic Places. Period furnishings decorate the guest rooms, suites and common areas. Each guest room is named after someone famous in Louisiana history, such as Louis Armstrong. The chateau is one mile from the French Quarter, and the St. Charles streetcar stops just three blocks away.

Innkeeper(s): Joanne C. Preston. $79-250. 5 rooms with PB, 2 suites and 2 conference rooms. Breakfast and snacks/refreshments included in rates. Types of meals: Cont plus and early coffee/tea. Beds: KQ. Modem hook-up, data port, cable TV, reading lamp, ceiling fan, clock radio, telephone, voice mail and data ports in room. Central air. Fax, copier, library and parlor games on premises. Weddings, small meetings, family reunions and seminars hosted. Antiquing, art galleries, bicycling, fishing, golf, live theater, museums, parks, shopping, sporting events, tennis, water sports, zoo, executive development meetings led by Joanne C. Preston PH.D and RODC nearby.

Columns Hotel

3811 Saint Charles Ave
New Orleans, LA 70115-4638
(504)899-9308 (800)445-9308 Fax:(504)899-8170
E-mail: columnshtl@aol.com
Web: www.thecolumns.com

Circa 1883. The Columns was built by Simon Hernsheim, a
tobacco merchant, who was the wealthiest philanthropist in
New Orleans. The two-story columned gallery and portico provide a grand entrance into this restored mansion. The estate was
selected by Paramount Studios for the site of the movie "Pretty
Baby," with Brooke Shields. The hotel is in the National Register
of Historic Places. Jazz performances are scheduled Tuesday,
Wednesday, Friday and during the Sunday champagne brunch.
Historic Interest: Garden District (one-half mile), aquarium (two miles), zoo (one-
half mile), universities (one-half mile), French Quarter (two miles on streetcar).
Innkeeper(s): Claire & Jacques Creppel. $90-200. 20 rooms with PB, 3
suites and 2 conference rooms. Breakfast included in rates. Types of meals:
Country bkfst. Telephone on premises.
Publicity: *Good Housekeeping, New York Times, Vogue, Good Morning
America, Elle, Forbes FYI, Travel Holiday and Conde Nast.*

*"...like experiencing life of the Old South, maybe more like living in a
museum. We came to New Orleans to learn about New Orleans, and
we did... at The Columns."*

Cornstalk Hotel

915 Royal St
New Orleans, LA 70116-2701
(504)523-1515 (800)759-6112 Fax:(504)522-5558
E-mail: info@cornstalkhotel.com
Web: www.cornstalkhotel.com

Circa 1816. This home belonged to Judge Francois Xavier-
Martin, the author of the first history of Louisiana and
Louisiana's first State Supreme Court Chief Justice. Andrew
Jackson stayed here and another guest, Harriet Beecher Stowe,
wrote Uncle Tom's Cabin after viewing the nearby slave markets.

The Civil War followed the widely
read publication. Surrounding the inn
is a 160-year-old wrought-iron cornstalk fence. Stained-glass windows,
Oriental rugs, fireplaces and antiques
grace the property. Breakfast and the
morning newspaper can be served in
your room or set up on the balcony,
porch or patio.

Innkeeper(s): Debi & David Spencer. $75-185. 14 rooms with PB. Beds:
KQDT. TV and telephone on premises.
Publicity: *London Sunday Times and Tampa Tribune.*

Fairchild House

1518 Prytania St
New Orleans, LA 70130-4416
(504)524-0154 (800)256-8096 Fax:(504)568-0063
E-mail: info@fairchildhouse.com
Web: www.fairchildhouse.com

Circa 1841. Situated in the oak-lined Lower Garden District of
New Orleans, this Greek Revival home was built by architect
L.H. Pilie. The house and its guest houses maintain a Victorian
ambiance with elegantly appointed guest rooms. Wine and
cheese are served upon guests' arrival. Afternoon tea can be
served upon request. The bed & breakfast, which is on the
Mardi Gras parade route, is 17 blocks from the French Quarter

and 12 blocks from the convention center. Streetcars are just
one block away, as are many local attractions, including paddleboat cruises, Canal Place and Riverwalk shopping, an aquarium, zoo, the St. Charles Avenue mansions and Tulane and
Loyola universities.
Innkeeper(s): Rita Olmo & Beatriz Aprigliano-Ziegler. $75-165. 20 rooms, 17
with PB and 3 suites. Breakfast included in rates. Types of meals: Cont plus.
Beds: KQDT. Clock radio, telephone, desk and voice mail in room. Air conditioning. TV, fax and copier on premises. Weddings and family reunions hosted. Antiquing, shopping and restaurants nearby.

"Accommodations were great; staff was great ... Hope to see y'all soon!"

The Frenchmen Hotel

417 Frenchmen
New Orleans, LA 70116-2003
(504)948-2166 (800)831-1781 Fax:(504)948-2258
E-mail: fm5678@aol.com
Web: french-quarter.org

Circa 1897. Ideally located in a quiet area of Fauborg Marigny
bridging the French Quarter, this historic small hotel offers
attentive service from friendly and knowledgeable staff 24 hours
a day. Complimentary parking is available and the river front
streetcar is nearby. Air-conditioned guest bedrooms boast a variety of sizes and décor. Some feature mini-refrigerators, decorative
fireplaces, canopy beds and exposed brick walls. A few have private balconies. Many rooms open onto an Old New Orleans
brick courtyard with marble and wrought iron tables. Lush tropical plants surround a petite pool and heated Jacuzzi. A local
bakery delivers fresh pastries and croissants every morning, and
Louisiana-roast coffee is brewed all day long.
Innkeeper(s): Brent Kovach. $59-175. 28 rooms. Breakfast included in rates.
Types of meals: Cont. Beds: QD. Cable TV, reading lamp, ceiling fan, clock
radio and telephone in room. Air conditioning. Fax, copier, swimming, fireplace and Jacuzzi on premises. Antiquing, fishing, golf, live theater, parks,
shopping and sporting events nearby.

Grand Victorian

2727 St. Charles Ave
New Orleans, LA 70130
(504)895-1104 (800)977-0008 Fax:(504)896-8688
E-mail: brabe2727@aol.com
Web: www.gvbb.com

Circa 1893. Thomas Sully, a celebrated New Orleans architect,
built this Queen Anne Victorian located at the edge of the
Garden District. Gables, porches, balconies, bay windows,
dormers, flower boxes and a wraparound porch have all been
carefully renovated. Furnishings are antique to complement the
inn's original millwork, pine floors and beautiful staircase.
Guest rooms feature romantic old beds and armoires and there
are suites with Jacuzzis and private balconies. The innkeeper is
a native of New Orleans and is enthusiastic about all that it
offers. She will be glad to help you plan your stay as well as
suggest tours to nearby plantations within an hour's drive. The
inn is located on the streetcar route.
Innkeeper(s): Bonnie Rabe. $150-300. 8 rooms, 6 with PB and 2 suites.
Breakfast and snacks/refreshments included in rates. Types of meals: Cont
plus and early coffee/tea. Beds: KQD. Data port, cable TV, reading lamp, ceiling fan, clock radio, telephone, hot tub/spa and voice mail in room. Central
air. Fax and parlor games on premises. Limited handicap access. Weddings,
small meetings and family reunions hosted. Amusement parks, antiquing, art
galleries, beach, fishing, golf, live theater, museums, parks, shopping and
sporting events nearby.
Publicity: *Travel, Channel-Mardi Gras 2001 and 2002, Times Picayune,
Southern Living, Detroit Free Press and Local Mayorial Press Conference.*

HH Whitney House on the Historic Esplanade

1923 Esplanade Ave
New Orleans, LA 70116-1706
(504)948-9448 (877)944-9448 Fax:(504)949-7939
E-mail: stay@hhwhitneyhouse.com
Web: www.hhwhitneyhouse.com

Circa 1865. The Civil War had barely ended when builders broke ground on this elegant Italianate mansion. More than a century later, much of its original charm has been maintained. The intricate molding and plasterwork are of the highest quality. Common rooms with Victorian furnishings and appointments complement the architecture. Distinctive antiques include an early 20th-century player piano. A decorative fireplace is featured in each guest bedroom. The Bride's Room, with a lace-draped canopy bed, makes a spacious two- or three-bedroom suite when combined with the Solarium or Groom's rooms. The romantic Honeymoon Suite in the former servants' quarters offers total privacy. Located in the Esplanade Ridge historic district, the French Quarter is just a half-mile walk.

Innkeeper(s): Glen Miller/ Randy Saizan. $75-225. 5 rooms, 2 with PB, 5 with FP and 1 suite. Snacks/refreshments included in rates. Types of meals: Full bkfst. Beds: Q. Cable TV, reading lamp, CD player, ceiling fan, clock radio, telephone, turn-down service, safes and bathrobes in room. Central air. VCR, fax, parlor games, fireplace, laundry facility and hot tub on premises. Weddings, small meetings and family reunions hosted. Amusement parks, antiquing, art galleries, bicycling, canoeing/kayaking, fishing, golf, horseback riding, live theater, museums, parks, shopping, sporting events, tennis and French Quarter nearby.

La Maison Marigny

1421 Bourbon St
New Orleans, LA 70116
(504)948-3638 (800)570-2014 Fax:(504)945-5012
E-mail: stay@lamaisonmarigny.com
Web: www.lamaisonmarigny.com

Circa 1898. At the end of world-famous Bourbon Street, this award-winning Queen Anne Victorian sits in the quiet residential section, three blocks from the historic French Market and Riverfront Streetcar lines. The inn is perfectly located for the convention-goer, business traveler or vacationer. Guest bedrooms and a suite are furnished in a delightful blend of historic eclectic decor, offering an assortment of amenities to ensure comfort. Partake of seasonal fruit, fresh-baked muffins or scones, croissants, granolas and cereals before embarking on the day's activities.

Innkeeper(s): John Ramsey and Dewey Donihoo. $99-250. 4 rooms with PB, 4 with FP and 1 suite. Breakfast included in rates. Types of meals: Cont plus and snacks/refreshments. Beds: Q. Modem hook-up, data port, cable TV, VCR, reading lamp, stereo, refrigerator, ceiling fan, clock radio, telephone and fireplace in room. Central air. Fax and parlor games on premises. Family reunions hosted. Amusement parks, beach, bicycling, live theater, museums, parks, shopping, sporting events, water sports, French Quarter, Aquarium/IMAX, Superdome, D-Day Museum and French Market and Frenchmen Street nearby.
Publicity: *Travel and Leisure Magazine and San Francisco Chronicle.*

Lafitte Guest House

1003 Bourbon St
New Orleans, LA 70116-2707
(504)581-2678 (800)331-7971 Fax:(504)581-2677
E-mail: lafitte@travelbase.com
Web: www.lafitteguesthouse.com

Circa 1849. This elegant French manor house has been meticulously restored. The house is filled with fine antiques and paintings collected from around the world. Located in the heart

of the French Quarter, the inn is near world-famous restaurants, museums, antique shops and rows of Creole and Spanish cottages. Between 5:30 p.m. and 7 p.m., there is a wine and cheese social hour on Friday and Saturday.

Historic Interest: Historic New Orleans Collection, Keyes House, Beauregard House, Gallier House (few blocks away), famous Jackson Square and Saint Louis Cathedral (4 blocks), French Market (3 blocks).
Innkeeper(s): Edward G. Dore & Andrew J. Crocchiolo. $159-229. 14 rooms with PB, 7 with FP and 2 suites. Cont plus. Beds: KQ. TV, refrigerator, ceiling fan, clock radio, telephone and desk in room. Air conditioning. Fax and copier on premises. Amusement parks, antiquing, fishing, live theater, parks, shopping, sporting events and water sports nearby.
Publicity: *Glamour, Antique Monthly, McCall's, Dixie and Country Living.*

"This old building offers the finest lodgings we have found in the city." — *McCall's Magazine*

Lamothe House

621 Esplanade Ave
New Orleans, LA 70116-2018
(504)947-1161 (800)367-5858 Fax:(504)943-6536
E-mail: lam5675842@aol.com
Web: new-orleans.org

Circa 1830. Stay at this 1830s townhouse with Creole-style façade, gracing Esplanade Avenue, a famous street with ancient oaks that shade horse-drawn carriages and some the state's oldest architecture. Furnished with Victorian antiques, decorative fireplaces accent many of the air-conditioned guest bedrooms and suites and some face the lush inner courtyard overlooking the fish pond. A few rooms can be adjoined for those traveling together. More accommodations are offered at the Marigny Guest House, a Creole cottage across the street. Louisiana-roast coffee, fresh-baked pastries and croissants are served for breakfast in the elegant dining room. Sip complimentary sherry in the afternoon. Feel refreshed after a swim in the outdoor pool or soak in the Jacuzzi.

Historic Interest: National Register.
Innkeeper(s): Carol Chauppette. $59-250. 20 rooms with PB, 1 with FP, 9 suites, 2 cottages and 1 conference room. Breakfast included in rates. Types of meals: Cont plus and afternoon tea. Beds: QDT. Cable TV, reading lamp, stereo, ceiling fan, clock radio, telephone, turn-down service and desk in room. Air conditioning. VCR, fax, copier, child care, free parking, swimming pool and Jacuzzi on premises. Weddings, small meetings and family reunions hosted. Amusement parks, antiquing, fishing, live theater, parks, shopping, sporting events and French Quarter nearby.
Publicity: *Southern Living (Cover), Los Angeles Times, Houston Post and Travel & Leisure.*

Le Chateau de Claudine

2127 Esplanade Ave
New Orleans, LA 70119
(504)943-8418 (866)515-7378 Fax:(504)943-6751
E-mail: chateauclaudine@aol.com
Web: www.lechateaudeclaudine.com

Circa 1800. A French Canadian landowner purchased the land that surrounds Le Chateau de Claudine in the early 1700s. The inn, built in Edwardian style, has accommodated guests for a century. Antiques grace the guest rooms and common areas. Each guest room has been appointed individually in authentic, period style. The grounds feature a pond, as well as wisteria, peach, pecan, pear and banana trees. The inn is located in the historic Esplanade Ridge District of New Orleans. The French Quarter, Riverwalk and many other popular attractions are just a few minutes away.

Innkeeper(s): Claudine Mechling. $95-199. 6 rooms with PB. Breakfast

included in rates. Types of meals: Full gourmet bkfst, early coffee/tea, afternoon tea and snacks/refreshments. Beds: KQT. Cable TV in room. Air conditioning. Library, parlor games, telephone and fireplace on premises. Amusement parks, antiquing, art galleries, beach, bicycling, canoeing/kayaking, fishing, golf, live theater, museums, parks, shopping, sporting events and tennis nearby.
Publicity: Soul of New Orleans, Pathfinders Magazine, Off Beat/Time Out, The African American Success Resource Guide and New Orleans Travel Planners Guide.

Magnolia Mansion

2127 Prytania Street
New Orleans, LA 70130
(504)412-9500 (888)222-9235 Fax:(504)412-9502
E-mail: info@magnoliamansion.com
Web: www.magnoliamansion.com

Circa 1857. Experience a high standard of opulence at this upscale, adults-only, non-smoking bed & breakfast. It is the perfect romantic getaway, quiet and peaceful weekend retreat, or a wonderful place to celebrate an anniversary, birthday, honeymoon or other special occasion. The Mansion is centrally located in what is considered to be "The Gateway To The Garden District." It is just one block from St. Charles Ave. streetcar on the Mardi Gras Parade Route and within minutes of the French Quarter. Relax with friends or read a good book on the wraparound veranda overlooking the enchanting courtyard surrounded by massive 150-year-old oak trees. Wake each morning from a great night's sleep in a luxurious themed guest bedroom to enjoy a continental breakfast in the formal dining room. Visit the area's major attractions, including the Superdome; enjoy fine dining and ride on a Mississippi River Paddlewheel.
Historic Interest: Historically Known as the Harris Maginnis House. Designed and built by James Calrow in 1857-58 who is the same architect who designed and built the home that Anne Rice currently lives in around the corner. The property became the Official Red Cross Headquarters during World War II from 1939-1954. Magnolia Mansion, formerly referred to as the Harris-Maginnis House, was purchased by internationally recognized entertainer Hollie Diann Vest and her mother, Wanda Marie Hansen, on the first of October, 2001. Prior to that, the home has had a magnificent and often turbulent history of owners, the most interesting of whom are the Harris family, the Maginnis family, and the New Orleans Chapter of the American Red Cross. The house now spans one and a half centuries of the social life of New Orleans.
Innkeeper(s): Hollie Vest. $125-750. 9 rooms with PB. Breakfast included in rates. Types of meals: Cont plus and early coffee/tea. Beds: KQT. Modem hook-up, cable TV, VCR, reading lamp, ceiling fan, clock radio, telephone, desk, robes, hair dryers, makeup mirrors, valet, iron and ironing board in room. Central air. Complimentary local calls, video and book library and data ports on premises. Weddings, small meetings, family reunions and seminars hosted. Amusement parks, antiquing, art galleries, beach, bicycling, canoeing/kayaking, fishing, golf, hiking, horseback riding, live theater, museums, parks, shopping, sporting events, tennis, water sports and wineries nearby.
Publicity: American Airlines, American Way Inflight Magazine, Times Picayune, Off Beat Publications, Weddings With Style, Chris Rose Times Picayune Columnist, Live on Internet Talk Show and New Orleans Bride on Cox Cable.

Maison Perrier B&B

4117 Perrier St
New Orleans, LA 70115
(504)897-1807 (888)610-1807 Fax:(504)897-1399
E-mail: innkeeper@maisonperrier.com
Web: www.maisonperrier.com

Circa 1892. Experience Southern hospitality and a casually elegant atmosphere at this bed & breakfast located in the Uptown Garden District. The historic Victorian mansion was built in 1892 with renovations carefully preserving ornamental woodwork, fireplace tiles, chandeliers and antique furnishings while adding modern conveniences. Distinctive guest bedrooms and

suites with parlors feature stunning beds, romantic touches that include candles and flowers, whirlpool tubs, terry cloth robes, and private balconies. Praline French toast, apple puff pancakes, creole eggs and potato casserole are among the incredible breakfast favorites that begin and end with New Orleans coffee. Relax in the brick courtyards surrounded by tropical plants.
Historic Interest: Built in 1892, renovated maintaining all original architectural details including cypress doors, hardwood floors, transoms and original tiles in fireplaces.
Innkeeper(s): Tracewell Bailey. $89-250. 16 rooms with PB, 10 suites and 4 conference rooms. Breakfast, afternoon tea and snacks/refreshments included in rates. Types of meals: Full gourmet bkfst, veg bkfst, early coffee/tea, picnic lunch and room service. Beds: KQT. Modem hook-up, data port, cable TV, reading lamp, refrigerator, ceiling fan, clock radio, telephone, turn-down service, desk, hot tub/spa, voice mail, fireplace, luxury bath amenities and terry cloth robes in room. Central air. VCR, fax, copier, spa, tennis, library, child care, parlor games, fireplace, laundry facility and gift shop on premises. Weddings, small meetings, family reunions and seminars hosted. Amusement parks, antiquing, art galleries, beach, bicycling, fishing, golf, live theater, museums, parks, shopping, sporting events, tennis and water sports nearby.
Publicity: Fodors, Frommers and Memphis PBS.

Olde Victorian Inn & Spa

914 N Rampart St
New Orleans, LA 70116
(504)522-2446 (800)725-2446 Fax:(504)522-8646
E-mail: oldeinn@aol.com
Web: www.oldevictorianinn.com

Circa 1842. Experience the romantic 1840s at this two-story Victorian inn in the historic French Quarter. It is one of the area's first homes owned by a free slave before the Civil War. Enjoy tea in the lush tropical courtyard or inside, surrounded by floor to ceiling windows, antiques and plenty of lace and ruffles. Large beds and private baths highlight the elegantly decorated guest bedrooms. Most feature fireplaces and some have balconies. Miss Celie's Spa Orleans provides on-site pampering. Schedule a facial and a couples massage. A gourmet breakfast begins an adventurous day from the front door steps onto Rampart Street.
Innkeeper(s): Keith & Andre West-Harrison. $150-275. 4 rooms with PB. Breakfast included in rates. Types of meals: Full gourmet bkfst, veg bkfst, early coffee/tea and gourmet dinner. Beds: D. Ceiling fan, clock radio, desk, fireplace and clawfoot tubs in room. Central air. TV, VCR, fax, copier, library, telephone and fireplace on premises. Weddings, small meetings, family reunions and seminars hosted. Amusement parks, antiquing, art galleries, live theater, museums, parks and shopping nearby.
Publicity: Vogue, Australian Travel Channel and MSN.com.

Rathbone Inn

1227 Esplanade Ave
New Orleans, LA 70116-1975
(504)947-2100 (800)947-2101 Fax:(504)947-7454
E-mail: rathboneinn@aol.com
Web: www.rathboneinn.com

Circa 1850. Built prior to the Civil War, Rathbone Inn appears just as a genteel New Orleans mansion should. Two stories, accentuated with stately columns, wrought-iron fencing, and delicate exterior trim create a perfect historic ambiance. Guests are just blocks from the French Quarter and famed Bourbon Street. The innkeepers can help arrange unique tours of the city. Guests are pampered with wine and cheese upon arrival, and each morning, a continental breakfast buffet is provided. There is a courtyard complete with a hot tub, a perfect place to relax after touring the Quarter. Rooms include helpful amenities such as data ports and coffeemakers. Some rooms have balconies, and others include a kitchenette.

Innkeeper(s): Levi & Tina. $59-300. 13 suites. Breakfast, afternoon tea and snacks/refreshments included in rates. Types of meals: Cont plus, veg bkfst and early coffee/tea. Beds: KQ. Data port, cable TV, reading lamp, refrigerator, ceiling fan, snack bar, clock radio, telephone, coffeemaker and hot tub/spa in room. Air conditioning. VCR, fax, copier, spa and laundry facility on premises. Weddings hosted. Amusement parks, antiquing, art galleries, bicycling, golf, hiking, horseback riding, live theater, museums, parks, shopping, French Quarter and Bourbon Street nearby.

St. Vincent Guest House

1507 Magazine St
New Orleans, LA 70130-4723
(504)566-1515 Fax:(504)566-1518
E-mail: peterschreiber@compuserve.com
Web: www.stvincentsguesthouse.com

Circa 1861. Built in 1861, this three-story Victorian-Colonial guest house is a recognized historic landmark within walking distance of New Orleans' French Quarter. Tall white pillars invite guests to enter through the doors and step into the traditional décor of wicker and pastels, followed by a stroll down wraparound, tiered balconies. Located in lower Garden District, guests can absorb rich Louisiana history in Coliseum Square or live it up in the New Orleans night life. Following a full Southern breakfast, spend a soothing day by the pool in the courtyard or with your friends in the tea room. With the variety of festivities that New Orleans has to offer, this guest house provides an optimum location for travelers seeking a comfortable place to stay in a city that is alive.
Innkeeper(s): Sally Leonard Schreiber, Peter Schreiber. $59-89. 76 rooms, 74 with PB and 2 suites. Breakfast included in rates. Types of meals: Full bkfst and early coffee/tea. Beds: KQDT. Data port, TV, reading lamp, ceiling fan, telephone, turn-down service and desk in room. Air conditioning. Fax, copier, swimming, bicycles, child care and laundry facility on premises. Limited handicap access. Weddings, small meetings and family reunions hosted. Amusement parks, antiquing, art galleries, bicycling, canoeing/kayaking, fishing, golf, horseback riding, live theater, museums, parks, shopping, sporting events, tennis, Convention Center and Garden District nearby.

St. Peter Guest House Hotel

1005 Saint Peter St
New Orleans, LA 70116-3014
(504)524-9232 (800)535-7815 Fax:(504)523-5198
E-mail: sptlj678z@aol.com
Web: www.crescent-city.org

Circa 1800. Comfort and convenience are offered at this popular retreat situated in a quiet area just two blocks from Bourbon Street. This quaint, historic hotel boasts inviting iron-lace balconies with great views and tropical brick courtyards that are so much a part of the French Quarter ambiance. Stay in a spacious, air-conditioned guest bedroom furnished with antiques or choose one with a more contemporary style decor. Wake up to enjoy freshly baked pastries and Louisiana-roast coffee. Ask the 24-hour front desk staff for tour recommendations or help in planning each day's fun and adventure.
Innkeeper(s): Brent Kovach. $59-225. 28 rooms with PB and 11 suites. Breakfast included in rates. Types of meals: Cont plus. Beds: KQDT. Cable TV, reading lamp, ceiling fan, telephone and desk in room. Air conditioning. Fax on premises. Amusement parks, antiquing, fishing, live theater, parks and shopping nearby.

Sully Mansion - Garden District

2631 Prytania St
New Orleans, LA 70130-5944
(504)891-0457 (800)364-2414 Fax:(504)269-0793
E-mail: sullym@bellsouth.net
Web: www.sullymansion.com

Circa 1890. This handsome Queen Anne Victorian, designed by its namesake, Thomas Sully, maintains many original features common to the architecture. A wide veranda, stained glass, heart-of-pine floors and a grand staircase are among the notable items. Rooms are decorated in a comfortable mix of antiques and more modern pieces. Sully Mansion is the only inn located in the heart of New Orleans' Garden District.
Innkeeper(s): Chris & Heather Black. $89-249. 7 rooms with PB, 5 with FP. Breakfast included in rates. Types of meals: Cont plus. Beds: KQ. Modem hook-up, data port, cable TV, reading lamp, stereo, refrigerator, clock radio, telephone and desk in room. Air conditioning. Fax, copier, library, parlor games and fireplace on premises. Amusement parks, antiquing, art galleries, bicycling, fishing, golf, hiking, horseback riding, live theater, museums, parks, shopping, sporting events, tennis and wineries nearby.
Publicity: *Houston Chronicle, Travel & Leisure, New Orleans Times Picayune, Los Angeles Times, Travel & Holiday and San Francisco Chronicle.*

"I truly enjoyed my stay at Sully Mansion—the room was wonderful, the pastries memorable."

Sun & Moon Bed & Breakfast

1037 N Rampart St
New Orleans, LA 70116-2405
(504)529-4652 (800)638-9169 Fax:(504)529-4652
E-mail: sunmoon4@bellsouth.net
Web: www.sunandmoonbnb.com

Circa 1819. Built in the early part of the 19th century, Sun & Moon offers a historic experience just blocks from Bourbon Street and many French Quarter attractions. The Sun Suite has a private balcony, and the Moon Suite has a private deck. Both suites include a private porch and balcony overlooking the lush courtyard. The Jazz Gallery is an excellent spot for a longer stay. It includes a bedroom, kitchen, living room with a sofa bed and a bathroom with a hand-painted clawfoot tub. In the mornings, guests are served a continental New Orleans-style breakfast with freshly brewed chicory coffee and pastries. Innkeeper Mary Pat Van Tine can point you to jazz clubs, restaurants and the best local attractions.
Innkeeper(s): MaryPat VanTine. $90-120. 4 rooms with PB. Types of meals: Cont. Beds: KQ. TV, reading lamp, ceiling fan, refrigerator and coffeemaker in room. Air conditioning. Fax, telephone and lush courtyard with fountain on premises. Antiquing, art galleries, live theater, museums, parks, shopping, local music and neighborhood festivals nearby.

Saint Francisville   E6

Butler Greenwood Plantation

8345 US Highway 61
Saint Francisville, LA 70775-6671
(225)635-6312 Fax:(225)635-6370
E-mail: butlergree@aol.com
Web: www.butlergreenwood.com

Circa 1795. Still owned and occupied by the original family, this beautiful English-country-style 1796 plantation offers more than 50 acres with hundreds of graceful ancient live oaks and blooming gardens on the landscaped grounds. Accommodations are in a variety of cottages offering privacy and seclusion. Each cottage offers a unique experience such as the Treehouse, which

features a king cypress four-poster bed, three-level deck and fireplace. The 1796 Old Kitchen cottage boasts skylights, the plantation's original well and a double Jacuzzi. On the National Register, the home offers a daily tour narrated by one of the plantation's family members. The formal Victorian parlor in the house is filled with original antiques and high Victorian decor. Each accommodation has its own kitchen, but the innkeeper, a historian and author, (her books are available in the gift shop) also provides a continental breakfast.
Historic Interest: Seven historic plantations are located within 10 miles.
Innkeeper(s): Anne Butler. $125. 7 rooms and 8 cottages. Breakfast included in rates. Types of meals: Cont plus. Beds: KQD. Cable TV, reading lamp, refrigerator, ceiling fan, snack bar, clock radio, telephone, coffeemaker, desk, hot tub/spa, kitchen, fireplaces, Jacuzzis and BBQ in room. Central air. Swimming on premises. Small meetings, family reunions and seminars hosted. Antiquing, bicycling, fishing, golf, hiking, horseback riding, museums, parks, shopping, water sports and wineries nearby.

Myrtles Plantation

PO Box 1100, 7747 US Hwy 61
Saint Francisville, LA 70775
(225)635-6277

Circa 1796. Sitting high on the rolling hills, this mansion is elegantly appointed with many pieces of artwork and furnishings. The entrance hall features an original 17th-century French chandelier of Baccarat crystal, as well as hand-painted and etched stained glass. Matching twin parlors boast chandeliers, Carrara marble mantels and French gilded mirrors. Myrtles is listed as "One of America's Most Haunted Houses." The Oxbow Carriage House Restaurant is located on the grounds of the plantation.
Innkeeper(s): Teeta & John Moss. $115-230. 10 rooms with PB. Types of meals: Cont. Beds: QD.
Publicity: *Wall Street Journal, Oprah, A&E, National Geographic Explorer, Travel Channel, History Channel, Unsolved Mysteries and Discovery Channel.*

St. Francisville Inn

5720 Commerce St, PO Box 1369
Saint Francisville, LA 70775-1369
(225)635-6502 (800)488-6502 Fax:(225)635-6421
E-mail: staff@wolfsinn.com
Web: www.stfrancisvilleinn.com

Circa 1880. Formerly known as the Wolf-Schlesinger House, this one-acre estate in the historic district features Victorian Gothic architecture and 100-year-old oak trees draped with moss. Antiques and reproductions blend with a touch of country decor for a pleasant appeal. Relaxation comes easy in the parlor and den. Guest bedrooms connect to the main house by wide covered porches in the front and back. They all open onto a New Orleans-style courtyard. One room boasts an oversized Jacuzzi. A breakfast buffet includes an assortment of egg dishes, breads and muffins, grits, blintz, fruit and sausage. Enjoy a swim in the pool. Ask about special packages available.
Innkeeper(s): Patrick & Laurie Walsh. $75-90. 10 rooms with PB and 1 conference room. Breakfast included in rates. Types of meals: Full gourmet bkfst and afternoon tea. Beds: KQD. Modem hook-up, cable TV, reading lamp, ceiling fan, clock radio, telephone and desk in room. Air conditioning. Fax, copier, swimming and gift shop on premises. Small meetings, family reunions and seminars hosted. Amusement parks, antiquing, art galleries, bicycling, golf, hiking, horseback riding, museums, parks, shopping, sporting events, water sports and wineries nearby.

Shreveport   B2

Fairfield Place

2221 Fairfield Ave
Shreveport, LA 71104-2040
(318)222-0048 Fax:(318)226-0631
E-mail: fairfldpl@aol.com
Web: www.fairfieldbandb.com/

Circa 1890. The historic district is an appropriate setting for these two elegant Victorian mansions that impart legendary Southern hospitality. Special amenities make this smoke-free inn ideal for the business or leisure traveler. Enjoy relaxing with an abundance of books and artwork. Guest bedrooms and suites feature quiet privacy, tasteful antiques, seductive lighting and feather beds made with fine linens. A daily breakfast menu includes fresh juice, rich Cajun coffee, fruit, pastries, herbed egg scrambles, Natchitoches meat pies, cereals and oatmeal. Savor each gourmet morsel in the formal dining room, the garden porch or New Orleans-style courtyard. A variety of gardens and koi ponds cover more than an acre of park-like grounds.
Innkeeper(s): Janie Lipscomb. $135-225. 12 rooms with PB, 4 suites, 1 cottage and 3 conference rooms. Breakfast included in rates. Types of meals: Full gourmet bkfst, veg bkfst, early coffee/tea and room service. Beds: KQT. Modem hook-up, cable TV, VCR, reading lamp, ceiling fan, clock radio, telephone, turn-down service, desk, hot tub/spa and voice mail in room. Central air. Fax, copier, library, parlor games and an acre of gardens on premises. Weddings, small meetings, family reunions and seminars hosted. Antiquing, art galleries, fishing, golf, horseback riding, live theater, museums, parks, shopping, sporting events, tennis and water sports nearby.
Publicity: *Dallas News and Shreveport Times.*

"We have been here many times and love it more each time we come."

Sunset   F4

La Caboose B&B

DR E 145 S Budd St
Sunset, LA 70584
(337)662-5401 Fax:(337)662-5401

Circa 1904. Huge pecan trees, orchards and gardens enhance three acres of enchantment. The unusual accommodations include a 1900s depot, caboose, ticket office and an 1800s mail/passenger railroad car. Enjoy private surroundings with patios or porches, antique furnishings, lace and stained glass. For breakfast Margaret proudly serves entrees like french toast with baked apples and sausage, fresh fruit and offers her own famous jellies and syrups. The bread is made from scratch and kneaded by hand. Central to many historic sites and interesting activities, visit antebellum homes, take a swamp tour and listen to Cajun music.
Innkeeper(s): Margaret Brinkhaus. $75-95. 4 rooms with PB. Breakfast and snacks/refreshments included in rates. Types of meals: Country bkfst. Beds: QDT. TV, reading lamp, refrigerator, ceiling fan, clock radio and desk in room. Air conditioning. Fax, copier and telephone on premises. Limited handicap access. Antiquing, art galleries, fishing, golf, live theater, museums, parks, shopping, sporting events, tennis and water sports nearby.

Maine

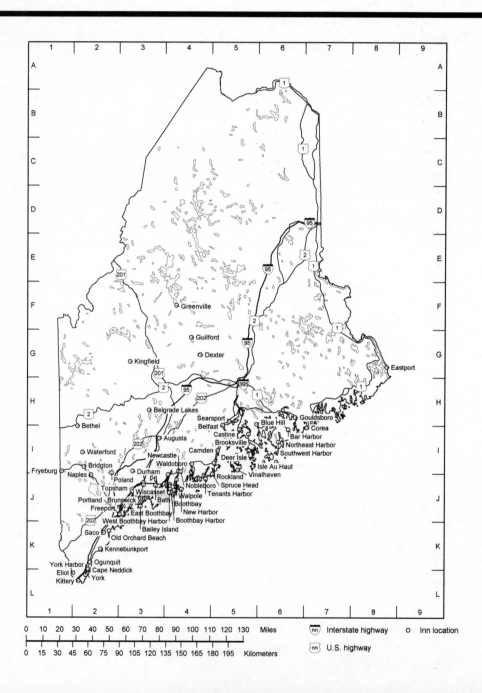

	⌐nn⌐ Interstate highway	o Inn location
	⌐nn⌐ U.S. highway	

Scale:
0 10 20 30 40 50 60 70 80 90 100 110 120 130 Miles

0 15 30 45 60 75 90 105 120 135 150 165 180 195 Kilometers

Acadia Schoodic   **H8**

Acadia Oceanside Meadows Inn

PO Box 90, Rt 195, Prospect Harbor Rd
Acadia Schoodic, ME 04669
(207)963-5557 Fax:(207)963-5928
E-mail: oceaninn@oceaninn.com
Web: www.oceaninn.com

Circa 1860. Dunes, a sandy beach, a salt marsh, ponds, tidal pools, bald eagles and 200 acres of forest and meadows surround this oceanfront classic New England home. The inn is comprised of two houses originally built as inns by sea captain George Allen. Enjoy a sunset stroll and a starlit sky, then cuddle up to sounds of the crashing waves and a roaring fire. Art from local artists are featured throughout, and the décor includes country furnishings and an occasional carved mahogany chest or table. Breakfast offerings feature freshly baked treats (strawberry-rhubarb bread is a favorite) and an entrée such as wild blueberry-filled crepes garnished with edible flowers from the inn's organic garden. The innkeepers have had careers in geology, marine biology and geography and offer a wealth of information to help you enjoy the area. They have created Oceanside Meadows Innstitute in a converted barn on the grounds for cultural and educational events. Hike the grounds, bird watch, visit the nearby lighthouse or take your camera in case you spot a moose.

Innkeeper(s): Ben Walker & Sonja Sundaram. $90-198. 14 rooms, 12 with PB, 2 suites and 1 conference room. Breakfast and afternoon tea included in rates. Types of meals: Full gourmet bkfst, veg bkfst and early coffee/tea. Beds: KQT. Modem hook-up, data port, reading lamp, ceiling fan, telephone, desk, table fans, fresh flowers, quilts, wingback chairs, rocking chairs and bedtime stories in room. Fax, swimming, library, parlor games, fireplace, refrigerator, coffeemaker, stereo, croquet, horseshoes, gardens and art gallery on premises. Weddings, small meetings, family reunions and seminars hosted. Antiquing, art galleries, beach, bicycling, canoeing/kayaking, fishing, golf, hiking, live theater, museums, parks, shopping and water sports nearby.

"This is our best bed and breakfast experience. Hope to return soon."

Augusta   **I3**

Maple Hill Farm B&B Inn

RR 1 Box 1145, Outlet Rd
Augusta, ME 04347
(207)622-2708 (800)622-2708 Fax:(207)622-0655
E-mail: stay@MapleBB.com
Web: www.MapleBB.com

Circa 1906. Visitors to Maine's capitol city have the option of staying at this nearby inn, a peaceful farm setting adjacent to a 600-acre state wildlife management area that is available for canoeing, fishing, hiking and hunting. This Victorian Shingle-style inn was once a stagecoach stop and dairy farm. Some rooms include large double whirlpool tubs and fireplaces. The inn, with its 130-acre grounds, easily accommodates conferences, parties and receptions. Guests are welcome to visit the many farm animals. Cobbossee Lake is a five-minute drive from the inn. Nearby downtown Hallowell is listed as a National Historic District and offers antique shops and restaurants.

Historic Interest: State capitol building, state museum, archives and Fort Western (5 miles).

Innkeeper(s): Scott Cowger & Vince Hannan. $70-185. 8 rooms with PB, 5 with FP and 1 conference room. Breakfast and afternoon tea included in rates. Types of meals: Full bkfst, early coffee/tea and snacks/refreshments. Beds: KQD. TV, VCR, reading lamp, telephone, three with private decks and four with large whirlpool tubs in room. Fireplace on premises. Limited handicap access. Weddings, small meetings, family reunions and seminars hosted. Antiquing, cross-country skiing, live theater, shopping and water sports nearby.

Publicity: *Family Fun, An Explorer's Guide to Maine, The Forecaster, Portland Press Herald, Kennebec Journal, Maine Times, Travel and Leisure "Special Hotels" issue as one of 30 Great U.S. Inns and Editor's Pick in the 2002 & 2003 Yankee Magazine Travel Guide to New England.*

"You add many thoughtful touches to your service that set your B&B apart from others, and really make a difference. Best of Maine, hands down!" — Maine Times

Bailey Island   **J3**

Captain York House B&B

Rt 24, PO Box 298
Bailey Island, ME 04003
(207)833-6224
E-mail: athorn7286@aol.com
Web: www.captainyorkhouse.com

Circa 1906. Bailey Island is the quaint fisherman's village of stories, poems and movies. Guests cross the world's only cribstone bridge to reach the island, where beautiful sunsets and dinners of fresh Maine lobster are the norm. This shingled, turn-of-the-century, Mansard-style B&B was then home of a famous Maine sea captain, Charles York. Now a homestay-style bed & breakfast, the innkeepers have restored the home to its former glory, filling it  with many antiques. Guests at Captain York's enjoy water views from all the guest rooms. Wild Maine blueberries often find a significant place on the breakfast menu.

Innkeeper(s): Alan & Jean Thornton. $70-130. 5 rooms with PB. Breakfast included in rates. Types of meals: Full bkfst. Beds: QT. Reading lamp in room. VCR and telephone on premises. Weddings, small meetings, family reunions and seminars hosted. Antiquing, live theater, parks, shopping, sporting events, water sports, P. McMilan Museum and Maine Maritime Museum nearby.

Publicity: *Tri-Town News and Palm Beach Post.*

"Bailey Island turned out to be the hidden treasure of our trip and we hope to return for your great hospitality again."

Bar Harbor   **I6**

Atlantic Oakes By-the-Sea

119 Eden Street
Bar Harbor, ME 04609
(207)288-5801 (800)336-2463 Fax:(207)288-8402
E-mail: oakes@barharbor.com
Web: www.barharbor.com

Circa 1913. Formerly the estate of Sir Harry Oakes, this 12-acre property has both a charming bed & breakfast inn and a motel complex that totals 153 guest bedrooms, including 150 ocean-view rooms with balconies. "The Willows," a 1913 colonial mansion has 10 guest bedrooms and is the structure closest to Frenchman's Bay. A continental breakfast is served each morning. The estate is a 20-minute walk from Bar Harbor's business and shopping district and a short drive to Acadia National Park's Visitor's Center.

Innkeeper(s): The Cough Family. $85-295. 153 rooms with PB and 6 conference rooms. Types of meals: Full bkfst, early coffee/tea and picnic lunch. Beds: KQD. Cable TV, reading lamp, clock radio, telephone and voice mail in room. Air conditioning. Fax, copier, spa, swimming, tennis and laundry facility on premises. Weddings, small meetings, family reunions and seminars hosted. Antiquing, art galleries, beach, bicycling, canoeing/kayaking, cross-country skiing, fishing, golf, hiking, live theater, museums, parks, shopping, tennis and breweries nearby.

Balance Rock Inn on The Ocean

21 Albert Meadow
Bar Harbor, ME 04609-1701
(207)288-2610 (800)753-0494 Fax:(207)288-5534
E-mail: barhbrinns@aol.com
Web: www.barharborvacations.com

Circa 1903. Built for a Scottish railroad tycoon, the Shingle-style structure was designed by a prestigious Boston architectural firm often used by wealthy summer residents of Bar Harbor. The inn is set on a secluded tree-covered property with views of the islands and Frenchman's Bay. Bar Harbor is two short blocks away. Off the back veranda, overlooking the pool, and past nearly an acre of sweeping lawns is the Historic Shore Path that winds its way around the waterfront.

Innkeeper(s): Mike & Nancy Cloud. $135-575. 20 rooms with PB, 12 with FP and 3 suites. Breakfast included in rates. Types of meals: Full bkfst, early coffee/tea and afternoon tea. Beds: KQ. Cable TV, reading lamp, clock radio, telephone, turn-down service and desk in room. Air conditioning. VCR, fax, swimming, many rooms with porches and gym on premises. Weddings hosted. Antiquing, live theater, parks, water sports, Acadia National Park and ocean activities nearby.

Bar Harbor Castlemaine Inn

39 Holland Ave
Bar Harbor, ME 04609-1433
(207)288-4563 (800)338-4563 Fax:(207)288-4525

Circa 1886. This Queen Anne charmer was once the summer home to the Austro-Hungarian ambassador to the United States. Rooms are decorated in a light, comfortable Victorian style. Five guest rooms include a whirlpool tub and most include a private balcony or deck and a fireplace. In the mornings, a generous breakfast buffet is presented, with freshly baked scones, muffins, breads and coffee cake, as well as bagels, cream cheese, fresh fruit, cereals and a variety of beverages.

Innkeeper(s): Terence O'Connell & Norah O'Brien. $50-225. 15 rooms with PB, 11 with FP and 5 suites. Breakfast included in rates. Types of meals: Cont plus. Beds: KQ. Cable TV, VCR, reading lamp, refrigerator and desk in room. Air conditioning. TV, fax, copier, parlor games, telephone and fireplace on premises. Antiquing, fishing, golf, live theater, parks, shopping, tennis and water sports nearby.

Publicity: *Country Inns and Arrington's Book of B&B's One of Top 10 on the Eastern Seaboard.*

"This year we celebrate our tenth anniversary in our relationship with Castlemaine."

Bar Harbor Hotel-Bluenose Inn

90 Eden Street (Rte 3)
Bar Harbor, ME 04609
(207)288-3348 (800)445-4077 Fax:(220)728-82183
E-mail: reservations@bluenoseinn.com
Web: www.bluenoseinn.com

Circa 1883. Sitting on top of a granite-terraced hillside with spectacular views of Frenchman Bay, this modern inn and hotel is luxury and elegance. Queen Anne-style furnishings further enhance the ambiance. Classically appointed guest bedrooms and suite style rooms offer gracious service and privacy. Some boast fireplaces and balconies with panoramic ocean views. Award-winning Rose Garden Restaurant serves breakfast and dinner. The culinary team includes an executive chef trained at the Ritz Carlton in Chicago. Enjoy the gorgeous Great Room lounge, heated indoor and outdoor pools, Jacuzzi and fitness center.

Innkeeper(s): Wil Gaines. $75-365. 97 rooms with PB, 46 with FP, 21 suites and 1 conference room. Types of meals: Full bkfst, early coffee/tea, gourmet dinner and room service. Restaurant on premises. Beds: KQD. Cable TV, refrigerator, clock radio, telephone, coffeemaker, turn-down service, desk, voice mail, fireplace and irons and ironing boards in room. Air conditioning. VCR, fax, copier, swimming, fireplace, laundry facility, Jacuzzi and gift shop on premises. Limited handicap access. Weddings, small meetings, family reunions and seminars hosted. Antiquing, art galleries, beach, bicycling, canoeing/kayaking, fishing, golf, hiking, live theater, museums, parks, shopping and Acadia National Park nearby.

Publicity: *Boston Globe and Portland Press Herald.*

Bar Harbor Tides B&B

119 West St
Bar Harbor, ME 04609-1430
(207)288-4968

Circa 1887. Sweeping views of Frenchmen Bay are seen from this exquisite four-diamond Greek Revival Inn, listed in the National Register of Historic Places. Gracious and personalized hospitality is offered in an intimate atmosphere. Luxurious suites boast elegant formal parlors and fireplaces. Enjoy a delicious gourmet breakfast before embarking on the day's activities. The Tides is conveniently located on the water, two blocks from downtown Bar Harbor and minutes away from Acadia National Park.

Historic Interest: Acadia National Park, the first national park established east of the Mississippi River, is nearby and includes the Abbe Museum, with its vast collection of Native American artifacts. The Islesford Museum on Little Cranberry Island offers many maritime exhibits. The Bar Harbor Historical Museum provides documents and photographs from Bar Harbor's heyday as grand resort for the country's wealthiest citizens.

Innkeeper(s): Ray & Loretta Harris. $225-395. 4 rooms with PB, 3 with FP and 3 suites. Breakfast included in rates. Types of meals: Full bkfst. Beds: KQ. Cable TV, reading lamp, telephone and 3 suites with fireplace in room. Parlor games and fireplace on premises. Antiquing, cross-country skiing, live theater, parks, shopping and water sports nearby.

Black Friar Inn

10 Summer St
Bar Harbor, ME 04609-1424
(207)288-5091 Fax:(207)288-4197

Circa 1900. When this three-story house was renovated in 1981, the owners added mantels, hand-crafted woodwork and windows gleaned from old Bar Harbor mansions that had been torn down. Victorian and country furnishings are accentuated with fresh flowers and soft carpets. Breakfast is presented in the greenhouse, a room that boasts cypress paneling and embossed tin recycled from an old country church.

Historic Interest: Acadia National Park, the second most popular park in the U.S. (nearby).

Innkeeper(s): Perry & Sharon Risley. $75-160. 7 rooms with PB, 4 with FP and 1 suite. Breakfast and afternoon tea included in rates. Types of meals: Full gourmet bkfst. Beds: KQ. Reading lamp, ceiling fan and clock radio in room. Air conditioning. TV, VCR, telephone and fireplace on premises. Antiquing, cross-country skiing, fishing, live theater, parks, shopping, water sports, concerts, art fairs and museums nearby.

"A great place and great innkeepers!"

Chiltern Inn

3 Cromwell Harbor Rd
Bar Harbor, ME 04609-1202
(207)288-0114 (800)404-0114 Fax:(207)288-0124
E-mail: pat@chilterninn.com
Web: www.chilterninn.com

Circa 1905. Originally an elaborate carriage house, this Edwardian Shingle-style inn has been extensively restored. The inn boasts the sophistication and privacy of a European-style hotel as well as the warm elegance of an English country manor home. Experience original 19th-century art, fine period antiques and rich fabrics. Guest bedrooms feature luxurious marble baths with two-person Jacuzzis. Breakfast may include Finnish pancakes baked with fresh apples and other homemade treats. Enjoy an indoor pool with spa and sauna in a columned room with fireplace. The formal and English cottage gardens exude an Oriental flair. Visit nearby Acadia National Park for outstanding vistas.

Innkeeper(s): Pat Monhollon/John Shaw. $275-395. 4 rooms with PB, 4 with FP. Breakfast, afternoon tea and snacks/refreshments included in rates. Types of meals: Full gourmet bkfst. Beds: KQ. Cable TV, VCR, reading lamp, clock radio, telephone, turn-down service, hot tub/spa and fireplace in room. Central air. Fax, spa, swimming, sauna, library, parlor games and fireplace on premises. Antiquing, art galleries, beach, canoeing/kayaking, cross-country skiing, fishing, golf, hiking, live theater, museums, parks, shopping, tennis, water sports and wineries nearby.

Publicity: *Country Inn Article, Bar Harbor Times, a fashion photography shoot for a New York department store and AAA 4 diamond.*

Cleftstone Manor

92 Eden St
Bar Harbor, ME 04609-1123
(207)288-8086 (888)288-4951 Fax:(207)288-2089
E-mail: innkeeper@cleftstone.com
Web: www.cleftstone.com

Circa 1880. Listed in the National Register, this historic Victorian mansion was one of the area's first summer cottages. Sitting on a terraced hillside with gardens on two sides, this inn has offered warm hospitality for more than 50 years. Enjoy games, puzzles and books or converse by the fire. In the afternoon, beverages are served with fresh-baked cookies. The spacious guest bedrooms and suites are traditionally decorated and elegantly furnished with antiques. Some feature fireplaces, balconies and beamed ceilings. Three hot entrees are served each morning with baked goods and fresh fruit. Choices may include rolled herb souffle, cinnamon raisin French toast and pancakes with bacon or sausage.

Innkeeper(s): Barbara. $70-200. 16 rooms with PB, 5 with FP, 2 suites and 1 conference room. Breakfast, afternoon tea and snacks/refreshments included

ed in rates. Types of meals: Full gourmet bkfst and early coffee/tea. Beds: KQD. Data port, cable TV, reading lamp, ceiling fan, clock radio, telephone and fireplace in room. Air conditioning. Fax, library, parlor games and fireplace on premises. Small meetings hosted. Antiquing, beach, bicycling, canoeing/kayaking, fishing, golf, hiking, parks and shopping nearby.

Coach Stop Inn

PO Box 266 Rt 3
Bar Harbor, ME 04609
(207)288-9886 Fax:(207)288-4241
E-mail: info@coachstopinn.com
Web: www.coachstopinn.com

Circa 1804. Built during Thomas Jefferson's presidency, this two-story, shingled building was previously known as "Halfway Tavern" and served the community as a stagecoach stop and tavern. Each of the five guest rooms offers a fireplace, sitting room, private porch or brick patio and a private bath. A full country breakfast and afternoon refreshment are served each day, featuring specialties such as Colonial bread pudding, blueberry corn pancakes and stuffed French toast with sauteed apples harvested from ancient apple trees on the property. Just two miles from the entrance to Acadia National Park, there are miles of carriage roads and hiking tails to explore, as well as canoeing, sailing, whale-watching or antiquing.

Innkeeper(s): Kathy Combs. $59-135. 5 rooms with PB, 2 with FP. Breakfast and snacks/refreshments included in rates. Types of meals: Full gourmet bkfst and early coffee/tea. Beds: Q. Ceiling fan in room. Air conditioning. TV, parlor games and fireplace on premises. Amusement parks, antiquing, art galleries, beach, bicycling, canoeing/kayaking, cross-country skiing, fishing, golf and hiking nearby.

Cove Farm Inn

25 Crooked Rd
Bar Harbor, ME 04609
(207)288-5355 (800)291-0952
E-mail: covefarm@acadia.net
Web: www.covefarm.com

Circa 1778. Watch the sun rise over the Atlantic from this 1778 two-story gabled farmhouse that sits off a winding, country road. Walk the five-acre grounds with a rolling lawn, groves of shade trees, colorful gardens and a pond. Guest bedrooms and suites are available in the historic farmhouse where breakfast is served in the kitchen by the wood stove. Fridge space is provided and guests can make lunches and dinners using fresh vegetables and herbs picked from the garden. A chalet-style three-bedroom cottage with fireplace, Jacuzzi, full kitchen and entertainment center in the living room offers more spacious seclusion. The perfect host, Jerry enjoys introducing others to the treasures of Mount Desert Island. Experience Japanese Gardens, a volcanic pond, musical beaches, seals, special hiking trails of Acadia National Park, museums and lakes.

Historic Interest: Part of the inn was built by the French Jesuits in 1778. It was moved by the original owners of the farm. The structure was two miles away on a hillside. They hooked up the oxen, put poles under it and pulled it to where it is now. They lived in it and built the rest of the farm around it.

Innkeeper(s): Jerry and Barbara Keene. $38-214. 13 rooms, 4 with PB, 1 suite and 2 cottages. Breakfast included in rates. Types of meals: Full bkfst. Beds: QDT. Cable TV, VCR, reading lamp, stereo, refrigerator, ceiling fan, clock radio, telephone, coffeemaker, hot tub/spa and fireplace in room. Air conditioning. Spa, child care and laundry facility on premises. Handicap access. Weddings and family reunions hosted. Antiquing, art galleries, beach, bicycling, canoeing/kayaking, cross-country skiing, fishing, golf, hiking, horseback riding, live theater, museums, parks, shopping, sporting events, tennis, water sports and wineries nearby.

Publicity: *Family Fun Magazine.*

Graycote Inn

40 Holland Ave
Bar Harbor, ME 04609-1432
(207)288-3044 Fax:(207)288-2719
E-mail: history@graycoteinn.com
Web: www.graycoteinn.com

Circa 1881. Hospitality is generous at this Victorian inn, originally built for the first rector of St. Saviour's Episcopal Church.
Sitting beside the living room fireplace or on the veranda is a
relaxing way to enjoy afternoon refreshments. Find a tray of hot

beverages placed near guest bedrooms every morning, before
savoring a gourmet breakfast on
the enclosed porch. Hammocks
beckon nappers, and the lawn is
ready for croquet. Free off-street
parking makes it easy to explore
opportunities for hiking, bird-
watching, biking, photography, and other local activities. The
innkeepers are happy to make recommendations.

Historic Interest: Acadia National Park is less than two miles from the inn.

Innkeeper(s): Pat & Roger Samuel. $75-175. 12 rooms with PB, 3 with FP.
Breakfast included in rates. Types of meals: Full bkfst. Beds: KQ. Reading
lamp, refrigerator, clock radio, ceiling fans in some rooms and some with air
conditioning in room. Telephone and fireplace on premises. Small meetings
and seminars hosted. Antiquing, cross-country skiing, golf, live theater, parks,
shopping, water sports, music, theatre, Acadia National Park, walk to excellent restaurants and concerts nearby.

Publicity: *Country Inns, Washington Post, Victorian Decorating & Lifestyles
and Arrington's Inn Traveler.*

Hatfield B&B

20 Roberts Ave
Bar Harbor, ME 04609-1820
(207)288-9655

Circa 1895. Located a short stroll from the waterfront in Bar
Harbor, this country Victorian inn offers a pleasant and welcoming atmosphere. St. Saviors Church, boasting original
stained glass Tiffany windows, is a block from the inn. Each of
the six guest rooms have private baths and names as individual
as their décor: Uncle Frank, John Wayne, Knotsberry, Rachel's
Retreat, Corner and Eldorado. Awaken each day to the aroma
of fresh coffee and a hearty hot entrée in addition to fresh fruit,
juice and fresh home-baked muffins and breads. Sip afternoon
iced tea on the porch or enjoy the view from the third floor sun
deck as you plan your next day's activities. Mt. Desert Island,
home to Acadia National park, boasts scenic vistas, hiking, biking, swimming, whale watching and sailing. During the winter
the surrounding area offers cross-country skiing, snowshoeing,
hiking, snowmobiling, ice-skating and ice fishing.

Innkeeper(s): Sandy & Jeff Miller. $70-130. 6 rooms with PB. Breakfast and
afternoon tea included in rates. Types of meals: Country bkfst, early coffee/tea
and picnic lunch. Beds: Q. Reading lamp and ceiling fan in room. Air conditioning. Parlor games, telephone and fireplace on premises. Family reunions hosted.
Antiquing, art galleries, beach, bicycling, canoeing/kayaking, cross-country skiing, fishing, golf, hiking, live theater, museums, parks, shopping, sporting
events, tennis, water sports, ocean, mountains and micro-breweries nearby.

Publicity: *Discovery Channel.*

*"Excellent in every way. Thanks for the fine food, accommodations
and company."*

Hearthside Bed & Breakfast

7 High St
Bar Harbor, ME 04609-1816
(207)288-4533
E-mail: bnbinns@hearthsideinn.com
Web: www.hearthsideinn.com

Circa 1907. Originally built for a doctor, this three-story shingled house sits on a quiet street in town. Guests enjoy four
working fireplaces and a porch. Three rooms include a
whirlpool bath. The parlor includes a library and fireplace.
Acadia National Park is five minutes away.

Innkeeper(s): Susan & Barry Schwartz. $100-150. 9 rooms with PB, 3 with
FP. Breakfast and afternoon tea included in rates. Types of meals: Full bkfst.
Beds: Q. Ceiling fan and whirlpool baths in room. Air conditioning. Bicycling,
canoeing/kayaking, cross-country skiing, golf, hiking and water sports nearby.

Publicity: *Philadelphia Jewish Exponent.*

*"I have only one word to describe this place, 'Wow!' My wife and I
are astonished at the splendor, the warmth of your care and the beauty of the surroundings."*

Holbrook House

74 Mount Desert St
Bar Harbor, ME 04609-1323
(207)288-4970
E-mail: info@holbrookhouse.com
Web: www.holbrookhouse.com

Circa 1876. A local landmark of hospitality for more than 100
years, this Victorian inn is in an ideal New England setting and
location. An ambiance of nostalgic elegance is enhanced by
antiques, chintz and flowers. Enchanting guest bedrooms offer
four-poster and lace-covered canopy beds. The two cottages
with welcoming window boxes feature private patios with hammocks and sitting rooms. Savor a wonderful breakfast served in
the cheery sunroom. Afternoon tea and refreshments are
enjoyed on the spacious front porch.

Historic Interest: Located one mile from Acadia National Park.

Innkeeper(s): Phil & Lesley DiVirgilio. $125-175. 10 rooms with PB and 2
suites. Types of meals: Full bkfst. Beds: QDT.

Publicity: *The Discerning Traveler.*

*"When I selected Holbrook House all my dreams of finding the per-
fect inn came true."*

Holland Inn

35 Holland Ave
Bar Harbor, ME 04609-1433
(207)288-4804
E-mail: info@hollandinn.com
Web: www.hollandinn.com

Circa 1895. Reflecting its humble beginnings as a New
England farmhouse, the hosts and 20-year Mount Desert Island
residents, Evin and Tom Hulbert, have paid every attention to
detail in the renovation of the old house. Each room is tastefully decorated in country shaker, resembling the ambiance of the
old Quaker farms. A full gourmet breakfast can be savored on
the sunny porch or outside on the patio. Lush gardens surround the grounds and many activities are within walking distance, including Acadia National Park and the many restaurants
and shops near historic Bar Harbor.

Innkeeper(s): Evin & Tom Hulbert. $55-145. 5 rooms with PB. Breakfast
included in rates. Types of meals: Full gourmet bkfst. Beds: Q. Cable TV,
reading lamp, ceiling fan and clock radio in room. Air conditioning. Parlor

games and telephone on premises. Small meetings and family reunions hosted. Antiquing, art galleries, beach, bicycling, canoeing/kayaking, cross-country skiing, fishing, golf, hiking, horseback riding, live theater, museums, parks, shopping, tennis, water sports and Acadia National Park nearby.

Ivy Manor Inn & Michelle Fine Dining

194 Main St
Bar Harbor, ME 04609-1742
(207)288-2138 (888)670-1997 Fax:(207)288-0038
E-mail: ivymanor@acadia.net
Web: www.ivymanor.com

Circa 1940. Sumptuous elegance is imparted at this French Country inn with a European flair. Authentic 18th and 19th century furnishings reflect the decor as well as offer comfort. Hardwood floors, mahogany paneling and rich wall coverings instill a warm and welcoming ambiance. Relax with late afternoon refreshments in the English pub-like Fleur de Lis Tavern that is accented with stained glass and a fireplace. Romantic guest suites are private getaways that boast balconies, fireplaces, designer tiles, marble-topped vanities, original clawfoot tubs and convenient amenities. Visit Michelle's Fine Dining Bistro, the delightful on-site restaurant, for a candlelit meal under the stars or by the fireside. The grounds feature an antique Japanese maple surrounded by multi-colored roses.

Historic Interest: Home was built by the original doctor on the island and is considered the most distinguished building in downtown Bar Harbor.

Innkeeper(s): Bob & Judy Stanley. $175-350. 9 rooms with PB, 7 with FP and 3 conference rooms. Breakfast included in rates. Types of meals: Full gourmet bkfst, veg bkfst, early coffee/tea, gourmet lunch and gourmet dinner. Restaurant on premises. Beds: KQ. Modem hook-up, data port, cable TV, reading lamp, clock radio, telephone, turn-down service, desk, fireplace and balconies in room. Air conditioning. Fax, copier, parlor games, laundry facility, four-diamond French restaurant and lounge on premises. Limited handicap access. Weddings, small meetings, family reunions and seminars hosted. Antiquing, art galleries, bicycling, fishing, golf, hiking, horseback riding, live theater, parks, shopping, water sports and wineries nearby.

Publicity: *Fodor's, Frommer's, Yankee Conde Naste, AAA and Bangor Times.*

The Kedge

112 West St
Bar Harbor, ME 04609-1429
(207)288-5180 (800)597-8306 Fax:(207)288-5180

Circa 1870. Originally this bed & breakfast was located at the edge of the harbor and served as a social club for gentlemen. In the 1880s it was moved to its current location. The home rests on a portion of the street that is listed in the National Register of Historic Places. The Victorian interior is enhanced and brightened by flowered wallpapers. Stay in a comfortable guest bedroom. One room features a whirlpool tub. Relax on wicker furnishings on the veranda.

Historic Interest: One of the areas first social clubs, built in 1870, one of the earlier luxury cottages of Bar Harbor. Mansard roof and arched windows highlight the victorian style.

Innkeeper(s): Lisa DeMuro & Rick Jewett. $65-195. 5 rooms with PB, 2 with FP. Breakfast and afternoon tea included in rates. Types of meals: Full bkfst and early coffee/tea. Beds: KQ. Cable TV, VCR, clock radio, fireplace, one with Jacuzzi tub and one with private deck in room. Air conditioning. Parlor games, telephone and fireplace on premises. Antiquing, art galleries, beach, bicycling, canoeing/kayaking, cross-country skiing, fishing, golf, hiking, horseback riding, live theater, museums, parks, shopping, water sports, museums, oceanarium, concerts, movies, ocean activities, Acadia National Park and microbreweries nearby.

Ledgelawn Inn

66 Mount Desert St
Bar Harbor, ME 04609-1324
(207)288-4596 (800)274-5334 Fax:(207)288-9968
E-mail: barhbrinns@aol.com
Web: www.barharborvacations.com

Circa 1904. Gables, a mansard roof, red clapboard, bays, columns and verandas characterize this three-story summer mansion located on an acre estate in the Historic Corridor. This elegant country inn offers lodging in the original house or the newly constructed Carriage House, made to look as if built at the same time. A grand wood staircase leads from a common area to upstairs guest bedrooms, many with whirlpool tubs. Some feature four-poster beds, saunas and working fireplaces. Relax in the lounge, or by the pool. The town and waterfront are within walking distance.

Innkeeper(s): Nancy Cloud & Mike Miles. $65-250. 33 rooms with PB, 12 with FP and 1 suite. Breakfast included in rates. Types of meals: Cont, early coffee/tea and afternoon tea. Beds: KQD. Cable TV, reading lamp, clock radio, telephone, turn-down service and desk in room. TV, fax, swimming, child care and fireplace on premises. Family reunions hosted. Antiquing, live theater, parks, water sports and Acadia National Park nearby.

Publicity: *New York Times.*

"A lovely place to relax and enjoy oneself. The area is unsurpassed in beauty and the people friendly."

Manor House Inn

106 West St
Bar Harbor, ME 04609-1856
(207)288-3759 (800)437-0088 Fax:(207)288-2974
E-mail: manor@acadia.net
Web: www.barharbormanorhouse.com

Circa 1887. Colonel James Foster built this 22-room Victorian mansion, now in the National Register. It is an example of the tradition of gracious summer living for which Bar Harbor was and is famous. In addition to the main house, there are several charming cottages situated in the extensive gardens on the property.

Innkeeper(s): Stacey & Ken Smith. $75-235. 18 rooms, 17 with PB, 11 with FP and 7 suites. Breakfast and afternoon tea included in rates. Types of meals: Full bkfst and early coffee/tea. Beds: KQT. TV, reading lamp, refrigerator, ceiling fan, clock radio, desk, air conditioning in all rooms and some with fireplaces in room. Fax, copier, telephone and fireplace on premises. Antiquing, fishing, parks, shopping, water sports and national park nearby.

Publicity: *Country Folks Art Magazine and Discerning Traveler.*

"Wonderful honeymoon spot! Wonderful inn, elegant, delicious breakfasts, terrific innkeepers. We loved it all! It's our fourth time here and it's wonderful as always."

The Maples Inn

16 Roberts Ave
Bar Harbor, ME 04609-1820
(207)288-3443 Fax:(207)288-0356
E-mail: info@maplesinn.com
Web: www.maplesinn.com

Circa 1903. This Victorian "summer cottage" once served wealthy summer visitors to Mt. Desert Island. Located on an attractive residential street, away from Bar Harbor traffic, it has been tastefully restored and filled with attractive, comfortable

furnishings. The inn is within walking distance of shops, boutiques and restaurants. Acadia National Park is less than two miles from our door. Hiking, kayaking and cycling are among the nearby activities.

Innkeeper(s): Tom & Sue Palumbo. $70-160. 6 rooms with PB, 1 with FP. Breakfast and afternoon tea included in rates. Types of meals: Full gourmet bkfst and early coffee/tea. Beds: Q. Reading lamp and clock radio in room. Air conditioning. Fax, library, parlor games, telephone and fireplace on premises. Family reunions and seminars hosted. Antiquing, cross-country skiing, live theater, parks, shopping, sporting events and water sports nearby.

Publicity: *Gourmet July 2002, Bon Appetit, The Discerning Traveler Newsletter July/August 2002 and Yankee Magazine's 54 Award Winning Recipe Cookbook 2002.*

"What a wonderful place this is. Warm, comfortable, friendly, terrific breakfasts, great tips for adventure around the island. I could go on and on."

Mira Monte Inn & Suites

69 Mount Desert St
Bar Harbor, ME 04609-1327
(207)288-4263 (800)553-5109 Fax:(207)288-3115
E-mail: mburns@miramonte.com
Web: www.miramonte.com

Circa 1864. A gracious 18-room Victorian mansion, the Mira Monte has been newly renovated in the style of early Bar Harbor. It features period furnishings, pleasant common rooms, a library and wraparound porches. Situated on estate grounds, there are sweeping lawns, paved terraces and many gardens. The inn was one of the earliest of Bar Harbor's famous summer cottages. The two-room suites each feature canopy beds, two-person whirlpools, a parlor with a sleeper sofa, fireplace and kitchenette unit. The two-bedroom suite includes a full kitchen, dining area and parlor. The suites boast private decks with views of the gardens.

Historic Interest: Acadia National Park is nearby. Many estates are still visible by water tours around the island.

Innkeeper(s): Marian Burns. $165-265. 16 rooms with PB, 14 with FP and 3 suites. Breakfast and afternoon tea included in rates. Types of meals: Full bkfst and early coffee/tea. Beds: KQT. Cable TV, VCR, reading lamp, clock radio, telephone, desk and hot tub/spa in room. Air conditioning. TV, fax, library, parlor games, fireplace, data ports and Internet access on premises. Limited handicap access. Small meetings hosted. Antiquing, fishing, live theater, parks, shopping and Acadia National Park nearby.

Publicity: *Los Angeles Times.*

"On our third year at your wonderful inn in beautiful Bar Harbor. I think I enjoy it more each year. A perfect place to stay in a perfect environment."

Primrose Inn

73 Mount Desert St
Bar Harbor, ME 04609-1327
(207)288-4031 (877)846-3424
E-mail: relax@primroseinn.com
Web: www.primroseinn.com

Circa 1878. One of the last remaining grand residences of its time, this impressive Stick-Style Victorian is situated in downtown's Historic Corridor. The inn offers spacious guest bedrooms furnished with antiques and period reproductions, plush carpeting and floral wallpaper. Many feature whirlpool tubs, gas fireplaces, private balconies or French doors leading onto the wraparound porches. A hearty breakfast and afternoon tea are served daily. Private off-street parking is available. For longer visits or for families, stay in the inn's self-catering apartments.

Innkeeper(s): Pamela & Bryan. $85-215. 15 rooms with PB, 4 with FP and 4 suites. Breakfast and afternoon tea included in rates. Types of meals: Full bkfst. Beds: QT. Cable TV, VCR, ceiling fan, telephone and fireplace in room. Central air. Fax and library on premises. Antiquing, art galleries, beach, bicycling, canoeing/kayaking, fishing, golf, hiking, live theater, museums, parks, shopping, Acadia National Park and whale/puffin watch nearby.

Stratford House Inn

45 Mount Desert St
Bar Harbor, ME 04609-1748
(207)288-5189
E-mail: info@stratfordinn.com
Web: www.stratfordinn.com

Circa 1900. Lewis Roberts, Boston publisher of Louisa Mae Alcott's "Little Women" constructed a 10-bedroom cottage for his guests. It was modeled on Shakespeare's birthplace in an English Tudor style with Jacobean period furnishings and motifs throughout. The rooms are all furnished with antiques such as four-poster mahogany and brass bow-bottom beds. The entrance and dining room are paneled in ornate black oak.

Innkeeper(s): Barbara & Norman Moulton. $75-175. 10 rooms, 8 with PB. Types of meals: Cont. Beds: KQD.

"Marvelous visit. Love this house. Great hospitality."

Town Motel & Moseley Cottage Inn

12 Atlantic Ave
Bar Harbor, ME 04609-1704
(207)288-5548 (800)458-8644 Fax:(207)288-9406
Web: www.townmotelmoseleycottageinn.com

Circa 1894. Although the innkeepers do offer simple, comfortable accommodations in their nine-room motel, they also offer a more historic experience in a late 19th-century Queen Anne Victorian. Bar Harbor has been a popular vacation spot for well over a century. This spacious house was built as a "cottage" for a wealthy family who spent their summers on Maine's scenic coast. The rooms are decorated with period furnishings, Oriental rugs, lacy curtains and flowery wallpapers. Each of nine rooms in the historic home has been decorated individually. Guests at the historic inn are treated to a full breakfast. Guests can walk to many attractions, and everything, from the harbor to Acadia National Park, is nearby.

Innkeeper(s): The Paluga Family. $120-185. 18 rooms with PB, 4 with FP. Breakfast included in rates. Types of meals: Full bkfst and early coffee/tea. Beds: QDT. Cable TV, reading lamp, refrigerator, ceiling fan and desk in room. Air conditioning. VCR, fax, copier and fireplace on premises. Small meetings and family reunions hosted. Antiquing, fishing, golf, live theater, parks, shopping, tennis and water sports nearby.

Bath   **J3**

Benjamin F. Packard House

45 Pearl St
Bath, ME 04530-2746
(207)443-6069 (800)516-4578

Circa 1790. Shipbuilder Benjamin F. Packard purchased this handsome home in 1870. The inn reflects the Victorian influence so prominent in Bath's busiest shipbuilding years. The Packard family, who lived in the house for five generations, left many family mementos. Period furnishings, authentic colors and shipbuilding memorabilia all reflect Bath's romantic past. The mighty Kennebec River is just a block away. A full breakfast is served daily.

Historic Interest: The inn is situated in a historic district, and nearby historic Front Street offers many antique stores and other commercial business in historic buildings. Maine Maritime Museum, 10-acre site on original shipyard (1 mile), Front Street (one-half mile), forts and lighthouses at Mouth of Kennebee River (12 miles south).

Innkeeper(s): Taylor & Stephen Kluckowski. $90-120. 3 rooms with PB and 1 suite. Breakfast included in rates. Types of meals: Full bkfst. Beds: KQT. Library, telephone and fireplace on premises. Antiquing, golf, live theater, parks, shopping and water sports nearby.

Publicity: *Coastal Journal, Times Record and Maine Sunday Telegram.*

"Thanks for being wonderful hosts."

Fairhaven Inn

118 N Bath Rd
Bath, ME 04530
(207)443-4391 (888)443-4391 Fax:(207)443-6412
E-mail: fairhvn@gwi.net
Web: www.mainecoast.com/fairhaveninn

Circa 1790. With its view of the Kennebec River, this site was so attractive that Pembleton Edgecomb built his Colonial house where a log cabin had previously stood. His descendants occupied it for the next 125 years. Antiques and country furniture fill the inn. Meadows and lawns, and woods of hemlock, birch and pine cover the inn's 16 acres.

Innkeeper(s): Susie & Dave Reed. $80-130. 8 rooms, 6 with PB, 1 suite and 1 cottage. Breakfast included in rates. Types of meals: Full gourmet bkfst and early coffee/tea. Beds: KQT. Reading lamp and clock radio in room. TV, VCR, fax, library, parlor games, telephone and fireplace on premises. Small meetings, family reunions and seminars hosted. Antiquing, art galleries, beach, bicycling, canoeing/kayaking, cross-country skiing, fishing, golf, hiking, live theater, museums, parks, shopping, sporting events, tennis and water sports nearby.

Publicity: *The State, Coastal Journal and Times Record.*

"The Fairhaven is now marked in our book with a red star, definitely a place to remember and visit again."

The Galen C. Moses House

1009 Washington St
Bath, ME 04530-2759
(207)442-8771 (888)442-8771
E-mail: stay@galenmoses.com
Web: www.galenmoses.com

Circa 1874. This Victorian mansion is filled with beautiful architectural items, including stained-glass windows, woodcarved and marble fireplaces and a grand staircase. The

innkeepers have filled the library, a study, morning room and the parlor with antiques. A corner fireplace warms the dining room, which overlooks the lawns and gardens. Tea is presented in the formal drawing room.

Historic Interest: The home is in the National Register of Historic Homes and has been featured in a number of publications, including the Bank of England's employees magazine "The Old Lady of Threadneedle Street," "The Insider's Guide: Maine's Southern Coast," "The Romantic Northeast" (Ken Christensen), "Maine, Off the Beaten Path" (Wayne Curtis), and all three major newspapers serving Bath.

Innkeeper(s): James Haught, Larry Kieft. $99-259. 4 rooms with PB and 1 suite. Breakfast and afternoon tea included in rates. Types of meals: Full gourmet bkfst. Beds: QT. Turn-down service and fans in room. Air conditioning. VCR, bicycles, library, telephone and fireplace on premises. Family reunions hosted. Antiquing, art galleries, beach, bicycling, canoeing/kayaking, cross-country skiing, fishing, golf, hiking, horseback riding, live theater, museums, parks, shopping, tennis, water sports and boats nearby.

Publicity: *Philadelphia, Back Roads USA, Ghost Stories of New England - Susan Smitten, "LC & Co" show and Home & Garden channel - "Restore America."*

"For our first try at B&B lodgings, we've probably started at the top, and nothing else will ever measure up to this. Wonderful food, wonderful home, grounds and wonderful hosts!"

Kennebec Inn

251 High St
Bath, ME 04530
(207)443-5324 (888)595-1664
E-mail: donlhseinn@clinic.net
Web: www.mainelodging.com

Circa 1850. From the cupola atop the roof of this Italianate home, guests may enjoy a moonlit view of the Kennebec River. The inn's exterior is elegantly painted in gray with white on the columns and trim. Inside are hardwood floors and antiques, set against cheerful wall colors and white woodwork. There are two front parlors, one a sunny yellow and white, and the other with marble fireplace, Oriental rug and a rose-patterned wallpaper. Guest bedrooms offer four-poster beds, and some have fireplaces. One room boasts a Roman spa tub. A three-course breakfast is served on Blue Willow china in the formal dining room.

Innkeeper(s): Kenneth & Rachel Parlin. $100-225. 4 rooms with PB, 2 with FP and 1 suite. Breakfast and afternoon tea included in rates. Types of meals: Full bkfst and early coffee/tea. Beds: Q. Cable TV, reading lamp and one with a fireplace and Roman spa tub whirlpool in room. Air conditioning. Fireplace, piano room and background stereo music on premises. Antiquing, art galleries, beach, bicycling, canoeing/kayaking, cross-country skiing, fishing, golf, hiking, live theater, museums, parks, shopping, tennis, Maine Maritime Museum and boat landing nearby.

"Your beautiful home offered the space and energy we all needed."

Belfast   **H5**

The Alden House Bed & Breakfast

63 Church St
Belfast, ME 04915-6208
(207)338-2151 (877)337-8151 Fax:(207)338-2151
E-mail: info@thealdenhouse.com
Web: www.thealdenhouse.com

Circa 1840. This pre-Civil War, pristinely restored Greek Revival manor was built for prominent Belfast citizen Hiram Alden. Alden was editor of the local paper, town postmaster and vice-president of American Telegraph. The interior still boasts grand features, such as marble fireplace mantels, tin ceilings and a hand-carved curved staircase. Early risers enjoy the view from the front porch as they sip a cup of freshly ground coffee. Breakfast begins with juice, fresh fruit and muffins, followed by a special entree.

Innkeeper(s): Bruce & Susan Madara. $90-130. 7 rooms, 5 with PB, 1 with FP. Breakfast and afternoon tea included in rates. Types of meals: Full bkfst and early coffee/tea. Beds: QDT. Reading lamp, natural body care products, hair dryers and robes in room. VCR, fax, library, parlor games, telephone and fireplace on premises. Weddings, small meetings and family reunions hosted. Antiquing, cross-country skiing, downhill skiing, fishing, golf, live theater, parks, shopping, tennis and water sports nearby.

Publicity: *Bangor Daily News and Waldo Independent.*

Belfast Bay Meadows Inn

192 Northport Ave
Belfast, ME 04915-6011
(207)338-5715 (800)335-2370
E-mail: bbmi@baymeadowsinn.com
Web: www.baymeadowsinn.com

Circa 1890. A shingled waterfront estate overlooking Penobscot Bay sits on eight acres of flowering meadows and woods. The Victorian decor is enhanced by high ceilings and ornate wood trim. Families and pets are welcome at the inn, where hospitality and comfort are in abundance. Many of the spacious guest bedrooms offer private entrances with decks boasting gorgeous ocean views. The gourmet country breakfast may include a lobster omelette, or scrambled eggs with smoked salmon, among other delights. Enjoy dining in the the inn's new restaurant, Mistral. The inn's own beach is only a short walk away on grassy paths.

Innkeeper(s): Karin Kane. $85-165. 20 rooms, 19 with PB, 1 with FP. Breakfast included in rates. Types of meals: Full gourmet bkfst. Restaurant on premises. Beds: KQ. Modem hook-up, cable TV, refrigerator, ceiling fan, clock radio, telephone and fireplace in room. Air conditioning. VCR, fax, copier, parlor games and fireplace on premises. Weddings, small meetings, family reunions and seminars hosted. Antiquing, art galleries, beach, bicycling, canoeing/kayaking, cross-country skiing, downhill skiing, fishing, golf, hiking, live theater, museums, parks, shopping, tennis and water sports nearby.

Belhaven Inn

14 John St
Belfast, ME 04915-6650
(207)338-5435
E-mail: stay@belhaveninn.com
Web: www.belhaveninn.com

Circa 1851. This 16-room 1851 Federal Victorian stands on an acre in the heart of Belfast, a historic harbor community with roots in shipbuilding. Mullioned windows, pumpkin pine floors and carved mantels are some of the many period features of the inn. A circular staircase leads to the four guest bedrooms, each appointed with period pieces. A three-course country breakfast is served daily on the side porch, weather permitting. It includes items such as fruit cup with yogurt or granola, freshly baked muffins, hot breads and a hot entrée of either eggs, pancakes, crepes or sausage. Locally grown berries and produce are used in season. After breakfast relax on the porch or head into Belfast to explore the many art galleries and shops. Take a ride on the vintage Belfast and Moosehead Train or arrange for a boat to explore the islands in the Penobscot Bay or take a drive and explore the nearby lighthouses.

Innkeeper(s): Anne & Paul Bartels. $85-125. 5 rooms, 3 with PB and 1 suite. Breakfast and snacks/refreshments included in rates. Types of meals: Country bkfst and early coffee/tea. Beds: KQDT. Reading lamp, clock radio, turn-down service and desk in room. TV, VCR, tennis, library, parlor games, telephone, fireplace, badminton and volleyball on premises. Family reunions hosted. Antiquing, art galleries, beach, bicycling, canoeing/kayaking, cross-country skiing, fishing, golf, hiking, horseback riding, live theater, museums, parks, shopping, tennis and wineries nearby.

The Jeweled Turret Inn

40 Pearl St
Belfast, ME 04915-1907
(207)338-2304 (800)696-2304
E-mail: info@jeweledturret.com
Web: www.jeweledturret.com

Circa 1898. This grand Victorian is named for the staircase that winds up the turret, lighted by stained- and leaded-glass panels and jewel-like embellishments. It was built for attorney James Harriman. Dark pine beams adorn the ceiling of the den, and the fireplace is constructed of bark and rocks from every state in the Union. Elegant antiques furnish the guest rooms. Guests can relax in one of the inn's four parlors, which are furnished with period antiques, wallpapers, lace and boast fireplaces. Some rooms have a ceiling fan and whirlpool tub or fireplace. The verandas feature wicker and iron bistro sets and views of the historic district. The inn is within walking distance of the town and its shops, restaurants and the harbor.

Historic Interest: The home, which is listed in the National Register, is near many historic homes. Walking tours are available.

Innkeeper(s): Cathy & Carl Heffentrager. $105-150. 7 rooms with PB, 1 with FP. Breakfast and afternoon tea included in rates. Types of meals: Full gourmet bkfst and early coffee/tea. Beds: QDT. TV, reading lamp and one room with whirlpool tub in room. Telephone and fireplace on premises. Small meetings and family reunions hosted. Antiquing, cross-country skiing, downhill skiing, fishing, live theater, shopping and water sports nearby.

Publicity: *News Herald, Republican Journal, Waterville Sentinel, Los Angels Times, Country Living, Victorian Homes and The Saturday Evening Post.*

"The ambiance was so romantic that we felt like we were on our honeymoon."

Londonderry Inn

133 Belmont Ave (Rt 3)
Belfast, ME 04915
(207)338-2763 (877)529-9566 Fax:(207)338-6303
E-mail: info@londonderry-inn.com
Web: www.londonderry-inn.com

Circa 1803. Built in 1803, this Maine farmhouse provides elegant comfort and spacious common areas to relax and enjoy a wonderful vacation. Choose from five delightful guest bedrooms with private modern baths. Wake up each morning to an old-fashioned farmer's breakfast featuring gourmet foods that may include blueberry pancakes and apple walnut muffins served in the large fireplaced country kitchen. Early risers can sip coffee on the screened porch or backyard deck overlooking the garden. Explore ten beautiful acres surrounding the inn, pick raspberries in season or catch a glimpse of deer or wild turkeys. Pick a complimentary in-room movie from the extensive video collection of more than 200 films. Visit the area's many historic sites like Fort Knox State Park.

Innkeeper(s): Marsha Oakes. $95-135. 5 rooms with PB. Breakfast and snacks/refreshments included in rates. Types of meals: Country bkfst, early coffee/tea and afternoon tea. Beds: KQD. Cable TV, VCR, reading lamp, clock radio, telephone, bathrobes, hair dryers and twin sleep sofa in room. Air conditioning. Fax, library, fireplace, laundry facility, backyard deck, evening dessert, 200+ video and periodical library and laundry facilities available for a nominal fee on premises. Antiquing, art galleries, bicycling, canoeing/kayaking, downhill skiing, fishing, golf, hiking, horseback riding, live theater, museums, parks, shopping, water sports and lighthouses nearby.

Belgrade Lakes H3

Wings Hill Inn
PO Box 386
Belgrade Lakes, ME 04918-0386
(207)495-2400 (866)495-2400
E-mail: wingshillinn@earthlink.net
Web: wingshillinn.com

Circa 1800. In a picturesque lakefront village setting, this post and beam farmhouse is an ideal romantic getaway. Relaxation comes easy by the fireplace in the Great Room or the extensive screened wraparound porch overlooking Long Pond. The guest bedrooms boast a comfortable elegance. Hospitality is abundant, as experienced in the optional breakfast basket delivered to the door, or join others in the dining area. Enjoy intimate candlelit dining Sunday-Thursday. Hiking, fishing, boating and golf are only steps away. Other popular New England sites and activities are an easy drive away.

Innkeeper(s): Christopher & Tracey Anderson. $95-145. 8 rooms with PB. Breakfast and afternoon tea included in rates. Types of meals: Full bkfst and early coffee/tea. Antiquing, cross-country skiing, downhill skiing, fishing, golf, hiking, shopping, sporting events and water sports nearby.

Bethel I2

Chapman Inn
PO Box 1067
Bethel, ME 04217-1067
(207)824-2657 (877)359-1498

Circa 1865. As one of the town's oldest buildings, this Federal-style inn has been a store, a tavern and a boarding house known as "The Howard." It was the home of William Rogers Chapman,

composer, conductor and founder of the Rubenstein Club and the Metropolitan Musical Society, in addition to the Maine Music Festival. The inn is a convenient place to begin a walking tour of Bethel's historic district.

Innkeeper(s): Sandra & Fred. $25-105. 10 rooms with PB and 2 suites. Breakfast included in rates. Types of meals: Full bkfst, early coffee/tea and afternoon tea. TV, reading lamp, refrigerator, telephone and desk in room. Air conditioning. VCR, fax, sauna, parlor games and fireplace on premises. Weddings, small meetings, family reunions and seminars hosted. Antiquing, cross-country skiing, downhill skiing, fishing, golf, live theater, parks, shopping, tennis and water sports nearby.

L'Auberge Country Inn
Mill Hill Rd, PO Box 21
Bethel, ME 04217-0021
(207)824-2774 (800)760-2774 Fax:(207)824-0806
E-mail: inn@laubergecountryinn.com
Web: www.laubergecountryinn.com

Circa 1850. In the foothills of the White Mountains, surrounded by five acres of gardens and woods, this former carriage house was converted to a guest house in the 1920s. Among its seven guest rooms are two spacious suites. The Theater Suite offers a four-poster queen bed and dressing room. The Family Suite can accommodate up to six guests. Mount Abrahms and Sunday River ski areas are just minutes away.

Historic Interest: 1850s renovated carriage house. Original restored barn floors, antiques and fine art.

Innkeeper(s): Alexandra & Adam Adler. $69-149. 7 rooms with PB and 2 suites. Breakfast and afternoon tea included in rates. Types of meals: Country bkfst, veg bkfst, early coffee/tea, picnic lunch, snacks/refreshments, gourmet dinner and room service. Restaurant on premises. Beds: K. Reading lamp, clock radio, turn-down service and desk in room. Air conditioning. TV, VCR, fax, bicycles, library, pet boarding, child care, telephone, fireplace, laundry facility and gift shop on premises. Weddings, small meetings, family reunions and seminars hosted. Antiquing, art galleries, beach, bicycling, canoeing/kayaking, cross-country skiing, downhill skiing, fishing, golf, hiking, horseback riding, live theater, museums, parks, shopping, tennis, water sports, Gould Academy and National Training Laboratories nearby.

Publicity: *Yankee, Gourmet and Canadian Life.*

Blue Hill H5

The Blue Hill Inn
Union St, Rt 177
Blue Hill, ME 04614-0403
(207)374-2844 (800)826-7415 Fax:(207)374-2829
E-mail: bluehillinn@hotmail.com
Web: www.bluehillinn.com

Circa 1830. Sitting on an acre in the heart of the historic town center, this Federalist-style inn has operated continuously for more than 160 years. Near Blue Hill Bay, it is distinguished by its shuttered windows, clapboards, brick ends and five chimneys. The wide pumpkin-pine floors are accented by antique period furnishings. Enjoy reading or socializing in two common rooms. Some of the romantic guest bedrooms feature comfortable sitting areas and fireplaces. The Cape House is a luxury suite that can accommodate a family of four. Breakfast includes a choice of entrees. Afternoon tea with refreshments as well as evening drinks with hors d'oeuvres are served in the garden or parlor. Ask about the seasonal Wine Dinners prepared by visiting chefs.

Historic Interest: Located close to Acadia National Park and the Maine coast.

Innkeeper(s): Mary & Don Hartley. $148-275. 11 rooms with PB, 4 with FP. Breakfast included in rates. Types of meals: Full gourmet bkfst and early coffee/tea. Beds: KQDT. Fax, parlor games, telephone, fireplace, one luxury suite-cottage, hors d'oeuvres, Wine Spectator award winning wine dinners presented May, June, September and October on premises. Limited handicap access. Family reunions hosted. Antiquing, cross-country skiing, fishing, golf, parks, boating and kayaking nearby.

Publicity: *Washington Post and Country Inn Cooking with Gail Greco-Second Series.*

Boothbay J4

Hodgdon Island Inn
PO Box 603, 374 Barter Island Rd
Boothbay, ME 04537
(207)633-7474 Fax:(207)633-0571
Web: www.hodgdonislandinn.com

Circa 1810. This early 19th-century Victorian still boasts many original features, including molding and windows. Antiques and wicker furnishings decorate the guest rooms. There is a heated swimming pool available to summer guests. The historic inn is minutes from downtown Boothbay Harbor.

Innkeeper(s): Peter Wilson & Peter Moran. $105-150. 8 rooms with PB. Breakfast included in rates. Types of meals: Full gourmet bkfst and early coffee/tea. Beds: KQ. Reading lamp, ceiling fan, clock radio, water views and some with fireplaces in room. TV, VCR, swimming, library, parlor games, telephone and fireplace on premises. Antiquing, art galleries, bicycling, canoeing/kayaking, cross-country skiing, fishing, golf, hiking, museums, parks, shopping, water sports and lobster bake on island cruise nearby.

Kenniston Hill Inn

Rt 27, PO Box 125
Boothbay, ME 04537-0125
(207)633-2159 (800)992-2915 Fax:(207)633-2159

Circa 1786. The elegant clapboard home is the oldest inn at Boothbay Harbor Region and was occupied by the Kenniston family for more than a century. Five of the antique-filled bedrooms have fireplaces. After a walk through the gardens or woods, warm up in the parlor next to the elegant, open-hearthed fireplace. Boothbay Harbor offers something for everybody, including whale-watching excursions and dinner theaters.

Innkeeper(s): Jim & Gerry Botti. $85-130. 10 rooms with PB, 5 with FP and 2 cottages. Breakfast and afternoon tea included in rates. Types of meals: Country bkfst and early coffee/tea. Beds: KQDT. Reading lamp, ceiling fan and clock radio in room. Air conditioning. TV, VCR, fax, copier, parlor games, telephone, fireplace and laundry facility on premises. Weddings and family reunions hosted. Antiquing, art galleries, beach, bicycling, canoeing/kayaking, fishing, golf, hiking, live theater, museums, parks, shopping and tennis nearby.

Publicity: *Boothbay Register.*

"England may be the home of the original bed & breakfast, but Kenniston Hill Inn is where it has been perfected!"

Boothbay Harbor   J4

1830 Admiral's Quarters Inn

71 Commercial St
Boothbay Harbor, ME 04538-1827
(207)633-2474 (800)644-1878 Fax:(207)633-5904
E-mail: loon@admiralsquartersinn.com
Web: www.admiralsquartersinn.com

Circa 1830. Set on a rise looking out to the ocean, this renovated sea captain's home commands a view of the harbor and its activities. Guest bedrooms are decorated with white wicker, antiques and quilts that enhance the ambiance. They all feature fireplaces and decks or patios with private entrances. Savor a

homemade breakfast served on the porch or in the glass solarium, complete with wood-burning stove, overlooking manicured lawns and the water beyond. Afternoon refreshments can be enjoyed in front of the fireplace or while watching the lobster boats glide by. Boat excursions and restaurants are within walking distance.

Historic Interest: Maine Maritime Museum.

Innkeeper(s): Les & Deb Hallstrom. $95-195. 7 rooms with PB, 7 with FP and 4 suites. Breakfast, afternoon tea and snacks/refreshments included in rates. Types of meals: Country bkfst, veg bkfst and early coffee/tea. Beds: KQT. Modem hook-up, cable TV, reading lamp, ceiling fan, snack bar, clock radio, telephone, desk, all with fireplaces, air conditioning and toiletries in room. Fax, copier, library, parlor games, fireplace, laundry facility and glider swing on premises. Weddings, small meetings, family reunions and seminars hosted. Antiquing, art galleries, beach, bicycling, canoeing/kayaking, cross-country skiing, downhill skiing, fishing, golf, hiking, horseback riding, live theater, museums, parks, shopping, sporting events, tennis, water sports, boat trips and pottery shops nearby.

Publicity: *Franklin Business Review, Down East Magazine and Yankee Traveler.*

"If you're looking to put down stakes in the heart of Boothbay Harbor, the Admiral's Quarters Inn provides an eagle's eye view on land and at sea." — Yankee Traveler

Anchor Watch Bed & Breakfast

9 Eames Rd
Boothbay Harbor, ME 04538-1882
(207)633-7565
E-mail: info@anchorwatch.com
Web: www.anchorwatch.com

Circa 1920. Listen to the lapping of the waves and the call of seabirds, smell the salt air and gaze out on the harbor from this Colonial inn on the waterfront in Boothbay Harbor. The inn has a private pier for swimming or fishing, a butterfly/azalea garden and a patio on the rocks. The comfortably appointed inn is decorated with quilts and stenciling. Its five guest rooms are each named for a Monhegan ferryboat from years gone by. Breakfast fare includes items like baked orange French toast, sausage and popovers with strawberry jam — all served in the sunny breakfast nook overlooking the sea. Walk to shops, restaurants, clambakes and boat trips. The innkeepers' Balmy Day Cruises include harbor tours, all-day excursions to Monhegan Island and sailing trips.

Innkeeper(s): Diane Campbell & Kathy Campbell-Reed. $105-175. 5 rooms with PB. Breakfast included in rates. Types of meals: Full bkfst. Beds: KQ. Telephone and fireplace on premises. Antiquing, art galleries, beach, canoeing/kayaking, cross-country skiing, fishing, golf, hiking, museums, parks, shopping and tennis nearby.

Five Gables Inn

PO Box 335
Boothbay Harbor, ME 04544
(207)633-4551 (800)451-5048
E-mail: info@fivegablesinn.com
Web: www.fivegablesinn.com

Circa 1896. One could hardly conjure up a more perfect setting than this Maine inn's location, just yards from Linekin Bay with wooded hills as a backdrop. For more than a century, guests have come here to enjoy the Maine summer. The porch offers a hammock and rockers, as well as a pleasing view. Guest rooms offer bay views, and five include a fireplace. Breakfasts offer a wide assortment of items, a menu might include puffed apple pancakes, grilled tomatoes, ham, freshly baked scones, fruit and homemade granola. The inn is open from mid-May to October.

Innkeeper(s): Mike & De Kennedy. $130-195. 16 rooms with PB, 5 with FP. Breakfast and afternoon tea included in rates. Types of meals: Full gourmet bkfst and early coffee/tea. Beds: KQT. Reading lamp, clock radio and telephone in room. Library, parlor games and fireplace on premises. Antiquing, fishing, golf, live theater, parks, shopping, tennis, water sports, whale watching and windjammers nearby.

Publicity: *Calendar, Atlanta Journal-Constitution, Down East Magazine and Yankee Traveler.*

Greenleaf Inn at Boothbay Harbor

65 Commercial St
Boothbay Harbor, ME 04538
(207)633-7346 (888)950-7724 Fax:(207)633-2642
E-mail: info@greenleafinn.com
Web: www.greenleafinn.com

Circa 1850. For well over a century, guests have stopped at Greenleaf Inn. The guest rooms are decorated in a cozy, New England-country style. The suites have the added luxury of a harbor view. In the mornings, the innkeeper provides a variety of breakfast items, including a special daily entrée. Guests can enjoy the meal in the cheerful country dining room or on the front porch where a view of the harbor may be enjoyed.

Boothbay offers a variety of festivals throughout the year, as well as plenty of outdoor activities.

Innkeeper(s): Jeff Teel. $105-185. 7 rooms with PB, 7 with FP, 1 suite and 1 conference room. Breakfast and snacks/refreshments included in rates. Types of meals: Full bkfst and early coffee/tea. Beds: QDT. Modem hook-up, cable TV, VCR, reading lamp, refrigerator, ceiling fan, clock radio, telephone, voice mail and fireplace in room. Fax, copier, bicycles, library, parlor games, fireplace and gift shop on premises. Weddings, small meetings, family reunions and seminars hosted. Antiquing, art galleries, beach, bicycling, canoeing/kayaking, fishing, golf, hiking, live theater, museums, parks, shopping and tennis nearby.

The Harborage Inn on the Edge of the Bay

75 Townsend Ave
Boothbay Harbor, ME 04538
(207)633-4640 (800)565-3742
E-mail: info@harborageinn.com
Web: www.harborageinn.com

Circa 1872. A family-run business for three generations, this Victorian is the oldest original inn in the harbor. Completely restored, it is decorated throughout with Laura Ashley fabrics and designs. The warm ambiance and country atmosphere reflect the local coastal area. Guest bedrooms and suites are romantic retreats featuring Colonial furnishings, antique stenciling and private entrances. Some offer bay views. The meticulous waterfront grounds with colorful flower boxes offer eye-pleasing scenes from the wraparound porches. Visit historical Fort William Henry, only 15 miles away. There are several local museums and sites, including the Maine Maritime Museum and Boothbay Railway Village.

Innkeeper(s): The Chapman & Wallace Family's. $65-160. 9 rooms, 5 with PB and 4 suites. Breakfast included in rates. Types of meals: Cont plus. Beds: KQD. Modem hook-up, cable TV, reading lamp, refrigerator, clock radio, telephone, coffeemaker, desk and wraparound porches with scenic views in room. Swimming and private waterfront lawn with seating on premises. Weddings, small meetings, family reunions and seminars hosted. Antiquing, art galleries, beach, bicycling, canoeing/kayaking, cross-country skiing, fishing, golf, hiking, horseback riding, live theater, museums, parks, shopping, tennis, water sports, deep sea fishing, aquarium, botanical gardens, nature preserves, lighthouses, sailboat rentals and festivals nearby.

Harbour Towne Inn on The Waterfront

71 Townsend Ave
Boothbay Harbor, ME 04538-1158
(207)633-4300 (800)722-4240 Fax:(207)633-2442
E-mail: gtme@gwi.net
Web: www.harbourtowneinn.com

Circa 1880. This Victorian inn's well-known trademark boasts that it is "the Finest B&B on the Waterfront." The inn's 12 air-conditioned rooms offer outside decks, and the Penthouse has an outstanding view of the harbor from its private deck.

Breakfast is served in the inn's Sunroom, and guests also may relax in the parlor, which has a miniature antique library and a beautiful antique fireplace. A conference area is available for meetings. The inn's meticulous grounds include flower gardens and well-kept shrubs and trees. A wonderful new addition is a dock and float for sunning, sketches/painting, reading or hopping aboard a canoe, kayak or small boat. It's a pleasant five-minute walk to the village and its art galleries, restaurants,

shops and boat trips. Special off-season packages are available. Ft. William Henry and the Fisherman's Memorial are nearby.

Historic Interest: Boothbay Region Historical Building (3 blocks), lighthouses (5 to 50 minutes).

Innkeeper(s): George Thomas & family. $69-299. 12 rooms with PB and 1 conference room. Breakfast included in rates. Types of meals: Cont. Beds: KQDT. Reading lamp, refrigerator, telephone, satellite TV and microwave in room. Air conditioning. Fax, copier, fireplace and outside decks and new waterfront dock on premises. Limited handicap access. Weddings, small meetings, family reunions and seminars hosted. Antiquing, fishing, live theater, parks, shopping, water sports and boating nearby.

Lion d'Or Bed & Breakfast

106 Townsend Ave
Boothbay Harbor, ME 04538-1835
(207)633-7367 (800)887-7367
E-mail: liondor@gwi.net
Web: www.liondorboothbay.com

Circa 1886. A five-minute walk from the sites and activities of the waterfront, this 1886 Victorian inn offers a picture-perfect in-town location. Comfortable yet elegant, guest bedrooms and a suite feature gas log fireplaces, cozy bathrobes and personal amenities like hair dryers, phones and clock radios for added convenience. Breakfast is a bountiful repast made from Lucy's popular recipes that she gladly shares upon request. Visit local shops and galleries. Enjoy afternoon treats and good conversation or read a book from the library. Take day excursions to experience the entire mid-coast. Gift certificates are available.

Innkeeper(s): Lucy & Gregory Barter. $65-135. 5 rooms with PB, 4 with FP and 1 suite. Breakfast and snacks/refreshments included in rates. Types of meals: Full bkfst. Beds: Q. Data port, cable TV, clock radio, telephone and fireplace in room. TV, library and fireplace on premises. Antiquing, art galleries, beach, canoeing/kayaking, fishing, golf, hiking, museums, parks and shopping nearby.

Newagen Seaside Inn

PO Box 29, Rt 27
Boothbay Harbor, ME 04576
(207)633-5242 (800)654-5242 Fax:(207)633-5340
E-mail: innkeeper@newageninn.com
Web: www.newagenseasideinn.com

Circa 1903. Europeans have inhabited Cape Newagen since the 1620s, and a fort built on this property was destroyed in the King Philips War in 1675. Rachel Carson sought refuge at this seaside inn, and it is here that her final resting place is located. The peaceful scenery includes vistas of islands and lighthouses, and guests can enjoy the view from an oceanside gazebo. There are both freshwater and saltwater swimming pools, nature trails, tennis courts and a mile of rocky shoreline to enjoy. Some rooms offer private decks, and each is decorated in traditional style. The innkeepers also offer three cottages. Maine Lobster is a specialty at the inn's restaurant

Innkeeper(s): Scott & Corinne Larson. $85-250. 26 rooms with PB, 3 suites, 3 cottages and 1 conference room. Breakfast included in rates. Types of meals: Full bkfst, early coffee/tea, lunch, picnic lunch and gourmet dinner. Restaurant on premises. Beds: KQT. Reading lamp and desk in room. VCR, fax, copier, swimming, tennis, library, parlor games, telephone, fireplace, lawn games, nature trails, rowboats, dock and tide pools on premises. Limited handicap access. Weddings, small meetings, family reunions and seminars hosted. Antiquing, fishing, golf, live theater, parks, shopping, tennis, water sports and whale watching nearby.

Publicity: *Down East, Yankee, New England Travel and CBS Sunday Morning.*

The Welch House Inn

56 McKown Street
Boothbay Harbor, ME 04538-1863
(207)633-3431 (800)249-7313
E-mail: info@welchhouseinn.com
Web: www.welchhouseinn.com

Circa 1889. Magnificent vistas of the seacoast and ocean are unsurpassed at this bed & breakfast atop McKown Hill. Soak up the 180-degree view of the harbor from the third-floor deck. A spacious living room boasts a stone fireplace and a library features videos, books and games. Comfortable guest bedrooms, several with fireplaces, are perfect for romantic getaways, family vacations or business trips. Start the day with scrambled eggs in spiced puff pastry with sweet roasted red pepper, cream and white wine sauce served with Canadian bacon in the sun-filled breakfast room. The grounds include lush perennial gardens and many hanging plants. Take a scenic boat tour or supper cruise.

Innkeeper(s): Susan Hodder & Michael Feldmann. $115-185. 14 rooms with PB, 6 with FP. Breakfast included in rates. Types of meals: Full gourmet bkfst and veg bkfst. Beds: KQDT. Data port, cable TV, VCR, reading lamp, clock radio, telephone and fireplace in room. Air conditioning. Library, parlor games, video library and wireless Internet access on premises. Small meetings, family reunions and seminars hosted. Antiquing, art galleries, beach, bicycling, canoeing/kayaking, fishing, golf, hiking, museums, parks, shopping and water sports nearby.

Bridgton 12

Noble House

37 Highland Road
Bridgton, ME 04009
(207)647-3733 Fax:(207)647-3733

Circa 1903. Located on Highland Lake, this inn is tucked among four acres of old oaks and a grove of pine trees, providing an estate-like view from all guest rooms and many with private porches. The elegant parlor contains a library, grand piano and hearth. Bed chambers are furnished with antiques, wicker

and quilts. Five rooms have whirlpool tubs; family suites are available. A hammock placed at the water's edge provides a view of the lake and Mt. Washington. The inn's lake frontage also allows for canoeing at sunset and swimming. Restaurants are nearby.

Historic Interest: Built by a senator in the turn of the century as a summer retreat.

Innkeeper(s): Rick & Julie Whelchel. $99-160. 9 rooms with PB and 4 suites. Breakfast and afternoon tea included in rates. Types of meals: Country bkfst, veg bkfst and early coffee/tea. Beds: QDT. Reading lamp, clock radio and five with whirlpool tubs in room. Antiquing, beach, bicycling, canoeing/kayaking, cross-country skiing, downhill skiing, fishing, golf, hiking, horseback riding, live theater, parks, shopping, tennis, water sports and wineries nearby.

Publicity: *Down East Magazine and April 2002 issue.*

"It's my favorite inn."

Brooksville I5

Oakland House Seaside Resort

435 Herrick Rd
Brooksville, ME 04617
(207)359-8521 (800)359-7352 Fax:(207)359-9865
E-mail: jim@oaklandhouse.com
Web: www.oaklandhouse.com

Circa 1907. It is easy to enjoy this historic inn and its 50 wooded acres with hiking trails, panoramic views and a half-mile of private oceanfront. One of the state's few remaining original coastal resorts, it is still family-owned, now by the fourth generation. Shore Oaks, the private summer home built in Arts and Crafts style, offers seaside accommodations. Relax on vintage furnishings by the weathered stone fireplace in the living room. Guest bedrooms are appointed with period antiques and fine linens. Savor a full breakfast in the dining room. Unwind on porch rockers overlooking the lighthouse and an island. One-to-five bedroom cottages are tucked among the trees or along the shore. Most offer living rooms with woodburning fireplaces and kitchens. The old homestead, the Oakland House, is an acclaimed on-site restaurant.

Historic Interest: The Brooksville area was a trading post of the Puritans of Plymouth in the early 1600s and was taken by the French in 1635, then captured by the Dutch and later abandoned. Fort George was the largest fort built by the British during the Revolutionary War. In the waters off nearby Castine, America suffered its greatest naval disaster until Pearl Harbor.

Innkeeper(s): Jim & Sally Littlefield. $95-295. 10 rooms, 7 with PB, 2 with FP, 15 cottages and 2 conference rooms. Breakfast and dinner included in rates. Types of meals: Full bkfst and picnic lunch. Beds: KQDT. Reading lamp and desk in room. VCR, fax, copier, swimming, library, row boats and recreation room on premises. Weddings and family reunions hosted. Antiquing, cross-country skiing, fishing, parks, shopping, water sports, concerts, musical events, boating and whale watching nearby.

Publicity: *"One of 12 Best Spots to Dine on the Coast of New England," Redbook, Yankee Magazine's Travel Guide to New England, Downeast Magazine's "Tasting the Cottage Life," Rhode Island Monthly's Bride issue, Maine Sunday Telegram and Maine Public Broadcasting's "Home; A Place Apart."*

"We have dreamt of visiting Maine for quite some time. Our visit here at Shore Oaks and the beautiful countryside surpassed our dreams. We will be back to enjoy it again."

Brunswick J3

Brunswick B&B

165 Park Row
Brunswick, ME 04011-2000
(207)729-4914 (800)299-4914
E-mail: inn@brunswickbnb.com
Web: www.brunswickbnb.com

Circa 1849. The Brunswick Bed & Breakfast, a Greek Revival-style home, overlooks the town green. Guests often relax in one of the two front parlors, with their inviting fireplaces. Summertime guests enjoy the wraparound front porch. Rooms are filled with antiques, collectibles and quilts. In the years that the bed & breakfast served as a family home for law professor Daniel Stanwood, the home was host to an array of famed personalities, including Edna St. Vincent Millay, Thornton Wilder and Admiral Richard Byrd. Ice skating in the "mall" across the street is a popular winter activity. Freeport, only a 10-minute drive, is perfect for shoppers, and several state parks are nearby. Bowdoin College is a short walk away from the inn.

Innkeeper(s): Mercie & Steve Normand. $110-175. 8 rooms with PB, 3 suites, 1 cottage and 1 conference room. Breakfast and snacks/refreshments included in rates. Types of meals: Full bkfst, veg bkfst and early coffee/tea. Beds: KQD. Modem hook-up, reading lamp, clock radio, telephone, desk, TV in suites, terry robes, hair dryers, iron/ironing board and wireless Internet connection in room. Air conditioning. TV, bicycles, library, parlor games, fireplace and 24-hour kitchenette on premises. Weddings, small meetings, family reunions and seminars hosted. Antiquing, art galleries, beach, bicycling, canoeing/kayaking, fishing, golf, live theater, museums, parks, shopping and sporting events nearby.
Publicity: *Times Record, Coastal Journal and Atlanta Journal.*

"Good bed, great shower, fine breakfast (nice mix of substance and sweets and excellent java) and of course convivial hosts."

Camden I5

A Little Dream

60 High Street
Camden, ME 04843-1768
(207)236-8742 (800)217-0109
E-mail: dreamers1@adelphia.net
Web: www.littledream.com

Circa 1888. This Victorian was built as a guest cottage on an estate that is the home to Norumberg Castle, a vast manor built by the inventor of the dual teletype, J.B. Stearns. The rooms are wonderfully romantic, displaying a divine English-country ambiance. One room features a pencil-post bed decorated with dried flowers. Another boasts a cozy sitting area with a fireplace. Whimsical touches include a collection of teddy bears and antique toys.  Views of the bay and islands add to the romance. Breakfasts are artfully displayed on fine china. Edible flowers decorate plates with items such as an apple-brie omelet or lemon-ricotta pancakes with a raspberry sauce. Guests, if they can tear themselves away from the inn, are sure to leave rejuvenated.
Innkeeper(s): JoAnn Ball. $159-285. 7 rooms with PB, 2 with FP and 3 suites. Breakfast and afternoon tea included in rates. Types of meals: Full gourmet bkfst and early coffee/tea. Beds: KQ. Cable TV, VCR, reading lamp, refrigerator, clock radio, telephone and turn-down service in room. Air conditioning. Library and fireplace on premises. Antiquing, cross-country skiing, downhill skiing, fishing, golf, live theater, parks, shopping, tennis and water sports nearby.
Publicity: *Country Inns, Glamour, Yankee Magazine and Country Living.*

Abigail's B&B By The Sea

8 High St
Camden, ME 04843-1611
(207)236-2501 (800)292-2501 Fax:(207)230-0657
E-mail: abigails@midcoast.com
Web: www.abigailsinn.com

Circa 1847. This Federal home was the former residence of Maine senator E.K. Smart. Each guest room is decorated with poster beds, antiques, quilts, fireplaces and Jacuzzis. English  chintzes and wicker abound. Enjoy breakfast in bed or share it with other guests in the sunny dining room. Everything from French toast, scones and fresh fruit to souffles and quiche highlight the meal. An afternoon tea is

served in the parlor, which boasts two fireplaces. Unique shops, galleries, restaurants and musical festivals and craft fairs are but a few ways to enjoy this harbor-side town.
Innkeeper(s): Donna & Ed Misner. $125-225. 4 rooms with PB. Breakfast and afternoon tea included in rates. Types of meals: Full bkfst. Beds: QT. Data port in room. Air conditioning. TV and telephone on premises. Antiquing, cross-country skiing, downhill skiing, fishing, golf, live theater and water sports nearby.

The Belmont Inn

6 Belmont Ave
Camden, ME 04843-2029
(207)236-8053 (800)238-8053 Fax:(207)236-9872
E-mail: info@thebelmontinn.com
Web: www.thebelmontinn.com

Circa 1890. Perfect for a vacation in mid-coast Maine, this intimate inn is situated on the quiet yet convenient harbor side of Camden, where walking everywhere is a delight. Built in 1890 as an elegant Edwardian summer home, it is fully restored and offers the architectural grace and detail of that earlier era combined with modern comforts appreciated today. Air-conditioned guest bedrooms are spacious retreats. Savor a hearty breakfast in the dining room or on one of the porches. Mornings might start with just-baked muffins or scones, fresh fruit and a savory entrée like tomato basil frittata or sweet peaches and cream French toast with bacon or sausage. Enjoy afternoon refreshments while overlooking the garden or relaxing in one of the comfortable living rooms after exploring the waterfront or taking a scenic drive.
Innkeeper(s): Sherry & Bruce Cobb. $85-175. 6 rooms with PB, 3 with FP. Breakfast and afternoon tea included in rates. Types of meals: Full bkfst. Beds: KQDT. Reading lamp, stereo, clock radio, telephone, desk and three with gas fireplaces in room. Air conditioning. Fax, fireplace, laundry facility, cable TV and in room massage therapist available on premises. Antiquing, art galleries, bicycling, canoeing/kayaking, cross-country skiing, downhill skiing, fishing, golf, hiking, horseback riding, live theater, museums, parks, shopping, tennis and schooner cruises nearby.

Blackberry Inn

82 Elm St
Camden, ME 04843-1907
(207)236-6060 (800)388-6000
E-mail: blkberry@midcoast.com
Web: www.blackberryinn.com

Circa 1860. Blackberry Inn is a true Painted Lady, the only Maine Inn featured in "Daughters of the Painted Ladies". The exterior of the Italianate Victorian-style home is highlighted by contrasting shades of Blackberry Purple outlining its bays and friezes. Original elaborate plaster ceiling designs, polished parquet floors, finely crafted fireplace mantels, and tin ceilings grace the spacious parlors. Guest rooms are decorated in authentic Victorian period style, blended with modern amenities. Two rooms offer whirlpool tubs and four have private garden entrances. Several also include a fireplace. The inn is within walking distance to shops, the harbor and restaurants.
Innkeeper(s): Jim & Cynthia Ostrowski. $99-235. 11 rooms with PB, 7 with FP. Types of meals: Full gourmet bkfst. Beds: KQDT. Some have whirlpools in room.
Publicity: *The Miami Herald, Daughters of Painted Ladies and Yankee.*

"Charming. An authentic reflection of a grander time."

Camden Maine Stay Inn

22 High St
Camden, ME 04843
(207)236-9636 Fax:(201)236-0621
E-mail: innkeeper@camdenmainestay.com
Web: www.camdenmainestay.com

Circa 1802. The innkeepers of this treasured colonial, that is one of the oldest of the 66 houses which comprise the High Street Historic District, take great pleasure in making guests feel at home. Antiques from the 17th, 18th and 19th centuries adorn the rooms. The center of the village and the Camden Harbor are a short five-minute walk away.

Historic Interest: The Camden Opera House, historic mill and manufacturing buildings, and the First Congregational Church are among the area's historic sites.

Innkeeper(s): Bob & Juanita Topper. $100-205. 8 rooms with PB, 4 with FP and 3 suites. Breakfast and afternoon tea included in rates. Types of meals: Full gourmet bkfst and veg bkfst. Beds: QT. Cable TV, VCR, reading lamp, stereo, ceiling fan, clock radio, coffeemaker, fireplace, patio and balcony in room. Fax, copier, parlor games, telephone and fireplace on premises. Antiquing, art galleries, beach, bicycling, canoeing/kayaking, cross-country skiing, downhill skiing, fishing, golf, hiking, horseback riding, live theater, museums, parks, shopping, sporting events, tennis and water sports nearby.

Publicity: *Frommer's, Discerning Traveler, Atlanta Journal Constitution, Boston Globe, Yankee Travel Guide, Down East Magazine, Featured on cover of Johansens Recommended Inns and Hotels and Resorts for North America 2003.*

"We've traveled the East Coast from Martha's Vineyard to Bar Harbor and this is the only place we know we must return to."

Camden Windward House B&B

6 High St
Camden, ME 04843-1611
(207)236-9656 (877)492-9656 Fax:(207)230-0433
E-mail: bnb@windwardhouse.com
Web: www.windwardhouse.com

Circa 1854. Each guest room at this Greek Revival home has been individually decorated and features names such as the Carriage Room, Trisha Romance Room, Brass Room, or Silver Birch Suite. Expansive views of Mt. Battie may be seen from its

namesake room. It offers a private balcony, skylights, cathedral ceilings, sitting area with fireplace, an extra large TV and a Jacuzzi and separate shower. All rooms include antiques and romantic amenities such as candles and fine linens. The innkeepers further pamper guests with a hearty breakfast featuring a variety of juices, freshly ground coffee and teas and a choice of items such as featherbed eggs, pancakes, French toast or Belgian waffles topped with fresh Maine blueberries. After the morning meal, guests are sure to enjoy a day exploring Camden, noted as the village where "the mountains meet the sea." The inn is open year-round.

Innkeeper(s): Phil & Liane Brookes. $99-269. 8 rooms with PB, 5 with FP. Breakfast and afternoon tea included in rates. Types of meals: Full gourmet bkfst and early coffee/tea. Beds: KQ. TV, reading lamp, ceiling fan, clock radio, desk, two with Jacuzzi whirlpool tubs, two with antique claw foot soaking tubs, phones with data port, individual air conditioning, some with private balcony or deck and some with VCRs and/or separate sitting rooms in room. Fax, copier, library, parlor games, telephone and fireplace on premises. Small meetings hosted. Antiquing, cross-country skiing, downhill skiing, fishing, live theater, parks, shopping, water sports, windjammer cruises and hiking nearby.

Captain Swift Inn

72 Elm St
Camden, ME 04843-1907
(207)236-8113 (800)251-0865 Fax:(207)230-0464

Circa 1810. This inviting Federal-style home remains much as it did in the 19th century, including the original 12-over-12 windows and a beehive oven. The innkeepers have worked diligently to preserve the historic flavor, and the home's original five fireplaces, handsome wide pine floors, restored moldings and exposed beams add to the warm and cozy interior. Guest rooms are filled with period antiques and reproductions and offer down pillows, handmade quilts and comfortable beds. The only addition

to the home was a new section, which includes the innkeeper's quarters, a kitchen and a guest room entirely accessible for guests with wheelchairs. A gourmet, three-course breakfast includes items that sound decadent, but are truly low in fat and cholesterol, such as an apple pancake souffle.

Innkeeper(s): Tom & Kathy Filip. $95-125. 4 rooms with PB. Breakfast and afternoon tea included in rates. Types of meals: Full gourmet bkfst and early coffee/tea. Beds: QT. Reading lamp, clock radio and table and chairs in room. Air conditioning. VCR, fax, copier, library, parlor games and telephone on premises. Limited handicap access. Small meetings and family reunions hosted. Antiquing, cross-country skiing, downhill skiing, fishing, golf, live theater, parks, shopping, tennis, water sports, schooners, lighthouses and museums nearby.

Publicity: *Maine Boats & Harbors, Boston Patriot Ledger, Tea-Time Journeys, Secrets of Entertaining and Wake Up & Smell the Coffee.*

"We came intending to stay for one night and ended up staying for five. . .need we say more!"

The Elms B&B

84 Elm St
Camden, ME 04843-1907
(207)236-6250 (800)755-3567 Fax:(207)236-7330
E-mail: info@elmsinn.net
Web: www.elmsinn.net

Circa 1806. Captain Calvin Curtis built this Colonial a few minutes' stroll from the picturesque harbor. Candlelight shimmers year round from the inn's windows. A sitting room, library and parlor are open for guests. Tastefully appointed bed chambers scattered with antiques are available in both the main house and the carriage house. A cottage garden can be seen beside the carriage house. A lighthouse theme permeates the decor, and there is a wide selection of lighthouse books, collectibles and artwork.

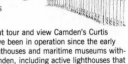

Historic Interest: Guests can take a boat tour and view Camden's Curtis Island lighthouse and others, which have been in operation since the early 19th century. There are a variety of lighthouses and maritime museums within an hour to an hour and a half of Camden, including active lighthouses that date back to the 1820s.

Innkeeper(s): Ted & Jo Panayotoff. $90-125. 6 rooms with PB, 3 with FP. Breakfast and afternoon tea included in rates. Types of meals: Full bkfst and early coffee/tea. Beds: QT. Telephone in room. Parlor games and fireplace on premises. Limited handicap access. Antiquing, cross-country skiing, downhill skiing, live theater, parks, shopping, windjammer trips, lighthouses, museums, sailing and hiking nearby.

"If something is worth doing, it's worth doing first class, and your place is definitely first class."

Hawthorn Inn Bed & Breakfast

9 High St
Camden, ME 04843-1610
(207)236-8842 Fax:(207)236-6181
E-mail: info@camdenhawthorn.com
Web: www.camdenhawthorn.com

Circa 1894. This handsome yellow and white turreted Victorian sits on an acre and a half of sloping lawns with a view of the harbor. The interior boasts a grand, three-story staircase and original stained-glass windows. The inn has 10 rooms with private baths. The Carriage House rooms offer harbor views, private decks, double Jacuzzi tubs and fireplaces. A three-course breakfast is served by fireside or, during warm weather, guests are invited to eat on the deck overlooking the harbor.

Historic Interest: Downtown Camden features many shops, galleries and restaurants nestled around its beautiful harbor.

Innkeeper(s): Maryanne Shanahan. $100-240. 10 rooms with PB, 5 with FP. Breakfast included in rates. Types of meals: Full bkfst and early coffee/tea. Beds: QDT. Reading lamp, clock radio, phone and TV and VCR in some rooms in room. Fax, parlor games, telephone and fireplace on premises. Small meetings hosted. Antiquing, bicycling, cross-country skiing, downhill skiing, hiking, shopping, sailing, ocean kayaking and island hopping nearby.

Publicity: *Glamour, Country Inns, Outside, Yankee, Down East, Cleveland Plain Dealer and Minneapolis Tribune.*

"The outstanding location, excellent rates and marvelous innkeeper make this one of the B&Bs we will frequent for years to come."

Lord Camden Inn

24 Main St
Camden, ME 04843-1704
(207)236-4325 (800)336-4325 Fax:(207)236-7141

Circa 1893. Lord Camden Inn, housed in a century-old brick building, offers the gentle warmth of a seaside inn with all the comforts and services of a modern downtown hotel. Located in the midst of Camden's fine shops and restaurants, the bustling waterfront and beautiful parks, Lord Camden Inn offers splendid views of the harbor, Camden Hills and the village. Amenities include private baths, cable TV, air conditioning, phones and elevator services.

Historic Interest: Conway House (1 mile), Fort Knox (45 minutes), Children Chapel (1-1/2 miles), Owls Head Museum Montpelier (8 miles), Lime Kilns Rockport Harbor.

Innkeeper(s): Stuart & Marianne Smith. $90-220. 31 rooms with PB, 4 suites and 1 conference room. Breakfast included in rates. Types of meals: Full bkfst and early coffee/tea. Beds: KQD. Clock radio, telephone, some microwaves and refrigerators in room. TV, fax, copier and valet service available in high season on premises. Weddings, small meetings, family reunions and seminars hosted. Antiquing, cross-country skiing, downhill skiing, fishing, live theater, parks, shopping, water sports, sailing, fine dining, bicycle rentals, kayaking and hiking nearby.

Publicity: *Portland Magazine and Thinner.*

Swan House B&B

49 Mountain St
Camden, ME 04843-1635
(207)236-8275 (800)207-8275 Fax:(207)236-0906
E-mail: hikeinn@swanhouse.com
Web: www.swanhouse.com

Circa 1870. Nestled on just under an acre of wooded grounds at the foot of Mt. Battie, this Victorian is a welcoming site inside and out. Antique-filled guest rooms are comfortable, each named for a different variety of swan. Four of the rooms offer private entrances. The Lohengrin Suite is a spacious room with its own sitting area, while the Trumpeter Room offers a private deck. Hearty breakfasts include country-style fare, fruit, homemade granola and special pastry of the day. The village of Camden and the surrounding area offer plenty of activities, and the innkeepers are happy to point guests in an interesting direction.

Innkeeper(s): Lyn & Ken Kohl. $110-175. 6 rooms with PB and 1 suite. Breakfast included in rates. Types of meals: Full bkfst, early coffee/tea and afternoon tea. Beds: QD. Clock radio and telephone in room. Fax, parlor games, gazebo and mountain hiking trails on premises. Small meetings and family reunions hosted. Antiquing, cross-country skiing, downhill skiing, fishing, live theater, parks, shopping, water sports and mountain hiking trails nearby.

"We loved our stay at the Swan House and our breakfast there was by far the most excellent breakfast we have ever had."

Cape Neddick   K2

Cape Neddick House

1300 Route 1
Cape Neddick, ME 03902
(207)363-2500
E-mail: capeneddickhouse@aol.com
Web: www.capeneddickhouse.com

Circa 1885. Rest assured, as the scent of fresh-baked blueberry poppyseed scones and ham and sticky buns drifts up upward, an alarm clock is not needed at this renovated Victorian farmhouse. Begin the day's breakfast feast with fresh flowers and settings of china and crystal in the dining room. For a more casual meal on the deck, overlook the 10 acres of gardens and woods. In winter, a fun treat is to gather by the Glenwood as Dianne has mastered the lost art of cooking with a real woodstove. Sustained for the day's adventures, explore York, Kittery and Ogunquit. The Diana Card Folk Gallery, a few steps away, is in what was the post office, run for 75 years by the Goodwins. The ocean, beaches, historic sites, Nubble Lighthouse and the Marginal Way are all just minutes away.

Innkeeper(s): Dianne Goodwin. $95-145. 5 rooms with PB, 1 with FP and 1 suite. Breakfast included in rates. Types of meals: Full gourmet bkfst and early coffee/tea. Beds: QD. Reading lamp and clock radio in room. Air conditioning. TV, VCR, library, parlor games, telephone, fireplace, coffeemaker, refrigerator in the hall and cooking classes available from November to May on premises. Small meetings and family reunions hosted. Amusement parks, antiquing, art galleries, beach, bicycling, canoeing/kayaking, cross-country skiing, fishing, golf, hiking, horseback riding, live theater, museums, parks, shopping, tennis, water sports and wineries nearby.

Publicity: *Boston Globe, York County Coast Star, WFBS Channel 3 from Hartford and CT.*

"A wonderful vacation from all. Breakfast was super."

Castine   I5

The Castine Harbor Lodge

PO Box 215
Castine, ME 04421-0215
(207)326-4335 (866)566-1550
E-mail: chl@acadia.net
Web: www.castinemaine.com

Circa 1893. Overlooking Penobscot Bay, relax on the expansive harbor-side verandas of this Edwardian mansion and listen to the sounds of the waves crashing on the shore. Spectacular ocean views are also seen from the guest bedrooms that exude a tranquil summer cottage ambiance. A Honeymoon Cottage sits on the water with a private deck and kitchen/living room area. Start the day with a continental breakfast buffet in the dining room or sunny porch. The Lodge's restaurant and wine bar offers spirits and Downeast cuisine in the evenings. A dock and guest moorings are available.

Historic Interest: Castine, which has been claimed as the property of four countries, is home to the Maine Maritime Academy. The academy includes old British barracks and the school keeps a training ship anchored at the town dock.

Innkeeper(s): Paul & Sara Brouillard. $75-245. 16 rooms, 10 with PB and 1 cottage. Breakfast included in rates. Types of meals: Cont plus. Beds: KQDT. Reading lamp and desk in room. Swimming, library, parlor games, telephone and fireplace on premises. Weddings, small meetings and family reunions hosted. Antiquing, fishing, golf, parks and tennis nearby.

Publicity: *Conde Nast Travel, Yankee, Boats & Harbors and Frommers.*

Center Lovell   I3

Center Lovell Inn

Rt 5
Center Lovell, ME 04016
(207)925-1575 (800)777-2698
E-mail: cox@centerlovellinn.com
Web: www.centerlovellinn.com

Circa 1805. Acclaimed by Architectural Digest and overlooking the White Mountain forest, this unusual Mississippi Steamboat-style inn is near Kezar Lake. Oriental rugs atop original wood floors and a variety of antiques decorate the rooms. A full country breakfast featuring Maine blueberries gathered by the innkeeper is served year-round in dishes such as blueberry cinnamon pancakes. New England Travel Guide listed the Center Lovell Inn as offering the best country inn dinner. Popular activities are hiking, boating, fishing and cycling along country lanes. In winter, guests can leave from the inn to 600 miles of trails for cross-country skiing and snowmobiling. A private land trust nearby also offers seven miles of trails for snowshoeing and skiing. It's 20-30 minutes to several major downhill ski areas.

Innkeeper(s): Janice & Richard Cox. $60-190. 10 rooms, 6 with PB and 1 conference room. Types of meals: Full bkfst and gourmet dinner. Beds: DT. TV and telephone in room. Spa on premises.

Publicity: *New York Magazine, Architectural Digest, Down East Magazine, Sunday Boston Globe Magazine, Wall Street Journal, London Times, Phil Donahue and Oprah Winfrey Show.*

Corea   I7

The Black Duck Inn on Corea Harbor

PO Box 39 Crowley Island Rd
Corea, ME 04624-0039
(207)963-2689 (877)963-2689 Fax:(207)963-7495
E-mail: bduck@acadia.net
Web: www.blackduck.com

Circa 1890. Two of the guest rooms at this turn-of-the-century farmhouse boast harbor views, while another offers a wooded scene out its windows. The innkeepers have decorated the home in an eclectic mix of old and new with antiques and contemporary pieces. There are two waterfront cottages for those who prefer more privacy. The full, gourmet breakfasts include house specialties, such as "eggs Black Duck" or items such as orange glazed French toast, blintzes or perhaps eggs Benedict.

Innkeeper(s): Barry Canner & Bob Travers. $105-160. 6 rooms, 4 with PB, 2 suites, 2 cottages and 1 conference room. Breakfast included in rates. Types of meals: Full gourmet bkfst and early coffee/tea. Beds: QDT. Reading lamp

and clock radio in room. TV, VCR, fax, copier, library, parlor games, telephone and fireplace on premises. Small meetings, family reunions and seminars hosted. Antiquing, art galleries, beach, bicycling, canoeing/kayaking, cross-country skiing, fishing, golf, hiking, live theater, parks, shopping and wineries nearby.

Publicity: *Boston Globe and Miami Herald.*

"Never could we have known how warmly received we would all four feel and how really restored we would be by the end of the week."

Cornish   J2

Cornish Inn

Main St
Cornish, ME 04020
(207)625-8501 (800)352-7235 Fax:(207)625-0992
E-mail: innkeeper@cornishinn.com
Web: cornishinn.com

Circa 1848. Between Maine's scenic shoreline and New Hampshire's majestic Mt. Washington Valley, sits this pleasant inn. Surrounded by the beauty of nature, the Great Ossipee and Saco rivers vie for attention from the White Mountains. The B&B's attractive country decor imparts a relaxing, casual atmosphere. Whether enjoying the lobby or one of the rockers on the large wraparound porch, any stress evaporates. Spacious guest bedrooms are cheerfully furnished in good taste. Suites easily accommodate families. Linger over a hearty, home-cooked breakfast. On Sundays, a jazz brunch is offered before venturing into the great outdoors.

Innkeeper(s): Shellie & Caleb Davis. $65-125. 16 rooms with PB and 2 suites. Breakfast included in rates. Types of meals: Country bkfst and early coffee/tea. Beds: KQDT. Reading lamp, ceiling fan and clock radio in room. Air conditioning. TV, fax, copier, library, parlor games, telephone and fireplace on premises. Weddings, small meetings, family reunions and seminars hosted. Antiquing, bicycling, canoeing/kayaking, cross-country skiing, fishing, golf, hiking, museums and shopping nearby.

Deer Isle   I5

Pilgrim's Inn

20 Main St
Deer Isle, ME 04627
(207)348-6615 (888)778-7505 Fax:(207)348-6615
E-mail: innkeeper@pilgrimsinn.com
Web: www.pilgrimsinn.com

Circa 1793. A quiet village surrounded by water is the idyllic backdrop of this meticulously restored and maintained island inn. Listed in the National Register, the massive wood-frame home boasts appealing details that reflect its historic integrity and character. All the spacious guest bedrooms feature sitting areas and overlook the Northwest Harbor and Penobscot Bay or the large mill pond across the three-acre rear lawn with 500 feet of waterfront. Three well-equipped cottages offer extra space and privacy. After a delicious breakfast, explore the area on bicycles, enjoy numerous other outdoor activities or visit nearby art galleries and a national park. Evening hors d'oeuvres by the eight-foot-wide fireplace instill idle bliss.

Historic Interest: Built in 1793.

Innkeeper(s): Dan & Michele Brown. $90-225. 12 rooms with PB and 3 cottages. Breakfast and snacks/refreshments included in rates. Types of meals: Country bkfst, veg bkfst, early coffee/tea, hors d'oeuvres and dinner. Restaurant on premises. Beds: KQDT. Reading lamp, clock radio, fireplace and water views in room. TV, fax, copier, bicycles, library, parlor games, telephone, fireplace and gift shop on premises. Weddings, small meetings, family reunions and seminars hosted. Antiquing, art galleries, beach, bicycling, canoeing/kayaking, fishing, golf, hiking, parks, shopping, tennis and water sports nearby.

Publicity: *Discerning Traveler, Travel & Leisure, Boston Globe and local TV.*

Dexter G4

Brewster Inn of Dexter, Maine

37 Zions Hill Rd
Dexter, ME 04930-1122
(207)924-3130 Fax:(207)924-9768
E-mail: innkeeper@brewsterinn.com
Web: www.brewsterinn.com

Circa 1934. Located on two acres with rose and perennial gardens, this handsome Colonial Revival-style house was built by architect John Calvin Stevens for Governor Ralph Brewster. It is in the National Register. Some guest rooms offer fireplaces, window seats, original tile bathrooms and views of the gardens. One has a whirlpool tub for two. Furnishings include antiques and reproductions. A breakfast buffet includes hot entrees such as quiche, gingerbread pancakes or stuffed apples.

Innkeeper(s): Ivy & Michael Brooks. $59-125. 10 rooms with PB, 3 with FP and 4 suites. Breakfast and snacks/refreshments included in rates. Types of meals: Full bkfst and early coffee/tea. Beds: KQDT. Cable TV, reading lamp, clock radio, telephone and books in room. Air conditioning. VCR, fax, copier, tennis, library, parlor games and fireplace on premises. Limited handicap access. Weddings, small meetings, family reunions and seminars hosted. Antiquing, cross-country skiing, fishing, golf, parks, shopping, tennis and water sports nearby.

Publicity: *Bangor Daily News, People and Places & Plants.*

Durham I3

The Bagley House

1290 Royalsborough Rd
Durham, ME 04222-5225
(207)865-6566 (800)765-1772 Fax:(207)353-5878
E-mail: bglyhse@aol.com
Web: www.bagleyhouse.com

Circa 1772. Six acres of fields and woods surround the Bagley House. Once an inn, a store and a schoolhouse, it is the oldest house in town. Guest rooms are decorated with colonial furnishings and hand-sewn quilts. For breakfast, guests gather in the country kitchen in front of a huge brick fireplace and beehive oven.

Historic Interest: Bowdoin College, Maritime Museum and Old Sea Captain Homes.

Innkeeper(s): Suzanne O'Connor & Susan Backhouse. $95-175. 8 rooms with PB, 4 with FP and 1 conference room. Breakfast and afternoon tea included in rates. Types of meals: Full bkfst, early coffee/tea, picnic lunch and snacks/refreshments. Beds: KQDT. Reading lamp, refrigerator and desk in room. Fax, telephone, fireplace and blueberry picking on premises. Small meetings and family reunions hosted. Antiquing, cross-country skiing, downhill skiing, live theater, shopping and sporting events nearby.

Publicity: *Los Angeles Times, New England Getaways, Lewiston Sun, Springfield Register and 2001 Yankee Magazine-Editors Pick.*

"I had the good fortune to stumble on the Bagley House. The rooms are well-appointed and the innkeepers are charming."

East Boothbay J4

Ocean Point Inn

Shore Rd
East Boothbay, ME 04544
(207)633-4200 (800)552-5554
E-mail: opi@oceanpointinn.com
Web: www.oceanpointinn.com

Circa 1898. Ocean Point Inn is comprised of a white clapboard main house, lodge, cottages, apartments and motel units located on three oceanfront acres. There are gardens and a lovely road along the bay where guests watch lobstermen, seals and passing windjammers. Four lighthouses may be viewed among the nearby islands. Boothbay Harbor is six miles away, but right at hand is the town pier and the inn's restaurant

with a view of the ocean. In addition to lobster dishes and crab cakes, the specialty of the house is fresh Maine salmon. Select from a wide choice of activities such as swimming, fishing and hiking, or simply settle into the Adirondack chairs and watch the soothing sea. Guests can rent motor boats or kayaks in Boothbay Harbor.

Innkeeper(s): Beth & Dave Dudley. $120-190. 61 rooms with PB, 3 with FP, 10 suites and 7 cottages. Types of meals: Full bkfst and dinner. Beds: KQDT. Cable TV, telephone and mini-refrigerators in room. Air conditioning. Outdoor heated pool and hot tub on premises. Family reunions hosted. Antiquing, fishing, golf, live theater, parks, shopping, tennis and kayaking nearby.

Eastport G8

The Milliken House B&B

29 Washington St
Eastport, ME 04631
(207)853-2955 (888)507-9370 Fax:(207)853-4830

Circa 1846. This inn is filled with beautiful furnishings and knickknacks, much of which belonged to the home's first owner, Benjamin Milliken. Ornately carved, marble-topped pieces and period decor take guests back in time to the Victorian era. Milliken maintained a wharf on Eastport's waterfront from which he serviced the tall trading ships that used the harbor as a port of entry to the United States. An afternoon glass of port or sherry and chocolate turn-down service are among the amenities. Breakfasts are a gourmet treat, served in the dining room with its carved, antique furnishings.

Historic Interest: The waterfront historic district is just two blocks away as is the Barracks Historical Museum.

Innkeeper(s): Bill & Mary Williams. $65. 6 rooms with PB. Breakfast and snacks/refreshments included in rates. Types of meals: Full bkfst, early coffee/tea and afternoon tea. Beds: QDT. TV, VCR, fax, copier, parlor games, telephone and fireplace on premises. Small meetings and family reunions hosted. Antiquing, art galleries, beach, canoeing/kayaking, fishing and hiking nearby.

"A lovely trip back in history to a more gracious time."

Todd House

Todd's Head
Eastport, ME 04631
(207)853-2328

Circa 1775. Todd House is a typical full-Cape-style house with a huge center chimney. In 1801, Eastern Lodge No. 7 of the Masonic Order was chartered here. It became temporary barracks when Todd's Head was fortified. Guests may use barbecue facilities overlooking Passamaquoddy Bay. Children and well-behaved pets are welcome.

Innkeeper(s): Ruth McInnis. $50-95. 6 rooms, 2 with PB, 3 with FP and 2 suites. Breakfast included in rates. Types of meals: Cont plus. Beds: QDT. Cable TV, VCR, reading lamp and refrigerator in room. Library, parlor games and telephone on premises. Limited handicap access. Antiquing, art galleries, beach, canoeing/kayaking, fishing, golf, hiking, live theater, museums, parks, shopping and tennis nearby.

Publicity: *Portland Press Herald.*

"Your house and hospitality were real memory makers of our vacation."

Weston House

26 Boynton St
Eastport, ME 04631-1305
(207)853-2907 (800)853-2907 Fax:(207)853-0981

Circa 1810. Jonathan Weston, an 1802 Harvard graduate, built this Federal-style house on a hill overlooking Passamaquoddy Bay. James Audubon stayed here as a guest of the Westons while awaiting passage to Labrador in 1833. Each guest room is furnished with antiques and Oriental rugs. The

Weston and Audubon rooms boast views of the bay and gardens. Breakfast menus vary, including such delectables as heavenly pancakes with hot apricot syrup or freshly baked muffins and coddled eggs. Seasonal brunches are served on weekends and holidays. The area is full of outdoor activities, including whale watching. Nearby Saint Andrews-by-the-Sea offers plenty of shops and restaurants.

Historic Interest: Nearby historic attractions include Campobello Island, where Franklin D. Roosevelt spent his summers. King's Landing, a restored Loyalist settlement dating back to 1780, is two hours away.

Innkeeper(s): Jett & John Peterson. $65-85. 3 rooms. Breakfast and afternoon tea included in rates. Types of meals: Full gourmet bkfst and picnic lunch. Beds: KQD. Cable TV, reading lamp, clock radio and desk in room. Parlor games, telephone and fireplace on premises. Weddings, small meetings and family reunions hosted. Fishing, live theater, shopping, tennis, whale watching and nature nearby.

Publicity: *Down East, Los Angeles Times, Boston Globe, Boston Magazine and New York Times.*

"All parts of ourselves have been nourished."

Edgecomb   J4

Cod Cove Farm B&B

117 Boothbay Road
Edgecomb, ME 04556
(207)882-4299 (800)293-7718
E-mail: stay@codcovefarm.com
Web: www.codcovefarm.com

Circa 1840. Distant views of the Sheepscot River and Wicasset are seen from this high-posted, cape-cod style farmhouse with post-and-beam barn on five acres. Cozy moments are spent

playing the Steinway, watching TV, reading, playing games and enjoying afternoon refreshments in the common areas. Gracious and imaginative guest bedrooms boast various whimsical themes. A variety of tasty breakfast fare includes Adirondack flapjacks and Scottish scones with homemade jams. Go on a whale watching adventure, or take a dinner sail out of nearby Boothbay Harbor.

Innkeeper(s): Don & Charlene Schuman. $95-115. 4 rooms, 2 with PB. Breakfast, afternoon tea and snacks/refreshments included in rates. Types of meals: Full gourmet bkfst, veg bkfst and early coffee/tea. Beds: KQ. Turndown service in room. Central air. TV, VCR, parlor games, telephone, fireplace and gift shop on premises. Weddings, small meetings, family reunions and seminars hosted. Antiquing, art galleries, beach, bicycling, canoeing/kayaking, fishing, golf, hiking, horseback riding, live theater, museums, parks, shopping, water sports, Chewonki Foundation Maine Coast Semester Program and Watershed Center for the Arts nearby.

Eliot   L2

High Meadows B&B

Rt 101
Eliot, ME 03903
(207)439-0590 Fax:(207)439-6343

Circa 1740. A ship's captain built this house, now filled with remembrances of colonial days. At one point, it was raised and a floor added underneath, so the upstairs is older than the downstairs. It is conveniently located to factory outlets in Kittery, Maine, and great dining and historic museums in Portsmouth, N.H.

Innkeeper(s): Elaine. $80-90. 4 rooms with PB. Breakfast and afternoon tea included in rates. Types of meals: Full bkfst and early coffee/tea. Beds: QDT. Reading lamp in room. Telephone and fireplace on premises. Weddings, small meetings and family reunions hosted. Antiquing, fishing, shopping and water sports nearby.

Publicity: *Portsmouth Herald and York County Focus.*

"High Meadows was the highlight of our trip."

Freeport   J3

Captain Briggs House B&B

8 Maple Ave
Freeport, ME 04032-1315
(207)865-1868 (888)217-2477 Fax:(207)865-6083
E-mail: briggsbb@suscom-maine.net
Web: www.captainbriggs.net

Circa 1853. This mid-19th-century home's most notable resident was John A. Briggs, a shipbuilder. There are six comfortable guest rooms, all with private baths. A full breakfast prepares guests for a day of outlet shopping in Freeport. The famous L.L. Bean factory store and other outlets are just minutes away. Harbor cruises, fishing, seal watching, hiking and just enjoying the scenery in this coastal town are other options.

Innkeeper(s): Celia & Rob Elberfeld. $85-140. 6 rooms with PB. Breakfast, afternoon tea and snacks/refreshments included in rates. Types of meals: Full gourmet bkfst. Beds: KQDT. Reading lamp and clock radio in room. Air conditioning. TV, VCR, fax, copier and telephone on premises. Family reunions hosted. Amusement parks, antiquing, art galleries, beach, bicycling, canoeing/kayaking, cross-country skiing, fishing, golf, hiking, live theater, museums, parks, shopping, water sports, LL Bean Outlets, seal watching and harbor cruises nearby.

Publicity: *New York Times.*

Captain Josiah Mitchell House B&B

188 Main St
Freeport, ME 04032-1407
(207)865-3289

Circa 1789. Captain Josiah Mitchell was commander of the clipper ship "Hornet." In 1866, en route from New York to San Francisco it caught fire, burned and was lost. The passengers and crew survived in three longboats, drifting for 45 days. When the boats finally drifted into one of the South Pacific Islands, Samuel Clemens was there, befriended the Captain and wrote his first story, under the name of Mark Twain and about the captain. The diary of Captain Mitchell parallels episodes of "Mutiny on the Bounty." Flower gardens and a porch swing on the veranda now welcome guests to Freeport and Captain Mitchell's House.

Historic Interest: Henry Wadsworth Longfellow house (13 miles), Admiral McMillan, polar explorer with Perry, Bowdoin College (7 miles) and Freeport.
Innkeeper(s): Alan & Loretta Bradley. $78-95. 7 rooms with PB. Breakfast included in rates. Types of meals: Full bkfst. Beds: QDT. Reading lamp, ceiling fan and clock radio in room. Air conditioning. TV and telephone on premises. Amusement parks, antiquing, cross-country skiing, downhill skiing, fishing, live theater, parks, shopping, sporting events and LL Bean nearby.
Publicity: *Famous Boats and Harbors.*

"Your wonderful stories brought us all together. You have created a special place that nurtures and brings happiness and love. This has been a dream!"

Harraseeket Inn

162 Main St
Freeport, ME 04032-1311
(207)865-9377 (800)342-6423 Fax:(207)865-1684
E-mail: harraseeke@aol.com
Web: www.stayfreeport.com

Circa 1889. The tavern and drawing room of this inn are decorated in the Federal style. Guest rooms are furnished with antiques and half-canopied beds. Some have whirlpools and fireplaces. The inn features two restaurants and offers a buffet breakfast. The L.L. Bean store is just two blocks away, with 130 outlet stores such as Ralph Lauren and Anne Klein nearby.
Innkeeper(s): Gray Family. $140-325. 93 rooms with PB, 16 with FP, 3 suites and 5 conference rooms. Breakfast and afternoon tea included in rates. Types of meals: Full gourmet bkfst, lunch, dinner and room service. Restaurant on premises. Beds: KQD. TV, fax, copier, swimming, telephone, wood fired oven and grill, exercise equipment, indoor pool and two restaurants on premises. Limited handicap access. Antiquing, cross-country skiing, fishing and live theater nearby.

Kendall Tavern B&B

213 Main St
Freeport, ME 04032-1411
(207)865-1338 (800)341-9572 Fax:(207)865-9213
E-mail: info@kendalltavern.com
Web: www.kendalltavern.com

Circa 1800. Kendall Tavern is a welcoming farmhouse painted in a cheerful, creamy yellow hue with white trim. The interior is appointed in an elegant New England country style. Each of the parlors has a fireplace. Our parlor is a perfect place to curl up with a book, the other has a television and VCR. Breakfasts are creative and plentiful. The morning meal might start off with poached pears topped with a French vanilla yogurt sauce and accompanied by blueberry muffins. From there, guests enjoy a broccoli and mushroom quiche, grilled ham and home

fries. Another menu might include baked apples stuffed with cranberries, cream cheese raspberry coffeecake, blueberry pancakes, scrambled eggs and crisp bacon. Whatever the menu, the breakfast is always a perfect start to a day of shopping in outlet stores, hiking, sailing or cross-country skiing, all of which are nearby.
Innkeeper(s): Carrie J. McBride. $95-155. 7 rooms with PB. Breakfast and afternoon tea included in rates. Types of meals: Country bkfst and early coffee/tea. Beds: QDT. Reading lamp in room. Air conditioning. TV, fax, copier, parlor games, telephone and fireplace on premises. Small meetings and family reunions hosted. Antiquing, art galleries, beach, bicycling, canoeing/kayaking, cross-country skiing, fishing, golf, hiking, horseback riding, live theater, museums, parks, shopping and tennis nearby.

Maple Hill B&B

18 Maple Ave
Freeport, ME 04032-1315
(207)865-3730 (800)867-0478 Fax:(207)865-6727
E-mail: mplhll@aol.com
Web: www.maplehillbedandbreakfast.com

Circa 1831. Maple Hill is comprised of a Greek Revival farmhouse and attached barn located on two tree-shaded acres of lawns and gardens. Furnished with antiques, the inn is in an amazing location two blocks from L. L. Bean. A family suite is offered (the innkeepers have raised six children and enjoy hosting families). Queen-size guest rooms are also available, and a romantic atmosphere is provided at the inn with its fireplace, candlelight, flowers and music. Hearty breakfasts are served in the morning, featuring fruit compotes, French toast, waffles, blueberry muffins or biscuits.
Innkeeper(s): Lloyd & Susie Lawrence. $110-170. 3 rooms with PB, 1 suite and 1 conference room. Types of meals: Country bkfst, veg bkfst, early coffee/tea, afternoon tea and snacks/refreshments. Beds: KQT. Cable TV, VCR, reading lamp, clock radio and desk in room. Air conditioning. Fax, copier, bicycles, library, parlor games, telephone, fireplace, laundry facility and child care available on premises. Weddings, small meetings, family reunions and seminars hosted. Antiquing, art galleries, beach, bicycling, canoeing/kayaking, cross-country skiing, fishing, golf, hiking, horseback riding, live theater, museums, parks, shopping, sporting events, tennis and water sports nearby.
Publicity: *McCalls.*

Fryeburg I1

Admiral Peary House

9 Elm St
Fryeburg, ME 04037-1114
(207)935-3365 (877)-4ADMPRY Fax:(207)935-3698

Circa 1865. Sitting on six and a half tranquil acres of lawns, perennial gardens and woods, this historic home is in the oldest village in the White Mountains. Admiral Robert E. Peary, an arctic explorer who discovered the North Pole, once resided here. Relax in tasteful and immaculate surroundings. A regulation billiards table and massive fireplace are showcased in the spacious living room with comfortable sitting areas. Take a nap or read on the three-season screened porch that overlooks the lush grounds. After a good night's sleep savor a well-presented gourmet breakfast in the kitchen. Rent snowshoes for on-site trails. Nearby lakes, rivers and mountains offer year-round activities to experience and enjoy.
Innkeeper(s): Hilary Jones & Derrek Schlottmann. $95-205. 7 rooms with PB. Breakfast included in rates. Types of meals: Full gourmet bkfst, veg bkfst, early coffee/tea and snacks/refreshments. Beds: KQT. Reading lamp, clock radio and desk in room. Air conditioning. TV, VCR, fax, spa, library, parlor games, telephone, fireplace, fireside living room, billiards, snowshoe trail and rentals on premises. Weddings, small meetings and seminars hosted.

Antiquing, beach, bicycling, canoeing/kayaking, cross-country skiing, downhill skiing, fishing, golf, hiking, horseback riding, live theater, museums, parks, shopping, tennis, water sports, snowshoeing and snowmobiling nearby.

Publicity: *Mountain Ear.*

Peace With-Inn Bed & Breakfast

Rte.113 West Fryburg Road
Fryeburg, ME 04037
(207)935-7363 (866)935-7322
E-mail: info@peacewithinn.com
Web: www.peacewithinn.com

Circa 1750. Simple pleasures and generous amenities highlight the tranquility and relaxation found at the historic Hardy Farm. Feel welcomed with complimentary refreshments upon check-in. Guest bedrooms feature antiques, fine linens on comfortable beds, Gilchrist and Soames toiletries, luxurious robes, bottled water, fresh flowers, European chocolates and towel heaters. Stay in the Notch room boasting a Select Comfort bed and Jacuzzi for two or choose the first-floor Fireside Room with a gas fireplace. Families appreciate the suite created by adjoining the Meadow and Forest rooms. Wake up hungry to feast on a multiple-course New England-style breakfast. Ask about special packages available. Most personal requests can be arranged from dietary needs to champagne to in-room massage. Enjoy numerous year-round activities.

Innkeeper(s): The Link Family. $90-125. 4 rooms with PB, 1 with FP and 1 suite. Breakfast and snacks/refreshments included in rates. Types of meals: Full gourmet bkfst, veg bkfst, early coffee/tea, picnic lunch and room service. Beds: Q. Cable TV, VCR, CD player, ceiling fan, clock radio, telephone and hot tub/spa in room. Spa, fax, copier, spa, bicycles, library, parlor games and fireplace on premises. Weddings, small meetings and family reunions hosted. Antiquing, beach, bicycling, canoeing/kayaking, cross-country skiing, downhill skiing, fishing, golf, hiking, horseback riding, live theater and shopping nearby.

Gouldsboro H6

Sunset House

Rt 186, HCR 60
Gouldsboro, ME 04607
(207)963-7156 (800)233-7156 Fax:(207)963-5859

Circa 1898. This coastal country farm inn is situated near Acadia National Park. Naturalists can observe rare birds and other wildlife in an unspoiled setting. Seven spacious bedrooms are spread over three floors. Four of the bedrooms have ocean views; a fifth overlooks a freshwater pond behind the house. During winter, guests can ice skate on the pond, while in summer it is used for swimming. The 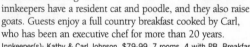 innkeepers have a resident cat and poodle, and they also raise goats. Guests enjoy a full country breakfast cooked by Carl, who has been an executive chef for more than 20 years.

Innkeeper(s): Kathy & Carl Johnson. $79-99. 7 rooms, 4 with PB. Breakfast included in rates. Types of meals: Full gourmet bkfst, veg bkfst and early coffee/tea. Beds: KQDT. Reading lamp, clock radio and turn-down service in room. TV, VCR, fax, copier, swimming, parlor games, telephone and fireplace on premises. Family reunions hosted. Antiquing, art galleries, bicycling, canoeing/kayaking, cross-country skiing, fishing, golf, parks, shopping, tennis and wineries nearby.

Greenville F4

Blair Hill Inn at Moosehead Lake

351 Lily Bay Rd
Greenville, ME 04441
(207)695-0224 Fax:(207)695-4324
E-mail: info@blairhill.com
Web: www.blairhill.com

Circa 1891. An impressive Queen Anne Victorian, this inn sits on a breathtaking 15-acre estate. Majestically situated on a tranquil hill, guarded by cannons and a high stone wall, there are spectacular panoramic views of Moosehead Lake, its islands and the surrounding mountains. Luxurious pleasures abound throughout the elegant inn with seven fireplaces, a 90-foot veranda, outdoor Jacuzzi, exercise room, massage therapy, art gallery and concierge. The plush guest bedrooms are filled with unexpected surprises. Encounter feather beds and fine linens, soft robes, aromatherapy candles and personal products, fresh flowers and bottled water. Breakfast is a gastronomical masterpiece, and dining at the inn's restaurant is a must. On-site seasonal activities include croquet, badminton, bocce ball, a catch-and-release trout pond, snowshoeing and hiking.

Historic Interest: The inn was built in 1891 at the center of Blair Hill with the best vantage point for dramatic views found in the entire area. Built atop a massive stone wall, with historic cannons guarding the estate and its beautiful gardens. The architectural beauty of the main home is significant. High, coved ceilings, large pocket doors, French doors, seven wood-burning fireplaces, winding staircase and Tiffany light fixtures are among the many historic details.

Innkeeper(s): Dan & Ruth McLaughlin. $200-450. 8 rooms with PB, 4 with FP and 1 conference room. Breakfast included in rates. Types of meals: Full gourmet bkfst. Restaurant on premises. Beds: KQ. Reading lamp, CD player, ceiling fan, clock radio, turn-down service, desk, CD players, plush terry robes, feather beds, down comforters and pillows, 312-count linens, all natural bath and body products produced locally especially for the Blair Hill Inn, candles, fresh flowers, hair dryers and fireplace in room. TV, VCR, fax, copier, spa, library, telephone, fireplace, spa towels and guest refrigerator with spring water and juices, hiking trails, snowshoeing, massage therapy, catch and release trout pond, Adirondack chairs, extensive gardens, wildflower fields, woodlands, exercise room, fine wines and cocktails on premises. Weddings, small meetings and family reunions hosted. Antiquing, art galleries, beach, bicycling, canoeing/kayaking, cross-country skiing, downhill skiing, fishing, golf, hiking, horseback riding, parks, shopping, tennis, water sports, moose safari, snowshoeing, dog sledding, sea plane tours, white water rafting and snowmobiling nearby.

Publicity: *Travel & Leisure, Boston Globe, Down East Magazine, Yankee Magazine-2000 Editor's Pick, The Garden Magazine of Maine, Architectural Digest, ESPN, NESN, Maine PBS and The Wild Wild Web Show.*

Greenville Inn

Norris St, PO Box 1194
Greenville, ME 04441-1194
(207)695-2206 (888)695-6000 Fax:(207)695-0335
E-mail: gvlinn@moosehead.net
Web: www.greenvilleinn.com

Circa 1895. Lumber baron William Shaw built this inn, which sits on a hill overlooking Moosehead Lake and the Squaw Mountains. The inn includes many unique features. Ten years were needed to complete the embellishments on the cherry and mahogany paneling, which is found throughout the inn. A spruce tree is painted on one of the leaded-glass windows on the stairway landing. The inn's six fireplaces are adorned with carved mantels, English tiles and mosaics. The inn's dining room is

ideal for a romantic dinner. Fresh, seasonal ingredients fill the ever-changing menu, and the dining room also offers a variety of wine choices.

Historic Interest: SS Katahdin, restored steamship offering daily cruises, in season (nearby), Moosehead Marine Museum (nearby), Evelyth Craft-Sheridan Historical House Museum (2 miles).

Innkeeper(s): Terry & Jeff Johannemann. $140-275. 12 rooms with PB, 2 with FP, 2 suites and 6 cottages. Types of meals: Full bkfst. Restaurant on premises. Beds: KQDT. TV and reading lamp in room. Hearty buffet breakfast and fine dining restaurant on premises. Weddings, small meetings and family reunions hosted.

Publicity: *Travel & Leisure, Travel Holiday, Maine Times, Portland Monthly, Bangor Daily News and Grays Sporting Journal.*

"The fanciest place in town. It is indeed a splendid place."

The Lodge at Moosehead Lake

Upon Lily Bay Rd, Box 1167
Greenville, ME 04441
(207)695-4400 Fax:(207)695-2281
E-mail: innkeeper@lodgeatmooseheadlake.com
Web: www.lodgeatmooseheadlake.com

Circa 1916. Westerly views of the lake can be enjoyed from four of the five lodge rooms, all of the suites, the living and dining rooms of this inn. Each of the lodge rooms have hand-carved, four-poster beds with dual-control electric blankets and fireplaces. At the end of the day, relax in a Jacuzzi tub found in each private bath. In 1997, the adjacent carriage house was transformed into three luxurious suites that offer a total retreat. Each of the suites feature the above as well as river-stone whirlpool baths, sunken living rooms and private decks and gardens. The Katahdin Suite has a King-size bed and a fireplace in the bathroom. The Allegash and Baxter Suites feature Queen-size beds that are suspended from the ceiling to gently rock visitors to sleep.

Innkeeper(s): Sonda & Bruce Hamilton. $205-475. 8 rooms with PB. Breakfast included in rates. Types of meals: Full bkfst. Beds: Q. Cable TV, VCR, reading lamp, clock radio, turn-down service, Jacuzzi, electric blankets, seven with lake views and mountain view in room. Air conditioning. Telephone, fireplace and guest pantry on premises. Small meetings and seminars hosted. Canoeing/kayaking, cross-country skiing, downhill skiing, fishing, golf, hiking, horseback riding and water sports nearby.

Publicity: *Country Inns, Getaways, Country Living, Country Home, Travel & Leisure, Travel Holiday, Globe and Great Country Inns TV program.*

Guilford   G4

Trebor Mansion Inn

11 A Golda Ct
Guilford, ME 04443
(207)876-4070 (888)280-7575
E-mail: info@trebormansioninn.com
Web: www.trebormansioninn.com

Circa 1830. High on a hill in the Lakes Region sits this archi-tectural treasure listed in the National Register, boasting the original slate roof, woodwork and stained-glass windows. Built in 1830, its Queen Anne Stick Jacobean style had not yet exist-ed, yet overwhelming evidence and photographs support this date. Relax on the veranda, wraparound porch or balconies. Stroll the three-acre grounds with benches and swings on land-scaped lawns, picnic areas, sugar maples and mature oaks over-looking the Piscataquis River. Elegant guest bedrooms feature comfortable furnishings, artwork and books that together create an informal ambiance. Breakfast is served daily at nine o'clock.

Extended visits are welcome depending on seasonal availability. Ask about Hunting Lodge specials.

Innkeeper(s): The Shaffer Family. $30-110. 8 rooms, 4 with PB. Types of meals: Cont. Beds: KQDT. VCR in room. Telephone, fireplace, breakfast avail-able at small premium and other meals may be available on premises. Weddings, small meetings, family reunions and seminars hosted. Antiquing, cross-country skiing, downhill skiing, fishing, golf, parks, shopping, tennis, water sports, hunting and snowmobiling nearby.

Isle Au Haut   I5

The Keeper's House

PO Box 26
Isle Au Haut, ME 04645-0026
(207)367-2261
Web: www.keepershouse.com

Circa 1907. Designed and built by the U.S. Lighthouse Service, the handsome 48-foot-high Robinson Point Light guid-ed vessels into this once-bustling island fishing village. Guests arrive on the mailboat. Innkeeper Judi Burke, whose father was a keeper at the Highland Lighthouse on Cape Cod, provides picnic lunches so guests may explore the scenic island trails. Dinner is served in the keeper's dining room. The lighthouse is adjacent to the most remote section of Acadia National Park. It's not uncommon to hear the cry of an osprey, see deer approach the inn, or watch seals and porpoises cavorting off the point. Guest rooms are comfortable and serene, with stunning views of the island's ragged shore line, forests and Duck Harbor.

Historic Interest: Acadia National Park, adjacent 18th-century one-room school house, church & town hall (1-mile walk away).

Innkeeper(s): Jeff & Judi Burke. $300-375. 5 rooms and 1 cottage. Breakfast and dinner included in rates. Types of meals: Full gourmet bkfst and early coffee/tea. Beds: D. Desk and wood stove in room. Swimming, bicycles, library, parlor games and fireplace on premises. Weddings, small meetings, family reunions and seminars hosted. Parks and shopping nearby.

Publicity: *New York Times, USA Today, Los Angeles Times, Ladies Home Journal, Christian Science Monitor, Down East, New York Woman, Philadelphia Inquirer, McCalls, Country, Men's Journal, Travel & Leisure, Gourmet, House Beautiful, PBS, CBS and CNN.*

"Simply one of the unique places on Earth."

Kennebunk Beach   K2

The Ocean View

171 Beach Ave
Kennebunk Beach, ME 04043-2524
(207)967-2750
E-mail: arena@theoceanview.com
Web: www.theoceanview.com

Circa 1900. Just steps from the beach, depart from the tradi-tional at this bright and cheery Painted Lady Victorian boasting a light and airy decor with hand-painted furniture and yards of colorful fabric. Enjoy the touch of whimsy and eclectic flair of the oceanfront guest bedrooms in the main house and in Ocean View Too, an extended wing that offers seaside junior suites with breakfast in bed. Baked pears with yogurt, honey and slivered almonds, followed by Belgian waffles topped with seasonal fresh fruit and a dollop of creme fraiche are some of the specialties served on colorful china in the seaside breakfast room. Visit the village of Kennebunkport, just one mile away.

Historic Interest: National Register Historic Walk.

Innkeeper(s): Carole & Bob Arena. $155-375. 9 rooms with PB and 5 suites. Breakfast and snacks/refreshments included in rates. Types of meals: Full gourmet bkfst and early coffee/tea. Beds: KQT. TV, VCR, reading lamp, CD player, ceiling fan, clock radio, telephone, desk, luxurious robes, fresh flowers, mini refrigerator, iron/ironing board, hair dryer, clock radio and CD player in room. Fax, library, parlor games, fireplace, fireplaced living room and TV room on premises. Antiquing, beach, fishing, live theater, parks, shopping, sporting events, water sports and ocean nearby.

Publicity: *New York Times, Boston, Boston Magazine, Entree and Elegance.*

Kennebunkport K2

1802 House

15 Locke Street
Kennebunkport, ME 04046-1646
(207)967-5632 (800)932-5632 Fax:(207)967-0780
E-mail: inquiry@1802inn.com
Web: www.1802inn.com

Circa 1802. The rolling fairways of Cape Arundel Golf Course, old shade trees and secluded gardens create the perfect setting for this historic 19th-century farmhouse. Located along the gentle shores of the Kennebunk River, the inn is accentuated by personal service and attention to detail. Romantic guest bedrooms offer four-poster canopy beds, two-person whirlpool tubs and fireplaces. The luxurious three-room Sebago Suite tucked into a private wing is a favorite choice. Homemade specialties and regional delights are part of a gourmet breakfast served in the sunlit dining room. Popular Dock Square is within walking distance for browsing in boutiques and art galleries. Golf packages are available.

Innkeeper(s): Edric & Mary Ellen Mason. $109-369. 6 rooms with PB, 5 with FP and 1 suite. Breakfast and snacks/refreshments included in rates. Types of meals: Full gourmet bkfst, early coffee/tea and picnic lunch. Beds: Q. Cable TV, VCR, reading lamp, CD player, clock radio, turn-down service, fireplace and whirlpool tubs in room. Air conditioning. Fax, parlor games, telephone, fireplace and gift shop on premises. Weddings, small meetings, family reunions and seminars hosted. Antiquing, art galleries, beach, bicycling, canoeing/kayaking, cross-country skiing, fishing, golf, hiking, horseback riding, live theater, museums, parks, shopping, tennis, water sports and wineries nearby.

Bufflehead Cove Inn

PO Box 499
Kennebunkport, ME 04046-0499
(207)967-3879 Fax:(207)967-3879
E-mail: info@buffaloheadcove.com
Web: www.buffleheadcove.com

Circa 1888. Travelers looking for solitude will find their dream come true at this Dutch Colonial cottage, which is tucked away in a wooded area at the edge of the tidal Kennebunk River. The busy village of Kennebunkport is within view of the inn and within walking distance. This rambling cottage takes guests back to a simple time with its full cookie jar, innkeepers' warmth and friendly conversation. Intimate breakfasts are served on a small deck. A porch filled with potted flowers is the perfect place to relax.

Historic Interest: The inn was built as a summer cottage in the late 1800s by a local boat builder. Bufflehead Cove is one of those shingle-style cottages Maine is known for. We are also on the Kennebunk River where ships were built for the King of England before the revolution.

Innkeeper(s): James & Harriet Golt. $115-350. 6 rooms with PB, 5 with FP and 1 cottage. Breakfast and snacks/refreshments included in rates. Types of meals: Full gourmet bkfst and early coffee/tea. Beds: KQ. Cable TV, reading lamp, refrigerator, ceiling fan, clock radio, turn-down service, desk, hot tub/spa and fireplace in room. Air conditioning. Fax, swimming, parlor games and telephone on premises. Family reunions hosted. Antiquing, art galleries, beach, bicycling, canoeing/kayaking, fishing, golf, hiking, live theater, parks, shopping, tennis and water sports nearby.

Publicity: *Country Inns Magazine, Discerning Traveler, New England Travel Guide and Yankee.*

Captain Fairfield Inn

8 Pleasant St
Kennebunkport, ME 04046-2690
(207)967-4454 (800)322-1928 Fax:(207)967-8537
E-mail: jrw@captainfairfield.com
Web: www.captainfairfield.com

Circa 1813. This romantic country inn is located in the heart of Kennebunkport, a seaside resort. An elegant sea captain's mansion, Captain Fairfield Inn overlooks the scenic Kennebunkport River Green. Shaded by tall trees, and on the National Register, the inn offers an enticing and gracious spot for celebrating anniversaries and honeymoons. Guest rooms are spacious, all with sitting areas, and boast period furnishings such as four-poster and canopy beds as well as fireplaces and views of the gardens or the neighborhood's historic homes. Down comforters and bouquets of fresh garden flowers are additional amenities. Ask for the Library for a special occasion and you'll enjoy a fireplace and a whirlpool tub for two. Breakfast is a lavish four-course affair and is served next to an open-hearth fireplace in the gathering room or in view of the inn's gardens. Guests enjoy the location's access to the ocean and beaches, boutique shops, art galleries and restaurants. Carriage rides and theater and spa packages are offered. Activities include kayaking, cycling, fishing, whale watching and sailing. Other activities include touring the Brick Store Museum, the Rachel Carson Preserve and the Seashore Trolley Museum.

Historic Interest: Brick Store Museum, Kennebunkport Historical Society.

Innkeeper(s): Janet & Rick Wolf. $110-295. 9 rooms with PB, 6 with FP. Breakfast, afternoon tea and snacks/refreshments included in rates. Types of meals: Full gourmet bkfst and early coffee/tea. Beds: QT. Modem hook-up, data port, reading lamp, ceiling fan, clock radio, telephone, bottled water, hair dryers, iron/ironing board and many with fireplace in room. Air conditioning. Fax, copier, library, parlor games, fireplace, piano, guest refrigerator, ice machine, maps, menus and concierge service on premises. Antiquing, art galleries, beach, bicycling, canoeing/kayaking, cross-country skiing, fishing, golf, hiking, live theater, museums and shopping nearby.

"It couldn't have been nicer...Your breakfasts were delicious and your hospitality unequaled...all in all a wonderful experience"

Captain Jefferds Inn

PO Box 691, 5 Pearl St
Kennebunkport, ME 04046-0691
(207)967-2311 (800)839-6844 Fax:(207)967-0721
E-mail: captjeff@captainjefferdsinn.com
Web: www.captainjefferdsinn.com

Circa 1804. This Federal-style home was given as a wedding gift from a father to his daughter and new son-in-law. It was constructed the same year Thomas Jefferson was re-elected to the presidency. Each guest room is different. Several offer two-person whirlpools, eight have a fireplace. Canopy, four-poster and sleigh beds are among the furnishings. In the afternoons, tea is served in the garden room. The breakfasts feature gourmet fare and are served by candlelight. The inn is located

in a local historic district, just minutes from shops and restaurants.

Innkeeper(s): Pat & Dick Bartholomew. $165-350. 16 rooms with PB, 8 with FP and 5 suites. Breakfast and afternoon tea included in rates. Types of meals: Full gourmet bkfst and early coffee/tea. Beds: KQDT. Reading lamp, refrigerator, clock radio and desk in room. Air conditioning. VCR, fax, library, parlor games, telephone and fireplace on premises. Weddings, small meetings and family reunions hosted. Antiquing, cross-country skiing, downhill skiing, fishing, golf, parks, shopping, water sports and whale watching nearby.

The Captain Lord Mansion

Corner Pleasant & Green, PO Box 800
Kennebunkport, ME 04046
(207)967-3141 (800)522-3141 Fax:(207)967-3172
E-mail: innkeeper@captainlord.com
Web: www.captainlord.com

Circa 1812. In the National Register, the Captain Lord Mansion was built during the War of 1812 and is one of the finest examples of Federal architecture on the coast of Maine. The home rests at the edge of the village green within view of the Kennebunk River and within walking distance of the town's many historic sites. The romantically appointed guest rooms include roomy four-poster beds, gas fireplaces and heated marble and tile floors in the bathrooms. Some rooms include a double Jacuzzi tub. Guests are further pampered with fresh flowers, a full breakfast and afternoon treats.

Innkeeper(s): Bev Davis & Rick Litchfield. $125-449. 16 rooms with PB, 16 with FP and 2 conference rooms. Breakfast included in rates. Types of meals: Full bkfst, early coffee/tea and afternoon tea. Beds: KQ. Reading lamp, refrigerator, clock radio, telephone and desk in room. Air conditioning. Fax, copier, library, parlor games and fireplace on premises. Small meetings, family reunions and seminars hosted. Antiquing, cross-country skiing, fishing, live theater and shopping nearby.

Publicity: *Andrew Harper's Hideaway Report, Colonial Homes, Yankee and New England Getaways.*

"A showcase of elegant architecture. Meticulously clean and splendidly appointed. It's a shame to have to leave."

Captains Hideaway

12 Pleasant St
Kennebunkport, ME 04046-2746
(207)967-5711 Fax:(207)967-3843
E-mail: hideaway@cybertours.com
Web: www.captainshideaway.com

Circa 1800. Each of the two guest rooms at this bed & breakfast has been decorated with romance in mind. The Captain's Room features a massive four-poster canopy bed dressed with luxurious linens. The room is further decorated with a Victorian fainting couch that rests at the foot of the bed and a fireplace warms the bedchamber. In addition to this, the spacious bathroom includes a two-person whirlpool tub and another fireplace. The Garden Room is another option, decorated with light lilac floral wallpaper, a lace canopy bed and iron furnishings. This room also includes a whirlpool tub. The innkeepers create a customized breakfast for their guests that might include muffins, croissants, scones and an entrée of waffles, French toast or eggs and bacon.

Innkeeper(s): Susan Jackson & Judith Hughes-Boulet. $179-279. 2 rooms with PB, 2 with FP. Breakfast, afternoon tea and snacks/refreshments included in rates. Types of meals: Full gourmet bkfst, veg bkfst and early coffee/tea. Beds: KQ. Cable TV, VCR, reading lamp, stereo, refrigerator, clock radio, desk and Jacuzzi in room. Air conditioning. Fax, parlor games, telephone and fireplace on premises. Weddings hosted. Amusement parks, antiquing, art galleries, beach, bicycling, canoeing/kayaking, cross-country skiing, downhill skiing, fishing, golf, hiking, horseback riding, live theater, museums, parks, shopping, sporting events, tennis and water sports nearby.

Publicity: *Patriot Ledger, Tourist News, Eagle Tribune and America's Favorite Inns & B&B.*

Crosstrees

6 South St
Kennebunkport, ME 04046
(207)967-2780 (800)564-1527 Fax:(207)967-2610
E-mail: info@crosstrees.com
Web: www.crosstrees.com

Circa 1818. Located in Maine's largest historic district, this Federal-style house was built by Daniel Walker, a descendant of an original Kennebunkport family. Later, Maine artist and architect Abbot Graves purchased the property and named it "Crosstrees" for its maple trees. The inn features New England antiques and brilliant flower gardens in view of the formal dining room in spring and summer. A full breakfast is provided. Art galleries, beaches, antiquing and golf are nearby.

Historic Interest: Built by one of the first four families in Kennebunkport.
Innkeeper(s): John & Merle Hoover. $120-250. 4 rooms with PB, 3 with FP. Breakfast included in rates. Types of meals: Full bkfst and early coffee/tea. Beds: KQ. Reading lamp, clock radio, desk and suite with Jacuzzi in room. Telephone on premises. Weddings, small meetings and family reunions hosted. Antiquing, fishing, live theater, shopping and ocean nearby.

"Absolutely gorgeous inn. You two were wonderful to us. What a great place to relax."

English Meadows Inn

141 Port Rd
Kennebunkport, ME 04043
(207)967-5766 (800)272-0698
E-mail: eminn@adelphia.net
Web: www.englishmeadowsinn.com

Circa 1860. For more than 100 years this Victorian farmhouse has warmly welcomed travelers, and has been lovingly maintained to stay in pristine condition. Peaceful surroundings include at least two acres of manicured lawns, flowers, trees and antique lilacs. The main house offers comfortable guest bedrooms furnished with antiques and lace curtains. The carriage house boasts a cozy fireplace in the large common room. A guest house has a screened porch amidst the trees. A hearty breakfast may include fresh fruit, Honey Nut Crunch French toast, sausage and egg casserole. Dock Square is just a short walk for shopping or restaurants, and there are many historic sites and nearby beaches.

Historic Interest: Walkers Pointe, President Bush's summer residence (1.5 miles).
Innkeeper(s): Kathy & Peter Smith. $90-165. 12 rooms, 10 with PB. Breakfast and snacks/refreshments included in rates. Types of meals: Country bkfst, early coffee/tea, afternoon tea and room service. Beds: KQDT. Reading lamp, clock radio and all rooms with air conditioning in room. TV, library, parlor games, telephone and fireplace on premises. Small meetings and family reunions hosted. Amusement parks, antiquing, art galleries, beach, bicycling, canoeing/kayaking, cross-country skiing, fishing, golf, hiking, horseback riding, live theater, museums, parks, shopping, tennis and water sports nearby.

"I didn't know what I was looking for until I found it here. "

Harbor Inn

Ocean Ave, PO Box 538 A
Kennebunkport, ME 04046-1838
(207)967-2074
E-mail: barry@covehouse.com
Web: www.harbor-inn.com

Circa 1903. This welcoming inn lies behind a white iron, Victorian fence. The large, rocker-lined veranda is a perfect place to relax and enjoy the sea air and an early morning cup of coffee. Period antiques and Oriental rugs decorate the well-appointed guest rooms. The innkeepers also offer Woodbine Cottage, which includes a private patio. A full breakfast is served in the formal dining room and garden room. After the morning meal, guests can take a short walk to the ocean or enjoy a leisurely stroll to the town's shopping area, about a half-mile from the inn.

Innkeeper(s): Bob & Kathy Jones. $99-165. 8 rooms with PB, 1 with FP, 2 suites and 1 cottage. Breakfast included in rates. Types of meals: Full gourmet bkfst and early coffee/tea. Beds: QDT. TV and reading lamp in room. Telephone and fireplace on premises. Antiquing, fishing, live theater, parks, shopping and water sports nearby.

Publicity: *Country Inns and Yankee Travel Guide.*

"Everything is beautifully done. It's the best we've ever been to."

Inn on South Street

5 South Street
Kennebunkport, ME 04046
(207)967-5151 (800)963-5151 Fax:(207)967-4385
E-mail: innkeeper@innonsouthst.com
Web: www.innonsouthst.com

Circa 1815. Stay within walking distance of the ocean, shops, and restaurants at this early 19th-century Federal-style manor. Listed in the National Register, it is situated in the historic dis-

trict. A unique "Good Morning" staircase is one of the first items noticed upon entering the inn. Richly appointed guest bedrooms and a suite with tradition-al furnishings are accented with splendid window dressings and pine plank floors. Enjoy generous amenities that include tele-phones and fireplaces. A full gourmet candlelit breakfast is served in the dining room or, if weather permits, in the tran-quil gardens.

Historic Interest: Kennebunkport boasts many two- and three-story wooden Federal-style dwellings, which date back to the early 19th century. Cape Arundel, one mile away, features the work of John Calvin Stevens, a noted 19th-century architect. Among the roomy summer cottages he created was the home of former President Bush.

Innkeeper(s): Tom & Patti Bond. $125-250. 4 rooms, 3 with PB, 4 with FP and 1 suite. Breakfast and snacks/refreshments included in rates. Types of meals: Full gourmet bkfst and early coffee/tea. Beds: Q. Cable TV, reading lamp, CD player, refrigerator, clock radio, telephone and fireplace in room. Air conditioning. Antiquing, art galleries, beach, bicycling, canoeing/kayaking, golf, hiking and shopping nearby.

Publicity: *Los Angeles Times, Summertime, Country Inns and Down East.*

"Superb hospitality. We were delighted by the atmosphere and your thoughtfulness."

Kennebunkport Inn

One Dock Sq
Kennebunkport, ME 04046
(207)967-2621 (800)248-2621 Fax:(207)967-3705
E-mail: stay@kennebunkportinn.com
Web: www.kennebunkportinn.com

Circa 1899. Intimate charm, excellent service and tasteful lux-ury are distinctively found at this elegant Victorian mansion. Choose from a variety of well-appointed guest bedrooms; some

feature sitting areas and fireplaces. Dining and lodging packages are available which include breakfast and/or dinner served in the dining rooms or al fresco on the patio. There is ample private parking, convenient for a pleasant walk to the historic harbor and shops of Dock Square. Or enjoy a refreshing swim in the outdoor pool. In the evening, the hotel's Victorian Pub offers live entertainment.

Historic Interest: Nott House.

Innkeeper(s): Debra Lennon & Tom Nill. $89-299. 34 rooms with PB, 3 with FP, 5 suites and 2 conference rooms. Types of meals: Country bkfst, picnic lunch and gourmet dinner. Restaurant on premises. Beds: KQDT. Modem hook-up, data port, cable TV, reading lamp, clock radio, telephone, desk and voice mail in room. Air conditioning. Fax, copier, swimming, bicycles, library, parlor games, fireplace, gift shop, wonderful restaurant serving regional cuisine, lively piano bar, outdoor garden patio serving dinner, outdoor pool and deck on premises. Weddings, small meetings, family reunions and seminars hosted. Antiquing, art galleries, beach, bicycling, fishing, golf, hiking, horseback riding, live theater, museums, shopping, tennis and water sports nearby.

Publicity: *Getaways for Gourmets and Coast Guide.*

"From check-in to check-out, from breakfast through dinner, we were treated like royalty."

Lake Brook Bed & Breakfast

57 Western Ave, Lower Village
Kennebunkport, ME 04046
(207)967-4069

Circa 1900. This pleasant old farmhouse is situated on a tidal brook. Comfortable rockers offer an inviting rest on the wrap-around porch where you can enjoy the inn's flower gardens that trail down to the marsh and brook. Gourmet breakfasts are served. Walk to Kennebunk-port's Dock Square and lower village to visit fine galleries, shops and restaurants.

Historic Interest: The Brick Store Museum and other historical sites are nearby.

Innkeeper(s): Carolyn A. McAdams. $95-150. 4 rooms with PB and 1 suite. Breakfast included in rates. Types of meals: Full gourmet bkfst. Beds: QD. Reading lamp, ceiling fan, clock radio and kitchen in suite available July and August only in room. Air conditioning. Telephone on premises. Antiquing, cross-country skiing, fishing, golf, live theater, parks, shopping, tennis, water sports and historical seaport nearby.

"Truly wonderful atmosphere."

Maine Stay Inn & Cottages at the Melville Walker House

PO Box 500A
Kennebunkport, ME 04046-6174
(207)967-2117 (800)950-2117 Fax:(207)967-8757
E-mail: innkeeper@mainestayinn.com
Web: www.mainestayinn.com

Circa 1860. In the National Register, this inn is a square-block Italianate contoured in a low hip-roof design. Later additions reflecting the Queen Anne period include a suspended spiral staircase, crystal windows, ornately carved mantels and moldings, bay windows and porches. A sea captain built the handsome cupola that became a favorite spot for making taffy. In the 1920s, the cupola was a place from which to spot offshore rumrunners. Guests enjoy afternoon tea with stories of the Maine Stay's heritage. Two suites and one room in the main building and six of the cottage rooms have working fireplaces.

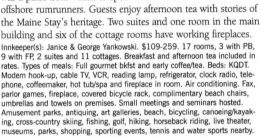

Innkeeper(s): Janice & George Yankowski. $109-259. 17 rooms, 3 with PB, 9 with FP, 2 suites and 11 cottages. Breakfast and afternoon tea included in rates. Types of meals: Full gourmet bkfst and early coffee/tea. Beds: KQDT. Modem hook-up, cable TV, VCR, reading lamp, refrigerator, clock radio, telephone, coffeemaker, hot tub/spa and fireplace in room. Air conditioning. Fax, parlor games, fireplace, covered bicycle rack, complimentary beach chairs, umbrellas and towels on premises. Small meetings and seminars hosted. Amusement parks, antiquing, art galleries, beach, bicycling, canoeing/kayaking, cross-country skiing, fishing, golf, hiking, horseback riding, live theater, museums, parks, shopping, sporting events, tennis and water sports nearby.

"We have traveled the East Coast from Martha's Vineyard to Bar Harbor, and this is the only place we know we must return to."

Old Fort Inn

Old Fort Ave, PO Box M 1
Kennebunkport, ME 04046-1688
(207)967-5353 (800)828-3678 Fax:(207)967-4547
E-mail: info@oldfortinn.com
Web: www.oldfortinn.com

Circa 1880. In a secluded setting of vintage summer estates, this country retreat is hidden away on fifteen landscaped and wooded acres. The peaceful, private environment blends with an old-world charm. Guest bedrooms exude an exquisite elegance, furnished in period antiques, canopy and four-poster beds with down comforters, distinctive fabrics and wall coverings. Some rooms boast fireplaces and Jacuzzis. Generous amenities include robes, Belgian chocolates and cookies. Enjoy a lavish breakfast buffet of fresh fruit, pastries and a hot entree. Browse through the antique shop, play tennis or swim in the pool. Located just a block from the ocean's rocky shore and crashing surf, the inn is only about a mile from popular Dock Square's art galleries, restaurants and boutiques.

Historic Interest: Trolly Car Museum, Brick Store Museum, historic homes and landmarks.
Innkeeper(s): Sheila & David Aldrich. $99-400. 16 rooms with PB and 1 conference room. Breakfast included in rates. Types of meals: Full bkfst. Beds: KQ. Cable TV, reading lamp, refrigerator, snack bar, clock radio, telephone, robe, hair dryer, iron, some with fireplace and Jacuzzi in room. Air conditioning. TV, fax, copier, swimming, tennis and fireplace on premises. Small meetings hosted. Antiquing, fishing, live theater, parks and shopping nearby.
Publicity: Country Inns and Down East Magazine.

"My husband and I have been spending the last two weeks in August at the Old Fort Inn for years. It combines for us a rich variety of what we feel a relaxing vacation should be."

Tides Inn By The Sea

252 King's Hwy, Goose Rocks Beach
Kennebunkport, ME 04046
(207)967-3757
E-mail: info@tidesinnbythesea.com
Web: www.tidesinnbythesea.com

Circa 1899. Adjacent to the three-mile-long, white sand and surf of Goose Rocks Beach, this Victorian inn was built in the authentic shingle-style popular in the state's seacoast towns. Teddy Roosevelt and Arthur Conan Doyle are two of the notables who have stayed here. This B&B boasts an atmosphere of tranquility while blending relaxed sophistication and timeless simplicity. Guest bedrooms feature antique furnishings and designer linens. Overlook the islands and the Atlantic from the sun porch where a continental breakfast is served. The on-site Belvidere Club, a vintage Victorian Bar, offers regional fare and libations in a richly romantic candlelit atmosphere with ocean views. Contemporary Tides Too Oceanfront Suites are available on a weekly basis.

Innkeeper(s): Marie & Kristin Henriksen. $195-325. 22 rooms, 19 with PB and 3 suites. Breakfast included in rates. Types of meals: Cont. Restaurant on premises. Beds: KQDT. Reading lamp, ceiling fan and clock radio in room. Fax, swimming, parlor games, telephone, fireplace, light continental included in non-kitchen units and cocktails and dinner served in the Inn's own Belvidere Club on premises. Family reunions hosted. Amusement parks, antiquing, fishing, golf, live theater, parks, shopping, sporting events, tennis and water sports nearby.
Publicity: Down East, Boston Sunday Herald, Conde Nast Traveler and Tourist News.

"Always a treat to visit here—so unique and pleasant."

The Welby Inn

92 Ocean Ave, PO Box 774
Kennebunkport, ME 04046-0774
(207)967-4655 (800)773-4085 Fax:(207)967-8654
E-mail: innkeeper@welbyinn.com
Web: www.welbyinn.com

Circa 1900. Built as a summer home in this seaport town at the turn of the last century, the inn's Dutch Gambrel architecture is typical of the era. A large common room with Victorian furnishings invites relaxing by the fire or conversing in the window seat. A guest pantry offers beverages and facilities for anytime refreshment. Air-conditioned guest bedrooms feature plush robes and fresh flowers. Sleep in a canopy bed by a fireplace in the Grantham Room overlooking the Kennebunk River, or stay in the cheery James Room with a view of the tidal water. A bountiful breakfast and afternoon tea are served in the dining room and breakfast porch. Stroll to the ocean, or to the shops and restaurants of Dock Square.

Innkeeper(s): Christopher Farr. $99-175. 7 rooms with PB, 1 with FP. Breakfast and afternoon tea included in rates. Types of meals: Full gourmet bkfst and early coffee/tea. Beds: KQDT. Reading lamp and clock radio in room. Air conditioning. TV, VCR, library, parlor games, telephone and fireplace on premises. Family reunions hosted. Amusement parks, antiquing, art galleries, beach, bicycling, cross-country skiing, fishing, golf, live theater, museums, parks, shopping, water sports, art galleries, museums and ocean nearby.

"I'm glad we found this place before Gourmet Magazine discovers it and the rates increase!"

Kingfield G3

Herbert Grand Hotel

PO Box 67
Kingfield, ME 04947-0067
(207)265-2000 (888)656-9922 Fax:(207)265-4594
E-mail: innkeeper@herbertgrandhotel.com
Web: www.herbertgrandhotel.com

Circa 1948. This three-story, Beaux-Arts-style hotel with its original terrazzo marble floors, brass fixtures and oak floors was built by Maine legislator Herbert Wing. A sink remaining on the dining room wall once provided stagecoach patrons a place to wash up before dining. A moosehead is the focal point above the fireplace. Simply furnished rooms are equipped with Jacuzzis or steam baths.

Innkeeper(s): Marcie Herrick. $69-169. 27 rooms with PB, 4 with FP, 3 suites and 1 conference room. Breakfast and afternoon tea included in rates. Types of meals: Cont plus and gourmet dinner. Restaurant on premises. Beds: KQDT. TV, clock radio, turn-down service, desk and some with fireplace in room. VCR, fax, copier, sauna, parlor games, telephone and fireplace on premises. Weddings, small meetings and family reunions hosted. Antiquing, art galleries, bicycling, canoeing/kayaking, cross-country skiing, downhill skiing, fishing, golf, horseback riding, museums, shopping, tennis and water sports nearby.

Publicity: *Public Broadcasting Station.*

Kittery L2

Enchanted Nights B&B

29 Wentworth St
Kittery, ME 03904-1720
(207)439-1489
Web: www.enchantednights.org

Circa 1890. The innkeepers bill this unique inn as a "Victorian fantasy for the romantic at heart." Each of the guest rooms is unique, from the spacious rooms with double whirlpool tubs and fireplaces to the cozy turret room. A  whimsical combination of country French and Victorian decor permeates the interior. Wrought-iron beds and hand-painted furnishings add to the ambiance. Breakfasts, often with a vegetarian theme, are served with gourmet coffee in the morning room on antique floral china.

Historic Interest: There are museums, forts, churches, historic homes and buildings all within five miles of the home.

Innkeeper(s): Nancy Bogenberger & Peter Lamandia. $52-300. 10 rooms with PB, 4 with FP and 2 conference rooms. Breakfast included in rates. Types of meals: Full gourmet bkfst, veg bkfst and early coffee/tea. Beds: KQDT. Cable TV, VCR, reading lamp, refrigerator, ceiling fan, clock radio, microwave, 5 have whirlpools and 4 have fireplaces in room. Air conditioning. Telephone and refrigerator on premises. Handicap access. Weddings, small meetings, family reunions and seminars hosted. Antiquing, art galleries, beach, bicycling, canoeing/kayaking, golf, hiking, horseback riding, live theater, museums, parks, shopping, sporting events, tennis, water sports, wineries, outlet shopping, historic homes, whale watching and harbor cruises nearby.

"The atmosphere was great. Your breakfast was elegant. The breakfast room made us feel we had gone back in time. All in all it was a very enjoyable stay."

Portsmouth Harbor Inn & Spa

6 Water St
Kittery, ME 03904
(207)439-4040 Fax:(207)438-9286
E-mail: info@innatportsmouth.com
Web: www.innatportsmouth.com

Circa 1879. Built during the Victorian era, this historic brick home features ornate exterior trim and a sweeping veranda. The five guest rooms are decorated with English antiques, and some rooms include a harbor view. A full breakfast is served in a dining room illuminated by firelight. The town offers antique shops, boutiques and more than 80 restaurants to enjoy.

Innkeeper(s): Paula Miller. $109-209. 5 rooms with PB. Breakfast included in rates. Types of meals: Full gourmet bkfst and early coffee/tea. Beds: KQ. Modem hook-up, data port, cable TV, reading lamp, ceiling fan, clock radio, telephone, desk and voice mail in room. Air conditioning. Library, parlor games, new day spa located in the renovated barn offers massage, facials, body treatments, manicures and pedicures on premises. Weddings, small meetings, family reunions and seminars hosted. Antiquing, art galleries, beach, bicycling, canoeing/kayaking, fishing, golf, hiking, horseback riding, live theater, museums, parks and shopping nearby.

Publicity: *Charlotte Observer.*

Naples J2

Augustus Bove House

Corner Rts 302 & 114, 11 Sebago Rd
Naples, ME 04055
(207)693-6365 (888)806-6249
E-mail: augbovehouse@pivot.net
Web: www.naplesmaine.com

Circa 1830. A long front lawn nestles up against the stone foundation and veranda of this house, once known as the Hotel Naples, one of the area's summer hotels in the 1800s. In the 1920s, the inn was host to a number of prominent guests, including Enrico Caruso, Joseph P. Kennedy and Howard Hughes. The guest rooms are decorated in a Colonial style and modestly furnished with antiques. Many rooms provide a view of Long Lake. A fancy country breakfast is provided.

Innkeeper(s): David & Arlene Stetson. $59-200. 10 rooms with PB and 3 suites. Breakfast and afternoon tea included in rates. Types of meals: Full bkfst and early coffee/tea. Beds: KQT. Cable TV and telephone in room. Air conditioning. VCR, fax and spa on premises. Weddings, small meetings and family reunions hosted. Antiquing, cross-country skiing, downhill skiing, fishing, live theater, parks, shopping and water sports nearby.

Publicity: *Brighton Times, Yankee Magazine and Quality Travel Value Award.*

"Beautiful place, rooms, and people."

Inn at Long Lake

Lake House Rd, PO Box 806
Naples, ME 04055
(207)693-6226 (800)437-0328 Fax:(207)693-7132
E-mail: info@innatlonglake.com
Web: www.innatlonglake.com

Circa 1906. Reopened in 1988, the inn housed the overflow guests from the Lake House resort about 90 years ago. Guests traveled to the resort via the Oxford-Cumberland Canal, and each room is named for a historic canal boat. The cozy rooms offer fluffy comforters and a warm, country decor in a romantic atmosphere. Warm up in front of a crack-

ling fire in the great room, or enjoy a cool Long Lake breeze on the veranda while watching horses in nearby pastures. The setting is ideal for housing guests for weddings or reunions.

Historic Interest: Songo Locks, Shaker Museum, Jones Glass Museum.

Innkeeper(s): Buddy Marcum. $99-200. 16 rooms with PB, 2 suites and 1 conference room. Breakfast, afternoon tea and snacks/refreshments included in rates. Types of meals: Full bkfst and early coffee/tea. Beds: QDT. TV, VCR, reading lamp, ceiling fan, clock radio, turn-down service and suites have fireplace in room. Air conditioning. Library, telephone and fireplace on premises. Weddings, family reunions and seminars hosted. Antiquing, cross-country skiing, downhill skiing, fishing, golf, hiking, horseback riding, live theater, parks, shopping and water sports nearby.

Publicity: *Bridgton News and Portland Press Herald.*

"Convenient location, tastefully done and the prettiest inn I've ever stayed in."

Lamb's Mill Inn

131 Lambs Mill Rd
Naples, ME 04055
(207)693-6253
E-mail: lambsmil@pivot.net
Web: www.lambsmillinn.com

Circa 1800. This cheery, yellow farmhouse offers six guest rooms, each filled with comfortable furnishings. Guests are pampered with down comforters, a hot tub and 20 peaceful acres of woods, fields and perennial gardens.
Fresh vegetable frittata with items picked from the garden and raspberry Belgian waffles  are among the breakfast entrees. Evening snacks are served as well. The home is close to cross-country and alpine skiing, golf, tennis, parasailing, shopping, restaurants and antiquing.

Innkeeper(s): Laurel Tinkham & Sandy Long. $80-125. 6 rooms with PB. Breakfast, afternoon tea and snacks/refreshments included in rates. Types of meals: Full gourmet bkfst, veg bkfst and early coffee/tea. Beds: KQD. Cable TV, VCR, reading lamp, stereo, refrigerator, clock radio and turn-down service in room. Air conditioning. Spa, bicycles, library, parlor games, telephone, fireplace, outside stone barbecue pit and horseback riding on premises. Weddings, small meetings and family reunions hosted. Amusement parks, antiquing, art galleries, beach, bicycling, canoeing/kayaking, cross-country skiing, downhill skiing, fishing, golf, hiking, horseback riding, live theater, museums, parks, shopping, tennis, water sports and wineries nearby.

"We really enjoyed our week in your lovely home."

New Harbor J4

Gosnold Arms

146 State Route 32
New Harbor, ME 04554
(207)677-3727 Fax:(207)677-2662
E-mail: info@gosnold.com
Web: www.gosnold.com

Circa 1840. Located on the historic Pemaquid peninsula, the Gosnold Arms includes a remodeled, saltwater farmhouse situated on a rise above the harbor. There are several cottages and many accommodations with views. A cozy lounge offers two large stone fireplaces and a glassed-in dining porch overlooking the water.

Historic Interest: Pemaquid archaeological dig at Pemaquid Beach; Pemaquid Lighthouse and Fisherman's Museum (1 mile), Summer boat to Monhegan Island from New Harbor (1 hour ride).

Innkeeper(s): The Phinney Family. $95-178. 25 rooms with PB and 14 cot-

tages. Breakfast included in rates. Types of meals: Full bkfst. Beds: QDT. Antiquing, fishing, boat trips, historic sites and restaurants nearby.

Publicity: *New York and Down East.*

Newcastle I4

The Harbor View Inn at Newcastle

34 Main St
Newcastle, ME 04553
(207)563-2900 Fax:(207)563-2900
E-mail: joe@theharborview.com
Web: www.theharborview.com

Circa 1841. The Harbor View Inn is a recently restored New England cape situated on a rise overlooking the villages of Newcastle and Damariscotta and just down the River Road from Boothbay Harbor, 20 minutes away. Two of the three guest rooms have their own private deck and fireplace. Innkeeper Joe McEntee was the chef and manager of several Philadelphia restaurants before he purchased the inn. Multi-course gourmet breakfasts include fresh orange juice, a fresh fruit plate, scrambled eggs, pancakes, mushrooms, ham, roasted potatoes, broiled tomatoes, homemade ginger-peach muffins, coffee and tea. On sunny mornings have your breakfast served on the spacious deck that provides views of the harbor. Shops, art galleries, restaurants and antique dealers are a short walk away. Guests can drive to Pemaquid to photograph the lighthouse and fort, or visit New Harbor for lobsters or cruises to Monhegan Island.

Innkeeper(s): Joe McEntee. $105-175. 3 rooms with PB. Breakfast included in rates. Types of meals: Full gourmet bkfst. Beds: KQT. Modem hook-up, data port, cable TV, reading lamp, ceiling fan, telephone and individual thermostat in room. Fax, copier and fireplace on premises. Antiquing, art galleries, beach, canoeing/kayaking, cross-country skiing, fishing, golf, hiking, museums, parks, shopping, tennis and lighthouses nearby.

The Newcastle Inn

60 River Rd
Newcastle, ME 04553-3803
(207)563-5685 (800)832-8669 Fax:(207)563-6877
E-mail: innkeeper@newcastleinn.com
Web: www.newcastleinn.com

Circa 1849. The Newcastle Inn is a Federal-style colonial picturesquely situated on a lawn that slopes down to the Damariscotta River. Most rooms feature antique beds and water views. Honeymooners like the room with the old-fashioned canopy bed. Breakfast consists of four courses and may include eggs with caviar on puff pastry or brioche with lemon curd. A four-course dinner is available by reservation.

Historic Interest: Built in 1860s. Exterior maintained to original design.

Innkeeper(s): Laura Barclay. $125-295. 15 rooms, 11 with PB, 6 with FP, 5 suites and 1 conference room. Breakfast included in rates. Types of meals: Full bkfst, early coffee/tea and gourmet dinner. Restaurant on premises. Beds: KQT. Reading lamp, clock radio, fireplace, turn-down service in season and eight with AC in room. Fax, copier, library, parlor games and telephone on premises. Weddings, small meetings, family reunions and seminars hosted. Antiquing, art galleries, bicycling, canoeing/kayaking, cross-country skiing, downhill skiing, fishing, golf, hiking, live theater, museums, parks, shopping, sporting events and water sports nearby.

Publicity: *One of the 12 "Romantic Hideaways" for 2001 by The Discerning Traveler, restaurant was awarded 4-1/2 stars by the Maine Sunday Telegram, Boston Globe, Yankee Magazine, Down East and Romantic Hideaways.*

"To eat and stay here is to know life to the fullest."

Nobleboro I4

Mill Pond Inn

50 Main St
Nobleboro, ME 04555
(207)563-8014

Circa 1780. The one acre of grounds surrounding this 18th-century home are packed with scenery. A pond with a waterfall flows into the adjacent Damariscotta Lake and trees offer plenty of shade. Rooms are decorated in a whimsical country style and they have pond views and fresh flowers. Breakfasts are served in a room that overlooks the pond and grounds. Innkeeper Bobby Whear is a registered Maine guide, and the innkeepers offer private fishing trips. Complimentary canoeing and biking are available.

Innkeeper(s): Bobby & Sherry Whear. $110. 6 rooms with PB, 3 with FP and 1 suite. Breakfast and afternoon tea included in rates. Types of meals: Full bkfst and early coffee/tea. Beds: KQT. Reading lamp, clock radio and desk in room. VCR, bicycles, telephone, fireplace, private fishing trips available with Registered Maine Guide and canoes on premises. Weddings, small meetings, family reunions and seminars hosted. Antiquing, cross-country skiing, downhill skiing, fishing, live theater, parks, shopping, sporting events, water sports and bird watching nearby.

Northeast Harbor I6

Maison Suisse

PO Box 1090
Northeast Harbor, ME 04662
(207)276-5223 (800)624-7668
E-mail: maison@acadia.net
Web: www.maisonsuisse.com

Circa 1892. Stay in the inviting comfort and quiet elegance of the landmark Early Shingle-style main house close to Bar Harbor in a timeless village setting. The recently built harbor-view annex is an adaptation of a century-old design by the same architect. Guest bedrooms and suites are furnished in antiques and boast oversized beds, historic or appropriately coordinated wallpapers. Two rooms include fireplaces. Breakfast is provided at the on-site bakery and restaurant across the street. Choose a hearty New England breakfast or a lighter continental with fresh pastries. The grounds boast a goldfish and iris water garden from the 1950s and a rustic garden with cranberry, blueberry, heather, fern and cedar thyme. Relax in one of the sitting areas and terraces. Visit the many popular attractions of nearby Acadia.

Innkeeper(s): White Family & Friends. $95-305. 16 rooms with PB, 2 with FP and 5 suites. Breakfast and afternoon tea included in rates. Types of meals: Full bkfst and early coffee/tea. Beds: KQT. Cable TV, reading lamp, clock radio, telephone, desk, fireplace, fans and tea/coffee available 24 hours/day in room. Library, parlor games, tennis, gold, laundry, fax, copy, gym, VCR and movie rentals on premises. Handicap access. Weddings, small meetings, family reunions and seminars hosted. Amusement parks, antiquing, art galleries, beach, bicycling, canoeing/kayaking, cross-country skiing, fishing, golf, hiking, horseback riding, live theater, museums, parks, shopping, tennis and water sports nearby.

Publicity: *Travel and Leisure, USA Weekend, Glamour, Woman's Day and Elle Decor.*

Ogunquit K2

Hartwell House Inn & Conference Center

312 Shore Rd, PO Box 1950
Ogunquit, ME 03907-0393
(207)646-7210 (800)235-8883 Fax:(207)646-6032
E-mail: info@hartwellhouseinn.com
Web: www.hartwellhouseinn.com

Circa 1921. Hartwell House offers suites and guest rooms furnished with distinctive early American and English antiques. Many rooms are available with French doors opening to private balconies overlooking sculpted flower gardens. Guests are treated to both a full, gourmet breakfast and afternoon tea. Seasonal dining packages are available. Restaurants, beaches, hiking and outlet shopping is nearby.

$110-265. 16 rooms with PB, 3 suites and 4 conference rooms. Types of meals: Full gourmet bkfst and afternoon tea. Beds: KQ. Reading lamp and refrigerator in room. Air conditioning. Parlor games, telephone and fireplace on premises. Weddings hosted. Antiquing, cross-country skiing, fishing, live theater, parks, shopping, sporting events, water sports, restaurants, outlet and boutique shopping and beaches nearby.

Publicity: *Innsider.*

"This engaging country inn will be reserved for my special clients."

Morning Dove B&B

13 Bourne Ln, PO Box 1940
Ogunquit, ME 03907-1940
(207)646-3891
E-mail: info@themorningdove
Web: www.themorningdove.com

Circa 1865. Surrounded by country gardens and a pond, this Victorian farmhouse was built by one of the area's first families. The inn offers delightful accommodations all year. In the warmer months, breakfast is served on the spacious porch, and in the fireplaced gathering room during winter. Expect to partake of hot and cold beverages, fruit, yogurt, cereals, as well as entrees such as stuffed French toast and omelettes. The ideal location is perfect for strolling the Marginal Way, a gorgeous one-mile walk along rugged ocean cliffs. Equally close is Perkins Cove, sandy beaches and the Ogunquit Playhouse.

Innkeeper(s): Jane & Fred Garland. $100-175. 6 rooms with PB. Breakfast included in rates. Types of meals: Full bkfst. Beds: KQ. Reading lamp, refrigerator, 3 with TV and one with private deck in room. Air conditioning. TV, parlor games, telephone and fireplace on premises. Amusement parks, antiquing, art galleries, beach, bicycling, fishing, horseback riding, live theater, museums, shopping and tennis nearby.

Nellie Littlefield House

27 Shore Rd
Ogunquit, ME 03907
(207)646-1692 Fax:(207)361-1206
E-mail: fhaselt@aol.com
Web: www.visit-maine.com/nellielittlefieldhouse/

Circa 1889. J.H. Littlefield had this grand three-story Victorian home built for his wife Nellie. It was a place that welcomed visitors who became friends. The inn continues that tradition today. Relax on one of the porches or the turreted balcony. Antiques and period furnishings are accented by window treatments and upholstery. Wonderfully decorated guest bedrooms access deck areas; some offer views of the water. Enjoy an indulgent breakfast buffet that includes cereals, an assortment of homemade breads and muffins, pancakes, waffles, egg dishes, fresh fruit and yogurt. The inn is conveniently located in an ocean community that offers a variety of related activities.

Innkeeper(s): Woody & Ethel Haselton. $90-220. 8 rooms with PB and 2 suites. Breakfast and afternoon tea included in rates. Types of meals: Full bkfst. Beds: QT. Cable TV, refrigerator, ceiling fan, clock radio, telephone, desk and one suite with Jacuzzi in room. Central air. TV, fax, library, parlor games and fireplace on premises. Limited handicap access. Family reunions hosted. Antiquing, art galleries, beach, bicycling, canoeing/kayaking, fishing, golf, hiking, live theater, museums, shopping, tennis and water sports nearby.

Rockmere Lodge

150 Stearns Rd
Ogunquit, ME 03907
(207)646-2985 Fax:(207)646-6947
E-mail: info@rockmere.com
Web: www.rockmere.com

Circa 1899. Offering an outstanding view of the Atlantic from its site on Marginal Way (the town's oceanside path), this shingle-style Victorian is enhanced by gardens, fountains and a wraparound veranda filled with white wicker. The inn is furnished with period antiques and Victorian collectibles. Every room except one enjoys an ocean view. Walk to galleries, boutiques and fine restaurants. Ten miles south is Kittery, a center for factory outlets.

Innkeeper(s): Andy Antoniuk & Bob Brown. $100-200. 8 rooms with PB. Types of meals: Cont plus. Beds: QD. Cable TV, VCR, reading lamp, CD player, refrigerator and clock radio in room. Fax, library, parlor games and telephone on premises. Antiquing, cross-country skiing, fishing, golf, live theater, parks, shopping, sporting events and water sports nearby.

Publicity: *York County Coast Star.*

Yardarm Village Inn

406 Shore Rd, PO Box 773
Ogunquit, ME 03907-0773
(207)646-7006 (888)927-3276 Fax:(207)646-9034
E-mail: yardarm@maine.rr.com
Web: www.yardarmvillageinn.com

Circa 1874. In the quiet part of town, just south of the entrance to Perkins Cove, this three-story classic New England inn offers a delightful selection of accommodations. The large veranda is the perfect spot for relaxing on a white wicker rocker. Comfortable guest bedrooms and two-room suites are furnished and decorated in a Colonial-country style. Start the day with homemade blueberry muffins, fruit and beverages. Take an afternoon or evening sailboat charter past the three-mile beach or along the rocky coast. The on-site wine and cheese shop is well-stocked to satisfy the most discriminating palate.

Innkeeper(s): Scott & Beverlee. $69-109. 8 rooms with PB and 4 suites. Types of meals: Cont. Beds: KQDT. Cable TV, reading lamp, refrigerator, clock radio, refrigerator and hair dryers in room. Air conditioning. Telephone, fireplace and private sailboat charters available on premises. Family reunions hosted. Amusement parks, antiquing, art galleries, beach, bicycling, canoeing/kayaking, fishing, golf, hiking, live theater, museums, parks, shopping, tennis and water sports nearby.

Old Orchard Beach   K2

Atlantic Birches Inn

20 Portland Ave Rt 98
Old Orchard Beach, ME 04064-2212
(207)934-5295 (888)934-5295
E-mail: info@atlanticbirches.com
Web: www.atlanticbirches.com

Circa 1903. The front porch of this Shingle-style Victorian and 1920s bungalow are shaded by white birch trees. The houses are a place for relaxation and enjoyment, uncluttered, simple havens filled with comfortable furnishings. The guest rooms are decorated with antiques and pastel wallcoverings. Maine's coast offers an endless amount of activities, from boating to whale watching. It is a five-minute walk to the beach and the pier.

Innkeeper(s): Ray & Kim Deleo. $69-135. 10 rooms with PB. Breakfast included in rates. Types of meals: Cont plus. Beds: KQDT. Reading lamp, ceiling fan and clock radio in room. Air conditioning. VCR, copier, swimming, library, parlor games and telephone on premises. Small meetings and family reunions hosted. Amusement parks, antiquing, fishing, parks, shopping, sporting events and water sports nearby.

"Your home and family are just delightful! What a treat to stay in such a warm & loving home."

Poland   I2

Wolf Cove Inn

5 Jordan Shore Dr
Poland, ME 04274-7111
(207)998-4976 Fax:(207)998-7049
E-mail: wolfcove@exploremaine.com
Web: www.wolfcoveinn.com

Circa 1910. The pristine lakeside setting of this inn calms the spirit of the busiest traveler, and there are more than two acres of grounds with perennial gardens, giant pine trees and an herb garden. The inn offers a variety of rooms, most with lake or garden views, period furnishings and queen or king beds. Request a third-floor room for a fireplace and whirlpool tub. The Calla Lily Suite includes a sitting area as well as a tub overlooking Tripp Lake. The inn's favorite guest space is the flagstone terrace overlooking the water. Breakfast offerings are provided in the glassed-in porch (also a great spot to watch the sunset).

Innkeeper(s): Rose Aikman. $73-250. 10 rooms, 8 with PB. Breakfast and snacks/refreshments included in rates. Types of meals: Full bkfst and early coffee/tea. Beds: KQT. Air conditioning. TV, VCR, fax, swimming, telephone and fireplace on premises. Weddings, small meetings, family reunions and seminars hosted. Antiquing, beach, bicycling, canoeing/kayaking, cross-country skiing, downhill skiing, golf, hiking, horseback riding and shopping nearby.

Portland J3

Inn At St John

939 Congress St
Portland, ME 04102-3031
(207)773-6481 (800)636-9127 Fax:(207)756-7629
E-mail: theinn@maine.rr.com
Web: www.innatstjohn.com

Circa 1897. Tucked on a city street, this Victorian inn is conveniently located near many Portland sites, including museums, restaurants and shops. The guest rooms feature antiques and traditional furnishings, and hardwood floors are topped with Oriental rugs. The inn is European in style, and some rooms have a shared bath. Children are welcome, and those younger than 12 can stay for free.

Innkeeper(s): Paul Hood. $46-186. 37 rooms, 27 with PB. Breakfast included in rates. Types of meals: Cont plus and early coffee/tea. Beds: KQDT. Cable TV, reading lamp, refrigerator, telephone, desk and HBO in room. Air conditioning. Fax, copier, bicycle storage and free parking on premises. Amusement parks, antiquing, cross-country skiing, fishing, golf, live theater, parks, shopping, sporting events, tennis, water sports and historic district nearby.

Publicity: *Down East, Portland Press Herald, Houston Chronicle, New York Times, Portland Magazine and Travel Holiday and WCSH/Fox/WGME.*

"We were surprised at how much charm there is tucked in to this building."

Inn on Carleton

46 Carleton St
Portland, ME 04102-3226
(207)775-1910 (800)639-1779 Fax:(207)761-2160
E-mail: innkeeper@innoncarleton.com
Web: www.innoncarleton.com

Circa 1869. One of the first to adorn the prestigious, tree-lined Western Promenade neighborhood, this restored 1869 Victorian home is an historic landmark and the area's oldest established bed and breakfast. Innkeepers Phil and Sue desire that each stay be relaxed and comfortable. An assortment of reading materials and local menus are placed in the parlor. Sit on period antiques by the fire or admire the amazing clock collection. Guest bedrooms provide a good night's rest, followed by a hot breakfast. Close to downtown, it is a short walk to the art museum and performing arts center. Take a nearby international ferry to visit Nova Scotia.

Historic Interest: Victorian Period Pieces.

Innkeeper(s): Phil & Sue Cox. $159-225. 6 rooms with PB. Breakfast and afternoon tea included in rates. Types of meals: Country bkfst, veg bkfst and early coffee/tea. Beds: KQDT. Cable TV, VCR, reading lamp, CD player, ceiling fan, clock radio, telephone, turn-down service and desk in room. Air conditioning. Fax, copier, bicycles, parlor games, fireplace and laundry facility on premises. Weddings, small meetings, family reunions and seminars hosted. Amusement parks, antiquing, art galleries, bicycling, canoeing/kayaking, cross-country skiing, downhill skiing, fishing, golf, hiking, horseback riding, live theater, museums, parks, shopping, sporting events and water sports nearby.

Percy Inn

15 Pine St
Portland, ME 04102
(207)871-7638 (888)417-3729 Fax:(207)775-2599
E-mail: innkeeper@percyinn.com
Web: www.percyinn.com

Circa 1830. Recently renovated, this historic three-story 1830 Brick Rowhouse in Federal style offers distinctive accommodations for business or leisure. Relax in the large brick courtyard or on the spacious sundeck. Snacks are available in the pantry any time. Bumbleberry Pie, a crumb concoction of raspberries, blueberries and blackberries, is a popular favorite. Amenity-rich guest bedrooms in the main inn include safes, candles, stocked refrigerators, fax machines, voice mail, coolers, beach bags and blankets. Satellite suites with full kitchens and living areas are perfect for families. Breakfast is served from 8-10 AM. The surrounding urban setting is generously endowed with landmark buildings and restaurants.

Historic Interest: Built in 1830, ten years after Maine became a state, the building survived Portland's Great Fire of 1866. Our Longfellow Square hosts five restaurants, the Center for Cultural Exchange and on the adjoining block are numerous landmark buildings.

Innkeeper(s): Dale Northrup, CTC. $89-259. 12 rooms with PB, 2 with FP, 7 suites and 1 cottage. Breakfast, afternoon tea and snacks/refreshments included in rates. Types of meals: Full bkfst and early coffee/tea. Beds: Q. Modem hook-up, data port, cable TV, VCR, reading lamp, CD player, refrigerator, ceiling fan, snack bar, clock radio, telephone, coffeemaker, desk, voice mail, fireplace, safes, complimentary stocked refrigerator, fax machine, coolers, beach bags, blankets, weather radios and candles in room. Air conditioning. Fax, library, parlor games, fireplace, bike and canoe/kayak storage and dedicated lit parking on premises. Family reunions and seminars hosted. Antiquing, art galleries, bicycling, live theater, museums, parks, shopping, Cultural Center and Portland Museum nearby.

Publicity: *Vogue, Travel & Leisure, National Geographic Traveler, Yankee, New York Times, Boston Globe, bestfares.com, Passport, NPR, PBS, Armchair Traveler, syndicated travel radio, The Touring Company and The Percy Inn Story (2002) produced by Houghton Mifflin Company as part of a series for university market.*

West End Inn

146 Pine St
Portland, ME 04102-3541
(207)772-1377 (800)338-1377 Fax:(207)828-0984
E-mail: innkeeper@westendbb.com

Circa 1871. Located in Portland's Western Promenade Historic District, this Georgian-style inn is one of many Victorian-era homes found there. Rooms are decorated with four-poster beds. The inn's full, New England-style breakfasts include such items as blueberry pancakes, sausage, eggs and fruit. The menu changes daily and guests may opt for lighter fare. An afternoon tea also is served and provides a perfect opportunity to relax after an activity-filled day. The Museum of Art and the Old Port are nearby and are accessible by foot or by car.

Innkeeper(s): Dan & Michele Brown. $99-209. 6 rooms with PB. Breakfast included in rates. Types of meals: Full bkfst. Beds: KQT. Cable TV, reading lamp, ceiling fan, clock radio, telephone, desk and air conditioning in room. Library and fireplace on premises. Small meetings hosted. Antiquing, cross-country skiing, downhill skiing, fishing, live theater, parks, shopping, sporting events and water sports nearby.

Publicity: *New York Times.*

Wild Iris Inn

273 State Street
Portland, ME 04101
(207)775-0224 (800)600-1557
E-mail: diane@wildirisinn.com
Web: www.wildirisinn.com

Circa 1892. Conveniently located within walking distance to the arts district, restaurants, shopping and activities, this Victorian inn graces an historic downtown neighborhood. Off-street parking is available. Relax in the common room with games, videos and books, or sit in the backyard garden and sitting area. A business center offers use of a computer, high-speed Internet connection, printer, copier and fax. Air-conditioned guest bedrooms feature comfortable furnishings. Enjoy a buffet breakfast that includes fresh seasonal fruit, homemade granola, yogurt, an assortment of baked breads and muffins as well as locally roasted coffee and tea. Visit nearby Henry Longfellow's house.

Historic Interest: Located in a historic neighborhood of downtown Portland.

Innkeeper(s): Diane Edwards. $85-125. 7 rooms, 5 with PB. Breakfast and afternoon tea included in rates. Types of meals: Cont plus. Beds: QD. Ceiling fan and clock radio in room. Air conditioning. TV, VCR, fax, copier, child care, parlor games, telephone and fireplace on premises. Small meetings hosted. Antiquing, art galleries, beach, bicycling, canoeing/kayaking, cross-country skiing, fishing, golf, live theater, museums, parks, shopping, sporting events, tennis and water sports nearby.

Rockland   I5

Berry Manor Inn

81 Talbot Ave
Rockland, ME 04841
(207)596-7696 (800)774-5692 Fax:(207)596-9958
E-mail: info@berrymanorinn.com
Web: www.berrymanorinn.com

Circa 1898. Romance is renewed at this stately Shingle-style mansion, located in a quiet neighborhood in the historic district. The elegant Victorian decor is enhanced by antiques and period reproductions. Morning juice and coffee is served in the library. Other comfortable gathering places include parlors and a front porch. All of the guest bedrooms feature fireplaces, whirlpool or clawfoot tubs, bathrobes, fine linens and candles, some also offer double shower heads and sitting areas. Enjoy a delicious, intimate breakfast served at individual tables with china, silver and crystal settings. A guest pantry provides daily snacks and refreshments. Tree-lined and well-manicured lawns accented by colorful perennial garden beds beckon a game of croquet.

Innkeeper(s): Cheryl Michaelsen. $95-240. 8 rooms with PB, 8 with FP and 2 conference rooms. Breakfast and snacks/refreshments included in rates. Types of meals: Full gourmet bkfst, early coffee/tea and picnic lunch. Beds: KQT. Modem hook-up, data port, cable TV, reading lamp, clock radio, telephone, turn-down service, desk, hot tub/spa and fireplace in room. Air conditioning. VCR, fax, copier, library, parlor games, fireplace, gift shop, refrigerator, guest pantry and porch on premises. Weddings, small meetings, family reunions and seminars hosted. Antiquing, art galleries, beach, bicycling, canoeing/kayaking, cross-country skiing, downhill skiing, fishing, golf, hiking, horseback riding, museums, parks, shopping and wineries nearby.

Publicity: *Discerning Traveler and Midcoast Maines only AAA 4-Diamond rated historic B&B inn.*

Old Granite Inn

546 Main St
Rockland, ME 04841-3341
(207)594-9036 (800)386-9036 Fax:(207)594-0099
E-mail: ogi@midcoast.com
Web: www.olstoniteinn.com

Circa 1790. The Old Granite Inn is a Federal Colonial-style inn built in 1790 with gray granite quarried nearby in St. George and hauled by oxen to the site. It's located on a half acre in the national historic district of Rockland. The inn's nine guest bedrooms are furnished with antiques and original art. A typical inn breakfast is quiche, fresh fruit and juice, coffeecake or muffins, toasts, jams, coffee and tea. Guests often request picnic lunches so they can eat outdoors and listen to the waves

break and take in the salt air. The local area is becoming known in art circles because of the Farnsworth Art Museum, including its newest addition, the Wyeth Center. Many art galleries and shops of all kinds are nearby, as are beaches, parks, lighthouses and mountains. Guest may take tour boats, go kayaking, or ferry to the nearby islands for a foot or bicycle tour.

Innkeeper(s): John & Ragan Cary. $75-155. 9 rooms with PB. Breakfast included in rates. Types of meals: Full bkfst, early coffee/tea and picnic lunch. Beds: KQT. Cable TV, reading lamp, CD player and ceiling fan in room. TV, VCR, bicycles, library, parlor games, telephone and fireplace on premises. Handicap access. Small meetings and seminars hosted.

Saco   K2

Crown 'n' Anchor Inn

121 North St, PO Box 228
Saco, ME 04072-0228
(207)282-3829 (800)561-8865 Fax:(207)282-7495
E-mail: cna@gwi.net

Circa 1827. This Greek Revival house, listed in the National Register, features both Victorian baroque and colonial antiques. Two rooms include whirlpool tubs. A collection of British coronation memorabilia displayed throughout the inn includes 200 items. Guests gather in the Victorian parlor or the formal library. The innkeepers, a college librarian and an academic bookseller, lined the shelves with several thousand volumes, including extensive Civil War and British royal family collections and travel, theater and nautical books. Royal Dalton china, crystal and fresh flowers create a festive breakfast setting.

Historic Interest: Kennebunkport, The George Bush Estate, The Victorian Mansion, Portland Head Lighthouse.

Innkeeper(s): John Barclay & Martha Forester. $80-130. 6 rooms with PB, 2 with FP. Breakfast included in rates. Types of meals: Full gourmet bkfst, early coffee/tea and afternoon tea. Beds: KQDT. Cable TV and two rooms with whirlpools in room. VCR, library, parlor games, telephone and fireplace on premises. Weddings, small meetings, family reunions and seminars hosted. Amusement parks, antiquing, cross-country skiing, downhill skiing, fishing, live theater, parks, shopping, sporting events and water sports nearby.

Publicity: *Yankee, Saco, Biddeford, Old Orchard Beach Courier, Country, Portland Press Herald, Editors Choice Southern Maine for 2001 and HGTV.*

"A delightful interlude! A five star B&B."

Searsport   H5

1794 Watchtide... by the Sea

190 W Main St, US Rt 1
Searsport, ME 04974-3514
(207)548-6575 (800)698-6575 Fax:(207)548-0938
E-mail: stay@watchtide.com
Web: www.watchtide.com

Circa 1794. Once owned by General Henry Knox, Washington's first Secretary of War, this acclaimed seaside inn has been operating since 1917 and is listed in the National Register. Updated suites and guest bedrooms feature luxurious amenities that include clock radios with sound therapy, quiet air conditioners, New England

Vermont Sweetwater, cozy robes and personal care products. Choose a suite with a double whirlpool tub and fireplace. Renowned for creating scrumptious meals, the inn's breakfast is served on the 60-foot sunporch overlooking a bird sanctuary and Penobscot Bay. Play croquet on the expansive lawn. Receive a discount at the inn's antique/gift shop. Walk to the beach at Moosepoint State Park. Bar Harbor and Rockland are easy day trips from this central location.

Historic Interest: Considered by visitors to have the best antique shopping in Maine. Near Acadia National Park, lighthouses, ocean and lakes, water sports, skiing, golf, theater and excellent restaurants.

Innkeeper(s): Nancy-Linn Nellis & Jack Elliott. $95-195. 5 rooms with PB, 5 with FP, 5 with HT. Breakfast and snacks/refreshments included in rates. Types of meals: Full bkfst and early coffee/tea. Beds: KQT. Turn-down service, robes, hair dryers, clock-radios, sound therapy units, Nan's Crans, Vermont Sweet Water and super quiet Quasar air conditioners in room. Library, guest lounge with large-screen TV, game table, piano, picnic tables, horseshoes, croquet, 60' year-round sun porch furnished in wicker with fireplace overlooking Penobscot Bay, sitting room with fireplace, 18 hour refreshment bar and picnic tables overlooking the bay on premises. Antiquing, fishing, golf, live theater, museums, parks, shopping, sporting events, water sports, lighthouses, concerts, whale watching, Acadia National Park and rail and sail trips nearby.

Publicity: Boston Globe, Green Bay Press Gazette, Maine- An Explorer's Guide, City Line News, Desert News, Asbury Park Press, Yankee Magazine Editor's Choice 2001, Berkshire Eagle, Patriot Ledger and Arrington's Book Of Lists-2004 "voted best to visit again and again."

Brass Lantern Inn

81 W Main St
Searsport, ME 04974-3501
(207)548-0150 (800)691-0150
E-mail: stay@brasslanternmaine.com
Web: www.brasslanternmaine.com

Circa 1850. This Victorian inn is nestled at the edge of the woods on a rise overlooking Penobscot Bay. Once a sea captain's elegant home, it has maintained its architectural detail and allure, which has earned it a place in the National Historic Registry.  Enjoy breakfast by candlelight in the dining room with its ornate tin ceiling, where you'll feast on Maine blueberry muffins and other sumptuous treats. Centrally located between Camden and Bar Harbor, Searsport is known as the antique capital of Maine. There are many local attractions, including the Penobscot Marine Museum, fine shops and restaurants, as well as a public boat facility.

Historic Interest: Fort Knox (8 miles).

Innkeeper(s): Patricia Ann Stewart. $95-125. 5 rooms with PB. Breakfast included in rates. Types of meals: Full gourmet bkfst. Beds: QDT. Reading lamp, clock radio, clock radio, sound spas and robes in room. TV, VCR, library, telephone, fireplace, Cable TV/VCR, guest refrigerator, games, two comfortable parlors, picnic areas and Maine map books for guests' use on premises. Small meetings and family reunions hosted. Antiquing, cross-country skiing, fishing, live theater, parks, shopping, art galleries, beaches, canoeing/kayaking, golf, hiking, museums, tennis, sailing trips, whale watching and Acadia National Park nearby.

Publicity: Country Living, Republication Journal, Travel Today, Down East, Saturday Evening Post, AAA Car & Travel, Inn Traveler, Yankee Magazine Bed & Breakfast Directory recipe section, Voted Best in the North and one of the top 15 B&Bs/Inns in Arrington Journal's 2003 Book of Lists.

"We had read about your B&B and were anxious to stay here. We were delighted that the reality is even better than the description. You have done a fabulous job with all the rooms in the house and have made each one special and cozy. Thank you so very much for a delightful stay - very relaxing. And thanks for the dinner suggestion, the food was great. But your breakfast - now that was something else, again! Thanks so very much."

Carriage House Inn

120 E. Main Street
Searsport, ME 04974
(207)548-2167 (800)578-2167 Fax:(207)548-2506
E-mail: carriagehouseinn@hotmail.com
Web: www.carriagehouseinmaine.com

Circa 1874. There is a rich history behind this popularly photographed Second Empire Victorian mansion sitting on two acres of landscaped grounds with ocean vistas. It was built in 1874 by a sea captain and later owned by impressionist painter Waldo Peirce whose lifelong friend, Ernest Hemingway, visited often. Play the baby grand piano in the elegant parlor showcasing an original marble fireplace or watch a video by firelight in the nautical den. On the second floor a library/sitting area with bay views extends a peaceful spot to read or listen to a book selection on tape. Guest bedrooms with floor-to-ceiling windows are graciously furnished with 19th-century antiques and artifacts. Honeymooners enjoy the spacious Captain's Quarters with a hand-carved cherry canopy bed, marble-top dresser and bay window. A bountiful breakfast is served in the dining room.

Innkeeper(s): Marcia L. Markwardt. $85-120. 3 rooms with PB, 2 with FP. Breakfast, afternoon tea and snacks/refreshments included in rates. Types of meals: Full bkfst, veg bkfst and early coffee/tea. Beds: QD. Reading lamp, clock radio, desk and fireplace in room. TV, VCR, fax, library, parlor games and telephone on premises. Small meetings, family reunions and seminars hosted. Antiquing, art galleries, beach, bicycling, canoeing/kayaking, cross-country skiing, downhill skiing, fishing, golf, hiking, live theater, museums, parks, shopping and water sports nearby.

Homeport Inn

RR 1 Box 647
Searsport, ME 04974-9728
(207)548-2259 (800)742-5814 Fax:(207)548-2259
E-mail: hportinn@acadia.net
Web: www.homeportbnb.com

Circa 1861. Captain John Nickels built this home on Penobscot Bay. On top of the two-story historic landmark is a widow's walk. A scalloped picket fence frames the property.  Fine antiques, black marble fireplaces, a collection of grandfather clocks and elaborate ceiling medallions add to the atmosphere. Landscaped grounds sweep out to the ocean's edge. Some rooms have an ocean view. There are Victorian cottages available for weekly rental.

Historic Interest: Fort Knox, Owl's Head Lighthouse, historical architecture homes.

Innkeeper(s): Dr. & Mrs. F. George Johnson. $70-125. 10 rooms, 7 with PB. Breakfast included in rates. Types of meals: Full bkfst. Beds: KQD. Reading lamp and clock radio in room. TV, library and fireplace on premises. Weddings, small meetings and family reunions hosted. Antiquing, art galleries, beach, canoeing/kayaking, cross-country skiing, golf, hiking, live theater, museums, parks, shopping and tennis nearby.

Publicity: Yankee and Down East.

"Your breakfast is something we will never forget."

Southwest Harbor   16

Central House Inn

51 Clark Point Road
Southwest Harbor, ME 04679
(207)244-0100 (877)205-0289
E-mail: info@centralhouseinn.com
Web: www.centralhouseinn.com

Circa 1889. Run as a rooming house more than 100 years ago, meticulous renovations have recently transformed this three-story house surrounded by flower and herb gardens into a luxury inn offering year-round, smoke-free enjoyment. Its central location on Clark Point Road makes it an easy walk to shops, restaurants and the free Island Explorer bus system. Tastefully furnished guest suites feature gas fireplaces, DVD players, cable Internet access, pillow-top beds and each room boasts a shower with three heads. The South Suite includes a whirlpool tub. Look forward to daily breakfast favorites like pecan orange Belgian waffles or fresh crabmeat and feta cheese omelet. The nearby Acadia National Park is a must-see scenic treasure.

Innkeeper(s): Terry Preble. $85-175. 3 rooms with PB, 3 with FP. Breakfast and snacks/refreshments included in rates. Types of meals: Full gourmet bkfst and afternoon tea. Beds: Q. Modem hook-up, data port, cable TV, reading lamp, ceiling fan, clock radio, desk, hot tub/spa, fireplace and DVD in room. Weddings and family reunions hosted. Amusement parks, antiquing, art galleries, beach, bicycling, canoeing/kayaking, cross-country skiing, fishing, golf, hiking, live theater, museums, parks, shopping and water sports nearby.

Harbour Cottage Inn

9 Dirigo Rd
Southwest Harbor, ME 04679
(207)244-5738 (888)843-3022 Fax:(207)244-5731
E-mail: info@harbourcottageinn.com
Web: www.harbourcottageinn.com

Circa 1870. Originally known as the Island House cottage, this historic inn served as an annex for a summer hotel. Eventually, it turned into a boarding house and was used as apartments. Now more than a century old, the inn has returned to its original purpose, accommodating the many guests who flock to Maine's idyllic seashore. Some guest rooms offer a harbor view, and room sizes range from a cozy little room with a whirlpool tub to rooms with king-size canopy beds and sitting areas. Clawfoot or whirlpool tubs are available in many rooms. For breakfast, guests enjoy items such as homemade granola and freshly baked muffins or breads with an entree of perhaps blueberry pancakes or eggs Benedict. Bar Harbor and Acadia National Park are about 20 minutes away, and museums, lighthouses, restaurants and shops are nearby.

Innkeeper(s): Don Jalbert & Javier Montesinos. $89-225. 11 rooms, 7 with PB, 2 suites and 2 cottages. Breakfast and snacks/refreshments included in rates. Types of meals: Full gourmet bkfst, early coffee/tea and picnic lunch. Beds: KQT. Modem hook-up, data port, cable TV, reading lamp, refrigerator, ceiling fan, clock radio, telephone, coffeemaker, hot tub/spa and fireplace in room. Fax, spa, bicycles, library, parlor games and fireplace on premises. Weddings, small meetings, family reunions and seminars hosted. Antiquing, art galleries, beach, bicycling, canoeing/kayaking, cross-country skiing, fishing, golf, hiking, horseback riding, live theater, museums, parks, shopping, water sports and Acadia National Park nearby.

Inn at Southwest

371 Main St, PO Box 593
Southwest Harbor, ME 04679-0593
(207)244-3835 Fax:(207)244-9879
E-mail: innatsw@acadia.net
Web: www.innatsouthwest.com

Circa 1884. Peaceful harbor views are abundant from this three-story Victorian bed and breakfast centrally located in an idyllic New England town. The new owners have lovingly restored its original grandeur while renovating with modern comforts. Each of the well-appointed guest bedrooms and suites are named after the state's historic lighthouses. They boast antique furnishings, fine linens and towels, and most have gas log fireplaces. Hospitality and service are highly evident in the savory gourmet breakfast served in the dining room or wraparound porch. Specialties such as crab potato bake and eggs Florentine complement the many regional dishes that include famous Maine blueberries. Coffee and tea are always available, and guests enjoy warm cookies every afternoon. Majestic Acadia National Park and Bar Harbor are among the many local sights to explore.

Innkeeper(s): Andrea Potapovs and Sandy Johnson. $75-185. 7 rooms with PB, 3 with FP and 2 suites. Breakfast and afternoon tea included in rates. Types of meals: Full gourmet bkfst and early coffee/tea. Beds: KQD. Reading lamp, ceiling fan, clock radio, desk, down comforters and fireplace in room. Fax, copier, library, parlor games, telephone and fireplace on premises. Family reunions hosted. Antiquing, bicycling, canoeing/kayaking, fishing, golf, hiking, horseback riding, museums, parks, shopping, tennis and Acadia National Park (5 minutes) nearby.

Publicity: *Yankee Travel Guide.*

"How could any place that serves dessert for breakfast be bad?"

The Island House

121 Clark Point Rd
Southwest Harbor, ME 04679
(207)244-5180

Circa 1850. The first guests arrived at Deacon Clark's door as early as 1832. When steamboat service from Boston began in the 1850s, the Island House became a popular summer hotel. Among the guests was Ralph Waldo Emerson. In 1912, the hotel was taken down and rebuilt as two separate homes using much of the woodwork from the original building.

Innkeeper(s): Ann and Charles Bradford. $75-130. 4 rooms with PB. Breakfast included in rates. Types of meals: Full bkfst and early coffee/tea. Beds: KQDT. TV, reading lamp, clock radio and refrigerator in Carriage House in room. VCR, library, parlor games, telephone, fireplace, cable TV, CD player, telephone and guest house with private bath on premises. Small meetings, family reunions and seminars hosted. Antiquing, art galleries, beach, bicycling, canoeing/kayaking, cross-country skiing, fishing, golf, hiking, horseback riding, live theater, museums, parks, shopping, tennis and water sports nearby.

"Island House is a delight from the moment one enters the door! We loved the thoughtful extras. You've made our vacation very special!"

Lindenwood Inn

PO Box 1328
Southwest Harbor, ME 04679-1328
(207)244-5335

Circa 1906. Sea Captain Mills named his home "The Lindens" after stately linden trees in the front lawn. Elegantly refurbished, this historic house features many items collected from the new innkeeper's world travels. The rooms have sun-drenched balconies overlooking the harbor and its sailboats and lobster boats. A hearty full breakfast is served in the dining room with a roaring fireplace in the winter. The inn has a heated, in-ground swimming pool and a spa. From the inn you may take a tree-lined path down to the wharf.

Innkeeper(s): Jim King. $95-275. 9 rooms. Breakfast included in rates. Types of meals: Full bkfst. Beds: QDT. Cable TV and telephone in room. Spa and swimming on premises. Small meetings and family reunions hosted. Amusement parks, antiquing, cross-country skiing, fishing, shopping and water sports nearby.

Publicity: *McCall's.*

"We had a lovely stay at your inn. Breakfast, room and hospitality were all first-rate. You made us feel like a special friend instead of a paying guest."

Spruce Head   J5

Craignair Inn

5 Third Street
Spruce Head, ME 04859
(207)594-7644 (800)320-9997 Fax:(207)596-7124

Circa 1930. Craignair originally was built to house stonecutters working in nearby granite quarries. Overlooking the docks of the Clark Island Quarry, where granite schooners  once were loaded, this roomy, three-story inn is tastefully decorated with local antiques. A bountiful continental plus breakfast is served in the inn's dining room which offers scenic ocean and coastline views.

Historic Interest: General Knox (Washington's Secretary of War) Mansion, called Montpelier (8 miles).

Innkeeper(s): Steve & Neva Joseph. $68-135. 20 rooms, 12 with PB. Breakfast included in rates. Types of meals: Cont plus and gourmet dinner. Restaurant on premises. Beds: KQDT. Cable TV and telephone in room. Fax, copier, parlor games and fireplace on premises. Weddings, small meetings, family reunions and seminars hosted. Antiquing, cross-country skiing, downhill skiing, fishing, live theater, parks, shopping and water sports nearby.

Publicity: *Boston Globe, Free Press, Tribune, Country Living Magazine* and selected as *"one of twenty five great glorious escapes in the United States."*

"A coastal oasis of fine food and outstanding service with colonial maritime ambiance!"

Tenants Harbor   J4

East Wind Inn

Mechanic St, PO Box 149
Tenants Harbor, ME 04860-0149
(207)372-6366 (800)241-8439 Fax:(207)372-6320
E-mail: info@eastwindinn.com
Web: www.eastwindinn.com

Circa 1860. This seaside inn affords vistas of the nearby harbor and islands. The inn is comprised of a former sail loft, a captain's house, the Meeting House and adjacent Wheeler Cottage, all restored. Rooms and suites are decorated with antiques. Breakfast is served in the dining room overlooking the harbor, also the location of evening dining by candlelight. Guests can relax on one of the wraparound porches and enjoy gentle sea breezes coming in over manicured lawns and bright flower beds, or stroll around 350 feet of waterfront.

Innkeeper(s): Tim Watts & Joy Taylor. $96-275. 26 rooms, 12 with PB, 3 suites and 1 conference room. Breakfast included in rates. Types of meals: Full bkfst and dinner. Beds: KQDT. Reading lamp and telephone in room. TV, VCR, fax, copier, library and grand piano on premises. Weddings, small meetings, family reunions and seminars hosted. Antiquing, fishing, golf, tennis, water sports, museums, Farnsworth and Owls Head transportation, sailing and island trips nearby.

Publicity: *Maine Sunday Telegram and Boston Globe.*

Topsham   J3

Black Lantern B&B

6 Pleasant St
Topsham, ME 04086
(207)725-4165 (888)306-4165 Fax:(207)725-4165
E-mail: innkeeper@blacklanternbandb.com
Web: www.blacklanternbandb.com

Circa 1810. Rev. Amos Wheeler, minister at Bowdoin College, once owned this welcoming Federal-style home, with its shuttered, many-paned windows, large lawn and shade trees. It is in the National Register of Historic Places. Plaid sofas next to a fireplace invite guests to relax, and there are cozy corners for conversation, games and quilting. Guest rooms feature country curtains, quilts and hardwood floors. A popular breakfast dish, often served fireside in the dining room, is puff pancakes with fresh fruit, omelettes and bacon. (In summer, the porch is the breakfast spot.) Fresh rhubarb crisp is offered for desert. Summer theater is offered at Bowdoin College, a mile away. Popham Beach and Freeport are nearby.

Innkeeper(s): Judy & Tom Connelie. $80-90. 3 rooms with PB. Breakfast included in rates. Types of meals: Full bkfst, veg bkfst and early coffee/tea. Beds: KQT. Reading lamp and clock radio in room. Fax, copier, parlor games, telephone, fireplace and cable modem on premises. Antiquing, art galleries, beach, bicycling, canoeing/kayaking, fishing, golf, live theater, museums and shopping nearby.

Vinalhaven   I5

Payne Homestead at the Moses Webster House

Atlantic Ave
Vinalhaven, ME 04863
(207)863-9963 (888)863-9963 Fax:(207)863-2295

Circa 1873. Situated on an island, a half-mile from the ferry, this handsome Second Empire French Victorian is at the edge of town. Enjoy a game room, reading nooks and a parlor. The

Coral Room boasts a view of Indian Creek, while shadows of Carver's Pond may be seen through the windows of Mama's Room. A favorite selection is the Moses Webster Room that features a marble mantel, tin ceiling and a bay window looking out at the town. Breakfast usually offers fresh fruit platters and egg dishes with either French toast or pancakes. Restaurants and Lane Island Nature Conservancy are close. Take scenic walks past private fishing boats, ponds and shoreline, all part of the hideaway quality noted by National Geographic in "America's Best Kept Secrets."

Innkeeper(s): Lee & Donna Payne. $90-145. 5 rooms, 1 with PB. Breakfast included in rates. Types of meals: Full bkfst and early coffee/tea. TV, VCR, fax, copier, parlor games and telephone on premises. Weddings and family reunions hosted. Antiquing, bicycling, canoeing/kayaking and parks nearby.

Publicity: *National Geographic's "Best kept secrets" and Boston's New England Travel Magazine.*

"Our first stay in a B&B contributed greatly to the perfection of our honeymoon."

Waldoboro   I4

Blue Skye Farm

1708 Friendship Road
Waldoboro, ME 04572
(207)832-0300

Circa 1774. Moses Eaton's original wall stencils in the entrance hall and stairway, as well as the Indian shutters and bread oven in one of the many fireplaces reflect the history of this recently converted 18th-century home. Games and books inspire entertainment in the sitting room, and music is provided from the English piano in the dining room. Spacious guest bedrooms with four-poster, iron and spoon-cut beds boast grand views. The large country kitchen is available for preparing dinner or a midnight snack. Roam 100 acres of gardens, ponds and woodland, perfect for long hikes, cross-country skiing or birdwatching.

Historic Interest: Extensive original Moses Eaton stencils.

Innkeeper(s): Jan and Peter Davidson. $85-125. 5 rooms, 3 with PB, 2 with FP. Breakfast included in rates. Types of meals: Country bkfst, veg bkfst and early coffee/tea. Beds: KQDT. Reading lamp and fireplace in room. Swimming, library, parlor games, telephone and fireplace on premises. Antiquing, art galleries, beach, bicycling, canoeing/kayaking, cross-country skiing, fishing, hiking, horseback riding, live theater, museums, parks, shopping and water sports nearby.

Broad Bay Inn & Gallery

1014 Main St
Waldoboro, ME 04572
(207)832-6668 (800)736-6769 Fax:(207)832-4632
E-mail: innkeeper@broadbayinn.com
Web: www.broadbayinn.com

Circa 1830. Sheltered by tall pines, this 1830 Colonial inn sits in a coastal community within walking distance of the Medomak River. Victorian furnishings adorn the guest bedrooms. Sleep in a canopy bed in Sarah's Room. The Lincoln boasts elaborately carved period pieces. Wake up to an elegant breakfast accented with delicious house specialties. Visit the Gallery and Gift Shop open in July and August, featuring the "Union of Maine Visual Artists" including watercolors painted by locals. Plan to attend an art show and workshop. Relax or picnic in the garden and back deck. Open year-round; ask about special packages such as Candlelight Dinner, Sleigh Rides, Theater Tickets and Sail on the Friendship Sloop.

Innkeeper(s): Libby Hopkins. $75-110. 5 rooms, 1 with PB. Breakfast included in rates. Types of meals: Full bkfst, veg bkfst, early coffee/tea and gourmet dinner. Beds: DT. Cable TV, VCR, reading lamp, stereo, clock radio, telephone, desk and voice mail in room. Air conditioning. Fax, copier, library, parlor games, fireplace, old movies, art library, art classes and gift shop on premises. Weddings, small meetings, family reunions and seminars hosted. Antiquing, art galleries, beach, bicycling, canoeing/kayaking, cross-country skiing, downhill skiing, fishing, golf, hiking, horseback riding, live theater, museums, parks, shopping, sporting events, tennis and water sports nearby.

Publicity: *Boston Globe, Ford Times, Courier Gazette, Princeton Packet and Better Homes & Gardens Cookbook.*

"Breakfast was so special - I ran to get my camera. Why, there were even flowers on my plate."

Walpole   J4

Brannon-Bunker Inn

349 S St Rt 129
Walpole, ME 04573
(207)563-5941 (800)563-9225

Circa 1820. This Cape-style house has been a home to many generations of Maine residents, one of whom was captain of a ship that sailed to the Arctic. During the '20s, the barn served as a dance hall. Later, it was converted into comfortable guest rooms. Victorian and American antiques are featured, and there are collections of WWI military memorabilia.

Innkeeper(s): Joe & Jeanne Hovance. $80-90. 7 rooms, 5 with PB and 1 suite. Breakfast included in rates. Types of meals: Cont plus. Beds: QDT. TV, reading lamp, clock radio and desk in room. VCR, library, child care, parlor games, telephone and fireplace on premises. Limited handicap access. Weddings, small meetings, family reunions and seminars hosted. Antiquing, art galleries, beach, bicycling, canoeing/kayaking, fishing, golf, hiking, horseback riding, museums, parks, shopping, tennis and water sports nearby.

Publicity: *Times-Beacon Newspaper.*

"Wonderful beds, your gracious hospitality and the very best muffins anywhere made our stay a memorable one."

Waterford   I2

Bear Mountain Inn

364 Waterford Rd
Waterford, ME 04088
(207)583-4404 Fax:(207)583-2437
E-mail: bearmtnin@megalink.net

Circa 1825. Sitting on the shores of Bear Lake, every season is a pleasure at this 52-acre, 180-year-old bed & breakfast that has been recently renovated and boasts country-style decor and furnishings. Relax on porch rockers or take a nap on a hammock. Watch television in the living room or play cards by the fireplace. Accommodations include luxurious one- and two-bedroom suites in the inn, private Sugar Bear Cottage and a Rustic Log Cabin with a view. After a hearty breakfast try ice fishing in the pond or swim, canoe, kayak or paddleboat. Snowmobile or hike Bear River Mountain. Ask about special package deals and pet arrangements.

Innkeeper(s): Lorraine Blais. $100-275. 10 rooms, 6 with PB, 3 with FP, 1 suite, 1 cottage, 1 cabin and 1 conference room. Beds: QDT. Cable TV, VCR, reading lamp, refrigerator, ceiling fan, snack bar, clock radio, telephone, coffeemaker, desk and 3 with fireplace in room. Air conditioning. Spa, swimming, fireplace and gift shop on premises. Weddings, small meetings, family reunions and seminars hosted.

Kedarburn Inn

Rt 35 Box 61
Waterford, ME 04088
(207)583-6182 (866)583-6182 Fax:(207)583-6424
E-mail: inn@kedarburn.com
Web: www.kedarburn.com

Circa 1858. The innkeepers of this Victorian establishment invite guests to try a taste of olde English hospitality and cuisine at their inn, nestled in the foothills of the White Mountains in Western Maine. Located in a historic village, the inn sits beside the flowing Kedar Brook, which runs to the shores of Lake Keoka. Each of the spacious rooms is decorated with handmade quilts and dried flowers. Explore the inn's shop and you'll discover a variety of quilts and crafts, all made by innkeeper Margaret Gibson. Ask about special quilting weekends. With prior reservation, the innkeepers will prepare an English afternoon tea.

Innkeeper(s): Margaret & Derek Gibson. $71-125. 7 rooms, 5 with PB and 1 suite. Breakfast included in rates. Types of meals: Full bkfst, early coffee/tea, afternoon tea and snacks/refreshments. Beds: KQDT. Reading lamp, clock radio and desk in room. Air conditioning. VCR, fax, parlor games, telephone and fireplace on premises. Antiquing, cross-country skiing, downhill skiing, fishing, live theater, shopping and water sports nearby.

Publicity: *Maine Times.*

Lake House

686 Waterford Rd.
Waterford, ME 04088
(207)583-4182 (800)223-4182 Fax:(207)583-2831
E-mail: info@lakehousemaine.com
Web: www.lakehousemaine.com

Circa 1790. Situated on the common, the Lake House was first a hotel and stagecoach stop. In 1817, granite baths were constructed below the first floor. The inn opened as "Dr. Shattuck's Maine Hygienic Institute for Ladies." It continued as a popular health spa until the 1890s. Now noted for excellent country cuisine, there are two dining rooms for non-smokers. There are seven guest rooms. The spacious Grand Ballroom Suite features curved ceilings and a sitting area with TV.

Innkeeper(s): Michael & Doreen Myers. $90-170. 7 rooms with PB, 2 suites and 1 conference room. Breakfast included in rates. Types of meals: Full bkfst and dinner. Restaurant on premises. Beds: KQ. Data port, reading lamp, ceiling fan, clock radio, coffeemaker and desk in room. Air conditioning. TV, library, parlor games, telephone and fireplace on premises. Weddings, small meetings and family reunions hosted. Antiquing, beach, canoeing/kayaking, cross-country skiing, downhill skiing, fishing, golf, hiking, live theater, parks, shopping and wineries nearby.

Publicity: *Bon Appetit, Downeast, Portland Press Herald and Travel & Leisure.*

"Your hospitality was matched only by the quality of dinner that we were served."

Wells Beach   K2

Haven By The Sea

59 Church St
Wells Beach, ME 04090
(207)646-4194 Fax:(207)646-6883

Circa 1920. Just steps away from the Atlantic's sandy beaches, enjoy the sea air at this inviting inn that was originally a post and beam church. Traditional and Victorian décor accent the inn. A variety of common areas with fireplaces and romantic lighting offer warm and welcoming places to relax. Guest bedrooms and a spacious suite feature comfortable furnishings. Larger accommodations include a furnished apartment called Haven's Heaven and A Bit of Haven, the adjacent guesthouse. A satisfying breakfast boasts an appetizer of fruit, sorbet, compote or baked goods, a gourmet egg entrée, specialty pancakes, quiches and meat dishes. The inn hosts special events from weddings to corporate meetings and retreats. Ask about available Getaway Packages.

Historic Interest: Once a vintage church.

Innkeeper(s): John and Susan Jarvis. $119-275. 5 rooms with PB, 1 with FP, 1 suite and 1 conference room. Breakfast included in rates. Types of meals: Full gourmet bkfst, early coffee/tea and room service. Beds: KQT. Modem hook-up, cable TV, reading lamp, ceiling fan, clock radio, turn-down service and fireplace in room. VCR, fax, copier, library, parlor games and gift shop on premises. Weddings, small meetings, family reunions and seminars hosted. Amusement parks, antiquing, art galleries, beach, bicycling, canoeing/kayaking, fishing, golf, hiking, horseback riding, live theater, museums, parks, shopping, tennis and water sports nearby.

Publicity: *Down East Magazine, York County Coast Star, Making It At Home and Portland Press Herald.*

West Boothbay Harbor   J4

Lawnmeer Inn

PO Box 505
West Boothbay Harbor, ME 04575-0505
(800)633-7645
E-mail: cooncat@lawnmeerinn.com
Web: www.lawnmeerinn.com

Circa 1899. This pleasant inn sits by the shoreline, providing a picturesque oceanfront setting. Located on a small, wooded island, it is accessed by a lift bridge. Rooms are clean and homey and there is a private honeymoon cottage in the Smoke House. The dining room is waterside and serves continental cuisine with an emphasis on seafood. Boothbay Harbor is two miles away.

Innkeeper(s): Lee & Jim Metzger. $95-195. 32 rooms with PB, 1 suite and 1 cottage. Types of meals: Full bkfst, early coffee/tea and gourmet dinner. Restaurant on premises. Beds: KQD. Reading lamp and desk in room. Parlor games, telephone and fireplace on premises. Weddings, small meetings and family reunions hosted. Antiquing, fishing, live theater, shopping and water sports nearby.

Publicity: *Los Angeles Times and Getaways for Gourmets.*

"Your hospitality was warm and gracious and the food delectable."

Wiscasset   J4

Snow Squall B&B

5 Bradford Rd
Wiscasset, ME 04578
(207)882-6892 (800)775-7245 Fax:(207)882-6832
E-mail: snowsquall@maine.com
Web: www.snowsquallinn.com

Circa 1848. A quarter mile from the water on Route 1 in mid-coast Maine stands this Colonial inn. Stone walkways cross the beautifully landscaped two-and-a-half acres set in the town of Wiscasset, known as "the prettiest village in Maine." The four main house guest bedrooms and two Carriage House suites are all named after clipper ships and are all decorated in Down East tradition. Guests enjoy a full breakfast in the dining room at individual tables. The menu includes cereal, juice, fresh fruit and one of the inn's specialty hot entrees such as Sausage Strata, baked French toast with blueberries or Baked Eggs Supreme. After this hearty meal guests may explore the natural beauty of the area, which is renowned for its rugged coastline, estuaries, peninsulas and islands. Other options include sea kayaking, sailing, fishing, bicycling, hiking or a whale/puffin cruise from Boothbay Harbor or Pemaquid. In the evening, relax in the den or watch videos that will help plan your next day's adventure.

Innkeeper(s): Anne & Steve Kornacki. $95-220. 6 rooms with PB, 2 with FP and 2 suites. Breakfast included in rates. Types of meals: Full bkfst. Beds: KQT. Modem hook-up, data port, reading lamp, ceiling fan, clock radio and fireplace in room. Air conditioning. TV, VCR, fax, copier, library, telephone and fireplace on premises. Seminars hosted. Antiquing, art galleries, beach, bicycling, canoeing/kayaking, fishing, hiking, museums, parks, shopping and water sports nearby.

The Squire Tarbox Inn

1181 Main Road
Wiscasset, ME 04578-3501
(207)882-7693 (800)818-0626 Fax:(207)882-7107
E-mail: squiretarbox@prexar.com
Web: squiretarboxinn.com

Circa 1763. Meadows, stone walls and woods surround this country inn. Squire Tarbox built this rambling farmhouse around a building originally constructed in 1763. Today, the rooms are

warm and comfortable in the inn and in the remodeled hayloft. A house-party atmosphere pervades the inn. Beaches, harbors and lobster shacks are some of the nearby visitor hot spots.

Historic Interest: Maritime Museum, old forts, lighthouses, sea captain's homes, abundant antique shops, fishing museums, windjammers, beaches, lobster shacks, etc. (30 minutes). World's finest Music Box Museum.

Innkeeper(s): Roni & Mario De Pietro. $122-190. 11 rooms with PB, 4 with FP. Breakfast included in rates. Types of meals: Full bkfst, early coffee/tea and gourmet dinner. Restaurant on premises. Beds: KQDT. Reading lamp in room. Air conditioning. Bicycles, telephone, fireplace and row boat on premises. Antiquing, fishing, live theater, parks, shopping, beaches, lobster shacks, museums and harbors nearby.

Publicity: *Washington Post, New York Times, Yankee, Bon Appetit, USA Today and Public.*

"Your hospitality was warm, friendly, well-managed and quite genuine. That's a rarity, and it's just the kind we feel best with."

York   L2

Dockside Guest Quarters

PO Box 205
York, ME 03909-0205
(207)363-2868 (800)270-1977 Fax:(207)363-1977
E-mail: info@docksidegq.com
Web: www.docksidegq.com

Circa 1900. This small resort provides a panoramic view of the Atlantic Ocean and harbor activities. Guest rooms are located in the classic, large New England home, which is the Maine House, and modern multi-unit buildings. All rooms have private balconies or porches with unobstructed views of the water. Some rooms have fireplaces. The on-premise restaurant is bi-level with floor to ceiling windows, affording each

table a view of the harbor. Child-care services are available.

Historic Interest: The York Historic District offers several interesting sites.

Innkeeper(s): Lusty Family. $85-215. 25 rooms, 2 with FP, 6 suites and 1 conference room. Types of meals: Cont plus, early coffee/tea, lunch and afternoon tea. Restaurant on premises. Beds: KQDT. Cable TV, reading lamp and refrigerator in room. TV, fax, bicycles, library, child care, parlor games, telephone and fireplace on premises. Amusement parks, antiquing, cross-country skiing, fishing, live theater, parks, shopping and water sports nearby.

Publicity: *Portland Press Herald, Boston Globe and Yankee Travel Guide.*

"We've been back many years. It's a paradise for us, the scenery, location, maintenance, living quarters."

York Harbor   L2

York Harbor Inn

PO Box 573, Rt 1A
York Harbor, ME 03911-0573
(207)363-5119 (800)343-3869 Fax:(207)363-7151
E-mail: info@yorkharborinn.com
Web: www.yorkharborinn.com

Circa 1800. Experience a relaxing coastal getaway or business retreat at this luxurious oceanfront inn, located in the historical district with period estates listed in the National Register. Gathering rooms include the Cabin room, originally a sail loft from the 1600s, showcasing a massive fieldstone fireplace. Many of the large guest bedrooms and suites feature fireplaces, Jacuzzi tubs, heated tile bathroom floors,

decks and seascapes. Taste award-winning gourmet dining overlooking the Atlantic, or enjoy a pub menu and entertainment in the Ship's Cellar Pub. A gift shop and outdoor hot tub offer pleasant indulgences.

Historic Interest: Old York Historical Society Museum buildings (1.5 miles), Strawberry Banke Colonial Village Museum (6 miles).

Innkeeper(s): Garry Dominguez. $99-329. 47 rooms with PB, 18 with FP, 10 suites and 7 conference rooms. Breakfast included in rates. Types of meals: Cont plus, early coffee/tea, lunch, gourmet dinner and room service. Restaurant on premises. Beds: KQD. Data port, cable TV, reading lamp, clock radio, telephone, climate control, ironing board, many with fireplaces, 19 with ocean views, Jacuzzi spa tubs and Internet access via data port in room. Air conditioning. VCR, fax, copier, hot tub, AV equipment, restaurant, pub and meeting and function rooms on premises. Weddings, small meetings, family reunions and seminars hosted. Antiquing, art galleries, beach, bicycling, canoeing/kayaking, cross-country skiing, fishing, golf, horseback riding, live theater, museums, parks, shopping, water sports, Kittery Outlet shopping, seaside drives, area lighthouses, whale watching, island and river boat tours, deep sea fishing, historic house tours, holiday festivals, seasonal dinner theatre and lobster nearby.

Publicity: *New York Times, Down East, Food & Wine, The Learning Channel, Ladies Home and Travel Channel-"Great Country Inns."*

"It's hard to decide where to stay when you're paging through a book of country inns. This time we chose well."

Maryland

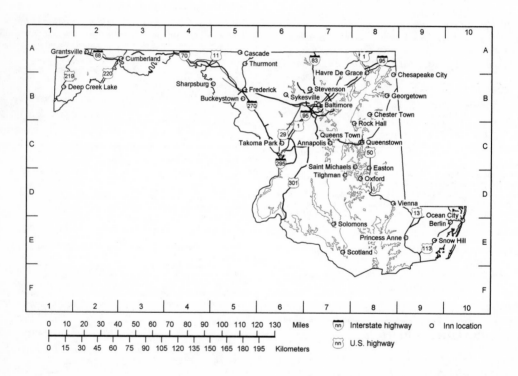

Annapolis C7

1908-William Page Inn B&B

8 Martin St
Annapolis, MD 21401-1716
(410)626-1506 (800)364-4160 Fax:(410)263-4841
E-mail: info@williampageinn.com
Web: www.williampageinn.com

Circa 1908. This turn-of-the-century cedar shingle home, immaculately renovated, offers a setting of Victorian elegance and comfort. For more than 50 years, the Four Square-style house served as the Democratic Club in the historic district. The inn now offers visitors five distinctively appointed guest rooms furnished with antiques and family collectibles. Crystal chandeliers, artwork, polished woodwork and an open stairway invite guests to a relaxing and pampered stay. The common room features a fireplace and wet bar service. Guests enjoy full breakfasts, often served on the wraparound porch or in one of the parlors.

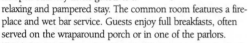

Historic Interest: For more then fifty years this home served as the local Democratic club.

Innkeeper(s): Robert L. Zuchelli. $120-250. 5 rooms, 3 with PB and 1 suite. Breakfast and snacks/refreshments included in rates. Types of meals: Full bkfst, veg bkfst and early coffee/tea. Beds: Q. Data port, reading lamp, CD player, refrigerator, snack bar, clock radio, telephone and some with whirlpools in room. Air conditioning. Fax, copier, parlor games, fireplace and off-street parking on premises. Small meetings and family reunions hosted. Amusement parks, antiquing, art galleries, beach, bicycling, canoeing/kayaking, fishing, golf, hiking, horseback riding, live theater, museums, parks, shopping, tennis and water sports nearby.

Publicity: *National Geographic Traveller, Our World International Travel Magazine, The Discerning Traveler and PBS series "Country Inn Cooking."*

"It was such a pleasure to see such a very elegantly appointed Victorian inn."

201 Bed & Breakfast

201 Prince George St
Annapolis, MD 21401
(410)268-8053 Fax:(410)263-3007
E-mail: bbat201@aol.com
Web: www.201bb.com

Circa 1800. Sitting amongst other fine historic homes, this grand house was built in the Georgian style of architecture. It is furnished with distinctive English and American period antiques, exuding a comfortable elegance. Overstuffed couches and a fireplace create a warm welcome in the double parlor that leads outdoors to a spacious garden with fish ponds and orchid house. Large guest suites are well-appointed with four-poster beds, refrigerators, sitting areas and double Jacuzzis. Some boast views of the Capitol building's dome. Bring a big appetite to the dining room in the morning for a full English breakfast. The delicious meal is highlighted by a vintage crystal chandelier. Stress-free, on-site parking is available. The U.S. Naval Academy and city dock are just a few blocks away.

Innkeeper(s): Robert Bryant & Graham Gardnerr. $130-225. 4 rooms with PB, 1 with FP and 2 suites. Breakfast included in rates. Types of meals: Full gourmet bkfst and early coffee/tea. Beds: Q. Modem hook-up, cable TV, VCR, reading lamp, refrigerator, clock radio, turn-down service, desk, hot tub/spa and fireplace in room. Central air. Fax, copier, library, telephone and fireplace on premises. Small meetings and family reunions hosted. Antiquing, art galleries, beach, bicycling, canoeing/kayaking, fishing, golf, hiking, live theater, museums, parks and shopping nearby.

55 East Bed and Breakfast

55 East St
Annapolis, MD 21401
(410)295-0202 Fax:(410)295-0203
E-mail: tricia@erols.com
Web: www.55east.com

Circa 1864. Experience a gracious interlude in the heart of the historic district at this Federal-period house with Victorian details. Relax in comfortably elegant living rooms accented by gas fireplaces with antique New Orleans mantles. Watch TV in the parlor, or borrow a book from the library. Heirlooms and original art highlight the serene guest bedrooms that feature a sitting room, computer hook-up, robes, fresh flowers and evening treats. The Russell and Johnson rooms boast French doors onto a covered balcony. Read the morning paper in the garden courtyard before breakfast. Ice and beverages are available at any time.

Historic Interest: It is a Federal period house restored to one of its historic uses, that of being a home, although built initially as a store/residence and used as a boarding house.

Innkeeper(s): Tricia & Mat Herban. $140-175. 3 rooms with PB. Breakfast included in rates. Types of meals: Full gourmet bkfst and early coffee/tea. Beds: KQT. Modem hook-up, data port, cable TV, reading lamp, clock radio, telephone, coffeemaker and fireplace in room. Central air. TV, fax, library and parlor games on premises. Small meetings hosted. Amusement parks, antiquing, art galleries, beach, bicycling, canoeing/kayaking, fishing, golf, hiking, live theater, museums, parks, shopping, sporting events, tennis and water sports nearby.

Publicity: *Recommended by the Los Angeles Times, Washington Post, Baltimore Sun, Baltimore Magazine, PGA Tour recommendation and PBS Cooking on the Chesapeake.*

The Barn on Howard's Cove

500 Wilson Rd
Annapolis, MD 21401-1052
(410)266-6840 Fax:(410)266-7293
E-mail: gdgutsche5@aol.com
Web: www.bnbweb.com/howards-cove.html

Circa 1850. This renovated 1850 horse barn is located just outside Annapolis on a cove of the Severn River. The six-and-a-half-acre grounds create a restful environment. The two guest rooms, which are decorated with antiques and handmade quilts, offer water and garden views. There is also a small kitchen area between the two guest rooms for preparing snacks and coffee. A private balcony adjoins one guest room. The innkeepers, a U.S. Naval Academy professor and an artist also keep a unique Noah's Ark collection on display. The innkeepers have canoes and kayaks on the premises for guests.

Historic Interest: U.S. Naval Academy, the Paca House, Saint Johns College.

Innkeeper(s): Graham & Libbie Gutsche. $125. 2 rooms with PB and 1 conference room. Breakfast included in rates. Types of meals: Full gourmet bkfst. Beds: Q. Cable TV, VCR, reading lamp, refrigerator, ceiling fan, snack bar, clock radio and coffeemaker in room. Central air. TV, fax, copier, swimming, parlor games, telephone, fireplace, canoe and dock on premises. Family reunions hosted. Antiquing, art galleries, beach, bicycling, canoeing/kayaking, fishing, golf, hiking, live theater, museums, parks, shopping, sporting events, tennis and water sports nearby.

Publicity: *Baltimore Sun, New York Times, Mid-Atlantic Country, Christian American, Washington Post, Annapolis Capital "Home of the Week" and Arrington's 2002 Book of Lists.*

"Thank you so much for your gracious hospitality and for making our wedding night special."

Chez Amis B&B

85 East St
Annapolis, MD 21401-1729
(410)263-6631 (888)224-6455
E-mail: stay@chezamis.com
Web: www.chezamis.com

Circa 1854. This historic bed & breakfast once served as a local grocery store, and the guest rooms were once the living quarters of the former store owner. Guest rooms are decorated with brass beds and antique quilts. The innkeepers can provide champagne or perhaps a heart-shaped cake for guests celebrating a special occasion. Guests can walk to the capitol and the U.S. Naval Academy, as well as shops, restaurants and the harbor. Innkeepers Don and Mickie Deline have interesting former careers. Don, a former army lawyer, was the head lawyer for the Senate Armed Services Committee. Mickie was a tour guide in Washington, D.C., for nearly a decade and is equally full of knowledge about Annapolis.

Innkeeper(s): Don & Mickie Deline. $135-165. 4 rooms with PB. Breakfast included in rates. Types of meals: Full gourmet bkfst. Beds: KQT. Cable TV, reading lamp and clock radio in room. Air conditioning. VCR, fax, copier and telephone on premises. Weddings, small meetings, family reunions and seminars hosted. Antiquing, fishing, live theater, parks, shopping, sporting events, water sports and sailing nearby.

Publicity: *Baltimore Sun, Tate County Democrat, Washington Post, Chesapeake Home, Baltimore Magazine, Cottage Style, Country Collectibles, Inns & Outs of Collecting and Channel 9 News.*

Flag House Inn Bed & Breakfast

26 Randall St
Annapolis, MD 21401-1720
(410)280-2721 (800)437-4825 Fax:(410)280-0133
E-mail: info@flaghouseinn.com
Web: www.flaghouseinn.com

Circa 1878. Reflecting its name, the state or national flag of each guest is hung outside this inn, located in the center of the National Historic District. Originally two Victorian townhouses, the traditional decor blends Oriental and nautical motifs with antiques and reproductions. The spacious guest library is a welcome spot to enjoy fireside reading of local area guides and related books and magazines. Comfortable seating, good lighting and privacy are appealing amenities of the guest bedrooms. Fruit, cereals, fresh-baked breads, pastries and hot entrees are prepared for a satisfying breakfast in the dining room. The full-length front porch offers swings and teak benches to linger in. Coveted off-street parking is available on-site, and the many attractions of this bayside Colonial town are an easy walk.

Innkeeper(s): Charlotte & Bill Schmickle. $120-250. 5 rooms with PB, 1 suite and 1 conference room. Breakfast included in rates. Types of meals: Full bkfst. Beds: KT. Cable TV, reading lamp, ceiling fan, clock radio and desk in room. Central air. Fax, copier, library, parlor games, telephone, fireplace, front porch with swings and off-street parking on premises. Small meetings and seminars hosted. Amusement parks, antiquing, art galleries, beach, canoeing/kayaking, fishing, golf, live theater, museums, parks, shopping, sporting events, water sports, historic homes and public buildings, sailing, boat tours, Naval museum and model shop gallery and historic walking tours nearby.

Georgian House B&B

170 Duke of Gloucester St
Annapolis, MD 21401-2517
(410)263-5618 (800)557-2068
E-mail: info@georgianhouse.com
Web: www.georgianhouse.com

Circa 1747. Stay in this 250-year-old home once used by signers of the Declaration of Independence as a clubhouse. Today this pre-Revolutionary home is a landmark in the heart of the historic district, renown for being a comfortable and elegant  bed and breakfast. Original yellow pine floors, 16-inch thick brick walls and six fireplaces are accented by fine oil paintings, period window treatments and bed covers. Guest bedrooms with private baths and other modern conveniences pamper and please. Read the paper in the double salon or relax in the garden. Listen to the mini-grand player piano during a satisfying breakfast. Videos, books, a stocked refrigerator and a microwave are found in the second floor library.

Historic Interest: Our house is in the federal government's Historic Register.
Innkeeper(s): Sandy & Hank Mayer. $145-190. 4 rooms with PB, 1 with FP and 1 suite. Breakfast included in rates. Types of meals: Full gourmet bkfst and early coffee/tea. Beds: Q. Modern hook-up, VCR, reading lamp, ceiling fan, clock radio, telephone and desk in room. Air conditioning. Copier, parlor games and fireplace on premises. Antiquing, fishing, golf, live theater, parks, shopping, sporting events, tennis and water sports nearby.
Publicity: *National Geographic Traveler and Chesapeake Life.*

Gibson's Lodgings

110 Prince George St
Annapolis, MD 21401-1704
(410)268-5555 (877)330-0057
E-mail: gibsonslodging@starpower.net
Web: www.gibsonslodgings.com

Circa 1774. This Georgian house in the heart of the Annapolis Historic District was built on the site of the Old Courthouse, circa 1680. Two historic houses make up the inn, and there was a new house built in 1988. All the rooms, old and new, are furnished with antiques. Only a few yards away is the City Dock Harbor and within two blocks is the Naval Academy visitor's gate.

Historic Interest: U.S. Naval Academy, Chesapeake Bay.
Innkeeper(s): Bev Snyder & John Lauer. $99-279. 21 rooms, 17 with PB, 6 suites and 1 conference room. Breakfast included in rates. Types of meals: Cont. Beds: QT. Air conditioning. Free parking on premises. Limited handicap access. Small meetings and seminars hosted. Antiquing, fishing, live theater, parks, shopping, sporting events and water sports nearby.
Publicity: *Mid-Atlantic Country and New York.*

"We had a delightful stay! We enjoyed the proximity to the waterfront, the fun atmosphere and the friendly people."

Jonas Green House B&B

124 Charles St
Annapolis, MD 21401-2621
(410)263-5892 (877)892-4845 Fax:(410)263-5895
E-mail: jghouse@erols.com
Web: www.bbhost.com/jghouse

Circa 1690. For those seeking a truly historic vacation, Jonas Green House is a perfect starting place. The kitchen building of this historic home was completed in the 1690s and still houses the original cooking fireplace and an original crane. From this point, more was added until its completion sometime in the 1740s. Much of the home's original floors, wainscoting, fireplace and a corner cabinet with original glass has survived through the years. The home is named for one of innkeeper Randy Brown's rela- 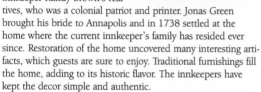 tives, who was a colonial patriot and printer. Jonas Green brought his bride to Annapolis and in 1738 settled at the home where the current innkeeper's family has resided ever since. Restoration of the home uncovered many interesting arti-facts, which guests are sure to enjoy. Traditional furnishings fill the home, adding to its historic flavor. The innkeepers have kept the decor simple and authentic.

Historic Interest: The National Landmark home rests in the middle of a his-toric district. The Colonial Capitol Building is three blocks north and all of Annapolis' historic structures and the U.S. Naval Academy are within five or six blocks of the inn.

Innkeeper(s): Randy & Dede Brown. $100-135. 3 rooms, 1 with PB, 2 with FP. Breakfast included in rates. Types of meals: Full bkfst. Beds: KQDT. Reading lamp and clock radio in room. Central air. Fax, copier, parlor games, telephone and fireplace on premises. Small meetings hosted. Antiquing, fish-ing, live theater, parks, shopping, sporting events and water sports nearby.

Publicity: *Annapolitan, Capital, Washington Post, National Geographic Traveler, New York Times and Baltimore Sun.*

"Thank you for your hospitality in a wonderful house so full of per-sonal and American history."

Baltimore B7

Abacrombie Fine Foods & Accommodations

58 W Biddle St
Baltimore, MD 21201-5534
(410)244-7227 (888)922-3437 Fax:(410)244-8415
E-mail: info@badger-inn.com
Web: www.badger-inn.com

Circa 1890. This five-story row house was once the home to Colonel Biddle of the Union Army. The home includes a dozen guest rooms with English appointments. Guests can relax in the first-floor parlor and enjoy dinner at the 80-seat fine dining restaurant and full bar, also located in the inn. The Meyerhoff Symphony Hall is across the street from the B&B, which is located in Baltimore's cultural center. Antique shops and an opera house are just a few blocks away, as is the streetcar line, which will take guests to the convention center, stadiums and other attractions.

Innkeeper(s): Mr. & Mrs. Edward M. Sweetman. $88-155. 12 rooms with PB. Breakfast included in rates. Types of meals: Cont plus. Restaurant on premises. Beds: Q. Modem hook-up, cable TV, reading lamp, clock radio,

telephone, desk and voice mail in room. Central air. Fax, copier, library and parking off street on premises. Antiquing, art galleries, canoeing/kayaking, golf, live theater, museums, parks, shopping and sporting events nearby.

Hopkins Inn

3403 St Paul St
Baltimore, MD 21218
(410)235-8600 (800)537-8483 Fax:(410)235-7051
E-mail: hopkinsinn@bichotels.com
Web: www.hopkinsinnbaltimore.com

Circa 1920. Major renovations have turned this inn with Spanish Revival architecture into uptown elegance. Victorian decor and antique furnishings reside with original artwork in tasteful luxury. A meeting room and a conference room are available for business or pleasure. The inviting guest bedrooms have a cozy ambiance. Start the day with a continental break-fast. Centrally located across from Johns Hopkins University on renown Homewood Campus, it is close to all the attractions this area has to offer.

Historic Interest: Built in the 1920s the building was originally part of a seven building residential project. In the 1980s it was restored and trans-formed into the inn and was part of a regional group of inns in Baltimore and Philadelphia. Today it is part of a collection of hotels owned by Baltimore International College.

Innkeeper(s): Mr. Jeff Lambert. $89-159. 25 rooms, 14 with PB, 11 suites and 2 conference rooms. Breakfast and afternoon tea included in rates. Types of meals: Cont plus and early coffee/tea. Beds: QT. Modem hook-up, cable TV, reading lamp, clock radio, telephone and desk in room. Air conditioning. Fax, copier and parlor games on premises. Weddings, small meetings and family reunions hosted. Antiquing, art galleries, bicycling, golf, hiking, muse-ums, parks, shopping, sporting events, Baltimore Inner Harbor, Union Memorial Hospital, Baltimore Museum of Art, Camden Yards, PSI Net Stadium and Convention Center nearby.

Inn at 2920

2920 Elliott St
Baltimore, MD 21224
(410)342-4450 (877)774-2920 Fax:(410)342-6436
E-mail: reservations@theinnat2920.com
Web: www.theinnat2920.com

Circa 1880. Decorated with an eclectic contemporary style, this large, old-fashioned Rowhouse features original details like exposed brick, a copper ceiling and wood staircase. The inn sits in Canton, a premier waterfront neighborhood located downtown. Each well-appointed guest bedroom provides an assortment of comforts including a Jacuzzi, fine linens, hypo-allergenic bedding and Kingsdown mattress. Tall ceilings, large windows, sleigh and wrought iron canopy beds accent a spa-cious ambiance. Sensitive to the needs of the business traveler, corporate packages are available, offering high-tech assistance. Chef David uses mostly farm fresh, organic ingredients to make delicious and well-presented breakfasts. He maintains an herb and vegetable garden in the dining room bay window. Exciting city life is within walking distance.

Innkeeper(s): David & Debbie Schwartz. $155-225. 4 rooms with PB. Breakfast and snacks/refreshments included in rates. Types of meals: Full gourmet bkfst and veg bkfst. Beds: KQ. Cable TV, VCR, reading lamp, CD player, ceiling fan, clock radio, turn-down service, desk, hot tub/spa, corpo-rate package includes high-speed and wireless internet access and mobile phone for the duration of stay in room. Central air. Fax, copier, parlor games, telephone and fireplace on premises. Small meetings hosted. Antiquing, art galleries, fishing, live theater, museums, parks, shopping, sporting events, Camden yards, Ravens stadium, inner harbor and Baltimore convention cen-ter nearby.

Mr. Mole B&B

1601 Bolton St
Baltimore, MD 21217-4317
(410)728-1179 Fax:(410)728-3379

Circa 1869. Set on a quiet, upscale street in the historic Bolton Hill neighborhood, this restored brick town house, named after the fastidious character in The Wind in the Willows, is a combination of whimsical romantic ambiance and old Baltimore society. Throughout the house, 18th- and 19th-century antiques enhance wainscoting, painted draped ivy and 14-foot ceilings. Each guest room and suite features a different theme. The Garden Suite, blooming with sunny floral prints and plaid, offers a bright, third-floor sun room, sitting room and a spacious private bath. The Explorer Suite features sophisticated leopard-print fabrics and a zebra-skin rug. This inn received Mobil's four-star rating from '95-'99. It is located six blocks from the Meyerhoff Symphony Hall, the Lyric Opera House, the Metro and the beginning of Baltimore's Antique Row.

Historic Interest: On historic Bolton Hill. Located close to Johns Hopkins University and the University of Baltimore. Downtown Baltimore, the Inner Harbor and Fells Point are five minutes away by car, Metro or trolley.

Innkeeper(s): Paul Bragaw & Collin Clarke. $119-175. 5 rooms with PB, 4 with FP and 2 suites. Breakfast included in rates. Types of meals: Cont plus. Beds: Q. Modem hook-up, reading lamp, clock radio, telephone, turn-down service, desk and voice mail in room. Air conditioning. Fax and library on premises. Antiquing, golf, live theater, parks, shopping and sporting events nearby.

Publicity: *Baltimore Magazine, Maryland Magazine, Travel Holiday, Mid-Atlantic, Washingtonian, New York Times and National Geographic.*

Berlin   E10

Merry Sherwood Plantation

8909 Worcester Hwy
Berlin, MD 21811-3016
(410)641-2112 (800)660-0358 Fax:(410)641-9528
E-mail: info@merrysherwood.com
Web: www.merrysherwood.com

Circa 1859. This magnificent pre-Civil War mansion is a tribute to Southern plantation architecture. The inn features antique period furniture, hand-woven, Victorian era rugs and a square grand piano. The ballroom, now a parlor for guests, boasts twin fireplaces and pier mirrors. (Ask to see the hidden cupboards behind the fireside bookcases in the library.) Nineteen acres of grounds are beautifully landscaped and feature azaleas, boxwoods and 125 varieties of trees.

Innkeeper(s): Kirk Burbage. $125-175. 8 rooms, 6 with PB, 4 with FP and 1 suite. Breakfast included in rates. Types of meals: Full gourmet bkfst and afternoon tea. Beds: QD. Air conditioning. Telephone and fireplace on premises. Weddings, small meetings, family reunions and seminars hosted. Amusement parks, antiquing, fishing, shopping and water sports nearby.

Publicity: *Washington Post, Baltimore Sun and Southern Living.*

"Pure elegance and privacy at its finest."

Buckeystown   B5

The Inn at Buckeystown

3521 Buckeystown Pike
Buckeystown, MD 21717
(301)874-5755 (800)272-1190 Fax:(301)831-1355
E-mail: info@innatbuckeystown.com
Web: www.innatbuckeystown.com

Circa 1897. Gables, bay windows and a wraparound porch are features of this grand Victorian mansion located on two-and-a-half acres of lawns and gardens (and an ancient cemetery). The inn features a polished staircase, antiques and elegantly decorated guest rooms. Ask for the Deja Vu Suite, which boasts a working fireplace and oak decor. A gourmet dinner is served by request. High tea and monthly murder mysteries are also offered. The inn also hosts weddings, rehearsals and retreats. The village of Buckeystown is in the National Register.

Historic Interest: Frederick, Barbara Fritchie and Francis Scott Key grave sites (4 miles), National Battle of the Monocacy Civil War Battlefield Park (3 miles), Camp David (15 miles).

Innkeeper(s): Janet Wells. $90-225. 8 rooms, 5 with PB. Breakfast and snacks/refreshments included in rates. Types of meals: Full gourmet bkfst, veg bkfst, early coffee/tea and dinner. Restaurant on premises. Beds: QD. Cable TV, reading lamp, refrigerator and desk in room. Air conditioning. TV, VCR, fax, parlor games, telephone, fireplace and tea room on premises. Weddings, small meetings, family reunions and seminars hosted. Antiquing, art galleries, bicycling, canoeing/kayaking, downhill skiing, fishing, golf, live theater, museums, parks, shopping, sporting events and wineries nearby.

Publicity: *Mid-Atlantic, Innsider, The Washingtonian, Washington Post and Baltimore Sun.*

"This was one of the best bed and breakfast experiences we have ever had."

Cascade   A5

Bluebird on the Mountain

14700 Eyler Ave
Cascade, MD 21719-1938
(301)241-4161 (800)362-9526

Circa 1900. In the mountain village of Cascade, this gracious shuttered Georgian manor is situated on two acres of trees and wildflowers. Three suites have double whirlpool tubs. There is an outdoor hot tub as well. The Rose Garden Room and Mt. Magnolia suites have fireplaces and porches overlooking the back garden. The inn is appointed with antiques, lace and white linens, and white wicker. On Sundays, a full breakfast is served. Cascade is located in between Frederick, Md., and Gettysburg, Pa.

Innkeeper(s): Eda Smith-Eley. $105-130. 5 rooms with PB, 2 with FP and 2 suites. Breakfast included in rates. Types of meals: Full bkfst, early coffee/tea and room service. Beds: KQT. Cable TV, VCR, reading lamp, refrigerator, ceiling fan, clock radio, turn-down service and hot tub/spa in room. Air conditioning. Spa, parlor games, telephone and fireplace on premises. Small meetings, family reunions and seminars hosted. Antiquing, downhill skiing, fishing, live theater, parks, shopping, sporting events, water sports and hiking nearby.

Publicity: *Warm Welcomes, Baltimore Sun, Frederick News and Washington Post.*

"A wonderful balance of luxury and at-home comfort."

Chesapeake City   B8

Blue Max

300 Bohemia Ave, PO Box 30
Chesapeake City, MD 21915-1244
(410)885-2781 (877)725-8362 Fax:(410)885-2809
E-mail: innkeeper@bluemaxinn.com
Web: www.bluemaxinn.com

Circa 1854. Known as "the house with generous porches," this
is one of the town's largest residences, built with Georgian
architecture by the owner of the sawmill. This elegant inn has
working fireplaces and a parlor with a grand player piano.
Elaborate upscale amenities in the romantic suites and guest
bedrooms include robes, flowers, chocolates and luxurious
linens. Whirlpool tubs, a private balcony and second-floor
verandas are also featured. Mouth-watering dishes like peaches
and kiwi with amaretto cream sauce, apple crisp pancakes and
country bacon, and eggs Benedict souffle are enjoyed in the fireside dining room or in the solarium overlooking gardens and a
fish pond. A waterfall and gazebo highlight lush landscaping.
Innkeeper(s): Wayne & Wendy Mercer. $100-225. 9 rooms with PB and 2
suites. Breakfast and afternoon tea included in rates. Types of meals: Full
gourmet bkfst, early coffee/tea and snacks/refreshments. Beds: KQ. Modem
hook-up, data port, cable TV, VCR, reading lamp, CD player, refrigerator, ceiling fan, clock radio, telephone, desk, Jacuzzi for two, fireplace and private
balcony in the honeymoon suite in room. Air conditioning. Fax, copier, bicycles, library, parlor games and fireplace on premises. Limited handicap
access. Small meetings, family reunions and seminars hosted. Antiquing, art
galleries, bicycling, canoeing/kayaking, fishing, golf, hiking, horseback riding,
museums, parks, shopping, tennis and water sports nearby.

Inn at The Canal

104 Bohemia Ave
Chesapeake City, MD 21915
(410)885-5995 Fax:(410)885-3585
E-mail: mary@innatthecanal.com
Web: www.innatthecanal.com

Circa 1870. A favorite activity here is watching the parade of
boats and ships from the waterfront porch. The Inn at the
Canal was built by the Brady family, who owned the tugboats
that operated on the canal. Rooms are furnished in antiques
and quilts. The dining room and parlor are
set off by original hand-painted and
elaborately designed ceilings. Guests
enjoy European soaking tubs and
fine amenities. The historic canal
town offers a fine collection of
restaurants and shops.
Innkeeper(s): Mary & Al Ioppolo. $85-185.
7 rooms with PB, 1 suite and 1 conference room. Breakfast, afternoon tea
and snacks/refreshments included in rates. Types of meals: Full gourmet
bkfst, veg bkfst and early coffee/tea. Beds: KQD. Cable TV, VCR, reading
lamp, refrigerator, ceiling fan, snack bar, clock radio, telephone, desk and
voice mail in room. Air conditioning. Fax, library and parlor games on premises. Small meetings hosted. Antiquing, art galleries, beach, bicycling, fishing,
golf, hiking, horseback riding, live theater, museums, parks, shopping, sporting events, tennis, water sports and wineries nearby.

Chestertown   B8

Brampton Inn

25227 Chestertown Rd.
Chestertown, MD 21620
(410)778-1860 (866)305-1860
E-mail: innkeeper@bramptoninn.com
Web: www.bramptoninn.com

Circa 1860. Situated on 35 acres of gardens, meadows and
woodland on Maryland's Eastern Shore between the Chester
River and Chesapeake Bay, Brampton is a graceful three-story
brick, Greek Italianate Revival house. Swiss innkeeper Danielle
Hanscom selected family antiques to furnish the parlor and
dining room. A massive walnut staircase winds to the upstairs
where spacious rooms feature canopied beds, antiques and
reproductions. A full country breakfast is served.
Innkeeper(s): Danielle & Michael Hanscom. $135-235. 10 rooms with PB, 9
with FP, 2 suites and 2 cottages. Breakfast and afternoon tea included in
rates. Types of meals: Full bkfst and early coffee/tea. Beds: KQT. Reading
lamp, clock radio, desk and fireplace in room. Air conditioning. TV, VCR,
library, parlor games, telephone, fireplace and gift shop on premises.
Weddings, small meetings and family reunions hosted. Antiquing, art galleries, beach, bicycling, canoeing/kayaking, fishing, golf, horseback riding, live
theater, museums, parks, shopping and tennis nearby.
Publicity: *Washington Post, New York Times and Baltimore Sun.*

"A stately beauty that exudes peace and tranquility."

Great Oak Manor

10568 Cliff Rd
Chestertown, MD 21620-4115
(410)778-5943 (800)504-3098 Fax:(410)810-2517
E-mail: innkeeper@greatoak.com
Web: www.greatoak.com

Circa 1938. This elegant Georgian mansion anchors vast lawns
at the end of a long driveway. Situated directly on the
Chesapeake Bay, it is a serene and picturesque country estate. A
library with fireplace, den and formal parlors are available to
guests. With its grand circular
stairway, bayside gazebo, private
beach and nearby marina, the
Manor is a remarkable setting
for events such as weddings
and reunions. Chestertown is
eight miles away.

Innkeeper(s): Cassandra and John Fedas. $140-275. 10 rooms with PB, 5
with FP, 1 suite and 2 conference rooms. Breakfast included in rates. Types
of meals: Full bkfst and early coffee/tea. Beds: KT. TV, reading lamp, clock
radio, telephone, desk, VCR and refrigerator (in suite) in room. Air conditioning. VCR, fax, copier, bicycles, library, parlor games, fireplace and two computer ready rooms on premises. Weddings, small meetings, family reunions
and seminars hosted. Antiquing, canoeing/kayaking, fishing, golf, live theater,
shopping, tennis and Historic Washington College nearby.
Publicity: *Philadelphia, Diversions, Road Best Traveled, Washingtonian, Country
Inns, Southern Living, New Choices, Chesapeake Life and Time Magazine.*

*"The charming setting, professional service and personal warmth we
experienced at Great Oak will long be a pleasant memory. Thanks
for everything!"*

The Inn at Mitchell House

8796 Maryland Pkwy
Chestertown, MD 21620-4209
(410)778-6500
E-mail: innkeeper@innatmitchellhouse.com
Web: www.innatmitchellhouse.com

Circa 1743. This pristine 18th-century manor house sits as a jewel on 12 acres overlooking Stoneybrook Pond. The guest rooms and the inn's several parlors are preserved and appointed in an authentic Colonial mood, heightened by handsome polished wide-board floors. Eastern Neck Island National

Wildlife Refuge, Chesapeake Farms, St. Michaels, Annapolis and nearby Chestertown are all delightful to explore. The Inn at Mitchell House is a popular setting for romantic weddings and small corporate meetings.

Innkeeper(s): Tracy & Jim Stone. $100-140. 5 rooms with PB, 4 with FP. Breakfast included in rates. Types of meals: Full bkfst and early coffee/tea. Beds: KQ. TV, VCR, reading lamp, refrigerator, turn-down service and desk in room. Air conditioning. Telephone and fireplace on premises. Weddings, small meetings, family reunions and seminars hosted. Antiquing, fishing, live theater, shopping, sporting events, water sports and private beach nearby.

Publicity: *Washingtonian, New York Magazine, Glamour, Philadelphia Inquirer, Baltimore Sun, Kent County News, Ten Best Inns in the Country, New York Times, Washington Post and National Geographic Traveler.*

Cumberland   A3

The Inn at Walnut Bottom

120 Greene St
Cumberland, MD 21502-2934
(301)777-0003 (800)286-9718 Fax:(301)777-8288
E-mail: iwb@iwbinfo.com
Web: www.iwbinfo.com

Circa 1820. Two historic homes comprise the Inn at Walnut Bottom: the 1820 Federal-style Cowden House and the 1890 Queen Anne Victorian-style Dent House, both located on Cumberland's oldest street. Antiques and reproduction furnish-

ings decorate the parlors, beautiful guest rooms and family suites. Each morning a delicious full breakfast is served and in the afternoon, tasty refreshments. Enjoy a stroll to the historic district

and restaurants or ask to borrow one of the inn's bicycles for exploring the C&O Canal Towpath.

Historic Interest: George Washington Headquarters, Fort Cumberland, Allegany County Courthouse and the scenic railroad are all within walking distance. Frank Lloyd Wright's Fallingwater is nearby.
Innkeeper(s): Grant M. Irvin & Kirsten O. Hansen. $93-147. 12 rooms, 8 with PB and 2 suites. Breakfast included in rates. Types of meals: Full bkfst and early coffee/tea. Beds: KQDT. Cable TV, reading lamp, clock radio, telephone, desk and hair dryers in room. Air conditioning. Fax, copier, bicycles, parlor games, 2 family suites and massage therapy on premises. Small meetings, family reunions and seminars hosted. Bicycling, cross-country skiing, downhill skiing, fishing, live theater, parks, scenic train ride and Frank Lloyd Wrights Falling Water nearby.

Publicity: *Washington Post, Mid-Atlantic Country, Southern Living, Baltimore Magazine and Blue Ridge Country Magazine.*

Deep Creek Lake   B1

Haley Farm B&B Spa and Retreat Center

16766 Garrett Hwy
Deep Creek Lake, MD 21550-4036
(301)387-9050 (888)231-3276 Fax:(301)387-9050
E-mail: info@haleyfarm.com
Web: www.haleyfarm.com

Circa 1920. Surrounded by 65 acres of rolling hills and mountains, this farmhouse has been graciously transformed. Chinese carpets, tapestries and European furnishings are some of the innkeepers' many elegant touches. Three luxury suites include a heart-shaped Jacuzzi, king bed, kitchenette and sitting room with a fireplace. There are also six mini-suites and one deluxe guest bedroom. A three-bedroom lakeside cottage includes a boat dock and gorgeous views. Croquet and badminton are set up on the grounds. Other popular activities are fishing in the trout pond, napping in the hammock or picnicking in the gazebo. Be pampered by the spa and sauna with a facial, massage, reflexology or sunless tanning. Ask about retreats and workshops. Located three hours from Washington, DC it is only minutes from the lake, state parks and a ski and golf resort.

Innkeeper(s): Eric & Joan Bair. $130-210. 11 rooms, 4 with PB and 7 suites. Breakfast included in rates. Types of meals: Full bkfst. Beds: KQ. Ceiling fan and 7 suites with fireplace and Jacuzzis in room. Air conditioning. VCR, spa, bicycles, library, parlor games, telephone and trout pond on premises. Weddings, small meetings, family reunions and seminars hosted. Antiquing, cross-country skiing, downhill skiing, fishing, parks, shopping, water sports and white water rafting nearby.

"A beautiful setting for a quiet, romantic escape."

Lake Pointe Inn Bed & Breakfast

174 Lake Pointe Drive
Deep Creek Lake, MD 21541
(301)387-0111 (800)523-5253 Fax:(301)387-0190

Circa 1890. A two-mile vista down the Marsh Run Cove is seen from rockers on the wraparound porch of this farmhouse at the edge of Deep Creek Lake. Read by the nine-foot stone fireplace surrounded by chestnut paneling in the Great Room. The inn's award-winning décor features Arts and Crafts Mission-style furnishings. Attractive guest bedrooms and suites with scenic views boast William Morris prints, fireplaces and spa tubs. A bountiful breakfast may include golden pineapple in ginger syrup, egg roulade with fresh corn and basil on a bed of roasted red pepper coulis, oven-roasted potatoes, hickory-smoked pepper bacon, muffins, cereals and homemade granola. Relax in the steam and sauna shower. Schedule a massage after a refreshing swim or bike ride. A croquet court overlooks the gardens. Gather for hors d'oeuvre each evening. Snacks and beverages are always available.

Innkeeper(s): Caroline McNiece. $148-249. 10 rooms, 8 with PB, 7 with FP, 2 suites and 1 conference room. Breakfast and snacks/refreshments included in rates. Types of meals: Full gourmet bkfst and early coffee/tea. Beds: Q. Cable TV, VCR, reading lamp, CD player, ceiling fan, clock radio, telephone, desk, hot tub/spa and fireplace in room. Central air. Fax, copier, swimming, sauna, bicycles, parlor games, swimming/boating dock, canoes, kayaks, access to community tennis court, croquet court, herb garden and outdoor firepit on premises. Small meetings and seminars hosted. Bicycling, canoeing/kayaking, cross-country skiing, downhill skiing, fishing, golf, hiking, horseback riding, parks, shopping, tennis and water sports nearby.

Publicity: *Washingtonian Magazine, Baltimore Magazine, Bungalow Magazine, Southern Living, New Jersey Southern Living, Washington Post and Baltimore Sun.*

Easton C8

Bishop's House Bed and Breakfast

214 Goldsborough St, PO Box 2217
Easton, MD 21601-2217
(410)820-7290 (800)223-7290 Fax:(410)820-7290
E-mail: bishopshouse@skipjack.bluecrab.org
Web: www.bishopshouse.com

Circa 1880. The innkeepers of this in-town Victorian lovingly restored it in 1988. The three-and-a-half-story clapboard and gabled roof home includes three spacious first-floor rooms with 14-foot-high ceilings and generously sized second- and third-floor guest rooms. With its period- style furnishings, working fireplaces and whirlpool tubs, the inn offers its guests both romance and the ambiance of the Victorian era with modern conveniences. A sumptuous full breakfast is served every morning. Located in Easton's Historic District, it is within three blocks of boutiques, antique shops, restaurants and historic sites. The inn provides private off-street parking and secured overnight storage for bicycles.

Historic Interest: Within 10 miles of historic Oxford and St. Michaels.

Innkeeper(s): John & Diane Ippolito. $110-130. 5 rooms with PB, 3 with FP. Breakfast and snacks/refreshments included in rates. Types of meals: Full bkfst and early coffee/tea. Beds: KQ. Modem hook-up, cable TV, reading lamp, CD player, ceiling fan, clock radio, fireplace, hair dryer, ironing board, down comforters, high-speed wireless connection and whirlpool tubs in room. Air conditioning. TV, VCR, fax, bicycles, library, telephone and video tapes on premises. Small meetings, family reunions and seminars hosted. Antiquing, art galleries, beach, bicycling, canoeing/kayaking, fishing, golf, hiking, live theater, museums, parks, shopping, tennis and water sports nearby.

Publicity: *Better Homes & Gardens Magazine and Country Roads of Maryland & Delaware.*

Chaffinch House B&B

132 S Harrison St
Easton, MD 21601-2928
(410)822-5074 (800)861-5074 Fax:(410)822-5074
E-mail: innkeeper@chaffinchhouse.com
Web: www.chaffinchhouse.com

Circa 1893. Chaffinch House is an outstanding example of the whimsy in Victorian architecture. The exterior boasts gables, a turret, bays, a keyhole window and a wrap around front porch. Inside, there are more than 60 windows, each a different size. The home is appointed with period furnishings. Guest rooms include the Wedding Room suite, with a four-poster rice bed, bathroom, sitting room and a screened-in porch. Easton, called one of the best small towns in America, is about an hour-and-a-half drive from Washington, D.C., and minutes from St. Michaels and Oxford. Fine restaurants, museums, boutique shops, antique stores and art galleries are within walking distance of the inn.

Historic Interest: The architecture is truly unique & much of it has been preserved. The woodwork, mouldings, high ceilings, wavy glass windows, huge wrap porch, gables, bays, turret and oriels make it exceptional. The original owners who built the home kept it in the family for over 50 years. They owned a Haberdashery in town. The design of the home is very original and a true stand-out. Many of the town folk call it the prettiest house in Easton. When the house was renovated and brought up to date, the interior was minimally disrupted. Many walls are still plaster, original stained woodwork is still gorgeous, wood floors are throughout with the exception of baths.

Innkeeper(s): Susan & Edward Hilyard. $110-140. 5 rooms with PB and 1 suite. Breakfast included in rates. Types of meals: Full gourmet bkfst and snacks/refreshments. Beds: KQ. Reading lamp, ceiling fan, clock radio, coffeemaker, turn-down service, beverage setups, robes, coffeemaker and sitting area in room. Central air. Fax, copier, library, parlor games, telephone, fireplace, gift shop, iron, blow dryer, TV/VCR, patio and porches on premises. Weddings, small meetings, family reunions and seminars hosted. Antiquing, art galleries, bicycling, canoeing/kayaking, fishing, golf, hiking, live theater, museums, parks, shopping and tennis nearby.

John S. McDaniel House B&B

14 N Aurora St
Easton, MD 21601-3617
(410)822-3704 (877)822-5702 Fax:(410)822-3704

Circa 1865. A wide veranda wraps around this three-story Queen Anne Victorian, complete with octagonal tower and dormers. Located in the historic district, considered to be the "Colonial Capital of the Eastern Shore," it's within walking distance to the classic Avalon Theater, Academy of Art, many good restaurants and unique shops.

Innkeeper(s): Mrs. Mary Lou Karwacki. $105-135. 6 rooms with PB and 1 suite. Breakfast included in rates. Types of meals: Full gourmet bkfst. Beds: KQ. Cable TV, VCR, ceiling fan and sitting area in room. Central air. Fax, copier, telephone, wraparound porch and large living room and breakfast room on premises. Family reunions hosted. Antiquing, art galleries, beach, bicycling, canoeing/kayaking, fishing, golf, hiking, horseback riding, live theater, parks, shopping, tennis and water sports nearby.

Publicity: *Public YV - Radio.*

Frederick B5

McCleery's Flat

121 E Patrick St
Frederick, MD 21701-5677
(301)620-2433 (800)774-7926

Circa 1876. Indulge in quiet European elegance at this French second empire-style townhouse. Located in the the heart of downtown on historic Antique Row, the decor blends period antiques and reproductions. Well-appointed guest bedrooms and suites offer a variety of delightful features. Choose from a whirlpool or soaking tub, private balcony or covered outdoor sitting area, and a touch of whimsy, Victorian or historical furnishings. Beds include canopy, sleigh, poster, cast-iron and wicker. Creative international recipes collected by the innkeepers are served for breakfast. The landscaped grounds and courtyard offer areas to relax and listen to the soft-flowing fountains and gaze at the colorful flowers.

Innkeeper(s): Jutta & George Terrell. $105-140. 5 rooms with PB and 2 suites. Breakfast and snacks/refreshments included in rates. Types of meals: Full gourmet bkfst, veg bkfst and early coffee/tea. Beds: KQD. Modem hook-up, reading lamp, ceiling fan, clock radio and desk in room. Air conditioning. TV, VCR, library, telephone and fireplace on premises. Weddings, small meetings and family reunions hosted. Antiquing, art galleries, bicycling, canoeing/kayaking, downhill skiing, fishing, golf, hiking, live theater, museums, parks, shopping, sporting events, tennis and wineries nearby.

Georgetown   B8

Kitty Knight House on the Sassafras

14028 Augustine Herman Hwy
Georgetown, MD 21930
(410)648-5200 Fax:(410)275-1800
E-mail: juan@kittyknight.com
Web: www.kittyknight.com

Circa 1755. Enjoy the view overlooking the scenic Georgetown
Yacht Basin while staying at this historic Colonial landmark that
commemorates the inn's namesake, an early American heroine.
Recently renovated, the inn offers quaint and comfortable
Traditional decor accented with heart-of-pine hardwood floors.
Spacious suites and guest bedrooms feature luxurious furnishings, fine linens and computer access. Other extras include gas
log fireplaces and two-person whirlpool tubs. A satisfying
breakfast offers family favorites and classic Eastern Shore fare.
The restaurant and the tavern provide dining opportunities for
lunch and dinner. Relax on the deck where weekend sunsets
are serenaded with music.

Innkeeper(s): Michael Sciota. $95-160. 10 rooms with PB, 5 with FP, 1
suite and 4 conference rooms. Breakfast included in rates. Types of meals:
Full gourmet bkfst, veg bkfst, early coffee/tea, gourmet lunch, picnic lunch,
snacks/refreshments and gourmet dinner. Restaurant on premises. Beds: KQ.
Modem hook-up, cable TV, reading lamp, ceiling fan, clock radio, telephone,
desk, hot tub/spa and fireplace in room. Central air. Fax, copier, and fireplace on premises. Limited handicap access. Weddings, small meetings, family reunions and seminars hosted. Antiquing, beach, canoeing/kayaking, fishing, hiking, horseback riding, museums, parks, shopping, sporting events,
water sports and Bird Watching/Wildlife Observatory nearby.

Publicity: *Philadelphia Magazine, DE Today and various local newspapers.*

Grantsville   A2

Walnut Ridge Bed & Breakfast

92 Main St, PO Box 128
Grantsville, MD 21536
(301)895-4248 (888)419-2568
E-mail: walnutridgebandb@aol.com
Web: www.walnutridge.net

Circa 1864. The new owners of this inn have lovingly renovated the historic farmhouse which offers a comfortable parlor to
gather for games or conversation. A selection of books and a
video library are located in the hallway. Elegant Colburn Room
and cheerful Gypsy's Garden both have a fireplace. The
Wilderness Suite boasts a rustic ambiance with a full kitchen,
fireplace, separate entrance and private hot tub. A gourmet
breakfast is served in the candlelit dining room or on the back
porch overlooking the gardens and mountains. For more privacy, stay in the spacious cabin for four or cozy cottage in the
woods. Relax with a glass of iced tea in the gazebo. Walk to the
Artisan Village or nearby Casselman River. The inn is centrally
located to an assortment of fun activities.

Innkeeper(s): Matthew & Paula Brown. $80-150. 5 rooms with PB, 4 with
FP, 1 suite, 1 cottage and 1 cabin. Breakfast included in rates. Types of
meals: Full gourmet bkfst and early coffee/tea. Beds: Q. Cable TV, VCR, CD
player, refrigerator, ceiling fan, clock radio, coffeemaker, desk, hot tub/spa
and fireplace in room. Air conditioning. Spa, bicycles, library, parlor games,
telephone and fireplace on premises. Family reunions hosted. Antiquing, bicycling, canoeing/kayaking, cross-country skiing, downhill skiing, fishing, golf,
hiking, horseback riding, museums, parks, shopping, sporting events, tennis,
water sports and wineries nearby.

Publicity: *Washington Post, Lancaster Farming and and The Country Register.*

"Best nights' sleep I've had this summer."

Havre De Grace   A8

La Cle D'Or Guesthouse

226 N Union Ave
Havre De Grace, MD 21078-2907
(410)939-6562 (888)HUG-GUEST Fax:(410)939-1833
Web: www.lacledorguesthouse.com

Circa 1868. Johns Hopkins' family built this Second Empire
Victorian-style home located in the canal town's historic district. The decor is reminiscent of eclectic post-Civil War. The
parlor features a domed recessed alcove, bay window and fireplace. Strauss crystal chandeliers, Ronald Redding wallpapers
and local artworks are found throughout the inn. Eastlake furnishings and reproductions fill exquisite guest bedrooms. An
all-you-can-eat breakfast includes traditional fare served in the
formal dining room. Stroll the brick-walled secret garden with
wrought iron gates, relax on the flagstone terrace, or enjoy the
river view.

Innkeeper(s): Ron Browning. $120-140. 3 rooms, 2 with PB. Breakfast and
snacks/refreshments included in rates. Types of meals: Full bkfst, veg bkfst,
early coffee/tea and room service. Beds: QD. Cable TV, VCR, reading lamp,
clock radio, turn-down service, desk and hair dryer in room. Central air. Fax,
copier, library, pet boarding, parlor games, fireplace, laundry facility and snack
bar/refrigerator on premises. Weddings, small meetings, family reunions and
seminars hosted. Antiquing, art galleries, bicycling, canoeing/kayaking, fishing,
golf, hiking, live theater, museums, parks, shopping, sporting events, tennis,
water sports, wineries and seafood restaurants nearby.

Publicity: *Country Extra Magazine and has received Arrington's B&B Journal
Award 2002 - B&B with the best garden and Arrington's B&B Journal Award
2003 - B&B with most historical charm.*

Spencer Silver Mansion

200 S Union Ave
Havre De Grace, MD 21078-3224
(410)939-1097 (800)780-1485
E-mail: spencersilver@erols.com
Web: www.spencersilvermansion.com

Circa 1896. This elegant granite Victorian mansion is graced
with bays, gables, balconies, a turret and a gazebo veranda. The
Victorian decor, with antiques and Oriental rugs, complements
the house's carved-oak woodwork, fireplace mantels and parquet floors. The Concord Point Lighthouse (oldest continuously operated lighthouse in America) is only a walk away. In addition to the four rooms in the main house,
a romantic carriage house suite is available, featuring an in-room fireplace,
TV, whirlpool bath and kitchenette.

Historic Interest: Fort McHenry (45
minutes), Concord Point Lighthouse
(1 minute).

Innkeeper(s): Carol Nemeth. $70-140.
5 rooms, 3 with PB, 1 with FP and 1 cottage. Breakfast included in rates.
Types of meals: Full bkfst and early coffee/tea. Beds: QDT. Cable TV, reading
lamp, clock radio, telephone, turn-down service and hot tub/spa in room. Air
conditioning. Parlor games and fireplace on premises. Weddings, small meetings and family reunions hosted. Antiquing, fishing, parks, shopping, water
sports, museums and restaurants nearby.

Publicity: *Mid-Atlantic Country and Maryland.*

*"A fabulous find. Beautiful house, excellent hostess. I've stayed at a
lot of B&Bs, but this house is the best."*

Vandiver Inn, Kent & Murphy Homes

301 S Union Ave
Havre De Grace, MD 21078-3201
(410)939-5200 (800)245-1655 Fax:(410)939-5202

Circa 1886. Three acres surround this three-story historic Victorian mansion. A chandelier lights the entrance. Some of the rooms offer gas fireplaces and clawfoot tubs, and all are furnished with Victorian antiques. For instance, a king-size Victorian bed, original to the house, is one of the features of the Millard E. Tydings Room, also offering a decorative fireplace and sitting area. The innkeeper creates gourmet breakfasts with freshly baked scones or muffins. Spend some time in the garden where a summer gazebo is supported by 12 cedar tree trunks.
Innkeeper(s): Susan Muldoon. $68-185. 17 rooms with PB, 4 with FP. Breakfast included in rates. Types of meals: Full gourmet bkfst, veg bkfst, early coffee/tea, picnic lunch and dinner. Beds: KQDT. Data port, cable TV, reading lamp, clock radio, telephone and desk in room. Central air. Fax, parlor games, fireplace, laundry facility and indoor and outdoor conference rooms on premises. Weddings, small meetings and family reunions hosted. Antiquing, art galleries, bicycling, canoeing/kayaking, fishing, golf, hiking, horseback riding, live theater, museums, parks, shopping, tennis, water sports and wineries nearby.

Ocean City   E10

An Inn on the Ocean

1001 Atlantic Avenue
Ocean City, MD 21842
(410)289-8894 (888)226-6223 Fax:(410)289-8215
E-mail: innonoc@aol.com
Web: www.InnOnTheOcean.com

Circa 1920. From the wraparound porch of this inn, guests can watch birds soar and ocean waters crash upon the shore.. The Inn includes six elegant guest rooms, each individually decorated with rich fabrics and designer linens. The Hunt and Tapestry rooms each boast an ocean view. The Oceana Suite includes a private balcony that looks out to the sea. The Veranda Room has its own oceanfront porch. Most rooms include a Jacuzzi tub. The gourmet breakfasts include homemade breads, fruit and special egg dishes, such as a frittata. The Inn is oceanfront, so guests need only walk a few steps to enjoy the beach and nearby Boardwalk. Golfing, outlet stores, fishing, water sports, antique shops and harness racing are other local attractions.
Innkeeper(s): The Barrett's. $125-300. 6 rooms with PB and 1 conference room. Breakfast and snacks/refreshments included in rates. Types of meals: Full bkfst, early coffee/tea and gourmet dinner. Beds: KQ. Cable TV, VCR, reading lamp, ceiling fan, clock radio, Jacuzzi and bathrobes in room. Air conditioning. Fax, copier, bicycles, parlor games, telephone, fireplace, beach chairs and umbrellas on premises. Weddings, small meetings, family reunions and seminars hosted. Amusement parks, antiquing, art galleries, beach, bicycling, canoeing/kayaking, fishing, golf, hiking, horseback riding, live theater, museums, parks, shopping, sporting events, tennis and water sports nearby.

Oxford   D8

The Robert Morris Inn

314 N Morris St, PO Box 70
Oxford, MD 21654
(410)226-5111 (888)823-4012 Fax:(410)226-5744
E-mail: bestcrabcakes@webtv.net
Web: www.robertmorrisinn.com

Circa 1710. Peace and relaxation are offered at this Eastern Shore country inn that is known for its tradition of quality. Stay in the one of the quaint, historic guest bedrooms at the Main inn or choose a waterfront room with private porch in the Sandaway Lodge. Ask for the romantic Sandaway Suite with a canopy bed and soaking tub for two. Sit by the Tred Avon River on adirondack chairs or rent a kayak. The inn's restaurant is highly acclaimed for its Chesapeake Bay crab cakes and seafood.
Historic Interest: Talbot Historic Society (15 minutes), Chesapeake Maritime Museum (25 minutes).
Innkeeper(s): Jay Gibson. $130-350. 35 rooms with PB and 1 conference room. Restaurant on premises. Beds: KQDT. Reading lamp in room. Air conditioning. Fax, copier, library, telephone, fireplace and 2 efficiencies on premises. Limited handicap access. Small meetings and seminars hosted. Antiquing, fishing, golf, live theater, parks and shopping nearby.
Publicity: *Southern Accents, The Evening Sun, Maryland, Mid-Atlantic Country, Bon Appetit and Select Registry.*

"Impressed! Unbelievable!"

Princess Anne   E9

Waterloo Country Inn

28822 Mount Vernon Rd
Princess Anne, MD 21853
(410)651-0883 Fax:(410)651-5592
E-mail: innkeeper@waterloocountryinn.com
Web: www.waterloocountryinn.com

Circa 1750. In the midst of 300 acres of land encircled by small cottages, brick walkways, century-old trees and flower beds, lies this pre-Revolutionary Georgian brick plantation house, beautifully restored and furnished with Swiss antiques. Listed in the National Register of Historical Places, the Waterloo Country Inn is situated on a tidal pond that is a habitat for wildlife and birds. Owners Theresa and Erwin Kraemer, natives to Switzerland, have brought "a taste of Europe to Maryland," according to a Maryland newspaper, with its elegant décor and European flair in dining. Enjoy the crisp Eastern Shore air while canoeing, bicycling, relaxing at the pool or strolling along Monie Creek. Ride the ferry to nearby antique shops and golf courses.
Innkeeper(s): Erwin & Theresa Kraemer. $125-255. 6 rooms with PB, 5 with FP and 2 suites. Breakfast and snacks/refreshments included in rates. Types of meals: Full gourmet bkfst. Beds: KQT. Cable TV, reading lamp, coffeemaker, desk, hot tub/spa, suites with Jacuzzi, fireplace, VCR, coffeemaker, bathrobes and clock radio in room. Central air. VCR, fax, copier, swimming, bicycles, library, parlor games, fireplace and canoes on premises. Limited handicap access. Weddings, family reunions and seminars hosted. Antiquing, beach, bicycling, canoeing/kayaking, fishing, golf, hiking, horseback riding, museums, parks, water sports, famous wild ponies on Assateague Island and Chesapeake Bay Island cruises nearby.
Publicity: *Gourmet Magazine, Baltimore Sun, Chesapeake Life Magazine and Daily Times.*

"What a find! We have traveled all over the world and this is really special."

Queenstown   C8

Queenstown Inn Bed & Breakfast

7109 Main St. PO Box 2012
Queenstown, MD 21658-2012
(410)827-3396 (888)744-3407 Fax:(410)827-3397
E-mail: qtbb@dmv.com
Web: www.queenstowninn.com

Circa 1830. Relaxation is easy at this comfortable inn, built with an original cast-iron front. Situated near Chesapeake Bay, take a short walk to a private beach. Boaters are welcome and can be picked up from a dock a few blocks away. The State Room is a spacious gathering place with wood stove, brick bar, stereo and an organ. It opens to a large screened-in porch overlooking flower gardens. Guest bedrooms and a suite are deliberately without electronics for a calm setting. A satisfying continental-plus breakfast is served in the Historic Room, which features vintage pictures of the Eastern shore and the inn's past. Visit the gift shop, an old storefront offering the work of local artists and craftsmen. Unique gift baskets can be made to order. An outlet mall and antique center are nearby.

Innkeeper(s): Josh Barns, Micheal Lydon. $95-155. 5 rooms, 4 with PB and 1 suite. Breakfast and snacks/refreshments included in rates. Types of meals: Cont plus, veg bkfst and early coffee/tea. Beds: QDT. Reading lamp, ceiling fan and tub with shower in room. Central air. TV, VCR, fax, copier, bicycles, library, parlor games, telephone, fireplace, laundry facility and gift shop on premises. Limited handicap access. Weddings, small meetings, family reunions and seminars hosted. Antiquing, art galleries, beach, bicycling, canoeing/kayaking, fishing, golf, hiking, live theater, museums, parks, shopping, sporting events, tennis, water sports, outlet shopping, Horsehead Wetlands Center and Wye Island Natural Resources Management area nearby.

Rock Hall   C8

Huntingfield Manor B&B

4928 Eastern Neck Rd
Rock Hall, MD 21661
(410)639-7779 (800)720-8788 Fax:(410)639-2924
E-mail: manorlord@juno.com
Web: www.huntingfield.com

Circa 1850. This 136-foot-long, telescope-type Colonial house is a working farm dating back to the mid-1600s when the property was called "The Prevention of Inconvenience." Today the inn sits on 67 secluded pastoral acres that include seven perennial gardens on six acres of lawn. Choose to stay in one of the guest bedrooms or the fully appointed cottage. A continental breakfast offers a scrumptious variety of fresh breads and fruits. Located on the shore of Chesapeake Bay and near the Chester and Sassafras rivers as well as many creeks, the inn boasts many excellent places to fish, crab and enjoy many water sports. The nearby Eastern Neck Wildlife Refuge has miles of hiking and bird-watching trails. Seafood is abundant, and nearly every weekend a local church has a fish-fry supper.

Innkeeper(s): George & Bernie Starken. $110-200. 6 rooms with PB. Breakfast and afternoon tea included in rates. Types of meals: Cont plus. Beds: KT. Reading lamp, clock radio and desk in room. Air conditioning. TV, fax, copier, bicycles, library, pet boarding, parlor games, telephone, fireplace, laundry facility and 40-foot swimming pool on premises. Weddings, small meetings, family reunions and seminars hosted. Antiquing, art galleries, beach, bicycling, canoeing/kayaking, fishing, golf, horseback riding, museums, parks and shopping nearby.

Moonlight Bay Marina & Inn

6002 Lawton Ave
Rock Hall, MD 21661-1369
(410)639-2660 Fax:(410)639-7739

Circa 1850. Moonlight Bay offers an ideal setting, right at the edge of the Chesapeake Bay. The pre-Civil War home includes a veranda lined with wicker furnishings and a swing, and the grounds boast a gazebo. Five rooms are located in the main inn, and several offer outstanding bay views. The West Wing includes five bay-front rooms, all with a whirlpool bath. Guests are pampered in Victorian style with a full breakfast and afternoon tea. Guests can rent boats, fish, golf or take a nature walk at one of two local wildlife preserves. Other local attractions include auctions and antique shops.

Innkeeper(s): Robert & Dorothy Santangelo. $125-165. 10 rooms with PB and 2 conference rooms. Breakfast and afternoon tea included in rates. Types of meals: Full bkfst and early coffee/tea. Beds: KQT. Reading lamp, ceiling fan, clock radio and whirlpool tub in room. Air conditioning. VCR, fax, bicycles and fireplace on premises. Limited handicap access. Weddings, small meetings, family reunions and seminars hosted. Antiquing, fishing, golf, live theater, shopping and tennis nearby.

Publicity: *Washingtonian* and *Washington Post.*

Saint Michaels   C8

Barrett's Bed & Breakfast

204 N Talbot St
Saint Michaels, MD 21663
(410)745-3322 Fax:(410)745-3888
E-mail: jwbarrett@yahoo.com
Web: www.barrettbb.com

Circa 1860. Located on Chesapeake Bay's eastern shore, this Colonial-style inn is perfect for a restful getaway or a romantic honeymoon. Furnished with antiques, the guest bedrooms boast fireplaces, handmade quilts, fresh flowers, candles, outside entrances and some feature double Jacuzzi tubs. A gourmet breakfast in the Tea Room may include bacon, egg and cheese souffle with fresh breads and jam, cereal and fruit. The rose garden is a pleasant diversion, or sit on the patio or shaded porch with wicker furniture. Ask about the many specialty packages offered that pamper and please.

$120-250. 7 rooms with PB, 7 with FP. Breakfast included in rates. Types of meals: Full gourmet bkfst, early coffee/tea, afternoon tea and snacks/refreshments. Beds: Q. Cable TV, refrigerator, snack bar, clock radio, hot tub/spa, fireplace and double Jacuzzi tub in room. Central air. Fax, copier, spa, fireplace and gift shop on premises. Family reunions hosted. Antiquing, art galleries, bicycling, canoeing/kayaking, fishing, golf, museums, parks and shopping nearby.

George Brooks House Inn and Spa

24500 Rolles Range Road
Saint Michaels, MD 21663
(410)745-0999 (866)218-1384
E-mail: brooksbb@dmv.com
Web: www.GeorgeBrooksHouse.com

Circa 1908. Designated a historic site, this restored Gothic Revival Victorian home is surrounded by more than seven acres of landscaped formal gardens. Sit on the front porch or chat over afternoon tea and cookies in the parlor. Enjoy evening wine and cheese by the fire. A DVD library offers selections for in-room use. Rich colors, hand-carved mahogany beds with Egyptian cotton sheets, Waverly comforters and window treatments highlight lavish guest bedrooms that may also feature a gas fireplace or a two-person whirlpool bath. Hot beverages and pastries are offered before a full breakfast with entrees like stuffed French toast, egg casserole or Belgium waffles. Relax in the outdoor pool or hot tub. Bikes are available to explore the scenic area.

Historic Interest: Designated historic site by Talbot County Historic Preservation Commission, the George Brooks House dates back to the Civil War period and was built by freed slaves for Captain Andrew C. Barkman. Purchased in 1900 by George and Mamie Brooks, they expanded the house in 1908 when they became the guardians for 11 children when his sister died. George may have been the most prosperous black man in the area, and boasted of having the largest home of any African-American in this area. In 1936, George published a famous document on race relations where he tells his fellow blacks "to go back to work and stop grumbling and growling about the white man." Carefully restored and expanded in 2001, the George Brooks house retains important elements from the time that George built the Gothic Revival Section that faces Route 33.

Innkeeper(s): Will Workman. $90-225. 6 rooms with PB, 5 with FP. Breakfast, afternoon tea and snacks/refreshments included in rates. Types of meals: Full gourmet bkfst and early coffee/tea. Beds: KQ. Cable TV, CD player, clock radio, fireplace and DVD player in room. Air conditioning. Spa, swimming, bicycles, parlor games, telephone, fireplace, DVD library, spa for manicures, pedicures and facials on premises. Limited handicap access. Weddings, small meetings, family reunions and seminars hosted. Antiquing, art galleries, bicycling, canoeing/kayaking, fishing, golf, horseback riding, museums, shopping, tennis and water sports nearby.

Publicity: *Shore Living Magazine, Easton Star-Democrat Newspaper and "Heritage Award" from Talbot County Historic Society as the best historic restoration in 2001.*

Kemp House Inn

412 Talbot St, PO Box 638
Saint Michaels, MD 21663-0638
(410)745-2243
E-mail: info@kemphouseinn.com
Web: www.kemphouseinn.com

Circa 1807. This two-story Georgian house was built by Colonel Joseph Kemp, a shipwright and one of the town forefathers. The inn is appointed in period furnishings accentuated by candlelight. Guest rooms include patchwork quilts, a collection of four-poster rope beds and old-fashioned night-shirts. There are several working fireplaces. Robert E. Lee is said to have been a guest.

Historic Interest: Listed in the National Register.

Innkeeper(s): Diane M. & Steve Cooper. $95-130. 7 rooms with PB, 4 with FP and 1 cottage. Breakfast included in rates. Types of meals: Cont plus. Beds: QDT. Reading lamp in room. Air conditioning. Telephone and fireplace on premises. Antiquing, fishing, shopping and water sports nearby.

Publicity: *Gourmet and Philadelphia.*

"It was wonderful. We've stayed in many B&Bs, and this was one of the nicest!"

Parsonage Inn

210 N Talbot St
Saint Michaels, MD 21663-2102
(410)745-5519 (800)394-5519
E-mail: parsinn@dmv.com
Web: www.parsonage-inn.com

Circa 1883. A striking Victorian steeple rises next to the wide bay of this brick residence, once the home of Henry Clay Dodson, state senator, pharmacist and brickyard owner. The house features brick detail in a variety of patterns and inlays, perhaps a design statement for brick customers. Porches are decorated with filigree and spindled columns. Waverly linens,

late Victorian furnishings, fireplaces and decks add to the creature comforts. Six bikes await guests who wish to ride to Tilghman Island or to the ferry that goes to Oxford. Gourmet breakfast is served in the dining room.

Historic Interest: Maritime Museum & Historic Boats (2 blocks), Town of Oxford (10 miles), Town of Easton (9 miles).

Innkeeper(s): Bill Wilhelm. $100-195. 8 rooms with PB, 3 with FP. Breakfast included in rates. Types of meals: Full gourmet bkfst. Beds: KQD. Reading lamp, ceiling fan, clock radio and TV (two rooms) in room. Air conditioning. TV, bicycles, telephone and fireplace on premises. Limited handicap access. Small meetings and family reunions hosted. Antiquing, fishing, shopping, water sports and Chesapeake Bay Maritime Museum nearby.

Publicity: *Philadelphia Inquirer Sunday Travel, Wilmington and Delaware News Journal.*

"Striking, extensively renovated."

Victoriana Inn

205 Cherry St
Saint Michaels, MD 21663
(410)745-3368 (888)316-1282
E-mail: info@victorianainn.com
Web: www.victorianainn.com

Circa 1873. Most everything about this inn is Victorian, from the style of architecture to the decor and ambiance. Parlor games can be played fireside. Guest bedrooms and suites are accented with fresh bouquets of flowers and boast high ceilings. Some feature canopy beds and fireplaces. The Junior Suite also includes a poster bed and private deck overlooking the harbor. Hunger is unheard of with a hearty breakfast, snacks and refreshments available. Almost one acre of landscaped lawns and two porches filled with wicker furnishings create a splendid bayside retreat. Visit the nearby Chesapeake Bay Maritime Museum, and tour the historic town by foot or bicycle.

Innkeeper(s): Charles & Maria McDonald. $129-319. 7 rooms. Breakfast and snacks/refreshments included in rates. Types of meals: Full gourmet bkfst and early coffee/tea. Beds: KQDT. Cable TV, reading lamp, ceiling fan, clock radio and fireplace in room. Central air. Bicycles, parlor games, telephone and fireplace on premises. Small meetings, family reunions and seminars hosted. Antiquing, art galleries, bicycling, canoeing/kayaking, fishing, golf, hiking, parks, shopping and tennis nearby.

Wades Point Inn on The Bay

PO Box 7, Wades Point Rd, McDaniel
Saint Michaels, MD 21663
(410)745-2500 (888)923-3466
E-mail: wadesinn@wadespoint.com
Web: www.wadespoint.com

Circa 1819. Experience country serenity at this historic bed & breakfast with sweeping views of Chesapeake Bay. The 120 acres of picturesque woodland and fields impart a peaceful setting. Watch the ever-changing scenery from a rocker on the porch. Guest bedrooms are decorated and furnished in traditional period style. Some of the rooms boast kitchenettes and waterside balconies. After a generous European continental breakfast, walk or jog along the one-mile nature trail. Recreation and relaxation are enjoyed in abundance at this inn on the Eastern Shore.

Weddings, retreats and seminars are accommodated easily.
Innkeeper(s): The Feiler Family. $130-250. 24 rooms with PB and 1 conference room. Breakfast included in rates. Beds: QDT. Weddings and seminars hosted. Hiking nearby.

Scotland E7

St. Michael's Manor B&B

50200 St Michael's Manor Way
Scotland, MD 20687-3107
(301)872-4025 Fax:(301)872-9330
E-mail: stmichaelsman@olg.com
Web: stmichaels-manor.com

Circa 1805. Twice featured on the Maryland House and Garden Tour, St. Michael's Manor is located on Long Neck Creek, a half-mile from Chesapeake Bay. The original handcrafted woodwork provides a handsome backdrop for the inn's

antique collection. A three-acre vineyard and swimming pool are on the property.
Historic Interest: Original woodwork, molding. Named St. Michael's Manor in 1637. Property originally 1,500 acres.

Innkeeper(s): Joe & Nancy Dick. $50-130. 4 rooms, 1 with PB. Breakfast included in rates. Types of meals: Full gourmet bkfst, veg bkfst, early coffee/tea, picnic lunch, afternoon tea and snacks/refreshments. Beds: QDT. Reading lamp, clock radio, telephone, desk and voice mail in room. Central air. Fax, copier, swimming, bicycles, library, parlor games, fireplace, laundry facility, rowboat, canoe, paddleboat and bird watching on premises. Weddings, small meetings, family reunions and seminars hosted. Antiquing, beach, bicycling, canoeing/kayaking, cross-country skiing, fishing, golf, hiking, live theater, museums, parks, shopping, sporting events, tennis, water sports, wineries, crabbing and boats nearby.
Publicity: *Washington Post and St. Mary's Co. Enterprise.*

"Your B&B was so warm, cozy and comfortable."

Sharpsburg B5

The Inn at Antietam

220 E Main St, PO Box 119
Sharpsburg, MD 21782-0119
(301)432-6601 (877)835-6011
E-mail: innatantietam@juno.com
Web: www.innatantietam.com

Circa 1908. Eight acres of meadows surround this gracious Victorian framed by English walnut trees. A columned veranda provides a view of the countryside, the town with its old stone churches and the Antietam Battlefield. Gleaming floors accentuate romantically designed Victorian guest rooms, all with sitting rooms. The Smokehouse Suite offers a wide brick fireplace, a sleeping loft, refrigerator, wet bar and television. The entire third floor comprises the Penthouse Suite, which features skylights, an enclosed balcony with views of the Blue Ridge Mountains, refrigerator, wet bar, TV/VCR and a spiral staircase that leads to a library. A solarium, library, parlor, patio and wide wraparound porches are gathering places.
Innkeeper(s): Bob LeBlanc & Charles Van Metre. $110-175. 5 suites, 1 with FP. Types of meals: Full bkfst. Beds: Q. TV on premises. Parks nearby.
Publicity: *Country Inns.*

"A romantic setting and a most enjoyable experience."

Snow Hill E9

Chanceford Hall B&B

209 W Federal St
Snow Hill, MD 21863-1159
(410)632-2900 Fax:(410)632-2479
E-mail: chancefordhall@chancefordhall.com
Web: www.chancefordhall.com

Circa 1759. Chanceford Hall is a gracious Greek Revival manor house. The inn is a National Historic Landmark that sits on an acre of landscaped grounds along the Pocomoke River. The gardens include one of the oldest black walnut trees in the state. Handsome architectural details are found throughout and include gleaming wide-plank floors and 10-foot-high ceilings. The inn has 10 working fireplaces and an inviting outdoor lap pool. The four large guest rooms-Chanceford, Chadwick, Cliveden and Conway-are decorated in antiques and include four-poster, queen-size beds. Elegantly served breakfasts include such fare as multi-grain pancakes, French toast, omelettes, fruit crisp, Italian strata and fresh scones.
Innkeeper(s): Alice Kesterson & Randy Ifft. $120-150. 4 rooms with PB, 3 with FP and 1 conference room. Breakfast and snacks/refreshments included in rates. Types of meals: Full gourmet bkfst and veg bkfst. Beds: Q. Reading lamp, desk, three with wood-burning fireplaces and sitting areas in room. Central air. Fax, copier, swimming, bicycles, library, telephone and fireplace on premises. Weddings, small meetings, family reunions and seminars hosted. Amusement parks, antiquing, art galleries, beach, bicycling, canoeing/kayaking, fishing, golf, hiking, museums, parks, shopping and water sports nearby.
Publicity: *Washington Post, Daily Times, Washingtonian Magazine, Southern Living, Chesapeake Life Magazine, Baltimore Sun and WBOC-CBS affiliate.*

River House Inn

201 E Market St
Snow Hill, MD 21863-2000
(410)632-2722 Fax:(410)632-2866
E-mail: innkeeper@riverhouseinn.com
Web: www.riverhouseinn.com

Circa 1860. This picturesque Gothic Revival house rests on the banks of the Pocomoke River and boasts its own dock. Its two acres roll down to the river over long tree-studded lawns. Lawn furniture and a hammock add to the invitation to relax as do the inn's porches. Some guest rooms feature faux marble fireplaces. The 17th-century village of Snow Hill boasts old brick sidewalks and historic homes. Canoes can be rented two doors from the inn.

Innkeeper(s): Larry & Susanne Knudsen. $140-250. 8 rooms with PB, 8 with FP, 3 cottages and 3 conference rooms. Breakfast and snacks/refreshments included in rates. Types of meals: Country bkfst, veg bkfst, early coffee/tea, gourmet dinner and room service. Beds: KQT. Modem hook-up, cable TV, VCR, reading lamp, refrigerator, ceiling fan, clock radio, coffeemaker, desk, hot tub/spa and fireplace in room. Central air. Fax, copier, spa, library, pet boarding, child care, parlor games, telephone, fireplace and laundry facility on premises. Handicap access. Weddings, small meetings, family reunions and seminars hosted. Amusement parks, antiquing, art galleries, beach, bicycling, canoeing/kayaking, fishing, golf, hiking, live theater, museums, parks, shopping and water sports nearby.
Publicity: *Washington Post, Baltimore Sun, Los Angeles Times, Philadelphia Inquirer, Washingtonian, Southern Living and Salisbury MD affiliates.*

Solomons E7

Back Creek B&B

PO Box 520
Solomons, MD 20688-0520
(410)326-2022 Fax:(410)326-2946
Web: www.bbonline.com/md/backcreek

Circa 1880. This delightful inn serves as a perfect respite or executive retreat for those visiting the charming village of Solomons. Located along the banks of Back Creek, the grounds offer water and garden views. Guests enjoy the garden spa where they can watch the boats go by. Many guests stroll along the river walk to watch the sunset. A country garden theme permeates the Inn, with bouquets of herbs and flowers decorating guest rooms. The innkeepers take pride in their well-presented breakfasts, which often include "one-of-a-kind" omelets topped with homemade salsa, fresh orange batter French toast and sausage or perhaps Back Creek "Eggs Benny." On Sunday, a buffet breakfast offers up the inn's famous crab quiche. Guests are welcomed by land or sea.

Innkeeper(s): Lin Cochran & Carol Pennock. $95-175. 7 rooms with PB, 2 with FP, 2 suites, 1 cottage and 1 conference room. Breakfast and snacks/refreshments included in rates. Types of meals: Full bkfst, early coffee/tea, picnic lunch and afternoon tea. Beds: KQ. Cable TV, reading lamp, ceiling fan, clock radio, telephone and desk in room. Air conditioning. VCR, fax, spa, bicycles, parlor games and lawn games on premises. Limited handicap access. Small meetings, family reunions and seminars hosted. Antiquing, fishing, live theater, parks, shopping, sporting events, water sports, museum and historic sites nearby.

Publicity: *Maryland, Washington Post and Mid-Atlantic Country.*

Solomons Victorian Inn

125 Charles Street
Solomons, MD 20688-0759
(410)326-4811 Fax:(410)326-0133
E-mail: info@solomonsvictorianinn.com
Web: www.solomonsvictorianinn.com

Circa 1906. The Davis family, renowned for their shipbuilding talents, constructed this elegant Queen Anne Victorian at the turn of the century. Each of the inn's elegant common rooms and bedchambers boasts special touches such as antiques, Oriental rugs and lacy curtains. The inn's suites include whirlpool tubs. The home affords views of Solomons Harbor and its entrance into the picturesque Chesapeake Bay. Guests are treated to an expansive breakfast in a dining room, which overlooks the harbor.

Historic Interest: Historic Saint Mary's City is a half hour from the inn, while Washington, D.C. is just an hour away.

Innkeeper(s): Richard & Helen Bauer. $95-195. 8 rooms with PB and 1 suite. Breakfast and snacks/refreshments included in rates. Types of meals: Full gourmet bkfst, veg bkfst and early coffee/tea. Beds: KQ. Modem hook-up, cable TV, reading lamp, refrigerator, ceiling fan, clock radio, telephone and hot tub/spa in room. Air conditioning. Fax, copier, library and parlor games on premises. Small meetings hosted. Antiquing, art galleries, beach, bicycling, canoeing/kayaking, fishing, golf, hiking, museums, parks, shopping and water sports nearby.

"Instead of guests at a place of lodging, you made us feel like welcome friends in your home."

Stevenson B7

Gramercy Mansion

1400 Greenspring Valley Rd
Stevenson, MD 21153-0119
(410)486-2405 (800)553-3404 Fax:(410)486-1765
E-mail: gramercy@erols.com
Web: www.gramercymansion.com

Circa 1902. Dreams come true at this English Tudor mansion and gardens that crown 45 acres of woodlands. A superb grand staircase, high ceilings, artwork, antiques and Oriental carpets exude historic elegance. Retire to handsome guest suites decorated with lavish comfort and style. Comparable to a master suite, they feature wood-burning fireplaces and whirlpool tubs. Wake up to birds singing and the aroma of a multi-course gourmet breakfast. Dine by the fire in the dining room or at a private table on the flower-filled porch by the Olympic-size swimming pool. The terraced lower garden, "Our Special Place," overlooking historic Greenspring Valley is long remembered. Downtown Baltimore is a 20-minute drive.

Historic Interest: Inner Harbor (20 minutes), Fort McHenry (20 minutes), Ladew Gardens (25 minutes), Baltimore Zoo (15 minutes).

Innkeeper(s): Anne Pomykala & Cristin Kline. $100-325. 11 rooms, 9 with PB, 7 with FP, 2 suites and 4 conference rooms. Breakfast and snacks/refreshments included in rates. Types of meals: Full gourmet bkfst and veg bkfst. Beds: KD. Modem hook-up, TV, VCR, reading lamp, refrigerator, ceiling fan, snack bar, telephone, coffeemaker, desk, hot tub/spa, voice mail and fireplace in room. Central air. Fax, copier, swimming, tennis, library, parlor games and laundry facility on premises. Limited handicap access. Weddings, small meetings, family reunions and seminars hosted. Antiquing, art galleries, golf, hiking, horseback riding, live theater, museums, parks, shopping, sporting events, tennis and wineries nearby.

Publicity: *Washington Post, Baltimore Sun, Country Folk Art, Vegetarian Times, Mid-Atlantic Country Magazine and Baltimore Magazine.*

"The hospitality, atmosphere, food, etc. were top-notch."

Sykesville B6

Inn at Norwood

7514 Norwood Ave
Sykesville, MD 21784
(410)549-7868
E-mail: kelly@innatnorwood.com
Web: www.innatnorwood.com

Circa 1906. Romance is the trademark of this Colonial Revival home that sits in the center of Sykesville, a quaint town on the National Register of Historic Places. The front porch and cozy parlor are both perfects spots for relaxation. The guest bedrooms and suite are tastefully decorated to reflect the four seasons. They boast two-person Jacuzzi and clawfoot tubs, canopy and poster beds and some fireplaces. A three-course breakfast features homemade baked goods such as cinnamon applesauce cake, a house specialty, fresh fruit, bacon or apple sausage and an entree. A refreshment bar with snacks and beverages is always available. Stroll the landscaped grounds with a deck and tranquil pond.

Innkeeper(s): Kelly & Steve Crum. $90-150. 5 rooms with PB, 3 with FP. Breakfast, afternoon tea and snacks/refreshments included in rates. Types of meals: Full gourmet bkfst. Beds: Q. Modem hook-up, cable TV, VCR, reading lamp, ceiling fan, clock radio, fireplace and four with hot tub in room. Central air. Bicycles, library, telephone and fireplace on premises. Antiquing, bicycling, fishing, golf, hiking, museums and parks nearby.

Publicity: *Baltimore Sun and Carroll County Times.*

Takoma Park C6

Davis Warner Inn

8114 Carroll Ave
Takoma Park, MD 20912-7348
(301)408-3989 (888)683-3989 Fax:(301)408-4840
E-mail: reservations@daviswarnerinn.com
Web: www.daviswarnerinn.com

Circa 1855. An imposing landmark, this huge historic mansion was built with rare, Stick Style architecture. The central location near the Metro, Washington, DC and the Capital Beltway makes it ideal for a business or pleasure stay. Gather in the large first-floor living room with two sets of bay windows, a fireplace and three separate seating areas. The library offers a varied collection of videos and books. Spacious guest bedrooms are furnished with gorgeous antiques and family heirlooms. The Mark and Kira Davis Suite boasts a Jacuzzi tub, sitting area and impressive views. Begin a satisfying breakfast with a cup of the inn's special blend signature coffee or herbal teas. Stroll the secluded rose gardens with fountains and lily ponds. A footbridge adds to the romantic setting.

Historic Interest: Built in about 1855, the inn's Stick Style of architecture is very rare. It is the oldest building in this area of Maryland.

Innkeeper(s): Robert Patenaude and Doug Harbit. $85-145. 4 rooms, 1 with PB and 1 suite. Breakfast included in rates. Types of meals: Full bkfst. Beds: QD. Clock radio in room. Central air. TV, VCR, fax, copier, library, parlor games, telephone, fireplace and laundry facility on premises. Weddings, small meetings, family reunions and seminars hosted. Amusement parks, antiquing, art galleries, live theater, museums, parks and shopping nearby.

Thurmont A5

Cozy Country Inn

103 Frederick Rd
Thurmont, MD 21788-1813
(301)271-4301 Fax:(301)271-4301
E-mail: cozyville@aol.com
Web: www.cozyvillage.com

Circa 1929. This Country Victorian-style inn has evolved into a unique destination point for travelers throughout the years. The six-acre village includes the inn, a restaurant with seating capacity for 700 and a craft and antique village. Still operated by the founding family, the Cozy features lodging that pleases a variety of travelers. Many of the rooms are themed after past presidents. Memorabilia from nearby Camp David, past presidents and political dignitaries are displayed throughout.

Innkeeper(s): Jerry & Becky Freeze. $47-150. 21 rooms with PB, 5 with FP, 4 suites, 5 cottages and 5 conference rooms. Breakfast included in rates. Types of meals: Full bkfst, lunch, picnic lunch, gourmet dinner and room service. Restaurant on premises. Beds: KQD. Cable TV, VCR, reading lamp, refrigerator, snack bar, clock radio, telephone, desk, hot tub/spa, Jacuzzi, robes, wet bars, hair dryers and towel warmers in room. Air conditioning. Fax, copier and fireplace on premises. Limited handicap access. Weddings, small meetings, family reunions and seminars hosted. Antiquing, cross-country skiing, downhill skiing, fishing, parks, tennis, village of shops and presidential golf course nearby.

Tilghman D7

Black Walnut Point Inn

Black Walnut Rd, PO Box 308
Tilghman, MD 21671
(410)886-2452 Fax:(410)886-2053
E-mail: mward@intercom.net
Web: www.tilghmanisland.com/blackwalnut

Circa 1843. Located on 57 beautiful acres set aside as a wildlife sanctuary, this handsome Colonial Revival manor commands waterfront views from its private peninsula location. Charter fishing and island river cruises can be arranged by the innkeepers. From its bayside hammock to its nature walk, swimming pool and tennis court, the inn provides an amazingly private getaway. Accommodations are in the main house as well as the Riverside Cottage. The Cove Cottage has its own kitchen and screened porch facing the river.

Innkeeper(s): Tom & Brenda Ward. $120-225. 7 rooms with PB, 2 cottages and 1 conference room. Types of meals: Cont plus and early coffee/tea. Beds: QDT. Reading lamp, refrigerator and clock radio in room. Central air. TV, VCR, fax, copier, spa, swimming, tennis, library, parlor games, telephone and fireplace on premises. Small meetings, family reunions and seminars hosted. Antiquing, art galleries, bicycling, canoeing/kayaking, fishing, golf, parks, shopping, tennis and water sports nearby.

Chesapeake Wood Duck Inn

Gibsontown Rd, PO Box 202
Tilghman, MD 21671
(410)886-2070 (800)956-2070 Fax:(413)677-7256
E-mail: woodduck@bluecrab.org
Web: www.woodduckinn.com

Circa 1890. This Tilghman Island Victorian overlooks Dogwood Harbor and a fleet of old wooden sailing vessels still used for oystering. A favorite breakfast is Jeff's fresh banana bread French toast with peaches and cinnamon cream and grilled smoked turkey sausage, served with fine china and fresh flowers in the formal dining room or the wicker-filled porch overlooking the water. Borrow bicycles or fishing gear or have the innkeepers arrange sunset sailing. The island is linked to the peninsula by a drawbridge.

Innkeeper(s): Kimberly, Jeffrey Bushey. $139-229. 7 rooms. Breakfast included in rates. Types of meals: Full gourmet bkfst and dinner. Beds: QD. Ceiling fan and clock radio in room. Air conditioning. TV, VCR, fax, telephone and fireplace on premises. Small meetings, family reunions and seminars hosted. Antiquing, bicycling, canoeing/kayaking, fishing, golf, horseback riding, museums, parks, shopping and water sports nearby.

Lazyjack Inn on Dogwood Harbor

5907 Tilghman Island Road
Tilghman, MD 21671
(410)886-2215 (800)690-5080 Fax:(410)886-2635
E-mail: mrichards@bluecrab.org
Web: www.lazyjackinn.com

Circa 1855. On the Chesapeake Bay, this Eastern Shore Colonial boasts a casual elegance and unpretentious luxury with Persian carpets, family heirlooms, original art and personal service. Relax on the sunny back deck or in a rocker on the covered porch. Romantic suites and guest bedrooms offer peaceful surroundings. Some feature scenic views, fireplaces and Jacuzzi tubs. In the Harbor Room incredible breakfasts may start with a mascarpone cheese-filled cream puff served on a berry coulis and pineapple garnish. Fresh sticky buns or muffins are treats between courses. Herbed eggs on a grilled portobello mushroom over a bed of spinach with diced tomatoes and parsley round off the gourmet meal. The island village location is perfect for walking to local shops and restaurants. Take a lighthouse tour then sail off into the sunset on The Lady Patty for a Champagne cruise.

Historic Interest: The original portion of the house was built around 1855 as a small watermans home of 2 rooms. It was located close to the waters of the Chesapeake Bay and has the original pine floors in the East room. Simple in form and straight forward in function the restoration efforts have maintained the architectural character of the original structure. It is typical of a home for a hardworking family of the middle 1800s.

Innkeeper(s): Mike & Carol Richards. $119-259. 4 rooms with PB, 2 with FP and 2 suites. Breakfast, afternoon tea and snacks/refreshments included in rates. Types of meals: Full bkfst, veg bkfst and early coffee/tea. Beds: KQ. Reading lamp, ceiling fan, turn-down service, hot tub/spa and fireplace in room. Central air. Fax, library, parlor games, telephone, fireplace, screened porches and lovely gardens on premises. Antiquing, art galleries, bicycling, canoeing/kayaking, fishing, golf, horseback riding, live theater, museums, parks, shopping and water sports nearby.

Publicity: *Miami Herald, Chesapeake Bay Magazine, Washingtonian and Pittsburgh Post Gazette.*

Tilghman Island Inn

PO Box B
Tilghman, MD 21671
(410)886-2141 (800)886-2214 Fax:(410)888-62216
E-mail: info@tilghmanislandinn.com
Web: tilghmanislandinn.com

Circa 1907. There is something for everyone at this inn. Conveniently located at the Knapp's Narrows Bayside entrance, the T-dock or transient slips make boat transit easy. Sit on Adirondack chairs on the Sunset Deck or swim in the pool. Charter a sailboat, rent a kayak or go fishing. Take an eco-tour, play tennis or take a nap. Bright and cheery guest bedrooms offer spacious accommodations. Some feature fireplaces and spa tubs. Chef David is renown for his delicious gourmet recipes. Corporate retreats and special occasions are organized with great attention to the details that will ensure a memorable and successful event or celebration.

Innkeeper(s): Jack Redmon and David McCallum. $200-300. 20 rooms with PB, 5 with FP. Breakfast, snacks/refreshments and dinner included in rates. Types of meals: Full gourmet bkfst, early coffee/tea and gourmet lunch. Restaurant on premises. Beds: KQD. Data port, cable TV, reading lamp, refrigerator, ceiling fan, telephone, desk, hot tub/spa, voice mail and fireplace in room. Central air. Fax, copier, swimming, tennis, parlor games, fireplace and gift shop on premises. Limited handicap access. Weddings, small meetings, family reunions and seminars hosted. Canoeing/kayaking, fishing, golf, museums, shopping, tennis and water sports nearby.

Publicity: *Gourmet Magazine, Santee Wine Spectator, Southern Living and Chesapeake Bay Cooking.*

Vienna   D8

Tavern House

111 Water St, PO Box 98
Vienna, MD 21869-0098
(410)376-3347

Circa 1730. Enjoy a wonderful view of the Nanticoke River and marshes while staying at this restored Colonial tavern. Authenticated colors and stark white lime, sand and hair plaster accent the carved details of the woodwork. The inn boasts six fireplaces including the cooking hearth in the cellar. More than a meal, the mouth-watering specialty breakfasts are a social affair. Explore the Eastern Shore from this excellent base. Visit interesting small towns, Blackwater Wildlife Refuge, the bay and the marshes of Dorchester.

Innkeeper(s): Harvey & Elise Altergott. $70-75. 4 rooms, 3 with PB, 2 with FP. Types of meals: Full bkfst. Ceiling fan in room. Air conditioning. Bicycling, canoeing/kayaking, fishing and bird watching nearby.

"Delightful and invigorating and as serene as the tide."

Whitehaven   E8

Whitehaven B&B

23844 River St
Whitehaven, MD 21856-2506
(410)873-3320 (888)205-5921 Fax:(410)873-2162
E-mail: whavnbb@dmv.com
Web: www.whitehaven.com

Circa 1850. Two historic properties comprise this bed & breakfast. The Charles Leatherbury House, which dates to 1886, includes two guest rooms, decorated in country Victorian style. The two rooms share a bath, perfect for couples traveling together. Book both rooms and you'll enjoy the utmost of privacy in a historic setting. The Otis Lloyd House, constructed prior to the Civil War, includes three guest rooms, each with a private bath. Guests at both houses enjoy a full breakfast, including farm-fresh eggs and homemade baked goods. The village of Whitehaven, originally chartered in 1685, includes 22 buildings listed in the National Register.

Innkeeper(s): Maryen & Mark Herrett. $70-100. 5 rooms, 3 with PB. Breakfast and snacks/refreshments included in rates. Types of meals: Full gourmet bkfst and veg bkfst. Beds: KQT. Air conditioning. TV, VCR, fax, copier, bicycles, library, parlor games, fireplace, gas and horseback riding on premises. Weddings and family reunions hosted. Antiquing, art galleries, bicycling, canoeing/kayaking, fishing, golf, museums, parks and Atlantic beaches nearby.

Massachusetts

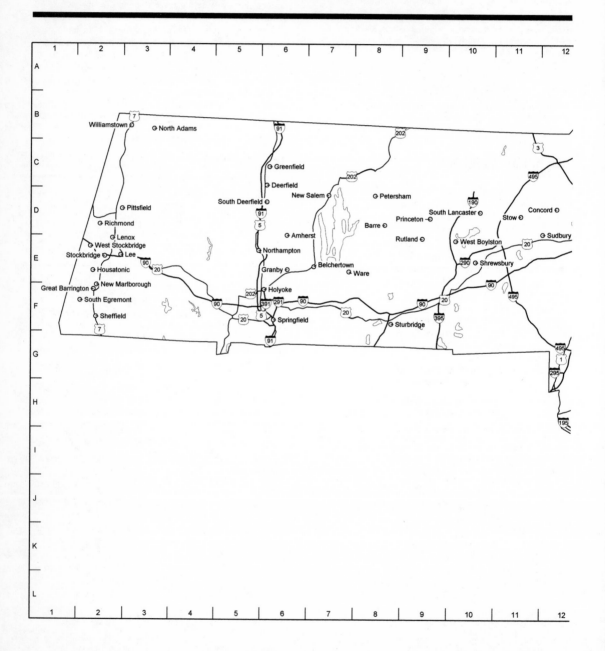

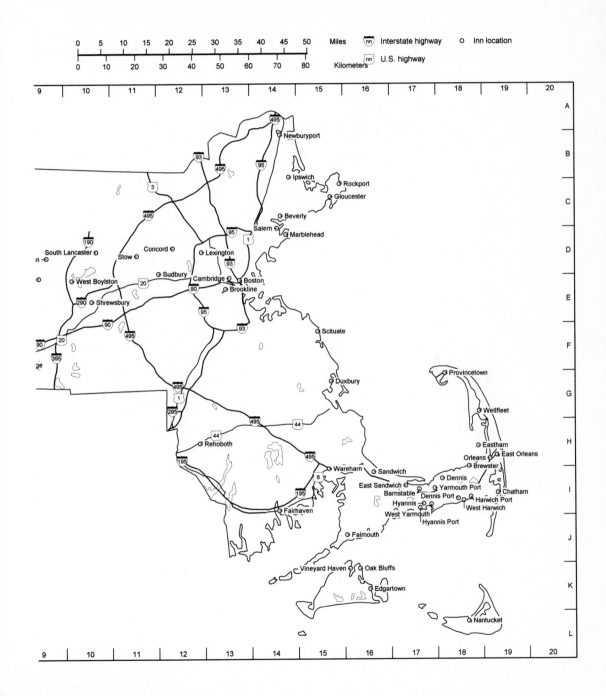

0   5   10   15   20   25   30   35   40   45   50   Miles   [nn] Interstate highway   o   Inn location

0   10   20   30   40   50   60   70   80   Kilometers   [nn] U.S. highway

Amherst D6

Allen House Victorian Inn

599 Main St
Amherst, MA 01002-2409
(413)253-5000
E-mail: allenhouse@webtv.net
Web: www.allenhouse.com

Circa 1886. This stick-style Queen Anne is much like a Victorian museum with guest rooms that feature period reproduction wallpapers, pedestal sinks, carved golden oak and brass beds, painted wooden floors and plenty of antiques. Among its many other treasures include Eastlake fireplace mantels. Unforgettable breakfasts include specialties such as eggs Benedict or French toast stuffed with rich  cream cheese. Afternoon tea is a treat, and the inn offers plenty of examples of poetry from Emily Dickinson, whose home is just across the street from the inn.

Historic Interest: Aside from the Dickinson home, the area offers many museums and the inn is within walking distance of Amherst College, Hampshire College and the University of Massachusetts. Emily Dickinson Homestead (less than one-fourth mile), historic Deerfield (18 miles north), Norman Rockwell Museum and Tanglewood (less that 1 hour away).

Innkeeper(s): Alan & Ann Zieminski. $75-175. 7 rooms with PB. Breakfast, afternoon tea and snacks/refreshments included in rates. Types of meals: Full bkfst and early coffee/tea. Beds: QDT. Modem hook-up, reading lamp, ceiling fan, clock radio, telephone, desk and down comforters & pillows in room. Air conditioning. Fax, copier, library, parlor games and fireplace on premises. Small meetings and seminars hosted. Amusement parks, antiquing, cross-country skiing, downhill skiing, fishing, golf, live theater, parks, shopping, sporting events, tennis and water sports nearby.

Publicity: *New York Times, Boston Magazine, Bon Appetit, Yankee Travel and Victorian Homes.*

"Our room and adjoining bath were spotlessly clean, charming, and quiet, with good lighting. Our meals were delicious and appetizing, and the casual, family-like atmosphere encouraged discussions among the guests."

Black Walnut Inn

1184 N Pleasant St
Amherst, MA 01002-1328
(413)549-5649 Fax:(413)549-5149
E-mail: info@blackwalnutinn.com
Web: www.blackwalnutinn.com

Circa 1745. This stately brick Federal-style inn is just three miles from Emily Dickinson's home and nine miles from the Smith College Museum of Art, which houses works by Picasso, Degas, Monet and Winslow. The inn sits on one and a half acres and is shaded by black walnut trees. Guests who stay there in October can have their fill of free walnuts. The yard is manicured and country flower gardens surround the home. The seven guest bedrooms are all soundproofed to accommodate children. Furnishings include antiques and period reproductions. Guests are served a continental plus breakfast that includes hot fruit pies and muffins, fresh squeezed orange juice and a choice of four different hot entrees. The inn has been featured in the New York Times; it received the 2000 Historical Preservation Award and it won The Maine Yankee Editor's Pick Award.

Innkeeper(s): Dan Burbine. $95-180. 10 rooms with PB, 3 with FP and 3

suites. Breakfast and snacks/refreshments included in rates. Types of meals: Full gourmet bkfst, veg bkfst, early coffee/tea and afternoon tea. Beds: KQT. Modem hook-up, cable TV, VCR, reading lamp, refrigerator, clock radio, telephone, coffeemaker, desk and one king suite with Jacuzzi tub in room. Central air. Fax, copier, pet boarding, parlor games, fireplace and outdoor fireplace on premises. Small meetings and family reunions hosted. Antiquing, art galleries, beach, bicycling, canoeing/kayaking, fishing, golf, hiking, live theater, museums, parks, shopping, sporting events and tennis nearby.

Publicity: *New York Times and Yankee Magazine.*

Barnstable I17

Ashley Manor Inn

3660 Main St, Rt 6A
Barnstable, MA 02630
(508)362-8044 (888)535-2246 Fax:(508)362-9927
E-mail: stay@ashleymanor.net
Web: www.ashleymanor.net

Circa 1699. This manor house has lived through a succession of expansions, the first addition built in 1750. The final effect is wonderful and mysterious. The inn, thought to be a hiding place for Tories during the Revolutionary War, features a huge open-hearth fireplace with beehive oven and a secret passageway connecting the upstairs and downstairs suites. The inn is reminiscent of a gracious English country house and is filled with Oriental rugs and antiques. All but one of the guest rooms boasts fireplaces, and four have large whirlpool baths. Two acres of manicured lawns include a regulation-size tennis court. Nature lovers will enjoy the landscape, dotted with cherry and apple trees. The romantic gazebo is the perfect location to view the fountain garden. A full gourmet breakfast is served on the brick terrace or fireside in the formal dining room.

Historic Interest: Nantucket and Martha's Vineyard, Chatham, the National Seashore and Provincetown on the Cape.

Innkeeper(s): Kathy Callahan. $120-225. 6 rooms with PB, 5 with FP and 4 suites. Breakfast included in rates. Types of meals: Full gourmet bkfst. Beds: KQ. Data port, reading lamp, clock radio, telephone, coffeemaker, hot tub/spa, voice mail, fireplace, four with whirlpool baths, flowers, chocolates, beverages and coffee in room. Air conditioning. Bicycles, tennis, library, parlor games and fireplace on premises. Weddings hosted. Antiquing, art galleries, beach, bicycling, canoeing/kayaking, fishing, golf, hiking, live theater, museums, parks, shopping and tennis nearby.

Publicity: *Chicago Tribune, Boston Globe, Bon Appetit, Tennis, New York Times, Pittsburgh Press, Gourmet, GBH and Newsday.*

"This is absolutely perfect! So many very special, lovely touches."

Beechwood Inn

2839 Main St, Rt 6A
Barnstable, MA 02630-1017
(508)362-6618 (800)609-6618 Fax:(508)362-0298
E-mail: info@beechwoodinn.com
Web: www.beechwoodinn.com

Circa 1853. Beechwood is a beautifully restored Queen Anne Victorian offering period furnishings, some rooms with fireplaces or ocean views. Its warmth and elegance make it a favorite hideaway for couples looking for a peaceful and romantic return to the Victorian era. The inn is named for rare old beech trees that shade the veranda.

Historic Interest: Plymouth Rock (30 minutes), Kennedy Compound and JFK Monument (10 minutes), oldest library in USA (walking distance).

Innkeeper(s): Debbie & Ken Traugot. $100-190. 6 rooms with PB, 3 with FP. Breakfast and afternoon tea included in rates. Types of meals: Full bkfst and early coffee/tea. Beds: KQD. TV, VCR, reading lamp, refrigerator, wine glasses and corkscrew in room. Air conditioning. Fax, copier, bicycles, parlor games, telephone and fireplace on premises. Antiquing, fishing, live theater, parks, shopping, sporting events, water sports, historic sites, whale watching, bird watching and horseback riding nearby.

Publicity: *National Trust Calendar, New England Weekends, Rhode Island Monthly, Cape Cod Life, Boston Magazine and Yankee Magazine.*

"Your inn is pristine in every detail. We concluded that the innkeepers, who are most hospitable, are the best part of Beechwood."

Honeysuckle Hill B&B

591 Old Kings Hwy, Rt 6A
Barnstable, MA 02668
(508)362-8418 (866)444-5522 Fax:(508)362-8386
E-mail: stay@honeysucklehill.com
Web: www.honeysucklehill.com

Circa 1810. This Queen Anne Victorian, which is listed in the National Register, is set on a picturesque acre with gardens. The interior is decorated with antiques and white wicker furnishings. The hearty breakfasts include items such as Captain's Eggs, homemade granola, fresh fruit and cranberry-orange muffins. Nearby are the dunes of Sandy Neck Beach. Hyannis is 10 minutes away.

Historic Interest: Plymouth Plantation, Hyannisport, Sandwich Village, Plymouth Rock and Mayflower II.

Innkeeper(s): Bill & Mary Kilburn. $100-219. 5 rooms, 4 with PB and 1 suite. Breakfast and snacks/refreshments included in rates. Types of meals: Full gourmet bkfst and early coffee/tea. Beds: QD. Ceiling fan, clock radio, feather beds, fresh flowers and terry cloth robes in room. Air conditioning. TV, VCR, fax, copier, library, parlor games, telephone, fireplace, beach towels, chairs and umbrellas, guest refrigerator, fish pond, porch and gardens on premises. Antiquing, art galleries, beach, bicycling, canoeing/kayaking, fishing, golf, hiking, live theater, museums, parks, shopping, tennis, wineries, beach, ferries and whale watching nearby.

Publicity: *Atlanta Constitution, Saint Louis Journal, Prime Time, Cape Cod Travel Guide, Cape Cod Life and Secondhome.*

"The charm, beauty, service and warmth shown to guests are impressive, but the food overwhelms. Breakfasts were divine!" — Judy Kaplan, St. Louis Journal

Lamb and Lion Inn

2504 Main St., Rt. 6A, PO Box 511
Barnstable, MA 02630-0511
(508)362-6823 (800)909-6923 Fax:(508)362-0227
E-mail: info@lambandlion.com
Web: www.lambandlion.com

Circa 1740. This rambling collection of Cape-style buildings sits on four acres overlooking the Old King's highway. Newly decorated, the inn offers a feeling of casual elegance. The Innkeeper's Pride is a romantic suite with sunken tub, fireplace, kitchenette and a deck overlooking a garden and woods. The Barn-stable is one of the original buildings and now offers three sleeping areas, a living and dining area and French doors to a private patio. A large central courtyard houses a generous sized heated pool and hot tub spa.

Innkeeper(s): Alice Pitcher. $145-250. 10 rooms with PB, 11 with FP, 1 cottage and 1 conference room. Breakfast included in rates. Types of meals: Cont plus. Beds: KQDT. Modem hook-up, cable TV, VCR, reading lamp, refrig-

erator, telephone, coffeemaker and fireplace in room. Air conditioning. Fax, copier, spa, swimming, parlor games and fireplace on premises. Weddings, small meetings, family reunions and seminars hosted. Antiquing, art galleries, beach, bicycling, canoeing/kayaking, cross-country skiing, fishing, golf, hiking, horseback riding, live theater, museums, parks, shopping, sporting events, tennis, water sports and wineries nearby.

Barre   D8

Stevens Farm B&B

Old Coldbrook Rd
Barre, MA 01005
(978)355-2227 Fax:(978)355-2234
E-mail: stevensfarminn@juno.com
Web: www.stevensfarminn.com

Circa 1789. Guests enjoy an old-fashioned country experience at Stevens Farm. The 18th-century farmhouse has been in the innkeepers' family for nine generations since 1789. Guests can take tours of the 350-acre working farm, enjoy a swimming pool or just relax and enjoy the view from the gazebo. During the winter months, guests can cross-country ski on the property or ice skate on the pond. Colorful, handmade afghans and comfortable antiques decorate the bedchambers. The parlor features Victorian furnishings, an upright piano and a tin ceiling. The innkeeper once worked as a cook and professional baker and prepares the savory full breakfasts. Dinner, featuring items such as Yankee pot roast, homemade bread and cranberry walnut pie, can be arranged. The inn recently received the Governors Hospitality Award.

Innkeeper(s): Richard & Irene Stevens. $75-95. 6 rooms, 1 with PB and 1 conference room. Breakfast and afternoon tea included in rates. Types of meals: Full bkfst, early coffee/tea, picnic lunch, snacks/refreshments and room service. Beds: D. Reading lamp, clock radio and window fans in room. Weddings, small meetings, family reunions and seminars hosted. Antiquing, art galleries, bicycling, canoeing/kayaking, cross-country skiing, downhill skiing, fishing, golf, hiking, horseback riding, live theater, museums, shopping, tennis and wineries nearby.

Belchertown   E7

Ingate Farms B&B

60 Lamson Ave-S. Amherst Line
Belchertown, MA 01007-9710
(413)253-0440 (888)464-2832 Fax:(413)253-0440

Circa 1740. This Cape-style home was built as a bobbin factory, and eventually it was moved and reassembled at its current location on a 400-acre equestrian center. The interior is homey, with an emphasis on early American decor. Guests can relax on the enclosed porch, which is filled with comfortable furnishings. From the porch, guests can watch horses and enjoy the countryside.  The grounds offer an Olympic-size swimming pool, hiking trails, and guests can rent a boat and fish at nearby Quabbin Reservoir. Amherst, Hampshire and Holyoke colleges are nearby, as well as the University of Massachusetts at Amherst.

Innkeeper(s): Virginia Kier & Bill McCormick. $70-95. 5 rooms, 3 with PB. Breakfast and afternoon tea included in rates. Types of meals: Cont plus and early coffee/tea. Beds: KQT. TV, reading lamp, refrigerator, ceiling fan, clock radio, telephone and ice water in room. Air conditioning. VCR, fax, copier, swimming, stable, library, fireplace, pressing/irons, hair dryers, riding and hiking trails and riding lessons on premises. Family reunions hosted.

Amusement parks, antiquing, cross-country skiing, downhill skiing, fishing, golf, live theater, parks, shopping, sporting events and tennis nearby.

"I've felt so at home here this week and also charmed by the calm and loveliness of this place."

Mucky Duck

38 Park St PO Box 1266
Belchertown, MA 01007-9590
(413)323-9657 Fax:(413)323-6997
E-mail: dukbb@aol.com
Web: www.muckyduckinn.com

Circa 1839. On the peaceful side of the Common, this 1846 Gothic Greek Revival cottage is the only one of its architectural type in the area. European antiques, artwork and stained glass highlight the ambiance and decor. Sit by the fire in the parlor with a good book and music playing softly. A refrigerator is available for use. The business room provides a modem hookup. Each distinctive guest bedroom boasts tasteful furnishings and decor, most include a walk-in closet. Stay in the white and delft blue Aylesbury Room with a four-poster bed and clawfoot tub or the Eider Suite with a sunny dormer and cozy sitting area. Enjoy a relaxed buffet-style breakfast in the dining room with fresh-baked breads, imported cheeses, fruits and a hot entree. Hiking trails are just two miles away at scenic Quabbin Reservoir.

Historic Interest: This house was built by Calvin Bridgman for his daughter as a wedding present. It was later used as the parsonage for the Congregational Church.

Innkeeper(s): Annie and Richard Steiner. $85-135. 4 rooms with PB and 1 suite. Breakfast included in rates. Types of meals: Full gourmet bkfst, veg bkfst and early coffee/tea. Beds: KQT. Cable TV, reading lamp, clock radio and desk in room. Air conditioning. Fax, telephone and fireplace on premises. Amusement parks, antiquing, art galleries, bicycling, canoeing/kayaking, cross-country skiing, fishing, golf, hiking, horseback riding, museums, parks, shopping, sporting events and pet boarding nearby.

Beverly   C14

Gordon's 1841 House B&B

15 Washington Street
Beverly, MA 01915
(978)921-2612 (888)927-2612 Fax:(978)927-7696
E-mail: gorfab@tiac.net
Web: www.gordons1841house.com

Circa 1841. Adults appreciate the quiet solitude and privacy of this historic Federal-style home built by a mariner. Located in the Cape Ann area just over the bridge from Salem, the inn is just a short walk from the ocean beach. The spacious Hannah Suite features a first-floor kitchenette with refrigerator and microwave, computer station with Internet access, TV/VCR, second-floor bedroom, double Jacuzzi, separate shower and private entrance. A continental breakfast is provided. Relax on a bench in the flower garden by the koi pond with waterfall. The shaded porch boasts inviting rockers. Bicycles are available for more active exploring.

Innkeeper(s): Juanita & George Gordon. $125-140. 2 rooms with PB, 1 with FP and 1 suite. Breakfast and refreshments included in rates. Types of meals: Cont and early coffee/tea. Beds: QD. Modem hook-up, data port, cable TV, VCR, reading lamp, refrigerator, clock radio, telephone, coffeemaker, desk, hot tub/spa, fireplace and double Jacuzzi in room. Central air. Fax, spa, bicycles, fireplace and porch rocking chairs on premises. Weddings and family reunions hosted. Antiquing, art galleries, beach, bicycling, canoeing/kayaking, fishing, golf, hiking, horseback riding, live theater, museums, parks, shopping, tennis and water sports nearby.

Boston   E13

Abigayle's Bed and Breakfast

PO Box 57166
Boston, MA 02457
(617)720-0522 (888)486-6021 Fax:(781)455-6745
E-mail: info@bnbboston.com
Web: www.bnbboston.com/boston-bnbs/b&bs_4c.htm

Circa 1896. Experience Victorian luxury at this elegant 1896 four-story Brownstone that has been lovingly renovated while preserving original woodwork, architectural details and period furnishings. Gracing a residential neighborhood on a tree-lined street adjacent to Kenmore Square near Boston University, it is conveniently located around the corner from the subway, shops and restaurants. Stay in smoke-free comfort in traditionally appointed and tastefully decorated guest bedrooms. Enjoy warm hospitality and a daily self-serve breakfast that is available when desired. Visit the many nearby historic sites of the city that include Fanueil Hall, Old South Church and Bunker Hill.

Innkeeper(s): Marie Kemmler. $110-150. 3 rooms with PB. Breakfast included in rates. Types of meals: Cont plus and early coffee/tea. Beds: KQT. Modem hook-up, data port, cable TV, clock radio, telephone and desk in room. Air conditioning. Art galleries, live theater, museums, parks, shopping, sporting events, Freedom Trail, Fenway Park, Fleet Center, Bunker Hill, USS Constitution and Quincy Market nearby.

Carruth House - A Private Home Bed & Breakfast in Boston

30 Beaumont St
Boston, MA 02124-5008
(617)436-8260 (888)838-8900 Fax:(617)436-5320

Circa 1877. Built in the Victorian Second Empire style around 1877, this landmark historic home graces the Ashmont section of Dorchester in a garden suburb setting. Many common areas invite relaxation for a quiet and peaceful getaway. Sit in the shade of the covered front porch or under an umbrella on the spacious back deck. Nap in the double-wide Pawleys Island hammock. Play eight ball on the vintage McGandy regulation-size pool table in the Great Room. Select from the collection of videos, DVDs, CDs and games. The first-floor Ashmont Suite features a private entrance, carved antique four-poster canopy bed and a mahogany fireplace mantle accented with Chelsea tile. Third-floor guest bedrooms share an open sitting area as well as a large bathroom with a whirlpool tub. Enjoy a self-serve breakfast with fresh baked goods from a local bakery, fruit, cereal and yogurt.

Historic Interest: Please refer to the history page on website for information on Herbert Carruth. www.carruthhouse.us.

Innkeeper(s): Heidi Kieffer. $85-125. 3 rooms, 1 with FP, 1 suite and 1 conference room. Breakfast and snacks/refreshments included in rates. Types of meals: Cont plus. Beds: QDT. TV, VCR, clock radio, desk and fireplace in room. Air conditioning. Fax, copier, library, parlor games, telephone and two dogs on premises. Small meetings and family reunions hosted. MBTA Ashmont Station on the red line nearby.

Charles Street Inn

94 Charles Street
Boston, MA 02114
(617)314-8900 (877)772-8900 Fax:(617)371-0009
E-mail: info@charlesstreetinn.com
Web: www.charlesstreetinn.com

Circa 1860. Elegantly gracing the historic district of Beacon Hill, this inn was built as a model home in 1860 featuring Second Empire decor. Exquisite luxury resonates from this meticulously renovated and refurbished delight. Each amenity-filled guest bedroom is named after a famous local Victorian who contributed to the arts and is tastefully furnished to reflect that character. Plush comforts include large air-jet whirlpool spa tubs, refrigerators stocked with complementary beverages, marble fireplaces, stereo CDs, DSL Internet access, Crabtree & Evelyn toiletries, Frette linens, robes and slippers, Turkish rugs, antiques, oil paintings and much more. A deluxe continental breakfast is savored in the privacy of the room. The sights of the city beckon and are even more enjoyable knowing what splendor awaits back at the inn.

Historic Interest: On National Registry of Historic Places, first model home in America, model for Back Bay Townhouses.

Innkeeper(s): Sally Deane & Louise Venden. $225-425. 9 rooms with PB, 9 with FP. Breakfast and snacks/refreshments included in rates. Types of meals: Cont plus, early coffee/tea and room service. Beds: KQD. Modem hook-up, data port, cable TV, VCR, reading lamp, stereo, refrigerator, snack bar, clock radio, telephone, coffeemaker, turn-down service, desk, hot tub/spa, voice mail and DSL in room. Central air. Fax, copier, spa, library, parlor games, fireplace and laundry facility on premises. Limited handicap access. Weddings and family reunions hosted. Antiquing, art galleries, live theater, museums, parks, shopping, sporting events and tennis nearby.

Publicity: *Washington Port, Boston Globe, Travel & Leisure, Conde Nast, Johansens Guide to North America, Karen Browns Guide to North American Inns, USA Today and ABC Good Morning America.*

Gryphon House

9 Bay State Rd
Boston, MA 02215-2101
(617)375-9003 (877)375-9003 Fax:(617)250-0716

Circa 1895. Ideally situated for pleasant strolls and easy access to historic city sites, this Richardson Romanesque Victorian, built in 1895, boasts original wood floors, moldings, tiles and Zuber wallpaper. The interior blends Victorian, Arts & Craft, Chinoiserie and Italianate decor. Browse the extensive video library in the lobby where an iMac computer is available to use. Each air-conditioned guest bedroom features a gas log fireplace, wet bar with refrigerator, voice mail and high-speed Internet access. Enjoy views of the Charles River from two of the spacious rooms. A generous continental breakfast is served daily. Convenient on-site parking is complimentary.

Historic Interest: Date built, original moldings, tiles, wood floors, decor, Zuber wallpaper.

Innkeeper(s): Teresa Blagg & Ed Hatfield. $129-235. 8 rooms with PB, 8 with FP. Breakfast included in rates. Types of meals: Cont, veg bkfst and early coffee/tea. Beds: Q. Modem hook-up, data port, cable TV, VCR, reading lamp, stereo, refrigerator, clock radio, telephone, coffeemaker, desk, voice mail and fireplace in room. Air conditioning. Fax, library, parlor games, video and CD library and free on-site parking on premises. Weddings, small meetings, family reunions and seminars hosted. Antiquing, art galleries, beach, bicycling, canoeing/kayaking, golf, live theater, museums, parks, shopping, sporting events and water sports nearby.

Host Homes of Boston

PO Box 117-Waban Branch
Boston, MA 02468-0001
(617)244-1308 (800)600-1308 Fax:(617)244-5156
E-mail: info@hosthomesofboston.com
Web: www.hosthomesofboston.com

Circa 1864. Perfect for leisure or business travel, this reliable reservation service offers convenient, comfortable and affordable accommodations. One of the many fine private homes available includes a stately townhouse on Commonwealth Avenue in Boston's chic Back Bay, less than one block away from the Boston Common and a short walk to Copley Square.

Choose from a variety of vacation possibilities throughout the Greater Boston area and suburbs. Walk the Freedom Trail, browse for antiques on Beacon Hill or people watch from a sidewalk café at Newbury Street. Savor fresh seafood along the waterfront, visit Charlestown's Old Ironsides, attend a concert at the Symphony or Boston Pops, browse through Harvard Square's bookshops or watch a ball game at Fenway Park.

Historic Interest: Boston and its surrounding areas are full of historic sites. Each of the accommodations is near something unique.

Innkeeper(s): Marcia Whittington. $80-160. 75 rooms. Breakfast included in rates. Types of meals: Cont plus. Beds: KQDT. Each bed and breakfast offers different amenities in room. Each bed and breakfast offers different amenities on premises. Antiquing, live theater, museums, shopping, sporting events, historic sites and whale watching nearby.

Publicity: *The Sunday Times, USA Today, What's Doing in Boston, BBC Holiday and Marie Claire.*

"Very special. I have never stayed at such an excellent, elegant B&B. Our hosts were delightful, the place, magnificent!"

The Newbury Guesthouse

261 Newbury Guesthouse
Boston, MA 02116
(617)437-7666 (800)437-7668 Fax:(617)670-6100
E-mail: lundy@hagopianhotels.com
Web: www.newburyguesthouse.com

Circa 1882. Originally built as a private residence in the fashionable Back Bay neighborhood in 1882, this elegant brick brownstone has been renovated for modern conveniences while retaining the vintage fixtures and floors. Tastefully appointed guest bedrooms offer privacy, comfort and a graceful décor. One large room features a bay window and a sleigh bed covered with a down-filled duvet. Breakfast includes fresh fruit, eggs, bacon, and home-baked muffins served in the parlor or on the patio overlooking Newbury Street. The historic landmarks and sites of the city are nearby. A short walk to the Charles River offers paths along panoramic views. Whether staying for business or pleasure, the location and amenities are accommodating. Ask about romantic getaway packages that are offered throughout the year.

Innkeeper(s): Lundy Carre. $99-195. 32 rooms with PB. Breakfast included in rates. Types of meals: Cont plus and early coffee/tea. Beds: Q. Data port, cable TV, reading lamp, clock radio, telephone and voice mail in room. Central air. Limited handicap access. Antiquing, art galleries, canoeing/kayaking, live theater, museums, parks, shopping and sporting events nearby.

Publicity: *New York Times.*

Oasis Guest House

22 Edgerly Rd
Boston, MA 02115-3007
(617)267-2262 (800)230-0105 Fax:(617)267-1920
E-mail: info@oasisgh.com
Web: www.oasisgh.com

Circa 1885. Located in the Back Bay area of Boston, this historic row house offers an excellent location from which to enjoy the city. More than one half of the guest rooms include a private bath, and all are comfortably furnished with antiques and contemporary pieces. The home still maintains some of its Victorian features, including a grand fireplace in one of the common areas. Continental fare is available in the mornings.

Innkeeper(s): Joe Haley. $80-140. 16 rooms, 10 with PB. Breakfast included in rates. Types of meals: Cont. Beds: QDT. Cable TV, reading lamp, clock radio, telephone and desk in room. Air conditioning. Fax and copier on premises. Antiquing, live theater, museums, parks, shopping and sporting events nearby.

Taylor House Bed & Breakfast

50 Burroughs St
Boston, MA 02130
(617)983-9334 (888)228-2956 Fax:(617)522-3852

Circa 1855. Sitting adjacent to popular Jamaica Pond in the Monument Square Historic District, this Italianate Victorian inn with Greek Revival elements has been recently restored. Go through the double doors into the main lobby where a gorgeous staircase leads to second-floor guest bedrooms. Original works of art grace the walls and colorful garden views enhance the serene ambiance. Sleep comes easy on a Queen-size sleigh bed. Amenities provide an assortment of comforts to meet most business or leisure needs. Enjoy fresh fruit, baked goods, cereals and yogurt for breakfast. Walk or jog the nearby 1.5 mile paved trail or visit the spectacular Arnold Arboretum only six blocks away.

Historic Interest: Built in 1855 by international merchant, George Taylor.

Innkeeper(s): Dave Elliott and Daryl Bichel. $125-190. 3 rooms, 1 suite and 1 conference room. Breakfast and snacks/refreshments included in rates. Types of meals: Cont plus and early coffee/tea. Beds: Q. Modem hook-up, TV, VCR, clock radio, telephone and voice mail in room. Air conditioning. Fax and copier on premises. Small meetings, family reunions and seminars hosted. Antiquing, art galleries, bicycling, fishing, golf, hiking, live theater, museums, parks and shopping nearby.

Publicity: *Boston Globe, Calendar Review, San Francisco Chronicle and Hartford Chronicle.*

The Tremont Boston - A Wyndham Historic Hotel

275 Tremont Street
Boston, MA 02116
(617)426-1400 Fax:(617)338-1893
E-mail: jtrout@wyndham.com

Circa 1925. Graciously restored to combine the classic elegance of the Roaring Twenties with eclectic contemporary decor, this Grand Style hotel is in the thriving downtown Theatre District near the government center and blocks from the Back Bay. Upscale amenities that include plush robes and personal products from the Golden Door Bath Care Collection as well as the latest technology with T1 high-speed Internet access are featured in the posh guest bedrooms. The hotel offers dining on French Mediterranean cuisine in the Caprice Restaurant, relaxation in the intimate atmosphere of the Encore Piano Lounge or the entertaining Roxy Night Club, Jukebox and Matrix. Walk to Boston's historic sites, shop Faneuil Hall Marketplace or take the underground transportation across the street to see a baseball game at Fenway Park.

Innkeeper(s): Jeanni Trout. $129-229. 322 rooms with PB, 1 suite and 9 conference rooms. Beds: KQDT. Cable TV, clock radio, telephone, coffeemaker, Wayport services, turn-down service is available for ByRequest Members and special requests and some with CD player in room. Air conditioning. Fax, copier, gift shop, business center available complete with fax, copy machine and PC on premises. Limited handicap access. Weddings, small meetings, family reunions and seminars hosted.

Verona's Bed and Breakfast

PO Box 57166
Boston, MA 02457
(617)720-0522 (800)486-6021 Fax:(781)455-6745
E-mail: info@bnbboston.com
Web: www.bnbboston.com/boston-bnbs/b&rbs_6b.htm

Circa 1900. Recently restored to provide modern comfort and convenience, yet having retained all of its historic charm, this Victorian four-story brick townhouse boasts original fireplaces with intricately carved marble mantles and wrought-iron filigree. Antique furnishings also reflect the home's heritage. Private access to the spacious guest bedrooms is from the central stairway. Features include granite-tiled baths, a wet bar and pantry, individually controlled air conditioning, direct-dial phones and distinctive color schemes. Stay in one room with a working fireplace. A continental breakfast is available every morning. Take a tour or walk the popular Freedom Trail and many other city sites.

Historic Interest: Victorian in Boston's Historic South End neighborhood.

Innkeeper(s): Marie Kemmler. $110-170. 5 rooms with PB, 1 with FP. Breakfast included in rates. Types of meals: Cont plus. Beds: Q. Modem hook-up, data port, cable TV, reading lamp, refrigerator, clock radio, telephone, coffeemaker and fireplace in room. Central air. Antiquing, art galleries, live theater, museums, parks, shopping and sporting events nearby.

Brewster   H18

The Beechcroft Inn

1360 Main St
Brewster, MA 02631-1724
(508)896-9534 (877)233-2446
E-mail: info@beechcroftinn.com
Web: www.beechcroftinn.com

Circa 1828. Hospitality has been a tradition for more than 140 years at this delightful Greek Revival inn, which before that time was a church meeting house in idyllic Cape Cod. Special attention is given to personal touches that pamper and please.

English antiques furnish the tastefully decorated guest bedrooms. Some boast a sitting area, private deck and offer a variety of views including the extensive gardens, famous beech tree and bay. A full breakfast is served on site in The Brewster Teapot, an authentic English tearoom. Complimentary evening wines and sherries are served in the living room. A croquet lawn is a new addition, and bicycles are available for local exploring.

Innkeeper(s): Jan & Paul Campbell. $115-165. 10 rooms with PB. Breakfast included in rates. Types of meals: Full bkfst, early coffee/tea, lunch and afternoon tea. Restaurant on premises. Beds: KQDT. Reading lamp and clock radio in room. VCR, bicycles, parlor games, telephone and fireplace on premises. Weddings, small meetings, family reunions and seminars hosted. Antiquing, fishing, golf, live theater, parks, shopping and water sports nearby.

Candleberry Inn

1882 Main St
Brewster, MA 02631-1827
(508)896-3300 (800)573-4769 Fax:(508)896-4016
E-mail: cmorse@cape.com
Web: www.candleberryinn.com

Circa 1750. The two-acre grounds of this 250-year-old inn feature gardens complete with lawn swings. Wainscoting is dominant in the guest rooms, which feature Oriental rugs on top of pine-planked floors. Antiques and family heirlooms decorate the inn. Three rooms include working fireplaces and one has a Jacuzzi. A full, gourmet breakfast is served in the dining room, which

is also the inn's oldest room. The beach is less than a mile away, and Brewster offers many shops and restaurants.

Innkeeper(s): Cheryl & Jeff Morse. $105-205. 9 rooms with PB, 3 with FP and 2 suites. Breakfast included in rates. Types of meals: Full gourmet bkfst. Beds: KQDT. Reading lamp, clock radio, desk, robes and hair dryers in room. Air conditioning. Fax, copier, parlor games, telephone and fireplace on premises. Family reunions hosted. Antiquing, fishing, golf, live theater, parks, shopping, tennis, water sports and bike and nature trails nearby.

Publicity: *Brewster Oracle and New York Times.*

"Wonderful, relaxing time, don't want to leave."

Captain Freeman Inn

15 Breakwater Rd
Brewster, MA 02631-1311
(508)896-7481 (800)843-4664 Fax:(508)896-5618
E-mail: stay@captainfreemaninn.com
Web: www.captainfreemaninn.com

Circa 1866. This Cape Cod mansion was designed with the architectural detail befitting its original owner's expensive taste. Captain William Freeman, an aristocratic shipmaster, imported the inn's ornate plaster moldings from Italy, and the floors were laid in a light and dark herringbone pattern. A commanding center staircase with a hand-carved banister leads to the inn's luxurious guest rooms, all decorated with period reproductions. Many of the rooms offer fireplaces, balconies and whirlpool tubs. Guests are invited to swim in the inn's pool surrounded by flower and herb gardens or play croquet and badminton on more than an acre of sweeping lawns. The inn offers a full breakfast served poolside in the warmer months or fireside in the dining room. Tea or hot chocolate is offered on cool days in the fall and spring. Walk to the beach on Cape Cod Bay or borrow a bicycle and explore the miles of bike paths. Tennis, golf, horseback riding, theater, antiquing, art galleries and shopping are located nearby.

Historic Interest: Built in 1866 by a local wealthy sea captain, the inn is located in the center of town overlooking the town green. Also, a short stroll down the old packet landing road leads you to Breakwater Beach on beautiful Cape Cod Bay.

Innkeeper(s): Donna & Peter Amadeo. $150-225. 12 rooms with PB, 6 with FP and 1 conference room. Breakfast and snacks/refreshments included in rates. Types of meals: Full gourmet bkfst. Beds: Q. Modem hook-up, cable TV, VCR, reading lamp, refrigerator, ceiling fan, clock radio, telephone, desk, hot tub/spa, voice mail and fireplace in room. Central air. Fax, copier, swimming, bicycles, parlor games, fireplace, laundry facility and gift shop on premises. Small meetings and seminars hosted. Antiquing, art galleries, beach, bicycling, canoeing/kayaking, fishing, golf, hiking, live theater, museums, parks, shopping, tennis, water sports and wineries nearby.

Publicity: *Yankee Magazine 1998 & 2000, Boston Globe, Boston Herald, LA Times, Houston Post, Cape Cod Times, Southwest Airlines inflight magazine, newsletter for Lincoln car owners, Fast & Healthy magazine, Betty Crocker cookbook, AAA monthly newsletter, Boston channel 5 and PBS Country Inn Cooking show.*

"We were in awe when we entered our room, and the charm, elegance and romantic decor instilled in us a memory we will cherish always."

Old Manse Inn

1861 Main St
Brewster, MA 02631-0745
(508)896-3149 Fax:(508)896-1546
E-mail: theoldmanseInn@verizon.net
Web: www.oldmanseinn.com

Circa 1801. Home to some of the most famous sea captains on Cape Cod, this mansion was built in 1801 on the site where the first Lutheran Chapel was built in this area of New

England. The inn is lavishly furnished with antique and period furnishings that are accented by high ceilings, hardwood floors, oriental rugs and artwork depicting life on the high seas. Luxurious guest bedrooms feature historic wall coverings, handmade drapes, fine linens, four-poster, canopy or sleigh beds. Hosts Paul and Joyce offer full concierge and vacation planning services as well as a fabulous gourmet breakfast. Superb tennis and golf facilities are available and enjoy easy access to the many dining, theater and recreational activities offered locally.

Innkeeper(s): Joyce & Paul Stier. $125-148. 9 rooms with PB and 2 conference rooms. Breakfast included in rates. Types of meals: Full gourmet bkfst, veg bkfst and afternoon tea. Beds: QDT. Cable TV, reading lamp, ceiling fan, clock radio and telephone in room. Air conditioning. VCR, fax, swimming, stable, tennis, library, pet boarding, parlor games and fireplace on premises. Weddings, small meetings and family reunions hosted. Antiquing, art galleries, beach, bicycling, canoeing/kayaking, fishing, golf, hiking, horseback riding, live theater, museums, parks, shopping, tennis, water sports, wineries, whale watching and lighthouse tours nearby.

Publicity: *Travel & Leisure, Boston Herald and Boston Globe.*

"Our stays at the Old Manse Inn have always been delightful. The innkeepers are gracious, the decor charming and the dining room has a character all its own."

Old Sea Pines Inn

2553 Main St, PO Box 1026
Brewster, MA 02631-1959
(508)896-6114 Fax:(508)896-7387
E-mail: innkeeper@oldseapinesinn.com
Web: www.oldseapinesinn.com

Circa 1900. Formerly the Sea Pines School of Charm and Personality for Young Women, this turn-of-the-century mansion sits on three-and-one-half acres of trees and lawns. Recently renovated, the inn displays elegant wallpapers and a grand sweeping stairway. On Sunday evenings, mid June through mid September, enjoy a dinner show in conjunction with Cape Cod Repertory Theatre. Beaches and bike paths are nearby, as are village shops and restaurants.

Historic Interest: Local Historic Registry.

Innkeeper(s): Michele & Stephen Rowan. $75-150. 24 rooms, 16 with PB, 3 with FP, 2 suites and 2 conference rooms. Breakfast and snacks/refreshments included in rates. Types of meals: Full bkfst, early coffee/tea, afternoon tea and room service. Beds: QDT. Cable TV and reading lamp in room. Air conditioning. TV, telephone and fireplace on premises. Limited handicap access. Weddings, small meetings, family reunions and seminars hosted. Antiquing, fishing, live theater, shopping, water sports and dinner theatre in summer nearby.

Publicity: *New York Times, Cape Cod Oracle, For Women First, Home Office, Entrepreneur, Boston Magazine, Redbook, Travel & Leisure and Better Homes & Gardens-British Edition.*

"The loving care applied by Steve, Michele and staff is deeply appreciated."

Ruddy Turnstone B&B

463 Main St
Brewster, MA 02631-1049
(508)385-9871 (800)654-1995
E-mail: info@theruddyturnstone.com
Web: www.theruddyturnstone.com

Circa 1810. This restored antique-filled farmhouse affords ocean views. Guests opt for rooms in the main house or in the restored carriage house, which was brought to the property from Nantucket. Each guest room offers something special. The Bayview Suite includes a fireplace and boasts ocean views. Both carriage house rooms include canopy beds and period furniture. The bed  & breakfast was named as the best B&B on the Lower Cape for three consecutive years by Cape Cod Life Magazine. Guests to this Cape Cod retreat can relax and enjoy views of the marsh and the bay or stroll to shops, museums and restaurants.

Innkeeper(s): Gordon & Sally Swanson. $125-195. 5 rooms with PB, 1 with FP and 2 suites. Breakfast included in rates. Types of meals: Full bkfst and early coffee/tea. Beds: Q. Reading lamp, clock radio, turn-down service and desk in room. Air conditioning. Parlor games, telephone and fireplace on premises. Weddings, small meetings, family reunions and seminars hosted. Antiquing, beach, fishing, golf, live theater, parks, shopping, tennis, galleries and whale watching nearby.

Publicity: *National Geographic Traveler, Victoria and Cape Cod Life Magazine.*

"Here lies the true New England, warm, comfortable and welcoming."

Brookline   E13

Beech Tree Inn

83 Longwood Ave
Brookline, MA 02446
(617)277-1620 (800)544-9660 Fax:(617)277-0657
E-mail: beechtreeinn@verizon.net

Circa 1885. Offering "Neighborhood Charm in the City" this delightful Victorian-style bed and breakfast was once a private home. The casual atmosphere and surroundings are ideal for relaxing or exploring. Air-conditioned guest bedrooms feature ceiling fans, Internet access, CD players, TV/VCRs and phones with voice mail. Three of the rooms with a shared bath include thick, fluffy robes. A video library and microwave popcorn are available. A continental breakfast is served daily. Located just minutes from downtown Boston, it is within walking distance to Harvard Medical School and Boston University.

Innkeeper(s): Nancy Sullivan. $79-150. 10 rooms, 7 with PB. Breakfast included in rates. Types of meals: Cont, early coffee/tea, afternoon tea and snacks/refreshments. Beds: KQDT. TV, VCR, reading lamp, CD player, ceiling fan, clock radio, telephone, desk, voice mail and Internet access in room. Air conditioning. Fax on premises. Antiquing, art galleries, golf, live theater, museums, parks, shopping and sporting events nearby.

Publicity: *Bed and Breakfast Journal's Book of List, 2004 as part of the Top 15 B&B/Country Inns and Regional Gold Medal Winner of the 2003 Reader's Choice Award for the Best Hotel/Motel/Inn/B&B.*

The Bertram Inn

92 Sewall Ave
Brookline, MA 02446-5327
(617)566-2234 (800)295-3822 Fax:(617)277-1887

Circa 1907. Antiques and authenticity are the rule at this turn-of-the-century Gothic Revival inn, found on a peaceful, tree-lined street two miles from central Boston. The Bertram Inn  features old-English stylings and Victorian decor. Guests can enjoy breakfast or afternoon tea by the fire in the common room or, if weather permits, on the front porch overlooking the garden. Boston College, Boston University, Fenway Park and the F.L. Olmstead National Historic Site all are nearby. Shops and restaurants are within walking distance, and the Boston area's many attractions are nearby. Parking is included in the rates.

Historic Interest: Faneuil Hall and the Freedom Trail (10 minutes).

Innkeeper(s): Bryan Austin. $99-239. 14 rooms with PB, 2 with FP and 4 suites. Breakfast included in rates. Types of meals: Cont plus and afternoon tea. Beds: KQDT. Cable TV, telephone and hair dryer in room. Air conditioning. Fax on premises. Sporting events nearby.

"The Bertram Inn is a gem, and you may be sure I will highly recommend it to anyone coming this way. So pleased to have discovered you!"

The Samuel Sewall Inn

143 St. Paul St
Brookline, MA 02446
(617)713-0123 (888)713-2566 Fax:(617)738-2685
E-mail: innkeeper@samuelsewallinn.com
Web: www.samuelsewallinn.com

Circa 1883. Elegant Old World charm mingles with modern conveniences at this comfortable Queen Anne Victorian house. More than 100 years old, the inn's original beauty has been restored featuring rich woodwork, high ceilings and large windows, some with stained glass. Fine wallpaper, draperies and period antiques enhance the splendor. Romance and tranquility are easily inspired. The spacious guest bedrooms and junior suites boast 21-inch-thick mattresses, TVs and dedicated modem lines. Some offer wood-burning fireplaces. A full breakfast displayed buffet style is sure to satisfy. Parking is available, and downtown Boston is just minutes away by trolley. Relax on the patio with fresh-baked cookies, cakes, pies, beverages and other snacks after sightseeing.

Innkeeper(s): Bryan Austin. $95-205. 14 rooms with PB, 5 with FP. Breakfast, afternoon tea and snacks/refreshments included in rates. Types of meals: Full bkfst and early coffee/tea. Beds: KQT. Modem hook-up, cable TV, VCR, reading lamp, clock radio, telephone, turn-down service, desk, fireplace, iron with ironing board and hair dryers in room. Central air. Fax, small guest refrigerators and parking on premises. Limited handicap access. Family reunions hosted. Antiquing, art galleries, beach, bicycling, canoeing/kayaking, golf, hiking, horseback riding, live theater, museums, parks, shopping, sporting events, tennis, 2 blocks from downtown Boston and 2 blocks from Coolidge Corner nearby.

Cambridge   E13

A Bed & Breakfast In Cambridge

1657 Cambridge St
Cambridge, MA 02138-4316
(617)868-7082 (800)795-7122 Fax:(617)876-8991
E-mail: doaneperry@yahoo.com
Web: www.cambridgebnb.com

Circa 1897. Located minutes from Harvard Square, this colonial revival house reflects the rich ambiance of the Cambridge historical district. Surround yourself in the finest New England culture, located walking distance from the house. Visit museums, theaters and fine restaurants. Rest under the voluminous trees in the park across the street, or hop on the Red Line for an excursion to Boston. After an active day of sight seeing, return to the warmth of turn-of-the-century antique decor at this three-story home away from home. Enjoy a savory breakfast featuring such delights as home-baked, sesame-orange spice bread and cranberry brody, and spend the afternoon relaxing in an overstuffed chair or Grandmother's cane rockers with some tea or sherry.

Innkeeper(s): Doane Perry. $95-160. 3 rooms. Breakfast and afternoon tea included in rates. Types of meals: Full gourmet bkfst, veg bkfst and early coffee/tea. Beds: KQT. Modem hook-up, data port, cable TV, reading lamp, clock radio, telephone, turn-down service, desk and voice mail in room. Air conditioning. Fax, copier and library on premises. Family reunions hosted. Antiquing, art galleries, beach, bicycling, canoeing/kayaking, cross-country skiing, live theater, museums, parks, shopping, sporting events, tennis and water sports nearby.

A Cambridge Cottage

237 Allston St.
Cambridge, MA 02139
(617)661-8156

Circa 1840. A quiet, cozy atmosphere is imparted at this restored 1840 Federal-style cottage. A pleasant mélange of country charm, works of art, Mexican tile and Oriental rugs accent the original wide pine floors, moldings and banister. Comfortable guest bedrooms feature quilts, fresh flowers and candles. Start the day with a continental breakfast of croissants, muffins and fresh fruit. Relax on the brick patio and perennial garden. The B&B is located one mile from Harvard Square. Nearby historic sites include Fort Washington, only six blocks away.

Historic Interest: A simple cottage built in 1840, situated in the Cambridgeport area. Original wide-pine floors, moldings and banister.

Innkeeper(s): Linda Selaya. $60-95. 2 rooms. Breakfast included in rates. Types of meals: Cont. Beds: KT. Modem hook-up, cable TV, reading lamp, refrigerator, clock radio and desk in room. Air conditioning. Fireplace on premises. Antiquing, art galleries, beach, bicycling, canoeing/kayaking, golf, live theater, museums, parks, shopping, sporting events, tennis and water sports nearby.

A Friendly Inn

1673 Cambridge St
Cambridge, MA 02138-4316
(617)547-7851 Fax:(617)547-7851
Web: www.afinow.com/afi

Circa 1893. Superbly located, this Queen Anne Victorian is a short walk to Harvard Square and the subway to MIT or downtown Boston. Local restaurants, stores and theaters are also nearby. Friendly is well-defined in the generous hospitality and amenities. Free parking is available and the front desk is accessible at any time. Air conditioned guest bedrooms feature Cable TV and DSL computer connections. Enjoy a daily continental breakfast before exploring the area's many historic sites.

Innkeeper(s): Lusa & Arnold. $97-137. 17 rooms with PB. Breakfast included in rates. Types of meals: Cont. Beds: QDT. Cable TV, reading lamp, telephone, desk, wake up call, answer machine and DSL in room. Air conditioning. Fax, copier, swimming, library and 24 hour security on premises. Antiquing, live theater, parks, shopping, sporting events, museums and book stores nearby.

Harding House

288 Harvard St
Cambridge, MA 02139
(617)876-2888 Fax:(617)497-0953

Circa 1867. Located in the mid-Cambridge area, this historic Victorian is within walking distance to Harvard Square, and guests can hop on the Red Line and head into Boston.

The guest rooms feature a comfortable decor and amenities include fax service and in-room hair dryers. A continental buffet is set up in the breakfast room. The owners also operate Irving House at Harvard.

Innkeeper(s): David Fishman. $79-290. 14 rooms with PB. Breakfast included in rates. Types of meals: Cont plus. Beds: QT. TV and telephone in room. Air conditioning. Fax and limited parking on premises. Antiquing, shopping, sporting events, historic tours and restaurants nearby.

Irving House at Harvard

24 Irving Street
Cambridge, MA 02138-3007
(617)547-4600 (877)547-4600 Fax:(617)576-2814
E-mail: reserve@irvinghouse.com
Web: www.irvinghouse.com

Circa 1893. Irving House is located in a historic, turn-of-the-century Colonial Revival and has been receiving guests since the 1940s. The simple, comfortable rooms feature a modern hotel decor, and more than half include a private bath. In the mornings, a continental buffet with fruit, pastries and cereals is set up for guests to enjoy. Harvard Square is just minutes away, and guests can walk to the Red Line stop that goes into Boston.

Innkeeper(s): Rachael Solem & Zoia Krastanova. $90-190. 44 rooms, 32 with PB and 1 conference room. Breakfast and afternoon tea included in rates. Types of meals: Cont plus and early coffee/tea. Beds: QDT. TV, reading lamp, clock radio and desk in room. Central air. Fax, laundry facility, off-street parking and DSL on premises. Small meetings and family reunions hosted. Antiquing, art galleries, bicycling, live theater, museums, parks, shopping, sporting events, tennis and downtown Boston nearby.

The Kendall Hotel

350 Main Street
Cambridge, MA 02142
(617)577-1300 (866)566-1300 Fax:(617)577-1377
E-mail: stay@kendallhotel.com
Web: www.kendallhotel.com

Circa 1894. The oldest building in Kendall Square, this historic Victorian Fire Station Engine 7 was used as such from 1893 until 1993. Now the area's only family-owned unique boutique hotel, it includes the renovated firehouse and a newly built seven-story tower. Guest bedrooms mix modern conveniences like high-speed Internet, voice mail and data ports with handmade American quilts, all-cotton sheets, custom-framed artwork, antiques and reproduction pieces. Some feature Jacuzzi tubs. Other upscale amenities enhance a pleasurable and relaxing stay. Indulge in a Fireman's Breakfast, hearty enough to last through the morning's sightseeing adventures in nearby downtown Boston. Parking is provided in the hotel's underground garage. Meeting rooms are available for small gatherings.

Innkeeper(s): Nicholas Fandetti. $119-299. 65 rooms with PB and 2 conference rooms. Breakfast included in rates. Types of meals: Full gourmet bkfst, veg bkfst, early coffee/tea, gourmet lunch, afternoon tea, snacks/refreshments, gourmet dinner and room service. Restaurant on premises. Beds: KQ. Modem hook-up, data port, cable TV, reading lamp, ceiling fan, clock radio, telephone, desk, hot tub/spa and voice mail in room. Central air. Fax, copier, parlor games, fireplace, laundry facility and gift shop on premises. Limited handicap access. Weddings, small meetings, family reunions and seminars hosted. Art galleries, live theater, museums, parks, shopping, sporting events and water sports nearby.

Publicity: *Boston Globe and Boston South Station Journal.*

The Mary Prentiss Inn

6 Prentiss St
Cambridge, MA 02140-2212
(617)661-2929 Fax:(617)661-5989
E-mail: stay@maryprentissinn.com
Web: www.maryprentissinn.com

Circa 1843. Only a half-mile from Harvard Square, this restored Greek Revival Inn features ionic fluted columns and Doric trim. During summer months, guests are treated to breakfast under umbrella-covered tables on the outdoor deck, while wintertime guests enjoy their morning fare in front of a roaring fire in the parlor room. Several of the unique guest rooms feature kitchenettes, three suites include a working fireplace. The inn was the winner of the Massachusetts Historic Commission Preservation Award.

Historic Interest: Cambridge offers no shortage of activities, including the Cambridge Common where George Washington took command of the Continental Army, and the church where he and wife, Martha, worshipped. Historic battlefields and Walden Pond are only a short drive away.

Innkeeper(s): Jennifer & Nicholas Fandetti. $99-229. 20 rooms with PB, 3 with FP and 5 suites. Breakfast and afternoon tea included in rates. Types of meals: Full bkfst. Beds: QT. Cable TV, reading lamp, refrigerator, ceiling fan, clock radio, telephone and desk in room. Air conditioning. Fax and fireplace on premises. Limited handicap access. Weddings and family reunions hosted. Antiquing, golf, live theater, parks, shopping, sporting events, tennis and water sports nearby.

Publicity: *Cambridge Chronicle, Travel & Leisure, Discerning Traveler and Cambridge Current.*

"We thank you for the special privilege of staying at such a magnificent inn. We had a wonderful time, and you helped to make it so."

Prospect Place

112 Prospect St
Cambridge, MA 02139-2503
(617)864-7500 (800)769-5303 Fax:(617)576-1159
E-mail: prospectb-b@juno.com
Web: www.prospectpl.com

Circa 1866. This 5,000-square-foot Italianate Victorian was owned by the same family for more than 100 years (until 1994). Located in the heart of Cambridge, the inn is within walking distance of Harvard University, MIT and the Boston Freedom Train Trolley Tours. The inn, including its three guest bedrooms, has a Victorian décor that makes the most of an eclectic collection of antiques, including two grand pianos in the parlor. Period details are evident throughout the charming inn, from classic archways to cut-glass windows and extraordinary marble fireplaces. The delightful breakfast is served in the Victorian dining room and includes a variety of freshly baked breads, pastries, scones and muffins, a fresh-fruit bowl, juices and eggs to order. Afternoon tea is available upon request. After breakfast, guests can head out on foot or grab the subway or bus, which are just a few minutes' walk from the inn, and explore the area's rich history. Metropolitan Boston is just across the river from the inn.

Innkeeper(s): Eric Huenneke. $90-175. 3 rooms, 2 with PB. Types of meals: Full gourmet bkfst. Beds: KDT. Clock radio, telephone and desk in room. Central air. TV, fax and laundry facility on premises. Antiquing, art galleries, beach, live theater, museums, parks, shopping and sporting events nearby.

Chatham   119

Captain's House Inn

369-377 Old Harbor Rd
Chatham, MA 02633
(508)945-0127 (800)315-0728 Fax:(508)945-0866
E-mail: info@captainshouseinn.com
Web: www.captainshouseinn.com

Circa 1839. A white picket fence opens to an inviting estate on two manicured acres of English gardens and perfect lawns. Romantic accommodations offer lavishly decorated rooms with amenities such as four-poster canopy beds, fireplaces, and Jacuzzis located in one of the inn's historic buildings: the Carriage House, the Captain's Cottage, the Mansion or the magically transformed Stables. A favorite choice is the Lydia Harding Suite in the former stables. It offers two rooms with French doors opening to a balcony, two fireplaces, a lavish bath and several sitting areas. Afternoon tea and a deluxe gourmet breakfast is served in the dining room with views to the fountain and gardens. The innkeepers, one a native of Britain, also own a 16th-century coaching inn near Oxford and enjoy sharing their experiences and knowledge of both areas with their guests. Specially prepared picnics are available along with beach chairs, towels and coolers. Be sure to take advantage of the innkeepers excellent concierge services to maximize your experience while on the Cape.

Innkeeper(s): Dave & Jan McMaster. $185-400. 16 rooms with PB, 16 with FP and 4 suites. Breakfast, afternoon tea and snacks/refreshments included in rates. Types of meals: Full gourmet bkfst, veg bkfst, early coffee/tea and room service. Beds: KQ. Data port, cable TV, VCR, reading lamp, CD player, refrigerator, ceiling fan, clock radio, telephone, coffeemaker, turn-down service, desk, hot tub/spa, voice mail and fireplace in room. Air conditioning. Fax, copier, spa, library, parlor games, fireplace, gift shop, outdoor swimming pool and workout facility on premises. Limited handicap access. Family reunions hosted. Antiquing, art galleries, beach, bicycling, canoeing/kayaking, fishing, golf, hiking, horseback riding, live theater, museums, parks, shopping, tennis, water sports, wineries and whale watching nearby.

Publicity: *Providence Journal, Cape Cod Life, Cape Cod Travel Guide, Country Inns, Toronto Sun, Cosmopolitan, Elle,* Featured on Best Inns of New England on Cable TV Network, HGTV and Food TV.

Carriage House Inn

407 Old Harbor Rd
Chatham, MA 02633-2322
(508)945-4688 (800)355-8868 Fax:(508)945-8909

Circa 1890. This charming Cape inn offers tasteful, traditional decor and pristine rooms with a light and airy ambiance. The carriage house rooms each include a fireplace and an entrance to an outside sitting area. Breakfast items such as pancakes, French toast, eggs Benedict, homemade muffins and scones, and fresh fruit juices can be enjoyed either in the dining room or on the sun porch. Guests can wander through Chatham's many shops and galleries, or just relax and enjoy the grounds, which include flower-filled gardens and shaded sitting areas. Beach towels and chairs are furnished for trips to the shore, located within walking distance from the inn.

Historic Interest: Cape Cod National Seashore (20 minutes).

Innkeeper(s): Jill & James Meyer. $105-195. 6 rooms with PB, 3 with FP.

Breakfast and snacks/refreshments included in rates. Types of meals: Full bkfst and early coffee/tea. Beds: Q. Cable TV, ceiling fan, coffeemaker, CD alarm clock, hair dryer, iron, ironing board, umbrella, morning newspaper delivered and some available with private entrance and fireplace in room. Air conditioning. Parlor games, telephone, fireplace, computer with high-speed Internet access, DVDs, CDs and books on premises. Antiquing, fishing, hiking, live theater, parks, shopping and water sports nearby.

"This might well have been our best B&B experience ever. It was the hosts who made it so memorable."

The Cranberry Inn of Chatham

359 Main St
Chatham, MA 02633-2425
(508)945-9232 (800)332-4667 Fax:(508)945-3769
E-mail: info@cranberryinn.com
Web: www.cranberryinn.com

Circa 1830. Continuously operating for over 150 years, this inn originally was called the Traveler's Lodge, then the Monomoyic after a local Indian tribe. An un-harvested cranberry bog adjacent to the property inspired the current name. Recently restored, the inn is located in the heart of the historic district. It's within walking distance of the lighthouse, beaches, shops and restaurants. Guest rooms feature four-poster beds, wide-planked floors and coordinated fabrics. Antique and reproduction furnishings throughout.

Innkeeper(s): Kay & Bill DeFord. $110-310. 18 rooms with PB, 8 with FP and 3 suites. Breakfast and afternoon tea included in rates. Types of meals: Full gourmet bkfst. Beds: QDT. Private balconies and wet bars and fireplaces in some rooms in room. Fully licensed tavern on premises. Antiquing, art galleries, bicycling, fishing, golf, live theater, parks and sporting events nearby.

Publicity: Country Inns, Cape Cod Life and Cape Cod Travel Guide.

Cyrus Kent House

63 Cross St
Chatham, MA 02633-2207
(508)945-9104 (800)338-5368 Fax:(508)945-6104
E-mail: cyrus@cape.com
Web: www.cyruskent.com

Circa 1877. Gardens with brick walkways surround this award-winning and stately 1877 inn, located in the village center. Extensive renovations during the last two years provide modern conveniences while retaining the historic Italianate architecture. Distinctive furnishings and significant antiques, new fixtures, carpets and chandeliers create an upscale ambiance. Fresh flowers are placed throughout the inn. Gracious guest bedrooms skillfully feature custom window treatments and artwork. Fine linens grace four-poster and canopy beds. Suites include sitting rooms with fireplaces. Beach chairs and towels are provided during the summer.

Innkeeper(s): Steve & Sandra Goldman. $95-290. 10 rooms with PB, 6 with FP and 4 suites. Breakfast and afternoon tea included in rates. Types of meals: Cont plus and early coffee/tea. Beds: KQT. Cable TV, reading lamp, clock radio, telephone, hair dryers, VCRs in all rooms and DVD players in suites in room. Air conditioning. TV, fax and fireplace on premises. Weddings, small meetings, family reunions and seminars hosted. Antiquing, beach, fishing, shopping and water sports nearby.

Publicity: Country Inns.

Moses Nickerson House

364 Old Harbor Rd
Chatham, MA 02633-2374
(508)945-5859 (800)628-6972 Fax:(508)945-7087
E-mail: tmnhi@attbi.comcast.net
Web: www.mosesnickersonhouse.com

Circa 1839. This historic, rambling sea captain's house, built in 1839, features wide pine floors, many fireplaces and colorful gardens. Unforgettably charming, the inn is decorated with antique furnishings and Oriental rugs, retaining the character of by-gone days. Each of the rooms offers its own distinctive decor. Breakfast is served in a glass-enclosed dining area that radiates morning sunlight. The inn provides an ambiance of simple elegance.

Innkeeper(s): Linda & George Watts. $99-209. 7 rooms with PB, 3 with FP. Breakfast included in rates. Types of meals: Full bkfst. Beds: KQ. Cable TV, reading lamp, ceiling fan, clock radio, telephone and fireplace in room. Air conditioning. VCR, library, parlor games, fireplace, hair dryer, beach towels and beach chairs on premises. Family reunions and seminars hosted. Antiquing, beach, fishing, golf, live theater, tennis, whale watching, National Seashore and seal tours nearby.

Publicity: Cape Cod Life and The Discerning Traveler.

"The attention to detail in unsurpassed."

Old Harbor Inn

22 Old Harbor Rd
Chatham, MA 02633-2315
(508)945-4434 (800)942-4434 Fax:(508)945-7665
E-mail: info@chathamoldharborinn.com
Web: www.chathamoldharborinn.com

Circa 1932. This pristine New England bed & breakfast was once the home of "Doc" Keene, a popular physician in the area. A meticulous renovation has created an elegant, beautifully appointed inn offering antique furnishings, designer linens and lavish amenities in an English country decor. A buffet breakfast, featuring Judy's homemade muffins, is served in the sunroom or on the deck. The beaches, boutiques and galleries are a walk away and there is an old grist mill, the Chatham Lighthouse and a railroad museum. Band concerts are offered Friday nights in the summer at Kate Gould Park.

Historic Interest: The Whit Tileston Band Stand Gazebo in Kate Gould Park (one-half mile), The Training Field of the Colonial Militia, Old Burial Grounds, Atwood House Museum.

Innkeeper(s): Judy & Ray Braz. $99-269. 8 rooms with PB, 2 with FP and 1 suite. Breakfast included in rates. Types of meals: Early coffee/tea and afternoon tea. Beds: KQT. Reading lamp, ceiling fan, clock radio, desk, Jacuzzi in suite, toiletries and welcome package in room. Air conditioning. Parlor games, telephone, fireplace, concierge and gift shop on premises. Antiquing, beach, fishing, golf, live theater, parks, shopping, tennis, water sports, art festivals and concerts nearby.

Publicity: Honeymoon, Cape Cod Life, Boston, Cape Cod Travel Guide, Country Inns, Cape Cod Dreams and Off Shore.

Port Fortune Inn

201 Main St
Chatham, MA 02633-2423
(508)945-0792 (800)750-0792

Circa 1910. The fronts of these charming Cape Cod buildings are decorated with colorful flowers and plants. The interior of each of the inn's two historic buildings is elegant and inviting with traditional furnishings, and most of the guest rooms are decorated with

four-poster beds. The breakfast room and some of the guest rooms have ocean views. The grounds include perennial gardens and a patio set up with furniture for those who wish to relax and catch a few sea breezes. The inn is featured on the walking tour through the historic Old Village, which is Chatham's oldest neighborhood. Port Fortune Inn is a short walk away from beaches and the historic Chatham Lighthouse.

Innkeeper(s): Mike & Renee Kahl. $100-210. 12 rooms with PB. Breakfast included in rates. Types of meals: Cont plus and early coffee/tea. Beds: Q. Reading lamp, clock radio, telephone and some with TV in room. Air conditioning. Fax, copier, library, parlor games, fireplace and beach towels and chairs on premises. Amusement parks, antiquing, fishing, golf, live theater, parks, shopping, tennis, water sports and whale watching nearby.

"Excellent. The entire experience was wonderful as usual."

Concord   D12

Concord Center B&B

15 Brooks Street
Concord, MA 01742
(978)369-8980
E-mail: concordcenterbb@aol.com
Web: www.concordcenterbb.com

Circa 1876. Recently renovated, this colonial-style house was the first to be built in the now historic area of New England, only 20 miles from Boston. A simple but elegant décor features colorful designer wallpaper and subtle lighting. The peaceful suite offers privacy and a terra cotta gas fireplace. A sunny sitting area boasts views of the backyard and Japanese garden. Built-in bookcases are filled with ballet and art books that reflect the innkeepers' interests. A generous continental breakfast is delivered to the room each morning. Visit nearby Walden Pond or the homes of Ralph Waldo Emerson and Louisa May Alcott. The Concord River provides a wonderful opportunity to rent a kayak or canoe.

Innkeeper(s): Jero & Marie Nesson. $115-130. 1 suite, 1 with FP. Breakfast included in rates. Types of meals: Cont plus and room service. Beds: Q. Modem hook-up, cable TV, VCR, reading lamp, ceiling fan, clock radio, telephone and fireplace in room. Air conditioning. Fireplace on premises. Antiquing, art galleries, beach, bicycling, canoeing/kayaking, cross-country skiing, downhill skiing, fishing, golf, hiking, live theater, museums, parks, shopping, tennis, water sports, wineries, Historic Walden Pond and home museums of Alcott & Emerson, Historic Old North Bridge and National Historic Park and great Meadows Wildlife Refuge nearby.

Hawthorne Inn

462 Lexington Rd
Concord, MA 01742-3729
(978)369-5610 Fax:(978)287-4949
E-mail: hawthorneinn@concordmass.com
Web: www.concordmass.com

Circa 1870. Share the joy of history, literature, poetry and artwork at this intimate New England bed & breakfast. For 25 years, the inn's ambiance has imparted the spirit of writers and philosophers such as the Alcotts, Emerson, Hawthorne and Thoreau, who once owned and walked the grounds. Antique furnishings, weavings, hardwood floors, a welcoming fireplace and stained-glass windows all exude a wonderful warmth and gentility.

Enjoy afternoon tea on a rustic garden bench in the shade of aged trees and colorful plants. The area offers woods to explore, rivers to canoe, a quaint village with museums, infamous Sleepy Hollow Cemetery, and untold treasures.

Historic Interest: Old North Bridge and Walden Pond are just a few minutes away.

Innkeeper(s): Marilyn Mudry & Gregory Burch. $175-275. 7 rooms with PB. Breakfast and afternoon tea included in rates. Types of meals: Cont plus. Beds: QDT. Data port, reading lamp, clock radio, telephone and desk in room. Air conditioning. Fax, library, parlor games, fireplace and piano on premises. Weddings, small meetings and family reunions hosted. Antiquing, cross-country skiing, fishing, parks, shopping and authors homes nearby.

Publicity: *Yankee, New York Times, Los Angeles Times, Le Monde, Early American Life, Evening and National Geographic Traveler.*

"Surely there couldn't be a better or more valuable location for a comfortable, old-fashioned country inn."

Deerfield   C6

Deerfield Inn

81 Old Main St
Deerfield, MA 01342-0305
(413)774-5587 (800)926-3865 Fax:(413)775-7221
E-mail: information@deerfieldinn.com
Web: www.deerfieldinn.com

Circa 1884. The village of Deerfield was settled in 1670. Farmers in the area still unearth bones and ax and arrow heads from French/Indian massacre of 1704. Now, 50 beautifully restored 18th- and 19th-century homes line the mile-long main street, considered by many to be the loveliest street in New England. Fourteen of these houses are museums of Pioneer Valley decorative arts and are open year-round to the public. The Memorial Hall Museum, open from May to November, is the oldest museum in New England and full of local antiquities. The inn is situated at the center of this peaceful village, and for those who wish to truly experience New England's past, this is the place. The village has been designated a National Historic Landmark.

Innkeeper(s): Jane & Karl Sabo. $188-255. 23 rooms with PB and 1 conference room. Breakfast and afternoon tea included in rates. Types of meals: Full bkfst and dinner. Restaurant on premises. Beds: KQT. TV in room. Fax, copier and telephone on premises. Limited handicap access. Antiquing, cross-country skiing, fishing and live theater nearby.

Publicity: *Travel Today, Colonial Homes, Country Living, Country Inns B&B, Yankee and Romantic Homes.*

"We've stayed at many New England inns, but the Deerfield Inn ranks among the best."

Dennis   I18

Isaiah Hall B&B Inn

152 Whig St.
Dennis, MA 02638
(508)385-9928 (800)736-0160 Fax:(508)385-5879
E-mail: info@isaiahhallinn.com
Web: www.isaiahhallinn.com

Circa 1857. Adjacent to the Cape's oldest cranberry bog is this Greek Revival farmhouse built by Isaiah Hall, a cooper. His grandfather was the first cultivator of cranberries in America and Isaiah designed and patented the original barrel for shipping cranberries. In 1948, Dorothy Gripp, an artist, established the inn. Many examples of her artwork remain. The inn is located in the heart of the Cape and within walking distance to beaches, Dennis village and the Cape Playhouse.

Historic Interest: Cape Playhouse (one-third mile), Old Kings Highway (one-third mile), Old Salt Works (2 miles).

Innkeeper(s): Dick & Marie Brophy. $111-188. 9 rooms, 10 with PB, 1 with FP and 1 suite. Breakfast included in rates. Types of meals: Cont plus and early coffee/tea. Beds: KQDT. Cable TV, reading lamp, clock radio, telephone, desk, hair dryers, robes and antiques in room. Air conditioning. Fax, parlor games, fireplace, surrounded by gardens and high-speed Internet access available on premises. Antiquing, fishing, golf, live theater, parks, shopping, water sports, whale watching and bike paths nearby.

Publicity: Cape Cod Life, New York Times, Golf, National Geographic Traveler, Yankee Travel Guide, Hartford Courant, Best Inn for Relaxing & Unwinding Book of Lists, 2003 Best Hospitality Book of Lists, "Best Mid-Cape B&B" - Silver Award, Cape Cod Life and voted "Best Place to Visit Again & Again."

"Your place is so lovely and relaxing."

Scargo Manor Bed & Breakfast

909 Main St, Rt 6A
Dennis, MA 02638-1405
(508)385-5534 (800)595-0034 Fax:(508)385-9791
E-mail: scargomanor@mediaone.net
Web: www.scargomanor.com

Circa 1895. A sea captain built this lakefront 19th-century home. The six guest rooms and two suites of this Cape Cod inn are decorated with New England-style furnishings, such as canopy or four-poster beds. The suites include a separate sitting area. All rooms include amenities such as mini refrigerators, irons and ironing boards and hair dryers. A gourmet breakfast is served with a variety of delicacies. The innkeepers can supply guests with kayaks, a canoe or a small sailboat. Lawn games, such as croquet and badminton are available, as well.

Innkeeper(s): Debbie & Larry Bain. $95-195. 6 rooms with PB, 1 with FP and 2 suites. Breakfast included in rates. Types of meals: Full gourmet bkfst, early coffee/tea and snacks/refreshments. Beds: KQT. Cable TV, reading lamp, refrigerator, clock radio, iron, ironing board, hair dryer and fireplace in room. Air conditioning. TV, fax, swimming, bicycles, parlor games, telephone, fireplace, kayaks, canoe, small sailboat and lawn games on premises. Weddings, small meetings, family reunions and seminars hosted. Antiquing, art galleries, beach, bicycling, canoeing/kayaking, fishing, golf, hiking, live theater, museums, parks, shopping, tennis and water sports nearby.

Dennisport   I18

By The Sea Guests Bed & Breakfast & Suites

57 Chase Ave
Dennisport, MA 02639-2627
(508)398-8685 (800)447-9202 Fax:(508)398-0334
E-mail: by.the.sea@comcast.net
Web: www.bytheseaguests.com

Circa 1890. On the private beach that adjoins this historic inn, guests can pass their time lounging. A huge wraparound porch is a favorite spot to enjoy views of Nantucket Sound. The porch is also the location where breakfast is served. The interior is decorated with a mix of traditional and New England country furnishings and appointments. Most rooms offer an ocean view. Several rooms can accommodate more than two guests. Two rooms include relaxing, soaking tubs. The current innkeepers are the second generation to welcome guests to this seaside home.

$90-195. 12 rooms with PB and 5 suites. Breakfast and snacks/refreshments included in rates. Types of meals: Cont plus, early coffee/tea and afternoon tea. Beds: QDT. Cable TV, reading lamp, refrigerator, ceiling fan and clock radio in room. Fax, copier, swimming, parlor games, telephone and fireplace on premises. Antiquing, art galleries, beach, bicycling, canoeing/kayaking, fishing, golf, hiking, horseback riding, live theater, museums, parks, shopping, tennis, water sports and wineries nearby.

Joy House Inc., B&B

181 Depot Street
Dennisport, MA 02639
(508)760-3663 (877)569-4687 Fax:(508)760-6618

Circa 1732. Remodeled for comfort and privacy, this Pre-Revolutionary War, Antique Colonial house is an ideal place to be pampered and served with joy. An old sea captain's home with wide pumpkin pine floors, the foyer gives access to a large common room and fireside sitting area. Listen to classical music or watch cable TV. Attractive guest bedrooms offer a restful stay. Sleep on a four-poster bed under a skylight in the romantic Lighthouse Suite with a decorative fireplace. Wake up to Chef Barbara's breakfast in the dining room. Splendidly landscaped gardens are resplendent with hollies, hydrangeas, roses, rhododendrons and cherry trees.

Historic Interest: Wide pumpkin pine floors which belonged to King George III.

Innkeeper(s): Barbara and Peter Bach. $90-150. 3 rooms with PB, 1 with FP and 1 suite. Breakfast and snacks/refreshments included in rates. Types of meals: Cont plus. Beds: KQD. Modem hook-up, cable TV, VCR, stereo, refrigerator, snack bar, clock radio, telephone, fireplace, Direct TV, DVD and daily newspaper in room. Air conditioning. Fax, copier, spa, library, parlor games and fireplace on premises. Weddings and family reunions hosted. Antiquing, art galleries, beach, bicycling, canoeing/kayaking, fishing, golf, hiking, live theater, museums, parks, shopping, tennis, water sports and wineries nearby.

Rose Petal B&B

152 Sea St PO Box 974
Dennisport, MA 02639-2404
(508)398-8470
E-mail: info@rosepetalofdennis.com
Web: www.rosepetalofdennis.com

Circa 1872. Surrounded by a white picket fence and picturesque gardens, the Rose Petal is situated in the heart of Cape Cod. The Greek Revival-style home was built for Almond Wixon, who was a Mayflower descendant and member of a prominent seafaring family. His homestead has been completely restored and offers guest rooms with spacious private baths. Home-baked pastries highlight a full breakfast served in the dining room. Walk through the historic neighborhood past century-old homes to Nantucket Sound's sandy beaches.

Historic Interest: JFK Museum, family compound (10 miles).

Innkeeper(s): Gayle & Dan Kelly. $79-119. 3 rooms with PB. Breakfast included in rates. Types of meals: Full gourmet bkfst and early coffee/tea. Beds: QT. Reading lamp and clock radio in room. Air conditioning. Parlor games and telephone on premises. Family reunions hosted. Antiquing, fishing, live theater, parks, shopping, water sports and whale watching nearby.

"Perfect. Every detail was appreciated."

Duxbury   G15

The Winsor House Inn

390 Washington St
Duxbury, MA 02332-4552
(781)934-0991 Fax:(781)934-5955
E-mail: info@winsorhouseinn.com
Web: www.winsorhouseinn.com

Circa 1803. A visit to this inn is much like a visit back in time
to Colonial days. The early 19th-century home was built by a
prominent sea captain and merchant, Nathaniel Winsor, as a
wedding gift for his daughter, Nancy. With an eye for the
authentic, the innkeepers have restored parts of the inn to look
much the way it might have when the young bride and groom
took up residence. Rooms are decorated with Colonial furnishings, canopied beds and fresh flowers. Guests may enjoy a
drink or a casual dinner at the inn's English-style pub. For a
romantic dinner, try the inn's Dining Room, which serves
everything from roasted venison with a juniper berry and
mushroom crust to herb-seared salmon with plum tomato saffron vinaigrette.

Historic Interest: Plimoth Plantation, Mayflower and Plymouth Rock, 15
minutes away. Twenty miles to Cape Cod.

Innkeeper(s): David and Patricia O'Connell. $140-210. 4 rooms with PB and
2 suites. Breakfast included in rates. Types of meals: Full bkfst, picnic lunch
and dinner. Restaurant on premises. Beds: QT. Reading lamp, clock radio and
desk in room. Fax, copier, telephone and fireplace on premises. Small meetings and family reunions hosted. Antiquing, cross-country skiing, fishing,
shopping, water sports and Plymouth nearby.

Publicity: *Colonial Homes.*

East Orleans   H19

The Nauset House Inn

143 Beach Rd, PO Box 774
East Orleans, MA 02643
(508)255-2195 (800)771-5508 Fax:(508)240-6276

Circa 1810. Located a 1/2 mile from Nauset Beach, this inn is
a renovated farmhouse set on three acres, which include an old
apple orchard. A Victorian conservatory was purchased from a
Connecticut estate and reassembled here, then filled with wicker furnishings, Cape
flowers and stained
glass. Hand-stenciling,
handmade quilts,
antiques and more bou-
quets of flowers decorate the
rooms. The breakfast room features a fireplace, brick floor and
beamed ceiling. Breakfast includes treats such as ginger pancakes or waffles with fresh strawberries. Wine and cranberry
juice are served in the evenings.

Innkeeper(s): Diane Johnson, John & Cindy Vessella. $75-160. 14 rooms, 8
with PB and 1 cottage. Breakfast and snacks/refreshments included in rates.
Types of meals: Full bkfst, early coffee/tea and afternoon tea. Beds: KQDT.
Reading lamp and terry robes for shared bath guests in room. Parlor games,
telephone and fireplace on premises. Antiquing, fishing, live theater, parks,
shopping, sporting events, water sports, biking, tennis, ocean and golf nearby.

Publicity: *Country Living, Glamour, West Hartford News and Travel & Leisure.*

"The inn provided a quiet, serene, comforting atmosphere."

The Parsonage Inn

202 Main St, PO Box 1501
East Orleans, MA 02643
(508)255-8217 (888)422-8217 Fax:(508)255-8216
E-mail: innkeeper@parsonageinn.com
Web: www.parsonageinn.com

Circa 1770. Originally a parsonage, this Cape-style home is
now a romantic inn nestled in the village of East Orleans and
only a mile and a half from Nauset Beach. Rooms are decorated
with antiques, quilts, Laura Ashley
fabrics and stenciling, and
they include the original pine
floors and low ceilings.
Cooked breakfasts are
served either in the dining
room or on the brick patio. The
innkeepers keep a selection of menus from local restaurants on
hand and in the summer season serve appetizers and refreshments each evening while guest peruse their dining choices.
The Parsonage is the perfect location to enjoy nature, with the
national seashore, Nickerson State Park and whale-watching
opportunities available to guests.

Historic Interest: Cape Cod offers plenty of historic homes and sites.

Innkeeper(s): Ian & Elizabeth Browne. $120-155. 8 rooms with PB and 2
suites. Breakfast included in rates. Beds: QDT. All with private en-suite bathrooms, one has a kitchen, all rooms have Queen beds & two also have a twin
bed, all have TVs and air conditioning and some have refrigerators in room.
Telephone, refrigerator, fax and grand piano on premises. Antiquing, live theater, shopping, restaurants and Nauset Beach nearby.

Publicity: *Conde Nast Traveler and Bon Appetit.*

*"Your hospitality was as wonderful as your home. Your home was as
beautiful as Cape Cod. Thank you!"*

Ship's Knees Inn

186 Beach Rd, PO Box 756
East Orleans, MA 02643
(508)255-1312 Fax:(508)240-1351
E-mail: skinauset@aol.com
Web: www.shipskneesinn.com

Circa 1820. This 180-year-old restored sea captain's home is a
three-minute walk to the ocean. Rooms are decorated in a nautical style with antiques. Several rooms feature authentic ship's
knees, hand-painted trunks, old clipper ship models and four-
poster beds. Some rooms
boast ocean views, and
the Master Suite has a
working fireplace. The
inn offers swimming and
tennis facilities on the
grounds. About three miles away, the innkeepers also offer three
rooms, a bedroom efficiency apartment and two heated cottages
on the Town Cove. Head into town, or spend the day basking in
the beauty of Nauset Beach with its picturesque sand dunes.

Innkeeper(s): Lesley & George Sloan. $65-200. 16 rooms, 14 with PB, 1
with FP. Breakfast included in rates. Types of meals: Cont. Beds: KQDT. TV
on premises. Weddings, small meetings and family reunions hosted.
Amusement parks, antiquing, fishing, live theater, parks, shopping and water
sports nearby.

Publicity: *Boston Globe.*

*"Warm, homey and very friendly atmosphere. Very impressed with
the beamed ceilings."*

East Sandwich 117

Wingscorton Farm Inn

Rt 6A, Olde Kings Hwy
East Sandwich, MA 02537
(508)888-0534

Circa 1763. Wingscorton is a working farm on 13 acres of lawns, gardens and orchards. It adjoins a short walk to a private ocean beach. This Cape Cod manse, built by a Quaker family, is a historical landmark on what once was known as the King's Highway, the oldest historical district in the United States. All the rooms are furnished with antiques and working fireplaces (one with a secret compartment where runaway slaves hid). Breakfast features fresh produce with eggs, meats and vegetables from the farm's livestock and gardens. Pets and children welcome.

Innkeeper(s): Sheila Weyers & Richard Loring. $175-210. 7 rooms, 7 with FP, 4 suites and 2 cottages. Breakfast included in rates. Types of meals: Full gourmet bkfst. Beds: QDT. TV, reading lamp, refrigerator and clock radio in room. Swimming, library, child care, parlor games, telephone, fireplace and private beach on premises. Weddings, small meetings, family reunions and seminars hosted. Antiquing, cross-country skiing, downhill skiing, fishing, live theater, parks, shopping, sporting events and water sports nearby.

Publicity: *US Air and Travel & Leisure.*

"Absolutely wonderful. We will always remember the wonderful time."

Eastham H18

Fort Hill B&B

75 Fort Hill Road
Eastham, MA 02642
(508)240-2870
E-mail: gordon@forthillbedandbreakfast.com
Web: www.forthillbedandbreakfast.com

Circa 1864. If spectacular ocean views and leisurely scenic walks sound inviting, then this Greek Revival Farmhouse located on three acres within the Cape Cod National Seashore is the perfect place to stay. It is surrounded by more than 100 acres of marsh, beach, forest and fields. Casually refined, this intimate inn is furnished with period antiques and reproductions, accented by Oriental carpets. Choose the romantic three-room Emma suite with a library/sitting room, canopy bed, mahogany piano, oversize tub and window seat. The Lucille suite boasts historic charm with original wide-pine floors, slanted-eaves ceiling and a wrought-iron bed. The private Nantucket Gallery Suite, just steps from the main house, offers a view of the ocean over rolling farm fields and features a fireplace, patio and private gardens. Partake of a hearty breakfast that may include cheesy-chive egg souffle, a Dutch apple pancake, or eggs Benedict.

Innkeeper(s): Gordon & Jean Avery. $165-250. 3 suites, 1 with FP. Breakfast included in rates. Types of meals: Full gourmet bkfst, veg bkfst, early coffee/tea and afternoon tea. Beds: Q. Cable TV, reading lamp, stereo, refrigerator, ceiling fan, clock radio, telephone, desk, fireplace, wet bar and soaking tub in room. Air conditioning. Library, parlor games, fireplace, piano, gardens and ocean views on premises. Antiquing, art galleries, beach, bicycling, canoeing/kayaking, fishing, golf, hiking, horseback riding, live theater, museums, parks, shopping, sporting events, tennis, water sports, wineries, birding, lighthouses and whale watching nearby.

Publicity: *Boston Globe, Better Homes and Gardens, Explorer's Guide to Cape Cod and the Islands, Cape Cod Travel Guide and Yankee Magazine.*

Over Look Inn

3085 County Road
Eastham, MA 02642
(508)255-1886 (877)255-1886 Fax:(508)240-0345
E-mail: stay@overlookinn.com
Web: www.overlookinn.com

Circa 1870. Gracing the Historic District, this Queen Anne Victorian listed in the National Register was originally a sea captain's home in 1870. Relax on a porch rocker or in the backyard hammock. Play pool in the Game Room or read by the fire in the parlor. The Garden Room is perfect for a romantic getaway with a wood-burning fireplace. Furnished in period antiques, the Captain's Room boasts a clawfoot tub. Families appreciate the accommodations in the Carriage House. Enjoy fine Danish hospitality reflected in the generous hot country breakfasts served in the dining room. Ebelskivers, Captain's Eggs, Apple-Cranberry Pancakes, Banana Walnut French Toast and Parmesan Baked eggs are popular rotating favorites. After exploring this ocean community, converse over afternoon tea.

Historic Interest: The inn was originally built in 1870 by Sea Captain Barnabus Chipman and his wife Sarah. The inn is located in the Eastham Center Historic District.

Innkeeper(s): Don & Pam Andersen. $115-220. 12 rooms with PB, 3 with FP, 3 suites and 1 conference room. Breakfast and afternoon tea included in rates. Types of meals: Full bkfst and early coffee/tea. Beds: QDT. Cable TV, reading lamp, ceiling fan, clock radio, telephone, fireplace and hair dryer in room. Air conditioning. VCR, fax, parlor games, fireplace and game room with pool table on premises. Weddings, small meetings, family reunions and seminars hosted. Antiquing, art galleries, beach, bicycling, canoeing/kayaking, fishing, golf, hiking, horseback riding, live theater, museums, parks, shopping, sporting events, tennis, water sports and wineries nearby.

"A delightful experience."—Max Nichols, Oklahoma City Journal Record

Penny House Inn

4885 County Rd, Rt. 6
Eastham, MA 02642
(508)255-6632 (800)554-1751 Fax:(508)255-4893
E-mail: pennyhouse@aol.com
Web: pennyhouseinn.com

Circa 1690. In the early 1980s, this former 17th-century sea captain's home was carefully restored and renovated into a memorable country inn. Retaining its Colonial heritage, the great room and dining room feature 300-year-old ceiling beams and traditional wide-plank floors. Choose among an assortment of amenities in some of the guest rooms, including fireplaces, whirlpool tubs, plush robes, VCRs, refrigerators and coffeemakers. Enjoy a hearty country breakfast each morning. Afternoon tea with fresh baked goods are served in the sunroom. Secluded on two picturesque acres, the inn is conveniently located near beaches, fishing, boating, bike trails, whale watching and Audubon Sanctuary.

Innkeeper(s): Margaret & Rebecca Keith. $195-350. 12 rooms with PB, 7 with FP and 2 suites. Breakfast and afternoon tea included in rates. Types of meals: Full bkfst and early coffee/tea. Beds: KQT. Cable TV, VCR, telephone, hair dryers, most with fireplace, coffeemakers, refrigerator and whirlpool tubs in room. Air conditioning. Fax, copier and spa on premises. Antiquing, bicycling, fishing, hiking, live theater, parks, shopping, tennis, boating, health club and restaurants nearby.

Publicity: *Cape Cod Life - voted "Best inn outer Cape 2003" and Cape Codder.*

"Enjoyed my stay tremendously. My mouth waters thinking of your delicious breakfast."

Edgartown

K16

The Arbor

222 Upper Main St, PO Box 1228
Edgartown, MA 02539
(508)627-8137

Circa 1880. Originally built on the adjoining island of Chappaquiddick, this house was moved over to Edgartown on a barge at the turn of the century. Located on the bicycle path, it is within walking distance from downtown and the harbor. Guests may relax in the hammock, have tea on the porch, or walk the unspoiled island beaches of Martha's Vineyard.

Historic Interest: Methodist Camp Meeting Ground.

Innkeeper(s): Lorna Giles. $135-175.
10 rooms, 8 with PB. Breakfast and afternoon tea included in rates. Types of meals: Cont. Beds: QD. Reading lamp in room. Air conditioning. Telephone, fireplace and guest refrigerator on premises. Antiquing, fishing, live theater, shopping, water sports and biking nearby.

Publicity: *Herald News and Yankee Traveler.*

"Thank you so much for your wonderful hospitality! You are a superb hostess. If I ever decide to do my own B&B, your example would be my guide."

Ashley Inn

129 Main St, PO Box 650
Edgartown, MA 02539-0650
(508)627-9655 (800)477-9655 Fax:(508)627-6629
E-mail: mail@ashleyinn.net
Web: www.ashleyinn.net

Circa 1860. A retired whaling captain built this gracious Georgian inn on Martha's Vineyard. Guest rooms are furnished in period antiques, brass and wicker. The inn is just four blocks from the beach, and its Main Street location offers easy access to Edgartown's many fine restaurants and shops. Breakfasts are served in the English tea room, and guests find the inn's grounds perfect for an after-meal stroll. Others like to relax in the hammock or in the comfortable sitting room. A special honeymoon package is available.

Historic Interest: Built in 1860 by Captain Crowell.

Innkeeper(s): Fred Hurley. $125-295. 10 rooms, 1 with FP and 1 suite. Breakfast included in rates. Types of meals: Cont. Beds: KQD. Cable TV and reading lamp in room. Air conditioning. Small meetings and seminars hosted. Antiquing, art galleries, beach, bicycling, canoeing/kayaking, fishing, golf, hiking, horseback riding, museums, shopping, tennis, water sports and wineries nearby.

Colonial Inn of Martha's Vineyard

38 N Water St, PO Box 68
Edgartown, MA 02539-0068
(508)627-4711 (800)627-4701 Fax:(508)627-5904
E-mail: info@colonialinnmvy.com
Web: www.colonialinnmvy.com

Circa 1911. Overlooking Edgartown Harbor, this impressive Colonial structure has served as an inn since opening its doors in 1911. Somerset Maugham and Howard Hughes were among the regulars at the inn. Guests at Colonial Inn can sit back and relax on a porch lined with rockers as they gaze at the harbor and enjoy refreshing sea breezes. Flowers, an atrium and court-yards decorate the grounds. The inn has a full-service restau-rant, a salon and day spa, fitness room, meeting facilities, art gallery and several boutiques on the premises. Some guest rooms boast harbor views, fireplaces and canopy beds. All rooms are decorated in an elegant country style. The inn is located in the heart of the town's historic district.

Innkeeper(s): CJ Rivard. $80-395. 43 rooms with PB, 5 suites and 2 confer-ence rooms. Breakfast included in rates. Types of meals: Cont and dinner. Restaurant on premises. Beds: QD. Data port, cable TV, reading lamp, clock radio, telephone, air conditioning and heat, some with refrigerators and VCRs in room. TV, fax, library and parlor games on premises. Limited handicap access. Small meetings and seminars hosted. Antiquing, art galleries, bicy-cling, fishing, golf, live theater, parks, shopping, tennis, water sports, con-certs and swimming nearby.

Publicity: *Glamour, Vineyard Gazette and Mitsubishi commercials.*

Daggett House

59 N Water
Edgartown, MA 02539
(508)627-4600 (800)946-3400 Fax:(508)627-4611
E-mail: innkeeper@the daggetthouse.com
Web: www.thedaggetthouse.com

Circa 1750. Experience a delightful seaside garden setting at this inn composed of four historic buildings with Federal-style architecture and antique furnishings. The main building and garden cottage overlook a manicured lawn and flower gardens that border Edgartown Harbor. The Henry Lyman Thomas House was renovated to easily accommodate families. It fea-tures junior suites and a Lightkeeper's Cottage with kitchen facilities. Cribs are available. The Restaurant at the Daggett House serves a country breakfast and lunch. The 1660 Captain's Tavern dining room was the first on the island of Martha's Vineyard. Sit back and relax in an Adirondack chair and watch the boats sail by.

Innkeeper(s): Judy Rogers. $90-585. 31 rooms with PB, 10 suites and 1 cottage. Afternoon tea included in rates. Types of meals: Early coffee/tea. Restaurant on premises. Beds: KQDT. Data port, cable TV, VCR, reading lamp, refrigerator, ceiling fan, clock radio, telephone, coffeemaker, desk and hot tub/spa in room. Central air. Fax, copier, parlor games, fireplace and gift shop on premises. Antiquing, art galleries, beach, bicycling, canoeing/kayak-ing, fishing, golf, museums, parks, shopping and tennis nearby.

Edgartown Inn

56 N Water
Edgartown, MA 02539
(508)627-4794 Fax:(508)627-9420

Circa 1798. The Edgartown Inn originally was built as a home for whaling Captain Thomas Worth. (Fort Worth, Texas, was named for his son.) The house was converted to an inn around 1820, when Daniel Webster was a guest. Nathaniel Hawthorne stayed here while writing much of his "Twice Told Tales." He pro-posed to the innkeeper's daughter Eliza Gibbs (who turned him down). Later, John Kennedy stayed at the inn as a young senator.

Innkeeper(s): Earle Radford. $110-240. 20 rooms, 16 with PB. Types of meals: Country bkfst and early coffee/tea. Beds: KQDT. Cable TV, reading lamp and ceiling fan in room. Air conditioning. TV, fax, copier, parlor games and tele-phone on premises. Antiquing, art galleries, beach, bicycling, canoeing/kayak-ing, fishing, hiking, live theater, museums, shopping and water sports nearby.

Publicity: *Vineyard Gazette.*

The Kelley House

23 Kelly Street
Edgartown, MA 02539-0037
(508)627-7900 (800)225-6005 Fax:(508)627-8142
Web: www.kelley-house.com

Circa 1742. Located in the heart of both downtown Edgartown and the historic district, this is one of the island's oldest inns. Over the years, five additional buildings have been added, all maintaining the inn's colonial style. It has recently been extensively restored and refurbished. Rooms include many modern amenities, such as television, radio and iron with ironing board. There is a swimming pool. Private parking is another plus. The inn is open from May through October.

Innkeeper(s): Michelle Dion . $185-800. 60 rooms. Breakfast included in rates. Types of meals: Cont. TV, irons and ironing boards in room. Air conditioning. Swimming and private parking on premises. "News from America" pub on site nearby.

Publicity: *Boston Globe and Boston Magazine.*

Point Way Inn

PO Box 128
Edgartown, MA 02539-0128
(508)627-8633 Fax:(508)627-8579
E-mail: info@pointway.com
Web: www.pointway.com

Circa 1850. The reception area of Point Way Inn is papered with navigational charts from a 4,000-mile cruise the innkeepers made with their two daughters. After the voyage, they discovered this old sea captain's house. They completely renovated it, filling it with New England antiques, period wallpapers, and canopied beds. There are working fireplaces and French doors opening onto private balconies. Complimentary laundry service and a guest car are available.

Innkeeper(s): John Glendon. $100-600. 15 rooms with PB, 10 with FP and 1 suite. Breakfast and afternoon tea included in rates. Types of meals: Cont plus and early coffee/tea. Beds: QDT. TV, reading lamp, ceiling fan and turn-down service in room. Air conditioning. Fax, copier, parlor games, telephone and fireplace on premises. Weddings, small meetings, family reunions and seminars hosted. Antiquing, fishing, live theater, parks, shopping and water sports nearby.

Publicity: *Boston Herald American.*

"One of the most pleasant old New England inns around."

Shiretown Inn on the Island of Martha's Vineyard

44 North Water St
Edgartown, MA 02539-0921
(508)627-3353 (800)541-0090 Fax:(508)627-8478
E-mail: Paradise@ShiretownInn.com
Web: www.ShiretownInn.com

Circa 1795. Listed in the National Register of Historic Places, Shiretown Inn is located in a historic district of whaling captain homes on Martha's Vineyard, the famed island seven miles off the coast of Massachusetts. Ask to stay in one of the inn's two 1795 houses where you can choose a traditionally furnished guest room with a variety of amenities such as a canopy bed and an Oriental rug. More modest rooms are available in the Carriage Houses, and there is a cottage with kitchen and living room that is particularly popular for families with small children. The inn's restaurant offers indoor dining or seating on a garden terrace. There's also a pub. Walk one block to the

Chappaquiddick Ferry and the harbor. (Make reservations in advance if you plan to bring your car, as there is limited space on the ferry.) Shops, galleries, restaurants and beaches are nearby. Cycling, golf, windsurfing, sailing, tennis and horseback riding are also close.

Innkeeper(s): Gene Strimling & Karen Harris. $79-750. 39 rooms with PB, 5 with FP, 5 suites and 1 cottage. Breakfast included in rates. Types of meals: Cont. Restaurant on premises. Beds: KQDT. Cable TV, clock radio and telephone in room. Air conditioning. Fax on premises. Weddings, small meetings, family reunions and seminars hosted. Antiquing, fishing, golf, parks, shopping, tennis and water sports nearby.

Tuscany Inn The Lodgings

22 N Water
Edgartown, MA 02539
(508)627-5999 Fax:(508)627-6605
E-mail: tuscany@vineyard.net
Web: www.tuscanyinn.com

Circa 1893. This Italianate Victorian inn overlooking Edgartown Harbor is located in the heart of this quaint sea-side village. Originally a sea captain's home, the inn has been lovingly restored to reflect the art, interior design and culinary skills of the current innkeepers. There are eight spacious rooms with private baths individually decorated in sophisticated country antiques. Guests are invited to relax in the garden with a cappuccino and enjoy one of the innkeeper's  homemade biscotti. A full breakfast features fresh fruit, homemade frittata and freshly baked breads. La Cucina ristorante, the inn's on-site restaurant, is open for dinner. Beaches, bicycle paths, museums and art galleries are a short walk away.

Historic Interest: The inn is home to Goldie Hawn, James Taylor, Carly Simon, and a favorite vacation spot for President Bill Clinton.

Innkeeper(s): Laura Scheuer. $90-325. 8 rooms with PB. Breakfast included in rates. Types of meals: Full gourmet bkfst. Beds: KQT. Cable TV and reading lamp in room. Air conditioning. Fax and library on premises. Antiquing, fishing, golf, parks, shopping, tennis and water sports nearby.

Fairhaven   I14

Edgewater B&B

2 Oxford St
Fairhaven, MA 02719-3310
(508)997-5512
E-mail: kprof@aol.com
Web: www.rixsan.com/edgewater

Circa 1760. On the historic Moby Dick Trail, Edgewater overlooks the harbor from the grassy slopes of the Acushnet River. The inn is in the charming, rambling, eclectic-style of the area. Its lawns and porches provide water views. Across the harbor in New Bedford, is Herman Melville's "dearest place in all New England." There, visitors immerse themselves in the history and lore of whaling. Near the B&B is the Gothic Revival-style Unitarian Church with stained glass by Tiffany.

Innkeeper(s): Kathy Reed. $85-135. 6 rooms with PB, 2 with FP. Types of meals: Cont plus. Beds: KQT. Cable TV and new wallpaper in room. TV and fireplace on premises.

Publicity: *Standard Times, Fairhaven Advocate, Syndicated Travel, Article Across Country Hatrford, CT, Sarasota, Fl and Kansas City.*

Fairhaven Harborside Inn & Spa

One Main St
Fairhaven, MA 02719-2907
(508)990-7760 (888)575-STAY Fax:(508)990-7722
E-mail: fhi@mediaone.net
Web: www.fairhavenharborsideinn.com

Circa 1912. As its name suggests, this red brick Colonial inn sits right on the waterfront. The Grand Foyer highlights a regal staircase with an Oriental carpet runner. The Bradford Sitting Room, named after world-renowned artist William Bradford who originally had his studio on this site, is ideal for chatting by the fire or watching TV. Period furniture including brass and four-poster wooden beds accent the spacious guest bedrooms that feature tasteful quilts and elegant wallpapers. A changing breakfast of the day is offered in addition to a continental breakfast served in the banquet-size formal dining room or glass-enclosed wraparound porch/function room where the views of the harbor are spectacular. Enjoy two acres of landscaped grounds. Plans are to add a Spa with Jacuzzi, sauna and pool.

Innkeeper(s): Sandra & Stephen Ledogar. $85-145. 6 rooms with PB and 1 suite. Breakfast included in rates. Types of meals: Full gourmet bkfst and afternoon tea. Beds: Q. Modem hook-up, reading lamp, ceiling fan, clock radio and hair dryer in room. TV, fax, copier, parlor games, telephone, fireplace and gift shop on premises. Antiquing, art galleries, beach, bicycling, canoeing/kayaking, fishing, golf, hiking, horseback riding, live theater, museums, parks, shopping, tennis, water sports and wineries nearby.

Falmouth *J16*

The Chapoquoit Inn

495 Route 28A, PO Box 367
Falmouth, MA 02574
(508)540-7232 Fax:(508)540-7295
E-mail: info@chapoquoit.com
Web: www.chapoquoit.com

Circa 1739. The breezes of Buzzards Bay, quality accommodations and a full continental breakfast greet guests at this Queen Anne Victorian inn. Chapoquoit Beach is a short walk and the grounds sport herb gardens and a romantic gazebo. Guests enjoy their 4 p.m. daily meeting time in the living room, where they may sample a complimentary glass of sherry. The Saconesset Homestead Museum is nearby, and South Cape Beach and Washburn Island State Parks are within easy driving distance.

Innkeeper(s): Kim & Time McIntyre. $95-225. 9 rooms, 7 with PB. Breakfast included in rates. Types of meals: Cont plus. Beds: QDT. Reading lamp in room. Fireplace on premises. Weddings, small meetings, family reunions and seminars hosted. Antiquing, fishing, live theater, shopping and water sports nearby.

Grafton Inn

261 Grand Ave S
Falmouth, MA 02540-3784
(508)540-8688 (800)642-4069 Fax:(508)540-1861
E-mail: alamkid@aol.com
Web: www.graftoninn.com

Circa 1870. If you want to enjoy grand ocean views while staying at an inn in Cape Cod, this is the place. Oceanfront and within walking distance to the ferries, the inn is an ideal place to hop on board a ferry and spend a day at Martha's Vineyard and return that evening to relax and watch the moon over the ocean from your bedroom window. Snacks of wine and cheese are served in the afternoon. The inn is often

seen on television and ESPN because of its unique location at the final leg of the Falmouth Road Race.

Historic Interest: Plimoth Plantation (30 miles), Heritage Plantation (15 miles), Bourne Farm (6 miles).
Innkeeper(s): Rudy Cvitan. $110-260. 11 rooms with PB. Breakfast included in rates. Beds: KQD. Cable TV, reading lamp, ceiling fan, clock and radio in room. Air conditioning. Fax, swimming, parlor games, telephone, fireplace and sand chairs on premises. Small meetings hosted. Antiquing, fishing, live theater, parks, shopping and water sports nearby.

Publicity: *Enterprise, At Your Leisure, Cape Cod Life, Cape Cod Times and Cape Cod Travel Guide.*

"You have certainly created a lovely inn for those of us who wish to escape the city and relax in luxury."

The Inn at One Main Street

1 Main St
Falmouth, MA 02540-2652
(508)540-7469 (888)281-6246
E-mail: innat1main@aol.com
Web: www.innatonemain.com

Circa 1892. In the historic district, where the road to Woods Hole begins, is this shingled Victorian with two-story turret, an open front porch and gardens framed by a white picket fence. It first became a tourist house back in the '50s. Cape Cod cranberry pecan waffles and gingerbread pancakes with whipped cream are favorite specialties. Within walking distance, you'll find the Shining Sea Bike Path, beaches, summer theater, tennis, ferry shuttle and bus station. The innkeepers are available to offer their expertise on the area.

Innkeeper(s): Christi and Ray Stoltz. $100-225. 6 rooms with PB, 1 with FP. Breakfast included in rates. Types of meals: Full bkfst. Beds: QT. Reading lamp, ceiling fan, clock radio and one with whirlpool tub and fireplace in room. Air conditioning. Parlor games, telephone and fireplace on premises. Antiquing, live theater, shopping, water sports, bike path, ferries to islands and Woods Hole Oceanographic Institute nearby.

"The art of hospitality in a delightful atmosphere, well worth traveling 3,000 miles for."

La Maison Cappellari at Mostly Hall

27 Main St
Falmouth, MA 02540-2652
(508)548-3786 (800)682-0565 Fax:(508)457-1572

Circa 1849. In the historic district off Falmouth Village green, a secluded Italianate Villa listed in the National Register sits on more than an acre of park-like gardens and landscaped grounds. Built for a seacaptain's bride, Mostly Hall was aptly named after the home's spacious central hallways. All of the guest bedrooms feature canopy beds, mural paintings, idyllic sitting areas and hand-painted furniture. In the fireplaced living room or on the veranda, feast on a delicious breakfast that may include seafood, European cheeses, pastries and fruit. Bicycles are available to explore the area, take the ferry to Martha's Vineyard or enjoy the many sites and activities of Cape Cod.

Historic Interest: The birthplace of Kathryn Lee Bates, author of "America the

Beautiful," is across the street. Plymouth and Plimoth Plantation is 35 miles, and the Kennedy Museum and Monument in Hyannisport is 23 miles.

Innkeeper(s): Christina & Bogdan Simcic. $185-225. 6 rooms with PB. Breakfast and afternoon tea included in rates. Types of meals: Full gourmet bkfst and early coffee/tea. Beds: Q. Reading lamp, ceiling fan, clock radio and two comfortable reading chairs in room. Central air. TV, VCR, fax, bicycles, library, parlor games, telephone, fireplace and gazebo on premises. Antiquing, art galleries, beach, bicycling, golf, live theater, shopping, tennis, Martha's Vineyard ferries, restaurants, island ferries and nature trails nearby.

Publicity: *Bon Appetit, Boston Globe, Yankee Magazine* "Editor's Pick" and *Discovery* "Seekers of Lost Treasure."

"Of all the inns we stayed at during our trip, we enjoyed Mostly Hall the most. Imagine, Southern hospitality on Cape Cod!"

Palmer House Inn

81 Palmer Ave
Falmouth, MA 02540-2857
(508)548-1230 (800)472-2632 Fax:(508)540-1878
E-mail: innkeepers@palmerhouseinn.com
Web: www.palmerhouseinn.com

Circa 1901. Just off the village green in Falmouth's historic district, sits this turn-of-the-century Victorian and its adjacent guest house. The polished woodwork, stained-glass windows and collection of antiques tie the home to a romantic, bygone era. Some guest rooms have fireplaces and whirlpool tubs. Innkeeper Joanne Baker prepares an opulent feast for the morning meal, which is served in traditional Victorian

style, by candlelight on tables set with fine china and crystal. Creamed eggs in puff pastry and chocolate-stuffed French toast are two of the reasons why the cuisine has been featured in Gourmet and Bon Appetit. Joanne also offers heart-healthy fare for those monitoring their fat and cholesterol. Afternoon refreshments quell those before-dinner hunger pangs.

Innkeeper(s): Ken & Joanne Baker. $90-269. 16 rooms with PB and 1 suite. Breakfast and snacks/refreshments included in rates. Types of meals: Full gourmet bkfst and early coffee/tea. Beds: KQDT. TV, reading lamp, refrigerator, ceiling fan, clock radio, telephone, coffeemaker, turn-down service, hot tub/spa, fireplace, robes, hair dryer and iron/ironing board in room. Air conditioning. Fax, copier, bicycles and parlor games on premises. Limited handicap access. Small meetings, family reunions and seminars hosted. Antiquing, fishing, live theater, parks, shopping and water sports nearby.

Publicity: *Country Inns, Gourmet, Bon Appetit, Runners World and Yankee Traveler.*

Village Green Inn

40 Main St
Falmouth, MA 02540-2667
(508)548-5621 (800)237-1119 Fax:(508)457-5051
E-mail: vgi40@aol.com
Web: www.villagegreeninn.com

Circa 1804. The inn, listed in the National Register, originally was built in the Federal style for Braddock Dimmick, son of Revolutionary War General Joseph Dimmick. Later, "cranberry king" John Crocker moved the house onto a granite slab foundation, remodeling it in the Victorian style. There are inlaid floors, large porches and gingerbread trim.

Historic Interest: Plimoth Plantation and Heritage Plantation are nearby.

Innkeeper(s): Diane & Don Crosby. $90-225. 5 rooms with PB, 2 with FP and 1 suite. Breakfast and afternoon tea included in rates. Types of meals: Full bkfst, early coffee/tea and

snacks/refreshments. Beds: Q. Cable TV, reading lamp, ceiling fan, clock radio, telephone, desk, hair dryers and robes in room. Air conditioning. Bicycles, parlor games and fireplace on premises. Small meetings and family reunions hosted. Antiquing, fishing, golf, live theater, parks, shopping, water sports and whale watching nearby.

Publicity: *Country Inns, Cape Cod Life, Yankee, London Observer, Escape and New York Magazine.*

"Tasteful, comfortable and the quintessential New England flavor ... You have turned us on to the B&B style of travel and we now have a standard to measure our future choices by."

Wildflower Inn

167 Palmer Ave
Falmouth, MA 02540-2861
(508)548-9524 (800)294-5459 Fax:(508)548-9524
E-mail: wldflr167@aol.com
Web: www.wildflower-inn.com

Circa 1898. This three-story Victorian combines modern amenities with the inn's original architectural character. Gleaming wood floors throughout are topped by Oriental rugs and period antiques. All second-floor and third-floor guest rooms are uniquely decorated for romance and comfort. For a more intimate stay, the inn offers its Loft-Cottage that boasts a private entrance, porch, a full kitchen and a spiral staircase leading to a romantic loft bedroom. Breakfast includes edible flowers and features stuffed lemon pancakes, blueberry country flower muffins and pansy butter. The inn is a short walk to the Village Green, restaurants and the shuttle to island ferries.

Innkeeper(s): Phil & Donna Stone. $150-275. 6 rooms with PB and 1 cottage. Breakfast and snacks/refreshments included in rates. Types of meals: Full gourmet bkfst, early coffee/tea and afternoon tea. Beds: QT. Reading lamp, ceiling fan, clock radio, desk and whirlpool in room. Air conditioning. VCR, fax, copier, bicycles, parlor games, telephone, fireplace, tea and wine on premises. Antiquing, fishing, golf, live theater, shopping, tennis, water sports and ferry to Martha's Vineyard nearby.

Publicity: *Cape Cod Times, Romantic Homes Magazine, Honeymoon Magazine, Yankee-Blue Ribbon, Cape Cod Life Magazine, Cape Cod Travel Guide - Top Ten Accommodations on Cape Cod, People Places Plants Magazine, Boston Globe - Best Breakfasts on Cape Cod, Boston Cooks and PBS.*

Woods Hole Passage B&B Inn

186 Woods Hole Rd
Falmouth, MA 02540-1670
(508)548-9575 (800)790-8976 Fax:(508)540-4771
E-mail: inn@woodsholepassage.com
Web: www.woodsholepassage.com

Circa 1880. This Cape Cod-style carriage house was moved more than 50 years ago to its present site, surrounded by trees and wild berry bushes. The home's common area provides a spacious, comfortable setting, while guest quarters feature country decor. Breakfasts often are served on the patio, which overlooks the one-and-a-half-acre grounds or in the garden. Items such as homemade breads, fresh fruit and quiche are among the fare. It's just a short walk through the woods to the beach. A bike path, Martha's Vineyard, an aquarium, shopping and restaurants are just a few of the nearby attractions.

Innkeeper(s): Deb Pruitt. $100-195. 5 rooms with PB. Breakfast and afternoon tea included in rates. Types of meals: Full gourmet bkfst and early coffee/tea. Beds: Q. Reading lamp, ceiling fan and sitting area in room. Air conditioning. Fax, copier, tennis, library, parlor games, telephone and fireplace on premises. Small meetings, family reunions and seminars hosted. Antiquing, fishing, golf, live theater, parks, shopping and water sports nearby.

Gloucester   C15

Lanes Cove House

6 Andrews Street
Gloucester, MA 01930
(978)282-4647 Fax:(978)283-1022
E-mail: lanescove@adelphia.net
Web: www.lanescovehouse.com

Circa 1860. Overlooking picturesque Lanes Cove, this historic Victorian home is only a ten-minute walk to the village beach. Relax and enjoy the year-round scenery from the large deck. Recently renovated for comfort and privacy, guest bedrooms and a suite with a fully equipped kitchen/sitting room boast ocean views and hardwood floors covered with Oriental rugs. An expanded continental breakfast is served in the dining room including a variety of juices, premium coffees and teas, cereals, fresh fruit, yogurt, local breads, scones and muffins with special spreads and toppings. Cape Ann offers numerous activities and sightseeing adventures. For a taste of city life, Boston is only an hour away.

Historic Interest: Lanes Cove House was built in the mid-1800s by schooner owner and housewright Enos Griffin on land sold by Nathaniel Haraden, sailmaster of the USS Constitution.

Innkeeper(s): Anna Andella. $100-150. 3 rooms with PB and 1 suite. Breakfast and afternoon tea included in rates. Types of meals: Cont plus and early coffee/tea. Beds: QT. Cable TV, VCR, reading lamp, refrigerator, ceiling fan, clock radio and desk in room. Air conditioning. Parlor games, telephone and fireplace on premises. Antiquing, art galleries, beach, bicycling, canoeing/kayaking, fishing, golf, hiking, horseback riding, live theater, museums, parks, shopping and water sports nearby.

Granby   E6

An Old Indian Trail Bed & Breakfast

664 Amherst Road
Granby, MA 01033
(413)467-3528
E-mail: reispd@attbi.com
Web: bbonline.com/ma/oit

Circa 1944. This impressive Colonial stone home and cottages are located in a quaint rural setting at the base of the Holyoke Mountain Range. The bed & breakfast offers the best of both worlds with its Amherst location and its proximity to the nearby Five College area of New England. A comfortable blend of contemporary country decor is interspersed with fine artwork throughout the inn. Plenty of good books are found in the living room for relaxed reading. The guest bedrooms, suites and cottages are bright and cheery, some with cozy fireplaces. A wonderful breakfast is served in the dining room of the main house or can be happily delivered. Choose the delicious special of the day from a menu that offers hot and cold selections.

Innkeeper(s): Peter & Dolores Reis. $85-135. 3 rooms with PB, 1 suite and 2 cottages. Breakfast included in rates. Types of meals: Full bkfst. Beds: QD. Modem hook-up, cable TV, VCR, reading lamp, refrigerator, ceiling fan, clock radio, coffeemaker and some with fireplace in room. Fax, copier, telephone and fireplace on premises. Small meetings and family reunions hosted. Amusement parks, antiquing, art galleries, bicycling, cross-country skiing, fishing, golf, hiking, horseback riding, live theater, museums, parks, shopping, sporting events, tennis, Six Flags, Big E Grounds and Mullin Center nearby.

Great Barrington   F2

Augusta House

49 South Street
Great Barrington, MA 01230
(413)528-3064

Circa 1863. Sitting in the historic hill section surrounded by other elegant homes, this 1863 Colonial is in a quiet neighborhood in a quaint but active town. Relax on a wicker loveseat or a rocking chair on the front porch, shaded by a 300-year-old Copper Beech tree. Sit by the fire in one of the common rooms. Family heirlooms, antiques and collectibles highlight each country-style guest bedroom. Diane's homemade bread is a favorite part of a healthy and generous continental breakfast. A guest kitchen includes spring water, ice and refreshments as well as use of a microwave and refrigerator.

Historic Interest: A house as old as Augusta House is bound to have a local history. History information on the house and area is in each room.

Innkeeper(s): Diane Humphrey. $80-140. 3 rooms with PB. Breakfast included in rates. Types of meals: Cont. Beds: Q. Reading lamp in room. TV, telephone, fireplace, guest kitchen with refrigerator, microwave, hot and cold spring water, refreshments and sitting area with games on premises. Family reunions hosted. Antiquing, art galleries, bicycling, canoeing/kayaking, cross-country skiing, downhill skiing, fishing, golf, hiking, horseback riding, live theater, museums, shopping, tennis, water sports, Tanglewood Music Festival, Norman Rockwell Museum and Berkshire Theatre Festival nearby.

Baldwin Hill Farm B&B

121 Baldwin Hill Rd N/S
Great Barrington, MA 01230-9061
(413)528-4092 (888)528-4092 Fax:(413)528-6365
E-mail: rpburds@aol.com
Web: www.baldwinhillfarm.com

Circa 1840. Several barns, dating back to the mid-18th century are still to be found on this 450-acre farm. The main house, a Victorian-style, New England farmstead, features a screened-in front porch where guests can enjoy the spectacular scenery of hills, fields, valleys, mountains, gardens and orchards. As the home has been in the family since 1912, the four guest rooms include  many family antiques. Homemade country breakfasts are served in the formal dining room. The inn is 20 minutes or less from many attractions, including museums, golf courses, ski areas, Tanglewood and antique shops.

Innkeeper(s): Richard & Priscilla Burdsall. $89-130. 4 rooms, 2 with PB and 2 conference rooms. Breakfast and afternoon tea included in rates. Types of meals: Full bkfst. Beds: KQT. Reading lamp and fans and clocks in room. Air conditioning. VCR, copier, swimming, stable, library, parlor games, telephone, fireplace and refrigerator on premises. Weddings, small meetings and family reunions hosted. Antiquing, cross-country skiing, downhill skiing, fishing, live theater, parks, shopping, sporting events, water sports, historical and cultural attractions, biking, hiking and camping nearby.

"We enjoyed your home immensely - from the wonderful views to your beautiful perennial flower beds to your sumptuous breakfasts."

Seekonk Pines

142 Seekonk Cross Rd
Great Barrington, MA 01230-1571
(413)528-4192 (800)292-4192 Fax:(413)528-1076

Circa 1832. Known as the Crippen Farm from 1835-1879, Seekonk Pines Inn now includes both the original farmhouse and a Dutch Colonial wing. Green lawns, gardens and meadows surround the inn. The name "Seekonk" was the local Indian name for the Canadian geese which migrate through this part of the Berkshires. The inn is an easy drive to Tanglewood.

Historic Interest: Chesterwood, Colonel Ashley House, and the Norman Rockwell Museum are within 10 miles. Hancock Shaker Village is approximately 19 miles away.

Innkeeper(s): Bruce, Roberta & Rita Lefkowitz. $90-175. 6 rooms with PB. Breakfast included in rates. Types of meals: Full bkfst. Beds: QDT. TV, reading lamp, ceiling fan, clock radio and desk in room. Air conditioning. VCR, fax, copier, swimming, bicycles, library, parlor games, telephone, fireplace and guest pantry on premises. Weddings and family reunions hosted. Antiquing, cross-country skiing, downhill skiing, fishing, golf, live theater, shopping, tennis, water sports and Tanglewood Music Festival nearby.

Publicity: *Los Angeles Times, Boston Sunday Globe, Country Inns and New York Newsday.*

"Of all the B&Bs we trekked through, yours was our first and most memorable! This has been our best ever Berkshire escape...thanks to your wonderful B&B."

Windflower Inn

684 S Egremont Rd
Great Barrington, MA 01230-1932
(413)528-2720 (800)992-1993 Fax:(413)528-5147
E-mail: wndflowr@windflowerinn.com
Web: www.windflowerinn.com

Circa 1850. Situated on 10 tranquil acres in the Berkshire Mountains, this Federal-style country inn was built for gracious living. The informal blend of antiques and comfortable decor make the public rooms perfect spots to gather for a board game, play the piano or read a good book in front of a crackling fire. Making new friends and sharing great conversations are regular occurrences at the Windflower. Several of the spacious guest bedrooms feature  working fireplaces. An organic garden provides fresh vegetables, herbs and berries that enhance a delicious breakfast including homemade pastries and breads. The four seasons offer beautiful scenery and a changing variety of activities. Guests can enjoy the private swimming pool bordered with perennials after playing golf across the street at the Egremont Country Club, or head to the local resorts for a day of skiing.

Historic Interest: Chesterwood, the home of Daniel Chester French, Herman Melville's home and the site of Shay's Rebellion are all nearby.

Innkeeper(s): Barbara & Gerald Liebert, Claudia & John Ryan. $100-200. 13 rooms with PB, 6 with FP. Breakfast and afternoon tea included in rates. Types of meals: Full bkfst and early coffee/tea. Beds: KQT. TV, reading lamp, clock radio, telephone, desk and fireplace in room. Air conditioning. Fax, copier, swimming, library and parlor games on premises. Weddings, small meetings, family reunions and seminars hosted. Antiquing, bicycling, cross-country skiing, downhill skiing, fishing, golf, live theater, parks, shopping and Tanglewood nearby.

Publicity: *Los Angeles Times, Boulevard, Redbook, Country Inns, Countryside, Road Best Traveled and Discerning Traveler.*

"Every creative comfort imaginable, great for heart, soul and stomach."

Greenfield   C6

The Brandt House

29 Highland Ave
Greenfield, MA 01301-3605
(413)774-3329 (800)235-3329 Fax:(413)772-2908

Circa 1890. Three-and-a-half-acre lawns surround this impressive three-story Colonial Revival house, situated hilltop. The library and poolroom are popular for lounging, but the favorite  gathering areas are the sunroom and the covered north porch. Ask for the aqua and white room with the fireplace, but all the rooms are pleasing. A full breakfast often includes homemade scones and is sometimes available on the slate patio in view of the expansive lawns and beautiful gardens. A full-time staff provides for guest needs. There is a clay tennis court and nature trails, and in winter, lighted ice skating at a nearby pond. Historic Deerfield and Yankee Candle Company are within five minutes.

Historic Interest: Poet's Seat Tower & Historic Homes (walking distance), Shelburne Falls & the Bridge of Flowers (15 minutes).

Innkeeper(s): Full time staff. $100-225. 9 rooms, 7 with PB, 2 with FP, 1 suite and 1 conference room. Breakfast included in rates. Types of meals: Full bkfst and early coffee/tea. Beds: KQT. Cable TV, reading lamp, refrigerator, ceiling fan, clock radio, telephone, desk, hot tub/spa, refrigerators, fireplaces in two rooms and microwave in room. Air conditioning. VCR, fax, copier, tennis, library, parlor games and fireplace on premises. Weddings, small meetings, family reunions and seminars hosted. Antiquing, cross-country skiing, downhill skiing, fishing, live theater, parks, shopping, sporting events, water sports, Old Deerfield and Lunt Silver nearby.

Harwich Port   I18

Augustus Snow House

528 Main St
Harwich Port, MA 02646-1842
(508)430-0528 (800)320-0528 Fax:(508)432-6638
E-mail: info@augustussnow.com
Web: www.augustussnow.com

Circa 1901. This gracious, Queen Anne Victorian is a turn-of-the-century gem, complete with a wide, wraparound veranda, gabled windows and a distinctive turret. Victorian wallpapers, stained glass and rich woodwork complement the interior, which is appropriately decorated in period style. Each of the romantic guest quarters offers something special. One room has a canopy bed and all rooms have fireplaces, while another  includes a relaxing clawfoot tub. Three rooms have Jacuzzi tubs. The beds are dressed in fine linens. As is the Victorian way, afternoon refreshments are served each day. The breakfasts include delectables, such as banana chip muffins, baked pears in raspberry cream sauce or, possibly, baked French toast with layers of homemade cinnamon bread, bacon and cheese.

Innkeeper(s): Joyce & Steve Roth. $105-275. 7 rooms with PB, 6 with FP. Breakfast included in rates. Types of meals: Full gourmet bkfst and early coffee/tea. Beds: KQ. Cable TV, reading lamp, ceiling fan, clock radio, telephone and fireplace in room. Air conditioning. Fax, copier, parlor games and fireplace on premises. Weddings, small meetings and family reunions hosted. Antiquing, fishing, golf, parks, shopping, water sports, private beach, restaurants, bike trails and bicycle rentals nearby.

Harbor Walk

6 Freeman St
Harwich Port, MA 02646-1902
(508)432-1675

Circa 1880. There's always a breeze on the front porch of this Victorian inn built originally as a summer guest house. Handmade quilts and antiques enhance the Cape Cod spirit of the inn. A few steps from the house will bring you into view of the Wychmere Harbor area. The greater community of Harwich offers a large conservation area for walking and birdwatching, which connects with a scenic bike path that stretches for 40 miles. There are two golf courses, three harbors for boating and fishing, and sandy beaches with warm-water swimming.

Innkeeper(s): Marilyn Barry. Call for rates. Breakfast included in rates. Reading lamp and turn-down service in room. VCR and telephone on premises. Family reunions hosted. Antiquing, live theater and shopping nearby.

Haydenville   E5

Penrose Victorian Inn

133 Main Street
Haydenville, MA 01060
(413)268-3014 (888)268-7711 Fax:(413)268-9232
E-mail: zimmer@penroseinn.com
Web: www.penroseinn.com

Circa 1820. Experience Victorian elegance at this distinctive Queen Anne that sits on two resplendent acres across from the river. Recently renovated, the inn's antique furnishings and period decor offer a warm hospitality. Common rooms include the music room and parlor. Most of the well-appointed guest bedrooms feature fireplaces. Savor Penrose French toast with fresh seasonal fruit, juice and hot beverages by candlelight. Stroll the perennial and rose gardens with fountain, relax on the porch or go for a swim. Explore Emily Dickens House, Old Deerfield and Calvin Coolidge House, each less than 10 miles away.

Innkeeper(s): Nancy & Dick Zimmer. $95-120. 3 rooms with PB. Breakfast included in rates. Types of meals: Full gourmet bkfst and veg bkfst. Beds: Q. Data port, reading lamp, clock radio, telephone, turn-down service and fireplace in room. Air conditioning. TV, VCR, fax, copier, swimming, library, fireplace and laundry facility on premises. Family reunions hosted. Amusement parks, antiquing, art galleries, bicycling, canoeing/kayaking, cross-country skiing, fishing, golf, hiking, horseback riding, live theater, museums, parks, shopping, sporting events, tennis and water sports nearby.

Publicity: *Arrington's Bed and Breakfast Journal (voted "Best in the North" and "Best Near a College or University") and Christmas special with Mark Twain House.*

Holyoke   F6

Yankee Pedlar Inn

1866 Northampton St
Holyoke, MA 01040-1997
(413)532-9494 Fax:(413)536-8877
E-mail: sales@yankeepedlar.com
Web: www.yankeepedlar.com

Circa 1875. Five buildings comprise this Pioneer Valley inn, located in western Massachusetts. In addition to the inn's restaurant, the Oyster Bar & Grill Room, there are seven ban-

quet facilities and a lounge where guests can enjoy lighter fare. Each of the guest rooms offers fine antiques and rich draperies. Museums, shopping and the volleyball and basketball halls of fame are among the many nearby attractions.

Innkeeper(s): The Clayton Family. $60-130. 30 rooms with PB and 12 suites. Breakfast included in rates. Types of meals: Cont, early coffee/tea, gourmet lunch and gourmet dinner. Restaurant on premises. Beds: KQT. Cable TV, reading lamp, clock radio, telephone and desk in room. Air conditioning. TV, fax, copier and fireplace on premises. Limited handicap access. Weddings, small meetings, family reunions and seminars hosted. Amusement parks, antiquing, cross-country skiing, downhill skiing, fishing, live theater, parks, shopping, sporting events, water sports, museums, antique carousel, ice skating, water park, hiking trail and bicycle trails nearby.

Publicity: *Reincarnation of Peter Proud.*

Housatonic   E2

Christine's Bed-Breakfast & Tearoom

325 N Plain Rd
Housatonic, MA 01236-9741
(413)274-6149 (800)536-1186 Fax:(413)274-6296
E-mail: innkeepers@christinesinn.com
Web: www.christinesinn.com

Circa 1780. Centrally located between Stockbridge and Great Barrington in the middle of the Berkshires, this country cottage farmhouse has sat at the foothill of Tom Ball Mountain for more than 200 years. Large, open beams, slant ceilings and wide pine floors reflect its original character. Check-in is at the back parlor, once a small barn. High poster and canopy beds highlight the Colonial-style guest bedrooms. A suite features a fireplace and private terrace. Enjoy breakfast crepes with strawberries or baked French toast with peaches and cream in the garden dining room. Afternoon tea is served on the screened-in porch.

Innkeeper(s): Christine Kelsey. $85-195. 4 rooms with PB, 1 with FP and 1 suite. Breakfast and afternoon tea included in rates. Types of meals: Country bkfst, veg bkfst, dinner and room service. Beds: QT. Cable TV, VCR, reading lamp, stereo, ceiling fan, clock radio, telephone, turn-down service, desk and fireplace in room. Air conditioning. Fax, copier, library, parlor games and fireplace on premises. Seminars hosted. Antiquing, art galleries, bicycling, canoeing/kayaking, cross-country skiing, downhill skiing, fishing, golf, hiking, horseback riding, live theater, museums, parks, shopping, sporting events and tennis nearby.

Hyannis   I17

Cape Cod Harbor House Inn

119 Ocean Street
Hyannis, MA 02601
(508)771-1880 (800)211-5551
E-mail: stay@harborhouseinn.net
Web: www.harborhouseinn.net

Circa 1851. Experience the sea breeze, salty air and picturesque views of the historic harbor while staying at this recently renovated captain's house with a modern wing. The inn is proud to offer smoke-free comfort, cleanliness and hospitality. Complimentary computer Internet access is provided for e-mail needs. Each well-appointed mini-suite shares a first-floor patio or second-floor balcony and features designer linens, a fully equipped kitchen and dining area. The Honeymoon Suite boasts a Jacuzzi tub and private balcony overlooking the water. Enjoy a generous continental-plus breakfast that includes breads, jam and jellies, pastries and doughnuts, fresh fruit, blueberry and cranberry muffins, bagels and cream cheese, oatmeal, cereals and beverages. Visit the nearby Kennedy Memorial and Museum.

Innkeeper(s): Ken Komenda. $79-350. 19 rooms with PB. Breakfast included in rates. Types of meals: Cont plus. Beds: KQD. Cable TV, reading lamp, refrigerator, clock radio, telephone, coffeemaker, desk and full separate kitchen in each unit in room. Central air. Fax, copier, child care and free Internet access daily for email for our guests on premises. Family reunions hosted. Antiquing, art galleries, beach, bicycling, canoeing/kayaking, fishing, golf, hiking, horseback riding, live theater, museums, parks, shopping, tennis, wineries and ferries to Martha's Vineyard and Nantucket nearby.

Publicity: *2002 Cape Cod Life Guide.*

Hyannis Port   I17

Marston Family Bed and Breakfast

70 Marston Ave.
Hyannis Port, MA 02647-0458
(508)775-3334

Circa 1786. In a quiet neighborhood near two beaches on Nantucket Sound, this Traditional Cape Cod home is one of the area's oldest. Recently renovated, the American Colonial decor is accented with antique furnishings. This B&B is pet and family friendly with an inviting yard. Watch TV in the common room. Complimentary use of the washer and dryer is a convenient amenity. Sleep on a four-poster canopy bed with luxurious linens in the Master Suite. The Middle Room boasts a fireplace and book collection. Alongside fresh baked goods, cold cereals and beverages, a satisfying hot breakfast is cooked to order. Enjoy the pleasure of a sailing excursion on the inn's 34-foot sailboat.

Historic Interest: This traditional Cape Cod home was built by colonial activist Judge Nymphus Marston in 1786 and is the oldest house in Hyannis Port.

Innkeeper(s): Marcus Sherman. $74-92. 3 rooms, 1 with PB and 1 suite. Breakfast included in rates. Types of meals: Cont plus. Beds: QT. Cable TV, VCR, clock radio, desk and fireplace in room. Library, pet boarding, parlor games, telephone, fireplace, laundry facility and free rides on 34-foot sailboat on premises. Antiquing, art galleries, beach, bicycling, canoeing/kayaking, fishing, golf, hiking, horseback riding, live theater, museums, parks, shopping, tennis, water sports, wineries and sailboat rides nearby.

The Simmons Homestead Inn

288 Scudder Ave
Hyannis Port, MA 02647
(508)778-4999 (800)637-1649 Fax:(508)790-1342
E-mail: simmonshomestead@aol.com
Web: www.simmonshomesteadinn.com

Circa 1805. This former sea captain's home features period decor and includes huge needlepoint displays and lifelike ceramic and papier-mache animals that give the inn a country feel. Some rooms boast canopy beds, and each is individually decorated. Traditional full breakfasts are served in the formal dining

room. Evening wine helps guests relax after a day of touring the Cape. There is a billiard room on the premises and an outdoor hot tub.

Innkeeper(s): Bill Putman. $140-360. 14 rooms with PB, 2 with FP and 2 suites. Breakfast included in rates. Types of meals: Full bkfst and early coffee/tea. Beds: KQT. Reading lamp, ceiling fan, clock radio and desk in room. VCR, fax, copier, bicycles, library, pet boarding, child care, parlor games, telephone, fireplace, billiard room and modem hook-up on premises. Weddings, small meetings and family reunions hosted. Antiquing, fishing, golf, live theater, parks, shopping, tennis and water sports nearby.

Publicity: *Bon Appetit, Cape Code Life and Yankee.*

"I want to say that part of what makes Cape Cod special for us is the inn. It embodies much of what is wonderful at the Cape. By Sunday, I was completely rested, relaxed, renewed and restored."

Ipswich   B14

Ipswich Bed & Breakfast

2 East Street
Ipswich, MA 01938
(978)356-2431 (866)477-9424 Fax:(978)356-5239
E-mail: raymorley@attbi.com
Web: www.ipswichbedbreakfast.com

Circa 1864. Stroll on walkways throughout this almost-one-acre estate that is accented by terraced perennial gardens. The Victorian home with Italianate detail was built by a Civil War veteran who became a general merchant. Accommodations include guest bedrooms in the main house and the restored Carriage House, which offers more privacy. The innkeepers will work with food restrictions and preferences. A wholesome breakfast is served in the formal dining room, on the garden deck, in the kitchen with the cook or brought to the room. A tranquil ambiance is imparted during a visit here.

Innkeeper(s): Ray & Margaret Morley. $100-140. 5 rooms, 4 with PB, 1 suite and 1 conference room. Breakfast included in rates. Types of meals: Full bkfst, veg bkfst and early coffee/tea. Beds: QT. Modem hook-up, cable TV, VCR, reading lamp, refrigerator, ceiling fan, snack bar, clock radio, telephone, coffeemaker and desk in room. Air conditioning. Fax, parlor games and laundry facility on premises. Weddings, small meetings, family reunions and seminars hosted. Antiquing, art galleries, beach, bicycling, canoeing/kayaking, cross-country skiing, downhill skiing, fishing, golf, hiking, live theater, museums, parks, shopping, tennis and water sports nearby.

Publicity: *Arrington's B&B Journal awarded best amenities.*

Lee   E2

Applegate

279 W Park St
Lee, MA 01238-1718
(413)243-4451 (800)691-9012
E-mail: lenandgloria@applegateinn.com
Web: www.applegateinn.com

Circa 1920. This romantic bed & breakfast is an ideal accommodation for those visiting the Berkshires. Well-dressed, four-poster beds rest atop polished wood floors. Gracious furnishings, Oriental rugs and soft lighting add to the ambiance. Most guest rooms offer fireplaces and whirlpool tubs, and several offer views of woods or gardens. Fresh flowers, brandy and Godiva chocolates are just a few extras that await guests. In the early evening, wine and cheese is served. Breakfasts are served by candlelight, with crystal stemware and antique china. The innkeepers offer several special getaway packages, such as a wine-tasting and dinner weekends. Golf and tennis facilities are located across the street.

Historic Interest: Norman Rockwell Museum is nearby.

Innkeeper(s): Len & Gloria Friedman. $115-310. 11 rooms with PB, 11 with FP and 1 cottage. Breakfast included in rates. Types of meals: Full bkfst. Beds: KQD. Reading lamp, clock radio, desk, steam shower, whirlpool tubs, flowers and brandy and chocolates in room. Air conditioning. VCR, fax, copier, swimming, bicycles, library, parlor games, telephone, fireplace, CD player, baby grand piano and screened porch overlooking gardens on premises. Weddings, small meetings, family reunions and seminars hosted. Antiquing, cross-country skiing, downhill skiing, live theater, parks, shopping, water sports, Norman Rockwell museum, Tanglewood concerts and Jacobs Pillow nearby.

Publicity: *Country Inns and Sep/Oct 95.*

Devonfield

85 Stockbridge Rd
Lee, MA 01238-9308
(413)243-3298 (800)664-0880 Fax:(413)243-1360
E-mail: innkeeper@devonfield.com
Web: www.devonfield.com

Circa 1800. The original section of this Federal inn was built by a Revolutionary War soldier. Guest rooms are spacious with charming furniture and patterned wallcoverings. Three of the rooms feature fireplaces. The one-bedroom cottage has both a fireplace and an efficiency kitchen. Guests are treated to a full breakfast. One need not wander far from the grounds to find

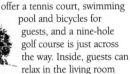

something to do. The innkeepers offer a tennis court, swimming pool and bicycles for guests, and a nine-hole golf course is just across the way. Inside, guests can relax in the living room

with its fireplace and library or in the television room. The area is full of boutiques, antique shops and galleries to explore, as well as hiking, fishing and skiing. Tanglewood, summer home of the Boston Symphony, is close by.

Historic Interest: Among the many historic sites offered in this part of Massachusetts are the Norman Rockwell Museum and the Hancock Shaker Village. There's no shortage of historic homes to visit.

Innkeeper(s): Jim & Pam Loring. $90-295. 10 rooms with PB, 4 with FP, 4 suites and 1 cottage. Beds: KQT. Cable TV, reading lamp and clock radio in room. Air conditioning. Fax, copier, swimming, bicycles, tennis, library, parlor games, telephone and fireplace on premises.

Publicity: *Discerning Traveler, New York Magazine and Karen Brown's Guides.*

"A special thank you for your warm and kind hospitality. We feel as though this is our home away from home."

The Parsonage on The Green B&B

20 Park Pl
Lee, MA 01238-1618
(413)243-4364 Fax:(413)243-2372
E-mail: parsonage@berkshire.net
Web: www.bbhost.com/parsonageonthegreen

Circa 1851. As the former parsonage to the first Congregational Church (known as having the highest wooden steeple in the country), this white colonial inn is tucked behind a white picket fence on a quiet side of the village common. The boughs of an old apple tree shade a pleasant wicker-filled side veranda. Family heirlooms, 18th-century American antiques and Oriental rugs are set against polished maple and oak hardwood floors. An elegant afternoon tea is served graciously from the teacart in the parlor and includes freshly made sweets such as Victorian lace cookies and scones. Homemade breads accompany a full breakfast served on fine china in the candle-lit dining room. Walk to restaurants, galleries and shops. Stockbridge and Lenox are nearby, as is outlet shopping. One mile from exit 2 of Mass. Pike.

Innkeeper(s): Barbara & Don Mahony. $80-175. 4 rooms with PB. Breakfast and afternoon tea included in rates. Types of meals: Full bkfst and early coffee/tea. Beds: QD. Reading lamp, ceiling fan, turn-down service, robes and hand-dipped chocolates in room. Air conditioning. VCR, bicycles, library, parlor games, telephone, fireplace, piano and newspapers on premises. Antiquing, bicycling, cross-country skiing, downhill skiing, fishing, golf, hiking, live theater, parks, shopping, sporting events, tennis, water sports and swimming in Laurel Lake nearby.

Publicity: *Berkshire Eagle and Inns and Outs of Collecting.*

"Our dream came true, the perfect romantic getaway."

Lenox E2

7 Hills Country Inn & Restaurant

40 Plunkett St
Lenox, MA 01240-2795
(413)637-0060 (800)869-6518 Fax:(413)637-3651

Circa 1911. Descendants of those who sailed on the Mayflower built this rambling, Tudor-style mansion. The inn's 27 acres of terraced lawns and stunning gardens often serve as the site for weddings, receptions and meetings. The grounds include two tennis courts and a swimming pool. Guest rooms are elegantly appointed with antiques, and the mansion still maintains its hand-carved fireplaces and leaded glass windows. In addition to the original elements, some rooms contain the modern amenities of a jet tub, fireplace and kitchenette. The inn's chef, whose cuisine has been featured in Gourmet magazine, prepares creative, continental specialties. Seven Hills offers close access to many attractions in the Berkshires.

Innkeeper(s): Patricia & Jim Eder. $85-350. 58 rooms with PB, 11 with FP, 2 suites and 4 conference rooms. Breakfast included in rates. Types of meals: Country bkfst, veg bkfst and gourmet dinner. Restaurant on premises. Beds: KQDT. Cable TV, reading lamp, clock radio, telephone and desk in room. Air conditioning. VCR, fax, copier, swimming, tennis, library, parlor games and fireplace on premises. Limited handicap access. Weddings, small meetings, family reunions and seminars hosted. Antiquing, art galleries, beach, bicycling, canoeing/kayaking, cross-country skiing, downhill skiing, fishing, golf, hiking, horseback riding, live theater, museums, parks, shopping and water sports nearby.

Publicity: *Gourmet, Entrepreneur and Boston Globe.*

Arbor Rose B&B

8 Yale Hill, Box 114
Lenox, MA 01262
(413)298-4744 (877)298-4744 Fax:(413)298-4235
E-mail: innkeeper@arborrose.com
Web: www.arborrose.com

Circa 1810. This New England farmhouse overlooks an 1800s mill, pond and gardens with the mountains as a backdrop. During the winter months, guests often relax in front of the wood stove in the inn's cozy front parlor. Four-poster beds, antiques and rural-themed paintings decorate the rooms. The inn's 19th-century mill now houses guests. The mill was one of five in the vicinity and was still in operation as late as the 1930s. The Berkshire Theatre, open for the summer season, is across the street. The Norman Rockwell Museum, Tanglewood Music Festival, ski areas and antique, outlet and specialty shops are all within a seven-mile radius.

Historic Interest: Mission House, the first mission set up for the Stockbridge Indians, and the historic Main Street of Stockbridge are among the nearby historic sites.

Innkeeper(s): Christina Alsop. $105-175. 6 rooms with PB. Breakfast included in rates. Types of meals: Country bkfst and early coffee/tea. Beds: KQT. Cable TV, reading lamp, ceiling fan, desk and some with TV in room. Air conditioning. TV, VCR, library, parlor games, telephone and fireplace on premises. Family reunions hosted. Antiquing, art galleries, bicycling, canoeing/kayaking, cross-country skiing, downhill skiing, fishing, golf, hiking, horseback riding, live theater, museums, parks, shopping, tennis, music festival and Tanglewood nearby.

Publicity: *Yankee Traveler.*

"If houses really do exude the spirit of events and feelings stored from their history, it explains why a visitor feels warmth and joy from the first turn up the driveway."

Birchwood Inn

7 Hubbard St, Box 2020
Lenox, MA 01240-4604
(413)637-2600 (800)524-1646 Fax:(413)637-4604
E-mail: innkeeper@birchwood-inn.com
Web: www.birchwood-inn.com

Circa 1767. Experience comfortable country elegance at this Colonial Revival mansion that has welcomed friends since 1767. The inn's antiques, collectibles, quilts, canopy beds

and nine fireplaces create an idyllic getaway. The inn is renowned for sumptuous breakfasts and afternoon tea. Enjoy Berkshire breezes and fireflies on the porch in summer, spring blossoms in stone-fenced gardens, vibrant fall foliage, and the welcome warmth of the firesides in winter. The oldest home in Lenox, it is a short walk from its tranquil hilltop setting to the village's restaurants, galleries and shops.

Historic Interest: Edith Wharton's home is two miles away, while Herman Melville's home is three miles from the inn. The Norman Rockwell Museum is about four miles away.

Innkeeper(s): Ellen Gutman Chenaux. $110-275. 11 rooms with PB, 6 with FP, 3 suites and 2 conference rooms. Breakfast and afternoon tea included in rates. Types of meals: Country bkfst and early coffee/tea. Beds: KQT. Modem hook-up, data port, TV, reading lamp, clock radio, telephone, desk and most with fireplace in room. Air conditioning. VCR, fax, copier, library, parlor games, gift shop and fireplaces on premises. Weddings, small meetings, family reunions and seminars hosted. Antiquing, art galleries, beach, bicycling, cross-country skiing, downhill skiing, fishing, golf, hiking, live theater, museums, parks, shopping, water sports, Tanglewood, music and theater festivals and the Norman Rockwell Museum nearby.

Publicity: *Country Inns and Country Living.*

"Thank you for memories that we will cherish forever."

Brook Farm Inn

15 Hawthorne St
Lenox, MA 01240-2404
(413)637-3013 (800)285-7638 Fax:(413)637-4751
E-mail: innkeeper@brookfarm.com
Web: www.brookfarm.com

Circa 1870. Brook Farm Inn is named after the original Brook Farm, a literary commune that sought to combine thinker and worker through a society of intelligent, cultivated members. In keeping with that theme, this gracious Victorian inn offers poetry and story telling and has a large volume poetry library. Canopy beds, Mozart and a swimming pool tend to the spirit.

Historic Interest: Home of Edith Wharton (the Mount), home of Herman Melville (Arrowhead), home of Daniel Chester French, Lincoln Memorial (Chesterwood).

Innkeeper(s): Linda & Phil Halpern. $100-350. 15 rooms with PB, 9 with FP. Breakfast and afternoon tea included in rates. Types of meals: Full bkfst and early coffee/tea. Beds: KQT. Reading lamp, ceiling fan, clock radio, telephone, fluffy towels, toiletries and 3 with whirlpools and TV in room. Air conditioning. Fax, copier, swimming, parlor games, fireplace, butler's pantry, round-the-clock coffee and tea on premises. Family reunions hosted. Antiquing, cross-country skiing, downhill skiing, fishing, live theater, museums, parks, shopping, sporting events, water sports and Tanglewood nearby.

Publicity: *Berkshire Eagle, Country Inns, Travel & Leisure and Boston Globe.*

"We've been traveling all our lives and never have we felt more at home."

Cornell Inn

203 Main St
Lenox, MA 01240-2384
(413)637-0562 (800)637-0562 Fax:(413)637-0927
E-mail: info@cornellinn.com
Web: www.cornellinn.com

Circa 1880. Located one-and-a-half miles from Tanglewood, this welcoming inn has a 70-year history. Originally, the Main House was a guest house and the adjacent Carriage house was a speakeasy. The MacDonald House was the former home of a Civil War veteran and U.S. Representative. The decor of each building, respectively, is Victorian, country primitive and Colonial. Many of the guest bedrooms feature fireplaces, whirlpool tubs, mini-bars and decks. The suites offer a fully equipped kitchen. Breakfast can be enjoyed overlooking the waterfall and Koi pond. Every evening a private full-service pub opens. Experience classic hospitality just minutes from New England's sites and activities.

Innkeeper(s): Billie & Doug McLaughlin. $100-300. 30 rooms with PB, 18 with FP. Breakfast included in rates. Types of meals: Cont plus. Beds: KQDT. Cable TV and telephone in room. Air conditioning. Spa and sauna on premises. Bicycling, cross-country skiing, downhill skiing, golf, hiking and cultural activities nearby.

The Gables Inn

81 Walker St, Rt 183
Lenox, MA 01240-2719
(413)637-3416 (800)382-9401 Fax:(413)637-3416

Circa 1885. At one time, this was the home of Pulitzer Prize-winning novelist, Edith Wharton. The Queen Anne-style Berkshire cottage features a handsome eight-sided library and Mrs. Wharton's own four-poster bed. An unusual indoor swimming pool with spa is available in warm weather.

Innkeeper(s): Mary & Frank Newton. $90-250. 17 rooms with PB, 15 with FP and 4 suites. Breakfast included in rates. Beds: Q. Cable TV, VCR, reading lamp, refrigerator, clock radio and desk in room. Air conditioning. Fax, swimming, tennis, telephone and fireplace on premises. Family reunions hosted. Antiquing, cross-country skiing, downhill skiing, fishing, live theater, parks, shopping, sporting events and water sports nearby.

Publicity: *P.M. Magazine and New York Times.*

"You made us feel like old friends and that good feeling enhanced our pleasure. In essence, it was the best part of our trip."

Hampton Terrace Bed and Breakfast

91 Walker Street
Lenox, MA 01240
(413)637-1773 (800)203-0656
E-mail: info@hamptonterrace.com
Web: www.hamptonterrace.com

Circa 1897. One of Berkshire County's oldest bed & breakfast inns, the 1897 Georgian Colonial Main House and Carriage House have been completely renovated and feature a 1930s decor. This in-town landmark was built during the Gilded Age between the Wharton and Morgan family estates. Common areas boast fireplaces, crystal sconces, elaborate moldings and a three-story suspended staircase. Vintage furniture, fireplaces, TV/VCRs, CD players, Jacuzzis or antique clawfoot tubs are found in most of the guest bedrooms. The innkeepers are originally from Georgia and offer a hearty Southern-style breakfast that changes daily. Listen to the Boston Symphony playing at nearby Tanglewood. Ask about off-season specials.

Historic Interest: Hampton Terrace is one of the official "Berkshire Cottages," mansions built by the likes of Morgan, Vanderbilt, Carnegie, Westinghouse, Astor, Tappan, Proctor and others in Lenox at the turn of the century. Hampton Terrace was owned by the Bonners, founders/owners of the New York Ledger and great-granddaughter of General Lafayette. It has been an inn since 1937.

Innkeeper(s): Stan and Susan Rosen. $140-240. 11 rooms with PB, 8 with FP and 1 suite. Breakfast included in rates. Types of meals: Full gourmet bkfst and early coffee/tea. Beds: KQDT. Modem hook-up, data port, cable TV, VCR, reading lamp, stereo, ceiling fan, clock radio, desk, hot tub/spa and fireplace in room. Air conditioning. Fax, spa, tennis, library, parlor games and telephone on premises. Weddings, small meetings, family reunions and seminars hosted. Antiquing, art galleries, bicycling, cross-country skiing, downhill skiing, fishing, golf, hiking, horseback riding, live theater, museums, parks, shopping, tennis and Tanglewood the summer home of the Boston Symphony nearby.

Publicity: *Michelin Green Guide.*

The Kemble Inn

2 Kemble St
Lenox, MA 01240-2813
(413)637-4113 (800)353-4113
Web: www.kembleinn.com

Circa 1881. Named for a famous 19th-century actress, Fanny Kemble, this three-story Georgian-style inn boasts an incredible view of the mountains in the Berkshires. The inn's 14 elegant guest rooms are named for American authors, including Nathaniel Hawthorne, Henry Wadsworth Longfellow, Herman Melville, Mark Twain and Edith Wharton. The impressive Fanny Kemble Room, which features mountain views, includes two fireplaces, a Jacuzzi tub and a king-size, four-poster bed. The inn is within minutes of five major ski areas, and Tanglewood is less than two miles away.

Historic Interest: Norman Rockwell Museum, Edith Wharton Restoration.

Innkeeper(s): J. Richard & Linda Reardon. $110-315. 14 rooms with PB, 6 with FP. Types of meals: Cont. Cable TV, reading lamp, clock radio and telephone in room. Air conditioning. Fireplace and refrigerator for guest use on premises. Limited handicap access. Antiquing, cross-country skiing, downhill skiing, fishing, parks, shopping, water sports and cultural attractions nearby.

Publicity: *Country Inns.*

"Kemble Inn was a showcase B&B - just what we had hoped for."

Rookwood Inn

11 Old Stockbridge Rd, PO Box 1717
Lenox, MA 01240-1717
(413)637-9750 (800)223-9750
E-mail: stay@rookwoodinn.com
Web: www.rookwoodinn.com

Circa 1885. This turn-of-the-century Queen Anne Victorian inn offers 20 elegant guest rooms, including suites. Among the amenities in the air-conditioned guest rooms are antiques and fireplaces. The public rooms and halls are decorated with the innkeepers' collection of antique handbags and Wallace Nutting prints. The day begins with a bountiful heart-healthy breakfast. The  beautiful Berkshires are famous for cultural and recreational opportunities, and guests can walk to shops and restaurants. Tanglewood is one mile away.

Innkeeper(s): Amy Lindner-Lesser. $85-300. 20 rooms with PB, 8 with FP, 3 suites and 2 conference rooms. Breakfast and snacks/refreshments included in rates. Types of meals: Full bkfst. Beds: KQT. Reading lamp, telephone and some with television in room. Air conditioning. Parlor games and fireplace on premises. Weddings, small meetings, family reunions and seminars hosted. Antiquing, cross-country skiing, downhill skiing, fishing, golf, live theater, parks, shopping, tennis and water sports nearby.

Publicity: *New York Times, Boston Globe, London Times, New York Magazine and Philadelphia Magazine.*

"Of all the inns I've visited, Rookwood, by far, was the most comfortable, with personable, friendly and obliging innkeepers, excellent breakfasts and cozy atmosphere."

The Village Inn

16 Church St
Lenox, MA 01240
(413)637-0020 (800)253-0917 Fax:(413)637-9756
E-mail: villinn@vgernet.net
Web: www.villageinn-lenox.com

Circa 1771. A few years after the Whitlocks built this 1771 Federal-style house they converted and joined it with two other buildings for lodging. It has operated as an inn ever since and is smoke-free. Luxurious amenities feature four-poster canopy beds, fireplaces, whirlpool tubs, VCRs and a video movie library. Furnishings include Oriental rugs, maple floors, antiques and reproductions. A complimentary continental-plus breakfast is offered midweek in winter and spring and a full breakfast is served in summer, fall and weekends throughout the year. Enjoy Saturday afternoon tea and freshly baked scones with English clotted cream. Candlelight dinners of regional American cuisine are available in summer, fall and on weekends throughout the year. Ask about special seasonal packages.

Historic Interest: The Mount (1 mile), Arrowhead (3 miles), Hancock Shaker Village (5 miles), Grandma Moses museum (20 miles), Clark Art Institute (10 miles), Tanglewood (1 mile).

Innkeeper(s): Clifford Rudisill & Ray Wilson. $65-285. 32 rooms with PB, 6 with FP, 1 suite and 2 conference rooms. Breakfast included in rates. Types of meals: Full gourmet bkfst, afternoon tea and gourmet dinner. Restaurant on premises. Beds: KQT. Data port, VCR, reading lamp, stereo, clock radio, telephone, desk, voice mail, hair dryers, magnifying mirror, satellite TV, complimentary VCR library, voice mail, air conditioning in summer and 25 with whirlpool tub in room. TV, fax, library, parlor games, cookies, coffee and tea available throughout the day and evening on premises. Limited handicap access. Weddings, small meetings, family reunions and seminars hosted. Antiquing, art galleries, beach, bicycling, cross-country skiing, downhill skiing, fishing, golf, hiking, live theater, museums, parks, shopping, sporting events, tennis, water sports, wineries, canoeing and Tanglewood summer music festival nearby.

Publicity: *The London Independent.*

"Kathy and I stayed at your beautiful inn in early October. It was the highlight of our trip to New England."

Walker House

64 Walker St
Lenox, MA 01240-2718
(413)637-1271 (800)235-3098 Fax:(413)637-2387
E-mail: walkerhouse.inn@verizon.net
Web: www.walkerhouse.com

Circa 1804. This beautiful Federal-style house sits in the center of the village on three acres of graceful woods and restored gardens. Guest rooms have fireplaces and private baths. Each is named for a favorite composer such as Beethoven, Mozart or Handel. The innkeepers' musical backgrounds include associations with the San Francisco Opera, the New York City Opera, and the Los Angeles Philharmonic. Walker House concerts are

scheduled from time to time. The innkeepers offer film and opera screenings nightly on a twelve-foot screen. With prior approval, some pets may be allowed.

Historic Interest: Tanglewood and The Mount are both nearby attractions.

Innkeeper(s): Peggy & Richard Houdek. $90-220. 8 rooms with PB, 5 with FP and 1 conference room. Breakfast and afternoon tea included in rates. Types of meals: Cont plus and early coffee/tea. Beds: QDT. Reading lamp, clock radio and desk in room. Air conditioning. VCR, fax, copier, library, parlor games, telephone, fireplace, theatre with Internet access and 100-inch screen on premises. Limited handicap access. Weddings, small meetings and family reunions hosted. Antiquing, cross-country skiing, downhill skiing, fishing, live theater, parks, shopping, water sports and music nearby.

Publicity: *Boston Globe, PBS, Los Angeles Times, New York Times and Dog Fancy.*

"We had a grand time staying with fellow music and opera lovers! Breakfasts were lovely."

Lexington   D12

Morgan's Rest

205 Follen Rd
Lexington, MA 02421
(781)652-8018 Fax:(781)240-4761

Circa 1942. This traditional New England home is a great place to rest as well as being conveniently located in the historic Lexington-Concord area just 12 miles west of Boston. Relax in a common room or play the piano. Choose from a selection of videos, CDs, games and books. A kitchen area provides use of a refrigerator, microwave and coffee pot. Stay in the spacious Pool Room that boasts a pool table and a master bath. The Follen Hill and Sunset Rooms feature stunning marble showers. Before embarking on the day's adventures, enjoy a continental breakfast served in the formal dining room.

Innkeeper(s): Alexandra Bartsch. $80-100. 3 rooms with PB. Breakfast included in rates. Types of meals: Cont. Beds: KDT. Modem hook-up, cable TV, VCR, reading lamp, stereo, refrigerator, ceiling fan, snack bar, clock radio, coffeemaker and desk in room. Air conditioning. Fax, library and parlor games on premises. Antiquing, bicycling, cross-country skiing, live theater, museums and parks nearby.

Marblehead   D14

A Nesting Place B&B

16 Village St
Marblehead, MA 01945-2213
(781)631-6655
E-mail: louisehir@aol.com
Web: www.anestingplace.com

Circa 1890. Tastefully furnished, this bright and cheerful home is embellished with colorful hand-painted furniture and a touch of whimsy. Homemade breakfasts may include seasonal fruits, fresh baked goods, bread pudding, apple crisp and french toast. Relax in the outdoor hot tub or on the deck. Ask about arranging personalized spa services. The renowned sailing harbor is within an easy walk, as are beaches, restaurants, shops, parks and historic sites. Boston airport and Cape Ann are 30 minutes away.

Innkeeper(s): Louise Hirshberg. $70-85. 2 rooms. Breakfast included in rates. Types of meals: Cont plus, early coffee/tea and afternoon tea. Beds: KQT. Reading lamp and clock radio in room. Air conditioning. VCR, spa and parlor games on premises. Antiquing, cross-country skiing, fishing, live theater, parks, shopping, sporting events, water sports, historic sites and bike path nearby.

Brimblecomb Hill

33 Mechanic St
Marblehead, MA 01945-3448
(781)631-3172
E-mail: garnould@gis.net
Web: www.brimblecomb.com

Circa 1721. This gracious pre-Revolutionary War Colonial home is a fun place to soak in New England's history and charm. The home was host to a variety tradesmen including a cooper and a wigmaker, not to mention a friend of Benjamin Franklin. The bed & breakfast is only about 20 miles from Boston and the town of Marblehead offers many fine galleries, shops and restaurants, and, of course, Marblehead Harbor.

Historic Interest: Marblehead was incorporated in 1649 and features an array of historic buildings and churches. Some of the highlights include the town's Old North Church, Abbot Hall. A walking tour can be arranged. The American Navy began in Marblehead's historic harbor, and the original painting "Spirit of '76," hangs in the town hall.

Innkeeper(s): Gene Arnould. $85-110. 3 rooms, 1 with PB. Breakfast included in rates. Types of meals: Cont plus. Beds: QD. Air conditioning. Antiquing, fishing, live theater and water sports nearby.

"Thank you for such wonderful hospitality. We really enjoyed our stay & loved the B&B atmosphere! We will definitely plan a trip back!"

Harbor Light Inn

58 Washington
Marblehead, MA 01945
(781)631-2186 Fax:(781)631-2216
E-mail: info@harborlightinn.com
Web: www.harborlightinn.com

Circa 1729. This early 18th-century inn is an elegant New England retreat. Oriental rugs, refined furnishings, fine paintings and items such as four-poster beds create a warm, inviting character. A dozen of the guest rooms include a fireplace, and some offer sunken Jacuzzi tubs. For three years, Vacations magazine ranked the inn as one of the nation's most romantic. The inn is located within walking distance of shops and restaurants, as well as Marblehead Harbor.

Innkeeper(s): Peter & Suzanne Conway. $125-295. 22 rooms with PB, 12 with FP, 2 suites, 1 cabin and 1 conference room. Breakfast included in rates. Types of meals: Cont plus. Beds: KQT. Cable TV, VCR, reading lamp, refrigerator, snack bar, clock radio, telephone and Jacuzzis in room. Air conditioning. Fax, copier, swimming, parlor games and fireplace on premises. Weddings, small meetings, family reunions and seminars hosted.

Publicity: *Vacations.*

Harborside House B&B

23 Gregory Street
Marblehead, MA 01945
(781)631-1032
E-mail: stay@harborsidehouse.com
Web: www.harborsidehouse.com

Circa 1850. Enjoy the Colonial charm of this home, which overlooks Marblehead Harbor on Boston's historic North Shore. Rooms are decorated with antiques and period wallpaper. A third-story sundeck offers excellent views. A generous continental breakfast of home-baked breads, muffins and fresh fruit is served each morning in the well-decorated dining room or on the open porch. The village of Marblehead provides many shops and restaurants. Boston and Logan airport are 30 minutes away.

Historic Interest: Lee Mansion (1768), King Hooper Mansion (1745) and St. Michael's Church (1714).

Innkeeper(s): Susan Livingston. $80-95. 2 rooms. Breakfast, afternoon tea and snacks/refreshments included in rates. Types of meals: Cont plus and veg bkfst. Beds: DT. Reading lamp, clock radio and desk in room. TV, bicycles, library, telephone and fireplace on premises. Antiquing, art galleries, bicycling, museums, parks, shopping and water sports nearby.

Publicity: *Marblehead Reporter.*

"Harborside Inn is restful, charming, with a beautiful view of the water. I wish we didn't have to leave."

Pheasant Hill Inn B&B

71 Bubier Rd
Marblehead, MA 01945-3630
(781)639-4799 (888)202-1705 Fax:(781)639-4799
E-mail: info@pheasanthill.com
Web: www.pheasanthill.com

Circa 1917. Stay in an authentic, shingled-style home with original woodwork, hardwood floors and built-in cabinets. Early antiques and painted furniture decorate the rooms, and some offer hand-painted ceilings with puffy white clouds. The artist innkeeper also has painted murals around the inn. A favorite accommodation is the spacious Garden Suite. It offers polished hardwood floors, a marbleized fireplace, handsome desk and plaid easy chairs. There's a door to the deck for views to the water. Homemade breads are a favorite breakfast item. An acre of lawns and gardens invite strolls and include a massive cluster of pink and red rhododendrons. The Spirit of '76 painting may be viewed within a half mile. Salem is five miles from the inn where whale watching and harbor/dinner cruises can be arranged. Boston is 18 miles away.

Historic Interest: An old summer house filled with light from numerous windows still with some of the original wavy glass and French doors. All original woodwork, flooring and cabinets. Original pedestal sinks still in use with modern updates.

Innkeeper(s): Nancy & Bill Coolidge. $95-175. 3 suites. Breakfast and afternoon tea included in rates. Types of meals: Cont plus and early coffee/tea. Beds: KQT. Modem hook-up, cable TV, reading lamp, CD player, refrigerator, clock radio, telephone, desk and fireplace in room. Air conditioning. VCR, fax, copier, parlor games, fireplace, lawn games, croquet, bocci, gardens, fountain, outside seating and decks with views to ocean on premises. Antiquing, art galleries, beach, bicycling, canoeing/kayaking, fishing, golf, live theater, museums, parks, shopping, tennis, whale watching and harbor cruise nearby.

Nantucket   L18

Centre Street Inn

78 Centre St
Nantucket, MA 02554-3604
(508)228-0199 (800)298-0199 Fax:(508)228-8676
E-mail: innkeeper@centrestreet.com
Web: www.centrestreetinn.com

Circa 1742. Considered on the island to be a typical Nantucket house in the Old Historic District, it is Quaker in design and was originally the home of a whale oil trader. Later converted into a boardinghouse, it became one of the area's earliest inns. Resident innkeeprs Sheila and Fred have made many pleasant changes to ensure a relaxing stay. Family heir-

looms, antiques and reproduction pieces create a warm and inviting ambiance of casual elegance. Make new friends in the spacious common room over a cup of tea. A thoughtful guest pantry has a refrigerator with ice maker and a microwave. Guest bedrooms, named after holidays, are accented with English pine, wicker, canopy beds, chintz, gingham, florals and a touch of whimsy. Indulge in a leisurely breakfast buffet by candlelight or on the brick garden patio.

Historic Interest: Inn was built as a residence for Peter Folger, a whale oil trader, and his family. In 1855 Joseph Swain bought the house and converted it to a "boarding house" establishing its history as one of the Island's earliest inns.

Innkeeper(s): Sheila & Fred Heap. $75-275. 13 rooms, 7 with PB. Breakfast included in rates. Types of meals: Cont plus. Beds: QDT. Reading lamp, clock radio and Non-working fireplaces in room. TV, VCR, library, parlor games, telephone, fireplace, gift items, guest pantry with refrigerator/ice maker and microwave on premises. Amusement parks, antiquing, art galleries, beach, bicycling, fishing, golf, hiking, live theater, museums, parks, shopping, tennis and wineries nearby.

Publicity: *Boston Globe.*

Century House

10 Cliff Rd
Nantucket, MA 02554-3640
(508)228-0530
E-mail: centurybnb@aol.com
Web: www.centuryhouse.com

Circa 1833. Captain Calder built this Federal-style house and supplemented his income by taking in guests when the whaling industry slowed down. According to late historian Edouard Stackpole, the house is the oldest continually operating guesthouse on the island. It is surrounded by other prestigious homes on a knoll in the historic district. Museums, beaches and restaurants are a short walk away. The inn's motto for about the last 100 years has been, "An inn of distinction on an island of charm." Cottages are also available.

Innkeeper(s): Husband & wife, Gerry Connick & Jeane Heron. $95-295. 14 rooms with PB. Breakfast included in rates. Types of meals: Cont plus. Beds: KQD. Free high-speed wireless Internet access 24/7 on premises.

Publicity: *Palm Beach Daily News, Boston Globe, Spur Magazine and Figaro.*

"Gerry's breakfast is outrageously great!"

La Roche

109 Orange Street
Nantucket, MA 02554-3947
(508)228-4482 (800)649-4482 Fax:(508)228-4752

Circa 1820. Light and airy with an intimate ambiance, this boutique inn is perfect for a New England island adventure. The new owners have refurbished and added upscale ameni-

ties. Stay in a guest bedroom with luxury 600 count linens, down pillows and floor-length spa robes. Families will appreciate the two-bedroom suite available. Wake up and start the day with a generous gourmet continental breakfast. Relax in one of the lawn chairs or play a game of croquet. Before going out to dinner, chat over wine, beer, cheese and hors d'oeuvres, served in the late afternoon to early evening. It is a ten-minute walk to the town.

Historic Interest: Nantucket Historical Association Exhibits (one-half mile).

Innkeeper(s): Arthur Holistin. $175-325. 8 rooms, 7 with PB and 1 suite. Breakfast included in rates. Types of meals: Cont plus, early coffee/tea, picnic lunch, hors d'oeuvres and wine. Beds: QT. Cable TV, VCR, reading lamp, refrigerator, ceiling fan, clock radio, telephone, turn-down service and voice mail in room. Air conditioning. Fax, bicycles, parlor games, fireplace and gift shop on premises. Small meetings, family reunions and seminars hosted. Antiquing, art galleries, beach, bicycling, canoeing/kayaking, fishing, golf, hiking, horseback riding, live theater, museums, parks, shopping, tennis, water sports, wineries and restaurants nearby.

Publicity: *Innsider and New York Times.*

"A relaxing, comfortable week with gracious hosts. Thanks for your Southern hospitality in the Northeast."

Pineapple Inn

10 Hussey St
Nantucket, MA 02554-3612
(508)228-9992 Fax:(508)325-6051
E-mail: info@pineappleinn.com
Web: www.pineappleinn.com

Circa 1838. Built for a prominent whaling ship captain, this classic colonial has been restored and refurnished to inspire the gracious and elegant standard of a time in history that most of us only read about in books. Reproduction and authentic 19th-century antiques, artwork and Oriental rugs are featured throughout the inn. Luxurious goose down comforters and Ralph Lauren linens top beautiful handmade, four-poster canopy beds in most of the 12 guest rooms. The innkeepers, seasoned restauranteurs, offer guests a delightful combination of steaming cappuccinos, freshly squeezed orange juice, hot or cold cereals, a fresh fruit plate and a selection of pastries served restaurant-style in the formal dining room or on the bricked garden patio.

Innkeeper(s): Caroline & Bob Taylor. $145-325. 12 rooms with PB, 3 with FP and 1 conference room. Breakfast included in rates. Types of meals: Cont plus and early coffee/tea. Beds: KQ. Cable TV, reading lamp, telephone and desk in room. Air conditioning. Fax, copier and fireplace on premises. Weddings, small meetings, family reunions and seminars hosted. Antiquing, fishing, golf, live theater, shopping, tennis, water sports, historic homes and whaling museum nearby.

"Our time here was more than just a lovely room. The patio breakfast was heavenly... and you always took time to chat and make us feel welcome. The essence of elegance—the most modern comforts and the charm of an old whaling Captain's house."

Sherburne Inn

10 Gay St
Nantucket, MA 02554-3650
(508)228-4425 (888)577-4425 Fax:(508)228-8114
E-mail: sherinn@nantucket.net
Web: www.sherburneinn.com

Circa 1835. This Greek Revival inn with Nantucket wood shingles once was home to the Atlantic Silk Company. On a quiet side street in the core historic district, it became an elegant guest house in 1872 and still retains its 19th-century charm while offering fine decor, furnishings and plush linens. Two parlors, both with fireplaces, are available for guests wishing to read, relax or watch TV. Continental plus breakfasts may be enjoyed in front of the fireplace, in the flower garden, or on the deck. The inn offers easy access to Nantucket's fine restaurants and shops and the beach is just 500 feet away. The Steamship Authority dock is also nearby.

Innkeeper(s): Dale & Susan Hamilton. $85-295. 8 rooms with PB, 1 with FP. Breakfast included in rates. Types of meals: Cont plus, early coffee/tea, afternoon tea and snacks/refreshments. Beds: KQ. Modem hook-up, data port, cable TV, VCR, reading lamp, refrigerator, ceiling fan, clock radio, telephone, fireplace, imported French & English wallcoverings, Oriental rugs and original artwork in room. Central air. Fax, copier, library, parlor games, fireplace, outside deck, flower garden with tables and chairs and bike rack on premises.

Small meetings and family reunions hosted. Antiquing, art galleries, beach, bicycling, canoeing/kayaking, fishing, golf, hiking, live theater, museums, parks, shopping, tennis, water sports, wineries, Nantucket Whaling Museum, cranberry bogs, bike paths, 83 miles of beaches, world-class boat basin, sailing and restaurants nearby.

Publicity: *New York Times, Town and Country and Travel and Leisure.*

The Woodbox Inn

29 Fair St
Nantucket, MA 02554-3798
(508)228-0587
E-mail: woodbox@nantucket.net
Web: www.woodboxinn.com

Circa 1709. In the heart of the historic district, the Woodbox Inn was built in 1709 by Captain George Bunker. Guest rooms are decorated with antiques and reproductions and some have

canopy beds. The six suites offer sitting rooms and fireplaces. Walk to Main Street and enjoy fine boutiques and art galleries. Other activities include biking, tennis, golf, whale watching and sandy beaches for sunning. The inn's award-winning gourmet dining room features an early American atmosphere with low-beamed ceilings and pine-paneled walls. (Meals are not included in room rates.)

Innkeeper(s): Dexter Tutein. $185-315. 9 rooms with PB, 6 with FP and 6 suites. Types of meals: Full bkfst. Restaurant on premises. Beds: KQDT. Reading lamp, refrigerator, clock radio and desk in room. Telephone and fireplace on premises. Weddings, small meetings and family reunions hosted. Antiquing, fishing, live theater, parks, shopping, tennis and water sports nearby.

Publicity: *Wharton Alumni, Cape Cod Life, Boston Magazine, Wine Spectator, James Beard Foundation and Phantom Gourmet.*

New Marlborough F2

Old Inn on The Green & Gedney Farm

Rt 57
New Marlborough, MA 01230
(413)229-3131 (800)286-3139 Fax:(413)229-8236
E-mail: brad@oldinn.com
Web: www.oldinn.com

Circa 1760. This former stagecoach stop, tavern, store and post office offers guest rooms in three locations. Gedney Farm, on 300 acres, is a short walk away from the main house. It accommodates the guest suites in two enormous Normandy-style barns, where Percheron stallions and Jersey cattle were once housed. The elegant country decor is warmed by hardwood floors, hand-hewn beams and granite fireplaces. There are tiled whirlpool tubs in some of the rooms. The dining room offers colonial elegance in candle-lit rooms. "Superb" is the most frequently stated complement about the inn's fine dining experience.

Innkeeper(s): Leslie Miller & Brad Wagstaff. $175-365. 43 rooms, 27 with PB, 17 with FP, 2 suites and 3 conference rooms. Breakfast included in rates. Types of meals: Cont plus, early coffee/tea and gourmet dinner. Restaurant on premises. Beds: KQT. Reading lamp, ceiling fan, clock radio, telephone, turn-down service, 11 with A/C and 11 with whirlpools in room. Fax, swimming, library, fireplace and pool on premises. Weddings, small meetings and family reunions hosted. Antiquing, cross-country skiing, downhill skiing, fishing, golf, hiking, live theater, parks, shopping, boating, spa and facials and massage nearby.

Publicity: *NYTm Country Inn, Country Living, Wine Spectator, Boston Globe, Atlantic Monthly, Travel & Leisure, Food & Wine, Zagat Survey and Travel Channel.*

New Salem D7

Bullard Farm B&B

89 Elm St
New Salem, MA 01355-9502
(978)544-6959 Fax:(978)544-6959

Circa 1793. This inn's four guest rooms are found in a farm-house containing six working fireplaces. The farm has been in the family of the innkeeper's mother since 1864, and guests are welcome to hike the inn's grounds, observing its history as a lumber mill and tannery. The inn features many original pieces used in its country-style decor. Full breakfasts may include banana sour cream coffee cake. Winter visitors may enjoy a sleigh ride or cross-country skiing on the inn's 300 acres. Quabbin Reservoir is a one-mile drive from the inn.

Innkeeper(s): Janet F. Kraft. $75-100. 4 rooms, 2 with FP and 2 conference rooms. Breakfast included in rates. Types of meals: Full bkfst. Beds: QDT. Reading lamp and telephone in room. Air conditioning. VCR, fax, parlor games and fireplace on premises. Small meetings, family reunions and seminars hosted. Antiquing, cross-country skiing, downhill skiing, fishing, shopping, sporting events, hiking and swimming nearby.

Publicity: *Boston Globe and Worcester Telegram.*

Newburyport B14

Clark Currier Inn

45 Green St
Newburyport, MA 01950-2646
(978)465-8363

Circa 1803. Once the home of shipbuilder Thomas March Clark, this three-story Federal-style inn provides gracious accommodations to visitors in the Northeast Massachusetts area. Visitors will enjoy the inn's

details added by Samuel McEntire, one of the nation's most celebrated home builders and woodcarvers. Breakfast is served in the dining room or garden room, with an afternoon tea offered in the garden room. The inn's grounds also boast a picturesque garden and gazebo. Parker River National Wildlife Refuge and Maudslay State Park are nearby, as well as Plum Island beaches.

Historic Interest: The Cushing House Museum, Firehouse Center, Custom House Museum and Market Square are within walking distance. Lowell's Boat Shop, a museum across the river, houses the Amesbury dory and highlights more than 200 years of boat building.

Innkeeper(s): Bob Nolan. $95-185. 8 rooms with PB. Breakfast and afternoon tea included in rates. Types of meals: Cont plus. Beds: QDT. Reading lamp, CD player, telephone and desk in room. Air conditioning. Parlor games, sherry and fruit are available in the library on premises. Amusement parks, antiquing, cross-country skiing, fishing, live theater, parks, shopping, water sports and many acclaimed and varied restaurants and shops nearby.

"We had a lovely stay in your B&B! We appreciated your hospitality!"

Garrison Inn

11 Brown Square
Newburyport, MA 01950
(978)499-8500 Fax:(978)499-8555

Circa 1809. This recently renovated four-story townhouse is located near Newburyport's restored downtown and waterfront areas. Originally built as a residence, the house served as a doc-

tor's office, boarding house, and embroidery business. At the turn of the century it became an inn. Exposed brick walls, hewn beams and furnishings that reflect the colonial era add character to the guest rooms. There is elevator service to all levels. The Moses Brown Pub boasts vaulted brick arches, a wood-burning stove and granite walls.

Historic Interest: This inn is in the National Register and is nationally certified.

Innkeeper(s): Hotel Management Degree (Joy MacFarlend). $130-250. 24 rooms with PB, 5 with FP, 6 suites and 1 conference room. Breakfast and afternoon tea included in rates. Types of meals: Cont plus and early coffee/tea. Restaurant on premises. Beds: KQDT. Modem hook-up, data port, cable TV, reading lamp, clock radio, telephone, coffeemaker, desk, voice mail and fireplace in room. Central air. Fax, copier, fireplace, restaurant and bar, 24-hour coffee and tea service and laundry service on premises. Limited handicap access. Weddings, small meetings, family reunions and seminars hosted. Antiquing, art galleries, beach, bicycling, canoeing/kayaking, cross-country skiing, fishing, golf, hiking, horseback riding, live theater, museums, parks, shopping, tennis and water sports nearby.

Publicity: *Yankee Travel Guide and New England Getaways.*

Windsor House

38 Federal St
Newburyport, MA 01950-2820
(978)462-3778 (888)873-5296 Fax:(978)465-3443
E-mail: windsorinn@earthlink.net
Web: www.bbhost.com/windsorhouse

Circa 1786. This brick Federal-style mansion was designed as a combination home and ship's chandlery (an outfitter and broker for cargo). The Merchant Suite was once the sales room and features a 14-foot ceiling with hand-hewn, beveled beams. The Bridal Suite was once the master suite. The newest suite, England's Rose, is a tribute to Princess Diana. The English innkeepers serve a hearty English-country breakfast and an English tea in the afternoon.

Historic Interest: William Lloyd Garrison birthplace (across the street), Newburyport Custom's House and Caleb Cushing House (walking distance).

Innkeeper(s): Judith & John Harris. $130-165. 4 rooms with PB. Breakfast and afternoon tea included in rates. Types of meals: Full bkfst. Beds: KQD. TV, reading lamp, ceiling fan, telephone, desk, fans, alarm clocks and tea and coffee facilities in room. Air conditioning. VCR, fax, copier and parlor games on premises. Small meetings and seminars hosted. Antiquing, cross-country skiing, fishing, golf, live theater, parks, shopping, tennis, water sports, bird watching and wildlife refuge nearby.

Publicity: *New York Times, Boston Globe, Boston Herald Sunday and Le Monde.*

"You will find what you look for and be met by the unexpected too. A good time!"

North Adams B3

The Porches Inn

231 River Street
North Adams, MA 01247
(413)664-0400 Fax:(413)664-0401

Circa 1900. Originally built as housing for mill workers, these classic Victorian rowhouses were retrofitted and recently renovated. The contemporary decor and generous amenities appeal to the senses. Guest bedrooms and suites feature cordless telephones, high-speed Internet access and cable TV with DVD players. Youngsters are treated to child-size canopy beds. A continental breakfast is available daily and can be delivered to the room in a factory worker's-style lunch box. Enjoy swimming, or relax in the hot tub.

Innkeeper(s): Olivier Glattfelder / The Fitzpatrick Family. $135-435. 52 rooms with PB, 21 suites and 2 conference rooms. Breakfast included in rates. Types of meals: Cont plus. Beds: KQ. Modem hook-up, data port, cable TV, reading lamp, refrigerator, snack bar, clock radio, turn-down service, desk, voice mail, cordless telephones, high-speed Internet access, self-serve honor bar, safe and DVD in room. Central air. Spa, swimming, sauna, child care, telephone, fireplace, gift shop and business center on premises. Limited handicap access. Weddings, small meetings, family reunions and seminars hosted. Antiquing, art galleries, beach, bicycling, canoeing/kayaking, cross-country skiing, downhill skiing, fishing, golf, hiking, horseback riding, live theater, museums, parks, shopping, sporting events and tennis nearby.

Publicity: *Boston Globe, Tatler(UK), Conde Nast Traveler, National Geographic Traveler, WRGB Channel 6 and Schenectady.*

Northampton   E5

Lupine House

185 North Main St
Northampton, MA 01060
(413)586-9766 (800)890-9766

Circa 1872. This Colonial offers a comfortable setting for those enjoying a New England getaway. Rooms are simply furnished with antiques adding to the ambiance. Continental-plus fare is served in the mornings, including homemade granola, fresh fruit, cereals, breads and muffins. The B&B is a short drive from downtown Northampton and many area schools, including Amherst, Smith, Hampshire and Mount Holyoke colleges and the University of Massachusetts.

Historic Interest: Old Deerfield is just a few minutes drive away.

Innkeeper(s): Evelyn & Gil Billings. $80-90. 3 rooms with PB. Breakfast included in rates. Types of meals: Cont plus and early coffee/tea. Beds: QDT. Reading lamp, clock radio, turn-down service and desk in room. Air conditioning. Library, parlor games, telephone and fireplace on premises. Antiquing, cross-country skiing, fishing, golf, live theater, parks, shopping, sporting events, tennis, biking and museums nearby.

Publicity: *Daily Hampshire Gazette.*

"You certainly provide 'the extra mile' of hospitality and service. Thank you."

Sugar Maple Trailside Inn

62 Chestnut Street
Northampton, MA 01062
(413)585-8559 (866)416-2753 Fax:(413)585-8559
E-mail: info@suger-maple-inn.com
Web: www.sugar-maple-inn.com

Circa 1865. Rich in historical context, this recently restored Colonial inn was originally built by Florence Sewing Company to house supervisory employees. Three years later, in 1868, the New Haven Railroad went in adjacent to the house. It is now a 14-mile rail trail for bike enthusiasts and hikers that will eventually extend some 80 miles to New Haven, Connecticut. Innkeeper Craig has authored four books on rail trails and their history. The inn boasts the region's largest collection of antique railroad maps, documents and history books. Peruse the vast library and relax on the three-season porch. Renovated to offer modern comforts, air-conditioned guest bedrooms feature wireless broadband Internet connections, quiet surroundings, antique furnishings, large closets and pleasant views.

Historic Interest: Canvas Ceilings installed by the railroad as a mitigation offer. Also was first house built by Florence Sewing Machine Company to house supervisory personnel.

Innkeeper(s): Craig and Kathy Della Penna. $60-90. 2 rooms with PB. Types

of meals: Cont and early coffee/tea. Beds: QD. Modem hook-up, reading lamp, clock radio and wireless broadband Internet capability in room. Air conditioning. Fax, library, telephone, fireplace and 14 miles of trails on premises. Antiquing, art galleries, bicycling, canoeing/kayaking, cross-country skiing, fishing, golf, hiking, horseback riding, live theater, museums, parks, shopping, tennis and wineries nearby.

Publicity: *Daily Hampshire Gazette and The Ride Magazine.*

Oak Bluffs   K16

Admiral Benbow Inn

81 New York Ave
Oak Bluffs, MA 02557
(508)693-6825 Fax:(508)693-7820
E-mail: innkeepers@admiral-benbow-inn.com
Web: www.admiral-benbow-inn.com

Circa 1883. Original carved oak woodwork, high ceilings, large windows and period furnishings add to the wonderful appeal of this turn-of-the-century Victorian bed & breakfast built in 1883 and recently renovated. Relax with a beverage and good conversation on the front porch wicker furniture or on the patio by the koi pond. Stay in a comfortable guest bedroom on the first or second floor that may have a canopy bed, sitting area or view of the gardens. Fresh fruits, pastries, bagels, yogurt and cereals are a great start to the day. Take a short walk to the harbor, shops and ferries or hop a bus for easy island transportation. Visit the historic Methodist Campground's Gingerbread Cottages and the Flying Horses, a vintage merry-go-round.

Historic Interest: Large Victorian built in 1883.

Innkeeper(s): Mary and Bill Moore. $105-209. 7 rooms with PB. Breakfast included in rates. Types of meals: Cont plus and early coffee/tea. Beds: QD. Reading lamp, ceiling fan and clock radio in room. TV, telephone and fireplace on premises. Family reunions hosted. Amusement parks, art galleries, beach, bicycling, canoeing/kayaking, fishing, golf, parks, shopping, Flying Horses (one of the oldest merry-go-rounds) and Methodist Campground gingerbread houses nearby.

"Full of beauty, charm and relaxation."

Nashua House

30 Kennebec Ave, PO Box 2221
Oak Bluffs, MA 02557-0803
(508)693-0043
E-mail: calebcaldwellmv@hotmail.com
Web: www.nashuahouse.com

Circa 1865. Affordable accommodations are found at this seaside hotel on Martha's Vineyard. Sunlit guest bedrooms blend the Victorian era with cottage-style furnishings accented by beadboard walls and ceilings. Many rooms with large bay windows offer ocean views, and there is a second-floor balcony that is perfect for relaxing in the sun. Besides the many beaches, there is much to explore in this historic area of New England. Centrally located, all the mainland ferry docks are within an easy walk. Transportation for getting around the island is just one block away.

Innkeeper(s): Caleb Caldwell, Chris Blake. $49-109. 15 rooms. Beds: DT. TV, VCR and telephone on premises. Amusement parks, antiquing, art galleries, beach, bicycling, canoeing/kayaking, fishing, golf, hiking, horseback riding, live theater, museums, parks, shopping, tennis, water sports and wineries nearby.

Publicity: *The Boston Sunday Globe and Newsday.*

The Oak Bluffs Inn

P.O. Box 2099
Oak Bluffs, MA 02557
(508)693-7171 (800)955-6235 Fax:(508)693-8787
E-mail: bmyguest@oakbluffsinn.com
Web: www.8009556235.com

Circa 1870. A widow's walk and gingerbread touches were added to this graceful home to enhance the Victorian atmosphere already prevalent throughout the inn. Rooms are decorated in Victorian style with antiques. Home-baked breads and fresh fruits start off the day. After enjoying the many activities Martha's Vineyard has to offer, return for a scrumptious afternoon tea with scones, tea sandwiches and pastries. Oak Bluffs originally was named Cottage City, and is full of quaint, gingerbread homes to view. Nearby Circuit Avenue offers shopping, ice cream parlors, eateries and the nation's oldest carousel.
Innkeeper(s): Erik & Rhonda Albert. $135-260. 9 rooms with PB. Breakfast included in rates. Types of meals: Cont plus. Beds: QD. Reading lamp, ceiling fan and clock radio in room. Air conditioning. Parlor games, telephone and refrigerator/ice maker on premises. Antiquing, fishing, golf, live theater, parks, shopping, tennis and water sports nearby.

The Oak House

PO Box 299AA Seaview Ave
Oak Bluffs, MA 02557
(508)693-4187 (800)245-5979

Circa 1872. Massachusetts Gov. William Claflin purchased this gingerbread cottage because of its fine location and splendid view of the ocean. He imported oak timbers and employed ship's carpenters to carve oak ceilings, wall panels and interior pillars. A servants' wing, an additional floor, and a wide veranda were added, all for the purpose of entertaining important Massachusetts leaders. As a bed & breakfast, the Oak House maintains the grand style with authentic Victorian furnishings and refined hospitality.
Innkeeper(s): Betsi Convery-Luce. $160-250. 10 rooms with PB. Breakfast included in rates. Types of meals: Cont plus and afternoon tea. Beds: KQ. TV and telephone in room.
Publicity: *Vineyard Gazette.*

"I feel like a guest in a friend's home."

Tivoli Inn, Martha's Vineyard

125 Circuit Ave.
Oak Bluffs, MA 02557
(508)693-7928
E-mail: tivoli@capecod.net

Circa 1890. Escape to the island charm of this renovated Victorian Gingerbread house. It was built during the era of great sailing ships and showcases a latticed wraparound porch and flowery balcony. Comfortable and clean, the inn offers a friendly atmosphere highlighted by cheerful guest bedrooms. One room features a balcony; another boasts a private entrance to the front porch. Breakfast is served each morning in season. Town beaches, ferries, shops, entertainment and public transportation are all within an easy walk from this inn, located just past the edge of town.
Innkeeper(s): Lori & Lisa Katsounakis. $65-165. 6 rooms, 3 with PB. Breakfast included in rates. Types of meals: Cont plus. Beds: QDT. Cable TV, reading lamp and refrigerator in room. Bicycles and telephone on premises. Small meetings, family reunions and seminars hosted. Antiquing, fishing, golf, parks, shopping, tennis and water sports nearby.
Publicity: *Boston Magazine.*

"I will recommend your inn to all who wish a pleasant stay at the Vineyard."

Orleans H19

Governor Prence Inn

66 Route 6A
Orleans, MA 02601
(508)255-1216 (800)342-4300 Fax:(508)240-1107
E-mail: info@governorprenceinn.com
Web: www.governorprenceinn.com

Circa 1930. Five secluded acres of flowering trees, pines and award-winning gardens surround this country inn located in the historic village of Orleans, gateway to the National Seashore. Spacious guest bedrooms feature cable television with HBO, microwaves, refrigerators and sun decks or courtyard. Enjoy hot coffee and baked goods in the morning. An Olympic-size outdoor swimming pool is an inviting amenity. Barbecue grills and picnic tables add to the relaxing atmosphere. Access the Rail Trail bike path directly behind the inn. Skaket Beach on Cape Cod Bay, Coast Guard Beach and Nauset Beach on the Atlantic Ocean are all popular and close by. Hyannis and Provincetown are a short drive away.
Historic Interest: The original building was a mid-19th century farmhouse built on the site of a windmill.
Innkeeper(s): Linda LeGeyt. $104-154. 56 rooms with PB and 1 conference room. Breakfast included in rates. Types of meals: Cont. Beds: KD. Cable TV, reading lamp, refrigerator, clock radio and telephone in room. Air conditioning. Fax, swimming, parlor games, picnic tables and BBQ on premises. Family reunions hosted. Antiquing, art galleries, beach, bicycling, canoeing/kayaking, fishing, golf, hiking, horseback riding, live theater, museums, shopping and tennis nearby.

Orleans Waterfront Inn

Rt 6A on Town Cove, PO Box 188
Orleans, MA 02653
(508)255-2222 Fax:(508)255-6722
E-mail: info@orleansinn.com
Web: www.orleansinn.com

Circa 1875. Recently refurbished, this Sea Captain Mansion, which was built by a descendant of the Mayflower Pilgrims, features a waterfront setting and a Victorian decor. The lobby showcases an original stone fireplace, vintage dolls and a grandfather clock. Expect gracious service that begins with a welcome box of fine chocolates. Quiet guest bedrooms boast custom furnishings and floral quilts. Enjoy a continental breakfast in bed or in the Snow Dining Room. A kitchenette with toaster oven, refrigerator and microwave is available for guest use. Casual fare can be found on-site at O'Hagan's Irish Pub. Relax on the deck with a cold beverage and watch the boats sail by.
Innkeeper(s): Ed & Laurie Maas and children. $125-250. 11 rooms with PB, 3 suites and 1 conference room. Breakfast, afternoon tea and snacks/refreshments included in rates. Types of meals: Cont plus, early coffee/tea, gourmet lunch, picnic lunch, gourmet dinner and room service. Restaurant on premises. Beds: KQT. Modem hook-up, data port, cable TV, reading lamp, clock radio, telephone and desk in room. Air conditioning. VCR, fax, copier, library, pet boarding and fireplace on premises. Antiquing, art galleries, beach, bicycling, canoeing/kayaking, fishing, golf, hiking, horseback riding, live theater, museums, parks, shopping, sporting events, tennis, water sports and wineries nearby.
Publicity: *Cape Codder, Cape Cod Life, Cape Cod Times and Albany Times Union.*

Petersham D8

The Inn at Clamber Hill

111 N Main St
Petersham, MA 01366-9501
(978)724-8800 (888)374-0007 Fax:(978)724-8829
E-mail: clamber@tiac.net
Web: www.clamberhill.com

Circa 1927. Sitting in the midst of 33 peaceful and secluded wooded acres this statuesque 1927 European country estate is just minutes from Quabbin Reservoir. The local forests, known for their dramatic seasonal color changes, draw many leaf peepers to the inn. Furnished with antiques and Oriental carpets, guest bedrooms are inviting retreats. Stay in a suite with a sitting room and fireplace. Breakfast is a gourmet delight with fresh fruit, homemade cinnamon rolls, muffins, waffles with strawberries, peach-filled French toast and wild blueberry pancakes. High tea is available by arrangement. A full-service restaurant serves dinner Sunday through Wednesday. Stroll through the colorful gardens and bird watch. Visit the Fisher Museum just three miles away at the 3000-acre Harvard Forest.
Innkeeper(s): Mark & Deni Ellis. $145-195. 5 rooms with PB, 4 with FP, 2 suites and 1 conference room. Breakfast and refreshments included in rates. Types of meals: Full bkfst, veg bkfst, early coffee/tea and afternoon tea. Beds: Q. Reading lamp, clock radio, coffeemaker, desk and fireplace in room. Air conditioning. Fax, copier, library, parlor games, telephone, fireplace, laundry facility, parlor, terraces, gardens and full service restaurant Sunday through Wednesday evenings available on premises. Weddings, small meetings, family reunions and seminars hosted. Antiquing, art galleries, beach, bicycling, canoeing/kayaking, cross-country skiing, downhill skiing, fishing, golf, hiking, live theater, museums, parks, shopping and water sports nearby.

Winterwood at Petersham

19 N Main St
Petersham, MA 01366
(978)724-8885
E-mail: winterwoodatpetersham@juno.com
Web: www.winterwoodinn.com

Circa 1842. The town of Petersham is often referred to as a museum of Greek Revival architecture. One of the grand houses facing the common is Winterwood. It boasts fireplaces in almost every room. Private dining is available for groups of up to 70 people. The inn is listed in the National Register.

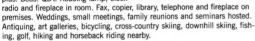

Innkeeper(s): Jean & Robert Day. $129. 6 rooms with PB, 5 with FP. Breakfast included in rates. Types of meals: Cont plus. Beds: QDT. Reading lamp, clock radio and fireplace in room. Fax, copier, library, telephone and fireplace on premises. Weddings, small meetings, family reunions and seminars hosted. Antiquing, art galleries, bicycling, cross-country skiing, downhill skiing, fishing, golf, hiking and horseback riding nearby.

Publicity: *Boston Globe and Yankee Magazine.*

"Between your physical facilities and Jean's cooking, our return to normal has been made even more difficult. Your hospitality was just a fantastic extra to our total experience."

Pittsfield D2

Olde White Horse Inn

378 South St
Pittsfield, MA 01201-6804
(413)442-2512 Fax:(413)443-0490
E-mail: whitehorsebb@yahoo.com
Web: www.whitehorsebb.com

Circa 1902. Innkeeping runs in the family at the White Horse, which features an elegant Colonial exterior set on an acre of manicured lawn. The current innkeeper's grandparents also were innkeepers, and two rooms are named in honor of them. The Colonial theme continues into the home and to its eight guest rooms, decorated with antiques and beds topped with cozy comforters. The innkeepers' daughters also pitch in and help run the inn; the oldest prepares the breakfasts. The morning meal includes such items as quiche, pancakes, homemade muffins or breads and fresh fruit.
Innkeeper(s): Joe & Linda Kalisz. $85-190. 8 rooms with PB, 2 with FP. Breakfast included in rates. Types of meals: Country bkfst, veg bkfst, early coffee/tea. Beds: QD. Modem hook-up, data port, cable TV, reading lamp, refrigerator, clock radio, telephone, coffeemaker, turn-down service, desk and fireplace in room. Air conditioning. Fax, copier and fireplace on premises. Weddings, small meetings and family reunions hosted. Antiquing, art galleries, beach, bicycling, canoeing/kayaking, cross-country skiing, downhill skiing, fishing, golf, horseback riding, live theater, parks, shopping, sporting events, water sports and wineries nearby.

Princeton D9

Fernside Inn

PO Box 303, 162 Mountain Rd
Princeton, MA 01541-0303
(978)464-2741 (800)545-2741 Fax:(978)464-2065
E-mail: innkeeper@fernsideinn.com
Web: www.fernsideinn.com

Circa 1835. Originally built by Capt. Benjamin Harrington, this elegant Federal mansion was transformed in 1870 into a tavern and boarding house for Harvard professors and students. In 1890, the home changed owners and served as a vacation house for working women for more than 100 years. In 1994, the Morrisons transformed it once again and meticulously restored  it. Situated on the eastern slope of Mount Wachusett, the inn is nestled on 15 acres with breathtaking sunrise views. Designed for entertaining, there are ten cozy fireplaces, numerous sitting rooms and a variety of porches. The common rooms as well as the guest rooms are elegantly decorated with antiques, period reproductions, and Oriental rugs. A home-cooked breakfast includes fresh fruit, pastries and a variety of entrees.
Innkeeper(s): Jocelyn & Richard Morrison. $125-230. 8 rooms with PB, 6 with FP, 2 suites and 1 conference room. Breakfast included in rates. Types of meals: Full gourmet bkfst and early coffee/tea. Beds: KQ. Reading lamp, clock radio, telephone and turn-down service in room. Fax, copier, parlor games, fireplace and refreshments served on premises. Limited handicap access. Small meetings and seminars hosted. Antiquing, cross-country skiing, downhill skiing, golf, parks, shopping and tennis nearby.

"You cannot help but feel at ease the moment you walk into the inn."

Provincetown G18

Archer Inn

26 Bradford St
Provincetown, MA 02657-1321
(508)487-2529 (800)263-6574
E-mail: archerinn@comcast.net
Web: www.archerinn.com

Circa 1800. From the top of a hill, this former sea captain's home affords a panoramic view of Cape Cod Bay. Two suites offer views of the bay, and two other rooms boast harbor views. The innkeepers also offer accommodations in a small cottage adjacent to the main house. A concierge service is available, and guests also can be shuttled to and from the airport or nearby docks.
Innkeeper(s): Brian Maginns. $85-235. 10 rooms, 6 with PB and 1 suite. Breakfast and snacks/refreshments included in rates. Types of meals: Cont and early coffee/tea. Beds: KQD. Cable TV, refrigerator, ceiling fan and turn-down service in room. Air conditioning. Copier and telephone on premises. Antiquing, fishing, live theater, parks, shopping, water sports, bicycling and sailing nearby.

Bradford Carver House

70 Bradford St
Provincetown, MA 02657-1363
(508)487-4966 (800)826-9083 Fax:(508)487-7213
E-mail: info@bradfordcarver.com
Web: www.bradfordcarver.com

Circa 1800. One block from Cape Cod Bay, this mid-1800s Victorian inn is painted Federal blue with a white picket fence, roses, gladioli and azaleas, creating a welcoming invitation. Inside, there's always a bowl of fruit and in summer, fresh cut flowers. The innkeeper's collections of Hummels, chandeliers and candelabras (Bill confesses to being a candelabra fanatic) are found throughout the parlor and guest rooms. Antiques such as a Victorian sofa and French settee furnish the living room with its handsome fireplace. The five rooms all offer large beds, phones with voice mail and data ports, VCRs and many other amenities. A 900-piece video library is cataloged, categorized and color coded for guests. Enjoy a complimentary continental breakfast in the parlor or on one of the patios and plan your day's activities. Located in the heart of historic Provincetown, it is located just one block from Commercial Street with its many unique shops, restaurants and stores. Try booking a boating excursion or visit Pilgrims' First Landing Park and Museum.
Historic Interest: The Pilgrims first landed at Provincetown and Pilgrims' First Landing Park is dedicated to commemorating that event.
Innkeeper(s): Bill & Jose. $49-199. 5 rooms with PB, 2 with FP. Types of meals: Cont. Beds: KQ. Modem hook-up, data port, cable TV, VCR, reading lamp, stereo, refrigerator, ceiling fan, clock radio, telephone and voice mail in room. Air conditioning. Fireplace on premises. Antiquing, art galleries, beach, bicycling, canoeing/kayaking, fishing, hiking, museums, parks, shopping, tennis and wineries nearby.

Carpe Diem

12 Johnson Street
Provincetown, MA 02657
(508)487-4242 (800)487-0132 Fax:(508)487-4242
E-mail: info@carpediemguesthouse.com
Web: www.carpediemguesthouse.com

Circa 1864. A neighborhood landmark, this Second Empire-style mansion with a mansard roof is furnished with European antiques and a French country decor. Sip complimentary sherry

or port by the fire in one of the common rooms. Guest bedrooms and suites are named after well-known poets and most feature whirlpool tubs, fireplaces and private entrances as well as a variety of amenities. In addition to the Main House and Carriage House rooms, a garden cottage and beach studio are also available. The inn is famous for Jurgen's homemade breakfasts that combine classic American with German bounty. Hospitality is abundant, offering bike storage, a beverage and ironing station, guest office with Internet access and much more. Soak in the spa, read on a secluded patio or relax in the garden.
Historic Interest: The inn is one of the few Second Empire style houses in Provincetown. It has all the original features and is a landmark on our street.
Innkeeper(s): Rainer Horn, Jurgen Herzog. $70-315. 14 rooms, 10 with PB, 6 with FP, 3 suites and 1 cottage. Breakfast, afternoon tea and snacks/refreshments included in rates. Types of meals: Full gourmet bkfst and early coffee/tea. Beds: Q. Modem hook-up, data port, cable TV, VCR, reading lamp, stereo, refrigerator, ceiling fan, clock radio, telephone, coffeemaker, hot tub/spa, voice mail and fireplace in room. Air conditioning. Fax, copier, spa, parlor games, fireplace, laundry facility, video library, guest office, 24-hour coffee/espresso station, refreshment, wine hour in afternoon and complimentary sherry and port on premises. Weddings, family reunions and seminars hosted. Antiquing, art galleries, beach, bicycling, canoeing/kayaking, fishing, golf, live theater, museums, parks, shopping, tennis, water sports and wineries nearby.
Publicity: *Frommer's Guide, Out & About, Haunted Inns of New England, Register of Haunted House in New England, Canal Vie and Quebec.*

Christopher's By The Bay

8 Johnson St
Provincetown, MA 02657
(508)487-9263 (877)487-9263 Fax:(508)487-9263
E-mail: christophers.bythebay@verizon.net
Web: www.christophersbythebay.com

Circa 1860. Overlooking the harbor, this three-story Victorian inn sits quietly on a side street in the heart of town. The fireplace in the front room is the perfect catalyst for relaxation. The guest bedrooms and suite, named after famous artists, have so much to offer. Some feature bay windows, wide plank hardwood floors, a fireplace and stunning views. Choose from an extensive video library for in-room use. Wake up to a delicious breakfast served in the sunny dining room. The garden is a delight, as is exploring the local sites just around the corner.
Innkeeper(s): Ash Calder & Jason Real. $50-170. 10 rooms, 5 with PB, 1 with FP and 1 suite. Breakfast included in rates. Types of meals: Cont and early coffee/tea. Beds: QD. Data port, cable TV, VCR, reading lamp, CD player, refrigerator, ceiling fan, clock radio, telephone and voice mail in room. Air conditioning. Fax, parlor games, fireplace and laundry facility on premises. Weddings, small meetings, family reunions and seminars hosted. Antiquing, art galleries, beach, bicycling, canoeing/kayaking, fishing, golf, hiking, horseback riding, live theater, museums, parks, shopping, tennis, water sports and wineries nearby.

Fairbanks Inn

90 Bradford St
Provincetown, MA 02657-1428
(508)487-0386 (800)324-7265 Fax:(508)487-3540
E-mail: info@fairbanksinn.com
Web: www.fairbanksinn.com

Circa 1776. Gardens and a picket fence surround the three historic buildings that comprise this gracious inn. The Federal-style main house offers many historic details, including wide-pine floors originally a part of the ship of the sea captain who built the home. Freshly baked cookies and an original wood-burning fireplace in the parlor (once the cooking fireplace) add to the inviting experience. Bed chambers are furnished in colonial antiques and reproductions and offer fluffy comforters. The dining room is the spot where the innkeepers serve an expanded continental breakfast buffet. There's a rooftop sun deck for summer tanning, a porch and patio. Enjoy whale watching, restaurants, shops, beaches and the Pilgrim Monument.

Innkeeper(s): Lynette Molnar, Sabrian Riddle. $50-250. 14 rooms, 12 with PB, 10 with FP. Breakfast included in rates. Types of meals: Cont plus. Beds: KQD. Cable TV, reading lamp, clock radio and telephone in room. Air conditioning. Fax, parlor games and fireplace on premises. Weddings, small meetings, family reunions and seminars hosted. Antiquing, art galleries, beach, bicycling, canoeing/kayaking, fishing, golf, hiking, horseback riding, live theater, museums, parks, shopping, tennis, water sports and wineries nearby.

Publicity: *Yankee Magazine, Cape Cod Life and Hidden New England.*

Gabriel's Apartments and Guest Rooms

104 Bradford St
Provincetown, MA 02657-1441
(508)487-3232 (800)969-2643 Fax:(508)487-1605
E-mail: gabrielsma@aol.com
Web: www.gabriels.com

Circa 1936. Experience Gabriel's heavenly setting and cozy hospitality that have been enjoyed by many since 1979. Restored homes are graced with sky-lit common areas to gather in as a group or an individual. Each guest bedroom and suite is distinguished by the name and character of a famous personality. Most feature fireplaces, many boast Jacuzzi tubs and some include kitchenettes, skylights, sleeping lofts and semi-private porches. Modern amenities include high-speed Internet access and computers, voice mail, VCRs and a video library. Savor a full breakfast each morning. Lounge on a sun deck with afternoon wine and cheese. After a work out in the exercise gym, relax in the sauna or steam room. Soak in one of the two soothing outdoor hot tubs. Conveniently located in the heart of quaint Provincetown, the beach is only one block away.

Innkeeper(s): Gabriel Brooke. $100-300. 22 rooms with PB, 12 with FP, 10 suites and 1 conference room. Breakfast included in rates. Types of meals: Full bkfst and afternoon tea. Beds: QD. Cable TV, VCR, reading lamp, refrigerator, ceiling fan, clock radio, telephone, desk and hot tub/spa in room. Air conditioning. Fax, copier, spa, sauna, bicycles, library, parlor games, fireplace and e-mail on premises. Weddings, small meetings, family reunions and seminars hosted. Antiquing, cross-country skiing, fishing, golf, live theater, parks, shopping, tennis, water sports and whale watching nearby.

Revere Guest House Inc

14 Court St
Provincetown, MA 02657-2114
(508)487-2292 (800)487-2292
E-mail: info@reverehouse.com
Web: www.reverehouse.com

Circa 1830. This restored Captain's home on Court Street was built in 1830 when Provincetown (where the Pilgrims landed in 1620) was still a thriving fishing port. It was awarded the 1998 Preservation Award by the Provincetown Historical Commission. The inn is surrounded by gardens and a picket fence, and it has eight guest rooms- all with private bath. Enjoy a continental breakfast before biking to the beach or walking across paths in the sand dunes.

Innkeeper(s): Gary Palochko. $75-275. 8 rooms with PB. Breakfast included in rates. Types of meals: Cont. Beds: QD. Cable TV, VCR, refrigerator and clock radio in room. Air conditioning. Telephone and fireplace on premises. Antiquing, art galleries, beach, bicycling, fishing, hiking, horseback riding, live theater, museums, parks, shopping and water sports nearby.

Snug Cottage

178 Bradford St
Provincetown, MA 02657-2498
(508)487-1616 (800)432-2334 Fax:(508)487-5123

Circa 1920. Framed by a split-rail fence, this Cape Cod house is conveniently located within a short walk of all of Provincetown. Behind the inn is the Loft Lodge with cathedral ceilings, a kitchen and its own fireplace. An informal New England decor with period furnishings is enhanced by a collection of original paintings. If your visit is in the spring, request the Cherry Tree Room and enjoy the delicate blossoms from your window.

In addition, the innkeeper also offers accommodations in five, two-bedroom townhomes and a penthouse with a view of Cape Cod Bay. The townhomes sleep six and include kitchens, working fireplaces and decks off the master bedroom.

Innkeeper(s): James Mack. $85-195. 8 rooms with PB, 6 with FP, 6 suites and 3 cottages. Types of meals: Full bkfst. Beds: Q. Data port, cable TV, VCR, reading lamp, CD player, refrigerator, ceiling fan, clock radio, telephone, turn-down service, voice mail, fireplace and high-speed wireless Internet access in room. Air conditioning. Fax, copier and library on premises. Weddings, small meetings, family reunions and seminars hosted.

Publicity: *Country Inns.*

"We return year after year for the gourmet breakfasts, incredibly beautiful gardens and the warm atmosphere."

Rehoboth   H12

Gilbert's Tree Farm B&B

30 Spring St
Rehoboth, MA 02769-2408
(508)252-6416
E-mail: gilbertsbb@aasp.net
Web: www.gilbertsbb.com

Circa 1835. This country farmhouse sits on 17 acres of woodland that includes an award-winning tree farm. Cross-country skiing and hiking are found right outside the door. If they choose to, guests can even help with the farm chores, caring for horses and gardening. A swimming pool is open during summer. Three antique-filled bedrooms share a second-floor sitting room. There are two first-floor rooms with a working fireplace and private bath. The nearby town of Rehoboth is 360 years old.

Historic Interest: Battleship Massachusetts (8 miles), Museum of Lizzie Borden artifacts (8 miles), Carpenter Museum (4 miles), Plymouth Plantation (1 hour), Newport mansions (45 minutes), Providence Waterfires (15 minutes).

Innkeeper(s): Jeanne Gilbert. $70-90. 5 rooms, 2 with PB and 1 conference room. Breakfast, afternoon tea and snacks/refreshments included in rates. Types of meals: Full bkfst and early coffee/tea. Beds: KQDT. Reading lamp, desk and two with fireplace in room. VCR, copier, swimming, stable, bicycles, library, telephone, fireplace and horse boarding only on premises. Small meetings and seminars hosted. Antiquing, cross-country skiing, fishing, live theater, parks, shopping, sporting events and water sports nearby.

Publicity: *Attleboro Sun Chronicle, Country, Somerset Spectator, Country Gazette and Pawtucket Times.*

"This place has become my second home. Thank you for the family atmosphere of relaxation, fun, spontaneity and natural surroundings."

Richmond D2

Inn At Richmond

802 State Rd
Richmond, MA 01254
(413)698-2566 (888)968-4748 Fax:(413)698-2100
E-mail: innkeepers@innatrichmond.com
Web: www.innatrichmond.com

Circa 1775. The inn at Richmond was built just a year prior to
the Revolutionary War. The property was part of a land grant
from King George. The inn has been restored impeccably, and
each room has been decorated individually with Waverly and
Schumacher fabrics and appointments. Furnishings include a
mix of antiques and reproductions, and five of the accommodations include a fireplace. The suites are especially luxurious,
and the Federal Suite includes a clawfoot tub. Three private,
one-bedroom cottages are available; each is decorated with
antiques, reproductions and family heirlooms. In addition to
the beautiful surroundings, which include views of the rolling
Berkshire Hills, guests are pampered with a gourmet breakfast.
The menu changes daily, but always includes Berkshire granola,
fruit yogurt, muffins or special pastries and a selection of fresh,
seasonal fruits. Entrees range from lemon, poppyseed pancakes
with fresh raspberries from the inn's garden to a savory
spinach, tomato and Brie tart with a cracked black pepper
crust. After this luscious meal, there's much for guests to do in
the Richmond area. Skiing, the Appalachian Trail, Tanglewood,
museums, auctions and Hancock Shaker Village are among the
many attractions.

Innkeeper(s): Jerri & Dan Buehler. $125-325. 9 rooms with PB, 5 with FP, 3
suites and 3 cottages. Breakfast and snacks/refreshments included in rates.
Types of meals: Full gourmet bkfst. Beds: KQ. Cable TV, VCR, reading lamp,
refrigerator, clock radio, telephone and coffeemaker in room. Air conditioning.
Fax, stable, library, parlor games, fireplace and books and videos on premises. Weddings, small meetings and family reunions hosted. Antiquing, art galleries, bicycling, canoeing/kayaking, cross-country skiing, downhill skiing,
fishing, golf, hiking, horseback riding, live theater, museums, parks, shopping, tennis, water sports, modern dance and concerts nearby.
Publicity: *New York Magazine and The Discerning Traveler.*

Rockport C15

Addison Choate Inn

49 Broadway
Rockport, MA 01966-1527
(978)546-7543 (800)245-7543 Fax:(978)546-7638
E-mail: info@addisonchoateinn.com
Web: www.addisonchoateinn.com

Circa 1851. Antiques and reproductions decorate the interior
of this mid-19th-century home. The guest rooms feature
antique and wicker furnishings, artwork and polished, pine
floors. Freshly ground coffee, homemade baked breads, fruit
and cereals are served each morning in the inn's dining room,
which still contains the original fireplace with a beehive oven. If
weather permits, breakfasts are served on the inn's wraparound
porch, offering a view of the garden. Shops, restaurants and art
galleries all are nearby.

Innkeeper(s): Cynthia Francis & Ed Cambron. $105-175. 8 rooms, 5 with
PB, 1 suite and 2 cottages. Breakfast and snacks/refreshments included in
rates. Types of meals: Cont plus, early coffee/tea and afternoon tea. Beds:
KQT. Cable TV, reading lamp, refrigerator, ceiling fan, clock radio, turn-down
service and fireplace in room. Air conditioning. VCR, fax, copier, bicycles,

library, parlor games, telephone and fireplace on premises. Antiquing, art galleries, beach, bicycling, canoeing/kayaking, cross-country skiing, fishing, golf,
hiking, live theater, museums, parks, shopping and water sports nearby.
Publicity: *Yankee Magazine.*

"Our stay was a delight!"

Emerson Inn By The Sea

One Cathedral Avenue
Rockport, MA 01966
(978)546-6321 (800)964-5550 Fax:(978)546-7043
E-mail: info@emersoninnbythesea.com
Web: www.emersoninnbythesea.com

Circa 1846. This Greek Revival inn's namesake, Ralph Waldo
Emerson, once called the place, "thy proper summer home."
As it is the oldest continuously operated inn on Cape Ann,
decades of travelers agree with his sentiment. The guest rooms
are comfortable, yet tastefully furnished, and some boast ocean
views. The grounds include a
heated, saltwater swimming
pool as well as landscaped gardens. Breakfast is included in
the rates. Guests also can enjoy
dinner at The Grand Cafe, the
inn's award winning restaurant.

Innkeeper(s): Bruce & Michele Coates. $95-350. 36 rooms with PB, 2 with
FP, 2 suites and 3 conference rooms. Breakfast included in rates. Types of
meals: Full gourmet bkfst, early coffee/tea, afternoon tea, snacks/refresh-
ments and gourmet dinner. Restaurant on premises. Beds: KQDT. Modem
hook-up, data port, cable TV, refrigerator, clock radio, telephone, desk, fireplace and 11 with spa tubs in room. Air conditioning. TV, copier, swimming
and parlor games on premises. Weddings, small meetings, family reunions
and seminars hosted. Beach, bicycling, canoeing/kayaking, fishing, golf, hiking and live theater nearby.
Publicity: *TV 40 Springfield.*

"We were very impressed with every aspect of the Emerson Inn."

The Inn on Cove Hill

37 Mount Pleasant St
Rockport, MA 01966-1727
(978)546-2701 (888)546-2701 Fax:(978)546-1095

Circa 1771. Pirate gold found at Gully Point paid for this
Georgian Federal-style house. A white picket fence and granite
walkway welcome guests. Inside, an exquisitely crafted spiral staircase, random-width, pumpkin-pine floors and hand-forged hinges
display the original artisan's handiwork. Furnishings include family
heirlooms, four-poster canopy beds, and paintings by area artists.
Muffin Du Jour is baked fresh each day by Betsy. Bicycles can be
rented, and you can enjoy whale watching, fishing the local
waters, or simply exploring the antique shops and village streets.

Historic Interest: For historic sites, Gloucester is just five miles away, offering
tours of Beauport, a historic 1907 home and the Hammond Castle Museum.
Innkeeper(s): Betsy Eck. $75-145. 8 rooms, 6 with PB. Breakfast included
in rates. Types of meals: Cont plus and early coffee/tea. Beds: QDT. Reading
lamp in room. Air conditioning. Telephone on premises. Antiquing, fishing,
live theater and parks nearby.

Linden Tree Inn

26 King St
Rockport, MA 01966-1444
(978)546-2494 (800)865-2122 Fax:(978)546-3297

Circa 1870. The breakfasts at this Victorian-style inn keep
guests coming back year after year. Guests feast on home-baked
treats such as scones, coffee cakes or Sunday favorites, French

toast bread pudding, asparagus frittatas and spinach quiche. Each of the bedchambers features individual decor, and the innkeepers offer a formal living room and sun room for relaxation. The cupola affords a view of Mill Pond and Sandy Bay.

Historic Interest: Motif No. 1 is less than one mile from the home, and Boston is about 40 miles away.

Innkeeper(s): Tobey and John Shepherd. $80-136. 17 rooms, 12 with PB. Breakfast included in rates. Types of meals: Cont plus. Beds: KQDT. TV and all with air conditioning in room. Fax, copier, parlor games, telephone, fireplace and four units are available in the carriage on premises. Amusement parks, antiquing, art galleries, beach, bicycling, fishing, golf, hiking, live theater, museums, parks, shopping, tennis and water sports nearby.

Publicity: *Boston Magazine.*

"Great coffee! Love that apple walnut bread. Thank you for making this home."

Sally Webster Inn

34 Mount Pleasant St
Rockport, MA 01966-1713
(978)546-9251 (877)546-9251

Circa 1832. William Choate left this pre-Civil War home to be divided by his nine children. Sally Choate Webster, the ninth child, was to receive several first-floor rooms and the attic chamber, but ended up owning the entire home. The innkeepers have filled the gracious home with antiques and period reproductions, which complement the original pumpkin pine floors, antique door moldings and six fireplaces. Shops, restaurants, the beach and the rocky coast

are all within three blocks of the inn. Whale watching, kayaking, antique shops, music festivals, island tours and museums are among the myriad of nearby attractions. In addition to these, Salem is just 15 miles away, and Boston is a 35-mile drive.

Innkeeper(s): John & Kathy Fitzgerald. $85-125. 7 rooms with PB. Breakfast included in rates. Types of meals: Cont plus. Beds: KQDT. TV, guest phone available and air conditioning in room.

"All that a bed and breakfast should be."

The Tuck Inn B&B

17 High St
Rockport, MA 01966-1644
(978)546-7260 (800)789-7260
E-mail: info@tuckinn.com
Web: www.tuckinn.com

Circa 1790. Two recent renovations have served to make this charming Colonial inn all the more enticing. Period antiques and paintings by local artists are featured throughout the spacious inn. A favorite gathering spot is the living room with its fireplace, wide pine floors, tasteful furnishings and a piano available for guest use. Buffet breakfasts feature homemade breads, muffins, cakes and scones, granola accompanied by fresh fruit and yogurt. Guests may

take a dip in the swimming pool or at local beaches. Located on a quiet secondary street within easy walking distance to many art galleries, restaurants and shops of Bearskin Neck. A nearby train station offers convenient access to Boston.

Historic Interest: The inn is 10 minutes from Gloucester. Other historic towns, such as Salem, Boston, Lexington and Concord, are within an hour's drive of the inn.

Innkeeper(s): Liz & Scott Wood. $75-155. 11 rooms with PB and 1 suite. Breakfast included in rates. Types of meals: Cont plus and early coffee/tea. Beds: KQDT. Cable TV, reading lamp, clock radio, desk, all private baths and no smoking in room. Air conditioning. VCR, swimming, bicycles, library, parlor games, telephone and fireplace on premises. Antiquing, cross-country skiing, fishing, live theater, parks, shopping, sporting events and water sports nearby.

Publicity: *Fall River Herald News, North Shore News, Cape Ann Weekly and San Francisco Chronicle.*

"Wonderful people, lovely scenery, and great food, all good for the soul! Your hospitality and service was wonderful and we look forward to returning very soon!"

Yankee Clipper Inn

127 Granite St.
Rockport, MA 01966
(978)546-3407 (800)545-3699 Fax:(978)546-9730
E-mail: info@yankeeclipperinn.com
Web: www.yankeeclipperinn.com

Circa 1929. Sweeping views of the ocean and the rocky shoreline are eye-pleasers at this white clapboard, Art Deco oceanfront mansion and quarter deck. Polished mahogany woodwork and fireplaces reside with fine antiques imparting an old-fashioned, elegant ambiance. Sitting on one-and-a-half acres of breathtaking beauty, every guest bedroom overlooks an expansive vista. Enjoy the heated salt-water pool and New England hospitality.

Historic Interest: Lexington (35 miles), Concord (35 miles), Salem (20 miles), Gloucester (5 miles), Boston (40 miles).

Innkeeper(s): Randy & Cathy Marks. $129-349. 16 rooms with PB and 1 conference room. Breakfast included in rates. Types of meals: Full gourmet bkfst. Beds: KQDT. Modem hook-up, cable TV, reading lamp, clock radio, telephone, desk, hot tub/spa, some with DVD players and wireless Internet access in room. Central air. Fax, copier, swimming and fireplace on premises. Weddings, small meetings, family reunions and seminars hosted. Antiquing, art galleries, beach, bicycling, canoeing/kayaking, fishing, golf, hiking, live theater, museums, parks, shopping, tennis, water sports, whale watching, snorkeling and boat cruises nearby.

Publicity: *Gloucester Daily Times, Los Angeles Times, North Shore Life, Country Living, Discerning Traveler, Country Inns, Travel Holidays, Arringtons 'Best Ocean View', Boston Magazine, Channel 5 Chronicle and Great Country Inns.*

"The rooms were comfortable, the views breathtaking from most rooms, and the breakfasts delicious, with prompt and courteous service."

Rutland E9

The General Rufus Putnam House

344 Main St
Rutland, MA 01543-1303
(508)886-0200 Fax:(508)886-4864

Circa 1750. This historic Georgian colonial house, listed in the National Register, was the home of General Rufus Putnam, founder of Marietta, Ohio. A memorial tablet on the house states that "to him it is owing ... that the United States is not now a great slaveholding empire." Surrounded by tall maples and a rambling stone fence, the inn rests on seven acres of woodlands and meadows. There are eight fireplaces, blue Delft tiles and a beehive oven. Afternoon tea and breakfast are served fireside in the keeping room.

Historic Interest: Inn is a National Historic Landmark.

Innkeeper(s): Chris & Marcia Warrington. $100-175. 3 rooms, 1 with PB, 3 with FP. Breakfast and snacks/refreshments included in rates. Types of meals: Full bkfst, picnic lunch and afternoon tea. Beds: KQT. TV, reading lamp, clock

291

radio and turn-down service in room. Fax, copier, swimming, library, parlor games, telephone and fireplace on premises. Weddings, small meetings, family reunions and seminars hosted. Amusement parks, antiquing, cross-country skiing, downhill skiing, fishing, golf, live theater, parks, shopping, sporting events, tennis and skating nearby.

Publicity: *Sunday Telegram, The Land Mark and Washusett People.*

"We were thrilled with the beauty and luxury of this B&B and especially the wonderful hospitality."

Salem   D14

Amelia Payson House

16 Winter St
Salem, MA 01970-3807
(978)744-8304
E-mail: bbamelia@aol.com
Web: www.ameliapaysonhouse.com

Circa 1845. This elegantly restored two-story house features four white columns and is a prime example of Greek Revival architecture. Period antiques and wallpapers decorate the guest rooms and the formal dining room. Located in the heart of the Salem Historic District, it is a short walk to shops, museums, Pickering Wharf and waterfront restaurants. Train service to Boston is four blocks away. This is a non-smoking establishment.

Historic Interest: House of Seven Gables (2 blocks), Peabody Museum (1 block), Witch Museum (1 block), Maritime Historic Site (2 blocks).

Innkeeper(s): Ada & Donald Roberts. $95-155. 4 rooms with PB. Breakfast included in rates. Types of meals: Cont plus. Beds: QT. TV on premises. Antiquing and water sports nearby.

"Your hospitality has been a part of my wonderful experience."

Coach House Inn

284 Lafayette St
Salem, MA 01970-5462
(978)744-4092 (800)688-8689 Fax:(978)745-8031

Circa 1879. Captain Augustus Emmerton, one of the last Salem natives to earn his living from maritime commerce, built this stately home. Emmerton's house is an imposing example of Second Empire architecture and situated just two blocks from the harbor in a Salem historic district. Guest rooms are cheerful and romantic, furnished with antiques, four-poster beds and Oriental rugs. The House of Seven Gables and the Salem Witch Museum are nearby. Boston is just a short drive away.

$95-155. 11 rooms, 9 with PB, 7 with FP. Breakfast included in rates. Types of meals: Cont. Beds: QT. TV on premises.

Publicity: *The North Shore and Gourmet.*

Inn on Washington Square

53 Washington Sq
Salem, MA 01970
(978)741-4997
E-mail: debd731@aol.com
Web: washingtonsquareinn.com

Circa 1850. Overlooking the other historical homes surrounding Salem Commons, this Greek Revival house has many original details including wood mouldings and windows. Offering privacy for romance and relaxation, deluxe guest bedrooms feature four-poster or canopy beds, candles, Jacuzzi tubs, a video

library for in-room VCRs, and one with a fireplace. A breakfast basket of baked goods is delivered to the door. Hot beverages can be made in the personal coffeemakers, or freshly brewed coffee is available in the inn's main sitting area. Perennial gardens and a small koi pond grace the grounds.

Innkeeper(s): Deb D'Alessandro. Call for rates. 3 rooms with PB, 1 with FP. Breakfast included in rates. Types of meals: Cont, early coffee/tea and snacks/refreshments. Beds: KQ. Cable TV, VCR, reading lamp, refrigerator, clock radio and coffeemaker in room. Air conditioning. Antiquing, art galleries, beach, fishing, golf, live theater, museums, parks and shopping nearby.

The Salem Inn

7 Summer St
Salem, MA 01970-3315
(978)741-0680 (800)446-2995 Fax:(978)744-8924
E-mail: reservations@saleminnma.com
Web: www.saleminnma.com

Circa 1834. Located in the heart of one of America's oldest cities, the inn's 42 individually decorated guest rooms feature an array of amenities such as antiques, Jacuzzi baths, fireplaces and canopy beds. Comfortable and spacious one-bedroom family suites with kitchenettes, are available. A complimentary continental breakfast is offered. Nearby are fine restaurants, shops, museums, Pickering Wharf and whale watching boats for cruises.

Historic Interest: Located 18 miles from Boston, the inn is the perfect base to explore nearby Concord and Lexington, as well as the coastal towns of Rockport and Gloucester. Historic Salem is home to the Salem Witch Museum, the Peabody Essex Museum, the House of Seven Gables, Salem Maritime National Historic Site, Pickering Wharf and whale watching cruises.

Innkeeper(s): Richard & Diane Pabich. $129-290. 42 rooms with PB, 18 with FP and 11 suites. Breakfast included in rates. Types of meals: Cont. Beds: KQT. Cable TV and telephone in room. Air conditioning. Fax and fireplace on premises. Antiquing, fishing, live theater, parks, shopping, sporting events and water sports nearby.

Publicity: *New York Times, Boston Sunday Globe and Country Living Magazine.*

Stephen Daniels House

1 Daniels St
Salem, MA 01970-5214
(978)744-5709

Circa 1667. This lovely 300-year-old captain's house is one of the few three-story homes of this vintage still intact. Two large walk-in fireplaces grace the common rooms, and each guest room includes antique furnishings, a canopy bed and a wood-burning fireplace. A pleasant English garden is filled with colorful blooms. Children and well-behaved pets are welcome.

Innkeeper(s): Catherine Gill. $85-135. 4 rooms, 3 with PB, 4 with FP. Breakfast and afternoon tea included in rates. Types of meals: Cont plus and early coffee/tea. Beds: DT. TV and reading lamp in room. Air conditioning. Library, parlor games and fireplace on premises. Amusement parks, antiquing, art galleries, beach, bicycling, fishing, hiking, museums, parks, shopping, Endicot and Gordon nearby.

Publicity: *Country Living.*

"Like going back to earlier times."

Sandisfield   F3

New Boston Inn

Jct Rt 8 & 57
Sandisfield, MA 01255-0120
(413)258-4477 Fax:(413)258-4477
E-mail: nbi@bgernet.net
Web: newbostoninn.com

Circa 1737. Reflecting the surrounding beauty of the Southern Berkshires, this Federal-style inn built in 1737 boasts a tranquil setting amidst landscaped lawn and gardens. It features a vibrant history as well as hosting many celebrities. A ballroom with vaulted ceilings is popular for special events. Watch a video on the big screen TV or play pool in the spacious Billiards Room with two fireplaces. Inviting guest bedrooms ensure restful respites from the many outdoor activities available. Dining is always a delight, offering a Pub Menu or, for a more refined gourmet meal, an ever-changing specials menu may include Shrimp Scampi, Sesame Encrusted Salmon, Chicken Francese and Balsamic Glazed Roast Pork. Visit the Sandisfield Art Center, or enjoy a concert at Tanglewood.

Innkeeper(s): Conrad and Susan Ringeisen. $95-110. 8 rooms with PB and 1 conference room. Types of meals: Full bkfst. Restaurant on premises. Beds: QDT. TV and telephone in room. Limited handicap access.

Publicity: *Springfield Union News and Yankee Magazine.*

"We appreciate all you did to make us feel special."

Sandwich   I16

Captain Ezra Nye House

152 Main St
Sandwich, MA 02563-2232
(508)888-6142 (800)388-2278 Fax:(508)833-2897
E-mail: captainnye@adelphia.net
Web: www.captainezranyehouse.com

Circa 1829. The inn's namesake was a distinguished clipper ship captain who built this large Federal house in 1829. Sitting in the heart of the historic village, it is within walking distance

to the many local museums, shops and Cape Cod beaches. Fully restored, the inn now reflects the warmth and generosity of innkeepers Mike and Becky. Comfortable and beautifully decorated, guest bedrooms and suites are inviting retreats. Start the day with a freshly prepared gourmet breakfast. Arrangements have been made with Sandwich Hollows Golf Club to offer golf access and schedule tee times in advance. For a fun day trip, take a whale-watching tour from Provincetown.

Innkeeper(s): Becky & Mike Hanson. $105-150. 6 rooms with PB, 1 with FP and 2 suites. Breakfast included in rates. Types of meals: Full gourmet bkfst and early coffee/tea. Beds: KQ. Reading lamp, clock radio and ironing boards in room. TV, VCR, fax, library, parlor games, telephone and fireplace on premises. Small meetings and family reunions hosted. Antiquing, art galleries, beach, bicycling, fishing, golf, live theater, museums, parks, shopping, water sports, museums, plantation, bike trails and tennis nearby.

Publicity: *Glamour, Cape Cod Life, Toronto, Life, Cape Cod Times and Ottawa Citizen.*

"The prettiest room and most beautiful home we have been to. We had a wonderful time."

The Dan'l Webster Inn

149 Main St
Sandwich, MA 02563-2231
(508)888-3622
E-mail: info@danlwebsterinn.com
Web: www.danlwebsterinn.com

Circa 1692. Originally built as a parsonage in the late 17th century, the inn offers the essence of Colonial charm and elegance. Each of the 54 guest rooms is individually appointed with period furnishings. Many rooms offer canopy and four-poster beds, working fireplaces and whirlpool tubs. Guests are invited to

enjoy their meals by the fireside, in the sun room or moon-lit conservatory. The inn is recognized for its outstanding service and innovative cuisine. Eight new rooms offer spectacular amenities such as heated tile baths.

Innkeeper(s): Robert Catania. $109-379. 54 rooms with PB, 15 with FP and 2 conference rooms. Types of meals: Full gourmet bkfst, lunch and dinner. Restaurant on premises. Beds: KQDT. 15 rooms have whirlpool tubs in room. TV, fax, copier, telephone and heated swimming pool on premises. Limited handicap access. Fishing, golf and tennis nearby.

Publicity: *Bon Appetit, New York Times, Great Weekends, Los Angeles Times and Good Housekeeping.*

"Excellent accommodations and great food."

Inn At Sandwich Center

118 Tupper Rd
Sandwich, MA 02563-1828
(508)888-6958 (800)249-6949 Fax:(508)888-2746
E-mail: info@innatsandwich.com
Web: www.innatsandwich.com

Circa 1750. In the National Register, this 18th Century Federal home has many original features including a keeping room with a beehive oven. There are hardwood floors and period antiques throughout, and the guest rooms are spacious, some with fireplaces and four-poster beds. Air conditioning is available in summer. Breakfast is served in the keeping room on the inn's handmade table. Across the street is the Sandwich Glass Museum and guests can also walk to antique and gift shops as well as historic attractions such as the Gristmill and Hoxie House. Heritage Plantation, with 76 acres of rhododendrons, is also within walking distance. Sandwich is Cape Cod's most historic town, founded in 1637.

Innkeeper(s): Tom O'Brien and Deborah O'Brien. $85-135. 5 rooms with PB, 3 with FP. Breakfast included in rates. Types of meals: Full gourmet bkfst. Beds: KQT. Reading lamp, clock and chocolates in room. Telephone and fireplace on premises. Small meetings and family reunions hosted. Antiquing, fishing, golf, live theater, parks, shopping, tennis, water sports and museums in village nearby.

Publicity: *The Sandwich Broadsider.*

"A warm inviting inn where you are 'at home.'"

Scituate   F15

Allen House

18 Allen Place
Scituate, MA 02066-1302
(781)545-8221 Fax:(781)544-3192
E-mail: allenhousebnb@aol.com
Web: www.allenhousebnb.com

Circa 1905. Located approximately 25 miles southeast of Boston in the historic fishing village of Scituate (pronounced sit-you-it), this shingle-style Colonial sits on a hill overlooking the harbor. Originally built in 1905 by local town merchant William Paley Allen as a wedding gift to his daughter, the house has recently been lovingly restored by

innkeeper Meredith Emmons. Each guest bedroom has a private bath, one features a double whirlpool tub. Several rooms boast views of the water and two have gas log stoves. The main floor Harbor View Room is wheelchair accessible and amenable. A full gourmet breakfast is served on the porch with garden and harbor views or in the fireside dining room. Special dietary needs are accommodated with advance notice. Walk to the local boutique shops and restaurants.

Innkeeper(s): Meredith Emmons. $109-219. 6 rooms with PB and 1 suite. Breakfast and snacks/refreshments included in rates. Types of meals: Full gourmet bkfst and early coffee/tea. Beds: KQT. Cable TV, VCR, reading lamp, clock radio, robes and amenities basket in room. Central air. Fax, telephone, fireplace, complimentary beverages and snacks, wheelchair ramp and video library on premises. Antiquing, art galleries, beach, bicycling, fishing, golf, museums, parks, shopping, tennis, beaches, harbor, ocean, national/state parks, sailing/boating, shopping, fine dining, live music, movie theater, gym, restaurants, lighthouses, whale watching, boat cruises, bowling, bike and nature trails and massage therapy nearby.

Publicity: *Kent Life.*

"Everything one could possibly wish for is provided here.. a wonderful weekend."

Sheffield F2

B&B at Howden Farm

303 Rannapo Road
Sheffield, MA 01257
(413)229-8481 Fax:(413)229-0443
E-mail: bhowden@rnetworx.com
Web: www.howdenfarm.com

Circa 1830. Follow a quiet country road to this recently renovated home reflecting Greek Revival architecture. This working farm spans 250 acres, including 40 acres of crops that include pumpkins, sweet corn, blueberries and raspberries. Decorated and furnished with antiques, this intimate bed & breakfast offers romantic accommodations. Linger over a hearty breakfast before embarking on the day's adventures. This picturesque mountain area provides many opportunities for activities ranging from photography to skiing.

Innkeeper(s): Bruce Howden, David Prouty. $89-119. 3 rooms. Breakfast included in rates. Types of meals: Full bkfst. Beds: QDT. Cable TV and reading lamp in room. Air conditioning. Parlor games on premises. Antiquing, art galleries, bicycling, canoeing/kayaking, cross-country skiing, downhill skiing, fishing, golf, hiking, live theater, museums and parks nearby.

Birch Hill Bed & Breakfast

254 S Undermountain Rd
Sheffield, MA 01257-9639
(413)229-2143 (800)359-3969 Fax:(413)229-3405
E-mail: info@birchhillbb.com
Web: birchhillbb.com

Circa 1780. A slice of history is felt at this Colonial home that was built during the American Revolution. Graciously situated on 20 scenic acres in the Berkshires, it is adjacent to the Appalachian Trail. The Chestnut Room has a fantastic view and invites gathering to play the piano or games in front of the fire, listening to a CD or watching TV. Guest bedrooms and suites offer total relaxation. Some feature sitting areas and fireplaces. Creative, mouth-watering breakfasts begin a day of serendipity. Swim in the pool,

try croquet and kayak or canoe in the lake across the street. Bicycles are available to explore the local area.

Historic Interest: Hancock Shaker Village, Norman Rockwell Museum and the Colonial Ashley House are all nearby.

Innkeeper(s): Wendy & Michael Advocate. $110-215. 7 rooms, 5 with PB, 3 with FP, 1 suite and 1 conference room. Breakfast and afternoon tea included in rates. Types of meals: Full gourmet bkfst, veg bkfst and early coffee/tea. Beds: KDT. Reading lamp, CD player, refrigerator, clock radio and fireplace in room. Central air. TV, VCR, fax, copier, swimming, bicycles, library, child care, parlor games, telephone and fireplace on premises. Weddings, small meetings, family reunions and seminars hosted. Amusement parks, antiquing, art galleries, beach, bicycling, canoeing/kayaking, cross-country skiing, downhill skiing, fishing, golf, hiking, horseback riding, live theater, museums, parks, shopping, tennis and water sports nearby.

"My experience at your B&B was among the most pleasant I've ever experienced, from the moment I walked in to hear classical music. It was all divine. I can't wait to come back!"

Broken Hill Manor

771 West Road
Sheffield, MA 01257
(413)528-6159 (877)535-6159 Fax:(413)644-8872
E-mail: Mail@BrokenHillManor.com
Web: www.BrokenHillManor.com

Circa 1900. Four years of careful renovation has restored this 1900 Edwardian country manor house to its glory. Sitting on twelve landscaped acres of lawns and gardens, it is surrounded by 100 more acres of trees and birds. Relax in one of the many public areas. Read the paper with a cup of tea in the Gallery or sit by the fire in the Great Room. Romantic guest bedrooms are named after some of opera's famous heroines and decorated to reflect that genre with antiques from around the world. Breakfast in the dining room or on the terrace offers changing house specialties that may include Cinnamon Pancakes, English Bread Pudding and Summer Souffle. Visit downtown Great Barrington, just three miles away and enjoy the splendor of the Berkshires.

Historic Interest: Highly authentic, almost all original 1900s Manor House Home.

Innkeeper(s): Gaeten and Mike. $145-185. 8 rooms with PB. Breakfast and snacks/refreshments included in rates. Types of meals: Full bkfst, early coffee/tea and afternoon tea. Beds: Q. VCR, reading lamp, CD player, ceiling fan, clock radio, turn-down service, desk and air conditioning in room. TV, fax, copier, library, parlor games, telephone and fireplace on premises. Small meetings and seminars hosted. Antiquing, art galleries, bicycling, canoeing/kayaking, cross-country skiing, downhill skiing, fishing, golf, hiking, horseback riding, live theater, museums, parks and shopping nearby.

Staveleigh House

59 Main St
Sheffield, MA 01257-9701
(413)229-2129

Circa 1821. The Reverend Bradford, minister of Old Parish Congregational Church, the oldest church in the Berkshires, built this home for his family. Afternoon tea is served and the inn is especially favored for its splendid breakfast and gracious hospitality. Located next to the town green, the house is in a historic district in the midst of several fine antique shops. It is also near Tanglewood, skiing and all Berkshire attractions.

Innkeeper(s): Ali A. Winston. $115-160. 7 rooms, 5 with PB. Breakfast and afternoon tea included in rates. Types of meals: Full bkfst and early coffee/tea. Beds: KQDT. Reading lamp, ceiling fan, clock radio, turn-down service and desk in room. Air conditioning. Telephone, fireplace and terrycloth bath robes on premises. Limited handicap access. Weddings, small meetings, family reunions and seminars hosted. Antiquing, cross-country skiing, downhill skiing, fishing, live theater, parks, shopping, water sports and art galleries nearby.

Publicity: *Los Angeles Times, Boston Globe and House and Garden Magazine.*

"The hospitality at Staveleigh House is deeper and more thoughtful than any you will find elsewhere." — House & Gardens Magazine

Shrewsbury   E10

Sumner House

5 Church Rd
Shrewsbury, MA 01545-1836
(508)845-6446 Fax:(508)846-6446
E-mail: info@sumnerhouse.com
Web: www.sumnerhouse.com

Circa 1797. Commissioned by Reverend Joseph Sumner, this sprawling Colonial home sits on two acres of shaded lawns and perennial gardens. Listed in the National Register, the inn's pristine character has been retained for all these years. A letter from George Washington to Artemus Ward was found in the home's safe in 1980. Furnished with family heirlooms, the array of common rooms includes a study, great room with fireplace, parlor, living room, sunroom boasting a TV and an antique tool collection. Sunny guest bedrooms feature wide plank and splatter-painted floors. The Ward Room boasts a deep soaker tub. Expect signature breakfast dishes like Sumner Eggs, blueberry and apple pancakes or French toast strata to round off the meal.

Innkeeper(s): Bill & Ellen Glascock. $85-100. 5 rooms, 3 with PB. Breakfast and snacks/refreshments included in rates. Types of meals: Full bkfst, veg bkfst and early coffee/tea. Beds: KD. Data port, snack bar, clock radio, turndown service, fireplace, some with modem hook-up and TV in room. Air conditioning. TV, VCR, fax, copier, library, parlor games, telephone, fireplace, upstairs sitting room with coffee and soda on premises. Weddings, small meetings, family reunions and seminars hosted. Antiquing, art galleries, bicycling, canoeing/kayaking, downhill skiing, fishing, golf, museums, parks, shopping, sporting events, tennis, water sports and wineries nearby.

South Deerfield   D6

Deerfield's Yellow Gabled House

111 N Main St
South Deerfield, MA 01373-1026
(413)665-4922

Circa 1800. Huge maple trees shade the yard of this historic house, four miles from historic Deerfield and one mile from Route 91. Decorated with antiques, the bed chambers feature coordinating bedspreads and window treatments. One suite includes a sitting room, and canopy beds are another romantic touch. Breakfasts include items such as three-cheese stuffed French toast, an apple puff and fresh fruit topped with a yogurt-cheese sauce. The home is near historic Deerfield, and guests can walk to restaurants. The battle of Bloody Brook Massacre in 1675 occurred at this site, now landscaped with perennial English gardens. Yankee Candle is only one-half mile away and Historic Deerfield is only three miles away.

Innkeeper(s): Edna Julia Stahelek. $80-150. 3 rooms. Breakfast included in rates. Types of meals: Full gourmet bkfst and early coffee/tea. Beds: QT. Cable TV, reading lamp, ceiling fan, clock radio and telephone in room. Air conditioning. VCR on premises. Small meetings and family reunions hosted. Antiquing, bicycling, cross-country skiing, downhill skiing, fishing, live theater, shopping, sporting events and restaurants nearby.

Publicity: *Recorder, Boston Globe and Springfield Republican.*

"We are still speaking of that wonderful weekend and our good fortune in finding you."

South Egremont   F2

Egremont Inn

Old Sheffield Rd
South Egremont, MA 01258
(413)528-2111 (800)859-1780 Fax:(413)528-3284
E-mail: egremontinn@taconic.net
Web: www.egremontinn.com

Circa 1780. This three-story inn, listed in the National Register of Historic Places, was once a stagecoach stop. Guest rooms are furnished with country antiques. Dinner is available Wednesday through Sunday in the elegant dining room, and there is also a tavern. Five fireplaces adorn the common rooms. A wraparound porch, tennis courts and a swimming pool are on the premises.

Historic Interest: Minutes from the site of Shays Rebellion, formerly a mustering-in location and hospital during the Revolutionary War.

Innkeeper(s): Karen & Steven Waller. $90-225. 20 rooms with PB, 2 suites and 3 conference rooms. Breakfast included in rates. Types of meals: Full bkfst and dinner. Restaurant on premises. Beds: KQDT. Reading lamp, telephone and desk in room. Air conditioning. TV, VCR, swimming, tennis, parlor games and fireplace on premises. Weddings, small meetings, family reunions and seminars hosted. Antiquing, cross-country skiing, downhill skiing, fishing, hiking, live theater, parks and shopping nearby.

"All the beauty of the Berkshires without the hassle, the quintessential country inn."

Weathervane Inn

Rt 23, Main St
South Egremont, MA 01258
(413)528-9580 (800)528-9580 Fax:(413)528-1713

Circa 1785. The original post-and-beam New England farmhouse with its beehive oven was added on to throughout its history. It has been restored to combine today's modern amenities with the charm of the inn's historic past. The inn's historic architectural features include broad plank floors, tree trunk supports and granite columns. A full breakfast is offered every morning.

Historic Interest: Norman Rockwell Museum, Berkshire Museum, The Clark Museum and Hoosac Railroad Tunnel built during the Civil War are all nearby.

Innkeeper(s): Maxine & Jeffrey Lome. $115-245. 8 rooms with PB and 2 suites. Breakfast included in rates. Types of meals: Full bkfst. Beds: KQD. Antiquing, cross-country skiing, downhill skiing, fishing, golf, live theater and water sports nearby.

Publicity: *New York Times, Berkshire Eagle, Boston Herald, Newsday and Daily News.*

Springfield   F6

Lathrop House

188 Sumner Avenue
Springfield, MA 01108
(413)736-6414 Fax:(413)736-6414
E-mail: dmh@dianamarahenry.com

Circa 1899. Sitting on one scenic acre in the midst of the historic residential district of Forest Park Heights, this 1899 Victorian is known as "The Mansion House." Recently restored, it features original carved mantels, wood paneling, stained glass and a formal staircase. Swing on a columned porch overlooking the wide lawn. Relax on the veranda, smell the scent of the rose garden or picnic under the shade trees in the back yard. Elegant guest bedrooms with high-ceilings are accented with contemporary art, in-room libraries, designer bathrooms with showers and clawfoot tubs. A two-bedroom apartment with bath, kitchen, living and dining rooms offers spacious privacy for families or larger groups. Experience a dream breakfast as requested. Across from a park, hike trails or swim in the public pool.

Innkeeper(s): Diana Henry. $80-125. 4 rooms with PB and 1 suite. Breakfast and snacks/refreshments included in rates. Types of meals: Cont plus, early coffee/tea, picnic lunch and afternoon tea. Beds: KQDT. Modem hook-up, cable TV, VCR, reading lamp, CD player, refrigerator, ceiling fan, snack bar, clock radio, coffeemaker, turn-down service and desk in room. Air conditioning. Fax, copier, library, parlor games, laundry facility and private boat for charter on premises. Weddings, small meetings, family reunions and seminars hosted. Amusement parks, antiquing, art galleries, beach, bicycling, canoeing/kayaking, fishing, golf, live theater, museums, parks, shopping, tennis, water sports, wineries, Basketball Hall of Fame, Big E (New England Regional Fair in September) and Six Flags nearby.

Stockbridge   E2

Historic Merrell Inn

1565 Pleasant St, Rt 102
Stockbridge, MA 01260
(413)243-1794 (800)243-1794 Fax:(413)243-2669
E-mail: info@merrell-inn.com
Web: www.merrell-inn.com

Circa 1794. This elegant stagecoach inn was carefully preserved under supervision of the Society for the Preservation of New England Antiquities. Architectural drawings of Merrell Inn have been preserved by the Library of Congress. Eight fire-

places in the inn include two with original beehive and warming ovens. An antique circular birdcage bar serves as a check-in desk. Comfortable rooms feature canopy and four-poster beds with Hepplewhite and Sheraton-style antiques. The Riverview Suite is tucked on the back wing of the building and has a private porch which overlooks the Housatonic River.

Historic Interest: Hancock Shaker Village and the Norman Rockwell Museum are all nearby.

Innkeeper(s): George Crockett. $95-270. 10 rooms with PB, 4 with FP. Breakfast included in rates. Types of meals: Full bkfst. Beds: KQT. Reading lamp, refrigerator, clock radio, telephone, desk and fireplaces (some rooms) in room. Air conditioning. Fax, parlor games and fireplace on premises. Family reunions and seminars hosted. Antiquing, cross-country skiing, fishing, hiking, live theater, parks, shopping, Tanglewood Music Festival and Norman Rockwell Museum nearby.

Publicity: *Americana, Country Living, New York Times, Boston Globe, Country Accents, Travel Holiday and USA Today.*

"We couldn't have chosen a more delightful place to stay in the Berkshires. Everything was wonderful. We especially loved the grounds and the gazebo by the river."

The Inn at Stockbridge

PO Box 618
Stockbridge, MA 01262-0618
(413)298-3337 (888)466-7865 Fax:(413)298-3406
E-mail: innkeeper@stockbridgeinn.com
Web: www.stockbridginn.com

Circa 1906. Twelve secluded acres surround this white-pillared Georgian-style mansion, restored to a delightful bed & breakfast. A comfortable elegance is enhanced by antiques and a

tasteful decor. Soft music, warm fires and good books are found in the library, living room and TV game room. The formal dining room is the perfect setting for a candlelight breakfast that includes culinary delights such as lemon cottage cheese pancakes. Spacious guest bedrooms offer charm and style for every taste. Some feature a porch with sweeping views of the meadow, or a deck overlooking the reflecting pond. Canopied four-poster beds, fireplaces, skylights and whirlpools instill a touch of romance and luxury. For an afternoon repose, enjoy varieties of wine and cheese. Visit the nearby Norman Rockwell Museum and attend concerts at Tanglewood.

Innkeeper(s): Alice & Len Schiller. $140-320. 16 rooms with PB, 9 with FP, 8 suites and 1 conference room. Breakfast and snacks/refreshments included in rates. Types of meals: Full gourmet bkfst and early coffee/tea. Beds: KQT. Cable TV, VCR, reading lamp, CD player, ceiling fan, clock radio, telephone and hot tub/spa in room. Air conditioning. Fax, copier, swimming, library, parlor games and fireplace on premises. Handicap access. Antiquing, art galleries, bicycling, canoeing/kayaking, cross-country skiing, downhill skiing, fishing, golf, hiking, horseback riding, live theater, museums, parks, shopping and tennis nearby.

Publicity: *Vogue, New York, New York Daily News, Country Inns Northeast, Arts & Antiques and Travel channel.*

"Classy & comfortable."

The Red Lion Inn

Main St
Stockbridge, MA 01262
(413)298-5545 Fax:(413)298-5130
E-mail: reservations@redlioninn.com
Web: www.redlioninn.com

Circa 1773. The venerable white clapboard Red Lion Inn has operated as a tavern and inn since its inception. The originator, Silas Pepoon, is said to have hosted a rally to protest the use of British goods. This meeting led to the approval of a document said to have been the first Declaration of Independence. A vital part of the area's history, the inn is one of the last of the 18th-century Berkshire hotels still in operation. The collection of fine antique furnishings, colonial pewter and Staffordshire china found in the inn's parlor was gathered in the late 19th century by proprietor Mrs. Charles Plumb. The inn is part of the Norman Rockwell "Stockbridge Main Street at Christmas" painting. Traditional decor extends to the comfortable guest rooms and some have four-poster and canopy beds, fireplaces, antique vanities and desks. The inn is home to three restaurants. Rocking on the long front porch is a favored activity, and one wonders if former visitors such as presidents Cleveland, McKinley, Theodore Roosevelt, Coolidge and Franklin Roosevelt enjoyed the privilege. Contemporary regional cuisine is the specialty of the inn's restaurants.

Innkeeper(s): Bruce Finn. Call for rates. 108 rooms, 94 with PB, 25 suites and 7 cottages. Types of meals: Full bkfst, early coffee/tea, lunch, picnic lunch, gourmet dinner and room service. Restaurant on premises. Beds: KQT. Cable TV, reading lamp, telephone, turn-down service and desk in room. VCR, fax, copier, swimming, library, fireplace and 7 meeting rooms on premises. Limited handicap access. Weddings, small meetings, family reunions and seminars hosted. Antiquing, cross-country skiing, downhill skiing, fishing, golf, live theater, shopping and tennis nearby.

Publicity: *Country Folk Art, The Age and USA Today.*

"My family and I travel quite a bit and your facility and employees top them all."

Seasons on Main B&B

47 Main St
Stockbridge, MA 01262
(413)298-5419 (888)955-4747 Fax:(413)298-0092
E-mail: info@seasonsonmain.com
Web: www.seasonsonmain.com

Circa 1862. Seasons on Main was built during the Civil War. The historic Greek Revival home includes a sweeping veranda where guests can relax on wicker chairs and loveseats. The interior is Victorian in style, and two of the rooms include a fireplace. Breakfasts include items such as fresh fruit, muffins or coffeecake and entrees such as baked French toast strata. The inn offers close access to Tanglewood, the Norman Rockwell Museum, Berkshire Botanical Gardens, Edith Wharton's home, hiking, skiing and biking.

Innkeeper(s): Pat O'Neill. $135-250. 4 rooms with PB, 2 with FP. Breakfast and snacks/refreshments included in rates. Types of meals: Full bkfst. Beds: KQD. Cable TV, VCR, reading lamp, refrigerator, ceiling fan, clock radio and turn-down service in room. Air conditioning. TV, fax, parlor games, telephone and fireplace on premises. Antiquing, art galleries, bicycling, cross-country skiing, downhill skiing, fishing, golf, hiking, live theater, museums, parks, shopping and tennis nearby.

The Stockbridge Country Inn

Rt 183, 26 Glendale Road
Stockbridge, MA 01262
(413)298-4015 Fax:(413)298-3413
E-mail: innkeeper@stockbridgecountryinn.com
Web: www.stockbridgecountryinn.com

Circa 1856. Shaded by tall trees, this Federal country house sits on a knoll overlooking four acres of private grounds with perennial beds, green lawns, an in-ground pool and a period carriage barn. Decorated in an American cottage style, the guest bedrooms feature four-poster canopy beds and upcountry antiques. A library and living room each offer a fireplace for cool weather. And in summer, a plentiful hot breakfast is enjoyed on the screened porch. The inn is close to Rockwell Museum, Stockbridge Center and minutes to all Berkshire attractions.

Innkeeper(s): Diane & Vernon Reuss. $145-389. 8 rooms with PB. Breakfast included in rates. Types of meals: Full bkfst and early coffee/tea. Beds: QT. Reading lamp and ceiling fan in room. Air conditioning. VCR, fax, copier, swimming, telephone and fireplace on premises. Small meetings and family reunions hosted. Antiquing, cross-country skiing, downhill skiing, shopping and upscale outlets nearby.

"A wonderful experience, please adopt me."

Stow   D11

Amerscot House

61 West Acton Rd
Stow, MA 01775-2112
(978)897-0666 Fax:(978)897-6914
E-mail: doreen@amerscot.com
Web: www.amerscot.com

Circa 1734. Gracing a rural New England town, this 1734 center chimney farmhouse sits on two and a half tranquil acres of lawns and gardens. Linger over sherry or tea and scones by the family room fireplace. Stay in a spacious guest bedroom with fresh flowers, antiques, quilts, a fireplace and cable TV. The Lindsay Suite features a canopy bed, sitting room and marble-walled bathroom with a Jacuzzi. Light eaters appreciate fresh fruit and homemade Amerscot granola or porridge. For a more substantial breakfast, muffins, raspberry swirl French toast, eggs Benedict or quiche can be also enjoyed in the Colonial dining room or the greenhouse. Shop in nearby Concord or Boston and visit the many historic sites. Seasonally, canoe the Sudbury or Assabet Rivers and ski local trails.

Historic Interest: The inn was built in 1734. It has wide floorboards, two bake ovens, six fireplaces, old window panes and antique furniture.

Innkeeper(s): Doreen Gibson. $130-150. 3 rooms with PB, 1 suite and 1 conference room. Breakfast and snacks/refreshments included in rates. Types of meals: Full gourmet bkfst, early coffee/tea and afternoon tea. Beds: KQ. Data port, cable TV, reading lamp, clock radio, telephone, turn-down service, voice mail, fireplace and suite has Jacuzzi in room. Air conditioning. Fax, copier, parlor games and fireplace on premises. Small meetings hosted. Antiquing, art galleries, bicycling, canoeing/kayaking, cross-country skiing, golf, hiking, museums, parks, shopping and historical sites nearby.

Sturbridge   F8

Publick House Historic Inn & Country Lodge

PO Box 187, On The Common Rte 131
Sturbridge, MA 01566-0187
(800)PUB-LICK Fax:(508)347-5073
E-mail: info@publickhouse.com
Web: www.publickhouse.com

Circa 1771. This property includes four lodging facilities, two restaurants, 12 meeting rooms and 60 acres of countryside. Many special events take place throughout the year, including a New England Lobster Bake, a Beer Dinner, Harvest Weekend and Yankee Winter Weekends. All the rooms in the main building are decorated with period furnishings.

Innkeeper(s): Albert Cournoyer. $79-165. 126 rooms with PB and 6 suites. Types of meals: Full gourmet bkfst, early coffee/tea, gourmet lunch, picnic lunch, snacks/refreshments and gourmet dinner. Restaurant on premises. Beds: KQDT. Cable TV, reading lamp and telephone in room. Air conditioning. Fax, swimming and fireplace on premises. Limited handicap access. Weddings, small meetings, family reunions and seminars hosted. Antiquing, cross-country skiing, fishing, live theater, parks, shopping and sporting events nearby.

Sturbridge Country Inn

PO Box 60, 530 Main St
Sturbridge, MA 01566-0060
(508)347-5503 Fax:(508)347-5319
E-mail: info@sturbridgecountryinn.com
Web: www.sturbridgecountryinn.com

Circa 1840. Shaded by an old silver maple, this classic Greek Revival house boasts a two-story columned entrance. The attached carriage house now serves as the parlor and displays the original post-and-beam construction and exposed rafters. All guest rooms have individual fireplaces and whirlpool tubs and include breakfast with champagne. They are appointed gracefully in colonial style furnishings, including queen-size and four-posters. A patio and gazebo are favorite summertime retreats. A five-star restaurant and outdoor heated pool are also on the premesis.

Innkeeper(s): Patricia Affenito. $59-179. 13 rooms with PB, 13 with FP, 2 suites and 1 conference room. Breakfast included in rates. Types of meals: Cont, early coffee/tea and room service. Restaurant on premises. Beds: KQ. Cable TV, VCR, reading lamp, refrigerator, ceiling fan, clock radio, telephone, desk and hot tub/spa in room. Air conditioning. TV, fax, copier, spa, swimming, fireplace, restaurant, luxury suites, hair dryer and iron on premises. Weddings, small meetings, family reunions and seminars hosted. Antiquing, cross-country skiing, downhill skiing, fishing, live theater, parks, shopping, water sports, casinos and old Sturbridge Village nearby.

Publicity: *Southbridge Evening News and Worcester Telegram & Gazette.*

"Best lodging I've ever seen."

Sudbury   D12

Arabian Horse Inn

277 Old Sudbury Rd
Sudbury, MA 01776-1842
(978)443-7400 (800)272-2426 Fax:(978)443-0234
E-mail: info@arabianhorseinn.com
Web: www.arabianhorseinn.com

Circa 1880. Secluded on nine wooded acres with a horse farm, this 1880 Queen Anne Victorian offers the ultimate in privacy and romance. This inn is the perfect retreat to celebrate birthdays, anniversaries or other special occasions. The three-room Tanah Suite with a canopy bed, two-person Jacuzzi and fireplace is a honeymoon favorite. A stay in the two-room Orlandra Suite featuring a draped four-poster bed, two-person Jacuzzi and huge balcony is also a popular pleaser. A complete breakfast is made at a flexible time to suit every taste with delicious entrees and accompaniments. Enjoy the meal in the Ye Old Worlde Café, on the veranda under the pergola or in-room. Lunch or dinner can be arranged with advance reservation. Tours are gladly given of the original four-story barn with post and beam ceiling and huge cupola.

Innkeeper(s): Joan & Richard Beers. $169-310. 3 suites, 1 with FP. Breakfast and afternoon tea included in rates. Types of meals: Full gourmet bkfst, early coffee/tea and room service. Beds: K. Cable TV, VCR, reading lamp, stereo, ceiling fan, clock radio, telephone and desk in room. Air conditioning. Fax, copier, stable, library, pet boarding, parlor games and fireplace on premises. Weddings, small meetings, family reunions and seminars hosted. Amusement parks, antiquing, cross-country skiing, downhill skiing, fishing, golf, live theater, parks, shopping, sporting events, tennis and water sports nearby.

Hunt House Inn

330 Boston Post Rd.
Sudbury, MA 01776
(978)440-9525 Fax:(978)440-9082
E-mail: mollyhunthouse@ix.netcom.com
Web: www.hunthouseinn.com

Circa 1850. Well-suited as a bed and breakfast, this early American farmhouse and barn is located in the King Philip Historic District. Fully restored, it is furnished with period antiques and boasts an eclectic decor. The air-conditioned guest bedrooms feature adjoining rooms. The Executive Suite includes a sitting area and separate entrance. Breakfast is a delight every morning, offering combinations of warm muffins, omelettes and egg dishes, fresh fruit, homemade waffles with Vermont maple syrup, sausages and an assortment of vegetarian entrees. Dietary restrictions are accommodated with ease. Visit the historic sites of nearby Boston.

Innkeeper(s): Molly Davidson. $85-100. 3 rooms with PB, 2 suites and 1 conference room. Breakfast, afternoon tea and snacks/refreshments included in rates. Types of meals: Full gourmet bkfst, veg bkfst and early coffee/tea.

Beds: QDT. Modem hook-up, TV, reading lamp, snack bar, clock radio and telephone in room. Air conditioning. VCR, fax and laundry facility on premises. Weddings, small meetings and family reunions hosted. Antiquing, art galleries, beach, canoeing/kayaking, golf, hiking, live theater, museums, parks, shopping, sporting events, tennis and wineries nearby.

Longfellow's Wayside Inn

Wayside Inn Rd
Sudbury, MA 01776
(978)443-1776 Fax:(978)443-8041
E-mail: innkeepers@wayside.org
Web: www.wayside.org

Circa 1716. Henry Ford founded the non-profit corporation that manages the Wayside Inn in 1944, to preserve it as a historic and literary shrine. The inn's second owner is known to have led the colonists of Sudbury on the march to Concord on April 19, 1775, toward the Old North Bridge. Originally opened as How's Tavern in 1716, it later became Red Horse Tavern. Finally, in 1897, a new owner, acknowledging the popular association with Longfellow's poem Tales of a Wayside Inn, changed the name. The Old Barroom, Longfellow's Parlor, the pianoforte and grandfather clock are all here. A reproduction Grist Mill, and the Redstone Schoolhouse are open for touring. Allow six to 12 months ahead for reservations.

Historic Interest: An authentic colonial for nearly three hundred years now, a historic site with exhibits and educators to teach about our colonial past.

Innkeeper(s): Bob Purrington. $96-155. 10 rooms with PB and 1 conference room. Breakfast included in rates. Types of meals: Full bkfst, veg bkfst and early coffee/tea. Beds: KQDT. Reading lamp, clock radio, telephone and desk in room. Central air. TV, fax, copier, stable, library, parlor games, fireplace and gift shop on premises. Limited handicap access.

"Charming! I'm glad the inn is still here after all these years! The Inn is just beautiful, and we love the food!"

Vineyard Haven   K16

The Crocker House Inn

12 Crocker Ave, PO Box 1658
Vineyard Haven, MA 02568
(508)693-1151 (800)772-0206 Fax:(508)693-1123
E-mail: crockerinn@aol.com
Web: www.crockerhouseinn.com

Circa 1900. Enjoy all that Martha's Vineyard has to offer at this historic inn, which has close access to beaches, restaurants, galleries, museums, shops and a winery. Guest rooms offer amenities such as fireplaces, Jacuzzi's, water views or private porches. The front porch is lined with rockers, a perfect spot for relaxation with a splendid harbor view. The innkeepers provide a continental breakfast to get guests started before heading out and enjoying the island. The inn is within walking distance to the ferry service.

Innkeeper(s): Jeff & Jynell Kristal. $115-365. 8 rooms, 7 with PB, 2 with FP and 1 suite. Breakfast and snacks/refreshments included in rates. Types of meals: Cont plus. Beds: KQDT. Modem hook-up, data port, cable TV, reading lamp, refrigerator, snack bar, clock radio, telephone, voice mail and suite with hot tub/spa in room. Air conditioning. TV, fax and fireplace on premises. Small meetings and family reunions hosted. Antiquing, art galleries, beach, bicycling, canoeing/kayaking, fishing, golf, hiking, horseback riding, live theater, parks, shopping, tennis and wineries nearby.

The Look Inn

Box 2195, 25 Look St
Vineyard Haven, MA 02568-2195
(508)693-6893

Circa 1806. Located three blocks from the beaches and ferry and in the Vineyard Haven Historic District, the Look Inn is a restored farmhouse, bordered by a fieldstone wall. Rooms are furnished with antiques and country pieces and have queen beds and private sinks. Guests can enjoy a good book from the library with its cozy fireplace or enjoy the night sky in the on-site hot tub. Breakfast is served on the sun porch overlooking an acre of lawn and gardens. There's a fishpond and hammock. Photo/hiking tours are offered, and massages can be scheduled with the innkeeper, who is a massage and yoga therapist.

Innkeeper(s): Freddy Rundlet, Catherine Keller. $80-100. 3 rooms. Breakfast included in rates. Types of meals: Cont plus and early coffee/tea. Beds: Q. Reading lamp and hot tub/spa in room. Bicycles, library, parlor games, telephone, fireplace, hot hub, massage and photo tours on premises. Family reunions hosted. Antiquing, fishing, golf, live theater, parks, shopping, sporting events, tennis, water sports, paradise, sailing and swimming nearby.

Martha's Place

114 Main
Vineyard Haven, MA 02568
(508)693-0253
E-mail: info@marthasplace.com
Web: www.marthasplace.com

Circa 1840. Pink roses surround this beautifully decorated inn offering a romantic setting in an elegant Greek Revival-style home. Polished wood floors, Oriental rugs, antiques, chandeliers and meticulously detailed decor provides a nestling place after a day of playing tennis on nearby clay courts, sailing, cycling the island or poking around nearby shops. Ask for the suite for special water view, velvet half-canopy bed and a sitting room separated by French doors. Floor-to-ceiling windows light the dining room where breakfast is served with crystal and silver. You may enjoy it brought to your room upon prior arrangement, as well. The inn is directly across from Owen Park Beach overlooking Vineyard Haven Harbor. The ferry is only a block away.

Innkeeper(s): Martin & Richard. $200-395. 6 rooms with PB, 3 with FP, 1 suite and 1 conference room. Types of meals: Cont plus. Beds: QD. Modem hook-up, data port, reading lamp, CD player, clock radio, telephone, desk and voice mail in room. Air conditioning. Bicycles and fireplace on premises. Weddings and family reunions hosted. Antiquing, art galleries, beach, bicycling, canoeing/kayaking, fishing, golf, hiking, horseback riding, live theater, museums, parks, shopping, tennis and water sports nearby.

Publicity: Boston Magazine, Frommer's Cape Cod, Out & About Magazine, Boston Sunday Herald, Our World Magazine, Cape Cod Travel Guide, Maisons Cote'Quest Magazine and AMC television.

Thorncroft Inn

460 Main St, PO Box 1022
Vineyard Haven, MA 02568-1022
(508)693-3333 (800)332-1236 Fax:(508)693-5419
E-mail: innkeeper@thorncroft.com
Web: www.thorncroft.com

Circa 1918. The Thorncroft Estate is a classic craftsman bungalow with a dominant roof and neo-colonial details. It was built by Chicago grain merchant John Herbert Ware as the guest house of a large oceanfront estate. Most guest rooms include working fireplaces and canopied beds. Some also boast two-person whirlpool tubs or private 300-gallon hot tubs. The

inn is situated in three buildings on three-and-one-half acres of lawns and woodlands. In its naturally romantic setting, the Thorncroft provides the perfect ambiance for honeymooners, anniversaries and special couples' getaways. Full breakfasts and afternoon teas are served in the dining rooms, but guests can opt for a continental breakfast served in their room.

Innkeeper(s): Karl & Lynn Buder. $200-550. 14 rooms with PB, 10 with FP and 1 cottage. Breakfast and afternoon tea included in rates. Types of meals: Full bkfst and room service. Beds: KQD. TV in room. Fax, copier and telephone on premises. Antiquing, fishing, live theater and water sports nearby.

Publicity: Cape Cod Life, Travel & Leisure, Wheel of Fortune, Hollywood Squares and Travel Channel-Great Country Inns.

"It's the type of place where we find ourselves falling in love all over again."

Twin Oaks Inn

28 Edgartown Rd
Vineyard Haven, MA 02568
(508)693-1066 (800)339-1066 Fax:(508)696-6099
E-mail: innkeeper@twinoaksinn.net
Web: www.twinoaksinn.net

Circa 1906. When visiting Martha's Vineyard, Twin Oaks offers two pleasurable places to choose from that are within walking distance to the beach, ferry or downtown shops. Stay at the award-winning Clark House, a classic bed & breakfast or the Hanover House, an elegant three-diamond country inn just next door. Gather on one of the porches, the large backyard or private brick patio and gazebo. Complimentary bikes and high-speed Internet access are available on a first come first serve basis. Each of the comfortable guest bedrooms offer Internet access. Join the "breakfast party" for a bountiful continental-plus morning meal.

Innkeeper(s): Steve and Judy Perlman. $99-315. 20 rooms. Breakfast included in rates. Types of meals: Cont plus. Beds: KQD. Cable TV, reading lamp, refrigerator, ceiling fan and two with fireplace in room. Air conditioning. Fax, copier, parlor games and telephone on premises. Antiquing, art galleries, beach, bicycling, canoeing/kayaking, fishing, golf, hiking, horseback riding, live theater, museums, parks, shopping, tennis, water sports and wineries nearby.

Publicity: New York Times.

Ware E7

The Wildwood Inn

121 Church St
Ware, MA 01082-1203
(413)967-7798 (800)860-8098
E-mail: website@wildwoodbb.net
Web: www.wildwoodinn.net

Circa 1891. This yellow Victorian has a wraparound porch and a beveled-glass front door. American primitive antiques include a collection of New England cradles and heirloom quilts, a saddlemaker's bench and a spinning wheel. The inn's two acres are dotted with maple, chestnut and apple trees. Through the woods, you'll find a river.

Historic Interest: Old Sturbridge Village (15 miles), Old Deerfield (30 miles), Amherst College (15 miles).

Innkeeper(s): Fraidell Fenster & Richard Watson. $60-110. 9 rooms, 7 with PB, 1 suite and 2 conference rooms. Breakfast and afternoon tea included in rates. Types of meals: Full bkfst and early coffee/tea. Beds: KQDT. Reading lamp, turn-down service and desk in room. Air conditioning. Library, parlor games, telephone, fireplace and canoe on premises. Limited handicap access. Weddings, small meetings, family reunions and seminars hosted. Amusement parks, antiquing, cross-country skiing, downhill skiing, fishing, hiking, live theater, parks, shopping, sporting events, kayaking and great restaurants nearby.

Publicity: *Boston Globe, National Geographic Traveler, Country and Worcester Telegram & Gazette.*

"Excellent accommodations, not only in rooms, but in the kind and thoughtful way you treat your guests. We'll be back!"

Wareham   I15

Mulberry B&B

257 High St
Wareham, MA 02571-1407
(508)295-0684 (866)295-0684

Circa 1847. This former blacksmith's house is in the historic district of town and has been featured on the local garden club house tour. Frances, a former school teacher, has decorated the guest rooms in a country style with antiques. A deck, shaded by a tall mulberry tree, looks out to the back garden.

Historic Interest: Plymouth (18 miles), New Bedford Whaling Capitol (17 miles), Provincetown/Eastham, where Pilgrims first landed (70 miles).

Innkeeper(s): Frances Murphy. $55-85. 3 rooms. Breakfast included in rates. Types of meals: Full bkfst and afternoon tea. Beds: KDT. TV, reading lamp, clock radio and turn-down service in room. Air conditioning. VCR, parlor games and telephone on premises. Antiquing, cross-country skiing, fishing, live theater, parks, shopping, sporting events, water sports and whale watching nearby.

Publicity: *Brockton Enterprise and Wareham Courier.*

"Our room was pleasant and I loved the cranberry satin sheets."

Wellfleet   G18

Blue Gateways

252 Main St
Wellfleet, MA 02667-7437
(508)349-7530
E-mail: info@bluegateways.com
Web: www.bluegateways.com

Circa 1712. Built by Squire Higgins in 1712 when George I was on the throne of England and Louis XIV was King of France, this Georgian inn is listed in the National Register. The house always has been a residence, but at times it also has served as a dry and fancy goods store, a pin and needle shop, a dressmaker's shop and a tearoom. Its three bedrooms are appointed with family antiques. The private back yard has an ornamental fish pond. A daily continental breakfast includes delights like juices, fruit, yogurt, specialty homemade granola and fresh to-die-for baked goods. Guest may go beach combing, biking, boating, golfing, hiking, swimming or whale watching. Or they may visit art galleries, museums, wineries or theaters. The inn was featured as Editor's Pick in the 1999 Yankee Magazine's Travel Guide to New England, and it was termed "elegant" in the Cape Cod Travel Guide.

Innkeeper(s): Richard & Bonnie Robicheau. $120-140. 3 rooms with PB. Breakfast and snacks/refreshments included in rates. Types of meals: Cont plus. Beds: KQ. Reading lamp and clock radio in room. Air conditioning. TV, VCR, fax, telephone and fireplace on premises. Small meetings and family reunions hosted. Antiquing, art galleries, beach, bicycling, canoeing/kayaking, fishing, golf, hiking, horseback riding, live theater, museums, parks, shopping, tennis, water sports, wineries and Audubon and National seashore nearby.

The Inn at Duck Creeke

70 Main St, PO Box 364
Wellfleet, MA 02667-0364
(508)349-9333
E-mail: info@innatduckcreeke.com
Web: www.innatduckcreeke.com

Circa 1815. The five-acre site of this sea captain's house features both a salt-water marsh and a duck pond. The Saltworks house and the main house are appointed in an old-fashioned style with antiques, and the rooms are comfortable and cozy. Some have views of the nearby salt marsh or the pond. The inn is favored for its two restaurants; Sweet Seasons and the Tavern Room. The latter is popular for its jazz performances.

Historic Interest: Marconi Station (first wireless Trans Atlantic radio transmission). Wellfleet Historical Museum.

Innkeeper(s): Bob Morrill & Judy Pihl. $70-115. 25 rooms, 17 with PB and 1 conference room. Breakfast included in rates. Types of meals: Cont plus and dinner. Restaurant on premises. Beds: QDT. Reading lamp and air conditioning in some rooms. Fax, parlor games and fireplace on premises. Weddings, small meetings, family reunions and seminars hosted. Antiquing, fishing, live theater, parks, shopping, water sports, National Seashore, Audubon Sanctuary and bike trails nearby.

Publicity: *Italian Vogue, Travel & Leisure, Cape Cod Life, Providence Journal, New York Times, Provincetown, Conde Nast Traveler, British Vogue and Bon a Parte (Denmark).*

"Duck Creeke will always be our favorite stay!"

Stone Lion Inn

130 Commercial Street
Wellfleet, MA 02667
(508)349-9565 Fax:(508)349-9697
E-mail: info@stonelioncapecod.com
Web: www.stonelioncapecod.com

Circa 1871. Built by a sea captain in the 1800s, this French Second Empire Victorian recently has been renovated and redecorated to offer modern indulgences with an old-fashioned charm. Feel right at home in the comfortable living room with games, puzzles, VCR and videotapes. A large selection of books on local history as well as fiction and non-fiction are available to read. Guest bedrooms are named for Brooklyn neighborhoods where the innkeepers once lived or worked. The Clinton Hill boasts a clawfoot tub and shower and a private deck. A hearty breakfast buffet served in the dining room is sure to please. Vegetarian diets are graciously accommodated with advance notice. An apartment and a cottage provide more space and privacy. The grounds feature fish ponds, fountains, a wisteria-covered gazebo and a hammock.

Innkeeper(s): Janet Lowenstein & Adam Levinson. $90-155. 4 rooms with PB and 1 cottage. Breakfast included in rates. Types of meals: Country bkfst. Beds: Q. Reading lamp, ceiling fan and clock radio in room. Air conditioning. TV, VCR, library, parlor games and telephone on premises. Antiquing, art galleries, beach, bicycling, canoeing/kayaking, fishing, golf, hiking, live theater, parks, shopping, tennis and water sports nearby.

Publicity: *Conde Nast Traveler May 02 and Cape Cod Traveler.*

West Boylston
E10

The Rose Cottage Bed & Breakfast

24 Worcester St, Rte 12 and 140
West Boylston, MA 01583-1413
(508)835-4034 Fax:(508)835-4034

Circa 1850. This landmark Gothic Revival with its classic gabled roof and gingerbread dormers overlooks Wachusett Reservoir. Elegant antique furnishings complement the white marble fireplaces, gaslight hanging lamps, lavender glass doorknobs, wide-board floors and floor-to-ceiling windows. The delightful guest bedrooms feature vintage quilts, white iron, brass, Art Deco or spool beds,ceiling fans and fluffy towels. With over 20 years of pampering guests, the innkeepers provide a breakfast with signature entrees and regional specialties guests will find delicious. The carriage house is available as a monthly rental- a secluded, fully equipped apartment with a skylight cathedral ceiling.

Innkeeper(s): Michael & Loretta Kittredge. $90. 5 rooms and 1 conference room. Breakfast included in rates. Types of meals: Full gourmet bkfst and early coffee/tea. Beds: DT. Ceiling fan, at additional cost ($20), an extra twin bed can be put in some rooms and some with private bath in room. Air conditioning. Cross-country skiing, downhill skiing, golf, tennis and public pool nearby.

Publicity: The Telegram Gazette, Item, Landmark and Banner.

"Your concern, your caring, your friendliness made me feel at home!"

West Harwich
I18

Cape Cod Claddagh Inn

77 Route 28 PO Box 667
West Harwich, MA 02671-0667
(508)432-9628 (800)356-9628 Fax:(508)432-6039
E-mail: claddagh@capecod.net
Web: www.capecodcladdaghinn.com

Circa 1890. The owner of Chase and Sanborn coffee built this historic inn, and its original use was as a parsonage. Rumor has it that friendly ghosts may inhabit the home. The interior is a whimsical mix of Victorian, Colonial and even a little Caribbean. Guest rooms include stately poster beds and traditional furnishings. As the name of the inn suggests, there is an Irish influence at work here, as well. This is ever apparent in the Claddagh Pub, where guests can enjoy a hearty, gourmet dinner, rich desserts or a fine selection of spirits.

Innkeeper(s): Eileen & Jack Connell. $95-175. 13 rooms with PB. Breakfast included in rates. Types of meals: Full bkfst. Restaurant on premises. Beds: KQDT. Cable TV, refrigerator, ceiling fan and fireplace in room. Central air. Fax, copier, swimming, fireplace, Irish pub, full restaurant and tiki bar by the pool on premises. Weddings, small meetings, family reunions and seminars hosted. Amusement parks, antiquing, art galleries, beach, bicycling, canoeing/kayaking, fishing, golf, hiking, horseback riding, live theater, museums, parks, shopping, tennis, water sports and wineries nearby.

West Stockbridge
E2

Card Lake Inn

PO Box 38
West Stockbridge, MA 01266-0038
(413)232-0272 Fax:(413)232-0294

Circa 1880. Located in the center of town, this Colonial Revival inn features a popular local restaurant on the premises. Norman Rockwell is said to have frequented its tavern. Stroll around historic West Stockbridge then enjoy the inn's deck cafe with its flower boxes and view of the sculpture garden of an art gallery across the street. Original lighting, hardwood floors and antiques are features of the inn. Chesterwood and Tanglewood are within easy driving distance.

Historic Interest: The Norman Rockwell Museum is approximately two miles away.

Innkeeper(s): Ed & Lisa Robbins. $100-150. 8 rooms. Breakfast included in rates. Types of meals: Cont and early coffee/tea. Restaurant on premises. Beds: KQ. Ceiling fan and clock radio in room. Air conditioning. VCR and telephone on premises. Weddings, small meetings, family reunions and seminars hosted. Amusement parks, antiquing, shopping and sporting events nearby.

West Yarmouth
I17

Inn at Lewis Bay

59 Maine Ave
West Yarmouth, MA 02673
(508)771-3433 (800)962-6679 Fax:(508)790-7089
E-mail: stay@InnatLewisBay.com
Web: www.innatlewisbay.com

Circa 1920. This Dutch Colonial bed & breakfast is located in a quiet seaside neighborhood on Cape Cod's south shore overlooking Lewis Bay, and just a block from the beach. Whale watching, golfing, bicycling and restaurants are just minutes away, as well as ferries to the islands. Guests can relax in the fireplaced sitting room or enjoy the stars and water views in the backyard.

Innkeeper(s): Janet & Dave Vaughn. $98-138. 6 rooms with PB. Breakfast and snacks/refreshments included in rates. Types of meals: Full bkfst, early coffee/tea and afternoon tea. Beds: QD. Reading lamp and clock radio in room. Air conditioning. VCR, library, parlor games, telephone and fireplace on premises. Antiquing, fishing, live theater, parks, shopping, water sports, whale watching and bicycling nearby.

"An experience I am anxious to repeat."

Williamstown
B3

The Guest House at Field Farm

554 Sloan Road
Williamstown, MA 01267
(413)458-3135 Fax:(413)458-3144
E-mail: guesthouseatfieldfarm@ttor.org
Web: www.guesthouseatfieldfarm.org

Circa 1948. In the middle of 316 acres of conserved land this authentic Bauhaus-inspired, American Modern house features impressive views of Mt. Greylock. The interior is adorned with retro-contemporary furnishings and artwork that exude a museum quality atmosphere boasting an original Eames chair, Noguchi coffee table and Kagan sofa in the living room. A guest pantry is easily accessible. Exceptional guest bedrooms include terry robes, soaps, and some feature a fireplace and private outdoor patio or deck. Savor a complete breakfast as well as afternoon refreshments. Request a tour of the Folly, a pinwheel-shaped shingled guest house designed by modernist architect Ulrich Franzen, that overlooks the pond. Four miles of walking or cross-country skiing trails and landscaped formal strolling gardens with thirteen sculptures are accented by pastures, forest, marshes, a pond and a stream. Snowshoes are available and a swimming pool is open in season.

Historic Interest: Authentic modern Bauhaus style house, with authentic and reproduction furniture from the era.

Innkeeper(s): Bob Chok. $145-225. 5 rooms with PB, 2 with FP. Breakfast and afternoon tea included in rates. Types of meals: Full bkfst, early coffee/tea and snacks/refreshments. Beds: KQ. Reading lamp, desk, fireplace and outdoor decks in room. Swimming, library, telephone, fireplace, snow-shoes and guest pantry access on premises. Weddings and small meetings hosted. Antiquing, art galleries, bicycling, cross-country skiing, golf, hiking, horseback riding, live theater, museums, parks, shopping and tennis nearby.

Publicity: *Fodor's Choice Property, Boston Globe and New York Times.*

Yarmouth Port   117

Colonial House Inn

Rt 6A, 277 Main St
Yarmouth Port, MA 02675
(508)362-4348 (800)999-3416 Fax:(508)362-8034

Circa 1730. Although the original structure was built in pre-revolutionary times, a third floor was later added and another section was shipped in from Nantucket. The innkeepers renovated the carriage house, creating 10 new rooms. Dining areas include the Colonial Room with hand-stenciled walls and a fireplace, and the Common Room, a recent glass-enclosed addition with a view of the veranda and town green. A traditional Thanksgiving dinner is served every year, and guests may enjoy other specialties, including murder-mystery, Las Vegas and wine-tasting weekends.

Innkeeper(s): Malcolm Perna. $80-120. 21 rooms with PB, 3 with FP, 2 suites and 3 conference rooms. Breakfast and dinner included in rates. Types of meals: Cont plus and lunch. Restaurant on premises. Beds: KQDT. VCR, reading lamp, ceiling fan, clock radio, telephone, desk, TV and canopy beds in room. Air conditioning. TV, fax, copier, spa, swimming, sauna, library, parlor games and fireplace on premises. Limited handicap access. Weddings, small meetings, family reunions and seminars hosted. Antiquing, cross-country skiing, fishing, golf, live theater, parks, shopping, sporting events, tennis and water sports nearby.

Publicity: *Country Living, New York Daily News, New York Times, Yankee, Cape Cod Life, Boston Globe, Newsday and Chronicle (Peter Mehegan).*

"The nicest place I've ever stayed."

Liberty Hill Inn

77 Main St, Rt 6A
Yarmouth Port, MA 02675
(508)362-3976 (800)821-3977
E-mail: libertyh@capecod.net
Web: www.libertyhillinn.com

Circa 1825. Just back from historic Old King's Highway, in a seaside village, this country inn is a restored Greek Revival mansion built by shipwrights. It is located on the site of the original Liberty Pole dating from Revolutionary times. A romantic decor includes fine antiques and original architectural features, enhancing the tall windows and high ceilings. Guests can request rooms with a fireplace

and whirlpool tub in a restored historic barn. Stroll past the inn's lawns for a brief walk to antique shops, restaurants and an old-fashioned ice cream parlor.

Historic Interest: Two historic restorations from the 18th century are within a half mile. Maritime history is celebrated each May with tours of historic buildings.

Innkeeper(s): Ann & John Cartwright. $100-210. 9 rooms with PB. Types of meals: Full gourmet bkfst and afternoon tea. Beds: KQT. Cable TV, reading lamp, clock radio, desk and honeymoon rooms with whirlpools in room. Air conditioning. Fax, copier, parlor games, telephone and guest refrigerator on premises. Small meetings and seminars hosted. Antiquing, fishing, golf, live theater, parks, shopping, tennis, water sports, whale watching, historic restorations and auctions nearby.

Publicity: *Cape Cod Life, Colonial Homes, Cape Cod Travel Guide and Yankee Magazine's "Editor's Pick"- 2002 Travel Guide.*

"Immaculate and incredibly clean. Plenty of information for one and all. Thank you for a delightful stay."

Olde Captain's Inn on The Cape

101 Main St Rt 6A
Yarmouth Port, MA 02675-1709
(508)362-4496 (888)407-7161
E-mail: general@oldecaptainsinn.com
Web: www.oldecaptainsinn.com

Circa 1812. Located in the historic district and on Captain's Mile, this house is in the National Register. It is decorated in a traditional style, with coordinated wallpapers and carpets, and there are two suites that include kitchens and living rooms. Apple trees, blackberries and raspberries grow on the acre of grounds and often contribute to the breakfast menus. There is a summer veranda overlooking the property. Good restaurants are within walking distance.

Historic Interest: Plymouth Rock and Plantation (30 miles).

Innkeeper(s): Sven Tilly. $60-120. 3 rooms, 1 with PB and 2 suites. Breakfast included in rates. Types of meals: Cont plus. Beds: QD. Cable TV, reading lamp and clock radio in room. TV on premises. Antiquing, fishing, live theater, shopping, sporting events and water sports nearby.

Michigan

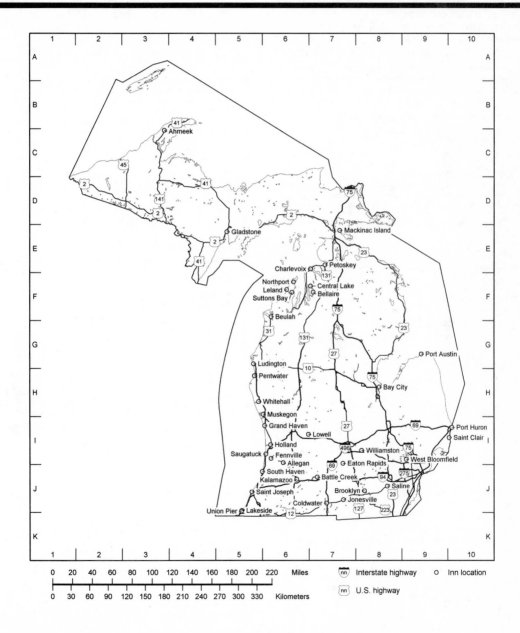

- **Miles:** 0 20 40 60 80 100 120 140 160 180 200 220
- **Kilometers:** 0 30 60 90 120 150 180 210 240 270 300 330

- (nn) Interstate highway
- (nn) U.S. highway
- o Inn location

Ahmeek   C3

Sand Hills Lighthouse Inn

5 Mile Point Road
Ahmeek, MI 49901
(906)337-1744
E-mail: frabotta@up.net
Web: www.sandhillslighthouseinn.com

Circa 1917. Located on 35 acres on the Keweenaw Peninsula, including 3,000 feet of private Lake Superior shoreline, this yellow-brick lighthouse was constructed around a seven-story, steel-beam core. Inside the massive structure are carved oak railings on the staircase, plaster medallions around all the light fixtures and antique Victorian furnishings throughout. The parlor offers a fireplace and walls that are covered in floor-to-ceiling oak wainscoting. For a special anniversary ask for the lavish King Room. It features 96 yards of purple velvet in a crown canopy that flows around the bed, and there is a fireplace and scenic water views. The inn is open year-round, and from mid-May to mid-August lighthouse guests enjoy the unique experience of both sunrise and sunset views over the water. Gourmet breakfasts are served, including melt-in-your-mouth English scones.

Innkeeper(s): William H. Frabotta. $125-185. 8 rooms with PB, 1 with FP and 1 suite. Breakfast included in rates. Types of meals: Full gourmet bkfst, early coffee/tea and snacks/refreshments. Beds: KQ. Reading lamp, clock radio and whirlpool (two rooms) in room. Air conditioning. Copier, swimming, library, telephone, fireplace and grand piano on premises. Antiquing, cross-country skiing, fishing, golf, live theater, parks, shopping, sporting events and water sports nearby.

Allegan   I6

Castle In The Country Bed and Breakfast

340 M 40 S
Allegan, MI 49010-9609
(269)673-8054 (888)673-8054 Fax:(269)686-0058
E-mail: info@castleinthecountry.com
Web: www.castleinthecountry.com

Circa 1906. Reflecting its nickname and castle-like appearance, a three-story turret and wide wraparound porch accent this 1906 Queen Anne Victorian adorning five acres of scenic countryside. Gather in one of the several common rooms or sitting areas. A Guest Refreshment Center has a coffee pot and refrigerator. Romantic guest bedrooms and a suite feature fresh flowers, candles, terry robes, handmade bath products, a video library and VCR. Several rooms include whirlpool tubs, fireplaces and CD players. Breakfast is specially prepared and served on fine china and vintage crystal. Innkeepers Herb and Ruth enjoy providing personalized service that ensures a pleasant stay. Ask for an Adventure Map, a helpful tool to enjoy local activities and sites. Many special packages are regularly offered.

Innkeeper(s): Herb & Ruth Boven. $85-205. 5 rooms with PB, 5 with FP and 1 suite. Breakfast included in rates. Types of meals: Full gourmet bkfst, veg bkfst, early coffee/tea, picnic lunch, afternoon tea, dinner and room service. Beds: KQT. Modem hook-up, data port, TV, VCR, reading lamp, stereo, refrigerator, ceiling fan, snack bar, clock radio, turn-down service, desk and hot tub/spa in room. Central air. Fax, copier, spa, parlor games, telephone and fireplace on premises. Weddings, family reunions and seminars hosted. Antiquing, art galleries, beach, bicycling, canoeing/kayaking, cross-country skiing, downhill skiing, fishing, golf, hiking, horseback riding, live theater, museums, parks, shopping, tennis, water sports and wineries nearby.

Publicity: *Cover of Arringtons B&B Journal and Arringtons B&B Journal Book of Lists 2002.*

Delano Inn Victorian Bed and Breakfast

302 Cutler St
Allegan, MI 49010-1210
(269)686-0240 (866)686-0240
E-mail: delanoinn@triton.net
Web: delanoinn.com

Circa 1863. Recently restored to its pristine condition, this ornate Cubical Italianate inn is listed in the State and National Registers of Historic Places. It boasts a Victorian elegance luxuriously reflected in the period antiques and furnishings of the 1800s. Stroll the one acre of English gardens before relaxing with a beverage on the wraparound veranda or in one of the parlors. Spacious guest bedrooms and suites feature exquisite decor. Sleep in a sleigh or full tester bed, lounge on a fainting couch and view the grounds through ten-foot windows. Linger over a satisfying breakfast before heading out for the day's activities.

Innkeeper(s): Scott and Karen Ehrich. $70-165. 4 rooms with PB, 2 with FP, 2 suites and 1 conference room. Breakfast and snacks/refreshments included in rates. Types of meals: Full gourmet bkfst, veg bkfst and early coffee/tea. Beds: Q. Modem hook-up, data port, cable TV, VCR, reading lamp, refrigerator, snack bar, clock radio, telephone, desk, fireplace and whirlpool tubs in room. Air conditioning. Fax, library, parlor games, fireplace and laundry facility on premises. Weddings, small meetings, family reunions and seminars hosted. Antiquing, art galleries, beach, bicycling, canoeing/kayaking, cross-country skiing, downhill skiing, fishing, golf, hiking, horseback riding, live theater, museums, parks, shopping, sporting events, tennis, water sports and wineries nearby.

"The world would be a much more peaceful place if we all celebrated hospitality the way you folks do."

Battle Creek   J7

Greencrest Manor

6174 Halbert Rd E
Battle Creek, MI 49017-9449
(616)962-8633 Fax:(616)962-7254

Circa 1934. Once used as monastery, this 13,000-square-foot French Normandy mansion rests on 20 acres. Extensive gardens are lush with apple orchards, tiered gardens, herb gardens, reflecting pools, Japanese maples and cherry trees. It is in the National Register as a rare example of Norman-style architecture in the United States. The inn's inviting drawing room boasts egg-and-dart molding, sofas and drapes in an English cabbage-rose print and floor-to-ceiling French windows. The dining room has a white marble fireplace, Parisian chandelier and Oriental carpet. Ask for the VIP Suite for a king bed, white marble fireplace and double whirlpool showers.

Innkeeper(s): Tom & Kathy VanDaff. $95-235. 8 rooms, 6 with PB, 1 with FP, 6 suites and 3 conference rooms. Breakfast included in rates. Types of meals: Cont. Beds: KQD. Cable TV, reading lamp, ceiling fan, clock radio, telephone, desk and hot tub/spa in room. Air conditioning. Fax, copier, library, fireplace and porch with snacks and beverages on premises. Weddings and small meetings hosted. Antiquing, cross-country skiing, golf, parks, shopping and tennis nearby.

Publicity: *Country Inns and Lifestyles.*

"I've been in Normandy many times, I've never seen anything like your 'French Chateau.'"

Bay City   H8

Clements Inn

1712 Center Ave M-25
Bay City, MI 48708-6122
(989)894-4600 (800)442-4605 Fax:(989)891-9442

Circa 1886. The amber-paned windows and oak ceilings of
this three-story Queen Anne Victorian inn are just a few of its
impressive features. Built by William Clements, the home
joined a number of other impressive estates on Center Avenue,
most of which were owned by lumber barons. The inn's well-
appointed guest rooms are named for famous authors or fic-
tional characters, continuing a strong tradition started by
Clements, a collector of rare books. A winding staircase, original gas lighting fixtures and hand-carved woodwork have
impressed many visitors.

Innkeeper(s): Dave & Shirley Roberts. $75-190. 6 rooms with PB, 3 with FP
and 2 suites. Breakfast included in rates. Types of meals: Cont. Beds: KQD.
Cable TV, VCR, reading lamp, clock radio, telephone, desk and two suites
have whirlpool in room. Air conditioning. Fax and parlor games on premises.
Antiquing, cross-country skiing, fishing, live theater, parks, shopping, planetarium and birding nearby.

Bellaire   F7

Applesauce Inn Bed & Breakfast

7296 Hwy M-88 South
Bellaire, MI 49615
(231)533-6448 (888)533-6448
E-mail: wendy@applesauceinn.com
Web: www.applesauceinn.com

Circa 1900. Original woodwork and floors accent this recently
restored, historic four-square farmhouse in the heart of the
scenic chain-of-lakes area. Relaxing is easy while swinging on a
hammock or rocking on the wraparound front porch. Enjoy fireside chats in comfortable surroundings. Stay in a tastefully decorated guest bedroom with a cherry or oak sleigh bed and robes.
The first-floor Grantz Room features a scrolled wrought iron bed
and an electric fireplace. Hearty breakfast favorites may include
blueberry cream cheese-stuffed french toast, morel mushroom
egg bake or applesauce porridge with whipped cream.

Innkeeper(s): David & Wendy Keene. $65-95. 3 rooms, 2 with PB, 2 with
FP. Breakfast and snacks/refreshments included in rates. Types of meals:
Country bkfst. Beds: Q. Cable TV, VCR, reading lamp, clock radio, fireplace
and plush robes in room. Library, parlor games, fireplace, evening desserts,
video library and relaxing wraparound porch with rockers and hammock on
premises. Antiquing, beach, bicycling, canoeing/kayaking, cross-country skiing, downhill skiing, fishing, golf, hiking, horseback riding, parks, shopping
and water sports nearby.

Bellaire Bed & Breakfast

212 Park St
Bellaire, MI 49615-9595
(231)533-6077 (800)545-0780

Circa 1879. Maple trees line the drive to this American
Gothic home. Relax on the porch swing, or enjoy the warmth
of a crackling fire in the English-style library. The fresh, family-style continental-plus breakfast is a treat. A nearby park
offers swimming, tennis, basketball, shuffleboard and a playground. Browse through the downtown shops or hunt for
antiques. Guests can take in 18 rounds at "The Legend" at

Shanty Creek golf course, and in winter, enjoy skiing.

Innkeeper(s): David Schulz & Jim Walker. $95-130. 5 rooms with PB. Types
of meals: Full bkfst and afternoon tea. Beds: Q.

Grand Victorian Inn

402 N Bridge St
Bellaire, MI 49615-9591
(231)533-6111 (800)336-3860 Fax:(231)533-4214
E-mail: innkeeper@grandvictorian.com

Circa 1895. Featured in Country Inns and Midwest Living
magazines, this Queen Anne Victorian mansion boasts three
original fireplaces, hand-carved mantels, intricate fretwork and
numerous architectural details. Relax with a glass of wine
before the fire in the formal front parlor, or listen to music while playing cards and games
in the back parlor. Guest bedrooms
offer an eclectic mix of antique furnishings including Victorian Revival,
Eastlake and French Provincial. Soak
in an 1890s clawfoot tub, or enjoy
the park view from a private balcony.
Be pampered with an incredible stay in one of the country's
most remarkable and unique inns. The gazebo is a perfect spot
to while away the day, or take advantage of the area's many
nearby activities.

$95-175. 5 rooms with PB. Beds: QD. Cable TV, reading lamp, private bath-
rooms, coffee and tea in room. Air conditioning. Telephone on premises.
Weddings, small meetings, family reunions and seminars hosted. Antiquing,
cross-country skiing, downhill skiing, fishing, golf, hiking, shopping, water
sports, fine dining restaurants and lounging nearby.

Publicity: *Midwest Living, Country Inns,* Featured on Nabisco
Crackers/Cookies Boxes Promotion, Grand Traverse Magazine and 2003
Book of Lists Award-Arrington's B&B Journal-Most Elegant.

*"We certainly enjoyed our visit to the Grand Victorian. It has been
our pleasure to stay in B&Bs in several countries, but never one more
beautiful and almost never with such genial hosts."*

Stone Waters Inn on the River

226 North Bridge St
Bellaire, MI 49615
(231)533-6131 (800)336-3860 Fax:(231)533-4214
E-mail: info@stonewatersinn.com
Web: www.stonewatersinn.com

Circa 1920. Located directly on the water, more than 700 feet
of serene river frontage awaits you at this inn that offers a
casual appeal blended with simple elegance. Linger by the
lobby's grand fieldstone fireplace, or play a game of billiards.
Custom-decorated guest bedrooms each reflect one of the distinct flavors of Northern Michigan. Choose the relaxed Cottage
Room or the rustic decor of The Lodge. For more luxurious
tastes, each of the riverside suites features a fireplace and two-
person Jacuzzi. The Vineyard Room boasts a four-poster
canopy bed and private deck overlooking the water. A front
porch invites people-watching, and a hot tub provides year-
round enjoyment.

Innkeeper(s): Romona Belanger. $95-175. 10 rooms with PB and 1 cot-
tage. Beds: QD. Cable TV, telephone, hair dryers, coffee and suites with fireplace and two-person Jacuzzi in room. Riverside hammock, grills, kayaks,
swimming and picnic area on premises. Antiquing, canoeing/kayaking,
cross-country skiing, downhill skiing, fishing, golf, hiking, parks, shopping,
sporting events, water sports, snowmobiling, ice fishing, fine dining and
lounging nearby.

Beulah   F6

Brookside Inn

115 US Hwy 31
Beulah, MI 49617-9701
(231)882-9688 Fax:(231)882-4600
E-mail: brookside@brooksideinn.com
Web: www.brooksideinn.com

Circa 1939. Experience the best of romance at this inn, located near Crystal Lake. Designed for couples, each guest bedroom features a mirrored canopy waterbed or conventional mattress, a three foot deep Polynesian spa and wood-burning stove. Some deluxe  rooms boast a loft and offer a larger spa as well as combinations of a sauna, steam bath and French suntanning solarium. Meals include breakfast and dinner, served on the outdoor deck or by the fireplace. Expect fresh flowers, fine wine and great food. The seven-acre grounds showcase a bridge to a flower and herb garden.

Innkeeper(s): Pam & Kirk Lorenz. $180-270. 31 rooms with PB, 31 with FP and 3 conference rooms. Breakfast and dinner included in rates. Types of meals: Full gourmet bkfst, early coffee/tea, gourmet lunch, picnic lunch and snacks/refreshments. Restaurant on premises. Beds: K. Cable TV, VCR, reading lamp, ceiling fan, hot tub/spa, some with sauna steam and tanning bed in room. Air conditioning. Fax, copier, spa, sauna, telephone and fireplace on premises. Limited handicap access. Weddings, small meetings, family reunions and seminars hosted. Downhill skiing, fishing, golf, live theater, parks, sporting events, tennis, water sports, snowmobiling, ice fishing and hot air balloons nearby.

Publicity: *AAA Travel, Detroit Free Press and Chicago Tribune.*

"Michigan's romantic retreat...works a spell." - Rick Sylvain, Detroit Free Press

Brooklyn   J8

Chicago Street Inn

219 Chicago St
Brooklyn, MI 49230-9781
(517)592-3888 Fax:(517)592-3241
E-mail: chiinn@aol.com
Web: www.chicagostreetinn.com

Circa 1886. Three acres of natural beauty surround this 1886 Queen Anne Victorian home that features original oak and cherry woodwork, stained-glass windows and fireplaces with English tiles. The main house offers tastefully decorated guest bedrooms with small stocked refrigerators and pampering extras. The 1920s bungalow is a separate building boasting two of the inn's four Jacuzzi suites with fireplaces. Savor home-cooked specialties like baked French toast, vegetarian omelette or egg-sausage casserole.

Historic Interest: Built in 1886, all the beautiful oak and cherry woodwork still boasts its original finish. Stained-glass windows and ceramic fireplace tiles were brought here from England when the first owner and his wife returned from their honeymoon. Mystery surrounds the rumors of a tunnel connecting several local houses, including Chicago Street Inn, and evidence indicates the strong possibility of a once-existing and much-used tunnel right in the basement of this beautiful structure.

Innkeeper(s): Carl & Mary Moore. $60-155. 6 rooms with PB, 3 with FP and 4 suites. Breakfast and snacks/refreshments included in rates. Types of meals: Full bkfst, veg bkfst and early coffee/tea. Beds: QD. Data port, cable TV, VCR, reading lamp, refrigerator, ceiling fan, clock radio, coffeemaker,

desk, hot tub/spa and fireplace in room. Central air. Spa, parlor games and fireplace on premises. Amusement parks, antiquing, beach, bicycling, fishing, golf, hiking, horseback riding, live theater and shopping nearby.

Dewey Lake Manor

11811 Laird Rd
Brooklyn, MI 49230-9035
(517)467-7122
E-mail: deweylk@frontiernet.net
Web: www.deweylakemanor.com

Circa 1868. This Italianate house overlooks Dewey Lake and is situated on 18 acres in the Irish Hills. The house is furnished in a country Victorian style with antiques. An enclosed porch is a favorite spot to relax and take in the views of the lake while having breakfast. Favorite pastimes include lakeside bonfires in the summertime and ice skating or cross-country skiing in the winter. Canoe and paddleboats are available to guests.

Historic Interest: The Great Saulk Trail (2 miles from U.S. 12), Walker Tavern, a stagecoach stop on the trail (2 miles), Saint Joseph Catholic Shrine (5 miles).

Innkeeper(s): Barb & Joe Phillips. $80-135. 5 rooms with PB, 5 with FP and 1 conference room. Breakfast included in rates. Types of meals: Full bkfst, early coffee/tea, picnic lunch and snacks/refreshments. Beds: QT. Cable TV, reading lamp, ceiling fan, clock radio, telephone, one with Jacuzzi and five with VCR in room. Air conditioning. Fireplace, VCR in sitting room and baby grand piano in parlor on premises. Weddings, small meetings and family reunions hosted. Antiquing, cross-country skiing, fishing, golf, live theater, shopping, sporting events and water sports nearby.

Publicity: *Ann Arbor News.*

"I came back and brought my friends. It was wonderful."

Central Lake   F7

Bridgewalk B&B

2287 S Main, PO Box 399
Central Lake, MI 49622-0399
(231)544-8122

Circa 1895. Secluded on a wooded acre, this three-story Victorian is accessible by crossing a foot bridge over a stream. Guest rooms are simply decorated with Victorian touches, floral prints and fresh flowers. The Garden Suite includes a clawfoot tub. Much of the home's Victorian elements have been restored, including pocket doors and the polished woodwork. Breakfasts begin with such items as a cold fruit soup, freshly baked muffins or scones accompanied with homemade jams and butters. A main dish, perhaps apple-sausage blossoms, tops off the meal.

Innkeeper(s): Janet & Tom Meteer. $85-105. 5 rooms with PB and 1 suite. Breakfast included in rates. Types of meals: Full bkfst and early coffee/tea. Beds: KQT. Reading lamp and ceiling fan in room. Parlor games, telephone and fireplace on premises. Small meetings hosted. Antiquing, cross-country skiing, downhill skiing, fishing, parks, shopping, golf and gourmet restaurants nearby.

Charlevoix   E7

Bridge Street Inn

113 Michigan Ave
Charlevoix, MI 49720-1819
(231)547-6606 Fax:(231)547-1812
E-mail: vmckown@voyager.net
Web: www.bridgestreetinn-chx.com

Circa 1895. This three-story Colonial Revival structure recalls the bygone era when Charlevoix was home to many grand hotels. Originally a guest "cottage" of one of those large hotels, this inn boasts seven gracious guest rooms, many of which are available with private bath. The rooms sport antique furnishings, floral rugs and wooden floors and some offer views of the surrounding lakes. Guests are within walking distance of Lake Michigan's beaches, Round Lake's harbor and Lake Charlevoix's boating and fishing. Be sure to inquire in advance about the inn's many discounts and special rate for small groups.

Historic Interest: Mrs. Baker's cottage.

Innkeeper(s): Vera & John McKown. $83-145. 7 rooms, 6 with PB and 1 suite. Breakfast included in rates. Types of meals: Full bkfst. Beds: QT. Cable TV, reading lamp and ceiling fan in room. VCR, fax, telephone and fireplace on premises. Weddings, small meetings and family reunions hosted. Antiquing, art galleries, beach, bicycling, canoeing/kayaking, cross-country skiing, downhill skiing, fishing, golf, hiking, horseback riding, museums, parks, shopping, tennis, water sports and wineries nearby.

The Inn at Grey Gables

306 Belvedere Ave
Charlevoix, MI 49720-1413
(231)547-2251 (800)280-4667 Fax:(231)547-1944

Circa 1887. Guests at this attractive two-story inn are just a short walk from a public beach. Visitors have their choice of seven rooms, including two suites. The Pine Suite features a

kitchen and private entrance, perfect for honeymooners or for those enjoying a longer-than-usual stay. All of the rooms offer private baths and most have queen beds. Guests may opt to relax and enjoy the beautiful surroundings or take advantage of the many recreational activities available in the Charlevoix area, including Fisherman's Island State Park.

Innkeeper(s): Gary & Kay Anderson. $110-135. 7 rooms, 5 with PB and 2 suites. Breakfast included in rates. Types of meals: Full bkfst. Beds: KQT. Reading lamp, ceiling fan, clock radio and desk in room. Parlor games and telephone on premises. Small meetings and family reunions hosted. Antiquing, cross-country skiing, downhill skiing, fishing, parks, shopping and water sports nearby.

Publicity: *USA Today.*

Coldwater   J7

Chicago Pike Inn

215 E Chicago St
Coldwater, MI 49036-2001
(517)279-8744 Fax:(517)278-8597

Circa 1903. This exquisite colonial mansion was built by an architect who designed many of the homes on Mackinac Island. Furnished with period antiques, the inn features chandeliers, stained glass, parquet flooring and a stunning cherry staircase. Its name is derived from Coldwater's midway location on the old Detroit-Chicago turnpike. Guests will enjoy exploring Coldwater's historic buildings or perhaps a visit to the Victorian-style Tibbits Opera House built in 1882.

Innkeeper(s): Becky Schultz. $100-195. 8 rooms with PB, 1 with FP, 2 suites and 1 conference room. Breakfast included in rates. Types of meals: Full bkfst, early coffee/tea and gourmet dinner. Beds: QT. Cable TV, VCR, reading lamp, refrigerator, ceiling fan, clock radio, telephone and turn-down service in room. TV, fax, copier, bicycles, library, parlor games and fireplace on premises. Weddings, small meetings, family reunions and seminars hosted. Antiquing, cross-country skiing, fishing, live theater, parks, shopping, sporting events and water sports nearby.

Publicity: *Midwest Living, Country and Michigan.*

"Your warmth and hospitality added so much to the time we spent with you."

Eaton Rapids   I7

English Inn

677 S Michigan Rd
Eaton Rapids, MI 48827-9273
(517)663-2500 (800)858-0598 Fax:(517)663-2643
E-mail: englishinn@arq.net
Web: www.englishinn.com

Circa 1927. Elegance, graciousness and personal attention are the hallmarks of this late 1920s two-story, L-shaped, cross-gabled Tudor Revival country manor that adorns an impressive 15-acre estate. Stay in a guest bedroom or suite in the main house and two cottages include even more spacious privacy. Enjoy breakfast in the Thames Room. For dinner, the award-winning restaurant and wine cellar offer a superb selection of fine food and drink. The English Pub and Terrace menu features less-formal fare. Wander along the riverside walking trails, by a fish pond, artesian well, pergola and gazebo overlooking colorful flower gardens. Play croquet on a tournament-size court or swim in the large pool. Two nearby golf courses boast special rates for inn guests.

Innkeeper(s): Gary and Donna Nelson. $95-175. 10 rooms, 8 with PB, 1 with FP, 2 suites and 1 conference room. Breakfast included in rates. Types of meals: Full gourmet bkfst, early coffee/tea, lunch, picnic lunch, gourmet dinner and room service. Restaurant on premises. Beds: QDT. Modem hook-up, cable TV, VCR, reading lamp, clock radio, telephone, desk, hot tub/spa and fireplace in room. Air conditioning. Fax, copier, spa, library, parlor games and local artists gallery/exhibit on premises. Handicap access. Weddings, small meetings, family reunions and seminars hosted. Antiquing, art galleries, cross-country skiing, fishing, golf, live theater, museums, shopping, sporting events and Boarshead Theater nearby.

Fennville   I6

J. Paules' Fenn Inn

2254 S 58th St
Fennville, MI 49408-9461
(269)561-2836 Fax:(269)561-2836
E-mail: jpaules@accn.org
Web: www.jpaulesfenninn.org

Circa 1900. This traditional bed and breakfast is peacefully situated in the countryside. Choose from a variety of impressive guest bedrooms, some with sun decks. There is a two-bedroom suite that is perfect for families. Starting with a gourmet breakfast, the hospitality continues throughout the day. Hot beverages, baked goods and fruit are available in the main dining room. Popcorn is offered as the perfect companion while watching a video. Pets are welcome.

Innkeeper(s): Paulette Clouse & Ewald Males. $85-175. 5 rooms with PB and 1 suite. Breakfast, afternoon tea and snacks/refreshments included in rates. Types of meals: Full gourmet bkfst, veg bkfst and early coffee/tea. Beds: KQDT. Refrigerator, ceiling fan and one with full kitchen in room. Air conditioning. TV, VCR, fax, copier, spa, bicycles, library, telephone and laundry facility on premises. Amusement parks, antiquing, art galleries, beach, bicycling, cross-country skiing, downhill skiing, fishing, golf, hiking, horseback riding, live theater, museums, parks, shopping, tennis, water sports and wineries nearby.

Georgetown   H9

The Grey Havens

96 Seguinland Rd
Georgetown, MI 04548-0308
(207)371-2616
E-mail: inn@greyhavens.com
Web: www.greyhavens.com

Circa 1906. For more than two decades, Haley and Bill Eberhart have welcomed guests to this handsome shingle-style hotel on Georgetown Island. From the wraparound porch and most of the rooms, guests may view the harbor, islands, lighthouses and the open ocean. The lounge features a huge rock fireplace and a 12-foot-tall window. Furnishings are antique. Ask for one of the four turret rooms for a 180-degree ocean view. Reid State Park, Bath, the Maine Maritime Museum and Freeport are nearby.

Innkeeper(s): Bill & Haley Eberhart. $100-220. 13 rooms with PB and 1 suite. Breakfast included in rates. Types of meals: Full bkfst, early coffee/tea and snacks/refreshments. Beds: KQD. Reading lamp in room. Fax, copier, library, parlor games, telephone, fireplace, guest canoes, "fully rockered" porch, great coffee and small "honor bar on premises. Weddings, small meetings, family reunions and seminars hosted. Antiquing, art galleries, beach, bicycling, canoeing/kayaking, fishing, golf, hiking, live theater, museums, parks, shopping, Audubon Bird Sanctuary, Nature Conservancy and fishing village nearby.

Publicity: *Victoria, Travel & Leisure, House Beautiful, Yankee Magazine, Coastal Living, Down East and Budget Living.*

"We keep coming back. This place is wonderful."

Gladstone   E5

Kipling House Bed & Breakfast

1716 N Lake Shore Dr
Gladstone, MI 49837-2751
(906)428-1120 (877)905-ROOM Fax:(906)428-4696

Circa 1897. Stay here and learn why this historical Four Square house is named after Rudyard Kipling. Relax on the front porch rockers or by the fire in the parlor. Choose a guest bedroom

with a whimsical or elegant decor. The cottage features a sleeping loft and a free-standing fireplace. Gourmet Chef Ralph takes great pride in presenting a splendid candlelight breakfast in the dining room, as well as a tasty dessert in the evenings. The grounds offer a gazebo, deck perennial and water garden. Bikes are available to explore the local Upper Peninsula area. Enjoy nearby Hiawatha National Forest boasting almost one million acres, or visit a restored mining village at Fayette State Park.

Innkeeper(s): Ann & Ralph Miller. $75-150. 6 rooms, 3 with PB. Breakfast, afternoon tea and snacks/refreshments included in rates. Types of meals: Full gourmet bkfst, early coffee/tea and picnic lunch. Beds: KQD. Modem hook-up, cable TV, VCR, reading lamp, refrigerator, ceiling fan, coffeemaker, turn-down service and fireplace in room. Air conditioning. Copier, bicycles, library, parlor games, telephone, fireplace, laundry facility and gift shop on premises. Weddings, small meetings and seminars hosted. Antiquing, art galleries, beach, bicycling, canoeing/kayaking, cross-country skiing, downhill skiing, fishing, golf, hiking, museums, parks, shopping and water sports nearby.

Publicity: *Daily Press and WLUC TV.*

Grand Haven   I6

Boyden House Bed & Breakfast

301 S 5th St
Grand Haven, MI 49417-1413
(616)846-3538 Fax:(616)847-4030
E-mail: boydenhouse@chartermi.net
Web: www.boydenhouse.com

Circa 1874. A lavish garden surrounds this nineteenth century Victorian/Dutch colonial home, filled with elegant, yet cozy rooms. Deep cherry wood furniture and hard wood floors encompass each visitor upon their first step over the threshold. Relax with friends on the porch or in the comfort of your own room as you snuggle up by the fireplace or enjoy the soothing bubbles of your private spa. Take a walk down the Grand River Boardwalk to the beaches of Lake Michigan, or enjoy a variety of attractions in Grand Haven, ranging from visiting shops and the museum in town to braving water sports on the beach.

Innkeeper(s): Gale Kowalski. $75-130. 7 rooms with PB, 3 with FP and 1 conference room. Breakfast and snacks/refreshments included in rates. Types of meals: Full gourmet bkfst, veg bkfst, early coffee/tea and room service. Beds: KQT. Modem hook-up, cable TV, reading lamp, ceiling fan, telephone and hot tub/spa in room. Central air. VCR, fax, copier, spa, library, child care, parlor games and fireplace on premises. Small meetings, family reunions and seminars hosted. Amusement parks, antiquing, art galleries, beach, bicycling, canoeing/kayaking, cross-country skiing, downhill skiing, fishing, golf, hiking, horseback riding, live theater, museums, parks, shopping, tennis, water sports and wineries nearby.

Khardomah Lodge

1365 Lake Ave
Grand Haven, MI 49417
(616)842-2990

Circa 1873. A favorite place for family gatherings, the inn's natural wooded surroundings and flower gardens instill an overall sense of well-being. Built in the late 1800s and sitting amongst other historic homes, the lodge's cottage-style decor and antiques create a delightful nostalgia. The great room fireplace is an instant socializer. Choose to stay in the lodge suites, guest bedrooms or a cottage. A hot tub is the highlight of the master suite. Create memorable meals in the fully-equipped kitchen and gas grill. A catering service also can be arranged. Relax by the fireplace, read a book from the library, watch a video or play a game.

Innkeeper(s): Mo & Patty Rave. $50-175. 20 rooms, 2 suites, 1 cottage and

1 conference room. Types of meals: Early coffee/tea. Beds: QDT. Ceiling fan, hot tub in master suite, A/C in suites and some rooms with central air in room. TV, VCR, library, parlor games, telephone, fireplace, laundry facility, furnished kitchen and gas grill on premises. Weddings, small meetings, family reunions and seminars hosted. Amusement parks, antiquing, art galleries, beach, bicycling, canoeing/kayaking, cross-country skiing, fishing, golf, hiking, horseback riding, live theater, museums, parks, shopping, tennis, water sports and wineries nearby.

Publicity: *Hunts Guide, Michigan Meetings, Events and Fox Local News for historical dedication.*

Holland   I6

Bonnie's Parsonage 1908 B&B

6 E 24th St/Central Ave
Holland, MI 49423-4817
(616)396-1316
Web: www.bbonline.com/mi/parsonage

Circa 1908. This historic American Four-Square parsonage was built in 1908 by one of Holland's early Dutch churches. It has housed seven ministers and their families through the years. Since 1984, it has served as a bed & breakfast. The inn features original oak woodwork, leaded glass windows and pocket doors. A delicious full breakfast is served in the formal dining room. Close to fine dining, shops and bike trails.

Historic Interest: Cappon House (a few blocks), Lake Michigan beaches, the historic Saugatuck Resort (12-mile drive). There are art shops and bike trails nearby.

Innkeeper(s): Bonnie McVoy-Verwys. $110-135. 3 rooms, 2 with PB. Breakfast included in rates. Types of meals: Full gourmet bkfst. Beds: DT. TV, reading lamp, ceiling fan, clock radio, turn-down service and desk in room. Air conditioning. VCR, library, telephone, fireplace, summer porch and outdoor garden patio on premises. Antiquing, art galleries, beach, bicycling, cross-country skiing, golf, hiking, live theater, museums, parks, shopping, tennis, wineries, Lake Michigan beaches, bike trails and fine dining nearby.

Publicity: *Detroit Free Press Travel Tales, Midwest Living and Fodors Best of the Upper Great Lakes.*

"Charming. We slept so well! Thank you again for a pleasant visit to a beautiful city in Michigan. And our special thanks to Ms. Verwys and her wonderful home."

Dutch Colonial Inn

560 Central Ave
Holland, MI 49423-4846
(616)396-3664 Fax:(616)396-0461
E-mail: dutchcolonialinn@juno.com
Web: www.dutchcolonialinn.com

Circa 1928. Originally this Dutch-inspired home was built as a wedding gift for a newlywed couple. Seventy years later, romantic getaways and honeymoons continue to be popular here all year-round. Enjoy the warm and inviting atmosphere with antiques and 1930s furnishings. Gather by the fire in the parlor or living room and relax on white wicker in the cheerful Sun Room. Air-conditioned guest bedrooms feature generous amenities that include phones with data ports, televisions and homemade cookies. Stay in the spacious Tulip or Jenny Lind Suites with fireplaces and Jacuzzi tubs. A hearty, healthy homemade breakfast is a pampering affair with delicious specialties. Innkeepers Pat and Bob are pleased to share their favorite recipes.

Historic Interest: The Cappon House Museum (5 minutes).

Innkeeper(s): Bob & Pat Elenbaas. $100-160. 4 rooms with PB, 4 with FP and 3 suites. Breakfast included in rates. Types of meals: Full bkfst and early coffee/tea. Beds: KQ. Cable TV, reading lamp, clock radio, telephone, desk and three with double-Jacuzzi tubs in room. Air conditioning. VCR, fax and fireplace on premises. Antiquing, cross-country skiing, fishing, parks, shopping and water sports nearby.

Publicity: *Shoreline Living and Country Folk Art.*

"Thank you again for your generous hospitality, Dutch cleanliness and excellent breakfasts."

Jonesville   J7

Horse & Carriage B&B

7020 Brown Rd
Jonesville, MI 49250-9720
(517)849-2732 Fax:(517)849-2732
E-mail: ccbrown@modempool.com
Web: www.hcbnb.com

Circa 1898. Enjoy a peaceful old-fashioned day on the farm. Milk a cow, snuggle shetland sheep, gather eggs and cuddle baby chicks. In the winter, families are treated to a horse-drawn sleigh ride at this 18th-century home, which is surrounded by a 700-acre cattle farm. In the warmer months, horse-drawn carriage rides pass down an old country lane past Buck Lake. The innkeeper's family has lived on the property for more than 150 years. The home itself was built as a one-room schoolhouse. A mix of cottage and Mission furnishings decorate the interior. The Rainbow Room, a perfect place for children, offers twin beds and a playroom. Guests are treated to hearty breakfasts made with farm-fresh eggs, fresh fruits and vegetables served on the porch or fireside.

Innkeeper(s): Keith Brown & family. $85-125. 4 rooms, 2 with PB. Breakfast and snacks/refreshments included in rates. Types of meals: Full gourmet bkfst and early coffee/tea. Beds: KQT. Reading lamp, telephone and desk in room. Air conditioning. Parlor games, fireplace, milk a cow, pet lambs, gather eggs and horse/carriage rides on premises. Small meetings and family reunions hosted. Antiquing, cross-country skiing, fishing, live theater, parks, shopping, sporting events, water sports, Jackson Space Center, Speedway and County Fair nearby.

Publicity: *Detroit Free Press, The Toledo Blade, Hillsdale Daily News and MSU Alumni.*

Munro House B&B Health & Day Spa

202 Maumee St
Jonesville, MI 49250-1247
(517)849-9292 (800)320-3792 Fax:(517)849-7685
E-mail: historicinn@munrohouse.com
Web: www.munrohouse.com

Circa 1834. "The Most Comfortable Lodging in South Central Michigan" is found at this historic 1834 bed & breakfast that was once a station on the Underground Railroad. Relax in an abundance of common areas, play the grand piano, read in the library or watch a video. Enjoy complimentary soft drinks and homemade cookies. Stay in a themed guest bedroom with a gas fireplace and two-person Jacuzzi tub. Wake up to a country-style breakfast. Murder Mystery Dinners, massage/spa services, Chef Night, Romantic Getaways, Holiday Dinners and Intimate Weddings are some of the specialty packages offered.

Innkeeper(s): Mike & Lori Venturini. $109-189. 7 rooms with PB, 5 with FP. Breakfast and snacks/refreshments included in rates. Types of meals: Full bkfst. Beds: Q. Cable TV, VCR, telephone, two rooms have Jacuzzi tubs and fireplace in room. Air conditioning. Fax, copier, library, 400 title video library and homemade cookies on premises. Weddings, small meetings and family reunions hosted. Antiquing, golf, horseback riding, live theater and museums nearby.

"Your home is a wonderful port for the weary traveler. I love it here. The rooms are great and the hospitality unsurpassed."

Kalamazoo   J6

Hall House

106 Thompson St
Kalamazoo, MI 49006-4537
(269)343-2500 (888)761-2525 Fax:(269)343-1374
E-mail: thefoxes@hallhouse.com
Web: www.hallhouse.com

Circa 1923. In a National Historic District, this Georgian
Colonial Revival-style house was constructed by builder H.L.
Vander Horst as his private residence. Special features include

polished mahogany wood-
work and marble stairs. The
living room boasts a domed
ceiling, while the Library
Room is graced with a hand-
painted mural. Other special
features of the house include
an early intercom system. The inn is located on the edge of
Kalamazoo College campus. Western Michigan University and
downtown are a few minutes away.

Innkeeper(s): Scott & Terri Fox. $79-155. 6 rooms with PB, 2 with FP and 2
suites. Breakfast included in rates. Types of meals: Full bkfst. Beds: KQDT. Cable
TV, VCR, telephone and one Jacuzzi in room. Air conditioning. Parlor games and
fireplace on premises. Antiquing, golf, live theater and shopping nearby.

*"A step into the grace, charm and elegance of the 19th century but
with all the amenities of the 21st century right at hand."*

The Henderson Castle Bed & Breakfast

100 Monroe Street
Kalamazoo, MI 49006-4433
(269)344-1827 Fax:(269)344-0620
E-mail: info@hendersoncastle.com
Web: www.hendersoncastle.com

Circa 1895. A local landmark since the 1800s, this regal Queen
Anne Victorian castle sits on a hill overlooking the city. The
home was painstakingly restored to retain its historical integrity
while offering elegant comfort in an earth-conscious manner.
Ornate woodwork, stained glass and incredible antiques create
an elegant ambiance. Themed guest bedrooms evoke a distinct
European flavor, with a hand-painted mural of the Taj Mahal,
heated Italian marble floors, Dutch tiles and French bath fixtures. Other accommodations include the Carriage House, a private bungalow with a kitchen. The morning meal may feature
eggless quiche potatoes with mixed peppers, onions, mushrooms and fresh rosemary; seasonal fruit plate with edible flowers; smoothies; organic coffee, tea and juices. Stroll the three
romantic acres of garden paths through the orchard and vineyard while passing by statues and fountains.

Innkeeper(s): Fred Royce. $200. 4 rooms with PB, 1 suite and 1 conference
room. Breakfast and snacks/refreshments included in rates. Types of meals:
Full gourmet bkfst, veg bkfst, early coffee/tea and room service. Beds: KQDT.
Data port, VCR, reading lamp, refrigerator and clock radio in room. Air conditioning. TV, fax, copier, spa, sauna, library, parlor games, telephone, fireplace,
laundry facility, steam room and discount to gym on premises. Antiquing, art
galleries, beach, bicycling, canoeing/kayaking, cross-country skiing, downhill
skiing, fishing, golf, hiking, horseback riding, live theater, museums, parks,
shopping, sporting events, tennis, water sports, wineries, rollerblading trails,
nature center and planetarium nearby.

Publicity: *Kalamazoo Gazette, Elite Magazine, WOTV, Positively Michigan,
House Sitter, The Night They Saved Sigfried's Brain In The Woods,
Kalamazoo Lost & Found and Historic Kalamazoo.*

Lakeside   J5

Lakeside Inn

15251 Lakeshore Rd
Lakeside, MI 49116-9712
(269)469-0600 Fax:(269)469-1914
E-mail: reservationslk@triton.net
Web: www.lakesideinns.com

Circa 1890. Totally renovated in 1995, the Lakeside Inn and
Spa features original wood pillars and rustic stone fireplaces in
the lobby and ballroom. The inn overlooks Lake Michigan,
located just across the street, and was recently featured in a
USA Today article "Ten Great Places to Sit on the Porch"
because of its view and 100-foot-long veranda. Each individual-

ly decorated room
combines the spe-
cial ambiance of
comfortable antique
furnishings with
modern amenities like TVs, air conditioning and private baths.
Many of the rooms are on the lake side, and some offer Jacuzzi
tubs. Besides board games or cards for indoor recreation, the
inn offers an exercise room, dry sauna and massage therapist.
Cycling, horseback riding, swimming, antique shops, art galleries and a state park are nearby.

Historic Interest: Located one hour from Chicago.

Innkeeper(s): Connie Williams. $75-175. 31 rooms with PB, 1 suite and 1
conference room. Types of meals: Full bkfst. Beds: KQDT. TV, reading lamp,
clock radio and hot tub/spa in room. Air conditioning. Fax, copier, swimming,
sauna, bicycles, parlor games, telephone, fireplace and cafe on premises.
Limited handicap access. Weddings, small meetings, family reunions and
seminars hosted. Antiquing, art galleries, bicycling, cross-country skiing, fishing, golf, parks, shopping and swimming nearby.

Publicity: *Chicago Tribune, USA Today, Midwest Living, Chicago Magazine
and Washington Post.*

Leland   F6

Manitou Manor B&B

PO Box 864
Leland, MI 49654-0864
(231)256-7712 Fax:(231)256-7941

Circa 1900. This sprawling farmhouse offers a glassed in porch
that looks out over the inn's cherry orchards. Traditional furnishings and antiques are found throughout, and there is a
granite fireplace in the living room. Manitou Manor's breakfasts
are served in the formal dining room and feature foods produced locally. Walk to a nearby winery for a self-guided tour, or
drive to herb, hydroponic and maple syrup farms. Take a ferry
from Leland to the Manitou islands, or visit the nearby Grand
Traverse Lighthouse Museum.

Historic Interest: Land was deeded to the Chippewa Indians by Ulysses S.
Grant in 1813 and since that time only 5 white families have owned the
land. At one time the inn was known as the Lattice Lodge. Visitors coming
from steamships in Good Harbour Bay via horse and buggy would stop for
tea and the ladies would freshen up.

Innkeeper(s): Mike and Sandy Lambdin. $125-140. 5 rooms with PB.
Breakfast included in rates. Types of meals: Full bkfst. Beds: KQT. Clock radio
in room. VCR, telephone and fireplace on premises. Weddings, small meetings, family reunions and seminars hosted. Antiquing, cross-country skiing,
downhill skiing, fishing, live theater, shopping and sporting events nearby.

Publicity: *Booth Newspaper and Outsider Magazine.*

Lowell   I6

McGee Homestead B&B

2534 Alden Nash NE
Lowell, MI 49331
(616)897-8142

Circa 1880. Just 18 miles from Grand Rapids, travelers will
find the McGee Homestead B&B, an Italianate farmhouse with
four antique-filled guest rooms. Surrounded by orchards, it is
one of the largest farm-
houses in the area.
Breakfasts feature the
inn's own fresh eggs.
Guests may golf at a
nearby course or enjoy
our hot tub on the screen porch. Lowell is home to Michigan's
largest antique mall, and historic covered bridges are found in
the surrounding countryside. Travelers who remain on the farm
may relax in a hammock or visit a barn full of petting animals.

Innkeeper(s): Chuck & Elaine Brinkert. $58-78. 4 rooms with PB and 1 con-
ference room. Breakfast and snacks/refreshments included in rates. Types of
meals: Full bkfst and early coffee/tea. Beds: KQDT. TV, reading lamp and ceiling fan in room. Air conditioning. VCR, library, parlor games, telephone, fireplace and refrigerator on premises. Small meetings hosted. Antiquing, cross-
country skiing, downhill skiing, fishing, parks and shopping nearby.

Ludington   G5

Abbey Lynn Inn B&B

603 E. Ludington Ave
Ludington, MI 49431
(231)845-7127 (800)795-5421
E-mail: abbeylynn@mishoreline.com
Web: www.abbeylynninn.com

Circa 1890. Tall ceilings, wide woodwork and Victorian furnishings at this 1890 Colonial home create an ambiance of yesterday. Built during the lumbering era, it has been completely
renovated to retain that period, yet the comforts of today
ensure a pleasant stay. Socialize in the large common room or
watch TV. A library of books and magazines will interest avid
readers. Romantic guest bedrooms are decorated in traditional
and country cottage styles. Sleep on a four-poster bed in the
classic Lacy Jo Room with a sitting area, or in the elegant
Kirstie Lynn Room with a jet tub. The mouth-watering aroma
of fresh sweet rolls is a daily invitation to a hearty breakfast of
favorite foods. The inn offers many special event and activity
packages throughout the year.

Historic Interest: The Abbey Lynn Inn Bed and Breakfast was built during the
lumbering era. Tall ceilings, wide woodwork and a beautiful staircase.

Innkeeper(s): Bill & Judy Trim. $65-130. 5 rooms with PB. Breakfast, after-
noon tea and snacks/refreshments included in rates. Types of meals: Full
gourmet bkfst and early coffee/tea. Beds: Q. Cable TV, VCR, clock radio and
hot tub/spa in room. Air conditioning. Fireplace on premises. Amusement
parks, antiquing, art galleries, beach, bicycling, canoeing/kayaking, cross-
country skiing, fishing, golf, hiking, horseback riding, live theater, museums,
parks, shopping, tennis, water sports and wineries nearby.

Schoenberger House

409 E Ludington Ave
Ludington, MI 49431
(231)843-4435

Circa 1903. The carved white columns of this elegant brick Greek
Revival mansion rise two stories to a beautifully designed pedi-
ment. A wide balcony with balustrades overlooks the front garden.
Inside, a variety of finely crafted woodwork is highlighted throughout the mansion starting with the white oak entrance hall. There's
a black walnut library, a cherry living room, American sycamore
dining room and mahogany music room. Original chandeliers and
five fireplaces are complemented with antique and reproduction
furnishings and contemporary art. An abundant, expanded continental breakfast is served. Ludington and this part of the Lake
Michigan shoreline offer beautiful uncrowded beaches.

Innkeeper(s): Mary Saucedo. $145-245. 5 rooms with PB and 1 suite.
Breakfast included in rates. Types of meals: Cont plus and early coffee/tea.
Beds: KQD. Reading lamp in room. Air conditioning. Fax, copier, library, tele-
phone and fireplace on premises. Small meetings and seminars hosted.
Antiquing, beach, bicycling, canoeing/kayaking, cross-country skiing, fishing,
golf, hiking, horseback riding, live theater, parks and shopping nearby.

Publicity: *The Saginaw News, Grand Rapids Press, Ann Arbor News,
Rockford Independent Flint Journal and Kalamazoo Gazette.*

Mackinac Island   E7

Bay View Bed & Breakfast

100 Huron St.
Mackinac Island, MI 49757
(906)847-3295 Fax:(906)847-6219
E-mail: bayviewbnb@aol.com
Web: www.mackinacbayview.com

Circa 1890. For a trip back in time, Bay View Cottage is the perfect Victorian retreat. No cars, neon signs or traces of modern
city life are in view on Mackinac Island. Inhabitants still traverse
the island with horses and bicy-
cles. Imagine taking a quiet
buggy ride to a quaint restaurant
for a candlelit dinner. Each guest
room is tastefully decorated and
boasts a beautiful water view. A
deluxe continental breakfast,
which includes home-baked pastries and a special Bay View
Blend coffee, is served in the dining room or on the veranda.

Innkeeper(s): Doug & Lydia Yoder. $95-345. 19 rooms with PB. Breakfast,
afternoon tea and snacks/refreshments included in rates. Types of meals: Full
gourmet bkfst, early coffee/tea and room service. Beds: KQT. Data port, cable
TV, VCR, reading lamp, stereo, refrigerator, ceiling fan, clock radio, telephone,
desk and fireplace in room. Air conditioning. Fax, bicycles, parlor games, fireplace and gift shop on premises. Handicap access. Weddings, small meetings
and family reunions hosted. Antiquing, art galleries, beach, bicycling, canoe-
ing/kayaking, fishing, golf, hiking, horseback riding, live theater, museums,
parks, shopping, tennis, water sports and wineries nearby.

Publicity: *Midwest Living and Traverse Magazine.*

"The most relaxing place I've ever been."

Cloghaun

PO Box 1540
Mackinac Island, MI 49757-0203
(906)847-3885 (888)442-5929

Circa 1884. Pronounced "Clah han," the inn's name is Gaelic
for "stoney ground" in reference to Mackinac Island's beaches.
Built spacious enough to house Thomas and Bridgett

Donnelly's large Irish family, this handsome Victorian home is owned and operated by their great grandson James Bond. The inn's gracious exterior boasts a front porch and upper balcony where guests enjoy watching the horse-drawn carriages pass by. Guest rooms are furnished in period antiques. Kelton Library is a welcoming retreat for reading or watching videos. Afternoon tea is served. The inn's location on Market Street affords easy access to parks, restaurants, ferries and shops.

Innkeeper(s): Marti & Paul Carey. $100-165. 11 rooms, 9 with PB. Breakfast included in rates. Types of meals: Cont plus. Beds: KQD. Reading lamp in room. VCR and library on premises. Parks, shopping and restaurants and ferry lines nearby.

Publicity: *Country Inns, Michigan Living and Country Discoveries.*

Muskegon   H6

Port City Victorian Inn, Bed & Breakfast

1259 Lakeshore Dr
Muskegon, MI 49441-1659
(231)759-0205 (800)274-3574 Fax:(231)759-0205
E-mail: pcvicinn@gte.net
Web: www.portcityinn.com

Circa 1877. Old world elegance characterizes this Queen Anne Victorian mansion gracing the bluff of Muskegon Lake. The front parlor boasts curved leaded-glass windows with views of the harbor. A paneled grand entryway is accented by the carved posts and spindles of an oak staircase leading up to a TV room and rooftop balcony overlooking the state park. Luxurious honeymoon suites boasts two-person whirlpool baths, and romantic guest bedrooms include desks, modems, refrigerators and ice buckets. Early risers sip morning coffee while reading the local newspaper. A hot breakfast can be delivered to the room, enjoyed in the formal dining room or served in the 14-window sunroom. Ask about special packages available.

Historic Interest: This 1877 Queen Ann mansion was built by Alexander Rodgers, founder of the Rodgers Iron Manufacturing Company in 1850. Alexander also became a lumber barron in 1872 following the great Chicago fire of 1871.

Innkeeper(s): Barbara Schossau & Fred Schossau. $80-155. 5 rooms with PB, 1 with FP and 2 suites. Breakfast included in rates. Types of meals: Country bkfst, early coffee/tea, snacks/refreshments and room service. Beds: Q. Modem hook-up, data port, cable TV, VCR, reading lamp, CD player, refrigerator, ceiling fan, clock radio, telephone, coffeemaker, turn-down service, desk, double whirlpool tubs, fireplace, hair dryers, robes and lake views in room. Central air. Fax, copier, bicycles, parlor games and fireplace on premises. Weddings, small meetings, family reunions and seminars hosted. Amusement parks, antiquing, art galleries, beach, bicycling, canoeing/kayaking, cross-country skiing, fishing, golf, hiking, live theater, museums, parks, shopping, sporting events, tennis, water sports, Lake Michigan, Muskegon Lake and Port City Princess cruise ship nearby.

Publicity: *Muskegon Chronicle, Detroit Free Press, Arrington's Bed & Breakfast Journal and Arrington's Bed & Breakfast Journal's award "Best In The Midwest."*

"The inn offers only comfort, good food and total peace of mind."

Northport   F6

Days Gone By Bed & Breakfast

201 N High St
Northport, MI 49670
(231)386-5114
E-mail: jane@daysgonebybnb.com
Web: www.daysgonebybnb.com

Circa 1868. Recently renovated, this Country Victorian home was built in 1868 for the area's first physician and his family. Dr. Hutchinson is known for being a caring man who cured the local Indian tribe of a smallpox epidemic. The enchanting acre is bordered by a stone fence and includes garden pathways and benches. The Garden Room boasts a Victorian floral décor in pastel greens, antiques, a whirlpool tub and a shower. Another guest bedroom is rich in Native American history and includes a clawfoot tub. The Buckboard Room depicts early settlers pulling up to their homestead in a vintage buckboard wagon. Tempting gourmet breakfast foods are served each morning. Enjoy local wine and cheese before stargazing by the large outdoor fireplace.

Innkeeper(s): Jane & Jack Poniatowski. $89-129. 3 rooms with PB. Breakfast included in rates. Types of meals: Full gourmet bkfst, veg bkfst and snacks/refreshments. Beds: KQT. Cable TV, reading lamp, ceiling fan, clock radio, one room with clawfoot tub and one with whirlpool tub in room. Central air. Fax, copier, library, parlor games and fireplace on premises. Antiquing, art galleries, beach, bicycling, canoeing/kayaking, cross-country skiing, fishing, golf, hiking, horseback riding, live theater, museums, parks, shopping, tennis, water sports and wineries nearby.

Oden   E7

The Inn At Crooked Lake

4407 US 31 North, Box 139
Oden, MI 49764
(231)439-9984 (877)644-3339 Fax:(231)347-3683
E-mail: Innatcrookedlake@aol.com
Web: www.innatcrookedlake.com

Circa 1906. An inviting wraparound porch beckons to this Victorian lake cottage inn. Fully restored, the original wavy glass windows, birch paneling, maple flooring and fireplaces in the common rooms retain the home's historical elements. Enjoy the casual and relaxed atmosphere in the Great Room. Comfortable guest bedrooms feature expensive linens, feather comforters, CD players, flowers and candy. Hearty three-course breakfasts served in the dining room, use fresh local ingredients. In the evening, indulge in a homemade dessert and fresh cup of Peet's coffee.

Historic Interest: Our home was built in 1906 when the railroad brought families from Chicago, Cincinnati and Indianapolis to northern Michigan for the summer. The old train gazebo is behind us. Our home has been fully restored leaving the most historical elements including the old wavy glass in the common rooms, original maple flooring and a large wraparound front.

Innkeeper(s): Mark and Diane Hansell. $90-195. 5 rooms, 3 with PB, 1 with FP and 1 suite. Breakfast and snacks/refreshments included in rates. Types of meals: Full gourmet bkfst, veg bkfst, early coffee/tea and picnic lunch. Beds: KQD. Reading lamp, stereo, ceiling fan, clock radio, hot tub/spa, fireplace, candy and fresh flowers in room. Air conditioning. TV, VCR, fax, copier, swimming, library, parlor games, telephone, fireplace and gift shop on premises. Small meetings and family reunions hosted. Antiquing, art galleries, beach, bicycling, canoeing/kayaking, cross-country skiing, downhill skiing, fishing, golf, hiking, horseback riding, live theater, museums, parks, shopping, tennis, water sports and wineries nearby.

Publicity: *Midwest Living Magazine their Best of the Midwest Poll and the Inn At Crooked Lake placed 3rd in the entire Midwest for Best B&B.*

Pentwater H5

Candlewyck House B & B

438 East Lowell St
Pentwater, MI 49449-9420
(231)869-5967

Circa 1868. Enjoy the homelike atmosphere that highlights this 1868 Colonial Farm House in an historic lakefront village. Restored to its original character, furnishings include primitive American antiques. Hundreds of videos are available to watch by the fire in the large living room. The library, with overstuffed chairs, boasts more than 1,000 books to peruse. Choose to stay in a suite with a fireplace. A mini kitchen is located in or near the guest bedrooms. Ask about special touches like flowers, champagne or candy. Wake up to a generous, country-style breakfast. Relax on the patio with snacks. Bikes are provided to further explore the scenic area.

Innkeeper(s): John and Mary Jo Neidow. $99-129. 6 rooms, 2 with FP and 2 suites. Breakfast and snacks/refreshments included in rates. Types of meals: Country bkfst. Beds: QDT. Cable TV, VCR, refrigerator, ceiling fan, snack bar, clock radio, desk and fireplace in room. Air conditioning. Bicycles, library, telephone and fireplace on premises. Weddings and family reunions hosted. Antiquing, art galleries, beach, bicycling, canoeing/kayaking, fishing, golf, hiking, parks, shopping and water sports nearby.

Petoskey E7

Stafford's Bay View Inn

PO Box 3
Petoskey, MI 49770-0003
(231)347-2771 (800)456-1917 Fax:(616)347-3413
E-mail: bayview@staffords.com
Web: www.staffords.com

Circa 1886. Stafford guests will find this inn not only a relaxing retreat, but a step back in time. The innkeepers have filled the inn with antiques and period decor, including a variety of unique wall coverings. There are plenty of beautiful places to relax, both indoors and outside, where guests can sip a tall glass of lemonade while watching breezes gently move waters at Little Traverse Bay. Expansive, country breakfasts are served on the Roselawn Porch, featuring dishes from a time-tested collection of family recipes. The innkeepers offer special events throughout the year, including an old-fashioned Fourth of July picnic. They close the summer season with hayrides, country-style harvest dinners and a fiddle band which serenades guests as they dance reels and waltzes.

Historic Interest: Historic Mackinac Island is an hour drive or boat ride from the inn. Petoskey's Gaslight District offers many shops and guests can enjoy one of the country's last active chautauquas, with a long list of summer lectures, concerts and theater productions.

Innkeeper(s): The Stafford Smith Family. $79-185. 31 rooms with PB and 13 suites. Breakfast included in rates. Types of meals: Full bkfst, lunch, picnic lunch and dinner. Restaurant on premises. Beds: KQDT. Reading lamp, refrigerator, ceiling fan, snack bar, clock radio, desk, hot tub/spa and fireplace in room. Central air. TV, VCR, fax, copier, swimming, bicycles, tennis, library, parlor games, telephone, gift shop and pet boarding on premises. Limited handicap access. Antiquing, cross-country skiing, downhill skiing, live theater and water sports nearby.

Publicity: *Country Inns, Michigan Living and Midwest Living.*

Terrace Inn

1549 Glendale
Petoskey, MI 49770
(231)347-2410 (800)530-9898 Fax:(231)347-2407
E-mail: info@theterraceinn.com
Web: www.theterraceinn.com

Circa 1911. This Victorian inn is located on what began as a Chautauqua summer resort, surrounded by more than 400 Victorian cottages. Terrace Inn was built in 1911, and most of its furnishings are original to the property. Guests will enjoy stunning views of Lake Michigan and Little Traverse Bay, and they can enjoy the shore at the private Bay View beach. In keeping with the surrounding homes, the guest rooms are decorated in a romantic-country cottage style. To take guests back in time, there are no televisions or telephones in the rooms. This historic resort town offers many attractions, from swimming and watersports to hiking to summer theater. During the summer season, the inn's restaurant (open all year) and outdoor veranda are great spots for dinner.

Innkeeper(s): Tom & Denise Erhart. $49-109. 43 rooms with PB, 1 suite and 2 conference rooms. Breakfast included in rates. Types of meals: Cont plus, snacks/refreshments and dinner. Restaurant on premises. Beds: QDT. Reading lamp, clock radio, 10 have A/C and suite with hot tub in room. TV, VCR, fax, copier, bicycles, tennis, library, parlor games, telephone, fireplace, beach and cross-country skiing on premises. Weddings, small meetings and family reunions hosted. Antiquing, art galleries, beach, bicycling, canoeing/kayaking, cross-country skiing, downhill skiing, fishing, golf, hiking, horseback riding, live theater, museums, parks, shopping, tennis, water sports, wineries and Chautauqua nearby.

Publicity: *Oakland Press & Observer Eccentric, Midwest Living, Michigan Magazine and Detroit News.*

Port Austin G9

Grindstone City School Bed & Breakfast

3173 Grindstone Rd
Port Austin, MI 48467
(989)738-6627
E-mail: selatyfam@yahoo.com
Web: www.huroncounty.com

Circa 1906. Now a fully restored Traditional Victorian bed & breakfast in a quiet country setting, it began as a three-story brick schoolhouse. One of the area's few remaining original structures, it sits just half a mile from the historic namesake city that milled grindstones and shipped them all over the world during the late 1800s and early 1900s. The huge Gathering Room boasts a large-screen TV, VCR and stereo. Munch on homemade cookies, snacks and beverages anytime. A guest kitchen is available as well. Stay in elegant yet comfortable guest bedrooms furnished with antiques. The spacious third-floor Bell Tower Suite features two baths, a dining area and full kitchen. Savor quiche or baked French toast, fresh fruit and bagels for breakfast. The backyard deck overlooks colorful flower gardens and farm fields.

Historic Interest: Our building was the school for historic Grindstone City, which has milled sharpening stones of all sizes which were shipped all over the world during the late 1800s and early 1900s.

Innkeeper(s): A.J. & Rebecca Sealty. $85-125. 5 rooms, 4 with PB, 1 suite and 1 conference room. Breakfast and snacks/refreshments included in rates. Types of meals: Full bkfst. Beds: KQT. Reading lamp, ceiling fan, clock radio and Bell Tower Suite has full kitchen in room. Air conditioning. TV, VCR and telephone on premises. Small meetings, family reunions and seminars hosted. Amusement parks, antiquing, beach, canoeing/kayaking, fishing, golf, hiking, horseback riding, live theater, parks, shopping and water sports nearby.

Publicity: *The Huron Country Press and Bay City Times.*

Lake Street Manor

8569 Lake St
Port Austin, MI 48467
(989)738-7720 (888)273-8987
Web: http://hometown.aol.com/lakestreetmanor

Circa 1875. As history has shown, the homes of lumber barons are often some of the most luxurious. This Victorian, with its peak roofs and gingerbread trim is no exception. The Culhane family, who made their fortune in the timber business, used this home as their summer retreat. In the 1930s, it was rented out as a summer guest house, and today the innkeeper, Carolyn, has once again opened the doors to visitors. The rooms have charming names: The Garden Basket Room, the Wedding Ring Room and the Raspberry Wine Room, to name a few. The Parlor Room, which includes a bay window, is accessed by double pocket doors, a characteristic feature in Victorian homes. The Bay Room, which is one of the inn's common rooms, includes a hot tub in front of a wood-burning stove.

Historic Interest: Registered.

Innkeeper(s): Carolyn and Jack. $60-80. 5 rooms, 3 with PB. Breakfast included in rates. Types of meals: Cont plus, picnic lunch and room service. Beds: D. Cable TV, VCR, reading lamp and ceiling fan in room. Spa, bicycles, parlor games, telephone, woodstove, stereo, BBQ, yard games and hot tub on premises. Weddings and family reunions hosted. Antiquing, cross-country skiing, fishing, golf, live theater, parks, shopping, tennis, water sports, horseback riding and canoe rental nearby.

Port Huron   I10

Victorian Inn

1229 7th St
Port Huron, MI 48060-5303
(810)984-1437 Fax:(810)984-5777

Circa 1896. This finely renovated Queen Anne Victorian house has both an inn and restaurant. Gleaming carved-oak woodwork, leaded-glass windows and fireplaces in almost every room reflect the home's gracious air. Authentic wallpapers and

draperies provide a background for carefully selected antiques. At the three-star, AAA-rated Pierpont's Pub & Wine Cellar, Victorian-inspired menus include such entrees as rack-o-lamb, filets, fish and seafood, all served on antique china.

Innkeeper(s): Dan Nichols & Christine Smith. $50-75. 4 rooms, 2 with PB, 2 with FP and 1 suite. Breakfast included in rates. Restaurant on premises. Beds: QDT. Reading lamp and clock radio in room. TV, parlor games, telephone, fireplace and pub on premises. Weddings and small meetings hosted. Antiquing, cross-country skiing, fishing, live theater, parks, shopping and water sports nearby.

Publicity: *Detroit News, Detroit Free Press, Heritage, Crains Business Magazine, Good Afternoon Detroit and HGTV-Bob Villa's Restore America.*

"In all of my trips, business or pleasure, I have never experienced such a warm and courteous staff."

Saint Clair   I10

William Hopkins Manor

613 N Riverside Ave
Saint Clair, MI 48079-5417
(810)329-0188 Fax:(810)329-6239

Circa 1876. This three-story Second Empire Victorian, encompasses 10,000 square feet and comes complete with tower, slate mansard roof, dormers, porches and an elaborate wrought iron fence. Its riverfront location across the street from the St. Clair River affords the pastime of watching freighters and barges pass by. Guest rooms feature reproductions and antiques, and some rooms have fireplaces. A billiard room and two parlors are available for relaxing. Breakfast is served family style in the dining room. The Historic St. Clair Inn, a five-minute walk away, offers an interesting dining option.

Innkeeper(s): Sharon Llewellyn & Terry Mazzarese. $80-100. 5 rooms, 1 with PB, 1 with FP. Breakfast included in rates. Types of meals: Full bkfst, veg bkfst and early coffee/tea. Beds: QD. Reading lamp and clock radio in room. Air conditioning. Fireplace and CD players on premises. Small meetings, family reunions and seminars hosted. Antiquing, art galleries, beach, canoeing/kayaking, fishing, golf, horseback riding, live theater, museums, parks, shopping and water sports nearby.

Publicity: *Southern Sunrise, Midwest Living, The Voice, Between the Lines, Detroit Free Press and Detroit News.*

Saint Joseph   J5

South Cliff Inn B&B

1900 Lakeshore Dr
Saint Joseph, MI 49085-1668
(269)983-4881 Fax:(269)983-7391

Circa 1915. Overlooking Lake Michigan is this charming English cottage, which features seven luxurious guest rooms. One of the most popular is the teal-toned Sunset Suite, with its panoramic lake view and custom marble tub. Many guests enjoy relaxing in front of the inn's living room fireplace, or on one of two decks that provide vistas of the lake. St. Joseph, a popular getaway for Chicago and Detroit residents, offers many opportunities for visitors. Guests may walk to the beach or downtown for shopping and dining. Several state parks are within easy driving distance.

Innkeeper(s): Bill Swisher. $85-225. 1 suite. Cable TV, reading lamp, refrigerator, ceiling fan, clock radio, telephone and desk in room. Air conditioning. VCR and fireplace on premises. Amusement parks, antiquing, cross-country skiing, live theater, shopping and sporting events nearby.

Saline   J8

The Homestead B&B

9279 Macon Rd
Saline, MI 48176-9305
(734)429-9625

Circa 1851. The Homestead is a two-story brick farmhouse situated on 50 acres of fields, woods and river. The house has 15-inch-thick walls and is furnished with Victorian antiques and family heirlooms. This was a favorite camping spot for Native Americans while they salted their fish, and many arrowheads have been found on the farm. Activities include long walks through meadows of wildflowers and cross-country skiing in season. It is 40 minutes from Detroit and Toledo and 10 minutes from Ann Arbor.

Innkeeper(s): Shirley Grossman. $70-75. 5 rooms and 1 conference room. Breakfast and snacks/refreshments included in rates. Types of meals: Full bkfst and early coffee/tea. Beds: DT. TV and reading lamp in room. Air conditioning. VCR, telephone and fireplace on premises. Small meetings, family reunions and seminars hosted. Antiquing, cross-country skiing, parks, shopping and sporting events nearby.

Publicity: *Ann Arbor News, Country Focus and Saline Reporter.*

"We're spoiled now and wouldn't want to stay elsewhere! No motel offers deer at dusk and dawn!"

Saugatuck   I6

Bayside Inn

618 Water St Box 186
Saugatuck, MI 49453
(269)857-4321 Fax:(269)857-1870
E-mail: info@baysideinn.net
Web: www.baysideinn.net

Circa 1926. Located on the edge of the Kalamazoo River and across from the nature observation tower, this downtown inn was once a boathouse. The common room now has a fire-

place and view of the water. Each guest room has its own deck. The inn is near several restaurants, shops and beaches. Fishing for salmon, perch and trout is popular.

Innkeeper(s): Kathy Wilson. $85-250. 10 rooms with PB, 4 with FP, 4 suites and 1 conference room. Breakfast included in rates. Types of meals: Cont plus. Beds: KQ. Cable TV, VCR, reading lamp, refrigerator and telephone in room. Air conditioning. TV, fax, copier, spa and fireplace on premises. Weddings, small meetings, family reunions and seminars hosted. Antiquing, cross-country skiing, fishing, live theater, shopping and water sports nearby.

"Our stay was wonderful, more pleasant than anticipated, we were so pleased. As for breakfast, it gets our A 1 rating."

Ivy Inn

421 Water
Saugatuck, MI 49453
(616)857-4643
Web: www.ivy-inn.com

Circa 1890. Relaxation begins when stepping onto the porch with an enticing swing. Originally a boarding house, it is now more than 100 years old and renovated for pleasurable get-aways. An inviting common room with fireplace features an extensive library. Gorgeous views of the Kalamazoo River or Village Park are seen from the well-decorated guest bedrooms. Hard-boiled eggs, sausage, cheese, muffins, cobbler, cereal and fruit are typical of the deluxe continental breakfast offered daily. A breakfast basket can be prepared for the room or for a picnic outdoors. Encounter friendly people and unique shops in the quaint village.

Innkeeper(s): Linda Brooks/Kay VanHorn. $100-135. 6 rooms with PB. Breakfast included in rates. Types of meals: Cont plus. Cable TV, reading lamp and ceiling fan in room. Air conditioning. Library, parlor games and fireplace on premises. Weddings, small meetings, family reunions and seminars hosted. Antiquing, art galleries, beach, bicycling, canoeing/kayaking, cross-country skiing, fishing, golf, hiking, horseback riding, live theater, parks, shopping, tennis, water sports and wineries nearby.

Maplewood Hotel

428 Butler St, PO Box 1059
Saugatuck, MI 49453-1059
(269)857-1771
E-mail: info@maplewoodhotel.com
Web: www.maplewoodhotel.com

Circa 1860. Maplewood Hotel stands on the quiet village green in the center of Saugatuck. Built during Michigan's lumber era, the elegant three-story Greek Revival hotel boasts four massive wooden pillars, each 25 feet high. The interiors include crystal chandeliers, period furniture and well-appointed lounge areas.

Innkeeper(s): Catherine Simon. $120-240. 15 rooms with PB and 1 conference room. Types of meals: Cont. Beds: KQ. Data port, TV and telephone in room. Outdoor pool on premises.

"Staying at the Maplewood provided the pleasure of listening to classical music on the player grand piano. It was so easy vacationing...steps from boutiques, art galleries and antique shops."

Newnham Suncatcher Inn

PO Box 1106
Saugatuck, MI 49453-1106
(616)857-4249 (800)587-4249
Web: www.suncatcherinn.com

Circa 1902. Just minutes from Lake Michigan, this 1902 Victorian inn with a wraparound porch, hardwood floor and country antiques, offers seven guest rooms and a double-suite cottage. Guests are offered a full breakfast from 9:30 to 10:30 a.m., including such fare as apple puff pancakes, stratas, peach French toast, cold strawberry soup and chocolate chip coffeecake. The nearby lake offers numerous outdoor activities, such as swimming, fishing and boating.

Innkeeper(s): Barb Wishon & Nancy Parker. $75-135. 7 rooms, 5 with PB, 3 with FP, 1 suite and 2 cottages. Breakfast included in rates. Types of meals: Full gourmet bkfst and veg bkfst. Beds: QDT. Cable TV, VCR, reading lamp, refrigerator, ceiling fan, clock radio, coffeemaker and hot tub/spa in room. Air conditioning. Copier, spa, swimming, parlor games, telephone and fireplace on premises. Family reunions hosted. Antiquing, art galleries, beach, bicycling, canoeing/kayaking, cross-country skiing, fishing, golf, hiking, horseback riding, live theater, museums, parks, shopping, sporting events, tennis, water sports and wineries nearby.

The Park House Inn

888 Holland St
Saugatuck, MI 49453-9607
(269)857-4535 (800)321-4535 Fax:(269)857-1065
E-mail: info@parkhouseinn.com
Web: www.parkhouseinn.com

Circa 1857. This Greek Revival-style home is the oldest residence in Saugatuck and was constructed for the first mayor. Susan B. Anthony was a guest here for two weeks in the 1870s,

and the local Women's Christian Temperance League was established in the parlor. A country theme pervades the inn, with antiques, old woodwork and pine floors. A cottage with a hot tub and a river-front guest house are also available.

Historic Interest: Listed in the National Register.

Innkeeper(s): Sallie & John Cwik. $65-235. 9 rooms with PB, 6 with FP, 3 suites, 4 cottages and 1 conference room. Breakfast included in rates. Types of meals: Full bkfst, veg bkfst, early coffee/tea, gourmet lunch, picnic lunch, snacks/refreshments, gourmet dinner and room service. Beds: KQDT. Cable

TV and reading lamp in room. Air conditioning. TV, VCR, fax, copier, tennis, library, child care, parlor games, telephone and fireplace on premises. Limited handicap access. Weddings, small meetings, family reunions and seminars hosted. Antiquing, art galleries, beach, bicycling, canoeing/kayaking, cross-country skiing, fishing, golf, hiking, live theater, museums, parks, shopping, water sports and wineries nearby.

Publicity: *Detroit News, Innsider, Gazette, South Bend Tribune and NBC.*

"Thanks again for your kindness and hospitality during our weekend."

Sherwood Forest B&B

938 Center St
Saugatuck, MI 49453
(269)857-1246 (800)838-1246 Fax:(269)857-1996
E-mail: sf@sherwoodforestbandb.com
Web: www.sherwoodforestbandb.com

Circa 1902. As the name suggests, this gracious Victorian is surrounded by woods. A large wraparound porch, gables, and leaded-glass windows add to the appeal. There are hardwood

floors and each guest room features antiques, wing chairs and queen-size beds. Two suites offer a Jacuzzi and fireplace. Another room boasts a gas fireplace and a unique hand-painted mural that transforms the room into a canopied tree-top loft. A breakfast of delicious coffees or teas and homemade treats can be enjoyed either in the dining room or on the porch. The outdoor heated pool features a hand-painted mural of a sunken Greek ship embedded in a coral reef and surrounded by schools of fish. The eastern shore of Lake Michigan is only a half block away.

Innkeeper(s): Keith & Sue Charak. $95-185. 5 rooms with PB, 3 with FP, 2 suites, 1 cottage and 1 conference room. Breakfast included in rates. Types of meals: Full gourmet bkfst, veg bkfst, early coffee/tea and gourmet dinner. Beds: Q. Reading lamp, CD player, refrigerator, ceiling fan, clock radio and wet bars in room. Central air. VCR, fax, swimming, bicycles, parlor games and telephone on premises. Weddings and family reunions hosted. Antiquing, art galleries, beach, bicycling, canoeing/kayaking, cross-country skiing, fishing, golf, hiking, horseback riding, live theater, museums, parks, shopping, sporting events, tennis, water sports and boat charters nearby.

Publicity: *Commercial Record, Chicago SunTimes, New York Times, Detroit Free Press, Sun-Time, Grand Rapids Press, Michigan Living and Voted #4 in Michigan by AAA.*

"We enjoyed our weekend in the forest, the atmosphere was perfect, and your suggestions on where to eat and how to get around was very appreciated. Thanks for remembering our anniversary."

Twin Gables Inn

PO Box 1150, 900 Lake St
Saugatuck, MI 49453-1150
(269)857-4346 (800)231-2185
E-mail: relax@twingablesinn.com
Web: www.twingablesinn.com

Circa 1865. Overlooking Lake Kalamazoo, this delightful inn is a state historic site. It is the area's only remaining original lumber mill. The home also has served as a brewery icehouse, a tannery and a boat-building factory. Embossed tin ceilings and walls are accented by antique furnishings. Some of the comfortable guest bedrooms boast a fireplace. After a day of cross-country skiing, golfing or a walk to the local shops, soak in the relaxing indoor hot tub or sit and watch the sunset from the porch. Enjoy swimming in the outdoor heated pool.

Historic Interest: Saugatuck has its own historical museum, and a retired Victorian cruiseliner is docked nearby. Guided tours are available.

Innkeeper(s): Bob Lawrence & Susan Schwaderer. $85-200. 14 rooms with PB and 3 cottages. Breakfast included in rates. Types of meals: Full bkfst. Beds: KQDT. Air conditioning. TV, VCR, fax, spa, swimming and bicycles on premises. Limited handicap access. Weddings, small meetings, family reunions and seminars hosted. Antiquing, beach, cross-country skiing, fishing, golf, live theater, parks, shopping, tennis, water sports and wineries nearby.

Twin Oaks Inn

PO Box 818, 227 Griffith St
Saugatuck, MI 49453-0818
(269)857-1600 (800)788-6188 Fax:(269)857-7440

Circa 1860. This large Queen Anne Victorian inn was a boarding house for lumbermen at the turn of the century. Now an old-English-style inn, it offers a variety of lodging choices, including a room with its own

Jacuzzi. There are many diversions at Twin Oaks, including a collection of videotaped movies numbering more than 700. Guests may borrow bicycles or play horseshoes on the inn's grounds.

Innkeeper(s): Willa Lemken. $105-145. 6 rooms with PB and 1 conference room. Types of meals: Full bkfst, early coffee/tea and snacks/refreshments. Beds: KQ. Cable TV, VCR, reading lamp, stereo, clock radio, desk and hot tub/spa in room. Air conditioning. Parlor games, telephone and fireplace on premises. Weddings, small meetings and family reunions hosted. Antiquing, cross-country skiing, fishing, live theater, parks, shopping and water sports nearby.

South Haven   J5

Martha's Vineyard Bed and Breakfast

473 Blue Star Hwy
South Haven, MI 49090
(269)637-9373 Fax:(269)639-8214
E-mail: donnans@marthasvy.com
Web: www.marthasvy.com

Circa 1852. In a park-like setting of more than four acres with a private beach, this 1852 Federal style estate offers pampered elegance and extravagant hospitality. Gather in the traditionally-decorated parlor. Each spacious guest bedroom boasts a fireplace, antiques, two-person shower, bathrobes and a veranda. A four-course breakfast with silver settings and cloth napkins may include caramel apple pancakes. Indulge in special packages designed as personally requested. Choose golf, massage or an assortment of getaway amenities.

Historic Interest: Built in 1852, it was the third home in the township.

Innkeeper(s): Paul & Pamela Donnan. $99-165. 8 rooms with PB, 8 with FP. Breakfast included in rates. Types of meals: Full gourmet bkfst, veg bkfst, early coffee/tea and picnic lunch. Beds: Q. Cable TV, VCR, reading lamp, CD player, refrigerator, ceiling fan, clock radio, hot tub/spa and fireplace in room. Central air. Fax, copier, swimming, parlor games, telephone, fireplace, gift shop, sun porches and five with Jacuzzi tubs on premises. Weddings, small meetings and family reunions hosted. Antiquing, art galleries, beach, bicycling, canoeing/kayaking, cross-country skiing, downhill skiing, fishing, golf, hiking, horseback riding, live theater, museums, parks, shopping, tennis, water sports and wineries nearby.

Publicity: *Winner of Inn Traveler Magazine Award for third consecutive year and voted "Most Romantic Hideaway" in North America for 2004.*

Sand Castle Inn

203 Dyckman Ave
South Haven, MI 49090
(269)639-1110 Fax:(269)637-1050
E-mail: innkeeper@thesandcastleinn.com
Web: www.thesandcastleinn.com

Circa 1898. Two towers, several balconies and a wraparound porch are features of this unique Queen Anne Victorian Its romantic location half way between the Black River walkway and Lake Michigan offers pleasant waterside strolls and close proximity to the beach. The inn is also across from Stanley Johnson Park. Request one of the three round guest rooms in the towers; all offer fireplaces and private balconies. The Tower Suite boasts splendid views as well. Breakfast features a gourmet entree such as wild rice quiche, creamy breakfast lasagna, or an egg casserole and includes fresh fruit and baked goods. The inn was built as part of a resort and during recent renovation, old love letters now on display, were found in the walls. Enjoy the white wicker swing on the porch underneath the soft breeze of ceiling fans. Evening snacks are served at 6 p.m. and bedtime cookies at 8.

Innkeeper(s): Mary Jane & Charles Kindred. $110-225. 9 rooms with PB, 6 with FP and 3 suites. Breakfast included in rates. Types of meals: Full gourmet bkfst, early coffee/tea and snacks/refreshments. Beds: K. Cable TV, VCR, reading lamp, ceiling fan and clock radio in room. Central air. Fax, telephone, fireplace and laundry facility on premises. Limited handicap access. Weddings hosted. Antiquing, art galleries, beach, bicycling, canoeing/kayaking, cross-country skiing, downhill skiing, fishing, golf, hiking, horseback riding, live theater, museums, parks, shopping, sporting events, tennis, water sports and wineries nearby.

Victoria Resort B&B

241 Oak St
South Haven, MI 49090-2302
(269)637-6414 (800)473-7376
E-mail: info@victoriaresort.com
Web: www.victoriaresort.com

Circa 1925. Less than two blocks from a sandy beach, this Classical Revival inn offers many recreational opportunities for its guests, who may choose from bicycling, beach and pool swimming, basketball and tennis, among others. The inn's  rooms provide visitors several options, including cable TV, fireplaces, whirlpool tubs and ceiling fans. Cottages for families or groups traveling together, also are available. A 10-minute stroll down tree-lined streets leads visitors to South Haven's quaint downtown, with its riverfront restaurants and shops.

Innkeeper(s): Bob & Jan. $59-185. 9 rooms with PB, 4 with FP, 2 suites and 5 cottages. Breakfast included in rates. Types of meals: Cont plus. Beds: KQ. Cable TV, VCR, reading lamp, refrigerator, ceiling fan, clock radio, telephone, desk and six with whirlpool in room. Air conditioning. Fax, swimming, bicycles, tennis, library, fireplace and basketball on premises. Antiquing, cross-country skiing, downhill skiing, fishing, parks, shopping, water sports and horseback riding nearby.

Yelton Manor Bed & Breakfast

140 N Shore Dr
South Haven, MI 49090-1135
(269)637-5220
E-mail: elaine@yeltonmanor.com
Web: www.yeltonmanor.com

Circa 1872. Sunsets over Lake Michigan, award-winning gardens and gourmet breakfasts are just a sampling of what guests will partake of at this restored Victorian. There are 11 guest rooms from which to choose, each named for a flower. The anniversary and honeymoon suites offer lakeside views. Most rooms include a Jacuzzi tub. Each of the guest rooms includes a TV and VCR, and there is a large video library to peruse. Bountiful breakfasts include items such as  blueberry pancakes or a homemade egg strata with salsa. Yelton Manor guests also enjoy evening hors d'oeuvres, and don't forget to sample one of the inn's signature chocolate chip cookies. During the Christmas season, a tree is placed in every room, and more than 15,000 lights decorate the inn. The innkeepers also offer six additional rooms in the Manor Guest House, a Victorian home built in 1993. Those staying at the guest house enjoy a continental breakfast delivered to their room door.

Innkeeper(s): Elaine Herbert & Robert Kripaitis. $95-270. 17 rooms with PB, 7 with FP and 1 conference room. Types of meals: Full bkfst. Beds: KQ. Cable TV, VCR, telephone, gardens, books and music in room. TV and library on premises.

Publicity: *Great Lakes Getaway, Adventure Roads, Chicago Tribune, New York Times, Hour Detroit, Chicago Sun Times and Country Living.*

"The Yelton Manor is a lovely place to unwind and enjoy the special amenities provided by the very friendly staff. We appreciate all your hard work and will definitely plan to be back! Thank You!"

Suttons Bay   F6

Korner Kottage B&B

503 N St Josephs Ave, PO Box 174
Suttons Bay, MI 49682-0174
(231)271-2711 Fax:(231)271-2712
E-mail: info@kornerkottage.com
Web: www.kornerkottage.com

Circa 1920. The lake stone screened porch of this restored vintage home reflects an idyllic quaintness. Located in a Nordic village on Leelanau Peninsula, it is within view of the bay and downtown. Relax in an inviting living room. Cheery guest bedrooms are clean and crisp with ironed bed linens. Enjoy a hearty breakfast in the dining room before taking a short walk to the public beach or unique shops.

Innkeeper(s): Sharon Sutterfield. $115-145. 3 rooms with PB. Types of meals: Full bkfst. Beds: KQ. Cable TV, refrigerator and refrigerator in room. Air conditioning. TV and telephone on premises. Antiquing, art galleries, beach, golf, live theater, shopping, casinos, dining, marina and National Parks nearby.

Publicity: *The Detroit News.*

"Thank you very much for making our stay here in your home a very pleasant experience."

Union Pier
J5

The Inn at Union Pier

9708 Berrien Street
Union Pier, MI 49129-0222
(269)469-4700 Fax:(269)469-4720
E-mail: theinn@qtm.net
Web: www.innatunionpier.com

Circa 1920. Set on a shady acre across a country road from Lake Michigan, this inn features unique Swedish ceramic wood-burning fireplaces, a hot tub and sauna, a veranda ringing the house and a large common room with comfortable overstuffed furniture and a grand piano. Rooms offer such

amenities as private balconies and porches, whirlpools, views of the English garden and furniture dating from the early 1900s. Breakfast includes fresh fruit and homemade jams made of fruit from surrounding farms.

Innkeeper(s): Bill & Joyce Jann. $155-230. 16 rooms with PB, 12 with FP, 2 with HT, 2 suites and 1 conference room. Breakfast and snacks/refreshments included in rates. Types of meals: Full gourmet bkfst and early coffee/tea. Beds: KQT. Ceiling fan, clock radio, telephone and wood burning fireplace in room. Air conditioning. VCR, fax, copier, spa, swimming, sauna, bicycles, library, parlor games and fireplace on premises. Limited handicap access. Weddings, small meetings, family reunions and seminars hosted. Antiquing, art galleries, bicycling, cross-country skiing, hiking, parks, sporting events, water sports, wineries and wine tasting nearby.

Publicity: *Chicago, Midwest Living, W, Country Living, Travel & Leisure, Bride's, Chicago Tribune, "Chicagoing" on WLS-TV and Romantic-Inns-The Travel Channel.*

"The food, the atmosphere, the accommodations, and of course, the entire staff made this the most relaxing weekend ever."

West Bloomfield
I9

The Wren's Nest Bed & Breakfast

7405 West Maple Rd.
West Bloomfield, MI 48322
(248)624-6874 Fax:(248)624-9869
E-mail: thewrensnest@comcast.net
Web: www.bbonline.com/mi/wrensnest/

Circa 1840. Tulips and a plethora of perennial and annual flower beds accent the professionally landscaped grounds surrounding this farmhouse adjacent to a woodland, in a country

setting. Numerous birdhouses, creations of the innkeeper, are scattered around the property, and the innkeeper has planted more than 60 varieties of heirloom tomatoes in a heritage vegetable garden. Ask for the cozy canopy room for a comfortable bed and floral wallpaper. A large breakfast is served in the dining room. The innkeeper raised all five of her children here and welcomes families.

Innkeeper(s): Irene Scheel. $95-115. 6 rooms, 3 with PB and 1 conference room. Breakfast, afternoon tea and snacks/refreshments included in rates. Types of meals: Full gourmet bkfst, veg bkfst and room service. Beds: KQDT. Modem hook-up, data port, cable TV, VCR, reading lamp, stereo, refrigerator, ceiling fan, snack bar, clock radio, telephone, coffeemaker, turn-down service, desk, voice mail and fireplace in room. Central air. Fax, copier, library, fireplace, laundry facility, heirloom vegetables in the summer and pygmy goats

in the back yard on premises. Weddings, small meetings, family reunions and seminars hosted. Antiquing, art galleries, beach, bicycling, cross-country skiing, downhill skiing, fishing, golf, hiking, horseback riding, live theater, museums, parks, shopping, sporting events, tennis and water sports nearby.

Publicity: *Detroit News, Midwest Living and Japanese Free Press.*

Whitehall
H5

White Swan Inn

303 S Mears Ave
Whitehall, MI 49461-1323
(231)894-5169 (888)948-7926 Fax:(231)894-5169
E-mail: info@whiteswaninn.com
Web: www.whiteswaninn.com

Circa 1884. Maple trees shade this sturdy Queen Anne home, a block from White Lake. A screened porch filled with white wicker and an upstairs coffee room are leisurely retreats. Parquet floors in the dining room, antique furnishings and chandeliers add to the comfortable decor. Chicken and broccoli quiche is a favorite breakfast recipe. Cross the street for summer theater or walk to shops and restaurants nearby.

Innkeeper(s): Cathy & Ron Russell. $95-155. 4 rooms with PB. Breakfast and snacks/refreshments included in rates. Types of meals: Full bkfst and early coffee/tea. Beds: KQDT. Cable TV, VCR, reading lamp, ceiling fan, clock radio, desk and one suite with whirlpool tub in room. Air conditioning. Fax, copier, parlor games, telephone, gift shop and beverage center on premises. Small meetings and family reunions hosted. Amusement parks, antiquing, art galleries, beach, bicycling, canoeing/kayaking, cross-country skiing, fishing, golf, hiking, live theater, museums, parks, sporting events, tennis, water sports, thoroughbred racing and seasonal festivals nearby.

Publicity: *White Lake Beacon, Muskegon Chronicle, Michigan Travel Ideas, Bed, Breakfast and Bike Midwest, Book of Lists, Arrington's B&B Journal, Cookbook-Great Lakes, Great Breakfasts, voted by inngoers "Best Guest Accommodations 2004", Cookbook-Inn Time for Breakfast and Voted by inngoers-Best in the Midwest 2003.*

"What a great place to gather with old friends and relive past fun times and create new ones."

Williamston
I8

Topliff's Tara Bed & Breakfast

251 Noble Road
Williamston, MI 48895
(517)655-8860 (800)251-1607
E-mail: info@topliffstara.com
Web: www.topliffstara.com

Circa 1905. The rural setting is perfect for this 50-acre llama farm with a grand country home and 1905 farmhouse. Videos, puzzles and magazines are found in the living room accented with a gas-log fireplace. The kitchen is available for limited use. Snacks, fruit and beverages also are provided. Tastefully decorated guest bedrooms reflect the innkeepers' interests in gardening, music, quilts, antiques and weaving. Attic Treasures is a premier suite with a whirlpool tub. Family-style breakfasts are served in the dining and eating areas. The open porch invites relaxation. Absorb the peaceful charm with a stroll through the gardens, or visit the wooly llamas in the barns and pastures. Swim in the outdoor pool, or relax in the hot tub.

Innkeeper(s): Don & Sheryl Topliff. $75-125. 5 rooms, 3 with PB. Breakfast and snacks/refreshments included in rates. Types of meals: Full bkfst. Beds: KQDT. TV, VCR, reading lamp, ceiling fan and clock radio in room. Central air. Spa, swimming, parlor games, telephone, gift shop and llamas on premises. Antiquing, bicycling, cross-country skiing, golf, hiking, museums, parks, shopping, sporting events and tennis nearby.

Minnesota

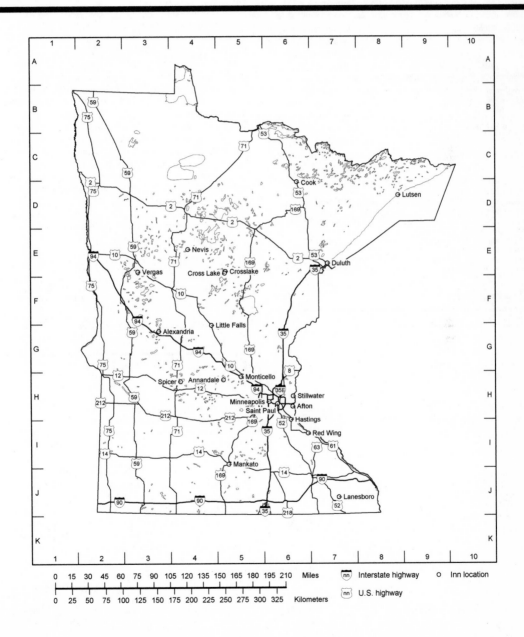

0 15 30 45 60 75 90 105 120 135 150 165 180 195 210 Miles

0 25 50 75 100 125 150 175 200 225 250 275 300 325 Kilometers

Interstate highway   Inn location

U.S. highway

Afton H6

The Historic Afton House Inn

3291 S. St. Croix Trail
Afton, MN 55001
(651)436-8883 (877)436-8883 Fax:(651)436-6859
E-mail: reservations@aftonhouseinn.com
Web: www.aftonhouseinn.com

Circa 1867. Located on two acres of waterfront on the St. Croix River, this historic inn reflects an old New England-style architecture. Guest rooms offer Jacuzzi tubs, fireplaces, water-

front balconies and are decorated with American country antiques. A restaurant on the premises provides candlelight dining in the Wheel Room. (Ask for Banana Foster, or any flaming dessert-a house special-

ty.) Or you might prefer to dine in the Catfish Saloon & Cafe, which has a more casual menu. Champagne Brunch cruises are offered on the Grand Duchess May-October. Three charter vessels are available for private cruises for weddings, birthdays, anniversaries, corporate getaways or for groups of 10-350. Visit the inn's web site for online availability.

Innkeeper(s): Gordy & Kathy Jarvis. $65-275. 25 rooms with PB, 19 with FP. Breakfast included in rates. Types of meals: Full bkfst, gourmet lunch, gourmet dinner and room service. Restaurant on premises. Beds: KQ. Cable TV, VCR, clock radio, telephone, desk, hot tub/spa and fireplace in room. Air conditioning. Fax, copier and spa on premises. Limited handicap access. Weddings, small meetings, family reunions and seminars hosted. Antiquing, art galleries, beach, bicycling, cross-country skiing, downhill skiing, fishing, golf, hiking, horseback riding, live theater, museums, parks, shopping, tennis, water sports and wineries nearby.

Alexandria G3

Cedar Rose Inn

422 7th Ave W
Alexandria, MN 56308
(320)762-8430 (888)203-5333 Fax:(320)762-8044
E-mail: aggie@cedarroseinn.com
Web: www.cedarroseinn.com

Circa 1903. Diamond-paned windows, gables, a wraparound porch with a swing for two and stained glass enhance the exterior of this handsome three-story Tudor Revival home in the National Register. Located in what was once referred to as the "Silk Stocking District," the home was built by the town's mayor. Arched doorways, Tiffany chandeliers, a glorious open staircase, maple floors and oak woodwork set the atmosphere. There's a library, a formal dining room and a parlor with fireplace and window seat. Request the Noah P. Ward room and enjoy the king-size bed and double whirlpool with mood lights for a special celebration. Wake to the aroma of freshly baked caramel rolls, scones or cinnamon buns. Entrees of sausage and quiche are favorites. In the evening, enjoy watching the sunset over Lake Winona. Private hiking trails are available for guests or enjoy a day of lake activities, shopping, antiquing or horseback riding.

Innkeeper(s): Aggie & Florian Ledermann. $85-140. 4 rooms with PB. Breakfast and snacks/refreshments included in rates. Types of meals: Full bkfst, early coffee/tea and room service. Beds: KQ. Reading lamp, CD player, clock radio and desk in room. Air conditioning. Bicycles, library, parlor games, telephone and fireplace on premises. Weddings, small meetings and family

reunions hosted. Antiquing, bicycling, cross-country skiing, downhill skiing, fishing, golf, hiking, live theater, parks, shopping, tennis and water sports nearby.

"The Cedar Rose Inn was more than we imagined it would be. We felt like royalty in your beautiful dining room."

Annandale H5

Thayer's Historic Bed n' Breakfast

PO Box 246 Hwy 55 60 West Elm St
Annandale, MN 55302
(320)274-8222 (800)944-6595 Fax:(320)274-5051
E-mail: thayers@hotmail.com
Web: www.thayers.net

Circa 1895. Gus Thayer, the town constable, school bus driver, thresher and mill operator, originally built this old railroad-style hotel to accommodate weary road and rail travelers. At that time, the inn epitomized the unique turn-of-the-century gaiety of dining, dancing, singing and sleeping all under one roof. Although there have been many changes throughout its 100 years, innkeeper, and psychic, Sharon Gammell, has restored the home to its original intended purpose. Richly appointed rooms feature authentic period furnishings, four-poster beds and hot tubs. On scheduled weekends Thayers offers packages such as "Mystery Dinners to Die For." All visitors will enjoy a gourmet breakfast with specialties such as raspberry cheese blintzes served on smoked bacon and hand-dipped chocolate covered strawberries. A cocktail lounge features 38 varieties of Scotch and a wide selection of beers. The home is listed on the National Register of Historic Places.

Innkeeper(s): Sharon Gammell. $99-225. 11 rooms with PB, 1 with FP and 1 conference room. Breakfast included in rates. Types of meals: Full gourmet bkfst, early coffee/tea, gourmet lunch, picnic lunch, afternoon tea, snacks/refreshments and gourmet dinner. Beds: QDT. Cable TV, VCR, reading lamp, clock radio and desk in room. Air conditioning. Fax, copier, spa, sauna, parlor games, telephone, fireplace, liquor lounge and dining on weekends on premises. Weddings, small meetings, family reunions and seminars hosted. Amusement parks, antiquing, cross-country skiing, downhill skiing, fishing, live theater, parks, shopping and water sports nearby.

Cook D6

Ludlow's Island Lodge

8166 Ludlow Dr
Cook, MN 55723
(218)666-5407 (877)583-5697 Fax:(218)666-2488
E-mail: info@ludlowsresort.com
Web: www.ludlowsresort.com

Circa 1939. A collection of 18 rustic cabins is nestled on two shores of the lake and a private island. They range in style and size and are from one to five bedrooms. All have fireplaces, kitchens and outdoor decks. All cabins have multiple baths and are equipped with tubs and showers. This resort is very private with many activities on the property that are free of charge including tennis, racquetball, canoeing and sailboating. A 24-hour convenience grocery store is also on premises. Children may enjoy watching movies that are shown every evening in the lodge, and there are daily activities that focus on the surrounding environment.

Innkeeper(s): Mark & Sally Ludlow. $200-525. 56 rooms. Types of meals: Dinner. Beds: KQDT. Cable TV, VCR, reading lamp, CD player, refrigerator, ceiling fan, clock radio, fireplace and kitchen in room. Fax, copier, swimming, sauna, tennis, library, child care, telephone, fishing, sailing, canoeing and racquetball on premises. Weddings, small meetings, family reunions and seminars hosted. Golf and shopping nearby.

Publicity: *Midwest Living, USA Today, Parents, Country Inns, Minnesota Monthly, Architecture Minnesota, Outside Magazine and Family Circle.*

Crosslake   E5

Birch Hill Inne Bed & Breakfast

PO Box 468
Crosslake, MN 56442
(218)692-4857
E-mail: stay@birchhillinne.com
Web: birchhillinne.com

Circa 1926. An immense screened-in front porch highlights
the exterior of this historic home, which offers five individually
decorated guest rooms. Each bedchamber contains something
unique. The Garden room includes a private sunroom. The
Norway Pine Room includes an unusual twig headboard and a
double Jacuzzi tub. The inn affords views of Ox Lake, and
guests can canoe across the lake in search of hiking trails and a
picnic area. The canoes, fishing boat and snowshoes all are
available for guests at the inn.

Innkeeper(s): David Senst. $99-135. 5 rooms with PB. Breakfast included in
rates. Types of meals: Full bkfst and early coffee/tea. Beds: QD. Cable TV, reading lamp, desk, hot tub/spa and 2 rooms with double Jacuzzis in room. Air
conditioning. VCR, swimming, bicycles, parlor games, telephone, fireplace and
snow shoes on premises. Limited handicap access. Small meetings hosted.
Amusement parks, antiquing, cross-country skiing, downhill skiing, fishing, golf,
parks, shopping, tennis, water sports and near Paul Bunyan bike trail nearby.

Duluth   E7

A Charles Weiss Inn- A Return to Victorian Duluth

1615 E Superior St
Duluth, MN 55812-1642
(218)724-7016 (800)525-5243
E-mail: dglee@uslink.net
Web: www.duluth.com/acw

Circa 1895. In summer, flower gardens frame this large three-
story turn-of-the-century home. Inside, gleaming wood paneling, carved woodwork, handsome tiled or marble fireplaces and
a beamed ceiling in the parlor are among the inn's historic features. Rooms are furnished with antiques and have features
such as a fireplace, whirlpool tub or bay window. White oak,
bird's-eye maple and cherry are among the fine woods selected
by the home's builder, A. Charles Weiss, original publisher of
the Duluth Herald. Located in the historic district, guests enjoy
viewing a variety of historic homes as they walk three blocks to
the boardwalk along Lake Superior and on to Canal Park and
the downtown area for shopping and restaurants.

Innkeeper(s): Dave & Peg Lee. $95-145. 5 rooms with PB, 2 with FP and 1
suite. Breakfast included in rates. Types of meals: Full bkfst and early coffee/tea.
Beds: QD. Reading lamp, clock radio, one with hot tub and five with A/C in
room. TV, VCR, spa, library, parlor games, telephone and fireplace on premises.
Antiquing, art galleries, beach, bicycling, canoeing/kayaking, cross-country skiing, downhill skiing, fishing, golf, hiking, horseback riding, live theater, museums, parks, shopping, sporting events, tennis and water sports nearby.

A.G. Thomson House

2617 E Third St
Duluth, MN 55812
(218)724-3464 (877)807-8077 Fax:(218)724-5177
E-mail: info@thomsonhouse.biz
Web: www.thomsonhouse.biz

Circa 1909. A Dutch Colonial Revival with a delightful history
of prominent owners, this inn was recently renovated to maximize comfort and style. Each guest bedroom has its own dis-

tinct personality. Choose from a variety of decor: classic elegance, Southwest, Northwoods or French Country. A double
whirlpool bath or deep clawfoot tub, private sunporch or deck,
gas fireplace and CD player add a touch of romance. A continental breakfast basket can be delivered to the room, or a full
breakfast can be enjoyed in the sunny dining room. Entrees may
include orange-spiced French toast or wild rice quiche. The
quiet one-and-a-half-acre property overlooks Lake Superior. A
well-manicured lawn accented with perennial beds, scotch pines
and spruce trees resides peacefully with wildflowers and sumac.

Innkeeper(s): Bill & Becky Brakken. $129-269. 7 rooms with PB, 7 with FP.
Breakfast and snacks/refreshments included in rates. Types of meals: Full
gourmet bkfst and early coffee/tea. Beds: KQ. Reading lamp, CD player, ceiling fan, clock radio, desk, hot tub/spa and fireplace in room. Air conditioning.
Library, parlor games, telephone, fireplace and gift shop on premises.
Weddings, small meetings, family reunions and seminars hosted. Antiquing,
art galleries, beach, bicycling, canoeing/kayaking, cross-country skiing, downhill skiing, fishing, golf, hiking, live theater, museums, parks, shopping, sporting events, tennis and water sports nearby.
Publicity: *Duluth News-Tribune, Inn Traveler, Duluth TV Channel 3, 6 and 10.*

The Cotton Mansion

2309 East 1st St
Duluth, MN 55812
(218)724-6405 (800)228-1997 Fax:(218)728-0952
E-mail: cottonmansion@msn.com
Web: www.cottonmansion.com

Circa 1908. Four blocks from Lake Superior in the historic East
Side, this 16,000-square-foot, three-story Italian Renaissance
mansion was once the home of Joseph Bell Cotton, John D.
Rockefeller's attorney. Its grand entrance, beautiful solarium,
library and elegant parlor with carved alabaster fireplace and
beamed ceiling offer a refined experience. Generous guest bedrooms and suites are distinctive, romantic retreats. Some feature
fireplaces, whirlpools, overstuffed lounge chairs and sofas,
Oriental rugs and antique furnishings. A candlelight breakfast is
served on fine china, crystal and silver in the exquisite dining
room. Eggs Benedict and stuffed French toast are among the
mouth-watering creations. Wine and cheese are enjoyed in the
evening. This gracious setting is perfect for small weddings or
other romantic occasions and corporate gatherings.

Innkeeper(s): Ken & Kimberly Aparicio. $125-245. 7 rooms with PB, 4 with FP
and 6 suites. Types of meals: Full bkfst and early coffee/tea. Beds: Q. CD player,
clock radio and hot tub/spa in room. Library, parlor games, telephone and fireplace on premises. Family reunions hosted. Antiquing, bicycling, canoeing/kayak-
ing, cross-country skiing, downhill skiing, fishing, golf, hiking, horseback riding,
live theater, museums, parks, shopping, tennis and water sports nearby.
Publicity: *HGTV's The Good Life.*

The Firelight Inn on Oregon Creek

2211 East Third St
Duluth, MN 55812
(218)724-0272 (888)724-0273 Fax:(218)724-0304
E-mail: info@firelightinn.com
Web: www.firelightinn.com

Circa 1910. This three-story red brick mansion boasts twelve fireplaces built of a variety of materials including marble, granite and
copper. A massive glassed-in porch overlooks the inn's creek,
which flows to Lake Superior a few blocks away. In addition to a
gas fireplace, five suites offer a Jacuzzi tub and a brass, canopy or
four-poster bed. The inn features beautifully preserved woodwork,
a carved staircase and polished wood floors. There's a baby grand
piano in the living room. Breakfast is brought to your room, and it
is usually eaten fireside. Specialties include dishes such as stuffed
strawberry French toast, bacon, fruit and lemon pecan bread.

Innkeeper(s): Jim & Joy Fischer. $170-250. 5 rooms with PB, 5 with FP. Breakfast and snacks/refreshments included in rates. Types of meals: Full bkfst, early coffee/tea and picnic lunch. Beds: KQ. Cable TV, VCR, stereo, ceiling fan, clock radio and hot tub/spa in room. Fax, copier, telephone, fireplace and massage therapy on premises. Weddings, small meetings, family reunions and seminars hosted. Antiquing, art galleries, beach, bicycling, canoeing/kayaking, cross-country skiing, downhill skiing, fishing, golf, hiking, museums, parks, shopping and sporting events nearby.

Publicity: *Minneapolis Star Tribune, Duluth Area Women Magazine and MSP Magazine.*

Manor On The Creek Inn/ Bed & Breakfast

2215 E 2nd St
Duluth, MN 55812-1864
(218)728-3189 (800)428-3189 Fax:(218)724-6227
Web: www.manoronthecreek.com

Circa 1907. Set on two wooded, park-like acres along Oregon Creek yet in the heart of the historic East End, this exquisite mansion is Duluth's third largest home. Built by architects Bray and Nystrom, who were originally influenced by Louis Sullivan and Frank Lloyd Wright, the home boasts finely crafted woodwork, a grand great hall, a unique parlor ceiling and a Tiffany fireplace in the dining room. Decorated with traditional furnishings appropriate to the period, the living room entices guests to relax. There are seven accommodations; most feature fireplaces and ceiling fans. There are five suites, three with double whirlpool tubs. Common rooms include a sunroom and billiards room. A full breakfast is served, and dinner and picnic lunches may be reserved ahead. Enjoy cultural events, concert and sports packages and a wide range of activities such as antiquing, fishing and shopping.

Innkeeper(s): Ernest & Helene Agne. $110-250. 8 rooms, 7 with PB, 7 with FP and 6 suites. Breakfast and afternoon tea included in rates. Types of meals: Full bkfst, early coffee/tea, picnic lunch, snacks/refreshments, dinner and room service. Beds: KQ. CD player, ceiling fan, clock radio, turn-down service, hot tub/spa, fireplace and turn-down service on request in room. Central air. TV, VCR, fax, parlor games, telephone, special-event dining and Internet access available on premises. Weddings, small meetings, family reunions and seminars hosted. Antiquing, cross-country skiing, downhill skiing, fishing, golf, hiking, live theater, parks, shopping, sporting events, tennis, water sports and symphony nearby.

Publicity: *MN Monthly, Rochester Press, St. Paul Pioneer Press and Duluth News-Tribune.*

Mathew S. Burrows 1890 Inn

1632 E 1st St
Duluth, MN 55812-1650
(218)724-4991 (800)789-1890
Web: www.visitduluth.com/1890inn

Circa 1891. Guests will know the meaning of love at first site when they visit this historic inn. The exterior's Victorian architecture is whimsical and welcoming, and the interior is truly a work of art. The woodwork is the very definition of spectacular. Carved mantels and a grand staircase are among the notable features, and the interior is proof positive that the Victorians understood the meaning of elegance. The romantic rooms include suites with a fireplace or a lace-enclosed, four-poster bed. The Rose and Morning Glory rooms each include a clawfoot tub. The Ballroom Suite, a must for all honeymooners, includes an opulent sitting room, two romantic bedrooms, a clawfoot tub and a view of Lake Superior. The home is located in a historic section of Duluth. The town offers plenty of lake-related activities, an aquarium, historic sites, a casino, railroad tours along the river and a unique library museum with one-of-a-kind manuscripts.

Olcott House Bed & Breakfast

2316 E 1st St
Duluth, MN 55812-1807
(218)728-1339 (800)715-1339
E-mail: info@olocotthouse.com
Web: www.olcotthouse.com

Circa 1904. Georgian Colonial architecture surrounded by brick and wrought iron creates an antebellum ambiance at this home and carriage house in the historic East End Mansion District. Soaring pillars, bay windows, beamed ceilings, hardwood floors, a grand center staircase and 11 fireplaces add a regal elegance to the stately inn. The multi-room suites and carriage house offer spacious grandeur with antique Victorian furnishings, four-poster and canopy beds, clawfoot or whirlpool tubs, fireplaces, private porches, CD players and other pleasures to enjoy. More than a meal, breakfast is a delicious luxury with candlelit table settings of silver, crystal, fine china and fresh flowers. Lake Superior and North Shore attractions are minutes away.

Innkeeper(s): Don & Barb Trueman. $125-185. 6 suites, 6 with FP. Breakfast and snacks/refreshments included in rates. Types of meals: Full gourmet bkfst and early coffee/tea. Beds: KQ. VCR, reading lamp, CD player, refrigerator, clock radio, telephone, desk, fireplace and one with hot tub in room. Air conditioning. TV, library, parlor games, fireplace and gift shop on premises. Antiquing, art galleries, beach, bicycling, canoeing/kayaking, cross-country skiing, downhill skiing, fishing, golf, hiking, horseback riding, live theater, museums, parks, shopping, sporting events, tennis and water sports nearby.

Publicity: *HGTV-"If Walls Could Talk."*

Hastings   H6

Thorwood & Rosewood Historic Inns

315 Pine St
Hastings, MN 55033-1137
(651)437-3297 (888)846-7966 Fax:(651)437-4129
E-mail: mrthorwood@aol.com
Web: www.thorwoodinn.com

Circa 1880. This Queen Anne Victorian has several verandas and porches. Grained cherry woodwork and fireplaces add elegance to the inn. All but two of the 15 rooms have fireplaces. In the Mississippi Under the Stars Room, a skylight shines down on the teak whirlpool tub. This 900-square-foot suite features tapestries, paisleys and a copper soaking tub as well as a round shower. The innkeepers serve a formal, five-course afternoon tea on Wednesday and Sundays, which guests can enjoy with a prior reservation.

Innkeeper(s): Dick & Pam Thorsen. $97-277. 14 rooms with PB, 12 with FP, 3 suites and 3 conference rooms. Breakfast and snacks/refreshments included in rates. Types of meals: Full bkfst, early coffee/tea, gourmet lunch, picnic lunch, gourmet dinner and room service. Beds: QDT. TV, VCR, reading lamp, stereo, refrigerator, snack bar, telephone, desk and fireplace in room. Central air. Fax, copier, library, parlor games, fireplace, laundry facility and gift shop on premises. Limited handicap access. Small meetings and seminars hosted. Amusement parks, antiquing, cross-country skiing, downhill skiing, golf, live theater, shopping, sporting events, nine hole golf course and mall of America nearby.

Publicity: *Travel Holiday, Midwest Living and Glamour.*

Lanesboro J7

Stone Mill Suites

100 Beacon Street East
Lanesboro, MN 55949
(507)467-8663 (866)897-8663 Fax:(507)467-2470
E-mail: stonemillsuites@hotmail.com
Web: www.stonemillsuites.com

Circa 1885. Combining an historical heritage with modern conveniences, this recently restored nineteenth-century stone building was built using limestone quarried from the area's surrounding bluffs. The original clay ceilings and stair railings accent the decor. Themed suites and guest bedrooms reflect local history and its undeniable charm. Relaxing amenities feature a fireplace, whirlpool tub, microwave and refrigerator. Children are welcome, ask about family packages. A generous continental breakfast may include breads, assorted muffins, cereal, fruit, beverages and French toast topped with strawberries, blueberries and whip cream. A variety of museums and the Laura Ingalls Wilder Site are all within a 30-minute drive.
Historic Interest: 1885 Limestone Building constructed from limestone quarried in bluffs surrounding Lanesboro. Renovated cold storage, egg and poultry processing and feed storage facility. Original clay ceilings, stair railings, and themes to past uses of the building.
$80-140. 10 rooms with PB, 4 with FP and 7 suites. Breakfast included in rates. Types of meals: Cont plus and early coffee/tea. Beds: KQDT. Modem hook-up, data port, cable TV, VCR, reading lamp, refrigerator, ceiling fan, clock radio, telephone, coffeemaker, desk, hot tub/spa, fireplace and microwave in room. Air conditioning. Fax and parlor games on premises. Limited handicap access. Weddings, small meetings and family reunions hosted. Antiquing, art galleries, bicycling, canoeing/kayaking, cross-country skiing, fishing, golf, hiking, live theater, museums, parks, shopping and wineries nearby.
Publicity: *MN Monthly, Midwest getaway, Wisconsin State Journal* and *Minneapolis Star Tribune.*

Little Falls G4

The Randall House

200 4th St SE
Little Falls, MN 56345
(320)616-5815

Circa 1890. Adorning an historic town that sits on the banks of the Mississippi River, this three-story Italianate Second Empire house offers comfortable and relaxing accommodations. Pickup is available from Little Falls Airport. Choose the romantic Rebecca Room with attached sitting room or the spacious first-floor Victoria Room highlighted by three six-foot windows. A generous breakfast is enjoyed daily in the dining room. The expansive grounds boast several gardens. Visit the childhood home of famous aviator Charles Lindbergh. Family owned and lived in, it is open for tours along with a restored interpretive center. After the tour, hike the state park across the street.
Innkeeper(s): June D. Belsvik Sucher. $65-75. 4 rooms. Breakfast and snacks/refreshments included in rates. Types of meals: Full gourmet bkfst, early coffee/tea and room service. Beds: QDT. Ceiling fan, clock radio and kitchen area in room. Air conditioning. Library and telephone on premises. Small meetings, family reunions and seminars hosted. Antiquing, art galleries, bicycling, canoeing/kayaking, cross-country skiing, fishing, golf, hiking, live theater, museums, parks, shopping and water sports nearby.

Lutsen D8

Cascade Lodge

3719 W Hwy 61
Lutsen, MN 55612
(218)387-1112 (800)322-9543 Fax:(218)387-1113
Circa 1939. Cascade River State Park surrounds these accommodations that span 14 acres on Lake Superior. Choose from a variety of lodgings, including rooms in the main house, log cabins, a house with spa, or a motel, at this distinctly family-oriented inn that features a playground, game room and restaurant with a children's menu. Recreation facilities are abundant with hiking, cross-country skiing, ping pong, pool table, video arcade games, volleyball, and table games. Explore and enjoy the area by renting mountain or ten-speed bikes; canoes, paddles and life preserves; cross-country skis, boots and poles; snowshoes; and even backpacks.
Innkeeper(s): Gene & Laurene Glader. $38-225. 27 rooms with PB, 11 with FP, 1 suite, 11 cabins and 1 conference room. Types of meals: Full bkfst, early coffee/tea, lunch, picnic lunch and dinner. Restaurant on premises. Beds: QDT. TV, VCR, reading lamp, refrigerator, clock radio, telephone, coffeemaker, desk, hot tub/spa, fireplace and whirlpool baths in room. Fax, copier, fireplace, gift shop, rental of mountain bikes and cross country skis and canoes on premises. Weddings, small meetings and family reunions hosted. Antiquing, art galleries, bicycling, canoeing/kayaking, cross-country skiing, downhill skiing, fishing, golf, hiking, horseback riding, museums, parks, shopping, tennis, alpine slide and gondola ride, swimming, whirlpool and sauna nearby.

Mankato I5

Butler House Bed and Breakfast

704 S Broad St.
Mankato, MN 56001-3820
(507)387-5055
E-mail: butler1@hickorytech.net
Web: www.butlerhouse.com

Circa 1903. Beamed ceilings and hand-painted frescoes grace the interior of this turn-of-the-century home. Fireplaces and window seats create the elegant feel of an English country manor. The main hall features a Steinway grand piano. Rooms are furnished with canopy beds and down comforters. One boasts its own fireplace, and two rooms have private Jacuzzis. A three-course gourmet breakfast is served in the formal dining room. The surrounding area provides many activities, including downhill and cross-country skiing, cycling, golf, antique shopping and college theater.
Innkeeper(s): Ron & Sharry Tschida. $89-139. 5 rooms with PB, 1 with FP. Types of meals: Full bkfst. Two with Jacuzzis and one with fireplace in room. TV and telephone on premises. Weddings hosted. Antiquing, bicycling, cross-country skiing, downhill skiing, golf and live theater nearby.

Minneapolis H6

1900 LaSalle Guest House

1900 LaSalle Ave
Minneapolis, MN 55403-3035
(612)874-1900
E-mail: c1900@sihope.com
Web: www.vandusencenter.com

Circa 1896. Part of the Van Dusen Center, these elegant accommodations in the fully restored 1892 turreted granite mansion are furnished with art and antiques. Original chandeliers adorn the three main floor formal parlors and a stained-glass skylight illuminates an impressive central staircase. The Music Room boasts a grand piano and one of the ten carved wood and tile fireplaces that grace the 12,000 square foot home. Distinctive guest bedrooms are spacious and lavishly appointed. The Carriage House and Grand Parlor have been renovated with state-of-the-art lighting and audiovisual equipment for meetings and events. A lushly landscaped brick courtyard with waterfall and pond sits between the mansion and Carriage House. Off-street parking is available, and the city's major arts venues and downtown shops and restaurants are just blocks away.

Historic Interest: Opulent Castle style built in 1892 for G.W. Van Dusen is restored to its original splendor.
Innkeeper(s): Christine Viken. $129-249. 4 rooms with PB, 2 with FP and 1 conference room. Breakfast included in rates. Types of meals: Full bkfst. Beds: KQ. TV and telephone in room. Guthrie Theatre, Walker Art Center, Minneapolis Institute of Art, Minneapolis Convention Center, Orchestra Hall and Minneapolis Downtown nearby.

Nan's B&B

2304 Fremont Ave S
Minneapolis, MN 55405-2645
(612)377-5118

Circa 1895. Guests at Nan's enjoy close access to downtown Minneapolis, including the Guthrie Theatre, shopping and restaurants. The Lake of the Isles with its scenic walking paths is just four blocks away, and a bus stop is just down the street. The late Victorian home is furnished with antiques and decorated in a country Victorian style. The innkeepers are happy to help guests plan their day-to-day activities.
Innkeeper(s): Nan & Jim Zosel. $60-70. 3 rooms. Breakfast included in rates. Types of meals: Full bkfst. Beds: QD. Reading lamp in room. Air conditioning. Telephone on premises. Antiquing, cross-country skiing, fishing, live theater, shopping, water sports, lakes, walking and biking nearby.

"I had a wonderful stay in Minneapolis, mostly due to the comfort and tranquility of Nan's B&B."

Monticello   H5

The Rand House

One Old Territorial Rd
Monticello, MN 55362
(612)295-6037 Fax:(612)295-6037
E-mail: info@randhouse.com
Web: www.randhouse.com

Circa 1884. Situated on more than three secluded acres in the historic district, this award-winning three-story Queen Anne Victorian is in the National Register as one of the last remaining country estates of its kind in the region. The estate, known as Random, offers extensive grounds with colorful gardens, wooded walking paths, a pond and fountains. There is a library and drawing room and the winter parlor features arched windows and a large fieldstone fireplace. A favorite guest bedroom is The Turret with a clawfoot tub, tiled fireplace and an octagonal sitting area boasting views of the city. Depending on the season, breakfast is served in the solarium, wraparound porch or in the dining room with linen, china, silver, flowers and candlelight. Specialties may include a fruit plate, freshly baked scones, a frittata or quiche with sausage. Downtown Minneapolis is 40 minutes away.
Innkeeper(s): Duffy & Merrill Busch. $105-165. 4 rooms with PB, 3 with FP and 1 suite. Breakfast included in rates. Types of meals: Full gourmet bkfst and early coffee/tea. Beds: KQ. Reading lamp, clock radio, telephone, turn-down service and desk in room. Central air. Fax, library, parlor games and fireplace on premises. Family reunions hosted. Antiquing, cross-country skiing, fishing, golf, live theater, parks, shopping, sporting events, tennis, water sports and outlet malls nearby.
Publicity: *The Old Times, Country Register, Minnesota Monthly* (cover story), *Minneapolis/St. Paul Magazine* and *Minneapolis Star Tribune.*

"We're glad we discovered the Rand House and are looking forward to visiting again."

Nevis   E4

The Park Street Inn

106 Park St
Nevis, MN 56467-9704
(218)652-4500 (800)797-1778

Circa 1912. This late Victorian home was built by one of Minnesota's many Norwegian immigrants, a prominent businessman. He picked an ideal spot for the home, which overlooks Lake Belle Taine and sits across from a town park. The suite includes an all-season porch and a double whirlpool tub. The Grotto Room, a new addition, offers an oversize whirlpool and a waterfall. Oak lamposts light the foyer, and the front parlor is highlighted by a Mission oak fireplace. Homemade fare such as waffles, pancakes, savory meats, egg dishes and French toast are served during the inn's daily country breakfast. Bicyclists will appreciate the close access to the Heartland Bike Trail, just half a block away.
Innkeeper(s): Irene & Len Hall. $75-125. 4 rooms with PB and 1 suite. Breakfast included in rates. Types of meals: Full bkfst, early coffee/tea and picnic lunch. Beds: KQD. Reading lamp and hot tub/spa in room. VCR, spa, bicycles, library, telephone and fireplace on premises. Weddings, small meetings and family reunions hosted. Amusement parks, antiquing, cross-country skiing, fishing, golf, parks, shopping and water sports nearby.

"Our favorite respite in the Heartland, where the pace is slow, hospitality is great and food is wonderful."

Red Wing   I6

The Candlelight Inn

818 W 3rd St
Red Wing, MN 55066-2205
(651)388-8034 (800)254-9194
E-mail: info@candlelightinn-redwing.com
Web: www.candlelightinn-redwing.com

Circa 1877. Listed in the Minnesota historic register, this modified Italianate Victorian was built by a prominent Red Wing businessman. The interior woodwork of Candlelight Inn is an impressive sight. Butternut, cherry, oak and walnut combine throughout the house to create the rich parquet floors and stunning grand staircase. A crackling fire in the library welcomes guests and its leather furnishings and wide selection of books make this a great location for relaxation. The wrap-around-screened porch offers comfortable wicker furnishings. Each of the guest rooms includes a fireplace, and three rooms also feature a whirlpool tub. Homemade scones, fresh peaches with custard sauce and wild rice quiche are some of the gourmet breakfast dishes. The Mississippi River town of Red Wing features many historic homes and buildings, as well as shops, restaurants and the restored Sheldon Theater. Hiking and biking trails are nearby, as well as Treasure Island Casino.
Historic Interest: The Candlelight Inn was occupied by five families before becoming an inn in 1989. The families included a doctor, a pharmacist, a dentist, and a school superintendent. No major structural changes have been made and all of the wood has its original finish, largely due to the 50-year occupancy of the Van Guilder family (1915-1965). In fact, before becoming The Candlelight Inn, it was known as The Van Guilder House. Original Quezal lighting fixtures are found throughout and the captain's wheel motif in the original stained-glass windows is repeated in the balustrade of the main staircase.
Innkeeper(s): Lynette and Zig Gudrais. $99-199. 5 rooms with PB, 5 with FP. Breakfast and snacks/refreshments included in rates. Types of meals: Full bkfst, early coffee/tea and picnic lunch. Beds: Q. Reading lamp, clock radio and hot tub/spa in room. Air conditioning. Library, parlor games, telephone and fireplace on premises. Weddings and small meetings hosted. Antiquing, bicycling, cross-country skiing, downhill skiing, golf, hiking, live theater, museums, parks, shopping, water sports, wineries and casino nearby.

Publicity: *Minnesota Monthly and Minneapolis-St. Paul Magazine.*

"Thanks very much for a very enjoyable stay. Your hospitality is wonderful and the breakfasts were the highlight of the wonderful meals we enjoyed this weekend. Thank you for sharing the history of this home and providing all the interesting suggestions of things to do and see in the area. A return visit will be a must!"

Golden Lantern Inn

721 East Ave
Red Wing, MN 55066-3435
(651)388-3315 (888)288-3315 Fax:(651)385-8509
E-mail: info@goldenlantern.com
Web: www.goldenlantern.com

Circa 1932. Follow the cobblestone path into the luxury of this Tudor revival manor, built in 1932 by the president of Red Wing Shoe Company. Within its 6,000 square feet lie five guest rooms and spacious common areas to relax with friends. Grab a book from the library to read on the stone porch, or take a break in the living room in front of the marble fireplace. Adjourn to a wooden bench beside the stone fireplace on the private patio, or unwind in the hot tub after an exciting day in Red Wing's historic district. Travel up the winding staircase to a room complete with canopy bed, soothing whirlpool bath and cozy fireplace to cap off a night of small-town fun near the Mississippi Bluffs.
Innkeeper(s): Rhonda & Timothy McKim. $99-205. 5 rooms with PB, 4 with FP, 3 suites and 2 conference rooms. Breakfast and snacks/refreshments included in rates. Types of meals: Full bkfst, early coffee/tea and room service. Beds: KQD. Cable TV, reading lamp, stereo, refrigerator, ceiling fan, snack bar, clock radio, desk and hot tub/spa in room. Central air. TV, VCR, fax, copier, spa, bicycles, library, parlor games, telephone, fireplace and outdoor patio with fireplace and hot tub on premises. Weddings, small meetings, family reunions and seminars hosted. Amusement parks, antiquing, art galleries, beach, bicycling, canoeing/kayaking, cross-country skiing, downhill skiing, fishing, golf, hiking, horseback riding, live theater, museums, parks, shopping, sporting events, tennis, water sports and casino nearby.

Moondance Inn

1105 W 4th St
Red Wing, MN 55066-2423
(651)388-8145 (866)388-8145 Fax:(651)388-9655
E-mail: info@moondanceinn.com
Web: www.moondanceinn.com

Circa 1874. Experience exquisite surroundings at this magnificent Italianate home sitting on two city lots in the historic district. Listed in the National Register, the inn has exterior walls made of thick limestone block, and massive butternut and oak pieces for beams, walls and window sills. A grand staircase, gilded stenciled ceiling, Steuben and Tiffany chandeliers, and a huge living room imparts a European influence. The great room showcases a Red Wing tile and oak fireplace. Each of the spacious guest bedrooms and the Garden Suite features a two-person whirlpool tub and antique furnishings. Luxurious fabrics include gold satin, red silk, brocade, damask and tapestry. A full breakfast buffet is offered on weekends, a hearty meal is served during the week. Appetizers are available mid-afternoon. Retreat to private gardens and a terraced hillside or relax on the front porch.
Innkeeper(s): Mikel Waulk & Chris Brown Mahoney. $110-199. 5 rooms with PB and 1 conference room. Breakfast and snacks/refreshments included in rates. Types of meals: Full gourmet bkfst, veg bkfst, early coffee/tea, gourmet lunch and gourmet dinner. Beds: KQ. Modem hook-up, reading lamp, hot tub and two-person whirlpools in room. Central air. TV, VCR, fax, copier, library, parlor games, telephone, fireplace and porch on premises. Weddings, small meetings, family reunions and seminars hosted. Amusement parks, antiquing, art galleries, bicycling, canoeing/kayaking, cross-country skiing, downhill skiing, fishing, golf, hiking, live theater, museums, parks, shopping, sporting events, tennis and water sports nearby.

Publicity: *Conde Nast Traveler, Minneapolis Star Tribune, Minneapolis St. Paul Magazine, Minnesota Monthly, Saint Paul, Pioneer Press and Wisconsin Public Radio.*

St. James Hotel

406 Main St
Red Wing, MN 55066-2325
(651)388-2846 (800)252-1875 Fax:(651)388-5226
E-mail: info@st-james-hotel.com
Web: www.st-james-hotel.com

Circa 1875. Experience the historic charm of this picturesque community, and enjoy the classic elegance of this hotel. Contemporary amenities blend distinctively with the Victorian guest bedrooms to provide a graceful comfort. There are four dining opportunities to choose from, including the Veranda for breakfast or the Summit Room with spectacular valley views for Sunday Brunch. The Port serves dinners in an intimate two-wine cellar ambiance, while Jimmy's Pub offers appetizers, beverages and music. Browse in the seven courtyard shops before embarking on a riverboat cruise or biking the Cannon Trail. A variety of other sports activities and antiquing are available nearby.
Innkeeper(s): Craig Scott. $99-190. 61 rooms with PB and 13 conference rooms. Types of meals: Full bkfst, early coffee/tea, lunch, dinner and room service. Restaurant on premises. Beds: QDT. Period-antique decor, two-line telephones with voicemail and data ports, remote control cable TV, individual climate control, hair dryers, irons and ironing boards and valet service and twice-daily maid service. Whirlpool rooms available in room. Fax and copier on premises. Limited handicap access. Weddings, small meetings, family reunions and seminars hosted. Antiquing, cross-country skiing, downhill skiing, fishing, golf, hiking, live theater, parks and shopping nearby.
Publicity: *Midwest Living.*

Saint Paul   H6

Covington Inn Bed and Breakfast

Pier #1 Harriet Island B3
Saint Paul, MN 55107
(651)292-1411
E-mail: towboat@mninter.net
Web: www.covingtoninn.com

Circa 1946. Buoyed by the Mississippi River, this romantic towboat is moored against a backdrop of the downtown skyline. Now a floating B&B, this authentic line boat was the prototype for modern-era towboats. Trimmed stem to stern in brass, bronze and mahogany, the authentic nautical theme is elegant. The comfortable salon, lit with clerestory windows, offers tables with a view, fireside couches and a library of historic books. Private staterooms feature built-in cabinets, antique fixtures and vintage art. The galley provides a breakfast blend of gourmet and hearty regional fare like wild rice French toast with fresh strawberries, organic maple syrup and bacon or sausage. Enjoy a quiet getaway or explore the active city life.
Innkeeper(s): Ann Holt & Tom Welna. $140-235. 4 rooms with PB, 2 suites and 1 conference room. Breakfast included in rates. Types of meals: Full bkfst. Beds: QD. Modem hook-up, reading lamp, CD player, refrigerator, clock radio, fireplace and decks in room. Air conditioning. Library, parlor games and fireplace on premises. Weddings, small meetings, family reunions and seminars hosted. Antiquing, bicycling, live theater, museums, parks and sporting events nearby.

Spicer   H4

Spicer Castle Inn

11600 Indian Beach Rd
Spicer, MN 56288-9694
(320)796-5870 (800)821-6675 Fax:(320)796-4076
E-mail: SpicerCastle@SpicerCastle.com
Web: www.spicercastle.com

Circa 1893. On the scenic shores of Green Lake, this Tudor castle with English Country decor is listed in the National and State Registers of Historic Places. Air conditioned suites and guest bedrooms feature a variety of delightful amenities. Choose Amy's Room, boasting a clawfoot tub and balcony overlooking gardens, woods and a lagoon. Stay in the masculine Mason's or romantic Eunice's Room each with a double whirlpool tub. John's Cottage also offers a refrigerator, microwave and coffeemaker. A lumberjack built Raymond's Cabin with rustic logs and a stone fireplace chimney. Hospitality includes full breakfast and afternoon tea. A Murder Mystery Dinner, Belle Dinner Cruise, and holiday festivities are some of the special events to ask about.

Historic Interest: Over a century ago, land baron John Spicer built a home on Green Lake now called the Spicer Castle. State of the art in its time, you can now get a sense of things a hundred years past. Furnishings in the Spicer are those used by the Spicer family as they enjoyed the tranquility of this fine old lake home.

Innkeeper(s): Mary Swanson. $80-145. 10 rooms with PB, 2 with FP, 3 suites, 1 cottage, 1 cabin and 3 conference rooms. Breakfast and afternoon tea included in rates. Types of meals: Full gourmet bkfst, veg bkfst, early coffee/tea, gourmet lunch, picnic lunch, snacks/refreshments, gourmet dinner and room service. Restaurant on premises. Beds: KQT. Reading lamp, refrigerator, ceiling fan, clock radio, coffeemaker, desk, hot tub/spa, fireplace and some with private balconies in room. Air conditioning. Fax, copier, swimming, library, telephone and fireplace on premises. Weddings, small meetings, family reunions and seminars hosted. Amusement parks, antiquing, beach, bicycling, canoeing/kayaking, cross-country skiing, fishing, golf, hiking, live theater, museums, parks, shopping, tennis and water sports nearby.
Publicity: *Minneapolis Star & Tribune.*

"What a wonderfully hospitable place!"

Stillwater   H6

Ann Bean Mansion

319 W Pine St
Stillwater, MN 55082-4933
(651)430-0355 Fax:(651)351-2152
Web: www.annbeanmansion.com

Circa 1878. This butter-colored, four-story Victorian beauty is just six blocks from the St. Croix River. It is the oldest surviving lumber baron mansion in Stillwater. Purchased in 1880 by lumber baron Jacob Bean, the mansion was the site of his daughter Ann's elaborate wedding, and then was given to her. It remained in the family until 1957. The inn has two towers with views of the river and the valley. The Victorian design includes items such as carved oak fireplace mantels and shutters that fold into 18-inch walls. Candle and lamplight, mirrors and flickering fireplaces reflect off the gleaming rich woodwork throughout the structure. The inn's five guest bedrooms all have fireplaces and double whirlpool baths. The 18-inch walls lend privacy and give a cozy ambiance to the rooms. The Tower Room is furnished in antique wicker and has a view of the St. Croix River. Ann and Albert's room is a 400-square-foot room with a large bay window and a hand-carved oak bedroom set. Jacob's Room offers an original marble shower, and Cynthia's

room boasts a cherry mantel. Breakfast is served on linens with china next to a cozy fireplace. The meal includes four courses of such gourmet delights as poached pears with vanilla custard, homemade caramel rolls, eggs Florentine and homemade sherbet. Or guests may request a gourmet continental breakfast in bed and enjoy fresh pastries and breads and piping hot coffee or tea in the privacy of their own rooms.

Innkeeper(s): Kari Stimac, John Wubbels. $99-209. 5 rooms. Breakfast and snacks/refreshments included in rates. Types of meals: Full gourmet bkfst and early coffee/tea. Beds: QD. Reading lamp, ceiling fan, clock radio and hot tub/spa in room. Central air. Fax, library, telephone and fireplace on premises. Weddings, small meetings, family reunions and seminars hosted. Antiquing, art galleries, bicycling, canoeing/kayaking, cross-country skiing, downhill skiing, fishing, golf, hiking, live theater, parks, shopping, water sports and wineries nearby.
Publicity: *Holiday Travel Magazine.*

Aurora Staples Inn

303 N 4th St
Stillwater, MN 55082
(651)351-1187 (800)580-3092 Fax:(651)351-9061
E-mail: info@aurorastaplesinn.com
Web: www.aurorastaplesinn.com

Circa 1892. This historic Queen Anne Victorian Inn was built in the 1890s for Isaac Staple's daughter, Aurora. Her husband, Adolphus Hospes, was a Civil War veteran and survivor of the famous first Minnesota charge at Gettysburg. The inn is elegantly decorated to reflect the Victorian era with five guest rooms offering a variety of amenities such as double whirlpool tubs, private baths and fireplaces. The Carriage House is also open as a guest room. A full breakfast is served, as well as wine and hors d'oeuvres during check-in. Enjoy our formal gardens or walk through the scenic St. Croix Valley.

Innkeeper(s): Cathy & Jerry Helmberger. $119-219. 5 rooms with PB, 5 with FP, 5 with HT. Breakfast included in rates. Types of meals: Full bkfst. Beds: KQD. Air conditioning. Library, parlor and dining room on premises. Weddings and family reunions hosted. Antiquing, art galleries, beach, bicycling, canoeing/kayaking, cross-country skiing, downhill skiing, fishing, golf, hiking, horseback riding, live theater, museums, parks, shopping, tennis, water sports, wineries, train rides and trolley rides nearby.

Brunswick Inn

114 East Chestnut Street
Stillwater, MN 55082
(651)430-8111
E-mail: info@brunswickinnstillwater.com
Web: www.brunswickinnstillwater.com

Circa 1849. Victorian elegance encompasses this Greek Revival inn that is the oldest wooden building and the only B&B in historic downtown. Expertly decorated guest bedrooms are furnished with well-placed period antiques. Each room offers romantic indulgences that include curling up by the fire and soaking in a private Jacuzzi for two. Enjoy breakfast in bed delivered to your room. Take a scenic paddleboat ride down the nearby St. Croix River, or enjoy a hot air balloon ride. Reservations can be made for supper in the dining cars of the Minnesota Zephyr.

Innkeeper(s): Marlin and Janine Eiklenborg, Joele Eiklenborg Hiers. $99-165. 3 rooms with PB, 3 with FP. Breakfast included in rates. Types of meals: Cont. Beds: QD. Reading lamp, clock radio, coffeemaker, hot tub/spa, shared telephone in hallway and fireplace in room. Air conditioning. Telephone and fireplace on premises. Weddings and family reunions hosted. Antiquing, art galleries, canoeing/kayaking, cross-country skiing, downhill skiing, fishing, golf, hiking, horseback riding, museums, parks, shopping, tennis, water sports and wineries nearby.

Cover Park Manor

15330 58th St N
Stillwater, MN 55082-6508
(651)430-9292 (877)430-9292 Fax:(651)430-0034
E-mail: coverpark@coverpark.com
Web: www.coverpark.com

Circa 1850. Cover Park, a historic Victorian home, rests adjacent to its namesake park on an acre of grounds. Two guest rooms offer a view of the park and the St. Croix River. Each room includes a fireplace and a whirlpool tub. Amenities include items such as refrigerators, stereos and TVs. In addition to the whirlpool and fireplace, Adell's Suite includes a king-size white iron bed, a sitting room and a private porch. Breakfasts include fresh fruit, one-half-dozen varieties of freshly baked pastries and special entrees. The manor is one mile from historic Stillwater's main street.

Innkeeper(s): Chuck & Judy Dougherty. $95-195. 4 rooms with PB, 4 with FP and 2 suites. Breakfast and snacks/refreshments included in rates. Types of meals: Full gourmet bkfst, early coffee/tea, picnic lunch, afternoon tea and room service. Beds: KQ. Cable TV, reading lamp, stereo, refrigerator, clock radio, telephone, desk and hot tub/spa in room. Air conditioning. Fax, copier, parlor games and fireplace on premises. Limited handicap access. Small meetings and seminars hosted. Amusement parks, antiquing, cross-country skiing, downhill skiing, fishing, golf, live theater, parks, shopping, sporting events, tennis and water sports nearby.

Publicity: *Pioneer Press, Star Tribune, Country Magazine and Courier.*

James A. Mulvey Residence Inn

622 W Churchill
Stillwater, MN 55082
(651)430-8008 (800)820-8008
E-mail: truettldem@aol.com
Web: www.jamesmulveyinn.com

Circa 1878. A charming river town is home to this Italianate-style inn, just a short distance from the Twin Cities, but far from the metro area in atmosphere. Visitors select from seven guest rooms, many decorated Victorian style. The three suites have Southwest, Art Deco or Country French themes, and there are double Jacuzzi tubs and fireplaces. The inn, just nine blocks from the St. Croix River,  is a popular stop for couples celebrating anniversaries. Guests enjoy early coffee or tea service that precedes the full breakfasts. A handsome great room in the vine-covered Carriage House invites relaxation. Antiquing, fishing and skiing are nearby, and there are many picnic spots in the area.

Innkeeper(s): Truett & Jill Lawson. $179-219. 7 rooms with PB, 7 with FP and 3 suites. Breakfast and afternoon tea included in rates. Types of meals: Full gourmet bkfst and early coffee/tea. Beds: QD. Reading lamp, clock radio, hot tub/spa and seven double whirlpool Jacuzzi tubs in room. Air conditioning. Bicycles, parlor games and telephone on premises. Small meetings and family reunions hosted. Antiquing, cross-country skiing, downhill skiing, fishing, live theater, parks, shopping, water sports and 30 minutes from Mall of America nearby.

Publicity: *Cover of Christian B&B Directory and Bungalow Magazine.*

Rivertown Inn

306 Olive St W
Stillwater, MN 55082-4932
(651)430-2955 Fax:(651)430-2206
E-mail: rivertown@rivertowninn.com
Web: www.rivertowninn.com

Circa 1882. This three-story Victorian mansion, built by lumberman John O'Brien, is the town's first bed & breakfast and has recently been renovated and restored by new owners.

Framed by a wrought iron fence, the inn boasts a wraparound veranda. Each guest room and suite has been named and decorated after 19th-century poets such as Lord Byron, Browning, Tennyson and Longfellow. Period antiques were chosen to represent the poets' unique styles. Carved or poster beds are featured, and all rooms offer fireplaces and double whirlpool tubs. Among the many amenities are Egyptian cotton bed linens and plush robes. The inn's chef prepares gourmet entrees for breakfast and in the evening light hors d'oeuvres and fine wines are offered. Historic downtown is three blocks away and overlooks the St. Croix River.

Innkeeper(s): Diane Savino, Jeff & Julie Anderson. $175-250. 9 rooms with PB, 9 with FP and 4 suites. Breakfast included in rates. Types of meals: Full gourmet bkfst, early coffee/tea and snacks/refreshments. Beds: QD. Reading lamp, desk, hot tub/spa, double whirlpool tubs, plush robes, hand milled soaps and Egyptian cotton bed linens in room. Air conditioning. Fax, copier, parlor games, telephone, fireplace, social hour with fine wine and light hors d'oeuvres and in-house chef to prepare gourmet meals (reservations required) on premises. Small meetings hosted. Antiquing, cross-country skiing, downhill skiing, fishing, golf, parks, shopping, sporting events, tennis and water sports nearby.

Publicity: *Country Magazine, Minneapolis Star Tribune, Pioneer Press and Minnesota Monthly.*

Vergas   E3

The Log House & Homestead on Spirit Lake

PO Box 130
Vergas, MN 56587-0130
(218)342-2318 (800)342-2318
E-mail: loghouse@tekstar.com
Web: www.loghousebb.com

Circa 1889. Either a 19th-century family log house or a turn-of-the-century homestead greets guests at this inn, situated on 115 acres of woods and fields. The inn overlooks Spirit Lake in the heart of Minnesota's lake country. Both houses have been carefully restored in a romantic, country style. Guest rooms are light and airy with colorful quilts, poster beds and elegant touches. Three rooms include fireplaces and whirlpool baths for two. The innkeepers recently added a penthouse suite, perfect for a romantic getaway. During the summer months, guests enjoy use of small boats and canoes equipped with parasols, and in the winter, snowshoes are available. Guests are welcomed with a tray filled with goodies. For an additional charge, the innkeepers offer a picnic lunch.

Historic Interest: Two state parks (30 miles), Itasca, source of the Mississippi (1 1/2 hours).

Innkeeper(s): Suzanne Tweten. $110-195. 5 rooms with PB, 3 with FP, 1 suite and 1 conference room. Breakfast included in rates. Types of meals: Full gourmet bkfst, early coffee/tea, picnic lunch and gourmet dinner. Beds: KQ. Reading lamp, ceiling fan, clock radio, desk, whirlpools, bathrobes and hair dryers in room. Air conditioning. Swimming, parlor games, telephone, fireplace, game & book shelves and refrigerators on premises. Weddings, small meetings and seminars hosted. Antiquing, cross-country skiing, live theater, parks, shopping, sporting events and water sports nearby.

Publicity: *Minneapolis/St. Paul, Minnesota Monthly, Forum, News Flashes, Minneapolis/St. Paul, Minnesota Monthly, House To Home, St. Paul Pioneer Press, Midwest Living and Mpls/St. Paul Magazine.*

"Our stay here has made our anniversary everything we hoped for!"

Mississippi

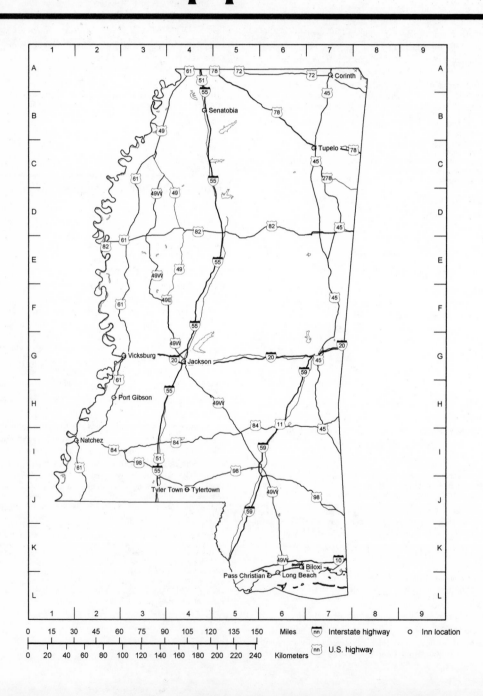

0   15   30   45   60   75   90   105   120   135   150   Miles

0   20   40   60   80   100   120   140   160   180   200   220   240   Kilometers

nn Interstate highway   o Inn location

nn U.S. highway

Biloxi   K6

Father Ryan House B&B

1196 Beach Blvd
Biloxi, MS 39530-3631
(228)435-1189 (800)295-1189 Fax:(228)436-3063
E-mail: frryan@datasync.com
Web: www.frryan.com

Circa 1841. Father Abram Ryan, once the Poet Laureate of the
Confederacy and a friend of Jefferson Davis, lived in this
Antebellum manor. The inn is in the National Historic Registry
and one of the oldest homes on the Gulf Coast. The Gulf of
Mexico sparkles just across the way, and guests can enjoy the
view from several guest rooms. There are 16 rooms to choose,
eight include a whirlpool tub. Several offer a porch or balcony.
Rooms are elegantly appointed, and the antique beds are
dressed with luxury linens. Down comforters and pillows are
other amenities. Father Ryan's poetry and books are placed
throughout the inn. There is much to see and do in Biloxi;
guests can tour historic homes, enjoy the beach and fine dining.
Innkeeper(s): Roseanne McKenney. $100-175. 16 rooms with PB, 2 with FP,
4 suites and 2 cottages. Breakfast included in rates. Types of meals: Full
gourmet bkfst and early coffee/tea. Beds: KQD. Cable TV, reading lamp, clock
radio, telephone, turn-down service, desk and some with whirlpool tubs in
room. Air conditioning. Fax, swimming and library on premises. Limited
handicap access. Weddings, small meetings and family reunions hosted.
Amusement parks, antiquing, fishing, golf, live theater, parks, shopping, tennis and water sports nearby.
Publicity: *Travel & Leisure, Southern Living and Mississippi Public Television.*

The Santini-Stewart House Bed and Breakfast Inn

964 Beach Blvd
Biloxi, MS 39530-3740
(228)436-4078 (800)686-1146 Fax:(228)392-9193

Circa 1837. This pre-Civil War home is named not for its first
resident, but for the residents that lived there for the longest
time. The Santini family lived in this historic home for more
than a century. The B&B is not only listed on the National
Register of Historic Places, but also with the Civil War
Preservation Trust. Each room is decorated with a different
theme. One room features a Western motif, one is African in
style, the third is decorated with an Oriental flair and the
fourth has European decor. In addition to the guest rooms in
the main house, the innkeepers also offer a private honeymoon
cottage with a Jacuzzi tub, wet bar and king-size bed. A full,
Southern-style breakfast is served in the formal dining room on
a table set with fine china, sterling silver and crystal. Among
the nearby attractions are Jefferson Davis' home, Beauvoir.
Charter boats, sunset cruises, walking tours, a lighthouse,
NASA and outlet shops are other options.
Historic Interest: The B&B is the last home of Confederate General Alexander
P. Stewart, the Soldier of Tennessee.
Innkeeper(s): James A & Patricia S Dunay. $75-175. 5 rooms with PB, 2
with FP, 1 cottage and 1 conference room. Breakfast and afternoon tea
included in rates. Types of meals: Full bkfst and early coffee/tea. Beds: KQ.
Modem hook-up, data port, cable TV, reading lamp, clock radio, telephone,
coffeemaker, turn-down service and hot tub/spa in room. Air conditioning.
Spa, bicycles, parlor games, fireplace, laundry facility, BBQ grills and picnic
area on premises. Weddings, small meetings and family reunions hosted.
Amusement parks, antiquing, art galleries, beach, bicycling, canoeing/kayak-
ing, fishing, golf, live theater, museums, parks, shopping, sporting events,
water sports and motorcoach luncheon tours nearby.

Corinth   A7

The Generals' Quarters B&B Inn

924 Fillmore St
Corinth, MS 38834-4125
(662)286-3325 (800)664-1866 Fax:(662)287-8188
E-mail: genqtrs@tsixroads.com
Web: www.thegeneralsquarters.com

Circa 1872. History buffs will enjoy this inn, located 22 miles
from Shiloh National Military Park and in the historic district of
Corinth, a Civil War village. Visitors to this Queen Anne
Victorian, with its quiet, tree-lined lot, enjoy a full breakfast
and grounds decorated with a pond and flowers. Five guest
rooms and four suites are available. Fort Robinette and Corinth
National Cemetery are nearby. The inn is within walking distance to shops, museums, historic sites, restaurants and more.
Innkeeper(s): Charlotte & Luke Doehner. $75-120. 10 rooms with PB, 5 with
FP, 4 suites and 1 conference room. Breakfast included in rates. Types of
meals: Full gourmet bkfst, early coffee/tea and picnic lunch. Beds: KQDT.
Data port, cable TV, VCR, reading lamp, ceiling fan, clock radio, telephone,
turn-down service and desk in room. Air conditioning. Fax, bicycles, fireplace
and private dining on premises. Limited handicap access. Weddings, small
meetings, family reunions and seminars hosted. Antiquing, bicycling, fishing,
hiking, live theater, parks, shopping, water sports and historical tours nearby.
"Ranks with the best, five stars. You have thought of many comforts."

Jackson   G4

Fairview Inn

734 Fairview St
Jackson, MS 39202-1624
(601)948-3429 (888)948-1908 Fax:(601)948-1203
E-mail: fairview@fairviewinn.com
Web: www.fairviewinn.com

Circa 1908. Elegant and romantic canopied beds are among
the enticements at this magnificent Colonial Revival mansion.
Designed by an associate of Frank Lloyd Wright, the home
boasts unforgettable polished hardwood floors, a beautiful marble floor, fine furnishings and tasteful decor. The
innkeepers, Carol and William
Simmons, pamper guests
with a plentiful cook-to-order
breakfast and fresh flowers
and have hosted many a wedding reception and party.
Underneath the shade of ancient oaks and graceful magnolia
trees, an inviting deck offers a quiet space to reflect or enjoy
conversation. History buffs will appreciate William's knowledge
of Mississippi's past. There are helpful business amenities here,
including in-room data ports. The inn has been hailed for its
hospitality and cuisine by Country Inns magazine and the
James Beard Foundation.
Historic Interest: The home, one of few of its kind remaining in Jackson, is
listed in the National Register. The Old Capitol Museum is just over a mile
from Fairview. Historic Manship House is only half a mile, and an art museum and agriculture and forestry museum are two miles away.
Innkeeper(s): Carol & William Simmons. $115-290. 18 rooms with PB and
4 conference rooms. Breakfast included in rates. Types of meals: Full gourmet
bkfst, early coffee/tea, gourmet lunch, snacks/refreshments and gourmet dinner. Beds: KQ. Cable TV, reading lamp, snack bar, clock radio, telephone,
turn-down service and desk in room. Air conditioning. VCR, fax, copier,
library, fireplace, voice mail and data ports on premises. Limited handicap
access. Weddings, small meetings, family reunions and seminars hosted.

Antiquing, live theater, parks, shopping, sporting events and tennis nearby.
Publicity: *Country Inns, Travel & Leisure, Southern Living,* "Most Outstanding Inn North America 2003" by Conde Nast Johansen and ETV Documentary.

"Fairview Inn is southern hospitality at its best." — Travel and Leisure

Millsaps-Buie House

628 N State St
Jackson, MS 39202-3303
(601)352-0221 (800)784-0221 Fax:(601)709-3315
E-mail: info@mbuiehouse.com
Web: millsapsbuiehouse.com

Circa 1888. Major Millsaps, founder of Millsaps College, built this stately mansion more than 100 years ago. Today the house remains in the family. A handsome, columned entrance, bays and gables are features of the house decorated by Berle Smith, designer for Mississippi's governor's mansion. The parlor features a grand piano. Some guest rooms are appointed in antiques and canopied beds.

Historic Interest: Listed in the National Register, Circa 1888, 4th generation family owners.

Innkeeper(s): Judy Loper, Vicky Lynn Wade & Walt Johnson. $116-195. 11 rooms with PB and 1 conference room. Breakfast included in rates. Types of meals: Full gourmet bkfst. Cable TV, turn-down service and complimentary high-speed Internet access in room. TV, fax, copier, telephone and parking on premises. Weddings, small meetings, family reunions and seminars hosted. Antiquing, golf, live theater, museums and fitness center nearby.

Publicity: *New York Times, Jackson Clarion Ledger, Mississippi Magazine, Travel & Leisure and Southern Living.*

Long Beach   L6

Red Creek Inn, Vineyard & Racing Stable

7416 Red Creek Rd
Long Beach, MS 39560-8804
(228)452-3080 (800)729-9670 Fax:(228)452-4450
E-mail: info@redcreekinn.com
Web: redcreekinn.com

Circa 1899. This inn was built in the raised French cottage-style by a retired Italian sea captain, who wished to entice his bride to move from her parents' home in New Orleans. There

are two swings on the 64-foot front porch and one swing that hangs from a 300-year-old oak tree. Magnolias and ancient live oaks, some registered with the Live Oak Society of the Louisiana Garden Club, on four acres. The inn features a parlor, six fireplaces, ceiling fans and antiques, including a Victorian organ, wooden radios and a Victrola. The inn's suite includes a Jacuzzi tub.

Historic Interest: The inn is near Beauvoir, Jefferson Davis' last home.

Innkeeper(s): Karl & Toni Mertz. $49-134. 6 rooms, 5 with PB, 1 with FP, 1 suite and 1 conference room. Breakfast included in rates. Types of meals: Cont plus and early coffee/tea. Beds: QDT. TV and reading lamp in room. Air conditioning. VCR, fax, copier, library, parlor games, telephone and fireplace on premises. Weddings, small meetings, family reunions and seminars hosted. Amusement parks, antiquing, fishing, golf, live theater, parks, shopping, water sports and casinos nearby.

Publicity: *Jackson Daily News, Innviews, Men's Journal, The Bridal Directory, TV Channel 13 and Mississippi ETV.*

"We loved waking up here on these misty spring mornings. The Old South is here."

Natchez   I2

The Briars Inn & Garden

PO Box 1245
Natchez, MS 39121-1245
(601)446-9654 (800)634-1818 Fax:(601)445-6037
E-mail: thebriarsinn@bkbank.com
Web: www.thebriarsinn.com

Circa 1814. Set on 19 wooded and landscaped acres overlooking the Mississippi River, the Briars is most noted for having been the family home of Varina Howell where she married Jefferson Davis in 1845. One can only imagine the romance evoked from the simple ceremony in the parlor in front of the carved wood Adam-style mantel. Everything about this elegant and sophisticated Southern  Planter-style home brings to life glorious traditions of the Old South, from the 48-foot drawing room with its twin staircases, five Palladian arches and gallery to the lush gardens with more than 1,000 azaleas and camellias. The current owners are interior designers, which is evident in their fine use of fabrics, wall coverings, tastefully appointed guest rooms decorated in period antiques, Oriental rugs and selected art. A gourmet breakfast is served each morning.

Innkeeper(s): R E Canon-Newton Wilds. $160-360. 16 rooms with PB, 6 with FP, 3 suites, 1 cottage and 1 conference room. Breakfast included in rates. Types of meals: Full gourmet bkfst and early coffee/tea. Beds: KQT. Cable TV, reading lamp, ceiling fan, clock radio, telephone, coffeemaker, turn-down service and desk in room. Central air. Fax, copier, swimming and fireplace on premises. Handicap access. Family reunions hosted. Antiquing, bicycling, fishing, golf, hiking, museums, parks, shopping, tennis and wineries nearby.

"We so enjoyed the splendor of your beautiful gardens. Breakfast was superb and the service outstanding! Thanks!"

The Burn

712 N Union St
Natchez, MS 39120-2951
(601)442-1344 (800)654-8859 Fax:(601)445-0606
E-mail: book@theburnbnb.com
Web: www.theburnbnb.com

Circa 1834. Sitting on a high bluff with two acres of terraced gardens that include dogwoods, azaleas and camellias, this Greek Revival mansion is located only five blocks from the Mississippi River and historic downtown. Owned by the original family for 101 years, this Antebellum bed & breakfast inn is listed in the National Register and showcases a freestanding spiral staircase. Lavish Southern hospitality is imparted now. Wine and refreshments are served upon arrival. Experience an intimate and romantic ambiance featuring period antique furnishings. After savoring a full plantation breakfast enjoy a memorable home tour. Relax in the outdoor cloistered brick patio boasting a courtyard fountain and pool.

Innkeeper(s): Ty & Sonja Taylor. $125-200. 9 rooms with PB, 2 suites and 1 conference room. Breakfast and snacks/refreshments included in rates. Types of meals: Country bkfst, veg bkfst and early coffee/tea. Beds: KQD. Modem hook-up, data port, cable TV, reading lamp, ceiling fan, clock radio, telephone, coffeemaker, desk and fireplace in room. Central air. Fax, copier, swimming, library, fireplace, laundry facility, Internet and gift shop on premises. Weddings, small meetings and family reunions hosted. Antiquing, art galleries,

bicycling, canoeing/kayaking, fishing, golf, hiking, horseback riding, live theater, museums, parks, shopping, tennis, water sports and wineries nearby.
Publicity: *Country Inns and Bon Appetit.*

"We are still basking in the pleasures we found at The Burn."

Cedar Grove Plantation-Natchez

617 Kingston Rd
Natchez, MS 39120-9561
(601)445-0585 (877)508-6800 Fax:(601)446-5150
E-mail: cedargroveplantation@bkbank.com
Web: www.cedargroveplantation.com

Circa 1830. A native of New Jersey built this plantation home in historic Natchez surrounded by 150 acres. The home is listed in the National Register of Historic Places. The drive to the front of the house is lined with trees, and the grounds include gardens and five ponds. Period antiques and reproductions grace the interior of the Greek Revival home. The innkeepers offer a variety of amenities and services. There is a swimming pool to enjoy and walking trails to meander along. There are even kennels available to guests traveling with pets.

Innkeeper(s): Kay Caraway. $120-225. 9 rooms with PB and 1 suite. Breakfast included in rates. Types of meals: Country bkfst, early coffee/tea and dinner. Beds: KQT. Data port, TV, reading lamp, clock radio and desk in room. Central air. VCR, fax, copier, spa, swimming, library, pet boarding, parlor games, telephone, five fishing ponds, hiking trails, croquet lawn and horseshoes on premises. Small meetings and family reunions hosted. Antiquing, art galleries, bicycling, fishing, golf, hiking, live theater, museums, parks, shopping, tennis, water sports and wineries nearby.
Publicity: *Country Roads and WYES TV12-New Orleans.*

Dunleith

84 Homochitto St
Natchez, MS 39120-3996
(601)446-8500 (800)433-2445 Fax:(601)446-8554
E-mail: dunleith@dunleithplantation.com
Web: www.dunleithplantation.com

Circa 1856. Elegant and luxurious, this magnificent Greek Revival plantation with white colonnade on the front and sides is surrounded by forty acres of landscaped gardens, lawns and wooded bayous. Quiet and intimate yet offering upscale amenities, renovated guest suites and bedrooms are located in the historic 1856 Main House, Dairy Barn and the 1840 Cotton Warehouse. Furnishings include period antiques, reproductions, fireplaces and some boast whirlpool tubs. Take a tour of the home after a hearty Southern breakfast. World-class dining of nouveau cuisine and a casual atmosphere is enjoyed at the Castle Restaurant & Pub in the restored 1790s carriage house. Live music in the evening with food and drink are offered at the more relaxed Bowie's Tavern. Swim in the seasonal pool. Ask about the Enchantment Package, sure to make any stay even more special.

Innkeeper(s): John Holyoak. $89-225. 11 rooms, 21 with PB, 21 with FP and 1 conference room. Breakfast included in rates. Types of meals: Full bkfst. Beds: KQDT. Modem hook-up, data port, cable TV, reading lamp, clock radio, telephone, coffeemaker, turn-down service, desk, hot tub/spa and fireplace in room. Central air. Swimming and gift shop on premises. Limited handicap access. Weddings, small meetings, family reunions and seminars hosted. Antiquing nearby.
Publicity: *Southern Accents, Unique Homes, Good Housekeeping and Country Inns.*

"The accommodations at the mansion were wonderful. Southern hospitality is indeed charming and memorable!"

Highpoint

215 Linton Ave
Natchez, MS 39120-2315
(601)442-6963 (800)283-4099

Circa 1890. Located just a block from the Mississippi River, this Queen Anne Victorian was named the 1997 Property of the Year by the Natchez Convention and Visitors Bureau and has been honored as BB/Inn with the Friendliest Innkeepers by an Arrington Publishing Company poll of more than 100,000 nationwide inngoers and owners. The home was the initial residence built in the state's first planned subdivision. Enjoy a tour upon arrival. A plentiful, plantation-style breakfast is served each morning. This inn, best suited for children over 12, is listed in the National Register of Historic Places.

Innkeeper(s): Frank Bauer, John Davis. $80-125. 3 rooms with PB, 2 with FP. Breakfast and snacks/refreshments included in rates. Types of meals: Full gourmet bkfst and early coffee/tea. Beds: KQT. Reading lamp, clock radio, turn-down service and desk in room. Air conditioning. Library, telephone and fireplace on premises. Small meetings and family reunions hosted. Antiquing, live theater and shopping nearby.

"You have a special gift for making others feel welcome. Thank you for such a good time."

Linden

1 Linden Pl
Natchez, MS 39120-4077
(601)445-5472 (800)254-6336 Fax:(601)442-7548

Circa 1800. Mrs. Jane Gustine-Connor purchased this elegant white Federal plantation home in 1849, and it has remained in her family for six generations. Nestled on seven wooded acres, the inn boasts one of the finest collections of Federal antique furnishings in the South. The stately dining room contains an original Hepplewhite banquet table, set with many pieces of family coin silver and heirloom china. Three Havell editions of John James Audubon's bird prints are displayed on the walls. Throughout the years, the inn has served as a respite for famous Mississippi statesmen, including the wife of Senator Percy Quinn. Each of the seven guest rooms features canopy beds and authentic Federal antiques. A full Southern breakfast is included in the rates. The Linden is on the Spring and Fall Pilgrimages.

Historic Interest: The inn is in the National Register.

Innkeeper(s): Jeanette Feltus. $105-135. 7 rooms with PB. Breakfast included in rates. Types of meals: Full gourmet bkfst and early coffee/tea. Beds: KQDT. Reading lamp, ceiling fan, desk and TV in some of the bedrooms in room. Air conditioning. TV, fax, copier, library, parlor games, telephone and TV on back gallery on premises. Limited handicap access. Antiquing, fishing, golf, live theater, parks, shopping, tennis and water sports nearby.

Monmouth Plantation

36 Melrose Ave
Natchez, MS 39120-4005
(601)442-5852 (800)828-4531 Fax:(604)446-7762
E-mail: luxury@monmouthplantation.com
Web: www.monmouthplantation.com

Circa 1818. Monmouth was the home of General Quitman who became acting Governor of Mexico, Governor of Mississippi, and a U.S. Congressman. In the National Historic

Landmark, the inn features antique four-poster and canopy beds, turndown service and an evening cocktail hour. Guests Jefferson Davis and Henry Clay enjoyed the same acres of gardens, pond and walking paths available today. Elegant, five-course Southern dinners are served in the beautifully appointed dining room and parlors.

Innkeeper(s): Ron & Lani Riches. $155-375. 31 rooms with PB, 18 with FP, 16 suites, 6 cottages and 1 conference room. Breakfast included in rates. Types of meals: Full bkfst, early coffee/tea and dinner. Restaurant on premises. Beds: KQDT. Cable TV, reading lamp, CD player, clock radio, turn-down service and desk in room. Air conditioning. TV, fax, copier, telephone and fireplace on premises. Weddings, small meetings, family reunions and seminars hosted. Antiquing and shopping nearby.

Publicity: *Nominated among the world's best places to stay. Achieving a rating of 88.5 Monmouth Plantation is on the 2003 Gold List. More than 28,000 Conde Nast Traveler subscribers voted in this year's Reader's Choice Poll to select the few best places to stay. The high score achieved is a reflection of the staff's dedication to our guests' comfort. Among our staff many have been at the property for over ten years.*

"The best historical inn we have stayed at anywhere."

Myrtle Corner

600 State St
Natchez, MS 39120
(601)455-5999 (866)488-5999 Fax:(601)304-4065
E-mail: myrtlecornerbnb@msn.com
Web: www.myrtlecorner.com

Circa 1897. The exterior of Myrtle Corner appears as a fanciful confection of light pink with snow-white trim along the streets of historic downtown Natchez. Antiques and reproductions decorate the interior. The Magnolia Suite includes two bedrooms, a gas-log fireplace and bathroom with a Jacuzzi tub. A carved mahogany, four-poster bed graces the Myrtle and Cypress rooms. The Raintree room has a marble bath. Guests are greeted with a bottle of wine. Each morning, a full breakfast is served in the formal dining room with traditional Southern items such as biscuits and grits and gourmet treats such as eggs Benedict or pecan waffles.

Innkeeper(s): Layne Taylor and Don Vesterse. $110-160. 4 rooms with PB, 4 with FP and 1 suite. Breakfast included in rates. Types of meals: Full gourmet bkfst and early coffee/tea. Beds: KQT. Cable TV, reading lamp, ceiling fan, clock radio, desk, hot tub/spa and fireplace in room. Central air. VCR, fax, copier, telephone, fireplace, laundry facility, private planted courtyard and galleries on premises. Weddings, small meetings, family reunions and seminars hosted. Antiquing, art galleries, bicycling, fishing, golf, hiking, live theater, museums, parks, shopping, tennis, water sports and wineries nearby.
Publicity: *Country Roads and WYES TV-12 New Orleans.*

Natchez Guest House Historic Inn

201 N Pearl St
Natchez, MS 39120-3240
(601)442-8848 (866)442-8848 Fax:(601)442-3323
E-mail: ghinn@bellsouth.net
Web: www.natchezguesthouse.com

Circa 1840. Just three blocks from the Mississippi River, in the heart of the historic district on Antique Row, this two-story Greek Revival Antebellum mansion features wraparound verandas with Ionic columns. Nineteenth century American Empire antiques and fine quality reproductions are accented by period art and prints. Exquisite guest bedrooms and suites boast 12-foot ceilings, rich draperies and wall treatments, fine bedding on canopy beds and lavish bath and grooming amenities. Regional breakfast dishes, lunches and candlelight dinners are prepared by the internationally acclaimed chef in the Garden Court Bistro, a glass-walled dining room and fountained courtyard. Enjoy listening to classical music with High Tea on The Veranda. A jazz and blues brunch is served on Sundays. Ask the concierge to arrange massage or spa treatments.

Historic Interest: Built in 1840 as a Greek Revival city mansion, converted to a gentleman's club after the war between the states, exquisite period antiques and furnishings. Surrounded by historic properties and sites.

Innkeeper(s): Layne Taylor. $60-200. 17 rooms with PB, 4 with FP, 2 suites and 1 conference room. Types of meals: Full gourmet bkfst, veg bkfst, gourmet lunch, afternoon tea and gourmet dinner. Restaurant on premises. Beds: KQD. Modem hook-up, data port, cable TV, reading lamp, ceiling fan, clock radio, telephone, coffeemaker, turn-down service, desk, voice mail, HBO, fireplace, hair dryers and 12-foot ceilings in room. Central air. Fax, copier, The Garden Court Bistro for fine Southern and international cuisine prepared by an internationally acclaimed chef, private planted courtyards with fountain, two floors of wraparound verandas and gallery overlooking Courtyard on premises. Handicap access. Weddings, small meetings, family reunions and seminars hosted. Antiquing, art galleries, bicycling, fishing, golf, hiking, live theater, museums, parks, shopping, tennis, water sports and wineries nearby.

Publicity: *County Roads Magazine, HGTV, television affiliate stations in Alexandria, La., Natchez, Miss., Baton Rouge, La. and New Orleans.*

Oakland Plantation

1124 Lower Woodville Rd
Natchez, MS 39120-8132
(601)445-5101 (800)824-0355 Fax:(601)442-5182

Circa 1785. Andrew Jackson courted his future wife, Rachel Robards, at this gracious 18th-century home. This working cattle plantation includes fishing ponds, a tennis court and canoeing. Rooms are filled with antiques, and the innkeepers provide guests with a tour of the main home and plantation. They also will arrange tours of Natchez.

Historic Interest: The historic mansions of Natchez are all within 10 miles of the inn.

Innkeeper(s): Jean & Andy Peabody. $90-100. 3 rooms, 2 with PB, 3 with FP and 1 conference room. Breakfast included in rates. Types of meals: Full bkfst. Beds: KT. Reading lamp and clock radio in room. Air conditioning. Tennis, telephone and fireplace on premises. Small meetings hosted. Antiquing, fishing, golf, live theater, parks, water sports and touring Natchez Mansions nearby.

Publicity: *Southern Living and Country Inns.*

"Best kept secret in Natchez! Just great!"

Pass Christian   L6

Harbour Oaks Inn

126 W Scenic Dr
Pass Christian, MS 39571-4420
(228)452-9399 (800)452-9399 Fax:(228)452-9321
E-mail: harbour@attg.net
Web: www.harbouroaks.com

Circa 1860. Three dormers rise from the roof of this two-and-a-half-story coastal cottage, listed in the National Register. Shaded by massive live oaks draped with Spanish moss, this is the only 19th-century hotel still operating in the area. It was formerly known as the Live Oaks House and later the Crescent Hotel. A double veranda stretches gracefully across the width of the inn. Decorated with interesting antiques and family heirlooms, the inn's white woodwork, French doors and multi-paned windows bring light and air to the guest rooms. Surviving both Union shelling and 200-mile Hurricane Camille, the inn stands beautifully maintained overlooking the harbor and Gulf of Mexico. Enjoy the Billiard room or stroll to galleries and antique shops.

Innkeeper(s): Tony & Diane Brugger. $88-128. 5 rooms with PB. Breakfast included in rates. Types of meals: Full bkfst and early coffee/tea. Beds: KQD. Data port, cable TV, reading lamp, ceiling fan, clock radio and telephone in room. Air conditioning. VCR, fax, copier and parlor games on premises. Small meetings hosted. Antiquing, fishing, golf, live theater, parks, shopping, tennis, water sports and museums nearby.

Publicity: *Southern Living, Chicago Bride, ABD and Mississippi PBS.*

"The last few days have been a marvelous experience. You welcomed me into your home and made me feel like family."

Inn At The Pass

125 E Scenic Dr
Pass Christian, MS 39571-4415
(228)452-0333 (800)217-2588 Fax:(228)452-0449
E-mail: innatpas@aol.com
Web: www.innatthepass.com

Circa 1885. Listed in the National Register, this Victorian is adorned by a veranda where guests can relax and catch a tranquil breeze wafting off the Mississippi Gulf Coast. Four of the rooms are located in the main house, but there is also a secluded cottage out back. The décor is Victorian in style, but the rooms include modern amenities. On the weekends, a full, Southern-style breakfast is served. A beach resort town for more than a century, Pass Christian and its surrounding area offers a variety of activities, including water sports, fishing and casinos.

Innkeeper(s): Phyllis Hines & Mimi Smith. $90-129. 4 rooms with PB, 3 with FP and 1 cottage. Breakfast included in rates. Types of meals: Full bkfst, veg bkfst and early coffee/tea. Beds: QDT. Cable TV, VCR, reading lamp, CD player, refrigerator, ceiling fan, clock radio, telephone, coffeemaker, desk and hot tub/spa in room. Central air. Fax, copier, fireplace and laundry facility on premises. Weddings hosted. Antiquing, art galleries, beach, fishing, golf and water sports nearby.

Port Gibson   H2

BernheimerHouse B&B

212 Walnut Street
Port Gibson, MS 39150
(601)437-2843 (800)735-3407 Fax:(601)437-2843
E-mail: innkeeper@bernheimerhouse.com
Web: www.bernheimerhouse.com

Circa 1901. Reflecting the picturesque design and materials typical of Queen Anne architecture, this historic home with original light fixtures, sliding doors, furniture and memorabilia is listed in the National Register. The main floor surrounds a large living hall that is a great gathering place. The Loft Multimedia Library on the third floor offers an extensive book collection, computer with Internet access, games, and a TV/VCR. Spacious guest bedrooms are well-appointed and tastefully decorated. Breakfast in the formal dining room or on the huge veranda includes orange juice, hot or cold cereal, two biscuits, two scrambled eggs, two Texas French toast, three strips of bacon, three sausage links, hash browns, a large cinnamon roll and hot beverage. Arrange to join Nancy and Loren for a family-style diner. The award-winning landscaped yard blooms almost year-round.

Historic Interest: The original home that was used by General U.S. Grant as his headquarters after the Battle of Port Gibson burnt in 1900. The present home was built on the basement of that home by Jacob Bernheimer the most prominent Jewish businessman in Claiborne County, MS. The home contains many original pieces of furniture and memorabilia.

Innkeeper(s): Loren & Nancy Ouart. $105-130. 4 rooms with PB. Breakfast included in rates. Types of meals: Country bkfst, early coffee/tea, picnic lunch and dinner. Beds: KD. Data port, cable TV, VCR, reading lamp, refrigerator,

clock radio, telephone and desk in room. Air conditioning. TV, fax, copier, spa, tennis, library and gift shop on premises. Weddings, small meetings, family reunions and seminars hosted. Antiquing, art galleries, bicycling, fishing, hiking, museums, parks and shopping nearby.

Oak Square Bed & Breakfast

1207 Church St
Port Gibson, MS 39150-2609
(601)437-4350 (800)729-0240 Fax:(601)437-5768

Circa 1850. Six 22-foot-tall fluted Corinthian columns support the front gallery of this 30-room Greek Revival plantation. The owners furnished the mansion with 18th- and 19th-century Mississippi heirloom antiques and the guest rooms offer beautiful canopy beds. The parlor holds a carved rosewood Victorian suite, original family documents and a collection of Civil War memorabilia. A hearty southern breakfast is served. Enormous oaks and magnolia trees grace the grounds.

Historic Interest: Listed in the National Register.

Innkeeper(s): Ms. William D. Lum. $105-135. 10 rooms with PB. Breakfast included in rates. Types of meals: Full bkfst. Beds: QT. Cable TV, reading lamp and telephone in room. Air conditioning. TV, VCR and fax on premises. Museums, state park and Civil War battlefields nearby.

Publicity: *Quad-City Times and Dallas Morning News.*

Senatobia   B4

Spahn House B&B

401 College St
Senatobia, MS 38668-2128
(662)562-9853 (800)400-9853 Fax:(662)562-6569
E-mail: dspahn@www.spahnhouse.com
Web: www.spahnhouse.com

Circa 1904. Originally built by a cotton and cattle baron, this 5,000-square-foot Neoclassical house sits on two acres and is listed in the National Register. Professionally decorated, it features fine antiques and luxuriously furnished rooms with elegant bed linens and Jacuzzi tubs. Separate from the main house, a brand new bridal suite offers a large Jacuzzi bath, a king bed and a kitchen. Private candle-

light dinners are available by advance request. Breakfasts feature gourmet cuisine as the inn also manages a full-time catering business. (Guests sometimes are invited to sample food in the kitchen before it makes its way to local parties and events.) Memphis is 30 minutes north.

Historic Interest: Elvis Presley's Graceland, Sun Studio, Clarksdale's Delta Blues Museum.

Innkeeper(s): Daughn Spahn. $75-225. 5 rooms with PB and 1 suite. Breakfast included in rates. Types of meals: Full bkfst. Beds: KQ. Cable TV, reading lamp, stereo, ceiling fan, clock radio, telephone, desk, hot tub/spa and abundant toiletries in room. Air conditioning. VCR, fax, library, parlor games, fireplace and full catering staff/floral supply on premises. Weddings, small meetings, family reunions and seminars hosted. Amusement parks, antiquing, fishing, live theater, parks, shopping, sporting events, water sports, hiking and wetlands nearby.

Publicity: *South Florida Magazine, Mississippi Magazine, B&B Management Magazine, ABC and PBS.*

"I hope everyone gets to experience that type of Southern hospitality just once in their lifetime."

Tupelo   C7

The Mockingbird Inn B&B

305 N Gloster St
Tupelo, MS 38801-3623
(662)841-0286 Fax:(662)840-4158
E-mail: sandbird@netdoor.com
Web: www.bbonline.com/ms/mockingbird

Circa 1925. This inn's architecture incorporates elements of
Colonial, Art Deco and Arts and Crafts styles. The interior is
decorated with white sofas, a plethora of green plants and
antiques. Guest rooms include Paris with a pewter canopy wedding bed and Victorian wicker chaise, and the Athens, which
boasts a lavish Grecian decor including columns and an L-
shaped whirlpool for two. Other rooms and corresponding
themes offered are Africa, Bavaria, Venice, Mackinac Island and
Sansabel Island. Several romantic packages are available including a Sweetheart Gift Basket. A porch, gazebo and back garden
invite relaxing conversation. Cross the street to three of the
area's favorite restaurants. Children 12 and over are welcome.

Innkeeper(s): Sharon Robertson. $89-139. 7 rooms with PB, 1 with FP and
2 suites. Breakfast and snacks/refreshments included in rates. Types of
meals: Full gourmet bkfst and early coffee/tea. Beds: Q. Cable TV, reading
lamp, ceiling fan, clock radio, telephone, desk, hot tub/spa and fireplace in
room. Central air. Fax, parlor games and one room full-handicap facility on
premises. Antiquing, art galleries, fishing, golf, hiking, live theater, museums,
parks, shopping and tennis nearby.

Publicity: *Southern Living, National Geographic Traveler, Travel and Leisure,
American's Best Bed and Breakfasts, The South's Best Bed and Breakfasts
and Blue Ribbon (Turner South Network) Best of Best B&B.*

Tylertown   J4

Merry Wood B&B, Vacation Sanctuary

26 Dillons Bridge Rd
Tylertown, MS 39667
(504)222-1415 (866)222-1415 Fax:(504)222-1449
E-mail: merrywoodcottage@aol.com
Web: www.merrywoodcottages.com

Circa 1940. A quiet "comfortable wilderness" surrounds this
country cottage and two guest houses that offer flexible accommodations, a tranquil pond and river frontage with a private
beach. Decorated in vintage furnishings, the old-fashioned
ambiance is enhanced by antique footed tubs, quilts, brick
floors, period-style stoves and tin ceilings. Modern amenities
include electric security gates, satellite TV, VCR, central air and
heat, microwaves and ceiling fans. Hair dryers, robes and fine
linens are additional luxuries. Enjoy a satisfying breakfast of
farm-fresh coddled eggs, homemade biscuits and gravy,
Mayhaw jelly, Southern cheese grits, vegetarian sausage, fruit
with cream and granola topping and beverages. Bikes are available. Guided nature walks, spa services, yoga/tai chi classes
and canoeing can be arranged.

Innkeeper(s): Drs. Merry & Ryck Caplan. $130-180. 5 rooms, 4 with PB, 5
with FP, 2 suites, 1 cottage and 2 conference rooms. Breakfast and
snacks/refreshments included in rates. Types of meals: Full gourmet bkfst,
veg bkfst, early coffee/tea, gourmet lunch, picnic lunch, afternoon tea,
gourmet dinner and room service. Beds: KT. Modem hook-up, data port,
cable TV, VCR, reading lamp, stereo, refrigerator, ceiling fan, snack bar, clock
radio, telephone, coffeemaker, turn-down service, desk, fireplace, terrycloth
robes, hair dryers, iron and ironing board in room. Central air. Fax, copier,
swimming, bicycles, library, parlor games, fireplace, laundry facility, exercise
room, reading room, canoes, BBQ, picnic supplies, beach supplies, organic

vegetable & flower garden for guest use, river trails and spa services on
premises. Weddings, small meetings, family reunions and seminars hosted.
Amusement parks, antiquing, art galleries, beach, bicycling, canoeing/kayak-
ing, fishing, golf, hiking, horseback riding, live theater, museums, parks and
shopping nearby.

Publicity: *Country Roads, St. Charles Magazine, Natural Awakenings and
WWLTV.*

Vicksburg   G3

Anchuca

1010 First East St
Vicksburg, MS 39183
(601)661-0111 (888)686-0111 Fax:(601)661-0111
E-mail: reservations@anchucamansion.com
Web: www.anchucamansion.com

Circa 1832. This early Greek Revival mansion rises resplendently above the brick-paved streets of Vicksburg. It houses
magnificent period antiques and artifacts. Confederate
President Jefferson Davis once addressed the townspeople from
the balcony while his brother was living in the home after the
Civil War. The turn-of-the-century guest cottage has been transformed into an enchanting hideaway and rooms in the mansion
are appointed with formal decor and four-poster beds. A swimming pool and Jacuzzi are modern amenities.

Historic Interest: Vicksburg National Military Park (5 minutes), Old
Courthouse Museum (2 blocks), Cairo Museum (one-half mile).

Innkeeper(s): Thomas Pharr & Christopher Brinkley. $95-175. 8 rooms with
PB, 4 with FP and 3 suites. Breakfast included in rates. Types of meals: Full
gourmet bkfst, veg bkfst, early coffee/tea, gourmet lunch, picnic lunch, afternoon tea, snacks/refreshments, gourmet dinner and room service. Beds: KQT.
Cable TV, reading lamp, clock radio, coffeemaker, turn-down service, hot
tub/spa, mini refrigerator stocked with snacks and beverages and coffee center in room. Central air. Fax, spa, swimming, library, parlor games, telephone,
fireplace and laundry facility on premises. Weddings, small meetings, family
reunions and seminars hosted. Antiquing, fishing, golf, museums, parks,
shopping, sporting events, tennis and National Military Park nearby.

Publicity: *Times Herald, Southern Living, Innsider, Country Inns,
Smithsonian, Conde Nast and Johansens.*

*"The 'Southern Hospitality' will not be forgotten. The best Southern
breakfast in town."*

Annabelle

501 Speed St
Vicksburg, MS 39180-4065
(601)638-2000 (800)791-2000 Fax:(601)636-5054
E-mail: annabelle@vicksburg.com
Web: www.annabellebnb.com

Circa 1868. From the outside, Annabelle looks like a friendly
mix of Victorian and Italianate architecture set on an unassuming lawn of magnolias and pecan trees. It is the gracious interi-
or and hospitality that has earned
this bed & breakfast consistently
high ratings. Walls are painted in
deep, rich hues, highlighting the
polished wood floors, Oriental
rugs and beautiful antiques. Some
of the furnishings are family heirlooms, and some rooms include a

whirlpool tub. Innkeepers George and Carolyn Mayer spent
many years in the restaurant business and offer delicious
Southern fare during the morning meal. Carolyn hails from
New Orleans and George, a native of Moravia, speaks German,
Portuguese and some Spanish.

Historic Interest: Antebellum homes and civil war history sites.
Innkeeper(s): Carolyn & George Mayer. $95-150. 8 rooms with PB, 2 with FP, 1 suite and 1 cottage. Breakfast and afternoon tea included in rates. Types of meals: Full gourmet bkfst and early coffee/tea. Beds: KQ. Cable TV, reading lamp, refrigerator, clock radio, telephone and turn-down service in room. Air conditioning. TV, fax, swimming, library and fireplace on premises. Family reunions hosted. Amusement parks, antiquing, fishing, live theater, parks, shopping, water sports, Civil War historic sites, casinos and antebellum homes nearby.
Publicity: *Southern Living, Country Inns and NBC Dateline.*

"You have a beautiful home. The history and decor really give the place flavor."

Cedar Grove Mansion Inn

2200 Oak St
Vicksburg, MS 39180-4008
(601)636-1000 (800)862-1300 Fax:(601)634-6126

Circa 1840. It's easy to relive "Gone With the Wind" at this grand antebellum estate built by John Klein as a wedding present for his bride. Visitors sip mint juleps and watch gas chandeliers flicker in the finely appointed parlors. Many rooms contain their original furnishings. Although Cedar Grove survived the Civil War, a Union cannonball is still lodged in the parlor wall. There is a magnificent view of the Mississippi from the terrace and front gallery. Four acres of gardens include fountains and gazebos. There is a bar, and the inn's restaurant opens each evening at 6 p.m.

Historic Interest: National Military Park (5 miles) and museums.
$100-205. 34 rooms with PB, 6 with FP, 15 suites, 8 cottages and 4 conference rooms. Breakfast and afternoon tea included in rates. Types of meals: Full bkfst, gourmet dinner and room service. Restaurant on premises. Beds: KQDT. Cable TV, reading lamp, refrigerator, clock radio, telephone, turn-down service and desk in room. Air conditioning. TV, fax, copier, swimming, bicycles, tennis, library and laundry facility on premises. Limited handicap access. Weddings, small meetings and family reunions hosted. Amusement parks, antiquing, fishing, live theater, parks, shopping, water sports and casino river boat gaming nearby.
Publicity: *Vicksburg Post, Southern Living, Victorian Homes, Country Inns and Miss Firecracker.*

"Love at first sight would be the best way to describe my feelings for your home and the staff."

Corners B&B Inn

601 Klein St
Vicksburg, MS 39180-4005
(601)636-7421 (800)444-7421 Fax:(601)636-7232

Circa 1873. Overlook the Mississippi and Yazoo Rivers from the porches and galleries of this elegant mansion gracing the Historic Garden District. The front looks like a Southern Louisiana Raised Cottage with a seventy foot elevated gallery

and hand pierced Vicksburg Columns. Classic Revival and Italianate architecture are also reflected in this bed & breakfast inn built during the period of Reconstruction. Take an informative tour by the innkeeper. Relax with refreshments in the morning room or large double parlor that boasts two fireplaces, floor to ceiling windows and a baby grand piano. Distinctive guest bedrooms and suites offer spacious privacy with a romantic ambiance. Some feature large whirlpool tubs, fireplaces and antique beds. Savor a plantation breakfast served by candlelight with silver and crystal in the formal dining room. Stroll the original Parterre Gardens or brick walkways of the walled back gardens with pink crepe myrtle trees.

Historic Interest: Original Par Terre Gardens, cast iron fence and pierced columns.
Innkeeper(s): Bettye Kilby & Cliff Whitney. $90-130. 17 rooms with PB, 10 with FP and 2 suites. Breakfast, afternoon tea and snacks/refreshments included in rates. Types of meals: Full gourmet bkfst and veg bkfst. Beds: KQDT. Modem hook-up, cable TV, refrigerator, ceiling fan, clock radio, telephone, desk, hot tub/spa and fireplace in room. Air conditioning. Fax, copier, library and parlor games on premises. Limited handicap access. Weddings, small meetings, family reunions and seminars hosted. Antiquing, art galleries, bicycling, fishing, golf, hiking, live theater, museums, parks, shopping, tennis and boat trips on the Mississippi River nearby.
Publicity: *Los Angeles Times and Southern Living.*

Stained Glass Manor - Oak Hall

2430 Drummond St
Vicksburg, MS 39180-4114
(601)638-8893 (888)VIC-KBNB Fax:(601)636-3055

Circa 1902. Billed by the innkeepers as "Vicksburg's historic Vick inn," this restored, Mission-style manor boasts 40 stained-glass windows, original woodwork and light fixtures. Period furnishings create a Victorian flavor. George Washington Maher, who employed a young draftsman named Frank Lloyd Wright, probably designed the home, which was built from 1902 to 1908. Lewis J. Millet did the art for 36 of the stained-glass panels. The home's first owner, Fannie Vick Willis Johnson, was a descendent of the first Vick in Vicksburg. All but one guest room has a fireplace, and all are richly appointed with antiques, reproductions and Oriental rugs. "New Orleans" breakfasts begin with cafe au lait, freshly baked bread, Quiche Lorraine and other treats.

Innkeeper(s): Bill & Shirley Smollen. $99-185. 5 rooms with PB, 3 with FP, 1 cottage, 1 cabin and 3 conference rooms. Breakfast included in rates. Types of meals: Full gourmet bkfst. Beds: KQDT. Modem hook-up, cable TV, VCR, clock radio, telephone, desk, fireplace and cast iron clawfoot tubs in room. Air conditioning. Fax, sauna, library, parlor games, fireplace and laundry facility on premises. Weddings, small meetings and family reunions hosted. Antiquing, art galleries, bicycling, fishing, golf, hiking, horseback riding, live theater, museums, parks, shopping, tennis, home tours and historic sites nearby.

Missouri

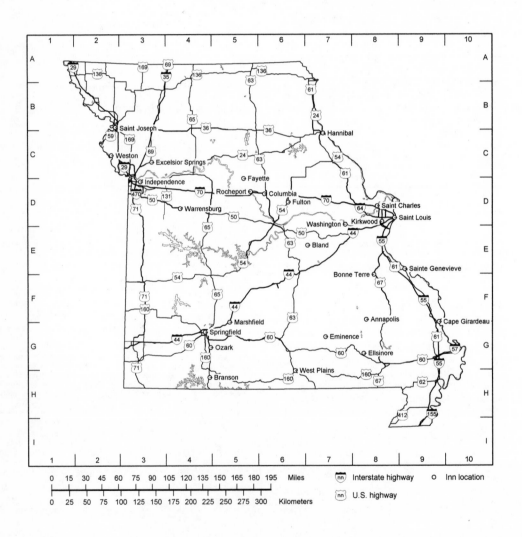

0 15 30 45 60 75 90 105 120 135 150 165 180 195   Miles

0   25   50   75   100 125 150 175 200 225 250 275 300   Kilometers

☐ nn Interstate highway   ○ Inn location

⬡ nn U.S. highway

Annapolis   F8

Rachel's B&B

202 West Second
Annapolis, MO 63620
(573)598-4656 (888)245-7771 Fax:(573)598-3439
E-mail: info@rachelsbb.com
Web: www.rachelsbb.com

Circa 1921. Formerly the Bolch Mansion, now this renovated
Arts and Craft-style B&B is named after the innkeepers'
youngest daughter. Annapolis' oldest home, with original glass
doorknobs, woodwork, built-in book cases and country elegance, sits on one acre surrounded by mountains and hills.
Perfect for a remote romantic getaway, enjoy two-person
Jacuzzis, bath salts, robes, fireplace, soft music, romantic in-
room videos and private decks. Some rooms are specifically
family friendly. In the common room an antique rocking horse
is available. There is a large video selection. Enjoy the landscaped grounds with garden pond, goldfish and waterfall, then
relax in the outdoor hot tub.

Innkeeper(s): Joe & Sharon Cluck. $65-130. 7 rooms with PB, 3 with FP, 5
suites, 1 cottage and 1 conference room. Breakfast and snacks/refreshments
included in rates. Types of meals: Full gourmet bkfst, veg bkfst, early
coffee/tea, picnic lunch and gourmet dinner. Beds: KQDT. Modem hook-up,
data port, cable TV, VCR, reading lamp, stereo, refrigerator, ceiling fan, clock
radio, telephone, coffeemaker, desk, hot tub/spa, fireplace, hot tub and snug-
gly robes in room. Central air. Fax, copier, spa, swimming, library, parlor
games, fireplace and laundry facility on premises. Limited handicap access.
Weddings, small meetings, family reunions and seminars hosted. Antiquing,
art galleries, beach, bicycling, canoeing/kayaking, fishing, golf, hiking, horseback riding, museums, parks, shopping and water sports nearby.
Publicity: *Journal Banner, Mountain Echo News, Mustang Club, Top 15
handicap accessible B&B by B&B Journal Book of List for 2001, Bed &
Breakfast and Bikes and KTJJ.*

Bland   E7

Caverly Farm & Orchard B&B

100 Cedar Ridge Lane
Bland, MO 65014
(573)646-3732 Fax:(573)646-5274

Circa 1850. Built prior to the Civil War, this farmhouse has
been renovated completely. The innkeepers preserved many
original features, and to keep the home authentic, they used
original accents within the home. Guest rooms are decorated in
Colonial style and include family antiques. Take a stroll around
the inn's 50-plus acres, and you'll find woods, a pond, a variety
of birds and perhaps a deer or two. Breakfasts include items
such as farm-fresh cheesy eggs with chives, Canadian bacon,
fresh fruit and homemade breads served with homemade preserves and jams. The home is within an hour's drive of antique
shops, craft stores, farm auctions, wineries and the state capital, Jefferson City. Hermann, a historic town about 45 miles
away, is an interesting place to visit, especially during its
famous Oktoberfest.

Innkeeper(s): David & Nancy Caverly. $55-60. 3 rooms with PB. Breakfast
included in rates. Types of meals: Country bkfst, veg bkfst and early cof-
fee/tea. Beds: QDT. Reading lamp, ceiling fan, clock radio and desk in
room. Central air. TV, VCR, library, parlor games and telephone on premises. Antiquing, canoeing/kayaking, fishing, golf, hiking, shopping and viner-
ies nearby.
Publicity: *Southern Living, St. Louis Post Dispatch, High Performance
People and Country Magazine.*

Bonne Terre   F8

Victorian Veranda

207 E School St
Bonne Terre, MO 63628
(573)358-1134 (800)343-1134
E-mail: info@victorianveranda.com
Web: www.victorianveranda.com

Circa 1868. A veranda encircles this blue and white Queen
Anne and there are finely crafted decorative details such as
porch columns and dentil work. Furnishings in the dining
room are country-style enhanced by light floral wallpaper, fine
wood paneling and woodwork around the doors, all painted
white. Egg casseroles, potatoes and coffee cakes are served
here. There are eight state parks in the area and Cherokee
Landing offers canoe trips along the river.

Innkeeper(s): Galen & Karen Forney. $70-110. 4 rooms with PB, 1 with FP
and 1 suite. Breakfast, afternoon tea and snacks/refreshments included in
rates. Types of meals: Full gourmet bkfst, early coffee/tea, picnic lunch and
room service. Beds: Q. Reading lamp, stereo, refrigerator, ceiling fan, snack
bar, clock radio, telephone and desk in room. Air conditioning. VCR, parlor
games and fireplace on premises. Weddings, small meetings and family
reunions hosted. Antiquing, fishing, golf, live theater, parks, shopping, sporting events, tennis, water sports and scuba diving/cave nearby.

Branson   H4

Branson Hotel B&B Inn

214 W Main St
Branson, MO 65616-2724
(417)335-6104 (800)933-0651 Fax:(417)339-3224
E-mail: info@bransonhotelbb.com
Web: www.bransonhotelbb.com

Circa 1903. A picket fence frames the Branson Hotel, a Four
Square style Victorian and a Branson Historic Landmark.
Adirondack chairs fill the fieldstone veranda and the front balcony, affording guests the pleasure of visiting and enjoying the
view. As Branson's oldest commercial structure, important gatherings here played a significant part in the history of Branson,
and the novel "Shepherd of the Hills" was written here. A harvest table in the glass-enclosed dining room is laden with
hearty gourmet breakfast offerings including bacon quiche, cinnamon spiced pears and broiled grapefruit.

Innkeeper(s): Randy & Cynthia Parker. $75-99. 7 rooms with PB. Breakfast
and snacks/refreshments included in rates. Types of meals: Full gourmet bkfst,
early coffee/tea and room service. Beds: KQ. Data port, cable TV, reading lamp,
ceiling fan, clock radio, telephone and robes in room. Central air. Fax and gift
shop on premises. Small meetings, family reunions and seminars hosted.
Amusement parks, antiquing, fishing, golf, hiking, horseback riding, live theater,
museums, parks, shopping, tennis, water sports and wineries nearby.
Publicity: *Southern living, Midwest Living, Glamour and Automobile Magazine.*

Cape Girardeau   G9

Bellevue B&B

312 Bellevue St
Cape Girardeau, MO 63701-7233
(573)335-3302 (800)768-6822 Fax:(573)332-7752

Circa 1891. Within three blocks of Mississippi River front
Park, this Queen Anne Victorian with gables and bay windows
is in the local historic register. The house is painted deep
hunter green with taupe and cranberry trim, emphasizing the

historic craftsmanship of its gables, bay windows, balustrades, cornices and stained glass windows. A glider and two wicker rocking chairs sit on the front porch. Inside, the original woodwork remains as well as several sets of original pocket doors and fireplaces. Ask for the Parkridge Room where a six-foot high antique headboard is the focal point or for the Shea Lorraine or Dearborn rooms, both with large whirlpool tubs. There's a fireplace on the patio for evening get-togethers. SEMO University is nearby.

Innkeeper(s): Marsha Toll. $75-115. 4 rooms with PB. Breakfast included in rates. Types of meals: Full bkfst. Beds: Q. Cable TV, ceiling fan, whirlpool and phones in some rooms in room. Air conditioning. Weddings, small meetings and family reunions hosted.

Columbia   D6

University Avenue B&B

1315 University Ave
Columbia, MO 65201
(573)499-1920 (800)499-1920
E-mail: stay@universityavenuebnb.com
Web: www.universityavenuebnb.com

Circa 1920. Just minutes from the University of Missouri campus, this bed & breakfast provides an excellent location from which to enjoy many nearby attractions. It's just a 15-minute drive into Jefferson City, the state capitol. Stephens College, University of Missouri, restaurants and shops in Columbia's downtown area also are nearby. The historic home is filled with antiques. Guest rooms include beds topped with quilts. Some guest baths include amenities such as a jetted or clawfoot tub. In addition to the four guest rooms, the innkeepers also can provide a meeting room for up to 40 people. Business amenities include in-room desks and modem ports. Breakfast at University Avenue begins with homemade muffins and fresh fruit, followed by an entrée such as caramel French toast.

Innkeeper(s): Willa Adelstein, Susan Schabilion. $80-95. 4 rooms with PB and 1 conference room. Breakfast, afternoon tea and snacks/refreshments included in rates. Types of meals: Full gourmet bkfst, veg bkfst and early coffee/tea. Beds: KQT. Modem hook-up, TV, reading lamp, ceiling fan, clock radio, telephone, one with hot tub and two with VCR in room. Central air. VCR, fax, bicycles, parlor games, fireplace and laundry facility on premises. Weddings, small meetings, family reunions and seminars hosted. Antiquing, art galleries, bicycling, golf, hiking, live theater, museums, parks, shopping, sporting events and wineries nearby.

Ellsinore   G8

Alcorn Corner B&B

HCR 3 Box 247
Ellsinore, MO 63937
(573)322-5297

Circa 1904. Surrounded by 20 acres, this simple Victorian farmhouse is the kind of bed & breakfast guests will enjoy sharing with their children. There are farm animals, and the innkeeper, a former teacher, is like a grandma to families. Early American furnishings are found in the two guest rooms, and a family-style breakfast with three menu choices is offered.

Innkeeper(s): Virgie Alcorn Evans. $35-50. 2 rooms. Beds: DT. Reading lamp and turn-down service in room. VCR, library, telephone and fireplace on premises. Family reunions hosted. Antiquing, parks, shopping and museums nearby.

Eminence   G7

Old Blue House B&B

301 S Main St
Eminence, MO 65466-0117
(573)226-3498
E-mail: oldbluehouseb-b@webtv.net
Web: www.missouri2000.net/oldbluehouse

Circa 1800. This old two-story frame house once was home to a beauty shop, grocery store and pharmacy. There are antiques throughout and framed prints, much of which is for sale. The garden is shaded by maple and magnolia trees and there are peonies, lilacs and roses. Breakfast is continental plus. However, if you'd like a country breakfast with sausage, gravy, scrambled eggs and homemade biscuits there is an extra charge. Eminence is located in the Ozark National Scenic Riverway.

Innkeeper(s): Wanda L. Pummill. $65-90. 3 rooms with PB. Breakfast and snacks/refreshments included in rates. Types of meals: Full bkfst and early coffee/tea. Beds: D. Cable TV, reading lamp, ceiling fan and desk in room. Air conditioning. Parlor games and telephone on premises. Antiquing, beach, bicycling, canoeing/kayaking, fishing, golf, hiking, horseback riding, parks, shopping, water sports and cross-country trail rides nearby.

Publicity: St. Louis Post Dispatch, Midwest Living, B&B Guest House and Inns of Missouri.

Excelsior Springs   C3

The Inn on Crescent Lake

1261 Saint Louis Ave
Excelsior Springs, MO 64024-2938
(816)630-6745 (866)630-LAKE
E-mail: info@crescentlake.com
Web: www.crescentlake.com

Circa 1915. Located on 22 acres of lush grounds with woodland and bucolic ponds, this three-story, Georgian-style house is just a half-hour drive from downtown Kansas City and the airport. Spacious suites and guest rooms all have private baths, and guests can choose to have either a whirlpool or clawfoot tub. Try the Train Room or the Treehouse Suite. Both innkeepers graduated from the French Culinary Institute in New York City, and guests are encouraged to book a dinner reservation at the inn's dining room. Try the paddle boats, or borrow a fishing rod and take out the bass boat.

Innkeeper(s): Bruce & Anne Libowitz. $115-250. 10 rooms with PB and 3 suites. Breakfast included in rates. Types of meals: Full bkfst. Beds: KQT. Cable TV, ceiling fan and telephone in room. Air conditioning. Copier, spa and swimming pool on premises. Weddings hosted. Antiquing, fishing, parks and shopping nearby.

Fayette   D5

Bedford House B&B

308 S Main St
Fayette, MO 65248
(660)248-2204
E-mail: gkoelker@coin.org
Web: www.bedfordhousebandb.com

Circa 1850. Feel like royalty at this B&B, built in the Federal style. Hardwood floors with inlays, and hand-carved doors and mantels are enhanced by antiques and traditional furnishings. A spacious guest bedroom and suite offer an intimate ambiance. A full breakfast is highlighted by silverplate and crystal. The large tree-shaded grounds with day lilies offer a tranquil setting. There are three historic districts within walking distance.

Innkeeper(s): Georgette & Rod Koelker. $50-65. 2 rooms, 1 with PB and 1 suite. Breakfast and snacks/refreshments included in rates. Types of meals: Full bkfst, veg bkfst, early coffee/tea and dinner. Beds: QD. Reading lamp, ceiling fan, clock radio, coffeemaker and desk in room. Central air. TV, VCR, library, parlor games, telephone and laundry facility on premises. Weddings, small meetings, family reunions and seminars hosted. Antiquing, art galleries, bicycling, fishing, hiking, live theater, museums, parks, sporting events, tennis, farmers market, Morrison Observatory and swimming pool nearby.

Fulton   D6

Romancing The Past Victorian B&B

830 Court St
Fulton, MO 65251
(573)592-1996 Fax:(573)592-1999
E-mail: innkeeper@sockets.net
Web: www.romancingthepast.com

Circa 1867. A porch wraps around this pristine Victorian home and offers white wicker furnishings. There's a hammock and hot tub with gazebo in the garden. Finely crafted and restored fretwork, brackets and bay windows decorate the exterior. Polished woodwork, a gracious staircase and parquet floors are highlighted with well-chosen Victorian antiques. The Renaissance Suite boasts a fainting couch and carved walnut canopy bed, a sitting room and a large bath decorated in the Neoclassical style. In fact, luxurious baths are the inn's hallmark and there are both indoor and outdoor spas and aromatherapy.

Innkeeper(s): Jim & ReNee Yeager. $100-170. 3 rooms, 4 with PB, 3 with FP. Breakfast included in rates. Types of meals: Full gourmet bkfst, early coffee/tea, picnic lunch and snacks/refreshments. Beds: Q. Reading lamp, stereo, ceiling fan, clock radio, telephone, turn-down service, desk and clock in room. VCR, fax, copier, spa, bicycles, library, parlor games, fireplace, CD player, TV and evening desserts on premises. Weddings, small meetings, family reunions and seminars hosted. Antiquing, fishing, golf, live theater, parks, shopping, sporting events, tennis, UMC and bike trails nearby.

Publicity: *Awards for Best Spa Bath and Best Interior Design in Arringtons Bed and Breakfast Journal.*

Hannibal   C7

Garth Woodside Mansion

11069 New London Rd
Hannibal, MO 63401-9644
(573)221-2789 (888)427-8409
E-mail: innkeeper@garthmansion.com
Web: www.garthmansion.com

Circa 1871. Thirty-nine acres of rolling meadows, ponds, woodland and flower gardens surround this Italian Renaissance Victorian mansion. Upon arrival, enjoy afternoon snacks and a beverage in one of the many antique-filled common rooms. An 1869 Steinway square grand piano offers musical interludes. The flying staircase with invisible support rises to three stories. Each air-conditioned guest bedroom includes a feather bed and vintage nightshirts. Ask for the Samuel Clemens Room where Mark Twain slept. Savor a full country breakfast. Relax on the front porch or second-floor balcony. A spacious stone cottage is available with a fireplace in the master bedroom and bathroom with two-person whirlpool and shower. The loft boasts a surround sound entertainment center, and the private deck overlooks the pond. Breakfast is served in the kitchenette/dining room.

Historic Interest: Mark Twain Boyhood Home (3 miles), a rare inland lighthouse lit by the President (3 miles).

Innkeeper(s): Julie & John Rolsen. $109-349. 8 rooms with PB, 6 with FP and 1 cottage. Breakfast and afternoon tea included in rates. Types of meals: Full gourmet bkfst and early coffee/tea. Beds: QD. Reading lamp, turn-down service, desk, fireplaces and two-person whirlpool tubs in room. Air conditioning. Parlor games, telephone and fireplace on premises. Small meetings hosted. Amusement parks, antiquing, fishing, live theater and parks nearby.

Publicity: *Inn Country USA, Country Inns, Chicago Sun-Times, Glamour, Victorian Homes, Midwest Living, Insider, Country Living, Conde Nast Traveler and Bon Appetit.*

"So beautiful and romantic and relaxing, we forgot we were here to work."— Jeannie and Bob Ransom, Innsider

Independence   D3

Serendipity B&B

116 S Pleasant St
Independence, MO 64050
(816)833-4719 (800)203-4299 Fax:(816)833-4719
E-mail: serendipitybandb@aol.com
Web: www.bbhost.com/serendipitybb

Circa 1887. This three-story brick home offers guests the ultimate Victorian experience. Antique furnishings and period appointments create an authentic period ambiance. Victorian children's books and toys, antique pictures, china figurines and a collection of antique colored glassware add to the home's charm. Stereoscopes and music box tunes are other special touches. A full breakfast is served by candlelight in the formal dining room. Outside gardens include arbors, Victorian gazing balls, birdhouses, birdbaths, a hammock, swing and fountain. If time and weather permit, guests may request a ride in an antique car and tour of the house.

Innkeeper(s): Susan & Doug Walter. $45-85. 6 rooms with PB. Types of meals: Full bkfst. Beds: KQD. Air conditioning. TV, VCR, fax and copier on premises. Amusement parks, antiquing, fishing, golf, live theater, parks, shopping, sporting events, tennis, water sports, historic sites and casinos nearby.

"It was so special to spend time with you and to share your lovely home."

Woodstock Inn B&B

1212 W Lexington Ave
Independence, MO 64050-3524
(816)833-2233 (800)276-5202 Fax:(816)461-7226
E-mail: tjustice@independence-missouri.com
Web: www.independence-missouri.com

Circa 1900. This home, originally built as a doll and quilt factory, is in the perfect location for sightseeing in historic Independence. Visit the home of Harry S Truman or the Truman Library and Museum. The Old Jail Museum is another popular attraction. A large country breakfast is served each morning featuring malted Belgian waffles and an additional entree. Independence is less than 30 minutes from Kansas City, where you may spend the day browsing through the shops at Country Club Plaza or Halls' Crown Center.

Innkeeper(s): Todd & Patricia Justice. $75-189. 11 rooms with PB and 2 suites. Breakfast included in rates. Types of meals: Full bkfst and early coffee/tea. Beds: KQD. Cable TV, VCR, reading lamp, stereo, refrigerator, clock radio, telephone, coffeemaker, desk, hot tub/spa, voice mail and fireplaces in room. Air conditioning. Fax and parlor games on premises. Limited handicap access. Weddings, small meetings, family reunions and seminars hosted. Amusement parks, antiquing, art galleries, fishing, golf, live theater, museums, parks, shopping and sporting events nearby.

Publicity: *Country, San Francisco Chronicle, Independence Examiner, Kansas City Star and New York Times.*

"Pleasant, accommodating people, a facility of good character."

Kirkwood D8

Fissy's Place

500 N Kirkwood Rd
Kirkwood, MO 63122-3914
(314)821-4494

Circa 1939. The innkeeper's past is just about as interesting as the history of this bed & breakfast. A former Miss Missouri celebrating her 10th year in the innkeeping business, the innkeeper has acted in movies with the likes of Burt Reynolds and Robert Redford, and pictures of many movie stars decorate the home's interior. A trained interior designer, she also shares this talent in the cheerfully decorated guest rooms. Historic downtown Kirkwood is within walking distance to the home, which also offers close access to St. Louis.

Innkeeper(s): Fay & Randy Sneed. $70-85. 3 rooms with PB and 1 conference room. Breakfast and snacks/refreshments included in rates. Types of meals: Full bkfst and early coffee/tea. Beds: QDT. Cable TV, VCR, reading lamp, ceiling fan, telephone, turn-down service and desk in room. Air conditioning. Copier, parlor games and fireplace on premises. Limited handicap access. Small meetings, family reunions and seminars hosted. Antiquing, live theater, parks, shopping, sporting events and many fine restaurants nearby.

Marshfield G5

The Dickey House B&B, Ltd.

331 S Clay St
Marshfield, MO 65706-2114
(417)468-3000 (800)450-7444 Fax:(417)859-2775

Circa 1913. This Greek Revival mansion is framed by ancient oak trees and boasts eight massive two-story Ionic columns. Burled woodwork, beveled glass and polished hardwood floors accentuate the gracious rooms. Interior columns soar in the parlor, creating a suitably elegant setting for the innkeeper's outstanding collection of antiques. A queen-size canopy bed,

fireplace and sunporch are featured in the Heritage Room. Some rooms offer amenities such as Jacuzzi tubs and a fireplace. All rooms include cable TV and a VCR. The innkeepers also offer a sun room with a hot tub.

Innkeeper(s): Larry & Michaelene Stevens. $75-165. 7 rooms, 3 with PB and 4 suites. Breakfast included in rates. Types of meals: Full gourmet bkfst. Beds: KQD. Cable TV, VCR, reading lamp, ceiling fan, clock radio, telephone and four with double Jacuzzi in room. New sun room with therapeutic hot tub on premises. Limited handicap access. Weddings, small meetings, family reunions and seminars hosted.

Ozark G4

BarnAgain Bed & Breakfast

904 W Church St
Ozark, MO 65721
(417)581-2276 (877)462-2276
E-mail: barnagain1@msn.com

Circa 1910. Listed in the Ozark Historical Register, this was the area's last dairy farm to bottle and sell white and chocolate milk. Situated on 40 acres, two converted barns and a Victorian farmhouse restored by Amish craftsmen offer elegant accommodations. Guest bedrooms are decorated in themes ranging from

rustic to romantic. Soft drinks and fresh-baked cookies are placed in each room. The romantic Rose Room features a whirlpool tub, poolside views and luxurious furnishings. Peaches and cream-stuffed French toast may be one of the entrees served for breakfast. The swimming pool is open May to September. Sit on the porch swing, hike the trails or play a game of horseshoes. Relax under the stars by the warm fire pit.

Innkeeper(s): Mark & Susan Bryant. $109-129. 4 rooms, 3 with PB, 1 with FP and 1 suite. Breakfast and snacks/refreshments included in rates. Types of meals: Full gourmet bkfst, veg bkfst and room service. Beds: Q. TV, VCR, reading lamp, refrigerator, ceiling fan, clock radio, coffeemaker, turn-down service and fireplace in room. Central air. Swimming, bicycles, parlor games, telephone, fireplace, walking trails, horseshoes and basketball court on premises. Amusement parks, antiquing, art galleries, bicycling, canoeing/kayaking, fishing, golf, hiking, live theater, museums, parks, shopping, tennis, water sports and wineries nearby.

Publicity: *Midwest Living and Springfield News-Leader.*

Rocheport D5

School House B&B Inn

504 Third Street
Rocheport, MO 65279
(573)698-2022
E-mail: innkeeper@schoolhousebandb.com
Web: www.schoolhousebb.com

Circa 1914. This three-story brick building was once a schoolhouse. Now luxuriously appointed as a country inn, it features 13-foot-high ceilings, small print wallpapers and a bridal suite with Victorian furnishings and a private spa. Rooms feature names such as The Spelling Bee and The Schoolmarm. The basement houses an antique bookshop, The Bookseller. Nearby is a winery and a trail along the river providing many scenic miles for cyclists and hikers.

Historic Interest: Historic Katy Trail (2 blocks), Missouri River (4 blocks), local museum (4 blocks), Rocheport, has 80 buildings in the National Register.

Innkeeper(s): Mike & Lisa Friedemann. $115-235. 10 rooms with PB, 1 suite and 1 conference room. Breakfast and snacks/refreshments included in rates. Types of meals: Full bkfst, early coffee/tea and afternoon tea. Beds: KQD. Reading lamp, ceiling fan, telephone and hot tub/spa in room. Air conditioning. Library and parlor games on premises. Small meetings and family reunions hosted. Antiquing, art galleries, fishing, live theater, parks, shopping, sporting events, hiking and bicycling nearby.

Publicity: *Midwest Living, Midwest Motorist, Successful Farming, Hallmark Greeting Cards, Romance of Country Inns, Southern Living, New York Times, Denver Post, St. Louis Post Dispatch, Romantic Homes, Rural Missouri Magazine and New York Post.*

"We are still talking about our great weekend in Rocheport. Thanks for the hospitality, the beautiful room and delicious breakfasts, they were really great."

Saint Charles D8

Boone's Lick Trail Inn

1000 South Main St
Saint Charles, MO 63301-3514
(636)947-7000 (888)940-0002

Circa 1840. This Federal-style brick and limestone house, overlooks the wide Missouri River and Katy Trail. Situated in an old river settlement with its brick street and green spaces, the inn is at the start of the Boone's Lick Trail. V'Anne's delicate lemon biscuits, fresh fruit and hot entrees are served amid regional antiques and Paul's working duck decoy collection. Because of its setting and decor, travelers have remarked at how close the inn resembles a European inn.

Historic Interest: Goldenrod Showboat (one-fourth mile), Missouri First State Capitol (one-half mile), Daniel Boone Homestead (25 miles), Gateway Arch (20 minutes), Jefferson Memorial Courthouse.

Innkeeper(s): V'Anne & Paul Mydler. $110-175. 6 rooms with PB. Breakfast included in rates. Types of meals: Full bkfst. Beds: QT. TV and telephone in room. Antiquing, golf, shopping, historic district, museums, wineries, casino, birding, biking, restaurants, swimming and hiking nearby.

Publicity: *New York Times, Southern Living, Country Home and Midwest Living.*

Geery's Bed & Breakfast

720 N 5th St
Saint Charles, MO 63301
(636)916-5344 Fax:(636)916-4702

Circa 1891. The neighborhood where this Four Square Colonial Revival home sits is a registered National Landmark in historic Frenchtowne. A delightful blend of Victorian elegance and Scottish culture creates a warm and inviting atmosphere. Distinctive reproductions and 19th-century antiques furnish the parlors and guest bedrooms. The Lindsay Room features a four-poster bed, double whirlpool, corner fireplace and private porch. A hearty breakfast is well presented on Royal Doulton china with gold silverware. Three sitting porches offer views of the flower and shade gardens.

Innkeeper(s): Peter & Mrilyn Geery. $70-125. 3 rooms with PB, 1 with FP and 2 conference rooms. Breakfast included in rates. Types of meals: Full gourmet bkfst, veg bkfst, early coffee/tea, picnic lunch and afternoon tea. Beds: KQ. Modem hook-up, cable TV, reading lamp, stereo, refrigerator, ceiling fan, snack bar, clock radio, telephone, desk, hot tub/spa and fireplace in room. Central air. Fax, copier, spa, bicycles, library, parlor games, fireplace, gardens, gazebo and Lewis and Clark spoken here on premises. Weddings, small meetings and seminars hosted. Amusement parks, antiquing, art galleries, bicycling, canoeing/kayaking, downhill skiing, fishing, golf, hiking, horseback riding, live theater, museums, parks, shopping, sporting events, tennis, water sports, wineries and Casino nearby.

Publicity: *The Sheffield Star from England, St. Louis Post-Dispatch, and Voted Best Bed and Breakfast in St. Charles City and County for 2001 and 2002 by the business record magazine in St. Charles.*

Saint Joseph   B2

Shakespeare Chateau B&B

809 Hall St
Saint Joseph, MO 64501
(816)232-2667 (888)414-4944 Fax:(816)232-0009
E-mail: chateau@ponyexpress.net
Web: www.shakespearechateau.com

Circa 1885. This gabled and turreted confection offers three stories of lavish antique furnishings, carved woodwork and at least 40 original stained-glass windows. The inn is in the Hall Street Historic District, known as "Mansion Hill". All the homes in this area are listed in the National Register. The fireplace in the inn's foyer has boasted a bronze of Shakespeare for more than 100 years and with this as a starting point, the innkeeper has created a Victorian, Shakespearean theme. Two of the inn's room offer whirlpools. A two-course breakfast is served in the romantic dining room.

Innkeeper(s): Kellie. $100-175. 6 rooms with PB, 3 suites and 1 conference

room. Breakfast and snacks/refreshments included in rates. Types of meals: Full bkfst, veg bkfst and early coffee/tea. Beds: KQ. Reading lamp, ceiling fan, clock radio, coffeemaker and hot tub in room. Air conditioning. TV, VCR, fax, library and telephone on premises. Family reunions hosted. Antiquing, art galleries, bicycling, downhill skiing, fishing, golf, live theater, museums, parks, shopping and tennis nearby.

Publicity: *Midwest Living, Victorian Decorating & Lifestyle Magazine and Kansas City Magazine.*

Saint Louis   D8

Eastlake Inn Bed & Breakfast

703 N Kirkwood Rd
Saint Louis, MO 63122-2719
(314)965-0066 Fax:(314)966-8615
E-mail: info@eastlakeinn.com
Web: www.eastlakeinn.com

Circa 1920. Tall trees shade this colonial-style inn on one acre of grounds. Eastlake antiques are found throughout along with an antique doll collection. Guest rooms include the Garden Room with a queen Eastlake bed and a view of the perennial gardens. The Magnolia Room has a fireplace and a double whirlpool tub. A full breakfast is offered in the dining room under the lights of a chandelier. Dishes include items such as peach French toast, maple sausage, and fruit from the local farmer's market. The inn's two golden retrievers may enjoy a garden tour with you or stroll through the pleasant neighborhood on a walk to Mudd Grove.

Innkeeper(s): Lori & Dean Murray. $70-165. 3 rooms, 2 with PB, 1 with FP and 1 suite. Breakfast included in rates. Types of meals: Full gourmet bkfst and early coffee/tea. Beds: KQD. Modem hook-up, data port, cable TV, VCR, reading lamp, ceiling fan, clock radio, telephone, coffeemaker, turn-down service, hot tub/spa and fireplace in room. Central air. Fax, copier, library, parlor games and fireplace on premises. Amusement parks, antiquing, art galleries, bicycling, canoeing/kayaking, downhill skiing, fishing, golf, hiking, horseback riding, live theater, museums, parks, shopping, sporting events, tennis and wineries nearby.

Lehmann House B&B

10 Benton Pl
Saint Louis, MO 63104-2411
(314)422-1483 Fax:(314)241-1597

Circa 1893. This National Register manor's most prominent resident, former U.S. Solicitor General Frederick Lehmann, hosted Presidents Taft, Theodore Roosevelt and Coolidge at this gracious home. Several key turn-of-the-century literary figures also visited the Lehmann family. The inn's formal dining room, complete with oak paneling and a fireplace, is a stunning place to enjoy the formal breakfasts. Antiques and gracious furnishings dot the well-appointed guest rooms. The home is located in St. Louis' oldest historic district, Lafayette Square.

Historic Interest: Presidents Taft, Roosevelt and Coolidge visited Lehmann House.

Innkeeper(s): Marie & Michael Davies. $100. 2 rooms with PB, 2 with FP. Breakfast included in rates. Types of meals: Full bkfst and early coffee/tea. Beds: KQDT. Reading lamp, ceiling fan and clock radio in room. Air conditioning. Swimming, tennis, library, parlor games, telephone and fireplace on premises. Weddings, small meetings, family reunions and seminars hosted. Amusement parks, antiquing, live theater, parks, shopping, sporting events, museums, zoos and botanical gardens nearby.

Publicity: *St. Louis Post Dispatch and KTVI-St. Louis.*

"Wonderful mansion with great future ahead. Thanks for the wonderful hospitality."

Napoleon's Retreat

1815 Lafayette Ave
Saint Louis, MO 63104
(314)772-6979 (800)700-9980 Fax:(314)772-7675
E-mail: info@napoleonsretreat.com
Web: www.napoleonsretreat.com

Circa 1880. This three-story, French-style Second Empire Victorian townhouse is located in Lafayette Square, a National Historic District that offers the largest collection of French Second Empire Victorians in the country. Pocket doors, twelve-foot ceilings, pine floors, artworks, collectibles and period antiques are features of the inn. The innkeeper offers egg dishes, Napoleon French Toast, quiche or Belgian waffles along with fruit and other freshly baked breads for breakfast. The inn is a mile and a half from the convention center and close to historic Soulard Market, the Missouri Botanical Gardens, the zoo, St. Louis Cathedral and Fox Theater.

Innkeeper(s): Jeff Archuleta & Michael Lance. $98-135. 5 rooms, 4 with PB, 1 with FP and 1 suite. Breakfast and snacks/refreshments included in rates. Types of meals: Full gourmet bkfst and early coffee/tea. Beds: Q. Cable TV, reading lamp, refrigerator, ceiling fan, clock radio, telephone and desk in room. Central air. Fax and copier on premises. Amusement parks, antiquing, art galleries, fishing, golf, hiking, horseback riding, live theater, museums, parks, shopping, sporting events and wineries nearby.
Publicity: *St. Louis Commerce and Show Me St. Louis.*

Sainte Genevieve   E9

Dr. Hertich's House

99 North Main Street
Sainte Genevieve, MO 63670
(800)818-5744
E-mail: stgemme@brick.net
Web: www.bbhost.com/drhertich

Circa 1850. The full-time physician's placard is still affixed to the front of this 1850 Second Empire French Chateau with mansard roof. Though the exterior has remained much the same, the interior has been meticulously renovated. Hardwood floors, antique furnishings and the original staircase with turned spindles and mahogany banister exude a gentile ambiance that is accented by rich wall coverings, carpeting and classical music playing in the background. Luxury air-conditioned suites feature fireplaces, whirlpool tubs, ceiling fans and robes. A complete breakfast is served in the dining area or in the room. Afternoon refreshments are also provided. Enjoy one of the best views of Main Street from the inviting front porch. The small historic community is the oldest French settlement west of the Mississippi.

$179-189. 5 rooms, 1 with PB, 4 with FP and 4 suites. Breakfast, afternoon tea and snacks/refreshments included in rates. Types of meals: Full gourmet bkfst and picnic lunch. Beds: KQ. Cable TV, VCR, reading lamp, refrigerator, ceiling fan, clock radio, coffeemaker, hot tub/spa and fireplace in room. Air conditioning. Antiquing, bicycling, golf, hiking, museums, parks, shopping and wineries nearby.

Inn St. Gemme Beauvais

78 N Main St
Sainte Genevieve, MO 63670-1336
(573)883-5744 (800)818-5744 Fax:(573)883-3899
E-mail: stgemme@brick.net
Web: www.bbhost.com/innstgemme

Circa 1848. This three-story, Federal-style inn is an impressive site on Ste. Genevieve's Main Street. The town is one of the oldest west of the Mississippi River, and the St. Gemme Beauvais is the oldest operating Missouri bed & breakfast. The

rooms are nicely appointed in period style, but there are modern amenities here, too. The Jacuzzi tubs in some guest rooms are one relaxing example. There is an outdoor hot tub, as well. The romantic carriage house includes a king-size bed, double Jacuzzi tub and a fireplace. Guests are pampered with all sorts of cuisine, including full breakfasts served at individual candle-lit tables with a choice of eight entrees. Later, tea, drinks, hors d'oeuvres and refreshments are also served.

Innkeeper(s): Janet Joggerst. $89-179. 9 rooms with PB, 1 with FP, 6 suites and 1 conference room. Breakfast, afternoon tea and snacks/refreshments included in rates. Types of meals: Full gourmet bkfst. Beds: KQD. Cable TV, reading lamp, stereo, ceiling fan, clock radio, desk and hot tub/spa in room. Air conditioning. VCR, fax, copier, parlor games, telephone and fireplace on premises. Weddings, small meetings, family reunions and seminars hosted. Antiquing, golf, parks, shopping and historic area nearby.

Main Street Inn

221 North Main St
Sainte Genevieve, MO 63670
(573)883-9199 (800)918-9199 Fax:(573)839-9911
E-mail: info@mainstreetinnbb.com
Web: www.rivervalleyinns.com

Circa 1882. This exquisite inn is one of Missouri's finest bed & breakfast establishments. Built as the Meyer Hotel, the inn has welcomed guests for more than a century. Now completely renovated, each of the individually appointed rooms includes amenities such as bubble bath and flowers. Rooms are subtly decorated. Beds are topped with vintage quilts and tasteful linens. Three rooms include a whirlpool tub. The morning meal is prepared in a beautiful brick kitchen, which features an unusual blue cookstove, and is served in the elegant dining room. The menu changes from day to day, apricot filled French toast with pecan topping is one of the inn's specialties.

Historic Interest: Built in 1882 as a luxury hotel with magnificent gardens, the building passed through hard times in the last century, but has now emerged fresh and newly appointed in this century.

Innkeeper(s): Ken & Karen Kulberg. $95-139. 8 rooms with PB, 1 with FP and 1 conference room. Breakfast and snacks/refreshments included in rates. Types of meals: Full gourmet bkfst and early coffee/tea. Beds: QDT. Modem hook-up, cable TV, VCR, reading lamp, refrigerator, ceiling fan, telephone, desk, hot tub/spa and fireplace in room. Central air. TV, fax, copier, library, parlor games and gift shop on premises. Weddings, small meetings, family reunions and seminars hosted. Antiquing, art galleries, bicycling, fishing, golf, hiking, museums, parks, shopping, tennis, wineries and historic sites nearby.

Southern Hotel

146 South Third Street
Sainte Genevieve, MO 63670
(573)883-3493 (800)275-1412 Fax:(573)883-9612
E-mail: mike@southernhotelbb.com
Web: www.southernhotelbb.com

Circa 1790. Located at the square in historic Sainte Genevieve, the Southern Hotel is a landmark and was known for providing the best accommodations between Natchez and St. Louis, as well as good food, gambling and pool. Guests now enjoy two parlors, a dining room and a game room on the first floor where a quilt is always underway. Guest rooms offer country

Victorian furnishings along with whimsical collectibles. Highlights include a rosewood tester bed, a unique iron bed, several hand-painted headboards and a delicately carved Victorian bed. The clawfoot tubs are hand-painted.

Guests also can browse the studio shop as they stroll through the gardens or relax on the long front porch.

Innkeeper(s): Mike & Barbara Hankins. $93-138. 8 rooms with PB, 4 with FP and 2 conference rooms. Breakfast included in rates. Types of meals: Full gourmet bkfst, early coffee/tea and snacks/refreshments. Beds: KQD. Reading lamp, ceiling fan, clock radio, fireplace and clock radios in room. Central air. Fax, copier, bicycles, parlor games, telephone, fireplace and gift shop on premises. Small meetings hosted. Antiquing, art galleries, bicycling, fishing, golf, hiking, museums, parks, shopping, tennis and wineries nearby.

Publicity: *Midwest Living, Southern Living, Country Inns, PBS, Country Inn Cooking, 25 Most Romantic B&B/Inn 2002 and in the top 15 B&B/Inn Best Cook Book 2003.*

"I can't imagine ever staying in a motel again! It was so nice to be greeted by someone who expected us. We felt right at home."

Springfield G4

The Mansion at Elfindale

1701 S Fort Ave
Springfield, MO 65807-1280
(417)831-5400
E-mail: mansion@cwoc.org
Web: www.mansionatelfindale.com

Circa 1800. The Mansion at Elfindale once served as the St. de Chantel Academy for girls. The gray stone structure features a turret observation room, ornate fireplaces, stained-glass windows, vaulted ceilings, marble-finish furnishings, wicker furniture and antiques. Breakfast includes foods from around the world.

Innkeeper(s): Ann Cook. $94-149. 13 rooms with PB, 2 with FP and 1 conference room. Breakfast included in rates. Types of meals: Dinner. Beds: KQDT. TV and telephone in room. Limited handicap access. Weddings, small meetings, family reunions and seminars hosted. Antiquing, shopping, sporting events and bass pro nearby.

"Many thanks for your warm hospitality."

Virginia Rose B&B

317 E Glenwood St
Springfield, MO 65807-3543
(417)883-0693 (800)345-1412

Circa 1906. Three generations of the Botts family lived in this home before it was sold to the current innkeepers, Virginia and Jackie Buck. The grounds still include the rustic red barn. Comfortable, country rooms are named after Buck family members and feature beds covered with quilts. The innkeepers also offer a two-bedroom suite, the Rambling Rose, which is decorated in a sportsman theme in honor of the nearby Bass Pro. Hearty breakfasts are served in the dining room, and the innkeepers will provide low-fat fare on request.

Historic Interest: Wild Bill Hickok shot Dave Tutt on the public square in Springfield, which is about two miles from the inn. Wilson's Creek National Battlefield is about eight miles away. Other Springfield attractions include Springfield National Cemetery, The Frisco Railroad Museum and the History Museum for Springfield and Greene County.

Innkeeper(s): Jackie & Virginia Buck. $70-120. 4 rooms, 2 with PB and 1 suite. Breakfast included in rates. Types of meals: Full bkfst, early coffee/tea, picnic lunch and snacks/refreshments. Beds: KQT. Reading lamp, clock radio, telephone and turn-down service in room. Air conditioning. VCR, fax and parlor games on premises. Family reunions and seminars hosted. Amusement parks, antiquing, fishing, live theater, parks, shopping, sporting events and water sports nearby.

Publicity: *Auctions & Antiques, Springfield Business Journal, Today's Women Journal and Springfield News-leader.*

"The accommodations are wonderful and the hospitality couldn't be warmer."

Walnut Street Inn

900 E Walnut St
Springfield, MO 65806-2603
(417)864-6346 (800)593-6346 Fax:(417)864-6184
E-mail: stay@walnutstreetinn.com
Web: www.walnutstreetinn.com

Circa 1894. This three-story Queen Anne gabled house has cast-iron Corinthian columns and a veranda. Polished wood floors and antiques are featured throughout. Upstairs you'll find the gathering room with a fireplace. Ask for the McCann guest room with two bay windows, or one of the five rooms with a double Jacuzzi tub. A full breakfast is served, including items such as strawberry-filled French toast.

Historic Interest: Springfield History Museum (3 blocks), Laura Ingalls Wilder Museum (40 minutes), Wilson's Creek National Battlefield (20 minutes), General Sweeney's Civil War Museum (20 minutes).

Innkeeper(s): Gary & Paula Blankenship. $89-169. 14 rooms, 12 with PB, 10 with FP and 2 suites. Breakfast included in rates. Types of meals: Full gourmet bkfst, early coffee/tea and afternoon tea. Beds: KQD. Cable TV, VCR, reading lamp, CD player, refrigerator, ceiling fan, clock radio, telephone, coffeemaker, turn-down service, desk, beverage bars and modem in room. Air conditioning. Fax and copier on premises. Limited handicap access. Amusement parks, antiquing, fishing, live theater, parks, shopping, sporting events and water sports nearby.

Publicity: *Southern Living, Women's World, Midwest Living, Victoria, Country Inns, Innsider, Glamour, Midwest Motorist, Missouri, Saint Louis Post, Kansas City Star and USA Today.*

"Rest assured your establishment's qualities are unmatched and through your commitment to excellence you have won a life-long client."

Warrensburg D4

Camel Crossing Bed & Breakfast

210 E Gay St
Warrensburg, MO 64093-1841
(660)429-2973 Fax:(660)429-2722

Circa 1906. This beautiful big inn has a huge front porch and dormers on the third floor. Birds, squirrels and cottontail rabbits often frequent the meticulously landscaped yard. The inn has four guest bedrooms, two with shared baths. The third-floor suite is an impressive 363 square feet. The Middle Eastern décor reflects the background of the innkeepers themselves, who are former Aramcons, while the exterior is traditional American architecture with beveled and stained glass. It serves a delicious breakfast with courses like fruit, bacon, ham, sausage, eggs, hotcakes and waffles.

Innkeeper(s): Joyce & Ed Barnes. $70-90. 4 rooms, 2 with PB, 1 with FP and 1 suite. Breakfast and snacks/refreshments included in rates. Types of meals: Full gourmet bkfst and early coffee/tea. Beds: Q. Modem hook-up, data port, cable TV, VCR, reading lamp, stereo, refrigerator, ceiling fan, snack bar, clock radio, telephone, coffeemaker, desk and fireplace in room. Air conditioning. Fax, copier, parlor games and fireplace on premises. Antiquing, fishing, golf, live theater, parks, shopping, sporting events, tennis, wineries and Amtrak train station (5 blocks) nearby.

Cottage on the Knoll at Cedarcroft Farm B&B

431 SE County Rd Y
Warrensburg, MO 64093-8316
(660)747-5728 (800)368-4944
E-mail: info@cedarcroft.com
Web: www.cedarcroft.com

Circa 1867. Escape to this luxuriously romantic hideaway cottage secluded on an 80-acre farm that is surrounded by woodlands, meadows and creeks where deer, coyotes and wild turkeys abound. Amenities include a four-poster bed, two-person thermal massage tub, dual nozzle shower, wood-burning fireplace, satellite TV, VCR with videos and a CD stereo. Waffle-weave robes, booties and personal products are available. A small refrigerator is stocked with snacks and beverages. Sandra prepares delicious home-cooked country breakfasts that are known for being bountiful. Relax on the porch overlooking the stream. Cedarcroft is inspected and approved by Bed & breakfast Inns of Missouri.

Innkeeper(s): Sandra & Bill Wayne. $175-225. 1 room with PB. Breakfast and snacks/refreshments included in rates. Types of meals: Full bkfst. Beds: K. VCR, telephone, satellite TV, fireplace and stereo in room. Air conditioning. Antiquing, fishing, hiking, live theater, parks, shopping, rodeos, bike trails, bird watching, music festivals and state fair nearby.

Publicity: *Midwest Motorist, Country America, Entrepreneur, Small Farm Today, Kansas City Star, Daily Star-Journal, Higginsville Advance, KCTV, KMOS, KSHB and CNN.*

"We enjoyed the nostalgia and peacefulness very much. Enjoyed your wonderful hospitality and great food."

Washington D7

Schwegmann House

438 W Front St
Washington, MO 63090-2103
(636)239-5025 (800)949-2262
E-mail: cathy@schwegmannhouse.com
Web: www.schwegmannhouse.com

Circa 1861. John F. Schwegmann, a native of Germany, built a flour mill on the Missouri riverfront. This stately three-story home was built not only for the miller and his family, but also to provide extra lodging for overnight customers who traveled long hours to the town. Today, weary

travelers enjoy the formal gardens and warm atmosphere of this restful home. Patios overlook the river, and the gracious rooms are decorated with antiques and handmade quilts. The new Miller Suite boasts a tub for two and breakfast can be delivered to their door. Guests enjoy full breakfasts complete with house specialties such as German apple pancakes or a three-cheese strata accompanied with homemade breads, meat, juice and fresh fruit. There are 11 wineries nearby, or guests can visit one of the historic districts, many galleries, historic sites, antique shops, excellent restaurants and riverfront park located nearby.

Historic Interest: The home is part of the historic downtown Washington area and full of homes and buildings to admire. Daniel Boone's home is 20 miles away. Old Bethel Church and Anna Belle Chapel are short drives. The house is 10 blocks from the Washington Historical Museum.

Innkeeper(s): Catherine & Bill Nagel. $110-160. 9 rooms with PB and 1 suite. Breakfast and snacks/refreshments included in rates. Types of meals: Full gourmet bkfst and early coffee/tea. Beds: QD. Reading lamp, ceiling fan, telephone and desk in room. Air conditioning. Parlor games and fireplace on premises. Small meetings, family reunions and seminars hosted. Antiquing, Missouri River Wine Country and Katy Bike Trail nearby.

Publicity: *St. Louis Post-Dispatch, West County Journal, Midwest Living, Country Inns, Midwest Motorist and Ozark.*

"Like Grandma's house many years ago."

West Plains H6

Pinebrook Lodge B&B

791 State Route T
West Plains, MO 65775
(417)257-7769 (888)892-7699

Circa 1924. Pinebrook Lodge originally served as a health resort for wealthy guests, including presidents and a few more notorious guests. Today, guests still flock here, drawn by the secluded Ozark setting and the hospitality. Each of the inviting guest rooms is unique and decorated with antiques or reproductions. Evening dessert is served and in the morning, breakfasts include entrees such as cheese-stuffed crepes with strawberry-rhubarb sauce. The lodge's ground encompasses 100 acres, which includes a four-acre lake where guests can enjoy catch-and-release fishing. The surrounding Ozarks offer a multitude of attractions, including float, canoe and kayak excursions, hunting, fishing, wilderness trails and several historic mills.

Innkeeper(s): Alice-Jean & Robert Eckhart. $60-85. 7 rooms, 5 with PB. Breakfast and snacks/refreshments included in rates. Types of meals: Full gourmet bkfst. Beds: KQDT. Reading lamp, ceiling fan and turn-down service in room. TV, VCR, library, parlor games, telephone, fireplace, fishing and hiking on premises. Weddings, small meetings, family reunions and seminars hosted. Antiquing, art galleries, canoeing/kayaking, fishing, golf, hiking, live theater, museums, parks, shopping, sporting events and tennis nearby.

Publicity: *Midwest Living Magazine and Ozark Mountaineer Magazine.*

"Thank you for providing the opportunity to relax and enjoy peacefulness."

Weston C2

The Hatchery House

618 Short St
Weston, MO 64098-1228
(816)640-5700
E-mail: hatcherybb@kc.rr.com
Web: www.hatcherybb.com

Circa 1845. This brick Federal home, built prior to the Civil War, was constructed by one of Weston's mayors. It derives its unusual name from its years serving as a boarding house. It seems that many young couples started their families in the house, and the townspeople began calling it the "hatchery," because of the hatching of babies. The inn is still family oriented, and there are antique dolls, toys and books for children to enjoy. Breakfasts include fanciful items such as homemade chocolate chip muffins baked in heart-shaped tins. Entrees include specialty items such as French toast almondine. Local wines are served in the early evenings. Weston offers a variety of antique shops, wineries, a brewery, and an orchard. Fort Leavenworth and the Snow Creek Ski Resort are other attractions. Kansas City is an easy drive to the south.

Innkeeper(s): Bill & Anne Lane. $100-150. 4 rooms with PB, 4 with FP and 1 suite. Breakfast and afternoon tea included in rates. Types of meals: Full gourmet bkfst, veg bkfst, early coffee/tea and picnic lunch. Beds: QT. TV, reading lamp, refrigerator, ceiling fan, clock radio, coffeemaker and one with Jacuzzi for two in room. Central air. Parlor games, telephone and fireplace on premises. Amusement parks, antiquing, art galleries, bicycling, downhill skiing, golf, hiking, museums, parks, shopping, wineries, festivals, orchards and farms nearby.

Montana

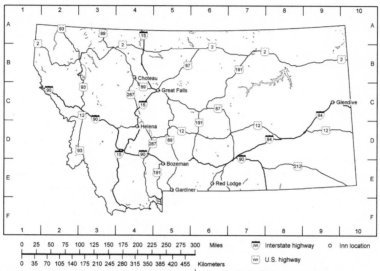

0 25 50 75 100 125 150 175 200 225 250 275 300 Miles

0 35 70 105 140 175 210 245 280 315 350 385 420 455 Kilometers

Interstate highway   o   Inn location

U.S. highway

Bozeman   E5

Gallatin Gateway Inn

Hwy 191
Bozeman, MT 59715
(406)763-4672
E-mail: gatewayinn@gallatingatewayinn.com
Web: www.gallatingatewayinn.com

Circa 1927. Just outside of Bozeman, and 75 miles north of
Yellowstone National Park, lies one of the grand railroad hotels of
the Rocky Mountains West. Stunningly restored, the original
hand-hewn beams, palatial windows and mahogany woodwork
still grace the common rooms. The inn is located in the heart of
Yellowstone Country amid spectacular scenery, hiking and fly-
fishing opportunities. The inn has its own casting pond, outdoor
swimming pool and outdoor Jacuzzi. The rooms are comfortable
and well appointed. The inn's historic dining room offers fine
dining and more casual fare is found in The Baggage Room Pub.
Innkeeper(s): John Power. $70-185. 33 rooms. Types of meals: Cont.
Restaurant on premises. Beds: KQT. TV, radios, coffee maker and hair dryer
in room. Fax, telephone, conference facilities, pool (summer only) and hot tub
on premises. Bicycling and casting pond nearby.
Publicity: *Travel & Leisure, Conde Naste Traveler, Country Living, House &
Garden, Diversions, Bon Appetit, Historic Gourmet, Travel Holiday and
Adventure West.*

Lehrkind Mansion

719 N Wallace Ave
Bozeman, MT 59715-3063
(406)585-6932 (800)992-6932
E-mail: lehrkindmansion@imt.net
Web: www.bozemanbedandbreakfast.com

Circa 1897. A captivating corner tower, peaked gables and
gingerbread trim are among the fanciful architectural elements
found in this Queen Anne Victorian. Original woodwork and
leaded- and stained-glass windows enhance the period
antiques and elegant décor. Located in the historic Brewery
District, the inn is listed in the National Register. Enjoy
refreshments in the afternoon while listening to an antique
music box in the parlor. Excellent local skiing at Bridger Bowl
and Big Sky ski resorts is a short drive away. The local downtown area offers a variety of interesting shops and restaurants.
The owners were former park rangers in Yellowstone National
Park, only one-and-a-half hours away.
Innkeeper(s): Jon Gerster & Christopher Nixon. $79-159. 8 rooms with PB and
2 suites. Breakfast and afternoon tea included in rates. Types of meals: Full
gourmet bkfst, veg bkfst and early coffee/tea. Beds: QD. Modem hook-up, reading lamp, refrigerator and desk in room. Fax, spa, library, parlor games, telephone, refrigerator, data ports, porch with garden and no smoking on premises.
Small meetings hosted. Antiquing, art galleries, bicycling, canoeing/kayaking,
cross-country skiing, downhill skiing, fishing, golf, hiking, horseback riding, live
theater, museums, parks, shopping and sporting events nearby.
Publicity: *Montana Living, Victorian Homes, At Home, Bozeman Daily
Chronicle, HGTV and If These Walls Could Talk.*

*"The entire mansion is beautiful and each room so nicely decorated.
The breakfast was excellent!"*

Silver Forest Inn

15325 Bridger Canyon Rd
Bozeman, MT 59715-8278
(406)586-1882 (877)394-9357 Fax:(406)582-0492
E-mail: info@silverforestinn.com
Web: www.silverforestinn.com

Circa 1932. This historic log home was originally built as a summer artist colony and school of drama. It later served as a hunting lodge. The unusual turret, stone and massive pine log construction makes for a unique accommodation and the secluded setting adds to the experience. Ask to stay in the Turret Room for an expansive view overlooking Bridger Mountains. It boasts a queen-size log bed. (The bath is shared.) A family suite is offered for families with children. Breakfast specialties include blueberry/cream cheese French toast, fresh fruit and chicken sausage.
Historic Interest: Bridger Bowl Ski Area (1/4 mile), Big Sky Ski Resort (short drive), Bohart Ranch Cross-Country Center (1 mile).
Innkeeper(s): Lorraine & Mike Conn. $50-130. 6 rooms, 4 with PB. Breakfast and snacks/refreshments included in rates. Types of meals: Full gourmet bkfst, early coffee/tea and picnic lunch. Beds: KQT. Reading lamp, clock radio and desk in room. TV, VCR, fax, telephone, fireplace, spa and DVD on premises. Small meetings, family reunions and seminars hosted. Antiquing, bicycling, canoeing/kayaking, cross-country skiing, downhill skiing, fishing, golf, hiking, horseback riding, museums, parks and shopping nearby.

Voss Inn

319 S Willson Ave
Bozeman, MT 59715-4632
(406)587-0982 Fax:(406)585-2964
E-mail: vossinn@bridgeband.com
Web: www.bozeman-vossinn.com

Circa 1883. The Voss Inn is a restored two-story Victorian mansion with a large front porch and a Victorian parlor. Antique furnishings include an upright piano and chandelier. Two of the inn's six rooms include air conditioning. A full breakfast is served, with freshly baked rolls kept in a unique warmer that's built into an ornate 1880s radiator.
Historic Interest: Little Big Horn (Custer battle site, 18 miles), Virginia City and Nevada City (60 miles), Madison Buffalo Jump (30 miles), Headwaters of Missouri (45 miles), Yellowstone National Park (90 miles), various Lewis & Clark sites (10-100 miles).
Innkeeper(s): Bruce & Frankee Muller. $105-125. 6 rooms with PB, 3 with FP, 1 suite and 1 conference room. Breakfast and afternoon tea included in rates. Types of meals: Full gourmet bkfst, veg bkfst, early coffee/tea and gourmet dinner. Beds: KQT. Modem hook-up, data port, reading lamp, clock radio, telephone, desk and fireplace in room. Air conditioning. TV, fax, copier, library, parlor games and gift shop on premises. Small meetings and family reunions hosted. Antiquing, art galleries, bicycling, canoeing/kayaking, cross-country skiing, downhill skiing, fishing, golf, hiking, horseback riding, live theater, museums, parks, shopping, sporting events, tennis, golf, hunting, hiking and biking nearby.
Publicity: *Sunset, Cosmopolitan, Gourmet, Countryside and Country Inns.*

"First class all the way."

Choteau   B4

Styren Guest House

961 20th Rd NW
Choteau, MT 59522
(406)466-2008 (888)848-2008

Circa 1912. Located in an area known as the Rocky Mountain Front, where the prairie meets the Rockies, this country guest house was built during the days of homesteading. It sits on a five-acre family ranch and farm with a cow calve herd, alfalfa hay and

barley grown. There are three bedrooms and twice that many beds. A kitchen and bath were added after the arrival of plumbing and electricity. Fully equipped, modern appliances include a microwave for cooking ease. A barbecue grill is outside. A second-story deck overlooking surroundings of green trees, a large lawn and flower beds is perfect for watching colorful sunsets.
Innkeeper(s): Deanna Styren. $450. 3 rooms. Beds: QDT. Cable TV, VCR, reading lamp, refrigerator, ceiling fan, clock radio, coffeemaker, desk and fireplace in room. Pet boarding, parlor games, telephone, laundry facility, gas grill and upper and lower deck on premises. Family reunions hosted. Antiquing, art galleries, bicycling, cross-country skiing, downhill skiing, fishing, hiking, horseback riding, museums, parks, shopping and birding nearby.
Publicity: *Travel Montana, Teton Co Visitor Guide and Chamber of Commerce.*

Gardiner   E5

Yellowstone Suites B&B

506 4th St
Gardiner, MT 59030
(406)848-7937 (800)948-7937
E-mail: bandb@montanadsl.net
Web: www.wolftracker.com/ys

Circa 1904. This three-story stone Victorian home is located just three blocks from the historic Roosevelt Arch, the original gateway to Yellowstone Park. Seasonal activities for the adventure-minded include whitewater rafting, fishing, horseback riding, hiking and canoeing in the summer and snowshoeing, snowmobiling and cross-country skiing in the winter. The road from Gardiner to Cooke City travels through the northern range where antelope, bison, elk, deer, big-horn sheep and wolves are commonly seen. At the end of the day, relax in a rocking chair on the inn's spacious, covered veranda, or soak in the hot tub.
Innkeeper(s): Dagan Klein. $49-108. 4 rooms, 2 with PB, 1 suite and 1 conference room. Breakfast and snacks/refreshments included in rates. Types of meals: Full gourmet bkfst and veg bkfst. Beds: QT. Cable TV, VCR, reading lamp, refrigerator, ceiling fan, snack bar, clock radio, telephone, coffeemaker and hot tub/spa in room. Spa, library, parlor games, landscaped garden and covered porch veranda on premises. Weddings and family reunions hosted. Art galleries, canoeing/kayaking, cross-country skiing, fishing, hiking, horseback riding, museums, parks and shopping nearby.
Publicity: *Sunset Magazine.*

Glendive   C9

The Hostetler House B&B

113 N Douglas St
Glendive, MT 59330-1619
(406)377-4505 (800)965-8456 Fax:(406)377-8456

Circa 1912. Casual country decor mixed with handmade and heirloom furnishings are highlights at this Prairie School home. The inn features many comforting touches, such as a romantic hot tub and gazebo, enclosed sun porch and sitting room filled with books and videos. The two guest rooms share a bath, and are furnished by Dea, an interior decorator. The full breakfasts may be enjoyed on Grandma's china in the dining room or on the sun porch. The historic Bell Street Bridge and the Yellowstone River are one block from the inn, and downtown shopping is two blocks away. Makoshika State Park, home of numerous fossil finds, is nearby.

Historic Interest: Guests are invited to tour Glendive's historic district on the innkeeper's tandem mountain bike.
Innkeeper(s): Craig & Dea Hostetler. $50. 2 rooms. Breakfast included in rates. Types of meals: Full gourmet bkfst and early coffee/tea. Beds: DT. Reading lamp, ceiling fan and air conditioning in room. VCR, fax, spa, bicycles, library,

parlor games, telephone and secretarial service on premises. Small meetings hosted. Antiquing, cross-country skiing, fishing, live theater, parks, shopping, sporting events, water sports and fossil and agate hunting nearby.
Publicity: *Ranger Review/Circle Banner.*

"Warmth and loving care are evident throughout your exquisite home. Your attention to small details is uplifting. Thank you for a restful sojourn."

Great Falls   C5

Collins Mansion B&B

1003 2nd Ave NW
Great Falls, MT 59401
(406)452-6798 (877)452-6798 Fax:(406)452-6787
E-mail: cmansionbb@aol.com
Web: www.collinsmansion.com

Circa 1891. Impressive to behold and a delight to stay at, this large Queen Anne with wraparound veranda, circular drive and landscaped grounds is listed in the National Register. Read by the fire in the library or front parlor, play piano in the music room or watch a video in the lounge upstairs. Complimentary baked goods and beverages always are available on the buffet in the formal dining room. After a restful sleep in one of the tasteful guest bedrooms, enjoy breakfast delicacies like banana muffins with baked apple, sausage patties and peach Dutch babies with whipped cream. Relax on the porch or patio overlooking flower beds and a gazebo.
Innkeeper(s): Connie Romain & Diana Unghire. $75-98. 5 rooms with PB, 1 with FP. Breakfast included in rates. Types of meals: Full bkfst & early coffee/tea. Beds: QDT. Modem hook-up, data port, reading lamp & ceiling fan in room. Air conditioning. TV, VCR, fax, copier, library, telephone, fireplace and laundry facility on premises. Weddings, small meetings and family reunions hosted. Antiquing, art galleries, cross-country skiing, downhill skiing, fishing, golf, horseback riding, museums, parks, shopping, sporting events, tennis & water sports nearby.

Helena   D4

The Sanders - Helena's Bed & Breakfast

328 N Ewing St
Helena, MT 59601-4050
(406)442-3309 Fax:(406)443-2361
E-mail: thefolks@sandersbb.com
Web: www.sandersbb.com

Circa 1875. This historic inn is filled with elegantly carved furnishings, paintings and collections that are original to the house. Wilbur Sanders, an attorney and a Montana senator and his wife Harriet, built their home in the heart of Helena. The three-story house features a front and side porch, and balconies and bay windows that provide views of the mountains and downtown Helena. In addition to the rich interior and hospitality, guests are pampered with gourmet breakfasts that might include items such as an orange souffle, sourdough or huckleberry pancakes, French toast with sauteed fruit or savory frittatas. The main dish is accompanied by fresh fruit, juice, freshly ground organically grown coffee and an assortment of homemade muffins, coffee cakes or breads.
Historic Interest: Montana State Historical Museum, Cathedral of St. Helena, Reeders Alley & Capital.
Innkeeper(s): Bobbi Uecker & Rock Ringling. $85-130. 7 rooms with PB and 2 conference rooms. Breakfast included in rates. Types of meals: Full gourmet bkfst, early coffee/tea, afternoon tea and room service. Beds: Q. Cable TV, reading lamp, ceiling fan, telephone, turn-down service, desk, fireplace, hair dryer and computer hook-up in room. Air conditioning. VCR, fax, copier, library, parlor games, fireplace, porch with garden, smoke-free, off-street parking, cookies, fruit, sherry and data port on premises. Weddings, small meetings, family reunions and seminars hosted. Antiquing, art galleries, cross-country skiing,

downhill skiing, fishing, live theater, museums, parks, shopping, sporting events, water sports, state capitol, Governor's mansion and Helena's Cathedral nearby.
Publicity: *National Geographic Traveler, Country Travels, Pacific Northwest, Washington Post, Boston Globe and New York Times.*

Red Lodge   E6

The Pollard

PO Box 650
Red Lodge, MT 59068
(406)446-0001 (800)765-5273 Fax:(406)446-0002
E-mail: pollard@pollardhotel.com
Web: www.pollardhotel.com

Circa 1893. A distinctive architectural landmark, this red brick building is a grand hotel listed in the National Register. Learn of its rich heritage and restorations in the oak-paneled History Room or relax by the fireplace in the gallery with coffered ceilings. Early guests included Calamity Jane, Buffalo Bill Cody and William Jennings Bryan. Stay in an upscale guest bedroom or suite with a balcony, hot tub, steambath or mountain view. Breakfast is made to order in the award-winning dining room. Enjoy the health club's exercise room, sauna, whirlpool and racquetball. After a beautiful ceremony at the Canyon Wedding Chapel, this is the perfect place for a lavish or intimate reception and honeymoon.
Historic Interest: Built in 1893, guests include Calamity Jane, Buffalo Bill Cody, Wild Bill Hickok.
Innkeeper(s): Sharon Nix. $74-265. 39 rooms with PB. Breakfast included in rates. Types of meals: Full bkfst, veg bkfst, early coffee/tea, lunch, picnic lunch, snacks/refreshments, dinner & room service. Restaurant on premises. Beds: KQD. Modem hook-up, cable TV, VCR, reading lamp, clock radio, telephone, hot tub/spa, voice mail, hair dryers, bathrobes & some with Jacuzzi & balconies in room. Air conditioning. Fax, copier, spa, sauna, fireplace & pub with fireplace on premises. Limited handicap access. Weddings, small meetings, family reunions & seminars hosted. Antiquing, art galleries, bicycling, canoeing/kayaking, cross-country skiing, downhill skiing, fishing, golf, hiking, horseback riding, museums, parks, shopping, tennis, health club, racquetball courts, hot tub & saunas nearby.
Publicity: *Carlson County News and ABC 6 and Fox 4.*

Willows Inn

224 S Platt Ave
Red Lodge, MT 59068
(406)446-3913
E-mail: willowinn@earthlink.net
Web: www.bbhost.com/willowsinn

Circa 1909. Dreams do come true at this three-story Queen Anne Victorian with gingerbread trim and white picket fence. An assortment of common rooms are accented with original wood molding, leaded-glass windows and boast reading nooks, a TV parlor with extensive videos and a living room. Two storybook cottages offer privacy. Antique furnishings and specialty bath products highlight the well-appointed guest bedrooms. Savor a gourmet breakfast and Elven's tasty afternoon refreshments in the cheery wicker-filled dining room. Relax on comfy chairs and enjoy the mountain view from the large front porch that overlooks the colorful flowerbeds and manicured lawn. Stroll down Main Street and stop for lunch or dinner cuisine at Bridge Creek Backcountry Kitchen and Wine Bar.
Innkeeper(s): Carolyn, Kerry & Elven Boggio. $65-85. 5 rooms, 3 with PB and 2 cottages. Breakfast and snacks/refreshments included in rates. Types of meals: Full gourmet bkfst and veg bkfst. Beds: KQDT. VCR, reading lamp, ceiling fan and cottages with television in room. Air conditioning. TV, sauna, bicycles, library, parlor games, telephone, cable TV and CD player on premises. Family reunions hosted. Antiquing, art galleries, bicycling, canoeing/kayaking, cross-country skiing, downhill skiing, fishing, golf, hiking, horseback riding, museums, parks, shopping and tennis nearby.
Publicity: *The Billings Gazette, Innsider, Travel & Leisure, National Geographic Traveler, Gourmet, Country, Forbes, Los Angeles Times and New York Times.*

"It was heavenly. The bed was comfortable and we loved the decor."

Nebraska

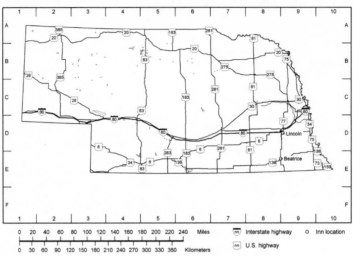

Beatrice   E9

The Carriage House B&B
25478 S 23rd Rd
Beatrice, NE 68310
(402)228-0356 (888)228-0356

Circa 1930. The two-story brick house and accompanying 10
acres are listed in the State Historic Register. A quiet and tranquil ambiance is enhanced by the elegantly furnished period
antiques. The Victorian Guest Parlor welcomes relaxation with
music and a fireplace. Choose from well-decorated, quaint
guest bedrooms like the Garden Room with French doors leading to a private veranda, or the Victorian Suite with antique
clawfoot tub, pedestal sink and dressing table. Enjoy a generous breakfast served in the large dining room. Hand-feed the
llamas in the 1887 barn, delight in the peaceful gazebo and
watch a gorgeous sunset from the wraparound porch.

Innkeeper(s): Jess & Wanda Enns. $55-105. 5 rooms and 2 suites. Breakfast
and snacks/refreshments included in rates. Types of meals: Full gourmet
bkfst. Beds: DT. Reading lamp and clock radio in room. Central air. TV, VCR,
stable, pet boarding, telephone, fireplace and private living room on premises. Weddings and family reunions hosted. Fishing, golf, hiking, parks, shopping and tennis nearby.

Lincoln   D9

The Atwood House B&B
740 S 17th St
Lincoln, NE 68508-3708
(402)438-4567 (800)884-6554 Fax:(402)477-8314

Circa 1894. Located two blocks from the state capitol, this
7,500-square-foot mansion, in the Neoclassical Georgian
Revival style, features four massive columns. Interior columns
are repeated throughout such as on the
dressing room vanity, on the staircase and on the parlor fireplace.
Classically appointed, the parlor
and entranceway set an elegant
yet inviting tone. Guest suites are
large and feature spacious sitting
rooms, fireplaces, massive bedsteads and Oriental carpets. The
800-square-foot bridal suite consists of three rooms, and it
includes a fireplace, a carved walnut bed and a large whirlpool
tub set off by columns. Breakfast is served on bone china with
Waterford crystal and sterling flatware.

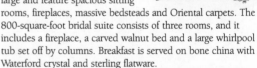

Innkeeper(s): Ruth & Larry Stoll. $85-179. 4 suites, 2 with FP and 1 conference
room. Breakfast and snacks/refreshments included in rates. Types of meals: Full
gourmet bkfst and early coffee/tea. Beds: KQ. Cable TV, VCR, reading lamp, clock
radio, telephone, turn-down service, desk and three with two-person whirlpool in
room. Air conditioning. Fax, copier, library and fireplace on premises. Weddings
and small meetings hosted. Antiquing, cross-country skiing, fishing, golf, live theater, parks, shopping, sporting events, tennis and water sports nearby.
Publicity: *Lincoln Journal Star and Channel 8 local.*

"Such a delightful B&B! It is such a nice change in my travels."

348

Nevada

Boulder City   J8

The Historic Boulder Dam Hotel Bed & Breakfast

1305 Arizona Street
Boulder City, NV 89005
(702)293-3510 Fax:(702)293-3093
E-mail: resinfo@boulderdamhotel.com
Web: www.boulderdamhotel.com

Circa 1933. Quaint yet comfortable, this Dutch Colonial-style hotel, listed in the National Register, has been carefully restored to offer a bygone era of hospitality with today's modern amenities. Guest bedrooms and suites feature voice-mail and computer jacks. Enjoy a full breakfast at the on-site Boulder Dam Cafe & Bakery. Evening wine and cheese is served as well as fresh-baked cookies and fruit. Room service items are available. Visit the unique gift shop and art gallery. Admission to the local museum and free use of the gym is included.

Innkeeper(s): Larry Kimball. $99-149. 22 rooms, 20 with PB, 2 suites and 1 conference room. Types of meals: Country bkfst, early coffee/tea, lunch, dinner and room service. Restaurant on premises. Beds: QD. Modem hook-up, cable TV, clock radio, telephone, desk and voice mail in room. Central air. Fax, copier, fireplace and gift shop on premises. Weddings, small meetings, family reunions and seminars hosted. Antiquing, art galleries, beach, bicycling, canoeing/kayaking, fishing, golf, hiking, museums, parks, shopping, tennis and water sports nearby.

Carson City   E2

Bliss Mansion B&B

608 Elizabeth Street
Carson City, NV 89703-3865
(775)887-8988 (800)887-3501 Fax:(775)887-0540
E-mail: innkeeper@blissmansion.com
Web: www.blissmansion.com

Circa 1879. Exquisitely restored, this mansion is one of Nevada's few historic bed & breakfast inns. Named after its original owner, the inn was the state's largest residence when built. Located in the historic district, it housed the first residential gas lighting and phone line. The B&B has been updated with modern comforts while retaining its character. Guest bedrooms feature pillow-top mattresses, Carrera marble and mahogany fireplaces, 10-foot windows, clawfoot tubs, plush towels, fine linens and robes. There is a spacious family suite available on the third floor. A hearty breakfast is served on the hand-carved 15-foot Honduras mahogany dining room table with 19th-century intricate French chairs. Enjoy the relaxation, comfort and indulgence

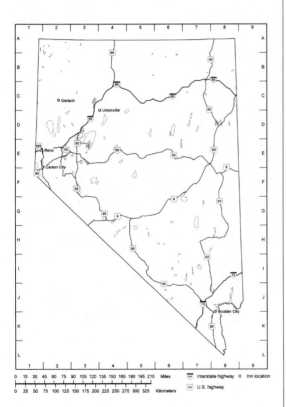

in this elegant setting. The state's capital offers many activities, sports and entertainment within close proximity.

$145-195. 5 rooms with PB. Breakfast included in rates. Types of meals: Full gourmet bkfst and early coffee/tea. Beds: KQ. TV, reading lamp, hair dryer and instant hot water in room. Air conditioning. VCR, fax, copier, library, telephone and fireplace on premises. Antiquing, cross-country skiing, downhill skiing, fishing, golf, parks, water sports, gambling and historical tours nearby.

"A Hearst Castle with air conditioning, pillowtop mattresses and instant hot water."

Gerlach   C2

Soldier Meadows Guest Ranch & Lodge

Soldier Meadows Rd
Gerlach, NV 89412
(530)279-4881 Fax:(530)279-2024
E-mail: soldier@direcway.com
Web: www.soldiermeadows.com

Circa 1865. Once known as Fort McGarry, this historic working ranch once housed the troops who were assigned to protect pioneers traveling the Applegate-Lassen Trail from the Paiute Indians of the area. The Estill family now runs cattle on the land. Green meadows and willow trees frame the ranch house and the bunkhouse. Stone stables erected by the U. S. Army are still in use, as well as the original Officers' Quarters. There are two natural hot springs for swimming. Wildlife is abundant in the area, including wild mustangs, mule deer and antelope. Guests may opt to work the range with the ranch's cowhands and enjoy trail riding, hunting, fishing or hiking. Some like to mine for opals at the adjacent opal mine, while others organize a camping experience at one of the two sheep camps in the aspen and mahogany forests of the foothills. For the complete experience, join the crew in the cookhouse early for breakfast or later for lunch. A ranch supper is offered in the evening where, after a day or two, you may find yourself spinning a yarn of your own about the Old West

Innkeeper(s): Mackey & Candi Hedges. $45-125. 10 rooms, 1 suite and 1 conference room. Breakfast, snacks/refreshments and dinner included in rates. Types of meals: Full bkfst, early coffee/tea and lunch. Beds: QT. Reading lamp, refrigerator and coffeemaker in room. Laundry facility, natural hot springs and BBQ supper almost every night on premises. Small meetings and family reunions hosted. Bicycling, canoeing/kayaking, hiking, horseback riding and historic Pioneer Trails nearby.

Reno   E1

Bed and Breakfast: South Reno

136 Andrew Ln
Reno, NV 89511-9740
(775)849-0772

Circa 1948. Look out upon mountain vistas and neighboring ranches at this bed & breakfast in a country setting just two blocks off 395 and only ten miles from Reno. Beamed ceilings,

original paintings and gorgeous antique furnishings create a pleasant atmosphere. Enjoy conversation in a large sitting room with a splendid view of Mount Rose. The private two-room suite is secluded upstairs and features a four-poster bed and wing chair. Breakfast is made to please with dietary preferences gladly accommodated. Relax on the landscaped lawns with forty trees, several patios and decks. Take a refreshing swim in the pool. Windsurf at nearby Washoe Lake or ski at Slide Mountain. Popular sledding and snowmobiling are also less than 20 miles away.

Innkeeper(s): Caroline Walters & Robert McNeill. $75-90. 2 rooms with PB. Breakfast included in rates. Types of meals: Cont plus and early coffee/tea. Beds: QDT. Cable TV, VCR, reading lamp, stereo, clock radio and telephone in room. Air conditioning. Swimming, library, fireplace and antique shop on premises. Weddings and seminars hosted. Amusement parks, antiquing, art galleries, cross-country skiing, downhill skiing, fishing, golf, hiking, horseback riding, live theater, museums, parks, shopping, sporting events, tennis, water sports and casinos nearby.

Publicity: *Denver, Reno, Carson and Newspaper articles.*

Unionville   D4

Old Pioneer Garden Country Inn

2805 Unionville Rd
Unionville, NV 89418-8204
(775)538-7585

Circa 1861. Once a bustling silver mining town, Unionville now has only a handful of citizens, and Old Pioneer Garden Guest Ranch is just down the road from town. Accommodations are in a renovated blacksmith's house, a farmhouse and across the meadow in the Hadley House. Samuel L. Clemens once stayed at this inn, and modern guests can still settle down in front of a fire in the inn's library. A Swedish-style gazebo rests beside a bubbling stream, and there are orchards, grape arbors, vegetable gardens, sheep and goats. A country supper is available. The innkeepers can accommodate visiting horses in their barn and corrals.

Innkeeper(s): Mitzi & Lew Jones. $85-95. 12 rooms, 7 with PB, 1 with FP, 1 suite and 1 conference room. Breakfast included in rates. Types of meals: Full gourmet bkfst, early coffee/tea, gourmet lunch, picnic lunch and dinner. Beds: D. Library, parlor games, telephone, fireplace and tournament-size pool table on premises. Limited handicap access. Antiquing and fishing nearby.

Publicity: *Denver Post.*

"An array of charm that warms the heart and delights the soul."

New Hampshire

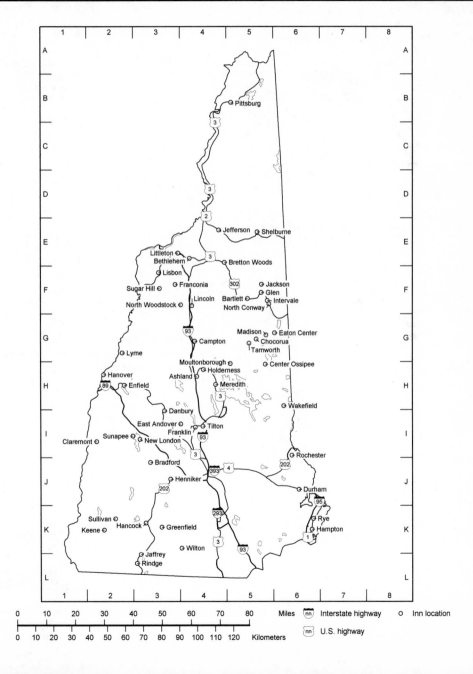

0 10 20 30 40 50 60 70 80   Miles [nn] Interstate highway   ○ Inn location

0 10 20 30 40 50 60 70 80 90 100 110 120   Kilometers   [nn] U.S. highway

Albany F5

The Darby Field Country Inn & Restaurant

185 Chase Hill Rd
Albany, NH 03818
(603)447-2181 (800)426-4147 Fax:(603)447-5726
E-mail: marc@darbyfield.com
Web: www.darbyfield.com

Circa 1826. This rambling, blue clapboard farmhouse has a huge fieldstone fireplace, stone patio and outstanding views of the Mt. Washington Valley and the Presidential Mountains. For

many years, it was called the Bald Hill Grand View Lodge, but was renamed to honor the first European to climb Mt. Washington, Darby Field. Bed & breakfast rates range from $100 to $280 per couple.

Innkeeper(s): Marc & Maria Donaldson. $100-280. 13 rooms with PB. Types of meals: Country bkfst and gourmet dinner. Beds: KQT. Deluxe rooms have TV, VCR, air conditioning, fireplace and Jacuzzi in room. Telephone, fireplace, cross-country nature trails, horse-drawn sleigh, heated swimming pool, spa services and six deluxe rooms available on premises. Weddings, small meetings, family reunions and seminars hosted. Amusement parks, antiquing, cross-country skiing, downhill skiing, live theater and shopping nearby.

Ashland H4

Anniversary Inn - A Glynn House Inn

59 Highland St, PO Box 719
Ashland, NH 03217-0719
(603)968-3775 (800)637-9599 Fax:(603)968-9415
E-mail: theglynnhouseinn@aol.com
Web: glynnhouse.com

Circa 1895. A three-story turret, gables and verandas frosted with Queen Anne gingerbread come together in an appealing mass of Victoriana in the Glynn House. Carved oak woodwork and pocket doors accentuate the foyer. Period furnishings and ornate Oriental wall coverings decorate the parlor. The

Circa 1895

village of Ashland is located in the "On Golden Pond" (Squam Lake) and the White Mountains area. The inn is about two hours from Boston and one hour from Manchester airport.

Historic Interest: Shaker Village (20 minutes), Polar Caves (10 minutes).

Innkeeper(s): Jim & Gay Dunlop. $119-239. 13 rooms with PB, 10 with FP and 7 suites. Breakfast and snacks/refreshments included in rates. Types of meals: Full gourmet bkfst and early coffee/tea. Beds: KQT. Cable TV, VCR, reading lamp, clock radio, desk, fireplace and two-person whirlpools in room. Air conditioning. Fax, parlor games, telephone and fireplace on premises. Weddings, small meetings, family reunions and seminars hosted. Amusement parks, antiquing, cross-country skiing, downhill skiing, fishing, parks, shopping, sporting events, water sports and discount stores nearby.

"Boston was fun, but the Glynn House is the place we'll send our friends."

Bartlett F5

The Bartlett Inn

Rt 302, PO Box 327
Bartlett, NH 03812
(603)374-2353 (800)292-2353 Fax:(603)374-2547
E-mail: stay@bartlettinn.com
Web: www.bartlettinn.com

Circa 1885. One mile from White Mountain National Forest, near Crawford Notch State Park and Mount Washington, stands an 1885 Stick Victorian Inn cottage on two-and-a-half acres. The inn has appeared in numerous publications, including Outside Magazine, because of its proximity to the wilderness. Guests may choose among 16 bedrooms and 10 cottages. A full country breakfast offers courses such as custom omelets, crepes, waffles, ham and

bacon. After a day enjoying the wilderness by hiking, canoeing or mountain biking, guests may relax in a rocking chair on the front porch, swing in the hammock or enjoy the stars as they soak in the hot tub. Moose, deer, fox and coyote have been spotted in nearby areas.

Historic Interest: Heritage, New Hampshire (6 miles), Crawford Notch State Park (10 miles), Mt. Washington (18 miles).

Innkeeper(s): Miriam Habert & Nick Jacques. $79-175. 16 rooms, 10 with PB, 4 with FP and 10 cottages. Breakfast included in rates. Types of meals: Country bkfst and early coffee/tea. Beds: D. Cable TV, refrigerator and coffeemaker in room. Air conditioning. VCR, fax, spa, library, parlor games, telephone and fireplace on premises. Family reunions hosted. Antiquing, art galleries, bicycling, canoeing/kayaking, cross-country skiing, downhill skiing, fishing, golf, hiking, horseback riding, live theater, museums, parks, shopping, tennis and water sports nearby.

Publicity: *Outside Magazine, Adventure Journal, Boston Herald, Backcountry, NH Explorers Guide, Family Camping and New Hampshire Handbook.*

"Walking through your door felt like stepping back in time."

Bethlehem E4

Adair Country Inn

80 Guider Lane
Bethlehem, NH 03574
(603)444-2600 (888)444-2600 Fax:(603)444-4823
E-mail: innkeeper@adairinn.com
Web: www.adairinn.com

Circa 1927. Representing all that a New England country inn is hoped to be, enjoy relaxation and tranquility on more than 200 picturesque acres with mountain views and perennial gardens. This four-diamond-rated inn was originally a wedding gift from Frank Hogan to his daughter, Dorothy Adair Hogan. Dorothy hosted many famed guests here, including presidential candidates, Supreme Court justices and actors. Just-baked popovers start the morning fare, followed by fresh fruit, yogurt and specialty dishes such as pumpkin pancakes with Vermont bacon. Homemade

cakes and cookies are served during the complimentary afternoon tea service. Make advance reservations for dinner at Tim-Bir Alley restaurant, as it is also open to the public.

Innkeeper(s): Judy & Bill Whitman. $175-345. 10 rooms with PB, 8 with FP, 2 suites and 1 cottage. Breakfast and afternoon tea included in rates. Types of meals: Full bkfst, early coffee/tea and gourmet dinner. Restaurant on premises. Beds: KQ. Reading lamp, clock radio, turn-down service and desk in room. Air conditioning. VCR, fax, copier, tennis, library, parlor games, telephone, fireplace and pool table on premises. Small meetings, family reunions and seminars hosted. Antiquing, cross-country skiing, downhill skiing, live theater, shopping and hiking nearby.

Publicity: *Travel & Leisure, Yankee Connecticut Magazine, New England Travel, Gourmet, Cosmopolitan* and *New Hampshire Magazine.*

"What can we say, we expected a lot — and got much more."

The Mulburn Inn

2370 Main St, Rt 302
Bethlehem, NH 03574
(603)869-3389 (800)457-9440

Circa 1908. This English Tudor mansion was once the summer estate of the Woolworth family. The home was built by notable architect Sylvanius D. Morgan, whose inspired design includes many intricate details. The home's romantic ambiance entices a multitude of visitors, and it is within these idyllic walls that Cary Grant and Barbara Hutton enjoyed their honeymoon. Today, guests also have use of a hot tub.

Historic Interest: Crawford Notch State Park, Franconia Notch State Park, Heritage, Mount Washington.

Innkeeper(s): Christina Ferraro & Alecia Loveless. $85-175. 7 rooms with PB. Breakfast included in rates. Types of meals: Full gourmet bkfst. Beds: KQ. Reading lamp, clock radio and desk in room. Air conditioning. TV, VCR, fax, spa, library, parlor games, telephone and fireplace on premises. Weddings, small meetings, family reunions and seminars hosted. Antiquing, bicycling, canoeing/kayaking, cross-country skiing, downhill skiing, fishing, golf, live theater, parks, shopping, tennis, water sports and romantic getaways nearby.

Publicity: *Cover of Yankee B&B Guide, NECN This is Your Dream House, The Today Show* and *Home & Garden Channel.*

"You have put a lot of thought, charm, beauty and warmth into the inn. Your breakfasts were oh, so delicious!!"

The Wayside Inn

Rt 302 at Pierce Bridge, 3738 Main Stree
Bethlehem, NH 03574
(603)869-3364 (800)448-9557 Fax:(603)869-5765
E-mail: info@thewaysideinn.com
Web: www.thewaysideinn.com

Circa 1825. The Ammonosuc River flows gently a few yards from this historic inn, which was built in the early 1800s. Additions were added in 1910 and again in the 1950s. The inn originally was the home of John Pierce, nephew of President Franklin Pierce. Of the 26 guest rooms, 14 are located in the inn. These rooms are decorated in traditional New England style with beds topped with quilts. Some rooms include a poster bed. The rest of the rooms have contemporary furnishings. Guests can enjoy the gardens and mountain views or head down to the sandy beach. In the winter, guests can go snowmobiling or cross-country skiing. Breakfast is included in the rates, and Chef Victor Hofmann was named Chef of the Year by the American Culinary Federation in 1994. The Hofmann family has owned and operated the Wayside Inn for more than a decade.

Innkeeper(s): Victor & Kathie Hofmann. $88-112. 26 rooms with PB. Breakfast included in rates. Types of meals: Full bkfst, early coffee/tea and dinner. Restaurant on premises. Beds: KQD. Reading lamp, desk, some with TV, refrigerator, whirlpool tub and balconies in room. Air conditioning. Fax, copier,

swimming, parlor games, telephone, fireplace and bocce court on premises. Limited handicap access. Weddings, small meetings and family reunions hosted. Amusement parks, antiquing, cross-country skiing, downhill skiing, fishing, golf, live theater, parks, shopping, tennis and water sports nearby.

Bradford   J3

Candlelite Inn

5 Greenhouse Ln
Bradford, NH 03221-3505
(603)938-5571 (888)812-5571
E-mail: candlelite@conknet.com
Web: www.candleliteinn.com

Circa 1897. Nestled on three acres of countryside in the valley of the Lake Sunapee region, this Victorian inn has all of the grace and charm of an era gone by. The inn offers a gazebo porch perfect for sipping lemonade on a summer day. On winter days, keep warm by the parlor's fireplace, while relaxing with a good book. Enjoy a three-course gourmet breakfast, including dessert, in the sun room overlooking the pond. Country roads invite fall strolls, cross-country skiing and snowshoeing.

Historic Interest: Close to the John Hay.

Innkeeper(s): Les & Marilyn Gordon.
$95-140. 6 rooms with PB. Breakfast included in rates. Types of meals: Full bkfst, early coffee/tea and snacks/refreshments. Beds: Q. Reading lamp, ceiling fan, some with sitting areas, glass front gas stove, large shower heads, hair dryers and air conditioning in room. Telephone, fireplace, piano and afternoon refreshments into the evening on premises. Antiquing, cross-country skiing, downhill skiing, live theater, shopping and sporting events nearby.

Publicity: *Grapevine, InterTown News, Sunday Monitor, N.H. Business Review, The Bradford Bridge, Antiques & Auction News, Concord Area Buywise, Taste of New England, Congressional Record, Country Extra Magazine, Arrington's Book of Lists, Accord Publishing B&B calendar* and Voted 2001 Inn of the Year.

The Rosewood Country Inn

67 Pleasant View Rd
Bradford, NH 03221-3113
(603)938-5253
E-mail: rosewood@conknet.com
Web: www.rosewoodcountryinn.com

Circa 1850. This three-story country Victorian inn in the Sunapee Region treats its guests to a candlelight and crystal breakfast and elegant accommodations that manage to avoid being stuffy. The inn prides itself on special touches. The innkeepers like to keep things interesting with ideas such as theme weekends and special breakfast fare, including cinnamon apple pancakes with cider sauce. Mount Sunapee Ski Area and Lake Sunapee are less than eight minutes away.

Historic Interest: Gish sisters, Gloria Swanson, Douglas Fairbanks, Charlie Chaplin and Mary Pickford stayed here.

Innkeeper(s): Lesley & Dick Marquis. $119-269. 11 rooms with PB, 8 with FP and 3 conference rooms. Breakfast included in rates. Types of meals: Full gourmet bkfst, veg bkfst and early coffee/tea. Beds: KQ. Cable TV, VCR, reading lamp, ceiling fan, clock radio, hot tub/spa, four with Jacuzzi tubs for two and all rooms have sherry in room. Air conditioning. Fax, spa, swimming, bicycles, parlor games, telephone, fireplace, cross-country skiing, hiking, snowshoeing, ice skating and fishing on premises. Limited handicap access. Weddings, small meetings, family reunions and seminars hosted. Antiquing, beach, bicycling, canoeing/kayaking, cross-country skiing, downhill skiing, fishing, golf, hiking, horseback riding, live theater, museums, parks, shopping, sporting events and water sports nearby.

Publicity: *Modern Bride, Country Inn, Boston Magazine, Boston Globe, New York Newsday, New York Times, Boston Herald,* Featured on "Chronicle"- NH & Boston and MA.

Thistle and Shamrock Inn & Restaurant

11 West Main St
Bradford, NH 03221
(603)938-5553 (888)938-5553 Fax:(603)938-5554
E-mail: stay@thistleandshamrock.com
Web: www.thistleandshamrock.com

Circa 1898. The front porch beckons with wicker furniture and hanging flower baskets. Originally a hotel accommodating traveling salesmen to area mill towns, this historic Federal-style inn with wide halls and stairways features quiet comfort. Relax by the fireplace in the large parlor, or read in the well-stocked library. Experience 19th-century furnishings and modern conveniences in the guest bedrooms, mini-suites or family suites. Chef Jim's culinary expertise is enjoyed for breakfast and dinner in the Roters Dining Room. The cozy Pub Room offers a beverage and hors d'oeuvre menu. Lake and Mount Sunapee are nearby, contributing to the area's many year-round activities.

Innkeeper(s): Jim & Lynn Horigan. $95-150. 10 rooms with PB and 7 suites. Breakfast included in rates. Types of meals: Full bkfst and gourmet dinner. Restaurant on premises. Beds: KQT. Reading lamp and ceiling fan in room. TV, library, parlor games, telephone and fireplace on premises. Weddings, small meetings, family reunions and seminars hosted. Antiquing, art galleries, beach, bicycling, canoeing/kayaking, cross-country skiing, downhill skiing, fishing, golf, hiking, live theater, museums, parks, shopping and water sports nearby.

Publicity: *Soonipi Magazine, Valley News, WMUR-TV, Manchester and Cook's Corner.*

Bretton Woods E4

Bretton Arms Country Inn

Route 302
Bretton Woods, NH 03575
(603)278-1000 (800)258-0330 Fax:(603)278-8838
E-mail: hotelinfo@mtwashington.com
Web: www.brettonarms.com

Circa 1896. This magnificent Victorian was once a private home and later served as lodging at the prestigious Mount Washington Resort. The inn eventually closed, but it now has been completely restored and reopened. The guest rooms and suites are appointed in Victorian style. The inn has been designated a National Historic Landmark. Guests enjoy use of all that the Mount Washington Resort has to offer, including 2,600 scenic acres. There are a dozen tennis courts, two golf courses, swimming pools, cross-country and alpine ski trails and a Jacuzzi and sauna. Sleigh and carriage rides can be arranged, or guests can simply stroll through the beautifully maintained gardens. Guests can enjoy a delicious breakfast or gourmet dinner in the inn's impressive dining room. Nightly entertainment is provided mid-May through mid-October and late November through early April at the resort's Cave Lounge, an intimate setting reminiscent of an old speakeasy.

Innkeeper(s): Eleanor Imrie. $55-195. 34 rooms with PB and 3 suites. Breakfast included in rates. Types of meals: Full bkfst and gourmet dinner. Restaurant on premises. Beds: KQ. Cable TV, clock radio, telephone, desk and high-speed Internet access in room. VCR, fax, copier, swimming, sauna, stable, bicycles, tennis, library, child care, parlor games, fireplace, downhill skiing and cross country skiing and golf on premises. Limited handicap access. Weddings, small meetings, family reunions and seminars hosted. Bicycling, downhill skiing, fishing, golf, hiking, live theater, parks, shopping and tennis nearby.

Campton G4

Colonel Spencer Inn

3 Colonel Spencer Rd
Campton, NH 03223
(603)536-3438
Web: www.colonelspencerinn.com

Circa 1764. This pre-Revolutionary Colonial boasts Indian shutters, gleaming plank floors and a secret hiding place. Joseph Spencer, one of the home's early owners, fought at Bunker Hill and with General Washington. Within view of the river and the mountains, the inn is now a cozy retreat with warm Colonial decor. A suite with a kitchen is also available.

Innkeeper(s): Carolyn & Alan Hill. $45-65. 7 rooms with PB and 1 suite. Breakfast and snacks/refreshments included in rates. Types of meals: Full bkfst. Beds: D. Reading lamp and fans in room. TV, parlor games, telephone and fireplace on premises. Small meetings and family reunions hosted. Antiquing, cross-country skiing, downhill skiing, fishing, live theater, parks, shopping, sporting events, water sports and water parks nearby.

"You have something very special here, and we very much enjoyed a little piece of it!"

Mountain-Fare Inn

Mad River Rd, PO Box 553
Campton, NH 03223
(603)726-4283
E-mail: mtnfareinn@cyberportal.net
Web: www.mountainfareinn.com

Circa 1830. Located in the White Mountains between Franconia Notch and Squam Lake, this white farmhouse is surrounded by flower gardens in the summer and unparalleled foliage in the fall. Mountain-Fare is an early 19th-century village inn in an ideal spot from which to enjoy New Hampshire's many offerings. Each season brings with it different activities, from skiing to biking and hiking or simply taking in the beautiful scenery. Skiers will enjoy the inn's lodge atmosphere during the winter, as well as the close access to ski areas. The inn is appointed in a charming New Hampshire style with country-cottage decor. There's a game room with billiards and a soccer field for playing ball. The hearty breakfast is a favorite of returning guests.

Historic Interest: Franconia Notch (Old Man of the Mountain), Squam Lake (Golden Pond), and drive the Scenic Kancamagus Highway.

Innkeeper(s): Susan & Nick Preston. $85-135. 10 rooms with PB. Breakfast and afternoon tea included in rates. Types of meals: Full bkfst. Beds: QDT. Reading lamp and clock radio in room. TV, VCR, sauna, telephone, fireplace, game room with billiards and soccer field on premises. Weddings, small meetings and family reunions hosted. Antiquing, cross-country skiing, downhill skiing, fishing, hiking, live theater, parks, sporting events and water sports nearby.

Publicity: *Ski, Skiing and Snow Country.*

"Thank you for your unusually caring attitude toward your guests."

Center Ossipee   H5

Hitching Post Village Inn

Grant Hill Rd
Center Ossipee, NH 03814
(603)539-3360 (800)482-POST Fax:(831)624-6229
Web: www.hitchingpostvillageinn.com

Circa 1830. Experience the lakes and mountains of central New Hampshire from this historic bed & breakfast that welcomes families with children. Socialize on the porch; relax by the fire in the library or living room. A third-floor lounge has a TV/VCR/DVD with a projection display. All of the guest bedrooms and suites are spacious and comfortable. Most offer views of the garden or the church's picturesque steeple and the historical society across the street. The French Suite features a four-poster Queen bed and whirlpool tub. The English Suite boasts a four-poster King bed and clawfoot tub. Enjoy a typical breakfast of fresh fruit, just-baked marmalade bread, bacon, omelette, home fries, pancakes or waffles with blueberry maple syrup and coffee cake in the fireside dining room. Ask for a tour of the barn's two-story outhouse and the kitchen's beehive oven.

Innkeeper(s): Michael & Linda Lee. $65-95. 5 rooms with PB and 1 conference room. Breakfast and afternoon tea included in rates. Types of meals: Country bkfst. Beds: KQDT. TV, VCR, parlor games and DVD on premises. Small meetings and family reunions hosted. Amusement parks, antiquing, beach, bicycling, canoeing/kayaking, cross-country skiing, downhill skiing, fishing, golf, hiking, horseback riding, parks, shopping, tennis and water sports nearby.

Chocorua   G5

Brass Heart Inn

PO Box 370
Chocorua, NH 03817-0370
(603)323-7766 Fax:(603)323-7531
E-mail: info@thebrassheartinn.com
Web: www.thebrassheartinn.com

Circa 1778. The main building of Harte's, home to a prosperous farm family for over 150 years, is Federal style. It became a guest house in the 1890s. An old apple orchard and sugar house remain, and there's a kitchen garden. A rocky brook still winds through the rolling fields, and in the adjacent woods, there's a natural swimming hole. Guest rooms are furnished in antiques and replicas.

Innkeeper(s): Don & Joanna Harte. $70-240. 11 rooms, 1 with FP and 4 cottages. Breakfast included in rates. Types of meals: Full gourmet bkfst. Restaurant on premises. Beds: KQDT. TV and telephone in room.

Publicity: *Esquire, Boston Globe, Seattle Times* and *Los Angeles Times.*

"Delicious food, delightful humor!"

Claremont   I2

Goddard Mansion B&B

25 Hillstead Rd
Claremont, NH 03743-3317
(603)543-0603 (800)736-0603 Fax:(603)543-0001
E-mail: info@goddardmansion.com
Web: www.goddardmansion.com

Circa 1905. This English-style manor house and adjacent garden tea house is surrounded by seven acres of lawns and gardens. Each of the guest rooms is decorated in a different style.

One features French Country decor, another sports a Victorian look. The living room with its fireplace, window seats and baby grand piano is a perfect place to relax. Homemade breakfasts, made using natural ingredients and fresh produce, include items such as souffles, pancakes, freshly baked muffins and fruit. The hearty breakfasts are served in the wood paneled dining room highlighted by an antique Wurlitzer jukebox.

Innkeeper(s): Debbie Albee. $75-135. 10 rooms, 3 with PB, 1 suite and 2 conference rooms. Breakfast included in rates. Types of meals: Full gourmet bkfst. Beds: KQDT. TV, reading lamp, clock radio, telephone, turn-down service and some desks in room. Air conditioning. VCR, fax, bicycles, library, parlor games, fireplace, child care available and Internet connection on premises. Weddings, small meetings, family reunions and seminars hosted. Antiquing, cross-country skiing, downhill skiing, fishing, live theater, parks, shopping and canoeing and kayaking on Connecticut River nearby.

Publicity: *Eagle Times, Yankee (editors pick), Boston Globe* and *Manchester Union Leader.*

"A perfect romantic getaway spot."

Danbury   I3

The Inn at Danbury

Rt 104
Danbury, NH 03230
(603)768-3318 Fax:(603)768-3773
E-mail: alex@innatdanbury.com
Web: www.innatdanbury.com

Circa 1870. Multilingual innkeeper Alexandra imparts a New England hospitality with a European flair at this cozy yet rambling country inn on five wooded acres. The original 1850 roadside farmhouse has evolved into comfortable accommodations with a carriage house and historic wing. Sit by the locally quarried mica stone fireplace in the living room, read a book from the secluded library, converse on the wraparound four-seasons porch, play games in the front game room or relax in the upstairs common room. All the suites and guest bedrooms feature scenic views and either a modern rustic or historically preserved decor. The Alpenglow Bistro dining room offers dinners and Sunday brunch. An adjacent sunroom opens onto a patio and English gardens.

Innkeeper(s): Alex Graf. Call for rates. Types of meals: Dinner. Reading lamp, ceiling fan and clock radio in room. VCR, child care, telephone and fireplace on premises. Weddings, small meetings, family reunions and seminars hosted. Antiquing, cross-country skiing, downhill skiing, live theater and shopping nearby.

Durham   J6

Three Chimneys Inn

17 Newmarket Rd
Durham, NH 03824
(603)868-7800 (888)399-9777 Fax:(603)868-2964
E-mail: chimney3@threechimneysinn.com
Web: www.threechimneysinn.com

Circa 1649. Valentine Hill, a 17th-century entrepreneur, was responsible for building this inn. Not surprisingly, the 1649 inn is listed in the National Register. After passing from owner to owner, the historic gem fell into disrepair, but fortunately has been restored to its former state. Most of the rooms include a fireplace. Although the inn is among the nation's most historic buildings, there are modern amenities to be found, including Jacuzzi tubs, data ports and fax services. If all the history isn't enough, the inn affords views of Oyster River and Little Bay. A traditional menu, featuring local items, is offered at the inn's restaurant.

Innkeeper(s): Ron & Jane Peterson. $119-199. 23 rooms with PB, 17 with FP and 2 conference rooms. Breakfast and afternoon tea included in rates. Types of meals: Full gourmet bkfst, early coffee/tea, gourmet lunch, snacks/refreshments, gourmet dinner and room service. Restaurant on premises. Beds: KQ. Cable TV, reading lamp, clock radio, telephone, turn-down service, desk, hot tub/spa, data port and Jacuzzi in room. Air conditioning. VCR, fax, copier, bicycles, library, parlor games, fireplace and formal gardens on premises. Limited handicap access. Weddings, small meetings, family reunions and seminars hosted. Amusement parks, antiquing, cross-country skiing, fishing, golf, live theater, parks, shopping, sporting events, tennis, water sports, museums and historic home tours nearby.

East Andover   I4

Highland Lake Inn B&B

32 Maple St, PO Box 164
East Andover, NH 03231-0164
(603)735-6426 Fax:(603)735-5355
E-mail: highlandlakeinn@msn.com
Web: www.highlandlakeinn.com

Circa 1767. This early Colonial-Victorian inn overlooks three mountains, and all the rooms have views of either the lake or the mountains. Many guest rooms feature handmade quilts and some have four-poster beds. Guests may relax with a book from the inn's library in front of the sitting room fireplace or walk the
seven-acre grounds and enjoy
old apple and maple trees, as
well as the shoreline of the
lake. Adjacent to a 21-acre
nature conservancy, there are

scenic trails and a stream to explore. Highland Lake is stocked with bass and also has trout. Fresh fruit salads, hot entrees, and homemade breads are featured at breakfast.

Historic Interest: Two Shaker Villages, old one-room school house.
Innkeeper(s): Steve & Judee Hodges. $89-129. 10 rooms with PB, 2 with FP. Breakfast and snacks/refreshments included in rates. Types of meals: Full gourmet bkfst and early coffee/tea. Beds: KQT. Reading lamp, ceiling fan, clock radio and fireplace in room. TV, VCR, fax, swimming, library, telephone, fireplace and gift shop on premises. Weddings, small meetings, family reunions and seminars hosted. Antiquing, art galleries, beach, bicycling, canoeing/kayaking, cross-country skiing, downhill skiing, fishing, golf, hiking and shopping nearby.
Publicity: *Intertown, Neighbors and Valley Business Journal.*

"New Hampshire at its most magical."

Eaton Center   G6

Rockhouse Mountain Farm Inn

PO Box 90
Eaton Center, NH 03832-0090
(603)447-2880

Circa 1900. This handsome old house is framed by maple trees on 450 acres of forests, streams, fields, wildflowers and songbirds. A variety of farm animals provide entertainment for city youngsters of all ages. Three
generations of the Edges have
operated this inn, and some
guests have been coming since
1946, the year it opened. A 250-
year-old barn bulges at times with

new-mown hay, and there is a private beach nearby with swimming and boating for the exclusive use of Rockhouse guests.
Innkeeper(s): Johnny & Alana Edge. $68. 15 rooms, 7 with PB, 1 with FP. Breakfast and dinner included in rates. Types of meals: Full bkfst. Beds: DT. TV and reading lamp in room. Swimming, library, parlor games, telephone, fireplace and farm animals on premises. Limited handicap access. Small meetings and family reunions hosted. Antiquing, fishing, golf, live theater, parks, shopping, tennis and water sports nearby.
Publicity: *New York Times, Family Circle, Woman's Day, Boston Globe and Country Vacations.*

"We have seen many lovely places, but Rockhouse remains the real high spot, the one to which we most want to return."

Enfield   H2

Shaker Hill Bed & Breakfast

259 Shaker Hill Road
Enfield, NH 03748
(603)632-4519 (877)516-1370 Fax:(603)632-4082
E-mail: info@shakerhill.com
Web: www.shakerhill.com

Circa 1793. Modified to provide the utmost comfort, this restored Colonial farmhouse boasts original wide-board floors accented by traditional furnishings. Enjoy games, books or television in the living room. Pleasant guest bedrooms are delightfully decorated with comforting amenities and computer access. Fresh-baked scones, fruit and a special entree highlight a scrumptious breakfast. Afternoon tea and an always-full cookie jar provide even more delightful treats. Relax on the huge wraparound porch, or walk the gardens and trails. Ski nearby slopes in the winter months.
Innkeeper(s): Allen & Nancy Smith. $75-95. 4 rooms with PB. Breakfast and afternoon tea included in rates. Types of meals: Full bkfst, veg bkfst, early coffee/tea and snacks/refreshments. Beds: KQDT. Modem hook-up, reading lamp, clock radio and desk in room. Air conditioning. TV, VCR, fax, parlor games, telephone and fireplace on premises. Antiquing, art galleries, beach, canoeing/kayaking, cross-country skiing, downhill skiing, fishing, golf, hiking, horseback riding, live theater, museums, parks, shopping, sporting events, tennis and water sports nearby.

Franconia   F3

Franconia Inn

1300 Easton Rd
Franconia, NH 03580-4921
(603)823-5542 (800)473-5299 Fax:(603)823-8078
E-mail: info@franconiainn.com
Web: www.franconiainn.com

Circa 1934. Beautifully situated on 117 acres below the White Mountain's famous Franconia Notch, this white clapboard inn is three stories high. An oak-paneled library, parlor, rathskeller lounge and two verandas offer relaxing retreats. The inn's
rooms are simply decorated
in a pleasing style and
there is a special honey-
moon suite with private
Jacuzzi. Bach, classic wines
and an elegant American
cuisine are featured in the

inn's unpretentious dining room. There's no shortage of activity here. The inn offers four clay tennis courts, horseback riding, a heated swimming pool, croquet, fishing, cross-country ski trails and glider rides among its outdoor amenities.

Innkeeper(s): Alec Morris. $103-188. 34 rooms, 29 with PB, 3 with FP, 4 suites, 1 cottage and 1 conference room. Breakfast included in rates. Types of meals: Full gourmet bkfst, early coffee/tea, picnic lunch and gourmet dinner. Restaurant on premises. Beds: KQDT. Reading lamp, clock radio and desk in room. TV, VCR, copier, spa, swimming, bicycles, tennis, child care, parlor games, telephone, fireplace, sleighs and ice skating on premises. Weddings, small meetings, family reunions and seminars hosted. Amusement parks, antiquing, cross-country skiing, downhill skiing, fishing, live theater, parks, shopping and sporting events nearby.

Publicity: *Philadelphia Inquirer, Boston Globe, Travel & Leisure and Powder.*

"The piece de resistance of the Franconia Notch is the Franconia Inn." — *Philadelphia Inquirer*

Lovetts Inn

1474 Profile Rd
Franconia, NH 03580
(603)823-7761 (800)356-3802 Fax:(603)823-7130
E-mail: innkeepers@lovettsinn.com
Web: www.lovettsinn.com

Circa 1784. In the heart of the White Mountains, this historic country inn continuously bestows warm hospitality and personalized attention. Listed in the National Register, the well-appointed rooms are accented with wonderful antiques. Gather by the fire to watch a video, play games or browse the library. Guest bedrooms in the main house feature CD players, hair dryers, sitting areas and views of the pond or Cannon Mountain. The cottages boast fireplaces, coffee makers, TVs and private porches with excellent vistas. A full country breakfast is served by candlelight for a romantic meal in the dining room. Ten acres of natural beauty await the day. Swim in the pool, visit the gift shop or enjoy the nearby Franconia Notch State Park.

Innkeeper(s): Janet & Jim Freitas. $99-235. 21 rooms with PB, 16 with FP and 5 suites. Breakfast and afternoon tea included in rates. Types of meals: Full gourmet bkfst, veg bkfst, early coffee/tea, picnic lunch, snacks/refreshments and gourmet dinner. Restaurant on premises. Beds: KQDT. Cable TV, reading lamp, clock radio, coffeemaker, hot tub/spa and fireplace in room. Air conditioning. VCR, fax, copier, swimming, library, parlor games, telephone, fireplace and gift shop on premises. Handicap access. Weddings, small meetings, family reunions and seminars hosted. Amusement parks, antiquing, art galleries, beach, bicycling, canoeing/kayaking, cross-country skiing, downhill skiing, fishing, golf, hiking, horseback riding, live theater, museums, shopping, tennis and water sports nearby.

"Room very pleasant, comfortable and clean. Delicious dinner. We appreciated being made to feel welcome and at home."

Franklin   I4

Maria Atwood Inn

71 Hill Road Rt 3A
Franklin, NH 03235
(603)934-3666
E-mail: info@atwoodinn.com
Web: www.atwoodinn.com

Circa 1830. Candles in the windows welcome guests to this handsome two-and-a-half story brick Federal home, which was built by Joseph Burleigh. Well-landscaped grounds with tall trees and green lawns frame the house. Many original features remain, including interior Indian shutters, old locks, Count Rumford fireplaces and wide-plank wood floors. Recently renovated, the rooms offer country furnishings, quilts, antiques and art. Full breakfasts are served by candlelight in the inn's library. Tilton School, Proctor Academy and New Hampton School are nearby. The Lakes Region provides a wide variety of outdoor recreation. Especially popular is canoeing and kayaking on the Pemigewasset and Merrimack Rivers. Theater,

antique shops, boutiques and restaurants are also at hand.

Historic Interest: Daniel Webster birthplace and Canterbury Shaker Village are close by.

Innkeeper(s): Fred & Sandi Hoffmeister. $90-100. 7 rooms with PB, 4 with FP. Breakfast, afternoon tea and snacks/refreshments included in rates. Types of meals: Full bkfst and early coffee/tea. Beds: QDT. Ceiling fan in room. Air conditioning. TV, parlor games, telephone and fireplace on premises. Small meetings and family reunions hosted. Antiquing, bicycling, cross-country skiing, downhill skiing, fishing, golf, hiking, live theater, parks, shopping, snowmobiling, outlets and boating nearby.

Publicity: *Concord, Monitor and Wiers Times.*

"Wouldn't stay anywhere else."

Glen   F5

Bernerhof Inn

Rt 302, PO Box 240
Glen, NH 03838-0240
(603)383-9132 (800)548-8007 Fax:(603)383-0809
E-mail: stay@bernerhofinn.com
Web: www.bernerhofinn.com

Circa 1880. Built in the late 19th century for travelers passing through Crawford Notch, this historic Victorian Inn was named by the Zumsteins, its proprietors known for providing fine accommodations, musical enjoyment and outstanding food. Today's innkeepers continue this hospitable commitment offering creative gourmet cuisine in the dining room and casual fare in the Black Bear Pub. Elegantly  decorated guest bedrooms are non-smoking, some feature brass beds, antiques, stained glass, spa tub Jacuzzis and a fireplace. Novice and experienced chefs alike enjoy learning tricks of the trade at A Taste of the Mountains Cooking School. Located in the foothills of the White Mountains, a variety of outdoor activities are easily accessible.

Innkeeper(s): George & June Phillips. $99-189. 9 rooms with PB and 2 suites. Breakfast included in rates. Types of meals: Country bkfst and gourmet dinner. Restaurant on premises. Beds: KQ. Cable TV, VCR, reading lamp, ceiling fan, clock radio, telephone, most with two-person spa/tub Jacuzzi, one with fireplace and one with sauna in room. Air conditioning. TV, fax, copier, sauna and fireplace on premises. Weddings, small meetings and family reunions hosted. Amusement parks, antiquing, bicycling, cross-country skiing, downhill skiing, fishing, golf, hiking, live theater, parks, shopping, rock climbing, ice climbing and snow shoeing nearby.

Publicity: *Yankee Magazine, Boston Globe, Bon Appetit, Good Housekeeping, Skiing, Gault Millau, Country New England Inns and Weekends for Two in New England: 50 Romantic Getaways Inn Spots & Special Places in New England.*

"When people want to treat themselves, this is where they come."

Covered Bridge House B&B

Rt 302
Glen, NH 03838
(603)383-9109 (800)232-9109 Fax:(603)383-8089
E-mail: info@coveredbridgehouse.com
Web: www.coveredbridgehouse.com

Circa 1910. The two-acre grounds at this inn boast the only privately owned covered bridge with a gift shop inside. The bridge, which dates to 1850, houses the inn's gift shop. The grounds also include a private beach area that rests along side a river where guests can go swimming or tubing. Guest rooms are decorated in a country Colonial style with quilts, floral comforters and stenciled walls. Breakfasts include fresh fruit, homemade muffins and made-to-order eggs or perhaps French toast. In warmer weather breakfast is served on the patio.

Innkeeper(s): Dan & Nancy Wanek. $59-109. 6 rooms, 4 with PB. Breakfast included in rates. Types of meals: Full bkfst and early coffee/tea. Beds: KQT. Reading lamp, ceiling fan and clock radio in room. Air conditioning. Spa, swimming and telephone on premises. Family reunions hosted. Amusement parks, antiquing, cross-country skiing, downhill skiing, fishing, golf, live theater, parks, shopping, tennis and water sports nearby.

Greenfield   K3

The Greenfield Inn

PO Box 400
Greenfield, NH 03047
(603)547-6327 (800)678-4144 Fax:(603)547-2418
E-mail: greenfield@earthlink.net
Web: www.greenfieldinn.com

Circa 1817. In the 1850s this inn was purchased by Henry Dunklee, innkeeper of the old Mayfield Inn across the street. When there was an overflow of guests at his tavern, Mr. Dunklee accommodated them here. This totally renovated Victorian mansion features veranda views of Crotched, Temple and Monadnock Mountains. There is a conference room with a lovely mountain view. The gracious innkeepers and comfortable interiors have been enjoyed by many well-traveled guests, including Dolores and Bob Hope.

Historic Interest: The inn is located near the historic town graveyard and the first town hall in New Hampshire.

Innkeeper(s): Barbara & Vic Mangini. $49-129. 15 rooms, 12 with PB, 3 with FP, 2 suites, 1 cottage and 2 conference rooms. Breakfast included in rates. Types of meals: Full gourmet bkfst and snacks/refreshments. Beds: KQDT. Modem hook-up, cable TV, VCR, reading lamp, stereo, refrigerator, ceiling fan, snack bar, clock radio, telephone, coffeemaker, desk, hot tub/spa and voice mail in room. Air conditioning. Fax, copier, spa and fireplace on premises. Weddings, small meetings, family reunions and seminars hosted. Antiquing, art galleries, bicycling, canoeing/kayaking, cross-country skiing, downhill skiing, fishing, golf, hiking, horseback riding, live theater, museums, parks, shopping and tennis nearby.

Publicity: *Manchester Union Leader and Innsider.*

"I'm coming back for more of this New Hampshire therapy."—Bob Hope

Hampton   K6

The Victoria Inn

430 High St
Hampton, NH 03842-2311
(603)929-1437 (800)291-2672
E-mail: Nyhans@thevictoriainn.com
Web: www.thevictoriainn.com

Circa 1865. Elegance and style are featured at this Queen Anne Victorian inn just a half-mile from the ocean. A romantic gazebo, spacious guest rooms and Victorian furnishings throughout the inn add to its considerable charm. The Honeymoon Suite and Victoria Room are popular with those seeking privacy and luxury. Guests may borrow the inn's bicycles for a relaxing ride or read a book in its deluxe morning room. Common areas include the living room and the sitting room, with its cozy fireplace.

Innkeeper(s): John & Pamela Nyhan. $100-150. 6 rooms with PB. Breakfast included in rates. Types of meals: Full bkfst and early coffee/tea. Beds: KQ. Cable TV, reading lamp, ceiling fan, clock radio, telephone and turn-down service in room. Air conditioning. VCR, bicycles, library, parlor games and fireplace on premises. Weddings, small meetings, family reunions and seminars hosted. Antiquing, cross-country skiing, downhill skiing, fishing, live theater, parks, shopping, sporting events and water sports nearby.

Hancock   K3

The Hancock Inn

33 Main St
Hancock, NH 03449-5321
(603)525-3318 (800)525-1789 Fax:(603)525-9301
E-mail: innkeeper@hancockinn.com
Web: www.hancockinn.com

Circa 1789. Considered the state's oldest inn, warm hospitality has been continuously offered at this classically stately house since 1789. Main Street is peacefully seen from the columned front porch. Converse by the fire in the common room. A historic integrity and ambiance is reflected throughout each Colonial guest bedroom. The Rufus Porter Room boasts an original hand painted mural from the 1820s. Some of the spacious rooms feature four-poster beds, gas fireplaces, sitting areas and deep soaking tubs. The sunny Garden Room is an enchanting setting for a resplendent breakfast with fruits, yogurt, granola, cereals, fresh-baked pastries and hot entrees. Award-winning and often-requested dinner recipes are served in the fireside Dining Room.

Historic Interest: Franklin Pierce Homestead (10 miles).

Innkeeper(s): Robert Short. $215-250. 11 rooms with PB. Breakfast included in rates. Types of meals: Full gourmet bkfst, early coffee/tea, picnic lunch, afternoon tea and dinner. Restaurant on premises. Beds: QDT. Cable TV, reading lamp, clock radio and telephone in room. Central air. Fax, swimming, library, parlor games, fireplace, deep soaking tubs, boating and swimming in nearby Norway pond on premises. Small meetings, family reunions and seminars hosted. Antiquing, beach, bicycling, cross-country skiing, downhill skiing, fishing, hiking, live theater, parks, shopping and water sports nearby.

Publicity: *New York Times, Country Accent, Folk Art, Country Inns, Boston Globe, Keene Sentinel and Yankee Homes.*

"The warmth you extended was the most meaningful part of our visit."

Hanover   H2

The Trumbull House Bed & Breakfast

40 Etna Road
Hanover, NH 03755
(603)643-1400 Fax:(603)643-2430
E-mail: bnb@valley.net
Web: www.trumbellhouse.com

Circa 1919. This handsome two-story farmhouse was concocted and built by Walter Trumbull from materials he gathered from old Dartmouth College buildings and fraternity houses. Presiding over 16 acres with stands of maple and pine, and a meandering brook, the inn offers a cozy refuge for all, including cross-country skiers and Dartmouth College alumni and parents. The parlor features Country English chairs, sofas and lace curtains.

Innkeeper(s): Hillary Pridgen. $120-275. 5 rooms with PB and 1 suite. Breakfast included in rates. Types of meals: Full gourmet bkfst and early coffee/tea. Beds: QT. Modem hook-up, cable TV, VCR, clock radio, telephone, desk, hot tub/spa, luxury feather pillows and down comforters in room. Air conditioning. Fax, copier, spa, swimming, fireplace, business center on second floor and scanning on premises. Cross-country skiing, golf, hiking, shopping, sporting events, water sports, River Valley Club and nearby health club available to guests nearby.

Publicity: *Boston Globe and Upper Valley News.*

"From the beautiful setting outdoors through every elegant and thoughtful detail indoors, including your exquisite sunlit breakfast, we were in heaven!"

Haverhill F3

Gibson House

341 Dartmouth College Highway
Haverhill, NH 03765
(603)989-3125 Fax:(603)989-5749
E-mail: gibsonhs@ix.netcom.com
Web: www.gibsonhousebb.com

Circa 1850. This 1850 Greek Revival inn near Dartmouth was a stagecoach inn and also part of the underground railway. It is listed in the National Register of Historic Places. Its 50-foot porches provide guests with views of the Vermont Green Mountains. The property also includes formal gardens with a central lily pond, gazebo and wildflower meadow. The gardens are romantically lit at night. There are six guest bedrooms, four with private baths. All are decorated by the artist-owner with special attention to color, texture, light and mood. A full gourmet breakfast includes courses like fresh fruit, Blueberry Cloud Cakes with warm local maple syrup, smokehouse bacon and homemade quiche. After breakfast, guests may head out for swimming, golf and tennis in the summer, and plenty of skiing in the winter. An afternoon snack welcomes them back to the comfort of the inn.

Innkeeper(s): Keita Colton. $120-175. 7 rooms, 4 with PB. Breakfast, afternoon tea and snacks/refreshments included in rates. Types of meals: Full gourmet bkfst, veg bkfst and early coffee/tea. Beds: KQDT. Modem hook-up, reading lamp, ceiling fan, telephone, turn-down service and desk in room. Fax, copier, bicycles, library, fireplace and laundry facility on premises. Weddings, small meetings, family reunions and seminars hosted. Antiquing, art galleries, beach, bicycling, canoeing/kayaking, cross-country skiing, downhill skiing, fishing, golf, hiking, horseback riding, parks, sporting events, tennis and water sports nearby.

Publicity: *Yankee Magazine Editors Choice and Unofficial Guide to New England Bed and Breakfast.*

Henniker J3

Colby Hill Inn

3 The Oaks, PO Box 779
Henniker, NH 03242-0779
(603)428-3281 (800)531-0330 Fax:(603)428-9218
E-mail: info@colbyhillinn.com
Web: www.colbyhillinn.com

Circa 1820. Located in an untouched village full of charm, this 18th-century Colonial inn boasts more than five peaceful acres. The romantic setting is accented with original barns, lush perennial gardens and a gazebo. Antique-filled guest bedrooms, some with working fireplaces and whirlpools for two, feature

down comforters and private baths. Anticipate acclaimed dining by intimate candlelight overlooking the pleasant grounds. Enjoy a refreshing swim in the in-ground pool.

Innkeeper(s): Cyndi & Mason Cobb. $115-265. 16 rooms with PB, 6 with FP and 1 conference room. Breakfast included in rates. Types of meals: Full gourmet bkfst, early coffee/tea, snacks/refreshments, gourmet dinner and room service. Restaurant on premises. Beds: KQDT. Reading lamp, telephone, data port and some with whirlpools for two in room. Air conditioning. Fax, copier, swimming, parlor games and fireplace on premises. Weddings, small meetings, family reunions and seminars hosted. Antiquing, cross-country skiing, downhill skiing, fishing, parks and Canterbury Shaker village nearby.

Publicity: *Wine Spectator Award of Excellence.*

The Meeting House Inn

35 Flanders Rd
Henniker, NH 03242-3313
(603)428-3228 (800)436-4200 Fax:(603)428-6334

Circa 1770. The simple abundance and elegance of this New England country farmstead is compelling to guests fortunate enough to discover it, just up the road from the site of the first meeting house in Henniker and across from Pats Peak Ski Mountain. Wide pine floors, brass beds and antique accessories decorate the rooms in the main house. A full, hot break-

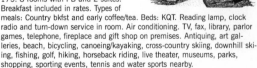

fast is delivered in a picnic basket to your room. Individually prepared New England cookery is offered in the 200-year-old barn, for a memorable dining experience.

Innkeeper(s): Mathew & Michele Mitnitsky. $85-125. 6 rooms, 4 with PB and 2 suites. Breakfast included in rates. Types of meals: Country bkfst, veg bkfst and gourmet dinner. Restaurant on premises. Beds: QD. Reading lamp, refrigerator, ceiling fan, clock radio and coffeemaker in room. Air conditioning. TV, fax, copier, parlor games, telephone, restaurant, brick oven pizza, specialties and wine bar on premises. Weddings, small meetings, family reunions and seminars hosted. Antiquing, beach, bicycling, canoeing/kayaking, cross-country skiing, downhill skiing, fishing, golf, hiking, horseback riding, museums, parks, shopping, sporting events, tennis, water sports and New England College nearby.

Publicity: *Manchester Union Leader - "A six star experience in a five star restaurant," Boston Globe, Concord Monitor, WJYY, WNNH and WKXL.*

"Thank you for giving us a honeymoon worth waiting eleven years for. Exceptional dining facility utilizing local ingredients."

Holderness H4

The Inn on Golden Pond

Rt 3, PO Box 680
Holderness, NH 03245
(603)968-7269 Fax:(603)968-9226
E-mail: innongp@lr.net
Web: www.innongoldenpond.com

Circa 1879. Framed by meandering stone walls and split-rail fences more than 100 years old, this inn is situated on 25 acres of woodlands. Most rooms overlook picturesque countryside and nearby is Squam Lake, setting for the film "On Golden Pond." An inviting, 60-foot screened porch provides a place to relax during the summer.

Innkeeper(s): Bill & Bonnie Webb. $105-175. 8 rooms with PB and 2 suites. Breakfast included in rates. Types of meals: Country bkfst and early coffee/tea. Beds: KQT. Reading lamp, clock radio and turn-down service in room. Air conditioning. TV, fax, library, parlor games, telephone, fireplace and gift shop on premises. Antiquing, art galleries, beach, bicycling, canoeing/kayaking, cross-country skiing, downhill skiing, fishing, golf, hiking, horseback riding, live theater, museums, parks, shopping, sporting events, tennis and water sports nearby.

Publicity: *Boston Globe, Baltimore Sun and Los Angeles Times.*

"Another sweet flower added to my bouquet of life."

Manor on Golden Pond

Rt 3 Box T
Holderness, NH 03245
(603)968-3348 (800)545-2141 Fax:(603)968-2116
E-mail: info@manorongoldenpond.com
Web: www.manorongoldenpond.com

Circa 1903. An Englishman and land developer had a boy-hood dream of living in a beautiful mansion high on a hill over-looking lakes and mountains. After he discovered these beauti-ful 13 acres, he brought craftsmen from around the world to build an English-style country mansion. Old world charm is reflected at this manor by marble fireplaces and the hand-carved mahogany lobby.

Innkeeper(s): Brian & Mary Ellen Shields. $175-395. 27 rooms with PB. Breakfast and afternoon tea included in rates. Types of meals: Full gourmet bkfst, early coffee/tea, picnic lunch, dinner and room service. Beds: KQ. Data port, cable TV, VCR, reading lamp, stereo, refrigerator, ceiling fan, clock radio, telephone, coffeemaker, turn-down service, desk and fireplace in room. Central air. Fax, copier, swimming, tennis, library, parlor games, fireplace and gift shop on premises. Weddings and small meetings hosted. Antiquing, art galleries, beach, canoeing/kayaking, downhill skiing, fishing, golf, hiking, horseback riding, shopping, tennis and water sports nearby.

Publicity: *The Best of New England "Hideaway Report" August 1999, Connecticut Magazine and Frommer's.*

"Out of a magazine on how the rich decorate but still comfortable and relaxing."

Intervale   F5

The Forest - A Country Inn

PO Box 37
Intervale, NH 03845-0037
(603)356-9772 (877)854-6535 Fax:(603)356-5652
E-mail: forest@ncia.net
Web: www.forest-inn.com

Circa 1830. Situated on 25 wooded acres with a stream, this country Victorian bed & breakfast offers easy access to the many attractions of Mt. Washington Valley. Relax while enjoying

afternoon refreshments on the screened-in porch or fireside in the living room. Well-decorated guest bedrooms are furnished with antique treasures. The romantic stone cottage rooms offer a private setting and boast four-poster beds and fireplaces. Morning brings the anticipation of fresh fruit, homemade baked goods, and entrees like Apple Pancakes, Spiced Belgian Waffles and Amaretto French Toast. Cross-country skiing, river canoeing and swimming in the pool are fun seasonal activities.

Innkeeper(s): Bill & Lisa Guppy. $70-169. 11 rooms with PB, 5 with FP and 3 cottages. Breakfast and snacks/refreshments included in rates. Types of meals: Full bkfst. Beds: Q. Reading lamp and ceiling fan in room. Fax, swimming, parlor games, telephone and fireplace on premises. Family reunions and seminars hosted. Amusement parks, antiquing, cross-country skiing, downhill skiing, fishing, live theater, parks, shopping, sporting events and water sports nearby.

Jackson   F5

Carter Notch Inn

Carter Notch Rd, Box 269
Jackson, NH 03846
(603)383-9630 (800)794-9434
E-mail: jimdunwell@earthnet.net
Web: www.carternotchinn.com

Circa 1900. This turn-of-the-century home rests on a wooded acre, offering views of the surrounding mountains, Eagle Mt. Golf Course and the Wildcat River. Guest rooms are charming, some have painted wood floors, throw rugs, quilts and wicker or oak furnishings. The innkeepers latest addition is "The Treehouse," which features suites with two-person Jacuzzi tubs, private decks and fireplaces. Breakfast is a treat; be sure to ask for Jim's Grand Marnier French toast. Cross-country ski trails begin right out the front door, as does golfing. Hiking and other outdoor activities abound in the area. After a day touring the area, return to the inn for a relaxing soak in the outdoor hot tub or sit on the wraparound front porch and enjoy the view.

Innkeeper(s): Jim & Lynda Dunwell. $79-199. 7 rooms, 6 with PB and 1 suite. Breakfast and afternoon tea included in rates. Types of meals: Full gourmet bkfst and early coffee/tea. Beds: KQD. Reading lamp and clock radio in room. Air conditioning. VCR, fax, spa, swimming, tennis, parlor games, telephone, fireplace, golf and fishing on premises. Weddings, small meetings, family reunions and seminars hosted. Antiquing, downhill skiing, live theater, parks, tennis, water sports and non-holiday free midweek cross country skiing nearby.

The Crowes' Nest

PO Box 427 Thorn Mountain Road
Jackson, NH 03846
(603)383-8913 (800)511-8383 Fax:(603)383-8241
E-mail: tcn@crowesnest.net
Web: www.crowesnest.net

Circa 1922. Each season brings a new adventure to this ele-gant Colonial inn surrounded by the tranquil beauty of White Mountain National Forest. There is room to roam outdoors as well as inside with spacious areas including the living room in the main house and the lodge's common room. The decor has an international flavor, in keeping with the innkeepers' exten-sive travels. Many of the guest bedrooms feature a fireplace, pri-vate balcony, Jacuzzi and breathtaking views. Breakfast in the dining room is an event to be savored. Poached pears in port wine, coffee cake made with fresh blueberries from the garden and florentine frittata with fresh herbs are some of the mouth-watering dishes served. Relax on the patio and gardens over-looking the village, and be sure to visit Jackson Falls.

Innkeeper(s): Myles & Christine Crowe. $99-209. 7 rooms with PB, 4 with FP and 2 suites. Breakfast and afternoon tea included in rates. Types of meals: Full bkfst. Beds: KQ. Reading lamp, ceiling fan, clock radio and fireplace in room. Air conditioning. TV, fax, library, parlor games, telephone, fireplace and gift shop on premises. Weddings, small meetings, family reunions and seminars hosted. Amusement parks, antiquing, art galleries, bicycling, canoeing/kayaking, cross-country skiing, downhill skiing, fishing, golf, hiking, horseback riding, live theater, museums, parks, shopping, tennis and water sports nearby.

Publicity: *Skeletons in the Closet.*

Ellis River House

Rt 16, Box 656
Jackson, NH 03846
(603)383-9339 (800)233-8309 Fax:(603)383-4142
E-mail: innkeeper@erhinn.com
Web: www.ellisriverhouse.com

Circa 1893. Andrew Harriman built this farmhouse, as well as the village town hall and three-room schoolhouse where the innkeepers' children attended school. Classic antiques and Laura Ashley prints decorate the guest rooms and riverfront "honeymoon" cottage, and each window reveals views of magnificent mountains, or spectacular Ellis River. In 1993, the

innkeepers added 18 rooms, 11 of which feature fireplaces and six offer two-person Jacuzzis. They also added three suites, a heated, outdoor pool, an indoor Jacuzzi, sauna and a cozy pub.

Historic Interest: The White Mountains School of Art is nearby. Artists such as Albert Bierstadt and Benjamin Champney were among the many to attend this school.

Innkeeper(s): Monica & Jim Lee. $95-255. 20 rooms with PB, 14 with FP, 4 suites, 1 cottage and 1 conference room. Breakfast included in rates. Types of meals: Full bkfst, early coffee/tea, picnic lunch, afternoon tea and dinner. Beds: KQD. Cable TV, reading lamp, telephone and hot tub/spa in room. Air conditioning. Fax, spa, swimming, sauna, parlor games and fireplace on premises. Limited handicap access. Weddings, small meetings, family reunions and seminars hosted. Amusement parks, antiquing, cross-country skiing, downhill skiing, fishing, live theater, parks, shopping, sporting events and water sports nearby.

Publicity: *Philadelphia Inquirer.*

"We have stayed at many B&Bs all over the world and are in agreement that the beauty and hospitality of Ellis River House is that of a world-class bed & breakfast."

The Inn at Jackson

PO Box 807, Main St at Thornhill Rd
Jackson, NH 03846
(603)383-4321 (800)289-8600 Fax:(603)383-4085
E-mail: info@innatjackson.com
Web: www.innatjackson.com

Circa 1902. Architect Stanford White designed this inn for the Baldwin family of New York (of piano fame) and served as their summer residence. The inn offers a grand foyer, spacious guest rooms, some with TV and air conditioning, private baths, hardwood floors, fireplaces and an outdoor hot tub

Jacuzzi. A full breakfast is served in our sunporch overlooking the mountains.

Historic Interest: Mount Washington (15 minutes) and Cog Railway (45 minutes).

Innkeeper(s): Lori Tradewell. $86-195. 14 rooms with PB, 6 with FP. Breakfast included in rates. Types of meals: Full bkfst. Beds: KQT. TV, reading lamp and clock radio in room. Air conditioning. VCR, fax, spa, library, telephone and fireplace on premises. Cross-country skiing, downhill skiing, fishing, live theater, parks and shopping nearby.

"We had a terrific time and found the inn warm and cozy and most of all relaxing."

The Inn at Thorn Hill

Thorn Hill Rd, PO Box A
Jackson, NH 03846-0800
(603)383-4242 (800)289-8990 Fax:(603)383-8062
E-mail: www.innatthornhill.com
Web: www.innatthornhill.com

Circa 1895. Follow a romantic drive through the Honeymoon Covered Bridge to Thorn Hill Road where this newly renovated country inn sits on a knoll overlooking Jackson Village. Guest bedrooms and suites in the main inn, carriage house and cottages are uniquely decorated with antique furnishings and boast

scenic vistas. Most feature a gas fireplace, TV and Jacuzzi. Spectacular views of the White Mountains are also seen from the dining room, lounge and porch. Award-

winning food and attentive service are much-appreciated amenities. After a workout in the exercise room, use the sauna or steam room, or schedule a massage or spa service.

Innkeeper(s): Jim & Ibby Cooper. $125-340. 25 rooms with PB, 6 suites, 3 cottages and 2 conference rooms. Breakfast, afternoon tea and dinner included in rates. Types of meals: Full bkfst, early coffee/tea and picnic lunch. Restaurant on premises. Beds: KQD. TV, reading lamp and turn-down service in room. Air conditioning. Fax, copier, swimming, library, parlor games, telephone and fireplace on premises. Weddings, small meetings, family reunions and seminars hosted. Antiquing, cross-country skiing, downhill skiing, fishing, live theater, parks and shopping nearby.

Publicity: *Mature Outlook, Reporter, Bon Appetit, Gourmet, Ski, Washington Post, Toledo Blade, GEO, Good Housekeeping, Mirabella, Conde Nast Traveler Reader's Choice Awards as the 45th Best Place to Stay in North America in their November 2002 issue, Conde Nast Traveler January 2003 issue, The Inn at Thorn Hill is the only listing in New Hampshire for the Gold List, the 700 World's Best Places to Stay and with the only perfect score of 100 for food.*

"Magnificent, start to finish! The food was excellent but the mountain air must have shrunk my clothes!"

Nestlenook Farm Resort

Dinsmore Rd
Jackson, NH 03846
(603)383-9443 (800)659-9443 Fax:(603)383-4515
E-mail: inn@lmgnh.com
Web: www.nestlenookfarm.com

Circa 1790. Experience romantic Victorian elegance at this 200-year-old inn and smoke-free resort that is cradled by the mountains on 65 pristine acres. Exquisite guest bedrooms feature period antiques, two-person Jacuzzis and a parlor stove or fireplace. The newly added Victorian Village overlooks the estate offering luxurious accommodations with kitch-

enettes. After breakfast, stroll through the award-winning gardens or relax in a poolside hammock. Watch the sunset from the lakeside gazebo. Enjoy biking, fly fishing and rowboating. Winter snowfall transforms the area into a Currier & Ives scene with ice skating, snowshoe trails and horse-drawn sleigh rides.

Innkeeper(s): Robert Cyr. $125-759. 21 rooms with PB. Types of meals: Full bkfst and snacks/refreshments. Beds: KQ. Telephone in room. Air conditioning. Fax, copier, swimming, bicycles, fireplace, recreation room with DVD, surround sound and antique billiard table on premises. Antiquing, cross-country skiing, downhill skiing, fishing, hiking, live theater, parks, shopping, water sports and carriage rides nearby.

Publicity: *Country Living, Country Inns, Ski, Friends, Manage Quebec, Discerning Traveler and Yankee Magazine.*

Jaffrey L3

The Benjamin Prescott Inn

Rt 124 E, 433 Turnpike Rd
Jaffrey, NH 03452
(603)532-6637 (888)950-6637 Fax:(603)532-6637
E-mail: innkeeper@benjaminprescottinn.com
Web: www.benjaminprescottinn.com

Circa 1853. Colonel Prescott arrived on foot in Jaffrey in 1775 with an ax in his hand and a bag of beans on his back. The family built this classic Greek Revival many years later. Now, candles light the windows, seen from the stonewall-lined lane adjacent to the inn. Each room bears the name of a Prescott family member and is furnished with antiques.

Innkeeper(s): Bob & Alice Seidel. $75-160. 10 rooms with PB and 3 suites. Breakfast included in rates. Types of meals: Country bkfst and early coffee/tea. Beds: KQDT. Modem hook-up, TV, reading lamp, ceiling fan, clock radio, telephone, desk, toiletries and private label glycerine soaps in room. Fax, copier, library, parlor games, fireplace, open cookie jar in winter and tea (on request) on premises. Weddings, small meetings and family reunions hosted. Antiquing, art galleries, bicycling, canoeing/kayaking, cross-country skiing, downhill skiing, fishing, golf, hiking, horseback riding, live theater, museums, parks, shopping, national Shrine, lectures and concerts nearby.

"We have a candle glowing in the window just for you."

The Grand View Inn & Resort

580 Mountain Road
Jaffrey, NH 03452
(603)532-9880 (888)984-7263 Fax:(603)532-6252

Circa 1797. Surrounded by 330 picturesque acres at the base of Mount Monadnock, this resort features a 19th century Colonial mansion, full service spa, world-class restaurant and an equestrian center. It is easy to relax in the warm and inviting country decor and furnishings. Spacious guest suites and bedrooms exude a comfortable, rustic elegance. A satisfying breakfast is served daily. Walk or hike beginner and advanced trails. Swim in an in-ground heated pool and fish or canoe the 30-acre beaver pond. Winter activities include cross country skiing, snowshoeing and snowmobile rentals. Ask about spa and horseback riding packages.

Historic Interest: The Grand View Inn & Resort was the first brick house built in Jaffrey, New Hampshire by Lt. Alexander Milliken. It was a popular tavern frequented by many weary travelers on the third New Hampshire Turnpike in 1800.

Innkeeper(s): Scott & Kelly Mitchell. $75-250. 9 rooms, 7 with PB, 4 with FP, 2 suites, 1 cottage and 2 conference rooms. Breakfast, afternoon tea and snacks/refreshments included in rates. Types of meals: Cont plus, veg bkfst, early coffee/tea, lunch, picnic lunch, gourmet dinner and room service. Restaurant on premises. Beds: KQT. Telephone, turn-down service and fireplace in room. TV, VCR, fax, copier, spa, swimming, sauna, stable, library, parlor games, fireplace, laundry facility, full service day spa, Restaurant Function Hall and climbing mountain on premises. Weddings, small meetings, family reunions and seminars hosted. Antiquing, art galleries, bicycling, canoeing/kayaking, cross-country skiing, fishing, golf, hiking, horseback riding, live theater, parks and shopping nearby.

Publicity: *Yankee Magazine 2002-Editor's Choice, named one of the most romantic inns in New Hampshire-2002 and NH Chronicle.*

Jefferson E4

Applebrook B&B

Rt 115A, PO Box 178
Jefferson, NH 03583-0178
(603)586-7713 (800)545-6504
E-mail: vacation@applebrook.com
Web: www.applebrook.com

Circa 1797. Panoramic views surround this large Victorian farmhouse nestled in the middle of New Hampshire's White Mountains. Guests can awake to the smell of freshly baked muffins made with locally picked berries. A comfortable, fire-lit sitting room boasts stained glass, a goldfish pool and a beautiful view of Mt. Washington. The romantic Nellie's Nook, includes a king-size bed and a balcony with views of the mountains and a two-person spa. Test your golfing skills at the nearby 18-hole championship course, or spend the day antique hunting. A trout stream and spring-fed rock pool are nearby. Wintertime guests can ice skate or race through the powder at nearby ski resorts or by way of snowmobile, finish off the day with a moonlight toboggan ride. After a full day, guests can enjoy a soak in the hot tub under the stars, where they might see shooting stars or the Northern Lights.

Historic Interest: The area boasts several covered bridges within 10 miles of the bed & breakfast. The Cog Railroad is 15 miles away, while the Jefferson Historical Museum is only one mile from the inn.

Innkeeper(s): Sandra Conley. $60-100. 14 rooms, 8 with PB and 1 conference room. Breakfast included in rates. Types of meals: Full bkfst and early coffee/tea. Beds: KQDT. Reading lamp, ceiling fan and desk in room. Spa, library, parlor games, telephone and fireplace on premises. Weddings, small meetings, family reunions and seminars hosted. Amusement parks, antiquing, cross-country skiing, downhill skiing, fishing, live theater, parks, shopping and water sports nearby.

Publicity: *Outside, PriceCostco Connection, New Hampshire Outdoor Companion and Outdoor.*

"We came for a night and stayed for a week."

Jefferson Inn

Rt 2
Jefferson, NH 03583
(603)586-7998 (800)729-7908 Fax:(603)586-7808
E-mail: jeffinn@ncia.net
Web: www.jeffersoninn.com

Circa 1896. A turret, gables and wraparound verandas characterize this romantic 19th-century Victorian home. Cradled in the White Mountain National Forest, the inn overlooks

Jefferson Meadows to Franconia Notch, Mt. Washington and the northern Presidential range. Each of the guest bedrooms and family suites boast a distinctively unique decor and offers privacy. Indulge in a leisurely full breakfast. Swim in the spring-fed pond across the street. During winter, it transforms into an ice skating rink. A horse-drawn wagon and sleigh rides are available. Afternoon beverages and homemade baked goods are served in the afternoon. The Weathervane Summer Theater provides nightly entertainment. Biking and golf are nearby.

Innkeeper(s): Mark & Cindy Robert and Bette Bovio. $75-175. 11 rooms with PB and 2 suites. Breakfast, afternoon tea and snacks/refreshments included in rates. Types of meals: Full gourmet bkfst and early coffee/tea. Beds: KQDT. Data port, TV, reading lamp, refrigerator and turn-down service in room. Fax, library, parlor games, telephone and laundry facility on premises. Weddings, small meetings, family reunions and seminars hosted. Amusement parks, antiquing, art galleries, bicycling, canoeing/kayaking, cross-country skiing, downhill skiing, fishing, golf, hiking, horseback riding, live theater, parks, shopping, tennis, moose tours, snowmobiling and horse drawn sleigh rides nearby.

"Marvelous breakfast and a warm, comfortable atmosphere."

Keene   K2

Carriage Barn Guest Room

358 Main St
Keene, NH 03431-4146
(603)357-3812
E-mail: carriagebarn@webryders.net
Web: www.carriagebarn.com

Circa 1870. Any season is the perfect time to visit New England, but if you come in the fall to Keene, you can see the most carved jack-o'lanterns ever assembled in one place—over 20,000 grinning pumpkins lining the streets and holding the current world record. Adding to this great experience is a stay at this renovated 19th-century barn, now a comfortable and homey B&B. All four guest rooms, decorated with antiques found in local shops, have private baths. Games, books and a refrigerator filled with cold drinks are available in the common room. A substantial continental breakfast includes muffins or coffee cake, bread, cereals, yogurt and fruit. If it's not Halloween, there's still plenty to do here. The nearby villages with their covered bridges, lakes and antique shops are postcard perfect. For the active visitor, hiking the popular Mount Monadnock, biking, canoeing, skiing and horseback riding are easily arranged.

Innkeeper(s): Dave & Marilee Rouillard. $75-110. 4 rooms with PB. Breakfast and snacks/refreshments included in rates. Types of meals: Cont plus. Beds: QT. Reading lamp, clock radio and coffeemaker in room. Central air. TV, VCR, parlor games and telephone on premises. Antiquing, bicycling, canoeing/kayaking, cross-country skiing, downhill skiing, fishing, golf, hiking, horseback riding, live theater, museums, parks, shopping, sporting events and tennis nearby.

Lincoln   F4

Red Sleigh Inn

PO Box 562
Lincoln, NH 03251-0562
(603)745-8517

Circa 1900. This 1900 Colonial home in the heart of the White Mountains has seven guest rooms and offers splendid views and easy access to the area's abundant recreation. After breakfasting on innkeeper Loretta's famous blueberry muffins, guests may explore the countryside and enjoy skiing, snowmobiling, golfing, swimming, hiking and biking. Or guests may choose to wander through the town of Lincoln, enjoying its charm and indulging in shopping and dinner theatre.

Innkeeper(s): Bill & Loretta Deppe. $85-110. 7 rooms, 3 with PB. Breakfast included in rates. Types of meals: Full bkfst. Beds: KQT. Reading lamp and desk in room. TV, VCR, parlor games, telephone and fireplace on premises. Weddings and family reunions hosted. Amusement parks, antiquing, cross-country skiing, downhill skiing, fishing, live theater, parks, shopping, sporting events and water sports nearby.

Publicity: *Newsday, Ski and Skiing.*

"Your ears must be ringing because we haven't stopped talking about the Red Sleigh Inn and its wonderful, caring owners."

Lisbon   F3

Ammonoosuc Inn

641 Bishop Road
Lisbon, NH 03585
(603)838-6118 (888)546-6118
E-mail: amminn@mail.com
Web: www.amminn.com

Circa 1880. Enjoy panoramic views at this 100-year-old Colonial inn with Early American decor sitting in the Ammonoosuc River Valley surrounded by the White Mountains. Relax on the padded wicker chairs on the wraparound porch and soak in the scenery. In cooler weather, snuggle up to the wood stove in the pub. A full breakfast is served in the honey-pine beamed dining room. Candlelight dinners with selections such as rack of lamb, salmon and steak are available. Fish for brook trout in the river, or in just minutes the National Forest attractions include Flume Gorge and Cannon Mountain Tramway. The inn overlooks a golf course with cross-country ski and hiking trails and a major snowmobile trail nearby. Ask about ski and golf packages.

Innkeeper(s): Jeni & Jim Lewis. $75-130. 9 rooms. Breakfast included in rates. Types of meals: Full bkfst, afternoon tea and dinner. Beds: KQDT. Reading lamp in room. TV, VCR, fax, copier, library, parlor games, telephone and fireplace on premises. Weddings, small meetings, family reunions and seminars hosted. Antiquing, bicycling, canoeing/kayaking, cross-country skiing, downhill skiing, fishing, golf, hiking, horseback riding, live theater, parks and tennis nearby.

Littleton   E3

Beal House Inn & Fine Dining Restaurant

2 W Main St
Littleton, NH 03561-3502
(603)444-2661 (866)616-BEAL Fax:(603)444-6224
E-mail: info@bealhouseinn.com
Web: www.bealhouseinn.com

Circa 1833. This Main Street landmark is centrally located in the White Mountains for year-round enjoyment. Refurbished and elegantly furnished with antiques, the suites feature four-poster and canopy beds, fireplaces, Jacuzzis and clawfoot tubs. Relax in luxury with down comforters, bathrobes, coffeemakers, CD players and satellite TV. A feta and fresh spinach frittata with home-baked wheat bread, banana buttermilk pancakes served with local maple syrup, or other delicious recipes may be served for breakfast. Enjoy the pleasant interlude of afternoon tea. The inn's award winning restaurant offers an extensive menu for fine dining.

Historic Interest: Located in the heart of the White Mountains. Littleton Opera House, Robert Frost House (1 mile).

Innkeeper(s): Jose Luis & Catherine Pawelek. $135-245. 8 rooms with PB, 4 with FP and 5 suites. Breakfast and afternoon tea included in rates. Types of meals: Full gourmet bkfst, dinner and room service. Restaurant on premises. Beds: KQD. Modem hook-up, data port, TV, VCR, reading lamp, stereo, refrigerator, clock radio, telephone, coffeemaker, air conditioning, ceiling fans (some rooms), fireplace, Jacuzzi tubs and hair dryer in room. Central air. Fax, copier, library, parlor games, fireplace and gift shop on premises. Weddings, small meetings, family reunions and seminars hosted. Antiquing, art galleries, bicycling, canoeing/kayaking, cross-country skiing, downhill skiing, fishing, golf, hiking, horseback riding, live theater, museums, parks, shopping, tennis, water sports and sleigh rides nearby.

Publicity: *Country Inns, Glamour, Le Soleil, Star Ledger, Miami Herald, Yankee, Courier and Ammonoosuc Times.*

"These innkeepers know and understand people, their needs and wants. Attention to cleanliness and amenities, from check-in to check-out, is a treasure."

Thayers Inn
111 Main St
Littleton, NH 03561-4014
(603)444-6469 Fax:(800)634-8179
E-mail: don@thayersinn.com
Web: www.thayersinn.com

Circa 1843. Ulysses Grant is said to have spoken from the inn's balcony in 1869. In those days, fresh firewood and candles were delivered to guest rooms each day as well as a personal thunderjug. The handsome facade features four 30-foot, hand-carved pillars and a cupola with views of the surrounding mountains.

Innkeeper(s): Don & Carolyn Lambert. $60-120. 41 rooms, 38 with PB and 6 suites. Breakfast included in rates. Types of meals: Lunch and dinner. Beds: KQDT. TV, fax, copier, telephone and movies on premises. Antiquing, cross-country skiing, downhill skiing, fishing, live theater and water sports nearby.

Publicity: *Business Life, Vacationer, Bon Appetit and Yankee.*

"This Thanksgiving, Russ and I spent a lot of time thinking about the things that are most important to us. It seemed appropriate that we should write to thank you for your warm hospitality as innkeepers."

Lyme   G2

Alden Country Inn
One Market St
Lyme, NH 03768
(603)795-2222 (800)794-2296 Fax:(603)795-9436
E-mail: info@aldencountryinn.com
Web: www.aldencountryinn.com

Circa 1809. This handsome country inn, standing at the village common, first became a stagecoach stop in the 1830s. It has been restored recently and is decorated in a traditional style with antiques. A full breakfast is served, and the inn's restaurant offers New England cookery. Guests staying on Saturday night especially will enjoy the next morning's Sunday brunch, included in the rates. Townsfolk mingle with guests on the porch or in the inn's tavern and restaurant.

Innkeeper(s): Frank & Darlene Godoy. $95-145. 15 rooms with PB, 4 with FP and 2 conference rooms. Breakfast included in rates. Types of meals: Country bkfst, early coffee/tea and dinner. Restaurant on premises. Beds: KQ. Modem hook-up, cable TV, telephone and TV upon request in room. Air conditioning. Fax, copier, fireplace and laundry facility on premises. Weddings, small meetings, family reunions and seminars hosted. Antiquing, art galleries, beach, bicycling, canoeing/kayaking, cross-country skiing, downhill skiing, fishing, golf, hiking, horseback riding, live theater, museums, shopping, sporting events, tennis and water sports nearby.

The Dowds' Country Inn
PO Box 58
Lyme, NH 03768
(603)795-4712 (800)482-4712 Fax:(603)795-4220
E-mail: reservations@dowdscountryinn.com
Web: www.dowdscountryinn.com

Circa 1780. This 18th-century inn offers pure New England elegance. The historic home, surrounded by a plentiful six

acres, rests on The Common in this charming historic village. The grounds include a duck pond, fountain and gardens- a perfect setting for the many parties and weddings held at the inn. The guest rooms are decorated in a warm, inviting style, many feature stencilled walls or country artwork. The innkeepers serve made-to-order breakfasts and an opulent afternoon tea. The staff will gladly help you plan a day trip to enjoy the charm of the surrounding village and nearby places of interest.

Historic Interest: The Lyme Congregational Church, a nearly 200-year-old house of worship with a bell fashioned by Paul Revere, is a popular historic site. The Hood Museum and Baker Library are other nearby historic attractions.

Innkeeper(s): Tami Dowd. $125-230. 22 rooms with PB and 3 suites. Breakfast and afternoon tea included in rates. Types of meals: Country bkfst. Beds: QT. Modem hook-up, reading lamp, clock radio, turn-down service and desk in room. Air conditioning. VCR, fax, copier, library, telephone and gift shop on premises. Limited handicap access. Weddings, small meetings, family reunions and seminars hosted. Antiquing, art galleries, beach, bicycling, canoeing/kayaking, cross-country skiing, downhill skiing, fishing, golf, hiking, live theater, museums, parks, shopping, sporting events, tennis and water sports nearby.

Madison   G5

Maple Grove House
21 Maple Grove Rd
Madison, NH 03849
(603)367-8208 (877)367-8208 Fax:(603)679-9217
E-mail: info@maplegrovehouse.com
Web: www.maplegrovehouse.com

Circa 1911. Alongside a quiet country road and across from an apple orchard, this white Victorian farmhouse offers a spacious wraparound porch with views of the White Mountains. A wood burning stove warms the living room, and there is an original guest register from the home's early years. Common rooms include a library and sunny dining room. Polished hardwood floors are highlights of the bedrooms. North Conway outlet shops and restaurants are nearby.

Innkeeper(s): Celia & Don Pray. $95-115. 6 rooms, 4 with PB and 1 suite. Breakfast and snacks/refreshments included in rates. Types of meals: Full bkfst and early coffee/tea. Beds: QT. Cable TV, VCR, reading lamp, ceiling fan, clock radio and window fans in room. Library and telephone on premises. Small meetings and family reunions hosted. Antiquing, cross-country skiing, downhill skiing, fishing, golf, live theater, parks, shopping and tennis nearby.

Meredith   H4

The Inns at Mill Falls
312 Daniel Webster Hwy #28
Meredith, NH 03253
(603)279-7006 (800)622-6455 Fax:(603)279-6797
E-mail: info@millfalls.com
Web: www.millfalls.com

Circa 1820. Three inns with a total of 101 guest rooms and suites sit on this property built around a forty-foot waterfall and restored linen mill from the 1800s. A glass bridge connects the inns with the mill, which now has 18 delightful shops, galleries and restaurants. Many of the spacious guest rooms have balconies, fireplaces, personal whirlpool spas, and views of the lake. The common grounds include an indoor pool, sauna and a fitness room. In the winter enjoy a horse-drawn wagon ride, skiing, ice-skating or ice boating. In the summer cruise on the lake or relax on the balcony.

Innkeeper(s): Gail Batstone. $79-289. 101 rooms with PB, 31 with FP, 3 suites and 6 conference rooms. Types of meals: Cont and early coffee/tea. Restaurant on premises. Beds: KQD. Cable TV, VCR, reading lamp, refrigerator, clock radio, telephone and desk in room. Air conditioning. Fax, copier, spa, swimming, sauna, parlor games and fireplace on premises. Limited handicap access. Weddings, small meetings, family reunions and seminars hosted. Antiquing, cross-country skiing, downhill skiing, fishing, golf, live theater, parks, shopping, tennis and water sports nearby.

Meredith Inn

2 Waukewan
Meredith, NH 03253
(603)279-0000 Fax:(603)279-4017
E-mail: inn1897@meredithinn.com
Web: www.meredithinn.com

Circa 1897. Located at the northwestern tip of Lake Winnipesaukee at the gateway to the White Mountains, the town of Meredith has the feel of a New England village. The Meredith Inn has a two-story turret and walk-out bay windows. The inn's exterior has three different styles of shingles and clapboard siding and interesting roof angles. Its eight guest bedrooms have fireplaces, whirlpool tubs, luxury linens, and brick fireplaces with recessed mantels of intricate Victorian design. The interior has lots of hard yellow pine trim and doors, etched brass doorknobs and doorplates, and a recessed china cabinet with a leaded-glass door. Breakfast includes such delightful courses as juice, fruits in season with yogurt, hot and cold cereals and a hot entrée of the day like plain or berry pancakes, French toast with pure maple syrup, eggs frittata, omelets and blueberry blintzes. The inn is a mile from the Anna Lee Doll Museum, two miles from the Old Paint Barn and half a mile from the Meredith Historical Society and Farm Museum.

Innkeeper(s): Janet Carpenter. $89-175. 8 rooms with PB, 2 with FP. Breakfast included in rates. Types of meals: Full gourmet bkfst and veg bkfst. Beds: KQT. Cable TV, reading lamp and telephone in room. Fax, copier, library, parlor games and fireplace on premises. Limited handicap access. Weddings and family reunions hosted. Amusement parks, antiquing, art galleries, beach, bicycling, canoeing/kayaking, cross-country skiing, downhill skiing, fishing, golf, hiking, horseback riding, live theater, museums, parks, shopping, tennis and water sports nearby.

Moultonborough   H5

Olde Orchard Inn

108 Lee Rd
Moultonborough, NH 03254-9502
(603)476-5004 (800)598-5845 Fax:(603)476-5004
E-mail: oldeorchardinn@myway.com
Web: www.oldeorchardinn.com

Circa 1790. Surrounded by twelve scenic acres, this historic 1790 Colonial farmhouse is a peaceful bed and breakfast inn that graces the Lakes Region. Experience year-round pampering and generous hospitality. Air-conditioned guest bedrooms are furnished with antiques and include an assortment of pleasing amenities. The popular upper and lower pond rooms feature woodburning fireplaces, whirlpool baths and one boasts a romantic canopy bed. Several rooms offer multiple beds and a fold-out couch which are perfect for families. After a large country breakfast, ride a bike to Lake Winnipesaukee or hike the trails at the Audubon Loon Center.

Innkeeper(s): Clark & Jo Hills. $75-185. 9 rooms with PB, 3 with FP. Breakfast and snacks/refreshments included in rates. Types of meals: Country bkfst, veg bkfst and early coffee/tea. Beds: QDT. TV, reading lamp, clock radio, desk, hot tub/spa, fireplace, three with whirlpools, fresh flowers and fine robes in room. Air conditioning. VCR, fax, copier, spa, bicycles, library, child care, parlor games, telephone, fireplace, sauna and gazebo on premises. Handicap access. Weddings, small meetings, family reunions and seminars hosted. Antiquing, art galleries, beach, bicycling, canoeing/kayaking, cross-country skiing, downhill skiing, fishing, golf, hiking, horseback riding,

live theater, museums, parks, shopping, tennis and water sports nearby.
Publicity: *Merideth News.*

"What a wonderful getaway we had at your lovely inn. We're so glad we found you on the Internet."

New London   I3

The Inn at Pleasant Lake

853 Pleasant St, PO Box 1030
New London, NH 03257-1030
(603)526-6271 (800)626-4907 Fax:(603)526-4111
E-mail: bmackenz@tds.net
Web: www.innatpleasantlake.com

Circa 1790. In its early days, this inn served as a farmhouse. By the late 1870s, it was serving guests as a summer resort. Its tradition of hospitality continues today with relaxing guest rooms, which offer lake or wood views. The five-acre grounds

face Pleasant Lake, which has a private beach. Guests may enjoy the lake on their own rowboat or canoe, but the innkeepers will lend theirs if requested. Meander over wooded trails or take a stroll around New London. Innkeeper and Culinary Institute of America graduate Brian MacKenzie prepares the inn's five-course, prix fixe dinners.

Innkeeper(s): Linda & Brian MacKenzie. $110-175. 10 rooms with PB and 1 conference room. Breakfast and afternoon tea included in rates. Types of meals: Full bkfst and dinner. Beds: KQD. Reading lamp, clock radio and three with whirlpool tub in room. Central air. Fax, copier, swimming, parlor games, telephone, fireplace and exercise room on premises. Weddings, small meetings, family reunions and seminars hosted. Antiquing, bicycling, canoeing/kayaking, cross-country skiing, downhill skiing, fishing, golf, hiking, live theater, museums, parks, shopping and water sports nearby.

Publicity: *Country Inns Magazine, James Beard Dinner and Yankee Magazine Travel Guide to New England.*

"What a perfect setting for our first ever visit to New England."

Newfound Lake   H4

The Inn on Newfound Lake

1030 Mayhew Tpke
Newfound Lake, NH 03222-5108
(603)744-9111 (800)745-7990 Fax:(603)744-3894
E-mail: inonlk@cyberportal.net
Web: www.newfoundlake.com

Circa 1840. Originally the mid-way stop on the stagecoach route from Boston to Montreal, this inn has continued to provide comfortable accommodations in the foothills of the White Mountains for more than 150 years. Recently completely renovated, the antique furnishings are accented by a variety of oil paintings and artwork. Relax in a common sitting room in the main inn. The adjoining

Elmwood Cottage offers additional guest bedrooms. Enjoy dining at the renowned Pasquaney Restaurant overlooking the lake. A private beach and boat dock enhance the many outdoor activities available. Inside, enjoy a TV and card room, Jacuzzi and weight room.

Historic Interest: Canterbury, an authentic Shaker village, is just 20 minutes away. Daniel Webster's birthplace and the state capital are about a half-hour drive from the inn.

Innkeeper(s): Phelps C. Boyce II. $105-345. 31 rooms, 29 with PB and 2 suites. Breakfast included in rates. Types of meals: Cont and dinner. Restaurant on premises. Beds: QT. Reading lamp, ceiling fan and clock radio in room. TV, VCR, fax, copier, spa, swimming, bicycles, library, parlor games, telephone and fireplace on premises. Weddings, small meetings and seminars hosted. Antiquing, beach, bicycling, canoeing/kayaking, cross-country skiing, downhill skiing, fishing, golf, hiking, horseback riding, parks, shopping and water sports nearby.

Publicity: *The Record Enterprise, Travel & Leisure* and *Yankee Magazine.*

"The rooms were quaint and cozy with just the right personal touches and always immaculate. The bed and pillows were so comfortable, it was better than sleeping at home! The inn itself is magnificent; elegance never felt so warm and homey."

North Conway F5

1785 Inn & Restaurant

3582 White Mountain Hwy
North Conway, NH 03860-1785
(603)356-9025 (800)421-1785 Fax:(603)356-6081
E-mail: the1785inn@aol.com
Web: www.the1785inn.com

Circa 1785. The main section of this center-chimney house was built by Captain Elijah Dinsmore of the New Hampshire Rangers. He was granted the land for service in the American Revolution. Original hand-hewn beams, corner posts, fireplaces, and a brick oven are still visible and operating. The inn is located at the historical marker popularized by the White Mountain School of Art in the 19th century.

Historic Interest: Mount Washington.

Innkeeper(s): Becky & Charlie Mallar. $69-219. 17 rooms, 12 with PB, 1 suite and 1 conference room. Breakfast included in rates. Types of meals: Country bkfst, early coffee/tea, afternoon tea, snacks/refreshments, gourmet dinner and room service. Restaurant on premises. Beds: KQDT. Cable TV, VCR, reading lamp, refrigerator, ceiling fan, snack bar, clock radio, coffeemaker and turn-down service in room. Air conditioning. Fax, copier, swimming, library, parlor games, telephone, fireplace, cross-country skiing and nature trails on premises. Weddings, small meetings, family reunions and seminars hosted. Amusement parks, antiquing, art galleries, beach, bicycling, canoeing/kayaking, cross-country skiing, downhill skiing, fishing, golf, hiking, horseback riding, live theater, museums, parks, shopping, tennis, water sports, walking, gardens, nature trails, rock climbing and ice climbing nearby.

Publicity: *Country, Bon Appetit, Travel & Leisure, Ski, Travel Holiday, Connecticut, Better Homes & Gardens* and *The Wedding Story.*

"Occasionally in our lifetimes is a moment so unexpectedly perfect that we use it as our measure for our unforgettable moments. We just had such an experience at The 1785 Inn."

Buttonwood Inn

Mount Surprise Rd
North Conway, NH 03860
(603)356-2625 (800)258-2625 Fax:(603)356-3140
E-mail: innkeeper@buttonwoodinn.com
Web: www.buttonwoodinn.com

Circa 1820. Sitting on six secluded acres of scenic mountain beauty, this New England farmhouse is located two miles from the village. Experience a memorable blend of hospitality and laughter at this delightful inn. The comfortable guest bedrooms feature antiques and Shaker furniture, quilts and stenciling. Award-winning perennial gardens are an eye-pleasing adven-

ture. Swim, hike or cross-country ski, as weather permits. An added treat during the holidays is the highly acclaimed seasonal decor.

Historic Interest: Mount Washington (20 minutes), Cog Railway (40 minutes), Heritage, N.H. (10 minutes).

Innkeeper(s): Elizabeth & Jeffrey Richards. $95-235. 10 rooms with PB, 1 with FP, 2 suites and 1 conference room. Breakfast and afternoon tea included in rates. Types of meals: Full gourmet bkfst and early coffee/tea. Beds: KQT. Clock and Jacuzzi (one room) and fireplace (two rooms) in room. Air conditioning. TV, VCR, fax, swimming and hiking on premises. Antiquing, cross-country skiing, downhill skiing, fishing, hiking, live theater, parks and shopping nearby.

Publicity: *Classic American Homes, Boston Globe, Boston Herald* and *Boston Magazine.*

"The very moment we spotted your lovely inn nestled midway on the mountainside in the moonlight, we knew we had found a winner."

Cranmore Inn

80 Kearsarge St
North Conway, NH 03860
(603)356-5502 (800)526-5502
E-mail: stay@cranmoreinn.com
Web: www.cranmoreinn.com

Circa 1863. Cranmore Inn is just what a White Mountains retreat ought to be. A gambrel roof, emerald shutters and a covered front porch accentuate the inn's historic ambiance. One easily can imagine the days when the travelers from the local railroad flocked to this spot. In fact, Cranmore is the oldest continuously operating inn in the Mt. Washington Valley. Its rooms are cozy with comfortable, country-style appointments. Most of the rooms and suites include a private bath. Three rooms have a private bath just down the hall. The innkeepers also offer two modern-style kitchen units. A full breakfast and afternoon refreshments are included in the rates. Guests can spend the day shopping at factory outlets or hunting for antiques. Outdoor activities include golfing, hiking, whitewater rafting, climbing, and fishing. There are more than half a dozen ski areas within 30 minutes of the inn.

Innkeeper(s): Chris & Virginia Kanzler. $59-108. 18 rooms, 8 with PB and 3 suites. Breakfast and afternoon tea included in rates. Types of meals: Country bkfst and veg bkfst. Beds: KQT. Reading lamp and telephone in room. TV, fax, swimming, library and parlor games on premises. Weddings, small meetings, family reunions and seminars hosted. Amusement parks, antiquing, beach, bicycling, canoeing/kayaking, cross-country skiing, downhill skiing, fishing, golf, hiking, horseback riding, live theater, parks, shopping, tennis and water sports nearby.

Eastman Inn

Route 16/302
North Conway, NH 03860
(603)356-6707 (800)626-5855 Fax:(603)356-7708
E-mail: lea@eastmaninn.com
Web: www.eastmaninn.com

Circa 1777. Award-winning gardens accent the beauty of this Georgian Colonial home. The sunny wraparound porch reflects the traditional Early American style. Furnishings include an eclectic combination of antiques and modern furnishings. Relax by the fire or absorb the view of the Moat Mountains from the parlor. A beverage station is available in the redecorated dining room. Just-baked cookies are served in the afternoon. Many of the elegant guest bedrooms feature gas-insert fireplaces, vintage clawfoot tubs, whirlpool baths, sitting areas and private balconies. Explore the local White Mountain attractions after a satisfying gourmet breakfast. Outdoor adventures are numerous. Year-round tax-free shopping is nearby.

Innkeeper(s): Lea Greenwood & Tom Carter. $90-260. 14 rooms with PB. Beds: KQ. Cable TV, hot tub/spa, fireplace and balconies in room. Air conditioning. Weddings and family reunions hosted. Amusement parks, antiquing, cross-country skiing, downhill skiing, live theater, shopping and sporting events nearby.

Kearsarge Inn

42 Seavey Street
North Conway, NH 03860
(603)356-8700 (800)637-0087 Fax:(603)356-8740
E-mail: innkeeper@kearsargeinn.com
Web: www.kearsargeinn.com

Circa 1884. Bearing the name of a famous local hotel, one of the stately peaks of the White Mountains that frames the village, and also a legendary Civil War sailing ship, this Victorian residence has undergone extensive restoration to become the area's first boutique hotel. Its name reflects a rugged luxury and its rich history is honored in the unique memorabilia that decorates the inn. Several different accommodations include guest bedrooms and suites or intimate cottages with period carpeting, colonial molding, gas fireplaces, and four-poster or sleigh beds. Stay in the Penthouse Suite with a living room, or choose a cottage with a Jacuzzi or soaker tub. Stroll the gardens and relax on the wraparound porch or in the gazebo. Ask about special packages and making advance dinner reservations for Decades Steak House.

Historic Interest: A modern rendition of North Conway's famous Kearsarge Hotel.
Innkeeper(s): Lucy Van Cleve. $79-249. 15 rooms with PB and 5 cottages. Types of meals: Early coffee/tea and dinner. Beds: KD. Modem hook-up, data port, cable TV, VCR, reading lamp, ceiling fan, clock radio, telephone, desk, hot tub/spa and fireplace in room. Air conditioning. Fax, copier, laundry facility and parlor on premises. Handicap access. Weddings, small meetings, family reunions and seminars hosted. Amusement parks, antiquing, art galleries, beach, bicycling, canoeing/kayaking, cross-country skiing, downhill skiing, fishing, golf, hiking, horseback riding, live theater, museums, parks, shopping, sporting events, tennis and water sports nearby.

Nereledge Inn

River Rd, Off Main St, PO Box 547
North Conway, NH 03860-0547
(603)356-2831 Fax:(603)356-7085
E-mail: info@nereledgeinn.com
Web: www.nereledgeinn.com

Circa 1787. Season after season, warm hospitality is offered at this big white house with a simple New England-style decor and informal atmosphere. Two large living rooms include a game room boasting a fireplace, darts and backgammon. Wood stoves warm the sitting and breakfast rooms, and guests can enjoy a cup of tea from the guest pantry. Comfortable guest bedrooms and a suite are air-conditioned. Walk to the village to shop, dine and attend the theatre, or stroll to the river to swim, canoe and fish. Hike, bike, ski, rock or ice climb nearby. Families and small groups are welcome.

Historic Interest: Dartmouth College is 2-1/2 hours away.
Innkeeper(s): Dave and Betsy. $59-159. 11 rooms, 7 with PB. Breakfast included in rates. Types of meals: Full bkfst. Beds: QDT. Reading lamp in room. Air conditioning. TV, VCR, fax, copier, swimming, library, parlor games, telephone, fireplace, guest pantry, tea, tea kettle, microwave, refrigerator and toaster on premises. Small meetings and family reunions hosted. Antiquing, cross-country skiing, downhill skiing, fishing, live theater, climbing and hiking nearby.

Publicity: *White Mountain Region Newspaper, Outside and Men's Journal.*

"Our home away from home."

Old Red Inn & Cottages

PO Box 467
North Conway, NH 03860-0467
(603)356-2642 (800)338-1356 Fax:(603)356-6626
E-mail: oldredinn@adelphia.net
Web: www.oldredinn.com

Circa 1810. Guests can opt to stay in an early 19th-century home or in one of a collection of cottages at this country inn. The rooms are decorated with handmade quilts and stenciling dots the walls. Several rooms include four-poster or canopy beds. Two-bedroom cottages feature a screened porch. A hearty, country meal accompanied by freshly baked breads, muffins and homemade preserves starts off the day. The inn is near many of the town's shops, restaurants and outlets.

Innkeeper(s): Dick & Terry Potochniak. $98-178. 17 rooms, 15 with PB, 1 suite and 10 cottages. Breakfast included in rates. Types of meals: Full bkfst and early coffee/tea. Beds: QDT. Cable TV, reading lamp and refrigerator in room. Air conditioning. Fax, copier, swimming, telephone and fireplace on premises. Weddings, small meetings, family reunions and seminars hosted. Amusement parks, antiquing, cross-country skiing, downhill skiing, fishing, golf, live theater, parks, shopping, sporting events, tennis and water sports nearby.

Spruce Moose Lodge and Cottages

207 Seavey St
North Conway, NH 03860
(603)356-6239 (800)600-6239 Fax:(603)356-7622
E-mail: mainmoose@sprucemooselodge.com
Web: www.sprucemooselodge.com

Circa 1850. Offering a heritage of hospitality for more than 150 years, this pet-friendly inn is warm and inviting in the heart of the White Mountains. Relax by the woodburning fire in the living room tastefully furnished with eclectic antiques. The two air-conditioned Spruce and Moose wings in the Lodge feature spacious guest bedrooms for individuals, couples or families. Private cottages and Jacuzzi apartments boast gas fireplaces, full kitchens and two-person hot tubs. A bountiful country breakfast may include blueberry or banana pancakes, French toast, eggs any style, sausage and bacon. The grounds are enclosed by a cedar post and rail fence. Ask about group rates and special packages. Mt. Cranmore ski area is 1/4 mile away.

Historic Interest: Built in 1850 and a haven for White Mountains travelers for more than 100 years.
Innkeeper(s): Robin and Emily Kinkopf. $79-300. 14 rooms, 11 with PB, 5 with FP and 3 cottages. Breakfast included in rates. Types of meals: Country bkfst. Beds: KQDT. TV, reading lamp, refrigerator, ceiling fan, telephone and cottages and Jacuzzi apartments have gas fireplaces and full kitchens in room. Air conditioning. Fax, copier and fireplace on premises. Small meetings, family reunions and seminars hosted. Amusement parks, antiquing, art galleries, beach, bicycling, canoeing/kayaking, cross-country skiing, downhill skiing, fishing, golf, hiking, horseback riding, live theater, museums, parks, shopping, tennis, water sports and Mt. Cranmore ski area nearby.

"I would just like to thank you both again for your tremendous hospitality. The accommodations were extremely cozy and comfortable."

Victorian Harvest Inn

28 Locust Ln, Box 1763
North Conway, NH 03860
(603)356-3548 (800)642-0749 Fax:(603)356-8430
E-mail: help@victorianharvestinn.com
Web: www.victorianharvestinn.com

Circa 1853. Mountain views, personalized attention and tranquility are available at this tastefully restored Victorian inn that sits on a hill in the Mt. Washington Valley. Relax in the library while listening to Beethoven, Bach or Vivaldi. Many guest bedrooms feature fireplaces and Jacuzzis. Breakfast may include Belgian waffles, Dutch pannekoukan, Italian frittatas, down-home pancakes or omelettes. Swim in the pool and enjoy the gardens. Nearby outlet shopping, hiking trails, horseback riding and kayaking beckon the more adventuresome.

Innkeeper(s): David & Judy Wooster. $90-220. 8 rooms with PB. Breakfast and afternoon tea included in rates. Types of meals: Full gourmet bkfst. Air conditioning. VCR, fax, copier, swimming, library, parlor games, telephone and fireplace on premises. Family reunions hosted. Antiquing, canoeing/kayaking, cross-country skiing, downhill skiing, golf, hiking, horseback riding, live theater, parks, shopping, water sports, tubing and outlet shopping nearby.

North Woodstock   F4

Wilderness Inn B&B

Rfd 1, Box 69, Rts 3 & 112
North Woodstock, NH 03262-9710
(603)745-3890 (888)777-7813
E-mail: info@thewildernessinn.com
Web: www.thewildernessinn.com

Circa 1912. Surrounded by the White Mountain National Forest, this charming shingled home offers a picturesque getaway for every season. Guest rooms, all with private baths, are furnished with antiques and Oriental rugs. The innkeepers also offer family suites and a private cottage with a fireplace, Jacuzzi and a view of Lost River. Breakfast is a delightful affair with choices ranging from fresh muffins to brie cheese omelets, French toast topped with homemade apple syrup, crepes or specialty pancakes. For the children, the innkeepers create teddy bear pancakes or French toast. If you wish, afternoon tea also is served.

Innkeeper(s): Michael & Rosanna Yarnell. $65-160. 7 rooms with PB and 1 cottage. Breakfast included in rates. Types of meals: Full gourmet bkfst. Beds: QDT. TV in room.

"The stay at your inn, attempting and completing the 3D jigsaw puzzle, combined with those unforgettable breakfasts, and your combined friendliness, makes the Wilderness Inn a place for special memories."

Orford   G2

White Goose Inn

Rt 10, PO Box 1
Orford, NH 03777-0017
(603)353-4812 (800)358-4267 Fax:(603)353-4543
E-mail: whitegooseinn@valley.net
Web: www.whitegooseinn.com

Circa 1773. Relax amidst the rolling hills and scenic country setting while staying at this Colonial Revival inn. More than a community conversation piece, the circular porch across the front and north sides is an inviting place to sit and enjoy the gorgeous view of the Green Mountains. The traditional décor and furnishings as well as the authentic wide-pine floors, beamed ceilings and fireplaces, enhance the New England ambiance. After a restful slumber in one of the comfortable guest bedrooms or the suite, satisfy morning hunger with a full breakfast. Glorious in any season, there are a variety of local attractions and activities from skating and skiing in winter, to leaf peeping in the fall to hiking in summer and spring among wildflowers. Dartmouth College is nearby.

Innkeeper(s): Marshall & Renee Ivey. $89-149. 10 rooms, 8 with PB and 1 suite. Breakfast included in rates. Types of meals: Full bkfst and early coffee/tea. Beds: QDT. Reading lamp, ceiling fan, clock radio and fireplace in room. Air conditioning. Fax, library, parlor games and telephone on premises. Weddings, small meetings, family reunions and seminars hosted. Antiquing, cross-country skiing, downhill skiing, fishing, live theater, shopping and sporting events nearby.
Publicity: *Country Living.*

Pittsburg   B5

The Glen

First Connecticut Lake, 77 The Glen Rd
Pittsburg, NH 03592
(603)538-6500 (800)445-GLEN Fax:(603)538-7121

Circa 1900. This lakeside mountain lodge is located on the 45th parallel, midway between the equator and the North Pole. More than 160 acres surround the lodge, offering a bounty of activities. Guests can fish in a lake stocked with trout and salmon, or they can fish at the river, which offers rainbow and brown trout. The surrounding area also provides opportunities for hunters. Birdwatchers can enjoy gazing at dozens of different species. The Glen provides stunning views of the mountains and First Connecticut Lake, as well as the vast expanse of forestland. The interior of the lodge features natural wood paneling and hardwood floors; rooms are decorated in a comfortable lodge style. In addition to the lodge rooms and suite, there are 10 cabins. Breakfast, lunch and dinner are included in the rates. The hosts have been welcoming guests for nearly 40 years.

Innkeeper(s): Betty Falton. Call for rates. 6 rooms with PB, 1 suite and 10 cabins. Beds: QDT. Fishing on lake nearby.

Tall Timber Lodge

231 Beach Road
Pittsburg, NH 03592
(603)538-6651 (800)835-6343 Fax:(603)538-6582
E-mail: relax@talltimber.com
Web: www.talltimber.com

Circa 1946. Explore the North Woods on Back Lake at this relaxed resort that offers deluxe accommodations, including a rustic lodge with air-conditioned guest bedrooms, lakeshore log cabins and luxury cottages. For delicious, economical meals, the Rainbow Grille is a highly acclaimed restaurant in the main lodge. Natural panoramic beauty is unparalleled in this wilderness region, and a variety of activities are available. Experience mountain biking, fishing, canoeing, hiking, kayaking, moose watching and loon listening.

Innkeeper(s): The Caron Family. $50-330. 26 rooms, 20 with PB, 9 with FP, 2 suites, 4 cottages and 12 cabins. Types of meals: Country bkfst, picnic lunch and gourmet dinner. Restaurant on premises. Beds: QDT. Cable TV, VCR, stereo, refrigerator, ceiling fan, clock radio, telephone, coffeemaker and hot tub/spa in room. Air conditioning. Fax, copier, swimming, bicycles, library, parlor games and fireplace on premises. Weddings and family reunions hosted. Bicycling, canoeing/kayaking, fishing, golf, hiking, moose watching and snowmobiling nearby.
Publicity: *Yankee Magazine, Boston Globe, Boston Magazine, Field & Stream and North America's Greatest Fishing Lodges.*

Rindge
L3

Cathedral House B&B

63 Cathedral Entrance
Rindge, NH 03461
(603)899-6790

Circa 1850. This pre-Civil War, Colonial-style farmhouse is surrounded by 450 acres with meadows, a fishing pond, nature trails and scenic vistas. The five, comfortable bedrooms have been decorated in Colonial style, with artwork and fresh flowers in season. Rooms offer views of mountains and Emerson Pond. A hearty country breakfast is served. The bed & breakfast is located on the grounds of the Cathedral of the Pines, a non-denominational place of worship, which offers solitude in natural surroundings. The grounds originally were selected by a young pilot and his wife as a location for their home upon his return from World War II. The pilot was killed in the line of duty, and his parents created the Cathedral of the Pines in his memory and others who served. The site has been recognized by the U.S. Congress as a national memorial.

Innkeeper(s): Donald & Shirley Mahoney. $45-125. 5 rooms. Breakfast included in rates. Types of meals: Full bkfst. Beds: QDT. Reading lamp and clock radio in room. Library, parlor games, telephone and fireplace on premises. Antiquing, cross-country skiing, downhill skiing, fishing, live theater, parks, shopping, sporting events and water sports nearby.

Publicity: *New York Times, Hartford Courant and Yankee.*

"Thank you for making our wedding day such a success and for making our family feel so welcome."

Woodbound Inn

62 Woodbound Rd
Rindge, NH 03461
(603)532-8341 (800)688-7770 Fax:(603)532-8341
E-mail: woodbound@aol.com
Web: www.woodbound.com

Circa 1819. Vacationers have enjoyed the Woodbound Inn since its opening as a year-round resort in 1892. The main inn actually was built in 1819, and this portion offers 19 guest rooms, all appointed with classic-style furnishings. The innkeep-ers offer more modern accommodations in the Edgewood Building, and there are eleven cabins available. The one- and two-bedroom cabins rest along the shore of Lake Contoocook. The inn's 162 acres include a private beach, fishing, hiking, nature trails, tennis courts, a volleyball court, a game room and a golf course. There is a full service restaurant, a cocktail lounge and banquet facilities on premises. If for some reason one would want to venture away from the inn, the region is full of activities, including ski areas, more golf courses and Mount Monadnock.

Innkeeper(s): Rick Kohlmorgen. $89-139. 48 rooms, 45 with PB, 13 cabins and 5 conference rooms. Breakfast included in rates. Types of meals: Full bkfst, lunch and dinner. Restaurant on premises. Beds: QDT. Clock radio, telephone, desk and cabins have fireplaces in room. Air conditioning. VCR, copier, swimming, tennis, library, parlor games and fireplace on premises. Limited handicap access. Weddings, small meetings, family reunions and seminars hosted. Amusement parks, antiquing, cross-country skiing, downhill skiing, fishing, live theater, parks, shopping and water sports nearby.

Rochester
I6

The Agnes Pease House

1 May Street
Rochester, NH 03867
(603)332-5509 Fax:(603)332-7276
E-mail: msclemons@ttlc.net
Web: www.agnespeasehouse.com

Circa 1930. The interior of this restored Victorian is eclectic — a mix of antique furnishings and modern pieces. Each room has its own special touch. The Sun Room is especially cheerful, encapsulated by two walls of leaded windows. It also features a bed topped with a hand-made quilt. The Lilac Room includes a king-size iron and wicker bed. This spacious room can be combined with the cozy Bay Room to form a suite, perfect for those traveling together. In addition to providing a hearty, full breakfast, the innkeepers provide plenty of helpful amenities, such as a modem jack and fax service for business clients. As well, inn-goers enjoy privileges at a local health club.

Innkeeper(s): Paul Bear Ross & M. Susan Clemons. $55-160. 5 rooms, 3 with PB and 1 suite. Breakfast included in rates. Types of meals: Full gourmet bkfst, veg bkfst and early coffee/tea. Beds: KQ. Cable TV, VCR, reading lamp, telephone and voice mail in room. Central air. Fax, copier, library and fireplace on premises. Amusement parks, antiquing, art galleries, beach, cross-country skiing, downhill skiing, fishing, golf, hiking, live theater, museums, parks, shopping, sporting events, tennis and water sports nearby.

Publicity: *Channel 12.*

Rye
K6

Rock Ledge Manor B&B

1413 Ocean Blvd
Rye, NH 03870-2207
(603)431-1413
E-mail: info@rockledgemanor.com
Web: www.rockledgemanor.com

Circa 1860. From its oceanfront location at Concord Point, Rock Ledge overlooks the Atlantic. The wraparound front porch boasts panoramic views, as well. Guests linger to watch  lobstermen plying the waters or the full sails of pleasure craft. The Isle of Shoal may be seen in the distance. All rooms have ocean views, private baths, air conditioning and ceiling fans. Breakfast may include fruit pancakes, French toast, waffles and homemade muffins and breads, served in the breakfast room, with a water view. After watching the sunrise over the water, explore the tide pools, the park or enjoy some local saltwater fishing. Whale watching trips depart from Rye Harbor and historic Portsmouth, five minutes away. The University of Hampshire is 20 minutes away in Durham. Golf, tennis, theater, museums and restaurants all are nearby.

Innkeeper(s): Phyllis Petruzziello, Paula Klane. $125-200. 3 rooms with PB. Breakfast included in rates. Types of meals: Cont plus. Beds: QD. Ceiling fan in room. Air conditioning. Telephone on premises. Antiquing, beach, fishing, golf, live theater, museums, parks, shopping, tennis, boating and whale watching nearby.

"A lovely peaceful oasis."

Shelburne   E5

Philbrook Farm Inn

881 North Rd
Shelburne, NH 03581-3212
(603)466-3831
Web: www.philbrookfarminn.com

Circa 1834. Genuine simplicity is offered at this country inn in
the Androscoggin River Valley, where guests are considered
extended family. Relax by the fire or on the porch. Enjoy table
games and wooden jigsaw puzzles hand-cut by by three generations of Philbrooks. Furnished with antiques, family treasures
and practical reproductions, choose between a variety of guest
bedrooms. Cottages with fireplaces and porches are available
on a weekly basis in summer. Breakfast and dinner are provided, featuring homestyle New England cooking. Special dietary
needs can be accommodated. Play billiards, ping-pong, shuffleboard, horseshoes, badminton or swim in the pool.
Surrounded by mountain ranges, try miles of hiking, snowshoeing or cross-country skiing trails.

Innkeeper(s): Philbrook/Leger Family. $120-150. 19 rooms, 11 with PB, 4
cottages and 2 cabins. Breakfast and dinner included in rates. Types of
meals: Full bkfst. Beds: KDT. Reading lamp and desk in room. TV, VCR,
swimming, parlor games, telephone and fireplace on premises. Weddings,
small meetings, family reunions and seminars hosted. Amusement parks,
antiquing, bicycling, canoeing/kayaking, cross-country skiing, downhill skiing,
fishing, golf, hiking, horseback riding, museums, parks and tennis nearby.

Wildberry Inn B&B

592 State Rt 2
Shelburne, NH 03581
(603)466-5049
E-mail: rec@ncia.net
Web: www.northernwhitemountains.com/wildberry

Circa 1877. This colonial salt-box home is located on seven
acres in the White Mountains National Forest with the
Appalachian Trail passing through part of the property. Rooms
are decorated in a fresh country style with quilts and Priscilla
curtains. There's a separate suite in the "barn" with fireplace,
upstairs bedroom and a downstairs living room with views of
the pond, waterfall and garden from its many windows. In winter, snowshoeing, cross-country skiing and snowmobiling are
popular activities. In summer and fall, guests enjoy canoeing
and fishing or simply hiking along the property to enjoy the
golden oaks, birches, and red and orange maple foliage.
Breakfast usually features freshly picked berries in season,
homemade breads and dishes to accommodate a lavish pouring
of local maple syrup.

Innkeeper(s): Bob & Jackie Corrigan. $75-125. 3 rooms with PB, 1 with FP
and 1 cottage. Breakfast and afternoon tea included in rates. Types of meals:
Full gourmet bkfst. Beds: QDT. Data port, TV, VCR, reading lamp, refrigerator,
clock radio and coffeemaker in room. Air conditioning. Swimming, telephone,
fireplace and laundry facility on premises. Weddings and family reunions
hosted. Antiquing, bicycling, canoeing/kayaking, cross-country skiing, downhill skiing, fishing, golf, hiking, parks, shopping, gourmet dining and snowmobiling nearby.

Publicity: *The Berlin Daily Sun.*

Snowville   G5

Snowvillage Inn

146 Stewart Rd, PO Box 68
Snowville, NH 03832
(603)447-2818 (800)447-4345 Fax:(603)447-5268
E-mail: info@snowvillageinn.com
Web: www.snowvillageinn.com

Circa 1915. Peacefully sitting on a secluded hillside with
panoramic views of the entire Presidential mountain range, this
Victorian inn is a wonderful blend of Apine flair and New
England charm. In the Main House, built by author Frank
Simonds, enjoy many common rooms to gather in, there are
books to read by the fireplace, or watch a gorgeous sunset on
the front porch. Each of the comfortable guest bedrooms in the
Chimney House and Carriage House are named after a writer,
in honor of the inn's heritage. Discover more breathtaking vistas, fireplaces and antique furnishings. Renown for its elegant
country dining, breakfast is a satisfying culinary delight.
Explore the award-winning gardens and nature trails.

Innkeeper(s): Kevin, Caitlin & Maggie Flynn. $99-249. 18 rooms with PB, 4
with FP. Breakfast included in rates. Types of meals: Full gourmet bkfst and
gourmet dinner. Restaurant on premises. Beds: KQD. Reading lamp, clock
radio, telephone, desk and fireplace in room. Fax, copier, library, parlor
games, fireplace, c ross-country skiing and showshoeing on premises.
Weddings, small meetings, family reunions and seminars hosted. Antiquing,
art galleries, bicycling, canoeing/kayaking, cross-country skiing, downhill skiing, fishing, golf, hiking, horseback riding, live theater, museums and water
sports nearby.

Publicity: *Yankee Magazine, Wine Spectator, Boston Globe, Bon Appetit and
WMUR New Hampshire.*

Sugar Hill   F3

A Grand Inn-Sunset Hill House

231 Sunset Hill Rd
Sugar Hill, NH 03585
(603)823-5522 (800)786-4455 Fax:(603)823-5738
E-mail: innkeeper@sunsethillhouse.com
Web: www.sunsethillhouse.com

Circa 1882. This Second Empire luxury inn has views of five
mountain ranges. Three parlors, all with cozy fireplaces, are
favorite gathering spots. Afternoon tea is served here. The inn's
lush grounds offer many opportunities for recreation or relaxing, and guests often enjoy special events here, such as the
Fields of Lupine Festival. The Cannon Mountain Ski Area and
Franconia Notch State Park are nearby, and there is 30 kilometers of cross-country ski trails at the inn. Be sure to inquire
about golf and ski packages. In the fall, a Thanksgiving package
allows guests to help decorate the inn for the holidays as well
as enjoy Thanksgiving dinner together. NH Magazine just
named Sunset Hill House — A Grand Inn the "Very Best in
NH for a Spectacular Meal."

Historic Interest: Robert Frost Cottage (1 mile), site of first ski school (one-
half mile), Sugar Hill Historic Museum (one-half mile).

Innkeeper(s): Lon, Nancy, Mary Pearl & Adeline Henderson. $100-350. 28
rooms with PB and 3 conference rooms. Breakfast included in rates. Types of
meals: Full bkfst, early coffee/tea, picnic lunch, snacks/refreshments and dinner. Restaurant on premises. Beds: KQDT. Reading lamp, clock radio, desk,
suites with fireplaces and/or whirlpools and many with ceiling fans in room.
Fax, parlor games, telephone, fireplace, tavern, golf course and clubhouse on
premises. Weddings, small meetings, family reunions and seminars hosted.
Antiquing, cross-country skiing, downhill skiing, fishing, live theater, parks,
shopping, water sports and golf course nearby.

Publicity: *Yankee Travel Guide, Courier, Caledonia Record, Boston Globe, Portsmouth Herald, Manchester Union Leader, Journal Enquirer, Sunday Telegraph, Boston Herald, New Hampshire Magazine, GeoSaison, National Geographic, Traveller, Small Meeting Marketplace, BBW Magazine, Ski Magazine, Peoples Places and Plants Magazine and Korean Times.*

"I have visited numerous inns and innkeepers in my 10 years as a travel writer, but have to admit that few have impressed me as much as yours and you did."

Sullivan   K2

The Post and Beam B&B

18 Centre St
Sullivan, NH 03445
(603)847-3330 (888)376-6262 Fax:(603)847-3306

Circa 1797. Situated on a hill above Otter Brook and the Sullivan countryside, this late 18th-century, Colonial post-and-beam farmhouse was home to the Union Store and first town telephone company. Today, the inn's rustic hand-hewn exposed beams are a prominent architectural feature of the main living room. The guest rooms feature fireplaces, wide pine floors and antiques collected throughout the area. Guests also can enjoy the hot tub in the outdoor gazebo. A family-style, three-course New England breakfast is served in the dining room each morning.

Historic Interest: The Monadnock region offers kayaking, fishing, horseback riding, downhill and cross country skiing. There are nearby covered bridges and nine state parks are a short drive away. Nearby Keene and Peterborough offers 30 local craft and gift shops.

Innkeeper(s): Darcy Bacall & Priscilla Hardy. $75-125. 7 rooms, 2 with PB, 5 with FP. Breakfast and afternoon tea included in rates. Types of meals: Full bkfst and early coffee/tea. Beds: KQ. Reading lamp, clock radio, coffeemaker and desk in room. VCR, fax, copier, spa, library, parlor games, telephone, fireplace, deck/gazebo, kayaks, data port, refrigerator and cable TV on premises. Limited handicap access. Family reunions and seminars hosted. Antiquing, cross-country skiing, downhill skiing, fishing, golf, live theater, parks, shopping, sporting events and water sports nearby.

Publicity: *Keene Shopper and Sunday Sentinel.*

"Warm, cozy, beautiful B&B run by special people! Thanks for taking such good care of us! We'll be back."

Sunapee   I2

Dexter's Inn

258 Stagecoach Rd
Sunapee, NH 03782
(603)763-5571 (800)232-5571
E-mail: dexters@tds.net
Web: www.dextersnh.com

Circa 1801. Proud of continuing its 50-year history of quality innkeeping, this Federalist-style inn was recently renovated. Tastefully furnished with a blend of antiques and country collectibles, it reflects the nostalgic essence of New England. The library is perfect for sipping a hot beverage while reading a good book by the fireplace; or play games and meet new friends in the family room. Choose one of the guest bedrooms in the main inn or annex, or stay in the Holly House Cottage-a home away from home. A generous country breakfast buffet, regaled for its Belgian waffles and French toast, is served in the dining room. Enjoy the scenic beauty of the gardens, lake and the surrounding mountains from the large screened porch, play a game of tennis or soak up the sun after a swim in the pool.

Innkeeper(s): Emily & John Augustine. $100-175. 19 rooms, 17 with PB, 1 suite, 1 cottage and 2 conference rooms. Breakfast and snacks/refreshments included in rates. Types of meals: Country bkfst, early coffee/tea and afternoon tea. Beds: KQDT. Reading lamp in room. Air conditioning. TV, VCR, fax, copier, swimming, tennis, library, parlor games, telephone and fireplace on premises. Weddings, small meetings, family reunions and seminars hosted. Antiquing, art galleries, beach, bicycling, canoeing/kayaking, cross-country skiing, downhill skiing, fishing, golf, hiking, horseback riding, live theater, museums, parks, shopping, tennis and water sports nearby.

"Just like being at home."

The Inn at Sunapee

PO Box 336
Sunapee, NH 03782-0336
(603)763-4444 (800)327-2466 Fax:(603)763-9456
E-mail: stay@innatsunapee.com
Web: www.innatsunapee.com

Circa 1875. Formerly part of a dairy farm, this spacious farmhouse inn also is home to a restaurant. The innkeepers, who spent nearly 30 years in the Far East and Southeast Asia, have blended an international flavor into the traditional antique furnishings and New England menu items. The inn offers two sit-  ting rooms, an impressive fieldstone fireplace, a library and swimming. The family-oriented inn also hosts meetings, reunions and weddings. Mt. Sunapee State Park and ski area are nearby.

Innkeeper(s): Ted & Susan Harriman. $90-175. 16 rooms with PB and 1 conference room. Types of meals: Full bkfst. Restaurant on premises. Telephone and fireplace on premises. Weddings, small meetings, family reunions and seminars hosted. Antiquing, cross-country skiing, downhill skiing, fishing, live theater and shopping nearby.

Publicity: *New London-Gadabouts and Yankee Magazine.*

Tamworth   G5

A B&B at Whispering Pines

Rt 113A & Hemenway Rd
Tamworth, NH 03886
(603)323-7337 Fax:(603)323-7337
E-mail: erickson@ncia.net
Web: www.WhisperingPinesNH.com

Circa 1900. Two farmhouses were joined more than a century ago to become what is now a delightful bed & breakfast that sits on 22 wooded acres in the foothills of the White Mountains near the Winnipesaukee Lakes Region. Sheltered by tall pines, the tranquil setting offers a peaceful getaway and the inn provides generous hospitality. Relax on the wicker-filled, screened-in porch or in the quaint living room with an antique soapstone stove. Each guest bedroom boasts a view of the gardens or woods. Linger over a hearty breakfast served in the large country kitchen. Cross-country ski or snowshoe from the back door to connect with Tamworth Outing Club Trails and Hemenway State Forest. Ask about special packages that are available.

Innkeeper(s): Karen & Kim Erickson. $80-145. 4 rooms, 2 with PB. Breakfast and snacks/refreshments included in rates. Types of meals: Country bkfst, veg bkfst, early coffee/tea and afternoon tea. Beds: KQD. Reading lamp and clock radio in room. Library, parlor games, telephone, fireplace, gift shop, guest refrigerator, screened-in guest porch, guest living room, coffeemaker and refreshments on premises. Amusement parks, antiquing, art galleries, beach, bicycling, canoeing/kayaking, cross-country skiing, downhill skiing, fishing, golf, hiking, horseback riding, live theater, parks, shopping, tennis and water sports nearby.

Publicity: *Summer Week.*

Tamworth Inn

Main Street
Tamworth, NH 03886-0189
(603)323-7721 (800)642-7352 Fax:(603)323-2026
E-mail: inn@tamworth.com
Web: www.tamworth.com

Circa 1833. Enjoy a bucolic setting and simple elegance in lodging, dining and spirits. Originally a stagecoach stop, Tamworth Inn is furnished with antiques and original artwork. The library and inn's living room both have cozy fireplaces to invite guests to

relax. There's a sparkling trout stream adjacent to the property and across the street is the Barnstormer's Theater, one of the country's oldest summer stock theaters, as well as Remick Country Doctor and Farm Museum.

Historic Interest: Grover Cleveland's summer home (2 miles), Chinook Kennels.

Innkeeper(s): Bob & Virginia Schrader. $115-300. 16 rooms with PB, 2 with FP, 5 suites and 1 conference room. Breakfast included in rates. Types of meals: Full gourmet bkfst, picnic lunch and gourmet dinner. Restaurant on premises. Beds: KQDT. Three with jetted tubs in room. Hiking and biking on premises. Small meetings hosted. Antiquing, cross-country skiing, downhill skiing, fishing and live theater nearby.

Publicity: *Boston Globe, Arts Around Boston, Wall Street Journal, Yankee, Country Inns Magazine, The Independant, Elle Magazine, New Hampshire Magazine and Food Channel.*

"It was great spending the day touring and returning to the quiet village of Tamworth and your wonderful inn."

Tilton   I4

Tilton Manor

40 Chestnut St
Tilton, NH 03276-5546
(603)286-3457 Fax:(603)286-3308

Circa 1862. This turn-of-the-century Victorian inn is just two blocks from downtown Tilton. The inn's comfortable guest rooms are furnished with your comfort in mind. Guests are treated to a hearty country breakfast. Visitors enjoy relaxing in the sitting room, where they can play games, read or watch TV after a busy day exploring the historic area. Gunstock and Lake Winnipesaukee are nearby, and the Daniel Webster Birthplace and Shaker Village are within easy driving distance. Shoppers will enjoy Tilton's latest addition-an outlet center.

Historic Interest: Historic Concord is just 15 minutes from the manor.

Innkeeper(s): Peggy Sheriff & Al Dravidzius. $90-200. 5 rooms with PB, 1 with FP and 1 suite. Breakfast included in rates. Types of meals: Full gourmet bkfst, veg bkfst and early coffee/tea. Beds: KDT. Data port, cable TV, VCR, reading lamp, ceiling fan, clock radio, hot tub/spa and some televisions in room. Air conditioning. Fax, copier, spa, library, parlor games, telephone, fireplace and laundry facility on premises. Weddings, small meetings, family reunions and seminars hosted. Antiquing, art galleries, beach, bicycling, canoeing/kayaking, cross-country skiing, downhill skiing, fishing, golf, hiking, horseback riding, parks, shopping, tennis, water sports and outlet mall nearby.

Wakefield   H6

Wakefield Inn Bed & Breakfast, Inc

2723 Wakefield Rd
Wakefield, NH 03872-4374
(603)522-8272 (800)245-0841

Circa 1804. Early travelers pulled up to the front door of the Wakefield Inn by stagecoach, and while they disembarked, their luggage was handed up to the second floor. It was brought in through the door, which is still visible over the porch roof. A spiral staircase, ruffled curtains, wallpapers and a wraparound porch all create the romantic ambiance of days gone by. In the living room, an original three-sided fireplace casts a warm glow on guests as it did more than 190 years ago.

Historic Interest: New Hampshire Farm Museum, Museum of Childhood.

Innkeeper(s): Lin & John Koch. $75-90. 7 rooms with PB. Breakfast included in rates. Types of meals: Full bkfst and early coffee/tea. Beds: QDT. Reading lamp and ceiling fan in room. VCR, parlor games and telephone on premises. Antiquing, cross-country skiing, fishing, golf and shopping nearby.

"Comfortable accommodations, excellent food and exquisite decor highlighted by your quilts."

Wilton   K4

Stepping Stones B&B

Bennington Battle Tr
Wilton, NH 03086
(603)654-9048 (888)654-9048

Circa 1790. Decks and terraces overlook the enormous gardens of this Greek Revival house, listed in the local historic register. Guest rooms feature white-washed pine, cherry or Shaker-style country pieces accented with botanical prints, handwoven throws, rugs, pillows and fresh flowers. Breakfast is served in the solar garden room. Poached eggs on asparagus with hollandaise sauce, blueberry Belgian waffles and jumbo apple muffins with streusel topping are guests' favorite breakfast choices. The innkeeper is both a garden designer and weaver, and there is a handweaving studio on the premises. The inn is an Editor's Pick in Yankee Magazine.

Innkeeper(s): D. Ann Carlsmith. $65-75. 3 rooms with PB. Breakfast included in rates. Types of meals: Full bkfst, early coffee/tea and afternoon tea. Beds: QDT. Reading lamp and desk in room. Library, parlor games, telephone and fireplace on premises. Weddings and family reunions hosted. Antiquing, cross-country skiing, downhill skiing, hiking, live theater, parks, handweaving studio, chamber music and tennis courts nearby.

Publicity: *Yankee Magazine.*

"A very relaxing and beautiful getaway. The color and fragrance of the gardens is stunning."

New Jersey

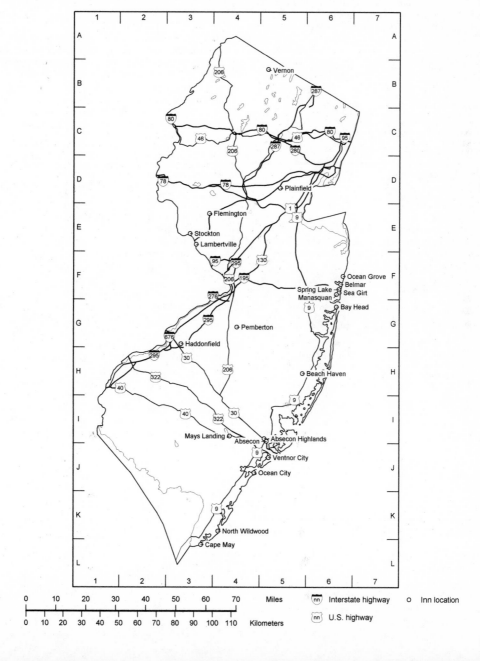

| | | | | | | |
|1|2|3|4|5|6|7|

A

B
- 206
- Vernon
- 287

C
- 80
- 46
- 80
- 80
- 95
- 287
- 46
- 280

D
- 78
- 78
- Plainfield
- 1
- 9

E
- Flemington
- Stockton
- Lambertville
- 1
- 9

F
- 95
- 295
- 130
- 206
- 195
- Ocean Grove
- Belmar
- Spring Lake
- Sea Girt
- Manasquan
- 276
- 9
- Bay Head

G
- 295
- Pemberton

H
- 676
- Haddonfield
- 295
- 30
- 40
- 322
- 206
- Beach Haven
- 9

I
- 40
- 322
- 30
- Mays Landing
- Absecon
- Absecon Highlands
- 9
- Ventnor City

J
- 9
- Ocean City

K
- 9
- North Wildwood

L
- Cape May

| | | | | | | |
|1|2|3|4|5|6|7|

| 0 | 10 | 20 | 30 | 40 | 50 | 60 | 70 | Miles |
| 0 | 10 | 20 | 30 | 40 | 50 | 60 | 70 | 80 | 90 | 100 | 110 | Kilometers |

nn Interstate highway   o Inn location

nn U.S. highway

Absecon 15

Dr. Jonathan Pitney House

57 North Shore Rd
Absecon, NJ 08201
(609)569-1799 (888)774-8639 Fax:(609)569-9224
E-mail: drpitney@pitneyhouse.com
Web: www.pitneyhouse.com

Circa 1799. A picket fence surrounds this recently renovated Italianate and Colonial inn. It was the home of Dr. Pitney, considered the Father of Atlantic City. Some of the inn's rooms feature Colonial decor, while others are in a Victorian motif. There are clawfoot tubs, whirlpools, ceiling fans and fireplaces. Breakfast is offered gourmet-style and features an entree, freshly baked breads and cakes. Nearby is Atlantic City, Smithville, a winery, beaches, boardwalk, the convention center and a bird sanctuary.

Innkeeper(s): Don Kelly & Vonnie Clark. $100-250. 10 rooms with PB, 10 with FP and 4 suites. Breakfast and afternoon tea included in rates. Types of meals: Full gourmet bkfst and early coffee/tea. Beds: QD. Cable TV, VCR, ceiling fan and desk in room. Air conditioning. Fax, library, parlor games, telephone and fireplace on premises. Limited handicap access. Weddings and small meetings hosted. Antiquing, fishing, golf, parks, shopping, sporting events, tennis, water sports and casinos nearby.

Absecon Highlands 15

White Manor Inn

739 S 2nd Ave
Absecon Highlands, NJ 08205-9542
(609)748-3996 Fax:(609)652-0073

Circa 1932. This quiet country inn was built by the innkeeper's father and includes unique touches throughout, many created by innkeeper Howard Bensel himself, who became a master craftsman from his father's teachings and renovated the home extensively. Beautiful flowers and plants adorn both the lush grounds and the interior of the home. Everything is comfortable and cozy at this charming

B&B, a relaxing contrast to the glitz of nearby Atlantic City.

Historic Interest: A short drive will take guests to a number of historic sites, including the Towne of Smithville, Atlantic City Boardwalk, Renault Winery, Wharton State Forest, the Somers Mansion, and Margate, home of Lucy the Elephant, a National Historic Landmark.

Innkeeper(s): Anna Mae & Howard R. Bensel Jr. $65-105. 7 rooms, 5 with PB, 1 suite and 1 conference room. Breakfast and snacks/refreshments included in rates. Types of meals: Cont plus and early coffee/tea. Beds: QDT. Ceiling fan in room. Air conditioning. Parlor games and telephone on premises. Small meetings, family reunions and seminars hosted. Amusement parks, antiquing, fishing, live theater, parks, shopping, sporting events, water sports, golf, bird watching and casinos nearby.

"We felt more like relatives than total strangers. By far the most clean inn that I have seen — spotless!"

Bay Head G6

Bay Head Harbor Inn Bed & Breakfast

676 Main Avenue
Bay Head, NJ 08742-5346
(732)899-0767 Fax:(732)899-0148
Web: www.bayhead.org/harborinn

Circa 1890. This three-story Shingle-style inn, just a block from the beach and the bay, boasts several rooms with porches. The inn is decorated with folk art and country antiques.

Afternoon tea and evening snacks are served. Walk to fine restaurants, unique shops and Twilight Lake.

Innkeeper(s): Janice & Dan Eskesen. $100-190. 9 rooms. Breakfast, afternoon tea and snacks/refreshments included in rates. Types of meals: Cont plus and early coffee/tea. Beds: QDT. Reading lamp and clock radio in room. Air conditioning. TV, parlor games, telephone, fireplace, refrigerator and reading material/areas on premises. Family reunions hosted. Amusement parks, antiquing, fishing, golf, parks, shopping, tennis, water sports and fine and casual dining nearby.

Beach Haven H5

Amber Street Inn

118 Amber St
Beach Haven, NJ 08008-1744
(609)492-1611

Circa 1885. Located on Long Beach Island, just six miles off the New Jersey Coast, this historic inn was one of Beach Haven's earliest homes. The Victorian rests within the town's historic district across from Bicentennial Park. Rooms are decorated in an eclectic Victorian style with refurbished antiques. A full breakfast is served buffet style. The beach is a short walk away, and the innkeepers provide beach passes, chairs and bicycles.

Innkeeper(s): Joan & Michael Fitzsimmons. $135-245. 6 rooms with PB and 1 suite. Breakfast included in rates. Types of meals: Full bkfst, early coffee/tea and snacks/refreshments. Beds: KQ. Reading lamp, ceiling fan and telephone in room. Air conditioning. Fax, bicycles, library, parlor games, fireplace, English garden and porch rockers on premises. Antiquing, beach, fishing, golf, live theater, parks, shopping, tennis, water sports and lighthouse nearby.
Publicity: *Gannett Travel.*

Island Guest House Bed and Breakfast

207 Third St.
Beach Haven, NJ 08008-1857
(609)492-2907 (877)LBI-STAY Fax:(609)492-2907
E-mail: islandguesthouse@lbinet.com
Web: lbinet.com/islandguesthouse

Circa 1902. Voted the Best Bed and Breakfast on Long Beach Island and the Mainland by the Times Beacon, this historic inn is located ocean side in the heart of Beach Haven. The island's white sandy beaches are only steps away, and restaurants and shops are just a leisurely stroll away. Stay in one of 15 beautifully decorated guest bedrooms, each with private bath, TV and air conditioning. Some feature private patios or decks, refrigerators or luxury double his and her showers. A cottage with a Jacuzzi tub and a fireplace sleeps four. An outside courtyard boasts wrought iron tables and chairs with market umbrellas for daytime shade, and candlelight café style for evening gatherings. Wind chimes and sea breezes invite relaxation on the large screened sunroom full of wicker furniture. Play checkers, chess, backgammon or other games in the common area.

Historic Interest: Our bed and breakfast was built 100 years ago as a boarding home.

Innkeeper(s): Joanne and Mark Spulock. $99-190. 15 rooms, 12 with PB, 2 suites and 1 cottage. Breakfast and afternoon tea included in rates. Types of meals: Cont plus. Beds: KQDT. Cable TV and clock radio in room. Central air. Bicycles, parlor games and telephone on premises. Weddings and family reunions hosted. Amusement parks, art galleries, beach, bicycling, fishing, live theater, museums, shopping, tennis and water sports nearby.
Publicity: *Times Beacon - Voted "Best Bed and Breakfast" on Long Beach Island and the Mainland.*

Belmar   F6

The Inn at The Shore Bed & Breakfast

301 4th Ave
Belmar, NJ 07719-2104
(732)681-3762 Fax:(732)280-1914

Circa 1880. This child friendly country Victorian actually is near two different shores. Both the ocean and Silver Lake are within easy walking distance of the inn. From the inn's wrap-around porch, guests can view swans on the lake. The innkeepers decorated their Victorian home in period style. The inn's patio is set up for barbecues.

Innkeeper(s): Rosemary & Tom Volker. $140-230. 10 rooms, 4 with PB and 1 conference room. Breakfast included in rates. Types of meals: Full bkfst. Cable TV, reading lamp, clock radio, telephone, modem, whirlpool tubs and fireplaces in room. Air conditioning. VCR, bicycles, parlor games, fireplace, aquarium, patio with gas grill, guest pantry with refrigerator and microwave on premises. Weddings, small meetings, family reunions and seminars hosted. Amusement parks, antiquing, fishing, live theater, parks, shopping, sporting events and water sports nearby.

"You both have created a warm, cozy and comfortable refuge for us weary travelers."

Morning Dove Inn

204 Fifth Ave.
Belmar, NJ 07719
(732)556-0777

Circa 1892. Watch the swans on Silver Lake from the front porch of this cheerful bed & breakfast while a sea breeze from the nearby Atlantic Ocean refreshes and soothes. A spacious living room provides assorted seating arrangements for fireside chats. Enjoy afternoon refreshments and a game of cards in the solarium. Aptly named after birds, the gracious suites and guest bedrooms offer an assortment of comfortable amenities. In the dining room, a satisfying breakfast featuring the inn's specialties is served.

Innkeeper(s): Carol Lee Tieman. $100-220. 8 rooms, 6 with PB and 2 suites. Breakfast and afternoon tea included in rates. Types of meals: Full bkfst and early coffee/tea. Beds: KQDT. Cable TV, reading lamp, ceiling fan, clock radio and hot tub/spa in room. Air conditioning. TV, telephone and fireplace on premises. Family reunions hosted. Amusement parks, antiquing, art galleries, beach, bicycling, fishing, golf, horseback riding, live theater, parks, shopping and water sports nearby.

Cape May   L3

The Abbey Bed & Breakfast

34 Gurney at Columbia Ave
Cape May, NJ 08204
(609)884-4506 (866)884-8800 Fax:(609)884-2379
E-mail: theabbey@bellatlantic.net
Web: www.abbeybedandbreakfast.com

Circa 1869. This historic inn consists of two buildings, one a Gothic Revival villa with a 60-foot tower, Gothic arched windows and shaded verandas. Furnishings include floor-to-ceiling mirrors, ornate gas chandeliers, marble-topped dressers and beds of carved walnut, wrought iron and brass. The cottage adjacent to the villa is a classic Second Empire-style cottage with a mansard roof. A full breakfast is served in the dining room in spring and fall and on the veranda in the summer. Late afternoon refreshments and tea are served each day at 5 p.m. The beauti-

ful inn is featured in the town's Grand Christmas Tour, and public tours and tea are offered three times a week in season.

Innkeeper(s): Jay & Marianne Schatz. $100-295. 14 rooms with PB, 2 suites and 2 conference rooms. Breakfast and afternoon tea included in rates. Types of meals: Full bkfst. Beds: KQD. Reading lamp, ceiling fan, some air conditioning, small refrigerator and desks and antiques in room. Parlor games, beach chairs, on- and off-site parking and house telephone on premises. Small meetings and seminars hosted. Antiquing, art galleries, beach, bicycling, canoeing/kayaking, fishing, hiking, live theater, museums, parks, shopping, tennis, wineries, birding and free zoo nearby.

Publicity: Richmond Times-Dispatch, New York Times, Glamour, Philadelphia Inquirer, National Geographic Traveler, Smithsonian and Victorian Homes Magazine.

"Staying with you folks really makes the difference between a 'nice' vacation and a great one!"

Abigail Adams B&B By The Sea

12 Jackson St
Cape May, NJ 08204-1418
(609)884-1371 (888)827-4354
E-mail: info@abigailadamsinn.com
Web: www.abigailadamsinn.com

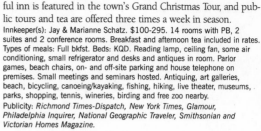

Circa 1888. This charming Victorian is only 100 feet from the beach which affords refreshing sea breezes and ocean views. There is a free-standing circular staircase, as well as original fireplaces and woodwork throughout. The decor is highlighted with flowered chintz and antiques, and the dining room is hand-stenciled. A full breakfast features the inn's homemade baked sweets.

Historic Interest: One of the "Seven Sisters of Cape May" built by Stephen Decatur Button.

Innkeeper(s): Kate Emerson. $85-215. 6 rooms, 4 with PB. Breakfast included in rates. Types of meals: Full bkfst and afternoon tea. Beds: QD. TV, ceiling fan and clock radio in room. Air conditioning. Telephone and fireplace on premises. Amusement parks, antiquing, fishing, live theater and water sports nearby.

"What a wonderful time. Comfortable & homey."

Albert Stevens Inn

127 Myrtle Ave
Cape May, NJ 08204-1237
(609)884-4717 (800)890-2287 Fax:(609)884-8320
E-mail: albertstevensinn@hotmail.com
Web: www.albertstevensinn.com

Circa 1898. Dr. Albert Stevens built this Queen Anne Free Classic house for his home and office. Carved woodwork and Victorian antiques enhance the delightful architectural details. The floating staircase and tower lead to spacious air-conditioned guest bedrooms. Enjoy a complete breakfast as well as afternoon tea and refreshments. Relax in the comfortably heated sunroom, or on the inviting veranda. The outside hot tub offers to soothe and rejuvenate. Free on-site parking is convenient for shopping, restaurants and the beach a short walk away. Beach towels and chairs are gladly provided.

Innkeeper(s): Jim & Lenanne Labrusciano. $90-220. 10 rooms, 7 with PB and 3 suites. Breakfast and afternoon tea included in rates. Types of meals: Full bkfst. Beds: KQD. TV and ceiling fan in room. Air conditioning. Telephone, fireplace, hot tub and on-site parking on premises. Weddings, small meetings, family reunions and seminars hosted. Amusement parks, antiquing, beach, bicycling, fishing, live theater, shopping, water sports and bird watching nearby.

Publicity: The Jersey Shore, Mid-Atlantic Country, Atlantic City Press, Cape May Star and Wave, The Herald, Washington Post, The New York Times, Philadelphia Inquirer and NBC News.

Alexander's Inn

653 Washington St
Cape May, NJ 08204-2324
(609)884-2555 Fax:(609)884-8883
E-mail: Larry@alexandersinn.com
Web: www.alexandersinn.com

Circa 1883. This mansard-roofed Victorian has been recently renovated and fitted with private baths and central air conditioning, yet the inn still maintains its elegant Victorian atmosphere. There are Oriental rugs, antiques and oil paintings in abundance. The gourmet dining room provides white-glove service with silver, crystal, linen and lace. Located on Washington Street are the trolley tours, horse-and-carriage rides, bicycle rentals, museums and shops. Saturday night guests at the inn are treated to a five-course Sunday brunch. During the rest of the week, guests are pampered with a continental-plus breakfast and buffet-style afternoon tea service.

Innkeeper(s): Larry & Diane Muentz. $110-160. 7 rooms with PB and 1 conference room. Breakfast and afternoon tea included in rates. Types of meals: Cont plus and gourmet dinner. Restaurant on premises. Beds: QD. Cable TV, VCR, reading lamp, ceiling fan, telephone and beach passes in room. Air conditioning. Fax, copier and parlor games on premises. Weddings, small meetings, family reunions and seminars hosted. Antiquing, fishing, live theater, shopping and water sports nearby.

Angel of The Sea

5 Trenton Ave
Cape May, NJ 08204-2735
(609)884-3369 (800)848-3369 Fax:(609)884-3331
Web: www.angelofthesea.com

Circa 1850. Views of the Atlantic are seen from almost half of the rooms in this renovated Victorian mansion with a mansard roof and tower. A double-tiered, oceanfront veranda stretches across the house. Each guest bedroom is uniquely furnished and some boast handsome antique beds. Afternoon tea is offered as well as wine and cheese. Complimentary bicycles, beach chairs, umbrellas and towels are available.

Innkeeper(s): Greg & Lorie Whissell. $135-315. 27 rooms with PB. Breakfast and afternoon tea included in rates. Types of meals: Full gourmet bkfst and early coffee/tea. Beds: KQD. Cable TV, reading lamp and turn-down service in room. Air conditioning. TV, bicycles, fireplace and wine and cheese which are included in rates are on premises. Weddings and family reunions hosted. Art galleries, beach, bicycling, canoeing/kayaking, fishing, golf, hiking, horseback riding, live theater, museums, shopping, tennis, water sports and wineries nearby.
Publicity: *Victoria, Mid Atlantic Country, Philadelphia Magazine* and *New Jersey Monthly.*

"We've travelled bed and breakfasts for years and this is by far the best."

Bayberry Inn B&B

223 Perry St
Cape May, NJ 08204
(609)884-9232 (877)923-9232
Web: www.bayberryinncapemay.com

Circa 1800. This Carpenter Gothic home, located just two blocks from the beach, was built by Joseph Q. Williams, a local builder and three-term mayor during the Civil War. Located one block from shopping and great restaurants and cafes, the inn features Victorian décor through most of the house. Original paintings created by local artists are displayed. Three-course breakfasts are served each morning, including a fruit dish, main dish and dessert. Homemade treats are served at tea time, which is 4 p.m..

Innkeeper(s): Andy & Toby Fontaine. $95-260. 6 rooms, 4 with PB and 1 suite. Breakfast and afternoon tea included in rates. Types of meals: Full bkfst and veg bkfst. Beds: Q. Air conditioning. Fax, copier, parlor games, telephone, fireplace, TV/VCR (on request), guest refrigerator, beach chairs and free parking on premises. Family reunions hosted. Amusement parks, antiquing, art galleries, beach, bicycling, canoeing/kayaking, fishing, golf, hiking, horseback riding, live theater, museums, parks, shopping, tennis, water sports, wineries and tours of historic district and homes nearby.

Bedford Inn

805 Stockton Ave
Cape May, NJ 08204-2446
(609)884-4158 Fax:(609)884-6320
E-mail: info@bedfordinn.com or cindy@bedfordinn.com
Web: www.bedfordinn.com

Circa 1880. The Bedford, decked in gingerbread trim with verandas on both of its two stories, has welcomed guests since its creation in the 19th century. Electrified gaslights, period wallcoverings and rich, Victorian furnishings create an air of nostalgia. The inn is close to many of Cape May's shops and restaurants, as well as the beach, which is just half a block away. Guests are pampered with breakfasts of quiche, gourmet egg dishes, French toast and freshly baked breads.

Innkeeper(s): Cindy & James Schmucker. $115-245. 10 rooms, 7 with PB and 3 suites. Breakfast included in rates. Types of meals: Full bkfst and snacks/refreshments. Beds: KQDT. Cable TV, VCR, reading lamp, ceiling fan and clock radio in room. Air conditioning. Library, telephone, fireplace, refrigerator, free limited driveway parking and afternoon refreshments on premises. Antiquing, fishing, live theater, parks, water sports, house tours, trolley tours, restaurants and beach nearby.

Brass Bed Inn

719 Columbia Ave
Cape May, NJ 08204-2307
(609)884-2302 Fax:(609)884-4826
Web: www.brassbedinn.com

Circa 1872. Nineteenth-century brass beds and antiques original to this three-story Carpenter Gothic Victorian give the Brass Bed Inn a particular uniqueness in its Historic District setting. Oriental carpets, vintage wallpapers and the old-fashioned wraparound veranda filled with rockers make it easy to envision the home's original life as a private seaside retreat. Guests enjoy watching the horses and carriages pass by or occasionally stop while an engagement ring or proposal is offered to a surprised beloved. Full stick-to-your-ribs breakfasts are served hearthside in the morning and include freshly baked cakes, scones or pineapple bread pudding, all made from scratch. Butterfly bushes, lilies, roses and baby's breath fill the garden. Most surprising is the unusual color of the hydrangeas — red — due to the iron in the hairpin lace fence that has encircled the home all these years. The water is one block away.

Innkeeper(s): Jim Huckleberry & Theresa McCarthy. $90-175. 9 rooms, 7 with PB. Breakfast and afternoon tea included in rates. Types of meals: Full bkfst, early coffee/tea and snacks/refreshments. Beds: KQDT. Reading lamp, ceiling fan and clock radio in room. Air conditioning. TV, fax, library, parlor games, telephone and fireplace on premises. Weddings, small meetings and family reunions hosted. Antiquing, art galleries, beach, bicycling, canoeing/kayaking, fishing, golf, horseback riding, live theater, parks, shopping, tennis, water sports, tours of B&Bs and wonderful restaurants nearby.

Buttonwood Manor

115 Broadway
Cape May, NJ 08204-1264
(609)884-4070
E-mail: ring@dandy.net
Web: www.buttonwoodmanorbb.com

Circa 1908. While most of us enjoy the usual silverware, plates and towels, Lizzie H. Richardson received this stately Colonial Revival manor as her wedding gift. The interior includes seven guest rooms, decorated with turn-of-the-century furnishings. A multi-course, gourmet breakfast is served each morning. Guests enjoy items such as baked fruit, egg puffs, and buttermilk biscuits. The inn is located slightly away from the hustle and bustle of downtown Cape May, yet close enough to walk to shops, restaurants and other attractions.
Innkeeper(s): Diane & Roger Ring. $100-200. 7 rooms with PB, 2 with FP. Breakfast and afternoon tea included in rates. Types of meals: Full gourmet bkfst, veg bkfst and early coffee/tea. Beds: KQT. Cable TV, reading lamp and ceiling fan in room. Air conditioning. Library, parlor games, telephone and fireplace on premises. Antiquing, art galleries, beach, bicycling, canoeing/kayaking, fishing, golf, hiking, live theater, museums, parks, shopping, tennis, water sports and birding nearby.

Captain Mey's B&B Inn

202 Ocean St
Cape May, NJ 08204-2322
(609)884-7793 (800)981-3702
E-mail: innkeeper@snip.net
Web: www.captainmeys.com

Circa 1890. Named after Dutch explorer Capt. Cornelius J. Mey, who named the area, the inn displays its Dutch heritage with table-top Persian rugs, Delft china and imported Dutch

lace curtains. The dining room features chestnut and oak Eastlake paneling and a fireplace. Two guest rooms have double whirlpool tubs. Some guest rooms include both a queen and a single bed. A hearty breakfast is served by candlelight or on the wraparound veranda in the summertime. The ferry and lighthouse are nearby.
Historic Interest: Cold Spring Village and the Cape May Lighthouse are five minutes away. Lewes, Del., is one hour by ferry.
Innkeeper(s): George & Kathleen Blinn. $95-235. 7 rooms with PB and 1 suite. Breakfast and afternoon tea included in rates. Types of meals: Full bkfst. Beds: QT. Reading lamp, refrigerator, ceiling fan, clock radio, some with two-person whirlpool tubs and TV in room. Air conditioning. Fireplace on premises. Small meetings and family reunions hosted. Amusement parks, antiquing, fishing, live theater, parks, shopping, water sports, bicycling, bird watching, lighthouse and ferry nearby.
Publicity: *Americana, Country Living, New Jersey Monthly, WKYW News (CBS) Philadelphia, WNJN (N.J. Network News Trenton), New Jersey Country Roads Magazine and Traveller.*

"The innkeepers pamper you so much you wish you could stay forever."

The Carroll Villa B&B

19 Jackson St
Cape May, NJ 08204-1417
(609)884-9619 Fax:(609)884-0264
E-mail: cvres@eticomm.net
Web: www.carrollvilla.com

Circa 1882. This Victorian hotel is located one-half block from the ocean on the oldest street in the historic district of Cape May. Breakfast at the Villa is a memorable event, featuring dish-

es acclaimed by the New York Times and Frommer's. Homemade fruit breads, Italian omelets and Crab Eggs Benedict are a few specialties. Meals are served in the Mad Batter Restaurant on a European veranda, a secluded garden terrace or in the sky-lit Victorian dining room. The restaurant serves breakfast, lunch, dinner and cocktails daily. The decor of this inn is decidedly Victorian with period antiques and wallpapers.
Innkeeper(s): Mark Kulkowitz & Pamela Ann Huber. $75-190. 22 rooms with PB and 2 conference rooms. Breakfast included in rates. Types of meals: Full bkfst, lunch and dinner. Beds: QD. TV, VCR, ceiling fan, clock radio and telephone in room. Air conditioning. Fax, copier and fireplace on premises. Weddings, small meetings, family reunions and seminars hosted. Amusement parks, antiquing, fishing, live theater, parks and shopping nearby.
Publicity: *Atlantic City Press, Asbury Press, Frommer's, New York Times and Washington Post.*

"Mr. Kulkowitz is a superb host. He strives to accommodate the diverse needs of guests."

The Chalfonte Hotel

301 Howard St, PO Box 475
Cape May, NJ 08204-0475
(609)884-8409 Fax:(609)884-4588
E-mail: chalfonte@snip.net
Web: www.chalfonte.com

Circa 1876. This 70-room hotel was built by Civil War hero Colonel Henry Sawyer. The hotel features wraparound porches, simply appointed rooms with marble-topped dressers and other original antiques. The fare in the Magnolia Room is Southern-style with fresh fish daily and vegetarian options. Children of all ages are welcome, and there is a supervised children's dining room for guests aged six and under. Much of the hotel's restoration and preservation is accomplished by dedicated volunteers and architectural students who have adopted the hotel as their own. Painting workshops, Elderhostel educational programs, weekly events and entertainment, group retreats, weddings and family reunions are offered.
Historic Interest: Cold Springs Village (4 miles).
Innkeeper(s): Anne LeDuc & Judy Bartella. $130-299. 70 rooms, 12 with PB, 2 cottages and 2 conference rooms. Breakfast and dinner included in rates. Types of meals: Full bkfst and early coffee/tea. Restaurant on premises. Beds: KQDT. TV, reading lamp and ceiling fan in room. VCR, fax and copier on premises. Weddings, small meetings, family reunions and seminars hosted. Amusement parks, antiquing, fishing, golf, live theater, parks, shopping, sporting events, tennis, water sports, nature trails, whale watching and birding nearby.
Publicity: *Dallas Morning News, Washington Post, Travel & Leisure, Washingtonian, Philadelphia Inquirer, New York Times, Country Inns, Richmond Times, Mid-Atlantic Country, Star and Wave, Virginian Pilot & Ledger-Star, USA Today, Los Angeles Times, National Public Radio, South Jersey Weddings, PBS Channel 12, Discovery Channel and Maryland Public TV.*

"We love the relaxed and genteel atmosphere, the feeling of having stepped into another time is delightful."

Cliveden B&B Inn & Cottage

709 Columbia Ave
Cape May, NJ 08204-2307
(609)884-4516 (800)884-2420
Web: www.clivedeninn.com

Circa 1884. This three-story Victorian boasts gingerbread trim on the gables and the front porch. The spacious wraparound porch is furnished with white antique wicker and is shaded by cranberry colored awnings. There are sitting areas and ceiling fans in the air-conditioned rooms. The inn is two blocks from the beach and a short stroll from the Victorian shopping area with its fine restaurants and shops. A full breakfast is served buffet-style. Guests enjoy taking breakfast on the veranda most of the time. There is a two-bedroom Victorian cottage popular for families with children.

Innkeeper(s): Susan & Al DeRosa. $115-175. 10 rooms with PB, 2 with FP and 1 cottage. Breakfast and afternoon tea included in rates. Types of meals: Full gourmet bkfst. Beds: QD. Reading lamp, refrigerator and ceiling fan in room. Air conditioning. Library, telephone and fireplace on premises. Weddings, small meetings, family reunions and seminars hosted. Amusement parks, antiquing, art galleries, beach, bicycling, canoeing/kayaking, fishing, golf, hiking, horseback riding, live theater, museums, parks, shopping, tennis, water sports and wineries nearby.

Dormer House

800 Columbia Ave
Cape May, NJ 08204-2310
(609)884-7446 (800)884-5052
Web: www.dormerhouse.com

Circa 1899. This three-story Colonial Revival estate is three blocks from the ocean and the historic walking mall. The inviting wraparound porch, with its red drapes and striped awnings, is often enjoyed as the site for afternoon tea. Originally built by marble-dealer John Jacoby, the inn retains much of the original marble and furniture.

Innkeeper(s): Lucille & Dennis Doherty. $80-210. 9 rooms, 2 suites and 1 cottage. Breakfast and afternoon tea included in rates. Types of meals: Full bkfst. Beds: Q. Cable TV, reading lamp, refrigerator, ceiling fan, clock radio, desk and some with Jacuzzi tubs in room. Air conditioning. Telephone, fireplace, beach chairs and outside showers on premises. Amusement parks, antiquing, fishing, live theater, parks, shopping and water sports nearby.
Publicity: *Cape May Star & Wave.*

The Duke of Windsor Inn

817 Washington St
Cape May, NJ 08204-1651
(609)884-1355 (800)826-8973
E-mail: innkeeper@dukeofwindsorinn.com
Web: www.dukeofwindsorinn.com

Circa 1896. This Queen Anne Victorian was built by Delaware River boat pilot Harry Hazelhurst and his wife, Florence. They were both six feet tall, so the house was built with large open rooms and doorways, and extra-wide stairs. The inn has a carved, natural oak open staircase with stained-glass windows at top and bottom. Five antique chandeliers grace the dining room. Parking is available on premises.

Historic Interest: National Register.
Innkeeper(s): Patricia Joyce. $125-235. 10 rooms with PB. Breakfast and afternoon tea included in rates. Types of meals: Full bkfst and early coffee/tea. Beds: QDT. Ceiling fan in room. Air conditioning. Telephone, fireplace, off-street parking, outside hot and cold shower and refrigerator available for guest use on premises. Antiquing, fishing, live theater, parks, shopping and water sports nearby.
Publicity: *Philadelphia Magazine, New Jersey Countryside Magazine, Endless Vacation and Shape.*

"Breakfast at a.m. and tea at p.m. were delicious and relaxing. We can't wait to come back."

Fairthorne B&B

111 Ocean St
Cape May, NJ 08204-2319
(609)884-8791 (800)438-8742 Fax:(609)898-6129
E-mail: fairthornebnb@aol.com
Web: www.fairthorne.com

Circa 1892. Antiques abound in this three-story Colonial Revival. Lace curtains and a light color scheme complete the charming decor. There is a new, yet historic addition to the B&B. The innkeepers now offer guest quarters (with fireplaces) in The Fairthorne Cottage, a restored 1880s building adjacent to the inn. The signature breakfasts include special daily entrees along with an assortment of home-baked breads and muffins. A light afternoon tea also is served with refreshments. The proximity to the beach will be much appreciated by guests, and the innkeepers offer the use of beach towels, bicycles and sand chairs. The nearby historic district is full of fun shops and restaurants.

Innkeeper(s): Diane & Ed Hutchinson. $190-275. 8 rooms with PB and 1 suite. Breakfast and afternoon tea included in rates. Types of meals: Full bkfst and early coffee/tea. Beds: KQ. Reading lamp, refrigerator, ceiling fan and clock radio in room. Air conditioning. Fax, telephone and fireplace on premises. Antiquing, fishing, live theater, parks, shopping, water sports and historic lighthouse & Victorian architectural tours nearby.
Publicity: *New Jersey Countryside, The Discerning Traveler, Arrington's and NJ Golf.*

"I feel as if I have come to stay with a dear old friend who has spared no expense to provide me with all that my heart can desire! ... I will savor the memory of your hospitality for years to come. Thanks so much."

Gingerbread House

28 Gurney St
Cape May, NJ 08204
(609)884-0211
E-mail: info@gingerbreadinn.com
Web: gingerbreadinn.com

Circa 1869. The Gingerbread is one of eight original Stockton Row Cottages, summer retreats built for families from Philadelphia and Virginia. It is a half-block from the ocean and breezes waft over the wicker-filled porch. The inn is listed in the National Register. It has been meticulously restored and decorated with period antiques and a fine collection of paintings. The inn's woodwork is especially notable, guests enter through handmade teak double doors.

Historic Interest: Historic tours are available.
Innkeeper(s): Fred & Joan Echevarria. $90-260. 6 rooms, 3 with PB and 1 suite. Breakfast and afternoon tea included in rates. Types of meals: Full bkfst. Beds: QD. Air conditioning. Telephone and fireplace on premises. Small meetings and family reunions hosted. Antiquing, fishing, live theater, parks, shopping, water sports, birding and Victorian homes nearby.
Publicity: *Philadelphia Inquirer, New Jersey Monthly and Atlantic City Press Newspaper.*

"The elegance, charm and authenticity of historic Cape May, but more than that, it appeals to us as 'home.'"

Hebenthal House

509 Franklin St.
Cape May, NJ 08204
(609)884-4516 (800)884-2420 Fax:(609)884-7943

Circa 1867. Lounge on the wraparound veranda of this 1862 Victorian guest house that is now part of the historic district. Originally the home of a stage coach driver, guest parking is now where the stables once were. Perfect for family reunions, the house boasts a front parlor, dining room, fully equipped retro '50s kitchen and seven guest bedrooms. A courtyard features a patio table and chairs. Enjoy use of a barbecue grill. Sand chairs and beach towels add to the pleasure experienced at one of America's top ten beaches and active seaport. A birding hot spot, Cape May is the birding migration capital of North America. From art to history to nature and even fine dining, Cape May has much to appreciate all through the year.
Historic Interest: The Hebenthals were stage coach drivers. Current guests have private parking on the previous site of the stables.
Innkeeper(s): Susan & Alex DeRosa. $2500-4200. 7 rooms. Beds: KQDT. Cable TV, VCR, reading lamp, CD player, refrigerator, ceiling fan, snack bar, clock radio, telephone, coffeemaker, fully equipped kitchen with dishwasher, microwave, toaster and blender in room. Central air. Sand chair, beach towels, enclosed courtyard with BBQ grill, table and chairs on premises. Weddings, small meetings, family reunions and seminars hosted. Amusement parks, antiquing, art galleries, beach, bicycling, canoeing/kayaking, fishing, golf, horseback riding, live theater, museums, parks, shopping, tennis, water sports and wineries nearby.

The Henry Sawyer Inn

722 Columbia Ave
Cape May, NJ 08204-2332
(609)884-5667 (800)449-5667 Fax:(609)884-9406

Circa 1877. This fully restored, three-story peach Victorian home boasts a gingerbread embellished veranda, brick-colored shutters and brown trim. Inside, the parlor features Victorian antiques, a marble fireplace, polished wood floors, an Oriental rug, formal wallcoverings, a crystal chandelier and fresh flowers. Guest rooms have been decorated with careful attention to a romantic and fresh Victorian theme, as well. One room includes a whirlpool tub, one includes a private porch, and another a fireplace.
Innkeeper(s): Mary & Barbara Morris. $85-240. 5 rooms with PB, 1 with FP and 2 suites. Breakfast and afternoon tea included in rates. Types of meals: Full bkfst and early coffee/tea. Beds: KQT. Cable TV, reading lamp, ceiling fan, clock radio, small refrigerator and one with whirlpool or private porch in room. Air conditioning. VCR, fax, telephone, fireplace and parking on premises. Weddings, small meetings, family reunions and seminars hosted. Antiquing, fishing, golf, live theater, parks, shopping, tennis, water sports, carriage and Victorian trolley nearby.

Humphrey Hughes House

29 Ocean St
Cape May, NJ 08204-2411
(609)884-4428 (800)582-3634

Circa 1903. Stained-glass windows mark each landing of the staircase, and intricately carved American chestnut columns add to the atmosphere in this 30-room mansion. The land was purchased by the Captain Humphrey Hughes family in the early 1700s. The majestic grandfather clock remains as one of many late-Victorian antiques.
Historic Interest: The inn is listed in National Register.
Innkeeper(s): Lorraine & Terry Schmidt.

$160-275. 7 rooms with PB and 4 suites. Breakfast and afternoon tea included in rates. Beds: KQ. Cable TV, reading lamp, ceiling fan and clock radio in room. Air conditioning. Parlor games and telephone on premises. Antiquing, live theater, shopping and water sports nearby.
Publicity: *New York Times and AM Philadelphia.*

"Thoroughly enjoyed our stay."

The Inn on Ocean

25 Ocean St
Cape May, NJ 08204-2411
(609)884-7070 (800)304-4477 Fax:(609)884-1384
E-mail: claytoninc@aol.com
Web: www.theinnonocean.com

Circa 1880. Centrally located, this inn is one of Cape May's most historic and distinctive. The unique design reflects a fully restored 1880s French Second Empire architecture. Considered the "Beacon of Cape May," the classic mansard roof is crowned with lighted cresting. Relax on the large porches or in the elegant Victorian splendor of antiques, fireplaces, high ceilings and tall windows with lace curtains. A parlor and grand billiard room are inviting places to gather. Choose a guest bedroom or suite that may include a clawfoot bathtub, fireplace, and refrigerator. A hearty country breakfast is served daily. It is only half a block to the beach, and chairs are available.
Innkeeper(s): Richard White & Victoria Clayton. $129-259. 4 rooms with PB, 1 with FP and 1 suite. Breakfast and afternoon tea included in rates. Types of meals: Full bkfst. Beds: KQ. Cable TV, ceiling fan and suite has fireplace in room. Air conditioning. Antiquing, fishing, live theater, parks, shopping, water sports, tennis and golf nearby.
Publicity: *Delta Airlines, United Airlines & Southwest Airlines In-Flight Magazines, Washington Post Sunday Magazine and Long Island Newsday Newspaper.*

"A wonderful and beautiful experience. Great comfort, great breakfast and great hospitality."

John F. Craig House

609 Columbia Ave
Cape May, NJ 08204-2305
(609)884-0100 (877)544-0314 Fax:(609)898-1307
E-mail: chipbarbara@comcast.net
Web: www.johnfcraig.com

Circa 1866. The deep red wine exterior reflects the overall warmth of this historic Carpenter Gothic Victorian that also boasts a touch of whimsy. Sit on one of the porches with afternoon refreshments and watch the horse and carriages go by. Fun and frivolity are found in the many games and puzzles. Laptop hookup is provided in the library next to the main parlor. Antique furnishings and period decor blend comfortably with modern amenities in each guest bedroom, some with fireplaces. Enjoy a generous buffet breakfast served daily. Bikes, beach towels and chairs are available. The concierge service offers year-round information for local activities and makes restaurant reservations.
Innkeeper(s): Barbara & Chip Masemore. Call for rates. 8 rooms, 7 with PB and 1 suite. Breakfast and snacks/refreshments included in rates. Types of meals: Veg bkfst, early coffee/tea and afternoon tea. Beds: KQT. Reading lamp, refrigerator and clock radio in room. Fax, copier, bicycles, library, parlor games, telephone, fireplace and laundry facility on premises. Small meetings, family reunions and seminars hosted. Amusement parks, antiquing, art galleries, beach, bicycling, canoeing/kayaking, fishing, golf, hiking, horseback riding, live theater, museums, parks, shopping, tennis, water sports and wineries nearby.

John Wesley Inn

30 Gurney St
Cape May, NJ 08204
(609)884-1012

Circa 1869. The innkeepers of this graciously restored Carpenter Gothic home have won awards for their captivating exterior Christmas decorations, and holidays at the inn are a seasonal delight. The interior decor preserves the Victorian era so treasured in this seaside village. Antiques are set in rooms decorated with bright, patterned wallpapers and windows decked in lace. The innkeepers also offer a restored carriage house, featuring the same period decor, but the modern amenity of a stocked kitchen.

Innkeeper(s): John & Rita Tice. $95-180. 6 rooms, 4 with PB, 2 cottages and 1 conference room. Breakfast included in rates. Types of meals: Cont plus. Beds: QD. Reading lamp, refrigerator, ceiling fan, clock radio, telephone and desk in room. Air conditioning. Fireplace on premises. Weddings, small meetings, family reunions and seminars hosted. Amusement parks, antiquing, fishing, live theater, parks, shopping and water sports nearby.

The King's Cottage

9 Perry St
Cape May, NJ 08204-1460
(609)884-0415 (877)258-1876 Fax:(609)884-1113
E-mail: kingscottage@snip.net
Web: www.kingscottage.com

Circa 1878. Enjoy the beautiful ocean views as you relax on antique wicker on the wraparound verandas at this architectural gem, designed by Frank Furness. The railings boast ceramic tiles that were part of a Japanese exhibition from the Philadelphia Centennial of 1876, and a measured drawing is recorded in the Library of Congress. Most of the guest rooms afford ocean views and two offer private verandas. All feature unique period decor and antiques. Breakfasts are served in the formal dining room on tables set with china, crystal and silver.

Historic Interest: The King's Cottage is listed in the National Register and located in Cape May's primary historic district. The Victorian Mall, restored Cape May Lighthouse and Physick Estate Museum are just a few of the nearby historic attractions.

Innkeeper(s): Roseann Baker & Barbara Preminger. $100-235. 9 rooms with PB, 1 with FP and 1 suite. Breakfast, afternoon tea and snacks/refreshments included in rates. Types of meals: Full gourmet bkfst, veg bkfst and early coffee/tea. Beds: Q. Reading lamp in room. Air conditioning. Telephone, private veranda with some accommodations and on-site parking on premises. Weddings, small meetings, family reunions and seminars hosted. Amusement parks, antiquing, art galleries, beach, bicycling, canoeing/kayaking, fishing, golf, hiking, horseback riding, live theater, museums, parks, shopping, tennis, water sports, wineries, dolphin watching, lighthouse and casinos nearby.

Publicity: *Victorian Affair, Atlantic City Press, Newark Star, New Jersey Savy Living and Cape May Videos.*

"Thanks so much for your warm and inviting hospitality. I never expected to feel so at home at a bed and breakfast. Your personal touch made this a memorable experience and not just "a place to stay." The views and ocean breezes were more than you described. Truly great."

Linda Lee Bed & Breakfast

725 Columbia Ave
Cape May, NJ 08204-2305
(609)884-1240 Fax:(609)884-6762
E-mail: lindale@bellatlantic.net
Web: www.thelindalee.com

Circa 1872. Built in Carpenter Gothic style, this recently renovated cottage still reflects its origins. Located in the National Historic Landmark District, it is appropriately furnished in authentic Victorian decor. Comfortable guest bedrooms offer

quiet relaxation; some feature fireplaces. A complete breakfast is served in the dining room on Wedgewood china and sterling silver settings at nine every morning. Don't miss afternoon tea at 5 p.m. with finger sandwiches and sweets. It is an easy walk to the beach in this waterfront community, and towels and chairs are provided for use. Free on-site parking is available, as is a bike rack to secure a personal or rented bike.

Innkeeper(s): Lynda and Corbin Cogswell. $100-195. 5 rooms with PB, 2 with FP. Breakfast and afternoon tea included in rates. Types of meals: Full bkfst and early coffee/tea. Beds: KQT. Reading lamp, ceiling fan, clock radio and fireplace in room. Air conditioning. Library, parlor games, telephone, fireplace, gift shop, shared refrigerator in kitchen and on-site parking on premises. Weddings and family reunions hosted. Amusement parks, antiquing, art galleries, beach, bicycling, canoeing/kayaking, fishing, golf, hiking, live theater, museums, parks, shopping, tennis, water sports and wineries nearby.

Mainstay Inn

635 Columbia Ave
Cape May, NJ 08204-2305
(609)884-8690

Circa 1872. This was once the elegant and exclusive Jackson's Clubhouse popular with gamblers. Many of the guest rooms and the grand parlor look much as they did in the 1870s. Fourteen-foot-high ceilings, elaborate chandeliers, a sweeping veranda and a cupola add to the atmosphere. Tom and Sue Carroll received the American Historic Inns award in 1988  for their preservation efforts, and have been making unforgettable memories for guests for decades. A writer for Conde Nast Traveler once wrote, "architecturally, no inn, anywhere, quite matches The Mainstay."

Historic Interest: Cape May Lighthouse & State Park Museum (2 miles). Innkeeper(s): Tom & Sue Carroll. $115-395. 16 rooms with PB, 4 with FP and 7 suites. Breakfast and afternoon tea included in rates. Types of meals: Full bkfst and early coffee/tea. Beds: KQD. Reading lamp, refrigerator, clock radio, telephone, desk, suites with phones and some with ceiling fans in room. Air conditioning. Library, parlor games and fireplace on premises. Limited handicap access. Small meetings and seminars hosted. Antiquing, fishing, live theater, parks, shopping, sporting events, water sports, historic attractions, tennis, golf, birding, biking, hiking and ocean boardwalk nearby. Publicity: *Washington Post, Good Housekeeping, New York Times, Conde Nast Traveler, Smithsonian, Americana, Travel & Leisure and National Geographic Traveler.*

"By far the most lavishly and faithfully restored guesthouse...run by two arch-preservationists—Travel & Leisure."

The Mission Inn

1117 New Jersey Ave
Cape May, NJ 08204-2638
(609)884-8380 (800)800-8390 Fax:(609)884-4191
E-mail: info@missioninn.net
Web: www.missioninn.net

Circa 1912. Renown for being the town's only house built with Spanish-style architecture and Mission-style decor, this historic inn is located in a gorgeous seashore setting. Tyrone Power, Errol Flynn and Robert Preston are some of the notables who have stayed here. Relax on oversized comfortable furnish-

ings by the fireplace in the Great Room. After a good nights rest, an artistically presented and abundant breakfast may include seasonal fruits, homemade breads and muffins, stuffed French toast, peppered ham, sausage patties or smoked bacon. The patio and veranda are resplendent with colorful flowers and indigenous fruit-bearing trees. Bikes are available for further exploring. Beach towels and chairs are also provided.

Historic Interest: Built in 1912, only Spanish Mission-style house in town. Several movie stars stayed here.

Innkeeper(s): Susan Babineau-Roberts. $110-255. 8 rooms with PB, 3 with FP. Breakfast and snacks/refreshments included in rates. Types of meals: Full gourmet bkfst and early coffee/tea. Beds: KQ. Cable TV, reading lamp, ceiling fan and clock radio in room. Air conditioning. VCR, bicycles, library, parlor games, fireplace, on-site parking, beach towels and beach chairs on premises. Family reunions hosted. Antiquing, art galleries, beach, bicycling, canoeing/kayaking, fishing, golf, hiking, horseback riding, live theater, museums, parks, shopping, tennis, water sports and wineries nearby.

Publicity: *Cape May County Herald, Atlantic City Press, Bright Side Newspaper, Cape May Chamber of Commerce (both local and county guidebook), KOOL 98.3 (Atlantic and Cape May Counties), Arrington's 2003 Book of Lists voted "Best on Eastern Seaboard" and 2004 Book of Lists voted "Best Interior Design and Decor."*

"Cape May's best kept secret."

Poor Richard's Inn

17 Jackson St
Cape May, NJ 08204-1417
(609)884-3536
Web: www.poorrichardsinn.com

Circa 1882. The unusual design of this Second-Empire house has been accentuated with five colors of paint. Arched gingerbread porches tie together the distinctive bays of the house's facade. The combination of exterior friezes, balustrades and fretwork has earned the inn an individual listing in the National Register. Some rooms sport an eclectic country Victorian decor with patchwork quilts and pine furniture, while others tend toward a more traditional turn-of-the-century ambiance. An apartment suite is available.

Innkeeper(s): Harriett Sosson. $65-165. 8 rooms, 6 with PB and 1 suite. Breakfast included in rates. Types of meals: Cont plus. Beds: QDT. Cable TV in room. Air conditioning. Copier and telephone on premises. Small meetings and family reunions hosted. Amusement parks, antiquing, fishing, live theater, parks, water sports and ocean beach nearby.

Publicity: *Washington Post, New York Times, National Geographic Traveler and New Jersey.*

"Hold our spot on the porch. We'll be back before you know it."

The Primrose B&B

1102 Lafayette St
Cape May, NJ 08204-1722
(609)884-8288 (800)606-8288 Fax:(609)884-2358
E-mail: primroseinn@comcast.net
Web: www.theprimroseinn.com

Circa 1850. The Primrose is an adorable country Victorian painted in shades of rose with gingerbread trim. The grounds are dotted with gardens, and a view of historic properties can be seen from all directions. The interior is decorated in country Victorian style, featuring five cozy guest rooms, each one individually decorated. The rates include both afternoon refreshments, as well as breakfast entrees such as baked oatmeal, stuffed French toast or a unique blueberry lasagna. Cape May is the oldest seaside resort in the U.S.A. and boasts over 600 Victorian homes. The main attractions, other than the homes, are the ocean, fine dining and antiquing. The innkeepers provide you with bicycles, beach chairs and towels in season.

Innkeeper(s): Sally & Bart Denithorne. $100-300. 5 rooms with PB. Breakfast and afternoon tea included in rates. Types of meals: Early coffee/tea. Beds: KQ. Cable TV, ceiling fan, clock radio, hair dryer and some

with fireplace or Jacuzzi in room. Air conditioning. Antiquing, art galleries, beach, bicycling, canoeing/kayaking, fishing, golf, hiking, live theater, museums, parks, shopping, tennis, water sports and wineries nearby.

Publicity: *Arrington's Book of Lists - voted 10th best inn on East Coast.*

The Queen Victoria

102 Ocean St
Cape May, NJ 08204-2320
(609)884-8702
E-mail: qvinn@bellatlantic.net
Web: www.queenvictoria.com

Circa 1881. This nationally acclaimed inn, a block from the ocean and shops in the historic district, is comprised of two beautiful Victorian homes, restored and furnished with antiques. "Victorian Homes" magazine featured 23 color photographs of The Queen Victoria, because of its décor and luxurious amenities. Guest rooms offer handmade quilts, antiques, air conditioning, mini-refrigerators and all have private baths. Luxury suites and many rooms have a whirlpool tub and some with handsome fireplace. Afternoon tea is enjoyed while rocking on the porch in summer or before a warm fireplace in winter. Breakfast is hearty buffet style and the inn has its own cookbook. The innkeepers keep a fleet of complimentary bicycles available for guests and there are beach chairs and beach towels as well. The inn is open all year with special Christmas festivities and winter packages.

Innkeeper(s): Dane & Joan Wells. $100-300. 21 rooms with PB and 6 suites. Breakfast and afternoon tea included in rates. Types of meals: Full bkfst and early coffee/tea. Beds: Q. Reading lamp, refrigerator, clock radio, phones (in some rooms) and TV in room. Air conditioning. Bicycles and fireplace on premises. Small meetings hosted. Amusement parks, antiquing, beach, golf, parks, water sports and historic tours nearby.

Publicity: *Philadelphia Inquirer and Travel channel.*

Queen's Hotel

601 Columbia Ave
Cape May, NJ 08204-2305
(609)884-1613
E-mail: qvinn@bellatlantic.net
Web: www.queenshotel.com

Circa 1876. This elegant Victorian hotel is located just a block from the beach in the center of Cape May's historic district. Period decor graces the luxurious guest rooms. The feeling is both romantic and historic. Many of the rooms and suites offer double whirlpool tubs or glass-enclosed marble showers. Other amenities include hair dryers, TV, heated towel bar, air conditioning, coffeemakers and mini refrigerators. Some have private balconies and ocean views. A continental breakfast buffet is included in the rates. Restaurants and cafes are within walking distance or you can ask for the continental breakfast tray for a small charge. The hotel's staff includes professional concierge service. Shops are one block away. There are bicycles on the premises to explore the town and scenic water views.

Historic Interest: Originally, the hotel was used for commercial purposes, and a large, second-story room once served as a gambling casino.

Innkeeper(s): Dane & Joan Wells. $90-280. 11 rooms with PB, 1 with FP and 1 suite. Breakfast included in rates. Types of meals: Cont. Beds: Q. Cable TV, reading lamp, refrigerator, ceiling fan, clock radio, telephone, hair dryer, coffeemaker and heated towel bar in room. Air conditioning. Bicycles on premises. Small meetings hosted. Amusement parks, antiquing, bicycling, fishing, golf, live theater, parks, water sports and historic tours nearby.

Publicity: *Philadelphia Inquirer.*

Rhythm of The Sea

1123 Beach Dr
Cape May, NJ 08204-2628
(609)884-7788
E-mail: rhythm@algorithms.com
Web: www.rhythmofthesea.com

Circa 1915. The apt name of this oceanfront inn describes the soothing sounds of the sea that lull many a happy guest into a restful night's sleep. Watching sunsets, strolling the beach, bird watching and whale watching are popular activities. Many of the features of a Craftsman home are incorporated in this seaside inn, such as light-filled spacious rooms, adjoining dining and living areas and gleaming natural wood floors. Mission oak furnishings compliment the inn's architecture. For guests seeking an especially private stay, ask for the three-room suite and arrange for a private dinner prepared by the innkeeper Wolfgang Wendt, a European trained chef. Full breakfasts are provided each morning. Guests are given complimentary beach towels and chairs. There is free parking and complimentary use of bicycles.

Innkeeper(s): Robyn & Wolfgang Wendt. $198-365. 7 rooms with PB, 2 with FP and 1 suite. Breakfast and snacks/refreshments included in rates. Types of meals: Full bkfst and dinner. Beds: Q. Reading lamp and clock radio in room. Air conditioning. VCR, bicycles, telephone and fireplace on premises. Small meetings and family reunions hosted. Amusement parks, antiquing, fishing, live theater, shopping and water sports nearby.
Publicity: *Atlantic City Press, New Jersey Monthly and POV.*

"Your home is lovely, the atmosphere is soothing."

Saltwood House

28 Jackson St
Cape May, NJ 08204-1465
(609)884-6754 (800)830-8232

Circa 1906. The peach-colored awnings and the Colonial Revival architecture of Saltwood House welcome guests to a Victorian experience in a setting of hand-carved antique oak furniture, Tiffany-style lamps and a collection of Victorian silver plate serving pieces. A favorite room is the Saratoga with a bay window view overlooking the street, a carved gargoyle oak bedstead, chrysanthemum wallpaper and a Larkin desk. Located one-half block from the beach and in the middle of Cape May's oldest street with gas lamps, sycamore trees and horse-drawn carriages, there are restaurants, shops and the walking mall on Washington Street to enjoy. Egg casseroles, bacon and fresh fruit are often served at breakfast.

Innkeeper(s): Don Schweikert. $80-310. 4 rooms with PB and 2 suites. Breakfast and afternoon tea included in rates. Types of meals: Full bkfst. Beds: KQ. Cable TV, VCR, reading lamp, ceiling fan, clock radio and desk in room. Air conditioning. Fax, copier, parlor games, telephone, fireplace and parking on premises. Amusement parks, antiquing, fishing, golf, live theater, parks, shopping, tennis and water sports nearby.
Publicity: *Newark Star-Ledger, Philadelphia's Channel 6 and QVC & PBS.*

"We're back. Every stay gets better and better. Thanks so much for your wonderful hospitality. See you again next year."

Summer Cottage Inn

613 Columbia Ave
Cape May, NJ 08204-2305
(609)884-4948
E-mail: summercottageinn@yahoo.com
Web: www.summercottageinn.com

Circa 1867. A cupola tops this Italianate-style inn located on a quiet tree-lined street in the historic district. It's close to the beach (one block) and the Victorian Mall. Period Victorian pieces are featured in the parlor and the veranda is filled with plants and rockers. There's a fireplace in the sitting room and a Baby Grand piano in the parlor.

Innkeeper(s): Linda & Skip Loughlin. $105-235. 9 rooms with PB. Breakfast and afternoon tea included in rates. Types of meals: Full bkfst. Beds: Q. Reading lamp, ceiling fan and clock radio in room. Air conditioning. Telephone and fireplace on premises. Antiquing, beach, fishing, live theater, shopping and water sports nearby.
Publicity: *Star Ledger and Philadelphia Inquirer.*

"Comfortable. Home away from home."

Velia's Seaside Inn

16 Jackson Street
Cape May, NJ 08204
(609)884-7004 Fax:(609)884-7884
E-mail: Kmendolia@comcast.net
Web: www.veliasinn.com

Circa 1890. The Jersey Shore is only 75 steps from the inviting wicker-filled front porch of this Italianate-style Victorian home, the fifth of the historic Seven Sisters on Atlantic Terrace. Off-street parking, beach chairs, towels and umbrellas are available. Cheery guest suites feature ocean views, a private sitting area, quilted King-size beds, in-room thermostat controls, microwave and refrigerator. Enjoy a home-cooked breakfast in the parlor. Bask in the sun and refreshing sea breeze while in the garden, or relax in the living room. Ask about specials and local seasonal events.

Innkeeper(s): Joy Phelps, Kathy Mendolia, John Mendolia. $95-269. 4 suites. Breakfast and afternoon tea included in rates. Types of meals: Full gourmet bkfst, veg bkfst, early coffee/tea, snacks/refreshments and room service. Beds: KQ. Cable TV, VCR, reading lamp, refrigerator, ceiling fan, telephone, coffeemaker, private parking, all beach amenities such as beach towels, chairs and umbrellas provided in room. Central air. Fax, copier, swimming, parlor games and fireplace on premises. Small meetings and family reunions hosted. Amusement parks, antiquing, art galleries, beach, bicycling, canoeing/kayaking, fishing, golf, hiking, live theater, museums, parks, shopping, tennis, water sports, wineries, Victorian shopping mall, protected bird sanctuary and fine dining restaurants nearby.

Windward House

24 Jackson St
Cape May, NJ 08204-1465
(609)884-3368 Fax:(609)884-1575
Web: www.windwardhouseinn.com

Circa 1905. Enter a tradition of hospitality and comfort at this gracious Edwardian seaside inn and feel welcomed by hosts Sandy, Owen and Vicki Miller. Museum-quality antiques, chestnut and oak woodwork, beveled and stained glass are complemented by collections of china and glass displays, bisque fig-

urines and period artwork. Relax on the wicker-filled wraparound front porch or the third-floor sun deck. Romance is easily recaptured in one of the elegantly furnished and tastefully decorated Victorian guest bedrooms or spacious suites. Generous amenities include mini refrigerators, TV/VCRs, ceiling fans, air conditioning and hair dryers. Walk to the beach, only half a block down the street, or stroll to nearby shops and restaurants.

Innkeeper(s): Owen & Sandy Miller. $100-205. 8 rooms with PB and 2 suites. Breakfast and afternoon tea included in rates. Types of meals: Full gourmet bkfst and early coffee/tea. Beds: KQ. TV, VCR, reading lamp, refrigerator, ceiling fan, clock radio, hair dryer and refrigerator in room. Air conditioning. Fax, library, parlor games, telephone and fireplace on premises. Small meetings and family reunions hosted. Antiquing, fishing, golf, live theater, parks, shopping, tennis, water sports and ocean beaches nearby.

Publicity: *New Jersey Monthly, Delaware Today, Mid-Atlantic Country, Country Inns, Victorian Homes, Innsider, Mainline Magazine and Princeton Packet.*

"The loveliest and most authentically decorated of all the houses we visited."

Woodleigh House

808 Washington St
Cape May, NJ 08204-1652
(609)884-7123 (800)399-7123
Web: www.bbgetaways.com/woodleighhouse

Circa 1866. Rocking chairs line the veranda of this 1866 Victorian. Its natural cedar siding is highlighted with burgundy and creme trim. Period antiques are featured. The dining room, for instance, boasts a carved antique sideboard from Brussels,

an Oriental carpet and an original chandelier. Guest rooms offer romantic, seven-foot-high, carved antique headboards and marble-top dressers. Popular breakfast dishes are Banana Blinni (a French toast made from banana bread) and breakfast casseroles featuring herbs from the garden. Afternoon tea is hot or cold depending upon the season and may feature Heath-nut crunch cookies or other homemade goodies. The innkeepers have developed a secret garden complete with pond and a wisteria arbor to add to the inn's inviting outdoor spaces.

Innkeeper(s): Joe & Joanne Tornambe. $110-185. 5 rooms with PB and 1 suite. Breakfast and afternoon tea included in rates. Types of meals: Full bkfst. Beds: KQ. TV in room. Air conditioning. Bike rack, off-street parking and beautiful gardens on premises. Antiquing, beach, fishing, live theater, shopping, tennis and water sports nearby.

"Clean and comfortable, delicious breakfast, charming hosts."

Flemington   E3

Main Street Manor B&B

194 Main St
Flemington, NJ 08822-1626
(908)782-4928

Circa 1901. Reflecting a gracious air, this elegantly restored Queen Anne Victorian adorns the historic district. Sip lemonade on the front porch, converse by the fire in the formal front parlor, or watch satellite TV in the quaint side parlor. Sip sherry while perusing the local restaurant menus. Through the grand foyer, past the crystal chandelier and up the sweeping staircase, romantic guest bedrooms feature an antique Empire mahogany sleigh and four-poster rice bed, clawfoot tub, and a balcony overlooking the wooded and landscaped grounds. Breakfast is served in the paneled dining room, with specialty dishes added on the weekends. Take a walking tour of the other 18th and 19th century buildings in the neighborhood.

Innkeeper(s): Margaret & Henry Ferreira. $110-170. 5 rooms with PB. Beds: Q. Modem hook-up, cable TV, VCR, reading lamp, refrigerator, ceiling fan, snack bar, clock radio, telephone, coffeemaker and desk in room. Central air. Fax and parlor games on premises. Small meetings, family reunions and seminars hosted.

Haddonfield   G3

Haddonfield Inn

44 West End Ave
Haddonfield, NJ 08033-2616
(856)428-2195 (800)269-0014 Fax:(856)354-1273
E-mail: innkeeper@haddonfieldinn.com
Web: www.haddonfieldinn.com

Circa 1865. This three-story Victorian house, complete with gabled roofs, a turret and veranda, is in the National Trust. Its location is historic Haddonfield, said by Philadelphia Magazine to be the most picturesque village in the Delaware Valley. Handsome heritage homes, fine museums, symphony orchestras, theater and more than 200 shops and restaurants are nearby. Parlors are furnished with antiques and chandeliers, and the guest rooms offer whirlpools and fireplaces, each in the theme of a European country or other culture. Upon arrival, guests are offered snacks and beverages. In the morning, a gourmet breakfast is served before a flickering fireplace in the dining room or on the wraparound veranda overlooking the inn's lawns. For guest convenience, there is an elevator, and the innkeeper provides concierge service. The inn is popular for small meetings and special events. Walk to the train to visit Philadelphia (17 minutes away) and connect to stadiums, the airport and Amtrak.

Innkeeper(s): Nancy & Fred Chorpita. $140-215. 8 rooms with PB and 1 suite. Breakfast and snacks/refreshments included in rates. Types of meals: Full gourmet bkfst. Beds: KQ. Modem hook-up, cable TV, telephone, hot tub/spa and voice mail in room. Central air. Spa, swimming, tennis, fireplace, Internet access and golf on premises. Limited handicap access. Weddings, small meetings and family reunions hosted. Amusement parks, golf, museums, parks, sporting events, tennis, swimming and health clubs nearby.

Lambertville   E3

Chimney Hill Farm Estate & The Ol' Barn Inn

207 Goat Hill Rd
Lambertville, NJ 08530
(609)397-1516 (800)211-4667 Fax:(609)397-9353
E-mail: info@chimneyhillinn.com
Web: www.chimneyhillinn.com

Circa 1820. Chimney Hill, in the hills above the riverside town of Lambertville, is a grand display of stonework, designed with both Federal and Greek Revival-style architecture. The inn's sunroom is particularly appealing, with its stone walls, fire-

places and French windows looking out to eight acres of gardens and fields. All eight of the guest rooms in the estate farmhouse

include fireplaces, and some have canopied beds. The Ol' Barn has four suites with fireplaces, Jacuzzis, steam rooms, guest pantries, spiral staircases and loft bedrooms. The innkeepers offer adventure, romance and special interest packages for their guests, and the inn is also popular for corporate retreats. There are plenty of seasonal activities nearby, from kayaking to skiing. New Hope is the neighboring town and offers many charming restaurants and shops, as well.

Innkeeper(s): Terry & Richard Anderson. $130-350. 12 rooms, 8 with PB, 10 with FP, 4 suites and 2 conference rooms. Breakfast and snacks/refreshments included in rates. Types of meals: Country bkfst and early coffee/tea. Beds: KQD. Modem hook-up, data port, cable TV, reading lamp, refrigerator, ceiling fan, snack bar, clock radio, telephone, coffeemaker, fireplace and Jacuzzi in room. Air conditioning. Fax, copier, parlor games and gift shop on premises. Weddings, small meetings and seminars hosted. Antiquing, art galleries, bicycling, canoeing/kayaking, fishing, golf, hiking, horseback riding, live theater, museums, parks, shopping, tennis and wineries nearby.
Publicity: *Country Inns (Cover), Colonial Homes Magazine, Country Roads Magazine, NY Times, NJ Magazine, and New Jersey Network.*

"We would be hard pressed to find a more perfect setting to begin our married life together."

York Street House

42 York St
Lambertville, NJ 08530-2024
(609)397-3007 (888)398-3199 Fax:(609)397-3299
E-mail: innkeeper@yorkstreethouse.com
Web: www.yorkstreethouse.com

Circa 1909. Built by early industrialist George Massey as a 25th wedding anniversary present for his wife, the gracious manor house is situated on almost an acre in the heart of the historic district. Common rooms are warmed by Mercer Tile fireplaces and an original Waterford Crystal chandelier. A winding three-story staircase leads to well-appointed guest bedrooms with period furnishings. Looking out on the lawn and sitting porch, breakfast is served in the dining room, showcasing built-in leaded-glass china and large oak servers. Art galleries, antique shops and restaurants are nearby. Enjoy mule-drawn barges and carriage rides. New Hope, Penn. is a short walk across the Delaware River Bridge, with many quaint shops.

Innkeeper(s): Laurie and Mark Weinstein. $100-215. 6 rooms with PB. Breakfast included in rates. Types of meals: Full gourmet bkfst, early coffee/tea and picnic lunch. Beds: KQ. Cable TV, reading lamp, ceiling fan, clock radio, desk, and fireplace and Jacuzzi in room. Air conditioning. VCR, fax, parlor games and telephone on premises. Small meetings hosted. Antiquing, fishing, live theater, parks and shopping nearby.

Manasquan   F6

Nathaniel Morris Inn

117 Marcellus Ave
Manasquan, NJ 08736
(732)223-7826

Circa 1882. The second-story porch is the perfect place to catch cool summer breezes at this restored Victorian manor, which was built by one of Manasquan's founding fathers. During the 1930s and throughout World War II, the inn served as a restaurant, tea room and lodging, popular with the many soldiers who visited the Jersey Shore. The interior is decorated in period style with antiques and floral comforters. Business guests will appreciate the use of phone, computer, Internet and modem services. Breakfasts are served buffet style in the formal dining room.

Innkeeper(s): Paul & Gail McFadden. $105-200. 6 rooms with PB, 2 suites and 1 conference room. Breakfast included in rates. Types of meals: Full gourmet bkfst and early coffee/tea. Beds: Q. Cable TV, reading lamp, refrigerator, ceiling fan and clock radio in room. Air conditioning. VCR, fax, copier, bicycles, library, parlor games and telephone on premises. Weddings, small meetings, family reunions and seminars hosted. Amusement parks, antiquing, art galleries, beach, bicycling, canoeing/kayaking, fishing, golf, hiking, horseback riding, live theater, museums, parks, shopping, sporting events, tennis, water sports and wineries nearby.
Publicity: *Coast Star, Bergen Record and Asbury Park Press.*

Mays Landing   I4

Abbott House

6056 Main St
Mays Landing, NJ 08330-1852
(609)625-4400
E-mail: theabbotthouse@email.msn.com
Web: www.bbianj.com/abbott

Circa 1865. Guests at this Victorian-style mansion can relax on the bluff overlooking the Great Egg Harbor River, read on the second-floor veranda with its intricate fretwork or take afternoon tea in the belvedere (cupola) with spectacular views of historic Mays Landing. The inn is within walking distance to Lake Lenape and its various summer attractions. Each room is individually decorated with antiques, wicker, handmade quilts and other special touches. The Victorian Parlor is a place for games, reading and conversation. Refreshments can be enjoyed on one of the many porches and verandas.

Innkeeper(s): Linda Maslanko. $89-129. 3 rooms and 1 suite. Breakfast included in rates. Types of meals: Full bkfst. Clock radio and turn-down service in room. Air conditioning. Telephone and fireplace on premises. Small meetings and family reunions hosted. Antiquing and shopping nearby.

North Wildwood   K4

Candlelight Inn

2310 Central Ave
North Wildwood, NJ 08260-5944
(609)522-6200 (800)992-2632 Fax:(609)522-6125
E-mail: info@candlelight-inn.com
Web: www.candlelight-inn.com

Circa 1905. Candlelight Inn offers ten guest rooms in a restored Queen Anne Victorian. The home is decorated with an assortment of period pieces. Among its antiques are a Victorian sofa dating to 1855 and an 1890 Eastlake piano. Breakfasts begin with a fresh fruit course, followed by fresh breads and a daily entrée, such as waffles, pancakes or a specialty egg dish. Candlelight Inn is about eight miles from the historic towns of Cape May and Cold Spring Village.

Innkeeper(s): Bill & Nancy Moncrief. $125-250. 10 rooms with PB, 2 with FP and 3 suites. Breakfast and afternoon tea included in rates. Types of meals: Full bkfst, early coffee/tea and snacks/refreshments. Beds: KQT. Cable TV, reading lamp, refrigerator, ceiling fan, clock radio, coffeemaker, desk, fireplace and four with double whirlpool tubs in room. Central air. Fax, copier, telephone, fireplace and hot tub on premises. Weddings, small meetings, family reunions and seminars hosted. Amusement parks, antiquing, art galleries, beach, bicycling, fishing, golf, live theater, museums, parks, shopping, tennis and water sports nearby.
Publicity: *Select Registry.*

Summer Nites "50's Theme B&B"

2110 Atlantic Ave.
North Wildwood, NJ 08260
(609)846-1955 (866)762-1950 Fax:(609)729-1045
E-mail: info@summernites.com
Web: www.summernites.com

Circa 1913. The 1950s décor and furnishings have completely transformed this 1913 Victorian home to reflect the era of early Rock and Roll. The quiet residential neighborhood at the Jersey Shore is within a mile of the surrounding nightlife. Bikes are available for a ride on the boardwalk. Play a game of pool or vintage pinball. Guest bedrooms feature original memorabilia related to each themed namesake. Stay in the two-room Elvis

Suite or spacious Marilyn Room with whirlpool tubs, hand-painted murals and VCR/DVD/CD players. Dine in a box car diner booth, complete with neon lights and a Seeburg jukebox, for a fantastic breakfast. A hot tub and sun deck add to the fun and relaxing atmosphere. Off-street parking is provided.

Innkeeper(s): Sheila & Rick Brown. $95-275. 5 rooms, 4 with PB and 1 suite. Breakfast and snacks/refreshments included in rates. Types of meals: Full bkfst, veg bkfst and early coffee/tea. Beds: KQ. Cable TV, VCR, reading lamp, CD player, ceiling fan, clock radio, hot tub/spa, comfortable chair, suite has mini refrigerator, wet bar, gold sofa, love seat and ottoman in room. Central air. Fax, spa, bicycles, parlor games, telephone and fireplace on premises. Amusement parks, antiquing, art galleries, beach, bicycling, canoeing/kayaking, fishing, golf, live theater, museums, parks, shopping, tennis and water sports nearby.

Ocean City   J4

Barnagate B&B

637 Wesley Ave
Ocean City, NJ 08226-3855
(609)391-9366 Fax:(609)399-5048

Circa 1896. Three-and-a-half blocks from the ocean, the Barnagate B&B offers Victorian-style guest rooms with paddle fans and country quilts. The top floor of the four-story inn features a private sitting room. Guests enjoy fresh fruit and homemade breads at breakfast.

Innkeeper(s): Lois & Frank Barna. $85-160. 5 rooms, 1 with PB and 1 suite. Breakfast included in rates. Types of meals: Cont plus and early coffee/tea. Beds: QDT. Reading lamp and ceiling fan in room. Air conditioning. TV, VCR, fax, library and parlor games on premises. Small meetings and family reunions hosted. Amusement parks, antiquing, fishing, golf, live theater, parks, shopping, tennis and water sports nearby.
Publicity: *The Star-Ledger, The Intelligencer-Record and The Press of Atlantic City.*

New Brighton Inn

519 5th St
Ocean City, NJ 08226-3940
(609)399-2829 (866)399-2829 Fax:(609)398-7786

Circa 1896. This home is a stunning example of Queen Anne architecture, and is one of the town's outstanding architectural landmarks, featuring a distinctive roofline and a wraparound open porch trimmed with royal blue awnings. The interiors offer all the cozy nooks fanciful historic Victorians are known for and are appointed with elegant and inviting furnishings. Guest rooms are decorated with antiques.

Historic Interest: One of the first properties in Ocean City.
Innkeeper(s): Sally & Roger Woodhull. $115-185. 6 rooms with PB. Breakfast, afternoon tea and snacks/refreshments included in rates. Types of meals: Full bkfst and early coffee/tea. Beds: Q. Cable TV, VCR, reading lamp, refrigerator, ceiling fan, clock radio and one with a two-person Jacuzzi in room. Air conditioning. Bicycles and fireplace on premises. Small meetings hosted. Amusement parks, art galleries, beach, bicycling, fishing, golf, parks, shopping, tennis, water sports, boardwalk and Atlantic City casinos nearby.
Publicity: *Philadelphia Inquirer and The Press of Atlantic City.*

Northwood Inn B&B

401 Wesley Ave
Ocean City, NJ 08226-3961
(609)399-6071 Fax:(609)398-5553
E-mail: info@northwoodinn.com
Web: www.northwoodinn.com

Circa 1894. This gracious three-story Queen Anne Victorian with Colonial Victorian touches has been restored by the innkeeper, who is a wooden boat builder and custom-home builder. There are gleaming plank floors, a sweeping staircase, a billiard room and a stocked library. The two-room Tower Suite

in the turret is a favorite, offering a luxurious bath with a double Jacuzzi tub and over-sized shower. The Magnolia Room is another popular choice with its taupe-colored walls, lace curtains and double Jacuzzi. There is a

rooftop, four-person spa where guests can relax and enjoy the sunset. The inn is within walking distance of the beach, boardwalk, shops and restaurants. The innkeepers offer bicycles and beach tags to their guests. Availability may be checked on line.

Historic Interest: Cape May (30 miles).
Innkeeper(s): Marj & John Loeper. $85-235. 8 rooms with PB and 2 suites. Types of meals: Full bkfst. Beds: KQT. TV, VCR, reading lamp, clock radio and suites with Jacuzzi in room. Air conditioning. Fax, library, parlor games, telephone, massage therapist and rooftop spa on premises. Weddings and small meetings hosted. Amusement parks, antiquing, fishing, live theater, parks, shopping, water sports and casino/Atlantic City nearby.
Publicity: *Philadelphia Magazine and NJN Discover New Jersey.*

"In all our years of staying at B&Bs - still our favorite. Comfortable, relaxing, wonderful breakfasts, and hosts who couldn't be more welcoming. In season, off season, or whenever a break is needed, we head for the Northwood to renew!"

Scarborough Inn

720 Ocean Ave
Ocean City, NJ 08226-3787
(609)399-1558 (800)258-1558 Fax:(609)399-4472
E-mail: info@scarboroughinn.com
Web: www.scarboroughinn.com

Circa 1895. Savor the vintage charm of this 19th century B&B that artfully offers modern conveniences. Guest bedrooms are tastefully decorated, featuring many amenities to make each stay a pampered one, including signature toiletries and the morning newspaper. Indulge in a tempting full breakfast and afternoon refreshments. The inn is located in the heart of the island community's historic district, featuring off-street parking. The boardwalk, beach, recreation park, dining and shopping are only 1.5 blocks away.

Historic Interest: Wheaten Village (1 hour), Cold Spring Village (40 minutes), Leemings Run Gardens (30 minutes), Atlantic City (20 minutes), Cape May (30 minutes).
Innkeeper(s): Gus & Carol Bruno. $80-220. 24 rooms, 18 with PB and 5 suites. Breakfast included in rates. Types of meals: Full gourmet bkfst, early coffee/tea and afternoon tea. Beds: KQDT. Modem hook-up, cable TV, reading lamp, clock radio, telephone, desk, suites have alarm clocks, morning newspaper, hair dryers and VCR in room. Air conditioning. VCR, fax, library, parlor games, laundry facility, parking and beach passes on premises. Small meetings and family reunions hosted. Amusement parks, antiquing, beach, fishing, golf, live theater, parks, shopping, sporting events, water sports, birding, casinos and cultural and historical sites nearby.

Serendipity B&B

712 E 9th St
Ocean City, NJ 08226-3554
(609)399-1554 (800)842-8544 Fax:(609)399-1527
E-mail: info@serendipitynj.com
Web: www.serendipitynj.com

Circa 1912. The beach and the boardwalk are less than half a block from this renovated Dutch Colonial bed & breakfast for a perfect weekend escape or vacation. Stay in a guest bedroom decorated in pastels and furnished with wicker. Healthy full breakfasts are served in the dining room or, in the summer, on a vine-shaded veranda. Choose from six entrees daily, including vegetarian and high protein selections. Relax on the garden veranda or soak in the spa/hot tub.

Innkeeper(s): Clara & Bill Plowfield. $83-195. 6 rooms, 4 with PB. Breakfast and snacks/refreshments included in rates. Types of meals: Full bkfst. Beds: KQDT. Cable TV, VCR, reading lamp, ceiling fan, bathrobes and bottled water in room. Air conditioning. Parlor games, telephone, fireplace, dressing rooms with showers and beach towels, beach chairs, guest refrigerator, microwave, video library and outdoor hot tub on premises. Amusement parks, antiquing, fishing, live theater, parks, shopping, water sports and ocean beach and boardwalk nearby.
Publicity: *Philadelphia Inquirer Magazine* and *"Best Weekend Escape"* Awarded by Arrington's Bed & Breakfast Journal 2004 Book of Lists.

"Serendipity is such a gift. For me it's a little like being adopted during vacation time by a caring sister and brother. Your home is a home away from home. You make it so."

Ocean Grove   F6

The Manchester Inn B&B and Secret Garden Restaurant

25 Ocean Pathway
Ocean Grove, NJ 07756-1645
(732)775-0616
E-mail: thenjinn@aol.com
Web: www.themanchesterinn.com

Circa 1875. Enjoy cool ocean breezes while you lounge on the front porch of this quaint Victorian, which is featured in the town's annual Victorian Holiday House Tour each December. The full-service restaurant has bright, flowery decor and offers plenty of choices for breakfast, lunch and dinner. Ocean Grove is an ideal spot to bask in the Victorian tradition. The beach is only one block and the inn looks out onto Ocean Parkway, one of Ocean Grove's finest streets. The town itself offers many festivals throughout the year, plus a variety of interesting shops to explore.
Historic Interest: The Great Auditorium is the pride of Ocean Grove. Built in 1894, it seats more than 6,000 people, and its speakers and visitors have included presidents Grant, Garfield, McKinley, Teddy Roosevelt, Taft, Wilson and Nixon. Surrounding the auditorium is the Tent Community, where descendants of the founding families spend their summers.
Innkeeper(s): Margaret & Clark Cate. $75-135. 35 rooms, 25 with PB and 1 conference room. Breakfast included in rates. Types of meals: Cont and dinner. Restaurant on premises. Beds: KQDT. Antiquing, fishing and water sports nearby.

Pemberton   G4

Isaac Hilliard House Bed, Breakfast...and Beyond

31 Hanover St
Pemberton, NJ 08068
(609)894-0756 (800)371-0756

Circa 1750. This 250-year-old Federal-era house is situated on the edge of the scenic Pine Barrens. The inn offers year-round, lighted, off-street parking. An entertainment center is provided in the first-floor parlor. Spacious accommodations include guest bedrooms and the Isaac Hilliard Suite, featuring a remote-controlled fireplace, four-poster canopy bed, dressing room, mini-fridge, cable TV/VCR with video selection

386

and garden tub. Enjoy a freshly prepared breakfast in the well-appointed dining room or quaint side porch. Swim in the private in-ground pool. Take a short walk to rent canoes on the Rancocas River, hike, golf or visit an amusement park nearby.
Historic Interest: Trenton, N.J., battlefield and buildings (25 minutes), Washington Crossing State Park (40 minutes), Ye Olde Lock Up Building (5-minute walk).
Innkeeper(s): Phyllis Davis & Gene R. O'Brien. $85-165. 3 rooms with PB and 1 suite. Breakfast included in rates. Types of meals: Full and veg bkfst. Beds: Q. Refrigerator, ceiling fan, turn-down service, hair dryer and suite has remote-controlled gas fireplace in room. Air conditioning. Swimming and refrigerator on premises. Weddings and small meetings hosted. Amusement parks, antiquing, fishing, live theater, parks, water sports and newly dedicated Pemberton Rail Trail with visitor center nearby.
Publicity: *New Jersey Travel Guide, New Jersey Monthly* and *Burlington County Times.*

"Every little detail was made so kind and warm. For even a short time, we both felt as if we traveled abroad. Your home is kept gorgeous and so tasteful."

Plainfield   D5

Pillars of Plainfield B&B

922 Central Ave
Plainfield, NJ 07060
(908)753-0922 (888)PIL-LARS
E-mail: info@pillars2.com
Web: www.pillars2.com

Circa 1870. Victorian and Georgian influences are mingled in the design of this grand historic mansion, which boasts majestic columns and a wraparound porch. An acre of well-manicured grounds and gardens surrounds the home, which is located in Plainfield's Van Wyck Historic District. Guest rooms and suites are appointed with traditional furnishings, and each room has its own special decor. The romantic Van Wyck Brooks Suite includes a wood-burning fireplace and a canopy bed topped with a down quilt. A wicker table and chairs are tucked into the bay window alcove of the Clementine Yates room. Another spacious room includes a full kitchen. Business travelers will appreciate the private in-room phones with voice mail and the separate data ports. Swedish home cooking highlights the morning meal, which is accompanied by freshly ground coffee. Plainfield, the first inland settlement in New Jersey, offers many historic attractions, including the Drake House Museum.
Innkeeper(s): Chuck & Tom Hale. $114-250. 7 rooms with PB, 2 with FP. Breakfast and snacks/refreshments included in rates. Types of meals: Full bkfst, veg bkfst and early coffee/tea. Beds: QT. Modem hook-up, data port, cable TV, VCR, reading lamp, ceiling fan, clock radio, telephone, coffeemaker, turn-down service, desk and voice mail in room. Air conditioning. Fax, copier, library, parlor games, fireplace and laundry facility on premises. Weddings, small meetings, family reunions and seminars hosted. Amusement parks, antiquing, art galleries, beach, golf, hiking, live theater, museums, parks, shopping, sporting events and tennis nearby.

Sea Girt   F6

Beacon House

100 & 104 Beacon Blvd
Sea Girt, NJ 08750-1609
(732)449-5835 Fax:(732)282-0974
E-mail: beaconhouse@aol.com
Web: www.beaconhouseinn.com

Circa 1879. Built in classic Victorian style, this recently renovated inn has been a relaxing getaway for more than a century. Splendidly furnished parlors with fireplaces, crystal chandeliers

and oak floors are pleasurable places to while away time. The two main houses, a cottage and a carriage house offer the best in casual elegance. Encounter wicker, brass and chintz in the sunny guest bedrooms. Some boast ocean or lake views, fireplaces and Jacuzzi tubs. Morning is a celebration when a memorable gourmet breakfast is served in the candle-lit dining room. Enjoy the colorful landscape from a rocker on one of the wraparound porches, lounge by the swimming pool, or take a bike ride to the popular boardwalk in this quaint seaside community.
Innkeeper(s): Candy Kadimik. $135-375. 17 rooms, 14 with PB, 6 with FP, 2 suites and 2 cottages. Breakfast and snacks/refreshments included in rates. Types of meals: Full gourmet bkfst, veg bkfst and early coffee/tea. Beds: QDT. Cable TV, reading lamp, ceiling fan, clock radio and fireplace in room. Central air. VCR, fax, copier, swimming, bicycles, library, parlor games, telephone, fireplace and gift shop on premises. Weddings, small meetings, family reunions and seminars hosted. Amusement parks, antiquing, art galleries, beach, bicycling, canoeing/kayaking, fishing, golf, hiking, live theater, museums, parks, shopping, tennis and water sports nearby.
Publicity: The Coast Star Newspaper.

Spring Lake   F6

Ashling Cottage Bed and Breakfast

106 Sussex Ave
Spring Lake, NJ 07762-1248
(732)449-3553 (888)274-5464
E-mail: beautifuldream@compuserve.com
Web: www.ashlingcottage.com

Circa 1877. Well-recommended and newly decorated, this historic bed & breakfast is half a block away from a "wedding-perfect" lake and one block from the ocean. After a peaceful night's rest, savor a delicious homemade breakfast that is pleasantly served on the glass-and-screen-enclosed atrium porch overlooking the water. Visit the quaint shopping village, just a short 2.5-block walk.

Relax on wicker rockers, chairs and loveseats on the tranquil open-air porch comfortably shaded by sycamore trees.
Historic Interest: Allaire State Park (5 miles).
Innkeeper(s): Joanie & Bill Mahon. $99-275. 11 rooms, 9 with PB. Breakfast included in rates. Types of meals: Full bkfst and early coffee/tea. Beds: Q. Reading lamp, ceiling fan, clock radio, desk and clock in room. Air conditioning. VCR, bicycles, library, parlor games, telephone, fireplace, beach chairs, beach passes, beach umbrellas and beach towels on premises. Weddings, small meetings, family reunions and seminars hosted. Amusement parks, antiquing, beach, fishing, live theater, parks, shopping, sporting events, water sports, race tracks, boardwalk, complimentary beverages and guest privileges to the best health & fitness center in New Jersey nearby.
Publicity: New York Times, New Jersey Monthly, Town & Country, Country Living, New York, Harrods of London and Travel & Leisure.

Chateau

500 Warren Ave
Spring Lake, NJ 07762-1293
(732)974-2000 Fax:(732)974-0007
E-mail: info@chateauinn.com
Web: www.chateauinn.com

Circa 1888. In addition to the lake, this village has a two-mile boardwalk along the ocean. The Chateau is a Victorian-era inn with many rooms providing scenic vistas of the park, lake and gazebo. Borders of flowers surround the white-pillared verandas, and there are brick patios, sun-filled balconies and private porches. The Spring Lake Trolley departs every half hour from the front door.

Innkeeper(s): Scott Smith. $49-132. 40 rooms with PB, 4 with FP and 1 conference room. Types of meals: Cont. Beds: KQDT. TV, fax, copier and telephone on premises. Limited handicap access.
Publicity: Great Water Escapes.

"One of the top five inns in New Jersey." — Mobil Travel Guide

Hollycroft Bed & Breakfast Inn

PO Box 448
Spring Lake, NJ 07762
(732)681-2254 (800)679-2254 Fax:(732)280-8145
E-mail: info@hollycroft.com
Web: www.hollycroft.com

Circa 1908. Overlooking Lake Como and only five minutes to sandy ocean beaches, this 1908 Arts & Crafts lodge with cedar log beams and massive stone fireplaces imparts a refined country elegance. Secluded in a rustic wooded setting, Hollycroft is the perfect romantic hideaway. The huge living room has space for a variety of relaxing activities. Air-conditioned guest bedrooms and suites, several with fireplaces, are furnished and decorated in a variety of inviting styles. Sleep on an antique iron and brass, handmade log, mahogany four-poster or pine canopy bed. Luxurious Lords of the Manor Suite is a stunning fantasy of opposites and the cheerful Windsor Suite reflects an English country cottage. Hunger is unheard of after a bountiful buffet that even entices those who never eat breakfast.
Innkeeper(s): Mark & Linda Fessler. $125-325. 7 rooms with PB, 4 with FP and 2 suites. Breakfast included in rates. Types of meals: Full gourmet bkfst, veg bkfst and early coffee/tea. Beds: D. Cable TV, VCR, reading lamp, CD player, refrigerator, ceiling fan, clock radio, coffeemaker and fireplace in room. Air conditioning. TV, fax, bicycles, library, parlor games, telephone, fireplace and gift shop on premises. Amusement parks, antiquing, art galleries, beach, bicycling, canoeing/kayaking, fishing, golf, horseback riding, live theater, museums, parks and water sports nearby.
Publicity: New York Magazine, Country Inns Magazine and New Jersey Monthly Magazine.

La Maison Inn

404 Jersey Ave
Spring Lake, NJ 07762-1437
(732)449-0969 (800)276-2088 Fax:(732)449-4860
E-mail: lamaisonnj@aol.com
Web: www.lamaisoninn.com

Circa 1870. A French Victorian with a wide wraparound veranda, this historic inn is located four blocks from the ocean. The French influence is repeated in romantic furnishings such as fluffy duvets, sleigh beds and Louis Philippe pieces. At breakfast, freshly squeezed juice, espresso or cappuccino complements gourmet entrees and freshly baked goods. A cottage, complete with a kitchen, fireplace, queen bed and clawfooted soaking tub is popular for a secluded getaway.
Innkeeper(s): Julianne Corrigan. $125-325. 8 rooms with PB, 2 suites and 1 cottage. Breakfast included in rates. Types of meals: Full gourmet bkfst and early coffee/tea. Beds: QT. Cable TV and telephone in room. Air conditioning. Fax, bicycles, health club passes, nightly hors d'oeuvres, beach passes, beach chairs and outside Teak shower on premises. Weddings, small meetings, family reunions and seminars hosted. Antiquing, fishing, live theater, parks, shopping and water sports nearby.
Publicity: Country Inns, Innspots & Special Places, Gourmet Magazine, New Jersey Countryside, The Star Ledger and News 12-New Jersey.

The Normandy Inn

21 Tuttle Ave
Spring Lake, NJ 07762-1533
(732)449-7172 (800)449-1888 Fax:(732)449-1070
E-mail: normandy@bellatlantic.net
Web: www.normandyinn.com

Circa 1888. In a picturesque seaside town, this historic Italianate Villa with Queen Anne details is just half a block from the ocean. Listed in the National Register, the Colonial Revival and Neoclassicism interior reflect its traditionally elegant Victorian heritage. Relax in spacious double parlours or play the 1886 trumpet-legged grand piano. Fine antiques adorn air-conditioned guest bedrooms. Some rooms feature cozy fireplaces, canopy beds and Jacuzzis. Choose from a selection of hearty country breakfast entrees to savor in the dining room. The inn's exceptional service, romantic ambiance and central location make it the perfect all-season getaway.

Innkeeper(s): The Valori family. $135-396. 17 rooms with PB, 7 with FP, 2 suites and 1 conference room. Breakfast and afternoon tea included in rates. Types of meals: Full gourmet bkfst, early coffee/tea, picnic lunch and snacks/refreshments. Beds: KQDT. Modem hook-up, data port, cable TV, VCR, reading lamp, refrigerator, clock radio, telephone, coffeemaker, desk and Jacuzzi tubs and fireplace in room. Central air. Fax, copier, bicycles, library, parlor games, fireplace and gift shop on premises. Weddings, small meetings, family reunions and seminars hosted. Amusement parks, antiquing, art galleries, beach, bicycling, canoeing/kayaking, fishing, golf, hiking, horseback riding, live theater, museums, parks, shopping, sporting events, tennis and water sports nearby.

Publicity: *New York Times.*

"The cozy and delicious accommodations of your inn were beyond expectations."

Ocean House

102 Sussex Ave
Spring Lake, NJ 07762-1215
(732)449-9090 (888)449-9094 Fax:(732)449-9092
E-mail: oceanhouse07762@aol.com
Web: www.theoceanhouse.net

Circa 1876. For more than 100 years the Ocean House has welcomed guests. You can't miss it across from the boardwalk. Pale pink with sage green window shutters, a canopied veranda wraps around the outside. The main interior feature is a grand staircase moved from the 1876 Philadelphia Exposition by the home's first owner. Eleven-foot-high ceilings, plaster moldings and antiques continue the Victorian atmosphere. Breakfast, served in either the dining room that is decorated in floral fabrics or on the outside veranda, consists of fresh baked scones and blueberry muffins, French toast, eggs and fruit. The innkeepers can supply you with a bicycle for a fun afternoon exploring the boardwalk and town, or for a more relaxing time, take one of the inn's beach chairs out on the sand.

Innkeeper(s): Dennis and Nancy Kaloostian. $80-325. 35 rooms with PB, 8 suites and 1 conference room. Breakfast, afternoon tea and snacks/refreshments included in rates. Types of meals: Country bkfst and early coffee/tea. Beds: KQDT. Cable TV, reading lamp, ceiling fan, clock radio and telephone in room. Air conditioning. VCR, fax, copier, swimming, bicycles, tennis, library, parlor games, fireplace and laundry facility on premises. Weddings, small meetings, family reunions and seminars hosted. Amusement parks, antiquing, art galleries, beach, bicycling, canoeing/kayaking, fishing, golf, hiking, horseback riding, live theater, museums, parks, shopping, sporting events, tennis, water sports and wineries nearby.

Sea Crest By The Sea

19 Tuttle Ave
Spring Lake, NJ 07762-1533
(732)449-9031 (800)803-9031 Fax:(732)974-0403
E-mail: capt@seacrestbythesea.com
Web: www.seacrestbythesea.com

Circa 1885. You can hear the surf from most rooms in this Victorian mansion, located an hour from New York city or Philadelphia. Guests will be pampered with Egyptian cotton and Belgian-lace linens, queen-size feather beds, fresh flowers and classical music. Six rooms have Jacuzzis for two and there are eight with fireplaces. Tunes from a player piano announce afternoon tea at 4 p.m.—a good time  to make dinner reservations at one of the area's fine restaurants. In the morning family china, crystal and silver add to the ambiance of a full gourmet breakfast. Bicycles are available and the beach is a half block away.

Innkeeper(s): Barbara & Fred Vogel. $300-450. 8 rooms with PB, 8 with FP, 5 suites and 1 conference room. Breakfast and afternoon tea included in rates. Types of meals: Full gourmet bkfst. Beds: Q. Cable TV, VCR, reading lamp, CD player, refrigerator, ceiling fan, clock radio, telephone, hot tub/spa, Jacuzzi for two, fireplace, robes, hair dryers and slippers in room. Central air. Fax, copier, bicycles, parlor games, fireplace, gift shop, evening cordials, passes to premier health fitness club and beach gear on premises. Small meetings and seminars hosted. Amusement parks, antiquing, art galleries, beach, bicycling, canoeing/kayaking, fishing, golf, hiking, live theater, museums, parks, shopping, tennis, water sports and Atlantic Beach nearby.

Publicity: *New York Times, Gourmet, Victoria, Star Ledger and New York Magazine.*

"This romantic storybook atmosphere is delightful! A visual feast."

Spring Lake Inn

104 Salem Ave
Spring Lake, NJ 07762-1040
(732)449-2010 Fax:(732)449-4020
E-mail: springlakeinn@aol.com
Web: www.springlakeinn.com

Circa 1888. Only a block from the beach, this historic Victorian inn boasts an informal seaside atmosphere. Relax on the 80-foot, rocker-lined porch or fireside in the parlor. Well-decorated guest bedrooms and suites offer a variety of peaceful settings including the Turret, surrounded by four windows, and the Tower View suite with sleigh bed and ocean views. Enjoy a leisurely breakfast served in the spacious dining room featuring a 12-foot ceiling. Walk to the town center, with more than 60 shops to explore.

Historic Interest: This charming bed and breakfast, formerly the Spring Lake Hotel, was originally the Grand Central Stables of Spring Lake Beach. Moved twice since it was built in 1888.

Innkeeper(s): Barbara & Andy Seaman. $99-495. 16 rooms with PB, 8 with FP, 2 suites and 1 conference room. Breakfast and afternoon tea included in rates. Types of meals: Full gourmet bkfst and early coffee/tea. Beds: QD. Modem hook-up, cable TV, VCR, reading lamp, stereo, refrigerator, ceiling fan, snack bar, clock radio, desk, hot tub/spa, fireplace, beach chairs, beach badges and beach towels in room. Air conditioning. Fax, copier, library, parlor games, telephone and fireplace on premises. Small meetings, family reunions and seminars hosted. Amusement parks, antiquing, art galleries, beach, bicycling, canoeing/kayaking, fishing, golf, hiking, horseback riding, live theater, museums, parks, shopping, sporting events, tennis, water sports and wineries nearby.

Publicity: *Asbury Press and NJ 12.*

White Lilac Inn

414 Central Ave
Spring Lake, NJ 07762-1020
(732)449-0211
E-mail: mari@whitelilac.com
Web: www.whitelilac.com

Circa 1880. The White Lilac looks like a sweeping Southern home with wide wraparound porches decorating its three stories. The first story veranda is lined with wicker rockers and baskets of flowering plants hang from the ceiling, creating an ideal spot for relaxation. Inside, the Victorian decor contains period furnishings, antiques, whirlpool tubs, fireplaces and canopy beds. Breakfast is served fireside on intimate tables for two in the Garaden Room and on the enclosed porch. The ocean is less than five blocks from the inn.

Innkeeper(s): Mari Kennelly. $139-329. 10 rooms with PB, 6 with FP. Breakfast and snacks/refreshments included in rates. Types of meals: Full bkfst and early coffee/tea. Beds: QT. Cable TV, reading lamp, ceiling fan, clock radio and desk in room. Air conditioning. Bicycles, library, parlor games, telephone and fireplace on premises. Small meetings and family reunions hosted. Amusement parks, antiquing, fishing, golf, live theater, parks, shopping, sporting events, tennis, water sports and ocean nearby.
Publicity: *The Star-Ledger, Asbury Park Press and Coast Star and Philadelphia Inquirer.*

Stockton   E3

Woolverton Inn

6 Woolverton Rd
Stockton, NJ 08559-2147
(609)397-0802 (888)264-6648 Fax:(609)397-0987
E-mail: sheep@woolvertoninn.com
Web: www.woolvertoninn.com

Circa 1792. Sitting on 10 park-like acres high above the Delaware River, this tranquil retreat features a stone manor, carriage house and two barns. The inn is surrounded by 300 acres of rolling farmland and forest, and panoramic vistas often are enjoyed from the welcoming

porches. All the guest bedrooms and suites offer fresh flowers, CD players and library, plush terry robes, feather beds with canopy, four-poster or twig headboards and Egyptian cotton linens and towels. Many also boast private entrances and two-person whirlpool tubs. Enjoy complimentary soft drinks and bottled water as well as afternoon refreshments and snacks. A satisfying country breakfast may include Grand Marnier French toast, vegetable frittata with homemade turkey sausage and apple-blueberry streusel en papillote. Breakfast in bed is available upon request. After a stroll through gardens and meadows, visit the nearby sites in Bucks County, Newhope and Lambertville.

Innkeeper(s): Mark Smith, Matthew Lovette and Carolyn McGavin. $120-395. 13 rooms with PB, 8 with FP, 2 suites and 5 cottages. Breakfast and snacks/refreshments included in rates. Types of meals: Country bkfst, early coffee/tea, lunch and gourmet dinner. Beds: KQD. Reading lamp, clock radio, CD players, CD library, terrycloth robes, complimentary soft drinks and bottled water, cottages have private outdoor sitting areas, phones and whirlpool tubs in room. Air conditioning. Fax, copier, parlor games, telephone and fireplace on premises. Limited handicap access. Weddings, small meetings, family reunions and seminars hosted. Antiquing, bicycling, fishing, golf, horseback riding, live theater, museums, parks, shopping, water sports, wineries, walking trails and breweries nearby.

Publicity: *New York Magazine, Travel & Leisure and Philadelphia Inquirer.*
"Thank you for providing a perfect setting and relaxed atmosphere for our group. You're terrific."

Ventnor City   J5

Carisbrooke Inn

105 S Little Rock Ave
Ventnor City, NJ 08406-2840
(609)822-6392 Fax:(609)822-2563
E-mail: info@carisbrookeinn.com
Web: www.carisbrookeinn.com

Circa 1918. Relaxation is easy at this enticing seaside bed & breakfast just a few steps away from the world-famous boardwalk and only one mile from Atlantic City. Delight in the ocean view from the front deck or the tranquility of the back patio. Afternoon refreshments are enjoyed in the sunny Main Parlor, or by the warmth of a winter fire. Pleasant guest bedrooms and a suite feature comfortable amenities and the romantic accents of plants, fresh flowers and lacy curtains. The innkeepers offer a huge breakfast that may include homemade waffles and fresh berries, banana pecan pancakes, Italian frittata with fresh herbs and cheese, Quiche Lorraine and French toast, accompanied by fruit and just-baked muffins and breads. Beach towels and tags are provided for fun in the sun at the shore.

Innkeeper(s): John and Julie Battista. $95-315. 8 rooms with PB and 1 suite. Breakfast and snacks/refreshments included in rates. Types of meals: Full gourmet bkfst and early coffee/tea. Beds: KQD. Cable TV, reading lamp, ceiling fan, clock radio and fresh flowers in room. Air conditioning. Fax, copier, parlor games, telephone, fireplace, complimentary tea/coffee/snacks in main parlor, beach tags and towels and chairs (in season) on premises. Weddings, small meetings and family reunions hosted. Amusement parks, antiquing, beach, bicycling, fishing, golf, live theater, parks, shopping, tennis, water sports and casinos nearby.
"You have a beautiful, elegant inn. My stay here was absolutely wonderful."

Vernon   B5

Alpine Haus B&B

217 State Rt 94
Vernon, NJ 07462
(973)209-7080 Fax:(973)209-7090
E-mail: alpinehs@warwick.net
Web: www.alpinehausbb.com

Circa 1887. A private hideaway in the mountains, this former farmhouse is more than 100 years old. The renovated Federal-style inn with Victorian accents offers comfortable guest bedrooms named after mountain flowers with a decor reflecting that theme. Antiques also highlight the inn. The adjacent Carriage House has two suites with four-poster beds, stone fireplace and Jacuzzi. A generous country breakfast is enjoyed in the dining room or a continental breakfast on the second-story covered porch with majestic views. The family room and formal sitting room with fireplace are wonderful gathering places for games or conversation. Located next to Mountain Creek Ski and Water Park.

Innkeeper(s): Jack & Allison Smith. $110-225. 10 rooms with PB, 3 with FP and 2 suites. Breakfast included in rates. Types of meals: Country bkfst, veg bkfst, early coffee/tea and snacks/refreshments. Beds: QDT. Modem hook-up, data port, cable TV, VCR, reading lamp, refrigerator, clock radio, telephone, coffeemaker, desk, hot tub/spa, Internet access and two suites with fireplace and Jacuzzi in room. Central air. Fax, parlor games and fireplace on premises. Limited handicap access. Weddings, small meetings and family reunions hosted. Antiquing, art galleries, canoeing/kayaking, cross-country skiing, downhill skiing, fishing, golf, hiking, horseback riding, museums, parks, shopping, water sports and wineries nearby.

New Mexico

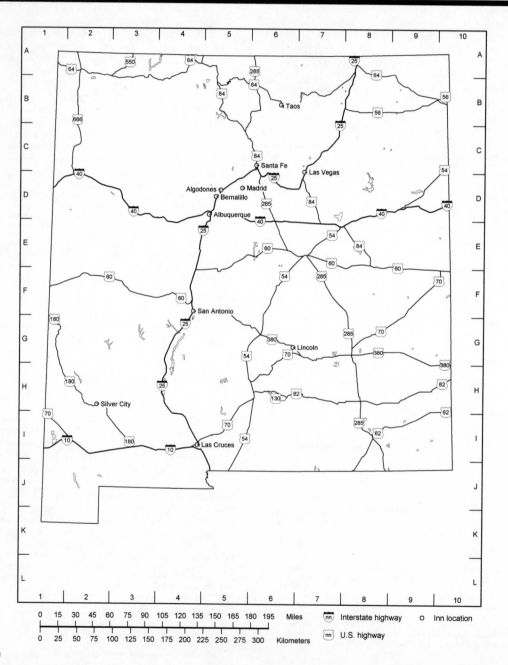

0 15 30 45 60 75 90 105 120 135 150 165 180 195   Miles

0 25 50 75 100 125 150 175 200 225 250 275 300   Kilometers

Interstate highway   o Inn location

U.S. highway

Albuquerque D5

Brittania & W.E. Mauger Estate B&B

701 Roma Ave NW
Albuquerque, NM 87102-2038
(505)242-8755 (800)719-9189 Fax:(505)842-8835
E-mail: maugerbb@aol.com
Web: www.maugerbb.com

Circa 1897. Now an elegantly restored Victorian, this former boarding house is listed in the National Register. Guest bedrooms offer amenities that include satellite television, refrigerators, a basket with snacks, voice mail and European down comforters on the beds. The inn is located four blocks from the convention center/business district and Historic Route 66. Old Town is less than one mile away. There are many interesting museums to visit locally, featuring topics from Native American culture to the atomic age.

Historic Interest: Albuquerque is full of unique museums, featuring topics from Native American culture to the atomic age.

Innkeeper(s): Mark Brown & Keith Lewis. $89-209. 8 rooms with PB and 1 conference room. Breakfast included in rates. Types of meals: Full bkfst and snacks/refreshments. Beds: KQDT. TV, reading lamp, refrigerator, ceiling fan, snack bar, clock radio, telephone, desk, voice mail, coffeemaker, iron and hair dryer in room. Air conditioning. Small meetings and family reunions hosted. Amusement parks, antiquing, live theater and shopping nearby.

Publicity: *Albuquerque Journal, Phoenix Home and Garden, Albuquerque Monthly, National Geographic Traveler, New Mexico Business Week and Golf Digest.*

"Because of your hospitality, kindness and warmth, we will always compare the quality of our experience by the W.E. Mauger Estate."

Casa Del Granjero & El Rancho Guest House

414 C De Baca Ln NW
Albuquerque, NM 87114-1600
(505)897-4144 (800)701-4144 Fax:(505)792-3118
E-mail: granjero@prodigy.net
Web: www.innewmexico.com

Circa 1890. Innkeepers Victoria and Butch Farmer, who appropriately named their home Casa del Granjero, or "the farmer's house," have designed their bed & breakfast to reflect Southwestern style with a hint of old Spanish flair. The adobe's guest rooms all include a rustic, kiva fireplace. Cuarto Allegre is the largest suite in the main house, and it includes a canopy bed covered in lace and French doors that open onto a small porch. Cuarto del Rey affords a mountain view and includes Mexican furnishings and handmade quilts. Cuarto de Flores also has quilts, Mexican tile and French doors leading to a private porch. The innkeepers have a hot tub room for guest use in a special garden area. The innkeepers also have restored a historic adobe ranch house across the road. The accommodations here include three suites and a guest room with a double bed. A kitchen, common area and wood-burning stove also are located in this house. A variety of baked goods, New Mexican-style recipes and fresh fruit are served each morning in the dining room or on the portal. Several recipes have been featured in a cookbook.

Innkeeper(s): Victoria & Butch Farmer. $79-179. 7 rooms, 2 with PB, 7 with FP and 5 suites. Breakfast included in rates. Types of meals: Full bkfst, picnic lunch, gourmet dinner and room service. Beds: KQT. Antiquing, cross-country skiing, downhill skiing, fishing, golf, hiking, live theater, shopping and water sports nearby.

Publicity: *Hidden SW.*

"Wonderful place, wonderful people. Thanks so much."

Cinnamon Morning Bed & Breakfast

2700 Rio Grande Blvd NW
Albuquerque, NM 87104-3228
(505)345-3541 (800)214-9481 Fax:(505)342-2283
E-mail: info@cinnamonmorning.com
Web: www.cinnamonmorning.com

Circa 1945. After a visit to this fully restored traditional New Mexico home on three acres in the Land of Enchantment, it will be hard to leave. The colorful Southwest décor with Mexican emphasis is accented with art and artifacts blending old and new. Relax in the inviting Great Room or by the outdoor fireplace in the courtyard with a garden, pond and fountains. Guest bedrooms in the Main House feature contemporary and antique furnishings sitting on hardwood floors. Two include fireplaces. A Guest House and Casita are also available. Indulge in a delicious breakfast that may offer a large selection of fruit, fresh-baked croissants and soufflé with raspberry chili sauce. Visit nearby Old Town or take a day trip to the Indian Pueblos.

Innkeeper(s): Sue & Dick Percilick. $85-190. 8 rooms, 5 with PB, 2 with FP, 2 cottages and 1 conference room. Breakfast and snacks/refreshments included in rates. Types of meals: Full gourmet bkfst, veg bkfst and early coffee/tea. Beds: KQT. Cable TV, VCR, reading lamp, stereo, refrigerator, ceiling fan, snack bar, clock radio, telephone, coffeemaker, desk and fireplace in room. Central air. Fax and parlor games on premises. Weddings, small meetings, family reunions and seminars hosted. Antiquing, art galleries, bicycling, downhill skiing, golf, hiking, horseback riding, live theater, museums, parks, shopping, sporting events, tennis and wineries nearby.

Hacienda Antigua B&B

6708 Tierra Dr NW
Albuquerque, NM 87107-6025
(505)345-5399 (800)201-2986 Fax:(505)345-3855
E-mail: info@haciendantigua.com
Web: www.haciendantigua.com

Circa 1780. In the more than 200 years since this Spanish Colonial-style hacienda was constructed, the current innkeeper is only the fifth owner. Once a stagecoach stop on the El Camino Real, it also served as a cantina and mercantile store. It was built by Don Pablo Yrisarri, who was sent by the King of Spain to search the area for gold. The home is elegant, yet maintains a rustic, Spanish charm with exposed beams, walls up to 30 inches thick, brick floors and adobe fireplaces. Along with a sitting room and kiva fireplace, the Don Pablo Suite includes a "ducking door" that leads onto the courtyard. Other rooms have clawfoot tubs, antique iron beds or a private patio. The cuisine is notable and one of the inn's recipes appeared in Culinary Trends magazine. Guests might sample a green chile soufflé along with bread pudding and fresh fruit. The inn has been featured on the TV series "Great Country Inns."

Innkeeper(s): Bob Thompson. $149-300. 8 rooms with PB, 7 with FP and 4 suites. Breakfast included in rates. Types of meals: Full bkfst and early coffee/tea. Beds: KQT. Reading lamp, refrigerator, ceiling fan, clock radio and telephone in room. Air conditioning. TV, VCR, fax, spa, swimming and fireplace on premises. Small meetings, family reunions and seminars hosted. Amusement parks, antiquing, cross-country skiing, downhill skiing, fishing, golf, live theater, parks, shopping, sporting events, tennis, hiking, biking and balloon fiesta nearby.

Publicity: *Culinary Trends, Cavalcade of Enchantment and Great Country Inns.*

Algodones   D5

Hacienda Vargas

PO Box 307
Algodones, NM 87001-0307
(505)867-9115 (800)261-0006 Fax:(505)867-0640
E-mail: stay@haciendavargas.com
Web: www.haciendavargas.com

Circa 1840. Nestled among the cottonwoods and mesas of the middle Rio Grande Valley, between Albuquerque and Santa Fe, Hacienda Vargas has seen two centuries of Old West history. It once served as a trading post for Native Americans as well as a 19th-century stagecoach stop between Santa Fe and Las Cruces. The grounds contain an adobe chapel, courtyard and gardens. The main house features five kiva fireplaces, Southwest antiques, Spanish tile, a library and suites with private Jacuzzis.

Historic Interest: Coronado Monument, Indian Ruins (5 miles), Bandelier National Park (40 miles), Chaco Canyon (80 miles).

Innkeeper(s): Cynthia & Richard Spence. $79-149. 7 rooms with PB, 6 with FP and 4 suites. Breakfast included in rates. Types of meals: Full bkfst. Beds: QT. Reading lamp, ceiling fan, clock radio, desk and suites have spa in room. Air conditioning. Parlor games, telephone and fireplace on premises. Weddings and family reunions hosted. Antiquing, downhill skiing, fishing, live theater, shopping, sporting events, Golf MECCA and car racing nearby.

Publicity: *Albuquerque Journal (Country Inns), Vogue and San Francisco Chronicle.*

"This is the best! Breakfast was the best we've ever had!"

Bernalillo   D5

La Hacienda Grande

21 Barros Rd
Bernalillo, NM 87004
(505)867-1887 (800)353-1887 Fax:(505)771-1436

Circa 1711. The rooms in this historic adobe inn surround a central courtyard. The first European trekked across the grounds as early as 1540. The land was part of a 1711 land grant from Spain, and owned by descendants of the original family until the innkeepers purchased it. The decor is Southwestern, and each bedchamber is filled with beautiful, handcrafted furnishings. One includes an iron high-poster bed and Jacuzzi tub, and others offer a kiva fireplace. Breakfasts are served in a dining room decorated with wood beams and a brick floor.

Innkeeper(s): Troy & Melody Scott. $109-139. 6 rooms with PB, 5 with FP and 1 conference room. Breakfast included in rates. Types of meals: Full bkfst and early coffee/tea. Beds: KQDT. Reading lamp, clock radio and sitting areas and TV on request in room. Air conditioning. VCR, fax, copier, library, parlor games, telephone, fireplace and phone on premises. Weddings, small meetings, family reunions and seminars hosted. Antiquing, cross-country skiing, downhill skiing, fishing, live theater, parks, shopping, sporting events and water sports nearby.

Las Cruces   I4

T.R.H. Smith Mansion B&B

909 N Alameda Blvd
Las Cruces, NM 88005-2124
(505)525-2525 (800)526-1914 Fax:(505)524-8227

Circa 1914. Surrounded by park-like grounds with tall pecan and sycamore trees, this beautifully preserved Prairie-style 5,700-square-foot mansion has a somewhat notorious past. The home was designed by prominent Southwest architect Henry Trost, and built by banker/embezzler TRH Smith. It was rumored to have served as a bordello and to have buried treasure somewhere within its walls. Four well-appointed guest bedrooms offer a variety of styles including Latin American, European, Southwest and Pacific Rim. Each one features both cable TV and a professional computer with DSL for always-on Internet and e-mail access. In the dining or garden rooms enjoy a hearty German-style breakfast of fresh fruit, home-baked breads, an egg entrée, imported meats and cheeses along with fresh-ground coffees and teas made from herbs grown on the grounds.

Innkeeper(s): Marlene & Jay Tebo. $85-150. 4 rooms with PB, 1 with FP. Breakfast included in rates. Types of meals: Full gourmet bkfst. Beds: KQ. Reading lamp, clock radio and desk in room. Parlor games, telephone and fireplace on premises. Weddings, small meetings, family reunions and seminars hosted. Antiquing, golf, live theater, parks, shopping, sporting events and tennis nearby.

Publicity: *Las Cruces Sun-News, Las Cruces Bulletin, Gateway Magazine and New Mexico Magazine.*

Las Vegas   C7

Carriage House B&B

925 6th St
Las Vegas, NM 87701-4306
(505)454-1784 (888)221-9689

Circa 1893. A prominent local attorney built this historic Queen Anne Victorian home. The innkeepers offer five comfortable guest rooms, and pamper their guests with a full breakfast and afternoon tea. Las Vegas has an amazing Wild West past, and there are more than 900 buildings in town that are listed in the National Register.

Innkeeper(s): Anne & John Bradford. $75-95. 12 rooms, 4 with PB. Breakfast included in rates. Types of meals: Cont plus, early coffee/tea and afternoon tea. Beds: Q. Ceiling fan in room. TV, fax, telephone and afternoon tea available by reservation on premises. Weddings and family reunions hosted. Antiquing, art galleries, cross-country skiing, downhill skiing, fishing, golf, hiking, museums, parks, shopping and wineries nearby.

Publicity: *Red Dawn.*

Lincoln   G6

Ellis Store & Country Inn

US Highway 380
Lincoln, NM 88338
(505)653-4609 (800)653-6460 Fax:(505)653-4610
E-mail: ellisstore@pvtnetworks.net
Web: www.ellisstore.com

Circa 1850. Experience the history of the Old West at the original site of the Lincoln County War, where Billy the Kid and his "Regulators" took refuge. Guests actually can stay in the room where Billy the Kid was held. The Main House, built in the mid-1800s in exquisite adobe offers wood-burning stoves, antiques and hand-made quilts in each guest room. The Mill house, built in the 1880s then used as nurses' quarters and a lodge hall, now serves as an ideal location for family reunions and retreats. The recently built Casa Nueva houses two private suites, allowing guests a private retreat of their own. The inn's critically acclaimed restaurant, Isaac's Table, offers candle-lit dining, a wine cellar and a menu with worldwide flair. Situated on six acres surrounded by fresh-cut green grass and lush gardens, this New Mexico territorial home combines the beauty of Victorian décor with the rugged West in a peaceful harmony that has been enjoyed by many happy returns.

Innkeeper(s): Virginia & David Vigil. $79-139. 10 rooms, 6 with PB, 3 with FP, 2 suites and 1 conference room. Types of meals: Full gourmet bkfst and gourmet dinner. Restaurant on premises. Beds: KQDT. Reading lamp and ceiling fan in room. VCR, fax, copier, stable, telephone and fireplace on premises. Weddings, small meetings, family reunions and seminars hosted. Antiquing, art galleries, cross-country skiing, downhill skiing, fishing, golf, hiking, horseback riding, live theater, museums and shopping nearby.

Madrid   D5

Java Junction

2855 State Highway 14 N, Turquoise Trail
Madrid, NM 87010
(505)438-2772 (877)308-8884 Fax:(505)474-4359
E-mail: heavenmadrid@hotmail.com
Web: www.java-junction.com

Circa 1916. A restored Victorian home in this once-famous railroad and coal mining town is the quaint setting for this delightful inn. Aptly named with its first-floor coffee and gift shop, a continental breakfast is served from here daily. The second story features a spacious suite with a kitchen, private porch and six-foot, clawfoot tub in the bathroom.

Innkeeper(s): Linda Dunnill. $69-89. 1 suite. Breakfast included in rates. Types of meals: Cont and early coffee/tea. Restaurant on premises. Beds: Q. TV, reading lamp, refrigerator, snack bar, clock radio, coffeemaker and stove in room. Air conditioning. Telephone and coffee shop on premises. Art galleries, horseback riding, live theater, museums and shopping nearby.

Publicity: *60 Minutes.*

San Antonio   F4

Casa Blanca Bed & Breakfast

13 Montoya Street, PO Box 31
San Antonio, NM 87832
(505)835-3027
E-mail: casablancabandb@hotmail.com
Web: www.casablancabedandbreakfast.com

Circa 1880. Constructed with 24-inch-thick double adobe walls, this Victorian farmhouse was the home of Territorial Senator Eutimio Montoya, a well-known politician. Since 1989 it has served as an intimate bed & breakfast for bird watchers and nature lovers visiting the Bosque del Apache National Wildlife Refuge. Displays of Southwestern Indian and Mexican art, original photography, framed historic documents and antiques highlight the inn. Accommodations in the Crane Room feature a wood-burning stove. The larger Heron Room boasts a whirlpool tub. The Egret Room holds a double and twin bed. A generous breakfast includes homemade breads, muffins, coffeecake, fresh fruit, yogurt, cereal, eggs and cheeses. The inn is closed June through September.

Innkeeper(s): Phoebe Wood. $60-90. 3 rooms with PB, 1 with FP. Breakfast included in rates. Types of meals: Full bkfst and early coffee/tea. Beds: QDT. Reading lamp, ceiling fan and alarm clocks in room. TV, VCR, sauna, bicycles, library, parlor games, telephone, fireplace, laundry facility and piano on premises. Bicycling, hiking and bird watching nearby.

Santa Fe   C6

Alexander's Inn

529 E Palace Ave
Santa Fe, NM 87501-2200
(505)986-1431 (888)321-5123 Fax:(505)982-8572
E-mail: alexandinn@aol.com
Web: www.alexanders-inn.com

Circa 1903. Twin gables and a massive front porch are prominent features of this Craftsman-style brick and wood inn. French and American country decor, stained-glass windows and a selection of antiques create a light Victorian touch. The inn also features beautiful gardens of roses and lilacs. The exquisite Southwest adobe casitas are a favorite for families and romantic getaways. Breakfast is often served in the backyard garden. Home-baked treats are offered to guests in the afternoon.

Historic Interest: Puye Cliffs, Bandalier and Pecos National Monument all are within one hour from the inn.

Innkeeper(s): Carolyn Lee. $85-195. 8 rooms with PB, 5 with FP, 1 suite and 4 cottages. Breakfast and afternoon tea included in rates. Types of meals: Full gourmet bkfst and early coffee/tea. Beds: KQT. Cable TV, VCR, reading lamp, refrigerator, clock radio, telephone, desk and hot tub/spa in room. Fax, spa, library, child care, parlor games and fireplace on premises. Weddings and family reunions hosted. Antiquing, cross-country skiing, downhill skiing, fishing, live theater, parks, shopping, water sports, museums and Pueblos nearby.

Publicity: *New Mexican, Glamour, Southwest Art and San Diego Union Tribune.*

"Thanks to the kindness and thoughtfulness of the staff, our three days in Santa Fe were magical."

Arius Compound

1018 Canyon Road
Santa Fe, NM 87501
(505)982-8859 (800)735-8453 Fax:(505)983-9531
E-mail: len@ariuscompound.com
Web: www.ariuscompound.com

Circa 1920. At the end of a private lane in the historic East Side, two homes and two guest houses sit on almost an acre surrounded by high adobe walls. Built in Old Mexican style around a central courtyard with lush gardens, fruit trees, fountains and patios, these Santa Fe-style adobe casitas feature tile and flagstone floors as well as fully-equipped kitchens. Wood is provided for the fireplaces. Relax in the outdoor red-cedar hot tub. Experience nearby Canyon Road's restaurants, shops and galleries. Up the hill, visit the Museum Complex offering International Folk Arts, Navajo Ceremonial and Indian Arts museums.

Innkeeper(s): Len & Robbie Goodman. $90-180. 3 cottages. Beds: QDT. Modem hook-up, TV, VCR, reading lamp, stereo, refrigerator, ceiling fan, snack bar, clock radio, telephone, coffeemaker, fireplace and satellite TV in room. Hot tub on premises. Weddings and family reunions hosted. Antiquing, art galleries, bicycling, cross-country skiing, downhill skiing, fishing, golf, hiking, horseback riding, live theater, museums, parks, shopping, tennis and wineries nearby.

Publicity: *Los Angeles Times.*

"You really feel like you're living in Old Santa Fe—not visiting. We loved it."

Casa de la Cuma B&B

105 Paseo de la Cuma
Santa Fe, NM 87501-1213
(505)983-1717 (888)366-1717 Fax:(505)983-2241
E-mail: info@casacuma.com
Web: www.casacuma.com

Circa 1940. Offering a warm and serene atmosphere, Casa de la Cuma B&B has three unique rooms and a suite decorated with Navajo textiles, original artwork and Southwestern-period furniture. Guests

enjoy breakfast on the glassed-in porch or simply relaxing on the shaded patio. During cooler weather, the fireplace in the living room is the gathering spot. The inn features views of the Sangre De Cristo Mountains and is within walking distance of the Plaza.

Historic Interest: The inn is located on the same hill as the original cross which honors Spanish priests killed during the 1680 pueblo revolt.

Innkeeper(s): Nancy & Alex Leeson. $95-170. 4 rooms with PB, 2 with FP and 1 suite. Breakfast and snacks/refreshments included in rates. Types of meals: Cont plus and afternoon tea. Beds: KQT. Cable TV, reading lamp, refrigerator, ceiling fan, clock radio, telephone, desk and suite has kitchenette in room. Spa, fireplace, gardens, fountain and sunset views on premises. Antiquing, downhill skiing, parks, museums, hiking and rafting nearby.

Don Gaspar Inn

623 Don Gaspar Avenue
Santa Fe, NM 87505
(505)986-8664 (888)986-8664 Fax:(505)986-0696
E-mail: info@dongaspar.com
Web: www.dongaspar.com

Circa 1912. This lush, peaceful hideaway is located within one of Santa Fe's first historic districts. Within the Compounds surrounding adobe walls are brick pathways meandering through beautiful gardens, emerald lawns, trees and a courtyard fountain. The elegant Southwestern decor is an idyllic match for the warmth and romance of the grounds. For those seeking privacy, the innkeepers offer the Main House, a historic Mission-style home perfect for a pair of romantics or a group as large as six. The house has three bedrooms, two bathrooms, a fully equipped kitchen and two wood-burning fireplaces. In addition to the main house, there are three suites in a Territorial-style home with thick walls and polished wood floors. There also are two private casitas, each with a gas-burning fireplace. The Fountain Casita includes a fully equipped kitchen, while the Courtyard Casita offers a double whirlpool tub. All accommodations include a TV, telephone, microwave and refrigerators.

Historic Interest: The inn is a short walk from Santa Fe's historic plaza, as well as several museums.

Innkeeper(s): Aggie, Trudi and Ana. $115-295. 10 rooms with PB, 8 with FP and 3 suites. Breakfast included in rates. Types of meals: Full bkfst. Beds: KQ. TV, VCR, reading lamp, refrigerator, ceiling fan, clock radio, telephone, coffeemaker, hot tub/spa, voice mail and fireplace in room. Air conditioning. Fax, copier, fireplace, laundry facility, gardens, courtyard, fountain and two casitas on premises. Limited handicap access. Weddings and family reunions hosted. Antiquing, art galleries, bicycling, cross-country skiing, fishing, golf, hiking, horseback riding, live theater, museums, parks, shopping and tennis nearby.

Publicity: *Sunset, Conde Nast Traveler and PBS.*

"Everything was simply perfect."

Dunshee's

986 Acequia Madre
Santa Fe, NM 87505-2819
(505)982-0988 Fax:(505)982-1547
E-mail: sdunshee@aol.com
Web: www.dunshees.com

Circa 1930. Where better could one experience Santa Fe's rich history than in an authentic adobe casita or a restored adobe home? Innkeeper Susan Dunshee offers accommodations in

both. Guests can stay in the adobe home's spacious suite or rent the casita by the day or week. The casita offers a continental-plus breakfast, two bedrooms, a kitchen, a living room warmed by a rustic, kiva fireplace and a private patio. The antique-filled rooms are decorated in a warm, Santa Fe style, and bedrooms sport a more country look. Guests who opt for the bed & breakfast suite are treated to Southwestern breakfasts with items such as a green chile souffle. The refrigerator at the casita is stocked with treats for the guests' breakfast.

Innkeeper(s): Susan Dunshee. $125-140. 3 rooms, 2 with PB, 3 with FP, 1 suite and 1 cottage. Breakfast included in rates. Types of meals: Full gourmet bkfst and early coffee/tea. Beds: QD. Cable TV, reading lamp, stereo, refrigerator, telephone, desk, fresh flowers and homemade cookies in room. Library on premises. Antiquing, cross-country skiing, downhill skiing, live theater, parks, shopping, opera and Indian pueblos nearby.

El Farolito B&B Inn

514 Galisteo St
Santa Fe, NM 87501
(505)988-1631 (888)634-8782 Fax:(505)988-4589
E-mail: innkeeper@farolito.com
Web: www.farolito.com

Circa 1900. El Farolito's seven guest rooms and one suite are spread among five adobe buildings, some of which date back to the 1900s. The beamed ceilings, tile or brick floors and kiva fireplaces enhance the Southwestern decor. The bed & breakfast is located within Santa Fe's historic district, and a 10-minute walk will take you to the famous plaza. Other sites, the Capitol building, shops and restaurants are even closer.

Innkeeper(s): Walt Wyss & Wayne Mainus. $150-220. 8 rooms with PB. Breakfast included in rates. Types of meals: Cont plus. Beds: KQD. Cable TV, reading lamp, refrigerator, clock radio, telephone and desk in room. Air conditioning. TV, fireplace, refrigerators and coffee service in some rooms on premises. Small meetings, family reunions and seminars hosted. Antiquing, cross-country skiing, downhill skiing, fishing, golf, live theater, parks, shopping and sporting events nearby.

Publicity: *New Mexican Newspaper, Albuquerque Journal, Romantic Southwest, Select Registry and Winner of "Best small property of the year" awarded in 1999 by the New Mexico Hotel & Motel Association.*

El Paradero

220 W Manhattan Ave
Santa Fe, NM 87501-2622
(505)988-1177
E-mail: info@elparadero.com
Web: www.elparadero.com

Circa 1820. This was originally a two-bedroom Spanish farmhouse that doubled in size to a Territorial style in 1860, was remodeled as a Victorian in 1912 and became a Pueblo Revival in 1920. All styles are present and provide a walk through many years of history. Located in historic downtown Santa Fe, the inn

is within easy walking distance to the Plaza and Canyon Road.

Innkeeper(s): Matt & Jen Laessig. $75-160. 14 rooms, 12 with PB, 7 with FP, 2 suites and 1 conference room. Breakfast and afternoon tea included in rates. Types of meals: Full gourmet bkfst and early coffee/tea. Beds: QT. Reading lamp, clock radio, telephone, cable TV, suite has refrigerator and fireplaces in room. Air conditioning. TV and fireplace on premises. Cross-country skiing, fishing, live theater, shopping, pueblos, opera and mountains nearby.

Publicity: *Denver Post, Insider, Country Inns, Outside, Sunset, New York Times, Los Angeles Times, Travel & Leisure, America West and Travel & Holiday.*

"I'd like to LIVE here."

Four Kachinas Inn

512 Webber St
Santa Fe, NM 87501-4454
(505)982-2550 (888)634-8782 Fax:(505)989-1323
E-mail: info@fourkachinas.com
Web: www.fourkachinas.com

Circa 1910. This inn is built in the Northern New Mexico pitched-tin roof style around a private courtyard. Appealing guest rooms are decorated with Southwestern art and crafts, including Navajo rugs, Kachina dolls and handmade regional furniture. Three bedrooms have individual garden patios, while a fourth offers a view from the second floor. An additional room is located in Digneo cottage, built in 1910. Breakfast is served in a separate adobe building and features home baked goods.

Historic Interest: Santa Fe Plaza (4 1/2 blocks).
Innkeeper(s): Walt Wyss & Wayne Manus. $110-190. 5 rooms with PB. Breakfast and afternoon tea included in rates. Types of meals: Cont plus. Beds: KQ. TV and telephone on premises. Limited handicap access. Antiquing, art galleries, cross-country skiing, downhill skiing, fishing, live theater and museums nearby.

Publicity: *Rocky Mountain News, New York Times, Travel & Leisure and Denver Post.*

"We found the room to be quiet and comfortable and your hospitality to be very gracious. We also really enjoyed breakfast, especially the baked goods!"

Grant Corner Inn

122 Grant Ave
Santa Fe, NM 87501-2031
(505)983-6678 (800)964-9003 Fax:(505)983-1526

Circa 1900. Judge Robinson and his family lived here for 30 years, and many couples were married in the parlor. A contin-

ually romantic setting, the inn is secluded by a garden with willow trees, and there is a white picket fence. Rooms are appointed with antique furnishings and the personal art collections of the innkeeper.

Historic Interest: Bandelier and Pecos National Monuments, Indian Pueblos.
Innkeeper(s): Louise Stewart. $130-240. 10 rooms with PB, 1 with FP. Breakfast and afternoon tea included in rates. Types of meals: Full gourmet bkfst, early coffee/tea, gourmet lunch, picnic lunch, gourmet dinner and room service. Restaurant on premises. Beds: KQT. Cable TV, reading lamp, refrigerator, ceiling fan, clock radio and telephone in room. Air conditioning. Fax and copier on premises. Limited handicap access. Weddings, small meetings, family reunions and seminars hosted. Antiquing, art galleries, cross-country skiing, downhill skiing, fishing, golf,

hiking, horseback riding, live theater, museums and shopping nearby.

Publicity: *New England Bride and Galveston Daily News.*

"The very best of everything — comfort, hospitality, food and T.L.C."

Hacienda Nicholas

320 East Marcy Street
Santa Fe, NM 87501
(505)992-8385 (888)284-3170 Fax:(505)982-8572
E-mail: haciendanicholas@aol.com
Web: www.haciendanicholas.com

Circa 1930. The Southwest meets Provence in this 1930 Adobe Hacienda built around a central garden courtyard full of wisteria, iris, daisies, pansies, geraniums and roses. Heated by an outdoor kiva fireplace on cool days and filled with birdsong on warm days, the courtyard is the perfect place to linger over a breakfast of homemade muffins and quiche or to return for afternoon tea. The high-ceilinged great room is warmed by a huge fireplace and furnished with overstuffed couches. Just blocks from Santa Fe's historic plaza, the inn's seven guest rooms are elegantly furnished in Mexican décor, each with a wrought iron or carved wood four-poster bed.

Innkeeper(s): Glennon Grush/Carolyn Lee. $95-160. 7 rooms with PB, 3 with FP, 3 suites and 1 conference room. Breakfast and afternoon tea included in rates. Types of meals: Full gourmet bkfst and early coffee/tea. Beds: KQ. Cable TV, reading lamp, telephone and fireplace in room. Air conditioning. Fax and fireplace on premises. Limited handicap access. Small meetings and seminars hosted. Antiquing, art galleries, bicycling, canoeing/kayaking, cross-country skiing, downhill skiing, fishing, golf, hiking, horseback riding, live theater, museums, parks, shopping, sporting events, tennis, water sports and wineries nearby.

Publicity: *Travel Holiday.*

Inn of The Turquoise Bear B&B

342 E Buena Vista St
Santa Fe, NM 87505
(505)983-0798 (800)396-4104 Fax:(505)988-4225
E-mail: bluebear@newmexico.com
Web: www.turquoisebear.com

Circa 1880. Tall ponderosa pines shade this rambling Spanish Pueblo Revival adobe, giving it the feeling of being in a mountain setting, although it's only blocks from the plaza. In the National Register, it was the home of poet and essayist Witter Bynner, when it hosted a myriad of celebrities including Edna St. Vincent Millay, Robert Frost, Ansel Adams, Rita Hayworth, Errol Flynn and Georgia O'Keeffe. The walled acre of grounds includes flagstone paths, wild roses, lilacs, rock terraces and stone benches and fountains. In a Southwest decor, there are kiva fireplaces and romantic courtyards. The Shaman room has a king bed, viga beams and a picture window with garden views. Guests are invited to enjoy wine and cheese in the afternoon. Museums, galleries, restaurants and shops are within walking distance. Among its accolades, the inn was the recipient of the Heritage Preservation Award from the city of Santa Fe in 1999, and from the state of New Mexicoin 2000.

Innkeeper(s): Robert Frost & Ralph Bolton. $95-315. 11 rooms, 8 with PB, 10 with FP, 1 suite and 1 conference room. Breakfast and snacks/refreshments included in rates. Types of meals: Cont plus. Beds: KQ. Modem hook-up, cable TV, VCR, reading lamp, clock radio, telephone and desk in room. Fax, library, child care, parlor games and fireplace on premises. Weddings, small meetings, family reunions and seminars hosted. Antiquing, art galleries, bicycling, canoeing/kayaking, cross-country skiing, downhill skiing, fishing, golf, hiking, horseback riding, live theater, museums, parks, shopping, tennis, wineries & opera nearby.

Publicity: *Santa Fean, Hidden New Mexico, Our World, New Mexico Magazine, selected by Sunset Magazine as one of the West's Best Inns, Out Magazine-as one of the 5 best B&B's in the USA and Southern Living.*

"Staying at your inn was a vacation and history lesson we will always remember!"

The Madeleine (formerly The Preston House)

106 Faithway St
Santa Fe, NM 87501
(505)982-3465 (888)877-7622 Fax:(505)982-8572
E-mail: madeleineinn@aol.com
Web: www.madeleineinn.com

Circa 1886. This gracious 19th-century home is the only authentic example of Queen Anne architecture in Santa Fe. This home displays a wonderful Victorian atmosphere with period furnishings, quaint wallpapers and beds covered with down quilts. Afternoon tea is a must, as Carolyn serves up a mouth-watering array of cakes, pies, cookies and tarts. The Madeleine, which is located in downtown Santa Fe, is within walking distance of the Plaza.

Innkeeper(s): Carolyn Lee. $70-180. 8 rooms, 6 with PB, 4 with FP and 2 cottages. Breakfast and afternoon tea included in rates. Types of meals: Full bkfst and early coffee/tea. Beds: KQDT. Cable TV, reading lamp, refrigerator, ceiling fan, clock radio, telephone and desk in room. Fax, copier and fireplace on premises. Weddings, small meetings, family reunions and seminars hosted. Antiquing, cross-country skiing, downhill skiing, fishing, live theater, parks and shopping nearby.

Publicity: *Country Inns.*

"We were extremely pleased — glad we found you. We shall return."

Pueblo Bonito

138 W Manhattan Ave
Santa Fe, NM 87501
(505)984-8001 (800)461-4599 Fax:(505)984-3155
E-mail: pueblo@cybermesa.com
Web: www.pueblobonitoinn.com

Circa 1880. A thick adobe wall surrounds the grounds of this estate, once the home of a circuit judge. An authentic Indian "orno" oven is attached to the main house. Red brick pathways, old elm trees and a private hot tub add to the atmosphere. In the late afternoon, guests are treated to complimentary margaritas, wine and afternoon tea fare. The inn was selected as Santa Fe's second best B&B for the year 2000 by The Reporter, a local newspaper.

Innkeeper(s): Amy & Herb Behm. $70-165. 18 rooms with PB, 18 with FP and 7 suites. Breakfast and afternoon tea included in rates. Types of meals: Cont plus and snacks/refreshments. Beds: QD. Cable TV, reading lamp, clock radio and telephone in room. Air conditioning. Fax, copier, spa, complimentary margaritas, wine, cheese/crackers, fruit and parking on premises. Limited handicap access. Cross-country skiing, downhill skiing, fishing, golf, live theater, parks, shopping and opera nearby.

Publicity: *Innsider and Country Inns.*

"You captured that quaint, authentic Santa Fe atmosphere, yet I didn't feel as if I had to sacrifice any modern conveniences."

Spencer House Bed & Breakfast

222 McKenzie St
Santa Fe, NM 87501-1831
(505)988-3024 (800)647-0530 Fax:(505)986-0991
E-mail: anna@spencerhousesantafe.com
Web: www.spencerhousesantafe.com

Circa 1923. Just around the corner from the new Georgia O'Keeffe Museum and just four blocks from the historic plaza, in the McKenzie Street corridor, this 1923 Mediterranean-style

adobe house reflects a mixture of Hispanic and early 20th century design motifs. Antiques, Oriental carpets and artwork create an intimate ambiance while central air conditioning provides modern comfort. Relax by the fire in the spacious living room accented with collectibles. Each graciously appointed guest bedroom and suite features a delightfully inviting décor. Stay in the Cottage Room with sleigh bed, fireplace, jetted tub, kitchen and walled patio. The Croft Room boasts a four-poster bed, gas fireplace and whirlpool bath. Start the day with a full gourmet breakfast in the dining room that is sure to please.

Innkeeper(s): Anna Randall. $107-175. 6 rooms with PB, 3 with FP and 1 suite. Breakfast and snacks/refreshments included in rates. Types of meals: Full gourmet bkfst, early coffee/tea and afternoon tea. Beds: QT. Cable TV, VCR, reading lamp, ceiling fan, telephone and two rooms have whirlpool tubs in room. Central air. Fireplace on premises. Antiquing, art galleries, canoeing/kayaking, cross-country skiing, downhill skiing, fishing, golf, hiking, horseback riding, live theater, museums, parks and shopping nearby.

Silver City   H2

Bear Mountain Lodge

2251 Cottage San Road, PO Box 1163
Silver City, NM 88061
(505)538-2538 (877)620-2327 Fax:(505)534-1827
E-mail: innkeeper@bearmountainlodge.com
Web: www.bearmountainlodge.com

Circa 1928. Bordering Gila National Forest, this just-renovated hacienda on 178 acres began as the Rocky Mountain Ranch School, became a country club hotel, a dude ranch, and then a guest house. Donated to the Nature Conservancy, it retains its historic integrity with hand-hewn beams, a distinctive pine staircase, stone fireplaces and hardwood floors, while offering luxurious accommodations. Located in three buildings, spacious guest bedrooms feature hand-crafted Southwestern and Mission-style furnishings and majestic balcony views. Nature in full glory is found here, with abundant plants, birds and wildlife. The lodge naturalist holds conservation workshops and activities.

Innkeeper(s): Maura Gonsior. $105-200. 11 rooms with PB. Breakfast included in rates. Types of meals: Full bkfst, veg bkfst, early coffee/tea, picnic lunch, snacks/refreshments and dinner. Beds: KQT. Reading lamp, ceiling fan, telephone, hot tub/spa, private balconies and handcrafted furniture in room. Fax, copier, stable, bicycles, library, fireplace, nature trails and staff naturalist on premises. Small meetings, family reunions and seminars hosted. Antiquing, art galleries, bicycling, canoeing/kayaking, fishing, hiking, horseback riding, museums, parks, shopping, archaeological ruins, Gila Cliff Dwellings and Gila National Forest nearby.

Publicity: *The Nature Conservancy Magazine, Albuquerque Journal, Los Angeles Times, Sunset, Las Cruces Sun News, National Geographic Traveler and San Diego Union Tribune.*

Taos   B6

Adobe & Pines Inn

4107 Highway 68
Taos, NM 87557
(505)751-0947 (800)723-8267 Fax:(505)758-8423
E-mail: adobepines@taosnet.com
Web: www.newmex.com/adobepines

Circa 1832. Set on several acres of pine, orchard and pasture-covered land near Taos, this restored adobe hacienda provides a peaceful, romantic getaway. A stream running through the grounds adds to the tranquility. Rooms feature Southwestern details, kiva fireplaces, down comforters and pillows. A separate

guest cottage includes a canopy bed, whirlpool bath, two fireplaces and a kitchen. Exotic evening hors d'oeuvres and gourmet breakfasts are enjoyed by guests. A flower-filled, stone-walled courtyard affords magnificent views of Taos Mountain.

Innkeeper(s): David & KayAnn Tyssee, Cathy Ann Connelly. $95-195. 9 rooms with PB, 8 with FP, 6 suites and 4 cottages. Breakfast and snacks/refreshments included in rates. Types of meals: Full gourmet bkfst, veg bkfst and early coffee/tea. Beds: KQ. Cable TV, VCR, reading lamp, stereo, refrigerator, ceiling fan, clock radio, coffeemaker, desk and hot tub/spa in room. Air conditioning. Fax, copier, library, pet boarding, parlor games, telephone, fireplace and laundry facility on premises. Weddings, small meetings, family reunions and seminars hosted. Antiquing, art galleries, bicycling, canoeing/kayaking, cross-country skiing, downhill skiing, fishing, golf, hiking, horseback riding, live theater, museums, parks, shopping, tennis and wineries nearby.

Publicity: *Yellow Brick Road, Denver Post, Los Angeles Times and San Francisco Examiner.*

"The Adobe & Pines Inn warms your soul and your senses with traditional New Mexican decor, hospitality and comfort."

Casa De Las Chimeneas Inn & Spa

405 Cordoba - 5303 NDCBU
Taos, NM 87571
(505)758-4777 (877)758-4777 Fax:(505)758-3976
E-mail: casa@newmex.com
Web: www.visittaos.com

Circa 1935. Innkeeper Susan has created a destination resort with an intimate atmosphere. Fountains, sitting areas, a large courtyard, kitchen herb and English cottage-style gardens impart a secluded setting behind adobe walls, yet the historic center of town is only two and a half blocks away. Translated House of Chimneys, this Southwestern inn is aptly named as each of the guest bedrooms features a fireplace as well as a mini-refrigerator stocked with complimentary beverages, robes, private entrance, custom toiletries and many more thoughtful amenities. A three-course breakfast includes award-winning recipes developed for the inn. A not-to-be-missed evening buffet supper is also included. Relax in the outdoor hot tub after a workout in the fitness facility and be sure to arrange for spa services.

Historic Interest: Much of the original building is adobe construction, all done by hand.

Innkeeper(s): Susan Vernon, Tracy Baker and Claude Bodson. $165-325. 8 rooms with PB, 8 with FP and 2 suites. Breakfast, snacks/refreshments and dinner included in rates. Types of meals: Full gourmet bkfst, early coffee/tea and picnic lunch. Beds: KQT. Data port, cable TV, VCR, reading lamp, CD player, refrigerator, clock radio, telephone, coffeemaker, turn-down service, desk and fireplace in room. Fax, spa, sauna, parlor games, fireplace, laundry facility and gift shop on premises. Limited handicap access. Family reunions hosted. Art galleries, bicycling, canoeing/kayaking, cross-country skiing, downhill skiing, fishing, golf, hiking, horseback riding, live theater, museums, parks, shopping, tennis and wineries nearby.

Publicity: *Gourmet, Bon Appetit, Women's Day, The Santa Fean, Ski, Skiing, New Mexico Magazine, Atlanta Homes, Sunset and Great Country Inns.*

Casa Encantada

416 Liebert St
Taos, NM 87571
(505)758-7477 (800)223-TAOS Fax:(505)737-5085
E-mail: encantada@newmex.com
Web: www.casaencantada.com

Circa 1930. Located only a few blocks from the historic Taos plaza, this historic adobe rests in a quiet neighborhood behind soft adobe walls. Secluded gardens, courtyards and patios add

to the serenity. Most guest accommodations include a fireplace, and all have been individually decorated with original local art. Some have kitchenettes. The Santa Fe Suite is popular for anniversaries and special occasions. It includes a living room with fireplace, dressing area, and king bedroom. The Anasazi offers Taos character with a sun room, loft bedroom, living room and gas kiva. The Casita, once the hacienda's chapel, is the most spacious suite and with Southwest style offers two queen bedrooms, two kiva fireplaces, a kitchenette, bath, laundry and a private courtyard. Skiing, shopping, galleries, restaurants and much more are all nearby.

Innkeeper(s): Sharon Nicholson. $100-185. 9 rooms with PB, 6 with FP, 6 suites and 1 conference room. Breakfast included in rates. Types of meals: Full gourmet bkfst and early coffee/tea. Beds: KQ. Cable TV, VCR, reading lamp, refrigerator, ceiling fan, clock radio and desk in room. Fax, copier, library, telephone and fireplace on premises. Weddings, small meetings, family reunions and seminars hosted. Antiquing, cross-country skiing, downhill skiing, fishing, golf, live theater, parks, shopping, sporting events, tennis and water sports nearby.

Casa Europa Inn & Gallery

HC 68, Box 3 F, 840 Upper Ranchito
Taos, NM 87571-9408
(505)758-9798 (888)758-9798
E-mail: casa-europa@travelbase.com
Web: www.casaeuropanm.com

Circa 1700. Guests will appreciate both the elegance and history at Casa Europa. The home is a 17th-century pueblo-adobe creation with heavy beams, walls three-feet thick and a dining room with a massive kiva fireplace. Freshly baked goodies are served in the afternoons, and during ski season, hors d'oeuvres are provided in the early evening. European antiques fill the rooms, which are decorated in an elegant, Southwestern style. The French Room offers an 1860 bed, kiva fireplace and French doors opening onto the courtyard. Other rooms offer a fireplace, whirlpool tub or private hot tub. The inn is 1.6 miles from Taos Plaza.

Innkeeper(s): Joe & Lisa McCutcheon. $75-175. 6 rooms with PB, 6 with FP. Breakfast included in rates. Types of meals: Full gourmet bkfst, early coffee/tea, afternoon tea and snacks/refreshments. Beds: KQT. Cable TV, reading lamp, refrigerator, ceiling fan, clock radio, telephone, turn-down service, desk and hot tub/spa in room. Spa, sauna and fireplace on premises. Small meetings and family reunions hosted. Antiquing, cross-country skiing, downhill skiing, fishing, live theater, parks, shopping and water sports nearby.

Dreamcatcher Bed & Breakfast

416 La Lomita Rd.
Taos, NM 87571
(505)758-0613 (888)758-0613 Fax:(505)751-0115
E-mail: dream@taosnm.com
Web: www.dreambb.com

Circa 1946. Encounter the essence of the area at this traditional New Mexican adobe with Southwestern decor. Accommodations include guest bedrooms, a suite and two cabins with amenities such as robes and hair dryers. Most rooms boast fireplaces and refrigerators. Start the day with a filling country-style breakfast of Belgian waffles with whipped cream and strawberries, an egg burrito with green chili and cheese or a mushroom cheese omelette. A fruit plate, cereal, granola or oatmeal are other options. Relax in the secluded wooded location bordered on one side by a small stream. A soak in the hot tub provides further pampering.

Innkeeper(s): Bob & Jill Purtee. $89-134. 7 rooms with PB, 7 with FP, 1 suite, 2 cabins and 1 conference room. Breakfast, afternoon tea and snacks/refreshments included in rates. Types of meals: Country bkfst and early coffee/tea. Beds: KQD. Cable TV, reading lamp, stereo, refrigerator, ceiling fan, clock radio, coffeemaker, desk, fireplace, robes and hair dryer in room. Fax, spa, parlor games, telephone, fireplace, gift shop and hammocks on premises. Weddings, small meetings and family reunions hosted. Antiquing, art galleries, bicycling, canoeing/kayaking, cross-country skiing, downhill skiing, fishing, golf, hiking, horseback riding, live theater, museums, parks, shopping, tennis, wineries, National Park, Taos Pueblo and Rio Grande Gorge nearby.

Hacienda Del Sol

PO Box 177
Taos, NM 87571-0177
(505)758-0287 (866)333-4459 Fax:(505)758-5895
E-mail: sunhouse@newmex.com
Web: www.taoshaciendadelsol.com

Circa 1810. Mabel Dodge, patron of the arts, purchased this old hacienda as a hideaway for her Native American husband, Tony Luhan. The spacious adobe sits among huge cottonwoods, blue spruce, and ponderosa pines, with an uninterrupt-

ed view of the Taos mountains across 95,000 acres of Native American Indian lands. Among Dodge's famous guests were

Georgia O'Keefe, who painted here, and D. H. Lawrence. The mood is tranquil and on moonlit nights guests can hear Indian drums and the howl of coyotes.

Historic Interest: Taos Pueblo (2 miles), Bandelier National Monument (60 miles), Puye Cliffs (53 miles).

Innkeeper(s): Dennis Sheehan. $95-260. 11 rooms with PB, 10 with FP and 2 suites. Breakfast and snacks/refreshments included in rates. Types of meals: Full bkfst and early coffee/tea. Beds: KQDT. Reading lamp, CD player, refrigerator, clock radio, hot tub/spa, cassette/CD player, fireplace, steam baths and Jacuzzi tubs in room. Fax, spa, library, parlor games, telephone and fireplace on premises. Limited handicap access. Weddings, small meetings, family reunions and seminars hosted. Antiquing, cross-country skiing, downhill skiing, fishing, live theater, parks, shopping, water sports, museums, art galleries, 1,500-year-old pueblo, art festivals, cultural programs and Indian ruins nearby.

Publicity: *Cleveland Plain Dealer, Houston Chronicle, Chicago Tribune, Los Angeles Daily News, Denver Post, Globe & Mail, Reunions Magazine, Santa Fe Magazine and Travel Channel.*

"Your warm friendliness and gracious hospitality have made this week an experience we will never forget!"

Inn on La Loma Plaza

PO Box 4159, 315 Ranchitos Rd
Taos, NM 87571
(505)758-1717 (800)530-3040 Fax:(505)751-0155
E-mail: laloma@vacationtaos.com
Web: www.VacationTaos.com

Circa 1800. Thick adobe walls, vigas and latillas comprise this restored inn which showcases Pueblo Revival architecture (Santa Fe style). Listed in the national and state registers, this landmark sits on a small hill in the historic district. Two blocks from downtown, an old world setting blends with a Southwest ambiance enhanced by hand-carved wood details, antiques and local art. All guest bedrooms include kitchenettes, patios and exceptional views. Savor a satisfying gourmet breakfast as well as afternoon snacks, beverages, and evening coffee with cookies. The park-like setting features fountains and gardens. Enjoy a children's playground and large outdoor hot tub. Privileges

are extended for use of the nearby health club, tennis court and pool. Try white-water rafting or skiing at a local resort.

Innkeeper(s): Jerry & Peggy Davis. $100-300. 7 rooms with PB, 7 with FP, 2 suites and 1 conference room. Breakfast and snacks/refreshments included in rates. Types of meals: Full gourmet bkfst and early coffee/tea. Beds: KQ. Cable TV, VCR, reading lamp, CD player, clock radio, telephone, desk and FM radios in room. Air conditioning. Fax, library, fireplace and a poured concrete 6-person hot tub on premises. Weddings, small meetings, family reunions and seminars hosted. Antiquing, cross-country skiing, downhill skiing, fishing, golf, parks, shopping, tennis and water sports nearby.

Publicity: *USA Today, Outside, Chicago Tribune, Denver Post, Romantic Getaways, Sunset and Mountain Living.*

"Your hospitality while we were there exceeded what we've ever experienced at a B&B."

La Posada De Taos

PO Box 1118
Taos, NM 87571-1118
(505)758-8164 (800)645-4803 Fax:(505)751-4696
E-mail: laposada@laposadadetaos.com
Web: www.laposadadetaos.com

Circa 1907. This secluded adobe is located just a few blocks from the plaza in the Taos historic district. Rooms are decorated in a romantic Southwestern style with antiques, quilts and polished wood or tile floors. All but one of the guest rooms

include a kiva fireplace, and some offer private patios, TVs and telephones. For those in search of solitude, ask about the innkeeper's separate honeymoon casita suite. Guests can walk to galleries, museums, shops and restaurants.

Innkeeper(s): Sandy & Alan Thiese. $99-234. 6 rooms with PB, 5 with FP and 1 conference room. Breakfast and snacks/refreshments included in rates. Types of meals: Full bkfst. Beds: KQ. Reading lamp, desk and some with phone and TV in room. VCR, fax, copier, library, parlor games, telephone, fireplace and private deck with waterfall on premises. Weddings, small meetings and family reunions hosted. Antiquing, cross-country skiing, downhill skiing, fishing, live theater, parks, shopping, water sports and art galleries nearby.

Publicity: *New York Times, Bon Appetit, Country Inns, Glamour and Los Angeles Times.*

"We had a wonderful stay in your beautiful B&B. Everything was excellent. I'm giving your name to my travel agent, with the highest recommendation for your B&B."

Old Taos Guesthouse B&B

1028 Witt Rd, 6552 NDCBU
Taos, NM 87571
(505)758-5448 (800)758-5448
E-mail: oldtaos@newmex.com
Web: taoswebb.com/hotel/oldtaoshouse/

Circa 1850. This adobe hacienda sits on a rise overlooking Taos and is surrounded by large cottonwood, blue spruce, apple, apricot and pinon trees. This estate, which offers panoramic views, originally served as a farmer's home, but later was home to an artist. As the years went by, rooms were added. Most rooms include special items such as kiva fireplaces, handwoven wall hangings, dried flowers, log four-poster beds and

hand-painted vanities. The Southwestern-style rooms all have private entrances. The outdoor hot tub boasts a wonderful view. Healthy, homemade breakfasts are served in a room filled with antiques. The home is set on more than seven acres, located less than two miles from the Plaza.

Historic Interest: There is a historic acequia irrigation ditch that runs through the grounds. Nearby attractions include a 1,000-year-old Taos Pueblo, Martinez Hacienda, the Kit Carson House and St. Francis de Assisi church. The Bandelier National Monument Cliff Dwellings are about an hour from Taos.

Innkeeper(s): Tim & Leslie Reeves. $70-125. 9 rooms with PB, 5 with FP and 2 suites. Breakfast included in rates. Types of meals: Cont plus and early coffee/tea. Beds: KQT. Reading lamp, refrigerator and clock radio in room. Spa, stable, library, parlor games, telephone and fireplace on premises. Antiquing, cross-country skiing, downhill skiing, fishing, live theater, parks and shopping nearby.

Publicity: *Denver Post Travel, Inn for the Night, Dallas Morning News, West, Country and Houston Chronicle.*

"We really enjoyed the authenticity of your guesthouse."

Orinda B&B

461 Valverde
Taos, NM 87571
(505)758-8581 (800)847-1837
E-mail: orinda@newmex.com
Web: www.orindabb.com

Circa 1935. Current innkeepers Adrian and Sheila Percival are only the fifth owners of this property, which was deeded to its original owners by Abraham Lincoln. The house itself, a traditional adobe with an outstanding view of Taos Mountain, was built years later, and features Southwestern touches such as kiva fireplaces,  original art and turn-of-the-century antiques. Sheila serves up a full breakfast such as green chile souffle, pecan French toast and bottomless cups of the inn's special coffee blend.

Historic Interest: The Kit Carson Home is a 15-minute walk from the bed & breakfast. Taos Pueblo and Martinez Hacienda are within easy driving distance, and the village of Taos offers many historic sites. Art galleries, museums, skiing, hiking, biking, riding, golf and fishing are all located nearby.

Innkeeper(s): Adrian & Sheila Percival. $89-145. 5 rooms with PB, 3 with FP and 1 suite. Breakfast included in rates. Types of meals: Full bkfst. Beds: KQT. TV, VCR and one has two-person whirlpool in room. Weddings and family reunions hosted. Antiquing, cross-country skiing, downhill skiing, fishing, golf, shopping, hiking, museums and biking nearby.

"It really is 'a B&B paradise' with your beautiful surroundings."

Taos Country Inn

PO Box 2331
Taos, NM 87571-2331
(505)758-4900 (800)866-6548 Fax:(505)758-0331
E-mail: taoscountryinn@newmex.com
Web: www.taos-countryinn.com

Circa 1850. Nestled among 200-year-old towering willows and cottonwoods on more than 20 acres of pasture land and cultivated gardens, this adobe-style inn offers both the luxury of modern amenities and the rustic charm of its historic past. There are nine spacious suites decorated in leather sofas, down comforters, and all featuring sweeping mountain or river views. Close to the historic Plaza, museums and Indian Pueblo.

Innkeeper(s): Yolanda Deveaux. $100-140. 8 rooms with PB, 8 with FP. Breakfast included in rates. Types of meals: Full gourmet bkfst and early coffee/tea. Beds: KQT. Cable TV, reading lamp, clock radio, telephone and desk in room. VCR, fax, copier, fireplace and refrigerator on premises. Weddings, small meetings and family reunions hosted. Antiquing, cross-country skiing, downhill skiing, fishing, golf, shopping and tennis nearby.

The Taos Inn

125 Paseo Del Pueblo Norte
Taos, NM 87571-5901
(505)758-2233 (800)826-7466 Fax:(505)758-5776
E-mail: taosinn@newmex.com
Web: www.taosinn.com

Circa 1880. Voted by National Geographic Traveler as one of "America's 54 Great Inns", The Taos Inn is a historic landmark with sections dating back to the 1600s. The inn's authentic adobe pueblo architecture enhances the inviting wood-burning fireplaces (kivas), vigas and wrought iron. Handsomely decorated rooms include reflections of the area's exotic tri-cultural heritage of Spanish, Anglo and Indian in the hand-loomed Indian bedspreads, antique armoires and Taos furniture. The well reviewed restaurant includes the legendary Adobe Bar. Ancient Taos Pueblo is nearby.

Innkeeper(s): Douglas Smith & Carolyn Haddock. $60-225. 33 rooms, 36 with PB and 3 suites. Types of meals: Full gourmet bkfst, veg bkfst, early coffee/tea, gourmet lunch, snacks/refreshments and gourmet dinner. Restaurant on premises. Beds: KQDT. Cable TV, clock radio, telephone and voice mail in room. Air conditioning. VCR, fax, copier, fireplace, outdoor pool, greenhouse, Jacuzzi, full bar with live music five nights per week (legendary margaritas) and live jazz venue on premises. Limited handicap access. Weddings, small meetings and family reunions hosted. Art galleries, bicycling, canoeing/kayaking, cross-country skiing, downhill skiing, fishing, golf, hiking, live theater, museums, parks, shopping and wineries nearby.

Publicity: *Travel & Leisure, Gourmet, Bon Appetit, National Geographic Traveler and New York Times.*

"It is charming, warm, friendly and authentic in decor with a real sense of history."

Touchstone Inn, Spa & Gallery

0110 Mabel Dodge Ln
Taos, NM 87571
(505)758-0192 (800)758-0192 Fax:(505)758-3498
E-mail: touchstone@taosnet.com
Web: www.touchstoneinn.com

Circa 1800. Touchstone Inn is a quiet, historic adobe estate secluded among tall trees at the edge of Taos Pueblo lands. The grounds have an unobstructed view of Taos Mountain. USA Today calls it "the place to stay in Taos." The inn, connected to a spa and a gallery, features cozy rooms with fireplaces, luxurious textiles, intimate patios and exquisite tiled baths (four of which have Jacuzzi tubs). The inn offers full gourmet vegetarian and continental breakfasts. The spa offers massages, yoga and art classes, facials and therapeutic baths and wraps. Guests enjoy the outdoor hot tub with choice vistas of Taos Mountain. Taos Ski valley is 18 miles to the north.

$135-350. 7 rooms with PB, 6 with FP. Types of meals: Full gourmet bkfst. Beds: KQD. Cable TV, VCR, ceiling fan, telephone, coffeemaker, bath robes, hair dryers and four with Jacuzzi in room. Day spa, piano and garden massages on premises. Downhill skiing nearby.

Publicity: *USA Today, Bride's Magazine, Modern Bride, Mountain Living and Getaways.*

New York

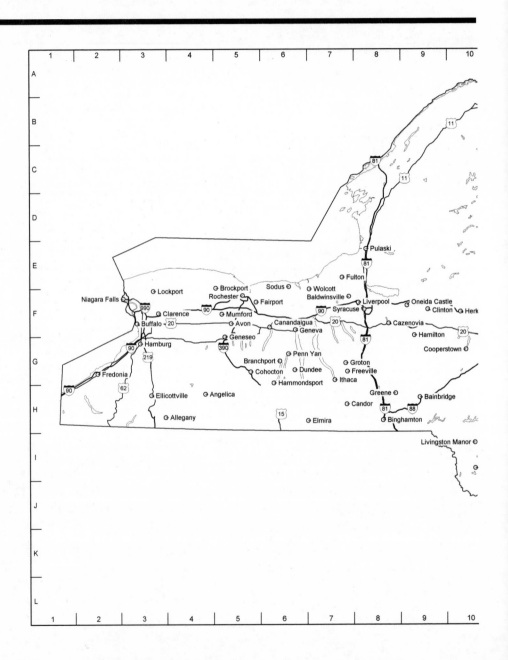

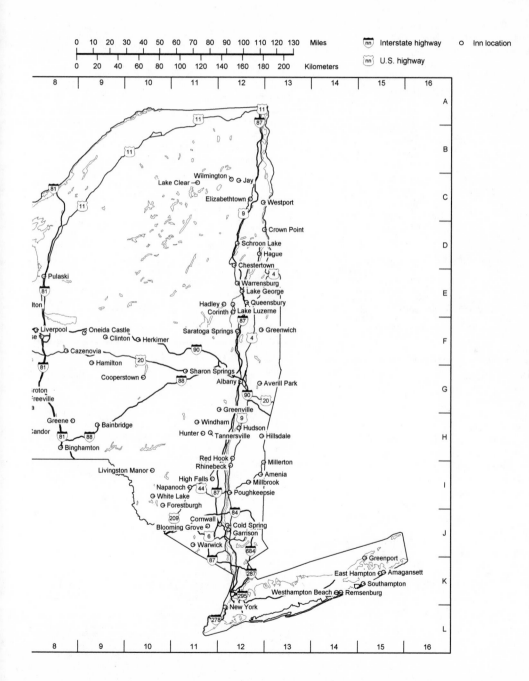

Miles
0 10 20 30 40 50 60 70 80 90 100 110 120 130

Kilometers
0 20 40 60 80 100 120 140 160 180 200

<table>
</table>

Interstate highway   o   Inn location

U.S. highway

Adirondack D12

Adirondack Pines Bed & Breakfast & Guest House

1257 Valentine Road
Adirondack, NY 12808
(518)494-5249 Fax:(518)494-5299
E-mail: stay@adirondackpines.com
Web: www.adirondackpines.com

Circa 1837. Surrounded by year-round scenic beauty, there is much to experience while staying at this historic 1837 Country Farmhouse, just two minutes from Schroon Lake's beach and boat launch. Relax in the living room with cable TV. Antiques and handmade quilts accent the pleasant décor of the air-conditioned guest bedrooms. The Master Suite boasts wide plank flooring, a refrigerator, gas stove and a two-person Jacuzzi tub. The spacious Balsam Room offers a Queen and a twin bed. A small room with a twin bed accommodates a fourth person. Linger over a candlelit country breakfast in the dining room by the wood stove. A private, newly renovated three-bedroom house with a gas fireplace is also available. Soak up nature while strolling the 100 acres of grounds. Ski nearby Gore Mountain or hike Pharaoh Mountain for breathtaking views.
Historic Interest: It is an 1837 farmhouse with modern amenities, 1st house in our village of Adirondack.

Innkeeper(s): Dan & Nancy Lindsley-Freebern. $65-125. 3 rooms, 2 with PB, 1 with FP. Breakfast and snacks/refreshments included in rates. Types of meals: Country bkfst. Beds: KQDT. Cable TV, VCR, refrigerator, clock radio, coffeemaker, two-person Jacuzzi tub and gas freestanding fireplace in room. Air conditioning. Fax, copier, parlor games, telephone and fireplace on premises. Amusement parks, antiquing, art galleries, beach, bicycling, canoeing/kayaking, cross-country skiing, downhill skiing, fishing, hiking, horseback riding, museums, shopping, water sports and wineries nearby.

Albany G12

Pine Haven B&B

531 Western Ave
Albany, NY 12203-1721
(518)482-1574
E-mail: pinehavenb@aol.com
Web: www.pinehavenbedandbreakfast.com

Circa 1896. This turn-of-the-century Victorian is located in Pine Hills, an Albany historic district. In keeping with this history, the innkeepers have tried to preserve the home's 19th-century charm. The rooms offer old-fashioned comfort with Victorian influences. The Capitol Building and other historic sites are nearby.

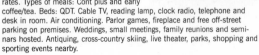

Innkeeper(s): Janice Tricarico. $69-99. 5 rooms with PB. Breakfast included in rates. Types of meals: Cont plus and early coffee/tea. Beds: QDT. Cable TV, reading lamp, clock radio, telephone and desk in room. Air conditioning. Parlor games, fireplace and free off-street parking on premises. Weddings, small meetings, family reunions and seminars hosted. Antiquing, cross-country skiing, live theater, parks, shopping and sporting events nearby.

Allegany H3

Gallets House B&B

1759 Four Mile Rd
Allegany, NY 14706-9724
(716)373-7493 Fax:(716)806-0384
E-mail: info@galletshouse.com
Web: www.galletshouse.com

Circa 1896. Once a summer retreat for Franciscan Friars, this 1896 Victorian inn was built by the current innkeeper's great uncle. Relax on the 100-foot wraparound porch and enjoy the view of the picturesque Alleghany hills. Choose among five guest rooms named after family members: Rose Clara, Mary Elizabeth, Grace Agatha , Regina Barbara and Christina Helen. Larger groups may prefer the Carriage House, which has three bedrooms with queen-size beds, a small kitchen and a spacious living room with a sofa bed. Innkeeper Joan prepares lavish gourmet breakfasts and serves them in the formal dining room by candlelight. Fruits, homemade breads and biscuits are the prelude to sumptuous hot entrees and Joan's memorable apple cinnamon pancakes. Joan also provides afternoon or evening beverages and freshly baked goods. The inn hosts murder mysteries and tea parties. Ask about their specialty packages.

Innkeeper(s): Joan & Gary Boser. $75-125. 5 rooms with PB, 1 with FP and 1 conference room. Breakfast and snacks/refreshments included in rates. Types of meals: Full gourmet bkfst, early coffee/tea and afternoon tea. Beds: KQD. Modem hook-up, cable TV, reading lamp, CD player, ceiling fan, clock radio, telephone, desk and two whirlpool tubs in room. Air conditioning. Fax, copier, spa and fireplace on premises. Weddings, small meetings and family reunions hosted. Antiquing, art galleries, bicycling, canoeing/kayaking, cross-country skiing, downhill skiing, fishing, golf, hiking, horseback riding, live theater, museums, parks, shopping and sporting events nearby.

Amagansett K15

The William Hand House

384 Main Street
Amagansett, NY 11930-1253
(631)267-2626 Fax:(631)267-1034

Circa 1829. One of the East End's first guest houses, this classic example of Greek Revival architecture has been recently renovated to impart modern comforts while retaining its original charm and Victorian decor. Relaxation comes easy on the porch, garden swing or hammock. Explore the area on a guest bicycle, or walk to the ocean beach. Guest bedrooms, many with fireplaces, feature country antiques, Jacuzzi tubs with bath salts, candles, fluffy robes, refrigerators and cable TV/VCR. Borrow a video from the collection in the dining room. Choose from an assortment of juices and cereals alongside carrot walnut raisin muffins and preserves, blueberry banana pancakes, mimosas or bloody marys for breakfast. Weather permitting, dine al fresco on picnic tables.
Historic Interest: The doorway of the William Hand House is the finest example of a Greek Revival doorway on the East coast.

Innkeeper(s): Steve and Doris Switsky. $125-450. 5 rooms with PB, 3 with FP and 1 suite. Breakfast, afternoon tea and snacks/refreshments included in rates. Types of meals: Full gourmet bkfst. Beds: KQDT. Cable TV, VCR, reading lamp, refrigerator, ceiling fan, coffeemaker and fireplace in room. Air conditioning. Bicycles, library, parlor games, telephone and fireplace on premises. Weddings and family reunions hosted. Antiquing, art galleries, beach, bicycling, canoeing/kayaking, fishing, golf, hiking, horseback riding, live theater, museums, parks, shopping, tennis, water sports and wineries nearby.
Publicity: *Home and Garden.*

Amenia I12

Troutbeck

Leedsville Rd
Amenia, NY 12501
(845)373-9681 Fax:(845)373-7080
E-mail: garret@troutbeck.com
Web: www.troutbeck.com

Circa 1918. This English country estate on 600 wooded acres enjoyed its heyday in the '20s. The NAACP was conceived here and the literati and liberals of the period, including Teddy Roosevelt, were overnight guests. Weekend room rates, $650 to $1050, include six meals and luxurious accommodations for two. On Sundays, brunch is served. The inn has a fitness center, billiard table, outdoor and indoor pools and tennis courts. During the week the inn is a corporate retreat and has been awarded Executive Retreat of the Year. In July, 1997, Troutbeck was the site of a United Nations Summit meeting. Many weddings are held here each year and a new Great Room/ballroom has been added, which accommodates weddings with up to 250 guests and corporate gatherings for about 70 people.

Innkeeper(s): Jim Flaherty & Garret Corcoran. $650-1050. 42 rooms, 37 with PB, 9 with FP, 8 suites and 3 conference rooms. Breakfast and dinner included in rates. Types of meals: Full bkfst, early coffee/tea and lunch. Restaurant on premises. Beds: KQDT. Reading lamp, clock radio, telephone, turn-down service, desk and some ceiling fans in room. Air conditioning. VCR, fax, copier, swimming, sauna, tennis, library, parlor games, fireplace and day spa on premises. Weddings, family reunions and seminars hosted. Antiquing, cross-country skiing, downhill skiing, fishing, live theater, parks, shopping and sporting events nearby.

Publicity: *New York Times, Good Housekeeping, New York Magazine, American Express and Vogue.*

"This 1920s-style estate makes you wish all life could be this way."

Angelica H4

Angelica Inn

64 E Main St. Box 686
Angelica, NY 14709-8710
(585)466-3063

Circa 1882. Located in the Allegany foothills, the Angelica Inn features stained glass, crystal chandeliers, parquet floors, an oak staircase, carved woodwork, antique furnishings and scent-

ed rooms. Guest rooms offer such amenities as fireplaces, a porch and a breakfast alcove area.

Innkeeper(s): Cynthia & Nicholas Petito. $75-125. 6 rooms with PB, 3 with FP and 1 conference room. Breakfast included in rates. Types of meals: Full bkfst. Beds: KQ. Cable TV, refrigerator, ceiling fan and desk in room. Weddings, small meetings, family reunions and seminars hosted. Antiquing, cross-country skiing, fishing, golf and parks nearby.

"Victorian at its best!"

Averill Park G12

La Perla at the Gregory House, Country Inn & Restaurant

Rt 43 PO Box 401
Averill Park, NY 12018-0401
(518)674-3774 Fax:(518)674-8916
E-mail: info@gregoryhouse.com
Web: www.gregoryhouse.com

Circa 1830. Stockbroker Elias Gregory built what is now the restaurant, as his Colonial home in the 1800s. The newer B&B inn, just twelve years old, blends well with the original house to retain the ambiance of its Victorian heritage. Gather by the dramatic fireplace in the common room which boasts vaulted ceilings, comfy furniture and a big-screen TV. The decor of each well-appointed guest bedroom is inviting. Award-winning La Perla offers Italian continental cuisine and is personally run by innkeeper Alfonso. This rural country town is surrounded by the Adirondacks, Berkshires, Hudson River, Saratoga and Albany with a variety of historic and scenic attractions.

Innkeeper(s): Anna Maria & Alfonso Acampora. $100-125. 12 rooms with PB and 1 conference room. Breakfast included in rates. Types of meals: Cont. Restaurant on premises. Beds: QDT. TV, reading lamp, clock radio, telephone and desk in room. Air conditioning. VCR, fax, copier and fireplace on premises. Weddings, small meetings, family reunions and seminars hosted. Amusement parks, antiquing, cross-country skiing, downhill skiing, fishing, live theater, parks, shopping, sporting events and water sports nearby.

Publicity: *Hudson Valley, Albany Times Union, Schenectady Gazette, Courier and Sunday Record.*

"We experienced privacy and quiet, lovely surroundings indoors and out, excellent service and as much friendliness as we were comfortable with, but no more."

Avon F5

Avon Inn

55 E Main St
Avon, NY 14414-1438
(716)226-8181 Fax:(716)226-8185

Circa 1820. This Greek Revival mansion, in both the state and national historic registers, has been providing lodging for more than a century. After 1866, the residence was turned into a health center that provided water cures from the local sulphur springs. The guest registry included the likes of Henry Ford, Thomas Edison and Eleanor Roosevelt. Though the inn is no longer a health spa, guests can still relax in the garden with its towering trees and fountain or on the Grecian-pillared front porch. A full-service restaurant and conference facilities are on the premises.

Historic Interest: 1820 Greek Revival initially the residence of Jonathan H. Gerry, a successful broom corn grower.

Innkeeper(s): Linda Moran. $75-115. 14 rooms with PB. Breakfast included in rates. Types of meals: Cont. Restaurant on premises. Beds: KQD. Clock radio, telephone and desk in room. Air conditioning. TV, fax and copier on premises. Weddings, small meetings, family reunions and seminars hosted. Amusement parks, antiquing, cross-country skiing, downhill skiing, fishing, golf, museums, parks and shopping nearby.

White Oak Bed and Breakfast

277 Genesee Street
Avon, NY 14414
(585)226-6735
E-mail: avon-bnb@frontiernet.net
Web: whiteoakbandb.com

Circa 1860. Built as a summer home in the 1860s, this distinctive Second Empire Victorian with a mansard roof and wraparound porch has been recently renovated to retain its original charm and traditional decor. A private den/parlor with TV/VCR and board games is a convenient gathering place. Well-placed period furnishings accent the guest bedrooms and spacious Pine Suite. Enjoy the expansive view from the dining room while savoring home-baked breads, fresh fruit, and perhaps a broccoli cheddar omelette with home fries and bacon for breakfast. The one acre of gardens, with flowers for every season, include private sitting areas to chat. Visit nearby Genesee Country Village or take day trips to explore the scenic Finger Lakes Region.

Historic Interest: A splendid example of Second Empire Victorian with a mansard roof, built circa 1860.

Innkeeper(s): Barbara Herman. Call for rates. 3 rooms with PB. Breakfast and snacks/refreshments included in rates. Types of meals: Country bkfst, veg bkfst, early coffee/tea and picnic lunch. Beds: QD. Antiquing, art galleries, bicycling, fishing, golf, hiking, horseback riding, live theater, museums, parks, shopping and wineries nearby.

Bainbridge H9

Berry Hill Gardens B&B

242 Ward Loomis Rd.
Bainbridge, NY 13733
(607)967-8745 (800)497-8745 Fax:(607)967-2227
E-mail: info@berryhillgardens.com
Web: www.berryhillgardens.com

Circa 1820. Surrounded by flower and herb gardens, this farmhouse presides over 180 acres. Guest rooms are furnished in antiques and decorated with bunches of fresh and dried flowers. Organic gardens provide 100 varieties of annuals and

perennials. There are tulips, poppies, lilacs, sweet peas and in May, the fruit trees are in bloom. A full country breakfast is served. By advance reservation you can arrange for a sleigh ride or horse-drawn wagon to take you through the woods and meadows of the Berry Hill Farm, or you may stroll through the gardens and woods on your own.

Innkeeper(s): Jean Fowler & Cecilio Rios. $75-125. 5 rooms, 2 with PB, 1 suite and 1 cottage. Types of meals: Country bkfst and early coffee/tea. Beds: QDT. Reading lamp, ceiling fan, clock radio and desk in room. TV, VCR, fax, copier, swimming, parlor games and telephone on premises. Weddings, small meetings, family reunions and seminars hosted. Antiquing, art galleries, bicycling, canoeing/kayaking, cross-country skiing, fishing, golf, hiking, horseback riding, live theater, museums, parks, shopping, sporting events, tennis and water sports nearby.

Publicity: *Country Living Gardener Magazine-August 2001 and Binghamton Press and Sun.*

"The house is just wonderful and our rooms were exceptionally comfortable."

Baldwinsville F7

Pandora's Getaway

83 Oswego St
Baldwinsville, NY 13027-1130
(315)635-9571 (888)638-8668

Circa 1845. Nestled amid large trees on a hill in a tranquil village setting, this Greek Revival inn is listed in the National Register of Historic Places. Homemade crafts are mingled with antiques and collectibles to decorate the inn. Families with children are welcomed with a variety of games and toys. Guests enjoy breakfasts of fresh fruit, homemade breads and quiche or a favorite family recipe in the formal dining room. The innkeeper collects depression glassware and uses it in her special table settings. Rockers on the porch afford quiet reading and visiting while listening to the breeze rustle the trees. Located a block from the center of town, the inn provides easy access to all the village offerings, including restaurants, shops, a working river lock of the Barge Canal System and a bakery.

Innkeeper(s): Sandra Wheeler. $65-90. 4 rooms. Breakfast included in rates. Types of meals: Full gourmet bkfst and early coffee/tea. Beds: KQD. TV, ceiling fan, clock radio and telephone in room. VCR and fireplace on premises. Family reunions and seminars hosted. Antiquing, bicycling, cross-country skiing, fishing, golf, hiking, horseback riding, museums, parks, shopping, sporting events, tennis and wineries nearby.

Binghamton H8

Pickle Hill B&B

795 Chenango St
Binghamton, NY 13901-1844
(607)723-0259
E-mail: trossi@stny.rr.com
Web: www.picklehill.net

Circa 1890. This folksy B&B is a haven for those tired of endless motel nights. Guests feel as if they've stepped into the home of a good friend, and innkeepers Tom Rossi and Leslie Kiersted have made many friends over the last few years. The environment is comfortable country, highlighted by stained-glass windows and rich woodwork. The grounds are equipped for a game of basketball or badminton, and guests are often found gathered around the piano singing old songs.

Innkeeper(s): Tom Rossi & Leslie Kiersted Rossi. $50-60. 3 rooms. Breakfast and snacks/refreshments included in rates. Types of meals: Full bkfst, early coffee/tea and room service. Beds: DT. Reading lamp, radio and tapes in room. VCR, bicycles, parlor games, telephone and piano on premises. Antiquing, cross-country skiing, downhill skiing, fishing, live theater, parks, shopping, sporting events and water sports nearby.

Bloomfield   F5

A Wolfpack Bed N' Breakfast

6700 State Rt 5 & 20
Bloomfield, NY 14469
(585)657-4863 Fax:(585)657-4576

Circa 1820. Relatives of President Taft built this Colonial farm-house, now restored and a peaceful place to stay while explor-ing the picturesque and historic Finger Lakes region. The guest bedrooms are decorated in a comfortable country charm. Most feature a fireplace and Jacuzzi for two to inspire romance. The Carriage House, perfect for family retreats, has a full kitchen, dining area, living room and private deck. A hearty breakfast is prepared to please. Enjoy gently swinging in the gazebo loveseat, while planning the day's events.

Innkeeper(s): Robin Grentus & Micheal. $95-165. 3 rooms with PB and 1 cottage. Breakfast and snacks/refreshments included in rates. Types of meals: Country bkfst and early coffee/tea. Beds: KQT. Reading lamp, ceiling fan, clock radio, fireplace and two with Jacuzzi in room. Air conditioning. TV, VCR, fax, copier, library, parlor games, telephone and fireplace on premises. Amusement parks, antiquing, art galleries, beach, cross-country skiing, down-hill skiing, fishing, golf, hiking, horseback riding, live theater, museums, parks, shopping, water sports and wineries nearby.

Blooming Grove   J11

The Dominion House

50 Old Dominion Road
Blooming Grove, NY 10914
(845)496-1826 Fax:(845)496-3492
E-mail: kathy@thedominionhouse.com
Web: www.thedominionhouse.com

Circa 1880. At the end of a country lane in the scenic Hudson Valley, this Victorian Farmhouse has been adorning four and a half acres since 1880. Original marble mantels, ornate cornice work, wide-plank floors, large pocket doors and eleven-foot ceilings with plaster medallions reflect a well-maintained ele-gance. The library offers a large book selection or relax by the fire in the oak den. Play a game of pool on the slate-top table and listen to music in the parlor. Large guest bedrooms and a private Honeymoon Cottage are furnished with antiques. A hearty breakfast is served in the dining room with specialty dishes that may include caramel sticky buns, featherlight scones, stuffed croissants, peach French toast and sausage. Swim in the inground pool, play horseshoes or relax on the wraparound porch.

Historic Interest: Built in 1880 it has charm and unique mouldings, marble mantels, plater cornice work, large rooms, high ceilings and original floor plans on parchment.

Innkeeper(s): Kathy & Joe Spear. $105-169. 4 rooms, 1 with PB and 1 cottage. Breakfast and snacks/refreshments included in rates. Types of meals: Country bkfst and early coffee/tea. Beds: QDT. Modem hook-up, cable TV, reading lamp, clock radio, telephone and robes in room. Air conditioning. Fax, copier, spa, swimming, library, parlor games, fireplace, slate-top pool table, horseshoes, guest refrigerator and complimentary snacks and drinks on premises. Weddings and family reunions hosted. Antiquing, art galleries, canoeing/kayaking, cross-country skiing, downhill skiing, fishing, golf, hiking, live theater, museums, parks, shopping and wineries nearby.

Branchport   G6

Gone With The Wind on Keuka Lake

14905 W Lake Rd, Rt 54 A
Branchport, NY 14418
(607)868-4603

Circa 1887. Breezes from Keuka Lake waft up to the front porch where guests often sit with a cup of coffee. The lakeside home, a Victorian, is decorated with an eclectic, uncluttered assortment of reproductions. Each of the bathrooms features unique decor, such as oak, brass or marble. One room includes a fireplace. There's a hot tub in the solarium, and the grounds offer a gazebo by the inn's private beach cove.

Innkeeper(s): Linda & Robert Lewis. $80-130. 10 rooms, 3 with PB, 1 with FP. Breakfast included in rates. Types of meals: Full bkfst. Beds: KQ. Reading lamp, refrigerator, clock radio and Jacuzzi in room. Air conditioning. Fax, spa, swimming, telephone and fireplace on premises. Antiquing, cross-country ski-ing, fishing, parks, shopping, tennis, water sports, Curtis Museum and nine wineries nearby.

Publicity: *Summer Pleasures, Outdoors, Travel and Wine Times.*

"Thanks once again for a delightful stay. You have a little bit of heaven here."

Brockport   E5

The Portico B&B

3741 Lake Rd N
Brockport, NY 14420-1415
(585)637-0220

Circa 1850. Named for its three porches, called porticos, this Greek Revival inn is situated amid blue spruce, maple and sycamore trees in a historic district. Tall columns and a cupola add to its charm. The interior features three fireplaces. Three antique-filled guest rooms are available to visitors, who enjoy a full Victorian breakfast and kettledrum, also known as after-noon tea. The inn is listed in the National Register, as are sever-al other structures in town. The surrounding area offers many attractions, including the Cobblestone Museum, Darien Lake Amusement Park, George Eastman House and Strasenburgh Planetarium. Several colleges, golf courses and parks are nearby. In winter, sleigh rides also are available nearby.

Innkeeper(s): Anne Klein. $70-80. 3 rooms with PB, 3 with FP. Breakfast included in rates. Types of meals: Full bkfst and early coffee/tea. Reading lamp and turn-down service in room. VCR, telephone and fireplace on premises. Amusement parks, antiquing, cross-country skiing, downhill skiing, live theater, shopping, sporting events and sleigh rides nearby.

The Victorian B&B

320 S Main St
Brockport, NY 14420-2253
(585)637-7519 Fax:(585)637-7519
E-mail: sk320@aol.com
Web: www.victorianbandb.com

Circa 1890. Within walking distance of the historic Erie Canal, this Queen Anne Victorian inn is located on Brockport's Main Street. Visitors select from five second-floor guest rooms, all with phones, private baths and TVs. Victorian furnishings are found through-out the inn. A favorite spot is the solarium, with its three walls of windows and fireplace, perfect for curling up with a book or magazine. Two first-floor sitting areas with fireplaces also provide relaxing havens for guests. Lake Ontario is just 10 miles away, and visitors will find much to explore in Brockport and Rochester. Brockport is home to the State University of New York and Niagara Falls is an hour away.

Innkeeper(s): Sharon Kehoe. $64-101. 5 rooms with PB. Breakfast and afternoon tea included in rates. Types of meals: Full bkfst. Beds: KQDT. Cable TV, reading lamp, clock radio, telephone, desk and Jacuzzi tub in room. Air conditioning. VCR, fax, fireplace and e-mail access on premises. Small meetings, family reunions and seminars hosted. Antiquing, cross-country skiing, live theater, shopping and sporting events nearby.

"Memories of another time; hospitality of another era."

Buffalo   F3

Beau Fleuve B&B Inn

242 Linwood Ave
Buffalo, NY 14209-1802
(716)882-6116 (800)278-0245
E-mail: beauflve@buffnet.net
Web: www.beaufleuve.com

Circa 1881. Each of the five rooms in this serene Victorian inn celebrates a different ethnic group that settled in the region. In the French Room, absolute comfort is found, from the Neoclassical feather bed to Louis XV chairs covered in champagne damask. The Irish Room features an antique brass bed and William Morris sage and celery chrysanthemum wallcovering. Other elegant rooms mark the contributions of German, Italian and Polish immigrants. To honor the land's first inhabitants, the upstairs Native American common area showcases Indian artifacts accented by stunning stained-glass windows. The inn is located in the five-block-long Linwood Historic District, an intact living museum of America's architecture where art galleries, antique shops and restaurants are just steps away. A friendly ambiance is a reminder that Buffalo is known as the "City of Good Neighbors." Niagara Falls is just 16 miles away, via a scenic riverside drive.

Historic Interest: Buffalo's Allentown Historic District is less than one mile away and the magnificent Niagara Falls is 16 miles from the Beau Fleuve.

Innkeeper(s): Ramona Pando Whitaker & Rik Whitaker. $90-135. 5 rooms, 3 with PB. Breakfast included in rates. Types of meals: Full bkfst. Beds: KQDT. Antiquing, cross-country skiing, downhill skiing, fishing, live theater, sporting events, water sports and concerts/music nearby.

Publicity: *Buffalo News, New York Daily News, Preservation Coalition Tour House, Boston Globe, WIVB, WKBW TV and Adelphia Cable TV.*

"Relaxing, comfortable hospitality in beautiful surroundings."

Campbell   H6

Halcyon Place Bed & Breakfast

11 Maple Lane
Campbell, NY 14821
(607)583-4311
E-mail: herbtique@aol.com
Web: www.bbonline.com/ny/halcyon

Circa 1840. Named after a Greek word that means peace and tranquility, this circa 1840 Greek Revival inn is a landmark Steuben County home surrounded by two acres of open fields and scenic vistas. Its classic six-over-six windows, graceful columns, pine floors and detailed woodwork are accented by

period antique furnishings. Relax by the fire in the parlor or sit on the wicker-filled porch. Browse the new herb and antique shop in the former harness shop. Gorgeous guest bedrooms with ample space feature four-poster, canopy and tiger maple beds, toile fabrics and rich paint colors. A gourmet breakfast is served in the dining room with favorites like rum sticky buns or pear gingerbread and satisfying seasonal entrees. Explore the Keuka Lake Wine Trail, or nearby Corning.

Historic Interest: This circa 1840 house was the home of a wealthy lumber and sawmill owner. Former farm of the US Ambassador to France and CEO of Corning Glass.

Innkeeper(s): Doug & Yvonne Sloan. $95-140. 3 rooms with PB, 1 with FP. Breakfast included in rates. Types of meals: Full gourmet bkfst, veg bkfst and afternoon tea. Beds: QD. Refrigerator, turn-down service and fireplace in room. Air conditioning. Bicycles, telephone, fireplace and gift shop on premises. Limited handicap access. Weddings and small meetings hosted. Antiquing, art galleries, bicycling, cross-country skiing, fishing, golf, hiking, museums, parks, shopping, sporting events, water sports and wineries nearby.

Publicity: *Star-Gazette Homes Section.*

Canandaigua   F6

1795 Acorn Inn

4508 Rt 64 S, Bristol Ctr
Canandaigua, NY 14424
(585)229-2834 (888)245-4134 Fax:(585)229-5046
E-mail: acorninn@rochester.rr.com
Web: www.acorninnbb.com

Circa 1795. Guests to this Federal Stagecoach inn can relax before the blazing fire of a large colonial fireplace equipped with antique crane and hanging iron pots. Guest rooms, two with fireplace, are furnished with period antiques, canopy beds, luxury linens and bedding, and each has a comfortable sitting area. Books are provided in each guest room as well as in the libraries. After a day of visiting wineries, skiing, hiking in the Finger Lakes area and dinner at a local restaurant, guests can enjoy the inn's outdoor Jacuzzi. Beds are turned down each night and chocolates are placed in each room. Complimentary beverages are always available.

Historic Interest: Erie Canal (10 miles), Ganodagan Indian Site, Grauger Homestead, Sonnenberg Gardens.

Innkeeper(s): Joan & Louis Clark. $135-215. 4 rooms with PB, 2 with FP. Breakfast included in rates. Types of meals: Full gourmet bkfst and early coffee/tea. Beds: Q. Cable TV, VCR, reading lamp, stereo, refrigerator, snack bar, clock radio, turn-down service, down quilt, bathrobe and hair dryer in room. Air conditioning. Fax, copier, spa, library, parlor games, telephone and fireplace on premises. Weddings, small meetings and family reunions hosted. Antiquing, cross-country skiing, downhill skiing, fishing, live theater, parks, shopping and water sports nearby.

Publicity: *New York, Mid-Atlantic, Great Destinations: Finger Lakes, The Unofficial Guide to Bed and Breakfasts and Country Inns in the Mid-Atlantic, Frommers and Travel City.*

1885 Sutherland House B&B Inn

3179 State Route 21 South
Canandaigua, NY 14424-8341
(585)396-0375 (800)396-0375 Fax:(585)396-9281
E-mail: innkeeper@sutherlandhouse.com
Web: www.sutherlandhouse.com

Circa 1885. Lovingly refurbished, this Second Empire Victorian has had more than forty new windows added. Most of the original elements are intact such as a winding cherry staircase, marble fireplaces, molding and window shutters to create an elegant 19th-century Victorian atmosphere and décor. Well-appointed guest bedrooms feature double Jacuzzis and fireplaces. Located just one mile from Main Street, visit nearby restaurants and wineries or go antique shopping. This scenic Finger Lakes region offers many outdoor activities.

Innkeeper(s): Bonnie & Gary Ross. $100-195. 5 rooms with PB, 5 with FP and 1 suite. Breakfast, afternoon tea and snacks/refreshments included in rates. Types of meals: Country bkfst, veg bkfst and early coffee/tea. Beds: KQT. TV, VCR, reading lamp, refrigerator, ceiling fan, snack bar, clock radio, telephone and desk in room. Air conditioning. Fax, parlor games, fireplace and three double Jacuzzi on premises. Family reunions hosted. Antiquing, beach, bicycling, canoeing/kayaking, cross-country skiing, downhill skiing, fishing, golf, hiking, horseback riding, live theater, parks, shopping, sporting events, water sports, wineries and festivals nearby.

Chambery Cottage Bed & Breakfast

6104 Monks Road
Canandaigua, NY 14424
(585)393-1405
E-mail: euroctge@frontiernet.net
Web: www.chamberycottage.com

Circa 1901. Experience European hospitality at this renovated 100-year-old farmhouse on 31 acres of meadows, streams, woodlands and groomed hiking trails. Old World French Country decor exudes a romantic ambiance with comfortable furnishings. Relax by the large fireplace in the drawing room boasting an extensive collection of Bohemian crystal. Browse the video, CD and book library. Snacks are available at the dining-room coffee-and-tea bar. Delightful guest bedrooms feature canopy beds, TV/VCRs and CD players. A whirlpool tub is enjoyed in Bohemian Rhapsody, and the Chambery Suite boasts a private deck. Linger over a lavish candlelight breakfast of fresh fruit, eggs Benedict, peach cobbler with whipped cream or other satisfying specialties. Visit nearby historic Granger Homestead and the must-see Sonnenberg Mansion and Gardens.

Innkeeper(s): Terry & Zora Molkenthin. $105-145. 4 rooms with PB, 2 with FP and 1 suite. Breakfast, afternoon tea and snacks/refreshments included in rates. Types of meals: Full gourmet bkfst and room service. Beds: KQ. TV, VCR, reading lamp, stereo, refrigerator, ceiling fan, snack bar, clock radio, hot tub/spa and fireplace in room. Air conditioning. Library, parlor games, telephone, fireplace, groomed hiking trails, video library and CD library on premises. Family reunions hosted. Amusement parks, antiquing, art galleries, beach, bicycling, canoeing/kayaking, cross-country skiing, downhill skiing, fishing, golf, hiking, horseback riding, live theater, museums, parks, shopping, tennis, water sports and wineries nearby.

Habersham Country Inn B&B

6124 State Route 5 And 20
Canandaigua, NY 14424-7938
(585)394-1510 (800)240-0644
E-mail: bandb@rochester.rr.com
Web: www.habershaminn.com

Circa 1843. A vast, sweeping front lawn and 11 peaceful acres surround this pre-Civil War home. Guests can relax on the front porch with Muff and Josie, the innkeepers' adorable canine friends, or, when there's a chill in the air, rest near the crackling fireplace of the living room. There are five guest rooms, including a suite with a two-person Jacuzzi. Bristol Ski Mountain, museums, galleries, Seneca Park Zoo, horse racing,

antique shopping and sporting activities are among the local attractions. Tour the many wineries in the fingerlakes region.

Innkeeper(s): Raymond & Sharon Lesio. $89-175. 5 rooms, 3 with PB. Breakfast and snacks/refreshments included in rates. Types of meals: Full gourmet bkfst and veg bkfst. Beds: QDT. Modem hook-up, cable TV, VCR, reading lamp and clock radio in room. Central air. Fax, parlor games, telephone and fireplace on premises. Antiquing, art galleries, beach, canoeing/kayaking, downhill skiing, fishing, golf, hiking, live theater, museums, parks, shopping, water sports and wineries nearby.

Morgan Samuels B&B Inn

2920 Smith Rd
Canandaigua, NY 14424-9558
(315)789-2447 Fax:(716)394-8044
E-mail: morsambb@aol.com
Web: www.morgansamuelsinn.com

Circa 1812. A luxurious Victorian estate on 46 acres of peaceful countryside, this inn offers elegance and comfort. Fireplaces, floor to ceiling windows, museum-quality furnishings, stained glass, and wide plank floors are delightful features found in both common and private areas. The guest bedrooms boast French doors leading to balconies that overlook landscaped gardens, fountains and a tennis court, or have a private entrance with an ivy-covered archway. Candlelight and soft music accentuate a lavish gourmet breakfast served in the formal dining room, intimate tea room or glass-enclosed stone porch. Afternoon tea and appetizers are welcome treats.

Innkeeper(s): Julie & John Sullivan. $129-355. 6 rooms with PB, 6 with FP, 1 suite and 1 conference room. Breakfast, afternoon tea and snacks/refreshments included in rates. Types of meals: Full gourmet bkfst, early coffee/tea and gourmet dinner. Beds: KQ. Reading lamp, clock radio, turn-down service and two rooms have refrigerator in room. Air conditioning. VCR, fax, copier, bicycles, tennis, library, child care, parlor games, telephone and fireplace on premises. Weddings, small meetings, family reunions and seminars hosted. Antiquing, cross-country skiing, downhill skiing, fishing, live theater, parks, shopping, sporting events, water sports, dozens of wineries, Sonnenburg Gardens, Cumming Nature Center, horse racing and Eastman House nearby.

Thendara Inn & Restaurant

4356 East Lake Road
Canandaigua, NY 14424
(585)394-4865
E-mail: info@thendarainn.com
Web: www.thendarainn.com

Circa 1900. Originally named by the Seneca Indians, Thendara means The Meeting Place. This historic nine-acre property was owned by Senator John Raines, who built the landmark Victorian home that has been lovingly preserved and maintained. Accented by family antiques that have adorned the rooms for more than 100 years, modern conveniences have been thoughtfully added. Gather for games, conversation or reading in one of the three common areas with wood-burning fireplaces. Spacious guest bedrooms are lavish and inviting. Enjoy a gorgeous view of the lake while savoring a homemade breakfast served in the dining room, patio or sun porch. Snacks and beverages are always available. Boat slips make good use of the 600 feet of lakefront. The adjacent Boathouse offers casual dining on the water.

Innkeeper(s): Lori Ferreira. $169-225. 4 rooms with PB. Breakfast included in rates. Types of meals: Full gourmet bkfst, early coffee/tea and snacks/refreshments. Restaurant on premises. Beds: KQ. Cable TV, reading lamp, ceiling fan, snack bar, telephone and desk in room. Air conditioning. Swimming and fireplace on premises. Beach, canoeing/kayaking, fishing, hiking, water sports and wineries nearby.

Candor   H7

The Edge of Thyme, A B&B Inn

6 Main St
Candor, NY 13743-1615
(607)659-5155 (800)722-7365 Fax:(607)659-5155

Circa 1840. Originally the summer home of John D. Rockefeller's secretary, this two-story Georgian-style inn offers gracious accommodations a short drive from Ithaca. The inn sports many interesting features, including an impressive stairway, marble fireplaces, parquet floors, pergola (arbor) and windowed porch with leaded glass. Guests may relax in front of the inn's fireplace, catch up with reading in its library or watch television in the sitting room. An authentic turn-of-the-century full breakfast is served, and guests also may arrange for special high teas.

Innkeeper(s): Prof. Frank & Eva Mae Musgrave. $75-135. 5 rooms, 3 with PB and 2 suites. Breakfast included in rates. Types of meals: Full gourmet bkfst, early coffee/tea and afternoon tea. Beds: KQDT. Reading lamp and desk in room. VCR, parlor games, telephone and fireplace on premises. Weddings, small meetings, family reunions and seminars hosted. Antiquing, cross-country skiing, downhill skiing, fishing, live theater, parks, shopping, sporting events and wineries nearby.

Publicity: *Historic Inns of the Northeast.*

Cazenovia   F8

Brae Loch Inn

5 Albany St
Cazenovia, NY 13035-1403
(315)655-3431 Fax:(315)655-4844
E-mail: braeloch1@aol.com
Web: www.braelochinn.com

Circa 1805. Hunter green awnings accentuate the attractive architecture of the Brae Loch. Since 1946 the inn has been owned and operated by the same family. A Scottish theme is evident throughout, including in the inn's restaurant. Four of the oldest rooms have fireplaces (non-working). Stickley, Harden and antique furniture add to the old-world atmosphere, and many rooms offer canopy beds. Guest rooms are on the second floor above the restaurant.

Historic Interest: Lorenzo (in village), Chittenango Falls (4 miles).

Innkeeper(s): Jim & Val Barr. $80-140. 12 rooms with PB and 1 conference room. Breakfast included in rates. Types of meals: Cont and gourmet dinner. Restaurant on premises. Beds: KQDT. Cable TV, reading lamp, clock radio, telephone, desk and three with Jacuzzis in room. Air conditioning. Fax, copier and fireplace on premises. Weddings, small meetings, family reunions and seminars hosted. Antiquing, cross-country skiing, downhill skiing, fishing, golf, parks, shopping, sporting events, tennis, water sports and swimming nearby.

Publicity: *The Globe and Mail, Traveler Magazine and CNY.*

"Everything was just perfect. The Brae Loch and staff make you feel as if you were at home."

The Brewster Inn

PO Box 507, 6 Ledyard Ave
Cazenovia, NY 13035-0507
(315)655-9232 Fax:(315)655-2130
Web: www.cazenovia.com/brewster

Circa 1890. This large Victorian mansion is located on three acres and offers a terrace and two dining rooms with views of Cazenovia Lake. Originally, the home was constructed by Benjamin Brewster, a partner of John Rockefeller in Standard Oil. Some guest rooms offer fireplaces and Jacuzzi tubs. The inn's renowned restaurant staffs seven chefs preparing gourmet meals with only the freshest ingredients. Dessert souffles are a specialty.

Innkeeper(s): Richard A. Hubbard. $60-225. 17 rooms with PB, 4 with FP and 1 suite. Breakfast included in rates. Types of meals: Cont plus, early coffee/tea and gourmet dinner. Restaurant on premises. Beds: KQD. Cable TV, reading lamp, stereo, ceiling fan, clock radio, telephone, desk, hot tub/spa and Internet access in room. Air conditioning. Fax, copier and fireplace on premises. Limited handicap access. Weddings, small meetings, family reunions and seminars hosted. Antiquing, cross-country skiing, downhill skiing, fishing, golf, parks, shopping, sporting events, tennis and water sports nearby.

Publicity: *New York Times, Conde Nast, PBS Travel Series and If Ever I Would See You Again.*

Chestertown   D12

Friends Lake Inn

963 Friends Lake Rd
Chestertown, NY 12817
(518)494-4751 Fax:(518)494-4616

Circa 1860. This Mission-style inn offers its guests elegant accommodations, fine dining and an award-winning wine list. Overlooking Friends Lake, the inn provides easy access to the entire Adirondack area. Guests are welcome to borrow a canoe for a lake outing and use the inn's private beach or in-ground swimming pool. Guest rooms are well-appointed and most include four-poster beds. Many have breathtaking lake views or Jacuzzis. Three rooms have a wood-burning fireplace. An outdoor sauna is a favorite spot after a busy day of recreation. The 25km Tubbs Snowshoe Center is on site with wilderness trails and rentals. Trails are available for hiking as well.

Innkeeper(s): Sharon & Greg Taylor. $295-425. 17 rooms with PB. Breakfast and dinner included in rates. Types of meals: Country bkfst, picnic lunch and room service. Restaurant on premises. Beds: KQ. Reading lamp, clock radio and turn-down service in room. Air conditioning. VCR, fax, copier, parlor games, telephone, fireplace, pool, beach and sauna on premises. Weddings, small meetings, family reunions and seminars hosted. Amusement parks, antiquing, cross-country skiing, downhill skiing, fishing, live theater, museums, parks, shopping, sporting events and water sports nearby.

Publicity: *Country Inns and New York Times.*

"Everyone here is so pleasant, you end up feeling like family!"

Landon Hill B&B

10 Landon Hill Rd
Chestertown, NY 12817
(518)494-2599 (888)244-2599 Fax:(518)494-7324

Circa 1860. Built during Civil War times, this historic Victorian was once known as Sunset Camp. The home includes five guest rooms. Adirondack-style furnishings and wicker pieces decorate the rooms. Beds are topped with quilts. Pedestal sinks in the bathrooms add to the historic flavor. Several rooms offer a view of the surrounding scenery. Guests can relax on the screened-in front porch, nap in the hammock or curl up in front of the fireplace in the living room. The acre-and-a-half of grounds includes a perennial rock garden and century-old maple trees. Adirondack quiche, eggs Benedict and blueberry pancakes are among the homemade entrees guests might enjoy during the morning breakfast service. Whatever the menu, the meal fortifies guests for a busy day in the Adirondacks. The innkeepers provide maps of the area, will make restaurant recommendations and offer several ski packages for nearby Gore and Whiteface ski areas.

Innkeeper(s): Judy & Carl Johnson. $75-175. 5 rooms with PB. Breakfast included in rates. Types of meals: Full gourmet bkfst, veg bkfst and early coffee/tea. Beds: KQ. Cable TV, reading lamp, ceiling fan and clock radio in room. Air conditioning. Bicycles, library, parlor games, telephone, fireplace, laundry facility and refrigerator in common area on premises. Limited handicap access. Weddings, small meetings and family reunions hosted. Amusement parks, antiquing, art galleries, beach, bicycling, canoeing/kayaking, cross-country skiing, downhill skiing, fishing, golf, hiking, horseback riding, live theater, museums, parks, shopping, tennis and water sports nearby.

Clarence   F3

Asa Ransom House

10529 Main St
Clarence, NY 14031-1684
(716)759-2315 (800)841-2340 Fax:(716)759-2791
E-mail: innfo@asaransom.com
Web: www.asaransom.com

Circa 1853. Set on spacious lawns, behind a white picket fence, the Asa Ransom House rests on the site of the first grist mill built in Erie County. Silversmith Asa Ransom constructed an inn and grist mill here in response to the Holland Land Company's offering of free land to anyone who would start and operate a tavern. A specialty of the dining room is "Veal Perrott" and "Pistachio Banana Muffins."

Historic Interest: Clarence Center Emporium (5 miles), Amherst Museum, Colony (8 miles), Theodore Roosevelt Inaugural National Historic Site (Wilcox Mansion) (16 miles).

Innkeeper(s): Robert & Abigail Lenz. $98-165. 9 rooms with PB, 8 with FP, 2 suites and 1 conference room. Breakfast included in rates. Types of meals: Full bkfst, early coffee/tea and dinner. Restaurant on premises. Beds: KQT. Reading lamp, stereo, clock radio, telephone, turn-down service, desk and old radio tapes in room. Air conditioning. TV, fax, copier, library, parlor games and fireplace on premises. Limited handicap access. Weddings and small meetings hosted. Antiquing, cross-country skiing, live theater, parks and shopping nearby.

Publicity: *Toronto Star, Buffalo News, Prevention Magazine, Country Living, Country Inns and Inn Country USA.*

"*Popular spot keeps getting better.*"

Clinton   F9

Artful Lodger

7 E Park Row
Clinton, NY 13323-1544
(315)853-3672 (888)563-4377 Fax:(315)853-1489
E-mail: artful@dreamscape.com
Web: www.innplace.com/inns/A002711.html

Circa 1835. For nearly two centuries, this handsome Federal-style residence has rested peacefully on Clinton's historic village green. Tastefully decorated guest rooms include traditional furnishings, and guests may enjoy a view of the green and fountain from their rooms. Gourmet breakfasts and freshly baked oatmeal bread are among the homemade amenities.

Shops and restaurants are within walking distance, and it's a short drive to Hamilton College and Colgate University.

Innkeeper(s): Susan & Tim Sweetland. $89-130. 5 rooms with PB. Breakfast included in rates. Types of meals: Full gourmet bkfst, veg bkfst and early coffee/tea. Beds: KQT. Data port, reading lamp, ceiling fan, clock radio and desk in room. Air conditioning. TV, VCR, fax, copier, library, parlor games, telephone, gift shop and art gallery on premises. Small meetings hosted. Amusement parks, antiquing, art galleries, canoeing/kayaking, golf, hiking, live theater, museums, parks, shopping and casino nearby.

Cohocton   G5

Ambroselli's Villa Serendip

10849 State Route 371
Cohocton, NY 14826
(585)384-5299 Fax:(585)384-9228
E-mail: inhost@yahoo.com
Web: www.villaserendip.com

Circa 1860. Country Victorian elegance awaits at this Italianate villa surrounded by rolling hills and scenic splendor. Non-smoking guest bedrooms and suites easily accommodate families and honeymooners alike. Cupid's Retreat with a canopy bed and fireplace is perfect for a private romantic getaway. The first-floor Victorian Bride's Dream features a four-poster rice bed and bay window alcove. The Empire Suite offers spaciousness and extra beds as well as a sitting room with a large screen television and VCR. Oven-baked bananas, French toast with glazed pecans, muffins, skillet potatoes with sausage and rosemary, and scrambled eggs with three cheeses are popular breakfast favorites. Visit Canandaigua Lake, Corning Glass Factory and award-winning wineries.

Innkeeper(s): Fran Ambroselli. $95-225. 5 rooms with PB and 2 suites. Breakfast included in rates. Types of meals: Full gourmet bkfst, veg bkfst, early coffee/tea, afternoon tea and snacks/refreshments. Beds: KQ. Modem hook-up, cable TV, VCR, reading lamp, refrigerator, ceiling fan, clock radio, telephone, turn-down service, fireplace and hot tub in room. Parlor games, fireplace and Jacuzzi on premises. Handicap access. Weddings, small meetings and family reunions hosted. Antiquing, beach, cross-country skiing, downhill skiing, fishing, golf, hiking, horseback riding, live theater, museums, parks, shopping, wineries, Mountain Ski Resort, Swain Ski Resort, Letworth State Park, Stony Brook State Park, Corning Museum of Glass and Keuka Lake nearby.

Cold Spring   J12

Pig Hill Inn

73 Main St
Cold Spring, NY 10516-3014
(845)265-9247 Fax:(845)265-4614
E-mail: pighillinn@aol.com
Web: www.pighillinn.com

Circa 1808. The antiques at this stately three-story inn can be purchased, and they range from Chippendale to chinoiserie style. Rooms feature formal English and Adirondack decor with special touches such as four-poster or brass beds, painted rockers and, of course, pigs. The lawn features a tri-level garden. The delicious breakfasts can be shared with guests in the Victorian conservatory, dining room or garden, or it may be served in the privacy of your room. The inn is about an hour out of New York City, and the train station is only two blocks away.

Innkeeper(s): Marcy Clemence. $120-220. 9 rooms, 5 with PB, 6 with FP and 1 conference room. Breakfast included in rates. Types of meals: Full bkfst. Beds: KQDT. Telephone on premises. Weddings, small meetings, family reunions and seminars hosted. Antiquing, live theater, shopping, sporting events and great restaurants nearby.

Publicity: *National Geographic, Woman's Home Journal, Country Inns and Getaways for Gourmets.*

"Some of our fondest memories of New York were at Pig Hill."

Cooperstown G10

Angelholm

14 Elm Street
Cooperstown, NY 13326-0705
(607)547-2483 Fax:(607)547-2309
E-mail: anglholm@telenet.net
Web: angelholmbb.com

Circa 1805. Built at the turn of the 19th century, Angelholm was constructed on land that was part of historic Phinney's Farm. It was on this farmland that the game of baseball was first played. The National Baseball Hall of Fame is within walking distance. However, Angelholm is not just a place for baseball fans. The guest rooms are decorated in a nostalgic style. Rooms include items such as the four poster bed in the Elihu Phinney Room or the antique lace curtains in the Glimmerglass Room. Breakfast is a formal affair with entrees such as a souffle or pecan waffles. After a day exploring the Hall of Fame, shopping, searching for antiques or perhaps golfing at a nearby course, return and enjoy afternoon tea on the veranda.

Innkeeper(s): Dan Lloyd. $80-125. 5 rooms with PB. Breakfast and afternoon tea included in rates. Types of meals: Full bkfst and early coffee/tea. Beds: KQT. Reading lamp in room. Air conditioning. VCR, fax, parlor games, telephone and fireplace on premises. Weddings, small meetings and family reunions hosted. Antiquing, cross-country skiing, fishing, golf, live theater, parks, shopping, sporting events, water sports and Glimmerglass Opera nearby.

Publicity: *New York Times and Country Inns.*

Cooper Inn

Main & Chestnut Streets
Cooperstown, NY 13326
(607)547-2567 (800)348-6222 Fax:(607)547-1271

Circa 1812. This Federal-style brick house opened as an inn in 1936, although it was built more than a century before that. It has been restored to the elegance of when it was first designed in the early 1800s. Guests can relax in the inn's main parlor. Decorative period woodwork and paintings from the Fenimore Art Museum adorn the main floor. Rooms have been redecorated recently, and the inn is within walking distance to most of Cooperstown's attractions.

Innkeeper(s): Steve Walker. $120-300. 20 rooms with PB, 5 suites and 1 conference room. Types of meals: Cont plus and early coffee/tea. Beds: QT. Modem hook-up, data port, cable TV, reading lamp, clock radio, telephone, desk and voice mail in room. Central air. Fax, copier, tennis, library and parlor games on premises. Weddings, small meetings, family reunions and seminars hosted. Antiquing, art galleries, beach, bicycling, canoeing/kayaking, cross-country skiing, fishing, golf, hiking, horseback riding, live theater, museums, parks, shopping, sporting events, tennis, water sports and driving range nearby.

The Country Lion

4 Glen Ave
Cooperstown, NY 13326
(607)547-8264 Fax:(607)547-8264
E-mail: countrylion@countrylion.com
Web: www.countrylion.com

Circa 1883. Experience comfort and gracious service at this Queen Anne Victorian home, located within walking distance to the area's historic sites and famous local attractions. Stress is easily erased upon entering into the old-world ambiance of this bed & breakfast. A wood-panelled foyer features stained-glass windows, an ornate staircase and a beckoning fireplace. The sunny parlor is a cozy spot with French doors opening onto a wraparound porch where afternoon tea is enjoyed. The library offers TV/VCR, games and of course, books to read by the fire. Spacious guest bedrooms are furnished with country antiques and canopy beds covered with quilts. Linger over a bountiful breakfast with a changing menu that may include creme brulee French toast, blueberry pancakes, bacon, sausage, breads and seasonal fruits. Off-street parking is conveniently available.

Innkeeper(s): Maureen & Richard Haralabatos. $135-159. 4 rooms, 3 with PB and 1 suite. Breakfast and afternoon tea included in rates. Types of meals: Country bkfst and early coffee/tea. Beds: KQT. Cable TV, reading lamp and high-speed Internet access available in room. Air conditioning. TV, VCR, fax, library, parlor games and telephone on premises. Weddings, small meetings and family reunions hosted. Antiquing, art galleries, beach, bicycling, canoeing/kayaking, cross-country skiing, fishing, golf, hiking, horseback riding, live theater, museums, parks, shopping, sporting events and water sports nearby.

The Inn at Cooperstown

16 Chestnut St
Cooperstown, NY 13326-1006
(607)547-5756 Fax:(607)547-8779
E-mail: info@innatcooperstown.com
Web: www.innatcooperstown.com

Circa 1874. This three-story, Second Empire hotel features a graceful porch filled with wicker furniture and rocking chairs. The inn is located in the center of the Cooperstown National Historic District. The guest rooms are decorated tastefully and comfortably. A block from Otsego Lake, the inn is within walking distance of most of Cooperstown's attractions.

Historic Interest: Baseball Hall of Fame (2 blocks), The Farmers' Museum & Fenimore Art Museum (1 mile), Glimmerglass Opera (8 miles).

Innkeeper(s): Marc and Sherrie Kingsley. $98-325. 17 rooms with PB, 1 suite and 1 conference room. Breakfast included in rates. Types of meals: Cont. Beds: QT. Reading lamp and clock radio in room. TV, fax, library, parlor games, telephone, fireplace and wireless Internet access on premises. Limited handicap access. Small meetings hosted. Antiquing, cross-country skiing, fishing, live theater, parks, shopping, sporting events, water sports, museum, opera and lake nearby.

Publicity: *Cleveland Plain Dealer, New York Times, Atlanta Journal, Los Angeles Times, New York Magazine, Conde Nast Traveler, USA Today, Travel & Leisure and Good Day New York.*

"An unpretentious country inn with 17 rooms, spotless on the inside and stunning on the outside." — Conde Nast Traveler

Thistlebrook B&B

316 County Hwy 28
Cooperstown, NY 13326
(607)547-6093 (800)596-9305
E-mail: bugonian@aol.com
Web: www.thistlebrook.com

Circa 1866. This sprawling barn with its rustic appearance belies the spacious and elegant rooms awaiting discovery inside. Fluted columns in the living room enhance the inn's original architectural details. Furnishings include American and European pieces, an Egyptian Revival mirror, Oriental rugs and crystal chandeliers. Just up the wide stairway is a library from which the guest rooms are reached. Breakfasts are hearty and may include fresh fruit salad and three-cheese omelets with biscuits and ham. Enjoy valley vistas from the inn's deck. A variety of wildlife such as deer, bullfrogs, wood ducks and an occasional blue heron, gather around the pond.

Innkeeper(s): Paula & Jim Bugonian. $155-175. 5 rooms with PB and 2 suites. Breakfast included in rates. Types of meals: Full bkfst and early coffee/tea. Beds: KQ. Reading lamp, ceiling fan and clock radio in room. Air conditioning. Telephone, fireplace and wheelchair access on premises. Small meetings and family reunions hosted. Antiquing, fishing, golf, live theater, shopping, sporting events, tennis, water sports and summer opera nearby.

Publicity: *Country Inns, New York Magazine and Home and Garden TV.*

Corinth   E12

Agape Farm B&B and Paintball

4839 Rt 9N
Corinth, NY 12822-1704
(518)654-7777 Fax:(518)654-7777

Circa 1870. Amid 33 acres of fields and woods, this Adirondack farmhouse is home to chickens and horses, as well as guests seeking a refreshing getaway. Visitors have their choice of six guest rooms, all with ceiling fans, phones, private baths and views of the tranquil surroundings. The inn's wraparound porch lures many visitors, who often enjoy a glass of icy lemonade. Homemade

breads, jams, jellies and muffins are part of the full breakfast served here, and guests are welcome to pick berries or gather a ripe tomato from the garden. A trout-filled stream on the grounds flows to the Hudson River, a mile away.

Historic Interest: Built on the site of a hundred-year-old dairy farm, outbuildings and animals keep this atmosphere alive.

Innkeeper(s): Fred & Sigrid Koch. $79-175. 6 rooms with PB and 1 conference room. Breakfast and snacks/refreshments included in rates. Types of meals: Full gourmet bkfst, veg bkfst and early coffee/tea. Beds: KQDT. Reading lamp, ceiling fan, clock radio, telephone and desk in room. TV, VCR, fax, swimming, child care, parlor games, laundry facility and downstairs HC room and bath on premises. Limited handicap access. Weddings, small meetings, family reunions and seminars hosted. Amusement parks, antiquing, art galleries, beach, bicycling, canoeing/kayaking, cross-country skiing, downhill skiing, fishing, golf, hiking, horseback riding, museums, parks, shopping, sporting events, tennis and water sports nearby.

"Clean and impeccable, we were treated royally."

Cornwall   J12

Cromwell Manor Inn B&B

174 Angola Rd
Cornwall, NY 12518
(845)534-7136
E-mail: cmi@hvc.rr.com
Web: www.cromwellmanor.com

Circa 1820. Listed in the National Register of Historic Places, this stunning Greek Revival mansion sits on seven lush acres with scenic Hudson Valley views. It is elegantly furnished with period antiques and fine reproductions. The Chimneys Cottage, built in 1764, offers romantic guest bedrooms with a country decor. Savor a bountiful gourmet breakfast before a stroll in the garden. The inn extends afternoon hospitality, while boasting spa and fitness

facilities. After a day of exploring, relax by the fireside or indulge in the Jacuzzi.

Historic Interest: West Point (5 miles), nearby mansions: Roosevelt, Vanderbilt and Boscobel. The Brotherhood Winery, the nation's oldest (15 miles). New Windsor Cantonment, Washington's and Knox's headquarters and many others.

Innkeeper(s): Jack & Cynthia Trowell. $165-370. 10 rooms with PB, 7 with FP, 2 suites and 1 conference room. Breakfast included in rates. Types of meals: Full gourmet bkfst, early coffee/tea, picnic lunch, afternoon tea and room service. Beds: KQD. Reading lamp, refrigerator, clock radio, turn-down service, desk and hot tub/spa in room. Air conditioning. VCR, copier, parlor games, telephone and fireplace on premises. Limited handicap access. Weddings, small meetings, family reunions and seminars hosted. Antiquing, fishing, hiking, horseback riding, live theater, parks, shopping, sporting events, water sports, wineries, Hudson Valley Mansion, outlets, art center, Renaissance Festival, West Point sports and mountain biking nearby.

Publicity: *Hudson Valley, Montreal Gazette, Washington Post, New York Magazine, Philadelphia Inquirer, USA Today, NY Times, Fox, CBS Early Show and Top 10 Inns of NY.*

Crown Point   D12

Crown Point Bed & Breakfast

2695 Main Street, Rt 9N
Crown Point, NY 12928
(518)597-3651 Fax:(518)597-4451
E-mail: mail@crownpointbandb.com
Web: www.crownpointbandb.com

Circa 1886. In the heart of the Adirondacks, this Queen Anne Victorian Painted Lady sits on five-and-a-half partially wooded acres. Recently renovated, stained-glass windows, eight varieties of wood flooring and paneling, pocket doors, four carved stone fireplaces and a Baldwin icebox are original details that blend perfectly with floral wallpapers, Oriental rugs, and fine antiques to enhance the luxurious ambiance. Each custom-decorated guest bedroom and suite features comfortable slippers, robes, shower massage, hair dryers and gourmet truffles with turn-down service. A satisfying breakfast is served on English bone china with vintage glassware. Three porches and a side sitting lawn with bistro tables invite relaxation amidst a fountain and flower gardens.

Innkeeper(s): Hugh & Sandy Johnson. $75-150. 6 rooms with PB. Breakfast included in rates. Types of meals: Full gourmet bkfst, veg bkfst, early coffee/tea and picnic lunch. Beds: QDT. Reading lamp, ceiling fan, turn-down service, desk, hot tub/spa, robes, slippers, shower massage, hair dryers and gourmet truffles in room. TV, fax, copier, bicycles, parlor games, telephone, fireplace and gift shop on premises. Weddings, small meetings, family reunions and seminars hosted. Antiquing, art galleries, beach, bicycling, canoeing/kayaking, fishing, golf, hiking, live theater, museums, parks, shopping, tennis and water sports nearby.

Publicity: *Mineville.*

Dundee   G6

The 1819 Red Brick Inn

2081 State Route 230
Dundee, NY 14837-9424
(607)243-8844
E-mail: redbrickinn@frontiernet.net
Web: www.bbonline.com/ny/redbrick

Circa 1819. Centrally located between scenic Keuka and Seneca Lakes on eight idyllic acres, this fully restored Federal-style inn features an impressive exterior with 15-inch-thick brick walls. The well-appointed interior is accented with antiques and period furnishings. Overlook the stream and pond in the three-season sun porch. Relax by the fire in the parlor or enjoy conversa-

tion in the country kitchen with a wood-burning stove. Air-conditioned guest bedrooms include a sound system. Savor a hearty breakfast in the morning and indulge in home-baked treats by candlelight in the evening. Complimentary beverages are available in the fully stocked refrigerator. It is an easy drive to Watkins Glens State Park and other scenic Finger Lakes attractions.

Historic Interest: The inn is near mineral springs that in the late 1800s attracted many health-conscious visitors.

Innkeeper(s): Robert & Wendy Greenslade. $95-115. 5 rooms with PB, 1 with FP. Breakfast included in rates. Types of meals: Full bkfst and early coffee/tea. Beds: D. Reading lamp and stereo in room. Telephone and fireplace on premises. Antiquing, cross-country skiing, fishing, golf, parks, shopping, sporting events and water sports nearby.

East Chatham   G12

Inn At Silver Maple Farm

1871 Rt 295
East Chatham, NY 12060
(518)781-3600 Fax:(518)781-3883
E-mail: info@silvermaplefarm.com
Web: www.silvermaplefarm.com

Circa 1820. Sprawled on 10 acres in the peaceful foothills of the Berkshires, this converted barn (adjacent to the the owner's home) exudes country bliss. Post and beam construction, wide pine board floors and a brick fireplace highlight the Great Room. A simple decor showing Shaker influence offers casual, open comfort. Hand-painted murals embellish the walls of the guest bedrooms and suites with pleasing views of the perennial gardens and open fields. A great day might begin with apple pie pancakes or baked peach French toast to round off a full breakfast. A hammock and Adirondack chairs are placed throughout the grounds.

Historic Interest: 1820 dairy farm; original slate roof barn.

Innkeeper(s): Nancy & Ross Audino. $80-290. 11 rooms with PB, 2 with FP, 2 suites and 1 conference room. Breakfast and snacks/refreshments included in rates. Types of meals: Full bkfst and afternoon tea. Beds: KQDT. Data port, cable TV, reading lamp, refrigerator, ceiling fan, clock radio, telephone, desk, two suites with soaking tubs and fireplaces, hair dryers and iron/ironing board in room. Air conditioning. Fax, copier and fireplace on premises. Weddings, small meetings, family reunions and seminars hosted. Antiquing, art galleries, bicycling, canoeing/kayaking, cross-country skiing, downhill skiing, fishing, golf, hiking, horseback riding, live theater, museums, parks, shopping, tennis, water sports and wineries nearby.

Publicity: *Boston Globe, NY Times, LA Times, NY Magazine and "best location to view fall foilage" by Arrington's Bed and Breakfast Journal.*

East Hampton   K15

East Hampton Village Bed & Breakfast

172 Newton Lane
East Hampton, NY 11937
(631)324-1858 Fax:(631)329-0762
E-mail: info@hamptonsvacations.com
Web: www.easthamptonvillagebandb.com

Circa 1904. Originally the home of a local whale boat captain, this century-old Victorian has been recently renovated for enhanced comfort. Gather for conversation or play games in a sitting room. Air-conditioned guest bedrooms feature Queen beds with quilts and comforters. The Oak Room's private bath boasts a clawfoot tub and shower. Bask in the serene surroundings of the sun-filled porch or lush one-acre grounds during a generous continental breakfast of fresh fruit, fresh-baked bagels, croissants, pastries, muffins and danish rolls. Relax on white, wrought iron furniture or Adirondack chairs under tall shade trees.

Historic Interest: The East Hampton Village B&B was originally built in 1904. It was originally the residence of a local whale boat captain.

Innkeeper(s): Marianne, Michael, Jeanne and Eric Kaufman. $150-300. 4 rooms with PB. Breakfast included in rates. Types of meals: Cont plus and early coffee/tea. Beds: QT. Reading lamp and clock radio in room. Air conditioning. Fax, copier, parlor games, telephone, refrigerator and coffee and tea on premises. Weddings and family reunions hosted. Antiquing, art galleries, beach, bicycling, canoeing/kayaking, fishing, golf, hiking, horseback riding, live theater, museums, parks, shopping, tennis, water sports and wineries nearby.

Publicity: *Inn Spots, Jodi's Shortcuts, Hamptons Survival Guide (4 stars), Hamptons Country Magazine and Away for the Weekend.*

J Harper Poor Cottage

181 Main St
East Hampton, NY 11937-2720
(631)324-4081 Fax:(631)329-5931
E-mail: info@jharperpoor.com
Web: www.jharperpoor.com

Circa 1910. Enjoy the luxury of a stately English manor at this elegant inn, located in one of the oldest communities in the United States. A colonial revival staircase leads upstairs to the guest rooms, which offer such unique features as exposed beams, antique wall paneling, fireplaces or clawfoot bathtubs. Rooms facing the front enjoy a view of the picture-perfect town pond and green, and rooms facing the back look over the formal English garden. Relax in the comfortable Great Room, with ample books and reading lamps, and grand piano. A sumptuous breakfast of apple tarts or lemon pancakes can be enjoyed inside or out in the garden. It's just a short walk to unusual shops, galleries, nature trails and some of the finest beaches on the Atlantic Coast.

Innkeeper(s): Gary & Rita Reiswig. $200-600. 5 rooms with PB, 4 with FP and 2 conference rooms. Breakfast included in rates. Types of meals: Full gourmet bkfst, early coffee/tea, picnic lunch, afternoon tea, snacks/refreshments and room service. Beds: KQT. Modem hook-up, data port, cable TV, VCR, reading lamp, refrigerator, ceiling fan, telephone, turn-down service, desk, hot tub/spa and voice mail in room. Central air. Fax, spa, sauna, library, parlor games, fireplace and laundry facility on premises. Weddings, small meetings, family reunions and seminars hosted. Antiquing, art galleries, beach, bicycling, canoeing/kayaking, fishing, golf, hiking, horseback riding, live theater, museums, parks, shopping, tennis, water sports and wineries nearby.

Publicity: *Town & Country and Travel & Leisure.*

Maidstone Arms

207 Main St
East Hampton, NY 11937-2723
(631)324-5006 Fax:(631)324-5037

Circa 1860. Situated on the village green, this classic inn has all the characteristics that epitomize this community of winding lanes and sandy white beaches. The inn's restaurant houses a world-class selection of wines in its own climate-controlled underground wine cellar. Nearby activities include whale-watching expeditions and local winery tours.

Historic Interest: The Maidstone Arms is located on Long Island, which offers many historic buildings and sites. New York City is about two hours away.

Innkeeper(s): Diane McIngvale. $215-535. 19 rooms with PB, 4 suites, 3 cottages and 1 conference room. Breakfast included in rates. Types of meals: Full bkfst, early coffee/tea, gourmet lunch, picnic lunch, snacks/refreshments, dinner and room service. Restaurant on premises. Beds: KQDT. Cable TV, reading lamp, refrigerator, telephone, turn-down service, desk and cottages with fireplace in room. Air conditioning. Fireplace on premises. Weddings, small meetings, family reunions and seminars hosted. Antiquing, fishing, live theater and water sports nearby.

Mill House Inn

31 N Main St
East Hampton, NY 11937-2601
(631)324-9766 Fax:(631)324-9793
E-mail: innkeeper@millhouseinn.com
Web: www.millhouseinn.com

Circa 1790. This Colonial house is just opposite the Old Hook Windmill. It is in the center of East Hampton, which has been called "America's most beautiful village." Guest rooms are decorated with a Hamptons' theme in mind, sporting names such

as Sail Away or Hampton Holiday. Romantic amenities abound, including fireplaces in six of the guest rooms. Several rooms also have whirlpool tubs. Families are welcome.

Innkeeper(s): Sylvia & Gary Muller.
$200-650. 8 rooms with PB, 4 with FP, 2 suites and 1 conference room. Breakfast and snacks/refreshments included in rates. Types of meals: Full bkfst and early coffee/tea. Beds: KQ. Cable TV, VCR, reading lamp, stereo, ceiling fan, clock radio, telephone, desk, hot tub/spa, voice mail, fireplace, feather beds and down quilts in room. Air conditioning. Fax, library, parlor games, fireplace and gift shop on premises. Limited handicap access. Small meetings and family reunions hosted. Antiquing, art galleries, beach, bicycling, canoeing/kayaking, fishing, golf, hiking, horseback riding, live theater, museums, parks, shopping, tennis, water sports, wineries, international film festival, classic horse show and polo nearby.

Publicity: *New York Magazine, Destinations, The New York Times, Newsday, Dan's Papers, The East Hampton Star, New York Living and HGTV.*

"Perfect everything, it's hard to leave."

Pink House Inn

26 James Ln
East Hampton, NY 11937-2710
(631)324-1122 (866)459-PINK Fax:(631)907-0493
E-mail: cnj@pinkhouseinn.com
Web: www.pinkhouseinn.com

Circa 1832. Perfectly situated on the historic Village green, this elegant bed & breakfast was built in 1832 by a sea captain. It has been newly refurbished to provide comfort, convenience and privacy for even the most sophisticated. Relax in the lush gardens or by the secluded pool. Sit by the fire in the drawing room or browse for a book in the library. Air-conditioned guest bedrooms are distinctive and luxuriously appointed with Frette linens and robes, splendid Kingsdown beds, TV and phones with voice mail. Walk to local galleries, shops and restaurants. The Atlantic Ocean beckons sea-lovers. Beach towels and passes are provided.

Historic Interest: Built in 1832 by a sea captain.
Innkeeper(s): Charley Buck & John Murtha. $200-475. 6 rooms with PB. Breakfast included in rates. Types of meals: Cont plus and early coffee/tea. Beds: KQT. Modem hook-up, cable TV, VCR, reading lamp, stereo, ceiling fan, telephone, voice mail, down comforters, Frette linens, towels, robes, spacious marble bathrooms and one with steam shower in room. Air conditioning. Fax, copier, swimming, sauna, library, parlor games, fireplace, laundry facility, beach passes and towels, elegant private garden, front porch and views of village green and historical buildings on premises. Weddings, small meetings, family reunions and seminars hosted. Antiquing, art galleries, beach, bicycling, canoeing/kayaking, fishing, golf, hiking, horseback riding, live theater, museums, parks, shopping, sporting events, tennis, water sports and wineries nearby.

Publicity: *Hamptons Cottages & Gardens.*

"The new owners have made the Pink House even rosier."

Elizabethtown   C12

The Old Mill Bed & Breakfast

136 River Street
Elizabethtown, NY 12932
(518)873-2294 (888)668-3009
E-mail: bbpushee@willex.com
Web: www.adirondackinns.com/oldmill

Circa 1850. More than a bed & breakfast, the historic Old Mill sits on two and a quarter acres consisting of the main house built in the 1800s, cottages and an art studio/gallery. Enjoy an unhurried stay while savoring the old-fashioned ambiance of this country inn. Homey guest bedrooms in the renovated mill house are accented with artwork and pleasing amenities. After a restful night's sleep indulge in an inviting and well-presented gourmet breakfast. The Mill Studio/Gallery is open for the public to browse through the art and antiques. Located between Albany and Montreal, it is only a ten-minute drive to Lake Champlain and Lake Placid is only a half an hour away. It is 20 minutes from Essex Ferry to Charlotte, Vermont.

Innkeeper(s): Bruce Pushee & Beki Maurello-Pushee. $72-95. 4 rooms. Types of meals: Full gourmet bkfst.

Publicity: *Recommended Country Inns.*

Ellicottville   H3

The Jefferson Inn of Ellicottville

3 Jefferson St, PO Box 1566
Ellicottville, NY 14731-1566
(716)699-5869 (800)577-8451 Fax:(716)699-5758
E-mail: jeffinn@eznet.net
Web: thejeffersoninn.com

Circa 1835. The Allegheny Mountains provide a perfect backdrop for this restored Victorian home built by Robert H. Shankland, an influential citizen who owned the local newspaper, along with other enterprises. The home's 100-foot wrap-

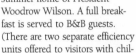

around Greek Revival porch was added in the 1920s and patterned after the summer home of President Woodrow Wilson. A full breakfast is served to B&B guests. (There are two separate efficiency units offered to visitors with children or pets.) The only bed & breakfast within the village, it is located in the center of town where you'll enjoy following the tree-lined streets to restaurants and shops.

Historic Interest: Historic Ellicottville offers plenty of historic buildings and sites. Also offers a walking tour.
Innkeeper(s): Jim Buchanan & Donna Gushue. $65-180. 7 rooms with PB, 3 with FP. Breakfast included in rates. Types of meals: Full gourmet bkfst, early coffee/tea and picnic lunch. Beds: KQDT. Modem hook-up, cable TV, reading lamp, CD player, clock radio, telephone and desk in room. Central air. TV, VCR, fax, library, parlor games and fireplace on premises. Limited handicap access. Weddings, small meetings, family reunions and seminars hosted. Antiquing, art galleries, bicycling, cross-country skiing, downhill skiing, fishing, golf, hiking, museums, parks, shopping and tennis nearby.

Publicity: *Genesse Country Magazine, Buffalo Spree Magazine, Olean Chronicle and Ellicottville News.*

"Even though we just met, we are leaving with the feeling we just spent the weekend with good friends."

Elmira   H7

The Painted Lady Bed and Breakfast

520 West Water Street
Elmira, NY 14905
(607)732-7515 Fax:(607)732-7515
E-mail: info@thepaintedlady.net
Web: www.thepaintedlady.net

Circa 1875. This rare but magnificent example of Second Empire Victorian architecture features a slate mansard roof and dormer windows, original Turkish-designed silk tufted in satin ceiling and wall treatments, period stained glass, etched- and cut-glass entry, Eastlake woodwork and pocket doors. Carved wood, marble and ceramic tile fireplaces are found in some common rooms and every guest bedroom. Smoked salmon roulade, crustless crab quiche, baked blueberry French toast, rosemary roasted potatoes, orange-glazed sausage and Southern scalloped pineapple are a few of the delicious breakfast items served. Relax in an oak-coffered billiard parlor. The flower and herb gardens provide beauty outside as well as inside the home.

Innkeeper(s): Laurie & Dorian Desmarais. $165-275. 5 rooms with PB, 5 with FP and 1 suite. Breakfast and afternoon tea included in rates. Types of meals: Full bkfst, veg bkfst, early coffee/tea, picnic lunch and snacks/refreshments. Beds: QT. Modem hook-up, cable TV, VCR, reading lamp, stereo, refrigerator, ceiling fan, snack bar, clock radio, telephone, coffeemaker, desk, hot tub/spa, fireplace, iron/board, hair dryer, spa robes and herbal bath products in room. Air conditioning. Fax, copier, library, parlor games, fireplace, laundry facility, gift shop, billiard parlor, furnished front porches and piano on premises. Weddings, small meetings, family reunions and seminars hosted. Amusement parks, antiquing, art galleries, beach, bicycling, canoeing/kayaking, cross-country skiing, fishing, golf, hiking, horseback riding, live theater, museums, parks, shopping, sporting events, tennis, water sports and wineries nearby.

Publicity: *"America's Painted Ladies,"* a renowned series of books, Los Angeles Times, The Star-Gazette, The Leader, breakfast menus featured on WETM-TVs Live at Five series and Voted #1 Best Country Inn/B&B in Northern USA for 2003.

Fairport   F5

Esten-Wahl Farm B & B

4394 Carter Rd
Fairport, NY 14450-8402
(585)388-1881 Fax:(585)377-6669
E-mail: carol@estenwahlfarm.com
Web: www.estenwahlfarm.com

Circa 1870. A local historical landmark, this restored vernacular farmhouse sits on 30 picturesque acres in the countryside. A casual decor accented with antiques and reproductions invites relaxation. Watch a movie in the living room, or play the piano. Cherry-shaker-pencil-post or iron frame beds are featured in the comfortable guest bedrooms. Indulge in Carol's breakfast treats such as gingerbread waffles, turkey sausage, muffins and fruit cup in the Victorian dining room. The original corn crib building next to the barn is now Pleasant View Cottage, fully renovated for handicap accessibility. Perfect for families, it provides privacy and more space. Two decks offer impressive views. Enjoy the basketball hoops, regulation-size tennis court and in-ground pool. Fairport Antiques in the nearby village on the Erie Canal is fun to explore. Visit Lorain at Rainy Day Mercantile for treasures and gifts.

Innkeeper(s): Carol Santos. $75-120. 3 rooms, 2 with PB and 1 cottage. Breakfast and snacks/refreshments included in rates. Types of meals: Country bkfst. Beds: QT. Reading lamp, refrigerator, ceiling fan, clock radio, telephone

and desk in room. Central air. TV, VCR, swimming, tennis and parlor games on premises. Limited handicap access. Antiquing, hiking, parks, shopping, tennis and wineries nearby.

Forestburgh   I10

The Inn at Lake Joseph

162 Saint Joseph Rd
Forestburgh, NY 12777
(845)791-9506 Fax:(845)734-1948
E-mail: inn2@lakejoseph.com
Web: www.lakejoseph.com

Circa 1863. Just 800 feet from private Lake Joseph is this 135-year-old Queen Anne Victorian Country Estate surrounded by a 2,000-acre wildlife preserve. Steven Crane wrote "The Red Badge of Courage" in a building on the original premises. Common rooms include the billiard and game rooms. The Inn's guest bedrooms feature working fireplaces and whirlpool baths. Manor House rooms are decorated with lacy linens, dried flowers, Persian rugs and period pieces. The estate also offers accommodations in the rustic Carriage House and Cottage where pets are welcome. Most include kitchens, cathedral ceilings, private sundecks, working fireplaces and whirlpools. A sumptuous breakfast is served on the Inn's seasonally screened-in or glassed veranda. Snacks are also provided. Enjoy the nearby health and fitness club as well as the area's many activities.

Innkeeper(s): Ivan & Ru Weinger. $150-405. 15 rooms with PB, 14 with FP, 3 suites and 1 conference room. Breakfast and snacks/refreshments included in rates. Types of meals: Country bkfst, veg bkfst and early coffee/tea. Beds: KQ. Modem hook-up, TV, VCR, reading lamp, stereo, refrigerator, ceiling fan, clock radio, telephone, coffeemaker, desk, voice mail, fireplace, some with full kitchens, satellite TV and whirlpool bath in room. Air conditioning. Fax, copier, swimming, bicycles, tennis, library, parlor games, fireplace, billiard room, game room, fishing, boating, kayaking, tennis, hiking and cross-country skiing on premises. Handicap access. Small meetings and seminars hosted. Antiquing, art galleries, bicycling, canoeing/kayaking, cross-country skiing, downhill skiing, fishing, golf, hiking, horseback riding, live theater, museums, shopping, tennis, wineries and rafting nearby.

Publicity: *New York Times and New York Magazine.*

"This is a secluded spot where every detail is attended to, making it one of the country's best inns."

Fredonia   G2

The White Inn

52 E Main St
Fredonia, NY 14063-1836
(716)672-2103 (888)FRE-DONI Fax:(716)672-2107
E-mail: res@whiteinn.com
Web: www.whiteinn.com

Circa 1868. Pleasantly blending the delightful ambiance of yesteryear with the modern elegance of today, this traditional Victorian inn sits in the center of a thriving cultural and historical community. Great attention is given to detail, and the qualities of service and warmth are a top priority. Meticulously restored, distinctive guest bedrooms provide comfort and style. The Presidential Suite boasts a fireplace and whirlpool tub. Linger over a leisurely breakfast. Known for its award-winning American cuisine, the inn offers fine dining, cocktails and casual fare in the lounge or on the 100-foot-long veranda.

Innkeeper(s): Robert Contiguglia & Kathleen Dennison. $69-179. 23 rooms with PB, 2 with FP, 11 suites and 4 conference rooms. Breakfast included in rates. Types of meals: Full bkfst, lunch and gourmet dinner. Restaurant on premises. Beds: KQD. Cable TV, reading lamp, refrigerator, clock radio, telephone, desk and hot tub/spa in room. Air conditioning. VCR, fax, copier and fireplace on premises. Weddings, small meetings, family reunions and seminars hosted. Antiquing, golf, live theater, parks, shopping and wineries nearby.

Publicity: *Upstate New York Magazine, Country Living, US Air Magazine and Buffalo News.*

Freeville   G7

Bountiful Blessings Bed and Breakfast

147 Lick St
Freeville, NY 13068
(607)898-3370 (877)224-8422 Fax:(607)898-3333
E-mail: tdonlick@mail.odyssey.net
Web: www.geocities.com/bbb_b2000

Circa 1840. The stately maple trees were planted when Scotsman John McKellar built this Victorian home more than 150 years ago. Now carefully restored and decorated with period furnishings, it imparts an elegant atmosphere by mingling modern amenities and old-fashioned charm. Romantic guest bedrooms offer an assortment of amenities including four-poster and sleigh goose down feather beds and pillows, luxury linens, terry robes and sitting areas. The Olde Homer Room boasts a Jacuzzi tub and a view of Owasco Valley. A leisurely candlelight breakfast is served in the dining room with fresh flowers. Enjoy the pond and gardens that embellish the grounds. A large deck and two sitting porches are easy places to sit and daydream. Take a swim in the refreshing pool before exploring the many facets of the Finger Lakes region.

Innkeeper(s): Terry Donlick. $95-165. 5 rooms, 3 with PB, 1 suite and 1 cottage. Breakfast included in rates. Types of meals: Country bkfst and early coffee/tea. Beds: KQDT. TV, reading lamp, ceiling fan, clock radio, telephone, coffeemaker and feather beds in room. Air conditioning. Fax, copier, swimming, library, parlor games, wood stove, genealogical library, large deck, two sitting porches, pond and gardens on premises. Weddings, small meetings, family reunions and seminars hosted. Antiquing, art galleries, bicycling, canoeing/kayaking, cross-country skiing, downhill skiing, golf, hiking, horseback riding, live theater, museums, parks, shopping, sporting events, tennis, water sports, wineries and Finger Lakes Wine Trail nearby.

Fulton   E7

Battle Island Inn

2167 State Route 48 N
Fulton, NY 13069-4132
(315)593-3699 Fax:(315)592-5071
E-mail: battleislandinn@usadatanet.net
Web: www.battle-island-inn.com

Circa 1840. Topped with a gothic cupola, this family farmhouse overlooks the Oswego River and a golf course. There are three antique-filled parlors. Guest accommodations are furnished in a variety of styles including Victorian and Renaissance Revival.

There are four wooded acres with lawns and gardens. Guests are often found relaxing on one of the inn's four porches and enjoying the views. The Honeymoon suite features a canopy bed, full bath and private Jacuzzi.

Innkeeper(s): Richard & Joyce Rice. $60-125. 5 rooms with PB and 1 suite. Breakfast included in rates. Types of meals: Full gourmet bkfst and early coffee/tea. Beds: QDT. Cable TV, reading lamp, ceiling fan, clock radio, telephone and desk in room. TV, VCR, fax, copier, fireplace and refrigerator on premises. Limited handicap access. Small meetings and seminars hosted. Cross-country skiing, fishing, live theater, parks, shopping, water sports, golf and fort nearby.

Publicity: *Lake Effect, Palladium Times, Travel, Journey, Oswego County Business and Valley News.*

"We will certainly never forget our wonderful weeks at Battle Island Inn."

Garrison   J12

The Bird & Bottle Inn

Old Albany Post Rd, Rt 9
Garrison, NY 10524
(845)424-3000 Fax:(845)424-3283

Circa 1761. Built as Warren's Tavern, this three-story yellow farmhouse served as a lodging and dining spot on the New York-to-Albany Post Road, now a National Historic Landmark. George Washington, Hamilton, Lafayette and many other historic figures frequently passed by. The inn's eight acres include secluded lawns, a babbling stream and Hudson Valley woodlands. Timbered ceilings, old paneling and fireplace mantels in the inn's notable restaurant maintain a Revolutionary War-era ambiance. Second-floor guest rooms have canopied or four-poster beds and each is warmed by its own fireplace.

Innkeeper(s): Ira Boyar. $210-260. 4 rooms with PB, 4 with FP, 1 suite and 1 cottage. Breakfast included in rates. Types of meals: Gourmet dinner. Restaurant on premises. Beds: Q. Reading lamp, clock radio, desk and $75 dinner credit for two in room. Air conditioning. Fax, copier, telephone and fireplaces on premises. Weddings, small meetings, family reunions and seminars hosted. Antiquing, cross-country skiing, fishing, live theater, parks and shopping nearby.

Publicity: *Colonial Homes, Hudson Valley, Spotlight, Travel Channel, The Learning Channel, Conde Nast Traveler Gazette, Country Living, Time Out New York, The News-Times-CT, The New York Times, MTV, Food Network and Kiss Me Goodbye.*

Geneseo   G5

Oak Valley Inn

4562 Millennium Dr
Geneseo, NY 14454
(585)243-5570
E-mail: keith@oakvalleyinn.com
Web: www.oakvalleyinn.com

Circa 1868. It's difficult to imagine that this enormous Federal-style building was once the location of the county's poor house. The building now contains an assortment of comfortably appointed guest rooms, decorated in early American style. The suites include a king-size bed, whirlpool tub and a fireplace. The grounds are decorated with gardens. In the mornings, guests are served continental-plus breakfasts that include breads, bagels, muffins, fresh fruit, cereal and a daily entree.

Innkeeper(s): Keith & Marilyn Hollis. $65-175. 15 rooms with PB, 4 with FP, 3 suites and 1 conference room. Breakfast and snacks/refreshments included in rates. Types of meals: Cont plus and early coffee/tea. Beds: KQT. TV, refrigerator, clock radio, telephone, coffeemaker, desk, hot tub/spa and fireplace in room. Air conditioning. Fax, copier, library and parlor games on premises. Weddings, small meetings, family reunions and seminars hosted. Amusement parks, antiquing, cross-country skiing, downhill skiing, fishing, golf, live theater, parks, shopping, sporting events, tennis and water sports nearby.

Publicity: *Rochester Paper and Country Magazine.*

Geneva F6

Belhurst Castle

PO Box 609
Geneva, NY 14456-0609
(315)781-0201 Fax:(315)781-0201
Web: www.belhurst.com

Circa 1889. The century old stone castle is situated in the heart of the finger lakes wine region that overlooks Seneca Lake. Belhurst Castle features dining in the library, parlor, center room, solarium or on the veranda that overlooks the expansive grounds and lake. There are 13 guest rooms with private baths and all are decorated in period furnishings. The Castle Ballroom, a favorite for receptions, accommodates up to 300 guests. Belhurst Castle is the recipient of the Wine Spectator Award for ten consecutive years and was voted "one of the most romantic places in New York State."

Historic Interest: In 1885, Carrie Harron Collins, a descendant of Henry Clay, hired an architect and 50 men to begin work on her dream. During construction one man lost his life, another lost his mind. Four years and more than $475,00 later, 48 men completed her dream - Belhurst Castle. In the century since the structure was built, Belhurst Castle has been, at various times, a private home, casino, speakeasy and restaurant. Tales persist of the romantic past, of secret tunnels, hidden treasures buried in the walls and on the grounds, of ghosts and hauntings. Fact or fancy? No one knows. Belhurst combines the romance of the past with the comforts of the present in an elegant, yet relaxed atmosphere. Listed in the National Register of Historic Places.

Innkeeper(s): Duane R. Reeder. $65-315. 13 rooms with PB, 4 with FP. Breakfast included in rates. Types of meals: Sun. brunch and room service. Restaurant on premises. Beds: QDT. TV, VCR, reading lamp, stereo, ceiling fan, snack bar, telephone, coffeemaker and hot tub/spa in room. Fax, copier, parlor games, fireplace and private Jacuzzis on premises. Limited handicap access. Weddings, small meetings, family reunions and seminars hosted. Antiquing, art galleries, cross-country skiing, downhill skiing, fishing, golf, live theater, museums, parks, shopping, sporting events, water sports and wineries nearby.

Geneva On The Lake

1001 Lochland Rd, Rt 14S
Geneva, NY 14456
(315)789-7190 (800)343-6382 Fax:(315)789-0322
E-mail: info@genevaonthelake.com
Web: www.genevaonthelake.com

Circa 1911. This opulent world-class inn is a replica of the Renaissance-era Lancellotti Villa in Frascati, Italy. It is listed in the National Register. Although originally built as a residence, it became a monastery for Capuchin monks. Now it is one of the finest resorts in the U.S. Renovated under the direction of award-winning designer William Schickel, there are 10 two-bedroom suites, some with views of the lake. Here, you may have an experience  as fine as Europe can offer, without leaving the country. Some compare it to the Grand Hotel du Cap-Ferrat on the French Riviera. The inn has been awarded four diamonds from AAA for more than a decade. Breakfast is available daily and on Sunday, brunch is served. Dinner is served each evening, and in the summer, lunch is offered on the terrace.

Historic Interest: The Corning Glass Center, where Steuben glass is created by hand, is nearby. The town of Elmira, another close attraction, is the site where "The Adventures of Tom Sawyer" and "Huckleberry Finn," were written by Mark Twain.

Innkeeper(s): William J. Schickel. $138-730. 58 rooms, 29 with PB, 3 with FP, 29 suites and 3 conference rooms. Breakfast included in rates. Types of

meals: Cont, gourmet dinner and room service. Restaurant on premises. Beds: KQDT. TV, refrigerator, clock radio, telephone, turn-down service and desk in room. Air conditioning. VCR, fax, copier, swimming, bicycles, parlor games, fireplace, sailing, fishing, lawn games and boats on premises. Weddings, small meetings, family reunions and seminars hosted. Antiquing, cross-country skiing, downhill skiing, live theater, parks, shopping, sporting events, water sports and wineries nearby.

Publicity: *Travel & Leisure, Bon Appetit, Country Inns, The New York Times, Bride's, Catholic Register, Pittsford-Brighton Post, New York, Glamour, Gourmet, Washingtonian, Toronto Star, Globe & Mail and Rochester Democrat & Chronicle.*

"The food was superb and the service impeccable."

Greene H8

Water's Edge Bed & Breakfast

1 Washington St
Greene, NY 13778
(607)656-4891 Fax:(607)656-4892

Circa 1851. Located on the bank of the Chenango River, this Italianate Victorian home is conveniently located in a picturesque village known for its arts and antiques. Decorated informally with country antiques, the original character is enhanced by modern conveniences. The inn features an exercise room, a big screen TV in the parlor and books to borrow. After a restful night in one of the comfortable guest bedrooms, enjoy a buffet breakfast with a view, boasting made-to-order eggs. Tourism advice is freely given, gifts and local products are for sale and a canoe and kayak are available to use.

Innkeeper(s): Candace, Rob, Andrew Harrington. $65-85. 4 rooms with PB. Breakfast and snacks/refreshments included in rates. Types of meals: Full gourmet bkfst, veg bkfst and early coffee/tea. Beds: QT. Reading lamp, ceiling fan, clock radio and coffeemaker in room. Central air. Fax, copier, telephone, fireplace and laundry facility on premises. Small meetings, family reunions and seminars hosted. Antiquing, art galleries, bicycling, canoeing/kayaking, cross-country skiing, downhill skiing, fishing, golf, hiking, museums, parks, shopping, sporting events, tennis, water sports and wineries nearby.

Publicity: *Binghamton Press and Norwich Sun.*

Greenport K15

The Bartlett House Inn

503 Front St
Greenport, NY 11944-1519
(631)477-0371
E-mail: degilmore@hotmail.com
Web: www.greenport.com/bartlett

Circa 1908. Built for Mr. John Bartlett, NY State Assemblyman and later serving as a convent, this large Victorian house became a bed & breakfast in 1982. Features include Corinthian columns, stained-glass windows, two fireplaces and a large front porch. Period antiques complement the rich interior. The inn is within walking distance of shops, restaurants, the harbor, wineries, the Shelter Island Ferry and train station.

Innkeeper(s): Diane Gilmore. $110-250. 10 rooms with PB, 1 with FP and 1 conference room. Breakfast included in rates. Types of meals: Cont plus and early coffee/tea. Beds: QDT. Reading lamp, clock radio, telephone, desk, fireplace and hair dryers in room. Air conditioning. TV, VCR and parlor games on premises. Weddings, small meetings, family reunions and seminars hosted. Antiquing, fishing, parks, shopping, water sports, maritime museum, outlet shopping, art galleries, golf and fine restaurants nearby.

Publicity: *Suffolk Times, Newsday, New York Times and New York Post.*

Stirling House Bed & Breakfast

143 Sterling Avenue
Greenport, NY 11944
(631)477-0654 Fax:(631)477-2885
E-mail: info@stirlinghousebandb.com
Web: www.stirlinghousebandb.com

Circa 1873. Offering Southern-style hospitality on Long Island, this Victorian home from the 1800s was a boarding house during the whaling era. It has been restored recently to its original integrity and renovated to provide modern pleasures. The elegant parlor is furnished with antiques accented by a hand-painted floral mural and an inlaid marble fireplace hearth. An eclectic-melange of guest bedrooms feature maritime, French, garden and old-fashioned decorating themes. Animation artwork graces the walls of the whimsical breakfast room that is filled with collectibles, vintage toys and a fireside TV/VCR. Ample wicker seating is available to enjoy a continental morning buffet or dine alfresco in the English garden beside the fish pond. Afternoon tea and lemonade are refreshing interludes after visiting local sites.

Innkeeper(s): Clayton Sauer. $125-195. 3 rooms, 2 with PB and 1 suite. Breakfast and snacks/refreshments included in rates. Types of meals: Country bkfst, veg bkfst and afternoon tea. Beds: QD. Reading lamp, ceiling fan and clock radio in room. Air conditioning. TV, VCR, fax, parlor games, telephone, fireplace, refrigerator, cable TV, VCR, fireplace, outdoor garden and dining area and front porch with view of water on premises. Antiquing, art galleries, beach, bicycling, canoeing/kayaking, fishing, golf, horseback riding, live theater, museums, parks, shopping, tennis, water sports and wineries nearby.

Greenville   G12

Greenville Arms 1889 Inn

PO Box 659, Route 32
Greenville, NY 12083
(518)966-5219 (888)665-0044 Fax:(518)966-8754
E-mail: stay@greenvillearms.com
Web: www.greenvillearms.com

Circa 1889. Built by William Vanderbilt, this pleasurable Queen Anne with Victorian details, antiques and original artwork has been a welcoming inn for fifty years. An atmosphere of warmth and relaxed comfort is found in the three buildings that grace six acres of lawns, shade trees and colorful gardens. After a restful night's sleep, don't miss a satisfying hot breakfast before heading out for Hudson Valley sightseeing. Hike, bike, relax on the porch or by the fifty-foot outdoor pool.

Innkeeper(s): Eliot & Letitia Dalton. $115-195. 15 rooms with PB, 2 with FP, 3 suites, 1 cottage and 2 conference rooms. Breakfast and afternoon tea included in rates. Types of meals: Full gourmet bkfst, veg bkfst, early coffee/tea and dinner. Beds: KQDT. Reading lamp, refrigerator, clock radio, some have fireplaces and whirlpools or private porches in room. Air conditioning. TV, VCR, swimming, library, parlor games, telephone, fireplace, gift shop and outdoor pool on premises. Small meetings, family reunions and seminars hosted. Antiquing, bicycling, downhill skiing, fishing, golf, hiking, horseback riding and parks nearby.

Publicity: *Victorian Homes, New York Magazine, Yankee, Sophisticated Traveler, Hudson Valley, Great Country Inns and The Learning Channel.*

"Just a note of appreciation for all your generous hospitality, and wonderful display of attention and affection!"

Greenwich   F12

Country Life B&B

67 Tabor Road
Greenwich, NY 12834
(518)692-7203 (888)692-7203 Fax:(518)692-9203
E-mail: stay@countrylifebb.com
Web: www.countrylifebb.com

Circa 1829. Near the Battenkill River in the Adirondack foothills, this Flat Front farmhouse sits on 118 acres surrounded by rolling hills. Filled with antiques and traditional furnishings, romantic guest bedrooms feature comfortable terry robes, sherry and candy. A free breakfast is a delicious way to begin the day. Relax on three acres of groomed lawn with flower gardens, a two-person hammock and a porch swing. The bridge across an old mill stream leads to woodland trails. Swim in the ponds with two waterfalls and a rock slide.

Innkeeper(s): Wendy & Richard Duvall. $85-175. 4 rooms with PB. Breakfast and snacks/refreshments included in rates. Types of meals: Country bkfst, veg bkfst and early coffee/tea. Beds: KQ. TV, reading lamp, clock radio, turn-down service, terry cloth robes, sherry, candy, extra blankets and pillows in room. Air conditioning. Fax, bicycles, library, child care, parlor games, telephone, fireplace and coffeemaker on premises. Weddings and family reunions hosted. Antiquing, art galleries, beach, bicycling, canoeing/kayaking, cross-country skiing, downhill skiing, fishing, golf, hiking, horseback riding, live theater, museums, parks and shopping nearby.

Publicity: *Long Island Newsday, Inn Times, NY Times, Country Extra, Long Island Lifestyles Magazine, Washington County Magazine, Glens Falls Business News, ABC TV-Weekend Report and CBS-TV This Morning.*

Groton   G7

Benn Conger Inn

206 W Cortland St
Groton, NY 13073-1008
(607)898-5817 (888)871-0220 Fax:(607)898-5818
E-mail: benncongerinn@yahoo.com
Web: www.benncongerinn.com

Circa 1920. Once home to namesake Benn Conger, founder of Smith-Corona typewriters and Dutch Schultz, notorious bootlegger, this majestic inn overlooks a picturesque village in the heart of the Finger Lakes. Sitting on 20 park-like acres, it includes a mansion reminiscent of Tara in "Gone With The Wind," as well as a delightful Victorian cottage. Spacious guest bedrooms and suites are a stunning collaboration of interior design, architecture and thoughtful amenities. Several feature whirlpool tubs, fireplaces and large porches. Choose from American or European menu selections for breakfast in the Morning Room or on the Terrace. Chef/owner Peter prepares renown Mediterranean cuisine for dinner, and offers an award-winning wine selection. He and his wife, innkeeper Alison instill an elegant ambiance steeped in tradition and hospitality.

Innkeeper(s): Alison van der Meulen. $90-250. 10 rooms, 9 with PB, 7 with FP and 1 suite. Breakfast and afternoon tea included in rates. Types of meals: Full gourmet bkfst, early coffee/tea, picnic lunch, snacks/refreshments, gourmet dinner and room service. Restaurant on premises. Beds: KQDT. Modem hook-up, data port, cable TV, reading lamp, ceiling fan, clock radio, telephone, turn-down service, desk, hot tub/spa, digital TV and Music Choice in room. Air conditioning. Fax, copier, spa, bicycles, library, pet boarding, parlor games, fireplace and laundry facility on premises. Weddings, small meetings, family reunions and seminars hosted. Antiquing, art galleries, beach, bicycling, canoeing/kayaking, cross-country skiing, downhill skiing, fishing, golf, hiking, horseback riding, live theater, museums, parks, shopping, sporting events, tennis, water sports and wineries nearby.

Publicity: *Syracuse New Times, Herald American, Ithaca Journal, Ithaca Times and Cortland Standard.*

Hadley E12

Saratoga Rose Inn & Restaurant

4274 Rockwell St
Hadley, NY 12835-0238
(518)696-2861 (800)942-5025 Fax:(518)696-5319
E-mail: saratogarose@adelphia.net
Web: www.saratogarose.com

Circa 1885. This romantic Queen Anne Victorian offers a small, candle-lit restaurant perfect for an evening for two. Breakfast specialties include Grand Marnier French toast and Eggs Anthony. Rooms are decorated in period style. The Queen Anne Room, decorated in blue, boasts a wood and tile fireplace and a quilt-covered bed. The Carriage House features an iron canopy bed, skylight, TV, fireplace and private deck with a Jacuzzi while the Garden Room offers a private sunporch and an outside deck with a Jacuzzi spa. Each of the rooms features something special. Guests can take in the mountain view or relax on the veranda while sipping a cocktail.

Innkeeper(s): Nancy Merlino, Chef Anthony. $160-190. 6 rooms with PB, 6 with FP. Breakfast included in rates. Types of meals: Full gourmet bkfst and gourmet dinner. Beds: KD. Ceiling fan, clock radio, hot tub/spa and four rooms with private hot tubs in room. Air conditioning. VCR, telephone and fireplace on premises. Weddings, small meetings, family reunions and seminars hosted. Amusement parks, antiquing, cross-country skiing, downhill skiing, fishing, live theater, parks, shopping and sporting events nearby.

Publicity: Getaways for Gourmets.

"A must for the inn traveler."

Hague D12

Ruah B&B

34 Lake Shore Dr
Hague, NY 12836-9705
(518)543-8816 (800)224-7549
E-mail: ruahbb@aol.com
Web: www.ruahbb.com

Circa 1907. Artist Harry Watrous built this Dutch Colonial mansion, and some of the property may have been acquired with an especially good poker hand. Be sure to ask the innkeepers about Watrous and the legend of the creature in the

lake. The inn is set on more than six acres, and offers wonderful views of Lake George. The innkeepers restored the turn-of-the-century inn and its four guest rooms. The two redecorated everything except for the living room. This room was chosen for a special redecorating project by House Beautiful magazine, which featured the inn in a six-page feature. The living room is stunning, the decor and furniture arrangement was selected carefully as not to overpower the lake views. There is a veranda lined with wicker for those who wish to relax and enjoy the sight of mountains and the water. A buffet breakfast is presented each morning with items such as souffles, frittatas, granola, cereal, fruit and homemade baked goods.

Innkeeper(s): Judy & Peter Foster. $90-205. 4 rooms with PB, 2 with FP and 1 suite. Breakfast included in rates. Types of meals: Full bkfst and early coffee/tea. Beds: KQT. Reading lamp and desk in room. Library, parlor games, telephone and fireplace on premises. Weddings, small meetings, family reunions and seminars hosted. Amusement parks, antiquing, cross-country skiing, downhill skiing, fishing, golf, parks, shopping, tennis and water sports nearby.

Publicity: House Beautiful, Forbes, FYI, Albany Times, Union Glens Falls, Post Star, Chronicle, New York News, Wall Street Journal, chosen as one of twelve "Best Undiscovered B&Bs in America" and Albany Channel 10 News.

"Wonderful, fantastic, romantic, comfortable, friendly and pretty!"

Trout House Village Resort

PO Box 510, Lake Shore Dr
Hague, NY 12836-0510
(518)543-6088 (800)368-6088 Fax:(518)543-6124
E-mail: info@trouthouse.com
Web: www.trouthouse.com

Circa 1920. On the shores of beautiful Lake George is this resort inn, offering accommodations in the inn, authentic log cabins or cottages. Many of the guest rooms in the inn boast lake views, while the log cabins offer jetted tubs and fireplaces. The guest quarters are furnished comfortably. The emphasis here is on the abundance of outdoor activities. Outstanding cross-country skiing, downhill skiing and snowmobiling are found nearby. The inn furnishes bicycles, canoes, kayaks, paddle boats, rowboats, sleds, shuffleboard, skis and toboggans. Summertime evenings offer games of capture-the-flag and soccer. Other activities include basketball, horseshoes, ping pong, a putting green and volleyball.

Historic Interest: Fort Ticonderoga (8 miles).

Innkeeper(s): Scott & Alice Patchett. $59-350. 42 rooms, 9 with PB, 15 with FP, 3 cottages, 17 cabins and 2 conference rooms. Beds: QDT. Modem hook-up, cable TV, VCR, reading lamp, CD player, refrigerator, clock radio, telephone, coffeemaker, desk, hot tub/spa, voice mail and hair dryer in room. Fax, copier, spa, swimming, bicycles, child care, parlor games, fireplace, canoes, rowboats, kayaks, shuffleboard, basketball, horseshoes, ping-pong, BBQ grills, volleyball and putting green on premises. Limited handicap access. Weddings, small meetings, family reunions and seminars hosted. Amusement parks, antiquing, art galleries, beach, bicycling, canoeing/kayaking, cross-country skiing, downhill skiing, fishing, golf, hiking, horseback riding, live theater, museums, parks, shopping, tennis, water sports and child care nearby.

"My wife and I felt the family warmth at this resort. There wasn't that coldness you get at larger resorts."

Hamburg G3

Sharon's Lake House B&B

4862 Lake Shore Rd
Hamburg, NY 14075-5542
(716)627-7561

Circa 1935. This historic lakefront house is located 10 miles from Buffalo and 45 minutes from Niagara Falls. Overlooking Lake Erie, the West Lake Room and the Upper Lake Room provide spectacular views. The home's beautiful furnishings offer additional delights.

Innkeeper(s): Sharon & Vince Di Maria. $110. 2 rooms, 1 with PB. Breakfast included in rates. Types of meals: Full gourmet bkfst and gourmet dinner. Beds: D. Cable TV, reading lamp, CD player, ceiling fan, clock radio and telephone in room. VCR, fax, spa, swimming, bicycles, library, parlor games, fireplace, hot tub room and computer room at an hourly rate available on premises. Antiquing, art galleries, beach, bicycling, canoeing/kayaking, cross-country skiing, downhill skiing, fishing, golf, hiking, live theater, museums, parks, shopping, water sports and wineries nearby.

"Spectacular view, exquisitely furnished."

Hamilton   F9

Lawrence Inn

72 Madison Street
Hamilton, NY 13346
(315)824-0382 (888)758-4749
E-mail: conni@lawrenceinn.com
Web: www.lawrence-inn.com

Circa 1860. Enjoy a refined and leisurely stay at this renovated Victorian home in scenic upstate New York. Watch TV, play games, just relax by the fire in the library or browse the bookshelves. The sitting room in the tower is perfect for reading and quiet meditation. Themed guest bedrooms are named and decorated to reflect the innkeepers' favorite places. Sleep in a wicker bed in The Tropics, or in a king-size canopy in Paris. London boasts sophisticated Country English furnishings and Munich features a Bavarian blue sky and a contemporary setting. Upscale pleasures include radiant heated floors, individual climate controls for air and heat, terry robes, down duvet comforters and ironed linens. The morning meal is served in the Breakfast Room. Walk to shops in the rural village or to Colgate's Seven Oaks Golf Course.

Innkeeper(s): Charlie & Conni Lawrence. $155-205. 3 rooms with PB. Breakfast included in rates. Types of meals: Full bkfst, early coffee/tea and room service. Beds: KQT. Reading lamp, ceiling fan, telephone, plush terry robes and down comforters in room. Air conditioning. Library, parlor games and fireplace on premises. Antiquing, art galleries, bicycling, golf, hiking, live theater, museums and shopping nearby.

Hammondsport   G6

The Amity Rose Bed & Breakfast

8264 Main St
Hammondsport, NY 14840-9701
(607)569-3402 (800)982-8818
Web: www.amityroseinn.com

Circa 1899. Relax on the two-story veranda at this country Victorian with shuttered windows. All guest bedrooms feature queen beds and most include a fireplace. Two rooms boast whirlpool soaking tubs. Stay in Sweet Emma's Suite, with a furnished sitting room. Savor a hearty country breakfast each morning. Walk to the historic village square to listen to a bandstand concert. Go fishing in a trout stream. Located in the scenic Finger Lakes region, tour what was the famous Taylor Winery, now Pheasant Valley Winery. Visit the interesting sites and attractions of nearby Corning and Bath.

Historic Interest: Museum (1 mile), Glen Curtis.

Innkeeper(s): Ellen & Frank Laufersweiler. $95-125. 4 rooms with PB, 3 with FP, 1 suite and 1 conference room. Breakfast and afternoon tea included in rates. Types of meals: Country bkfst, veg bkfst and early coffee/tea. Beds: Q. Reading lamp, CD player, clock radio, coffeemaker and 2 whirlpool Jacuzzis in room. Air conditioning. Fax, bicycles, tennis, parlor games, telephone and fireplace on premises. Small meetings and seminars hosted. Antiquing, art galleries, beach, bicycling, canoeing/kayaking, fishing, golf, hiking, horseback riding, museums, parks, shopping, sporting events, tennis, water sports and wineries nearby.

"How nice, a bathroom big enough to waltz in, well almost!"

Hector   G7

Magnolia Place

5240 State Route 414
Hector, NY 14841-9707
(607)546-5338 Fax:(607)546-5339
E-mail: Magplace414@aol.com
Web: www.MagnoliaPlace414.com

Circa 1837. Overlooking Seneca Lake in the midst of scenic Finger Lakes Wine Country, this 1830s farmhouse has been renovated to offer year-round hospitality and relaxation. Luxurious guest suites with central air conditioning were individually designed for the utmost in comfort. Several feature canopy beds, Jacuzzi tubs, fireplaces, and private porches with views of the water. Linger over a country breakfast in the kitchen or on the veranda. Arrange for a lunch, dinner or sightseeing cruise; parasail, rent a boat, jet ski or kayak. Watkins Glen State Park is just seven miles away. Ask about special packages available.

Innkeeper(s): Theresa Kelly Remmers and Ted Palevsky. $130-200. 8 suites, 2 with FP. Beds: KQ. Fireplace and suites have private baths in room. Central air, TV, VCR, fax, copier, parlor games and telephone on premises. Small meetings, family reunions and seminars hosted.

Herkimer   F10

Bellinger Rose Bed & Breakfast

611 W German St
Herkimer, NY 13350
(315)867-2197
E-mail: bellingerrose@hotmail.com
Web: www.bellingerrose.com

Circa 1865. Originally built in 1865 by the prominent Bellinger family, this recently renovated inn exudes Victorian grace and charm. The exquisite decor and splendid antique furnishings invite pleasantries and relaxation. The common rooms include a formal parlor with a perfectly tuned piano, and a sitting room offering modern entertainment such as videos or DVD with surround sound. Both areas provide the warmth and ambiance of wood-burning marble fireplaces. In keeping with the name, a romantic theme of roses adorns the two unique guest bedrooms with spacious sitting areas. A full breakfast is served daily in the elegant dining room. The pampering continues with plush robes, a year-round hot tub, and a chair massage that is included with each night's stay.

Innkeeper(s): Chris & Leon Frost. $85-95. 2 rooms with PB. Breakfast included in rates. Types of meals: Full bkfst. Beds: Q. Modem hook-up, cable TV, VCR, reading lamp, clock radio and turn-down service in room. Air conditioning. Spa, bicycles, child care, telephone, fireplace and professional massage on premises. Small meetings hosted. Antiquing, art galleries, bicycling, canoeing/kayaking, cross-country skiing, fishing, golf, hiking, live theater, museums and shopping nearby.

High Falls   I11

1797 Depuy Canal House

Route 213 Box 96
High Falls, NY 12440
(845)687-7700 Fax:(845)687-7073
Web: www.depuycanalhouse.net

Circa 1870. The proprietors of the nationally acclaimed 1797 Depuy Canal House restaurant also offer overnight accommodations at Locktender Cottage across the street — an excellent solution to solve the dilemma of those who sometimes drive three hours to enjoy chef John Novi's culinary skills. Located beside the historic Delaware and Hudson Canal, there are three guest rooms (one with a fireplace), and what is called the Chef's Quarters with its own whirlpool, kitchenette and laundry. Pick-your-own orchards and vegetable farms are nearby. Other activities are winery tours, fishing, skiing, taking a Hudson River cruise, riding the Delaware and Ulster Rail Ride or tubing on Esopus Creek.

Historic Interest: FDR's Hyde Park home, Vanderbilt Mansion, Mohonk Preserve.

Innkeeper(s): John N Novi. $75-145. 3 rooms. Beds: QD. Air conditioning. Cross-country skiing, downhill skiing, fishing, hiking, museums, wineries, pick your own fruit and vegetable farms nearby.

Publicity: *Time Magazine, Hudson Valley HJournal and Poughkeepsie Journal.*

"A great home away from home."

Hillsdale H12

The Inn at Green River

9 Nobletown Rd
Hillsdale, NY 12529-5712
(518)325-7248 Fax:(518)325-1474
E-mail: deborah@iagr.com
Web: www.iagr.com

Circa 1830. A former farmhouse, this inn was once used as a parsonage for the former Lutheran Church next door. The charming side-hall colonial rests on an acre of lush lawn and gardens and is surrounded by mead-

ows and an ancient, abandoned cemetery. Antiques, paintings and old family photographs combine with wool and chintz draperies to create warmth and elegance. Breakfast is served on "grandmother's" china on the screened porch or candlelit dining room. Scones and fresh fruit are staples, with entrees such as lemon-Ricotta pancakes adding a gourmet touch.

Innkeeper(s): Deborah Bowen. $95-185. 7 rooms with PB. Breakfast included in rates. Types of meals: Full gourmet bkfst, veg bkfst and early coffee/tea. Beds: KQD. Hot tub/spa in room. Air conditioning. Fireplace on premises. Limited handicap access. Fishing nearby.

Publicity: *Gourmet, New York Magazine, The South Florida and Martha Stewart Living magazine loved the Inn's kitchen and grounds so much that they used them for several location photo shoots.*

"A very lovely interlude."

Hudson H12

Hudson City B&B

326 Allen St
Hudson, NY 12534
(518)822-8044 Fax:(518)828-9139
E-mail: hcbb98@aol.com
Web: www.hudsoncitybnb.com

Circa 1865. The view from the tower, the warmth of the fireplace, the comfort of the canopy beds and the sway of the porch swing become favorite memories of guests who stay at this three-story Second Empire Victorian home. Joshua T. Waterman, railroad baron and mayor of the town in the mid-1800s, built the mansion, and he and his wife watched their 12 children grow up here. Today, guests seek out the same cozy nooks once enjoyed by the original family. In the morning,

breakfasts of waffles, pancakes or French toast are served in the dining room before the fireplace. Nearby is The Daughter's of the American Revolution Museum, "Olana," a fireman's museum and many antique shops and galleries.

Historic Interest: Hudson City was the first town to be chartered after the Declaration of Independence.

Innkeeper(s): Kenneth Jacobs. $109-189. 5 rooms with PB, 2 suites and 1 conference room. Types of meals: Country bkfst, early coffee/tea, afternoon tea and snacks/refreshments. Beds: KQ. Cable TV, VCR, reading lamp, refrigerator, ceiling fan, snack bar, desk and antiques in room. Air conditioning. Fax, copier, library, parlor games, telephone, fireplace and laundry facility on premises. Weddings, small meetings, family reunions and seminars hosted. Antiquing, art galleries, cross-country skiing, downhill skiing, horseback riding, live theater, museums, shopping, tennis, wineries, Fireman's Museum and Catskill Game Farm nearby.

Publicity: *Winner of Columbia County competition for window box and yard design.*

Union Street Guest House

349 Union Street
Hudson, NY 12534
(518)828-0958
E-mail: info@unionstreetguesthouse.com
Web: www.unionstreetguesthouse.com

Circa 1830. Surrounded by Columbia County's Catskill Mountains, this 1830 Greek Revival mansion is just off the Courthouse Square within a delightful stroll of world-class antique shops, fine restaurants, and a park gazebo. Private guest suites are furnished with antiques and mid-century pieces. Stay in the Library Suite with a sitting room and house library or choose the more spacious two-bedroom Bainbridge Suite with a sitting room and large screened porch. Snacks and refreshments are available. The grounds and gardens feature a country ambiance with lush green lawns that are fenced in front and boast views of barns in the back. The Hudson River is only five blocks away. Visit the popular Berkshires in Massachusetts in just 20 minutes.

Innkeeper(s): Chris Wagoner. $90-200. 2 suites. Snacks/refreshments included in rates. Types of meals: Early coffee/tea and afternoon tea. Beds: KQD. Cable TV, reading lamp, refrigerator, ceiling fan, clock radio, coffeemaker, turn-down service, desk and fireplace in room. Air conditioning. Library, parlor games and refrigerators on premises. Antiquing, art galleries, bicycling, canoeing/kayaking, cross-country skiing, downhill skiing, fishing, golf, hiking, horseback riding, live theater, museums, parks, shopping, tennis, water sports and wineries nearby.

Hunter H11

Fairlawn Inn

7872 Main Street, PO Box 182
Hunter, NY 12442
(518)263-5025 Fax:(518)263-5025
E-mail: finn1@hvc.rr.com
Web: www.fairlawninn.com

Circa 1902. A three-story turret, large wraparound front porch and sweeping two-story covered veranda with gazebo accentuate the exterior of this historic Victorian. The interior has original woodwork and light fixtures restored to reflect its original grandeur. Period-style wallpapers, an incredible art collection and many antiques add to the ambiance. Guest bedrooms are elegantly decorated and furnished with reproduction beds, comfortable seating, and modern amenities. Some include vintage oversized clawfoot tubs, and one is handicapped accessible. Breakfast features fresh fruit, baked goods, eggs, pancakes, souffles or French toast. The Catskill Mountains offer scenic outdoor activities. Viewed from the front porch, Hunter Mountain ski resort is a half-mile away. Take a trolley to one of the three local villages with two movie screens, a performing arts center, organic produce market and many places to shop or eat.

Innkeeper(s): Chuck Tomajko. $99-199. 9 rooms with PB. Breakfast included in rates. Beds: Q. Clock radio and all rooms with private en-suite baths in room. TV, VCR, fax and copier on premises. Weddings, small meetings, family reunions and seminars hosted. Antiquing, bicycling, canoeing/kayaking, cross-country skiing, downhill skiing, fishing, golf, hiking, horseback riding, parks, shopping, tennis, hunting and rock/ice climbing nearby.

"This was a wonderful romantic getaway as well as a great chance to meet and make new friends."

The Redcoat's Country Inn & Restaurant

50 Dale Lane
Hunter, NY 12427
(518)589-9858
E-mail: info@redcoatsonline.com
Web: www.redcoatsonline.com

Circa 1910. Styled as a charming English country inn, this delightful four-story lodging sits on 15 acres in the northern Catskill Mountains in the center of the Game Preserve. Relax on the front porch or outdoor deck. Elegant cuisine is served in the dinner restaurant that is open to the public. Gather by the stone fireplace in the lounge and linger over a great meal in one of the two cozy dining rooms. Playing golf and skiing are favorite seasonal activities.

Innkeeper(s): Steve and Carol Fink. $95-125. 14 rooms, 7 with PB. Types of meals: Full gourmet bkfst. Beds: DT. Reading lamp in room. Fireplace on premises. Weddings, small meetings, family reunions and seminars hosted. Antiquing, cross-country skiing, downhill skiing, fishing, golf, hiking and shopping nearby.

Publicity: *New York Times, Ski Magazine and Golf Magazine.*

"Loved the place even more than last time."

Ithaca   G7

A Slice of Home B&B

178 N Main St
Ithaca, NY 14883
(607)589-6073

Circa 1850. This Italianate inn's location, approximately equidistant from Ithaca and Watkins Glen, offers a fine vantage point for exploring the Finger Lakes winery region. Although the area is well-known for its scenery, many recreational opportunities also are available. The innkeeper is happy to help guests plan tours and has a special fondness for those traveling by bicycle. The inn offers four guest rooms, and a two-bedroom cottage, a hot tub and bicycles for all guests. Guests may relax by taking a stroll on the inn's 10 acres, mountain hiking, biking or having a cookout in the inn's backyard. Guests can begin a cross-country ski excursion right from the back porch.

Innkeeper(s): Bea & Sterling Fulmer. $75-200. 4 rooms with PB and 1 cottage. Types of meals: Full bkfst and early coffee/tea. Beds: KQD. Cable TV in

room. Air conditioning. VCR, copier, bicycles, parlor games, telephone, fireplace, horseshoes, badminton and hot tubs on premises. Weddings, small meetings, family reunions and seminars hosted. Antiquing, downhill skiing, fishing, live theater, parks, shopping, sporting events, water sports, wineries and swimming nearby.

The Federal House B&B

Po Box 4914
Ithaca, NY 14882
(607)533-7362 (800)533-7362

Circa 1815. As its name suggests, this historic home was built in the Federal style of architecture. It features spacious antique-filled rooms, original woodwork and hand-carved fireplaces that are reportedly made by Brigham Young, an apprentice carpenter at the time. Nearby Salmon Creek is considered one of the best fishing spots in the Ithaca area. Sit on the porch or in the garden gazebo and listen to the soothing sounds of the creek and falls. Stay in the air-conditioned Lincoln Suite boasting a four-poster canopy bed, sitting area with a gas fireplace and a private staircase. Enjoy a lavish daily breakfast in the formal dining room and afternoon refreshments. Located in the heart of the Finger Lakes, Cayuga Lake is just two miles away.

Innkeeper(s): Stephanie Levy & James Mason. $75-180. 3 rooms with PB, 1 with FP and 1 suite. Breakfast included in rates. Types of meals: Full bkfst and early coffee/tea. Beds: KQT. Modem hook-up, cable TV, reading lamp, ceiling fan, clock radio, coffeemaker, turn-down service and fireplace in room. Air conditioning. Fax, bicycles, parlor games and telephone on premises. Antiquing, bicycling, fishing, hiking, parks, wineries, Cayuga Lake and state parks nearby.

Publicity: *Ithaca Journal and Cortland Paper.*

"Your inn is so charming and your food was excellent."

Rose Inn

Rt 34N, Box 6576
Ithaca, NY 14851-6576
(607)533-7905 Fax:(607)533-7908
E-mail: info@roseinn.com
Web: www.roseinn.com

Circa 1842. This classic Italianate mansion has long been famous for its circular staircase of Honduran mahogany. It is owned by Sherry Rosemann, a noted interior designer specializing in mid-19th-century architecture and furniture, and her husband Charles, a hotelier from Germany. On 14 landscaped acres with a large formal garden and wedding chapel, it is 10 minutes from Cornell University. The inn has been the recipient of many awards for its lodging and dining, including a four-star rating nine years in a row.

Historic Interest: National Women's Hall of Fame (1 hour), Steuben Glass (1 hour), Cornell University.

Innkeeper(s): Charles & Sherry Rosemann. $130-340. 20 rooms with PB and 2 conference rooms. Breakfast included in rates. Types of meals: Full gourmet bkfst, early coffee/tea and gourmet dinner. Restaurant on premises. Beds: KQD. Modem hook-up, data port, cable TV, ceiling fan, telephone, turn-down service, twelve suites have Jacuzzi, seven with fireplace, TV and VCR in room. Air conditioning. TV, VCR, fax, copier, library, parlor games and fireplace on premises. Weddings, small meetings, family reunions and seminars hosted. Antiquing, art galleries, beach, bicycling, canoeing/kayaking, cross-country skiing, downhill skiing, fishing, golf, hiking, horseback riding, live theater, museums, parks, shopping, sporting events, tennis, water sports and wineries nearby.

Publicity: *New York Times, Toronto Globe and Mail and Inn Country USA.*

"The blending of two outstanding talents, which when combined with your warmth, produce the ultimate experience in being away from home. Like staying with friends in their beautiful home."

Stone Quarry House

26 Quarry Road
Ithaca, NY 14850
(607)273-4692
E-mail: nnorton@twcny.rr.com
Web: stonequarryhouse.com

Circa 1880. Sitting on a reclaimed stone quarry, this newly custom-built house compliments the historic farmhouse that sits 300 yards from a one-room schoolhouse still in use. The private accommodations feature Arts and Crafts decor with Stickley and Amish furniture accented by hand-knotted Persian carpets. A full kitchen with dishwasher, a dining area, washer and dryer and a library offer comfort and ease. Luxuriously comfortable surroundings include a hot tub. The quiet hillside setting boasts a flagstone walk with bench and bird feeders, a meadow, fragrant cutting gardens and a fountain. Sit in an Adirondack chair by the spring-fed pond, or take an invigorating dip in the cool water. Dine at the famous Moosewood Restaurant in town.

Historic Interest: Custom built to compliment turn-of-the-century farmhouse. 300 yards from only one-room schoolhouse still in daily use as a school building. On the grounds of a reclaimed stone quarry which has been supplying stone to Cornell University and Ithaca College since their inceptions.

Innkeeper(s): Buzz Dolph and Nancy Norton. $125-175. 3 rooms. Beds: KQ. Modem hook-up, data port, cable TV, VCR, reading lamp, refrigerator, clock radio, telephone, coffeemaker, voice mail, washer and dryer, dishwasher, full kitchen and dining area, stickley and Amish furniture, hand-knotted Persian carpets and library in room. Central air. Spa and parlor games on premises. Antiquing, art galleries, bicycling, canoeing/kayaking, cross-country skiing, downhill skiing, fishing, golf, hiking, horseback riding, live theater, museums, parks, shopping, tennis, water sports, wineries, Paleontolgy Research Institute, Sapsucker Woods Ornithology Lab, Friends of the Library book sale, Angelhart Barn Sale and Grassroots Music Festival nearby.

Jay C12

Book and Blanket B&B

Rt 9N, PO Box 164
Jay, NY 12941-0164
(518)946-8323

Circa 1860. This Adirondack bed & breakfast served as the town's post office for many years and also as barracks for state troopers. Thankfully, however, it is now a restful bed & breakfast catering to the literary set. Guest rooms are named for authors and there are books in every nook and cranny of the house. Guests may even take a book home with them. Each of the guest rooms is comfortably furnished. The inn is a short walk from the Jay Village Green and the original site of the Historic Jay covered bridge.

Innkeeper(s): Kathy, Fred, Sam & Zoe the Basset Hound. $70-90. 3 rooms, 1 with PB. Breakfast, afternoon tea and snacks/refreshments included in rates. Types of meals: Full bkfst, veg bkfst and early coffee/tea. Beds: QDT. Reading lamp and clock radio in room. TV, VCR, library, parlor games, telephone, fireplace, fireplace and whirlpool tub on premises. Family reunions hosted. Antiquing, art galleries, beach, bicycling, canoeing/kayaking, cross-country skiing, downhill skiing, fishing, golf, hiking, parks, sporting events, tennis, water sports, Olympic venues i.e. bobsled, luge, ski jump and ice skating nearby.

Lake Clear C11

Hohmeyer's Lake Clear Lodge

RR1 Box 221
Lake Clear, NY 12945
(518)891-1489 (800)442-2356 Fax:(518)891-9954
E-mail: thelodge@northnet.org
Web: www.lodgeonlakeclear.com

Circa 1886. Surrounded by 25 acres of Adirondack scenery, this German-style lodge with 175 feet of private beachfront is awash in Old World ambiance. The Lodge, run by the same family for more than a century, originally accommodated those traveling along the New York to Montreal rail line. Old tracks still run through the property. The German cuisine served at the inn's restaurant is highly recommended, and knotty pine woodwork and exposed beams add to the dining room's European atmosphere. Guest rooms feature a combination of Adirondack/European style decor with pine floors, Adirondack antiques and custom woodwork. Accommodations are available in the woodland chalet or the Sunwater Guesthaus, as well. The Guesthaus offers two units with lake views, a wood-burning fireplace, kitchen, two bedrooms and a bath with a whirlpool tub. The Lodge, with its location in the St. Regis Wilderness area, provides a multitude of recreational possibilities right at your doorstep. Not far from the Lake Placid Olympic sites, it is also a perfect spot for those enjoying a ski vacation. Lakeside weddings, seminars and reunions are popular here.

Innkeeper(s): Cathy & Ernest Hohmeyer. $149-289. 13 rooms, 4 with PB, 5 with FP, 5 suites, 4 cottages and 3 conference rooms. Types of meals: Full gourmet bkfst, gourmet lunch, picnic lunch, afternoon tea and gourmet dinner. Restaurant on premises. Beds: KQDT. VCR, reading lamp, stereo, refrigerator, ceiling fan, clock radio, coffeemaker, desk, hot tub/spa, fireplace, applies to most lodgings, modem available at main lodge and TV/VCR by request only in room. Fax, copier, spa, swimming, bicycles, library, child care, parlor games, fireplace and gift shop on premises. Weddings, small meetings, family reunions and seminars hosted. Antiquing, art galleries, beach, bicycling, canoeing/kayaking, cross-country skiing, downhill skiing, fishing, golf, hiking, horseback riding, live theater, museums, parks, shopping, sporting events, tennis, water sports, wineries, Olympic & international events, wilderness areas, natural history and secluded lakes nearby.

Publicity: *Birnbaum's, Adirondack Cookbook, Discerning Traveler Magazine - Adirondack edition, National Geographic Traveler, Outside Magazine, Albany Times Union, Ski Magazine, Skiing Magazine, New York Alive, Adirondack Life, Adirondack Guidebook, PBS Dining Series - Adirondacks North, Forbes Art Magazine, Adirondack Cuisine Cookbook and Country Inns Cookbook.*

"Great as it was 20 years ago."

Lake George E12

Lake George Boathouse B&B

44 Sagamore Rd
Lake George, NY 12814
(518)644-2554 Fax:(775)320-9648

Circa 1917. When one thinks of a houseboat, the images of Cary Grant and Sophia Loren might arise. Lake George Boathouse offers all of the romance of Grant and Loren without the rustic surroundings. This early 20th-century gem is more manor home than boathouse, located along prestigious Millionaires Row. The home rests at the edge of Lake George, providing panoramic views of the water and the Adirondack Region. There is a veranda filled with wicker furnishings where guests can enjoy the view. Each morning, breakfasts are served in the massive, unique great room, which features exposed beams and fine woodwork. The area offers historic sites, festivals, horse racing and plenty of outdoor activities.

Innkeeper(s): Joe Silipigno/Patti Gramberg. $125-375. 7 rooms with PB and 3 suites. Breakfast included in rates. Types of meals: Country bkfst. Beds: KQ. Cable TV, reading lamp, stereo, ceiling fan, telephone, lake view walk-out porches and clock in room. Fax, swimming, fireplace and membership to fitness center and pool at four-star resort on premises. Small meetings and family reunions hosted. Amusement parks, antiquing, art galleries, beach, bicycling, canoeing/kayaking, cross-country skiing, downhill skiing, fishing, golf, hiking, horseback riding, museums, parks, shopping, tennis and water sports nearby.

Publicity: *Post Star Newspaper, Wall Street Journal and Unique Homes.*

Lake Luzerne   E12

Lamplight Inn Bed & Breakfast

231 Lake Avenue
Lake Luzerne, NY 12846
(518)696-5294 (800)262-4668
E-mail: stay@lamplightinn.com
Web: www.lamplightinn.com

Circa 1890. Howard Conkling, a wealthy lumberman, built this Victorian Gothic estate. The home was designed for entertaining since Conkling was a very eligible bachelor. It has 12-foot beamed ceilings, chestnut wainscoting and moldings, and a chestnut keyhole staircase crafted in England. Six rooms boast Jacuzzi tubs.

Historic Interest: Fort William Henry (10 miles), Fort Ticonderoga (1 hour), Saratoga Battlefield (30 minutes).

Innkeeper(s): Gene & Linda Merlino. $89-239. 13 rooms with PB, 7 with FP, 7 suites and 1 conference room. Breakfast included in rates. Types of meals: Full gourmet bkfst, veg bkfst, early coffee/tea and snacks/refreshments. Beds: KQ. Modem hook-up, data port, cable TV, reading lamp, ceiling fan, clock radio, telephone, hot tub/spa, voice mail and fireplace in room. Central air. VCR, fax, copier, library, parlor games, fireplace and gift shop on premises. Limited handicap access. Small meetings and seminars hosted. Amusement parks, antiquing, art galleries, beach, bicycling, canoeing/kayaking, cross-country skiing, downhill skiing, fishing, golf, hiking, horseback riding, live theater, museums, parks, shopping, sporting events, tennis, water sports and white water rafting and snowmobiling is in town nearby.

Publicity: *The Complete Guide To Bed and Breakfast Inns and Guest Houses in U.S. and Canada, New York Magazine, Newark Star-Ledger, Newsday, Country Inns and Country Victorian.*

"Rooms are immaculately kept and clean. The owners are the nicest, warmest, funniest and most hospitable innkeepers I have ever met."

Liverpool   F8

Ancestor's Inn at The Bassett House

215 Sycamore St
Liverpool, NY 13088
(888)866-8591
E-mail: innkeeper@ancestorsinn.com
Web: www.ancestorsinn.com

Circa 1862. Early local residents, George and Hannah Bassett built this Italianate home. The innkeepers call the home Ancestor's Inn because guest rooms are named after a special relative. Valentine's Room includes a double whirlpool tub. A hearty, full breakfast is served each morning. Homemade granola, pastries and breads accompany the daily breakfast entree. Complimentary beverages are available in a guest refrigerator.

Innkeeper(s): Mary & Dan Weidman. $70-115. 4 rooms with PB. Breakfast included in rates. Types of meals: Full gourmet bkfst, early coffee/tea and afternoon tea. Beds: Q. TV, VCR, reading lamp, ceiling fan and clock radio in

room. Air conditioning. Library, parlor games, telephone, fireplace, movies available and porch on premises. Weddings hosted. Antiquing, cross-country skiing, golf, live theater, parks, shopping, sporting events, water sports and New York State Fair nearby.

Livingston Manor   I10

De Bruce Country Inn on The Willowemoc

982 De Bruce Rd
Livingston Manor, NY 12758
(845)439-3900

Circa 1890. This inn is located on the banks of the Willowemoc stream, not far from where the first dry fly was cast in the United States. This early 20th-century retreat, with its excellent trout fishing, secluded woodlands, views of the valley and mountains continues to draw visitors today. The inn, situated in the Catskill Forest Preserve, offers wooded trails, wildlife and game, a stocked pond, swimming pool, sauna and whirlpool. Guests enjoy hearty breakfasts and fine dinners on the dining terrace overlooking the valley and romantic evenings in the Dry Fly Lounge.

Innkeeper(s): Ron & Marilyn Lusker. $100-250. 13 rooms with PB and 2 suites. Breakfast and dinner included in rates. Types of meals: Full bkfst. Restaurant on premises. Beds: KQDT. Ceiling fan in room. TV, VCR, fax, copier, spa, swimming, sauna, library, fireplace, hiking, bar and wine cellar on premises. Weddings, small meetings, family reunions and seminars hosted. Antiquing, golf, museums, state park and horseback riding nearby.

Lockport   F3

Hambleton House B&B

130 Pine St
Lockport, NY 14094-4402
(716)439-9507
E-mail: hambletbb@aol.com
Web: www.niagarabedandbreakfast.com

Circa 1850. A carriage maker was the first owner of this mid-19th-century home, and it remained in his family for several generations. The home maintains a delicate blend of the past and present. Main Street and the Erie Barge Canal locks are a short walk away, and Buffalo and Niagara Falls are within a half-hour drive.

Innkeeper(s): Joan Hambleton. $65-105. 3 rooms with PB. Breakfast included in rates. Types of meals: Cont plus. Beds: DT. Reading lamp in room. Air conditioning. Telephone on premises. Weddings, small meetings and family reunions hosted. Parks, Lewiston, Art Park, Old Fort Niagara, Barge Canal Trips and Lake Ontario nearby.

Millbrook   I12

Parc Brook Farms

303 North Tower Hill Rd
Millbrook, NY 12545
(845)677-5950 Fax:(845)677-5528
E-mail: parcbrook@cybermax.net
Web: www.parcbrook.com

Circa 1869. Just one and a half hours north of New York City, this 34-acre country estate features four manor homes with fireplaces and 1 to 8 bedrooms. They can each be rented as a whole or enjoyed as a bed & breakfast. Amenities are varied. The Swiss Cottage is perfect for families and has impressive views of the countryside. The romantic French Chateau boasts a baby grand piano, sauna, steam and exercise rooms, indoor heated pool, spa, two-person Jacuzzis, and spectacular sunset vistas of the valley, and the Berkshire and Catskill mountains. Gaze out at ponds and horses grazing from the windows of The English Manor, also with a spa and two-person Jacuzzis. The Italian Villa includes spacious rooms and a fully equipped kitchen to easily prepare meals. Edible flowers, fruits and vegetables are gathered from the farm's gardens.

$149-495. 25 rooms, 15 with PB, 13 with FP and 1 conference room. Breakfast, afternoon tea and snacks/refreshments included in rates. Types of meals: Full gourmet bkfst, veg bkfst, early coffee/tea and picnic lunch. Beds: KQT. Modem hook-up, TV, VCR, reading lamp, stereo, refrigerator, ceiling fan, clock radio, telephone, coffeemaker, desk, hot tub/spa, satellite TV and modem access in room. Central air. Fax, copier, spa, swimming, sauna, library, parlor games, fireplace, laundry facility, fireplace, indoor pool, spa, kitchen stocked with wine, cheese, fruit, soft drinks and English breakfast on premises. Handicap access. Weddings and family reunions hosted. Antiquing, art galleries, bicycling, canoeing/kayaking, cross-country skiing, downhill skiing, fishing, golf, hiking, horseback riding, live theater, parks, shopping, sporting events, tennis, water sports, wineries, hot air balloon and bowling nearby.

Publicity: *New York Magazine and Millbrook Round Table Newspaper.*

"Thank you for a delightful, utterly relaxing vacation in your beautiful home!"

Millerton
I12

Simmons' Way Village Inn
53 Main Street Rt 44E
Millerton, NY 12546
(518)789-6235 Fax:(518)789-6236
E-mail: swvi@taconic.net
Web: www.simmonsway.com

Circa 1854. Enjoy warm American hospitality and a charming European tradition in this 50-year-old Victorian in the Berkshire foothills. Simmon's Way Village Inn is located in the village of Millerton near Poughkeepsie, the birthplace of Eddie Collins. The inn was chosen by American Express/Hertz as the "Quintessential County Inn 1991." Recently, the inn and restaurant were acclaimed by Gannett papers. Its nine guest bedrooms and one suite, some with fireplaces, are decorated with antiques and international collections. An extensive continental breakfast and afternoon tea are included in the tariff. Picnic lunches, dinners, banquets and catering can be arranged through the restaurant on premises. The frequently changing menu includes a variety of fare from seasonal game to pasta to vegetarian and international specialties. Outdoor activities abound, including fishing, hiking, tennis, golf, swimming, boating, cross-country skiing, biking and horseback riding. The inn is near the Baseball Hall of Fame.

Innkeeper(s): Jay & Martha Reynolds. $160-190. 9 rooms with PB, 2 with FP and 1 suite. Breakfast and afternoon tea included in rates. Types of meals: Cont plus, early coffee/tea, picnic lunch, snacks/refreshments and gourmet dinner. Restaurant on premises. Beds: KQDT. Cable TV, reading lamp, stereo and clock radio in room. Central air. TV, VCR, fax, copier, library, parlor games, telephone and fireplace on premises. Weddings, small meetings, family reunions and seminars hosted. Antiquing, art galleries, bicycling, canoeing/kayaking, cross-country skiing, downhill skiing, fishing, golf, hiking, horseback riding, live theater, museums, parks, shopping, tennis and wineries nearby.

Mumford
F5

Genesee Country Inn
948 George St
Mumford, NY 14511-0340
(585)538-2500 (800)697-8297 Fax:(585)384-4565

Circa 1833. Amid eight and a half serene acres of ponds, waterfalls, woods and gardens, this peaceful bed & breakfast offers quiet country elegance and hospitality. In 1883 it was a stone mill with two and a half foot thick limestone walls. Today this historic haven is a getaway for leisure and business travelers. Savor afternoon tea and home-baked cookies upon arrival and relax in the living room. Air-conditioned guest bedrooms are tastefully furnished with antiques and reproductions. Authentic period patterns have been hand-stenciled to accent the decor. Assorted amenities in some of the rooms include a gas fireplace, canopy bed, designer linens, handstitched New York Amish quilts, a sitting area and view of the mill ponds. Award-winning recipes are served to satisfy in the Breakfast Room with a morning newspaper. Soak in the Sun Room spa, sit in the gazebo or fish for trout.

Innkeeper(s): Hal Robinson. $95-175. 9 rooms, 10 with PB, 3 with FP. Breakfast and afternoon tea included in rates. Types of meals: Full bkfst. Beds: Q. Reading lamp, clock radio, telephone and desk in room. Air conditioning. TV, fax, copier, fireplace and fly fishing on premises. Small meetings, family reunions and seminars hosted. Museums, Genesee Country Museum, Rochester, Letchworth State Park, Erie Canal and Susan B. Anthony house nearby.

"You may never want to leave."

Napanoch
I11

Catskill Mountain House
44 Continental Road
Napanoch, NY 12458
(845)647-4288 Fax:(845)647-4288

Circa 1860. Surrounded by trees and forests and cradled by mountains, this restored Victorian B&B was built as an inn in the 1800s. Original woodwork and floors, stained-glass windows and a wraparound porch reflect its rich heritage. Spacious guest bedrooms and a suite feature antique furnishings, luxurious linens and fine quilts. The chef/innkeeper will take personal preferences into consideration when preparing a gourmet breakfast that is sure to please. Enjoy homemade treats in the afternoon on the back deck overlooking the herb garden.

Innkeeper(s): Karen Leitstein. $110-175. 6 rooms, 3 with PB, 2 suites and 1 cottage. Breakfast included in rates. Types of meals: Full gourmet bkfst, afternoon tea and gourmet dinner. Beds: KQDT. Cable TV, reading lamp, CD player, ceiling fan, turn-down service, desk and hot tub/spa in room. Air conditioning. VCR, fax, copier, spa, telephone and fireplace on premises. Weddings, small meetings, family reunions and seminars hosted. Antiquing, art galleries, beach, bicycling, canoeing/kayaking, cross-country skiing, downhill skiing, fishing, golf, hiking, horseback riding, live theater, museums, parks, shopping, sporting events, tennis, water sports and wineries nearby.

New York
L12

1871 House
East 60s between Park & Lexington Ave
New York, NY 10021
(212)756-8823 Fax:(212)588-0995
E-mail: infobnbinns@1871house.com
Web: www.1871house.com

Circa 1871. On a tree-lined street on the fashionable Upper East Side, this classic Brownstone offers stylishly elegant accommodations. Old World charm is evident in the decorative ironwork covering the front door, ornate moldings around windows, high ceilings and floors, and ornate marble and wood fireplace mantelpieces. The Cottage was a turn-of-the-century carriage house. Beds of antique iron and brass, a sleigh bed with netting, a Tuscan cottage bed and a cherry sheaf of wheat bed grace the guest bedrooms decorated with lace curtains and country quilts. A pleasant cedar terrace has colorful potted plants, teak furniture and a cafe table and chair set.

Innkeeper(s): Lia & Warren Raum. $139-249. 11 rooms with PB, 6 with FP, 3 suites and 1 cottage. Beds: QDT. Modem hook-up, cable TV, reading lamp, refrigerator, clock radio, telephone, coffeemaker, voice mail and fireplace in room. Air conditioning. Fireplace on premises. Antiquing, art galleries, bicycling, canoeing/kayaking, fishing, hiking, horseback riding, live theater, museums, parks and shopping nearby.

Publicity: *Japanese Esquire Magazine, awarded four stars by Frommer's the "Unofficial Guide to Bed & Breakfasts and Country Inns in the Mid-Atlantic," Joan Hamburg Show on 710 AM radio in New York, 2004 voted most intimate inn by Inngoers, 2003 voted best for pampering oneself by Inngoers and 2003 100 best little hotels in New York City.*

Incentra Village House

32 Eighth Avenue
New York, NY 10014
(212)206-0007 Fax:(212)604-0625

Circa 1841. Historic Greenwich Village sets the tone for these two, red-brick, landmark townhouses. The trademark Victorian double parlor boasts two fireplaces and a baby grand piano from the 1930s. Antiques and artwork reflect an old-world charm. Pleasantly appointed guest bedrooms offer an assortment of amenities. Most studios feature kitchenettes and fireplaces. Choose from a four-poster, sleigh, ornate iron and brass bed or a sleeping loft with a double futon. The inn is centrally located to all the city has to offer, and gays are welcome here.

Innkeeper(s): Jeff Pica. $119-199. 12 rooms, 11 with PB and 1 suite. Beds: DT. Cable TV, refrigerator, clock radio, telephone, coffeemaker and fireplace in room. Air conditioning. Fax and fireplace on premises. Antiquing, art galleries, live theater, museums, parks and shopping nearby.

Publicity: *Channel 4 News and WNBC.*

Niagara Falls   F3

The Cameo Manor North

3881 Lower River Rd, Rt 18-F
Niagara Falls, NY 14174
(716)745-3034
E-mail: cameoinn@adelphia.net
Web: www.cameoinn.com

Circa 1860. This Colonial Revival inn offers a restful setting ideal for those seeking a peaceful getaway. The inn's three secluded acres add to its romantic setting, as does an interior that features several fireplaces. Visitors select from three suites, which feature private sun rooms, or two guest rooms that share a bath. Popular spots with guests include the library, great room and solarium. Fort Niagara and several state parks are nearby, and the American and Canadian Falls are within easy driving distance of the inn. The inn is actually located about eight miles north of Niagara Falls near the village of Youngstown.

Innkeeper(s): Gregory Fisher. $75-175. 5 rooms. Breakfast included in rates. Types of meals: Full bkfst. Beds: QDT. TV in room. Air conditioning. Amusement parks, antiquing, cross-country skiing, downhill skiing, fishing, live theater, shopping, sporting events and water sports nearby.

Publicity: *Country Folk Art, Esquire, Journey, Seaway Trail, Waterways and Buffalo News.*

"I made the right choice when I selected Cameo."

The Red Coach Inn

Two Buffalo Avenue
Niagara Falls, NY 14303-1133
(716)282-1459 (800)282-1459 Fax:(716)282-2650
E-mail: info@redcoach.com
Web: www.redcoach.com

Circa 1923. Located 1,500 feet from Niagara Falls, this Old English Tudor inn offers a splendid view of the Rapids from most of its rooms. Furnished with antiques and reproductions suitable to English Country décor, most accommodations are view suites and the majority have fireplaces as well. The Fireside Room is a popular gathering spot for cocktails or an after-dinner drink. Or enjoy the roaring wood fire in the main dining room. The Rapids Room offers a panoramic view of the rapids. A welcoming offering of champagne, fruit and cheese is provided in your room.

Innkeeper(s): Tom Reese. $89-179. 20 rooms with PB, 16 with FP, 18 suites and 1 conference room. Breakfast included in rates. Types of meals: Cont plus, gourmet lunch, gourmet dinner and room service. Restaurant on premises. Beds: KQ. Data port, cable TV, VCR, reading lamp, stereo, refrigerator, clock radio, telephone, coffeemaker, turn-down service, desk, hot tub/spa and voice mail in room. Central air. Fax, copier, spa, library and fireplace on premises. Weddings, small meetings, family reunions and seminars hosted. Bicycling, cross-country skiing, fishing, golf, hiking, horseback riding, museums, parks, shopping, tennis and wineries nearby.

Publicity: *Fortune Magazine, AAA Today, New York Times, Chicago Tribune, Kansas City Star, Toledo Blade, San Diego Union Tribune and Boston Globe.*

Oneida Castle   F9

Governors House Bed & Breakfast

50 Seneca Ave
Oneida Castle, NY 13421-2558
(315)363-5643 (800)437-8177 Fax:(315)363-5643

Circa 1848. Built in the hopes of becoming the first residence for the Governor of New York State, this brick Federal house sits on two acres. The inn's finely crafted architecture includes features such as a mansard roof, elegant cupola and handsome porches. Antiques and canopy beds enhance most of the guest rooms, and there are two parlors, a library and a guest kitchen.

Innkeeper(s): Bernadette and David Peck. $97-161. 5 rooms with PB, 3 with FP and 2 suites. Breakfast, afternoon tea and snacks/refreshments included in rates. Types of meals: Full bkfst and early coffee/tea. Beds: Q. Cable TV, VCR, reading lamp, stereo, refrigerator, snack bar, clock radio, telephone, coffeemaker, turn-down service, desk and fireplace in room. Central air. Copier, library, parlor games, fireplace, fully stocked guest kitchen with homemade cakes and sweets, wine and cheese available on weekend evenings upon request, full and hot candlelight breakfast available on weekends and deluxe Continental breakfast available on weekdays on premises. Limited handicap access. Amusement parks, antiquing, cross-country skiing, downhill skiing, fishing, golf, live theater, parks, shopping, sporting events, tennis, water sports, rural driving and walking routes, Turning Stone Casino and pro golf courses nearby.

Otto   G3

R & R Dude Ranch

8940 Lange Rd
Otto, NY 14766
(716)257-5663 Fax:(716)257-5664

Circa 1880. Three hundred acres of trails and breathtaking scenery provide a tranquil setting for this 19th-century farmhouse and log cabin. Horseback riding is a must during a stay here. Each season offers delights to experience, and almost every outdoor activity imaginable awaits the interested enthusiast. Boasting a central location upstate, the ranch is minutes away from Holiday Valley Ski Resort. A trip to Niagara Falls is an easy excursion that shouldn't be missed.

Innkeeper(s): Alice Ferguson. $80-100. 6 rooms, 4 with PB, 3 with FP, 1 suite and 1 cabin. Breakfast included in rates. Types of meals: Full gourmet bkfst and veg bkfst. Beds: KQT. TV, VCR, reading lamp, ceiling fan, snack bar, telephone, coffeemaker, hot tub/spa, fireplace and refrigerator in room. Fax, copier, spa, swimming, stable, bicycles, pet boarding, fireplace, laundry facility, gift shop, Jacuzzi, volleyball, ping pong, badminton, horseback riding, horseshoes, beaches, fishing, tubing, hiking, cross-country skiing, camping, hunting, hay rides, sleigh rides, sled hill and water tubing on premises. Handicap access. Weddings, small meetings, family reunions and seminars hosted. Downhill skiing, golf, parks, shopping, water sports, wineries and sailing nearby.

Penn Yan   G6

Fox Inn

158 Main St
Penn Yan, NY 14527-1201
(315)536-1100 (800)901-7997

Circa 1820. Experience the pleasant elegance of a fine, historic home at this Greek Revival Inn. Furnished with Empire antiques, the accommodations include a living room with marble fireplace, sun porch, parlor with billiards table and formal rose gardens. Five guest rooms and one two-bedroom suite each have private baths. The gourmet breakfast provides a selection of six different types of pancakes served with fresh blueberries or raspberries and four varieties of French toast. Located near the Windmill Farm Market, the largest farm market in New York, you can spend a casual day shopping or visiting nearby museums or wineries. Or, enjoy more active alternatives such as biking, hiking and picnicking or boating on Keuka Lake.

Innkeeper(s): Cliff & Michele Orr. $95-169. 6 rooms with PB, 1 with FP, 1 suite and 1 conference room. Breakfast included in rates. Types of meals: Full gourmet bkfst and early coffee/tea. Beds: QD. Cable TV, VCR, clock radio, telephone, turn-down service and hot tub/spa in room. Air conditioning. Library, parlor games, fireplace and billiard table on premises. Weddings, small meetings, family reunions and seminars hosted. Amusement parks, antiquing, art galleries, beach, bicycling, canoeing/kayaking, cross-country skiing, downhill skiing, fishing, golf, hiking, horseback riding, live theater, museums, parks, shopping, tennis, water sports and wineries nearby.

Publicity: *Inn Times "Top 50 Inns in America Award."*

Trimmer House Bed & Breakfast

145 E Main St
Penn Yan, NY 14527-1633
(315)536-8304 (800)968-8735 Fax:(315)536-8304
E-mail: innkeeper@trimmerhouse.com
Web: www.trimmerhouse.com

Circa 1891. Built in 1891, this Queen Anne-style Victorian is complemented by period furnishings, and features such elegant accents as marble and oak floors, ornate ceilings and hand-crafted chandeliers. The guest rooms offer many special options to choose from, including a sleigh bed, vintage clawfoot bathtubs, fireplace or private veranda. Two public parlors, the Library and Music Room, provide cozy areas to relax, read or enjoy a cup of tea. A variety of restaurants, shops and boutiques are within walking distance. Several wineries, craft and farm markets, hiking and bike trails, and public parks are nearby, or guests can pass a quiet afternoon on the front porch swing.

Innkeeper(s): Gary M Smith. $75-185. 5 rooms with PB, 3 with FP and 1 suite. Breakfast included in rates. Types of meals: Full gourmet bkfst. Beds: Q. Modem hook-up, data port, cable TV, VCR, reading lamp, stereo, ceiling fan, clock radio, telephone and hot tub/spa in room. Central air. Fax, copier, spa, library, parlor games and fireplace on premises. Small meetings and

seminars hosted. Antiquing, art galleries, beach, bicycling, canoeing/kayaking, cross-country skiing, downhill skiing, fishing, golf, hiking, museums, parks, shopping, tennis, water sports and wineries nearby.

The Wagener Estate B&B

351 Elm St
Penn Yan, NY 14527-1446
(315)536-4591 Fax:(315)531-8142
E-mail: wagener-estate@wagenerestate.com
Web: www.wagenerestate.com

Circa 1794. Nestled in the Finger Lakes area on four shaded acres, this 15-room house features a wicker-furnished veranda where guests can relax in solitude or chat with others. Some of the early hand-hewn framing and the original brick fireplace and oven can be seen in the Family Room at the north end of the house. Most of the land, which is known as Penn Yan, was once owned by the original occupants of the home, David Wagener and his wife, Rebecca. David died in 1799, leaving this property to his son, Squire Wagener, who is considered to be the founder of Penn Yan. Some rooms include air conditioning and a television. Gift certificates are available.

Historic Interest: Near the Oliver House and Birkett Mills.

Innkeeper(s): Lisa & Ken Greenwood. $75-95. 6 rooms, 4 with PB. Breakfast included in rates. Types of meals: Full bkfst. Beds: KQDT. Some with TV in room. Parlor games on premises. Antiquing, cross-country skiing, fishing, parks, water sports and wineries nearby.

Publicity: *Finger Lakes Times, Chronicle Express and New York Times.*

"Thanks so much for the wonderful hospitality and the magnificent culinary treats."

Poughkeepsie   I12

Copper Penny Inn

2406 New Hackensack Rd
Poughkeepsie, NY 12603-4207
(845)452-3045
E-mail: innkeeper@copperpennyinn.com
Web: www.copperpennyinn.com

Circa 1860. Find yourself lost somewhere in time at this 1860s colonial farmhouse located minutes away from several historical landmarks, such as the Morse (Morse Code) Historic Home and the Franklin D. Roosevelt Library, Home and Museum. You'll wonder where the afternoon went as you find yourself gazing upon a clear, blue sky while resting beneath a tree on the home's 12 wooded acres of rolling pasture. Enjoy breakfast on the stone terrace or screened porch before venturing out on one of the many trails leading to streams and a pond. During winter months, snuggle up by the fire in the living room, or enjoy a fireside meal in the dining room. Surrounded by the beauty of nature and the rich culture of the Hudson Valley, guests can explore the Shawangunk Mountains and local wineries, while experiencing the life of the town home to the prestigious Vassar College.

Innkeeper(s): Michael & Anna de Cordova. $90-150. 4 rooms with PB. Breakfast included in rates. Types of meals: Full gourmet bkfst and early coffee/tea. Beds: KQT. Modem hook-up, data port, cable TV, VCR, reading lamp, clock radio, telephone, turn-down service and desk in room. Central air. Fax, bicycles, library, parlor games and fireplace on premises. Small meetings and family reunions hosted. Antiquing, art galleries, bicycling, canoeing/kayaking, cross-country skiing, downhill skiing, fishing, golf, hiking, horseback riding, live theater, museums, parks, shopping, tennis and wineries nearby.

Pulaski   E8

Woodlawn Bed & Breakfast

4677 Salina St.
Pulaski, NY 13142
(315)298-3573
E-mail: mail@woodlawnbb.com
Web: www.woodlawnbb.com

Circa 1839. In a country setting on 17 acres within the village limits, this historic white farm home and red barn is Federal style with Greek Revival trim. Six Tuscan columns support the large, open porch. Completely renovated, the traditional decor blends well with the hand carved woodwork in the parlor, study and front hall. Tastefully furnished guest bedrooms feature paddle fans and heated bath towels. The Rose Room suite boasts an attached living area. After breakfast, explore the garden surrounded by fields. The nearby Salmon River offers world-class, year-round fishing. Snowmobilers appreciate exploring the Oswego County trail system that goes right by the inn.

Historic Interest: The house was built in 1839 and remained in the same family until purchased in 1997. Woodwork is original. Minor renovations were made to the original floor plan.

Innkeeper(s): Steve & Joanna Young. $80-115. 3 rooms, 2 with PB and 1 suite. Breakfast included in rates. Types of meals: Full bkfst. Beds: QT. Cable TV, ceiling fan, clock radio, coffeemaker and desk in room. Air conditioning. VCR, telephone and fireplace on premises. Antiquing, beach, bicycling, canoeing/kayaking, cross-country skiing, downhill skiing, fishing, golf, shopping and sporting events nearby.

Queensbury   E12

The Crislip's B&B

693 Ridge Rd
Queensbury, NY 12804-6901
(518)793-6869
E-mail: nedbc@capital.net

Circa 1802. This Federal-style house was built by Quakers and was once owned by the area's first doctor, who used it as a training center for young interns. There's an acre of lawns and annual gardens and a Victorian Italianate veranda overlooks the Green Mountains. The inn is furnished with 18th-century antiques and reproductions, including four-poster canopy beds and highboys. There's a keeping room with a huge fireplace. Historic stone walls flank the property.

Innkeeper(s): Ned & Joyce Crislip. $65-90. 3 rooms with PB. Breakfast included in rates. Types of meals: Full bkfst and early coffee/tea. Beds: KD. Reading lamp in room. Air conditioning. Telephone and fireplace on premises. Small meetings hosted. Amusement parks, antiquing, cross-country skiing, downhill skiing, fishing, live theater, parks, shopping, sporting events, water sports and civic center nearby.

Red Hook   H12

The Grand Dutchess

7571 Old Post Rd
Red Hook, NY 12571-1403
(845)758-5818 Fax:(845)758-3143
E-mail: grandut@worldnet.att.net
Web: www.granddutchess.com

Circa 1874. This Second Empire Victorian was originally built as the Hoffman Inn. It later served as the town school, a speakeasy and then a lonely hearts club. Twin parlors behind etched-glass and wood sliding doors feature hardwood floors, antique chandeliers, arched marble fireplaces with massive carved mirrors, Oriental rugs and heirloom antiques. Lace curtains decorate the floor-to-ceiling windows. Most of the rooms have queen-size beds and private baths and are located at the corners of the home to maximize the use of natural light. A full breakfast of homemade breads, a main dish, cereal and fruit is offered. For young guests, the innkeeper will prepare chocolate chip pancakes.

Innkeeper(s): Elizabeth Pagano & Harold Gruber. $95-155. 6 rooms, 4 with PB, 1 suite and 1 conference room. Breakfast included in rates. Types of meals: Full gourmet bkfst, early coffee/tea and snacks/refreshments. Beds: KQDT. Reading lamp and clock radio in room. Air conditioning. VCR, fax, copier, library, parlor games and telephone on premises. Weddings, small meetings and family reunions hosted. Antiquing, cross-country skiing, fishing, golf, live theater, parks, shopping, tennis, historic homes and Rhinebeck Aerodrome nearby.

Publicity: *Northeast, Gazette Advertiser, Poughkeepsie Journal* and *"The Eleanor Affair"* an award-winning short film.

"This place is outrageous! We love this place!"

Remsenburg   K14

Hidden Mill Bed & Breakfast

139 South County Road, PO Box 611
Remsenburg, NY 11960
(631)325-8622
E-mail: jenaug@msn.com
Web: www.hiddenmill.com

Circa 1796. Casual elegance is imparted at this handsome Colonial home that was built in 1796 and has been recently restored. A vine-covered water mill and small red barn accent the landscaped grounds that include Japanese gardens, a hot tub and pond-like heated granite swimming pool. Public rooms boast comfortable chairs and sofas. Enjoy scenic views and gracious amenities. Stay in the Balcony Suite with a jetted tub and French doors opening to a private balcony. The Library Suite features a gas fireplace and screened porch with a private entrance. The romantic Tea House with cathedral ceilings is an inviting hideaway with a wisteria-covered pergola. Creme Brulee French toast or egg strata with fresh spinach, cheese and tomatoes are popular breakfast favorites that may be accompanied by a fresh fruit plate and homemade muffins.

Innkeeper(s): Jennifer Truscott-Augustin. $135-350. 5 rooms, 2 with PB, 1 with FP, 2 suites and 1 cottage. Breakfast and snacks/refreshments included in rates. Types of meals: Full gourmet bkfst. Beds: KQ. Cable TV, reading lamp, CD player, refrigerator, ceiling fan, clock radio, coffeemaker, hot tub/spa and fireplace in room. Air conditioning. Copier, spa, swimming, bicycles, parlor games and fireplace on premises. Weddings and family reunions hosted. Antiquing, art galleries, beach, bicycling, canoeing/kayaking, golf, live theater, parks, shopping, tennis, water sports and wineries nearby.

Rhinebeck 112

Beekman Arms-Delamater Inn

Rt 9
Rhinebeck, NY 12572
(845)876-7077
E-mail: beekmanarm@aol.com
Web: www.beekmandelaterinn.com

Circa 1766. Said to be the oldest landmark inn in America, some walls of the Beekman Arms are two- and three-feet-thick. It has seen a variety of guests-including pioneers, trappers, Indians and Dutch farmers. Among the famous were Aaron Burr, William Jennings Bryan, Horace Greeley, Franklin Roosevelt, Neil Armstrong and Elizabeth Taylor. Like most old taverns and inns, it provided a meeting place for leaders of the day. The Delamater House, an Alexander Jackson Gothic home, was built in 1844 and is in the National Register of Historic Places.

Innkeeper(s): George Banta. $95-220. 67 rooms with PB, 33 with FP and 1 conference room. Breakfast included in rates. Types of meals: Cont. Restaurant on premises. Beds: KQDT. TV and telephone in room. Limited handicap access.

Publicity: *New York Times.*

"If this is any indication of your general hospitality, it is very easy to see why you have stayed in the business for so long."

Olde Rhinebeck Inn

340 Wurtemburg Rd
Rhinebeck, NY 12572
(845)871-1745 Fax:(845)876-8809
E-mail: innkeeper@rhinebeckinn.com
Web: www.rhinebeckinn.com

Circa 1745. Located on three acres, this is a beautifully maintained early colonial farmhouse. The original buttermilk blue finishes remain and there is original hardware throughout. The innkeeper provides fine linens, antiques, fresh flowers and a breakfast that is served in the historic dining room. Offerings include sweet potato frittata, baked French pear and apple butter maple pecan muffins. There are miniature goats and a bass-stocked pond on the property.

Innkeeper(s): Jonna Paolella. $195-295. 3 rooms with PB. Breakfast included in rates. Types of meals: Full bkfst and afternoon tea. Beds: Q. Cable TV, reading lamp and satellite TV in room. Air conditioning. VCR, fax, parlor games, telephone and fireplace on premises. Antiquing, golf, parks and shopping nearby.

Publicity: *Country Living.*

Veranda House B&B

6487 Montgomery St
Rhinebeck, NY 12572-1113
(845)876-4133 (877)985-6800 Fax:(845)876-4133
E-mail: visit@verandahouse.com
Web: www.verandahouse.com

Circa 1845. For nearly a century, this Federal-style home served as the parsonage for an Episcopal church. The home is located in a Rhinebeck historic district among many notable houses. The home is decorated in a comfortable mix of styles, with many antiques. If weather permits, breakfasts are served on the terrace, featuring items such as freshly baked pastries or maple walnut coffee cake and a daily entree. The scenic area offers much in the way of activities. Woodstock is a short drive away.

Innkeeper(s): Yvonne Sarn. $130-150. 5 rooms with PB. Breakfast included in rates. Types of meals: Full gourmet bkfst. Beds: QT. Reading lamp, ceiling fan, telephone and clocks in room. Air conditioning. VCR, library, parlor games and fireplace on premises. Small meetings, family reunions and semi-nars hosted. Antiquing, cross-country skiing, downhill skiing, fishing, golf, hiking, live theater, parks, shopping, tennis and water sports nearby.

"Beautiful rooms, terrific breakfast! We will recommend you highly."

Rochester F5

428 Mount Vernon

428 Mount Vernon Ave
Rochester, NY 14620-2710
(585)271-0792 (800)836-3159

Circa 1917. Victorian furnishings and decor grace the interior of this stately Irish manor house. Set on two lush acres of shade trees and foliage, this secluded spot is perfect for guests in search of relaxation. Guests can create their morning meals from a varied breakfast menu. The inn is adjacent to Highland Park, great walking park and conservatory.

Innkeeper(s): Philip & Claire Lanzatella. $125. 7 rooms with PB and 1 conference room. Breakfast included in rates. Types of meals: Full gourmet bkfst and early coffee/tea. Beds: QDT. Cable TV, reading lamp, ceiling fan, clock radio, telephone, turn-down service and desk in room. Air conditioning. Parlor games and fireplace on premises. Weddings, small meetings and seminars hosted. Antiquing, cross-country skiing, live theater, parks, shopping, Annual Lilac Festival, University of Rochester and Rochester Institute of Technology and Museum nearby.

"Everything was wonderful, they took care in every detail."

A B&B at Dartmouth House

215 Dartmouth Street
Rochester, NY 14607-3202
(585)271-7872 (800)724-6298 Fax:(585)473-0778
E-mail: stay@DartmouthHouse.com
Web: www.DartmouthHouse.com

Circa 1905. The lavish, four-course breakfasts served daily at this beautiful turn-of-the-century Edwardian home are unforgettable. Innkeeper and award-winning, gourmet cook Ellie Klein starts off the meal with special fresh juice, which is served in the parlor. From this point, guests are seated at the candlelit dining table to enjoy a series of delectable dishes, such as poached pears, a mouth-watering entree, a light, lemon ice and a rich dessert. And each of the courses is served on a separate pattern of Depression Glass. If the breakfast isn't enough, Ellie and husband, Bill, an electrical engineer, have stocked the individually decorated bathrooms with fluffy towels and bathrobes and guests can soak in inviting clawfoot tubs. Each of the bedchambers boasts antique collectibles and fresh flowers. The inn is located in the prestigious turn-of-the-century Park Avenue Historical and Cultural District. The entire area is an architect's dream. Museums, colleges, Eastman School of Music, Highland Park, restaurants and antique shops are among the many nearby attractions.

ca. 1905

Historic Interest: George Eastman's Mansion and International Museum of Photography is a 10-minute walk from the inn. The High Falls Brown's Race Historic Center is two miles, the graves of Susan B. Anthony and Frederick Douglass are two miles away at Mount Hope Cemetery. The Rochester Historical Society is a 10-minute walk.

Innkeeper(s): Ellie & Bill Klein. $125-150. 4 rooms with PB. Breakfast included in rates. Types of meals: Full bkfst and early coffee/tea. Beds: KQT. TV, VCR, reading lamp, ceiling fan, clock radio, telephone, desk, robe, tape deck and lighted makeup mirror in room. Air conditioning. Fax, bicycles and library on premises. Antiquing, live theater, museums, parks, shopping and George Eastman International Museum of Photography within walking distance nearby.

Publicity: *Democrat & Chronicle, DAKA, Genesee Country, Seaway Trail, Oneida News, Travelers News, Country Living and The New York Times Travel Section.*

"The food was fabulous, the company fascinating, and the personal attention beyond comparison. You made me feel at home instantly."

The Edward Harris House B&B Inn

35 Argyle Street
Rochester, NY 14607
(585)473-9752 (800)419-1213 Fax:(585)473-9752
E-mail: ehhbb@aol.com
Web: www.edwardharrishousebb.com

Circa 1896. Acclaimed as one of the finest early examples of architect Claude Bragdon's work, this Georgian mansion is a restored Landmark home. Its history only enhances the rich warmth, and the immense size reflects a cozy ambiance. Relax in a leather chair in the traditional library. Antiques and collectibles combine well with florals and chintz for a touch of romance. Two guest bedrooms and the Garden Suite boast fireplaces. Four-poster rice beds and hand-painted furniture add to the individual decorating styles. A gourmet candlelight breakfast is served in the formal dining room on crystal and china or on the brick garden patio. The night before, choose a main entree from a seasonal menu offering seven or eight items. Enjoy afternoon tea on the wicker-filled front porch. A plethora of historic sites, including The George Eastman House and Strong Museum, are within a one-mile range.

Innkeeper(s): Susan Alvarez. $125-150. 5 rooms, 4 with PB, 3 with FP, 2 suites and 1 conference room. Breakfast included in rates. Types of meals: Full gourmet bkfst, veg bkfst, early coffee/tea, afternoon tea, snacks/refreshments and room service. Beds: KQDT. Data port, cable TV, reading lamp, stereo, refrigerator, ceiling fan, clock radio, telephone, coffeemaker, turn-down service, desk and fireplace in room. Air conditioning. VCR, fax, copier, library, parlor games, fireplace, laundry facility and small kitchen on guest room level on premises. Small meetings and seminars hosted. Amusement parks, antiquing, art galleries, beach, bicycling, canoeing/kayaking, cross-country skiing, downhill skiing, fishing, golf, hiking, horseback riding, live theater, museums, parks, shopping, sporting events, tennis, water sports and wineries nearby.

Saint Johnsville   F10

INn By The Mill

1679 Mill Rd
Saint Johnsville, NY 13452-3911
(518)568-2388 (866)568-2388
E-mail: Romance@innbythemill.com
Web: www.innbythemill.com

Circa 1830. This authentic 1835 gristmill is located in a park-like setting with cascading waterfalls and gardens with thousands of herbs and perennials. The inn was once a station of the underground railroad. The richly decorated rooms are located in the century-old miller's home where there is a kitchen stocked with breakfast goodies, sitting room and game parlor. During the summer, guests create ice cream delights and enjoy gourmet desserts in an ice cream parlor. Additional accommodations include the Cliffside Cottage and seasonally available Hog'n'Haus Cottage with views of a private gorge and roaring waterfall. Local attractions range from the Saratoga Race Track to the Cooperstown Baseball Hall of Fame.

Innkeeper(s): Judith & Ron Hezel. $110-300. 6 rooms, 5 with PB, 6 with FP, 2 suites and 2 cottages. Breakfast and afternoon tea included in rates. Types of meals: Cont plus, early coffee/tea and snacks/refreshments. Beds: KQDT. Modem hook-up, data port, cable TV, VCR, reading lamp, CD player, refrigerator, ceiling fan, snack bar, clock radio, telephone, coffeemaker, desk, fireplace, Godiva chocolates, gourmet juices, glycerin soaps and Nexxus Shampoos in room. Air conditioning. Fax, copier, spa, swimming, parlor games, laundry facility, complimentary gourmet desserts in museum-like Emporium Gift shop and ice cream parlor on premises. Small meetings and family reunions hosted. Amusement parks, antiquing, art galleries, bicycling, cross-country skiing, fishing, golf, horseback riding, live theater, museums, parks, shopping, sporting events, water sports and wineries nearby.

Salisbury Mills   J11

The Caldwell House

25 Orrs Mills Rd.
Salisbury Mills, NY 12577-0425
(845)496-2954 Fax:(845)496-5924
E-mail: info@caldwellhouse.com
Web: www.caldwellhouse.com

Circa 1803. Sheltered by weeping cherry trees with an apple and fruit orchard in the back, this elegantly restored Colonial home is filled with exquisite antiques. The original lockboxes remain on all doors. Gather by the fire in the parlor or dining room. After a comfortable nights rest in one of the guest bedrooms, savor breakfast favorites like Peach Toast, Ginger Scones and Creme Brulee French Toast. Relax on the multi-pillared wraparound porch. The property is surrounded by stone walls and a flowering landscape with ample places to sit and soak up the scenic beauty. Visit nearby Storm King Arts Center, the country's largest outdoor sculpture park or relive our nation's history; many sites are within 15 minutes.

Historic Interest: Elegantly restored 1803 home of the Caldwell Family, who lived here for 150 years. Lovely antiques. Original lockboxes on all doors. Fireplaces in parlor and dining room.

Innkeeper(s): Carmela Turco and Gene Sheridan. $135-245. 4 rooms with PB. Breakfast and snacks/refreshments included in rates. Types of meals: Full bkfst. Beds: Q. Modem hook-up, cable TV, VCR and clock radio in room. Air conditioning. Fax, copier and gift shop on premises. Weddings and family reunions hosted. Antiquing, art galleries, bicycling, hiking, horseback riding, live theater, museums, parks, shopping and wineries nearby.

Publicity: *The Times Herald Record, Orange County Post, Cornwall Local News of the Hudson Highlands and WAMC Northeast Public Radio.*

Saratoga Springs   F12

Adelphi Hotel

365 Broadway
Saratoga Springs, NY 12866-3111
(518)587-4688 Fax:(518)587-0851

Circa 1877. This Victorian hotel is one of two hotels still remaining from Saratoga's opulent spa era. A piazza overlooking Broadway features three-story columns topped with Victorian fretwork. Recently refurbished with lavish turn-of-the-century decor, rooms are filled with antique furnishings, opulent draperies and wall coverings, highlighting the inn's high ceilings and ornate woodwork. A continental breakfast is served buffet-style each morning. There is an inviting swimming pool in the back garden.

Innkeeper(s): Sheila Parkert. $105-400. 39 rooms with PB, 18 suites and 1 conference room. Breakfast included in rates. Types of meals: Cont plus. Beds: QDT. Cable TV, reading lamp, telephone, turn-down service and desk in room. Air conditioning. TV on premises. Weddings and small meetings hosted. Antiquing, golf, live theater, parks and shopping nearby.

Publicity: *New York Times, Country Inns, Back Roads, Conde Nast and Victorian Homes.*

Apple Tree B&B

49 W High St
Saratoga Springs, NY 12020-1912
(518)885-1113 Fax:(518)885-9758
E-mail: mail@appletreebb.com
Web: www.appletreebb.com

Circa 1878. A pond, waterfall and a garden decorate the entrance to this Second Empire Victorian, which is located in the historic district of Ballston Spa, a village just a few minutes from Saratoga

Springs. Guest rooms feature Victorian and French-country decor, and each has antiques and whirlpool tubs. Guests enjoy fresh fruit, homemade baked goods, a selection of beverages and a daily entree during the breakfast service.

Innkeeper(s): Dolores & Jim Taisey. $100-175. 5 rooms with PB. Breakfast included in rates. Types of meals: Full bkfst and early coffee/tea. Beds: Q. Cable TV, VCR, reading lamp, refrigerator, clock radio and whirlpool in room. Central air. Parlor games, telephone and fireplace on premises. Small meetings and family reunions hosted. Amusement parks, antiquing, cross-country skiing, downhill skiing, fishing, live theater, parks, shopping, sporting events, water sports and Saratoga Race Course nearby.

Publicity: *Country Folk Art Magazine.*

Chestnut Tree Inn

9 Whitney Pl
Saratoga Springs, NY 12866-4518
(518)587-8681 (888)243-7688

Circa 1870. Linger over breakfast as you sit and enjoy the view from a wicker-filled veranda at this Second Period Empire-style house. The grounds boast what is thought to be the last live chestnut tree in the city. The innkeepers are antique dealers, who operate a local antique shop. They have filled the home with turn-of-the-century pieces and have won awards for the preservation of their inn and for having the "best front porch" in Saratoga. The home is within walking distance of the race track, downtown shopping, only a mile from the Saratoga Performing Arts Center and the State Park where guests can enjoy mineral baths.

Historic Interest: The Canfield Casino, a restored local gambling house with a museum on the second floor, is two blocks from the inn. Saratoga Battlefield is about 10 miles away.

Innkeeper(s): Cathleen & Bruce De Luke. $95-165. 7 rooms with PB. Breakfast included in rates. Types of meals: Cont plus. Beds: QDT. Antiquing, fishing, live theater and water sports nearby.

Publicity: *New York Times.*

Fox 'n' Hound Bed and Breakfast

142 Lake Ave.
Saratoga Springs, NY 12866
(518)584-5959 (866)369-1913 Fax:(518)584-2594
E-mail: marlena@foxnhoundbandb.com
Web: www.foxnhoundbandb.com

Circa 1904. An architectural marvel, this restored Colonial mansion in the historic district features a facade of narrow gray brick, triple-rounded bay windows, gables and stained glass. Enter the foyer's large sliding doors to be comfortably surrounded by bird's-eye maple-paneled walls. A fireplace with a hand-carved mantle graces the living room. Enjoy complimentary refreshments and Saratoga mineral water and relax in the game/music room. Take the spiral staircase to bright, spacious guest bedrooms and suites with Victorian decor and antique furnishings; several have canopy beds. The cheery Lilac Room includes a balcony. Bathrooms boast Italian tile floors, and some include whirlpool tubs. After a generous breakfast of creative entrees in the formal dining room, sit on the porch overlooking the garden. Ask about special packages.

Historic Interest: The mansion was designed and built in 1904 by the renowned architect Newton Breeze and designated as a historic house. The Fox 'n' Hound is located in the Historic District of Saratoga Springs.

Innkeeper(s): Marlena Sacca. $135-335. 5 rooms with PB, 2 suites and 2 conference rooms. Breakfast and snacks/refreshments included in rates. Types of meals: Full gourmet bkfst and early coffee/tea. Beds: KQ. Data port, cable TV, reading lamp, clock radio, telephone, desk, hot tub/spa, complimentary Saratoga mineral water and snacks in room. Central air. VCR, fax, copier, parlor games and fireplace on premises. Small meetings, family reunions and seminars hosted. Amusement parks, antiquing, art galleries, beach, cross-country skiing, fishing, golf, hiking, live theater, museums, parks, shopping, sporting events, water sports and The Balloon Festival at Lake George nearby.

Six Sisters B&B

149 Union Ave
Saratoga Springs, NY 12866-3518
(518)583-1173 Fax:(518)587-2470
E-mail: stay@sixsistersbandb.com
Web: www.sixsistersbandb.com

Circa 1880. The unique architecture of this Victorian home features a large second-story bay window, a tiger oak front door decked with stained glass and a veranda accentuated with rock-

ing chairs. Inside, the marble and hardwoods combine with antiques and Oriental rugs to create an elegant atmosphere. During racing season, guests can rise early and take a short walk to the local race track to watch the horses work out. Upon their return,

guests are greeted with the aroma of a delicious, gourmet breakfast. A 10-minute walk to Saratoga Springs' downtown area offers antique shops, boutiques and many restaurants.

Historic Interest: Saratoga Battlefield (15 minutes), Spa State Park (5 minutes), Saratoga Racetrack (across street).

Innkeeper(s): Kate Benton. $85-350. 4 rooms with PB. Breakfast included in rates. Types of meals: Full gourmet bkfst and early coffee/tea. Beds: KQ. Cable TV, reading lamp, refrigerator, ceiling fan, clock radio, three rooms with private balcony and whirlpool in room. Air conditioning. TV, fax and telephone on premises. Amusement parks, antiquing, cross-country skiing, downhill skiing, fishing, live theater, parks, shopping, sporting events, water sports, spa and mineral baths and museums nearby.

Publicity: *Gourmet, Country Inns, Country Folk Art, Country Victorian, McCalls and New York Times.*

Westchester House B&B

102 Lincoln Ave
Saratoga Springs, NY 12866-4536
(518)587-7613 (800)581-7613 Fax:(518)583-9562
E-mail: innkeepers@westchesterhousebandb.com
Web: www.westchesterhousebandb.com

Circa 1885. This gracious Queen Anne Victorian has been welcoming vacationers for more than 100 years. Antiques from four generations of the Melvin family grace the high-ceilinged rooms. Oriental rugs top gleaming wood floors, while antique clocks and lace curtains set a graceful tone. Guests gather on the wraparound porch, in the parlors or gardens for an afternoon refreshment of old-fashioned lemonade. Most attractions are within walking distance.

Historic Interest: Built by master carpenter Almeron King in 1885.

Innkeeper(s): Bob & Stephanie Melvin. $125-325. 7 rooms with PB and 1 conference room. Breakfast and afternoon tea included in rates. Types of meals: Cont plus and early coffee/tea. Beds: KQT. Reading lamp, ceiling fan, clock radio, telephone, desk, data port and voice mail in room. Air conditioning. TV, fax, copier, library and baby grand piano on premises. Small meetings, family reunions and seminars hosted. Antiquing, cross-country skiing, fishing, live theater, parks, shopping, sporting events, water sports, opera, ballet, horse racing, race track and Saratoga Performing Arts Center nearby.

Publicity: *Getaways for Gourmets, Albany Times Union, Saratogian, Capital, Country Inns, New York Daily News, WNYT, Newsday and Hudson Valley.*

"I adored your B&B and have raved about it to all. One of the most beautiful and welcoming places we've ever visited."

Schroon Lake   D12

Schroon Lake B&B

1525 US Rt 9, PO Box 638
Schroon Lake, NY 12870
(518)532-7042 (800)523-6755

Circa 1922. Sitting on a grassy knoll on two acres, this Victorian farmhouse overlooks the breathtaking Adirondack Mountains. Polished hardwood floors, antiques, Tiffany-style lamps and Oriental rugs create a tastefully elegant inn renovated for comfort and convenience. Guest bedrooms feature a casual sophistication with designer bed linens, terry robes and cozy chairs. Rita takes great pleasure in presenting a bountiful, mouth-watering breakfast that may include zucchini-dill puffed omelettes, apple-walnut French toast with fresh berry fruit sauce or spinach-apple and feta cheese timbales. Savor every bite in the formal dining room or on the porch.

Innkeeper(s): Rita & Bob Skojec. $115-195. 4 rooms with PB and 1 suite. Breakfast and snacks/refreshments included in rates. Types of meals: Full gourmet bkfst, veg bkfst and early coffee/tea. Beds: KQT. Reading lamp, ceiling fan and clock radio in room. Air conditioning. TV, fax, copier, library, parlor games and telephone on premises. Small meetings, family reunions and seminars hosted. Amusement parks, antiquing, art galleries, beach, bicycling, canoeing/kayaking, cross-country skiing, downhill skiing, fishing, golf, hiking, horseback riding, live theater, museums, parks, shopping, sporting events, tennis, water sports and fine dining nearby.

Publicity: *Country Register, New York Newsday Magazine and Post Star News.*

"Great food, great atmosphere, comfy bed, heaven on earth!"

Sharon Springs   G11

Edgefield

Washington St, PO Box 152
Sharon Springs, NY 13459
(518)284-3339
E-mail: dmwood71@hotmail.com
Web: www.sharonsprings.com/edgefield.htm

Circa 1865. This home has seen many changes. It began as a farmhouse, a wing was added in the 1880s, and by the turn of the century, sported an elegant Greek Revival facade. Edgefield is one of a collection of nearby homes used as a family compound for summer vacations. The rooms are decorated with traditional furnishings in a formal English-country style. In the English tradition, afternoon tea is presented with cookies and tea sandwiches. Sharon Springs includes many historic sites, and the town is listed in the National Register.

Innkeeper(s): Daniel Marshall Wood. $135-185. 5 rooms with PB. Types of meals: Full gourmet bkfst, early coffee/tea, afternoon tea and snacks/refreshments. Beds: QT. Reading lamp, ceiling fan, clock radio, turn-down service and desk in room. Library, fireplace, drawing room and veranda on premises. Antiquing, golf, live theater, museums, parks, shopping, water sports and opera nearby.

Publicity: *Colonial Homes Magazine, Philadelphia Inquirer and Boston Globe.*

"Truly what I always imagined the perfect B&B experience to be!"

Sodus   E6

Maxwell Creek Inn

7563 Lake Rd
Sodus, NY 14551-9309
(315)483-2222 (800)315-2206

Circa 1846. Located on the shores of Lake Ontario, this historic cobblestone house rests on six acres and is surrounded by a woodland wildlife preserve and apple orchards. On the Seaway Trail near Sodus Bay, the property includes a historic grist mill and is rumored to have been a part of the Underground Railroad. Stroll through the apple orchards to the lake or enjoy the fishing stream, tennis courts and hiking trails. There are kayak and canoes rentals on the premises. Maxwell Creek's spacious accommodations are comprised of five guest rooms in the main house, including a honeymoon suite. The Cobblestone Cottage, a former carriage house, offers two efficiency suites popular for families and groups. Guests are treated to a full breakfast served by candlelight in a rustic wood-paneled dining room warmed by a unique fireplace.

Innkeeper(s): Patrick & Belinda McElroy. $85-150. 7 rooms with PB, 2 suites, 1 cottage and 1 conference room. Breakfast included in rates. Types of meals: Full gourmet bkfst. Beds: KQDT. Reading lamp and desk in room. Tennis, library, parlor games, telephone, fishing creek and hiking on premises. Family reunions hosted. Amusement parks, antiquing, canoeing/kayaking, cross-country skiing, downhill skiing, fishing, hiking, parks, shopping, water sports, fall foliage train rides and snowmobiling nearby.

Publicity: *Atlanta Journal and Newman Times.*

"The best food I've ever tasted."

South Worcester   G10

Charlotte Valley Inn

Charlotte Creek Rd
South Worcester, NY 12197
(607)397-8164
E-mail: charlottevalley@yahoo.com
Web: www.cooperstownchamber.org/cvinn

Circa 1832. This elegant, imposing Federal Greek Revival stands on two pastoral acres in this historic hamlet surrounded by a glorious valley. Built as a stagecoach stop, the inn is decorated in period antiques, available for purchase. The five guest bedrooms have antique beds, some with canopies. Guests are served a full country breakfast in the Hepplewhite dining room. The meal includes such items as omelettes, homemade breads, muffins and scones, bacon, sausage, toast and quiches. After breakfast, guests can enjoy the common rooms: the parlor, the Empire Reading Room or the sunroom with the natural flagstone floor and the view of Charlotte Valley. Or they may head out for the local attractions: Hanford Mills Museum, Fenimore Art Museum and the Baseball Hall of Fame.

Historic Interest: Charlotte Valley is a stagecoach stop built in 1832 that was on the route for travelers from Albany to Oneonta to Binghamton, carefully preserved and restored Federal Greek Revival architecture. Stepping into the Inn is to step back in time, the furnishings and atmosphere bring you back to the 19th century.

Innkeeper(s): Lawrence & Joanne Kosciusko. $90-125. 5 rooms, 3 with PB and 1 suite. Breakfast, afternoon tea and snacks/refreshments included in rates. Types of meals: Country bkfst and early coffee/tea. Beds: D. Reading lamp and clock radio in room. TV, VCR, parlor games, telephone and fireplace on premises. Antiquing, art galleries, bicycling, canoeing/kayaking, cross-country skiing, downhill skiing, fishing, golf, hiking, horseback riding, live theater, museums, parks, shopping, sporting events, tennis, water sports and wineries nearby.

Publicity: Otsego County Times, Oneonta Daily Star and Images of America: Tri-Valley from Cobleskill to Colliersville by Marilyn E. Dufresne.

Southampton K15

Evergreen On Pine

89 Pine St
Southampton, NY 11968-4945
(631)283-0564 (877)824-6600
E-mail: info@evergreenonpine.com
Web: www.evergreenonpine.com

Circa 1860. Guests enjoy a short walk to the beach from this two-and-a-half-story cottage, tucked behind an arched hedge and shaded by tall trees. Located in the middle of the village, the bed and breakfast offers guests a front porch and a patio for relaxing. Guest rooms are comfortable and welcoming. Breakfast is continental style and features cereal, muffins and fruit. Nearby Main Street is lined with unique shops and restaurants and a number of antique shops. Visit the area's wineries or glean fresh local produce from the popular fruit and vegetable stands when not strolling the beach.

Innkeeper(s): Peter & Joann Rogoski. $100-325. 5 rooms with PB and 1 suite. Breakfast included in rates. Types of meals: Cont and early coffee/tea. Beds: QD. Cable TV, refrigerator, ceiling fan, clock radio, telephone and coffeemaker in room. Air conditioning. Fax, copier and fireplace on premises. Weddings hosted. Antiquing, art galleries, beach, bicycling, canoeing/kayaking, fishing, golf, hiking, horseback riding, live theater, museums, parks, shopping and wineries nearby.

Mainstay

579 Hill St
Southampton, NY 11968-5305
(631)283-4375 Fax:(631)287-6240

Circa 1870. This Colonial has served as a guest house, country store and now a bed & breakfast with eight guest rooms. Antiques, including iron beds, decorate the bedchambers. One suite includes a clawfoot tub. A decanter of sherry has been placed in each guest room. Several walls feature hand-painted murals. There is a swimming pool for guest use, as well as beach access.

Innkeeper(s): Elizabeth Main. $100-450. 8 rooms, 5 with PB and 2 suites. Breakfast included in rates. Types of meals: Cont. Beds: KQDT. Reading lamp and ceiling fan in room. Fax, telephone and fireplace on premises. Antiquing, fishing, golf, live theater, parks, shopping, tennis and water sports nearby.

Publicity: New York Times.

Stone Ridge I11

Sparrow Hawk Bed & Breakfast

4496 Rte 209
Stone Ridge, NY 12484
(845)687-4492
E-mail: sparrowhawkbb@aol.com
Web: www.sparrowhawkbandb.com

Circa 1770. Situated on five acres in the picturesque Hudson Valley, this 1770 Registered Brick Colonial with wood shake roof and wide plank floors sits beneath majestic 200-year-old locust trees. Wide hallways lead to the five large air-conditioned guest rooms furnished with special antiques, some with original fireplaces. Behind the old house is the air-conditioned Grand Room, with cathedral windows on three sides and a balcony library full of books, magazines, videos and music for leisurely entertainment. A full gourmet breakfast of freshly baked muffins and special egg dishes with homemade sausage or bacon made by chef Howard, a graduate of the New York Restaurants School, can be enjoyed on the blue stone patio. The surrounding countryside affords many activities such as hiking, skiing, golf or exploring antique shops, wineries or local artisan's pottery shops.

Innkeeper(s): Howard & Betsy Mont. $115-170. 5 rooms, 4 with PB, 1 suite and 1 conference room. Breakfast and afternoon tea included in rates. Types of meals: Full gourmet bkfst. Beds: KQDT. Reading lamp in room. Air conditioning. TV, VCR, fax, copier, bicycles, library, parlor games, telephone and fireplace on premises. Weddings, small meetings and family reunions hosted. Antiquing, art galleries, bicycling, canoeing/kayaking, cross-country skiing, downhill skiing, fishing, golf, hiking, horseback riding, live theater, parks, shopping, tennis and wineries nearby.

Publicity: Blue Stone Press, Hudson Valley Magazine and Hudson Valley Guide.

Syracuse F8

Bed & Breakfast Wellington

707 Danforth St
Syracuse, NY 13208
(315)474-3641 (800)724-5006 Fax:(315)474-2557
E-mail: innkeepers@bbwellington.com
Web: www.bbwellington.com

Circa 1914. Built as a stucco and brick Tudor home and listed in the National and State registers, the inn has architecture and furnishings that reflect an Arts & Crafts influence. A tasteful combination of old and new is found in the Stickley and Mission-style antiques, Oriental carpets and modern technology with in-room DSL Internet access, data ports, central air conditioning and VCRs. Complimentary drinks are available around the clock. Sip a cup of tea by the fire, browse through the Wallace Nutting book collection or play on a one-of-a-kind chess board. Many of the well-appointed guest bedrooms feature a screened-in sleeping porch with wicker furniture or a private balcony. The Lakeview Room also boasts vistas of Onondaga Lake. The Gang Suite includes a dining area, living room with gas-log fireplace, library and efficiency kitchen. Located in Central New York, the rich heritage of this region offers many activities and historic sites.

Historic Interest: Erie Canal Museum, Salt City Museum, Everson Art Museum.

Innkeeper(s): Wendy Wilber & Ray Borg. $95-135. 5 rooms, 4 with PB, 1 with FP, 1 suite and 2 conference rooms. Breakfast included in rates. Types of meals: Full gourmet bkfst and veg bkfst. Beds: KQ. Modem hook-up, data port, cable TV, VCR, reading lamp, refrigerator, clock radio, telephone, coffeemaker, desk and fireplace in room. Central air. Fax, copier, fireplace and laundry facility on premises. Weddings, small meetings, family reunions and seminars hosted. Antiquing, art galleries, beach, bicycling, canoeing/kayaking, cross-country skiing, downhill skiing, fishing, golf, hiking, live theater, museums, parks, shopping, sporting events, tennis, water sports and wineries nearby.

Bed and Breakfast at Giddings Garden

290 W Seneca Tpke
Syracuse, NY 13207-2639
(800)377-3452
E-mail: giddingsb-b@webtv.net
Web: www.giddingsgarden.com

Circa 1810. Once a prestigious tavern, this two-hundred-year-old Federal-style inn has been restored to include the many original chandeliers and rich douglas fir floors while adding upscale details and amenities. Spacious guest bedrooms feature handpicked antique furnishings and collectibles. Marble baths and floor-to ceiling mirrored showers add to the elegance. Savor a creative gourmet breakfast and enjoy refreshments any time at the complimentary guest station with well-stocked refrigerator and microwave. Sip a glass of wine on the old stone patio or stroll the one-acre grounds that are accented by beautifully landscaped gardens, fish ponds and park benches. Downtown and the university are just five minutes away. Skaneateles Lake and the many wineries of the Finger Lakes are also nearby.

Innkeeper(s): Pat & Nancy Roberts. $90-200. 5 rooms with PB. Breakfast included in rates. Types of meals: Full gourmet bkfst and early coffee/tea. Beds: Q. Cable TV, reading lamp, clock radio, telephone, desk, HBO, Internet access, VCR/DVD in West Wing and some with microwave in room. Air conditioning. VCR, fax, copier, fireplace, complimentary refreshment center, free local calls, off-street parking and concierge services on premises. Small meetings hosted. Antiquing, cross-country skiing, downhill skiing, fishing, golf, live theater, parks, shopping, sporting events, tennis and water sports nearby.

Dickenson House On James

1504 James St
Syracuse, NY 13203-2814
(315)423-4777 (888)423-4777
E-mail: innkeeper@dickensonhouse.com
Web: www.dickensonhouse.com

Circa 1924. As pretty as a picture from a long ago era, this crisp, tidy ornate Tudor home stands in a prestigious urban neighborhood in Syracuse's preservation district. The inn has stained glass, a beautiful beveled mirror foyer, crystal chandeliers, a stone front porch and a porte-cochere. It has four guest bedrooms and a 1300-square-foot loft suite with vaulted ceilings and skylights. All the guest rooms are named for British poets. The literary themed living room includes an old violin, a Victrola, antique cameras, kaleidoscopes and a fireplace.

Breakfast is a taste sensation of entrees with fruits juices, coffee, almond scones, fruit parfait, yogurt, granola, and orange/pecan crusted French toast.

Innkeeper(s): Pam & Ed Kopiel. $105-350. 4 rooms with PB and 1 suite. Breakfast, afternoon tea and snacks/refreshments included in rates. Types of meals: Full gourmet bkfst, veg bkfst and early coffee/tea. Beds: KQT. Modem hook-up, data port, cable TV, VCR, reading lamp, stereo, refrigerator, ceiling fan, snack bar, clock radio, telephone, coffeemaker, desk and robes in room. Central air. Fax, copier, library, parlor games, fireplace, laundry facility and guest kitchen on premises. Small meetings and family reunions hosted. Amusement parks, antiquing, art galleries, beach, bicycling, canoeing/kayaking, cross-country skiing, downhill skiing, fishing, golf, hiking, horseback riding, live theater, museums, parks, shopping, sporting events, tennis, water sports and wineries nearby.

Tannersville   H11

The Eggery Inn

County Rd 16
Tannersville, NY 12485
(518)589-5363 (800)785-5364
E-mail: eggeryinn@aol.com
Web: www.eggeryinn.com

Circa 1900. Year-round delight is enjoyed at this bed & breakfast inn located on a 12-acre mountainside in the Catskill Forest Preserve. The restored 100-year-old, three-story Dutch Colonial was an historic Boarding House. Relax on the wrap-around porch with the south lawn facing Hunter Mountain and the adjacent range. The cozy fireside lounge is a perfect rest stop after a day of skiing, biking or hiking. Air-conditioned guest bedrooms and baths have been remodeled to offer comfort and ease with a voice mail phone system and cable TV. Select a made-to-order breakfast from the full-choice menu of classic favorites that is sure to satisfy. Group dinner parties can be arranged. Visit nearby North and South Lake State Park, scenic waterfalls and trails.

Innkeeper(s): Julie & Abraham Abramczyk. $95-125. 15 rooms with PB. Breakfast included in rates. Types of meals: Full bkfst. Beds: KQD. Data port, cable TV, reading lamp, clock radio and telephone in room. Air conditioning. Parlor games and fireplace on premises. Family reunions hosted. Antiquing, bicycling, cross-country skiing, downhill skiing, fishing, golf, hiking, live theater, parks, shopping, tennis and swimming nearby.

Publicity: Kaatskill Life, Newsday, Skiing and AAA Mobil Guide.

Thompson Ridge   I11

Hopewell Farm B&B

PO Box 45 #680 Rt 302
Thompson Ridge, NY 10985
(845)361-2197
E-mail: hopewellfarm@hotmail.com
Web: bbonline.com/ny/hopewell

Circa 1780. Thirteen scenic acres of gardens, woods and fields are bordered by the Pakanasink Creek and overlooked by the Shawangunk Mountains at this landmark Colonial farmstead that also includes the original barn, carriage house and four more outbuildings. The 18th-century residence, listed in the National and State Registers, is now a B&B. It features American and Asian antiques. Relax in the Green Room with a library, TV and woodburning stove. Sleep in air-conditioned comfort in the Crawford and Victorian rooms. An elaborate gourmet breakfast is served in the summer kitchen with a beamed ceiling, huge stone fireplace and beehive oven. Toasted grapefruit with fresh strawberries, blueberry pancakes, cereals, smoked salmon with bagels and cream cheese are just some of the foods to enjoy. Explore the area on an available bike then swim in the large in-ground pool. New York City is just 70 miles away.

Historic Interest: Original 18th-century farmstead of the Crawford family, after whom the town was named. The adjacent Hopewell Farm Cemetery is the burial site of 2 Revolutionary Soldiers.

Innkeeper(s): A. Kees Jordan. $105-160. 4 rooms, 1 with PB. Breakfast and snacks/refreshments included in rates. Types of meals: Full gourmet bkfst, veg bkfst, afternoon tea and gourmet dinner. Beds: QT. Cable TV, reading lamp, desk and antique furniture in room. Air conditioning. TV, bicycles, library, pet boarding, laundry facility and 20x40' swimming pool on premises. Weddings and family reunions hosted. Antiquing, art galleries, bicycling, cross-country skiing, golf, hiking, horseback riding, museums, parks, shopping, tennis, wineries, DIA Arts Center, Beacon, Storm King Art Center, The Landing, Hudson River front restaurants, cruise ships and Newburgh nearby.

Warrensburg E12

Alynn's Butterfly Inn B&B

69 State Route 28
Warrensburg, NY 12885
(518)623-9390

Circa 1750. A visit to the Adirondacks should include a stay at this pristine 18th-century, French-country farmhouse sitting on 176 acres of nature's beauty. The sprawling wraparound porch invites relaxation. Spacious yet intimate, the comfortable ambiance is accented with thoughtful amenities. Guest bedrooms feature jetted tubs and soft, terry robes to linger in. View Moon Mountain from the great room while indulging in an abundant gourmet breakfast. After a full day of hiking or cross-country skiing the inn's trails, soak in the outdoor hot tub. Lake George and Gore Mountain Ski Center are 10-15 minutes away.

Historic Interest: The site for the novel "Last of the Mohicans" is nearby, as are French & Indian and Revolutionary War sites.

Innkeeper(s): Al & Lynn Smith. $119-149. 5 rooms with PB. Breakfast included in rates. Types of meals: Full gourmet bkfst. Beds: KQ. Refrigerator, coffeemaker and terry robes in room. Air conditioning. Spa, telephone and hot tub on premises. Weddings, small meetings, family reunions and seminars hosted. Amusement parks, antiquing, fishing, hiking, parks and shopping nearby.

Publicity: *Post Star, Chronicle, G.F. Business Journal, Adirondack Journal, Veterans Travel and Travel.*

The Cornerstone Victorian B&B

3921 Main St, Route 9
Warrensburg, NY 12885-1149
(518)623-3308 Fax:(518)623-3979
E-mail: stay@cornerstonevictorian.com
Web: www.cornerstonevictorian.com

Circa 1904. Replete with gleaming woodwork and polished interior columns, this large wood and stone Victorian home has a wraparound porch overlooking Hackensack Mountain. Inside are stained-glass windows, Victorian furnishings, three terra-cotta fireplaces and a beautiful cherry staircase. Awake each morning to a candlelight breakfast complete with homemade morning cakes, Louise's famous granola and other gourmet entrees. Simply ask the innkeepers, with their 25-year experience in the hospitality field, and they can help you plan your leisure activities in the Lake George/Adirondack and Saratoga Springs area.

Innkeeper(s): Doug & Louise Goettsche. $85-175. 5 rooms with PB, 1 with FP and 1 conference room. Breakfast included in rates. Types of meals: Full bkfst and early coffee/tea. Beds: Q. Ceiling fan and hair dryer in room. Air conditioning. VCR, fax, copier and bicycles on premises. Amusement parks, antiquing, cross-country skiing, downhill skiing, fishing, golf, hiking, live theater, museums, parks, shopping, tennis and water sports nearby.

Country Road Lodge B&B

115 Hickory Hill Rd
Warrensburg, NY 12885-3912
(518)623-2207 Fax:(518)623-4363
E-mail: mail@countryroadlodge.com
Web: www.countryroadlodge.com

Circa 1929. Originally built for a local businessman as a simple "camp," this bed & breakfast has expanded to offer comfortable accommodations. At the end of a short country road in a secluded setting on the Hudson River, 35 acres of woodlands and fields are surrounded by a state forest preserve. Common rooms boast panoramic views of the river and the Adirondack Mountains. After a restful night's sleep, enjoy homemade bread and muffins in the dining room while selecting from the breakfast menu. Nature walks, bird watching, hiking and cross-country skiing are just out the front door.

Historic Interest: French and Indian War battlefields, Fort William Henry, Ticonderoga, and Defiance, Millionaire's Row on Lake George.

Innkeeper(s): Sandi & Steve Parisi. $72-82. 4 rooms with PB and 1 suite. Breakfast included in rates. Types of meals: Country bkfst and early coffee/tea. Beds: QT. Reading lamp and ceiling fan in room. Air conditioning. Library, parlor games and telephone on premises. Small meetings and family reunions hosted. Amusement parks, antiquing, art galleries, beach, bicycling, canoeing/kayaking, cross-country skiing, downhill skiing, fishing, golf, hiking, horseback riding, live theater, museums, parks, shopping, tennis, whitewater rafting, snowshoeing, scenic drives, lake cruises, colonial history sites and garage sales nearby.

Publicity: *North Jersey Herald & News.*

"Homey, casual atmosphere. We really had a wonderful time. You're both wonderful hosts and the Lodge is definitely our kind of B&B! We will always feel very special about this place and will always be back."

Emerson House Bed & Breakfast

3826 Main Street
Warrensburg, NY 12885
(518)623-2758 Fax:(518)623-5121

Circa 1830. Scenic beauty and a variety of activities are enjoyed year-round at this stately Greek Revival mansion in the Adirondack Mountains near Lake George. Built in the 1830s, it has been meticulously restored and boasts a Colonial decor. Gather for conversation in the living room, read in the library or be entertained in the TV room. Distinctive guest bedrooms and a suite offer an assortment of delightful amenities that may include a double whirlpool or clawfoot tub, dual showerheads, a decorative fireplace and a private upstairs porch. Fresh-baked blueberry muffins, mixed fruit, Southwestern Breakfast Omelet, Caramel French Toast and locally smoked bacon are some of the favorite foods served in the mornings. Ask about Ski and Stay packages that feature lift tickets at Gore Mountain.

Historic Interest: Built by a prominent family who started the first bank in town.

Innkeeper(s): Faith Buck. $90-150. 6 rooms, 5 with PB, 1 with FP and 1 suite. Breakfast included in rates. Types of meals: Full bkfst, veg bkfst and early coffee/tea. Beds: KQT. Reading lamp, refrigerator, ceiling fan, snack bar, coffeemaker and hot tub/spa in room. TV, VCR, spa, library, parlor games, telephone and fireplace on premises. Weddings and family reunions hosted. Amusement parks, antiquing, art galleries, beach, bicycling, canoeing/kayaking, cross-country skiing, downhill skiing, golf, hiking, horseback riding, museums, parks, shopping and water sports nearby.

The Merrill Magee House

3 Hudson St PO Box 391
Warrensburg, NY 12885-0391
(518)623-2449 (888)664-4661 Fax:(518)623-3990
E-mail: mmhinn1@capital.net
Web: www.merrillmageehouse.com

Circa 1834. This stately Greek Revival home offers beautiful antique fireplaces in every guest room. The Sage, Rosemary, Thyme and Coriander rooms feature sitting areas. The decor is romantic and distinctly Victorian. Romantic getaway packages include candlelight dinners. The local area hosts art and craft festivals, an antique car show, white-water rafting and Gore Mountain Oktoberfest. Tour the Adirondacks from the sky during September's balloon festival or browse through the world's largest garage sale in early October.

Historic Interest: Fort William Henry, Fort George Battlegrounds (5 miles), Schuyler Heights Battle (30 miles).

Innkeeper(s): Pam Converse. $125-165. 10 rooms with PB, 10 with FP and 1 conference room. Breakfast included in rates. Types of meals: Full gourmet bkfst, veg bkfst, early coffee/tea, picnic lunch and gourmet dinner. Restaurant on premises. Beds: KQT. Reading lamp, clock radio and fireplace in room. Central air. TV, VCR, swimming, library, parlor games and telephone on premises. Limited handicap access. Weddings, small meetings, family reunions and seminars hosted. Amusement parks, antiquing, art galleries, beach, bicycling, canoeing/kayaking, cross-country skiing, downhill skiing, fishing, golf, hiking, horseback riding, live theater, museums, parks, shopping, sporting events, tennis and water sports nearby.

"A really classy and friendly operation—a real joy."

Seasons B&B

3822 Main Street
Warrensburg, NY 12885
(518)623-3832 (866)322-2632 Fax:(518)623-3916
E-mail: eileen@seasons-bandb.com
Web: seasons-bandb.com

Circa 1820. Listed in the National Register, this Italianate home sits on a small hill in the scenic Adirondacks surrounded by blue spruce, hemlocks and fir trees. Noted author James Fenimore Cooper stayed here during the 1830s. Relax and enjoy afternoon tea on the wraparound porch or in the living room. Renovated and refurbished, antiques and contemporary furnishings reside comfortably together, fusing the old and the new in spacious guest bedrooms and suites. In-room massage is available. A satisfying breakfast is served in the casually elegant ambiance of the dining room. Visit the historic sites of Fort William Henry and Ticonderoga.

Historic Interest: The house was built in the early 1820s and the Italian-style villas section was added in the 1830s. James Fenimore Cooper, the author of Last of the Mohicans, stayed at the house in the 1830s. It is listed as one of the most distinguished homes in the area.

Innkeeper(s): Eileen M. Frasier. $95-175. 5 rooms, 3 with PB, 1 with FP and 2 suites. Breakfast and afternoon tea included in rates. Types of meals: Full bkfst and early coffee/tea. Beds: Q. Cable TV, reading lamp, ceiling fan and clock radio in room. Air conditioning. TV, VCR, spa, library, fireplace and massage therapist on premises. Amusement parks, antiquing, art galleries, beach, bicycling, canoeing/kayaking, cross-country skiing, downhill skiing, fishing, golf, hiking, horseback riding, live theater, museums, parks, shopping, sporting events, tennis and water sports nearby.

Publicity: *Local newspapers and public radio and television support.*

Warwick J11

Glenwood House B&B and Cottage Suites

49 Glenwood Rd
Warwick, NY 10969
(845)258-5066
E-mail: info@glenwoodhouse.com
Web: www.glenwoodhouse.com

Circa 1855. Built prior to the Civil War, this restored Victorian farmhouse is secluded on more than two picturesque acres in New York's Pochuck Valley. The spacious front veranda is filled with comfortable wicker furnishings, inviting guests to relax and enjoy the country setting. Guest rooms are decorated with a romantic flair. Three rooms include canopied beds. Deluxe cottage suites include a whirlpool tub for two and a fireplace. Seasonal, farm-fresh fruits start off the breakfast service, which

might include an entrée such as Texas-style French toast or buttermilk pancakes accompanied by bacon or sausage. The home is close to ski areas, golf courses, wineries, historic home tours and antique stores. The Appalachian Trail, Hudson River and Greenwood Lake are other nearby attractions.

Historic Interest: The Glenwood House was built by a wealthy farming family and served as an active dairy farm until the 1960s. Portraits of the original owners, Margaret Moorehouse and Lynn Roy can be found in the library. Their descendants still own all of the fields and valley which surround the B&B. The Lenape Indians settled in the valley in front of the house over 10,000 years ago and artifacts are still being unearthed by the plows to this day.

Innkeeper(s): Andrea & Kevin Colman. $110-295. 7 rooms with PB, 2 with FP, 3 suites and 2 cottages. Breakfast included in rates. Types of meals: Country bkfst. Beds: KQD. Modem hook-up, cable TV, VCR, reading lamp, CD player, refrigerator, ceiling fan, clock radio, desk, hot tub/spa, fireplace and Jacuzzi for two in room. Air conditioning. Copier, spa, library, parlor games and telephone on premises. Weddings, small meetings, family reunions and seminars hosted. Antiquing, art galleries, beach, downhill skiing, fishing, golf, hiking, horseback riding, live theater, parks, shopping, tennis, water sports, wineries, Mountain Creek Ski Resort and Water Park, Appalachian Trail, Holly Trail, Artist's Open Studio Tour, Walkill River Wildlife Refuge and Famous Black Dirt Region and 'Onion Capital of The World' nearby.

Warwick Valley Bed & Breakfast

24 Maple Ave
Warwick, NY 10990-1025
(845)987-7255 (888)280-1671 Fax:(845)988-5318

Circa 1900. This turn-of-the-century Colonial Revival is located in Warwick's historic district among many of the town's other historic gems. The B&B includes five guest rooms decorated with antiques and country furnishings. Breakfasts are a treat with entrees such as eggs Benedict, apple pancakes or a savory potato, cheese and egg bake. Wineries, antique shops and many outdoor activities are nearby, and innkeeper Loretta Breedveld is happy to point guests in the right direction.

Innkeeper(s): Loretta Breedveld. $100-145. 5 rooms with PB. Breakfast included in rates. Types of meals: Full gourmet bkfst and early coffee/tea. Beds: KQT. TV, telephone, desk, fireplace, sitting area and high-speed Internet access in room. Central air. VCR, fax, copier and bicycles on premises. Family reunions hosted. Amusement parks, antiquing, cross-country skiing, downhill skiing, fishing, golf, live theater, parks, shopping, sporting events, tennis, water sports and wineries nearby.

Publicity: *Warwick Advertiser.*

Westhampton Beach K14

1880 House Bed & Breakfast

PO Box 648
Westhampton Beach, NY 11978-0648
(516)288-1559 (800)346-3290 Fax:(516)288-7696

Circa 1880. On Westhampton Beach's exclusive Seafield Lane, this country estate includes a pool and tennis court, and it is just a short walk to the ocean. The inn is decorated with Victorian antiques, Shaker benches, and Chinese porcelain, creating a casual, country inn atmosphere.

Innkeeper(s): Elsie Collins. $150-250. 3 rooms and 2 suites. Breakfast included in rates. Types of meals: Full bkfst, veg bkfst and afternoon tea. Beds: QD. Cable TV, reading lamp, refrigerator, clock radio and desk in room. Air conditioning. Fax, swimming, tennis, library, telephone and fireplace on premises. Weddings, small meetings, family reunions and seminars hosted. Antiquing, art galleries, beach, bicycling, fishing, golf, hiking, horseback riding, live theater and wineries nearby.

Publicity: *Mid-Atlantic Getaways and Country Inns.*

"From the moment we stepped inside your charming home we felt all the warmth you sent our way which made our stay so comfortable and memorable."

Westport C12

The Victorian Lady

6447 Main St
Westport, NY 12993
(518)962-2345 Fax:(518)962-2345
E-mail: victorianlady@westelcom.com
Web: www.victorianladybb.com

Circa 1856. This Second Empire home features all the delicate elements of a true "Painted Lady," from the vivid color scheme to the Eastlake porch that graces the exterior. Delicate it's not, however, having stood for more than a century. Its interior is decked in period style with antiques from this more gracious era. A proper afternoon tea is served, and breakfasts are served by candlelight. More than an acre of grounds, highlighted by English gardens, surround the home. Lake Champlain is a mere 100 yards from the front door.

Innkeeper(s): Doris & Wayne Deswert. $110-125. 4 rooms with PB. Breakfast and afternoon tea included in rates. Types of meals: Full gourmet bkfst and early coffee/tea. Beds: KQT. Reading lamp, ceiling fan, clock radio and desk in room. VCR, fax, copier, library, parlor games and telephone on premises. Weddings and family reunions hosted. Antiquing, cross-country skiing, downhill skiing, fishing, golf, live theater, parks, shopping, tennis and water sports nearby.
Publicity: *Victorian Homes Magazine.*

White Lake I10

Bradstan Country Hotel

1561 Rte 17B PO Box 312
White Lake, NY 12786
(845)583-4114 Fax:(845)583-5106
E-mail: brad57@aol.com
Web: www.bradstancountryhotel.com

Circa 1925. If the innkeepers start to sing, "Come to the cabaret," it's not simply because of their love for the theater. There actually is a cabaret on the premises, drawing some of the world's top performers. In addition to this unique offering, guests will admire the award-winning restoration of this historic hotel. Guest rooms and

suites are decorated with antiques and vintage furnishings, and there are three cottages, as well. Guests often enjoy relaxing on the wicker-filled porch. After an evening at the cabaret, the audience usually wanders into the hotel's piano bar. In the mornings, a huge breakfast is served, buffet-style, with fruits, cereals, coffeecake, freshly baked muffins, eggs, quiche, savory meats and the likes.

Innkeeper(s): Scott Samuelson & Edward Dudek. $90-175. 7 rooms, 2 with PB, 3 suites, 3 cottages and 1 conference room. Breakfast included in rates. Types of meals: Cont plus. Beds: Q. Ceiling fan, clock radio and hair dryers in room. Central air. TV, fax, copier, swimming, parlor games, telephone, fireplace and world class cabaret and entertainment piano bar on premises. Weddings, small meetings, family reunions and seminars hosted. Antiquing, art galleries, beach, bicycling, canoeing/kayaking, cross-country skiing, downhill skiing, fishing, golf, hiking, horseback riding, live theater, museums, parks, shopping, tennis, water sports and wineries nearby.
Publicity: *The Times Herald, Cabaret Scenes, Sullivan County Democrat and Weekender.*

"The beautiful surroundings were ideal for a romantic getaway and we plan on returning very soon."

Wilmington C12

Willkommen Hof

Rt 86, PO Box 240
Wilmington, NY 12997
(518)946-7669 (800)541-9119 Fax:(518)946-7626
E-mail: willkommen@whiteface.net
Web: www.lakeplacid.net/willkommenhof

Circa 1910. This turn-of-the-century farmhouse served as an inn during the 1920s, but little else is known about its past. The innkeepers have created a cozy atmosphere, perfect for relaxation after a day exploring the Adirondack Mountain area. A large selection of books and a roaring fire greet guests who choose to settle down in the reading room. The innkeepers also offer a large selection of movies. Relax in the sauna or outdoor spa or simply enjoy the comfort of your bedchamber.

Historic Interest: Visit a covered bridge in Jay, just four miles away or cruise the Whiteface Memorial Highway, which is just a few miles away. Lake Placid, the site of the 1932 and 1980 Olympics, offers much to see and do.
Innkeeper(s): Heike & Bert Yost. $50-165. 8 rooms, 3 with PB and 1 suite. Breakfast and afternoon tea included in rates. Types of meals: Full bkfst and dinner. Restaurant on premises. Beds: KQDT. TV, VCR, reading lamp, refrigerator, ceiling fan, clock radio, coffeemaker, hot tub/spa and fireplace in room. Fax, copier, spa, sauna, library, parlor games, telephone, fireplace and baby grand piano on premises. Weddings, small meetings, family reunions and seminars hosted. Amusement parks, antiquing, art galleries, beach, bicycling, canoeing/kayaking, cross-country skiing, downhill skiing, fishing, golf, hiking, horseback riding, live theater, museums, shopping and water sports nearby.

"Vielen Dank! Alles war sehr schoen and the breakfasts were delicious."

Windham H11

Albergo Allegria B&B

#43 Route 296, PO Box 267
Windham, NY 12496-0267
(518)734-5560 Fax:(518)734-5570
E-mail: mail@albergousa.com
Web: www.albergousa.com

Circa 1892. Two former boarding houses were joined to create this luxurious, Victorian bed & breakfast whose name means "the inn of happiness." Guest quarters, laced with a Victorian theme, are decorated with period wallpapers and antique furnishings. One master suite includes an enormous Jacuzzi tub.

There are plenty of relaxing options at Albergo Allegria, including an inviting lounge with a large fireplace and overstuffed couches. Guests also can choose from more than 300 videos in the innkeeper's movie collection.

Located just a few feet behind the inn are the Carriage House Suites, each of which includes a double whirlpool tub, gas fireplace, king-size bed and cathedral ceilings with skylights. The innkeepers came to the area originally to open a deluxe, gourmet restaurant. Their command of cuisine is evident each morning as guests feast on a variety of home-baked muffins and pastries, gourmet omelettes, waffles and other tempting treats. The inn is a registered historic site.

Historic Interest: Blenheim Bridge, the longest covered wooden bridge of its kind in the United States, is about a half hour from the inn, as is Olana Castle.

Innkeeper(s): Leslie & Marianna Leman. $73-299. 21 rooms with PB, 8 with FP and 9 suites. Breakfast included in rates. Types of meals: Full gourmet bkfst. Beds: KQT. Cable TV, VCR, reading lamp, refrigerator, ceiling fan, clock radio, telephone and desk in room. Air conditioning. Fax, copier, bicycles, parlor games, fireplace, afternoon tea on Saturdays, 24-hour guest pantry with soft drinks and hot beverages and sweets on premises. Limited handicap access. Weddings, small meetings and seminars hosted. Amusement parks, antiquing, bicycling, cross-country skiing, downhill skiing, fishing, hiking, parks, shopping, tennis, water sports, bird watching and waterfalls nearby.

Publicity: *Yankee.*

Wolcott   F7

Bonnie Castle Farm B&B

PO Box 188

Wolcott, NY 14590-0188

(315)587-2273 (800)587-4006 Fax:(315)587-4003

Circa 1887. This large, waterfront home is surrounded by expansive lawns and trees, which overlook the east side of Great Sodus Bay, a popular resort at the turn of the century. Accommodations include a suite and large guest rooms with water views. Other rooms feature wainscoting and cathedral ceilings. A full, gourmet breakfast includes a cereal bar, fresh fruit and juices and an assortment of entrees such as Orange Blossom French toast, sausages, a creamy potato casserole and fresh-baked pastries topped off with teas and Irish creme coffee. Guests can visit many nearby attractions, such as the Renaissance Festival, Erie Canal and Chimney Bluffs State Park.

Historic Interest: Dozens of historic sites await guests at the Bonnie Castle Farm, including the Everson Museum, Susan B. Anthony House, National Women's Hall of Fame, William Phelps General Store Museum, the Sodus Point Maritime Museum, Renaissance Faire and others.

Innkeeper(s): Eric & Georgia Pendleton. $99-165. 8 rooms with PB and 1 suite. Breakfast included in rates. Types of meals: Full gourmet bkfst. Beds: KQD. Cable TV, VCR, ceiling fan and clock radio in room. Air conditioning. TV, fax, copier, spa, swimming, telephone and fireplace on premises. Small meetings, family reunions and seminars hosted. Antiquing, cross-country skiing, downhill skiing, fishing, live theater, parks, shopping, sporting events and water sports nearby.

"We love Bonnie Castle. You have a magnificent establishment. We are just crazy about your place. Hope to see you soon."

North Carolina

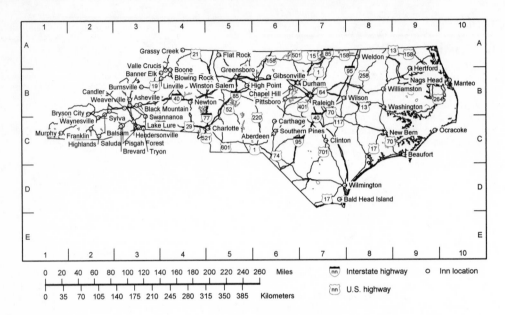

		Miles
0 20 40 60 80 100 120 140 160 180 200 220 240 260		
0 35 70 105 140 175 210 245 280 315 350 385		Kilometers

🛡 Interstate highway   ○ Inn location

🛡 U.S. highway

Aberdeen   C6

The Inn at Bryant House

214 N Poplar St
Aberdeen, NC 28315-2812
(910)944-3300 (800)453-4019 Fax:(910)944-8898
E-mail: lsteele@eclipsetel.com
Web: innatbryanthouse.com

Circa 1913. This Colonial Revival inn has been completely
restored to its original Southern splendor. Pastel colors flow
through the entire house, and the sitting, dining and living
rooms open to one another for easy access. Breakfast is served
in the dining or garden room. With advance notice, lunches
and dinners can be served for small business meetings, wedding parties, family gatherings, club activities and weekend
retreats. The Pinehurst area is known for its quiet rolling hills
and more than 30 championship-quality golf courses.
Historic Interest: Pinehurst Village (5 miles), Raleigh Durham (55 miles),
Cameron Historic District and antique shops (15 miles).
Innkeeper(s): Lee & Sharon Steele. $70-105. 9 rooms, 8 with PB. Breakfast
included in rates. Types of meals: Full bkfst. Beds: QDT. Reading lamp in
room. Air conditioning. VCR, telephone and fireplace on premises. Weddings,
small meetings, family reunions and seminars hosted. Antiquing, golf, live
theater and shopping nearby.

Asheville   B3

1889 WhiteGate Inn & Cottage

173 E Chestnut St
Asheville, NC 28801-2339
(828)253-2553 (800)485-3045 Fax:(828)281-1883
E-mail: innkeeper@whitegate.net
Web: www.whitegate.net

Circa 1889. A white picket fence surrounds this historic home
that prominent businessman Frederick Kent transformed from
Victorian to an English shingle-style structure. Relax in front of
the fire or enjoy the warmth of the solarium. Guest bedrooms
and suites are named to honor
American poets and are decorated
with antiques and collectibles. The
Cottage includes a living room
with working fireplace and full
kitchen. A lavish breakfast may
include a starter course of peach
halves poached in vanilla syrup filled with ricotta mousse, a main
course of crab and artichoke heart egg puff in a white wine and
parsley sauce and a sweet course of chocolate torte in orange
caramel sauce. Afterwards, roam the exotically landscaped yard
with waterfalls, or visit the greenhouse of orchids and tropicals.

Innkeeper(s): Frank Salvo & Ralph Coffey. $155-295. 5 rooms with PB, 3 with FP, 3 suites and 1 cottage. Breakfast included in rates. Types of meals: Full bkfst, early coffee/tea and snacks/refreshments. Beds: KQ. Reading lamp, ceiling fan and clock radio in room. Air conditioning. TV, VCR, fax, copier, parlor games, telephone and fireplace on premises. Weddings, small meetings and family reunions hosted. Antiquing, art galleries, bicycling, canoeing/kayaking, cross-country skiing, downhill skiing, fishing, golf, hiking, horseback riding, live theater, museums, parks, shopping, tennis and wineries nearby.

1900 Inn on Montford

296 Montford Ave
Asheville, NC 28801-1660
(828)254-9569 (800)254-9569 Fax:(828)254-9518
E-mail: info@innonmontford.com
Web: www.innonmontford.com

Circa 1900. This National Register home was one of a few local homes designed by Richard Sharpe Smith, the supervising architect for the nearby Biltmore Estate. The simple exterior and pleasing Arts & Crafts style is flanked by a wide veranda for relaxing and enjoying the neighborhood. English and American antiques fill the elegant inn. Well-appointed guest bedrooms feature King-size beds and fireplaces. Some have whirlpool tubs, and one boasts a clawfoot tub. A secluded, deluxe five-room whirlpool suite also offers a sitting room and private entrance with balcony. Breakfasts include a special fruit dish such as baked banana souffle, a daily entree and dessert. The inn hosts a social hour from 6-7 p.m. daily. Spend the day touring historic homes, or hike and raft in nearby wilderness areas.

Innkeeper(s): Ron and Lynn Carlson. $125-345. 5 rooms with PB, 5 with FP and 1 suite. Breakfast included in rates. Types of meals: Full gourmet bkfst and early coffee/tea. Beds: KQ. Data port, TV, VCR, reading lamp, refrigerator, clock radio, telephone, desk and high-speed Internet access in room. Air conditioning. Fax, copier, library and fireplace on premises. Weddings, small meetings and seminars hosted. Antiquing, downhill skiing, fishing, golf, live theater, parks, shopping, sporting events, tennis, water sports, Biltmore Estate and Chimney Rock nearby.

A Bed Of Roses

135 Cumberland Ave
Asheville, NC 28801
(828)258-8700
E-mail: info@abedofroses.com
Web: www.abedofroses.com

Circa 1897. Expect no thorns at this splendid Victorian bed & breakfast on a quiet tree-lined street in the Montford Historic District. Built in 1897 and recently restored, the meticulous renovations have retained the wood floors and other details to keep its original ambiance. Relax by the fire in the parlor. Well-appointed guest bedrooms are named after previous owners. Most feature fireplaces and Jacuzzis, and one boasts a clawfoot tub. The turret suite includes a sitting room, fireplace and private balcony. Savor a two-course gourmet breakfast served in the dining room. Plan the day's adventures while enjoying the landscaped yard from the wicker-filled front porch. Tea and homemade goodies are available each afternoon. Ask about weekend packages with tickets to the Biltmore Estate.

Innkeeper(s): Chris & Janis Ortwein. $105-200. 5 rooms with PB, 3 with FP, 1 suite and 1 cottage. Breakfast included in rates. Types of meals: Full gourmet bkfst. Beds: Q. Modem hook-up, data port, cable TV, reading lamp, ceiling fan, clock radio, telephone, desk, hot tub/spa, fireplace and four rooms have whirlpool tubs in room. Central air. Spa and fireplace on premises. Weddings hosted. Antiquing, art galleries, bicycling, canoeing/kayaking, fishing, golf, hiking, horseback riding, live theater, museums, parks, shopping and wineries nearby.

A Hill House B&B

120 Hillside St
Asheville, NC 28801-1206
(828)232-0345 (800)379-0002 Fax:(828)253-1092
E-mail: withzak@charter.net
Web: www.hillhousebb.com

Circa 1885. Ancient oak trees surround this Victorian house set on a hill overlooking downtown Asheville. After spending the day exploring the nearby Biltmore Estate and Great Smoky Mountains, you'll welcome returning to your own comfortable home at Hill House. One of the rocking chairs on the veranda that wraps around the house makes a good place to relax and meet other guests. Many guest rooms offer whirlpool baths, fireplaces and views of the garden and mountains. Rooms are individually named and decorated. The Flat Iron Suite boasts a fireplace, clawfoot tub and a small kitchen with stove top, refrigerator and sink. A canopy bed hung with white gauzy drapes highlights the Jackson Room; for something completely different, there is the S & W Room, with a black lacquer bed, African animal prints, and an Oriental carpet atop a hardwood floor. Frittatas, English muffins, coffee cake and fruit can be brought to your room for breakfast. Snacks are served on arrival.

Innkeeper(s): Terry & Bill Erickson. $125-250. 9 rooms with PB, 4 with FP, 5 suites and 1 cottage. Breakfast and afternoon tea included in rates. Types of meals: Full gourmet bkfst and veg bkfst. Beds: QD. Cable TV, VCR, reading lamp, ceiling fan and hot tub/spa in room. Air conditioning. TV, fax, telephone and fireplace on premises. Antiquing, art galleries, canoeing/kayaking, cross-country skiing, downhill skiing, golf, hiking, horseback riding, live theater, museums, shopping and wineries nearby.

Abbington Green B&B

46 Cumberland Cir
Asheville, NC 28801-1718
(828)251-2454 (800)251-2454 Fax:(828)251-2872

Circa 1908. Innkeeper Valerie Larrea has definitely put her heart and soul into this bed & breakfast. When she discovered the home, located in Asheville's Montfort Historic District, it was desperately in need of a facelift. Through hard work, which included putting in nine bathrooms and replacing the electrical system and all the plumbing, she earned an award for the restoration. The home sports an English decor, and each guest room is named for a park or garden in England. Antiques and reproductions furnish the home. An inventive breakfast menu is prepared each morning, featuring gourmet tidbits such as homemade pumpkin bread, a warm cherry soup and quiche Florentine with grilled sausage. The home was designed by a supervising architect during the building of the Biltmore Estate, which is nearby and open for tours. The inn also features award-winning English gardens. The Blue Ridge Parkway and University of North Carolina also are near.

Innkeeper(s): Valerie, Julie & Gabrielle Larrea. $135-295. 8 rooms with PB, 6 with FP. Breakfast included in rates. Types of meals: Full bkfst. Beds: KQT. Reading lamp, ceiling fan, desk and two and one bedroom suites with whirlpool tubs in room. Air conditioning. VCR, fax, bicycles, library, parlor games, telephone and fireplace on premises. Antiquing, downhill skiing, fishing, golf, live theater, parks, shopping, tennis and white water rafting nearby. Publicity: *Asheville Citizen-Times, Summer Magazine, The Plain Dealer, Gazette* and *Blue Ridge Peak Magazine.*

"Our stay will always be a memorable part of our honeymoon. The breakfasts were outstanding."

Albemarle Inn

86 Edgemont Rd
Asheville, NC 28801-1544
(828)255-0027 (800)621-7435 Fax:(828)236-3397
E-mail: info@albemarleinn.com
Web: www.albemarleinn.com

Circa 1907. In the residential Grove Park area, this AAA four-diamond elegant Greek Revival Mansion graces almost an acre of landscaped grounds. The inn features an exquisite carved-oak staircase and period furnishings. Enjoy late afternoon

refreshments on the veranda overlooking award-winning English gardens or fireside in the parlor. Spacious guest bedrooms and suites boast fine linens, antique clawfoot tubs and showers, televisions and phones. Some rooms include a whirlpool tub and a fireplace. A sumptuous candlelight breakfast is served at individual tables in the dining room or on the plant-filled sun porch. Gourmet dishes may include poached cinnamon pears, stuffed French toast with orange sauce and sausages. Inspired by the singing birds, composer Bela Bartok wrote his third piano concerto while staying here. The inn is a member of Select Registry.

Innkeeper(s): Cathy & Larry Sklar. $165-295. 11 rooms with PB, 1 with FP and 2 suites. Breakfast and snacks/refreshments included in rates. Types of meals: Full gourmet bkfst, early coffee/tea and afternoon tea. Beds: KQDT. Modem hook-up, cable TV, reading lamp, ceiling fan, clock radio, telephone, coffeemaker, turn-down service and suite has 2-person marble whirlpool tub in room. Air conditioning. Parlor games and fireplace on premises. Antiquing, art galleries, bicycling, canoeing/kayaking, downhill skiing, fishing, golf, hiking, horseback riding, live theater, museums, parks, shopping, sporting events, tennis, wineries, golf and Biltmore Estate nearby.

Publicity: *AAA Four-Diamond Award, National Geographic Traveler, Travel Holiday, Charleston Living & Home Design and WLOS TV (ABC).*

"Most outstanding breakfast I've ever had. We were impressed to say the least!"

Applewood Manor Inn

62 Cumberland Cir
Asheville, NC 28801-1718
(828)254-2244 (800)442-2197 Fax:(828)254-0899
E-mail: innkeeper@applewoodmanor.com
Web: www.applewoodmanor.com

Circa 1910. This is a spacious Colonial Revival house furnished comfortably with antiques. Guests can relax in front of the wood-burning fireplace or stroll the inn's two-acre grounds. Accommodations include four guest rooms and a

cottage. Cream-cheese omelets, orange French toast, blueberry pancakes or homemade waffles are some of the delectables that appear on the breakfast menu along with fresh fruits, juices and homemade muffins.

Innkeeper(s): Coby & Johan Verhey. $110-130. 4 rooms with PB, 3 with FP and 1 cottage. Breakfast included in rates. Types of meals: Full bkfst and early coffee/tea. Beds: Q. Reading lamp, ceiling fan and clock radio in room. Air conditioning. Fax, copier, bicycles, parlor games and fireplace on premises. Family reunions hosted. Antiquing, live theater, parks, shopping and Biltmore Estate nearby.

Publicity: *Country Inns and Innsider.*

"It goes without saying—the accommodations and breakfasts are outstanding!"

At Cumberland Falls B&B

254 Cumberland Ave
Asheville, NC 28801
(828)253-4085 (888)743-2557 Fax:(828)253-5566

Circa 1903. This Victorian inn stands on nearly an acre in the historic Montford area of Asheville. The grounds have gardens, waterfalls and ponds with koi and lilies. Inside, hardwood floors, Oriental rugs and spacious light-filled rooms with fresh flowers create a serene ambiance perfect for relaxing. The inn has five guest bedrooms with fireplaces and Jacuzzis. A four-course gourmet breakfast can be served bedside. Guests enjoy delightful offerings like a fresh fruit bowl, pineapple muffins and Belgian waffles with fresh blueberry sauce topped with whipped cream. Home-baked cookies and pastries are available throughout the day. Golfing, biking, horseback riding, hiking and white-water rafting are popular activities. Less rigorous pastimes include touring antique shops, art galleries and wineries. The innkeepers help guests plan day trips to sites like the Thomas Wolfe Memorial.

Innkeeper(s): Patti & Gary Wiles. $125-250. 5 rooms with PB, 5 with FP. Breakfast included in rates. Types of meals: Full gourmet bkfst, early coffee/tea, afternoon tea, snacks/refreshments and room service. Beds: Q. Cable TV, VCR, reading lamp, CD player, ceiling fan, snack bar, clock radio, telephone, turn-down service and hot tub/spa in room. Central air. Spa and fireplace on premises. Weddings and family reunions hosted. Antiquing, art galleries, bicycling, canoeing/kayaking, fishing, golf, hiking, horseback riding, live theater, museums, parks, shopping, tennis, wineries, Biltmore Estates and white-water rafting nearby.

Beaufort House Victorian B&B

61 N Liberty St
Asheville, NC 28801-1829
(828)254-8334 (800)261-2221 Fax:(828)251-2082

Circa 1894. In the Queen Anne Victorian style, this inn rests on two acres of beautifully landscaped grounds, including a tea garden. Offering views of the mountains, the full wraparound porch is festooned with gingerbread trim. Most guest rooms feature Jacuzzi tubs. Ask for the Sarah Davidson Suite where light streams through a handsome fan window onto a king-size canopy bed decked in white Battenburg Lace. There is a sitting area with wing back chairs and a Queen Anne desk. Guests are pampered with a lavish, gourmet breakfast.

Innkeeper(s): Robert & Jacqueline Glasgow. $125-285. 11 rooms. Breakfast and afternoon tea included in rates. Types of meals: Full gourmet bkfst, early coffee/tea and picnic lunch. Beds: KQ. Cable TV, VCR, reading lamp, refrigerator, ceiling fan, snack bar, clock radio, telephone, desk and CD in room. Air conditioning. Fax, parlor games and fireplace on premises. Weddings, small meetings, family reunions and seminars hosted. Amusement parks, antiquing, downhill skiing, fishing, golf, live theater, parks, shopping, sporting events and tennis nearby.

Biltmore Village Inn

119 Dodge St.
Asheville, NC 28803
(828)274-8707 (866)274-8779
E-mail: info@biltmorevillageinn.com
Web: www.biltmorevillageinn.com

Circa 1892. As the gentle breeze blows, enjoy the mountain views from the porch of this historic Queen Anne Victorian. The inn is a county landmark listed in the National Register. Collections of paintings and antique furnishings appropriately reside together. Afternoon tea is served fireside in the parlor for a relaxing respite. Spacious guest bedrooms boast canopy and poster beds, double whirlpool tubs and fireplaces. A satisfying breakfast offers specialties like Caribbean pears, orange raspberry croissants in almond custard, and parmesan souffle with an apple and bacon confit. The enchanting grounds are graced with flowering bushes and trees, boxwoods and perennial gardens. Innkeeper(s): Owen Sullivan and Ripley Hotch. $175-285. 5 rooms with PB, 5 with FP, 1 suite and 1 cottage. Breakfast and afternoon tea included in rates. Types of meals: Full gourmet bkfst, veg bkfst and early coffee/tea. Beds: KQ. Modem hook-up, data port, cable TV, VCR, reading lamp, refrigerator, clock radio, telephone, coffeemaker, desk, hot tub/spa and fireplace in room. Central air. Fax, copier, spa, library, parlor games and fireplace on premises. Antiquing, art galleries, canoeing/kayaking, fishing, golf, hiking, horseback riding, live theater, museums, parks, shopping, tennis, water sports and wineries nearby.

Blake House Inn

150 Royal Pines Dr
Asheville, NC 28704
(828)681-5227 (888)353-5227 Fax:(828)681-0420
E-mail: blakeinn@aol.com
Web: www.blakehouse.com

Circa 1847. Built prior to the Civil War, this Gothic Italianate home was used as a Confederate field hospital during the Civil War. It also is rumored to have been a stop on the Underground Railroad. Each guest room is decorated with antiques, and three rooms include a fireplace. The Lilac Room includes both a fireplace and a clawfoot tub. Gourmet breakfasts include fresh fruit and homemade baked goods followed by an entrée such as crepes stuffed with Chevre, asparagus and Canadian bacon sauced with a sun-dried tomato cream, eggs Charleston or French toast Grand Marnier. The inn is close to the Biltmore Estate and the scenic Blue Ridge Parkway.
Innkeeper(s): Nancy & Terry Rice. $155-225. 6 rooms with PB, 3 with FP, 1 suite and 3 conference rooms. Breakfast included in rates. Types of meals: Full gourmet bkfst, veg bkfst, early coffee/tea, picnic lunch and snacks/refreshments. Beds: KQD. Data port, cable TV, VCR, reading lamp, telephone, desk and voice mail in room. Fax, copier, parlor games, fireplace and laundry facility on premises. Weddings, small meetings, family reunions and seminars hosted. Antiquing, art galleries, bicycling, canoeing/kayaking, downhill skiing, fishing, golf, hiking, horseback riding, live theater, museums, parks, shopping, sporting events, tennis, water sports and wineries nearby.
Publicity: *Lifetime-Intimate Portraits with Andie MacDowell.*

"Wonderful time, wonderful friends, and magnificent food every meal. This is a place to return to many times."

Bridle Path Inn

30 Lookout Rd
Asheville, NC 28804
(828)252-0035 Fax:(828)252-0221
E-mail: fjhalton3@aol.com
Web: www.bridlepathinn.com

Circa 1910. Recently renovated, this secluded English-style country inn is surrounded by mountains and offers a quiet setting overlooking the city. Relax in front of the fireplace in the great room. All the guest bedrooms feature small refrigerators stocked with beverages and Wisconsin cheeses and include a porch or private entrance to a veranda. The Lexington Room also boasts a four-poster bed, clawfoot tub and antique shower. Savor a satisfying breakfast in the dining room or on the third-floor veranda with a panoramic view. The nearby Appalachian Trail is full of adventures.
Innkeeper(s): Fred & Carol Halton. $98-150. 4 rooms with PB. Breakfast included in rates. Types of meals: Full gourmet bkfst, veg bkfst and early coffee/tea. Beds: KQT. Cable TV, reading lamp, refrigerator, ceiling fan, clock radio and telephone in room. Air conditioning. Fax, copier and fireplace on premises. Small meetings and family reunions hosted. Antiquing, art galleries, beach, bicycling, canoeing/kayaking, downhill skiing, fishing, golf, hiking, horseback riding, live theater, museums, parks, shopping, sporting events, tennis and wineries nearby.
Publicity: *Atlanta Magazine.*

Carolina B&B

177 Cumberland Ave
Asheville, NC 28801-1736
(828)254-3608 (888)254-3608
E-mail: info@carolinabb.com
Web: www.carolinabb.com

Circa 1900. Architect Richard Sharp Smith, whose credits include creating homes for such tycoons as George Vanderbilt, designed this home in Asheville's historic Montford district. Bay windows and porches decorate Carolina's exterior. Inside, rooms feature pine floors, high ceilings and many fireplaces. Guest rooms are furnished with antiques and unique collectibles. The expansive breakfasts include fresh breads, fruits, egg dishes and breakfast meats.

Historic Interest: Historic homes abound in the area, including the famed Biltmore House, Thomas Wolfe home and the Carl Sandburg home.
Innkeeper(s): Sue Birkholz & David Feinstein. $95-200. 6 rooms with PB, 5 with FP and 1 cottage. Breakfast and afternoon tea included in rates. Types of meals: Full gourmet bkfst and early coffee/tea. Beds: KQ. Cable TV, reading lamp, ceiling fan and clock radio in room. Air conditioning. Parlor games and telephone on premises. Weddings, small meetings and family reunions hosted. Antiquing, downhill skiing, golf, live theater, parks, shopping and tennis nearby.
Publicity: *Orange County Register, Asheville Citizen-Times, Charlotte and Mid-Atlantic Country.*

"It was like a dream, exactly as we pictured the perfect honeymoon. Excellent host & hostess, very helpful and informative as to local area. Food was wonderful. Rated an A-plus."

Cedar Crest Victorian Inn

674 Biltmore Ave
Asheville, NC 28803-2513
(828)252-1389 (800)252-0310 Fax:(828)253-7667
E-mail: stay@cedarcrestinn.com
Web: www.cedarcrestinn.com

Circa 1891. This Queen Anne mansion is one of the largest and most opulent residences surviving Asheville's 1890s boom. A captain's walk, projecting turrets and expansive verandas welcome guests to lavish interior woodwork created by artisans employed by the Vanderbilts. All rooms are furnished in antiques with satin and lace trappings.
Historic Interest: The inn is in the National Register and is three blocks to the Biltmore Estate.
Innkeeper(s): Rita & Bruce Wightman. $150-285. 12 rooms with PB, 6 with FP, 4 suites and 1 cottage. Breakfast and snacks/refreshments included in rates. Types of meals: Full bkfst. Beds: KQDT. TV, reading lamp, ceiling fan, clock radio, telephone, turn-down service and desk in room. Air conditioning. Fax, parlor games and fireplace on premises. Antiquing, art galleries, fishing, live theater, parks and shopping nearby.
Publicity: *Travel Holiday, New York Times, New Woman, Southern Living, Good Housekeeping, House Beautiful, Country Inns, National Geographic Traveler, Victorian Decorating Magazine, Charlotte Taste Magazine and Smokey Mountain Living Magazine.*

"Cedar Crest is a real beauty and will hold a special place in our hearts."

The Colby House

230 Pearson Dr
Asheville, NC 28801-1614
(828)253-5644 (800)982-2118
E-mail: colbyhouse@cs.com

Circa 1924. This Dutch Colonial home, framed by a white picket fence, welcomes guests to the Montford Historic District, in the National Register. The first level offers a traditional decor with period antiques and hardwood floors. Guest rooms feature queen beds, pretty linens and antiques. The inn's colorful gardens are an inviting place for conversation. Local wildflowers grown within a rock-walled garden provide a setting for relaxation.

Innkeeper(s): Bonnie and Peter Marsh. $125-165. 4 rooms with PB. Types of meals: Full bkfst. Beds: Q. TV on premises.

Publicity: *Asheville Citizen-Times.*

Corner Oak Manor

53 Saint Dunstans Rd
Asheville, NC 28803-2620
(828)253-3525 (888)633-3525
E-mail: info@corneroakmanor.com
Web: www.corneroakmanor.com

Circa 1920. Surrounded by oak, maple and pine trees, this English Tudor inn is decorated with many fine oak antiques and handmade items. Innkeeper Karen Spradley has handstitched something special for each room, and the house features handmade items by local artisans. Breakfast delights include entrees such as Blueberry Ricotta Pancakes, Four Cheese and Herb Quiche and Orange French Toast. When you aren't enjoying local activities, you can sit on the shady deck, relax in the Jacuzzi, play a few songs on the piano or curl up with a good book.

Historic Interest: Biltmore House and Gardens (1/2 mile).

Innkeeper(s): Karen & Andy Spradley. $125-195. 3 rooms with PB and 1 cottage. Breakfast included in rates. Types of meals: Full gourmet bkfst. Beds: Q. Reading lamp, refrigerator, ceiling fan and one cottage with fireplace in room. Air conditioning. Parlor games, telephone, fireplace and Jacuzzi (outdoor) on premises. Family reunions hosted. Antiquing, fishing, live theater, parks and shopping nearby.

"Great food, comfortable bed, quiet, restful atmosphere, you provided it all and we enjoyed it all!"

Dogwood Cottage Inn

40 Canterbury Rd N
Asheville, NC 28801-1560
(828)258-9725

Circa 1910. This Carolina mountain home is located a mile-and-a-half from downtown Asheville, on Sunset Mountain. The veranda, filled with white wicker and floral chintz prints, is the focal point of the inn during summer. It affords tree-top views of the Blue Ridge Mountains. Wing chairs and country pieces accent the inn's gleaming hardwood floors. Breakfast is served in the formal dining room or on the covered porch.

Innkeeper(s): Joan & Don Tracy. $110-125. 4 rooms with PB, 3 with FP. Breakfast included in rates. Types of meals: Full gourmet bkfst and early coffee/tea. Beds: Q. Reading lamp, ceiling fan and desk in room. Air conditioning. TV, pet boarding, telephone and fireplace on premises. Limited handicap access. Weddings and family reunions hosted. Antiquing, downhill skiing, fishing, live theater, parks, shopping, sporting events and water sports nearby.

"Cozy, warm and gracious."

Katherine's Bed & Breakfast

43 Watauga Street
Asheville, NC 28801
(828)236-9494 (888)325-3190 Fax:(828)236-2218
E-mail: lstrongman@earthlink.net
Web: www.katherinesbandb.com

Circa 1904. Honored with The Griffin Award by the preservation society, this 2.5 story Queen Anne Vernacular boasts Colonial Revival details. Innkeeper Ineke's talent for historical restoration, skill in creating a rich, high style and taste for international travel is reflected in the elegant and comfortable decor. Each guest bedroom offers picture-perfect furnishings, air conditioning, robes, down comforter, fireplace and a welcoming teddy bear. The Pine Room boasts a canopy bed, clawfoot tub, hand-stenciled walls and bay window accented with lace and silk. Mahogany pieces in the spacious Sandalwood Room are highlighted by red and camel tones with a blue porcelain collection. Linger over a sumptuous morning meal in the cheery breakfast room before exploring the local area.

Innkeeper(s): Ineke Strongman & Michael Pewther. $110-185. 6 rooms with PB and 1 conference room. Breakfast and snacks/refreshments included in rates. Types of meals: Full gourmet bkfst, early coffee/tea and picnic lunch. Beds: KQD. TV, VCR, reading lamp, stereo, refrigerator, ceiling fan, clock radio, telephone and turn-down service in room. Central air. Fax, tennis, library and gift shop on premises. Weddings, small meetings, family reunions and seminars hosted. Antiquing, art galleries, bicycling, canoeing/kayaking, cross-country skiing, downhill skiing, fishing, golf, hiking, horseback riding, live theater, museums, parks, shopping, tennis, water sports and wineries nearby.

Publicity: *Charlotte Parent Magazine.*

The Lion & The Rose

276 Montford Ave
Asheville, NC 28801-1660
(828)255-7673 (800)546-6988
E-mail: info@lion-rose.com
Web: www.lion-rose.com

Circa 1895. Asheville's Montford Historic District wouldn't be complete without this Queen Anne Georgian, listed in the National Register. Innkeepers Jim and Linda preserve the history of this home with the period decor. The interior is gracious, showcasing the original leaded- and stained-glass windows and tiger oak wood. Afternoon refreshments are served each day, often on the inn's veranda. Memorable breakfasts are served on English china with silver. Fresh flowers and chocolates welcome guests to their well-appointed rooms.

Innkeeper(s): Jim & Linda Palmer. $155-255. 5 rooms with PB and 1 suite. Breakfast and snacks/refreshments included in rates. Types of meals: Full gourmet bkfst. Beds: Q. Cable TV, reading lamp, ceiling fan, clock radio, telephone and robes in room. Air conditioning. Parlor games and fireplace on premises. Small meetings hosted. Antiquing, live theater, parks, shopping, water sports and restaurants nearby.

North Lodge on Oakland

84 Oakland Rd
Asheville, NC 28801-4818
(828)252-6433 (800)282-3602 Fax:(828)252-3034
E-mail: stay@northlodge.com
Web: www.northlodge.com

Circa 1904. Built by an old Asheville family who were descendants of the owners of Smith Plantation, this 1904 three-story stone lodge is only one mile from the Biltmore Estate. Indulge in the pleasures of a cookie bar on the weekends. Comfortable guest bedrooms offer a variety of amenities that include fire-

places, plush terry robes, chocolates and in-room massage.
Crepes, Belgian waffles and
stuffed French toast are enjoyed
for breakfast along with fruits
and fresh-baked breads.

Innkeeper(s): Peggy & Patrick Irwin.
$110-160. 6 rooms with PB. Breakfast
included in rates. Types of meals: Full gourmet bkfst. Beds: KQDT. Cable TV,
reading lamp, clock radio, massages, chocolates and plush terry robes in room.
Air conditioning. Fireplace and cookie bar on weekends on premises. Antiquing,
cross-country skiing, downhill skiing, fishing, golf, live theater, parks, shopping,
sporting events, tennis, water sports and Biltmore Estate nearby.

*"The room was marvelous, breakfasts were delicious, and you cer-
tainly were gracious hosts."*

Old Reynolds Mansion

100 Reynolds Hgts
Asheville, NC 28804
(828)254-0496 (800)709-0496
E-mail: innkeeper@oldreynoldsmansion.com
Web: www.oldreynoldsmansion.com

Circa 1855. This handsome, three-story brick antebellum
mansion is situated on a four-acre knoll of Reynolds Mountain.
Rescued from near ruin by innkeepers Fred and Helen Faber,

the home has been restored
to its former glory as a gracious Southern manor. Each
of the guest quarters reflects a
different style from early
American to Oriental. Guests
can enjoy mountain views
from their own room, by a wood-burning fireplace or on a
rocking chair on the inn's wraparound porch. The mansion
offers use of a swimming pool set among pine trees.

Historic Interest: Several historic homes, including the Biltmore Estate,
Thomas Wolfe home and Carl Sandburg home are a short drive.
Innkeeper(s): Fred & Helen. $90-150. 11 rooms with PB, 5 with FP, 1 suite
and 1 cottage. Breakfast and afternoon tea included in rates. Types of meals:
Full bkfst and veg bkfst. Beds: QDT. Reading lamp, ceiling fan and clock
radio in room. Air conditioning. TV, swimming, library, parlor games, telephone and fireplace on premises. Amusement parks, antiquing, art galleries,
bicycling, canoeing/kayaking, downhill skiing, fishing, golf, hiking, horseback
riding, live theater, museums, parks, shopping, tennis and wineries nearby.
Publicity: Greensboro News & Record and Blue Ridge Country.

*"This was one of the nicest places we have ever stayed. We spent
every sundown on the porch waiting for the fox's daily visit."*

Pinecrest Bed & Breakfast

249 Cumberland Ave.
Asheville, NC 28801-1735
(828)281-4275 (888)811-3053 Fax:(828)281-2215
E-mail: innkeeper@pinecrestbb.com
Web: www.pinecrestbb.com

Circa 1905. Designed by the lead architect for the Biltmore
Estate, this English Tudor features turrets, a front porch and
symmetrical front facade. Common rooms offer comfortable
places to watch videos, relax by the fire or play games.
Afternoon desserts are a pleasurable interlude. Romantic guest
bedrooms reflect a European decor and boast fine linens and
robes. A typical breakfast might include a fresh berry compote topped with custard sauce and granola, apple-stuffed
pancakes with raspberry sauce and apple-cider syrup with
bacon. Relax on the large stone patio that overlooks more

than an acre of lush grounds with native trees and foliage.

Innkeeper(s): Barbara & Richard Newell. $145-175. 4 rooms with PB.
Breakfast and snacks/refreshments included in rates. Types of meals: Full
gourmet bkfst, veg bkfst, early coffee/tea and afternoon tea. Beds: Q. Cable
TV, reading lamp, ceiling fan, turn-down service, desk, guest refrigerator, fine
linens, hair dryers and robes in room. Air conditioning. VCR, fax, copier, parlor games, telephone and fireplace on premises. Weddings hosted. Antiquing,
art galleries, canoeing/kayaking, fishing, golf, hiking, horseback riding, live
theater, museums, parks, shopping and sporting events nearby.

Richmond Hill Inn

87 Richmond Hill Dr
Asheville, NC 28806-3912
(828)252-7313 (800)545-9238 Fax:(828)252-8726
E-mail: info@richmondhillinn.com
Web: www.richmondhillinn.com

Circa 1889. This renovated Victorian mansion was designed
for the Pearson family by James G. Hill, architect of the U.S.
Treasury buildings. The elegant estate features a grand entry
hall, ballroom, library and
10 master fireplaces with
Neoclassical mantels.
Guests may choose from
accommodations in the
luxurious mansion, charm-
ing cottages on a croquet

court, or the garden rooms amid a striking landscape and facing a waterfall. Gabrielle's Restaurant, which is on the premises, serves gourmet cuisine each evening. The inn is listed in the
National Register of Historic Places.

Historic Interest: The Biltmore House and Gardens are 20 minutes away.
The Thomas Wolfe Memorial is about 15 minutes from the home, while Carl
Sandburg home is an hour away.
Innkeeper(s): Susan Michel. $195-495. 36 rooms with PB, 26 with FP, 3
suites and 3 conference rooms. Breakfast and afternoon tea included in rates.
Types of meals: Full bkfst and gourmet dinner. Restaurant on premises. Beds:
KQD. TV, fax, copier, telephone and croquet court on premises. Limited hand-
icap access.
Publicity: Atlanta Journal & Constitution, Southern Living, Victoria, Inn
Country USA, Inn Country Chefs, Robb Report and Southern Accents.

*"A great adventure into history. I am moved to tell you how grateful
we are that you had the foresight and courage to rescue this wonderful place. The buildings and grounds are elegantly impressive ...
and the staff superb! You have created a total experience that fulfills
and satisfies."*

Wright Inn & Carriage House

235 Pearson Dr
Asheville, NC 28801-1613
(828)251-0789 (800)552-5724 Fax:(828)251-0929
E-mail: info@wrightinn.com
Web: www.wrightinn.com

Circa 1899. A true landmark that is timeless in the old-fashioned graciousness and modern conveniences offered, this
gabled Queen Anne boasts an award-winning restoration and
lavish gardens. Gather in the Coleman Parlor and the Drawing
Room with period decor, fireplaces
and inviting activities. Romantic
suites and guest bedrooms feature
distinctive designs; several feature
fireplaces and high-speed Internet.
The three-bedroom Carriage House
is perfect for larger groups or families. Enjoy a gourmet breakfast and

an afternoon social hour. Relax on the large wraparound porch and gazebo.

Historic Interest: The inn and carriage house are listed in the local and national historic registers. The Blue Ridge Parkway, Biltmore House and Smith-McDowell House are only minutes away.

Innkeeper(s): Vicki & Mark Maurer. $140-325. 10 rooms with PB, 4 with FP. Breakfast included in rates. Types of meals: Full gourmet bkfst, early coffee/tea and afternoon tea. Beds: KQDT. Cable TV, reading lamp, clock radio and telephone in room. Central air. Fax, library, parlor games, fireplace, afternoon social hour is included in rates, high-speed Internet and cable TV on premises. Hiking, shopping and water sports nearby.

Bald Head Island   D7

Theodosia's B&B

2 Keelson Row
Bald Head Island, NC 28461
(910)457-6563 (800)656-1812 Fax:(910)457-6055
E-mail: stay@theodosias.com
Web: www.theodosias.com

Circa 1817. For a romantic getaway or a quiet retreat, this historic barrier island at the mouth of the Cape Fear River offers a tranquil beauty. Exquisite accommodations are found at this modern Victorian bed & breakfast inn that boasts a southern elegant decor. Stay in the main inn, Carriage House, or three-story Cottage. Delightful guest bedrooms feature splendid views of the harbor, river, marshes and lighthouse from balconies. In the dining room, breakfast entrees may include favorites such as Eggs Benedict, Caramel Soaked French Toast, Egg Souffle and Belgian Waffles. Relax on porch rockers or swings, explore the sites and trips to the beach by bike or electric golf cart. Enjoy use of the golf course, tennis courts and other club facilities. Chat with new friends over afternoon refreshments. Weddings and special events are popular at this idyllic setting. Innkeeper Gary is also a minister, available for planning and performing a wedding ceremony.

Innkeeper(s): Thompson & Brandy Higgins. $170-275. 13 rooms with PB and 1 suite. Breakfast and snacks/refreshments included in rates. Types of meals: Full bkfst. Beds: KQD. Cable TV, reading lamp, clock radio, telephone and desk in room. Air conditioning. Fax, bicycles and fireplace on premises. Limited handicap access. Weddings, small meetings and family reunions hosted. Fishing, golf, parks, tennis and water sports nearby.

Publicity: *The Thomasville Times, Southern Living, Raleigh News and Observer, Charlotte Observer, Money Magazine and Coastal Living.*

Balsam   B2

Balsam Mountain Inn

PO Box 40
Balsam, NC 28707-0040
(828)456-9498 (800)224-9498 Fax:(828)456-9298
E-mail: balsaminn@earthlink.net
Web: www.balsaminn.com

Circa 1905. This inn, just a quarter mile from the famed Blue Ridge Parkway, is surrounded by the majestic Smoky Mountains. The inn was built in the Neoclassical style and overlooks the scenic hamlet of Balsam. The inn is listed in the National Register of Historic Places and is designated a Jackson County Historic Site. It features a mansard roof and wraparound porches with mountain views. A complimentary full breakfast is served daily, and dinner also is available daily.

Innkeeper(s): Merrily Teasley. $120-180. 50 rooms with PB and 8 suites. Breakfast included in rates. Types of meals: Full gourmet bkfst, early coffee/tea, picnic lunch and gourmet dinner. Restaurant on premises. Beds: KD. Reading lamp and desk in room. Fax, copier, parlor games, fireplace, hiking trails and

wildflower walks on premises. Limited handicap access. Weddings, small meetings, family reunions and seminars hosted. Antiquing, downhill skiing, fishing, parks, shopping, whitewater rafting, hiking and Blue Ridge Pkwy nearby.

"What wonderful memories we have of this beautiful inn."

Banner Elk   B4

1902 Turnpike House

317 Old Turnpike Rd
Banner Elk, NC 28604-7537
(828)898-5611 (888)802-4487 Fax:(828)898-5612
E-mail: info@1902turnpikehouse.com
Web: www.1902turnpikehouse.com

Circa 1902. Located at the foot of Beech Mountain in the high country near Daniel Boone's historic area, this restored farmhouse is also just minutes from Sugar and Grandfather Mountains. Spacious guest bedrooms feature down comforters and are appointed with an eclectic blend of antiques and family treasures. Enjoy an early morning cup of freshly brewed coffee on the covered front porch, or by the fireside when it's cool. Then gather for breakfast around a large farm table set with heirloom china, crystal and vintage sterling silver. Specialty juices, breads and meats accompany chef-prepared gourmet recipes such as Bananas Foster French Toast, Turnpike House Egg Casserole, Fresh Blueberry Pancakes, Ham and Three-cheese Omelets.

Innkeeper(s): Paul & Cindy Goedhart. $79-134. 5 rooms with PB. Breakfast and snacks/refreshments included in rates. Types of meals: Full gourmet bkfst and early coffee/tea. Beds: QDT. Cable TV, reading lamp, ceiling fan, clock radio and desk in room. VCR, fax, spa, telephone, fireplace and guest pantry on premises. Weddings, small meetings and family reunions hosted. Antiquing, art galleries, bicycling, canoeing/kayaking, cross-country skiing, downhill skiing, fishing, golf, hiking, horseback riding, live theater, parks, shopping, sporting events, tennis and water sports nearby.

The Banner Elk Inn B&B and Cottages

407 Main St, E
Banner Elk, NC 28604
(828)898-6223
E-mail: info@bannerelkinn.com
Web: www.bannerelkinn.com

Circa 1912. This rose-colored farmhouse was built originally as a church, but later was remodeled by artist Edna Townsend who transformed it into an inn. The home was abandoned eventually and refurbished by current innkeeper Beverly Lait, who decorated it with international flair, filling each room with antiques and pieces from around the world. Individually decorated rooms feature special items such as an antique brass bed or pewter twin beds, down comforters and bright, airy wallcoverings, lace window dressings and a fabulous new addition room/cottage. For breakfast, Beverly prepares a feast of homemade breads, fresh fruit and mouthwatering entrees such as her sausage and egg casserole and soft cheese pancakes. The inn is a perfect spot to enjoy the natural surroundings of Banner Elk and the Blue Ridge Parkway trails.

Historic Interest: The Mast General Store in Valle Crucis is more than 100 years old.

Innkeeper(s): Beverly Lait. $90-190. 6 rooms, 5 with PB, 2 suites and 4 cottages. Breakfast and afternoon tea included in rates. Types of meals: Full bkfst and room service. Beds: KQT. Cable TV and telephone in room. 2 honeymoon suites on premises. Antiquing, cross-country skiing, downhill skiing, fishing and live theater nearby.

Publicity: *Mountain Getaways, Southern Living, Blue Ridge Country Magazine* and *Atlanta Magazine.*

"You surely have five-star accommodations with five-star attention."

Perry House Bed & Breakfast

153 Klonteska Dr
Banner Elk, NC 28604
(828)898-3535 (877)806-4280 Fax:(828)898-6881
E-mail: perryhouse@skybest.com
Web: www.perryhouse.com

Circa 1910. Enjoy the relaxed ambiance of this Victorian country inn with custom designed furnishings made by local master craftsmen. Relax on a rocker on the wraparound porch looking out on both Grandfather and Sugar Mountains. Choose from a newspaper or magazine to read in the comfortable living room or select a video to watch. Refreshments are always available in the guest refrigerator stocked with snacks and beverages. Spacious guest bedrooms are accented with colorful quilts on beds with down comforters. Stay in the Jennifer Room on the first floor that features a canopy bed, hardwood floor and a scenic view. Some of the popular breakfast favorites include Crunchy French Toast, cheese soufflé, and a variety of egg casseroles. Located just above downtown, it is an easy walk to the village shops and restaurants. The inn's Dunn's Deli serves specialty sandwiches, soups and salads. Ski or play golf nearby.

Historic Interest: Built in the early 1900s, Mr. & Mrs. Frank Perry lived in this home from about 1930 until their deaths in the 1980s. They were well-loved citizens of Banner Elk.

Innkeeper(s): Robin & Mike Dunn. $55-129. 5 rooms with PB. Breakfast and snacks/refreshments included in rates. Types of meals: Full bkfst, veg bkfst and room service. Beds: QDT. Cable TV, VCR, reading lamp and clock radio in room. Fax, copier, parlor games, telephone, fireplace, laundry facility, guest refrigerator, snacks and drinks on premises. Weddings, small meetings, family reunions and seminars hosted. Antiquing, art galleries, bicycling, downhill skiing, fishing, golf, hiking, horseback riding, live theater, parks, shopping and sporting events nearby.

Beaufort   C9

The Cedars Inn

305 Front St
Beaufort, NC 28516-2124
(252)728-7036 Fax:(252)728-1685
Web: www.cedarsinn.com

Circa 1768. The Cedars is comprised of two historic houses, of which, the Main House dates back to 1768. Five of the guest rooms are located in the Main House, and an additional six are located in a restored 1851 house next door. The guest rooms include amenities such as fireplaces, clawfoot tubs, four-poster beds and antiques. All rooms include a private bath, and suites also have a sitting room. The innkeepers also have a honeymoon cottage, which includes a Jacuzzi tub. Both houses include front porches, lined with rocking chairs, on the first and second floors. Hearty breakfasts include such items as banana-walnut pancakes, French toast, croissants, pastries, sausage, bacon, fresh fruit, juices, coffee and tea. The inn has a wine bar featuring a variety of vintages, champagne, beer and non-alcoholic options. The Cedars is located in Beaufort's historic district, and bicycles are available for guests who wish to tour the state's third oldest town.

Historic Interest: The Beaufort Historical Association offers tours of a two-acre complex of historic buildings, including an 1829 jail and a 1796 county courthouse.

Innkeeper(s): Sam & Linda Dark. $135-170. 11 rooms with PB, 5 with FP, 1 cottage and 1 conference room. Breakfast included in rates. Types of meals: Full gourmet bkfst and early coffee/tea. Beds: KQDT. Data port, cable TV, reading lamp, hair dryers and high-speed Internet access in room. Central air.

Fax, copier, bicycles, telephone and fireplace on premises. Weddings, small meetings, family reunions and seminars hosted. Antiquing, art galleries, beach, bicycling, canoeing/kayaking, fishing, golf, horseback riding, live theater, museums, shopping, water sports and diving nearby.
Publicity: *The Washington Post, Greensboro News & Record, Raleigh News & Observer* and *Chatham News.*

Delamar Inn

217 Turner St
Beaufort, NC 28516-2140
(252)728-4300 (800)349-5823
Web: www.bbonline.com/nc/delamarinn/

Circa 1866. The innkeepers, who have lived in Africa, Denmark, Hawaii and Scotland, lend an international touch to this hospitable two-story home, which features wide porches on each level. Each of the guest rooms is decorated to reflect a different style. One of the rooms has an original clawfoot tub.

The innkeepers keep plenty of coffee and tea around and stock comfortable sitting rooms with cookies and fruit for late-night snacking. They also can provide beach chairs and bicycles for guests heading to the beach.

Historic Interest: The Delamar Inn is located in North Carolina's third-oldest town, and historic Fort Macon, built in 1834, guards Beaufort's harbor. The inn is within walking distance of a collection of old buildings preserved by the local historical society. The Maritime Museum is another nearby historic attraction.

Innkeeper(s): Tom & Mabel Steepy. $88-124. 3 rooms with PB. Breakfast included in rates. Types of meals: Cont plus and early coffee/tea. Beds: KQ. Reading lamp, ceiling fan, clock radio and desk in room. Air conditioning. Bicycles, parlor games, telephone, fireplace, beach chairs and coolers and towels on premises. Small meetings and family reunions hosted. Antiquing, fishing, parks, shopping and water sports nearby.

Langdon House

135 Craven St
Beaufort, NC 28516-2116
(252)728-5499
E-mail: innkeeper@costalnet.com
Web: www.langdonhouse.com

Circa 1734. With Colonial Federal design and generous hospitality this 1734 house is Beaufort's oldest running bed and breakfast. Relax on either of the two-story porches with hammocks and rockers. Sit by the fire in the sitting room with polished heartpine flooring. An 1800s Estey organ highlights the parlor. Each first-floor guest bedroom reflects the traditional ambiance of the inn with antique furnishings and decor. Hallmark candlelight breakfasts are served at the huge dining room table on the second floor. Two courses, fresh fruit and yogurt and a house specialty alongside delectable accompaniments are sure to please. Personal preferences and dietary restrictions are gladly accommodated. Stroll through the landscaped country-style garden.

Historic Interest: National Register.

Innkeeper(s): Jimm & Lizzet Prest. $85-142. 4 rooms with PB and 1 conference room. Breakfast and snacks/refreshments included in rates. Types of meals: Full gourmet bkfst, veg bkfst and early coffee/tea. Beds: Q. Reading lamp and clock radio in room. Central air. Fax, bicycles, library, parlor games, telephone, fireplace, laundry facility and beach equipment on premises. Small meetings and family reunions hosted. Amusement parks, antiquing, art galleries, beach, bicycling, canoeing/kayaking, fishing, golf, hiking, horseback riding, museums, parks, shopping, tennis and water sports nearby.
Publicity: *McCalls, Lookout Magazine, Mid-Atlantic Country Magazine, Atlanta Journal* and *Florida Home Journal.*

"Prest is a historian, a guide, a maitre d', a confidant. Your friend."

Pecan Tree Inn B&B

116 Queen St
Beaufort, NC 28516-2214
(252)728-6733 Fax:(252)728-3909
E-mail: innkeeper@pecantree.com
Web: www.pecantree.com

Circa 1866. A few steps from the scenic yacht harbor, this
landmark inn is located in the heart of the historic district.
Built in 1866, the Victorian architecture is enhanced by light-
filled bay windows, antique furnishings and handsome, unclut-

tered decor. Sleep well in distinctive yet comfortable guest
bedrooms. The romantic
Queen Anne bridal suite and
the Beaufort Suite feature King-
size canopy beds and two-person Jacuzzi tubs. Relax on one
of the three porches or stroll through the renowned flower and
herb gardens. Innkeepers David and Allison DuBuisson will
personalize each stay to help you discover all that this delightful seaport has to offer.

$85-160. 7 rooms with PB and 2 suites. Breakfast included in rates. Types
of meals: Cont plus and early coffee/tea. Beds: KQ. Cable TV, reading lamp,
ceiling fan, clock radio, desk and two King/two-person Jacuzzi suites in room.
Air conditioning. Bicycles, library, parlor games and telephone on premises.
Weddings, small meetings and family reunions hosted. Amusement parks,
antiquing, bicycling, fishing, parks, shopping, water sports, beaches, shelling,
boating, kayaking, ecological excursions, jogging and historic tours nearby.
Publicity: *Raleigh News & Observer, Rocky Mtn Telegram, Jacksonville
Scale, Southern Getaway, This Week, Conde Nast, State, Coaster Magazine-
Reader's Choice Award 1998-2001, Southern Living, Birds and Blooms,
ABC - Greenville NC and Video - NC's Best 50 Inns.*

Black Mountain   B3

Red Rocker Inn

136 N Dougherty St
Black Mountain, NC 28711-3326
(828)669-5991 (888)669-5991
E-mail: info@redrockerinn.com
Web: www.redrockerinn.com

Circa 1896. Voted as the best B&B in Asheville, Black
Mountain and all of Western North Carolina for the past four
years, this three-story inn sits on one acre of pristinely landscaped grounds. Located just 14 miles east of Asheville and the
famous Biltmore Estate, discover why the Atlanta Journal
named this inn one of its "Top 12 Favorites in the Southeast."
Elegant, air-conditioned guest bedrooms exude an inviting
ambiance. Many feature fireplaces and whirlpool tubs. Each
morning sit down to a heaping Southern breakfast that is sure
to satisfy. Stroll through gorgeous gardens with a view of the
mountains or relax in front of a roaring fire. Red rockers line
the expansive wraparound porch, a perfect spot to enjoy tea
and hand-dipped macaroons. Special dining packages are available year-round which include homemade specialties and
award-winning desserts.

Innkeeper(s): The Lindberg family. $95-155. 17 rooms with PB, 3 with FP.
Breakfast, afternoon tea and snacks/refreshments included in rates. Types of
meals: Full bkfst, early coffee/tea and dinner. Restaurant on premises. Beds:
KQD. Reading lamp, ceiling fan, desk and five with whirlpool tubs in room.
Air conditioning. Fax, library, parlor games, telephone and fireplace on
premises. Weddings, small meetings, family reunions and seminars hosted.
Antiquing, downhill skiing, fishing, golf, live theater, parks, shopping, tennis
and water sports nearby.

Renee Allen House

303 Montreat Rd
Black Mountain, NC 28711-3119
(828)669-1124 (888)393-7829

Circa 1910. Discover the scenic splendor of this Country
Victorian bed & breakfast that sits in a gorgeous mountain setting. Overlook the gardens while relaxing in the gazebo or on a
front porch rocker. Stay in the Treehouse, a deluxe suite with a
sitting room, fireplace, Roman soaking tub and skylight for
stargazing. A spacious cabin and cottage are also available. Jog
around Lake Tomahawk, play tennis or golf and swim in the
public pool. Browse through the variety of galleries and shops
after a short walk into town. Ask for a brochure from the on-
site Bone-A-Fide Bakery, which makes and ships homemade
treats for pampered pets.

Innkeeper(s): Sandi Rector/Betty Beahan. $115-150. 3 rooms, 3 with FP, 1
suite, 1 cottage and 1 cabin. Beds: QT. Cable TV, VCR, refrigerator, telephone, coffeemaker and central heat in room. Fireplace on premises.
Antiquing, art galleries, bicycling, canoeing/kayaking, cross-country skiing,
downhill skiing, fishing, golf, hiking, horseback riding, live theater, museums,
parks, shopping, sporting events, tennis and wineries nearby.
Publicity: *Black Mountain News.*

Blowing Rock   B4

Blowing Rock Victorian Inn

242 Ransom St
Blowing Rock, NC 28605
(828)295-0034 Fax:(828)263-0200
E-mail: info@blowingrockvictorianinn.com
Web: www.blowingrockvictorianinn.com

Circa 1932. Located in the heart of Blowing Rock, a short walk
from Main Street's shops and a variety of restaurants, this elegantly restored inn offers gables, balconies, porches and a turret, all
set off with white trim and borders of white impatiens. A fetching
Victorian flower garden adds to
the appeal and draws passers-by
to pause and take in the picture-
perfect scene. Baskets of flowers
hang from the balconies, and
each suite has a private entrance,
ceiling fan, deluxe bath, luxurious

comforter and small refrigerator. Two rooms have large Jacuzzi
baths as well as separate showers and there are four rooms with
fireplaces. Spacious decks offer large rockers overlooking the garden. Blowing Rock has been a Blue Ridge resort for more than
100 years and is named for a rock that hangs over a cliff.

Innkeeper(s): Ron & Deb Branch. $99-149. 6 rooms with PB. Beds: KQ.
Cable TV, reading lamp, ceiling fan, snack bar, fireplace, refrigerator and two-
person Jacuzzi tubs in room. Air conditioning. Telephone on premises.
Weddings and family reunions hosted. Amusement parks, antiquing, canoe-
ing/kayaking, cross-country skiing, downhill skiing, fishing, golf, hiking, horseback riding, live theater, parks, shopping, sporting events, tennis, water
sports and craft shows nearby.

Maple Lodge

152 Sunset Dr
Blowing Rock, NC 28605
(828)295-3331
E-mail: innkeeper@maplelodge.net
Web: www.maplelodge.net

Circa 1943. Guests at this village B&B enjoy a 50-year tradition of innkeeping during their stay. Country antiques and family heirlooms fill the rooms. Lace, handmade quilts and down

comforters create a warm, romantic atmosphere in the guest rooms, some of which include canopy beds and fireplaces. The buffet breakfasts are served in the unique Garden Room, which includes a wood-burning stove and stone floor.

Innkeeper(s): Marilyn & David Bateman. $100-200. 11 rooms with PB, 1 suite and 3 conference rooms. Breakfast included in rates. Types of meals: Full bkfst and early coffee/tea. Beds: KQDT. Refrigerator, ceiling fan, clock radio, some with fireplace and TV in room. Air conditioning. Fax, library, parlor games, telephone and fireplace on premises. Weddings, small meetings and family reunions hosted. Amusement parks, antiquing, cross-country skiing, downhill skiing, fishing, live theater, parks, shopping, sporting events and water sports nearby.

Boone   B4

Lovill House Inn

404 Old Bristol Rd
Boone, NC 28607-7678
(828)264-4204 (800)849-9466
E-mail: innkeeper@lovillhouseinn.com
Web: www.lovillhouseinn.com

Circa 1875. A romantic setting, old world charm, southern comfort and hospitality combine at this carefully restored historic farmhouse on eleven secluded acres conveniently located in the heart of the High Country Mountains. Updated guest bedrooms have double-built insulated walls for privacy, robes, oversized towels, turndown service, and an assortment of pleasing amenities. The Spring House is a retreat cottage behing the main farmhouse. Early risers enjoy coffee and tea on the wraparound porch before savoring a breakfast that may include fresh fruit, breads, buttermilk pancakes, eggs with sausage and grits. Dietary requests are honored. Share refreshments by the fire with the innkeepers at the evening hosted social hour.

Innkeeper(s): Scott & Anne Peecook. $115-185. 6 rooms with PB, 3 with FP. Breakfast, afternoon tea and snacks/refreshments included in rates. Types of meals: Full gourmet bkfst, early coffee/tea and picnic lunch. Beds: KQT. Cable TV, VCR, reading lamp, refrigerator, ceiling fan, clock radio, telephone, turn-down service, desk and goose down comforters in room. Spa, library, parlor games, fireplace, streams, waterfalls and gazebo on premises. Weddings, small meetings, family reunions and seminars hosted. Amusement parks, antiquing, cross-country skiing, downhill skiing, fishing, hiking, live theater, parks, shopping, sporting events, water sports, Blue Ridge Parkway, Grandfather Mountain and Appalachian State University nearby.

Publicity: *Raleigh News & Observer, Asheville Citizen-Times, Charlotte Observer, Charlotte Taste and NY Times.*

"From the moment we walked in the door, we were treated and pampered like royalty! We will return."

Brevard   C3

Red House Inn B&B

412 W Probart St
Brevard, NC 28712-3620
(828)884-9349

Circa 1851. Originally built as a trading post, this inn was also the county's first post office and railroad station. It survived the Civil War and years of neglect. Recently renovated, it is furnished with Victorian antiques. The center of town is four blocks away.

Innkeeper(s): Peter & Marilyn Ong. $69-125. 5 rooms, 4 with PB, 1 with FP, 2 suites and 1 cottage. Breakfast included in rates. Types of meals: Full bkfst and afternoon tea. Beds: QDT. TV, reading lamp, ceiling fan and desk in room. Air conditioning. VCR, telephone and fireplace on premises. Limited handicap access. Weddings, small meetings and family reunions hosted. Antiquing, fishing, golf, live theater, parks, tennis, horseback riding and hiking nearby.

Publicity: *The Transylvania Times.*

"Lovely place to stay - clean and bright."

Bryson City   B2

Folkestone Inn

101 Folkestone Rd
Bryson City, NC 28713-7891
(828)488-2730 (888)812-3385 Fax:(828)488-0722
E-mail: innkeeper@folkestone.com
Web: www.folkestone.com

Circa 1926. This farmhouse is constructed of local stone and rock. Pressed-tin ceilings, stained-glass windows and clawfoot tubs remain. The dining room, where breakfast and Saturday night dinner is served, features floor-to-ceiling windows on all sides with views of the mountains. There is a stream with a rock bridge on the property as well
as a garden, and you can walk 10 minutes to waterfall views in the Great Smoky Mountains National Park. All day cookies, snacks, coffee, tea, soft drinks and an optional multi-course dinner available Saturday nights.

Innkeeper(s): Kay Creighton and Peggy Myles. $88-148. 10 rooms with PB. Breakfast included in rates. Types of meals: Full bkfst and snacks/refreshments. Beds: KQ. Reading lamp and central heat in room. Central air. Fax, copier and telephone on premises. Weddings, small meetings, family reunions and seminars hosted. Antiquing, fishing, horseback riding, shopping, tubing, rafting, hiking, scenic train and mountain biking nearby.

Publicity: *Asheville Citizen-Times, Atlanta Journal, Lakeland and Palm Beach Post.*

Randolph House Country Inn

223 Fryemont Rd, PO Box 816
Bryson City, NC 28713-0816
(828)488-3472 (800)480-3472
Web: www.randolphhouse.com

Circa 1895. Randolph House is a mountain estate tucked among pine trees and dogwoods, near the entrance of Great Smoky Mountain National Park. Antiques, some original to the house, fill this National Register home. Each guest room is appointed in a different color scheme. The house provides an unforgettable experience, not the least of which is the gourmet dining provided on the terrace or in the dining room.

Historic Interest: In the National Register.

Innkeeper(s): Bill & Ruth Randolph Adams. $75-150. 7 rooms, 3 with PB, 4 with FP, 1 cottage and 1 conference room. Breakfast included in rates. Types of meals: Country bkfst and dinner. Restaurant on premises. Beds: KQD. Reading lamp and desk in room. Air conditioning. TV, library, parlor games, telephone and fireplace on premises. Small meetings, family reunions and seminars hosted. Amusement parks, antiquing, bicycling, canoeing/kayaking, fishing, golf, hiking, horseback riding, parks, shopping and tennis nearby.

Publicity: *New York Times and Tourist News.*

"Very enjoyable, great food."

Burnsville   B3

The Nuwray Inn

Town Square PO Box 156
Burnsville, NC 28714
(828)682-2329 (800)368-9729 Fax:(828)682-1113
E-mail: nuwrayinn@aol.com
Web: www.nuwrayinn.com

Circa 1833. Surrounded by the scenic Blue Ridge Mountains, this Colonial Revival is the oldest continuously operated inn in the western part of the state. The quaint atmosphere is enhanced by the lobby's large fireplace and the comfortable parlor. The elegant guest bedrooms are decorated with country furnishings. Breakfast includes authentic Southern regional fare. Relax in the rocking chairs on the first- and second-floor porches while planning the day's delightful explorations. The changing seasons offer extraordinary beauty and an array of sites, sports and activities.

Historic Interest: Thomas Wolfe Home, Biltmore Estate (Asheville, 45 minutes), Jonesborough, Tennessee (1 hour).

Innkeeper(s): Rosemary & Chuck Chandler. $80-100. 26 rooms, 21 with PB. Breakfast included in rates. Types of meals: Country bkfst, early coffee/tea, afternoon tea and dinner. Restaurant on premises. Beds: KQDT. Cable TV, reading lamp, ceiling fan and antiques in room. Fax, parlor games, telephone and fireplace on premises. Limited handicap access. Weddings, small meetings, family reunions and seminars hosted. Antiquing, art galleries, bicycling, canoeing/kayaking, downhill skiing, fishing, golf, hiking, horseback riding, live theater, parks, shopping, tennis, water sports, Scottish festival, Gemstone festival, arts and crafts fairs and Cherokee casino nearby.

Publicity: *Our State, Blue Ridge Mountains Guide, 20/20 and North Carolina Now.*

Candler   B3

Owl's Nest Inn at Engadine

2630 Smokey Park Hwy
Candler, NC 28715-9365
(828)665-8325 (800)665-8868 Fax:(878)667-2539
E-mail: info@engadine.com

Circa 1885. This Queen Anne Victorian has been gloriously preserved, still featuring the original heart-of-pine woodwork that in some rooms runs from floor to ceiling. A few of the rooms still contain the original marble-topped sinks. The home was built and designed by a Confederate cavalry officer. The sur-

rounding mountains and forests create a peaceful setting, and guests can enjoy the scenery from a veranda or perhaps on a stroll through the four-acre grounds. Four-poster beds, clawfoot or whirlpool tubs, canopies and stunning views are what guests might find in their rooms. Frittatas, stuffed French toast, Caribbean pears and freshly baked muffins are among the breakfast fare, which is served on fine china in the gracious dining room. The home is minutes away from Asheville, and guests can visit the Biltmore Estate or take a drive down the Blue Ridge Parkway.

Historic Interest: The home was built in 1885 and it had running water, central heat, direct electricity and refrigeration. It was built by a Captain in the Civil War.

Innkeeper(s): Marg Dente & Gail Kinney. $120-195. 5 rooms, 4 with PB, 1 with FP, 1 suite and 1 conference room. Breakfast, afternoon tea and snacks/refreshments included in rates. Types of meals: Country bkfst, veg bkfst, early coffee/tea, gourmet lunch, picnic lunch and room service. Beds: KQT. Modem hook-up, data port, cable TV, VCR, reading lamp, stereo, refrigerator, ceiling fan, snack bar, clock radio, telephone, coffeemaker, desk, hot tub/spa, fireplace and views in room. Central air. Fax, copier, spa, library, parlor games and fireplace on premises. Weddings, small meetings, family reunions and seminars hosted. Antiquing, art galleries, bicycling, canoeing/kayaking, cross-country skiing, downhill skiing, fishing, golf, hiking, horseback riding, live theater, museums, parks, shopping, sporting events, tennis, water sports and wineries nearby.

Publicity: *Received 2002 Award for best top 15 best B&Bs that perform Murder Mysteries by Arrington, accepted into Fodor's Best B&B of America Book for 2001, HGTV and If Walls Could Talk.*

Carthage   C6

Lauren's Haven

108 W Barrett St
Carthage, NC 28327
(910)947-2633
E-mail: laurens-haven@mindspring.com
Web: www.laurens-haven.com

Circa 1893. This late 1800s Colonial Revival home celebrates early America with its traditional décor. Also known as The Rose-Hurwitz House, the home received its second story in 1930 and became a bed & breakfast in 1996. The home derives its name from the two families who built and remodeled it — the Roses and the Hurwitzes. Arrangements are delicately crafted for honeymoons and anniversaries, including a private couple's breakfast in the upstairs sun room. Each guest room is tastefully decorated in its own distinct color scheme and style, complete with a private sitting room and bath. A continental breakfast of muffins, biscuits, poached eggs and seasonal fruit helps start each morning off on the right foot. Just as enjoyable as the house itself are the grounds it rests upon, featuring a small walking garden and fishpond.

Innkeeper(s): Richard & Shaw Oldham. $75. 3 rooms with PB. Breakfast and snacks/refreshments included in rates. Types of meals: Full bkfst. Beds: QT. Cable TV, reading lamp, clock radio and telephone in room. Central air. VCR, fax and parlor games on premises. Small meetings hosted. Antiquing, golf and Asheboro Zoo nearby.

Publicity: *The Pilot.*

Chapel Hill   B6

The Inn at Bingham School

PO Box 267
Chapel Hill, NC 27514-0267
(919)563-5583 (800)566-5583 Fax:(919)563-9826
E-mail: fdeprez@aol.com
Web: www.chapel-hill-inn.com

Circa 1790. This inn served as one of the locations of the famed Bingham School. This particular campus was the site of a liberal arts preparatory school for those aspiring to attend the University at Chapel Hill. The inn is listed as a National Trust

property and has garnered awards for its restoration. The property still includes many historic structures including a 1790s log home, an 1801 Federal addition, an 1835 Greek Revival

home, the headmaster's office, which was built in 1845, and a well house, smokehouse and milk house. Original heart of pine floors are found throughout the inn. Guests can opt to stay in the Log Room, located in the log cabin, with a tight-winder staircase and fireplace. Other possibilities include Rusty's Room with two antique rope beds. The suite offers a bedroom glassed in on three sides. A mix of breakfasts are served, often including pear almond Belgian waffles, quiche or souffles.

Historic Interest: The Orange County Historical Museum is 12 miles from the inn. The Durham Homestead is 20 miles away, and the Horace Williams House and North Carolina Collection Gallery are 10 miles away.

Innkeeper(s): Francois & Christina Deprez. $85-135. 5 rooms with PB, 4 with FP, 1 suite, 1 cottage and 1 conference room. Breakfast and snacks/refreshments included in rates. Types of meals: Full gourmet bkfst and early coffee/tea. Beds: QD. Reading lamp, clock radio, telephone, desk, hair dryers and robes in room. Air conditioning. VCR, fax, library, parlor games, fireplace, trails and hammocks on premises. Weddings and small meetings hosted. Antiquing, fishing, live theater, parks, shopping, sporting events and water sports nearby.

Publicity: *Southern Inns, Mebane Enterprise, Burlington Times, Times News and Washington Post.*

Charlotte C5

The Homeplace B&B

5901 Sardis Rd
Charlotte, NC 28270-5369
(704)365-1936 Fax:(704)366-2729

Circa 1902. Follow the winding drive to a storybook setting and enchanting home on two and one-half wooded acres in South Charlotte, just six miles from uptown. Sitting amidst the trees, this restored 1902 Country/Victorian was established as a bed & breakfast twenty years ago by owners and innkeepers, Frank and Peggy. Relax on the wraparound porch with a soft drink. Inside the home, a grand foyer has an unusual front and back stairway. Ten-foot ceilings, intricately carved mantels, heart pine floors and woodwork are  featured throughout. Inviting guest bedrooms offer a comfortable décor and spaciousness. Before breakfast, sip early morning coffee while strolling down brick walkways to sit in the garden gazebo overlooking the pond. SouthPark and Phillips Place are popular major shopping and dining areas less than three miles away.

Innkeeper(s): Peggy and Frank Dearien. $95-125. 3 rooms with PB. Breakfast included in rates. Types of meals: Full bkfst and early coffee/tea. Beds: Q. Cable TV, reading lamp, ceiling fan, clock radio, desk, non-working fireplace and comfortable seating with reading lamp in room. Central air. Fax and telephone on premises. Antiquing, art galleries, golf, live theater, museums, parks, shopping and sporting events nearby.

Publicity: *Charlotte Observer, Birmingham News, Country, Southern Living's Weekend Vacations and American Historic Cookbook.*

"Everything was perfect. The room was superb, the food excellent!"

The Morehead Inn

1122 E Morehead St
Charlotte, NC 28204-2815
(704)376-3357 (888)667-3432 Fax:(704)335-1110

Circa 1917. This old-fashioned Southern house is set on a huge corner lot dotted with oaks and azaleas. Guests gather in the great room, library and dining room, all furnished with English and American antiques. Balconies, canopy and four-poster beds and whirlpool tubs are among the amenities offered in some of the rooms. The Solarium Suite is a favorite choice.

Historic Interest: Reed Gold Mine (20 miles), Latta Plantation (5 miles), James K. Polk Memorial (8 miles).

Innkeeper(s): Billy Maddalon, Helen Price. $120-190. 12 rooms with PB, 1 with FP. Breakfast included in rates. Types of meals: Cont plus and early coffee/tea. Beds: KQ. Cable TV, reading lamp, ceiling fan, clock radio, telephone, turn-down service, desk, fireplace and voice mail on phones and database ports in rooms in room. Air conditioning. TV, VCR, fax, copier, parlor games, fireplace and passes to YMCA on premises. Weddings, small meetings, family reunions and seminars hosted. Antiquing, fishing, golf,

live theater, parks, shopping, sporting events and tennis nearby.
Publicity: *Business Journal, New York Times, Charlotte Observer and Carolina Bride.*

"What a great historic neighborhood."

Clinton C7

Courthouse Inn

102 E. Faison Street
Clinton, NC 28328-3402
(910)592-3933 (800)463-9817 Fax:(910)592-2929
Web: www.clintonlodging.com

Circa 1818. Serving the county as a courthouse for almost a century, this Classic Greek Revival building was restored using many original details including the hand-hewn front door and wooden tongue-in-groove ceiling. Renovations have allowed for handicap accessibility, modern amenities and technology in the impressive guest bedrooms. Each accommodation boasts computer phone lines, microwave, refrigerator, hair dryer, iron and board. A laundry facility is available. Savor a breakfast that reflects Southern hospitality at its best. Relax on the wraparound porch. Enjoy golf privileges at a local course.

Innkeeper(s): Glenn & Juanita McLamb and Anita Green. $75-150. 8 rooms with PB and 1 cottage. Breakfast and snacks/refreshments included in rates. Types of meals: Country bkfst, veg bkfst and early coffee/tea. Beds: KQD. Cable TV, VCR, reading lamp, refrigerator, ceiling fan, clock radio, telephone, coffeemaker, desk, microwave, hair dryer and iron/ironing board in room. Central air. Fax, copier, laundry facility, concrete parking area, drinks and snacks on premises. Limited handicap access. Antiquing, canoeing/kayaking, fishing, golf and live theater nearby.

Publicity: *Sampson Independent, Fayetteville Observer and WECT-Wilimington.*

Durham B6

Blooming Garden Inn

513 Holloway St
Durham, NC 27701-3457
(919)687-0801 (888)687-0801 Fax:(919)688-1401
E-mail: bloominggardeninn@msn.com
Web: www.bloominggardeninn.com

Circa 1890. Blooming Garden is an apt name for this bed & breakfast, as the inn is surrounded by colorful gardens. The exterior is dotted with a bright mix of perennials and annuals. The inn is located in the Holloway Historic District in downtown Durham. Each guest room is artfully appointed with a different, colorful theme. For instance, the Tiffany Room is accentuated with stained-glass pieces. The Moroccan Room is dressed in dramatic hues of dark green, gold and red. Each room offers a special bed, as well. Most impressive is the mid-19th-century carved Rosewood bed in the Morning Glory Suite. The inn's luxury suites include a double Jacuzzi tub. Homemade ginger waffles topped with a creamy lemon curd are among the specialties served for breakfast. For guests planning an extended stay in the area, the innkeepers offer accommodations in Holly House, a nicely furnished, restored Victorian home. The home includes a suite and three guest rooms, common areas, access to a kitchen, phone, washer and dryer. Although the beds are topped with goose down pillows, the innkeepers are sensitive to those with allergies and can accommodate guests' needs.

Innkeeper(s): Dolly & Frank Pokrass. $110-225. 4 rooms with PB, 4 with FP and 2 suites. Breakfast included in rates. Types of meals: Full gourmet bkfst and early coffee/tea. Beds: QD. Cable TV, reading lamp, stereo, ceiling fan, clock radio, telephone, desk and suites have 2-person Jacuzzi in room. Air conditioning. VCR, fax, copier, library, parlor games and fireplace on premises. Weddings, small meetings and family reunions hosted. Antiquing, live theater, parks, sporting events, many excellent restaurants and Durham Bulls ball park nearby.

Publicity: *Southern Living, Travel & Leisure, National Geographic, Travel Magazine* and Mobil Guide Book.

Flat Rock   A5

Highland Lake Inn - A Country Retreat

180 Highland Lake Rd.
Flat Rock, NC 28731
(828)693-6812 (800)635-5101 Fax:(828)696-8951
E-mail: btaylor@HLInn.com
Web: www.HLInn.com

Circa 1900. A great place for families, this country farm setting features acres of activities. Besides a visit to the goat barn or watching for the resident peacock, canoe the lake, hike, swim, bike, play volleyball or horseshoes. The inn offers romantic guest bedrooms, some with whirlpool tubs or French doors leading to a porch with rockers. A rustic lodge with cozy rooms and private baths boasts a river rock fireplace in the lobby, billiards and table tennis in the recreation room. There are ten cabin rooms. Cottages with two to four bedrooms have kitchen facilities and some include a washer, dryer and large outside deck. The restaurant boasts an award-winning wine list and meals are made with fresh organic ingredients from the gardens. Explore local Carl Sandburg's home or Flat Rock Playhouse and historic sites in nearby Hendersonville. The Biltmore Estate is 28 miles away.

Innkeeper(s): Jack & Linda Grup. $89-399. 63 rooms, 36 with PB, 17 with FP, 1 suite, 16 cottages, 10 cabins and 3 conference rooms. Breakfast included in rates. Types of meals: Country bkfst, gourmet lunch, picnic lunch and gourmet dinner. Restaurant on premises. Beds: KQT. Modem hook-up, data port, cable TV, reading lamp, refrigerator, ceiling fan, clock radio, telephone, coffeemaker, desk, voice mail and some with fireplace in room. Air conditioning. VCR, fax, copier, swimming, bicycles, tennis, parlor games, fireplace, gift shop, a variety of conference facilities, yoga studio and in-room massage available by appointment on premises. Weddings, small meetings, family reunions and seminars hosted. Antiquing, art galleries, bicycling, canoeing/kayaking, fishing, golf, hiking, horseback riding, live theater, parks, shopping and wineries nearby.

Publicity: *Southern Living, The Southern Gardener, Wine Spectator Magazine (recipient of "Award of Excellence" for having one of the best restaurant wine lists in the world)* and PBS.

Franklin   C2

Franklin Terrace

159 Harrison Ave
Franklin, NC 28734-2913
(704)524-7907 (800)633-2431

Circa 1887. This plantation home, built originally to house a school, is listed in the National Register of Historic Places. Each of the guest rooms features period antiques. The innkeepers also offer a cottage that can sleep up to four quite comfortably. Those opting to stay in the historic home are treated to a lavish, breakfast buffet with home-baked muffins, french toast, cereals, juices, fruit, melon, sausages, poached eggs and several different breads. The home is within walking distance to shops, clothing boutiques and a variety of restaurants, but guests are welcome to simply sit and relax on the veranda, which is lined with wicker rocking chairs.

Innkeeper(s): Ed & Helen Henson. $52-75. 9 rooms with PB and 1 cottage.

Breakfast included in rates. Types of meals: Full bkfst and early coffee/tea. Beds: KQD. Cable TV, reading lamp and ceiling fan in room. Air conditioning. Telephone and fireplace on premises. Small meetings, family reunions and seminars hosted. Downhill skiing, fishing, live theater, parks and water sports nearby.

"We just 'discovered' this wonderful B&B on a trip home from the mountains of North Carolina. The inn offers privacy, porches, unique rooms, comfort, cleanliness and is very pretty."

Fuquay-Varina   B7

Fuquay Mineral Spring Inn and Garden

333 South Main Street
Fuquay-Varina, NC 27526
(919)552-3782 (866)552-3782 Fax:(919)552-5229
E-mail: jbyrne@fuquayinn.com
Web: www.fuquayinn.com

Circa 1927. Sitting on a hill across from the historic mineral springs and town park, this Colonial Revival bed & breakfast is a landmark in the National Register District. The formal main parlor, perfect for chess, cards or social gatherings, boasts a crafted brass chandelier, fluted Doric columns, a grand staircase and a warm fireplace. The sunroom provides a large-screen TV as well as views of the side garden and gazebo. Antique furnishings, large windows with plantation shutters and delightful decorative touches highlight the guest bedrooms. The spacious Cardinal Suite and adjoining sitting room boast original artwork and a nostalgic ambiance. Savor a traditional Southern breakfast in the formal dining room or adjacent library. Casual fare may be enjoyed on the porch for a more intimate setting. Special diets are accommodated.

Innkeeper(s): John & Patty Byrne. $90-150. 4 rooms, 3 with PB, 1 suite and 1 conference room. Breakfast, afternoon tea and snacks/refreshments included in rates. Types of meals: Full gourmet bkfst, veg bkfst, early coffee/tea and room service. Beds: QDT. Modem hook-up, data port, cable TV, VCR, reading lamp, stereo, refrigerator, ceiling fan, snack bar, clock radio, telephone, coffeemaker, turn-down service, desk, hot tub/spa and fireplace in room. Central air. Fax, copier, spa, bicycles, library, parlor games, fireplace, laundry facility, gift shop and gardens on premises. Weddings, small meetings, family reunions and seminars hosted. Amusement parks, antiquing, art galleries, bicycling, canoeing/kayaking, fishing, golf, hiking, horseback riding, live theater, museums, parks, shopping, sporting events, tennis, water sports and wineries nearby.

Gibsonville   B6

Burke Manor Inn

303 Burke Street
Gibsonville, NC 27249
(336)449-6266 (888)BUR-KE11 Fax:(336)449-9440
E-mail: info@burkemanor.com
Web: www.burkemanor.com

Circa 1906. Blending the warmth of exceptional hospitality with prestigious service, this historic Victorian bed & breakfast inn features luxurious surroundings, quality reproductions and a comfortable atmosphere. Lavish suites include upscale amenities for the leisure and business traveler alike. Breakfast reflects the quality of food that has given the inn's restaurant a reputation for fine dining. Play tennis, then swim in the heated pool or soak tired muscles in the hot tub. The 3.5 acres provide a peaceful setting for beautiful garden weddings. It is an easy walk from the inn to downtown sites and shops.

Historic Interest: Built in 1906 by the Cone Family, textile magnates. Mr. JW Burke funded the Gibsonville bank during the depression. Mrs. PT Burke founded the NC PTA and had the state office here. Nat King Cole and Natalie (as a little girl) stayed in the Burke home on numerous occassions.

Innkeeper(s): Vernon & Lynn Brady. $89-199. 7 rooms with PB, 1 suite and 2 conference rooms. Breakfast and snacks/refreshments included in rates. Types of meals: Full gourmet bkfst, veg bkfst and early coffee/tea. Beds: KQ. Modem hook-up, cable TV, reading lamp, stereo, ceiling fan, snack bar, clock radio, telephone, desk, hot tub/spa, voice mail, high thread count pressed linens, plush robes, candles, heated pool and breakfast in room. Central air. Fax, copier, swimming, tennis, parlor games, 4,800-square-foot wedding reception pavilion and gift shop on premises. Weddings, small meetings, family reunions and seminars hosted. Amusement parks, antiquing, art galleries, bicycling, canoeing/kayaking, fishing, golf, hiking, live theater, museums, parks, shopping, sporting events, tennis and water sports nearby.
Publicity: *Greensboro News and Record, Burlington Times News, Crossroads Journal, WFMY TV 2 and WBAG 1150AM.*

Grassy Creek   A4

River House

1896 Old Field Creek Rd
Grassy Creek, NC 28631
(336)982-2109
E-mail: riverhouse@skybest.com
Web: www.riverhousenc.com

Circa 1870. Cradled in the Blue Ridge Mountains overlooking the New River, this country inn and restaurant is an ideal place for weekend getaways, honeymoons, vacations, corporate retreats and business seminars. Open year-round, relax on front

porch rockers or in a comfy chair by a warm log fire. Choose a guest bedroom with a Jacuzzi and a private porch in the 1870 farmhouse, or stay in a secluded, spacious cabin by the millpond. After waking up to morning coffee or tea, a sublime breakfast is

served in the renowned restaurant. A mile of riverfront offers wading, fishing, tubing and canoeing. Play tennis on one of the two full-size courts or walk the landscaped trails that meander through the 180 acres. A full service bar offers an extensive wine selection to enhance a wonderful dinner. Live music and entertainment is an occasional treat.
Innkeeper(s): Gayle Winston, John Stewart. $115-150. 9 rooms with PB, 6 with FP, 4 suites, 1 cottage, 2 cabins and 3 conference rooms. Breakfast included in rates. Types of meals: Full gourmet bkfst, early coffee/tea, gourmet lunch, picnic lunch, afternoon tea, gourmet dinner and room service. Restaurant on premises. Beds: KQT. Reading lamp, refrigerator, ceiling fan, clock radio, desk, hot tub/spa and whirlpool tubs in room. VCR, fax, copier, spa, swimming, tennis, library, parlor games, telephone and fireplace on premises. Weddings, small meetings, family reunions and seminars hosted. Antiquing, canoeing/kayaking, cross-country skiing, downhill skiing, fishing, golf, hiking, live theater, parks, shopping, sporting events, tennis and water sports nearby.

Greensboro   B6

Andrea's Troy-Bumpas Inn B&B

114 S Mendenhall St
Greensboro, NC 27403
(336)370-1660 (800)370-9070 Fax:(336)370-1970
E-mail: troybumpas@earthlink.net
Web: www.troy-bumpasinn.com

Circa 1847. As General Sherman marched through the South on his way to Atlanta, some of his Union soldiers occupied this home. The grand Greek Revival home was built by Rev. Sidney Bumpas, and for 20 years, a Methodist newspaper was published here. The interior, often showcased on local historic home tours, has been restored to its former glory. The four

guest rooms are decorated in a nostalgic, romantic style. One room contains a 19th-century mahogany bed with beautifully carved woodwork, another room offers a fireplace, clawfoot tub and bed draped in luxurious linens.

The innkeepers offer two breakfast choices, one a light meal with fruits and homemade breads or a full Southern feast featuring items such as banana waffles topped with praline sauce. The home, listed in the National Register, is located in Greensboro's historic College Hill district.
Innkeeper(s): Andrea Wimmer. $95-120. 3 rooms with PB, 1 with FP and 1 conference room. Breakfast and snacks/refreshments included in rates. Types of meals: Full bkfst and early coffee/tea. Beds: KQ. Clock radio, telephone, turn-down service and desk in room. Air conditioning. VCR and fireplace on premises. Weddings, small meetings and family reunions hosted. Antiquing, golf, live theater, parks, shopping and sporting events nearby.
Publicity: *News & Record and North Carolina Tastefull Magazine.*

"You both know how to spoil people rotten."

Hendersonville   C3

Claddagh Inn

755 N Main St
Hendersonville, NC 28792-5079
(828)697-7778 (800)225-4700 Fax:(828)697-8664
E-mail: innkeepers@claddaghinn.com
Web: www.claddaghinn.com/

Circa 1898. Claddagh has been host for more than 90 years to visitors staying in Hendersonville. The wide, wraparound veranda is filled with rocking chairs, while the library is filled with inviting books. Many of North Carolina's finest craft and antique shops are just two blocks from the inn. Carl Sandburg's house and the Biltmore Estate are nearby, and within a short drive are spectacular sights in the Great Smoky Mountains.
Historic Interest: National Register.
Innkeeper(s): Vanessa Mintz. $100-150. 14 rooms with PB and 2 suites. Breakfast included in rates. Types of meals: Full bkfst and early coffee/tea. Beds: KQDT. Reading lamp, ceiling fan, telephone and TVs in room. Air conditioning. TV, fax, library, parlor games, fireplace, refrigerator and TV on premises. Weddings, small meetings and family reunions hosted. Antiquing, fishing, live theater, parks, shopping, water sports, tennis and golf nearby.
Publicity: *Country Inn, Blue Ridge Country and Southern Living.*

"Excellent food, clean, home-like atmosphere."

Inn on Church Street

201 3rd Ave W
Hendersonville, NC 28739
(828)693-3258 (800)330-3836 Fax:(828)693-7263
E-mail: innonchurch@innspiredinns.com
Web: www.innspiredinns.com

Circa 1920. Restored to its original splendor, this classy yet cozy Craftsman and Art Deco inn sits in the heart of historic downtown, just one block from Main Street. Guests are greeted with fresh-baked cookies around check-in time, and the pleasures continue with a late afternoon social and turndown service. Guest bedrooms and suites offer a plethora of decor including folk art, French Country, Americana, bunnies, golf, Christmas, jungle, horses, birds and teddy bears. An upscale breakfast may include almond croissant French toast, Church Street eggs of the day, or spiced pancakes. Relax on the wide, wraparound porch and enjoy the whimsically decorated gardens.

Innkeeper(s): Mike & Rhonda Horton. $89-199. 21 rooms with PB, 2 suites and 2 conference rooms. Breakfast, afternoon tea and snacks/refreshments included in rates. Types of meals: Full gourmet bkfst, veg bkfst, early coffee/tea, gourmet lunch and gourmet dinner. Beds: KQ. Modem hook-up, data port, cable TV, reading lamp, CD player, refrigerator, ceiling fan, clock radio, telephone, coffeemaker, turn-down service, desk, voice mail and hot tub in room. Air conditioning. Fax, copier, spa, parlor games, fireplace, afternoon social hour, cookies upon check-in and lunch and dinner served Tuesday-Saturday on premises. Limited handicap access. Weddings, small meetings, family reunions and seminars hosted. Antiquing, art galleries, bicycling, canoeing/kayaking, downhill skiing, fishing, golf, hiking, horseback riding, live theater, museums, parks, shopping, sporting events, tennis and wineries nearby.

Publicity: *Our State Magazine, Times News and Asheville Citizen Times.*

Melange Bed & Breakfast

1230 5th Ave W
Hendersonville, NC 28739-4112
(828)697-5253 (800)303-5253 Fax:(828)697-5751
E-mail: mail@melangebb.com
Web: www.melangebb.com

Circa 1920. Classical gardens and fountains bordered by hemlock hedges and century-old trees accent this stately New England Colonial home with an elegant European flair. Listed in the National Register, it is furnished with antiques and boasts an eclectic melange of French Mediterranean decor. Luxurious guest bedrooms are named after their color scheme and feature posh wall and window coverings, colorful Anatolian rugs, Turkish bathrobes, refrigerators and feather beds with down comforters. The romantic, two-bedroom Rose Suite includes a Jacuzzi, big screen TV, surround stereo/CD as well as a large living and sitting area. Stay in the art deco Green Room with private porch and wood fireplace. Gourmet breakfasts are a delightful experience served alfresco in the rose garden patio or by candlelight in the greenhouse room.

Innkeeper(s): Lale & Mehmet Ozelsel. $105-185. 5 rooms, 4 with PB, 1 suite and 1 conference room. Breakfast, afternoon tea and snacks/refreshments included in rates. Types of meals: Full gourmet bkfst, veg bkfst, gourmet lunch, picnic lunch and room service. Beds: KQD. Modem hook-up, cable TV, VCR, reading lamp, stereo, refrigerator, ceiling fan, clock radio, coffeemaker, desk, hot tub/spa, fireplace, DVD and balcony in room. Central air. Fax, copier, library, parlor games, telephone, fireplace, gardens and patio/porch on premises. Weddings, small meetings, family reunions and seminars hosted. Antiquing, art galleries, bicycling, canoeing/kayaking, fishing, golf, hiking, horseback riding, live theater, museums, parks, shopping, tennis and wineries nearby.

Publicity: *Hendersonville Times News.*

Hertford   B9

Beechtree Inn

948 Pender Rd
Hertford, NC 27944-9801
(252)426-7815 Fax:(252)426-7815
E-mail: hobbs@beechtreeinn.net
Web: www.beechtreeinn.net

Circa 1776. Experience the 1700s era while enjoying modern amenities during a stay in one of three private small houses at this inn's assembled collection of pre-Civil War buildings on 37 scenic acres of woods, gardens, lawn and farmland. Each restored house is furnished with reproduction furniture made on site, has central air conditioning and heat, a working fireplace, cable TV, VCR, refrigerator, microwave and coffeemaker. Pets are allowed in Flat Branch and Bear Swamp House for an extra fee. Wake up hungry to fully appreciate the hearty coun-

try breakfast served each morning. Complimentary refreshments are also provided. A canoe is available to use on Bethel Creek. Several restaurants are nearby.

Innkeeper(s): Ben and Jackie Hobbs. $90. 4 rooms, 3 with FP and 3 cottages. Breakfast, afternoon tea and snacks/refreshments included in rates. Types of meals: Full gourmet bkfst. Restaurant on premises. Beds: QT. Modem hook-up, data port, cable TV, VCR, reading lamp, refrigerator, snack bar, clock radio, telephone, coffeemaker, desk and fireplace in room. Central air. Fax, copier, bicycles, pet boarding and parlor games on premises. Small meetings hosted. Antiquing, art galleries, beach, bicycling, canoeing/kayaking, fishing, golf, hiking, parks, shopping and tennis nearby.

Publicity: *Virginia Pilot, Fine Woodworking and Woodworker's Journal.*

High Point   B5

J.H. Adams Inn

1108 North Main St
High Point, NC 27262
(336)882-3267 (888)256-1289 Fax:(336)882-1920
E-mail: dblakely@jhadamsinn.com

Circa 1918. A romantic ambiance surrounds this Italian Renaissance inn that was built in 1918 as a private home. It is listed in the National Register and has been completely restored into a 30-room inn with a grand staircase, richly carved moldings, wood floors and a marble fireplace. Gracious hospitality, outstanding comfort, attention to detail and exquisite interiors are central to the inn's heritage. Elegant guest bedrooms and a spacious suite feature Frette linens on premium Sealy mattresses and plush robes. The lavish décor and furnishings reflect the history of the area. Cereals, fruit, muffins, bagels and assorted breads, yogurt and beverages are offered for a continental breakfast. Southern Roots, the inn's restaurant, serves lunch and dinner.

Historic Interest: Built in 1918 and listed on the National Register of Historic Places, the J.H. Adams Inn features a grand staircase, richly carved moldings, marble fireplace, beautiful wood floors and elegantly furnished rooms.

Innkeeper(s): Donna Blakely. $129-229. 30 rooms with PB, 1 with FP, 1 suite and 1 conference room. Breakfast included in rates. Types of meals: Cont. Restaurant on premises. Beds: KQ. Modem hook-up, data port, cable TV, reading lamp, refrigerator, clock radio, telephone, coffeemaker, desk and voice mail in room. Central air. Fax, copier, fireplace and two handicap-accessible rooms in the South Wing on premises. Weddings, small meetings, family reunions and seminars hosted. Golf, live theater, museums, parks, shopping and furniture shopping nearby.

Publicity: *Restore America Fall 2003.*

Highlands   C2

Colonial Pines Inn

541 Hickory St
Highlands, NC 28741
(828)526-2060

Circa 1937. Secluded on a hillside just half a mile from Highlands' Main Street, this inn offers relaxing porches that boast a mountain view. The parlor is another restful option, offering a TV, fireplace and piano. Rooms, highlighted by knotty pine, are decorated with an eclectic mix of antiques. The guest pantry is always stocked with refreshments for those who need a little something in the afternoon. For breakfast, freshly baked breads accompany items such as a potato/bacon casserole and baked pears topped with currant sauce. In addition to guest rooms and suites, there are two cottages available, each with a fire-place and kitchen.

Innkeeper(s): Chris & Donna Alley. $85-160. 8 rooms with PB, 3 suites and 2 cottages. Breakfast, afternoon tea and snacks/refreshments included in rates. Types of meals: Full gourmet bkfst and early coffee/tea. Beds: KQDT. Data port, cable TV, VCR, reading lamp, refrigerator, ceiling fan, snack bar, telephone and fireplace in room. Small meetings, family reunions and seminars hosted. Antiquing, art galleries, canoeing/kayaking, downhill skiing, fishing, golf, hiking, horseback riding, live theater, shopping and tennis nearby.

Publicity: *Greenville News, Atlanta Journal, Highlander, Atlanta Constitution and Birmingham News.*

"There was nothing we needed which you did not provide."

Highlands Inn & Kelsey Place Restaurant

420 Main Street
Highlands, NC 28741
(828)526-9380 (800)964-6955 Fax:(828)526-8072
E-mail: info@highlandsinn-nc.com
Web: www.highlandsinn-nc.com

Circa 1880. The breathtaking backdrop of the mountains complements the impressive interior of this historic Colonial inn. Antique furnishings sit on original heartpine floors, while period fabrics, stencils and paints accent the walls and windows. Stay in a well-appointed guest bedroom, suite or cottage, some with fireplaces and patios or balconies overlooking the garden. A hearty country breakfast with southern specialties like grits and biscuits with sausage gravy is included and served in the inn's Kelsey Place Restaurant. Midweek lunches are offered, as well dinners on Fridays and Saturdays. Beverages and ice are available in the Sequoyah Room, and an evening nightcap of homemade cookies and coffee, tea or milk is enjoyed in the Bird Room.

Historic Interest: Placed on the National Register in 1990, the inn was built in 1880. Furnishings, stenciling and fabrics are of the period. Antiques throughout the period. Original heartpine flooring from 1880.
Innkeeper(s): Sabrina Hawkins. $79-225. 37 rooms with PB, 6 with FP, 10 suites and 2 cottages. Breakfast and snacks/refreshments included in rates. Types of meals: Country bkfst, early coffee/tea and lunch. Restaurant on premises. Beds: KQT. Cable TV, reading lamp, refrigerator, clock radio, telephone, coffeemaker, desk and fireplace in room. Air conditioning. VCR, fax, copier, library, parlor games and gift shop on premises. Weddings, small meetings, family reunions and seminars hosted. Antiquing, art galleries, bicycling, canoeing/kayaking, downhill skiing, fishing, golf, hiking, horseback riding, live theater, museums, parks, shopping, tennis and water sports nearby.
Publicity: *Southern Living, Southern Bride, Appalachian Life, Points North, Atlanta Homes & Magazine and Romantic Destinations.*

"Exceeded our expectations - we loved it."

Main Street Inn

270 Main St
Highlands, NC 28741-8446
(828)526-2590 (800)213-9142 Fax:(828)787-1142
E-mail: maininn@dnet.net
Web: www.mainstreet-inn.com

Circa 1885. A careful restoration retained the warm character of this Federal farmhouse built more than 100 years ago. Cathedral ceilings exposed hand-hewn beams. Original sand-forged windows were reinstalled as interior windows. Stone fireplaces in the dining room and lobby enhance the mountain ambiance. Most of the guest bedrooms in the Main House and the Guest House feature balconies and walk-in showers. Some offer antique clawfoot tubs and sitting areas. The first-floor Terrace Room boasts a private entrance and patio. Enjoy a hot country breakfast and afternoon tea. Landscaped grounds afford impressive photo opportunities as the seasons change.

Innkeeper(s): Farrel & Jan Zehr. $85-185. 19 rooms with PB. Breakfast and afternoon tea included in rates. Types of meals: Full gourmet bkfst and early coffee/tea. Beds: KQDT. Cable TV and telephone in room. Central air. Fax, copier and fireplace on premises. Weddings, small meetings, family reunions and seminars hosted. Antiquing, art galleries, canoeing/kayaking, fishing, golf, hiking, horseback riding, live theater, museums and shopping nearby.

Horseshoe   A9

Big Creek Lodge

5289 North Mills River Rd
Horseshoe, NC 28742
(828)891-3261 Fax:(828)891-2288
E-mail: bcreeklodge@yahoo.com
Web: www.bigcreeklodge.com

Circa 1890. Surrounded by the Pisgah National Forest, this historic two-level lodge was built in 1890. It graces 80 pristine acres that offer enchanting opportunities for nature lovers or those needing a respite from city life. Relax in the living room by the river rock fireplace. A pond and mountain streams are filled with rainbow trout for fishing enthusiasts. Go rafting or take a refreshing swim. Enjoy the view from the screened-in porch. Guest bedrooms feature a rustic decor with comfortable amenities. A fully equipped kitchen as well as a washer and dryer are available any time. A rock grill and picnic area are also provided. Rates are for entire lodge.

Innkeeper(s): Carolyn Edmundson. $300. 12 rooms and 1 conference room. Beds: Q. Data port, reading lamp, stereo, refrigerator, ceiling fan, clock radio, coffeemaker and linens in room. Central air. VCR, parlor games, telephone, fireplace, laundry facility, living room, 3 complete baths, large screened porch, river rock fireplace and mountain streams stocked with trout on premises. Limited handicap access. Weddings, small meetings, family reunions and seminars hosted. Amusement parks, antiquing, art galleries, bicycling, canoeing/kayaking, downhill skiing, fishing, golf, hiking, horseback riding, live theater, museums, parks, shopping, tennis, water sports, wineries and swimming nearby.

Lake Lure   B3

The Chalet Club

532 Washburn Rd
Lake Lure, NC 28746-0100
(828)625-9315 (800)336-3309 Fax:(828)625-9373
E-mail: reservations@chaletclub.com
Web: www.chaletclub.com

Circa 1926. Just 25 miles from Asheville, this compound of chalets and cottages sits on 300 secluded acres on the eastern slope of the Blue Ridge Mountains. It's a mile and a half from Lake Lure. The main chalet has five guest bedrooms and a main living room. Seven cottages are nearby, some with fireplaces stocked with seasoned wood and balconies with views of Hickory Nut Gorge and Chimney Rock. The log cabin Honeymoon Cottage is a favorite for lovers, and Stonehenge 1 and Stonehenge 2 share a pool and are a favorite for reunions. The inn has earned four Mobil Stars, and it is operated by second and third generation innkeepers. Meals are served in the main building, but all cottages have refrigerators and coffee makers. The price includes three meals a day served on the terrace or in the dining room next to the fireplace. A typical dinner consists of delectable courses such as pork loin, sweet potatoes, green beans, wild rice and blackberry cobbler with ice cream. Guests also have free use of the club's "On the Mountain," "Indoor" and "Water Sports" facilities. Guests may use without charge the club's wet suits, four kayaks, two canoes and fishing boat. The site also has tennis courts, pools, seven miles of hiking trails and a recreation house at the lake that has a pool table and low-impact exercise equipment.

Innkeeper(s): Anne & Bob Washburn. $122-326. 20 rooms, 17 with PB. Breakfast, snacks/refreshments and dinner included in rates. Types of meals: Full bkfst, veg bkfst, early coffee/tea and lunch. Restaurant on premises. Beds: KQT. Reading lamp, refrigerator, telephone, coffeemaker, desk, some with fireplaces and decks in room. Central air. TV, VCR, fax, swimming, tennis, library, fireplace, laundry facility, canoeing, sea kayaks, waterskiing, shuffleboard game room and recreation house by lake on premises. Small meetings, family reunions and seminars hosted. Antiquing, art galleries, bicycling, canoeing/kayaking, fishing, golf, hiking, horseback riding, parks, shopping, tennis, water sports, wineries, Biltmore House and gardens, Chimney Rock Park, Blue Ridge Parkway, Flat Rock Playhouse and Folk Art Center nearby.

Publicity: Tampa Tribune, Waterski Magazine and Blue Ridge Country Magazine.

Linville   B4

Linville Cottage Bed & Breakfast

PO Box 508
Linville, NC 28646-0508
(828)733-6551
Web: www.highsouth.com/linville

Circa 1910. Choose from a variety of comfortable year-round accommodations. Stay in the restored farm house surrounded by a white picket fence and English country gardens for a traditional bed & breakfast. Enchanting but casual guest bedrooms are filled with antiques and collectibles. The morning meal is served in the fireside Breakfast Room overlooking Grandfather Mountain. Granny's Suite is ideal for children and pets. Upscale Grandfather's Nook boasts a fireplace, Jacuzzi, kitchenette and TV. The secluded Falls Cabin is tucked away in a rhododendron forest with stone fireplace and is perfect for a romantic getaway or honeymoon. Ski slopes and hiking are just minutes away.

Innkeeper(s): Fran Feely. $85-150. 6 rooms with PB. Breakfast included in rates. Types of meals: Country bkfst. Beds: QD. Peace and quiet in room. Library, parlor games, telephone, fireplace, herb and flower garden and tours on premises. Weddings and family reunions hosted. Amusement parks, antiquing, cross-country skiing, downhill skiing, fishing, live theater, parks, shopping, sporting events, water sports, Grandfather Mountain and herb walks nearby.

Manteo   B10

White Doe Inn

319 Sir Walter Raleigh St
Manteo, NC 27954-9421
(252)473-9851 (800)473-6091 Fax:(252)473-4708
E-mail: whitedoe@whitedoeinn.com
Web: www.whitedoeinn.com

Circa 1910. For a romantic stay in the Outer Banks, this renovated Queen Anne Victorian on Roanoke Island is enchanting. Formerly called The Theodore Meekins House and listed in the National Register, its extraordinary architectural details are frequently photographed. The interior is also an eye-pleaser, enhanced by comfortable decor and furnishings. Spacious guest bedrooms are pampering retreats with private garden areas, bedside fireplaces, two-person whirlpools or an antique clawfoot tub, aromatherapy bath products, fluffy robes, plush Egyptian cotton linens and towels, CD players and Godiva chocolates. Southern hospitality excels with a hearty breakfast garnished with edible flowers and herbs grown on-site, served in the dining room or on the veranda. Afternoon tea, coffee and

desserts are enjoyed in the library/TV room, and evening sherry in the parlor. Relax on the wraparound porch with a swing and rockers or explore the area on a bike.

Historic Interest: Fort Raleigh National Historic Site, The Elizabethan Gardens (2 miles), NC Maritime Museum (2 blocks), Cape Hatteras National Seashore (10 miles), Wright Brothers National Memorial (20 miles).

Innkeeper(s): Bebe & Bob Woody. $140-340. 10 rooms, 8 with PB and 2 suites. Breakfast and afternoon tea included in rates. Types of meals: Full gourmet bkfst, early coffee/tea, picnic lunch and snacks/refreshments. Beds: KQ. Reading lamp, CD player, ceiling fan, clock radio, telephone, desk, hot tub/spa, gas fireplace and whirlpools in room. Central air. Fax, copier, bicycles, library, parlor games, fireplace and gift shop on premises. Weddings, small meetings, family reunions and seminars hosted. Antiquing, art galleries, beach, bicycling, canoeing/kayaking, fishing, golf, live theater, museums, parks, shopping, tennis and water sports nearby.

Murphy   C1

Huntington Hall B&B

272 Valley River Ave
Murphy, NC 28906-2829
(828)837-9567 (800)824-6189 Fax:(828)837-2527
E-mail: huntington@grove.net
Web: bed-breakfast-inn.com/

Circa 1881. This two-story country Victorian home was built by J.H. Dillard, the town mayor and twice a member of the House of Representatives. Clapboard siding and tall columns accent the large front porch. An English country theme is highlighted throughout. Afternoon refreshments and evening turndown service are included. Breakfast is served on the sun porch. Murder-mystery, summer-theater, and white-water-rafting packages are available.

Innkeeper(s): Curt & Nancy Harris. $65-125. 5 rooms with PB. Breakfast included in rates. Types of meals: Full gourmet bkfst and early coffee/tea. Beds: KQDT. Cable TV, reading lamp, ceiling fan, clock radio, turn-down service and desk in room. Air conditioning. TV, VCR, fax, copier, library, parlor games, telephone and fireplace on premises. Weddings, small meetings, family reunions and seminars hosted. Antiquing, fishing, live theater, parks, shopping, tennis and water sports nearby.

Publicity: Atlanta Journal, Petersen's 4-Wheel and New York Times.

"A bed and breakfast well done."

Nags Head   B10

First Colony Inn

6720 S Va Dare Tr
Nags Head, NC 27959
(252)441-2343 (800)368-9390 Fax:(252)441-9234
E-mail: innkeeper@firstcolonyinn.com
Web: www.firstcolonyinn.com

Circa 1932. This Shingle-style inn features two stories of continuous verandas on all four sides. It is the last of the original beach hotels built on the Outer Banks. To save it from destruction, the Lawrences moved it to family property three miles south. During the midnight move, townsfolk lined the streets cheering and clapping to see the preservation of this historic building. First Colony boasts a pool, croquet court, private beach access and ocean and sound views from the

second and third floors. Furnishings include antiques and traditional reproductions. There are Jacuzzis, kitchenettes, an elegant library and a sunny breakfast room.

Historic Interest: Chicamacomico Lifesaving Station (20 miles), Wright Brothers Memorial (9 miles), the Outer Banks is the "Graveyard of the Atlantic," with many shipwrecks from the 16th century on. Elizabeth II, replica 16th-century ship (9 miles), Fort Raleigh, site of first English colony in the New World.

Innkeeper(s): The Lawrences. $80-310. 26 rooms with PB, 6 suites and 1 conference room. Breakfast and afternoon tea included in rates. Types of meals: Full bkfst, early coffee/tea and room service. Beds: KQT. Cable TV, VCR, reading lamp, refrigerator, clock radio, telephone, desk, hot tub/spa, wet bars, kitchenettes, Jacuzzi and hair dryers in room. Air conditioning. TV, fax, copier, swimming, library, parlor games, BBQ, beach chairs, towels on heated towel bars, umbrellas, modem ports and guests passes to the local YMCA on premises. Limited handicap access. Weddings, small meetings, family reunions and seminars hosted. Beach, fishing, live theater, parks, water sports, historic sites and lighthouses nearby.

Publicity: Southern Living, Washington Post, Carolina Style, Greensboro News & Record, Discerning Traveler, Raleigh News & Observer, High Point Enterprise, Lexington Dispatch, Coast, Norfolk Virginian, USA Today, Outer Banks Magazine and Our State Magazine.

"Great, well done, nothing to change."

New Bern   C8

Aerie Inn Bed & Breakfast
509 Pollock St
New Bern, NC 28562-5611
(252)636-5553 (800)849-5553 Fax:(252)514-2157
E-mail: Aerieinn@aol.com
Web: www.aerieinn.com

Circa 1882. Experience the charm of the historic district and the shops of downtown while staying at this comfortable 1880s Victorian "Inn of Distinction." Whether on business or for pleasure, such personal attention is given that it is hard to leave and easy to return. Relax with evening refreshments in the parlor that features a player piano. Gracious guest bedrooms are furnished with period antiques. A full country breakfast offers a choice of three hot entrees. Visit the Tryon Palace Historic Sites and Gardens, just one block away. Ride a horse-drawn carriage or sail on the Neuse River.

Innkeeper(s): Michael & Marty Gunhus. $99-129. 7 rooms with PB, 5 with FP. Breakfast included in rates. Types of meals: Full bkfst and early coffee/tea. Beds: KQT. TV and telephone in room. Air conditioning. Fax, player piano and refreshments available on premises. Antiquing, beach, golf and museums nearby.

Harmony House Inn
215 Pollock St
New Bern, NC 28560-4942
(252)636-3810 (800)636-3113 Fax:(252)636-3810
E-mail: harmony@cconnect.net
Web: www.harmonyhouseinn.com

Circa 1850. Long ago, this two-story Greek Revival was sawed in half and the west side moved nine feet to accommodate new hallways, additional rooms and a staircase. A wall was then built to divide the house into two sections. The rooms are decorated with antiques, the innkeeper's collection of handmade crafts and other collectibles. Two of the suites include a heart-shaped Jacuzzi tub. Offshore breezes sway blossoms in the lush garden. Cross the street to an excellent restaurant or take a picnic to the shore.

Historic Interest: The inn was occupied by Company K of the 45th Massachusetts Infantry during the Civil War.

Innkeeper(s): Ed & Sooki Kirkpatrick. $89-160. 10 rooms with PB, 3 suites

and 2 conference rooms. Breakfast included in rates. Types of meals: Full bkfst and early coffee/tea. Beds: KQT. Modem hook-up, data port, cable TV, reading lamp, ceiling fan, clock radio and telephone in room. Central air. Fax, copier, parlor games and gift shop on premises. Small meetings and family reunions hosted. Antiquing, art galleries, beach, bicycling, golf, live theater, museums, parks and shopping nearby.

"We feel nourished even now, six months after our visit to Harmony House."

Meadows Inn a Colonial B&B
212 Pollock St.
New Bern, NC 28560
(252)634-1776 (877)551-1776 Fax:(252)634-1776

Circa 1847. In the heart of the historic district, this Greek Revival/Federal-style home is considered to be the town's first inn. Boaters enjoy the close proximity to the dock of the Neuse and Trent Rivers with the Intercoastal Waterway only 30 miles away. The Gathering Room is a favorite place to play the baby grand piano or work on a puzzle. Hot and cold beverages always are available. Themed guest bedrooms are spacious and comfortable with non-working fireplaces. Ask about a romantic package in the Victorian Room, or choose the family-friendly two-room suite on the third floor. The morning meal may include quiche, breakfast pizza, scrambled egg enchiladas, or baked French toast to enjoy with fresh fruit, hot breads or muffins and juice.

Innkeeper(s): John & Betty Foy. $90-155. 7 rooms with PB, 1 suite and 1 conference room. Breakfast included in rates. Types of meals: Full bkfst, early coffee/tea and afternoon tea. Beds: QDT. Cable TV, reading lamp, ceiling fan, telephone and fireplace in room. Air conditioning. Fax, copier, parlor games, CD player and refrigerator on premises. Small meetings and family reunions hosted. Antiquing, art galleries, beach, bicycling, canoeing/kayaking, fishing, golf, hiking, parks and wineries nearby.

Newton   B4

The Trott House Inn, Inc
802 N Main Ave
Newton, NC 28658-3148
(828)465-0404 Fax:(828)465-5753
Web: www.trotthouse.com

Circa 1897. Trott House was built originally as a hunting lodge, the section that houses the inn guest rooms was part of a later addition. Room choices include four guest rooms decorated with Victorian accents and a spacious suite. The suite includes an in-room Jacuzzi. For honeymooners, the innkeepers can provide breakfast in the privacy of your bedchamber, as well as providing fresh flowers and champagne. In addition to the gourmet breakfasts, guests are pampered with afternoon refreshments and turndown service.

Innkeeper(s): Anne. $85-135. 5 rooms with PB and 1 suite. Breakfast and snacks/refreshments included in rates. Types of meals: Full gourmet bkfst and early coffee/tea. Beds: KQT. Modem hook-up, cable TV, reading lamp, refrigerator, ceiling fan, snack bar, clock radio, telephone, coffeemaker and hot tub/spa in room. Central air. Fax, copier, spa, parlor games and fireplace on premises. Small meetings, family reunions and seminars hosted. Antiquing, art galleries, fishing, golf, live theater, museums and parks nearby.

Ocracoke C9

The Castle on Silver Lake

PO Box 908
Ocracoke, NC 27960
(252)928-3505 (800)471-8848 Fax:(252)928-3501
E-mail: innkeeper@thecastlebb.com
Web: www.thecastlebb.com

Circa 1948. Standing on the Outer Banks just yards from the harbor, this historic Colonial American/Williamsburg mansion, listed in the National and Local Registers, was built by decoy carvers and boat builders over three decades. Accented by cedar shakes and seven cozy dormers with gables, the 9,000 square foot castle is on two meticulously landscaped acres with flowers in bloom almost all year. Large windows in the parlor overlook the water and the den features warm woods and a custom-built pool table. Enjoy afternoon tea and snacks. Stay in one of the B&B's well-appointed guest bedrooms or third-floor Lighthouse Suite. The adjacent Courtyard Villas provide more lodging choices. Linger over a hearty country breakfast in the kitchen or dining room. A 40-foot jasmine arbor leads to the heated swimming pool and follow a lantana-lined walkway to the sundeck on the dock. Fish from the pier or explore the area on an available bike. Just two blocks away, Ocracoke Lighthouse is one of America's oldest working beacons. It is a short drive to Norfolk, Virginia and Raleigh, North Carolina.

Innkeeper(s): Dave & Ginny Foss and Jamie Tunnell. $169-249. 10 rooms with PB, 1 suite and 1 conference room. Breakfast, afternoon tea and snacks/refreshments included in rates. Types of meals: Country bkfst and early coffee/tea. Beds: QT. Cable TV, VCR, stereo, refrigerator, snack bar, clock radio, telephone, coffeemaker, fireplace and some with water view in room. Central air. Fax, copier, swimming, sauna, bicycles, parlor games, day spa with masseuse and steamrooms and heated pool on premises. Small meetings and family reunions hosted. Antiquing, art galleries, beach, bicycling, canoeing/kayaking, fishing, hiking, museums, shopping, water sports, offshore fishing and the Castle has docks on the harbor nearby.

Publicity: *Metro Magazine.*

Pisgah Forest C3

Key Falls Inn

151 Everett Rd
Pisgah Forest, NC 28768-8621
(828)884-7559 Fax:(828)885-8342

Circa 1860. The back section of this fascinating Victorian farmhouse was constructed prior to the Civil War and the front section after the war. The meadow in front of the home is reputed to have been a Civil War encampment area. The inn sits on 35 acres near Blue Ridge Parkway and Pisgah National forest with hiking and bike trails and numerous waterfalls.

Accommodations include two suites, decorated in Victorian and other antiques and reproductions. In addition to the guest rooms at Key Falls Inn, there is now a guest room with a private entrance at River Bend, which is a historic reproduction home near the inn on five wooded acres overlooking the French Broad River. The spacious guest bedroom has a fireplace and refrigerator. A breakfast basket with fresh baked good and fruit is placed in the room each day. Guests in the farmhouse feast on a full breakfast that includes dishes such as breakfast bacon or sausage with eggs or a hot casserole. Juice, fruit compote, biscuits, sweet rolls, French toast, cereal and bananas are additional offerings. The Key Falls Trail begins at the inn and climbs

toward a waterfall. A pond on the property, fed by a cascading stream, has two docks for sunning or fishing for bass or bream. There's also a waterfall on the property. A porch with the requisite rockers boasts a spectacular view of the mountains. The inn is 45 minutes from Biltmore Estate, 15 miles from the Carl Sandburg Home and 35 miles from the Thomas Wolfe Home.

Innkeeper(s): Clark & Patricia Grosvenor & Janet Fogleman. $60-105. 6 rooms, 4 with PB, 1 with FP and 2 suites. Breakfast and snacks/refreshments included in rates. Types of meals: Country bkfst and early coffee/tea. Beds: KQ. Cable TV, VCR, reading lamp, refrigerator, ceiling fan, clock radio, telephone and coffeemaker in room. Central air. TV, fax, tennis, parlor games and fireplace on premises. Family reunions hosted. Antiquing, art galleries, bicycling, canoeing/kayaking, fishing, golf, hiking, horseback riding, live theater, museums, parks, shopping, tennis and Brevard music center nearby.

Pittsboro B6

The Fearrington House Inn

2000 Fearrington Village Ctr
Pittsboro, NC 27312-8502
(919)542-2121 Fax:(919)542-4202
E-mail: fhouse@fearrington.com
Web: www.fearrington.com

Circa 1927. The Fearrington is an old dairy farm. Several of the original outbuildings, including the silo and barn, have been converted into a village with a potter's shop, bookstore, jewelry shop, and a Southern garden shop. The original homestead houses an award-winning restaurant. The inn itself is of new construction and its rooms overlook pasture land with grazing Belted Galloway cows, as well as a courtyard. Polished pine floors, fresh floral prints and amenity-filled bathrooms are among the inn's offerings.

Innkeeper(s): Richard Delany. $220-450. 32 rooms with PB, 5 with FP, 12 suites and 5 conference rooms. Breakfast and afternoon tea included in rates. Types of meals: Full gourmet bkfst, early coffee/tea, lunch, picnic lunch, snacks/refreshments, gourmet dinner and room service. Restaurant on premises. Beds: KQDT. Cable TV, VCR, reading lamp, stereo, snack bar, clock radio, telephone, turn-down service and heated towel racks in room. Air conditioning. TV, fax, copier, swimming, bicycles, tennis and fireplace on premises. Limited handicap access. Weddings, small meetings and seminars hosted. Antiquing, fishing, golf, live theater, parks, shopping, sporting events, tennis and water sports nearby.

Publicity: *Bon Appetit, Southern Living, Gourmet, Country Inns, Living It Up and North Carolina Homes and Gardens.*

"There is an aura of warmth and caring that makes your guests feel like royalty in a regal setting!"

Raleigh B7

The Oakwood Inn B&B

411 N Bloodworth St
Raleigh, NC 27604-1223
(919)832-9712 (800)267-9712 Fax:(919)836-9263
E-mail: innkeepers@oakwoodinnbb.com
Web: www.oakwoodinnbb.com

Circa 1871. Presiding over Raleigh's Oakwood Historic District, this lavender and gray Victorian beauty is in the National Register. A formal parlor is graced by rosewood and burgundy velvet, while guest rooms exude an atmosphere of vintage Victoriana.

Innkeeper(s): Gary & Doris Jurkiewicz. $99-175. 6 rooms with PB, 6 with FP and 1 conference room. Types of meals: Full bkfst. Beds: KQ. Cable TV in room. Fax, copier, telephone, afternoon refreshments,

complimentary beverage alcove and lighted off-street parking on premises.
Publicity: *Business Digest, Connoisseur, Southern Living* and *The Inside Scoop*.

*"Resplendent and filled with museum-quality antique furnishings." -
Kim Devins, Spectator*

Saluda   C3

Orchard Inn

PO Box 725
Saluda, NC 28773-0725
(828)749-5471 (800)581-3800 Fax:(828)749-9805
E-mail: orchard@saluda.tds.net
Web: www.orchardinn.com

Circa 1926. This inn combines the casual feel of a country
farmhouse with the elegance of a Southern plantation. The spacious living room features Oriental rugs, original artwork, quilts
and a cozy stone fireplace. In addition to the nine comfortably
furnished guest rooms, there are three cottages with fireplaces,
whirlpool baths and private decks. A full breakfast is
served every morning, and dinner is
available by reservation Tuesday
through Saturday. Guests can
explore the area on superb
country roads recently designated a scenic by-way.

Historic Interest: Carl Sandburg's home and grounds are about 15 minutes
from the inn. The Biltmore Estate is 35 minutes away.
Innkeeper(s): Kathy & Bob Thompson. $119-245. 12 rooms, 9 with PB, 5
with FP, 4 cottages and 1 conference room. Breakfast included in rates.
Types of meals: Full bkfst, early coffee/tea, picnic lunch, afternoon tea and
dinner. Beds: KQT. Ceiling fan and cottages have TV in room. VCR, fax, parlor
games, telephone, fireplace and hiking trails on premises. Small meetings
and seminars hosted. Antiquing, fishing, golf, parks, shopping, tennis, water
sports and Biltmore Estate nearby.
Publicity: *Southern Living, Raleigh News & Observer, Tryon Daily Bulletin
and State.*

*"We enjoyed the peace and tranquility, the fine food and good friends
we made."*

Southern Pines   C6

Knollwood House

1495 W Connecticut Ave
Southern Pines, NC 28387-3903
(910)692-9390 Fax:(910)692-0609

Circa 1925. Fairway dreams await golfers at this English-
manor-style inn where upstairs sitting rooms overlook the 14th
and 15th holes of the beautiful Mid-Pines golf course. The
inn's lawns roll down 100 feet or so to the course, which is a
masterpiece by Scottish golf course architect Donald Ross.
More than 30 golf courses are
within 20 miles. There have
been many celebrations under
the crystal chandelier and 10-
foot ceilings, and the Glenn
Miller Orchestra once played on
the back lawn.

Innkeeper(s): Dick & Mimi Beatty. $115-175. 6 rooms with PB, 1 with FP, 1
cottage and 1 conference room. Breakfast included in rates. Types of meals:
Full gourmet bkfst, veg bkfst and early coffee/tea. Beds: KQT. Cable TV, reading lamp, refrigerator, ceiling fan, clock radio, coffeemaker, turn-down service,
desk and fireplace in room. Central air. Fax, copier, swimming, tennis, library,
parlor games, telephone and fireplace on premises. Weddings, small meetings, family reunions and seminars hosted. Amusement parks, antiquing, art
galleries, bicycling, golf, horseback riding, live theater, museums, parks,
shopping, tennis and major pottery center nearby.

Swannanoa   B3

Sleepy Hollow B&B

132 Old Jim's Branch Rd
Swannanoa, NC 28778
(828)298-1115 (866)708-1115 Fax:(828)298-7188
E-mail: sleepyhollowinn@charter.net
Web: www.ashevillebbinn.com

Circa 1902. Original carved wooden mantels on massive stone
fireplaces, stained-glass windows, chandeliers, an ornate oak
staircase and antique furnishings highlight this completely renovated mountain home on five scenic acres. Admire the working pump organ on the way to the parlor for wine or beer and
other refreshments served during the hosted social hour. Watch
TV or play board games in the lounge. Porch rockers provide a
relaxing outdoor respite. Decorative fireplaces adorn the guest
bedrooms and suites. Stay in the two-bedroom Rosebud Suite
with a Jacuzzi or the English Ivey Suite with a clawfoot tub.
Linger over a hearty southern breakfast in the dining room or
on the outdoor covered stone terrace. A popular wedding site,
the landscaped grounds boast flowers, shrubs and a pond. Visit
nearby Biltmore Estate.

Historic Interest: Our Inn was built in the early 1900s. It originally had
5,000 square feet of space. Fireplaces are in all but two of our bedrooms.
The original plaster has been restored and period wallpaper and colors have
been used to keep in the period decor.
Innkeeper(s): Clayton & Danrae Babbitt. $125-175. 7 rooms with PB, 3
suites and 1 conference room. Breakfast included in rates. Types of meals:
Country bkfst and early coffee/tea. Beds: KQ. Cable TV, reading lamp, ceiling
fan, clock radio, desk and fireplace in room. Central air. Fax, copier, swimming, tennis, library and telephone on premises. Weddings, small meetings,
family reunions and seminars hosted. Antiquing, art galleries,
canoeing/kayaking, downhill skiing, golf, hiking, horseback riding, live theater,
museums, parks, shopping, tennis and wineries nearby.

Sylva   C2

Mountain Brook

208 Mountain Brook Rd #19
Sylva, NC 28779-9659
(828)586-4329
E-mail: AHI@mountainbrook.com
Web: www.mountainbrook.com

Circa 1930. Located in the Great Smokies, Mountain Brook in
western North Carolina consists of 14 cabins on a hillside amid
rhododendron, elm, maple and oak trees. The resort's 200-acre
terrain is crisscrossed with brooks and waterfalls, contains a
trout-stocked pond and nature
trail. Two cabins are constructed
with logs from the property,
while nine are made from native
stone. They feature fireplaces,
full kitchens, porch swings and
some have Jacuzzi.

Innkeeper(s): Gus, Michele, Maqelle McMahon. $90-140. 12 cottages with
PB, 12 with FP. Types of meals: Early coffee/tea. Beds: KD. Reading lamp,
refrigerator and clock radio in room. Game room and spa/sauna bungalow on
premises. Limited handicap access. Weddings and family reunions hosted.
Amusement parks, antiquing, downhill skiing, fishing, golf, live theater, shop-
ping, sporting events, tennis, water sports, casino, Great Smokies National
Park, railroad and nature trail nearby.
Publicity: *Brides Magazine, Today* and *The Hudspeth Report.*

*"The cottage was delightfully cozy, and our privacy was not interrupt-
ed even once."*

Tryon C3

Foxtrot Inn

PO Box 1561, 210 Fox Trot Lane
Tryon, NC 28782-1561
(828)859-9706 (888)676-8050
E-mail: wim@foxtrotinn.com
Web: www.foxtrotinn.com

Circa 1915. Located on six acres in town, this turn-of-the-century home features mountain views and large guest rooms. There is a private two bedroom guest cottage with its own kitchen and a hanging deck. The rooms are furnished with antiques. The Cherry Room in the main house has a four-poster, queen-size canopy bed with a sitting area overlooking the inn's swimming pool. The Oak Suite includes a wood-paneled sitting room with cathedral ceiling. A cozy fireplace warms the lobby.

Innkeeper(s): Wim Woody. $85-150. 4 rooms with PB, 2 suites and 1 cottage. Breakfast included in rates. Types of meals: Full bkfst. Beds: QDT. Reading lamp, clock radio and desk in room. Air conditioning. Swimming, parlor games, telephone and fireplace on premises. Weddings, small meetings, family reunions and seminars hosted. Antiquing, fishing, parks, shopping and water sports nearby.

Pine Crest Inn

85 Pine Crest Ln
Tryon, NC 28782
(828)859-9135 (800)633-3001 Fax:(828)859-9135
E-mail: info@pinecrestinn.com
Web: www.pinecrestinn.com

Circa 1906. Once a favorite of F. Scott Fitzgerald, this inn is nestled in the foothills of the Blue Ridge Mountains. Opened in 1917 by famed equestrian Carter Brown, the inn offers guests romantic fireplaces, gourmet dining and wide verandas that offer casual elegance. The Blue Ridge Parkway and the famous Biltmore House are a short drive away. Rooms are available in the Main Lodge and cottages. Original buildings include a 200-year-old log cabin, a woodcutter cottage and a stone cottage. Elegant meals are served in a Colonial tavern setting for full breakfasts and gourmet dinners.

Historic Interest: The Biltmore Estate is a 40-minute drive.

Innkeeper(s): Debby & Barney DuBois. $110-550. 35 rooms with PB, 27 with FP, 17 suites, 5 cottages, 3 cabins and 3 conference rooms. Breakfast, afternoon tea and snacks/refreshments included in rates. Types of meals: Full gourmet bkfst, early coffee/tea, picnic lunch, gourmet dinner and room service. Restaurant on premises. Beds: KQDT. Modem hook-up, data port, cable TV, VCR, reading lamp, refrigerator, ceiling fan, clock radio, telephone, coffeemaker, turn-down service, desk and hot tub/spa in room. Central air. Fax, copier, spa, library, child care, parlor games, fireplace, laundry facility and gift shop on premises. Weddings, small meetings, family reunions and seminars hosted. Antiquing, art galleries, bicycling, canoeing/kayaking, fishing, golf, hiking, horseback riding, live theater, parks, shopping, tennis, water sports and wineries nearby.

Publicity: *Southern Living and Wine Spectator.*

"We felt pampered and at home in your lovely Pine Crest Inn."

Tryon Old South B&B

27 Markham Rd
Tryon, NC 28782-3054
(828)859-6965 (800)288-7966 Fax:(828)859-6965
E-mail: pat@tryonoldsouth.com
Web: www.tryonoldsouth.com

Circa 1910. This Colonial Revival inn is located just two blocks from downtown and Trade Street's antique and gift shops. Located in the Thermal Belt, Tryon is known for its pleasant, mild weather. Guests don't go away hungry from innkeeper Pat Grogan's large Southern-style breakfasts. Unique woodwork abounds in this inn and equally as impressive is a curving staircase. Behind the property is a large wooded area and several waterfalls are just a couple of miles away. The inn is close to Asheville attractions.

Innkeeper(s): Tony & Pat Grogan. $75-105. 4 rooms with PB and 2 cottages. Breakfast included in rates. Types of meals: Full bkfst and early coffee/tea. Beds: QDT. Reading lamp and clock radio in room. Air conditioning. VCR, fax, copier, parlor games, telephone and fireplace on premises. Family reunions hosted. Antiquing, fishing, live theater, parks and shopping nearby.

Valle Crucis B4

The Baird House

PO Box 712
Valle Crucis, NC 28691
(828)297-4055 (800)297-1342 Fax:(828)297-3506
E-mail: bairdhouse@boone.net
Web: www.bairdhouse.com

Circa 1790. Warm hospitality has been offered since 1790 at this Colonial Farmhouse sitting on 16 secluded acres of riverfront coupled with rolling hills, wooded pastures and cool mountain breezes. The front porch rocking chairs invite relaxation and conversation. Enjoy sodas and homemade treats from the bottomless cookie jar. Fully restored, the hand-planed hardwood and other original details are accented by antiques, family heirlooms and a contemporary country decor. Several of the spacious guest bedrooms in the main house and carriage house feature gas log or wood-burning fireplaces, whirlpool baths, a balcony or wrap-around porch. A continental breakfast is available before a hearty meal that may include creamy style eggs, hashbrown casserole, hot biscuits, thick hickory smoked bacon, butter pecan coffee cake, fresh granola and fruit cups. Step outside the front door to swim, fish or tube on the river. Linville Falls, Grandfather Mountain, golf and ski resorts provide a variety of local activities.

Historic Interest: In the late 1780s Ezekiel and Susannah Baird, the second couple to move into the area, built their cabin here. Their descendants lived here for over 150 years.

Innkeeper(s): Deede & Tom Hinson. $119-159. 7 rooms with PB, 4 with FP. Breakfast and snacks/refreshments included in rates. Types of meals: Country bkfst and early coffee/tea. Beds: Q. Cable TV, VCR, reading lamp, refrigerator, ceiling fan, clock radio, coffeemaker, desk, fireplace, whirlpool tubs, bottomless cookie jar filled with homemade chocolate or pecan cookies, complimentary Coca-Colas and Diet Cokes, local maps and restaurant information in room. Fax, swimming, parlor games, telephone, fireplace and 2 acres of riverfront property for fishing and wading on premises. Weddings, small meetings and family reunions hosted. Amusement parks, antiquing, art galleries, bicycling, downhill skiing, fishing, hiking, horseback riding, live theater, parks and shopping nearby.

Publicity: *Carolina Mountain Living and Recommended in Romantic North Carolina a Hill Street Press Book.*

The Mast Farm Inn

PO Box 704
Valle Crucis, NC 28691-0704
(828)963-5857 (888)963-5857 Fax:(828)963-6404
E-mail: stay@mastfarminn.com
Web: www.mastfarminn.com

Circa 1812. Listed in the National Register of Historic Places, this 18-acre farmstead includes a main house and ten outbuildings, one of them a log cabin built in 1812. The inn features a wraparound porch with rocking chairs, swings and a view of the mountain valley. Fresh flowers gathered from the garden add fragrance throughout the inn. Rooms are furnished with antiques, quilts and mountain crafts. In addition to the inn rooms, there are seven cottages  available, some with kitchens. Before breakfast is served, early morning coffee can be delivered to your room. Organic home-grown vegetables are featured at dinners, included in a contemporary regional cuisine.

Historic Interest: Saint John's Church (2 miles), Mast General Store (1 mile), Maple Spring (on premises).

Innkeeper(s): Wanda Hinshaw & Kay Philipp. $125-275. 8 rooms with PB and 7 cottages. Breakfast included in rates. Types of meals: Full bkfst and dinner. Restaurant on premises. Beds: KQ. Reading lamp, ceiling fan, cottages with fireplaces, refrigerator and one with full kitchen in room. Air conditioning. Fax, parlor games, telephone and fireplace on premises. Limited handicap access. Antiquing, art galleries, bicycling, downhill skiing, fishing, golf, hiking, live theater, water sports, river sports, Blue Ridge Pkwy and Grandfather Mt nearby.

Publicity: *Travel & Leisure, Cooking Light, Blue Ridge Country, Southern Living, New York Times* and *Our State.*

"We want to live here!"

Washington   B8

Carolina House Bed & Breakfast

227 E. 2nd Street
Washington, NC 27889
(252)975-1382

Circa 1880. The character and charm of this Victorian bed & breakfast are highlighted by the Southern hospitality and European flair. Listed in the National Register of Historic Homes, the B&B has high ceilings, heirloom antiques and modern furnishings which accent a pleasant decor of yesteryear. The parlor boasts a pewter chess set. A two-person Jacuzzi is featured in the Queen's Room. Other guest bedrooms and a suite offer spacious comfort. Savor a delicious three-course candlelight breakfast with soft music setting a relaxing mood. Special diets are accommodated easily. Sit by the river and watch the boats, take a bike ride or visit the Estuarian, exhibiting science, art, nature and history.

Innkeeper(s): Toni & Peter Oser. $75-95. 4 rooms with PB and 1 suite. Breakfast, afternoon tea and snacks/refreshments included in rates. Types of meals: Full gourmet bkfst, veg bkfst and early coffee/tea. Beds: KQDT. Modem hook-up, data port, cable TV, VCR, CD player, refrigerator, ceiling fan, clock radio, telephone, coffeemaker, desk, hot tub/spa and fireplace in room. Air conditioning. Bicycles, library, parlor games, snacks, complimentary sodas and coffee/tea in the evening on request on premises. Antiquing, art galleries, bicycling, canoeing/kayaking, fishing, golf, hiking, museums, parks, shopping, sporting events, tennis, water sports and wineries nearby.

The Moss House Bed & Breakfast

129 Van Norden St
Washington, NC 27889-4846
(252)975-3967 (888)975-3393 Fax:(252)975-1148
E-mail: info@themosshouse.com
Web: www.themosshouse.com

Circa 1902. High ceilings and heart pine floors impart a light and airy ambiance to this Victorian home that is steeped in family history and filled with heirlooms and original artwork. The B&B is owned and operated by the great-granddaughter of Mr. & Mrs. Frank A. Moss, its builders. Fresh flowers and greenery cut from the gardens are thoughtful details in the elegant guest bedrooms. A satisfying Southern gourmet breakfast is served. Listed in the National Register and located in the historic district at the start of the self-guided walking tour, it is also one block from the Pamlico River, and a short walk to downtown shops, restaurants and a sailboat marina.

Innkeeper(s): Mary Havens Cooper. $85-95. 4 rooms with PB and 1 suite. Breakfast included in rates. Types of meals: Full gourmet bkfst. Beds: KQT. Modem hook-up, TV, ceiling fan, telephone and central heat in room. Central air. Fax on premises. Weddings, small meetings, family reunions and seminars hosted. Antiquing, golf, live theater, parks, shopping, tennis, water sports, boating and library nearby.

"We really enjoyed the comfortable atmosphere and the food was delectable."

Waynesville   B2

Adger House Bed & Breakfast

127 Balsam Drive
Waynesville, NC 28786
(828)452-0861 (866)234-3701 Fax:(828)452-0847

Circa 1906. Cradled by three wooded acres, this recently renovated neo-classical revival home has retained much of its original architectural details. High ceilings, hardwood floors and paneled wainscoting complement the period antiques and reproductions. There is ample room to roam, whether enjoying afternoon refreshments in the Eagle's Nest Parlor, reading in a well-stocked library or relaxing in the sunroom. Oversize guest bedrooms are splendidly furnished. Choose a room with a fireplace, loft or double shower. A generous breakfast is served in the Adgerwood Room or alfresco on the patio. Stroll the gardens, or visit the quaint historic village nearby.

Innkeeper(s): Leslie & Bruce Merrell. $95-150. 5 rooms with PB, 2 with FP. Breakfast and afternoon tea included in rates. Types of meals: Full gourmet bkfst, early coffee/tea and snacks/refreshments. Beds: KQT. Reading lamp, ceiling fan, clock radio, turn-down service and fireplace in room. TV, library, parlor games and telephone on premises. Weddings, small meetings, family reunions and seminars hosted. Antiquing, art galleries, bicycling, canoeing/kayaking, downhill skiing, fishing, golf, hiking, horseback riding, museums, parks, shopping and water sports nearby.

Andon House Bed & Breakfast

92 Daisey Ave
Waynesville, NC 28786
(828)452-3089 (800)293-6190 Fax:(828)452-7003
E-mail: info@andonhouse.com
Web: www.andonhouse.com

Circa 1902. Designated as one of the town's historic properties, this turn-of-the-century home reflects a traditional style of architecture and interior decor. Large windows, oak floors and tall ceilings are original features that add to the charm of this B&B. The garden room with glass surround invites conversation by the fire or enjoying the impressive landscape and mountain view. A large-screen TV offers further entertainment. Guest bedrooms boast private temperature controls and choices of fireplace, clawfoot or whirlpool tub and private balcony. Partake of a four-course, candlelight breakfast with fresh flowers on the dining room table. Plan the day's excursions on the veranda. The inn is close to downtown and within easy access of many year-round attractions.

Historic Interest: Former "Speakeasy" during prohibition.

Innkeeper(s): Ann & Don Rothermel. $85-135. 5 rooms with PB, 4 with FP and 2 suites. Breakfast and snacks/refreshments included in rates. Types of meals: Full gourmet bkfst, veg bkfst and early coffee/tea. Beds: KQT. Modem hook-up, reading lamp, stereo, refrigerator, ceiling fan, clock radio, coffeemaker, fireplace and hot tub in room. Air conditioning. TV, fax, copier, parlor games, telephone, fireplace, hot tub, game tables, mountain views, 2 balconies and cable TV on premises. Family reunions hosted. Amusement parks, antiquing, art galleries, canoeing/kayaking, cross-country skiing, downhill skiing, fishing, golf, hiking, horseback riding, live theater, museums, parks, shopping and tennis nearby.

Publicity: *Hendersonville News, Blue Ridge Country, Discovery Channel and Lynette Jennings Show.*

"Our weekend was wonderful. Having stayed at several B & Bs yours hit the top rating. The atmosphere, hospitality, food and fellowship were all top of the line. What a great way to relax."

Herren House

94 East St
Waynesville, NC 28786-3836
(828)452-7837 (800)284-1932
E-mail: herren@brinet.com
Web: www.herrenhouse.com

Circa 1897. Pink and white paint emphasize the Victorian features of this two-story inn with wraparound porch. Inside, the Victorian decor is enhanced with the innkeepers' paintings and handmade furniture. Soft music and candlelight set the tone for breakfast, which often features the inn's homemade chicken sausage and a baked egg dish along with freshly baked items such as apricot scones. (Saturday evening dinners are available by prior arrangement.) A garden gazebo is an inviting spot with an overhead fan and piped in music. A block away are galleries, antique shops and restaurants. The Great Smoky Mountains National Park and the Blue Ridge Parkway begin a few minutes from the inn.

Innkeeper(s): Jackie & Frank Blevins. $85-150. 6 rooms with PB. Breakfast, afternoon tea and snacks/refreshments included in rates. Types of meals: Full gourmet bkfst and early coffee/tea. Beds: KQT. Cable TV, VCR, reading lamp, ceiling fan and desk in room. Air conditioning. Fax, copier, library, parlor games, telephone and gourmet dinner served at additional charge Saturday evenings on premises. Limited handicap access. Small meetings hosted. Antiquing, cross-country skiing, downhill skiing, fishing, golf, live theater, parks, shopping and water sports nearby.

"The two of you have mastered the art of sensory pleasures! Nothing was left unattended."

The Swag Country Inn

2300 Swag Rd
Waynesville, NC 28785-9623
(828)926-0430 (800)789-7672 Fax:(828)926-2036
E-mail: letters@theswag.com
Web: www.theswag.com

Circa 1795. The Swag is composed of six hand-hewn log buildings, one dating to 1795. They were moved to the site and restored. An old church was reassembled and became the cathedral-ceilinged common room. The fireplace in this room was constructed of fieldstones with no mortar to maintain authenticity. The inn's 250 acres feature a nature trail with five

hideaways along the trail, a spring-fed pond, hammocks and thick forests. A two-and-a-half-mile gravel road winds through a heavily wooded hillside to the inn. In the evening, dinner is served on pewter ware at long walnut tables. Listening to folk music and mountain storytelling afterwards is popular. A full list of special events is available each month.

Innkeeper(s): Deener Matthews. $295-640. 15 rooms with PB, 7 with FP, 3 cabins and 1 conference room. Breakfast, afternoon tea, snacks/refreshments and dinner included in rates. Types of meals: Full bkfst and lunch. Restaurant on premises. Beds: KQT. Reading lamp, refrigerator, clock radio, telephone, desk, Bose CD players and radio satellite in room. TV, VCR, copier, spa, sauna and fireplace on premises. Limited handicap access. Small meetings, family reunions and seminars hosted. Antiquing and shopping nearby.

Publicity: *The Atlanta Journal, Mid-Atlantic Country, Southern Living, Hideaway Report, Gourmet and Travel & Leisure.*

"The Swag gives us both a chance to relax our bodies and revitalize our brains."

Yellow House on Plott Creek Road

89 Oakview Dr
Waynesville, NC 28786-7110
(704)452-0991 (800)563-1236 Fax:(704)452-1140

Circa 1885. This manor, which boasts views of the Blue Ridge Mountains, was built as a summer home to a family from Tampa, Fla. The interior of the home is decidedly French country done in romantic colors. Each room is special, from the Batternburg bedding in the Carolina and S'conset rooms to the four-poster bed and mountain view in the Montecito room. Each of the rooms and suites has a fireplace. The Carriage House, S'conset St. Paul de Vence Suite offer whirlpool tubs. Special amenities, such as bathrobes, fresh flowers, a decanter of port, coffee, hair dryers and toiletries thoughtfully have been placed in each room and suite. Each evening, the innkeepers offer wine and cheese, and in the mornings, a gourmet breakfast is served. Guests are free to enjoy their meal on the veranda or in the privacy of their room.

Innkeeper(s): Sharon & Ron Smith. $125-250. 6 rooms with PB, 6 with FP, 4 suites and 1 cottage. Breakfast and snacks/refreshments included in rates. Types of meals: Full gourmet bkfst, early coffee/tea and picnic lunch. Beds: KQT. Reading lamp, CD player, refrigerator, ceiling fan, telephone, turn-down service, desk and hot tub/spa in room. Air conditioning. Fax, copier and library on premises. Small meetings, family reunions and seminars hosted. Antiquing, fishing, golf, hiking, live theater, parks, shopping, tennis, water sports and mountain biking nearby.

Publicity: *Asheville Citizen Times, Mountainee., WRAL - Raleigh and NC.*

"The scenery and quaintness of this community was only surpassed by the gracious surroundings and hospitality here at the Yellow House."

Weaverville   B3

Dry Ridge Inn

26 Brown St
Weaverville, NC 28787-9202
(828)658-3899 (800)839-3899
E-mail: innkeeper@dryridgeinn.com
Web: www.dryridgeinn.com

Circa 1849. This house was built as the parsonage for the Salem Campground, an old religious revival camping area. Because of the high altitude and pleasant weather, it was used as a camp hospital for Confederate soldiers suffering from pneumonia during the Civil War. The area was called Dry Ridge by the Cherokee Indians before the campground was established.

Innkeeper(s): Howard & Kristen Dusenbery. $95-155. 8 rooms with PB. Types of meals: Full bkfst. Beds: QD. TV, reading lamp, CD player, ceiling fan and clock radio in room. Air conditioning. VCR, telephone, fireplace and outdoor hot tub on

premises. Antiquing, art galleries, hiking, live theater, Biltmore Estate, fine arts, white water rafting, gift shop and Blue Ridge Parkway outdoor spa nearby.
Publicity: *Asheville Citizen Times and Marshall News Record.*

"Best family vacation ever spent."

Inn on Main Street

88 S Main Street
Weaverville, NC 28787
(828)645-4935 (877)873-6074
E-mail: relax@innonmain.com
Web: www.innonmain.com

Circa 1900. Atop a ridge in Blue Ridge Mountains, this 1900 Country Victorian inn has been a retreat from the hustle and bustle of daily life for the past 100 years. Built as a doctor's home and office, the downstairs was used to care for the sick and the upstairs to house paying guests who came to the area for the healthy mountain air. The gardens include rhododendrons, perennials, herbs and vegetables. Its seven comfortably furnished guest rooms are perfect for relaxing after a day of sightseeing, shopping, golfing, hiking, skiing, rafting, trail rides or partaking of local natural hot mineral baths. Breakfasts include such treats as the inn's signature frittata, homemade bread and muffins.
Innkeeper(s): Dan & Nancy Ward. $85-155. 7 rooms with PB. Breakfast and snacks/refreshments included in rates. Types of meals: Full gourmet bkfst, veg bkfst and early coffee/tea. TV, ceiling fan, clock radio, desk and some with fireplace and whirlpool tub in room. Central air. Fax, parlor games, telephone and fireplace on premises. Small meetings, family reunions and seminars hosted. Antiquing, art galleries, bicycling, canoeing/kayaking, cross-country skiing, downhill skiing, fishing, golf, hiking, horseback riding, live theater, parks, shopping, wineries, Biltmore Estate and Blue Ridge Parkway nearby.

Weldon   A8

Weldon Place Inn

500 Washington Ave
Weldon, NC 27890-1644
(252)536-4582 (800)831-4470 Fax:(252)536-4582

Circa 1914. Blueberry buckle and strawberry blintzes are a pleasant way to start your morning at this Colonial Revival home. Located in a National Historic District, it is two miles from I-95. Wedding showers and other celebrations are popular here. There are beveled-glass windows, canopy beds and Italian fireplaces. Most of the inn's antiques are original to the house, including a horse-hair stuffed couch with its original upholstery. Select the Romantic Retreat package and you'll enjoy sweets, other treats, a gift bag, sparkling cider, a whirlpool tub and breakfast in bed.
Innkeeper(s): Bill & Cathy Eleczko. $60-89. 4 rooms with PB. Breakfast included in rates. Types of meals: Full bkfst and early coffee/tea. Beds: D. Cable TV, reading lamp, clock radio and coffeemaker in room. Air conditioning. VCR and telephone on premises. Weddings and small meetings hosted. Antiquing, fishing, live theater and shopping nearby.

Williamston   B8

Big Mill Bed & Breakfast

1607 Big Mill Rd
Williamston, NC 27892-8032
(252)792-8787
E-mail: info@bigmill.com
Web: www.bigmill.com

Circa 1918. Originally built as a small arts and crafts frame house, the many renovations conceal its true age. The historic farm outbuildings that include the chicken coop, smokehouse,

pack house, tobacco barns and potato house, were built from on-site heart pine and cypress trees that were felled and floated down the streams of this 250-acre woodland estate. The Corncrib guest bedroom is in the pack house that originally housed mules. Each of the guest bedrooms feature climate control, stenciled floors, faux-painted walls, hand-decorated tiles on the wet bar and a private entrance. The suite also boasts a stone fireplace and impressive view. The countryside setting includes a three-acre lake with bridges, fruit orchard, vegetable and flower gardens. Eighty-year-old pecan trees planted by Chloe's parents provide nuts for homemade treats as well as shade for the inn.
Innkeeper(s): Chloe Tuttle. $58-75. 4 rooms with PB, 1 with FP, 1 suite, 1 cottage and 1 conference room. Breakfast included in rates. Types of meals: Cont and picnic lunch. Beds: QDT. TV, VCR, reading lamp, refrigerator, ceiling fan, telephone, desk, private entrances, individual climate control, wet bars, kitchenettes with sinks, refrigerators, toaster ovens and coffee pots in room. Air conditioning. Fax, bicycles, parlor games, fireplace, laundry facility, lake fishing and off-street parking for any size vehicle on premises. Antiquing, bicycling, canoeing/kayaking, fishing, golf, hiking, horseback riding, sporting events, water sports, horse shows, nature trails, nature preserves, boating access, Roanoke River Refuge, Gardner's Creek camping platforms and Bob Martin Agriculture Center nearby.
Publicity: *WRAL-TV.*

Wilmington   D7

C.W. Worth House B&B

412 S 3rd St
Wilmington, NC 28401-5102
(910)762-8562 (800)340-8559 Fax:(910)763-2173
E-mail: relax@worthhouse.com
Web: www.worthhouse.com

Circa 1893. This beautifully detailed three-story Queen Anne Victorian boasts two turrets and a wide veranda. From the outside, it gives the appearance of a small castle. The inn was renovated around 1910, and it retains many of the architectural details of the original house, including the paneled front hall. Victorian decor is found throughout the inn, including period antiques. The Rose Suite offers a king four-poster bed, sitting room and bath with a clawfoot tub and separate shower. Guests are treated to gourmet breakfasts. Freshly baked muffins and entrees such as eggs Florentine, rosemary and goat cheese strata and stuffed French toast are served. A second-story porch overlooks the garden with dogwood, ponds and pecan trees.
Innkeeper(s): Margi & Doug Erickson. $115-150. 7 rooms with PB. Breakfast and snacks/refreshments included in rates. Types of meals: Full bkfst. Beds: KQT. Reading lamp, ceiling fan, telephone and one with two-person whirlpool in room. Air conditioning. TV, wireless high-speed Internet access, fax, TV/VCR and copier service on premises. Small meetings and family reunions hosted. Antiquing, fishing, golf, museums, parks, shopping, tennis, water sports, performing arts and fine dining nearby.

Front Street Inn

215 S Front St
Wilmington, NC 28401-4414
(910)762-6442 (800)336-8184 Fax:(910)762-8991
E-mail: jay@frontstreetinn.com
Web: www.frontstreetinn.com

Circa 1923. The Front Street Inn is in the heart of Wilmington's historic district. The Brick Italianate structure has a European ambiance and is full of American art. There are nine guest bedrooms, including six spacious suites some with Jacuzzis and fireplaces. All have wet-bars, private baths, hard-

461

wood floors and private entrances. The second-floor suites open directly onto the balcony. Guests return to the inn for the delicious extensive continental breakfasts, which include healthy items such as fresh bran muffins, whole-grain cereals, hard-boiled eggs, assorted cheeses, smoked salmon, fresh fruit, yogurt and a variety of coffee cakes, breads and biscotti with accompaniments such as jam and local honey. Breakfast is served in the Sol y Sombra Bar and Breakfast Room or in the guest's suite upon request. The inn has an exercise room, bicycles, a wine and beer bar and a game room with a pool table. It is less than a block from Chandler's Wharf, Cape Fear River, half a mile from the USS N.C. Battleship and six miles from Orton Plantation. Guests may stroll along the River Walk, visit St. John's Museum of Art or meander through an extensive residential section of restored homes and delightful gardens.

Innkeeper(s): Jay & Stefany Rhodes. $98-180. 12 suites. Breakfast included in rates. Types of meals: Cont plus, veg bkfst, early coffee/tea, snacks/refreshments and room service. Beds: KQDT. Modem hook-up, data port, cable TV, VCR, reading lamp, CD player, refrigerator, ceiling fan, snack bar, clock radio, telephone, coffeemaker, desk, hot tub/spa, voice mail, robes, hair dryer, individual heat/AC control and some with Jacuzzi and fireplace in room. Fax, copier, bicycles, parlor games, laundry facility, CD player, wine & beer bar and game/exercise room on premises. Small meetings, family reunions and seminars hosted. Amusement parks, antiquing, art galleries, beach, bicycling, canoeing/kayaking, fishing, golf, horseback riding, live theater, museums, parks, shopping, sporting events, tennis, water sports, river cruises and historic sightseeing nearby.

Graystone Inn

100 S 3rd St
Wilmington, NC 28401-4503
(910)763-2000 (888)763-4773 Fax:(910)763-5555
E-mail: reservations@graystoneinn.com
Web: www.graystoneinn.com

Circa 1906. If you are a connoisseur of inns, you'll be delighted with this stately mansion in the Wilmington Historic District and in the National Register. Recently chosen by American Historic Inns as one of America's Top Ten Romantic Inns, towering columns mark the balconied grand entrance. Its 14,000 square feet of magnificent space includes antique furnishings, art and amenities. A staircase of hand-carved red oak rises three stories. Guests lounge in the music room, drawing room and library. A conference room and reception area with a fireplace and sitting area are on the third floor, once a grand ballroom. The elegant guest rooms are often chosen for special occasions, especially the 1,300-square-foot Bellevue, which offers a sitting room, king bed, sofa and handsome period antiques.

Innkeeper(s): Paul & Yolanda Bolda. $159-329. 7 rooms with PB, 6 with FP, 2 suites and 1 conference room. Breakfast included in rates. Types of meals: Full gourmet bkfst and early coffee/tea. Beds: KQ. Data port, TV, reading lamp, ceiling fan, clock radio, telephone, turn-down service, desk, computer jacks and many with four-poster beds in room. Air conditioning. Fax, copier, library, parlor games, fireplace, weight training room and PC data ports on premises. Weddings, small meetings and family reunions hosted. Antiquing, fishing, golf, live theater, parks, shopping, sporting events, tennis, water sports and museums nearby.

Publicity: *Country Inns, TV series Young Indiana Jones, Matlock, Dawsons Creek, Movie Rambling Rose and Mary Jane's Last Dance and Cats Eye.*

Inn on Orange

410 Orange St.
Wilmington, NC 28401
(910)815-0035 (800)381-INNN Fax:(910)762-2279
E-mail: frani@innonorange.com
Web: www.innonorange.com

Circa 1875. Burgundy paint accentuates the trim of this blue and cream Italianate Victorian B&B. The inn's landscaping is enhanced by azaleas, roses and 40-foot-tall crepe myrtle. Spacious guest rooms feature canopy beds, antiques, fireplaces, ceiling fans and Persian carpets. Twelve-foot ceilings are found throughout, including the dining room where four-course breakfasts are served by candlelight with fine china, silver and crystal. Walk to restaurants,  nightclubs and shops, or enjoy the Riverwalk, a waterfront park. In addition to the neighborhoods of stately homes, guests often ride the sternwheel paddleboat or horse-drawn carriage to further enjoy the Southern atmosphere.

Innkeeper(s): Francesca Sperrazza-King. $75-150. 4 rooms with PB, 4 with FP. Breakfast and snacks/refreshments included in rates. Types of meals: Full gourmet bkfst, veg bkfst and early coffee/tea. Beds: KQT. Cable TV, VCR, ceiling fan, clock radio and fireplace in room. Central air. Fax, copier and stocked refrigerators on premises. Weddings and family reunions hosted. Amusement parks, antiquing, art galleries, beach, bicycling, canoeing/kayaking, fishing, golf, horseback riding, live theater, museums, parks, shopping and sporting events nearby.

Publicity: *Travelhost.*

"A relaxing atmosphere with a touch of elegance."

Rosehill Inn Bed & Breakfast

114 S 3rd St
Wilmington, NC 28401-4556
(910)815-0250 (800)815-0250 Fax:(910)815-0350
E-mail: rosehill@rosehill.com
Web: www.rosehill.com

Circa 1848. Architect Henry Bacon Jr., most famous for designing the Lincoln Memorial in Washington, D.C., lived here in the late 19th century. Located in the largest urban historic district in the country, this  Neoclassical Victorian was completely renovated in 1995. The guest rooms are spacious and decorated in period furnishings. Breakfast treats include eggs Benedict with Cajun Crab Hollandaise and stuffed French toast with orange syrup.

Innkeeper(s): Laurel Jones. $99-229. 6 rooms with PB. Breakfast included in rates. Types of meals: Full gourmet bkfst and early coffee/tea. Beds: KQD. Modem hook-up, data port, cable TV, VCR, reading lamp, clock radio, telephone, desk, data port and iron and ironing board in room. Fax on premises. Family reunions hosted. Antiquing, fishing, golf, live theater, parks, shopping, sporting events, tennis, water sports, battleship memorial and beaches nearby.

Publicity: *Southern Living, Wilmington Star News, Wilmington Magazine, Washington Post, Insiders Guide to Wilmington, Atlanta Sun, Philadelphia Inquirer and Oprah Winfrey "The Wedding."*

The Wilmingtonian

101 South Second St
Wilmington, NC 28401
(919)343-1800 (800)525-0909 Fax:(919)251-1149
E-mail: mail@thewilmingtonian.com
Web: www.thewilmingtonian.com

Circa 1841. Unwind and relax at this historic downtown location of five elegant buildings only two blocks from the river in Cape Fear country. The de Rosset House is a luxuriously restored antebellum mansion with aged heart of pine floors. The Dram Tree House, originally a vegetable dye factory, has a rustic Southern ambiance with a Charleston-style courtyard and fish pond. The Maritime Building, once a convent, boasts a nautical theme reflecting this seaport city. The Clarenden, named after a local Earl, is perfect for groups or reunions as some of the suites can interconnect through a conservatory. The Cinema House, a tribute to the area's active movie industry, offers specially designed suites showcasing themes of a classical movie or star. Most of these romantic lodgings feature private entrances and balconies with rockers overlooking gardens.
Innkeeper(s): Mike Compton. $110-285. 42 rooms, 7 with FP, 40 suites and 3 conference rooms. Breakfast included in rates. Types of meals: Cont plus, gourmet lunch, snacks/refreshments, gourmet dinner and room service. Restaurant on premises. Beds: KQD. Data port, cable TV, VCR, reading lamp, stereo, refrigerator, ceiling fan, snack bar, clock radio, telephone, coffeemaker, hot tub/spa, voice mail, microwaves, toasters, hair dryers, irons, ironing boards, fireplace, some with full kitchens and washers/dryers in room. Central air. Fax, copier, library, laundry facility, video tape library, lounge, bar, grill and room/pub on premises. Weddings, small meetings, family reunions and seminars hosted. Amusement parks, antiquing, art galleries, beach, bicycling, canoeing/kayaking, fishing, golf, live theater, museums, parks, shopping, tennis and water sports nearby.

Verandas

202 Nun St
Wilmington, NC 28401-5020
(910)251-2212 Fax:(910)251-8932
E-mail: verandas4@aol.com
Web: www.verandas.com

Circa 1854. It's difficult to believe that this graceful three-story Victorian ever featured shag carpeting and linoleum floors. Hardly a fitting ending for a home that once belonged to a Confederate ship-builder and blockade runner, who burned his shipyard rather than let Union soldiers capture it. Innkeepers Charles Pennington and Dennis Madsen transformed Verandas from an ill-decorated, fire-damaged wreck into an elegant bed & breakfast. The restoration process included two years of painstaking work. For their efforts, they have been awarded a historic preservation award from the Historic Wilmington Foundation. The romantic guest rooms are filled with American, French and English antiques. Most rooms include a fireplace, and the beds are topped with luxurious, hand-ironed linens. Bathrooms now feature oversized tubs and marble floors and vanities. Gourmet coffees and teas accompany the lavish breakfasts, which feature delectable entrees such as a croissant stuffed with smoked salmon and cream cheese and baked in an egg custard. There are many amenities for business travelers, including modem hook-ups, fax service and corporate midweek rates.
Innkeeper(s): Charles Pennington & Dennis Madsen. $150-200. 8 rooms with PB. Breakfast and snacks/refreshments included in rates. Types of meals: Full gourmet bkfst and early coffee/tea. Beds: KQ. Modem hook-up, data port, cable TV, VCR, reading lamp, clock radio, telephone and desk in room. Central air. Fax and fireplace on premises. Family reunions hosted.

Antiquing, art galleries, beach, bicycling, canoeing/kayaking, fishing, golf, live theater, museums, parks, shopping, tennis and water sports nearby.
Publicity: Select Registry and Conde Naste Johannsens Guide.

"You have done a magnificent job with your property, and you certainly make your guests feel welcome with your food and hospitality."

Wilson   B7

Miss Betty's B&B Inn

600 West Nash St
Wilson, NC 27893-3045
(252)243-4447 (800)258-2058 Fax:(252)243-4447

Circa 1858. Located in a gracious setting in the downtown historic district, the inn is comprised of several restored historic homes, chief of which is the two-story National Register Italianate building called the Davis-Whitehead Harris House.

Here there are 12-foot high ceilings, heart-pine and oak floors and wonderful collections of antiques. Breakfast is served in the Victorian dining room of the main house, with its walnut antique furniture and clusters of roses on the wallpaper. All the extras, such as lace tablecloths and hearty meals, conjure up the Old South. Smoking is allowed on the outside porches — there are six of them — and the deck. Four golf courses, numerous tennis courts and many fine restaurants are nearby. Wilson is known as the antique capitol of North Carolina.
Historic Interest: The inn is listed in the National Register and located on Nash Street, which once was described as one of the most beautiful streets in the country.
Innkeeper(s): Betty & Fred Spitz. $60-80. 14 rooms with PB, 11 with FP and 3 suites. Breakfast included in rates. Types of meals: Full bkfst. Beds: KQDT. Cable TV, reading lamp, ceiling fan, clock radio, telephone and desk in room. Air conditioning. TV, fax, copier, parlor games and fireplace on premises. Limited handicap access. Family reunions hosted. Live theater and sporting events nearby.
Publicity: Wilson Daily Times-1996, The Philadelphia Enquirer-1999, Southern Living-1997, Mid-Atlantic Country-1995, Our State/NC-1995 and Washington Post-1998.

"Yours is second to none. Everything was perfect. I can see why you are so highly rated."

Winston-Salem   B5

Augustus T. Zevely Inn

803 S Main St
Winston-Salem, NC 27101-5332
(336)748-9299 (800)928-9299 Fax:(336)721-2211
E-mail: ctheal@dddcompany.com
Web: www.winston-salem-inn.com

Circa 1844. The Zevely Inn is the only lodging in Old Salem. Each of the rooms at this charming pre-Civil War inn have a view of historic Old Salem. Moravian furnishings and fixtures permeate the decor of each of the guest quarters, some of which boast working fireplaces. The home's architecture is reminiscent of many structures built in Old Salem during the second quarter of the 19th century. The formal dining room and parlor have wood burning fireplaces. The two-story

porch offers visitors a view of the period gardens and a beautiful magnolia tree. A line of Old Salem furniture has been created by Lexington Furniture Industries, and several pieces were created especially for the Zevely Inn.

Historic Interest: Winston-Salem abounds with historic activity. Old Salem, founded in 1766, is a restored, Moravian community. Among the sites are the Historic Bethabara Park, the Piedmont Craftsman, Inc. and Mesda, the nation's only museum dedicated to researching Southern materials and styles. The museum features a variety of furniture, textiles, ceramics and paintings dating back to the 17th century.

Innkeeper(s): Steven Kellam. $80-205. 12 rooms with PB, 3 with FP and 1 suite. Breakfast and snacks/refreshments included in rates. Beds: KQDT. Cable TV, reading lamp, refrigerator, clock radio, telephone, desk and whirlpool tub in room. Air conditioning. Fax, copier, parlor games and fireplace on premises. Antiquing, live theater, shopping, sporting events and Old Salem Historic District nearby.

Publicity: *Washington Post Travel, Salem Star, Winston-Salem Journal, Tasteful, Country Living, National Trust for Historic Preservation, Homes and Gardens, Homes Across America, Southern Living, Heritage Travel, Top 25 Historic Inns & Hotels and Home & Gardens Network Show.*

"Colonial charm with modern conveniences, great food. Very nice! Everything was superb."

Brookstown Inn B&B

200 Brookstown Ave
Winston-Salem, NC 27101-5202
(336)725-1120 (800)845-4262 Fax:(336)773-0147

Circa 1837. Originally constructed as a cotton mill, located on one acre, this four-story building now offers gracious accommodations to travelers. The old brick walls, exposed wood beams and high ceilings add warmth and character to all of the rooms, including the parlor and conference room. Guest rooms are decorated with attractive colonial reproductions such as poster beds, and there are spacious suites with decorative fireplaces, sitting areas and a garden tub. Breakfast is served in the dining room, which features a large colonial fireplace set against a sunny yellow wallcovering. Evening receptions offer wine and cheese in the parlor. Just a short walk away is Williamsburg-style Old Salem Moravian Village, built in 1766.

Innkeeper(s): Carol Hogan, GM. $125-155. 71 rooms with PB, 31 suites and 2 conference rooms. Breakfast included in rates. Types of meals: Cont plus, afternoon tea and snacks/refreshments. Restaurant on premises. Beds:

KQD. Data port, cable TV, reading lamp, clock radio, telephone, coffeemaker, desk, voice mail, garden tubs, hair dryers and iron/ironing board in room. Air conditioning. Fax, copier and wine and cheese in the afternoon featuring wines from a local winery on premises. Weddings, small meetings, family reunions and seminars hosted. Antiquing, art galleries, live theater, museums, sporting events and wineries nearby.

Henry F. Shaffner House

150 S Marshall St
Winston-Salem, NC 27101-2833
(336)777-0052 (800)952-2256 Fax:(336)777-1188
Web: www.shaffnerhouse.com

Circa 1907. Located near the historic Old Salem area, this elaborate Queen Anne Tudor-style Victorian has been carefully renovated and was awarded the city's restoration award. Handsome gables, copper roof shingles and an elegant iron fence establish the house's unique appeal. Built by Henry Shaffner, one of the founders of Wachovia Bank, the mansion features tiger oak woodwork, fireplaces and several common rooms: the parlor, tea room, library and sun room. The inn is popular for holding special events and weddings. Each room is distinctively decorated with tastefully selected furnishings and fabrics. A favored guest room is the private top-floor Piedmont Room with Jacuzzi, wet bar, king-size bed and sitting room. Breakfast features gourmet omelets and home-baked breads, fruits and specialty coffees. Murder-mystery weekends are also offered. Wine and cheese are offered in the evening. There is a horse-drawn carriage service available.

$99-239. 9 rooms with PB, 3 suites and 2 conference rooms. Breakfast included in rates. Types of meals: Full bkfst, snacks/refreshments, dinner and room service. Beds: KQT. Cable TV, reading lamp, refrigerator, ceiling fan, snack bar, clock radio, telephone, turn-down service, desk and whirlpool tubs in room. Air conditioning. Fax, copier, library, parlor games, fireplace and fitness club passes on premises. Weddings, small meetings, family reunions and seminars hosted. Antiquing, golf, live theater, parks, shopping, sporting events and tennis nearby.

Publicity: *Southern Living, Triad Business News, Winston-Salem Journal, Life & Leisure, Winston-Salem, Buena Vista and Great Country Inns.*

North Dakota

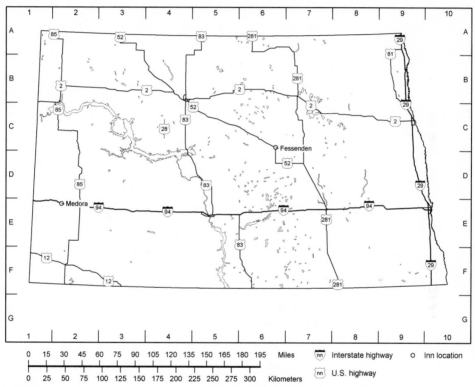

0 15 30 45 60 75 90 105 120 135 150 165 180 195 Miles

0 25 50 75 100 125 150 175 200 225 250 275 300 Kilometers

(nn) Interstate highway   o Inn location

(nn) U.S. highway

Fessenden   C6

Beiseker Mansion
1001 2nd St NE
Fessenden, ND 58438-7409
(701)547-3411

Circa 1899. Situated on nearly a city block, this 15-room Queen Anne Victorian is bordered by an old-fashioned wrought iron fence. Features include a splendid wraparound veranda and two turrets. The original golden oak woodwork is seen in the staircase, fireplace and dining room wainscoting. The turret room, with its king-size sleigh bed and marble-topped dresser, is a favorite choice. A third-floor library, open to guests, contains 3,000 volumes. The house is in the National Register of Historic Places.

Innkeeper(s): Paula & Jerry Tweton. $55-95. 6 rooms, 2 with PB. Breakfast included in rates. Types of meals: Full bkfst. Cable TV and VCR in room. Air conditioning. TV and fireplace on premises.

Publicity: *Grand Forks Herald* and *Fessenden Herald Press.*

"What a beautiful house! The food and atmosphere were lovely."

Medora   E2

The Rough Riders Hotel B&B
Medora, ND
Medora, ND 58645
(701)623-4444 (800)633-6721 Fax:(701)623-4494

Circa 1865. This old hotel has the branding marks of Teddy Roosevelt's cattle ranch as well as other brands stamped into the rough-board facade out front. A wooden sidewalk helps to maintain the turn-of-the-century cow-town feeling. Rustic guest rooms are above the restaurant and are furnished with homesteader antiques original to the area. In the summer, an outdoor pageant is held complete with stagecoach and horses. In October, deer hunters are accommodated. The hotel, along with two motels, is managed by the non-profit Theodore Roosevelt Medora Foundation.

Innkeeper(s): Randy Hatzenbuhler. $45-58. 9 rooms with PB. Breakfast included in rates.

Ohio

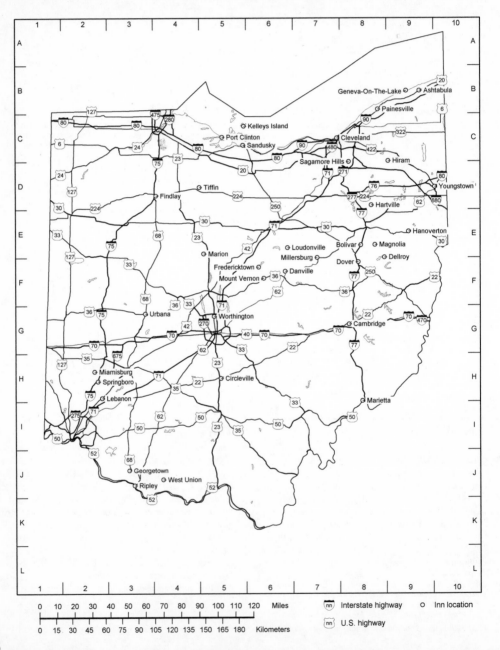

0 10 20 30 40 50 60 70 80 90 100 110 120 Miles

0 15 30 45 60 75 90 105 120 135 150 165 180 Kilometers

nn Interstate highway   ○ Inn location

nn U.S. highway

Ashtabula   B9

Peggy's B&B

8721 Munson Hill Road
Ashtabula, OH 44004
(440)969-1996 Fax:(440)964-5767
E-mail: peggy@peggysbedandbreakfast.com
Web: www.peggysbedandbreakfast.com

Circa 1945. Enjoy the privacy of a getaway cottage amid an
area of covered bridges, woodlands, wineries, beaches and
restaurants. Located an hour east of Cleveland, the cottage sits
on the edge of a forest and offers a porch, fireplace, loft bedroom and full kitchen. Decorated with knotty pine, there's a
lodge atmosphere with comfortable furnishings, making the
cottage feel like your own second home. Breakfasts can be
catered according to guest's wishes and picnic lunches and
dinners may also be arranged. Recommended restaurants in the
surrounding area includes Ferrante's Winery and Ristorante
and Lou's Billow Beach.

Innkeeper(s): Peggy Huggins. $95-125. 1 cottage. Breakfast included in
rates. Types of meals: Full gourmet bkfst, veg bkfst, early coffee/tea, picnic
lunch and dinner. Beds: Q. TV, VCR, reading lamp, stereo, refrigerator, ceiling
fan, clock radio, telephone, coffeemaker, desk and fireplace in room. Air conditioning. Parlor games on premises. Small meetings hosted. Amusement
parks, antiquing, art galleries, beach, bicycling, canoeing/kayaking, cross-
country skiing, fishing, golf, hiking, horseback riding, live theater, museums,
parks, shopping, sporting events, tennis, water sports and wineries nearby.

Publicity: *Chamber of Commerce (two areas).*

Bolivar   E8

Springhouse Bed & Breakfast

10903 St. Route 212, NE
Bolivar, OH 44612
(330)874-4255 (800)796-9100 Fax:(330)874-1106
E-mail: bnb@wilkshire.net
Web: www.springhousebnb.com

Circa 1857. Overlooking picturesque Tuscarawas River Valley,
this peaceful six-acre estate is composed of a main house and
seven outbuildings in the middle of 50 acres of trees and corn-
fields. The historic Modern Greek Revival home, a smokehouse and springhouse are listed in the National Register.
Antique furnishings and country accents highlight 11-foot ceilings, massive woodwork and original floors. Spacious guest
bedrooms and the Bell Tower Suite boast comfort and luxury.
Lounge in a plush robe on a canopy or brass bed. A candlelight breakfast is served with soft music playing. Stroll the gardens, relax by the pond or stone fountain, soak in the hot tub
or sit on the balcony.

Innkeeper(s): Tim & Elise Shuff. $85-150. 5 rooms, 4 with PB and 1 suite.
Breakfast and snacks/refreshments included in rates. Types of meals: Full
gourmet bkfst, veg bkfst, early coffee/tea and picnic lunch. Beds: KQD. Data
port, TV, VCR, reading lamp, refrigerator, ceiling fan, snack bar, clock radio,
telephone, coffeemaker, turn-down service, desk, plush robes, blow dryers
and satellite dish in room. Central air. Fax, copier, spa, library and parlor
games on premises. Weddings, small meetings, family reunions and seminars
hosted. Antiquing, bicycling, canoeing/kayaking, fishing, golf, hiking, horseback riding, museums, parks, shopping, wineries, Canton Pro-Football Hall of
Fame (15 minutes), "Trumpet in the Land" outdoor drama (20 minutes) and
Amish Country nearby.

Publicity: *Akron Beacon Journal.*

Cambridge   G8

Colonel Taylor Inn B&B and Gift Shop

633 Upland Rd
Cambridge, OH 43725
(740)432-7802 Fax:(740)435-3152
E-mail: coltaylr@coltaylorinnbb.com
Web: www.coltaylorinnbb.com

Circa 1878. The namesake who built this Victorian Painted
Lady was a Civil War veteran and congressman. The spacious
mansion imparts an intimate ambiance. The Grand Foyer showcases a carved staircase, oak paneling, 11-foot ceilings, hardwood floors and stained-glass windows. A large sitting room
boasts a big screen TV and table games. The parlor and library
provide quiet places to read or chat. The inns boasts 11 fireplaces, and one of the guest bedrooms even has a fireside
whirlpool tub in the bath. Apple French toast, sausage, coffee
cake and fresh fruit is one of the delightful breakfasts served
daily. The historic downtown district is seven blocks away.

Innkeeper(s): Jim & Patricia Irvin. $135-195. 4 rooms with PB, 4 with FP, 1
suite and 2 conference rooms. Breakfast included in rates. Types of meals:
Full gourmet bkfst, early coffee/tea and afternoon tea. Beds: Q. Cable TV,
reading lamp, ceiling fan, clock radio, fireplace and one with bathroom
whirlpool tub/fireplace in room. Central air. TV, VCR, library, parlor games,
fireplace, large-screen TV, two parlors, formal dining room and three porches
on premises. Weddings, small meetings and seminars hosted. Antiquing, art
galleries, beach, bicycling, cross-country skiing, fishing, golf, hiking, horseback riding, live theater, museums, parks, shopping, water sports, wineries,
glass factories, potteries, festivals and concerts nearby.

Publicity: *Arrington's Bed & Breakfast Journal, Inn Traveler and voted "Best in
the USA" & awarded "The Inn with the most Hospitality" 2003 by inngoers.*

Misty Meadow Farm Bed & Breakfast and Resort

64878 Slaughter Hill Rd.
Cambridge, OH 43725
(740)439-5135 Fax:(740)439-5408
E-mail: misty@cambridgeoh.com
Web: www.mistymeadow.com

Circa 1940. Romance is easily kindled at this 150-acre private
natural paradise. The low-ranch home blends country decor
and antique furnishings. Comfortable yet lavish guest bedrooms boast soft robes for the spa, fresh flowers, homemade
cookies and vistas that overlook the apple orchard and visiting
deer. A cozy historic cottage also is available. Savor a bountiful
breakfast served in the glass Octagon Room with panoramic
views or on the sunny patio deck. Two acres of spring-fed water
offer swimming, fishing, paddle boating or soaking in the sun
on the dock. Hike one of the trails, and then relax in the spa,
sauna or pool. Ask about the popular hayride to the hilltop
sunset dinner in the meadow.

Innkeeper(s): Jim & Vicki Goudy. $140-190. 4 rooms, 3 with PB, 1 with FP,
1 cottage and 1 conference room. Breakfast and snacks/refreshments included in rates. Types of meals: Full gourmet bkfst, early coffee/tea and gourmet
dinner. Beds: QT. VCR, reading lamp, stereo, refrigerator, ceiling fan, clock
radio, telephone, coffeemaker, desk, hot tub/spa, fireplace, thick robes, fresh
flowers and homemade cookies in room. Central air. Fax, copier, spa, swimming, sauna, library, parlor games, fireplace, boating, fishing, swimming
pool, pond swim dock, hiking and hattaras hammocks on premises.
Weddings, small meetings, family reunions and seminars hosted. Amusement
parks, antiquing, art galleries, beach, bicycling, canoeing/kayaking, cross-
country skiing, fishing, golf, hiking, horseback riding, live theater, museums,
parks, shopping, sporting events, tennis, water sports and wineries nearby.

Publicity: *Daily Jeffersonian, Columbus Dispatch, Ohio Magazine and Travel
Show Channel 8 Cleveland.*

Morning Glory B&B

5637 Fairdale Dr
Cambridge, OH 43725-9454
(740)439-2499

Circa 1859. This two-story farmhouse set on five acres along the Old National Road is conveniently located between Cambridge and New Concord. The original staircase, construct-

ed of chestnut and walnut, leads to the three guest rooms that offer private baths and ceiling fans. The inn features hardwood floors, antiques and many handmade items, influenced by the Amish, whose enclave is just an hour away. Guests can enjoy a full

breakfast in the pantry kitchen by the warmth of the hearth or in the dining room. Shopping, antiques, crafts, museums and parks are located nearby.

Historic Interest: Located close to the Wild Animal Preserve, Salt Fork State Park and the Pritchard-Laughlin Civic Center.

Innkeeper(s): Jim & Jane Gibson. $65-85. 3 rooms with PB. Breakfast and snacks/refreshments included in rates. Types of meals: Full bkfst and early coffee/tea. Beds: Q. Ceiling fan and clock radio in room. Central air. Parlor games, telephone and fireplace on premises. Antiquing, bicycling, fishing, golf, hiking, horseback riding, live theater, museums, parks, shopping, tennis, water sports, wineries, "The Wilds" animal preserve and glass factories nearby.

Publicity: *Daily Jeffersonian and Midwest Living.*

"Outstanding, we give it '5 stars.'"

Circleville   H5

Braeburn Farm B&B

6768 Zane Trail Rd
Circleville, OH 43113-9761
(740)474-7086
E-mail: braeburn@bright.net

Circa 1853. Braeburn, a bucolic 300-acre working farm is located in the Ohio countryside. Originally a land grant to veterans of the Revolutionary War, it was part of the first "Northwest Territory." The brick farmhouse has been renovated

and offers antique furnishings. Guest rooms feature a variety of beds, such as a canopy bed, sleigh bed, and a high-back bedstead topped with a featherbed. There is an iron bed on the sleeping porch, popular on summer nights. Clawfoot tubs are outfitted with

showers. Innkeeper Tony Ellis is a master banjo and fiddle player and can be coaxed to offer renditions for guests. A library and two living rooms with fireplaces are common rooms which compete with the two pillared porches for guests' attention. A hammock hangs from two elm trees in the yard. In addition to the smokehouse, spring house and summer kitchen, there's a historic hand-hewn post and beam barn where cats, goats, sheep, cows and llamas reside. An abundance of wildlife populates the farm along the creeks and wooded paths, and there are dogs, chickens and geese on the property. Hocking Hills, Chillicothe and the outdoor drama, Tecumseh, are nearby attractions. Braeburn has its own summer concert series held at

the farm's outdoor pavilion. (Check the web site for the dates of musical events.)

Historic Interest: The Mound City Group National Monument is a unique historic site, highlighting the Hopewell Indian culture. The Hopewell were prevalent in the Circleville area nearly 2,000 years ago, and their artwork, tools and weapons are on display.

Innkeeper(s): Louise Adkins & Tony Ellis. $85. 4 rooms, 1 with FP and 1 cottage. Breakfast included in rates. Types of meals: Full bkfst. Beds: D. Air conditioning. TV, VCR, library and fireplace on premises. Weddings and family reunions hosted. Hiking, live theater and Cumseh an outdoor drama nearby.

Penguin Crossing B&B

3291 Sr 56 W
Circleville, OH 43113-9622
(740)477-6222 (800)736-4846 Fax:(740)420-6060
E-mail: innkeeper@penguin.cc
Web: www.penguin.cc

Circa 1820. This romantic country getaway on 300 acres offers heart-shaped personal Jacuzzis for two, antique appointed rooms, gourmet hot chocolate served fireside, candlelight breakfasts and room amenities such as a wood-burning fire-

place or brass bed. Bright colors and original walnut woodwork add to the decor in this 1820s brick farmhouse, once a stage-coach stop. As the name might suggest, the inn has a collection of penguins on display. In the

evenings, guests enjoy moon-lit walks along the old country lane and in the daytime, exploring the inn's farmland, watching the kittens playing in the barn, or cycling to downtown Circleville, four miles away. Breakfasts include a selection of natural foods, and the innkeeper is happy to cater to special dietary needs.

Historic Interest: Ted Lewis Museum (4 miles), Circleville Pumpkin Show (4 miles), Deer Creek State Park (20 miles).

Innkeeper(s): Allan Colgan & Carol Jones. $100-225. 5 rooms with PB, 2 with FP. Breakfast included in rates. Types of meals: Cont and early coffee/tea. Beds: KQDT. Reading lamp, telephone, desk and Jacuzzi (four rooms) in room. Air conditioning. VCR, fax, parlor games and fireplace on premises. Limited handicap access. Weddings, small meetings, family reunions and seminars hosted. Antiquing, fishing, live theater, parks, shopping and water sports nearby.

"If I had to describe this home in one word, it would be — enchanting."

Cleveland   C7

Bourbon House

6116 Franklin Boulevard
Cleveland, OH 44102
(216)939-0535
E-mail: Robert_Bourbon_House@msn.com
Web: bedandbreakfast.worldres.com/script/gen_prop.asp?hotel_id=27458&front_end_id=706

Circa 1901. Boasting three stories, a balconied turret and a pillared front porch, this eclectic-style house is located in the heart of the historic district. Just minutes from Edgewater Park Beach on the shores of Lake Erie, or equally close to downtown, the 24-hour front desk or concierge can assist in activity planning. The air-conditioned Turkin-Roberts Suite features a fireplace, refrigerator, sitting room and walk-in closet. Sleep in a four-poster bed and relax on the sofa while watching TV in Mathews Suite. The Berger Room can be adjoined with either suite. Other amenities include turndown service, iron/ironing board and free local calls. Enjoy a complimentary breakfast, snacks and free parking.

Innkeeper(s): Robert Lonzer. $65-150. 3 rooms, 2 with PB, 1 with FP and 2 suites. Breakfast and snacks/refreshments included in rates. Types of meals: Full gourmet bkfst and early coffee/tea. Beds: KQD. Cable TV, reading lamp, refrigerator, snack bar, clock radio, telephone, turn-down service, desk and fireplace in room. Air conditioning. Library, parlor games and fireplace on premises. Amusement parks, antiquing, art galleries, beach, bicycling, down-hill skiing, fishing, golf, hiking, horseback riding, live theater, museums, parks, shopping, sporting events and water sports nearby.

Publicity: *Crains Cleveland Business.*

Danville   F6

Red Fox Country Inn

26367 Danville Amity Rd, PO Box 717
Danville, OH 43014-0746
(740)599-7369 (877)600-7310
E-mail: sudsimp@aol.com
Web: www.redfoxcountryinn.com

Circa 1830. This inn, located on 15 scenic central Ohio acres, was built originally to house those traveling on the Danville-Amity Wagon Road and later became a farm home. Amish woven rag rugs and country antiques decorate the guest rooms. Some of the furnishings belonged to early owners, and some date to the 18th century. Four rooms include Amish-made oak beds and the fifth an 1880s brass and iron double bed. Breakfasts include fresh pastries, fruits, coffee and a variety of delectable entrees. Special dietary needs usually can be accommodated. There are books and games available in the inn's sitting room, and guests also are invited to relax on the front porch. Golfing, canoeing, fishing, horseback riding, hiking, biking, skiing and Mohican State Park are nearby, and the inn is 30 minutes from the largest Amish community in the United States.

Historic Interest: Amish settlements, Malibar Farm, historic Roscoe Village and the National Heisey Glass Museum are less than an hour from the inn.

Innkeeper(s): Sue & Denny Simpkins. $65-105. 5 rooms with PB. Breakfast included in rates. Beds: QD. Reading lamp and clock radio in room. Air conditioning. Library, telephone and great place for retreats on premises.

Publicity: *Dealers Automotive, Columbus Dispatch, Mount Vernon News and Cincinnati Enquirer.*

"Our dinner and breakfast were '5 star.' Thank you for the gracious hospitality and special kindness you showed us."

The White Oak Inn

29683 Walhonding Rd, SR 715
Danville, OH 43014
(740)599-6107
E-mail: info@whiteoakinn.com
Web: www.whiteoakinn.com

Circa 1915. Large oaks and ivy surround the wide front porch of this three-story farmhouse situated on 13 green acres. It is located on the former Indian trail and pioneer road that runs along the Kokosing River, and an Indian mound has been discovered on the property. The inn's woodwork is all original white oak, and guest rooms are furnished in antiques. Visitors often shop for maple syrup, cheese and handicrafts at

nearby Amish farms. Three cozy fireplace rooms and two cottages provide the perfect setting for romantic evenings.

Historic Interest: Roscoe Village, restored Erie Canal Town (30 minutes).

Innkeeper(s): Yvonne & Ian Martin. $80-185. 12 rooms with PB, 6 with FP and 1 conference room. Breakfast and snacks/refreshments included in rates. Types of meals: Full bkfst, early coffee/tea and gourmet dinner. Beds: KQDT. Reading lamp, ceiling fan, clock radio, telephone, TV jacks and three with whirlpool tub in room. Air conditioning. Library, parlor games, fireplace, guest refrigerator and piano on premises. Weddings, small meetings, family reunions and seminars hosted. Antiquing, fishing, horseback riding, parks, shopping, water sports and Amish area/museums nearby.

Publicity: *Ladies Home Journal, Columbus Monthly, Cleveland Plain Dealer, Country, Glamour, Columbus Dispatch, Midwest Living and PBS - Country Inn Cooking.*

"The dinner was just fabulous and we enjoyed playing the antique grand piano."

Dellroy   E8

Whispering Pines Bed and Breakfast

1268 Magnolia Rd SW
Dellroy, OH 44620
(330)735-2824 (866)4LAKEVU Fax:(330)735-7006
E-mail: whisperingpines@atwoodlake.com
Web: www.atwoodlake.com

Circa 1880. Blissful memories are made at this Victorian Italianate inn sitting on seven lush acres of rolling hills. Exquisitely furnished with antiques and period pieces, the decor is relaxing and elegant. Romantic guest bedrooms and honeymoon suite offer gorgeous lake views, fluffy robes and CD players to enhance any mood. Some feature fireplaces, private balconies and Jacuzzis. Breakfast is such a delight, the frequently requested mouth-watering recipes are now in a cookbook. Each season brings an eye-pleasing adventure to the surrounding area for an ultimate getaway, perfect for any occasion.

Innkeeper(s): Bill & Linda Horn. $150-225. 9 rooms with PB, 7 with FP. Breakfast, afternoon tea and snacks/refreshments included in rates. Types of meals: Full gourmet bkfst, veg bkfst and early coffee/tea. Beds: KQ. Reading lamp, CD player, refrigerator, ceiling fan, snack bar, clock radio, hot tub/spa, fireplace and seven rooms with 2-person spa tub in room. Central air. Fax, spa, parlor games and telephone on premises. Weddings hosted. Antiquing, art galleries, beach, bicycling, canoeing/kayaking, fishing, golf, hiking, horseback riding, live theater, museums, parks, shopping, tennis, water sports and wineries nearby.

Dover   F8

Olde World Bed & Breakfast & Tea Room

2982 State Route 516 NW
Dover, OH 44622-7247
(330)343-1333 (800)447-1273 Fax:(330)364-8022
E-mail: owbb@tusco.net
Web: www.oldeworldbb.com

Circa 1881. A quaint atmosphere is imparted at this red brick Victorian farmhouse. The tea parlor features beautifully preserved woodwork found in the pocket doors and fireplace mantel. Themed guest bedrooms and a suite include Parisian, Alpine, Mediterranean and the signature Victorian decor which boasts a carved bed and clawfoot tub. Enjoy an elegant breakfast in the floral-wallpapered dining room with chandelier. The meal may include Swiss eggs, rhubarb muffins, cream scones and grilled local whole hog sausage. Queen's tea is served every Wednesday through Saturday afternoon. The veranda is a favorite retreat while munching on warm, homemade cookies. The Amish countryside and an abundance of antiquing opportunities are nearby.

Innkeeper(s): Jonna Cronebaugh. $80-120. 5 rooms, 4 with PB, 1 suite and 1 conference room. Breakfast included in rates. Types of meals: Full gourmet bkfst, lunch, afternoon tea, snacks/refreshments and dinner. Beds: KQ. Reading lamp and clock radio in room. Air conditioning. VCR, fax, spa, parlor games, telephone and fireplace on premises. Family reunions and seminars hosted. Antiquing, fishing, golf, live theater, shopping, tennis, water sports and Amish Country historical sites nearby.

Publicity: *Ohio Magazine, Columbus Dispatch, Canton Repository, Cleveland Plain Dealer, Ohio Pass Magazine, Country Discovers and Ohio Home and Away.*

Findlay   D4

Rose Gate Cottage Bed & Breakfast

423 Western Ave
Findlay, OH 45840-2447
(419)424-1940 (877)614-4577 Fax:(419)424-1940
E-mail: rosegate@rosegateinn.com
Web: www.rosegateinn.com

Circa 1900. Original hardwood floors, trim and high ceilings accentuate this two-story home of rose-colored stucco. Experience an inviting Victorian atmosphere with warm and friendly innkeepers. The parlor features a piano and offers local restaurant menus to peruse. Antique beds in the wallpapered guest bedrooms include an oak highback, pine cone posted and four poster. The Garden Villa room boasts a double whirlpool tub, fireplace, cable, TV, VCR and robes. Tea Rose rooms has a single whirlpool tub, cable TV, VCR and robes. In our Carriage house we have two lovely banquet rooms catering for small elegant affairs seating for up to 50 people. Breakfast may include the inn's signature dish, a hot apple puff pancake baked in a ramekin. History is very evident in this quaint midwestern town. Presidents McKinley, Hayes and Harding all have memorial sites within driving distance.

Innkeeper(s): John & Belinda Nesler. $75-95. 4 rooms with PB and 1 conference room. Breakfast included in rates. Types of meals: Full gourmet bkfst. Beds: QD. Desk and whirlpool tubs in room. Air conditioning. VCR and telephone on premises. Antiquing, art galleries, bicycling and golf nearby.

Fredericktown   F6

Heartland Country Resort

2994 Township Rd 190
Fredericktown, OH 43019
(419)768-9300 (800)230-7030 Fax:(419)768-9133
E-mail: heartbb@bright.net
Web: www.heartlandcountryresort.com

Circa 1878. This remodeled farmhouse and luxury log cabin offer guests a serene country setting with hills, woods, pastures, fields, wooded trails, barns, horse stables and riding arenas.  The four suites include a fireplace and Jacuzzi tub. With full run of the huge house, guests also have their choice of a wide variety of recreation. Horseback riding is the recreation of choice for most visi-

tors. Innkeeper Dorene Henschen tells guests not to miss the beauty of the woods as seen on the guided trail rides.

Historic Interest: Malabar Farm, where Humphrey Bogart & Lauren Bacall were married (20 miles).

Innkeeper(s): Dorene Henschen. $105-195. 6 rooms with PB and 5 suites. Breakfast and afternoon tea included in rates. Types of meals: Cont plus, picnic lunch, dinner and room service. Beds: QT. Jacuzzis in suites in room. Antiquing, cross-country skiing, downhill skiing, fishing and water sports nearby.

Publicity: *Columbus Dispatch, Country Extra, One Tank Trips, Getaways, Home and Away and Ohio Magazine.*

"Warm hospitality . . . Beautiful surroundings and pure peace & quiet. What more could one want from a B&B in the country? Thank you for an excellent memory!"

Geneva On The Lake   B9

Eagle Cliff Inn

5254 Lake Road East
Geneva On The Lake, OH 44041
(440)466-1110 Fax:(440)466-0315
E-mail: beachclub5@adelphia.net
Web: www.beachclubbandb.com

Circa 1880. Catering to adults, this recently renovated 1880 Victorian inn graces one acre of the Strip in the state's first resort village. It is listed in the National Register, noted as significantly reflecting the dominant recreation history of Geneva On The Lake. Enjoy the relaxed atmosphere while sitting on white wicker cushioned chairs and rockers or a porch swing. Elegantly functional guest bedrooms and a suite offer views of the Strip. The cottages are situated privately in the back. Savor a satisfying daily breakfast. Magnificent sunsets are best viewed from the inn's easy beach access. Sip a local wine from famed Ashtabula County while chatting by the fireplace. Visit the nearby Jenny Munger Museum.

Historic Interest: In 1995, the inn was nominated and placed on the National Registry of Historic Places under Criterian A as a significant resource reflecting the recreation history that is the dominant theme in the history of Geneva On The Lake.

Innkeeper(s): LuAnn & Jerry Busch. $80-140. 6 rooms with PB, 1 suite and 3 cottages. Breakfast, afternoon tea and snacks/refreshments included in rates. Types of meals: Full gourmet bkfst and early coffee/tea. Beds: KQ. Reading lamp, ceiling fan and heat in room. Air conditioning. Fax, copier, telephone, fireplace, laundry facility, parlor and library with fireplaces on premises. Amusement parks, antiquing, art galleries, beach, bicycling, cross-country skiing, fishing, golf, hiking, parks, shopping, tennis, water sports and wineries nearby.

Publicity: *"Superior Small Lodging."*

Georgetown   J3

Bailey House

112 N Water St
Georgetown, OH 45121-1332
(937)378-3087

Circa 1830. The stately columns of this three-story Greek Revival house once greeted Ulysses S. Grant, a frequent visitor during his boyhood when he was sent to buy milk from the Bailey's. A story is told that Grant accidentally overheard that the Bailey boy was leaving West Point. Grant immediately ran through the woods to the home of Congressman Thomas Hamer and petitioned an appointment in Bailey's place which he received, thus launching his military career. The inn has

double parlors, pegged oak floors and Federal-style fireplace mantels. Antique washstands, chests and beds are found in the large guest rooms.

Innkeeper(s): Nancy Purdy. $60. 4 rooms, 2 with FP. Breakfast included in rates. Types of meals: Full bkfst and early coffee/tea. Beds: QD. Reading lamp, clock radio, telephone, desk, fireplace (two rooms) and desk (one room) in room. Air conditioning. Library, parlor games, fireplace and herb garden on premises. Weddings, small meetings, family reunions and seminars hosted. Antiquing, fishing, golf, parks, shopping, tennis, water sports, private tours of U.S. Grant Home, historic sites and John Ruthven Art Gallery nearby.

"Thank you for your warm hospitality, from the comfortable house to the delicious breakfast."

Hanoverton E9

The Spread Eagle Tavern & Inn

10150 Plymouth St, PO Box 277
Hanoverton, OH 44423
(330)223-1583 Fax:(330)223-1445
E-mail: dpeterson@spreadeagletavern.com
Web: www.spreadeagletavern.com

Circa 1837. For nearly two centuries, this three-story brick inn has graced historic Plymouth Street. The interior has been meticulously restored and maintains its early 19th-century ambiance. The restoration effort included repairing brick parts of the inn with bricks that came from an Ohio house more than 30 years older than the inn. Exposed beams, refurbished wood floors and period decor and furnishings adorn the interior. Original fireplaces still showcase color tile. The inn's restaurant offers a variety of dinner specials served in a room with authentic Federal-style decor. Guests might start off with clam chowder or an appetizer of baked Brie. As an entree, guests might choose rainbow trout, shrimp scampi or maybe a hearty porterhouse or New York strip steak.

Innkeeper(s): Peter & Jean Johnson. $150-200. 5 rooms with PB, 4 with FP. Breakfast included in rates. Types of meals: Full bkfst, gourmet lunch and gourmet dinner. Restaurant on premises. Beds: KQD. Cable TV, reading lamp, clock radio and telephone in room. Air conditioning. Fax, copier and fireplace on premises. Weddings and small meetings hosted. Antiquing, fishing, golf and parks nearby.

Publicity: *Midwest Living, Colonial Homes and Ohio Magazine.*

Hartville D8

Ivy & Lace

415 S Prospect Ave
Hartville, OH 44632-9401
(330)877-6357
E-mail: suzbnb@juno.com

Circa 1920. Large trees shade the exterior of Ivy & Lace, a historic home built in the Mission and four-square architectural styles, both of which were popular when the property was being constructed. Hartville's blacksmith built this home. Guest rooms feature antique furnishings, including a few pieces from the innkeepers' family. Rates include a full breakfast, and the artfully presented morning specialties include garnishes of fresh flowers or fresh fruit. Crepes and French toast are among the entrees. Guests can walk from the home to the Town

Square with its charming shops. French and Flea markets, Quail Hollow State Park, Pro Football Hall of Fame and First Ladies Library are popular attractions in the area.

Innkeeper(s): Sue & Paul Tarr. $65-75. 3 rooms, 1 with PB. Breakfast included in rates. Types of meals: Full bkfst. Beds: QDT. Cable TV, reading lamp, refrigerator, ceiling fan, clock radio and phones can be arranged in room. Air conditioning. TV, parlor games and fireplace on premises. Antiquing, cross-country skiing, golf, live theater, museums, parks, shopping and sporting events nearby.

Hiram C9

The Lily Ponds B&B

PO Box 322, 6720 Wakefield Rd
Hiram, OH 44234-0322
(330)569-3222 (800)325-5087 Fax:(330)569-3223
E-mail: lilypondsbb@aol.com
Web: www.lilypondsbedandbreakfast.com

Circa 1940. This homestay is located on 20 acres of woodland dotted with rhododendron and mountain laurel. There are two large ponds and an old stone bridge. Your hostess works with a tour company and has traveled around the world. The inn's decor includes her collections of Eskimo art and artifacts and a variety of antiques. Pecan waffles served with locally harvested maple syrup are a favorite breakfast. Guests enjoy borrowing the canoe or hiking the inn's trails. Sea World and Six Flags are 15-minute drive away.

Innkeeper(s): Marilane Spencer. $75-95. 3 rooms with PB. Breakfast included in rates. Types of meals: Full bkfst and early coffee/tea. Beds: KQT. Cable TV, reading lamp and clock radio in room. Air conditioning. TV, VCR, bicycles, library, child care, parlor games, telephone, fireplace, canoeing and skiing on premises. Small meetings and family reunions hosted. Amusement parks, antiquing, canoeing/kayaking, cross-country skiing, downhill skiing, fishing, golf, parks, shopping, water sports, Six Flags and Sea World nearby.

Publicity: *Local newspaper, Record-Courier and Record-News.*

"We felt like we were staying with friends from the very start."

Kelleys Island C5

Himmelblau B&B

337 Shannon Way
Kelleys Island, OH 43438
(419)746-2200

Circa 1893. This secluded Queen Anne Victorian on the Eastern Shore of Kelleys Island rests on more than eight acres of lake front lawns and cedar groves. Its front yard tree swing and slate blue and white gabled entrance offer an inviting introduction to a pleasant stay. Once the summer home of an Ohio governor, the property was also an early 1900s vineyard. Inside are a screened porch and a second-floor reading corner, which offers expansive Lake Erie views. A favorite activity of guests is to walk along the pristine shoreline at sunrise. The more adventurous enjoy snorkeling around an old shipwreck yards from the shoreline. Watching for white-tail deer after a moonlight swim, sunbathing and stargazing are popular activities, as well.

Innkeeper(s): Marvin Robinson. $95-150. 4 rooms, 1 with PB. Breakfast included in rates. Types of meals: Full gourmet bkfst. Beds: KQD. Reading lamp, ceiling fan and fireplace in room. Air conditioning. TV, VCR, swimming, bicycles, library, parlor games and fireplace on premises. Weddings, small meetings, family reunions and seminars hosted. Amusement parks, antiquing, art galleries, beach, bicycling, canoeing/kayaking, fishing, hiking, parks, shopping, water sports and wineries nearby.

Lakeshore Landing

229 Lakeshore Drive
Kelleys Island, OH 43438
(419)746-2210

Circa 1928. Whether arriving by boat, ferry or plane, this waterfront bed & breakfast on the south side of the picturesque island will captivate and please. Situated just west of Seaway Marina, a lookout offers a scenic setting for magnificent sunsets; the private beach and dock are added conveniences. Air-conditioned guest bedrooms are cheery and bright with antique furnishings and lake views. After an expanded continental breakfast, rent a bike or golf cart to explore the local area. Downtown is only one and a half blocks away.

Innkeeper(s): Caroline DeBoard. $95-125. 3 rooms, 2 with PB. Breakfast included in rates. Types of meals: Cont. TV, VCR, reading lamp and ceiling fan in room. Central air. Swimming, telephone and fireplace on premises. Amusement parks, antiquing, beach, bicycling, fishing, hiking, parks, shopping and wineries nearby.

Lebanon   H2

Burl Manor

230 S Mechanic St
Lebanon, OH 45036-2212
(513)934-0400 (800)450-0401
E-mail: burl_manor@yahoo.com
Web: www.burlmanor.com

Circa 1847. This handsome mansion was originally built for William Denney, an early editor and publisher for Ohio's oldest weekly newspaper, the Western Star. In addition to the parlors and formal dining room, the manor has an unusual center staircase.There are Oriental rugs, period wallpapers and carved fireplaces. A swimming pool, lawn croquet, volleyball and basketball are among the activities that can be enjoyed on the premises. Guests can ride a bike or rent a canoe and enjoy the sites of the Little Miami River. Tennis and golf are just minutes away.

Innkeeper(s): Mark & Beth Lewis. $100. 2 rooms with PB. Breakfast included in rates. Types of meals: Full bkfst. Beds: Q. Fireplace, workout room and pool on premises.

Loudonville   E6

Blackfork Inn

303 N Water St
Loudonville, OH 44842-1273
(419)994-3252
E-mail: bfinn@bright.net
Web: www.blackforkinn.com

Circa 1865. A Civil War businessman, Philip Black, brought the railroad to town and built the Blackfork. Its well-preserved Second Empire style has earned it a place in the National Register. Noted preservationists have restored the inn with care and it is filled with a collection of Ohio antiques. Located in a scenic Amish area, the three-course breakfasts feature local produce. The innkeepers also offer two large three-room suites in a restored 1847 house, one suite includes a gas fireplace.

Historic Interest: Accurate restoration. Extensive collection of Ohio-made 19th-century furniture, glass, pottery and huge library.

Innkeeper(s): Sue & Al Gorisek. $70-125. 8 rooms with PB and 2 suites. Breakfast included in rates. Types of meals: Country bkfst, veg bkfst and early coffee/tea. Beds: KQDT. Reading lamp, CD player and desk in room.

Central air. Sauna, bicycles, library, parlor games and masseuse on call on premises. Weddings, small meetings, family reunions and seminars hosted. Antiquing, art galleries, beach, bicycling, canoeing/kayaking, cross-country skiing, downhill skiing, fishing, golf, horseback riding, live theater, museums, parks, shopping, sporting events, tennis, water sports and wineries nearby.

Magnolia   E8

Elson Inn

225 North Main St (Rt 183)
Magnolia, OH 44643
(333)866-9242 Fax:(330)866-3398
E-mail: jelson@neo.rr.com
Web: www.elsoninn.com

Circa 1879. Experience small-town America at this brick Victorian Italianate. This stately home's elegant sense of history is felt from the 10-foot, leaded-glass double doors to the marble fireplaces. Climb the staircase to the romantic guest rooms, furnished in antiques and quilts, with spacious ceilings and private baths. Each day begins with a delicious breakfast featuring specialties such as crème brulee French toast, fresh fruit and muffins with the inn's own special label jams and jellies. A shady, wraparound porch provides the perfect place to relax in a swing or one of the rocking chairs. A free tour is offered of the 1834 flour mill next door to the inn. There are ducks to be fed on the pond, and other activities include fishing, hiking, tennis, golf and fine dining across the street.

Innkeeper(s): Jo Lane & Gus Elson. $100-120. 5 rooms, 4 with PB and 1 conference room. Breakfast included in rates. Types of meals: Full bkfst. Beds: KQD. Modem hook-up, reading lamp and clock in room. Central air. TV, VCR, fax, copier, tennis, library, parlor games, telephone, fireplace and laundry facility on premises. Weddings, small meetings, family reunions and seminars hosted. Amusement parks, antiquing, art galleries, beach, bicycling, canoeing/kayaking, fishing, golf, hiking, live theater, museums, parks, shopping, sporting events, tennis, water sports, National Football Hall of Fame, National 1st Ladies Library and Amish Settlement nearby.

Publicity: *Times Reporter, Canton Repository, Free Press News, Cleveland Plain Dealer, Akron Beacon Journal, Inspected and Approved by the Ohio B&B Association and Voted "Most Historical Inn" by Arrington's B&B Journal.*

Marietta   H8

The Buckley House

332 Front St
Marietta, OH 45750-2913
(740)373-3080 (888)282-5540

Circa 1879. Conveniently located in the downtown historic district, this Southern-style home features impressive views of Muskingum Park, Lookout Point and Valley Gem, a traditional stern-wheel boat. After a peaceful night's rest in the well-appointed guest bedrooms, begin a new day with a delicious breakfast. A New Orleans-style garden with gazebo and fish pond grace the grounds that include a spa. Ponder fond memories while relaxing on the double porches or decks. The coveted Pineapple Award for excellence was bestowed on this inn by the Ohio Bed and Breakfast Association.

Innkeeper(s): Dell & Alf Nicholas. $85-95. 3 rooms with PB. Breakfast included in rates. Types of meals: Full bkfst and early coffee/tea. Beds: KDT. Reading lamp and ceiling fan in room. Central air. VCR, fax, spa, library, parlor games, telephone and fireplace on premises. Weddings, small meetings, family reunions and seminars hosted. Antiquing, fishing, live theater, parks, shopping and water sports nearby.

Marion   E5

Hide Away Country Inn

1601 SR 4
Marion, OH 43302
(419)562-3013 (800)570-8233 Fax:(419)562-3003
E-mail: innkeeper@hideawayinn.com
Web: www.hideawayinn.com

Circa 1938. Experience a refreshing getaway while staying at
this remarkable inn. Because of the inn's outrageous service,
even the business traveler will feel rejuvenated after embarking
on a rendezvous with nature here. Exquisite guest suites feature
private Jacuzzis, fireplaces and amenities that pamper. Savor a
leisurely five-course breakfast. Enjoy fine dining in the restaurant, or ask for an intimate picnic to be arranged. A productive
conference room instills a personal quiet and inspires the mind.
Innkeeper(s): Steve & Debbie Miller. $87-287. 12 rooms with PB, 7 with FP,
8 suites and 2 conference rooms. Breakfast included in rates. Types of meals:
Full gourmet bkfst, early coffee/tea, gourmet lunch, picnic lunch, afternoon
tea, snacks/refreshments, gourmet dinner and room service. Restaurant on
premises. Beds: KQD. TV, VCR, ceiling fan, snack bar, telephone, turn-down
service, voice mail, fireplace, satellite TV and Jacuzzi in room. Air conditioning. Fax, copier, swimming, bicycles, library and child care on premises.
Weddings, small meetings, family reunions and seminars hosted. Amusement
parks, antiquing, bicycling, downhill skiing, fishing, golf, hiking, horseback
riding, live theater, parks, shopping, sporting events, water sports and Baja
boats nearby.
Publicity: *New York Times, Columbus Dispatch, Ohio Country Journal, Akron
Beacon Journal, Cleveland Plain Dealer, Travel & Leisure, Neil Zurcker One
Tank-Trips-Cleveland, Akron WKBN, Del's Folks and Del's Feasts Cleveland
and Cleveland WKYC.*

Miamisburg   H2

English Manor B&B

505 E Linden Ave
Miamisburg, OH 45342-2850
(937)866-2288 (800)676-9456
E-mail: englishmanor@englishmanorbandb.com
Web: www.englishmanorbandb.com

Circa 1924. This is a beautiful English Tudor mansion situated
on a tree-lined street of Victorian homes. Well-chosen antiques
combined with the innkeepers' personal heirlooms added to the

inn's polished floors, sparkling lead-
ed-and stained-glass windows and
shining silver, make this an elegant
retreat. Breakfast is served in the formal dining room. Fine restaurants, a
water park, baseball, air force museum and theater are close by, as is
The River Corridor bikeway on the
banks of the Great Miami River.
Historic Interest: 10 minutes south of Dayton.
Innkeeper(s): Julie & Larry Chmiel. $79-95. 5 rooms and 1 conference room.
Breakfast included in rates. Types of meals: Full bkfst. Clock radio, telephone
and turn-down service in room. Air conditioning. VCR and fireplace on premises. Weddings, small meetings, family reunions and seminars hosted.
Amusement parks, antiquing, live theater, shopping and sporting events nearby.

Millersburg   F7

Hotel Millersburg

35 West Jackson Street
Millersburg, OH 44654
(330)674-1457 (800)822-1457 Fax:(330)674-4487
E-mail: hotelmillersburg@valkyrie.net
Web: www.hotelmillersburg.com

Circa 1847. Built in the state's earliest frontier, this hotel is the
area's oldest large building and was a welcome improvement
over the era's stagecoach inns. Listed in the National Register,
extensive renovations have retained its historical integrity while
adding modern refinements. The pristine exterior and rooms
with tin ceilings reflect yesterday's virtues while an elaborate
fire safety system and private bathrooms offer today's comforts.
Smoking and non-smoking guest bedrooms feature air conditioning, cable TV and a coffeemaker. Handmade Amish quilts
grace many of the beds. Two-room suites include a large sitting
room. Dine in the Tavern with an ornate brass and oak bar and
a full menu with daily specials and Certified Angus Beef. The
Courtyard boasts live entertainment and fresh grilled meats.
The elegant Formal Dining Room is perfect to reserve for private banquets or parties.
Historic Interest: Built in 1847 and renovated to retain historical flavor.
Innkeeper(s): Bill Robinson. $35-109. 24 rooms with PB, 2 suites and 1
conference room. Types of meals: Lunch and dinner. Restaurant on premises.
Beds: QDT. Private bath, air conditioning, cable TV with remote, coffeemaker,
telephone and daily housekeeping service in room. TV, fax, copier, parlor
games and telephone on premises. Small meetings, family reunions and seminars hosted. Antiquing, bicycling, canoeing/kayaking, fishing, golf, hiking,
horseback riding and shopping nearby.

Mount Vernon   F6

The Chaney Manor

7864 Newark Road
Mount Vernon, OH 43050-9569
(740)392-2304
E-mail: chaney@ecr.net

Circa 1823. Spanning six gorgeous rural acres, the grounds
evoke an arboretum ambiance with theme gardens, benches,
fountains, life-size statues, a pond, bridge and covered dock.
The Federal style architecture with Greek Revival elements was
built in 1823 for the Ohio state representative, James
McFarland. Let creativity flow in the fully supplied art loft. Avid
readers will enjoy the bookbarn. Guest suites and common
rooms reflect a variety of decor that include Victorian, British
Colonial, Early American, rustic and modern. Enjoy pleasurable
amenities such as robes, videos, bath and spa products, a
refrigerator, coffee pot and oversized Jacuzzi. A gourmet breakfast is included and custom dinners can be ordered in advance.
Browse the gift shop to buy the James McFarland House 180th
Anniversary Brew custom coffee and the House Blessings book.
Three historic districts are all nearby.
Innkeeper(s): Freda & Norman Chaney. $90-100. 2 suites. Breakfast, after-
noon tea and snacks/refreshments included in rates. Types of meals: Full
gourmet bkfst and gourmet dinner. Beds: Q. TV, VCR, reading lamp and desk
in room. Central air. Spa, library, parlor games, telephone, fireplace, laundry
facility, refrigerator in Jacuzzi room, coffee pot, free bath and spa supplies,
robes for guest use, stereos, free VCR movies, art loft with free supplies for
guests, original art, gift baskets and "House Blessings" book is sold in the gift
shop on premises. Small meetings hosted. Antiquing, art galleries, beach,

bicycling, canoeing/kayaking, downhill skiing, fishing, golf, hiking, horseback riding, live theater, museums, parks, shopping, sporting events, tennis and wineries nearby.

Publicity: *Mount Vernon News, 2004 Arrington's B and B Inn Traveler Guide and Time-Warner TV.*

The Russell-Cooper House

115 E Gambier St
Mount Vernon, OH 43050-3509
(740)397-8638 Fax:(740)397-3839
E-mail: mdvorak@jdsi.net
Web: www.russell-cooper.com

Circa 1829. Dr. John Russell and his son-in-law, Colonel Cooper, modeled a simple brick Federal house into a unique Victorian. Its sister structure is the Wedding Cake House of Kennebunk,

 Maine. There is a hand-painted plaster ceiling in the ballroom and a collection of Civil War items and antique medical devices. Woodwork is of cherry, maple and walnut, and there are etched and stained-glass windows. Hal Holbrook called the town "America's Hometown."

Historic Interest: In 2004 The Russell-Cooper House will be 175 years old. It is located in historic Mount Vernon, and the area offers numerous state and national historic sites.

Innkeeper(s): Tom & Mary Dvorak. $65-100. 6 rooms with PB and 1 conference room. Breakfast and snacks/refreshments included in rates. Types of meals: Full gourmet bkfst. Beds: QDT. Cable TV, reading lamp, ceiling fan and clock radio in room. Air conditioning. Fax, copier, telephone and fireplace on premises. Weddings, small meetings, family reunions and seminars hosted. Antiquing, golf, parks, shopping and bike trails nearby.

Publicity: *Ohio Business, Victorian Homes, Columbus Monthly, Innsider, Country, Americana, Columbus Dispatch, Ohio, Midwest Living, New York Times and Washingtonian.*

"A salute to the preservation of American history and culture. Most hospitable owners! A romantic memory we will always remember!"

Painesville   B8

Rider's 1812 Inn

792 Mentor Ave
Painesville, OH 44077-2516
(440)354-8200 Fax:(440)350-9385
E-mail: ridersinn@ncweb.com
Web: www.ridersinn.com

Circa 1812. In the days when this inn and tavern served the frontier Western Reserve, it could provide lodging and meals for more than 100 overnight guests. Restored in 1988, the pub features an original fireplace and wavy window panes. Most of the inn's floors are rare, long-needle pine. A passageway in the cellar is said to have been part of the Underground Railroad. An English-style restaurant is also on the premises. Guest rooms are furnished with antiques. Breakfast in bed is the option of choice.

Historic Interest: President Garfield's Home, Shadybrook, Lake County Historical Museum, Harbor Lighthouse.

Innkeeper(s): Elaine Crane & Gary Herman, Bob Beauvais- General Manager. $75-101. 10 rooms, 9 with PB, 1 suite and 3 conference rooms. Breakfast included in rates. Types of meals: Full gourmet bkfst, veg bkfst, early coffee/tea, lunch, picnic lunch, afternoon tea, dinner and room service. Beds: KQDT. Cable TV, reading lamp, CD player, refrigerator, ceiling fan, snack bar, clock radio, telephone, turn-down service, desk and voice mail in room. Central air. Fax, copier, library, pet boarding, child care, parlor games, fireplace and laundry facility on premises. Weddings, small meetings, family

reunions and seminars hosted. Antiquing, art galleries, beach, cross-country skiing, fishing, golf, horseback riding, live theater, museums, parks, shopping, sporting events, tennis and wineries nearby.

Publicity: *Business Review, News-Herald, Midwest Living, WEWS, Haunted Ohio V and Channel 5.*

Port Clinton   C5

SunnySide Tower Bed & Breakfast Inn

3612 NW Catawba Rd
Port Clinton, OH 43452-9726
(419)797-9315 (888)831-1263
E-mail: ssidetowr@cros.net
Web: www.sunnysidetower.com

Circa 1879. One of Catawba Island's original landmarks, this classic Victorian farmhouse is the innkeeper's ancestral family home. The hilltop inn and tower with a fourth-story widow's watch sits on 19 acres of wooded nature trails, herb gardens and landscaping. A glacial rock fireplace is showcased in the great room, or relax in the sunroom, a screened porch with wicker furniture. Distinctive country antique guest bedrooms feature comfortable period furnishings. Appetites are awakened with the aroma of gourmet coffee and teas accompanying a country breakfast. Share a romantic moment in a double hammock, or soak in the hot tub. The area offers easy access to a variety of Lake Erie activities and several state parks.

Innkeeper(s): John Davenport. $69-159. 10 rooms, 4 with PB and 1 conference room. Breakfast included in rates. Types of meals: Country bkfst. Beds: KQD. Reading lamp, ceiling fan and clock radio in room. Central air. TV, parlor games, telephone, fireplace, laundry facility, hot tub and children's play area on premises. Handicap access. Weddings, small meetings, family reunions and seminars hosted. Amusement parks, antiquing, art galleries, beach, bicycling, canoeing/kayaking, fishing, golf, hiking, live theater, museums, parks, shopping, tennis, water sports, wineries, basketball courts, baseball/soccer fields and sledding hill nearby.

Ripley   J3

The Signal House

234 N Front St
Ripley, OH 45167-1015
(937)392-1640 Fax:(937)392-1640

Circa 1830. This Greek Italianate home is said to have been used to aid the Underground Railroad. A light in the attic told Rev. John Rankin, a dedicated abolitionist, that it was safe to transport slaves to freedom. Located within a 55-acre historical

 district, guests can take a glance back in time, exploring museums and antique shops. Twelve-foot ceilings with ornate plaster-work grace the parlor, and guests can sit on any of three porches anticipating paddlewheelers traversing the Ohio River.

Innkeeper(s): Vic & Betsy Billingsley. $95-150. 2 rooms and 1 suite. Breakfast included in rates. Types of meals: Full bkfst and early coffee/tea. Beds: Q. Reading lamp, ceiling fan, clock radio and iron in room. Central air. TV, VCR, fax, copier, library, parlor games, telephone and fireplace on premises. Small meetings hosted. Antiquing, bicycling, fishing, golf, hiking, museums, parks, shopping, tennis, water sports, wineries and canoeing nearby.

Publicity: *Cincinnati Enquirer, Ohio Columbus Dispatch, Ohio Off the Beaten Path, Cincinnati Magazine, Cincinnati Post, Dayton Daily News, Ohio Magazine, Cleveland Plain Dealer, Channel 12, WKRC- "One Tank Trip" and Husband's first car in "Lost in Yonkers."*

Sagamore Hills   D8

The Inn at Brandywine Falls

8230 Brandywine Rd
Sagamore Hills, OH 44067-2810
(330)467-1812 (888)306-3381 Fax:(330)467-2162
E-mail: brandywinefallsinn@prodigy.net
Web: www.innatbrandywinefalls.com

Circa 1848. Overlooking Brandywine Falls and situated snug-
gly on National Parkland, this National Register Greek Revival
farmhouse has been meticulously renovated. Antiques made in
Ohio are featured in the Greek Revival-style rooms and include
sleigh and four-poster beds. Some suites include a double
whirlpool tub. The kitchen has been designed to allow guests
to chat with the innkeepers while sipping coffee in front of a
crackling fireplace and watching breakfast preparations. The
Waterfall and hiking trails are just past the gate. Cleveland is a
short drive, offering attractions such as the Rock 'n' Roll Hall of
Fame and the Cleveland Orchestra.

Innkeeper(s): Katie & George Hoy. $108-295. 6 rooms with PB, 3 with FP
and 3 suites. Breakfast included in rates. Types of meals: Full gourmet bkfst,
veg bkfst and snacks/refreshments. Beds: KDT. Modem hook-up, TV, VCR,
reading lamp, stereo, refrigerator, ceiling fan, clock radio, telephone, coffeemaker, hot tub/spa and fireplace in room. Central air. Fax, copier, spa,
library, pet boarding, parlor games, fireplace, laundry facility and gift shop on
premises. Limited handicap access. Weddings, small meetings, family
reunions and seminars hosted. Amusement parks, antiquing, art galleries,
bicycling, canoeing/kayaking, cross-country skiing, downhill skiing, fishing,
golf, hiking, museums, parks, shopping and wineries nearby.

Publicity: *Ohio Magazine, Countryside, Innsider, Western Reserve, Cleveland
Plain Dealer, Akron Beacon Journal, Vindicator, Dayton Daily News and
Michigan Living.*

"The magic of the inn was not forgotten. We will be back to enjoy."

Sandusky   C5

Wagner's 1844 Inn

230 E Washington St
Sandusky, OH 44870-2611
(419)626-1726 Fax:(419)626-0002

Circa 1844. This inn originally was constructed as a log cabin.
Additions and renovations were made, and the house evolved
into Italianate style accented with brackets under the eaves and
black shutters on the second-story windows. A wrought-iron
fence frames the house, and there are ornate wrought-iron
porch rails. A billiard room and screened-in porch are available
to guests. The ferry to Cedar Point and Lake Erie Island is within walking distance.

Innkeeper(s): Barb Wagner. $70-120. 3 rooms with PB, 2 with FP. Breakfast
included in rates. Types of meals: Cont. Beds: Q. Reading lamp, clock radio
and desk in room. Air conditioning. Library, parlor games, telephone, fireplace and TV on premises. Amusement parks, antiquing, fishing, parks, shopping, Lake Erie Islands and golf nearby.

Publicity: *Lorain Journal and Sandusky Register.*

"This B&B rates in our Top 10."

Springboro   H2

Wright House Bed & Breakfast

80 W. State Street
Springboro, OH 45066
(937)748-0801 (866)748-0801 Fax:(937)748-1550

Circa 1815. One of the area's 27 documented Underground
Railroad sites, this historic Federal brick home was built in
1815. Antique furnishings blend well with recent renovations
to provide modern conveniences. Watch television or play
games by the fire in a common room. Comfortable guest bedrooms offer peaceful privacy. Breakfast may include fresh fruit,
hot muffins, quiche and an assortment of beverages. Stroll
through the grounds featuring English-style gardens.

Historic Interest: Home was built in 1815. Documented Underground
Railroad sites.

Innkeeper(s): Burt Correll. $75-95. 2 rooms with PB. Breakfast and after-
noon tea included in rates. Types of meals: Full gourmet bkfst and early coffee-
fee/tea. Beds: KD. Cable TV, reading lamp, stereo, ceiling fan, clock radio,
turn-down service and desk in room. Central air. Fax, parlor games, telephone
and fireplace on premises. Amusement parks, antiquing, art galleries, beach,
bicycling, canoeing/kayaking, fishing, golf, hiking, live theater, museums,
parks, shopping and tennis nearby.

Tiffin   D5

Fort Ball Bed & Breakfast

25 Adams St
Tiffin, OH 44883-2208
(419)447-0776 (888)447-0776 Fax:(419)448-8415

Circa 1894. The prominent front turret and wraparound porch
are classic details of this Queen Anne Revival house built by
John King, builder of the Tiffin Court House and College Hall
at Heidelberg College. The innkeepers dedicated more than a

year restoring this turn-of-the-century
Victorian to its original elegant state.
The renovation yielded rich hardwood
flooring, wood paneling and many
additional architectural details like the
elaborate woodwork in the parlor,
front entryway and sitting room. Guest
rooms are comfortably decorated to
accommodate business travelers, families or honeymooners, and offer pri-
vate and shared baths while some feature whirlpool tubs for
two. Breakfast can be enjoyed in the dining room with its elegantly restored woodwork. The inn is within walking distance
of the downtown business district, restaurants, antiques, shopping, museums and theater.

Innkeeper(s): Charles & Lenora Livingston. $65-105. 4 rooms, 2 with PB.
Breakfast and snacks/refreshments included in rates. Types of meals: Full
bkfst and early coffee/tea. Beds: KQDT. TV, VCR, reading lamp, ceiling fan,
clock radio, telephone and hot tub/spa in room. Air conditioning. Fax, library,
parlor games and fireplace on premises. Small meetings hosted. Amusement
parks, antiquing, golf, live theater, parks, tennis and historical sites nearby.

Publicity: *Advertiser-Tribune.*

Urbana G3

Northern Plantation B&B

3421 E RR 296
Urbana, OH 43078
(937)652-1782 (800)652-1782

Circa 1913. This Victorian farmhouse, located on 100 acres, is occupied by fourth-generation family members. (Marsha's father was born in the downstairs bedroom in 1914.) The

Homestead Library is decorated traditionally and has a handsome fireplace, while the dining room features a dining set and a china cabinet made by the innkeeper's great-grandfather. Most of the guest rooms

have canopy beds. A large country breakfast is served. On the property is a fishing pond, corn fields, soybeans and woods with a creek. Nearby are Ohio Caverns and Indian Lake.

Innkeeper(s): Marsha J. Martin. $85-105. 4 rooms, 1 with PB. Breakfast included in rates. Types of meals: Full bkfst and snacks/refreshments. Beds: KD. Reading lamp and clock radio in room. Air conditioning. VCR, library, parlor games, telephone and fireplace on premises. Weddings and family reunions hosted. Antiquing, cross-country skiing, parks, shopping and Pratt Castle nearby.

West Union J4

Murphin Ridge Inn

750 Murphin Ridge Rd
West Union, OH 45693-9734
(937)544-2263 (877)687-7446
E-mail: murphinn@bright.net
Web: www.murphinridgeinn.com

Circa 1810. The inn is contemporary, yet situated on an historic 142-acre woodland farm imparting a tranquil atmosphere. Some of the guest bedrooms feature fireplaces and/or porches.

Three new Amish-built log cabins boast two-person showers and double whirlpool tubs. A romantic ambiance is enhanced by three-sided open fireplaces. Meals are served in an 1810 red-brick farmhouse. Visit a

neighboring Amish community, Serpent Mound and the Edge of Appalachia Nature Preserve.

Innkeeper(s): Sherry & Darryl McKenney. $90-185. 10 rooms with PB and 3 cabins. Breakfast included in rates. Types of meals: Full bkfst, lunch and gourmet dinner. Restaurant on premises. Beds: Q. Antiquing nearby.

Publicity: *Midwest Living, Ohio Magazine, National Geographic Traveler, Cincinnati Enquirer, Midwest Living and Ohio Magazine.*

"Restful, relaxing escape. Outstanding autumn color, trails, hospitality."

Worthington G5

The Worthington Inn

649 High St
Worthington, OH 43085-4144
(614)885-2600 Fax:(614)885-1283
E-mail: reservations@worthingtoninn.com
Web: www.worthingtoninn.com

Circa 1831. One of the area's most significant landmarks, this extensively restored and expanded inn features architecture and decor that reflects Early American Colonial, Federalist and Victorian styles. Considered a distinguished small hotel, expect to find luxurious accommodations, attentive service and generous upscale amenities. Each well-appointed suite and guest bedroom boasts authentic American antiques. Meals are enjoyed in the on-site Seven Seas Restaurant, highly acclaimed for its cuisine and extensive wine list. An intimate pub offers a more casual ambiance and live entertainment. The Van Loon Ballroom is perfect for weddings, meetings or special events. Executive services with cutting-edge technology easily meet business needs. Shop at specialty stores just an inviting stroll from this quaint, historic location.

Historic Interest: The inn was built in 1831 and was fully restored to its Victorian character in 1983. We preserved the character of the original inn by appointing all rooms with genuine antiques from its original period.

$150-260. 26 rooms, 22 with PB, 4 suites and 5 conference rooms. Breakfast included in rates. Types of meals: Full gourmet bkfst, lunch, snacks/refreshments, dinner and room service. Restaurant on premises. Beds: QD. Data port, cable TV, reading lamp, clock radio, telephone, turn-down service, desk and voice mail in room. Air conditioning. Fax, copier and gift shop on premises. Weddings, small meetings, family reunions and seminars hosted. Amusement parks, antiquing, art galleries, bicycling, golf, hiking, live theater, parks, shopping and sporting events nearby.

Publicity: *Country Inns, Columbus Dispatch, Columbus Monthly, Ohio and Midwest Living.*

Youngstown D10

The Inn at the Green

500 S Main St
Youngstown, OH 44514-2032
(330)757-4688

Circa 1876. Main Street in Poland has a parade of historic houses including Connecticut Western Reserve colonials, Federal and Greek Revival houses. The Inn at the Green is a Classic Victorian Baltimore townhouse. Two of the common rooms, the greeting room and parlor have working marble fireplaces. Interiors evoke an authentic 19th-century atmosphere with antiques and Oriental art and rugs that enhance the moldings, 12-foot ceilings and poplar floors.

Innkeeper(s): Ginny & Steve Meloy. $60-70. 4 rooms with PB, 3 with FP. Breakfast included in rates. Types of meals: Cont. Beds: QDT. Cable TV, VCR, reading lamp, stereo, clock radio, telephone and desk in room. Air conditioning. Fireplace on premises. Antiquing, golf, live theater, parks, shopping, biking trails, Amish country and Butler Institute of American Art nearby.

Publicity: *The Vindicator.*

"Thank you for a comfortable and perfect stay in your beautiful Victorian home."

Oklahoma

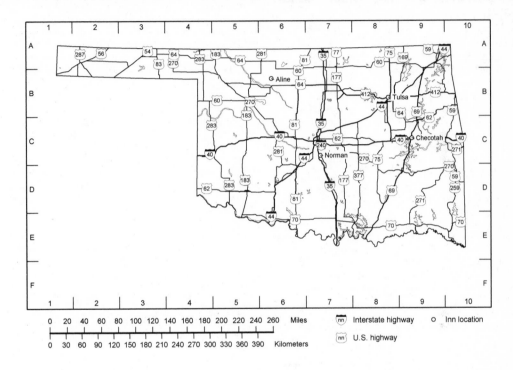

	1	2	3	4	5	6	7	8	9	10

Scale:
0 20 40 60 80 100 120 140 160 180 200 220 240 260 Miles
0 30 60 90 120 150 180 210 240 270 300 330 360 390 Kilometers

Interstate highway
U.S. highway
Inn location

Aline   B6

Heritage Manor

33 Heritage Road
Aline, OK 73716-9118
(580)463-2563 (800)295-2563

Circa 1903. This inn provides a way to enjoy and experience the ambiance of the turn of the century. Explore and relax in the inn's peaceful gardens and 80-acre wildlife habitat and watch song birds, butterflies, long-haired cattle, donkeys, llamas and ostriches. The inn invites visitors to enjoy its more than 5,000-volume library and more than a 100 channels on Dish TV. Guests can walk the suspension bridge to two rooftop decks and a widow's walk to view the stars and sunsets. There is also an out-door hot tub for soaking. Dine in the parlor, gazebo, courtyard or tree-top-level deck where the choice of time and menu is entirely up to the guest.

Innkeeper(s): A.J. & Carolyn Rexroat. $55-150. 4 rooms, 2 suites and 2 conference rooms. Breakfast and snacks/refreshments included in rates. Types of meals: Full bkfst, early coffee/tea, gourmet lunch, picnic lunch, afternoon tea and gourmet dinner. Restaurant on premises. Beds: QD. Cable TV, reading lamp, telephone and desk in room. Air conditioning. VCR, spa, library, parlor games and fireplace on premises. Limited handicap access. Weddings, small meetings, family reunions and seminars hosted. Antiquing, fishing, live theater, parks, shopping, sporting events and water sports nearby.

Publicity: *Country, Enid Morning News, Daily Oklahoman, Cherokee Messenger, Republican, Fairview Republican* and *Discover Oklahoma.*

Checotah   C9

Sharpe House

301 NW 2nd St
Checotah, OK 74426-2240
(918)473-2832

Circa 1911. Built on land originally bought from a Creek Indian, this Southern plantation-style inn was a teacherage—the rooming house for single female teachers. It is furnished with heirlooms from the innkeepers' families and hand-crafted accessories. The look of the house is antebellum, but the specialty of the kitchen is Mexican cuisine. Family-style evening meals are available upon request. Checotah is located at the junction of I-40 and U.S. 69. This makes it the ideal base for your day trips of exploration or recreation in Green Country.

Innkeeper(s): Kay Kindt. $35-50. 3 rooms with PB and 1 suite. Breakfast included in rates. Types of meals: Full bkfst and early coffee/tea. Beds: D. Cable TV, reading lamp and ceiling fan in room. Air conditioning. Library, child care, parlor games, telephone and fireplace on premises. Weddings and small meetings hosted. Amusement parks, antiquing, fishing, parks, shopping and water sports nearby.

Norman   C7

Holmberg House B&B
766 Debarr Ave
Norman, OK 73069-4908
(405)321-6221 (877)621-6221 Fax:(405)321-0400
E-mail: info@holmberghouse.com
Web: www.holmberghouse.com

Circa 1914. Professor Fredrik Holmberg and his wife Signy built this Craftsman-style home across the street from the University of Oklahoma. Each of the antique-filled rooms has its own individual decor and style.

The Blue Danube and Bed & Bath rooms are romantic retreats and both include a two-person whirlpool tub. The Garden Room includes a clawfoot tub. The Sundance Room is ideal for  friends traveling together, as it includes both a queen and twin bed. The parlor and front porch are perfect places to relax with friends, and the lush grounds include a cottage garden. Aside from close access to the university, Holmberg House is within walking distance to more than a dozen restaurants.

Historic Interest: The Oklahoma Museum of Natural History is six blocks from the inn. The Cleveland County Historical Society and Lindsey Moor House are about a mile from the home. Jacobson House, a Native American museum, is six blocks away.

Innkeeper(s): Yvonne Brame & Rayma Macy. $95-120. 4 rooms with PB. Breakfast included in rates. Types of meals: Full gourmet bkfst and early coffee/tea. Beds: QT. Cable TV, reading lamp, ceiling fan and desk in room. Air conditioning. Fax, copier, library, parlor games, telephone and fireplace on premises. Weddings, small meetings and family reunions hosted. Antiquing, live theater, parks, shopping and sporting events nearby.

Publicity: *Metro Norman, Oklahoma City Journal Record, Norman Transcript and Country Inns.*

"Your hospitality and the delicious food were just super."

Tulsa   B8

McBirney Mansion B&B
1414 S Galveston Ave
Tulsa, OK 74127-9116
(918)585-3234 Fax:(918)585-9377
Web: www.mcbirneymansion.com

Circa 1927. An oil baron built this immense Tudor mansion, which is listed in the National Register. The home rests on three acres, adjacent to Tulsa River Parks. The countryside, with its spring-fed ponds, was a common gathering spot for local native tribes and early settlers. Washington Irving once camped out on the grounds and later wrote about his experience in "Tour of the Prairies." Winding stone paths lead down to the banks of the Arkansas River, and the grounds are dotted with gardens. The manor's interior is equally impressive. Bedchambers boast fine antiques, some include a marble bath or whirlpool tub. For a romantic getaway, consider the Carriage House Retreat, a private cottage with a bedroom, sitting room, small kitchen area and a bath with a jetted shower. Guests are treated to a multi-course, gourmet breakfast. The morning meal begins with fresh fruit, perhaps poached pears, strawberry compote or baked apple. The main course might include eggs Benedict, huevos rancheros, a spinach quiche served with cheese grits in a baked tomato and homemade English muffins. McBirney Mansion is close to museums, shops, antique stores, galleries, restaurants and Tulsa's business district and civic center.

Innkeeper(s): Kathy Collins & Renita Shofner. $119-225. 8 rooms with PB, 1 with FP, 3 suites and 3 conference rooms. Breakfast and snacks/refreshments included in rates. Types of meals: Full gourmet bkfst, veg bkfst, early coffee/tea and picnic lunch. Beds: KQ. Data port, cable TV, VCR, reading lamp, refrigerator, clock radio, telephone, coffeemaker, desk, voice mail and data ports in room. Central air. Fax, copier, library and parlor games on premises. Weddings, small meetings, family reunions and seminars hosted. Amusement parks, antiquing, art galleries, bicycling, fishing, golf, hiking, live theater, museums, parks, shopping and tennis nearby.

Publicity: *Southern Living, OK Today, Dallas Morning News and Tulsa People.*

Oregon

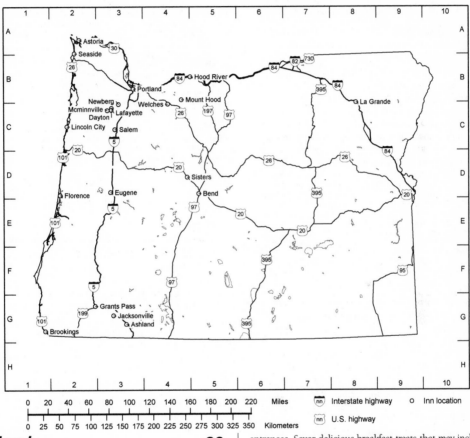

0 20 40 60 80 100 120 140 160 180 200 220   Miles

0 25 50 75 100 125 150 175 200 225 250 275 300 325 350   Kilometers

- (nn) Interstate highway   ○ Inn location
- (nn) U.S. highway

Ashland   G3

Cowslip's Belle

159 N Main St
Ashland, OR 97520-1729
(541)488-2901 (800)888-6819 Fax:(541)482-6138
E-mail: stay@cowslip.com
Web: www.cowslip.com

Circa 1913. Experience old-fashioned hospitality and romantic luxury at this Craftsman bungalow and carriage house. Recently renovated, the decor reflects an eclectic mix of comfortable period furnishings. Guest bedrooms and suites, one boasting a fireplace and Jacuzzi, feature English spa toiletries, fine linens, turndown service with chocolate truffles and private entrances. Savor delicious breakfast treats that may include green-chili egg puff, corn pudding and homemade baked goods highlighted by Maxfield Parrish artwork in the vintage dining room. A large koi pond, soothing waterfalls and brick walkways with arbors accent an enchanting ambiance. The garden patio is perfect for reading while devouring cookies made from the City Dunkers Gourmet Cookie Company.

Historic Interest: Cowslip's Belle is located in the heart of Ashland's historic district, and it is only 20 minutes from Jacksonville, an entire town listed in the National Register.

Innkeeper(s): Jon & Carmen Reinhardt. $125-205. 5 rooms with PB, 1 with FP, 2 suites and 1 cottage. Breakfast and snacks/refreshments included in

479

rates. Types of meals: Full gourmet bkfst and early coffee/tea. Beds: KQT. Data port, cable TV, reading lamp, ceiling fan, turn-down service, desk, fireplace, English Spa toiletries and Jacuzzi in room. Central air. Fax, copier, library, parlor games, telephone, fireplace, koi pond with waterfall, complimentary use of Ashland Racquet Club with indoor pool, indoor tennis courts, Jacuzzis, saunas, weight room, exercise machines and scrumptious cookies from our very own City Dunkers Gourmet Cookie Company on premises. Antiquing, art galleries, bicycling, canoeing/kayaking, cross-country skiing, downhill skiing, fishing, golf, hiking, horseback riding, live theater, museums, parks, shopping, sporting events, tennis, water sports and wineries nearby.
Publicity: *Northwest Best Places, Best Places to Kiss in the Northwest, San Francisco Chronicle, Oregonian, Weekends for Two in the Pacific Northwest: 50 Romantic Getaways, America's Favorite Inns, McCalls Magazine and Country Accents Magazine.*

"The atmosphere was delightful, the decor charming, the food delicious and the company grand. Tony says he's spoiled forever."

Wolfe Manor Inn

586 B St
Ashland, OR 97520
(541)488-3676 (800)801-3676 Fax:(541)488-4567
E-mail: wolfebandb@aol.com
Web: www.wolfemanor.com

Circa 1910. A glass door with sidelights welcomes guests to this massive Craftsman-style home. A grand parlor/ballroom with original lighting fixtures and fine woodwork is the combination sitting area and dining room. Bedrooms offer views of the mountains or the inn's pleasantly landscaped lawns and gardens. Guests often enjoy relaxing on the inn's porches.
Innkeeper(s): Sybil & Ron Maddox. $89-150. 5 rooms with PB. Breakfast and snacks/refreshments included in rates. Types of meals: Full gourmet bkfst, veg bkfst and early coffee/tea. Beds: QD. Reading lamp, ceiling fan and clock radio in room. Central air. TV, fax, copier, library, telephone, refrigerator, snack bar and coffeemaker on premises. Family reunions hosted. Antiquing, art galleries, bicycling, canoeing/kayaking, cross-country skiing, downhill skiing, fishing, golf, hiking, horseback riding, live theater, museums, parks, shopping, tennis, water sports and wineries nearby.
Publicity: *Getaways Magazine, PNW "Best Places to Stay" and Conde Nast Magazine.*

Astoria   A2

Astoria Inn Bed & Breakfast

3391 Irving Ave
Astoria, OR 97103-2632
(503)325-8153 (800)718-8153

Circa 1890. Perched on the hillside, this stately Victorian inn is just five blocks from the Columbia River and has views of the forest and the river. It offers four guest bedrooms. A country breakfast is served each morning and it includes egg dishes, bacon, sausage or ham, potatoes, fruit and juices. Astoria is rich in historical and natural beauty. It was the first settlement west of the Rockies and was discovered in 1806 by John Jacob Astor. The inn is eight miles from Ft. Clatsop. Guests enjoy watching ships passing in the Columbia River and in the evening, the ships that anchor in the river basin in front of the inn create a wonderland of twinkling lights.
Innkeeper(s): Ms. Mickey Cox. $60-85. 4 rooms with PB. Breakfast and snacks/refreshments included in rates. Types of meals: Country bkfst, veg bkfst and early coffee/tea. Beds: Q. Reading lamp and clock radio in room. TV, VCR, library, parlor games and telephone on premises. Family reunions hosted. Antiquing, art galleries, beach, bicycling, canoeing/kayaking, fishing, golf, hiking, horseback riding, museums, shopping, tennis, water sports and wineries nearby.
Publicity: *VIA (AAA) and Los Angeles Times.*

Grandview B&B

1574 Grand Ave
Astoria, OR 97103-3733
(503)325-0000 (800)488-3250
E-mail: grandviewbnb@freedom.usa.com
Web: www.pacifier.com/~grndview/

Circa 1896. To fully enjoy its views of the Columbia River, this Victorian house has both a tower and a turret. Antiques and white wicker furnishings contribute to the inn's casual, homey feeling. The Bird Meadow Room is particularly appealing to bird-lovers with its birdcage, bird books and bird wallpaper. Breakfast, served in the main-floor turret, frequently includes smoked salmon with bagels and cream cheese.
Historic Interest: Flavel House (8 blocks), Heritage Museum (1 block), Firefighters Museum (18 blocks).
Innkeeper(s): Charleen Maxwell. $61-103. 9 rooms, 7 with PB, 3 with FP and 2 suites. Breakfast and snacks/refreshments included in rates. Types of meals: Full bkfst. Beds: QT. Reading lamp and snack bar in room. Parlor games, telephone and fireplace on premises. Weddings, small meetings and family reunions hosted. Antiquing, fishing, live theater, parks, shopping, water sports, historic homes tour, old-fashioned trolley, river walk, aqua center, movie complex and forts nearby.
Publicity: *Pacific Northwest Magazine, Northwest Discoveries, Los Angeles Times, Oregonian and Daily Astorian.*

"I have travelled all over the world and for the first time I found in the country of the computers such a romantic house with such poetic rooms at the Grandview Bed & Breakfast. Thanks." - MD from Paris, France

Bend   D5

The Sather House B&B

7 NW Tumalo Ave
Bend, OR 97701-2634
(541)388-1065 (888)388-1065 Fax:(541)330-0591

Circa 1911. This Craftsman-style home is listed in the local, county and national historic registers. One room includes a clawfoot tub that dates to 1910. Period furnishings are found in the nicely appointed guest rooms, which feature touches of Battenburg and lace. The front porch is lined with wicker for those who wish to relax and enjoy the surroundings. For breakfast, innkeeper Robbie Giamboi serves items such as apple and banana pancakes topped with her own homemade blackberry, raspberry maple or apple syrup. Guests also enjoy afternoon tea.
Innkeeper(s): Robbie Giamboi. $88-126. 4 rooms with PB. Breakfast and afternoon tea included in rates. Types of meals: Full gourmet bkfst and early coffee/tea. Beds: KQDT. Reading lamp, ceiling fan and desk in room. VCR, library, parlor games, telephone and fireplace on premises. Small meetings and family reunions hosted. Antiquing, cross-country skiing, downhill skiing, fishing, golf, live theater, parks, shopping, sporting events, tennis & water sports nearby.
Publicity: *Bend Bulletin and Oregonian.*

Brookings   G1

South Coast Inn B&B

516 Redwood St
Brookings, OR 97415-9672
(541)469-5557 (800)525-9273 Fax:(541)469-6615

Circa 1917. Enjoy panoramic views of the Pacific Ocean at this Craftsman-style inn designed by renowned San Francisco architect Bernard Maybeck. All rooms are furnished with antiques, ceiling fans, CD player, VCRs and TVs. Two guest rooms afford panoramic views of the coastline and there is a separate cottage. A floor-to-ceiling stone fireplace and beamed ceilings make the parlor a great place to gather with friends. There are sun decks and a strolling garden. The Brookings area offers something for everyone. Outdoor activities include hiking, boating, golfing, digging for clams or simply enjoying a stroll along the spectacular coastline. Concerts, galleries, museums, antiques, specialty shops and fine restaurants all can be found within the area.

Innkeeper(s): Sheldon & Gro Lent. $99-139. 4 rooms with PB and 1 cottage. Breakfast included in rates. Types of meals: Full gourmet bkfst and early coffee/tea. Beds: KQ. Cable TV, VCR, reading lamp, ceiling fan, clock radio, desk, hair dryers in baths and 1 with gas fireplace/stove in room. Fax, spa, sauna, library, parlor games, telephone, fireplace and continental breakfast in cottage on premises. Weddings, small meetings, family reunions and seminars hosted. Antiquing, fishing, live theater, parks, shopping and water sports nearby.

"Thank you for your special brand of magic. What a place!"

Dayton C3

Wine Country Farm

6855 NE Breyman Orchards Rd
Dayton, OR 97114-7220
(503)864-3446 (800)261-3446 Fax:(503)864-3109
E-mail: winecountryfarm@webtv.net
Web: www.winecountryfarm.com

Circa 1910. Surrounded by vineyards and orchards, Wine Country Farm is an eclectic French house sitting on a hill overlooking the Cascade Mountain Range. Arabian horses are raised here, and five varieties of grapes are grown. Request the master bedroom and you'll enjoy a fireplace. The innkeepers can arrange for a horse-drawn buggy ride and picnic or horseback through the vineyards and forests to other wineries. There are outdoor wedding facilities and a new wine tasting room, where guests can sample wine from the vineyard. Downtown Portland and the Oregon coast are each an hour away.

Innkeeper(s): Joan Davenport. $105-175. 9 rooms with PB, 4 with FP, 3 suites and 1 conference room. Breakfast included in rates. Types of meals: Full gourmet bkfst, early coffee/tea and room service. Beds: KQDT. Reading lamp and desk in room. Air conditioning. VCR, fax, copier, stable, library, parlor games, telephone and fireplace on premises. Weddings, small meetings, family reunions and seminars hosted. Antiquing, cross-country skiing, downhill skiing, fishing, live theater, parks, shopping, sporting events and water sports nearby.

Publicity: Wine Spectator.

Eugene D3

Campbell House, A City Inn

252 Pearl St
Eugene, OR 97401-2366
(541)343-1119 (800)264-2519 Fax:(541)343-2258
E-mail: campbellhouse@campbellhouse.com
Web: www.campbellhouse.com

Circa 1892. Fully restored, this gracious Victorian inn sits on one acre of landscaped beauty. Classic elegance and comfort combine with generous hospitality and service to ensure a pleasant visit. Suites and guest bedrooms feature private covered balconies or a patio with pond. Gas fireplaces, jetted or clawfoot tubs and four-poster beds are featured in some rooms.

For more space, stay in Celeste Cottage, a full-size house next door. Hunger is far from the mind after a satisfying breakfast each morning. Downtown is within a short walk. Ride the

riverside bike paths, or jog the renowned Pre's Trail. Enjoy wine or cider in the evenings.

Historic Interest: The historic Shelton McMurphy Johnson House, which was built in 1882 and now is owned by the city, is located at the base of the driveway, and tours are available. The innkeepers will provide guests with walking maps of the historic district.

Innkeeper(s): Myra Plant. $92-349. 19 rooms with PB, 8 with FP, 1 suite and 2 conference rooms. Breakfast included in rates. Types of meals: Full bkfst, early coffee/tea and room service. Beds: KQDT. Cable TV, VCR, reading lamp, refrigerator, ceiling fan, snack bar, telephone, turn-down service, desk and jetted or clawfoot tubs in room. Air conditioning. Fax, copier, library, parlor games, fireplace and complimentary evening wine and beverages on premises. Limited handicap access. Weddings, small meetings, family reunions and seminars hosted. Antiquing, bicycling, fishing, golf, hiking, live theater, parks, shopping, sporting events, water sports and rock climbing nearby.

Publicity: Oregon Business, American Travels, B&B Innkeepers Journal, Eugene Register Guard, Country Inns, Oregonian, Sunset, Good Evening Show and KVAL & KAUW News.

"I guess we've never felt so pampered! Thank you so much. The room is beautiful! We had a wonderful getaway."

Kjaer's House In Woods

814 Lorane Hwy
Eugene, OR 97405-2321
(541)343-3234 (800)437-4501

Circa 1910. This handsome Craftsman house on two landscaped acres was built by a Minnesota lawyer. It was originally accessible by streetcar. Antiques include a square grand piano of rosewood and a collection of antique wedding photos. The house is attractively furnished and surrounded by flower gardens.

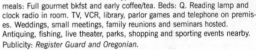

Historic Interest: Wayne Moore Historical Park (4 blocks), covered bridges (3 miles). Innkeeper(s): George & Eunice Kjaer. $65-80. 2 rooms with PB and 1 conference room. Breakfast included in rates. Types of meals: Full gourmet bkfst and early coffee/tea. Beds: Q. Reading lamp and clock radio in room. TV, VCR, library, parlor games and telephone on premises. Weddings, small meetings, family reunions and seminars hosted. Antiquing, fishing, live theater, parks, shopping and sporting events nearby.

Publicity: Register Guard and Oregonian.

"Lovely ambiance and greatest sleep ever. Delicious and beautiful food presentation."

Pookie's B&B on College Hill

2013 Charnelton St
Eugene, OR 97405-2819
(541)343-0383 (800)558-0383 Fax:(541)431-0967
E-mail: pookiesbandb@aol.com
Web: www.pookiesbandblodging.com

Circa 1918. Pookie's is a charming Craftsman house with "yester-year charm." Surrounded by maple and fir trees, the B&B is located in an older, quiet neighborhood. Mahogany and oak antiques decorate the rooms. The innkeeper worked for many years in the area as a concierge and can offer you expert help with excursion planning or business needs.

Historic Interest: Historic downtown (1 1/2 mile).

Innkeeper(s): Pookie & Doug Walling. $80-115. 3 rooms, 2 with PB and 1 suite. Breakfast included in rates. Types of meals: Full bkfst and early coffee/tea. Beds: KQT. Cable TV, reading lamp, ceiling fan, clock radio, telephone and desk in room. VCR, fax, copier and parlor games on premises. Antiquing, fishing, live theater, parks, shopping, sporting

events, water sports and baseball stadium nearby.
Publicity: *Oregon Wine.*

"I love the attention to detail. The welcoming touches: flowers, the 'convenience basket' of necessary items . . . I'm happy to have discovered your lovely home."

Florence   D2

The Blue Heron Inn

6563 Hwy 126, PO Box 1122
Florence, OR 97439-0055
(541)997-4091 (800)997-7780

Circa 1940. From the porch of this bed & breakfast inn, guests can gaze at rolling, forested hills and watch as riverboats ease their way down the Siuslaw River. Aside from the spectacular view, the inn is located within a few yards of a marina where docking and

mooring is available. The ocean, the dunes and historic Florence are just minutes away as well. The Bridal Suite offers king-size bed, sitting area, whirlpool tub and view of the river and grounds. Fresh, seasonal fare highlights the breakfast menu. Treats such as fresh fruit smoothies, muffins topped with homemade blackberry jam or a smoked salmon and avocado quiche are not uncommon.

Innkeeper(s): Maurice & Stella Souza. $65-140. 5 rooms with PB. Breakfast and afternoon tea included in rates. Types of meals: Full bkfst. Beds: KQT. Reading lamp, ceiling fan, desk and jetted tubs in room. VCR, library, parlor games, telephone and video room on premises. Weddings, small meetings and family reunions hosted. Antiquing, fishing, parks, shopping, water sports, dune buggies and horseback riding nearby.
Publicity: *Best Places to Kiss, Oregon Lodgings Association and KLSR.*

"The entire place was decorated with great taste. Our room was beautiful and relaxing. It made us feel at ease and at peace."

Grants Pass   G2

Lawnridge House

1304 N W Lawnridge Ave
Grants Pass, OR 97526-1218
(541)476-8518

Circa 1909. This inn, a graceful, gabled clapboard house is shaded by 200-year-old oaks. The home features spacious rooms with comfortable antiques, canopy beds and beamed ceilings. Mini refrigerators, TVs and VCRs are among the amenities. A family suite accommodates up to six people and includes one or two bedrooms, a sitting room and bathroom. The innkeeper serves Northwest regional cuisine for the full breakfasts. The Rogue River is five minutes away, and the Ashland Shakespearean Festival is a 45-minute drive.

Innkeeper(s): Barbara Head. $85-95. 4 rooms with PB and 2 suites. Breakfast included in rates. Types of meals: Full bkfst. Beds: KQ. Reading lamp, refrigerator and desk in room. Air conditioning. Parlor games, telephone and fireplace on premises. Antiquing, fishing, live theater and water sports nearby.
Publicity: *Grants Pass Courier, This Week and CBS TV.*

"Thank you for your incredible friendliness, warmth, and energy expended on our behalf! I've never felt so nestled in the lap of luxury - what a pleasure!"

Weasku Inn

5560 Rogue River Hwy
Grants Pass, OR 97527
(541)471-8000 (800)493-2758 Fax:(541)471-7038
E-mail: info@weasku.com
Web: www.weasku.com

Circa 1924. Built as a secluded fishing lodge, this historic inn once hosted the likes of President Herbert Hoover, Zane Grey, Walt Disney, Clark Gable and Carole Lombard. It is said that after Lombard's death, Gable spent several weeks here lamenting the loss of his beloved wife. A complete restoration took place in the late 1990s, reviving the inn back to its former glory. The log exterior, surrounding by towering trees and 10 fragrant acres, is a welcoming site. Inside, crackling fires from the inn's rock fireplaces warm the common rooms. Vaulted ceilings and exposed log beams add a cozy, rustic touch to the pristine, airy rooms all decorated in Pacific Northwest style. Many rooms include a whirlpool tub and river rock fireplace, and several offer excellent views of the Rogue River, which runs through the inn's grounds. In addition to the inn rooms, there are riverfront cabins, offering an especially romantic setting. In the evenings, guests are treated to a wine and cheese reception, and in the mornings, a continental breakfast is served. The staff can help plan many activities, including fishing and white-water rafting trips.

Innkeeper(s): Sue Price. $110-295. 17 rooms with PB, 12 with FP, 3 suites, 12 cabins and 1 conference room. Breakfast and snacks/refreshments included in rates. Types of meals: Cont plus. Beds: KQT. Data port, cable TV, reading lamp, ceiling fan, clock radio, telephone and hot tub/spa in room. Central air. Fax, parlor games and fireplace on premises. Limited handicap access. Weddings, small meetings, family reunions and seminars hosted. Antiquing, canoeing/kayaking, fishing, golf, hiking, live theater, museums, parks, shopping, water sports, wineries, jet boat excursions and wildlife park nearby.
Publicity: *Travel & Leisure Magazine, LA Magazine, Sunset and SF Magazine.*

Hood River   B5

Columbia Gorge Hotel

4000 Westcliff Dr
Hood River, OR 97031-9799
(541)386-5566 (800)345-1921 Fax:(541)386-9141
E-mail: cghotel@gorge.net
Web: www.columbiagorgehotel.com

Circa 1921. This posh hotel is a gem among gems in the National Register of Historic Places. Idyllic guest quarters offer such ornate furnishings as a hand-carved canopy bed that once graced a French castle. The beautifully landscaped grounds, champagne and caviar social hour, turndown service with rose. Outdoor river-view dining terrace and a gourmet restaurant are favorite amenities. Last, but not least, are spectacular views of the majestic Columbia River. Guests are treated to the opulent "World Famous Farm Breakfast." The hotel is close to ski areas, golfing and popular windsurfing spots. Pets are welcome!

Innkeeper(s): Boyd & Halla Graves. $189-275. 40 rooms with PB, 2 with FP and 3 conference rooms. Breakfast included in rates. Types of meals: Full bkfst, early coffee/tea, lunch, picnic lunch, afternoon tea, gourmet dinner and room service. Restaurant on premises. Beds: KQD. Cable TV, reading lamp, telephone and turn-down service in room. VCR, fax, copier and fireplace on premises. Weddings, small meetings, family reunions and seminars hosted. Antiquing, cross-country skiing, downhill skiing, fishing, live theater, parks, shopping, water sports and windsurfing nearby.

Jacksonville   G3

Historic Orth House B&B

105 W Main St, PO Box 1437
Jacksonville, OR 97530
(541)899-8665 (800)700-7301 Fax:(541)899-9146
E-mail: orthbnb@orthbnb.com
Web: www.orthbnb.com

Circa 1880. Surrounded by a white picket fence and a half acre
of landscaped grounds, this historic, two-story brick Italianate

home was built during the Gold
Rush and is now listed in the
National Register. Large guest
bedrooms feature period furnishings and clawfoot tubs. After a
satisfying breakfast, stroll among
the blooming flower gardens.
Innkeeper(s): Lee & Marilyn Lewis. $95-
250. 4 rooms, 3 with PB and 1 suite. Breakfast included in rates. Types of
meals: Full bkfst. Beds: KQT. Reading lamp, ceiling fan and clock radio in
room. Air conditioning. Fax, copier, bicycles, parlor games and telephone on
premises. Antiquing, downhill skiing, fishing, golf, live theater, parks, shopping, Britt Music Festival and Ashland Shakespeare Festival nearby.
Publicity: *American Profile and Country Discoveries.*

La Grande   C8

Stang Manor Inn

1612 Walnut St
La Grande, OR 97850-1553
(541)963-2400 (888)286-9463
E-mail: innkeeper@stangmanor.com
Web: www.stangmanor.com

Circa 1923. Accented with detailed woodwork, original light
fixtures and tiles throughout, this elegant Georgian Colonial
mansion was built and owned by August Stange, a northeast
Oregon lumber baron. Each of the guest bedrooms is unique in
size, décor and history; while offering excellent views of the rose
garden, grounds, local hills and mountains. Breakfast includes
fresh fruits, homemade breads, granola, a specialty entrée, juices
and coffee served in the formal dining room. History buffs can
study the Oregon Trail or tour many local sites in La Grande
and nearby Baker City, Pendleton and Joseph.
Historic Interest: History buffs can study the Oregon Trail or tour the many
historic sites in La Grande and nearby Baker City, Pendleton and Joseph.
Innkeeper(s): Ron & Carolyn Jensen. $98-115. 4 rooms with PB and 2
suites. Breakfast included in rates. Types of meals: Full bkfst. Beds: QT.
Antiquing, cross-country skiing, downhill skiing, fishing and hiking nearby.
Publicity: *Oregon B&B Gazette and Observer.*

"Absolutely charming. So pleasant."

Lafayette   C3

Kelty Estate B&B

675 Third St
Lafayette, OR 97127
(800)867-3740

Circa 1872. An early pioneer couple, one a local druggist and
county sheriff and the other, the first woman elected to the
Lafayette School Board, built this home. The grounds are well-
landscaped with gardens, trees and lush plants. Guests can
enjoy the tranquility from the swing on the home's front porch.
There are two guest rooms, decorated in pastels. Furnishings

include period antiques. Breakfasts feature fresh Oregon-grown
items, with specialties such as strawberry-kiwi juice, fresh
strawberries and bananas in a cream sauce, homemade breads
and eggs Benedict accompanied by herbed potatoes. Wineries,
a museum and antiquing are among the nearby attractions.
Innkeeper(s): Ron & JoAnn Ross. $95. 2 rooms with PB. Breakfast and after-
noon tea included in rates. Types of meals: Full bkfst. Beds: Q. Reading lamp
and desk in room. VCR, library, parlor games, telephone and fireplace on premises. Weddings, small meetings, family reunions and seminars hosted. Amusement
parks, antiquing, fishing, live theater, parks, shopping and water sports nearby.

Lincoln City   C2

Brey House

3725 NW Keel Ave
Lincoln City, OR 97367
(541)994-7123
E-mail: breysinn@webtv.net
Web: www.breyhouse.com

Circa 1941. The innkeepers at this three-story, Cape Cod-style
house claim that when you stay with them it's like staying with
Aunt Shirley and Uncle Milt. Guest rooms include some with
ocean views and private entrances, and the Deluxe Suite offers
a living room with fireplace, two baths and a kitchen. The
Admiral's Room on the third floor has knotty pine walls, a skylight, fireplace and the best view.
Innkeeper(s): Milt & Shirley Brey. $90-160. 4 rooms with PB, 3 with FP and
2 suites. Breakfast included in rates. Types of meals: Full gourmet bkfst and
early coffee/tea. Beds: KQ. Cable TV, VCR, reading lamp, refrigerator, ceiling
fan, clock radio, desk and hot tub/spa in room. Parlor games, telephone and
fireplace on premises. Antiquing, fishing, golf, live theater, parks, shopping,
tennis, water sports and Indian casino nearby.

McMinnville   C3

Baker Street B&B

129 S Baker St
McMinnville, OR 97128-6035
(503)472-5575 (800)870-5575
E-mail: cheryl@bakerstreetinn.com
Web: www.bakerstreetinn.com

Circa 1914. Restored to its natural beauty, this Craftsman inn
offers three guest bedrooms all year-round. The décor includes
vintage Victorian memorabilia, antiques and a clawfoot or jetted
tub. Perfect for longer stays or couples traveling together, Le
Petite Chateau is a renovated, private two-bedroom cottage
with tub/shower bath combination, living room, kitchen and
laundry facilities. Situated in the heart of wine country,
gourmet restaurants and wineries are nearby. Visit Salem,
Portland and the coast, just one hour away.
Innkeeper(s): Cheryl Hockaday. $95-125. 4 rooms, 3 with PB and 1 cottage.
Breakfast included in rates. Types of meals: Full bkfst. Beds: KQDT. Cable TV,
VCR, reading lamp, refrigerator, ceiling fan, clock radio and coffeemaker in
room. Central air. Telephone and laundry facility on premises. Small meetings
and family reunions hosted. Antiquing, art galleries, golf, live theater, parks,
shopping, restaurants and 70 wineries nearby.

Mattey House

10221 N E Mattey Ln
McMinnville, OR 97128-8219
(503)434-5058 Fax:(503)434-6667
E-mail: mattey@matteyhouse.com
Web: www.matteyhouse.com

Circa 1892. Windows rimmed with stained glass and gingerbread trim decorate the exterior of this Queen Anne Victorian.
The home is nestled on 10 acres of vineyards, orchards and

stately, old cedar trees. Visitors may even pick a few of the succulent grapes. Guest rooms are decorated in period style with antiques, and each is named appropriately for a variety of wine. Upon returning from a day of sightseeing, guests are treated to late afternoon refreshments. Breakfasts are a treat, and the innkeepers serve dishes such as a baked peach with a stuffing of raspberries and cream, baked herbed eggs or perhaps an Italian frittata. Homemade scones are a specialty.

Innkeeper(s): Denise & Jack Seed. $95-125. 4 rooms with PB. Breakfast and afternoon tea included in rates. Types of meals: Full bkfst, early coffee/tea and snacks/refreshments. Beds: Q. Reading lamp, turn-down service, clocks and robes in room. Parlor games, telephone, fireplace and stereo on premises. Family reunions hosted. Antiquing, fishing, live theater, parks, shopping, sporting events, water sports, wine tasting and golf nearby.

Publicity: *Conde Nast, Sunset, Oregon Wine Press, Oregonian, Anchorage Daily News, Tacoman News Tribune and Orange County Register.*

"What a lovely home and what thoughtful innkeepers you both are. We enjoyed our cozy room with all of your nice touches."

Mount Hood   B4

Brightwood Guesthouse B&B

64725 E Barlow Trail Rd
Mount Hood, OR 97011-0189
(503)622-5783 (888)503-5783

Circa 1932. Peaceful, private and romantic, this guesthouse in the woods is decorated with Asian art, artifacts and fresh flowers. A Feng Shui retreat secluded on two forested acres, it includes a kitchen/dining room, large bath, and two sleeping areas. A feather bed is in the loft and the sunny living room comfortably sleeps four. The stocked cupboards include coffee, cider, cocoa, spices, popcorn and an abundant tea selection. An excellent five-course breakfast that may include Savory brioche, roasted potatoes, fresh fruit plate, seared vegetable frittata and Amaretto trifle is served at a desired time to the inside table or on the private deck that is surrounded by a Japanese water garden and waterfall. A year-round creek adjoins the forested hillside in back. Complimentary beverages are offered for special occasions. Ask about available packages and a keepsake basket.

Innkeeper(s): Jan Estep. $125. Breakfast included in rates. Types of meals: Full gourmet bkfst, veg bkfst and room service. Beds: DT. VCR, stereo, telephone, turn-down service, well-stocked kitchenette, kimonos, slippers, bath lotions, hair dryers and videos in room. TV, fax, copier, bicycles, library, parlor games, laundry facility, gazebo with fireplace, one guest house available with: kitchenette/dining room, large bath, living room, sleeping loft and private deck & parking on premises. Family reunions hosted. Antiquing, bicycling, canoeing/kayaking, cross-country skiing, downhill skiing, fishing, golf, hiking, horseback riding, live theater, museums, parks, shopping, tennis, water sports, wineries, snowboarding, slug races at Brightwood Tavern (seasonal), national forest, brewery, waterfalls, Indian reservation, windsurfing, orchards and Portland nightlife nearby.

Publicity: *Sunset, Mountain Times, Weekend Viaggi, Bridal Resource Guide, Best Places to Kiss in Oregon, Arrington's Inn Traveler, Hot Showers, Soft Beds, Dayhikes in the Central Cascades, The Unofficial Guide to B&B's & Small Inns of the Pacific Northwest, Recommended Bed & Breakfasts: The Pacific Northwest, Fodor's Staying in Cascades & Columbia River Gorge and Absolutely Every Bed & Breakfast in Oregon.*

Newberg   C3

Springbrook Hazelnut Farm

30295 N Hwy 99 W
Newberg, OR 97132
(503)538-4606 (800)793-8528

Circa 1912. An ancient silver maple tree shades the main house, one of four Craftsman-style buildings on this farm. There

are 10 acres of gardens, a pool, tennis court and a 60-acre hazelnut orchard. A blue heron monitors the inn's pond and you may paddle around in the canoe. Walking through the orchard to the adjoining winery is a must, as is a bicycle ride to other wineries in the area. Ask for the Carriage House or the Cottage, and you'll enjoy a pond and garden view. The inn's cottages have kitchens and private baths.

Historic Interest: Champoeg Park (6 miles).

Innkeeper(s): Charles & Ellen McClure. $100-200. 4 rooms, 2 with PB and 2 cottages. Breakfast included in rates. Types of meals: Full bkfst. Beds: QD. Reading lamp in room. Air conditioning. Telephone, fireplace, orchard, pond and gardens on premises. Small meetings and seminars hosted. Antiquing, live theater, shopping, sporting events and wine touring nearby.

Publicity: *Travel & Leisure, Wine Spectator, Money Magazine, National Geographic Traveler and Wall St. Journal.*

"An incredible, wonderful refuge! We are beautifully surprised!"

Portland   B3

Terwilliger Vista B&B

515 SW Westwood Dr
Portland, OR 97201-2791
(503)244-0602 (888)244-0602 Fax:(503)293-8042

Circa 1940. Bay windows accentuate the exterior of this stately Georgian Colonial home. A mix of modern and Art Deco furnishings decorate the interior. The home has an airy, uncluttered feel with its polished floors topped with Oriental rugs and muted tones. There is a canopy bed and fireplace in the spacious Garden Suite, and the Rose Suite overlooks the Willamette Valley. Other rooms offer garden views, bay windows or wicker furnishings. There is a library, and an area set up with refreshments. The house is located in what will be the Historical Terwilliger Boulevard Preserve.

Innkeeper(s): Dick & Jan Vatert. $85-150. 5 rooms with PB, 1 with FP and 2 suites. Breakfast included in rates. Types of meals: Full bkfst. Beds: KQT. Cable TV, reading lamp, clock radio and desk in room. Air conditioning. Parlor games, fireplace, guest refrigerator, telephone and data port and fax available on premises. Family reunions hosted. Antiquing, live theater, parks, shopping, sporting events and wine country nearby.

"Like staying in House Beautiful."

Salem   C3

A Creekside Garden Inn

333 Wyatt Ct NE
Salem, OR 97301-4269
(503)391-0837
E-mail: rickiemh@open.org
Web: www.salembandb.com

Circa 1938. Each room in this Mt. Vernon Colonial replica of George Washington's house has a garden theme. Consider the Picket Fences room. This gracious view room features a fireplace, Queen-size plus daybed, antique toys and a private bath. The four other upstairs guest rooms offer similar themes. There are regular evening movie screenings complete with popcorn in the common room. The extensive gardens offer guests an opportunity to stroll along historic Mill Creek or enjoy a round of croquet in the spacious backyard, weather permitting.

Hazelnut waffles, confetti hash and oatmeal custard are a few of the breakfast specialties. The inn is just two blocks from the Court-Chemeketa Historic District.

Historic Interest: Located close to the state capitol and Willamette University.
Innkeeper(s): Ms. Rickie Hart. $65-95. 5 rooms, 3 with PB, 1 with FP. Breakfast and snacks/refreshments included in rates. Types of meals: Full gourmet bkfst and early coffee/tea. Beds: QT. Reading lamp and desk in room. VCR, bicycles, parlor games, telephone and fireplace on premises. Weddings, small meetings and family reunions hosted. Amusement parks, antiquing, golf, live theater, parks, shopping, sporting events, wine country tours and wineries nearby.
Publicity: *Statesman Journal, Sunset, The Oregonian, The Christian Science Monitor and Carlton Food Network (United Kingdom).*

"We all agreed that you were the best hostess yet for one of our weekends!"

Seaside   A2

10th Avenue Inn Bed & Breakfast & Vacation Rental

125 10th Ave
Seaside, OR 97138-6241
(503)738-0643 (800)745-2378 Fax:(503)738-0172

Circa 1908. Sunlight fills this cozy home, once owned by a circuit court judge. Splendid ocean views are provided through the panoramic windows and guests look out to the Promenade and the coastal mountain range and shoreline. An inviting parlor offers a baby grand piano and a warm fireplace. Guests gather here for evening refreshments and to watch the sunsets. The guest rooms are modern and pleasant, and some of the furnishings are antiques. The innkeepers serve a variety of appetizing breakfast entrees and after breakfast, guests can stroll downtown Seaside or spend the day enjoying the ocean. Next door, the Doll House vacation rental is perfect for small families.
Innkeeper(s): Jack & Leslie Palmeri. $89-150. 3 rooms with PB and 1 suite. Breakfast included in rates. Types of meals: Full bkfst and early coffee/tea. Beds: KDT. Cable TV, reading lamp, refrigerator, clock radio, sitting tub, soaking tub and one suite with fireplace in room. VCR, fax, copier, parlor games, telephone, fireplace, vacation rental and easy beach access on premises. Weddings, small meetings and family reunions hosted. Amusement parks, antiquing, beach, fishing, golf, live theater, parks, shopping, tennis, water sports and Pacific Ocean nearby.

"Very clean, cozy house with comfortable beds. Pleasing ocean view, convenient parking."

The Gilbert Inn, B&B

341 Beach Dr
Seaside, OR 97138-5707
(503)738-9770 (800)410-9770 Fax:(503)717-1070
E-mail: gilbertinn@seasurf.net
Web: www.gilbertinn.com

Circa 1892. This yellow Victorian with its turret and third-story garret is framed with a white picket fence and gardens of lilies, roses and tulips. There are down quilts, antiques, and fresh country fabrics in the guest rooms. A house specialty is stuffed French toast topped with apricot sauce. The ocean and the historic promenade, which stretches for a mile and a half along the sand, are a block away.
Innkeeper(s): Dick & Carole Rees. $89-125. 10 rooms with PB, 1 suite and 2 cottages. Breakfast included in rates. Types of meals: Full bkfst and early coffee/tea. Beds: QT. Cable TV, reading lamp, clock radio and telephone in room. Fax, copier and fireplace on premises. Weddings, small meetings and seminars hosted. Antiquing, art galleries, beach, bicycling, canoeing/kayaking, fishing, golf, hiking, horseback riding, live theater, museums, parks, shopping, tennis, water sports, wineries, on the beach

volleyball, kite-flying, surfing, beach bikes and sandcastles nearby.
Publicity: *The Oregonian, Romantic Homes Magazine, VIA, "Romantic Getaways," Northwest Best Places and Best Places to Kiss.*

Sisters   D4

Conklin's Guest House

69013 Camp Polk Rd
Sisters, OR 97759-9705
(541)549-0123 (800)549-4262 Fax:(541)549-4481
Web: www.conklinsguesthouse.com

Circa 1910. The original portion of this Craftsman-style house was constructed in 1910, with later additions in 1938 and more recent changes in 1992 and 1996. Mountain views and four-and-a-half peaceful acres invite relaxation and romance. There are several ponds on the property stocked with trout for those wanting to try their hand at catch and release fishing. There is also a heated swimming pool. Three guest rooms have clawfoot tubs, and the Suite and Forget-Me-Not rooms offer a pleasing view. For those in a larger group, the inn's Heather room includes a queen bed and two single beds. Sisters' airport is across the street from the home.
Innkeeper(s): Frank & Marie Conklin. $70-150. 5 rooms with PB, 1 with FP and 1 suite. Breakfast and snacks/refreshments included in rates. Types of meals: Full gourmet bkfst, veg bkfst and early coffee/tea. Beds: QT. Modem hook-up, reading lamp, stereo, refrigerator, ceiling fan, snack bar, clock radio, telephone and desk in room. Central air. Fax, copier, swimming, parlor games, fireplace and laundry facility on premises. Limited handicap access. Weddings, small meetings and family reunions hosted. Antiquing, art galleries, bicycling, canoeing/kayaking, cross-country skiing, downhill skiing, fishing, golf, hiking, horseback riding, live theater, museums, parks, shopping, tennis, water sports, whitewater rafting and rock climbing nearby.

"A wonderful and romantic time for our wedding anniversary. Thanks so much. Oh - great fishing too."

Welches   C4

Old Welches Inn B&B

26401 E Welches Rd
Welches, OR 97067-9701
(503)622-3754 Fax:(503)622-5370

Circa 1890. This two-story colonial building, behind a picket fence, was originally the first hotel to be built in the Mt. Hood area. Reconstructed in the '30s, the building now has shutters and French windows. The inn's two acres offer a plethora of flower beds and views of the Salmon River and Hunchback Mountain. Rooms are named for wildflowers and include antiques. If traveling with children or friends try Lilybank, a private cottage which overlooks the first hole of Three Nines. There are two bedrooms, a kitchen and a river rock fireplace.

Innkeeper(s): Judith & Ted Mondun. $96-163. 4 rooms and 1 cottage. Breakfast and snacks/refreshments included in rates. Types of meals: Full bkfst and early coffee/tea. Beds: QD. Reading lamp and turn-down service in room. VCR, fax, pet boarding, parlor games, telephone and fireplace on premises. Weddings, small meetings and family reunions hosted. Antiquing, cross-country skiing, downhill skiing, fishing, golf, parks, shopping, sporting events and tennis nearby.
Publicity: *Oregonian, Sunset and Northwest Best Places.*

Pennsylvania

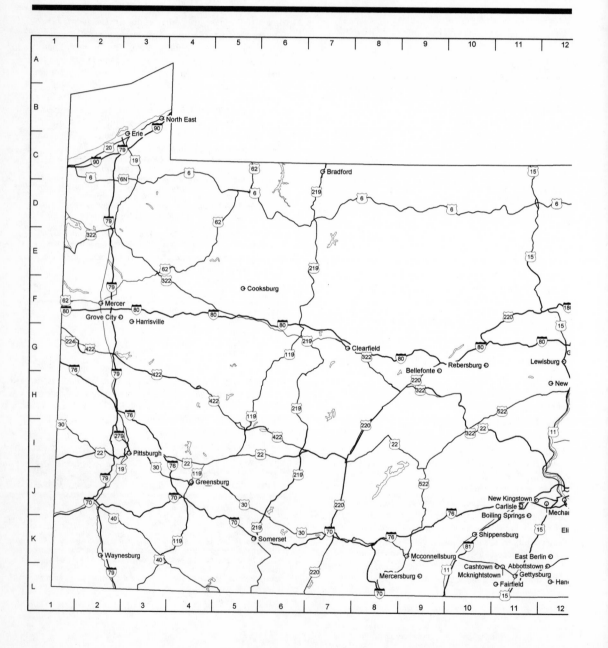

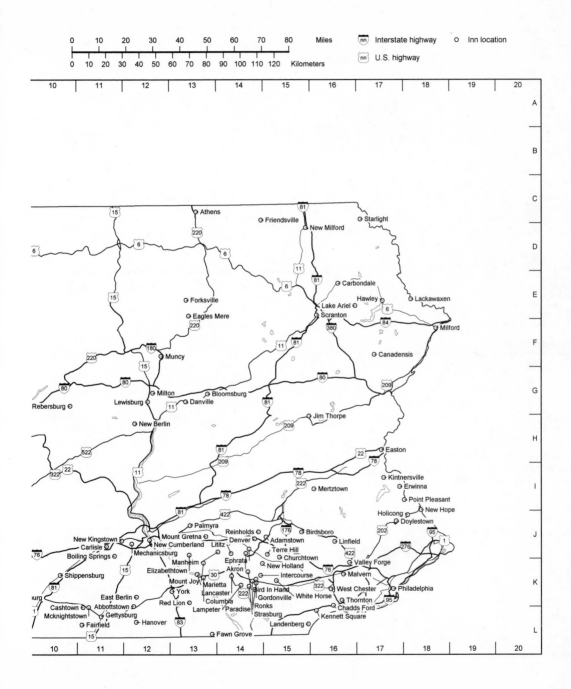

	0	10	20	30	40	50	60	70	80	Miles

0 10 20 30 40 50 60 70 80 90 100 110 120 Kilometers

(nn) Interstate highway   o   Inn location

(nn) U.S. highway

Abbottstown   K12

The Altland House

Rt 30 Center Square
Abbottstown, PA 17301
(717)259-9535
E-mail: stacey_myers@altlandhouse.com
Web: www.altlandhouse.com

Circa 1790. A French mansard roof sits atop this three-story
country inn and tavern known for its excellent cuisine and gracious hospitality. Located halfway between York and
Gettysburg, it is on an old Conestoga route.
The spacious guest rooms offer high
ceilings and chestnut woodwork.
Whirlpool tubs add pleasure to
several deluxe rooms. On the
third floor, one room offers a
sunroom with a deck and hot
tub while another includes a comfy sofa, an extra-large
whirlpool tub and a kitchenette. The inn's two restaurants present a variety of house specialties. The Underside Pub & Eatery
has a more casual atmosphere serving sandwiches as well as
entrees, while the Berwick Room Restaurant is noted for more
elegant cuisine. A popular Sunday brunch buffet is served from
11:30 a.m. to 2 p.m. Golf and Getaway packages are available,
some including wine and dinner.

Innkeeper(s): Ryan Haugh. $99-150. 10 rooms with PB and 2 conference
rooms. Breakfast included in rates. Types of meals: Cont plus, lunch, gourmet
dinner and room service. Beds: KQ. Cable TV, reading lamp, clock radio, telephone, desk, whirlpool tubs and free HBO in room. Air conditioning. Fax,
copier and fireplace on premises. Weddings and family reunions hosted.
Antiquing, downhill skiing, fishing, golf, live theater, shopping, tennis, history
and Gettysburg battlefield nearby.

Adamstown   J15

Adamstown Inn

62 W Main St
Adamstown, PA 19501
(717)484-0800 (800)594-4808
E-mail: stay@adamstown.com
Web: www.adamstown.com

Circa 1830. This restored Victorian with its 1850s pump organ
found in the large parlor and other local antiques, fits right into
this community known as one of the antique capitals of
America (3,000 antique dealers).
Other decorations include family
heirlooms, Victorian wallpaper,
handmade quilts and lace curtains.
For outlet mall fans, Adamstown is
10 miles from Reading, which
offers a vast assortment of top-
quality merchandise.

Historic Interest: The Ephrata Cloister is just seven miles away.
Innkeeper(s): Tom & Wanda Berman. $70-169. 4 rooms with PB and 1
suite. Breakfast, afternoon tea and snacks/refreshments included in rates.
Types of meals: Cont plus and early coffee/tea. Beds: KQ. Reading lamp, ceil-
ing fan, clock radio, desk, hot tub/spa, fireplace and two with Jacuzzi in
room. Air conditioning. TV, copier, library, parlor games, telephone and fire-
place on premises. Small meetings, family reunions and seminars hosted.
Amusement parks, antiquing, fishing, live theater, parks and shopping nearby.
Publicity: *Country Victorian, Lancaster Intelligencer, Reading Eagle, Travel &
Leisure, Country Almanac, Lancaster Magazine* and *Chester County Magazine.*

*"Your warm hospitality and lovely home left us with such pleasant
memories."*

Akron   J14

Bella Vista Bed & Breakfast

1216 Main St
Akron, PA 17501-1635
(717)859-4227 (888)948-9726 Fax:(717)859-4071
E-mail: info@bellavistabandb.com
Web: www.bellavistabandb.com

Circa 1905. Translated, this historical post Victorian inn's name
means "beautiful view," appropriately sitting across from 51
acres of parkland with ponds and trails. A comfortable country
coziness is enhanced by antique furnishings. The Family/TV
Room boasts a fireplace and large beamed ceiling, the Sitting
Room/Parlor is stocked with books and local maps. A queen
canopy bed and clawfoot tub are some of the guest bedrooms'
highlights. A generous family-style breakfast that may include
Lancaster County sausage and peach French toast is enjoyed in
the dining room. Venturing beyond the porch swings and rockers, there is much to explore in the surrounding areas.

Innkeeper(s): Sarah & Jeff Shirk. $85-95. 6 rooms with PB. Breakfast includ-
ed in rates. Types of meals: Country bkfst, veg bkfst, early coffee/tea and
snacks/refreshments. Beds: KQDT. Reading lamp, some with data port and
cable TV in room. Air conditioning. TV, fax, copier, spa, bicycles, parlor
games, telephone and fireplace on premises. Small meetings and family
reunions hosted. Amusement parks, antiquing, bicycling, golf, hiking, live theater, museums, parks, shopping and tennis nearby.

Athens   C13

Failte Inn B&B and Antique Shoppe

RR #2 Box 323 SR 1043
Athens, PA 18810
(570)358-3899 Fax:(570)358-3387

Circa 1925. During its heyday, parties with hundreds of guests
were not uncommon at this Gatsby-era estate. The inn's name
derives from the innkeepers' Scottish heritage and means welcome in Gaelic. The inn is decorated with a variety of antiques,
including some family pieces. One special decoration is an 18th-
century quilt designed by the innkeeper's great-great-great grandmother. The innkeeper also has her father's World War I uniform
on display and her mother's wedding dress. Complimentary
wine, brandy and other beverages are provided in the inn's pub,
which formerly served as a speakeasy during the days of
Prohibition. Breakfasts, served either in the formal dining room or
on the screened wraparound verandas, include baked goods such
as homemade sourdough bread, sticky buns or Amish friendship
bread accompanied by homemade jams and jellies. The daily
entrée might be cheesy eggs with Canadian bacon or perhaps
thick slices of sourdough French toast with Pennsylvania maple
syrup. The surrounding area offers lakes, parks and outdoor activities in the Endless Mountains, as well as antique shops, wineries,
the Corning Glass Museum and New York's Finger Lakes.

Innkeeper(s): Jim, Sarah & Jamie True. $75-105. 5 rooms with PB and 2
suites. Breakfast and snacks/refreshments included in rates. Types of meals:
Full gourmet bkfst, veg bkfst and early coffee/tea. Beds: KQDT. Cable TV,
reading lamp, ceiling fan, coffeemaker, one suite with sunken garden tub,
fireplace and a complimentary carafe of mead (wine made from honey) in
room. Air conditioning. VCR, fax, copier, library, parlor games, telephone, fireplace, huge screened veranda, microwave, web TV and pool table on premises. Weddings, small meetings, family reunions and seminars hosted.
Antiquing, bicycling, fishing, golf, hiking, horseback riding, museums, parks,
shopping, tennis, water sports and wineries nearby.
Publicity: *Happenings Magazine, Towanda Daily Review, Inn Traveler
Magazine* - winner of "Most Romantic Hideaway of 2004", WNEP Home
and garden show and PBS special.

Bear Creek F15

Bischwind B&B

Box 7 One Coach Road
Bear Creek, PA 18602-0007
(570)472-3820
E-mail: renglish@epix.net
Web: www.bischwind.com

Circa 1886. This spacious Tudor estate was built on prime acreage above the waterfall in Bear Creek Village by lumber and ice baron Albert Lewis. Dr. & Mrs. A.H. Von Dran have spent many years restoring the mansion. Filled with antiques, some rooms boast furnishings original to the house. An elegant four-course breakfast is served in the Presidential dining room with choice of filet mignon, salmon or shrimp scampi. Horses are raised on the property.

Innkeeper(s): Bill & Ralph English. $125-235. 9 rooms with PB. Breakfast included in rates. Types of meals: Full gourmet bkfst and early coffee/tea. Beds: KQD. Cable TV, reading lamp, ceiling fan, desk, some with Jacuzzi, fireplace and refrigerator in room. Central air. TV, VCR, fax, copier, library, parlor games, telephone, fireplace and in ground swimming pool on premises. Weddings, small meetings and seminars hosted. Antiquing, cross-country skiing, downhill skiing, fishing, golf, live theater, parks, shopping, sporting events & water sports nearby.
Publicity: People's Press.

"Beautiful home, scrumptious breakfast."

Bellefonte G9

Reynolds Mansion B&B

101 W Linn St
Bellefonte, PA 16823-1622
(814)353-8407 (800)899-3929
E-mail: innkeeper@reynoldsmansion.com
Web: www.reynoldsmansion.com

Circa 1885. Bellefonte is a town with many impressive, historic homes, and this exquisite stone mansion is no exception. The home, a combination of late Victorian and Gothic styles, features extraordinary, hand-crafted woodwork and intricately laid wood floors, as well as 10 fireplaces. Five guest rooms include a fireplace and a Jacuzzi tub. All enjoy a romantic atmosphere, heightened by candles, fresh flowers and the poshest of furnishings and decor. There also is a billiards room and library for guests to enjoy. Baked, stuffed French toast served with bacon or sausage  is among the breakfast specialties accompanied by muffins, juices, cereals and a fruit compote created with more than a half dozen different fresh fruits. For an excellent lunch or dinner, the innkeepers suggest the nearby Gamble Mill Tavern, a 200-year-old mill listed in the National Register.

Innkeeper(s): Joseph & Charlotte Heidt. $105-215. 6 suites, 6 with FP. Breakfast included in rates. Types of meals: Full gourmet bkfst and early coffee/tea. Beds: KQ. Reading lamp, stereo, clock radio, desk, Jacuzzi tubs and Jacuzzi steam shower in room. Central air. TV, VCR, fax, copier, library, parlor games, telephone, fireplace and billiards room on premises. Weddings, small meetings, family reunions and seminars hosted. Antiquing, bicycling, canoeing/kayaking, cross-country skiing, downhill skiing, fishing, golf, hiking, live theater, museums, parks, shopping, sporting events, water sports and Victorian architecture nearby.
Publicity: Country Victorian, Pennsylvania Magazine, Town & Gown, Arrington's B&B Journal voted "Best Inn Near a College or University," hosted National Governors' Meeting tour and tea for spouses and on the cover of Select Registry.

"Your bed & breakfast is such an inspiration to us."

Bird-in-Hand K14

Mill Creek Homestead B&B

2578 Old Philadelphia Pike
Bird-in-Hand, PA 17505-9796
(717)291-6419 (800)771-2578 Fax:(717)291-2171
E-mail: valfone@yahoo.com
Web: www.millcreekhomestead.com

Circa 1790. This 18th-century fieldstone farmhouse is one of the oldest homes in Bird-in-the-Hand. Located in the Pennsylvania Dutch Heartland, the inn is decorated for comfort with Amish influences represented throughout. There are four guest rooms with private baths and fireplaces or stoves. Guests are invited to lounge by the outdoor pool or sit on the porch and watch the horse-drawn buggies go by. A full breakfast is served in the formal  dining room, while afternoon refreshments are in the common rooms. The inn is within walking distance of shops, museums, farmers market, antiques and crafts.

Innkeeper(s): Vicki & Frank Alfone. $109-195. 4 rooms with PB. Breakfast, afternoon tea and snacks/refreshments included in rates. Types of meals: Full bkfst and early coffee/tea. Beds: QT. Stereo, ceiling fan and turn-down service in room. Air conditioning. Swimming, library, parlor games, telephone and fireplace on premises. Amusement parks, antiquing, fishing, golf, live theater, parks, shopping, tennis and water sports nearby.
Publicity: Country Inns and Lancaster County Magazine.

"Thank you for sharing your wonderful home with us. I knew this place would be perfect!"

The Village Inn of Bird-In-Hand

PO Box 253
Bird-In-Hand, PA 17505-0253
(717)293-8369 (800)914-2473 Fax:(717)768-1511
E-mail: lodging@bird-in-hand.com
Web: www.bird-in-hand.com/villageinn

Circa 1734. The history of this property dates back to the 18th century when it served as a hotel for weary guests traveling the Pennsylvania Turnpike. The original inn was destroyed by fire in 1851 and the present, three-story hotel was built in its place. Today, guests will enjoy the inn's historic sense of ambiance and Victorian decor. Breakfasts are served on the sun porch with its paddle fans and wicker furnishings. Two  of the guest rooms feature a large Jacuzzi, and another room boasts a fireplace. Swimming and tennis facilities are within walking distance of the inn. The inn is adjacent to a farmers' market, country store, bakery, restaurant and several shops and outlets.

Historic Interest: The inn offers a complimentary two-hour tour of the surrounding Amish farm lands, and the Pennsylvania Dutch Convention and Visitors Bureau is only a few miles away.
Innkeeper(s): Rick Meshey. $69-155. 11 rooms with PB, 1 with FP and 6 suites. Breakfast and snacks/refreshments included in rates. Types of meals: Cont plus. Beds: KQ. Cable TV, reading lamp, clock radio and telephone in room. Air conditioning. Two hour complimentary tour of farm lands on premises. Amusement parks, antiquing, golf, live theater, parks, shopping, tennis, PA Dutch Amish Country and miniature golf nearby.
Publicity: Country Folk Art.

"The Village Inn offers the charm and coziness of a B&B with the privacy of a hotel."

Birdsboro J15

Brooke Mansion Victorian Inn

Washington St
Birdsboro, PA 19508
(610)582-9775 (800)544-1094
E-mail: brookemansion@worldlynx.net
Web: www.brookemansion.com

Circa 1888. Designed by celebrated Victorian architect Frank
Furness, the Brooke Mansion, a stunning Victorian, is the only
B&B in the country designed by Mr. Furness, who was recently
named one of the Top Ten Architects by the American Institute of

Architects. It is one of those
exquisite homes you might pass by
and wish you could see inside. The
home is a fanciful display of
Victorian architecture, the first
owner built it as a wedding gift for
his bride. Stained glass, ornate
hand-carved woodwork, a circular library and a grand staircase are
among the gems guests will marvel at in this 42-room manor. The
interior includes fine antiques, some of which are family heirlooms. One suite is located in the mansion's turret. The area offers
much to do, from antiquing to exploring Amish country. The inn
is an hour's drive from Philadelphia and minutes from Reading.
Innkeeper(s): Marci & Pete Xenias. $99-140. 4 rooms with PB and 1 suite.
Breakfast included in rates. Types of meals: Full bkfst and early coffee/tea.
Beds: K. Reading lamp and ceiling fan in room. Air conditioning. Library and
telephone on premises. Antiquing, golf, live theater, parks, shopping, tennis
and outlets nearby.
Publicity: *News of Southern Berks, Washington Flyer, Antiques & Auction
News, Routers, Boston Globe, Book of Quilts are Forever, Acord publishing
and B&B Calendar of Days.*

"Incredible, we are glad we found you!"

Bloomsburg G13

The Inn at Turkey Hill

991 Central Rd
Bloomsburg, PA 17815-8990
(570)387-1500 Fax:(570)784-3718
E-mail: info@innatturkeyhill.com
Web: www.innatturkeyhill.com

Circa 1839. Turkey Hill is an elegant, white brick farmhouse. All
the guest rooms are furnished with hand-crafted reproductions
from Habersham Plantation in Georgia and most overlook the
duck pond and gazebo. Two rooms provide wood-burning fire-

places and two-person whirlpool
tubs. The five stable rooms also
include a gas fireplace and two-
person whirlpool tub. The mural
room features hand-painted
murals of the rolling
Pennsylvania countryside.
Innkeeper(s): Andrew B. Pruden. $107-225. 23 rooms with PB, 7 with FP and
2 conference rooms. Breakfast included in rates. Types of meals: Cont, gourmet
dinner and room service. Restaurant on premises. Beds: KQ. Data port, refrigerator, coffeemaker and DVD library in room. TV, fax, copier and telephone on
premises. Limited handicap access. Antiquing, fishing and live theater nearby.
Publicity: *Baltimore Sun, Tempo and Philadelphia Inquirer.*

*"How nice to find an enclave of good taste and class, a special place
that seems to care about such old-fashioned virtues as quality and the
little details that mean so much." — Art Carey, Philadelphia Inquirer*

Boiling Springs J11

Gelinas Manor Victorian B&B

219 Front Street
Boiling Springs, PA 17007
(717)258-6584 Fax:(717)245-9328
E-mail: lee@gelinas-manor.com
Web: www.gelinas-manor.com

Circa 1869. One of the first homes in the quiet historic village
by the lake, this 1869 Victorian is listed in the National
Register. Enjoy comfortable accommodations and a satisfying
breakfast before embarking on the day's activities. The well-
stocked lake and crystal-clear Yellow Breeches Creek are considered some of the country's best trout fishing areas. The nearby
Fly Shop features locally tied flys, fishing gear, clothing and
gifts as well as offering experienced tips for any interested fisherman. The famous Allenberry Resort and Playhouse is minutes
away for fine dining and entertainment in the evening. Visit the
sites of Gettysburg within a 30-minute drive, or savor the flavors of Hershey in an hour. The inn is about 1 1/2 hours away
from Pennsylvania Dutch Country in Lancaster County.
Innkeeper(s): Lee & Kitty Gelinas. $60-145. 3 rooms and 1 suite. Breakfast
included in rates. Types of meals: Full gourmet bkfst. Beds: QDT. Cable TV, refrigerator, ceiling fan, clock radio, telephone and turn-down service in room. Air conditioning. Fax, copier, library and fireplace on premises. Amusement parks,
antiquing, art galleries, cross-country skiing, downhill skiing, fishing, golf, hiking,
live theater, museums, parks, shopping, sporting events and tennis nearby.

Bradford C7

Mountain Laurel Inn

136 Jackson Avenue
Bradford, PA 16701
(814)362-8006 Fax:(814)362-4208
E-mail: info@mountainlaurelbradford.com
Web: www.mountainlaurelbradford.com

Circa 1894. Subtly combining Greek and Colonial Revival architecture, this stately inn for adults is an impressive example of hospitality and elegance. Past the grand circular staircase, the living
room is perfect for relaxing with complimentary beverages. The
luxurious guest bedrooms, decorated with charm and sophistication, offer many special touches to pamper and please. Innkeepers
Carolyn and Bob create extraordinary culinary delights each morning served in the intimate breakfast room or formal dining room.
The garden is always in bloom and the landscaped grounds are
best appreciated from the comfort of the cushioned wicker furniture on the large pillared front porch. Centrally located in the
Allegheny Mountains, there is a variety of year-round activities.
Innkeeper(s): Bob & Carolyn Krebs. $95-105. 7 rooms with PB. Breakfast
and snacks/refreshments included in rates. Types of meals: Full gourmet
bkfst, veg bkfst and early coffee/tea. Beds: KQ. Cable TV, reading lamp, clock
radio, telephone, turn-down service and desk in room. Air conditioning. Fax,
copier, parlor games, fireplace, beverage, snack and refrigerator area on
premises. Weddings, small meetings, family reunions and seminars hosted.
Antiquing, bicycling, canoeing/kayaking, cross-country skiing, downhill skiing,
fishing, golf, hiking, live theater, museums, parks, shopping, tennis, water
sports, wineries, Zippo Lighter Museum, Case Knive Museum, University of
Pittsburgh at Bradford and St. Bonaventure University nearby.

Canadensis F17

Brookview Manor Inn

RR 2 Box 2960, Route 447
Canadensis, PA 18325
(570)595-2451 (800)585-7974

Circa 1901. By the side of the road, hanging from a tall evergreen, is the welcoming sign to this forest retreat on five acres adjoining 250 acres of woodland and hiking trails. The expansive wraparound porch overlooks a small stream. There are

 brightly decorated common rooms and four fireplaces. Ten guest rooms include two with Jacuzzis and two deluxe suites. The carriage house has three additional rooms. One of the inn's dining rooms is surrounded by original stained glass, a romantic location for the inn's special five-course dinners prepared by a New York city chef now on staff. The innkeepers like to share a "secret waterfall" within a 30-minute walk from the inn.

Historic Interest: Pocono Mountains.

Innkeeper(s): Gaile & Marty Horowitz. $130-250. 10 rooms with PB, 5 with FP and 2 suites. Breakfast and afternoon tea included in rates. Types of meals: Full gourmet bkfst, early coffee/tea and dinner. Beds: KQ. TV, reading lamp, two rooms with Jacuzzi and suites have sitting rooms and private porches in room. Air conditioning. Fax, copier, telephone, fireplace, swing, wraparound porch overlooking small stream, hiking and gourmet dinner available by reservation on premises. Weddings, small meetings and family reunions hosted. Amusement parks, antiquing, cross-country skiing, downhill skiing, fishing, live theater, parks, shopping, water sports and hiking nearby.

Publicity: Mid-Atlantic Country, Bridal Guide and New York Times.

"Thanks for a great wedding weekend. Everything was perfect."

Pine Knob Inn

Rt 447, PO Box 295
Canadensis, PA 18325-0295
(570)595-2532 (800)426-1460 Fax:(717)595-6429
E-mail: innkeepers @pineknobinn.com
Web: pineknobinn.com

Circa 1847. Enjoy history and the beauty of the Poconos at Pine Knob, which was built by a man who owned the largest tannery in the United States. By 1886, the sprawling Victorian became an inn, long before the area became a hot spot for vacationers. The interior is charming, filled with antiques and country furnishings, as well as Arts & Crafts-style pieces. The innkeepers' collection of birdhouses is found here and there, both inside and hanging from trees throughout the six-and-a-half-acre spread. As a true country inn, both breakfast and dinner are included in the rates. Dinner includes five courses and is served by candlelight. The Poconos offer plenty of activities for nature-lovers and shoppers alike.

Innkeeper(s): Cheryl & John Garman. $158-190. 28 rooms, 19 with PB, 5 with FP, 3 cottages and 1 conference room. Breakfast and dinner included in rates. Types of meals: Full bkfst. Restaurant on premises. Beds: KQDT. Reading lamp and ceiling fan in room. Air conditioning. VCR, fax, copier, swimming, tennis, library, parlor games, telephone, fireplace, trout stream and gazebos on premises. Weddings, small meetings, family reunions and seminars hosted. Antiquing, cross-country skiing, downhill skiing, fishing, golf, live theater, parks, shopping, sporting events, tennis, water sports, waterfalls, shuffleboard, hiking and picnic area nearby.

Carbondale E16

Heritage House on the Park

5 Park Place
Carbondale, PA 18407-2330
(570)282-7477 Fax:(570)282-8698

Circa 1912. Built in Victorian style, Heritage House offers four guest rooms all decorated with elegant, period décor. The Ivy Suite includes a fireplace and whirlpool tub. Lacy curtains, clawfoot tubs and roses are other romantic amenities. Breakfasts are served by candlelight and include homemade breads and muffins and items such as crepes with fresh fruit, oven-baked pancakes or baked oatmeal. The house overlooks Memorial Park and Carbondale's city hall. The inn offers close access to ski areas, golfing, hunting, fishing, horseback riding, tennis and snowmobiling.

Innkeeper(s): Darlene Ferraro-Ploch. $75-105. 4 rooms, 3 with PB, 1 with FP and 1 suite. Breakfast and snacks/refreshments included in rates. Types of meals: Full gourmet bkfst, veg bkfst and picnic lunch. Beds: QD. Cable TV, reading lamp, refrigerator, clock radio, telephone, coffeemaker, desk and garden tub in room. Central air. TV, fax, parlor games and fireplace on premises. Antiquing, art galleries, bicycling, cross-country skiing, downhill skiing, fishing, golf, hiking, horseback riding, live theater, museums, parks, shopping, sporting events, tennis, water sports and wineries nearby.

Carlisle J11

Jacobs Resting Place

1007 Harrisburg Pike
Carlisle, PA 17013-1616
(717)243-1766 (888)731-1790 Fax:(781)459-6592
E-mail: jacobsrest@pa.net
Web: www.jacobsrestingplace.com

Circa 1790. Three acres surround this pristine heritage home, located on land purchased from the William Penn Land Grant. The gracious brick Georgian with its white shutters and original floors, doors, woodwork and seven fireplaces offered respite to travelers more than two centuries ago when it was called The Sign of the Green Tree. It is said that George Washington met his army on this site in 1794. You will enjoy a four-poster rice bed and whirlpool bath if you request the 1700 Suite, but each room at the inn is steeped in history and decorated in a different period. The Blue and Gray Room, combined with the old tavern-keeper's quarters, provides for a family or friends traveling together when they need two bedrooms. Breakfast is served with china, crystal and silver on white linens and may include a crepe dish or stuffed French toast and home-baked breads. Terry is a Civil War historian, a wonderful resource for enjoying the Civil War battlefields and Military History Institute nearby. There is a trout stream on the property as well as a hot tub and pool, or you might enjoy a quarter of a mile walk to the 1800 Indian School.

Historic Interest: William Penn Museum.

Innkeeper(s): Terry & Marie Hegglin. $75-130. 5 rooms with PB, 4 with FP, 4 suites and 1 conference room. Breakfast and snacks/refreshments included in rates. Types of meals: Full gourmet bkfst. Beds: KQDT. Modem hook-up, TV, reading lamp, ceiling fan, clock radio, telephone, turn-down service, desk and voice mail in room. Central air. VCR, fax, copier, spa, parlor games, fireplace, swimming pool, trout fishing and refrigerator on premises. Small meetings, family reunions and seminars hosted. Amusement parks, antiquing, art galleries, canoeing/kayaking, cross-country skiing, downhill skiing, fishing, golf, hiking, live theater, museums, parks, shopping, sporting events, tennis, water sports and wineries nearby.

Pheasant Field B&B

150 Hickorytown Rd
Carlisle, PA 17013-9732
(717)258-0717 (877)258-0717 Fax:(717)258-0717
E-mail: stay@pheasantfield.com
Web: www.pheasantfield.com

Circa 1800. Located on 10 acres of central Pennsylvania farmland, this brick, two-story Federal-style farmhouse features wooden shutters and a covered front porch. Rooms include a TV and telephone. An early 19th-century stone barn is on the property, and horse boarding is available. The Appalachian Trail is less than a mile away. Fly-fishing is popular at Yellow Breeches and Letort Spring. Dickinson College and Carlisle Fairgrounds are other points of interest.

Historic Interest: Gettysburg National Historical Park (32 miles), Molly Pitcher gravesite.
Innkeeper(s): Denise Fegan. $90-175. 7 rooms with PB. Breakfast included in rates. Types of meals: Full bkfst and early coffee/tea. Beds: KQT. Cable TV, reading lamp, clock radio, telephone and desk in room. Air conditioning. VCR, fax, fireplace and piano on premises. Weddings, small meetings and family reunions hosted. Amusement parks, antiquing, cross-country skiing, downhill skiing, fishing and live theater nearby.
Publicity: *Outdoor Traveler and Harrisburg Magazine.*

"You have an outstanding, charming and warm house. I felt for the first time as being home."

Cashtown   L11

Cashtown Inn

1325 Old Rt 30, PO Box 103
Cashtown, PA 17310
(717)334-9722 (800)367-1797

Circa 1797. Cashtown Inn's history alone will inspire a visit. The inn was built as a stagecoach stop and has welcomed guests for more than two centuries. It also served as a stop along the Underground Railroad and curiously, also served as a Confederate headquarters prior to the Battle of Gettysburg. The inn's rooms are decorated in country Victorian style with four-poster beds. One room includes a lace canopy bed. In addition to the gourmet breakfasts, which are included in the rates, the inn also serves lunch and includes a renowned restaurant with dinners prepared by a chef. Dinners are served in the rustic bar, which was the inn's original tavern or in the more elegant main dining room. The chef's menus feature starters such as a baked brie in pastry or savory artichoke dip with focaccia bread. From there, guests can partake of homemade soups or salads with freshly prepared dressings. The menu is ever changing, but might include entrees such as pecan-crusted chicken with maple butter sauce or perhaps beef medallions with bourbon walnut sauce. The inn is eight miles from Gettysburg Military Park, and also offers close access to many historic sites, museums, a winery, art galleries and shopping.

Innkeeper(s): Dennis & Eileen Hoover. $76-145. 7 rooms, 4 with PB and 3 suites. Breakfast included in rates. Types of meals: Full gourmet bkfst, early coffee/tea, lunch and dinner. Restaurant on premises. Beds: KQD. Cable TV, VCR, reading lamp, ceiling fan and clock radio in room. Central air. Fax, copier, telephone and fireplace on premises. Weddings, small meetings, family reunions and seminars hosted. Antiquing, art galleries, downhill skiing, golf, hiking, horseback riding, live theater, museums, parks, shopping, sporting events and wineries nearby.

Publicity: *Philadelphia.*

"We were impressed with your inn, but more importantly with your personal touch toward all your guests...many thanks for your generosity and hospitality."

Chadds Ford   K16

Fairville Inn

506 Kennett Pike
Chadds Ford, PA 19317
(610)388-5900 Fax:(610)388-5902
E-mail: info@fairvilleinn.com
Web: www.fairvilleinn.com

Circa 1826. This federal-style country inn offers a fine base to explore the Brandywine Valley—an area known for its stately homes and rural back roads. Guest rooms feature various combinations of cathedral ceilings, fireplaces, king- and queen-size beds (some with canopies). They are found in three different buildings: The Main House, which dates back to 1820, the Springhouse, and the Carriage House. Suites have an additional sitting area and French doors that open onto a private deck. Full breakfasts consist of a hot entree, fruit, fresh-squeezed juice and baked goodies. They also offer an afternoon tea. Nearby activities include canoeing, biking, golf, art galleries, museums and parks.

Innkeeper(s): Noel and Jane McStay. $150-250. 15 rooms with PB, 8 with FP and 2 suites. Breakfast and afternoon tea included in rates. Beds: KQT. Cable TV, reading lamp, telephone, desk, iron, ironing board and hair dryer in room. Fax, copier, library and fireplace on premises. Limited handicap access. Antiquing, art galleries, bicycling, canoeing/kayaking, golf, horseback riding, museums, parks, wineries, Andrew Wyatt Museum, Longwood Gardens and Winterthur Mansion and Gardens nearby.

Hamanassett B&B

725 Darlington Road
Chadds Ford, PA 19017
(610)459-3000 (877)836-8212 Fax:(610)558-7366
E-mail: visitus@hamanassett.com
Web: www.hamanassett.com

Circa 1856. Located in Brandywine Valley, this Federalist mansion offers romantic accommodations with thoughtful extras. Inside the impressive three-story manor there is a spacious living room with wood-burning fireplace and a baby grand piano. A billiards room features fireside contemporary and antique games as well as a pool table. Relax in the cozy solarium with separate sitting areas. Appealing guest bedrooms provide upscale amenities that pamper and please. A Rosewood half-tester bed is showcased in the Windsor Room. The carriage house is perfect for children and pets. Candlelight gourmet breakfasts are served in the formal dining room that boasts a floor-to-ceiling fireplace and looks out on spacious lawns, trees and a stone terrace. A guest refrigerator is stocked with snacks and beverages.

Historic Interest: Located near many of the Brandywine Valley attractions, including Longwood Gardens, Winterthur, Brandywine Museum (Wyeth), and Nemours. Local dining and historic restaurants are nearby.
Innkeeper(s): Ashley & Glenn Mon. $130-350. 6 rooms with PB, 1 with FP and 2 suites. Breakfast, afternoon tea and snacks/refreshments included in rates. Types of meals: Full gourmet bkfst, veg bkfst and picnic lunch. Beds: KQT. Data port, cable TV, VCR, reading lamp, CD player, refrigerator, ceiling fan, clock radio, telephone, coffeemaker, desk, fireplace, fluffy robes and hair dryer in room. Air conditioning. Fax, copier, library, parlor games, fireplace and gift shop on premises. Small meetings, family reunions and seminars hosted. Antiquing, art galleries, canoeing/kayaking, fishing, golf, hiking, horseback riding, live theater, museums, parks, shopping, sporting events, wineries and Brandywine Valley attractions nearby.
Publicity: *Philadelphia, Back Roads USA, Mid-Atlantic Country and*

Philadelphia and Its Countryside.

"For our first try at B&B lodgings, we've probably started at the top, and nothing else will ever measure up to this. Wonderful food, wonderful home, grounds and wonderful hostess!"

Pennsbury Inn

883 Baltimore Pike
Chadds Ford, PA 19317-9305
(610)388-1435 Fax:(610)388-1436
E-mail: info@pennsburyinn.com
Web: www.pennsburyinn.com

Circa 1714. Listed in the National Register, this country farm-house with hand-molded Flemish Bond brick facade was built originally with Brandywine Blue Granite rubble stone and later enlarged. Retaining its colonial heritage with slanted doorways, winding wood staircases and huge fireplaces, it boasts modern conveniences. There are elegant public sitting areas such as the living room, music room, library with an impressive book collection and breakfast in the dining room. The comfortable guest bedrooms feature antique feather beds and unique architectural details. The eight-acre estate boasts formal gardens that include a fish pond and reflection pool in a serene woodland setting.
Innkeeper(s): Cheryl. $100-225. 7 rooms, 6 with PB, 1 suite and 3 conference rooms. Breakfast, afternoon tea and snacks/refreshments included in rates. Types of meals: Country bkfst, veg bkfst and early coffee/tea. Beds: KQDT. Modem hook-up, data port, cable TV, reading lamp, CD player, clock radio, telephone, turn-down service, desk and three with decorative fireplaces in room. Central air. VCR, fax, copier, library, parlor games and fireplace on premises. Weddings, small meetings and family reunions hosted. Antiquing, art galleries, bicycling, canoeing/kayaking, golf, hiking, live theater, museums, parks, shopping, sporting events, tennis and wineries nearby.

Churchtown   J15

The Inn at Twin Linden

2092 Main St # 23
Churchtown, PA 17555-9514
(717)445-7619
Web: www.innattwinlinden.com

Circa 1840. Experience luxurious elegance at this historic country manor estate. Towering linden trees, the inn's namesake, overlook the brick courtyard. Romantic guest bedrooms and suites feature two-person Jacuzzis or clawfoot tubs, fireplaces and feather beds, some with canopies. Breakfast and afternoon tea are culinary creations by a nationally renowned chef and author of two cookbooks. Relax on wicker-filled porches. The 2.5 acres boast colorful gardens overlooking Mennonite and Amish farm valleys. Play golf at a nearby course, or shop and browse through antiques.
Innkeeper(s): Donna & Bob Leahy. $125-265. 8 rooms with PB, 7 with FP and 1 conference room. Breakfast and afternoon tea included in rates. Types of meals: Full gourmet bkfst. Beds: KQDT. Cable TV in room. Copier on premises. Publicity: *Early American Life, Los Angeles Times, Country Home, Country Living, USA Today, National Geographic Traveler, Travel Holiday, Food & Wine and Victoria.*

"Your inn exceeds all others."

Clearfield   G7

Christopher Kratzer House

101 E Cherry St
Clearfield, PA 16830-2315
(814)765-5024 (888)252-2632

Circa 1840. This inn is the oldest home in town, built by a carpenter and architect who also started Clearfield's first newspa-

per. The innkeepers keep a book of history about the house and town for interested guests. The interior is a mix of antiques from different eras, many are family pieces. There are collections of art and musical instruments. Two guest rooms afford views of the Susquehanna River. Refreshments and a glass of wine are served in the afternoons. The inn's Bridal Suite Special includes complimentary champagne, fruit and snacks, and breakfast may be served in the privacy of your room. Small wedding receptions, brunches and parties are hosted at the inn.
Innkeeper(s): Bruce & Ginny Baggett. $65-90. 4 rooms, 2 with PB. Breakfast, afternoon tea and snacks/refreshments included in rates. Types of meals: Full gourmet bkfst and early coffee/tea. Beds: KQT. Cable TV, reading lamp, ceiling fan, clock radio, telephone and desk in room. Air conditioning. Library, parlor games and fireplace on premises. Antiquing, cross-country skiing, fishing, live theater, parks, shopping, sporting events, hiking, biking and playground across street nearby.
Publicity: *Local PA newspapers.*

"Past and present joyously intermingle in this place."

Columbia   K13

The Columbian

360 Chestnut St
Columbia, PA 17512-1156
(717)684-5869 (800)422-5869
E-mail: inn@columbianinn.com
Web: www.columbianinn.com

Circa 1897. This stately three-story mansion is a fine example of Colonial Revival architecture. Antique beds, a stained-glass window and home-baked breads are among its charms.

Guests may relax on the wrap-around sun porches.
Historic Interest: The National Watch and Clock Museum (one-half block), The Wrights Ferry Mansion (4 blocks), The Bank Museum (4 blocks).
Innkeeper(s): Chris & Becky Will. $75-125. 8 rooms with PB, 4 with FP and 2 suites. Breakfast included in rates. Types of meals: Full bkfst. Beds: KQT. Cable TV, reading lamp, ceiling fan, clock radio and fruit/candy/flowers in room. Air conditioning. TV, parlor games, telephone and fireplace on premises. Weddings, small meetings and family reunions hosted. Amusement parks, antiquing, art galleries, cross-country skiing, downhill skiing, fishing, live theater, museums, parks, shopping, sporting events, water sports and Elizabethtown nearby.
Publicity: *Philadelphia Inquirer, Lancaster Intelligencer Journal, Columbia News, Washington Post, Potomac and Allentown Morning Call.*

"In a word, extraordinary! Truly a home away from home. First B&B experience but will definitely not be my last."

Cooksburg   F5

Gateway Lodge

Rt 36, Box 125
Cooksburg, PA 16217-0125
(814)744-8017 (800)843-6862 Fax:(814)744-8017
E-mail: info@gatewaylodge.com
Web: www.gatewaylodge.com

Circa 1934. This well-reviewed rustic log lodge was built to accommodate visitors to Cook Forest State Park, a National Natural Landmark. Gateway Lodge borders the park, which offers a multitude of outdoor activities. Guests may opt for cozy rooms in the main lodge, a spacious fireside, whirlpool suite, or a cottage for two to eight people, ideal for families with children. All accommodations are decorated in a comfortable country style. Inn, suite and BB/MAP cottage guests are offered full access to all the inn's amenities, including afternoon tea. Picnic lunches are available and a wine room with more than 300 varieties of domestic and imported wines is on the premises. Each of the three common rooms, including the library, has a fireplace. Popular for conferences (up to 40 people), there is also a full service restaurant on the premises. The innkeepers offer several different packages.

Innkeeper(s): Joe & Linda Burney. $95-250. 34 rooms, 2 with PB, 24 suites, 8 cottages and 1 conference room. Types of meals: Country bkfst, early coffee/tea, lunch, picnic lunch, afternoon tea and gourmet dinner. Restaurant on premises. Beds: KD. Turn-down service, refrigerator, clock radios and suites have Jacuzzis in room. Air conditioning. Fax, copier, spa, swimming, sauna, library, parlor games, fireplace, wine room offering more than 300 varieties of domestic and imported wines, exercise room and Hospitality Hour on premises. Limited handicap access. Weddings, small meetings, family reunions and seminars hosted. Amusement parks, antiquing, cross-country skiing, fishing, golf, live theater, parks, shopping, sporting events, tennis and water sports nearby.

Publicity: *Erie Daily Times, PM Magazine, KDKA Magazine, Sharon Herald, Money Magazine and Innsider Magazine.*

Danville   G13

The Pine Barn Inn

1 Pine Barn Pl
Danville, PA 17821-1299
(570)275-2071 (800)627-2276 Fax:(570)275-3248
E-mail: innkpr@pinebarninn.com
Web: pinebarninn.com

Circa 1860. The inn is a restored Pennsylvania German barn. Original stone walls and beams accent the restaurant and a large stone fireplace warms the tavern. It is believed to be the first all-electric residence in the state.

Innkeeper(s): Susan Dressler. $50-90. 102 rooms with PB and 2 conference rooms. Types of meals: Full bkfst. Restaurant on premises. Beds: KQDT. TV and telephone on premises.

"For four years we have stayed at the Pine Barn Inn. I thought then, and still think, it is truly the nicest inn I have been in and I've been in many."

Denver   J14

Cocalico Creek B&B

224 S Fourth St
Denver, PA 17517
(717)336-0271 (888)208-7334
E-mail: cocalicocrk@dejazzd.com
Web: www.cocalicocrk.com

Circa 1927. Casual elegance is found at this tranquil retreat in a country setting. Overlooking gardens and pastures, the B&B is accented with the sounds of splashing ducks in the creek or ponds and an occasional buggy passing by. Comfortably decorated guest bedrooms, most with a view and some with a fireplace, are named for local wildlife. Blending traditional and antique furnishings, the rooms are enhanced with wallpapers, lace curtains and Oriental rugs. Enjoy a four-course breakfast made with many local seasonal ingredients, served in the candlelit dining room or on the side porch. Dietary requests are accommodated. Relax by the large stone fireplace or on the stenciled porch with wicker furniture. Schedule an in-room massage or dinner at an Amish home.

Innkeeper(s): Charlene Sweeney. $99-125. 4 rooms with PB, 2 with FP. Breakfast and snacks/refreshments included in rates. Types of meals: Full

bkfst, veg bkfst and early coffee/tea. Beds: Q. Reading lamp, clock radio, turn-down service, heated beds, robes, hair dryer and one with fireplace in room. Air conditioning. TV, VCR, library, telephone, fireplace, gift shop, TV, stereo, board/card games and puzzles on premises. Amusement parks, antiquing, art galleries, bicycling, cross-country skiing, fishing, golf, hiking, horseback riding, live theater, museums, parks, shopping, sporting events, tennis and wineries nearby.

Doylestown   J17

Doylestown Inn

18 W State St
Doylestown, PA 18901-4269
(215)345-6610 Fax:(215)348-9940
E-mail: deauville1234 @aol.com
Web: www.doylestowninn.com

Circa 1902. At the center of downtown, this historic inn has been a popular home away from home since 1902. Fully restored in 2001, a four-story atrium is capped by a skylight, flooding the main lobby and hallways with sunshine. Take the elevator to individually heated and air-conditioned guest bedrooms that also feature elegant furnishings, jetted tubs and a mini bar. Spacious Premium Rooms include fireplaces and sitting areas. ADA rooms are available. Enjoy complimentary coffee, tea and pastries with the morning newspaper. Walk to dozens of nearby shops and restaurants, watch a movie at the art deco theatre, visit the James A. Michener Art and Mercer museums.

$135-220. 11 rooms with PB, 3 with FP and 3 suites. Breakfast included in rates. Types of meals: Early coffee/tea. Beds: KQ. Modem hook-up, cable TV, VCR, reading lamp, snack bar, telephone, desk and fireplace in room. Air conditioning. Fax and copier on premises. Limited handicap access. Weddings hosted. Antiquing, art galleries, bicycling, cross-country skiing, golf, horseback riding, museums, shopping and wineries nearby.

Publicity: *Destination Doylestown.*

Eagles Mere   E13

Eagles Mere Inn

Box #356 Corner of Mary & Sullivan Avenues
Eagles Mere, PA 17731-0356
(570)525-3273 (800)426-3273 Fax:(570)525-3731
E-mail: relax@eaglesmereinn.com
Web: www.eaglesmereinn.com

Circa 1887. Developed as a resort in the 1800s, Eagles Mere sits in the mountains of Northeastern Pennsylvania near a pristine lake and surrounded by the unspoiled beauty of a nature conservancy. As the last full-service inn built for guests of the 1800s, the Eagles Mere Inn is part of the town's history, retaining its Victorian architecture and charm. Accommodations include guest rooms with private baths, sunny breakfast room, cozy living room with fireplace and pub. The restaurant serves breakfast and five-course gourmet dinners. The location offers year-round recreation and activities, from boating and swimming at the lake in the summer and viewing the autumn colors of the mountains to ice-skating, cross-country skiing and a famous toboggan slide.

Innkeeper(s): Susan & Peter Glaubitz. $159-259. 19 rooms with PB and 3 suites. Breakfast, snacks/refreshments and dinner included in rates. Types of meals: Country bkfst, veg bkfst and early coffee/tea. Restaurant on premises. Beds: KQDT. Modem hook-up, reading lamp, ceiling fan, desk and hot tub/spa in room. Air conditioning. TV, VCR, fax, copier, bicycles, library, parlor games, telephone, fireplace and gift shop on premises. Handicap access. Weddings, small meetings, family reunions and seminars hosted. Antiquing, beach, bicycling, canoeing/kayaking, cross-country skiing, fishing, golf, hiking, horseback riding, live theater, museums, parks, shopping and tennis nearby.

East Berlin   K12

Bechtel Victorian Mansion B&B Inn

400 W King St
East Berlin, PA 17316
(717)259-7760 (800)579-1108
E-mail: bechtelvictbb@aol.com
Web: www.bbonline.com/pa/bechtel/

Circa 1897. The town of East Berlin, near Lancaster and 18 miles east of Gettysburg, was settled by Pennsylvania Germans prior to the American Revolution. William Leas, a wealthy banker, built this many-gabled romantic Queen Anne mansion, now listed in the National Register. The inn is furnished with an abundance of museum-quality antiques and collections. Rooms are decorated in country Victorian style with beautiful quilts and comforters, lace, dolls and teddy bears.
Historic Interest: Gettysburg (18 miles).
Innkeeper(s): Richard & Carol Carlson. $100-150. 7 rooms with PB and 2 suites. Breakfast included in rates. Types of meals: Full bkfst, early coffee/tea and snacks/refreshments. Beds: KQD. Reading lamp and turn-down service in room. Air conditioning. TV, VCR, parlor games, telephone and fireplace on premises. Weddings, small meetings and family reunions hosted. Amusement parks, antiquing, bicycling, downhill skiing, fishing, golf, hiking, live theater, museums, shopping and wineries nearby.
Publicity: *Washington Post and Richmond Times.*

Lion and The Lamb

530 W King St
East Berlin, PA 17316
(717)259-9866

Circa 1810. Folk art and period furnishings create an authentic early 19th-century ambiance at this red brick Federal bed & breakfast. The 1810 home is listed in the National Register of Historic Places, and the innkeepers have earned an award for the home's restoration from Historic Gettysburg. Breakfasts are served in a dining room warmed by a crackling fire. Homemade scones or muffins, fresh fruit and a daily special entree fortify guests for a day of exploring the area. Gettysburg, Amish country, a plethora of antique shops and the Appalachian Trail all are nearby.
Innkeeper(s): Gretchen & Jim Davis. $88-100. 3 rooms, 2 with PB. Breakfast and snacks/refreshments included in rates. Types of meals: Full bkfst. Reading lamp and clock radio in room. Air conditioning. Telephone and fireplace on premises. Antiquing, cross-country skiing, downhill skiing, fishing, golf, parks, shopping and historic Gettysburg nearby.

Easton   H17

The Lafayette Inn

525 West Monroe St
Easton, PA 18042-1737
(610)253-4500 Fax:(610)253-4635
E-mail: lafayinn@fast.net
Web: www.lafayetteinn.com

Circa 1895. For distinctive accommodations on College Hill, this 1895 Georgian-style mansion offers an elegant comfort. Relax by the fire in the lounge or play the grand piano. The light and airy Sunroom makes a perfect setting for special events or business meetings. Antique-filled suites feature a balcony, fireplace and whirlpool tubs. Sit at common or individual tables for an upscale breakfast served family-style. Purchase mugs and aprons with the inn's logo at the Gift Shoppe. Take a mule-drawn canal boat ride on the Lehigh River. The one-acre estate includes a garden patio with fountain, waterfall and Adirondack chairs.
Historic Interest: Once a fraternity house of Lafayette College, this was once a single family home built in 1895 by the Wagner family and inhabited by the Filmore family of presidential fame.
Innkeeper(s): Scott and Marilyn Bushnell. $110-250. 18 rooms with PB, 5 with FP, 5 suites and 2 conference rooms. Breakfast and snacks/refreshments included in rates. Types of meals: Full bkfst. Beds: KQD. Data port, cable TV, VCR, reading lamp, CD player, refrigerator, clock radio, telephone, coffeemaker, desk and fireplace in room. Air conditioning. Fax, copier, parlor games, fireplace and gift shop on premises. Weddings, small meetings and family reunions hosted. Amusement parks, antiquing, art galleries, canoeing/kayaking, downhill skiing, fishing, golf, hiking, live theater, parks, shopping, sporting events, wineries, Crayola factory, mule-drawn canal boat rides and Martin Guitar factory tours nearby.
Publicity: *Lehigh Valley Magazine and Lehigh Valley Style Magazine.*

Elizabethtown   J13

West Ridge Guest House

1285 W Ridge Rd
Elizabethtown, PA 17022-9739
(717)367-7783 (877)367-7783 Fax:(717)367-8468
E-mail: wridgeroad@aol.com
Web: www.westridgebandb.com

Circa 1890. Guests at this country home have many choices. They may opt to relax and enjoy the view from the gazebo, or perhaps work out in the inn's exercise room. The hot tub provides yet another soothing possibility. Ask about rooms with whirlpool tubs. The innkeepers pass out a breakfast menu to their guests, allowing them to choose the time they prefer to eat and a choice of entrees. Along with the traditional fruit, muffins or coffeecake and meats, guests choose items such as omelets, waffles or pancakes.
Innkeeper(s): The Millers. $80-140. 8 rooms with PB, 5 with FP and 3 suites. Breakfast included in rates. Types of meals: Full bkfst. Beds: KQ. TV, VCR, ceiling fan, telephone, some with fireplaces, decks and whirlpool tubs in room. Spa and air conditioning on premises. Family reunions hosted. Antiquing, fishing, parks and shopping nearby.

Ephrata   J14

Doneckers, The Inns

318-324 N State St
Ephrata, PA 17522
(717)738-9502 Fax:(717)738-9554
E-mail: inns@doneckers.com

Circa 1777. Jacob Gorgas, a devout member of the Ephrata Cloister and a clock maker, noted for crafting 150 eight-day Gorgas grandfather clocks, built this stately Dutch Colonial-style home. Guests can opt to stay in one of three antique-filled homes. The 1777 House, which includes 12 rooms, features hand-stenciled walls, suites with whirlpool baths, fireplaces, original stone masonry and an antique tiled floor. The home served as a tavern in the 1800s and an elegant inn in the early 1900s. The Homestead includes

four rooms, some with fireplaces and amenities such as Jacuzzis, sitting areas and four-poster beds. The Guesthouse features a variety of beautifully decorated rooms each named and themed in honor of local landmarks or significant citizens. All guests enjoy an expansive breakfast with freshly squeezed juice, fruits, breakfast cheeses and other delicacies. The homes are part of the Donecker Community, which features upscale fashion stores, furniture galleries and a restaurant within walking distance of the 1777 House.

Historic Interest: The Ephrata Cloister, a communal religious society that was instrumental in the Colonial era's development of printing, music and Germanic architecture, is less than a mile away. Wheatland, the home of President James Buchanan, is nearby in Lancaster.

Innkeeper(s): Kelly Snyder. $79-210. 35 rooms, 33 with PB and 15 suites. Breakfast included in rates. Types of meals: Cont plus, gourmet lunch and gourmet dinner. Restaurant on premises. Beds: KQDT. Reading lamp, refrigerator, clock radio, telephone, hot tub/spa and personal CD players in room. Central air. VCR, fax, parlor games and fireplace on premises. Weddings, small meetings, family reunions and seminars hosted. Amusement parks, antiquing, art galleries, golf, live theater, museums, parks, shopping and wineries nearby.
Publicity: *Daily News and Country Inns.*

"A peaceful refuge."

Historic Smithton Inn

900 W Main St
Ephrata, PA 17522-1328
(717)733-6094
Web: www.historicsmithtoninn.com

Circa 1763. Family run for 236 years, this enchanting inn offers a peaceful and relaxing stay in Lancaster County, just one hour west of Philadelphia. Gather by the fire in the common room. Refreshments on the sideboard include eggnog, hot mulled wine or cider and just-baked apple pie. Inviting guest bedrooms and a luxurious three-room suite are spacious with an intimate ambiance enhanced by well-appointed furnishings, candlelight, chamber music and working fireplaces. Feather beds are gladly provided when requested in advance. Linger leisurely over a satisfying breakfast served daily in the dining room.

Historic Interest: The Ephrata Cloister Museum is only one block away.
Innkeeper(s): Dorothy Graybill. $85-175. 8 rooms with PB, 8 with FP and 1 suite. Breakfast and snacks/refreshments included in rates. Types of meals: Full bkfst. Beds: KQDT. Reading lamp, desk, whirlpools and feather beds in room. Air conditioning. Parlor games, telephone, fireplace, flower gardens and candlelight on premises. Amusement parks, antiquing, art galleries, golf, hiking, live theater, museums, shopping, tennis, wineries, farmland, handcrafts and farmers market nearby.

Publicity: *New York, Country Living, Early American Life, Washington Post and Philadelphia Inquirer.*

"After visiting over 50 inns in four countries, Smithton has to be one of the most romantic, picturesque inns in America. I have never seen its equal!"

Erie   C3

Spencer House B&B

519 W 6th St
Erie, PA 16507-1128
(814)454-5984 (800)890-7263 Fax:(814)456-5091

Circa 1876. This romantic Victorian mansion sits on Millionaire's Row in historic Erie. The original woodwork, 12-foot ceilings and pocket shutters reflect the distinctive quality of yesteryear. Peruse the well-stocked library. Some of the guest bedrooms feature fireplaces and clawfoot tubs. The Tree Top Room offers a floor-to-ceiling canopy bed and reading nook. Enjoy a relaxing rocking chair on the wraparound porch.

Innkeeper(s): Laurie Lawrence. $85-149. 5 rooms with PB. Breakfast included in rates. Types of meals: Full bkfst and early coffee/tea. Beds: Q. Cable TV, reading lamp, ceiling fan, clock radio, telephone and desk in room. Air conditioning. VCR, fax, copier, parlor games and fireplace on premises. Weddings, small meetings and family reunions hosted. Amusement parks, antiquing, bicycling, cross-country skiing, downhill skiing, fishing, hiking, live theater, parks, shopping, sporting events and water sports nearby.

Erwinna   117

Evermay-On-The-Delaware

River Rd, PO Box 60
Erwinna, PA 18920
(610)294-9100 Fax:(610)294-8249
E-mail: moffly@evermay.com
Web: www.evermay.com

Circa 1700. Twenty-five acres of Bucks County at its best — rolling green meadows, lawns, stately maples and the silvery Delaware River, surround this three-story manor. Serving as an inn since 1871, it has hosted such guests as the Barrymore family. Rich walnut wainscoting, a grandfather clock and twin fireplaces warm the parlor, scented by vases of roses or gladiolus. Antique-filled guest rooms overlook the river or gardens.

Historic Interest: Washington Crossing State Park, Mercer Museum, Pearl S. Buck House.

Innkeeper(s): Bill & Danielle Moffly. $145-275. 18 rooms with PB, 1 suite, 2 cottages and 2 conference rooms. Breakfast and afternoon tea included in rates. Types of meals: Cont plus, picnic lunch and gourmet dinner. Restaurant on premises. Beds: KQ. Reading lamp, telephone and turn-down service in room. Air conditioning. VCR, fax, copier, library, parlor games and fireplace on premises. Weddings, small meetings and seminars hosted. Antiquing, cross-country skiing, fishing, live theater, parks, shopping, sporting events and water sports nearby.
Publicity: *New York Times, Philadelphia, Travel & Leisure, Food and Wine, Child, Colonial Homes and USAir Magazine.*

"It was pure perfection. Everything from the flowers to the wonderful food."

Golden Pheasant Inn on the Delaware

763 River Rd
Erwinna, PA 18920-9254
(610)294-9595 (800)830-4474 Fax:(610)294-9882
E-mail: barbara@goldenpheasant.com
Web: www.goldenpheasant.com

Circa 1857. The Golden Pheasant is well established as the location of a wonderful, gourmet restaurant, but it is also home to six charming guest rooms decorated by Barbara Faure. Four-poster canopy beds and antiques decorate the rooms, which offer views of the canal and river. The fieldstone inn was built as a mule-barge stop for travelers heading down the Delaware Canal. The five-acre grounds resemble a French-country estate, and guests can enjoy the lush surroundings in a plant-filled greenhouse dining room. There are two other dining rooms, including an original fieldstone room with exposed beams and stone walls with decorative copper pots hanging here and there. The restaurant's French cuisine, prepared by chef Michel Faure, is outstanding. One might start off with Michel's special pheasant pate, followed by a savory onion soup baked with three cheeses. A mix of greens dressed in vinaigrette cleanses the palate before one samples roast duck in a luxurious raspberry, ginger and rum sauce or perhaps a sirloin steak flamed in cognac.

Innkeeper(s): Barbara & Michel Faure. $95-225. 6 rooms with PB, 4 with FP,

1 suite, 1 cottage and 3 conference rooms. Breakfast included in rates. Types of meals: Cont plus, early coffee/tea, picnic lunch, snacks/refreshments, gourmet dinner and room service. Restaurant on premises. Beds: Q. Reading lamp, CD player, refrigerator, ceiling fan, clock radio, telephone, coffeemaker, desk, hot tub/spa and fireplace in room. Air conditioning. Fax, copier, swimming, library, parlor games and canal path for walking on premises. Small meetings, family reunions and seminars hosted. Antiquing, art galleries, bicycling, canoeing/kayaking, cross-country skiing, fishing, golf, hiking, horseback riding, live theater, museums, parks, shopping, tennis, water sports, wineries, historic Doylestown, New Hope and Washington Crossing nearby.

Publicity: *The Philadelphia Inquirer, New York Times, Philadelphia Magazine, Food Network and Fox.*

"A more stunningly romantic spot is hard to imagine. A taste of France on the banks of the Delaware."

Fairfield   L11

The Fairfield Inn 1757

15 West Street (Rt. 116 West)
Fairfield, PA 17320
(717)642-5410 Fax:(717)642-5920
E-mail: innkeeper@thefairfieldinn.com
Web: www.thefairfieldinn.com

Circa 1757. Rich in history, this authentic American treasure has been a continuously operating tavern, restaurant and inn for 180 years and its origins as the Mansion House of the town's founder date back 245 years. Tour the Gettysburg battlefield then retreat to the hospitality and refinement expected from a small luxury hotel yet enjoyed at this inn. Sip a hot beverage by one of the eight fireplaces. Squire Miller's Tavern offers conversation and libations. Renovated guest bedrooms and suites boast air conditioning and cable television. The Mansion House Restaurant serves an imaginative menu of classically prepared and artistically presented dishes. A patio garden is bordered with privacy hedges and filled with flowers. Cooking classes, special dinners and holiday activities are among the many events planned throughout the year.
Innkeeper(s): Joan & Sal Chandon. Call for rates. 6 rooms with PB. Cable TV in room. Air conditioning.

Farmington   L4

Quiet House Bed & Breakfast

Highway 381 S
Farmington, PA 15437
(724)329-8120 (800)784-8187 Fax:(724)329-0797
E-mail: quiethousebnb.com
Web: www.quiethousebnb.com

Circa 1800. Relaxing pleasures are available year-round at this 234-acre country estate in a Laurel Highlands Mountain village. A variety of bed & breakfast accommodations are offered. Stay in the Majestic, Battonburg or Crystal Rooms in the Pre-Civil War Georgian Farm House, the romantic Carriage House Loft, or choose one of three spacious cottages: Spring House, Cozy or John's Cottages. Grandma Judy serves a hot gourmet breakfast with homemade treats and culinary delights delivered to the door. Ask about gift certificates and special packages with in-room massage and reflexology. The scenic grounds include a privately stocked trout pond. Nearby Yough Lake and a state park feature hiking, boating, white water rafting, skiing and sporting clays.
Innkeeper(s): Marty Anker. $98-168. 7 rooms with PB, 1 with FP, 3 cottages and 1 conference room. Breakfast and afternoon tea included in rates. Types of meals: Full gourmet bkfst, veg bkfst and early coffee/tea. Beds: QDT. Cable TV, VCR, reading lamp, refrigerator, ceiling fan, telephone, coffeemaker, turn-down service and desk in room. Air conditioning. Fax, swimming, stable, tennis, library, parlor games, fireplace and laundry facility on premises. Weddings, small meetings, family reunions and seminars hosted. Antiquing, art galleries, canoeing/kayaking, cross-country skiing, downhill skiing, fishing, golf, hiking, horseback riding, live theater, parks, shopping, sporting events, tennis, water sports, wineries and white water rafting nearby.

Fawn Grove   L13

Horse Lovers B&B

405 Throne Rd
Fawn Grove, PA 17321
(717)382-4171 Fax:(717)382-4171
E-mail: barb@ixiusa.com
Web: www.horseloversb-b.com

Circa 1840. Guests at this bed & breakfast and stables can enjoy a guided trail ride, take a riding lesson or help with grooming and feeding chores. The 400-acre grounds offer plenty of places to explore. The innkeepers care for a variety of different horse breeds, from Arabians to Belgians. Much of the farmhouse was built in the 1840s, and the home still includes the original plank floor. The home is decorated in country style with antiques. The Victorian Room, ideal for a special occasion, includes a king-size poster bed and a Jacuzzi tub. Breakfasts are served by candlelight and include homemade muffins with fruit from the B&Bs berry patch.
Innkeeper(s): Barb & Dale Torbert. $90-180. 5 rooms. Breakfast and afternoon tea included in rates. Types of meals: Full bkfst, early coffee/tea and room service. Beds: KQDT. Reading lamp, CD player, ceiling fan, clock radio, turn-down service and hot tub/spa in room. Air conditioning. VCR, fax, copier, spa, swimming, stable, bicycles, tennis, library, parlor games, telephone, fireplace, guided trail rides, exercise room and riding lessons on premises. Weddings, small meetings, family reunions and seminars hosted. Amusement parks, antiquing, downhill skiing, fishing, golf, live theater, parks, shopping, sporting events, tennis, wineries, museums and farm markets nearby.

Forksville   E13

Morgan Century Farm B&B

RR 1, Box 1145
Forksville, PA 18616
(570)924-4909 (888)335-1583 Fax:(570)924-4841

Circa 1850. This pre-Civil War farmhouse rests at the edge of a two-lane country road with acres of forests surrounding it. The farmhouse has seen many important uses: as a family home, the village post office, and it was also a stop along the Underground Railroad. The home has remained in the family since its earliest days. Innkeeper Linda Morgan Florentine now opens the family home to guests, offering cozy, comfortable rooms decorated with antiques. There's also a two-story cottage with a wood stove, kitchenette and a furnished barn loft. In the mornings, three-course breakfasts are presented. Fresh seasonal fruits, homemade breads and country entrees make up the fare. In the afternoons, wine and cheese are served. Guests can spend the day relaxing on the 35-acre property or perhaps fishing in the creek. Hiking, golfing and skiing are among the local outdoor activities, and auctions and antique shops abound.
Innkeeper(s): Ken & Linda Florentine. $85-125. 6 rooms, 3 with PB and 1 cottage. Breakfast and afternoon tea included in rates. Types of meals: Country bkfst and early coffee/tea. Beds: DT. Cable TV, reading lamp and clock radio in room. Central air. TV, fax, copier, library, parlor games, telephone and gift shop on premises. Weddings and family reunions hosted. Antiquing, art galleries, beach, bicycling, canoeing/kayaking, cross-country skiing, downhill skiing, fishing, golf, hiking, horseback riding, live theater, museums, parks, shopping and water sports nearby.

Friendsville C14

Addison House B&B

Rural Route 267
Friendsville, PA 18818
(570)553-2682
E-mail: info@1811addison.com
Web: www.1811addison.com

Circa 1811. Addison House was built by one of Choconut's earliest settlers, an Irish immigrant who purchased the vast homestead for just under a dollar an acre. The early 19th-century house is built in Federal style, but its interior includes many Victorian features, from the rich décor to the hand-carved marble fireplaces. A creek rambles through the 260-acre property, and guests will enjoy the secluded, wilderness setting. In the guest rooms, fluffy comforters top antique beds and floral wallcoverings add to the country Victorian ambiance. Breakfasts begin with items such as fresh berries with cream, followed by a rich entrée. The innkeepers are happy to help guests plan their days. The area offers a multitude of outdoor activities, as well as historic sites, antique shops, covered bridges and much more.
Innkeeper(s): Dennis & Gloria McLallen. $65-95. 3 rooms and 1 suite. Breakfast included in rates. Types of meals: Full gourmet bkfst, early coffee/tea and afternoon tea. Beds: D. Turn-down service, ice water and chocolates in room. Central air. TV, VCR, swimming, library, parlor games, telephone and fireplace on premises. Weddings and small meetings hosted. Antiquing, art galleries, bicycling, canoeing/kayaking, cross-country skiing, fishing, golf, hiking, live theater, museums, parks, shopping, sporting events, wineries, zoo and house tours by appointment nearby.

Gettysburg L11

A Sentimental Journey B&B

433 Baltimore St
Gettysburg, PA 17325
(717)337-0779 (888)337-0779 Fax:(717)337-0769
E-mail: aceshigh@supernet.com
Web: www.aceshighgallery.com

Circa 1928. It is easy to take a sentimental journey while staying at this three-story 1928 burgundy brick B&B conveniently located on Lincoln's Pathway in the heart of Gettysburg's Historic District. It was built on the site that was the town tannery, and it is within a short walk to the visitor center, battlefields, shops, attractions and restaurants. Gather with new friends in the vintage living room by the fireplace or relax on the porch glider. Nostalgic guest bedrooms reflect the early 20th century. Experience the romance of yesteryear mixed with today's modern comforts that include air conditioning and cable TV. Wake up when desired and enjoy a continental breakfast in the 1950s kitchen. Off-street parking is included. Special seasonal rates are available.
Innkeeper(s): Barbara & Steve Shultz. $75-90. 5 rooms, 4 with PB. Beds: QD.

Baladerry Inn at Gettysburg

40 Hospital Rd
Gettysburg, PA 17325
(717)337-1342
E-mail: baladerry@blazenet.net
Web: www.baladerryinn.com

Circa 1812. The quiet and private setting on the edge of the Gettysburg Battlefield, this brick country manor was used as a hospital during the Civil War. Additions were added in 1830 and

1977, and the inn has been completely restored. Guests can snuggle up with a book in their comfortable rooms or in the great room, which includes a fireplace. Some guest rooms include a private patio or a fireplace. The spacious grounds offer gardens, a gazebo, a tennis court and terraces. Guided tours of the battlefield can be arranged, and guests also can plan a horseback riding excursion on the battlefield.
Historic Interest: Gettysburg Battlefield National Park is just 100 yards from the inn. The area is full of historic sites, including the popular Eisenhower Farm tour.
Innkeeper(s): Suzanne Lonky. $125-250. 9 rooms with PB, 3 with FP and 3 conference rooms. Breakfast included in rates. Types of meals: Full bkfst, early coffee/tea and snacks/refreshments. Beds: KQT. Reading lamp, clock radio, telephone, desk and private patio overlooking grounds in room. Air conditioning. VCR, tennis and fireplace on premises. Small meetings, family reunions and seminars hosted. Antiquing, cross-country skiing, downhill skiing, fishing, golf, horseback riding, live theater, parks, shopping, sporting events and horseback riding or bicycling on Battlefield nearby.
Publicity: *Gettysburg Times, Allentown Morning Call, Pennsylvania Magazine and US Air Magazine.*

Battlefield Bed & Breakfast Inn

2264 Emmitsburg Rd
Gettysburg, PA 17325-7114
(717)334-8804
E-mail: info@gettysburgbattlefield.com
Web: www.gettysburgbattlefield.com

Circa 1809. Enjoy a Civil War Theme bed & breakfast on the Gettysburg Battlefield. Ponds, woods and streams fill the 30 acres of this historic estate. This stone farmhouse boasts four Confederate-themed guest rooms and four Union rooms. Hart's Battery provides a canopy bed and granite walls, while General Merritt's Headquarters takes up an entire floor of the Cornelius Houghtelin farmhouse and includes a fireplace and sitting room. Daily programs offer history demonstrations such as firing muskets and handling cavalry equipment, or artillery ammunition. Friday night ghost stories are another activity. The farm was occupied by Union cavalry and artillery units during the Battle of Gettysburg.
Innkeeper(s): Charlie & Florence Tarbox. $160-250. 8 rooms with PB, 2 with FP, 2 suites and 2 conference rooms. Breakfast and snacks/refreshments included in rates. Types of meals: Full gourmet bkfst, early coffee/tea, afternoon tea and room service. Beds: QDT. Reading lamp, telephone and desk in room. Air conditioning. TV, VCR, fax, copier, library, parlor games, fireplace, living history presentations and overnight horse boarding on premises. Small meetings, family reunions and seminars hosted. Antiquing, cross-country skiing, downhill skiing, fishing, golf, live theater, parks, shopping, sporting events, tennis, battlefield and national park nearby.
Publicity: *US Air Magazine, Country Collectibles, New Jersey Monthly, USA Weekend and New York Times.*

The Brafferton Inn

44 York St
Gettysburg, PA 17325-2301
(717)337-3423
E-mail: innkeepers@brafferton.com
Web: www.brafferton.com

Circa 1786. Aside from its notoriety as the first deeded house in what became the town of Gettysburg, The Brafferton bears a bullet shot into the fireplace mantel during the Civil War battle. The rooms are appointed with 18th- and 19th-century antiques

that belonged to the owners' ancestors. The dining room boasts a unique mural painted on all four walls depicting the early town of Gettysburg.

Lavish breakfasts are served in the colorful room on tables set with English china, old silver and crystal. Guest quarters are available in the original house or in the old carriage house across the brick atrium. Carriage house rooms feature stenciling and skylights. The garden area offers a large wooden deck to relax on as guests take in a variety of spring and summer flowers. The National Register inn is near all of Gettysburg's historic attractions, including the Gettysburg National Military Park.

Historic Interest: The inn is listed in the National Register and Gettysburg, site of the Civil War's most infamous battles, offers much history.

Innkeeper(s): Maggie & Bill Ward. $90-160. 14 rooms and 5 suites. Breakfast included in rates. Types of meals: Full bkfst, early coffee/tea and snacks/refreshments. Beds: QDT. Reading lamp, desk and alarm clocks in room. Air conditioning. Parlor games and telephone on premises. Weddings, small meetings and family reunions hosted. Antiquing, cross-country skiing, downhill skiing, fishing, live theater, parks, shopping, sporting events and Gettysburg National Park nearby.

Publicity: *Local newspapers, Early American Life, Country Living and Gettysburg Times.*

Brickhouse Inn

452 Baltimore St
Gettysburg, PA 17325-2623
(717)338-9337 (800)864-3464 Fax:(717)338-9265
E-mail: stay@brickhouseinn.com
Web: www.brickhouseinn.com

Circa 1898. Walk to local shops and restaurants while staying at this conveniently located 1898 inn that graces the downtown historic district. Private, off-street parking is available. The warm and inviting ambiance is accented with chestnut woodwork, family heirlooms and selected antiques. Relax on the porch with lemonade and homemade cookies or sip hot-spiced cider in one of the two parlors. Distinctive guest bedrooms including a two-room suite with a private porch and clawfoot tub are named after the states represented in the battle at Gettysburg. An adjacent 1830 home has been recently restored and boasts two rooms, a fireplace, porch and private entrance. Savor a complete breakfast each morning that includes a hot entrée, homemade muffins, fresh fruits and the inn's signature Pennsylvania Dutch Shoo Fly Pie. Visit nearby Civil War art galleries and the National Park Visitors Center.

Innkeeper(s): Craig & Marion Schmitz. $95-150. 10 rooms with PB and 2 suites. Breakfast and snacks/refreshments included in rates. Types of meals: Full bkfst. Beds: QD. Cable TV, ceiling fan, clock radio and two with fireplace in room. Air conditioning. Fax, parlor games and telephone on premises. Weddings, small meetings, family reunions and seminars hosted. Amusement parks, antiquing, cross-country skiing, downhill skiing, fishing, golf, parks, shopping and tennis nearby.

Publicity: *Washington Post, Washington Flyer, Hanover Sun, Gettysburg Times, Pittsburgh Post Gazette and WGAL Channel 8-Lancaster.*

The Doubleday Inn

104 Doubleday Ave
Gettysburg, PA 17325-8519
(717)334-9119
E-mail: doubledayinn@blazenet.net
Web: www.doubledayinn.com

Circa 1929. This Colonial Inn is situated directly on the Gettysburg Battlefield. From its wooded grounds, flower gardens and patios, guests enjoy panoramic views of historic Gettysburg and the National Military Park. The innkeepers have a significant collection of Civil War relics and books on hand, and on selected evenings they feature presentations with battlefield historians. Rooms are furnished with antiques and decorated in English-country style. A full, country-style breakfast is served each morning, and the innkeepers offer a selection of teas in the afternoon.

Historic Interest: Aside from the inn's location on the battlefield, the inn is close to the General Dwight D. Eisenhower Farm.

Innkeeper(s): Ruth Anne & Charles Wilcox. $95-130. 10 rooms, 8 with PB. Breakfast and afternoon tea included in rates. Types of meals: Full bkfst and early coffee/tea. Beds: DT. Reading lamp in room. Parlor games, telephone and fireplace on premises. Weddings, small meetings and family reunions hosted. Amusement parks, antiquing, cross-country skiing, downhill skiing, fishing, live theater, parks, shopping, sporting events and battlefield tours nearby.

Publicity: *Innsider, New York, State College, Washingtonian and Potomac.*

"A beautiful spot on an historic site that we'll long remember."

The Gaslight Inn

33 E Middle St
Gettysburg, PA 17325
(717)337-9100 (800)914-5698
E-mail: info@thegaslightinn.com
Web: www.thegaslightinn.com

Circa 1872. Gaslights illuminate the brick pathways leading to this 130-year-old Italianate-style, expanded farmhouse. The inn boasts two elegant parlors separated by original pocket doors, a spacious dining room and a first-floor guest room with wheelchair access that opens to a large, brick patio. An open switchback staircase leads to the second- and third-floor guest rooms, all individually decorated in traditional and European furnishings. Some of the rooms feature covered decks, fireplaces, whirlpool tubs and steam showers for two. Guests are invited to enjoy a hearty or heart-healthy breakfast and inn-baked cookies and brownies and refreshments in the afternoon. Winter weekend packages are available and carriage rides, private guides and a variety of activities can be arranged with the help of the innkeepers.

Innkeeper(s): Denis & Roberta Sullivan. $100-190. 9 rooms with PB, 6 with FP. Breakfast and snacks/refreshments included in rates. Types of meals: Full gourmet bkfst and early coffee/tea. Beds: KQT. Cable TV, reading lamp, ceiling fan, clock radio, telephone, desk, hot tub/spa and steam baths in room. Air conditioning. VCR, spa, parlor games, fireplace and spa facilities on premises. Limited handicap access. Weddings, small meetings, family reunions and seminars hosted. Antiquing, cross-country skiing, downhill skiing, fishing, golf, live theater, parks, shopping, tennis, water sports and historic educational tours and lectures nearby.

Publicity: *Tyler Texas Times, Hanover Sun, Los Angeles Times, Southern Living and Country Inns.*

Herr Tavern & Publick House

900 Chambersburg Rd
Gettysburg, PA 17325-3312
(717)334-4332 (800)362-9849 Fax:(717)334-3332
E-mail: info@herrtavern.com
Web: www.herrtavern.com

Circa 1815. Originally built as a Publick House, this Federal-style building became the site of the first Confederate stand and hospital during the Civil War. Listed in the National Register, the inn's 19th-century heritage and glory has now been faithfully restored, and a new wing added. Two common rooms overlook the historic area from Peace Light to Little Round Top. Each of the romantic suites feature a fireplace, most offer single or double Jacuzzis. The Garden Room also boasts a round bed, microwave, refrigerator and private deck. An additional area for business needs is included in the Presidential Suite. Enjoy a wonderful country breakfast in the sunroom, as well as afternoon tea and snacks. Stroll the landscaped grounds with two ponds.
Innkeeper(s): Steven & Sharon Wolf. $89-210. 17 rooms with PB, 17 with FP and 3 conference rooms. Breakfast and afternoon tea included in rates. Types of meals: Country bkfst, veg bkfst, early bkfst/tea, lunch, snacks/refreshments, dinner and room service. Restaurant on premises. Beds: QD. Modem hook-up, data port, cable TV, VCR, reading lamp, ceiling fan, clock radio, telephone, coffeemaker, desk, voice mail, fireplace, 15 with Jacuzzi and two with refrigerator and microwave in room. Central air. Fax, copier, spa, library, parlor games, fireplace and massage by appointment on premises. Limited handicap access. Weddings, small meetings, family reunions and seminars hosted. Antiquing, art galleries, bicycling, canoeing/kayaking, cross-country skiing, downhill skiing, fishing, golf, hiking, horseback riding, live theater, museums, parks, shopping, sporting events, tennis and wineries nearby.
Publicity: *PBS.*

Hickory Bridge Farm

96 Hickory Bridge Rd
Gettysburg, PA 17353-9734
(717)642-5261
E-mail: hickory@innbook.com
Web: www.hickorybridgefarm.com

Circa 1750. The oldest part of this farmhouse was constructed of mud bricks and straw on land that once belonged to Charles Carroll, father of a signer of the Declaration of Independence. Inside, there is an attractive stone fireplace for cooking. The farmhouse rooms include whirlpool baths. There are several country cottages in addition to the rooms in the farmhouse, and each includes a fireplace. Fine, country dining is offered in the restored barn on the weekends. The host family members have been innkeepers for more than 25 years.
Historic Interest: Gettysburg (9 miles).
Innkeeper(s): Mary Lynn Martin. $85-145. 9 rooms, 5 with PB, 4 with FP and 1 conference room. Breakfast included in rates. Types of meals: Full bkfst. Restaurant on premises. Beds: QD. TV and three with whirlpool in room. Antiquing, downhill skiing and fishing nearby.
Publicity: *Hanover Times, The Northern Virginia Gazette and Taste of Home.*

"Beautifully decorated and great food!"

James Gettys Hotel

27 Chambersburg St
Gettysburg, PA 17325
(717)337-1334 Fax:(717)334-2103
E-mail: info@jamesgettyshotel.com
Web: www.jamesgettyshotel.com

Circa 1803. Listed in the National Register, this newly renovated four-story hotel once served as a tavern through the Battle of Gettysburg and was used as a hospital for soldiers. Outfitted with cranberry colored awnings and a gold painted entrance, the hotel offers a tea room, nature store and gallery on the street level. From the lobby, a polished chestnut staircase leads to the guest quarters. All accommodations are suites with living rooms appointed with home furnishings, and each has its own kitchenette. Breakfasts of home-baked scones and coffee cake are brought to your room.
Innkeeper(s): Stephanie McSherry. $125-145. 11 suites. Breakfast included in rates. Types of meals: Cont. Beds: QD. Cable TV, reading lamp, refrigerator, clock radio, telephone, coffeemaker and turn-down service in room. Air conditioning. VCR and fax on premises. Limited handicap access. Weddings, small meetings and family reunions hosted. Amusement parks, antiquing, art galleries, bicycling, cross-country skiing, downhill skiing, fishing, golf, hiking, horseback riding, museums, parks, shopping, tennis and wineries nearby.

Keystone Inn B&B

231 Hanover St
Gettysburg, PA 17325-1913
(717)337-3888

Circa 1913. Furniture maker Clayton Reaser constructed this three-story brick Victorian with a wide-columned porch hugging the north and west sides. Cut stone graces every door and window sill, each with a keystone. A chestnut staircase ascends the full three stories, and the interior is decorated with comfortable furnishings, ruffles and lace.
Historic Interest: National Military Park, Eisenhower Farm (1 mile).
Innkeeper(s): Wilmer & Doris Martin.
$89-129. 5 rooms with PB and 1 suite. Breakfast and afternoon tea included in rates. Types of meals: Full bkfst and early coffee/tea. Beds: KQDT. TV, reading lamp and desk in room. Air conditioning. Library, parlor games and telephone on premises. Family reunions hosted. Amusement parks, antiquing, cross-country skiing, downhill skiing, fishing, live theater, parks, shopping, Civil War Battlefield and historic sites nearby.
Publicity: *Lancaster Sunday News, York Sunday News, Hanover Sun, Allentown Morning Call, Gettysburg Times, Pennsylvania and Los Angeles Times.*

"We slept like lambs. This home has a warmth that is soothing."

Glen Mills   K16

Sweetwater Farm

50 Sweetwater Road
Glen Mills, PA 19342
(610)459-4711 (800)793-3892 Fax:(610)358-4945
E-mail: info@sweetwaterfarmbb.com
Web: www.sweetwaterfarmbb.com

Circa 1734. Sitting on 50 acres off a quiet country road in the scenic Brandywine Valley, this 1734 stone mansion has been wonderfully restored to its Quaker Farmhouse tradition as well as the more formal 1815 Georgian wing, The Manor House. Its rich history includes being a Civil War infirmary and part of the Underground Railroad. Relax by the fire in the living, dining or billiard room. Guest bedrooms and a suite feature four-poster canopy beds, fine linens, antiques and some fireplaces. Private fireplace cottages are available with fully equipped kitchens, private patios, washers and dryers. After a hearty gourmet breakfast enjoy peaceful tranquility sitting on the porch overlooking gardens and horse pastures. Relax in the heated spa or swim in the pool.
Historic Interest: Built in 1734 by Quakers, expanded in 1815 with Georgian wing. Infirmary during the Civil War and part of the underground railroad. Original 1734 barn on property.
Innkeeper(s): Peggy & John Roethel. $125-225. 12 rooms with PB, 7 with

FP, 4 suites, 5 cottages and 1 conference room. Breakfast included in rates. Types of meals: Full gourmet bkfst and early coffee/tea. Beds: Q. TV, reading lamp, radio, telephone, coffeemaker, desk, voice mail and fireplace in room. Air conditioning. Fax, copier, spa, swimming, stable, library, pet boarding, parlor games, fireplace and in-ground pool on premises. Weddings, small meetings, family reunions and seminars hosted. Antiquing, art galleries, bicycling, golf, hiking, live theater, museums, parks, shopping and wineries nearby.

Gordonville   K14

1766 Osceola Mill House

313 Osceola Mill Rd
Gordonville, PA 17529
(717)768-3758 (800)878-7719
E-mail: elalahr@epix.net
Web: www.lancaster-inn.com

Circa 1766. In a quaint historic setting adjacent to a mill and a miller's cottage, this handsome limestone mill house rests on the banks of Pequea Creek. There are deep-set windows and wide pine floors. Guest bedrooms and the keeping room feature working fireplaces that add to the warmth and charm. Breakfast fare may include tasty regional specialties like locally made Pennsylvania Dutch sausage, and Dutch babies- an oven-puffed pancake filled with fresh fruit. Amish neighbors farm the adjacent fields, their horse and buggies enhance the picturesque ambiance.

Innkeeper(s): John & Elaine Lahr. $82-149. 5 rooms with PB, 4 with FP. Types of meals: Full gourmet bkfst. Beds: Q. TV and VCR on premises. Publicity: *The Journal, Country Living, Washington Times, Gourmet and BBC.*

"We had a thoroughly delightful stay at your inn. Probably the most comfortable overnight stay we've ever had."

Greensburg   J4

Huntland Farm B&B

RD 9, Box 21
Greensburg, PA 15601-9232
(724)834-8483 Fax:(724)838-8253

Circa 1848. Porches and flower gardens surround the three-story, columned, brick Georgian manor that presides over the inn's 100 acres. Corner bedrooms are furnished with English antiques. Fallingwater, the Frank Lloyd Wright house, is nearby. Other attractions include Hidden Valley, Ohiopyle water rafting, Bushy Run and Fort Ligonier.

Innkeeper(s): Robert & Elizabeth Weidlein. $75-85. 4 rooms, 2 with FP. Breakfast included in rates. Types of meals: Full bkfst. Beds: KQDT. Reading lamp, ceiling fan, clock radio and desk in room. VCR, fax, copier, library, parlor games, telephone and fireplace on premises. Small meetings and family reunions hosted. Antiquing, live theater, parks and shopping nearby. Publicity: *Tribune Review.*

Grove City   F2

Snow Goose Inn

112 E Main St
Grove City, PA 16127
(724)458-4644 (800)317-4644

Circa 1895. This home was built as a residence for young women attending Grove City College. It was later used as a family home and offices for a local doctor. Eventually, it was transformed into an intimate bed & breakfast, offering four cozy guest

rooms. The interior is comfortable, decorated with antiques and touches country with stenciling, collectibles and a few of the signature geese on display. Museums, shops, Amish farms, colleges and several state parks are in the vicinity, offering many activities.

Innkeeper(s): Orvil & Dorothy McMillen. $70. 4 rooms with PB. Breakfast and snacks/refreshments included in rates. Types of meals: Full gourmet bkfst and early coffee/tea. Beds: QD. Reading lamp, stereo, refrigerator and clock radio in room. Air conditioning. VCR, parlor games, telephone and fireplace on premises. Small meetings and family reunions hosted. Amusement parks, antiquing, cross-country skiing, downhill skiing, fishing, golf, live theater, parks, shopping, sporting events, tennis and water sports nearby. Publicity: *Allied News.*

"Your thoughtful touches and homey atmosphere were a balm to our chaotic lives."

Hanover   L12

The Beechmont B&B Inn

315 Broadway
Hanover, PA 17331-2505
(717)632-3013 (800)553-7009 Fax:(717)632-2769
E-mail: innkeeper@thebeechmont.com
Web: www.thebeechmont.com

Circa 1834. Feel welcomed by centuries of charm at this gracious Georgian inn, a witness to the Battle of Hanover, Civil War's first major battle on free soil. A 130-year-old magnolia tree shades the flagstone patio, and wicker furniture invites a lingering rest on the front porch. The romantic Magnolia Suite features a marble fireplace and queen canopy bed. The inn is noted for its sumptuous breakfasts.

Historic Interest: Gettysburg (13 miles).

Innkeeper(s): Kathryn & Thomas White. $85-150. 7 rooms with PB, 3 with FP and 3 suites. Breakfast and snacks/refreshments included in rates. Types of meals: Full gourmet bkfst and early coffee/tea. Beds: QD. Cable TV, ceiling fan, clock radio, telephone, desk and fireplace in room. Air conditioning. Fax, copier, library and parlor games on premises. Weddings, small meetings and family reunions hosted. Antiquing, bicycling, cross-country skiing, fishing, golf, hiking, horseback riding, live theater, parks, shopping, sporting events, water sports and wineries nearby. Publicity: *Evening Sun and York Daily Record.*

"I had a marvelous time at your charming, lovely inn."

Sheppard Mansion B&B

117 Frederick St
Hanover, PA 17331
(717)633-8075 (877)762-6746 Fax:(717)633-8074
E-mail: reservations@sheppardmansion.com
Web: www.sheppardmansion.com

Circa 1913. Indulge in luxury and elegance at this Neoclassical, Greek revival inn. This historic landmark was restored by descendants of the prominent Sheppard family. Decorated with the original antiques and furnishings, mostly Edwardian and some late Victorian, an air of sophistication and hospitality is evident. The spacious public rooms offer amenities that enhance business or pleasure. Appreciate the pampered feeling of fine linens, soaking tubs, marble floors, English toiletries, color TV and PC data ports in the splendid suites. Freshly brewed private blend coffee begins each morning's culinary masterpiece. The formal gardens and English boxwoods reside comfortably with holly, hemlock, copper beech, star and tulip magnolia trees.

Innkeeper(s): Kathryn Sheppard-Hoar & Timothy Bobb. $140-220. 9 rooms, 5 with PB, 1 with FP, 1 suite, 1 cottage and 2 conference rooms. Breakfast and snacks/refreshments included in rates. Types of meals: Full gourmet bkfst and early coffee/tea. Beds: QT. Modem hook-up, cable TV, VCR, reading lamp,

stereo, refrigerator, clock radio, telephone, desk and voice mail in room. Central air. Fax, copier, library, parlor games, fireplace, laundry facility and gift shop on premises. Weddings, small meetings and seminars hosted. Amusement parks, antiquing, art galleries, cross-country skiing, downhill skiing, fishing, golf, horseback riding, live theater, museums, parks and shopping nearby.
Publicity: *The Discerning Traveler, Girl Interrupted and Select Registry 2002.*

Harrisville   F3

As Thyme Goes By B&B

214 N Main St, PO Box 493
Harrisville, PA 16038
(724)735-4003 (877)278-4963
E-mail: asthymegoesby@pathway.net
Web: www.asthymegoesby.com

Circa 1846. This country Victorian is furnished with a unique blend of antiques, Art Deco and Oriental decorative arts. The inn features movie memorabilia and guests can spend an evening enjoying old films in the Bogart library or relaxing by the fire in the China Clipper parlor. Guest rooms are decorated with antique beds and offer private baths and air conditioning. A candlelight breakfast is highlighted by the innkeeper's homemade jams. Close to factory outlet shopping, local colleges and historic Volant Mills.
Innkeeper(s): Susan Haas. $60-80. 3 rooms with PB. Breakfast and snacks/refreshments included in rates. Types of meals: Full bkfst, early coffee/tea and afternoon tea. Beds: KQD. Reading lamp and ceiling fan in room. Air conditioning. VCR, library, parlor games, telephone and fireplace on premises. Antiquing, cross-country skiing, fishing, golf, parks, shopping and outlet mall nearby.
Publicity: *Allied News and KDKA Pittsburgh.*

"We have been trying for years to make the time to get away for our first B&B experience and you have exceeded all of our expectations for the visit."

Hawley   E17

The Falls Port Inn & Restaurant

330 Main Ave
Hawley, PA 18428-1330
(570)226-2600 Fax:(570)226-6409

Circa 1902. Constructed by Baron von Eckelberg, this three-story grand brick Victorian is reminiscent of the civility and sophistication of an era gone by. Relax in the elegant ambiance and fine decor. Guest bedrooms feature antique furnishings, polished brass fixtures and rich window treatments. The inn's

well-established restaurant boasts 14-foot-high original windows. The proprietor has been honored with the National Register's Who's Who in Executives and Professionals as well as the Gourmet Diners Society of North America Golden Fork Award for excellence in the food industry. Gourmet dinners include Chicken Remi and live lobster. Daily lunch specials, Sunday brunch and banquet facilities are available. The inn is a popular favorite for any special occasion from weddings, reunions and graduation parties to club meetings and corporate dinners.
Innkeeper(s): Dorothy Fenn. $75-120. 9 rooms, 5 with PB and 1 conference room. Breakfast included in rates. Types of meals: Cont, Sunday brunch, lunch and gourmet dinner. Restaurant on premises. Beds: QD. Reading lamp, clock radio and some with cable TV and desks in room. Central air. TV, VCR, fax, copier, telephone, fireplace, banquet facilities, weddings, rehearsal din-

ners, anniversary parties, baby showers, sweet 16 birthdays, bar/bat mitzvah, graduation parties, family reunions, Christmas parties, seminars, corporate dinners and retirement dinners on premises. Limited handicap access. Antiquing, beach, bicycling, canoeing/kayaking, cross-country skiing, downhill skiing, fishing, golf, hiking, horseback riding, live theater, museums, parks, shopping, tennis, water sports, movie theater, waterparks, rafting, tubing, hunting and local playhouse theater nearby.

Settlers Inn at Bingham Park

4 Main Ave
Hawley, PA 18428-1114
(570)226-2993 (800)833-8527 Fax:(570)226-1874
E-mail: settler@thesettlersinn.com
Web: www.thesettlersinn.com

Circa 1927. When the Wallenpaupack Creek was dammed up to form the lake, the community hired architect Louis Welch and built this Grand Tudor Revival-style hotel featuring chestnut beams, leaded-glass windows and an enormous stone fireplace. The dining room, the main focus of the inn, is decorated with antique prints, hanging plants and chairs that once graced a Philadelphia cathedral. If you're looking for trout you can try your luck fishing the Lackawaxen River, which runs behind the inn.

Historic Interest: Zane Gray Home & Museum (15 miles), Stourbridge Lion Train (10 miles), Dorflinger Glass Museum (5 miles).
Innkeeper(s): Jeanne & Grant Genzlinger. $85-150. 22 rooms with PB and 1 conference room. Breakfast included in rates. Types of meals: Full bkfst, early coffee/tea, lunch, picnic lunch and gourmet dinner. Restaurant on premises. Beds: KQD. Cable TV, reading lamp, clock radio, telephone and desk in room. Air conditioning. VCR, fax, copier, tennis, library, parlor games and fireplace on premises. Weddings, small meetings, family reunions and seminars hosted. Antiquing, cross-country skiing, downhill skiing, fishing, live theater, parks, shopping and water sports nearby.
Publicity: *Philadelphia, New York Newsday, Philadelphia Inquirer, Washington Post and Gail Greco - Country Inn Cooking.*

"Country cozy with food and service fit for royalty."

Holicong   J18

Ash Mill Farm

5358 York Rd
Holicong, PA 18928
(215)794-5373 Fax:(215)794-0763
E-mail: info@ashmillfarm.com
Web: www.ashmillfarm.com

Circa 1790. The oldest portion of this farmhouse dates to the 18th century and includes an original walk-in fireplace. Guest rooms and suites are decorated with handmade furniture and reproductions. Each room is individually decorated. The Library is a cozy guest room with built-in bookcases and king-size bed. The Ash Mill Suite includes a four-poster king bed and sitting room. The veranda is lined with benches and wicker furnishings. The innkeepers serve a gourmet breakfast, featuring items such as French toast stuffed with poached pears and Stilton cheese.
Historic Interest: Close proximity to New Hope, Doylestown and Lambertville.
Innkeeper(s): Larry & Toby Sue Steinhouse. $115-190. 5 rooms with PB and 2 suites. Breakfast included in rates. Types of meals: Full gourmet bkfst, veg bkfst, early coffee/tea and snacks/refreshments. Beds: KQ. Modem hook-up, data port, cable TV, ceiling fan and Internet in room. Air conditioning. Fax, copier, telephone, fireplace and fireplaces on premises. Weddings, small meetings and family reunions hosted. Amusement parks, antiquing, art galleries, bicycling, canoeing/kayaking, fishing, golf, hiking, horseback riding, live theater, museums, parks, shopping, tennis, water sports and wineries nearby.

Barley Sheaf Farm

5281 York Rd, Rt 202 Box 10
Holicong, PA 18928
(215)794-5104 Fax:(215)794-5332
E-mail: info@barleysheaf.com
Web: www.barleysheaf.com

Circa 1740. Situated on part of the original William Penn land grant, this beautiful stone house with ebony green shuttered windows and mansard roof is set on 30 acres of farmland. Once owned by noted playwright George Kaufman, it was the gathering place for the Marx Brothers, Lillian Hellman and S.J. Perlman. The bank barn, pond and majestic old trees round out a beautiful setting.

Innkeeper(s): Peter Suess. $105-285. 15 rooms with PB, 6 with FP, 7 suites and 3 conference rooms. Breakfast and afternoon tea included in rates. Types of meals: Full bkfst and early coffee/tea. Beds: KQD. Reading lamp, telephone, desk and Jacuzzis in room. Air conditioning. VCR, fax, copier, swimming, parlor games and fireplace on premises. Limited handicap access. Weddings, small meetings, family reunions and seminars hosted. Amusement parks, antiquing, cross-country skiing, downhill skiing, fishing, live theater, parks, shopping, water sports and museums nearby.
Publicity: *Country Living, Romantic Inns of America and CNC Business Channel.*

Intercourse   K14

Intercourse Village B&B Suites

Rt 340-Main Street, Box 340
Intercourse, PA 17534
(717)768-2626 (800)664-0949
E-mail: ivbbs@aol.com
Web: www.amishcountryinns.com

Circa 1909. The Amish country of Pennsylvania abounds in turn-of-the-century, Victorian houses. The Intercourse Village B&B Suites offers four guest rooms in a two-story home that dates to 1909 and eight suites in three, more contemporary buildings to the rear. This B&B caters to couples. The guest rooms in the main house remain true to their Victorian origins: Floral and stripped fabrics and wallpaper cover the walls, while lacy curtains give peeks to the grounds outside; fringed lamps stand to either side of rosewood settees and Oriental carpets cover the hardwood floors. Simpler in decor are the Homestead Suites that feature bright Amish quilts on the beds. Each suite has a fireplace, cable TV, VCR, refrigerator and microwave. Among these suites is the Summer House, which stands alone in its own building and boasts a heart-shaped whirlpool for two. A gourmet five-course breakfast is served by candlelight in the dining room of the main house. Nearby activities include visits to the town's craft, quilt and antique shops or tours through the candle and pretzel factories. You'll find the town of Hershey only an hour away and the Civil War Battlefield site of Gettysburg an hour and a half. Closer to home, you can relax on the white wicker furniture on the front porch and watch the Amish pass by in horse-drawn carriages. This inn has been awarded a four-diamond rating with AAA.

Innkeeper(s): Ruthann Thomas. $119-189. 8 suites. Breakfast included in rates. Types of meals: Full gourmet bkfst. Beds: KQ. Data port, cable TV, VCR, refrigerator, telephone and coffeemaker in room. Central air. Fireplace on premises. Antiquing, art galleries, golf, live theater and shopping nearby.

Jim Thorpe   H15

Arbor Glen

Packer Hill, PO Box 458
Jim Thorpe, PA 18229
(570)325-8566
E-mail: hpmbb@ptd.net
Web: www.arborglenbb.com

Circa 1850. Relax next to an idyllic stream and pond on the 65 acres where this spacious three-story Victorian farmhouse rests. Sister inn to the Harry Packer Mansion, this estate offers similarly romantic rooms with amenities such as fireplaces, four-poster beds, granite bathrooms and Jacuzzi tubs. Jim Thorpe is five miles away.

Innkeeper(s): Patricia & Robert Handwerk. $250-300. 4 suites, 4 with FP, 1 cottage and 1 conference room. Types of meals: Cont plus. Beds: Q. Modem hook-up, data port, cable TV, VCR, reading lamp, stereo, refrigerator, snack bar, clock radio, telephone, coffeemaker, desk and hot tub/spa in room. Air conditioning. Swimming, bicycles, library, parlor games and fireplace on premises. Weddings, small meetings, family reunions and seminars hosted. Antiquing, art galleries, beach, bicycling, canoeing/kayaking, cross-country skiing, downhill skiing, fishing, golf, hiking, horseback riding, live theater, museums, parks, shopping, sporting events, tennis, water sports and wineries nearby.

Harry Packer Mansion

Packer Hill, PO Box 458
Jim Thorpe, PA 18229
(570)325-8566
E-mail: mystery@murdermansion.com
Web: www.murdermansion.com

Circa 1874. This extravagant Second Empire mansion was used as the model for the haunted mansion in Disney World. It

was constructed of New England sandstone, and local brick and stone trimmed in cast iron. Past ornately carved columns on the front veranda, guests enter 400-pound, solid walnut doors. The opulent interior includes marble mantels, hand-painted ceilings and elegant antiques. Murder-mystery weekends are a mansion specialty.

Historic Interest: National Register. In historic district.
Innkeeper(s): Robert & Patricia Handwerk. $150-250. 12 rooms with PB, 3 suites and 3 conference rooms. Breakfast included in rates. Types of meals: Full gourmet bkfst. Beds: Q. Reading lamp, refrigerator, clock radio, turndown service and desk in room. Air conditioning. TV, parlor games, telephone, fireplace and Murder Mystery Weekends on premises. Weddings, small meetings, family reunions and seminars hosted. Antiquing, cross-country skiing, downhill skiing, fishing, parks, shopping and water sports nearby.
Publicity: *Philadelphia Inquirer, New York, Victorian Homes, Washington Post, Conde Nast Traveler and winner Best Murder Mystery by Arringtons Book of Lists.*

"*What a beautiful place and your hospitality was wonderful. We will see you again soon.*"

The Inn at Jim Thorpe

24 Broadway
Jim Thorpe, PA 18229
(570)325-2599 (800)329-2599 Fax:(570)325-9145
E-mail: innjt@ptd.net
Web: www.innjt.com

Circa 1848. This massive New Orleans-style structure, now restored, hosted some colorful 19th-century guests, including Thomas Edison, John D. Rockefeller and Buffalo Bill. All rooms

503

are appointed with Victorian furnishings and have private baths with pedestal sinks and marble floors. The suites include fireplaces and whirlpool tubs. Also on the premises are a Victorian dining Room, Irish pub and a conference center. The inn is situated in the heart of Jim Thorpe, a quaint Victorian town that was known at the turn of the century as the "Switzerland of America." Historic mansion tours, museums and art galleries are nearby, and mountain biking and whitewater rafting are among the outdoor activities.

Historic Interest: Switchboard Railroad, first railroad in U.S. (walking distance), Asa Packer Mansion, Millionaire's Row, Jim Thorpe final resting place (walking distance).
Innkeeper(s): David Drury. $99-299. 34 rooms with PB, 11 suites and 2 conference rooms. Breakfast included in rates. Types of meals: Cont plus, lunch, dinner and room service. Beds: KQ. Cable TV, reading lamp, clock radio, telephone, 11 suites with whirlpools and some with fireplaces in room. Air conditioning. Fax, copier, fireplace, game room, exercise room and elevator on premises. Limited handicap access. Weddings, small meetings, family reunions and seminars hosted. Antiquing, art galleries, bicycling, canoeing/kayaking, downhill skiing, fishing, golf, hiking, horseback riding, museums, parks, shopping and wineries nearby.
Publicity: *Philadelphia Inquirer, Pennsylvania Magazine and Allentown Morning Call.*

"We had the opportunity to spend a weekend at your lovely inn. Your staff is extremely friendly, helpful, and courteous. I can't remember when we felt so relaxed, we hope to come back again soon."

Kennett Square   L16

B&B at Walnut Hill

541 Chandler's Mill Rd
Kennett Square, PA 19311-9625
(610)444-3703
E-mail: millsjt@magpage.com
Web: www.bvbb.com/walnuthill.html

Circa 1840. The family who built this pre-Civil War home ran a grist mill on the premises. Innkeepers Sandy and Tom Mills moved into the home as newlyweds. Today, Sandy, a former

caterer and Winterthur docent, serves up gourmet breakfasts such as cottage cheese pancakes with blueberry sauce and homemade teas, lemon butter and currant jam. Her cooking expertise was recognized in Good Housekeeping's Christmas issue. The guest rooms are cozy, welcoming and filled with antiques. One room features a Laura Ashley canopy bed. Another boasts Victorian wicker. The house overlooks horses grazing in a meadow, and a nearby creek is visited by Canadian geese, deer and an occasional fox.

Historic Interest: Winterthur Museum, Brandywine Battlefield, Museum of Natural History, Longwood Gardens, Brandywine River Museum, Hagley Museum, Chaddsford Winery, Barnes Foundation.
Innkeeper(s): Tom & Sandy Mills. $75-115. 2 rooms with PB. Breakfast and snacks/refreshments included in rates. Types of meals: Full gourmet bkfst and afternoon tea. Beds: KDT. Cable TV, reading lamp, clock radio, turn-down service and desk in room. Central air. TV, VCR, copier, spa, parlor games, telephone, fireplace and porch overlooking meadow and stream on premises. Family reunions hosted. Canoeing/kayaking, golf, horseback riding, shopping and hot air balloons nearby.
Publicity: *Times Record, Suburban Advertiser, Four Seasons of Chester County, Country Inns, Good Housekeeping and Country Magazine.*

Inn at Whitewing Farm

370 Valley Road
Kennett Square, PA 19348
(610)388-2664 Fax:(610)388-3650
E-mail: info@whitewingfarm.com
Web: www.whitewingfarm.com

Circa 1796. Experience the beauty of Discerning Traveler magazine's "1999 Best Romantic Hideaway of Pennsylvania." This late-1700s English country farmhouse offers spacious luxury throughout, including the 43 acres it rests upon. The ultimate in privacy is found in the Gate House where guests can experience the comfort of a private guest house, complete with a sky light, fireplace and warm country décor, overlooking a gentle fountain pond. Visit the farm with the entire family and interact with and feed the animals. Travel to the Whitewing Farm throughout the year to experience the majesty of nature as it changes from vivid greens and blues to autumn reds and oranges, and the often-white winters. Savor each meal by the fireplace in the dining room overlooking the green rolling hills and pond.

Innkeeper(s): Ed & Wanda DeSeta. $135-259. 10 rooms with PB, 4 with FP, 4 suites and 1 conference room. Breakfast included in rates. Types of meals: Full gourmet bkfst, early coffee/tea and afternoon tea. Beds: KQT. Modem hook-up, TV, reading lamp, ceiling fan, clock radio and desk in room. Central air. Fax, spa, swimming, tennis, library, parlor games, fireplace, 10-hole chip and putt course and fishing on premises. Limited handicap access. Antiquing, art galleries, canoeing/kayaking, fishing, golf, hiking, horseback riding, museums, parks, shopping, sporting events, tennis and wineries nearby.

Kennett House Bed and Breakfast

503 W State St
Kennett Square, PA 19348-3028
(610)444-9592 (800)820-9592 Fax:(610)444-7633
E-mail: innkeeper@kennetthouse.com
Web: www.kennetthouse.com

Circa 1910. This granite American four-square home features an extensive wraparound porch, a front door surrounded by leaded-glass windows and magnificent chestnut woodwork. Beyond the foyer are two downstairs parlors with fireplaces, while a second-floor parlor provides a sunny setting for afternoon tea. Rooms are furnished with period antiques and Oriental carpets. An elegant gourmet breakfast is served each morning.

Innkeeper(s): Carol & Jeff Yetter. $119-149. 4 rooms with PB and 1 suite. Breakfast and snacks/refreshments included in rates. Types of meals: Full gourmet bkfst and early coffee/tea. Beds: Q. Cable TV, reading lamp, ceiling fan and high-speed Internet access in room. Central air. VCR, fax, copier, library, parlor games, telephone and fireplace on premises. Antiquing, art galleries, bicycling, canoeing/kayaking, fishing, golf, hiking, horseback riding, museums, parks, shopping, wineries, longwood Gardens, Brandywine Valley attractions and Amish country nearby.

"Truly an enchanting place."

Meadow Spring Farm Traditions at Longwood

96 Violet Dr
Kennett Square, PA 19348
(610)444-3903

Circa 1836. You'll find horses grazing in the pastures at this 245-acre working farm, as well as colorful perennial flowers. The two-story, white-brick house is decorated with old family pieces and collections of whimsical animals and antique wedding gowns. A Victorian doll collection fills one room. Breakfast is hearty country style, specialties include mushroom omelettes and freshly baked breads. Afterwards, guests may gather eggs or feed rabbits and horses. Carriage rides, through the fields and back roads, are available.

Historic Interest: Longwood Gardens and the Brandywine Museum are nearby.

Innkeeper(s): Anne Hicks. $95. 6 rooms, 5 with PB, 1 with FP and 1 suite. Breakfast, afternoon tea and snacks/refreshment s included in rates. Types of meals: Full gourmet bkfst, veg bkfst and early coffee/tea. Beds: QT. TV, reading lamp, refrigerator, ceiling fan and desk in room. Air conditioning. Swimming, tennis, parlor games, telephone and fireplace on premises. Limited handicap access. Family reunions hosted. Antiquing, art galleries, bicycling, canoeing/kayaking, fishing, golf, hiking, horseback riding, live theater, museums, parks, shopping, sporting events, tennis and wineries nearby.

Publicity: *Country Inn Magazine, Washington Post, New York Times and Channel 7.*

Kintnersville — I17

Bucksville House

4501 Durham Rd Rt 412
Kintnersville, PA 18930-1610
(610)847-8948 (888)617-6300 Fax:(610)847-8948

Circa 1795. For over two centuries, Bucksville House served as a stagecoach stop. It also enjoyed use as a tavern and a speakeasy. For nearly two decades, the historic Colonial-Federal home has welcomed guests in the form of a country inn. The five guest rooms have been appointed in a sophisticated style with Colonial and country furnishings. In one room, quilts are neatly stacked on armoire shelves. A quilt tops the bed and still another decorates a wall. All rooms include a fireplace. Flowers decorate the exterior, and the grounds include a large deck and a gazebo where guests can enjoy breakfast. A pond and herb garden are other items guests will find while strolling the four-and-a-half-acre grounds. Several friendly, albeit somewhat mischievous, ghosts are said to haunt the inn.

Innkeeper(s): Barb & Joe Szollosi. $125-150. 5 rooms with PB, 5 with FP and 1 suite. Breakfast and afternoon tea included in rates. Types of meals: Full bkfst. Beds: Q. Reading lamp in room. Air conditioning. VCR, fax, copier, library, parlor games, telephone, fireplace, pond and water garden on premises. Limited handicap access. Amusement parks, antiquing, fishing, golf, live theater, parks, shopping, tennis and water sports nearby.

Publicity: *Country Living, Bucks Country Town & Country, Country Decorating, Delaware Today, Lehigh Valley Magazine, Country Inns Magazine, New York Magazine, Country Accents Magazine and Voted Inn with best Antiques by Arrington's B&B Journal.*

Lackawaxen — E18

Roebling Inn on The Delaware

Scenic Dr, PO Box 31
Lackawaxen, PA 18435-0031
(570)685-7900 Fax:(570)685-1718
E-mail: roebling@ltis.net
Web: www.roeblinginn.com

Circa 1870. In the National Register of Historic Places, this Greek Revival-style home was once the home of Judge Ridgway, tallyman for the Delaware and Hudson Canal Company. The inn offers country furnishings and antiques. Guest rooms are comfortably furnished and some have fireplaces. There's a cottage, which is popular for families with children. The inn's long front porch is the favorite place to relax, but the sitting room is inviting as well with its cozy fireplace. Full country breakfasts are provided. Afterward, ask the innkeepers for directions to

nearby hidden waterfalls, or walk to the Zane Grey Museum. Roebling's Delaware Aqueduct is 100 yards downstream from the inn, now the oldest suspension bridge in North America. The scenic Delaware River is fun to explore, and there is a boat launch. Canoe, raft and tube rentals are available nearby. Fishing is a few steps from the inn's front porch or ask about guides for drift boat fishing. In the winter, look for bald eagles or ski at Masthope or Tanglewood. It's a two hour drive from New York City and two-and-a-half hours from Philadelphia.

Historic Interest: Minisink Battleground Park.

Innkeeper(s): Don & JoAnn Jahn. $75-150. 6 rooms, 5 with PB and 1 cottage. Breakfast included in rates. Types of meals: Full bkfst. Beds: QDT. Cable TV and some rooms with fireplace in room. Air conditioning. Fax and fireplace on premises. Antiquing, cross-country skiing, downhill skiing, fishing, live theater, parks and water sports nearby.

Publicity: *New York Magazine and New York Daily News.*

Lake Ariel — E16

Beech Tree Gardens B&B

RR #10 Box 3100
Lake Ariel, PA 18436
(570)226-8677 Fax:(570)226-7461
E-mail: beech@ptd.net
Web: www.beechtreegardens.com

Circa 1876. Sitting on 81 forested acres in the Pocono Mountains, this Victorian inn is just two hours from New York City and Philadelphia. Mahogany woodwork is showcased throughout the parlor. The well-appointed guest bedrooms boast clawfoot tubs, highback beds, marble washstands and pedestal sinks. Breakfast is served in the dining room beneath a ceiling mural adorned with cherubs. Fresh fruit, banana bread, apple dumplings, baked pears and omelettes are some of the delicious fare offered. Relax on the wraparound porch's swing and rocking chairs, or enjoy the fountain in the formal garden. Trails offer bird watching and wildlife observation. Walk the lighted paths at night through the woods and sit on the balcony of the Pond House. Steamtown National Historic Park, Lackawanna Coal Mine, Montage Mountain ski area and Dorflinger Glass Museum are within driving distance.

Innkeeper(s): Lynn & Kevin Schultz. $85-115. 3 rooms, 2 with PB and 1 suite. Breakfast included in rates. Types of meals: Full bkfst, veg bkfst and snacks/refreshments. Beds: QD. Reading lamp and clock radio in room. Air conditioning. Fax, parlor games, telephone, cylinder stove, hiking trails, ponds and snowshoeing on premises. Antiquing, beach, bicycling, canoeing/kayaking, cross-country skiing, downhill skiing, fishing, golf, hiking, horseback riding, live theater, museums, parks, shopping, sporting events and water sports nearby.

Publicity: *Meet the Chamber-local radio.*

Lampeter — K14

The Australian Walkabout Inn

837 Village Rd, PO Box 294
Lampeter, PA 17537-0294
(717)464-0707 Fax:(717)464-2501

Circa 1925. The inn, situated on beautifully landscaped grounds with an English garden and a lily pond, features a wraparound porch, where guests can watch Amish buggies pass by. Bedchambers have antique furniture, canopy beds, fireplaces and whirlpool tubs.

Historic Interest: The historic 1719 Hans Herr House is just one mile away.
Innkeeper(s): Jay & Valerie Petersheim. $99-289. 5 suites, 5 with FP and 1 cottage. Breakfast included in rates. Types of meals: Full gourmet bkfst. Beds: KQ. Cable TV, VCR, reading lamp, snack bar, clock radio, desk, hot tub or whirlpools and mini-fridge in room. Air conditioning. TV, parlor games, telephone and fireplace on premises. Family reunions hosted. Amusement parks, antiquing, live theater, parks, shopping, sporting events and Amish dinner nearby.
Publicity: *Gourmet, New York Post, Intelligencer Journal and Holiday Travel.*

"The Walkabout Inn itself and its surroundings are truly relaxing, romantic and quaint. It's the kind of place that both of us wanted and pictured in our minds, even before we decided to make reservations."

Lancaster K14

E.J. Bowman House

2672 Lititz Pike
Lancaster, PA 17601
(717)519-0808 (877)519-1776 Fax:(717)519-0774
E-mail: alice.ey@ejbowmanhouse.com
Web: www.ejbowmanhouse.com

Circa 1860. Known locally as the "big yellow house," this award-winning Italianate Victorian is in the heart of Amish Country. Reflecting its historical significance, exquisite murals are showcased in the foyer and formal staircase depicting the county's late 1800s seasonal life. Watch the big screen TV in the library, sit by the hearth in the parlor, and enjoy tea and treats in the music room. Comfortably luxurious guest bedrooms are decorated with soft hues and boast antiques, stove fireplaces, CD players, VCRs, data ports and heated tile floors in the bath. The Bowman Suite also features adjoining third-floor rooms with many family heirlooms, a whirlpool, exposed beam ceiling and impressive views. A hearty gourmet breakfast is served in the dining room. Relax on porches or on the second-floor balcony. Walk the well-lit paths that lead to the lush perennial and herb gardens, a dollhouse pond and places to reflect on nature's beauty.

Historic Interest: Built in 1860 to house a prominent Lancaster physician. One of only 5 Italianate Victorian country homes in Lancaster.
Innkeeper(s): Alice & E.Y. Murphey. $80-150. 5 rooms with PB and 1 suite. Types of meals: Full gourmet bkfst, veg bkfst, early coffee/tea and snacks/refreshments. Beds: KQDT. Modem hook-up, cable TV, VCR, reading lamp, CD player, ceiling fan, clock radio, turn-down service, desk, hot tub/spa, fireplace and heated tile floors in all baths in room. Central air. Fax, copier, library, parlor games, telephone, fireplace, guest kitchenette and music room on premises. Small meetings and seminars hosted. Amusement parks, antiquing, art galleries, golf, live theater, museums, parks and wineries nearby.
Publicity: *Intelligencier Journal, Lancaster New Era, Lancaster Magazine, WGAL TV and inspected by PA Tourism & Lodging.*

Flowers & Thyme B&B

238 Strasburg Pike
Lancaster, PA 17602-1326
(717)393-1460 Fax:(717)399-1986
E-mail: americaninnsinquiry@flowersandthyme.com
Web: www.flowersandthyme.com

Circa 1941. This 1941 brick property overlooks a working farm. Picturesque cottage gardens, as well as an herb garden, were featured in Birds and Blooms Magazine. An Amish carpenter built the home and the present innkeepers grew up here among the Amish and Mennonite communities. They are knowledgeable about the area and its history. The inn offers antiques and quilts and you can

choose from a variety of amenities such as a canopy bed, a Jacuzzi or a fireplace. The Gathering Room hosts the full country breakfast that is served each morning. A few minutes away are outlet stores, farmers markets, antique shops, craft and boutique shops.

Historic Interest: The Central Market in Lancaster is one of the oldest enclosed markets in the country featuring everything from fresh fruits and vegetables to flowers and baked goods. The Hans Herr House, the county's oldest building and second oldest Mennonite meeting house, is four miles from the home. For something unique, try the scenic 45-minute journey through Amish country on America's oldest short line, the Strasburg Railroad.
Innkeeper(s): Don & Ruth Harnish. $89-149. 3 rooms with PB. Breakfast included in rates. Types of meals: Full bkfst. Beds: Q. Ceiling fan and clock radio in room. Air conditioning. Library, parlor games, telephone and Jacuzzi in one room on premises. Amusement parks, antiquing, live theater, parks, shopping, sporting events and water sports nearby.
Publicity: *Lancaster newspapers, Allentown Morning Call and Birds & Bloom Magazine.*

Gardens of Eden

1894 Eden Rd
Lancaster, PA 17601-5526
(717)393-5179 Fax:(717)393-7722
E-mail: info@gardens-of-eden.com
Web: www.gardens-of-eden.com

Circa 1867. Wildflowers, perennials and wooded trails cover the three-and-a-half-acre grounds surrounding Gardens of Eden. The home, which overlooks the Conestoga River, is an example of late Federal-style architecture with some early

Victorian touches. The innkeepers have won awards for their restoration. Their guest cottage was featured on the cover of a decorating book. The interior, laced with dried flowers, handmade quilts, baskets and country furnishings, has the feel of a garden cottage. This cottage is ideal for families and includes a working fireplace and an efficiency kitchen. Gardens of Eden is within minutes of downtown Lancaster. The innkeepers can arrange for personalized tours of Amish and Mennonite communities and sometimes a dinner in an Amish home.

Innkeeper(s): Marilyn & Bill Ebel. $115-165. 4 rooms with PB, 1 with FP and 1 cottage. Breakfast included in rates. Types of meals: Full bkfst and afternoon tea. Beds: KQD. Reading lamp, stereo, refrigerator, clock radio, telephone, turn-down service and desk in room. Air conditioning. VCR, fax, copier, parlor games, fireplace, garden tours, canoe and bike maps and storage on premises. Amusement parks, antiquing, live theater, museums, shopping, amish culture and craft shows nearby.

Hollinger House

2336 Hollinger Rd
Lancaster, PA 17602-4728
(717)464-3050 (866)873-7370 Fax:(717)464-3053
E-mail: mywillow99@aol.com

Circa 1870. Become part of the family while staying at this elegant B&B in the heart of Amish Country just 35 miles from Harrisburg, 60 miles from Philadelphia. Hospitality is generous with homemade chocolates, tea, and evening pastries. Comfortable guest bedrooms include turndown service and romantic amenities like candles and bedside poetry. Indulge in a bountiful breakfast. Dietary needs can be accommodated upon prior request. Walk through the garden or lush forest. For day trips, it is just a 2-hour drive to Baltimore and 2 1/2 hours to New York.

Innkeeper(s): Gina & Jeff Trost. $100-125. 5 rooms with PB, 1 with FP, 1 suite and 1 cottage. Breakfast, snacks/refreshments and dinner included in rates. Types of meals: Full gourmet bkfst, veg bkfst, early coffee/tea, gourmet lunch and picnic lunch. Beds: KQT. Reading lamp, clock radio and fireplace in room. Air conditioning. TV, VCR, fax, copier, library, pet boarding, parlor games, telephone, fireplace and gift shop on premises. Small meetings, family reunions and seminars hosted. Amusement parks, antiquing, art galleries, beach, bicycling, canoeing/kayaking, cross-country skiing, downhill skiing, fishing, golf, hiking, horseback riding, live theater, museums, parks, shopping, sporting events, tennis, water sports, wineries, Amish attractions and historic sites nearby.

Publicity: *Victoria Magazine, Hallmark Greeting Cards photo shoot, People's Place photo shoot, Eisenhart Wallpaper photo shoot, Lancaster Magazine, Awarded the "Property of Distinction" award, Centennial (Novel, too) and by James Michener.*

The King's Cottage, A B&B Inn

1049 E King St
Lancaster, PA 17602-3231
(717)397-1017 (800)747-8717 Fax:(717)397-3447
E-mail: info@kingscottagebb.com
Web: www.kingscottagebb.com

Circa 1913. This Spanish Mission Revival house features a red-tile roof and stucco walls, common in many stately turn-of-the-century houses in California and New Mexico. Its elegant interiors include a sweeping staircase, a library with marble fireplace, stained-glass windows and a solarium. The inn is appointed with Oriental rugs and antiques and fine 18th-century English reproductions. Three guest rooms have Jacuzzi/whirlpool tubs and four have fireplaces. The formal dining room provides the location for gourmet morning meals.

Historic Interest: Landis Valley Farm Museum (5 miles), Railroad Museum of Pennsylvania (8 miles), Hans Herr House (5 miles).

Innkeeper(s): Janis Kutterer and Ann Willets. $150-260. 8 rooms with PB. Breakfast and afternoon tea included in rates. Types of meals: Full bkfst. Beds: KQ. Cable TV, reading lamp, clock radio, telephone, turn-down service, desk, VCR or DVD and some with whirlpools in room. Parlor games and fireplace on premises. Small meetings and seminars hosted. Amusement parks, antiquing, fishing, golf, live theater, shopping, sporting events, outlet shopping, Amish dinners and quilts nearby.

Publicity: *Country, USA Weekend, Bon Appetit, Intelligencer Journal, Times, New York Magazine, Forbes, Washingtonian, Long Island Wine Gazette and Discerning Traveler.*

"I appreciate your attention to all our needs and look forward to recommending your inn to friends."

Landenberg   L15

Cornerstone B&B Inn

300 Buttonwood Rd
Landenberg, PA 19350-9398
(610)274-2143 Fax:(610)274-0734
E-mail: corner3000@aol.com
Web: www.cornerstoneinn.net

Circa 1704. The Cornerstone is a fine 18th-century country manor house filled with antique furnishings. Two fireplaces make the parlor inviting. Wing chairs, fresh flowers and working fireplaces add enjoyment to the guest rooms. Award-win-

ning perennial gardens, a water garden and swimming pool are additional amenities.

Historic Interest: Brandywine River Museum, Brandywine Battlefield State Park, Franklin Mint, Valley Forge National Historical Park, Longwood Gardens, Winterthur Museum.

Innkeeper(s): Linda Chamberlin & Marty Mulligan. $100-250. 9 rooms, 5 with FP, 1 suite and 8 cottages. Breakfast included in rates. Types of meals: Full bkfst and early coffee/tea. Beds: KQT. Cable TV, reading lamp and clock radio in room. Air conditioning. VCR, fax, telephone and fireplace on premises. Small meetings and family reunions hosted. Amusement parks, antiquing, live theater, parks, shopping and sporting events nearby.

Lewisburg   G12

Anni's Inn & Outings

302 North Third St
Lewisburg, PA 17837
(570)523-7163
E-mail: anni@anni-bnb.com
Web: www.anni-bnb.com

Circa 1850. Built prior to the Civil War, Anni's has had a rich assortment of owners. For several decades, the home was owned by a native Indian medicine doctor who dried and prepared his own medicine on site. The five guest rooms are named for members of the innkeeper's family and are decorated with antiques and some Asian influences. Guests have the option of enjoying a hearty, full breakfast or selecting lighter fare such as homemade muffins and fresh fruit. Historic Lewisburg offers unique shops and restaurants and is home to Bucknell University. Plenty of outdoor activities are available at the many state parks in the area. The innkeeper also helps guests plan interesting bicycle treks that range from 15 to 45 miles in length, taking in country farms, covered bridges and historic villages along the way.

Innkeeper(s): Ann Longanbach. $85-100. 5 rooms, 3 with PB. Breakfast included in rates. Types of meals: Full bkfst, veg bkfst, early coffee/tea and picnic lunch. Beds: QT. Reading lamp and clock radio in room. Air conditioning. TV, VCR, parlor games and telephone on premises. Small meetings and seminars hosted. Amusement parks, antiquing, art galleries, bicycling, canoeing/kayaking, cross-country skiing, fishing, golf, hiking, live theater, museums, parks, shopping, sporting events, tennis and water sports nearby.

Publicity: *WBRE-Home and backyard.*

Linfield   J16

Shearer Elegance

1154 Main St
Linfield, PA 19468-1139
(610)495-7429 (800)861-0308 Fax:(610)495-7814
E-mail: shirley@shearerelegance.com
Web: www.shearerelegance.com

Circa 1897. This stone Queen Anne mansion is the height of Victorian opulence and style. Peaked roofs, intricate trim and a stenciled wraparound porch grace the exterior. Guests enter the home via a marble entry, which boasts a three-story staircase. Stained-glass windows and carved mantels are other notable features. The Victorian furnishings and decor complement the ornate workmanship, and lacy curtains are a romantic touch. The bedrooms feature hand-carved, built-in wardrobes. The grounds are dotted with gardens. The inn is located in the village of Linfield, about 15 minutes from Valley Forge.

Innkeeper(s): Shirley & Malcolm Shearer. $100-155. 7 rooms with PB, 3

suites and 3 conference rooms. Types of meals: Full bkfst and early coffee/tea. Beds: KQ. Cable TV, VCR, reading lamp, stereo, refrigerator, ceiling fan, clock radio and desk in room. Air conditioning. Fax, copier, library, parlor games and telephone on premises. Weddings, small meetings, family reunions and seminars hosted. Amusement parks, antiquing, downhill skiing, fishing, golf, live theater, parks, shopping, sporting events, tennis and outlets nearby.
Publicity: *Reading, Norristown, Pottstown and Local.*

"Thank you for creating such a beautiful place to escape reality."

Lititz   J14

The Alden House

62 E Main St
Lititz, PA 17543-1947
(717)627-3363 (800)584-0753
E-mail: inn@aldenhouse.com
Web: www.aldenhouse.com

Circa 1850. For more than 200 years, breezes have carried the sound of church bells to the stately homes lining Main Street. This Federal-style brick home in the center of the historic dis-

trict is within an easy walk to the country's first pretzel factory, unique shops, fine restaurants, chocolate factory and museums. Relax on one of the many porches. Spacious guest bedrooms and suites are furnished with distinctive antiques. Old-fashioned hospitality includes a gourmet breakfast.

Innkeeper(s): Bob & Shirley McCarthy. $90-120. 5 rooms with PB, 1 with FP and 3 suites. Breakfast included in rates. Types of meals: Full gourmet bkfst, early coffee/tea and snacks/refreshments. Beds: Q. Cable TV, VCR, clock radio and desk in room. Air conditioning. Telephone and off-street parking on premises. Small meetings hosted. Amusement parks, antiquing, live theater, parks and shopping nearby.
Publicity: *Mobile Travel Guide, American Historic Inns, Official Vacation Guide Lancaster County, Christian Bed and Breakfast Directory, Stash Tea Guide Bed and Breakfast Inns, San Francisco Chronicle, Litiz 2003 and Lititz Record Express.*

"Thanks for all the personal touches and for the warmth. We appreciated the wonderful breakfasts—all the touches of home!"

Casual Corners B&B

301 N Broad St
Lititz, PA 17543
(717)626-5299 (800)464-6764
E-mail: stay@casualcornersbnb.com
Web: www.casualcornersbnb.com

Circa 1904. Experience small-town charm in the heart of Pennsylvania Dutch Country mingled with elegant touches for enjoyment and comfort. Gather in the second-floor sitting room for conversation, evening wine and brandy and early morning coffee. Watch TV, read or use a data port connection to access the Internet. Air-conditioned guest bedrooms with a private entrance are tastefully decorated and furnished with antiques. Some of the many breakfast favorites include French coffee cake, blueberry buckle, Belgian waffles and egg strata. Browse the Gift Gallery featuring an assortment of crafts and treasures to buy. Relax on the large wraparound front porch or the backyard swing amidst the the flower and herb garden.

Innkeeper(s): Carol Beaupre. $80-95. 5 rooms, 3 with PB and 1 suite. Breakfast included in rates. Types of meals: Country bkfst, veg bkfst and early coffee/tea. Beds: QD. Reading lamp, ceiling fan and turn-down service in room. Air conditioning. Parlor games, telephone and fireplace on premises. Amusement parks, antiquing, art galleries, bicycling, golf, hiking, live theater, museums, parks, shopping, tennis and wineries nearby.

General Sutter Inn

14 E Main St
Lititz, PA 17543-1900
(717)626-2115 (717)626-2115 Fax:(717)626-0992
E-mail: brophyinn@attglobal.net
Web: www.generalsutterinn.com

Circa 1764. Built by the Moravian Church, the inn is considered the oldest continuously operating inn in Pennsylvania. Shaded now by tall trees, the inn's three-story brick facade is warmed by a white solarium with Palladian windows. There are banquet rooms, two restaurants, a tavern and outdoor patio. The decor is colonial. With its central location, the inn marks the beginning of the town's historic walking tour. The Wilbur Chocolate Candy Museum, Sturgis Pretzel House and Lititz Springs Park are close.

Innkeeper(s): Ed & Dolores Brophy. $87-120. 14 rooms with PB, 2 suites and 2 conference rooms. Types of meals: Full bkfst, lunch and gourmet dinner. Restaurant on premises. Beds: QDT. Cable TV, reading lamp, clock radio, telephone and desk in room. Air conditioning. Fax, library, parlor games and fireplace on premises. Weddings, small meetings, family reunions and seminars hosted. Amusement parks, antiquing, fishing, golf, live theater, parks, shopping and sporting events nearby.
Publicity: *Washington Post and Philadelphia Enquirer.*

Stauffer House B&B

14 Landis Valley Rd
Lititz, PA 17543-8628
(717)627-5663

Circa 1940. This comfortable Colonial inn sits on a park-like acre in the small town of Lititz in the heart of Amish country. The three guest bedrooms are furnished with family antiques such as a tall pencil-post bed and a ball-post bed. Innkeeper Hagar Scott serves a delightful full breakfast including her wonderful specialties of blueberry French toast, Belgian waffles with fresh fruit and whipped cream or blintzes with sour cream and jam. Tea and coffee are always available in the dining room and home-baked snacks and fruit are offered often, as well. Most guests head out after breakfast to Lancaster, Wheatland (the home of President James Buchanan) or Central Market, which is one of the oldest continual markets in the country, with Amish stands, great food, crafts and flowers. Wilbur Chocolates, located in Lititz, has a chocolate museum and a chocolate factory that flavors the air. After a day of site seeing, guests like to sit and rock on the back porch that overlooks a manicured lawn with flower and vegetable gardens, or play a quiet game of croquet.

Innkeeper(s): Hagar Scott. $65. 3 rooms. Breakfast and snacks/refreshments included in rates. Types of meals: Full bkfst. Beds: QDT. Reading lamp, snack bar and clock radio in room. Parlor games and telephone on premises. Amusement parks, antiquing, art galleries, fishing, golf, hiking, live theater, museums, parks and shopping nearby.

Malvern   K16

General Warren Inne

Old Lancaster Hwy
Malvern, PA 19355
(610)296-3637 Fax:(610)296-8084
E-mail: suites@generalwarren.com
Web: www.generalwarren.com

Circa 1745. This 250-year-old inn, once owned by the grandson of William Penn, is surrounded by three wooded acres and is filled with 18th-century charm. The rooms are simple and elegant, featuring chandeliers, painted woodwork, quilts and period reproductions. Each of the guest rooms offers a special touch. The Presidential Suite features a sitting room with a fireplace, while the William Penn

Suite boasts an original cathedral window. Other rooms include four-poster beds and fireplaces. Meals at the General Warren are a delight in one of the inn's three elegant candle-lit dining rooms. Start with a Caesar salad, prepared tableside or with a stuffed Portabello mushroom. Follow that with Beef Wellington and complete the meal with homemade Grand Marnier ice cream. Summer dishes feature locally grown produce and herbs from the inn's organic gardens. Gourmet magazine rated the inn's restaurant as one of Philadelphia's Top Tables.

Innkeeper(s): Karlie Davies. $120-190. 8 suites. Breakfast included in rates. Types of meals: Cont, lunch and gourmet dinner. Restaurant on premises. Beds: KQD. Live theater and historical sites nearby only. Publicity: *Colonial Homes and Gourmet Magazine.*

Manheim   J14

Manheim Manor

140 S Charlotte St
Manheim, PA 17545-1804
(717)664-4168 (888)224-4346 Fax:(717)664-0445
E-mail: Avellat@aol.com
Web: www.manheimmanor.com

Circa 1856. Adorning a quiet neighborhood in a quaint town, this Victorian home is listed in the National Register. Built from stone and wood, it boasts a pillared front porch with lacy fretwork embellishments. Chestnut wood creates a rich setting for elegant furnishings of double-brocaded love seats and a Louis XV medallion-backed, red-velvet sofa. Offering a variety of decorating styles, well-appointed guest bedrooms feature coordinated wall coverings, window treatments, luxurious fabrics and comfortable furnishings. Indulge in bedside cordials, English toffee, mints and Hershey's chocolates. A bountiful multi-course breakfast is a culinary event, creating a variety of dishes including the all-homemade: granola, yogurt, applesauce and signature Victorian brown bread pudding. Arrangements can be made to join an Amish family for dinner, take a buggy or winter sleigh ride. There is much to explore in Pennsylvania Dutch Country with historical sites and shops within walking distance.

Innkeeper(s): Alfred & Alice Avella. $85-250. 8 rooms with PB, 1 with FP and 1 conference room. Breakfast included in rates. Types of meals: Full gourmet bkfst and early coffee/tea. Beds: KQDT. Modem hook-up, cable TV, VCR, reading lamp, stereo, refrigerator, ceiling fan, clock radio, telephone, coffeemaker, desk, hot tub/spa, voice mail and fireplace in room. Central air. Fax, spa, fireplace and laundry facility on premises. Weddings, small meetings and family reunions hosted. Amusement parks, antiquing, art galleries, fishing, golf, hiking, horseback riding, live theater, museums, parks, shopping and wineries nearby.

Rose Manor B&B and Tea Room

124 S Linden St
Manheim, PA 17545-1616
(717)664-4932 (800)666-4932 Fax:(717)664-1611
E-mail: inn@rosemanor.net
Web: www.rosemanor.net

Circa 1905. A local mill owner built this manor house, and it still maintains original light fixtures, woodwork and cabinetry. The grounds are decorated with roses and herb gardens. An

herb theme is played out in the guest rooms, which feature names such as the Parsley, Sage, Rosemary and Thyme rooms. The fifth room is named the Basil, and its spacious quarters encompass the third story and feature the roof's angled ceiling. One room offers a whirlpool and another a fireplace. The decor is a comfortable English-manor style with some antiques. Afternoon tea is available by prior reservation, and there is a gift shop on the premises. The inn's location provides close access to many Pennsylvania Dutch country attractions.

Innkeeper(s): Susan Jenal. $70-130. 5 rooms, 3 with PB, 1 with FP. Breakfast included in rates. Types of meals: Full bkfst, picnic lunch and afternoon tea. Beds: QDT. Cable TV, reading lamp, ceiling fan and one with whirlpool in room. Air conditioning. Fax, copier, library, telephone and fireplace on premises. Family reunions hosted. Amusement parks, antiquing, fishing, live theater, parks and shopping nearby. Publicity: *Harrisburg Patriot, Lancaster County Magazine* and *Central Pennsylvania Life.*

Marietta   K13

The Noble House Bed & Breakfast

113 W Market St
Marietta, PA 17547-1411
(717)426-4389 (888)271-6426 Fax:(717)426-4012
E-mail: info@thenoblehouse.com
Web: www.thenoblehouse.com

Circa 1810. A 12-foot-high ceiling and stenciled front hallway greet guests at this restored Federal-style brick home. Family heirlooms, original art and fresh flowers decorate the home. All three guest rooms offer fireplaces and two have two-person soaking tubs with showers. The first-floor guest room, decorated to look like a 1950s pullman car, has its own private entrance. A full breakfast is served before the fireplace by candlelight. The living room, which has a piano and fireplace, and the garden are popular places to relax.

Historic Interest: Almost half of the buildings in this village have been placed in the National Register. Because of Marietta's close proximity to Gettysburg, two from the inn, the city graces its annual tour of historic homes with a Civil War theme.

Innkeeper(s): Elissa & Paul Noble. $95-145. 4 rooms with PB, 4 with FP, 1 suite and 1 cottage. Breakfast and snacks/refreshments included in rates. Types of meals: Full gourmet bkfst, veg bkfst, early coffee/tea, afternoon tea and room service. Beds: KQDT. Data port, cable TV, VCR, reading lamp, CD player, refrigerator, clock radio, desk, fireplace and 2 with two-person soaking tubs in room. Air conditioning. Fax, copier, library, parlor games, telephone and fireplace on premises. Weddings, small meetings, family reunions and seminars hosted. Amusement parks, antiquing, art galleries, bicycling, canoeing/kayaking, fishing, golf, hiking, horseback riding, live theater, museums, parks, shopping, sporting events, tennis, water sports and wineries nearby. Publicity: *Early American Life, Pennsylvania Dutch Hollydays, Elizabethtown Mount Joy Merchandiser, Lancaster Magazine* and *Favorite Garden Award for the Marietta Garden Tour.*

"Thank you for your hospitality. We felt like royalty, and enjoyed the detail in your beautiful home."

Railroad House Restaurant B&B

280 W Front St
Marietta, PA 17547-1405
(717)426-4141
Web: www.therailroadhouse.com

Circa 1820. The Railroad House, a sprawling old hotel, conjures up memories of the days when riding the rail was the way to travel. The house was built as a refuge for weary men who were

working along the Susquehanna River. When the railroad finally made its way through Marietta, the rail station's waiting room and ticket office were located in what's now known as the Railroad House. The restored rooms feature antiques, Oriental rugs, Victorian decor and rustic touches such as exposed brick walls. The chefs at the inn's restaurant create a menu of American and continental dishes using spices and produce from the beautifully restored gardens. The innovative recipes have been featured in Bon Appetit. The innkeepers also host a variety of special events and weekends, including murder mysteries and clambakes serenaded by jazz bands. Carriage rides and special walking tours of Marietta can be arranged.

Historic Interest: Wheatland, the home of President Buchanan, is 15 minutes from the Railroad House. The John Wright and Haldeman mansions are just 10 minutes away, and the Old Town Hall is a few blocks from the inn.
Innkeeper(s): Richard & Donna Chambers. $89-129. 8 rooms with PB, 1 cottage and 1 conference room. Breakfast included in rates. Types of meals: Full gourmet bkfst, early coffee/tea, gourmet lunch, picnic lunch, afternoon tea, snacks/refreshments and gourmet dinner. Restaurant on premises. Beds: QDT. Reading lamp, refrigerator, clock radio and desk in room. Air conditioning. Copier, bicycles, parlor games, telephone, fireplace, gardens and yard games on premises. Weddings, small meetings, family reunions and seminars hosted. Amusement parks, antiquing, downhill skiing, fishing, live theater, parks, shopping, sporting events, water sports and music box museum nearby.

McConnellsburg   K9

The McConnellsburg Inn

131 W Market St
McConnellsburg, PA 17233-1007
(717)485-5495 Fax:(717)485-5495
E-mail: Mconburgin@innernet.net
Web: www.innernet.net/mconburgin/

Circa 1903. Located in the historic district, this turn-of-the-century inn was built for a retired Union officer of the Civil War. Guest bedrooms include four-poster canopy beds. Gettysburg, East Broad Top Railroad, Cowans Gap State Park and Buchanan State Forest are nearby, as are Great Cove Golf Course and Whitetail Ski Resort.

Innkeeper(s): Kathryn Beckman. $70-85. 3 rooms with PB. Breakfast included in rates. Types of meals: Cont. Beds: Q. Modem hook-up, cable TV, reading lamp and clock radio in room. Air conditioning. Telephone on premises. Small meetings hosted. Antiquing, cross-country skiing, downhill skiing, fishing, golf, water sports, nature photography, country auctions, hiking and country auctions nearby.
Publicity: *Pennsylvania.*

McKnightstown   L11

Country Escape

275 Old Rt 30, PO Box 195
McKnightstown, PA 17343
(717)338-0611 (800)484-3244 Fax:(717)334-5227
E-mail: merry@countryescape.com
Web: www.countryescape.com

Circa 1867. This country Victorian, a brick structure featuring a porch decked in gingerbread trim, rests on the route that Confederate soldiers took on their way to nearby Gettysburg. The home itself was built just a few years after the Civil War. There are three comfortable guest rooms decorated in country style. For an extra fee, business travelers can use the inn's typing, copying, fax-

ing or desktop publishing services. There is also a children's play area outside. A traditional American breakfast is served, with such hearty items as eggs, pancakes, bacon and sausage. The inn offers close access to the famous battlefield, as well as other historic sites.

Innkeeper(s): Merry Bush & Ross Hetrick. $85-125. 3 rooms, 1 with PB and 1 suite. Breakfast and snacks/refreshments included in rates. Types of meals: Country bkfst and veg bkfst. Beds: Q. Reading lamp and clock radio in room. Air conditioning. TV, VCR, fax, copier, spa, parlor games, telephone, fireplace, children's play area and gardens on premises. Antiquing, bicycling, downhill skiing, golf, horseback riding, live theater, museums, parks, shopping, wineries, crafts and Gettysburg battlefield nearby.
Publicity: *Gettysburg Times and Hanover Evening Sun.*

Mechanicsburg   J12

Ashcombe Mansion B&B

1100 Grantham Rd
Mechanicsburg, PA 17055
(717)766-6820 Fax:(717)790-0723
E-mail: ashcombe@pa.net
Web: www.ashcombemansion.com

Circa 1892. This extraordinary century-old Queen Anne stands on 23 country acres just 25 miles from Gettysburg. Stained-glass windows cast jeweled light into the staircase leading to the eight guest bedrooms. Parquet floors, carved woodwork and murals create an elegant ambiance. Common rooms include the drawing room, music room and library. You may recognize the distinctive front of the inn from the NBC comedy series called "Grand." An unusual circular porch, dramatic roof lines, chimneys and gables as well as an interesting use of a variety of construction materials (brick, stucco, wood, stone and shingles) make this inn a destination in itself. After a full breakfast that includes items such as fruits, eggs and crepes with strawberries, guests may settle in on the porch and enjoy the pastoral views and watch the heron, geese and wild ducks that make the pond and stream their home. The inn is less than two hours from Washington, D.C., and Philadelphia, and it's only three-and-a-half hours from New York City.

Historic Interest: The inn was built as a summer home for Margaret Moser, the widow of Honorable Henry G. Moser, a well-known iron manufacturer, legislator and county judge.
Innkeeper(s): Mira Stanokovic. $120-180. 8 rooms, 6 with PB, 3 with FP and 4 conference rooms. Breakfast included in rates. Types of meals: Full gourmet bkfst and early coffee/tea. Beds: KQT. Modem hook-up, cable TV, VCR, reading lamp, stereo, clock radio, telephone, desk and hot tub/spa in room. Air conditioning. Fax, copier, fireplace and fireplaces on premises. Weddings, small meetings, family reunions and seminars hosted. Amusement parks, antiquing, art galleries, bicycling, canoeing/kayaking, fishing, golf, hiking and horseback riding nearby.
Publicity: *Baltimore Sun, Patriot News, Apprise Magazine, The Sentinel, Antiques and Auction News and Grand Mira sitcom.*

Mercer   F2

The John Orr Guest House

320 E Butler St
Mercer, PA 16137
(724)662-0839 (877)849-0839 Fax:(724)662-3883
E-mail: innkeeper@jorrbandb.com
Web: www.jorrbandb.com

Circa 1905. A prominent local businessman built this turn-of-the-20th-century home, which is constructed in Greek Revival style. The home has been restored, leaving in place the original woodwork and other architectural features. Guest rooms and common areas include period-style furnishings and some antiques. The front porch is set up for those who wish to relax, offering comfortable wicker chairs and a porch swing. The innkeepers serve a full breakfast with items such as stuffed French toast, Belgian waffles, a hearty egg casserole and scones. Mercer is a quaint Victorian town with many historic homes, fine restaurants and attractions to visit.

Innkeeper(s): Ann & Jack Hausser. $70-85. 3 rooms with PB, 2 with FP. Breakfast and snacks/refreshments included in rates. Types of meals: Full bkfst, veg bkfst and early coffee/tea. Beds: QD. Reading lamp, ceiling fan and clock radio in room. Central air. TV, VCR, fax, copier, telephone, fireplace, CD player, stereo and refrigerator on premises. Small meetings and seminars hosted. Antiquing, bicycling, fishing, golf, museums, parks, shopping, lakes and Amish crafts nearby.

Mercersburg   L9

The Mercersburg Inn
405 S Main St
Mercersburg, PA 17236-9517
(717)328-5231 Fax:(717)328-3403
E-mail: sandy@mercersburginn.com
Web: www.mercersburginn.com

Circa 1909. Situated on a hill overlooking the Tuscorora Mountains, the valley and village, this 20,000-square-foot Georgian Revival mansion was built for industrialist Harry Byron. Six massive columns mark the entrance, which opens to a majestic hall featuring chestnut wainscoting and an elegant double stairway and rare scagliola (marbleized) columns. All the rooms are furnished with antiques and reproductions. A local craftsman built the inn's four-poster, canopied king-size beds. Many of the rooms have their own balconies and a few have fireplaces. Thursday through Sunday evening, the inn's chef prepares noteworthy, elegant dinners, which feature an array of seasonal specialties.

Historic Interest: Gettysburg, Harpers Ferry, Antietam, James Buchanan's birthplace are less than one hour from the inn.
Innkeeper(s): Walt & Sandy Filkowski. $135-275. 15 rooms with PB, 3 with FP and 1 conference room. Breakfast included in rates. Types of meals: Full gourmet bkfst, picnic lunch and gourmet dinner. Restaurant on premises. Beds: KQT. Reading lamp, telephone and desk in room. Air conditioning. VCR, bicycles, parlor games and fireplace on premises. Weddings, small meetings, family reunions and seminars hosted. Antiquing, cross-country skiing, downhill skiing, fishing, golf, live theater, shopping and water sports nearby.
Publicity: *Mid-Atlantic Country, Washington Post, The Herald-Mail, Richmond News Leader, Washingtonian, Philadelphia Inquirer and Pittsburgh.*

"Elegance personified! Outstanding ambiance and warm hospitality."

Mertztown   I16

Longswamp Bed & Breakfast
1605 State St
Mertztown, PA 19539-8912
(610)682-6197 Fax:(610)682-4854
E-mail: innkeeper@longswamp.com
Web: www.longswamp.com

Circa 1789. Country gentleman Colonel Trexler added a mansard roof to this stately 1789 Federal mansion in 1860. Inside the three-story main house is a magnificent walnut staircase, pegged wood floors and 10-foot ceilings. The separate Guest House served as a post office and general store in the 1800s as well as a safe house on the Underground Railroad. A suite was created recently from two horse stalls in the original

barn. Stroll through spectacular herb and flower gardens or the fruit orchards. Enjoy a complimentary basket of in-season fruits.
Innkeeper(s): JoAnn & John Swenson. $93-125. 10 rooms with PB, 2 with FP and 3 suites. Breakfast included in rates. Types of meals: Full bkfst. Beds: Q. Modem hook-up, cable TV, VCR, reading lamp, ceiling fan, clock radio, desk and fireplace in room. Air conditioning. Fax, copier, parlor games, telephone, bocci, horseshoes, spectacular floral and herb gardens, fruit orchards from which guests may take a complimentary basket of in-season fruits, business dinners, luncheons and other special services by request and massage services available on premises. Small meetings, family reunions and seminars hosted. Amusement parks, antiquing, bicycling, cross-country skiing, downhill skiing, fishing, golf, hiking, horseback riding, parks, shopping, sporting events, wineries, fine dining, spas, Lehigh Valley Velodrome, major area festivals, car shows and Lehigh Valley wineries nearby.
Publicity: *Arringtons Journal "Best B&B in Wine Region," Washingtonian, Weekend Travel, The Sun and Food Network's Food 911 show.*

"The warm country atmosphere turns strangers into friends."

Milford   F18

Black Walnut Inn
179 Firetower Rd
Milford, PA 18337-9802
(570)296-6322 Fax:(570)296-7696
E-mail: stewart@theblackwalnutinn.com
Web: theblackwalnutinn.com

Circa 1897. Situated on 162 wooded acres, it's hard to imagine that this rustic English Tudor-style inn is less than two hours away from Manhattan. The woods, fields and four-acre lake offer guests a variety of on-site activities like picking fresh berries (in season), fishing for bass, horseback riding or mountain biking on endless trails. The grounds also include a petting zoo, a hot tub and paddle boats. The guest rooms are all furnished with brass beds and antique furniture. After a day of activities, guest can relax in front of the historic European fireplace or enjoy a drink while viewing the lake. There is also a game room. Guests begin their day with a hearty breakfast with items such as eggs, hot cakes, French toast, breakfast meats, fresh fruit salads and breads. The inn is often used for weddings, meetings and family reunions. Antique shopping, flea markets, museums, restaurants and canoeing down the Delaware are close by.

Historic Interest: Located near Grey Towers National Historic Landmark, the Appalachian Trail and High Point Monument.
Innkeeper(s): Robin & William. $85-175. 12 rooms, 4 with PB and 1 cabin. Breakfast included in rates. Types of meals: Full bkfst and early coffee/tea. Beds: QD. Reading lamp, cabin with full kitchen, full bathroom and living room with TV/VCR and fireplace in room. VCR, spa, swimming, parlor games, telephone, fireplace, paddle boats, horseback riding, petting zoo and game room on premises. Weddings, small meetings and family reunions hosted. Antiquing, bicycling, canoeing/kayaking, fishing, golf, hiking, museums, shopping, tennis, water sports, boating (row and paddle), antique cars, rafting, lawn games, bird watching and overnight camp-out nearby.

Cliff Park Inn & Golf Course
155 Cliff Park Rd
Milford, PA 18337-9708
(570)296-6491 (800)225-6535 Fax:(570)296-3982
E-mail: info@cliffparkinn.com
Web: www.cliffparkinn.com

Circa 1820. This historic country inn is located on a 600-acre family estate, bordering the Delaware River. It has been in the Buchanan family since 1820. Rooms are spacious with individual climate control, telephone and Victorian-style furnishings. Cliff Park features both a full-service restaurant and golf school. The inn's golf course, established in 1913, is one of the oldest in the United States. Cliff Park's picturesque setting is popular for country weddings and private business conferences. Both B&B or MAP plans are offered.

Historic Interest: Grey Towers National Landmark (2 miles).

Innkeeper(s): Harry W. Buchanan III. $93-160. 18 rooms with PB and 1 conference room. Breakfast included in rates. Types of meals: Full bkfst, lunch, picnic lunch and dinner. Restaurant on premises. Beds: KQDT. TV, fax and telephone on premises. Limited handicap access. Cross-country skiing and water sports nearby.

"Cliff Park Inn is the sort of inn I look for in the English countryside. It has that authentic charm that comes from history."

Laurel Villa Country Inn & Restaurant

Second & E Ann St
Milford, PA 18337
(570)296-9940 Fax:(570)296-7469
E-mail: info@laurelvilla.com
Web: www.laurelvilla.com

Circa 1876. Originally built 125 years ago as an inn and stage-coach stop, the Muhlhauser family has welcomed guests to this traditional Queen Anne for almost 60 years. Set in the picturesque northern Pocono Mountains, Laurel Villa is the second-oldest inn in Victorian Milford. Recently renovated, expect a casual country atmosphere with stylish elegance. The lounge offers fireside relaxation. Enjoy the rocking chairs on the front porch, or venture down a winding path to the side patio. Beyond that, encounter a koi pond and waterfall in an English garden offering benches for lingering. The restaurant, open to the public for lunch and dinner, serves Chef Carl's culinary specialties.

Innkeeper(s): Janice Halsted & Carl Muhlhauser. $70-135. 10 rooms, 9 with PB, 1 with FP, 1 suite and 1 conference room. Breakfast included in rates. Types of meals: Cont plus, veg bkfst and gourmet dinner. Restaurant on premises. Beds: KQD. Cable TV, reading lamp, ceiling fan and clock radio in room. Air conditioning. Fax, copier, telephone, fireplace, restaurant, bar, lounge, outdoor patio dining, English Gardens with waterfall and koi pond on premises. Weddings, small meetings, family reunions and seminars hosted. Antiquing, art galleries, beach, bicycling, canoeing/kayaking, cross-country skiing, fishing, golf, hiking, horseback riding, live theater, museums, parks, shopping, tennis, rafting and water tubing nearby.
Publicity: *NJ Herald*.

Pine Hill Farm B&B

181 Pine Hill Farm Rd
Milford, PA 18337
(570)296-5261
E-mail: getaway@pinehillfarm.com
Web: www.pinehillfarm.com

Circa 1870. Drive through scenic woodland before arriving at this 227-acre estate sitting high above the town in the Pocono Mountains. Inescapable vistas of the Kittatinny Mountains and the Delaware River Valley are breathtaking. The late 1800s Main House offers two guest bedrooms separated by a common room with satellite TV and mini refrigerator. The Caretaker Cottage boasts spacious suites with living rooms, and one features a private screened porch. The deluxe Adirondack and Country suites in the Hen House include large stone fireplaces, two-person Jacuzzis, and outdoor patios. A hearty country-style breakfast is served in the fireside dining room or on the terrace with a view. Hike or bike more than five miles of private trails or arrange for a variety of outdoor activities.

Innkeeper(s): James & Yvonne Klausmann. $140-210. 4 rooms with PB and 2 suites. Breakfast and snacks/refreshments included in rates. Types of

meals: Country bkfst, veg bkfst, early coffee/tea and picnic lunch. Beds: K. TV, reading lamp, refrigerator, ceiling fan and turn-down service in room. Air conditioning. Telephone on premises. Bicycling, canoeing/kayaking, cross-country skiing, fishing, golf, hiking and shopping nearby.

Milton   G12

Pau-Lyn's Country B&B

1160 Broadway Rd
Milton, PA 17847-9506
(570)742-4110

Circa 1850. This Victorian brick home offers a formal dining room with a fireplace and antique musical instruments. This restful haven offers a porch and patio overlooking the large lawn. Nearby are working farms and dairies, covered bridges, mountains, rivers and valleys.

Innkeeper(s): Paul & Evelyn Landis. $65-75. 7 rooms. Breakfast included in rates. Types of meals: Full bkfst. Beds: QDT. Reading lamp and clock radio in room. Air conditioning. Telephone, fireplace and large lawn and patio on premises. Amusement parks, antiquing, bicycling, golf, hiking, shopping, museums, underground railroad and little league museum and field nearby.

Mount Gretna   J13

Mount Gretna Inn

16 Kauffman Ave
Mount Gretna, PA 17064
(717)964-3234 (800)277-6602 Fax:(717)964-1887
E-mail: inn@mtgretna.com
Web: www.mtgretna.com

Circa 1921. This original Arts & Crafts-style home is set in the wooded mountains of historic Mt. Gretna, located conveniently close to a unique variety of attractions such as a lake, stream, cross-country skiing and miles of trails for mountain biking and hiking. Each of the inn's seven guest rooms features a sampling of antiques purchased by the innkeeper at local auctions. All rooms offer private baths, while some feature a private porch, gas fireplace or whirlpool and steam massage shower. Breakfast fare may include baked peaches, egg puff, sausage, homemade coffee cakes and muffins.

Historic Interest: Built in 1921 by Abraham Lincoln Kauffman, one of the founding entrepreneurs at the turn of the century.

Innkeeper(s): Keith & Robin Volker. $105-145. 7 rooms with PB, 6 with FP and 2 conference rooms. Breakfast and snacks/refreshments included in rates. Types of meals: Full bkfst, veg bkfst and early coffee/tea. Beds: KQT. Reading lamp, CD player, refrigerator, ceiling fan, clock radio, desk, hot tub/spa and fireplace in room. Air conditioning. Spa, bicycles, library, parlor games, telephone, fireplace, cross-country skiing, gift shop, Baby Grand Piano, large front porch, two rooms with private porches, kitchenette with ice maker, refrigerator, microwave, instant hot water, instant tea, coffee and hot chocolate available 24 hours on premises. Weddings, small meetings, family reunions and seminars hosted. Amusement parks, antiquing, art galleries, bicycling, canoeing/kayaking, fishing, golf, hiking, parks and Lebanon Valley nearby.
Publicity: *Daily News, Patriot News and Delaware Today*.

"What a wonderful respite from this hustle and bustle world. Quite like visiting an earlier time."

Mount Joy   K13

Cedar Hill Farm

305 Longenecker Rd
Mount Joy, PA 17552-8404
(717)653-4655 Fax:(717)653-9242
E-mail: cedarhillbnb@comcast.net
Web: www.cedarhillfarm.com

Circa 1817. Situated on 51 acres overlooking Chiques Creek, this stone farmhouse boasts a two-tiered front veranda affording pastoral views of the surrounding fields. The host was born

in the house and is the third generation to have lived here since the Swarr family first purchased it in 1878. Family heirlooms and antiques include an elaborately carved walnut bedstead, a marble-topped washstand and a "tumbling block" quilt. In the kitchen, a copper kettle, bread paddle and baskets of dried herbs accentuate the walk-in fireplace, where guests often linger over breakfast. Cedar Hill is a working poultry and grain farm.

Innkeeper(s): Russel & Gladys Swarr. $85-105. 5 rooms with PB. Breakfast included in rates. Types of meals: Cont plus and early coffee/tea. Beds: KQDT. Central air. VCR, fax, spa, parlor games, telephone, Internet access, picnic table and meadows and stream on premises. Small meetings and family reunions hosted. Amusement parks, antiquing, cross-country skiing, fishing, live theater, parks, shopping, sporting events, water sports and Amish country nearby.
Publicity: *Women's World, Lancaster Farming, Philadelphia, New York Times, Ladies Home Journal and Lancaster County Heritage.*

"Dorothy can have Kansas, Scarlett can take Tara, Rick can keep Paris — I've stayed at Cedar Hill Farm."

Hillside Farm Bed & Breakfast

607 Eby Chiques Road
Mount Joy, PA 17552-8819
(717)653-6697 (888)249-3406 Fax:(717)653-9775
E-mail: innkeeper@hillsidefarmbandb.com
Web: www.hillsidefarmbandb.com

Circa 1860. This comfortable farm has a relaxing homey feel to it. Rooms are simply decorated and special extras such as handmade quilts and antiques add an elegant country touch. Two

guest cottages each offer a king bed, whirlpool tub for two, fireplace, wet bar and deck overlooking a bucolic meadow. The home is a true monument to the cow. Dairy antiques, cow knickknacks and antique milk bottles abound.

Some of the bottles were found during the renovation of the home and its grounds. Spend the day hunting for bargains in nearby antique shops, malls and factory outlets, or tour local Amish and Pennsylvania Dutch attractions. The farm is a good vacation spot for families with children above the age of 10.
Historic Interest: It was built sometime in the 1840s as a very simple Mennonite farmhouse. Fireplace foundations can be seen in the basement, but they were never finished. There is a small brick bread oven built in the wall of the basement. Milk was bottled and distributed to local neighbors from the 1920s through the 1940s.
Innkeeper(s): Gary & Deb Lintner. $90-215. 5 rooms with PB, 3 with FP, 1 suite and 2 cottages. Breakfast included in rates. Types of meals: Country bkfst, veg bkfst, early coffee/tea and snacks/refreshments. Beds: KQT. TV, VCR, reading lamp, stereo, refrigerator, ceiling fan, snack bar, clock radio, coffeemaker and fireplace in room. Central air. Fax, copier, spa, library, parlor games, tele-

phone and gift shop on premises. Weddings, small meetings and seminars hosted. Amusement parks, antiquing, art galleries, bicycling, fishing, golf, hiking, live theater, museums, parks, shopping, tennis and wineries nearby.
Publicity: *Washingtonian Magazine.*

The Victorian Rose Bed & Breakfast

214 Marietta Ave
Mount Joy, PA 17552-3106
(717)492-0050 (888)313-7494

Circa 1896. Central to Hershey and Gettysburg battlefield, The Victorian Rose in Mount Joy is an elegant but comfortable place from which to explore beautiful Lancaster County. Enjoy the stately guest rooms and a number of elegant areas including the library and a formal living room. Guests are treated to innkeeper Doris Tyson's home-baked treats for breakfast, and to her homemade candies at other times. Pennsylvania Dutch Country is just 12 miles from the inn.
Innkeeper(s): Doris L. Tyson. $75-95. 4 rooms, 3 with PB. Breakfast included in rates. Types of meals: Country bkfst. Beds: Q. TV, VCR, reading lamp, ceiling fan and clock radio in room. Air conditioning. Library, telephone and fireplace on premises. Amusement parks, antiquing, golf, live theater, museums, shopping and wineries nearby.
Publicity: *Lancaster Historic Preservation Trust Featured Home 2001 tour and PA Dutch Visitor & Convention Bureau of Authentic B&B Association.*

Muncy   F12

The Bodine House B&B

307 S Main St
Muncy, PA 17756-1507
(570)546-8949 Fax:(570)546-0607

Circa 1805. This Federal-style townhouse, framed by a white picket fence, is in the National Register. Antique and reproduction furnishings highlight the inn's four fireplaces, the parlor, study and library. A favorite guest room features a walnut canopy bed, hand-stenciled and bordered walls, and a framed sampler

by the innkeeper's great-great-grandmother. Candlelight breakfasts are served beside the fireplace in a gracious Colonial dining room. Also available is a guest cottage with kitchenette.

Historic Interest: The Pennsdale Quaker Meeting House.
Innkeeper(s): David & Marie Louise Smith. $70-125. 3 rooms with PB, 1 with FP and 1 cottage. Breakfast included in rates. Types of meals: Full bkfst, early coffee/tea and afternoon tea. Beds: QDT. Cable TV, reading lamp and turn-down service in room. Air conditioning. TV, VCR, fax, bicycles, library, telephone and fireplace on premises. Small meetings and family reunions hosted. Antiquing, canoeing/kayaking, cross-country skiing, fishing, parks, shopping and sporting events nearby.
Publicity: *Colonial Homes and Philadelphia Inquirer.*

"What an experience, made special by your wonderful hospitality."

New Berlin   H12

The Inn at New Berlin

321 Market St
New Berlin, PA 17855-0390
(570)966-0321 Fax:(570)966-9557
E-mail: lodging@innatnewberlin.com
Web: www.innatnewberlin.com

Circa 1906. Built as a summer home for wealthy Philadelphian Jacob Schoch, experience the inn's splendid blending of Victorian elegance and contemporary convenience. Luxuriate in the comfort of elegantly appointed guest bedrooms. Savor mod-

ern American cuisine with a Pennsylvania flourish at the inn's award-winning Gabriel's restaurant, home base of Executive Chef Scott Brouse. Stroll the herb and vegetable gardens or browse through gourmet food items, home accents and the Christopher Radko ornament gallery in Gabriel's Gifts. Angeline's Garden Spa is newly opened in the restored carriage house, offering professional Swedish massage and a whirlpool tub. Visit nearby attractions and activities that include antiquing, golfing, biking, canoeing and hiking.

Historic Interest: The Slifer House Museum, Packwood House Museum, Mifflinburg Buggy Museum and Bucknell University are only a short drive away. Innkeeper(s): John & Nancy Showers. $109-209. 10 rooms with PB, 3 in FP, 4 with HT & 1 conference room. Breakfast included in rates. Types of meals: Full bkfst, gourmet lunch and gourmet dinner. Restaurant on premises. Beds: Q. Telephone & five with TV (otherwise available upon request) in room. Air conditioning. VCR, fax, copier, brunch & dinner available Wednesday through Sunday & massage on premises. Weddings, small meetings, family reunions & seminars hosted. Antiquing, bicycling, golf, hiking, shopping, yoga & state parks nearby. Publicity: *Philadelphia Inquirer, Washington Post, Country Inns Magazine, Wine Spectator Award of Excellence and PBS (Country Inn Cooking with Gail Greco).*

"I left feeling nurtured and relaxed. You've created a very caring, rich place for regenerating."

New Cumberland J12

Farm Fortune

204 Limekiln Rd
New Cumberland, PA 17070-2429
(717)774-2683 (888)774-2683
E-mail: frmfortune@aol.com
Web: www.farmfortune.com

Circa 1750. This limestone farmhouse boasts an intriguing history that stretches back to its construction in the mid-18th century. The house may even have been a part of the Underground Railroad. With antiques tastefully placed throughout the home, guests will be reminded of the charming times of years past. The innkeepers invite guests to make themselves at home in the keeping room in front of the huge walk-in fireplace. While relaxing, notice the interesting woodwork that makes this farmhouse so unique. Ski the nearby slopes at Ski Roundtop or relax along the banks of the Yellow Breeches Creek and enjoy some local trout fishing.

Historic Interest: The farmhouse is located within 45 minutes of the historic towns of Gettysburg, Carlise, York, Harrisburg, Hershey and Lancaster. Innkeeper(s): Phyllis Combs. $85-185. 4 rooms with PB and 1 cottage. Breakfast included in rates. Types of meals: Full bkfst. Beds: KQDT. Data port, cable TV, VCR, reading lamp, CD player, clock radio, telephone, desk, cottage with fireplace and kitchenette in room. Central air. Fax, copier, parlor games, fireplace and laundry facility on premises. Weddings, small meetings, family reunions and seminars hosted. Antiquing, art galleries, cross-country skiing, downhill skiing, fishing, hiking, live theater, museums and water sports nearby. Publicity: *Early American Life, Patriot and Evening News, Pennsylvania Magazine, Carlisle, Sentinel and York Dispatch.*

New Holland K14

Dilworth Rocking Horse Bed & Breakfast

285 West Main Street
New Holland, PA 17557
(717)354-8674 (800)208-9156 Fax:(717)355-5348
E-mail: info@rockinghorsebb.com
Web: www.rockinghorsebb.com

Circa 1793. Gracing the heart of Amish Country in Lancaster County, this historic two-hundred year-old Federal Stone

Colonial boasts original working fireplaces, wide windowsills and random width wood floors. Play games, do puzzles, watch TV or play the piano in the Gathering Room. Elegant guest bedrooms feature canopy or hand-carved beds and two-person Jacuzzi tubs. The spacious Country Suite also includes a sitting room and private balcony. Begin the morning in the dining room with a hearty candlelight breakfast by the walk-in fireplace. Take a tour of the carving studio in the carriage house behind the inn and watch the owner create reproduction carousel and rocking horses.

Historic Interest: Built in 1793. Walk-in fireplace in dining room, fire in winter months. Original corner cabinets. Innkeeper(s): Millice and Fred Dilworth. $90-149. 4 rooms with PB, 4 with FP and 1 suite. Breakfast and snacks/refreshments included in rates. Types of meals: Country bkfst and veg bkfst. Beds: KQT. Modem hook-up, cable TV, VCR, reading lamp, clock radio, fireplace and Jacuzzi tubs in room. Central air. Fax, copier, bicycles, parlor games and gift shop on premises. Family reunions hosted. Amusement parks, antiquing, art galleries, bicycling, golf, live theater, museums, parks, shopping and wineries nearby.

New Hope I18

Cordials B&B of New Hope

143 Old York Road
New Hope, PA 18938
(215)862-3919 (877)219-1009 Fax:(215)862-3917
Web: www.cordialsbb.com

Circa 1949. The name of this two-and-a-half-story inn reflects the cordial way of life imparted here. On Friday and Saturday afternoons a light snack with wine or a nonalcoholic beverage in crystal stemware is served. Request a wake-up call after a comfortable night's sleep in one of the air conditioned guest bedrooms. Relax on private decks and balconies with views of the colorful annuals, statuary, hemlocks and pines. Fresh flowers adorn the tables where a daily continental-plus breakfast is enjoyed. Fresh fruit, cake, cookies and candy are available throughout the day. It is a short walk to local antique shops and four-star restaurants. Historical landmarks are seen on a train ride or a mule-drawn barge along the Delaware Canal.

Innkeeper(s): Ciro. $73-145. 66 rooms, 6 with PB. Breakfast, afternoon tea and snacks/refreshments included in rates. Types of meals: Cont plus and veg bkfst. Beds: Q. Cable TV, VCR and refrigerator in room. Central air. Fax, copier, spa, telephone and fireplace on premises. Family reunions hosted. Amusement parks, antiquing, art galleries, bicycling, canoeing/kayaking, fishing, golf, hiking, horseback riding, live theater, museums, parks, shopping, tennis, water sports and wineries nearby. Publicity: *Delaware Today Magazine.*

Hollyhedge B&B

6987 Upper York Rd
New Hope, PA 18938-9511
(215)862-3136 Fax:(215)862-0960

Circa 1700. This handsome stone manor rests on 20 acres with green lawns, a natural pond and a small stream. French, American and English antiques are found throughout the inn. Some rooms have private entrances and some feature fireplaces. The owners are former restaurateurs and provide a notable breakfast. Catered weddings and corporate retreats are popular here.

Innkeeper(s): Diane Malloy. $105-200. 15 rooms with PB, 2 with FP, 2 suites and 1 conference room. Types of meals: Full bkfst. Beds: K. Reading lamp and ceiling fan in room. Air conditioning. VCR, bicycles, child care, telephone and fireplace on premises. Weddings, small meetings, family reunions and seminars hosted. Amusement parks, antiquing, live theater and shopping nearby.

Hollyleaf Inn

677 Durham Rd (Rt 413)
New Hope, PA 18940
(215)598-3100 Fax:(215)598-3423
E-mail: info@hollyleaf.com
Web: www.hollyleaf.com

Circa 1700. More than five rolling acres of scenic Bucks County countryside surround this handsome former farmhouse named for the welcoming 35-foot holly trees at the entrance. Enjoy afternoon refreshments in the parlor or on the patio. Romantic guest bedrooms are appointed with antiques, lace and fresh flowers. Evening turn-down service with bedtime chocolate is provided. In the morning, feel full after a satisfying breakfast. Relax in the hammock, pitch horseshoes, stroll along the Delaware River or browse through quaint shops downtown.

Historic Interest: Washington Crossing State Park (5 miles), Parry Mansion (6 miles), Pennsbury Manor (20 miles).
Innkeeper(s): Janice Sullivan. $95-175. 5 rooms with PB, 2 with FP and 1 conference room. Breakfast and afternoon tea included in rates. Types of meals: Full gourmet bkfst, early coffee/tea and snacks/refreshments. Beds: QD. Cable TV, reading lamp, clock radio and turn-down service in room. Central air. VCR, fax, copier, library, parlor games, telephone and fireplace on premises. Family reunions hosted. Antiquing, art galleries, bicycling, canoeing/kayaking, cross-country skiing, downhill skiing, fishing, golf, hiking, horseback riding, live theater, museums, parks, shopping, tennis, water sports and wineries nearby.
Publicity: Long Island Newsday, Bucks County Courier Times, Trentonian, Bucks County Courier Times and Philadelphia Inquirer.

"The accommodations were lovely and the breakfasts delicious and unusual, but it is really the graciousness of our hosts that made the weekend memorable."

Logan Inn

10 W Ferry St
New Hope, PA 18938-1312
(215)862-2300 Fax:(215)862-3931

Circa 1727. This classic colonial is Bucks County's oldest continuously run inn, and one of the five oldest in the country. Recently renovated, old and new are carefully blended to offer intimate luxury and comfort. Tasteful guest bedrooms are furnished with antiques and period pieces. The tavern's original woodwork, fireplace and restored murals offer a warm and inviting taste of history and late-night menu selections. Choose to dine in the enclosed stained glass Garden Dining Room, the glass-enclosed dining porches or alfresco on the tented patio. Experience the area's quaint sites and pleasurable activities. Ask about taking a horse-drawn carriage ride.

Innkeeper(s): Pam & Carl Asplundh. $115-230. 16 rooms with PB and 1 conference room. Breakfast included in rates. Types of meals: Cont, lunch and dinner. Restaurant on premises. Beds: KQD. Modem hook-up, data port, cable TV, reading lamp, telephone and voice mail in room. Air conditioning. Small meetings, family reunions and seminars hosted. Amusement parks, antiquing, art galleries, bicycling, canoeing/kayaking, fishing, hiking, horseback riding, live theater, museums, parks, shopping, tennis and wineries nearby.
Publicity: The Philadelphia Inquirer and The Home News.

"...the food was PERFECTION and served in a gracious and extremely courteous manner...our intentions had been to explore different restaurants, but there was no reason to explore, we had found what we wanted."

Pineapple Hill

1324 River Rd
New Hope, PA 18938
(215)862-1790 (888)866-8404
E-mail: innkeeper@pineapplehill.com
Web: www.pineapplehill.com

Circa 1790. The pineapple always has been a sign of friendship and hospitality, and guests at Pineapple Hill are sure to experience both. The inn is secluded on six private acres, yet it's just four miles from town. Antique shops, flea markets, auctions and plenty of outdoor activities are all close by. All rooms and suites include a fireplace, cable TV, phone and private bath. A full breakfast is served at individual tables, afternoon refreshments and evening sherry are also offered. Inside the walls of a stone barn is a tiled swimming pool.

Innkeeper(s): Kathy & Charles. $116-249. 9 rooms with PB, 3 suites and 1 conference room. Breakfast and afternoon tea included in rates. Types of meals: Full bkfst, early coffee/tea and snacks/refreshments. Beds: KQ. Cable TV, reading lamp, clock radio, telephone, desk, living room and private deck in room. Air conditioning. Fax, swimming, parlor games and fireplace on premises. Weddings, small meetings, family reunions and seminars hosted. Antiquing, fishing, live theater, parks, shopping, water sports and museums nearby.

"It was a delightful stay in every way. The clicking door latches and the smells of breakfast cooking wafting up to the bedroom were reminiscent of my childhood stays at my grandparents' farmhouse."

Porches on the Towpath

20 Fishers Aly
New Hope, PA 18938-1313
(215)862-3277 Fax:(215)862-1833
E-mail: info@porchesnewhope.com
Web: www.porchesnewhope.com

Circa 1815. Carefully preserved yet fully renovated, this whitewashed Federal brick house was originally built as a granary. Relax in tranquil elegance on the two-story wraparound porch that fronts the historic Delaware Canal in scenic Bucks County, or sit and admire the perennial gardens. Watch the mule barges float by from a comfy overstuffed chair in the library. Appealing guest bedrooms blend French, American and English antiques. The attic suite, on the entire third floor, boasts a clawfoot tub, and dormer sitting area with a view. Cottages are also available. Savor a complete country breakfast in the dining room that may include fresh fruit with Grand Marnier sauce, blueberry pancakes, French toast and a variety of meats. Private off-street parking is provided, and it is an easy walk to the local attractions.

Innkeeper(s): John, Billy and Chrissie. $95-195. 6 rooms with PB and 2 cottages. Breakfast and snacks/refreshments included in rates. Types of meals: Full gourmet bkfst, early coffee/tea and room service. Beds: QD. Reading lamp in room. Central air. TV, fax, bicycles, library and parlor games on premises. Family reunions hosted. Antiquing, art galleries, bicycling, canoeing/kayaking, fishing, golf, hiking, horseback riding, live theater, museums, parks, shopping, water sports and wineries nearby.

New Kingstown   J11

Kanaga House B&B Inn

6940 Carlisle Pike (US Rt 11)
New Kingstown, PA 17072
(717)766-8654 (877)9KA-NAGA Fax:(717)697-3908
E-mail: stay@kanagahouse.com
Web: www.kanagahouse.com

Circa 1775. Stay in this restored 1775 stone house while visiting the area's many tourist attractions such as Gettysburg Civil

War Battlefield, Hershey Chocolate World, Lancaster Dutch Country or Harrisburg (the state capital). The well-appointed guest bedrooms offer canopy beds, and one boasts a fireplace. Tree-studded grounds and a large gazebo are perfect for weddings. The first-floor rooms and catering staff also enhance business meetings and retreats. Walk the nearby Appalachian Trail, or fly fish in the Yellow Breeches and Letort Springs. Innkeeper(s): Mary Jane & Dave Kretzing. $85-125. 6 rooms with PB, 1 with FP and 1 conference room. Breakfast included in rates. Types of meals: Full bkfst and early coffee/tea. Beds: Q. TV, reading lamp, refrigerator, clock radio, telephone and desk in room. Air conditioning. VCR, copier, fireplace and gazebo with table and chairs on premises. Weddings, small meetings and seminars hosted. Amusement parks, antiquing, downhill skiing, live theater and shopping nearby.

New Milford   D15

Lynn-Lee House Bed & Breakfast

143 Main St
New Milford, PA 18834-2111
(570)465-3505
Web: www.lynn-lee.com

Circa 1868. An ageless warmth and gracious hospitality are found all year at this Second Empire Victorian bed & breakfast, only two and a half hours from Philadelphia and New York City. Wide board pine floors, original full-length windows, antiques and period furnishings enhance the ambiance of a tranquil and refined way of life. Converse around the tiled fireplace in the living room or play a game. Fresh flowers, quilts, down pillows and scented linens appeal to the senses in the guest bedrooms. Enjoy soaking in the seven-foot clawfoot tub. Awake to indulge in breakfast favorites and specialties in the formal dining room or front porch. In the side yard, Adirondack chairs are great for butterfly watching.
Innkeeper(s): Eleanor & Chuck Lempke. Call for rates. 4 rooms with PB. Breakfast, afternoon tea and snacks/refreshments included in rates. Types of meals: Full gourmet bkfst and early coffee/tea. Beds: Q. Modem hook-up, reading lamp, ceiling fan and turn-down service in room. TV, VCR, parlor games, telephone and fireplace on premises. Small meetings and family reunions hosted. Antiquing, bicycling, canoeing/kayaking, cross-country skiing, downhill skiing, fishing, golf, hiking, parks and shopping nearby.
Publicity: New York Times, WNEP and Channel 16.

North East   B3

Grape Arbor Bed and Breakfast

51 East Main St
North East, PA 16428-1340
(814)725-0048 (866)725-0048 Fax:(814)725-5740
E-mail: info@grapearborbandb.com
Web: www.grapearborbandb.com

Circa 1832. Two side-by-side brick Federal mansions with Victorian embellishments have been restored to preserve their antiquity yet provide today's conveniences. Built in the early 1830s as private homes, their history includes having served as a stagecoach tavern, primary school, and possibly a stop on the Underground Railroad. Watch videos, play games or read a book by the fire in the library. Socialize over hors d'oeuvres in the parlor. Elegant guest bedrooms and suites are named for local varieties of grapes and feature antiques, reproductions, data ports, VCRs and fine toiletries. Two main breakfast dishes, pastries and breads, a hot or cold fruit sampler, juice and freshly ground coffee are enjoyed in the formal Dining Room or the

light and airy Sun Porch. A guest refrigerator is stocked with beverages and homemade treats are always available.
Historic Interest: The Grape Arbor consists of two of the oldest brick buildings in town which have been a tavern, the town's first kindergarten and possibly a stop on the Underground Railroad.
Innkeeper(s): Dave and Peggy Hauser. $80-130. 7 rooms with PB, 1 with FP and 3 suites. Breakfast and snacks/refreshments included in rates. Types of meals: Full gourmet bkfst and early coffee/tea. Beds: KQD. Data port, cable TV, reading lamp, refrigerator, ceiling fan, clock radio, telephone, coffeemaker, turn-down service, desk, voice mail, fireplace and Jacuzzi in room. Central air. VCR, fax, copier, library, parlor games and fireplace on premises. Weddings, small meetings, family reunions and seminars hosted. Amusement parks, antiquing, beach, bicycling, cross-country skiing, downhill skiing, fishing, golf, hiking, horseback riding, live theater, parks and wineries nearby.

Palmyra   J13

The Hen-Apple B&B

409 S Lingle Ave
Palmyra, PA 17078-9321
(717)838-8282
Web: www.henapplebb.com

Circa 1825. Located at the edge of town, this Georgian farmhouse is surrounded by an acre of lawns and gardens. There are antiques and country pieces throughout. Breakfast is served to guests in the dining room or on the screened veranda. Hershey is two miles away, Lancaster and Gettysburg are nearby.
Innkeeper(s): Flo & Harold Eckert. $85-95. 6 rooms with PB. Breakfast included in rates. Types of meals: Full bkfst. Beds: QDT. Reading lamp, ceiling fan and clock radio in room. Air conditioning. Parlor games on premises. Amusement parks, antiquing, fishing, live theater, parks, shopping, sporting events and water sports nearby.
Publicity: Pennsylvania Magazine.

Paradise   K14

Creekside Inn

44 Leacock Rd
Paradise, PA 17562-0435
(717)687-0333 (866)604-2574
E-mail: cathy@thecreeksideinn.com
Web: www.thecreeksideinn.com

Circa 1781. This 18th-century Georgian home was built by David Witmer, a prominent citizen and member of one of the first families to settle in the area. The stone exterior features a gable roof with five bay windows. Relaxing guest quarters feature special amenities such as four-poster beds with Amish

quilts. The Cameo and Creekside rooms boast fireplaces. A hearty, full breakfast is served each morning. Antique and outlet shopping, as well as a variety of sporting activities are nearby.
Historic Interest: The inn is located in the heart of Lancaster County's Amish area, and the innkeepers say it's not uncommon to hear the sounds of Amish buggies as they travel down the road. Longwood Gardens and the Winterthur museum are 30 minutes away, and Hershey Park is a 45-minute drive.
Innkeeper(s): Catherine & Dennis Zimmermann. $85-110. 5 rooms with PB. Breakfast included in rates. Types of meals: Full gourmet bkfst and afternoon tea. Beds: Q. Antiquing, fishing and live theater nearby.

Philadelphia   K17

1011 Clinton B&B

1011 Clinton Street
Philadelphia, PA 19107
(215)923-8144 Fax:(215)923-7007
E-mail: 1011@concentric.net
Web: www.teneleven.com

Circa 1836. Just a five-minute walk to the historic sites of the city, this 1836 restored brick Federal Townhouse sits on a quiet, tree-lined street. Innkeeper Judith takes pride in providing the utmost service, comfort, convenience and privacy. Relax in the secluded, flower-filled courtyard. Each spacious suite features a fully equipped kitchen stocked with breakfast foods and beverages. Most have reclining chairs, sofas and fireplaces in the living rooms. Business is easily handled with individual phone lines, computer access and large workspaces. Well-behaved dogs are welcome.
Historic Interest: Our street, Clinton Street, is a registered historic street, the brick townhouses were built in 1836. You feel like you have stepped back in time.
Innkeeper(s): Judith Seraphin. $145-200. 5 suites, 3 with FP. Breakfast and snacks/refreshments included in rates. Types of meals: Cont, veg bkfst, early coffee/tea and room service. Beds: KQ. Modem hook-up, cable TV, VCR, reading lamp, refrigerator, ceiling fan, clock radio, telephone, coffeemaker, desk, voice mail, fireplace, full kitchens and living rooms in room. Air conditioning. Fax, parlor games and fireplace on premises. Amusement parks, antiquing, art galleries, bicycling, live theater, museums, parks, shopping, sporting events, tennis, Liberty Bell and Independence Hall National Park nearby.
Publicity: *National Geographic's Travelers Magazine, Elle Decor Magazine and Philadelphia Magazine.*

Alexander Inn

Spruce at 12th Street
Philadelphia, PA 19107-5908
(215)923-3535 (877)253-9466 Fax:(215)923-1004
E-mail: info@alexanderinn.com
Web: www.alexanderinn.com

Circa 1898. The Alexander Inn has resided in the center of Philadelphia for more than a century. Today, the historic building offers 48 guest rooms decorated in contemporary style and each room features a variety of artwork. Some of the amenities offered to guests include a buffet-style continental breakfast, use of the inn's 24-hour fitness center and telephones with modem ports. For an extra fee, parking is available at a nearby garage. The inn is close enough to walk to many city center locations, including the Betsy Ross House and the Liberty Bell, both of which are a 10-minute walk from the inn.
Innkeeper(s): Mark Najera. $89-149. 48 rooms with PB. Breakfast included in rates. Types of meals: Cont plus and early coffee/tea. Beds: KQDT. Modem hook-up, data port, cable TV, reading lamp, clock radio, telephone, hair dryers and irons/ironing boards in room. Air conditioning. Fax, fireplace and fitness center on premises. Weddings, small meetings & seminars hosted. Antiquing, art galleries, bicycling, live theater, museums, parks, shopping & sporting events nearby.
Publicity: *Ch. 29 and Ch. 06.*

Gables B&B

4520 Chester Ave
Philadelphia, PA 19143-3707
(215)662-1918 Fax:(215)662-1918
E-mail: gablesbb@aol.com
Web: www.gablesbb.com

Circa 1889. Located in the University City section, this red-brick Queen Anne Victorian has three stories and offers off-street parking. Chestnut and cherry woodwork, a grand entry hall and sitting rooms furnished with antiques make this a popular site. A

wraparound porch overlooks the inn's gardens of perennials, roses, dogwood and Japanese cherry and magnolia trees. The Christmas Room has mahogany antiques and a queen four-poster bed, while the Tower Room has a working fireplace and a settee tucked into the turret. Another room offers a soaking tub and sun porch. This inn received Philadelphia Magazine's four-heart award and the "Best of Philly 1996" award as an urban getaway.
Innkeeper(s): Don Caskey & Warren Cederholm. $85-135. 10 rooms with PB, 2 with FP & 1 suite. Breakfast included in rates. Types of meals: Full bkfst. Beds: QD. Cable TV, reading lamp, clock radio, telephone & desk in room. Air conditioning. Fax, library, parlor games, fireplace, Internet hookup & computer station on premises. Antiquing, live theater, parks, shopping & sporting events nearby.
Publicity: *Philadelphia, Victorian Homes and WGBH Documentary.*

Gaskill House Bed & Breakfast

312 Gaskill Street
Philadelphia, PA 19147
(215)413-0669
E-mail: gaskillbnb@aol.com
Web: www.gaskillhouse.com

Circa 1828. Located in the heart of Society Hill's Historic District, this urban oasis is listed in the National Register. A double townhouse built with Federal architecture, the home has been restored recently. Equipped with modern comforts, the gracious furnishings and decor of the 18th century have been retained. Elegant guest bedrooms offer spacious tranquility, whirlpool baths, fireplaces and and abundance of useful amenities. A made-to-order American breakfast is a welcome way to start the day. Guests can explore the many sites of the city.
Innkeeper(s): Guy Davis. $120-200. 4 rooms with PB, 3 with FP. Breakfast included in rates. Types of meals: Full bkfst. Beds: Q. Modem hook-up, cable TV, VCR, reading lamp, CD player, ceiling fan, telephone, desk, hot tub/spa and fireplace in room. Central air. Fax, copier, spa, library, fireplace and laundry facility on premises. Family reunions hosted. Antiquing, art galleries, bicycling, live theater, museums, parks, shopping and sporting events nearby.
Publicity: *Philadelphia Magazine.*

The Penn's View Hotel

Front & Market Streets
Philadelphia, PA 19106
(215)922-7600 (800)331-7634 Fax:(215)922-7642
Web: www.pennsviewhotel.com

Circa 1828. The original portion of Penn's View Hotel dates to 1828. Today, the elegant hotel includes 52 guest rooms and suites, some of which include a fireplace and whirlpool tub. Ristorante Panorama, the hotel's gourmet restaurant, offers acclaimed Italian cuisine, as well as a wine bar with more than 120 different varieties. The hotel looks out to the Delaware River and is situated within walking distance to many historic sites.
Innkeeper(s): The Sena Family. $120-225. 52 rooms. Breakfast included in rates. Types of meals: Cont plus, lunch and dinner. Restaurant on premises. Beds: KQ. Cable TV, reading lamp, clock radio, telephone, desk and lighted vanity mirror in room. Air conditioning. Fax and copier on premises. Small meetings and family reunions hosted. Antiquing, live theater, parks, shopping, sporting events and tennis nearby.
Publicity: *New York Times.*

Rittenhouse Square B&B

1715 Rittenhouse Square
Philadelphia, PA 19103
(215)546-6500 (877)791-6500 Fax:(215)546-8787
E-mail: innkeeper@rittenhousebb.com
Web: www.rittenhousebb.com

Circa 1911. Experience elegant luxury at this comfortably renovated carriage house, internationally renown for business or pleasure. Impressive art, impeccable decor, lavish furnishings and extraordinary service are the hallmarks of this inn. The guest bedrooms are spectacular, tranquil retreats. Distinctive amenities include CD players, triple sheeting, turndown service, computer workstations, plush robes and marble bathrooms. Enjoy breakfast in The Cafe and early evening wine and snacks in the gorgeous lobby.

Innkeeper(s): Harriet S. Seltzer. $209-299. 10 rooms with PB, 1 with FP, 2 suites and 1 conference room. Breakfast and snacks/refreshments included in rates. Types of meals: Cont plus. Beds: KQD. Modem hook-up, data port, cable TV, CD player, telephone, coffeemaker, turn-down service, voice mail and fireplace in room. Central air. Fax, copier, parlor games, fireplace and laundry facility on premises. Small meetings hosted. Antiquing, art galleries, museums, shopping and sporting events nearby.

Thomas Bond House

129 S 2nd St
Philadelphia, PA 19106-3039
(215)923-8523 (800)845-2663 Fax:(215)923-8504
E-mail: ctheal@dddcompany.com
Web: www.winston-salem-inn.com/philadelphia

Circa 1769. One way to enjoy the history of Philadelphia is to treat yourself to a stay at this Colonial-period, Georgian-style residence in Independence National Historical Park. White shutters and cornices accentuate the brick exterior, often draped in red, white and blue bunting. A finely executed interior renova-

tion provides a handsome background for the inn's collection of Chippendale reproductions, four-poster beds and drop front desks. Working fireplaces, phones, hair dryers, television and whirlpool tubs provide additional comforts.

Innkeeper(s): Rita McGuire. $95-175. 12 rooms with PB, 2 with FP, 2 suites and 1 conference room. Breakfast included in rates. Types of meals: Full bkfst and early coffee/tea. Beds: QDT. Reading lamp, clock radio, telephone, desk and some with whirlpool tubs in room. Air conditioning. TV, fax, copier, fireplace, free local calls and evening wine and cheese and freshly baked cookies on premises. Weddings, small meetings, family reunions and seminars hosted. Amusement parks, antiquing, fishing, live theater, parks, shopping, sporting events and historic sites nearby.

Publicity: *Mid-Atlantic Country, Washingtonian, Washington Post, Philadelphia Inquirer, Home & Garden, Boston Globe, Heritage Travel and Top 25 Historical Inns & Hotels.*

"Your service was excellent, congenial, made us feel comfortable and welcome."

Pittsburgh I3

The Priory

614 Pressley St
Pittsburgh, PA 15212-5616
(412)231-3338 Fax:(412)231-4838

Circa 1888. The Priory, now a European-style hotel, was built to provide lodging for Benedictine priests traveling through

Pittsburgh. It is adjacent to Pittsburgh's Grand Hall at the Priory in historic East Allegheny. The inn's design and maze of rooms and corridors give it a distinctly Old World flavor. All rooms are decorated with Victorian furnishings.

Historic Interest: Mexican War Streets Neighborhood, Fort Pitt Blockhouse & Point State Park.

Innkeeper(s): John and Suzanne Graf. $119-155. 24 rooms with PB, 3 suites and 1 conference room. Breakfast included in rates. Types of meals: Cont plus. Beds: KQD. Limited handicap access.

Publicity: *Pittsburgh Press, US Air, Country Inns,*

Innsider, Youngstown Vindicator, Travel & Leisure, Gourmet, Mid-Atlantic Country and National Geographic Traveler.

"Although we had been told that the place was elegant, we were hardly prepared for the richness of detail. We felt as though we were guests in a manor."

Point Pleasant I18

Tattersall Inn

River Road & Cafferty Road
Point Pleasant, PA 18950
(215)297-8233 (800)297-4988 Fax:(215)297-5093
E-mail: tattersallinn@aol.com
Web: www.tattersallinn.com

Circa 1750. This Bucks County plastered fieldstone house with its 18-inch-thick walls, broad porches and wainscoted entry hall was the home of local mill owners for 150 years. Today it offers a peaceful place to relax, rebuild and enjoy the bucolic surroundings in Olde Bucks. Breakfast is served in the dining room or on the porch. The Colonial-style common room features a beamed ceiling and walk-in fireplace. Guests gather there or on the porch for snacks and a glass of wine in the late afternoon.

Historic Interest: Washington Crossing Park (12 miles), William Penn's Pennsbury Manor (25 miles), Valley Forge (40 miles), 11 covered bridges (15 miles).

Innkeeper(s): John & Lori Gleason. $120-155. 6 rooms with PB, 2 with FP and 1 suite. Breakfast and afternoon tea included in rates. Types of meals: Full bkfst. Beds: Q. Air conditioning. Fax, copier, library, parlor games, telephone, fireplace and refrigerator on premises. Small meetings and family reunions hosted. Antiquing, canoeing/kayaking, cross-country skiing, fishing, live theater, parks, shopping, water sports, bike paths and quaint towns nearby.

Publicity: *Courier Times, Philadelphia, New York Times and WYOU.*

"Thank you for your hospitality and warm welcome. The inn is charming and has a wonderful ambiance."

Rebersburg G10

Centre Mills Enterprises

461 Smullton Road
Rebersburg, PA 16872
(814)349-8000 Fax:(814)349-5340
E-mail: maria@centremills.com
Web: www.centremills.com

Circa 1813. Discover the special pleasures of country life at this fully restored stone house and 1840 addition in the heart of an Amish farm community. Now listed in the National Register, this 26-acre estate was originally owned by a Pennsylvania German miller. The large and inviting Great Room is highlighted by a walk-in fireplace. Relax on a deck overlooking the meadow and Elk Creek at the foot of Brush Mountain. Comfortable guest bedrooms are furnished with period antiques. Share a wholesome breakfast around a sawbuck table in the dining room. Savor recipes made from fresh, local ingredients. Walk along the limestone stream or fly fish for wild trout.

Innkeeper(s): Maria Davison. $85-125. 4 rooms with PB. Breakfast and snacks/refreshments included in rates. Types of meals: Full gourmet bkfst, veg bkfst, early coffee/tea, picnic lunch and afternoon tea. Beds: Q. Reading lamp and clock radio in room. Central air. TV, VCR, fax, copier, library, pet boarding, parlor games, telephone and fireplace on premises. Weddings, small meetings and family reunions hosted. Antiquing, art galleries, bicycling, canoeing/kayaking, cross-country skiing, downhill skiing, fishing, golf, hiking, live theater, museums, parks, shopping, sporting events, tennis and wineries nearby.

Red Lion   K13

Red Lion Bed & Breakfast

101 S Franklin St
Red Lion, PA 17356
(717)244-4739 Fax:(717)246-9202
E-mail: staywithus@redlionbandb.com
Web: www.redlionbandb.com

Circa 1920. Explore one of the more popular regions of the state while staying at this unpretentious and quiet three-story brick, Federal-style home. Snuggle up next to the fireplace in the living room with a book from the well-stocked collection of reading material. Sip a cool iced tea on the enclosed sun porch or outside garden patio. Half of the six quaint and comfortable guest bedrooms offer a full bath and queen-size bed. Twin beds and cots are also available for families or groups traveling together. Breakfasts are substantial with quiche, pancakes, stuffed French toast, fresh baked rolls and muffins served alongside fruit or granola. The town has antique and craft shops and is within a 45-minute drive of vineyards, the Amish country of Lancaster, Hershey and the Gettysburg Battlefield.
Innkeeper(s): George & Danielle Sanders. $65-85. 6 rooms, 3 with PB and 1 conference room. Breakfast included in rates. Types of meals: Full bkfst. Beds: QT. TV, VCR, ceiling fan and clock radio in room. Air conditioning. Library, parlor games, telephone, fireplace, off-street parking and modem hook-up on premises. Small meetings hosted. Amusement parks, antiquing, canoeing/kayaking, fishing, golf, hiking, horseback riding, live theater, parks, water sports and wineries nearby.

Reinholds   J14

Brownstone Colonial Inn

590 Galen Hall Rd
Reinholds, PA 17569-9420
(717)484-4460 (877)464-9862 Fax:(717)484-4460
E-mail: info@brownstonecolonialinn.com
Web: www.brownstonecolonialinn.com

Circa 1790. Early German Mennonite settlers built this sandstone farmhouse in 1790. It graces seven scenic acres amidst Amish countryside. Feel relaxed and pampered at this fully restored inn. Guest bedrooms and a suite boast random-width plank floors, locally handcrafted period-authentic furniture, sleigh or pencil post beds and antique Shaker peg boards. Enjoy a hearty country breakfast in the homestead's original smokehouse with brick floor, ceiling beams and open hearth fireplace. Start the day with fresh juices, homemade pastries and jams, a hot entree and fruits grown on-site. Stroll by the fish pond and gardens, or walk the nearby nature trails. An abundance of outlet and antique malls as well as historical and cultural sites are minutes away.
Historic Interest: Once thought to have been a stage coach stop between Lancaster and Reading.
Innkeeper(s): Brenda & Mark Miller. $85-115. 3 rooms, 2 with PB and 1 suite. Breakfast and snacks/refreshments included in rates. Types of meals: Full bkfst, early coffee/tea and afternoon tea. Beds: QDT. Modem hook-up, reading lamp, clock radio and desk in room. Central air. VCR, telephone and fireplace on premises. Small meetings hosted. Amusement parks, antiquing, cross-country skiing, fishing, golf, hiking, horseback riding, live theater, museums, parks, shopping, sporting events, water sports and wineries nearby.

"We can't wait to tell friends and family about your paradise."

Ronks   K14

Candlelight Inn B&B

2574 Lincoln Hwy E
Ronks, PA 17572-9771
(717)299-6005 (800)772-2635 Fax:(717)299-6397
E-mail: candleinn@aol.com
Web: www.candleinn.com

Circa 1920. Located in the Pennsylvania Dutch area, this Federal-style house offers a side porch for enjoying the home's acre and a half of tall trees and surrounding Amish farmland. Guest rooms feature Victorian decor. Three rooms include a Jacuzzi tub and fireplace. The inn's gourmet breakfast, which might include a creme caramel French toast, is served by candlelight. The innkeepers are professional classical musicians. Lancaster is five miles to the east.
Innkeeper(s): Tim & Heidi Soberick. $85-169. 7 rooms with PB, 3 with FP, 3 with HT. Breakfast included in rates. Types of meals: Full gourmet bkfst. Beds: KQT. Reading lamp, clock radio, desk, amaretto, robes, three with Jacuzzi and fireplaces in room. Air conditioning. Fax, parlor games, telephone, fireplace, badminton and croquet on premises. Weddings, small meetings, family reunions and seminars hosted. Amusement parks, antiquing, cross-country skiing, downhill skiing, fishing, live theater, parks, shopping, sporting events and water sports nearby.
Publicity: *Lancaster Daily News, Pennsylvania Dutch Traveler and Pennsylvania Intelligencer Journal.*

Scranton   E16

The Weeping Willow Inn

308 N Eaton Rd
Scranton, PA 18657
(570)836-7257

Circa 1836. This Colonial, set on 22 acres, is filled with beautiful antiques and an elegant traditional decor. The home's original pine floor is topped with Oriental rugs. Breakfasts, with a fresh fruit parfait and perhaps apple-cinnamon French toast, are served by candlelight. The nearby Susquehanna River and mountains provide ample activities, from hiking to fishing and canoeing. Antique and craft shops also are plentiful in the area.

Innkeeper(s): Patty & Randy Ehrenzeller. $75-95. 3 rooms with PB. Breakfast included in rates. Types of meals: Full bkfst. Beds: QD. Reading lamp, clock radio, telephone and turn-down service in room. Air conditioning. Parlor games and fireplace on premises. Antiquing, cross-country skiing, downhill skiing, fishing, golf, parks, shopping, tennis and water sports nearby.
Publicity: *WNEP TV and local travel agency.*

Shippensburg   K10

Field & Pine B&B

2155 Ritner Hwy
Shippensburg, PA 17257-9756
(717)776-7179
E-mail: fieldpine@aol.com
Web: www.cvbednbreakfasts.com/field

Circa 1790. Local limestone was used to build this stone house, located on the main wagon road to Baltimore and Washington. Originally, it was a tavern and weigh station. The house is surrounded by stately pines, and sheep graze on the inn's 80 acres. The bedrooms are hand-stenciled and furnished with quilts and antiques.

Innkeeper(s): Mary Ellen & Allan Williams. $70-85. 3 rooms, 1 with PB, 1 with FP and 1 suite. Breakfast and snacks/refreshments included in rates. Types of meals: Full gourmet bkfst and early coffee/tea. Beds: QDT. TV, reading lamp, stereo, clock radio, turn-down service and desk in room. Air conditioning. VCR, telephone and fireplace on premises. Weddings, small meetings and family reunions hosted. Antiquing, fishing, parks and shopping nearby. Publicity: *Central Pennsylvania Magazine.*

"Our visit in this lovely country home has been most delightful. The ambiance of antiques and tasteful decorating exemplifies real country living."

McLean House B&B

80 W King St
Shippensburg, PA 17257-1212
(717)530-1390 (800)610-0330 Fax:(717)530-1390

Circa 1798. This inn is filled with an eclectic collection of furnishings, gathered from the innkeepers' 30 years of moves while in the army. Located in the historic district, the house features Italianate-style architecture. Trout-filled Branch Creek borders the property and attracts mallard ducks, often seen

from the dining area during breakfast. The innkeepers will advise you on visiting the dozens of antique and flea markets in the area. If you'd like, they also will arrange to escort you to your first auction.

Innkeeper(s): Bob & Jan Rose. $55. 3 rooms with PB. Breakfast included in rates. Types of meals: Full bkfst. Beds: D. Reading lamp, ceiling fan, clock radio and desk in room. Air conditioning. VCR, fax, swimming, parlor games, telephone, fireplace and piano for guests on premises. Weddings and small meetings hosted. Antiquing, fishing, parks and shopping nearby.

Somerset   K5

Quill Haven Country Inn

1519 North Center Ave
Somerset, PA 15501-7001
(814)443-4514 (866)784-5522 Fax:(814)445-1376
E-mail: quill@quillhaven.com
Web: www.quillhaven.com

Circa 1918. Set on three acres that were once part of a chicken and turkey farm, this historic Arts & Crafts-style home offers guest rooms, each individually appointed. The Bridal Suite includes a four-poster wrought iron bed and sunken tub in the bath. The Country Room includes a decorative pot-bellied stove. Antiques, reproductions and stained-glass lamps decorate the rooms. Guests are treated to a full breakfast with items such as baked grapefruit or apples, homemade breads and entrees such as stuffed French toast or a specialty casserole of ham, cheese and potatoes. Guests can spend the day boating or swimming at nearby Youghiogheny Reservoir, take a whitewater-rafting trip, bike or hike through the scenic countryside, ski at one of three ski resorts in the area or shop at antique stores, outlets and flea markets. Frank Lloyd Wright's Fallingwater is another nearby attraction.

Innkeeper(s): Carol & Rowland Miller. $85-115. 4 rooms with PB. Breakfast and snacks/refreshments included in rates. Types of meals: Full bkfst and

early coffee/tea. Beds: KQ. Cable TV, VCR, reading lamp, ceiling fan, clock radio, turn-down service and heated mattress pad in room. Air conditioning. Library, parlor games, telephone, outdoor hot tub, common room with fireplace and mini kitchenette on premises. Small meetings and family reunions hosted. Amusement parks, antiquing, bicycling, canoeing/kayaking, cross-country skiing, downhill skiing, fishing, golf, hiking, horseback riding, live theater, parks, shopping, tennis, water sports, wineries and skiing at Seven Springs and Hidden Valley. Located in the Laurel Highlands nearby. Publicity: *Westsylvania Magazine.*

"What a beautiful memory we will have of our first B&B experience! We've never felt quite so pampered in all our 25 years of marriage."

South Sterling   F16

French Manor

Huckleberry Rd
South Sterling, PA 18460
(570)676-3244 (800)523-8200
E-mail: info@thefrenchmanor.com
Web: www.thefrenchmanor.com

Circa 1932. In a storybook setting this country inn and restaurant sits atop Huckleberry Mountain with views of the northern Poconos. Built by local craftsman and artisans of German and Italian descent, the impressive architecture of this fieldstone chateau includes an imported Spanish slate roof, Romanesque arched entrance and cypress interior. Luxuriously romantic accommodations offer a generous variety of upscale amenities. Manor house guest rooms boast period furnishings. The unique two-story Turret Suite boasts a living room and private staircase to the bedroom. Stay in a fireplace or Jacuzzi suite in the adjacent Carriage House with private wrought-iron balconies. Savor breakfast in the elegant dining room with a forty-foot vaulted ceiling and twin fireplaces. Schedule an appointment with the in-house massage therapist after hiking or biking the miles of trails on the grounds.

Innkeeper(s): Ron and Mary Kay Logan. $139-285. 15 rooms with PB, 8 with FP, 9 suites and 1 conference room. Breakfast included in rates. Types of meals: Full gourmet bkfst, picnic lunch, afternoon tea, snacks/refreshments, gourmet dinner and room service. Beds: KQ. Modem hook-up, data port, cable TV, VCR, reading lamp, refrigerator, ceiling fan, snack bar, clock radio, telephone, coffeemaker, turn-down service, desk, voice mail, fireplace and Jacuzzi in room. Air conditioning. Fax, copier, spa, swimming, tennis, library, parlor games, gift shop, Some amenities are available at nearby sister inn and The Sterling Inn on premises. Limited handicap access. Weddings, small meetings and seminars hosted. Antiquing, art galleries, bicycling, canoeing/kayaking, cross-country skiing, downhill skiing, fishing, golf, hiking, horseback riding, live theater, museums, parks, shopping, tennis, water sports and wineries nearby.

Publicity: *Featured as "Exceptional Restaurant of PA" in Gourmet Magazine-February 2003 and featured in the Philadelphia Inquirer as "Dinner Fit for a King" Rated by "Country Inns Magazine" as one of the Top Ten Country Inns of America.*

Sterling Inn

Rt 191
South Sterling, PA 18460
(570)676-3311 (800)523-8200 Fax:(570)676-9786
E-mail: info@thesterlinginn.com
Web: www.thesterlinginn.com

Circa 1857. Relaxation and enjoyment are experienced inside as well as outdoors at this wonderful country inn that sits on more than 100 acres in the Pocono Mountains. Landscaped lawns and gardens, woods, creeks, lake and miles of hiking trails create a park-like setting. Living rooms and libraries provide pleasant places to read or chat with friends. Entertainment is offered every weekend and occasionally during the week.

Gracious accommodations include guest bedrooms and suites in the main inn, lodge, guest house or spacious cottages. A two-person Jacuzzi, fireplace, front porch and kitchenette are some of the amenities to choose from. A hearty breakfast is served in the Hearthstone Dining Room. Lounge by a pool, or walk along a path to two crystal-clear streams and a waterfall, a perfect spot for a picnic lunch.

Innkeeper(s): Ron & Mary Kay Logan. $114-239. 67 rooms with PB, 25 with FP, 13 with HT, 25 suites, 5 cottages and 3 conference rooms. Types of meals: Full bkfst. Beds: KQDT. Cable TV, reading lamp, clock radio, telephone and desk in room. Air conditioning. Tennis, parlor games, fireplace, swimming pool, hot tub, hiking trail, paddle boats, shuffleboard, cross country skiing, snowshoeing, sledding, ice skating and weekend entertainment on premises. Limited handicap access. Weddings, small meetings, family reunions and seminars hosted. Cross-country skiing, fishing, tennis, hiking, boating, picnic area, ice skating, tobogganing and horse-drawn sleigh rides nearby.

Publicity: *Philadelphia Inquirer, New Jersey Monthly and The Washington Post.*

"Your 'touch of elegance,' both in service and gourmet food, made all of our guests feel very special."

Starlight C17

The Inn at Starlight Lake

PO Box 27
Starlight, PA 18461-0027
(570)798-2519 (800)248-2519 Fax:(570)798-2672

Circa 1909. Acres of woodland and meadow surround the last surviving railroad inn on the New York, Ontario and Western lines. Originally a boarding house, the inn was part of a little village that had its own store, church, blacksmith shop and creamery. Platforms, first erected to accommodate tents for the

summer season, were later replaced by three small cottage buildings that now include a suite with a double whirlpool. A modern three-bedroom house is available for family reunions and conferences. The inn is situated on the 45-acre, spring-fed Starlight Lake, providing summertime canoeing, swimming, fishing and sailing. (No motorboats are allowed on the lake.) Breakfast is served in the lakeside dining area where dinner is also available.

Innkeeper(s): Jack & Judy McMahon. $165-195. 26 rooms, 20 with PB, 1 with FP, 1 suite, 3 cottages and 1 conference room. Breakfast and dinner included in rates. Types of meals: Full gourmet bkfst, veg bkfst, early coffee/tea, gourmet lunch, picnic lunch and snacks/refreshments. Restaurant on premises. Beds: KQDT. Reading lamp and ceiling fan in room. TV, fax, copier, bicycles, tennis, library, parlor games, fireplace and laundry facility on premises. Weddings, small meetings, family reunions and seminars hosted. Antiquing, bicycling, canoeing/kayaking, downhill skiing, fishing, golf, horseback riding, live theater, tennis and water sports nearby.

Publicity: *New York Times, Philadelphia Inquirer, Newsday, Discerning Traveler, Freeman and Travel Network.*

Strasburg K14

Limestone Inn B&B

33 E Main St
Strasburg, PA 17579-1427
(717)687-8392 (800)278-8392 Fax:(717)687-8366

Circa 1786. The Limestone Inn housed the first Chief Burgess and later became the Headmaster's House for Strasburg Academy. It is a handsome five-bay formal Georgian plan. Located in the Strasburg Historic District, the house is on the National Register. The surrounding scenic Amish farmlands offer sightseeing and antique and craft shopping.

Innkeeper(s): Denise & Richard Waller & family. $79-115. 5 rooms with PB, 1 with FP. Breakfast and snacks/refreshments included in rates. Types of meals: Full gourmet bkfst and early coffee/tea. Beds: KQDT. Reading lamp, clock radio and desk in room. Central air. TV, fax, copier, library, parlor games, telephone and fireplace on premises. Small meetings and family reunions hosted. Amusement parks, antiquing, golf, hiking, live theater, museums, parks, shopping, sporting events, tennis, wineries and outlet shopping nearby.

Publicity: *Lancaster New Era, Intelligencer Journal, Strasburg Weekly, Washingtonian Magazine, New York Times and Country Magazine.*

"A beautiful restoration, great innkeepers and a fantasy location."

Terre Hill J15

The Artist's Inn & Gallery

117 E Main St
Terre Hill, PA 17581
(717)445-0219 (888)999-4479
E-mail: info@artistinn.com
Web: www.artistinn.com

Circa 1853. Four-course breakfasts and warm and inviting guest rooms are offered at this Federal-style inn. Watch Amish buggies clip clop by from the Victorian veranda and listen to the chimes from the church across the way. Then plan your day with the help of innkeepers Jan and Bruce, avid adventurers who cross-country ski and explore the area's best offerings to share insights with guests. There's an art gallery with works by the resident artist. Guest accommodations are inviting with antiques, gas fireplaces, hardwood floors and decorative painting, wallpapers and borders. The Rose Room offers a Jacuzzi bath. The Garden Suite offers a whirlpool bath for two, massage shower, fireplace, king-size featherbed, private balcony and sitting room. Breakfasts feature breads such as scones or muffins, fruit parfaits, crepes or egg dishes and a luscious dessert-perhaps a pie, cake or tart.

Innkeeper(s): Jan & Bruce Garrabrandt. $105-179. 3 rooms with PB, 3 with FP and 2 suites. Breakfast and snacks/refreshments included in rates. Types of meals: Full gourmet bkfst, veg bkfst, early coffee/tea and afternoon tea. Beds: KQ. Reading lamp, ceiling fan, turn-down service, hot tub/spa, hair dryers, robes, feather beds, CD players, clock radios and whirlpool baths in room. Central air. Library, parlor games, telephone, fireplace and art gallery on premises. Amusement parks, antiquing, art galleries, bicycling, cross-country skiing, fishing, golf, hiking, live theater, museums, parks, shopping, tennis and wineries nearby.

Thornton K16

Pace One Restaurant and Country Inn

341 Thornton Rd
Thornton, PA 19373
(610)459-3702 Fax:(610)558-0825

Circa 1740. This beautifully renovated stone barn has two-and-a-half-foot-thick walls, hand-hewn wood beams and many small-paned windows. Just in front of the inn was the Gray family home used as a hospital during the Revolutionary War when Washington's army crossed nearby Chadd's Ford.

Innkeeper(s): Ted Pace. $95-130. 5 rooms, 4 with PB, 1 suite and 3 conference rooms. Breakfast included in rates. Types of meals: Cont plus, lunch, picnic lunch and gourmet dinner. Restaurant on premises. Beds: Q. Clock radio and telephone in room. Air conditioning. Fax, copier and fireplace on premises. Weddings, small meetings, family reunions and seminars hosted. Antiquing, fishing, live theater, parks, shopping and sporting events nearby.

"Dear Ted & Staff, we loved it here!! The accommodations were great. Thanks for making it a beautiful weekend."

Valley Forge — K16

The Great Valley House of Valley Forge

1475 Swedesford Road
Valley Forge, PA 19355
(610)644-6759
E-mail: info@greatvalleyhouse.com
Web: www.greatvalleyhouse.com

Circa 1691. This 300-year-old Colonial stone farmhouse sits on four acres just two miles from Valley Forge Park. Boxwoods line the walkway, and ancient trees surround the house. Each of the three antique-filled guest rooms is hand-stenciled and features a canopied or brass bed topped with handmade quilts. Guests enjoy a full breakfast before a 14-foot fireplace in the "summer kitchen," the oldest part of the house. On the grounds are a swimming pool, walking and hiking trails and the home's original smokehouse.
Historic Interest: The grounds have an original keep and tunnel, which was part of the Underground Railroad. Historic Philadelphia, Longwood Gardens and Brandywine River Museum are other nearby attractions. Lancaster Country, famous for its Amish communities, is a popular area to visit.
Innkeeper(s): Pattye Benson. $85-115. 3 rooms with PB. Breakfast included in rates. Types of meals: Full gourmet bkfst & early coffee/tea. Beds: QDT. Cable TV, reading lamp, refrigerator, clock radio, telephone, turn-down service and desk in room. Air conditioning. TV, fax, swimming, parlor games, fireplace & grand piano on premises. Weddings and small meetings hosted. Antiquing, cross-country skiing, fishing, live theater, parks, shopping, sporting events & water sports nearby.
Publicity: *Main Line Philadelphia, Philadelphia Inquirer, Washington Post, New York Times, Suburban Newspaper and Travel cable network.*

"As a business traveler, Patty's enthusiasm and warm welcome makes you feel just like you're home."

Waynesburg — K2

Castle Victoria

618 E Greene St
Waynesburg, PA 15370-1758
(724)627-5545
Web: www.castlevictoria.com

Circa 1902. Immerse yourself in another era at this stately, century-old Victorian. Elegantly appointed guest rooms include such special amenities as ceiling fans, hurricane lamps and snack bars. A traditional breakfast of eggs, pancakes or waffles and an assortment of fruit and cereal are served every day, as well as afternoon tea. Located on a quiet street in small-town America, the historic ambiance lends itself to activities such as a stroll through the garden, a game of croquet on the lawn, or a game of cards in the third-floor billiards parlor. Those interested in more active pursuits will also find plenty of opportunities to play golf, shop, or visit local museums and parks.
Innkeeper(s): Michael & Doreen Klipsic. $95. 4 rooms and 1 conference room. Breakfast, afternoon tea & snacks/refreshments included in rates. Types of meals: Country bkfst. Beds: Q. Cable TV, VCR, reading lamp, ceiling fan, snack bar and desk in room. Air conditioning. Fireplace on premises. Weddings, small meetings, family reunions and seminars hosted. Golf, museums, parks & shopping nearby.

West Chester — K16

1732 Folke Stone Bed and Breakfast

777 Copeland School Road
West Chester, PA 19380
(610)429-0310 (800)884-4666 Fax:(610)918-9228

Circa 1732. A carefully restored William Penn land grant home, this stone manor house was part of the historical Underground Railroad. It boasts random-width wood floors and open beam ceilings. The former winter kitchen is now a welcoming area with original stone crane fireplace and beehive

oven. A hospitality center offers beverages and snacks. Antiques and family heirlooms, including a Steinway piano, highlight the inn. Choose from guest bedrooms featuring a choice of Amish quilts on brass beds, a Jenny Lind spindle bed set, and French Provincial furniture with porcelain lamps and Victorian lace. Enjoy breakfast in the great room, and relaxing moments on the side porch or the veranda overlooking the pond.
Innkeeper(s): Walter & Marcy Schmoll. $75-100. 3 rooms with PB and 1 conference room. Breakfast and snacks/refreshments included in rates. Types of meals: Full gourmet bkfst, veg bkfst and early coffee/tea. Beds: KQT. Cable TV, reading lamp, clock radio and desk in room. Central air. VCR, fax, copier, library, parlor games, telephone and fireplace on premises. Family reunions and seminars hosted. Antiquing, art galleries, canoeing/kayaking, golf, hiking, live theater, museums, parks, shopping, sporting events, wineries, Longwood Gardens, Brandywine River Museum and Winterthur nearby.

White Horse — K15

Across The Way Bed and Breakfast at the Fassitt Mansion

6051 Old Philadelphia Pike - Gap
White Horse, PA 17527
(717)442-0453 (800)484-7554
E-mail: innkeeper@acrossthewaybb.com
Web: www.fassittmansion.com

Circa 1845. Once a safe-house on the Underground Railroad and a rest stop for tired travelers halfway between Philadelphia and Harrisburg, this elegant Victorian mansion is situated in the heart of picturesque Pennsylvania Dutch Amish Country. It features twelve-foot ceilings, deep window sills and decorative molding. Spacious guest bedrooms boast fireplaces and comfortable antique furnishings. The Masters Chamber is a romantic, oversized room adorned with a canopy bed and sitting area. A generous continental-plus breakfast is available when desired or a hearty country breakfast is served family-style at the large dining room tables. Enjoy relaxing with afternoon refreshments. Sit in the garden gazebo or on a front porch rocker.
Historic Interest: The Fassitt Mansion, once a safe-house on the Underground Railroad, was built by Captain William Fassitt in 1845 as a way to throw lavish parties.
Innkeeper(s): Thomas & Christie Starr. $69-109. 4 rooms with PB, 3 with FP and 1 conference room. Types of meals: Country bkfst, veg bkfst and snacks/refreshments. Beds: KQ. Spa, fireplace, living room, garden gazebo, water garden and outdoor fireplace on premises. Amusement parks, antiquing, art galleries, bicycling, canoeing/kayaking, fishing, golf, hiking, horseback riding, live theater, museums, parks, shopping and wineries nearby.

York — K13

Friendship House B&B

728 E Philadelphia St
York, PA 17403-1609
(717)843-8299

Circa 1897. A walk down East Philadelphia Street takes visitors past an unassuming row of 19th-century townhouses. The Friendship House is a welcoming site with its light blue shutters and pink trim. Innkeepers Becky Detwiler and Karen Maust have added a shot of Victorian influence to their charming townhouse B&B, decorating with wallcoverings and lacy curtains. A country feast is prepared some mornings with choices ranging from quiche to French toast accompanied with items such as baked apples, smoked sausage and homemade breads. Most items are selected carefully from a nearby farmer's market. A cozy gathering place is in the living room with its gas log fireplace.
Innkeeper(s): Becky Detwiler & Karen Maust. $65. 3 rooms, 2 with PB and 1 suite. Breakfast and snacks/refreshments included in rates. Types of meals: Full bkfst. Beds: Q. Air conditioning. VCR and telephone on premises. Antiquing, golf, live theater, parks, shopping and museums nearby.

Rhode Island

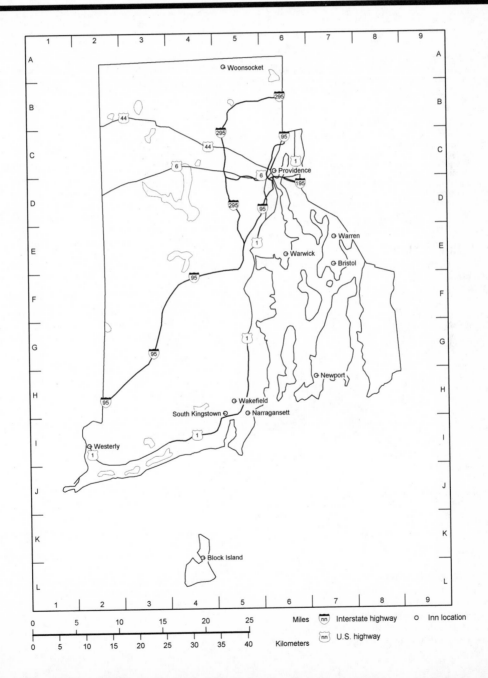

1	2	3	4	5	6	7	8	9

○ Woonsocket

295

295

44

44

95

6

○ Providence

6

1

195

295

95

1

○ Warren

○ Warwick

○ Bristol

95

1

95

○ Newport

95

○ Wakefield

South Kingstown ○   ○ Narragansett

1

○ Westerly

1

○ Block Island

0	5	10	15	20	25	Miles

0	5	10	15	20	25	30	35	40	Kilometers

Interstate highway   ○ Inn location

U.S. highway

523

Block Island K4

1661 Inn & Hotel Manisses

1 Spring St, PO Box I
Block Island, RI 02807-0001
(401)466-2421 (800)626-4773 Fax:(401)466-3162
E-mail: biresorts@riconnect.com
Web: www.blockisland.com/biresorts

Circa 1875. Seven buildings comprise this island inn and overlook grassy lawns and the ocean. Common rooms and guest rooms are furnished with antiques and art. The luxury rooms in the Nicholas Ball Cottage (a replica of an Episcopal church) offer both Jacuzzis and fireplaces. Dinner is available each night in the summer. Visit the inn's animal farm to watch the antics of the Indian runner ducks, black swans, pygmy goats, llamas and Sicilian donkeys. Flower, vegetable and herb gardens are adjacent to the farm.
Historic Interest: Historic Old Harbor.
Innkeeper(s): Justin Abrams, Rita & Steve Draper. $50-390. 57 rooms, 53 with PB and 5 conference rooms. Breakfast included in rates. Types of meals: Full gourmet bkfst, early coffee/tea, lunch, snacks/refreshments and gourmet dinner. Restaurant on premises. Beds: KQDT. Reading lamp, refrigerator and hot tub/spa in room. Child care, telephone and fireplace on premises. Weddings, small meetings, family reunions and seminars hosted. Fishing, shopping and water sports nearby.
Publicity: Newsday, New England Weekends, The Day, Detroit Free Press, US Air, USA Today, Block Island, New England Travel, Yankee, Gourmet and Bon Appetit.

The Bellevue House

PO Box 1198, High St
Block Island, RI 02807-1198
(401)466-2912 Fax:(401)466-2912
E-mail: bellevue@riconnect.com
Web: www.blockisland.com/bellevue

Circa 1882. Offering a hilltop perch, meadow-like setting and ocean views, this Colonial Revival farmhouse inn in the Block Island Historic District has served guests for more than a century. A variety of accommodations includes six guest rooms, one with private bath, four suites and two cottages. The Old Harbor Ferry, restaurants and shops are just a five-minute walk from the inn. Guests may use ferries from New London, Conn., Montauk Point, N.Y., and Point Judith, R.I., to reach the island. Beaches, Block Island National Wildlife Reserve and Rodmans Hollow Nature Area are nearby. Children are welcome.
Innkeeper(s): Neva Flaherty. $65-285. 6 rooms, 4 suites and 2 cottages. Breakfast included in rates. Types of meals: Cont. Beds: KQD. Reading lamp in room. Library, telephone, gas grills and picnic tables on premises. Family reunions hosted. Fishing, parks, shopping and water sports nearby.

Blue Dory Inn

PO Box 488, Dodge St
Block Island, RI 02807-0488
(401)466-5891 (800)992-7290 Fax:(401)466-9910
E-mail: rundezvous@aol.com
Web: www.blockislandinns.com

Circa 1887. This Shingle Victorian inn on Crescent Beach offers many guest rooms with ocean views. The Cottage, The

Doll House and The Tea House are separate structures for those desiring more room or privacy. Antiques and Victorian touches are featured throughout. Year-round car ferry service, taking approximately one hour, is found at Point Judith, R.I. The island also may be reached by air on New England Airlines or by charter. Mohegan Bluffs Scenic Natural Area is nearby.
Historic Interest: The Blue Dory is located in the Block Island Historic District, which includes many historic homes dating back 150 years.
Innkeeper(s): Ann Law. $65-245. 12 rooms with PB, 3 suites, 4 cottages and 1 conference room. Breakfast and afternoon tea included in rates. Types of meals: Cont plus and early coffee/tea. Beds: KQDT. Reading lamp, CD player, telephone, desk, some with air conditioning, VCRs and cable TV in room. TV, VCR, fax, copier, swimming, child care and parlor games on premises. Weddings, small meetings, family reunions and seminars hosted. Antiquing, beach, fishing, live theater, parks, shopping and water sports nearby.

"The Blue Dory is a wonderful place to stay. The room was lovely, the view spectacular and the sound of surf was both restful and tranquil."

Gothic Inn

PO Box 537
Block Island, RI 02807
(401)466-2918 (800)944-8991 Fax:(401)466-5028
E-mail: bennetbirx@cs.com
Web: www.blockisland.com/gothic/

Circa 1860. Built for a sea captain who was a late 18th-century druggist, this Victorian Gothic Inn is now owned by the Wohl family, also pharmacists on this small island. Situated in the center of the historic district, the inn boasts spectacular ocean views of Crescent Beach. Guests can watch pleasure and commercial boats enter and leave Old Harbor. Relax with a deluxe continental breakfast served in the cheery sitting rooms or large porch overlooking the lawn or the sea.
Innkeeper(s): Toube & Bennet Wohl. $65-285. 13 rooms, 1 with PB and 2 suites. Breakfast included in rates. Types of meals: Cont plus and early coffee/tea. Beds: DT. Modem hook-up, TV, VCR, refrigerator, ceiling fan, telephone, coffeemaker and fireplace in room. Parlor games and fireplace on premises. Handicap access. Small meetings and family reunions hosted. Art galleries, beach, bicycling, canoeing/kayaking, fishing, hiking, horseback riding, museums, parks, shopping, tennis and water sports nearby.

Rose Farm Inn

Roslyn Rd
Block Island, RI 02807-0895
(401)466-2034 Fax:(401)466-2053
E-mail: rosefarm@riconnect.com
Web: www.rosefarminn.com

Circa 1897. This romantic inn is comprised of two buildings, the turn-of-the-century farmhouse and the newer Captain Rose House. Canopy beds, sitting areas and whirlpool tubs are among the elegant touches that grace the rooms at the Captain Rose House. Most rooms afford either an ocean or countryside view; and there's always a light sea breeze to be enjoyed from the decks and front porch of the Farm House. A continental-plus buffet is served each morning on the enclosed sun porch, which overlooks the ocean.
Historic Interest: The farmhous is the original family name, renovated and furnished with antiques.
Innkeeper(s): Judith B Rose. $129-250. 19 rooms, 17 with PB. Breakfast and afternoon tea included in rates. Types of meals: Cont plus. Beds: KQDT. Reading lamp and telephone in room. VCR, fax, copier and bicycles on premises. Limited handicap access. Antiquing, beach, fishing, shopping, tennis and water sports nearby.
Publicity: Block Island and Getaways.

The Sheffield House, A Bed & Breakfast Inn

PO Box 1387, High St
Block Island, RI 02807
(401)466-2494 (866)466-2494 Fax:(401)466-7745
E-mail: info@thesheffieldhouse.com
Web: www.thesheffieldhouse.com

Circa 1888. Step off the ferry and step into a bygone era at this Queen Anne Victorian, which overlooks the Old Harbor district. Relax on one of the front porch rockers or enjoy the fragrance as you stroll through the private garden. Guest rooms are furnished with antiques and family pieces; each is individually decorated.

Historic Interest: The Old Harbor district is a historic area with plenty of places to explore. Built in 1888, located in Historic District.
Innkeeper(s): Nancy Sarah. $55-205. 6 rooms, 4 with PB. Breakfast and afternoon tea included in rates. Types of meals: Full gourmet bkfst. Beds: Q. Reading lamp, refrigerator, ceiling fan, clock radio and some have small library in room. TV, VCR, fax, copier, library, parlor games, telephone, fireplace, laundry facility and outdoor shower on premises. Weddings, small meetings, family reunions and seminars hosted. Antiquing, art galleries, beach, bicycling, canoeing/kayaking, fishing, hiking, horseback riding, shopping, water sports, ocean, nature hikes and restaurants nearby.

Bristol   E7

Governor Bradford House Country Inn at Mount Hope Farm

PO Box 66
Bristol, RI 02809
(401)254-9300 (877)254-9300 Fax:(401)254-1270
E-mail: reservations@mounthopefarm.com
Web: www.mounthopefarm.com

Circa 1745. Overlooking Mount Hope and Narragansett Bays, this inn is a medley of historic buildings on 200 acres of meadows, fields, woodlands, ponds and streams. Named a National Register landmark, President George Washington stayed at the two and a half-story Gambrel Roof Colonial for a week in the late 1700s while visiting William Bradford, a senator at that time. A Cape-style guest house is in the north pasture. Furnished with antiques and reproductions, some of the guest bedrooms feature fireplaces. Savor a satisfying breakfast and afternoon tea. Though not a working farm, about sixty acres are hayed each season and it is home to a variety of pheasant and other livestock. Walk a winding trail to Adirondack-type Cove Cabin, adjacent to a boat dock. Bicycles are available for exploring the scenic area. The recently renovated barn is perfect for special events. Catering services can be provided.
Innkeeper(s): Jim Farley. $100-250. 8 rooms with PB, 3 with FP and 5 conference rooms. Breakfast and afternoon tea included in rates. Types of meals: Country bkfst. Beds: KQDT. Clock radio and turn-down service in room. Air conditioning. TV, VCR, fax, copier, bicycles, library, parlor games, telephone, fireplace, walking trails, paths and running on site on premises. Small meetings and seminars hosted. Antiquing, art galleries, beach, bicycling, canoeing/kayaking, cross-country skiing, fishing, golf, hiking, horseback riding, live theater, museums, parks, shopping, sporting events, tennis, water sports and wineries nearby.

Rockwell House Inn B&B

610 Hope St
Bristol, RI 02809-1945
(401)253-0040 (800)815-0040 Fax:(401)253-1811
E-mail: rockwellinn@ids.net
Web: www.rockwellhouseinn.com

Circa 1809. Situated on a half-acre with pond, this Federal and Greek Revival home boasts eight-foot pocket doors, Italianate mantels and working gas-log fireplaces. Double parlors open to the dining room and its inlaid parquet floors. The sun porch features a stone turret and leaded-glass windows. Two guest rooms include working fireplaces, and antiques abound in each of the elegant quarters. The inn is only one block from Narragansett Bay and a 15-mile bike path. Guests can walk to restaurants and museums.

Historic Interest: Historic Newport and Providence are 12 miles away. The Blithewold Mansion and Gardens, Americas' Cup Hall of Fame, Haffenreffer Museum of Anthropology, Linden Place and Coggeshall Historic Farm Museum are all within a mile and a half of Rockwell House.
Innkeeper(s): Debra & Steve Krohn. $100-175. 4 rooms with PB, 2 with FP and 1 conference room. Breakfast and afternoon tea included in rates. Types of meals: Full gourmet bkfst and early coffee/tea. Beds: KQT. Reading lamp, ceiling fan, clock radio, iron/ironing board, terrycloth robes and hair blowers in room. Air conditioning. VCR, fax, copier, parlor games, telephone, fireplace and guest refrigerator on premises. Small meetings and seminars hosted. Antiquing, bicycling, cross-country skiing, fishing, museums, parks, shopping and water sports nearby.
Publicity: *New York Times, Los Angeles Times, Country Almanac Magazine and "Beautiful Inns of New England."*

Narragansett   H5

The 1900 House B&B

59 Kingstown Rd
Narragansett, RI 02882-3309
(401)789-7971

Circa 1900. For more than a century, Narragansett has been a hot spot for summer vacationers. Guests at the 1900 House enjoy both close access to the town's restaurants and shops as well as a nostalgic look back at the Victorian era. The innkeepers keep a stereoscope, hat boxes filled with antique post cards and other collectibles on hand for guests to discover. You might spot the wedding certificate of the home's original owner. Waffles topped with fresh fruit and cream are typical of the rich treats served at breakfast.

Innkeeper(s): Sandra & Bill Panzeri. $85-125. 3 rooms with PB. Breakfast included in rates. Types of meals: Full gourmet bkfst and early coffee/tea. Beds: D. TV and reading lamp in room. Telephone and fireplace on premises. Antiquing, fishing, live theater, parks, shopping, sporting events, water sports, Foxwoods Casino, bird sanctuary and South County Museum nearby.

"Wonderful! So relaxing and lovely, lovely breakfasts."

The Richards

144 Gibson Ave
Narragansett, RI 02882-3949
(401)789-7746

Circa 1884. J.P. Hazard, an influential member of one of the county's most prominent families, built this home, which resembles a English-country stone manor. The rooms are appointed with a beautiful collection of antiques, and each guest room has a fireplace and sitting area. Down comforters, carafes of sherry and candles are among the romantic amenities. After a restful night's sleep, guests are presented with a gourmet breakfast. French toast, made from Portuguese sweet bread, or rich, chocolate pancakes topped with an orange sauce might appear as the daily entree. The home is listed in the National Register of Historic Places.

Innkeeper(s): Nancy & Steven Richards. $95-200. 5 rooms, 4 with PB, 5 with FP and 2 suites. Breakfast included in rates. Types of meals: Full gourmet bkfst. Beds: KQ. Reading lamp in room. Library, telephone, fireplace, guest refrigerator, water garden with koi and winter garden on premises. Antiquing, fishing, golf, live theater, tennis and water sports nearby.
Publicity: Yankee Traveler, Home, Providence Journal-Bulletin, Narragansett Times and Rhode Island Monthly.

Newport   H7

1855 Marshall Slocum Guest House

29 Kay St
Newport, RI 02840-2735
(401)841-5120 (800)372-5120 Fax:(401)846-3787
E-mail: info@marshallslocuminn.com
Web: www.marshallslocuminn.com

Circa 1855. Victorian homes line the streets in the Historic Hill District of Newport, where this two-and-a-half-story house is situated on an acre of grounds. Architectural features include shutters, a hip roof with dormer windows and a front porch. The inn is furnished with antiques and contemporary pieces. A favorite breakfast is Fluffy Belgian Waffles served with freshly picked strawberries and mountains of whipped cream.

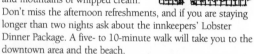

Don't miss the afternoon refreshments, and if you are staying longer than two nights ask about the innkeepers' Lobster Dinner Package. A five- to 10-minute walk will take you to the downtown area and the beach.

Innkeeper(s): Joan Wilson. $79-195. 5 rooms with PB, 2 with FP. Breakfast and snacks/refreshments included in rates. Types of meals: Full gourmet bkfst, early coffee/tea, gourmet lunch, picnic lunch and gourmet dinner. Beds: KQT. Reading lamp, clock radio and desk in room. Air conditioning. TV, VCR, fax, copier, library, parlor games, telephone and fireplace on premises. Weddings, small meetings, family reunions and seminars hosted. Antiquing, bicycling, fishing, golf, hiking and horseback riding nearby.
Publicity: Newport Daily News, Providence Journal, Washington Post, LA Times, PBS and WB2-TV.

Abigail Stoneman Inn

102 Touro Street
Newport, RI 02840
(401)847-1811 (800)845-1811 Fax:(401)848-5850
E-mail: innkeeper@legendaryinnsofnewport.com
Web: www.abigailstonemaninn.com

Circa 1866. Renowned architect George Champlin Mason built this classic Victorian home in the Historic Hill section just two blocks from the harbor front. Experience relaxed hospitality and intimate luxury at this extraordinary bed & breakfast inn. Well-appointed and very spacious guest bedrooms and suites are named to reflect significant eras of local history and are furnished with related artifacts and decor. Upscale amenities include a pillow menu with 18 styles to choose from, a variety of personal bath products and a selection of 24 international brands of bottled water. Read one of 11 newspapers with morning coffee delivered to each room. Savor a full breakfast in bed, at romantic tables for two in the parlor or alfresco on the patio.

Indulge in an English afternoon tea. The pampering continues with evening turndown service and homemade dessert treats.

Historic Interest: Home was built by renowned Newport architect George Champlin Mason, who designed and built a number of historic homes in Newport, including some of its famous Gilded Age mansions.

$425-675. 5 rooms with PB, 5 with FP and 3 suites. Breakfast and afternoon tea included in rates. Types of meals: Full gourmet bkfst, early coffee/tea and room service. Beds: K. Data port, cable TV, VCR, reading lamp, stereo, ceiling fan, clock radio, telephone, turn-down service, desk, hot tub/spa, fireplace, complimentary Luxury Amenity Menus: Pillow Menu, choose from 18 different types to sleep on, Bathing and Spa Menu: 30 of the world's best soaps, salts, foams and spa products, Tea Menu: 35 of the world's finest loose leaf teas, Water Menu and Water Pub: Rhode Island's only all water bar features 24 international still and sparkling waters, marble fireplaces, concealed media centers (with cable TV, CD, VCR, built-in room speakers), marble baths, two-person whirlpool tubs, some suites also have double steam baths, living rooms, second bedroom, dining room, bathing salon, library, reading areas and multiple fireplaces in room. Air conditioning. Spa, library, parlor games and fireplace on premises. Weddings, small meetings and family reunions hosted. Antiquing, art galleries, beach, bicycling, canoeing/kayaking, fishing, golf, horseback riding, live theater, museums, parks, shopping, tennis, water sports and wineries nearby.
Publicity: Wall Street Journal, New England's Best Guidebook (2002), Child Magazine, Getaways For Gourmets, USA Today and Rhode Island Monthly.

Adele Turner Inn

93 Pelham St
Newport, RI 02840
(401)847-1811 (800)845-1811 Fax:(401)848-5850
E-mail: innkeeper@legendaryinnsofnewport.com
Web: www.adeleturnerinn.com

Circa 1855. Architecturally significant, this recently restored inn is listed in the National Register. Located in a historic residential neighborhood, it sits on the country's first gaslit street. Two fireplaces highlight the elegant parlor, where classic English afternoon tea is served in Victorian tradition. Books and videos also are available there. Well-appointed guest bedrooms and suites reflect regional themes and events. Encounter period furnishings and fireplaces, with some rooms boasting two-person whirlpool tubs. Ask for the Harborview Spa which includes French doors leading to a rooftop deck with private hot tub and panoramic harbor view. Morning coffee or tea is brought to each room. In the parlor, a generous breakfast buffet begins a delicious meal followed by a hot entree.

Innkeeper(s): Susan Mauro. $175-525. 13 rooms with PB, 13 with FP and 3 suites. Breakfast and afternoon tea included in rates. Types of meals: Full bkfst and early coffee/tea. Beds: Q. Cable TV, VCR, clock radio, telephone, turn-down service, some with whirlpool baths and one with rooftop deck with hot tub spa in room. Air conditioning. Fax, library, video library, on-site parking and high-speed Internet access on premises. Weddings, small meetings, family reunions and seminars hosted. Antiquing, art galleries, beach, bicycling, canoeing/kayaking, fishing, golf, hiking, horseback riding, live theater, museums, parks, shopping, tennis, water sports, wineries, restaurants, sailing, International Tennis Hall of Fame and historic Redwood Library nearby.

Admiral Fitzroy

389 Thames St
Newport, RI 02840
(401)848-8000 (866)848-8780 Fax:(401)848-8006

Circa 1854. In Newport's waterfront district stands this European-style inn. Designed by renowned architect Dudley Newton, the inn was named for Admiral Fitzroy who commanded the HMS Beagle on Charles Darwin's historic voyage that preceded the writing of his famous book. Fitzroy also was famous for developing a barometer. Several examples of working antique barometers are on display in the inn. The inn has 17 attractive hand-painted rooms. A full breakfast is served each morning in the breakfast room. Breakfast fare includes such delights as cheese blintzes, pancakes, bacon, eggs, French toast, scones, cereal and fruits. After breakfast, guests will want to head out on foot to explore the historic waterfront district, which has excellent restaurants, antiquing and harbor activities. Newport boasts more occupied colonial houses than anywhere else in America. It also has the oldest Episcopal church and the first synagogue.

Innkeeper(s): Heather Reeves. Call for rates. 17 rooms with PB. Types of meals: Full bkfst. Beds: KQDT. Telephone in room. Fax and copier on premises. Antiquing and shopping nearby.

Agincourt Inn

120 Miantonomi Ave
Newport, RI 02842-5450
(401)847-0902 (800)352-3750 Fax:(401)848-6529
E-mail: randy@shadowlawn.com
Web: www.agincourtinn.com

Circa 1856. This elegant, three-story Stick Victorian inn, listed in the National Register, offers a glimpse of fine living in an earlier age. The innkeepers' attention to detail is evident throughout, with French crystal chandeliers, stained-glass windows and parquet floors in the library as a few of the highlights. Parlors are found on each of the inn's floors. Newport's many attractions, including the Art Museum, sailing and the world famous Newport mansions are just a short drive from the inn.

Historic Interest: Mansions from "Gilded Age" (5 minutes).

Innkeeper(s): Randy & Selma Fabricant. $79-225. 8 rooms with PB, 8 with FP. Breakfast included in rates. Types of meals: Full bkfst. Beds: KQ. Cable TV and VCR in room. Air conditioning. Library on premises. Weddings, small meetings, family reunions and seminars hosted. Antiquing, mansions and sailing nearby.

Publicity: *Newport Daily News, Providence Journal, West Essex Tribune, Victorian Homes and Mr. Smith.*

"A dream come true! Thanks for everything! We'll be back."

Almondy Inn

25 Pelham Street
Newport, RI 02840
(401)848-7202 (800)478-6155 Fax:(401)848-7299
E-mail: info@almondyinn.com
Web: www.almondyinn.com

Circa 1890. Fully restored to its original elegance, this 1890 Victorian, listed in the National Register, offers luxurious accommodations in a perfect location. Relax with afternoon tea and refreshments in the parlor. Newly decorated guest bedrooms with central air conditioning feature fine antiques, period furnishings, bathrobes, Jacuzzis, irons, data ports, VCRS and CD players. Many boast bedside fireplaces and scenic bay views. Spacious one-bedroom suites also include separate living rooms. Start the day with a gourmet breakfast served in the dining room. Feast on fresh fruit salad, freshly baked muffins and Eggs Almondy, the inn's signature version of eggs Benedict. Browse the gift shop before walking to the nearby galleries and boutiques. Relax on a beach or tour a famous Newport mansion.

Innkeeper(s): Evelyne Valkenberg. $110-300. 5 rooms with PB, 3 with FP and 2 suites. Breakfast and afternoon tea included in rates. Types of meals: Full gourmet bkfst and early coffee/tea. Beds: KQ. Data port, cable TV, VCR, reading lamp, CD player, clock radio, telephone, turn-down service, hot tub/spa, voice mail, fireplace, bathrobes, iron and ironing board in room. Central air. Fax, copier, library, parlor games and gift shop on premises. Antiquing, art galleries, beach, bicycling, fishing, golf, hiking, horseback riding, museums, parks, shopping, tennis, water sports and wineries nearby.

Attwater Villa

22 Liberty St
Newport, RI 02840-3221
(401)846-7444 (800)392-3717 Fax:(401)849-6429
E-mail: innkeeper@attwatervilla.com
Web: www.attwatervilla.com

Circa 1910. Built in 1910 as a place of respite for weary travelers, this historic inn blends the warmth and intimacy of a bed & breakfast with the upscale elegance of a hotel. Lovingly renovated with modern amenities make each stay a pleasant one, yet the hospitable traditions of the past still remain. Lavish air-conditioned suites and guest bedrooms feature comfortable furnishings, cable TV and phones. Cottage Suites are perfect for families or larger groups. Begin the day with a leisurely breakfast, then relax in the quiet privacy of the secluded sundeck. Centrally located, it is a short stroll past impressive 17th century homes to the waterfront. Behind the villa take the scenic Cliff Walk to the beach.

Innkeeper(s): Roland Caron. $89-225. 15 rooms with PB, 4 suites, 1 cottage and 1 conference room. Breakfast, afternoon tea and snacks/refreshments included in rates. Types of meals: Cont plus. Beds: KQ. Data port, cable TV, VCR, refrigerator, clock radio, telephone, coffeemaker and desk in room. Air conditioning. Fax, copier, library and parlor games on premises. Weddings, small meetings and family reunions hosted. Antiquing, art galleries, beach, bicycling, canoeing/kayaking, fishing, golf, hiking, horseback riding, live theater, museums, parks, shopping, tennis, water sports and wineries nearby.

Beech Tree Inn

34 Rhode Island Ave
Newport, RI 02840-2667
(401)847-9794 (800)748-6565 Fax:(401)847-6824
E-mail: cmquilt13@cox.net
Web: www.beechtreeinn.com

Circa 1897. This inn's location in historic Newport offers close access to the famous local mansions, and the turn-of-the-century home is within walking distance of the harbor. Most of the guest rooms include a fireplace. Special furnishings include canopy or poster beds, and suites offer the added amenity of a whirlpool tub. The innkeepers provide a breakfast feast, and guests enjoy made-to-order fare that might include eggs, pancakes, waffles, omelets, ham, bacon and more. In the winter months, guests are further pampered with homemade clam chowder in the evenings. Snacks, such as freshly baked cookies, are always on hand to curb one's appetite.

Innkeeper(s): Cindy Mahood. $79-295. 5 rooms with PB, 3 with FP, 1 suite and 1 conference room. Breakfast, afternoon tea and snacks/refreshments included in rates. Types of meals: Full bkfst and early coffee/tea. Beds: KQ. Cable TV, reading lamp, refrigerator, ceiling fan, clock radio, telephone, desk and fireplaces and Jacuzzi in room. Air conditioning. Fax, copier and fireplace on premises. Weddings, small meetings, family reunions and seminars hosted. Antiquing, cross-country skiing, downhill skiing, fishing, golf, live theater, parks, shopping, sporting events, tennis and water sports nearby.

Black Duck Inn

29 Pelham St
Newport, RI 02840-3018
(401)841-5548 (800)206-5212 Fax:(401)846-4873
E-mail: maryA401@aol.com
Web: www.blackduckinn.com

Circa 1870. This inn derives its name from a ship that smuggled liquor into Newport during the days of Prohibition. The inn is located in the downtown area and within walking distance of the harbor and famed mansions of Newport. In the guest rooms, English country fabrics and coordinating curtains and wallcoverings complete the romantic look. For those celebrating a special occasion, the innkeeper offers rooms with whirlpool tubs and fireplaces. Six of the rooms include a private bath. Two other rooms are joined by a bathroom, creating an ideal family suite. One of the rooms includes a queen bed, the other includes two twin beds. The continental-plus breakfasts include cereals, granola, fresh fruit, croissants, muffins and coffee cake.

Innkeeper(s): Mary A. Rolando. $100-210. 8 rooms, 6 with PB, 2 with FP. Breakfast included in rates. Types of meals: Cont plus. Beds: QT. TV, reading lamp, clock radio, telephone and hot tub/spa in room. Central air. Fax and copier on premises. Antiquing, art galleries, beach, bicycling, canoeing/kayaking, fishing, golf, horseback riding, museums, parks, shopping, sporting events, tennis, water sports and wineries nearby.

The Brinley Victorian Inn

23 Brinley St
Newport, RI 02840-3238
(401)849-7645 (800)999-8523
E-mail: thesweetmans@brinleyvictorian.com
Web: www.brinleyvictorian.com

Circa 1870. This is a three-story Victorian with a mansard roof and long porch. A cottage on the property dates from 1850. There are two parlors and a library providing a quiet haven from the bustle of the Newport wharfs. Each room is decorated with period wallpapers and furnishings. There are fresh flowers and mints on the pillows. The brick courtyard is planted with bleeding hearts, peonies and miniature roses, perennials of the Victorian era.

Historic Interest: Touro Synagogue (5-minute walk), Trinity Church (5-minute walk).

Innkeeper(s): John & Jennifer Sweetman. $89-229. 15 rooms with PB and 3 suites. Breakfast included in rates. Beds: KQDT. TV and suite has Jacuzzi and fireplace in room. Parlor games and telephone on premises.
Publicity: *New Hampshire Times, Boston Woman, Country Victorian and Yankee.*

"Ed and I had a wonderful anniversary. The Brinley is as lovely and cozy as ever! The weekend brought back lots of happy memories."

Castle Hill Inn & Resort

Ocean Ave
Newport, RI 02840
(401)849-3800 (888)466-1355

Circa 1874. Sitting on 40 oceanfront acres overlooking Narragansett Bay, this rambling Victorian inn was built as a summer home for scientist Alexander Agassiz. An on-site laboratory was a forerunner of the Woods Hole Marine Lab. Many original furnishings remain, and there are spectacular views from every room. Luxurious guest bedrooms and suites feature large whirlpool tubs, fireplaces and fine decor. Some boast French doors that open to sweeping water vistas. Enjoy a gourmet breakfast, and on Sundays a sumptuous buffet is part of the restaurant's special Jazz Brunch. Complimentary afternoon tea also is served daily. Dinner specialties include striped bass with clams and Vidalia onions, duck and grilled lamb. The grounds include a private beach, lighthouse, walking trails and a cutting garden.

Innkeeper(s): Natalie Ward. $145-795. 25 rooms with PB. Types of meals: Full bkfst, lunch, afternoon tea and dinner. Restaurant on premises. Beds: KD. Phones with data ports in room. 10 seasonal beach cottages on premises.

Chestnut Inn

99 Third Street
Newport, RI 02840
(401)847-6949
E-mail: chstnut99@aol.com
Web: www.newportchestnutinn.com

Circa 1904. In the historic Point section, one block from Narragansett Bay, this Victorian inn is an ideal year-round destination for a private romantic getaway or a family vacation that can include the pets. The spacious living room provides a welcoming place to gather for a movie, converse or find something to read from the library. Oversize first-floor guest bedrooms feature air conditioning and a bath with a jet tub. Enjoy a continental breakfast in the large country kitchen or alfresco on the front porch with morning ocean breezes. The landscaped grounds boast colorful flower gardens, shade trees and an adjacent playground with basketball and tennis courts.

Innkeeper(s): Bill & Eileen Nimmo. $75-150. 2 rooms. Breakfast included in rates. Types of meals: Country bkfst. Beds: K. Desk in room. Air conditioning. TV, VCR, swimming, tennis, library, pet boarding, parlor games, telephone and laundry facility on premises. Antiquing, art galleries, beach, bicycling, canoeing/kayaking, fishing, golf, hiking, horseback riding, live theater, museums, parks, shopping, sporting events, tennis, water sports and wineries nearby.

Cliffside Inn

2 Seaview Ave
Newport, RI 02840-3627
(401)847-1811 (800)845-1811 Fax:(401)848-5850
E-mail: innkeeper@legendaryinnsofnewport.com
Web: www.cliffsideinn.com

Circa 1876. The governor of Maryland, Thomas Swann, built this Newport summer house in the style of a Second Empire Victorian. It features a mansard roof and many bay windows. The rooms are decorated in a Victorian motif. Suites have marble baths, and all rooms have fireplaces. Fourteen rooms have a double whirlpool tub. The Cliff Walk is located one block from the inn.

Innkeeper(s): Stephan Nicolas. $245-625. 16 rooms with PB, 16 with FP, 8 suites and 1 cottage. Breakfast and afternoon tea included in rates. Types of meals: Full gourmet bkfst and early coffee/tea. Beds: KQ. Cable TV, VCR, reading lamp, stereo, ceiling fan, clock radio, telephone, turn-down service and desk in room. Air conditioning. Fax, parlor games and fireplace on premises. Antiquing, fishing, live theater, shopping and water sports nearby.
Publicity: *Conde Naste, Boston, New York Times, Zagat Survey, Bride's Magazine, Frommer's, Discerning Traveler and Good Morning America.*

"...it captures the grandeur of the Victorian age."

Francis Malbone House

392 Thames St
Newport, RI 02840-6604
(401)846-0392 (800)846-0392 Fax:(401)848-5956

Circa 1760. Newport, during the 18th century, was one of the busiest harbors in the Colonies. A shipping merchant, Colonel Francis Malbone, built the historic portion of this home, which includes nine of the inn's 20 guest rooms. The newer addition was completed in 1996. Fine furnishings fill the rooms, most of which offer a fireplace. Twelve rooms include a Jacuzzi tub. The inn's location, on the harborfront, is another wonderful feature. The breakfasts, heralded by Bon Appetit, include entrees such as pecan waffles with maple whipped cream or eggs Benedict with a roasted red pepper hollandaise. Guests are sure to be busy exploring Newport with its

abundance of historic sites and spectacular mansions.
Innkeeper(s): Will Dewey & Mark & Jasminka Eads. $165-475. 16 rooms, 17 with PB, 18 with FP, 3 suites and 6 conference rooms. Breakfast and afternoon tea included in rates. Types of meals: Full gourmet bkfst. Beds: KQ. TV, CD player, clock radio, telephone, turn-down service and desk in room. Air conditioning. Fax and fireplace on premises. Limited handicap access. Small meetings hosted. Antiquing, golf, parks, shopping, tennis and mansion tours nearby.
Publicity: *Colonial Homes, Bon Appetit, Country Inns, Gourmet, In-Style and HGTV.*

Hammett House Inn

505 Thames St
Newport, RI 02840-6723
(401)846-0400 (800)548-9417 Fax:(401)274-2690
E-mail: Check-In@HammettHouseInn.Com
Web: hammetthouseinn.com

Circa 1758. After a gracious welcome, enjoy the warm, relaxed ambiance of this historic three-story Georgian Federal home. Built in 1785, it boasts post and beam construction and beaded clapboard exterior. Completely renovated with thoughtful attention to detail, the tranquil intimate setting and comfortable surroundings instill a sense of timelessness. Air-conditioned guest bedrooms feature antique furnishings and a touch of romance. Many include harbor views. Walk to nearby shops, restaurants and the waterfront.
Innkeeper(s): Marianne Spaziano. $95-195. 5 rooms with PB. Breakfast included in rates. Types of meals: Cont plus and gourmet dinner. Restaurant on premises. Beds: Q. Cable TV, reading lamp and clock radio in room. Air conditioning. TV, fax and telephone on premises. Antiquing, fishing, live theater, parks, shopping, water sports and Newport mansion tours nearby.

Jailhouse Inn

13 Marlborough St
Newport, RI 02840-2545
(401)847-4638 (800)427-9444 Fax:(401)849-0605
E-mail: vacation@jailhouse.com
Web: www.historicinnsofnewport.com

Circa 1772. Listed in the National Register, this renovated inn was built in 1772 as a Colonial jail. Comfort, convenience and a stylish decor permeate the atmosphere today. Bright and cheery guest bedrooms and spacious suites offer air conditioning, tasteful furnishings, compact refrigerators and cable TV. Wake up to a continental breakfast buffet before exploring the harbor shops and restaurants only one block away. Relax on the porch with afternoon tea. Visit nearby historic Fort Adams. White Horse Tavern is across the street.
Historic Interest: The inn is located one block from harbor restaurants and shops.
Innkeeper(s): Susan Mauro. $45-280. 23 rooms with PB and 4 suites. Breakfast and afternoon tea included in rates. Types of meals: Cont and early coffee/tea. Beds: KQ. Data port, cable TV, reading lamp, refrigerator, clock radio, telephone and desk in room. Air conditioning. Fax on premises. Limited handicap access. Small meetings and family reunions hosted. Antiquing, art galleries, beach, bicycling, canoeing/kayaking, fishing, golf, hiking, horseback riding, live theater, museums, parks, shopping, tennis, water sports and wineries nearby.
Publicity: *Providence Journal.*

"I found this very relaxing and a great pleasure."

The Melville House

39 Clarke St
Newport, RI 02840-3023
(401)847-0640 Fax:(401)847-0956
E-mail: innkeeper@ids.net
Web: www.melvillehouse.com

Circa 1750. During the American Revolution this attractive National Register Colonial inn once housed aides to General Rochambeau. Reflecting its historical heritage, the interior

decor features early American furnishings. Stay in the spacious Fireplace Suite. A full breakfast is served each morning that may include homemade scones, muffins or coffee cakes and stuffed French toast, pepper frittata or whole wheat pancakes. Take a pleasant walk from this 1750 inn to the waterfront and local sites.

Historic Interest: On Clarke Street: Vernon House, Simon Pease House (c.1700), the Newport Artillery Company. Within one block: Touro Synagogue, Trinity Church (c.1726), Thames Street & Washington Square.
Innkeeper(s): Bob & Priscilla Peretti. $110-175. 5 rooms with PB, 1 with FP and 1 suite. Breakfast and afternoon tea included in rates. Types of meals: Full gourmet bkfst, early coffee/tea and picnic lunch. Beds: KDT. Air conditioning. Fax, bicycles, parlor games, telephone and fireplace on premises. Small meetings, family reunions and seminars hosted. Antiquing, fishing, live theater, parks, shopping and water sports nearby.
Publicity: *Country Inns, "Lodging Pick" for Newport, Good Housekeeping and New York Post.*

"Comfortable with a quiet elegance."

Old Beach Inn

19 Old Beach Rd
Newport, RI 02840-3237
(401)849-3479 (888)303-5033 Fax:(401)847-1236
E-mail: info@oldbeachinn.com
Web: oldbeachinn.com

Circa 1879. Stroll through the backyard at this enchanting Gothic Victorian bed & breakfast and you'll find a garden, lily pond and romantic gazebo. Innkeepers Luke and Cyndi Murray have kept a whimsical, romantic theme running inside and outside. Each of the guest rooms, two of which are located in the carriage house, bears the name of a flower. Delightful decor with bright wall coverings and linens accent the beautiful furnishings. The recently renovated Lily Room has a music theme, while the blue and yellow Forget-Me-Not Room is filled with wicker. Every item in the room is color-coordinated and features special painting and stenciling created by Cyndi. An expanded continental breakfast is served daily, and on Sundays, the innkeepers offer items such as an egg casserole, quiche or stuffed French toast. The area abounds with shops and restaurants, including a famous eatery managed by Luke.
Historic Interest: Several mansions in the area are open for tours. The Redwood Library is a short walk from the inn, as is the Tennis Hall of Fame. The historic harborfront is a seven-minute stroll.
Innkeeper(s): Luke & Cynthia Murray. $85-195. 7 rooms, 6 with PB, 6 with FP. Breakfast included in rates. Types of meals: Cont plus. Beds: KQT. Reading lamp, ceiling fan, clock radio, desk and one with Jacuzzi in room. Air conditioning. Fax, copier, parlor games, telephone and fireplace on premises. Weddings, small meetings, family reunions and seminars hosted. Antiquing, fishing, golf, live theater, parks, shopping and water sports nearby.
Publicity: *Canadian Leisure Ways and Seaway Trail.*

"Thanks for your exceptional and stylish innkeeping. We never wanted for one comfort."

The Pilgrim House

123 Spring St
Newport, RI 02840-6805
(401)846-0040 (800)525-8373 Fax:(401)848-0357

Circa 1879. This Victorian inn, located in the heart of Newport, has a rooftop deck with a panoramic view of the harbor. The home is within walking distance of shops, restaurants, the Cliff Walk and the Newport mansions. In the cooler months, the innkeepers serve sherry in the living room, which often is warmed by a crackling fire.

Historic Interest: Touro Synagogue, Trinity Church, Newport Harbor (1 block), Tennis Hall of Fame (3 blocks).

Innkeeper(s): Barry & Debbie Fonseca. $85-230. 10 rooms, 8 with PB and 1 conference room. Breakfast included in rates. Types of meals: Cont plus. Beds: QD. Air conditioning. Fax, copier, telephone, afternoon sherry and big screen TV on premises. Small meetings, family reunions and seminars hosted. Antiquing, fishing, live theater, parks, shopping and restaurants nearby.

Publicity: The Times.

"What can I say, it's a perfect hideaway. Great time was had by all."

Queen Anne Inn

16 Clarke St
Newport, RI 02840-3024
(401)846-5676 (888)407-1616 Fax:(401)841-8509
E-mail: queenanne@cox.net
Web: www.QueenAnneInnNewport.com

Circa 1900. Located in one of Newport's oldest neighborhoods, this Victorian is just a few blocks from the waterfront and the downtown area. The garden-covered grounds and peaceful residential setting create a pleasing serenity for those in search of relaxation. As it is just steps from the water, the innkeepers chose to decorate the inn in a nautical theme. In addition to the continental breakfast, which features items such as croissants and fresh pastries, afternoon tea is served each day. Museums and the famed mansions of Newport are among the town's attractions.

Innkeeper(s): Flavia Gardiner. $125-180. 10 rooms, 8 with PB and 1 suite. Breakfast and afternoon tea included in rates. Types of meals: Cont and early coffee/tea. Beds: KQT. Reading lamp in room. Air conditioning. TV, fax, copier, telephone and modem hook-up and parking on premises. Weddings and family reunions hosted. Antiquing, art galleries, beach, bicycling, canoeing/kayaking, golf, hiking, horseback riding, live theater, museums, parks, shopping, tennis, water sports, wineries and 12 meter sailing and power yachting nearby.

Reed Rose Cottage

8 Loyola Terrace
Newport, RI 02840
(401)846-8790
E-mail: reedrosecottage@cox.net
Web: www.reedrosecottage.com

Circa 1947. Quaint and cozy, this home was built in the style of Cape Cod cottages in a quiet neighborhood. It features a two-bedroom suite with open living, dining and kitchen areas. There is also a new French Country suite which has a private poolside porch. Antiques and wicker furnishings are embellished with a floral decor of cabbage roses. Cheery and comfortable suites overlook the in-ground swimming pool and perennial gardens. This ocean community offers many water sports and historic sites. Beach towels are provided.

Innkeeper(s): Charron K. Reed. $75-250. 2 suites. Breakfast included in rates. Types of meals: Cont plus. Beds: QD. Reading lamp, refrigerator, snack bar, clock radio, coffeemaker, suite has cable TV and central air in room. TV, swimming, library, child care, telephone and in-ground pool on premises. Weddings, small meetings and family reunions hosted. Amusement parks, antiquing, art galleries, beach, bicycling, canoeing/kayaking, cross-country skiing, downhill skiing, fishing, golf, hiking, horseback riding, live theater, museums, parks, shopping, sporting events, tennis, water sports and wineries nearby.

Stella Maris Inn

91 Washington
Newport, RI 02840
(401)849-2862

Circa 1861. Made of stone with black walnut woodwork inside, this is a French Victorian with mansard roof and wraparound veranda. The inn's two acres are landscaped with flower beds. Bright yet elegant wall coverings and fabrics set off the antiques, paintings and interior architectural points of interest. In the National Register, the inn is an early Newport mansion that was originally called "Blue Rocks." It later became a convent at which time it was renamed Stella Maris, "star of the sea." Several of the inn's lavishly appointed rooms offer ocean views, and some have fireplaces.

Innkeeper(s): Dorothy & Ed Madden. $85-225. 9 rooms with PB, 9 with FP and 1 cottage. Breakfast and afternoon tea included in rates. Types of meals: Cont plus and early coffee/tea. Beds: KQDT. Reading lamp, ceiling fan and clock radio in room. Library, telephone, fireplace and elevator on premises. Small meetings and family reunions hosted. Antiquing, fishing, golf, live theater, parks, shopping, tennis and water sports nearby.

"Rejuvenation for the soul!"

Victorian Ladies Inn

63 Memorial Blvd
Newport, RI 02840-3629
(401)849-9960
E-mail: info@victorianladies.com
Web: www.victorianladies.com

Circa 1851. Innkeepers Donald and Helene have created a comfortable and welcoming atmosphere at this restored three-story Victorian inn and cottage. Intimate and inviting, this traditional New England bed & breakfast features spacious guest bedrooms furnished with period pieces, fine reproductions, rich fabrics and wallcoverings. Linger over a gracious breakfast in the dining room. Stroll through the award-winning gardens, walk over the small bridge and gaze at the koi pond. Relax in the living room while planning activities for the day. Walk to nearby beaches, the Colonial town and harbor front.

Innkeeper(s): Donald & Helene O'Neill. $125-275. 11 rooms with PB, 1 with FP. Breakfast included in rates. Types of meals: Full gourmet bkfst and veg bkfst. Beds: KQ. Cable TV, VCR, reading lamp, clock radio, telephone, desk and one with fireplace in room. Central air. Library, parlor games and fireplace on premises. Family reunions hosted. Antiquing, art galleries, beach, bicycling, canoeing/kayaking, fishing, golf, hiking, horseback riding, live theater, museums, parks, shopping, tennis, water sports and wineries nearby.

Publicity: Country Inns, Glamour, Bride Magazine, L.A. Times, Country Victorian, Yankee Magazine, Newport Life Magazine and Voted Best Hotel/B&B by Newport Voters for 5 years.

"We want to move in!"

The White House on Catherine

73 Catherine Street
Newport, RI 02840
(401)841-0009 (877)841-0009 Fax:(401)846-7903
E-mail: cmquilt13@cox.net
Web: www.NewportsFirstFamily.com

Circa 1883. Feel like one of the First Family at this Victorian home that reflects a stately presidential motif. Relax by the fire with a glass of wine in the Diplomatic Reception Room. Large guest bedrooms and a suite are named after past commanders in chief and include amenities fit for foreign dignitaries. Enjoy a satisfying breakfast delivered to each room. The landscaped grounds feature trees, shrubs, white picket fences and the Rose Garden, a pleasant spot to to sit and reflect or read. Towels are available for excursions to a nearby beach. Visit an assortment of local historical sites.

Historic Interest: Owned in the 1920s by Rear Admiral and Mrs. Wm. Sowden Simms, past president of the Naval War College and good friend to Teddy Roosevelt. He was very integral in the early formation years of our US Navy.
Innkeeper(s): Jim and Cindy. $150-280. 4 rooms with PB, 4 with FP, 1 suite and 2 conference rooms. Breakfast, afternoon tea and snacks/refreshments included in rates. Types of meals: Full gourmet bkfst, veg bkfst and early coffee/tea. Beds: KQT. Modem hook-up, data port, cable TV, VCR, reading lamp, refrigerator, desk, fireplace, water bubbler, hair dryers, beach towels, iron and ironing board in room. Air conditioning. Fax, copier, library, parlor games, telephone and fireplace on premises. Weddings, small meetings, family reunions and seminars hosted. Antiquing, art galleries, beach, bicycling, canoeing/kayaking, cross-country skiing, fishing, golf, hiking, horseback riding, live theater, museums, parks, shopping, sporting events, tennis, water sports and wineries nearby.
Publicity: Boston Globe, Advocate Paper, New Haven Register and B&Bs of New England.

Willows of Newport - Romantic Inn & Garden

8-10 Willow St, Historic Point
Newport, RI 02840-1927
(401)846-5486 Fax:(401)849-8215
E-mail: thewillowsofnewport@cox.net
Web: www.thewillowsofnewport.com

Circa 1740. There's little wonder why this inn is known as The Romantic Inn. The spectacular secret garden, with its abundance of foliage, colorful blooms and a heart-shaped fish pond, is a popular stop on Newport's Secret Garden Tour. The inn is a three-time recipient of the
Newport Best Garden Award. The
French Quarter Queen room and
Canopy Room both boast views
of the gardens, and guests awake
to the fragrances of the many
flowers. The romantic Victorian
Wedding Room, decorated in pastel greens and rose, offers a queen canopy bed, hand-painted furniture and a fireplace. The Colonial Wedding Room features lace accents, a hand-crafted king bed and an original 1740s fireplace. A continental breakfast is delivered to your room on bone china with silver services. Innkeeper Pattie Murphy, aside from her gardening and decorating skills, is a native Newporter and is full of information about the city. Ask about the inn's new "Silk & Chandelier" collection.
Historic Interest: The home is listed as National Landmark. Newport is the home of the Touro Synagogue, the oldest Jewish house of worship in North America. The Tennis Hall of Fame and the nation's oldest library, Redwood, are popular attractions. Don't forget to visit the nation's oldest operating tavern, The White Horse Tavern, which first opened in 1687.
Innkeeper(s): Patricia 'Pattie' Murphy. $129-278. 5 rooms with PB. Breakfast and snacks/refreshments included in rates. Types of meals: Cont plus. Beds: KQD. Reading lamp, CD player, refrigerator and clock radio in room. Air conditioning. Telephone and award-winning secret garden on premises. Antiquing, fishing, parks, shopping, water sports, mansions and sunset sailing nearby nearby.
Publicity: Bostonia, New Woman, PM Magazine, Wedding Day NE, Travel America, Country Inn and HGTV.

"We enjoyed our getaway in your inn for its peace, elegance and emphasis on romance."

Providence   C6

AAA Jacob Hill Inn

PO Box 41326
Providence, RI 02940
(508)336-9165 (888)336-9165 Fax:(508)336-0951
E-mail: host@jacobhill.com
Web: www.inn-providence.com

Circa 1722. This historic Colonial home overlooks 50 acres and is located three miles outside Providence. In the '20s and '30s, it was the Jacob Hill Hunt Club and hosted the

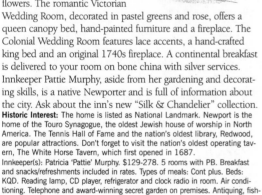

Vanderbilts during hunts and horse shows. Beamed ceilings, wall paintings of horse and hunting scenes and rare Southern long-leaf pine floors create the gracious setting.
Guest rooms may include a canopy bed, fireplace or whirlpool tub. Enjoy the inn's in-ground pool or tennis court or take a riding lesson, then relax in the gazebo at sunset. Stuffed French toast with whipped cream and strawberries is often served in the original kitchen area with its large beehive fireplace. Recently received the prestigious four diamond award by AAA.
Innkeeper(s): Bill & Eleonora Rezek. $179-299. 6 rooms, 10 with PB, 10 with FP and 2 suites. Breakfast and snacks/refreshments included in rates. Types of meals: Full gourmet bkfst and early coffee/tea. Beds: KQDT. Cable TV, VCR, reading lamp, clock radio, telephone, turn-down service and whirlpools in room. Air conditioning. Fax, swimming, tennis, library, parlor games and fireplace on premises. Limited handicap access. Small meetings hosted. Antiquing, fishing, golf, live theater, parks and sporting events nearby.

Edgewood Manor B&B

232 Norwood Ave
Providence, RI 02905
(401)781-0099 (800)882-3285 Fax:(401)467-6311
E-mail: edgemanor@aol.com
Web: www.providence-lodging.com

Circa 1905. Built as a private home, this 18-room Greek Revival Colonial mansion has served as a convent, an office, a rooming house and is now restored as an magnificent bed and breakfast. An elegant era is reflected in the coffered, beamed and domed-foyer ceilings, leaded- and stained-glass windows, hand-carved mantels and blend of Victorian and Empire decor. Romantic guest bedrooms feature Jacuzzi tubs and wood-burning fireplaces. Savor a satisfying gourmet breakfast served in the dining room or on the patio. The inn is within walking distance to Narragansett Bay and Roger Williams Park and Zoo, with 230 acres of magnificent gardens, sculptures and historic buildings.
Innkeeper(s): Joy Generali. $99-225. 8 rooms with PB. Breakfast included in rates. Types of meals: Full gourmet bkfst. Beds: KQ. TV, VCR, reading lamp, ceiling fan, clock radio, telephone, hot tub/spa, Jacuzzi tubs and wood-burning fireplaces in room. Air conditioning. Fax, copier, library, fireplace and bicycles for rent on premises. Antiquing, art galleries, beach, bicycling, canoeing/kayaking, fishing, golf, hiking, horseback riding, live theater, museums, parks, shopping, sporting events and wineries nearby.

Old Court B&B

144 Benefit St
Providence, RI 02903-1226
(401)751-2002 Fax:(401)272-4830

Circa 1863. Adjacent to the historic Rhode Island Courthouse, this Italianate building originally served as an Episcopal rectory. Indoor shutters, chandeliers hanging from 12-foot ceilings and elaborate Italian marble mantelpieces provide the gracious setting for antique Victorian beds. Some rooms overlook the capitol. Brown University, Rhode Island School of Design and downtown Providence are a short walk away.
Innkeeper(s): Jon Rosenblatt. $115-260. 10 rooms with PB. Breakfast included in rates. Types of meals: Full gourmet bkfst. Beds: KQDT. Reading lamp, clock radio, telephone, desk and some refrigerators in room. Air conditioning. TV, fax, copier and fireplace on premises. Weddings and small meetings hosted. Antiquing, live theater, parks, shopping and sporting events nearby.
Publicity: New York Times.

"My only suggestion is that you do everything in your power not to change it."

South Kingstown   H5

Admiral Dewey Inn

668 Matunuck Beach Rd
South Kingstown, RI 02879-7053
(401)783-2090 (800)457-2090
E-mail: admiraldeweyinn@cox.net
Web: www.admiraldeweyinn.com

Circa 1898. Although the prices have risen a bit since this inn's days as a boarding house (the rate was 50 cents per night), this Stick-style home still offers hospitality and comfort. The National Register inn is within walking distance of Matunuck Beach. Guests can enjoy the sea breeze from the inn's wraparound porch. Period antiques decorate the guest rooms, some of which offer ocean views.
Historic Interest: One half mile to Historic Theatre By The Sea.
Innkeeper(s): Joan Lebel. $100-150. 10 rooms, 8 with PB. Breakfast included in rates. Types of meals: Cont plus, early coffee/tea and picnic lunch. Beds: QDT. VCR, fax, copier, parlor games, telephone and fireplace on premises. Weddings, small meetings, family reunions and seminars hosted. Antiquing, fishing, live theater, parks, shopping and water sports nearby.
Publicity: Yankee Traveler and Rhode Island Monthly.

Wakefield   H5

Brookside Manor

380-B Post Rd
Wakefield, RI 02879
(401)788-3527 Fax:(401)788-3530
E-mail: allyson@brooksidemanor.net
Web: www.brooksidemanor.net

Circa 1690. Both architecturally and historically, this Colonial manor house fits in the category of great country homes. Formerly part of a large estate, it has been converted into a luxurious inn. The original one-and-a-half-story, post and beam structure with hearth and chimney still stands. Enjoy public gathering rooms splendidly decorated and furnished with antiques and Oriental rugs. Dramatic guest bedrooms offer an escape to a relaxing yet refined elegance. Homemade sausage, scones, fruit and a frittata are typical af the breakfasts served. Eight acres of professionally landscaped gardens are bordered by brick and stone terraces. A pond and brook add a park-like setting.
Innkeeper(s): Allyson Huskisson & Bob Vitale. $150-250. 5 rooms with PB, 5 with FP. Breakfast, afternoon tea and snacks/refreshments included in rates. Types of meals: Full gourmet bkfst, veg bkfst, early coffee/tea and gourmet dinner. Beds: KQT. Modem hook-up, cable TV, reading lamp, clock radio, telephone, turn-down service, desk, voice mail and fireplace in room. Central air. Fax, copier, library, parlor games and fireplace on premises. Weddings, small meetings and family reunions hosted. Amusement parks, antiquing, art galleries, beach, bicycling, canoeing/kayaking, fishing, golf, hiking, horseback riding, live theater, museums, parks, shopping, sporting events, tennis, water sports and wineries nearby.
Publicity: The Italian Travel Magazine, Dove, Harper & Queens and Country Living.

Larchwood Inn

521 Main St
Wakefield, RI 02879-4003
(401)783-5454 (800)275-5450 Fax:(401)783-1800
E-mail: larchwoodinn@xpos.com
Web: www.larchwoodinn.com

Circa 1831. The Larchwood Inn and its adjacent sister inn, Holly House, were both constructed in the same era. The two are sprinkled with antiques and are family-run, with 20th-century amenities. Scottish touches are found throughout the inn and

the Tam O'Shanter Tavern. Three dining rooms offer breakfast, lunch and dinner. (Breakfast is an extra charge.) The tavern offers dancing on weekends. Beaches, sailing and deep sea fishing all are nearby.
Innkeeper(s): Francis & Diann Browning. $40-150. 19 rooms, 13 with PB, 3 with FP and 1 conference room. Types of meals: Full bkfst, lunch and dinner. Reading lamp, telephone and desk in room. Fax and copier on premises. Weddings, small meetings, family reunions and seminars hosted. Antiquing, cross-country skiing, downhill skiing, live theater, shopping, beaches, fishing and boating nearby.
Publicity: Recommended Country Inns Yankee Magazine - Editors Pick.

Warren   E7

Nathaniel Porter Inn & Restaurant

125 Water St
Warren, RI 02885-3023
(401)245-6622 Fax:(401)247-2277
Web: www.nathanielporterinn.com

Circa 1750. Built by a sea captain in 1795 this Federal Colonial, listed in the National Register, was recently renovated and restored to offer modern improvements while retaining its historical integrity and New England traditions. Relax in the sitting room. Well-placed antique furnishings grace the tastefully decorated guest bedrooms that feature fireplaces. Some boast canopy beds. A continental breakfast is included. The inn's restaurant is known for fine dining in a romantic setting with fireplaces and works of art. Experience creative cuisine by candlelight in wing back chairs in one of the formal dining rooms, or enjoy the informal tavern with hand hewn beams. Take a walking tour, visit a museum or explore the many sites of the region.
Innkeeper(s): David W.Perry, Executive Chef & Alan E.Ramsay General Manager. $80. 3 rooms with PB, 3 with FP and 1 conference room. Breakfast included in rates. Types of meals: Full gourmet bkfst, veg bkfst, early coffee/tea, gourmet lunch, picnic lunch, afternoon tea, snacks/refreshments, gourmet dinner and room service. Restaurant on premises. Beds: KQT. Data port, cable TV, reading lamp, CD player, refrigerator, clock radio and telephone in room. Central air. VCR, swimming, bicycles, tennis and fireplace on premises. Weddings, small meetings, family reunions and seminars hosted. Amusement parks, antiquing, art galleries, beach, bicycling, canoeing/kayaking, cross-country skiing, downhill skiing, fishing, golf, hiking, horseback riding, live theater, museums, parks, shopping, sporting events, tennis, water sports and wineries nearby.
Publicity: Colonial Homes, Country Living, Yankee and Providence Journal.

Warwick   E6

Henry L. Johnson House

131 Post Rd
Warwick, RI 02888
(401)781-5158 Fax:(401)781-5158

Circa 1860. Named after the man who built this Greek Revival/early Victorian home for his residence, this gable-roofed, one-and-a-half story is located in historic Pawtuxet Village on Narragansett Bay. Recently renovated, the warm ambiance is inviting and intimate. Antique furnishings enhance a tasteful decor. Each guest bedroom features classic comfort, cable TV and a well-lit sitting area. Enjoy the welcome basket that provides bottled water, light snacks and toiletries. A full gourmet breakfast is served in the formal dining room. Embark on a New England adventure, offering something for everyone.
Innkeeper(s): Eric Gilbert & Richard LaNinfa. $90-100. 2 rooms. Breakfast included in rates. Types of meals: Full bkfst and snacks/refreshments. Beds: Q. Cable TV, reading lamp and clock radio in room. Air conditioning. VCR, fax, copier, swimming, library, parlor games, telephone, fireplace and laundry

facility on premises. Antiquing, art galleries, beach, bicycling, canoeing/kayaking, fishing, golf, hiking, live theater, museums, parks, shopping, sporting events, tennis, water sports and wineries nearby.

Westerly   I2

Grandview B&B

212 Shore Rd
Westerly, RI 02891-3623
(401)596-6384 (800)447-6384 Fax:(401)596-3036
E-mail: info@grandviewbandb.com

Circa 1910. An impressive wraparound stone porch highlights this majestic Shingle Victorian inn, which also boasts a lovely ocean view from its hilltop site. The inn features 9 guest rooms, a family room with cable TV, a spacious living room with a handsome stone fireplace, and a sun porch where visitors enjoy a hearty breakfast buffet. Antiquing, fishing, golf, swimming and tennis are found nearby as are Watch Hill, Mystic and Newport. The Foxwoods and Mohegan Sun casinos also are nearby.
Historic Interest: 1910 Building.
Innkeeper(s): Patricia Grand. $85-115. 9 rooms, 4 with PB & 1 suite. Breakfast included in rates. Types of meals: Cont plus & early coffee/tea. Beds: KQDT. Reading lamp, refrigerator, clock radio, 6 with ceiling fans & 2 with air conditioning in room. TV, fax, copier, bicycles, library, parlor games, telephone & fireplace on premises. Weddings, small meetings, family reunions & seminars hosted. Antiquing, fishing, live theater, parks, shopping, water sports & casinos nearby.

Langworthy Farm Bed & Breakfast

308 Shore Road
Westerly, RI 02891
(401)322-7791 (888)355-7083 Fax:(401)322-6040

Circa 1875. Enter this Victorian farmhouse from the side porch, facing the state's largest Norway Maple tree that was planted in 1875. Extensive renovations have been made to ensure comfortable furnishings and a tasteful decor. Several daily newspapers are available to read by the fireplace in the library. Appealing guest bedrooms and spacious suites feature antiques, most offer Jacuzzi tubs. Some boast views of the Atlantic Ocean, only one-half mile away. Savor a complete New England breakfast in the dining room. The walls depict hand painted scenes of local landmarks. Ride a bike to Misquamicut Beach, or scenic Watch Hill. Mystic Aquarium and Seaport are just a short drive.
Innkeeper(s): Joe and Gail Sharry. $85-175. 6 rooms, 4 with PB and 2 suites. Breakfast included in rates. Types of meals: Full bkfst and early coffee/tea. Beds: KQT. Modem hook-up, data port, cable TV, reading lamp, ceiling fan, clock radio, desk, hot tub/spa and fireplace in room. Central air. Fax, bicycles, library, telephone and fireplace on premises. Weddings and family reunions hosted. Amusement parks, antiquing, art galleries, beach, bicycling, canoeing/kayaking, fishing, golf, hiking, horseback riding, live theater, museums, parks, shopping, sporting events, tennis, water sports and wineries nearby.

Shelter Harbor Inn

10 Wagner Rd
Westerly, RI 02891-4701
(401)322-8883 (800)468-8883 Fax:(401)322-7907
E-mail: shelterharborinn@cox.net
Web: www.shelterharborinn.com

Circa 1810. This farmhouse at the entrance to the community of Shelter Harbor has been renovated and transformed to create a handsome country inn. Rooms, many with fireplaces, are in the main house, the barn and a carriage house. A third-floor deck with a hot tub, overlooks Block Island Sound. The dining room features local seafood and other traditional New England dishes.

Nearby are secluded barrier beaches, stone fences and salt ponds.
Innkeeper(s): Jim Dey. $78-178. 24 rooms with PB and 1 conference room. Breakfast included in rates. Types of meals: Full bkfst, lunch and dinner. Restaurant on premises. Beds: QD. Reading lamp, telephone and desk in room. Air conditioning. VCR, fireplace, Jacuzzi, croquet court and two paddle tennis courts on premises. Weddings, small meetings and family reunions hosted. Amusement parks, antiquing, beach, fishing, golf, shopping and tennis nearby.
Publicity: *Rhode Island Monthly and The Day.*

"This inn was, on the whole, wonderful."

The Villa

190 Shore Rd
Westerly, RI 02891-3629
(401)596-1054 (800)722-9240 Fax:(401)596-6268
E-mail: villa@riconnect.com
Web: www.thevillaatwesterly.com

Circa 1938. A lush landscape frames this three-story shuttered Dutch Colonial villa and its Italian-style porticos and verandas. Secluded on an acre and a half, the inn offers both a pool and outdoor hot tub. A queen-size bed and private sitting room is provided in La Sala di Venezia, while the Blue Grotto features natural stone walls as well as a fireside Jacuzzi. La Sala del Cielo has skylights and an ocean view in the distance. A breakfast buffet is served poolside or in the dining room. Some guests take their breakfast tray to their rooms. An 18-hole golf course is next door or you can drive to Mystic Seaport, Watch Hill or Foxwoods Casino. Newport is also a short drive away.
Innkeeper(s): Barbara Cardiff. $95-255. 7 suites, 2 with FP. Breakfast included in rates. Types of meals: Full bkfst and early coffee/tea. Beds: KQ. Cable TV, VCR, CD player, ceiling fan, clock radio, telephone, coffeemaker, microwave, refrigerator, coffeemaker, robes, hair dryer, four with Jacuzzi and two with gas fireplace in room. Air conditioning. Fax, spa, swimming, library and fireplace on premises. Family reunions hosted. Antiquing, art galleries, beach, bicycling, canoeing/kayaking, fishing, golf, horseback riding, live theater, museums, parks, shopping, tennis, water sports and wineries nearby.

Woonsocket   A5

Pillsbury House Bed & Breakfast

341 Prospect Street
Woonsocket, RI 02895
(401)766-7983 (800)205-4112
E-mail: rogerwnri@prodigy.net
Web: www.pillsburyhouse.com

Circa 1875. On an historic street in the fashionable North End, this restored Victorian mansion is one of the area's oldest. Boasting original parquet floors, high ceilings and furnished with antiques and period pieces, a grand elegance is imparted. Sit by the fire in the evenings or on the shaded porch during the day. A guest kitchenette on the second floor includes a microwave, refrigerator stocked with beverages, hair dryer and ironing board. Tastefully decorated guest bedrooms and a suite offer comfort and character. Breakfast in the gracious dining room is a satisfying meal with fresh fruit, homemade baked goods and a hot entree. Located in the heart of the Blackstone River Valley National Heritage Corridor, there is much to see and do.
Historic Interest: One of the area's oldest mansions, the Pillsbury House has been restored to its pre-turn-of-the-century elegance.
Innkeeper(s): Susan & Roger Bouchard. $95-135. 4 rooms with PB. Breakfast included in rates. Types of meals: Full bkfst and veg bkfst. Beds: KQDT. Clock radio in room. Air conditioning. TV, VCR, fax, telephone, fireplace, complimentary juices, beer and water available in second floor refreshment area on premises. Weddings and family reunions hosted. Antiquing, canoeing/kayaking, live theater, museums, parks, shopping, wineries, commuter train station to Boston 20 minutes away, 59 minute train ride to South Station and Museum of Work & Culture highlights the arrival of French Canadians Woonsocket and their merging into local culture nearby.

South Carolina

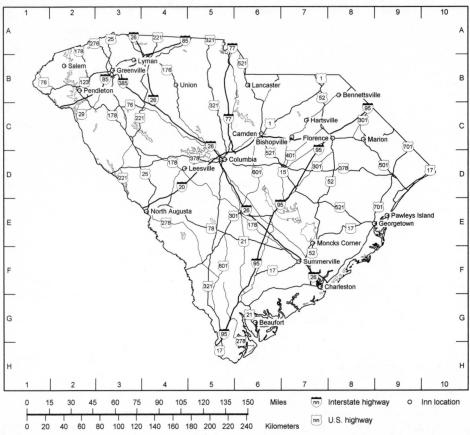

	Miles									
0	15	30	45	60	75	90	105	120	135	150

	Kilometers											
0	20	40	60	80	100	120	140	160	180	200	220	240

Interstate highway ○ Inn location
U.S. highway

Beaufort   G6

The Beaufort Inn

809 Port Republic St
Beaufort, SC 29901-1257
(843)521-9000 Fax:(843)521-9500
E-mail: bftinn@hargray.com
Web: www.beaufortinn.com

Circa 1897. Every inch of this breathtaking inn offers something special. The interior is decorated to the hilt with lovely furnishings, plants, beautiful rugs and warm, inviting tones. Rooms include four-poster and canopy beds combined with the modern amenities such as fireplaces, wet bars and stocked refrigerators. Enjoy a complimentary full breakfast at the inn's gourmet restaurant. The chef offers everything from a light breakfast of fresh fruit, cereal and a bagel to heartier treats such as pecan peach pancakes and Belgium waffles served with fresh fruit and crisp bacon.

Historic Interest: History buffs can visit Secession House, where the first ordinance for Southern secession was drawn up. Tabby Manse and Old Sheldon Church, burned in both the Revolutionary and Civil wars, still stand today. Penn Center, the first school for freed slaves, is located on St. Helena Island.

Innkeeper(s): Associated Luxury Inns of Beaufort. $145-350. 21 rooms with PB, 9 with FP, 6 suites and 1 conference room. Breakfast included in rates. Types of meals: Full gourmet bkfst, early coffee/tea, gourmet dinner and room service. Restaurant on premises. Beds: KQ. Data port, cable TV, VCR, reading lamp, refrigerator, ceiling fan and telephone in room. Air conditioning. Fax and copier on

534

premises. Weddings, small meetings, family reunions and seminars hosted. Antiquing, fishing, live theater, parks, shopping and water sports nearby.

Publicity: *Beaufort, Southern Living, Country Inns, Carolina Style, US Air and Town & Country.*

The Cuthbert House Inn B&B

1203 Bay St
Beaufort, SC 29902-5401
(843)521-1315 (800)327-9275 Fax:(843)521-1314
E-mail: cuthbert@hargray.com
Web: www.cuthberthouseinn.com

Circa 1790. This 18th-century waterfront mansion, listed in the National Register, boasts a veranda overlooking Beaufort Bay. The home was built during Washington's presidency, and General W.T. Sherman was once a guest here. The home has been lovingly restored to its original grandeur. Rich painted walls are highlighted by fine molding. Hardwood floors are topped with Oriental rugs and elegant 19th-century furnishings. The morning meal is served in a breakfast room that overlooks the water. The surrounding area offers plenty of activities in every season, and for those celebrating a new marriage, a honeymoon suite is available.

Historic Interest: Located in the National Landmark District.

Innkeeper(s): Gary & Sharon Groves. $155-265. 7 rooms with PB and 2 suites. Breakfast and snacks/refreshments included in rates. Types of meals: Country bkfst. Beds: KQ. Data port, cable TV, VCR, CD player, refrigerator, clock radio, telephone, voice mail, hair dryer, robes and some with fireplace or whirlpool in room. Air conditioning. Fax, bicycles, library, off-street parking and loaner beach towels and chairs on premises. Weddings, small meetings, family reunions and seminars hosted. Antiquing, fishing, parks, water sports, Parris Island USMC Depot, Ace Basin Tours and National Historic District tours nearby.

Publicity: *Beaufort Gazette, Atlanta Journal-Constitution, Glamour, Travel & Leisure, Delta Airlines Sky Magazine, Shape Magazine, Coastal Living, House & Garden Channel, White Squall and Top 10 Most Romantic Inns for 2002.*

Old Point Inn

212 New Street
Beaufort, SC 29902-5540
(843)524-3177 Fax:(843)525-6544
E-mail: oldpointinn@islc.net
Web: www.oldpointinn.com

Circa 1898. Built by William Waterhouse as a wedding present for his wife, Isabelle Richmond, this Queen Anne Victorian has wraparound verandas and a traditional southern garden. Guests can relax in the hammock while watching boats ply the Intracoastal Waterway. Four pillared fireplaces, pocket doors and eyebrow windows are features of the house. The inn is located in the residential historic district, with a waterfront park, a marina, restaurants and downtown shopping nearby.

Historic Interest: Santa Elena Archaeological Dig, Penn Center, Sheldon Ruins.

Innkeeper(s): Paul & Julie Michau. $95-165. 5 rooms with PB. Breakfast included in rates. Types of meals: Full gourmet bkfst. Beds: KQ. Air conditioning. Bicycles, baby grand piano, evening wine, Internet connection and kayaks on premises. Antiquing, fishing, golf, live theater, shopping, tennis and water sports nearby.

Publicity: *Islander, Southern Living, Southern Inns and Bed & Breakfast, Garden Tour, A Guide to Historic Beaufort, Historic Resources of the Low*

Country and Beaufort Lowcountry Magazine.

"Like walking backwards in time. It's rare to find a bed, more comfortable than your own. Breakfast — perfect! We're saddened to leave; like leaving on old friend."

TwoSuns Inn Bed & Breakfast

1705 Bay St
Beaufort, SC 29902-5406
(843)522-1122 (800)532-4244 Fax:(843)522-1122
E-mail: twosuns@islc.net
Web: www.twosunsinn.com

Circa 1917. The Keyserling family built this Neoclassical Revival-style home, which was later used by the local board of education as housing for single, female teachers. The home has been completely refurbished, a difficult task, considering the home had been the victim of two fires. The U.S. Department of the Interior noted the renovation with a Historic Building Certification in 1996. Guest rooms boast bay views, and each has its own theme. A gourmet breakfast and "Tea and Toddy Hour" are included in the rates.

Historic Interest: Beaufort has hosted film crews for many popular movies, including "Great Santini," "The Big Chill," "The Prince of Tides," "Forrest Gump" and "The Last Dance."

Innkeeper(s): Henri & Patricia Safran. $110-168. 6 rooms with PB. Breakfast and afternoon tea included in rates. Types of meals: Full gourmet bkfst, veg bkfst and early coffee/tea. Beds: KQ. Modem hook-up, cable TV, VCR, reading lamp, ceiling fan, clock radio, telephone and hair dryer in room. Central air. Fax, copier, bicycles, library, parlor games and fireplace on premises. Limited handicap access. Small meetings and family reunions hosted. Antiquing, art galleries, beach, bicycling, canoeing/kayaking, fishing, golf, hiking, live theater, museums, parks, shopping, tennis and water sports nearby.

Publicity: *Beaufort Gazette, Sandlapper, BBC 2 Travel Show December 19 and 1996.*

"One could not wish for a better experience."

Bennettsville   B8

Breeden Inn, Carriage House & Garden Cottage

404 E Main St
Bennettsville, SC 29512
(843)479-3665 (888)335-2996 Fax:(843)479-7998
E-mail: info@breedeninn.com
Web: www.breedeninn.com

Circa 1886. Three historic buildings in a village-like setting comprise this inn: the 1886 Southern mansion, the Carriage House and the Garden Cottage. One especially bountiful cotton crop paid for the construction of the mansion, which local attorney Thomas Bouchier presented to his bride as a wedding gift. The Main House exterior is graced with more than two dozen columns. The interior of each house features many interesting and varied architectural details. Suites and guest bedrooms delight with exquisite linens, antiques, collectibles, needlework and art. A satisfying morning meal is served in the dining room, breakfast parlor or on the veranda. Porch swings, rockers and ceiling fans are an inviting setting while overlooking the backyard wildlife habitat with trees and woodlands beyond.

Innkeeper(s): Wesley & Bonnie Park. $130-150. 10 rooms with PB, 9 with FP, 3 suites, 2 cottages and 1 conference room. Breakfast included in rates. Types of meals: Full bkfst and early coffee/tea. Beds: QDT. Cable TV, VCR, reading lamp, refrigerator, ceiling fan, telephone, desk, one suite with sunken whirlpool, five with private phone line, data port, central heating, hair dryer, iron/ironing board, full-length mirror, alarm clock, plush bed linens including down comforter and feather bed and fresh cut florals from the gardens of the inn in room. Central air. Fax, copier, parlor games, in-ground swimming pool, period Koi pond, antique/collectibles shop, hammock, binoculars/field guide books for birding, bicycles, volleyball, piano, refreshment drink upon arrival, two parlors, gathering room, two laundry rooms and two fully equipped period kitchens on premises. Small meetings hosted. Antiquing, fishing, golf, live theater, museums, shopping, tennis, local antiquing, 600-acre Lake Wallace, walking trails, swimming, historic touring, birding, volleyball and board games nearby.

"We were absolutely speechless at how lovely and comfortable our room was. Every detail was exquisite, especially the bedding. We had a wonderful romantic weekend. It was just what we were looking for and more. The gardens, your porches, the delicious food and your warm and friendly ways. Staying here was the highlight of our trip."

Bishopville   C7

The Foxfire B&B

416 N Main St
Bishopville, SC 29010-1442
(803)484-5643 (803)484-4489
E-mail: jeanwoodsc@sc.rr.com
Web: www.foxfirebnb.com

Circa 1922. A cotton broker built this unusual home, tinged with Spanish influences such as its tile roof. The home is fashioned from bricks, and the front exterior is decorated with a wraparound porch with tile floors and ceiling fans. Guests often choose this location to relax, as it's lined with rockers, chairs and a porch swing. The four rooms are comfortable, with pieces collected from around the world. Children are welcome and the innkeepers have games and swings. For breakfast, the innkeepers serve Swedish coffee, homemade muffins, fresh fruit and special items such as flannel cakes or stuffed French toast.
Innkeeper(s): Harry & Jean Woodmansee. $65-75. 4 rooms, 3 with FP. Breakfast included in rates. Types of meals: Full bkfst and early coffee/tea. Beds: KQT. Cable TV, reading lamp, ceiling fan and clock radio in room. Air conditioning. VCR, spa, bicycles, library, parlor games, telephone and fireplace on premises. Small meetings hosted. Antiquing, fishing, golf, museums, parks, tennis, Darlington raceway and South Carolina Cotton Museum nearby.
Publicity: *Lee County Observer.*

"True Southern hospitality, we will be back with our family to enjoy your home again."

Camden   C6

Candlelight Inn

1904 Broad St
Camden, SC 29020-2606
(803)424-1057

Circa 1933. Two acres of camellias, azaleas and oak trees surround this Cape Cod-style home. As per the name, the innkeepers keep a candle in each window, welcoming guests to this homey bed & breakfast. The decor is a delightful and tasteful mix of country, with quilts, hand-crafted samplers, poster beds, family antiques and traditional furnishings. Each of the rooms is named for someone significant in the innkeeper's life, and a picture of the special person decorates each room. Guests will enjoy the hearty breakfast, which changes daily. Several of innkeeper Jo Ann Celani's recipes have been featured in a cookbook, and one recipe won a blue ribbon at the Michigan State Fair.
Innkeeper(s): Jo Ann & George Celani. $90-125. 3 rooms, 2 with PB and 1

suite. Breakfast and snacks/refreshments included in rates. Types of meals: Full bkfst and early coffee/tea. Beds: QT. Reading lamp, clock radio, telephone, turn-down service and desk in room. Air conditioning. Library, parlor games and fireplace on premises. Antiquing, fishing, golf, live theater, parks, shopping, tennis and two steeplechase races nearby.
Publicity: *Chronicle-Independent, Sandlapper and Southern Inns and B&Bs.*

"You have captured the true spirit of a bed & breakfast."

Greenleaf Inn

1308 Broad St
Camden, SC 29020-3506
(803)425-1806 (800)437-5874 Fax:(803)425-5853
E-mail: info@greenleafinncamden.com
Web: www.greenleafinncamden.com

Circa 1805. Taste fine Southern living at this inn that consists of two historic homes, recently refurbished to reflect their original character and elegance. The 1805 Joshua Reynolds House is a Charleston-style home featuring a classic side veranda and traditional furnishings. The 1890 McLean House is Victorian in design and decor boasting ornate mantles, 14-foot ceilings, plantation shutters and a wraparound porch. Four-poster canopy beds and fireplaces are romantic amenities in many of the rooms. After breakfast, visit the local Revolutionary War Museum or Camden Archives, or attend a polo match at the fair grounds.
Innkeeper(s): Jim and Julie McIntyre. $89-129. 10 rooms with PB, 6 with FP. Breakfast included in rates. Types of meals: Full bkfst, early coffee/tea and dinner. Restaurant on premises. Beds: KQD. Cable TV, reading lamp, ceiling fan, clock radio, telephone, desk and voice mail in room. Central air. Fax, copier, parlor games and fireplace on premises. Weddings, small meetings, family reunions and seminars hosted. Antiquing, art galleries, fishing, golf, horseback riding, museums, parks and tennis nearby.

Charleston   F7

1843 Battery Carriage House Inn

20 S Battery St
Charleston, SC 29401-2727
(843)727-3100 (800)775-5575 Fax:(843)727-3130
E-mail: bch@mymailstation.com
Web: www.batterycarriagehouse.com

Circa 1843. Just outside the door of this antebellum house, guests can enjoy the serenity of a Charleston garden. And outside the wrought iron gates lies White Point Gardens, the Battery and Charleston Harbor, enticing guests to romantic moonlight walks and sultry daytime strolls in one of Charleston's most beautiful locations. Guest rooms are in both the Carriage House and in the ground floor of the Stephen Lathers House, a private residence. Renovations in many rooms have preserved the charm of the past, while increasing amenities, including cable television and steam baths or Jacuzzis that add to the inn's romantic atmosphere. Silver Tray Continental Breakfast service is provided and evening turndown adds to the pampering, as well. The inn was featured in the filming of "North and South" and the interior rooms have been filmed for "Queen." In the afternoon, visitors often enjoy a glass of wine in the gardens.
Historic Interest: Fort Sumter and Plantations are nearby.
$99-269. 11 rooms with PB. Types of meals: Cont. Beds: QT. Cable TV, reading lamp, ceiling fan, clock radio, telephone, turn-down service and some

with steam bath showers in room. Air conditioning. Fax on premises. Antiquing, art galleries, beach, bicycling, fishing, golf, live theater, museums, parks, shopping and water sports nearby.

Publicity: *New York Times, Los Angeles Times and South Carolina Touring.*

21 East Battery Bed and Breakfast

21 East Battery
Charleston, SC 29401
(843)577-8289
E-mail: info@21eastbattery.com
Web: www.21eastbattery.com

Circa 1825. Cradled within the urban compound of the historic 1825 Edmondston-Alston House, this bed & breakfast includes a renovated and sequestered carriage house and servants' quarters. Enjoy off-street parking and a personable welcome from the helpful resident manager. Original beamed ceilings and heart-pine floors are accented with attractive antiques in the roomy carriage house. Gaze at the Charleston Harbor from the second-floor balcony. The two-story quarters boasts two bedrooms and a downstairs fireplace. A prestocked kitchen features fresh fruit, juices, pastries, and a gourmet breakfast.

Historic Interest: 21 East Battery was built in 1825, one of the first dwellings constructed along the High Battery, during the tenure of the property's first owner, Charles Edmondston. Later, in 1838, second-owner Charles Alston extensively remodeled the house, adding significant Greek Revival details. The rear dependency originally served as a stable and livery for the wealthy rice planter's fine horses and handsome town carriages. The quarters once housed the servants who helped make 21 East Battery one of the city's showplaces of style and gracious entertaining. Today, the property once again welcomes visitors to the city where hospitality has always been an art.

Innkeeper(s): Laughton Chandler. $200-400. 3 rooms with PB, 2 with FP. Breakfast included in rates. Types of meals: Cont plus. Beds: Q. Data port, cable TV, reading lamp, stereo, refrigerator, clock radio, telephone, coffeemaker, desk and fireplace in room. Central air. Library, parlor games and fireplace on premises. Amusement parks, antiquing, art galleries, beach, bicycling, canoeing/kayaking, fishing, golf, hiking, horseback riding, live theater, museums, parks, shopping, tennis and water sports nearby.

A B&B At 4 Unity Alley

4 Unity Alley
Charleston, SC 29401
(843)577-6660 Fax:(843)723-3346

Circa 1820. Although George Washington never actually slept here, he did keep his horses on the premises while he dined in a restaurant next door. Today, the bed & breakfast is certainly fit for more than a horse. In fact, the innkeepers bill the place as an "antique warehouse." Rooms are pristine and airy with the signature antiques as well as a few modern pieces. The manicured grounds include a small garden filled with orchids. Charleston is known for its outstanding cuisine, and there are many restaurants within walking distance. Guests also can stroll to shops and boutiques or take a walking tour past historic homes. Plantation tours and golf are other nearby attractions just a short drive away.

Innkeeper(s): Rick Schneider, Don Smith. $125-165. 3 suites. Breakfast included in rates. Types of meals: Full gourmet bkfst. Beds: KQ. Cable TV, reading lamp, ceiling fan, clock radio, telephone and desk in room. Central air. Fax, copier and bicycles on premises. Antiquing, art galleries, beach, bicycling, fishing, golf, live theater, museums, shopping, tennis and water sports nearby.

Ansonborough Inn

21 Hasell St
Charleston, SC 29401-2601
(843)723-1655 (800)522-2073 Fax:(843)577-6888
E-mail: info@ansonboroughinn.com
Web: www.ansonboroughinn.com

Circa 1901. Once a stationer's warehouse won in a poker game by a British admiral, this three-story, all-suite inn sits in the middle of the historic district. Decorated and furnished in period antiques and reproductions, the inn boasts heart-pine beams, exposed brick walls and a three-story atrium. A delightful continental breakfast is served each morning in the library. It may include fresh raisin bread, danishes, bagels, fruits and juices. Each afternoon, wine and cheese with a homemade pimento cheese dip is served. The SC Aquarium and Waterfront Park are nearby. The Battery, open-air Old City Market and many historic tours are just a short walk away.

Innkeeper(s): Allison Fennell. $149-339. 37 rooms with PB, 5 with FP and 2 conference rooms. Types of meals: Cont plus, early coffee/tea, afternoon tea and snacks/refreshments. Beds: KQT. Modem hook-up, cable TV, reading lamp, refrigerator, clock radio, telephone, desk, voice mail and data ports in room. Central air. VCR, fax, copier and modem hook-up on premises. Limited handicap access. Weddings, small meetings and seminars hosted. Antiquing, art galleries, beach, bicycling, fishing, golf, live theater, museums, parks, shopping, sporting events, Historic city tours and aquarium nearby.

Publicity: *Southern Living, Travel Host, Seabreeze Magazine, Charleston Post and Courier, Spirit of the Carolinas Magazine, Charleston Regional Business Journal and Conde' Nast Johansens.*

"Thank you for such charm and hospitality. Elegantly decorated. Warm and friendly staff."

Antebellum B&B at The Thomas Lamboll House

19 King St
Charleston, SC 29401-2734
(843)723-3212 (888)874-0793 Fax:(843)723-5222

Circa 1735. A Colonial South Carolina judge, Thomas Lamboll, was the first resident of this impressive Colonial, located in Charleston's historic district. The home features two stories of piazzas set up with wicker furnishings, where guests can catch a cool breeze in the afternoon. The rooms are appointed with fine antiques, including Chippendale chairs and an early 19th-century sideboard in the dining room. There are two guest rooms, each with French doors leading to the piazzas, that overlook rooftops and the Charleston Harbor in the distance.

Innkeeper(s): Marie & Emerson Read. $125-185. 2 rooms with PB, 2 with FP and 1 suite. Breakfast included in rates. Types of meals: Cont. Beds: QT. Cable TV, reading lamp, ceiling fan, clock radio and telephone in room. Air conditioning. Fireplace on premises. Amusement parks, antiquing, fishing, live theater, parks, shopping, sporting events and water sports nearby.

Ashley Inn B&B

201 Ashley Ave
Charleston, SC 29403-5810
(843)723-1848 (800)581-6658 Fax:(843)579-9080
E-mail: ashleyinnbb@aol.com
Web: www.charleston-sc-inns.com

Circa 1832. Pampering guests is the specialty of the house at this bed & breakfast. The rose exterior has green shutters and porches on the first and second stories. Bright, colorful rooms

are accented by polished, hardwood floors, beautiful rugs and glorious furnishings and collectibles. Guest rooms boast antique four-poster, pencil-post or canopied rice beds. Breakfasts at Ashley Inn create culinary memories. Savory sausage pie, peaches and cream stuffed waffles with praline sauce or eggs Benedict Ashley are only a few of the mouth-watering specialties. An afternoon complete with plenty of homemade treats and evening sherry also is served. The innkeepers also provide bicycles for touring scenic Charleston.

Historic Interest: The inn is located in the Charleston historic district, full of interesting sites and shops. Ft. Sumter, The Battery, cabbage row, carriage tours and the market are nearby.

Innkeeper(s): Barry Carroll. $85-265. 6 rooms with PB and 1 suite. Breakfast and afternoon tea included in rates. Types of meals: Full gourmet bkfst. Beds: KQD. Home baked treats on premises. Antiquing, beach, fishing, golf, live theater, water sports and aquarium nearby.

Publicity: *Charleston Post & Courier, LA Times and Country Inn Cooking.*

"A truly pampering experience for both of us!"

Belvedere B&B

40 Rutledge Ave
Charleston, SC 29401-1702
(843)722-0973 (800)816-1664
E-mail: innkeeper@belvedereinn.com
Web: www.belvedereinn.com

Circa 1900. This Colonial Revival home with its semicircular portico, Ionic columns and four piazzas boasts a beautiful view of Charleston's Colonial Lake. Bright, airy rooms feature high ceilings with fans, polished wood floors, fireplaces, antique furnishings and Oriental rugs. Relax and enjoy the view on the piazzas or in one of the inn's public rooms. Belvedere B&B is close to many wonderful restaurants and shops.

Historic Interest: Belvedere is located in the downtown historic district and within walking distance to many historical sites, including museums, points of interest and Civil War landmarks.

Innkeeper(s): David S. Spell. $99-195. 3 rooms with PB. Breakfast included in rates. Types of meals: Cont plus. Beds: Q. Cable TV, ceiling fan, clock radio, desk and ornamental fireplaces in room. Air conditioning. VCR, telephone and refrigerator on premises. Antiquing, fishing, live theater, parks, shopping, sporting events and water sports nearby.

Publicity: *Discerning Traveler and Southern Brides.*

Cannonboro Inn

184 Ashley Ave
Charleston, SC 29403-5824
(803)723-8572 (800)235-8039 Fax:(803)723-8007
E-mail: cannonboroinn@aol.com
Web: www.charleston-sc-inns.com

Circa 1853. Enjoy a breakfast feast of Cannonboro Inn Eggs Benedict served with warm French puff muffins and local fresh fruit on the columned piazza overlooking the country garden and fountain. Guest rooms feature luxurious furnishings and antique four-poster and canopy beds. After a day in the city on the inn's touring bicycles, return for a scrumptious afternoon tea of home-baked treats and sherry. Cannonboro Inn has been rated as one of the best places to stay in the South.

Historic Interest: The Charleston Museum, Gibbes Museum and Plantations are nearby.

Innkeeper(s): Barry Carroll. $85-220. 5 rooms with PB and 1 suite. Breakfast and afternoon tea included in rates. Types of meals: Full gourmet bkfst. Beds: KQD. Cable TV, reading lamp, ceiling fan and clock radio in room. Air conditioning. TV, bicycles, parlor games, telephone, fireplace, free off-street parking and home baked treats on premises. Antiquing, beach, fishing, golf, live theater, parks, shopping, sporting events, tennis, water sports, carriage rides, harbor tours and aquarium nearby.

Publicity: *Chicago Sun-Times.*

"A brochure cannot convey the friendly, warm atmosphere created by their friendly innkeepers."

Charleston Governor's House

117 Broad St
Charleston, SC 29401-2435
(843)720-2070 (800)720-9812
E-mail: innkeeper@governorshouse.com
Web: www.governorshouse.com

Circa 1760. One of the most classic of Southern cities, Charleston's grace and beauty can be experienced at one of its most historic and gracious inns. At the Charleston Governor's House, civility and romance are a tradition. Declared a National Historic Landmark, the former Governor's Mansion was built in 1760 and was the home of Edward Rutledge, one of South Carolina's representatives to the First Continental Congress in 1775 and the youngest person to ratify and sign the Declaration of Independence a year later. After his capture and imprisonment by the British, he became governor of South Carolina and lived in this stately home. Today, one of the finest suites in the inn bears his name. Antique Italian chandeliers look down upon a king-size, arched-canopy bed, and a fireplace warms an elegant sitting area. When the weather is fine, a private porch makes a good spot for conversation. Three other suites also feature fireplaces, canopy beds, marble whirlpools and showers, while four standard rooms have combinations of 12-foot-high ceilings, canopy beds, sitting areas and porches. Hardwood floors extend throughout the inn. Homemade Charleston muffins and fresh local fruit are presented each morning in the dining room or on the spacious double veranda — also the locations for the inn's Lowcountry afternoon tea and evening sherry. Within walking distance of the inn are the other magnificent homes and gardens of the historic district of Charleston, the Battery and the Old Market.

Innkeeper(s): Karen Shaw. $179-345. 11 rooms with PB, 5 with FP, 4 suites and 2 conference rooms. Breakfast, afternoon tea and snacks/refreshments included in rates. Types of meals: Cont plus, early coffee/tea and room service. Beds: KQ. Modem hook-up, cable TV, refrigerator, ceiling fan, clock radio and telephone in room. Central air. TV, fax, fireplace, complimentary parking, low country afternoon tea and evening sherry on premises. Small meetings hosted. Antiquing, art galleries, beach, bicycling, fishing, golf, horseback riding, live theater, museums, parks, shopping, tennis, water sports, historic sites and plantations nearby.

Publicity: *Southern Living, Travel Holiday, Golf Digest, Discerning Traveler and Southern Living Favorites/Best of the South.*

Fulton Lane Inn

202 King Street
Charleston, SC 29401-3109
(843)720-2600 (800)720-2688 Fax:(843)720-2940

Circa 1870. The family of Confederate blockade runner John Rugheimer built this charming brick building after the Civil War ended. Bright cheery decor and fine furnishings highlight the architecture, which includes cathedral ceilings and several fireplaces. The inn affords views of the city skyline, full of historic sites and gracious, Southern buildings. Guest rooms boast canopy beds draped with hand-strung netting and large, whirlpool tubs. The innkeeper includes a refrigerator in each room, and delivers breakfast on a silver tray. Wine and sherry are served in the lobby.

Historic Interest: Fulton Lane Inn is located in Charleston's historic district and the area abounds with historic sites.

Innkeeper(s): Michelle Woodhull. $150-295. 27 rooms with PB, 8 with FP, 4 suites and 2 conference rooms. Breakfast included in rates. Types of meals: Cont and room service. Beds: KQ. Cable TV, reading lamp, refrigerator, clock radio, telephone and turn-down service in room. Air conditioning. Fax and child care on premises. Limited handicap access. Weddings, small meetings, family reunions and seminars hosted. Antiquing, fishing, live theater, parks, shopping and water sports nearby.

Publicity: *Southern Accents.*

Hayne House B&B

30 King St
Charleston, SC 29401-2733
(843)577-2633 Fax:(843)577-5906
E-mail: haynehouse@yahoo.com
Web: www.haynehouse.com

Circa 1730. Located one block from the Battery in one of Charleston's premiere private residential areas, this handsome clapboard house is in the National Register of Historic Places. Surrounded by a wrought-iron garden fence, it has an 1820 addition. It was built three stories tall to capture the harbor

breeze. The inn is furnished in antiques, and there is an appealing back porch with rockers and a swing. In addition to the six tastefully decorated guest rooms, there are two romantic suites that feature individual whirlpool tubs. The inn is a neighbor to some of the finest 18th- and 19th-century houses in America, including the Miles Brewton House, directly across the street, and the Nathaniel Russell House, just one block away. A full Southern breakfast is offered every morning.

Historic Interest: One of Charleston's oldest houses and one of 73 pre-Revolutionary buildings in the city. Listed in the National Register; restoration certified by the U.S Department of the Interior. Home of the illustrious Hayne family in the early 19th century, as well as of Basil Manly, Chaplain to the Confederacy.

Innkeeper(s): Brian & Jane McGreevy. $129-295. 6 rooms with PB, 4 with FP, 2 suites and 1 conference room. Breakfast included in rates. Types of meals: Full bkfst. Beds: KQT. Reading lamp, refrigerator, coffeemaker, hot tub/spa and fireplace in room. Central air. Fax, spa, library, telephone and fireplace on premises. Small meetings, family reunions and seminars hosted. Antiquing, art galleries, beach, bicycling, fishing, golf, live theater, museums, parks, shopping, tennis and water sports nearby.

Publicity: *InStyle Magazine, one of top five inns 5/01 Travel Holiday, one of top three inns 2/02 Fodor's Best Bed & Breakfasts in the South, one of only three highly recommended inns in Charleston Fodor's America's Best Bed and Breakfasts InnSpots and Special Places Recommended Bed & Breakfasts: The South and HGTV Charleston Roadtrip.*

"A fantasy realized. What a wonderful gift of hospitality."

John Rutledge House Inn

116 Broad St
Charleston, SC 29401
(843)723-7999 (800)476-9741 Fax:(843)720-2615

Circa 1763. John Rutledge, first governor of South Carolina, Supreme Court Justice, and an author and signer of the Constitution of the United States, wrote first drafts of the docu-

ment in the stately ballroom of his Charleston home. In 1791 George Washington dined in this same room. Both men would be amazed by the house's recent restoration, which includes three lavish suites with elaborately carved Italian marble fireplaces, personal refrigerators, spas, air conditioning and televisions along with fine antiques and reproductions. Exterior ironwork on the house was designed in the 19th century and features palmetto trees and American eagles to honor Mr. Rutledge's service to the state and country.

Innkeeper(s): Kathy Leslie. $190-385. 19 rooms with PB, 8 with FP, 3 suites and 1 conference room. Breakfast and afternoon tea included in rates. Types of meals: Full bkfst and room service. Beds: KQD. Cable TV, reading lamp, refrigerator, clock radio, telephone, turn-down service and desk in room. Air conditioning. TV, fax, child care and two carriage houses on premises. Limited handicap access. Weddings, small meetings, family reunions and seminars hosted. Antiquing, fishing, live theater, parks, shopping and water sports nearby.

Publicity: *Innsider, Colonial Homes, New York Times, Southern Living, Southern Accents, Gourmet, Bon Appetit, Deadly Pursuit and NBC.*

"Two hundred years of American history in two nights; first-class accommodations, great staff. John Rutledge should've had it so good!"

King George IV Inn

32 George St, Historic District
Charleston, SC 29401-1416
(843)723-9339 (888)723-1667 Fax:(843)723-7749
E-mail: info@kinggeorgeiv.com
Web: www.kinggeorgeiv.com

Circa 1792. This inn is a four-story Federal-style home with three levels of Charleston porches. All the rooms have decorative fireplaces, high ceilings, original wide-planked hardwood floors and finely crafted original moldings and architectural detail. Peter Freneau, who was a prominent Charleston journalist, merchant, ship owner and Jeffersonian politician, occupied the house for many years. The inn offers a hearty continental breakfast every morning. There is off-street parking available and King Street shopping and restaurants are just a short walk away.

Historic Interest: The inn is located in the United States' largest historic district with more than 3,000 historic homes and mansions.

Innkeeper(s): Debra, Terry. $99-185. 10 rooms, 8 with PB, 9 with FP and 4 suites. Breakfast included in rates. Types of meals: Cont plus and afternoon tea. Beds: QDT. Reading lamp, refrigerator, clock radio, telephone, television and decorative fireplace in room. Air conditioning. Fax and fireplace on premises. Small meetings and family reunions hosted. Antiquing, fishing, live theater, parks, shopping, sporting events, water sports and aquarium nearby.

The Kitchen House

126 Tradd St
Charleston, SC 29401-2420
(843)577-6362 Fax:(843)965-5615

Circa 1732. This elegant, pre-Revolutionary War house was once the home of Dr. Peter Fayssoux, who served as Surgeon General in the Continental Army during the Revolutionary War. His descendant Bernard Elliot Bee became the Confederate general who bestowed the nickname of "Stonewall" to General Stonewall Jackson. The kitchen building has been restored around its four original fireplaces using antique materials. The inn's patio overlooks a Colonial herb garden, pond and fountain. The pantry and refrigerator are stocked with breakfast items. Juice, cereals, eggs, fresh fruit, specialty teas and coffee are provided for guests. Afternoon sherry awaits guests on arrival and a concierge service is offered.

Historic Interest: Located in the heart of Charleston's historic district, the inn offers close access to many museum homes and antique shopping.

Innkeeper(s): Lois Evans. $150-400. 4 rooms with PB. Breakfast included in rates. Types of meals: Full bkfst. Beds: QT. Cable TV, VCR, reading lamp, refrigerator, clock radio, telephone and desk in room. Air conditioning. TV, fax, copier, library, fireplace and concierge Service on premises. Antiquing, fishing, golf, live theater, parks, shopping, sporting events, tennis and water sports nearby.

Publicity: *New York Times and Colonial Homes.*

"By all comparisons, one of the very best."

The Palmer Home B&B

5 East Battery
Charleston, SC 29401
(843)853-1574 (888)723-1574 Fax:(843)723-7983
E-mail: palmerbnb@aol.com
Web: www.palmerhomebb.com

Circa 1849. Considered one of the city's fifty most famous homes, this Italianesque mansion is known as "The Pink Palace." The hosts of this highly acclaimed bed & breakfast are third-generation owners. Incredible views of the Charleston Harbour and historic Fort Sumter are easily enjoyed throughout the home. Gather in the elegant drawing room, or sit on one of the covered front porches. Romantic guest bedrooms in the main house feature even more spectacular views from the third floor. A separate carriage house is also available. Take a relaxing swim in the pool. Weddings in the splendid garden or on the piazza are popular here.

Innkeeper(s): Francess Palmer Hogan. $175-300. 3 rooms with PB and 1 suite. Breakfast included in rates. Types of meals: Cont. Beds: KQD. Cable TV, VCR, reading lamp, refrigerator, ceiling fan, clock radio and telephone in room. Air conditioning. Fax, swimming, fireplace and free parking on premises. Weddings and small meetings hosted. Antiquing, fishing, golf, live theater, parks, sporting events, tennis and water sports nearby.

Phoebe Pember House

26 Society Street
Charleston, SC 29401-1532
(843)722-4186 Fax:(843)722-0557
E-mail: info@phoebepemberhouse.com
Web: www.phoebepemberhouse.com

Circa 1807. Acclaimed in Charleston as one of the most unique heritage properties in town, and located in the Historic District, East Bay is a Single House with a carriage house in the Federal style. Two large piazzas overlook the walled garden and the harbor. Phoebe Pember, Civil War heroine, was born here. Spacious guest rooms are filled with original art, antiques and fine fabrics. Some rooms offer canopied beds while others have a fully draped poster bed. Breakfast is provided on a silver tray that may be enjoyed in the guest rooms, the dining room or on the piazza.

Historic Interest: 1807 construction, with original hand carved, gouged woodwork, and fireplaces with Egyptian marble (not available after 1807) mantles dress the rooms. The Blue Room is virtually unchanged from 200 years ago. Other rooms still have original fireplaces. Phoebe Pember (Charleston's favorite daughter) was born on the third floor of the main house.

Innkeeper(s): Carolyn Rivers & Shannon Reardon. $125-215. 6 rooms with PB, 6 with FP, 1 suite and 1 conference room. Breakfast included in rates. Types of meals: Cont plus, veg bkfst, early coffee/tea and room service. Beds: KQT. Cable TV, reading lamp, CD player, ceiling fan, clock radio, telephone,

coffeemaker, turn-down service, desk, voice mail, fireplace and Jacuzzi bath in one room in room. Central air. VCR, fax, copier, fireplace, meditation gardens, yoga center, arbor and piazzas and balconies on premises. Weddings, small meetings, family reunions and seminars hosted. Antiquing, art galleries, beach, bicycling, canoeing/kayaking, fishing, golf, live theater, parks, shopping, sporting events, tennis, water sports and restaurants nearby.

Publicity: *Victoria Magazine, Charleston's City Paper and Skirt Magazine.*

Planters Inn

112 N Market St
Charleston, SC 29401-3118
(843)722-2345 (800)845-7082 Fax:(843)577-2125
E-mail: reservations@plantersinn.com
Web: www.plantersinn.com

Circa 1844. Prepare for a getaway of romance, elegance and history at this opulent, four-diamond-rated inn, located in historic Charleston. Built decades prior to the Civil War, the inn has watched Charleston grow and change. The interior displays the height of Southern elegance and charm. Rooms are decorated with rich wallcoverings, elegant furnishings and four-poster beds topped with the finest of linens. The inn's restaurant, Peninsula Grill, has been named one of the best new restaurants in the country by Esquire magazine, and the dining room serves a hearty breakfast including scrumptious pastries freshly baked in the kitchen and waffles and omelets. Guests, if they choose, may dine al fresco in a landscaped courtyard. Rated "Blue Shield" by Relais & Chateaux and 4 Diamond by AAA, the inn also offers romance and history packages.

Innkeeper(s): Larry Spelts, Jr. $195-350. 62 rooms with PB. Types of meals: Full bkfst. Restaurant on premises. Beds: KQ. Reading lamp, clock radio and turn-down service in room. Air conditioning. Fax, copier and telephone on premises. Small meetings hosted. Antiquing, live theater and shopping nearby.

Two Meeting Street Inn

2 Meeting St
Charleston, SC 29401-2799
(843)723-7322
Web: www.twomeetingstreet.com

Circa 1890. In the center of the historic district overlooking prestigious South Battery, this turreted Queen Anne was built as a wedding gift from a father to his daughter. It is one of the area's oldest bed & breakfast inns, offering Southern hospitality and a romantic heritage. Tiffany  stained-glass windows, crystal chandeliers and English oak woodwork are accented by fresh flowers, Oriental rugs and family heirlooms. Traditional antiques furnish the elegant guest bedrooms. Enjoy a deluxe continental breakfast in the courtyard or oval dining room. The famous arched piazza features rockers that invite relaxation while gazing beyond the century-old live oaks to the harbor. Low country afternoon tea is served with sherry and regional delicacies.

Historic Interest: The inn is located in Charleston's historic district overlooking Battery Park, where shots were fired during the Civil War. There are several museum homes around the inn, and Charleston offers many other historical sites.

Innkeeper(s): The Spell Family. $170-310. 9 rooms with PB, 5 with FP. Breakfast and afternoon tea included in rates. Types of meals: Cont plus and early coffee/tea. Beds: Q. TV, reading lamp, ceiling fan, clock radio and low country afternoon tea in room. Central air. Telephone and fireplace on premises. Antiquing, art galleries, beach, bicycling, fishing, golf, live theater, museums, parks, shopping and water sports nearby.

Publicity: *Innsider, Southern Accent and Gourmet.*

"Were there such an award as the - Ultimate Hosting Award — it would without question go to the Two Meeting Street Inn. The graciousness of your friendly ways in such a wonderful setting are unsurpassable."

Vendue Inn

19 Vendue Range
Charleston, SC 29401-2129
(843)577-7970 (800)845-7900
E-mail: info@vendueinn.com
Web: www.vendueinn.com

Circa 1864. In the Historic District near Waterfront Park and the harbor, this elegant inn was a series of 1860s warehouses before refurbishing into distinctive lodgings. Romantic guest bedrooms feature canopy or sleigh beds, open beam ceilings, reproduction wallpaper, antiques, original artwork, newspaper delivery and two-line telephones with data port. Spacious suites boast working fireplaces, travertine marble baths with whirlpool tubs and separate showers. Indulge in a traditional Southern breakfast buffet complete with grits. Enjoy afternoon wine and cheese in the lobby and after-dinner cordials or milk and cookies. Borrow a bike to tour the scenic French Quarter. The Rooftop Terrace offers panoramic views. A concierge will arrange carriage rides, tours or reservations.

Innkeeper(s): Coyne & Linda Edmison. $145-299. 65 rooms with PB, 26 with FP and 4 conference rooms. Breakfast included in rates. Types of meals: Full bkfst, lunch and dinner. Restaurant on premises. Beds: KQD. Cable TV, ceiling fan and turn-down service in room. Air conditioning. TV, VCR, fax, copier and telephone on premises. Beach, golf and live theater nearby.
Publicity: *Southern Living, Bon Appetit, Travel, New York Times and In-Style Magazine.*

Victoria House Inn

208 King St
Charleston, SC 29401
(843)720-2944 (800)933-5464 Fax:(843)720-2930

Circa 1898. Enjoy the gracious decor of the Victorian era while staying at this Romanesque-style inn, located in the heart of Charleston's historic district along King Street's famed Antique Row. Some rooms boast working fireplaces, while others feature romantic whirlpool baths. Champagne breakfasts are delivered to the bedchambers each morning, and the nightly turndown service includes chocolates on your pillow. Enjoy a glass of sherry before heading out to one of Charleston's many fine restaurants. The Victoria House Inn is close to a variety of antique shops and fashionable boutiques.

Historic Interest: The inn is within walking distance of plenty of historic homes and museums, and walking tours are available.
Innkeeper(s): Michelle Woodhull. $150-270. 18 rooms with PB, 4 with FP, 4 suites and 1 conference room. Breakfast included in rates. Types of meals: Cont plus and room service. Beds: KD. Cable TV, reading lamp, refrigerator, clock radio, telephone, turn-down service and desk in room. Air conditioning. Fax, copier and child care on premises. Limited handicap access. Weddings, small meetings, family reunions and seminars hosted. Antiquing, fishing, live theater, parks, shopping and water sports nearby.
Publicity: *Washington Post and Great Country Inns.*

Villa De La Fontaine B&B

138 Wentworth St
Charleston, SC 29401-1734
(843)577-7709
Web: charleston.cityinformation.com/villa/

Circa 1838. This magnificent Greek Revival manor is among Charleston's finest offerings. The grounds are lush with gardens and manicured lawns, and ionic columns adorn the impressive exterior. The innkeeper is a retired interior designer, and his elegant touch is found throughout the mansion, including many 18th-century antiques. A fully trained chef prepares the gourmet breakfasts, which are served in a solarium with a hand-painted mural and 12-foot windows. The chef's recipe for cornmeal waffles was featured in a Better Homes & Gardens' cookbook. The inn is located in the heart of Charleston's historic district, three blocks from the market area.

Innkeeper(s): Aubrey Hancock. $125-200. 4 rooms with PB and 1 cottage. Breakfast included in rates. Types of meals: Full gourmet bkfst. Beds: KQT. Reading lamp and TV in room. Central air. Telephone on premises. Antiquing, fishing, live theater, parks, shopping, sporting events, water sports and Medical U nearby.
Publicity: *New York Times.*

"What a wonderful vacation we had as recipients of your lavish hospitality."

Columbia   D5

Chestnut Cottage B&B

1718 Hampton St
Columbia, SC 29201-3420
(803)256-1718 (888)308-1718

Circa 1850. This inn was originally the home of Confederate General James Chesnut and his wife, writer Mary Boykin Miller Chesnut. She authored "A Diary From Dixie," written during the Civil War but published posthumously in 1905. The white frame one-and-a-half-story house has a central dormer with an arched window above the main entrance. The small porch has four octagonal columns and an ironwork balustrade. Hearty breakfasts are served in the privacy of your room, on the porch or in the main dining room. The innkeepers can provide you with sightseeing information, make advance dinner reservations, as well as cater to any other special interests you might have.

Historic Interest: Historic homes, Robert Mills Mansion, Hampton-Preston Mansion, The Woodrow Wilson Home (1 1/2 blocks).
Innkeeper(s): Gale Garrett. $75-225. 5 rooms with PB, 3 with FP and 1 suite. Breakfast and snacks/refreshments included in rates. Types of meals: Full gourmet bkfst, early coffee/tea, picnic lunch, gourmet dinner and room service. Beds: KQ. Modem hook-up, data port, cable TV, VCR, reading lamp, stereo, refrigerator, ceiling fan, snack bar, clock radio, telephone, coffeemaker, turn-down service, desk and fireplace in room. Central air. Fax and copier on premises. Weddings, small meetings, family reunions and seminars hosted. Antiquing, fishing, live theater, parks, shopping, sporting events and water sports nearby.
Publicity: *Sandlapper, London Financial Times and TV show "Breakfast with Christie."*

"You really know how to pamper and spoil. Chestnut Cottage is a great place to stay."

Florence   C8

Abingdon Manor

307 Church St
Florence, SC 29565-1359
(843)752-5090 (888)752-5090 Fax:(843)752-6034

Circa 1905. Boasting a four-diamond rating for both the inn
and the on-site restaurant, this lavish country inn was originally
built as an opulent private residence. Situated on three acres in
the historic district of a quaint village, this Greek Revival mansion is luxuriously appointed. Bask
in the elegant yet unpretentious
atmosphere, and enjoy the
attention to detail that
instills relaxation. Guest bed-
rooms feature an abundance
of pampering amenities. A full breakfast is served daily. Six-
course prix fixe dinners are presented at intimately lit tables for
two with fresh flowers, settings of silver, china and crystal.
Subtle sounds of jazz add to the warm ambiance. Cocktails,
wines, liqueurs and cordials are available.

Innkeeper(s): Michael & Patty Griffey. $130-185. 6 rooms with PB, 5 with
FP, 1 suite and 1 conference room. Breakfast included in rates. Types of
meals: Full gourmet bkfst, early coffee/tea and dinner. Beds: KQD. Cable TV,
VCR, reading lamp, turn-down service, desk, robes, feather beds, chocolates
and bath amenities in room. Air conditioning. Fax, parlor games, telephone,
fireplace and Internet access on premises. Weddings, small meetings, family
reunions and seminars nearby. Antiquing, fishing, golf, parks, shopping, tennis and water sports nearby.

Publicity: State, Pee Dee, Sandlapper, Southern Inns, Travel and SC Wildlife.

Georgetown   E8

1790 House B&B Inn

630 Highmarket St
Georgetown, SC 29440
(843)546-4821 (800)890-7432 Fax:(843)520-0609

Circa 1790. Feel pampered and refreshed at this wonderfully
restored three-story, hipped-roof West Indies Colonial with a
full-length veranda. It is historic as well as filtered with new
hypoallergenic heating and cooling systems and ozone ioniz-
ers. Relax by the original fireplace in the drawing room furnished with international art and antiques. Spacious guest
bedrooms and suites offer upscale
delights that include fresh flowers, 400 thread count
Egyptian cotton sheets,
plush robes, oversized
towels, and a sherry
nightcap. Some rooms
feature fireplaces, refrigerators, whirlpool tubs, private
entrances and patios. Savor breakfast in the well-appointed
dining room and afternoon treats in the proper English Tea
Room adjoining the expansive library. Cruise on the inn's
intracoastal yacht, ride a bike, or play in the ocean with beach
towels, chairs, umbrellas or boogie boards.

Historic Interest: The Prince George Episcopal Church, the first church established in the district, is across the street from the home. The area offers several historic homes, some dating back to the 1740s, including the Kaminski
House Museum and Hopsewee Plantation.

Innkeeper(s): Denise Heurich & Bill Gower. $99-195. 6 rooms with PB, 3
with FP, 3 suites, 1 cottage and 1 conference room. Breakfast, afternoon tea,
snacks/refreshments and dinner included in rates. Types of meals: Full

gourmet bkfst, veg bkfst, early coffee/tea, picnic lunch and room service.
Beds: KQ. Modem hook-up, data port, cable TV, VCR, reading lamp, refrigerator, ceiling fan, snack bar, clock radio, telephone, coffeemaker, turn-down service, desk, hot tub/spa, voice mail, fireplace, bath robes, hair dryers, fresh
flowers and 400 thread-count Egyptian cotton sheets in room. Central air. Fax,
copier, spa, bicycles, library, parlor games, fireplace and laundry facility on
premises. Weddings, small meetings, family reunions and seminars hosted.
Amusement parks, antiquing, art galleries, beach, bicycling, canoeing/kayak-
ing, fishing, golf, hiking, horseback riding, live theater, museums, parks, shopping, tennis, water sports, wineries, yachting and spa weekends nearby.

Publicity: Brides, Georgetown Times, Sun News, Charlotte Observer,
Southern Living, USAir, Augusta, Pee Dee and Sandlapper.

*"The 1790 House always amazes me with its beauty. A warm welcome
in a lovingly maintained home. Breakfasts were a joy to the palate."*

Alexandra's Inn

620 Prince St
Georgetown, SC 29440
(843)527-0233 (888)557-0233 Fax:(843)520-0718

Circa 1890. This stunning Georgian Colonial stands on half an
acre in the historic district of Georgetown on the Intracoastal
Waterway near Myrtle Beach. Built shortly after the Civil War, it
is decorated in a Gone with the Wind style, and all the guest
rooms are named after characters in the movie. The grounds
are a beautiful mixture of English gardens, brickwork, Magnolia
trees and walkways lined with boxwoods. Inside are pine floors
and a fireplace in each of the five guest bedrooms. Breakfast
includes such tasty entrees as fruit, juice, fresh-baked muffins,
coffee cake or breads and hot egg puffs, baked French toast,
waffles or pancakes. Georgetown is the "Ghost Capital of the
South" and tours of the town may be taken by boat or tram.

Innkeeper(s): Vit & Diane Visbaras. $99-145. 5 rooms with PB, 5 with FP.
Breakfast and snacks/refreshments included in rates. Types of meals: Full
gourmet bkfst, early coffee/tea and afternoon tea. Beds: KQ. Cable TV, reading lamp, ceiling fan, clock radio, telephone, turn-down service, desk, hot
tub/spa and fireplace in room. Central air. Fax, copier, swimming and fireplace on premises. Weddings hosted. Amusement parks, antiquing, art galleries, beach, canoeing/kayaking, fishing, golf, live theater, parks, shopping
and water sports nearby.

Harbor House

15 Cannon St
Georgetown, SC 29440
(843)546-6532 (877)511-0101
E-mail: info@harborhousebb.com
Web: www.harborhousebb.com

Circa 1765. Sitting proudly on the banks of the Sampit River,
this impressive three-story Georgian house with distinctive red
roof has been a welcoming beacon of hospitality for almost
two-and-a-half centuries. Winyah Bay's blue waters and the
ocean beyond are easily seen from this immaculately restored
B&B. Original Colonial moldings, heart pine floors and eight
fireplaces reside with early American antiques, family heirlooms
and Oriental rugs. Guest bedrooms include a choice of a four-
poster rice, pencil-post or sleigh bed. Served in the formal dining room, a Southern-style breakfast may include low country
shrimp and grits, fresh melon, ham biscuits, sweet potato pancakes with bananas and rum, bacon and baked apples. Enjoy
hors d'oeuvres in the parlor or while rocking riverside on the
front porch.

Innkeeper(s): Meg Tarbox. $135-175. 4 rooms with PB. Breakfast and
snacks/refreshments included in rates. Types of meals: Full gourmet bkfst and
early coffee/tea. Beds: KQ. Cable TV, reading lamp, clock radio, telephone
and fireplace in room. Central air. Bicycles and fireplace on premises.
Amusement parks, antiquing, art galleries, beach, bicycling, canoeing/kayak-
ing, fishing, golf, museums, parks, shopping and water sports nearby.

Live Oak Inn B&B

515 Prince St
Georgetown, SC 29440
(843)545-8658 (888)730-6004 Fax:(843)545-8948
E-mail: info@liveoakinn.com
Web: www.liveoakinn.com

Circa 1905. Said to have lived five centuries, two live oaks spread their branches over this recently renovated Victorian. Some of the turn-of-the-century treasures in the home are its grand carved stairway, its columned entry and inlaid hardwood floors. There's a whirlpool in most of the guest rooms, and furnishings include family antiques and collections. (Sam's Rooms features quilts made by the family's grandmothers.)

Historic Interest: Site of the State Champion live oak tree. Over 700 years old.
Innkeeper(s): Fred & Jackie Hoelscher. $85-150. 5 rooms with PB, 5 with FP. Breakfast and snacks/refreshments included in rates. Types of meals: Full gourmet bkfst and early coffee/tea. Beds: KQDT. Modem hook-up, cable TV, VCR, reading lamp, clock radio, telephone, desk and fireplace in room. Central air. Fax, copier, bicycles, library, parlor games, fireplace and laundry facility on premises. Weddings, family reunions and seminars hosted. Amusement parks, antiquing, art galleries, beach, bicycling, canoeing/kayaking, fishing, golf, hiking, live theater, museums, parks, shopping, sporting events, tennis, water sports and wineries nearby.
Publicity: *Southern Living, Sandlapper, Sun News, Charlotte Observer, A Taste of Charlotte, Georgetown Times and Southern Style.*

Greenville   B3

Pettigru Place Bed & Breakfast

302 Pettigru St.
Greenville, SC 29601
(864)242-4529 (877)362-4644 Fax:(864)242-1231
E-mail: info@pettigruplace.com
Web: www.pettigruplace.com

Circa 1920. Former classmates Gloria Hendershot and Janice Beatty reunited after two decades apart and created a charming bed & breakfast out of this Georgian Federalist home. Their labor of love created an inviting atmosphere full of color and comfort. Gloria, a professional caterer, creates the gourmet breakfasts, and Janice tends to the beautiful English garden. After a day of meetings or sightseeing, afternoon refreshments are a welcome treat. The innkeepers offer plenty of amenities for business travelers and plenty of romantic touches. Rooms feature special details such as ceiling fans, feather mattresses and writing desks. The suite includes a fireplace and separate sitting area. Some baths include whirlpool or clawfoot tubs. The Greenville area, with its close access to Clemson, Furman and Bob Jones Universities, offers plenty of activities from outdoor excursions to cultural events. Free high-speed wireless Internet access is available.

Historic Interest: The inn is located in a Greenville historic district.
Innkeeper(s): Sherry & Fred Smid. $99-185. 5 rooms with PB, 2 with FP and 2 conference rooms. Breakfast, afternoon tea and snacks/refreshments included in rates. Types of meals: Full gourmet bkfst, early coffee/tea and picnic lunch. Beds: KQ. Modem hook-up, data port, cable TV, reading lamp, refrigerator, ceiling fan, clock radio, telephone, coffeemaker, desk, hot tub/spa, fireplace and free high-speed wireless Internet access in room. Central air. Fax, copier and fireplace on premises. Weddings, small meetings and family reunions hosted. Antiquing, art galleries, canoeing/kayaking, golf, hiking, live theater, museums, parks, shopping, sporting events, tennis, water sports, short stroll to 50 fine restaurants, six live performance theaters and concert venues, world class art museum and free outdoor concerts three nights per week nearby.
Publicity: *Greenville Magazine.*

Hartsville   C7

Missouri Inn B&B

314 E Home Ave
Hartsville, SC 29550-3716
(843)383-9553 Fax:(843)383-9553

Circa 1901. It is from the third owners of this Federal-style inn that it derives its name. The home was at that time owned by the innkeepers' grandparents, F.E. and Emily Fitchett, and "Missouri" was the nickname given to Emily by her son-in-law. The entire house, including the five guest rooms, are decorated with antiques, and features wallpaper original to the home. The full breakfasts are hearty and homemade. The home, located in the town historic district, is across the street from Coker College and four blocks from downtown Hartsville.

Innkeeper(s): Kyle & Kenny Segars. $75-85. 5 rooms with PB, 3 with FP. Breakfast included in rates. Types of meals: Full gourmet bkfst, early coffee/tea, lunch, afternoon tea and gourmet dinner. Beds: KQT. Cable TV, reading lamp, ceiling fan, clock radio, telephone, desk, robes, flowers, mints and heated towel racks in room. Air conditioning. VCR, fax, copier, library, parlor games and fireplace on premises. Limited handicap access. Weddings, small meetings, family reunions and seminars hosted. Antiquing, fishing, golf, parks, tennis and water sports nearby.

Lancaster   B6

Kilburnie, the Inn at Craig Farm

1824 Craig Farm Road
Lancaster, SC 29720
(803)416-8420 Fax:(803)416-8429
E-mail: jtromp@infoave.net
Web: www.kilburnie.com

Circa 1828. The area's oldest surviving antebellum home, this Greek Revival was saved from demolition, moved to this 400-acre estate and extensively restored. Listed in the National Register, its historic and architectural significance is seen in the intricate details found in the public rooms. Experience Southern hospitality accented by European charm in a quiet and secluded setting with a classic elegance. Each guest bedroom and suite boasts a fireplace, as do two bathrooms. An unsurpassed two-course breakfast may include fresh-baked bread and muffins, a fruit appetizer of Poached Pears with Blueberries or Southern Pecan Peaches and a main entree of Oven-Shirred Eggs or Herbed Goat Cheese Omelette. Relax on one of the piazza rockers after a stroll on the nature path through the wildlife backyard habitat with bridges spanning the woodlands.

Historic Interest: Built in 1828. Lancaster's oldest surviving antebellum home. Owners hid in attic when the Sherman troops occupied "Lancasterville." Placed on the National Register in 1979. Slated for demolition in 1998. Moved and faithfully restored in 1999. Dedicated by SC Governor Jim Hodges on May 21, 2000.
Innkeeper(s): Johannes Tromp. $125-175. 5 rooms with PB, 7 with FP, 1 suite and 1 conference room. Breakfast included in rates. Types of meals: Full gourmet bkfst and gourmet dinner. Beds: KQ. Modem hook-up, cable TV, VCR, reading lamp, clock radio, telephone, turn-down service, desk, hot tub/spa and fireplace in room. Central air. Fax, copier, library, fireplace and laundry facility on premises. Weddings, small meetings and family reunions hosted. Amusement parks, antiquing, golf, parks and shopping nearby.
Publicity: *Sandlapper Magazine and Winner of the 2003 South Carolina Heritage Tourism Award.*

Leesville D4

The Able House Inn

244 E Columbia Ave
Leesville, SC 29070-9284
(803)532-2763 Fax:(803)532-2763

Circa 1939. This elegant, white brick home was built by a local druggist. Relax in the tastefully decorated living room or lounge on a comfy wicker chair among the large plants in the sunroom. Guest rooms, named after various relatives, boast beautiful amenities such as a canopied bed or window seats.

Jennifer's Room opens into a sitting room with a window seat so large, some guests have snuggled down for a restful night's sleep instead of the large, brass and enamel four-poster bed. Innkeepers offer guests snacks/refreshments in the evening and turndown service each night. Wake to freshly ground coffee before taking on the day. During the warmer months, innkeepers offer guests the use of their swimming pool.

Historic Interest: Historic Charleston is three hours from the inn.

Innkeeper(s): Jack & Annabelle Wright. $75-90. 5 rooms with PB and 1 suite. Breakfast and snacks/refreshments included in rates. Types of meals: Cont plus and early coffee/tea. Beds: QD. Cable TV, reading lamp, ceiling fan, clock radio, telephone, turn-down service and desk in room. Air conditioning. VCR, fax, copier, swimming, parlor games and fireplace on premises. Weddings, small meetings and family reunions hosted. Antiquing, fishing, golf, live theater, shopping, sporting events, tennis and water sports nearby.

Publicity: Sandlapper and State Newspaper.

"Thank you for the warm Southern welcome. Your place is absolutely beautiful, very inviting. The food was extraordinary!"

Lyman B3

Walnut Lane Inn

110 Ridge Rd
Lyman, SC 29365
(864)949-7230 Fax:(864)949-1633
E-mail: walnutlaneinn@charter.net
Web: www.walnutlaneinn.com

Circa 1902. This three-story Greek Revival manor was once the headquarters for a working cotton plantation. Some of the home's original furnishings including mantel tops, a bed, and mirrors are mixed with other antique pieces in the parlor and spacious guest rooms. There's a special suite available for families. Breakfast is offered in the formal dining room, which boasts vintage-style wallpapers, wood paneling, a fireplace and chandelier. A hearty Southern menu is served. The eight acres that surround the inn include a peach orchard as well as other fruit trees. Outlet shopping is particularly popular in the area, but there are also galleries, concerts and live theatre. The innkeepers can help with golf arrangements and reservations for country club dining.

Innkeeper(s): David Ades & Hoyt Dottry. $90-105. 6 rooms with PB, 1 suite and 1 conference room. Breakfast included in rates. Types of meals: Full bkfst, early coffee/tea and snacks/refreshments. Beds: QDT. Cable TV, reading lamp, clock radio, turn-down service and desk in room. Central air. VCR, fax, copier, library, parlor games, telephone, fireplace and two-bedroom suite on premises. Weddings, small meetings, family reunions and seminars hosted. Antiquing, art galleries, bicycling, canoeing/kayaking, fishing, golf, hiking, horseback riding, live theater, museums, parks, shopping and sporting events nearby.

Marion C8

Montgomery's Grove

408 Harlee St
Marion, SC 29571-3144
(843)423-5220 (877)646-7721

Circa 1893. The stunning rooms of this majestic Eastlake-style manor are adorned in Victorian tradition with Oriental rugs, polished hardwood floors, chandeliers and gracious furnishings. High ceilings and fireplaces in each room complete the elegant look. Guest rooms are filled with antiques and magazines or books from the 1890s. Hearty full breakfasts are served each day, and candlelight dinner packages can be arranged. Guests will appreciate this inn's five acres of century-old trees and gardens. The inn is about a half-hour drive to famous Myrtle Beach and minutes from I-95.

Historic Interest: Brittons Neck (15 minutes), Camden, S.C., (40 minutes), Charleston (70 minutes).

Innkeeper(s): Coreen & Richard Roberts. $90-120. 5 rooms, 3 with PB and 1 suite. Breakfast included in rates. Types of meals: Full bkfst, lunch, picnic lunch, afternoon tea and gourmet dinner. Beds: KQ. Antiquing, fishing, live theater and water sports nearby.

Publicity: Pee Dee Magazine, Sandlapper, Marion Star, Palmetto Places TV and Country Living.

Moncks Corner E7

Rice Hope Plantation Inn Bed & Breakfast

206 Rice Hope Dr
Moncks Corner, SC 29461-9781
(843)761-4832 (800)569-4038 Fax:(843)884-5020
E-mail: lou@ricehope.com
Web: www.ricehope.com

Circa 1840. Resting on 285 secluded acres of natural beauty, this historic mansion sits among oaks on a bluff overlooking the Cooper River. A stay here is a visit to yesteryear, where it is said to be 45 short minutes and three long centuries from downtown Charleston. Formal gardens boast a 200-year-old camellia and many more varieties of trees and plants, making it a perfect setting for outdoor weddings or other special occasions. Nearby attractions include the Trappist Monastery at Mepkin Plantation, Francis Marion National Forest and Cypress Gardens.

Historic Interest: 1696 rice plantation, 1795 garden, Loutrell Briggs garden, 1920s hunting lodge.

Innkeeper(s): Jamie Edens. $85-165. 5 rooms with PB and 1 conference room. Breakfast included in rates. Types of meals: Full bkfst and early coffee/tea. Beds: KQD. TV, reading lamp, ceiling fan, clock radio and coffeemaker in room. Air conditioning. Copier, tennis, library, parlor games, telephone and fireplace on premises. Weddings, small meetings, family reunions and seminars hosted. Antiquing, art galleries, beach, bicycling, canoeing/kayaking, fishing, golf, museums, parks, shopping and tennis nearby.

Publicity: "W" Fasion Magazine photo shoot, Green Power commercial, Japanese TV Documentary, Travel Channel, Haunted Inns and film location for "Consenting Adults" with Kevin Costner.

North Augusta   E4

Rosemary & Lookaway Halls

804 Carolina Ave
North Augusta, SC 29841
(803)278-6222 (803)642-9259 Fax:(803)278-4877
E-mail: innkeeper@sandhurstestate.com
Web: www.augustainns.com

Circa 1902. These historic homes are gracious examples of
Southern elegance and charm. Manicured lawns adorn the exterior of both homes, which appear almost as a vision out of
"Gone With the Wind." The Rosemary Hall boasts a spectacular heart-of-pine staircase. The homes stand as living museums,
filled to the brim with beautiful furnishings and elegant decor,
all highlighted by stained-glass windows, chandeliers and lacy
touches. Some guest rooms include Jacuzzis, while others offer
verandas. A proper afternoon tea is served each afternoon at
Rosemary Hall. The Southern hospitality begins during the
morning meal. The opulent gourmet fare might include baked
orange-pecan English muffins served with Canadian bacon or,
perhaps, a Southern strata with cheese and bacon. The catering
menu is even more tasteful, and many weddings, showers and
parties are hosted at these inns.

Innkeeper(s): Sandra Croy. $125-225. 23 rooms with PB and 2 conference
rooms. Breakfast and snacks/refreshments included in rates. Types of meals:
Full bkfst and early coffee/tea. Beds: KQDT. Cable TV, reading lamp, clock
radio, telephone, turn-down service and desk in room. Air conditioning. Fax,
copier and fireplace on premises. Limited handicap access. Weddings, small
meetings, family reunions and seminars hosted. Antiquing, fishing, parks,
shopping, sporting events and water sports nearby.
Publicity: Conde' Naste preferred hotel and inn and Top 10 Bed and
Breakfast in South Carolina.

Pawleys Island   E9

Litchfield Plantation

King's River Rd, PO Box 290
Pawleys Island, SC 29585
(843)237-9121 (800)869-1410 Fax:(843)237-1041
E-mail: vacation@litchfieldplantation.com
Web: www.litchfieldplantation.com

Circa 1750. Live oaks line the drive that leads to this antebellum mansion, and in one glance guests can imagine a time
when this 600-acre estate was a prosperous rice plantation. The
interior boasts many original features, and although the decor is
more modern than it was in
1750, it still maintains charm
and elegance. Four-poster and
canopy beds, as well as a collection of traditional furnishings,
grace the guest rooms, which are
located in a variety of lodging
options. Guests can stay in a
plantation house suite or opt for a room in the Guest House.
There are two and three-bedroom cottages available, too. The
cottages are particularly suited to adult families or couples traveling together and include amenities such as a fireplace, kitchen
and washer and dryer. The inn's dining room, located in the
Carriage House, is a wonderful place for a romantic dinner. Start
off with appetizers such as Terrine al Fresco, followed by a
Caesar salad and an entree such as medallions of pork or the

Carriage House Grouper. Guests enjoy privileges at the oceanfront Pawleys Island Beach House, and there are tennis courts
and a swimming pool on the plantation premises. Many golf
courses are nearby. Be sure to ask about the inn's packages.

Innkeeper(s): Karl W Friedrich. $186-620. 38 rooms with PB, 7 with FP, 3
suites, 8 cottages and 3 conference rooms. Breakfast included in rates. Types
of meals: Full bkfst and gourmet dinner. Restaurant on premises. Beds: KQT.
Cable TV, reading lamp, refrigerator, clock radio and telephone in room. Air
conditioning. Fax, copier, swimming, tennis, library and fireplace on premises. Weddings, small meetings, family reunions and seminars hosted.
Amusement parks, antiquing, fishing, golf, live theater, parks, shopping,
water sports and oceanfront beach clubhouse nearby.
Publicity: Tales of the South Carolina Low Country, Golf Week, Augusta
Magazine, PeeDee Magazine, Hidden Carolinas and Rice Plantations of
Georgetown.

*"What a wonderful, relaxing place to stay! Your accommodations
were excellent-first class."*

Pendleton   B2

Rocky Retreat Bed and Breakfast

1000 Milwee Creek Rd
Pendleton, SC 29670
(864)225-3494
E-mail: jtligon@aol.com
Web: www.bbonline.com/sc/rockyretreat/

Circa 1849. Locally called the Boone-Douthit House for the
area's prominent leaders who were previous owners, this classic
upcountry plantation house with tin roof has been accurately
restored and honored to be in the National Register. Original
heart pine floors and wall paneling accent the front hall, parlor
and guest rooms. Spacious guest bedrooms with large windows
feature eclectic antiques, clawfoot tubs and gas fireplaces. A
two-bedroom suite is great for families. Stone-ground grits and
sausage strata are regional dishes served with breakfast at an
old round table in the dining room. Among the foothills of the
Blue Ridge Mountains, farms and woodland views are appreciated from the large front porch, screened side porch and back
deck. Enjoy the native flora and fauna while on an exercise trail
that circles the grounds.

Innkeeper(s): Jim Ligon. $75-115. 4 rooms, 2 with PB, 4 with FP and 1
suite. Breakfast and snacks/refreshments included in rates. Types of meals:
Country bkfst and early coffee/tea. Beds: QD. Reading lamp, desk and fireplace in room. Central air. Fax, copier, library, parlor games, telephone, fireplace and guest refrigerator available on premises. Limited handicap access.
Weddings, small meetings and family reunions hosted. Antiquing, art galleries, fishing, golf, hiking, live theater, museums, parks, shopping, sporting
events and water sports nearby.

Salem   B2

Sunrise Farm B&B

325 Sunrise Dr
Salem, SC 29676-3444
(864)944-0121 (888)991-0121

Circa 1890. Situated on the remaining part of a 1,000-acre
cotton plantation, this country Victorian features large porches
with rockers and wicker. Guest rooms are furnished with period antiques, thick comforters, extra pillows and family heirlooms. The "corn crib" cottage is located in the original farm
structure used for storing corn. It has a fully equipped
kitchen, sitting area and bedroom with tub and shower. The
June Rose Garden Cottage includes a river rock fireplace and
full kitchen, as well as pastoral and mountain views. The inn

offers a full breakfast, snacks and country picnic baskets. Children and pets are welcome.

Innkeeper(s): Barbara Laughter. $90-125. 4 rooms with PB and 2 cottages. Breakfast and snacks/refreshments included in rates. Types of meals: Full bkfst and picnic lunch. Beds: Q. TV, VCR, ceiling fan and free movies in room. Air conditioning. Telephone, fireplace, llamas, miniature horses, goats, a pot belly pig, cats and dog on premises. Antiquing, fishing, parks, sporting events, water sports and boating nearby.

Publicity: *National Geographic Traveler, Southern Living, Country Extra and Palmetto Places.*

Summerville   F7

Linwood Historic Home & Gardens Bed & Breakfast

200 South Palmetto St
Summerville, SC 29483-6042
(843)871-2620 Fax:(843)875-2515
E-mail: linwoodbb@aol.com
Web: bbonline.com/sc/linwood

Circa 1883. Recently renovated, this historic Victorian plantation was built in 1883. It majestically graces two acres of landscaped gardens in a quaint town. The owners' collection of oriental rugs and fine English and American antiques are complemented by the heart of pine floors, Victorian bay and triple sash windows, high ceilings and chandeliers. Elegant suites include fine linens, down comforters, private label toiletries, computer hookups, TVs, phones, individual heat and air-conditioning. Some feature working fireplaces and four-poster beds. A refrigerator and ice are easily accessible. Enjoy a satisfying and healthy continental breakfast in the dining room at a personally designated time. Swim in the pool, relax on a wide porch or stroll the gardens. Afternoon English tea is available by arrangement.

Historic Interest: Home of Julia Drayton Hastie, owner of Magnolia Plantation the first public gardens in the United States.

Innkeeper(s): Linda & Peter Shelbourne. $95-150. 4 suites, 3 with FP and 2 cottages. Breakfast and afternoon tea included in rates. Types of meals: Cont plus, veg bkfst and early coffee/tea. Beds: QT. Modem hook-up, data port, cable TV, reading lamp, refrigerator, clock radio, telephone, desk, fireplace, stationery, toiletries and magazines in room. Central air. VCR, fax, copier, swimming, library, fireplace and laundry facility on premises. Weddings, small meetings, family reunions and seminars hosted. Antiquing, art galleries, beach, bicycling, canoeing/kayaking, fishing, golf and horseback riding nearby.

Publicity: *SandLapper, State Newspaper, Kipplinger Report and Walgreen commercials.*

Woodlands Resort & Inn

125 Parsons Rd
Summerville, SC 29483-3347
(843)875-2600 (800)774-9999 Fax:(843)875-2603
E-mail: reservations@woodlandsinn.com
Web: www.woodlandsinn.com

Circa 1906. Upon check-in, Woodlands guests are greeted with a sparkling glass of Alfred Gratien Champagne, a sure sign that one's stay will prove memorable. A turn-of-the-century estate, Woodlands was built as a winter home for Robert W. Parsons and his family. The magnificent home rests on 42 acres that include tennis courts, a swimming pool, croquet lawn, conference center and the Pavilion, a popular spot for wedding receptions. The intimate inn offers 19 rooms, each individually designed by a New York interior designer. Thoughtful items such as monogrammed robes and luxurious soaps have been placed in your room. In the evenings, turndown is accompanied with handmade chocolates or freshly baked cookies. The inn's spa offers massages. Once one has pampered both body and spirit, invigorate your palate at the inn's five-diamond dining room.

Innkeeper(s): Marty Wall. $295-395. 19 rooms with PB. Afternoon tea included in rates. Types of meals: Full gourmet bkfst, early coffee/tea, gourmet lunch, picnic lunch, snacks/refreshments, gourmet dinner and room service. Restaurant on premises. Beds: KT. Cable TV, VCR, reading lamp, ceiling fan, clock radio, telephone, turn-down service, desk, hot tub/spa, whirlpool tubs and heated towel racks in room. Air conditioning. Fax, copier, swimming, bicycles, tennis, parlor games, fireplace and day spa on premises. Limited handicap access. Weddings and small meetings hosted. Fishing, golf, hiking, parks, shopping, sporting events, tennis, Middleton Place, Magnolia gardens and croquet nearby.

Publicity: *Country Inns, Gourmet, Southern Accents, Relais & Chateaux, Instyle and Harper Collection.*

Union   B4

The Inn at Merridun

100 Merridun Pl
Union, SC 29379-2200
(864)427-7052 (888)892-6020 Fax:(864)429-0373

Circa 1855. Nestled on nine acres of wooded ground, this Greek Revival inn is in a small Southern college town. During spring, see the South in its colorful splendor with blooming azaleas, magnolias and wisteria. Sip an iced drink on the inn's marble verandas and relive memories of a bygone era. Soft strains of Mozart and Beethoven, as well as the smell of freshly baked cookies and  country suppers, fill the air of this antebellum country inn. In addition to a complimentary breakfast, guest will enjoy the inn's dessert selection offered every evening.

Historic Interest: Rose Hill Plantation State Park (8 miles), historic Brattonsville (35 miles).

Innkeeper(s): Peggy Waller & JD, the inn cat. $99-125. 5 rooms with PB and 3 conference rooms. Breakfast included in rates. Types of meals: Full gourmet bkfst, early coffee/tea, gourmet lunch, picnic lunch, afternoon tea, gourmet dinner and room service. Beds: KQT. Reading lamp, ceiling fan, clock radio, telephone, desk, TV/VCR and hair dryers in room. Air conditioning. Fax, copier, library, parlor games, fireplace, refrigerator on each floor for guest use, evening dessert and Miss Fannie's Tea Room on premises. Weddings, small meetings, family reunions and seminars hosted. Amusement parks, antiquing, fishing, parks, shopping, sporting events and water sports nearby.

Publicity: *Charlotte Observer, Spartanburg Herald, Southern Living, Atlanta Journal-Constitution, Sandlapper Magazine, SCETV, Prime Time Live, BBC Documentary and Marshall Tucker Band Music Video.*

South Dakota

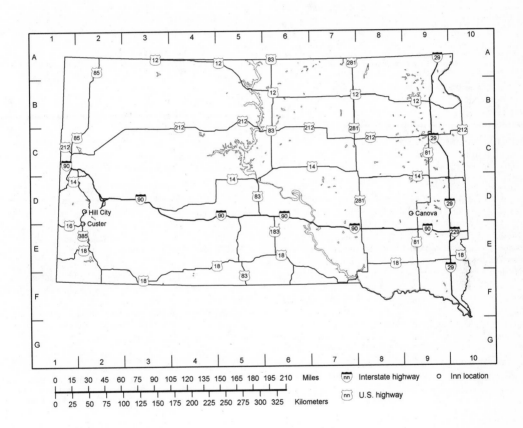

0 15 30 45 60 75 90 105 120 135 150 165 180 195 210   Miles

0 25 50 75 100 125 150 175 200 225 250 275 300 325   Kilometers

nn Interstate highway   o Inn location

nn U.S. highway

Canova   D9

B&B at Skoglund Farm

24375 438 Avenue
Canova, SD 57321-9726
(605)247-3445

Circa 1917. This is a working farm on the South Dakota prairie. Peacocks stroll around the farm along with cattle, chickens, emu and other fowl. Guests can enjoy an evening meal with the family. The innkeepers offer special rates for families with children. The farm's rates are $30 per adult, $25 per teenager and $20 per child. Children age five and younger stay for free.

Innkeeper(s): Alden & Delores Skoglund. $60. 4 rooms. Breakfast and dinner included in rates. Types of meals: Full bkfst, early coffee/tea and snacks/refreshments. Beds: QDT. TV, reading lamp and clock radio in room. VCR, library and telephone on premises. Antiquing, fishing, parks, shopping, sporting events and water sports nearby.

"Thanks for the down-home hospitality and good food."

Custer   D2

Custer Mansion B&B

35 Centennial Dr
Custer, SD 57730-9642
(605)673-3333 (877)519-4948 Fax:(605)673-6696

Circa 1891. Situated on one and a half acres of gardens and aspens, this two-story Gothic Victorian was built by one of the original Black Hills homesteaders. Architectural features include Eastlake stick trim, seven gables and stained-glass windows. Antiques fill the guest bedrooms and honeymoon or anniversary suites and family suites. Enjoy a hearty breakfast of fresh fruits, home-baked goods, meats, creative egg dishes, pancakes, waffles and French toast before venturing out for a day of activities in the Black Hills. Conveniently located, all area attractions are close by. After a day of sightseeing, relax in the outdoor hot tub. Pastries and hot and cold beverages are always available.

Innkeeper(s): Bob & Patricia Meakim. $65-125. 6 rooms, 5 with PB and 1 suite. Breakfast, afternoon tea and snacks/refreshments included in rates. Types of meals: Full gourmet bkfst, veg bkfst and early coffee/tea. Beds: KQDT. Cable TV, VCR, reading lamp, ceiling fan, clock radio and hot tub/spa in room. Air conditioning. Spa, library, parlor games and telephone on premises. Weddings, small meetings and family reunions hosted. Antiquing, art galleries, beach, bicycling, canoeing/kayaking, fishing, golf, hiking, horseback riding, live theater, museums, parks, shopping, tennis and water sports nearby.

Publicity: *Country Extra Magazine, National Historic Society, Midwest Living Magazine and Classic American Home.*

State Game Lodge

HC 83 Box 74
Custer, SD 57730-9705
(605)255-4541 (800)658-3530 Fax:(605)255-4706

Circa 1921. The State Game Lodge is listed in the National Register of Historic Places. It served as the summer White House for presidents Coolidge and Eisenhower. Although not a bed and breakfast, the lodge boasts a wonderful setting in the Black Hills. Ask for a room in the historic lodge building. (There are cottages and motel units, as well.) A favorite part of the experience is rocking on the front porch while watching buffalo graze. Breakfast is paid for separately in the dining room, where you may wish to order a pheasant or buffalo entree in the evening.

Innkeeper(s): Wade Lampert. $90-400. 68 rooms with PB, 3 with FP. Types of meals: Full gourmet bkfst, lunch and dinner. Restaurant on premises. Beds: QDT. TV and telephone on premises. Fishing and buffalo safari Jeep tours nearby.

Publicity: *Bon Appetit, Midwest Living and Sunset.*

"Your staff's cheerfulness and can-do attitude added to a most enjoyable stay."

Hill City   D2

Pine Rest Cabins

PO Box 377
Hill City, SD 57745-0377
(605)574-2416 (800)333-5306
E-mail: pinerestcabins@aol.com
Web: www.pinerestcabins.com

Circa 1911. Surrounded by Black Hills National Forest, these simple country cabins offer a variety of lodgings. Once located on the site of the Harney Peak Tin mining camp, one cabin is over 100 years old with a handmade stone fireplace and decorative bark walls. Several have knotty pine inside and out, wood floors and a gas fireplace. All the cabins feature kitchenettes and an outside barbecue grill and picnic table. A hot tub and gazebo is a relaxing treat. A sandbox, playground and games provide entertainment for the young at heart. The local setting is perfect for nature and outdoor enthusiasts. It is only a few minutes to historic Mt. Rushmore National Monument.

Innkeeper(s): Jan & Steve Johnson. $65-250. 12 cabins, 5 with FP. Beds: KQDT. Cable TV, reading lamp, refrigerator, ceiling fan, coffeemaker, fireplace and cabins all have kitchenettes in room. Spa, parlor games, telephone, volleyball, access to National Forest for hiking and kettle-style charcoal grill/picnic table outside each cabin on premises. Antiquing, art galleries, beach, bicycling, cross-country skiing, fishing, golf, hiking, horseback riding, live theater, museums, parks, shopping, tennis, water sports and canoeing nearby.

Tennessee

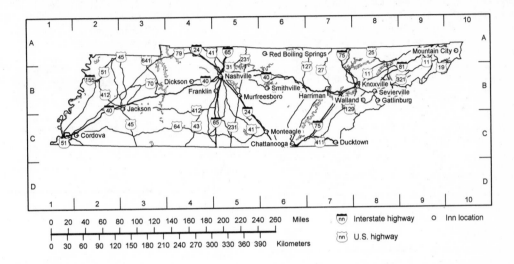

0 20 40 60 80 100 120 140 160 180 200 220 240 260 Miles

0 30 60 90 120 150 180 210 240 270 300 330 360 390 Kilometers

[nn] Interstate highway   ○ Inn location

[nn] U.S. highway

Chattanooga   C6

Mayor's Mansion Inn and Restaurant

801 Vine St
Chattanooga, TN 37403-2318
(423)265-5000 Fax:(423)265-5555
E-mail: innjoy@worldnet.att.net
Web: www.innjoy.com

Circa 1889. This former mayor's mansion of Tudor and Romanesque design was presented with the 1997 award for Excellence in Preservation by the National Trust. The interior of this gracious home boasts 16-foot ceilings and floors patterned from three different woods. The large entrance hall features carved cornices, a coiffured ceiling and a fireplace. Every room offers something special, from Tiffany windows and beveled glass to the mansion's eight fireplaces and luxurious ballroom. The cornerstone of the Fortwood Historic District, Chattanooga's finest historic residential area, the mansion also has received the coveted City Beautiful Award.

Historic Interest: The Chickamauga Battlefields are 15 minutes from the inn and other battle sites, museums and cemeteries are nearby.

Innkeeper(s): Carmen & Gene Drake. $150-295. 11 rooms with PB, 4 with FP and 3 suites. Breakfast included in rates. Types of meals: Full bkfst and gourmet dinner. Restaurant on premises. Beds: KQD. Data port, cable TV, VCR, reading lamp, CD player, snack bar, clock radio, telephone, turn-down service and desk in room. Air conditioning. Fax, copier, library, parlor games and fireplace on premises. Weddings, small meetings, family reunions and seminars hosted. Amusement parks, antiquing, fishing, live theater, parks, shopping, sporting events and water sports nearby.

Publicity: Chattanooga News Free, Nashville Tennessean, Southern Accents, National Geographic, Preservation Magazine, Traveler, News Free Press, Blue Ridge Magazine, PBS, CBS and NBC.

Cordova   C2

The Bridgewater House

7015 Raleigh Lagrange Rd
Cordova, TN 38018-6221
(901)384-0080 (800)466-1001 Fax:(901)372-3413

Circa 1890. This century-old schoolhouse sits on more than two acres shaded by stately oak trees. Upon entering, you will find the original hardwood floors, leaded-glass windows and hand-marbleized moldings. Awake to a gourmet breakfast prepared by the innkeeper, a certified chef, caterer and former manager of corporate test kitchens. Specialities include Strawberries Romanoff, Broccoli with Hollandaise, Merinque a la Grapefruit, Bridgewater Eggs Benedict, Greek Omelet or a Cheese Blintz souffle.

Innkeeper(s): Steve & Katherine Mistilis. $120. 2 rooms with PB. Breakfast included in rates. Types of meals: Full gourmet bkfst and early coffee/tea. Beds: QT. Data port, TV, reading lamp, CD player, ceiling fan, turn-down service and desk in room. Central air. VCR, fax, copier, library, parlor games, telephone and fireplace on premises. Weddings, small meetings and seminars hosted. Antiquing, art galleries, bicycling, canoeing/kayaking, fishing, golf, hiking, horseback riding, museums, parks, shopping, water sports and wineries nearby.

Dickson B4

East Hills Bed & Breakfast Inn

100 E Hills Ter
Dickson, TN 37055-2102
(615)441-9428 (866)613-3414 Fax:(615)446-2181
E-mail: jaluther@comcast.net
Web: www.easthillsbb.com

Circa 1948. This traditional Southern home, built by the owner's father, offers 5,000 square feet of gracious common rooms, porches and handsomely decorated guest rooms. The library-den has black and white tiles, book-lined walls, a fireplace and comfortable furniture. There are rocking chairs and swings on the porches. Four acres of lawns and gardens provide privacy for two cottages tucked into a thicket of oaks. Breakfast offerings include favorites such as blueberry pancakes and scrambled eggs or country ham, cheese grits, hot biscuits and potatoes. Walk to nearby Luther Lake or visit Cumberland Furnace or Historic Charlotte.

Innkeeper(s): John & Anita Luther. $75-125. 4 rooms with PB and 2 cottages. Breakfast, afternoon tea and snacks/refreshments included in rates. Types of meals: Full bkfst and early coffee/tea. Beds: QD. Modem hook-up, cable TV, VCR, reading lamp, stereo, refrigerator, ceiling fan, clock radio, telephone, coffeemaker, turn-down service and desk in room. Central air. Fax, bicycles, library, parlor games, fireplace and laundry facility on premises. Limited handicap access. Small meetings, family reunions and seminars hosted. Antiquing, art galleries, bicycling, canoeing/kayaking, fishing, golf, hiking, horseback riding, museums, parks, shopping, tennis, water sports and Renaissance Center nearby.

Ducktown C7

The White House B&B

104 Main St, PO Box 668
Ducktown, TN 37326-0668
(423)496-4166 (800)775-4166 Fax:(423)496-9778

Circa 1898. This Queen Anne Victorian boasts a wraparound porch with a swing. Rooms are decorated in traditional style with family antiques. Innkeepers pamper their guests with Tennessee hospitality, a hearty country breakfast and a mouthwatering sundae bar in the evenings. The innkeepers also help guests plan daily activities, and the area is bursting with possibilities. Hiking, horseback riding, panning for gold and driving tours are only a few choices. The Ocoee River is the perfect place for a river float trip or take on the challenge of roaring rapids. The river was selected as the site of the 1996 Summer Olympic Whitewater Slalom events.

Historic Interest: The Ducktown Mining Museum is a popular local attraction. Fields of the Wood, a biblical theme park, is 20 minutes away and free of charge.

Innkeeper(s): Dan & Mardee Kauffman. $75-85. 3 rooms. Breakfast, afternoon tea and snacks/refreshments included in rates. Types of meals: Full gourmet bkfst and early coffee/tea. Beds: QT. Reading lamp, ceiling fan, clock radio and central heat in room. Central air. VCR, fax, library, parlor games, telephone and fireplace on premises. Weddings, small meetings and family reunions hosted. Antiquing, fishing, golf, parks, shopping and water sports nearby.

Publicity: *Southern Living.*

"From the moment we walked into your home, we sensed so much hospitality and warmth. You took such good care of us in every way and lavished so much love on us - and the food!!! Oh, my goodness!!! We'll just have to come back!"

Franklin B5

Magnolia House B&B

1317 Columbia Ave
Franklin, TN 37064-3620
(615)794-8178
E-mail: magtenn@cs.com
Web: www.bbonline.com/tn/magnolia

Circa 1905. In summer, a blooming Magnolia tree shades the wicker-filled front porch of this gabled Craftsman cottage. The land is where the Battle of Franklin was fought. Furnishings range from 19th-century Victorian pieces to period antiques. Walk five blocks through a maple shaded neighborhood of historic houses to downtown Franklin, 15 blocks of which are in the National Register of Historic Places.

Innkeeper(s): Jimmy & Robbie Smithson. $85-100. 4 rooms. Breakfast included in rates. Types of meals: Full bkfst and early coffee/tea. Reading lamp, ceiling fan, telephone, turn-down service and desk in room. Air conditioning. VCR and fireplace on premises. Amusement parks, antiquing, live theater and shopping nearby.

Gatlinburg B8

Buckhorn Inn

2140 Tudor Mountain Rd
Gatlinburg, TN 37738-6014
(865)436-4668 Fax:(865)436-5009
E-mail: buckhorninn@msn.com
Web: www.buckhorninn.com

Circa 1938. Set high on a hilltop, Buckhorn is surrounded by more than 25 acres of woodlands and groomed meadows. There are inspiring mountain views and a spring-fed lake on the grounds. Original paintings enhance the antique-

filled guest rooms and the cottages and guest houses have wood burning fireplaces, Jacuzzi's and porches.

Innkeeper(s): John & Lee Mellor. $95-250. 9 rooms with PB and 10 cottages. Breakfast included in rates. Types of meals: Full gourmet bkfst, early coffee/tea, lunch, picnic lunch, afternoon tea and dinner. Beds: KDT. TV, reading lamp, stereo, refrigerator, coffeemaker, fireplace, Jacuzzi, coffeemaker and refrigerator in room. Air conditioning. VCR, fax, copier, library, telephone and fireplace on premises. Weddings, small meetings, family reunions and seminars hosted. Amusement parks, antiquing, cross-country skiing, downhill skiing, fishing, live theater, parks, shopping, sporting events, water sports and Great Smoky Arts & Crafts Community nearby.

Publicity: *Atlanta Journal & Constitution, Country, Brides, British Vogue, Birmingham News, New York Times, Travel & Leisure and Travel Holiday.*

Laurel Springs Lodge

204 Hill St
Gatlinburg, TN 37738-3012
(865)430-9211 (888)430-9211
E-mail: laurelspringslodge@msn.com
Web: www.laurelspringslodge.com

Circa 1932. Cradled on a wooded hillside overlooking the Little Pigeon River this authentic 1930s mountain lodge was built with lots of windows, a rough cedar shake exterior and knotty pine random boards. Relax by the fire in one of the inviting common rooms that exude an old world ambiance. Pampering amenities from fine linens to botanical bath products are enjoyed in each guest bedroom and suite that is furnished with antiques and tastefully decorated in a variety of styles. Savor a hearty southern-style breakfast with a mini-loaf of lemon poppy seed bread, fresh seasonal fruit, eggs made to order, biscuits and gravy and fried potatoes. Sit in the garden gazebo accented by ferns and flowers. Smoky Mountain National Park and Pigeon Forge are just five miles away.

Historic Interest: The B&B was built before the Smoky Mountain National Park was designated and has been a boarding house, guest house and now a B&B.

Innkeeper(s): Garth & Belinda Birdsey. $89-139. 5 rooms with PB and 3 suites. Breakfast included in rates. Types of meals: Country bkfst. Beds: QDT. Cable TV, VCR, clock radio, premium linens and botanical bath products in room. Central air. Fax, spa, library, parlor games, telephone and fireplace on premises. Weddings and family reunions hosted. Amusement parks, antiquing, art galleries, bicycling, canoeing/kayaking, downhill skiing, fishing, golf, hiking, horseback riding, live theater, museums, parks, shopping, sporting events, tennis, water sports and wineries nearby.

Harriman   B7

Bushrod Hall B&B

422 Cumberland St, NE
Harriman, TN 37748
(865)882-8406 (888)880-8406 Fax:(865)882-8489

Circa 1892. Bushrod Hall was built as part of a competition to see which town resident could build the most beautiful home, so its original owners spared little expense. Among the home's most notable features are its exquisite restored woodwork and stained glass. Harriman was founded as a utopia for those following the Temperance Movement. Bushrod Hall once served as the Hall of Domestic Science for the American Temperance University. Period-era furnishings add to the historic ambiance. Gourmet breakfast entrees include items such as an egg soufflé or caramel French toast. Guests can take a guided walking tour and see some of the town's historic sites. Antique shops, museums and recreation areas offer other possibilities. Bushrod Hall is located in Harriman's Cornstalk Heights Historic District and is listed in the National Register of Historic Places.

Innkeeper(s): Nancy & Bob Ward. $80-100. 3 rooms with PB. Breakfast and snacks/refreshments included in rates. Types of meals: Full gourmet bkfst, veg bkfst and early coffee/tea. Beds: KQ. Reading lamp, ceiling fan and clock radio in room. Central air. VCR, fax, library, parlor games, telephone and TV on premises. Weddings, small meetings and family reunions hosted. Antiquing, canoeing/kayaking, fishing, golf, hiking and water sports nearby.

Publicity: *Oak Ridge, Knoxville News Sentinel, Ronne Co News, Nashville Tennessean, WVLT and WBIR.*

Jackson   B3

Highland Place B&B

519 N Highland Ave
Jackson, TN 38301-4824
(731)427-1472

Circa 1911. Whether traveling for business or pleasure, a stay at this elegant Colonial Revival mansion will relax and inspire. Conveniently located in a quiet downtown historical district, the perfect blend of old and new furnishings provide luxurious comfort and modern convenience. Spacious barely describes the 10-foot-wide hallways, high ceilings, marble fireplace and many exquisite common rooms to gather in and dine together.

An audio center enhances the gracious ambiance, and a video library offers further entertainment. The impressive guest bedrooms are well-appointed. Special attention is given to meet personal or corporate needs.

Innkeeper(s): Cindy & Bill Pflaum. $105-195. 4 rooms with PB, 2 with FP and 1 conference room. Cable TV and VCR in room. Library, telephone, fireplace and Internet access on premises. Weddings, small meetings, family reunions and seminars hosted. Antiquing, art galleries, live theater, shopping and sporting events nearby.

Knoxville   B8

Maple Grove Inn

8800 Westland Dr
Knoxville, TN 37923-6501
(865)690-9565 (800)645-0713 Fax:(865)690-9385
E-mail: info@maplegroveinn.com
Web: www.maplegroveinn.com

Circa 1805. Enjoy real Southern hospitality in this late 18th-century, 12,000-square-foot, Georgian-style mansion on 16 acres in the foothills of the Great Smoky Mountains. Antiques, hand-carved fireplaces, Oriental rugs, and family heirlooms create a delightful ambiance in this inn that is one of Knoxville's oldest residence. Common rooms include the library, living room, sitting room and sunroom. The inn has eight guest bedrooms including some spacious suites that have Jacuzzis. Gourmet breakfasts can be served in the guest's bedroom or in the dining room. Items include such fare as homemade scones with strawberry jam, vegetable quiche with hollandaise sauce, country ham, skillet potatoes and fresh fruit. The gourmet restaurant is open for dinner Thursday through Saturday by reservation.

Historic Interest: James White Fort, William Blount Mansion (10-15 miles).

Innkeeper(s): Gina Buchanon, Beth Griffis. $125-250. 8 rooms, 6 with PB, 3 with FP, 2 suites and 1 conference room. Breakfast and snacks/refreshments included in rates. Types of meals: Full gourmet bkfst, early coffee/tea, lunch and dinner. Restaurant on premises. Beds: QD. Modem hook-up, data port, cable TV, reading lamp, refrigerator, telephone, coffeemaker, desk, hot tub/spa and voice mail in room. Air conditioning. VCR, fax, copier, swimming and tennis on premises. Weddings, small meetings and family reunions hosted. Antiquing, art galleries, golf, museums, parks, shopping, sporting events and tennis nearby.

Publicity: *Knoxville News Sentinel and Tennessee Getaways.*

Maplehurst Inn

800 W Hill Ave
Knoxville, TN 37902
(865)523-7773 (800)451-1562

Circa 1917. This townhouse, located in the downtown neighborhood of Maplehurst, is situated on a hill that overlooks the Tennessee River. A parlor with fireplace and piano invites guests to mingle in the evening or to relax quietly with a book. The inn's favorite room is the Penthouse with king bed, cherry furnishings and a sky lit Jacuzzi. The Anniversary Suite offers a double Jacuzzi and canopy bed. A light informal breakfast is served in the Garden Room overlooking the river, while breakfast casseroles, country potatoes, quiches and breads are offered buffet-style in the dining room. Check there for brownies and cookies if you come back in the middle of the day. The inn is within two blocks of the Convention Center and City Hall as well as several fine restaurants. The University of Tennessee and Neyland Stadium are nearby.

Innkeeper(s): Sonny & Becky Harben. $79-149. 11 rooms with PB and 1 suite. Breakfast and snacks/refreshments included in rates. Types of meals: Full gourmet bkfst, veg bkfst and early coffee/tea. Beds: KD. Cable TV, VCR, reading lamp, ceiling fan, clock radio, telephone, desk and some with Jacuzzi in room. Air conditioning. Laundry facility on premises. Small meetings and family reunions hosted. Antiquing, canoeing/kayaking, live theater, museums and parks nearby.

Monteagle   C6

Adams Edgeworth Inn

Monteagle Assembly
Monteagle, TN 37356
(931)924-4000 Fax:(931)924-3236
E-mail: innjoy@blomand.net
Web: www.adamsedgeworthinn.com

Circa 1896. Built in 1896 this National Register Victorian inn recently has been refurbished in a country-chintz style. Original paintings, sculptures and country antiques are found through-

out. Wide verandas are filled with wicker furnishings and breezy hammocks, and there's an award-winning chef who will prepare delicious candle-lit dinners. You can stroll through the 96-acre Victorian village that surrounds the inn and enjoy rolling hills, creeks and Victorian cottages. Waterfalls, natural caves and scenic overlooks are along the 150 miles of hiking trails of nearby South Cumberland State Park.

Historic Interest: University of the South, Jack Daniels Distillery, Civil War sites.

Innkeeper(s): Wendy Adams. $125-275. 10 rooms with PB, 10 with FP, 3 suites and 1 conference room. Breakfast included in rates. Types of meals: Full bkfst and gourmet dinner. Beds: KQD. Phone, air-conditioning and ceiling fan and some with TV in room. VCR, fax, copier, telephone and fireplace on premises. Weddings, small meetings, family reunions and seminars hosted. Antiquing, fishing, hiking, live theater, parks, shopping, sporting events, spelunking and historic architecture nearby.

Publicity: *Country Inns, Chattanooga News Free Press, Tempo, Gourmet, Victorian Homes, Brides, Tennessean, Southern Living, National Geographic, Inn Country, PBS Crossroads, ABC TV, CBS TV and Travel Channel.*

Monteagle Inn

204 West Main Street
Monteagle, TN 37356
(931)924-3869 (888)480-3245 Fax:(931)924-3867
E-mail: suites@monteagleinn.com
Web: www.monteagleinn.com

Circa 1942. Offering European elegance and comfort, this recently renovated inn is classical in style and design. Adjacent to the courtyard, a large wood-burning fireplace accents the great room that showcases a 1923 baby grand piano family heirloom. Guest bedrooms boast a variety of comfortable furnishings and amenities. Choose a four-poster, iron or sleigh bed with soft linens. Many include balconies. The two-bedroom Cottage boasts a fully equipped kitchen, front porch, dining and living rooms. Enjoy a homemade breakfast in the dining room. The garden gazebo is surrounded by year-round color, designed by a local horticulturist and a prominent landscape architect. Ask about romance and anniversary packages.

Innkeeper(s): Jim & Donna Harmon. $140-175. 15 rooms with PB, 1 cottage and 1 conference room. Breakfast and snacks/refreshments included in rates. Types of meals: Full gourmet bkfst, early coffee/tea, gourmet lunch, picnic lunch and gourmet dinner. Beds: KQT. Data port, reading lamp, ceiling

fan, telephone, desk, voice mail, down pillows, European linens, antiques and modern reproductions in room. Central air. TV, VCR, fax, copier, library and parlor games on premises. Handicap access. Weddings, small meetings, family reunions and seminars hosted. Antiquing, art galleries, bicycling, canoeing/kayaking, fishing, golf, hiking, parks, shopping and wineries nearby.

Mountain City   A10

Prospect Hill B&B Inn

801 W Main St (Hwy 67)
Mountain City, TN 37683
(423)727-0139 (800)339-5084
E-mail: judy@prospect-hill.com
Web: www.prospect-hill.com

Circa 1889. This three-story shingle-style Victorian manor garners a great deal of attention from passersby with its appealing architecture and commanding hilltop location. Romantic rooms offer tall arched windows, 11-foot ceilings and spectacular views. Fashioned from handmade bricks, it was once home to Major Joseph Wagner, who, like many of his neighbors in far northeastern Tennessee, served on the Union side. The restored home features five guest rooms. A 1910 oak Craftsman dining set complements the oak Stickley furniture (circa 1997) that decorates the living room. Fireplaces, whirlpools and stained glass add luxury to the guest rooms. Prospect Hill boasts views of the Appalachian and Blue Ridge Mountains. From the front window, guests can see three states: Tennessee, Virginia and North Carolina. The inn is within an hour of the Blue Ridge Parkway, Appalachian Trail and Roan and Grandfather mountains, and the Virginia Creeper Trail.

Historic Interest: Rare shingle style in brick. Built by a Union major after the Civil War in one of the most Republican counties in the U.S. One of only two historic homes in the town. Always owned by upper-class people who held jobs while maintaining a small working farm as their home. A grand feeling of "house on the hill" which speaks of the stature of the Wagner family which built it.

Innkeeper(s): Judy & Robert Hotchkiss. $89-179. 5 rooms with PB, 4 with FP and 1 conference room. Breakfast and snacks/refreshments included in rates. Types of meals: Full gourmet bkfst and early coffee/tea. Beds: KQT. Modem hook-up, data port, cable TV, VCR, reading lamp, ceiling fan, clock radio, telephone, turn-down service, desk, historic stained glass, balcony or porch, private entrance, bed for one child and fireplace in room. Central air. Fax, copier, library, fireplace and laundry facility on premises. Weddings, small meetings and family reunions hosted. Antiquing, bicycling, canoeing/kayaking, cross-country skiing, downhill skiing, fishing, golf, hiking, horseback riding, live theater, museums, parks, shopping, water sports, wineries, mountain views and scenery nearby.

Publicity: *Marquee Magazine, Old-House Journal, Haunted Inns of the Southeast, Voted Most Romantic Hideaway (Arrington's-2003) and Best Southern Inn.*

"The most wonderful thing I'll always remember about our stay is, by far, the wonderful home we came back to each night."

Murfreesboro   B5

Byrn-Roberts Inn

346 East Main Street
Murfreesboro, TN 37130
(615)867-0308 (888)877-4919 Fax:(615)867-0280
E-mail: byrnrobert@aol.com
Web: www.byrn-roberts-inn.com

Circa 1900. Rich in architectural detail, this majestic brick Queen Anne Victorian mansion has been meticulously restored to pamper you with present-day comforts and the quality craftsmanship of the past. Original oak woodwork, 11 ornate fireplaces, marble lavatories and gas lights reside with state-of-the-art technology. Suite-size guest bedrooms are more than spacious, with an elegant ambiance imparted by the rich decor, antiques and special touches like fresh flowers and plush robes. A wonderful gourmet breakfast is sure to please. An on-site fitness center has a refrigerator and snacks available 24 hours. Make a reservation for a massage after taking a leisurely bike ride in this historic district.

Innkeeper(s): David & Julie Becker. $115-175. 5 rooms with PB, 5 with FP. Types of meals: Full gourmet bkfst, veg bkfst, early coffee/tea and snacks/refreshments. Beds: KQ. Modem hook-up, data port, cable TV, VCR, reading lamp, ceiling fan, clock radio, telephone, turn-down service, desk, voice mail and fireplace in room. Central air. Fax, copier, bicycles, parlor games, fireplace, laundry facility, complimentary refrigerator & snacks located in fitness center open 24 hours a day and massage therapy available by reservation on premises. Antiquing, art galleries, bicycling, fishing, golf, hiking, horseback riding, live theater, museums, parks, shopping, sporting events and downtown Nashville (30 minutes) nearby.

Carriage Lane Inn

411 N Maney Ave
Murfreesboro, TN 37130-2920
(615)890-3630 (800)357-2827
E-mail: info@carriagelaneinn.com
Web: www.carriagelaneinn.com

Circa 1900. Carriage Lane, a century-old home, is situated in a local historic district. The guest rooms include amenities such as fireplaces, whirlpool tubs and feather beds. In the mornings, guests are served a full breakfast. The inn is just 20 minutes away from Nashville and is close to Civil War battlefields and historic sites.

Innkeeper(s): Sharon & Ted Petty. $100-155. 7 rooms with PB, 4 with FP, 1 cottage and 5 conference rooms. Breakfast and snacks/refreshments included in rates. Types of meals: Country bkfst, veg bkfst, early coffee/tea, lunch, picnic lunch and room service. Beds: QD. Modem hook-up, data port, cable TV, VCR, reading lamp, CD player, ceiling fan, snack bar, clock radio, telephone, desk, fireplace, breakfast and early coffee delivered in room. Central air. Fax, copier, parlor games, fireplace and laundry facility on premises. Weddings, small meetings, family reunions and seminars hosted. Antiquing, art galleries, bicycling, fishing, golf, hiking, horseback riding, live theater, museums, parks, shopping, sporting events, tennis and water sports nearby.

Nashville   B5

Crocker Springs B&B

2382 Crocker Springs Road
Nashville, TN 37072
(615)876-8502 (888)382-9397

Circa 1880. Once a working farm, the grounds that surround this historic home still include the old barn and outbuildings. Spacious, comfortable guest rooms are decorated with an elegant country style. Todd's Paisley Room includes a masculine paisley comforter atop an antique high-backed oak bed. Stefanie's Quilt Room includes antique furnishings and a feather bed topped with a colorful quilt. The Rose Room, also furnished with antiques, is especially spacious and can accommodate up to four guest, when reserved as a suite. The aroma of freshly brewed coffee wafts throughout the house, a gentle promise to wonderful culinary things to come. The innkeepers prepare a variety of different breakfasts, each ending with a breakfast desert. One guest favorite is a unique tomato pudding that is served along with egg dishes, breakfast meats, orchard-fresh juice and scrumptious orange biscuits. Guests can stroll the 58 acres or take the short drive into Nashville where historic

homes, Civil War battlefields and the Grand Old Opry await.

Innkeeper(s): Jack & Bev Spangler. $110-200. 3 rooms with PB, 1 suite and 1 conference room. Breakfast and snacks/refreshments included in rates. Types of meals: Country bkfst, veg bkfst and early coffee/tea. Beds: Q. Central air. TV, VCR, fax, stable, library, parlor games, telephone and fireplace on premises. Weddings, small meetings, family reunions and seminars hosted. Antiquing, art galleries, canoeing/kayaking, fishing, golf, hiking, horseback riding, live theater, museums, parks, shopping, sporting events, tennis, water sports and wineries nearby.

Publicity: *Goodlettsville Gazette and Channel 5-Talk of the Town.*

Red Boiling Springs   A6

Armours Hotel

321 E Main St
Red Boiling Springs, TN 37150-2322
(615)699-2180 Fax:(615)699-5111
E-mail: armourshotel@yahoo.com
Web: www.armourshotel.com

Circa 1924. As Tennessee's only remaining mineral bathhouse, this two-story, National Historic Register house is tucked away in the rolling hills of the Cumberland Plateau. Whether resting in one of the 23 antique-furnished guest rooms, listening to the babbling creek from the second-floor veranda, strolling under covered bridges, or simply enjoying the sunrise in a rocking chair on the porch before breakfast, tranquillity awaits each guest. Spend the afternoon in the gazebo with your favorite book from the library next door, or get in a game of tennis at the park across the street before dinner.

Innkeeper(s): Reba Hilton. $59-149. 21 rooms, 18 with PB and 3 suites. Breakfast and dinner included in rates. Types of meals: Country bkfst and lunch. Beds: KQDT. Reading lamp, clock radio, desk and bath house (mineral and steam) in room. Air conditioning. TV, VCR, fax, copier, spa, telephone, fireplace and massage room on premises. Weddings, small meetings, family reunions and seminars hosted. Antiquing, fishing, golf, hiking, horseback riding, parks, tennis, water sports and wineries nearby.

Publicity: *Southern Living, Tennessean and Country Crossroads.*

Sevierville   B8

Little Greenbrier Lodge

3685 Lyon Springs Rd
Sevierville, TN 37862-8257
(865)429-2500 (800)277-8100
E-mail: littlegreenbrier@worldnet.att.net
Web: www.littlegreenbrierlodge.com

Circa 1939. The spectacular, forested setting at Little Greenbrier is worth the trip. The rustic lodge is set on five, wooded acres less than a quarter mile from Great Smoky Mountains National Park. Rooms have valley or mountain views and are decorated with Victorian-style furnishings and antiques. The lodge served guests from 1939 until the 1970s when it became a religious retreat. When the innkeepers purchased it in 1993, they tried to preserve some of its early history, including restoring original sinks and the first bathtub ever installed in the valley. A copy of the lodge's original "house rules" is still posted. Within 30 minutes are Dollywood, outlet malls, antiquing, craft stores and plenty of outdoor activities.

Innkeeper(s): Charles & Susan LeBon. $100-135. 9 rooms with PB, 1 cabin and 1 conference room. Breakfast and snacks/refreshments included in rates. Types of meals: Full bkfst and early coffee/tea. Beds: QD. Reading lamp, ceiling fan, clock radio and desk in room. Air conditioning. VCR, fax, library, parlor games, telephone and fireplace on premises. Small meetings, family reunions and seminars hosted. Amusement parks, antiquing, cross-country skiing, downhill skiing, fishing, golf, live theater, shopping, sporting events, tennis and National parks nearby.

Publicity: *Knoxville News Sentinel, Miami Herald, Detroit Free Press and Tennessee Crossroads.*

Smithville B6

The Inn at Evins Mill

1535 Evins Mill Road
Smithville, TN 37166
(615)269-3740 (800)383-2349 Fax:(615)269-3771
E-mail: info@evinsmill.com
Web: www.evinsmill.com

Circa 1939. More than a country inn, this 40-acre secluded retreat includes a main log lodge, three award-winning cottages and a working gristmill. Poplar floors, fieldstone fireplaces and cedar porches invoke a comfortable ambiance for gathering. Resort amenities are offered in a comfortable bed & breakfast style. The Millstone Restaurant provides the perfect mealtime setting. Groups, families, couples and individuals can find team building, personal renewal, romance and rejuvenation. There are rolling hills, creeks and streams, hiking trails, fishing ponds, a ropes course and a swimming hole beneath a cascading waterfall.

Innkeeper(s): William Cochran, Jr.. $100-220. 14 rooms with PB and 2 conference rooms. Breakfast, snacks/refreshments and dinner included in rates. Types of meals: Full gourmet bkfst, veg bkfst, early coffee/tea and lunch. Restaurant on premises. Beds: KT. Reading lamp, ceiling fan, clock radio, coffeemaker, desk and private deck in room. Air conditioning. TV, VCR, fax, copier, swimming, library, parlor games, telephone, fireplace, laundry facility, waterfalls, gristmill, hiking trails, fishing ponds, dart boards, cigars and restaurant on premises. Weddings, small meetings, family reunions and seminars hosted. Antiquing, art galleries, canoeing/kayaking, fishing, golf, hiking, parks, shopping, water sports, wineries and Smithville Fiddler's Jamboree nearby.

Publicity: *Nashville Business Journal, The Review Appeal and Tennessean.*

Walland B8

Blackberry Farm

1471 W Millers Cove Rd
Walland, TN 37886-2649
(865)984-8166 Fax:(865)681-7753
E-mail: info@blackberryfarm.com
Web: www.blackberryfarm.com

Circa 1939. Gracious furnishings, spectacular scenery and gourmet cuisine are three of the reasons why guests return to Blackberry Farm. The 2,500 lush acres offer miles of nature to enjoy, complete with areas perfect for hiking, biking and fly fishing. The front terrace is lined with rocking chairs perfect for relaxing and enjoying the wonderful views. Guests are treated to deluxe breakfasts, lunches and  dinners. The rooms are exquisitely decorated and furnished with great attention to detail. The original 1870 farmhouse now houses a new spa facility. After a few days of being mercilessly pampered, guests won't want to leave.

Historic Interest: If the bounty of activities available at the inn fails to keep you busy, try visiting Gatlinburg. A 45-minute drive takes guests to this scenic mountain village. Another 40 minutes or so will take guests to Pigeon Forge. The inn backs up onto the Great Smoky Mountains National Park, which includes Cades Cove, a primitive settlement about 30 minutes from the inn.

Innkeeper(s): Kreis Beall and son Sam. $495-945. 44 rooms with PB, 16 with FP, 16 suites, 2 cottages and 4 conference rooms. Breakfast, afternoon tea and dinner included in rates. Types of meals: Full gourmet bkfst, veg bkfst, early coffee/tea, gourmet lunch, snacks/refreshments and room service. Restaurant on premises. Beds: KQDT. Modem hook-up, data port, cable TV, VCR, reading lamp, stereo, refrigerator, snack bar, clock radio, telephone, coffeemaker, turn-down service, desk, voice mail, hair dryer, iron/ironing board, umbrella and flashlight in room. Air conditioning. Fax, copier, spa, swimming, stable, bicycles, tennis, parlor games, fireplace, horseback riding, cooking school and fly fishing on premises. Limited handicap access. Weddings, small meetings, family reunions and seminars hosted. Amusement parks, antiquing, art galleries, bicycling, canoeing/kayaking, downhill skiing, golf, museums, parks, shopping, sporting events and water sports nearby.

Publicity: *Country Inns, Town & Country, Travel & Leisure, Southern Living, Conde Nast Traveler, Andrew Harper's Hideaway Report, Bon Appetit and Gourmet.*

"Everything was spectacular! A wonderful weekend getaway!"

Texas

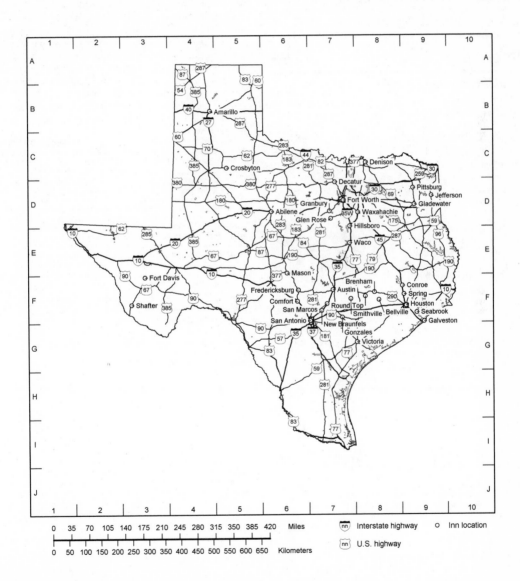

Abilene
D6

BJ's Prairie House B&B

508 Mulberry St
Abilene, TX 79601-4908
(325)675-5855 (800)673-5855 Fax:(325)677-4694

Circa 1902. This B&B was completely redesigned in 1920, omitting all references to the previous Victorian architecture and transforming into a prairie-style home. The home is filled with antiques and modern luxuries. Rooms bear the names Love, Joy, Peace and Patience, all clues to the relaxing, hospitable atmosphere. Peace includes a huge clawfoot tub.

Innkeeper(s): BJ Fender. $75-85. 4 rooms, 2 with PB. Breakfast included in rates. Types of meals: Full bkfst. Beds: KQDT. Reading lamp, ceiling fan and clocks in room. Central air. VCR and telephone on premises. Antiquing, fishing, live theater, parks, shopping, sporting events and water sports nearby.

Amarillo
B4

Parkview House B&B

1311 S Jefferson St
Amarillo, TX 79101-4029
(806)373-9464 Fax:(806)373-3166
E-mail: parkviewbb@aol.com
Web: members.aol.com/parkviewbb

Circa 1908. Ionic columns support the wraparound wicker-filled front porch of this Prairie Victorian. Antique mahogany, oak and walnut furnishings highlight the inviting interior. Gather by the fireplace in the eclectic country kitchen with a hot beverage. Themed guest bedrooms and a cozy cottage feature fabric-draped bedsteads and a romantic ambiance. A delicious continental-plus breakfast is served in the formal dining room.

Herb and rose gardens are accented by statuary and gazing balls. Relax on the tree-shaded porch, or enjoy the tranquility of the Koi pond. Borrow a bicycle to explore the neighborhood. Shop along Historic Route 66, hike in Palo Duro Canyon or watch an award-winning outdoor musical play, to name just a few of the many area attractions and cultural activities. At the end of the day, soak in the hot tub under a canopy of stars.

Historic Interest: Panhandle Plains Museum (15 minutes), Palo Duro State Park (23 miles), Alibates Flint Monument (16 miles), historic route 66, the longest segment of this historic highway that passes through Texas. Additionally, Amarillo is the closest city to the historical musical drama, "Texas" (Canyon, TX), performed for 36 years in the Palo Duro Canyon, and close to Texas' newest outdoor western musical, "Lone Star Rising" showcasing Texas culture.

Innkeeper(s): Carol & Nabil Dia. $75-135. 5 rooms, 3 with PB, 1 suite and 1 cottage. Breakfast included in rates. Types of meals: Full gourmet bkfst, early coffee/tea and snacks/refreshments. Beds: QD. TV, reading lamp, clock radio, hot tub/spa, some ceiling fans, desks and telephones in room. Air conditioning. VCR, fax, bicycles, parlor games, telephone and fireplace on premises. Weddings and small meetings hosted. Amusement parks, antiquing, bicycling, hiking, horseback riding, live theater, parks, shopping, tennis, water sports and bird watching nearby.

Publicity: *Lubbock Avalanche, Amarillo Globe News, Accent West, Sunday Telegraph Review and Channel 7.*

"You are what give B&Bs such a wonderful reputation. Thanks very much for the wonderful stay! The hospitality was warm and the ambiance incredible."

Austin
F7

1888 Miller Crockett House Bed & Breakfast

112 Academy Drive
Austin, TX 78704
(512)441-1600 (888)441-1641 Fax:(512)447-6532
E-mail: kat@millercrockett.com
Web: www.millercrockett.citysearch.com

Circa 1888. Verandas encompass all sides of this New Orleans-style Queen Anne Victorian. Considered a well-kept secret, this bed and breakfast is a historical landmark and has been used for a film location. Enjoy an award-winning view of the downtown skyline beyond the meticulously landscaped one-and-a-half acre lawn. High ceilings and preserved architectural details accent elegant period antiques, a baby grand piano and eclectic modern furnishings. The main house offers lovely guest bedrooms and a grand suite. Two cottages include kitchens and sitting rooms. A generous weekday breakfast is served, and a gourmet brunch is enjoyed on the weekends. Hike or bike the nearby trail at Town Lake. Nap in hammocks under the shade of an old oak tree.

Historic Interest: Inn was built in 1888 by a prominent local family as a wedding gift for their daughter who married a direct descendant of Davy Crockett.

Innkeeper(s): Kathleen Mooney. $99-169. 6 rooms, 3 with PB, 3 cottages and 2 conference rooms. Breakfast and snacks/refreshments included in rates. Types of meals: Full gourmet bkfst, veg bkfst, early coffee/tea and gourmet dinner. Beds: KQ. Modem hook-up, data port, cable TV, VCR, reading lamp, CD player, refrigerator, ceiling fan, clock radio, telephone, coffeemaker, turn-down service, desk, voice mail and fireplace in room. Central air. Fax, copier, swimming, bicycles, tennis, pet boarding, parlor games, fireplace and laundry facility on premises. Weddings, small meetings, family reunions and seminars hosted. Antiquing, art galleries, bicycling, canoeing/kayaking, fishing, golf, horseback riding, live theater, museums, parks, shopping, sporting events, tennis, water sports and wineries nearby.

Publicity: *Frommer's, Fodor's, Travel and Leisure, San Francisco Herald, Austin American Statesman, Austin Chronicle, the movie Newton Boys and Russell Crowe's "Texas" documentary.*

Austin Governors' Inn

611 W 22nd St
Austin, TX 78705-5115
(512)477-0711 (800)871-8908 Fax:(512)476-4769
E-mail: governorsinn@earthlink.net
Web: www.governorsinnaustin.com

Circa 1897. This Neoclassical Victorian is just a few blocks from the University of Texas campus and three blocks from the State Capitol. Guests can enjoy the view of two acres of trees and foliage from the porches that decorate each story of the inn. The innkeepers have decorated the guest rooms with antiques and named them after former Texas governors. Several of the bathrooms include clawfoot tubs.

Innkeeper(s): Lisa Wiedemann. $59-139. 10 rooms with PB, 5 with FP and 1 conference room. Breakfast, afternoon tea and snacks/refreshments included in rates. Types of meals: Full gourmet bkfst, early coffee/tea and picnic lunch. Beds: KQ. Cable TV, reading lamp, ceiling fan, clock radio, telephone, turn-down service, desk, hair dryers and robes in room. Air conditioning. VCR, fax, copier, parlor games and fireplace on premises. Limited handicap access. Weddings, small meetings, family reunions and seminars hosted. Antiquing, fishing, live theater, parks, shopping, sporting events and water sports nearby.

Publicity: *USA Today, Instyle, Voted best B&B in 1997, 1998, 1999, 2000, 2001 by the Austin Chronicle and Romantic Inns of America.*

Austin's Wildflower Inn B&B

1200 W 22 1/2 St
Austin, TX 78705-5304
(512)477-9639 (800)995-6171 Fax:(512)474-4188
E-mail: csims@io.com
Web: www.austinswildflowerinn.com

Circa 1936. This Colonial-style home fits right into its woodsy street, located in a quiet Austin neighborhood just a few blocks from the University of Texas. Three of the rooms are named for relatives of innkeeper Kay Jackson, who is related to a former president of the Republic of  Texas. Lacy curtains, stenciling, pedestal sinks, quilts and antiques create a homey country atmosphere. One room has a canopy bed, another includes a four-poster, oak bed. Each morning, a new Wildflower specialty is served at breakfast, along with homemade breads or muffins and fresh fruit. The State Capitol Complex is a few minutes from the home.

Innkeeper(s): Chris Sims. $94-159. 3 rooms with PB. Breakfast included in rates. Types of meals: Full bkfst and early coffee/tea. Beds: QD. Reading lamp, ceiling fan, clock radio, desk and telephones (two rooms) in room. Air conditioning. Fax and telephone on premises. Antiquing, fishing, live theater, parks, shopping, sporting events and water sports nearby.

"I was enchanted by your very friendly reception and personal care for my well-being."

Austins Inn at Pearl Street

809 W Martin Luther King Jr Blvd
Austin, TX 78701-1015
(512)478-0051 (800)494-2261 Fax:(512)478-0033
E-mail: lodging@sprintmail.com
Web: www.innpearl.com

Circa 1911. Porches and a 1,600-square-foot deck, surround this turn-of-the-century Greek Revival inn in downtown Austin. One-hundred-year-old oak and pecan trees enhance the landscape. Ten guest bedrooms include two suites and one cottage. The innkeeper is a hotel owner and operator in Austin for over 20 years. She serves a delightful European breakfast Monday through Friday. Full breakfasts on weekends include treats such as waffles with fruit, Egg Delight, eggs Benedict and Canadian bacon. On Sunday, champagne is added to the menu.

Innkeeper(s): Jill Bickford. $70-200. 10 rooms with PB, 1 with FP, 2 suites, 1 cottage and 2 conference rooms. Breakfast and snacks/refreshments included in rates. Types of meals: Full gourmet bkfst, veg bkfst, early coffee/tea, gourmet lunch, picnic lunch, afternoon tea, dinner and room service. Beds: KQT. Cable TV, VCR, ceiling fan, telephone, coffeemaker, turn-down service, voice mail, toiletries, clock radio, robes and hair dryer in room. Central air. Fax, copier, spa, bicycles, library, parlor games, fireplace and laundry facility on premises. Weddings, small meetings, family reunions and seminars hosted. Amusement parks, antiquing, art galleries, beach, bicycling, canoeing/kayaking, fishing, golf, hiking, horseback riding, live theater, museums, parks, shopping, sporting events, tennis, water sports and wineries nearby. Publicity: KXAN.

Brava House

1108 Blanco Street
Austin, TX 78703
(512)478-5034 (888)545-8200 Fax:(800)706-2054

Circa 1889. Considered a boutique bed & breakfast inn, this Victorian home is one of the first to be built here, and graces a very historic neighborhood. Hardwood floors, high ceilings, crown moldings, original fireplaces and clean lines reflect its heritage while meticulous restoration has added modern comforts. Well-appointed, uncluttered guest bedrooms and suites feature elegant antiques, a workspace with wireless Internet access, assorted personal care amenities, a microwave and mini refrigerator. The daily breakfast buffet includes a variety of fresh fruit, breads, yogurt and hot and cold cereals. It is expanded with more delights on weekends. Relax on the front porch or in the colorful back garden. Walk to local sites from this serene retreat.

Historic Interest: This home was one of the first Victorian homes. Built in 1889 in Clarksville, a neighborhood first settled by freed slaves.
Innkeeper(s): Shelley Seale. $89-195. 5 rooms with PB, 2 with FP and 3 suites. Breakfast, afternoon tea and snacks/refreshments included in rates. Types of meals: Full gourmet bkfst, veg bkfst and early coffee/tea. Beds: Q. Modem hook-up, cable TV, reading lamp, refrigerator, ceiling fan, clock radio, telephone, coffeemaker, desk and some with fireplace in room. Central air. Small meetings, family reunions and seminars hosted. Antiquing, art galleries, bicycling, canoeing/kayaking, fishing, golf, hiking, live theater, museums, parks, shopping, sporting events, water sports and Texas State Capitol nearby.

Carrington's Bluff

1900 David St
Austin, TX 78705-5312
(512)479-0638 (888)290-6090 Fax:(512)478-2009
E-mail: phoebe@carringtonsbluff.com
Web: www.carringtonsbluff.com

Circa 1877. Situated on a tree-covered bluff in the heart of Austin, this inn sits next to a 500-year-old oak tree. The innkeepers combine down-home hospitality with English charm. The house is filled with English and American antiques and handmade quilts. Rooms are carefully decorated with dried flowers, inviting colors and antique beds, such as the oak barley twist bed in the Martha Hill Carrington Room. After a hearty breakfast, relax on a 35-foot-long porch that overlooks the bluff. The Austin area is booming with things to do.

Innkeeper(s): Phoebe & Jeff Williams. $89-149. 8 rooms with PB and 1 conference room. Breakfast and snacks/refreshments included in rates. Types of meals: Full gourmet bkfst and early coffee/tea. Beds: KQDT. Cable TV, reading lamp, ceiling fan, clock radio, telephone and desk in room. Air conditioning. TV, VCR, fax, copier, library, child care, parlor games and fireplace on premises. Weddings, small meetings, family reunions and seminars hosted. Amusement parks, antiquing, fishing, live theater, parks, shopping, sporting events and water sports nearby.
Publicity: PBS Special.

"Victorian writer's dream place."

Healthy Quarters

1215 Parkway
Austin, TX 78703-4132
(512)476-7484 (800)392-6566 Fax:(512)480-9356
E-mail: healthyquarters@webtv.net
Web: www.healthyquarters.com

Circa 1935. This homestay is located near the State Capitol and the University of Texas on the edge of the downtown area. The comfortable accommodations include the Sun Room, which features an arched ceiling, a quilt-topped bed and country décor. The Ivy Room boasts a Jacuzzi shower bathtub, Elizabeth Ashley bed linens and a long series of shuttered windows adorns one wall. The guest refrigerators are stocked with milk, eggs, yogurt, English muffins and organic coffee. Juice, purified water and fresh organic fruit are also provided.

Innkeeper(s): Marilyn Grooms. $65-85. 2 rooms with PB. Breakfast included in rates. Beds: QD. Cable TV, VCR, telephone, private entrances and kitchen area in room. Central air. Laundry facility on premises. Antiquing, art galleries, bicycling, canoeing/kayaking, golf, hiking, live theater, museums, parks, shopping, sporting events, State Capitol and LBJ Library nearby.

Lazy Oak B&B

211 W Live Oak St
Austin, TX 78704-5114
(512)447-8873 (877)947-8873 Fax:(512)912-1484
E-mail: lazyoakinn@aol.com
Web: www.lazyoakbandb.com

Circa 1911. For a fun getaway, this historic plantation-style farmhouse offers an airy and relaxed ambiance. The mix of eclectic antique furnishings and decor imparts a casual country feel. Luxurious amenities are found in the comfortable guest bedrooms. Arrange for a massage, or soak in the hot tub. Linger over a scrumptious homemade breakfast enjoyed in-room, on the spacious front porch or in the kitchen. Gaze at the fish pond while strolling the landscaped acre or take a short walk to the sites and activities of Town Lake and Congress Avenue.

Innkeeper(s): Renee & Kevin Buck. $89-125. 5 rooms with PB. Breakfast and snacks/refreshments included in rates. Types of meals: Full gourmet bkfst, veg bkfst and early coffee/tea. Beds: KQD. Data port, cable TV, reading lamp, ceiling fan, clock radio and telephone in room. Central air. VCR, fax, copier, bicycles, library, parlor games, laundry facility and hot tub on premises. Small meetings and seminars hosted. Amusement parks, antiquing, art galleries, bicycling, canoeing/kayaking, fishing, golf, hiking, live theater, museums, parks, shopping, sporting events, tennis, water sports and wineries nearby.
Publicity: *Austin Chronicle.*

"The most relaxing and wonderful time. Breakfast was great and the accommodations were the nicest we've stayed in."

Woodburn House B&B

4401 Avenue D
Austin, TX 78751-3714
(512)458-4335 (888)690-9763 Fax:(512)458-4319
E-mail: woodburnhouse@yahoo.com
Web: www.woodburnhouse.com

Circa 1909. This stately home was named for Bettie Hamilton Woodburn, who bought the house in 1920. Hamilton's father was once the provisional governor of Texas and a friend of Abraham Lincoln. The home once was slated for demolition and saved in 1979 when George Boutwell bought the home for $1

and moved it to its present location. Guests will be taken immediately by the warmth of the home surrounded by old trees. The home is furnished with period antiques. Breakfasts are served formally in the dining room.

Historic Interest: The Elisabeth Ney Sculpture Museum is three blocks from Woodburn House. The bed & breakfast is within a district listed in the National Register and walking tours are offered.

Innkeeper(s): Herb & Sandra Dickson. $90-140. 4 rooms with PB and 1 suite. Breakfast included in rates. Types of meals: Full gourmet bkfst and early coffee/tea. Beds: KQT. Reading lamp, ceiling fan, clock radio, telephone, desk, whirlpool for two, double vanity, sitting room with sofa and suite has TV in room. Air conditioning. VCR, fax and amenities for the deaf on premises. Antiquing, fishing, live theater, parks, shopping, sporting events and museum nearby.
Publicity: *Austin Chronicle, Dallas Morning News, USA Today and Hard Promises.*

"The comfort, the breakfasts and the hospitality were excellent and greatly appreciated."

Bellville   F8

Bluebonnet Inn

214 S Live Oak St
Bellville, TX 77418-2340
(979)865-0027

Circa 1906. Fresh flowers, antique furnishings, gorgeous woodwork and curved corner windows create an inviting ambiance at this fully restored, 1906 Victorian bed & breakfast. Year-round relaxation is found at this country escape where raiding the bottomless cookie jar is encouraged. Watch satellite television, read or enjoy conversation in the upstairs sitting room. Stay in a comfortable guest bedroom or The Oaks, a private and separate honeymoon suite that features an authentic Victorian Iron Wedding Ring Bed and vintage clawfoot tub. Gather

in the old family dining room for a not-to-be-missed, generous southern-style breakfast served around 8:30 each morning. Swings are strategically located on the front porch, balcony and under the mature wisteria arbor. Swim in the fenced swimming pool surrounded by 100-year-old oaks and pecan trees. Family-style lunch and dinner meals are served to groups by advance reservation. Ask the innkeepers about excursions to Winedale, two state parks, Blue Bell Creamery, Festival Hill and Round Top.

Innkeeper(s): John and Debbie Marchak. $75-125. 6 rooms and 1 suite. Breakfast included in rates. Types of meals: Full bkfst. Beds: QDT. TV, reading lamp, ceiling fan and clock radio in room. Central air. VCR, swimming, telephone and laundry facility on premises. Weddings, small meetings, family reunions and seminars hosted. Antiquing, fishing, golf, live theater, museums, shopping, wineries and state parks nearby.

"We have thoroughly enjoyed our stay here. It is a wonderful and beautiful place to enjoy."

Brenham   F8

Mariposa Ranch B&B

8904 Mariposa Ln
Brenham, TX 77833-8906
(979)836-4737 (877)647-4774

Circa 1865. Several buildings comprise the inn: a Victorian, an 1820 log cabin, a quaint cottage, a farmhouse and a 1836 Greek Revival home. Guests relax on the veranda, stroll through the Live Oaks or explore the ranch's 100 acres of

fields and meadows. The inn is furnished with fine antiques. Ask for the Texas Ranger Cabin and enjoy a massive stone fireplace, sofa, clawfoot tub and loft with queen bed. Jennifer's Suite boasts a king canopy bed and two fireplaces. The "Enchanted Evening"

package offers champagne, fruit, flowers, candlelight, candy and an optional massage. Guests can select a room with a Jacuzzi for two or a clawfoot tub for additional luxury.

Innkeeper(s): Johnna & Charles Chamberlain. $79-250. 11 rooms with PB, 7 with FP, 2 suites, 2 cottages, 4 cabins and 2 conference rooms. Breakfast included in rates. Types of meals: Full bkfst, veg bkfst, early coffee/tea, gourmet lunch, picnic lunch, snacks/refreshments, gourmet dinner and room service. Beds: KQDT. TV, VCR, reading lamp, CD player, refrigerator, ceiling fan, clock radio, hot tub/spa and fireplace in room. Central air. Fax, copier, library, parlor games, telephone, fireplace and laundry facility on premises. Weddings, small meetings, family reunions and seminars hosted. Antiquing, fishing, golf, live theater, parks, shopping, tennis and water sports nearby. Publicity: *Southern Living, Texas Monthly, "D" Magazine and Austin American.*

Comfort   F6

Idlewilde

115 Hwy 473
Comfort, TX 78013
(830)995-3844

Circa 1902. Known as a "Haven in the Hills" this Western-style farmhouse and surrounding grounds were a girls' summer camp for more than sixty years. Experience a quiet privacy in one of the two air-conditioned cottages that feature kitch-enettes and wood-burning stoves. The innkeepers offer a morn-ing meal in the main house dining area or wherever desired, even breakfast in bed. Tennis courts, a pool and a pavilion provide pleas-ant diversions.

Innkeeper(s): Hank Engel & Connie Engel & Nicholas Engel. $85-115. 2 cot-tages. Breakfast included in rates. Types of meals: Full bkfst and picnic lunch. Beds: Q. Weddings, small meetings, family reunions and seminars hosted. Amusement parks, antiquing, fishing, golf, shopping, sporting events and water sports nearby.
Publicity: *Austin Chronicle and Hill Country Recorder.*

Conroe   F9

Heather's Glen . . . A B&B & More

200 E Phillips St
Conroe, TX 77301-2646
(936)441-6611 (800)665-2643 Fax:(936)441-6603
E-mail: heathersbb@aol.com
Web: www.heathersglen.com

Circa 1900. This turn-of-the-century mansion still maintains many of its original features, such as heart-of-pine flooring, gra-cious staircases and antique glass windows. Verandas and covered porches decorate the exterior, creating ideal places to relax. Guest rooms are decorated in a romantic, country flavor. One room has a bed draped with a lacy canopy, and five rooms include double Jacuzzi tubs. Antique shops, an outlet mall and Lake Conroe are nearby, and the home is within an hour of Houston.
Innkeeper(s): Ed & Jamie George. $90-250. 13 rooms, 8 with PB, 3 with FP and 3 conference rooms. Breakfast, afternoon tea and snacks/refreshments included in rates. Types of meals: Full gourmet bkfst and early coffee/tea. Beds: QD. Cable TV, reading lamp, CD player, refrigerator, ceiling fan, clock radio, telephone, turn-down service, desk and hot tub/spa in room. Air condi-tioning. Fax, copier, parlor games and fireplace on premises. Limited handi-cap access. Weddings, small meetings, family reunions and seminars hosted. Amusement parks, antiquing, downhill skiing, fishing, live theater, parks, shopping, sporting events, water sports and auctions weekly nearby.
Publicity: *HGTV-If Walls Could Talk.*

Crosbyton   C5

Smith House Inn

306 W Aspen St
Crosbyton, TX 79322-2506
(806)675-2178
E-mail: smithhousebnb@texasonline.net
Web: www.smithhousebnb.com

Circa 1921. Built as a boarding house, this inn proudly shares much of its original furnishings in its transformation to a bed & breakfast inn. A guest register that dates to 1921 is fun to

peruse and the original player piano still is the focal point of entertainment in the parlor. The dining room, with capacity for 35, is the location for a full Texan breakfast of homemade bread, meat and egg dishes. A variety of rooms include the Bridal suite with private sitting room and large bath.
Innkeeper(s): Terry & Karen Ellison. $60-125. 11 rooms, 7 with PB, 1 suite and 2 conference rooms. Breakfast included in rates. Types of meals: Full bkfst. Beds: KQDT. Air conditioning. VCR, parlor games and telephone on premises. Small meetings, family reunions and seminars hosted. Antiquing, fishing, parks and water sports nearby.

Decatur   D7

Abbercromby Penthouse Suites

103 W Main St
Decatur, TX 76234
(940)627-7005 (888)677-7737
E-mail: txabby@aol.com
Web: www.4romanticweddings.com

Circa 1895. Enter a time of nostalgic fantasy in this Victorian building on historic Town Square. The inn's three, second-story suites are lavish re-creations of a bygone era. Distinctly different in style and theme, they are impressive encounters with old-fashioned pampering, grand luxury or romantic seclusion. Fully furnished to meet modern needs, thoughtful attention also has been given to providing amenities. Each morning a delicious gourmet continental breakfast is delivered for private dining pleasure. For a delightful splurge, schedule an individual or couple's massage.
Innkeeper(s): Bob & Margaret Atkinson. $99-135. 3 suites and 1 conference room. Breakfast included in rates. Types of meals: Full bkfst. Beds: KQT. Modem hook-up, cable TV, VCR, reading lamp, stereo, refrigerator, ceiling fan, snack bar, clock radio, telephone, coffeemaker, desk, hot tub/spa and fireplace in room. Central air. Fax, copier, spa, pet boarding, parlor games, three massage therapists on staff and complete wedding packages from harp music to make-up artist on premises. Weddings, small meetings, family reunions and seminars hosted. Amusement parks, antiquing, art galleries, hiking, museums and shopping nearby.

Denison   C8

Inn of Many Faces Victorian Bed & Breakfast

412 W Morton St
Denison, TX 75020-2422
(903)465-4639 Fax:(903)465-3328
E-mail: theinn@texoma.net
Web: www.innofmanyfaces.com

Circa 1897. Resplendently sitting in the middle of towering pecan trees on two wooded acres, this restored Queen Anne Victorian provides rest and relaxation. A collection of whimsical faces are displayed throughout the house and gardens. Themed guest bedrooms offer spacious accommodations. The Katy Room is a romantic retreat that boasts a fireplace and whirlpool bath. The Cabbage Rose Room overlooks the lawn and gardens, gazebo and gold fish pond. In the morning, savor fresh fruit, a baked entree, breakfast meats, hot breads and muffins. Located near Lake Texoma allows for easy access to boating and fishing. Play golf on one of several area courses, shop for antiques or browse local art galleries.
Innkeeper(s): Charlie & Gloria Morton. $109-139. 4 rooms with PB, 2 with FP and 1 conference room. Breakfast and snacks/refreshments included in rates. Types of meals: Full gourmet bkfst, veg bkfst and early coffee/tea. Beds: KQD. Cable TV, VCR, reading lamp, ceiling fan, clock radio, hot

tub/spa and fireplace in room. Central air. Fax, copier, parlor games, telephone, fireplace and massages available on premises. Weddings, small meetings and seminars hosted. Antiquing, art galleries, fishing, golf, hiking, horseback riding, live theater, museums, parks, shopping, sporting events, tennis, water sports and wineries nearby.
Publicity: *Dallas Morning News and Texas Highways.*

Fort Davis   F3

The Veranda Country Inn B&B

PO Box 1238
Fort Davis, TX 79734-1238
 (888)383-2847
E-mail: info@theveranda.com
Web: www.theveranda.com

Circa 1883. A mile above sea level sits this historic inn, which first opened as the Lempert Hotel, a stopping point for travelers on the nearby Overland Trail. An owner later used the

building for apartments, but current innkeepers Paul and Kathie Woods returned the home into a place for hospitality. Paul and Kathie have restored their bed & breakfast's high ceilings, wood floors and beaded wood ceilings back to their original condition. The interior is furnished with antiques and collectibles. All rooms have a private bath, and the separate Carriage House and Garden Cottage are available in addition to the 11 inn rooms. The grounds offer the serene setting of gardens, quiet courtyards and large covered porches with rocking chairs.
Historic Interest: The Fort Davis area is full of historic places to visit, including the Fort Davis Historic Site, an 1854 restored frontier fort. The largest original unpaved portion of the Overland Trail is just a block away, and the Overland Trail Museum is another popular historic attraction. The Neill Doll Museum, which is located in a turn-of-the-century home, features more than 300 antique dolls.
Innkeeper(s): Paul & Kathie Woods. $85-120. 14 rooms with PB, 4 suites and 2 cottages. Breakfast included in rates. Types of meals: Full bkfst. Beds: KQ. Small meetings hosted. Horseback riding, parks, shopping and historic sites nearby.

Fort Worth   D7

Miss Molly's Bed & Breakfast, Inc

109 1/2 W Exchange Ave
Fort Worth, TX 76106-8508
(817)626-1522 (800)996-6559 Fax:(817)625-2723

Circa 1910. An Old West ambiance permeates this hotel, which once was a house of ill repute. Miss Josie's Room, named for the former madame, is decked with elaborate wall and ceiling coverings and carved oak furniture. The Gunslinger Room is filled with pictures of famous and infamous gunfighters. Rodeo memorabilia decorates the Rodeo Room, and twin iron beds and a pot belly stove add flair to the Cowboy's Room. Telephones and TV sets are the only things missing from the rooms, as the innkeeper hopes to preserve the flavor of the past.
Innkeeper(s): Dawn Street. $125-200. 7 rooms, 1 with PB. Breakfast included in rates. Types of meals: Full bkfst and early coffee/tea. Beds: DT. Reading lamp and ceiling fan in room. Air conditioning. Fax, copier, parlor games and telephone on premises. Small meetings, family reunions and seminars hosted. Amusement parks, antiquing, live theater, shopping, sporting events and stockyards National Historic district nearby.
Publicity: *British Bulldog, Arkansas Gazette, Dallas Morning News, Fort Worth Star-Telegram, Continental Profiles, Fort Worth Gazette and Eyes Of Texas.*

Texas White House B&B

1417 8th Ave
Fort Worth, TX 76104-4111
(817)923-3597 (800)279-6491 Fax:(817)923-0410
E-mail: txwhitehou@aol.com
Web: www.texaswhitehouse.com

Circa 1910. A spacious encircling veranda shaded by an old elm tree, graces the front of this two-story home located within five minutes of downtown, TCU, the zoo and many other area attractions. The inn's parlor and living room with fireplace and gleaming hardwood floors are the most popular spots for relaxing when not lingering on the porch. Guest rooms are equipped with phones and television, and early morning coffee is provided before the inn's full breakfast at a time convenient to your personal schedule. Suites include hot tub, sauna and fireplace. Baked egg casseroles and freshly made breads are served to your room or in the dining room. The owners are Fort Worth experts and keep abreast of cultural attractions and are happy to help with reservations and planning. The inn is popular with business travelers — secretarial services are available, etc. — during the week and appealing to couples on weekends.
Innkeeper(s): Grover & Jamie McMains. $105-185. 5 rooms with PB and 1 conference room. Breakfast and snacks/refreshments included in rates. Types of meals: Full gourmet bkfst, early coffee/tea and room service. Beds: Q. Modem hook-up, data port, cable TV, VCR, reading lamp, ceiling fan, clock radio, telephone, coffeemaker, turn-down service and desk in room. Central air. Fax, fireplace and laundry facility on premises. Small meetings hosted. Antiquing, art galleries, golf, live theater, museums and parks nearby.

Fredericksburg   F6

Alte Welt Gasthof (Old World Inn)

PO Box 628
Fredericksburg, TX 78624
(830)997-0443 (888)991-6749 Fax:(830)997-0040
E-mail: stay@texas-bed-n-breakfast.com
Web: www.texas-bed-n-breakfast.com

Circa 1915. Located on the second floor above a Main Street shop, Alte Welt is in a Basse Block building in the historic district. The entryway opens to an antique-filled foyer. A three-room suite offers a white sofa, silver accents including a silver, tin ceiling, wood floors and an antique iron four-poster bed draped in soft gauze. An armoire with TV and a small refrigerator and microwave add convenience. The innkeeper collects antique, crocheted and embroidered linens for the guest rooms. There is a spacious deck with hot tub adjoining one of the suites. Together, the two suites can accommodate as many as 10 people, so it is popular with families and small groups, who enjoy the freedom of simply going downstairs to Main Street and all its boutiques, shops and restaurants.
Innkeeper(s): Ron & Donna Maddux. $150-165. 2 suites. Breakfast included in rates. Types of meals: Cont and early coffee/tea. Beds: Q. Cable TV, reading lamp, refrigerator, ceiling fan, clock radio, telephone, desk, hot tub/spa, microwave and coffee bar in room. Air conditioning. Small meetings, family reunions and seminars hosted. Antiquing, fishing, golf, parks, shopping, tennis, museums and hunting nearby.

Camp David B&B

708 W. Main
Fredericksburg, TX 78624
(830)997-7797 (866)427-8374
E-mail: cottages@ktc.com
Web: www.campdavidbb.com

Circa 1929. Enjoy one of the only traditional Hill Country bed and breakfasts in the area that offers private cottages with fire-

places and whirlpool tubs. Front porches with rockers and bistro tables invite relaxation. The cottages sit behind the main house, are named after local trees and feature an English Country decor with American and European antique furnishings. Coffee, tea and cold drinks are provided in each room. A gourmet breakfast is delivered every morning to the door. The pecan tree-shaded courtyard features tables, chairs and a barbecue pit. Visit local wineries, attend the many festivals and tour the Pioneer Museum to learn of the town's history and heritage.
Innkeeper(s): Molly & Bob Sagebiel. $99-135. 7 rooms, 5 with FP and 1 suite. Breakfast and snacks/refreshments included in rates. Types of meals: Full gourmet bkfst and veg bkfst. Beds: KQT. Cable TV, reading lamp, refrigerator, ceiling fan, clock radio, telephone, coffeemaker and fireplace in room. Central air. Small meetings, family reunions and seminars hosted. Antiquing, art galleries, bicycling, golf, hiking, horseback riding, live theater, museums, parks, shopping and wineries nearby.
Publicity: *Texas Monthly.*

Magnolia House

101 E Hackberry St
Fredericksburg, TX 78624-3915
(830)997-0306 (800)880-4374 Fax:(830)997-0766

Circa 1923. This Craftsman-style home is listed as a Texas Historic Landmark and was built by Edward Stein, the designer of the Gillespie County Courthouse as well as many other local buildings. There are porches filled with wicker furnishings for those who wish to relax. Guest rooms are decorated with antiques and reproductions. The Bluebonnet Suite includes a wood-burning fireplace, antique clawfoot tub and a vintage refrigerator in the small kitchen. Southern-style breakfasts are served on tables set with antique china, silver and fresh flowers. The home is located about seven blocks from the main shopping area, which also offers museums, art galleries and wine tasting rooms. The Lyndon Johnson State and National Park are 16 miles away and there are several wineries in the area.
Innkeeper(s): Dee & David Lawford. $95-140. 5 rooms with PB, 2 with FP and 2 suites. Breakfast and snacks/refreshments included in rates. Types of meals: Full gourmet bkfst and early coffee/tea. Beds: KQ. Cable TV, VCR, ceiling fan and robes in room. Air conditioning. Small meetings and family reunions hosted. Antiquing, fishing, parks and shopping nearby.
Publicity: *Houston Chronicle.*

Galveston   F9

The Inn at 1816 Post Office

1816 Post Office St
Galveston, TX 77550
(409)765-9444 (888)558-9444 Fax:(409)762-8920

Circa 1886. This Victorian inn is a highlight of Galveston's East End Historical District. Each room is decorated in a different style. The Garden Room, so named for its view of the inn's garden, is light and airy with wicker furnishings, a wrought iron bed, stained-glass window, lacy curtains and a cast-iron tub in the bathroom. The Gain Room features a Jacuzzi tub and china pedestal sink. The inn's newest addition, the Studio "1816" Suite also boasts a Jacuzzi tub, as well as a queen-size sleigh bed. Antiques and clawfoot tubs, poster beds and family heirlooms are among the surprises you'll find in other rooms. Guests have use of a pool table and TV in the game room, and there are a variety of board games to enjoy. In the afternoons, refreshments are served in the inn's parlor. In the mornings, a gourmet breakfast is served in the dining room; eggs Benedict is a house specialty. There's much to do in Galveston, includ-

ing viewing historic homes, shopping, visiting the Arts District or enjoying a meal at one of the area's many restaurants. Houston and all of its attractions are a short drive away.
Innkeeper(s): Judy Wilkie & Bettye Hall. $100-195. 7 rooms with PB and 1 suite. Breakfast included in rates. Types of meals: Full gourmet bkfst, veg bkfst, early coffee/tea, picnic lunch and snacks/refreshments. Beds: KQ. Reading lamp, ceiling fan, coffeemaker, some with cable TV, some with refrigerator and some with hot tub/spa in room. Central air. TV, fax, copier, bicycles, parlor games and telephone on premises. Weddings, small meetings and seminars hosted. Antiquing, art galleries, beach, bicycling, canoeing/kayaking, fishing, golf, horseback riding, live theater, museums, parks and shopping nearby.

Gladewater   D9

Honeycomb Suites

111 N Main St
Gladewater, TX 75647-2333
(903)845-4430 (800)594-2253 Fax:(903)844-1859
E-mail: gloryb@cox-internet.com
Web: honeycombsuites.com

Circa 1932. Amid pine-covered rolling hills in the heart of East Texas' antique capital, these lavish accommodations were designed for intimate getaways. Several suites are popular for honeymooners with Victorian, white wicker or cottage motifs. For a manlier décor, the Gentleman's Quarters offers spacious luxury. A bed with a red iron headboard highlights another impressive suite and the Captain's Quarters on the first floor includes a refrigerator, microwave and coffeepot. All feature fine linens and remote cable TV; several boast whirlpools for two. Indulge in a gourmet breakfast served in the downstairs bakery dining room. Ask about special romance packages that provide fresh flowers, candlelight dinners and carriage rides. In addition to local activities, take a day trip to Dallas just two hours away or visit Shreveport, Louisiana within an hour's drive.
Innkeeper(s): Bill & Susan Morgan. $95-150. 7 rooms with PB, 6 suites and 1 conference room. Breakfast and snacks/refreshments included in rates. Types of meals: Full gourmet bkfst, early coffee/tea, lunch and picnic lunch. Restaurant on premises. Beds: Q. Cable TV, VCR, reading lamp, refrigerator, ceiling fan, telephone and hot tub/spa in room. Air conditioning. Weddings, small meetings, family reunions and seminars hosted. Antiquing, fishing, golf, parks, shopping, tennis, water sports, horseback riding and hot air ballooning nearby.
Publicity: *Dallas Morning News, Southern Living, Houston Chronicle, Shreveport Times and Longview News-Journal.*

Glen Rose   D7

Bussey's Something Special B&B

202 Hereford St
Glen Rose, TX 76043-4640
(254)897-4843 (877)426-2233 Fax:(254)897-3456

Circa 1896. Private guest cottages were built with a barn style, two-story wood frame near historic Downtown Square. The Cozy Victorian Cottage features a romantic whirlpool jet tub and the Cajun/Cowboy Bunk House is highlighted by ceramic tiles and weathered wood. Both boast front porch entrances with enclosed yards as well as a shared back porch and yard. Fully equipped and well-stocked kitchens include breakfast ingredients. Books, magazines and games provide indoor entertainment. It is a short walk to the Paluxy River, or to visit a nearby museum.
Innkeeper(s): Susan and Morris Bussey. $80-95. 2 rooms with PB. Breakfast, afternoon tea and snacks/refreshments included in rates. Types of meals: Cont plus, veg bkfst, early coffee/tea, picnic lunch and room service. Beds: KD. Reading lamp, refrigerator, ceiling fan, clock radio, coffeemaker, turn-down service, whirlpool jet tub, radio, cassette player, personal library, private

entrances, snacks and breakfast, microwave, toaster, coffee pot, electric skillet, sink and utensils in room. Central air. Fax, library, telephone, private fenced yard, paved off-street parking and fishing poles on premises. Antiquing, art galleries, bicycling, canoeing/kayaking, fishing, golf, hiking, horseback riding, live theater, museums, parks, shopping, water sports, wildlife endangered species conservation drive-through park and Dinosaur Texas State Park nearby.

Country Woods Inn

420 Grand Ave.
Glen Rose, TX 76043
(817)279-3002

Circa 1900. Family friendly, these Texas hill country accommodations offer scenic surroundings within a short walk of the historic downtown square. Exuding a rustic ambiance, lodgings in the Main House, Prairie House, Farm House, Bunk House, Saddle House, Carriage House and Railroad Car are perfect for large groups, weddings or reunions. Whether staying in one of the guest bedrooms or in the privacy of the small cottage, comfortable furnishings and tasteful decorating create pleasant memories. Nature enthusiasts enjoy the extensive walking and river trails as well as bird watching.

Innkeeper(s): Helen Kerwin. $90-150. 13 rooms with PB, 2 with FP, 4 suites, 3 cottages, 3 cabins and 2 conference rooms. Types of meals: Cont plus, early coffee/tea and snacks/refreshments. Beds: QDT. Modem hook-up, cable TV, VCR, reading lamp, refrigerator, ceiling fan, clock radio, telephone, coffeemaker, desk and drop fireplace in room. Central air. Swimming, stable, bicycles, pet boarding, parlor games, fireplace, laundry facility, walking trails, fishing, recreational area, barnyard and wedding chapel on premises. Weddings, small meetings, family reunions and seminars hosted. Antiquing, art galleries, bicycling, canoeing/kayaking, fishing, golf, hiking, horseback riding, museums, parks, shopping and tennis nearby.

Publicity: *Texas Highways, Dallas Morning News, Texas Monthly,* Voted Top Child Friendly B&B, 2002 Arrington's B&B Journal and Show Me Texas.

Gonzales   F7

Belle Oaks Inn

PO Box 57
Gonzales, TX 78629
(830)857-8613 Fax:(830)857-8624

Circa 1912. Transformed by a collaboration of Southern charm and hospitality, this Antebellum Greek Revival-Louisiana Plantation Style mansion is a tribute to the elegant grace of yesterday and the modern comforts appreciated today. Landscaped lawns and formal gardens are accented by large oak and pecan trees scattered over two scenic acres. Guest bedrooms and suites, some with fireplaces, boast lavish amenities that enhance the luxurious experience. A generous, self-serve continental-plus breakfast is available when desired. In-room massages and herbal body wraps are by appointment. Relax on the large rock terrace by the koi pond, swim in the pool or ride a bike.

Historic Interest: Was built in 1912 and designed by famous architect J. Gordon Riley who designed over 66 public buildings across the U.S. with 16 of them being Texas courthouses. The home was built by the local Dilworth banking family who has a very colorful history, as does the chain of ownership of the home and the stories that go with it. Gonzales is considered the "Lexington of Texas" as this is where the first shot of the Texas revolution was fired. We have local museums and monuments commemorating the rich and colorful history of the area which played a major role in Texas' fight for independence. We are located a short one hour drive from the Alamo in San Antonio and the forts in Goliad.

Innkeeper(s): Clint Hille & Richard Tiller. $75-125. 5 rooms with PB, 2 with FP and 2 suites. Breakfast and snacks/refreshments included in rates. Types of meals: Cont plus. Beds: QT. Cable TV, VCR, reading lamp, refrigerator, ceiling fan, clock radio, coffeemaker, turn-down service, fireplace, hair dryers, robes, down comforters and pillows and two with down mattresses in room. Central air. Fax, copier, swimming, bicycles, library, parlor games, telephone and fireplace on premises. Weddings, small meetings, family reunions and seminars hosted. Antiquing, art galleries, bicycling, canoeing/kayaking, fishing, golf, hiking, museums, parks and shopping nearby.

John Fauth Guest Cottage

521 Saint Peter Street
Gonzales, TX 78629-4067
(830)857-8091 (866)563-2884 Fax:(888)901-8668

Circa 1868. Completely restored, this premier guest house is a rare example of Steamboat Gothic architecture that reflects a German craftsman's building skills and a Victorian decor. It is perfect for a romantic getaway or a shopping excursion for antiques. Relax in the comfort of central heating and air conditioning as well as a Ben Franklin stove in the parlor. Sit by the fire in a spacious country kitchen with a 20-foot-high ceiling. The master bedroom boasts a fireplace with a mantel carved and signed by Mr. Fauth. Soak in the sunken whirlpool tub for two. The front and back sitting porches are inviting spots to pass the time chatting or daydreaming.

Innkeeper(s): Mayron & Bill Cole. $150-200. 2 rooms with PB, 1 with FP. Beds: QT. Cable TV, reading lamp, ceiling fan, clock radio and fireplace in room. Central air. TV, spa, telephone, laundry facility, full kitchen stocked with breakfast items and front & back porches on premises. Limited handicap access. Weddings, small meetings, family reunions and seminars hosted. Antiquing, museums, parks and shopping nearby.

Granbury   D7

Baker St. Harbour Bed & Breakfast

511 S. Baker St.
Granbury, TX 76048
(817)578-3684 (877)578-3684 Fax:(817)578-3689
E-mail: info@BakerStHarbour.com
Web: www.BakerStHarbour.com

Circa 1892. A white picket fence accents this Queen Anne Victorian home on a quiet cul-de-sac on Lake Granbury. Two acres of scenic beauty include a double-decked dock that is perfect for fishing and a large garden gazebo surrounded by 100-year-old oaks and colorful flowers. Play horseshoes or croquet. Relax on a porch rocker or a book in the library. Family heirlooms and antiques furnish the delightful guest bedrooms that boast waterfront views and many baths include a clawfoot tub. The spacious Dr. Doyle Suite also features a sitting area, fireplace and private entrance. Feel pampered with evening in-room desserts and fresh flowers. Family-style breakfasts are enjoyed in the dining room.

Historic Interest: Built in 1892, and owned by the Postmaster in 1894. Was built on the banks of the Brazos River. Lake Granbury was established beginning in 1968, when the Brazos was dammed up at DeCordova Bend. Many settlers & pioneers gathered on the banks of the Brazos, just a few feet from our home.

Innkeeper(s): Betty & Bill Moss. $115-175. 4 rooms with PB, 1 with FP, 1 suite and 1 conference room. Breakfast and snacks/refreshments included in rates. Types of meals: Full bkfst. Beds: KQ. Modem hook-up, cable TV, reading lamp, ceiling fan, clock radio, coffeemaker, desk, hair dryer, iron, ironing board, in-room desserts and fresh flowers in room. Central air. VCR, fax, copier, library, parlor games, telephone, fireplace, dock for relaxing, fishing, boating, gazebos, horseshoes and croquet on premises. Weddings, small meetings, family reunions and seminars hosted. Amusement parks, antiquing, art galleries, beach, bicycling, canoeing/kayaking, fishing, golf, hiking, horseback riding, live theater, museums, parks, shopping, sporting events, tennis and water sports nearby.

Dabney House B&B

106 S Jones St
Granbury, TX 76048-1905
(817)579-1260 (800)566-1260
E-mail: safe-dabney@flash.net
Web: www.flash.net/~safe-dabney

Circa 1907. Built during the Mission Period, this Craftsman-style country manor boasts original hardwood floors, stained-glass windows and some of the original light fixtures. The par-

lor and dining rooms have large, exposed, wooden beams and the ceilings throughout are 10-feet high. The Dabney Suite has a private entrance into an enclosed sun porch with rattan table and chairs that allow for a private breakfast or a candlelight dinner by advance reservation. The bedroom of this suite is furnished with a four-post tester bed with drapes and an 1800 wardrobe.

Historic Interest: Historic Town Square (one-half mile), Dinosaur Valley State Park (18 miles), Texas Dr. Pepper Plant (45 miles), Elizabeth Crockett (5 miles).
Innkeeper(s): John & Gwen Hurley. $75-110. 4 rooms with PB and 1 suite. Breakfast and snacks/refreshments included in rates. Types of meals: Full bkfst. Beds: Q. Reading lamp, ceiling fan, clock radio and desk in room. Air conditioning. VCR, spa, library, parlor games, telephone, hot tub, evening beverage and dinner available with 48 hour notice on premises. Small meetings, family reunions and seminars hosted. Antiquing, fishing, live theater, parks, shopping and water sports nearby.
Publicity: *Fort Worth Star Telegram and Dallas Morning News.*

Hillsboro   D7

Windmill Bed & Breakfast

441 HCR 2421E
Hillsboro, TX 76645
(254)582-7373 (800)951-0033
E-mail: WindmillBB@aol.com
Web: www.windmillbb.com

Circa 1872. Elegant and serene, this historic Victorian farmhouse is decorated in antiques and traditional furnishings. Enjoy complimentary refreshments and snacks after check-in. Romantic garden suites feature Jacuzzi tubs and a spacious guest bedroom includes a sitting area. Made from a special recipe, breakfast in the dining room boasts the best French toast ever eaten, bacon, potatoes, fresh fruit and muffins. Relax in the hammock for two, walk the trail to the pond, take the kids to feed apples to the horses in the pasture or just enjoy the garden and fountain view from the side veranda. Transportation into town, boat rentals, golf tee times and fishing guides can be arranged. Ask about special occasion packages and gift certificates.

Historic Interest: French Garden Suite and library were built in 1872. Remainder of house built in 1910 and the barn was built in 1896.
Innkeeper(s): Ruben & Gerry Marentes. $90-110. 3 rooms with PB, 2 suites and 1 conference room. Breakfast, afternoon tea and snacks/refreshments included in rates. Types of meals: Full gourmet bkfst, veg bkfst and early coffee/tea. Beds: KQT. Cable TV, reading lamp, CD player, ceiling fan, clock radio, desk and hot tub/spa in room. Central air. VCR, bicycles, library, parlor games, telephone and hammock in backyard patio on premises. Small meetings, family reunions and seminars hosted. Antiquing, art galleries, beach, bicycling, canoeing/kayaking, fishing, golf, hiking, horseback riding, museums, parks, shopping and water sports nearby.

Houston   F9

The Lovett Inn

501 Lovett Blvd
Houston, TX 77006-4020
(713)522-5224 (800)779-5224 Fax:(713)528-6708

Circa 1924. Built by former Houston Mayor and Judge Joseph C. Hutcheson, this gracious Colonial-style home remained with its owner until his death in 1973. Located on a tree-lined street in the center of town, the home has been meticulously restored to blend its elegant architectural character with today's modern amenities. Most guest rooms overlook the beautifully landscaped grounds with its gazebo, pool and spa. Gleaming hardwood floors and distinctive reproduction period antique furnishings are just a few of the features that enhance the inn's natural charm. The inn is available for weddings, receptions, retreats and meetings.

Innkeeper(s): Tom Fricke. $75-175. 8 rooms with PB, 3 suites and 1 conference room. Breakfast included in rates. Types of meals: Cont. Beds: KQD. Cable TV, VCR, reading lamp, refrigerator, clock radio, telephone, desk, coffeemakers, microwaves and refrigerators in room. Air conditioning. Fax, spa, swimming and library on premises. Weddings, small meetings, family reunions and seminars hosted. Amusement parks, antiquing, golf, live theater, parks, sporting events and museum of Fine Arts nearby.
Publicity: *Houston Chronicle, Dallas Morning News, Texas Monthly, Houston Business Journal, New York Times Travel Section and Independent Means.*

Palms on West Main

807 W Main St #1
Houston, TX 77006
(713)522-7987 Fax:(713)522-3150
E-mail: meadeandsmith@pdq.net
Web: www.palmsonwestmain.com

Circa 1914. Centrally located in Houston's historic museum district, this early 20th-century Dutch Colonial home can be found in the same neighborhood where Howard Hughes grew up, possessing unique architecture and mature trees. The inn's host, Tom Meade, a member of the Greater Houston Preservation Alliance, has restored many original designs of the house and enjoys providing ample information on Houston's history and attractions. Private access to each suite is located off the "Key West" deck, filled with tropical plants and fountains. Fireplaces and individual design distinguish each room. With many activities in the Houston area, guests get prepared each morning with a country breakfast delivered to their room offering ham frittata, apple cinnamon muffins, fresh fruit, juice and coffee.

Innkeeper(s): Tom Meade, Rick Smith. $99. 3 suites, 2 with FP. Breakfast included in rates. Types of meals: Full bkfst. Beds: KQ. Cable TV, VCR, reading lamp, ceiling fan, telephone and desk in room. Air conditioning. Fax, bicycles and fireplace on premises. Amusement parks, antiquing, art galleries, bicycling, golf, live theater, museums, parks, shopping and sporting events nearby.

Patrician B&B Inn

1200 Southmore Blvd
Houston, TX 77004-5826
(713)523-1114 (800)553-5797 Fax:(713)523-0790
E-mail: southmore@ev1.net
Web: www.texasbnb.com

Circa 1919. Built in 1919 by attorney George S. King, the Patrician B&B Inn makes a more intimate choice of accommodation over Houston's large, impersonal hotels. This three-story, Colonial Revival mansion, located near the museum district, Rice University and downtown, caters to both leisure and business travelers. Antique accents distinguish the guest rooms. Kathleen's Room features a clawfoot tub, and Lollie Dee's Room offers a turn-of-the-century burled walnut bed and a whirlpool tub. Breakfast, served in the large dining room or the solarium, usually consists of pear compote, French toast with a generous portion of cream cheese and marmalade, mandarin orange coffee cake and broccoli cornbread.

Innkeeper(s): Patricia Thomse. $100-165. 5 rooms, 7 with PB and 1 conference room. Breakfast and snacks/refreshments included in rates. Types of meals: Full gourmet bkfst and early coffee/tea. Beds: Q. Cable TV, VCR, reading lamp, CD player, ceiling fan, clock radio and telephone in room. Central air. Fax, copier and fireplace on premises. Weddings and small meetings hosted. Amusement parks, antiquing, art galleries, golf, hiking, live theater, museums, parks, sporting events and water sports nearby.

Robin's Nest

4104 Greeley St
Houston, TX 77006-5609
(713)528-5821 (800)622-8343 Fax:(713)529-4821
E-mail: robin@therobin.com
Web: www.therobin.com

Circa 1898. Robin's Nest is the oldest home in Houston's historic Montrose District. A two-story wooden Queen Anne Victorian, the historic home features original pine hardwoods, tall windows, high ceilings and a wraparound veranda. Luxurious fabrics, all custom sewn, warm the interior, which also boasts wall murals. The home originally was a dairy farm and now rests on an urban lot surrounded by dozens of rose bushes and azaleas. Located in the city's museum and arts district, the inn offers close proximity to downtown Houston, theaters and gourmet restaurants. Galveston and Johnson Space Center are about an hour away.

Historic Interest: The San Jacinto Monument and Armannd Bayou are 30 minutes from the home. Bayou Bend Gardens are 15 minutes away, Theatre District, Port of Houston, Museum and Arts District.

Innkeeper(s): Robin Smith. $89-150. 5 rooms with PB and 1 conference room. Breakfast included in rates. Types of meals: Full bkfst. Beds: QT. Cable TV, refrigerator, ceiling fan, telephone and baths in room. Air conditioning. TV on premises. Weddings, small meetings, family reunions and seminars hosted. Amusement parks, antiquing, fishing, live theater, museums, shopping, sporting events and water sports nearby.

Publicity: *Houston Home and Garden, Houston Business Journal, Woman's Day, Houston Metropolitan, Houston Post, Southern Living, Texas Monthly, Houston Chronicle, Inside Houston and Houston Press "Best Houston B & B 2002."*

"Fanciful and beautiful, comfortable and happy. We saw a whole new side of Houston, thanks to you."

Sara's B&B Inn

941 Heights Blvd
Houston, TX 77008-6911
(713)868-1130 (800)593-1130 Fax:(713)868-3284

Circa 1898. This mauve and white, gingerbread Victorian is located in the Houston Heights, one of the first planned suburbs in Texas. Book the Tyler Room and climb the stairs that wind up to the cupola. In the Austin Suite, located in the turret, guests will enjoy a balcony overlooking the street. The rooms and suites are decorated with antiques and collectibles. Downtown Houston is five minutes away, and the inn is a good location to visit the Galleria, Minute Maid Park, Reliant Stadium, the museum district or the Arts and Medical center. The inn is a popular spot for retreats, weddings and business meetings.

Innkeeper(s): Connie & Bob McCreight. $70-200. 12 rooms with PB and 4

suites. Breakfast included in rates. Types of meals: Full bkfst. Beds: KQD. TV, fax and telephone on premises. Antiquing and museums nearby.

Publicity: *Houston Chronicle, Texas Homes, Elle, Travellife and Debra Duncan Show-live.*

Jefferson D9

1st Bed & Breakfast in Texas Pride House

409 Broadway
Jefferson, TX 75657
(800)894-3526 Fax:(903)665-3901
E-mail: jefftx@mind.net
Web: www.jeffersontexas.com

Circa 1889. Mr. Brown, a sawmill owner, built this Victorian house using fine hardwoods, sometimes three layers deep. The windows are nine-feet tall on both the lower level and upstairs. The rooms include amenities such as fireplaces, balconies, canopy beds and private entrances. Most boast original stained-glass windows, and each room is named after a steamboat that once docked in Jefferson. One room is decorated in crimson reds and features a gigantic clawfoot tub that has received an award from Houston Style Magazine for "best bathtub in Texas." A wide veranda stretches around two sides of the house.

Innkeeper(s): Carol Abernathy & Bonnie Timmins. $85-200. 11 rooms with PB, 3 with FP, 1 suite and 1 cottage. Types of meals: Full gourmet bkfst. Beds: KQT. Reading lamp, ceiling fan, clock radio, telephone, desk, TV and some with fireplaces in room. Air conditioning. TV, parlor games, fireplace and complimentary refreshments on premises. Limited handicap access. Small meetings, family reunions and seminars hosted. Antiquing, canoeing/kayaking, fishing, live theater, steamboat tours, home tours, water skiing, antebellum home tours and steam train nearby.

Publicity: *Woman's Day, Country Home, Texas Highways and Texas Homes.*

"No five star hotel can compare to the hospitality of Pride House."

Claiborne House

312 S Alley Street
Jefferson, TX 75657
(903)665-8800 (877)385-9236 Fax:(903)665-9335
E-mail: stay@claibornehousebnb.com
Web: www.claibornehousebnb.com

Circa 1872. Retreat to the romantic ambiance of this modified Greek Revival with a front gabled roof. Wicker furniture, a Victorian swing and wood rockers invite relaxation and conversation on one of the four porches. The inn still retains the original flooring, baseboards, molding and stairway, as well as being tastefully decorated with 1800s American Empire furnishings. A refrigerator in one of the common areas is stocked with complimentary beverages. Guest bedrooms are named after classic romantic poets and include a variety of pampering amenities. The spacious first-floor Browning Room features a private entrance, woodburning fireplace and double whirlpool. Strawberry Soup, Eggs Benedict in puff pastry and blueberry coffee cake are typical of a gourmet Southern breakfast served in the dining room. Schedule massages and body treatments at the day spa.

Innkeeper(s): Steve & Elaine Holden. $100-185. 6 rooms with PB, 1 with FP. Breakfast and snacks/refreshments included in rates. Types of meals: Full gourmet bkfst, veg bkfst, early coffee/tea and gourmet dinner. Beds: KQ. Cable TV, reading lamp, refrigerator, ceiling fan, snack bar, clock radio, hot tub/spa and fireplace in room. Central air. Fax, copier, parlor games, tele-

phone, laundry facility and day spa on premises. Weddings, small meetings, family reunions and seminars hosted. Antiquing, art galleries, bicycling, canoeing/kayaking, fishing, golf, hiking, horseback riding, museums, parks and water sports nearby.
Publicity: *Ft. Worth Star Telegram.*

Falling Leaves Inn

304 E Jefferson St
Jefferson, TX 75657-2020
(903)665-8803

Circa 1855. Not only is Falling Leaves Inn located in Jefferson's historic district, it also has the distinction of being a Texas Historical Landmark and is listed in the National Register. Century-old trees shade the exterior of the Greek Revival home, which was built prior to the Civil War. Antiques and reproductions decorate the four guest rooms. The innkeepers offer afternoon treats and serve up a full breakfast with items such as Cajun eggs and orange-pecan French toast. Jefferson's downtown area is just a few blocks away.

Innkeeper(s): Lisa & Michael Barry. $100. 4 rooms with PB. Types of meals: Full bkfst, early coffee/tea and snacks/refreshments. Beds: K. Cable TV and clock radio in room. Central air. Antiquing, fishing, golf, museums, parks, shopping and water sports nearby.

Kennedy Manor Bed & Breakfast

217 West Lafayette St
Jefferson, TX 75657-2207
(903)665-2528
E-mail: kennedymanor@jeffersontx.com
Web: www.kennedy-manor.com

Circa 1860. Built before the Civil War, original cypress floors and 14-foot decorative ceilings grace this historic Greek Revival with Victorian decor. Listen to the Packard pump organ and antique piano in the music parlor or read from a large assortment of magazines. Clawfoot tubs, vintage furnishings, ceiling fans and individual climate control add to the comfort and charm of the guest bedrooms. Popular breakfast favorites are served in the formal dining room and may include baked caramel-apple pancakes with locally made Blackburn's Syrup, bananas praline and carmelized bacon. Schedule a massage then relax on a wicker rocking chair on one of the wraparound porches. Stroll the private gardens on the one-acre grounds.

Historic Interest: Kennedy Manor was built in 1860 before the Civil War.
Innkeeper(s): Chris & Laura Graham. $79-149. 6 rooms with PB. Breakfast and snacks/refreshments included in rates. Types of meals: Full gourmet bkfst and early coffee/tea. Beds: KQDT. Cable TV, reading lamp, ceiling fan and telephone in room. Central air. Library and parlor games on premises. Weddings, small meetings, family reunions and seminars hosted. Antiquing, art galleries, canoeing/kayaking, fishing, hiking, horseback riding, live theater, museums, parks, shopping, water sports, antique steam engine train rides, horse-drawn carriage tours through historic neighborhoods and live music every weekend nearby.
Publicity: *Arrington B&B Book of List - 2003 Best Literary Selection and Arrington B&B Book of List - 2004 Best Weekend Getaway.*

McKay House

306 E Delta St
Jefferson, TX 75657-2026
(903)665-7322 (800)468-2627
E-mail: innkeeper@mckayhouse.com
Web: www.mckayhouse.com

Circa 1851. For more than 15 years, the McKay House has been widely acclaimed for its high standards, personal service and satisfied guests. Both Lady Bird Johnson and Alex Haley have enjoyed the gracious Southern hospitality offered at the

McKay House. Accented by a Williamsburg-style picket fence, the Greek Revival cottage features a front porch with pillars. Heart-of-pine floors, 14-foot ceilings and documented wallpapers complement antique furnishings. A full "gentleman's" breakfast is served in the garden conservatory by the gable fireplace. Orange-pecan French toast, home-baked muffins and shirred eggs are a few of the house specialties. In each of the seven bedchambers you find a Victorian nightgown and old-fashioned nightshirt laid out for you. History abounds in Jefferson, considered the "Williamsburg of the Southwest."

Innkeeper(s): Hugh & Becky Lewis. $89-149. 7 rooms with PB, 6 with FP and 1 cottage. Breakfast included in rates. Types of meals: Full gourmet bkfst and early coffee/tea. Beds: KQD. Cable TV, ceiling fan, clock radio, telephone, suites and Internet also in room. Air conditioning. Parlor games, fireplace and refrigerator in common rooms on premises. Weddings, small meetings, family reunions and seminars hosted. Antiquing, fishing, live theater, parks, shopping and water sports nearby.
Publicity: *Southern Accents, Dallas Morning News, Country Home and Bride.*

"The facilities of the McKay House are exceeded only by the service and dedication of the owners."

Mason   E6

Hasse House and Ranch

1471 Ischar
Mason, TX 76856
(888)414-2773

Circa 1883. Guests may explore the 320-acre Hasse ranch, which is a working ranch where deer, wild turkey, feral hogs, quail and a bounty of wildflowers and bluebonnets are common sights. After purchasing the land, Henry Hasse and his wife lived in a log cabin on the property before building the sandstone home 23 years later. Three generations of Hasses have lived here, and today it is owned by a great-granddaughter who restored the home in 1980. The house is located in the small German village of Art, Texas, which is located six miles east of Mason. The innkeepers rent the two-bedroom National Register home out to only one group or guest at a time, host free. The home is filled with period furniture and accessories, yet offers the modern convenience of an on-site washer and dryer and a fully stocked kitchen. The ranch grounds include a two-mile nature trail perfect for nature lovers.

Innkeeper(s): Laverne Lee. $100. 2 rooms with PB. Types of meals: Cont plus. Beds: D. TV, reading lamp, refrigerator, ceiling fan, snack bar, coffeemaker, dishwasher and microwave in room. Air conditioning. Library, parlor games, washer, dryer, stove, microwave and patio on premises. Limited handicap access. Weddings, small meetings and family reunions hosted. Antiquing, parks, shopping, water sports, bicycle routes, 2 mile nature trail on ranch, bird-watching and wildflower viewing nearby.
Publicity: *San Angelo and Tx Special & "Eyes of Texas."*

"We enjoyed every aspect of our stay; the atmosphere, sense of history, rustic setting with a touch of class. We would love to return the same time next year!"

New Braunfels   F7

Gruene Homestead Inn

832 Gruene Rd
New Braunfels, TX 78130
(830)606-0216 (800)238-5534 Fax:(830)625-6390
E-mail: staff@gruenehomesteadinn.com
Web: www.gruenehomesteadinn.com

Circa 1850. The inn is composed of several historic buildings, five that have been moved to a peaceful country setting on eight acres. There are several farmhouses, a cabin, barn and cottage. Rose Cottage, for instance, is an 1800s farm home. It offers the Lady Banks Suite and The Belinda Suite. The inn's accommodations offer a variety of amenities, including Jacuzzi tubs, phones and private porches. The landscaped grounds feature a hot tub and pool and are less than a mile from the Gruene Historic District. In town, the Redbrick Gastehaus is located a half block from Gruene Hall in the Gruene Historic District. Tucked behind a handsome white wrought iron fence there are six guest rooms. The area is noted for its rafting, tubing, fishing, scenic hill country and shopping.

Innkeeper(s): Ed & Billie Miles. $95-162. 23 rooms with PB and 1 conference room. Breakfast included in rates. Types of meals: Cont and early coffee/tea. Beds: KQDT. Modem hook-up, data port, cable TV, refrigerator, ceiling fan, clock radio, coffeemaker and desk in room. Central air. Spa, swimming, telephone and laundry facility on premises. Weddings, small meetings, family reunions and seminars hosted. Amusement parks, antiquing, canoeing/kayaking, fishing, golf, hiking, museums, parks, shopping, tennis, water sports and wineries nearby.
Publicity: *Time Magazine and Texas Highways.*

Gruene Mansion Inn

1275 Gruene Rd
New Braunfels, TX 78130-3003
(830)629-2641 Fax:(830)629-7375
E-mail: frontdesk@gruenemansioninn.com
Web: www.gruenemansioninn.com

Circa 1872. Overlook the Guadalupe River from the porches of this Victorian mansion located on three acres in Hill Country, adjacent to the state's oldest dance hall. The inn has been designated a Historic Landmark and is listed in the National Register. The Mansion, barns, corn crib, carriage house and other outbuildings have all been refurbished to offer quiet and private guest bedrooms, cottages and guest houses. A rustic Victorian elegance is the ambiance and style of decor that blends antiques, fine fabrics and wall coverings. Savor breakfast entrees that boast a Mexican flair and flavor. For a day trip, visit the Alamo, 30 miles away.

Historic Interest: Built in 1872, home of founder of Gruene, Texas.
Innkeeper(s): Jackie Walcott. $119-219. 30 rooms with PB, 1 cottage and 1 conference room. Breakfast included in rates. Beds: KQDT. Cable TV, reading lamp, refrigerator, ceiling fan, clock radio, coffeemaker and fireplace in room. Central air. Fax, copier, telephone, porch with rocking chairs looking at Guadalupe River and gift shop on premises. Limited handicap access. Weddings, small meetings, family reunions and seminars hosted. Amusement parks, antiquing, art galleries, bicycling, canoeing/kayaking, fishing, golf, hiking, horseback riding, live theater, museums, parks, shopping, sporting events, tennis, water sports, wineries and oldest dance hall in Texas nearby.
Publicity: *San Antonio Express News, Austin American Statesmen and New Braunfels Herald Zietung.*

Historic Kuebler Waldrip Haus and Danville Schoolhouse B&B

1620 Hueco Springs Loop
New Braunfels, TX 78132
(830)625-8300 (800)299-8372
E-mail: kwbandb@compuvision.net
Web: www.kueblerwaldrip.com

Circa 1847. Friendship, food and hospitality are found in abundance at these historic accommodations sitting on 43 acres of hill country. Both main buildings are from the 1800s. The hand-hewn limestone and rock house was built by a German pioneer. The Danville Schoolhouse was moved here in 1990 and restored while retaining original floors, walls, roof and design. Table games are enjoyed in the common room. Some guest bedrooms feature whirlpools and are wheelchair accessible. Deer Haven is a spacious five-room cottage boasting a full kitchen, whirlpool tub, deck and large patio area. A hearty country breakfast may include homemade breads and baked goods, egg entrees, hash brown potatoes, grits and pancakes. Breakfast is served family style, so no one leaves the table hungry as heaping second helpings often keep guests full until dinner. Horseshoes, croquet, walking trails and fishing are popular outside activities.

Innkeeper(s): Margaret Kuebler Waldrip & Darrell Waldrip. $115-175. 10 rooms with PB, 3 suites, 1 cottage and 2 conference rooms. Breakfast and snacks/refreshments included in rates. Types of meals: Country bkfst, veg bkfst and early coffee/tea. Beds: KQDT. Modem hook-up, cable TV, VCR, reading lamp, CD player, refrigerator, ceiling fan, snack bar, clock radio, telephone, coffeemaker, desk, hot tub/spa and several units have full kitchens in room. Central air. Fax, copier, library, parlor games, fireplace, laundry facility, gift shop, picnic tables, barbecue pits, horseshoes, balls, badminton and computer for guest use on premises. Weddings, small meetings, family reunions and seminars hosted. Amusement parks, antiquing, art galleries, bicycling, canoeing/kayaking, fishing, golf, horseback riding, live theater, museums, parks, shopping, sporting events, tennis, water sports and wineries nearby.
Publicity: *Houston Chronicle, Auto Motor and Sport and New Braunfels Herald.*

The Hotel Faust

240 So. Seguin
New Braunfels, TX 78130
(830)625-7791 (800)913-2878 Fax:(830)620-1530
E-mail: innkeeper@thehotelfaust.com
Web: www.thehotelfaust.com

Circa 1929. Architectural German craftsmanship with a Spanish flair imparts an Old World charm at this National Landmark Hotel in the heart of Hill Country near historic Gruene. The unusual brick building has been renovated several times since its opening just before the stock market crash of 1929, yet it still contains many original furnishings, woodwork and fixtures. The lobby features a baby grand piano, Victrolas, specially-made cash register, vintage photos and even a Model A. Choose from a variety of guest bedrooms or a two-room suite with a brass postered bed, marble-topped wet bar and a fourth-floor view of downtown. Handicapped, smoking and non-smoking rooms are available. After a continental breakfast arrange a horse carriage ride, visit a water park or tour the Natural Bridge Caverns. Enjoy the on-site microbrewery and Bavarian-style restaurant.

Innkeeper(s): Bob Abbey. $59-400. 62 rooms with PB, 1 suite and 2 conference rooms. Breakfast and afternoon tea included in rates. Types of meals: Cont plus, early coffee/tea, dinner and room service. Restaurant on premises. Beds: KQD. TV, fax, copier, telephone, New Braunfels only microbrewery on premises and also a true German Restaurant on premises. Weddings, small meetings, family reunions and seminars hosted. Antiquing, art galleries, bicycling, canoeing/kayaking, fishing, golf, hiking, horseback riding, live theater, museums, parks, shopping, water sports and wineries nearby.

Pittsburg D9

Carson House Inn & Grille

302 Mount Pleasant St
Pittsburg, TX 75686-1335
(903)856-2468 (888)302-1878 Fax:(903)856-0709
E-mail: mailus@carsonhouse.com
Web: www.carsonhouse.com

Circa 1878. The city's oldest occupied home, this bed & breakfast with manicured lawns, a Koi pond and patio, also features a highly acclaimed restaurant. The interior was built using more than one mile of curly pine. The milled lumber, known for its interesting grain pattern, came from diseased trees, now thought to be extinct. The Carson Room boasts a sleigh bed, sitting area and private entrance. It adjoins the Abernathy Room with a brass bed. The Camp Room offers a relaxing two-person whirlpool tub. The private Carson and Barnes Railroad Car, decorated with artifacts, is a fitting tribute to local history. A refrigerator, two-person shower and a Jacuzzi just outside make this a perfect retreat. A cooked-to-order breakfast is made when desired.

Innkeeper(s): Eileen & Clark Jesmore. $85-145. 8 rooms, 6 with PB, 1 suite and 1 cottage. Breakfast included in rates. Types of meals: Full gourmet bkfst, veg bkfst, gourmet lunch, snacks/refreshments, gourmet dinner and room service. Restaurant on premises. Beds: KQD. Modem hook-up, data port, cable TV, VCR, reading lamp, refrigerator, ceiling fan, clock radio, telephone, coffeemaker, turn-down service, desk, hot tub/spa and voice mail in room. Central air. Fax, fireplace and laundry facility on premises. Weddings, small meetings, family reunions and seminars hosted. Antiquing, bicycling, fishing, golf, hiking, horseback riding, live theater, museums, parks, shopping and water sports nearby.

Publicity: *Dallas Morning News, Gourmet Magazine, Texas Parks & Wildlife and Romantic America.*

Round Top F8

Outpost

5808 Wagner Rd.
Round Top, TX 78954
(979)836-4975 (888)433-5791
E-mail: stay@outpostatcedarcreek.com
Web: www.outpostatcedarcreek.com

Circa 1880. Follow the quiet, secluded country road to this German prairie farmstead on a gentle hilltop surrounded by 51 acres of hay meadow. The compound includes historical structures creatively restored by recycling wood and treasures found in the abandoned homestead. Stay in the cypress Main House, with original stenciling in the parlor, pressed-tin dining room walls and five porches. The batten barn, used as a smokehouse with a water tower and cistern, offers a romantic guest bedroom and Victorian conservatory for a delightful suite. The Prairie Cottage in pure Texana style, boasts a Jacuzzi for two. Double log cabins feature mountain rustic decor with vintage artifacts and furnishings; one has a stone fireplace. Indulge in a mouth-watering breakfast in the Rangers' Lounge before exploring the native gardens.

Innkeeper(s): Lenore Prud'Homme. $100-300. 9 rooms, 5 with PB, 1 with FP, 2 suites, 1 cottage, 2 cabins and 1 conference room. Breakfast and snacks/refreshments included in rates. Types of meals: Full gourmet bkfst, veg bkfst, early coffee/tea, gourmet lunch, picnic lunch, afternoon tea, gourmet dinner and room service. Beds: QDT. TV, VCR, reading lamp, CD player, refrigerator, clock radio, coffeemaker, hot tub/spa, fireplace and satellite TV in room. Central air. Fax, copier, library, telephone and laundry facility on premises. Weddings, small meetings, family reunions and seminars hosted. Antiquing, art galleries, bicycling, golf, hiking, horseback riding, live theater, museums and wineries nearby.

Publicity: *New York Times, Country Home, Cowboys & Indians and Home Companion.*

San Antonio F7

A Beckmann Inn and Carriage House Bed and Breakfast

222 E Guenther Street
San Antonio, TX 78204-1405
(210)229-1449 (800)945-1449 Fax:(210)229-1061
E-mail: beckinn@swbell.net
Web: www.beckmanninn.com

Circa 1886. A wraparound porch with white wicker furniture warmly welcomes guests to the main house of this Victorian inn, where quiet elegance and gracious hospitality abound.

Through the entrance and into the living room, guests stand on an intricately designed wood mosaic floor imported from Paris. Arch-shaped pocket doors with framed opaque glass open to the formal dining room where breakfast is served. All the guest rooms feature 12- to 14-foot ceilings with fans, tall, ornately carved queen-size antique Victorian beds, colorful floral accessories and antiques.

Historic Interest: Alamo, Spanish Governor's Place, Riverwalk, missions, King William Historic District.

Innkeeper(s): Betty Jo & Don Schwartz. $110-150. 5 rooms with PB. Breakfast included in rates. Types of meals: Full gourmet bkfst. Beds: Q. Cable TV, reading lamp, ceiling fan, clock radio, telephone, desk, robes, hair dryers, irons/ironing boards and refrigerator in room. Air conditioning. Fax, copier, library and fireplace on premises. Family reunions hosted. Amusement parks, antiquing, golf, live theater, parks, shopping, sporting events, Alamo, Riverwalk, missions, Mexican market and Spanish Governor's Palace nearby.

Publicity: *Texas Monthly, Country Folk Art, Country Inns, Dallas Morning News, Southern Living, Texas Highways, Vacations, Country and Select Registry.*

"The Beckmann Inn & Carriage House is truly a home away from home for all who stay there. Don and Betty Jo put their heart and soul into making every guest's stay a memorable experience."

A Yellow Rose

229 Madison
San Antonio, TX 78204
(210)229-9903 (800)950-9903 Fax:(210)229-1691
E-mail: yellowrose@ddc.net
Web: www.ayellowrose.com

Circa 1878. Stay at this 130-year-old Victorian bed & breakfast located in the historic King William District, a quiet downtown neighborhood. Providing quality and comfort, the spacious rooms boast high ceilings and a relaxed sophistication. Each guest bedroom features non-allergen feather toppers, private entrances and porches. An assortment of pampering amenities adds pleasure and ease to traveling. The famous River Walk is two blocks away. Ask about packages for birthdays, golf or special events.

Historic Interest: Alamo (8 blocks), St. Francis Church (8 blocks), San Antonio Riverwalk (2 blocks), Mission Trail (one-half mile).

Innkeeper(s): Kit Walker & Deb Walker. $100-175. 5 rooms with PB and 1 suite. Beds: Q. Cable TV, reading lamp, ceiling fan, clock radio, desk and robes in room. Air conditioning. VCR, parlor games and telephone on premises. Amusement parks, antiquing, live theater, parks, shopping, sporting events and water sports nearby.

Publicity: *Aurum, Express News, Dallas Morning News, Fiesta Magazine, Patsy Swehnson's Cooking At Noon and The Today Show.*

"Recommendations will be forthcoming. Best Christmas gift we gave ourselves coming here! Thanks."

Adams House B&B

231 Adams St
San Antonio, TX 78210-1104
(210)224-4791 (800)666-4810 Fax:(210)223-5125
E-mail: nora@adams-house.com
Web: www.adams-house.com

Circa 1902. Southern tradition and hospitality abound at this bed & breakfast, decorated with sweeping verandas on both its first and second stories. The historic home has been painstakingly restored, including Oriental rugs, period antiques and handmade reproductions. Adams House is located in the King William Historic District. The River Walk is just two blocks away, and The Alamo is a 15-minute walk.
Innkeeper(s): Nora Peterson & Richard Green. $99-149. 4 rooms with PB. Cable TV, reading lamp, ceiling fan, clock radio and telephone in room. Air conditioning. VCR and spa on premises. Amusement parks, golf, live theater, shopping, sporting events and Alamo nearby.

An Oge' House Inn on the River Walk

209 Washington
San Antonio, TX 78204-1336
(210)223-2353 (800)242-2770 Fax:(210)226-5812
E-mail: ogeinn@swbell.net
Web: www.ogeinn.com

Circa 1857. This impressive antebellum mansion is a Texas Historic Landmark. It rests on the banks of the beautiful San Antonio Riverwalk on an acre-and-a-half of gardens. Shaded by graceful oak and pecan trees, the inn has a gazebo and double-tiered veranda. There are nine fireplaces. Queen- and king-size beds are provided and all the rooms are distinguished with period antiques, handsomely upholstered sofas and chairs and Oriental carpets. The trolley, convention center and the Alamo are steps away.
Innkeeper(s): Sharrie & Patrick Magatagan. $110-325. 10 rooms with PB, 7 with FP and 1 conference room. Breakfast included in rates. Types of meals: Full gourmet bkfst and early coffee/tea. Beds: KQ. Modem hook-up, cable TV, VCR, reading lamp, stereo, refrigerator, ceiling fan, snack bar, clock radio, telephone, desk, voice mail and fireplace in room. Central air. Fax, copier, library and parlor games on premises. Small meetings, family reunions and seminars hosted. Amusement parks, antiquing, live theater, parks, shopping, sporting events and water sports nearby.
Publicity: *Victoria, McCalls, Texas Monthly, Texas Highways, London Times, New York Times, Glamour, Travel & Leisure and Southern Living.*

"Wonderfully relaxing weekend in an elegant home with pure Southern hospitality."

Arbor House

540 N Saint Marys St
San Antonio, TX 78205-1706
(210)472-2005 (888)272-6700 Fax:(210)472-2007
E-mail: arborhaus@aol.com
Web: arborhouse.citysearch.com

Circa 1903. You'll remember far more than the Alamo when you stay in this Queen Anne Victorian compound in historic San Antonio. A Swiss cabinetmaker built the first part of the structure for his family in 1903. Recent renovations earned this home the coveted San Antonio Conservation Society Plaque. Four houses cluster around a beautiful garden and each has three suites with high ceilings, pine floors and balconies. The inn has 19 guest bedrooms including eight bedrooms and 11 suites. The open-air "potting room" offers a cool, breezy spot for reading or just relaxing. After breakfast, guests may head out to tour the city. The inn is five minutes from the Henry B.

Gonzales Convention Center, two minutes from The San Antonio River Walk and 10 minutes from the Alamo.
Innkeeper(s): Jerry Karkoska. $85-175. 19 rooms, 7 with PB and 11 suites. Breakfast included in rates. Types of meals: Cont. Beds: KQD. Modem hook-up, data port, cable TV, reading lamp, refrigerator, ceiling fan, telephone, coffeemaker, desk, hot tub/spa and voice mail in room. Central air. Fax, child care and laundry facility on premises. Weddings, small meetings, family reunions and seminars hosted. Amusement parks, antiquing, art galleries, golf, live theater, museums, parks, shopping, sporting events, tennis and wineries nearby.

Beauregard House

215 Beauregard
San Antonio, TX 78204-1304
(210)222-1198 (888)667-0555 Fax:(210)222-9338
E-mail: info@beauregardhouse.com
Web: www.beauregardhouse.com

Circa 1900. This historic Victorian is located on a quiet street within San Antonio's King William Historic District. The Riverwalk is just a block away, and the home is near shops, restaurants and other attractions. Relaxation and comfort is the theme at Beauregard House. Room amenities include cable TV, VCR, hair dryers, bathrobes, refrigerator and coffee service. Victorian period European furniture with old world charm decorates the bedchambers. Guests can relax on the front porch or play a game or watch movies in the home's living room. Homemade treats are served to guests upon arrival, and each morning brings with it the promise of a full gourmet breakfast. Fresh fruit dishes and homemade breads accompany entrees such as baked French toast.
Innkeeper(s): Al & Lisa Fittipaldi. $109-189. 6 rooms, 5 with PB, 1 with FP and 1 conference room. Breakfast included in rates. Types of meals: Full gourmet bkfst, veg bkfst, early coffee/tea, picnic lunch and snacks/refreshments. Beds: KQT. Reading lamp, refrigerator, ceiling fan and clock radio in room. Central air. TV, library, parlor games, telephone, fireplace and laundry facility on premises. Weddings, small meetings and family reunions hosted. Amusement parks, antiquing, art galleries, bicycling, fishing, golf, horseback riding, live theater, museums, parks, shopping, sporting events, tennis and water sports nearby.
Publicity: *Disney Channel, Discovery Channel, PAX TV, BBC World News and Oprah Winfrey Show.*

Bonner Garden

145 E Agarita Ave
San Antonio, TX 78212-2923
(210)733-4222 (800)396-4222 Fax:(210)733-6129
E-mail: noels@onr.com
Web: www.bonnergarden.com

Circa 1910. Mary Bonner was internationally renowned for her etchings and printmaking skills. Selected Bonner prints and works by other artists, including the Bonner House's owner, are displayed throughout the house. This Italian Renaissance inn has a rooftop patio and wet bar. The house made history when it was constructed by Atlee Ayres, who was one of the foremost architects of the era. The home was built of concrete, reinforced with steel and cast iron, and clad in stucco. Exercise facilities include a 50-foot pool, Nordic Track exerciser and bicycles.
Innkeeper(s): Jan & Noel Stenoien. $85-125. 5 rooms with PB, 3 with FP. Breakfast included in rates. Types of meals: Full bkfst. Beds: KQ. Cable TV, VCR, reading lamp, ceiling fan, clock radio, telephone and desk in room. Air conditioning. Fax, copier, swimming, bicycles, library, fireplace, exercise room and rooftop spa on premises. Small meetings and family reunions hosted. Amusement parks, golf, live theater, parks, shopping, sporting events and tennis nearby.

"Second time was as great as the first."

Brackenridge House

230 Madison
San Antonio, TX 78204-1320
(210)271-3442 (800)221-1412 Fax:(210)226-3139
E-mail: benniesueb@aol.com
Web: www.brackenridgehouse.com

Circa 1901. Each of the guest rooms at Brackenridge House is individually decorated. Clawfoot tubs, iron beds and a private veranda are a few of the items that guests might discover. Several rooms include kitchenettes. Blansett Barn, often rented by families or those on an extended stay, includes two bedrooms, a bathroom, a full kitchen and living and dining areas. Many of San Antonio's interesting sites are nearby. The San Antonio Mission Trail begins just a block away, and trolleys will take you to the Alamo, the River Walk, convention center and more. Coffeehouses, restaurants and antique stores all are within walking distance. Small pets are welcome in Blansett Barn.

Innkeeper(s): Bennie & Sue Blansett. $110-250. 6 rooms with PB, 2 suites and 1 cottage. Breakfast included in rates. Types of meals: Full gourmet bkfst and early coffee/tea. Beds: KQD. Cable TV, VCR, reading lamp, refrigerator, ceiling fan, clock radio, telephone, coffeemaker, microwave, iron, ironing board and hair dryer in room. Air conditioning. Fax, copier, spa and parlor games on premises. Family reunions hosted. Amusement parks, antiquing, fishing, golf, live theater, parks, shopping, sporting events and tennis nearby.

"Innkeeper was very nice, very helpful."

The Bullis House Inn

621 Pierce St, PO Box 8059
San Antonio, TX 78208-0059
(210)223-9426 (877)477-4100 Fax:(210)223-9426
E-mail: HISanAnton@aol.com
Web: www.BullisHouseInn.com

Circa 1909. A two-story portico supported by six massive columns accentuates the Neoclassical architecture of this home built for General Bullis who was instrumental in the capture of Chief Geronimo. Features include stairways and paneling of tiger's eye oak, marble fireplaces, chandeliers and parquet floors. There are contemporary and antique furnishings.

Historic Interest: Fort Sam Houston (across the street), Alamo (1 miles), Spanish Missions (5 miles).

Innkeeper(s): Steve & Alma Cross. $59-99. 10 rooms, 2 with PB, 5 with FP, 2 cottages and 4 conference rooms. Breakfast included in rates. Types of meals: Cont plus and early coffee/tea. Beds: KQDT. Cable TV, reading lamp, refrigerator, ceiling fan, clock radio, telephone, coffeemaker, desk, fireplace and some phones and refrigerators in room. Central air. VCR, swimming, fireplace, piano, tourist information and VCR rental available on premises. Weddings, small meetings, family reunions and seminars hosted. Antiquing, art galleries, bicycling, golf, hiking, live theater, museums, parks, shopping, restaurants and Riverwalk Amusement Park nearby.
Publicity: *New York Times, Fodors, Frommers, San Antonio Light Newspaper, San Antonio Express News, Hill Country Sun Times and Fiesta.*

"Loved your home and your hospitality very much."

Christmas House B&B

2307 McCullough
San Antonio, TX 78212
(210)737-2786 (800)268-4187 Fax:(210)734-5712

Circa 1908. Located in Monte Vista historic district, this two-story white inn has a natural wood balcony built over the front porch. The window trim is in red and green, starting the

Christmas theme of the inn. (There's a Christmas tree decorated all year long.) Guest rooms open out to pecan-shaded balconies. The Victorian Bedroom offers pink and mauve touches mixed with the room's gold and black decor. The Blue & Silver Room is handicap accessible and is on the first floor. Antique furnishings in the inn are available for sale.

Innkeeper(s): Penny & Grant Estes. $85-125. 4 rooms with PB and 1 suite. Breakfast and snacks/refreshments included in rates. Types of meals: Full bkfst, veg bkfst and early coffee/tea. Beds: KQ. Reading lamp, ceiling fan, clock radio and desk in room. Central air. TV, fax, library, parlor games, fireplace, laundry facility and ADA room on premises. Limited handicap access. Family reunions hosted. Amusement parks, antiquing, art galleries, bicycling, golf, live theater, museums, parks and shopping nearby.
Publicity: *Fort Worth Star Telegram.*

"What a treat to rise to the sweet smell of candied pecans and a tasty breakfast."

The Columns on Alamo

1037 S Alamo St
San Antonio, TX 78210-1109
(210)271-3245 (800)233-3364 Fax:(210)271-3245
E-mail: artlink@columnsSanAntonio.com
Web: www.columnsSanAntonio.com

Circa 1892. This bed & breakfast is located in an impressive Greek Revival home and a 1901 guest house in the King William Historic District. Victorian antiques and reproductions decorate the guest rooms, including pieces such as brass beds and fainting couches, four-poster beds, gas log fireplaces and several two-person Jacuzzis. The trolley stops a half block from the house, transporting guests to many of San Antonio's attractions. The River Walk and the Alamo are within walking distance, and the innkeepers recommend several restaurants that are right in the neighborhood.

Innkeeper(s): Ellenor & Arthur Link. $92-255. 13 rooms with PB, 5 with FP and 1 conference room. Breakfast included in rates. Types of meals: Full bkfst and early coffee/tea. Beds: KQ. Cable TV, reading lamp, ceiling fan, telephone and clocks in room. Air conditioning. Fax, copier, library and fireplace on premises. Amusement parks, antiquing, live theater, parks, shopping, sporting events, riverwalk and Alamo nearby.

"The house has been an inspiration. Very friendly and helpful host and hostess."

Gardenia Inn

307 Beauregard Street
San Antonio, TX 78204
(210)223-5875 (800)345-1605
E-mail: relax@gardenia-inn.com
Web: www.gardenia-inn.com

Circa 1905. An old fountain surrounded by boxwood accents the front yard that leads to this stately Victorian home with columns and two-story covered porches. This classic inn has been recently renovated and is perfectly situated in the historic King William district. Pastel colors blend with antique furnishings to impart an elegant and romantic ambiance. Relax fireside in one of the common rooms. A variety of delightful accommodations are offered that include guest bedrooms, a suite and a cottage. Linger over the generous morning meal served in the breakfast room. In the backyard the fragrant gardenia hedge is highlighted by climbing roses and a gazebo. Visit the famous Riverwalk nearby.

Historic Interest: King William is a historic district. Gardenia Inn is a wonderful Victorian house with beautiful columns in front.

Innkeeper(s): Peter & Nicki Luescher. $90-170. 5 rooms, 3 with PB, 1 suite and 1 cottage. Breakfast included in rates. Types of meals: Full gourmet bkfst. Beds: KQD. Cable TV, reading lamp, ceiling fan, clock radio, telephone, desk and hot tub/spa in room. Air conditioning. Fax and copier on premises. Amusement parks, antiquing, art galleries, live theater, museums, parks and shopping nearby.

Inn at Craig Place

117 West Craig Place
San Antonio, TX 78212
(210)736-1017 (877)427-2447
E-mail: stay@craigplace.com
Web: www.craigplace.com

Circa 1891. A collaboration of casual elegance and comfort creates a warm and welcoming atmosphere at this early showpiece of Arts and Crafts design in the historic Monte Vista neighborhood. Listed in the National Register, the inn has maintained the exquisite original 1891 woodwork that features five-foot wainscoting and yellow and red oak floors. Wraparound twin porches invite relaxation, a well-stocked library beckons readers and the parlor encourages conversation. A hospitality corner offers round-the-clock refreshments. Romantic background music sets the tone in the luxurious guest bedrooms that feature fireplaces, down blankets, feather pillows, robes and slippers. The spacious Happily Ever After suite is perfect for honeymooners. Choose when and where to eat Chef Tamra's incredible breakfasts. Ask about the creative assortment of packages available.

Historic Interest: The home, built in 1891, was the third house in the neighborhood, first on the street, and was built for one of San Antonio's city fathers. The architect, Alfred Giles, was a premier architect in Texas is the late 1800s. The home was one of the first examples of very early arts and crafts and showcases many fine examples of incredible woodwork. We are extremely fortunate that no one ever decided to paint the five-foot wainscotting in the foyer, dining room and parlor. The yellow and red oak flooring show master craftsmanship with each floor showcasing a different design. All floors are still original. The dining room has a four-wall mural above the five-foot wainscotting attributed to well-known south Texas artist Julian Onderdonk (it would have been around 1905). The house was also home to several other well known local historical figures.

Innkeeper(s): Tamra Black, Sandy & John Black. $115-200. 4 rooms with PB, 3 with FP, 1 suite and 1 conference room. Breakfast and snacks/refreshments included in rates. Types of meals: Full gourmet bkfst and veg bkfst. Beds: QT. Modem hook-up, data port, cable TV, reading lamp, CD player, refrigerator, ceiling fan, snack bar, clock radio, telephone, coffeemaker, turn-down service, desk, fireplace, iron/ironing board, hair dryers, aromatherapy soaps and bath scents in room. Central air. Fax, library, parlor games, fireplace and gift shop on premises. Weddings, small meetings and family reunions hosted. Amusement parks, antiquing, art galleries, bicycling, golf, hiking, live theater, museums, parks, shopping, sporting events, tennis and wineries nearby.

Publicity: *"Labour of Love" - San Antonio Express News and "Chef Whips Up Gourmet Breakfasts at Monte Vista B&B" - North San Antonio Times.*

Little Flower Inn

225 Madison
San Antonio, TX 78204-1321
(210)354-3116 Fax:(210)354-3116
E-mail: littleflower@satexas.com
Web: www.littleflowerinn.com

Circa 1907. The innkeepers of this elegant American Four Square house in historic King William District are dedicated to making every stay a memorable one. The inn is filled with early

1900s antiques, Oriental rugs, 14-foot floor-to-ceiling damask drapes, and rich wallcolors. The guest bedroom and suite boast private verandas. Read the paper with a cup of coffee on the front porch before indulging in fresh fruit, just-baked patisseries, and egg entrees seasoned with herbs from the garden. Eat breakfast in bed on a tray, in the formal dining room or poolside. Tea and delicacies are served every afternoon. A trolley goes to the Alamo and other sites, the Riverwalk is just two blocks away, and bikes can be rented to ride the Mission Trail.

Innkeeper(s): Phil & Christine. $99. 2 rooms, 1 with PB and 1 suite. Breakfast and afternoon tea included in rates. Types of meals: Full gourmet bkfst, veg bkfst, early coffee/tea, picnic lunch and room service. Beds: QT. Cable TV, VCR, reading lamp, refrigerator, ceiling fan, snack bar, clock radio, telephone, coffeemaker, turn-down service and desk in room. Central air. Library and swimming pool on premises. Weddings hosted. Antiquing, art galleries, bicycling, hiking, live theater, museums, parks, shopping, tennis and wineries nearby.

Publicity: *Houston Chronicle.*

"What a peaceful vacation. We couldn't wait to get to Texas and do all of the fun stuff. When we arrived, the accommodations were so complete it was hard to venture out."

Noble Inns

107 Madison
San Antonio, TX 78204-1319
(210)225-4045 (800)221-4045 Fax:(210)227-0877
E-mail: stay@nobleinns.com
Web: www.nobleinns.com

Circa 1894. Two historic homes, both designated city historic structures, comprise the Noble Inns collection. Both are located in the King William Historic District. The Jackson House is a brick and limestone Victorian. It offers a conservatory of stained and leaded glass enclosing a heated spa. Breakfast is served in the dining room and there is a parlor. The Pancoast Carriage House provides individual suites with full kitchens and stocked continental breakfasts. There is a swimming pool as well as spa. Both inns are furnished with Victorian-era antiques. There are fireplaces, marble baths, clawfoot tubs or whirlpools. Fresh flowers and fluffy monogrammed robes greet guests when they enter their rooms. Transportation in a classic 1960 Rolls Royce Silver Cloud II is available upon request. Call ahead for rates.

Innkeeper(s): Don & Liesl Noble. $120-250. 9 rooms with PB, 9 with FP, 4 with HT and 4 suites. Breakfast and afternoon tea included in rates. Types of meals: Full bkfst, veg bkfst and early coffee/tea. Beds: KQ. Data port, cable TV, reading lamp, ceiling fan, clock radio, telephone and turn-down service in room. Air conditioning. Fax, spa, library, parlor games, fireplace and voice mail on premises. Small meetings and family reunions hosted. Antiquing, live theater, parks, shopping and sporting events nearby.

San Marcos   F7

Crystal River Inn

326 W Hopkins St
San Marcos, TX 78666-4404
(512)396-3739 (888)396-3739 Fax:(512)396-6311
E-mail: info@crystalriverinn.com
Web: www.crystalriverinn.com

Circa 1883. Tall white columns accent this Greek Revival inn that features a fireside dining room with a piano and wet bar. Innkeepers encourage a varied itinerary, including sleeping until noon and having breakfast in bed to participating in a hilarious murder mystery. Rock the afternoon away on the veranda or curl up by the fireplace in a guest bedroom by the headwaters of crystal-clear San Marcos River. Clawfoot tubs, four-poster and canopied beds add to the pleasing ambiance. Shop at the state's largest outlet mall that features more than 200 designer stores.

Innkeeper(s): Mike, Cathy & Sarah Dillon. $90-160. 13 rooms with PB, 4 with FP, 3 suites, 1 cabin and 1 conference room. Breakfast included in rates. Types of meals: Full bkfst, early coffee/tea, lunch and dinner. Beds: KQDT. Cable TV, reading lamp, stereo, refrigerator, ceiling fan, clock radio, telephone and desk in room. Air conditioning. Fax, copier, bicycles, child care, fireplace, gardens, fish pond and veranda on premises. Limited handicap access. Weddings, small meetings, family reunions and seminars hosted. Amusement parks, antiquing, fishing, golf, live theater, parks, shopping, sporting events and water sports nearby.

Publicity: *Texas Monthly, USA Today, Country Inns, Southern Living, Dallas Morning News, Houston Chronicle, Boston Globe and Texas Highways.*

"Thanks for a smashing good time! We really can't remember having more fun anywhere, ever!"

Seabrook   F9

Pelican House B&B Inn

1302 First St
Seabrook, TX 77586-3802
(281)474-5295 Fax:(281)474-7840

Circa 1902. An acre of lawns with live oak and pecan trees stretch to the banks of Old Seabrook's Back Bay from this cozy white country house. Just beyond a white picket fence, the inn's salmon shutters and inviting front porch welcome guests. Inside, there are two dining areas and a sitting room. Bed chambers feature Queen-size beds and a nautical, whimsical decor. Stuffed french toast with apricot glaze is a favorite morning entree. In April and September, great white pelicans assemble on the bay and fish for mullet. Ospreys and other shore birds are seen most of the year. Within walking distance are antique shops and restaurants. The Nasa Space Center is three miles away and the Kemah Boardwalk is just a short drive.

Innkeeper(s): Suzanne Silver. $110-120. 4 rooms with PB. Breakfast included in rates. Types of meals: Full gourmet bkfst. Beds: Q. Reading lamp, ceiling fan, clock radio and desk in room. Air conditioning. VCR, fax, copier, parlor games and telephone on premises. Small meetings hosted. Antiquing, fishing, golf, parks, shopping, tennis and water sports nearby.

Publicity: *Houston Life and Texas Highways.*

Shafter   F3

Cibolo Creek Ranch

PO Box 44
Shafter, TX 79843
(915)229-3737 (866)496-9460 Fax:(915)229-3653
E-mail: pgleason@cibolocreekranch.com
Web: www.cibolocreekranch.com

Circa 1857. Secluded on more than 30,000 scenic acres of Chinati and Cienega Mountains in Big Bend region, this working longhorn ranch is surrounded by lush, spring-fed orchards. Three historic forts: El Cibolo, La Cienega and La Morita are listed in the National Register. Now fully restored, the adobe walls, cottonwood beams, saltillo tile floors and period antiques reflect traditional Mexican architecture and style. Romantic guest bedrooms and suites offer extensive amenities, fireplaces, down comforters and hand-stitched quilts. Three highly acclaimed, gourmet meals are served in the dining room, veranda or poolside. Enjoy a breakfast trail ride on horseback, or a lunch can be packed for hiking excursions. Archery, mountain bikes, clay target shooting, a stocked lake with bass and perch, cattle drives, paddle boats, a stargazing telescope, hammocks and 4-wheel drive tours are among the many activities offered.

Spa services include a full resort staff. Visit the on-site pioneer ruins, museum, ranger camp, Indian caves and pictographs.

Historic Interest: Three forts built in 1857.

$450. 36 rooms with PB, 35 with FP and 2 suites. Breakfast, snacks/refreshments and dinner included in rates. Types of meals: Full gourmet bkfst, veg bkfst, gourmet lunch, picnic lunch and afternoon tea. Restaurant on premises. Beds: KQT. Reading lamp, stereo, clock radio, coffeemaker, turn-down service and desk in room. Central air. TV, VCR, fax, copier, spa, swimming, stable, bicycles, library, pet boarding, child care, parlor games, telephone, laundry facility and air strip on premises. Weddings, small meetings, family reunions and seminars hosted. Art galleries, bicycling, canoeing/kayaking, fishing, hiking, horseback riding, museums and parks nearby.

Publicity: *Town & Country, Southern Living, New York Times, Oprah, Texas Country Reporter and Grand Champion.*

Smithville   F7

The Katy House Bed & Breakfast

201 Ramona St, PO Box 803
Smithville, TX 78957-0803
(512)237-4262 (800)843-5289 Fax:(512)237-2239
E-mail: thekaty@onr.com
Web: www.katyhouse.com

Circa 1909. Shaded by tall trees, the Katy House's Italianate exterior is graced by an arched portico over the bay-windowed living room. Georgian columns reflect the inn's turn-of-the-century origin. Long leaf pine floors, pocket doors and a graceful stairway accent the completely refurbished interior. The inn is decorated almost exclusively in American antique oak and railroad memorabilia. A 1909 caboose is being restored to be used as a guest room. Historic Main

Street is one block away with a fine collection of antique shops. Guests usually come back from walking tours with pockets full of pecans found around town. Smithville was the hometown location for the movie "Hope Floats."

Innkeeper(s): Bruce & Sallie Blalock. $95-125. 5 rooms with PB, 1 suite and 2 cottages. Breakfast included in rates. Types of meals: Full bkfst and early coffee/tea. Beds: Q. TV, VCR and ceiling fan in room. Air conditioning. Family reunions hosted. Antiquing, fishing, parks and shopping nearby.

Spring   F9

Janeves Old Town Bed and Breakfast

2438 Spring Creek Dr.
Spring, TX 77373
(281)288-8888 (866)526-3837

Circa 1920. Recently restored, this 80-year-old Victorian home sits on two delightful acres. The intimate setting features a private entry, living room, kitchen, dining room, two bedrooms and a secluded deck. Start the day with fresh-baked danishes and muffins, seasonal fruit, gourmet coffee, herbal teas and juices. The landscaped grounds include flagstone walkways, gardens, a gazebo, waterfall with pond, fountains and towering oaks.

Innkeeper(s): Evelyn De Chiro. $95-115. 2 rooms with PB. Breakfast and snacks/refreshments included in rates. Types of meals: Cont. Beds: QT. Cable TV, VCR, reading lamp, stereo, refrigerator, ceiling fan, snack bar, clock radio and coffeemaker in room. Central air. Gift shop, gazebo, entire house to yourself, private entry, private deck, yard, front porch, fountains, waterfall with pond, kitchen, dining room, towering oaks and and beautifully landscape on premises. Amusement parks, antiquing, bicycling, fishing, golf, live theater, museums, parks, shopping, water sports, wineries and Old Town Spring nearby.

Publicity: *Bed and breakfast has been on television.*

Victoria G8

Friendly Oaks B&B

210 E Juan Linn St
Victoria, TX 77901-8145
(361)575-0000
E-mail: innkpr@aol.com
Web: www.bbhost.com/friendlyoaks

Circa 1916. Listed in the National Register of Historic Places, this handsome home is embraced by six massive live oaks, offering an enchanting adventure for first-time guests as well as repeats. Full of Texas country charm, there are several themed guest rooms including the Ranch, Thrifty Scot, the Preservation Room and the Boudoir, a favorite of couples celebrating anniversaries. Breakfasts, like everything else in Texas, are big. Guests start off with a variety of fruits, then might sample Texas-shaped scones and entrees such as pecan waffles or French toast. The grounds are covered with the namesake oak trees and the historic street known as the "Street of Ten Friends" is in the heart of historic downtown Victoria.

Innkeeper(s): Bill & CeeBee McLeod. $55-85. 4 rooms with PB and 1 conference room. Breakfast and afternoon tea included in rates. Types of meals: Full gourmet bkfst and early coffee/tea. Beds: QD. TV, reading lamp, ceiling fan, clock radio, turn-down service and desk in room. Air conditioning. VCR, fax, library, parlor games, telephone and fireplace on premises. Limited handicap access. Weddings, small meetings, family reunions and seminars hosted. Antiquing, fishing, golf, live theater, parks, shopping, tennis, water sports, symphony, ballet and fine arts nearby.

Publicity: *Country Extra and Lifestyle.*

"Thanks so much for the great food, the tour of the town and the step back in history."

Waco E7

The Judge Baylor House

908 Speight Ave
Waco, TX 76706-2343
(254)756-0273 (888)522-9567 Fax:(254)756-0711

Circa 1940. This home was built by the head of the chemistry department at Baylor University, which is just one block away. There are five well-appointed guest rooms, each decorated with English antiques. Each room has something special. In one room, guests will discover French doors leading out to a patio. In another, there is a poster bed and hand-painted pedestal sink. Aside from the university and Elizabeth Barrett & Robert Browning Library, the home is near the Brazos Riverwalk, Lake

Waco, the Texas Sports Hall of Fame, antique shops, historic homes and more.

Innkeeper(s): Bruce & Dorothy Dyer. $72-105. 5 rooms, 4 with PB and 1 suite. Breakfast and afternoon tea included in rates. Types of meals: Full bkfst and early coffee/tea. Beds: KQT. Ceiling fan, clock radio and desk in room. Air conditioning. VCR, fax, copier, library, parlor games, telephone and fireplace on premises. Weddings, small meetings, family reunions and seminars hosted. Antiquing, fishing, golf, live theater, parks, shopping, sporting events and tennis nearby.

Publicity: *Fort Worth Star-Telegram, Dallas Morning News, Arrington's B&B Journal and Country Extra.*

Waxahachie D8

Baroness Inn & B&B

206 South Main Street
Waxahachie, TX 76670
(972)493-9393 (877)993-4924 Fax:(972)493-3100
E-mail: evelyn@baronessinn.com
Web: www.baronessinn.com

Circa 1850. Dedicated to romance and perfect for grown-up getaways, this renovated 1850s Victorian inn is elegantly appointed with antiques and detailed woodwork. Relax in one of the two spectacular parlors. Luxuriously enchanting guest bedrooms feature plush robes and turndown service. Many have Jacuzzi or clawfoot soaking tubs, fireplaces and canopy beds. An outstanding three-course breakfast menu includes beverages, freshly baked pastries, eggs served any style, buttermilk pancakes, specialty omelette, crepe of the day, hot oatmeal or cold cereal, bacon or sausage and home-fried potatoes. Stroll brick garden paths, play croquet or just sit on a balcony or porch. Bicycles are provided to explore the historic area. Ask about the variety of special packages, tea parties, and picnics that are available.

Innkeeper(s): Evelyn Williams. $100-160. 9 rooms, 8 with PB, 4 with FP and 4 conference rooms. Breakfast and snacks/refreshments included in rates. Types of meals: Full gourmet bkfst, veg bkfst, early coffee/tea, lunch, picnic lunch, afternoon tea, dinner and room service. Beds: Q. Data port, TV, VCR, reading lamp, refrigerator, ceiling fan, clock radio, telephone, turn-down service, desk, hot tub/spa and fireplace in room. Air conditioning. Fax, copier, spa, bicycles, library, parlor games, laundry facility and gift shop on premises. Weddings, small meetings, family reunions and seminars hosted. Antiquing, bicycling, fishing, hiking, horseback riding, live theater, museums, parks, shopping and water sports nearby.

Publicity: *Dallas Morning News, Texas Highways, Call to Courage, Ft. Worth Star Telegram, Waxahachie Daily Light, Texas Women, Channel 8 Country Reporter, Russ Martin Radio Talk Show and Operation Kindness.*

Utah

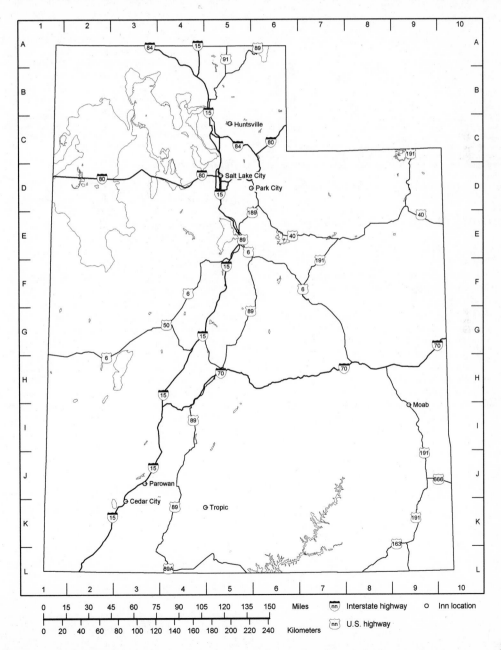

0 15 30 45 60 75 90 105 120 135 150 Miles

0 20 40 60 80 100 120 140 160 180 200 220 240 Kilometers

[nn] Interstate highway   o Inn location

[nn] U.S. highway

Cedar City K3

A Garden Cottage Bed & Breakfast

16 North 200 West
Cedar City, UT 84720
(435)586-4919 (866)586-4919
E-mail: romance@thegardencottagebnb.com
Web: www.thegardencottagebnb.com

Circa 1920. Taste the gracious ambiance of Merrie Olde England at this quaint English cottage across from the Utah Shakespearean Festival. At the top of a winding staircase, antique-filled guest bedrooms feature Victorian furnishings and handmade vintage linens with embroidery and lace. A pleasing breakfast usually includes home-baked breads, fresh fruit, quiche, juice smoothies, hot chocolate, tea, cider and coffee. The B&B is surrounded by an award-winning, old-fashioned garden to enjoy. Arrington's Bed and Breakfast Journal recently named the inn as one of the Top 15 B&B/Country Inns.

Innkeeper(s): Gary & Diana Simkins. $70-150. 3 rooms with PB, 1 with HT. Breakfast included in rates. Types of meals: Full bkfst. Beds: Q. Reading lamp and one with 75 gallon jetted tub in room. Central air. Parlor games and fireplace on premises. Antiquing, art galleries, bicycling, cross-country skiing, downhill skiing, fishing, golf, hiking, horseback riding, live theater, museums, parks, shopping, sporting events, tennis, water sports and Utah Shakespearean Festival nearby.

Publicity: *The Spectrum Newspaper, Cedar City Magazine and American Breakfast with Phil Paleologos.*

Cherished Memories Bed & Breakfast

170 N. 400 W.
Cedar City, UT 84720
(435)867-6498 (866)867-6498
E-mail: memories@cherishedmemoriesbnb.com
Web: www.cherishedmemoriesbnb.com

Circa 1906. Built with adobe brick and trimmed in gingerbread and lattice, this 1906 Victorian home is furnished with unusual pieces and distinctive antiques. Formerly known as the Paxman Summer House, it has been recently renovated to pamper and please. The warm and inviting parlor invites conversation. Relax on spacious front and rear porches. Air-conditioned guest bedrooms are delightfully decorated and feature comfortable Queen pillowtop beds. After a restful sleep, linger over a satisfying breakfast in the elegant formal dining room. Historic downtown and the Utah Shakespearean Festival are just two blocks away. Take a shuttle to Brian Head Ski Resort or plan a scenic day trip to Bryce Canyon or Zion National Parks. Box lunches can be arranged.

Historic Interest: Built in 1906 of adobe brick with gingerbread and lattice trim. High ceilings, original grain painting on interior wood.

Innkeeper(s): Larry & Rae Overson. $89. 4 rooms with PB. Breakfast included in rates. Types of meals: Full gourmet bkfst, early coffee/tea, picnic lunch and room service. Beds: QT. Reading lamp and ceiling fan in room. Air conditioning. TV, VCR, parlor games and telephone on premises. Antiquing, art galleries, bicycling, cross-country skiing, downhill skiing, fishing, golf, hiking, horseback riding, live theater, museums, parks, shopping, sporting events, tennis and water sports nearby.

Stratford Bed & Breakfast

161 South 200 West
Cedar City, UT 84720
(435)867-5280 (877)530-5280
E-mail: marybeth@stratfordbb.com
Web: www.stratfordbb.com

Circa 1934. Just two blocks from Main Street, this whimsical bed & breakfast adorns a quiet, tree-lined neighborhood in the historic downtown area. Sit on the inviting front porch with a glass of lemonade overlooking the hummingbirds in the garden. Watch cable TV or a video in the parlor. After sleeping under a quilt in a comfortable bed, read the morning paper before breakfast. Enjoy a family-style meal in front of the bay window of the breakfast room that includes fruit, an entree and just-baked breads with homemade jams and jellies. Take a shady one-block stroll to the Utah Shakespeare Festival.

Innkeeper(s): Mary Beth Cook. $75-120. 5 rooms with PB and 1 suite. Breakfast and snacks/refreshments included in rates. Types of meals: Full bkfst and early coffee/tea. Beds: KQT. Modem hook-up, data port, ceiling fan, clock radio, feather beds and iron/ironing board in room. Central air. TV, VCR, telephone and fireplace on premises. Antiquing, art galleries, bicycling, cross-country skiing, downhill skiing, fishing, golf, hiking, live theater, museums, parks and Utah Shakespearean Festival nearby.

Huntsville C5

Jackson Fork Inn LLC

7345 E 900 S
Huntsville, UT 84317-9778
(801)745-0051 (800)255-0672
E-mail: vjfi@softcom.net
Web: www.jacksonforkinn.com

Circa 1938. Surrounded by scenic mountains, pine and aspen trees, the location in the Ogden Valley Recreation Area is ideal for nature enthusiasts. The inn is named after the large hayfork that hauled hay into the loft of this former modern dairy barn and hangs on display outside. Two-story guest bedrooms are cozy and comfortable boasting lofts and spiral staircases. Several rooms include two-person whirlpool tubs. A self-serve continental breakfast is prepared each day with muffins and fresh coffee. A first-floor restaurant offers fish, chicken, steak, pasta and vegetarian dishes. Skiers appreciate the nearby Powder Mountain, Nordic Valley and Snowbasin ski resorts.

Innkeeper(s): Vicki Petersen. $75-125. 7 rooms with PB. Breakfast included in rates. Types of meals: Cont. Restaurant on premises. Beds: Q. Reading lamp and ceiling fan in room. Air conditioning. TV, fireplace and full breakfast on Sunday on premises. Weddings and small meetings hosted. Cross-country skiing, downhill skiing, fishing, parks, shopping and water sports nearby.

Moab I9

Cali Cochitta Bed & Breakfast Inn

110 S 200 East
Moab, UT 84532
(435)259-4961 (888)429-8112 Fax:(435)259-4964

Circa 1870. This two-story sandstone brick Victorian is in Red Rock Country, which is known for its beautiful panoramas. Innkeeper Kim's beautiful garden has a fountain and is lit by torches at night. She grows both flowers and herbs. The inn is decorated with period Victorian pieces and is full of music and candlelight at night. It has five guest bedrooms including one suite and one cottage. Innkeeper David Boger has 20 years in food management at country clubs and fine restaurants and has catered for international organizations and dignitaries including President George Bush. He cooks with fresh herbs from Kim's garden. Breakfasts include such gourmet fare as crab quiche, homemade blueberry muffins, banana bread, coffee cakes and fresh seasonal berries with the inn's secret Grand Marnier sauce. Other culinary requests, from picnic lunches to candlelight dinners, can be accommodated upon request. The inn is near Arches and Canyonlands National Park and not far from the town of Moab. Guests may enjoy antiquing, shopping touring museums and visiting wineries. Or they may go bicycling, canoeing, fishing, golfing, hiking or horseback riding. David and Kim suggest that guests get up early at least one morning during their stay, and sit on the front porch with a cup of coffee, tea or juice and soak in the magnificent Southern Utah sunrise.

Innkeeper(s): David & Kim Boger. $69-150. 5 rooms with PB, 1 suite and 1 cottage. Breakfast, afternoon tea and snacks/refreshments included in rates. Types of meals: Full gourmet bkfst, early coffee/tea, lunch, picnic lunch and gourmet dinner. Beds: QDT. Cable TV, reading lamp, ceiling fan, clock radio, turn-down service and desk in room. Central air. Spa, library, child care, parlor games and telephone on premises. Handicap access. Weddings, small meetings and family reunions hosted. Antiquing, art galleries, bicycling, canoeing/kayaking, cross-country skiing, fishing, golf, hiking, horseback riding, live theater, museums, parks, shopping, tennis, water sports, wineries, rock climbing and river rafting nearby.

Publicity: *PBS*.

Sunflower Hill B&B

185 N 300 E
Moab, UT 84532-2421
(435)259-2974 (800)662-2786 Fax:(435)259-3065

Circa 1895. Guests at Sunflower Hill stay either in a restored adobe farmhouse or a garden cottage. The one-and-a-half-acre grounds, dotted with gardens and wooded pathways, create a secluded environment, yet the home is only three blocks from downtown Moab. Guest rooms are decorated in country style with antiques and stenciled walls. A hearty breakfast buffet is served on an antique sideboard. Guests choose from a multitude of items, such as vegetable frittata, poached eggs with mushrooms and smoked turkey, lemon poppy seed scones, muffins, fresh fruit, honey-almond granola and more. There is an outdoor hot tub on the premises, as well as a laundry facility. Sunflower Hill is close to Arches and Canyonlands national parks.

Innkeeper(s): The Stucki Family. $89-199. 12 rooms with PB and 3 suites. Breakfast included in rates. Types of meals: Full bkfst, early coffee/tea, picnic lunch and snacks/refreshments. Beds: QD. Cable TV, reading lamp, ceiling fan, snack bar, clock radio, hot tub/spa and deluxe rooms have jet tubs and private balconies or patios in room. Air conditioning. VCR, fax, copier, spa, library, parlor games, telephone, fireplace and laundry facility on premises. Bicycling, cross-country skiing, fishing, golf, hiking, horseback riding, parks, shopping, tennis, water sports and white water rafting nearby.

Publicity: *Aspen Times, NBC Tonight Show with Jay Leno, Smart Money Magazine, Shape Magazine and Cowboys and Indians Magazine.*

"This place is awesome. We will be back."

Park City D6

The 1904 Imperial Hotel-A B&B

221 Main St, PO Box 1628
Park City, UT 84060-1628
(435)649-1904 (800)669-8824 Fax:(435)645-7421
E-mail: stay@1904imperial.com
Web: www.1904imperial.com

Circa 1904. Too much of a good thing can be wonderful. That's what they'll tell you at the Imperial, a historic turn-of-the-century hotel decorated in a "Western" Victorian style. Several guest rooms include amenities like clawfoot or Roman tubs and sitting areas. A few overlook Park City's historic Main Street. The inn's largest suite includes a bedroom and a spiral staircase leading up to a cozy loft area. There are ski lockers and a Jacuzzi on-site. Transportation to area ski lifts are located nearby.

Innkeeper(s): Marie Sheppard. $80-245. 10 rooms with PB and 2 suites. Breakfast included in rates. Types of meals: Full bkfst and snacks/refreshments. Beds: KQT. Cable TV, reading lamp, clock radio, telephone and desk in room. Fax, copier, parlor games and fireplace on premises. Antiquing, cross-country skiing, downhill skiing, fishing, live theater, parks, shopping, sporting events and water sports nearby.

Angel House Inn

PO Box 159
Park City, UT 84060-0159
(435)647-0338 (800)264-3561
E-mail: jrush@ditell.com
Web: www.angelhouseinn.com

Circa 1889. With the Wasatch Mountains in view, this 6,000-square-foot historic Park City mansion offers a welcoming invitation close to ski resorts. Each room is named after an angel and has been designed to highlight the inn's historic architecture and romantic setting. Antiques, fine linens and brocade appointed bedsteads are part of the décor. The Michael & Faith room for instance, comes with a fireplace and fainting couch. Other rooms include four-poster or canopy beds, and some offer the relaxing amenity of clawfoot tubs. A massage service is available, a perfect treat after a day on the slopes. The innkeepers serve a full breakfast with dishes such as Eggs Benedict or fresh berry pancakes in the dining room with inviting upholstered chairs and a crystal chandelier. Appetizers are served in the evenings.

Innkeeper(s): Jan & Joe Fisher-Rush. $85-250. 9 rooms with PB, 1 with FP and 1 conference room. Breakfast, afternoon tea and snacks/refreshments included in rates. Types of meals: Full gourmet bkfst, veg bkfst, early coffee/tea and picnic lunch. Beds: KQ. Modem hook-up, cable TV, VCR, reading lamp, ceiling fan, telephone, turn-down service and clawfoot tubs in room. Fax, spa, library, parlor games, fireplace and snow sleds on premises. Weddings, small meetings, family reunions and seminars hosted. Amusement parks, antiquing, art galleries, bicycling, canoeing/kayaking, cross-country skiing, downhill skiing, fishing, golf, hiking, horseback riding, live theater, museums, parks, shopping, tennis, water sports, site of 2002 Olympics, Sundance Film Festival, balloons, gliding and snowmobiles nearby.

Publicity: *Instyle, Sunset, Wine Spectator, Southern Living, San Francisco Chronicle and German Dating Game.*

The Old Miners' Lodge - A B&B Inn

615 Woodside Ave, PO Box 2639
Park City, UT 84060-2639
(435)645-8068 (800)648-8068 Fax:(435)645-7420
E-mail: stay@oldminerslodge.com
Web: www.oldminerslodge.com

Circa 1889. This originally was established as a miners' boarding house by E. P. Ferry, owner of the Woodside-Norfolk silver mines. A two-story Victorian with Western flavor, the lodge is a significant structure in the Park City National Historic District. Just on the edge of the woods is a deck and a steaming hot tub.

Historic Interest: Mining artifacts from the silver mining industry.

Innkeeper(s): Susan Wynne & Liza Simpson. $70-275. 12 rooms with PB, 3 suites and 3 conference rooms. Breakfast and snacks/refreshments included in rates. Types of meals: Full bkfst and early coffee/tea. Beds: KQDT. Reading lamp, refrigerator, ceiling fan, turn-down service, robes and clock in room. Fax, copier, spa, library, parlor games, telephone and fireplace on premises. Small meetings, family reunions and seminars hosted. Antiquing, cross-country skiing, downhill skiing, fishing, live theater, parks and shopping nearby.

Publicity: *Boston Herald, Los Angeles Times, Detroit Free Press, Washington Post, Ski, Bon Appetit and ESPN.*

"This is the creme de la creme. The most wonderful place I have stayed at bar none, including ski country in the U.S. and Europe."

Old Town Guest House

1011 Empire Ave
Park City, UT 84060
(435)649-2642 (800)290-6423 Fax:(435)649-3320
E-mail: Dlovci@cs.com
Web: www.oldtownguesthouse.com

Circa 1900. Centrally located, this historic inn is perfect for hikers, skiers and bikers to enjoy all that the mountains offer. Experience convenience and affordability accented with adventure and inspiration. Some of the comfortable guest bedrooms and suites feature lodge-pole pine furnishings and a jetted tub or fireplace. A Park City Breakfast is included and sure to please hungry appetites. The innkeepers' motto of "play hard, rest easy" is pleasantly fulfilled. Assistance is offered in making the most of any stay. Refuel with afternoon snacks and relax in the hot tub.

Historic Interest: Park City is full of great silver mining history, and Old Town Guest House was the residence of one of the famous characters of the day.

Innkeeper(s): Deb Lovci. $59-209. 4 rooms with PB, 1 with FP and 1 suite. Breakfast, afternoon tea and snacks/refreshments included in rates. Types of meals: Country bkfst, veg bkfst and early coffee/tea. Beds: QT. Modem hookup, data port, cable TV, VCR, reading lamp, stereo, refrigerator, ceiling fan, snack bar, clock radio, telephone, desk, hot tub/spa, fireplace and robes in room. Fax, spa, parlor games, fireplace, laundry facility, ski boot dryers, video library, afternoon snacks, bike storage, ski storage, computer and day packs on premises. Small meetings and family reunions hosted. Antiquing, art galleries, bicycling, canoeing/kayaking, cross-country skiing, downhill skiing, fishing, golf, hiking, horseback riding, live theater, museums, parks, shopping, tennis, Park City Mountain Resort (walking distance), Deer Valley (free shuttle), The Canyons (free shuttle) and snowshoeing nearby.

Publicity: *Utah Outdoor Magazine, Utah Outdoors July 2002 and voted inn "with best activities."*

Parowan   J3

Victoria's Bed & Breakfast

94 North 100 East
Parowan, UT 84761
(435)477-0075 (866)477-0090 Fax:(435)477-0079
E-mail: info@utahretreat.com
Web: utahretreat.com

Circa 1870. Revel in the gorgeous views of the surrounding mountains while staying at this 1870 Victorian home that sits at the base of Brian Head Ski Resort. Furnished with antiques that are easy to fall in love with, and each one is available to purchase and take home. Comfortable guest bedrooms and a suite feature pretty colors and pleasing amenities. Take the private entrance to Rhett's Room with a fireplace and double-headed shower. Aunt Pitty Pat's Suite features a soft green and blue décor with a sitting room. A hearty breakfast boasts favorites like homemade biscuits with country gravy, hash browns, sausage, bacon, muffins, cereal and yogurt. Winter sports are popular as well as hiking, biking, fishing and hunting. Stroll the well-maintained gardens and lawns and relax on the wraparound veranda.

Historic Interest: Built in 1870 By the Bishop of the 3rd Ward of the LDS Church.

Innkeeper(s): Sharon Gordon. $89-129. 4 rooms with PB, 1 with FP and 1 suite. Breakfast included in rates. Types of meals: Country bkfst, early coffee/tea and picnic lunch. Beds: KQ. Data port, cable TV, reading lamp, ceiling fan, clock radio and fireplace in room. Central air. Fax, telephone and laundry facility on premises. Family reunions hosted. Antiquing, bicycling, cross-country skiing, downhill skiing, fishing, golf, live theater and Shakespearean Festival nearby.

Salt Lake City   D5

Armstrong Mansion Inn

667 E 100 S
Salt Lake City, UT 84102-1103
(801)531-1333 (800)708-1333 Fax:(801)531-0282
E-mail: innkeeper@armstrongmanor.com
Web: www.Armstrongmanor.com

Circa 1893. A former Salt Lake City mayor built this Queen Anne-style home for his young bride. This beautiful mansion features the original carved-oak staircase and ornate woodwork. Guest rooms are decorated with Victorian furnishings and walls feature stenciling that was designed after looking at old photographs of the home. Each room is decorated to reflect a different month of the year. The home is within walking distance to downtown shopping, businesses and other attractions. The area offers many outdoor activities, such as hiking and skiing.

Historic Interest: The home is located in Salt Lake's historic district. Tree oldest of kind in SLC Valley.

Innkeeper(s): Judy & Dave Savage. $89-239. 15 rooms, 13 with PB, 2 suites and 1 conference room. Breakfast and snacks/refreshments included in rates. Types of meals: Full gourmet bkfst, early coffee/tea, gourmet dinner and room service. Beds: KQ. Cable TV, VCR, clock radio, telephone and jetted tubs in room. Central air. Fax, copier, parlor games, fireplace and laundry facility on premises. Limited handicap access. Weddings, small meetings, family reunions and seminars hosted. Amusement parks, antiquing, art galleries, bicycling, cross-country skiing, downhill skiing, fishing, golf, hiking, horseback riding, live theater, museums, parks, shopping, sporting events, tennis, water sports, historic Temple Square and ski resorts and summer watersports nearby.

Ellerbeck Mansion B&B

140 North B St
Salt Lake City, UT 84103-2482
(801)355-2500 (800)966-8364 Fax:(801)530-0938
E-mail: ellerbeckmansion@qwest.net
Web: www.ellerbeckbedandbreakfast.com

Circa 1892. Pleasantly located in the city's downtown historic district, this Victorian inn has been renovated for modern comfort and lovingly restored with original moldings, hardwood floors and stained glass. Impressive fireplaces can be found in the splendid main floor and upstairs galleries as well as in several of the six guest bedrooms. Different seasonal motifs adorn the bedrooms, so every day is a holiday in Christmas Wishes, complete with a sleigh bed. Autumn Winds and Spring Breeze can serve as an ideal suite for families. Enjoy a continental breakfast that is delivered to each room at an agreed-upon time. After exploring the local sites and nearby attractions, the turndown service, evening chocolates and complimentary soft drinks are welcome additions.

Historic Interest: Old Deseret Village, Historic Temple Square.

Innkeeper(s): Debbie Spencer. $115-135. 6 rooms with PB, 3 with FP. Breakfast and snacks/refreshments included in rates. Types of meals: Full bkfst. Beds: KQ. Modem hook-up, cable TV, reading lamp, clock radio, telephone, turn-down service and fireplace in room. Central air. Fax and fireplace on premises. Family reunions hosted. Antiquing, art galleries, bicycling, downhill skiing, hiking, horseback riding, live theater, museums, parks, shopping, sporting events and Historic Temple Square nearby.

Saltair B&B

164 S 900 E
Salt Lake City, UT 84102-4103
(801)533-8184 (800)733-8184 Fax:(801)595-0332
E-mail: saltair@saltlakebandb.com
Web: www.saltlakebandb.com

Circa 1903. The Saltair is the oldest continuously operating bed & breakfast in Utah and offers a prime location to enjoy Salt Lake City. The simply decorated rooms include light, airy window dressings, charming furnishings and special touches. Breakfasts, especially the delicious Saltair Eggs Benedict topped with avocado, sour creme and salsa, are memorable. The inn is within walking distance to four historic districts and only one mile from Temple Square and the Governor's Mansion. Day trips include treks to several national and state parks and the Wasatch Front ski areas.

Innkeeper(s): Nancy Saxton & Jan Bartlett. $79-149. 7 rooms, 4 with PB. Breakfast and snacks/refreshments included in rates. Types of meals: Full gourmet bkfst and early coffee/tea. Beds: QT. Reading lamp, clock radio and fresh flowers in room. Air conditioning. VCR, fax, spa, parlor games and telephone on premises. Seminars hosted. Antiquing, cross-country skiing, downhill skiing, fishing, live theater, parks, shopping, sporting events and water sports nearby.

Publicity: *Mobil, Logan Sun and Sunset.*

"Your swing and Saltair Muffins were fabulous."

Tropic   K4

Bryce Point B&B

61 N, 400 West
Tropic, UT 84776-0096
(435)679-8629 (888)200-4211 Fax:(435)679-8629
Web: www.brycepointlodging.com

Circa 1931. The innkeepers of this comfortable bed & breakfast have owned the home since 1951 and renovated it in the late '80s and soon after opened for guests. Each of the guests rooms is named for the innkeepers' children and their spouses, and each room feature comfortable furnishings and large picture windows. Relax on the wraparound porch or pick a movie from the innkeepers' library and snuggle up in your room to watch an old favorite. Six national parks surround the Tropic area, offering plenty of seasonal activities.

Historic Interest: Historic Bryce Canyon Lodge is nearby and offers hiking, horseback riding, hunting and fishing.

Innkeeper(s): Lamar & Ethel LeFevre. $60-120. 6 rooms, 5 with PB and 1 cottage. Breakfast included in rates. Types of meals: Full gourmet bkfst. Beds: KQT. TV, VCR, reading lamp, refrigerator, ceiling fan and telephone in room. Central air. Fax, spa, library and laundry facility on premises. Cross-country skiing, fishing, hiking, horseback riding and parks nearby.

Publicity: *The Toronto Sun, The Daily Spectrum, Country Hight and Atlanta Constitution (article by Clark Howard).*

"So many amenities abound: a comfortable, cheerful room, great sleeping, thoughtful touches, stargazing, scenery from your spacious deck, gracious hosts and so much more. We've been to many B&B's, Bryce Point is among the winners."

Vermont

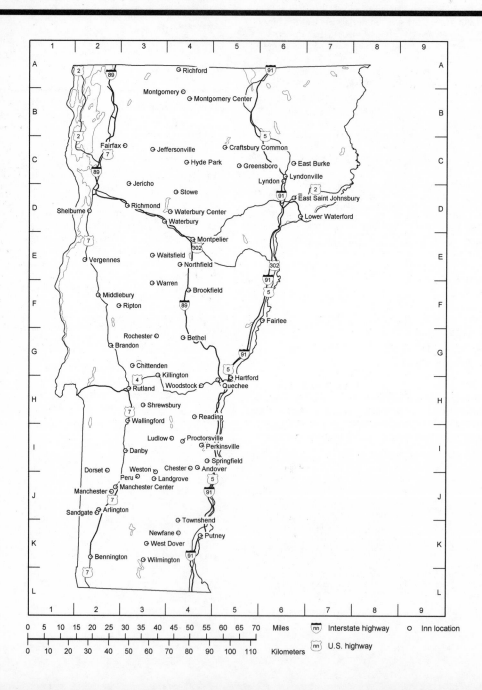

Andover   I4

Historic Rowells Inn

1834 Simonsville Rd
Andover, VT 05143
(802)875-3658 (800)728-0842 Fax:(802)875-3680
E-mail: innkeep@rowellsinn.com
Web: www.rowellsinn.com

Circa 1820. Experience the heritage of New England hospitality at this Greek Revival brick inn that is listed in the National Register. Built as a stagecoach stop and part of the Underground Railroad, historic details and lavish antiques combine with generous service in a splendid setting. Rockers on the front porch and a fire in the parlor or Sun Room provide comfortable relaxation. The Tavern Room, an English-style pub is ideal for working on puzzles with new friends and a cold drink. Authentically furnished guest bedrooms and suites feature canopy feather beds, fresh flowers, air conditioning or ceiling fans. Some boast clawfoot tubs, wood-burning fireplaces and balcony access. The country breakfasts are always a satisfying delight. Dinner service is available. Play horseshoes, badminton or croquet on the one and a half acres with flower gardens and a small fish pond.

Historic Interest: Built in 1820 as a stage coach stop, the Simonsville post office is still here along with intact guest registers dating back to 1870, part of the underground railroad at one time, was a speakeasy during prohibition, was the town post office, city hall, general store and always a working inn since the beginning.

Innkeeper(s): Michael Brengolini, Susan McNulty. $89-175. 7 rooms with PB, 2 with FP, 2 suites and 1 conference room. Breakfast and snacks/refreshments included in rates. Types of meals: Country bkfst, veg bkfst, early coffee/tea, picnic lunch, afternoon tea and gourmet dinner. Restaurant on premises. Beds: KQDT. Reading lamp, ceiling fan, clock radio, desk and fireplace in room. Air conditioning. TV, VCR, fax, copier, library, parlor games, telephone and fireplace on premises. Handicap access. Weddings, small meetings, family reunions and seminars hosted. Antiquing, art galleries, bicycling, canoeing/kayaking, cross-country skiing, downhill skiing, fishing, golf, hiking, horseback riding, live theater, museums, parks, shopping, tennis, water sports, wineries, foliage and bird watching nearby.

The Inn at High View

753 East Hill Rd
Andover, VT 05143
(802)875-2724 Fax:(802)875-4021
E-mail: hiview@aol.com
Web: www.innathighview.com

Circa 1789. Relaxation is stressed at this spacious farmhouse inn in the Green Mountains. A fireplace, rock garden, swimming pool and gazebo add to guests' enjoyment. Cross-country ski trails are found on the grounds, hooking up with a series of others to provide up to 15 kilometers of uninterrupted skiing. The inn offers advance-reservation dinner service for its guests on weekends and specializes in Italian fare.

Innkeeper(s): Gregory Bohan & Salvatore Massaro. $135-195. 8 rooms with PB, 2 suites and 1 conference room. Breakfast included in rates. Types of meals: Full bkfst, early coffee/tea, lunch and dinner. Beds: KQT. Reading lamp, desk and two rooms have hot tub on deck in room. VCR, telephone, fireplace, cross-country skiing and sauna on premises. Weddings, small meetings, family reunions and seminars hosted. Antiquing, downhill skiing, fishing, live theater and shopping nearby.

Arlington   J2

The Arlington Inn

Historic Rt 7A, PO Box 369
Arlington, VT 05250-0369
(802)375-6532 (800)443-9442
E-mail: arlinn@sover.net
Web: www.arlingtoninn.com

Circa 1848. The Arlington Inn is one of Vermont's finest examples of Greek Revival architecture. Guest rooms are thoughtfully decorated in a traditional style with period antiques suiting the elegance of the inn. Marshall's Library, for instance, offers both a tall canopy bed and sofa, while Sylvester's Study features a handsome fireplace, sitting area, maple ceiling and a private porch. Jacuzzi suites with fireplaces and private patios with pond views are very popular.

Breakfast is served in the solarium with green lawn and flower garden stretching out before you. In the evening, candlelight dinners are available in the inn's fine dining room. Norman Rockwell once used the carriage house as a studio. Nearby activities include fishing, canoeing, downhill and cross-country skiing, snow shoeing and hiking. (Ask about the inn's fly fishing package that includes a visit to the American Museum of Fly Fishing and fishing venues at Batten Kill, Roaring Branch and Deerfield Rivers.)

Innkeeper(s): Eric & Elizabeth Berger. $100-265. 18 rooms with PB, 10 with FP, 5 suites and 1 conference room. Breakfast included in rates. Types of meals: Full gourmet bkfst, picnic lunch and gourmet dinner. Beds: KQDT. TV, reading lamp, telephone, hot tub/spa and Jacuzzi in room. Air conditioning. VCR, fax, copier, bicycles, parlor games and fireplace on premises. Weddings, small meetings, family reunions and seminars hosted. Antiquing, cross-country skiing, downhill skiing, fishing, live theater, shopping, sporting events and water sports nearby.

Publicity: *San Diego Times, Bon Appetit, Country Inns, Vermont Life, Gourmet and New York Magazine.*

Arlington's West Mountain Inn

River Road, PO Box 40
Arlington, VT 05250-0481
(802)375-6516 Fax:(802)375-6553
E-mail: info@westmountainn.com
Web: www.westmountainn.com

Circa 1850. Llamas graze the hillside of this sprawling New England farmhouse situated on 150 acres of meadows and woodland. The inn overlooks the Battenkill River. Each room boasts amenities such as a lace canopied bed, a balcony or a fireplace. The Rockwell Kent Suite graced with a cathedral ceiling, features a fireplace and king-size bed. Back porches and decks are filled with Adirondack lawn chairs.

Innkeeper(s): The Carlson Family. $169-305. 18 rooms, 9 with PB, 10 with FP, 9 suites and 2 conference rooms. Breakfast and dinner included in rates. Types of meals: Full gourmet bkfst, veg bkfst, early coffee/tea and picnic lunch. Restaurant on premises. Beds: KQT. Modem hook-up, reading lamp, ceiling fan, desk and fireplace in room. Air conditioning. TV, VCR, fax, copier, swimming, library, child care, parlor games, telephone, fireplace and hiking trails on premises. Weddings, small meetings, family reunions and seminars hosted. Antiquing, art galleries, bicycling, canoeing/kayaking, cross-country skiing, downhill skiing, fishing, golf, hiking, horseback riding, live theater, museums, parks, shopping and tennis nearby.

Publicity: *Family Circle, Schenectady Gazette, New York Post, Daily News, Vermont Life, New York Times, Yankee, National Geographic, Vermont Magazine, Boston Globe, Glamour, Ski Magazine, Dove Magazine and Philadelphia Enquirer.*

"Excellent, warm, friendly, relaxing, absolutely the best!"

Country Willows

332 E. Arlington Rd
Arlington, VT 05250
(802)375-0019 (800)796-2585 Fax:(802)375-8054
E-mail: cw@sover.net
Web: www.countrywillows.com

Circa 1850. History envelops this traditional Queen Anne Victorian, a village landmark that is listed in the National Register. Comfortably furnished in period antiques, public rooms include the parlor with fireside seating areas. Each guest bedroom and suite offers a different delight. Sleep on a cherry wood sleigh bed in the first-floor Arlington Room, or a four-poster mahogany bed in the Manchester, with a clawfoot soaking tub and mountain view. Silver, crystal and china are set in the dining room to accent award-winning breakfast recipes made from fresh local ingredients that may include baked egg in herbed tomato and baked French toast. Relax on the wrap-around porch overlooking rolling lawn and gardens or nap in a hammock for two.

Innkeeper(s): Anne & Ron Weber. $110-165. 5 rooms with PB, 2 with FP and 1 suite. Breakfast and snacks/refreshments included in rates. Types of meals: Full gourmet bkfst, veg bkfst, early coffee/tea and picnic lunch. Beds: KQT. Cable TV, reading lamp, ceiling fan, clock radio, coffeemaker, turn-down service, desk, fireplace and guest robes in room. Central air. Fax, copier, library, parlor games, telephone, fireplace, wraparound porch, spacious lawns and gardens, picnic tables, lawn chairs and gift shop on premises. Family reunions hosted. Antiquing, art galleries, bicycling, canoeing/kayaking, cross-country skiing, downhill skiing, fishing, golf, hiking, horseback riding, live theater, museums, parks, shopping, tennis, water sports and wineries nearby.

Publicity: *Yankee Magazine, Time Magazine and Vermont Public Radio.*

Hill Farm Inn

458 Hill Farm Rd
Arlington, VT 05250-9311
(802)375-2269 (800)882-2545 Fax:(802)375-9918
E-mail: stay@hillfarminn.com
Web: www.hillfarminn.com

Circa 1790. One of Vermont's original land grant farmsteads, Hill Farm Inn has welcomed guests since 1905 when the widow Mettie Hill opened her home to summer vacationers.

The farm is surrounded by 50 peaceful acres that border the Battenkill River. Guests can relax and enjoy the simple life and visit the inn's sheep, goats and chickens or soak in the 360-degree views of the mountains.

Accommodations are charming and cozy, and summer guests have the option of staying in one of four cabins. A large, country breakfast of homemade fare starts off each day.

Historic Interest: The inn is one of Vermont's original farmsteads, granted to the Hill family from King George III in 1775. It has been operating as an inn since 1905.

Innkeeper(s): Al & Lisa Gray. $80-185. 15 rooms with PB, 3 with FP, 6 suites and 4 cabins. Breakfast and afternoon tea included in rates. Types of meals: Full bkfst. Beds: KQDT. Cable TV, VCR, reading lamp, refrigerator, ceiling fan, clock radio and two kitchenettes in room. Air conditioning. Fax, copi-

er, parlor games, telephone, fireplace and farm animals on premises. Weddings, small meetings, family reunions and seminars hosted. Amusement parks, antiquing, art galleries, bicycling, cross-country skiing, downhill skiing, fishing, golf, hiking, horseback riding, live theater, museums, parks, shopping and families welcome nearby.

Publicity: *Providence Journal, Boston Globe, Innsider and Country.*

"I have already taken the liberty of changing the meaning of relaxation in the dictionary to 'Hill Farm Inn.' Thank you. . . It was great."

The Inn on Covered Bridge Green

3587 River Rd
Arlington, VT 05250-9723
(802)375-9489 (800)726-9480
E-mail: cbg@sover.net
Web: www.coveredbridgegreen.com

Circa 1792. A quaint red covered bridge over the Battenkill River leads to this colonial inn, home to Norman Rockwell for 12 years. The artist was inspired by Arlington's scenes and people, and the six guest rooms at the inn are named for famous Rockwell paintings. The rooms are filled with comfortable chairs, old-fashioned dressers, antique armoires, desks and fireplaces, all in a Norman Rockwell style. A hearty New England breakfast reinforces your enjoyment of the countryside. The artist's actual two-bedroom studio may be rented as well as the one-bedroom art studio, both on the inn grounds.

Innkeeper(s): Clint & Julia Dickens. $125-280. 6 rooms with PB. Types of meals: Full gourmet bkfst. Beds: Q. Fireplaces in room. Air conditioning.

Publicity: *Vermont Life, The San Diego Union and The Boston Globe.*

"We find it difficult to leave. Everything is perfect."

Bennington   K2

Alexandra B&B

Rt 7A Orchard Rd
Bennington, VT 05201
(802)442-5619 (888)207-9386 Fax:(802)442-5592
E-mail: alexandr@sover.net
Web: www.alexandrainn.com

Circa 1859. Located on two acres at the edge of town, Alexandra is a Colonial-style inn. There are king or queen beds in all the rooms, as well as fireplaces and views of Bennington Monument and the Green Mountains. Each bath offers water jets and showers. A full gourmet breakfast is served. Bennington College and the business district are five minutes from the inn.

Innkeeper(s): Alex Koks & Andra Erickson. $100-150. 13 rooms with PB, 12 with FP, 7 suites and 1 conference room. Breakfast included in rates. Types of meals: Full gourmet bkfst and early coffee/tea. Beds: KQ. Modem hook-up, cable TV, VCR, reading lamp, clock radio, telephone, desk and hot tub/spa in room. Air conditioning. Fax and copier on premises. Small meetings, family reunions and seminars hosted. Antiquing, art galleries, bicycling, canoeing/kayaking, cross-country skiing, downhill skiing, fishing, golf, hiking, horseback riding, live theater, museums, parks, shopping, tennis, water sports and wineries nearby.

Four Chimneys Inn & Restaurant

21 West Rd (route 9)
Bennington, VT 05201-6100
(802)447-3500 (800)649-3503 Fax:(802)447-3692
E-mail: innkeeper@fourchimneys.com
Web: www.fourchimneys.com

Circa 1783. Four distinctive chimneys rise from the roofline of this three-story Georgian Revival manor on 11 acres. Recently redecorated, most guest bedrooms offer fireplaces and jetted tubs; one features an enclosed porch. Accommodations also are available in the carriage house and ice house. Formal gardens with a fountain are often the setting for elegant weddings. Try the Lamb Rack at the well-known restaurant on site. Nearby activities include a museum, live theater, art center, historic sites and canoeing.

Innkeeper(s): Christine & Harold Cullison. $105-205. 11 rooms with PB, 8 with FP. Breakfast included in rates. Types of meals: Cont plus and gourmet dinner. Restaurant on premises. Beds: KQ. Cable TV, reading lamp, clock radio, telephone, desk, hair dryers, individual heat controls, most with ceiling fans and jetted tubs in room. Air conditioning. VCR, fax, copier, parlor games and fireplace on premises. Weddings, small meetings, family reunions and seminars hosted. Antiquing, canoeing/kayaking, cross-country skiing, downhill skiing, fishing, golf, live theater, museums, parks, shopping, tennis, water sports, art center and historic sites nearby.

Molly Stark Inn

1067 Main St
Bennington, VT 05201-2635
(802)442-9631 (800)356-3076 Fax:(802)442-5224
E-mail: mollyinn@vermontel.net
Web: www.mollystarkinn.com

Circa 1890. This attractive Queen Anne Victorian inn has been serving travelers for more than 50 years. Careful restoration has enabled it to retain its Victorian charm, while offering the comforts today's guests have come to expect. Features include

antique furnishings, claw-foot tubs, hardwood floors, handmade quilts and a wood stove. The inn's convenient Main Street location puts it within walking distance of many restau-

rants and shops and just minutes from Historic Old Bennington. The Bennington Museum boasts paintings by Grandma Moses.

Innkeeper(s): Reed Fendler. $70-175. 9 rooms with PB, 3 with FP, 2 suites and 1 cottage. Breakfast and snacks/refreshments included in rates. Types of meals: Full gourmet bkfst. Beds: KDT. Cable TV, reading lamp, stereo, refrigerator, ceiling fan, telephone and desk in room. Air conditioning. Bicycles, fireplace and Jacuzzi on premises. Weddings, small meetings and family reunions hosted. Antiquing, cross-country skiing, downhill skiing, fishing, live theater, parks, shopping and water sports nearby.

Publicity: *Yankee Traveler, Colonial Homes, Albany Times Union and Saratogian.*

"...like my grandma's house, only better."

South Shire Inn

124 Elm St
Bennington, VT 05201-2232
(802)447-3839 Fax:(802)442-3547
E-mail: relax@southshire.com
Web: www.southshire.com

Circa 1887. Built in the late 1800s, this inn boasts a mahogany-paneled library, soaring 10-foot ceilings, and three of the guest rooms include one of the home's original fireplaces. Guest rooms feature antiques and Victorian décor. Rooms in the restored carriage house include both a fireplace and a whirlpool tub. Guests are pampered with a full breakfast, as well as afternoon tea. Local attractions include the Bennington Museum, antique shops, craft stores, covered bridges and skiing.

Innkeeper(s): George & Joyce Goeke. $110-190. 9 rooms with PB, 7 with FP and 1 suite. Breakfast and afternoon tea included in rates. Types of meals: Full bkfst, veg bkfst and early coffee/tea. Beds: KQD. Cable TV, VCR, reading lamp, ceiling fan, clock radio, telephone and whirlpool tubs in room. Central air. Fax, copier, library, parlor games, fireplace and guest refrigerator on premises. Weddings, small meetings, family reunions and seminars hosted. Antiquing, art galleries, bicycling, canoeing/kayaking, cross-country skiing, downhill skiing, fishing, golf, hiking, horseback riding, live theater, museums and shopping nearby.

Bethel   G4

Greenhurst Inn

88 North Rd
Bethel, VT 05032-9404
(802)234-9474 (800)510-2553

Circa 1890. In the National Register of Historic Places, Greenhurst is a gracious Victorian mansion built for the Harringtons of Philadelphia. Overlooking the White River, the inn's opulent interiors include etched windows once featured on the cover of Vermont Life. There are eight masterpiece fireplaces and a north and south parlor.

Innkeeper(s): Carl Follo. $50-100. 13 rooms, 7 with PB, 4 with FP. Breakfast included in rates. Types of meals: Cont plus and early coffee/tea. Beds: QDT. Reading lamp, clock radio and desk in room. TV, VCR, library, parlor games, telephone and fireplace on premises. Weddings, small meetings, family reunions and seminars hosted. Antiquing, cross-country skiing, downhill skiing, fishing, live theater, parks, shopping and water sports nearby.

Publicity: *Best Country Inns of New England, Victorian Homes, Washington Post, Boston Globe, Bride's Magazine, Los Angeles Times, Time, New York Times, Vermont Life and The Man Who Corrupted Hadleyburg.*

"The inn is magnificent! The hospitality unforgettable."

Brandon   G2

Churchill House Inn

3128 Forest Dale Rd, Rte 73 E
Brandon, VT 05733-9202
(802)247-3078 (877)297-2831 Fax:(802)247-0113
E-mail: innkeeper@churchillhouseinn.com
Web: www.churchillhouseinn.com

Circa 1871. Caleb Churchill and his son, Nathan, first built a three-story lumber mill, a grist mill and a distillery here, all water powered. Later, with their milled lumber, they constructed this 20-room house. Because of its location, it became a stagecoach stop and has served generations of travelers with comfortable accommodations. The inn is adjacent to Green Mountain National Forest, and excellent hiking, biking, skiing and fishing are just steps away. The inn serves a four-course dinner and a full breakfast.

Historic Interest: Shelburn Museum, Billings Farm, Fort Ticonderoga (less than 1 hour away).

Innkeeper(s): Linda & Richard Daybell. $90-220. 9 rooms with PB. Breakfast and dinner included in rates. Types of meals: Full bkfst and picnic lunch. Beds: QDT. Family reunions hosted. Antiquing, cross-country skiing, downhill skiing, parks, shopping and water sports nearby.

Publicity: *Country and Yankee.*

"We felt the warm, welcoming, down-home appeal as we entered the front hall. The food was uncommonly good — home cooking with a gourmet flair!"

The Gazebo Inn

On Rt 7 (25 Grove St)
Brandon, VT 05733
(802)247-3235 (888)858-3235
E-mail: gazebo@sover.net
Web: www.brandon.org/gazebo.htm

Circa 1865. Cozy elegance is found year-round at this classic New England clapboard home, which is listed in the National Register. Located in the foothills of the Green Mountain National Forest, the inn abounds with pastoral scenes and panoramic vistas. Furnished with Victorian antiques, common rooms include a library with TV/VCR, parlor, reading alcove and screened porch. Distinctive guest bedrooms offer air conditioning and feather beds with down comforters. Mother-daughter hostesses Donna and Lindsay provide a four-course scrumptious breakfast and daily refreshments. There is much to enjoy with two acres of private landscaped grounds and a gazebo. Walk into town or swim or boat at Lake Dunmore, only 10 minutes away. During winter try cross-country skiing at Blueberry Hill.

Historic Interest: The entire village of Brandon, where the inn is located, is listed on the National Register of Historic Places. Stephen A. Douglas' birthplace is a few doors away.

Innkeeper(s): Donna & Lindsay Taylor. $85-115. 4 rooms with PB. Breakfast and snacks/refreshments included in rates. Types of meals: Full gourmet bkfst and veg bkfst. Beds: QDT. Reading lamp and clock radio in room. Parlor games, telephone and fireplace on premises. Antiquing, art galleries, bicycling, cross-country skiing, downhill skiing, hiking, water sports, swimming, summer concerts and fine dining nearby.

"Thank you for your New England-style hospitality. We had a wonderful time. We will try to make this an annual event."

Lilac Inn

53 Park St
Brandon, VT 05733-1121
(802)247-5463 (800)221-0720 Fax:(802)247-5499
E-mail: lilacinn@sover.net
Web: www.lilacinn.com

Circa 1909. For some, the scenery is enough of a reason to visit Vermont. For those who need more, try the Lilac Inn. The restored inn's beautiful furnishings, polished woodwork and fireplaces add to the ambiance. Canopy beds dressed with fine linens, flowers, whirlpool tubs and sitting areas grace the guest rooms. A full, gourmet breakfast is included in the rates. The

inn is a popular site for unforgettable romantic weddings. The landscaped, two-acre grounds include ponds, a gazebo and hundreds of perennials and annuals. Flowers decorate the ground's stone walls.

Historic Interest: Originally built as a summer cottage this 11,000 square foot Renaissance style mansion is the centerpiece of Park Street, the prettiest street in Vermont.

Innkeeper(s): Shelly & Doug Sawyer. $135-300. 9 rooms with PB, 3 with FP and 3 conference rooms. Breakfast included in rates. Types of meals: Country bkfst and gourmet dinner. Restaurant on premises. Beds: QT. Cable TV, reading lamp, ceiling fan, clock radio, desk and fireplace in room. Air conditioning. Fax, library, telephone and fireplace on premises. Limited handicap access. Weddings, small meetings, family reunions and seminars hosted. Antiquing, art galleries, beach, bicycling, canoeing/kayaking, cross-country skiing, downhill skiing, fishing, golf, hiking, horseback riding, live theater, museums, parks, shopping, water sports and Warren Kimble nearby.

Publicity: *Yankee and Vermont & Country Inns.*

"Tasteful, charming and personable."

Brookfield   F4

Green Trails Inn

PO Box 494
Brookfield, VT 05036-0494
(802)276-3412 (800)243-3412 Fax:(802)276-3412
E-mail: greentrails@innevi.com
Web: www.greentrailsinn.com

Circa 1760. Two historic buildings, one constructed in 1790 and the other in 1830, comprise this inn. The innkeepers have an impressive clock collection, and clock sales, restoration and

repair are located on the premises. Many guest rooms offer views of the lake. One suite has a fireplace and others feature private Jacuzzis. The inn

is across the street from Sunset Lake and the Floating Bridge. Cross-country skiing, snowshoeing, hiking, biking and swimming are right outside the door, and there are a number of outdoor activities nearby.

Innkeeper(s): Nina Gaby & Craig Smith. $90-160. 13 rooms, 9 with PB, 1 with FP and 3 suites. Breakfast included in rates. Types of meals: Full gourmet bkfst, veg bkfst, early coffee/tea, lunch, afternoon tea and gourmet dinner. Beds: QDT. TV, reading lamp, clock radio, desk, hot tub/spa and Jacuzzi in room. VCR, fax, spa, swimming, library, child care, parlor games, telephone, fireplace and snowshoes on premises. Weddings, small meetings, family reunions and seminars hosted. Antiquing, art galleries, beach, bicycling, canoeing/kayaking, cross-country skiing, downhill skiing, fishing, golf, hiking, horseback riding, live theater, museums, parks, shopping and water sports nearby.

Publicity: *Sunday Republican, Yankee Magazine. Vermont Magazine and Simple.*

"The inn is really lovely, the welcome very warm and food is scrumptious."

Chester   I4

Henry Farm Inn

2206 Green Mountain Turnpike
Chester, VT 05143
(802)875-2674 (800)723-8213
E-mail: info@henryfarminn.com
Web: www.henryfarminn.com

Circa 1770. Fifty acres of scenic meadows, lawns and woods provide the setting for this handsomely restored three-story former stagecoach stop in the Green Mountains. There are original wide-pine floors and carefully selected early American furnishings. Fireplaces and twelve-over-twelve windows reflect the colonial heritage. A pond and river add to the beauty of the property.

Historic Interest: Chester Stone Village.

Innkeeper(s): Patricia & Paul Dexter. $80-155. 9 rooms with PB. Breakfast included in rates. Types of meals: Full bkfst. Beds: KQT. Reading lamp, clock radio and desk in room. VCR, library, parlor games, telephone and quilting workshops on premises. Weddings and family reunions hosted. Antiquing, bicycling, cross-country skiing, downhill skiing, fishing, golf, hiking, live theater, parks, shopping and tennis nearby.

"Fantastic old house and wonderful hospitality - one of our favorites!"

Hugging Bear Inn & Shoppe

244 Main St
Chester, VT 05143
(802)875-2412 (800)325-0519

Circa 1850. Among the 9,000 teddy bear inhabitants of this white Victorian inn, several peek out from the third-story windows of the octagonal tower. There is a teddy bear shop on the premises and children and adults can borrow a bear to take to bed with them. Rooms are decorated with antiques and comfortable furniture. A bear puppet show is often staged during breakfast.

Innkeeper(s): Georgette Thomas. $65-145. 6 rooms with PB. Breakfast included in rates. Types of meals: Full gourmet bkfst and early coffee/tea. Beds: KQDT. Reading lamp and teddy bear in room. Air conditioning. TV, VCR, library, parlor games, telephone, fireplace, 10,000

teddy bears on premises. Small meetings and family reunions hosted. Antiquing, cross-country skiing, downhill skiing, fishing, golf, parks, shopping and swimming nearby.
Publicity: *Rutland Daily Herald, Exxon Travel, Teddy Bear Review, Teddy Bear Scene and Boston Globe.*

Inn Victoria

On The Green, PO Box 788
Chester, VT 05143-0788
(802)85-4288 (800)732-4288 Fax:(802)875-2504

Circa 1850. This elegant Victorian inn is located On The Green in the heart of Chester. Rooms are furnished with antiques and queen size beds. Guests enjoy the pleasures of fireside reading, soaking by candlelight in a warm Jacuzzi and strolls to nearby restaurants and shops. The Second Empire Victorian is among several historic houses and seven church-es found in Chester's On the Green area. Many weekends include Victorian fairs and festi-

vals. Overture to Christmas is a festive time for townspeople and visitors who dress in Victorian attire and go carolling door-to-door. Two summer theater groups are nearby.
Innkeeper(s): Jack & Janet Burns. $110-195. 7 rooms with PB, 3 with FP and 1 suite. Breakfast and afternoon tea included in rates. Types of meals: Full gourmet bkfst and early coffee/tea. Beds: Q. Cable TV, reading lamp and fireplace in room. Air conditioning. Spa, parlor games and fireplace on premises. Weddings, small meetings, family reunions and seminars hosted. Antiquing, art galleries, canoeing/kayaking, cross-country skiing, downhill ski-ing, fishing, golf, hiking, horseback riding, shopping, water sports and special town-wide events nearby.

Stone Hearth Inn & Tavern

698 Rt 11 West
Chester, VT 05143
(802)875-2525 (888)617-3656 Fax:(802)875-1588
E-mail: info@thestonehearthinn.com
Web: www.thestonehearthinn.com

Circa 1810. Sheltered behind tall pines, this Federal-style farm-house sits on six acres of tranquility. The historic inn was built with bricks made on-site in a kiln, and it features wide board pine floors and exposed beams from its Colonial days. Relax with a book from the library in front of the fire, enjoy a movie, play a game or soak in the hot tub. Several relaxing guest bedrooms fea-ture fireplaces with candelabras. A hearty country breakfast over-looking the lawns and flower gardens may include blueberry but-termilk pancakes with locally made Vermont maple syrup and bacon or sausage. The Tavern menu is popular in the evenings.
Innkeeper(s): Christopher Clay & The Inn Cats. $69-159. 10 rooms with PB, 3 with FP and 1 conference room. Breakfast included in rates. Types of meals: Country bkfst, early coffee/tea and snacks/refreshments. Beds: KQDT. Reading lamp, clock radio, some with A/C and fireplace in room. TV, VCR, fax, spa, library, parlor games, telephone and fireplace on premises. Weddings, small meetings and family reunions hosted. Antiquing, art galleries, bicycling, canoe-ing/kayaking, cross-country skiing, downhill skiing, fishing, golf, hiking, horse-back riding, live theater, museums, parks, shopping, tennis and wineries nearby.

Chittenden G3

Fox Creek Inn

49 Chittenden Dam Rd
Chittenden, VT 05737
(802)483-6213 (800)707-0017
E-mail: foxcreek@sover.net
Web: www.foxcreekinn.com

Circa 1830. Thomas Edison was a regular guest here when the house was the country home of William Barstow. The inn is surrounded by the Green Mountains on three sides with a stream flowing a few yards away. The guest rooms feature antiques and Vermont country decor. Most rooms offer Jacuzzis and some boast fireplaces. Guests enjoy both breakfast and dinner at the inn. Buttermilk pancakes topped with Vermont

maple syrup are typical breakfast fare, and dinners include such items as medallions of pork topped with an orange-apricot sauce and white chocolate cheesecake.
Innkeeper(s): Ann & Alex Volz. $190-409. 9 rooms with PB. Breakfast and dinner included in rates. Types of meals: Full bkfst and early coffee/tea. Restaurant on premises. Beds: KQ. Reading lamp, some with fireplaces and most with Jacuzzis in room. Library, telephone and fireplace on premises. Weddings and small meetings hosted. Amusement parks, antiquing, cross-country skiing, downhill skiing, fishing, live theater, parks, shopping and water sports nearby.
Publicity: *New England Getaways.*

Mountain Top Inn & Resort

195 Mountain Top Rd
Chittenden, VT 05737
(802)483-2311 (800)445-2100 Fax:(802)483-6373
E-mail: info@mountaintopinn.com
Web: www.mountaintopinn.com

Circa 1870. Breathtaking views are among the endless pleasures enjoyed at this four-season post and beam Colonial-style inn that sits on a high meadow hilltop in the Green Mountains National Forest. On-site cross-country ski and equestrian centers as well as beachfront access to a pristine lake are some of the recreational activities available at this 345-acre resort. The new owners have renovated for comfort and style. Stay in a luxury suite with fine linens and two-person whirlpool tub; or a rustic cottage or ski chalet with a fireplace. The Petite Day Spa offers in-room massage. Linger over a candlelit meal of exceptional New American cuisine made with fresh local ingre-dients while surrounded by a refined mountain lodge ambiance. Enjoy a horse-drawn sleigh ride, snowshoeing, ice skating, sled-ding, bike riding, shooting clay birds or playing tennis.
Historic Interest: Made famous by President Eisenhower's visit in 1955 dur-ing a fishing expedition, the Inn was originally the barn for the Long family's turnip farm in the 1870s. In the 1940s, William Barstow, an associate of Thomas Edison, purchased the farm as an overflow lodging option for guests. Throughout the ensuing years, improvements and additions to the original building were made, however still maintained the integrity of its Yankee origin and the beauty and ecology of its natural surroundings.
$115-395. 41 rooms with PB, 9 with FP, 6 suites, 6 cottages and 2 confer-ence rooms. Afternoon tea included in rates. Types of meals: Full gourmet bkfst, veg bkfst, early coffee/tea, gourmet lunch, picnic lunch, snacks/refresh-

ments and gourmet dinner. Restaurant on premises. Beds: KQDT. Modem hook-up, data port, cable TV, VCR, reading lamp, CD player, refrigerator, clock radio, telephone, coffeemaker, desk, hot tub/spa, voice mail and fireplace in room. Air conditioning. Fax, copier, swimming, sauna, stable, bicycles, tennis, pet boarding, child care, parlor games, fireplace, laundry facility, gift shop, petite day spa and limited stalls available for boarding guest horses on premises. Weddings, small meetings, family reunions and seminars hosted. Amusement parks, antiquing, art galleries, bicycling, canoeing/kayaking, cross-country skiing, downhill skiing, fishing, golf, hiking, horseback riding, live theater, museums, parks, shopping, tennis, water sports and wineries nearby.
Publicity: *New York Times, Vermont Magazine, Washington Post, National Geographic, Traveler.com, Newsday, Select Registry and Johansens.*

"Twenty years ago we spent a very enjoyable week here with our daughter. The inn, the service and atmosphere were superior at that time and we are glad to report that it hasn't changed."

Craftsbury Common C5

The Inn on The Common

PO Box 75
Craftsbury Common, VT 05827-0075
(802)586-9619 (800)521-2233 Fax:(802)586-2249
E-mail: info@innonthecommon.com
Web: www.innonthecommon.com

Circa 1795. The Inn on the Common, built by the Samuel French family, is an integral part of this picturesque classic Vermont village. With its white picket fence and graceful white clapboard exterior, the inn provides a quietly elegant retreat.

Pastoral views are framed by the inn's famous perennial gardens. The inn also includes a notable wine cellar.

Historic Interest: Stonehouse Museum (20 miles), Saint Johnsbury-Atheneum museum, Fairbanks Museum (25 miles).

Innkeeper(s): Jim Lamberti. $149-340. 16 rooms with PB, 5 with FP, 2 suites and 1 conference room. Breakfast and dinner included in rates. Types of meals: Full bkfst. Restaurant on premises. Beds: KQDT. Reading lamp, ceiling fan, clock radio, desk and fireplace in room. TV, VCR, fax, copier, swimming, library, pet boarding, parlor games, telephone, laundry facility, upscale restaurant and wine cellar on premises. Cross-country skiing, downhill skiing, fishing, golf and water sports nearby.
Publicity: *New York Times, Craftsbury Common, Harper's Hideaway Report and Discerning Travel.*

"The closest my wife and I came to fulfilling our fantasy of a country inn was at The Inn on the Common." — Paul Grimes

Danby I3

Silas Griffith Inn

178 S Main St
Danby, VT 05739
(802)293-5567 (800)545-1509 Fax:(802)293-5559
E-mail: stay@silasgriffith.com
Web: www.silasgriffith.com

Circa 1891. Originally on 55,000 acres, this stately Queen Anne Victorian mansion features solid cherry, oak and bird's-eye maple woodwork. Considered an architectural marvel, an eight-foot, round, solid-cherry pocket door separates the original music room from the front parlor.

Historic Interest: Hildene, Coolidge Homestead (30 minutes).

Innkeeper(s): George & Carol Gaines. $159-359. 15 rooms with PB. Breakfast and afternoon tea included in

rates. Types of meals: Full gourmet bkfst, early coffee/tea, picnic lunch and gourmet dinner. Restaurant on premises. Beds: KQT. Reading lamp in room. VCR, fax, swimming, library, parlor games, telephone and fireplace on premises. Weddings, small meetings, family reunions and seminars hosted. Antiquing, cross-country skiing, downhill skiing, fishing, golf, live theater, parks, shopping, tennis and water sports nearby.
Publicity: *Vermont Weathervane, Rutland Business Journal, Vermont and Country.*

"Never have I stayed at a B&B where the innkeepers were so friendly, sociable and helpful. They truly enjoyed their job."

Dorset I2

Cornucopia of Dorset

Rt 30 Box 307
Dorset, VT 05251
(802)867-5751
E-mail: innkeepers@cornucopiaofdorset.com
Web: www.cornucopiaofdorset.com

Circa 1880. Window boxes overflow with seasonal flowers inviting guests to this comely 19th-century colonial home. Shaded by tall trees, it is set on a peaceful lawn near the village green. All the guest rooms have poster or canopy beds and fireplaces. A handsome cottage tucked in the trees has its own kitchen and living room with a fireplace and cathedral ceiling. Dorset summer theater is within a five-minute walk.
Historic Interest: National Register.

Innkeeper(s): Donna Butman. $150-270. 5 rooms with PB. Types of meals: Full bkfst. Beds: KQT. Telephone in room.
Publicity: *West Hartford News, New York Times and Country Inn Magazine.*

East Burke C6

The Inn At Mountain View Farm

Darling Hill Road, Box 355
East Burke, VT 05832
(802)626-9924 (800)572-4509 Fax:(802)626-3625
E-mail: innmtnview@kingcon.com
Web: www.innmtnview.com

Circa 1890. Surrounded by mountain splendor, this historic country inn sits on a 440-acre farm that includes part of the Kingdom Trails network of more than 100 miles of hiking, biking and cross-country skiing. Spectacular views, pristine lakes and rolling hills highlight the peaceful setting. Stay in the main inn, the Creamery, a restored 1890 red brick Georgian Colonial that features luxury suites and casually elegant guest bedrooms. Relax or read in the English manor-style parlor. Savor a generous morning meal in the spacious dining room. Afternoon tea and treats are offered in the Willoughby Room. Within a short walk, the Farmhouse has sophisticated suites with Jacuzzi tubs or a fireplace. The Westmore Wing is the perfect retreat for families or friends traveling together. Spa services are available by appointment. Burke Mountain ski resort is only ten minutes away.

Historic Interest: See website http://www.innmtnview.com/history.html.

Innkeeper(s): Marilyn Pastore. $150-385. 14 rooms with PB, 1 with FP, 4 suites and 1 conference room. Breakfast, afternoon tea and snacks/refreshments included in rates. Types of meals: Full gourmet bkfst, veg bkfst, early coffee/tea, picnic lunch and gourmet dinner. Restaurant on premises. Beds: QDT. Reading lamp, desk and fireplace in room. Air conditioning. TV, VCR, sauna, stable, library, pet boarding, parlor games, telephone, fireplace, laundry facility, gift shop, cross-country skiing, snowshoeing, horseback riding (if bring own horse) and mountain biking on premises. Weddings, small meetings, family reunions and seminars hosted. Antiquing, art galleries, beach, bicycling, canoeing/kayaking, cross-country skiing, downhill skiing, fishing, golf, hiking, horseback riding, museums, parks and shopping nearby.

Publicity: *Yankee* ("Editors' Pick"), *Country Living* ("Inn of the Month"), *Travel & Leisure* ("30 Great Inns" for July 2001 and June 2002), *Wine Spectator*, Johansens and Select Registry.

East Saint Johnsbury — D6

Echo Ledge Farm Inn

PO Box 75
East Saint Johnsbury, VT 05838-0046
(802)748-4750
E-mail: echoledgeinn@charter.net
Web: www.echoledgefarminn.com

Circa 1793. Phineas Page settled here on the banks of the Moose River. Later, his son supervised the farm and made it a political meeting place where representatives were chosen for Congress. The innkeepers have created a warm, cozy atmosphere, pampering guests as if they were at Grandma's house. An all-you-can-eat breakfast is served as is afternoon tea and evening cocktails. The inn offers plenty of opportunities for relaxation. Guests can sit on the porch and enjoy the view or stroll the grounds on walking trails and watch for moose, deer and other creatures. The area is rich for those wishing to hunt or fish. Innkeepers can also help guests find hay and sleigh rides.
Historic Interest: Vermont is full of historic sites and the area offers plenty of antique shopping.
Innkeeper(s): Ruth Anne Perkins. $85-95. 6 rooms with PB. Breakfast included in rates. Types of meals: Full bkfst, picnic lunch and afternoon tea. Beds: DT. Snowmobiles available for rent or trailer space available to bring your own on premises. Antiquing, cross-country skiing, downhill skiing, fishing and live theater nearby.
Publicity: *Vermont Country Sampler.*

"Great. We'll come back again! Very much like being at home."

Fairfax — C3

Inn at Buckhollow Farm

2150 Buck Hollow Road
Fairfax, VT 05454-9202
(802)849-2400 (800)849-7985 Fax:(802)849-9744
E-mail: inn@buckhollow.com
Web: www.buckhollow.com

Circa 1790. For a taste of quiet coziness, this classic Vermont farmhouse, carriage house and historic barn offer irresistible country living. Play games by the fire when not visiting local historic sites. Guest bedrooms are decorated in early American and primitives mixed with folk art. Enjoy a generous breakfast that may include Brad's Patriotic Pancakes with ham, meatless sausage or turkey bacon and fruit. Kids are especially delighted with the play area, horses and pool with slide. After a fun day, relax under the canopy of stars while soaking in the hot tub.
Historic Interest: Burlington (35 minutes), Shelburne Museum (45 minutes).
Innkeeper(s): Brad Schwartz. $73-93. 4 rooms. Breakfast included in rates. Types of meals: Full bkfst and veg bkfst. Beds: Q. Cable TV, reading lamp and clock radio in room. Air conditioning. VCR, fax, copier, spa, swimming, parlor games and fireplace on premises. Weddings, small meetings, family reunions and seminars hosted. Antiquing, art galleries, bicycling, canoeing/kayaking, cross-country skiing, downhill skiing, fishing, golf, hiking, horseback riding, live theater, museums, parks, shopping, tennis and water sports nearby.

"Song without end, you did it all!! Your home is beautiful and most comfortable."

Fairlee — F6

Silver Maple Lodge & Cottages

520 US Rt 5 South
Fairlee, VT 05045
(802)333-4326 (800)666-1946
E-mail: scott@silvermaplelodge.com
Web: www.silvermaplelodge.com

Circa 1790. This old Cape farmhouse was expanded in the 1850s and became an inn in the '20s when Elmer & Della Batchelder opened their home to guests. It became so successful that several cottages, built from lumber on the property, were added. For 60 years, the Batchelder family continued the operation. They misnamed the lodge, however, mistaking silver poplar trees on the property for what they thought were silver maples. Guest rooms are decorated with many of the inn's original furnishings, and the new innkeepers have carefully restored the rooms and added several bathrooms. A screened-in porch surrounds two sides of the house. Three of the cottages include working fireplaces and one is handicap accessible.
Historic Interest: The Quechee Gorge, Maple Grove Maple Museum, Billings Farm & Museum and the Saint Gauden's National Historic Site are among the area's historic sites.
Innkeeper(s): Scott & Sharon Wright. $69-99. 16 rooms, 14 with PB, 3 with FP and 8 cottages. Breakfast included in rates. Types of meals: Cont. Beds: KQDT. TV, reading lamp, refrigerator, clock radio and desk in room. VCR, copier, bicycles, parlor games, telephone and fireplace on premises. Limited handicap access. Small meetings and family reunions hosted. Antiquing, cross-country skiing, downhill skiing, fishing, live theater, parks, shopping and water sports nearby.
Publicity: *Boston Globe, Vermont Country Sampler, Travel Holiday, Travel America* and *New York Times.*

"Your gracious hospitality and attractive home all add up to a pleasant experience."

Greensboro — C5

Highland Lodge

1608 Craftsbury Road
Greensboro, VT 05841-8085
(802)533-2647 Fax:(802)533-7494

Circa 1865. With a private beach and 120 acres to enjoy, guests rarely have trouble finding a way to pass the time at this lodge. The lodge is located in a mid-19th-century farmhouse, and visitors either room here in country guest rooms or in a collection of cottages. The cottages have from one to three bedrooms, a living room, bathroom and a porch. All guests are welcome to use the lodge's common areas or simply relax on the porch, but there's sailing, swimming, fishing, boating and nature trails. In the winter, the lodge grooms 60 kilometers of cross-country ski trails and has a ski shop renting all the necessary gear. The breakfast choices include French toast, waffles, pancakes, eggs or muffins, and at dinner, guests choose from four entrees accompanied by salad, homemade bread and dessert.
Historic Interest: Greensboro Historical Society.
Innkeeper(s): Wilhelmina & David Smith. $230-300. 11 cottages with PB. Breakfast and dinner included in rates. Types of meals: Full bkfst, early coffee/tea, lunch, picnic lunch and afternoon tea. Restaurant on premises. Beds: QDT. Reading lamp and refrigerator in room. Fax, copier, swimming, bicycles, tennis, library, child care, parlor games, telephone, fireplace, sailing, cross-country skiing and Internet access on premises. Limited handicap access.

Weddings, small meetings, family reunions and seminars hosted. Antiquing, downhill skiing, golf, live theater and nature trail nearby.

Publicity: *New England Skiers Guide, Vermont Magazine, Hardwick Gazette, Rural New England Magazine, Better Homes & Gardens, Providence Sunday Journal, Yankee, Vermont Life and US Air Attache.*

"We had a great time last weekend and enjoyed everything we did— hiking, climbing, swimming, canoeing and eating."

Hartford   H5

House of Seven Gables Inn

1625 Maple Street Box 526
Hartford, VT 05047
(802)295-1200 (800)947-1200 Fax:(802)295-8949
E-mail: house7gables@email.com

Circa 1891. This historic inn is said to have been one of the first homes in Hartford to have electricity. It also served as the Bible Institute of New England and later as a restaurant bearing the name the inn retains today. Its unique architecture, a blend of Georgian, Gothic Revival and Stick Victorian, only adds to its charm. Victorian touches are found throughout the guest rooms, each featuring its own unique decor, and including brass, highback and poster beds. Luscious homemade breakfasts sometimes feature apple-filled pancakes or maple-cured bacon. Guests enjoy use of an outdoor pool, recreation room and a "rain forest" Jacuzzi room. Dartmouth College is four miles to the east.

Historic Interest: Listed in the National Register.
Innkeeper(s): Lani & Kathy Janisse. $95-150. Types of meals: Early coffee/tea. VCR, reading lamp, ceiling fan, clock radio, turn-down service and desk in room. Swimming, pet boarding, telephone, fireplace, grand piano, recreation room and Jacuzzi room on premises. Weddings, small meetings and seminars hosted. Antiquing, cross-country skiing, downhill skiing, live theater, shopping, sporting events, sleigh rides and skating nearby.

Hyde Park   C4

Governor's House in Hyde Park

100 Main St
Hyde Park, VT 05655
(802)888-6888 (866)800-6888
E-mail: info@OneHundredMain.com
Web: www.OneHundredMain.com

Circa 1893. High on a bluff, Governor Carroll Page built this historic 1893 copy of a 1759 Georgian mansion. He added gas lighting, made-to-order mirrored mantlepieces and an Italian marble foyer. Completely restored, retaining many original details as well as elegant period Georgian and Victorian decor, this seven-acre estate is the centerpiece of the quiet village. Play croquet on the landscaped lawn. Browse through videos and books in the library or choose from an assortment of games and toys for all ages. Relax in the parlor, sip an afternoon beverage in the portico or daydream in a cozy reading nook with panoramic mountain view. Sleep in a sleigh bed by a gas fireplace, soak in a whirlpool or antique clawfoot tub in one of the tastefully furnished guest bedrooms. Take in the majestic vistas while enjoying a multi-course breakfast served in the dining room.

Historic Interest: Built for Carroll Page in 1893 while he was governor of Vermont. Copy of 1759 Longfellow House in Cambridge, Mass. Restored and decorated in 2001 with period appropriate furnishings. Some appropriate historic memorabilia on display.
Innkeeper(s): Suzanne Boden. $110-185. 7 rooms, 5 with PB, 5 with FP. Breakfast and snacks/refreshments included in rates. Types of meals: Full gourmet bkfst, veg bkfst, gourmet lunch, picnic lunch, afternoon tea, gourmet dinner and room service. Beds: QDT. Modem hook-up, data port, cable TV,

VCR, reading lamp, CD player, ceiling fan, clock radio, telephone, turn-down service, desk, fireplace, breakfast hot chocolate at bedtime and Ben & Jerry's ice cream in room. Library, parlor games, fireplace, gift shop, video library, tournament croquet and full English afternoon tea on premises. Weddings, small meetings and family reunions hosted. Antiquing, art galleries, bicycling, canoeing/kayaking, cross-country skiing, downhill skiing, fishing, golf, hiking, horseback riding, live theater, shopping, water sports and wineries nearby.

Jeffersonville   C3

Jefferson House

PO Box 288, 71 Main St
Jeffersonville, VT 05464-0288
(802)644-2030 (800)253-9630 Fax:(802)644-6306
E-mail: jeffersonhouse@pwshift.com
Web: www.jeffersonhouseb-b.com

Circa 1800. Three comfortable guest rooms, decorated in a country Victorian style, are the offerings at this turn-of-the-century home. As one might expect, pancakes topped with Vermont maple syrup are often a staple at the breakfast table, accompanied by savory items such as smoked bacon. Each season brings a new activity to this scenic area. In the winter, it's just a few minutes to Smugglers' Notch ski area, and Stowe isn't far. Biking or hiking to the top of Mt. Mansfield are popular summer activities.

Innkeeper(s): Debbi Brundage. $60-110. 4 rooms with PB and 1 suite. Breakfast and snacks/refreshments included in rates. Types of meals: Full gourmet bkfst, veg bkfst, early coffee/tea, picnic lunch and dinner. Beds: KQDT. Data port, cable TV, reading lamp, refrigerator, snack bar, clock radio, telephone, desk, fireplace and alarm clock in room. Air conditioning. Fax, copier, library, pet boarding, child care, parlor games, laundry facility and gift shop on premises. Weddings, small meetings and family reunions hosted. Amusement parks, antiquing, art galleries, beach, bicycling, canoeing/kayaking, cross-country skiing, downhill skiing, fishing, golf, hiking, horseback riding, live theater, museums, parks, shopping, tennis, water sports and wineries nearby.

Nye's Green Valley Farm B&B

8976 Rt 15W
Jeffersonville, VT 05464
(802)644-1984
E-mail: nyesgvf@yahoo.com
Web: www.nyesgreenvalleyfarm.com

Circa 1811. Built as a stagecoach tavern in 1811, this Colonial brick home on four acres of farmland has welcomed visitors for nearly two centuries. Now owned by the fourth generation of Nyes, this classic bed & breakfast has been lovingly restored and tastefully decorated with early Vermont antiques. Gather by one of the two fireplaces, watch a video, listen to a CD or play the piano in one of the many common rooms. Air-conditioned guest bedrooms are comfortable and inviting. After a hearty country breakfast stroll the flower-filled grounds or pet the sheep, goats and llamas in the pasture. Cool off with a swim in the pond and in the evening sit by a summer campfire.

Historic Interest: The house was built as a stagecoach tavern in 1811 and purchased by the owner's grandfather in 1867. It was farmed by the Nye family until 1874. It may have been part of the underground railroad.
Innkeeper(s): David Lane and Marsha Nye Lane. $75-95. 3 rooms, 1 with PB. Breakfast, afternoon tea and snacks/refreshments included in rates. Types of meals: Country bkfst, veg bkfst and early coffee/tea. Beds: QD. Cable TV, VCR, reading lamp and clock radio in room. Central air. Telephone, pond for swimming, farm roads for walking and sheep, goats and llamas for petting on premises. Small meetings and family reunions hosted. Antiquing, art galleries, bicycling, canoeing/kayaking, cross-country skiing, downhill skiing, fishing, golf, hiking, horseback riding, museums, parks, shopping, tennis and wineries nearby.

Jericho C3

Sinclair Inn B&B

389 Vermont Route 15
Jericho, VT 05465
(802)899-2234 (800)433-4658 Fax:(802)899-2007
E-mail: Innkeeper@sinclairinnbb.com
Web: www.sinclairinnbb.com

Circa 1890. Enjoy the ambiance of a bygone era in this fully restored Queen Anne Victorian inn. Built by Edward Sinclair to showcase his craftsmanship, the inn's stained glass, turrets, fretwork, wainscoting and woodwork retain the home's original splendor. Guests have been welcome since the late 1800s when it was first opened to travelers. Sally and Bruce continue that tradition, offering a complimentary beverage, homemade sweets and information on

local events. Relax by a cozy fire in the living room before retiring to a guest bedroom with modern amenities, comfortable bed and sitting chairs. A generous four-course breakfast is made from scratch. The grounds include surrounding trees, a river, extensive gardens and a pond with a waterfall. Gaze at the mountains from an Adirondack chair or wrought iron lawn furniture.
Historic Interest: Old Red Grist Mill in Jericho Village (3 miles), historical houses, barns, covered bridges (nearby).
Innkeeper(s): Sally Gilbert-Smith. $100-160. 6 rooms with PB. Breakfast and snacks/refreshments included in rates. Types of meals: Full bkfst and early coffee/tea. Beds: KQT. Air conditioning. Fax, copier, data port and one handicap equipped room on premises. Limited handicap access. Antiquing, cross-country skiing, downhill skiing, fishing, live theater, parks, shopping, sporting events and water sports nearby.
Publicity: *Burlington Free Press, Champlain Valley Business News, Emerging Horizons and Arrington's Book of Lists 2002 & 2003.*

Killington G3

The Vermont Inn

Rt 4
Killington, VT 05751
(802)775-0708 (800)541-7795 Fax:(802)773-5810
E-mail: relax@vermontinn.com
Web: www.vermontinn.com

Circa 1840. Surrounded by mountain views, this rambling red and white farmhouse has provided lodging and superb cuisine for many years. Exposed beams add to the atmosphere in the living and game rooms. The award-winning dining room provides candlelight tables beside a huge fieldstone fireplace.
Historic Interest: Calvin Coolidge birthplace and Bennington, Vt., Civil War exhibits.
Innkeeper(s): Megan & Greg Smith.
$50-185. 18 rooms with PB, 5 with FP, 2 with HT. Breakfast and afternoon tea included in rates. Types of meals: Full bkfst, early coffee/tea and gourmet dinner. Beds: QDT. Ceiling fan, clock radio, two with Jacuzzi tub and 5 with fireplace in room. Air conditioning. VCR, fax, copier, spa, swimming, sauna, tennis, library, parlor games, telephone, fireplace and screened porch on premises. Limited handicap access. Weddings, small meetings, family reunions and seminars hosted. Antiquing, cross-country skiing, downhill skiing, fishing, live theater, parks, shopping and water sports nearby.
Publicity: *New York Daily News, New Jersey Star Leader, Rutland Business Journal, Bridgeport Post Telegram, New York Times, Boston, Vermont and Asbury Park Press.*

"We had a wonderful time. The inn is breathtaking. Hope to be back."

Landgrove J3

Landgrove Inn

132 Landgrove Rd
Landgrove, VT 05148
(802)824-6673 (800)669-8466 Fax:(802)824-6790
E-mail: vtinn@sover.net
Web: www.landgroveinn.com

Circa 1810. This rambling inn is located along a country lane in the valley of Landgrove in the Green Mountain National Forest. Breakfast and dinner are served in the newly renovated and stenciled dining room. Evening sleigh or hay rides often are arranged. Or guests can relax in the gathering room with fireplace and pub. Rooms vary in style and bedding arrangements, including some newly decorated rooms with country decor, so inquire when making your reservation.

Historic Interest: Hildene, Robert Todd Lincoln's Georgian Revival mansion is nearby, as is the Norman Rockwell Museum.
Innkeeper(s): Tom & Maureen Checchia. $95-235. 18 rooms, 16 with PB and 1 conference room. Breakfast included in rates. Types of meals: Full bkfst, afternoon tea and dinner. Restaurant on premises. Beds: KQD. Reading lamp and some with fireplace and hot air massage tub in room. VCR, fax, copier, tennis, parlor games, telephone, fireplace, heated pool, fishing pond and hiking trails on premises. Weddings, small meetings, family reunions and seminars hosted. Antiquing, cross-country skiing, downhill skiing, fishing, live theater, parks and shopping nearby.

"A true country inn with great food — we'll be back."

Lower Waterford D6

Rabbit Hill Inn

Lower Waterford Rd
Lower Waterford, VT 05848
(802)748-5168 (800)762-8669 Fax:(802)748-8342

Circa 1795. Above the Connecticut River overlooking the White Mountains, Samuel Hodby opened this tavern and provided a general store and inn to travelers. As many as 100 horse teams traveled by the inn each day. The ballroom, constructed in 1855, was supported by bent-wood construction giving the dance floor a spring effect. The classic Greek Revival exterior features solid pine Doric columns. Romance abounds in every nook and cranny. Rooms are

decorated to the hilt with beautiful furnishings and linens. The Loft room, which overlooks the garden, includes cathedral ceilings and a hidden staircase. The Jonathan Commings Suite offers two fireplaces, a whirlpool and a mountain view from its third-story private porch. Turndown service and afternoon tea are only a couple of the amenities. Glorious breakfasts and gourmet, five-course, candlelit dinners add to a memorable stay.
Historic Interest: There are several historic churches in the area. The Fairbanks Museum, Planetarium and Art Gallery is 10 minutes away, while the Robert Frost Museum is a 25-minute drive.
Innkeeper(s): Brian & Leslie Mulcahy. $275-435. 19 rooms with PB, 15 with FP. Breakfast, afternoon tea and dinner included in rates. Types of meals: Full bkfst, early coffee/tea and picnic lunch. Beds: KQ. Nine rooms with whirlpool tubs for two in room. Fax, copier and five-course dinners available on premises. Antiquing, bicycling, canoeing/kayaking, cross-country ski-

ing, downhill skiing, fishing, golf, hiking, horseback riding, parks, shopping, sleigh rides and massage services nearby.

Publicity: *New York Times, Los Angeles Herald Examiner, Today Show, Innsider, USA Today, Boston, Yankee, Bridal Guide, For the Bride, Country Living, Ski Magazine, National Geographic Traveler, NBC Today, Inn Country USA and Great Country Inns.*

"It is not often that one experiences one's vision of a tranquil, beautiful step back in time. This is such an experience. Everyone was so accommodating and gracious."

Ludlow   I4

The Combes Family Inn

953 E Lake Rd
Ludlow, VT 05149-9532
(802)228-8799 (800)822-8799 Fax:(802)228-8704
E-mail: billcfi@tds.net
Web: www.combesfamilyinn.com

Circa 1891. For many years this dairy farm supplied milk to the local communities, and maple syrup was produced from the sugar bushes. Now the 50 acres feature a renovated family-friendly farmhouse surrounded by meadows of wildflowers, apple trees, perennials and herb gardens. Furnished with turn-of-the-century oak, the lounge features barnboard paneling and a fireplace. Large, comfortable guest bedrooms and suites are decorated in early American country style. Okemo Mountain is seen from the bay window of the dining room, which features exposed beams. The rural setting and scenic beauty instills a return to carefree living. Children and the young at heart will enjoy games, videos and good food. Relax on the front porch, visit the neighbor's llamas or explore nearby lakes. Ask about special ski and seasonal packages.

Innkeeper(s): Ruth & Bill Combes. $65-160. 11 rooms with PB and 3 suites. Breakfast included in rates. Types of meals: Country bkfst, veg bkfst, early coffee/tea, dinner and room service. Beds: QDT. Reading lamp, clock radio and desk in room. Air conditioning. TV, VCR, fax, copier, library, parlor games, telephone and fireplace on premises. Weddings, small meetings and family reunions hosted. Antiquing, art galleries, bicycling, canoeing/kayaking, cross-country skiing, downhill skiing, fishing, golf, hiking, horseback riding, live theater, museums, parks, shopping, tennis and water sports nearby.

The Governor's Inn

86 Main St
Ludlow, VT 05149-1113
(802)228-8830 (800)GOVERNOR
E-mail: info@thegovernorsinn.com
Web: www.thegovernorsinn.com

Circa 1890. Governor Stickney built this house for his bride, Elizabeth Lincoln, and it retains the intimate feeling of an elegant country house furnished in Victorian fashion. Extraordinary details include slate fireplaces, polished woodwork and stained-glass windows that reside well with a tea cart and silver tea service, replica 1898 telephone, heirloom china, silver, crystal and oil lanterns on the dinner tables. Some of the antique-filled bed chambers boast gas fireplaces or Vermont Castings gas stoves, and all enhance the romantic ambiance. Enjoy a full hot breakfast with a coffee pot on each well-set table. Afternoon tea and turndown service add to the inn's gracious hospitality. Multi-course gourmet dinners and picnics are also offered. Discover Vermont from this delightful location.

Innkeeper(s): Cathy & Jim Kubec. $109-329. 8 rooms with PB, 5 with FP and 1 suite. Breakfast and afternoon tea included in rates. Types of meals: Full gourmet bkfst, picnic lunch and gourmet dinner. Beds: KQDT. Culinary Magic Seminars on premises. Antiquing, bicycling, canoeing/kayaking, cross-country skiing, downhill skiing, fishing, golf, hiking, horseback riding, live theater, parks,

shopping, historical sites, priory, sleigh rides and snowmobiling nearby.
Publicity: *Select Registry, Yankee Travel Guide (Editor's Pick) and earned Mobil 4-star rating 13 consecutive years.*

Lyndon   C6

Branch Brook B&B

PO Box 217
Lyndon, VT 05849-0217
(802)626-8316 (800)572-7712

Circa 1850. Filled with charm, this Federal home is accented with exposed beams and antique furnishings. The pleasant atmosphere is enhanced by friendly service. Fine country accommodations are reflected in the comfortable guest bedrooms. Order breakfast from a selection of fresh fruit, juices, locally-made yogurt, farm fresh eggs, bacon or sausage and French toast or pancakes topped with pure Vermont maple syrup. The made-to-please meal is prepared on an English AGA Cooker. Explore the nearby lakes and rivers or enjoy winter skiing. Antique shops, flea markets and auctions are in the area.

Innkeeper(s): Ann Tolman. $72-94. 5 rooms, 3 with PB. Breakfast included in rates. Types of meals: Full bkfst and early coffee/tea. Beds: KQT. Telephone in room. VCR, copier and library on premises. Weddings, small meetings and family reunions hosted. Antiquing, cross-country skiing, downhill skiing, fishing, golf, parks, shopping, water sports and five covered bridges nearby.

Lyndonville   C6

The Wildflower Inn

2059 Darling Hill Rd
Lyndonville, VT 05851
(802)626-8310 Fax:(802)626-3039
E-mail: info@wildflowerinn.com
Web: www.wildflowerinn.com

Circa 1796. Located on 500 scenic acres in northeast Vermont, this farmhouse is situated on a hillside providing pristine countryside views. Guests can stay in either the farmhouse or in the carriage barn. The School House cottage, once the former school building, offers a private deck and a two-person Jacuzzi. The Grand Meadow is a two-bedroom suite with its own living room, dining table, two baths and a washer and dryer. A full country breakfast is served with menu items such as blueberry-baked goods, fresh eggs and ham and teddy bear pancakes. Cross-country skiing is popular and other activities include donning snowshoes and enjoying the trails, taking horse-drawn sleigh rides or hay rides, skating and sledding down the hill. There's a petting barn and a children's playroom, and the home base for the Vermont's Children's Theatre is here.

Innkeeper(s): James & Mary O'Reilly. $85-230. 21 rooms with PB and 1 conference room. Types of meals: Full bkfst. Restaurant on premises. Spa, swimming, sauna, parlor games and pool on premises.
Publicity: *The Caledonian-Record.*

"Every aspect of our short stay was absolute perfection."

Manchester   J2

1811 House

Historic Rt 7A, PO Box 39
Manchester, VT 05254
(802)362-1811 (800)432-1811 Fax:(802)362-2443
E-mail: house1811@adelphia.net
Web: www.1811house.com

Circa 1775. Since 1811, the historic Lincoln Home has been operated as an inn, except for one time. It was the private resi-

dence of Mary Lincoln Isham, granddaughter of President Lincoln. It has been authentically restored to the Federal period with antiques and canopy beds. The gardens look out over a golf course, and it's just a short walk to tennis or swimming.
Historic Interest: Owned by Mary Lincoln Isham (granddaughter of Abraham Lincoln) for 30 years.
Innkeeper(s): Bruce & Marnie Duff, Cathy & Jorge Veleta. $140-280. 13 rooms, 11 with PB, 7 with FP and 2 suites. Breakfast included in rates. Types of meals: Full gourmet bkfst, early coffee/tea and afternoon tea. Beds: KQ. Reading lamp in room. Air conditioning. TV, VCR, fax, library, parlor games, telephone, fireplace and laundry facility on premises. Antiquing, art galleries, bicycling, canoeing/kayaking, cross-country skiing, downhill skiing, fishing, golf, hiking, horseback riding, live theater, museums, shopping and tennis nearby.
Publicity: *New York.*

Manchester Highlands Inn

216 Highland Ave, Box 1754
Manchester, VT 05255
(802)362-4565 (800)743-4565 Fax:(802)362-4028
E-mail: relax@highlandsinn.com
Web: www.highlandsinn.com

Circa 1898. This Queen Anne Victorian mansion sits proudly on the crest of a hill overlooking the village. From the three-story turret, guests can look out over Mt. Equinox, the Green Mountains and the valley below. Feather beds and down comforters adorn the beds in the guest rooms. Many with canopy beds and fireplaces. A game room with billiards and a stone fireplace are popular in winter, while summertime guests enjoy the outdoor pool, croquet lawn and veranda. Gourmet country breakfasts and home-baked afternoon snacks are served.

Historic Interest: Hildene, summer home of Robert Todd Lincoln (1 mile), Bennington Monument (20 miles), Southern Vermont Arts Center (1 mile). Innkeeper(s): Patricia & Robert Eichorn. $110-185. 15 rooms with PB. Breakfast and afternoon tea included in rates. Types of meals: Full gourmet bkfst. Beds: KQDT. Reading lamp, clock radio and several rooms with gas fireplaces in room. Air conditioning. TV, VCR, fax, swimming, library, parlor games, telephone, fireplace, game room, guest bar, bottomless cookie jar and Saturday wine & hors d'oeuvres on premises. Weddings, small meetings, family reunions and seminars hosted. Antiquing, bicycling, canoeing/kayaking, cross-country skiing, downhill skiing, fishing, golf, hiking, horseback riding, live theater, parks, shopping, ice skating and sleigh rides nearby.
Publicity: *Bennington Banner, Gourmet, Toronto Sun, Vermont Magazine, Asbury Park Press, Vermont Weathervane, Yankee Traveler, Boston Globe, Cat Fanciers Magazine, NY Times and Miami Herald.*

"We couldn't believe such a place existed. Now, we can't wait to come again."

The Reluctant Panther Inn & Restaurant

39 West Rd
Manchester, VT 05254
(802)362-2568 (800)822-2331 Fax:(802)362-2586
E-mail: stay@reluctantpanther.com
Web: www.reluctantpanther.com

Circa 1850. Designed for romance, this elegant country inn sits at the base of Mount Equinox in the Manchester Village Historic District. Exquisite gardens and patios offer stunning mountain views. The experienced owners, fluent in four languages, and the friendly staff extend attentive service to welcome and pamper. Three historic buildings feature luxurious suites and upscale guest bedrooms with a sophisticated European flair. Many rooms boast at least one wood-burning or

gas log fireplace. Other amenities include fresh flowers, Jacuzzi tubs for two, plush linens, antiques and private porches. A sumptuous three-course breakfast is served to Inn guests. Considered a truly memorable and delectable dining experience, European specialties complemented by a fine wine list are served in the main dining room by the fieldstone fireplace. Enjoy drinks on the patio or in the intimate Panther Bar.
Innkeeper(s): Robert & Maye Bachofen. $139-439. 21 rooms with PB, 15 with FP and 11 suites. Breakfast included in rates. Types of meals: Full gourmet bkfst and gourmet dinner. Restaurant on premises. Beds: KQT. Data port, cable TV, reading lamp, clock radio, telephone, coffeemaker, desk, fireplace, 2-person Jacuzzi tub, hair dryer and central air or window unit in room. Fax, copier and parlor games on premises. Family reunions hosted. Antiquing, art galleries, bicycling, canoeing/kayaking, cross-country skiing, downhill skiing, fishing, golf, hiking, horseback riding, live theater, museums, parks, shopping and tennis nearby.
Publicity: *New York Times, Gourmet, Country Inns and CNN.*

"We enjoyed our stay so much that now we want to make it our yearly romantic getaway."

Village Country Inn

PO Box 408, Rt 7A
Manchester, VT 05254-0408
(802)362-1792 (800)370-0300 Fax:(802)362-7238
E-mail: vci@vermontel.net
Web: www.villagecountryinn.com

Circa 1889. Townsfolk refer to the Village Country Inn as the old summer house of the Kellogg cereal family. A Grecian-columned porch spans 100 feet across the front of the house and is filled with chintz-covered rockers and pots of flowers. Decorated in a French-country style, rooms feature French lace and antiques. Dinner is served in a garden dining room, which overlooks marble terraces and fountains.
Historic Interest: Robert Todd Lincoln's Hildene (2 miles), Norman Rockwell Museum (10 minutes).
Innkeeper(s): Anne & Jay Degen.
$129-345. 31 rooms, 30 with PB and 12 suites. Beds: KQ. Telephone and suites with cable TV in room. Air conditioning. Fax on premises. Weddings, small meetings, family reunions and seminars hosted. Antiquing, canoeing/kayaking, cross-country skiing, downhill skiing, fishing, live theater, shopping, sleigh rides, sledding, ice skating, snowmobiling, tubing and Manchester Music Festival nearby.
Publicity: *Country Inns, Albany Times Union, Gourmet, Vacations, USA Today, Country Decorating Ideas, Victorian, Country Living, Garden Designs, Bedrooms and Baths, Romantic Homes, Flowers and Gardens and ABC-TV.*

"Absolutely charming. So much attention to detail. We loved it."

Wilburton Inn

PO Box 468
Manchester, VT 05254-0468
(802)362-2500 (800)648-4944 Fax:(802)362-1107
E-mail: wilbuinn@sover.net
Web: www.wilburton.com

Circa 1902. Shaded by tall maples, this three-story brick mansion sits high on a hill overlooking the Battenkill Valley, which is set against a majestic mountain backdrop. In addition to the mansion, the inn offers four villas and a five-bedroom reunion house. Carved moldings, mahogany paneling, Oriental carpets and leaded-glass windows are complemented by carefully chosen antiques.

The inn's 20 acres provide three tennis courts, a pool, green lawns, sculpture gardens and panoramic views. Country weddings are a Wilburton Inn's specialty. Gourmet dining is served in the billiard room with European ambiance. Gleneagles golf courses provide the inn with golf privileges.

Historic Interest: The inn was built in 1902 as a summer estate for a friend of Robert Todd Lincoln.
Innkeeper(s): Georgette Levis. $105-235. 35 rooms, 8 with FP and 1 conference room. Breakfast included in rates. Types of meals: Full gourmet bkfst, afternoon tea, gourmet dinner and room service. Restaurant on premises. Beds: KQ. TV in room. Air conditioning. Fax, copier, parlor games and telephone on premises. Antiquing, cross-country skiing, downhill skiing, fishing, golf, live theater and water sports nearby.
Publicity: *Great Escapes TV, Travelhost, Getaways For Gourmets, Country Inns, Bed & Breakfast, Gourmet, Best Places to Stay In New England and New York Times July 2002.*

"Simply splendid! Peaceful, beautiful, elegant. Ambiance & ambiance!"

Manchester Center   J2

The Inn at Ormsby Hill

1842 Main St
Manchester Center, VT 05255-9518
(802)362-1163 (800)670-2841 Fax:(802)362-5176
E-mail: stay@ormsbyhill.com
Web: www.ormsbyhill.com

Circa 1764. During the Revolutionary War, hero Ethan Allen reportedly hid out in the smoke room at this Federal-style mansion. Robert Todd Lincoln and President Taft are among the other notable guests at this historic treasure. The town's first jail cell still exists in the inn's basement, complete with steel bars and the marble slab where prisoners slept. The inn offers beautiful views of the nearby Green

Mountains. Inside, guests will marvel at the inn's conservatory, which was built to resemble a ship and looks out to the gardens and the mountains. Antique-filled rooms offer four-poster or canopy beds decked in fine linens. All rooms include fireplaces and two-person whirlpool tubs. Four of the rooms include steam saunas for two. Innkeeper Chris Sprague's culinary talents, in addition to writing a cookbook, have been heralded in such publications as Food & Wine, Yankee and Colonial Homes. Vermont is bustling with activities, dozens of which are just a short drive from the inn.

Historic Interest: The adjoining estate to the inn, which itself is listed in the Vermont Register of Historic Places, was home to Robert Todd Lincoln, the son of Abraham Lincoln.
Innkeeper(s): Ted & Chris Sprague. $190-370. 10 rooms with PB, 10 with FP. Breakfast and afternoon tea included in rates. Beds: KQ. Reading lamp, clock radio and two-person whirlpool in room. Air conditioning. Fax, library, parlor games and telephone on premises. Antiquing, cross-country skiing, downhill skiing, fishing, live theater and hiking nearby.
Publicity: *Gourmet, Getaways for Gourmets, Country Inns, Discerning Traveler, Colonial Homes, Yankee Traveler and Boston Globe.*

"After 17 years of visiting B&Bs in Vermont, we can truly say you are the best. On a scale of 1-10, you are a 12."

River Meadow Farm

PO Box 822
Manchester Center, VT 05255-0822
(802)362-1602

Circa 1797. The oldest portion of this New England farmhouse was built in the late 18th century, and in keeping with

that era, Colonial-style furnishings decorate the interior. During one part of its history, the home served as Manchester Poor Farm. The living room with its grand piano and fireplace is an ideal place for those seeking relaxation. At breakfast, fresh fruit, coffee, teas and juice accompany traditional entrees such as eggs and bacon or pancakes topped with blueberries. There are 90 acres to explore at this farm, some of which border the Battenkill River.

Historic Interest: Hildene, the summer home of Robert Todd Lincoln, can be seen on a hill on the farm. The 1906 home is open for tours from May to October.
Innkeeper(s): Patricia J. Dupree. $70. 5 rooms. Breakfast included in rates. Types of meals: Full bkfst. Beds: DT. Reading lamp in room. VCR, library, telephone and fireplace on premises. Antiquing, cross-country skiing, downhill skiing, fishing, live theater, parks, shopping and water sports nearby.

"We really loved our stay and are planning to return as soon as possible."

Mendon   H3

Red Clover Inn

7 Woodward Rd
Mendon, VT 05701
(802)775-2290 (800)752-0571 Fax:(802)773-0594
E-mail: innkeepers@redcloverinn.com
Web: www.redcloverinn.com

Circa 1840. Ideal for a romantic getaway or a mountain vacation, this relaxing country inn was built by General John Woodward in 1840 as a private retreat. Exposed wood beams and a fieldstone fireplace in the large Keeping Room accent the warm and inviting atmosphere. Deluxe guest bedrooms in the Main House and the Carriage House offer elegant, air-conditioned comfort, picturesque views and an assortment of amenities. Many include a whirlpool tub for two and a fireplace. The inn's creative chef creates sumptuous breakfasts and exquisite cuisine for dinner with an award-winning wine list. Hike the Appalachian Trail before a refreshing swim in the pool. Located in the Green Mountains, Killington Ski Resort is only five miles away.
Innkeeper(s): Melinda Davis, Dave & Mary Strelecki. $145-350. 14 rooms with PB, 6 with FP. Breakfast included in rates. Types of meals: Country bkfst and dinner. Restaurant on premises. Beds: KQ. TV, VCR, ceiling fan, hot tub/spa and fireplace in room. Air conditioning. Fax, copier, parlor games, gift shop and fine dining restaurant on premises. Weddings, small meetings, family reunions and seminars hosted. Antiquing, art galleries, bicycling, canoeing/kayaking, cross-country skiing, downhill skiing, fishing, golf, hiking, horseback riding, live theater, museums, parks and shopping nearby.
Publicity: *The Discerning Traveler - Romantic Hideaways.*

Middlebury   F2

Middlebury Inn

14 Courthouse Sq
Middlebury, VT 05753
(802)388-4961 (800)842-4666 Fax:(802)388-4563
E-mail: midinnvt@sover.net
Web: www.middleburyinn.com

Circa 1827. This red brick, white-shuttered inn that has hosted weary travelers for many generations, is celebrating its 176th-year anniversary this year. Guests can choose from several options when selecting a room. The grounds include three different properties aside from the Middlebury Inn, which is an amazing structure to behold. The Porter Mansion boasts a porch with wicker furnishings, marble fireplaces and a curving staircase. At the Middlebury Inn, guests enjoy delectable afternoon

teas on the veranda while viewing the Village Greens. The innkeepers include plenty of special touches such as stocking rooms with books, bath soaps and lotions.

Complimentary continental breakfast and afternoon tea is served daily. The inn offers ski and bicycle storage and will help guests make arrangements for walking tours, a popular activity.

Historic Interest: The Middlebury Inn is a community landmark, listed in the National Register, and in the center of Middlebury's historic district, which offers 155 architectural gems within walking distance. Vermont State Craft Center, museums and a waterfall are nearby.

Innkeeper(s): Emanuel Family. $88-395. 75 rooms with PB and 3 conference rooms. Breakfast and afternoon tea included in rates. Types of meals: Cont, early coffee/tea, picnic lunch and dinner. Restaurant on premises. Beds: KQDT. Cable TV, refrigerator, clock radio, telephone, desk, hair dryers in bathroom and heat units in room. Air conditioning. TV, VCR, fax, copier and fireplace on premises. Limited handicap access. Small meetings, family reunions and seminars hosted. Antiquing, cross-country skiing, downhill skiing, fishing, parks, shopping, sporting events, water sports and guest privileges to nearby fitness center nearby.

Publicity: *Vermont, Country Inns, Chicago Tribune, Glamour, Burlington Free Press and New York Times.*

Montgomery   B4

Black Lantern Inn

Rt 118
Montgomery, VT 05470
(802)326-4507 (800)255-8661 Fax:(802)326-2024
E-mail: blantern@together.net
Web: www.blacklantern.com

Circa 1803. Originally this brick inn and restaurant served as a stagecoach stop. Carefully decorated throughout, the gracious inn's ambiance is enhanced by Vermont antiques. Some of the suites feature fireplaces and whirlpool tubs. The inn's restaurant offers a variety of entrees such as filet mignon, roast duck and rack of lamb. Seafood and vegetarian entrees are available as well. A hot tub is popular on starry nights. A few minutes away, ride the tramway to the top of Jay Peak for novice and expert skiers. Montgomery Village is known for its seven covered bridges. Hike the Long Trail, fish or mountain bike.

Innkeeper(s): Deb & Bob Winders. $93-176. 8 rooms with PB and 7 suites. Breakfast included in rates. Types of meals: Full bkfst and gourmet dinner. Restaurant on premises. Beds: KQDT. TV, VCR, reading lamp and ceiling fan in room. Fax, telephone and fireplace on premises. Weddings, small meetings, family reunions and seminars hosted. Antiquing, cross-country skiing, downhill skiing and fishing nearby.

Publicity: *Burlington Free Press, Los Angeles Times, Bon Appetit, Ottawa Citizen and Travel - CJCF Montreal.*

"...one of the four or five great meals of your life."-Jay Stone, Ottawa Citizen

Montgomery Center   B4

The Inn On Trout River

Main St, PO Box 76
Montgomery Center, VT 05471-0076
(802)326-4391 (800)338-7049
E-mail: info@troutinn.com
Web: www.troutinn.com

Circa 1895. Both a fine country inn and restaurant, The Inn on Trout River, offers an ideal location for enjoying Vermont's Jay Peak region and the historic district of Montgomery Center. Antiques and comfortable furnishings decorate the inn. Feather pillows and

down comforters top the queen-size beds. The innkeepers offer adventure packages and new packages are added throughout the year. The inn's location provides close access to downhill and cross-country ski areas, snowmobiling,

snowshoeing, hiking, biking, golf courses, swimming, fishing and hunting. Museums, shops, antique stores and auctions are other amusements. The area boasts seven covered bridges and endless acres of scenery perfect for shutterbugs and nature lovers alike.

Historic Interest: Covered bridges in Montgomery and within an hour circumference.

Innkeeper(s): Michael & Lee Forman. $58-125. 10 rooms with PB, 1 with FP and 1 suite. Breakfast included in rates. Types of meals: Full bkfst and gourmet dinner. Restaurant on premises. Beds: KQT. Antiquing, bicycling, cross-country skiing, downhill skiing, fishing, golf, hiking, museums, parks, water sports, snowmobiling, snowshoeing and snowboarding nearby.

Publicity: *Caledonia-Record, Vermont Magazine, Cycle Canada Magazine and Yankee Magazine.*

"A superb place to stay."

Montpelier   E4

Betsy's B&B

74 E State St
Montpelier, VT 05602-3112
(802)229-0466 Fax:(802)229-5412
E-mail: BetsysBnB@adelphia.net
Web: www.BetsysBnB.com

Circa 1895. Within walking distance of downtown and located in the state's largest historic preservation district, this Queen Anne Victorian with romantic turret and carriage house features lavish Victorian antiques throughout its interior. Bay windows, carved woodwork, high ceilings, lace curtains and wood floors add to the authenticity. The full breakfast varies in content but not quality, and guest favorites include orange pancakes.

Innkeeper(s): Jon & Betsy Anderson. $65-105. 12 rooms with PB. Breakfast included in rates. Types of meals: Full bkfst. Beds: QDT. Cable TV, reading lamp, clock radio, telephone and desk in room. VCR, fax, parlor games, fireplace, laundry facility and refrigerator on premises. Antiquing, cross-country skiing, downhill skiing, fishing, live theater, parks, shopping and water sports nearby.

The Inn at Montpelier

147 Main St
Montpelier, VT 05602-2937
(802)223-2727 Fax:(802)223-0722
E-mail: innatmontpelier@adelphia.net
Web: www.innatmontpelier.com

Circa 1828. Two Federal-style homes comprise the Inn at Montpelier. Ten fireplaces, Greek Revival woodwork and glass-fronted china cupboards are original. A favorite guest room is number two with a lace-canopy bed. A block from the inn are restaurants, business districts and the 100-acre Hubbard Park. The inn holds a AAA three-diamond award.

Innkeeper(s): Rick & Rita Rizza. $90-177. 19 rooms with PB, 6 with FP and 1 conference room. Types of meals: Cont plus. Beds: KT. Modem hook-up, data port, cable TV, refrigerator, clock radio, telephone, coffeemaker and desk in room. Central air. TV, fax, copier and fireplace on premises. Weddings, small meetings, family reunions and seminars hosted.

Publicity: *Glamour Magazine and The Times Argus.*

"My hunch that the Inn at Montpelier would be ideal was well-founded."

Newfane K4

West River Lodge & Stables

117 Hill Rd
Newfane, VT 05345-9606
(802)365-7745 Fax:(802)365-4450
E-mail: capite@artacseel.com
Web: westriverlodge.com

Circa 1829. West River Lodge includes a picturesque white farmhouse next door to a big red barn, surrounded by meadows and hills. Flower gardens in view of the long front porch invite guests to linger. Many enjoy horseback riding nearby. Horse boarding is offered and a riding ring is available. The home was built in the early 19th century as part of a horse farm, and it has served as a horse farm for nearly two centuries. The cozy farmhouse offers comfortable guest rooms decorated with country antiques. A hearty breakfast with items such as blueberry pancakes, country sausage, eggs, homemade muffins and fresh fruit is included in the rates. Newfane offers everything from hiking to fishing, tubing, kayaking and canoeing, as well as antique shops and wonderful fall foliage. The West River is across the field from the lodge.

Innkeeper(s): Ellen & James Wightman. $75-140. 8 rooms, 4 with PB. Breakfast included in rates. Types of meals: Country bkfst. Beds: QDT. Reading lamp and clock radio in room. TV, fax, copier, swimming, stable, parlor games, telephone, fireplace and laundry facility on premises. Weddings, small meetings, family reunions and seminars hosted. Antiquing, art galleries, bicycling, canoeing/kayaking, cross-country skiing, downhill skiing, fishing, golf, hiking, horseback riding, museums, parks, shopping, tennis and water sports nearby.

Northfield E4

Northfield Inn

228 Highland Ave
Northfield, VT 05663-5663
(802)485-8558
E-mail: TheNorthfieldInn@aol.com
Web: www.TheNorthfieldInn.com

Circa 1901. A view of the Green Mountains can be seen from this Victorian inn, which is set on a mountainside surrounded by gardens and overlooking an apple orchard and pond. The

picturesque inn also affords a view of the village of Northfield and historic Norwich University. Rooms are decorated with antiques and Oriental rugs, and bedrooms feature European feather bedding and brass and carved-wood beds. Many outdoor activities are available on the three-acre property, including croquet, horseshoes, ice skating and sledding. Visitors may want to take a climb uphill to visit the Old Slate Quarry or just relax on one of the porches overlooking the garden with bird songs, wind chimes and gentle breezes.

Historic Interest: Norwich University, the oldest private military college in the country, is a half mile away. The state capitol is 10 miles away.
Innkeeper(s): Aglaia Stalb. $95-278. 12 rooms with PB and 2 suites. Breakfast and snacks/refreshments included in rates. Types of meals: Full bkfst. Beds: QDT. Cable TV, reading lamp, ceiling fan, clock radio, telephone and central cooling system available in room. TV, VCR, bicycles, library, parlor games, fireplace, lounge and fitness center on premises. Small meetings, family reunions and seminars hosted. Antiquing, cross-country skiing, downhill skiing, fishing, golf, hiking, live theater, parks,

shopping, sporting events, water sports, sledding, flying, fairs, auctions. Veteran's and Labor Day Festivals and Parade, Vermont Quilt Festival and 5 covered bridges in Northfield nearby.
Publicity: *Conde Nast Traveler and Gentlemen's Quarterly.*

"There's no place like here."

Perkinsville I4

The Inn at Weathersfield

1342 Route 106
Perkinsville, VT 05151
(802)263-9217 Fax:(802)263-9219
E-mail: stay@weathersfieldinn.com
Web: www.weathersfieldinn.com

Circa 1792. Perfectly suited for a quiet getaway, this stately Georgian-style inn with post and beam interior was built in 1792 and thought to have been a stop on the Underground Railroad. Decorated in a rustic elegance, each guest bedroom and suite includes cozy robes and slippers. Many feature fireplaces, four-poster or canopy beds, CD stereos, whirlpool or clawfoot tubs and private rooftop decks. Choose a hot, made-to-order breakfast from a menu. Roam the 21 wooded acres with a pond, walking trails, gardens, back roads and an outdoor starlit amphitheater. The candle-lit dining room offers New Vermont cuisine, and lighter fare is available in the Pub on select nights. Relax by the fire in the study after a full day of skiing. A computer provides high-speed Internet access for guest use.

Historic Interest: Built in 1792. Inn is said to have been a stop on the underground railroad.
Innkeeper(s): Jane and David Sandelman. $117-210. 12 rooms with PB, 6 with FP, 3 suites and 1 conference room. Breakfast, afternoon tea and snacks/refreshments included in rates. Types of meals: Full gourmet bkfst, veg bkfst, early coffee/tea, picnic lunch and gourmet dinner. Restaurant on premises. Beds: KQDT. Modem hook-up, cable TV, reading lamp, stereo, clock radio, desk, fireplace, robes and slippers in room. VCR, fax, copier, sauna, stable, library, pet boarding, parlor games, fireplace, high-speed Internet, gift shop and full service restaurant on premises. Weddings, small meetings, family reunions and seminars hosted. Antiquing, art galleries, bicycling, canoeing/kayaking, cross-country skiing, downhill skiing, fishing, golf, hiking, horseback riding, live theater, museums, parks and shopping nearby.

Peru J3

Wiley Inn

Rt 11 PO Box 37
Peru, VT 05152-0037
(802)824-6600 (888)843-6600 Fax:(802)824-4195
E-mail: historicinn@wileyinn.com
Web: www.wileyinn.com

Circa 1835. The innkeepers at Wiley Inn offer guests a choice of rooms, from romantic bedchambers with canopy beds and clawfoot tubs to family suites that can accommodate up to five people. For honeymooners or those celebrating a special occasion, there are two luxury rooms with a fireplace and double Jacuzzi. The nine-and-a-half acre grounds include a swimming pool and hot tub. The innkeepers offer winter ski packages.

Innkeeper(s): Judy & Jerry Goodman. $75-185. 12 rooms with PB, 4 with FP, 2 suites and 1 conference room. Breakfast and afternoon tea included in rates. Types of meals: Full bkfst. Restaurant on premises. Beds: KQDT. Reading lamp in room. VCR, fax, copier, spa, swimming, telephone, fireplace, Internet and e-mail on premises. Weddings, small meetings, family reunions and seminars hosted. Antiquing, cross-country skiing, downhill skiing, fishing, golf, hiking, shopping, tennis, biking trails, family amusement area, canoeing, skating, snowmobiles and sleigh rides nearby.

Proctorsville   I4

Golden Stage Inn

399 Depot St, PO Box 218
Proctorsville, VT 05153
(802)226-7744 (800)253-8226 Fax:(802)226-7882
E-mail: goldenstageinn@tds.net
Web: www.goldenstageinn.com

Circa 1788. The Golden Stage Inn was a stagecoach stop built
shortly before Vermont became a state. It served as a link in the
Underground Railroad and was the home of Cornelia Otis
Skinner. Cornelia's Room still offers its original polished wide-
pine floors and view of Okemo Mountain, and now there's a
four-poster cherry bed, farm ani-
mal border, wainscoting and a
comforter filled with wool from
the inn's sheep. Outside are
gardens of wildflowers, a little
pen with two sheep, a swim-
ming pool and blueberries and
raspberries for the picking. Breakfast offerings include an often-
requested recipe, Golden Stage Granola. Home-baked breakfast
dishes are garnished with Johnny-jump-ups and nasturtiums
from the garden. Guests can indulge anytime by reaching into
the inn's bottomless cookie jar. The inn offers stay & ski packages at Okemo Mountain with 48 hours advance notice, and
it's a 20 minute drive to Killington access.

Innkeeper(s): Sandy & Peter Gregg. $79-250. 10 rooms with PB and 1 suite.
Breakfast included in rates. Types of meals: Full bkfst and dinner. Beds:
KQDT. Central air. VCR, fax, copier, swimming, library, parlor games, tele-
phone, fireplace and one handicapped-equipped room on premises. Limited
handicap access. Weddings, small meetings and family reunions hosted.
Antiquing, cross-country skiing, downhill skiing, fishing, golf, live theater and
shopping nearby.
Publicity: *Journal Inquirer, Gourmet and Los Angeles Times.*

"The essence of a country inn!"

Whitney Brook B&B

2423 Twenty Mile Stream Rd
Proctorsville, VT 05153-9703
(802)226-7460
E-mail: whitney_brook@yahoo.com
Web: www.whitneybrook.com

Circa 1870. Stone walls encompass the 200 acres that surround this historic farmhouse. The grounds include streams,
meadows and woods. The guest rooms are decorated in country style. For example, the Newport room includes two poster
beds topped with white and blue comforters. The walls are
decorated with blue and white wallpaper and blue trim. The
innkeepers keep books and games on hand, as well as information about local activities. The Vermont Country Store is a
nearby attraction.

Innkeeper(s): Jim & Ellen Parrish. $62-102. 4 rooms, 2 with PB. Breakfast
included in rates. Types of meals: Full bkfst. Beds: QDT. Reading lamp and
ceiling fan in room. VCR, parlor games, telephone and fireplace on premises.
Antiquing, cross-country skiing, downhill skiing, fishing, golf, live theater,
shopping and water sports nearby.
Publicity: *Philadelphia Enquirer, Newark Ledger Star and Boston Globe.*

Putney   K4

Beckwood Pond Country Inn

1107 Route 5
Putney, VT 05346
(802)254-5900 (877)670-5900 Fax:(802)254-8456
E-mail: beckwood@sover.net
Web: www.beckwoodpond.com

Circa 1803. Fifteen acres of tiered gardens, lush lawns, stone
walls, a pond, woodland paths and an apple orchard surround
this English Colonial inn. Furnished with family heirlooms,
including European and American antiques, it is easy to enjoy
all the amenities offered. The Common Room features satellite
TV, music, books and games. Complimentary refreshments
always are available. Spacious guest bedrooms boast down-
filled duvets and rich fabrics. Some offer sitting rooms, a private
entrance and adjoining porch. Impressive three-course breakfasts include fresh local fruit, homemade baked goods and
entrees like creme brulee French toast, blueberry bake and
Italian vegetable frittata accompanied by potatoes. Seasonal
activities enhance this inn's year-round pleasure.

Innkeeper(s): Alan & Helene Saxby. $100-160. 5 rooms with PB and 1 suite.
Breakfast, afternoon tea and snacks/refreshments included in rates. Types of
meals: Full gourmet bkfst, veg bkfst, early coffee/tea and picnic lunch. Beds:
QDT. TV, VCR, fax, copier, bicycles, library, parlor games, telephone, fireplace, gift shop, porches overlooking gardens and hammocks in the apple
orchard on premises. Small meetings, family reunions and seminars hosted.
Antiquing, art galleries, bicycling, canoeing/kayaking, cross-country skiing,
downhill skiing, fishing, golf, hiking, horseback riding, live theater, museums,
parks, shopping, sporting events, tennis, water sports and wineries nearby.
Publicity: *The Gazette, The Great Outdoors, Australia's Internation Travel
Show and An Explorer's Guide: Vermont.*

Hickory Ridge House

53 Hickory Ridge Rd S
Putney, VT 05346-9326
(802)387-5709 (800)380-9218 Fax:(802)387-4328
E-mail: mail@hickoryridgehouse.com
Web: www.hickoryridgehouse.com

Circa 1808. This brick Federal house originally was built as an
elegant farmhouse on a 500-acre Merino sheep farm. Palladian
windows, and six Rumford fireplaces are original features.
Rooms are painted in bright Federal colors, such as rose,
salmon, blue and yellow.
Hickory Ridge House is listed
in the National Register of
Historic Places.
Historic Interest: First brick residence
in county, homesite to local farm fam-
ily for over 100 years.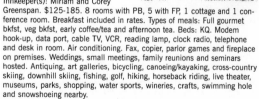
Innkeeper(s): Miriam and Corey
Greenspan. $125-185. 8 rooms with PB, 5 with FP, 1 cottage and 1 con-
ference room. Breakfast included in rates. Types of meals: Full gourmet
bkfst, veg bkfst, early coffee/tea and afternoon tea. Beds: KQ. Modem
hook-up, data port, cable TV, VCR, reading lamp, clock radio, telephone
and desk in room. Air conditioning. Fax, copier, parlor games and fireplace
on premises. Weddings, small meetings, family reunions and seminars
hosted. Antiquing, art galleries, bicycling, canoeing/kayaking, cross-country
skiing, downhill skiing, fishing, golf, hiking, horseback riding, live theater,
museums, parks, shopping, water sports, wineries, crafts, swimming hole
and snowshoeing nearby.
Publicity: *Philadelphia Inquirer and Boston Globe.*

*"We love your serene and peaceful house and we thank you for your
hospitality and warmth, good food and good company."*

The Putney Inn

PO Box 181
Putney, VT 05346-0181
(802)387-5517 (800)653-5517 Fax:(802)387-5211

Circa 1790. The property surrounding this New England farmhouse was deeded to an English Army Captain by King George in 1790. The grounds' first home burned in a fire, and this inn was constructed on the original foundation. Eventually it became a Catholic seminary, and then an elegant country inn. Rooms are located in a 1960s building, adjacent to the main historic farmhouse. The rooms are decorated in a Colonial style with antiques. The inn's dining room, headed by renown chef Ann Cooper, features New England cuisine. The ingredients are fresh and locally produced, and might include appetizers such as smoked salmon on Johnnycakes with an apple cider vinaigrette. Entrees such as a mixed grill of local venison and game hen flavored by an apple-horseradish marinade follow. Craft and antique shops, hiking, skiing and biking are among the local activities.
Innkeeper(s): Randi Ziter. $78-158. 25 rooms with PB and 4 conference rooms. Breakfast included in rates. Types of meals: Full gourmet bkfst, early coffee/tea, gourmet lunch, picnic lunch, afternoon tea, snacks/refreshments and gourmet dinner. Restaurant on premises. Beds: Q. Cable TV, reading lamp, clock radio, telephone and desk in room. Air conditioning. VCR, fax, copier and full dining restaurant on premises. Limited handicap access. Weddings, small meetings, family reunions and seminars hosted. Amusement parks, antiquing, bicycling, cross-country skiing, downhill skiing, fishing, golf, live theater, shopping, tennis, water sports, national forest and nature hikes nearby.
Publicity: *Chicago Tribune, Boston Herald, Culinary Arts, US Air, Travel & Leisure, Vermont Life, Vermont Magazine and Dine-Around.*

Quechee   H5

Herrin House Inn

984 Quechee-Hartland Rd.
Quechee, VT 05059
(802)296-7512 (800)616-4415 Fax:(802)295-6147
E-mail: jherrin@aol.com
Web: www.herrinhouseinn.com

Circa 1800. Leave the fast pace of city life behind while staying at this renovated country house built in Colonial/Federal style. The gracious setting boasts clean air and magnificent views of the rolling hills and surrounding scenery, easily enjoyed from the wraparound porch. Common areas offer gathering places with old brick and stone fireplaces. Family heirlooms and original works of art accent tasteful guest bedrooms and suites. The romantic Enchanted Cottage provides more spacious privacy, a four-poster rice bed, fireplace and a large bathroom with a clawfoot tub and shower. After breakfast, stroll the grounds to the sun-washed pond. Ask about the Quechee Club.
Innkeeper(s): Joe & Vicki Herrin. $140-230. 5 rooms with PB, 1 with FP, 2 suites and 1 cottage. Breakfast included in rates. Types of meals: Cont plus, early coffee/tea and afternoon tea. Beds: KQT. Cable TV, VCR, reading lamp, ceiling fan, clock radio, telephone and turn-down service in room. Air conditioning. Fax, copier, parlor games and fireplace on premises. Weddings, small meetings, family reunions and seminars hosted. Amusement parks, antiquing, art galleries, bicycling, canoeing/kayaking, cross-country skiing, downhill skiing, fishing, golf, hiking, horseback riding, live theater, museums, parks, shopping, sporting events, tennis and water sports nearby.

Reading   H4

Greystone B&B

Rt 106
Reading, VT 05062
(802)484-7200 (888)473-9222 Fax:(802)484-3716
E-mail: chmiller@thegreystone.com
Web: www.thegreystone.com

Circa 1830. Originally built by the Hammond brothers as a shoe factory, this beautiful gray stone building has been a B&B for almost 100 years. Located on two acres, the inn offers an elegant yet comfortable atmosphere. The Fox & Hounds Room is extra large and features a queen-size oak bed, antique armoire and skylights. The lovely Magnolia Room has a queen-sized canopy bed. A full country breakfast is cheerfully served by the owner with a main entree and homemade muffins. The inn is 11 miles south of Woodstock on RT106, and Dartmouth College is 35 minutes away. Guests often rent horses at the Kedron Valley Stables or attend a horse show nearby at the Green Mountain Horse Association.
Historic Interest: Built circa 1820 of Snecked Ashlar; originally housed a shoe factory.
Innkeeper(s): Connie Miller. $65-120. 4 rooms, 3 with PB and 1 suite. Breakfast included in rates. Types of meals: Full gourmet bkfst and early coffee/tea. Beds: KQDT. Reading lamp and clock radio in room. Fax, copier, library and fireplace on premises. Weddings, small meetings and family reunions hosted. Antiquing, cross-country skiing, downhill skiing, fishing, golf, parks, shopping, sporting events, tennis and water sports nearby.

Richford   A4

Grey Gables Mansion

122 River Street
Richford, VT 05476
(802)848-3625 Fax:(802)848-3629
E-mail: info@greygablesmansion.com
Web: www.greygablesmansion.com

Circa 1888. A stately balloon frame, classic asymmetrical multi-gables and ornate exterior highlight this 1888 Queen Anne Victorian listed in the National Register. Hand-carved woodwork, molded cornices, walnut and mahogany grand staircases grace the interior. Sit by the fire to watch TV in the library that boasts a video collection, games and books. Each of the lavish guest bedrooms feature colorful stained-glass windows, wood floors, cable TV and Gilchrist & Soames toiletries. Families appreciate the available Kids Room. Breakfast favorites may include blueberry pancakes with Vermont maple syrup, eggs Benedict, fruit, cereals, breads and muffins. Enjoy baked treats with afternoon tea while watching the Missisiquoi River flow by from the front porch. Ski nearby Jay Peak, Mount Sutton or Stowe. Located on the Canadian border, Montreal is an hour away.
Historic Interest: The rather elaborate design and decorative detailing of the house was taken from a popular late 19th-century architectural pattern book entitled, Pallister's American Cottage Homes (1878) and then adapted, by Richford builder M.E. Dodge, to both suit the needs of the Borights and to make use of the locally-available materials. The original house design, found on the cover of Pallister's 1878 pattern book, was actually used by George Pallister himself in the construction of his home in Seaside Park, a suburb of Bridgeport, CT. This building, however, is no longer standing, leaving the Boright House as perhaps the only surviving example of its kind in the coun-

try, and certainly the only one of its kind in the state of Vermont.
Innkeeper(s): Pam Montgomery. $79-139. 5 rooms with PB. Breakfast and afternoon tea included in rates. Types of meals: Country bkfst. Beds: QDT. Cable TV, reading lamp, ceiling fan, clock radio and hair dryers in room. VCR, fax, library, parlor games and video library on premises. Weddings, small meetings, family reunions and seminars hosted. Antiquing, bicycling, canoeing/kayaking, cross-country skiing, downhill skiing, fishing, golf, hiking, parks and shopping nearby.

Richmond D3

The Richmond Victorian Inn

191 East Main St, PO Box 652
Richmond, VT 05477-0652
(802)434-4410 (888)242-3362 Fax:(802)434-4411
E-mail: innkeeper@richmondvictorianinn.com
Web: www.richmondvictorianinn.com

Circa 1850. This Queen Anne Victorian, with a three-story tower, is accented with green shutters, a sunburst design, fish scale shingles and a gingerbread front porch. The Tower Room is filled with white wicker, delicate flowered wallpaper and an antique brass bed. The Gold Room features a Queen-size bed and a Jacuzzi, while the Pansy Room features an antique bed, white walls and a stenciled pansy border. There are hardwood floors and leaded-glass windows throughout. From the tree-shaded porch, enjoy the inn's lawns and flower gardens after a full breakfast.

Innkeeper(s): Frank & Joyce Stewart. $90-125. 6 rooms with PB. Breakfast included in rates. Types of meals: Full bkfst and early coffee/tea. Beds: QD. Reading lamp and clock radio in room. VCR, parlor games, telephone and afternoon tea September-May on Sundays 2-5 PM on premises. Weddings, small meetings, family reunions and seminars hosted. Antiquing, cross-country skiing, downhill skiing, fishing, golf, parks, shopping, sporting events and water sports nearby.

"Thanks for making us feel like part of your family."

Ripton F2

Chipman Inn

Rt 125
Ripton, VT 05766
(802)388-2390 (800)890-2390

Circa 1828. This was the home of Daniel Chipman, a prominent legislator and founder of Middlebury College. Chipman also managed the "Center Turnpike" (now Route 125) through the Green Mountains. A replica of the tariff board stands near the inn. The inn's lounge/bar is in the original kitchen, with its old fireplace and bread oven.

Historic Interest: Shelburne Museum (50 minutes), Fort Ticonderoga (1 hour).
Innkeeper(s): Joyce Henderson & Bill Pierce. $85-150. 8 rooms with PB. Breakfast included in rates. Types of meals: Full bkfst. Beds: QDT. Air conditioning. Parlor games, telephone and fireplace on premises. Small meetings and family reunions hosted. Antiquing, cross-country skiing, downhill skiing, fishing, parks, shopping and water sports nearby.

Publicity: *Gourmet, Food & Wine, New York Times* and *Addison County Independent.*

"Cozy, warm and friendly."

Rochester G3

Liberty Hill Farm

511 Liberty Hill Rd
Rochester, VT 05767-9501
(802)767-3926 Fax:(802)767-6056
E-mail: beth@libertyhillfarm.com
Web: www.libertyhillfarm.com

Circa 1825. A working dairy farm with a herd of registered Holsteins, this farmhouse offers a country setting and easy access to recreational activities. The inn's location, between the White River and the Green Mountains, is ideal for outdoor enthusiasts and animal lovers. Stroll to the barn, feed the calves or climb up to the hayloft and read or play with the kittens. Fishing, hiking, skiing and swimming are popular pastimes of guests, who are treated to a family-style dinner and full breakfast, both featuring many delicious homemade specialties.

Historic Interest: Calvin Coolidge birthplace (35 miles), Billmes Farm Museum, Rockefeller home (30 minutes), Shelburne Museum (50 minutes).
Innkeeper(s): Robert & Beth Kennett. $150. 7 rooms. Breakfast and dinner included in rates. Types of meals: Full bkfst and early coffee/tea. Beds: QDT. Reading lamp, clock radio and desk in room. VCR, swimming, library, child care, parlor games, telephone, working dairy farm and private beach for swimming and fishing on premises. Weddings, small meetings, family reunions and seminars hosted. Antiquing, art galleries, beach, bicycling, canoeing/kayaking, cross-country skiing, downhill skiing, fishing, golf, hiking, live theater, museums, parks, shopping, sporting events, water sports and wineries nearby.
Publicity: *New York Times, Boston Globe, Vermont Life, Family Circle, Family Fun, Woman's Day, Country Home, Boston Chronicle, Yankee* and *Good Morning America.*

"We had a wonderful time exploring your farm and the countryside. The food was great."

Rutland H3

The Inn at Rutland

70 N Main St
Rutland, VT 05701-3249
(802)773-0575 (800)808-0575 Fax:(802)775-3506
E-mail: relax@innatrutland.com
Web: www.innatrutland.com

Circa 1889. This distinctive Victorian mansion is filled with many period details, from high, plaster-worked ceilings to leather wainscotting in the dining room. Leaded windows and interesting woodwork are found throughout. Guest rooms have been decorated to maintain Victorian charm without a loss of modern comforts. A wrap around porch and common rooms are available to guests. Located in central Vermont, The Inn at Rutland is only 15 minutes from the Killington and Pico ski areas.

Historic Interest: Wilson Castle (10 minutes), Coolidge birthplace (30 minutes), Hildene (30 minutes), Norman Rockwell Museum (5 minutes).
Innkeeper(s): Steven & Leslie Brenner. $90-205. 11 rooms with PB, 2 with FP. Breakfast and afternoon tea included in rates. Types of meals: Full gourmet bkfst and veg bkfst. Beds: KQD. Cable TV, reading lamp, ceiling fan, clock radio, telephone, hair dryers and some with fireplace in room. Air con-

ditioning. TV, library, parlor games, fireplace and wraparound front porch with great views on premises. Family reunions hosted. Antiquing, art galleries, bicycling, canoeing/kayaking, cross-country skiing, downhill skiing, fishing, golf, hiking, horseback riding, live theater, museums, parks, shopping, tennis, water sports and museums nearby.

"A lovely page in the 'memory album' of our minds."

Sandgate   J2

Green River Inn

2480 Sandgate Rd
Sandgate, VT 05250
(802)375-2272 (888)648-2212 Fax:(802)375-2272
E-mail: stay@greenriverinn.com
Web: www.greenriverinn.com

Circa 1935. Since the 1930s, guests have visited this secluded country inn on more than 400 acres. The inn affords views of the surrounding valley and mountains. Innkeepers Jim and

Betsy Gunn offer 14 beautifully restored guest rooms, some with a fireplace or whirlpool tub. The rooms are decorated with antiques and hand-painted furnishings. Guests are treated to a full country breakfast.

Local attractions include hiking, nature trails, skiing, snowshoeing, canoeing and fishing area rivers, golfing, horseback riding or just enjoying the surrounding scenery.

Innkeeper(s): Jim & Betsy Gunn. $90-210. 14 rooms. Breakfast included in rates. Types of meals: Country bkfst and dinner. Beds: KQDT. Whirlpools and fireplaces in room. Air conditioning. VCR, telephone and fireplace on premises. Limited handicap access. Weddings, small meetings, family reunions and seminars hosted. Antiquing, canoeing/kayaking, cross-country skiing, downhill skiing, fishing, golf, hiking, horseback riding, live theater, parks, shopping and tennis nearby.

Shelburne   D2

Heart of the Village Inn

5347 Shelburne Road
Shelburne, VT 05482
(802)985-2800 (877)808-1834 Fax:(802)985-2870
E-mail: innkeeper@heartofthevillage.com
Web: www.heartofthevillage.com

Circa 1886. One of the historic village centerpieces, this white clapboard Queen Anne Victorian, listed in the National Register, was built in the late 1800s by a prosperous merchant. Gather in one of the two living rooms boasting overstuffed chairs. Casually elegant bed & breakfast accommodations are offered in the main house and the luxurious carriage barn. Comfortable guest bedrooms feature sunny village views, fine linens and period furnishings. Some rooms feature clawfoot tubs and pedestal sinks. The two-room Webb Suite includes an oversize whirlpool bath. Hungry appetites are fully satisfied after a filling breakfast. Savor the relaxation of afternoon tea. Rocking chairs overlook colorful gardens on the wraparound veranda.

Innkeeper(s): Pat Button. $115-225. 9 rooms with PB and 1 suite. Breakfast, afternoon tea and snacks/refreshments included in rates. Types of meals: Full gourmet bkfst and early coffee/tea. Beds: KQT. Modem hook-up, cable TV, reading lamp, CD player, clock radio, telephone and one with Jacuzzi in room. Air conditioning. Library, parlor games and gift shop on premises. Small meetings, family reunions and seminars hosted. Antiquing, art galleries, beach, bicycling, canoeing/kayaking, cross-country skiing, fishing, golf, hiking, live theater, museums, parks, shopping and tennis nearby.
Publicity: *New York Times, The Washington Post, The Gazette, Weekend, The Vermont Standard and Burlington Free Press.*

Shrewsbury   H3

Crisanver House

1434 Crown Point Road
Shrewsbury, VT 05738
(802)492-3589 (800)492-8089 Fax:(802)402-3480
E-mail: info@crisanver.com
Web: www.crisanver.com

Circa 1850. Listed in the state historic register, this completely renovated inn offers an ideal location, boasting views of mountains and sunsets and surrounded by 117 acres. The guest rooms, decorated in an elegant country style, feature original artwork, down comforters and carefully chosen antiques. Breakfasts are healthy and scrumptious, often featuring low-fat and low-cholesterol fare. Homemade muffins, scones, entrees made from farm-fresh eggs, seasonal fruits and pancakes topped with Vermont maple syrup might appear on the breakfast table, set with English china, silver, crystal and fresh flowers from the inn's gardens.

Innkeeper(s): Carol & Michael Calotta. $90-140. 8 rooms, 6 with PB and 1 conference room. Breakfast, afternoon tea and snacks/refreshments included in rates. Types of meals: Full gourmet bkfst, early coffee/tea and picnic lunch. Beds: QT. Reading lamp, desk and robes in room. TV, VCR, fax, copier, swimming, bicycles, tennis, library, telephone, fireplace, lawn games, grand piano, player piano, ping pong and flower gardens on premises. Weddings, small meetings, family reunions and seminars hosted. Antiquing, bicycling, cross-country skiing, downhill skiing, fishing, golf, hiking, horseback riding, live theater, parks, shopping, tennis and water sports nearby.
Publicity: *Country Inns.*

"Our expectation was great, but I must tell you the reality exceeded the expectation. I really cannot believe all the nice things you have done, big and small to make Crisanver House a comfortable, charming and elegant place to spend some quality time."

Springfield   I4

Hartness House Inn and Restaurant

30 Orchard St
Springfield, VT 05156-2612
(802)885-2115 (800)732-4789 Fax:(802)885-2207
E-mail: innkeeper@hartnesshouse.com
Web: www.hartnesshouse.com

Circa 1904. There are many inns where star-gazing is a popular nighttime activity. At Hartness House, it is taken to a whole new level. The original owner not only served as the state's governor, but inventor/astronomer James Hartness also created the historic observatory that remains at the home today. Aside from this uncommon amenity, the house itself is impressive. Guests who stay in the home's original portion reach their well-appointed rooms via a three-story staircase. Two newer wings also offer elegant accommodations. There is a Victorian-styled dining room on the premises as well, offering dinners by candlelight. The home is often the site of weddings, receptions and parties. Country Inns magazine chose Hartness House as one of its top inns, and in another article made note of the inn's wonderful holiday decorations and festivities.

Innkeeper(s): Alla and Alex Leone. $90-185. 43 rooms with PB, 1 with FP, 3 suites and 2 conference rooms. Breakfast included in rates. Types of meals: Full gourmet bkfst, early coffee/tea, lunch, afternoon tea and gourmet dinner. Restaurant on premises. Beds: QD. Modem hook-up, data port, cable TV, reading lamp, telephone, voice mail and wireless Internet in room. Air conditioning. Fax, copier, library, fireplace, gift shop, astronomy museum, telescope observatory, nature trails and art gallery on premises. Limited handicap access. Family reunions hosted. Antiquing, art galleries, bicycling, canoeing/kayaking, cross-country skiing, downhill skiing, fishing, golf, hiking, horseback riding, live theater, museums, shopping, lovely farms and covered bridges nearby.

Publicity: *Country Inn, Dorset Country Journal and Journal for Innkeepers.*

"A wonderful place to stop and remember simple elegance and all that is important."

Stowe   D4

Brass Lantern Inn B&B

717 Maple St
Stowe, VT 05672-4250
(802)253-2229 (800)729-2980 Fax:(802)253-7425
E-mail: info@brasslanterninn.com
Web: www.brasslanterninn.com

Circa 1810. This rambling farmhouse and carriage barn rests at the foot of Mt. Mansfield. A recent award-winning renovation has brought a new shine to the inn, from the gleaming plank floors to the polished woodwork and crackling fireplaces and soothing whirlpool tubs. Quilts and antiques fill the guest rooms, and many, like the Honeymoon Room, have their own fireplace, whirlpool tub and mountain view. A complimentary afternoon and evening tea is provided along with a full Vermont-style breakfast. A new two-bedroom cottage is now available, as well. The inn is a multi-time winner of the Golden Fork Award from the Gourmet Dinners Society of North America.

Innkeeper(s): Andy Aldrich. $85-225. 9 rooms with PB, 6 with FP, 6 with HT. Breakfast and afternoon tea included in rates. Types of meals: Full bkfst and early coffee/tea. Beds: Q. Reading lamp, clock radio and six with whirlpool tubs and fireplace in room. Air conditioning. VCR, fax, copier, library, parlor games, telephone, fireplace, gardens and patio on premises. Weddings and small meetings hosted. Antiquing, cross-country skiing, downhill skiing, fishing, live theater, parks, shopping, sporting events, water sports and tours nearby.

Publicity: *Vermont, Vermont Life, Insider, Discerning Traveler, Ski and Vermont B&B Innkeeper of the Year 2001.*

"The little things made us glad we stopped."

Foxfire Inn & Italian Restaurant

1606 Pucker S
Stowe, VT 05672
(802)253-4887 Fax:(802)253-7016
Web: www.foxfireinn.com

Circa 1850. This inn and 90-seat restaurant is in a restored farmhouse, bordered with colorful perennials. Shingles and many-paned windows add to the welcoming feeling. The inn is best known among Stowe visitors and locals as the best place for Italian food. Try the Chicken Ripieno stuffed with gorgonzola, pancetta and figs in a creamy Marsala sauce. For dessert you'll want to order the espresso/rum-soaked pound cake with chocolate mousse filling. Rated three diamonds by AAA, the guest rooms are furnished in a country decor with antiques.

Innkeeper(s): Robert Neilson. $65-90. 5 rooms with PB. Breakfast included in rates. Types of meals: Full bkfst and dinner. Restaurant on premises. Beds: QDT. Air conditioning. Fax, copier, parlor games, telephone and fireplace on premises. Antiquing, cross-country skiing, downhill skiing, fishing, golf, live theater, shopping, sporting events and tennis nearby.

"A wonderful evening for the third straight year!"

The Gables Inn

1457 Mountain Rd
Stowe, VT 05672-4750
(802)253-7730 (800)422-5371 Fax:(802)253-8989
E-mail: inngables@aol.com
Web: www.gablesinn.com

Circa 1856. This inn originally served as a farmhouse, but opened as an inn in the 1930s. Guest rooms feature Colonial decor with canopy beds and comfortable furnishings. The front porch and several guest rooms afford a view of Mount Mansfield. Rooms with a fireplace or Jacuzzi tub are available. The two-and-a-half-acre grounds include a swimming pool, hot tub and a little bridge that leads to a pond. Guests can relax in the solarium, in front of a fire in the living room or they can play a game in the den. The inn's restaurant serves breakfast throughout the year, and guests can choose an entree from a menu that offers everything from pancakes with Vermont maple syrup to "Two on a Raft," an English muffin with tomato, sprouts, poached eggs and Vermont cheddar cheese. Dinners are available in winter, and a lunch menu is offered during the summer months. Skiing, snowshoeing, ice skating, hiking, golf and shopping are among the many local attractions.

Innkeeper(s): Annette Manachelli & Randy Stern. $78-240. 18 rooms with PB, 7 with FP and 2 suites. Breakfast and afternoon tea included in rates. Types of meals: Full gourmet bkfst and early coffee/tea. Restaurant on premises. Beds: KQDT. Cable TV, reading lamp, refrigerator, clock radio, telephone, hot tub/spa and some with ceiling fan in room. Air conditioning. VCR, fax, swimming, bicycles, parlor games, fireplace and hot tubs on premises. Limited handicap access. Weddings, small meetings and family reunions hosted. Antiquing, cross-country skiing, downhill skiing, fishing, golf, live theater, parks, shopping, sporting events and tennis nearby.

Publicity: *Vermont Life Magazine.*

Green Mountain Inn

PO Box 60, 1 Main St
Stowe, VT 05672-0060
(802)253-7301 (800)253-7302 Fax:(802)253-5096
E-mail: info@gminn.com
Web: www.greenmountaininn.com

Circa 1833. This early 19th century inn is a member of the Historic Hotels of America. The main inn and adjacent depot building are listed in the National Register of Historic Places. Completely restored and decorated in early-American style with antiques and reproductions, the inn also boasts  original Walton Blodgett paintings. Guest bedrooms feature canopy beds, whirlpools and fireplaces. The health club offers a sauna, steam room and Jacuzzi. Enjoy the year-round outdoor pool and game room.

Historic Interest: The State House, Vermont's 114 covered bridges, Hubbardton Battlefield.

Innkeeper(s): Patricia Clark. $99-359. 100 rooms with PB, 49 with FP and 1 conference room. Types of meals: Full gourmet bkfst, early coffee/tea, gourmet lunch, afternoon tea, snacks/refreshments and dinner. Restaurant on premises. Beds: KQDT. Cable TV, reading lamp, refrigerator, clock radio, telephone, desk and hot tub/spa in room. Air conditioning. TV, VCR, fax, copier, sauna, parlor games, fireplace, game room, health club, Jacuzzi and year-round outdoor pool on premises. Limited handicap access. Weddings, small meetings, family reunions and seminars hosted. Antiquing, bicycling, cross-country skiing, downhill skiing, fishing, hiking, live theater, shopping and water sports nearby.

Publicity: *Snow Country, Elle, National Geographic Traveler and Ski Magazine.*

Ski Inn

Rt 108
Stowe, VT 05672
(802)253-4050

Circa 1941. This traditional New England inn, on 27-tree-studded acres, was the first ski lodge in Stowe. The Heyer family have operated the inn since 1941. Rooms are large and colorful with comfortable furnishings. Guests gather around the fieldstone fireplace, the dinner table and the mountain-view windows to discuss skiing and the Vermont countryside.
Innkeeper(s): Harriet Heyer. $35-65. 10 rooms, 5 with PB, 1 with FP and 1 conference room. Types of meals: Cont. Beds: DT. Telephone in room. TV and parlor games on premises.
Publicity: *The Stowe Reporter, New York Times and Ski Magazine.*

"Thanks again for a great time and providing a nice place to stay. The friendliness of hosts and guests make this the best inn we have ever stayed in."

Ten Acres Lodge

14 Barrows Rd
Stowe, VT 05672-4733
(802)253-7638 (800)327-7357
E-mail: tenacres@stowevt.net
Web: www.tenacreslodge.com

Circa 1848. For the comfortable feeling of home, this elegant and intimate country inn promises an unforgettable stay. The main lodge, boasting antique furnishings, is one of Stowe's most historic farmhouses. Guest bedrooms in the Hill House feature fireplaces, cathedral ceilings, a sitting area for watching TV and a private balcony. Two- and three-bedroom cottages offer woodburning fireplaces, a full kitchen and large living area. Taste buds are tantalized at the inn's award-winning restaurant. After a game of tennis, enjoy a swim in the pool or soak in the hot tub.
Innkeeper(s): Grace & Albert Obarzanek. $99-460. 18 rooms with PB, 10 with FP and 1 conference room. Types of meals: Full gourmet bkfst and afternoon tea. Restaurant on premises. Beds: KQT. TV, fax, spa, swimming, bicycles, tennis and telephone on premises. Fishing nearby.
Publicity: *Travel & Leisure, Bon Appetit, New York Times, Gourmet and Ski Magazine.*

Three Bears at The Fountain

1049 Pucker St
Stowe, VT 05672-9802
(802)253-7671 (800)898-9634 Fax:(802)253-8804
E-mail: threebears@stowevt.net
Web: www.threebearsbandb.com

Circa 1820. A spring-fed fountain on the grounds and the innkeepers' Three Bears Restaurant inspired the name for this Vermont country inn. The historic home was built by the first couple married in the village of Stowe, and it is the oldest guest house in town, opening its doors for travelers in the 1920s. The main house dates to the 1820s, but an adjacent carriage house was built in 1796. Original fireplaces, restored wood floors and exposed beams add a historic ambiance. Guest rooms are decorated in country style with quilts and antiques. Vermont's highest peak, Mount Mansfield, is just six miles away and guests are afforded the wonderful views from the wraparound porch or while relaxing in the hot tub. The King Room includes a gas fireplace, cathedral ceilings and mountain views. The breakfast room is warmed by a fireplace; and the morning meal is served on country oak tables set with linen and fine china.

Historic Interest: This is the first guest house in Stowe, built by the first couple married in Stowe. It has the original floors, the basement with the flagstone floor, original fireplaces and in winter, the "fountain" that freezes is a landmark in town.
Innkeeper(s): Goldilocks & Papa Bear. $95-225. 6 rooms with PB, 4 with FP and 2 suites. Breakfast, afternoon tea and snacks/refreshments included in rates. Types of meals: Full gourmet bkfst, veg bkfst and early coffee/tea. Beds: KQDT. Cable TV, VCR, reading lamp, stereo, refrigerator, clock radio, hot tub/spa and fireplace in room. Air conditioning. Fax, copier, spa, swimming, library, parlor games, telephone, gift shop and gazebo with mountain view for beautiful sunsets on premises. Weddings, small meetings and family reunions hosted. Antiquing, art galleries, bicycling, canoeing/kayaking, cross-country skiing, downhill skiing, fishing, golf, hiking, horseback riding, live theater, museums, parks, shopping, sporting events, tennis and wineries nearby.
Publicity: *Burlington Free Press, Stowe Reporter and Everybody Loves Raymond.*

Winding Brook... A Classic Mountain Lodge

199 Edson Hill Rd
Stowe, VT 05672
(802)253-7354 (800)426-6697 Fax:(802)253-8429

Circa 1939. Set beside a mountain stream on five wooded acres, Winding Brook is Stowe's oldest existing ski lodge. After skiing, relax in the living room with its inviting fieldstone fireplace or enjoy a long soak in the outdoor hot tub. During warmer months, guests can enjoy a swim in the pool. Stowe is famous for its skiing and Mount Mansfield, Vermont's highest mountain. The resort village also offers many shops, galleries and restaurants.
Innkeeper(s): Patrick J DiDomenico. $65-195. 15 rooms with PB. Breakfast included in rates. Types of meals: Full bkfst. Beds: KQT. Reading lamp and hot tub/spa in room. Air conditioning. TV, VCR, copier, swimming, library, telephone, fireplace, game room and pool table on premises. Weddings, small meetings, family reunions and seminars hosted. Antiquing, cross-country skiing, downhill skiing, fishing, golf, parks, shopping, tennis and water sports nearby.
Publicity: *Stowe Reporter.*

Townshend   K4

Boardman House

PO Box 112
Townshend, VT 05353-0112
(802)365-4086

Circa 1840. This stately Greek Revival is located on the village green of Townshend in Southeast Vermont. Guests enjoy a full breakfast before beginning their day, which could include antiquing, canoeing or kayaking in the West River or skiing at Bromley, or Stratton ski areas, all within easy driving distance. The inn boasts a large, lush lawn and gardens, a parlor with a library and a refreshing sauna. Early coffee or tea is served and picnic lunches are available.

Innkeeper(s): Paul Weber & Sarah Messenger. $70-80. 6 rooms, 5 with PB and 1 suite. Breakfast included in rates. Types of meals: Full gourmet bkfst. Beds: QT. Reading lamp in room. Air conditioning. VCR, sauna, library, parlor games and telephone on premises. Small meetings and family reunions hosted. Antiquing, cross-country skiing, downhill skiing, fishing, golf, parks, shopping, tennis and water sports nearby.
Publicity: *Boston Globe, Chronicle and Funny Farm.*

Troy   B4

Victorian Manor

1430 Vermont Route 101
Troy, VT 05868
(908)928-9061 (802)988-9880 Fax:(908)928-9062
E-mail: kkjohnsen@att.net
Web: www.snobowl.com

Circa 1837. Sitting on 22 acres overlooking the Missiquoi
River Valley, this 1837 Victorian offers a comfortable stay in the
country. Common rooms include a formal living and dining
room, family room and fully equipped kitchen. Enjoy use of
the sauna, VCR, woodstove, washer and dryer. Six guest bedrooms can comfortably accommodate groups of 15. Ride the
aerial tramway at nearby Jay Peak Ski and Summer Resort, ski
or play golf. Snowmobiles and nature hikes are accessible on
VAST corridor trails. It is only three miles to the Canadian border. Stowe and Burlington, Vermont are only one hour away.
North Troy Village Restaurant & Pub, The Lodge and The
Belfry are nearby restaurants to try.
Innkeeper(s): Karen & Henry Johnsen and Arthur Bonnell. Call for rates. 6
rooms with PB and 3 conference rooms. Beds: KQDT. Ceiling fan in room.
TV, VCR, sauna, stable, parlor games, telephone, laundry facility and currently unoccupied nine stall horse barn on premises. Weddings, small meetings,
family reunions and seminars hosted. Cross-country skiing, downhill skiing,
fishing, golf, horseback riding, parks, Jay Peak Resort, six golf courses, beautiful Lake Memphremagog (Mewport) Vermont and Canadian border nearby.

Vergennes   E2

Emerson Guest House

82 Main St
Vergennes, VT 05491-1155
(802)877-3293 Fax:(802)877-3293
E-mail: emersons@sover.net
Web: www.emersonhouse.com

Circa 1850. This historic 1850s Victorian home is situated on
three-and-a-half acres near downtown Vergennes in the heart of
Lake Champlain Valley. Choose from six spacious, airy guest
rooms, filled with antiques and personal collections. Start the
day with a fresh breakfast of frittatas and homemade muffins,
or French toast with apple praline topping. Then relax in the
large backyard and flower gardens or walk to nearby antique
shops and restaurants. The historic city of Vergennes is a welcome getaway, with activities such as swimming, boating or
fishing in Lake Champlain and biking or hiking along mountain trails. At the end of the day relax on the large front porch
and watch the sun set over the Adirondack Mountains.
Innkeeper(s): Christopher & Suzanne Wyckoff. $65-140. 6 rooms, 2 with PB,
1 suite and 1 conference room. Breakfast and snacks/refreshments included
in rates. Types of meals: Full gourmet bkfst and early coffee/tea. Beds: KQDT.
Reading lamp, ceiling fan and clock radio in room. TV, fax, copier, bicycles,
library, parlor games, telephone, fireplace, croquet and trails on premises.
Weddings and family reunions hosted. Antiquing, art galleries, bicycling,
canoeing/kayaking, cross-country skiing, downhill skiing, fishing, golf, hiking,
horseback riding, museums, parks, shopping, sporting events, tennis, water
sports, wineries and Lake Champlain nearby.

Strong House Inn

94 W Main St
Vergennes, VT 05491-9531
(802)877-3337 Fax:(802)877-2599
E-mail: innkeeper@stronghouseinn.com
Web: www.stronghouseinn.com

Circa 1834. This Federal-style home boasts views of the Green
Mountains and the Adirondack range. Several rooms offer working fireplaces and all are richly appointed. Country breakfasts
and afternoon refreshments are served, and on selected Sundays
don't miss the expansive
afternoon tea, complete
with pastries, tea sandwiches, and of course, a wide
selection of teas. Nearby
Lake Champlain offers boating and fishing. Golf, hik-
ing, skiing and some of the finest cycling in Vermont are all part
of the area's myriad of outdoor activities. Innkeeper Mary
Bargiel is an avid gardener and decorates the grounds with flowers and herb gardens. The innkeepers offer a selection of special
weekends from a Valentine's Day to a quilter's weekend.

Historic Interest: The area has no shortage of antique shopping, and the inn
itself is listed in the National Register of Historic Places.
Innkeeper(s): Hugh & Mary Bargiel. $95-305. 14 rooms with PB, 4 with FP,
1 suite and 1 conference room. Breakfast and snacks/refreshments included
in rates. Types of meals: Country bkfst and early coffee/tea. Beds: KQDT.
Modem hook-up, data port, cable TV, VCR, reading lamp, stereo, refrigerator,
clock radio, telephone, coffeemaker, desk, hot tub/spa and voice mail in
room. Central air. TV, fax, copier, spa, library, parlor games, fireplace and gift
shop on premises. Limited handicap access. Weddings, small meetings, family reunions and seminars hosted. Antiquing, art galleries, bicycling, canoe-
ing/kayaking, cross-country skiing, downhill skiing, fishing, golf, hiking, horseback riding, museums, parks, shopping and tennis nearby.
Publicity: *New York Times, Vermont Magazine, Addison County Independent
and RETN.*

"Blissful stay...Glorious breakfast!"

Waitsfield   E3

Featherbed Inn

Route 100, 5864 Main St
Waitsfield, VT 05673
(802)496-7151 Fax:(802)496-7933
E-mail: featherbedinn@madriver.com
Web: www.featherbedinn.com

Circa 1806. Surrounded by 25 acres of woods and meadows,
this New England farmhouse has been renovated with extreme
attention to preserving its historic integrity. Wide pine floors
with square head nails, post and beam construction, mullion
windows and Colonial decor retain the inn's quaint heritage.
The common areas offer a formal living room with grand piano,
an open, fieldstone fireplace in the lodge room (which has
games and books), and a TV/VCR in the den. Spacious guest
bedrooms and suites in the main house and cottage boast
warm, comfy feather beds. Breakfast begins in the sunny dining
room with different items that may include cider-poached pears,
strawberry bread, baked puff pancakes with orange-apricot
sauce and featherbed eggs. Relax in the gazebo overlooking the
pond, then explore the year-round activities of Mad River Valley.
Innkeeper(s): Tracey & Clive Coutts. $95-150. 10 rooms with PB and 2
suites. Breakfast, afternoon tea and snacks/refreshments included in rates.
Types of meals: Full gourmet bkfst, veg bkfst and early coffee/tea. Beds: QDT.
Reading lamp in room. Air conditioning. TV, VCR, fax, library, parlor games,

telephone and fireplace on premises. Small meetings and family reunions hosted. Antiquing, art galleries, bicycling, canoeing/kayaking, cross-country skiing, downhill skiing, fishing, golf, hiking, live theater, parks, shopping and tennis nearby.

Publicity: *Ski Magazine, Montreal Gazette, Ski America and Boston Globe.*

Lareau Farm Country Inn

PO Box 563, Rt 100
Waitsfield, VT 05673-0563
(802)496-4949 (800)833-0766
E-mail: lareau@lareaufarminn.com
Web: www.lareaufarminn.com

Circa 1794. This Greek Revival house was built by Simeon Stoddard, the town's first physician. Old-fashioned roses, lilacs, delphiniums, iris and peonies fill the gardens. The inn sits in a wide meadow next to the crystal-clear Mad River. A canoe trip or a refreshing swim are possibilities here.

Innkeeper(s): Susan Easley.
$80-135. 13 rooms, 11 with PB, 1 suite and 1 conference room. Breakfast included in rates. Types of meals: Full gourmet bkfst and early coffee/tea. Beds: QD. Reading lamp and desk in room. Swimming, library and fireplace on premises. Weddings, small meetings, family reunions and seminars hosted. Antiquing, cross-country skiing, downhill skiing, fishing, live theater and shopping nearby.

Publicity: *Pittsburgh Press, Philadelphia Inquirer and Los Angeles Times.*

"Hospitality is a gift. Thank you for sharing your gift so freely with us."

Mad River Inn

Tremblay Rd, PO Box 75
Waitsfield, VT 05673
(802)496-7900 (800)832-8278 Fax:(802)496-5390
E-mail: madriverinn@madriver.com
Web: www.madriverinn.com

Circa 1860. Surrounded by the Green Mountains, this Queen Anne Victorian sits on seven scenic acres along the Mad River. The charming inn boasts attractive woodwork throughout, highlighted by ash, bird's-eye maple and cherry. Guest rooms feature European feather beds and include the Hayden Breeze Room, with a King brass bed, large windows and sea relics, and the Abner Doubleday Room, with a Queen ash bed and mementos of baseball's glory days. The inn sports a billiard table, gazebo, organic gardens and a Jacuzzi overlooking the mountains.

Guests can walk to a recreation path along the river.

Historic Interest: The Historic Round Barn and Shelbourne Farm & Museum are a short distance.

Innkeeper(s): Luc & Karen Maranda. $95-135. 9 rooms with PB. Breakfast and afternoon tea included in rates. Types of meals: Full gourmet bkfst. Beds: KQ. Reading lamp, ceiling fan, turn-down service and desk in room. VCR, fax, spa, parlor games, telephone and fireplace on premises. Small meetings and family reunions hosted. Antiquing, cross-country skiing, downhill skiing, fishing, live theater, shopping, sporting events and water sports nearby.

Publicity: *Innsider, Victorian Homes, Let's Live, Skiing, AAA Home & Away, Tea Time at the Inn, Travel & Leisure and Ski Magazine.*

"Your hospitality was appreciated, beautiful house and accommodations, great food & friendly people, just to name a few things. We plan to return and we recommend the Mad River Inn to friends & family."

Waitsfield Inn

5267 Main St.
Waitsfield, VT 05673
(802)496-3979 (800)758-3801 Fax:(802)496-3970
E-mail: lodging@waitsfieldinn.com
Web: www.waitsfieldinn.com

Circa 1825. This Federal-style inn once served as a parsonage and was home to several state senators of the Richardson family. The 1839 barn offers a Great Room with fireplace and wood-plank floors, or in winter you may enjoy sipping spiced Vermont apple cider and munching on fresh cookies in the sitting room. Guest quarters are furnished with period antiques, quilts or comforters and some rooms have exposed beams or hand stenciling. A full breakfast is served in the dining room, with a choice of 14 delicious items as prepared by the inns chef. As the inn is in the village of Waitsfield, the entire town's sites are nearby including a beautiful covered bridge. Visit Glen Moss Waterfall, fly fish, canoe, try a glider, golf or watch a polo match. Snowshoeing, skiing and visits to the New England Culinary Institute and Ben & Jerry's Ice Cream Factory are popular activities.

Historic Interest: Ethan Allen's estate is 35 miles from the inn and Montpelier is 20 miles away.

Innkeeper(s): Mike & Rhonda Kelley. $105-150. 14 rooms with PB. Breakfast included in rates. Types of meals: Full bkfst. Beds: QDT. Fax, copier, library, telephone, fireplace and modem on premises. Small meetings, family reunions and seminars hosted. Antiquing, cross-country skiing, downhill skiing, fishing, golf, live theater, shopping and canoeing nearby.

Wilder Farm Inn

1460 Main St.
Waitsfield, VT 05673
(802)496-9935 (800)496-8878 Fax:(802)496-9954
E-mail: info@wilderfarminn.com
Web: www.wilderfarminn.com

Circa 1850. Affectionately called an oasis, this Gothic Revival farmhouse has been renovated recently to offer modern comfort mingled with the memory of days gone by. Furnished in country antiques, the inn offers easy relaxation. Enjoy fireside chats in the study with a hot beverage, or read a book in the living room. After a restful night in one of the delightful guest bedrooms, enter the dining room for a mouthwatering breakfast by a warm fire. Located in the Mad River Valley, the inn is surrounded by the grandeur of the Green Mountains.

Innkeeper(s): Ash Calder & Jason Real. $100-150. 8 rooms with PB. Breakfast and afternoon tea included in rates. Types of meals: Full bkfst, veg bkfst and early coffee/tea. Beds: KQDT. Reading lamp, ceiling fan, clock radio, desk and hair dryer in room. TV, VCR, fax, copier, library, parlor games, telephone and fireplace on premises. Small meetings hosted. Antiquing, art galleries, bicycling, canoeing/kayaking, cross-country skiing, downhill skiing, fishing, golf, hiking, horseback riding, live theater, parks, shopping, sporting events, tennis, water sports and wineries nearby.

Wallingford   **H3**

I. B. Munson House

37 S Main St, PO Box 427
Wallingford, VT 05773-0427
(802)446-2860 (888)519-3771 Fax:(802)446-3336
E-mail: stay@ibmunsoninn.com
Web: www.ibmunsoninn.com

Circa 1856. An Italianate Victorian bed & breakfast, the inn was meticulously restored as the innkeepers preserved many original elements, such as the wood floors, ornately carved mantels and

woodwork. Period antiques and Waverly wallcoverings are featured in the guest rooms, three of which include a fireplace. All seven guest rooms have private baths. Wallingford is a designated historic village, so there are many interesting old homes and buildings to see. Ski areas, shops and restaurants are within a couple of blocks. Innkeeper(s): Charles & Lisa McClafferty. $120-195. 7 rooms with PB, 3 with FP and 2 suites. Breakfast included in rates. Types of meals: Full bkfst, early coffee/tea, afternoon tea and dinner. Beds: QDT. Reading lamp, ceiling fan and turn-down service in room. VCR and fax on premises. Weddings, small meetings, family reunions and seminars hosted. Antiquing, cross-country skiing, downhill skiing, fishing, parks, shopping and water sports nearby. Publicity: *The Rotarian and Mill River Area Current.*

"It was a pleasure to stay at your beautiful historic Bed and Breakfast. Wonderful hospitality! Delicious breakfast - a very special treat!! We will be back."

Warren   F3

West Hill House

1496 West Hill Rd
Warren, VT 05674-9620
(802)496-7162 (800)898-1427
E-mail: westhill@madriver.com
Web: www.westhillhouse.com

Circa 1850. This attractive inn boasts a great location, on a scenic country road, just a mile from the Sugarbush Ski Area and next to the Sugarbush Golf Course/Cross-Country Ski Center. The nine-acre grounds include four ponds, meadows, perennial gardens, a uniquely designed gazebo and winter mountain views. All rooms offer a Jacuzzi and/or steam bath, and there are fireplaces in all of the bedchambers. Guests enjoy early coffee or tea before breakfast in one of the three spacious common areas, and later are served afternoon tea and bedtime snacks. Candlelight dinners, served in the English antique dining room, are available for six or more guests by prior arrangement. Summer weddings here can accommodate up to 150 with a wedding tent, while indoor winter weddings are popular for smaller parties.

Innkeeper(s): Dotty Kyle & Eric Brattstrom. $115-190. 8 rooms with PB, 8 with FP. Types of meals: Full bkfst, early coffee/tea, afternoon tea, snacks/refreshments and dinner. Beds: KQT. Cable TV, VCR, reading lamp, clock radio, all guestrooms have telephones with voicemail, DSL Internet access, double Jacuzzi and/or steam bath in room. Telephone, fireplace, three large common areas, front porch and back deck on premises. Weddings and family reunions hosted. Antiquing, bicycling, cross-country skiing, downhill skiing, fishing, hiking, live theater and shopping nearby. Publicity: *Yankee Magazine, Insider Magazine, Quilt Mania Magazine, UK Ski Magazine, Boston Globe and Washington Post.*

Waterbury   D3

Old Stagecoach Inn

18 N Main St
Waterbury, VT 05676-1810
(802)244-5056 (800)262-2206 Fax:(802)244-6956
E-mail: lodging@oldstagecoach.com
Web: www.oldstagecoach.com

Circa 1826. For many years, this inn served as both a stagecoach stop and meeting house. In the 1880s, an Ohio millionaire used the home as his summer retreat. He added the Victorian touches that are still present, including the polished woodwork, stained glass and elegant fireplaces. Today, guests stay in restored rooms decorated in Victorian style. Stowe, Sugarbush, Mad River Glen and Bolton Valley ski areas are nearby, and guests can also partake in fishing, swimming and water sports at Winooski River, Waterbury Reservoir or Lake Champlain.

Innkeeper(s): John & Jack Barwick. $60-180. 11 rooms, 8 with PB, 1 with FP. Breakfast included in rates. Types of meals: Full gourmet bkfst. Beds: KQDT. Data port, cable TV, VCR, reading lamp, stereo, refrigerator, ceiling fan, clock radio and telephone in room. Air conditioning. Copier, tennis, library, parlor games and fireplace on premises. Weddings, small meetings and family reunions hosted. Antiquing, art galleries, canoeing/kayaking, cross-country skiing, downhill skiing, fishing, golf, hiking, horseback riding, live theater, museums, parks, shopping, sporting events, tennis, water sports, wineries and Ben & Jerry's nearby.

"This place was first class all the way."

The Inn at Blush Hill

784 Blush Hill Rd
Waterbury, VT 05676
(802)244-7529 (800)736-7522 Fax:(802)244-7314
E-mail: inn@blushhill.com
Web: www.blushhill.com

Circa 1790. This shingled Cape-style house was once a stagecoach stop en route to Stowe and is the oldest inn in Waterbury. A 12-foot-long pine farmhand's table is set near the double fireplace and the kitchen bay window, revealing views of the Worcester Mountains. A favorite summertime breakfast, served gardenside, is pancakes with fresh blueberries, topped with ice cream and maple syrup.

Historic Interest: The inn has a 1760 fireplace with adjacent brick oven. Innkeeper(s): Pam Gosselin. $89-160. 5 rooms with PB, 1 with FP. Breakfast, afternoon tea and snacks/refreshments included in rates. Types of meals: Full gourmet bkfst and early coffee/tea. Beds: QT. TV, reading lamp, refrigerator, ceiling fan, clock radio, turn-down service and hot tub/spa in room. Air conditioning. Fax, library, parlor games, telephone and fireplace on premises. Antiquing, cross-country skiing, downhill skiing, fishing, golf, live theater, parks, shopping, water sports and Ben & Jerry's ice cream factory nearby. Publicity: *Vermont, Charlotte Observer, Yankee, New York Times, Ski, New York Post and WCAX Television.*

"Our room was wonderful — especially the fireplace. Everything was so cozy and warm."

Thatcher Brook Inn

PO Box 490, Rt 100 N
Waterbury, VT 05676-0490
(802)244-5911 (800)292-5911 Fax:(802)244-1294
E-mail: info@thatcherbrook.com
Web: www.thatcherbrook.com

Circa 1899. Listed in the Vermont Register of Historic
Buildings, this restored Victorian mansion features a rambling
porch with twin gazebos and a covered walkway leading to
the historic Wheeler House. Guest rooms are decorated in
classic country style. Four rooms have fireplaces, and six have
whirlpool tubs. The inn's
restaurant and tavern are located in the main inn. Guests can
dine fireside by candlelight, or
on the porch in summer.
Historic Interest: The inn is listed in
the National Register.

Innkeeper(s): Lisa & John Fischer. $80-
195. 22 rooms with PB, 4 with FP, 1 suite and 1 conference room. Breakfast
included in rates. Types of meals: Full bkfst and gourmet dinner. Restaurant
on premises. Beds: KQD. Reading lamp, ceiling fan, clock radio, telephone,
most rooms have A/C and 6 have whirlpools in room. Fax, copier, parlor
games, fireplace and Internet access on premises. Limited handicap access.
Weddings, small meetings, family reunions and seminars hosted. Antiquing,
bicycling, cross-country skiing, downhill skiing, fishing, hiking, horseback riding, live theater, parks, shopping and water sports nearby.

*"I'd have to put on a black tie in Long Island to find food as good as
this, and best of all it's in a relaxed country atmosphere."*

Waterbury Center   D4

The Black Locust Inn

5088 Waterbury-Stowe Rd, Rt 100
Waterbury Center, VT 05677
(802)244-7490 (800)366-5592 Fax:(802)244-8473
E-mail: innkeeper@blacklocustinn.com
Web: www.blacklocustinn.com

Circa 1832. Set on a hill graced with tall black locust trees is
this recently restored three-gabled farmhouse. The home once
presided over a 200-acre dairy farm and looks out to the Green
Mountain range and Camel's Hump. Guest rooms offer inviting
beds with duvets, down comforters, and piles of pillows.
Bathrobes, thick towels and hand-made soaps are among the
amenities. Wooden rocking chairs line the porch and situated
in scenic spots are gatherings of Vermont-made country furniture. A hammock swings between two locust trees. Afternoon
appetizers and drinks are served, and in the morning a three-
course candlelight breakfast might offer items such as freshly
baked maple muffins, poached pear served with Ben & Jerry's
sorbet and Vermont summer vegetable quiche with maple-
cured sausage.

Innkeeper(s): Len, Nancy & Valerie Vignola. $125-225. 6 rooms with PB.
Breakfast and snacks/refreshments included in rates. Beds: KQ.
Publicity: New York Times, Yankee, Ski Magazine, Vermont Magazine and
Discovery TV: "Best Places to Kiss."

*"Vermont's best kept secret! You are not just a bed and breakfast...
you go far beyond. The amenities and attention that we received
was nothing like we have ever experienced at any other B&B. You
made our stay so special. Memories that will last us for a lifetime.
Thank you."*

West Dover   K3

Austin Hill Inn

Rt 100, Box 859
West Dover, VT 05356
(802)464-5281 (800)332-7352 Fax:(802)464-1229

Circa 1930. This family-owned and operated inn is situated
between Mt. Snow and Haystack Mountains just outside the
historic village of West Dover. Guest rooms feature country
decor and furnishings. Romantic amenities include in-room
fireplaces and votive candles at turndown. Guests are treated
to a hearty New England breakfast, as well as afternoon wine
and cheese or home-baked
treats. In cool weather, guests
enjoy the warm glow of the
inn's fireplaces in the common
rooms. The Austin Hill Inn is
notable for its attention to detail
and superior hospitality.

Innkeeper(s): John & Deborah Bailey. $115-195. 10 rooms with PB, 1 suite
and 1 conference room. Breakfast and snacks/refreshments included in rates.
Types of meals: Full bkfst and gourmet dinner. Beds: KQDT. TV, fax, copier
and fireplace on premises. Antiquing, bicycling, canoeing/kayaking, cross-
country skiing, downhill skiing, fishing, golf, hiking, live theater, parks and
chamber music nearby.
Publicity: Country Inns, Getaways and Greenwich Magazine.

West Townshend   K4

Windham Hill Inn

311 Lawrence Drive
West Townshend, VT 05359-9701
(802)874-4080 (800)944-4080 Fax:(802)874-4702
E-mail: windham@sover.net
Web: www.windhamhill.com

Circa 1825. Originally a working dairy farm with a three-
story house, this peaceful Green Mountain home boasts
upscale country decor with Oriental carpets, period antiques
and fine locally made furnishings. The large music room was
built with the help of Will Ackerman, founder of Windham
Hill Records. It features an 1911 restored Steinway piano,
entertainment center and extensive CD collection. Wood-
burning brick fireplaces add a warm ambiance to the two
parlors. The main house and White Barn guest bedrooms
and lofts all offer great views. Many feature fireplaces or
Vermont Castings stoves, window seats, Jacuzzis or soaking
tubs and private porches. Scrumptiously satisfying cuisine is
served in the Frog Pond Dining Room. Play tennis on a
native-clay court, and then enjoy a swim in the brick-terraced
heated pool. Hike the four-mile network of trails through
160 acres of pine and maple forest. In the winter, the trails
are groomed for cross-country skiing and snowshoeing, with
ice skating on the pond.

Innkeeper(s): Joe & Marina Coneeny. $170-395. 21 rooms with PB, 16 with
FP. Breakfast and snacks/refreshments included in rates. Types of meals: Full
bkfst, early coffee/tea and afternoon tea. Beds: KQ. CD player, telephone,
turn-down service, radio/CD player, bathrobe, some with private decks and
some with soaking tub or whirlpool bath in room. Air conditioning. TV, fax,
copier, swimming, tennis, Internet access, gardens, walking trails, complimentary use of XC skis and snowshoes, trail network, fine dining, award winning wine list and evening cheese and crackers on premises. Weddings, small
meetings and family reunions hosted. Antiquing, downhill skiing, fishing, live
theater, water sports and countryside exploring nearby.
Publicity: New York, Ski, Vermont Ski Magazine, Yankee and Country

Inns Bed & Breakfast and Discerning Traveler.

"...enhanced. That's how I felt after not very long at all at the end of this particular road. Enhanced by exquisite views, extraordinary food and amiable hosts." — *James Tabor, Vermont Life*

Weston J3

The Darling Family Inn

815 Rt 100
Weston, VT 05161-5404
(802)824-3223

Circa 1830. This two-story inn also features two cottages. Located in the Green Mountains, just minutes from Bromley, Okemo, Magic and Stratton ski areas, the inn provides a taste of life from the early Colonial days. Guest rooms feature handmade quilts crafted locally. The cottages include kitch-enettes, and pets are welcome in the cottages if prior arrangements are made.

Innkeeper(s): Chapin & Joan Darling.
$85-145. 5 rooms with PB and 2 cottages. Breakfast included in rates. Types of meals: Full bkfst. Reading lamp and turn-down service in room. VCR, swimming, telephone and fireplace on premises. Small meetings and family reunions hosted. Antiquing, cross-country skiing, downhill skiing, live theater and shopping nearby.

The Inn at Weston

Scenic Route 100
Weston, VT 05161-0056
(802)824-6789 Fax:(802)824-3073
E-mail: info@innweston.com
Web: www.innweston.com

Circa 1848. Elegance and luxury reside at this historic 19th century Colonial inn, with award-winning restaurant and cozy pub with a wood-burning fireplace. Relax on Adirondack chairs in the field, gaze at the West River from the deck gazebo or sit on the porch rockers. Seasonal refreshments are enjoyed every afternoon. Posh guest bedrooms and suites in the inn, Coleman House and Carriage House boast fine linens and Ralph Lauren comforters on feather beds, fresh flowers, Lindt chocolate truffles, Saratoga Sparkling Water and European toiletries. Combinations of steam showers, saunas, two-person whirlpool or thermal massage tubs are available. A sumptuous breakfast is served al fresco or fireside. Tour the Greenhouse and learn all about orchids.

Historic Interest: Listed in the National Register of Historic Places.
Innkeeper(s): Bob & Linda Aldrich. $155-335. 13 rooms with PB, 9 with FP and 2 suites. Breakfast included in rates. Types of meals: Full gourmet bkfst, afternoon tea and gourmet dinner. Restaurant on premises. Beds: KQDT. Modem hook-up, data port, cable TV, VCR, reading lamp, stereo, ceiling fan, clock radio, telephone, desk, hot tub/spa, fireplace, steam shower and two-person whirlpool or thermal massage tubs in room. Central air. Fax, copier, library, child care, parlor games, fireplace and laundry facility on premises. Weddings, small meetings, family reunions and seminars hosted. Antiquing, art galleries, bicycling, canoeing/kayaking, cross-country skiing, downhill skiing, fishing, golf, hiking, horseback riding, live theater, museums, parks, shopping, Vermont country store and Weston Playhouse nearby.
Publicity: *Discerning Traveler (Awarded one of the twelve "Romantic Hideaways" in 2002) and Wine Spectator ("Award of Excellence").*

"Your staff was very attentive and courteous. Bill and I cannot stop talking about the delicious meals we were served both at breakfast and dinner. I'm sure our friends and family have committed to memory each meal we ate."

The Judge Wilder Inn

25 Lawrence Hill Rd
Weston, VT 05161-5600
(802)824-8172 Fax:(802)824-5054
E-mail: wilder@sover.net
Web: www.wilderhomestead.com

Circa 1827. Carrying on the tradition of friendly hospitality, this historic brick home with Federal and Greek Revival stylings is a short stroll from the picturesque village green. It is surrounded by the scenic beauty of the Green Mountains, situated at the edge of the forest by a meadow and two waterfalls. Relaxing guest bedrooms offer great views and most feature original Moses Eaton stenciling. A generous breakfast buffet includes a hot entree. Linger over afternoon tea and good conversation. The pub and dining room are open to the public.

Historic Interest: Museum Tavern in Weston, Old Grist Mill, Coolidge home (25 miles), Lincoln's home (20 miles).
Innkeeper(s): Paul Mazgelis & Roland Labrie. $95-165. 7 rooms. Breakfast and afternoon tea included in rates. Types of meals: Full bkfst. Beds: KQDT. Reading lamp in room. TV and VCR on premises. Weddings, small meetings and family reunions hosted. Antiquing, cross-country skiing, downhill skiing, fishing, live theater, shopping and sporting events nearby.
Publicity: *Country, Boston Globe and New York Times.*

Williston D2

Catamount B&B

592 Governor Chittenden Rd
Williston, VT 05495
(802)878-2180 (888)680-1011 Fax:(802)879-6066
E-mail: lucy@catamountoutdoor.com
Web: www.catamountoutdoor.com

Circa 1796. This huge Federal Colonial Revival inn on 500 acres has been in the McCullough family since 1873. In its early years, the elegant homestead sponsored many grand balls, and today the home exudes a sense of rich family history. The inn is the oldest standing building in Williston, and it has been a Williston landmark for more than 200 years. It is located on the family farm where the family owns and operates a recreation center that includes many outdoor activities. The grounds have one of the finest mountain bike facilities available. It has a professionally designed trail network that includes flat, rolling and steep trails that range from single-track to wide. And it has an acre of groomed ice for ice skating and a tree-free sledding hill. Guests who stay in the inn's three guest bedrooms (including one suite) enjoy a hearty continental breakfast each morning with courses such as homemade muffins, seasonal fruits, cereals, coffee and tea and sometimes waffles.

Innkeeper(s): Lucy & Jim McCullough. $75-105. 3 rooms, 1 suite and 1 conference room. Breakfast included in rates. Types of meals: Cont plus, veg bkfst and early coffee/tea. Beds: D. TV, VCR, fax, copier, bicycles, library, parlor games, telephone, fireplace, cross-country skiing, snowshoes, ice skating and 20 miles of trails on premises. Weddings, small meetings and seminars hosted. Amusement parks, antiquing, art galleries, beach, bicycling, canoeing/kayaking, cross-country skiing, downhill skiing, fishing, golf, hiking, horseback riding, live theater, museums, parks, shopping, sporting events, tennis, water sports, wineries and Burlington- the cultural hub of Vermont nearby.

Wilmington K3

The Red Shutter Inn

41 West Main
Wilmington, VT 05363
(802)464-3768 (800)845-7548 Fax:(802)464-5123
E-mail: innkeeper@redshutterinn.com
Web: www.redshutterinn.com

Circa 1894. This colonial inn sits on a five-acre hillside amid maples, pin oaks and evergreens. Tucked behind the inn is the renovated carriage house; among its charms is a cozy fireplace suite. In the summer, guests can enjoy gourmet dining by candlelight on an awning-covered porch. The Red Shutter Inn, with its fireplaces in the sitting room and dining room, antique furnishings and view of a rushing river, provide a congenial atmosphere. Antique shops, galleries and craft shops are within walking distance.

Innkeeper(s): Lucylee and Gerard Gingras. $105-260. 9 rooms with PB, 3 with FP and 2 suites. Breakfast included in rates. Types of meals: Full bkfst and gourmet dinner. Restaurant on premises. Beds: QD. Cable TV, reading lamp, ceiling fan, whirlpool tub and some with air conditioning in room. TV, library, telephone and fireplace on premises. Weddings, small meetings, family reunions and seminars hosted. Antiquing, cross-country skiing, downhill skiing, fishing, parks, shopping and water sports nearby.
Publicity: *USA Weekend.*

"You've made The Red Shutter Inn a cozy and relaxing hideaway."

Woodstock H4

Applebutter Inn

Happy Valley Rd
Woodstock, VT 05091
(802)457-4158 (800)486-1734 Fax:(802)457-4158
Web: www.applebutterinn.com

Circa 1850. Gracious hospitality and comfort are equally enjoyed at this elegant 1854 country home. Authentically restored, this Federal gabled inn listed in the National Register boasts original wide pine floors, Oriental rugs and rare antiques. Relax by the fire in the Yellow Room or browse through the extensive book collection. Play the Mason & Hamlin grand piano in the Music Room. Several of the spacious and romantic guest bedrooms feature fireplaces. The Cameo Room also has a separate entrance. Sleep well on an 18th century pencil-post bed in the King David Room with a private porch. Sit in the morning sun of the breakfast room and savor a gourmet meal highlighted by Barbara's own applebutter. Play croquet on the expansive lawn, or sit on the porch with afternoon tea and fresh-baked cookies. Located in the tranquil hamlet of Taftsville, seasonal activities and fine dining are close by.

Innkeeper(s): Barbara & Michael. $95-195. 6 rooms with PB and 1 conference room. Breakfast, afternoon tea and snacks/refreshments included in rates. Types of meals: Country bkfst, veg bkfst and early coffee/tea. Beds: KQDT. Cable TV, VCR and clock radio in room. Air conditioning. Fax, copier, library, parlor games, telephone and fireplace on premises.
Publicity: *Los Angeles Times and recommended in Yankee and Food & Wine.*

Ardmore Inn

23 Pleasant St, PO Box 466
Woodstock, VT 05091
(802)457-3887 (800)497-9652 Fax:(802)457-9006
E-mail: ardmoreinn@aol.com
Web: www.ardmorein.com

Circa 1850. This Greek Revival-style inn offers a gentle welcome with its pretty shutters and graceful entrance. Located on an acre in a village setting, it is furnished elegantly. For instance, the Tully Room has four eyebrow windows shedding sunlight on its four-poster queen bed, and there's a sitting area and marble bath. Enjoy breakfasts of Vermont flat bread served with truffle eggs, apple-smoked sausage and asparagus spears.
$110-175. 5 suites, 1 with FP. Breakfast and afternoon tea included in rates. Types of meals: Full gourmet bkfst. Beds: KQD. Reading lamp, refrigerator, clock radio and desk in room. Air conditioning. Fax, copier, bicycles, telephone and fireplace on premises. Weddings, small meetings and family reunions hosted. Antiquing, cross-country skiing, downhill skiing, fishing, golf, live theater, parks, shopping, tennis, mountain biking and fly fishing nearby.

Canterbury House

43 Pleasant St
Woodstock, VT 05091-1129
(802)457-3077 (800)390-3077
E-mail: innkeeper@thecanterburyhouse.com
Web: www.thecanterburyhouse.com

Circa 1880. National Geographic tabbed Woodstock as one of America's most beautiful villages, and this Victorian inn offers a lovely stopping place for those exploring the area. Visitors find themselves within easy walking distance of antique stores, art galleries, museums, restaurants and shopping. Ski lifts at Killington, Pico and Okemo are only minutes away.

Historic Interest: The Dana Museum and Billings Farm Museum are some of the historic sites. Walking tours are available.

Innkeeper(s): Bob & Sue Frost. $120-180. 7 rooms with PB, 1 with FP. Breakfast included in rates. Types of meals: Full gourmet bkfst. Beds: KQT. Air conditioning. VCR, parlor games, telephone and fireplace on premises. Weddings, small meetings and family reunions hosted. Antiquing, cross-country skiing, downhill skiing, fishing, live theater, parks, shopping, sporting events, water sports and mountain bikes nearby.
Publicity: *Boston Globe, Glamour Magazine and Travel & Leisure.*

Carriage House of Woodstock

455 Woodstock Road, Rt 4 West
Woodstock, VT 05091-1253
(802)457-4322 (800)791-8045 Fax:(802)457-4322

Circa 1860. This century-old home has been generously refurbished and features rooms filled with period antiques and individual decor. Those in search of relaxation will find plenty of

possibilities, from quiet music and conversation in the parlor to relaxing on the wraparound porch overlooking the picturesque views. Antique shopping, galleries, the historic Billings Farm Museum and plenty of outdoor activities are found in the Woodstock area. Fall and spring bring an explosion of color, and scenic drives will take you under covered bridges.

Innkeeper(s): Debbe & Mark Stanglin. $95-180. 9 rooms with PB, 1 with

FP. Breakfast and snacks/refreshments included in rates. Types of meals: Country bkfst. Beds: KQT. Cable TV, VCR, reading lamp, clock radio, desk, 1 with fireplace, 4 with cable TV, 3 with whirlpool tub and individual heat in room. Air conditioning. Telephone and fireplace on premises. Antiquing, art galleries, bicycling, canoeing/kayaking, cross-country skiing, downhill skiing, fishing, golf, hiking, horseback riding, live theater, museums, parks and shopping nearby.

Charleston House

21 Pleasant St
Woodstock, VT 05091-1131
(802)457-3843
E-mail: charleston@adelphia.net
Web: charlestonhouse.com

Circa 1835. This authentically restored brick Greek Revival town house, in the National Register, welcomes guests with shuttered many-paned windows and window boxes filled with pink blooms. Guest rooms are appointed with period antiques and reproductions, an art collection and Oriental rugs. Some of the rooms boast four-poster beds, and some feature fireplaces and Jacuzzis. A hearty full breakfast starts off the day in the candlelit dining room, and the innkeepers serve afternoon refreshments, as well. Area offerings include winter sleigh rides, snow skiing, auctions, fly fishing, golfing and summer stock theater, to name a few.

Historic Interest: The Billings/Marsh National Historic Park and Calvin Coolidge Homestead are nearby attractions.

Innkeeper(s): Dieter & Willa Nohl. $115-220. 9 rooms with PB. Breakfast included in rates. Types of meals: Full bkfst. Beds: QT. TV in room. Jacuzzis and fireplaces on premises. Antiquing, cross-country skiing, downhill skiing, fishing and golf nearby.

Publicity: *Harbor News, Boston Business Journal, Weekend Getaway, Inn Spots and Special Places.*

Village Inn of Woodstock

41 Pleasant St
Woodstock, VT 05091-1146
(802)457-1255 (800)722-4571 Fax:(802)457-3109
E-mail: stay@villageinnofwoodstock.com
Web: www.villageinnofwoodstock.com

Circa 1899. In a historic village location, this Queen Anne Victorian inn and intimate tavern create the perfect setting for a romantic interlude, weekend getaway or family reunion. Period antique furnishings are accented by original wood floors, oak molding and wainscoting, heavy beveled glass and ornate tin ceilings. Some guest bedrooms feature marble washstands, clawfoot tubs, Oriental rugs, brass and four-poster cherry beds. One boasts a stained-glass window and fireplace. Savor a three-course breakfast in the dining room showcasing antiques, art work and folk art. Relax in the garden, resplendent with pond and fountain.

Innkeeper(s): Evelyn & David Brey. $85-240. 7 rooms with PB, 1 with FP. Breakfast included in rates. Types of meals: Full bkfst, early coffee/tea, lunch, picnic lunch and dinner. Beds: KQD. Cable TV, reading lamp, clock radio and fireplace in room. Air conditioning. VCR, parlor games, telephone and fire-place on premises. Weddings, small meetings and family reunions hosted. Antiquing, art galleries, bicycling, canoeing/kayaking, cross-country skiing, downhill skiing, fishing, golf, hiking, horseback riding, live theater, museums, parks, shopping and tennis nearby.

The Woodbridge Inn of Woodstock

546 Woodstock Road
Woodstock, VT 05091
(802)672-1800 (866)966-3274

Circa 1870. Sitting alongside the scenic Ottaquechee River, this post Civil War Victorian home is cradled by the majestic Green Mountains. Relax in the private guest lounge with an open front wood stove and comfortable seating to watch a DVD on the 52-inch projection television. French doors open onto a sunny deck with a gorgeous view and an outdoor stone fireplace. Elegantly appointed guest bedrooms feature antique furnishings, warm colors and individual climate controls. Bring a big appetite to breakfast each morning in the dining room. An assortment of delicious food is well presented on white linen tablecloths with candles lit for a romantic ambiance. Shop the historic Marketplace at the Bridgewater Mill, just 300 yards away. Ski at nearby Killington Resort.

Innkeeper(s): Amy Audsley. $69-159. 6 rooms with PB. Beds: KQ. Modem hook-up, reading lamp, clock radio, high-speed Internet access available and large screen TV in guest lounge in room. Air conditioning. TV, VCR, fax, copier, telephone, fireplace and satellite and DVD viewing on large screen TV in guest lounge on premises. Weddings, small meetings and family reunions hosted.

Woodstocker B&B

61 River St Route 4
Woodstock, VT 05091-1227
(802)457-3896 (866)662-1439 Fax:(802)457-3897
E-mail: woodstocker@valley.net
Web: www.woodstockervt.com

Circa 1830. This early 19th-century, Cape-style inn is located at the base of Mt. Tom at the edge of the village of Woodstock. Hand-hewn wooden beams create a rustic effect. The seven guest rooms and two suites are individually appointed. Buffet-style, full breakfasts get the day off to a great start. Guests can take a short walk across a covered bridge to reach shops and restaurants. Hikers will enjoy trails that wind up and around Mt. Tom. After a busy winter day, come back and enjoy a soak in the five-person whirlpool.

Historic Interest: Billings Farm and Museum, the Calvin Coolidge Homestead and Dana House Museum are some of the historic sites. Four of Woodstock's churches boast bells made by Paul Revere.

Innkeeper(s): Tom & Nancy Blackford. $85-205. 9 rooms with PB and 2 suites. Breakfast included in rates. Types of meals: Full bkfst and early coffee/tea. Beds: QD. Cable TV, reading lamp and ceiling fan in room. Air conditioning. VCR, fax, copier and telephone on premises. Weddings and family reunions hosted. Antiquing, cross-country skiing, downhill skiing, fishing, live theater, shopping, sporting events and water sports nearby.

"You have truly opened your home and heart to create a comfortable and memorable stay."

Virginia

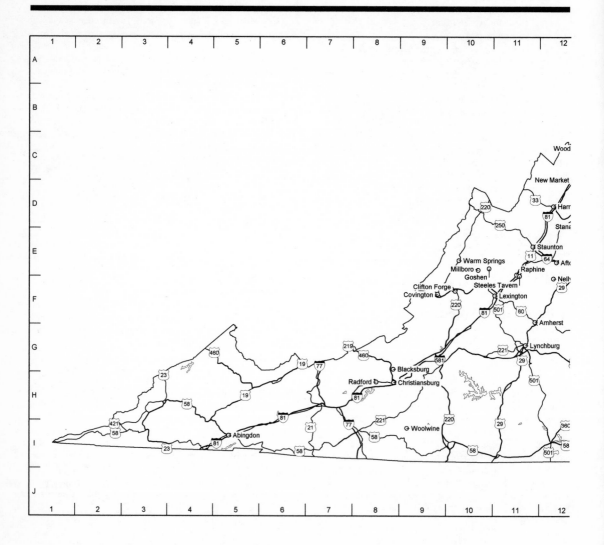

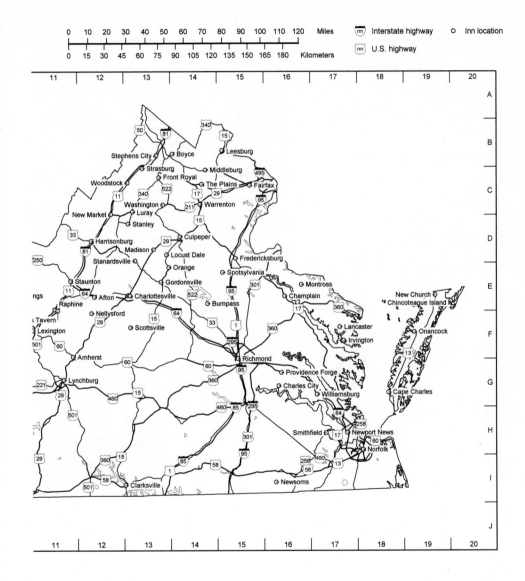

Miles
0 10 20 30 40 50 60 70 80 90 100 110 120

Kilometers
0 15 30 45 60 75 90 105 120 135 150 165 180

Interstate highway
U.S. highway
Inn location

Abingdon I5

Victoria & Albert B&B

224 Oak Hill St NE
Abingdon, VA 24210-2824
(800)475-5494
E-mail: v&rainn@naxs.com
Web: www.abingdon-virginia.com

Circa 1892. Awarded AAA's coveted 4 Diamonds (1996-2001), this handsome green and white, three-story Victorian inn is situated on a quiet street within walking distance to Abingdon's celebrated theaters, museums, galleries and historic homes. Shaded porches, bay windows and tasteful decor are among the inn's special features. Guest rooms offer ceiling fans and finely crafted traditional furnishings; all have gas fireplaces or whirlpool tubs. There are plenty of amenities such as hair dryers and CD players. In the late evening, desserts and wine are served, and the innkeepers pamper guests with evening turndown service. Full formal breakfasts are served in the dining room or guests can opt to enjoy the meal on the porches.
Historic Interest: The Victoria and Albert is located in Abingdon's historic district and within walking distance of shops and the Barter Theatre.
Innkeeper(s): Hazel Ramos-Cano & Richard Cano. $99-135. 5 rooms with PB. Breakfast included in rates. Types of meals: Full bkfst, early coffee/tea, snacks/refreshments and dinner. Beds: KQ. Cable TV, VCR, reading lamp, CD player, ceiling fan, clock radio, telephone, turn-down service, robes, gas fireplace and hair dryers in room. Air conditioning. Library, fireplace and gift shop on premises. Weddings, small meetings and family reunions hosted. Bicycling, fishing, hiking, live theater, shopping and Ballooning nearby.

"With all of the luxuries that you provide for your guests, I truly felt like royalty! My hat off to you and what you have accomplished at the Victoria and Albert."

Afton E12

Afton Mountain Bed & Breakfast

10273 Rockfish Valley Hwy
Afton, VA 22920-2771
(540)456-6844 (800)769-6844 Fax:(540)456-7255

Circa 1848. Surrounded by 140-year-old silver maples adorning 10 acres in the foothills of the Blue Ridge Mountains, this Victorian farmhouse features original heart pine floors and staircase, a stained-glass entryway and a variety of antiques. Air-conditioned guest bedrooms boast luxurious beds for the ultimate in comfort and include unique furnishings. A sumptuous breakfast begins with fresh fruit, homemade baked goods and an entree specialty. Stroll in the formal rose garden or swim in the pool. Relax on one of the spacious porches with just-baked cookies and a beverage. Tour scenic Skyline Drive, sample wines at local award-winning vineyards, golf or ski. Ask about special packages. Gift certificates are available for the perfect anniversary, birthday, or romantic getaway. Charlottesville and Monticello are nearby.
Innkeeper(s): Orquida and Dan Ingraham. $70-140. 5 rooms with PB. Breakfast, afternoon tea and snacks/refreshments included in rates. Types of meals: Full gourmet bkfst and early coffee/tea. Beds: KQDT. Ceiling fan and AM/FM CD player in room. Air conditioning. Fax, copier, swimming, library and VCR/DVD on premises. Weddings, small meetings and family reunions hosted. Antiquing, cross-country skiing, downhill skiing, fishing, golf, hiking, horseback riding, parks, shopping, sporting events, tennis, water sports and wineries nearby.

Amherst F11

Dulwich Manor B&B Inn

550 Richmond Hwy
Amherst, VA 24521-3962
(434)946-7207 (800)571-9011
E-mail: mfarmer@iwinet.com
Web: www.thedulwichmanor.com

Circa 1912. This red Flemish brick and white columned English Manor sits on five secluded acres at the end of a country lane and in the midst of 97 acres of woodland and meadow. The Blue Ridge Parkway is minutes away. The entry fea-

tures a large center hall and a wide oak staircase. Walls are 14 inches thick. The 18 rooms include a 50-foot-long ballroom on the third floor. The inn is decorated with a creative mix of antiques, traditional furniture and collectibles.
Innkeeper(s): Mark & Gail Moore. $95-120. 5 rooms with PB, 2 with FP. Breakfast included in rates. Types of meals: Full bkfst and early coffee/tea. Beds: KQ. Reading lamp, clock radio and two rooms with whirlpool tub in room. Air conditioning. Parlor games, telephone and fireplace on premises. Weddings, small meetings, family reunions and seminars hosted. Antiquing, downhill skiing, fishing, hiking, parks, shopping, sporting events, water sports, wineries, historic sites, Monticello and Appomattox Court House and Natural Bridge nearby.
Publicity: *Country Inn and Scene.*

Blacksburg G8

Clay Corner Inn

401 Clay St SW
Blacksburg, VA 24060
(540)953-2604 Fax:(540)951-0541

Circa 1929. Clay Corner Inn is comprised of four houses on a corner one block from Virginia Tech and a couple blocks from downtown. There are 12 guest rooms, three of which are two-bedroom suites. Each room is decorated with a different theme; all guest rooms have a private bath, cable TV, telephone and a queen or king bed. Two houses were built early in the century, two are a decade old and two others, circa 1940, are private residences. A full breakfast is served in the main house or covered deck outside. The inn also features an on-site heated swimming pool and a hot tub.

Historic Interest: Smithfield Plantation is one mile away, Blacksburg is over 200 years old.
Innkeeper(s): Joanne Anderson. $89-155. 12 rooms with PB. Breakfast included in rates. Types of meals: Full bkfst and early coffee/tea. Beds: KQ. Modem hook-up, data port, cable TV, reading lamp, ceiling fan, clock radio, telephone and desk in room. Central air. Fax, copier, spa, swimming, library, parlor games, fireplace and laundry facility on premises. Antiquing, art galleries, bicycling, canoeing/kayaking, fishing, golf, hiking, live theater, museums, shopping, sporting events, tennis and wineries nearby.

Boyce   B14

L'Auberge Provencale

13630 Lord Fairfax Highway
Boyce, VA 22620
(540)837-1375 (800)638-1702 Fax:(540)837-2004
E-mail: cborel@shentel.net
Web: www.laubergeprovencale.com

Circa 1753. This farmhouse was built with fieldstones gathered from the area. Hessian soldiers crafted the woodwork of the main house, Mt. Airy. As the name suggests, a French influence is prominent throughout the inn. Victorian and European antiques fill the elegant guest rooms, several of which include fireplaces. Innkeeper Alain Borel hails from a long line of master chefs, his expertise creates many happy culinary memories guests cherish. Many of the French-influenced items served at the inn's four-diamond restaurant, include ingredients from the inn's gardens, and Alain has been hailed by James Beard as a Great Country Inn Chef. The innkeepers also offer accommodations three miles away at Villa La Campagnette, an 1890 restored home. The home includes two suites and the Grand Master bedroom. Guests enjoy 18 acres with a swimming pool, hot tub and stables.

Historic Interest: Waterford, Luray Caverns, Holy Cross Abbey (Historic Long Branch).

Innkeeper(s): Alain & Celeste Borel. $145-275. 14 rooms, 10 with PB, 6 with FP, 4 suites and 1 conference room. Breakfast included in rates. Types of meals: Full gourmet bkfst, veg bkfst, early coffee/tea, picnic lunch, gourmet dinner and room service. Restaurant on premises. Beds: KQD. Reading lamp, ceiling fan, clock radio, coffeemaker and hot tub/spa in room. Central air. Fax, copier, spa, swimming, parlor games, telephone and fireplace on premises. Weddings, small meetings, family reunions and seminars hosted. Antiquing, art galleries, bicycling, canoeing/kayaking, fishing, golf, hiking, horseback riding, live theater, museums, parks, shopping, tennis and wineries nearby.
Publicity: *Food & Wine, Romantic Homes, Bon Appetit, Glamour, Washington Dossier, Washington Post, Baltimore, Richmond Times, Southern Living, Travel & Leisure, Great Chefs of the East and Great Country Inns.*

"A magical place to spend a birthday. Wonderful food an ambiance. Very romantic."

Bumpass   E14

Rockland Farm Retreat

3609 Lewiston Rd
Bumpass, VA 23024-9659
(540)895-5098

Circa 1820. The 75 acres of Rockland Farm include pasture land, livestock, vineyard, crops and a farm pond for fishing. The grounds here are said to have spawned Alex Haley's "Roots." Guests can study documents and explore local cemeteries describing life under slavery in the area surrounding this historic home and 18th-century farmlands.

Historic Interest: Some of the oldest slave cemeteries are nearby.
Innkeeper(s): Roy E. Mixon. $79-89. 4 rooms, 3 with PB, 1 suite and 2 conference rooms. Breakfast included in rates. Types of meals: Full bkfst, lunch and dinner. Beds: DT. Reading lamp, clock radio and desk in room. Air conditioning. VCR, parlor games, telephone and fireplace on premises. Weddings, small meetings, family reunions and seminars hosted. Amusement parks, antiquing, fishing, parks, shopping and water sports nearby.
Publicity: *Washington Post and Free Lance-Star.*

Cape Charles   G18

Cape Charles House

645 Tazewell Ave
Cape Charles, VA 23310-3313
(757)331-4920 Fax:(757)331-4960
E-mail: stay@capecharleshouse.com
Web: capecharleshouse.com

Circa 1912. A local attorney built this 1912 Colonial Revival home on the site of the town's first schoolhouse. The Cape Charles House is the recipient of the Governor's Award for Virginia Bed and Breakfast Hospitality. Oriental rugs cover lovingly restored hardwood floors. The owners have skillfully combined antiques, heirlooms, artwork, fabrics and collections.
Spacious guest bedrooms are named after historically significant townspeople. The premier Julia Wilkins Room features a whirlpool tub/shower and balcony. Gourmet breakfasts served in the formal dining  room may include favorites like fresh mango-stuffed croissants in an egg custard with grated nutmeg and orange liqueur. Enjoy late afternoon wine and cheese as well as tea and sweets. Visit the historic Victorian village and swim the quiet bay beach. Bikes, beach towels, chairs and umbrellas are available.

Innkeeper(s): Bruce & Carol Evans. $95-150. 5 rooms with PB. Breakfast, afternoon tea and snacks/refreshments included in rates. Types of meals: Full gourmet bkfst and early coffee/tea. Beds: KQ. Reading lamp, ceiling fan, clock radio, desk and Jacuzzi (two rooms) in room. Air conditioning. VCR, fax, copier, bicycles, parlor games, telephone and fireplace on premises. Weddings, small meetings, family reunions and seminars hosted. Antiquing, fishing, golf, live theater, parks, shopping, tennis and water sports nearby.
Publicity: *Southern Inns.*

"We'll rave, recommend, and we'll return. The culinary magic of your enchanting breakfasts are beyond comparison, unless you consider the charming effects of your warm and generous spirits."

Chesapeake Charm B&B

202 Madison Ave
Cape Charles, VA 23310
(757)331-2676 (800)546-9215 Fax:(757)331-3983
E-mail: info@chesapeakecharmbnb.com
Web: www.chesapeakecharmbnb.com

Circa 1921. Proudly situated in a large historic district on the banks of Chesapeake Bay, this American Revival inn maintains its original design construction. The hardwood floors, natural heart pine windows and architectural accents blend well with the period antiques and family furnishings that have been cherished since the house was first occupied. Families are welcome here and easily accommodated. The guest bedrooms are comfortably elegant with gorgeous wallpapers and draperies. The private Bay Loft features a sitting area and whirlpool tub. Breakfast is always a treat, with a specialty gourmet entree, meat dish and homemade baked goods. Gather in one of the common rooms for afternoon refreshments and non-alcoholic beverages. Bikes are available for exploring the local sites.

Innkeeper(s): Phyllis S. Tyndall. $75-120. 4 rooms with PB. Breakfast, afternoon tea and snacks/refreshments included in rates. Types of meals: Full gourmet bkfst. Beds: QT. Cable TV, VCR, refrigerator, ceiling fan and clock radio in room. Air conditioning. Fax, copier, bicycles, parlor games, telephone and fireplace on premises. Family reunions hosted. Antiquing, art galleries, beach, fishing, golf, hiking, museums, parks, shopping, tennis and water sports nearby.

Wilson-Lee House B&B on Virginia's Eastern Shore

403 Tazewell Ave
Cape Charles, VA 23310
(757)331-1954 Fax:(757)331-8133

Circa 1906. For a romantic retreat or relaxing getaway, this restored 1906 Colonial Revival inn reflects the style of homes built in this historic area on the Eastern Shore and an eclectic blend of Victorian and contemporary classic decor. Well-appointed guest bedrooms offer comfort and some feature a whirlpool tub. Both innkeepers are superb cooks, boasting creative gourmet breakfast menus that may include Leon's Broiled Grapefruit and Huevos Rancheros or David's Oven-baked Pancake with Apple and Creme Brulee French Toast. Vegan or vegetarian diets can be accommodated with advance notice. The landscaped corner lot features indigenous plantings, flowers, pampas grass and a magnolia tree. The side yard includes an herb garden. After a day of sightseeing, water sports, tennis or golf, soak in the large hot tub.

Historic Interest: All of Cape Charles is a National Historic District. Wilson-Lee House is typical of the houses being built at the turn of the century. It was built by the Wilson family who owned and operated the largest department store (Wilson's) on the Eastern Shore. It was designed by Norfolk architect, James W.

Innkeeper(s): David Phillips & Leon Parham. $105-160. 6 rooms with PB and 1 conference room. Breakfast and snacks/refreshments included in rates. Types of meals: Full gourmet bkfst, veg bkfst and early coffee/tea. Beds: Q. Cable TV, reading lamp, CD player, clock radio, desk and hot tub/spa in room. Central air. TV, VCR, fax, spa, bicycles and telephone on premises. Small meetings, family reunions and seminars hosted. Antiquing, art galleries, beach, bicycling, canoeing/kayaking, fishing, golf, hiking, live theater, museums, parks, shopping, tennis and water sports nearby.

Publicity: *Travel and Leisure Magazine April 1997, Chesapeake Magazine, Article and Recipes in Celebrate Virginia Cookbook by Rowena J. Fullinwider, James A. Crutchfield and Winette Sparkman Jeffre.*

Champlain   E16

Linden House B&B & Plantation

PO Box 23
Champlain, VA 22438-0023
(804)443-1170 (800)622-1202
Web: www.lindenplantation.com

Circa 1750. This restored planters home is designated a state landmark and listed in the National Register. The lush grounds boast walking trails, a pond, an English garden, patio with fountain, gazebo, arbor and five porches. Each of the accommodations offers something special. The Carriage Suite features country decor, antiques, a private porch and a fireplace. The Robert E. Lee room has a high-poster bed, fireplace and private bath. The Jefferson Davis room has a luxurious bath with a Jacuzzi and steam room. The fourth-floor Linden room affords a view of the countryside and features a queen-size bed and an alcove with a day bed adjoining the private bath. Other rooms also promise an enchanting experience. All rooms have their own television and refrigerator. With its new reception hall and verandas, the inn is popular for weddings, conferences and meetings.

Innkeeper(s): Ken & Sandra Pounsberry. $95-175. 5 rooms with PB and 2 suites. Breakfast included in rates. Types of meals: Full gourmet bkfst, early coffee/tea, snacks/refreshments and dinner. Beds: KQ. Reading lamp, refriger-

ator, clock radio, desk and some with ceiling fan in room. Central air. VCR, library, parlor games, telephone, fireplace and ballroom with large patio overlooking pond for catered receptions on premises. Limited handicap access. Weddings, small meetings, family reunions and seminars hosted. Amusement parks, antiquing, fishing, live theater, parks, shopping, water sports and boarding school nearby.

Publicity: *Rappahannock-Journal, Richmond Times Dispatch and Cable TV.*

Charles City   G16

Edgewood Plantation

4800 John Tyler Memorial Hwy
Charles City, VA 23230
(804)829-6908 (800)296-3343 Fax:(804)829-2962
E-mail: edgewoodplantation@williamsburg-virginia.com
Web: www.williamsburg-virginia.com/edgewood

Circa 1849. Among its expansive 7,000 square feet, this Gothic Revival mansion includes high ceilings, a double parlor, 10 fireplaces and a double spiral staircase. The plantation has an incredible history. It rests along the oldest highway in the United States, and it was once part of the Berkeley Plantation, the ancestral home of President William Henry Harrison. The inn's Civil War history is as fascinating as the authentic Victorian decor. Both innkeepers are antique dealers, and among the vintage pieces they've included in the inn are canopy beds dating back to 1790, 1818 and 1820. Breakfasts are served with fine silver, china and pewter on a Queen Anne table surrounded by Chippendale chairs. The innkeepers attention to detail is impressive, especially during the Christmas season when 18 decorated trees are placed throughout the inn. A few yards from the inn is a three-story mill with an unusual inside mill wheel built in 1725.

Innkeeper(s): Dot & Julian Boulware. $125-198. 8 rooms, 6 with PB, 3 with FP, 2 suites, 2 cottages and 1 conference room. Breakfast included in rates. Types of meals: Full gourmet bkfst, early coffee/tea, picnic lunch, afternoon tea and gourmet dinner. Beds: KQD. TV, VCR, reading lamp, refrigerator, ceiling fan, turn-down service and desk in room. Fax, swimming, parlor games and fireplace on premises. Weddings, small meetings, family reunions and seminars hosted. Amusement parks, antiquing, fishing, live theater, parks, shopping, sporting events, water sports and horseback riding nearby.

Publicity: *Country Home, Southern Living, Country, Victoria and Country Inns.*

"A feast for the eyes and wonderful manner in which things are displayed and put together."

North Bend Plantation

12200 Weyanoke Rd
Charles City, VA 23030-3632
(804)829-5176 Fax:(804)829-6828
E-mail: ridgely37@aol.com
Web: www.northbendplantation.com

Circa 1819. Civil war relics and southern hospitality await guests at this cultivated plantation located between Williamsburg and Richmond. Owned by the great, great grandson of Edwin Ruffin, the man who fired the first shot of the Civil War, the 1819 mansion has original mantels and stair carvings, as well as a number of Greek Revival features from the 1853 remodeling. The mansion is full of antiques, including the plantation desk used by General Sheridan when the Union Troops occupied the area in 1864. The desk still has the labels Sheridan placed on pigeonholes, and the eastern edge of the property still has Civil War breastworks. The five guests rooms, each spacious and complemented with family antiques and collectibles, range from the quaint Maids Quarters to The Sheridan Room with a Queen tester bed circa 1810 and Sheridan's desk. After a full country breakfast including delights like homemade waffles, omelets, biscuits, bacon, sausage, fruit and juice, guests may venture out on the grounds to swim or play croquet, horseshoes or volleyball. A park with nature trails and a fishing pier is just three miles from the mansion and a public golf course is 20 minutes away.

Historic Interest: The inn is a designated Virginia Historic Landmark and listed in the National Register of Historic Places. Charles City County is the home of the historic James River Plantations.

Innkeeper(s): George & Ridgely Copland. $135-160. 4 rooms with PB, 2 with FP and 1 suite. Breakfast included in rates. Types of meals: Full bkfst, early coffee/tea and afternoon tea. Beds: QD. Cable TV, reading lamp, ceiling fan, desk and refrigerator in room. Air conditioning. TV, fax, copier, swimming, bicycles, library, parlor games, telephone, fireplace, croquet, volleyball, horseshoes and hammocks on premises. Weddings, small meetings and family reunions hosted. Amusement parks, antiquing, golf, parks, shopping, colonial Williamsburg, Jamestown, Yorktown and horse racing nearby.

Publicity: *Daily Press, Richmond Times Dispatch, New York Times, Mid-Atlantic Country, Washington Post, Travel Talk, Southern Hospitality and Channel 12.*

"Your hospitality, friendship and history lessons were all priceless. Your love of life embraced us in a warmth I shall never forget."

Charlottesville   E13

200 South Street Inn

200 W South St
Charlottesville, VA 22902-5041
(434)979-0200 (800)964-7008 Fax:(434)979-4403
E-mail: southst@cstone.net
Web: www.southstreetinn.com

Circa 1844. This house was built for Thomas Jefferson Wertenbaker, son of Thomas Jefferson's librarian at the University of Virginia. It is furnished with English and Belgian antiques. Guests may choose rooms with whirlpool baths, fireplaces and canopy beds.

Historic Interest: Jefferson Home, Monticello (4 miles), Monroe Home, Ashlawn (6 miles), Madison Home, Montpelier (20 miles).

Innkeeper(s): Brendan & Jenny Clancy. $130-240. 19 rooms with PB, 10 with FP and 3 suites. Breakfast, afternoon tea and snacks/refreshments included in rates. Types of meals: Cont plus and early coffee/tea. Beds: KQT. Data port, cable TV, reading lamp, clock radio, telephone and turn-down service in room. Central air. VCR, fax, copier, library, parlor games and fireplace on premises. Weddings, small meetings, family reunions and seminars hosted. Antiquing, art galleries, bicycling, downhill skiing, fishing, golf, hiking, horseback riding, live theater, museums, parks, shopping, sporting events, tennis and wineries nearby.

Publicity: *New York Times, Gourmet, Vogue, Food & Wine, Los Angeles Times, Bon Appetit, Gourmet, Mid-Atlantic Country, Martha Stewart Living and In Style.*

"True hospitality abounds in this fine inn which is a neatly turned complement to the inspiring history surrounding it."

Chester

243 James River Rd
Charlottesville, VA 24590
(434)286-3960
E-mail: info@chesterbed.com
Web: www.chesterbed.com

Circa 1847. This historic Greek Revival house sits on seven acres of natural splendor. Beckoning from the front porch are traditional rocking chairs. Gracious Southern elegance is found throughout the inn. Visit the library or play the grand piano in the living

room. The guest bedrooms and suite boast fireplaces, four-poster beds, Oriental rugs, down comforters, plush towels and fresh flowers. Enjoy breakfast served on china with fine linens. The grounds are an informal sanctuary for people and wildlife alike. A large holly tree, lily pond, fountains, English boxwoods and pondside patio reside impressively in extensive gardens.

Innkeeper(s): Jean & Craig Stratton. $165-225. 5 rooms with PB, 5 with FP. Breakfast included in rates. Types of meals: Full gourmet bkfst and early coffee/tea. Beds: Q. Reading lamp, snack bar and turn-down service in room. Air conditioning. Fax, library, parlor games, telephone, fireplace and gourmet dinner available for groups of 6 or more on premises. Weddings, small meetings, family reunions and seminars hosted. Antiquing, cross-country skiing, downhill skiing, fishing, live theater, parks, shopping, sporting events and water sports nearby.

Guesthouses B&B Reservations

PO Box 5737
Charlottesville, VA 22905-5737
(434)979-7264
E-mail: info@va-guesthouses.com
Web: www.va-guesthouses.com

Circa 1815. Guesthouses is thought to be America's first reservation service for bed & breakfast accommodations. It appropriately originated in an area with a centuries-old tradition of outstanding hospitality. Some of the homes are in the National Register. Other homes are located near the University of Virginia and throughout Albemarle County and have been inspected carefully to assure a pleasant stay. Most accommodations offer one or two bedrooms in private homes or farms, but there is also a collection of private cottages including old renovated log houses. Mary Hill Caperton is the director.

Historic Interest: National Register.

Innkeeper(s): Mary Hill Caperton. $68-200.

Publicity: *Roanoke Times & World-News and Good Housekeeping.*

"The nicest B&B experience we had on our trip."

The Inn at Monticello

Rt 20 S, 1188 Scottsville Rd
Charlottesville, VA 22902
(434)979-3593 (877)-RELAX-VA
E-mail: stay@innatmonticello.com
Web: www.innatmonticello.com

Circa 1850. Thomas Jefferson built his own home, Monticello, just two miles from this gracious country home. The innkeepers have preserved the historic ambiance of the area. Rooms boast such pieces as four-poster beds covered with fluffy, down comforters. Some of the guest quarters have private porches or fireplaces. Breakfast at the inn is a memorable gourmet-appointed affair. Aside from the usual homemade rolls, coffee cakes and muffins, guests enjoy such entrees as pancakes or French toast with seasonal fruit, egg dishes and a variety of quiche. The front porch is lined with chairs for those who wish to relax, and the grounds feature several gardens to enjoy.

Historic Interest: Aside from its close access to Monticello, the inn is five miles from James Monroe's home, Ashlawn Highland. The historic Michie Tavern is just one mile from the inn, and the University of Virginia, which was founded by Jefferson, is about seven miles away.

Innkeeper(s): Norman & Rebecca Lindway. $100-190. 5 rooms with PB, 2 with FP. Breakfast and afternoon tea included in rates. Types of meals: Full gourmet bkfst and early coffee/tea. Beds: KQT. Reading lamp and desk in room. Air conditioning. Fax, parlor games, fireplace and afternoon tea with Virginia wine on premises. Small meetings and family reunions hosted. Antiquing, downhill skiing, live theater, parks, shopping, sporting events, Blue Ridge Parkway Sky Line Drive and wineries nearby.

Publicity: *Washington Post, Country Inns, Atlantic Country Magazine, Gourmet and Bon Appetit.*

"What a magnificent room at an extraordinary place. I can't wait to tell all my friends."

Prospect Hill Plantation Inn

PO Box 6909
Charlottesville, VA 22906
(540)967-0844 (800)277-0844 Fax:(540)967-0102
E-mail: innkeeper@prospecthill.com
Web: www.prospecthill.com

Circa 1732. Experience this authentic historic plantation complex listed in the National Register. Accommodations include the manor house, overseer's house, former slaves' quarters, summer kitchen, smokehouse, groom's quarters, log cabin and carriage house. Whether staying in one of the restored outbuildings or in one of the suites or guest bedrooms of the manor house, a variety of amenities are offered such as fireplaces, antique furnishings, Jacuzzi tubs and private decks. Relish a hearty country breakfast in bed or in the dining room. After a full day of swimming, playing golf, gathering for afternoon tea or visiting nearby Monticello, Thomas Jefferson's home, stroll the 50 acres of landscaped grounds before a candlelit five-course dinner.

Historic Interest: 1732 manor house with original dependencies dating from 1699 to 1850 converted guest rooms.

Innkeeper(s): The Sheehan family. $195-420. 13 rooms with PB, 13 with FP, 6 suites, 5 cottages, 1 cabin and 1 conference room. Breakfast, afternoon tea, snacks/refreshments and dinner included in rates. Types of meals: Full gourmet bkfst, veg bkfst, early coffee/tea, lunch, picnic lunch and room service. Restaurant on premises. Beds: KQ. Reading lamp, stereo, refrigerator, ceiling fan, clock radio, coffeemaker, desk, hot tub/spa, fireplace, fireplace and 7 with Jacuzzis in room. Air conditioning. TV, VCR, fax, copier, swimming, bicycles, library, parlor games, telephone, laundry facility and gift shop on premises. Weddings, small meetings, family reunions and seminars hosted. Amusement parks, antiquing, art galleries, bicycling, canoeing/kayaking, cross-country skiing, downhill skiing, fishing, golf, hiking, horseback riding, live theater, museums, parks, shopping, sporting events, tennis and wineries nearby.

Publicity: *The Washington Post, Better Homes and Garden, New York Times, Southern Living, LA Times, Country Inns, Country Living and Country Inns.*

"We've been to many wonderful inns - this is the nicest!"

Silver Thatch Inn

3001 Hollymead Dr
Charlottesville, VA 22911-7422
(434)978-4686 Fax:(434)973-6156
E-mail: info@silverthatch.com
Web: www.silverthatch.com

Circa 1780. This white clapboard inn, shaded by tall elms, was built by Hessian soldiers who were prisoners during the Revolutionary War. Before its present life as a country inn, Silver Thatch was a boys' school, a melon farm and a tobacco plantation. Many additions have been made to the original house. The original 1780 section is now called the Hessian Room. The inn is filled with antiques. There are three intimate dining rooms featuring contemporary cuisine.

Historic Interest: Charlottesville, Thomas Jefferson's Monticello, James Madison's Montpelier, James Monroe's Ashlawn.

Innkeeper(s): Jim & Terri Petrovits. $135-170. 7 rooms with PB, 4 with

FP. Breakfast included in rates. Types of meals: Country bkfst. Restaurant on premises. Beds: QDT. Reading lamp and clock radio in room. Air conditioning. Telephone and fireplace on premises. Antiquing, fishing, live theater, shopping and sporting events nearby.

Publicity: *Travel & Leisure, Washington Post, Los Angeles Times and New York Magazine.*

"Everything was absolutely perfect! The room, the food and above all, the people!"

Chincoteague Island   E20

The Watson House

4240 Main St
Chincoteague Island, VA 23336-2801
(757)336-1564 (800)336-6787 Fax:(757)336-5776

Circa 1898. Situated in town, this "painted lady" Victorian has a large front porch overlooking Main Street. The porch is a favorite spot of guests and often the location for afternoon tea and refreshments. Beach towels, chairs and bicycles are complimentary, and there is an outdoor shower for cleaning up after sunning.

Innkeeper(s): Tom & Jacque Derrickson, David & Jo Anne Snead. $79-129. 6 rooms with PB and 2 cottages. Breakfast included in rates. Beds: QD. Reading lamp, ceiling fan, clock radio and some with whirlpool tubs in room. Air conditioning. Fax, bicycles and telephone on premises. Antiquing, fishing, parks, shopping and water sports nearby.

Christiansburg   H8

Evergreen The Bell-Capozzi House

201 E. Main St.
Christiansburg, VA 24073
(540)382-7372 (888)382-7372 Fax:(540)382-0034
E-mail: evrgrninn@aol.com
Web: www.evergreen-bnb.com

Circa 1890. In the heart of the Blue Ridge Highlands sits this 1890 Victorian brick bed & breakfast. It has four guest bedrooms and one cottage, all decorated with comfort and elegance in mind. The inn's traditional Southern breakfasts are a hearty meal consisting of courses such as homemade biscuits, country ham, cheese grits, scrambled eggs, pancakes, Gevalia coffee and teas. Guests can enjoy the in-ground pool and gazebo in the back yard.

Historic Interest: Built in 1890. 1887 Bechstein concert grand piano.

Innkeeper(s): Rocco Capozzi & Barbara Bell-Capozzi. $125-175. 4 rooms with PB. Breakfast included in rates. Types of meals: Full gourmet bkfst, early coffee/tea and snacks/refreshments. Beds: KQD. Modem hook-up, data port, cable TV, reading lamp, stereo, refrigerator, snack bar, clock radio, coffeemaker and desk in room. Central air. Swimming, library, parlor games, telephone, fireplace, laundry facility, gazebo, rocking chairs on front porch, concert grand piano and local artwork on premises. Small meetings and seminars hosted. Antiquing, art galleries, bicycling, canoeing/kayaking, fishing, golf, hiking, live theater, museums, parks, shopping, sporting events, tennis, water sports and wineries nearby.

Publicity: *Roanoke Times, PBS, Fodors and Inn to Inn.*

Clarksville   I13

Century Manor Bed & Breakfast

PO Box 506
Clarksville, VA 23927
(434)374-5414

Circa 1898. In grand Victorian style, this two-story turreted manor sits on one-and-a-half acres in the middle of Lake Country. Filled with antiques and period furnishings, an

ambiance of welcoming warmth is evident. There are many common areas for conversation or private reflection that include a parlor, upstairs foyer with turret and a balcony. Romantic guest bedrooms are dressed with textured wallpapers, lace, canopy and iron beds, whirlpool and clawfoot tubs. Enjoy a typical country gourmet breakfast of apple crisp, crab quiche, bacon, oven-roasted potatoes and home-baked muffins served on the porch or in the dining room. Swing in the hammock or stroll through the courtyard and gazebos in the gardens.
Innkeeper(s): Pam & Mike Gentry. $75-99. 4 rooms. Breakfast included in rates. Types of meals: Full bkfst and early coffee/tea. Beds: KQD. Cable TV, VCR, ceiling fan, clock radio, king and double with Jacuzzi tub in room. Air conditioning. Telephone on premises. Antiquing, art galleries, canoeing/kayaking, fishing, golf, hiking, museums, parks and water sports nearby.

Clifton Forge   F10

Firmstone Manor

6209 Longdale Furnace Rd
Clifton Forge, VA 24422-3618
(540)862-0892 Fax:(540)862-0158
E-mail: charles@firmstonemanor.com
Web: www.firmstonemanor.com

Circa 1873. This Victorian was built by the ironmaster of the Longdale Furnace Company and is located in a state historic district named for the firm. The home boasts many unusual fea-

tures, including a wraparound porch that includes a built-in gazebo. There are more than 12 acres to enjoy, as well as views of the surrounding Shenandoah Valley and the Allegheny Mountains. Rooms are cheerfully appointed in a Victorian style and include ceiling fans and fireplaces. Civil War sites, museums, plantations, zoos, shopping and plenty of outdoor activities are in the area.
Innkeeper(s): Barbara Jarocka & Charles Towle. $80-140. 11 rooms, 6 with PB, 5 with FP, 1 suite and 1 cottage. Breakfast included in rates. Types of meals: Full bkfst, early coffee/tea and afternoon tea. Beds: KQDT. Reading lamp, ceiling fan and telephone in room. VCR, fax, copier, bicycles, library, parlor games and fireplace on premises. Weddings, small meetings and family reunions hosted. Antiquing, cross-country skiing, downhill skiing, fishing, golf, live theater, parks, shopping and water sports nearby.

"We'll catch your dreams."

Covington   F9

Milton Hall B&B Inn

207 Thorny Ln
Covington, VA 24426-5401
(540)965-0196 (877)7MILTON
E-mail: milton_h@cfw.com
Web: www.milton-hall.com

Circa 1874. This regal manor house, fashioned from handmade brick and boasting gothic details, is located in Virginia's western highlands. The historic 44-acre estate adjoins the George Washington National Forest, where guests can enjoy hiking, biking and fishing. The home was commissioned in 1874 by the Fitzwilliams, an English noble family. Guest rooms are furnished with

Victorian antiques and reproductions, creating an authentic Victorian ambiance. Each guest room includes a sitting area and fireplace. Guests are treated to both a gourmet breakfast and afternoon refreshments. The grounds include an English country garden. Guests can peruse through gifts and antiques at Lady Milton's Attic, a shop located in the carriage house.
Historic Interest: Humpback Bridge (2 miles), Falling Springs Waterfall (5 miles), Natural Bridge (45 miles), Lost World Caverns (25 miles), Greenbrier Resort (16 miles), VMI (48 miles).
Innkeeper(s): Suzanne & Eric Stratmann. $130-150. 5 rooms with PB, 5 with FP. Types of meals: Full bkfst. Beds: KQ. Turn-down service in room. TV, VCR, fax, telephone and fireplace on premises. Antiquing, downhill skiing, fishing, live theater and parks nearby.

"A lovely place, a relaxing atmosphere, delicious breakfasts, gracious hospitality. We thank you."

Culpeper   D14

Fountain Hall B&B

609 S East St
Culpeper, VA 22701-3222
(540)825-8200 (800)298-4748 Fax:(540)825-7716
E-mail: visit@fountainhall.com
Web: www.fountainhall.com

Circa 1859. The well-appointed, oversized guest bedrooms and suites offer comforts galore. Some feature a private porch, whirlpool tub, plush robes and sweeping views of neighboring farms. Enjoy a leisurely breakfast of just-baked flaky croissants with butter and jam, fresh fruits, yogurt, hot and cold cereals and beverages. The surrounding area is steeped in rich American history, and the meticulously landscaped grounds feature seasonal gardens and a lawn groomed for croquet and bocce ball.
Historic Interest: Brandy Station (5-10 miles), Chancellorsville, Wilderness (20 miles), Civil War battlefields.
Innkeeper(s): Steve & Kathi Walker. $95-150. 6 rooms with PB and 2 suites. Breakfast and snacks/refreshments included in rates. Types of meals: Cont plus and early coffee/tea. Beds: QDT. Modem hook-up, data port, cable TV, VCR, reading lamp, CD player, refrigerator, ceiling fan, clock radio, telephone and desk in room. Air conditioning. Fax, parlor games and fireplace on premises. Handicap access. Antiquing, art galleries, bicycling, canoeing/kayaking, fishing, golf, hiking, horseback riding, museums, parks, shopping and wineries nearby.
Publicity: *Culpeper Star Exponent, New York Times, Washington Post, Richmond Channel 8 and Local TV.*

"A great inn you run. We still look back on our stay at Fountain Hall as a standout."

Fairfax   C15

Bailiwick Inn

4023 Chain Bridge Rd.
Fairfax, VA 22030
(703)691-2266 Fax:(703)934-2112
E-mail: theinn@bailiwickinn.com
Web: www.bailiwickinn.com

Circa 1802. Located across from the county courthouse where George Washington's will is filed, this distinguished three-story Federal brick house recently has been renovated. The first Civil War casualty occurred on what is now the inn's lawn. The elegant, early Virginia decor is reminiscent of the state's fine plantation mansions. Ask to stay in the Thomas Jefferson Room, a

replica of Mr. Jefferson's bedroom at Monticello. Six-course "Wine Master Dinners" at the inn are featured once a month and include the opportunity for a special package rate for rooms. Every Tuesday and Sunday afternoon teas are featured. $165-225. 14 rooms, 13 with PB and 1 suite. Breakfast and afternoon tea included in rates. Types of meals: Full gourmet bkfst, gourmet lunch and gourmet dinner. Restaurant on premises. Beds: KQT. Modem hook-up, data port, cable TV, reading lamp, CD player, refrigerator, snack bar, clock radio, telephone, coffeemaker, turn-down service, desk, hot tub/spa, fireplace, Frette towels, sheets, bathrobes and hair dryers in room. Central air. VCR, fax, copier, library, fireplace, 26 seat AAA rated four diamond restaurant serving breakfast, lunch, tea, cocktails and dinner on premises. Weddings, small meetings, family reunions and seminars hosted. Amusement parks, antiquing, art galleries, bicycling, canoeing/kayaking, golf, hiking, horseback riding, live theater, museums, parks, shopping, sporting events, tennis, wineries, Mount Vernon, Woodlawn Plantation and Montpelier and many other plantations and historic sites nearby.
Publicity: *Washington Post, Washingtonian Magazine, North American Inns, Fairfax Connection, Inn Times, Mid-Atlantic Country, Victoria, Country Inns, Colonial Homes, The Food Network, Romancing America TV Program and Great Country Inns TV Program.*

"A visit to your establishment clearly transcends any lodging experience that I can recall."

Fredericksburg   D15

La Vista Plantation

4420 Guinea Station Rd
Fredericksburg, VA 22408-8850
(540)898-8444 (800)529-2823
E-mail: info@lavistaplantation.com
Web: www.lavistaplantation.com

Circa 1838. La Vista has a long and unusual past, rich in Civil War history. Both Confederate and Union armies camped here, and this is where the Ninth Cavalry was sworn in. It is no wonder then that the house is listed in the National Register of

Historic Places. The house, a Classical Revival structure with high ceilings and wide pine floors, sits on 10 acres of pasture and woods. The grounds include a pond stocked with bass. Guest quarters include a spacious room with a king-size, four-poster bed, fireplace and Empire furniture or a two-bedroom apartment that can accommodate up to six guests and includes a fireplace. Breakfasts feature homemade egg dishes from hens raised on the property.
Historic Interest: The plantation is within 15 miles of battlefields, museums, historic homes and within an hour from historic spots such as Monticello, Mt. Vernon and Washington, D.C.
Innkeeper(s): Michele & Edward Schiesser. $125-150. 3 rooms with PB. Breakfast included in rates. Types of meals: Full bkfst and early coffee/tea. Beds: KQDT. Reading lamp, refrigerator, clock radio, telephone, satellite TV and VCR in room. Air conditioning. Copier, parlor games, fireplace, fresh brown eggs from resident hens, modem, video and book library and children's library on premises. Amusement parks, antiquing, fishing, live theater, parks, shopping, sporting events, water sports, pond and rowboat and bird-watching nearby.
Publicity: *Mid-Atlantic Country, Free Lance Star and Richmond Times Dispatch.*

"Coming here was an excellent choice. La Vista is charming, quiet and restful, all qualities we were seeking. Breakfast was delicious."

On Keegan Pond Bed & Breakfast

11315 Gordon Rd
Fredericksburg, VA 22407-1725
(540)785-4662 (888)785-4662

Circa 1918. Visit historic Fredericksburg from this early 20th-century farm house located on five acres with a secluded spring-fed pond. The inn sits between two Civil War battle-

fields, both within biking distance. Artifacts found on the property indicate it was once a Union Sharpshooter campsite. The bed & breakfast features three well-appointed guest rooms, one of which is a large suite. Start the day with a hearty breakfast before striking out on day trips to see historical sites like Montpelier, Strafford Hall, Mount Vernon, Manassas, Gunston Hall and King's Dominion.
Innkeeper(s): Sandra Wallace. $65-125. 3 rooms, 2 with PB, 1 suite and 1 conference room. Breakfast and snacks/refreshments included in rates. Types of meals: Full gourmet bkfst and veg bkfst. Beds: QT. TV, VCR, CD player, refrigerator, ceiling fan, snack bar, clock radio and telephone in room. Central air. Library, fireplace and stocked pond on premises. Weddings, small meetings, family reunions and seminars hosted. Amusement parks, antiquing, art galleries, beach, bicycling, canoeing/kayaking, fishing, golf, hiking, live theater, museums, parks, shopping and wineries nearby.
Publicity: *Freelance Star Webb Site.*

Front Royal   C13

Chester House Inn

43 Chester St
Front Royal, VA 22630-3368
(540)635-3937 (800)621-0441 Fax:(540)636-8695
E-mail: mail@chesterhouse.com
Web: www.chesterhouse.com

Circa 1905. In the heart of the Historic District, this stately Italian Renaissance estate rests on two acres of terraced gardens, which include vast plantings of boxwood, wisteria arbors and a fountain fishpond. The main home features many original interior details, including an elaborately carved marble mantel. Walk to downtown restaurants and shops, the Confederate Museum and the Civil War home of Belle Boyd. The inn is just minutes from Skyline Drive, wineries, caverns, golf and hiking, or canoeing on the Shenandoah River.

Innkeeper(s): Phillip Inge, Allen & Barbara Hamblin. $120-225. 6 rooms with PB, 3 with FP, 2 suites and 1 cottage. Breakfast included in rates. Types of meals: Full bkfst and early coffee/tea. Beds: KQ. TV, reading lamp, clock radio and cottage with 2-person whirlpool bath in room. Air conditioning. VCR, fax, parlor games, telephone, fireplace, 2 TV parlors, VCR, complimentary wine, beer, sherry, soft drinks and secure wireless high-speed Internet access on premises. Small meetings and seminars hosted. Antiquing, canoeing/kayaking, fishing, golf, hiking, live theater, parks, shopping and wineries nearby.
Publicity: *Washington Entertainment Magazine, Blue Ridge Country Magazine, Rural Living Magazine, Winchester Star, Northern Virginia Daily, Inns of the Blue Ridge, EPM Publications, Winchester Star, Northern Virginia Daily and Blue Ridge Country.*

"A home of greater charm would be hard to find."

Killahevlin B&B Inn

1401 N Royal Ave
Front Royal, VA 22630-3625
(540)636-7335 (800)847-6132 Fax:(540)636-8694
E-mail: kllhvln@shentel.net
Web: www.vairish.com

Circa 1905. This Edwardian Mansion is in the National Register due in part to its builder, William Carson, creator of Skyline Drive, Williamsburg, Jamestown and Yorktown. A Civil War encampment once was located on the property. Each guest room enjoys mountain views, handsome decor and a working fireplace with antique mantels. Five rooms offer whirlpool tubs. The innkeeper shares a common Irish heritage with Will Carson. Antiques, 19th-century

Irish cottage furniture, wallpapers and Killahevlin's private Irish Pub add to the atmosphere. In addition to views of the Blue Ridge Mountains, the inn's three acres include two restored gazebos and an ornamental fish pool with a waterfall.

Innkeeper(s): Susan O'Kelly. $135-235. 6 rooms with PB, 6 with FP and 2 suites. Breakfast included in rates. Types of meals: Full bkfst and early coffee/tea. Beds: Q. Reading lamp, ceiling fan, telephone, turn-down service, desk, whirlpool baths and cable TV (suites) in room. Air conditioning. Library, parlor games, fireplace and Oriental fish pond on premises. Weddings, small meetings, family reunions and seminars hosted. Antiquing, canoeing/kayaking, fishing, golf, hiking, horseback riding, live theater, parks, shopping, water sports, wineries and fine dining nearby.

Publicity: *Washington Times, Boston Globe, Warren Sentinel, Winchester Star, Northern Virginia Daily, Ski Country and Washington Post.*

Gordonsville   E13

Sleepy Hollow Farm B&B

16280 Blue Ridge Tpke
Gordonsville, VA 22942-8214
(540)832-5555 (800)215-4804 Fax:(540)832-2515
E-mail: shfbnb@ns.gemlink.com
Web: www.sleepyhollowfarmbnb.com

Circa 1785. Many generations have added to this brick farmhouse creating somewhat of an optical illusion, as the historic home appears much smaller from a distance. The pink and white room often was visited by a friendly ghost, believed to be a Red Cross nurse during the Civil War, according to local stories. She hasn't been seen since the house was blessed in 1959. Accommodations also are available in Chestnut Cottage, which offers two suites with downstairs  sitting areas and bedrooms and baths upstairs. One suite has a fireplace. The other suite includes a deck, full kitchen, whirlpool room and Franklin wood stove. The grounds include abundant wildlife, flower gardens, an herb garden, a gazebo and pond for swimming and fishing.

Historic Interest: Montpelier (5 miles), James Madison Museum (6 miles), Wilderness Battlefields (30 miles), Civil War Exchange Hotel (4 miles), Fredricksburg (30 miles).

Innkeeper(s): Beverley Allison & Dorsey Comer. $65-150. 6 rooms with PB, 2 with FP. Breakfast included in rates. Types of meals: Full bkfst, early coffee/tea and snacks/refreshments. Beds: QDT. Cable TV, VCR, reading lamp, refrigerator, clock radio, telephone and desk in room. Air conditioning. Fax, swimming, library, two rooms with whirlpools. In the main house cake and cookies available on sideboard on premises. Weddings, small meetings and family reunions hosted. Antiquing, art galleries, downhill skiing, fishing, golf, hiking, live theater, museums, parks, shopping, sporting events, tennis, wineries, steeplechase race and historic homes nearby.

Publicity: *Orange County Review, City Magazine, Town & County, Washington Post, New York Times and Country Inn Magazine.*

"This house is truly blessed."

Goshen   E10

The Hummingbird Inn

PO Box 147, 30 Wood Ln
Goshen, VA 24439-0147
(540)997-9065 (800)397-3214
E-mail: hmgbird@hummingbirdinn.com
Web: www.hummingbirdinn.com

Circa 1853. This early Victorian villa is located in the Shenandoah Valley against the backdrop of the Allegheny Mountains. Both the first and second floors offer wraparound

verandas. Furnished with antiques, the inn features a library and sitting room with fireplaces. The rustic den and one guest room comprise the oldest portions of the inn, built around 1780. Four-course dinners, which include wine, are available by advance reservation (Friday and Saturday). An old barn and babbling creek are on the grounds. Lexington, the Virginia Horse Center, Natural Bridge, the Blue Ridge Parkway and antiquing are all nearby.

Historic Interest: Historic Lexington, Stonewall Jackson House & Museum, Lee Chapel (23 minutes). Monticello (70 minutes).

Innkeeper(s): Pam Miller & Dick Matthews. $120-165. 4 rooms with PB, 4 with FP. Breakfast included in rates. Types of meals: Full bkfst and early coffee/tea. Beds: KQ. Reading lamp and ceiling fan in room. Air conditioning. VCR, fax, library, parlor games, telephone, fireplace and satellite TV on premises. Limited handicap access. Antiquing, cross-country skiing, downhill skiing, fishing, live theater and shopping nearby.

Publicity: *Blue Ridge Country and Inn Spots and Special Places.*

"We enjoyed our stay so much that we returned two weeks later on our way back for a delicious home-cooked dinner, comfortable attractive atmosphere, and familiar faces to welcome us after a long journey."

Harborton   F19

Harborton House

28044 Harborton Road
Harborton, VA 23389
(757)442-6800 (800)882-0922

Circa 1900. Reflecting the quaint ambiance of the local bayside fishing village, this restored Victorian bed & breakfast is filled with family heirlooms, antiques and collectibles. Games and puzzles as well as a book and video library offer indoor activities. Comfortable guest bedrooms and a suite boast a nostalgic decor with modern comforts and luxuries. Enjoy breakfast in bed, in the dining room, on one of the two-story porches, or in the garden. Boats can be launched at the nearby public ramp. Try fishing or crabbing from the local dock. Bikes are available for further exploration of the scenic area.

Innkeeper(s): Helen & Andy Glenn. $89-109. 3 rooms with PB. Breakfast and snacks/refreshments included in rates. Types of meals: Full gourmet bkfst and veg bkfst. Beds: KQT. Cable TV, VCR, reading lamp, ceiling fan, clock radio and turn-down service in room. Central air. Fax, copier, bicycles, library, parlor games, telephone and fireplace on premises. Weddings, small meetings and family reunions hosted. Antiquing, art galleries, beach, bicycling, canoeing/kayaking, fishing, golf, hiking, live theater, museums, parks, shopping, tennis and water sports nearby.

Harrisonburg   D12

Joshua Wilton House

412 S Main St
Harrisonburg, VA 22801-3611
(540)434-4464 Fax:(540)432-9525
E-mail: jwhouse@rica.net
Web: www.joshuawilton.com

Circa 1888. This beautifully restored Victorian has served as a variety of dwellings. First a family home, it was later used by a fraternity and then converted into apartments. Today, the inn offers a wonderful glimpse back into the Victorian era. Light, airy rooms are elegant, full of antiques, and each room includes access to a small reading area. Meals at the Wilton House are a treat. A typical breakfast at the home includes fresh fruit, pas-

tries, delectable entrees and gourmet coffees. Guests need not stray far from their rooms to enjoy gourmet cuisine, the innkeepers run a highly recommended restaurant on the premises. Don't forget to ask about special events.

Historic Interest: The inn, surrounded by the Blue Ridge Mountains, is within walking distance of historic downtown Harrisonburg and James Madison University.

Innkeeper(s): Roberta & Craig Moore. $105-145. 5 rooms with PB, 1 with FP. Breakfast included in rates. Types of meals: Full gourmet bkfst, early coffee/tea and gourmet dinner. Restaurant on premises. Beds: Q. Reading lamp, ceiling fan, clock radio, telephone and desk in room. Air conditioning. Fax, copier and fireplace on premises. Weddings, small meetings, family reunions and seminars hosted. Amusement parks, antiquing, downhill skiing, fishing, parks, shopping and sporting events nearby.

Publicity: *Richmond Times Dispatch, Bon Appetit, Sunday New York Times, Harrisonburg Daily News Record, Southern Living and Washingtonian.*

Irvington F17

The Hope and Glory Inn

634 King Carter Dr
Irvington, VA 22480
(804)438-6053 (800)497-8228 Fax:(804)438-5362
E-mail: inquiries@hopeandglory.com
Web: www.hopeandglory.com

Circa 1890. Checkerboard wood floors and interior columns add an elegant touch to this eclectic inn, which once served as a small school. A cheerful, yellow exterior with unique windows and second-story porch is accentuated by two front doors, one for the girls and one for the boys. The decor is whimsical and romantic. One guest room features a bed dressed with a flowery comforter and a headboard that appears as a picket fence. Another room has a hidden passageway, which leads to the private bath. Tucked behind the inn are five garden cottages, and a path leading to a private outdoor shower and secluded clawfoot tub. One of the cottages is the Meeting House, popular for small retreats and meetings. (Catered lunches and dinners are available for groups.) After enjoying a full breakfast, guests can partake in sailing, fishing, shopping and all the other surprises this Chesapeake Bay area town has to offer. Cunard Travel has selected Hope and Glory as one of its 101 best hotels.

Innkeeper(s): Je Depew. $145-280. 7 rooms with PB and 4 cottages. Breakfast included in rates. Types of meals: Full bkfst and early coffee/tea. Beds: QD. Reading lamp and stereo in room. Air conditioning. TV, VCR, fax, copier, bicycles, tennis, parlor games, telephone, fireplace, massages and stereo on premises. Weddings, small meetings and family reunions hosted. Antiquing, bicycling, fishing, golf, horseback riding, live theater, museums, parks, shopping, water sports, sailing, bocce, croquet and historic tours nearby.

Publicity: *Coastal Living Magazine, Forbes FYI, Washington Post, Victoria, 10 Most Romantic by AHII, Travel & Leisure and Conde Nast Traveler.*

Lancaster F17

The Inn at Levelfields

10155 Mary Ball Road
Lancaster, VA 22503
(804)435-6887 (800)238-5578
E-mail: cahjcd@crosslink.net
Web: www.innatlevelfields.com

Circa 1857. This hip-roofed Georgian Colonial house stands a quarter of a mile from the road bordered by hedges of 250-year-old English boxwood. Once the center of a large plantation, the

mansion has been completely refurbished and filled with family antiques and Oriental rugs, offering the finest in Virginia tradition.

Innkeeper(s): Charlotte Hollings & John Dunn. $90-140. 4 rooms with PB, 4 with FP. Types of meals: Full bkfst. Beds: KQD. Ceiling fan in room. Air conditioning. Fireplace, swimming pool and walking trails on 45 acres of woods on premises. Weddings, small meetings, family reunions and seminars hosted. Antiquing and live theater nearby.

Publicity: *Richmond Times-Dispatch, Newport News Daily Press, Woman's Day and Colonial Homes.*

"Your hospitality far exceeds any we've experienced and truly made our stay one we'll treasure."

Leesburg B15

Leesburg Colonial Inn

19 S King St
Leesburg, VA 20175-2903
(703)777-5000 (800)392-1332 Fax:(703)777-7000

Circa 1830. In the historic district of Leesburg just 25 miles from Washington, D.C., stands this Colonial inn with polished wood floors, antique poster beds, Persian and Oriental rugs. It offers 10 guest bedrooms, some with fireplaces. A full gourmet breakfast with authentic 18th-century cuisine is served each morning in the dining room at candle-lit tables. The inn is located in scenic Loudoun County, which is bordered by the Blue Ridge Mountains and Potomac River. Named for the Earl of Loudoun, John Campbell, who was both Governor of Virginia and the British commander in the early stages of the French and Indian War, the county and historic Leesburg are full of historic buildings and sites.

Innkeeper(s): Fabian Saeidi. $88-175. 10 rooms with PB, 4 with FP and 1 conference room. Breakfast included in rates. Types of meals: Full gourmet bkfst, veg bkfst, early coffee/tea, gourmet lunch, afternoon tea, snacks/refreshments, gourmet dinner and room service. Restaurant on premises. Beds: QDT. Modem hook-up, cable TV, reading lamp, snack bar, telephone, voice mail and fireplace in room. Central air. Fax, copier, bicycles, fireplace, laundry facility, cafe and restaurant on premises. Weddings, small meetings, family reunions and seminars hosted. Antiquing, art galleries, bicycling, canoeing/kayaking, fishing, golf, hiking, horseback riding, live theater, museums, parks, shopping, sporting events, water sports and wineries nearby.

Lexington F11

The Inn at Lexington

408 South Main St
Lexington, VA 24450-2346
(540)463-4715 (866)288-4715 Fax:(540)463-4888
E-mail: innatlexington@yahoo.com
Web: www.theinnatlexington.com

Circa 1922. Rockbridge County's luxurious bed & breakfast is well-furnished with an enticing blend of eclectic elegance. It is centrally located to the historic downtown district as well as both local colleges. Listen to music or read by the fire in the spacious first-floor living room or relax in the adjacent sunroom accented with plants and a book and video library. An upstairs parlor includes a phone and computer to use. Guest suites are pampering retreats that feature Gilchrist and Soames personal products, plush towels, VCRs and an abundance of pillows. Savor a gourmet Bistro breakfast in the dining room each morning. Innkeeper Natalie is an experienced chef. Visit the area's many attractions and sites.

Historic Interest: The home itself takes you back in time to when southern life was easy. The inn has the look of an old plantation, but is located within walking distance of downtown historic Lexington Virginia.

Innkeeper(s): Natalie Boldurian. $120-160. 4 rooms with PB. Breakfast and snacks/refreshments included in rates. Types of meals: Full gourmet bkfst. Beds: Q. Cable TV, VCR, reading lamp and clock radio in room. Central air. Fax, copier, library, parlor games, telephone, fireplace and Internet access on premises. Weddings hosted. Antiquing, art galleries, canoeing/kayaking, fishing, golf, hiking, live theater, museums, parks, shopping and wineries nearby.

"It's like visiting a favorite aunt."

Inn at Union Run

Union Run Rd
Lexington, VA 24450
(540)463-9715 (800)528-6466 Fax:(540)463-3526

Circa 1883. This inn was named for the spring-fed creek that meanders in front of this restored farmhouse. Union troops, specifically the 2nd and 4th Michigan Calvary, camped on the grounds during the Civil War. The home is surrounded by 10 acres with a fishing pond and brook. The innkeepers have traveled extensively throughout Europe and have brought the influence into their inn. The furnishings, many of which were fashioned out of oak, are a mix of American and Victorian styles.

Innkeeper(s): Roger & Jeanette Serens. $95-120. 8 rooms with PB, 4 with FP and 1 conference room. Breakfast and afternoon tea included in rates. Types of meals: Full bkfst, early coffee/tea, lunch, picnic lunch, snacks/refreshments, dinner and room service. Restaurant on premises. Beds: Q. Reading lamp, refrigerator, ceiling fan, snack bar, clock radio, telephone, turn-down service, desk and Jacuzzis (6 rooms) in room. Air conditioning. Parlor games and fireplace on premises. Limited handicap access. Weddings, small meetings, family reunions and seminars hosted. Antiquing, cross-country skiing, fishing, live theater, museums, parks, shopping, water sports and Civil War sites nearby.

Publicity: *News Gazette, Blue Ridge Country and Insider Guide of Virginia.*

Magnolia House Inn B&B

501 South Main Street
Lexington, VA 24450-2307
(540)463-2567 Fax:(540)463-4358
E-mail: magnolia@rockbridge.net
Web: www.magnoliahouseinn.com

Circa 1868. This classic Shenandoah Victorian, with its huge magnolia tree, several dogwoods and many azaleas is comfortable and casual yet elegant. One of the first homes built after the Civil War in what is now the heart of the historic district, it is an easy walk to colleges and the town center. Sit on a front porch rocking chair amid cottage gardens and imagine that bygone era. Relax by the fire in the living room. Inviting suites and guest bedrooms feature luxurious linens and sitting areas. Some boast porches and working fireplaces. Enjoy a memorable, several-course breakfast creatively presented in the classic dining room. Equestrian lovers will want to visit the 600-acre Virginia Horse Center. The Appalachian Trail is nearby for hiking.

Innkeeper(s): Antonia Albano & Barney Brown. $105-160. 5 rooms with PB, 3 with FP and 3 suites. Breakfast and snacks/refreshments included in rates. Types of meals: Full gourmet bkfst, veg bkfst and early coffee/tea. Beds: QT. Cable TV, VCR, reading lamp, ceiling fan, turn-down service and fireplace in room. Air conditioning. Fax, copier, library and telephone on premises. Family reunions hosted. Antiquing, art galleries, bicycling, canoeing/kayaking, cross-country skiing, downhill skiing, fishing, golf, hiking, horseback riding, live theater, museums, shopping, sporting events, tennis, water sports and wineries nearby.

Stoneridge Bed & Breakfast

PO Box 38, Stoneridge Lane
Lexington, VA 24450
(540)463-4090 (800)491-2930 Fax:(540)463-6078
E-mail: stoneridge@ntelos.net
Web: www.webfeat-inc.com/stoneridge

Circa 1829. The Shenandoah Valley is the setting for this bed & breakfast, located on 32 secluded acres of woods, streams and rolling fields. The inn was built using bricks made on the property, and once served as a plantation home and possibly a stagecoach stop. The home still maintains original heart-of-pine floors, ornate mantels and other period features. Guest rooms feature antiques, some are family heirlooms. Four guest rooms include fireplaces; three offer double Jacuzzi tubs. All rooms have a mountain view. A variety of reading material is available in the library. Stoneridge offers a large selection of Virginia wines to its guests for purchase. The gourmet breakfasts might include blueberry buckle, stuffed French toast and baked eggs. The meal is served either in the candlelit dining room or on the back patio.

Historic Interest: Once the center of a small plantation, Stoneridge Bed & Breakfast offers a glimpse of antebellum life. The original house, built in 1829 with bricks made on the property, features the living room, library, and two of the five bedrooms. The dining room and Summer kitchen with its large, open fireplace were added shortly thereafter. Explore the grounds and find a restored spring house, a time-worn corn crib, the chimney ruin of a former servant cabin, and the spring in the woods that once provided water for the inhabitants. The house is rumored to have been a stagecoach stop for weary travelers. Enter through the original Adams-style double doors and find restored rooms with high ceilings, intricate mouldings, heart-of-pine floors, ornate mantels and other period features.

Innkeeper(s): Jim, Evelyn and John Stallard. $90-150. 5 rooms with PB, 4 with FP and 1 suite. Breakfast included in rates. Types of meals: Full bkfst, veg bkfst, early coffee/tea, picnic lunch and snacks/refreshments. Beds: Q. Reading lamp, ceiling fan, clock radio, three with two-person Jacuzzi and four with gas log fireplace in room. Central air. VCR, fax, copier, library, parlor games, telephone, fireplace and Direct TV on premises. Small meetings, family reunions and seminars hosted. Antiquing, bicycling, canoeing/kayaking, fishing, golf, hiking, horseback riding, live theater, museums, shopping, wineries, carriage rides, Blue Ridge Parkway, Virginia Horse Center, Natural Bridge, Washington and Lee University and VMI nearby.

Publicity: *News-Gazette, Blue Ridge Country and Gourmet Magazine.*

Locust Dale **D13**

The Inn at Meander Plantation

2333 North James Madison Hwy.
Locust Dale, VA 22948-9701
(540)672-4912 (800)385-4936 Fax:(540)672-0405
E-mail: inn@meander.net
Web: www.meander.net

Circa 1766. This historic country estate was built by Henry Fry, close friend of Thomas Jefferson who often stopped here on his way to Monticello. The mansion is serenely decorated with elegant antiques and period reproductions, including four-poster beds. Healthy gourmet breakfasts are prepared by Chef Suzie. Enjoy views of the Blue Ridge Mountains from the rockers on the back porches. Ancient formal boxwood gardens, surrounding natural woodlands, meadows, pastures

and Robinson River frontage are part of Meander Conservancy, offering educational programs and back-to-nature packages.

Historic Interest: Prehistoric Native American site on the property near the Robinson River. James and Dolley Madison's home (10 miles), Civil War battlefields: Cedar Mountain (4 miles), Brandy Station (15 miles), Manassas and Bull Run (50 miles).

Innkeeper(s): Suzie Blanchard, Suzanne Thomas. $120-200. 8 rooms with PB, 5 with FP, 4 suites and 1 conference room. Breakfast included in rates. Types of meals: Full bkfst, early coffee/tea, lunch, picnic lunch, snacks/refreshments and gourmet dinner. Beds: KQD. Reading lamp, clock radio and desk in room. Air conditioning. VCR, fax, stable, library, pet boarding, child care, parlor games, telephone, fireplace, restaurant service Thursday and Friday and Saturday on premises. Weddings, small meetings, family reunions and seminars hosted. Antiquing, cross-country skiing, downhill skiing, fishing, live theater, parks, shopping, sporting events and wineries nearby.

"Staying at the Inn at Meander Plantation feels like being immersed in another century while having the luxuries and amenities available today."

Luray   C13

The Ruffner House

440 Ruffner House Rd
Luray, VA 22835-9704
(540)743-7855 (800)969-7855

Circa 1739. This 23-acre estate offers scenic pastures with grazing horses in the heart of the Shenandoah Valley. Peter Ruffner, the first settler of Page Valley and Luray, built the inn, a stately manor. Ruffner family members discovered a cavern opposite the entrance to the Luray Caverns, which were later discovered. In 1840 the house was sold and no Ruffners occupied it until this year when an 8th-generation Ruffner purchased it. The inn offers handsome antiques, two parlors and two enticing porches. Guest rooms feature a selection of amenities including some with fireplaces, Victorian tubs, ceiling fans and pastoral views. Afternoon tea is offered. A gourmet breakfast is served in the manor's elegant dining room and will provide sustenance for a full day of recreation. Visit wineries, battlefields, the Shenandoah National Park and Luray Caverns or enjoy horseback riding, canoeing, cycling, golfing or browsing the antique and boutique shops.

Innkeeper(s): Sonia Croucher. $98-150. 6 rooms with PB, 3 with FP. Breakfast included in rates. Types of meals: Full gourmet bkfst, early coffee/tea, picnic lunch, snacks/refreshments and gourmet dinner. Beds: QD. TV, reading lamp, ceiling fan and Victorian soaking tubs (two rooms) in room. Air conditioning. VCR, parlor games, telephone, fireplace and porches with rocking chairs and swings on premises. Weddings, small meetings, family reunions and seminars hosted. Antiquing, canoeing/kayaking, cross-country skiing, downhill skiing, fishing, golf, hiking, horseback riding, parks, shopping, sporting events and wineries nearby.

Publicity: *Page News & Courier and Washingtonian Magazine.*

"This is the loveliest inn we have ever stayed in. We were made to feel very welcome and at ease."

South Court Inn Bed and Breakfast

160 South Court Street
Luray, VA 22835-1217
(540)843-0980 (888)749-8055
E-mail: inn@southcourtinn.com
Web: www.southcourtinn.com

Circa 1870. Lovingly renovated to reflect the grandeur of an elegant Victorian mansion, this bed & breakfast features elaborate moldings, vintage chandeliers, antiques, Oriental carpets, rich color schemes and window treatments. Built in the 1870s, the two-acre grounds bloom with informal gardens in the heart of historic Shenandoah Valley, just two hours from Washington,

DC. Romantic guest bedrooms with fireplaces are pampering retreats. Sleep in a four-poster canopy bed and soak in a claw foot tub. Lunch is rarely needed after an incredible breakfast that may start with fresh peaches and lavender honey or warm apple tart with cheese. Blueberry pancakes, lemon waffles, herb omelets and cheese soufflés are favorite entrees. Baked goods are hot from the oven and topped with homemade jams and syrups. Fruit sorbet tops off the meal. Relax in the outdoor hot tub.

Historic Interest: The house was built by the town pharmacist in the 1870s as a white clapboard farmhouse setting at the front of his 300+ acre farm. His son-in-law, a local hero from WWI who became Appointments Secretary to Senator Harry Bryd, renovated the house in the 1930s, moving the house to facilitate the "mining" of a full basement, then moving it back to its current location and adding the brick veneer, wraparound porch, sunroom, garage and summer porch. Anita and Tom renovated the interior of the house from 1997 to 2000, adding elaborate moldings, window treatments, paint and color schemes, furnishings and decor to match what might have been seen in a fine town home of the 1890s.

Innkeeper(s): Anita and Tom Potts. $100-250. 3 rooms with PB. Breakfast included in rates. Types of meals: Full gourmet bkfst, early coffee/tea and afternoon tea. Modem hook-up, reading lamp, refrigerator, desk and fireplace in room. Central air. TV, VCR, fax, copier, spa, library, parlor games, telephone and private off-street parking on premises. Amusement parks, antiquing, art galleries, canoeing/kayaking, cross-country skiing, downhill skiing, fishing, golf, hiking, horseback riding, live theater, museums, parks, shopping, water sports and wineries nearby.

The Woodruff Collection of Victorian Inns

138 E Main St
Luray, VA 22835
(540)743-1494 Fax:(540)743-1722
E-mail: woodruffinns@woodruffinns.com
Web: www.woodruffinns.com

Circa 1882. Prepare to be pampered. The Woodruffs entered the B&B business after years of experience in hotel management and restaurant businesses. They have not missed a detail, ensuring a perfect, relaxing visit. The Rooftop Skylight Fireside Jacuzzi Suite is often the room of choice because of its interesting shape and architecture, located where the attic was before restoration. The suite boasts skylights, Jacuzzi tub for two and antique stained glass. Tasteful antiques and fresh bouquets of flowers framed by candlelight add a special ambiance. Besides the extra attention and comfortable accommodations, the Woodruffs include coffee and afternoon dessert tea, in-room coffee or tea and a full fireside breakfast in the rates. Candlelight sets the mood for the gourmet dinner, and none of the spectacular meals are to be missed. A romantic finish to each evening is a private dip in one of the garden hot tubs.

Historic Interest: New Market Battlefield (20 minutes), the famous underground Luray Caverns discovered in the late 1800s (minutes away).

Innkeeper(s): Lucas & Deborah Woodruff. $119-289. 5 rooms with PB, 9 with FP, 4 suites and 1 conference room. Breakfast included in rates. Types of meals: Full bkfst, afternoon tea and gourmet dinner. Beds: KQ. Reading lamp, clock radio, coffeemaker, desk and coffeemaker in room. Air conditioning. Fax, spa, parlor games, telephone, fireplace, two outdoor gardens, Jacuzzi tubs for two and afternoon dessert tea & coffee included in rates on premises. Weddings, small meetings and family reunions hosted. Antiquing, downhill skiing, fishing, parks, shopping, water sports, caverns, Shenandoah River and Skyline Drive nearby.

Publicity: *Potomac Living, Cascapades Magazine, Blue Ridge Country Magazine, Cooperative Living, Virginia Wine Gazette, Food and Wine Magazine, Gourmet Magazine, Washington Times and recipient of Virginia's gold three cluster wine award.*

Lynchburg   G11

Federal Crest Inn

1101 Federal St
Lynchburg, VA 24504-3018
(434)845-6155 (800)818-6155 Fax:(434)845-1445
E-mail: inn@federalcrest.com
Web: www.federalcrest.com

Circa 1909. The guest rooms at Federal Crest are named for the many varieties of trees and flowers native to Virginia. This handsome red brick home, a fine example of Georgian Revival architecture, features a commanding front entrance flanked by columns that hold up the second-story veranda. A grand staircase, carved woodwork, polished floors topped with fine rugs and more columns create an aura of elegance. Each guest room offers something special and romantic, from a mountain view to a Jacuzzi tub. Breakfasts are served on fine china, and the first course is always a freshly baked muffin with a secret message inside. **Historic Interest:** Appomattox Court House and Jefferson's Poplar Forest. Innkeeper(s): Ann & Phil Ripley. $135-200. 5 rooms, 4 with PB, 3 with FP, 2 suites and 1 conference room. Breakfast, afternoon tea and snacks/refreshments included in rates. Types of meals: Full bkfst and early coffee/tea. Beds: Q. Cable TV, VCR, reading lamp, clock radio, turn-down service, desk and telephone in room. Air conditioning. Fax, copier, parlor games, telephone, fireplace, gift shop, conference theater with 60-inch TV (Ballroom) with stage, '50s cafe with antique jukebox and video library on premises. Weddings, small meetings, family reunions and seminars hosted. Antiquing, fishing, golf, live theater, parks, shopping, sporting events and tennis nearby. Publicity: *Washington Post, News & Advance, Scene and Local ABC.*

"What a wonderful place to celebrate our birthdays and enjoy our last romantic getaway before the birth of our first child."

Norvell-Otey House B&B

1020 Federal St
Lynchburg, VA 24504
(434)528-1020 (877)320-1020 Fax:(434)528-8811
E-mail: norvellotey@aol.com
Web: www.norvelloteyhouse.com

Circa 1817. This 1817 Federal-style manor house near Charlottesville, Richmond and Roanoke has porches, gardens and a lovely patio as well as four guest rooms appointed with antiques. After a hearty breakfast, strike out for Monticello, National D-Day Memorial, Patrick Henry's home, Appomattox and other historical sites. Innkeeper(s): Jenny West. $125-145. 4 rooms, 3 with PB, 1 with FP and 2 conference rooms. Breakfast, afternoon tea and snacks/refreshments included in rates. Types of meals: Full gourmet bkfst, veg bkfst, early coffee/tea, gourmet lunch, picnic lunch, gourmet dinner and room service. Beds: QT. Cable TV, reading lamp, clock radio, turn-down service and desk in room. Central air. VCR, fax, copier, spa, library, parlor games, telephone, fireplace, laundry facility, refrigerator, coffee, soft drinks, snacks, chocolates, card room, music room and newspaper on premises. Weddings, small meetings, family reunions and seminars hosted. Antiquing, art galleries, bicycling, canoeing/kayaking, cross-country skiing, downhill skiing, fishing, golf, hiking, horseback riding, live theater, museums, parks, shopping, sporting events, tennis, water sports, wineries and many historic sites nearby. Publicity: *New York Times, Lynchburg News & Advance, Roanoke Times, Channel 13 and 7 10.*

Peacock Manor Bed & Breakfast, Inc.

1115 Federal St
Lynchburg, VA 24504
(434)528-0626 Fax:(434)528-6007
E-mail: peacockmanor@hotmail.com
Web: www.peacockmanorbb.com

Circa 1890. Sitting high on a bluff in Federal Hill Historic District, at the foot of Virginia's Blue Ridge Mountains, this intimate European-style bed & breakfast is a Queen Anne Victorian with spectacular views of downtown and across the James River. Trudi and Dennis extend generous Southern hospitality with a New Orleans flair that reflects their upbringing. Swing or rock on the large front porch. Original hardwood floors, Tiffany reproduction stained-glass windows, eight slate fireplaces, Bradbury and Bradbury hand-blocked wallpaper, 11 crystal chandeliers, a heart of pine curved staircase, tall ceilings, and double parlors highlight the impressive interior. Jewel-colored guest bedrooms are a restful retreat and a creative breakfast is prepared from scratch. Sit near a fountain or gazebo on the well-landscaped grounds. Innkeeper(s): Trudi & Dennis Malik. $110-125. 4 rooms with PB. Breakfast and snacks/refreshments included in rates. Types of meals: Full gourmet bkfst, veg bkfst, early coffee/tea and afternoon tea. Beds: KQDT. Cable TV, VCR, reading lamp, stereo, refrigerator, ceiling fan, snack bar, coffeemaker, turn-down service and fireplace in room. Central air. Fax, copier, bicycles, pet boarding, parlor games and telephone on premises. Family reunions hosted. Antiquing, art galleries, bicycling, canoeing/kayaking, fishing, golf, hiking, live theater, museums, parks, shopping and wineries nearby. Publicity: *New York Times, Arrington's Bed & Breakfast Journal, News and Advance* and voted past two years "Best Antiques" by *Arrington's B&B Journal.*

Madison   D13

Dulaney Hollow at Old Rag Mountain B&B Inn

3932 South F.T. Valley Rd - Scenic VA Byway, Rt 231
Madison, VA 22727
(540)923-4470 Fax:(540)923-4841

Circa 1903. Period furnishings decorate this Victorian manor house on 15 acres of the Blue Ridge Mountains. There is also a cabin, cottage and hayloft suite available amid the shaded lawns and old farm buildings. Enjoy a delicious country breakfast. Take a bicycle jaunt or hike the hills around the Shenandoah River and National Park. Monticello, Charlottesville and Montpelier are within an hour's drive. Innkeeper(s): Susan & Louis Cable. $85-135. 6 rooms with PB, 1 suite and 2 cottages. Breakfast included in rates. Types of meals: Full gourmet bkfst, early coffee/tea, gourmet lunch, picnic lunch, afternoon tea and gourmet dinner. Beds: QDT. Ceiling fan and desk in room. Air conditioning. VCR, fax, copier, swimming, pet boarding, telephone and Internet access on premises. Weddings, small meetings, family reunions and seminars hosted. Antiquing, cross-country skiing, downhill skiing, fishing, golf, live theater, parks, shopping, sporting events, tennis, water sports, wineries, Civil War sites, historic sites and battlefields, Shenandoah National Park and wildlife preserve nearby. Publicity: *Madison Eagle and Charlottesville Daily Progress.*

McGaheysville   D12

Cave Hill Farm B&B

9875 Cave Hill Rd
McGaheysville, VA 22840
(540)289-7441 (888)798-3985 Fax:(540)289-5948
E-mail: info@cavehillfarmbandb.com
Web: www.cavehillfarmbandb.com

Circa 1830. Steeped in history, this English Manor house in the Shenandoah Valley has amazing stories to reveal. Recent restorations uncovered hidden letters written during and about Civil War battles. The basement housed the original kitchen and dining room. They now display an assortment of antique farm tools. The furnishings and decor exquisitely befit the ambiance and era of the home's heritage. Using fresh ingredients from the herb and vegetable garden, breakfast may include an Amaretto cream sauce fruit and nut appetizer, berry-stuffed

French toast, quiche, garlic pepper parmesan potatoes and a regional meat selection. There are 400 acres of landscaped grounds, flower gardens, fields and hills on this farm.
Innkeeper(s): Becky Sharp. $159-189. 5 rooms with PB, 5 with FP and 1 conference room. Breakfast included in rates. Types of meals: Full gourmet bkfst, veg bkfst and early coffee/tea. Beds: Q. Data port, cable TV, reading lamp, telephone, turn-down service and fireplace in room. Central air. VCR, fax, parlor games and fireplace on premises. Weddings, small meetings, family reunions and seminars hosted. Antiquing, bicycling, canoeing/kayaking, downhill skiing, golf, hiking, horseback riding, live theater, museums, parks, shopping, wineries, Massanutten Resort and Shenandoan National Park nearby.
Publicity: *Villager and Local Talk Radio.*

Middleburg C14

Briar Patch Bed & Breakfast

23130 Briar Patch Lane
Middleburg, VA 20117
(703)327-5911 (866)327-5911 Fax:(703)327-5933
E-mail: info@briarpatchbandb.com
Web: www.briarpatchbandb.com

Circa 1805. Leave stress behind when staying at this historic farm that sits on 47 rolling acres of land that once was where the Civil War's Battle of the Haystacks was fought in 1863. Located in the heart of horse, antique and wine country, it is just 20 minutes from Dulles Airport and 45 minutes from Washington, DC. Overlook the Bull Run Mountains while sitting on the front porch. Antique-filled guest bedrooms in the main house are named after the flowers and feature canopy or four-poster beds. Two rooms can adjoin to become a suite. A separate one-bedroom cottage includes a fully equipped kitchen, dining area and living room. Breakfast is provided in the large kitchen or outside patio. Swim in the pool or soak in the year-round hot tub.
Historic Interest: The house was built in 1805. A Civil War battle, The Battle of Haystacks, was fought on Briar Patch land in June of 1863.
Innkeeper(s): Virginia Hester, Manager. $95-225. 9 rooms, 2 with PB, 3 with FP and 1 cottage. Breakfast included in rates. Types of meals: Full gourmet bkfst. Beds: KQ. Modem hook-up, reading lamp, ceiling fan and fireplace in room. Air conditioning. TV, VCR, fax, copier, spa, swimming, parlor games and telephone on premises. Weddings, small meetings and family reunions hosted. Antiquing, bicycling, canoeing/kayaking, fishing, golf, hiking, horseback riding, parks, shopping, tennis and wineries nearby.

The Longbarn

37129 Adams Green Ln
Middleburg, VA 20118
(540)687-4137 Fax:(540)687-4044
E-mail: thlongbarn@aol.com
Web: www.members.aol.com/thlongbarn/

Circa 1889. Built in the late 1800s, this recently renovated barn offers private comfort amid eight acres of serene woodlands. Art lovers will appreciate the details of the Italian-European country décor inside, coupled with its picturesque surroundings. There is a large fireplace in the living room that guests can relax near. Take a walk through the European gardens to the gazebo for a picnic lunch and enjoy the pond. Rise each morning with fresh fruits, juice, omelets and grilled vegetables, homemade breads and breakfast meats. Nearby are many activities for the whole family, such as swimming, horseback riding, bicycling and golf.
Innkeeper(s): Chiara Langley. $130. 3 rooms with PB. Breakfast included in rates. Types of meals: Full gourmet bkfst, veg bkfst, afternoon tea and dinner. Beds: KQT. Reading lamp, ceiling fan, clock radio and desk in room. Central air. TV, bicycles, library, parlor games, telephone, fireplace and exercise room on premises. Weddings and small meetings hosted. Amusement parks, antiquing, art galleries, bicycling, golf, hiking, horseback riding, museums, parks, shopping, tennis and wineries nearby.

Millboro E10

Fort Lewis Lodge

HCR 3 Box 21A
Millboro, VA 24460
(540)925-2314 Fax:(540)925-2352
E-mail: ftlewis@tds.net
Web: www.fortlewislodge.com

Circa 1840. Colonel Charles Lewis, under the command of George Washington, built one of the string of forts on this property to protect the southern pass of the Shenandoah Mountains from Indian raids. It is easy to revel in the natural beauty of this 3,000-acre mountain farm. Stay in quaint lodge rooms, including "sleeping in the round," a silo with spiral stair- case. Two historic hand-hewn log cabins boast stone fireplaces. The newly restored Riverside House offers five spacious guest bedrooms. Enjoy Caryl's plentiful homemade meals served in the refurbished 19th-century grist mill. The local area features many opportunities to hike, hunt, bike and fish.
Historic Interest: A half-hour drive takes guests to Warm Springs, which includes soothing mineral baths designed by Thomas Jefferson. The famed Homestead Resort is five miles farther in Hot Springs.
Innkeeper(s): John & Caryl Cowden. $165-210. 18 rooms with PB. Breakfast and dinner included in rates. Types of meals: Full bkfst and picnic lunch. Restaurant on premises. Beds: KQT. Weddings, small meetings, family reunions and seminars hosted. Antiquing, fishing and water sports nearby.
Publicity: *Outside, AAA Today, Mid-Atlantic Country, Tasteful, Rural Living, Country, Washington Post, Washingtonian, Frommers Budget Travel and Better Homes and Gardens.*

"We have stayed at many inns in France, England and Germany, none have impressed me as much as yours. You have made the most of a beautiful piece of property and I feel privileged to share it with you."

Nellysford F12

The Mark Addy

56 Rodes Farm Dr
Nellysford, VA 22958-9526
(434)361-1101 (800)278-2154
E-mail: info@mark-addy.com
Web: www.mark-addy.com

Circa 1837. It's not hard to understand why Dr. John Everett, the son of Thomas Jefferson's physician, chose this picturesque, Blue Mountain setting for his home. Everett expanded the simple, four-room farmhouse already present into a gracious manor. The well-appointed guest rooms feature double whirlpool baths, double showers or a clawfoot tub. Beds are covered with vintage linens, feather pillows and cozy, down comforters. There are plenty of relaxing possibilities, including five porches and a hammock set among the trees.
Historic Interest: Dr. John Coleman Everett (son of Thomas Jefferson's physician) bought the estate in 1884.
Innkeeper(s): John Storck Maddox. $100-195. 10 rooms with PB and 1 suite. Types of meals: Full gourmet bkfst, early coffee/tea, gourmet lunch, picnic lunch and gourmet dinner. Beds: KQDT. Reading lamp, ceiling fan and Jacuzzi in room. Air conditioning. VCR, library, parlor games and telephone on premises. Limited handicap access. Weddings, small meetings and family reunions hosted. Antiquing, downhill skiing, fishing, live theater, parks, shopping, sporting events, horseback riding and hiking nearby.
Publicity: *Local paper.*

New Church   E19

The Garden and The Sea Inn

4188 Nelson Rd, #275
New Church, VA 23415-0275
(757)824-0672 (800)824-0672
E-mail: innkeeper@gardenandseainn.com
Web: www.gardenandseainn.com

Circa 1802. Gingerbread trim, a pair of brightly colored gables and two, adjacent verandas adorn the exterior of this Victorian. A warm, rich Victorian decor permeates the antique-filled guest rooms, an ideal setting for romance. Most rooms include whirlpool tubs. The inn's dining room serves gourmet dinners by reservation. Pets are very welcome.

Innkeeper(s): Tom & Sara Baker. $75-195. 8 rooms with PB and 1 conference room. Breakfast included in rates. Types of meals: Full bkfst, snacks/refreshments and gourmet dinner. Restaurant on premises. Beds: KQ. TV, reading lamp, ceiling fan, clock radio and some with fireplace in room. Air conditioning. VCR, fax, copier, library, parlor games, telephone and outdoor heated pool on premises. Limited handicap access. Antiquing, beach, fishing, parks, shopping and water sports nearby.

Publicity: *Washington Post, Modern Bride and Southern Living.*

New Market   C12

Cross Roads Inn B&B

9222 John Sevier Rd
New Market, VA 22844-9649
(540)740-4157 (888)740-4157
E-mail: lsmith18@juno.com
Web: www.crossroadsinnva.com

Circa 1925. This Victorian is full of Southern hospitality. Bountiful breakfasts and homemade treats are served as an afternoon refreshment. The home is decorated with English floral wallpapers, antiques and old family furnishings. Four-poster and canopy beds are topped with fluffy, down comforters. The historic downtown area is within walking distance.

Innkeeper(s): Sharon & Larry Smith. $95-135. 6 rooms with PB. Breakfast included in rates. Types of meals: Full bkfst, early coffee/tea, afternoon tea and snacks/refreshments. Beds: KQDT. Reading lamp, clock radio and several with Jacuzzi or fireplace in room. Air conditioning. VCR, fax, parlor games, telephone and fireplace on premises. Limited handicap access. Weddings, small meetings, family reunions and seminars hosted. Antiquing, downhill skiing, fishing, live theater, parks, shopping, sporting events, water sports and musical summer festivals nearby.

Newport News   H17

Boxwood Inn

10 Elmhurst St
Newport News, VA 23603-1138
(757)888-8854 Fax:(757)887-3986
Web: www.boxwood-inn.com

Circa 1896. Formerly a Warwick County Hall of Records, a post office, a general store, and then home of the prominent Curtis family, this historic plantation-style inn has hosted many important political and social events. Antiques found in the sprawling attic are found in every room as part of the period decor. Local museums display the remaining cherished memorabilia. The guest bedrooms are eye-pleasing and hold stories of their own,

housing soldiers and their families during both World War I and II. A savory breakfast is served in the Blue Willow Tea Room. Located in Historic Lee Hall Village, Colonial Williamsburg, as well as Revolutionary and Civil War battlefields are an easy drive.

Innkeeper(s): Barbara & Bob Lucas. $95-125. 4 rooms with PB. Breakfast included in rates. Types of meals: Full gourmet bkfst, early coffee/tea and afternoon tea. Restaurant on premises. Beds: Q. Reading lamp, ceiling fan, clock radio, coffeemaker and one with refrigerator in room. Air conditioning. Telephone and fireplace on premises. Weddings, small meetings, family reunions and seminars hosted. Amusement parks, antiquing, beach, hiking, museums, parks and wineries nearby.

Newsoms   I16

Sunnyside Plantation Bed & Breakfast

27549 Grays Shop Rd
Newsoms, VA 23874
(757)654-9075 Fax:(757)654-9040
E-mail: info@sunnysideplantationbb.com
Web: www.sunnysideplantationbb.com

Circa 1810. Secluded in Virginia Tidewater cotton country, this historic plantation now graces eight acres. Totally restored, original mill work, mantels, doors, windows, heart pine floors and 12-foot ceilings complement the 18th and 19th century antiques and fine reproductions in the Greek Revival Main House. The Guest Cottage is furnished and decorated in a Williamsburg casual style. Other outbuildings that remain standing are the smoke house, dairy house, privy, one-room school house and servants quarters. Sip evening wine and sherry in the parlor. Sleep on canopy or poster beds made up with fine linens in guest bedrooms that feature fireplaces. The romantic cottage offers more privacy and a kitchen. A full breakfast is served in the elegant dining room or delivered to the room. Enjoy the formal English garden. Take a midnight swim in the illuminated in-ground pool.

Historic Interest: Situated on land owned by the Pope family as early as 1732, the Greek Revival Plantation house was built between 1790 and 1810. The Plantation, exceeding 6,000 acres in 1870, supported cotton, peanut, corn and tobacco crops. Many original outbuildings still remain, including kitchen house/servants quarters, smokehouse, schoolhouse, dairy house, milk house and schoolmaster's house (now the guest cottage). The Main house retains original woodwork, doors, windows, fireplaces, magnificent heart pine floors and has been largely unaltered.

Innkeeper(s): Rod and Joan Lenahan. $95-195. 3 rooms, 2 with PB, 3 with FP and 1 cottage. Breakfast and snacks/refreshments included in rates. Types of meals: Full gourmet bkfst, early coffee/tea, afternoon tea and room service. Beds: Q. Reading lamp, CD player, refrigerator, ceiling fan, clock radio, coffeemaker, turn-down service, fireplace, ice buckets and glasses in room. Central air. TV, VCR, fax, copier, library, parlor games, telephone, fireplace, laundry facility, in-ground swimming pool and evening sherry on premises. Weddings hosted. Antiquing, art galleries, fishing, museums, parks, shopping, country antique auctions and historic homes and sites nearby.

Norfolk   H18

Page House Inn

323 Fairfax Ave
Norfolk, VA 23507-2215
(757)625-5033 (800)599-7659 Fax:(757)623-9451
E-mail: innkeeper@pagehouseinn.com
Web: www.pagehouseinn.com

Circa 1899. This pristinely renovated Georgian Revival inn, a 4-Diamond rated property in the National Register, is located in the Ghent Historic District. The parlor features polished wood floors, an Oriental carpet, period antiques, paintings and an elegant fireplace. Ask for the room with the King-size canopy bed, fireplace, sunken hot tub, bidet and steam shower for two. Amenities

include luxury linens and robes, and turndown service is available by request. There are solid oak doors, insulated walls and floors, valet laundry and daily maid service. Breakfast options include candlelight breakfasts for suite guests by advance notice, continental breakfast served in your room or a formal breakfast in the dining room. Nearby is the Chrysler Museum of Art with original works by Andy Warhol and Edward Hopper. Antique shoppers will enjoy Virginia's largest concentration of antique shops.
Innkeeper(s): Carl Albero/ Stormi Weathers. $130-220. 7 rooms with PB, 4 with FP and 3 suites. Breakfast, afternoon tea and snacks/refreshments included in rates. Types of meals: Full bkfst, early coffee/tea and room service. Beds: KDT. VCR, reading lamp, CD player, refrigerator, ceiling fan, telephone, turn-down service, desk and hot tub/spa in room. Air conditioning. TV, fax, copier, parlor games and fireplace on premises. Small meetings hosted. Amusement parks, antiquing, fishing, golf, live theater, museums, parks, shopping, sporting events, tennis, water sports, opera and symphony nearby.
Publicity: *Country Inns, Mid-Atlantic, Travel & Leisure and Southern Living.*

"What a treat this is to write a thank you note regarding 'quality,' which I define as giving someone more than they expect."

Onancock   F19

Creekside Inn B&B

37 King Street
Onancock, VA 23417
(757)787-7578 (888)858-7578
E-mail: dkukk@intercom.net
Web: www.creeksideinn.biz

Circa 1900. A block from the wharf, this Victorian inn was built in 1900 and recently underwent extensive renovations to provide a new roof, windows, porches, staircase, heating and air conditioning. Newly decorated guest bedrooms feature colorful window treatments, rich fabrics and luxury bath accessories for an added measure of comfort and style. Turndown service accents the hospitality. Savor a satisfying gourmet breakfast before relaxing at the nearby Assateague Island National Seashore. Bikes are available to explore the scenic area further.
Innkeeper(s): Diana Kukk. $95-110. 3 rooms with PB. Breakfast, afternoon tea and snacks/refreshments included in rates. Types of meals: Full gourmet bkfst and early coffee/tea. Beds: Q. Cable TV, VCR, reading lamp, CD player, clock radio, turn-down service and desk in room. Central air. TV, fax, copier, bicycles, library and parlor games on premises. Antiquing, art galleries, beach, bicycling, canoeing/kayaking, fishing, golf, hiking, live theater, museums, parks, shopping, water sports, wineries, Onancock Wharf and excursions to Tangier Island and the Barrier Islands nearby.

Orange   E13

The Holladay House

155 W Main St
Orange, VA 22960-1528
(540)672-4893 (800)358-4422 Fax:(540)672-3028
E-mail: jgearyhh@aol.com
Web: www.holladayhousebandb.com

Circa 1830. Experience quintessential Virginia at this Federal-style bed & breakfast in the Piedmont region with a commanding view of the Blue Ridge Mountains. Select a book from the library in the parlor, enjoy a cup of tea or glass of local wine and let all cares fade away. Heirloom period furnishings grace the common areas and guest bedrooms. Leisurely three-course gourmet breakfasts are not to be missed. Soft music, candle-light, antique Haviland china,

sterling silver and Fostoria crystal create an elegant ambiance in the formal dining room. Nearby vineyards offer wine-tasting tours. Visit Civil War battlefields and Montpelier, home of President James Madison, only four miles away.
Historic Interest: The immediate area played a prominent part in the Civil War; one skirmish was actually fought in the town's streets and, according to legend, a Confederate soldier died on the porch steps of the Holladay House.
Innkeeper(s): Judy Geary. $95-205. 6 rooms with PB, 2 suites and 1 conference room. Breakfast, afternoon tea and snacks/refreshments included in rates. Types of meals: Full gourmet bkfst. Beds: Q. Cable TV, VCR, reading lamp, refrigerator, ceiling fan, clock radio, desk, fireplace and two-person Jacuzzi in room. Air conditioning. Fax, copier, library, telephone, phone, air conditioning, port and sherry cordials included in rates, wine and cheese on weekends and dinner served on weekends by reservation $45/person on premises. Small meetings, family reunions and seminars hosted. Antiquing, art galleries, bicycling, fishing, golf, hiking, horseback riding, live theater, museums, shopping, sporting events and wineries nearby.

"My husband and I have traveled from Florida to Long Island for nine years. We always stay at B&Bs. The Holladay House is truly one of the finest."

Mayhurst Inn

12460 Mayhurst Ln
Orange, VA 22960
(540)672-5597 (888)672-5597 Fax:(540)672-7447
E-mail: info@mayhurstinn.com
Web: www.mayhurtinn.com

Circa 1859. Romance and relaxation await at this stunning 1859 plantation mansion. Meticulously restored to offer the best of contemporary comforts, it has retained yesterday's enchantment. Enjoy wine and cheese upon arrival. Ascend the four-story oval staircase to the fanciful cupola. Stately guest bedrooms boast double whirlpool tubs, fine linens, original Italian marble fireplaces, antique furnishings and period décor. Satisfying plantation breakfasts are served in front of the fireplace in the dining room, on the rear veranda or on the brick courtyard. Wander the 37 acres with summer kitchen, smokehouse and schoolhouse still standing amongst 200-year-old trees. Generals Lee, Jackson and Hill were guests when the Army's Northern Virginia Corps III headquartered here. Visit local wineries, three presidential homes and several major Civil War battlefields, all within 25 miles.

Historic Interest: National Register, Virginia Historic Landmark.
Innkeeper(s): Bob & Peg Harmon. $135-210. 7 rooms with PB, 6 with FP and 2 suites. Breakfast and wine included in rates. Types of meals: Full bkfst and early coffee/tea. Beds: KQT. Data port, reading lamp, clock radio, telephone, desk and hair dryer in room. Air conditioning. VCR, fax, copier and fireplace on premises. Limited handicap access. Small meetings, family reunions and seminars hosted. Antiquing, bicycling, fishing, golf, wineries, Civil War battlefields and Presidential homes nearby.
Publicity: *Old House Journal.*

"The beauty of this Inn is exceeded only by the graciousness of Mayhurst hosts: Peg and Bob."

Providence Forge   G16

Jasmine Plantation B&B Inn

4500 N Courthouse Rd
Providence Forge, VA 23140-3428
(804)966-9836 (800)639-5368 Fax:(804)966-5679

Circa 1750. Few travelers can boast that they have stayed at a mid-18th-century plantation. Jasmine Plantation is just such a place. Surrounded by more than 40 acres of Virginia countryside, it's not difficult to understand why the Morris family chose this spot for their home. The property's first dwelling was built as early as the 1680s. Several guest rooms are named for members of the Morris Family, and all are decorated with antiques. The Rose Room features

Victorian furnishings and a whirlpool bath. The George Morris Room includes 19th-century pieces, king size bed, a fireplace and clawfoot tub. Memorabilia from multiple centuries add special charm to the place. The innkeepers have antique irons, old books and magazines, antique dolls and a sampling of vintage advertising signs for Philip Morris or Coca-Cola.

Innkeeper(s): Scott & Rebecca Wagar. $120-165. 5 rooms with PB, 4 with FP and 1 suite. Breakfast and snacks/refreshments included in rates. Types of meals: Full bkfst and early coffee/tea. Beds: KQD. Ceiling fan in room. Air conditioning. VCR, telephone and fireplace on premises. Weddings, small meetings, family reunions and seminars hosted. Amusement parks, antiquing, fishing, golf, parks, shopping, water sports, sporting clays and horse racing nearby.
Publicity: Area newspapers and Area TV stations.

"We were charmed by the plantation accommodations and the kindness of the beautiful host and hostess."

Radford   H8

Nesselrod On The New Gardens and Guesthouse

7535 Lee Highway
Radford, VA 24141-8896
(540)731-4970 Fax:(540)731-4864
E-mail: innkeeper@nesselrod.com
Web: www.nesselrod.com

Circa 1939. Noted architect Everette Fauber designed Nesselrod, a historic Colonial Revival home. The well-appointed grounds include gardens that have been in existence since the home's earliest days. Inside there are four guest rooms; each was given a special name to honor the home's gardens. The rooms include many luxurious amenities, from fine, European linens to specialty bath products to heated towel racks. Guests also are pampered with a lavish, three-course gourmet breakfast. A sample menu might begin with baked pears in custard, followed by Scottish oatmeal with Scotch whiskey, and topped off with baked eggs with locally prepared goat cheese or perhaps blueberry French toast.

Innkeeper(s): Eric Hanson. $105-250. 4 rooms with PB, 3 with FP, 2 suites and 1 conference room. Breakfast included in rates. Types of meals: Full gourmet bkfst, early coffee/tea, afternoon tea and snacks/refreshments. Beds: QT. Data port, cable TV, reading lamp, stereo, refrigerator, clock radio, telephone, turn-down service, desk and fireplace in room. Central air. VCR, fax, fireplace and laundry facility on premises. Weddings, small meetings, family reunions and seminars hosted. Antiquing, bicycling, canoeing/kayaking, fishing, golf, hiking, horseback riding, museums, parks, shopping, sporting events, tennis, wineries, Smithfield Plantation, Claytor Lake, Cascades and new river trail nearby.
Publicity: Roanoke Times and Blue Ridge Country Magazine.

Raphine   E11

Willow Pond Farm Country House

137 Pisgah Rd
Raphine, VA 24472
(540)348-1310 (800)945-6763 Fax:(540)348-1359
E-mail: Willowpondfm@rockbridge.net
Web: www.willowpondfarminn.com

Circa 1800. If visions of rolling hills, woods and the picturesque Shenandoah Valley are what you have in mind for a

peaceful getaway, this Victorian farmhouse is an ideal location. Surrounded by more than 170 acres, guests are sure to enjoy this secluded bed & breakfast. There are four well-appointed, romantically styled guest rooms, featuring traditional furnishings and a few Victorian pieces. In addition, there are two suites available. The suites include double whirlpool tubs and private entrances that lead

out to the pool and garden. The innkeepers pamper guests with a gourmet breakfast and afternoon tea. In addition, the hosts will arrange for guests to enjoy a five-course dinner served by candlelight on a table set with fine linens, china and crystal.

Innkeeper(s): Carol Ann & Walter P. Schendel. $115-190. 6 rooms, 3 with PB, 2 suites and 1 cottage. Breakfast, afternoon tea and snacks/refreshments included in rates. Types of meals: Full gourmet bkfst, veg bkfst, early coffee/tea and picnic lunch. Beds: KQD. TV, VCR, reading lamp, refrigerator, ceiling fan, clock radio, turn-down service and desk in room. Air conditioning. Fax, copier, swimming, library, parlor games, telephone and fireplace on premises. Weddings and family reunions hosted. Antiquing, art galleries, bicycling, canoeing/kayaking, fishing, golf, hiking, horseback riding, live theater, museums, parks, shopping, sporting events, water sports, wineries, hiking, natural wonders and mountains nearby.
Publicity: Special 2001 Womens Day Decorating Ideas, Summer 2001 Bedroom & Bath, 2001 Country Victorian Restored with Pride, Spring 2001 Country Almanac, a B&B that keeps its promise, 2002 Richmond Magazine Pastoral Charm and "A true escape from stress."

"A jewel in the country! A perfect 10...many thanks!"

Richmond   F15

The William Miller House

1129 Floyd Avenue
Richmond, VA 23220-4822
(804)254-2928 Fax:(804)254-2928
E-mail: innkeeper@ourfanhomes.com
Web: www.ourfanhomes.com

Circa 1869. Built with clapboard in Greek Revival style, this intimate bed & breakfast has been totally renovated while retaining original marble mantles, period windows and architectural details. Decorated in Southern Traditional style, antiques and reproductions blend nicely with European pieces collected during the owners' travels. Relax in the spacious living room highlighted with a fireplace, or on the porch or patio. Lavishly decorated guest bedrooms boast garden views. The Regency Room boasts a whirlpool bath, and the Touch of France features a clawfoot tub. An elegant gourmet breakfast is served in the formal dining room under a crystal chandelier with original artwork gracing the walls and an Oriental rug underfoot.

Innkeeper(s): Patricia R. Daniels & Michael C. Rohde. $119-135. 2 rooms with PB. Breakfast included in rates. Types of meals: Full gourmet bkfst. Beds: KQ. Cable TV, reading lamp, ceiling fan, clock radio, telephone and desk in room. Central air. Fax and fireplace on premises. Antiquing, art galleries, bicycling, canoeing/kayaking, golf, live theater, museums, parks, shopping, sporting events, State Capitol, Civil War sites, Monument Avenue and Library of Virginia nearby.
Publicity: Style Weekly, Richmond Magazine in the annual "Best & Worst" issue (chosen as the "best in-town getaway"), Channel 12 - Showcase of Homes and Fan District Association's Holiday House Tour.

Scottsville F13

High Meadows Vineyard Inn

55 High Meadows Ln
Scottsville, VA 24590
(434)286-2218 (800)232-1832 Fax:(434)286-2124

Circa 1832. Minutes from Charlottesville on the Constitution Highway (Route 20), High Meadows stands on 25 acres of gardens, forests, ponds, a creek and a vineyard. Listed in the National Register, it is actually two historic homes joined by a breezeway as well as three private cottages. The inn is furnished in Federal and Victorian styles. Guests are treated to gracious Virginia hospitality in an elegant and peaceful setting with wine tasting and a romantic candlelight dinner every evening. There are two private hot tubs on the grounds.
Historic Interest: Jefferson, Monroe, Madison homes (15-20 miles), a Civil War trail site nearby.
Innkeeper(s): Peter Sushka, Mary Jae Abbitt. Rose Farber & Jon Storey. $99-390. 12 rooms with PB, 8 with FP, 5 suites and 1 conference room. Restaurant on premises. Beds: KQDT. Reading lamp, refrigerator, clock radio, desk and hot tub/spa in room. Air conditioning. Telephone and fireplace on premises. Weddings, small meetings, family reunions and seminars hosted. Antiquing, bicycling, cross-country skiing, downhill skiing, fishing, hiking, shopping, sporting events, water sports and theater nearby.
Publicity: *Daily Progress, Washington Post, Richmond Times Dispatch, Mid-Atlantic, Washingtonian, Gourmet Magazine and Arrington's Bed & Breakfast Journal.*

Smithfield H17

Four Square Plantation

13357 Foursquare Rd
Smithfield, VA 23430-8643
(757)365-0749 Fax:(757)365-0749
E-mail: foursquareplantation@att.net
Web: www.innvirginia.com

Circa 1807. Located in the historic James River area, the original land grant, "Four Square" was established in 1664 and consisted of 640 acres. Now in the National Register and a Virginia Historic Landmark, the Federal style home is called Plantation Plain by Virginia preservationists. The inn is furnished with family period pieces and antiques. The Vaughan Room offers a fireplace, Empire furnishings and access by private staircase. Breakfast is served in the dining room. The inn's four acres provide a setting for weddings and special events. Tour Williamsburg, Jamestown, the James River Plantations and Yorktown nearby.
Innkeeper(s): Roger & Donna. $75-85. 3 rooms with PB, 3 with FP. Breakfast included in rates. Types of meals: Full gourmet bkfst and early coffee/tea. Beds: KQT. Cable TV, reading lamp, ceiling fan, telephone and turn-down service in room. Air conditioning. VCR, fax, copier and parlor games on premises. Weddings, small meetings and family reunions hosted. Antiquing, golf and shopping nearby.
Publicity: *Daily Press and Virginia Pilot.*

Spotsylvania E15

Roxbury Mill B&B

6908 S Roxbury Mill Rd
Spotsylvania, VA 22553-2438
(540)582-6611

Circa 1723. Once a working mill for the Roxbury Plantation, this early 18th-century home has seen the formation of a nation and the wars that would follow. Civil War relics have been found on the property, which includes a dam and millpond. The innkeepers strive to maintain a sense of history at their B&B, keeping the decor in Colonial to pre-Civil War styles. The large master suite affords a view of the river from its private deck, and the bed is an 18th-century antique. All guest rooms offer a view, private porch and antique furnishings. Traditional Southern-Colonial fare, from family recipes, fills the breakfast menu. Cornpone topped with slab bacon or country ham and biscuits are some of the appetizing choices. For late risers, the innkeepers also offer brunch.
Innkeeper(s): Joyce B. Ackerman. $75-150. 3 rooms, 2 with PB and 1 suite. Breakfast and afternoon tea included in rates. Types of meals: Full gourmet bkfst, early coffee/tea and gourmet dinner. Beds: QD. Cable TV, reading lamp, refrigerator, ceiling fan, snack bar, clock radio and turn-down service in room. Air conditioning. VCR, telephone and fireplace on premises. Weddings, small meetings, family reunions and seminars hosted. Amusement parks, antiquing, fishing, parks, shopping, water sports, Civil War battlefields and museum nearby.

Stanardsville D13

South River Country Inn

3011 S River Rd
Stanardsville, VA 22973
(434)985-2901 (877)874-4473 Fax:(434)985-3833
E-mail: cbraun@sprintmail.com
Web: www.southrivercountryinn.com

Circa 1900. In the heart of South River Valley, this original Virginia-style farmhouse has been restored to provide modern comforts while retaining its authentic charm. The spectacular Blue Ridge Mountains are seen from each of the guest bedrooms, some of which feature Jacuzzi tubs for two. A wholesome country breakfast starts the day on this working farm. Hike, fish in one of the ponds or relax in a front porch swing, rocker or hammock. Shenandoah River activities are just a short drive away.
Innkeeper(s): Judy & Cliff Braun. $110-195. 3 rooms with PB and 1 suite. Breakfast included in rates. Types of meals: Country bkfst, veg bkfst, early coffee/tea, lunch, picnic lunch and dinner. Beds: QDT. Reading lamp, stereo, refrigerator, clock radio, telephone, coffeemaker and satellite TV in room. Central air. TV, fax, parlor games, laundry facility, fishing, DVD and swimming pool on premises. Weddings, small meetings, family reunions and seminars hosted. Antiquing, art galleries, bicycling, canoeing/kayaking, downhill skiing, fishing, golf, hiking, horseback riding, live theater, museums, parks, shopping, sporting events and wineries nearby.

Stanley D13

Jordan Hollow Farm Inn

326 Hawksbill Park Rd
Stanley, VA 22851-4506
(540)778-2285 (888)418-7000 Fax:(540)778-1759
E-mail: jhf@jordanhollow.com
Web: www.jordanhollow.com

Circa 1790. Nestled in the foothills of the Blue Ridge Mountains, this delightful 145-acre horse farm is ideal for those who love riding and country living. The colonial farm

house is a full-service restaurant decorated with antiques and artifacts. Horse boarding is available as is five miles of walking trails on the property.

Historic Interest: New Market Battlefield Museum, Luray Caverness, Skyline Drive.

Innkeeper(s): Gail Kyle . $140-190. 15 rooms with PB, 11 with FP and 1 conference room. Breakfast included in rates. Types of meals: Full gourmet bkfst, picnic lunch and gourmet dinner. Restaurant on premises. Beds: KQ. Cable TV, telephone, coffeemaker and hot tub/spa in room. Central air. Fax, copier, parlor games and fireplace on premises. Weddings, small meetings, family reunions and seminars hosted. Art galleries, canoeing/kayaking, cross-country skiing, downhill skiing, fishing, golf, hiking, horseback riding, parks, shopping, tennis, water sports and wineries nearby.

Publicity: *Country, Southern Living, Conde Nast, New York Times, Country Accents, Family Circle, Glamour, Vogue, Palm Beach and Washingtonian.*

"I keep thinking of my day at your lovely inn and keep dreaming of that wonderful lemon mousse cake!"

Staunton   E11

Frederick House

28 N New St
Staunton, VA 24401-4306
(540)885-4220 (800)334-5575 Fax:(540)885-5180
E-mail: stay@frederickhouse.com
Web: www.frederickhouse.com

Circa 1810. Adjacent to Mary Baldwin College, this inn consists of six renovated town houses, the oldest of which is believed to be a copy of a home designed by Thomas Jefferson. A full breakfast is served in Chumley's Tea Room. Guest rooms (some with fireplaces) are furnished with antiques and feature robes and ceiling fans. Original staircases and woodwork are highlighted throughout. Suites are available.

Historic Interest: Blue Ridge Parkway, Skyline Drive (12 miles), Woodrow Wilson birthplace (2 blocks), Museum of American Frontier Culture (2 miles), Shenadoah Shakespeare Black Friars Play House.

Innkeeper(s): Joe & Evy Harman. $85-170. 23 rooms with PB, 6 with FP, 8 suites and 1 conference room. Breakfast included in rates. Types of meals: Full gourmet bkfst and early coffee/tea. Beds: KQDT. Cable TV, reading lamp, telephone and desk in room. Air conditioning. TV and fireplace on premises. Weddings, small meetings, family reunions and seminars hosted. Antiquing, cross-country skiing, downhill skiing, fishing, live theater, parks, shopping, sporting events, water sports and Skyline Drive Blue Ridge Parkway nearby.

Publicity: *Daily News Leader, Richmond Times-Dispatch, News Journal, Washington Post and Blue Ridge Country.*

"Thanks for making the room so squeaky-clean and comfortable! I enjoyed the Virginia hospitality. The furnishings and decor are beautiful."

Steeles Tavern   E11

Steeles Tavern Manor Country Inn

30 Butler Circle
Steeles Tavern, VA 24476
(540)377-9261 (800)743-8666
E-mail: hoernlei@cfw.com
Web: www.steelestavern.com

Circa 1916. With a fascinating history of hospitality, this Georgian manor home and two secluded cottages offer comfortable elegance. Accented with antiques, thoughtfully decorat-

ed guest bedrooms and spacious suites feature fireplaces, two-person Jacuzzis and VCRs. Morning coffee is delivered to the door. Enjoy breakfast in bed or in the candlelit dining room. The published chef creates a meal that may include the signature Snowflake Waffles with fresh strawberries, and bacon. Explore 55 natural acres of wildflowers with streams and a pond. After experiencing the pleasure of birding, take a refreshing swim in the pool. Refreshments are available all day.

Innkeeper(s): Bill & Eileen Hoernlein. $120-185. 5 rooms with PB, 5 with FP, 2 suites and 2 cottages. Breakfast, afternoon tea and snacks/refreshments included in rates. Types of meals: Full gourmet bkfst, early coffee/tea, picnic lunch, gourmet dinner and room service. Beds: KQ. TV, VCR, reading lamp, ceiling fan, clock radio, coffeemaker, fireplace, robes, extra pillows, blankets and towels in room. Central air. Fax, copier, swimming, telephone, fireplace, gift shop, swimming pool, fishing pond and stream on premises. Weddings hosted. Antiquing, art galleries, bicycling, canoeing/kayaking, fishing, golf, hiking, horseback riding, live theater, museums, parks, shopping and wineries nearby.

Publicity: *Blue Ridge Country and WDBJ7-TV.*

Stephens City   B13

The Inn at Vaucluse Spring

231 Vaucluse Spring Ln
Stephens City, VA 22655
(540)869-0200 (800)869-0525 Fax:(540)869-9546
E-mail: mail@vauclusespring.com
Web: www.vauclusespring.com

Circa 1785. Set amid 100 scenic acres in Northern Shenandoah Valley, this inn consists of a variety of vintage guest houses that surround the crystal clear spring. Accommodations include the carefully restored Federal manor house, a walnut log home and cottages. One was originally an art gallery, another an artist's studio on the site of the former gristmill and the other an old tobacco barn. The Cottage on the hill offers two bedrooms. All rooms feature a fireplace, most have Jacuzzi tubs and several boast water or mountain views. Stroll the grounds that include a stream and waterfall.

Innkeeper(s): Neil & Barry Myers. $140-275. 15 rooms with PB, 15 with FP, 2 suites, 3 cottages and 2 conference rooms. Breakfast included in rates. Types of meals: Full bkfst, early coffee/tea and gourmet dinner. Beds: KQ. Reading lamp and clock radio in room. Air conditioning. Fax, copier, swimming, parlor games, telephone and fireplace on premises. Weddings and small meetings hosted. Antiquing, golf, live theater, parks and water sports nearby.

Publicity: *Washingtonian, Country Home and Southern Living.*

Strasburg   C13

Hotel Strasburg

213 S Holliday St
Strasburg, VA 22657-2213
(540)465-9191 (800)488-327 Fax:(540)465-4788
E-mail: thehotel@shentel.net
Web: www.hotelstrasburg.com

Circa 1902. Experience the romance of the Victorian era at this three-story hotel, situated on two acres, just one block from Main Street. Built in 1902 as a hospital, the building was converted into a hotel in 1915 after a doctor ran off with a nurse. Since then, it has been the social hub of Strasburg and offers luxurious accommodations and an exquisite dining area. Each room of the Victorian Clapboard inn holds the finest array of antique furnishings, all of which are for sale. Period pieces are continually brought into the inn from the innkeepers' travels. During their stay, guests enjoy hiking, canoeing, fishing and visiting nearby Civil War battlefields or taking an hour-long drive to Washington, D.C. Enjoy the elegance of Victorian

gourmet dining in the hotel's dining room throughout the day.
Innkeeper(s): Gary & Carol Rutherford. $79-175. 29 rooms with PB and 1
conference room. Types of meals: Full bkfst, early coffee/tea, lunch,
snacks/refreshments and gourmet dinner. Restaurant on premises. Beds:
KQDS. Data port, cable TV, reading lamp, telephone and some with hot tubs
in room. Air conditioning. Fax and copier on premises. Weddings, small meetings, family reunions and seminars hosted. Antiquing, beach, bicycling,
canoeing/kayaking, downhill skiing, fishing, golf, hiking, horseback riding, live
theater, museums, parks, shopping, tennis and wineries nearby.
Publicity: *Blue Ridge Country, Washington Post, Washingtonian, Country
Victorian and BBC.*

The Plains   C14

Grey Horse Inn

4350 Fauquier Ave.
The Plains, VA 20198
(540)253-7000 (877)253-7020 Fax:(540)253-7031

Circa 1880. Built as a Victorian tourist hotel on four acres in
the heart of hunting country, this exclusive yet intimate inn is
well-suited for both the leisure and business traveler. Furnished
with antebellum-era family heirlooms, a refined ambiance is
reflected. Enjoy afternoon tea on one of the relaxing porches
with unspoiled views of the Blue Ridge Mountains beyond the
garden and farmland. Each of the spacious guest bedrooms features a canopy bed, fine linens and personal amenities. Start
the day with a country breakfast before exploring the quaint village setting, nearby wineries or historic Civil War sites.
Innkeeper(s): John & Ellen Hearty. $105-195. 6 rooms. Breakfast included in
rates. Types of meals: Full gourmet bkfst and early coffee/tea. Beds: KQ.
Modem hook-up, data port, cable TV, VCR, reading lamp, refrigerator, clock
radio, telephone, turn-down service, desk and hot tub/spa in room. Central
air. Fax, copier, library, pet boarding, parlor games, fireplace and laundry
facility on premises. Limited handicap access. Weddings, small meetings,
family reunions and seminars hosted. Antiquing, art galleries, bicycling,
canoeing/kayaking, fishing, golf, hiking, horseback riding, museums, parks,
shopping and wineries nearby.

Warm Springs   E10

The Inn at Gristmill Square

PO Box 359
Warm Springs, VA 24484-0359
(540)839-2231 Fax:(540)839-5770

Circa 1800. The inn consists of five restored buildings. The
old blacksmith shop and silo, the hardware store, the Steel
House and the Miller House all contain guest rooms. (The old
mill is now the Waterwheel Restaurant.) There are three vacation apartment rentals ranging from
$125-$150. A few antiques
and old prints appear in
some rooms, while others
are furnished in a contemporary style. There are tennis
courts and a swimming pool
at the inn. A short walk over Warm Springs Mill Stream and
down the road brings travelers to historic Warm Springs Pools.
Innkeeper(s): The McWilliams family. $85-125. 17 rooms with PB, 8 with FP,
5 suites and 1 conference room. Breakfast included in rates. Types of meals:
Cont, picnic lunch, dinner and room service. Restaurant on premises. Beds:
KQDT. Cable TV, reading lamp, refrigerator, clock radio, telephone and desk in
room. Air conditioning. VCR, fax, copier, swimming, sauna and tennis on
premises. Weddings, small meetings, family reunions and seminars hosted.
Downhill skiing, fishing, golf, parks, shopping, tennis and water sports nearby.
Publicity: *New York Times, Bon Appetit and Colonial Homes.*

*"You have such a wonderful inn — such attention to detail and such
a considerate staff."*

Meadow Lane Lodge

HCR 01 Box 110
Warm Springs, VA 24484-9709
(540)839-5959 Fax:(540)839-2135
E-mail: meadowln@tds.net
Web: meadowlanelodge.com

Circa 1922. Meadow Lane Lodge boasts a colorful history. The
lodge is located on a vast, 1,600-acre spread in the Allegheny
Mountains, and its acreage was once part of a land grant made
by King George III to Charles Lewis, a pioneer settler. The farm
also is the site of Fort Dinwiddie, which was visited by George
Washington on two occasions. Although the fort is no longer
standing, a restored slave cabin still exists and is used as a reading room. An Indian village once rested on the property, and
guests might discover an arrowhead while meandering the
grounds. There are five guest rooms in the main lodge, decorated with a mix of comfortable furnishings and antiques. In addition to breakfast each day, Saturday night dinners are available
by prior arrangement. Guests will find walking and biking trails
on the grounds, a swimming hole and perhaps a beaver bog.
Deer, fox and a variety of birds are other sights you're sure to
see. Guests also can stay in nearby Warm Springs at a restored
log house, which dates to 1820. A late 19th-century grain barn,
located along the Jackson River, is another lodging option.
Innkeeper(s): Carter & Michelle Ancona. $105-260. 11 rooms with PB, 3
with FP and 1 conference room. Breakfast included in rates. Types of meals:
Country bkfst and picnic lunch. Beds: KQDT. Some with cable TV, coffeemaker, refrigerator and telephone in room. Air conditioning. TV, fax, swimming,
stable, bicycles, tennis, library, parlor games, telephone, fireplace, fishing,
hiking, massage, canoes, croquet and barn animals on premises. Weddings,
small meetings, family reunions and seminars hosted. Antiquing, art galleries,
canoeing/kayaking, cross-country skiing, downhill skiing, fishing, golf, hiking,
horseback riding, parks, shopping and tennis nearby.

"This 1,600-acre farm was very private and nice."

Warrenton   C14

Black Horse Inn

8393 Meetze Rd
Warrenton, VA 20187
(540)349-4020 Fax:(540)349-4242
E-mail: relax@blackhorseinn.com
Web: www.blackhorseinn.com

Circa 1850. Rich in history, the inn is named after an elite
Confederate cavalry unit. Resting on 20 acres of rolling countryside, the inn boasts a decor reflecting a horse-country theme.
Upon check-in, indulge in an afternoon tea with a sampling of
sherry and port wines. Romantic guest bedrooms are appointed
with four-poster canopy beds, fireplaces and Jacuzzi tubs. One
room is noted for inspiring more than three dozen marriage pro-
posals. Gourmet breakfasts include specialties such as Inn at
Little Washington French toast, a rich entree stuffed with pecans
and mascarpone cheese. Visit The Gilded Fox, an elegant and
stately reception facility that seats up to 200 people. Hike along
the Appalachian Trail, go horseback riding, paddling or cycling.
Innkeeper(s): Lynn A. Pirozzoli. $125-295. 8 rooms with PB, 4 with FP, 2
suites and 2 conference rooms. Breakfast and afternoon tea included in rates.
Types of meals: Full bkfst, early coffee/tea, picnic lunch and snacks/refresh-
ments. Beds: Q. Modem hook-up, reading lamp, CD player, ceiling fan, snack
bar, coffeemaker, turn-down service, desk and hot tub/spa in room. Air conditioning. TV, fax, copier, stable, bicycles, library, parlor games, telephone, fireplace and laundry facility on premises. Weddings, small meetings and family
reunions hosted. Antiquing, art galleries, bicycling, canoeing/kayaking, cross-
country skiing, fishing, golf, hiking, horseback riding, live theater, museums,

parks, sporting events, tennis, wineries and health club nearby.
Publicity: *Washingtonian, Fauquier Magazine, Washington Post, Washington Life, Total Living Network and Arrington's - voted inn with best wedding arrangements in the nation.*

Washington   C13

Caledonia Farm - 1812 B&B

47 Dearing Rd (Flint Hill)
Washington, VA 22627
(540)675-3693 (800)262-1812

Circa 1812. This gracious Federal-style stone house in the National Register is beautifully situated on 52 acres adjacent to Shenandoah National Park. It was built by a Revolutionary War officer, and his musket is displayed over a mantel. The house, a Virginia Historic Landmark, has been restored with the original Colonial color scheme retained.

All rooms have working fireplaces and provide views of Skyline Drive and the Blue Ridge Mountains. The innkeeper is a retired broadcaster.

Innkeeper(s): Phil Irwin. $140. 2 suites, 2 with FP and 1 conference room. Breakfast and snacks/refreshments included in rates. Types of meals: Full gourmet bkfst and early coffee/tea. Beds: D. VCR, reading lamp, refrigerator, snack bar, clock radio, telephone, turn-down service, desk, hot tub/spa and skyline Drive View in room. Air conditioning. TV, fax, copier, spa, bicycles, library, parlor games, fireplace, hay ride and lawn games on premises. Small meetings, family reunions and seminars hosted. Antiquing, cross-country skiing, downhill skiing, fishing, live theater, parks, shopping, water sports, wineries, caves, stables and battlefields nearby.
Publicity: *Country, Country Almanac, Country Living, Blue Ridge Country, Discovery, Washington Post, Baltimore Sun and Pen TV/Cable 15/PBS X3.*

"We've stayed at many, many B&Bs. This is by far the best!"

The Foster-Harris House

189 Main St
Washington, VA 22747
(540)675-3757 (800)666-0153

Circa 1900. This Victorian farmhouse stands on a lot laid out by George Washington and is located at the edge of the village. The streets of the town are exactly as surveyed 225 years ago. The village has galleries and craft shops as well as the Inn at Little Washington's five-star restaurant.
Historic Interest: Civil War battlefields & museums (less than an hour's drive).
Innkeeper(s): Patrick Corbett. $125-275. 5 rooms with PB, 2 with FP and 1 suite. Breakfast and afternoon tea included in rates. Types of meals: Full bkfst. Beds: QD. Reading lamp and ceiling fan in room. Air conditioning. Telephone and fireplace on premises. Small meetings hosted. Antiquing, cross-country skiing, fishing, live theater and shopping nearby.
Publicity: *Richmond Times-Dispatch, Southern Living and Washingtonian.*

Gay Street Inn

PO Box 237, 160 Gay St
Washington, VA 22747
(540)675-3288
E-mail: gaystinn@shentel.net
Web: www.gaystreetinn.com

Circa 1855. After a day of Skyline Drive, Shenandoah National Park and the caverns of Luray and Front Royal, come home to this stucco, gabled farmhouse. If you've booked the fireplace room, a canopy bed will await you. Furnishings include period Shaker pieces. The innkeepers will be happy to steer you to the most interesting vineyards, organic "pick-your-own" fruit and vegetable farms and Made-In-Virginia food and craft shops.

Breakfast and afternoon tea are served in the garden conservatory. Five-star dining is within walking distance at The Inn at Little Washington. The innkeepers can arrange for child care.

Historic Interest: Manassas Battlefield & Park and Chancellorsville are some of the area's many Civil War sites. The University of Virginia, historic Charlottesville and Monticello are other sites in the area, Mosby Country.
Innkeeper(s): Robin & Donna Kevis. $110-135. 4 rooms with PB, 1 with FP and 1 suite. Breakfast and afternoon tea included in rates. Types of meals: Full gourmet bkfst and early coffee/tea. Beds: Q. Reading lamp, clock radio and suite has TV in room. Air conditioning. Fireplace on premises. Weddings, small meetings and family reunions hosted. Antiquing, fishing, golf, horseback riding, live theater, parks, shopping, water sports and vineyards nearby.
Publicity: *Blue Ridge Country and Food Art.*

"Thank you for a wonderful visit. Your hospitality was superb."

Heritage House B&B

291 Main St , PO Box 427
Washington, VA 22747
(540)675-3207 (888)819-8280 Fax:(540)675-2004
E-mail: hhbb@shentel.net
Web: heritagehousebb.com

Circa 1837. Superbly located in a small village, it is easy to escape the city at this historic 1837 rural Colonial manor house. The house is purported to have served as a Confederate headquarters during the Civil War. Air-conditioned guest bedrooms are tastefully decorated and comfortably furnished with antiques and reproductions. The popular Garden Suite features an extra sunroom overlooking the summer garden with spectacular views of the Blue Ridge Mountains beyond. Enjoy a delectable breakfast before visiting local galleries, shops or award-winning wineries. Explore nearby Skyline Drive, hike Old Rag Mountain, go horseback riding, kayaking or canoeing. Innkeepers Gary and Michelle desire to help make each stay a memorable one.
Innkeeper(s): Michelle & Gary Schwartz. $120-155. 5 rooms with PB. Breakfast, afternoon tea and snacks/refreshments included in rates. Types of meals: Full gourmet bkfst, veg bkfst, early coffee/tea, lunch and dinner. Beds: KQDT. Reading lamp, ceiling fan, clock radio, turn-down service and desk in room. Air conditioning. TV, fax, copier, library, parlor games, telephone, fireplace and snack bar on premises. Weddings and family reunions hosted. Antiquing, art galleries, bicycling, canoeing/kayaking, fishing, golf, hiking, live theater, museums, parks, shopping, tennis, water sports, wineries, caverns, birding and world-class dining nearby.
Publicity: *Country Almanac and Washington Post.*

"Having been to a number of bed & breakfasts, yours is No. 1 in its setting, the wonderful food and your hospitality."

Middleton Inn

176 Main St
Washington, VA 22747-1915
(540)675-2020 (800)816-8157 Fax:(540)675-1050
E-mail: innkeeper@middleton-inn.com
Web: www.middleton-inn.com

Circa 1850. On a knoll facing the Blue Ridge Mountains, this historic, award-winning country estate is listed in the Virginia Landmarks Register. Built in the Federal style, the inn boasts the old summer kitchen, smoke house and stables on six rural acres of meadow and pasture. Accommodations include guest bedrooms in the brick manor house and the slaves' quarters, now a romantic two-story cottage. All of the delightfully decorated rooms have working fireplaces, terry cloth robes and marble baths. The cottage offers more spacious privacy, a Jacuzzi for two and a small kitchen. Savor a generous gourmet breakfast served on china and linens in the formal dining room or al fresco on one of the porches. Enjoy afternoon wine and cheese in the drawing room.

Innkeeper(s): Mary Ann Kuhn. $195-525. 5 rooms with PB, 5 with FP and 1 conference room. Breakfast, afternoon tea and snacks/refreshments included in rates. Types of meals: Full gourmet bkfst, veg bkfst, early coffee/tea, gourmet lunch, dinner and room service. Beds: KQT. Modem hook-up, data port, cable TV, VCR, reading lamp, stereo, refrigerator, ceiling fan, clock radio, telephone, coffeemaker, turn-down service, desk, hot tub/spa, voice mail, twice daily maid service, afternoon wine, Waterford crystal water glasses and sterling silver ice buckets in each room, service on silver trays at all times and thick terrycloth robes in room. Central air. Fax, copier, spa, stable, bicycles, library, pet boarding, child care, parlor games, fireplace and laundry facility on premises. Weddings, small meetings, family reunions and seminars hosted. Antiquing, art galleries, bicycling, canoeing/kayaking, fishing, golf, hiking, horseback riding, live theater, parks, shopping, tennis, wineries, Civil War battlefields, historic Monticello, Montpelier, gourmet dining, apple orchards and organic farms nearby.

Publicity: *Southern Living, The Washington Post, Washingtonian Magazine, Innspots & Special Places, Recommended Country Inns, Georgetown and Country and CBS News.*

Williamsburg   G17

A Williamsburg White House

718 Jamestown Rd
Williamsburg, VA 23185
(757)229-8580 (866)229-8580
E-mail: info@awilliamsburgwhitehouse.com
Web: www.awilliamsburgwhitehouse.com

Circa 1904. Just four blocks from historic downtown, this spacious century-old Colonial estate graces a picturesque neighborhood. Decorated around an elegant and traditional presidential theme, the common rooms include the JFK library, where a fireside game of chess can be played while sipping sherry in a leather chair, and the Diplomatic Reception Room where afternoon wine and delicious treats are served. Guest bedrooms are considered Presidential Suites with four-poster and canopy feather beds, robes, sitting areas and motif-matching memorabilia. Enjoy a sumptuous full breakfast in the Reagan Dining Room.

Innkeeper(s): Debbie & John Keane. $125-185. 4 rooms with PB and 3 suites. Breakfast, snacks/refreshments and wine included in rates. Types of meals: Full gourmet bkfst and early coffee/tea. Beds: KQ. Cable TV, telephone and two with fireplaces in room. Central air. Fax, library and fireplace on premises. Family reunions hosted. Amusement parks, antiquing, art galleries, bicycling, golf, hiking, horseback riding, live theater, museums, parks, shopping, sporting events and wineries nearby.

An American Inn - Williamsburg Manor B&B

600 Richmond Rd
Williamsburg, VA 23185
(757)220-8011 (800)422-8011 Fax:(757)220-0245
E-mail: Williamsburg@occassions.hrcoxmail.com
Web: www.williamsburg-manor.com

Circa 1927. Built during the reconstruction of Colonial Williamsburg, this Georgian brick Colonial is just three blocks from the historic village. A grand staircase, culinary library, Waverly fabrics, Oriental rugs and antiques are featured. Breakfasts begin with fresh fruits and home-baked breads, followed by a special daily entree. Gourmet regional Virginia dinners also are available.
Historic Interest: Historic Williamsburg

(3 blocks), Jamestown (5 miles), Yorktown (20 miles), William & Mary College (1 block).
Innkeeper(s): Laura & Craig Reeves. $79-169. 6 rooms, 4 with PB and 1 suite. Breakfast included in rates. Types of meals: Full gourmet bkfst, veg bkfst, early coffee/tea, gourmet lunch, picnic lunch, afternoon tea, snacks/refreshments and gourmet dinner. Beds: QT. Modem hook-up, cable TV, reading lamp, CD player, ceiling fan, clock radio, telephone and voice mail in room. Central air. VCR, spa, child care, parlor games, fireplace, freshly baked cookies and lemonade on premises. Amusement parks, antiquing, art galleries, beach, bicycling, canoeing/kayaking, fishing, golf, hiking, horseback riding, live theater, museums, parks, shopping, sporting events, tennis, water sports and wineries nearby.

Publicity: *Virginia Gazette, Williamsburg Magazine, Gourmet Magazine, San Francisco Reader and Daily Press.*

"Lovely accommodations - scrumptious breakfast."

Applewood Colonial B&B

605 Richmond Rd
Williamsburg, VA 23185-3539
(757)229-0205 (800)899-2753 Fax:(757)229-2873
E-mail: info@williamsburgbandb.com
Web: www.williamsburgbandb.com

Circa 1928. This stately home was built by the craftsman chosen to meticulously restore and reconstruct Colonial Williamsburg. Using the same high standards and hand-crafted architectural details, it is perfectly located along the Historic Corridor. The classic decor of the Colonial era is evident throughout the well-appointed rooms. Guest bedrooms and suites offer high four-poster canopy beds and boast modern conveniences. A magnificent candlelight breakfast is served on a pedestal table under a crystal chandelier in the dining room. Complimentary afternoon refreshments include fresh baked cookies, Virginia peanuts and beverages. In keeping with its name and extensive apple collection, delicious slices of apple pie are available every evening.
Historic Interest: Colonial Williamsburg (3 blocks away).
Innkeeper(s): Marty Jones. $90-175. 4 rooms with PB, 1 with FP and 1 suite. Breakfast and snacks/refreshments included in rates. Types of meals: Full bkfst and early coffee/tea. Beds: Q. Cable TV, VCR, stereo, refrigerator, telephone and hair dryer in room. Air conditioning. Weddings, small meetings, family reunions and seminars hosted. Amusement parks, antiquing, fishing, live theater, parks, shopping, sporting events, water sports, Colonial Williamsburg and historic sites nearby.
Publicity: *Discerning Traveler.*

"Our accommodations were the best, and you were most kind."

Cedars

616 Jamestown Rd
Williamsburg, VA 23185-3945
(757)229-3591 (800)296-3591 Fax:(757)229-0756
E-mail: btubbs@cedarsbandb.com
Web: www.cedarsofwilliamsburg.com

Circa 1933. This three-story brick Georgian home is a short walk from Colonial Williamsburg and is located across from William and Mary College. Rooms are decorated with traditional antiques, Colonial reproductions, fireplaces and four-poster or canopy beds. The bountiful breakfasts include a hearty entree, fresh fruits, breads, muffins and cereals.
Innkeeper(s): Thomas Mansfield. $110-275. 8 rooms with PB, 2 with FP, 2 suites and 1 cottage. Breakfast included in rates. Types of meals: Full bkfst and early coffee/tea. Beds: KQT. TV, reading lamp, ceiling fan and clock radio in room. Air conditioning. Library, parlor games, telephone and fireplace on premises. Family reunions hosted. Amusement parks, antiquing, parks, shopping and historic sites nearby.

Colonial Capital B&B

501 Richmond Rd
Williamsburg, VA 23185-3537
(757)229-0233 (800)776-0570 Fax:(757)253-7667
E-mail: ccbb@widomaker.com
Web: www.ccbb.com

Circa 1926. Conveniently located in the Architectural
Preservation District, this three-story Colonial Revival house is
a three-block walk to the outdoor living museum of Colonial
Williamsburg's Duke of Gloucester Street. Jamestown,
Yorktown and Busch Gardens
are less than 15 miles away.
Elegantly blending antiques
and oriental rugs, the
ambiance of warmth and style
is felt throughout the inn.
The classic plantation parlor
is an inviting place to relax by the wood-burning fireplace or in
air-conditioned comfort. Light and airy guest bedrooms feature
canopy beds. A screened porch, patio and deck provide outdoor enjoyment.

Innkeeper(s): Barbara & Phil Craig. $140-155. 5 rooms with PB and 1 suite.
Breakfast and afternoon tea included in rates. Types of meals: Full gourmet
bkfst and early coffee/tea. Beds: KQT. VCR, reading lamp, clock radio, desk,
hair dryer, remote controlled ceiling fans and phone with data port in room.
Air conditioning. Fax, copier, library, parlor games, afternoon wine, free bicycles, videos and table games on premises. Weddings, small meetings and
family reunions hosted. Amusement parks, antiquing, fishing, live theater,
parks, shopping, water sports, biking, living museums and bird watching
trails nearby.
Publicity: *Washington Post, Country Inns, Mid-Atlantic and The Romantic
Southeast.*

""Love, warmth, great room & southern hospitality.""

The Fife & Drum Inn

441 Prince George St
Williamsburg, VA 23185
(757)345-1776 (888)838-1783 Fax:(757)253-1675
E-mail: bscruggs@fifeanddruminn.com
Web: www.fifeanddruminn.com

Circa 1933. Having the distinction of being the only inn in the
historic downtown area, the inn occupies the second floor of the
Hitchens Building, which is noted for being instrumental in the
restoration of Colonial Williamsburg. Furnished with the decor
and ambiance of the 18th century with a modern streak, the
common room includes a library of local interest publications, a
relaxing sitting area and Colonial games to play by the fireplace.
Beverages are available around the clock. Guest bedrooms and
suites feature upscale amenities like fragrant imported bath products, cotton linens, fluffy duvets and plush robes. Folk art, signed
originals, family heirlooms, maps, prints and local archaeological
artifacts showcase attention to detail. Southern hospitality is generous, offering a breakfast buffet with a fresh fruit bowl, hot, flaky
biscuits stuffed with thinly sliced Virginia ham and entrees ranging from an egg and cheese strata to blueberry French toast.
Innkeeper(s): Sharon, Billy Scruggs. $155-175. 9 rooms, 7 with PB and 2
suites. Breakfast and snacks/refreshments included in rates. Types of meals:
Country bkfst and early coffee/tea. Beds: KQT. Modem hook-up, data port,
cable TV, VCR, reading lamp, ceiling fan, clock radio and telephone in room.
Central air. Library and parlor games on premises. Small meetings and family
reunions hosted. Amusement parks, antiquing, art galleries, beach, bicycling,
fishing, golf, hiking, live theater, museums, parks, shopping, tennis, water
sports and wineries nearby.
Publicity: *The Virginia Gazette.*

Liberty Rose B&B

1022 Jamestown Rd
Williamsburg, VA 23185-3434
(757)253-1260 (800)545-1825
Web: www.libertyrose.com

Circa 1922. This cozy retreat, located on the historic corridor,
is tucked among tall trees only a mile from Colonial
Williamsburg. The owner of Jamestown constructed this two-
story clapboard home. The entry porch is marked with the
millstone from one of Williamsburg's old mills. Antiques and
collectibles abound in each of the rooms. The innkeepers have
merged modern amenities with turn-of-the-century atmosphere. All rooms include telephones, TVs and VCRs with an
excellent selection of movies. A gourmet country breakfast is
served each morning. Each of the romantic guest rooms features something unique such as a lush canopy bed.
Honeymooners — the inn is often full of newlyweds — often
return to celebrate their anniversaries.
Historic Interest: Colonial Williamsburg (1 mile), Jamestown 1607 (4 miles),
Yorktown (12 miles), College of William & Mary (1/2 mile).
Innkeeper(s): Brad & Sandi Hirz. $175-235. 4 rooms with PB, 2 with FP
and 3 suites. Breakfast included in rates. Types of meals: Full bkfst. Beds: Q.
Cable TV, VCR and telephone in room. TV on premises. Antiquing, live the-
ater and water sports nearby.
Publicity: *Country Inns, Washington Post, Rural Living, Los Angeles Times,
Glamour, Country Victoria, Bedrooms & Baths and Travel Magazine
(Romantic Weekends).*

*"More delightful than we could possibly have imagined. Charm &
romance abounds when you walk into the house."*

Piney Grove at Southall's Plantation-1790

PO Box 1359
Williamsburg, VA 23187-1359
(804)829-2480
E-mail: info@pineygrove.com
Web: www.pineygrove.com

Circa 1790. Family heirlooms and antiques furnish the 1857
Ladysmith House, the Antebellum plantation home that provides guest accommodations. Spacious guest bedrooms and
suites offer modern amenities including coffee makers, refrigerators and hair dryers, which are appreciated as much as the
historic artifacts and decor. After the farm bell rings, a hearty
plantation breakfast is served by candlelight in the 1790 Log
Room, a rare Tidewater log building listed in the National
Register. Walk the nature trails, and then take a refreshing dip
in the pool. Enjoy a barnyard of farm animals, a gazebo, gardens and lawn games. Relax with a mint julep on the front
porch or a vintage selection from the Piney Grove wine cellar,
enjoyed fireside.
Historic Interest: Colonial Williamsburg, James River Plantations and Civil
War battlefields are some of the area's many historic attractions.
Innkeeper(s): Gordineer Family. $130-260. 5 rooms with PB, 5 with FP, 2
suites and 1 conference room. Types of meals: Full bkfst and
snacks/refreshments. Beds: DT. TV, reading lamp, refrigerator, clock radio,
turn-down service and desk in room. Air conditioning. VCR, fax, swimming,
parlor games, telephone, fireplace and James River Plantation Progressive
Candlelight Tour and Dinner on premises. Amusement parks, antiquing,
fishing, live theater, parks, shopping, sporting events, water sports and
plantation tours nearby.
Publicity: *New York Times, Richmond Times-Dispatch, Washington Post and
Southern Living.*

*"Thank you for your warm, gracious hospitality. We really enjoyed
ourselves and look forward to returning."*

Wolftown D13

Historic Old Rose Tavern Bed & Breakfast

Route 741, PO Box 100
Wolftown, VA 22748
(540)948-5771 Fax:(540)948-5771

Circa 1835. Originally a stopping point in Madison County where aristocrats would stay, this historic inn is still a popular place to visit and feel pampered "The Old Virginia Way." Gracing the foothills of the Blue Ridge Mountains, the Federal style architecture boasts Victorian accents. Recently renovated for modern comfort, elegant country antiques reside comfortably with European ones. Stay in the ground level Yellow Rose Suite with a sitting room, kitchen and private entrance. The Pink Rose Suite features a clawfoot tub and handheld brass shower. Ample seating in the Red Rose Suite is perfect for friends or family to gather. Indulge in a generous five-course breakfast of family favorites and old world recipes served in-room, on the enclosed porch, veranda or in the formal ballroom.

Innkeeper(s): Jacklyn & Brer Gallihugh. $75-250. 6 rooms, 3 suites and 3 conference rooms. Breakfast and afternoon tea included in rates. Types of meals: Full gourmet bkfst, veg bkfst, early coffee/tea, picnic lunch, snacks/refreshments and room service. Beds: QDT. Modem hook-up, TV, VCR, reading lamp, stereo, refrigerator, ceiling fan, clock radio, telephone, coffeemaker, turn-down service, desk, hot tub/spa, fireplace, elegant and private suites that accommodate 4-5 persons, private bath, private sitting room and one suite with private kitchen in room. Air conditioning. Fax, copier, spa, bicycles, library, pet boarding, parlor games, laundry facility and gift shop on premises. Weddings, small meetings, family reunions and seminars hosted. Antiquing, art galleries, bicycling, canoeing/kayaking, cross-country skiing, downhill skiing, fishing, golf, hiking, horseback riding, museums, parks, shopping, sporting events, tennis, water sports, wineries and Shenandoah National Park, Skyline drive, Virginia wine country, Civil War sites, Monticello, Ashlawn, Montpelier, Historic Michie Tavern, Historic districts of Charlottesville, Madison, Orange and Culpeper nearby.

Publicity: *Charlottesville Real Estate Weekly, Washington Post, Civil War publications and Bloomberg Radio.*

Woodstock C13

The Inn at Narrow Passage

PO Box 608
Woodstock, VA 22664-0608
(540)459-8000 (800)459-8002 Fax:(540)459-8001
E-mail: innkeeper@innatnarrowpassage.com
Web: www.innatnarrowpassage.com

Circa 1740. This log inn has been welcoming travelers since the time settlers took refuge here against the Indians. Later, it served as a stagecoach inn on the old Valley Turnpike, and in 1862, it was Stonewall Jackson's headquarters. Most guest rooms feature working fireplaces and views of the Shenandoah River and Massanutten Mountains.

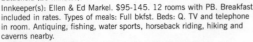

Historic Interest: Shenandoah County Courthouse (5 minutes), Cedar Creek Battlefield (15 minutes), New Market Battlefield (20 minutes).

Innkeeper(s): Ellen & Ed Markel. $95-145. 12 rooms with PB. Breakfast included in rates. Types of meals: Full bkfst. Beds: Q. TV and telephone in room. Antiquing, fishing, water sports, horseback riding, hiking and caverns nearby.

Publicity: *Southern Living, Washington Post, Washington Times and Richmond Times-Dispatch.*

Woolwine I9

The Mountain Rose B&B Inn

1787 Charity Hwy
Woolwine, VA 24185
(276)930-1057 Fax:(276)930-2165
E-mail: info@mountainrose-inn.com
Web: www.mountainrose-inn.com

Circa 1901. This historic Victorian inn, once the home of the Mountain Rose Distillery, sits on 100 acres of forested hills with plenty of hiking trails. A trout-stocked stream goes through the property and a swimming pool provides recreation. Each room has an antique mantled fireplace, which have been converted to gas logs. Guests can relax by the pool or in rocking chairs on one of the six porches. The innkeepers look forward to providing guests with casually elegant hospitality in the Blue Ridge Mountains. The Blue Ridge Parkway, Chateau Morrisette Winery, Mabry Mill, The Reynolds Homestead, Laurel Hill J. EB Stuart Birthplace, Patrick County Courthouse and the Patrick County Historical Museum are located nearby. A three-course breakfast is offered every morning.

Innkeeper(s): Melodie Pogue & Reeves Simms. $105-125. 5 rooms with PB, 5 with FP. Breakfast and snacks/refreshments included in rates. Types of meals: Full gourmet bkfst and early coffee/tea. Beds: KQT. Reading lamp, desk, five working fireplaces, satellite TV and access to porch in room. Air conditioning. VCR, fax, copier, swimming, parlor games, telephone, fireplace, trout-stocked creek and hiking trails on premises. Weddings, small meetings, family reunions and seminars hosted. Antiquing, fishing, golf, hiking, parks, shopping, tennis, water sports, wineries and Nascar racing nearby.

Publicity: *Enterprise, Bill Mountain Bugle, New York Times, The Parkway Edition and "Best Romantic Getaway" City Magazine.*

Old Spring Farm Bed & Breakfast, Ltd.

7629 Charity Hwy (Hwy 40)
Woolwine, VA 24185
(276)930-3404
Web: www.oldspringfarm.com

Circa 1883. Experience the perfect year-round mountain getaway just 50 miles south of Roanoke in Blue Ridge Wine Country. The farmhouse, Country Retreat House and Studio feature Country French décor accented with period pieces and collectibles. Stay in a themed guest bedroom. The Honeymoon Suite offers romantic accommodations with a Jacuzzi and a gas-log stove. Savor a hearty gourmet breakfast of homemade breads, jams and delectable specialties with farm-raised eggs, meat, fruit and vegetables. Take a farm tour after the morning meal. Picnic at Fairy Stone State Park or hike the Rocky Knob Trails. Visit local wineries and enjoy the peaceful countryside.

Innkeeper(s): Suzanne V. Pabst. $100-150. 6 rooms, 4 with PB and 1 conference room. Types of meals: Full gourmet bkfst, early coffee/tea, picnic lunch, snacks/refreshments and gourmet dinner. Beds: KQDT. TV, reading lamp, ceiling fan and clock radio in room. Central air. VCR, telephone, laundry facility and decks on premises. Small meetings and family reunions hosted. Antiquing, art galleries, canoeing/kayaking, fishing, golf, hiking, horseback riding, museums, shopping, sporting events, wineries, swimming and Winston Cup stock car race nearby.

Washington

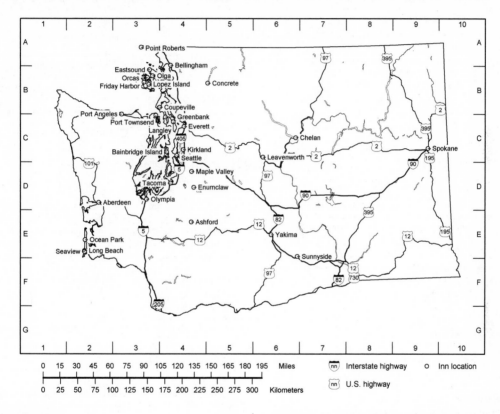

Map of Washington with grid reference (columns 1–10, rows A–G):

- Point Roberts
- Eastsound
- Orcas
- Olga
- Friday Harbor
- Lopez Island
- Bellingham
- Concrete
- Port Angeles
- Coupeville
- Greenbank
- Port Townsend
- Langley
- Everett
- Chelan
- Kirkland
- Bainbridge Island
- Seattle
- Leavenworth
- Spokane
- Maple Valley
- Tacoma
- Enumclaw
- Aberdeen
- Olympia
- Ashford
- Yakima
- Ocean Park
- Long Beach
- Seaview
- Sunnyside

Highways marked: 97, 395, 2, 405, 101, 5, 90, 195, 82, 12, 730, 205, 730

| 0 15 30 45 60 75 90 105 120 135 150 165 180 195 | Miles |
| 0 25 50 75 100 125 150 175 200 225 250 275 300 | Kilometers |

☐ (nn) Interstate highway   ○ Inn location
☐ (nn) U.S. highway

Aberdeen   D2

A Harbor View B&B

113 W 11th St
Aberdeen, WA 98520
(360)533-7996 (877)533-7996 Fax:(360)533-0433
E-mail: info@aharborview.com
Web: www.aharborview.com

Circa 1905. Just as its name suggests, enjoy spectacular views of Gray's Harbor as well as the Wiskah and Chehalis rivers from this historical Colonial Revival home built in 1905 atop Broadway Hill. Relax in the living room and feel free to use the guest kitchen or dining room. Victorian decorated guest bedrooms are comfortably furnished with antiques and boast sitting areas. A clawfoot tub is also featured in the Josephine Paine Room. Linger over a three-course gourmet breakfast feast each morning on the sun porch. Stroll the herb, butterfly and flower gardens; stop at the patios with a gazebo and a swing. Take a walking tour of the many restored homes in the neighborhood.

Historic Interest: First house built at top of Broadway hill. Built out of old growth lumber by one of the first pharmacy owners in Aberdeen. House built by Dr. W.B. Paine to house all of his servants. They were known as the formal family of Aberdeen. Turn-of-the-century architecture.

Innkeeper(s): Cindy Lonn. $69-119. 4 rooms with PB, 1 suite and 1 conference room. Breakfast, afternoon tea and snacks/refreshments included in rates. Types of meals: Full gourmet bkfst, veg bkfst, early coffee/tea and room service. Beds: QT. Cable TV, VCR, reading lamp, clock radio, desk, water views, sitting areas, snack table and chairs in room. Fax, copier, library, parlor games, telephone, fireplace, gift shop, full kitchen, video library and historical books on premises. Limited handicap access. Weddings, small meetings, family reunions and seminars hosted. Antiquing, art galleries, beach, bicycling, canoeing/kayaking, fishing, golf, hiking, horseback riding, live theater, museums, parks, shopping, tennis, water sports, birding and historic home tour nearby.

Publicity: *Daily World (Best Location and View)* and *Grays Harbor Chamber of Commerce (Business of the Month).*

"Thank you for the warm hospitality, comfortable and spacious accommodations and lovely breakfast. We felt totally spoiled."

Aberdeen Mansion B & B

807 N M St
Aberdeen, WA 98520-3324
(360)533-7079 (888)533-7079 Fax:(360)537-0378
E-mail: Al-joan@aberdeenmansionbb.com
Web: www.aberdeenmansionbb.com

Circa 1905. Exquisite best describes this Queen Anne Victorian mansion that was built for a lumber baron. Recently refurbished and in pristine condition, the inn boasts a graceful decor and delightful indulgences. The impressive entry hall showcases a magnificent staircase. Large, quiet guest bedrooms and a suite offer romantic flourishes and pampering amenities that include fluffy robes, soothing lotions and wine glasses with which to toast each other. The spacious carriage house is great for families. A wonderful two-course breakfast is served in the formal dining room with settings of gold, crystal and china. Relax on the wraparound porch, or stroll among the acre of flowering trees and gardens. Enjoy an evening beverage and dessert while reflecting on the day's adventures.

Historic Interest: Lumber baron's home, built in 1905. It still has the original woodwork that was all hand-crafted.

Innkeeper(s): Al & Joan Waters. $100-150. 4 rooms with PB, 1 suite and 2 conference rooms. Breakfast and snacks/refreshments included in rates. Types of meals: Full gourmet bkfst, veg bkfst, early coffee/tea and room service. Beds: KT. Modem hook-up, data port, cable TV, VCR, reading lamp, refrigerator, clock radio, telephone, coffeemaker and desk in room. Fax, copier, library, parlor games and fireplace on premises. Weddings, small meetings, family reunions and seminars hosted. Antiquing, beach, bicycling, canoeing/kayaking, fishing, golf, hiking, horseback riding, live theater, museums, parks and water sports nearby.

Publicity: *Grit/San Francisco Travel section, Sunset, Northwest Best Places, Kasin Brown's Travel Book and Business of the month for Grays Harbor County.*

Ashford   E4

National Park Inn

Mt Rainier Guest Services
Ashford, WA 98304
(360)569-2275 Fax:(360)569-2770
Web: www.guestservices.com/rainier

Circa 1920. Mt. Rainier National Park boasts a spectacular scenery of mountains and seemingly endless forests. For more than half a century, visitors from around the world have chosen National Park Inn for their park lodging. Old hickory and twig furnishings decorate the rustic, comfortable guest rooms. Breakfast, lunch and dinner service are available at the inn's dining room. From late October to May 1, rates include breakfast. Breakfast is not included during the high season, from May through October..

Innkeeper(s): David Wilde. $92-180. 25 rooms, 18 with PB. Breakfast included in rates. Types of meals: Full bkfst, lunch, afternoon tea and dinner. Restaurant on premises. Beds: QDT. Reading lamp, clock radio, desk and coffee in room. Parlor games and fireplace on premises. Limited handicap access. Small meetings hosted. Cross-country skiing, hiking and mountain climbing nearby.

Bainbridge Island   C4

Buchanan Inn

8494 NE Oddfellows Rd
Bainbridge Island, WA 98110
(206)780-9258 (800)598-3926 Fax:(206)842-9458

Circa 1912. A short ferry ride will take you from Seattle's harbor to quaint Bainbridge Island and this New England-style barn house. The acre-and-a-half of grounds are dotted with gardens. Each of the guest rooms includes beds topped with luxu-

rious Egyptian cotton linens, and two rooms include a fireplace. Guests are pampered with a glass of wine in the evenings and a full breakfast each morning. The breakfasts are served on fine china and include gourmet coffee, fresh fruit, homemade baked goods and entrees such as Northwest Eggs Benedict or a ham and brie strata. Bainbridge Island offers many restaurants, shops and galleries. Guests can explore the island or head into Seattle. After a day in the city, return to the serenity of the island and inn, relaxing perhaps in the inn's hot tub, which is located in a little cedar cottage.

Innkeeper(s): Ron & Judy Gibbs. $119-169. 4 rooms with PB, 2 with FP and 2 suites. Breakfast and snacks/refreshments included in rates. Types of meals: Full gourmet bkfst. Beds: KQ. Reading lamp, CD player, refrigerator, ceiling fan, clock radio, coffeemaker, desk, hair dryers and robes in room. TV, fax, spa, library, telephone and fireplace on premises. Weddings, small meetings and family reunions hosted. Antiquing, art galleries, beach, bicycling, canoeing/kayaking, cross-country skiing, fishing, golf, hiking, live theater, museums, parks, shopping, tennis, water sports and wineries nearby.

"Would you adopt me so I can stay here."

Bellingham   A4

Schnauzer Crossing

4421 Lakeway Dr
Bellingham, WA 98229
(360)734-2808 (800)562-2808
E-mail: schnauzerx@aol.com
Web: www.schnauzercrossing.com

Circa 1938. This contemporary Northwest house, nestled among tall evergreens and overlooking Lake Whatcom, is an outdoor lover's delight, with fishing, boating and swimming nearby. Maple, dogwood and birch trees abound, and fresh raspberries and blueberries can be picked from the garden. Guests enjoy lake or garden views from their comfortable rooms and the cottage. All rooms feature fresh flowers. The inn offers extensive gardens including a new tea house, a wisteria covered pergola and a koi pond.

Innkeeper(s): Vermont & Donna McAllister. $140-225. 3 rooms with PB, 1 suite and 1 cottage. Types of meals: Full bkfst. Beds: KQ. Spa and telephone on premises.

Publicity: *Seattle Post-Intelligencer and Oregonian.*

"A lovely retreat. We'll be sure to return."

Chelan   C6

A Quail's Roost Inn

121 E Highland Ave, PO Box 2089
Chelan, WA 98816
(509)682-2892 (800)681-2892
E-mail: m_henderson20@msn.com
Web: www.aquailsroostinn.com

Circa 1902. Formerly named Highland Guest House, this turn-of-the-century Victorian is decorated in period style with antiques. Each of the guest rooms has its own theme. For instance, one room offers a romantic canopy bed topped with a quilt. The Rose & Wicker Room includes a private porch that affords a beautiful view of Lake Chelan. The inn's parlor and dining room feature handstenciled ceilings, which duplicate original turn-of-the-century painting done by the home's original owner. A number of collectibles, including a spinning wheel, deco-

rate the common areas. Strawberries and cream French toast is a typical breakfast specialty. The innkeepers offer a variety of seasonal packages and can put together picnic and gift baskets. A Quail's Roost Inn is the site of a juried Victorian arts and crafts show, which takes place during the Christmas season.
Historic Interest: Listed in the National Register.
Innkeeper(s): Marilee Stolzenburg. $75-145. 3 rooms with PB. Breakfast included in rates. Types of meals: Full gourmet bkfst, picnic lunch and room service. Beds: QD. Reading lamp, ceiling fan, clock radio and desk in room. Air conditioning. Library, parlor games and telephone on premises. Small meetings, family reunions and seminars hosted. Amusement parks, antiquing, cross-country skiing, fishing, live theater, parks, shopping and water sports nearby.
Publicity: *Los Angeles Times.*

"Always liked Chelan...now we love it! We'll be back!"

Concrete   B5

Ovenell's Heritage Inn B&B

46276 Concrete Sauk Valley Rd
Concrete, WA 98237-9217
(360)853-8494 Fax:(360)853-8279

Circa 1910. Boasting views of the Cascade Mountains, this historic farmhouse is part of a working cattle ranch that was established in the late 19th century and spans more than 500 acres. The inn is decorated in period-style decor with antique-filled guest bedrooms. Guests in the main house will enjoy a full-country breakfast. Guesthouse accommodations boast spectacular views of Mt. Baker. New, pine-log cabins feature country furnishings and a mini-lodge for gatherings and catering services. There is much to enjoy in this breathtaking region, from river rafting to eagle watching.
Innkeeper(s): Eleanor, Norm, Cindy & Kris Ovenell. $85-120. 12 rooms, 9 with FP, 7 with FP and 4 cabins. Breakfast and snacks/refreshments included in rates. Types of meals: Country bkfst and early coffee/tea. Beds: QDT. Cable TV, VCR, reading lamp, refrigerator, ceiling fan, clock radio, telephone, coffeemaker and fireplace in room. Central air. Fax, copier, library, parlor games, fireplace and laundry facility on premises. Weddings, small meetings, family reunions and seminars hosted. Antiquing, bicycling, canoeing/kayaking, cross-country skiing, fishing, hiking, horseback riding, museums, parks, shopping, eagle watching and river rafting nearby.
Publicity: *Sunset Magazine, Country Magazine, People's Choice Skagit County Business Pulse Winner: Best B&B 2001 and Concrete Chamber of Commerce Small Business of the Year 2001.*

Coupeville   B4

Captain Whidbey Inn

2072 W Captain Whidbey Inn Rd
Coupeville, WA 98239
(360)678-4097 (800)366-4097 Fax:(360)678-4110
E-mail: captain@whidbey.net
Web: www.captainwhidbey.com

Circa 1907. Overlooking Whidbey Island's Penn Cove, this log inn has comfortable rooms featuring down comforters, feather beds and views of lagoons and gardens. The Cove Restaurant has a magnificent view and guests can enjoy their meals by the fireplace. Chef/owner James Roberts utilizes local products such as salmon and Penn Cove mussels. The proprietor is also a sailing captain, and guests can book an afternoon on his 52-foot ketch, Cutty Sark. The proprietor's family has run the inn for more than 30 years.

Innkeeper(s): Mendy Mclean-Stone. $95-300. 32 rooms, 20 with PB, 7 with FP and 1 conference room. Types of meals: Full bkfst, lunch, picnic lunch, snacks/refreshments and gourmet dinner. Restaurant on premises. Beds: KQD. Reading lamp, refrigerator, telephone and desk in room. Fax, copier, fireplace, sailing and fishing on premises. Small meetings and family reunions hosted. Antiquing, shopping and museums nearby.
Publicity: *Gourmet Magazine and USA-Weekend.*

"I visit and stay here once a year and love it."

Colonel Crockett Farm

1012 S Fort Casey Rd
Coupeville, WA 98239-9753
(360)678-3711 Fax:(360)678-3707
E-mail: email@crockettfarm.com
Web: www.crockettfarm.com

Circa 1855. Snowcapped mountains, scenic shoreline vistas and coastal cliffs are some of the visual pleasures experienced at this comfortable 1855 Victorian Farmhouse listed in the National Register. Overlooking Admiralty Inlet on Puget Sound and the Olympic Mountains, this inn graces the north shore of Crockett Lake in the heart of the Ebey's Landing National Historic Reserve on Whidbey Island. It is surrounded by nearly two acres of landscaped lawns, flower beds and orchards. Relax by the slate fireplace in the oak-paneled library or in the solarium.  Tastefully decorated guest bedrooms are named after original, local pioneer families. Sleep in a custom-made four-poster canopy, antique tiger maple, American oak or white wicker bed. Spectacular garden weddings and receptions in the two-story barn auditorium are popular.
Innkeeper(s): Bob & Beulah Whitlow. $85-115. 5 rooms with PB and 1 conference room. Breakfast included in rates. Types of meals: Country bkfst, veg bkfst, early coffee/tea and snacks/refreshments. Beds: KQT. TV, reading lamp, telephone and coffeemaker in room. Fax, copier, swimming, library, pet boarding, parlor games and fireplace on premises. Limited handicap access. Weddings, small meetings, family reunions and seminars hosted. Amusement parks, antiquing, art galleries, beach, bicycling, canoeing/kayaking, fishing, golf, hiking, horseback riding, live theater, museums, parks, shopping, tennis, water sports and wineries nearby.
Publicity: *Peninsula, Portland Oregonian, Country Inns and Glamour.*

"Everyone felt quite at home...such a beautiful spot."

Inn at Penn Cove

702 N Main
Coupeville, WA 98239
(360)678-8000 (800)688-2683

Circa 1887. Two restored historic houses, one a fanciful white and peach Italianate confection in the National Register, comprise the inn. Each house contains only three guest rooms affording a variety of small parlors for guests to enjoy. The most romantic accommodation is Desiree's Room with a fireplace, a whirlpool tub for two and mesmerizing views of Puget Sound and Mt. Baker.
Innkeeper(s): Gladys & Mitchell Howard. $60-125. 6 rooms, 4 with PB, 3 with FP. Breakfast and afternoon tea included in rates. Types of meals: Full gourmet bkfst and veg bkfst. Beds: KQ. Cable TV, reading lamp, ceiling fan, clock radio and hot tub/spa in room. TV, VCR, library, parlor games, telephone, fireplace, pump organ and music box on premises. Small meetings and family reunions hosted. Antiquing, beach, bicycling, fishing, golf, hiking, horseback riding, live theater, museums, parks, shopping and wineries nearby.
Publicity: *Whidbey News-Times, Country Inns and Glamour.*

"Our hosts were warm and friendly, but also gave us plenty of space and privacy - a good combination."

Eastsound   B3

Turtleback Farm Inn

1981 Crow Valley Rd
Eastsound, WA 98245
(360)376-4914 (800)376-4914

Circa 1895. Guests will delight in the beautiful views afforded from this farmhouse and the newly constructed Orchard House, which overlooks 80 acres of forest and farmland, duck ponds and Mt. Constitution to the east. Rooms feature antique furnishings and many boast views of the farm, orchard or sheep

pasture. Beds are covered with wool comforters made from sheep raised on the property. Bon Appetit highlighted some of the breakfast recipes

served at Turtleback; a breakfast here is a memorable affair. Tables set with bone china, silver and fresh linens make way for a delightful mix of fruits, juice, award-winning granola, homemade breads and specialty entrees. Evening guests can settle down with a game or a book in the fire-lit parlor as they enjoy sherry, tea or hot chocolate.

Historic Interest: Orcas Island, once the apple capital of Washington, features many historic sites. The Orcas Island Historical Museum and Crow Valley School Museum are among several options.
Innkeeper(s): William & Susan C. Fletcher. $80-225. 11 rooms with PB, 4 with FP. Breakfast included in rates. Types of meals: Full bkfst, early coffee/tea and picnic lunch. Beds: KQD. Reading lamp and clock radio in room. Library, parlor games, telephone, fireplace, refrigerator and self-serve beverage bar in dining room on premises. Limited handicap access. Weddings and family reunions hosted. Fishing, live theater, parks, shopping and water sports nearby.
Publicity: *Los Angeles Times, USA Today, Travel & Leisure, Contra Costa Sun, Seattle Times, Northwest Living, Sunset, Food & Wine, Gourmet, Northwest Travel, New York Times and Alaska Air.*

"A peaceful haven for soothing the soul."

Enumclaw   D4

White Rose Inn

1610 Griffin Ave
Enumclaw, WA 98022-2824
(360)825-7194 (800)404-7194 Fax:(360)802-2472
E-mail: info@whiteroseinnbb.com
Web: www.whiteroseinnbb.com

Circa 1920. Axel Hanson, owned the White River Lumber Company, built this 22-room, 8,500-square-foot Colonial mansion with Honduran mahogany and quarter-sawn oak. A large canopied four-poster cherry bed, crystal chandelier, and original

fresco ceilings appropriately adorn the Paradise Room. There is a rose garden, sunroom and formal dining room. Guests enjoy walking to town for dinner and shopping.

Innkeeper(s): Michael & Tami Dunn.
$89-99. Breakfast included in rates. Reading lamp in room. Telephone and fireplace on premises. Weddings, small meetings, family reunions and seminars hosted. Antiquing, cross-country skiing, downhill skiing, shopping, hiking and biking nearby.

Everett   C4

Gaylord House

3301 Grand Ave
Everett, WA 98201
(425)339-9153 (888)507-7177 Fax:(425)303-9713

Circa 1908. A shaded front porch surrounded by lush greenery is an inviting way to enjoy the serenity of this two-story Craftsman home, recently added to the city's historic overlay register. Find a secluded spot amid the 4,000-square-foot house, or listen to Gaylord play the clarinet in the parlor. Guest bedrooms offer different decor that match a variety of tastes, from nautical to floral, Mediterranean or old-fashioned English royalty. Select a teacup from the collection gathered by three generations, then enjoy a gourmet breakfast that may include cheese blintzes, baked apple, pork-apple sausage and fresh raspberries. This historic region is known as the gateway to all the wonders of the Pacific Northwest, between the Cascade Mountains and Puget Sound.

Innkeeper(s): Gaylord, ShirleyAnne, Theresa Schaudies. $68-135. 4 rooms with PB, 1 with FP. Breakfast included in rates. Types of meals: Full gourmet bkfst, veg bkfst, early coffee/tea, gourmet lunch, afternoon tea and gourmet dinner. Beds: Q. Modem hook-up, cable TV, VCR, reading lamp, clock radio, telephone, desk, hot tub/spa and Jacuzzi in room. Central air. Fax, copier, library, parlor games and fireplace on premises. Weddings, small meetings, family reunions and seminars hosted. Antiquing, art galleries, cross-country skiing, downhill skiing, fishing, golf, hiking, live theater, parks, tennis and wineries nearby.

Friday Harbor   B3

Panacea Bed & Breakfast

595 Park St
Friday Harbor, WA 98250
(360)378-3757 (800)639-2762 Fax:(360)378-8543
E-mail: stay@panacea-inn.com
Web: www.panacea-inn.com

Circa 1907. As the name promises, a getaway to this San Juan Island retreat should lift the spirits, relieve the stress of everyday life and inspire romance. Industrialist Peter Kirk, who later founded the town of Kirkland, built this early 20th-century Craftsman as a vacation home. The Concord family purchased and meticulously restored the home, maintaining the original woodwork and stained glass. Each of the four guest rooms has a private entrance. Two romantic rooms include a Jacuzzi tub and fireplace. Arts and Crafts furnishings and decor are a perfect complement to the Craftsman architecture. In the afternoons, refreshments are served on the veranda. After dinner, return to the bed & breakfast and you'll find chocolates and cordials set up on the sideboard. Breakfasts include the height of gourmet cuisine. One menu includes caviar, a summer fruit medley with pecan toffee and an entree such as eggs Florentine.

Innkeeper(s): Laura & Eric Concord. $100-180. 5 rooms with PB, 1 with FP and 2 suites. Breakfast, afternoon tea and snacks/refreshments included in rates. Types of meals: Full gourmet bkfst, early coffee/tea, picnic lunch and room service. Beds: KQ. Cable TV, reading lamp, ceiling fan, clock radio and turn-down service in room. Fax, parlor games, telephone and fireplace on premises. Small meetings hosted. Antiquing, fishing, golf, live theater, parks, shopping, tennis and water sports nearby.

San Juan Inn B&B

50 Spring St, Box 776
Friday Harbor, WA 98250-0776
(360)378-2070 (800)742-8210 Fax:(360)378-2027
E-mail: sanjuaninn@rockisland.com
Web: www.san-juan.net/sjinn

Circa 1873. In the National Register, this old European-style hotel is filled with stained glass, old photographs and flowers picked from the inn's garden. A Victorian settee is situated under a cherry tree within sniffing distance of the lilacs and roses. It's a half-block to the ferry landing.

Innkeeper(s): Steve Judson. $65-225. 10 rooms, 4 with PB and 2 suites. Breakfast included in rates. Types of meals: Cont plus. Beds: KQDT. Cable TV, VCR, reading lamp, refrigerator, ceiling fan, clock radio and hot tub/spa in room. Fax, spa and fireplace on premises. Small meetings and family reunions hosted. Fishing, live theater, parks, shopping and water sports nearby.

States Inn

2687 West Valley Rd
Friday Harbor, WA 98250-8164
(360)378-6240 (866)602-2737 Fax:(360)378-6241
E-mail: info@statesinn.com
Web: www.statesinn.com

Circa 1910. This sprawling ranch home has ten guest rooms, each named and themed for a particular state. The Arizona and New Mexico rooms, often booked by families or couples travel-

ing together, can be combined to create a private suite with two bedrooms, a bathroom and a sitting area. The oldest part of the house was built as a country school and later used as a dance hall, before it was relocated to its current 60-acre spread. Baked French toast, accompanied by fresh fruit topped with yogurt sauce and homemade muffins are typical breakfast fare.

Innkeeper(s): Cole & Amy Hull. $68-195. 10 rooms, 8 with PB, 1 with FP and 1 suite. Breakfast included in rates. Types of meals: Full gourmet bkfst, veg bkfst, early coffee/tea and snacks/refreshments. Beds: KQDT. Reading lamp and clock radio in room. Fax, stable, library, parlor games, telephone, fireplace and working ranch on premises. Limited handicap access. Weddings, small meetings, family reunions and seminars hosted. Antiquing, art galleries, beach, bicycling, canoeing/kayaking, fishing, golf, hiking, horseback riding, live theater, museums, parks, shopping, tennis, water sports, wineries, kayaks and whale watching nearby.
Publicity: *Glamour, Conde Naste and USA Today.*

Tucker House Bed & Breakfast

260 B Street
Friday Harbor, WA 98250
(360)378-2783 (800)965-0123 Fax:(360)378-6437
E-mail: reservations@rockisland.com
Web: www.tuckerhouse.com

Circa 1898. Only one block from the ferry landing, the white picket fence bordering Tucker House is a welcome sight for guests. The spindled entrance leads to the parlor. The home includes three guest rooms that share a bath. The rooms are decorated with antiques. The innkeepers also offer self-contained cottages that include private baths, kitchenettes, queen beds, TVs and VCRs. All guests enjoy use of the outdoor hot tub. The inn's breakfasts are served in the solarium.

Innkeeper(s): Alan Paschal . $125-300. 10 rooms with PB, 4 with FP, 2 suites, 2 cottages and 1 conference room. Breakfast and snacks/refreshments included in rates. Types of meals: Full gourmet bkfst, veg bkfst, early

coffee/tea, gourmet lunch, picnic lunch and room service. Beds: KQDT. Cable TV, VCR, reading lamp, refrigerator, ceiling fan, clock radio, coffeemaker, hot tub/spa, fireplace, private balcony, private entrance, microwave, convection oven and range in room. Spa, parlor games, telephone, fireplace, videos, sun room and sun deck on premises. Small meetings, family reunions and seminars hosted. Antiquing, art galleries, beach, bicycling, canoeing/kayaking, fishing, golf, hiking, horseback riding, live theater, museums, parks, shopping, water sports, wineries and dining nearby.
Publicity: *Travel Holiday magazine.*

"A lovely place, the perfect getaway. We'll be back."

Greenbank   C4

Guest House Log Cottages

24371-SR 525, Whidbey Island
Greenbank, WA 98253
(360)678-3115
E-mail: guesthse@whidbey.net
Web: www.guesthouselogcottages.com

Circa 1925. These storybook cottages and log home are nestled within a peaceful forest on 25 acres. The log cabin features stained-glass and criss-cross paned windows that give it the feel of a gingerbread house. Four of

the cottages are log construction. Ask for the Lodge and enjoy a private setting with a pond just beyond the deck. Inside are two Jacuzzi tubs, a stone fireplace, king bed, antiques and a luxurious atmosphere.

Innkeeper(s): Don & Mary Jane Creger. $165-325. 6 cottages. Breakfast included in rates. Types of meals: Full bkfst. Beds: KQ. TV, VCR, reading lamp, stereo, refrigerator, ceiling fan, clock radio, telephone, desk, hot tub/spa, kitchen and Jacuzzi in room. Air conditioning. Fax, copier, spa and swimming pool on premises. Antiquing, fishing, golf, parks, shopping and tennis nearby.
Publicity: *Los Angeles Times, Woman's Day, Sunset, Country Inns and Bride's.*

"The wonderful thing is to be by yourselves and rediscover what's important."

Kirkland   C4

Shumway Mansion

11410 99th Pl NE
Kirkland, WA 98033
(425)823-2303 Fax:(425)822-0421
E-mail: info@shumwaymansion.com
Web: www.shumwaymansion.com

Circa 1909. This resplendent 24-room, 10,000-square-foot mansion is situated on more than two acres overlooking Juanita Bay. With a large ballroom and veranda, few could guess that a short time ago, the building was hoisted

on hydraulic lifts. It was then pulled three miles across town to its present site, near the beach.

Innkeeper(s): Richard & Salli Harris, Julie Blakemore. $85-120. 7 rooms, 8 with PB and 1 suite. Breakfast included in rates. Types of meals: Full bkfst. Beds: Q. Data port, TV, reading lamp, clock radio, telephone, desk and fans in room. Fireplace on premises. Weddings, small meetings, family reunions and seminars hosted. Antiquing, fishing, live theater, shopping, sporting events and water sports nearby.
Publicity: *Northgate Journal, Journal American and Northwest Living.*

"Guests enjoy the mansion so much they don't want to leave." — *Northwest Living*

Langley   C4

Country Cottage of Langley

215 6th St
Langley, WA 98260-9623
(360)221-8709 (800)713-3860
E-mail: stay@acountrycottage.com
Web: www.acountrycottage.com

Circa 1926. Outstanding views of the Cascades, Saratoga
Passage and the village of Langley by the Sea can be seen from
the two acres that surround these cottages. All five cottages are
distinctly decorated reflecting a variety of themes with original
oil paintings, elegant country antiques, sitting areas with comfortable lounge chairs and dining with a view of the water.
Several cottages feature two-person Jacuzzis, terry robes and
private patios. One of the accommodations was an old creamery, now converted to comfortable luxury. After breakfast, relax
on the extensive garden deck and in the gazebo overlooking
Puget Sound.

Historic Interest: Our inn is the oldest B&B on Whidbey Island.
Innkeeper(s): Jacqueline Stewart. $129-179. 5 cottages, 3 with FP and 1
conference room. Types of meals: Full gourmet bkfst, veg bkfst and
snacks/refreshments. Beds: KQ. Cable TV, VCR, reading lamp, stereo, refrigerator, ceiling fan, coffeemaker, hot tub/spa and 3 Jacuzzis in room. Spa, bicycles, parlor games and fireplace on premises. Weddings, small meetings,
family reunions and seminars hosted. Amusement parks, antiquing, art galleries, beach, bicycling, canoeing/kayaking, fishing, golf, hiking, live theater,
museums, parks, shopping, water sports, wineries, County Fair, street, music
and art festivals, Christmas tours and mystery weekends nearby.

"Hospitality plus! Nicely decorated rooms. Beautiful breakfasts."

Leavenworth   C6

Mrs. Andersons Lodging House

917 Commercial St
Leavenworth, WA 98826-1413
(509)548-6173 (800)253-8990 Fax:(509)548-9113
E-mail: info@quiltersheaven.com
Web: www.quiltersheaven.com

Circa 1895. This historic home is named for the widow that
purchased the place just a few years after its 1895 construction. In order to support herself and two daughters, Mrs.
Anderson transformed the place into a boarding house. Today,
it still provides a cozy, relaxing haven for guests. Rooms feature
whimsical names, such as the Double Wedding Ring,
Grandmother's Flower Garden, Moon Over the Mountain and
Leavenworth Nine Patch. As one might deduct, quilters are
welcome here. In fact, quilting getaways are available and the
home includes a shop filled with quilting supplies, quilting
books, fabrics, stencils and other like items. Non-quilters can
relax on the sun deck and enjoy the view. Leavenworth is
known for its German heritage, and you'll find plenty of shops
and boutiques, as well as many outdoor activities.

Innkeeper(s): Dee & Al Howie. $46-80. 10 rooms, 8 with PB and 1 confer-
ence room. Breakfast and afternoon tea included in rates. Types of meals:
Cont plus and early coffee/tea. Beds: Q. Cable TV in room. Central air.
Library and parlor games on premises. Cross-country skiing, downhill skiing,
fishing, golf, hiking, horseback riding, live theater, museums, parks and
shopping nearby.

Long Beach   E2

Boreas Bed & Breakfast Inn

607 Ocean Beach Blvd, PO Box 1344
Long Beach, WA 98631-1344
(360)642-8069 (888)642-8069 Fax:(360)642-5353
E-mail: boreas@boreasinn.com
Web: www.boreasinn.com

Circa 1920. This oceanfront inn started as a beach house and
was remodeled eclectically with decks and two fireplaces. There
are two living rooms that offer views of the dunes. All of the
five guest rooms feature ocean, garden or mountain views.
Guests can enjoy private time in the hot tub in the enclosed
gazebo, take the private path that winds through the dunes to
the surf or walk to the boardwalk, restaurants and shopping.
There is also a three-bedroom cottage available. Breakfast and
spa is not available at the cottage.

Innkeeper(s): Susie Goldsmith & Bill Verner. $145-155. 5 suites and 1 cot-
tage. Types of meals: Full bkfst. Beds: KQT. Reading lamp, clock radio, desk
and one with jetted tub in room. VCR, fax, spa, library, parlor games, telephone and fireplace on premises. Weddings, small meetings and family
reunions hosted. Antiquing, fishing, golf, hiking, horseback riding, parks,
shopping, tennis, water sports, birding, lighthouses and Lewis & Clark historical sites nearby.

Publicity: *Arrington's 2003 & 2004 Most Romantic Hideaway Top 15 in the
nation, Business of the Year 2002, Customer Service Award honored by the
Better Business Bureau and Enterprise Rent-A-Car for Oregon and SW
Washington, Best Places to Kiss in the NW - three Kiss Rating, NW Best
Places and Sunset.*

Lopez Island   B3

MacKaye Harbor Inn

949 MacKaye Harbor Rd
Lopez Island, WA 98261
(360)468-2253 (888)314-6140 Fax:(360)468-2393
E-mail: mckaye@rockisland.com
Web: www.mackayeharborinn.com

Circa 1927. Launching a kayak from the inn's sandy beach is a
favorite activity here, as well as watching otters, seals and eagles
from the waterfront parlor. Four of the guest rooms boast views
of the bay, and there are eight acres to explore, including a
quarter mile of beach. The home was the first house on the
island to have electric lights, as well as its first inn. In the
evenings, guests are treated to chocolate truffles and an aperitif
to enhance the sunset views. The innkeepers also take care of
two luxurious carriage houses next door, popular for families
with children and for couples seeking more seclusion.
Complimentary mountain bikes are offered for cycling around
the island.

Innkeeper(s): Robin & Mike. $89-175. 5 rooms, 3 with PB, 1 with FP, 1
suite and 1 conference room. Breakfast included in rates. Types of meals:
Cont plus, early coffee/tea, picnic lunch and afternoon tea. Beds: KQDT.
Reading lamp, clock radio, turn-down service and desk in room. Fax, copier,
telephone, fireplace and BBQs on premises. Weddings, small meetings, family reunions and seminars hosted. Antiquing, bicycling, canoeing/kayaking,
fishing, golf, parks and tennis nearby.

Publicity: *Los Angeles Times, Sunset, Northwest and Coastal Living.*

Maple Valley   **D4**

Olson Mansion

21401 244th Ave SE
Maple Valley, WA 98038
(425)433-0711 (877)433-0711 Fax:(425)433-0701
E-mail: olsonmansion@aol.com
Web: www.olsonmansion.com

Circa 1907. Spanning 62 acres of scenic countryside, this Craftsman home with detailed woodwork was built by a Norwegian immigrant and is a rare example of concrete construction in a residence. Once a dairy farm with a large barrel vaulted barn, the 10,000 square foot mansion is now a European-style bed & breakfast that is surrounded by a nine-hole links golf course. Sit on the porch overlooking flowers, trees and orchards. Well-appointed guest bedrooms offer privacy and quiet without in-room phones or televisions. Enjoy gorgeous views of the mountains, a waterfall, tees and driving range. The spacious bathrooms feature heated floors. After breakfast, play one of the two rounds of golf that are included with a power cart. Miniature golf, catch and release fly-fishing and batting cages are also available activities.

Historic Interest: Rare example of concrete construction in a residential home. Also large barrel vaulted barn.
Innkeeper(s): Jerry and Collen Solomon. $99-165. 4 rooms. Types of meals: Full bkfst, early coffee/tea, lunch, afternoon tea and snacks/refreshments. Restaurant on premises. Beds: KQD. Reading lamp and clock radio in room. TV, fax, copier, library, parlor games, telephone and 9-hole links-style golf course on premises. Antiquing, downhill skiing, golf, parks, water sports and wineries nearby.

Ocean Park   **E2**

Charles Nelson Guest House

26205 Sandridge Road
Ocean Park, WA 98640
(360)665-3016 (888)862-9756 Fax:(360)665-5962
E-mail: cnbandb@charlesnelsonbandb.com
Web: www.charlesnelsonbandb.com

Circa 1928. Originally purchased from a Sears & Roebuck catalog, this Dutch Colonial home that overlooks Willapa Bay and Long Island's wildlife refuge has been impressively restored. Relax by firelight in the living room on the lambskin rug, or enjoy the view from the sunroom. Guest bedrooms are furnished with a blend of antiques and period furnishings. Homemade muffins, scones or sweet rolls with honey butter and jam accompany sausage and a double-cheese-and-bacon quiche for a typical breakfast in the dining room. Bird watch from the back deck, or gaze at the goldfish and koi in the pond. A nap on a nearby hammock is an inviting respite.

Innkeeper(s): Curt and Ginger Bish. $120-140. 3 rooms with PB. Breakfast and snacks/refreshments included in rates. Types of meals: Full gourmet bkfst, veg bkfst and early coffee/tea. Beds: KQT. Reading lamp, CD player, clock radio and turn-down service in room. TV, VCR, fax, copier, library, parlor games, telephone, fireplace and laundry facility on premises. Family reunions hosted. Antiquing, art galleries, beach, bicycling, canoeing/kayaking, fishing, golf, hiking, horseback riding, museums, parks and shopping nearby.
Publicity: *Seattle Home and Lifestyles.*

Olga   **B3**

Buck Bay Farm

716 Pt Lawrence Rd
Olga, WA 98279
(360)376-2908 (888)422-2825
E-mail: Buckbayfarm@centurytel.net
Web: www.buckbayfarm.com

Circa 1920. This farmhouse is secluded on five acres and is decorated in country style. Down pillows and comforters are a few homey touches. Homemade breakfasts include items like freshly baked muffins, scones and biscuits still steaming from the oven.

Innkeeper(s): Sheri Marzolf. $99-135. 5 rooms, 4 with PB and 1 suite. Breakfast included in rates. Types of meals: Full bkfst and early coffee/tea. Beds: Q. Reading lamp and clock radio in room. Spa, parlor games and telephone on premises. Limited handicap access. Weddings, small meetings, family reunions and seminars hosted. Antiquing, canoeing/kayaking, fishing, hiking, live theater, parks, shopping and whale watching nearby.
Publicity: *Island's Sounder.*

Olympia   **D3**

Swantown Inn B&B

1431 11th Ave SE
Olympia, WA 98501
(360)753-9123 Fax:(360)943-8047
E-mail: swantown@olywa.net
Web: www.swantowninn.us

Circa 1893. Explore the Puget Sound area from this historical Queen Anne/Eastlake Victorian mansion situated in a peaceful neighborhood. Listed in the state and city registers, this local landmark features distinctive woodwork inside and out. Common rooms offer pleasurable pursuits that include gameboards, piano or television by a warm fire. A writing desk, fax and phone line provides a workspace for computer use. Relax in elegantly appointed guest bedrooms. The spacious Astoria Room boasts a four-poster bed, sitting area with Capitol view and a two-person Jacuzzi tub. Ask about an accompanying Relaxation Package. A continental breakfast can be brought to the door, or linger over a splendid multi-course meal in the grand dining room. Organic vegetable and flower gardens span a half acre with an orchard and gazebo.

Historic Interest: Distinctive woodwork inside and out has made Swantown Inn a local landmark for over 100 years.
Innkeeper(s): Lillian & Ed Peeples. $75-120. 4 rooms with PB. Breakfast included in rates. Types of meals: Full gourmet bkfst, veg bkfst and early coffee/tea. Beds: KQT. Reading lamp, clock radio, desk and hot tub/spa in room. TV, VCR, fax, copier, parlor games, telephone, fireplace, sumptuous gourmet breakfast, organic gardens and orchard, gazebo and piano on premises. Weddings, small meetings, family reunions and seminars hosted. Antiquing, art galleries, beach, bicycling, canoeing/kayaking, golf, hiking, live theater, museums, parks, shopping, tennis, Washington State Capitol Campus, Olympia Farmer's Market and Wolf Haven International nearby.
Publicity: *The Olympian.*

Orcas   **B3**

Orcas Hotel

PO Box 155
Orcas, WA 98280-0155
(360)376-4300 (888)672-2792 Fax:(360)376-4399

Circa 1901. Listed in the National Register, this three-story Victorian inn across from the ferry landing has been a landmark to travelers and boaters since the early 1900s. The inn offers scenic views of terraced lawns and English gardens, as well as vistas of the water and harbor, making it an ideal site for business meetings, retreats, wedding receptions and family reunions. Breakfast, lunch and dinner are available in the hotel's bakery, cafe and restaurant.

Innkeeper(s): Laura & Doug Tidwell. $75-189. 12 rooms, 5 with PB. Types of meals: Full gourmet bkfst, veg bkfst, early coffee/tea, lunch, picnic lunch, snacks/refreshments and gourmet dinner. Restaurant on premises. Beds: QT. Two rooms with hot tub/spa in room. Fax, copier, parlor games and fireplace on premises. Weddings, small meetings and seminars hosted.
Publicity: *Los Angeles Times, Seattle Times, New York Times, Coastal Living, Northwest Best Places to Kiss and Pilots Getaway.*

Point Roberts   A3

Maple Meadow B&B

101 Goodman Rd
Point Roberts, WA 98281
(360)945-5536 Fax:(360)945-2855
E-mail: mplmedbb@whidbey.com
Web: www.travel-wise.com/maple/index.html

Circa 1910. Maple trees, including one that's more than 200 years old, give the name to this 1910 farmhouse. Pastures, a creek, trees and horses cast a peaceful country atmosphere.

Separate from the main farmhouse is the Old Pumphouse Room, decorated in a blend of Victorian and 1940s furnishings. The Rosewood Room features a king-size rosewood bed and a clawfoot tub. Two of the other rooms share a bath and shower. The morning begins with the smell of hot cinnamon buns, followed by crab omelets (cooked with fresh local crab), strawberries and pan-fried potatoes. In the evening, you can enjoy an outdoor Jacuzzi while looking at the stars. Only a block away is Boundary Bay where you can observe bird and sea life and, if the weather is fine, see all the way from Mount Baker to the San Juan Islands. Located near the Canadian border, ferries to Victoria are only 15 minutes away, and downtown Vancouver can be reached by car in 40 minutes.

Innkeeper(s): Terrie & Keith LaPorte. $75-140. 4 rooms, 2 with PB. Breakfast and snacks/refreshments included in rates. Types of meals: Full gourmet bkfst, veg bkfst and early coffee/tea. Beds: KQT. Reading lamp, ceiling fan, clock radio and turn-down service in room. TV, VCR, fax, spa, stable, bicycles, library, parlor games, telephone and fireplace on premises. Weddings and family reunions hosted. Antiquing, art galleries, beach, bicycling, canoeing/kayaking, fishing, golf, hiking, parks, shopping and water sports nearby.
Publicity: *Calgary Herald, San Francisco Chronicle, Vancouver Sun and Seattle Post Intelligencer.*

Port Angeles   C3

Domaine Madeleine B&B

146 Wildflower Ln
Port Angeles, WA 98362-8138
(360)457-4174 (888)811-8376 Fax:(360)457-3037
E-mail: romance@domainemadeleine.com
Web: www.domainemadeleine.com

Circa 1947. This unique inn blends French with Oriental decor and offers a romantic and very private setting on five acres with 168 feet of waterfront. The inviting landscape includes more than 100 rhododendrons and numerous wild and cultivated flowers. Huge Douglas firs, cedars, Japanese Maples and bamboo add to the garden's serenity and majesty.

Deer often stroll by, whales can sometimes be seen off shore, and eagles can be spotted soaring above. The innkeepers take pride in helping guests plan their day's events so they can enjoy the area fully. There are maps, books and videos on hand for visiting the Olympic Peninsula hiking trails, waterfalls and explorations along the coast. Choosing a restaurant for dinner is made easier by browsing the inn's menu collection. Victoria, B.C., is a short hour and a half away by ferry.

Innkeeper(s): Jeri, Victor, Ann, Noi & Ryan. $145-225. 5 rooms with PB, 5 with FP, 2 suites and 1 cottage. Breakfast included in rates. Types of meals: Full gourmet bkfst and afternoon tea. Beds: KQ. Cable TV, VCR, reading lamp, stereo, clock radio, telephone, desk, hot tub/spa and whirlpool in room. Air conditioning. Fax, copier, library, parlor games and fireplace on premises. Weddings and small meetings hosted. Antiquing, bicycling, cross-country skiing, downhill skiing, fishing, golf, hiking, live theater, parks, shopping, tennis and water sports nearby.
Publicity: *Northwest Travel.*

"Nowhere have I found lodgings that compared to Domaine Madeleine. I consider four criteria in determining where to stay when I travel: accommodations, food, uniqueness and hospitality. Domaine Madeleine excels in all these categories."

Five SeaSuns Bed & Breakfast

1006 S Lincoln St
Port Angeles, WA 98362-7826
(360)452-8248 (800)708-0777 Fax:(360)417-0465
E-mail: info@seasuns.com
Web: www.seasuns.com

Circa 1926. Take a respite from the rush of today at this restored, historic home that reflects the 1920s era of sophistication with a sense of romance and refinement. Guest bedrooms depict the seasons of the year and are furnished with period antiques. Pleasing amenities include whirlpool or soaking tubs, balconies and water or mountain views. Artfully presented gourmet breakfasts are served by candlelight with fine china and silver. Relax on the porch or wander the picturesque gardens that highlight the estate-like grounds. Explore nearby Olympic National Park and the Ediz Hook Coast Guard Station. The Underground History Walk is ten blocks. Visit the Makah Indian Museum 75 miles away.

Historic Interest: The Federal Building dedicated by Abraham Lincoln and Olympic National Park created by Franklin Roosevelt are nearby. Lincoln designated Port Angeles as a second national city.

Innkeeper(s): Jan & Bob Harbick. $75-145. 5 rooms with PB, 1 suite and 1 cottage. Breakfast, afternoon tea and snacks/refreshments included in rates. Types of meals: Full bkfst, veg bkfst, early coffee/tea and picnic lunch. Beds: QD. Reading lamp and turn-down service in room. TV, VCR, fax, parlor games, telephone and fireplace on premises. Weddings and family reunions hosted. Antiquing, art galleries, beach, bicycling, canoeing/kayaking, cross-country skiing, fishing, hiking, live theater, museums, parks, shopping and wineries nearby.
Publicity: *Arrington B&B Journal "Best Breakfast" award for 2003 and "Best Garden" for 2004.*

Tudor Inn

1108 S Oak St
Port Angeles, WA 98362-7745
(360)452-3138
E-mail: info@tudorinn.com
Web: www.tudorinn.com

Circa 1910. This English Tudor inn has been tastefully restored to display its original woodwork and fir stairway. Guests enjoy stone fireplaces in the living room and study. A terraced flower garden with 100-foot oak trees graces the property.

Innkeeper(s): Betsy Schultz. $85-145. 5 rooms with PB, 1 with FP. Breakfast and afternoon tea included in rates. Types of meals: Full bkfst. Beds: KQ. CD player and desk in room. TV, VCR, library, parlor games, telephone, fireplace and English gardens on premises. Weddings hosted. Antiquing, cross-country skiing, downhill skiing, fishing, live theater, parks, shopping, water sports and scenic flights nearby.
Publicity: *Seattle Times, Oregonian, Los Angeles Times* and *Olympic Magazine.*

"Delicious company and delicious food. Best in hospitality and warmth. Beautiful gardens!"

Port Townsend   C3

Ann Starrett Mansion

744 Clay St
Port Townsend, WA 98368-5808
(888)385-3205
E-mail: edel@starrettmansion.com
Web: www.starrettmansion.com

Circa 1889. George Starrett came from Maine to Port Townsend and became the major residential builder. By 1889, he had constructed one house a week, totaling more than 350 houses. The Smithsonian believes the Ann Starrett's elaborate free-hung spiral staircase is the only one of its type in the United States. A frescoed dome atop the octagonal tower depicts four seasons and four virtues. On the first day of each season, the sun causes a ruby red light to point toward the appropriate painting. The mansion won a "Great American Home Award" from the National Trust for Historic Preservation.
Historic Interest: The inn is located in the Port Townsend National Historic District near Fort Worden and Fort Townsend state parks.
Innkeeper(s): Edel Sokol. $133-225. 11 rooms with PB, 2 with FP, 2 suites, 2 cottages and 2 conference rooms. Breakfast included in rates. Types of meals: Full bkfst and afternoon tea. Beds: KQDT. Cable TV, reading lamp, refrigerator, clock radio, telephone, desk and hot tub/spa in room. VCR, fax, parlor games and fireplace on premises. Antiquing, cross-country skiing, fishing, live theater, parks, shopping and water sports nearby.
Publicity: *Peninsula, New York Times, Vancouver Sun, San Francisco Examiner, London Times, Colonial Homes, Elle, Leader, Japanese Travel, National Geographic Traveler, Victorian, Historic American Trails, Sunset Magazine, PBS* and *Day Boy Night Girl.*

"Staying here was like a dream come true."

Bishop Victorian Hotel

714 Washington St
Port Townsend, WA 98368-5718
(360)385-6122 (800)824-4738

Circa 1890. Located in downtown Port Townsend's historic district, this Victorian originally served as the Owl Cigar Company. Today, it holds 16 guest suites, all include a fireplace. Each of the suites includes a sitting room with sleeper sofas and antiques. Although each suite also includes a kitch-

enette, a continental breakfast is delivered each morning. Guests have privileges at a fitness club one block away.
Innkeeper(s): Joe & Cindy Finnie. $89-199. 16 suites, 14 with FP and 2 conference rooms. Types of meals: Cont plus. Beds: QD. Cable TV, reading lamp, refrigerator, ceiling fan, clock radio, telephone and desk in room. VCR, fax, copier, fireplace and health club access on premises. Weddings, small meetings, family reunions and seminars hosted. Antiquing, cross-country skiing, fishing, golf, live theater, parks, shopping, tennis and water sports nearby.

Blue Gull Inn B&B

1310 Clay Street
Port Townsend, WA 98368
(360)379-3241 (888)700-0205 Fax:(360)379-5498

Circa 1868. Proudly gracing the heart of the historic district between uptown and downtown, this Gothic Revival home boasts a Country Victorian decor. Absorb the peaceful ambiance from a rocker on the pillared front porch. Stylish guest bedrooms offer a variety of comfortable amenities. Two rooms can be made adjoining. Private bathrooms boast an oversize shower, clawfoot or whirlpool tub. Breakfast is a culinary treat of gourmet specialties and down-home favorites served in the dining room with an inspiring garden view.
Innkeeper(s): John & Renee Eissinger. $95-185. 6 rooms with PB and 1 suite. Breakfast and snacks/refreshments included in rates. Types of meals: Full bkfst, early coffee/tea and afternoon tea. Beds: QT. Two rooms with whirlpool tubs, spacious bathrooms and one room with private sun porch in room. Charming guest parlor and large dining room on premises. Weddings and family reunions hosted. Antiquing, art galleries, beach, bicycling, canoeing/kayaking, golf, hiking, live theater, museums, parks, shopping, water sports, wineries, downtown and waterfront nearby.

The English Inn

718 F St
Port Townsend, WA 98368-5211
(360)385-5302 (800)254-5302
E-mail: stay@english-inn.com
Web: www.English-Inn.com

Circa 1885. There is much to enjoy at this distinctive Italianate-style Victorian inn. The parlor's large bay window seat overlooks the impressive Olympic Mountains. Sit by the fire and choose from a diverse selection of music to listen to. An English pub atmosphere is imparted in the TV lounge and game room. Take the grand staircase to the spacious corner guest bedrooms named after British historical eras. Indulge in a long soak in a clawfoot tub. An

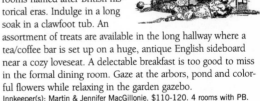

assortment of treats are available in the long hallway where a tea/coffee bar is set up on a huge, antique English sideboard near a cozy loveseat. A delectable breakfast is too good to miss in the formal dining room. Gaze at the arbors, pond and colorful flowers while relaxing in the garden gazebo.
Innkeeper(s): Martin & Jennifer MacGillonie. $110-120. 4 rooms with PB. Breakfast included in rates. Types of meals: Full gourmet bkfst, early coffee/tea and afternoon tea. Beds: Q. Reading lamp and desk in room. Parlor games and telephone on premises. Weddings, small meetings, family reunions and seminars hosted. Antiquing, bicycling, fishing, hiking, live theater, parks, shopping, water sports and beaches nearby.

Holly Hill House B&B

611 Polk St
Port Townsend, WA 98368-6531
(360)385-5619 (800)435-1454 Fax:(360)385-3041
E-mail: hollyhillhouse@olympus.net
Web: www.hollyhillhouse.com/rooms.html

Circa 1872. There are 17 holly trees surround this aptly named bed & breakfast, built by Robert C. Hill, the co-founder of the First National Bank of Port Townsend. The cozy, romantic rooms are decorated with florals and lace. Billie's Room affords a view of Admiralty Inlet and Mt. Baker, while Lizette's Room offers Victorian decor and a view of the garden. The Skyview Room includes a wonderful skylight. The spacious Colonel's Room features a picture window with water and mountain views, and the Morning Glory Room is a cozy retreat with lace-trimmed quilts. Expansive breakfasts are served in the dining room, and coffee and tea are always available. The inn's gardens are surrounded by a picket fence and nearly 90 rose bushes.

Historic Interest: The Holly Hill House is one of the few Victorian houses in the Pacific Northwest that displays original "faux bois" which is a stippling done to the wood. It has original fireplaces with marble surrounds and Italian brass inserts. Many of the light fixtures are original and have been converted from oil to gas to electric. The house was built in 1872 and still has a majority of its original architecture.

Innkeeper(s): Nina & Greg Dortch. $94-165. 5 rooms with PB and 1 suite. Breakfast and afternoon tea included in rates. Types of meals: Full bkfst, veg bkfst, early coffee/tea and picnic lunch. Beds: KQ. Reading lamp and clock radio in room. TV, VCR, library, parlor games, fireplace and DVD on premises. Weddings, small meetings, family reunions and seminars hosted. Antiquing, art galleries, beach, bicycling, canoeing/kayaking, fishing, golf, museums, parks, shopping, water sports and wineries nearby.

Publicity: *Washington State Visitors' Guide, PT Guide, Port Townsend Chamber of Commerce Guide, The Official Guide to American Historic Inns, Bed & Breakfast USA, Bed & Breakfast Homes Best of the West Coast, National Trust Guide, Romantic Getaway Guide and Stash Tea Guide of B&B Inns.*

Manresa Castle

PO Box 564, 7th & Sheridan
Port Townsend, WA 98368-0564
(360)385-5750 (800)732-1281 Fax:(360)385-5883

Circa 1892. When businessman Charles Eisenbeis built the largest private residence in Port Townsend, locals dubbed it "Eisenbeis Castle," because it resembled the castles in Eisenbeis' native Prussia. The home is truly a royal delight to behold, both inside and out. Luxurious European antiques and hand-painted wall coverings decorate the dining room and many of the castle's stately guest rooms. The turret suites are unique and many of the rooms have mountain and water views, but beware of the third floor. Rumors of ghosts in the upper floor have frightened some, but others seek out the "haunted" rooms for a spooky stay. Port Townsend offers a variety of galleries, gift shops and antiquing.

Historic Interest: Port Townsend and Manresa Castle are listed in the National Register. The town includes many examples of Victorian-style buildings and a historic district.

Innkeeper(s): Roger O'Connor. $70-175. 40 rooms with PB, 2 suites and 1 conference room. Breakfast included in rates. Types of meals: Gourmet dinner. Restaurant on premises. Beds: KQD. Cable TV, reading lamp, clock radio and telephone in room. Fax, copier and library on premises. Weddings, small meetings, family reunions and seminars hosted. Antiquing, art galleries, beach, bicycling, canoeing/kayaking, fishing, golf, hiking, live theater, museums, parks, shopping, tennis, water sports and wineries nearby.

Publicity: *Island Independent, Leader News, Province Showcase, Sunset Magazine, Oregonian, Northwest Palate Magazine, History Channel and Sightings.*

Palace Hotel

1004 Water St
Port Townsend, WA 98368-6706
(360)385-0773 (800)962-0741 Fax:(360)385-0780

Circa 1889. This old brick hotel has been restored and refurbished in a Victorian style. The Miss Rose Room has a Jacuzzi tub and is on the third floor. Some rooms have kitchenettes. Miss Kitty's Room, with its antique bed and wood-burning stove has great views of Puget Sound and downtown.

Innkeeper(s): Gary Schweitzer. $49-189. 17 rooms. Breakfast included in rates. Types of meals: Cont. Beds: KQDT. TV in room.

Seattle   C4

Amaranth Inn

1451 S Main St
Seattle, WA 98144
(206)720-7161 (800)720-7161 Fax:(206)323-0772
E-mail: visitus@amaranthinn.com
Web: www.amaranthinn.com

Circa 1906. Explore all the city sights from this elegantly restored Grand Craftsman home built by a lumber baron. Spacious rooms feature high ceilings with crown moldings, Oriental carpets on hardwood floors, gentle wall colors graced with original Pacific Northwest artwork, and well-placed antique furnishings. All but one of the guest bedrooms or suites have fireplaces. Clean and comfortable, enjoy hand-pressed cotton bedding, handmade soaps, terry robes, jetted tubs and tiled baths. Made-to-order gourmet breakfasts are served on settings of crystal and china in the formal dining room. The sunroom and front porch are pleasant places for relaxing.

Innkeeper(s): Herman & Alea Foster. $75-170. 8 rooms, 6 with PB, 7 with FP. Breakfast included in rates. Types of meals: Full gourmet bkfst, veg bkfst and early coffee/tea. Beds: QT. Data port, cable TV, reading lamp, clock radio, telephone, hot tub/spa, voice mail, fireplace, down comforters, handmade soaps and terry robes in room. VCR, fireplace, sun porch with fresh fruit available and reclining chairs on premises. Small meetings and family reunions hosted. Antiquing, art galleries, beach, bicycling, canoeing/kayaking, fishing, golf, hiking, live theater, museums, parks, shopping, sporting events, tennis, water sports, wineries, train station and freeway access nearby.

Bacon Mansion Bed & Breakfast

959 Broadway E.
Seattle, WA 98102
(206)329-1864 (800)240-1864 Fax:(206)860-9025
E-mail: info@baconmansion.com
Web: www.baconmansion.com

Circa 1909. Pass through the gates to see the family crest of red and white shields on the round stained-glass windows at this Edwardian-style Tudor mansion. The classic decor boasts original woods, marble fireplaces, a 3,000-crystal chandelier and pocket doors. The main house features day rooms for social or business events and a treasured library. Stately suites and guest bedrooms are well-furnished with private voicemail, data ports and hair dryers; some include fireplaces and soaking tubs. A large outside patio with fountain and rose garden leads to the historical Carriage House that offers two separate quarters adjoined through a double-locked door. An assortment of breakfast cereals, fruit, yogurt, hot & fresh muffins, Seattle coffee and tea are available daily.

Innkeeper(s): Daryl King. $82-179. 11 rooms, 9 with PB, 2 with FP, 3 suites and 1 cottage. Breakfast and afternoon tea included in rates. Types of meals: Cont plus and early coffee/tea. Beds: QDT. Modem hook-up, data port, TV, reading lamp, refrigerator, ceiling fan, clock radio, telephone, desk, voice mail and fireplace in room. Fax, copier, library and fireplace on premises. Small meetings hosted. Antiquing, art galleries, bicycling, canoeing/kayaking, live theater, museums, parks, shopping, sporting events, tennis and wineries nearby.

Chambered Nautilus B&B Inn

5005 22nd Ave NE
Seattle, WA 98105
(206)522-2536 (800)545-8459 Fax:(206)528-0898
E-mail: stay@chamberednautilus.com
Web: www.chamberednautilus.com

Circa 1915. This blue, Georgian Colonial Revival home was built on a hill in the university district by Dr. Herbert Gowen of the University of Washington. Georgian Colonial Revival architecture reflects the first owner's English heritage. Three dormers and Palladian doors grace the front of the inn and an enclosed sunporch that offers views of the garden. The large airy guest rooms are furnished with Persian rugs and antiques. Many have porches and views of

the Cascade mountains. Tea is served by the fire in the living room, while guests can enjoy freshly baked cookies on the sunporch or relax with a book from the inn's well-stocked shelves.
Historic Interest: Built in 1915 and an excellent example of Georgian architecture typical of homes built around the University of WA in that era. The home was built by Dr Gowan, an early University professor and founder of the Department of Asian Studies.
Innkeeper(s): Joyce Schulte & Steve Poole. $89-154. 10 rooms with PB, 2 with FP and 4 suites. Breakfast and snacks/refreshments included in rates. Types of meals: Full gourmet bkfst, veg bkfst and early coffee/tea. Beds: KQT. Modem hook-up, data port, cable TV, VCR, reading lamp, CD player, refrigerator, ceiling fan, snack bar, clock radio, telephone, coffeemaker, desk, voice mail, fireplace, bathrobes, bottled water and teddy bears in room. Air conditioning. Fax, copier and fireplace on premises. Weddings, small meetings, family reunions and seminars hosted. Antiquing, art galleries, beach, bicycling, canoeing/kayaking, hiking, live theater, museums, parks, shopping, sporting events, tennis and wineries nearby.

"I think you've spoiled us for any other inn, any place. We felt like royalty and family members all at the same time."

Chelsea Station on The Park

4915 Linden Ave N
Seattle, WA 98103-6536
(206)547-6077 (800)400-6077 Fax:(206)632-5107

Circa 1929. Chelsea Station on the Park is a gracious Federal Colonial home nestled between Fremont and Woodland Park, just north of downtown. The inn's uniquely decorated rooms include some spacious suites with peek-a-boo mountain views. Antiques and Mission-style furnishings add to the atmosphere. Guests are treated to a full Northwest breakfast, and there's a bottomless cookie jar. Guests can walk to the park, Seattle's rose garden and excellent restaurants. It's ten minutes to the heart of the city.
Historic Interest: Minutes from Seattle's historic Pioneer Square district.
Innkeeper(s): Eric & Carolanne Watness. $95-175. 9 rooms with PB and 7 suites. Breakfast included in rates. Types of meals: Full bkfst. Beds: KQT. Clock radio and telephone in room. Fax and parlor games on premises. Live theater, Many museums and art galleries nearby.
Publicity: *Innviews, Seattle Press, Puget Sound Business Journal, Journal Newspaper, National Geographic Traveler's, Seattle's Best Places, Northwest Best Places and Best Places to Kiss.*

"We're back...the food and lodging remains first class. We look forward to another visit soon."

Gaslight Inn

1727 15th Ave
Seattle, WA 98122-2614
(206)325-3654 Fax:(206)328-4803
E-mail: innkeepr@gaslight-inn.com
Web: www.gaslight-inn.com

Circa 1906. Stay at this Four Square, large Arts and Crafts bungalow offering quality, comfort and a relaxed yet elegant atmosphere. Impeccably decorated with mission-style furniture, Turkish rugs, artwork and antique lamps, the interior has been restored in exacting detail with rich oak paneling, a wide staircase and an enormous entryway. Showcased in the living room is a big, oak fireplace. Another pleasant common room is the library. Guest bedrooms include refrigerators. Many feature gas fireplaces, and some have decks boasting wonderful views. A koi pond and perennial garden grace the grounds that also have a private, heated, inground pool surrounded by several decks and tropical foliage.
Innkeeper(s): Steve Bennett & Trevor Logan. $88-198. 16 rooms. Breakfast included in rates. Types of meals: Cont. Beds: QD. Modem hook-up, data port, cable TV, reading lamp, refrigerator, ceiling fan, clock radio, telephone, coffeemaker, voice mail and fireplace in room. Fax, copier, swimming, fireplace and laundry facility on premises. Amusement parks, antiquing, art galleries, beach, bicycling, canoeing/kayaking, cross-country skiing, downhill skiing, fishing, golf, hiking, live theater, museums, parks, shopping, sporting events, tennis, water sports and wineries nearby.

Mildred's B&B

1202 15th Ave E
Seattle, WA 98112-3309
(206)325-6072 (800)327-9692 Fax:(206)325-6072
E-mail: mildredsbb@wwdb.org
Web: www.mildredsbnb.com

Circa 1898. Coffee and juice comes to your room half an hour before breakfast at this large, white Victorian inn. Making the trip-to-Grandmother's fantasy come alive are a grand piano, lace curtains, red carpets and a wrap-around veranda. A sitting area adjacent to the guest rooms has a pull-down ironing board. Across the street is historic, 44-acre Volunteer Park with a flower conservatory and tennis courts. An electric trolley stops right out the front door and the surrounding area is one of stately old homes and tree-lined streets.
Innkeeper(s): Mildred & Melodee Sarver. $115-175. 4 rooms with PB. Breakfast included in rates. Types of meals: Full gourmet bkfst, veg bkfst, early coffee/tea and afternoon tea. Beds: QT. Modem hook-up, data port, cable TV, VCR, reading lamp, refrigerator, clock radio, coffeemaker, desk and coffee and juice 1/2 hour prior to full breakfast in room. Fax, copier, telephone and fireplace on premises. Amusement parks, antiquing, art galleries, beach, bicycling, canoeing/kayaking, cross-country skiing, downhill skiing, fishing, golf, hiking, live theater, museums, parks, shopping, sporting events, tennis and wineries nearby.

Pioneer Square Hotel

77 Yesler Way
Seattle, WA 98104-3401
(206)340-1234 (800)800-5514 Fax:(206)467-0707
E-mail: sales@pioneersquare.com
Web: www.pioneersquare.com

Circa 1914. The estate of Seattle's founding father, Henry Yesler, built this historic waterfront hotel. The three-diamond hotel is well-appointed and elegant rooms feature coordinating prints. Business travelers will appreciate the direct dial telephones with data ports, and individual climate controls in each room. A generous continental breakfast is included in the hotel's rates. Restaurants and cafes are nearby, as is Historic Pioneer Square, Pike Place Market, ferries and shopping.

Innkeeper(s): Jo Thompson. $119-229. 75 rooms with PB and 3 suites. Types of meals: Cont and room service. Beds: KQDT. Cable TV, reading lamp, clock radio, telephone, turn-down service and desk in room. Air conditioning. Fax, copier, library and fireplace on premises. Limited handicap access. Weddings, small meetings, family reunions and seminars hosted. Cross-country skiing, downhill skiing, live theater, parks, shopping, sporting events and water sports nearby.

Seaview E2

Shelburne Inn

4415 Pacific Way, PO Box 250
Seaview, WA 98644
(360)642-2442 Fax:(360)642-8904
E-mail: innkeeper@theshelburneinn.com
Web: www.theshelburneinn.com

Circa 1896. The Shelburne is known as the oldest continuously operating hotel in the state of Washington, and it is listed in the National Register. The front desk at the hotel is a former church altar. Art nouveau stained-glass windows rescued

from a church torn down in Morecambe, England, now shed light and color on the dining room. The guest rooms are appointed in antiques. Just a 10-minute walk from the ocean, the inn is situated on the Long Beach Peninsula, a 28-mile stretch of seacoast that includes bird sanctuaries and lighthouses. The inn offers a full gourmet breakfast.
Innkeeper(s): David Campiche & Laurie Anderson. $119-199. 15 rooms with PB, 2 suites and 1 conference room. Breakfast included in rates. Types of meals: Full gourmet bkfst, lunch, gourmet dinner and room service. Restaurant on premises. Beds: QD. Fax and copier on premises. Limited handicap access. Antiquing and fishing nearby.
Publicity: *Better Homes & Gardens, Bon Appetit, Conde Nast Traveler, Esquire, Gourmet, Food & Wine and Travel & Leisure.*

"Fabulous food. Homey but elegant atmosphere. Hospitable service, like being a guest in an elegant home."

Spokane C9

Angelica's Mansion

1321 W 9th Ave
Spokane, WA 99204-3211
(509)624-5598 (800)987-0053 Fax:(509)624-5598
E-mail: info@angelicasbb.com
Web: www.angelicasbb.com

Circa 1907. Built in 1907, this elegant brick mansion is a romantic getaway located on Spokane's South Hill, and listed in the National Register of Historic Places. A European Arts and Crafts influence is demonstrated throughout the home in warm woodwork, antique furnishings and diamond-paned, leaded-glass windows. Four guest rooms each have private baths and offer individual features such as canopy bed, wicker furniture or tiled fireplace. Enjoy a breakfast of broccoli and goat cheese quiche, and a croissant with a slice of country ham before heading out to explore the city. Just five minutes from downtown, it's easy to visit the Opera House, arena, museum or Riverfront Park. At the end of the day, savor a cup of coffee or afternoon snack in the Sunroom, or relax on the spacious veranda.
Innkeeper(s): Lynette & Ted Gustafson. $95-115. 4 rooms with PB, 1 with FP, 2 suites and 1 conference room. Breakfast and snacks/refreshments included in rates. Types of meals: Full gourmet bkfst, veg bkfst, early coffee/tea, picnic lunch and afternoon tea. Beds: Q. Modem hook-up, cable TV, reading lamp, CD player, clock radio, telephone, turn-down service and desk in room. Air conditioning. VCR, fax, copier, library, parlor games and

fireplace on premises. Weddings, small meetings, family reunions and seminars hosted. Antiquing, art galleries, bicycling, cross-country skiing, downhill skiing, fishing, golf, hiking, live theater, museums, parks, sporting events, tennis, water sports and wineries nearby.
Publicity: *Romantic Decorating.*

Fotheringham House

2128 W 2nd Ave
Spokane, WA 99204-0916
(509)838-1891 Fax:(509)838-1807

Circa 1891. A vintage Victorian in the National Register, this inn was built by the first mayor of Spokane, David Fotheringham. There are tin ceilings, a carved staircase, gabled porches and polished woodwork. Victorian furnishings and stained-glass pieces are featured. Across the street is Coeur d'Alene Park and the Patsy Clark Mansion. Walk two blocks to the Elk Public House.

Historic Interest: 1891 home of Spokane's first mayor.
Innkeeper(s): Irene & Paul Jensen. $95-115. 4 rooms. Breakfast included in rates. Types of meals: Full bkfst and early coffee/tea. Reading lamp, clock radio, chocolates and amenities in room. Telephone and fireplace on premises. Weddings, small meetings, family reunions and seminars hosted. Antiquing, live theater, museums, shopping and sporting events nearby.

Waverly Place B&B

709 W Waverly Place
Spokane, WA 99205
(509)328-1856 (866)328-1856 Fax:(509)326-7059
E-mail: waverly@waverlyplace.com
Web: www.waverlyplace.com

Circa 1900. The first home built in what is now the Corbin Park Historical District, this storybook Victorian offers quiet relaxation and a central location. An inviting parlor boasts beaded pillars and window seats. Choose from spacious park-view rooms or the romantic third-floor turret suite. Wake to hot coffee just outside the door before savoring a full gourmet breakfast in the dining room. Swedish pancakes with huckleberry sauce, sausage, fresh fruit and yogurt are some of the favorite items served. Sit on the veranda with afternoon tea, or swim in the refreshing pool. The sites and shops of downtown are five minutes away.
Historic Interest: Our inn was the first house built in the Corbin Park Historic District on Corbin Park. The original owner was superintendent of building and bridges for Mr. Corbin.
Innkeeper(s): Marge & Tammy Arndt. $85-125. 4 rooms, 2 with PB and 1 suite. Breakfast and afternoon tea included in rates. Types of meals: Full gourmet bkfst, veg bkfst and early coffee/tea. Beds: Q. Reading lamp, clock radio and desk in room. Central air. Fax, swimming, telephone and fireplace on premises. Antiquing, art galleries, bicycling, cross-country skiing, downhill skiing, golf, hiking, live theater, museums, parks, shopping, sporting events, tennis, water sports and wineries nearby.

Sunnyside E6

Sunnyside Inn B&B

800 E Edison Ave
Sunnyside, WA 98944-2206
(509)839-5557 (800)221-4195
E-mail: sunnyside@sunnysideinn.com
Web: www.sunnysideinn.com

Circa 1919. This wine country inn offers spacious rooms, decorated in a comfortable, country style. Most of the rooms include baths with double Jacuzzi tubs. The one bedroom without a Jacuzzi, includes the home's original early 20th-century fixtures. Two rooms offer fireplaces. A full breakfast is served, as well as evening snacks.

Innkeeper(s): Karen & Don Vlieger. $89-119. 13 rooms with PB, 2 with FP. Breakfast and snacks/refreshments included in rates. Types of meals: Full bkfst. Beds: KQ. Cable TV, reading lamp, refrigerator, ceiling fan, clock radio and telephone in room. Air conditioning. Fireplace on premises. Small meetings and family reunions hosted. Antiquing, cross-country skiing, fishing, golf, live theater, parks and shopping nearby.

Tacoma D4

DeVoe Mansion

208 133rd St East
Tacoma, WA 98445-1420
(253)539-3991 (888)539-3991
E-mail: innkeeper@devoemansion.com
Web: www.devoemansion.com

Circa 1911. Women in Washington have great reason to thank the first owner of this National Register mansion. Emma Smith DeVoe, a dedicated suffragist, lobbied and fought to have Washington become the fifth state to give women the right to vote. She also founded what is now known as the League of Women Voters. Guest rooms are named in honor of people who were important in Emma's life, such as the Susan B. Anthony Room. Another room is named for her husband, John Henry DeVoe. All of the rooms are decorated with period antiques, affording a nostalgic charm, as do newspaper clippings from Emma's era. There are porches to relax on and more than an acre of landscaped grounds to enjoy. Each day, the innkeepers prepare a different breakfast entree, accompanied by fresh fruit and homemade muffins. Tacoma offers much to do, and Seattle is nearby.

Historic Interest: The DeVoe Mansion is the home of Emma Smith DeVoe, a member of the National Women's Hall of Fame. The home is on the National Historic Register as a tribute to the work she did in the suffrage movement. She was a highly organized speaker and lecturer and contributed to the passage of the 19th Amendment in 1920.

Innkeeper(s): Dave & Cheryl Teifke. $105-140. 4 rooms with PB and 1 conference room. Breakfast and snacks/refreshments included in rates. Types of meals: Full gourmet bkfst, early coffee/tea, picnic lunch and afternoon tea. Beds: QT. Modem hook-up, data port, TV, VCR, reading lamp, stereo, telephone, turn-down service, desk, luxurious terry cloth bath robes, classic movies, bottled water, ice and chocolates in room. Central air. Fax, parlor games, fireplace, gift shop and hot beverage bar with fresh fruit and homemade cookies on premises. Weddings, small meetings, family reunions and seminars hosted. Amusement parks, antiquing, art galleries, beach, bicycling, canoeing/kayaking, fishing, golf, hiking, live theater, museums, parks, shopping, sporting events, tennis, water sports, Western Washington Fairgrounds, McChord Air force Base, Fort Lewis and Spanaway Horse Arena nearby.

Publicity: *The Best Places to Kiss in the NW, American Historic Inns, Sweethearts Getaway Guide, The Unofficial Guide to B&B's in the NW, Washington Handbook and Absolutely Every B&B.*

"I felt like a princess in grandma's house."

Dutch Embassy

1601 N 8th St
Tacoma, WA 98403-1013
(253)627-4192 Fax:(253)627-4192

Circa 1893. Named after entertaining a brother who was a diplomat from the Netherlands, this two-story Queen Anne is tastefully furnished in antiques and collectibles. Greeted in the entry hall with leaded- and stained-glass windows on the stairway landing, the parlor fireplace is a relaxing gathering spot.

Guest bedrooms feature interesting curved footboard, half-canopy and four-poster beds. The Tower Suite with adjoining sitting room is in the finished attic and offers terry robes, as do all the other rooms. A satisfying breakfast is served in the dining room. Play badminton, basketball, pickle ball or paddle tennis on the outdoor court. It is an easy stroll to view the historic districts surrounding the inn.

Innkeeper(s): Kenneth & Velda McDonald. $55-90. 5 rooms, 1 with PB. Breakfast included in rates. Types of meals: Full bkfst. Beds: QDT. TV, VCR, reading lamp, clock radio and desk in room. Fax, copier, library, parlor games, telephone, fireplace and sport court on premises. Amusement parks, antiquing, beach, bicycling, golf and museums nearby.

Publicity: *Tacoma Weekly.*

Yakima E6

A Touch Of Europe™ B&B Inn Yakima

220 N 16th Ave
Yakima, WA 98902-2461
(509)454-9775 (888)438-7073
E-mail: atoeurope@msn.com
Web: www.winesnw.com/toucheuropeb&b.htm

Circa 1889. A lumber baron built this Queen Anne Victorian as his residence, which still maintains period elements such as stained glass and rich woodwork. The home was purchased by the Williams family in 1904, and Mrs. Ina Philips Williams was the first woman member of the Washington State House of Representatives. Theodore Roosevelt, whose portrait is displayed among other historical photographs, was a guest of the Williams family. Elegant guest bedrooms feature period decor and classic Victorian furnishings. A signature, multi-course, candlelit breakfast is prepared by innkeeper, European chef and cookbook author Erika Cenci, who also creates recipes and demonstrates them on local and international TV. This inn also offers fine dining, specializing in a variety of international cuisine. Private luncheons, traditional high teas or memorable multi-course dinners can be developed exclusively to fit almost any occasion or theme.

Innkeeper(s): Erika G. and James A. Cenci. $85-120. 3 rooms with PB, 1 with FP, 1 cottage and 1 conference room. Breakfast included in rates. Types of meals: Full bkfst. Beds: Q. Telephone in room. Air conditioning. Library on premises. Small meetings hosted. Antiquing, bicycling, golf, hiking, live theater, museums, wineries, Convention Center and skiing nearby.

Publicity: *"Touring & Tasting," Best Chef Award USA "Inn Traveler," Yakima Herald-Republic and KIMA-TV/Fisher Broadcasting.*

"Thank you for your warmth and friendliness and outstanding food! Your home is beautiful."

Birchfield Manor Country Inn

2018 Birchfield Rd
Yakima, WA 98901-9580
(509)452-1960 (800)375-3420 Fax:(509)452-2334

Circa 1910. Guests at this Prairie-style inn, once the centerpiece of a large sheep ranch, enjoy elegant decor and the tranquil scenery of seven rural acres. Four guest rooms have fireplaces, and some have double whirlpool tubs or a sauna shower. The innkeepers have won awards for their breakfasts, and for an additional charge, dinners are served on Thursday, Friday and Saturday nights.

Innkeeper(s): The Masset Family. $119-219. 11 rooms with PB, 4 with FP. Breakfast included in rates. Types of meals: Full gourmet bkfst, early coffee/tea, gourmet dinner and room service. Restaurant on premises. Beds: KQ. VCR, reading lamp, refrigerator, ceiling fan, clock radio, telephone and desk in room. Air conditioning. Swimming on premises. Limited handicap access. Weddings, small meetings, family reunions and seminars hosted. Antiquing, downhill skiing, fishing, live theater, parks and water sports nearby.

Washington, D.C.

Aaron Shipman House

13th and Q Streets NW
Washington, DC 20009
(202)328-3510 (877)893-8233 Fax:(413)582-9669
E-mail: bnbaccom@aol.com
Web: www.aaronshipmanhouse.com

Circa 1887. This three-story Victorian townhouse was built by Aaron Shipman, who owned one of the first construction companies in the city. The turn-of-the-century revitalization of Washington began in Logan Circle, considered to be the city's first truly residential area. During the house's restoration, flower gardens, terraces and fountains were added. Victorian antiques, original wood paneling, stained glass, chandeliers, as well as practical amenities such as air conditioning and laundry facilities, make this a comfortable stay. There is a furnished apartment available, as well.

Historic Interest: U.S. Capitol, Congress, Smithsonian Museums, White House, all national monuments.

Innkeeper(s): Charles & Jackie Reed. $75-165. 6 rooms, 5 with PB, 2 with FP. Breakfast included in rates. Types of meals: Full bkfst. Beds: QDT. Modem hook-up, data port, TV, clock radio, telephone, desk, hot tub/spa and fireplace in room. Central air. Spa, library, child care, fireplace and laundry facility on premises. Weddings, small meetings and family reunions hosted. Antiquing, art galleries, bicycling, museums, shopping, tennis and national monuments and Smithsonian nearby.

"This home was the highlight of our stay in Washington! This was a superb home and location. The Reeds treated us better than family."

Adams Inn

1744 Lanier Pl NW
Washington, DC 20009-2118
(202)745-3600 (800)578-6807 Fax:(202)319-7958
E-mail: adamsinn@adamsinn.com
Web: www.adamsinn.com

Circa 1908. These restored town houses have fireplaces, a library and parlor, all furnished home-style, as are the guest rooms. Former residents of this neighborhood include Tallulah Bankhead, Woodrow Wilson and Al Jolson. The Adams-Morgan area is home to diplomats, radio and television personalities and government workers. A notable firehouse across the street holds the record for the fastest response of a horse-drawn fire apparatus. Located in the restaurant area, over 100 restaurants and shops are within walking distance.

Historic Interest: Washington, D.C., it goes without saying, is full of national treasures and the Smithsonian museums.

Innkeeper(s): Anne Owens. $70-115. 25 rooms, 15 with PB. Breakfast included in rates. Types of meals:

Cont plus and early coffee/tea. Beds: QDT. Reading lamp and clock radio in room. Air conditioning. Parlor games, telephone and fireplace on premises. Antiquing, parks and walking distance to Metro and buses nearby.
Publicity: *Travel Host.*

"We enjoyed your friendly hospitality and the home-like atmosphere. Your suggestions on restaurants and help in planning our visit were appreciated."

Doolittle Guest House

506 E Capitol St SE
Washington, DC 20003-1141
(202)546-6622 Fax:(202)546-5046
E-mail: doolittlehouse@yahoo.com
Web: www.doolittlehouse.com

Circa 1866. Experience a taste of elegance while staying at this Richardsonian Romanesque house in the residential Capitol Hill historic district. Federalist and Centennial decor is enhanced by stained-glass windows, period antiques, marble fireplaces, chestnut and walnut paneling. Well-appointed guest bedrooms and a suite offer pure cotton bed and bath linens and robes for personal comfort. A healthy breakfast is served in the sunny dining room. Keep abreast of current world events with major daily newspapers and various magazines in the foyer and library. The second-floor library offers a fully equipped business center. Washington's political, historic and cultural sites are all nearby.

Innkeeper(s): Bernadine & Raymond Prince. $115-175. 3 rooms with PB, 1 suite and 1 conference room. Breakfast included in rates. Types of meals: Cont plus, veg bkfst and early coffee/tea. Beds: KQD. Modem hook-up, data port, reading lamp, ceiling fan, clock radio, telephone, turn-down service and desk in room. Central air. VCR, fax, copier, library, parlor games, fireplace and laundry facility on premises. Weddings, small meetings, family reunions and seminars hosted. Antiquing, art galleries, bicycling, canoeing/kayaking, golf, live theater, museums, parks, shopping, White House, U.S. Capitol, Washington Monument, Jefferson Memorial, Lincoln Memorial, Vietnam Memorial, Arlington National Cemetery and Holocaust Museum nearby.
Publicity: *Lonely Planet, Washington Traveler, Washington Print Club News and National Geographic and PBS documentaries.*

Dupont At The Circle

1604 19th St NW
Washington, DC 20009
(202)332-5251 (888)412-0100 Fax:(202)332-3244

Circa 1883. Completely restoring this Victorian townhouse infused this urban B&B inn with enhanced modern technology while retaining its historical flavor and integrity. Common areas include cozy parlors and a front patio. Antique furniture, fine ironed linens and upscale amenities offer luxurious comfort. Some guest bedrooms feature handcrafted reproduction stained-glass windows, four-poster canopy beds and whirlpool tubs. The Plum Suite spans an entire floor and boasts a living room with entertainment center, marble bath and whirlpool tub. The

English Basement is a spacious studio apartment with a kitchenette and private entrance. Concierge services can arrange transportation, dinner reservations and access to a local health club.

Innkeeper(s): Ines de Azcarate. $140-300. 8 rooms with PB, 1 suite and 1 conference room. Breakfast included in rates. Types of meals: Cont. Beds: QD. Modem hook-up, data port, cable TV, reading lamp, clock radio, telephone, desk, voice mail, some with CD player, refrigerator, stereo and VCR in room. Central air. TV, VCR, fax, library, parlor games and fireplace on premises. Small meetings and seminars hosted. Antiquing, art galleries, bicycling, golf, live theater, museums, parks, shopping, sporting events and tennis nearby.

Publicity: *Travel & Leisure, Washington Times and Latina Style & Travel Holiday.*

The Embassy Inn

1627 16th St NW
Washington, DC 20009-3063
(202)234-7800 (800)423-9111 Fax:(202)234-3309

Circa 1910. This restored inn is furnished in a Federalist style. The comfortable lobby offers books and evening sherry. Conveniently located, the inn is seven blocks from the Adams Morgan area of ethnic restaurants. The Embassy's philosophy of innkeeping includes providing personal attention and cheerful hospitality. Concierge services are available. The inn does not have an elevator or parking on site.

Innkeeper(s): Susan Stiles. $79-150. 38 rooms with PB. Breakfast included in rates. Types of meals: Cont plus and snacks/refreshments. Beds: DT. Cable TV, reading lamp, clock radio, telephone and free HBO in room. Air conditioning. Fax, copier and Washington Post daily on premises. Antiquing, live theater, museums, parks and White House nearby.

Publicity: *Los Angeles Times, Inn Times, Business Review and N.Y. Times.*

"When I return to D.C., I'll be back at the Embassy."

Maison Orleans Bed'n Breakfast on the Hill

414 Fifth St, SE
Washington, DC 20003-2051
(202)544-3694

Circa 1902. Maison Orleans is located less than two blocks from Pennsylvania Avenue on historic Capitol Hill. The interior features family antiques from the 1930s and 1940s, as well as antiques that once resided in other Capitol Hill homes. In the winter, guests in the Raspberry-Creole Room enjoy a view of the Washington Monument. Guests can walk the half-dozen blocks that lead to the Capitol building, Library of Congress and other important historic attractions.

Innkeeper(s): William Rouchell. $95-135. 3 rooms with PB, 1 with FP. Breakfast included in rates. Types of meals: Cont plus. Beds: KQT. TV, reading lamp, ceiling fan, clock radio, telephone, desk and voice mail in room. Central air. Parlor games and fireplace on premises. Family reunions hosted. Antiquing, art galleries, bicycling, live theater, museums, parks, shopping, Nation's Capitol and Whitehouse nearby.

Publicity: *Voice of the Hill.*

Swann House

1808 New Hampshire Ave NW
Washington, DC 20009-3206
(202)265-4414 Fax:(202)265-6755
E-mail: stay@swannhouse.com
Web: www.swannhouse.com

Circa 1883. Swann House is a splendid example of Richardson Romanesque architecture and all its glory. The gothic brick home includes a turret and an arched, covered front porch and a lavish, second-story balcony. The interior includes the original crown moldings, hardwood floors, a carved marble fireplace and original doors and paneling. The guest rooms and suites are decorated with an eclectic mix of antiques and contemporary furnishings. Several include a fireplace. Guests can take in the city view from a rooftop deck or enjoy the backyard garden, which includes a pool. The home is located in Dupont Circle, with Washington, D.C.'s, myriad of attractions all close by.

Innkeeper(s): Mary & Richard Ross, Rick Verkler. $140-295. 9 rooms with PB, 6 with FP and 2 conference rooms. Breakfast and snacks/refreshments included in rates. Types of meals: Cont plus. Beds: KQ. Data port, cable TV, telephone and voice mail in room. Central air. VCR, fax, copier, swimming, fireplace, laundry facility, pool, roof deck, balconies and gardens on premises. Weddings, small meetings, family reunions and seminars hosted. Antiquing, art galleries, bicycling, live theater, museums, parks, shopping, Congress, memorials and historical attractions nearby.

The Windsor Inn

1842 16th St NW
Washington, DC 20009-3316
(202)667-0300 (800)423-9111 Fax:(202)667-4503

Circa 1910. Recently renovated and situated in a neighborhood of renovated townhouses, the Windsor Inn is the sister property to the Embassy Inn. It is larger and offers suites as well as a small meeting room. The refurbished lobby is in an Art Deco style and a private club atmosphere prevails. It is six blocks to the Metro station at Dupont Circle. There are no elevators or parking on site.

Historic Interest: White House (12 blocks), Arlington House (3 miles), Hillwood House (2 miles), Mount Vernon (14 miles).

Innkeeper(s): Susan Stiles. $89-199. 45 rooms with PB, 2 suites and 1 conference room. Breakfast included in rates. Types of meals: Cont plus and snacks/refreshments. Beds: QDT. TV, reading lamp, clock radio, telephone and some with refrigerators in room. Air conditioning. Fax, copier and daily Washington Post on premises. Weddings, small meetings and family reunions hosted. Antiquing, live theater and parks nearby.

Publicity: *Los Angeles Times, Inn Times, Sunday Telegram, WCUA Press Release and New York Times.*

"Being here was like being home. Excellent service, would recommend."

Woodley Park Guest House

2647 Woodley Road, NW
Washington, DC 20008
(202)667-0218 (866)667-0218 Fax:(202)667-1080
E-mail: info@woodleyparkguesthouse.com
Web: www.woodleyparkguesthouse.com

Circa 1908. Conveniently located in a delightful historic neighborhood near the metro station, this renovated bed & breakfast inn was built using Federal architecture in 1908. People-watch from the front porch on comfortable white wicker furniture or relax in the centrally air-conditioned interior. Nicely decorated guest bedrooms are furnished in antiques. Internet access and voice mail service is provided. A generous continental-plus breakfast starts each day in the Breakfast/Fellowship Room. Walk two blocks to the zoo or go for a run in Rock Creek Park. Visit Capitol Hill and experience the nightlife of Georgetown.

Innkeeper(s): Laura and Raymond Saba. $65-150. 17 rooms, 11 with PB. Breakfast included in rates. Types of meals: Cont plus. Beds: QDT. Library and parlor games on premises. Art galleries, live theater, museums and parks nearby.

West Virginia

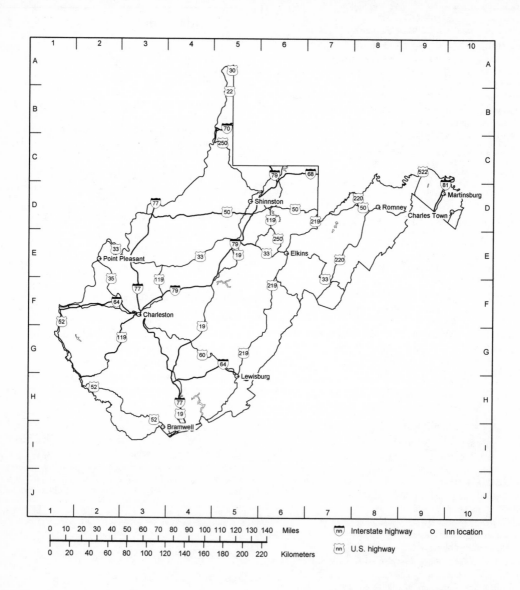

Bramwell   I3

Perry House B&B

Main St, PO Box 188
Bramwell, WV 24715-0248
(304)248-8145 (800)328-0248

Circa 1902. This brick Victorian was built by a bank cashier and remained in the family for 80 years. The rooms are decorated in period style with antiques. Although a small village, Bramwell once was home to more than a dozen millionaires, and some of these families' homes are located on the town walking tour. The inn is listed in the National Register.

Innkeeper(s): Joyce & Jim Bishop. $75. 4 rooms, 1 with PB. Breakfast included in rates. Types of meals: Full bkfst. Beds: QDT. Reading lamp and desk in room. Air conditioning. Parlor games, telephone and fireplace on premises. Weddings and family reunions hosted. Antiquing, downhill skiing, fishing, live theater, parks, shopping and water sports nearby.

Charles Town   D10

Gilbert House B&B of Middleway

PO Box 1104
Charles Town, WV 25414-7104
(304)725-0637

Circa 1760. A magnificent graystone of early Georgian design, the Gilbert House is located in one of the state's oldest European settlements. Elegant appointments include fine Oriental rugs, tasteful art and antique furnishings. During restoration, graffiti

found on the upstairs bedroom walls included an 1832 drawing of the future President James Polk and a child's growth chart from the 1800s. The inn is located in the Colonial era mill village of Middleway, which contains one of the country's best collections of log houses. The village is a mill site on the original settlers' trail into Shenandoah Valley ("Philadelphia Waggon Road" on Peter Jefferson's 1755 map of Virginia). Middleway was also the site of "wizard clip" hauntings during the last decade of the 1700s. The region was home to members of "Virginia Blues," commanded by Daniel Morgan during the Revolutionary War.

Historic Interest: Charles Town, Bunker Hill, Leetown (10 minutes), Antietam Battlefield (20 minutes), Winchester, Va. (25 minutes), Harpers Ferry (20 minutes).

Innkeeper(s): Bernie Heiler. $100-140. 3 rooms with PB, 2 with FP and 1 suite. Breakfast included in rates. Types of meals: Full gourmet bkfst. Beds: QT. Clock radio in room. Air conditioning. TV, VCR, library, parlor games, telephone and fireplace on premises. Antiquing, live theater, parks, shopping, sports car racing and slots nearby.

"We have stayed at inns for 15 years, and yours is at the top of the list as best ever!"

Hillbrook Inn

Summit Point Rd (Route 13)
Charles Town, WV 25414
(304)725-4223 (800)304-4223 Fax:(304)725-4455
E-mail: info@hillbrookinn.com
Web: www.hillbrookinn.com

Circa 1700. This graceful English Tudor inn meanders down the hillside overlooking a pond framed by daffodils and 18 acres of estate grounds that include streams, gardens and wooded

walks. The land once belonged to George Washington, and although most of the current structure was built in 1920, part began in the 1700s. Decorated in a European country-house style, the inn is replete with rich dark woods and interesting pieces that demand a lengthy stay to fully enjoy. The inn is often the location for elegant events and is known for its seven-course, prix-fixe candlelight dinners served at 8 p.m. Dinners are $75 per person and include house wines. The innkeepers do not accept single-night reservations without dinner.

Innkeeper(s): Gretchen Carroll. $200-325. 11 rooms with PB, 5 with FP. Breakfast included in rates. Types of meals: Full gourmet bkfst, veg bkfst, early coffee/tea, gourmet lunch, afternoon tea, snacks/refreshments, gourmet dinner and room service. Restaurant on premises. Beds: KQD. Modem hook-up, data port, cable TV, VCR, reading lamp, CD player, ceiling fan, telephone, coffeemaker and desk in room. Central air. Fax, library, parlor games and fireplace on premises. Weddings, small meetings, family reunions and seminars hosted. Antiquing, art galleries, bicycling, canoeing/kayaking, fishing, golf, live theater, museums, parks, shopping, sporting events, water sports, wineries and horse and car race tracks nearby.

Publicity: *Great Country Inn Dining Out.*

The Washington House Inn

216 S George St
Charles Town, WV 25414-1632
(304)725-7923 (800)297-6957 Fax:(304)728-5150
E-mail: emailus@washingtonhouseinnwv.com
Web: www.washingtonhouseinnwv.com

Circa 1899. This three-story brick Victorian was built by the descendants of President Washington's brothers, John Augustine and Samuel. Carved oak mantels, spacious guest rooms, antique furnishings and refreshments served on the wraparound veranda or gazebo make the inn memorable. For business travelers, data ports are available. Harpers Ferry National Historic Park, Antietam, and the Shenandoah and Potomac rivers are all within a 15-minute drive. Thoroughbred racing, slot machines and car racing are some of the popular area attractions.

Innkeeper(s): Mel & Nina Vogel. $99-175. 7 rooms with PB, 1 suite and 1 conference room. Breakfast and snacks/refreshments included in rates. Types of meals: Full bkfst and early coffee/tea. Beds: QT. Cable TV, reading lamp, ceiling fan, clock radio, telephone and desk in room. Air conditioning. VCR, fax, copier, parlor games, Internet and antiques and collectibles for sale on premises. Small meetings, family reunions and seminars hosted. Antiquing, fishing, golf, live theater, parks, shopping, water sports, history, museums, horse racing, car racing and slots nearby.

Publicity: *Washington Post - Feb 03, Good Housekeeping - April 03, Travel Holiday - May 03, Recreation News - May 03, Woman's Day and The Today Show.*

Charleston   F3

Brass Pineapple B&B

1611 Virginia St E
Charleston, WV 25311-2113
(304)344-0748 (800)CAL-LWVA Fax:(304)344-0748
E-mail: pineapp104@aol.com
Web: www.wvweb.com/brasspineapplebandb

Circa 1910. Original oak paneling, leaded and stained glass are among the architectural highlights at this smoke-free inn that graces the historic district near the Capitol Complex. Guest bedrooms feature thoughtful amenities including terry robes and hair dryers as well as technology for business needs. A full breakfast consisting of tea, juices, fruit, muffins, waffles, quiche, basil tomatoes and cottage fries, is served in the dining room. Dietary requirements can be met upon request.

Innkeeper(s): Lisa. $89-129. 6 rooms with PB and 1 suite. Breakfast, afternoon tea and snacks/refreshments included in rates. Types of meals: Full bkfst and early coffee/tea. Beds: KQT. Cable TV, VCR, reading lamp, clock radio, telephone, desk, robes and voice mail in room. Air conditioning. Fax, copier and parlor games on premises. Small meetings hosted. Antiquing, fishing, golf, live theater, parks, shopping, sporting events, tennis, water sports, horseback riding and river cruises nearby.

Publicity: *Mid-Atlantic Country, Country Inns, Gourmet, Charlestonian, Charleston Daily Mail, Gourmet, Southern Living, Recommended Country Inns and News 8.*

"Charming, convenient location, lovely antiques, appealing decor. Extremely clean; excellent service from Lisa and the staff."

Elkins   E6

The Post House Bed & Breakfast

306 Robert E Lee Ave
Elkins, WV 26241-3210
(304)636-1792

Circa 1930. Experience down-home hospitality at this brick, Cape Cod-style country home. Socialize by the fireplace in the large gathering room with TV and VCR. Comfortable guest bedrooms feature spacious accommodations. Linger over a generous continental-plus breakfast. Relax on the front porch. The park-like setting of the backyard includes a children's playhouse. Be sure to schedule an appointment for a certified massage. Nearby Canaan Valley offers year-round activities and mountain scenery.

Innkeeper(s): JoAnn Post Barlow. $65. 4 rooms, 2 with PB and 1 suite. Types of meals: Early coffee/tea. Beds: DT. Cable TV, VCR, reading lamp, stereo, refrigerator, snack bar, clock radio, telephone, coffeemaker and desk in room. Central air. Library, fireplace and gift shop on premises. Small meetings hosted. Antiquing, downhill skiing and shopping nearby.

Tunnel Mountain B&B

Rt 1, Box 59-1
Elkins, WV 26241-9711
(304)636-1684 (888)211-9123

Circa 1939. Nestled on five acres of wooded land, this three-story Fieldstone home offers privacy in a peaceful setting. Rooms are tastefully decorated with antiques, collectibles and crafts. Each bedroom boasts a view of the surrounding mountains.

The chestnut and knotty pine woodwork accentuate the decor. The fireplace in the large common room is a great place for warming up after a day of touring or skiing. The area is home to a number of interesting events, including a Dulcimer festival and the state's largest festival, the Mountain State Forest Festival.

Historic Interest: Rich Mountain Battlefield (20 miles), Halliehurst Mansion (4 miles), Beverly Museum (10 miles), Historic Elkins Walking Tour (4 miles), Beverly Historic Cemetery (10 miles), Old Mill (20 miles).

Innkeeper(s): Anne & Paul Beardslee. $80-85. 3 rooms with PB. Breakfast included in rates. Types of meals: Country bkfst. Beds: QD. Cable TV, reading lamp and clock radio in room. Air conditioning. Parlor games, telephone, fireplace and one great room on premises. Antiquing, art galleries, beach, bicycling, canoeing/kayaking, cross-country skiing, downhill skiing, fishing, golf, hiking, horseback riding, live theater, museums, parks, shopping, sporting events, tennis, water sports, rock climbing and mountain biking nearby.

Publicity: *Blue Ridge Country, Washington Post and WBOY.*

Lewisburg   H5

The General Lewis

301 E Washington St
Lewisburg, WV 24901-1425
(304)645-2600 (800)628-4454 Fax:(304)645-2600

Circa 1834. This gracious Federal-style inn boasts a columned veranda, flower gardens and long lawns. Patrick Henry and Thomas Jefferson registered at the inn's walnut desk, which was retrieved from an old hot springs resort in the area. A stagecoach that once delivered travelers to springs on the James River and Kanawha Turnpike, rests under an arbor. American antiques are featured throughout the inn, and

Memory Hall displays household items and tools once used by local pioneers. Nearby are state parks, national forests, streams and rivers, as well as sites of the Revolutionary and Civil wars.

Historic Interest: Civil War Cemetery, Carnegie Hall, Pearl S. Buck's Birthplace.

Innkeeper(s): The Morgan Family. $99-145. 23 rooms with PB and 2 suites. Types of meals: Early coffee/tea. Restaurant on premises. Beds: QD. Cable TV, reading lamp, clock radio, telephone and desk in room. Air conditioning. Fax, copier, parlor games and fireplace on premises. Limited handicap access. Weddings hosted.

Publicity: *National Geographic Traveler, Colonial Homes and Travel & Leisure.*

"Personality, charm and gracious service."

Martinsburg   D9

Boydville, The Inn at Martinsburg

601 S Queen St
Martinsburg, WV 25401-3103
(304)263-1448

Circa 1812. This Georgian estate was saved from burning by Union troops only by a specific proclamation from President Lincoln dated July 18, 1864. Tall maples line the long driveway leading up to the house. Guests can relax in rockers original to the inn on the spacious porch while gazing at 10 acres of lawns. The entry hall retains the original wallpaper brought from England in 1812 and hand-painted murals, fireplaces, and antiques adorn the spacious guest rooms. Sunlight filters through tree tops onto estate-sized lawns and gardens.

Historic Interest: Antietam Battlefield, Harpers Ferry, Berkeley Springs.

Innkeeper(s): LaRue Frye. $145. 7 rooms with PB and 1 conference room. Breakfast included in rates. Types of meals: Cont plus and early coffee/tea. Beds: QDT. Air conditioning. Library, parlor games and fireplace on premises. Weddings and family reunions hosted. Antiquing, downhill skiing, golf, live theater, shopping and Civil War sites nearby.

Publicity: *Washington Post, Mid-Atlantic Country and Colonial Homes.*

"Your gracious home, hospitality and excellent amenities were enjoyed so much. Such a fine job of innkeeping."

Point Pleasant   E2

Stone Manor

12 Main St
Point Pleasant, WV 25550-1026
(304)675-3442

Circa 1887. This stone Victorian sits on the banks of the Kanawha River with a front porch that faces the river. Point Pleasant Battle Monument Park, adjacent to the inn, was built to commemorate the location of the first battle of the Revolutionary War. In the National Register, the inn was once the home of a family who ran a ferry boat crossing for the Ohio and Kanawha rivers. Now restored, the house is decorated with Victorian antiques and offers a pleasant garden with a Victorian fish pond and fountain.

Innkeeper(s): Janice & Tom Vance. $50. 3 rooms, 3 with FP. Breakfast included in rates. Types of meals: Full bkfst. Beds: QD. VCR and reading lamp in room. Air conditioning. Telephone and fireplace on premises.

Romney   D8

Hampshire House 1884

165 N Grafton St
Romney, WV 26757-1616
(304)822-7171

Circa 1884. Located near the south branch of the Potomac River, the garden here has old boxwoods and walnut trees. The inn features ornate brickwork; tall, narrow windows; and fireplaces with handsome period mantels. A sitting room with a well-stocked library, a cozy patio and a music room with an antique pump organ are favorite places. On-site massage available. One guest room has been renovated to allow full wheelchair accessibility.

Innkeeper(s): Jane & Scott Simmons. $75-95. 5 rooms with PB, 3 with FP and 1 conference room. Breakfast included in rates. Types of meals: Full bkfst, early coffee/tea and snacks/refreshments. Beds: QDT. Cable TV, VCR, reading lamp, clock radio, telephone and desk in room. Air conditioning. TV, bicycles, parlor games, fireplace and therapeutic massage on premises. Small meetings hosted. Antiquing, canoeing/kayaking, fishing, hiking, museums, shopping, water sports, massage and Civil War museum nearby.

Publicity: *Hampshire Review, Mid-Atlantic Country and Weekend Journal.*

"Your personal attention made us feel at home immediately."

Shinnston   D5

Gillum House Bed & Breakfast

35 Walnut St
Shinnston, WV 26431
(304)592-0177 (888)592-0177 Fax:(304)592-1882

Circa 1912. The architectural style of a 1912 house is reflected in this comfortable inn. Original works of art, painted by the one of the innkeepers, grace the walls. The second-floor library offers books to savor and finish reading at home. Antique-filled guest bedrooms pamper with fresh flowers, candles, Egyptian cotton or flannel linens, down comforters and fluffy robes. Breakfast is a healthy, low-fat culinary delight, accented with locally made maple syrup. The nearby West Fork River Trail entertains hikers, bicyclists and equestrians.

Historic Interest: It was the home of the second and last B&O Railroad Station Agent who was also a mayor.

Innkeeper(s): Kathleen A. Panek. $57-67. 3 rooms and 1 conference room. Breakfast included in rates. Types of meals: Full bkfst, veg bkfst, early coffee/tea and picnic lunch. Beds: QD. Cable TV, VCR, reading lamp, clock radio and decorative fireplace in room. Air conditioning. Fax, copier, bicycles, library, parlor games, telephone, laundry facility, gift shop, overnight stabling 2.5 miles away and escort service provided from I-79 exit on premises. Antiquing, bicycling, fishing, golf, hiking, museums, parks, shopping, sporting events, wineries, 9 covered bridges, 7 state parks, Chapel of Perpetual Adoration, 2 drive-in theaters, several hand-blown glass factories with tours, historic sites, Mother's Day shrine, rail-trails and birding nearby.

Publicity: *Pittsburgh Post-Gazette, Clarksburg Exponent-Telegram, Shinnston News, Akron Beacon Journal, Blue Ridge Outdoors, C-FAX, WBOY, "Inn to Inn Hiking Guide to the Virginias," Off the Beaten Path- West Virginia, Fourth Edition (vignette), Good Morning West Virginia and Vol. II.*

Wisconsin

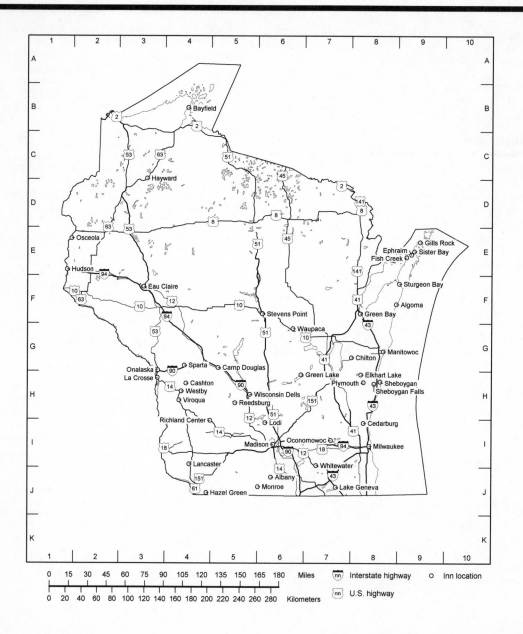

0 15 30 45 60 75 90 105 120 135 150 165 180 Miles

0 20 40 60 80 100 120 140 160 180 200 220 240 260 280 Kilometers

⌐nn⌐ Interstate highway   ○ Inn location

⌐nn⌐ U.S. highway

Albany J6

Albany House

405 S Mill St
Albany, WI 53502-9502
(608)862-3636 (866)977-7000 Fax:(608)862-1837
E-mail: innkeeper@albanyhouse.com
Web: www.albanyhouse.com

Circa 1908. The brick walkway, French-tiled foyer, over-stuffed furniture and abundance of flowers both inside and out set the comfortable tone for this three-story inn. A baby grand piano in the large foyer and fireplace in the living room also add to the

pleasant atmosphere. The guest rooms have large windows overlooking the garden and are furnished with many antiques and collectibles. Outside, maple and black walnut trees and various gardens grace the inn's three-acre property. Guests can tour New Glarus, a village known as America's Little Switzerland, which is a short drive away. Guests also can enjoy a bicycle ride on the nearby Sugar River Trail or canoe on the Sugar River.

Historic Interest: The Tallman House, the last existing house where Lincoln slept, is 25 miles away. The original Green County Courthouse with its restored clock tower is in Monroe, a 15-mile drive. The state capitol is 30 miles north.

Innkeeper(s): Ken & Margie Stoup. $65-170. 6 rooms, 4 with PB, 2 with FP and 1 suite. Breakfast and snacks/refreshments included in rates. Types of meals: Full gourmet bkfst, veg bkfst and early coffee/tea. Beds: KQD. Cable TV, VCR, reading lamp, CD player, refrigerator, ceiling fan, clock radio and telephone in room. Air conditioning. Fax, copier, library, parlor games, fireplace, swings, hammock, horseshoe and croquet on premises. Weddings, small meetings, family reunions and seminars hosted. Antiquing, bicycling, canoeing/kayaking, cross-country skiing, fishing, golf, hiking, parks, shopping and wineries nearby.

Publicity: *Madison, Monroe Evening Times, Silent Sports and Video: A Video Tour of Wisconsin's Bed & Breakfasts.*

"Was even more than I expected."

Algoma F8

Amberwood Inn

N7136 Hwy 42, Lakeshore Dr
Algoma, WI 54201
(920)487-3471
E-mail: innkeeper@amberwoodinn.com
Web: www.amberwoodinn.com

Circa 1925. With 300 feet of Lake Michigan beach front before them, guests at this beautifully renovated Cape Cod home can enjoy a sunrise over the lake from their rooms. Rooms are furnished with antiques and include French doors opening to private decks.

Breakfast is served in the dining room, although "breakfast in bed" requests are honored, as well. Afterwards spend the day on the beach or visit the villages of Door County. Then come home to Amberwood's Jacuzzi or sauna, sit around a beach side campfire or read by your private fireplace. The

favorite activity is listening to the waves and watching the stars. Nearby are marinas and boat ramps, hiking, cycling and cross-country ski trails. Sturgeon Bay is 20 minutes away. Algoma offers antique and craft shops also, as well as winery tours, festivals and fine restaurants.

Historic Interest: Historic Door County Wisconsin and Packer Hall of Fame are among the area's historic offerings.

Innkeeper(s): Mark & Karen Rittle. $89-139. 7 rooms with PB, 7 with FP. Breakfast included in rates. Types of meals: Full bkfst. Beds: KQT. TV, reading lamp, refrigerator, clock radio, hot tub/spa, whirlpool and wet bars in room. Telephone, fireplace, refrigerators and private entrances on premises. Antiquing, fishing, live theater, parks, shopping and water sports nearby.

"Very personable, friendly, down-to-earth."

Bayfield B4

Old Rittenhouse Inn

301 Rittenhouse Ave, PO Box 584
Bayfield, WI 54814-0584
(715)779-5111 (800)779-2129
E-mail: frontdsk@rittenhouseinn.com
Web: www.rittenhouseinn.com

Circa 1892. Two historic Queen Anne mansions, a guest house and a private cottage comprise this elegant Victorian inn and gourmet restaurant just a few blocks from downtown. Under massive gables, a wraparound veranda is filled with white wicker furniture, geraniums and petunias. The inn boasts 22 working fireplaces amidst antique furnishings. Well-appointed guest bedrooms and luxury suites offer a variety of romantic amenities that may include whirlpools as well as views of Madeline Island and Lake Superior. The two-story Fountain Cottage is just uphill. For breakfast indulge in baked muffins and breads served with Rittenhouse Jams and Jellies accompanied by Wild Bayfield Blueberry Crisp or Moonglow Pears Poached in White Zinfandel.

Innkeeper(s): Larry E. Cicero. $99-299. 24 rooms with PB, 19 with FP and 4 suites. Breakfast included in rates. Types of meals: Cont plus, gourmet lunch, gourmet dinner and room service. Restaurant on premises. Beds: KQD. Reading lamp and 14 luxury rooms/suites with whirlpool in room. Telephone and fireplace on premises. Limited handicap access. Weddings, small meetings and family reunions hosted. Shopping nearby.

Publicity: *Wisconsin Trails, Midwest Living, National Geographic Traveler, Country Inns, Minnesota Monthly, Bon Appetit, Gourmet and Better Homes and Gardens.*

"The whole decor, the room, the staff and the food were superb! Your personalities and talents give a great warmth to the inn."

Camp Douglas G5

Sunnyfield Farm B&B

N6692 Batko Rd
Camp Douglas, WI 54618
(608)427-3686 (888)839-0232
E-mail: soltvedt@mwt.net
Web: www.sunnyfield.net

Circa 1899. Scenic bluffs and rich land surround this 100-year-old, three-story farmhouse boasting 10-foot ceilings. Lovingly restored, the original hardwood floors and hand-carved oak woodwork reside easily with brass ceiling tiles and family heirlooms. Guest bedrooms feature a country decor with handmade quilts and stenciling. The Rose Room has an adjoining room that is perfect for families or groups. A private studio apartment on the third floor offers a cozy yet spacious suite with living room, kitchen and sky windows for stargazing. Wake up to a complete country breakfast served in the spacious dining room. Three of the 160 acres are manicured lawns to enjoy. Wisconsin Dells is just 30 minutes away.

Innkeeper(s): Susanne & John Soltvedt. $65-110. 4 rooms, 1 with PB. Breakfast included in rates. Types of meals: Country bkfst. Beds: QT. Reading lamp and ceiling fan in room. Library, parlor games and telephone on premises. Antiquing, art galleries, bicycling, cross-country skiing, fishing, golf, hiking, parks, shopping and water sports nearby.

Cashton   H4

Ages Past Country House B&B

1223 Front Street
Cashton, WI 54619
(608)654-5950 (888)322-5494 Fax:(608)543-5709
E-mail: innkeeper@agespast.net
Web: www.agespast.net

Circa 1898. Once a Catholic Rectory, this Country Victorian house near the Elroy Sparta Trail has been painstakingly restored and furnished with antiques and chandeliers from Belgium. An oak staircase is accented by stained-glass skylight. Relax in the lounge with a selection of videos and reading materials. Elegant guest bedrooms feature clawfoot tubs, showers, terry robes and slippers. Thoughtful details include cut flowers, CD players and VCRs. Fresh-baked muffins, almond coconut French toast, honey baked ham and Amish maple syrup are some of the breakfast treats to indulge in. The Back Door Cafe dining room is transformed in the evening with a European flair. The one-acre grounds are well-landscaped with garden benches, fountains, Grecian statues, lawn swings and grape arbors.

Historic Interest: The home was the Catholic Rectory for 80 years and has always been a focal point for the community.

Innkeeper(s): Carl & Barbara Bargabos. $95-115. 4 rooms with PB. Breakfast included in rates. Types of meals: Full gourmet bkfst, early coffee/tea, lunch, picnic lunch, snacks/refreshments, dinner and room service. Restaurant on premises. Beds: KQ. Modem hook-up, data port, cable TV, VCR, reading lamp, CD player, clock radio, telephone, turn-down service, bathrobes, slippers and hair dryers in room. Central air. TV, fax, copier, library, parlor games, fireplace and full service restaurant and bar on premises. Weddings, small meetings, family reunions and seminars hosted. Antiquing, art galleries, bicycling, canoeing/kayaking, cross-country skiing, downhill skiing, fishing, golf, hiking, horseback riding, parks, hunting and snowmobiling nearby.

Cedarburg   I8

Stagecoach Inn B&B

W 61 N 520 Washington Ave
Cedarburg, WI 53012
(262)375-0208 (888)375-0208 Fax:(262)375-6170
E-mail: info@stagecoach-inn-wi.com
Web: www.stagecoach-inn-wi.com

Circa 1853. This historic Greek Revival inn has been welcoming travelers since its earliest days, when it served as a stagecoach stop between Milwaukee and Green Bay. The innkeepers used 19th-century photographs to help authenticate the inn's meticulous restoration. In addition to the nine

guest rooms, the inn houses a pub where the continental-plus breakfasts are served in the mornings and complimentary wine in the afternoon. The innkeepers have owned Stagecoach Inn since the early 1980s. In 1991, they restored Weber Haus, an 1847 house across the street from the inn. Weber Haus offers three suites with whirlpool tubs. Two of the suites include a fireplace, and there is a secret garden to explore and enjoy. Many attractions are within walking distance, including a historic district, antique shops, cultural center, galleries, a winery and restaurants.

Historic Interest: Cedarburg, known as the antique capital of Wisconsin, is listed in the National Register. Milwaukee, about 20 minutes north of the inn, offers many museums and historic buildings.

Innkeeper(s): Brook & Liz Brown. $80-145. 12 rooms with PB, 2 with FP, 6 suites and 1 conference room. Breakfast included in rates. Types of meals: Cont plus and room service. Beds: QDT. Cable TV, reading lamp, CD player, telephone and suite has whirlpool tub in room. Air conditioning. Fax on premises. Antiquing, art galleries, shopping, wineries, Cedar Creek Settlement and Pioneer village nearby.

Publicity: *Milwaukee, Visions, Midwest Living, Travel Host, Innsider, Wisconsin Trails, Country Life, Business Journal, Country Living, Chicago Tribune, Country Crafts and Better Homes/Crafts.*

"Cedarburg is a lovely town and this is a great place from which to explore it. We hope to return."

The Washington House Inn

W 62 N 573 Washington Ave
Cedarburg, WI 53012-1941
(262)375-3550 (800)554-4717 Fax:(262)375-9422
E-mail: whinn@execpc.com
Web: www.washingtonhouseinn.com

Circa 1886. Completely renovated, this three-story cream city brick building is in the National Register. Rooms are appointed in a country Victorian style and feature antiques, whirlpool baths, vases of flowers and fireplaces. The original guest registry, more than 100 years old, is displayed proudly in the lobby, and a marble trimmed fireplace is often lit for the afternoon wine and cheese hour. Breakfast is continental and is available in the gathering room, often including recipes from a historic Cedarburg cookbook for items such as homemade muffins, cakes and breads.

Historic Interest: National Register.

Innkeeper(s): Wendy Porterfield. $92-232. 34 rooms with PB, 3 suites and 1 conference room. Breakfast included in rates. Types of meals: Cont plus and snacks/refreshments. Beds: KQD. Cable TV, VCR, reading lamp, ceiling fan, clock radio and telephone in room. Air conditioning. TV, fax, copier and sauna on premises. Weddings, small meetings, family reunions and seminars hosted. Antiquing, cross-country skiing, fishing, live theater, parks, shopping and sporting events nearby.

Publicity: *Country Home and Chicago Sun-Times.*

Chilton   G8

East Shore Inn

N3049 US Highway 151
Chilton, WI 53014-9445
(920)849-4230 Fax:(920)849-8521
E-mail: eastshorebub@aol.com
Web: www.bbinternet.com/eastshore

Circa 1895. The Bub family purchased this working farm in 1965 and offers guests a truly unique farm atmosphere. The guest cottage is rented out to one group or family at a time, insuring privacy. Relaxation is a priority. Quarters include a kitchen area and game room. Plenty of animals roam the grounds, and you're sure to see foxes, rabbits or deer. The surrounding area offers plenty of attractions, including cheese factories, boutiques, fruit farms and many outdoor activities.

Historic Interest: The inn is situated on what was a Native American reservation. Indian burial grounds are about five miles from the inn.

Innkeeper(s): Janice, Henry, Neil Bub. $75. 4 rooms with PB. Beds: DT. TV, VCR, reading lamp, stereo, refrigerator, ceiling fan, clock radio, telephone and coffeemaker in room. Central air. Library and parlor games on premises. Antiquing, cross-country skiing, fishing, water sports and snow tubes nearby.

Publicity: *Appleton Post Crescent, Chilton Times, Milwaukee Journal, Channel 11 and selected by Arrington's B&B Journal as a winner in their top 15 B&B/Country Inns for Family Vacations Award.*

"Our third trip. The kids love the kittens and feeding the calves. Beautiful sunset over the lake."

Eau Claire   F3

Otter Creek Inn

2536 Hwy 12, PO Box 3183
Eau Claire, WI 54702-3183
(715)832-2945 Fax:(715)832-4607

Circa 1920. On a hillside overlooking a creek is this Tudor-style inn, surrounded by oaks and pines. Visitors immediately feel welcome as they make their way up the inn's curved pebblestone walk and step into a house with country Victorian

decor. Each of the guest rooms includes a double whirlpool tub, and many have a fireplace. The Rose Room, often the choice of honeymooners, features a cloverleaf-shaped whirlpool tub that overlooks

the gardens and gazebo. The spacious inn provides many spots for relaxation, including a gazebo, the great room with its inviting fireplace and a roomy patio surrounding the in-ground heated swimming pool.

Innkeeper(s): Shelley & Randy Hansen. $100-190. 6 rooms with PB, 4 with FP. Breakfast included in rates. Types of meals: Full bkfst, early coffee/tea and snacks/refreshments. Beds: KQ. Modem hook-up, cable TV, VCR, reading lamp, refrigerator, clock radio, telephone, coffeemaker and double whirlpools in room. Air conditioning. Swimming, parlor games and fireplace on premises. Antiquing, beach, bicycling, canoeing/kayaking, cross-country skiing, fishing, golf, live theater, museums, parks, shopping, tennis and water sports nearby.

Publicity: *Country, Country Inns, Milwaukee Journal, St. Paul Pioneer Press, Country Gazette and Wisconsin West.*

"This is the perfect place to recharge your 'couple batteries.'"

Elkhart Lake   H8

Boarding House B&B

121 S East, PO Box 746
Elkhart Lake, WI 53020
(920)876-3616

Circa 1923. Typical of the local architecture in the early 1900s, this house was built in the Four-Square style. It was named after its service of housing many of the surrounding area's resort workers. Comfortable places to gather include the living room and game room, both furnished with antiques. Guest bedrooms feature terry robes and toiletry baskets. The main dining room showcases a full breakfast that offers dishes like custard French toast with warm berries. The famous Road

America racetrack is just two miles away.

Innkeeper(s): Bob & Cindy Roska. $85-130. 5 rooms. Breakfast included in rates. Types of meals: Country bkfst. Beds: KQDT. Cable TV, clock radio and telephone in room. Central air. Copier on premises. Antiquing, beach, fishing, golf, hiking and sports car racing nearby.

Ephraim   E9

Eagle Harbor Inn

9914 Water St
Ephraim, WI 54211-0588
(920)854-2121 (800)324-5427 Fax:(920)854-2121

Circa 1946. The Eagle Harbor Inn is located in the Historic District and offers a variety of accommodations. Rooms in the inn are decorated with antiques. Relax in one and two-bedroom suites with six-foot whirlpool tubs and two-sided fire-

places, full kitchens and private decks. Breakfast (optional for guests in the suites) is home cooked and served next to the garden in summertime. Afternoon refreshments are offered to all guests. There is an

indoor current pool, sauna and fitness room. A scenic sandy beach is a block away. Nearby are shops and galleries, and a half-hour drive leads guests to Rock Island, home of Wisconsin's first settlers. Door County Peninsula offers the largest selection of lighthouses in any U.S. county.

Innkeeper(s): Nedd & Natalie Neddersen. $74-238. 41 rooms, 7 with PB, 3 with FP and 32 suites. Types of meals: Full gourmet bkfst, early coffee/tea and afternoon tea. Beds: Q. Cable TV, VCR, reading lamp, stereo, refrigerator, ceiling fan, clock radio, telephone, desk, hot tub/spa, suites have whirlpool and fireplaces and kitchen in room. Air conditioning. Fax, copier, spa, swimming, sauna, library, parlor games, gardens, croquette, playground and picnic areas with woods and stream on premises. Limited handicap access. Weddings, small meetings, family reunions and seminars hosted. Cross-country skiing, fishing, golf, live theater, parks, shopping, tennis, water sports, antique shopping, historic walking tours, horse-drawn carriage rides and art classes nearby.

Publicity: *Door County Advocate, Milwaukee Business Journal, Chicago Sun Times, Wisconsin Trails and Travel Holiday.*

"From the friendly greeting when we arrived, to the elegant room, to the wonderful four-poster bed, our stay has been everything we hoped."

Fish Creek   E9

Thorp House Inn & Cottages

4135 Bluff Ln, PO Box 490
Fish Creek, WI 54212
(920)868-2444
E-mail: innkeeper@thorphouseinn.com
Web: www.thorphouseinn.com

Circa 1902. Every season surrounds this bed & breakfast inn and its cottages with a natural beauty. Listed in the National Register, an extensive restoration has preserved details like

authentic lighting and documentary wallcoverings. Fine antique furnishings and accessories accented with European lace enhance the gracious ambiance. Relax in the library or by the fire in the double parlor. Warm hos-

pitality is enjoyed on the summer sitting porch with refreshments from the stocked pantry. Choose a well-appointed guest bedroom or stay in one of the quaint country cottages. A beach house is also available.

Historic Interest: The Asa Thorp Log Cabin and Noble House Museum are one block away. The Church of the Attonement is three blocks away, and the Peninsula Park Lighthouse is four miles from the inn.

Innkeeper(s): Christine & Sverre Falck-Pedersen. $95-195. 5 rooms with PB and 6 cottages. Types of meals: Cont plus and early coffee/tea. Beds: KQDT. Reading lamp, refrigerator, three with whirlpool and two with fireplace in room. Central air. Parlor games, telephone and fireplace on premises. Antiquing, cross-country skiing, fishing, live theater, parks, shopping, water sports, summer art school and music festival nearby.

Publicity: *Green Bay Press-Gazette, Milwaukee Journal/Sentinel, McCall's, Minnesota PM and Madison PM.*

"Amazing attention to detail from restoration to the furnishings. A very first-class experience."

Gills Rock   E9

Harbor House Inn

12666 Hwy 42
Gills Rock, WI 54210
(920)854-5196
Web: www.door-county-inn.com

Circa 1904. Built by the Weborgs more than 100 years ago, the inn has stayed in the family and been carefully restored. The main house features suites and guest bedrooms with classic Victorian and Scandinavian country decor. Danish Cottage continues that theme, and Troll Cottage is a nautical cabin. The Lighthouse overlooks the quaint fishing village. A gazebo and private decks offer sunset and harbor views. A generous continental-plus breakfast is served in the sitting room. Enjoy a Norwegian sauna and spa or take a short walk along the beach road.

Historic Interest: Nautical Museum, many lighthouses.

Innkeeper(s): David & Else Weborg. $69-185. 15 rooms with PB, 2 with FP and 2 cottages. Breakfast included in rates. Types of meals: Cont plus and early coffee/tea. Beds: KQDT. TV, reading lamp, refrigerator, ceiling fan, clock radio, microwaves, kitchenettes and decks in room. Air conditioning. Spa, sauna, bicycles, parlor games, telephone, fireplace, gas grills, hot tub and bike rentals on premises. Limited handicap access. Antiquing, art galleries, bicycling, fishing, golf, hiking, live theater, museums, parks, shopping, water sports, island ferry, sunset cruise, Nautical Museum and historical lighthouses nearby.

Publicity: *Wisconsin State Journal and Travel & Leisure.*

"Lovely inn. Thank you for your hospitality."

Green Bay   F8

The Astor House B&B

637 S Monroe Ave
Green Bay, WI 54301-3614
(920)432-3585 (888)303-6370
E-mail: astor@execpc.com
Web: www.astorhouse.com

Circa 1888. Located in the Astor Historic District, the Astor House is completely surrounded by Victorian homes. Guests have their choice of five rooms, each uniquely decorated for a range of ambiance, from the Vienna Balconies to the Marseilles Garden to the Hong Kong Retreat. The parlor, veranda and many suites feature a grand view of City Centre's lighted church towers. This home is also the first and only

B&B in Green Bay and received the Mayor's Award for Remodeling and Restoration. Business travelers should take notice of the private phone lines in each room, as well as the ability to hook up a modem.

Historic Interest: Green Bay City Centre (8 blocks), Lambeau Field, 1837 Hazelwood Historic Home museum.

Innkeeper(s): Greg & Barbara Robinson. $115-152. 5 rooms with PB, 4 with FP and 3 suites. Breakfast included in rates. Types of meals: Cont plus. Beds: KQDT. Cable TV, VCR, reading lamp, stereo, refrigerator, clock radio, telephone, gas fireplaces and double whirlpool tub (4 of 5 rooms) in room. Air conditioning. Amusement parks, antiquing, cross-country skiing, fishing, live theater, parks, shopping, sporting events and water sports nearby.

Publicity: *Chicago Sun-Times and Corporate Reports.*

Green Lake   H6

McConnell Inn

497 S Lawson Dr
Green Lake, WI 54941-8700
(920)294-6430 (888)238-8625
E-mail: info@mcconnellinn.com
Web: www.mcconnellinn.com

Circa 1901. This stately home features many of its original features, including leaded windows, woodwork, leather wainscoting and parquet floors. Each of the guest rooms includes beds covered with handmade quilts and clawfoot tubs. The grand, master suite comprises the entire third floor and boasts 14-foot vaulted beam ceilings, Victorian walnut furnishings, a Jacuzzi and six-foot oak buffet now converted into a unique bathroom vanity. Innkeeper Mary Jo Johnson, a pastry chef, creates the wonderful pastries that accompany an expansive breakfast with fresh fruit, granola and delectable entrees.

Innkeeper(s): Mary Jo Johnson and Scott Johnson. $60-175. 5 rooms with PB, 2 with FP and 1 suite. Breakfast included in rates. Types of meals: Full gourmet bkfst and early coffee/tea. Beds: KQ. TV, VCR, reading lamp, refrigerator, ceiling fan, clock radio and hot tub/spa in room. Central air. Library, parlor games and telephone on premises. Antiquing, art galleries, beach, bicycling, canoeing/kayaking, cross-country skiing, fishing, golf, hiking, horseback riding, live theater, museums, parks, shopping, sporting events, tennis and water sports nearby.

Hayward   C3

Ross' Teal Lake Lodge & Teal Wing Golf Club

12425 N Ross Rd
Hayward, WI 54843
(715)462-3631
E-mail: amhisinn@teallake.com
Web: www.teallake.com

Circa 1908. Located on 250 acres bordering Teal Lake and Teal River, this is a great vacation spot for families, golfers and fishermen. Most of the Northwoods cabins here are of vertical log construction, and most feature fireplaces and kitchens. There are two beds in each room. Most rooms offer ceiling fans. Fishing guides and a fishing school for both children and adults offers fishing expertise and local folklore. (You'll learn how to catch the prized muskie, a fierce freshwater game fish.) An 18-hole golf course winds through the woods and has been recognized by Wisconsin Golf Magazine as one of the upper Midwest's best courses. Bicycles, tricycles and water bicycles are available to use. A family of eagles nest on the island, and you can watch them feed and learn to fly. Early springtime guests enjoy the otters that scramble around the inn's docks. Picnic and basket lunches are available. Breakfast and dinner are available in the lodge's dining room.

Innkeeper(s): Prudence & Tim Ross. $120-590. 2 suites and 1 conference room. Types of meals: Full bkfst, picnic lunch and dinner. Restaurant on premises. Beds: KDT. Reading lamp, refrigerator, desk and some with ceiling fans in room. Swimming, sauna, bicycles, tennis, library, parlor games, fireplace and golf on premises. Small meetings and family reunions hosted. Antiquing, cross-country skiing, fishing, golf, parks, shopping and water sports nearby.

Hazel Green   J4

Wisconsin House Stagecoach Inn

2105 Main, PO Box 71
Hazel Green, WI 53811-0071
(887)854-2233
E-mail: wishouse@mhtc.net
Web: www.wisconsinhouse.com

Circa 1846. Located in southwest Wisconsin's historic lead mining region, this one-time stagecoach stop will delight antique-lovers. The spacious two-story inn once hosted Ulysses S. Grant, whose home is just across the border in Illinois. One of the inn's guest rooms bears his name and features a walnut four-poster bed. Don't miss the chance to join the Dischs on a Saturday evening for their gourmet dinner, served by reservation only.

Innkeeper(s): Ken & Pat Disch. $75-125. 8 rooms, 6 with PB and 2 suites. Breakfast included in rates. Types of meals: Full gourmet bkfst, early coffee/tea and gourmet dinner. Beds: KQDT. Air conditioning. Copier, library, parlor games and telephone on premises. Weddings, small meetings, family reunions and seminars hosted. Antiquing, bicycling, cross-country skiing, downhill skiing, fishing, live theater and parks nearby.

Publicity: *Travel & Leisure, Milwaukee Magazine, Chicago Magazine, Milwaukee Journal and Wisconsin Trails.*

Hudson   E1

Baker-Brewster, A Victorian Inn

904 Vine St
Hudson, WI 54016
(715)381-2895 (877)381-2895
E-mail: bbinns@bakerbrewster.com
Web: www.bakerbrewster.com

Circa 1882. An outstanding landmark, this 1882 Victorian home has been painstakingly restored. The ambiance of relaxed elegance accents period antiques. Converse with new friends in the parlor. Air-conditioned guest bedrooms feature down-filled pillows and pillow top mattresses. Stay in the namesake Baker Brewster Room with original imported marble fireplace, clawfoot whirlpool tub and Louis XV bed. The Megan Lee Room and The Jessica Rose boast double whirlpool tubs. Savor an incredible four-course breakfast in the dining room. Stroll through the historic rivertown. Massage therapy and laundry services are available.

Innkeeper(s): Robert & Karen Eno. $99-169. 5 rooms with PB. Breakfast and snacks/refreshments included in rates. Types of meals: Full gourmet bkfst, veg bkfst and early coffee/tea. Beds: QD. Cable TV, VCR, reading lamp, clock radio, hot tub/spa and whirlpool in room. Central air. Spa, telephone,

fireplace, smoking on outside porch and cable TV on premises. Weddings, small meetings, family reunions and seminars hosted. Antiquing, art galleries, beach, canoeing/kayaking, cross-country skiing, downhill skiing, fishing, golf, hiking, horseback riding, live theater, museums, parks, shopping, water sports and wineries nearby.

Jefferson-Day House

1109 Third St
Hudson, WI 54016-1220
(715)386-7111
E-mail: jeffersn@pressenter.com
Web: www.jeffersondayhouse.com

Circa 1857. Near the St. Croix River and 30 minutes from Mall of America, the Italianate Jefferson-Day House features five guest rooms with both double whirlpool tubs and gas fireplaces. Antique art and furnishings fill the rooms, and there is a formal dining room and living room. Ask for the Captain's Room and you'll be rewarded with a cedar-lined bathroom, over-sized shower, antique brass bed, and a gas fireplace visible from the whirlpool tub for two. A four-course breakfast is served fireside every morning, and complimentary spirits are offered.

Innkeeper(s): Tom & Sue Tyler. $99-179. 5 rooms with PB, 5 with FP. Breakfast and snacks/refreshments included in rates. Types of meals: Full bkfst. Beds: Q. Reading lamp, clock radio, desk and 5 with double whirlpools in room. Telephone and fireplace on premises. Weddings, small meetings and family reunions hosted. Amusement parks, antiquing, cross-country skiing, downhill skiing, fishing, live theater, parks, shopping, sporting events and water sports nearby.

"Absolute perfection! That's the only way to describe our stay in the wonderful St. Croix suite!"

The Phipps Inn

1005 3rd St
Hudson, WI 54016-1261
(715)386-0800 (888)865-9388
Web: www.phippsinn.com

Circa 1884. In the National Register of Historic Places, Phipps Inn is an outstandingly beautiful example of delicate Queen Anne Victorian architecture. The mansion offers wraparound porches, fluted pilasters, gabled dormers and an octagonal tower that rises three stories high. Located on a historic street in Wisconsin's St. Croix Valley, an appropriate Victorian decor compliments the interior's oak and maple woodwork. Guest rooms and suites offer romantic furnishings and amenities such as brass, canopy or four-poster feather beds, and all feature large whirlpool tubs and fireplaces. There are a variety of rooms to wander into and enjoy, including the music room, billiards room and the inn's two parlors. Four-course breakfasts include a fresh fruit course, a pastry course, an entrée and a dessert. Antique shops, galleries, boutiques and a good selection of restaurants are nearby, as are parks and the St. Croix River. Octagon House, a museum in an 1855 house, is across the street from the inn.

Innkeeper(s): Rich & Mary Ellen Cox. $129-209. 6 rooms with PB. Types of meals: Full gourmet bkfst and early coffee/tea. Beds: Q. Reading lamp, clock radio, double whirlpool and fireplaces in room. Air conditioning. Bicycles on premises. Antiquing, art galleries, museums, parks, shopping and water sports nearby.

La Crosse   H3

Chateau La Crosse

410 Cass St
La Crosse, WI 54601-4508
(608)796-1090 (800)442-7969 Fax:(608)796-0700

Circa 1854. Enter a personal fairy tale when you visit this inviting yet stately stone castle. A destination unto itself, it is the oldest stone house in the state that has been continuously occupied since it was built. In the National Register, the finely crafted interior offers elegant fireplaces, gleaming woodwork and elaborately detailed wood floors, renovated at a cost of more than $1 million. Relax in the elegant common rooms, which include a main parlor, drawing room, dining room, library and music room. If it's a special occasion, request the Master Bedroom to enjoy its masterful hand-painted mural ceiling and faux-painted marble walls complete with gold leaf trim. There's a marble wood-burning fireplace, as well. The bath boasts marble floors and a tub of faux marble with a hand-painted mural of cherubs. The gardens offer a fountain, pond and variety of flowering trees such as a Japanese lilac tree. Red hibiscus, lilac, potted palms, elephant ears, hydrangeas and an arbor with roses completes the garden. A full champagne breakfast includes dishes such as quiche, cinnamon toast, French cashew waffles and usually a breakfast dessert such as cheesecake or peach pie. A gourmet restaurant on the premises offers six private dining rooms.

Innkeeper(s): JoAn Lambert Smith. $125-225. 7 rooms with PB and 1 conference room. Breakfast included in rates. Types of meals: Full gourmet bkfst, veg bkfst, early coffee/tea, gourmet lunch, picnic lunch, afternoon tea, snacks/refreshments, gourmet dinner and room service. Beds: KQ. Modem hook-up, data port, cable TV, reading lamp, stereo, ceiling fan, clock radio, telephone, coffeemaker, desk and hot tub/spa in room. Air conditioning. VCR, fax, copier, spa, library, parlor games, fireplace, laundry facility and full champagne breakfast on premises. Limited handicap access. Antiquing, art galleries, beach, bicycling, canoeing/kayaking, cross-country skiing, downhill skiing, fishing, golf, hiking, live theater, museums, parks, shopping, sporting events and tennis nearby.

Publicity: *LaCrosse Tribune and Home & Garden.*

Lake Geneva   J7

Eleven Gables Inn on Lake Geneva

493 Wrigley Dr
Lake Geneva, WI 53147-2115
(262)248-8393
E-mail: egi@lkgeneva.com
Web: www.lkgeneva.com

Circa 1847. Built as a summer estate, this Carpenter Gothic inn does feature nearly a dozen of its namesake gables. Accommodations include rooms in the main house, as well as the restored coach house that is ideal for families or couples traveling together. The innkeeper has lived in the house since the 1950s and has decorated the historic home with what she describes as "Jackie O"-era furnishings. The innkeeper has been opening her home to guests since the 1960s. The homemade breakfasts include entrees such as a soufflé or perhaps eggs Benedict.

Innkeeper(s): A.F. Milliette. $105-219. 8 rooms with PB, 8 with FP, 2 suites, 2 cottages and 2 conference rooms. Breakfast included in rates. Types of meals: Full bkfst and veg bkfst. Beds: KQ. Cable TV, VCR, reading lamp, stereo, refrigerator, ceiling fan, snack bar, coffeemaker, desk, hot tub/spa and

some with A/C in room. Fax, copier, fireplace and swimming in lake on premises. Handicap access. Weddings, small meetings and seminars hosted. Amusement parks, antiquing, beach, bicycling, canoeing/kayaking, cross-country skiing, fishing, golf, hiking, horseback riding, parks, shopping, tennis and water sports nearby.

Publicity: *Chicago Tribune and Lifestyles.*

General Boyd's B&B

W2915 County Trunk BB
Lake Geneva, WI 53147
(262)248-3543 Fax:(262)248-3362
E-mail: morton4u@execpc.com
Web: www.generalboydsbb.com

Circa 1843. Five acres with white oaks, old barns, perennial gardens and a meadow of wild flowers surround this Colonial Revival farmhouse. Notable for its fourth generation owner, Sue Morton, the great granddaughter to General Boyd, the home has always remained in the Boyd family. The collections of generations, including letters and handiwork, are available for guests to enjoy, and there are a number of antique furnishings original to the home. Guest rooms include the General's Room with a sitting area and views of the garden. Quiche, home-baked breads and fresh cobbler are menu items at breakfast, often featuring fruit and vegetables raised on the premises. It's a five-minute walk to the lake and Big Foot State Park, and restaurants are also within walking distance. The innkeepers will allow you to park your boat trailer on the property and are available to help arrange fishing guides.

Innkeeper(s): Bob & Sue Morton. $95-140. 4 rooms with PB. Breakfast and afternoon tea included in rates. Types of meals: Full gourmet bkfst, veg bkfst, early coffee/tea and snacks/refreshments. Beds: KQ. Cable TV, VCR, reading lamp, ceiling fan and clock radio in room. Central air. Fax, copier, library, parlor games, telephone, fireplace and laundry facility on premises. Weddings, small meetings, family reunions and seminars hosted. Antiquing, art galleries, beach, bicycling, cross-country skiing, downhill skiing, fishing, golf, hiking, horseback riding, live theater, museums, parks, shopping, tennis, water sports, boating and snowmobiling nearby.

Publicity: *The Week, Lake Geneva Regional News November 21 and 2002.*

Lazy Cloud Lodge B&B

W4033 Hwy 50
Lake Geneva, WI 53147
(262)275-3322 Fax:(262)275-8340
E-mail: love@lazycloud.com
Web: www.lazycloud.com

Circa 1920. Romance is the innkeepers' passion at this secluded Cape Cod inn built as a polo lodge in the 1920s. Author J.D. Salinger stayed here while writing Catcher in the Rye, and Paul Newman is another celebrity guest. The lodge features spacious guest suites and private cottages that all include a whirlpool for two in the sitting or living room within view of the fireplace. An intimate ambiance is inspired by canopy beds, fine linens and candles. Enjoy the inn's signature sticky pecan rolls, fresh fruit and homemade granola for breakfast on the cobblestone patio or brought to the room. Flowers, chocolates, and in-room massages can be arranged. Order the Enchanted Evening Picnic Basket for a quiet fireside dinner for two. Sitting on three gorgeous acres, the gazebo in the English Country gardens, or the hammocks among the trees are favorite spots to share with a loved one. Lake Geneva is just minutes away.

Innkeeper(s): Keith & Carol Tiffany. $120-240. 19 rooms with PB, 19 with FP and 17 suites. Breakfast and snacks/refreshments included in rates. Types of meals: Cont plus and picnic lunch. Beds: KQ. Reading lamp, refrigerator, snack bar, clock radio, whirlpool tub and fireplace in room. Air conditioning.

VCR, fax, copier, library, telephone and fireplace on premises. Limited handicap access. Antiquing, cross-country skiing, downhill skiing, fishing, golf, live theater, parks, shopping, sporting events, tennis and water sports nearby.

Publicity: *Walworth Week, Press Publications and Channel 58 Milwaukee Evening News.*

"This room is by far a wonderful "cloud" in the heavens of the Lazy Cloud."

Roses A Bed & Breakfast

429 S Lake Shore Dr
Lake Geneva, WI 53147-2128
(262)248-4344 Fax:(262)248-5766
E-mail: roses@rosesbnb.com
Web: www.rosesbnb.com

Circa 1926. A welcoming place to relax in casual comfort, this American Box-style home is only one block from the lake. The main level offers many common areas including a large living room/library and a deck for relaxing and enjoying the lake breezes. The cheerful guest bedrooms with modern conveniences are each named after the hosts' grandmothers. An English Country décor complements the oak or pine furnishings. Some rooms feature fireplaces and a large balcony. More than just a meal, a two-course breakfast is served on the wraparound porch with wicker furniture. Private parking, beach passes and bicycles ensure a stress-free stay.

Innkeeper(s): Ruth Ann Bae. $120-165. 4 rooms with PB, 3 with FP. Breakfast included in rates. Types of meals: Full gourmet bkfst, veg bkfst, early coffee/tea, picnic lunch, snacks/refreshments and dinner. Beds: KQ. Cable TV, VCR, reading lamp, stereo, ceiling fan, clock radio and fireplace in room. Central air. Fax, library, parlor games and telephone on premises. Weddings, small meetings and family reunions hosted. Antiquing, art galleries, beach, bicycling, canoeing/kayaking, cross-country skiing, downhill skiing, fishing, golf, hiking, horseback riding, parks, shopping, tennis, water sports, snowmobiling and petting zoo nearby.

Lancaster   14

Maple Harris Guest House

445 W Maple St
Lancaster, WI 53813-1611
(608)723-4717
E-mail: maplehgh@pcii.net
Web: www.mapleharris.com

Circa 1895. Enter the grand front door of this 1895 Queen Anne home to experience fine architectural features like detailed cherry, maple and oak woodwork, double wide pocket doors, the city's only residential elevator, hardwood floors, an open staircase with raised sitting alcove, a beveled, leaded window in the parlor and original gas fixtures. Sit by the coal-burning fireplace in the double living room. Each guest bedroom includes a sitting area and boasts original lace curtains, antiques, family heirlooms and handmade comforters and quilts. Sleep in a wrought-iron bed in the Turret Room with access to a balcony. Special rates are available for extended stays in the private Carriage House suites. Linger over a leisurely breakfast in the dining room that opens into a three-season porch. Visit year-round historic sites and area attractions.

Innkeeper(s): Bernadette & Leo Abing. $69-99. 5 rooms and 1 suite. Breakfast and afternoon tea included in rates. Types of meals: Full gourmet bkfst and veg bkfst. Beds: QT. Modem hook-up, cable TV, reading lamp, refrigerator, clock radio and telephone in room. Air conditioning. TV, fax and copier on premises. Handicap access. Weddings and family reunions hosted. Antiquing, bicycling, fishing, golf, hiking, museums, parks, shopping, tennis and wineries nearby.

Lodi   16

Victorian Treasure Inn

115 Prairie St
Lodi, WI 53555-1240
(608)592-5199 (800)859-5199 Fax:(608)592-7147
E-mail: innkeeper@victoriantreasure.com
Web: www.victoriantreasure.com

Circa 1897. Victorian Treasure features seven individually decorated guest rooms spread among two 19th-century Queen Anne Victorians. The interiors boast stained- and leaded-glass windows, pocket doors, rich restored woods and expansive porches. Five suites include a whirlpool tub, fireplace, wet bar, TV/VCR and stereo. Guests are greeted with a wine and cheese reception. Full, gourmet  breakfasts may include specialties such as eggs Florentine, herb vegetable quiche, or stuffed French toast topped with a seasonal fruit sauce. Guests enjoy hiking along the National Scenic Ice Age Trail which passes beside the inn.

Historic Interest: The Capitol Square in Madison (24 miles), Circus World Museum (20 miles), Wollersheim Winery (12 miles), Merrimac Car Ferry (5 miles), Frank Lloyd Wright Museum (35 miles).

Innkeeper(s): Renee & Eric Degelau. $119-219. 7 rooms with PB, 4 with FP, 6 suites and 1 conference room. Breakfast, afternoon tea and snacks/refreshments included in rates. Types of meals: Full gourmet bkfst, veg bkfst, early coffee/tea and room service. Beds: Q. Modem hook-up, data port, cable TV, VCR, reading lamp, stereo, refrigerator, ceiling fan, snack bar, clock radio, telephone, coffeemaker, turn-down service, desk, hot tub/spa and six with whirlpools in room. Central air. Fax, copier, library, parlor games, fireplace and gift shop on premises. Weddings, small meetings, family reunions and seminars hosted. Antiquing, art galleries, beach, bicycling, canoeing/kayaking, cross-country skiing, downhill skiing, fishing, golf, hiking, horseback riding, live theater, museums, parks, shopping, sporting events, tennis, water sports, bird watching and Taliesen nearby.

Publicity: *Recommended Romantic Inns, Wisconsin State Journal, Chicago Sun-Times, Milwaukee Magazine, Wisconsin Trails, Victorian Homes and Country Inn Cooking with Gail Greco.*

"An elegant, romantic getaway that everyone wants to return to again and again."

Madison   16

Arbor House, An Environmental Inn

3402 Monroe St
Madison, WI 53711-1702
(608)238-2981
Web: www.arbor-house.com

Circa 1853. Nature-lovers not only will enjoy the inn's close access to a 1,280-acre nature preserve, they will appreciate the innkeepers' ecological theme. Organic sheets and towels are offered for guests as well as environmentally safe bath products. Arbor House is one of Madison's oldest existing homes and features plenty of historic features, such as romantic reading chairs and antiques, mixed with modern amenities and unique touches. Five guest rooms include a whirlpool tub and three have fireplaces. The Annex guest rooms include private balconies. The innkeepers offer many amenities for business travelers, including value-added corporate rates. The award-winning inn has been recognized as a model of urban ecology. Lake Wingra is within walking distance as are biking and nature trails, bird watching and a host of other outdoor activities. Guests enjoy complimentary canoeing and use of mountain bikes.

Historic Interest: Frank Lloyd Wright designed many homes in Madison, and the Mansion Hill Historic District is nearby.

Innkeeper(s): John & Cathie Imes. $110-220. 8 rooms with PB, 3 with FP, 1 suite and 1 conference room. Breakfast included in rates. Types of meals: Full bkfst. Beds: KQ. Cable TV, VCR, reading lamp, stereo, ceiling fan, clock radio, telephone and desk in room. Air conditioning. Fax, copier, sauna and fireplace on premises. Limited handicap access. Weddings, small meetings, family reunions and seminars hosted. Antiquing, cross-country skiing, fishing, parks, shopping, sporting events and water sports nearby.

Publicity: *Money Magazine, Coop America, E, New York Times, Natural Home and Offspring.*

"What a delightful treat in the middle of Madison. Absolutely, unquestionably, the best time I've spent in a hotel or otherwise. B&Bs are the only way to go! Thank you!"

Mansion Hill Inn

424 N Pinckney St
Madison, WI 53703-1472
(608)255-3999 (800)798-9070 Fax:(608)255-2217
E-mail: info@mansionhillinn.com
Web: www.mansionhillinn.com

Circa 1858. The facade of this Romanesque Revival sandstone mansion boasts magnificent arched windows, Swedish railings, verandas and a belvedere. There are marble floors, ornate moldings and a magnificent mahogany and walnut staircase that

winds up four stories. Lovingly restored and lavishly decorated, the inn easily rivals rooms at the Ritz for opulence. A special occasion warrants requesting the suite with the secret passageway behind a swinging bookcase.

Historic Interest: State Capitol (3 blocks).

Innkeeper(s): Betty Blanchard. $150-340. 11 rooms with PB, 4 with FP and 2 suites. Breakfast and snacks/refreshments included in rates. Types of meals: Cont plus, early coffee/tea, picnic lunch and room service. Beds: KQ. Modem hook-up, data port, cable TV, VCR, reading lamp, stereo, refrigerator, telephone, turn-down service, whirlpool bath and some with desks in room. Central air. Fax, copier, library, parlor games and fireplace on premises. Weddings and small meetings hosted. Fishing, live theater, museums, parks, shopping, sporting events and state Capitol nearby.

Publicity: *Glamour, Country Inns, Chicago Sun-Times, Americana, Chicago Tribune, New York Times and Conde Nast Traveler.*

"The elegance, charm and superb services made it a delightful experience."

University Heights B&B

1812 Van Hise Ave
Madison, WI 53705
(608)233-3340 Fax:(608)233-3255
E-mail: simplybet@aol.com
Web: www.madison-lodging.com

Circa 1923. This Four-Square home offers a quiet residential neighborhood. Craftsman decor highlights the home's Frank Lloyd Wright influence. A large common area includes a fireplace and the two larger suites offer whirlpool tubs.
Breakfast may include poached pears with raspberry Grand Marnier sauce, sorrel, leek and mushroom quiche and cherry almond scones.

Innkeeper(s): Betty Humphries. $85-155. 4 rooms with PB, 2 suites and 1 conference room. Breakfast included in rates. Types of meals: Full bkfst and

early coffee/tea. Beds: QD. Reading lamp, CD player, ceiling fan, clock radio, telephone and desk in room. Air conditioning. VCR, fax, copier, bicycles and fireplace on premises. Small meetings and family reunions hosted. Golf, live theater, museums, parks, shopping, sporting events, capitol, UW Arboretun and Olbrich Botanical Gardens nearby.

Manitowoc   G8

Birch Creek Inn

4626 Calumet Avenue
Manitowoc, WI 54220
(920)684-3374 (800)424-6126 Fax:(920)684-9464

Circa 1940. Originally a farmstead that evolved into a motor inn, this cottage-style bungalow of wood and stone has been completely renovated and tastefully decorated. A cozy, country-like atmosphere is imparted here, though the inn is situated within the city limits. Watch the sunset, or browse through the lending library. There are many sitting areas for quiet relaxation. Each guest bedroom and suite is on one level with a private outside entrance and boasts a distinctive Wisconsin ethnic country charm. Most rooms feature fireplaces. After breakfast, stroll through the in-process, bird-and-butterfly-friendly walking garden.

Innkeeper(s): Dean and Jan Graunke. $50-265. 19 suites, 10 with FP and 1 conference room. Breakfast and snacks/refreshments included in rates. Types of meals: Cont plus, early coffee/tea, picnic lunch and afternoon tea. Beds: QDT. Data port, cable TV, VCR, reading lamp, refrigerator, ceiling fan, snack bar, clock radio, telephone, coffeemaker, turn-down service, desk and fireplace in room. Air conditioning. Fax, parlor games, fireplace and gift shop on premises. Antiquing, art galleries, beach, bicycling, canoeing/kayaking, cross-country skiing, fishing, golf, hiking, horseback riding, live theater, museums, parks, shopping, tennis, water sports, Green Bay Packers (45 minutes away) and Door County (less than an hour away) nearby.

Publicity: *Chicago Daily Herald, Midwest Travel and Herald Times Reporter.*

WestPort B&B, LLC

635 North Eighth St
Manitowoc, WI 54220
(920)686-0465 (888)686-0465

Circa 1879. This two-story Italianate-style bed and breakfast, built in 1879, was originally the home of a Civil War surgeon who had his practice in town. Renovated in 2003, four luxurious bedrooms provide ample private sitting space, fireplaces and double whirlpools to relax in. Start each morning with breakfast in bed or perhaps listening to birds chirping while sitting on the porch with a warm cup of coffee and a good book. Take a ride on the ferry across Lake Michigan, or enjoy the beaches of Wisconsin in the summer. Catch a show at the theater, shop in town or see a live sporting event at nearby Green Bay. Hosts Keith and Kim Lazansky Philippi provide the comfort and local knowledge that guests need to thoroughly enjoy their stay in Manitowoc.

Innkeeper(s): Kim Lazansky Philippi & Keith Philippi. $120-180. 4 rooms with PB, 3 with FP and 2 suites. Breakfast included in rates. Types of meals: Country bkfst, veg bkfst, early coffee/tea and room service. Beds: Q. Cable TV, reading lamp, refrigerator, ceiling fan, clock radio, hot tub/spa, refrigerator, fireplaces and double whirlpool tubs in room. Air conditioning. Telephone and fireplace on premises. Antiquing, art galleries, beach, bicycling, cross-country skiing, downhill skiing, fishing, golf, hiking, live theater, museums, parks, shopping, sporting events, tennis, water sports and Lake Michigan car ferry nearby.

Publicity: *Herald Times, Wisconsin Trails, Great Lakes Cruiser and Chicago Daily Herald.*

Milwaukee 18

The Brumder Mansion

3046 W Wisconsin Ave
Milwaukee, WI 53208
(414)342-9767 (866)793-3676 Fax:(414)342-4772
E-mail: brumder@execpc.com
Web: www.brumdermansion.com

Circa 1910. Built in the English Arts & Crafts style, this majestic brick home with Victorian and Gothic elements is furnished with elegant antiques. Common rooms feature huge oak fireplaces and exquisite woodwork, like the foyer's massive Gothic oak stairway. The lavish parlor's comfortable chairs invite relaxation, and the library has a large selection of games, magazines and books. A friendly atmosphere is enhanced with complimentary wine or beverages and homemade snacks or chocolates. Spacious guest bedrooms offer romantic settings with decorative painting and fine linens. Three suites include a double whirlpool, exquisite marble showers, CD player and TV/VCR. Enjoy the many flowers and view of the boulevard from the front porch.

Innkeeper(s): Carol & Bob Hirschi. $79-215. 5 rooms with PB, 3 with FP, 3 suites and 1 conference room. Breakfast and snacks/refreshments included in rates. Types of meals: Cont plus, veg bkfst and early coffee/tea. Beds: KQT. Cable TV, VCR, reading lamp, CD player, ceiling fan, clock radio, hot tub/spa, fireplace and 3 with whirlpools in room. Central air. Fax, copier, spa, library, parlor games, telephone and fireplace on premises. Small meetings hosted. Antiquing, art galleries, beach, live theater, museums, parks, shopping, sporting events, water sports and wineries nearby.

Publicity: *Milwaukee Magazine and HBO.*

Kilbourn Guesthouse B&B

2825 W Kilbourn Ave
Milwaukee, WI 53208-3523
(414)344-3167 Fax:(414)291-2185
E-mail: info@kilbournguesthouse.com
Web: www.kilbournguesthouse.com

Circa 1888. Adorning the historic Milwaukee neighborhood of Concordia, this grand brick Victorian is just two miles from the Festival Grounds on Lake Michigan. Relax in one of the three splendid parlors with period furnishings. Play the baby grand piano or choose a board game. Watch a video or DVD from the vast selection. A business center is available and wireless Internet access is provided throughout the house. Guest bedrooms have been completely renovated and redecorated. Stay in a room with a double whirlpool or a romantic fireplace. A specially prepared morning meal is served in the impressive dining room. Personal schedules can be accommodated with a breakfast basket or continental buffet. Enjoy the large backyard with a small garden and a pond.

Innkeeper(s): Pete Schwartz & Mike Schwan. $79-149. 5 rooms, 1 with PB, 1 with FP and 1 suite. Types of meals: Full bkfst, veg bkfst, early coffee/tea and snacks/refreshments. Beds: KQT. Cable TV, VCR, CD player, ceiling fan, snack bar, clock radio, hot tub/spa and fireplace in room. Air conditioning. Copier, library and telephone on premises. Small meetings, family reunions and seminars hosted. Antiquing, art galleries, beach, hiking, live theater, museums, parks, tennis and wineries nearby.

Monroe J6

Victorian Garden B&B

1720 16th St
Monroe, WI 53566-2643
(608)328-1720 (888)814-7909

Circa 1890. The original charm of this blue and white three-story Victorian home still remains today. Antiques and collectibles are found throughout the house, along with a vintage doll and teddy bear collection.  Wraparound porches and flower gardens are great for relaxing. Accommodations include the White Lace and Roses Suite featuring a clawfoot tub and shower for two. The Rosebud Room overlooks the hand-carved Italian fountain, and the Ivy Room is a quiet corner setting. A full breakfast is served in the formal dining room. Local attractions include the Monroe Depot and historic square. Come stay and visit with us, the pleasure is all ours.

Innkeeper(s): Judy & Ron Marsh. $79-99. 3 rooms with PB. Breakfast included in rates. Types of meals: Full bkfst. Beds: QD. Air conditioning. Antiquing, bicycling, cross-country skiing, fishing, golf, hiking, parks and sporting events nearby.

Oconomowoc 17

The Inn at Pine Terrace

351 E Lisbon Rd
Oconomowoc, WI 53066-2838
(262)567-7463 (888)526-0588

Circa 1879. This inn's convenient location, two hours from Chicago, midway between Madison and Milwaukee and just north of the interstate that connects them, makes it equally appealing to business travelers and those seeking a romantic retreat. The innkeeper bills the inn as a combination of a Victorian mansion and a small European hotel. Some rooms boast whirlpool tubs, and visitors are welcome to use the exercise room and the inn's in-ground swimming pool. A conference room is available for meetings, seminars and special occasions.

Innkeeper(s): Rich Borg. $75-175. 13 rooms with PB and 1 conference room. Breakfast included in rates. Types of meals: Cont plus. Beds: QT. Cable TV, reading lamp, telephone and desk in room. Air conditioning. Fax, copier, heated pool in summer, dining room and exercise room on premises. Weddings, small meetings, family reunions and seminars hosted. Antiquing, cross-country skiing, downhill skiing, fishing, golf, live theater, parks, shopping, sporting events, water sports, excellent dining and nature trails nearby.

Publicity: *Milwaukee Magazine.*

Onalaska   G3

Rainbow Ridge Farms B&B

N5732 Hauser Rd
Onalaska, WI 54650-8912
(608)783-8181

Circa 1902. Horses, llamas, goats, sheep and ducks are the primary occupants of Rainbow Ridge's 35 acres. Pleasant pond-view guest rooms are offered in the old farmhouse. Woodland, meadow and surrounding wooded bluffs create a picturesque setting and explains why this was the site for one of Onalaska's original farms. Guests are offered the opportunity to enjoy the working farm with a hands-on experience by feeding the animals and collecting eggs. A hearty farm breakfast is offered on weekends and an expanded continental during the week. The farm is popular for family reunions and weddings.

Innkeeper(s): Donna Murphy & Cindy Hoehne. $65-105. 4 rooms with PB. Breakfast and snacks/refreshments included in rates. Types of meals: Country bkfst, veg bkfst and early coffee/tea. Beds: QDT. Reading lamp and clock radio in room. Central air. TV, VCR, spa, bicycles, library, parlor games, telephone, satellite dish, fire pit, refrigerator and grill on premises. Weddings and family reunions hosted. Antiquing, art galleries, beach, bicycling, canoeing/kayaking, cross-country skiing, downhill skiing, fishing, golf, hiking, horseback riding, live theater, museums, parks, shopping, sporting events, tennis and water sports nearby.

Osceola   E1

St. Croix River Inn

305 River St, PO Box 356
Osceola, WI 54020-0356
(715)294-4248 (800)645-8820
E-mail: innkeeper@stcroixriverinn.com
Web: www.stcroixriverinn.com

Circa 1908. Timeless elegance is imparted at this meticulously restored stone house that blends old world charm with new world luxuries. Indulge in dramatic vistas from this gorgeous setting on the bluffs of the river. A comfortable ambiance embraces this inn where complimentary coffee is always found in the sitting room. There is also a wine and beverage bar. Select a book or game from the entertainment closet. Videos and CDs are also available for use in the private suites that all feature a fireplace and a hydromassage tub. A sumptuous breakfast served to each room is highlighted with spectacular views of the water.

Innkeeper(s): Vicki LaBelle. $100-200. 6 suites. Breakfast and snacks/refreshments included in rates. Types of meals: Full gourmet bkfst and early coffee/tea. Beds: Q. Cable TV, VCR, reading lamp, stereo, refrigerator, snack bar, clock radio, telephone, coffeemaker, hot tub/spa, fireplace, ultimate bathing experience with premier Acryline tubs and wine in room. Central air. Deck on premises. Handicap access. Weddings, small meetings, family reunions and seminars hosted. Antiquing, beach, bicycling, canoeing/kayaking, cross-country skiing, downhill skiing, golf, hiking, live theater, parks, shopping, water sports, snowmobile trails, scenic train ride, dinner cruises, dog sledding, spa services, casino and fine dining nearby.
Publicity: *Chicago Sun-Times, Skyway News and St. Paul Pioneer Press.*

Plymouth   H8

Hillwind Farm B&B

N 4922 Hillwind Rd
Plymouth, WI 53073
(920)892-2199 (877)892-2199
E-mail: info@hillwindfarm.com
Web: www.hillwindfarm.com

Circa 1856. One of the oldest farmhouses in the county, this romantic Victorian on five country acres was built prior to the Civil War. Air-conditioned guest bedrooms and a suite are distinctively decorated with colorful wallpapers, luxurious linens and furnished with antiques. Double whirlpool tubs, fireplaces and outdoor sitting porches are some of the features offered as well as pampering amenities that include Swiss chocolates, English soaps, terry robes, complimentary beverages, videos and CDs. Enjoy wine and home-baked cookies each evening. Savor a candlelit breakfast served at individual tables in the quaint dining area. Play golf or visit nearby state parks, Road America, Door County and Kettle Moraine Forest. Choose from a variety of activities available each season.

Innkeeper(s): Kim & Art Jasso. $99-178. 4 rooms with PB, 4 with FP and 1 suite. Breakfast included in rates. Beds: Q. Cable TV, VCR, reading lamp, ceiling fan, clock radio, 3 rooms have double whirlpool tubs and 4 have outside sitting porches in room. Air conditioning. Telephone and fireplace on premises. Family reunions hosted. Antiquing, cross-country skiing, fishing, golf, parks, shopping, tennis and water sports nearby.

"Thank you for a weekend we'll both never forget. We're engaged!"

Reedsburg   H5

Lavina Inn

325 Third Street
Reedsburg, WI 53959
(608)524-6706
E-mail: info@lavinainn.com
Web: www.lavinainn.com

Circa 1901. Rocking chairs, a glider and a loveseat beckon for spending quiet moments on the inviting wraparound porch of this Queen Anne Colonial Victorian. Located in the historic district, the gracious interior features original chandeliers, hardwood floors, leaded-glass windows and ornate woodwork. Gather for conversation in one of the two sitting parlors or enjoy the games and reading materials in the second-floor library. Seasonal refreshments and beverages are provided. Centrally air-conditioned guest bedrooms include antique furnishings, refrigerators, bathrobes and turndown service. Select a satisfying breakfast from a menu, and rest assured that special dietary needs are considered upon request. The many toys easily entertain children. Bicycle and ski storage is available. Area attractions are within walking distance.

Innkeeper(s): Lorinda Broughton & Michael Manning. $80-85. 3 rooms. Breakfast and snacks/refreshments included in rates. Types of meals: Full bkfst, veg bkfst and early coffee/tea. Beds: QD. Reading lamp, refrigerator, clock radio, turn-down service, homemade cookies, seasonal beverage upon arrival and wake-up coffee in room. Central air. Library, parlor games, telephone, laundry facility and storage for bikes on premises. Weddings, small meetings and family reunions hosted. Amusement parks, antiquing, art galleries, bicycling, canoeing/kayaking, cross-country skiing, downhill skiing, fishing, golf, hiking, horseback riding, live theater, shopping, tennis and wineries nearby.

Parkview B&B

211 N Park St
Reedsburg, WI 53959-1652
(608)524-4333 Fax:(608)524-1172
E-mail: info@parkviewbb.com
Web: www.parkviewbb.com

Circa 1895. Tantalizingly close to Baraboo and Spring Green, this central Wisconsin inn overlooks a city park in the historic district. The gracious innkeepers delight in tending to their guests' desires and offer wake-up coffee and a morning paper. The home's first owners were in the hardware business, so there are many original, unique fixtures, in addition to hardwood floors, intricate wood-work, leaded and etched windows and a suitors' window. The downtown business district is just a block away.

Historic Interest: It was built in 1895 and most of the original features are still present and enhanced by renovations.

Innkeeper(s): Tom & Donna Hofmann. $75-90. 4 rooms, 2 with PB, 1 with FP. Breakfast and snacks/refreshments included in rates. Types of meals: Full gourmet bkfst, veg bkfst and early coffee/tea. Beds: QT. Reading lamp, CD player, refrigerator, ceiling fan, clock radio and 1 with fireplace in room. Central air. TV, fax and parlor games on premises. Antiquing, art galleries, bicycling, canoeing/kayaking, cross-country skiing, downhill skiing, fishing, golf, hiking, horseback riding, live theater, parks, shopping, wineries and state parks nearby.

Publicity: *Reedsburg Report and Reedsburg Times-Press.*

"Your hospitality was great! You all made us feel right at home."

Richland Center   I4

Lambs Inn B&B

23761 Misslich Rd
Richland Center, WI 53581-4409
(608)585-4301
E-mail: lambsinn@mwt.net
Web: www.lambs-inn.com

Circa 1800. An old-fashioned family farm in a scenic hidden valley is the setting for this inn, with four guest rooms and an adjacent cottage. Ann's Room, with its cream walls, lace curtains and rose carpet, is highlighted by a quilt hand-pieced by Donna's grandmother. Marie's Room, with its yellow and blue

tones, offers a stunning view of the valley. The country kitchen is a favorite gathering place. Breakfast fare sometimes features bread pudding or kringle.

Innkeeper(s): Donna & Dick Messerschmidt. $90-250. 6 rooms, 4 with PB. Breakfast included in rates. Types of meals: Full bkfst. Beds: KQT. Reading lamp, CD player, ceiling fan, clock radio and telephone jack in room. Central air. VCR, library, parlor games, telephone, fireplace, goats, cats and trout in spring on premises. Small meetings, family reunions and seminars hosted. Antiquing, bicycling, canoeing/kayaking, cross-country skiing, fishing, golf, live theater, parks, shopping, tennis, water sports, wineries, Amish, Frank Lloyd Wright's Taliesen, American Players Theater and House on the Rock nearby.

Sheboygan   H8

Brownstone Inn

1227 No 7th Street
Sheboygan, WI 53081
(920)451-0644 Fax:(920)457-3426
E-mail: brwnstninn@aol.com
Web: www.brownstoneinn.com

Circa 1907. The descendants of the original owners of this handsome brownstone mansion have restored the property and added amenities for the pleasure of guests. A handsome polished and carved staircase, arched ceiling in the parlor and original chandeliers are some of the gracious appointments which remain. Each guest room offers a whirlpool tub and a shower, and some have beautifully carved fireplaces. There are porches, cozy reading areas and parlors. A billiards table is available. Walk to the lakefront, a sandy beach, marina, board-walk or shops and restaurants. In summer plan to arrange for an excursion on the inn's sailboat.

Innkeeper(s): Frank A Ribich Jr. $100-250. 7 rooms, 5 with PB and 1 conference room. Breakfast and snacks/refreshments included in rates. Types of meals: Cont plus, veg bkfst, early coffee/tea and room service. Beds: KQ. Cable TV, VCR, reading lamp, stereo, refrigerator, clock radio, telephone, turn-down service, desk, hot tub/spa and voice mail in room. Central air. Fireplace and billiards on premises. Weddings, small meetings and family reunions hosted. Amusement parks, antiquing, art galleries, beach, bicycling, canoe-ing/kayaking, fishing, golf, hiking, horseback riding, live theater, parks, sporting events, tennis, water sports and wineries nearby.

Sheboygan Falls   H8

The Rochester Inn

504 Water St
Sheboygan Falls, WI 53085-1455
(920)467-3123 Fax:(920)467-9729
E-mail: rochesterinn@excel.net
Web: www.rochesterinn.com

Circa 1848. This Greek Revival inn is furnished with Queen Anne Victorian antiques, wet bars and four-poster beds. The most romantic offerings are the 600-square-foot suites. They include living rooms with camel back couches and wing back chairs on the first floor and bedrooms with double whirlpool tubs on the second floor. Sheboygan Falls is one mile from the village of Kohler.

Innkeeper(s): Sean & Jacquelyn O'Dwanny. $99-160. 6 suites. Breakfast included in rates. Types of meals: Full gourmet bkfst, early coffee/tea and pic-nic lunch. Beds: Q. Cable TV, VCR, reading lamp, refrigerator, clock radio, telephone, desk and whirlpool in room. Air conditioning. Small meetings hosted. Antiquing, cross-country skiing, fishing, golf, parks, shopping, tennis, water sports, black Wolf Run, Kohler and WI nearby.

Sister Bay   E9

The Inn on Maple

414 Maple Dr
Sister Bay, WI 54234-9423
(920)854-5107

Circa 1902. Located on a quiet side street, a half block off Bay Shore Drive, this cozy inn is in the National Register of Historic Places because of its stovewood architecture. The inn is decorated with English antiques, ceiling fans and quilts. Full breakfasts are served on an enclosed front porch. Relax on the deck or in front of the fireplace in the Gathering Room. Door County offers 250 miles of shoreline, and there are state parks, antique shops and art galleries near the inn.

Innkeeper(s): Bill & Louise Robbins. $85-105. 6 rooms with PB. Breakfast included in rates. Types of meals: Full bkfst and early coffee/tea. Beds: QDT. Reading lamp, ceiling fan and clock radio in room. Air conditioning. TV, VCR, library, parlor games, telephone, fireplace, back yard deck, birdwatching and afternoon cookies and beverage on premises. Antiquing, art galleries, bicycling, cross-country skiing, fishing, golf, live theater, shopping, tennis and water sports nearby.

Sparta   G4

Justin Trails B&B Resort

7452 Kathryn Ave
Sparta, WI 54656-9729
(608)269-4522 (800)488-4521 Fax:(608)269-3280
E-mail: info@justintrails.com
Web: www.justintrails.com

Circa 1920. Do as little or as much as desired during a visit to this B&B resort in a peaceful valley surrounded by forested hills that invites daydreaming while lounging in an Amish bentwood rocker on private decks, or makes dreams come true of hiking, cross-country skiing, snowshoeing, bird watching, disc golfing and so much more. Cabins and 1920s farmhouse suites feature two-person whirlpool tubs and fireplaces. Kathryn's Room is the first-floor corner garden view room offering easy access to a common area with a coffeemaker, microwave and refrigerator. Enjoy Donna's hearty farm breakfasts that can be delivered to the cabins. The Justin Trails Eatery is open by advance reservation for lunch or dinner made with local produce.

Innkeeper(s): Don & Donna Justin. $95-275. 6 rooms with PB, 5 with FP, 2 suites, 3 cottages and 1 conference room. Breakfast included in rates. Types of meals: Full bkfst. Beds: KQT. TV, VCR, reading lamp, CD player, refrigerator, ceiling fan, coffeemaker, hot tub/spa and microwave in suites in room. Air conditioning. Spa, telephone, fireplace, snowshoe trails, cross-country skiing and disc golf, massage, Amish country shopping nearby and dogsledding on premises. Weddings, small meetings, family reunions and seminars hosted. Antiquing, canoeing/kayaking, cross-country skiing, downhill skiing, fishing, golf, hiking, horseback riding, parks, shopping and Amish country nearby.

Publicity: *Milwaukee Journal/Sentinel, Wisconsin Trails, Travel America, Family Fun, Family Life and Midwest Living and Chicago Tribune.*

Stevens Point   F6

A Victorian Swan on Water

1716 Water St
Stevens Point, WI 54481-3550
(715)345-0595 (800)454-9886
E-mail: victorian@g2a.net
Web: bbinternet.com/victorian-swan

Circa 1889. This Victorian is located a block and a half from the Wisconsin River. Black walnut inlays in the wood floors, crown moldings, walnut paneling and interior shutters are among the inn's architectural elements. The suite features a mural of a pastoral Mediterranean scene, a ceiling fan, whirlpool tub, fireplace and a balcony overlooking the garden. There are antique furnishings and lace curtains. Breakfast items may include rum-baked fresh pineapple and "turtle" French toast stuffed with chocolate and pecans and served with caramel sauce.

Innkeeper(s): Joan Ouellette. $70-140. 4 rooms, 3 with PB, 1 with FP and 1 suite. Breakfast included in rates. Types of meals: Full gourmet bkfst and early coffee/tea. Beds: KQDT. Ceiling fan, desk and whirlpool and suite has fireplace in room. Air conditioning. VCR, library, parlor games, telephone and fireplace on premises. Weddings, small meetings, family reunions and seminars hosted. Antiquing, cross-country skiing, downhill skiing, fishing, live theater, parks, shopping, sporting events and water sports nearby.

"Thanks, you made a business trip away from home feel like a vacation. Your place is beautiful and inviting."

Dreams of Yesteryear B&B

1100 Brawley St
Stevens Point, WI 54481-3536
(715)341-4525 Fax:(715)341-4248
E-mail: bonnie@dreamsofyesteryear.com
Web: dreamsofyesteryear.com

Circa 1901. This elegant, three-story, 4,000-square-foot Queen Anne home is within walking distance of downtown, the Wisconsin River and the University of Wisconsin. The inn features golden oak woodwork, hardwood floors and leaded glass. Each guest room offers exquisite decor; the third-floor Ballroom Suite boasts a whirlpool. Gourmet breakfasts are served in the inn's formal dining room. An excellent hiking trail is just a block from the inn.

Historic Interest: Historic downtown Stevens Point is nearby, and the inn is only a short trip from dozens of historical sites.

Innkeeper(s): Bonnie & Bill Maher. $62-149. 6 rooms, 4 with PB and 2 suites. Breakfast, afternoon tea and snacks/refreshments included in rates. Types of meals: Full gourmet bkfst and early coffee/tea. Beds: KQDT. Cable TV, reading lamp, clock radio, telephone and desk in room. Air conditioning. VCR, library, parlor games, fireplace, piano and victrolas on premises. Weddings, small meetings and family reunions hosted. Amusement parks, antiquing, cross-country skiing, downhill skiing, fishing, live theater, parks, shopping, sporting events, water sports, historical attractions and hiking trails nearby.

Publicity: *Victorian Homes, Reach, Stevens Point Journal and News WAOW Channel 9.*

"Something from a Hans Christian Anderson fairy tale."

Sturgeon Bay   F9

Chanticleer Guest House

4072 Cherry Rd (Hwy HH)
Sturgeon Bay, WI 54235
(920)746-0334 Fax:(920)746-1368
E-mail: chanticleer@itol.com
Web: www.chanticleerguesthouse.com

Circa 1916. Although Chanticleer is secluded on 70 acres boasting woods and fields of wildflowers, the home is just one mile from Sturgeon Bay. Each of the ten guest rooms, which consist of two cabins and eight bed and breakfast suites, has a fireplace and double whirlpool tub. Poster and sleigh beds are topped with country comforters. Delicate floral wallcoverings, exposed wood beams and paneled wood walls accentuate the elegant country decor. Breakfast is brought to your door, including such items as homemade muffins and fruit with fresh cream. Door County offers a multitude of attractions, including theater productions, musical festivals, watersports and hiking on trails in one of five state parks.

Innkeeper(s): Darrin Day & Bryon Groeschl. $120-210. 10 rooms, 10 with FP, 8 suites and 2 cottages. Breakfast and snacks/refreshments included in rates. Types of meals: Cont plus, veg bkfst and early coffee/tea. Beds: KQ. TV, VCR, reading lamp, stereo, refrigerator, ceiling fan, coffeemaker and antiques in room. Central air. Fax, copier, swimming, sauna, telephone, fireplace and laundry facility on premises. Handicap access. Antiquing, art galleries, beach, bicycling, canoeing/kayaking, cross-country skiing, downhill skiing, fishing, golf, hiking, horseback riding, live theater, museums, parks, shopping, sporting events, tennis, water sports and wineries nearby.

Publicity: *New York Times Travel Section.*

Hearthside B&B Inn

2136 Taube Rd
Sturgeon Bay, WI 54235
(920)746-2136
E-mail: hearthside@itol.com
Web: www.hearthside-farm-bb.com

Circa 1880. Experience country comfort at this vintage farmhouse that boasts an impressive night view of a Lake Michigan lighthouse two miles away. The inn is decorated with quilts and cozy furnishings, and features a fireplace with a floor-to-ceiling mirrored mantel. The guest bedrooms and suite are suitable for singles, couples or families. After a hearty all-you-can-eat breakfast, lunch is seldom needed. Stroll the gardens, or venture out to explore the local sites. Weddings and reunions are welcome events.

Innkeeper(s): Don & Lu Klussendorf. $65-70. 4 rooms with PB, 1 suite and 1 cottage. Breakfast included in rates. Types of meals: Full gourmet bkfst. Beds: QDT. Cable TV, VCR and reading lamp in room. Air conditioning. Stable, parlor games, telephone and fireplace on premises. Weddings, small meetings, family reunions and seminars hosted. Antiquing, cross-country skiing, golf, live theater, parks, shopping, sporting events, water sports and Green Bay Packers nearby.

Publicity: *Green Bay Gazette.*

The Reynolds House B&B

111 So 7th Ave
Sturgeon Bay, WI 54235
(920)746-9771 (877)269-7401 Fax:(920)746-9441

Circa 1900. A three-story, red-roofed Queen Anne Victorian house, the Reynolds House is painted in two shades of teal and yellow with white trim on its balustrades and brackets. Leaded-glass windows and a stone veranda that wraps around the front of the house are features. Rooms are cheerfully decorated and offer antique beds, attractive bed coverings and wallpapers.

Tucked under the gable, the Winesap Suite includes a whirlpool, sitting room and fireplace. The innkeeper's kitchen garden furnishes fresh herbs to accent breakfast dishes, as well as flowers for the table.

Innkeeper(s): Heather Hull. $65-165. 4 rooms with PB, 3 with FP and 1 suite. Breakfast and snacks/refreshments included in rates. Types of meals: Full gourmet bkfst and early coffee/tea. Beds: Q. Cable TV, ceiling fan, clock radio and some with whirlpool in room. Central air. TV, VCR, fax, copier, library, parlor games, telephone and fireplace on premises. Weddings and family reunions hosted. Antiquing, art galleries, beach, bicycling, cross-country skiing, fishing, golf, hiking, horseback riding, live theater, museums, parks, shopping, tennis and wineries nearby.

Publicity: *Door County Magazine, Midwest Living Magazine-Voted Best in the Midwest June 2001 & 2002 and Arrington Inn Traveler's Best Breakfast 2004.*

"Sometimes the last minute things in life are the best!"

Scofield House B&B

908 Michigan St
Sturgeon Bay, WI 54235-1849
(920)743-7727 (888)463-0204 Fax:(920)743-7727
E-mail: scofldhs@charterinternet.net
Web: www.scofieldhouse.com

Circa 1902. Mayor Herbert Scofield, prominent locally in the lumber and hardware business, built this late-Victorian house with a sturdy square tower and inlaid floors that feature intricate borders patterned in cherry, birch, maple, walnut, and red and white oak. Oak moldings throughout the house boast raised designs of bows, ribbons, swags and flowers. Equally lavish decor is featured in the guest rooms with fluffy flowered comforters and cabbage rose wallpapers highlighting romantic  antique bedsteads. Baked apple-cinnamon French toast is a house specialty. Modern amenities include many suites with fireplaces and double whirlpools. "Room at the Top" is a sky-lit 900-square-foot suite occupying the whole third floor and furnished with Victorian antiques.

Historic Interest: Door County Lighthouses, Maritime Museum, Door County Museum (within walking distance).

Innkeeper(s): Mike & Carolyn Pietrek. $84-220. 6 rooms with PB, 5 with FP. Breakfast and afternoon tea included in rates. Types of meals: Full gourmet bkfst. Beds: Q. Cable TV, VCR, reading lamp, stereo, refrigerator, ceiling fan, clock radio and double whirlpools in room. Air conditioning. TV, fax, copier, parlor games, telephone, fireplace and movie library (free) on premises. Antiquing, cross-country skiing, downhill skiing, fishing, live theater, parks, shopping, sporting events and water sports nearby.

Publicity: *Innsider, Glamour, Country, Wisconsin Trails, Green Bay Press Gazette, Chicago Tribune, Milwaukee Sentinel-Journal, Midwest Living, Victorian Decorating & Lifestyle, Country Inns and National Geographic Traveler.*

"You've introduced us to the fabulous world of B&Bs. I loved the porch swing and would have been content on it for the entire weekend."

White Lace Inn

16 N 5th Ave
Sturgeon Bay, WI 54235-1795
(920)743-1105 (877)948-5223
E-mail: romance@whitelaceinn.com
Web: www.WhiteLaceInn.com

Circa 1903. The romantic White Lace Inn is composed of four beautifully restored Victorian houses connected by meandering garden paths. Inviting rooms and suites offer fine antiques and ornate Victorian or canopy beds. The inn's suites include oversized whirlpool baths, fireplaces, white linens, down comforters and many other amenities. Often the site for romantic anniversary celebrations, a favorite suite has a two-sided fireplace, magnificent walnut Eastlake bed, English country fabrics and a whirlpool. Lemonade or hot chocolate and cookies are offered upon arrival. In the morning, the delectable offerings include items such as cherry apple crisp and creamy rice pudding. Year-round activities invite frequent visits - the Festival of Blossoms, the Lighthouse Walk, Cherry Festival and the Classic Wooden Boat event, for instance. Take museums and gallery strolls, and enjoy the area's great restaurants.

Innkeeper(s): Dennis & Bonnie Statz. $70-235. 18 rooms with PB, 15 with FP and 5 suites. Breakfast included in rates. Types of meals: Full bkfst. Beds: KQ. 12 with whirlpool tubs and 9 with fireplace and whirlpool in room.

Limited handicap access. Antiquing, cross-country skiing, fishing, live theater and water sports nearby.

Publicity: *Milwaukee Sentinel, Brides, National Geographic Traveler, Wisconsin Trails, Milwaukee, Country Home and Midwest Living.*

"Each guest room is an overwhelming visual feast, a dazzling fusion of colors, textures and beautiful objects. It is one of these rare gems that established a tradition the day it opened." - Wisconsin Trails

Viroqua   H4

Viroqua Heritage Inn B&B's

217 & 220 E Jefferson St
Viroqua, WI 54665
(608)637-3306 (888)443-7466
E-mail: rhodsent@mwt.net
Web: www.herinn.com

Circa 1890. Formerly the Boyle House, named for its original owner, this Queen Anne Victorian is an architectural jewel showcasing a three-story turret, turned balusters and columns, leaded beveled glass and circle-top windows. Embellishments continue with hardwood floors, ornate oak fireplace mantles and staircase and brass and crystal chandeliers. The nostalgic ambiance is enhanced by antique furnishings and Oriental rugs. A parlor-music room features a victrola and baby grand piano. Enjoy a leisurely breakfast in the formal dining room, on the front porch or on the balcony overlooking the garden. Ask about the pampering products and services of Day Lily Spa.

Innkeeper(s): Nancy Rhodes. $60-120. 8 rooms, 5 with PB, 1 with FP. Breakfast included in rates. Types of meals: Full bkfst and early coffee/tea. Beds: KQD. TV, reading lamp, clock radio, telephone, coffee pots and one with whirlpool bath in room. Air conditioning. VCR, bicycles, library, child care, parlor games, fireplace, refrigerator, exercise club, whirlpool tub, organic cooking and healing and nurturing spa on premises. Weddings, small meetings, family reunions and seminars hosted. Antiquing, cross-country skiing, downhill skiing, fishing, live theater, parks, shopping, water sports, Amish shopping and community built city park nearby.

Publicity: *Smithsonian Magazine, Readers' Digest and Milwaukee Magazine.*

"Wonderful house, great hosts."

Waupaca   G6

Crystal River Inn B&B

E1369 Rural Rd
Waupaca, WI 54981-8246
(715)258-5333
E-mail: crystalriverinn@charter.net
Web: www.crystalriver-inn.com

Circa 1853. The stately beauty of this historic Greek Revival farmhouse is rivaled only by its riverside setting. Each room features a view of the water, garden, woods or all three. A Victorian gazebo, down comforters and delicious breakfasts, with pecan sticky buns, a special favorite, add to guests' enjoyment. A recent addition to the inn's offerings include a newly restored historic cottage. With luxurious decor it includes two bedrooms, a living room with fireplace and private porches. It may be reserved singly or together. Exploring the village of Rural, which is in the National Register, will delight those interested in bygone days. Recreational activities abound, with the Chain O'Lakes and a state park nearby.

Historic Interest: National Register.

Innkeeper(s): Lois Sorenson. $68-138. 7 rooms, 5 with PB. Breakfast included in rates. Types of meals: Full bkfst. Beds: Q. TV, reading lamp, ceil-

ing fan, clock radio, telephone, desk and hot tub/spa in room. Air conditioning. Fireplace on premises. Weddings, small meetings and family reunions hosted. Antiquing, cross-country skiing, downhill skiing, shopping and sporting events nearby.

Publicity: *Resorter, Stevens Point Journal and Wisconsin Trail.*

"It was like being king for a day."

Westby   H4

Westby House Victorian Inn

200 W State St
Westby, WI 54667-1253
(608)634-4112 (800)434-7439 Fax:(608)634-2565
Web: www.westbyhouse.com

Circa 1890. This late 19th-century Victorian was completely refurbished in 1985, but the innkeepers left the original woodwork, stained glass and light fixtures. The rooms are filled with antiques. The main floor includes a full-service restaurant that features a variety of American cuisine. Westby, which is located between the Mississippi River and the Kickapoo River Valley, presents an unusual Norwegian celebration each May and a 90-meter international ski jump in February. Guests also might enjoy the nearby Norwegian and Amish farms.

Innkeeper(s): Mike & Marie Cimino. $75-185. 9 rooms with PB, 3 with FP. Types of meals: Full gourmet bkfst. Restaurant on premises. Beds: KQ. Two with whirlpools in room. TV and telephone on premises.

Publicity: *Pequote Press and Wisconsin Trails.*

Whitewater   I7

Hamilton House Bed & Breakfast

328 W Main St
Whitewater, WI 53190-1958
(262)473-1900
E-mail: kathie@bandbhamiltonhouse.com
Web: www.bandbhamiltonhouse.com

Circa 1861. Local citizens saved Hamilton House, a fanciful Second Empire home, from the wrecking ball. The home is now listed in the National Register of Historic Places. The interior boasts original mantels, woodwork and stained glass. Most of the rooms include a fireplace, and some include a whirlpool tub. A full breakfast is served fireside on tables lit with candles. The Whitewater area offers four lakes and an abundance of outdoor activities, as well as shopping and theater.

Historic Interest: Links to underground railroad.

Innkeeper(s): Jim & Kathleen Fleming. $90-175. 8 rooms with PB, 6 with FP, 1 suite and 1 conference room. Breakfast and snacks/refreshments included in rates. Types of meals: Full bkfst and early coffee/tea. Beds: KQDT. Data port, reading lamp, CD player, refrigerator, clock radio, telephone, desk, hot tub/spa and fireplace in room. Central air. Fax, copier and parlor games on premises. Weddings and small meetings hosted. Antiquing, beach, bicycling, cross-country skiing, fishing, golf, hiking, horseback riding, live theater, parks, shopping, sporting events and water sports nearby.

Victoria-On-Main B&B

622 W Main St
Whitewater, WI 53190-1855
(262)473-8400

Circa 1895. This graceful Queen Anne Victorian, shaded by a tall birch tree, is in the heart of Whitewater National Historic District, adjacent to the University of Wisconsin. It was built for Edward Engebretson, mayor of Whitewater. Yellow tulip and sunny daffodils fill the spring flower beds, while fuchsias and geraniums bloom in summertime behind a picket fence. The inn's gables, flower-filled veranda and three-story turret feature a handsome green tin roof. Each guest room is named for a Wisconsin hardwood. The Red Oak Room, Cherry Room and Bird's Eye Maple Room all offer  handsome antiques in their corresponding wood, Laura Ashley prints, antique sheets, pristine heirloom-laced pillowcases and down comforters. A hearty breakfast is sometimes served on the wraparound veranda, and there are kitchen facilities available for light meal preparation. Whitewater Lake and Kettle Moraine State Forest are five minutes away.

Innkeeper(s): Nancy Wendt. $75-85. 3 rooms, 1 with PB, 1 with FP. Breakfast included in rates. Types of meals: Full bkfst and early coffee/tea. Beds: D. Reading lamp and ceiling fan in room. Air conditioning. Telephone on premises. Antiquing, cross-country skiing, fishing, live theater, parks, shopping and water sports nearby.

"We loved it. Wonderful hospitality."

Wisconsin Dells   H5

Wisconsin Dells Thunder Valley B&B Inn

W15344 Waubeek Rd
Wisconsin Dells, WI 53965-9005
(608)254-4145

Circa 1870. The Wisconsin Dells area is full of both Scandinavian and Native American heritage, and the innkeepers of this country inn have tried to honor the traditions. The inn even features a Scandinavian gift shop. Chief Yellow Thunder, for whom this inn is named, often camped out on the grounds and surrounding area. The inn's restaurant is highly acclaimed. Everything is homemade, including the wheat the innkeepers grind for the morning pancakes and rolls. There is a good selection of Wisconsin beer and wine, as well. Guests can stay in the Farmhouse, Swedish Guest Hus, or Wee Hus, all of which offer microwaves and refrigerators.

Historic Interest: Chief Yellow Thunder, a Winnebago Indian Chief, had a pow-wow behind the barn. He is buried nearby.

Innkeeper(s): Anita, Kari & Sigrid Nelson. $65-135. 10 rooms with PB. Breakfast included in rates. Types of meals: Full bkfst. Beds: KQD. Air conditioning. Limited handicap access. Weddings, small meetings, family reunions and seminars hosted. International Crane Foundation, Circus Museum, House on Rock, casino, farm animals and dairy nearby.

Publicity: *Wisconsin Trails Magazine, Country Inns, Midwest Living Magazine, Chicago Sun-Times, Milwaukee Journal-Sentinel and National Geographic Travel Magazine.*

"Thunder Valley is a favorite of Firstar Club members — delicious food served in a charming atmosphere with warm Scandinavian hospitality."

Wyoming

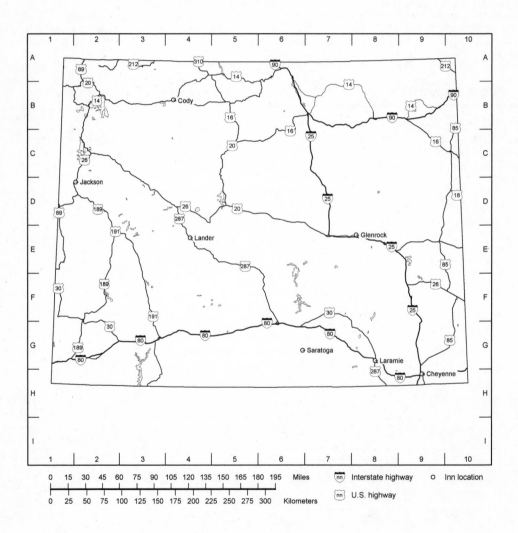

0 15 30 45 60 75 90 105 120 135 150 165 180 195   Miles

0 25 50 75 100 125 150 175 200 225 250 275 300   Kilometers

(nn) Interstate highway   ○ Inn location

(nn) U.S. highway

Cheyenne H9

Nagle Warren Mansion B&B

222 E 17th St
Cheyenne, WY 82001
(307)637-3333 (800)811-2610 Fax:(307)638-6879
E-mail: jim@nwmbb.com
Web: www.naglewarrenmansion.com

Circa 1888. When this Victorian mansion was constructed, Cheyenne was the richest town in the world for its size. The home's brilliant architecture serves as a reminder of this grand time in the city's history. The home boasts meticulously restored woodwork, including a grand staircase adorned with an ornate gaslight. The cast bronze fireplaces are topped with mirrors that reach the ceilings. Bronze medallions were set in the front doors, and guests will find stained glass throughout the home. The home's parlor still includes two paintings commissioned by the home's first owner, Erasmus Nagle. Nagle made his fortune in both the grocery and cattle businesses. From 1915 until 1933, the home belonged to Senator F.E. Warren and his wife. The mansion is in the National Register as well as being listed in the Smithsonian Guide to Historic America.

$108-178. 12 rooms with PB, 6 with FP, 1 suite and 3 conference rooms. Breakfast included in rates. Types of meals: Full gourmet bkfst. Beds: KQD. Cable TV, reading lamp, clock radio, telephone, desk, iron and ironing board in room. Air conditioning. Fax, copier, library, parlor games, fireplace, masseuse on call, hot tub gazebo and traditional English high tea is served Friday and Saturday on premises. Limited handicap access. Weddings, small meetings and family reunions hosted. Antiquing, golf, live theater, parks, shopping and eight restaurants within walking distance nearby.

"Thanks so much for your attention to the fine details of beauty in an old house. The food was great, the atmosphere was romantic."

Cody B4

Mayor's Inn Bed & Breakfast

1413 Rumsey Ave
Cody, WY 82414
(307)587-0887 (888)217-3001 Fax:(307)587-0890

Circa 1909. Considered the town's first mansion, this stylish two-story, turn-of-the-century home was built for Cody's first elected mayor. A romantic Victorian ambiance is achieved with warm hospitality, antiques, soft lighting, chandeliers and splendid wall and ceiling papers. The parlor inspires nostalgia. The guest bedrooms feature either a brass bed and clawfoot tub, a lodge pole pine bed, jetted tub and western art, or an open, sunny room with double shower. The suite boasts a fresh water hot tub and CD player. Offering private seating, breakfast is served in both of the dining rooms. The Carriage House is a cottage with a fully equipped kitchen.

Innkeeper(s): Bill & Daielee Delph. $95-205. 5 rooms, 4 with PB and 1 cottage. Breakfast included in rates. Types of meals: Full gourmet bkfst and early coffee/tea. Restaurant on premises. Beds: KQD. Cable TV, reading lamp, CD player, clock radio and hot tub/spa in room. Central air. Fax, parlor games, telephone and lounge on premises. Weddings, small meetings, family reunions and seminars hosted. Antiquing, art galleries, bicycling, canoeing/kayaking, cross-country skiing, downhill skiing, fishing, golf, hiking, horseback riding, museums, parks, shopping and water sports nearby.

Publicity: *Cody Enterprise and The Telegraph Travel.*

Glenrock E8

Hotel Higgins

PO Box 741
Glenrock, WY 82637-0741
(307)436-9212 (800)458-0144 Fax:(307)436-9213

Circa 1916. Elm trees and juniper frame this restored hotel, listed in the National Register. Located on the Oregon Trail, it is near the home station of the Pony Express. There are many period furnishings original to the hotel, including brass and iron beds. Polished tile floors and beveled-glass doors add to the inn's ambiance. Each morning a full gourmet breakfast is served with champagne. The Paisley Shawl is a restaurant on the premises.

Innkeeper(s): Judy Colling. $45-90. 10 rooms, 8 with PB, 2 suites and 1 conference room. Breakfast included in rates. Types of meals: Cont, gourmet lunch and gourmet dinner. Restaurant on premises. Beds: KQDT. Cable TV, reading lamp, ceiling fan and desk in room. Air conditioning. Fax, library, telephone and gift shop on premises. Handicap access. Weddings, small meetings, family reunions and seminars hosted. Antiquing, art galleries, beach, canoeing/kayaking, cross-country skiing, downhill skiing, fishing, golf, hiking, horseback riding, museums, parks, shopping, sporting events and water sports nearby.

Publicity: *Travel & Leisure, Rapid City Journal and Bon Appetit.*

Jackson D2

The Huff House Inn

240 E Deloney, PO Box 1189
Jackson, WY 83001-1189
(307)733-4164 (307)739-9091 Fax:(307)739-9091

Circa 1917. Originally built for the town's first medical doctor and town mayor, this Craftsman-style home served as both an office for seeing patients and a residence. The innkeepers have dedicated themselves to retaining the inn's historic character. Beveled-glass doors, chandeliers, antiques and brocade fabrics add to the inn's comfortable atmosphere. In addition to the three guest rooms in the main house, the inn features four separate cottages that boast hand-stenciled walls, Jacuzzi tubs and fireplaces. Breakfast is served in the formal dining room or breakfast room. Baked apple French toast with a spicy applesauce topping is a house favorite. The inn is a block from the historic district, restaurants, shops and museums.

Innkeeper(s): Jackie & Weldon Richardson. $119-225. 7 rooms, 3 with PB and 4 cottages. Breakfast included in rates. Types of meals: Full gourmet bkfst and early coffee/tea. Beds: KQ. Cable TV, VCR, reading lamp, clock radio, telephone, desk and cottages have fireplaces and whirlpool tubs in room. Air conditioning. Fax, copier, spa, library, parlor games and fireplace on premises. Small meetings and family reunions hosted. Antiquing, cross-country skiing, downhill skiing, fishing, golf, live theater, parks, shopping, tennis, water sports, dog sledding, snowmobiling, horse back riding and hiking nearby.

Publicity: *Denver Post, Los Angeles Times and St. Louis Dispatch.*

"Our honeymoon could not have been nicer! The food was incredible and the cottage was perfect."

Parkway Inn

125 North Jackson Ave
Jackson, WY 83001
(307)733-3143 (800)247-8390 Fax:(307)733-0955
E-mail: info@parkwayinn.com
Web: www.parkwayinn.com

Circa 1915. Quietly sheltered by pine and aspen, this
Victorian bed & breakfast sits only three blocks from the
Historic Town Square. Modern comfort, classic charm, warm
hospitality, personal service and generous amenities create an
inviting and relaxing atmosphere. Spacious guest suites and
bedrooms are available in the two-story main building furnished with American antiques and brass beds with quilts or
comforters. A separate cottage offers more suites with separate
sitting rooms and dressing areas. Some boast views of the park
and the Cache Creek Mountain from balconies. Work out in
the fully equipped gym, swim in the indoor pool, relax in
whirlpool tubs and saunas. Visit nearby Grand Teton National
Park or arrive at Yellowstone within an hour.

Historic Interest: One building on premises dates to approximately 1915.
One of the oldest structures in Jackson Hole, Wyoming.

Innkeeper(s): Tom & Carmen Robbins. $99-249. 49 rooms with PB and 12
suites. Breakfast included in rates. Types of meals: Cont plus. Beds: KQ.
Modem hook-up, data port, cable TV, reading lamp, clock radio, telephone,
coffeemaker, desk and hot tub/spa in room. Central air. Fax, spa, sauna, parlor games, indoor pool and full athletic gym on premises. Weddings and family reunions hosted. Art galleries, bicycling, canoeing/kayaking, cross-country
skiing, downhill skiing, fishing, golf, hiking, horseback riding, live theater,
museums, parks, shopping, Jackson Hole ski area, Grand Teton National Park
and Yellowstone National Park nearby.

Lander   E4

Blue Spruce Inn

677 S 3rd St
Lander, WY 82520-3707
(307)332-8253

Circa 1919. Five blue spruce trees mark this large Arts and
Crafts-influenced home that is accented by mission-style furnishings and listed in the National Register of Historic Places.
Original chandeliers, stained glass, oak crown molding and
woodwork add to the appeal. Ask for the Spotted Elk Room for
a Native American themed accommodation. Relax on the sun
porch or front porch. Fish in a mountain trout stream just a
block away. Lander is adjacent to the Wind River Indian
Reservation, where the grave site of Sacajawea is located. The
Oregon/Mormon/California Trail is about 20 miles away.

Historic Interest: In addition to small museums and cultural sites on the
Wind River Indian Reservation, South Pass, a significant portion of the
Oregon Trail is nearby. The Oregon/Mormon/California Trail is about 20
miles away. Historic South Pass City, a Wyoming State Historic Site, is 45
minutes away.

Innkeeper(s): Marvin & JoAnne Brown. $85. 4 rooms with PB. Breakfast
included in rates. Types of meals: Full bkfst and early coffee/tea. Beds: QT.
Reading lamp, desk, two rooms with phone and one with TV in room. TV,
VCR, bicycles, library, telephone and fireplace on premises. Small meetings
and family reunions hosted. Antiquing, cross-country skiing, fishing, parks,
shopping, Wind River Indian Reservation and museum nearby.

Laramie   G8

Vee Bar Guest Ranch

2091 State Hwy 130
Laramie, WY 82070-9734
(307)745-7036 (800)483-3227 Fax:(307)745-7433

Circa 1896. Experience the Old West on this 800-acre guest
ranch nestled on Little Laramie River at the base of the Snowy
Range Mountains. Once the private residence of an English cattle baron, the main lodge was the home station for a stagecoach company. Today, the authentic western character of the
lodge and its log cabins are preserved in the Ralph Lauren-style
rustic furnishings, wood floors and stone fireplaces. A full
country breakfast is included. The inn offers a variety of on-site
recreational activities.

Innkeeper(s): Jim "Lefty" & Carla Cole. $100-150. 9 cabins and 1 confer-
ence room. Breakfast included in rates. Types of meals: Full bkfst. Restaurant
on premises. Beds: KQDT. Reading lamp, refrigerator, coffeemaker and most
with washer and dryer in room. Fax, copier, stable, parlor games, telephone,
fireplace and hot tub on premises. Limited handicap access. Small meetings,
family reunions and seminars hosted. Cross-country skiing, downhill skiing,
fishing, snowmobiling and horseback riding nearby.

Publicity: *Log Home Design Ideas Magazine* and *National Geographic Traveler.*

Saratoga   G6

Far Out West B&B

304 N Second St
Saratoga, WY 82331
(307)326-5869 Fax:(307)326-9864

Circa 1920. Located two blocks from downtown, this historic
home maintains many original features, and there are two guest
rooms located in the main house. There is also a unique room
accessible only by a tiny,
four-foot-high door. Inside,
children will find toys,
books and other goodies.
Out back, there are several
accommodations with spe-
cial names such as The
Calamity Jane or The James Gang. The Hideout, located in a
separate house, includes a kitchen, dining area and living
room. Breakfast entrees, such as Gunfighter eggs, are accompanied by freshly baked biscuits, bacon and fresh fruit.

Innkeeper(s): Bill & BJ Farr. $100-130. 5 rooms with PB and 1 cottage.
Breakfast included in rates. Types of meals: Full bkfst and early coffee/tea.
Beds: KDT. Cable TV, reading lamp, ceiling fan, clock radio and robes in
room. VCR, fax, copier, library, telephone and fireplace on premises. Limited
handicap access. Weddings, small meetings, family reunions and seminars
hosted. Antiquing, cross-country skiing, fishing, golf, parks, shopping, tennis,
water sports, snowmobiling, natural hot springs and pet boarding nearby.

Publicity: *Saratoga Sun.*

"An absolutely wonderful place for comfort, friendliness and food."

U.S. Territories

Puerto Rico

San German

Parador Oasis

PO Box 1063
San German, PR 00683
(787)892-1175 (800)223-9815 Fax:(787)892-4546

Circa 1798. This 200-year-old mansion is located in the middle of the historic town of San German, near beaches, shops and restaurants. Rooms offer two or more beds, and there is a swimming pool on the grounds. The inn provides the opportunity for an in-house dining experience with items such as skirt steak, rice, beans, garlic bread and papaya and cheese.

Innkeeper(s): Ivette Acosta. $60-63. 52 rooms with PB and 1 conference room. Types of meals: Full bkfst, dinner and room service. Restaurant on premises. Beds: D. Cable TV, reading lamp, clock radio, telephone, desk and hair dryers in room. Air conditioning. Fax and swimming on premises. Weddings, small meetings, family reunions and seminars hosted. Live theater, shopping, water sports, cinema and shopping center nearby.

San Juan

El Canario Inn

1317 Ashford Ave
San Juan, PR 00907
(787)722-3861 (800)533-2649 Fax:(787)722-0391
E-mail: canariopr@aol.com
Web: www.canariohotels.com

Circa 1938. This three-story inn is only a block from San Juan's glorious white-sand beaches. Rooms are decorated in a tropical theme with rattan and wicker furnishings and Bermuda ceiling fans. Guests can relax on one of the patios. The inn is a charming escape from the multitude of high rise hotels along the coast. Casinos and discotheques are nearby, and sightseeing tours and boating trips can be arranged at the hotel.

Historic Interest: Old San Juan is only three miles away, and features forts, a museum, cathedrals and plenty of gracious Spanish architecture set among cobblestone streets.

Innkeeper(s): Jude & Keith Olson. $75-114. 25 rooms with PB. Breakfast included in rates. Types of meals: Cont plus and early coffee/tea. Beds: DT. Cable TV, reading lamp, ceiling fan, clock radio and telephone in room. Air conditioning. Fax on premises. Fishing, parks, shopping and water sports nearby.

Publicity: *USA Today, Conde Naste Traveler and New York Times.*

Canada

Alberta

Calgary

Calgary Historic Bed and Breakfast at Twin Gables

611-25 Avenue SW
Calgary, AB T2S 0L7
(403)271-7754 (866)271-7754
E-mail: twingables@shaw.ca
Web: www.twingables.ca

Circa 1910. Be immersed in the ambiance of the Arts and Crafts movement in this classic 1910 period home. Preserved and restored to retain historic authenticity yet offer modern luxury, original details include fine woodwork and wainscoting, leaded and stained glass, beveled windows and vintage fixtures accented by Tiffany lamps and antique furnishings. Gather in the Parlour to check e-mail, chat with new friends by the fire or read a book selected from the library. Watch television or listen to music in the Living Room. Overlook the gardens and enjoy city views by the fountain in the Solarium or on the terrace. Luxurious air-conditioned guest suites include fine linens and down duvets, high-speed data ports, stocked refrigerators, VCRs and stunning vistas. The spacious Mount Royale Suite features a Jacuzzi, fireplace and sitting area. Enjoy a breakfast favorite of Belgium waffles smothered in seasonal berries with chicken apple sausage.

Historic Interest: Built in 1910 with the Arts and Crafts Style alive in every piece of wood and timber.
Innkeeper(s): Deirdre and Henry Brost. $85-150. 3 suites, 1 with FP. Breakfast and snacks/refreshments included in rates. Types of meals: Full gourmet bkfst, veg bkfst, early coffee/tea and room service. Beds: KQDT. Modem hook-up, data port, cable TV, VCR, reading lamp, CD player, refrigerator, snack bar, clock radio, telephone, coffeemaker, turn-down service, desk, fireplace and computer in room. Air conditioning. Fax, copier, library and laundry facility on premises. Weddings, small meetings, family reunions and seminars hosted. Amusement parks, antiquing, art galleries, bicycling, canoeing/kayaking, cross-country skiing, downhill skiing, fishing, golf, hiking, live theater, museums, parks, shopping, sporting events and tennis nearby.

Calgary Westways Guest House

216-25 Ave SW
Calgary, AB T2S 0L1
(403)229-1758 Fax:(403)228-6265
E-mail: calgary@westways.ab.ca
Web: www.westways.ab.ca

Circa 1912. Pampered luxury begins when leaving the airport in a Rolls Royce Silver Shadow Mark 1 to arrive at this Heritage house in the historic Mission district. It features Victorian

details, hardwood floors, leaded-glass windows, box-beam ceilings and built-in cabinets. Specializing in romantic escapes, the guest bedrooms offer many relaxing amenities including robes, candles, jetted or soaker clawfoot tubs, entertainment centers and gas fireplaces. A satisfying breakfast is served in the dining room on bone china and cut crystal. Walk to the nearby city centre or visit Fort Calgary only one mile away.
Innkeeper(s): Jonathon Lloyd. $70-130. 5 suites, 4 with FP. Breakfast included in rates. Types of meals: Full gourmet bkfst and early coffee/tea. Beds: KQ. Modem hook-up, data port, cable TV, VCR, reading lamp, stereo, ceiling fan, clock radio, telephone, desk, hot tub/spa and fireplace in room. Central air. Fax, bicycles, library, pet boarding, parlor games, fireplace, laundry facility, free Internet access and video library on premises. Small meetings and family reunions hosted. Amusement parks, antiquing, art galleries, bicycling, canoeing/kayaking, fishing, golf, hiking, horseback riding, live theater, museums, parks, shopping, sporting events and tennis nearby.
Publicity: *Calgary Herald.*

British Columbia

Crawford Bay

Wedgwood Manor Country Inn

16002 Crawford Creek Rd
Crawford Bay, BC V0B 1E0
(250)227-9233 (800)862-0022 Fax:(250)227-9233
E-mail: wedgwood@netidea.com
Web: www.bctravel.net/wedgwood

Circa 1912. Set against a magical forest on 50 acres, this English manor house boasts gables, multi-paned windows and a steep red roof. It was built for a member of the Wedgwood china family. Favorite spots include the library, veranda and parlor. Breakfast is served fireside in the dining room and often features just-picked berries with whipped cream, freshly baked scones and Eggs Wedgwood (poached eggs over Black Forest ham over English muffins with an herb sauce from the inn's gardens). The innkeeper is a botanist and is a resource for the area's birds and wildlife. Wedgwood's park-like grounds include flower beds, wildflowers, a streams, ponds and a fountain. Across the road is the Kokanee springs Golf Resort.
Innkeeper(s): Joan Huiberts & John Edwards. $85-140. 7 rooms, 6 with PB, 1 with FP and 1 cottage. Breakfast included in rates. Types of meals: Full gourmet bkfst and snacks/refreshments. Beds: QD. Reading lamp, clock radio, desk, hot tub/spa, fireplace and hot tub in room. Fax, library, parlor games, telephone and fireplace on premises. Family reunions hosted. Art galleries, beach, bicycling, canoeing/kayaking, cross-country skiing, downhill skiing, fishing, golf, hiking, horseback riding, live theater, museums, parks, shopping, tennis and water sports nearby.
Publicity: *Calgary Herald and Vancouver Sun.*

"We really appreciate the way you spoil and pamper us. Wish we could just move in."

Sooke

Ocean Wilderness Inn & Spa Retreat

109 W Coast Rd, RR 2
Sooke, BC V0S 1N0
(250)646-2116 (800)323-2116 Fax:(250)646-2317
E-mail: info@oceanwildernessinn.com
Web: www.oceanwildernessinn.com

Circa 1940. The hot tub spa of this log house inn is in a
Japanese gazebo overlooking the ocean. Reserve your time for a
private soak, terry bathrobes are supplied. Experience massage

and mud treatments, ocean treatments and herbal wraps while
meditation enhances your creative expression. The inn will
arrange fishing charters, nature
walks, wilderness treks and
beachcombing. Coffee is delivered to your room each morning
on a silver service. Guests are invited to enjoy breakfast in their
room or in the dining lounge. Rooms include antiques, sitting
areas and canopy beds. Two of the rooms have hot tubs for two
with spectacular ocean and Olympic Mountain views. Rates are
in Canadian funds.

Historic Interest: Botanical Beach and Hatley Castle are 15 miles from the
inn, while Moss Cottage is only eight miles away. Butchart Gardens and the
Royal B.C. Museum are within 35 miles.

Innkeeper(s): Marion J. Rolston. $99-180. 9 rooms with PB. Breakfast
included in rates. Types of meals: Full bkfst and early coffee/tea. Beds: KQT.
Reading lamp and refrigerator in room. Fax and telephone on premises.
Limited handicap access. Weddings, small meetings, family reunions and
seminars hosted. Antiquing, fishing, live theater, parks, shopping, whale
watching and Galloping Goose biking trail nearby.

Publicity: *Puget Sound Business Journal, Getaways from Vancouver, Travel
Holiday Magazine and Seattle Times.*

*"Thank you for the most wonderful hospitality and accommodations
of our entire vacation."*

Vancouver

Kenya Court Ocean Front Guest House

2230 Cornwall Ave
Vancouver, BC V6K 1B5
(604)738-7085
E-mail: h&dwilliams@telus.net
Web: www.mondaytourism/kenyacourt.com

Circa 1927. Enjoy a piping hot cup of fresh, gourmet coffee as
you gaze out over the ocean at this scenic bed & breakfast.
Innkeeper Dorothy Williams not only provides a delectable
spread of fresh breads, croissants, cereals and fruits, she serves
it in a rooftop solarium. Williams, in charge of the piano
department at Vancouver Academy, will serenade guests with
piano concerts on some days. Roomy suites feature antiques,
separate entrances and boast ocean views. The home is within
walking distance to the Granville Market, the planetarium, city
centres, 10 minutes from the University of British Columbia
and 20 miles from the U.S. border. The athletically inclined will
enjoy the use of tennis courts, walking and jogging trails and a
heated outdoor saltwater pool across the street.

Historic Interest: A maritime museum is a five-minute walk from the bed &
breakfast. An anthropology museum is 10 minutes by car.

Innkeeper(s): Dr. & Mrs. H. Williams. $95-110. 7 rooms with PB, 4 with FP
and 5 suites. Breakfast included in rates. Types of meals: Full gourmet bkfst

and early coffee/tea. Beds: KQT. Cable TV, reading lamp, stereo, refrigerator,
clock radio, telephone and desk in room. VCR, library and fireplace on
premises. Weddings and family reunions hosted. Antiquing, cross-country skiing, downhill skiing, fishing, live theater, parks, shopping, sporting events and
water sports nearby.

Publicity: *Washington Times and Rocky Mountain News.*

"Beautiful home; we enjoyed the unsurpassed hospitality."

The Manor Guest House

345 W 13th Ave
Vancouver, BC V5Y 1W2
(604)876-8494 Fax:(604)876-5763
E-mail: info@manorguesthouse.com
Web: www.manorguesthouse.com

Circa 1902. This turn-of-the-century Edwardian still features
many original elements, including carved banisters, polished
wood floors and ornate wainscoting. The home is one of the
city's oldest. The innkeeper has decorated it with a collection
of English antiques. The penthouse
suite, which includes a bedroom, loft,
deck and kitchen, boasts a spectacular view of the city. Fresh fruits,
home-baked breads and specialties
such as a cheese and mushroom
souffle or blueberry cobbler highlight the breakfast menu.

Innkeeper(s): Brenda Yablon. $65-125. 10 rooms, 6 with PB, 1 with FP, 1
suite and 1 conference room. Types of meals: Full gourmet bkfst. Beds:
KQDT. Cable TV, reading lamp, clock radio and desk in room. VCR, fax, copier, parlor games, telephone, fireplace, free local calls, free Internet access
and free parking on premises. Weddings, small meetings, family reunions and
seminars hosted. Antiquing, downhill skiing, live theater, parks, shopping,
sporting events and water sports nearby.

'O Canada' House

1114 Barclay St
Vancouver, BC V6E 1H1
(604)688-0555 (877)688-1114 Fax:(604)488-0556
E-mail: info@ocanadahouse.com
Web: www.ocanadahouse.com

Circa 1897. The first version of the Canadian national anthem
was written in this Queen Anne Victorian, thus its unusual
name. The home is furnished with an upscale mix of Arts and
Crafts and Victorian pieces. The richly painted walls, fine
woodwork and luxurious carpeting add to the elegant interior.
In addition to the guest rooms, there is a private cottage available. The innkeepers offer many amenities for business travelers, including fax and copy services. A pantry is stocked with
snacks and refreshments, and breakfasts include gourmet coffee, homemade muffins, croissants or scones, fresh fruit and
entrees such as seafood crepes or eggs Florentine. The home is
minutes from many of Vancouver's popular attractions, including shopping, restaurants, Stanley Park and the beach.

Innkeeper(s): Helene Barton. $135-255. 6 rooms with PB, 1 with FP and 1
cottage. Breakfast and snacks/refreshments included in rates. Types of meals:
Full gourmet bkfst, veg bkfst and early coffee/tea. Beds: KQ. Cable TV, VCR,
reading lamp, refrigerator, ceiling fan, clock radio, telephone, desk and robes
in room. Central air. Fax, copier, library, fireplace, complimentary sherry
served in the parlor each evening and complimentary parking on premises.
Antiquing, art galleries, beach, bicycling, canoeing/kayaking, cross-country
skiing, downhill skiing, fishing, golf, hiking, live theater, museums, parks,
shopping, sporting events, tennis and water sports nearby.

Publicity: *Fodors and 4 1/2 Star Canada Select.*

The West End Guest House

1362 Haro St
Vancouver, BC V6E 1G2
(604)681-2889 (888)546-3327 Fax:(604)688-8812
E-mail: wegh@trilli.com
Web: www.westendguesthouse.com

Circa 1906. Among the hustle and bustle of Vancouver sits this pink Victorian, which transports its guests out of the modern metropolis and back to the turn-of-the-century days. The gracious home used to house a family of musicians and photogra-

phers. Innkeeper Evan Penner has preserved their past, placing lithographs and historical photos owned by the family throughout the house. Each of the rooms is individually decorated with glorious prints and beautiful antiques. The guest rooms are cozy and welcoming, the perfect place to snuggle down after a long day and sink into brass beds decked in fine linens and down comforters. Guests will enjoy relaxing on the second-story deck or strolling past the many plants and flowers in the back garden. A gourmet, country-style breakfast is served each morning, and homemade chocolates await guests as they arrive.

Historic Interest: The home is located in the heart of Vancouver, close to many historic sites, including Canada Place, the Canadian Pacific Railway Station and Gastown, a restored area full of interesting shops, restaurants and a unique steam-powered clock.

Innkeeper(s): Evan Penner. $118-250. 8 rooms with PB, 2 with FP. Breakfast included in rates. Types of meals: Full bkfst. Beds: KQDT. Cable TV, ceiling fan, clock radio, telephone, turn-down service and desk in room. Small meetings hosted. Amusement parks, antiquing, cross-country skiing, downhill skiing, fishing, live theater, shopping, sporting events and water sports nearby.

Publicity: *New York Times, Province News and 2002 Recipient Western Canada Bed & Breakfast Innkeepers Association Hospitality Award.*

"Quiet, comfort, convenience, homey, delicious food and good conversations with other guests. I will do nothing but sing the praises of B&Bs from now on, and I'm sure we will meet again."

Victoria

A B&B A Beautiful Island Away...Binners' B&B

58 Linden Avenue
Victoria, BC V8V 4C8
(250)383-5442 (888)409-5800 Fax:(250)383-5885
E-mail: ili-hosts@binners.com
Web: www.abeautifulislandaway.com

Circa 1945. A pretty seaside neighborhood surrounds this upscale Post Art Deco bed & breakfast that was built in the historic Fairfield Farm district. Experience a peaceful privacy after arriving and getting acquainted with this upscale and light-filled inn. Pristine yet comfortable guest bedrooms and a suite are spacious. Some include a fireplace, and each room boasts a mini-refrigerator and CD player. An artfully presented breakfast is served on colorful table linens with gorgeous place settings and fresh flowers. Linger over a meal which includes a delectable fruit course, a tempting pastry course, and artfully presented entree du jour (such as a chantarelle omelet, asparagus with 3-cheese sauce and multigrain toast) and assortment of low-fat yogurts, cereals, toast, coffee and teas. Wander

through the English country garden with a small pond and waterfall, or relax on the deck in cedar rockers. Walk the short half-block to scenic ocean waterways with majestic Olympic Mountain views, or stroll through Beacon Hill Park.

Historic Interest: The land was once the great side garden of a huge manor home built in historic Fairfield. In the 1940s the side garden was sold and a four room cottage was built there. In 1994 we purchased the severed property and cottage and converted it to a charming incarnation as a spacious, comfortable and light-filled bed and breakfast.

Innkeeper(s): Binners & Edward Davidson. $99-225. 3 rooms with PB, 3 with FP. Breakfast included in rates. Types of meals: Full bkfst, veg bkfst and early coffee/tea. Beds: Q. Cable TV, reading lamp, CD player, refrigerator, ceiling fan, clock radio, voice mail, jetted tubs and showers and instant on gas fireplaces in room. VCR, fax, copier, telephone and fireplace on premises. Antiquing, art galleries, beach, bicycling, canoeing/kayaking, fishing, golf, hiking, horseback riding, live theater, museums, parks, shopping, tennis, water sports and wineries nearby.

Abigail's Hotel

906 McClure St
Victoria, BC V8V 3E7
(250)388-5363 (800)561-6565 Fax:(250)388-7787
E-mail: innkeeper@abigailshotel.com
Web: www.abigailshotel.com

Circa 1930. Abigail's, a Tudor-style hotel, boasts three gabled stories, stained-glass windows, crystal chandeliers and tasteful decor. It holds a five-star rating as a heritage inn with Canada Select. Complimentary hors d'oeuvres and beverages are offered in the library, also a popular area for small weddings. Rooms feature a variety of ameni-

ties such as canopied beds, fire-
places, Jacuzzi baths and antiques.
The inn is located three blocks
from Victoria's inner harbor,
shops and restaurants. Rates are
quoted in Canadian dollars.

Innkeeper(s): Ellen & Russ Cmolik. $167-389. 23 rooms with PB, 14 with FP and 6 suites. Breakfast and snacks/refreshments included in rates. Types of meals: Full gourmet bkfst and early coffee/tea. Beds: KQD. Reading lamp, refrigerator, clock radio, telephone and hot tub/spa in room. Fax, copier, library, parlor games and fireplace on premises. Weddings, small meetings, family reunions and seminars hosted. Antiquing, fishing, live theater, parks, shopping and water sports nearby.

Publicity: *Seattle Magazine, Victoria Times Colonist and Country Inns.*

Amethyst Inn at Regents Park

1501 Fort Street
Victoria, BC V8S 1Z6
(250)595-2053 (888)265-6499 Fax:(250)595-2054
E-mail: innkeeper@amethyst-inn.com
Web: www.amethyst-inn.com

Circa 1885. Befitting its name, this Victorian mansion is a gorgeous gem. The inn is showcased in the prestigious heritage neighborhood of Rocklands, and it is the first home to be designated a heritage property in British Columbia. It has the original 13-foot ceilings, stained glass, wallpaper borders, and a freestanding double staircase in the wood-paneled foyer. The mansion was lovingly restored for comfort, elegance and romance, with great attention given to details. The decor, fixtures and furnishings authentically reflect the Victorian era. Impressive guest suites exude luxury and offer two-person clawfoot, soaker or hydrotherapy spa tubs. Most rooms feature Minton-tiled fireplaces. A full breakfast is prepared each morning by the chef and served in the dining room where tables are set with fine antique china and crystal.

$65-245. 16 rooms with PB, 13 with FP, 1 suite and 1 conference room. Types

of meals: Full gourmet bkfst. Beds: KQ. Modem hook-up, data port, reading lamp, refrigerator, ceiling fan, clock radio, hot tub/spa, most with bar refrigerator and fireplace in room. Parlor games on premises. Weddings hosted. Antiquing, art galleries, bicycling, canoeing/kayaking, fishing, golf, hiking, live theater, museums, parks, shopping, tennis, wineries and whale watching nearby.
Publicity: *Seattle Times, Readers Digest New Choices and LA Times.*

Beaconsfield Inn

998 Humboldt St
Victoria, BC V8V 2Z8
(250)384-4044 (888)884-4044 Fax:(250)384-4052
E-mail: info@beaconsfieldinn.com
Web: www.beaconsfieldinn.com

Circa 1905. Beautiful grounds accentuate this turn-of-the-century English manor. Rooms are light and airy with antiques, original woodwork, Oriental carpets and stained-glass windows. Many of the rooms feature fireplaces and Jacuzzi tubs and all include cozy, down comforters. A luxurious gourmet breakfast is served in the dining room or conservatory and afternoon tea is sure to delight. Evening sherry is served in the library. There's plenty to do in this seaside town, and The Beaconsfield is only four blocks from downtown and the oceanfront.
Historic Interest: Butchart Gardens are 25 miles away, and Victoria has many historic buildings, homes and other sites. Old Town and several museums are close by.
Innkeeper(s): Bob & Dawna Bailey. $129-359. 9 rooms with PB and 4 suites. Breakfast and afternoon tea included in rates. Types of meals: Full bkfst and early coffee/tea. Beds: Q. Reading lamp, CD player, clock radio, desk, fireplace and Jacuzzi tubs in room. Fax, copier, library, parlor games, telephone, evening sherry and tea and cookies on premises. Antiquing, fishing, live theater and water sports nearby.
Publicity: *Equity, Globe & Mail, New York Times, Country Inns, Seattle Times, Horizon Air, Dallas Morning News, Northwest Travel, Arkansas Democrat Gazette, Wichita Eagle, Look Travel, Vancouver Sun, Vancouver Province and 5 Star Canada Select.*

"This place is about as close to heaven as one can get."

Dashwood Seaside Manor

One Cook St
Victoria, BC V8V 3W6
(800)667-5517 Fax:(250)383-1760

Circa 1912. Dashwood Manor is a historic listed Edwardian Tudor Revival mansion with a rare oceanfront location. Choose between a first-floor suite with a fireplace, chandelier and beamed ceilings; a second-story "special occasion" suite; or a top-floor suite for spectacular balcony views of the ocean and the Olympic Mountains. Four suites include a Jacuzzi tub. To reach downtown Victoria, take a short walk through the park. The inn offers a self-catered full breakfast. Rates are quoted in Canadian dollars.
Innkeeper(s): Derek Dashwood Family & Staff. $95-385. 28 rooms, 14 with PB, 3 with FP and 14 suites. Breakfast included in rates. Types of meals: Full bkfst. Beds: Q. Cable TV, refrigerator, snack bar and clock radio in room. Telephone and fireplace on premises. Antiquing, fishing, live theater and shopping nearby.
Publicity: *San Francisco Chronicle.*

"Enchanting, very soothing."

Dreemskerry Heritage Inn

1509 Rockland Ave
Victoria, BC V8S 1W3
(250)384-4014 (888)464-2620 Fax:(250)598-4239
E-mail: dreemskerry@msn.com
Web: www.dreemskerry.bc.ca

Circa 1920. Three blocks from the water, this Georgian Revival mansion is located in a beautiful old historic neighborhood. Guest rooms and baths are spacious and include large beds,

Jacuzzi tubs, and some offer splendid views of sea and mountain. The Coach House Suite includes a private balcony. The family is retired from hotel management and now enjoys guests in the gracious setting of their own dining room at their English style-breakfast. Enjoy the garden with its flowers, water gardens and park-like grounds or stroll past other estate homes on a walk to Craigdarroch Castle, Antique Row or the gardens of Government House, all nearby.
Innkeeper(s): Bryan & Maureen Stoodlry. $85-150. 4 rooms with PB. Breakfast included in rates. Beds: KQ. Reading lamp, desk and fans in room. TV, fax, copier, parlor games, telephone, fireplace and laundry facility on premises. Amusement parks, antiquing, art galleries, beach, bicycling, canoeing/kayaking, fishing, golf, hiking, horseback riding, live theater, museums, parks, tennis, child care, pet boarding, swimming, sauna and stables nearby.
Publicity: *Rated Canada Select 5 Stars by Tourism BC and AAA 3 Diamonds for your assurance and security.*

"Thank you for letting us share this dream house with you; beautiful!"

Gregory's Guest House

5373 Patricia Bay Hwy
Victoria, BC V8Y 2N9
(250)658-8404 (888)658-8404 Fax:(250)658-4604

Circa 1919. The two acres of this historic flower farm are just across the street from Elk Lake, six miles from downtown Victoria and near Butchart Gardens. All the rooms are decorated in antiques and duvets, and they feature garden and lake views. The grounds include water gardens, a waterfall and a pond. A traditional, full Canadian breakfast is served, and after the meal, guests can enjoy the hobby farm and exotic birds or perhaps rent a boat at the lake.
Innkeeper(s): Paul & Elizabeth Gregory. $89-120. 3 rooms, 2 with PB. Breakfast included in rates. Types of meals: Full bkfst. Beds: QDT. Fax, library, parlor games, telephone, fireplace and parlor with fireplace on premises. Antiquing, fishing, live theater, parks, sporting events, water sports and Victoria Butchart Gardens nearby.

"Our family felt very welcome, loved the house and especially liked the super breakfasts."

Humboldt House Bed & Breakfast

867 Humboldt St
Victoria, BC V8V 2Z6
(250)383-0152 (888)383-0327 Fax:(250)383-6402
E-mail: rooms@humboldthouse.com
Web: www.humboldthouse.com

Circa 1893. Just two blocks from the magnificent Empress Hotel and Victoria's Inner Harbor and one block from Beacon Hill Park with views of mountains and water sits this 5,000 square-foot 1893 Victorian inn. The bed & breakfast is owned and managed by a former restaurant owner and pastry chef. Its six guest bedrooms each have their own fireplace and Jacuzzi tub. Oft-mentioned by enthusiastic travel reviewers is the gourmet champagne breakfast tucked into a basket and delivered to the privacy of the room each morning. It includes such courses as eggs Benedict, seafood crepes, French toast, fruit and home-baked croissants. In the afternoon, guests may enjoy a glass of wine and homemade delicacies in the common room.
Innkeeper(s): David & Vlasta Booth, Mila Werbik. $93-210. 6 rooms with PB, 6 with FP. Breakfast and snacks/refreshments included in rates. Types of meals: Full gourmet bkfst, early coffee/tea and picnic lunch. Beds: KQ. Reading lamp, CD player, refrigerator, clock radio, turn-down service and hot tub/spa in room. Library, telephone and fireplace on premises. Antiquing, art galleries, beach, bicycling, canoeing/kayaking, fishing, golf, hiking, horseback riding, live theater, museums, parks, shopping and tennis nearby.
Publicity: *Country Inns, Los Angeles Times, Western Living, Arringtons Bed & Breakfast Journal Awarded one of the Top 15 Inns in Canada and 4 Star Canada Select Rating.*

Oak Bay Guest House

1052 Newport Ave
Victoria, BC V8S 5E3
(250)598-3812 (800)575-3812 Fax:(250)598-0369

Circa 1912. Said to be the oldest continuously operated bed & breakfast in Victoria, Oak Bay is an English Tudor-style inn on a half acre of grounds. Features of the inn include beamed ceilings, diamond-shaped leaded-glass windows, built-in cupboards, a sun lounge and a parlor. Furnishings include antiques. Breakfasts are served in the dining room, complete with fireplace. There are four courses, including favorites as eggs Benedict and freshly baked muffins such as cranberry-walnut or rhubarb muffins. The inn's gardens are inviting, but so is downtown Victoria, a double-decker bus away (or you can walk). There are tea rooms, antique shops and turn-of-the-century Victorian homes in the gracious tree-shaded neighborhood. The ocean and beach walks are a block away. Rates are quoted in Canadian dollars.

Innkeeper(s): Herb Mueller. $90-205. 11 rooms with PB, 2 suites and 1 conference room. Breakfast included in rates. Types of meals: Country bkfst and early coffee/tea. Beds: KQDT. Modem hook-up, reading lamp, refrigerator, clock radio and coffeemaker in room. TV, VCR, fax, copier, bicycles, library, parlor games, telephone, fireplace and laundry facility on premises. Weddings, family reunions and seminars hosted. Antiquing, beach, bicycling, canoeing/kayaking, fishing, golf, shopping, tennis and water sports nearby.

Rosewood Victoria Inn

595 Michigan St
Victoria, BC V8V 1S7
(250)384-6644 (866)986-2222 Fax:(250)384-6117
E-mail: rvi@aviawest.com
Web: www.rosewoodvictoria.com

Circa 1932. Refurbished in a pristine English country style, this three-story inn is accentuated with a white picket fence, pillared balconies and colorful flower boxes. Luxurious accommodations have been designed individually and include fireplaces, sitting areas, a balcony or patio, handsome antiques and unique pieces, matching wallpapers and draperies, goose down duvets and full baths (four with double soaking tubs). The Conservatory or patio is the site for the inn's lavish breakfast. Victoria's Inner Harbor, downtown and the Seattle and Port Angeles ferry terminals are within three blocks.

Innkeeper(s): Jay Smith. $100-210. 17 rooms with PB. Breakfast included in rates. Types of meals: Full bkfst. Beds: KQT. Cable TV, reading lamp and telephone in room. Fireplace on premises. Weddings, small meetings and family reunions hosted. Antiquing, live theater and shopping nearby. Publicity: *Northwest Special Places.*

Scholefield House B&B

731 Vancouver St
Victoria, BC V8V 3V4
(250)385-2025 (800)661-1623 Fax:(250)383-3036
E-mail: mail@scholefieldhouse.com
Web: scholefieldhouse.com

Circa 1892. Located on a quiet street downtown and three blocks from the Empress Hotel, this authentically restored Victorian B&B is shaded by tall trees that line the wide boulevards. A picket fence and gabled front entrance provide an inviting welcome to guests. Rooms are furnished with antiques and period decor, and each has a private bath. The five-course champagne breakfast is served fireside in the

Parlor and edible flowers decorate the abundant servings of eggs Florentine, French toast with Brie, smoked salmon and other entrees. Two favorite spots are the private library where guests may enjoy a glass of sherry or tea and coffee and outside, an English herb and rose garden. The innkeeper is an author, who enjoys the historic register home's connection to the original owner, who founded the library in the Legislature Building. Stroll to the Inner Harbour, restaurants, antique shops, and theater in Victoria's flower-filled environment sometimes called "more English than England."

Innkeeper(s): Tana Dineen. $100-150. 3 rooms with PB, 1 with FP and 1 suite. Breakfast included in rates. Types of meals: Full gourmet bkfst. Beds: KQ. Reading lamp, ceiling fan, clock radio, turn-down service, 1 with Jacuzzi for two and 1 with fireplace and clawfoot tub in room. VCR, fax, library, parlor games, telephone and fireplace on premises. Antiquing, canoeing/kayaking, fishing, golf, live theater, museums, shopping, whale watching, salmon fishing, gardens and English high tea nearby.

West Vancouver

Beachside B&B

4208 Evergreen Ave
West Vancouver, BC V7V 1-H1
(604)922-7773 (800)563-3311 Fax:(604)926-8073
E-mail: info@beach.bc.ca
Web: www.beach.bc.ca

Circa 1947. Enjoy a warm Canadian welcome at this beachfront inn with breathtaking views. Surrounded by natural beauty in a quiet and secluded setting; the attractions of downtown are 20 minutes away. Stay in a spacious guest bedroom with an assortment of amenities that are sure to pamper and please including a fresh flower bouquet and fruit basket. The Oceanfront Honeymoon and Seaside Guest Suite feature large Jacuzzis, mini kitchens and glass doors leading to private patios. A generous continental-plus breakfast tray is provided for in-room privacy. Relax in the outdoor whirlpool while watching for orca whales, sea lions, seals and otters playing in the shore.

Innkeeper(s): Gibbs Family. $70-165. 3 rooms with PB, 1 with FP and 1 suite. Types of meals: Cont. Beds: QT. Cable TV, VCR, reading lamp, refrigerator, clock radio, coffeemaker, desk, Jacuzzi tubs, refrigerator and microwave in room. Fax, copier, swimming, parlor games, telephone, fireplace, laundry facility, e-mail and Jacuzzi on beach on premises. Small meetings and family reunions hosted. Antiquing, cross-country skiing, downhill skiing, fishing, golf, live theater, parks, shopping, sporting events, tennis and water sports nearby. Publicity: *Pacific Northwest, Frommers and Canada Select.*

"Our second stay was even more wonderful than our first."

New Brunswick

Edmundston

Auberge-LeFief Inn

87 Rue De L'Eglise
Edmundston, NB E3V 1J6
(506)735-0400 Fax:(506)735-0402

Circa 1920. This red brick Victorian offers rooms decorated in a variety of cultural themes, reflecting the pioneer heritage of New Brunswick. There's Irish Mist, The Highland, The French Vineyard and The Malobiannah, to name a few. Among the inn's regional dishes is the local "ploye," a buckwheat type crepe occasionally offered at breakfast. The inn has a four-star rating from Mobile.

Innkeeper(s): Sharon Belanger. $80-140. 9 rooms. Breakfast, afternoon tea and snacks/refreshments included in rates. Types of meals: Early coffee/tea. Beds: KQD. Modem hook-up, cable TV, VCR, reading lamp, refrigerator, ceiling fan, snack bar, clock radio, telephone, coffeemaker and desk in room. Air conditioning. Fax, copier, library, parlor games and fireplace on premises. Weddings, small meetings, family reunions and seminars hosted. Amusement parks, antiquing, art galleries, bicycling, canoeing/kayaking, cross-country skiing, downhill skiing, golf, hiking, horseback riding, live theater, museums, parks, shopping, sporting events, tennis and water sports nearby.

Nova Scotia

Bridgewater

Fairview Inn Bridgewater

25 Queen Street
Bridgewater, NS B4V 1P1
(902)423-1102 (800)725-8732 Fax:(902)423-8329
E-mail: info@nsinns.com
Web: www.nsinns.com

Circa 1863. Recently restored, this plantation-style inn is the area's oldest continually operating, and boasts a quiet, relaxed setting for business or leisure. Memorable suites feature historical themes and are enhanced with hardwood floors, antique furnishings, local original artwork and data ports. Stay in a suite with a canopy bed, fireplace and Jacuzzi tub. A satisfying breakfast starts the day. Dine on the covered veranda or fireside in the dining room. Room service is available. Swim in the heated outdoor pool and hot tub.

Innkeeper(s): Mr. Stephen O'Leary. $48-108. 26 rooms with PB and 4 suites. Breakfast included in rates. Types of meals: Full bkfst, lunch and dinner. Restaurant on premises. Beds: QDT. Modem hook-up, data port, cable TV, VCR, reading lamp, ceiling fan, clock radio, telephone, turn-down service, desk, hot tub/spa, voice mail and fireplace in room. Fax, copier, spa, swimming, fireplace, laundry facility and pool on premises. Weddings, small meetings, family reunions and seminars hosted. Antiquing, art galleries, beach, bicycling, canoeing/kayaking, cross-country skiing, fishing, golf, hiking, horseback riding, live theater, museums, parks, shopping, water sports and wineries nearby.

Centreville

Delft Haus B&B

1942 Hwy 359, PO Box 88
Centreville, NS B0P 1J0
(902)678-4333 (866)851-4333 Fax:(902)678-4333
E-mail: info@delfthaus.com
Web: www.delfthaus.com

Circa 1890. A romantic experience is offered at this 1910 Victorian manor with a gingerbread veranda, natural wood interiors and period furnishings. Surrounded by Annapolis Valley's apple orchard countryside, this heritage bed & breakfast, just minutes from major attractions, is situated on an acre of gardens with century-old ash and oak trees, a lush greenhouse and flowered walkways. Well-appointed guest bedrooms are very spacious with private ensuite baths and some include fireplaces. Lunch may not be needed after a hearty breakfast served on settings of Delft China. Owner and artist Daniel Richards' internationally published works are displayed. The secrets of his success are enthusiastically shared in fluent English or French.

Innkeeper(s): Daniel and Lesley Richards. $70-110. 4 rooms with PB, 2 with FP. Breakfast and snacks/refreshments included in rates. Types of meals: Full bkfst. Beds: Q. Modem hook-up, cable TV, VCR, reading lamp, CD player, ceil-

ing fan, clock radio, telephone, desk and fireplace in room. Air conditioning. Fax, bicycles, parlor games, fireplace and laundry facility on premises. Antiquing, art galleries, beach, bicycling, canoeing/kayaking, cross-country skiing, fishing, golf, hiking, horseback riding, live theater, museums, parks, shopping, sporting events, water sports, wineries and eagle watching nearby.

Publicity: *4 star Canada Select.*

Chester

Mecklenburgh Inn

78 Queen St
Chester, NS B0J 1J0
(902)275-4638
E-mail: suzi@mecklenburghinn.ca
Web: www.mecklenburghinn.ca

Circa 1903. Guests to this Edwardian Mission-style inn have plenty to see and do in the seaside village, which has catered to summer visitors for more than 150 years. Favorite activities include touring the historic streets, watching a yacht race, tennis, golf, and browsing the craft shops and boutiques. The living room is a popular place for sitting by the fireplace to talk and read from the selection of  travel books and magazines. Local theater productions can be seen at the Chester Playhouse. Guests will be happy to know that the innkeeper is a Cordon Bleu chef. Rates are quoted in Canadian dollars.

Historic Interest: Oak Island (5 miles).

Innkeeper(s): Suzi Fraser. $85-135. 4 rooms with PB. Breakfast included in rates. Types of meals: Full bkfst and early coffee/tea. Beds: QDT. Data port, reading lamp, clock radio, telephone, feather beds, down duvets and some with TV in room. VCR and fireplace on premises. Antiquing, fishing, live theater, shopping, sporting events and water sports nearby.

Publicity: *Georgetown Times, Life Channel Network, Brides, Toronto Sun and Power & Motor Yacht Magazine.*

"Lovely experience, great hospitality, yummy breakfast."

Clyde River

Clyde River Inn

10525 Highway 103
Clyde River, NS B0W 1R0
(902)637-3267 (877)262-0222 Fax:(902)637-1512

Circa 1874. This beautifully restored Victorian, once a stagecoach stop, features an inviting red exterior trimmed in a creamy shade of saffron. The interior is decorated with antiques in period, Victorian style. Guests are treated to an evening snack, as well as a full breakfast with items such as fresh fruit, homemade muffins and croissants, homemade preserves, yogurt and entrees such as blueberry pancakes. Golfing, fishing and beaches all are nearby.

Innkeeper(s): Michael & Pat Nickerson. $60-100. 4 rooms with PB and 1 suite. Breakfast and snacks/refreshments included in rates. Types of meals: Full bkfst and early coffee/tea. Beds: QDT. Reading lamp, ceiling fan and clock radio in room. TV, VCR, fax, library, parlor games, telephone and laundry facility on premises. Antiquing, beach, bicycling, canoeing/kayaking, fishing, golf, museums, parks and shopping nearby.

Digby County

Bear River Inn

1894 Clemeatvale Rd, Bear River
Digby County, NS
(902)543-2233 (800)725-8732 Fax:(902)530-3323
E-mail: info@NSinns.com
Web: www.NSinns.com

Circa 1870. Originally the family home of wealthy Captain Hettrick in the 1870s, the four-story Main House and two and a half-story Carriage House have been completely renovated for modern comfort while retaining the original wood floors, ten-foot ceilings, wide moldings, slate fireplaces and a grand staircase. Well-appointed guest bedrooms and suites of the Main House feature a classic country décor, antique furnishings and Simmons mattresses. A full breakfast is served in the dining room. Self-contained side-by-side suites with a whimsical country décor are available in the Carriage House. Each includes a fully equipped kitchen and a gas barbecue. Relax on a balcony overlooking the tidal brook. Ask about special packages and day adventures to best enjoy the sites and attractions of this scenic area.

Innkeeper(s): Monika & Willie. $65-145. 9 rooms, 2 with PB, 1 suite and 3 cottages. Breakfast included in rates. Types of meals: Country bkfst and early coffee/tea. Beds: Q. Reading lamp, refrigerator, clock radio, coffeemaker, desk, gas barbecue, balconies and antiques in room. TV, fax, copier, telephone and fireplace on premises. Weddings and family reunions hosted. Amusement parks, antiquing, art galleries, beach, bicycling, canoeing/kayaking, cross-country skiing, fishing, golf, hiking, live theater, museums, parks, shopping, water sports and wineries nearby.

Halifax

Welcome Inn Halifax

1984 Connaught Ave.
Halifax, NS B3H 4E1
(902)446-6500 (877)288-2999 Fax:(902)835-3805
E-mail: info@welcomeinnhalifax.com
Web: www.welcomeinnhalifax.com

Circa 1948. Leave stress at home and experience all the comforts and luxuries that are in abundance at this Dutch Colonial-style inn. An appealing ambiance is imparted from the blend of modern and traditional decor. Hardwood and ceramic floors enhance the clean interior. A fireplace highlights the spacious sitting room. Most of the guest bedrooms feature a fireplace, data port, Jacuzzi tub and balcony. A hearty breakfast makes lunch almost unnecessary. Fax and photocopying services are available.

Innkeeper(s): Angela Kidston. $105-155. 3 rooms with PB, 3 with FP. Breakfast included in rates. Types of meals: Full bkfst. Beds: Q. Cable TV, VCR, reading lamp, clock radio, telephone, fireplace and two rooms have a Jacuzzi tub in room. Fax on premises. Art galleries, bicycling, canoeing/kayaking, golf and hiking nearby.

Lunenburg

Lunenburg Inn

26 Dufferin Street
Lunenburg, NS B0J 2C0
(902)634-3963 (800)565-3963 Fax:(902)634-9419
E-mail: gail.don@lunenburginn.com
Web: www.lunenburginn.com

Circa 1893. Recently restored to maintain its classic Victorian beauty, this registered Heritage Property from the late 1800s sits on the edge of the UNESCO World Heritage Site of Old Town.

Original woodwork, period colors, decor and antiques blend well with modern conveniences to offer comfort and gracious accommodations. A sun deck and veranda provide relaxing interludes. Guest suites feature whirlpool baths and sitting rooms. Savor a hot breakfast accompanied by seasonal fruit, fresh baked goods and preserves. Year-round activities within a short walk include seasonal festivals, waterfront shops, jogging and cycling trails. Whale watching and harbour tours are available.

Innkeeper(s): Gail and Don Wallace. $80-180. 7 rooms, 5 with PB and 2 suites. Breakfast and afternoon tea included in rates. Types of meals: Full bkfst, veg bkfst and snacks/refreshments. Beds: QT. Data port, cable TV, reading lamp, ceiling fan, clock radio, desk, suites have air conditioning, whirlpool baths, refrigerator, TV and VCR in room. TV, VCR, fax, copier, library, parlor games, telephone and data port for guest use on premises. Weddings and family reunions hosted. Antiquing, art galleries, beach, bicycling, canoeing/kayaking, fishing, golf, hiking, horseback riding, museums, parks, shopping, tennis, water sports, wineries, waterfront, the Fisheries Museum of the Atlantic, scallop draggers, pleasure boats, tall ships, BlueNose II, wooden churches, art galleries, puffins and seals nearby.

Peggy's Cove

Peggy's Cove Bed & Breakfast

19 Church Road
Peggy's Cove, NS B3Z 3R7
(902)423-1102 (800)725-8732 Fax:(902)423-8329
E-mail: info@NSinns.com
Web: www.NSinns.com

Circa 1940. Walk to the world famous Peggy's Cove lighthouse from this yellow farm house with wraparound veranda. Situated in the fishing village, it is on two acres of grounds. Enjoying the sunset views from a private balcony, sipping local wines and soaking in an outdoor hot tub are among the favorite experiences at the inn. A full stick-to-your-ribs breakfast is offered. Once owned by artist Bill de Garthe, the home was originally a fisherman's house. The art studio now features contemporary landscapes and marine art by local Nova Scotian artisans including the resident artist. Carvings and local crafts are also on exhibit.

Innkeeper(s): Paul Matte & Bee Gibson. $95-145. 5 rooms with PB. Breakfast included in rates. Types of meals: Full bkfst. Beds: Q. Cable TV, reading lamp, clock radio and telephone in room. Outdoor hot tub on premises. Antiquing, canoeing/kayaking, fishing, golf, hiking and shopping nearby.

Prospect

Prospect Bed and Breakfast

1758 Prospect Bay Road
Prospect, NS B3H 4E1
(902)423-1102 (800)725-8732 Fax:(902)423-8329
E-mail: info@NSinns.com
Web: www.NSinns.com

Circa 1854. Surrounded by ocean with magnificent views in all directions, this Victorian home is at the end of a point in the quaint fishing village of Prospect. Originally built as a summer home for the Premiere of Nova Scotia, the large, comfortable rooms feature private baths and are furnished with antiques and original art. Kayak or canoe in the shelter of the bay, or explore one of the nearby, uninhabited islands with gull rookeries and secluded coves. Numerous nature trails on the cliffs along the coast provide opportunities for hiking and bird or whale watching, accompanied by a stunning view of the sunset. Meals include gourmet breakfasts featuring home-baked goods and complimentary afternoon tea.

Innkeeper(s): Helena Prsala. $95-145. 5 rooms with PB. Breakfast included in rates. Types of meals: Full gourmet bkfst and early coffee/tea. Beds: Q. Cable TV, reading lamp, clock radio and telephone in room. Swimming and beach on premises. Weddings and family reunions hosted. Antiquing, art galleries, beach, canoeing/kayaking, golf and hiking nearby.
Publicity: *National Geographic, Doctors Review, NS Tourism TV, Red Rose and Baby.*

Ontario

Gananoque

Manse Lane B&B

465 Stone St S
Gananoque, ON K7G 2A7
(613)382-8642 (888)565-6379

Circa 1860. Four comfortable guest rooms, two with a private bath, are available at this bed & breakfast. Breakfasts include items such as cereal, fruit, yogurt, cheeses, breads, bacon and eggs. Guests are within walking distance of local attractions.

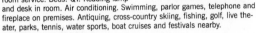

Innkeeper(s): Jocelyn & George Bounds. $55-160. 4 rooms, 2 with PB. Breakfast included in rates. Types of meals: Full bkfst, early coffee/tea, afternoon tea and room service. Beds: QT. Reading lamp and desk in room. Air conditioning. Swimming, parlor games, telephone and fireplace on premises. Antiquing, art galleries, beach, cross-country skiing, fishing, golf, live theater, parks, tennis, water sports, boat cruises and festivals nearby.

"Thoroughly enjoyed the stay. It was great to see you again."

The Victoria Rose Inn

279 King St. West
Gananoque, ON K7G 2G7
(613)382-3368 (888)246-2893 Fax:(613)382-8803
E-mail: vr@victoriaroseinn.com
Web: www.victoriaroseinn.com

Circa 1872. Two acres of award-winning landscaped grounds surround this Victorian Italianate mansion situated in the historic region of the Thousand Islands. This elegant country home was originally built for the area's first mayor and now serves as a pleasurable retreat or romantic getaway. Curl up in front of the fire in the cozy parlor, play a game or put together a puzzle and converse with a companion. The deluxe guest bedrooms and suites offer privacy and tasteful period-style reproductions and antique furnishings. The Tower, Victoria and American Beauty suites each boast champagne, a double Jacuzzi and fireplace. Enjoy breakfast in the dining room or on the veranda. The English-style gardens have a waterfall leading to a lily pond and are terraced to an old stone wall. Take advantage of the inn's new mini-spa with therapeutic massage, available by appointment.
$85-205. 11 rooms with PB, 2 with FP, 5 suites and 2 conference rooms. Breakfast and snacks/refreshments included in rates. Types of meals: Full gourmet bkfst, veg bkfst, lunch and gourmet dinner. Restaurant on premises. Beds: KQDT. Modem hook-up, cable TV, clock radio, coffeemaker, fireplace and five with Jacuzzi baths in room. Central air. VCR, fax, copier, library, parlor games, telephone, fireplace and mini-spa with therapeutic massage on premises. Weddings, small meetings, family reunions and seminars hosted. Antiquing, art galleries, beach, bicycling, canoeing/kayaking, cross-country skiing, fishing, golf, hiking, horseback riding, live theater, museums, parks, shopping, sporting events, tennis and water sports nearby.
Publicity: *GM car commercial.*

Lakefield

Tranquility Bed & Breakfast

1364 Third Line Road, RR #2
Lakefield, ON K0L 2H0
(705)652-1639 (800)551-4128 Fax:(705)652-3861

Circa 1832. Fifty-five scenic acres overlooking the Indian River inspire tranquility at this 170-year-old Georgian stone house with a log addition. Well-maintained and refurbished, the Victorian decor is accented by antiques. Luxurious and romantic queen suites feature four-poster beds with down-filled comforters, Jacuzzis, fireplaces and TV/VCRs. The top floor of the log addition is especially suited for families and is outfitted with cribs. A huge breakfast with choices of hot and cold cereal, yogurt, fresh fruit, sour cream blueberry pancakes with lemon sauce, bacon, sausage or ham and at least two baked goods provides fuel for the day. Walk the two miles of mowed trails, lounge in a hammock by the water and flower gardens, or borrow a canoe. Cross-country equipment and snowshoes are also available. Browse the gift shop or visit the spa for a massage and beauty treatment.
Historic Interest: One of the first families to the area, The Paynes, built the house.
Innkeeper(s): Maureen Carson. $80-160. 5 rooms, 3 with PB, 2 with FP. Breakfast, afternoon tea and snacks/refreshments included in rates. Types of meals: Full gourmet bkfst, early coffee/tea, gourmet lunch and picnic lunch. Beds: QT. Cable TV, VCR, reading lamp, CD player, refrigerator, ceiling fan, clock radio, coffeemaker, hot tub/spa, fireplace, bar fridges and tea service in room. Central air. Spa, library, parlor games, fireplace, gift shop, canoes, spa for massages and beauty treatments, walking trails, cross country equipment and snowshoes on premises. Antiquing, art galleries, beach, bicycling, canoeing/kayaking, cross-country skiing, fishing, golf, hiking, horseback riding, live theater, museums, parks, shopping and water sports nearby.
Publicity: *Two page article in North American Country Inns. Nominated to be in "The Best Places to Bed & Breakfast in Ontario" book.*

New Hamburg

The Waterlot

17 Huron St
New Hamburg, ON N3A 1K1
(519)662-2020 Fax:(519)662-2114

Circa 1844. Located beside a mill pond, this Victorian home boasts an imaginative architecture with gothic gables frosted with gingerbread trim and an unusual cupola. It houses the inn's most important asset, a French-country restaurant, Le Bistro, which seats 125 people. Overlooking the Nith River as it flows through the backyard, the restaurant has been well-known for more than two decades. Guest rooms are simple and housed beneath each of the inn's twin gables.
Innkeeper(s): Gord & Leslie Elkeer. $80-120. 3 rooms and 1 suite. Breakfast included in rates. Types of meals: Cont plus, lunch, picnic lunch and gourmet dinner. Restaurant on premises. Beds: KQD. Clock radio in room. Fax, copier, parlor games, telephone and fireplace on premises. Weddings, small meetings, family reunions and seminars hosted. Amusement parks, antiquing, cross-country skiing, downhill skiing, fishing, golf, live theater, parks, shopping and tennis nearby.

Niagara On The Lake

Acute B&B

127 Mary St
Niagara On The Lake, ON L0S 1J0
(905)468-1328 (888)208-2340 Fax:(905)468-1862
E-mail: info@acutebedandbreakfast.com
Web: www.acutebedandbreakfast.com

Circa 1843. Built in the first half of the 19th century, this bed
& breakfast features salt-box architecture and Victorian
ambiance both inside and out. The three guest suites feature
Victorian-style wallcoverings and floral comforters. The
Churchill Suite has a parlor with a fireplace. The Champlain
Suite is a cozy retreat with a sloped ceiling. The Chablis Suite
includes a sitting area with a sofa bed, and the room can
accommodate three guests comfortably. Fresh fruit, homemade
scones, eggs, breakfast meats and hash browns or pierogis comprise the country breakfast menu. Bicycles are among the
amenities offered to guests. Wineries are among the area's most
popular attractions with more than two dozen to visit.

Innkeeper(s): Jen Coburn. $70-130. 3 rooms with PB. Breakfast included in
rates. Types of meals: Full gourmet bkfst and veg bkfst. Beds: KQT. Cable TV,
reading lamp, ceiling fan, clock radio and fireplace in room. Central air. TV,
bicycles, parlor games and fireplace on premises. Family reunions hosted.
Antiquing, art galleries, bicycling, golf, hiking, live theater, parks, shopping
and wineries nearby.

Regent House

278 Regent Street
Niagara On The Lake, ON L0S 1J0
905-468-4361 Fax:(905)468-4813

Circa 1836. Gracing the Heritage District of Old Town, this
1836 home offers a pleasant ambiance to relax in while exploring this scenic and historic area throughout the year. Two
patios are inviting respites. The lush flower garden boasts a fish
pond and waterfall. Air-conditioned guest bedrooms include
refrigerators and cable TV. Enjoy a full breakfast that may
include fresh local fruits with yogurt and muesli, muffins and
scones, egg, leek and Brie strata with Canadian back bacon.
Located at the mouth of the Niagara River on Lake Ontario,
visit Fort George, the site of the War of 1812. Quaint boutiques
and antique shopping are favorite activities. An excursion to
Niagara Falls is a must.

Historic Interest: Built in 1836, located in the Heritage District of the Old
Town of Niagara on the Lake.

Innkeeper(s): John Hudson & Linda Smith. $110-150. 3 rooms with PB.
Types of meals: Full gourmet bkfst and early coffee/tea. Beds: KQT. Cable TV,
refrigerator, ceiling fan and clock radio in room. Central air. Amusement
parks, antiquing, art galleries, bicycling, golf, live theater, museums, parks,
shopping and wineries nearby.

Ottawa

Albert House Inn

478 Albert St
Ottawa, ON K1R 5B5
(613)236-4479 (800)267-1982 Fax:(613)237-9079
E-mail: contact@albertinn.com
Web: www.albertinn.com

Circa 1875. Albert House was built by Canadian architect
Thomas Scott in 1875, and he lived there until
1895. Scott was appointed to the governmental post of Chief
Architect and as such was responsible for the design, construc-

tion and maintenance of all federal buildings in Canada from
1871 to 1881. He designed part of the Parliament buildings
and supervised the construction of the Library of Parliament.
After Scott left Albert House, the structure was used by the
Victorian Order of Nurses and then it became Rosary Hall, a
convent of The Sisters of Service. The inn is half a mile from
the Parliament buildings and many other historic buildings in
Ottawa. It has a cobblestone parking area. The inn is renowned
for its large custom breakfast, which has an extensive menu,
including fruits, cereals, and a choice of griddle and egg
delights like French toast, blueberry pancakes, custom omelets,
fried egg sandwiches, fried tomatoes, fried potatoes and numerous fresh breads.

Innkeeper(s): Catherine & John Delroy. $88-158. 17 rooms with PB.
Breakfast and snacks/refreshments included in rates. Types of meals: Full
bkfst, early coffee/tea and room service. Beds: KQDT. Data port, cable TV,
reading lamp, clock radio, telephone, desk and hot tub/spa in room. Air conditioning. Fax, copier, fireplace, laundry facility and high-speed Internet
access desk free to guests is on premises. Antiquing, art galleries, beach,
bicycling, canoeing/kayaking, cross-country skiing, downhill skiing, fishing,
golf, hiking, horseback riding, live theater, museums, parks, shopping, sporting events, water sports and ten minutes from Rideau Canal nearby.

The Carmichael Inn & Spa

46 Cartier St
Ottawa, ON K2P 1-J3
(613)236-4667 (877)416-2417 Fax:(613)563-7529
E-mail: info@carmichaelinn.com
Web: www.carmichaelinn.com

Circa 1901. Carmichael Inn and Spa was built as the gracious
residence of Supreme Court Justice Thibodeau Rinfret. Situated
in a quiet residential area, the inn is conveniently close to the
Parliament buildings and the shops and restaurants of Elgin
Street. Guest rooms are appointed
in antiques such as mirrored
armoires, mahogany desks,
scrolled chairs and massive
headboards. The inn also offers
a range of spa services from
soothing massages to herbal
body wraps.

Innkeeper(s): Brian C. Fewster. $149. 10 rooms with PB and 1 conference
room. Breakfast included in rates. Types of meals: Cont. Beds: Q. Telephone
and desk in room. TV, fax, copier and spa on premises. Ice skating, museums, galleries and festivals nearby.

Gasthaus Switzerland Inn

89 Daly Ave
Ottawa, ON K1N 6E6
(613)237-0335 (888)663-0000 Fax:(613)594-3327
E-mail: switzinn@gasthausswitzerlandinn.com
Web: www.gasthausswitzerlandinn.com

Circa 1872. Constructed from limestone, this Vernacular
Classical Revival home served as a military rehabilitation facility
during World War I. The inn has welcomed guests since 1985,
and proud innkeepers Josef and Sabina provide splendid hospitality with a distinctively European flair. The well-appointed
guest bedrooms and romantic suites are comfortably elegant.
Some feature fireplaces, double Jacuzzis, CD stereos, four-
poster canopy beds and sparkling wine. A traditional Swiss, full
breakfast is served buffet style or delivered to the room.
Parliament Hill is within an easy walk, as are interesting shops,
museums and restaurants.

Innkeeper(s): Sabina & Josef Sauter. $98-248. 22 rooms, 20 with PB, 6 with FP and 2 suites. Breakfast included in rates. Types of meals: Full bkfst. Beds: KQDT. Modem hook-up, data port, cable TV, reading lamp, stereo, clock radio, telephone, desk and some with fireplace in room. Central air. TV, fax, copier, bicycles, fireplace, laundry facility and limited free parking on premises. Antiquing, beach, bicycling, cross-country skiing, downhill skiing, fishing, golf, hiking, horseback riding, live theater, museums, parks, shopping, tennis and cycling nearby.

Publicity: *The Washington Post, Arrington's Inn Traveler and Travel Travel CFCFTV.*

Inn on Somerset

282 Somerset St W
Ottawa, ON K2P 0J6
(613)236-9309 (800)658-3564 Fax:(613)237-6842
E-mail: info@innonsomerset.com
Web: www.innonsomerset.com

Circa 1895. Enjoy a delightful stay at this grand Victorian home built in 1895. Relax in front of the fireplace in the living room or take a leisurely stroll beside the Rideau Canal. Well-appointed guest bedrooms are furnished with period antiques and feature Internet access. Two rooms boast a fireplace and one has a sun porch. A hearty breakfast is served in the gracious dining room from 7:30 to 9 a.m. Work out in the exercise room, use the sauna or be entertained by the home theatre. A washer and dryer are available. The inn is located in the heart of Ottawa, an easy walk to Parliament Hill, shopping and fine restaurants.

Historic Interest: Parliament, Museum of Nature (5 minutes).

Innkeeper(s): George & Richard. $95-130. 11 rooms, 5 with PB, 1 with FP. Breakfast included in rates. Types of meals: Full bkfst. Beds: QDT. Reading lamp, clock radio, telephone and desk in room. Air conditioning. VCR, fax, copier, fireplace and sauna on premises. Weddings, small meetings and family reunions hosted. Antiquing, cross-country skiing, downhill skiing, live theater, parks, shopping, sporting events and tourist attractions nearby.

Publicity: *Ottawa Citizen.*

Peterborough

King Bethune Guest House & Spa

270 King St
Peterborough, ON K9J 2S2
(705)743-4101 (800)574-3664

Circa 1893. This brick Victorian is downtown on a quiet tree-shaded street. Restored hardwood floors, original trim throughout, tall ceilings and handsome windows grace the interiors. Guest rooms are large with ensuite baths and offer antiques, as well as desks, data ports, TVs and VCRs. The Spa Suite has a king bed and private entrance as well as a private hot tub, sauna, steam bath and massage therapy room. There's a restful walled garden with fireplace and patio, a favorite spot for breakfast.

Innkeeper(s): Marlis Lindsay. $104-220. 2 rooms with PB, 1 with HT and 1 suite. Breakfast included in rates. Types of meals: Full bkfst and room service. Beds: KQ. Cable TV, VCR, reading lamp, ceiling fan, clock radio, telephone, turn-down service and desk in room. Sauna, parlor games, fireplace, steambath, massage therapy room and private outdoor garden hot tub on premises. Small meetings and family reunions hosted. Amusement parks, antiquing, bicycling, cross-country skiing, downhill skiing, fishing, golf, live theater, parks, shopping, sporting events, tennis and water sports nearby.

Publicity: *Canadian Country and Examiner.*

"We still have not found better accommodations anywhere."

Toronto

213 Carlton - Toronto Townhouse B&B

213 Carlton Street
Toronto, ON M5A 2K9
(416)323-8898(877)500-0466
E-mail: houseboy@toronto-townhouse.com
Web: www.toronto-townhouse.com

Circa 1876. Conveniently located within walking distance to downtown and near public transit for city attractions, this flagship Edwardian house is a meticulously restored 125-year-old Heritage home. Many interesting architectural details include the original archways and moldings. Guest accommodations offer generous amenities and a smoke-free environment. The Peaches and Dreams Room is spacious and bright with a queen sleigh bed. Stay in the Upper Deck Suite with a separate entrance and a private deck with an incredible view of the Toronto skyline. Stroll the English garden and gaze at the colorful Japanese koi and goldfish in the built-in pond. Visit the quaint shops and historic sites of Niagara on the Lake.

Innkeeper(s): Frank. $51-148. 7 rooms, 3 with PB. Breakfast included in rates. Types of meals: Cont plus. Beds: KQ. Modem hook-up, data port, cable TV, VCR, reading lamp, refrigerator, clock radio, telephone, desk, hot tub/spa and voice mail in room. Central air. Spa and fireplace on premises. Amusement parks, antiquing, art galleries, beach, bicycling, golf, live theater, museums, parks, shopping, sporting events, public transit, train station, bus station and CN Tower nearby.

Publicity: *Toronto Tourism Award Winners - Sponsored by Diners Club International.*

Aberdeen Guest House

52 Aberdeen Ave
Toronto, ON M4X 1A2
(416)922-8697 Fax:(416)922-5011
E-mail: info@aberdeenguesthouse.com
Web: www.aberdeenguesthouse.com

Circa 1907. Nestled in the heart of Toronto's historic Cabbagetown, Aberdeen Guest House provides accommodations within walking distance to many Toronto attractions. The Victorian Row House is located in a neighborhood filled with historic Victorian homes. Guest rooms are decorated in a cheerful, cozy style featuring names such as the Magnolia Room or the Water Lily Room. The Sunflower Room includes artwork representing the signature flower, a sunflower comforter atop a four-poster bed, sunflower curtains and walls painted in a warm saffron tone. During the week, a continental breakfast is provided. On weekends, a full breakfast is served in the home's dining room.

Innkeeper(s): Gary Stothers. $100-140. 4 rooms, 1 with PB, 1 with FP and 1 conference room. Breakfast included in rates. Types of meals: Full gourmet bkfst. Beds: KQT. Cable TV, refrigerator, ceiling fan, clock radio, hot tub/spa, fireplace, robes, slippers and keyed security in room. Central air. Telephone, fireplace and laundry facility on premises. Weddings, small meetings and seminars hosted. Amusement parks, antiquing, art galleries, beach, bicycling, fishing, golf, hiking, horseback riding, live theater, museums, parks, shopping, sporting events, tennis and water sports nearby.

Woodstock

Chateau "Carbide" Willson

210 Vansittart Ave
Woodstock, ON N4S 6E9
(519)533-0800 Fax:(519)421-0842
E-mail: info@chateaucarbidewillson.com
Web: www.chateaucarbidewillson.com

Circa 1895. Deserving of its many accolades, this historic Richardsonian Romanesque mansion graces the heart of town in a perfect setting for a country inn bed & breakfast. Pearson International Airport and the sites of Toronto are less than an hour and a half away. Surrounded by exquisite detailed wood interiors, eight fireplaces, fine antiques and artwork, it is easy to be absorbed and charmed by the impressive ambiance of this palatial estate that has become an international landmark. Enjoy the peaceful library, parlor and intimate reading rooms. Luxurious guest bedrooms and suites offer a variety of styles and amenities. Stay in an executive suite with a sitting room, private tower balcony and whirlpool soaking tub. In the formal dining room an incredible breakfast might include the inn's signature four-mushroom omelet, toast, bacon, fresh fruit, Dutch cheese, yogurt, cereal and just-baked buns with homemade jam.

Historic Interest: Located in the rolling farmlands West of Kitchener, Woodstock can be counted as one of Ontario's better preserved historic communities. But it is on the aptly named Vansittart Street where Woodstock boasts one of Ontario's best collections of grand historic homes. Several claim high gables and towers, but it is the house built by Thomas "Carbide" Willson in 1895 that many claim to be the most castle-like in appearance. The cost, $90,000, was the most any house had cost in Woodstock up to that time.

Innkeeper(s): Felicio Loeffen. $69-249. 6 rooms with PB, 2 with FP, 3 suites and 1 conference room. Breakfast included in rates. Types of meals: Full gourmet bkfst, veg bkfst, early coffee/tea, snacks/refreshments and dinner. Beds: KQ. Cable TV, VCR, reading lamp, ceiling fan, clock radio, hot tub/spa, fireplace, Jacuzzi and whirlpool in room. Air conditioning. Fax, bicycles, library and parlor games on premises. Weddings, small meetings and family reunions hosted. Amusement parks, antiquing, art galleries, beach, bicycling, canoeing/kayaking, cross-country skiing, downhill skiing, fishing, golf, hiking, horseback riding, live theater, museums, parks, shopping, sporting events, tennis, water sports, wineries, Brantford Casino, horseracing, Canada games and Canada's largest wood show and largest outdoor farm show nearby. Publicity: *North American Inns Magazine, Ulysses and Dim Reaper.*

Quebec

Ayer's Cliff

Ripplecove Inn

700 Rue Ripplecove, PO Box 246
Ayer's Cliff, QB J0B 1-C0
(819)838-4296 (800)668-4296 Fax:(819)838-5541
E-mail: info@ripplecove.com
Web: www.ripplecove.com

Circa 1945. This exquisite Victorian inn, located on the shores of Lake Massawippi, is one of only 10 establishments in Quebec to earn a Four-Diamond award from the American Automobile Association. Some of the well-appointed rooms offer whirlpool tubs, fireplaces and private balconies. The 12-acre grounds include a heated swimming pool and private beach, and guests can partake of skating, skiing and ice fishing without leaving the property. Meals at Ripplecove are a special treat, set on tables with sterling silver, fine linens, crystal and Royal Doulton china. Our Chef combines classical and nouvelle French artistry with local produce to create an array of mouth-watering specialties.

Innkeeper(s): Jeffrey & Debra Stafford. $280-450. 26 rooms with PB, 11 with FP, 5 suites, 1 cabin and 2 conference rooms. Breakfast and dinner included in rates. Types of meals: Full bkfst, lunch and room service. Beds: KQDT. Cable TV, reading lamp, clock radio, telephone and turn-down service in room. Air conditioning. VCR, fax, copier, swimming, bicycles, tennis, library, child care, parlor games and fireplace on premises. Limited handicap access. Weddings, small meetings, family reunions and seminars hosted. Antiquing, cross-country skiing, downhill skiing, fishing, golf, live theater, parks, shopping, tennis and water sports nearby.
Publicity: *Country Inns and Gazette.*

"We shall never forget Ripplecove Inn. Its elegant and intimate setting provided the perfect place to hold the kind of wedding we had dreamed of. The refined cuisine, the superb service and your own personal hospitality made our dream a reality."

Montreal

Armor-Manoir Sherbrooke

157 Sherbrooke Est
Montreal, QB H2X 1-C7
(514)845-0915 (800)203-5485 Fax:(514)284-1126

Circa 1882. Montreal's bustling Latin Quarter is the location of this historic Victorian hotel. The elegant guest rooms and suites are individually decorated and boast fine woodwork and soaring ceilings with intricate designs. The three suites include a Jacuzzi. Guests can walk to many shops, restaurants and cafes. Old Montreal is a 15-minute walk from the hotel. Rates are quoted in Canadian dollars.

Innkeeper(s): Annick Morvan. $79-129. 25 rooms, 16 with PB and 3 suites. Breakfast included in rates. Types of meals: Cont. Beds: QD. Cable TV, telephone, desk and Jacuzzi in room. Air conditioning. Fax on premises.

Saint-Eugene, L'islet

Auberge des Glacis

46 Route Tortue
Saint-Eugene, L'islet, QB G0R 1X0
(418)247-7486 Fax:(418)247-7182

Circa 1840. The stone walls of this graceful former flour mill add unusual character and warmth to the inviting rooms offered by Auberge des Glacis. Breakfast is served buffet style, or you can arrange for it to be delivered to your room. The inn's restaurant is notable for its gourmet French cuisine. Twelve acres of scenic grounds include a lake and landscaped lawns. Swimming, golfing, cycling, skiing, birdwatching and cruising are favored activities.

Innkeeper(s): Micheline et Pierre Watters. $57. 10 rooms, 8 with PB and 2 suites. Breakfast and dinner included in rates. Types of meals: Full gourmet bkfst. Beds: QD. Reading lamp in room. Air conditioning. Fax, swimming, bicycles and telephone on premises. Antiquing, art galleries, bicycling, canoeing/kayaking, cross-country skiing, golf, hiking, live theater, museums and parks nearby.

Inns of Interest

African-American History

Wingscorton Farm Inn
.... East Sandwich, Mass.
Munro House B&B Health & Day Spa
.... Jonesville, Mich.
Troutbeck ....Amenia, N.Y.
The Signal House ....Ripley, Ohio
1790 House B&B Inn ... .Georgetown, S.C.
Golden Stage Inn ..... .Proctorsville, Vt.
Rockland Farm Retreat .... .Bumpass, Va.
Sleepy Hollow Farm ... .Gordonsville, Va.

Barns

Old Church House Inn .... .Mossville, Ill.
1794 Watchtide....by the Sea
.... Searsport , Maine
Brannon-Bunker Inn .... .Walpole, Maine
BarnAgain B&B Inn .... .Ozark, Mo.
Candlelite Inn ....Bradford, N.H.
Pine Barn Inn ....Danville, Pa.
Cornerstone B&B Inn .... .Landenberg, Pa.
Pace One Restaurant and Country Inn
.... Thornton, Pa.
Jackson Fork Inn ...... .Huntsville, Utah
Waitsfield Inn ....Waitsfield, Vt.

Castles

Castle Marne-A Luxury Urban Inn
.... Denver, Colo.
Castle Inn Riverside ...... .Wichita, Kan.
Manresa Castle .... .Port Townsend, Wash.

Churches & Parsonages

The Parsonage B&B ... .Nevada City, Calif.
Fourteen Lincoln Street, a Chef-Owned
Bed & Breakfast ..... .Niantic, Conn.
Old Church House Inn .... .Mossville, Ill.
Christopher's B&B .... .Bellevue, Ky.
Parsonage Inn ....St. Michaels, Md.
The Beechcroft Inn ..... .Brewster, Mass.
The Parsonage Inn .... .East Orleans, Mass.
The Parsonage on the Green .... .Lee, Mass.
The Dan'l Webster Inn .... .Sandwich, Mass.
Graycote Inn .... .Bar Harbor, Maine
The Abbey ....Cape May, N.J.
The Wilmingtonian .... .Wilmington, N.C.

Civil War

Myrtledene .... .Lebanon, Ky.
Old Manse Inn .... .Brewster, Mass.
The General Rufus Putnam House
.... Rutland, Mass.
Munro House B&B Health & Day Spa
.... Jonesville, Mich.
Anchuca .... .Vicksburg, Miss.
Cedar Grove Mansion Inn
.... Vicksburg, Miss.
Red House Inn B&B ..... .Brevard, N.C.
Andrea's Troy-Bumpas Inn B&B
.... Greensboro, N.C.
La Vista Plantation .... .Fredericksburg, Va.
Baladerry Inn at Gettysburg
.... Gettysburg, Pa.
The Brafferton Inn ...... .Gettysburg, Pa.
The Doubleday Inn ..... .Gettysburg, Pa.
James Getty Hotel ...... .Gettysburg, Pa.
The Beechmont B&B Inn .... .Hanover, Pa.
Chestnut Cottage B&B .... .Columbia, S.C.
The Inn at Narrow Passage
.... Woodstock, Va.
Boydville, Inn at Martinsburg
.... Martinsburg, W.Va.

Cookbooks Written By Innkeepers

Heartstone Inn & Cottages
.... Eureka Springs, Ark.
The Old Yacht Club Inn
.... Santa Barbara, Calif.
Blue Spruce Inn .... .Soquel, Calif.
Dockside Guest Quarters .... .York, Maine
Garth Woodside Mansion
.... Hannibal, Mo.
Mainstay Inn ....Cape May, N.J.
Fearrington House ..... .Fearrington, N.C.
White Oak Inn .... .Danville, Ohio
Whispering Pines B&B ..... .Delroy, Ohio
MacKaye Harbor Inn
.... Lopez Island, Wash.
Roses B&B .... .Lake Geneva, Wis.

Farms and Orchards

Scarlett's Country Inn .... .Calistoga, Calif.
The Inn at Shallow Creek Farm
.... Orland, Calif.
Howard Creek Ranch .... .Westport, Calif.
Homespun Farm B&B ..... .Jewett, Conn.
Applewood Farms Inn .... .Ledyard, Conn.
Canaan Land Farm B&B ... .Harrodsburg, Ky.
Maple Hill Farm B&B Inn
.... Augusta, Maine
Cove Farm Inn ....Bar Harbor, Maine
Baldwin Hill Farm B&B
.... Great Barrington, Mass.
Gilbert's Tree Farm B&B
.... Rehoboth, Mass.
Wingscorton Farm Inn .... .Sandwich, Mass.
Horse & Carriage B&B .... .Jonesville, Mich.
Caverly Farm & Orchard ..... .Bland, Mo.
Brass Heart Inn .... .Chocorua, N.H.
Rockhouse Mountain Farm Inn
.... Eaton Center, N.H.
Colby Hill Inn .... .Henniker, N.H.
Ellis River House .... .Jackson, N.H.
Olde Orchard Inn
.... Moultonborough, N.H.
Berry Hill Gardens B&B
.... Bainbridge, N.Y.
Agape Farm B&B ....Corinth, N.Y.
Inn at Silver Maple Farm
.... East Chatham, N.Y.
Fearrington House Inn .... .Pittsboro, N.C.
The Mast Farm Inn .... .Valle Crucis, N.C.
Old Pioneer Garden Guest Ranch
.... Unionville, Nev.
Wine Country Farm ...... .Dayton, Ore.
Springbrook Hazelnut Farm
.... Newberg, Ore.
Huntland Farm .... .Greensburg, Pa.
Barley Sheaf Farm .... .Holicong, Pa.
Meadow Spring Farm Traditions
at Longwood .... .Kennett Square, Pa.
Cedar Hill Farm .... .Mount Joy, Pa.
Hollyleaf Inn ....New Hope, Pa.
Field & Pine B&B ..... .Shippensburg, Pa.
B&B at Skogland Farm ..... .Canova, S.D.
Rockland Farm Retreat .... .Bumpass, Va.
Cave Hill Farm B&B
.... McGaheysville, Va.
Old Spring Farm B&B .... .Woolwine, Va.
Hill Farm Inn ....Arlington, Vt.
River Meadow Farm
.... Manchester Center, Vt.

681

Inns of Interest

West River Lodge & Stables
. . . . Newfane, Vt.
Liberty Hill Farm . . . . Rochester, Vt.
Colonel Crockett Farm
. . . . Coupeville, Wash.
Turtleback Farm . . . . . . Eastsound, Wash.
Justin Trails B&B Resort . . . . Sparta, Wisc.

Gold Mines & Gold Panning

Dunbar House, 1880 . . . . . Murphys, Calif.
Hotel Nipton . . . . Nipton, Calif.

Hot Springs

Rainbow Tarns B&B at Crowley Lake
. . . . . Mammoth/Crowley Lake, Calif.
Vichy Hot Springs Resort . . . . Ukiah, Calif.
Wiesbaden Hot Springs Spa & Lodgings
. . . . Ouray, Colo.
Boulder Hot Springs . . . . . . Boulder, Mont.
Soldier Meadows Guest Ranch
. . . . Gerlach, Nev.

Inns Built Prior to 1800

1649 Three Chimneys Inn
. . . . Durham, N.H.
1667 Stephen Daniels House
. . . . Salem, Mass.
1682 William Penn Guest House
. . . . New Castle, Del.
1690 Penny House Inn . . . . Eastham, Mass.
1690 Jonas Green House B&B
. . . . Annapolis, Md.
1690 Brookside Manor . . . . Wakefield, R.I.
1691 The Great Valley House of Valley Forge
. . . . Valley Forge, Pa.
1692 The Dan'l Webster Inn
. . . . Sandwich, Mass.
1699 Ashley Manor Inn
. . . . Barnstable, Mass.
1700 Elias Child House B&B
. . . . Woodstock, Conn.
1700 Casa Europa Inn & Gallery
. . . . Taos, N.M.
1700 Evermay-On-The-Delaware
. . . . Erwinna, Pa.
1700 Hollyleaf Inn . . . . . . New Hope, Pa.
1700 Hollyhedge B&B . . . . New Hope, Pa.
1700 Hillbrook Inn . . . Charles Town, W.Va.
1704 Cornerstone B&B Inn
. . . . Landenberg, Pa.
1709 The Woodbox Inn
. . . . Nantucket, Mass.
1710 Another Second Penny Inn
. . . . Stonington, Conn.
1710 The Robert Morris Inn
. . . . Oxford, Md.
1711 La Hacienda Grande
. . . . Bernalillo, N.M.
1712 Blue Gateways . . . . Wellfleet, Mass.

1714 Pennsbury Inn . . . . Chadds Ford, Pa.
1716 Longfellow's Wayside Inn
. . . . Sudbury, Mass.
1720 Butternut Farm . . . Glastonbury, Conn.
1721 Brimblecomb Hill
. . . . Marblehead, Mass.
1722 AAA Jacob Hill Inn
. . . . Providence, R.I.
1723 Roxbury Mill B&B
. . . . Spotsylvania, Va.
1727 Logan Inn . . . . New Hope, Pa.
1729 Harbor Light Inn . . Marblehead, Mass.
1730 Colonial House Inn
. . . . Yarmouth Port, Mass.
1730 Tavern House . . . . . . Vienna, Md.
1730 Hayne House B&B
. . . . Charleston, S.C.
1731 Bird-In-Hand . . . . . Coventry, Conn.
1732 Joy House Inc., B&B
. . . . Dennisport, Mass.
1732 1732 Folke Stone Bed and Breakfast
. . . . West Chester, Pa.
1732 The Kitchen House
. . . . Charleston, S.C.
1732 Prospect Hill Plantation Inn
. . . . Charlottesville, Va.
1734 Amerscot House . . . . . . Stow, Mass.
1734 Langdon House . . . . . Beaufort, N.C.
1734 The Village Inn of Bird-In-Hand
. . . . Bird-In-Hand, Pa.
1734 Sweetwater Farm . . . . Glen Mills, Pa.
1735 Antebellum B&B at The Thomas
Lamboll House . . . . Charleston, S.C.
1737 New Boston Inn . . . . Sandisfield, Mass.
1739 The Chapoquoit Inn
. . . . Falmouth, Mass.
1739 The Ruffner House . . . . . Luray, Va.
1740 Homespun Farm Bed and Breakfast
. . . . Jewett City, Conn.
1740 Red Brook Inn . . . Old Mystic, Conn.
1740 Lamb and Lion Inn
. . . . Barnstable, Mass.
1740 Ingate Farms B&B
. . . . Belchertown, Mass.
1740 High Meadows B&B . . . . Eliot, Maine
1740 Barley Sheaf Farm . . . . Holicong, Pa.
1740 Pace One Restaurant and
Country Inn . . . . Thornton, Pa.
1740 Willows of Newport - Romantic
Inn & Garden . . . . . . Newport, R.I.
1740 The Inn at Narrow Passage
. . . . Woodstock, Va.
1742 The Kelley House
. . . . Edgartown, Mass.
1742 Centre Street Inn
. . . . Nantucket, Mass.
1743 The Inn at Mitchell House
. . . . Chestertown, Md.

1745 Black Walnut Inn . . . . Amherst, Mass.
1745 Olde Rhinebeck Inn
. . . . Rhinebeck, N.Y.
1745 General Warren Inne
. . . . Malvern, Pa.
1745 Governor Bradford House Country Inn
at Mount Hope Farm . . . Bristol, R.I.
1746 Deacon Timothy Pratt Bed &
Breakfast Inn C.1746
. . . . Old Saybrook, Conn.
1747 Georgian House B&B
. . . . Annapolis, Md.
1750 Candleberry Inn . . . . Brewster, Mass.
1750 Daggett House . . . Edgartown, Mass.
1750 The General Rufus Putnam House
. . . . Rutland, Mass.
1750 Inn At Sandwich Center
. . . . Sandwich, Mass.
1750 Waterloo Country Inn
. . . . Princess Anne, Md.
1750 Peace With-Inn Bed & Breakfast
. . . . Fryeburg, Maine
1750 Isaac Hilliard House Bed, Breakfast...
and Beyond . . . . Pemberton, N.J.
1750 Alynn's Butterfly Inn B&B
. . . . Warrensburg, N.Y.
1750 Hickory Bridge Farm
. . . . Gettysburg, Pa.
1750 Farm Fortune
. . . . New Cumberland, Pa.
1750 Tattersall Inn . . . . Point Pleasant, Pa.
1750 The Melville House . . . Newport, R.I.
1750 Nathaniel Porter Inn & Restaurant
. . . . Warren, R.I.
1750 Litchfield Plantation
. . . . Pawleys Island, S.C.
1750 Linden House B&B & Plantation
. . . . Champlain, Va.
1750 Jasmine Plantation B&B Inn
. . . . Providence Forge, Va.
1753 L'Auberge Provencale . . . . Boyce, Va.
1755 Kitty Knight House on the Sassafras
. . . . Georgetown, Md.
1757 The Fairfield Inn 1757
. . . . Fairfield, Pa.
1758 Hammett House Inn
. . . . Newport, R.I.
1759 Chanceford Hall B&B
. . . . Snow Hill, Md.
1760 Edgewater B&B . . . . Fairhaven, Mass.
1760 Old Inn on The Green &
Gedney Farm
. . . . New Marlborough, Mass.
1760 Francis Malbone House
. . . . Newport, R.I.
1760 Charleston Governor's House
. . . . Charleston, S.C.

682

1760 Green Trails Inn . . . . .Brookfield, Vt.

1760 Gilbert House B&B of Middleway
. . . . Charles Town, W.Va.

1761 The Bird & Bottle Inn
. . . . Garrison, N.Y.

1763 Blackberry River Inn
. . . . Norfolk, Conn.

1763 Causey Mansion Bed & Breakfast
. . . . Milford, Del.

1763 Casa De Solana, B&B Inn
. . . . Saint Augustine, Fla.

1763 Wingscorton Farm Inn
. . . . East Sandwich, Mass.

1763 The Squire Tarbox Inn
. . . . Wiscasset, Maine

1763 Historic Smithton Inn
. . . . Ephrata, Pa.

1763 John Rutledge House Inn
. . . . Charleston, S.C.

1764 Colonel Spencer Inn
. . . . Campton, N.H.

1764 General Sutter Inn . . . . . . .Lititz, Pa.

1764 The Inn at Ormsby Hill
. . . . Manchester Center, Vt.

1765 Harbor House . . . .Georgetown, S.C.

1766 Beekman Arms-Delamater Inn
. . . . Rhinebeck, N.Y.

1766 1766 Osceola Mill House
. . . . Gordonville, Pa.

1766 The Inn at Meander Plantation
. . . . Locust Dale, Va.

1767 Birchwood Inn . . . . . . .Lenox, Mass.

1767 Highland Lake Inn B&B
. . . . East Andover, N.H.

1768 The Cedars Inn . . . . .Beaufort, N.C.

1769 Thomas Bond House
. . . . Philadelphia, Pa.

1770 The Parsonage Inn
. . . . East Orleans, Mass.

1770 The Meeting House Inn
. . . . Henniker, N.H.

1770 A Sparrow Hawk Bed & Breakfast
. . . . Stone Ridge, N.Y.

1770 The Richard Johnston Inn
. . . . Fredericksburg, Va.

1770 Henry Farm Inn . . . . . . .Chester, Vt.

1771 The Village Inn . . . . . .Lenox, Mass.

1771 The Inn on Cove Hill
. . . . Rockport, Mass.

1771 Publick House Historic Inn &
Country Lodge . . .Sturbridge, Mass.

1772 The Bagley House . . . .Durham, Maine

1772 Jailhouse Inn . . . . .Newport, R.I.

1773 The Red Lion Inn
. . . . Stockbridge, Mass.

1773 White Goose Inn . . . . .Orford, N.H.

1774 Gibson's Lodgings . . . .Annapolis, Md.

1774 Blue Skye Farm
. . . . Waldoboro, Maine

1775 Pinecrest Cottage and Gardens - A
Bed and Breakfast . . . .Louisville, Ky.

1775 Inn At Richmond
. . . . Richmond, Mass.

1775 Todd House . . . . . . .Eastport, Maine

1775 Kanaga House B&B Inn
. . . . New Kingstown, Pa.

1775 1811 House . . . . . .Manchester, Vt.

1776 Griswold Inn . . . . .Essex, Conn.

1776 Fairbanks Inn . . . .Provincetown, Mass.

1776 Beechtree Inn . . . . .Hertford, N.C.

1777 Eastman Inn . . . .North Conway, N.H.

1777 Doneckers, The Inns . . . .Ephrata, Pa.

1778 The Inn at Chester . . . .Chester, Conn.

1778 Cove Farm Inn . . . .Bar Harbor, Maine

1778 Brass Heart Inn . . . .Chocorua, N.H.

1779 Old Talbott Tavern . . . .Bardstown, Ky.

1780 Christine's Bed-Breakfast & Tearoom
. . . . Housatonic, Mass.

1780 Birch Hill Bed & Breakfast
. . . . Sheffield, Mass.

1780 Egremont Inn
. . . . South Egremont, Mass.

1780 Mill Pond Inn . . . .Nobleboro, Maine

1780 The Dowds' Country Inn
. . . . Lyme, N.H.

1780 Hacienda Antigua B&B
. . . . Albuquerque, N.M.

1780 Hopewell Farm B&B
. . . . Thompson Ridge, N.Y.

1780 Silver Thatch Inn
. . . . Charlottesville, Va.

1781 Creekside Inn . . . . . . .Paradise, Pa.

1783 The Towers B&B . . . . .Milford, Del.

1783 Four Chimneys Inn & Restaurant
. . . . Bennington, Vt.

1784 The Old Mystic Inn
. . . . Old Mystic, Conn.

1784 Lovetts Inn . . . . . . .Franconia, N.H.

1785 The Homestead B&B
. . . . Bardstown, Ky.

1785 Weathervane Inn
. . . . South Egremont, Mass.

1785 Oakland Plantation . . . .Natchez, Miss.

1785 1785 Inn & Restaurant
. . . . North Conway, N.H.

1785 Sleepy Hollow Farm B&B
. . . . Gordonsville, Va.

1785 The Inn at Vaucluse Spring
. . . . Stephens City, Va.

1786 Marston Family Bed and Breakfast
. . . . Hyannis Port, Mass.

1786 Windsor House
. . . . Newburyport, Mass.

1786 Kenniston Hill Inn
. . . . Boothbay, Maine

1786 The Brafferton Inn . . . .Gettysburg, Pa.

1786 Limestone Inn B&B . . . .Strasburg, Pa.

1787 Nereledge Inn
. . . . North Conway, N.H.

1788 Golden Stage Inn
. . . . Proctorsville, Vt.

1789 Stevens Farm B&B
. . . . Barre, Mass.

1789 Captain Josiah Mitchell House B&B
. . . . Freeport, Maine

1789 The Hancock Inn . . . .Hancock, N.H.

1789 Longswamp Bed & Breakfast
. . . . Mertztown, Pa.

1789 The Inn at High View
. . . . Andover, Vt.

1790 Riverwind . . . . . .Deep River, Conn.

1790 Silvermine Tavern . . . .Norwalk, Conn.

1790 Tolland Inn . . . . .Tolland, Conn.

1790 Darley Manor Inn
. . . . Wilmington, Del.

1790 17 Hundred 90 Inn . . . .Savannah, Ga.

1790 The Tuck Inn B&B
. . . . Rockport, Mass.

1790 Benjamin F. Packard House
. . . . Bath, Maine

1790 Fairhaven Inn . . . . .Bath, Maine

1790 Old Granite Inn . . . .Rockland, Maine

1790 Lake House . . . . . .Waterford, Maine

1790 Southern Hotel
. . . . Sainte Genevieve, Mo.

1790 The Inn at Bingham School
. . . . Chapel Hill, N.C.

1790 The Baird House
. . . . Valle Crucis, N.C.

1790 Nestlenook Farm Resort
. . . . Jackson, N.H.

1790 Olde Orchard Inn
. . . . Moultonborough, N.H.

1790 The Inn at Pleasant Lake
. . . . New London, N.H.

1790 Stepping Stones B&B
. . . . Wilton, N.H.

1790 Mill House Inn
. . . . East Hampton, N.Y.

1790 The Altland House
. . . . Abbottstown, Pa.

1790 Mill Creek Homestead B&B
. . . . Bird-in-Hand, Pa.

1790 Jacobs Resting Place . . . .Carlisle, Pa.

1790 Ash Mill Farm . . . . . . .Holicong, Pa.

1790 Pineapple Hill . . . . . .New Hope, Pa.

1790 Brownstone Colonial Inn
. . . . Reinholds, Pa.

1790 Field & Pine B&B
. . . . Shippensburg, Pa.

1790 The Cuthbert House Inn B&B
. . . . Beaufort, S.C.

1790 1790 House B&B Inn
. . . . Georgetown, S.C.

1790 Jordan Hollow Farm Inn
. . . . Stanley, Va.

1790 Piney Grove at Southall's
Plantation-1790 . . .Williamsburg, Va.

1790 Hill Farm Inn . . . . . . .Arlington, Vt.

1790 Inn at Buckhollow Farm
. . . . Fairfax, Vt.

1790 Silver Maple Lodge & Cottages
. . . . Fairlee, Vt.

1790 The Putney Inn . . . . . . .Putney, Vt.

1790 The Inn at Blush Hill
. . . . Waterbury, Vt.

1791 St. Francis Inn
. . . . Saint Augustine, Fla.

1792 Woolverton Inn . . . . .Stockton, N.J.

1792 King George IV Inn
. . . . Charleston, S.C.

1792 The Inn on Covered Bridge Green
. . . . Arlington, Vt.

1792 The Inn at Weathersfield
. . . . Perkinsville, Vt.

1793 Bullard Farm B&B
. . . . New Salem, Mass.

1793 Pilgrim's Inn . . . . . .Deer Isle, Maine

1793 Shaker Hill Bed & Breakfast
. . . . Enfield, N.H.

1793 Dilworth Rocking Horse Bed
& Breakfast . . . . .New Holland, Pa.

1793 Echo Ledge Farm Inn
. . . . East Saint Johnsbury, Vt.

1794 Historic Merrell Inn
. . . . Stockbridge, Mass.

1794 1794 Watchtide... by the Sea
. . . . Searsport, Maine

1794 The Wagener Estate B&B
. . . . Penn Yan, N.Y.

1794 Lareau Farm Country Inn
. . . . Waitsfield, Vt.

1795 Canaan Land Farm B&B
. . . . Harrodsburg, Ky.

1795 Butler Greenwood Plantation
. . . . Saint Francisville, La.

1795 Shiretown Inn on the Island of
Martha's Vineyard . . .Edgartown, Mass.

1795 The Swag Country Inn
. . . . Waynesville, N.C.

1795 1795 Acorn Inn
. . . . Canandaigua, N.Y.

1795 Bucksville House
. . . . Kintnersville, Pa.

1795 The Inn on The Common
. . . . Craftsbury Common, Vt.

1795 Rabbit Hill Inn
. . . . Lower Waterford, Vt.

1796 Old Riverton Inn . . . .Riverton, Conn.

1796 Myrtles Plantation
. . . . Saint Francisville, La.

1796 Hidden Mill Bed & Breakfast
. . . . Remsenburg, N.Y.

1796 Inn at Whitewing Farm
. . . . Kennett Square, Pa.

1796 The Wildflower Inn
. . . . Lyndonville, Vt.

1796 Catamount B&B . . . . .Williston, Vt.

1797 Sumner House . . . .Shrewsbury, Mass.

1797 The Grand View Inn & Resort
. . . . Jaffrey, N.H.

1797 Applebrook B&B . . . .Jefferson, N.H.

1797 The Post and Beam B&B
. . . . Sullivan, N.H.

1797 Cashtown Inn . . . . . .Cashtown, Pa.

1797 River Meadow Farm
. . . . Manchester Center, Vt.

1798 Edgartown Inn . . . .Edgartown, Mass.

1798 McLean House B&B
. . . . Shippensburg, Pa.

1798 Parador Oasis . . . .San German, P.R.

1799 Dr. Jonathan Pitney House
. . . . Absecon, N.J.

Jail House

Jailer's Inn . . . . .Bardstown, Ky.

Jailhouse Inn . . . . .Newport, R.I.

Inn at Ormsby Hill
. . . . Manchester Center, Vt.

Lighthouse

East Brother Light Station Inc
. . . . Isle Point Richmond, Calif.

Keeper's House . . . . .Isle Au Haut, Maine

Chesapeake Bay Lighthouse B&B
. . . . .Annapolis, Md.

Harbor House Inn . . . . . .Gills Rock, Wis.

Literary Figures Associated With Inns

Louisa May Alcott
Hawthorne Inn . . . . .Concord, Mass.

Susan B. Anthony
The Park House . . . . . .Saugatuck, Mich.

Henry Beston
Over Look Inn
. . . . Eastham (Cape Cod), Mass.

Rachel Carson
Newagen Seaside Inn
. . . . Boothbay Harbor, Maine

Ralph Waldo Emerson
Island House . . .Southwest Harbor, Maine

Hawthorne Inn . . . . .Concord, Mass.

Emerson Inn By the Sea
. . . . Rockport, Mass.

Nathaniel Hawthorne
Hawthorne Inn . . . . .Concord, Mass.

Island House . . . .Southwest Harbor, Maine

Emerson Inn By the Sea
. . . . Rockport, Mass.

D.H. Lawrence
Hacienda del Sol . . . . .Taos, N.M.

Jack London
Vichy Hot Springs Resort Inn
. . . . Ukiah, Calif.

James A. Michene
Robert Morris Inn . . . . .Oxford, Md.

Becky Thatcher
Fifth Street Mansion B&B
. . . . Hannibal, Mo.

Mark Twain/Samuel Clemnes
Vichy Hot Springs Resort Inn
. . . . Ukiah, Calif.

Garth Woodside Mansion
. . . . Hannibal, Mo.

Edith Wharton
The Gables Inn . . . . .Lenox, Mass.

Llama Ranches

Rockhouse Mountain Farm Inn
. . . . Eaton Center, N.H.

1661 Inn & Hotel Manisses
. . . . Block Island, R.I.

Rainbow Ridge Farms B&B
. . . . Onalaska, Wis.

Log Houses/Cabins

Ocean Wilderness Country Inn
. . . . Sooke, B.C.

Anniversary Inn . . . . . .Estes Park, Colo.

Tall Timber Lodge . . . . . .Pittsburg, N.H.

Trout House Village Resort . . . .Hague, N.Y.

The Swag Country Inn
. . . . Waynesville, N.C.

The Inn at Evins Mill . . . .Nashville, Tenn.

Arlington's West Mountain Inn
. . . . Arlington, Vt.

Fort Lewis Lodge . . . . .Millboro, Va.

Piney Grove at Southall's Plantation
. . . . Williamsburg, Va.

The Inn at Narrow Passage
. . . . Woodstock, Va.

Movie Locations

"Criss Cross"
Eden House . . . . .Key West, Fla.

"Girl, Interrupted"
Sheppard Mansion B&B . . . .Hanover, Pa.

"Pretty Baby"
Columns Hotel . . . . . . .New Orleans, La.

Old Mills

Silvermine Tavern ...... Norwalk, Conn.
Arbor Rose B&B .... Stockbridge, Mass.
Twin Gables Inn .... Saugatuck, Mich.
Asa Ransom House .... Clarence, N.Y.
Brookstown Inn B&B
.... Winston-Salem, N.C.
1766 Osceola Mill House
.... Gordonsville, Pa.
The Inn at Evins Mill .... Nashville, Tenn.
Roxbury Mill B&B ..... Spotsylvania, Va.

Oldest Continuously Operated Inns

1859 Historic National Hotel, A Country Inn
.... Jamestown, Calif.
The Cranberry Inn at Chatham
.... Chatham, Mass.
Emerson Inn By the Sea . .Rockport, Mass.
Candlelite Inn .... Bradford, N.H.
Wakefield Inn .... Wakefield, N.H.
The Fairfield Inn 1757 ...... Fairfield, Pa.
The Bellevue House .... Block Island, R.I.
Smith House Inn ..... Crosbyton, Texas

On the grounds of a U.S. National Monument

Cathedral House B&B ..... Rindge, N.H.

Plantations

Poipu Inn & Kauai Inn .... Koloa, Hawaii
Poipu Plantation .... Koloa, Hawaii
The Lodge on Little St. Simons Island
...... Little St. Simons Island, Ga.
Melhana, the Grand Plantation
.... Thomasville, Ga.
Inglewood Plantation .... Alexandria, La.
Madewood Plantation House
.... Napoleonville, La.
Merry Sherwood Plantation .... Berlin, Md.
La Maison Cappellari at Mostly Hall
.... Falmouth, Mass.
Dunleith .... Natchez, Miss.
Monmouth Plantation .... Natchez, Miss.
Oakland Plantation ...... Natchez, Miss.
Rice Hope Plantation Inn
.... Moncks Corner, S.C.
Edgewood Plantation ... .Charles City, Va.
La Vista Plantation .... Fredericksburg, Va.
The Inn at Meander Plantation
.... Locust Dale, Va.
Mayhurst Inn .... Orange, Va.
Four Square Plantation .... Smithfield, Va.

Post Offices

The Goose & Turrets B&B
.... Montara, Calif.

Boxwood Inn .... Newport News, Va.

Ranches

Wit's End Guest Ranch .... Bayfield, Colo.
Soldier Meadows Guest Ranch & Lodge
.... Gerlach, Nev.
Wine Country Farm .... Dayton, Ore.
Hasse House and Ranch .... Mason, Texas

Revolutionary War

The Robert Morris House .... Oxford, Md.
Ashley Manor Inn
...... Barnstable/Cape Cod, Mass.
Village Green Inn ..... Falmouth, Mass.
Pace One Restaurant & Country Inn
.... Thornton, Pa.
The Melville House ..... Newport, R.I.
John Rutledge House Inn
.... Charleston, S.C.
The Kitchen House ..... Charleston, S.C.
Silver Thatch Inn .... Charlottesville, Va.
Inn at Ormsby Hill
.... Manchester Center, Vt.
Gilbert House B&B of Middleway
.... Charles Town, W.Va.

Schoolhouses

Old Riverton Inn .... Riverton, Conn.
The Roosevelt Inn
.... Coeur d'Alene, Idaho
The Bagley House ...... Durham, Maine
Old Sea Pines Inn .... Brewster, Mass.
School House B&B Inn .... Rocheport, Mo.
Bear Mountain Lodge .... Silver City, N.M.
The Inn at Bingham School
.... Chapel Hill, N.C.

Stagecoach Stops

The Dorrington Hotel & Restaurant
.... Dorrington, Calif.
Simpson House Inn
.... Santa Barbara, Calif.
Tidewater Inn .... Madison, Conn.
Maple Hill Farm B&B Inn
.... Augusta, Maine
Historic Merrell Inn .... South Lee, Mass.
Egremont Inn .... South Egremont, Mass.
Alden Country Inn .... Lyme, N.H.
Wakefield Inn .... Wakefield, N.H.
Hacienda Antigua B&B
.... Albuquerque, N.M.
Hacienda Vargas
.... Algodones/Santa Fe, N.M.
The Inn at Bingham School
.... Chapel Hill, N.C.
Penguin Crossing B&B .... Circleville, Ohio
Laurel Villa Country Inn ..... Milford, Pa.

The Inn at Narrow Passage
.... Woodstock, Va.
Churchill House Inn .... Brandon, Vt.
Golden Stage Inn ..... Proctorsville, Vt.
The Inn at Blush Hill ..... Waterbury, Vt.
Old Stagecoach Inn ..... Waterbury, Vt.
The General Lewis .... Lewisburg, W.Va.
Wisconsin House Stagecoach Inn
.... Hazel Green, Wis.

Still in the Family

Inglewood Plantation .... Alexandria, La.
Oakland House Seaside Resort
.... Brooksville, Maine
The Grey Havens .... Georgetown, Maine
Cedarcroft Farm/Cottage on the Knoll B&B
.... Warrensburg, Mo.
The Sanders-Helena's Bed & Breakfast
.... Helena, Mont.
Rockhouse Mountain Farm Inn
.... Eaton Center, N.H.
The Chalfonte Hotel ..... Cape May, N.J.
Brae Loch Inn .... Cazenovia, N.Y.
Northern Plantation B&B ... Urbana, Ohio
Cedar Hill Farm .... Mount Joy, Pa.
Castle Hill Inn & Resort ... Newport, R.I.
Hasse House and Ranch .... Mason, Texas
North Bend Plantation .Charles City, Va.
Catamount B&B .... Williston, Vt.
The General Lewis .... Lewisburg, W.Va.
Harbor House Inn ..... Gills Rock, Wis.

Taverns

Bird-In-Hand .... Coventry, Conn.
Griswold Inn .... Essex, Conn.
Silvermine Tavern ..... Norwalk, Conn.
Red Brook Inn .... Old Mystic, Conn.
Chapman Inn .... Bethel, Maine
Kendall Tavern B&B .... Freeport, Maine
Birchwood Inn .... Lenox, Mass.
Alden Country Inn .... Lyme, N.H.
The Bird & Bottle Inn ..... Garrison, N.Y.
Giddings Garden Bed & Breakfast
.... Syracuse, N.Y.
Rider's 1812 Inn .... Painesville, Ohio
Smithton Inn .... Ephrata, Pa.
James Getty Hotel .... Gettysburg, Pa.
Rabbit Hill Inn .... Lower Waterford, Vt.

Train Stations & Renovated Rail Cars

Inn at Depot Hill
.... Capitola-by-the-Sea, Calif.
Trout City Berth & Breakfast
.... Buena Vista, Colo.
Red House Inn B&B ...... Brevard, N.C.
Green Mountain Inn .... Stowe, Vt.

Tunnels, Secret Passageways, Caves

Merry Sherwood Plantation
.... Berlin, Maine
Ashley Manor Inn
.... Barnstable/Cape Cod, Mass.
Wingscorton Farm Inn
.... East Sandwich, Mass.
Munro House B&B Health & Day Spa
.... Jonesville, Mich.
Lehrkind Mansion ......Bozeman, Mont.
Colonel Spencer Inn .....Campton, N.H.
Mansion Hill Inn ....Madison, Wis.

Underground Railroad

The Great Valley House of Valley Forge
.... Valley Forge, Pa.
1732 Folke Stone Bed & Breakfast
.... West Chester, Pa.

Unusual Sleeping Places

In a water tower
John Doughtery House
.... Mendocino, Calif.

Above a gold mine
Chichester-McKee House B&B
.... Placerville, Calif.

In a bank
Landmark Inn at the Historic Bank of Oberlin
.... Oberlin, Kan.

In a trading post
Hacienda Vargas ....Algodones, N.M.

On or next to an archaeological dig site
The White Oak Inn ......Danville, Ohio

By waterfalls
Inn at Brandywine Falls
.... Sagamore Hills, Ohio

Waterfalls

Inn at Brandywine Falls
.... Sagamore Hills, Ohio

Who Slept/Visited Here

Ethan Allen
Inn at Ormsby Hill
.... Manchester Center, Vt.
Neil Armstrong
Beekman Arms ....Rhinebeck, N.Y.
John James Audubon
Weston House ....Eastport, Maine
Barrymore family
Evermay-on-the-Delaware
.... Erwinna/Bucks County, Pa.
Sarah Bernhardt
Abigail's "Elegant Victorian Mansion"
.... Eureka, Calif.

Buffalo Bill Cody
The Pollard ....Red Lodge, Mont.
The Inn at Jim Thorpe ....Jim Thorpe, Pa.
Calamity Jane
The Pollard ....Red Lodge, Mont.
Clara Bow
Hotel Nipton ....Nipton, Calif.
Aaron Burr
Beekman Arms ....Rhinebeck, N.Y.
Henry Clay
Monmouth Plantation ....Natchez, Miss.
Samuel Clemens (Mark Twain)
Vichy Hot Springs Resort & Inn
.... Ukiah, Calif.
Garth Woodside Mansion ..Hannibal, Mo.
Calvin Coolidge
Lehman House B&B ......St. Louis, Mo.
State Game Lodge ....Custer, S.D.
Jefferson Davis
Monmouth Plantation ....Natchez, Miss.
Anchuca .... Vicksburg, Miss.
Danny DeVito
Colonel Crockett Farm
.... Coupeville, Wash.
Emma DeVoe
DeVoe Mansion ....Tacoma, Wash.
Michael Douglas
Colonel Crockett Farm
.... Coupeville, Wash.
Thomas Edison
The Inn at Jim Thorpe ....Jim Thorpe, Pa.
Dwight D. Eisenhower
State Game Lodge ....Custer, S.D.
Errol Flynn
The Mission Inn ....Cape May, N.J.
Clark Gable
Gold Mountain Manor Historic B&B
.... Big Bear, Calif.
The Willows Historic Palm Springs Inn
.... Palm Springs, Calif.
Cary Grant
Mulburn Inn ....Bethlehem, N.H.
Ulysses S. Grant
Thayers Inn ....Littleton, N.H.
Horace Greely
Beekman Arms-Delameter Inn
.... Rhinebeck, N.Y.
Alex Haley
McKay House ....Jefferson, Texas
Alexander Hamilton
Bird & Bottle Inn ....Garrison, N.Y.

Mrs. Warren Harding
Watchtide, B&B By the Sea
.... Searsport, Maine
Lillian Hellman
Barley Sheaf Farm ....Holicong, Pa.
Patrick Henry
General Lewis ....Lewisburg, Va.
Mrs. Herbert Hoover
Watchtide, B&B By the Sea
.... Searsport, Maine
Howard Hughes
Colonial Inn of Martha's Vineyard
.... Edgartown, Mass.
Barbara Hutton
Mulburn Inn ....Bethlehem, N.H.
Bob Hope
The Greenfield Inn .....Greenfield, N.H.
Andrew Jackson
Oakland Plantation ......Natchez, Miss.
General Stonewall Jackson
Inn at Narrow Passage ....Woodstock, Va.
Thomas Jefferson
Inn at Meander Plantation
.... Locust Dale, Va.
The General Lewis .....Lewisburg. W.Va.
William Jennings Bryan
The Pollard ....Red Lodge, Mont.
Beekman Arms ....Rhinebeck, N.Y.
Lady Bird Johnson
McKay House ....Jefferson, Texas
General Lafayette
The Bird & Bottle Inn .....Garrison, N.Y.
Lillie Langtry
Abigail's "Elegant Victorian Mansion"
.... Eureka, Calif.
D.H. Lawrence
Hacienda Del Sol ....Taos, N.M.
Robert E. Lee
The President's Quarters
.... Savannah, Ga.
Robert Todd Lincoln
Inn at Ormsby Hill
.... Manchester Center, Vt.
Carole Lombard
Gold Mountain Manor Historic B&B
.... Big Bear, Calif.
Willows Historic Palms Springs Inn
.... Palm Springs, Calif.
Jack London
Vichy Hot Springs Resort & Inn
.... Ukiah, Calif.
Marx brothers
Barley Sheaf Farm ....Holicong, Pa.

Somerset Maugham
Colonial Inn of Martha's Vineyard
. . . . Edgartown, Mass.

President William McKinley
Cheshire Cat Inn & Spa
. . . . Santa Barbara, Calif.

Captain Cornelius J. Mey
Captain Mey's B&B Inn . . . .Cape May, N.J.

Paul Newman
Lazy Cloud Lodge B&B
. . . . Lake Geneva, Wisc.

Georgia O'Keefe
Hacienda del Sol . . . . .Taos, N.M.

S.J. Perlman
Barley Sheaf Farm . . . . .Holicong, Pa.

Tyrone Power
The Mission Inn . . . . .Cape May, N.J.

Robert Preston
The Mission Inn . . . . .Cape May, N.J.

General Quitman
Monmouth Plantation . . . .Natchez, Miss.

John D. Rockefeller
The Inn at Jim Thorpe . . . .Jim Thorpe, Pa.

Eleanor Roosevelt
Watchtide, B&B By the Sea
. . . . Searsport, Maine

Franklin Roosevelt
Beekman Arms . . . . .Rhinebeck, N.Y.

Theodore Roosevelt
Vichy Hot Springs Resort & Inn
. . . . Ukiah, Calif.
Lehman House B&B . . . . . .St. Louis, Mo.
Troutbeck . . . . .Amenia, N.Y.
A Touch of Europe B&B Inn
. . . . Yakima, Wash.

John Rutledge
John Rutledge House Inn
. . . . Charleston, S.C.

J.D. Salinger
Lazy Cloud Lodge B&B
. . . . Lake Geneva, Wisc.

Jane Seymour
Pink House Inn . . . . .East Hampton, N.Y.

General W.T. Sherman
Cuthbert House Inn B&B . . . .Beaufort, S.C.

Martin Short
Pink House Inn . . . . .East Hampton, N.Y.

Carly Simon
Pink House Inn . . . . .East Hampton, N.Y.

William H. Taft
Inn at Ormsby Hill
. . . . Manchester Center, Vt.

Elizabeth Taylor
Beekman Arms . . . . .Rhinebeck, N.Y.

Kathleen Turner
Colonel Crockett Farm
. . . . Coupeville, Wash.

Mark Twain (Samuel Clemens)
Vichy Hot Springs Resort & Inn
. . . . Ukiah, Calif.

George Washington
Bird & Bottle Inn . . . . .Garrison, N.Y.
Jacob's Resting Place . . . . . . .Carlisle, Pa.
John Rutledge House Inn . .Charleston, S.C.

Stanford White
The Inn at Jackson . . . . . .Jackson, N.H.

Robin Williams
Pink House Inn . . . . .East Hampton, N.Y.

Woolworth family
Mulburn Inn . . . . .Bethlehem, N.H.

World War II

Kilaeua Lodge . . . . .Volcano, Hawaii

INN EVALUATION FORM

Please copy and complete this form for each stay and mail to the address shown. Since 1981 we have maintained files that include thousands of evaluations from inngoers who have sent this form to us. This information helps us evaluate and update the inns listed in this guide.

Name of Inn: _____

City and State: _____

Date of Stay: _____

Your Name: _____

Address: _____

City/State/Zip: _____

Phone: (___ ___ ___) ___ ___ ___ – ___ ___ ___ ___

E-mail: _____

Please use the following rating scale for the next items.
1: Outstanding.   2: Good.   3: Average.   4: Fair.   5: Poor.

Location	1	2	3	4	5
Cleanliness	1	2	3	4	5
Food Service	1	2	3	4	5
Privacy	1	2	3	4	5
Beds	1	2	3	4	5
Bathrooms	1	2	3	4	5
Parking	1	2	3	4	5
Handling of reservations	1	2	3	4	5
Attitude of staff	1	2	3	4	5
Overall rating	1	2	3	4	5

Comments on Above: _____

_____

_____

_____

_____

_____

MAIL THE COMPLETED FORM TO:
American Historic Inns, Inc.
PO Box 669
Dana Point, CA 92629-0669
(949) 497-2232
www.iLoveInns.com

INN EVALUATION FORM

Please copy and complete this form for each stay and mail to the address shown. Since 1981 we have maintained files that include thousands of evaluations from inngoers who have sent this form to us. This information helps us evaluate and update the inns listed in this guide.

Name of Inn: _____

City and State: _____

Date of Stay: _____

Your Name: _____

Address: _____

City/State/Zip: _____

Phone: (_ _ _) _ _ _ – _ _ _ _

E-mail: _____

Please use the following rating scale for the next items.
1: Outstanding.   2: Good.   3: Average.   4: Fair.   5: Poor.

	1	2	3	4	5
Location	1	2	3	4	5
Cleanliness	1	2	3	4	5
Food Service	1	2	3	4	5
Privacy	1	2	3	4	5
Beds	1	2	3	4	5
Bathrooms	1	2	3	4	5
Parking	1	2	3	4	5
Handling of reservations	1	2	3	4	5
Attitude of staff	1	2	3	4	5
Overall rating	1	2	3	4	5

Comments on Above: _____

_____

_____

_____

_____

MAIL THE COMPLETED FORM TO:
American Historic Inns, Inc.
PO Box 669
Dana Point, CA 92629-0669
(949) 497-2232
www.iLoveInns.com

Publications From American Historic Inns

Bed & Breakfast and Country Inns, 15th Edition

By Deborah Edwards Sakach

Imagine the thrill of receiving this unique book with its FREE night certificate as a gift. Now you can let someone else experience the magic of America's country inns with this unmatched offer. *Bed & Breakfasts and Country Inns* is the most talked about guide among inngoers.

This fabulous guide features nearly 1,600 inns from across the United States and Canada. Best of all, no other bookstore guide offers a FREE night certificate.* This certificate can be used at any one of the inns featured in the guide.

American Historic Inns, Inc. has been publishing books about bed & breakfasts since 1981. Its books and the FREE night offer have been recommended by many travel writers and editors, and featured in: *The New York Times, Washington Post, Los Angeles Times, Boston Globe, Chicago Sun Times, USA Today, Orange County Register, Baltimore Sun, McCalls, Good Housekeeping, Cosmopolitan, Consumer Reports* and more.

*With purchase of one night at the regular rate required. Subject to limitations.

440 pages, paperback, 500 illustrations   **Price $21.95**

The Official Guide to American Historic Inns

Completely Revised and Updated, Ninth Edition

By Deborah Sakach

A Book of the Month Club and History Book Club Selection

Open the door to America's past with this fascinating guide to historic inns that reflect our colorful heritage. From Dutch Colonials to Queen Anne Victorians, these bed & breakfasts and country inns offer experiences of a lifetime.

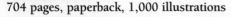

This special edition guide includes more than 2,650 certified American Historic Inns that provide the utmost in hospitality, beauty, authentic restoration and preservation. Inns have been carefully selected so as to provide readers with the opportunity to visit genuine masterpieces.

With inns dating back to as early as 1600, this guide is filled with treasures waiting to be discovered. Full descriptions, illustrations, guest comments and recommendations all are included to let you know what's in store for you before choosing one of America's Historic Inns.

704 pages, paperback, 1,000 illustrations   **Price $16.95**

How To Start & Run Your Own Bed & Breakfast Inn

By Ripley Hotch & Carl Glassman

In this book you'll discover the secrets of the best inns. Learn how to decide whether owning or leasing an inn is right for you. Find out what business strategies characterize a successful inn and learn how to incorporate them in your own business.

If you've always dreamed of owning a bed & breakfast, then this book is for you!

182 pages, paperback   **Price $15.95**

The Bed & Breakfast Encyclopedia

Completely Revised and Updated, Third Edition

By Deborah Edwards Sakach & Tiffany Crosswy

This massive guide is the most comprehensive guide on the market today. Packed with detailed listings to more than 2,600 bed & breakfasts and country inns, the Encyclopedia also includes an index to an additional 14,000 inns, detailed state maps and more than 1,200 illustrations. Recipes, helpful phone numbers, information about reservation services and informative articles about bed & breakfast hot spots, the best bed & breakfasts, inns of interest, how to start your own B&B and much, much more.

If you're planning a getaway, this all-inclusive guide is a must!

1,056 pages, paperback, 1,200 illustrations   **Price $18.95**

Bed & Breakfast and Country Inn Travel Club
Membership From American Historic Inns, Inc.

SAVE! SAVE! SAVE! We offer an exclusive discount club that lets you enjoy the excitement of bed & breakfast and country inn travel again and again. As a member of this special club, you'll receive benefits that include savings of 25% to 50% off every night's stay!

Your membership card will entitle you to tremendous savings at some of the finest inns in America. <u>Members receive a guide with more than 1,000 participating bed & breakfasts and country inns to choose from.</u> Plan affordable getaways to inns nearby or visit an area of the country you've always wanted to experience.

The best part of being an American Historic Inns Travel Club Member is that the card can be used as many times as you like.

In addition to your card, you will get a FREE night's stay certificate—truly a club membership that's hard to pass up!

All travel club members receive:
- Travel club card entitling holder to 25% to 50% off lodging.
- FREE night's stay certificate.
- Guide to more than 1,000 participating inns across America.
- 50% off at participating Hotels & Resorts

Membership is good for one year. Free night's stay with purchase of one night at the regular rate. Discount and certificate cannot be combined.

Introductory price with full benefits (Reg. $59.95)   **$49.95**

Golf Across America Club Membership

Introducing the best way to get free greens fees and other discounts at more than 700 courses nationwide! A one-year Golf Across America membership includes substantial discounts, such as:

- Free greens fees
- Buy-One-Get-One-Free greens fees
- 50% off greens fees.
- Plus More!

Plus, your Golf Across America membership card can be used as many times as you like. The average Golf Across America club member saves between $200-$400 each year. Get your one-year club membership and start saving today!

Introductory price with full benefits   **$39.95**

AMERICAN HISTORIC INNS
INCORPORATED

PO Box 669
Dana Point
California
92629-0669
(949) 497-2232
Fax (949) 497-9228
www.iLoveInns.com

Order Form

Date: __ __ / __ __ / __ __   Shipped: __ __ / __ __ / __ __

Name: _____

Street: _____

City/State/Zip: _____

Phone: (__ __ __) __ __ __ __ – __ __ __ __   E-mail: _____

QTY.	Prod. No.	Description	Amount	Total
_____	AHI15	Bed & Breakfasts and Country Inns	$21.95	_____
_____	AHIH9	The Official Guide to American Historic Inns	$16.95	_____
_____	AHIE3	Bed & Breakfast Encyclopedia	$18.95	_____
_____	AHIC2	Bed & Breakfast and Country Inn Travel Club	$49.95	_____
_____	CB03	How to Start Your Own B&B	$15.95	_____
_____	GOLF	Golf Across America Club Membership	$39.95	_____

Subtotal _____

California buyers add 7.75% sales tax _____

Shipping and Handling on Encyclopedia Book Orders
STANDARD (10-20 days): $3.50 for first book. Add $1 for each additional copy.
PRIORITY (3-5 days): $8.00. Add $5 each add'l copy. 2ND-DAY AIR: $11.00. Add $3.50 each add'l copy.

Shipping and Handling on Other Book and Travel Club Orders
STANDARD (10-20 days): $3 for first book. Add 75¢ for each additional copy.
PRIORITY (3-5 days): $5.75. Add $3.50 each add'l copy. 2ND-DAY AIR: $11.00. Add $3.50 each add'l copy _____

TOTAL _____

❏ Check/Money Order   ❏ Discover   ❏ Mastercard   ❏ Visa   ❏ American Express

Account Number __ __ __ __ __ __ __ __ __ __ __ __ __ __ __ __   Exp. Date __ __ / __ __

Name on card _____

Signature _____

AMERICAN HISTORIC INNS

INCORPORATED

PO Box 669
Dana Point
California
92629-0669
(949) 497-2232
Fax (949) 497-9228
www.iLoveInns.com

Order Form

Date: _ _ / _ _ / _ _   Shipped: _ _ / _ _ / _ _

Name: _____

Street: _____

City/State/Zip: _____

Phone: (_ _ _) _ _ _ – _ _ _ _   E-mail: _____

QTY.	Prod. No.	Description	Amount	Total
_____	AHI15	Bed & Breakfasts and Country Inns	$21.95	_____
_____	AHIH9	The Official Guide to American Historic Inns	$16.95	_____
_____	AHIE3	Bed & Breakfast Encyclopedia	$18.95	_____
_____	AHIC2	Bed & Breakfast and Country Inn Travel Club	$49.95	_____
_____	CB03	How to Start Your Own B&B	$15.95	_____
_____	GOLF	Golf Across America Club Membership	$39.95	_____

Subtotal _____

California buyers add 7.75% sales tax _____

Shipping and Handling on Encyclopedia Book Orders
STANDARD (10-20 days): $3.50 for first book. Add $1 for each additional copy.
PRIORITY (3-5 days): $8.00. Add $5 each add'l copy. 2ND-DAY AIR: $11.00. Add $3.50 each add'l copy.

Shipping and Handling on Other Book and Travel Club Orders
STANDARD (10-20 days): $3 for first book. Add 75¢ for each additional copy.
PRIORITY (3-5 days): $5.75. Add $3.50 each add'l copy. 2ND-DAY AIR: $11.00. Add $3.50 each add'l copy _____

TOTAL _____

❑ Check/Money Order   ❑ Discover   ❑ Mastercard   ❑ Visa   ❑ American Express

Account Number _ _ _ _ _ _ _ _ _ _ _ _ _ _ _ _ _ _ _   Exp. Date _ _ / _ _

Name on card _____

Signature _____

693

www.iLoveInns.com

"The only online bed & breakfast guide you will ever need.™"

"Best B&B Site" — Yahoo! Internet Magazine

- More than 17,000 bed & breakfasts and country inns.

- Color photos and line illustrations.

- Use our easy Innfinder Search to quickly access inns near your destination.

- Or use our Advanced Search to look for inns that meet your specific needs.

- Search for inns in our Free Night program.

- Make reservations via e-mail.

- See our specially selected Inn of the Week.

- Learn about bed & breakfast hot spots across the country.

- Find out where the top inns are, including our famous picks for the 10 Most Romantic Inns.